CHEVROLET

CHEVY S10/GMC S15 PICK-UPS 1982-91 REPAIR MANUAL

CHILTON'S

President, Chilton Enterprises David S. Loewith
Senior Vice President Ronald A. Hoxter

Publisher and Editor-In-Chief Kerry A. Freeman, S.A.E.
Managing Editors Peter M. Conti, Jr. □ W. Calvin Settle, Jr., S.A.E.
Assistant Managing Editor Nick D'Andrea
Senior Editors Debra Gaffney □ Ken Grabowski, A.S.E., S.A.E.
Michael L. Grady □ Richard J. Rivele, S.A.E.
Richard T. Smith □ Jim Taylor
Ron Webb
Director of Manufacturing Mike D'Imperio
Editor James R. Marotta

CHILTON BOOK COMPANY
ONE OF THE DIVERSIFIED PUBLISHING COMPANIES,
A PART OF CAPITAL CITIES/ABC, INC.

Manufactured in USA

Chilton Way Radnor, Pa. 19089
ISBN 0-8019-8141-7
Library of Congress Catalog Card No. 90-056131

345678901 2109876543

Contents

Contents

SAFETY NOTICE

Proper service and repair procedures are vital to the safe, reliable operation of all motor vehicles, as well as the personal safety of those performing repairs. This manual outlines procedures for servicing and repairing vehicles using safe, effective methods. The procedures contain many NOTES, CAUTIONS and WARNINGS which should be followed along with standard safety procedures to eliminate the possibility of personal injury or improper service which could damage the vehicle or compromise its safety.

It is important to note that the repair procedures and techniques, tools and parts for servicing motor vehicles, as well as the skill and experience of the individual performing the work vary widely. It is not possible to anticipate all of the conceivable ways or conditions under which vehicles may be serviced, or to provide cautions as to all of the possible hazards that may result. Standard and accepted safety precautions and equipment should be used when handling toxic or flammable fluids, and safety goggles or other protection should be used during cutting, grinding, chiseling, prying, or any other process that can cause material removal or projectiles.

Some procedures require the use of tools specially designed for a specific purpose. Before substituting another tool or procedure, you must be completely satisfied that neither your personal safety, nor the performance of the vehicle will be endangered

Although information in this manual is based on industry sources and is complete as possible at the time of publication, the possibility exists that some car manufacturers made later changes which could not be included here. While striving for total accuracy, Chilton Book Company cannot assume responsibility for any errors, changes or omissions that may occur in the compilation of this data.

PART NUMBERS

Part numbers listed in this reference are not recommendations by Chilton for any product by brand name. They are references that can be used with interchange manuals and aftermarket supplier catalogs to locate each brand supplier's discrete part number.

SPECIAL TOOLS

Special tools are recommended by the vehicle manufacturer to perform their specific job. Use has been kept to a minimum, but where absolutely necessary, they are referred to in the text by the part number of the tool manufacturer. These tools can be purchased under the appropriate part number, from your Chevrolet or GMC dealer or regional distributor or an equivalent tool can be purchased locally from a tool supplier or parts outlet. Before substituting any tool for the recommended one, read the SAFETY NOTICE at the top of this page.

ACKNOWLEDGMENTS

The Chilton Book Company expresses its appreciation to Chevrolet Motor Division, General Motors Corporation, Detroit, Michigan for their generous assistance.

1 General Information and Maintenance

QUICK REFERENCE INDEX

GENERAL INDEX

HOW TO USE THIS BOOK

Chilton's Total Car Care for the S-10/S-15 Pickups is intended to help you learn more about the inner working of your truck and save you money in it's upkeep and operation.

The first two Sections will be the most used, since they contain maintenance and tune-up information and procedures. Studies have shown that a properly tuned and maintained truck can get at least 10% better gas mileage than an out-of-tune truck. Other Sections deal with the more complex systems of your truck. Operating systems from engine through brakes are covered. This book will give you detailed instructions to help you perform minor to major repairs on your truck that in turn will save you money, give you personal satisfaction and help you avoid expensive repair bills.

A secondary purpose of this book is a reference for owners who want to understand their truck and/or their mechanics better. In this case, no tools at all are required.

Before removing any bolts, read through the entire procedure. This will give you the overall view of what tools and supplies will be required. There is nothing more frustrating than having to walk to the bus stop on Monday morning because you were short one bolt on Sunday afternoon. So read ahead and plan ahead. Each operation should be approached logically and all procedures thoroughly understood before attempting any work.

All Sections contain adjustments, maintenance, removal/installation and repair or overhaul procedures. When repair is not considered practical, we tell you how to remove the part and then how to install the new or rebuilt replacement. In this way, you at least save the labor costs. Backyard repair of some components is just not practical.

Two basic mechanic's rules should be mentioned: One, the left-side of the truck or engine is the driver's side of the truck. Conversely, the right-side of the truck means the passenger's side. Secondly, most screws and bolts are removed by turning them counterclockwise and tightened by turning them clockwise.

Safety is always the most important rule. Constantly be aware of the dangers involved in working on a truck and take the proper precautions. (See the section in this Section, Servicing Your Vehicle Safely and the SAFETY NOTICE on the acknowledgment page).

Pay attention to the instructions provided. There are 3 common mistakes in mechanical work:

1. Incorrect order of assembly, disassembly or adjustment: When taking something apart or putting it together, doing things in the wrong order usually costs extra time, however, it CAN break something. Read the entire procedure before beginning disassembly. Do everything in the order in which the instructions say you should do it, even if you can't immediately see a reason for it. When you're taking something apart that is very intricate (for example, a carburetor), you might want to draw (or take) a picture of how it looks when assembled at one point, in order to make sure you get everything back in its proper position. (We will supply exploded views whenever possible). When making adjustments, especially tune-up adjustments, do them in order. Often, one adjustment affects another and you cannot expect satisfactory results unless each adjustment is made only when it cannot be changed by any other.

2. Overtorquing (or undertorquing): While it is more common for overtorquing to cause damage, undertorquing can cause a fastener to vibrate loose causing serious damage. Especially, when dealing with aluminum parts, pay attention to torque specifications and utilize a torque wrench in assembly. If a torque figure is not available, remember that if you are using the right tool to do the job, you will probably not have to strain yourself to get a fastener tight enough. The pitch of most threads is so slight that the tension you put on the wrench will be multiplied many times (in actual force) on the fastener you are tightening. A good example of how critical torque is can be seen in the case of spark plug installation, especially where you are putting the plug into an aluminum cylinder head. Too little torque can fail to crush the gasket, causing leakage of combustion gases and consequent overheating of the plug and engine parts. Too much torque can damage the threads or distort the plug, which changes the spark gap.

NOTE: There are many commercial products available for ensuring that fasteners won't come loose, even if they are not torqued just right (a very common brand is Loctite®). If you're worried about getting something together tight enough to hold but loose enough to avoid mechanical damage during assembly, one of these products might offer substantial insurance. Read the label on the package and make sure the product is compatible with the components involved before choosing one.

3. Crossthreading: Crossthreading occurs when a part such as a bolt is screwed into a nut or casting at the wrong angle. It is more likely to occur if access is difficult. To help prevent crossthreading, clean and lubricate the fasteners, then start threading with the part to be installed going straight in. Start the bolt or spark plug with your fingers. If you encounter resistance, unscrew the part and start over again at a different angle until it can be inserted and turned several turns without much effort. Keep in mind that many parts, especially spark plugs, use tapered threads so that gentle turning will automatically bring the part you're threading to the proper angle if you don't force it or resist a change in angle. Don't put a wrench on the part until it's been turned a couple of turns by hand. If you suddenly encounter resistance, and the part has not been fully seated, don't force it. Pull it back out and make sure it's clean and threading properly.

NOTE: Always take your time and be patient. Once you have some experience working on your truck, it will become an enjoyable hobby.

TOOLS AND EQUIPMENT

Naturally, without the proper tools and equipment, it is impossible to properly service your truck. It would be impossible to catalog each tool that you would need to perform each and every operation in this book. It would also be unwise for the amateur to rush out and buy an expensive set of tools on the theory that he may need one or more of them at sometime.

The best approach is to proceed slowly, gathering a good quality set of tools that are used most frequently. Don't be misled by the low cost of bargain tools. It is far better to spend a little more for better quality. Forged wrenches, 6 or 12 point sockets and fine tooth ratchets are by far preferable to their less expensive counterparts. As any good mechanic can tell you, there are few worse experiences than trying to work on a truck with bad tools. Your monetary savings will be far outweighed by frustration and mangled knuckles.

Begin accumulating tools that are used most frequently; those associated with routine maintenance and tune-up.

In addition to the normal assortment of screwdrivers and pli-

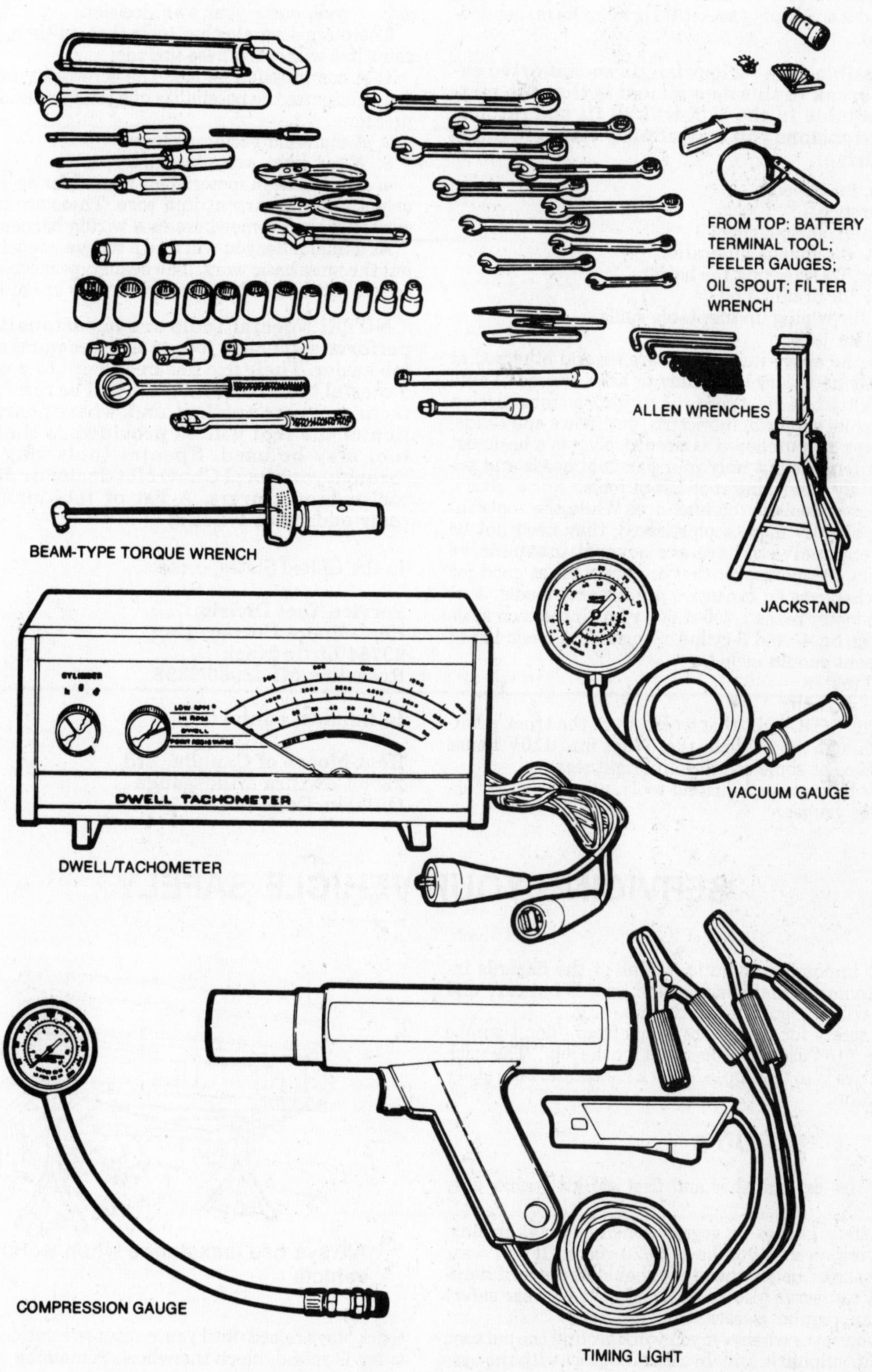
FROM TOP: BATTERY TERMINAL TOOL; FEELER GAUGES; OIL SPOUT; FILTER WRENCH
ALLEN WRENCHES
BEAM-TYPE TORQUE WRENCH
JACKSTAND
VACUUM GAUGE
DWELL TACHOMETER
DWELL/TACHOMETER
COMPRESSION GAUGE
TIMING LIGHT

You only need a basic assortment of hand tools and test instruments for most maintenance and repair jobs

ers you should have the following tools for routine maintenance jobs:

1. SAE and Metric wrenches and sockets in sizes from 1/8–3/4 in. (6–19mm) and a spark plug socket (13/16 in. or 5/8 in. depending on plug type).

NOTE: If possible, buy various length socket drive extensions. One break in this department is that the metric sockets available in the U.S. will all fit the ratchet handles and extensions you may already have (1/4 in., 3/8 in. and 1/2 in. drive).

2. Jackstands, for support
3. Oil filter wrench
4. Oil filler spout, for pouring oil
5. Grease gun, for chassis lubrication
6. Hydrometer, for checking the battery
7. A container for draining oil
8. Many rags for wiping up inevitable spills.
9. A quality floor jack.

In addition to the above items there are several others that are not absolutely necessary but handy to have around. These include oil dry (kitty litter is a good substitute), a transmission funnel and the usual supply of lubricants, antifreeze and fluids, although these can be purchased as needed. This is a basic list for routine maintenance but only your personal needs and desires can accurately determine your list of tools.

The second list of tools is for tune-ups. While the tools involved here are slightly more sophisticated, they need not be outrageously expensive. There are several inexpensive tach/dwell meters on the market that are every bit as good for the average mechanic as an expensive professional model. Just be sure that the meter reads 1,200–1,500 rpm on the tach scale and that it works on 4- and 6-cylinder engines. A basic list of tune-up equipment should include:

1. Tach/dwell meter.
2. Spark plug wrench.
3. Timing light (a DC light that works from the truck's battery is best, although an AC light that plugs into 110V house current will suffice at some sacrifice in brightness).
4. Wire spark plug gauge/adjusting tools.
5. Set of feeler gauges.

Here again, be guided by your own needs. A feeler gauge will set the points as easily as a dwell meter will read dwell, but slightly less accurately. Since you will need a tachometer anyway ... well, make your own decision.

There are several other tools that, in time, you will find you can't live without. These include:

1. A compression gauge. The screw-in type is slower to use but eliminates the possibility of a faulty reading due to escaping pressure.
2. A manifold vacuum gauge.
3. A test light, volt/ohm meter.
4. An induction meter. This is used for determining whether or not there is current in a wire. These are handy for use if a wire is broken somewhere in a wiring harness.

As a final note, you will find a torque wrench necessary for all but the most basic work. The beam type models are perfectly adequate, although the newer click type are more precise.

NOTE: Special tools are occasionally necessary to perform a specific job or are recommended to make a job easier. Their use has been kept to a minimum. When a special tool is indicated, it will be referred to by manufacturer's part number, and, where possible, an illustration of the tool will be provided so that an equivalent tool may be used. Special tools may be purchased through your local Chevrolet dealer or directly from the tool manufacturers. A list of tool manufacturers and their addresses follows:

In the United States, contact:

Service Tool Division
Kent-Moore Corporation
29784 Little Mack
Roseville, MI 48066-2298

In Canada, contact:

Kent-Moore of Canada, Ltd.
2395 Cawthra Mississauga
Ontario, Canada L5A 3P2.

SERVICING YOUR VEHICLE SAFELY

It is virtually impossible to anticipate all of the hazards involved with automotive maintenance and service but care and common sense will prevent most accidents.

The rules of safety for mechanics range from "don't smoke around gasoline," to "use the proper tool for the job." The trick to avoiding injuries is to develop safe work habits and take every possible precaution.

Do's

• Do keep a fire extinguisher and first aid kit within easy reach.

• Do wear safety glasses or goggles when cutting, drilling, grinding or prying, even if you have 20/20 vision. If you wear glasses for the sake of vision, then they should be made of hardened glass that can serve also as safety glasses or wear safety goggles over your regular glasses.

• Do shield your eyes whenever you work around the battery. Batteries contain sulphuric acid. In case of contact with the eyes or skin, flush the area with water or a mixture of water and baking soda, then get medical attention immediately.

• Do use safety stands for any under truck service. Jacks are for raising the truck. Safety stands are for making sure the truck stays raised until you want it to come down. Whenever the truck is raised, block the wheels remaining on the ground and set the parking brake.

Always use jackstands when working under the vehicle

• Do use adequate ventilation when working with any chemicals. Like carbon monoxide, the asbestos dust resulting from brake lining wear can be poisonous in sufficient quantities.

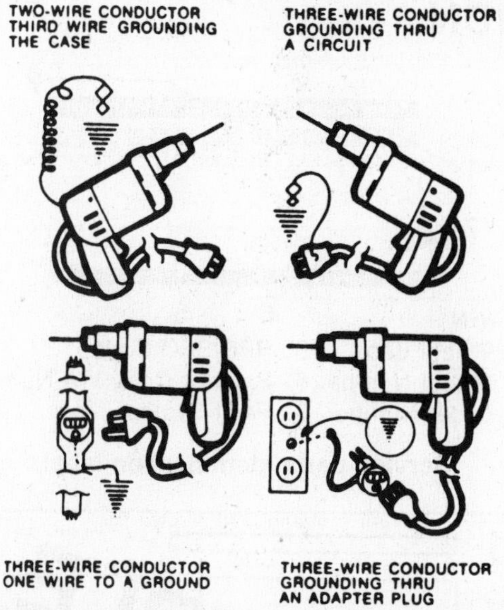
TWO-WIRE CONDUCTOR THIRD WIRE GROUNDING THE CASE
THREE-WIRE CONDUCTOR GROUNDING THRU A CIRCUIT
THREE-WIRE CONDUCTOR ONE WIRE TO A GROUND
THREE-WIRE CONDUCTOR GROUNDING THRU AN ADAPTER PLUG

When using electric tools, make sure they are properly grounded

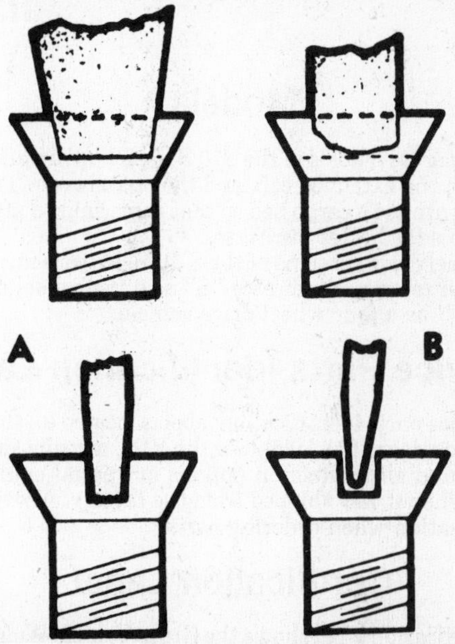
A
B

Keep screwdriver tips in good condition. They should fit the slot as in "A". If they look like those in "B", they need grinding or replacement

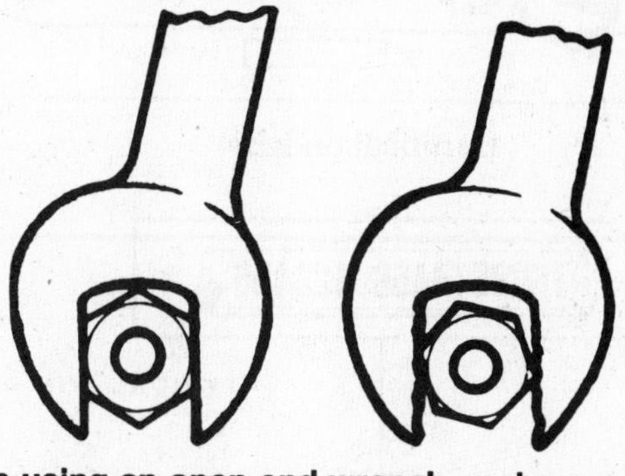

When using an open end wrench, make sure it is the correct size

- Do disconnect the negative battery cable when working on the electrical system. The primary ignition system can contain up to 40,000 volts.
- Do follow the manufacturer's instructions when working with potentially hazardous materials. Both brake fluid and antifreeze are poisonous if taken internally.
- Do properly maintain your tools. Loose hammer heads, mushroomed punches/chisels, frayed or poorly grounded electrical cords, excessively worn screwdrivers, spread wrenches (open end), cracked sockets, slipping ratchets and/or faulty droplight sockets cause accidents.
- Do use the proper size and type of tool for the job being done.
- Do pull on a wrench handle rather than push on it and adjust your stance to prevent a fall.
- Do be sure that adjustable wrenches are tightly adjusted on the nut or bolt and pulled so that the face is on the side of the fixed jaw.
- Do select a wrench or socket that fits the nut or bolt. The wrench or socket should sit straight, not cocked.
- Do strike squarely with a hammer—avoid glancing blows.
- Do set the parking brake and block the drive wheels if the work requires that the engine be running.

Dont's

- Don't run an engine in a garage or anywhere else without proper ventilation—EVER! Carbon monoxide is poisonous. It takes a long time to leave the body and can build up a deadly supply of it in your system by simply breathing in a little every day. You may not realize you are slowly poisoning yourself. Always use power vents, windows, fans or open the garage doors.
- Don't work around moving parts while wearing a necktie or other loose clothing. Short sleeves are much safer than long, loose sleeves and hard-toed shoes with neoprene soles protect your toes and give a better grip on slippery surfaces. Jewelry such as watches, fancy belt buckles, beads or body adornment or any kind is not safe working around a truck. Long hair should be hidden under a hat or cap.
- Don't use pockets for tool boxes. A fall or bump can drive a screwdriver deep into your body. Even a wiping cloth hanging from the back pocket can wrap around a spinning shaft or fan.
- Don't smoke when working around gasoline, cleaning solvent or other flammable material.
- Don't smoke when working around the battery. When the battery is being charged, it gives off explosive hydrogen gas.
- Don't use gasoline to wash your hands. There are excellent soaps available. Gasoline may contain lead, and lead can enter the body through a cut, accumulating in the body until you are very ill. Gasoline also removes all the natural oils from the skin so that bone dry hands will suck up oil and grease.
- Don't service the air conditioning system unless you are equipped with the necessary tools and training. The refrigerant, R-12, is extremely cold and when exposed to the air, will instantly freeze any surface it comes in contact with, including your eyes. Although the refrigerant is normally non-toxic, R-12 becomes a deadly poisonous gas in the presence of an open flame. One good whiff of the vapors from burning refrigerant can be fatal.
- Don't release refrigerant into the atmosphere. In most states it is now illegal to discharge refrigerant into the atmosphere due to the harmful effects Freon (R-12) has on the ozone layer. Check with local authorities about the laws in your state.

IDENTIFICATION

Models

Three separate models of the S10/S15 pickup are offered—the regular cab, the extended cab, and the chassis cab. The chassis cab comes without a cargo bed so that a specialized aftermarket bed may be added after purchase.

Four wheel drive versions of the S-10/S-15 were introduced in 1983. Model reference indicates "S" as a two wheel drive vehicle, and "T" as a four wheel drive vehicle.

Service Parts Identification Label

The service parts identification label is located on the inside of the glove box door. The label lists the VIN, wheelbase, paint information and all production options or special equipment on the truck when it was shipped from the factory. Always refer to this information when ordering parts.

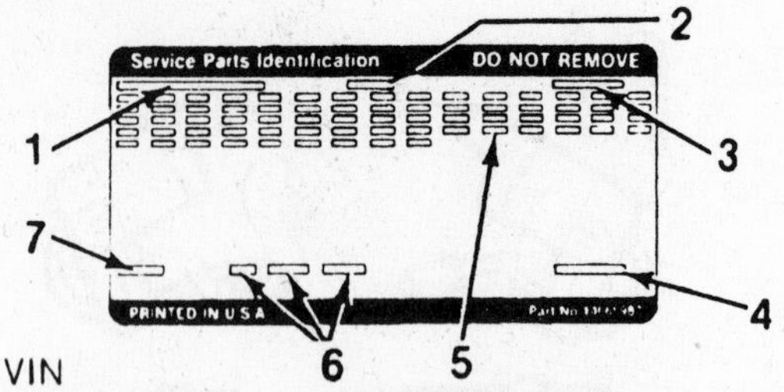
Service Parts Identification
DO NOT REMOVE
PRINTED IN U S A
1
2
3
4
5
6
7

1. VIN
2. Wheel Base
3. Model Number
4. Order Number
5. RPO/SEO Codes
6. Exterior Color WA Number
7. Paint System

Service parts identification label

Certification Label

The certification label shows the Gross Vehicle Weight Rating (GVWR), the front and rear Gross Axle Weight Rating (GAWR) and the Payload Rating.

Gross Vehicle Weight (GVW) is the weight of the originally equipped truck and all items added to it after leaving the factory. The GVW must not exceed the Gross Vehicle Weight Rating (GVWR) of your truck.

The Payload Rating shown on the label is the maximum allowable cargo load (including the weight of the occupants) that the truck can carry. The payload rating is decreased if any accessories or other equipment is added to the truck after delivery from the factory. Deduct the weight of any added accessories from the original payload rating to determine the new payload rating.

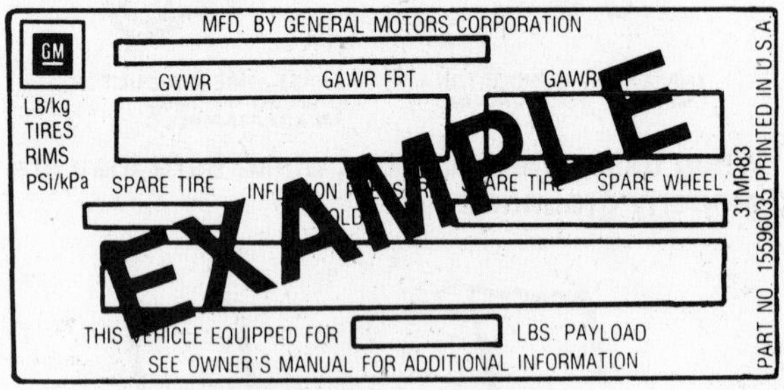
MFD. BY GENERAL MOTORS CORPORATION
GM
GVWR
GAWR FRT
LB/kg
TIRES
RIMS
PSI/kPa
SPARE TIRE
SPARE WHEEL
EXAMPLE
LBS. PAYLOAD
SEE OWNER'S MANUAL FOR ADDITIONAL INFORMATION
PART NO. 15596035 PRINTED IN U S A
31MR83

Certification label

Serial Number

Vehicle

The Vehicle Identification Number (VIN) is on a plate attached to the left hand top of the instrument panel, visible through the windshield. See the illustration for an explanation of the coding.

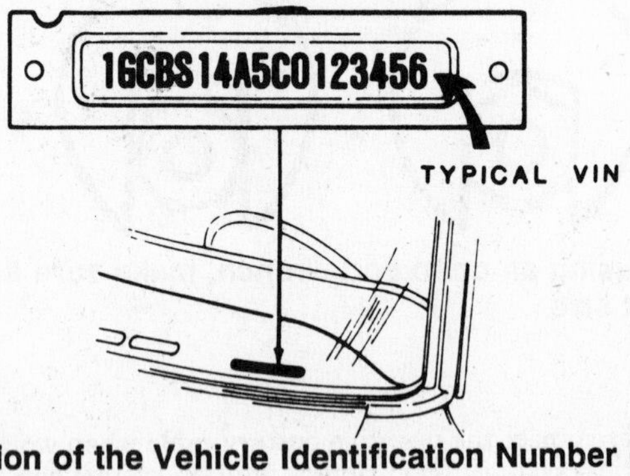
1GCBS14A5C0123456
TYPICAL VIN

Location of the Vehicle Identification Number (VIN)

ENGINE IDENTIFICATION CHART

Year	V.I.N. Code	Number of Cylinders Displacement in Liters	cu. in.	Engine Manufacturer	Fuel System
1982-85	A	4-1.9	118.9	Isuzu	2-bbl
	B	6-2.8	173	Chevrolet	2-bbl
1983-84	Y	4-2.0	121	Chevrolet	2-bbl
1983-85	S	4-2.2	136.6	Isuzu	Diesel
1985-91	E	4-2.5	151	Pontiac	TBI
1986-91	R	6-2.8	173	Chevrolet	TBI
1988-91	Z	6-4.3	262	Chevrolet	TBI

TBI—Throttle Body Injection

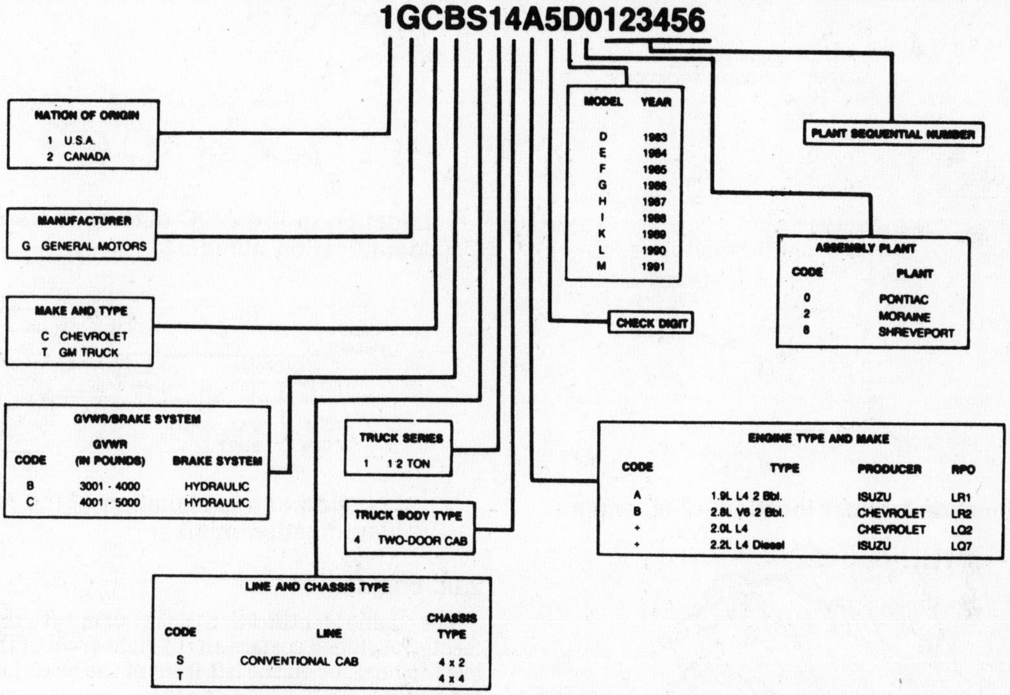
1GCBS14A5D0123456
NATION OF ORIGIN
1 U.S.A.
2 CANADA
MANUFACTURER
G GENERAL MOTORS
MAKE AND TYPE
C CHEVROLET
T GM TRUCK
GVWR/BRAKE SYSTEM
CODE GVWR (IN POUNDS) BRAKE SYSTEM
B 3001 - 4000 HYDRAULIC
C 4001 - 5000 HYDRAULIC
TRUCK SERIES
1 1 2 TON
TRUCK BODY TYPE
4 TWO-DOOR CAB
LINE AND CHASSIS TYPE
CODE LINE CHASSIS TYPE
S CONVENTIONAL CAB 4 x 2
T 4 x 4
MODEL YEAR
D 1983
E 1984
F 1985
G 1986
H 1987
I 1988
K 1989
L 1990
M 1991
CHECK DIGIT
PLANT SEQUENTIAL NUMBER
ASSEMBLY PLANT
CODE PLANT
0 PONTIAC
2 MORAINE
8 SHREVEPORT
ENGINE TYPE AND MAKE
CODE TYPE PRODUCER RPO
A 1.9L L4 2 Bbl. ISUZU LR1
B 2.8L V6 2 Bbl. CHEVROLET LR2
+ 2.0L L4 CHEVROLET LQ2
+ 2.2L L4 Diesel ISUZU LQ7

Explanation of the Vehicle Identification Number (VIN)

Engine

1.9L Engine

The engine identification number is on a machined flat surface, on the lower left-side of the block, near the flywheel.

2.0L Engine

The engine identification number is stamped on a flat, machined surface, facing forward, on the front of the engine block, just below the head.

2.2L Diesel Engine

The engine identification number is stamped on a flat, machined surface, facing forward, on the left-front of the engine block, just below the water pump.

2.5L Engine

The engine identification number is stamped on a flat, machined surface, on the left rear-side of the engine block, near the flywheel.

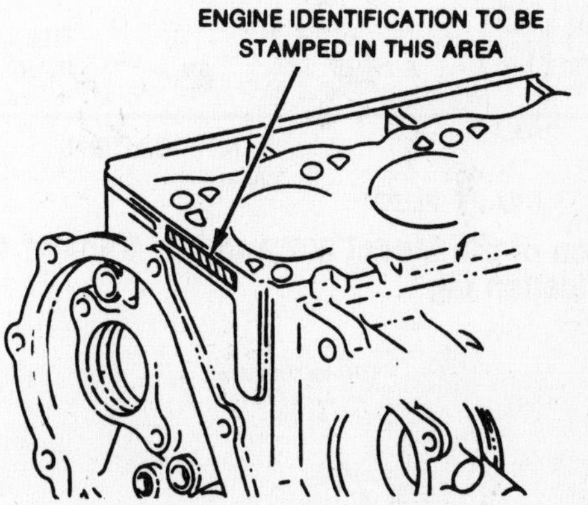
ENGINE IDENTIFICATION TO BE STAMPED IN THIS AREA

Engine identification number location—2.0L engine

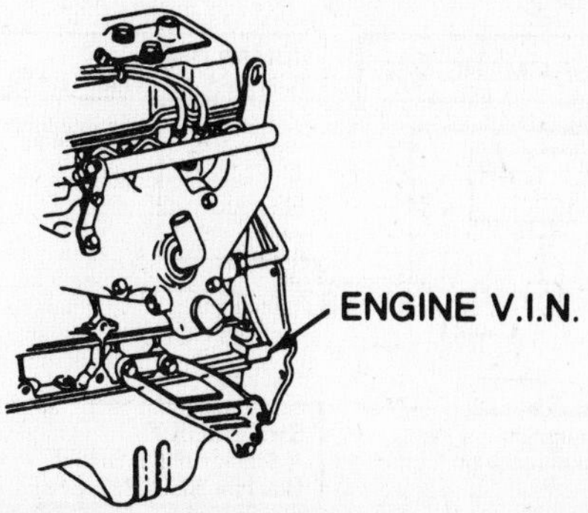
ENGINE V.I.N.

Engine identification number location—1.9L engine

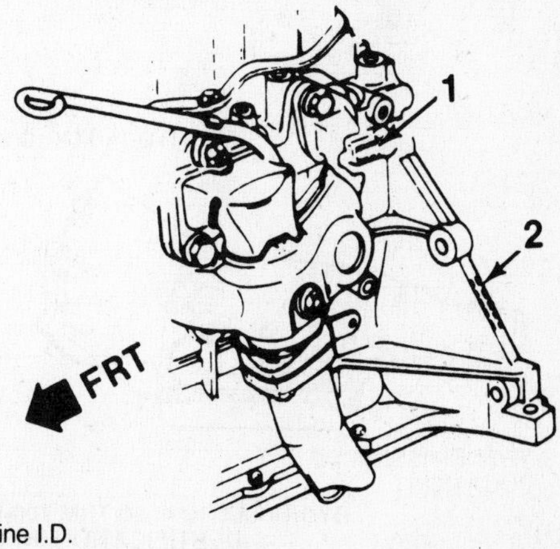
1
2
FRT

1. Engine I.D.
2. Engine I.D. (optional location)

Engine identification number location—2.5L engine

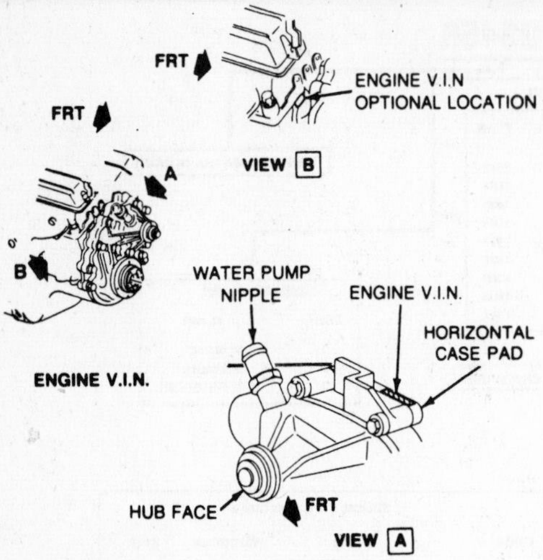
FRT
FRT
ENGINE V.I.N
OPTIONAL LOCATION
VIEW B
A
B
WATER PUMP
NIPPLE
ENGINE V.I.N.
HORIZONTAL
CASE PAD
ENGINE V.I.N.
HUB FACE
FRT
VIEW A

Engine identification number location—2.8L engine

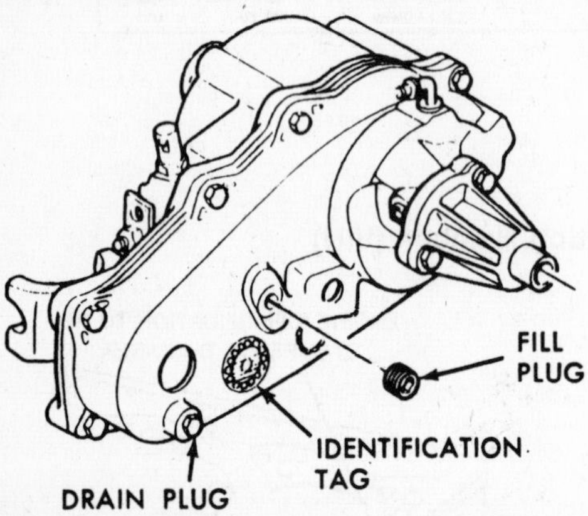
FILL
PLUG
IDENTIFICATION
TAG
DRAIN PLUG

Location of the Model 207 and 231 transfer case identification tag

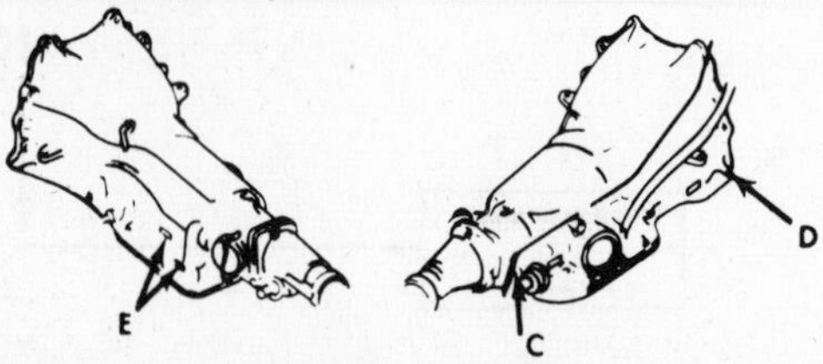
E
C
D

Location of the 220C automatic transmission identification numbers

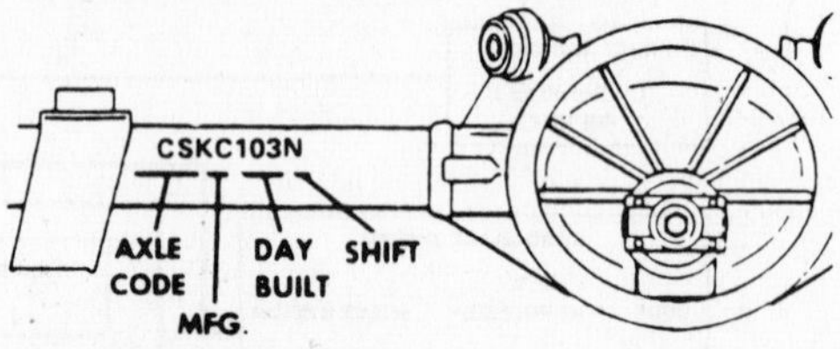
CSKC103N
AXLE
CODE
MFG.
DAY
BUILT
SHIFT

Location and explanation of the rear axle identification number

2.8L Engine

The engine identification code is stamped either on an upward facing, machined surface on the right-front of the block, just below the head, or on the left front of the block just above the water pump.

4.3L Engine

The engine identification number is stamped either on a flat, machined surface, on the right-front of the engine block, just above the water pump, or on the left-rear side of the engine block, where the transmission is joined to the engine.

Transmission

Manual

The transmission identification number is stamped on a met-

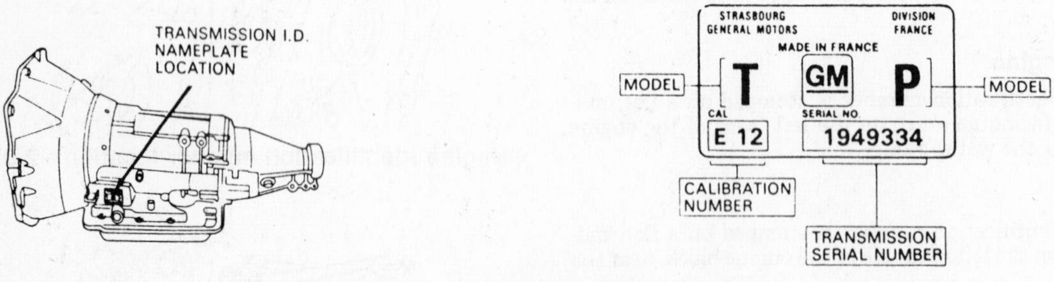
TRANSMISSION I.D.
NAMEPLATE
LOCATION
STRASBOURG
GENERAL MOTORS
DIVISION
FRANCE
MADE IN FRANCE
MODEL
T
GM
P
MODEL
CAL
SERIAL NO.
E 12
1949334
CALIBRATION
NUMBER
TRANSMISSION
SERIAL NUMBER

HYDRA-MATIC 3L30 TRANSMISSION I.D. NAMEPLATE

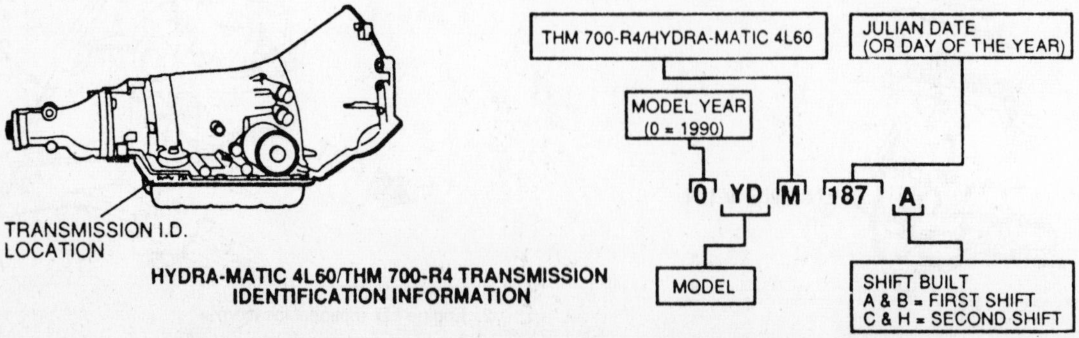
TRANSMISSION I.D.
LOCATION
THM 700-R4/HYDRA-MATIC 4L60
JULIAN DATE
(OR DAY OF THE YEAR)
MODEL YEAR
(0 = 1990)
0 YD M 187 A
MODEL
SHIFT BUILT
A & B = FIRST SHIFT
C & H = SECOND SHIFT

HYDRA-MATIC 4L60/THM 700-R4 TRANSMISSION IDENTIFICATION INFORMATION

180C and 700-R4 automatic transmission identification numbers

al plate which is attached to the extension housing case bolt, on the left-side.

Automatic

- The idenification number for the 180C is located on a metal tag attached to the left-front of the transmission case.
- The identification number, for the 200C (3-spd), is stamped on the right rear-side of the transmission case, behind the modulator.
- The identification number, for the 700-R4, is stamped on the right or left rear-side of the transmission pan rail.

Drive Axle

On rear axles, the identification number is stamped on the right-front side of the axle tube, next to the differential. On front axles, the ID number is stamped on a tag, attached to the differential cover by a cover bolt.

Transfer Case

The model 207 and 231 transfer cases are equipped with an identification tag which is attached to the rear half of the case; the tag gives the model number, the low range reduction ratio and the assembly part number. If for some reason it becomes dislodged or removed, reattach it with an adhesive sealant.

ROUTINE MAINTENANCE

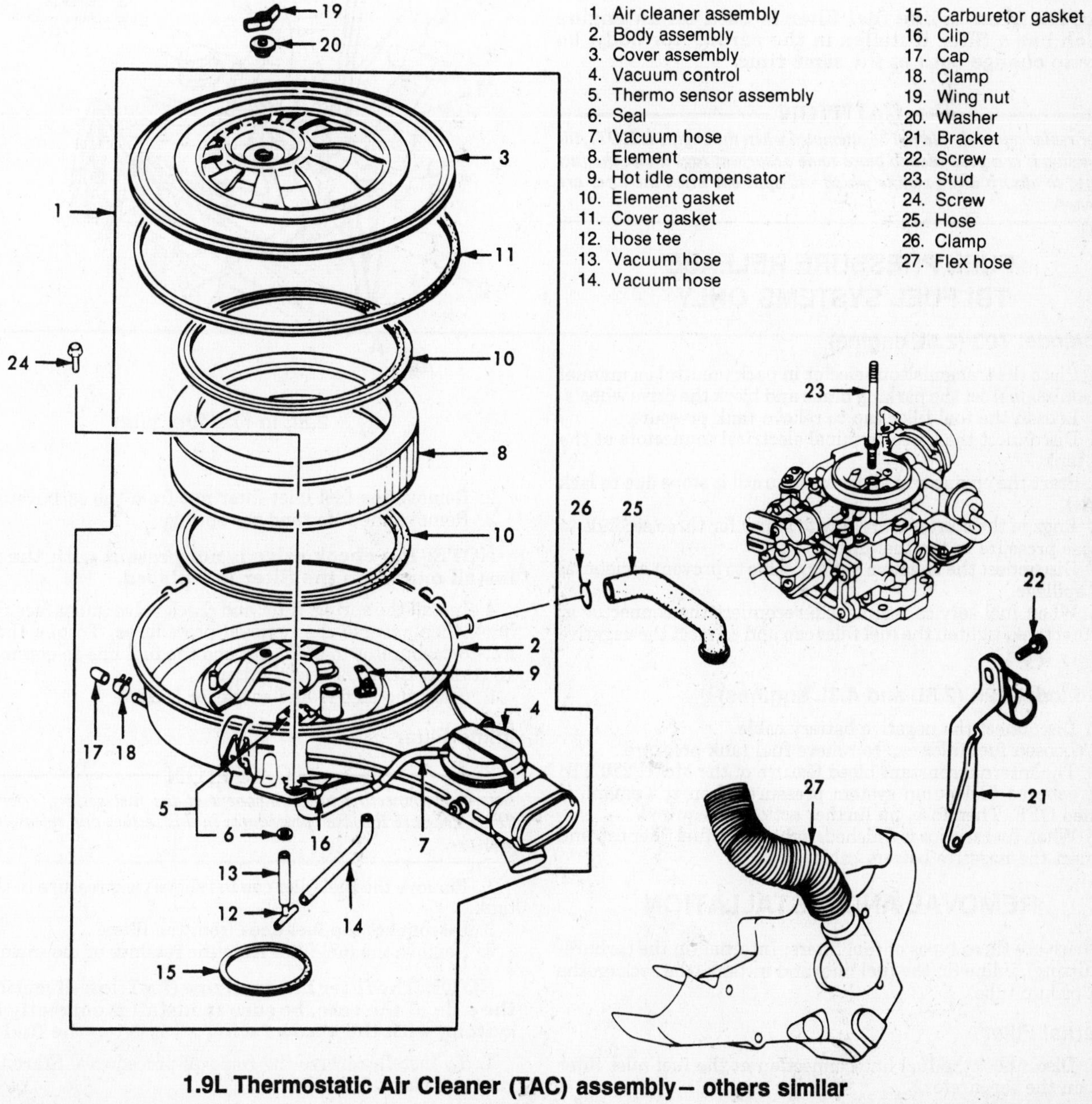

1. Air cleaner assembly
2. Body assembly
3. Cover assembly
4. Vacuum control
5. Thermo sensor assembly
6. Seal
7. Vacuum hose
8. Element
9. Hot idle compensator
10. Element gasket
11. Cover gasket
12. Hose tee
13. Vacuum hose
14. Vacuum hose
15. Carburetor gasket
16. Clip
17. Cap
18. Clamp
19. Wing nut
20. Washer
21. Bracket
22. Screw
23. Stud
24. Screw
25. Hose
26. Clamp
27. Flex hose

1.9L Thermostatic Air Cleaner (TAC) assembly— others similar

Air Cleaner

The air cleaner element is a paper cartridge type, it should be replaced every year or 30,000 miles; if the truck is operated in heavy traffic or under dusty conditions, replace the element at more frequent intervals.

REMOVAL AND INSTALLATION

1. Remove the top of the air cleaner.
2. Remove and discard the paper element.
3. Using a new element, reverse the removal procedures.

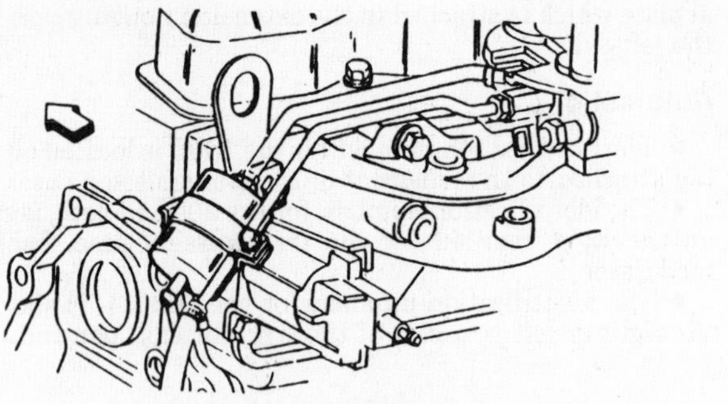

2.5L in-line fuel filter

Gasoline Fuel Filter

The fuel filter should be serviced every 15,000 miles; if operated under severe conditions, change it more often. Three types of fuel filters are used, a pleated-paper element type (with a internal check valve), an in-line type and an in-tank type.

NOTE: If an in-line fuel filter is used on an engine which has a filter installed in the carburetor body, be sure to change both at the same time.

CAUTION

Filter replacement should not be attempted when the engine is HOT. Additionally, it is a good idea to place some absorbent rags under the fuel fittings to absorb any gasoline which will spill out when the lines are loosened.

FUEL PRESSURE RELEASE
TBI FUEL SYSTEMS ONLY

TBI Model 700 (2.5L engine)

1. Place the transmisison selector in park (neutral on manual transmissions) set the parking brake and block the drive wheels.
2. Loosen the fuel filler cap to relieve tank pressure.
3. Disconnect the three terminal electrical connectors at the fuel tank.
4. Start the engine and allow to run until it stops due to lack of fuel.
5. Engage the starter (turn key to start) for three seconds to release pressure in the fuel lines.
6. Disconnect the negative battery cable to prevent accidental fuel spillage.
7. When fuel service is finished, reconnect the connector at the fuel tank, tighten the fuel filler cap and connect the negative battery cable.

TBI Model 220 (2.8L and 4.3L engines)

1. Disconnect the negative battery cable.
2. Loosen fuel filler cap to relieve fuel tank pressure.
3. The internal constant bleed feature of the Model 220 TBI unit relieves fuel pump system pressure when the engine is turned OFF. Therefore, no further action is required.
4. When fuel service is finished, tighten the fuel filler cap and connect the negative battery cable.

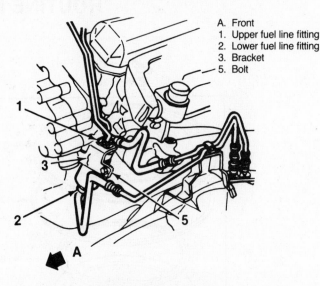

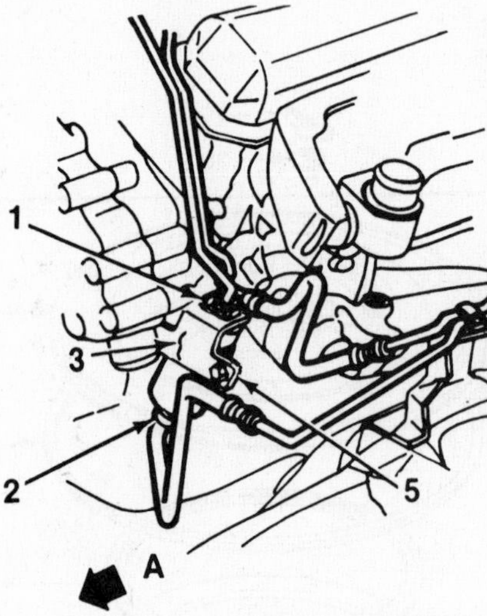
A. Front
1. Upper fuel line fitting
2. Lower fuel line fitting
3. Bracket
5. Bolt
1
2
3
5
A

2.8L in-line fuel filter

REMOVAL AND INSTALLATION

There are three types of fuel filters: Internal (in the carburetor fitting), inline (in the fuel line) and in-tank (the sock on the fuel pickup tube).

Internal Filter

1. Disconnect the fuel line connection at the fuel inlet filter nut on the carburetor.
2. Remove the fuel inlet filter nut from the carburetor.
3. Remove the filter and the spring.

NOTE: If a check valve is not present with the filter, install one when the filter is replaced.

4. Install the spring, filter and check valve (must face the fuel line), then reverse the removal procedures. Torque the filter nut-to-carburetor to 25 ft. lbs. and the fuel line-to-connector to 18 ft. lbs.; DO NOT overtighten.
5. Start the engine and check for leaks.

Inline Filter

CAUTION

Before disconnecting any component of the fuel system, refer to the "Fuel Pressure Release" procedures in this section and release the fuel pressure.

1. Remove the fuel filler cap to relieve the pressure in the fuel tank.
2. Disconnect the fuel lines from the filter.
3. Remove the fuel filter from the retainer or mounting bolt.

NOTE: The filter has an arrow (fuel flow direction) on the side of the case, be sure to install it correctly in the system, with the arrow facing away from the fuel tank.

4. To install, reverse the removal procedures. Start the engine and check for leaks.

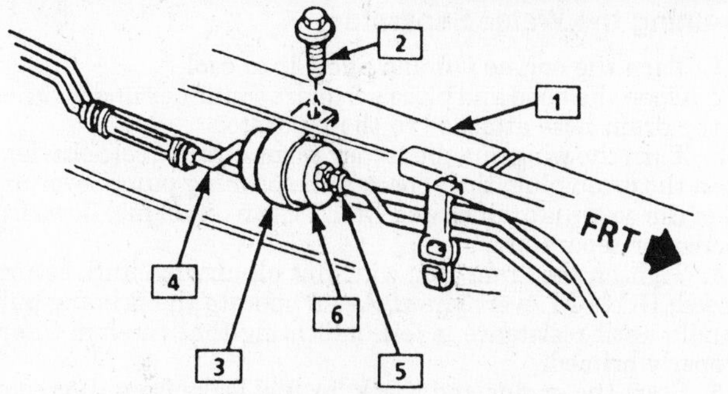
2
1
FRT
4
6
3
5

1 LEFT FRAME SIDE MEMBER

2 BOLT - TIGHTEN 16 N·m (24 lb. ft.)

3 CLAMP

4 REAR FUEL FEED PIPE
TIGHTEN 26 N·m (20 lb. ft.)

5 INTERMEDIATE FUEL FEED PIPE
TIGHTEN 26 N·m (20 lb. ft.)

6 IN - LINE FUEL FILTER

4.3L in-line fuel filter

10. Liquid-vapor separator
11. Return tube
12. Fuel tube
13. Coupler and sound insulator
14. Fuel level sender
15. Electric fuel pump
16. Filter strainer

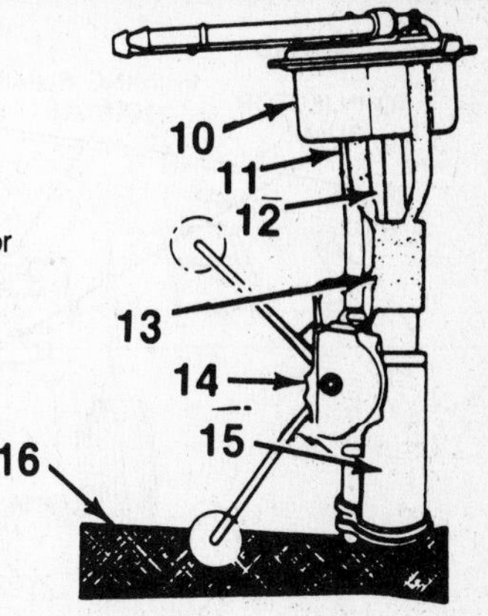
10
11
12
13
14
15
16

Fuel injected engine in-tank fuel filter

In-Tank Filter

To service the in-tank fuel filter, refer to the "Electric Fuel Pump Removal and Installation" procedures in Section 4.

Diesel Fuel Filter

REMOVAL AND INSTALLATION

Filter Element

1. Disconnect the negative battery terminal.
2. Disconnect the water sensor wire connector from the filter assembly.
3. Disconnect the water sensor-to-main body hose.
4. Using a filter band wrench, remove the fuel filter element by turning the cartridge counterclockwise, while being careful not to spill diesel fuel from the element.
5. Drain the fuel from the element into a container and discard it. Take precautions to avoid the risk of fire during replacement procedures.
6. Remove the water and heater sensor from the bottom of the used filter element.
7. Apply a thin coat of diesel fuel to the water sensor O-ring, then install the water and heater sensor on the bottom of the replacement filter element and tighten.
8. Wipe all filter sealing surfaces clean before installing the new filter and apply a thin coat of diesel fuel to the gasket on the new fuel filter element.
9. Install the new filter element by turning it clockwise until the gasket contacts the sealing surfaces on the main filter body. Hand tighten another ⅔ of a turn after the gasket contacts the sealing surface; DO NOT overtighten.
10. Reconnect the water sensor wiring connector, then disconnect the fuel outlet hose from the injection pump and place the end in a clean container.
11. Operate the priming pump handle on the injection pump several times to fill the new filter with fuel, until fuel flows from

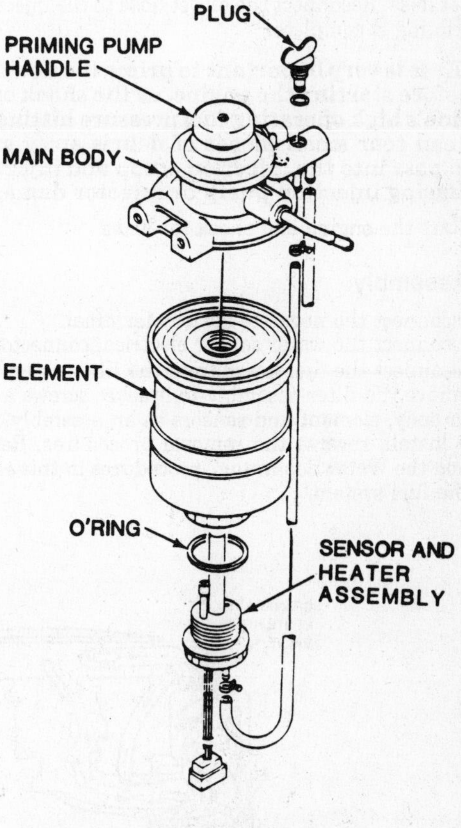
PLUG
PRIMING PUMP HANDLE
MAIN BODY
ELEMENT
O'RING
SENSOR AND HEATER ASSEMBLY

MOUNTED ON FILTER BRACKET

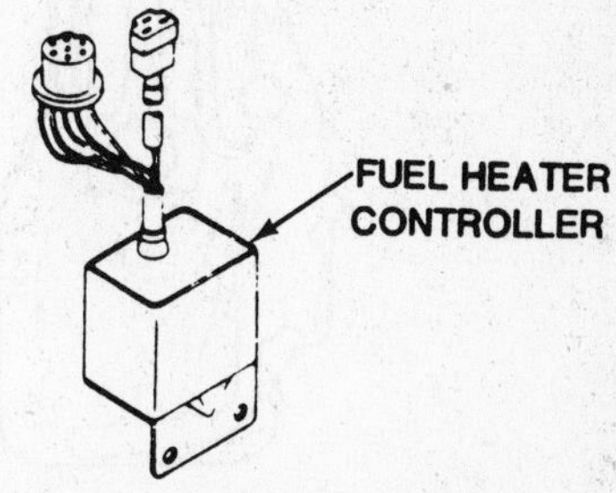
FUEL HEATER CONTROLLER

2.2L diesel fuel heater controller

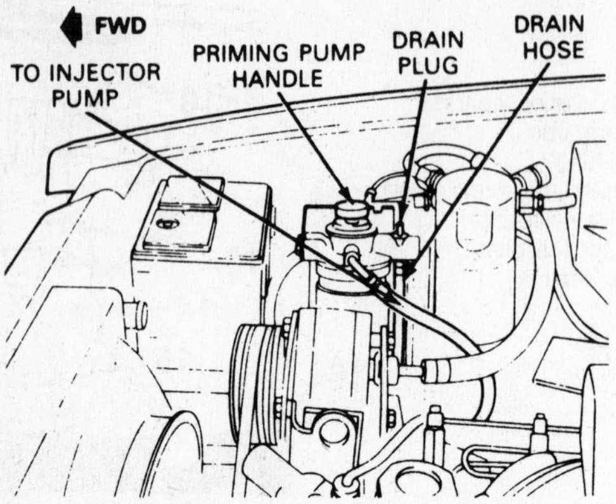
FWD
TO INJECTOR PUMP
PRIMING PUMP HANDLE
DRAIN PLUG
DRAIN HOSE

Typical diesel fuel filter assembly

the outlet hose. Reconnect the outlet hose to the injection pump when priming is complete.

NOTE: It is very important to prime the new filter element before starting the engine, as the shock of the diesel engine's high operating fuel pressure hitting a dry element can tear small pieces of debris away and allow them to pass into the injection pump and injectors, possibly causing injection pump or injector damage.

12. Start the engine and check for leaks.

Filter Assembly

1. Disconnect the negative battery terminal.
2. Disconnect the water sensor electrical connector.
3. Disconnect the fuel hoses from the filter assembly.
4. Remove the filter assembly-to-bracket screws and the filter main body, element and sensors as an assembly.
5. To install, reverse the removal procedures. Refer to the "Draining the Water Separator" procedures in this section and prime the fuel system.

Draining the Water Separator

1. Turn the engine Off and allow it to cool.
2. Open the hood and place a 2 quart container under the end of the drain hose attached to the separator.
3. Turn the wing nut about four turns **counterclockwise** to open the drain plug, then operate the priming pump lever until all of the water is drained and ONLY clean diesel fuel flows from the water separator.
4. Tighten the drain plug wing nut **clockwise** until securely closed; DO NOT overtighten. Again operate the priming pump handle until resistance is felt, indicating that the fuel filter is properly primed.
5. Start the engine and check for fuel leaks from the separator and fuel lines. Make sure the "Water In Fuel" light is Off; if the light remains On, the fuel tank must be purged of water with a siphon hose and hand pump fed into the tank through the fuel filter.

CAUTION

DO NOT attempt to siphon any fuel tank contents by using mouth suction to start the siphon effect. Diesel fuel is poisonous and is by far the worst tasting stuff you can imagine. Use a hand siphon pump or power drill attachment to pull the water from the fuel tank.

Positive Crankcase Ventilation (PCV)

The PCV valve is attached to the valve cover by a rubber grommet and connected to the intake manifold through a ventilation hose. Inspect the PCV system and replace the PCV valve and filter (located in the air cleaner) every 30,000 miles.

FUNCTIONAL CHECK

If the engine is idling rough, check for a clogged PCV valve, dirty vent filter or air cleaner element, or plugged hose. Test the system using the following procedure and replace components as necessary.

1. Remove the PCV valve from the rocker cover.
2. Run the engine at idle and place your thumb over the end of the valve to check for vacuum.

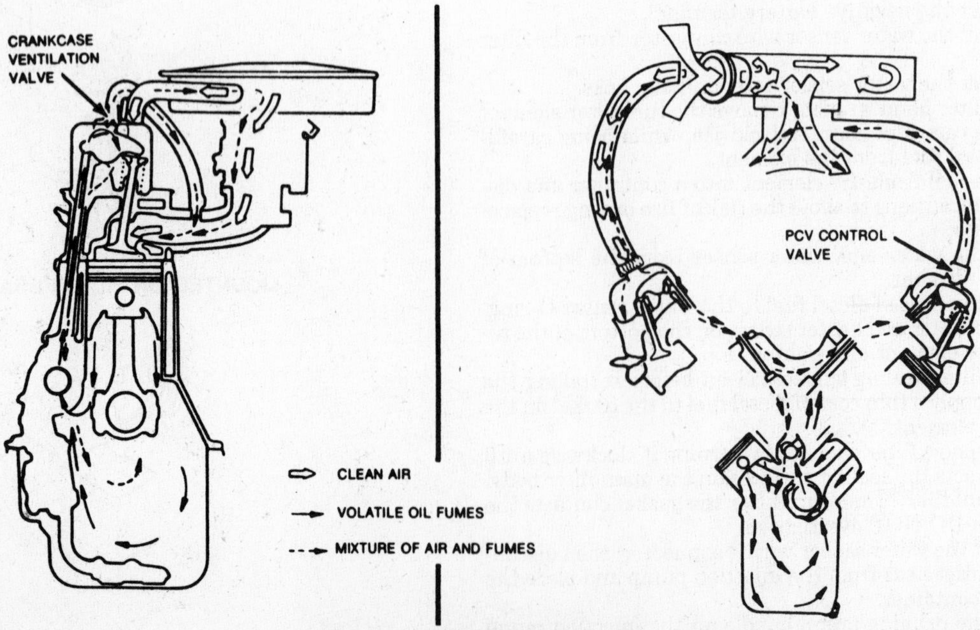
CRANKCASE VENTILATION VALVE
CLEAN AIR
VOLATILE OIL FUMES
MIXTURE OF AIR AND FUMES
PCV CONTROL VALVE

PCV flow through the engine

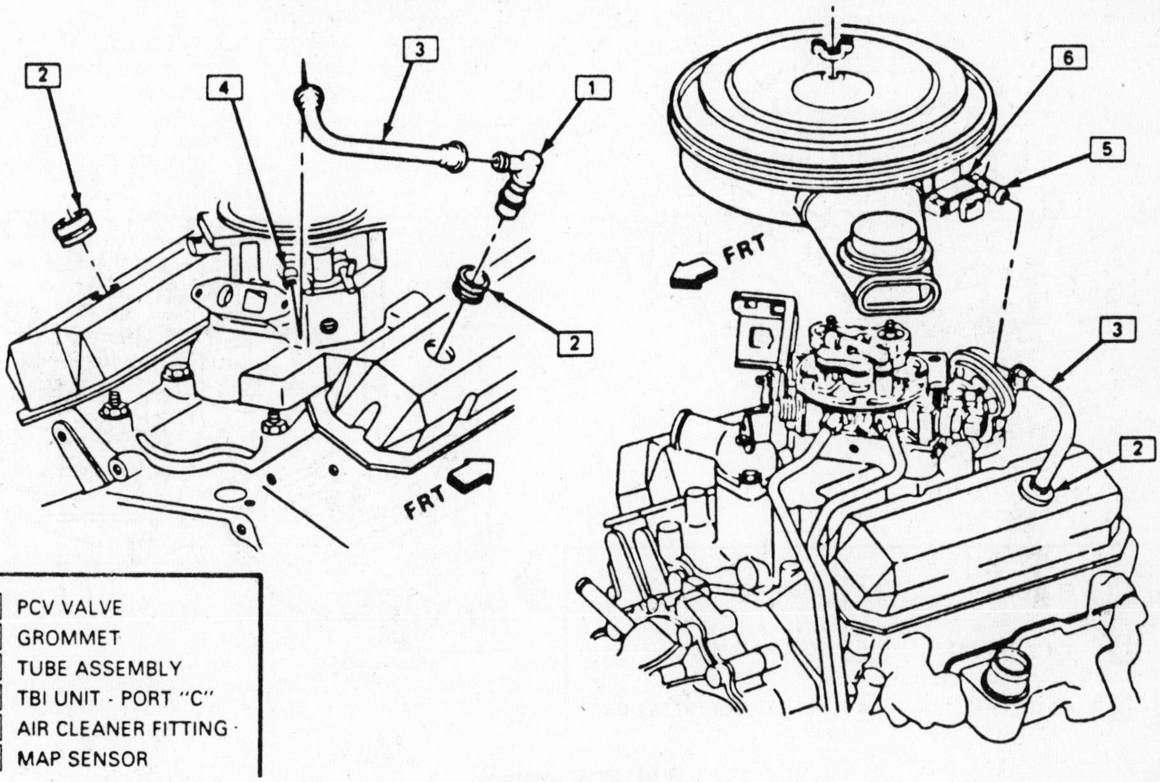
FRT
FRT
1 PCV VALVE
2 GROMMET
3 TUBE ASSEMBLY
4 TBI UNIT - PORT "C"
5 AIR CLEANER FITTING
6 MAP SENSOR

2.8L PCV system

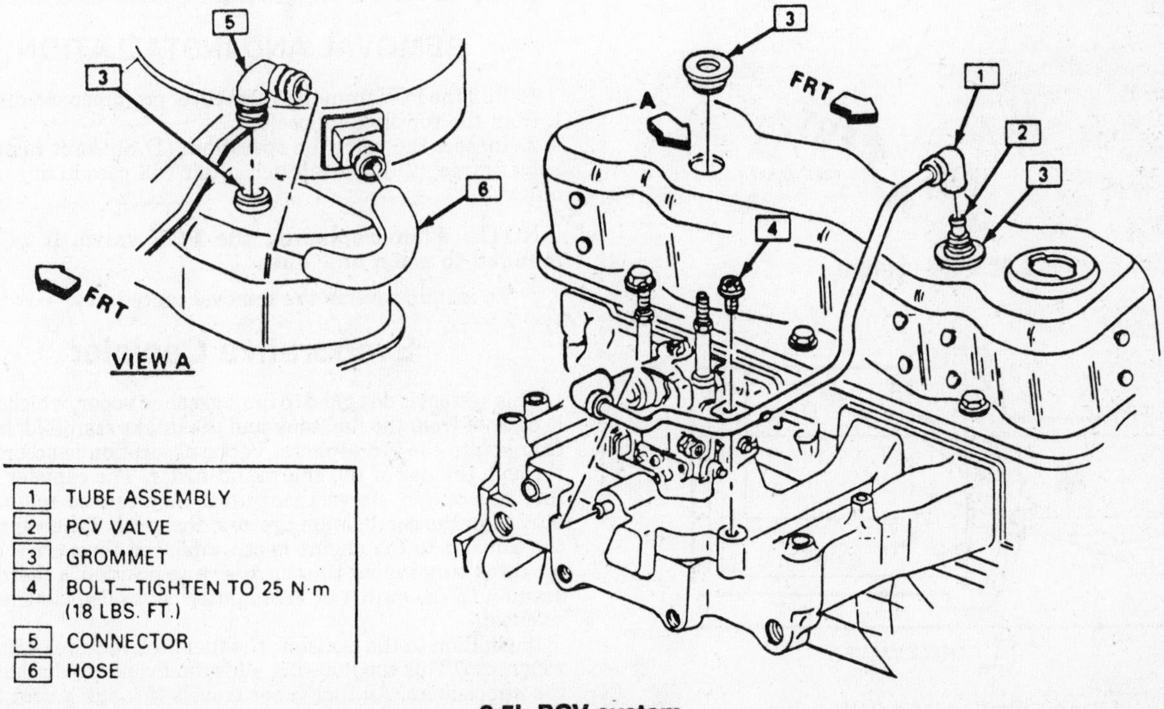
A
FRT
FRT
VIEW A
1 TUBE ASSEMBLY
2 PCV VALVE
3 GROMMET
4 BOLT—TIGHTEN TO 25 N·m (18 LBS. FT.)
5 CONNECTOR
6 HOSE

2.5L PCV system

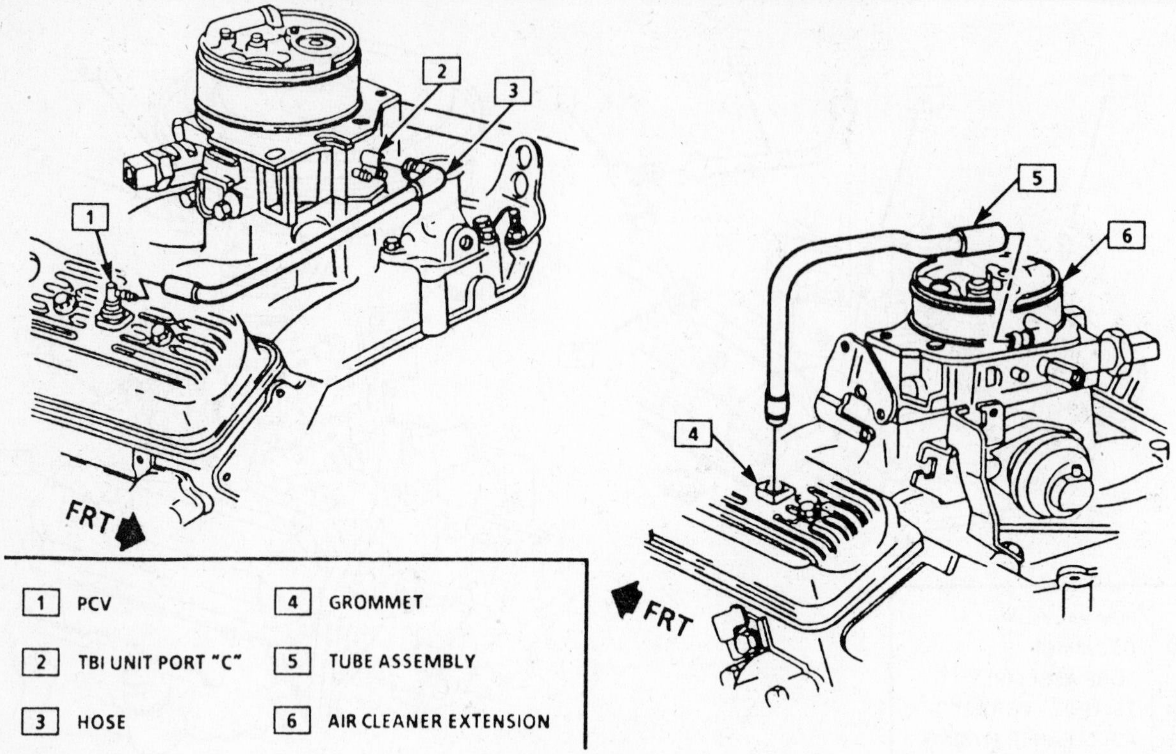
1
2
3
4
5
6
FRT
FRT
1 PCV
2 TBI UNIT PORT "C"
3 HOSE
4 GROMMET
5 TUBE ASSEMBLY
6 AIR CLEANER EXTENSION

4.3L PCV system

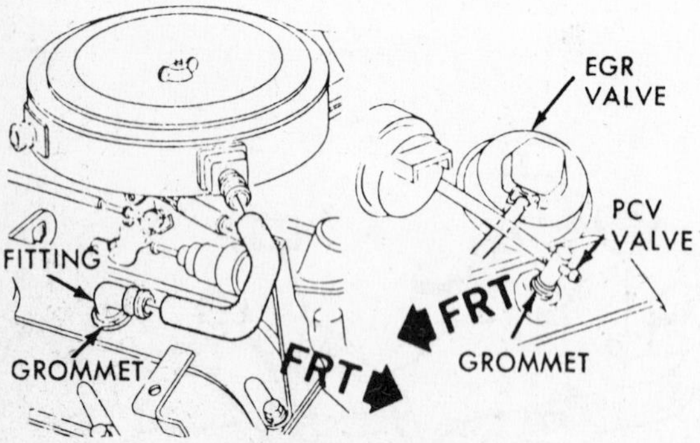
EGR
VALVE
PCV
VALVE
FITTING
GROMMET
FRT
FRT
GROMMET

2.0L PCV system

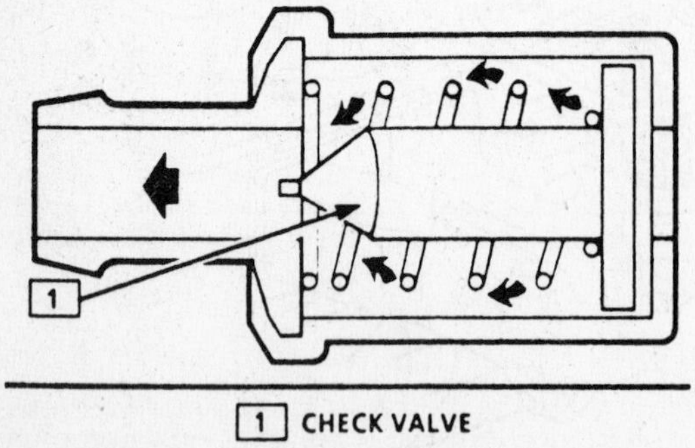
1
1 CHECK VALVE

Cross section of a PCV valve

3.If no vacuum exists, check for plugged hoses, manifold port vacuum at the carburetor or TBI unit, or a defective PCV valve.
4.To check PCV valve, remove the valve from the hose and shake it. If a rattling noise is heard, the valve is good. If no noise is heard, the valve is plugged and replacement is necessary.

REMOVAL AND INSTALLATION

1. Pull the PCV from the valve cover grommet and disconnect it from the ventilation hose(s).
2. Inspect the valve for operation: (1) Shake it to see if the valve is free; (2) Blow through it (air will pass in one direction only).

NOTE: When replacing the PCV valve, it is recommended to use a new one.

3. To install, reverse the removal procedures.

Evaporative Canister

This system is designed to limit gasoline vapor, which normally escapes from the fuel tank and the intake manifold, from discharge into the atmosphere. Vapor absorption is accomplished through the use of the charcoal canister. The canister absorbs fuel vapors and stores them until they can be removed and burned in the combustion process. Removal of the vapors from the canister to the engine is accomplished through: a canister mounted purge valve, the throttle valve position, a thermostatic vacuum (TVS) switch or a computer controlled canister purge solenoid.

In addition to the canister, the fuel tank requires a non-vented gas cap. This cap does not allow fuel vapor to discharge into the atmosphere. All fuel vapor travels through a vent line, inserted high into the domed fuel tank, directly to the canister.

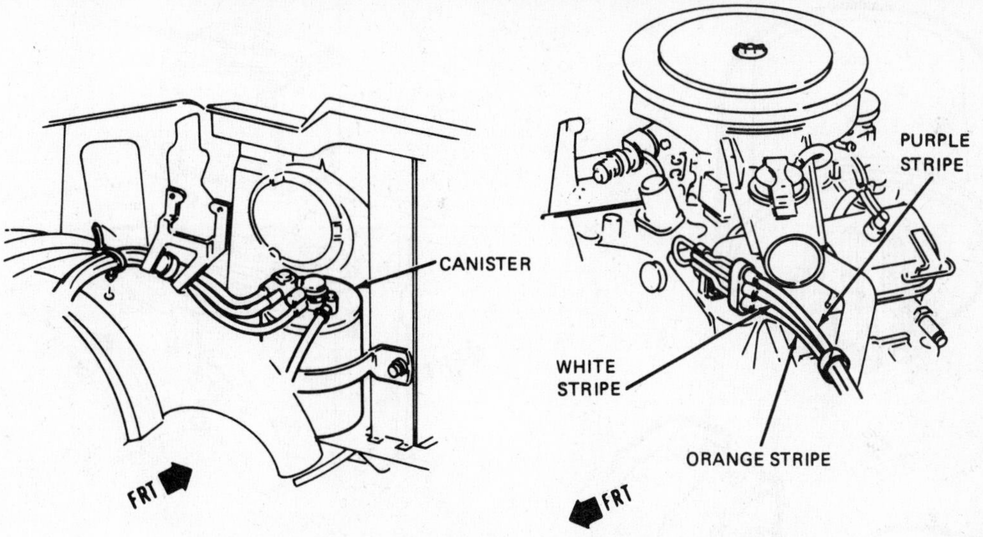
CANISTER
PURPLE
STRIPE
WHITE
STRIPE
ORANGE STRIPE
FRT
FRT

4-cylinder engine evaporative canister and hoses

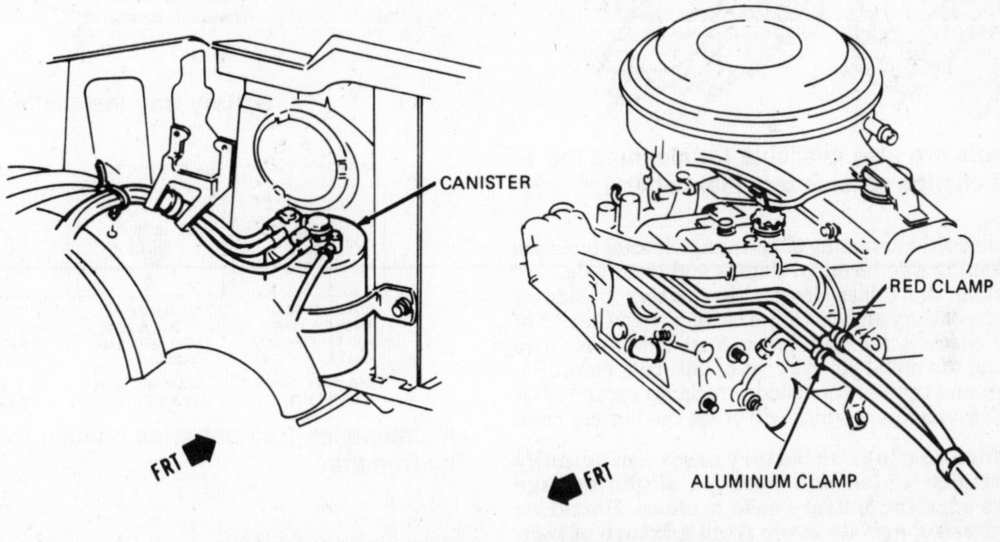
CANISTER
RED CLAMP
ALUMINUM CLAMP
FRT
FRT

6-cylinder evaporative canister and hoses

SERVICING

Every 30,000 miles or 24 months, check all fuel, vapor lines and hoses for proper hookup, routing and condition. If equipped, check that the bowl vent and purge valves work properly. Remove the canister and check for cracks or damage and replace (if necessary).

FUNCTIONAL TEST

1. Apply a short length of hose to the lower tube of the purge valve and attempt to blow through it. Little or no air should pass into the canister.
2. With a hand vacuum pump, apply a vacuum of 15 in. Hg to the control valve tube (upper tube). If the diaphragm does not hold vacuum for at least 20 seconds, the diaphragm is leaking and the canister must be replaced.
3. If the diaphragm holds vacuum, again try to bolw through the hose connected to the lower tube while vacuum is still being applied. An increased flow of air should be observed. If not, the canister must be replaced.

REMOVAL AND INSTALLATION

1. Label and disconnect the charcoal canister vent hoses.
2. Remove the canister-to-bracket bolt.
3. Lift the canister from the bracket.
4. To install, reverse the removal procedures.

Battery

All S-10/S-15 Pickups have a Maintenance Free battery as standard equipment, eliminating the need for fluid level checks and the possibility of specific gravity tests. Nevertheless, the battery does require some attention.

At least once a year, the battery terminals and the cable clamps should be cleaned. Remove the side terminal bolts and the cables, negative cable first. Clean the cable clamps and the battery terminals with a wire brush until all corrosion, grease, etc. is removed and the metal is shiny. It is especially important to clean the inside of the clamp thoroughly. A small deposit of foreign material or oxidation will prevent a sound electrical con-

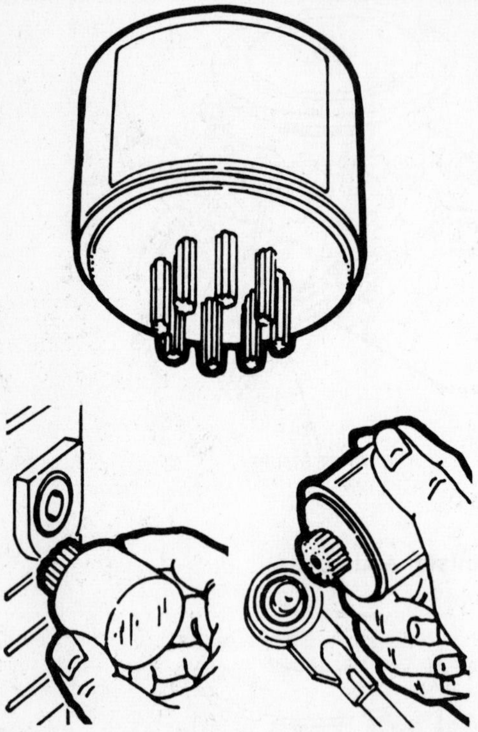

Special tools are also available for cleaning the posts and clamps on side terminal batteries

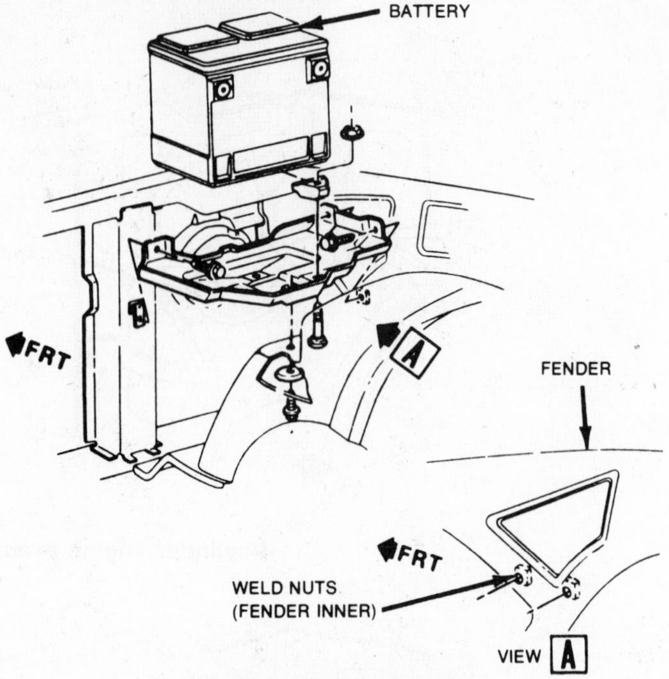
BATTERY
FRT
A
FENDER
FRT
WELD NUTS
(FENDER INNER)
VIEW A

Battery tray installation

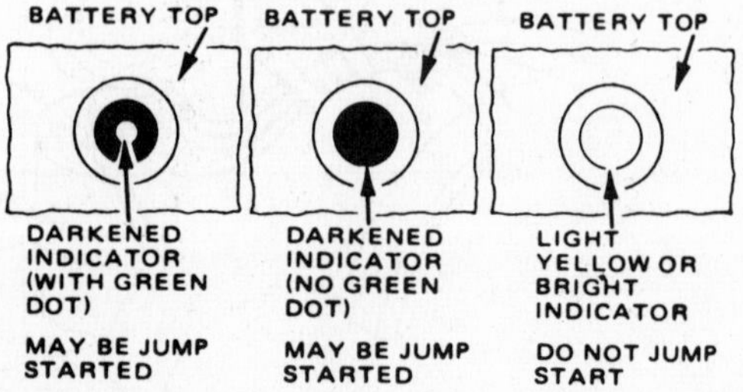
BATTERY TOP
BATTERY TOP
BATTERY TOP
DARKENED INDICATOR (WITH GREEN DOT)
MAY BE JUMP STARTED
DARKENED INDICATOR (NO GREEN DOT)
MAY BE JUMP STARTED
LIGHT YELLOW OR BRIGHT INDICATOR
DO NOT JUMP START

Maintenance-free batteries contain their own built in hydrometer

nection and inhibit either starting or charging. Special tools are available for cleaning side terminal clamps and terminals.

Before installing the cables, loosen the battery holddown clamp, remove the battery and check the battery tray. Clear it of any debris and check it for soundness. Rust should be wire brushed away and the metal given a coat of anti-rust paint. Replace the battery and tighten the holddown clamp securely but be careful not to overtighten, which will crack the battery case.

NOTE: Surface coatings on battery cases can actually conduct electricity which will cause a slight voltage drain, so make sure the battery case is clean. Batteries can be cleaned using a paste made from mixture of baking soda and water. Spread the paste on any corrosion, wait a few minutes, and rinse with water. Finish the job by cleaning metal parts with a wire brush.

After the clamps and terminals are clean, reinstall the cables, negative cable last. Give the clamps and terminals a thin external coat of nonmetallic grease after installation, to retard corrosion.

Check the cables at the same time that the terminals are cleaned. If the cable insulation is cracked, broken or the ends are frayed, the cable should be replaced with a new one of the same length and gauge.

CAUTION

Keep flames or sparks away from the battery. It gives off explosive hydrogen gas. The battery electrolyte contains sulphuric acid. If you should get any on your skin or in your eyes, flush the affected areas with plenty of clear water. If it lands in your eyes, seek medical help immediately.

Testing the Maintenance Free Battery

Maintenance free batteries, do not require normal attention as far as fluid level checks are concerned. However, the terminals require periodic cleaning, which should be performed at least once a year.

The sealed top battery cannot be checked for charge in the normal manner, since there is no provision for access to the electrolyte. To check the condition of the battery:

1. If the indicator eye on top of the battery is dark, the battery has enough fluid. If the eye is lit, the electrolyte fluid is too low and the battery must be replaced.
2. If a green dot appears in the middle of the eye, the battery is sufficiently charged. Proceed to Step 4. If no green dot is visible, go to Step 3.
3. Charge the battery.

NOTE: DO NOT charge the battery for more than 50 amp-hours. If the green dot appears or if the electrolyte squirts out of the vent hole, stop the charge and proceed to Step 4.

It may be necessary to tip the battery from side-to-side to get the green dot to appear after charging.

CAUTION

When charging the battery, the electrical system and control unit can be quickly damaged by improper connections, high output battery chargers or incorrect service procedures.

4. Connect a battery load tester and a voltmeter across the battery terminals (the battery cables should be disconnected

Battery	Test Load (Amps)
83–50	150
83-60	180
85A-60	170
87A-60	230
89A-60	270
1981103	200
1981104	250
1981105	270
1981577	260

Battery test load specifications chart

Charging Rate Amps	Time
75	40 min
50	1 hr
25	2 hr
10	5 hr

Battery charging rates chart

Temperature (°F)	Minimum Voltage
70 or above	9.6
60	9.5
50	9.4
40	9.3
30	9.1
20	8.9
10	8.7
0	8.5

Battery minimum voltage chart

from the battery). Apply a 300 amp load to the battery for 15 seconds to remove the surface charge. Remove the load.

5. Wait 15 seconds to allow the battery to recover. Apply the appropriate test load, as specified in the chart:

Apply the load for 15 seconds while reading the voltage. Disconnect the load.

6. Check the results against the chart. If the battery voltage is at or above the specified voltage for the temperature listed, the battery is good. It the voltage falls below what's listed, the battery should be replaced.

Early Fuel Evaporation (EFE) Heater

The EFE heating system is used on all carbureted engines. The purpose of the heating unit is to further vaporize the fuel droplets as they enter the intake manifold; vaporization of the air/fuel mixture ensures complete combustion which provides the maximum power and minimum emissions output for the fuel used.

REMOVAL AND INSTALLATION

Heater Unit

The EFE heater unit is located directly under the carburetor and is electrically operated.

1. Disconnect the negative battery terminal. Remove the air cleaner.
2. From the carburetor, disconnect the vacuum hoses, electrical connectors and fuel hoses. Disconnect the EFE Heater electrical connector from the wiring harness.

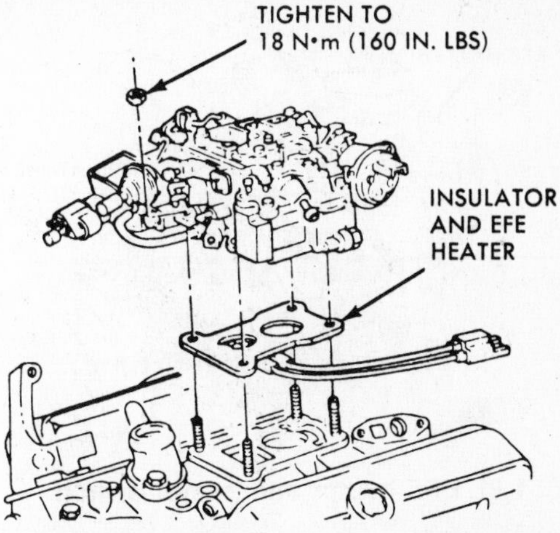
TIGHTEN TO
18 N•m (160 IN. LBS)
INSULATOR
AND EFE
HEATER

Carbureted 2.8L EFE heater assembly

3. Remove the carburetor-to-intake manifold nuts and the carburetor from the manifold. Lift the EFE Heater from the intake manifold.
4. Using a putty knife, clean the gasket mounting surfaces.
5. To install, use new gaskets and reverse the removal procedures. Torque the carburetor-to-intake manifold nuts to 13 ft. lbs.

Heater Switch

The heater switch is located near the thermostat housing (2.8L carbureted engine), on the bottom rear-side of the intake manifold (2.0L carbureted engine) or on the top right-side of the engine (1.9L carbureted engine).

1. Using a drain pan, position it under the radiator, then open the drain cock and drain the coolant to a level below the heater switch.

CAUTION

When draining the coolant, keep in mind that cats and dogs are attracted by the ethylene glycol antifreeze, and are quite likely to drink any that is left in an uncovered container or in puddles on the ground. This will prove fatal in sufficient quantity. Always drain the coolant into a sealable container. Coolant should be reused unless it is contaminated or several years old.

2. Disconnect the wiring harness connector from the EFE heater switch.
3. Remove the EFE heater switch (turn it counterclockwise) from the intake manifold.
4. To install the new EFE heater switch, coat the threads with a soft setting sealant and torque it to 10 ft. lbs. Reconnect the wiring harness connector to the EFE heater switch. Refill the cooling system.

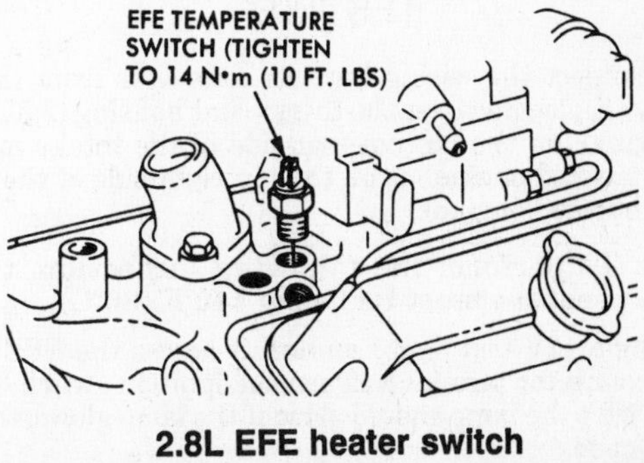
EFE TEMPERATURE
SWITCH (TIGHTEN
TO 14 N•m (10 FT. LBS)

2.8L EFE heater switch

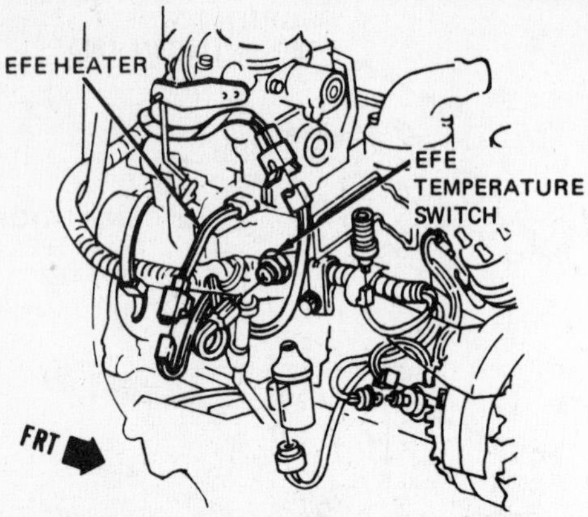
EFE HEATER
EFE TEMPERATURE SWITCH
FRT

1.9L EFE heater and heater switch

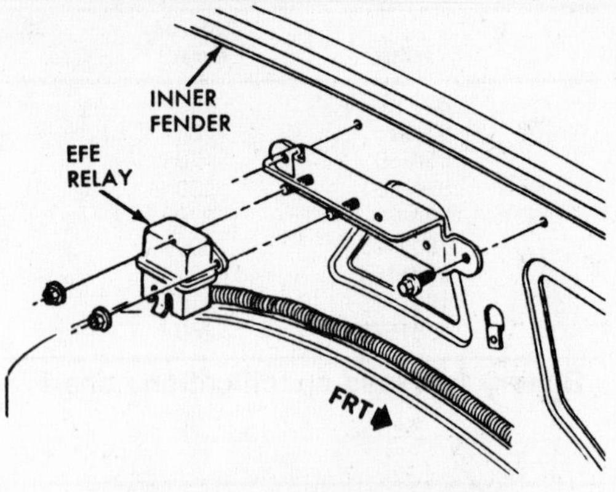
INNER FENDER
EFE RELAY
FRT

2.8L EFE heater switch relay

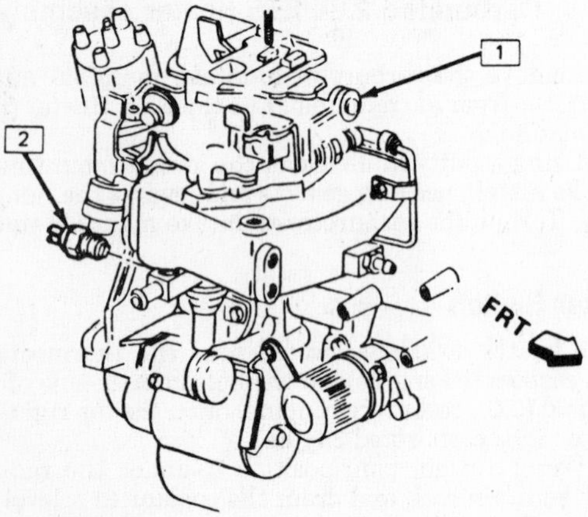
1
2
FRT

1. Carburetor
2. EFE heater switch

2.0L EFE heater switch on the 2.0L engine

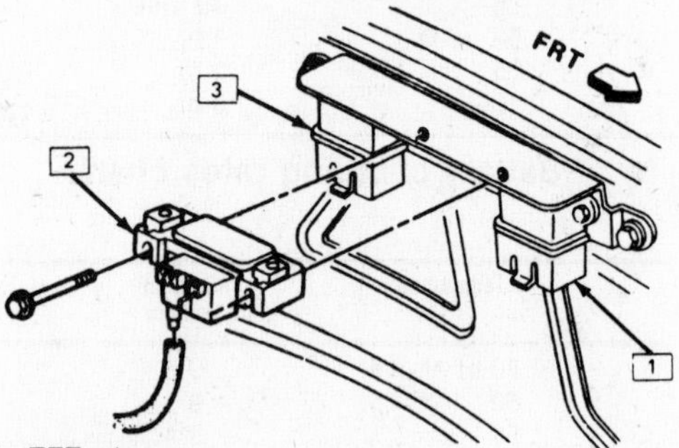
FRT
3
2
1

1. EFE relay
2. Manifold differential pressure sensor
3. W.O.T. relay

1984–85 EFE heater switch relay

NOTE: When applying sealant to the EFE heater, be careful not to coat the sensor and/or the switch.

Heater Switch Relay

The heater switch relay is located on the left-fender.

1. Disconnect the negative battery terminal.
2. Disconnect the wiring harness connector(s) from the heater switch relay.
3. Remove the heater switch relay-to-bracket screw and the relay from the truck.
4. To install, use a new relay and reverse the removal procedures.

TESTING

1. Disconnect the wiring harness connector from the EFE heater switch, located near the thermostat housing (2.8L carbureted engine), on the bottom rear-side of the intake manifold (2.0L carbureted engine) or on the top right-side of the engine (1.9L carbureted engine).

NOTE: To perform the following inspection, the engine temperature must be below 140°F (60°C).

2. Using a 12V test lamp, connect it across the EFE wiring harness connector terminals. Turn the ignition switch On (the engine is Off), the lamp should glow; if the lamp glows, the EFE heater is good.
3. If the lamp does not glow, reconnect the wiring harness connector to the EFE heater switch.
4. Using a DC voltmeter, place it on the 0–15V scale, insert the test probes into the rear of the wiring harness connector body (the black wire is to be grounded) and measure the voltage; it should read 11–13V.
5. If the voltage is not 11–13V, insure that the black wire is grounded; if the voltage is not 0V, the black (grounded) wire is an Open circuit, repair it.
6. If the voltage is 0V, check for voltage-to-ground at each heater switch terminal—the voltage at each switch terminal should be 11–13V.
7. If one terminal measures 11–13V and the other is low or 0V, check the connector for deformed terminals and repair, as necessary.
8. If the electrical connector is making proper contact, replace the EFE heater switch.
9. If the voltage is not 11–13V at each switch terminal, check the wiring harness circuit between the heater switch and the ignition switch, then repair as necessary.
10. Start the engine, allow it to warm to 170°F (76.7°C), then check the voltage across the EFE heater terminals; it should be 0V. If the voltage is not 0V, replace the EFE heater switch.

Accessory Drive Belts

INSPECTION

Check the drive belt(s) every 15,000 miles/12 months (heavy usage) or 30,000 miles/24 months (light usage) for evidence of wear such as cracking, fraying and incorrect tension. Determine the belt tension at a point halfway between the pulleys by pressing on the belt with moderate thumb pressure. The belt should

HOW TO SPOT WORN V-BELTS

V–Belts are vital to efficient engine operation—they drive the fan, water pump and other accessories. They require little maintenance (occasional tightening) but they will not last forever. Slipping or failure of the V–belt will lead to overheating. If your V–belt looks like any of these, it should be replaced.

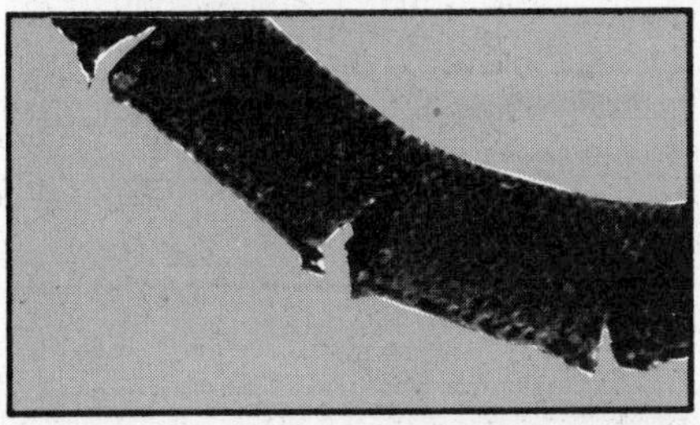

Cracking or Weathering

This belt has deep cracks, which cause it to flex. Too much flexing leads to heat build–up and premature failure. These cracks can be caused by using the belt on a pulley that is too small. Notched belts are available for small diameter pulleys.

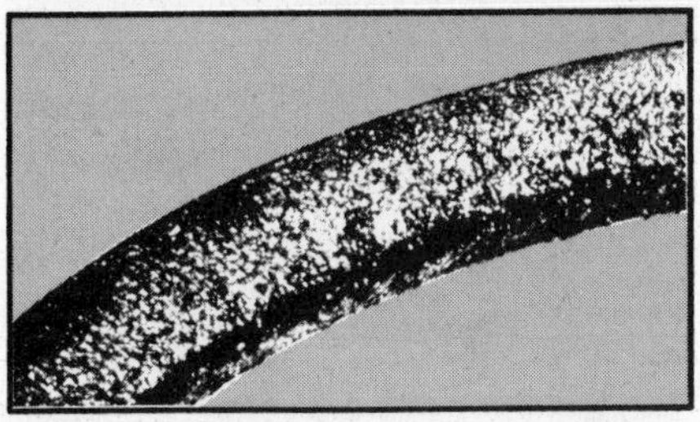

Softening (Grease and Oil)

Oil and grease on a belt can cause the belt's rubber compounds to soften and separate from the reinforcing cords that hold the belt together. The belt will first slip, then finally fail altogether.

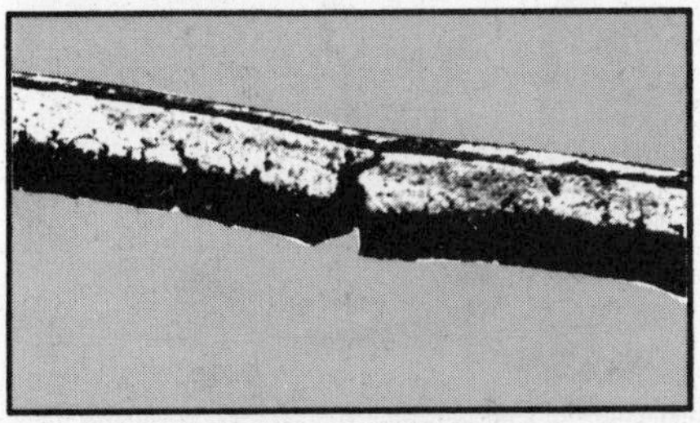

Glazing

Glazing is caused by a belt that is slipping. A slipping belt can cause a run-down battery, erratic power steering, overheating or poor accessory performance. The more the belt slips, the more glazing will be built up on the surface of the belt. The more the belt is glazed, the more it will slip. If the glazing is light, tighten the belt.

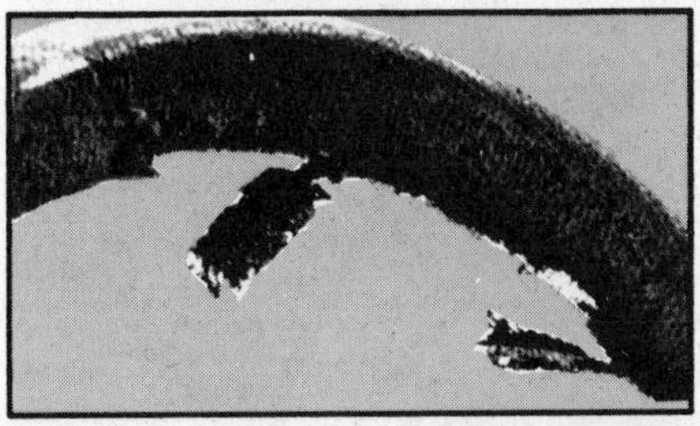

Worn Cover

The cover of this belt is worn off and is peeling away. The reinforcing cords will begin to wear and the belt will shortly break. When the belt cover wears in spots or has a rough jagged appearance, check the pulley grooves for roughness.

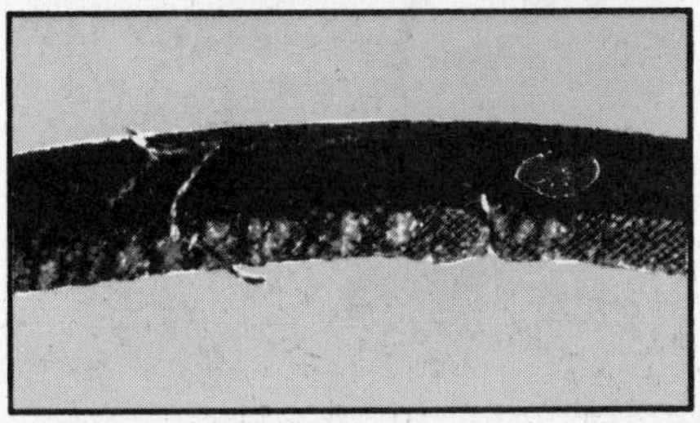

Separation

This belt is on the verge of breaking and leaving you stranded. The layers of the belt are separating and the reinforcing cords are exposed. It's just a matter of time before it breaks completely.

BELT TENSION SPECIFICATIONS

(all measurements in lbs.)

Year	Engine No. Cyl. Displacement Liters (cu. in.)	VIN Code	Tensioning	Alternator	Power Steering	Air Conditioning	Air Pump
1982-85	4-1.9 (118.9)	A	New	135	135	157	135
			Used	67	67	90	67
	6-2.8 (173)	B	New	146	135	146	135
			Used	67	67	67	67
1983-84	4-2.0 (121)	Y	New	146	146	169	146
			Used	67	67	90	67
1983-85	4-2.2 (136.6)	S	New	135	135	135	135
			Used	79	79	79	79
1985-91	4-2.5 (151)	E	New	146	146	169	—
			Used	67 ① ②	67 ① ②	90 ②	— ②
1986-91	6-2.8 (173)	R	New	135	135	146	146
			Used	67 ②	67 ②	67 ②	67 ②
1988-91	6-4.3 (262)	Z	New	②	②	②	②
			Used				

① With A/C: (new) 169 lbs. (used) 90 lbs.

② 1987–91 engines are equipped with serpentine belts and automatic tensioners; no adjustments are necessary.

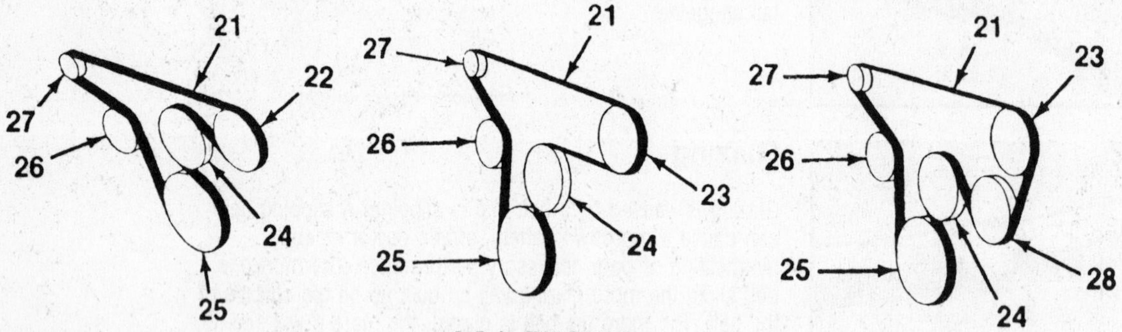
21
22
27
26
24
25
27
21
26
23
24
25
21
23
27
26
25
28
24

2.5 L ENGINE

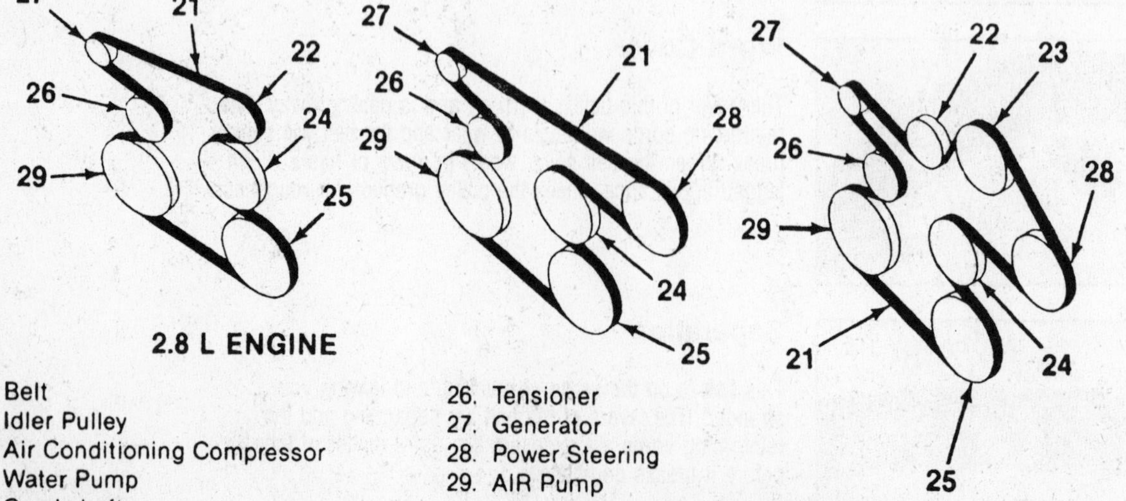
27
21
22
26
24
29
25
27
26
21
29
28
24
25
27
22
23
26
28
29
21
24
25

2.8 L ENGINE

21. Belt
22. Idler Pulley
23. Air Conditioning Compressor
24. Water Pump
25. Crankshaft
26. Tensioner
27. Generator
28. Power Steering
29. AIR Pump

2.5L and 2.8L serpentine drive belt routing

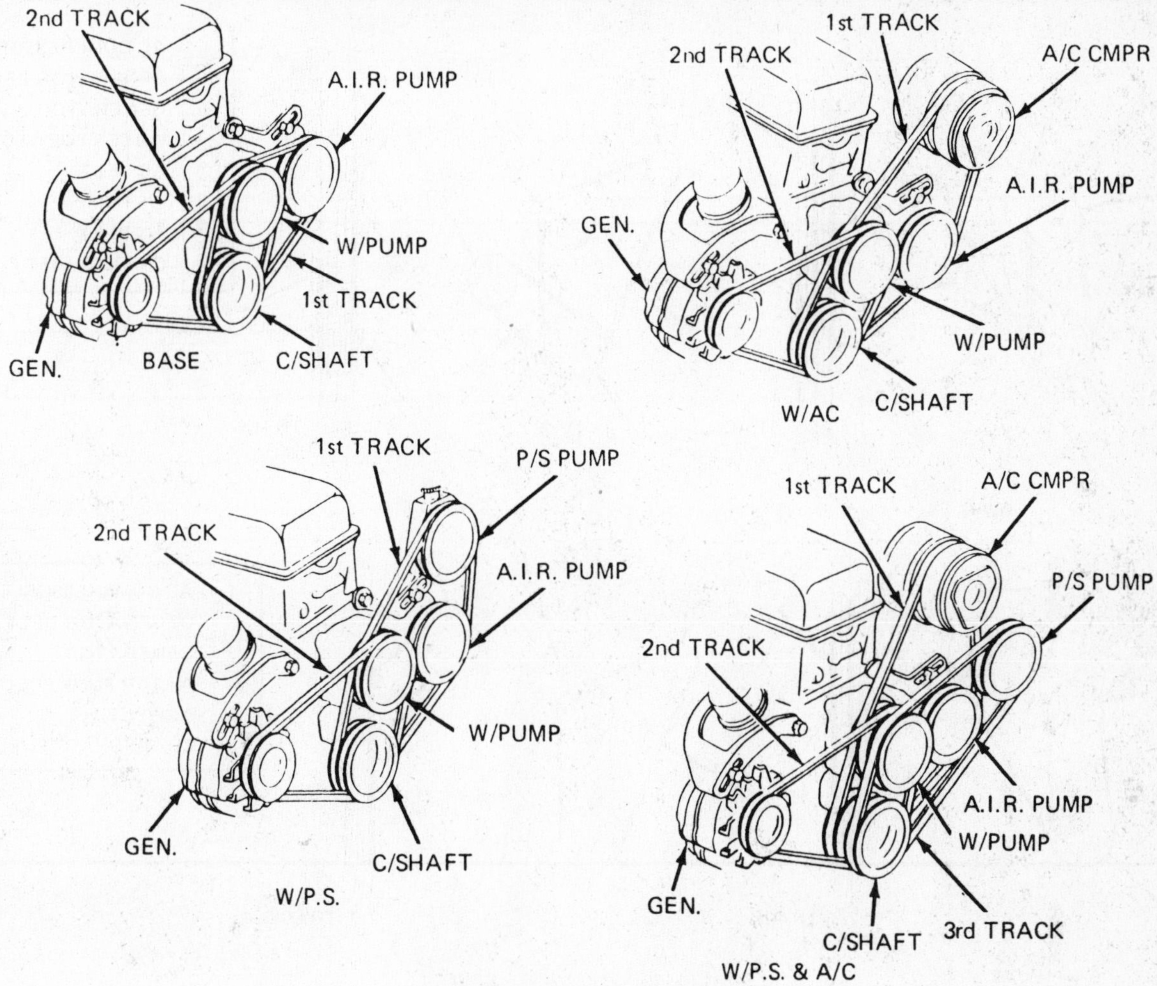
2nd TRACK
A.I.R. PUMP
W/PUMP
1st TRACK
GEN.
BASE
C/SHAFT
1st TRACK
2nd TRACK
A/C CMPR
A.I.R. PUMP
GEN.
W/PUMP
W/AC
C/SHAFT
1st TRACK
P/S PUMP
2nd TRACK
A.I.R. PUMP
W/PUMP
GEN.
C/SHAFT
W/P.S.
1st TRACK
A/C CMPR
P/S PUMP
2nd TRACK
A.I.R. PUMP
W/PUMP
GEN.
C/SHAFT
3rd TRACK
W/P.S. & A/C

1.9L V-Belt and pulley diagram

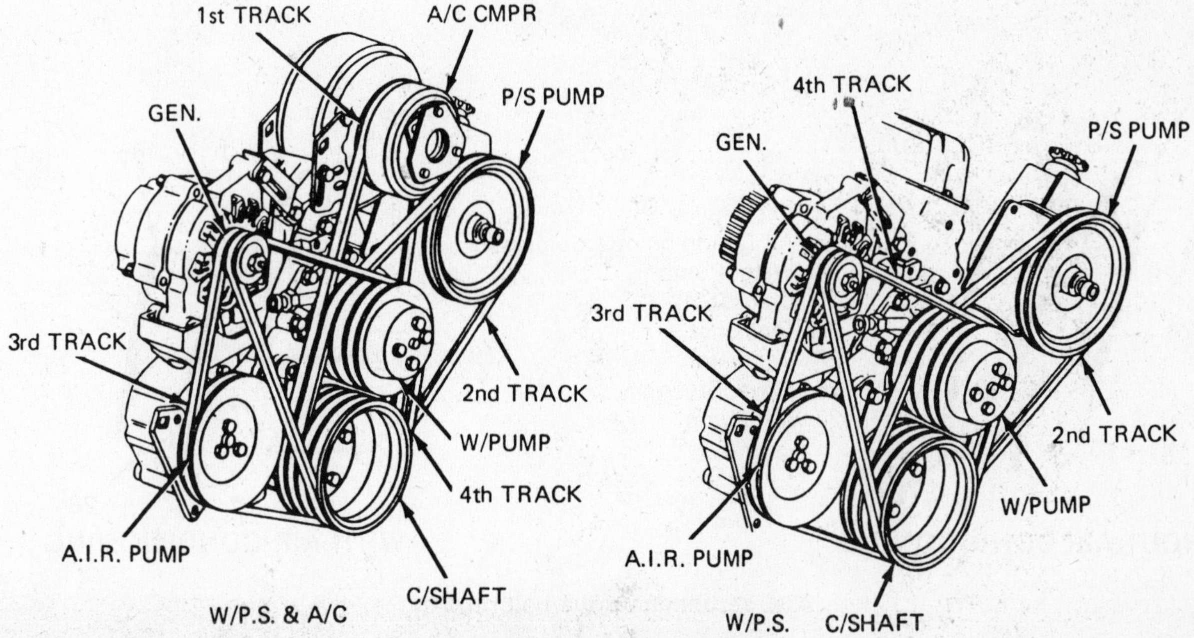
1st TRACK
A/C CMPR
GEN.
P/S PUMP
3rd TRACK
2nd TRACK
W/PUMP
4th TRACK
A.I.R. PUMP
C/SHAFT
W/P.S. & A/C
4th TRACK
GEN.
P/S PUMP
3rd TRACK
2nd TRACK
W/PUMP
A.I.R. PUMP
W/P.S.
C/SHAFT

2.8L V-Belt and pulley diagram

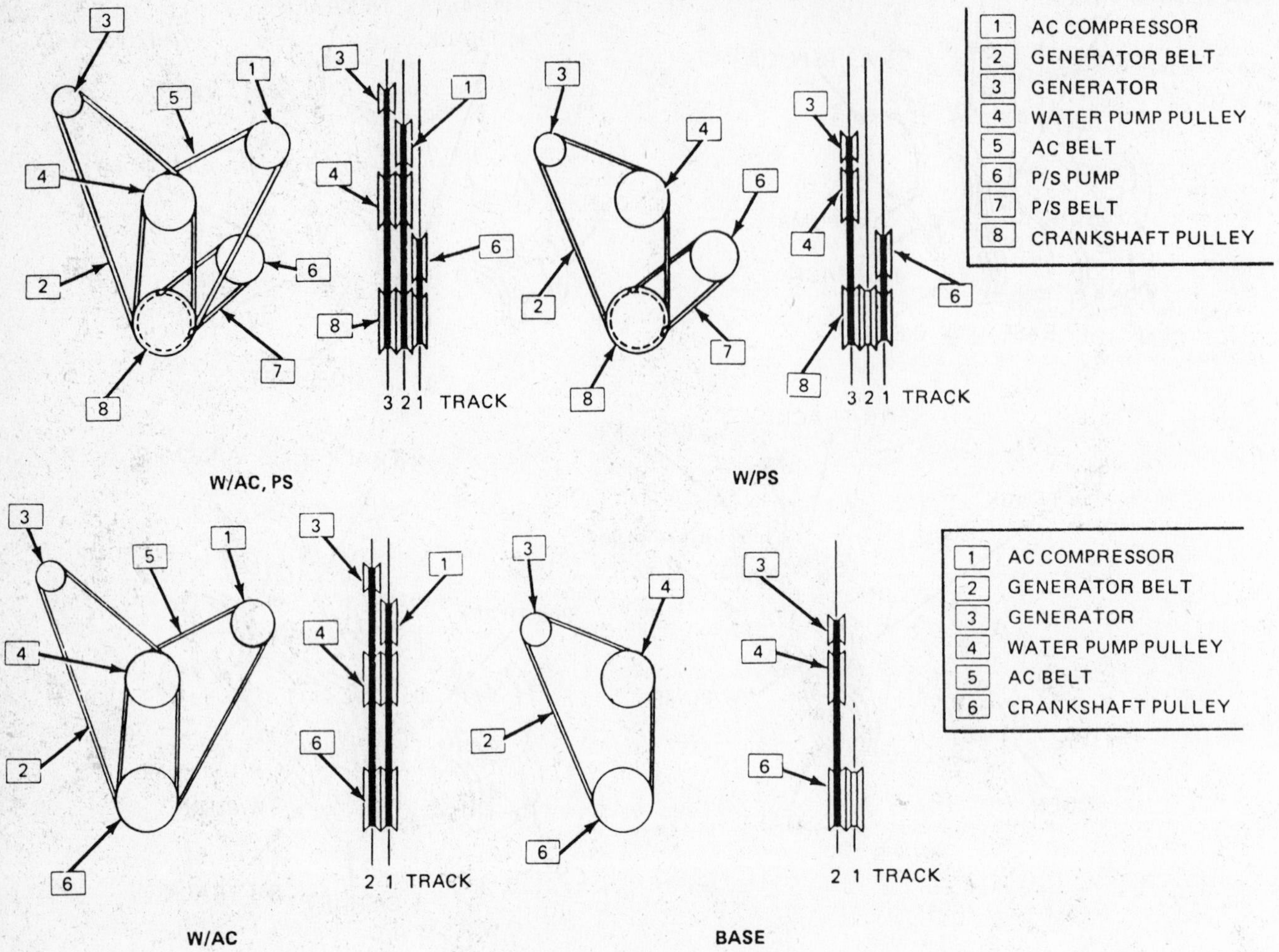
1 AC COMPRESSOR
2 GENERATOR BELT
3 GENERATOR
4 WATER PUMP PULLEY
5 AC BELT
6 P/S PUMP
7 P/S BELT
8 CRANKSHAFT PULLEY
3 2 1 TRACK
3 2 1 TRACK
W/AC, PS
W/PS
1 AC COMPRESSOR
2 GENERATOR BELT
3 GENERATOR
4 WATER PUMP PULLEY
5 AC BELT
6 CRANKSHAFT PULLEY
2 1 TRACK
2 1 TRACK
W/AC
BASE

2.5L V-Belt and pulley diagram

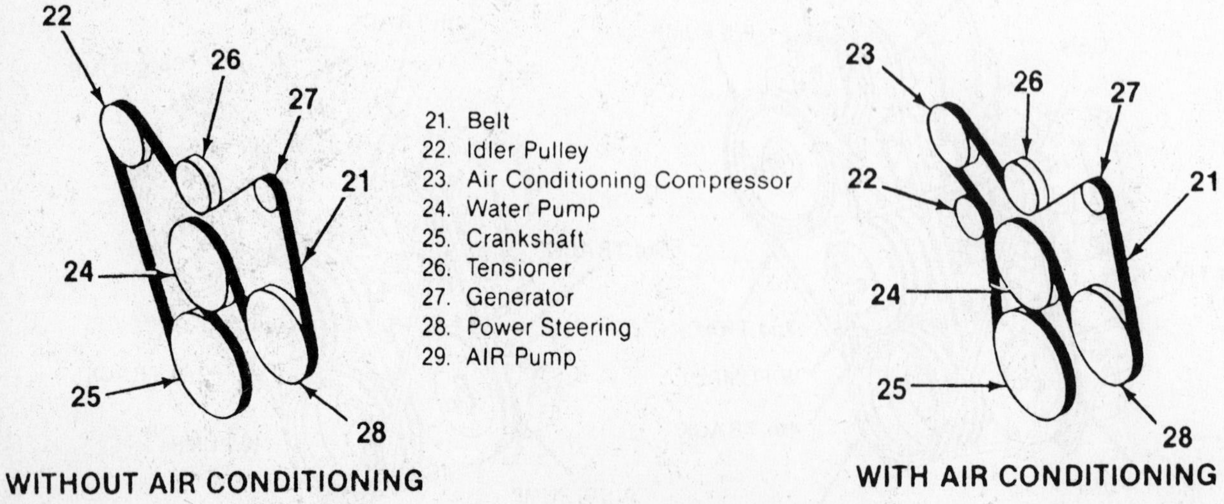
21. Belt
22. Idler Pulley
23. Air Conditioning Compressor
24. Water Pump
25. Crankshaft
26. Tensioner
27. Generator
28. Power Steering
29. AIR Pump
WITHOUT AIR CONDITIONING
WITH AIR CONDITIONING

4.3L serpentine drive belt routing

deflect about 1/4 in. (6mm) over a 7–10 in. (178–254mm) span, or 1/2 in. (12.7mm) over a 13–16 in. (330–406mm) span. If the deflection is found to be too much or too little, perform the tension adjustments.

ADJUSTING TENSION

When adjusting belt tension note the following:

- A used belt is one that has been rotated at least one complete revolution on the pulleys. This begins the belt seating process and it must never be tensioned to the new belt specifications.
- It is better to have belts too loose than too tight, because overtight belts will lead to bearing failure, particularly in the water pump and alternator. However, loose belts place an extremely high impact load on the driven components due to the whipping action of the belt.
- A GM Belt Tension Gauge No. BT-33-95-ACBN (regular V-belts), BT-33-97M (poly V-belts) or equivalent is required for tensioning accessory drive belts on 1982–86 trucks.

V-Belt tensioning (1982–86)

1. If the belt is cold, operate the engine (at idle speed) for 15 minutes; the belt will seat itself in the pulleys allowing the belt fibers to relax or stretch. If the belt is hot, allow it to cool, until it is warm to the touch.
2. Loosen the component-to-mounting bracket bolts.
3. Using a GM Belt Tension Gauge No. BT-33-95-ACBN (standard V-belts), BT-33-97M (poly V-belts) or equivalent, place the tension gauge at the center of the belt between the longest span.
4. Applying belt tension pressure on the component, adjust the drive belt tension to the correct specifications.
5. While holding the correct tension on the component, tighten the component-to-mounting bracket bolt.
6. When the belt tension is correct, remove the tension gauge.

Serpentine Belt Tensioning (1987–91)

1987–91 trucks are equipped with an automatic tensioner. No belt tensioning is necessary as the tensioner adjusts by spring action.

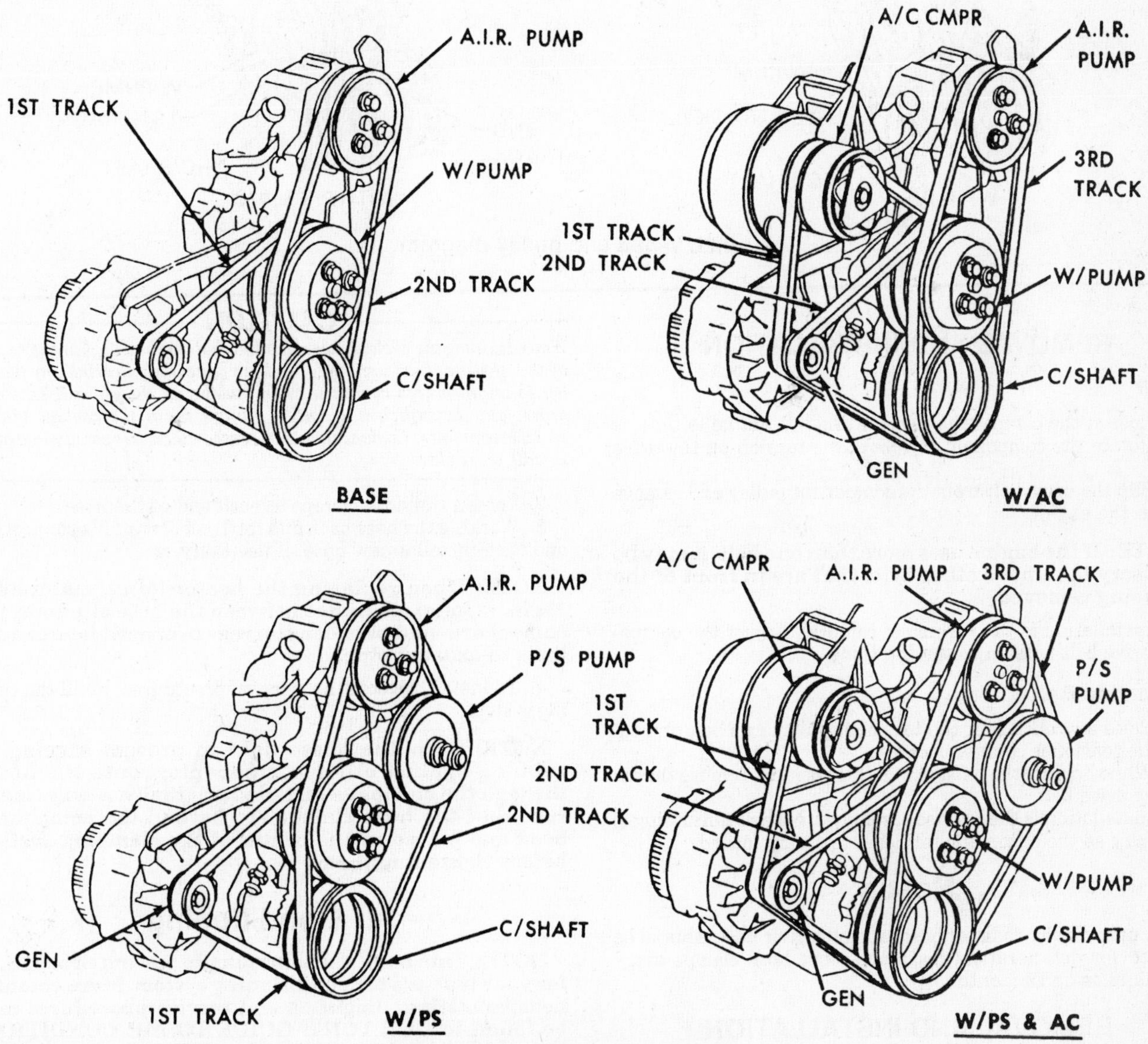
A.I.R. PUMP
1ST TRACK
W/PUMP
2ND TRACK
C/SHAFT
BASE
A/C CMPR
A.I.R. PUMP
3RD TRACK
1ST TRACK
2ND TRACK
W/PUMP
C/SHAFT
GEN
W/AC
A.I.R. PUMP
P/S PUMP
2ND TRACK
C/SHAFT
GEN
1ST TRACK
W/PS
A/C CMPR
A.I.R. PUMP
3RD TRACK
P/S PUMP
1ST TRACK
2ND TRACK
W/PUMP
C/SHAFT
GEN
W/PS & AC

2.0L V-Belt and pulley diagram

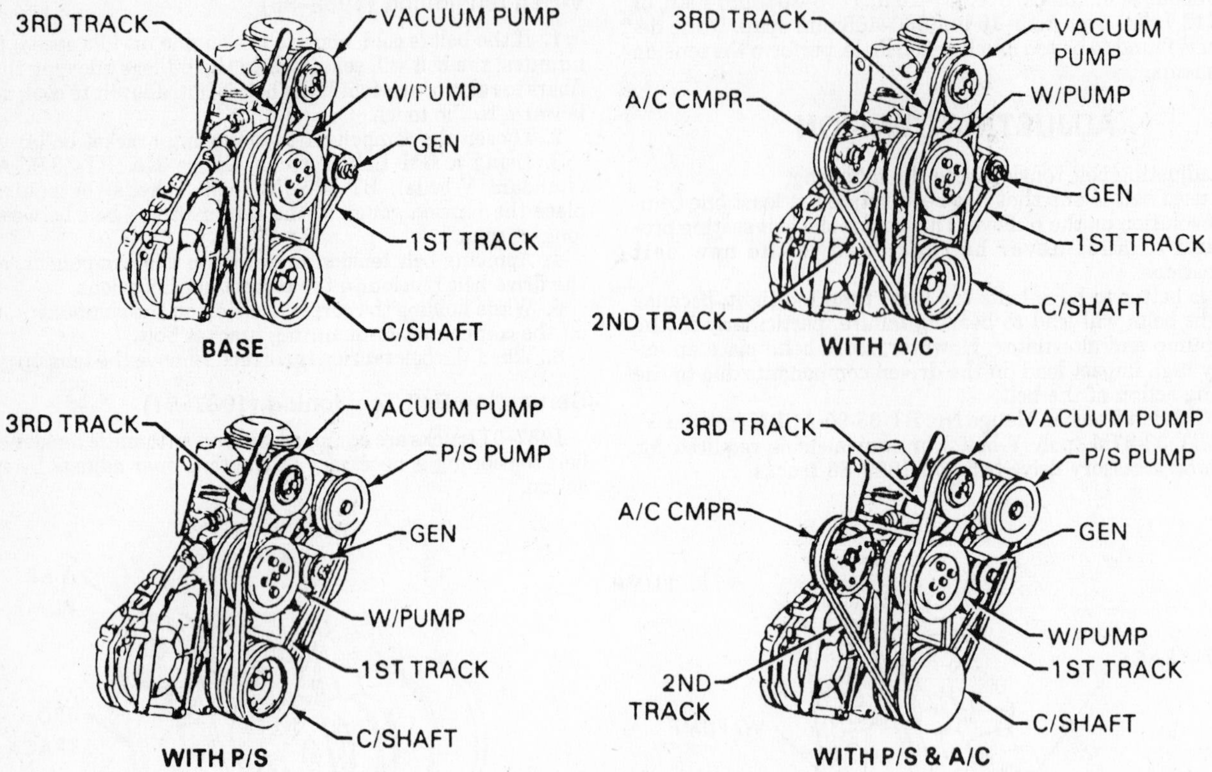
3RD TRACK
VACUUM PUMP
W/PUMP
GEN
1ST TRACK
C/SHAFT
BASE
3RD TRACK
VACUUM PUMP
A/C CMPR
W/PUMP
GEN
1ST TRACK
C/SHAFT
2ND TRACK
WITH A/C
3RD TRACK
VACUUM PUMP
P/S PUMP
GEN
W/PUMP
1ST TRACK
C/SHAFT
WITH P/S
3RD TRACK
VACUUM PUMP
P/S PUMP
A/C CMPR
GEN
W/PUMP
1ST TRACK
2ND TRACK
C/SHAFT
WITH P/S & A/C

2.2L V-Belt and pulley diagram

REMOVAL AND INSTALLATION

V-Belt

1. Loosen the component-to-mounting bracket bolts.
2. Rotate the component to relieve the tension on the drive belt.
3. Slip the drive belt from the component pulley and remove it from the engine.

NOTE: If the engine uses more than one belt, it may be necessary to remove other belts that are in front of the one being removed.

4. Installation is the reverse of removal. Adjust the component drive belt tension to specifications.

Serpentine Belt

1. Place a wrench over the tensioner pulley axis bolt and rotate the tensioner counterclockwise.
2. While holding the tensioner in this position, remove the accessory drive belt.
3. Installation is the reverse of removal. No belt tensioning is necessary as the automatic tensioner is spring loaded.

Hoses

The upper/lower radiator hoses and all heater hoses should be checked for deterioration, leaks and loose hose clamps every 15,000 miles or 12 months.

REMOVAL AND INSTALLATION

1. Drain the cooling system.

CAUTION

When draining the coolant, keep in mind that cats and dogs are attracted by the ethylene glycol antifreeze, and are quite likely to drink any that is left in an uncovered container or in puddles on the ground. This will prove fatal in sufficient quantity. Always drain the coolant into a sealable container. Coolant should be reused unless it is contaminated or several years old.

2. Loosen the hose clamps at each end of the hose.
3. Working the hose back and forth, slide it off it's connection and then install a new hose, if necessary.

NOTE: When replacing the heater hoses, maintain a 1½ in. (38mm) clearance between the hose clip-to-upper control arm and between the rear overhead heater core lines-to-exhaust pipe.

4. To install, reverse the removal procedures. Refill the cooling system.

NOTE: Draw the hoses tight to prevent sagging or rubbing against other components; route the hoses through the clamps as installed originally. Always make sure that the hose clamps are beyond the component bead and placed in the center of the clamping surface before tightening them.

Air Conditioning

NOTE: This book contains simple testing procedures for your trucks's air conditioning system. More comprehensive testing, diagnosis and service procedures may be found in CHILTON'S GUIDE TO AIR CONDITIONING SERVICE AND REPAIR, available at your local retailer.

HOW TO SPOT BAD HOSES

Both the upper and lower radiator hoses are called upon to perform difficult jobs in an inhospitable environment. They are subject to nearly 18 psi at under hood temperatures often over 280°F, and must circulate nearly 7500 gallons of coolant an hour—3 good reasons to have good hoses.

Swollen Hose

A good test for any hose is to feel it for soft or spongy spots. Frequently these will appear as swollen areas of the hose. The most likely cause is oil soaking. This hose could burst at any time, when hot or under pressure.

Cracked Hose

Cracked hoses can usually be seen but feel the hoses to be sure they have not hardened; a prime cause of cracking. This hose has cracked down to the reinforcing cords and could split at any of the cracks.

Frayed Hose End (Due to Weak Clamp)

Weakened clamps frequently are the cause of hose and cooling system failure. The connection between the pipe and hose has deteriorated enough to allow coolant to escape when the engine is hot.

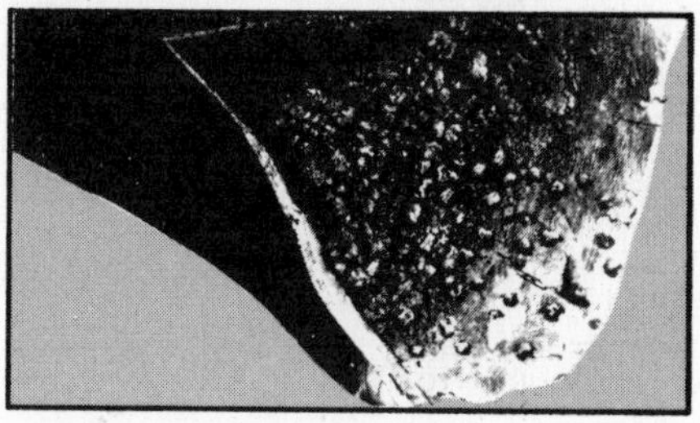

Debris in Cooling System

Debris, rust and scale in the cooling system can cause the inside of a hose to weaken. This can usually be felt on the outside of the hose as soft or thinner areas.

SAFETY WARNINGS

Because of the importance of the necessary safety precautions that must be exercised when working with air conditioning systems and R-12 refrigerant, a recap of the safety precautions are outlined.

- Avoid contact with a charged refrigeration system, even when working on another part of the air conditioning system or truck. If a heavy tool comes into contact with a section of copper tubing or a heat exchanger, it can easily cause the relatively soft material to rupture.
- When it is necessary to apply force to a fitting which contains refrigerant, as when checking that all system couplings are securely tightened, use a wrench on both parts of the fitting involved, if possible. This will avoid putting torque on the refrigerant tubing. It is recommended that tube or line wrenches be used when tightening these flare nut fittings.
- DO NOT attempt to discharge the system by merely loosening a fitting or removing the service valve caps and cracking these valves. Precise control is possible only when using the service gauges. Place a rag under the open end of the center charging hose while discharging the system to catch any drops of liquid that might escape. Wear protective gloves when connecting or disconnecting service gauge hoses.
- In most states it is now illegal to discharge refrigerant into the atmosphere due to the harmful effects Freon (R-12) has on the ozone layer. Check with local authorities about the laws in your state.
- Discharge the system only in a well ventilated area, as high concentrations of the gas can exclude oxygen and act as an anaesthetic. When leak testing or soldering, this is particularly important, as toxic gas is formed when R-12 contacts any flame.
- Never start a system without first verifying that both service valves are back-seated (if equipped) and that all fittings throughout the system are snugly connected.
- Avoid applying heat to any refrigerant line or storage vessel. Charging may be aided by using water heated to less than 125° to warm the refrigerant container. Never allow a refrigerant storage container to sit out in the sun or near any other heat source, such as a radiator.
- Always wear goggles when working on a system to protect the eyes. If refrigerant contacts the eyes, it is advisable in all cases to see a physician as soon as possible.
- Frostbite from liquid refrigerant should be treated by first gradually warming the area with cool water and then gently applying petroleum jelly. A physician should be consulted.
- Always keep the refrigerant drum fittings capped when not in use. Avoid any sudden shock to the drum, which might occur from dropping it or from banging a heavy tool against it. Never carry a drum in the passenger compartment of a truck.
- Always completely discharge the system before painting the truck (if the paint is to be baked on), or before welding anywhere near the refrigerant lines.

NOTE: Any repair work to an air conditioning system should be left to a professional. DO NOT, under any circumstances, attempt to loosen or tighten any fittings or perform any work other than that outlined here.

SYSTEM INSPECTIONS

NOTE: The Cycling Clutch Orfice Tube (CCOT) A/C system does not use a sight glass.

Checking For Oil Leaks

Refrigerant leaks show up as oily areas on the various components because the compressor oil is transported around the entire system along with the refrigerant. Look for oily spots on all the hoses and lines, especially on the hose and tubing connections. If there are oily deposits, the system may have a leak, have it checked by a qualified repairman.

NOTE: A small area of oil on the front of the compressor is normal and no cause for alarm.

Keep The Condenser Clear

Periodically inspect the front of the condenser for bent fins or foreign material (dirt, buts, leaves, etc.). If any cooling fins are bent, straighten them carefully with needlenose pliers. You can remove any debris with a stiff bristle brush or hose.

Operate The A/C System Periodically

A lot of A/C problems can be avoided by simply running the air conditioner at least once a week regardless of the season. Simply let the system run for at least 5 minutes a week (even in the winter) and you'll keep the internal parts lubricated as well as preventing the hoses from hardening.

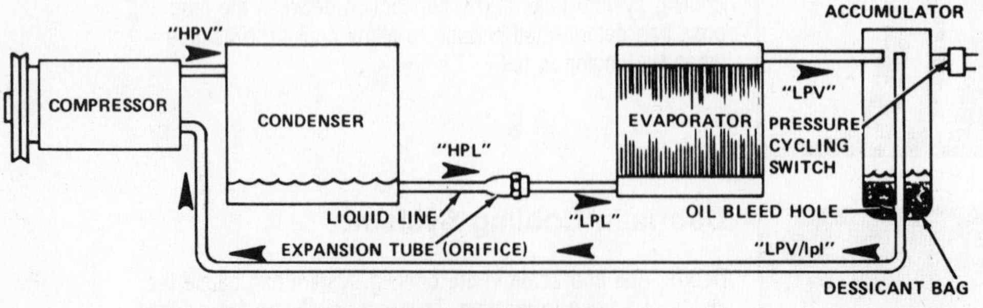
ACCUMULATOR
"HPV"
COMPRESSOR
CONDENSER
"LPV"
EVAPORATOR
PRESSURE
CYCLING
SWITCH
"HPL"
LIQUID LINE
"LPL"
OIL BLEED HOLE
EXPANSION TUBE (ORIFICE)
"LPV/lpl"
DESSICANT BAG
PRESSURE CYCLING SYSTEM

"HPV" – HIGH PRESSURE VAPOR LEAVING COMPRESSOR.

"HPL" – VAPOR IS COOLED DOWN BY CONDENSER AIR FLOW AND LEAVES AS HIGH PRESSURE LIQUID.

"LPL" – ORIFICE METERS THE LIQUID R-12, INTO EVAPORATOR, REDUCING ITS PRESSURE, AND WARM BLOWER AIR ACROSS EVAPORATOR CORE CAUSES BOILING OFF OF LIQUID INTO VAPOR.

"LPV" – LEAVES EVAPORATOR AS LOW PRESSURE VAPOR AND RETURNS WITH THE SMALL AMOUNT OF . . .

"lpl" – . . . LOW PRESSURE LIQUID THAT DIDN'T BOIL OFF COMPLETELY BACK TO THE COMPRESSOR TO BE COMPRESSED AGAIN.

Air conditioning system schematic

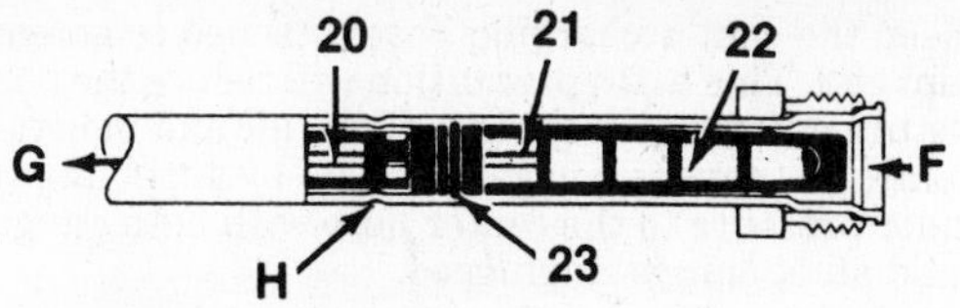
20
21
22
G
F
H
23

F. Inlet
G. Outlet (to evaporator)
H. Dent on tube (retains the expansion tube)
20. Outlet Screen
21. Expansion tube
22. Inlet screen
23. Seal

Sectional view of the air conditioning system orifice tube

Leak Testing the System

There are several methods of detecting leaks in an air conditioning system; among them, the two most popular are (1) halide leak detection or the open flame method and (2) electronic leak detector.

The Halide Leak Detection tool No. J-6084 or equivalent, is a torch like device which produces a yellow-green color when refrigerant is introduced into the flame at the burner. A purple or violet color indicates the presence of large amounts of refrigerant at the burner.

An Autobalance Refrigerant Leak Detector tool No. J-29547 or equivalent, is a small portable electronic device with an extended probe. With the unit activated, the probe is passed along those components of the system which contain refrigerant. If a leak is detected, the unit will sound an alarm signal or activate a display signal depending on the manufacturer's design. It is advisable to follow the manufacturer's instructions as the design and function of the detection may vary significantly.

CAUTION

Care should be taken to operate either type of detector in well ventilated areas, so as to reduce the chance of personal injury, which may result from coming in contact with poisonous gases produced when R-12 is exposed to flame or electric spark.

GAUGE SETS (USE)

Most of the service work performed in air conditioning requires the use of a two gauge set. The gauges on the set monitor the high (head) pressure side and the low (suction) side of the system.

The low side gauge records both pressure and vacuum. Vacuum readings are calibrated from 0–30 in. Hg, and the pressure graduations read from 0–60 psi. The high side gauge measures pressure from 0–600 psi.

Both gauges are threaded into a manifold that contains two hand shut-off valves. Proper manipulation of these valves and the use of the attached test hoses allow the user to perform the following services:

- Test high and low side pressures.
- Remove air, moisture and/or contaminated refrigerant.
- Purge the system of refrigerant.
- Charge the system with refrigerant.

The manifold valves are designed so they have no direct effect on the gauge readings but serve only to provide for or cut off the flow of refrigerant through the manifold. During all testing and hook-up operations, the valves are kept in a closed position to avoid disturbing the refrigeration system. The valves are opened ONLY to purge the system of refrigerant or to charge it.

When purging the system, the center hose is uncapped at the lower end and both valves are cracked (opened) slightly. This allows the refrigerant pressure to force the entire contents of the system out through the center hose. During charging, the valve on the high side of the manifold is closed and the valve on the low side is cracked (opened). Under these conditions, the low pressure in the evaporator will draw refrigerant from the relatively warm refrigerant storage container into the system.

Service Valves

For the user to diagnose an air conditioning system he or she must gain entrance to the system in order to observe the pressures; the type of terminal for this purpose is the familiar Schrader valve.

The Schrader valve is similar to a tire valve stem and the process of connecting the test hoses is the same as threading a hand pump outlet hose to a bicycle tire. As the test hose is threaded to the service port the valve core is depressed, allowing the refrig-

80. Low side valve
81. High side valve
82. Vacuum pump
83. 12 or 30 Lb. drum
84. Disposable cans
4. Accumulator

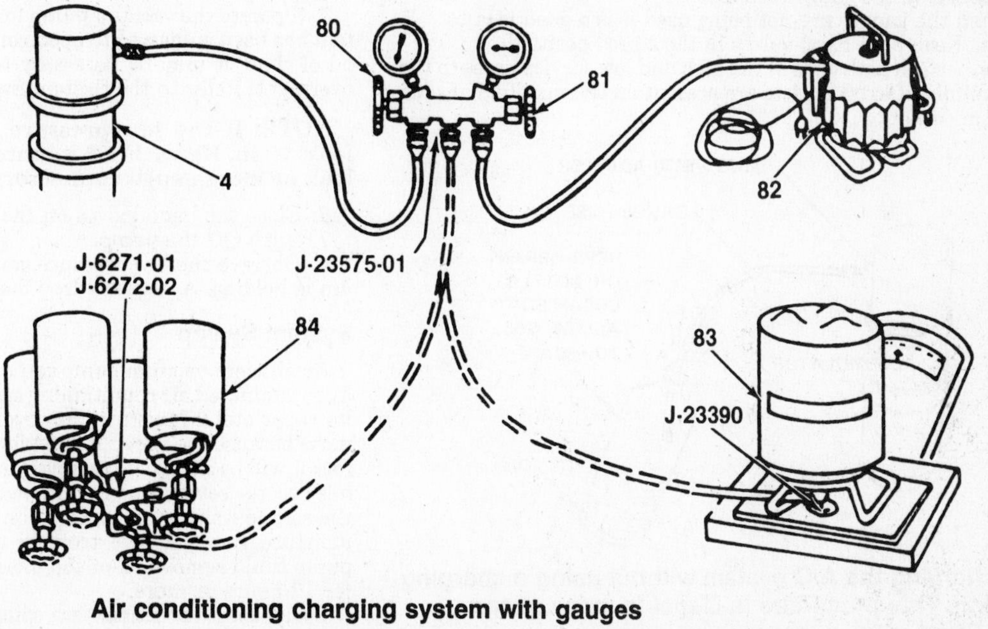
80
81
4
82
J-6271-01
J-6272-02
J-23575-01
84
83
J-23390

Air conditioning charging system with gauges

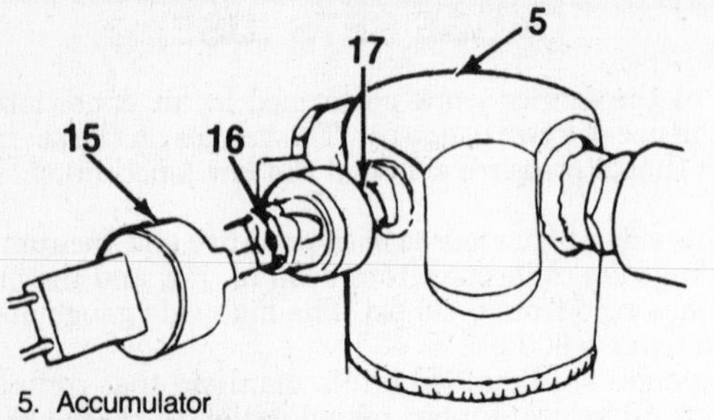
5
17
15
16

5. Accumulator
15. Electrical connector
16. Pressure cycling switch adjusting screw
17. "Schrader" type valve

A/C accumulator with Schrader valve

erant to enter the test hose outlet. Removal of the test hose automatically closes the system.

Extreme caution must be observed when removing test hoses from the Schrader valves as some refrigerant will normally escape.

Using The Manifold Gauges

The following are step-by-step procedures to guide the user in the correct usage of the gauge set:

CAUTION

Wear goggles or face shield during all testing operations. Backseat hand shut-off type service valves.

1. Remove the caps from the high and low side service ports. Make sure both gauge valves are closed.
2. Connect the low side test hose to the service valve that leads to the evaporator (located between the evaporator outlet and the compressor).
3. Attach the high side test hose to the service valve that leads to the condenser.
4. Mid-position the hand shutoff type service valves.
5. Start the engine and allow it to warm-up. All testing and charging of the system should be done after the engine and system has reached normal operating temperatures (except when using certain charging stations).
6. Adjust the air conditioner controls to MAX-COLD.
7. Observe the gauge readings.

When the gauges are not being used it is a good idea to:

a. Keep both hand valves in the closed position.

b. Attach both ends of the high and low service hoses to the manifold, if extra outlets are present on the manifold or plug them (if not).

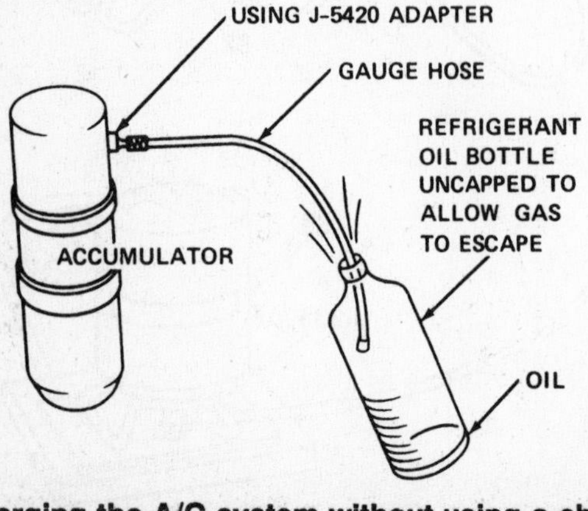
USING J-5420 ADAPTER
GAUGE HOSE
REFRIGERANT OIL BOTTLE UNCAPPED TO ALLOW GAS TO ESCAPE
ACCUMULATOR
OIL

Discharging the A/C system without using a charging station. This procedure is illegal in many states

c. Keep the center charging hose attached to an empty refrigerant can. This extra precaution will reduce the possibility of moisture entering the gauges. If the air and moisture have gotten into the gauges, purge the hoses by supplying refrigerant under pressure to the center hose with both gauge valves open and all openings unplugged.

DISCHARGING THE SYSTEM

CAUTION

In most states it is now illegal to discharge refrigerant into the atmosphere due to the harmful effects Freon (R-12) has on the ozone layer. Check with local authorities about the laws in your state.

1. Operate the air conditioner for at least 10 minutes.
2. Attach the gauges, turn Off the engine and the air conditioner.
3. Place a container or rag at the outlet of the center charging hose on the gauge. The refrigerant will be discharged there and this precaution will avoid its uncontrolled exposure.
4. Open the low side hand valve on gauge slightly.
5. Open the high side hand valve slightly.

NOTE: Too rapid a purging process will be identified by the appearance of an oily foam. If this occurs, close the hand valves a little more until this condition stops.

6. Close both hand valves on the gauge set when the pressures read 0 and all the refrigerant has left the system.

Evacuating the System

Before charging any system it is necessary to purge the refrigerant and draw out the trapped moisture with a suitable vacuum pump. Failure to do so will result in ineffective charging and possible damage to the system.

1. Connect both service gauge hoses to the high and low service outlets.
2. Open the high and low side hand valves on the gauge manifold.
3. Open both service valves a slight amount (from the back seated position), then allow the refrigerant to discharge from the system.
4. Install the center charging hose of the gauge set to the vacuum pump.
5. Operate the vacuum pump for at least one hour. If the system has been subjected to open conditions for a prolonged period of time, it may be necessary to "pump the system down" overnight. Refer to the System Sweep procedure.

NOTE: If the low pressure gauge does not show at least 28 in. Hg within 5 minutes, check the system for a leak or loose gauge connectors.

6. Close the hand valves on the gauge manifold.
7. Turn Off the pump.
8. Observe the low pressure gauge to determine if the vacuum is holding. A vacuum drop may indicate a leak.

System Sweep

An efficient vacuum pump can remove all the air contained in a contaminated air conditioning system very quickly, because of its vapor state. Moisture, however, is far more difficult to remove because the vacuum must force the liquid to evaporate before it will be able to be removed from the system. If the system has become severely contaminated, as it might become after all the charge was lost in conjunction with truck accident damage, moisture removal is extremely time consuming. A vacuum pump could remove all of the moisture only if it were operated for 12 hours or more.

Under these conditions, sweeping the system with refrigerant will speed the process of moisture removal considerably. Use the followign procedure to sweep the system:

1. Connect the vacuum pump to the gauges, operate it until the vacuum ceases to increase, then continue the operation for ten more minutes.
2. Charge the system with 50% of its rated refrigerant capacity.
3. Operate the system at fast idle for ten minutes.
4. Discharge the system.
5. Repeat (twice) the process of charging to 50% capacity, running the system for ten minutes, then discharging it for a total of three sweeps.
6. Replace the drier.
7. Pump the system down as in Step 1.
8. Charge the system.

CHARGING

CAUTION

Never attempt to charge the system by opening the high pressure gauge control while the compressor is operating. The compressor accumulating pressure can burst the refrigerant container, causing severe personal injury.

1. Start the engine, operate it with the choke Open and normal idle speed, then position the A/C control lever on the Off.
2. Using drum or 14 oz. cans of refrigerant, in the inverted position, allow about 1 lb. of refrigerant to enter the system through the low side service fitting on the accumulator.
3. After 1 lb. of refrigerant enters the system, position the control lever on Norm (the compressor will engage) and the blower motor on Hi speed; this operation will draw the remainder of the refrigerant into the system.

NOTE: To speed up the operation, position a fan in front of the condenser; the lowering of the condenser temperature will allow refrigerant to enter the system faster.

4. When the system is charged, turn Off the refrigerant source and allow the engine to run for 30 seconds to clear the lines and gauges.
5. With the engine running, remove the hose adapter from the accumulator service fitting (unscrew the hose quickly to prevent refrigerant from escaping).

CAUTION

Never remove the gauge line from the adapter when the line is connected to the system; always remove the line adapter from the service fitting first.

6. Replace the accumulator protective caps and turn the engine Off.
7. Using a leak detector, inspect the A/C system for leaks. If a leak is present, repair it.

Windshield Wipers

For maximum effectiveness and longest element life, the windshield and wiper blades should be kept clean. Dirt, tree sap, road tar and so on will cause streaking, smearing and blade deterioration if left on the glass. It is advisable to wash the windshield carefully with a commercial glass cleaner at least once a month. Wipe off the rubber blades with the wet rag, afterwards.

If the blades are found to be cracked, broken or torn, they should be replaced immediately. Replacement intervals will vary with usage, although ozone deterioration usually limits blade life to about one year. If the wiper pattern is smeared, streaked or if the blade chatters across the glass, the elements should be replaced. It is easiest and most sensible to replace the elements in pairs.

BLADE REPLACEMENT

1. Lift the wiper arm assembly from the windshield.
2. Depress the wiper arm-to-blade assembly pin to disconnect the blade assembly from the wiper arm.
3. To install, use new 16 in. blade assemblies and reverse the removal procedures.

Tires and Wheels

TIRE ROTATION

Tire wear can be equalized by switching the position of the tire about every 6,000 miles. Including a conventional spare in the rotation pattern can give up to 20% more tire life.

CAUTION

DO NOT include the new Space Saver® or temporary spare tires in the rotation pattern.

There are certain exceptions to tire rotation, however. Studded snow tires should not be rotated and radials should be kept on the same side of the truck (maintain the same direction of rotation). The belts on radial tires get set in a pattern. If the direction of rotation is reversed, it can cause rough ride and vibration.

NOTE: When radials or studded snows are taken off the truck, mark them, so you can maintain the same direction of rotation.

TIRE TYPES

For maximum satisfaction, tires should be used in sets of five. Mixing of different types (radial, bias-belted, fiberglass belted) should be avoided. Conventional bias tires are constructed so that the cords run bead-to-bead at an angle. This type of construction gives rigidity to both tread and sidewall. Bias-belted

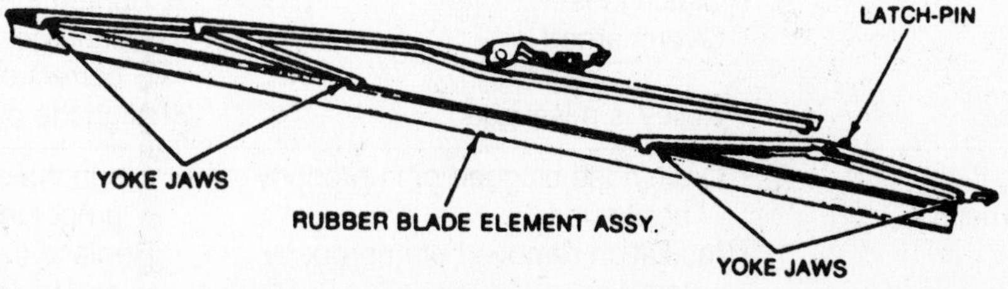
LATCH-PIN
YOKE JAWS
RUBBER BLADE ELEMENT ASSY.
YOKE JAWS

Typical windshield wiper assembly

Troubleshooting Basic Air Conditioning Problems

Problem	Cause	Solution
There's little or no air coming from the vents (and you're sure it's on)	• The A/C fuse is blown • Broken or loose wires or connections • The on/off switch is defective	• Check and/or replace fuse • Check and/or repair connections • Replace switch
The air coming from the vents is not cool enough	• Windows and air vent wings open • The compressor belt is slipping • Heater is on • Condenser is clogged with debris • Refrigerant has escaped through a leak in the system • Receiver/drier is plugged	• Close windows and vent wings • Tighten or replace compressor belt • Shut heater off • Clean the condenser • Check system • Service system
The air has an odor	• Vacuum system is disrupted • Odor producing substances on the evaporator case • Condensation has collected in the bottom of the evaporator housing	• Have the system checked/repaired • Clean the evaporator case • Clean the evaporator housing drains
System is noisy or vibrating	• Compressor belt or mountings loose • Air in the system	• Tighten or replace belt; tighten mounting bolts • Have the system serviced
Sight glass condition		
Constant bubbles, foam or oil streaks	• Undercharged system	• Charge the system
Clear sight glass, but no cold air	• No refrigerant at all	• Check and charge the system
Clear sight glass, but air is cold	• System is OK	
Clouded with milky fluid	• Receiver drier is leaking dessicant	• Have system checked
Large difference in temperature of lines	• System undercharged	• Charge and leak test the system
Compressor noise	• Broken valves • Overcharged • Incorrect oil level • Piston slap • Broken rings • Drive belt pulley bolts are loose	• Replace the valve plate • Discharge, evacuate and install the correct charge • Isolate the compressor and check the oil level. Correct as necessary. • Replace the compressor • Replace the compressor • Tighten with the correct torque specification
Excessive vibration	• Incorrect belt tension • Clutch loose • Overcharged • Pulley is misaligned	• Adjust the belt tension • Tighten the clutch • Discharge, evacuate and install the correct charge • Align the pulley
Condensation dripping in the passenger compartment	• Drain hose plugged or improperly positioned • Insulation removed or improperly installed	• Clean the drain hose and check for proper installation • Replace the insulation on the expansion valve and hoses

Troubleshooting Basic Air Conditioning Problems (cont.)

Problem	Cause	Solution
Frozen evaporator coil	• Faulty thermostat • Thermostat capillary tube improperly installed • Thermostat not adjusted properly	• Replace the thermostat • Install the capillary tube correctly • Adjust the thermostat
Low side low—high side low	• System refrigerant is low • Expansion valve is restricted	• Evacuate, leak test and charge the system • Replace the expansion valve
Low side high—high side low	• Internal leak in the compressor—worn	• Remove the compressor cylinder head and inspect the compressor. Replace the valve plate assembly if necessary. If the compressor pistons, rings or
Low side high—high side low (cont.)		cylinders are excessively worn or scored replace the compressor
	• Cylinder head gasket is leaking • Expansion valve is defective • Drive belt slipping	• Install a replacement cylinder head gasket • Replace the expansion valve • Adjust the belt tension
Low side high—high side high	• Condenser fins obstructed • Air in the system • Expansion valve is defective • Loose or worn fan belts	• Clean the condenser fins • Evacuate, leak test and charge the system • Replace the expansion valve • Adjust or replace the belts as necessary
Low side low—high side high	• Expansion valve is defective • Restriction in the refrigerant hose	• Replace the expansion valve • Check the hose for kinks—replace if necessary
Low side low—high side high	• Restriction in the receiver/drier • Restriction in the condenser	• Replace the receiver/drier • Replace the condenser
Low side and high normal (inadequate cooling)	• Air in the system • Moisture in the system	• Evacuate, leak test and charge the system • Evacuate, leak test and charge the system

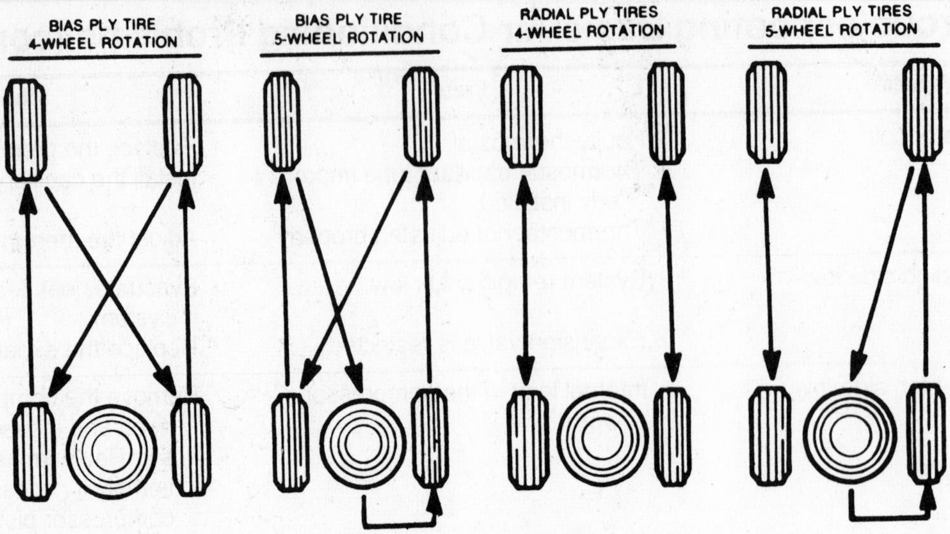
BIAS PLY TIRE
4-WHEEL ROTATION
BIAS PLY TIRE
5-WHEEL ROTATION
RADIAL PLY TIRES
4-WHEEL ROTATION
RADIAL PLY TIRES
5-WHEEL ROTATION

Tire rotation patterns

tires are similar in construction to conventional bias ply tires. Belts run at an angle and also at a 90° angle to the bead, as in the radial tire. Tread life is improved considerably over the conventional bias tire. The radial tire differs in construction, but instead of the carcass plies running are an angle of 90° to each other, they run at an angle of 90° to the bead. This gives the tread a great deal of rigidity and the sidewall a great deal of flexibility and accounts for the characteristic bulge associated with radial tires.

Chevrolet and GMC trucks are capable of using radial tires and they are recommended. If they are used, tire sizes and wheel diameters should be selected to maintain ground clearance and tire load capacity equivalent to the minimum specified tire. Radial tires should always be used in sets of five, but in an emergency, radial tires can be used with caution on the rear axle only. If this is done, both tires on the rear should be of radial design.

CAUTION

Radial tires should never be used on ONLY the front axle.

Snow tires should not be operated at sustained speeds over 70 mph.

On four wheel drive trucks, all tires must be of the same size, type, and tread pattern, to provide even traction on loose surfaces, to prevent driveline bind when conventional four wheel drive is used, and to prevent excessive wear on the center differential with full time four wheel drive.

TREAD DEPTH

All tires have 8 built-in tread wear indicator bars that show up as ½ in. (12.7mm) wide smooth bands across the tire when $^1/_{16}$ in. (1.5mm) of tread remains. The appearance of tread wear indicators means that the tires should be replaced. In fact, many states have laws prohibiting the use of tires with less than $^1/_{16}$ in. (1.5mm) tread.

You can check your own tread depth with an inexpensive gauge or by using a Lincoln head penny. Slip the Lincoln penny into several tread grooves. If you can see the top of Lincoln's head in 2 adjacent grooves, the tires have less than $^1/_{16}$ in. (1.5mm) tread left and should be replaced. You can measure snow tires in the same manner by using the tails side of the Lincoln penny. If you can see the top of the Lincoln memorial, it's time to replace the snow tires.

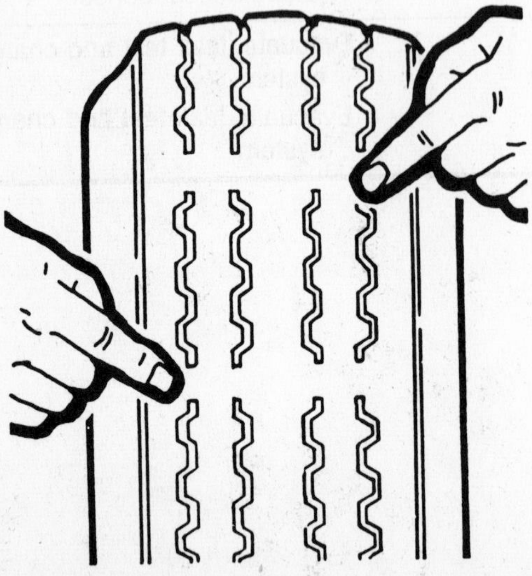

Tread wear indicators appear when the tire needs replacement

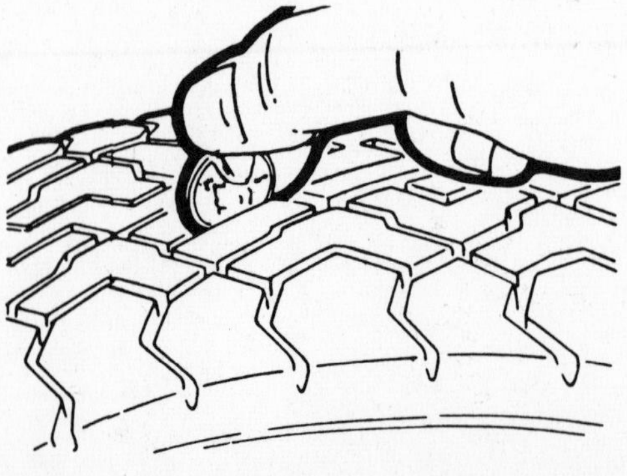

An quicker way to check tread depth is with a penny. If all of Lincoln's head is visible in two or more adjacent grooves, the tire should be replaced

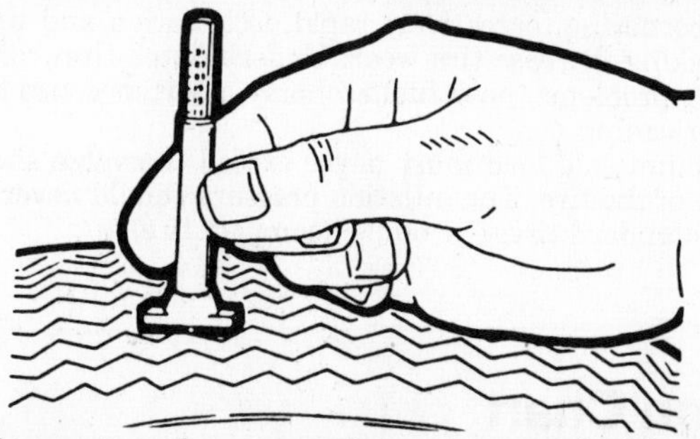

Tread wear can be accurately measured with a tread depth gauge

TIRE STORAGE

Store the tires at proper inflation pressures if they are mounted on wheels. All tires should be kept in a cool, dry place. If they are stored in the garage or basement, DO NOT let them stand on a concrete floor, set them on strips of wood.

ALUMINUM WHEELS

CAUTION

If your truck has aluminum wheels, be very careful when using any type of cleaner on either the wheels or the tires. Read the label on the package of the cleaner to make sure that it will not damage aluminum.

TIRE INFLATION

The inflation is the most ignored item of auto maintenance. Gasoline mileage can drop as much as 0.8% for every 1 pound/square inch (psi) of under inflation.

Two items should be a permanent fixture in every glove compartment: a tire pressure gauge and a tread depth gauge. Check the tire air pressure (including the spare) regularly with a pocket type gauge. Kicking the tires won't tell you a thing and the gauge on the service station air hose is notoriously inaccurate.

The tire pressures recommended for your truck are usually found on the glove box door or in the owner's manual. Ideally, inflation pressure should be checked when the tires are cool. When the air becomes heated it expands and the pressure increases. Every 10° rise (or drop) in temperature means a difference of 1 psi, which also explains why the tire appears to lose air on a very cold night. When it is impossible to check the tires cold, allow for pressure build-up due to heat. If the hot pressure exceeds the cold pressure by more than 15 psi, reduce your speed, load or both. Otherwise internal heat is created in the tire. When the heat approaches the temperature at which the tire was cured during manufacture, the tread can separate from the body.

CAUTION

Never counteract excessive pressure build-up by bleeding off air pressure (letting some air out). This will only further raise the tire operating temperature.

Troubleshooting Basic Wheel Problems

Problem	Cause	Solution
The car's front end vibrates at high speed	· The wheels are out of balance · Wheels are out of alignment	· Have wheels balanced · Have wheel alignment checked/adjusted
Car pulls to either side	· Wheels are out of alignment · Unequal tire pressure · Different size tires or wheels	· Have wheel alignment checked/adjusted · Check/adjust tire pressure · Change tires or wheels to same size
The car's wheel(s) wobbles	· Loose wheel lug nuts · Wheels out of balance · Damaged wheel · Wheels are out of alignment · Worn or damaged ball joint · Excessive play in the steering linkage (usually due to worn parts) · Defective shock absorber	· Tighten wheel lug nuts · Have tires balanced · Raise car and spin the wheel. If the wheel is bent, it should be replaced · Have wheel alignment checked/adjusted · Check ball joints · Check steering linkage · Check shock absorbers
Tires wear unevenly or prematurely	· Incorrect wheel size · Wheels are out of balance · Wheels are out of alignment	· Check if wheel and tire size are compatible · Have wheels balanced · Have wheel alignment checked/adjusted

Before starting a long trip with lots of luggage, you can add about 2–4 psi to the tires to make them run cooler, but never exceed the maximum inflation pressure on the side of the tire.

Factory installed wheels and tires are designed to handle loads up to and including their rated load capacity when inflated to the recommended inflation pressures. Correct tire pressures and driving techniques have an important influence on tire life. Heavy cornering, excessively rapid acceleration and unnecessary braking increase tire wear. Underinflated tires can cause handling problems, poor fuel economy, shortened tire life and tire overloading.

Maximum axle load must never exceed the value shown on the side of the tire. The inflation pressure should never exceed 35 psi (standard tires) or 60 psi (compact tire).

Tire Size Comparison Chart

"Letter" sizes			Inch Sizes	Metric-inch Sizes		
"60 Series"	"70 Series"	"78 Series"	1965–77	"60 Series"	"70 Series"	"80 Series"
			5.50-12, 5.60-12	165/60-12	165/70-12	155-12
		Y78-12	6.00-12			
		W78-13	5.20-13	165/60-13	145/70-13	135-13
		Y78-13	5.60-13	175/60-13	155/70-13	145-13
			6.15-13	185/60-13	165/70-13	155-13, P155/80-13
A60-13	A70-13	A78-13	6.40-13	195/60-13	175/70-13	165-13
B60-13	B70-13	B78-13	6.70-13	205/60-13	185/70-13	175-13
			6.90-13			
C60-13	C70-13	C78-13	7.00-13	215/60-13	195/70-13	185-13
D60-13	D70-13	D78-13	7.25-13			
E60-13	E70-13	E78-13	7.75-13			195-13
			5.20-14	165/60-14	145/70-14	135-14
			5.60-14	175/60-14	155/70-14	145-14
			5.90-14			
A60-14	A70-14	A78-14	6.15-14	185/60-14	165/70-14	155-14
	B70-14	B78-14	6.45-14	195/60-14	175/70-14	165-14
	C70-14	C78-14	6.95-14	205/60-14	185/70-14	175-14
D60-14	D70-14	D78-14				
E60-14	E70-14	E78-14	7.35-14	215/60-14	195/70-14	185-14
F60-14	F70-14	F78-14, F83-14	7.75-14	225/60-14	200/70-14	195-14
G60-14	G70-14	G77-14, G78-14	8.25-14	235/60-14	205/70-14	205-14
H60-14	H70-14	H78-14	8.55-14	245/60-14	215/70-14	215-14
J60-14	J70-14	J78-14	8.85-14	255/60-14	225/70-14	225-14
L60-14	L70-14		9.15-14	265/60-14	235/70-14	
	A70-15	A78-15	5.60-15	185/60-15	165/70-15	155-15
B60-15	B70-15	B78-15	6.35-15	195/60-15	175/70-15	165-15
C60-15	C70-15	C78-15	6.85-15	205/60-15	185/70-15	175-15
	D70-15	D78-15				
E60-15	E70-15	E78-15	7.35-15	215/60-15	195/70-15	185-15
F60-15	F70-15	F78-15	7.75-15	225/60-15	205/70-15	195-15
G60-15	G70-15	G78-15	8.15-15/8.25-15	235/60-15	215/70-15	205-15
H60-15	H70-15	H78-15	8.45-15/8.55-15	245/60-15	225/70-15	215-15
J60-15	J70-15	J78-15	8.85-15/8.90-15	255/60-15	235/70-15	225-15
	K70-15		9.00-15	265/60-15	245/70-15	230-15
L60-15	L70-15	L78-15, L84-15	9.15-15			235-15
	M70-15	M78-15				255-15
		N78-15				

NOTE: Every size tire is not listed and many size comaprisons are approximate, based on load ratings. Wider tires than those supplied new with the vehicle should always be checked for clearance

Troubleshooting Basic Tire Problems

Problem	Cause	Solution
The car's front end vibrates at high speeds and the steering wheel shakes	• Wheels out of balance • Front end needs aligning	• Have wheels balanced • Have front end alignment checked
The car pulls to one side while cruising	• Unequal tire pressure (car will usually pull to the low side) • Mismatched tires • Front end needs aligning	• Check/adjust tire pressure • Be sure tires are of the same type and size • Have front end alignment checked
Abnormal, excessive or uneven tire wear See "How to Read Tire Wear"	• Infrequent tire rotation • Improper tire pressure • Sudden stops/starts or high speed on curves	• Rotate tires more frequently to equalize wear • Check/adjust pressure • Correct driving habits
Tire squeals	• Improper tire pressure • Front end needs aligning	• Check/adjust tire pressure • Have front end alignment checked

FLUID AND LUBRICANTS

Engine Oil and Fuel Recommendations

ENGINE OIL

Use ONLY SG or SG/CE rated oils of the recommended viscosity.

Under the classification system developed by the American Petroleum Institute, the SG rating designates the highest quality oil for use in passenger vehicles. In addition, Chevrolet recommends the use of an SG/Energy Conserving oil. Oils labeled Energy Conserving (or Saving), Fuel (Gas or Gasoline) Saving, etc. are recommended due to their superior lubricating qualities (less friction – easier engine operation) and fuel saving characteristics.

Pick oil viscosity with regard to the anticipated temperatures during the period before your next oil change. Using the accompanying chart, choose the oil viscosity for the lowest expected temperature. You will be assured of easy cold starting and sufficient engine protection.

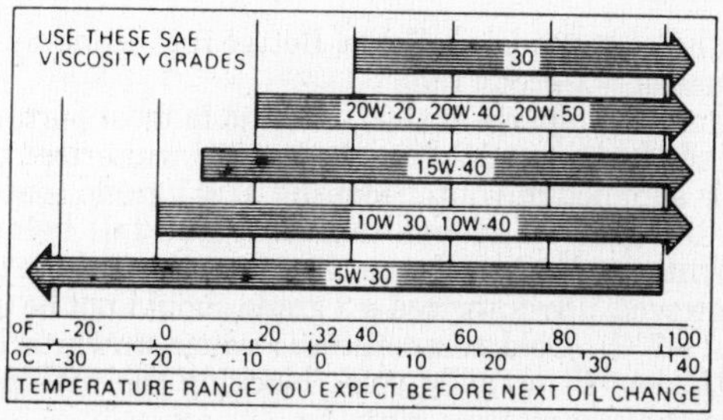
USE THESE SAE VISCOSITY GRADES
30
20W 20, 20W 40, 20W 50
15W 40
10W 30, 10W 40
5W 30
°F -20 0 20 32 40 60 80 100
°C -30 -20 -10 0 10 20 30 40
TEMPERATURE RANGE YOU EXPECT BEFORE NEXT OIL CHANGE

Gasoline engine oil viscosity recommedations

FUEL

Gasoline

NOTE: Some fuel additives contain chemicals that can damage the catalytic converter and/or oxygen sensor. Read all of the labels carefully before using any additive in the engine or fuel system.

Fuel should be selected for the brand and octane which performs best with your engine. Judge a gasoline by its ability to prevent pinging, it's engine starting capabilities (cold and hot) and general all weather performance.

As far as the octane rating is concerned, refer to the General Engine Specifications chart in Section 3 to find your engine and its compression ratio. If the compression ratio is 9.0:1 or lower, in most cases a regular unleaded grade of gasoline can be used. If the compression ratio is 9.0:1–9.3:1, use a premium grade of unleaded fuel.

NOTE: Your truck's engine fuel requirement can change with time, due to carbon buildup, which changes the compression ratio. If your truck's engine knocks, pings or runs on, switch to a higher grade of fuel (if possible) and check the ignition timing. Sometimes changing brands of gasoline will cure the problem. If it is necessary to retard the timing from specifications, don't change it more than a few degrees. Retarded timing will reduce the power output and the fuel mileage, plus it will increase the engine temperature.

Diesel

Diesel-engine pick-ups require the use of diesel fuel. Two grades are manufactured, #1 and #2 – although #2 grade is

NOTE: Fluids and lubricants identified below by name, part number or specification may be obtained from your GM Truck Dealer.

USAGE	FLUID/LUBRICANT
Engine Oil	GM Goodwrench Motor Oil or equivalent for API Service SG or SG/CE of the recommended viscosity
Engine Coolant	Mixture of water and a good quality ethylene glycol base antifreeze conforming to GM-6038-M (GM Part No. 1052103).
Hydraulic Clutch System	Hydraulic Clutch Fluid (GM Part No. 12345347) or DOT-3 brake fluid.
Hydraulic Brake Systems	Delco Supreme 11 brake fluid (GM Part No. 1052535 or DOT-3).
Parking Brake Cables	Chassis grease meeting requirements of GM-6031-M (GM Part No. 1052497).
Power Steering System	GM Power Steering Fluid (GM Part No. 1050017) or equivalent conforming to GM spec 9985010.
Manual Steering Gear	GM Lubricant (GM Part No. 1052182) or equivalent.
Automatic Transmission	DEXRON® II Automatic Transmission Fluid (GM Part No. 1051855).
Manual Transmission:	
4-Speed (RPO MC9, MF2)	DEXRON® II Automatic Transmission Fluid (GM Part No. 1051855).
4-Speed (RPO M20)	SAE-80W-90 gear lubricant (GM Part No. 12345577).
4-Speed Overdrive (RPO MY6)	DEXRON® II Automatic Transmission Fluid (GM Part No. 1051855).
5-Speed (RPO ML2, ML3 and MH3)	DEXRON® II Automatic Transmission Fluid (GM Part No. 1051855).
5-Speed (RPO MG5)	Manual Transmission Fluid (GM Part No. 1052931).
Differential:	
Standard - Front and Rear Axle	SAE-80W-90 GL-5 gear lubricant (GM Part No. 1052271).
Locking	SAE-80W-90 gear lubricant (GM Part No. 1052271).
Transfer Case	Dexron® II Automatic Transmission Fluid (GM Part No 1051855).

Recommended fluids and lubricants

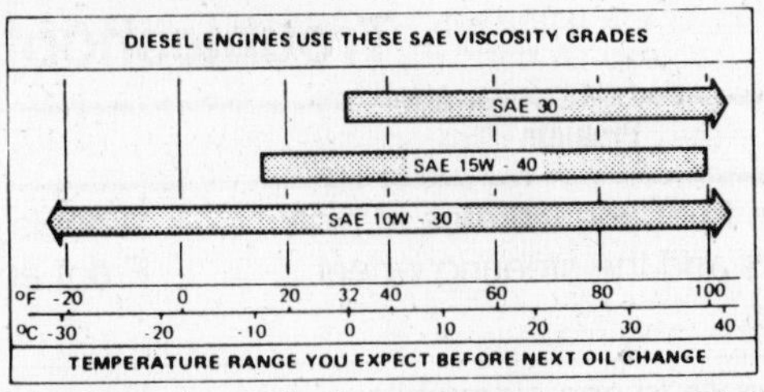
DIESEL ENGINES USE THESE SAE VISCOSITY GRADES
SAE 30
SAE 15W - 40
SAE 10W - 30
°F -20 0 20 32 40 60 80 100
°C -30 -20 -10 0 10 20 30 40
TEMPERATURE RANGE YOU EXPECT BEFORE NEXT OIL CHANGE

Diesel engine oil viscosity recommendation

ADD
1QT
FULL

The full level should be between the "add" and "full" marks on the dipstick

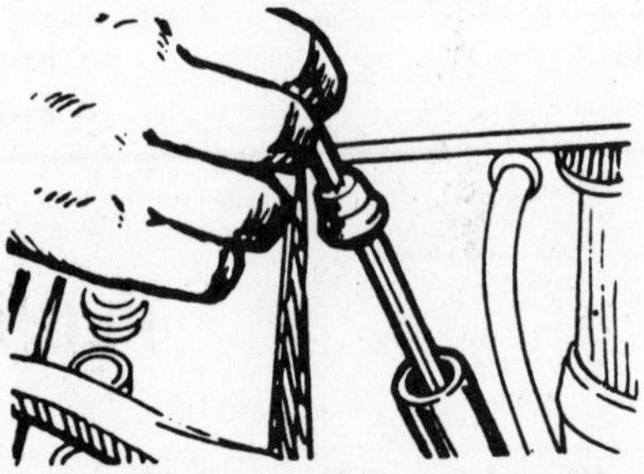

The oil level is checked with the dipstick. When checking engine oil level, note the color and smell of the oil. Oil that is black or has a gas smell indicates a need for engine service

generally the only grade available. Better fuel economy results from the use of #2 grade fuel.

In some northern parts of the USA, and in most parts of Canada, #1 grade fuel is available in winter, or a winterized blend of #2 grade is supplied in winter months. If #1 grade is available, it should be used whenever temperatures fall below 20°F (−7°C). Winterized #2 grade may also be used at these temperatures. However, unwinterized #2 grade should not be used below 20°F (−7°C). Cold temperatures cause unwinterized #2 grade to thicken (it actually gels), blocking the fuel lines and preventing the engine from running.

CAUTION

DO NOT use home heating oil or gasoline in the diesel truck. DO NOT attempt to "thin" unwinterized #2 diesel fuel with gasoline. Gasoline or home heating oil will damage the engine and void the manufacturer's warranty. A mixture of gasoline and diesel fuel produces an extremely potent explosive that is more volatile than gasoline alone.

Engine

OIL CHECK LEVEL

The engine oil should be checked on a regular basis, ideally at each fuel stop. If the truck is used for trailer towing or for heavy-duty use, it is recommended to check the oil more frequently.

When checking the oil level, it is best that the oil be at operating temperature. Checking the level immediately after stopping will give a false reading due to oil left in the upper part of the engine. Be sure that the truck is resting on a level surface, allowing time for the oil to drain back into the crankcase.

1. Open the hood and locate the dipstick. Remove it from the tube (The oil dipstick is located on the driver's side).
2. Wipe the dipstick with a clean rag.
3. Insert the dipstick fully into the tube and remove it again.
4. Hold the dipstick horizontally and read the oil level. The level should be between the FULL and ADD marks.
5. If the oil level is at or below the ADD mark, oil should be added as necessary. Oil is added through the capped opening on the valve cover(s) on gasoline engines. Diesel engines have a capped oil fill tube at the front of the engine. Refer to the "Engine Oil and Fuel Recommendations" in this section for the proper viscosity oil to use.
6. Replace the dipstick and check the level after adding oil. Be careful not to overfill the crankcase. Approximately one quart of oil will raise the level from ADD to FULL.

OIL AND FILTER CHANGE

Engine oil should be changed every 3,000 miles on gasoline engines and every 3,000 miles on diesel engines. The oil change and filter replacement interval should be cut in half under conditions such as:

- Driving in dusty conditions.
- Continuous trailer pulling or RV use.
- Extensive or prolonged idling.
- Extensive short trip operation in freezing temperatures (when the engine is not thoroughly warmed-up).
- Frequent long runs at high speed and high ambient temperatures.
- Stop-and-go service such as delivery trucks.

Operation of the engine in severe conditions such as a dust storm may require an immediate oil and filter change.

Chevrolet and GMC recommend changing both the oil and filter during the first oil change and the filter every other oil change thereafter. For the small price of an oil filter, it's cheap insurance to replace the filter at every oil change. One of the larger filter manufacturers points out in its advertisements that not changing the filter leaves one quart of dirty oil in the engine. This claim is true and should be kept in mind when changing your oil.

NOTE: The oil filter on the diesel engine must be changed every oil change.

To change the oil, the truck should be on a level surface and the engine should be at operating temperature. This is to ensure that the foreign matter will be drained away along with the oil and not left in the engine to form sludge. You should have available a container that will hold a minimum of 8 quarts of liquid, a wrench to fit the old drain plug, a spout for pouring in new oil and a rag or two, which you will always need. If the filter is being replaced, you will also need a band wrench or filter wrench to fit the end of the filter.

NOTE: If the engine is equipped with an oil cooler, this will also have to be drained, using the drain plug. Be sure to add enough oil to fill the cooler in addition to the engine.

1. Position the truck on a level surface and set the parking brake or block the wheels. Slide a drain pan under the oil drain plug.
2. From under the truck, loosen, but do not remove the oil drain plug. Cover your hand with a rag or glove and slowly unscrew the drain plug.

CAUTION

The engine oil will be HOT. Keep your arms, face and hands clear of the oil as it drains out.

3. Remove the plug and let the oil drain into the pan. Do not drop the plug into the drain pan.
4. When all of the oil has drained, clean off the drain plug and reinstall it into pan. Torque the drain plug to 20 ft. lbs. (gasoline) or 30 ft. lbs. (diesel) engines.
5. Using an oil filter wrench, loosen the oil filter. On most Chevrolet engines, especially the V6s, the oil filter is next to the

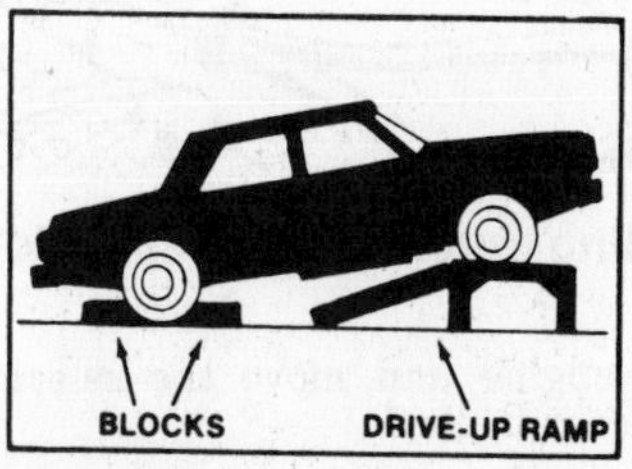
BLOCKS
DRIVE-UP RAMP

1. Warm the car up before changing your oil. Raise the front end of the car and support it on drive-on ramps or jackstands.

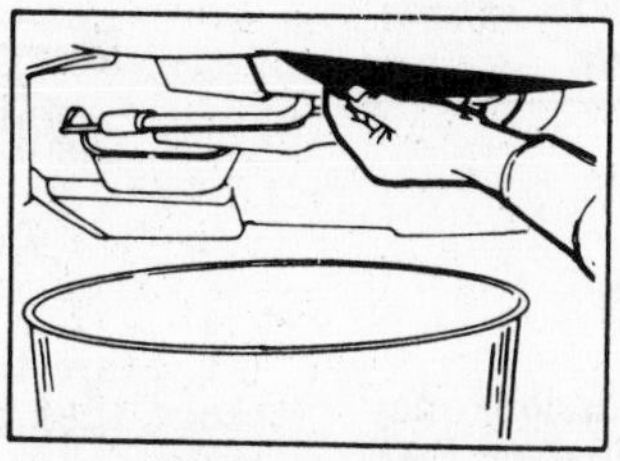

2. Locate the drain plug on the bottom of the oil pan and slide a low flat pan of sufficient capacity under the engine to catch the oil. Loosen the plug with a wrench and turn it out the last few turns by hand. Keep a steady inward pressure on the plug to avoid hot oil from running down your arm.

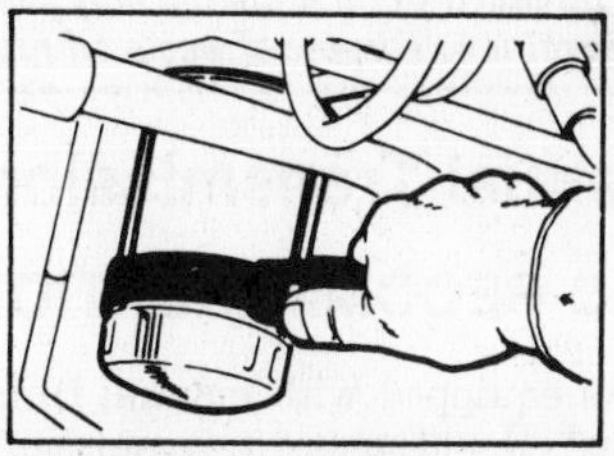

3. Remove the oil filter with a filter wrench. The filter can hold more than a quart of oil, which will be hot. Be sure the gasket comes off with the filter and clean the mounting base on the engine.

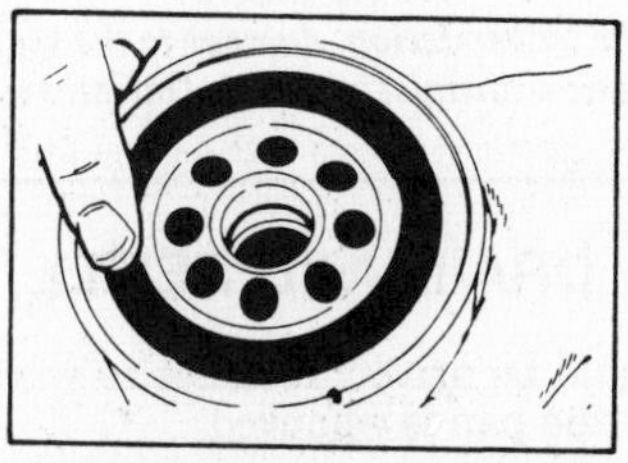

4. Lubricate the gasket on the new filter with clean engine oil. A dry gasket may not make a good seal and will allow the filter to leak.

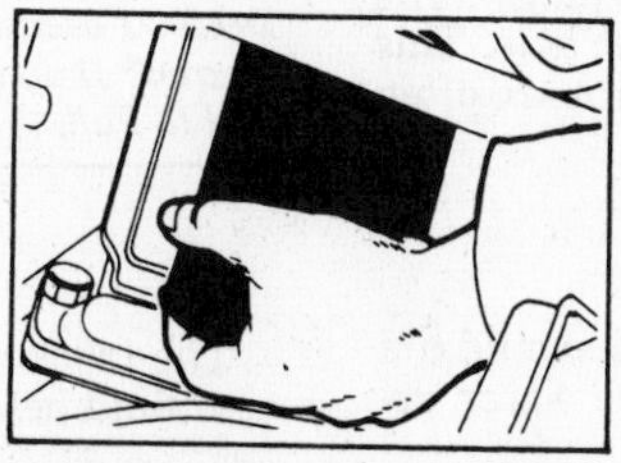

5. Position a new filter on the mounting base and spin it on by hand. Do not use a wrench. When the gasket contacts the engine, tighten it another ½–1 turn by hand.

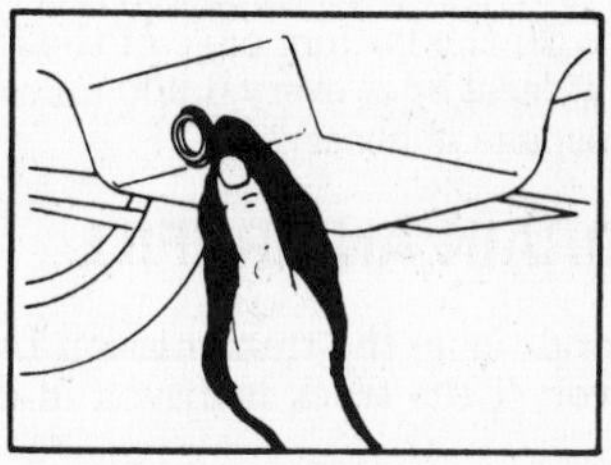

6. Using a rag, clean the drain plug and the area around the drain hole in the oil pan.

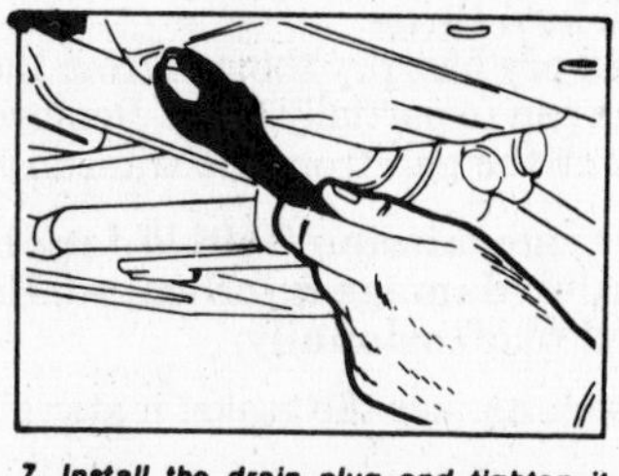

7. Install the drain plug and tighten it finger-tight. If you feel resistance, stop and be sure you are not cross-threading the plug. Finally, tighten the plug with a wrench.

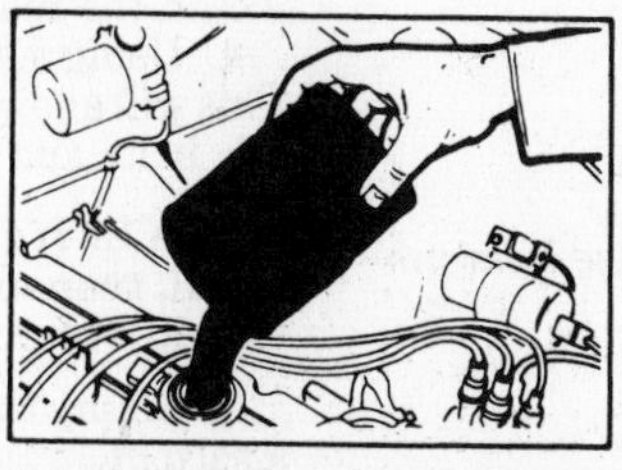

8. Locate the oil cap on the valve cover. An oil spout is the easiest way to add oil, but a funnel will do just as well.

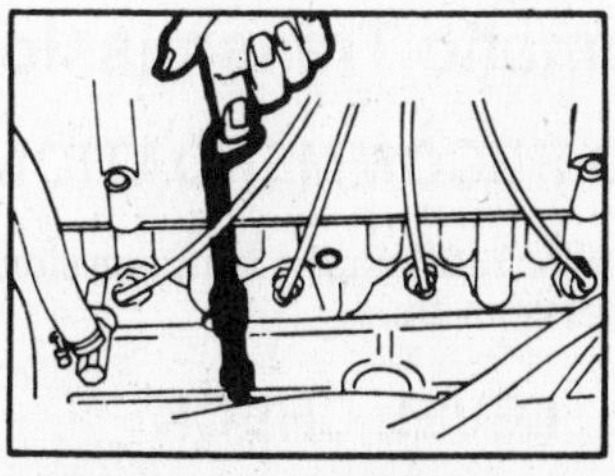

9. Start the engine and check for leaks. The oil pressure warning light will remain on for a few seconds; when it goes out, stop the engine and check the level on the dipstick.

exhaust pipes. Stay clear of these, since even a passing contact will result in a painful burn.

NOTE: On trucks equipped with catalytic converters, stay clear of the converter. The outside temperature of a hot catalytic converter can approach 1200°F.

6. Cover your hand with a rag and spin the filter off by hand; turn it slowly.
7. Coat the rubber gasket on a new filter with a light film of clean engine oil. Screw the filter onto the mounting stud and tighten it according to the directions on the filter (usually hand-tight one turn past the point where the gasket contacts the mounting base); DO NOT overtighten the filter.
8. Refill the engine with the specified amount of clean engine oil.
9. Run the engine for several minutes, checking for leaks. Check the level of the oil and add oil if necessary.

When you have finished this job, you will notice that you now possess four or five quarts of dirty oil. The best thing to do with it is to pour it into plastic jugs, such as milk or antifreeze containers. Then, locate a service station where you can pour it into their used oil tank for recycling.

CAUTION

Pouring used motor oil into a storm drain not only pollutes the environment, it violates Federal law. Dispose of waste oil properly.

Manual Transmission

FLUID RECOMMENDATIONS

S-10/S-15 trucks equipped with manual transmissions may use either Dexron® II automatic transmission fluid or SAE 80W-90 gear oil. Check the Recommended Fluids and Lubricants Chart to determine which type of lubricant your transmission uses.

LEVEL CHECK

Remove the filler plug from the passenger's-side of the transmission (the upper plug if the transmission has two plugs). The oil should be level with the bottom edge of the filler hole. This should be checked at least once every 6,000 miles or more often if any leakage or seepage is observed.

DRAIN AND REFILL

Under normal conditions, the transmission fluid should not be changed. However, if the truck is driven in deep water, replace the fluid.

1. Raise and support the vehicle on jackstands.
2. Place a fluid catch pan under the transmission.
3. Remove the bottom plug and drain the fluid.
4. Install the bottom plug and refill the transmission housing.

Automatic Transmission

FLUID RECOMMENDATIONS

When adding fluid or refilling the transmission, use Dexron® II automatic transmission fluid.

LEVEL CHECK

Before checking the fluid level of the transmission, drive the truck for at least 15 miles to warm the fluid.

1. Place the truck on a level surface, apply the parking brake and block the front wheels.

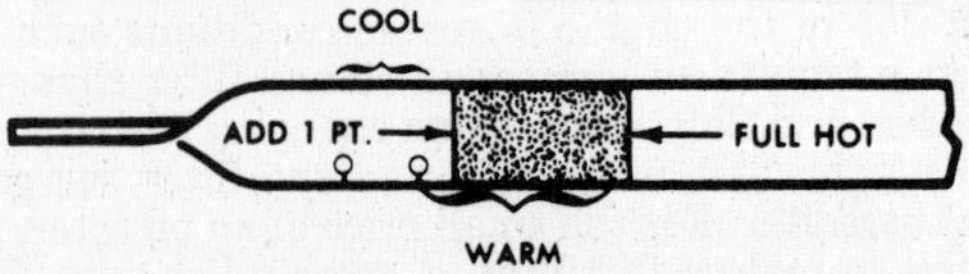
COOL
ADD 1 PT.
FULL HOT
WARM

Automatic transmission fluid dipstick. When checking transmission oil, note the color and smell of the oil. Oil that is brown or has a burnt smell indicates a need for transmission service

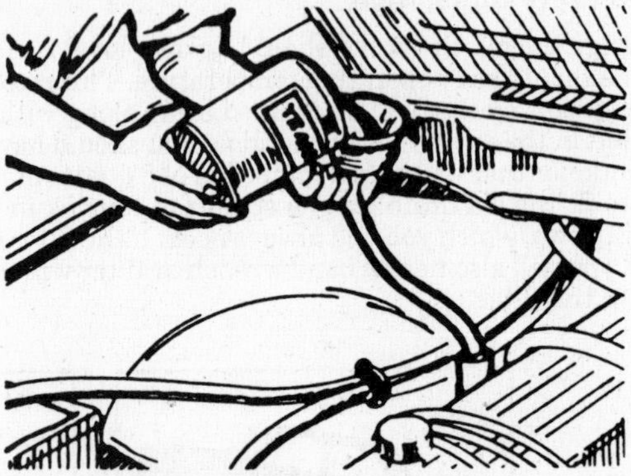

Adding automatic transmission fluid

2. Start the engine and move the selector through each range, then place it in Park.

NOTE: When moving the selector through each range, DO NOT race the engine.

3. With the engine running at a low idle, remove the transmission's dipstick to check the fluid level.
4. The level should be at the Full Hot mark of the dipstick. If not, add fluid.

CAUTION

DO NOT overfill the transmission, damage to the seals could occur. Use Dexron® II automatic transmission fluid. One pint raises the level from Add to Full.

DRAIN AND REFILL

The truck should be driven 15 miles to warm the transmission fluid before the pan is removed.

NOTE: The fluid should be drained while the transmission is warm.

1. Raise and support the front of vehicle on jackstands.
2. Place a drain pan under the transmission pan.
3. Remove the pan bolts from the front and the sides, then loosen the rear bolts 4 turns.
4. Using a small pry bar, pry the pan from the transmission. This will allow the pan to partially drain. Remove the remaining pan bolts and lower the pan from the transmission.

NOTE: If the transmission fluid is dark or has a burnt smell, transmission damage is indicated. Have the transmission checked professionally.

5. Empty the pan, remove the gasket material and clean with a solvent.
6. Using a putty knife, clean gasket mounting surfaces.
7. To install the oil pan, use a new gasket and sealant, then reverse the removal procedures. Torque the pan bolts to 8 ft. lbs. in a criss-cross pattern.

8. Using Dexron® II automatic transmission fluid, add it through the filler tube. See the Capacities Chart to determine the proper amount of fluid to be added.

CAUTION

DO NOT OVERFILL the transmission. Foaming of the fluid and subsequent transmission damage due to slippage will result.

9. With the gearshift lever in PARK, start the engine and let it idle. DO NOT race the engine.
10. Apply the parking brake and move the gearshift lever through each position. Return the lever to Park and check the fluid level with the engine idling. The level should be between the two dimples on the dipstick, about ¼ in. (6mm) below the ADD mark. Add fluid, if necessary.
11. Check the fluid level after the truck has been driven enough to thoroughly warm the transmission.

PAN AND FILTER SERVICE

1. Refer to the Drain and Refill procedures in this section and remove the oil pan.
2. Remove the screen and the filter from the valve body.
3. Install a new filter using a new gasket or O-ring.

NOTE: If the transmission uses a filter having a fully exposed screen, it may be cleaned and reused.

4. To install the oil pan, use a new gasket and sealant, then reverse the removal procedures. Torque the pan bolts to 8 ft. lbs. in a criss-cross pattern. Refill the transmission.

Transfer Case

FLUID RECOMMENDATIONS

When adding fluid or refilling the transfer case, use Dexron® II automatic transmission fluid.

LEVEL CHECK

1. Raise and support the vehicle (level) on jackstands.
2. At the rear-side of the transfer case, remove the filler plug.
3. Using your finger, check the fluid level, it should be level with the bottom of the filler hole.
4. If the fluid level is low, use Dexron® II automatic transmission fluid to bring the fluid up to the proper level.
5. Install the filler plug and torque it to 30–40 ft. lbs.

DRAIN AND REFILL

1. Raise and support the front of the vehicle on jackstands.
2. Position drain pan under transfer case.
3. Remove drain and fill plugs, then drain the lubricant into the drain pan.
4. Install drain plug. Torque the plug to 30–40 ft. lbs.
5. Remove the drain pan and dump the fluid into a used oil storage tank, for recycling purposes.
6. Using Dexron® II automatic transmission fluid, fill transfer case to edge of fill plug opening.
7. Install fill plug and torque it to 30–40 ft. lbs.
8. Lower vehicle and check the operation of the transfer case.

Drive Axles

If the truck is equipped with a front drive axle, perform the same procedures as for the standard rear drive axle. Replace the fluid at the first oil change. If the truck is operated in dusty areas or used in trailer towing applications, replace the fluid every 15,000 miles. Check fluid and add as needed to maintain a Full fluid level of ⅜ in. below the filler plug hole every oil change.

FLUID RECOMMENDATIONS

Standard Axle

Always use SAE-80W or SAE 80W-90 GL5.

Locking Axle

CAUTION

Never use standard differential lubricant in a positraction differential.

Always use GM Rear Axle Fluid No. 1052271. Before refilling the rear axle, add 4 ounces of GM Fluid No. 1052358.

LEVEL CHECK

The lubricant level should be checked at each oil change and maintained at ⅜ in. below the bottom of the filler plug hole.

1. Raise and support the vehicle on jackstands; be sure that the vehicle is level.
2. Remove the filler plug, located at the side of the differential carrier.
3. Check the fluid level, it should be ⅜ in. below the bottom of the filler plug hole, add fluid (if necessary).
4. Replace the filler plug.

DRAIN AND REFILL

Refer to Fluid Recommendations in this section for information on when to change the fluid.

1. Run the vehicle until the lubricant reaches operating temperature.
2. Raise and support the vehicle on jackstands; be sure that the vehicle is level.
3. Using a floor jack, support the drive axle. Position a drain pan under the rear axle.
4. Remove the cover from the rear of the drive axle and drain the lubricant.
5. Using a putty knife, clean the gasket mounting surfaces.
6. To install, use a new gasket, sealant and reverse the removal procedures.
7. Torque the cover-to-rear axle bolts in a criss-cross pattern to 20 ft. lbs. Using a suction gun or a squeeze bulb, install the fluid through the filler plug hole. Install the filler plug.

Cooling System

At least once every 2 years or 30,000 miles, the engine cooling system should be inspected, flushed and refilled with fresh coolant. If the coolant is left in the system too long, it loses its ability to prevent rust and corrosion. If the coolant has too much water, it won't protect against freezing.

FLUID RECOMMENDATIONS

Using a good quality of ethylene glycol antifreeze (one that will not effect aluminum), mix it with water until a 50–50 antifreeze solution is attained.

LEVEL CHECK

NOTE: When checking the coolant level, the radiator cap need not be removed, simply check the coolant tank.

Check the coolant recovery bottle (see through plastic bottle). With the engine Cold, the coolant should be at the ADD mark (recovery tank ¼ full). With the engine warm, the coolant

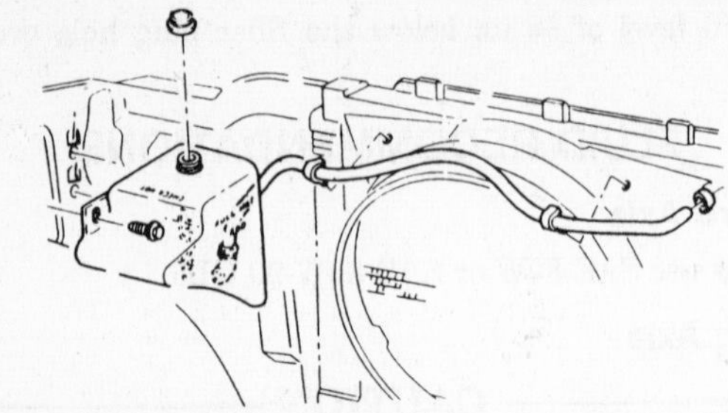

Coolant recovery system see-through bottle

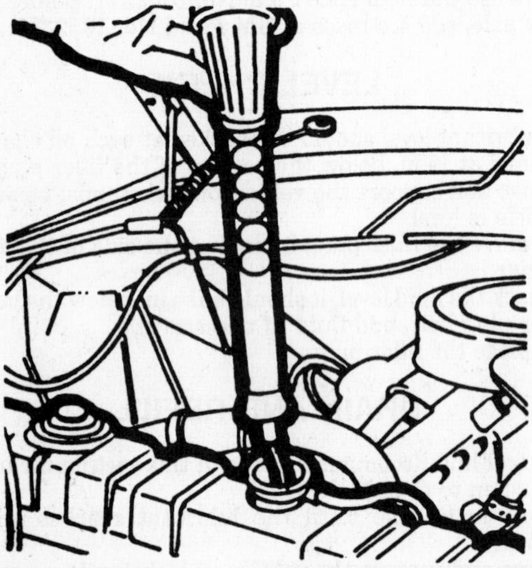

Coolant protection can be checked with a simple float-type tester

should be at the FULL mark (recovery tank ½ full). If necessary, add fluid to the recovery bottle.

DRAIN AND REFILL

CAUTION

To avoid injuries from scalding fluid and steam, DO NOT remove the radiator cap while the engine and radiator are still HOT.

1. When the engine is cool, remove the radiator cap using the following procedures.
   a. Slowly rotate the cap counterclockwise to the detent.
   b. If any residual pressure is present, WAIT until the hissing noise stops.
   c. After the hissing noise has ceased, press down on the cap and continue rotating it counterclockwise to remove it.
2. Place a fluid catch pan under the radiator, open the radiator drain valve and the engine drain plugs, then drain the coolant.

CAUTION

When draining the coolant, keep in mind that cats and dogs are attracted by the ethylene glycol antifreeze, and are quite likely to drink any that is left in an uncovered container or in puddles on the ground. This will prove fatal in sufficient quantity. Always drain the coolant into a sealable container. Coolant should be reused unless it is contaminated or several years old.

3. Close the drain valve and install the engine drain plugs.
4. Empty the coolant reservoir and flush it.
5. Using the correct mixture of antifreeze, fill the radiator to

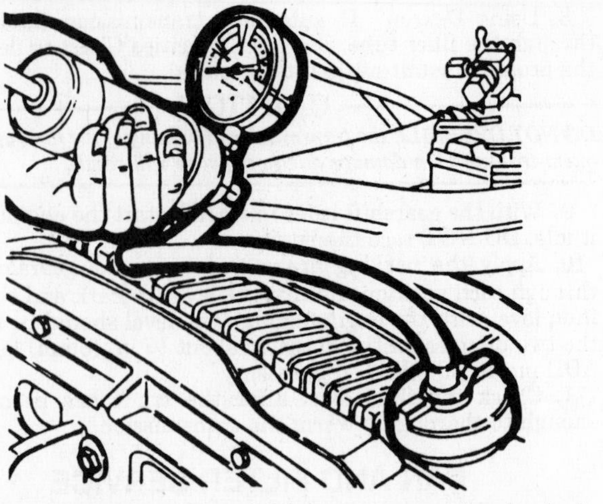

The coolant system should be pressure checked at least once a year

the bottom of the filler neck and the coolant tank to the FULL mark.

6. Install the radiator cap (make sure that the arrows align with the overflow tube).
7. Run the engine until it reaches the operating temperatures, allow it to cool, then check the fluid level and add fluid (if necessary).

FLUSHING AND CLEANING THE SYSTEM

1. Refer to the Drain and Refill procedures in this section, then drain the cooling system.

CAUTION

When draining the coolant, keep in mind that cats and dogs are attracted by the ethylene glycol antifreeze, and are quite likely to drink any that is left in an uncovered container or in puddles on the ground. This will prove fatal in sufficient quantity. Always drain the coolant into a sealable container. Coolant should be reused unless it is contaminated or several years old.

2. Close the drain valve and install the engine drain plugs, then add sufficient water to the cooling system.

CAUTION

When draining the coolant, keep in mind that cats and dogs are attracted by the ethylene glycol antifreeze, and are quite likely to drink any that is left in an uncovered container or in puddles on the ground. This will prove fatal in sufficient quantity. Always drain the coolant into a sealable container. Coolant should be reused unless it is contaminated or several years old.

3. Run the engine, then drain and refill the system. Perform this procedure several times, until the fluid (drained from the system) is clear.
4. Empty the coolant reservoir and flush it.
5. Using the correct mixture of antifreeze, fill the radiator to the bottom of the filler neck and the coolant tank to the FULL mark.
6. Install the radiator cap (make sure that the arrows align with the overflow tube).

Master Cylinder

NOTE: Refer to Anti-Lock Brake System in Section 8 for special service procedures.

Chevrolet and GMC trucks are equipped with a dual braking system, allowing a truck to be brought to a safe stop in the event of failure in either the front or rear brakes. The dual master cylinder has two separate reservoirs, one connected to the front brakes and the other connected to the rear brakes. In the event of failure in either portion, the remaining portion is unaffected.

FLUID RECOMMENDATIONS

Use only heavy-duty Delco Supreme 11 or DOT-3 brake fluid.

CAUTION

Brake fluid damages paint. It also absorbs moisture from the air; never leave a container or the master cylinder uncovered any longer than necessary. All parts in contact with the brake fluid (master cylinder, hoses, plunger assemblies and etc.) must be kept clean, since any contamination of the brake fluid will adversely affect braking performance.

LEVEL CHECK

The brake fluid level should be inspected every 6 months.

1. Remove the master cylinder reservoir cap.

NOTE: If equipped with a see through reservoir, it is not necessary to remove the reservoir cap unless you are adding fluid.

2. The fluid should be ¼ in. (6mm) from top of the reservoir, if necessary, add fluid.
3. Replace the reservoir caps.

Hydraulic Clutch

NOTE: The clutch master cylinder is mounted on the firewall next to the brake master cylinder.

FLUID RECOMMENDATIONS

Use only heavy duty Delco Supreme 11 or DOT-3 brake fluid.

LEVEL CHECK

The hydraulic clutch reservoir should be checked at least every 6 months. Fill to the line on the reservoir.

Power Steering Pump

The power steering pump reservoir is located at the front left-side of the engine.

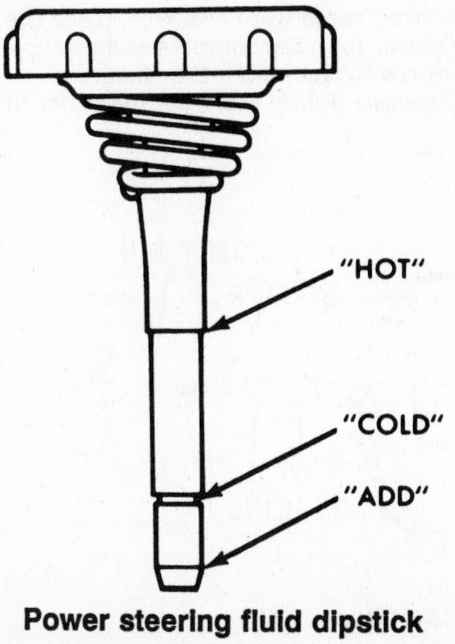
"HOT"
"COLD"
"ADD"

Power steering fluid dipstick

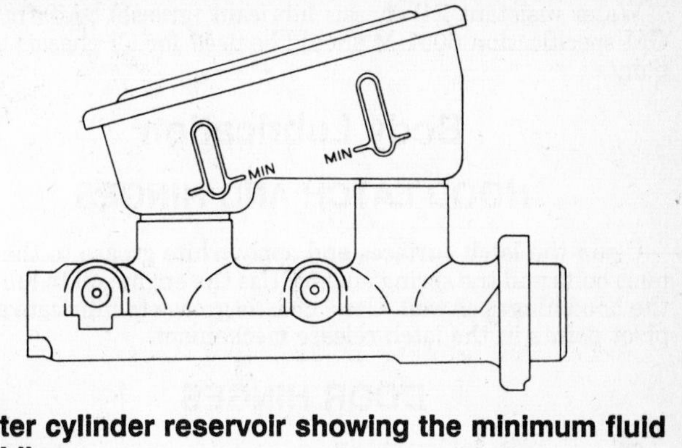
MIN
MIN

Master cylinder reservoir showing the minimum fluid level line

FLUID RECOMMENDATIONS

Use GM Power Steering Fluid No. 1050017 or equivalent.

NOTE: Avoid using automatic transmission fluid in the power steering unit, except in an emergency.

LEVEL CHECK

The power steering fluid should be checked at least every 6 months. There is a Cold and a Hot mark on the dipstick. The fluid should be checked when the engine is warm and turned OFF. If necessary, add fluid to the power steering pump reservoir.

NOTE: On models equipped with a remote reservoir, the fluid level should be ½–1 in. (25.4mm) from the top when the wheels are turned to the extreme left position.

Manual Steering Gear

The steering gear is factory-filled with a lubricant which does not require seasonal change. The housing should not be drained; no lubrication is required for the life of the gear.

FLUID RECOMMENDATIONS

Use GM steering gear lubricant No. 1052182 or equivalent.

LEVEL CHECK

The steering lubricant should be checked every 6 months or 7,500 miles. The gear should be inspected for seal leakage when specified in the Maintenance Interval chart. Look for solid grease, not an oily film. If a seal is replaced or the gear overhauled, it should be refilled with lubricant.

Chassis Greasing

Chassis greasing should be performed every 6 months or 7,500 miles, it can be performed with a commercial pressurized grease gun or at home by using a hand operated grease gun. Wipe the grease fittings clean before greasing in order to prevent the possibility of forcing any dirt into the component.

The four wheel drive front driveshaft requires special attention for lubrication. The large constant velocity joint at the front of the transfer case has a special grease fitting in the centering ball. A special needle nose adapter for a flush type fitting is required, as well as a special lubricant (GM part No. 1050679). You can only get at this fitting when it is facing up toward the floorboard, so you need a flexible hose, too.

Water resistant EP chassis lubricant (grease) conforming to GM specification 6031-M should be used for all chassis grease points.

Body Lubrication

HOOD LATCH AND HINGES

Clean the latch surfaces and apply white grease to the latch pilot bolts and the spring anchor. Use the engine oil to lubricate the hood hinges as well. Use a chassis grease to lubricate all the pivot points in the latch release mechanism.

DOOR HINGES

The gas tank filler door, the front doors and rear door hinges should be wiped clean and lubricated with white grease. The door lock cylinders can be lubricated easily with a shot of GM silicone spray No. 1052276 or one of the many dry penetrating lubricants commercially available.

PARKING BRAKE LINKAGE

Use chassis grease on the parking brake cable where it contacts the guides, links, levers and pulleys. The grease should be a water resistant for durability under the truck.

ACCELERATOR LINKAGE

Lubricate the throttle body lever, the cable and the accelerator pedal lever (at the support inside the truck) with white grease.

TRANSMISSION SHIFT LINKAGE

Lubricate the shift linkage with water resistant chassis grease which meets GM specification No. 6031M or equivalent.

Front Wheel Bearings—2WD Only

Once every 30,000 miles, clean and repack wheel bearings with a GM Wheel Bearing Grease No. 1051344 or equivalent. Use only enough grease to completely coat the rollers. Remove any excess grease from the exposed surface of the hub and seal.

REMOVAL, PACKING AND INSTALLATION

NOTE: The following procedures require the use of GM tools No. J-29117, J-8092, J-8850, J-8457, J-9746-02 or equivalent.

1. Raise and support the front of the vehicle on jackstands.

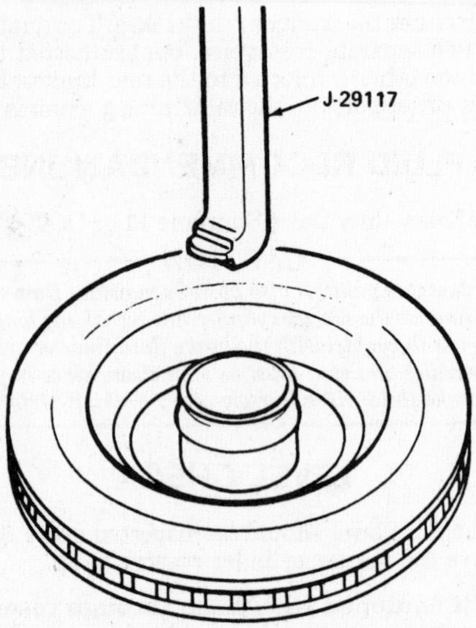
J-29117

Removing the bearing and race from the front wheel hub—2WD

2. Remove the tire/wheel assembly.
3. Remove the caliper-to-steering knuckle bolts and the caliper from the steering knuckle. Using a wire, support the caliper from the vehicle; DO NOT disconnect the brake line.
4. From the hub/disc assembly, remove the dust cap, the cotter pin, the spindle nut, the thrust washer and the outer bearing.
5. Grasping the hub/disc assembly firmly, pull the assembly from the axle spindle.
6. Using a small pry bar, pry the grease seal from the rear of the hub/disc assembly, then remove the inner bearing.

NOTE: DO NOT remove the bearing races from the hub, unless they show signs of damage.

7. If it is necessary to remove the wheel bearing races, use the GM front bearing race removal tool No. J-29117 or equivalent, to drive the races from the hub/disc assembly.
8. Using solvent, clean the grease from all of the parts, then wipe dry with a clean cloth. Blowing bearing dry with compressed air may damage them
9. Inspect all of the parts for scoring, pitting or cracking and replace if necessary.
10. If the bearing races were removed, place the replacement races in the freezer for a few minutes and then perform the following procedures to the install the them:
    a. Using grease, lightly lubricate the inside of the hub/disc assembly.

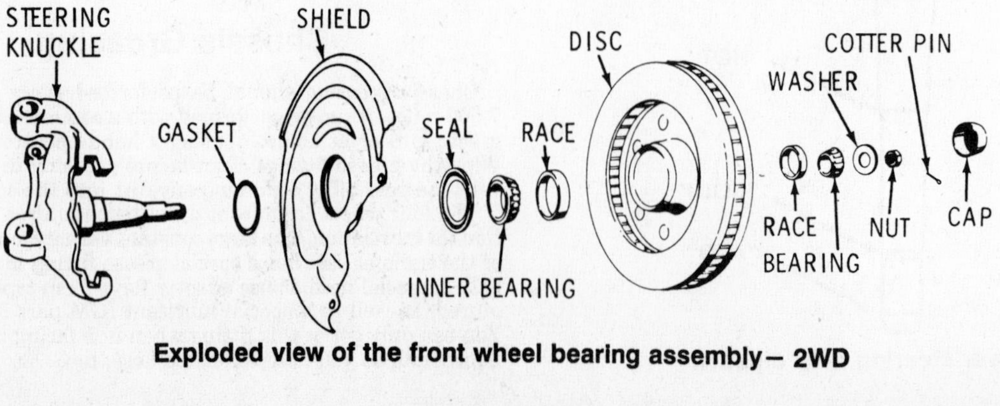
STEERING KNUCKLE
SHIELD
DISC
COTTER PIN
WASHER
GASKET
SEAL
RACE
RACE
NUT
CAP
BEARING
INNER BEARING

Exploded view of the front wheel bearing assembly— 2WD

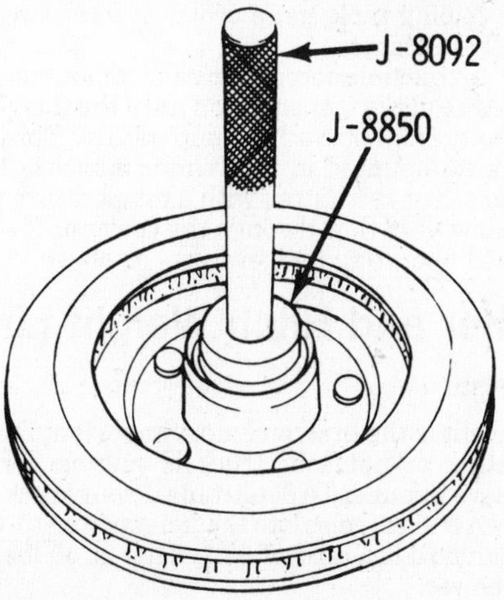
J-8092
J-8850

Installing the inner bearing race—2WD

b. Using the GM seal installation tools No. J-8092 and J-8850 or equivalent, drive the inner bearing race into the hub/disc assembly until it seats.

NOTE: When installing the bearing races, be sure to support the hub/disc assembly with GM tool No. J-9746-02 or equivalent.

c. Using the GM seal installation tools No. J-8092 and J-8457 or equivalent, drive the outer race into the hub/disc assembly until it seats.

11. Using wheel bearing grease, lubricate the bearings, the races and the spindle; be sure to place a gob of grease (inside the hub/disc assembly) between the races to provide an ample supply of lubricant.

NOTE: To lubricate each bearing, place a gob of grease in the palm of the hand, then roll the bearing through the grease until it is well lubricated.

12. Place the inner wheel bearing into the hub/disc assembly. Using a flat plate, drive the new grease seal into the rear of the hub/disc assembly until it is flush with the outer surface.

13. Onto the spindle, install the hub/disc assembly, the thrust washer and the hub nut. While turning the wheel, torque the hub nut to 16 ft. lbs. until the bearings seat. Loosen the nut, retighten it and back it off until the nearest nut slot aligns with a spindle hole (not more than a ½ turn).

14. Install a new cotter pin through the nut and the spindle, then bend the ends and cut off the excess pin. Install the grease cap.

15. If necessary, use a dial indicator to the check the rotor endplay. The endplay should be 0.001–0.005 in. (0.025–0.127mm); if not, readjust the hub/disc assembly.

16. Install the caliper onto the steering knuckle and torque the bolts to 37 ft. lbs. Road test the vehicle.

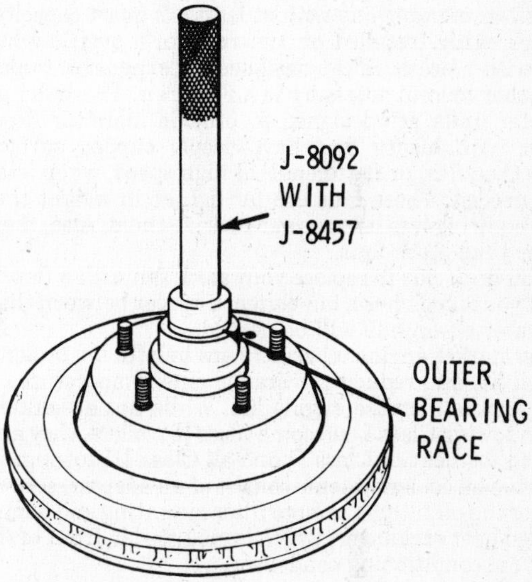
J-8092
WITH
J-8457
OUTER
BEARING
RACE

Installing the outer bearing race—2WD

TRAILER TOWING

Trucks are popular as trailer towing vehicles. Their strong construction and variety of power train combinations make them ideal for towing campers, boat and utility trailers.

Factory trailer towing packages are available on most trucks. However, if you are installing a trailer hitch and wiring on your truck, there are a few things you ought to know.

General Recommendations

Wiring

Wiring the truck for towing is fairly easy. There are a number of good wiring kits available and these should be used, rather than trying to design your own. All trailers will need brake lights, turn signals, tail lights and side marker lights. Most states require extra marker lights for overwide trailers. Also, most states have recently required back-up lights for trailers, and most trailer manufacturers have been building trailers with back-up lights for several years.

Additionally, some Class I, most Class II and all Class III trailers will have electric brakes.

Add to this number an accessories wire, to operate the trailer internal equipment or to charge the trailer's battery, and you can have as many as seven wires in the harness.

Determine the equipment on your trailer and buy the wiring kit necessary. The kit will contain all the wires needed, plus a plug adapter set which included the female plug, mounted on the bumper or hitch, and the male plug, wired into, or plugged into the trailer harness.

When installing the kit, follow the manufacturer's instructions. The color coding of the wires is standard throughout the industry.

One point to note: some domestic vehicles and most imported vehicles, have separate turn signals. On most domestic vehicles, the brake lights and rear turn signals operate with the same bulb. For those vehicles with separate turn signals, you can purchase an isolation unit so that the brake lights won't blink whenever the turn signals are operated, or, you can go to your local electronics supply house and buy four diodes to wire in series with the brake and turn signal bulbs. Diodes will isolate the brake and turn signals. The choice is yours. The isolation units are simple and quick to install, but far more expensive than the diodes. The diodes, however, require more work to install properly, since they require the cutting of each bulb's wire and soldering in place of the diode.

One, final point, the best kits are those with a spring loaded cover on the vehicle mounted socket. This cover prevents dirt and moisture from corroding the terminals. Never let the vehicle socket hang loosely; always mount it securely to the bumper or hitch.

Cooling

ENGINE

The most common problem associated with trailer towing is engine overheating.

With factory installed trailer towing packages, a heavy duty cooling system is usually included. Heavy duty cooling systems are available as optional equipment on most trucks, with or without a trailer package. If you have one of these extra capacity systems, you shouldn't have overheating problems.

If you have a standard cooling system, without an expansion tank, you'll definitely need to get an aftermarket expansion tank kit, preferably one with at least a 2 quart capacity. These kits are easily installed on the radiator's overflow hose, and come with a pressure cap designed for expansion tanks.

Another helpful accessory is a Flex Fan. These fan are large diameter units are designed to provide more air flow at low speeds, with blades that have deeply cupped surfaces. The blades then flex, or flatten out, at high speed, when less cooling air is needed. These fans are far lighter in weight than stock fans, requiring less horsepower to drive them. Also, they are far quieter than stock fans.

If you do decide to replace your stock fan with a flex fan, note that if your truck has a fan clutch, a spacer between the flex fan and water pump hub will be needed.

Aftermarket engine oil coolers are helpful for prolonging engine oil life and reducing overall engine temperatures. Both of these factors increase engine life. While not absolutely necessary in towing Class I and some Class II trailers, they are recommended for heavier Class II and all Class III towing.

Engine oil cooler systems consist of an adapter, screwed on in place of the oil filter, a remote filter mounting and a multi-tube, a finned heat exchanger, which is mounted in front of the radiator or air conditioning condenser.

TRANSMISSION

An automatic transmission is usually recommended for trailer towing. The increased load of trailer towing causesn increase in the temperature of the automatic transmission fluid—heat is the worst enemy of an automatic transmission. As the temperature of the fluid increases, the life of the fluid decreases. It is essential, therefore, that you install an automatic transmission cooler.

The cooler, which consists of a multi-tube, finned heat exchanger, is usually installed in front of the radiator or air conditioning compressor, and hooked inline with the transmission cooler tank inlet line. Follow the cooler manufacturer's installation instructions and select a cooler of at least adequate capacity, based upon the combined gross weights of the truck and trailer.

Cooler manufacturers recommend that you use an aftermarket cooler in addition to, and not instead of, the present cooling tank in your trucks radiator. If you do want to use it in place of the radiator cooling tank, get a cooler at least two sizes larger than normally necessary.

One note: A transmission cooler can, sometimes, cause slow or harsh shifting in the transmission until the fluid has a chance to come up to normal operating temperature. This condition is usually more pronounced in the Winter months. Some coolers can be purchased or retrofitted with a temperature bypass valve which will allow fluid flow through the cooler only when the fluid has reached operating temperature, or above.

Trailer and Hitch Weight Limits

Trailer Weight

Trailer weight is the first, and most important factor in determining whether or not your truck is suitable for towing the trailer you have in mind. To determine if your truck is capable of towing a given trailer, calculate the horsepower-to-weight ratio. The basic standard is a ratio of 35:1. That is, 35 lbs. of GVW for every horsepower.

To calculate this ratio, multiply you engine's rated horsepower by 35, then subtract the weight of the truck, including passengers and luggage. The resulting figure is the ideal maximum trailer weight that you can tow. One point to consider: a numerically higher axle ratio can offset what appears to be a low trailer weight. If the weight of the trailer that you have in mind is somewhat higher than the weight you just calculated, you might consider changing your rear axle ratio to compensate.

Hitch Weight

There are three kinds of hitches: bumper mounted, frame mounted and load equalizing.

Bumper mounted hitches are those which attach solely to the truck's bumper. Many states prohibit towing with this type of hitch, when it attaches to the truck's stock bumper, since it subjects the bumper to stresses for which it was not designed. Aftermarket rear step bumpers, designed for trailer towing, are acceptable for use with bumper mounted hitches.

Frame mounted hitches can be of the type which bolts to two or more points on the frame, plus the bumper, or just to several points on the frame. Frame mounted hitches can also be of the tongue type, for Class I towing, or, of the receiver type, for classes II and III.

Load equalizing hitches are usually used for large trailers. Most equalizing hitches are welded in place, they use equalizing bars and chains to level the truck after the trailer is connected.

Check the gross weight rating of your trailer. Tongue weight is usually figured as 10% of gross trailer weight. Therefore, a trailer with a maximum gross weight of 2,000 lbs. will have a maximum tongue weight of 200 lbs. Class I trailers fall into this category. Class II trailers are those with a gross weight rating of 2,000–3,500 lbs., while Class III trailers fall into the 3,500–6,000 lbs. category. Class IV trailers are those over 6,000 lbs. and are for use with fifth wheel trucks, only.

When you've determined the hitch that you'll need, follow the manufacturer's installation instructions exactly, especially when it comes to fastener torques. The hitch will subjected to a lot of stress and good hitches come with hardened bolts. Never substitute an inferior bolt for a hardened bolt.

PUSHING AND TOWING

CAUTION

Pushing or towing your truck to start it may result in unusually high catalytic converter and exhaust system temperatures, which under extreme conditions may ignite the interior floor covering material above the converter.

Pushing

Chevrolet and GMC trucks with manual transmissions can be push started. To push start, make sure that both bumpers are in reasonable alignment. Turn the ignition switch ON and engage High gear. Depress the clutch pedal. When a speed of about 10 mph is reached, slightly depress the gas pedal and slowly release the clutch. The engine should start.

NOTE: Automatic transmission equipped trucks cannot be started by pushing.

Towing

Chevrolet and GMC trucks can be towed on all four wheels (flat towed) at speeds of less than 35 mph for distances less than 50 miles, providing that the axle, driveline and engine/transmission are operable. The transmission should be in Neutral, the engine should be Off, the steering column unlocked, and the parking brake released.

Do not attach chains to the bumpers or bracketing. All attachments must be made to the structural members. Safety chains should be used. it should also be remembered that power steering and brake assists will not be working with the engine off.

The rear wheels must be raised off the ground or the driveshaft disconnected when the transmission is not operating properly, or when speeds or over 35 mph will be used or when towing more than 50 miles.

CAUTION

If a truck is towed on its front wheels only, the steering wheel must be secured with the wheels in a straight ahead position.

JUMP STARTING

The following procedure is recommended by the manufacturer. Be sure that the booster battery is 12 volt with negative ground. Follow this procedure exactly to avoid possible damage to the electrical system, especially on models equipped with computerized engine controls.

CAUTION

DO NOT attempt this procedure on a frozen battery – it will probably explode. DO NOT attempt it on a sealed Delco Freedom battery showing a light color in the charge indicator. Be certain to observe correct polarity connections. Failure to do so will result in almost immediate computer, alternator and regulator destruction. Never allow the jumper cable ends to touch each other.

1. Position the vehicles so that they are not touching. Set the parking brake and place automatic transmission in Park and manual transmission in Neutral. Turn Off the lights, heater and other electrical loads. Turn both ignition switches Off.
2. Remove the vent caps from both the booster and discharged battery. Lay a cloth over the open vent cells of each battery. This isn't necessary on batteries equipped with sponge type flame arrestor caps, and it isn't possible on sealed batteries.
3. Attach one cable to the positive terminal of the booster battery and the other end to the positive terminal of the discharged battery.

NOTE: If you are attempting to start a Chevrolet or GMC pick-up with the diesel engine, it is suggested that this connection be made to the battery on the driver's side of the truck, because this battery is closer to the starter, and thus the resistance of the electrical cables is lower. From this point on, ignore the other battery in the truck.

CAUTION

DO NOT attempt to jump start the truck with a 24 volt power source.

4. Attach one end of the remaining cable to the negative terminal of the booster battery and the other end to a good ground. Do not attach to the negative terminal of discharged batteries. Do not lean over the battery when making this last connection.
5. Start the engine of the truck with the booster battery. Start the engine of the truck with the discharged battery. If the engine will not start, disconnect the batteries as soon as possible. If this is not done, the two batteries will soon reach a state of equilibrium, with both too weak to start an engine. This will not be a problem of the engine of the booster truck is kept running fast enough. Lengthy cranking can also overheat and damage the starter.
6. Reverse the above steps to disconnect the booster and discharge batteries. Be certain to remove negative connections first.
7. Reinstall the vent caps. Dispose of the cloths; they may have battery acid on them.

CAUTION

The use of any "hot shot" type of jumper system in excess of 12 volts can damage the electronic control units or cause the discharged battery to explode.

JACKING AND HOISTING

The jack supplied with the truck is meant for changing tires. It was not meant to support the truck while you crawl under it and work. Whenever it is necessary to get under a truck to perform service operations, always be sure that it is adequately supported, by jackstands at the proper points. Always block the wheels when changing tires.

If your truck is equipped with a Positraction rear axle, do not run the engine for any reason with one rear wheel off the ground. Power will be transmitted through the rear wheel remaining on the ground, possibly causing the truck to drive itself off the jack.

Some of the service operations in this book require that one or both ends of the truck be raised and supported safely. The best arrangement for this, of course, is a grease pit or a vehicle lift, but these items are seldom found in the home garage. Hydraulic jacks and jackstands are next best thing to a vehicle lift. Spend a little extra time to make sure that your truck is lifted and supported safely. Remember! the truck you are laying under weighs ½ ton.

CAUTION

Concrete blocks are not recommended for supporting a vehicle; they may crumble if the load is not evenly distributed. Boxes and milk crates of any description must not be used. Shake the truck a few times to make sure the jackstands are securely supporting the weight before crawling under.

JUMP STARTING A DEAD BATTERY

The chemical reaction in a battery produces explosive hydrogen gas. This is the safe way to jump start a dead battery, reducing the chances of an accidental spark that could cause an explosion.

Jump Starting Precautions

1. Be sure both batteries are of the same voltage.
2. Be sure both batteries are of the same polarity (have the same grounded terminal).
3. Be sure the vehicles are not touching.
4. Be sure the vent cap holes are not obstructed.
5. Do not smoke or allow sparks around the battery.
6. In cold weather, check for frozen electrolyte in the battery. Do not jump start a frozen battery.
7. Do not allow electrolyte on your skin or clothing.
8. Be sure the electrolyte is not frozen.

CAUTION: Make certin that the ignition key, in the vehicle with the dead battery, is in the OFF position. Connecting cables to vehicles with on-board computers will result in computer destruction if the key is not in the OFF position.

Jump Starting Procedure

1. Determine voltages of the two batteries; they must be the same.
2. Bring the starting vehicle close (they must not touch) so that the batteries can be reached easily.
3. Turn off all accessories and both engines. Put both vehicles in Neutral or Park and set the handbrake.
4. Cover the cell caps with a rag—do not cover terminals.
5. If the terminals on the run-down battery are heavily corroded, clean them.
6. Identify the positive and negative posts on both batteries and connect the cables in the order shown.
7. Start the engine of the starting vehicle and run it at fast idle. Try to start the car with the dead battery. Crank it for no more than 10 seconds at a time and let it cool for 20 seconds in between tries.
8. If it doesn't start in 3 tries, there is something else wrong.
9. Disconnect the cables in the reverse order.
10. Replace the cell covers and dispose of the rags.

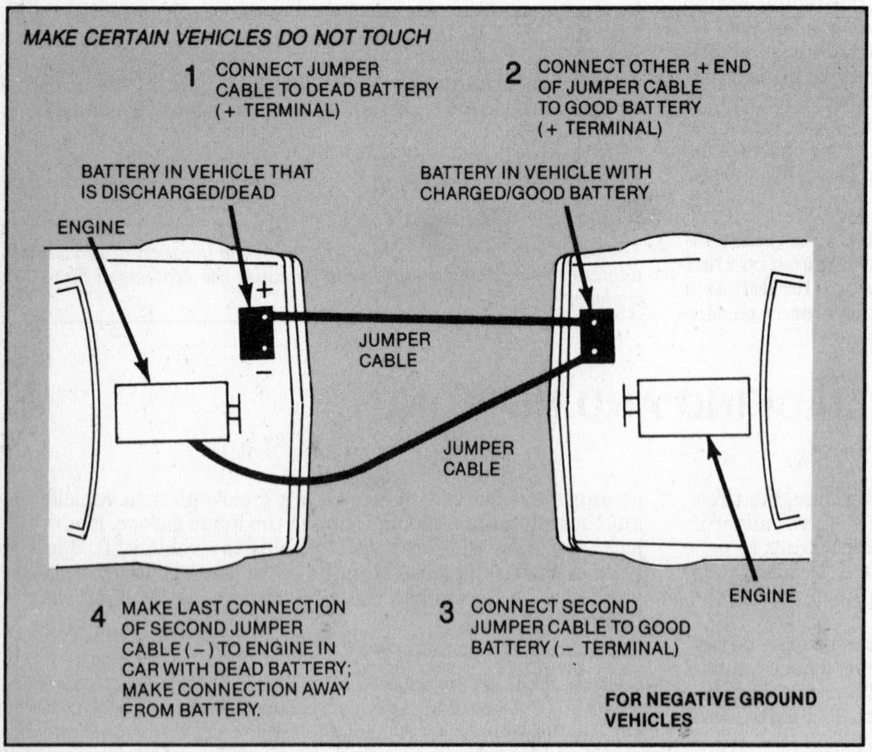
MAKE CERTAIN VEHICLES DO NOT TOUCH
1 CONNECT JUMPER CABLE TO DEAD BATTERY (+ TERMINAL)
2 CONNECT OTHER + END OF JUMPER CABLE TO GOOD BATTERY (+ TERMINAL)
BATTERY IN VEHICLE THAT IS DISCHARGED/DEAD
BATTERY IN VEHICLE WITH CHARGED/GOOD BATTERY
ENGINE
+
−
JUMPER CABLE
JUMPER CABLE
ENGINE
4 MAKE LAST CONNECTION OF SECOND JUMPER CABLE (−) TO ENGINE IN CAR WITH DEAD BATTERY; MAKE CONNECTION AWAY FROM BATTERY.
3 CONNECT SECOND JUMPER CABLE TO GOOD BATTERY (− TERMINAL)
FOR NEGATIVE GROUND VEHICLES

Side terminal batteries occasionally pose a problem when connecting jumper cables. There frequently isn't enough room to clamp the cables without touching sheet metal. Side terminal adaptors are available to alleviate this problem and should be removed after use

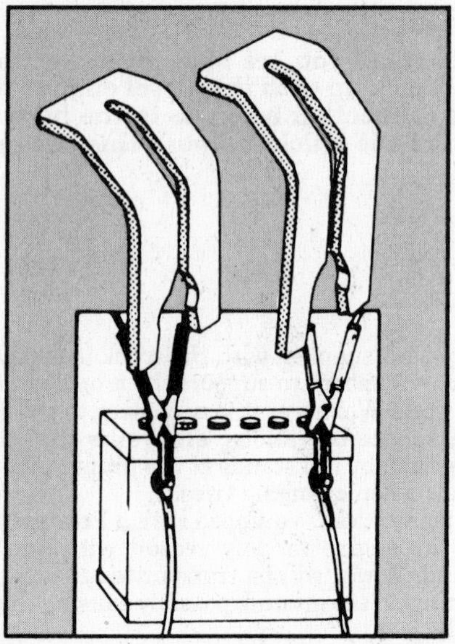

CAPACITIES

Year	Engine No. Cyl. cc. (Cu. In.) Displacement	Engine Crankcase (qts.)	Transmission Pts. To Refill After Draining Manual 4-Speed	Transmission Manual 5-Speed	Transmission Automatic	Transfer Case (pts.)	Rear Drive Axle (pts.)	Front Drive Axle (pts.)	Gasoline Tank (gals.)	Cooling System (qts.) With Heater	Cooling System (qts.) With A/C
1982-85	4-1.9 (118.9)	4.0	3.0	3.0	7.0②③	5.2	3.5	2.6	13.0①	9.4	9.5
	6-2.8 (173)	4.0	3.0	3.0	7.0②③	5.2	3.5	2.6	13.0①	12.0	12.0
1983-84	4-2.0 (121)	4.0	3.0	3.0	7.0②③	5.2	3.5	2.6	13.0①	9.6	9.6
1983-85	4-2.2 (136.6)	5.0	3.0	3.0	7.0②③	5.2	3.5	2.6	13.0①	10.0	10.0
1985-91	4-2.5 (151)	3.0	3.0	3.0	7.0②③	5.2	3.5	2.6	13.0①	10.5	10.5
1986-91	6-2.8 (173)	4.0	3.0	3.0	7.0②③	5.2	3.5	2.6	13.0①	11.6	11.6
1988-91	6-4.3 (262)	4.0	3.0	3.0	7.0②③	5.2	3.5	2.6	13.0①	12.1	12.1

① Optional: 20.0 gal.
② Figure shown is for pan removal only. Total overhaul is 19.0 pts.
③ If equipped with a 700-R4: Pan removal 10 pts. Overhaul 23 pts.

Maintenance Intervals Schedule I ①

Item No.	To Be Serviced	When to Perform Miles of Months, Whichever Occurs First Miles (000)	3	6	9	12	15	18	21	24	27	30	33	36	39	42	45	48
			The services shown in this schedule up to 48,000 miles are to be performed after 48,000 miles at the same intervals															
1	Every Oil and Oil filter Change	Every 3,000 Miles or 3 Months	•	•	•	•	•	•	•	•	•	•	•	•	•	•	•	•
2	Chassis Lubrication	Every oil change	•	•	•	•	•	•	•	•	•	•	•	•	•	•	•	•
3	Carburetor Choke and Hose Inspection	At 6,000 Miles, then at 30,000 Miles		•								•					•	
4	Carburetor or T.B.I. Mounting Bolt Torque Check			•								•						
5	Engine Idle Speed Adjustment			•								•						
6	Engine Accessory Drive Belts Inspection	Every 12 Months or 15,000 Miles					•					•					•	
7	Cooling System Service	Every 24 Months or 30,000 Miles										•						
8	Front Wheel Bearing Repack	Every 15,000 Miles					•					•					•	
9	Transmission Service	15,000 Miles					•					•						
10	Vacuum Advance System Inspection	Check at 6,000 Miles at 30,000 Miles, and at 45,000 Miles		•								•					•	
11	Spark Plugs and Wire Service	Every 30,000 Miles										•						
12	PCV System Inspection	Every 30,000 Miles										•						
13	EGR System Check	Every 30,000 Miles										•						
14	Air Cleaner and PCV Filter Replacement	Every 30,000 Miles										•						
15	Engine Timing Check	Every 30,000 Miles										•						
16	Fuel Tank, Cap and Lines Inspection	Every 12 Months or 15,000 Miles					•					•					•	
17	Early Fuel Evaporation System Inspection	At 6,000 Miles then at 30,000 Miles		•								•						
18	Evaporative Control System Inspection	At 30,000 Miles										•						
19	Fuel Filter Replacement	Every 15,000 Miles					•					•					•	
20	Valve Lash Adjustment	Every 15,000 Miles					•					•					•	
21	Thermostatically Controlled Air Cleaner Inspection	Every 30,000 Miles										•						

Schedule II ②

Item No.	To Be Serviced	When to Perform Miles or Months, Whichever Occurs First Miles (000)	The services shown in this schedule up to 60,000 miles are to be performed after 60,000 miles at the same intervals							
			7.5	15	22.5	30	37.5	45	52.5	60
1	Engine Oil Change	Every 7,500 Miles or 12 Months	•	•	•	•	•	•	•	•
	Oil Filter Change	At First and Every Other Oil Change or 12 Months	•		•		•		•	
2	Chassis Lubrication	Every oil change	•	•	•	•	•	•	•	•
3	Carburetor Choke and Hoses Inspection	At 6 Months or 7,500 Miles and at 60,000 Miles	•			•				•
4	Carburetor or T.B.I. Mounting Bolt Torque Check	At 6 Months or 7,500 Miles and at 60,000 Miles	•							•
5	Engine Idle Speed Adjustment	At 6 Months or 7,500 Miles and at 60,000 Miles	•							•
6	Engine Accessory Drive Belts Inspection	Every 24 Months or 30,000 Miles				•				•
7	Cooling System Service	Every 24 Months or 30,000 Miles				•				•
8	Front Wheel Bearing Repack	Every 30,000 Miles				•				•
9	Transmission Service	30,000 miles				•				•
10	Vacuum Advance System Inspection	Check at 6 Months or 7,500 Miles, then at 30,000 Miles, and then at 15,000 Mile intervals.	•			•		•		•
11	Spark Plugs and Wire Service	Every 30,000 Miles				•				•
12	PCV System Inspection	Every 30,000 Miles				•				•
13	ERG System Check	Every 30,000 Miles				•				•
14	Air Cleaner and PCV Filter Replacement	Every 30,000 Miles				•				•
15	Engine Timing Check	Every 30,000 Miles				•				•
16	Fuel Tank, Cap and Lines Inspection	Every 24 Months 30,000 Miles				•				•
17	Early Fuel Evaporation System Inspection	At 7,500 Miles and at 30,000 Miles than at 30,000 Mile intervals.	•			•				•
18	Evaporative Control System Inspection	Every 30,000 Miles				•				•
19	Fuel Filter Replacement	Every 30,000 Miles				•				•
20	Valve Lash Adjustment	Every 15,000 Miles		•		•		•		•
21	Thermostatically Controlled Air Cleaner Inspection	Every 30,000 Miles				•				•

① Severe service
② Normal service

2 Engine Performance and Tune-Up

QUICK REFERENCE INDEX

GENERAL INDEX

GASOLINE ENGINE TUNE-UP SPECIFICATIONS

Year	V.I.N. Code	Eng. No. Cyl. Disp. Liters (Cu. in.)	Eng. Mfg.	hp	Spark Plugs Orig. Type	Spark Plugs Gap (in.)	Ignition Timing (deg.) Man. Trans.	Ignition Timing (deg.) Auto. Trans.	Intake Valve Opens (deg.)	Fuel Pump Pressure (psi)	Idle Speed (rpm) Man. Trans.	Idle Speed (rpm) Auto. Trans.
1982-85	A	4-1.9 (118.9)	Isuzu	84	R42LXS	0.040	6B	6B	21B	3.0	800	900
	B	6-2.8 (173)	Chev.	110	R42TS	0.040	6B	10B	7B	7.0	1,000	750
1983-84	Y	4-2.0 (121)	Chev.	83	R42CTS	0.035	12B	12B	30B	5.0	750	700
1985-91	E	4-2.5 (151)	Pontiac	98	R43CTS6	①	②	②	—	9–13	②	②
1986-91	R	6-2.8 (173)	Chev.	125	R43CTS	①	②	②	—	9–13	②	②
1988-91	Z	6-4.3 (262)	Chev.	125	R45TS	①	②	②	—	9–13	②	②

① Refer to the information on the underhood sticker.
② This function is controlled by the emissions computer; no adjustment is necessary.

DIESEL ENGINE TUNE-UP SPECIFICATIONS

Year	VIN	Eng. No. Cyl. Displ. cc (Cu. In.)	Injection Timing (deg.)	Intake Valve Opens (deg.)	Low Idle (rpm)	Compression Pressure (psi)	Valve Clearance (In.) Intake	Valve Clearance (In.) Exhaust	Firing Order
1983-85	S	4-2238 (136.6)	15B	16B	750	441①	0.016C	0.016C	1-3-4-2

NOTE: The underhood specifications sticker often reflects tune-up specification changes made in production. Sticker figures must be used if they disagree with those in this chart.
① @ 200 rpm

TUNE-UP PROCEDURES

In order to extract the full measure of performance and economy from your engine it is essential that it is properly tuned at regular intervals. A regular tune-up will keep your truck's engine running smoothly and will prevent the annoying breakdowns and poor performance associated with an untuned engine.

A complete tune-up should be performed every 30,000 miles. This interval should be halved if the vehicle is operated under severe conditions such as trailer towing, prolonged idling, start-and-stop driving, or if starting or running problems are noticed. It is assumed that the routine maintenance described in Chapter 1 has been kept up, as this will have a decided effect on the results of a tune-up. All of the applicable steps of a tune-up should be followed in order, as the result is a cumulative one.

NOTE: Diesel engines do not require tune-ups per se, as they do not have an ignition system.

If the specifications on the underhood tune-up sticker in the engine compartment disagree with the Tune-Up Specifications chart in this Section, the figures on the sticker must be used. The sticker often reflects changes made during the production run.

Spark Plugs

Normally, a set of spark plugs requires replacement about every 20,000–30,000 miles, on vehicles equipped with an High Energy Ignition (HEI) system. Any vehicle which is subjected to severe conditions will need more frequent plug replacement.

Under normal operation, the plug gap increases about 0.001 in. (0.0254mm) for every 1,000–2,000 miles. As the gap increases, the plug's voltage requirement also increases. It requires a greater voltage to jump the wider gap and about 2–3 times as much voltage to fire a plug at high speeds than at idle.

When you are removing the spark plugs, work on one at a time. Don't start by removing the plug wires all at once, for unless you number them, they may become mixed up. Take a minute before you begin and number the wires with tape. The best location for numbering the wires is near the distributor cap.

REMOVAL

When removing the spark plugs, work on one at a time. Don't start by removing the plug wires all at once because unless you

Diagnosis of Spark Plugs

Problem	Possible Cause	Correction
Brown to grayish-tan deposits and slight electrode wear.	• Normal wear.	• Clean, regap, reinstall.
Dry, fluffy black carbon deposits.	• Poor ignition output.	• Check distributor to coil connections.
Wet, oily deposits with very little electrode wear.	• "Break-in" of new or recently overhauled engine. • Excessive valve stem guide clearances. • Worn intake valve seals.	• Degrease, clean and reinstall the plugs. • Refer to Section 3. • Replace the seals.
Red, brown, yellow and white colored coatings on the insulator. Engine misses intermittently under severe operating conditions.	• By-products of combustion.	• Clean, regap, and reinstall. If heavily coated, replace.
Colored coatings heavily deposited on the portion of the plug projecting into the chamber and on the side facing the intake valve.	• Leaking seals if condition is found in only one or two cylinders.	• Check the seals. Replace if necessary. Clean, regap, and reinstall the plugs.
Shiny yellow glaze coating on the insulator.	• Melted by-products of combustion.	• Avoid sudden acceleration with wide-open throttle after long periods of low speed driving. Replace the plugs.
Burned or blistered insulator tips and badly eroded electrodes.	• Overheating.	• Check the cooling system. • Check for sticking heat riser valves. Refer to Section 1. • Lean air-fuel mixture. • Check the heat range of the plugs. May be too hot. • Check ignition timing. May be over-advanced. • Check the torque value of the plugs to ensure good plug-engine seat contact.
Broken or cracked insulator tips.	• Heat shock from sudden rise in tip temperature under severe operating conditions. Improper gapping of plugs.	• Replace the plugs. Gap correctly.

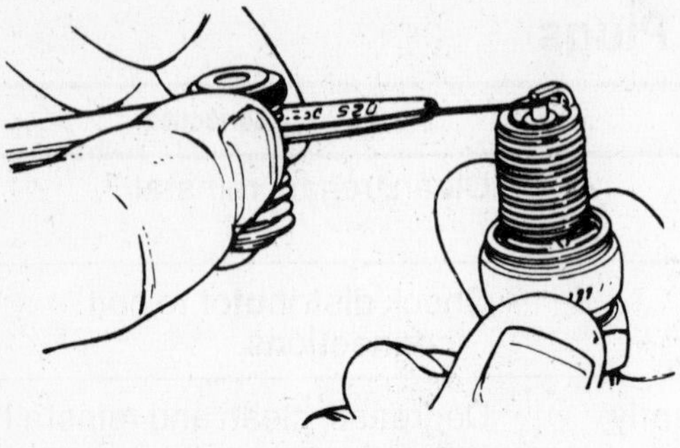

Checking spark plug gap

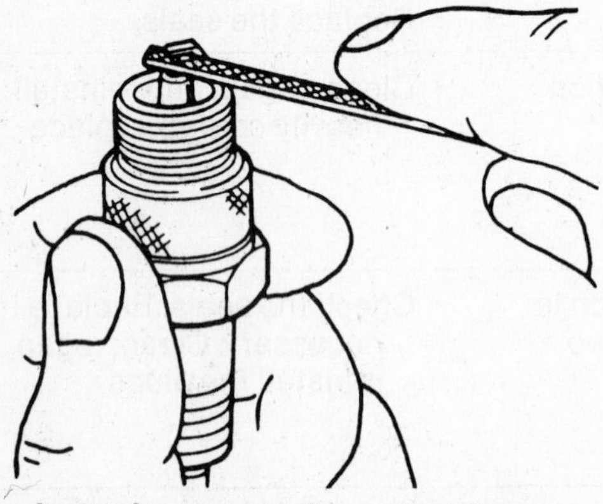

Filing an electrode square with an ignition points file

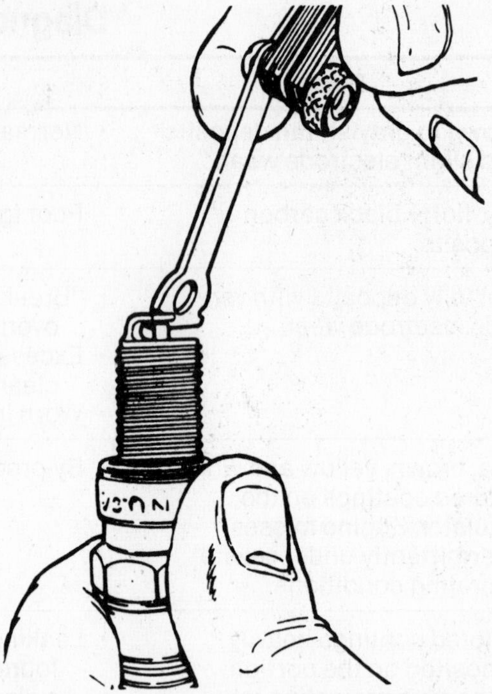

Bending the side electrode to adjust spark plug gap

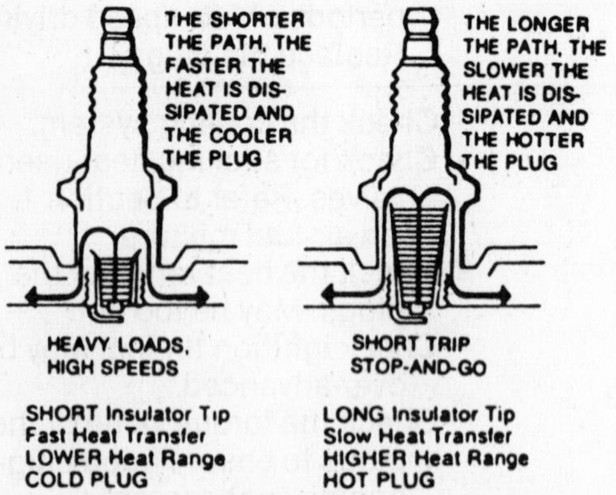
THE SHORTER THE PATH, THE FASTER THE HEAT IS DISSIPATED AND THE COOLER THE PLUG
THE LONGER THE PATH, THE SLOWER THE HEAT IS DISSIPATED AND THE HOTTER THE PLUG
HEAVY LOADS, HIGH SPEEDS
SHORT TRIP STOP-AND-GO
SHORT Insulator Tip
Fast Heat Transfer
LOWER Heat Range
COLD PLUG
LONG Insulator Tip
Slow Heat Transfer
HIGHER Heat Range
HOT PLUG

Illustration of spark plug heat range

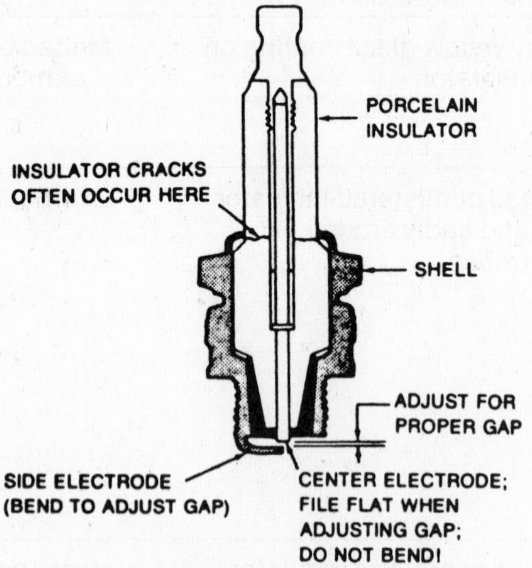
PORCELAIN INSULATOR
INSULATOR CRACKS OFTEN OCCUR HERE
SHELL
ADJUST FOR PROPER GAP
SIDE ELECTRODE (BEND TO ADJUST GAP)
CENTER ELECTRODE; FILE FLAT WHEN ADJUSTING GAP; DO NOT BEND!

Cross-section of a spark plug

number them, they're going to get mixed up. On some models, it will be more convenient for you to remove all of the wires before you start to work on the plugs. If this is necessary, take a minute before you begin and number the wires with tape before you take them off. The time you spend here will pay off later on.

1. Twist the spark plug boot ½ turn and remove the boot from the plug. You may also use a plug wire removal tool designed especially for this purpose. DO NOT pull on the wire itself. When the wire has been removed, take a wire brush and clean the area around the plug. Make sure that all the grime is removed so that none will enter the cylinder after the plug has been removed.
2. Remove the plug using the proper size socket, extensions and universals as necessary.
3. If removing the plug is difficult, drip some penetrating oil (Liquid Wrench®, WD-40®) on the plug threads, allow it to work, then remove the plug. Also, be sure that the socket is straight on the plug—especially on those hard to reach plugs.

INSPECTION

Check the plugs for deposits and wear. If they are not going to be replaced, clean the plugs thoroughly. Remember that any kind of deposit will decrease the efficiency of the plug. Plugs can be cleaned on a spark plug cleaning machine or with a stiff brush.

After the plugs are cleaned, the electrodes must be filed flat. Use an ignition points file, not an emery board or the like, which will leave deposits. The electrodes must be filed perfectly flat with sharp edges; rounded edges reduce the spark plug voltage by as much as 50%.

Check the spark plug gap before installation. The ground electrode (the L-shaped wire connected to the body of the plug) must be parallel to the center electrode and the specified size wire gauge (see Tune-Up Specifications) should pass through the gap with a slight drag. Always check the gap on the new plugs, they are not always set correctly at the factory. DO NOT use a flat feeler gauge when measuring the gap, because the reading will be inaccurate.

Wire gapping tools usually have a bending tool attached. Use that to adjust the side electrode until the proper distance is obtained. Absolutely, never bend the center electrode. Also, be careful not to bend the side electrode too far or too often; it may weaken and break off within the engine, requiring removal of the cylinder head to retrieve it.

Heat range is a term used to describe the cooling characteristics of spark plugs. Plugs with longer nosed insulators take a longer time to dissipate heat than plugs with shorter nosed insulators. These are termed "hot" or "cold" plugs, respectively. It is generally advisable to use the factory recommended plugs. However, in conditions of extremely hard use (cross-country driving in summer) going to the next cooler heat range may be advisable. If most driving is done in the city or over short distances, go to the next hotter heat range plug to eliminate fouling. If in doubt concerning the substitution of spark plugs, consult your Chevrolet or GMC dealer.

INSTALLATION

1. Lubricate the threads of the spark plugs with a drop of oil. Install the plugs and tighten them hand tight. Take care not to cross thread them.
2. Tighten the spark plugs with the socket. DO NOT apply the same amount of force you would use for a bolt; just snug them in. If a torque wrench is available, tighten to 11–15 ft. lbs.
3. Install the ignition wires on their respective plugs. Make sure the wires are firmly connected—you will be able to feel them click into place.

HEI Plug Wire Resistance Chart

Wire Length	Minimum	Maximum
0–15 inches	3000 ohms	10,000 ohms
15–25 inches	4000 ohms	15,000 ohms
25–35 inches	6000 ohms	20,000 ohms
Over 35 inches	6000 ohms	25,000 ohms

Spark Plug Wires

Every 15,000 miles, visually inspect the spark plug cables for burns, cuts or breaks in the insulation. Check the spark plug boots and the nipples on the distributor cap and coil. Replace any damaged wiring.

Every 30,000 miles or so, the resistance of the wires should be checked with an ohmmeter. Wires with excessive resistance will cause misfiring and may make the engine difficult to start in damp weather. Generally, the useful life of the cables is 30,000–45,000 miles.

To check spark plug wire resistance, remove the distributor cap, leaving the wires in place. Connect one lead of an ohmmeter to an electrode within the cap; connect the other lead to the corresponding spark plug terminal (remove it from the spark plug for this test). Replace any wire which shows a resistance over 30,000Ω. Generally speaking, resistance should not be over 25,000Ω.

It should be remembered that resistance is also a function of length; the longer the wire the greater the resistance. Thus, if the wires on your truck are longer than the factory originals, resistance will be higher, quite possibly outside these limits.

When installing a new set of spark plug wires, replace the wires one at a time so there will be no confusion. Start by replacing the longest cable first. Install the boot firmly over the spark plug. Route the wire exactly the same as the original. Insert the distributor end of the wire firmly into the distributor cap tower, then seat the boot over the tower. Repeat the process for each wire.

FIRING ORDERS

NOTE: To avoid confusion, replace spark plug wires one at a time.

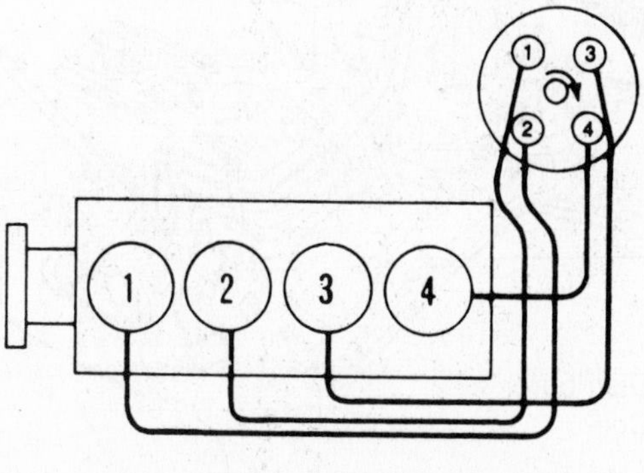
1
3
2
4
1
2
3
4
Firing order — 2.0L engine

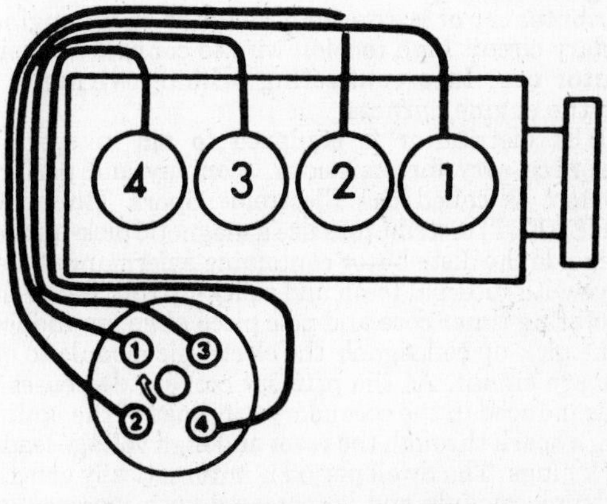
4
3
2
1
1
3
2
4
Firing order — 2.5L engine

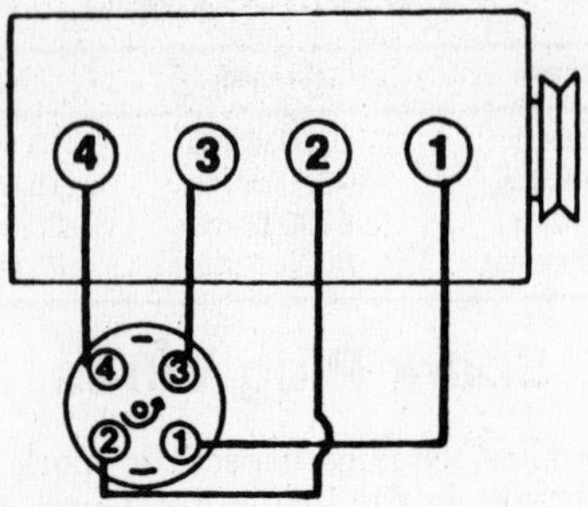
4
3
2
1

Firing order – 1.9L engine

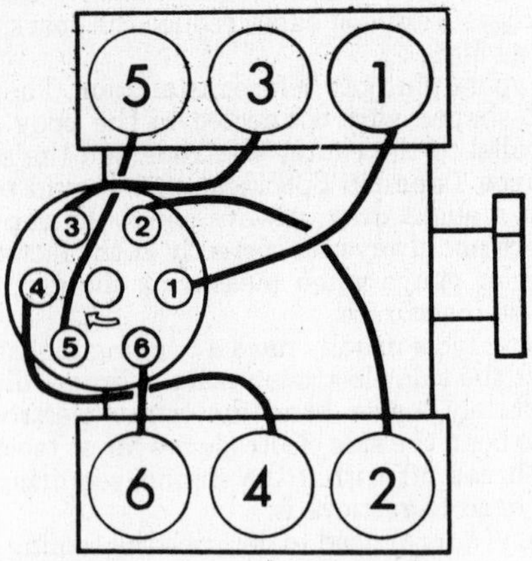
5
3
1
6
4
2

Firing order – 4.3L engine

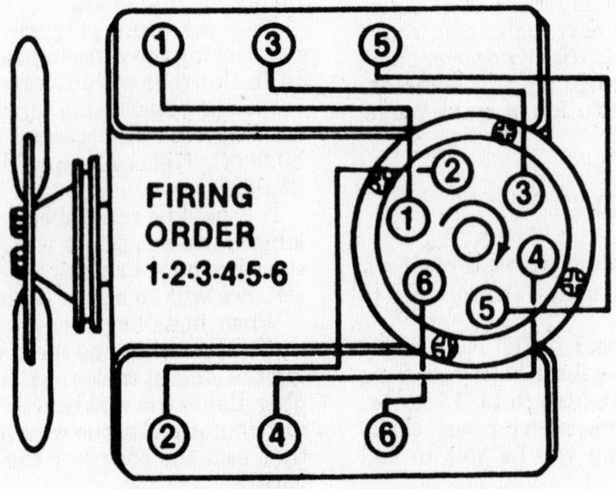
1
3
5
FIRING
ORDER
1-2-3-4-5-6
2
4
6

Firing order – 2.8L engine

ELECTRONIC IGNITION

General Information

The High Energy Ignition (HEI) distributor is used on all gasoline engines. The ignition coil is either mounted to the top of the distributor cap or is externally mounted on the engine, using a secondary circuit high tension wire to connect the coil to the distributor cap. Interconnecting primary wiring is routed through the engine harness.

The HEI distributor is equipped to aid in spark timing changes, necessary for emissions, economy and performance. This system is called the Electronic Spark Timing Control (EST). HEI(EST) distributors use a magnetic pick-up assembly, located inside the distributor containing a permanent magnet, a pole piece with internal teeth and a pick-up coil. When the teeth of the rotating timer core and pole piece align, an induced voltage in the pick-up coil signals the electronic module to open the coil primary circuit. As the primary current decreases, a high voltage is induced in the secondary windings of the ignition coil, directing a spark through the rotor and high voltage leads to fire the spark plugs. The dwell period is automatically controlled by the electronic module and is increased with increasing engine rpm. The HEI system features a longer spark duration which is instrumental in firing lean and EGR (Exhaust Gas Recircula-

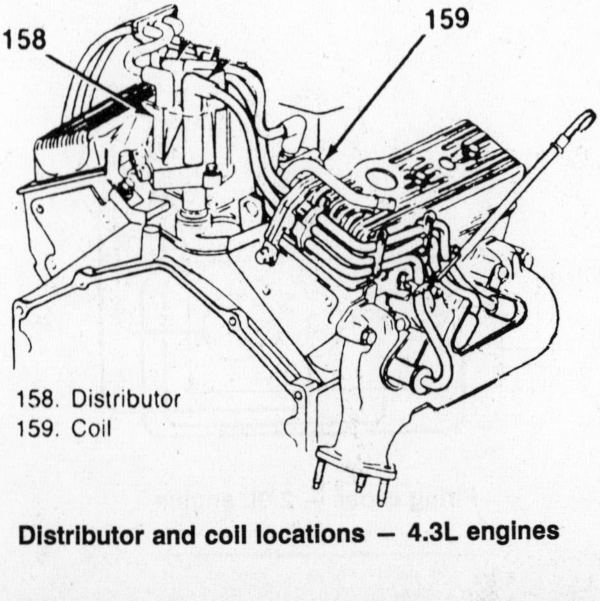
158
159
158. Distributor
159. Coil

Distributor and coil locations – 4.3L engines

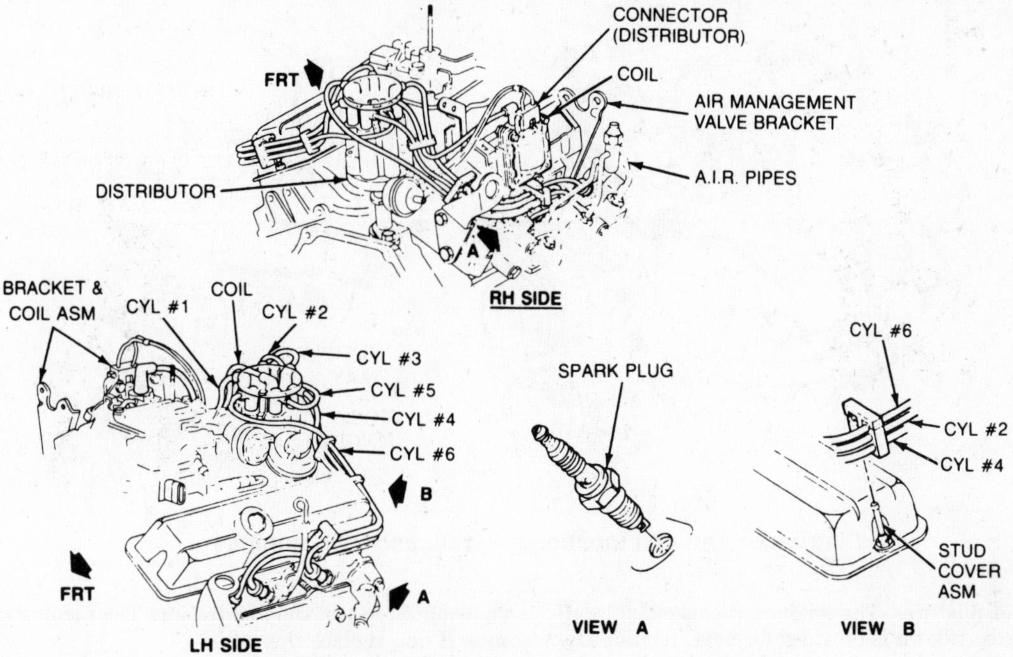
CONNECTOR
(DISTRIBUTOR)
COIL
AIR MANAGEMENT
VALVE BRACKET
A.I.R. PIPES
FRT
DISTRIBUTOR
A
RH SIDE
BRACKET &
COIL ASM
COIL
CYL #1
CYL #2
CYL #3
CYL #5
CYL #4
CYL #6
B
FRT
A
LH SIDE
SPARK PLUG
VIEW A
CYL #6
CYL #2
CYL #4
STUD
COVER
ASM
VIEW B

Distributor and coil locations — 2.8L engines

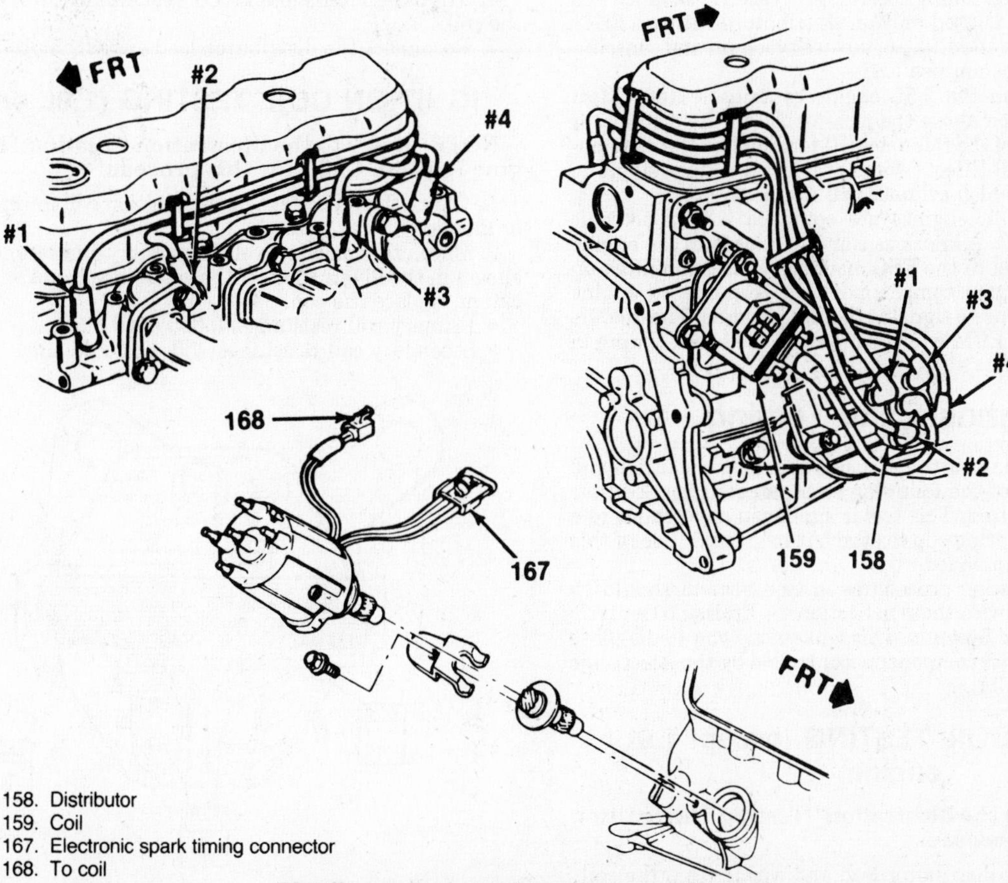
FRT
#2
#4
#1
#3
168
167
FRT
#1
#3
#4
#2
159
158
FRT

158. Distributor
159. Coil
167. Electronic spark timing connector
168. To coil

Distributor and coil locations — 2.5L engines

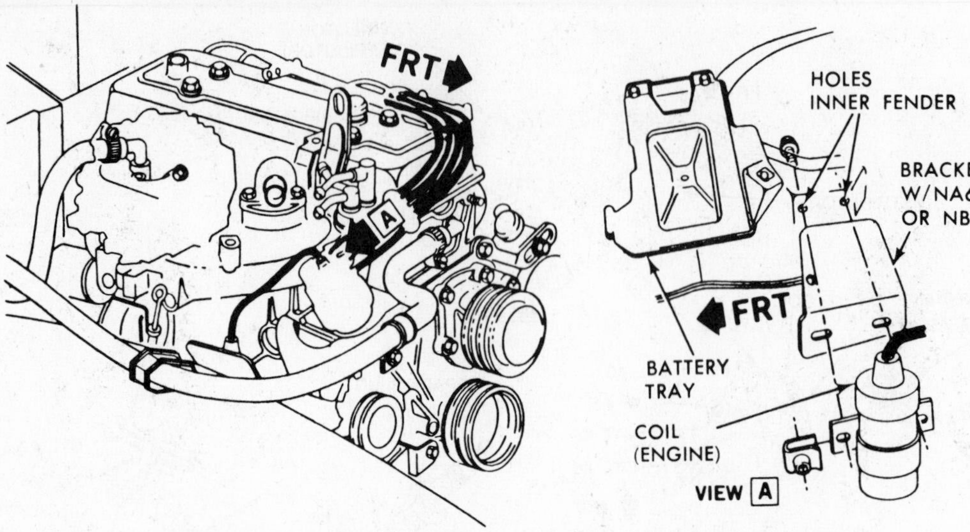
FRT
A
HOLES
INNER FENDER
BRACKET
W/NA6
OR NB2
FRT
BATTERY
TRAY
COIL
(ENGINE)
VIEW A

Distributor and coil locations — 1.9L and 2.0L engines

tion) diluted fuel/air mixtures. The condenser (capacitor) located within the HEI distributor is provided for noise (static) suppression purposes only and is not a regularly replaced ignition system component.

All spark timing changes in the HEI(EST) distributors are performed electronically by the Electronic Control Module (ECM), which monitors information from the various engine sensors, computes the desired spark timing and signals the distributor to change the timing accordingly. Vacuum advance and centrifugal advance is used only on distributors without EST.

The distributor on the 1.9L engine uses vacuum and centrifugal advance and does not use EST.

The distributor on the 2.5L engine contains a Hall Effect Switch. It is mounted above the pick-up coil in the distributor and takes the place of the reference (R) terminal on the distributor module. The Hall Effect Switch provides a voltage signal to the ECM to tell it which cylinder will fire next.

The 2.8L and 4.3L engines are equipped with Electronic Spark Control (ESC). A knock sensor is mounted in the engine block. It is connected to the ESC module which is mounted on the cowl in the engine compartment. In response to engine knock, the sensor sends a signal to the ESC module. The module will then signal the ECM which will retard the spark timing in the distributor.

Diagnosis and Testing

An accurate diagnosis is the first step to problem solution and repair. For several of the following steps, an HEI spark tester (tool ST 125) is utilized. This tool is similar in appearance to a spark plug, with a spring clip to attach it to ground. Use of this tool is highly recommended.

Diagnosis and testing procedures in this Section should be used in conjunction with those in Section 4—Emission Controls and Section 5—Fuel Systems. This will enable you to diagnose problems involving all components controlled by the Electronic Control Module (ECM).

IGNITION COIL TESTING (except 1.9L engine)

NOTE: Refer to the illustration "Testing The Ignition Coil" for this procedure.

1. Disconnect the distributor lead and wiring from the coil.
2. Using the HIGH scale, connect an ohmmeter to the coil as shown in Step 1 of the illustration. The reading should be infinite. If not, replace the coil.
3. Using the LOW scale, connect the ohmmeter as shown in Step of the illustration.
4. The reading should be very low or zero. If not, replace the coil.
5. Using the HIGH scale, connect the ohmmeter as shown in Step 3 of the illustration.
6. The ohmmeter should **NOT** read infinite. If it does, replace the coil.
7. Reconnect the distributor lead and wiring to the coil.

IGNITION COIL TESTING (1.9L engine)

NOTE: Refer to the illustration "Testing The 1.9L Engine Ignition Coil" for this procedure.

1. Check the outer face of the ignition coil for cracking, rust or damage.
2. Check the resistance of the primary and secondary coils as shown in the illustration. If the resistance is not within specification, replace the coil.

- Primary coil resistance: 0.090–1.40 ohms
- Secondary coil resistance: 7.3–11.1 kilo-ohms

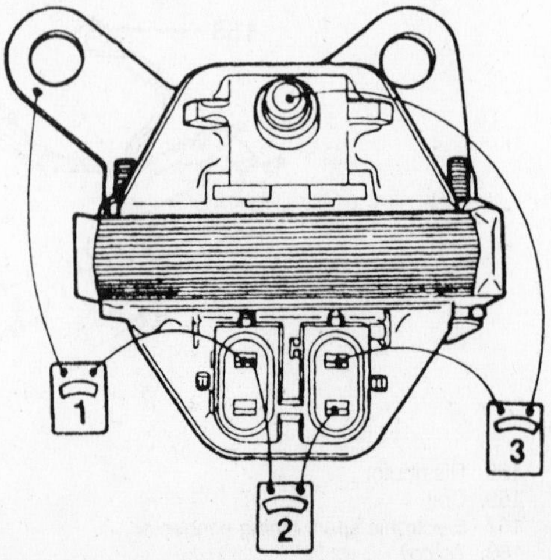
1
2
3

Testing the ignition coil

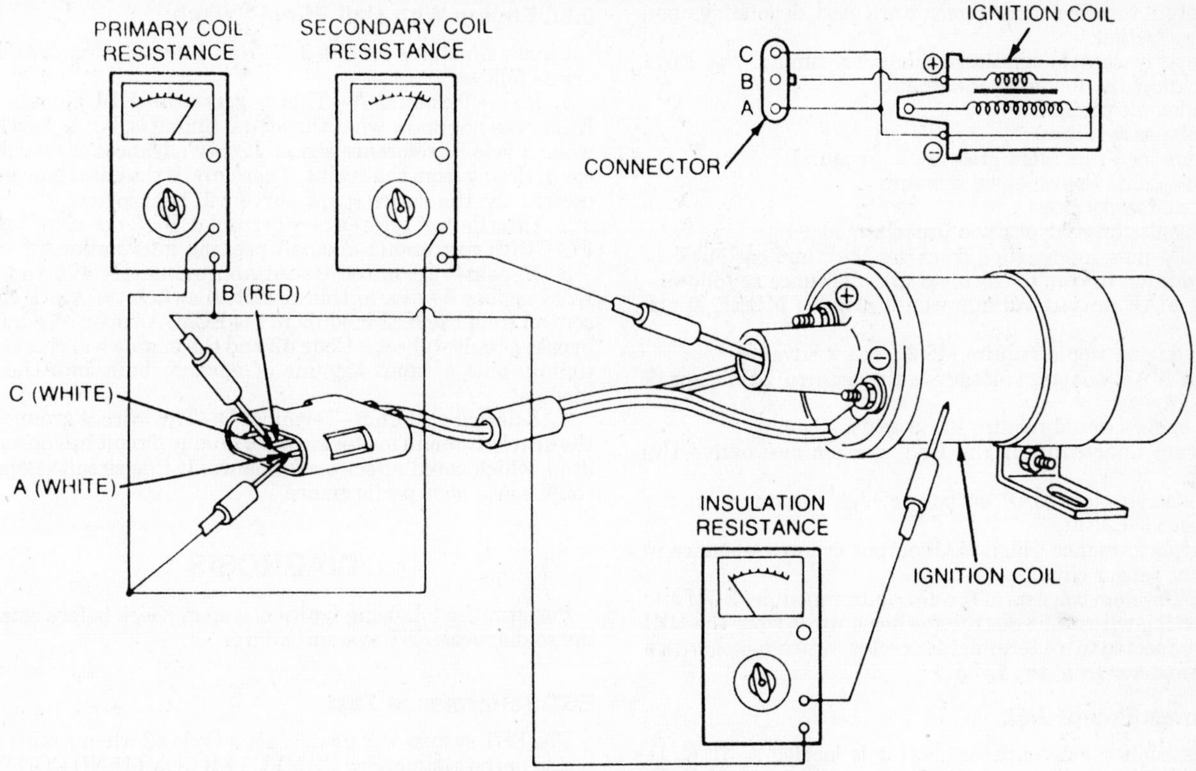
PRIMARY COIL RESISTANCE
SECONDARY COIL RESISTANCE
IGNITION COIL
C
B
A
CONNECTOR
B (RED)
C (WHITE)
A (WHITE)
INSULATION RESISTANCE
IGNITION COIL
Testing the 1.9L engine ignition coil

- Insulation resistance: 10 megohms or more

3. When testing the insulation resistance, if the ohmmeter needle deflects even slightly, the ignition coil is poorly insulated and should be replaced.

PICK-UP COIL TESTING (except 1.9L engine)

NOTE: Refer to the illustration "Testing The Pick-Up Coil" for this procedure.

1. Disconnect the negative battery cable.
2. Remove the distributor cap and disconnect the pick-up coil connector from the module.
3. Connect an ohmmeter to either pick-up coil lead and the housing as shown in Step 1 of the illustration. The reading should be infinite. If not, replace the pick-up coil.
4. Connect an ohmmeter to both pick-up coil leads as shown in Step 2 of the illustration. Flex the wires by hand at the coil and the connector to locate any intermittent opens.
5. The ohmmeter should read a constant number in the 500–1500 ohms
range. In not, replace the pick-up coil.

PICK-UP COIL TESTING (1.9L engine)

The pick-up coil and ignition module on the 1.9L engine must be tested as a unit. The use of an ignition module tester to perform this function is highly recommended.

Electronic Spark Timing (EST) System

The High Energy Ignition (HEI) system controls fuel combustion by providing the spark to ignite the compressed air/fuel mixture in the combustion chamber at the correct time. To provide improved engine performance, fuel economy and control of

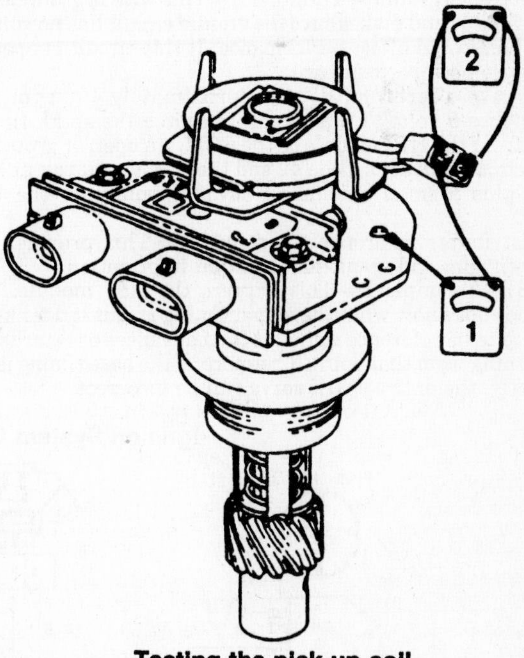
2
1
Testing the pick-up coil

the exhaust emissions, the ECM controls distributor spark advance (timing) using the Electronic Spark Timing (EST) system.

OPERATION

The HEI(EST) distributor uses a modified module. The module has seven terminals instead of the four used without EST.

Two different terminal arrangements are used, depending upon engine application.

To properly control ignition/combustion timing, the ECM needs to know the following information:

- Crankshaft position
- Engine speed (rpm)
- Engine load (manifold pressure or vacuum)
- Atmospheric (barometric) pressure
- Engine temperature
- Transmission gear position (certain models)

The ECM uses information from the MAP and coolant sensors in addition to rpm to calculate spark advance as follows:

- Low MAP output voltage would require MORE spark advance.
- Cold engine would require MORE spark advance.
- High MAP output voltage would require LESS spark advance.
- Hot engine would require LESS spark advance.

Incorrect operation of the EST system can cause the following:

- Detonation—low MAP output or high resistance in the coolant sensor circuit.
- Poor performance—high MAP output or low resistance in the coolant sensor circuit.

The EST system consists of the distributor module, ECM and its connecting wires. The distributor has 4 wires from the HEI module connected to a 4 terminal connector, which mates with a 4 wire connector from the ECM.

All Engines Except 2.5L

The distributor 4-terminal connector is labeled A, B, C, D. Circuit functions for these terminals (except the 2.5L Hall Effect Switch model) are as follows:

1. Reference ground—Terminal A—This wire is grounded in the distributor and makes sure the ground circuit has no voltage drop, which could affect performance. If this circuit is open, it could cause poor performance.
2. Bypass—Terminal B—At approximately 400 rpm, the ECM applies 5 volts to this circuit to switch the spark timing control from the HEI module to the ECM. An open or grounded bypass circuit will set a Code 42 and the engine will run at base timing, plus a small amount of advance built into the HEI module.
3. Distributor reference—Terminal C—This provides the ECM with rpm and crankshaft position information.
4. EST—Terminal D—This triggers the HEI module. The ECM does not know what the actual timing is, but it does know when it gets its reference signal. It then advances or retards the spark timing from that point. Therefore, if the base timing is set incorrectly, the entire spark curve will be incorrect.

2.5L Engine With Hall Effect Switch

Circuit functions for the 2.5L Hall Effect Switch distributor are as follows:

1. EST—Terminal A—This triggers the HEI module. The ECM does not know what the actual timing is, but it does know when it gets its reference signal. It then advances or retards the spark timing from that point. Therefore, if the base timing is set incorrectly, the entire spark curve will be incorrect.
2. Distributor reference—Terminal B—This provides the ECM with rpm and crankshaft position information.
3. Bypass—Terminal C—At approximately 400 rpm, the ECM applies 5 volts to this circuit to switch the spark timing control from the HEI module to the ECM. An open or grounded bypass circuit will set a Code 42 and the engine will run at base timing, plus a small amount of advance built into the HEI module.
4. Reference ground—Terminal D—This wire is grounded in the distributor and makes sure the ground circuit has no voltage drop, which could affect performance. If this circuit is open, it could cause poor performance.

DIAGNOSIS

Perform the following ignition system check before attempting to diagnose EST system failures.

EST Performance Test

The EST system will usually set a Code 42 when a fault is detected in the system. See COMPUTER COMMAND CONTROL SYSTEM in this section to determine how to retrieve codes from the ECM and for further diagnostic procedures.

2.5L ENGINE

The ECM will set a specified value timing when the ALDL diagnostic terminal is grounded. To check the EST operation, record the timing at 2000 rpm with the diagnostic terminal not grounded. Then, ground the diagnostic terminal (use a paper clip to ground terminals A and B) and the timing should change at 2000 rpm, indicating the EST is operating.

ALL EXCEPT 2.5L ENGINE

The ignition timing should change if the Set Timing connector is disconnected. To check the EST operation, record the timing at 2000 rpm with the Set Timing connector connected. Then, disconnect the Set Timing connector and recheck the timing. The timing should change at 2000 rpm, indicating the EST is operating.

Ignition System Check (except 4.3L engine)

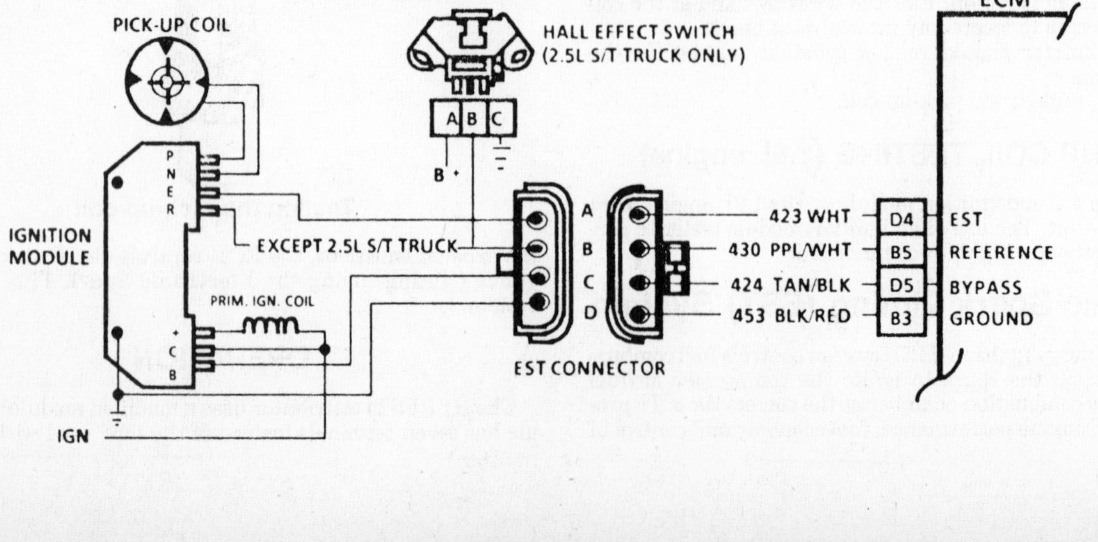
ECM
PICK-UP COIL
HALL EFFECT SWITCH
(2.5L S/T TRUCK ONLY)
A B C
P
N
E
R
B+
IGNITION
MODULE
EXCEPT 2.5L S/T TRUCK
PRIM. IGN. COIL
+
C
B
IGN
A
B
C
D
EST CONNECTOR
423 WHT
430 PPL/WHT
424 TAN/BLK
453 BLK/RED
D4
B5
D5
B3
EST
REFERENCE
BYPASS
GROUND

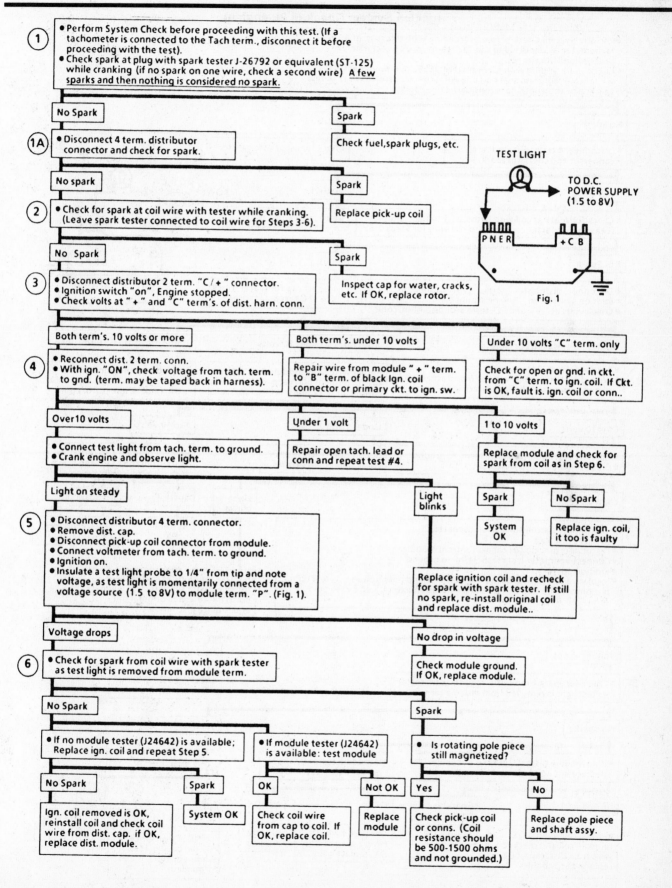

(1)
- Perform System Check before proceeding with this test. (If a tachometer is connected to the Tach term., disconnect it before proceeding with the test).
- Check spark at plug with spark tester J-26792 or equivalent (ST-125) while cranking (if no spark on one wire, check a second wire) A few sparks and then nothing is considered no spark.

→ **Spark**: Check fuel, spark plugs, etc.

→ **No Spark**:

(1A)
- Disconnect 4 term. distributor connector and check for spark.

→ **Spark**: Replace pick-up coil

→ **No spark**:

(2)
- Check for spark at coil wire with tester while cranking. (Leave spark tester connected to coil wire for Steps 3-6).

→ **Spark**: Inspect cap for water, cracks, etc. If OK, replace rotor.

→ **No Spark**:

(3)
- Disconnect distributor 2 term. "C/+" connector.
- Ignition switch "on", Engine stopped.
- Check volts at "+" and "C" term's. of dist. harn. conn.

→ **Both term's. under 10 volts**: Repair wire from module "+" term. to "B" term. of black Ign. coil connector or primary ckt. to ign. sw.

→ **Under 10 volts "C" term. only**: Check for open or gnd. in ckt. from "C" term. to ign. coil. If Ckt. is OK, fault is. ign. coil or conn..

→ **Both term's. 10 volts or more**:

(4)
- Reconnect dist. 2 term. conn.
- With ign. "ON", check voltage from tach. term. to gnd. (term. may be taped back in harness).

→ **Under 1 volt**: Repair open tach. lead or conn and repeat test #4.

→ **1 to 10 volts**: Replace module and check for spark from coil as in Step 6.
- **Spark**: System OK
- **No Spark**: Replace ign. coil, it too is faulty

→ **Over 10 volts**:
- Connect test light from tach. term. to ground.
- Crank engine and observe light.

→ **Light blinks**: Replace ignition coil and recheck for spark with spark tester. If still no spark, re-install original coil and replace dist. module..

→ **Light on steady**:

(5)
- Disconnect distributor 4 term. connector.
- Remove dist. cap.
- Disconnect pick-up coil connector from module.
- Connect voltmeter from tach. term. to ground.
- Ignition on.
- Insulate a test light probe to 1/4" from tip and note voltage, as test light is momentarily connected from a voltage source (1.5 to 8V) to module term. "P". (Fig. 1).

→ **No drop in voltage**: Check module ground. If OK, replace module.

→ **Voltage drops**:

(6)
- Check for spark from coil wire with spark tester as test light is removed from module term.

→ **Spark**:
- Is rotating pole piece still magnetized?
  - **Yes**: Check pick-up coil or conns. (Coil resistance should be 500-1500 ohms and not grounded.)
  - **No**: Replace pole piece and shaft assy.

→ **No Spark**:
- If no module tester (J24642) is available; Replace ign. coil and repeat Step 5.
  - **No Spark**: Ign. coil removed is OK, reinstall coil and check coil wire from dist. cap. if OK, replace dist. module.
  - **Spark**: System OK
- If module tester (J24642) is available: test module
  - **OK**: Check coil wire from cap to coil. If OK, replace coil.
  - **Not OK**: Replace module

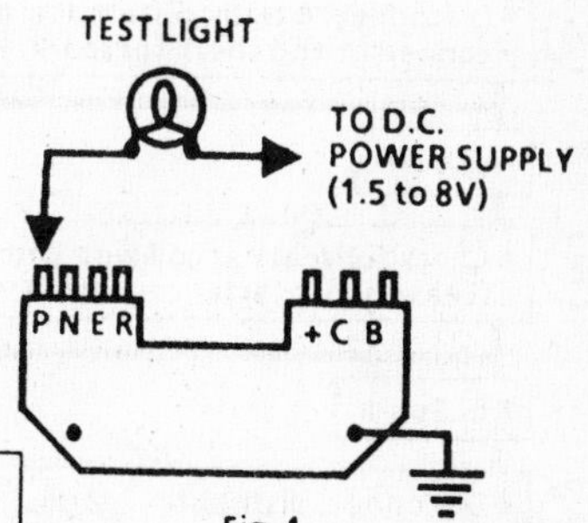
TEST LIGHT
TO D.C. POWER SUPPLY (1.5 to 8V)
P N E R
+ C B

Fig. 1

Ignition System Check (4.3L engine)

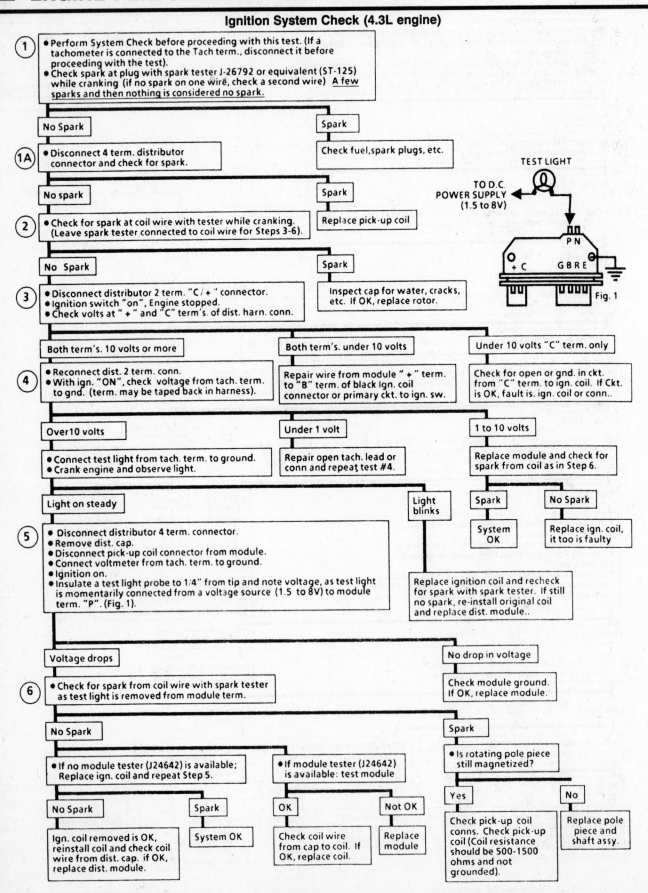

1
- Perform System Check before proceeding with this test. (If a tachometer is connected to the Tach term., disconnect it before proceeding with the test).
- Check spark at plug with spark tester J-26792 or equivalent (ST-125) while cranking (if no spark on one wire, check a second wire) A few sparks and then nothing is considered no spark.

Spark → Check fuel,spark plugs, etc.

No Spark →

1A
- Disconnect 4 term. distributor connector and check for spark.

Spark → Replace pick-up coil

No spark →

2
- Check for spark at coil wire with tester while cranking. (Leave spark tester connected to coil wire for Steps 3-6).

Spark → Inspect cap for water, cracks, etc. If OK, replace rotor.

No Spark →

3
- Disconnect distributor 2 term. "C/+" connector.
- Ignition switch "on", Engine stopped.
- Check volts at "+" and "C" term's. of dist. harn. conn.

Both term's. under 10 volts → Repair wire from module "+" term. to "B" term. of black Ign. coil connector or primary ckt. to ign. sw.

Under 10 volts "C" term. only → Check for open or gnd. in ckt. from "C" term. to ign. coil. If Ckt. is OK, fault is. ign. coil or conn..

Both term's. 10 volts or more →

4
- Reconnect dist. 2 term. conn.
- With ign. "ON", check voltage from tach. term. to gnd. (term. may be taped back in harness).

Under 1 volt → Repair open tach. lead or conn and repeat test #4.

1 to 10 volts → Replace module and check for spark from coil as in Step 6.
- Spark → System OK
- No Spark → Replace ign. coil, it too is faulty

Over10 volts →
- Connect test light from tach. term. to ground.
- Crank engine and observe light.

Light blinks → Replace ignition coil and recheck for spark with spark tester. If still no spark, re-install original coil and replace dist. module..

Light on steady →

5
- Disconnect distributor 4 term. connector.
- Remove dist. cap.
- Disconnect pick-up coil connector from module.
- Connect voltmeter from tach. term. to ground.
- Ignition on.
- Insulate a test light probe to 1/4" from tip and note voltage, as test light is momentarily connected from a voltage source (1.5 to 8V) to module term. "P". (Fig. 1).

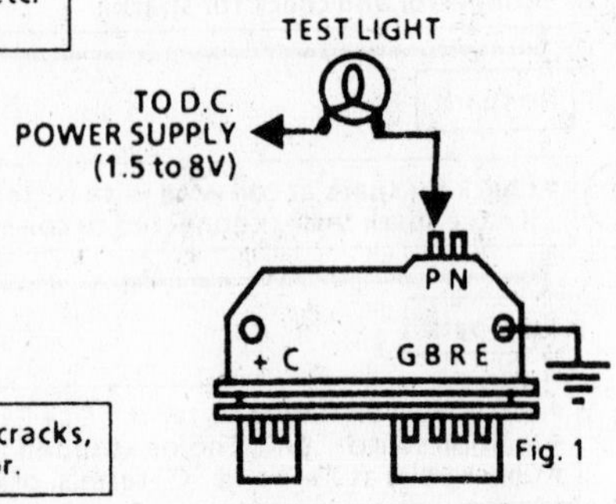
TEST LIGHT
TO D.C. POWER SUPPLY (1.5 to 8V)
P N
+ C
G B R E

Fig. 1

No drop in voltage → Check module ground. If OK, replace module.

Voltage drops →

6
- Check for spark from coil wire with spark tester as test light is removed from module term.

Spark →
- Is rotating pole piece still magnetized?
  - Yes → Check pick-up coil conns. Check pick-up coil (Coil resistance should be 500-1500 ohms and not grounded).
  - No → Replace pole piece and shaft assy.

No Spark →
- If no module tester (J24642) is available; Replace ign. coil and repeat Step 5.
  - No Spark → Ign. coil removed is OK, reinstall coil and check coil wire from dist. cap. if OK, replace dist. module.
  - Spark → System OK
- If module tester (J24642) is available: test module
  - OK → Check coil wire from cap to coil. If OK, replace coil.
  - Not OK → Replace module

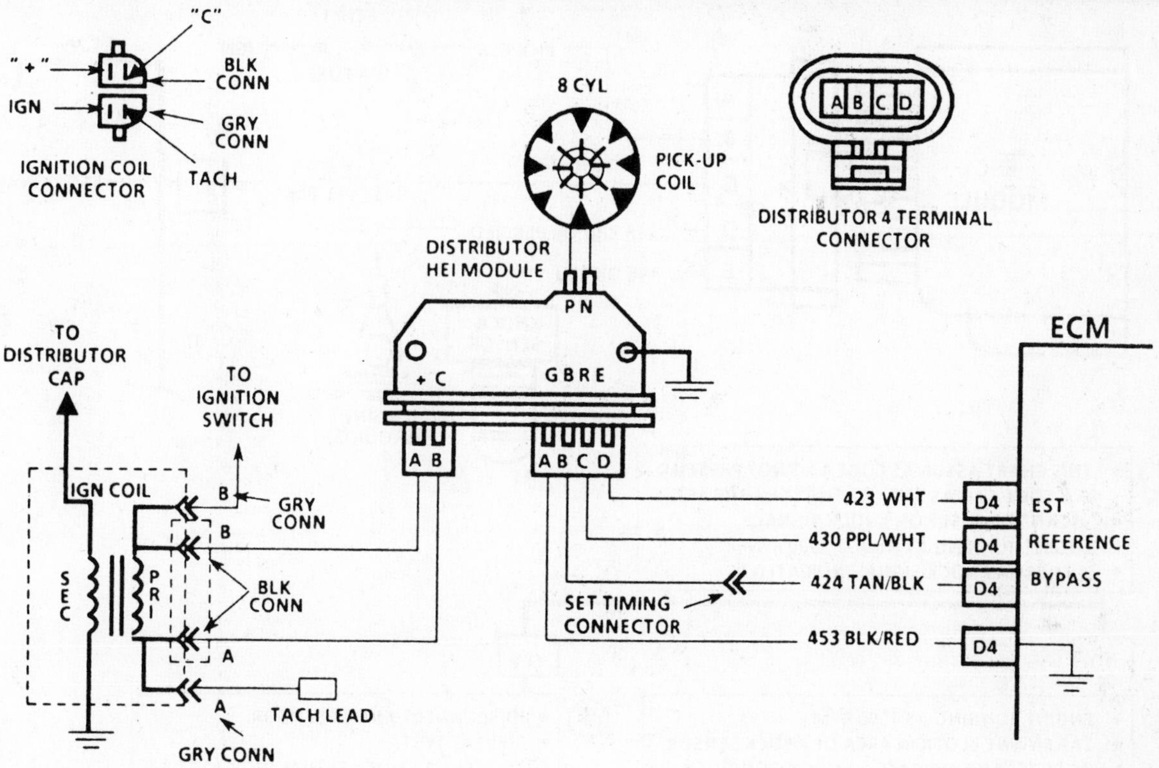
"C"
"+"
BLK CONN
IGN
GRY CONN
IGNITION COIL CONNECTOR
TACH
8 CYL
PICK-UP COIL
A B C D
DISTRIBUTOR 4 TERMINAL CONNECTOR
DISTRIBUTOR HEI MODULE
P N
TO DISTRIBUTOR CAP
+ C
G B R E
ECM
TO IGNITION SWITCH
A B
A B C D
IGN COIL
GRY CONN
B
423 WHT
D4
EST
430 PPL/WHT
REFERENCE
424 TAN/BLK
BYPASS
SEC
PRI
BLK CONN
SET TIMING CONNECTOR
453 BLK/RED
A
TACH LEAD
GRY CONN

Hall Effect Switch Test

1. Disconnect and remove the hall effect switch from the distributor.
2. Noting the polarity marked on the switch, connect a 12 volt battery and voltmeter as shown in the illustration.
3. Insert a thin bladed tool as shown in the illustration.
4. Voltmeter reading should be less than 0.5 volts without the blade against the magnet. Replace the switch if above 0.5 volts.
5. With the blade against the magnet, voltage should be within 0.5 volts of battery voltage. Replace the switch if not with specification.

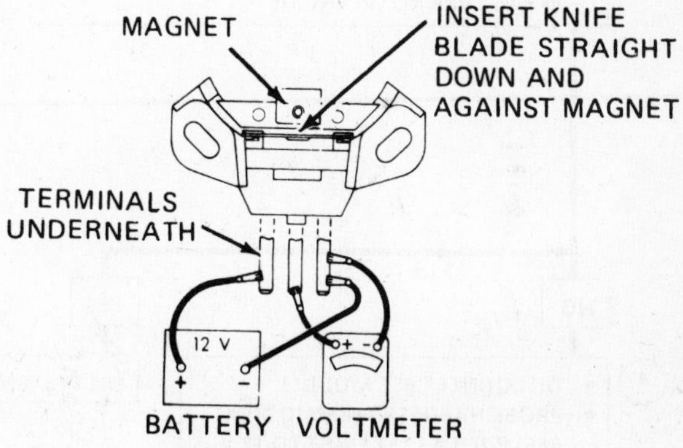
MAGNET
INSERT KNIFE BLADE STRAIGHT DOWN AND AGAINST MAGNET
TERMINALS UNDERNEATH
12 V
BATTERY
VOLTMETER

Hall Effect Switch testing

Electronic Spark Control (ESC) System

The Electronic Spark Control (ESC) system is designed to retard spark timing up to 20° to reduce detonation in the engine. This allows the engine to use maximum spark advance to improve driveability and fuel economy. Varying octane levels in gasoline can cause detonation (spark knock) in any engine.

OPERATION

The ESC system has three components:

- ESC Module
- ESC Knock Sensor
- ECM

The knock sensor detects abnormal vibration in the engine. The sensor is mounted in the engine block near the cylinders. The ESC module receives the knock sensor information and sends a signal to the ECM. The ECM then adjusts the Electronic Spark Timing (EST) to reduce spark knocking.

The ESC module sends a voltage signal to the ECM when no spark knocking is detected by the ESC knock sensor, and the ECM provides normal spark advance. When the knock sensor detects spark knock, the module turns off the circuit to the ECM. The ECM then retards EST to reduce spark knock.

DIAGNOSIS

Loss of the ESC knock sensor signal or loss of ground at the ESC module would cause the signal to the ECM to remain high. This condition would cause the ECM to control EST as if there was no spark knock. No retard would occur, and spark knocking could become severe under heavy engine load.

Spark retard without the knock sensor connected could indicate a noise signal on the wire to the ECM or a malfunctioning ESC module.

Loss of the ESC signal to the ECM would cause the ECM to constantly retard EST. This could result in sluggish performance and cause a Code 43 to be set. Code 43 indicates that the ECM is receiving less than 6 volts for a 4 second period with the engine running. See COMPUTER COMMAND CONTROL SYSTEM in this section to determine how to retrieve codes from the ECM and for further diagnostic procedures.

Electronic Spark Control (ESC) System Test

Electronic spark control is accomplished with a module that

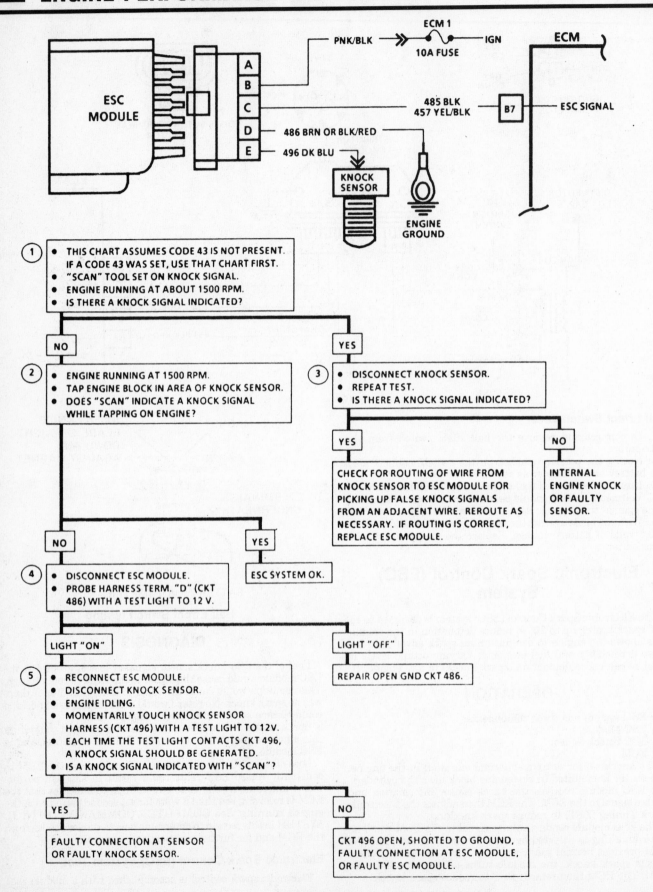

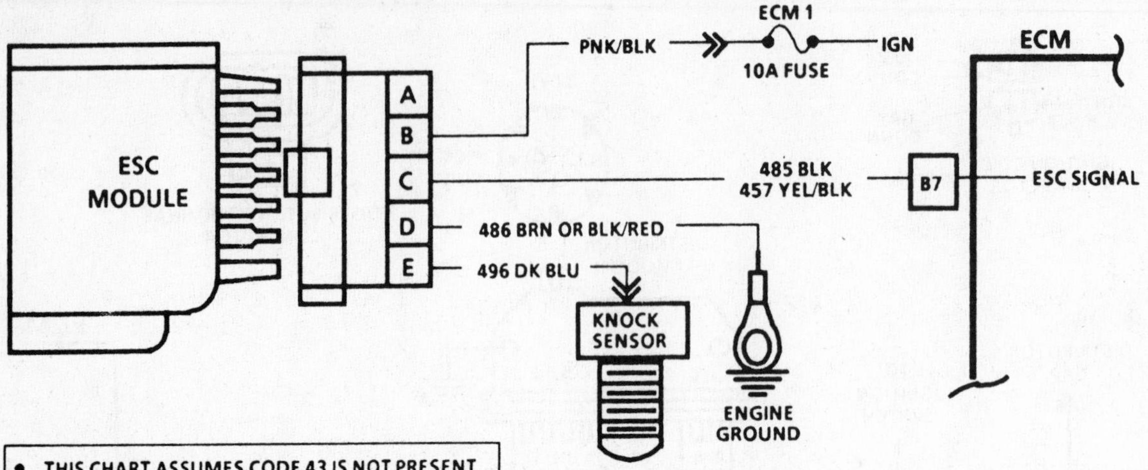
ECM 1
PNK/BLK
10A FUSE
IGN
ECM
ESC MODULE
A
B
C
D
E
485 BLK
457 YEL/BLK
B7
ESC SIGNAL
486 BRN OR BLK/RED
496 DK BLU
KNOCK SENSOR
ENGINE GROUND

(1)
- THIS CHART ASSUMES CODE 43 IS NOT PRESENT. IF A CODE 43 WAS SET, USE THAT CHART FIRST.
- "SCAN" TOOL SET ON KNOCK SIGNAL.
- ENGINE RUNNING AT ABOUT 1500 RPM.
- IS THERE A KNOCK SIGNAL INDICATED?

NO → (2)
- ENGINE RUNNING AT 1500 RPM.
- TAP ENGINE BLOCK IN AREA OF KNOCK SENSOR.
- DOES "SCAN" INDICATE A KNOCK SIGNAL WHILE TAPPING ON ENGINE?

YES → (3)
- DISCONNECT KNOCK SENSOR.
- REPEAT TEST.
- IS THERE A KNOCK SIGNAL INDICATED?

(3) YES → CHECK FOR ROUTING OF WIRE FROM KNOCK SENSOR TO ESC MODULE FOR PICKING UP FALSE KNOCK SIGNALS FROM AN ADJACENT WIRE. REROUTE AS NECESSARY. IF ROUTING IS CORRECT, REPLACE ESC MODULE.

(3) NO → INTERNAL ENGINE KNOCK OR FAULTY SENSOR.

(2) YES → ESC SYSTEM OK.

(2) NO → (4)
- DISCONNECT ESC MODULE.
- PROBE HARNESS TERM. "D" (CKT 486) WITH A TEST LIGHT TO 12 V.

(4) LIGHT "OFF" → REPAIR OPEN GND CKT 486.

(4) LIGHT "ON" → (5)
- RECONNECT ESC MODULE.
- DISCONNECT KNOCK SENSOR.
- ENGINE IDLING.
- MOMENTARILY TOUCH KNOCK SENSOR HARNESS (CKT 496) WITH A TEST LIGHT TO 12V.
- EACH TIME THE TEST LIGHT CONTACTS CKT 496, A KNOCK SIGNAL SHOULD BE GENERATED.
- IS A KNOCK SIGNAL INDICATED WITH "SCAN"?

(5) YES → FAULTY CONNECTION AT SENSOR OR FAULTY KNOCK SENSOR.

(5) NO → CKT 496 OPEN, SHORTED TO GROUND, FAULTY CONNECTION AT ESC MODULE, OR FAULTY ESC MODULE.

sends a voltage signal to the ECM. As the knock sensor detects engine knock, the voltage from the ESC module to the ECM is shut off and this signals the ECM to retard timing, if the engine is over 900 rpm.

6-Cylinder Distributor Overhaul

DISASSEMBLY

NOTE: Any time a distributor is disassembled, the retainer must be replaced. DO NOT attempt to reuse the old retainer.

Distributor With Sealed Module Connectors

1. Matchmark the distributor rotor and shaft for installation reference.
2. Remove the distributor from the engine. Remove the cap and rotor.
3. Using a punch, remove the roll pin that holds the drive gear in place at the bottom of the distributor shaft. Matchmark the drive gear for installation reference.
4. Remove the drive gear, washer or spring and spring retainer, or tan washer.
5. Remove the distributor shaft with the pole piece and plate from the housing.

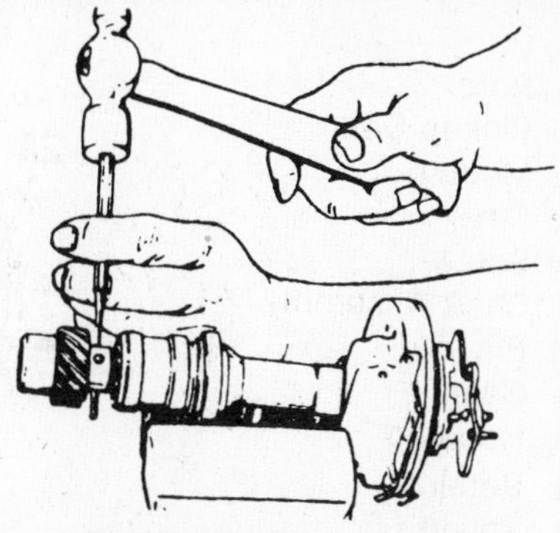

Removing the roll pin

6. Remove the retainer from the housing by prying gently with a pry bar. Remove the shield.
7. Remove the pick-up coil connector by lifting the locktab. Remove the pick-up coil.
8. Remove the two screws holding the ignition module to the housing and remove the module.

Distributor Without Sealed Module Connectors

1. Matchmark the distributor rotor and shaft for installation reference.

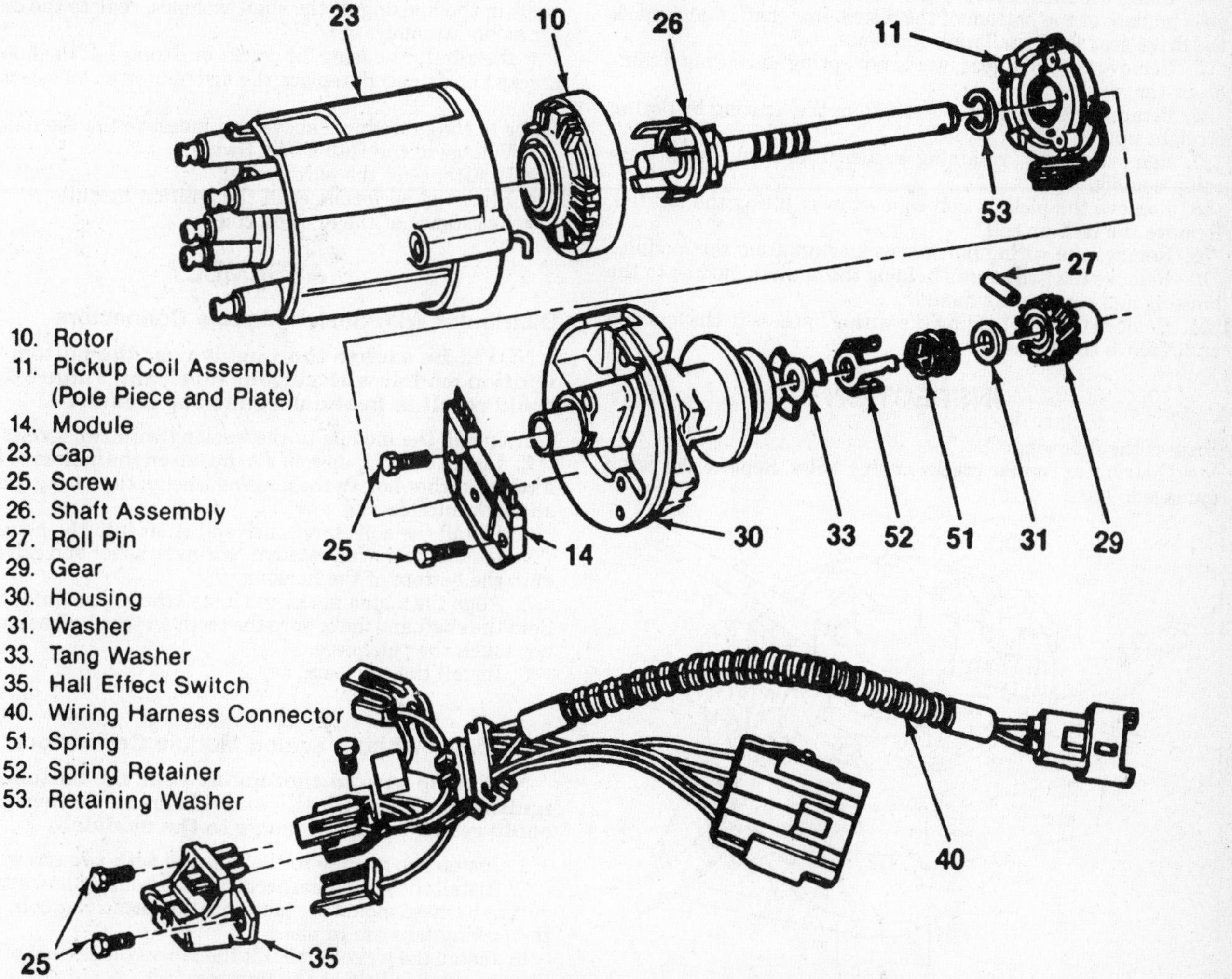
23
10
26
11
53
27
30
33
52
51
31
29
25
14
40
25
35
10. Rotor
11. Pickup Coil Assembly (Pole Piece and Plate)
14. Module
23. Cap
25. Screw
26. Shaft Assembly
27. Roll Pin
29. Gear
30. Housing
31. Washer
33. Tang Washer
35. Hall Effect Switch
40. Wiring Harness Connector
51. Spring
52. Spring Retainer
53. Retaining Washer

Distributor components — without sealed module connectors

10. Rotor
11. Pickup Coil
14. Module
23. Cap
25. Screw
26. Shaft Assembly
27. Pin
29. Gear
30. Housing
49. Retainer
50. Shield
51. Spring
52. Spring Retainer

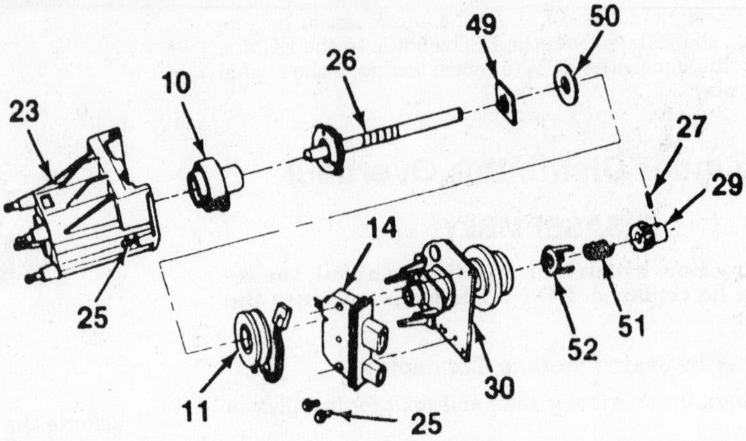
49
50
26
10
23
27
29
14
25
51
52
30
11
25

Distributor components — with sealed module connectors

2. Remove the distributor from the engine. Remove the cap and rotor.
3. If equipped, remove the two bolts holding the Hall Effect Switch to the housing. Lift away the locking tab of the connector to the switch, then remove the switch by lifting straight up.
4. Using a punch, remove the roll pin that holds the drive gear in place at the bottom of the distributor shaft. Matchmark the drive gear for installation reference.
5. Remove the drive gear, washer or spring and spring retainer, or tan washer.
6. Remove the distributor shaft from the housing by prying straight up.
7. Remove the "C" retaining washer from inside the pick-up coil assembly.
8. Remove the pick-up coil connector by lifting the locktab. Remove the pick-up coil.
9. Remove the wiring harness connectors from the module.
10. Remove the two screws holding the ignition module to the housing and remove the module.
11. Remove the bolt holding the wiring harness to the housing and remove the harness.

INSPECTION

Inspect the following:

- Distributor cap for cracks or tiny holes. Replace the cap if damaged.

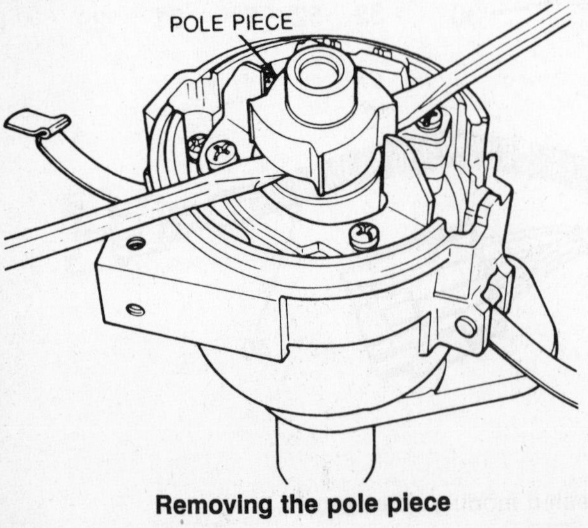
POLE PIECE

Removing the pole piece

- Metal terminals in the cap for corrosion. Scrape terminals clean or replace the cap.
- Rotor for wear or burning at the outer terminal. The presence of carbon on the terminal indicates rotor wear and the need for replacement..
- Distributor shaft for shaft-to-housing looseness. Insert the shaft in the housing. If the shaft wobbles, replace the distributor as an assembly.
- Distributor housing for cracks or damage. If the housing is cracked or damaged, replace the distributor as an assembly.

Refer to the procedures above and measure the the following:

- Voltage of the Hall Effect Switch.
- Resistance of the pick-up coil.
- Electrical performance of the ignition module.
- Resistance of the ignition coil.

ASSEMBLY

Distributor With Sealed Module Connectors

NOTE: Be sure to thoroughly coat the bottom of the ignition module with silicone lubricant. Failure to do so could result in heat damage to the module.

1. Install the module to the housing with two screws.
2. Install the pick-up coil. Fit the tab on the bottom of the coil into the anchor hole in the housing. Install the wiring connector and lock into place.
3. Install the shield, retainer and shaft into the housing.
4. Install the spring retainer, spring, washer and driven gear onto the bottom of the housing.
5. Align the matchmarks and install the roll pin into the gear. Spin the shaft and make sure the teeth on the shaft assembly do not touch the pole piece.
6. Install the rotor and cap.

Distributor Without Sealed Module Connectors

NOTE: Be sure to thoroughly coat the bottom of the ignition module with silicone lubricant. Failure to do so could result in heat damage to the module.

1. Install the module to the housing with two screws.
2. Install the wiring harness into the housing and attach the wiring harness mounting tabs with the attaching bolt. Ensure the locking tabs are in place.
3. Install the pick-up coil. Fit the tab on the bottom of the coil into the anchor hole in the housing.
4. Install the pick-up coil wiring connector to the module.

1. Cap assembly
2. Carbon point
3. Rotor head
4. Packing
5. Cover
6. Screw
7. Vacuum control assembly
8. Screw
9. Harness assembly
10. Pole piece
11. Roll pin
12. Screw
13. Breaker plate assembly
14. Screw
15. P/U coil module assembly
16. Spacer
17. Screw
18. Stator
19. Magnet set
20. Roll pin
21. Collar
22. Shaft assembly
23. Rotor shaft assembly
24. Packing
25. Screw
26. Governor weight
27. Governor spring

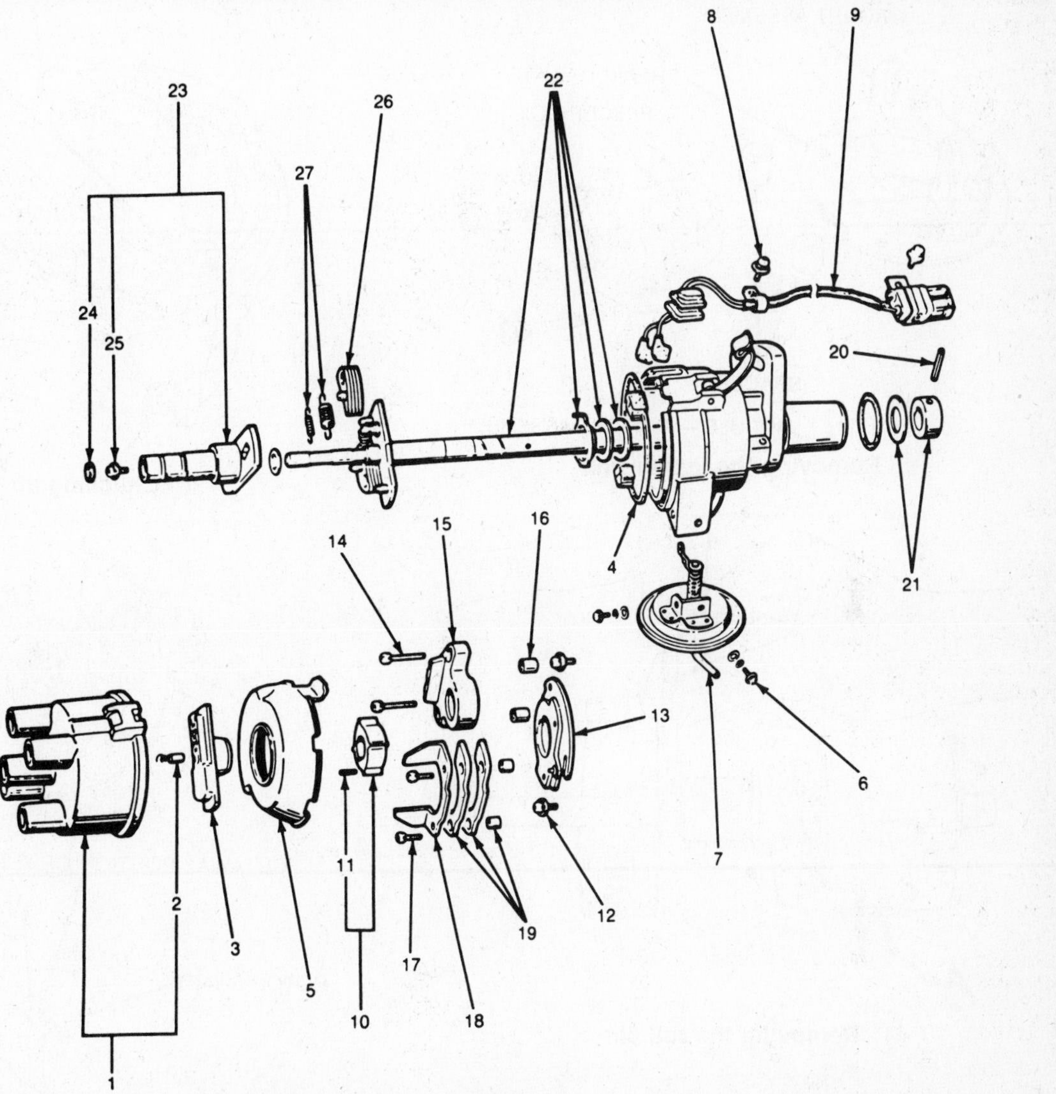

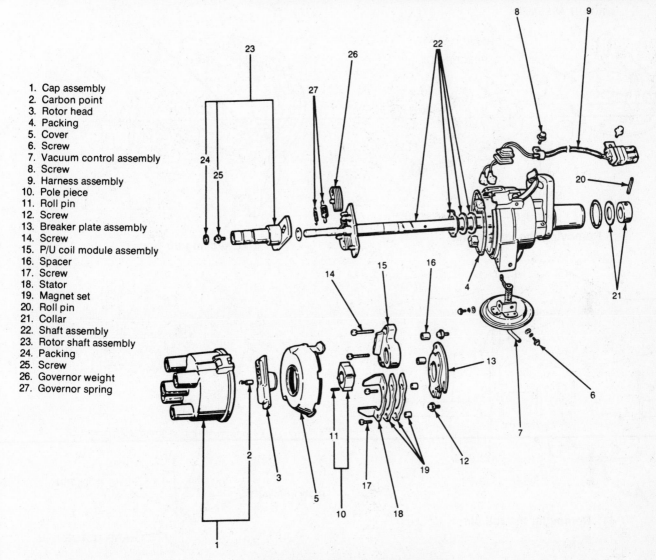

4-Cylinder distributor components

5. Install the "C" washer into the coil and the shaft into the housing.

6. Install the tan washer, spring retainer, spring and drive gear onto the shaft. Align the matchmarks on the drive gear and shaft.

7. Install the roll pin into the gear. Turn the shaft by hand to check tooth clearance between the shaft and pick-up coil assembly. If clearance needs adjustment, loosen and retighten the three pick-up coil bolts.

8. If equipped, install the wiring connector for the Hall Effect Switch and install the switch with two attaching bolts. The teeth of the switch should rotate between the back plate and the magnet of the switch without touching.

9. Install the rotor and cap.

4-Cylinder Distributor Overhaul

DISASSEMBLY

1. Remove the cap, rotor, packing and cover.

2. Remove the screws attaching the vacuum controller then remove the vacuum controller from the housing.

3. Remove the screws attaching the harness assembly.

4. Disconnect connectors of harness assembly from the igniter unit, then remove the harness assembly from the housing.

5. Remove the reluctor from the rotor shaft by prying up.

6. Remove the screws attaching the breaker plate assembly, then remove the breaker plate assembly from the housing.

7. Remove the module from the breaker plate assembly. The module is an integral construction and cannot be disassembled.

8. Drive out the roll pin using a punch.

9. Remove the governor shaft assembly from the housing.

NOTE: Matchmark the rotor shaft and governor shaft before disassembly.

10. Remove the packing from the governor shaft and remove the screw attaching the rotor shaft assembly. Remove the rotor shaft assembly from the governor shaft.

11. Remove the governor weights and springs from the shaft assembly.

INSPECTION

Clean disassembled parts in solvent and check for ewar or damage. Inspect the distributor cap for cracks or corrosion on terminals. Replace components as necessary.

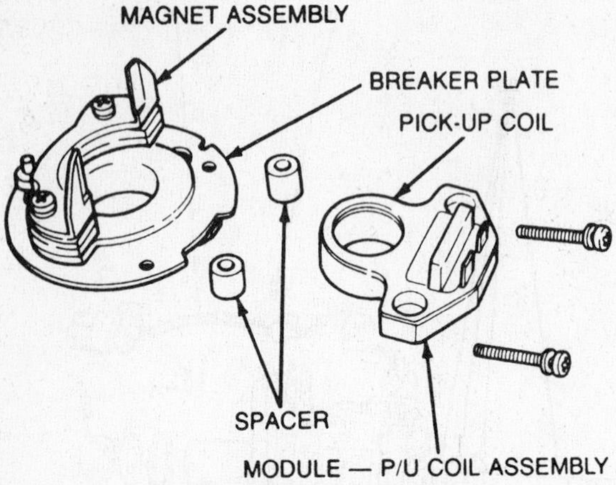
MAGNET ASSEMBLY
BREAKER PLATE
PICK-UP COIL
SPACER
MODULE — P/U COIL ASSEMBLY
Removing the igniter unit

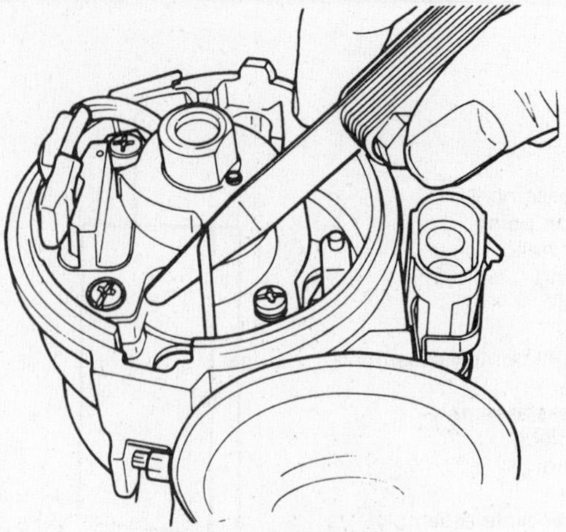
Checking air gap

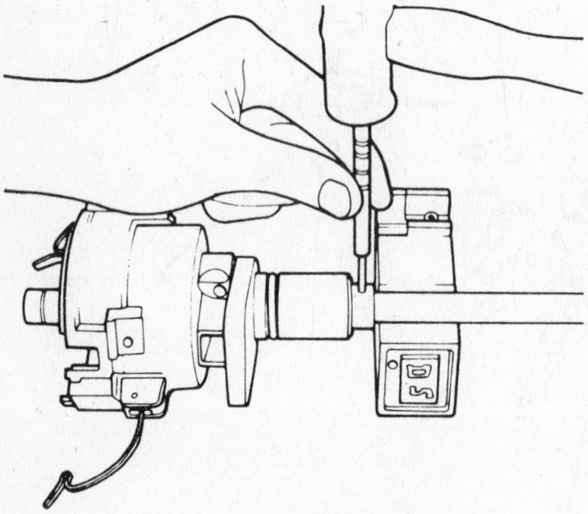
Removing the roll pin

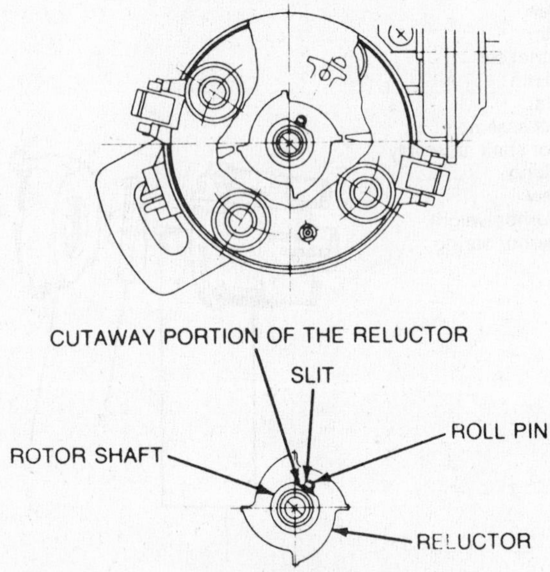
CUTAWAY PORTION OF THE RELUCTOR
SLIT
ROLL PIN
ROTOR SHAFT
RELUCTOR
Installing the roll pin

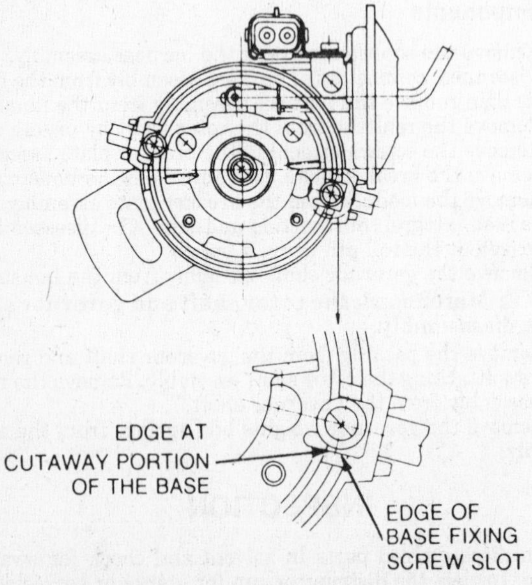
EDGE AT
CUTAWAY PORTION
OF THE BASE
EDGE OF
BASE FIXING
SCREW SLOT
Installing the breaker plate assembly

ADJUSTMENT

Air Gap

Using a non-magnetic feeler gauge, measure the air gap between the pole piece and the stator. Air gap should be 0.3–0.5mm. Adjust by loosening the two screws and moving the pole piece until the gap is correct. Tighten the two screws and recheck the air gap. Screws are made of non-magnetic stainless steel.

Govenor Advance

Normal operation is indicated if the rotor shaft returns to normal state when released after turning it counterclockwise with hour hand.

Vacuum Advance

Check vacuum controller for leaks by testing with a hand vacuum pump. Apply vacuum to the controller and test for proper operation. Hold vacuum for a few minutes to test the diaphragm. If the controller holds vacuum, it is good.

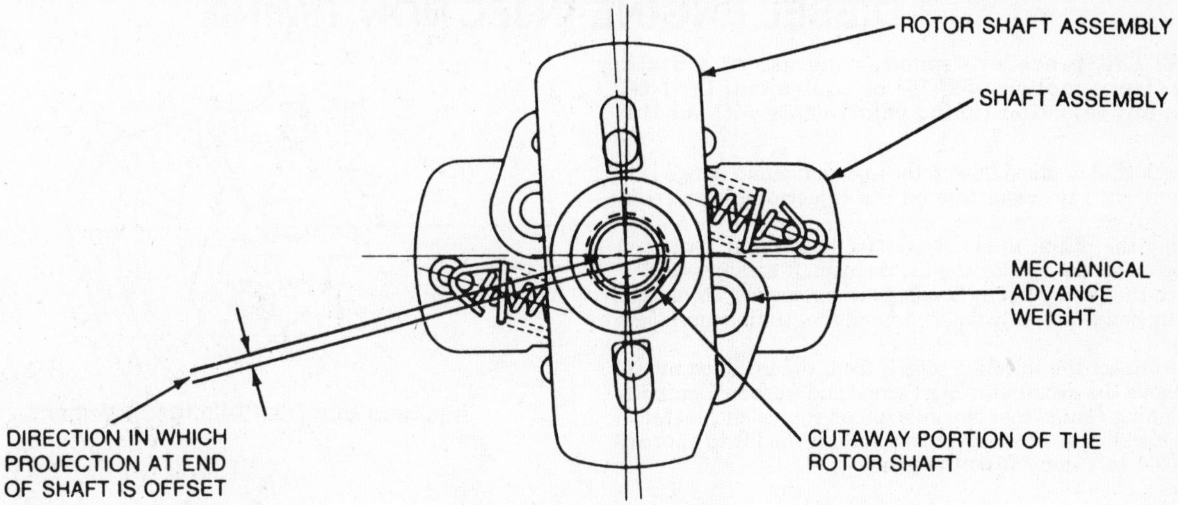
ROTOR SHAFT ASSEMBLY
SHAFT ASSEMBLY
MECHANICAL ADVANCE WEIGHT
DIRECTION IN WHICH PROJECTION AT END OF SHAFT IS OFFSET
CUTAWAY PORTION OF THE ROTOR SHAFT
Installing the rotor shaft

ASSEMBLY

Reassemble the distributor by following the disassembly procedure in reverse order. Note the following:

- The governor springs should be fitted to the spring hanger pin on the shaft assembly with the smaller hook end turned downward.
- The relation between the cutaway portion of the rotor shaft and the offset of projection at the end of the governor shaft should be carefully noted when install the rotor shaft to the housing.
- Use a new roll pin when installing the dollar.
- The edge at the cutaway portion of the base must be flush with the edge of the base fixing screw slot when installing the breaker plate assembly.
- The roller pin should be installed so that the slot is in parallel with the cutaway portion of the reluctor as viewed from above.

IGNITION TIMING ADJUSTMENT

The following procedure requires the use of a distributor wrench and a timing light. When using a timing light, be sure to consult the manufacturer's recommendations for installation and usage.

Gasoline Engine

- On 2.5L engines, ground the "A" and "B" terminals on the ALDL connector under the dash before adjusting the timing.
- On all other engines using the EST distributor, disconnect the timing connector wire, located below the heater case in the engine compartment or coming out of the the wiring harness near the distributor, before adjusting the timing.

1. Timing specifications are listed on the Vehicle Emissions Control Information label, located on the radiator support. Use the timing specifications specific to your vehicle.
2. Using a timing light, connect it to the engine by performing the following procedures:
   a. If using a non-inductive type, connect an adapter between the No. 1 spark plug and the spark plug wire; DO NOT puncture the spark plug wire, for this will cause a voltage leak.
   b. If using an inductive type, clamp it around the No. 1 spark plug wire.
   c. If using a magnetic type, place the probe in the connector located near the damper pulley; this type must be used with special electronic timing equipment.
3. If equipped with Electric Spark Timing (EST), disconnect the timing connector wire; this allows the engine to operate in the by-pass timing mode.

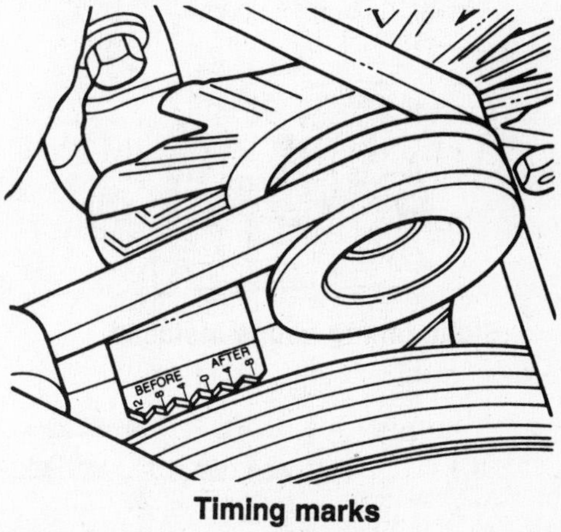
BEFORE
AFTER
Timing marks

4. Start the engine aim the timing light at the timing mark on the damper pulley; a line on the damper pulley will align the timing mark. If necessary (to adjust the timing), loosen the distributor hold down clamp and slowly turn the distributor slightly to align the marks. When the alignment is correct, tighten the hold down bolt.
5. Turn the engine OFF, remove the timing light and reconnect the timing connector wire (if disconnected).

DIESEL ENGINE INJECTION TIMING

NOTE: This procedure requires the use of a Static Timing Gauge tool No. J-29763 or equivalent; DO NOT attempt any injection timing adjustments without this tool.

1. Check that notched line on the injection pump flange is in alignment with notched line on the injection pump front bracket.
2. Bring the piston in No. 1 cylinder to top dear center on compression stroke by turning the crankshaft as necessary.
3. With the timing pulley housing cover removed, check that the timing belt is properly tensioned and that timing marks are aligned.
4. Disconnect the injection pipe(s) from the injection pump, then remove the distributor head screw and washer. Using the Static Timing Gauge tool No. J-29763 or equivalent, install it into the distributor head screw hole and set the lift to approximately 0.04 in. (1mm) from the plunger.

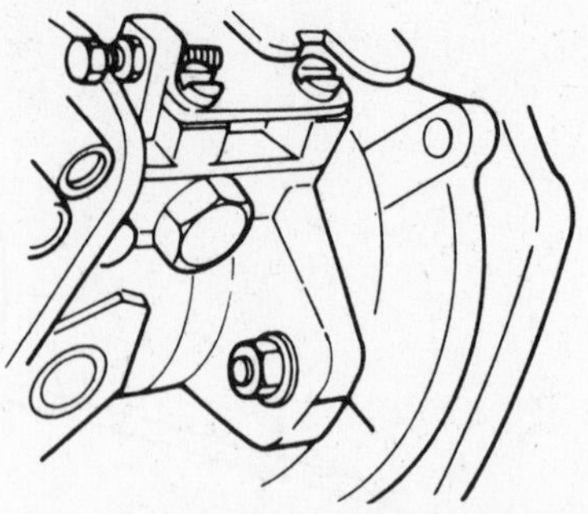

Injection pump and flange alignment

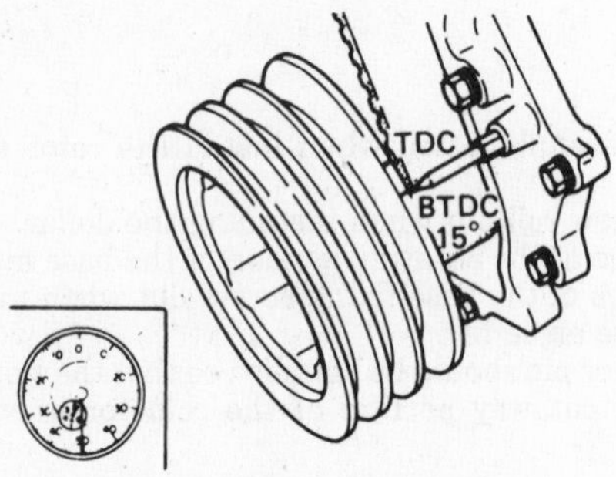
TDC
BTDC
15°

No. 1 piston 15° BTDC

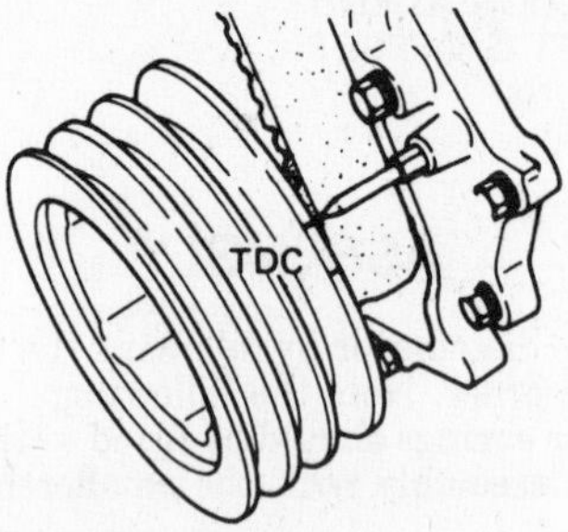
TDC

Number 1 piston at TDC

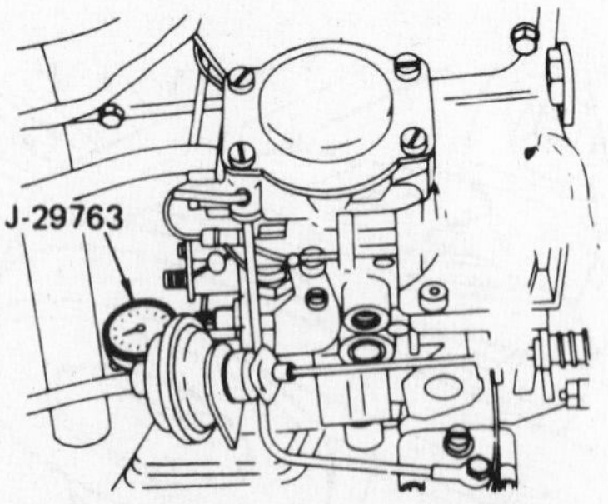
J-29763

Static timing gauge installed

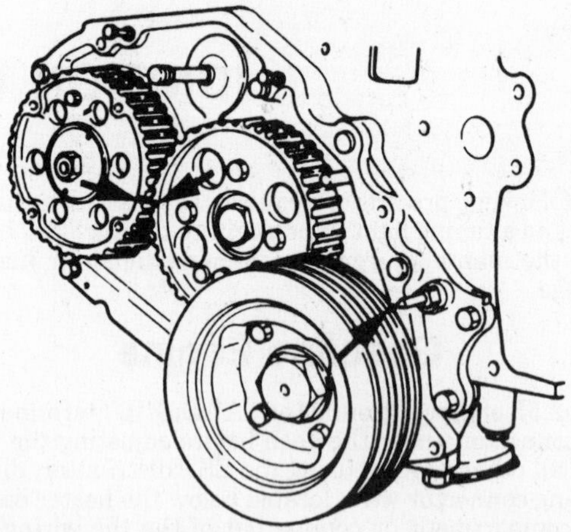

Aligning the timing marks – diesel engine

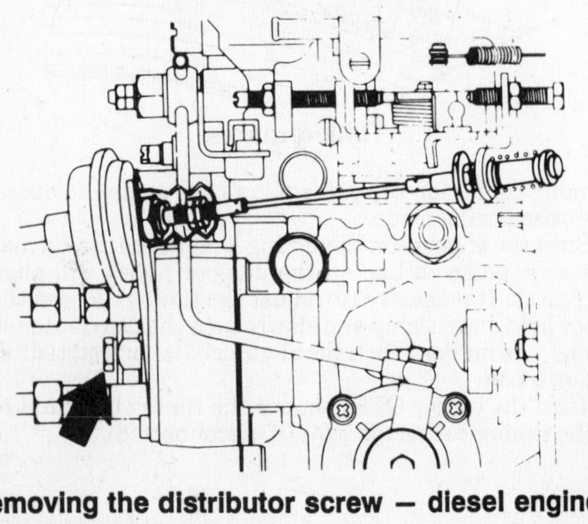

Removing the distributor screw – diesel engine

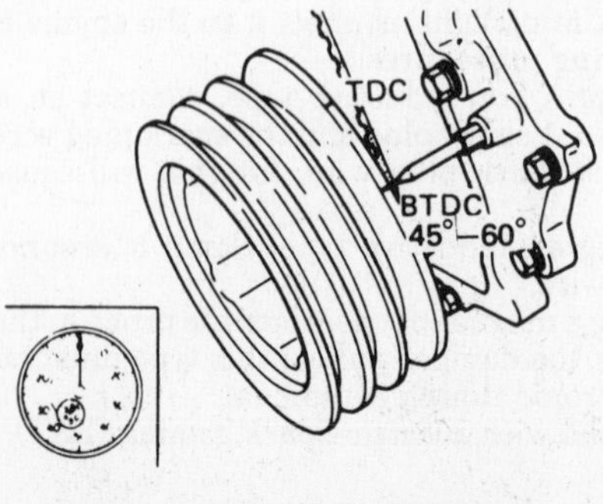
TDC
BTDC
45°–60°

No. 1 piston 45–60° BTDC

5. Use a wrench to hold the delivery holder when loosening the sleeve nuts on the injection pump side.
6. Bring the piston in No. 1 cylinder to a point 45–60° before top dead center (TDC) by turning the crankshaft, then calibrate the dial indicator to zero.
7. Turn the crankshaft pulley slightly in both directions and check that gauge indication is stable.
8. Turn the crankshaft in the normal direction of rotation, then record the reading of the dial indicator when the timing mark (15°) on the crankshaft pulley is in alignment with the pointer; the reading should be 0.020 in. (0.5mm).
9. If the reading of dial indicator deviates from the specified range, hold the crankshaft in position 15° BTDC and loosen two nuts on injection pump flange.
10. Move the injection pump to a point where dial indicator gives reading of 0.020 in. (0.5mm), then tighten pump flange nuts.

VALVE LASH ADJUSTMENT

Valve adjustment determines how far the valves enter the cylinder and how long they stay open and/or closed.

NOTE: While all valve adjustments must be made as accurately as possible, it is better to have the valve adjustment slightly loose than slightly tight, as a burned valve may result from overly tight adjustments.

1.9L and 2.2L Diesel

NOTE: The valves are adjusted with the engine Cold.

1. Remove the rocker arm cover.
2. Make sure that the rocker arm shaft nuts/bolts are torqued to 16 ft. lbs.
3. Using a wrench on the damper pulley bolt or a remote starter button, turn the crankshaft until the No. 1 piston is at TDC of the compression stroke.

NOTE: You can tell when the piston is coming up on the compression stroke by removing the spark plug and placing your thumb over the hole, you will feel the air being forced out of the spark plug hole. Stop turning the crankshaft when the TDC timing mark on the crankshaft pulley is directly aligned with the timing mark pointer.

4. With the No. 1 piston at TDC of the compression stroke, perform the following valve setting procedures:
   a. If working on the 1.9L engine, use a 0.006 in. (0.152mm) feeler gauge, to set intake valves of cylinders No. 1 & 2. Using a 0.010 in. (0.254mm) feeler gauge, set the exhaust valves of cylinders No. 1 & 3.
   b. If working on the 2.2L engine, use a 0.016 in. (0.40mm) feeler gauge, to set the intake valves of cylinders No. 1, 2 & 3, then set the exhaust valve of cylinder No. 1.
5. Rotate the engine one complete revolution, so that cylinder No. 4 is on the TDC of its compression stroke and the timing marks are aligned.

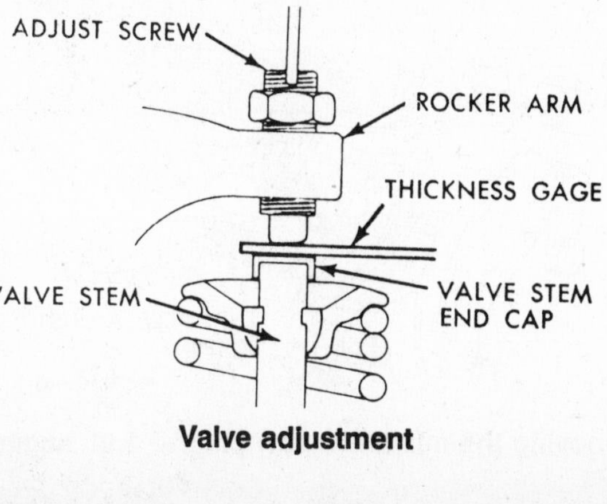
ADJUST SCREW
ROCKER ARM
THICKNESS GAGE
VALVE STEM
VALVE STEM END CAP

Valve adjustment

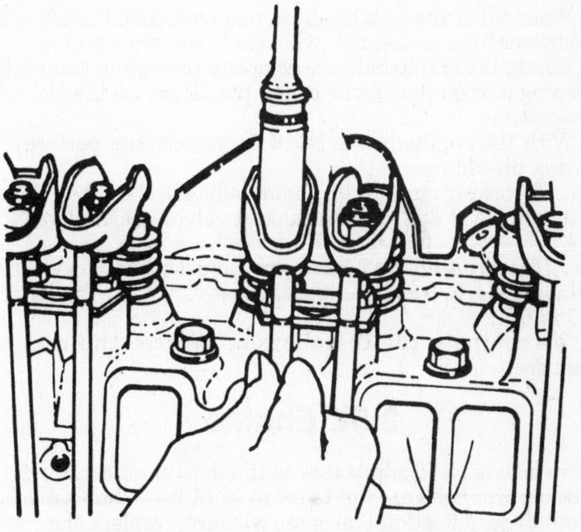

Valve adjustment – 2.0L and 2.8L engine

6. With cylinder No. 4 on the TDC of the compression stroke, perform the following valve setting procedures:
   a. If working on the 1.9L engine, use a 0.006 in. (0.152mm) feeler gauge, to set intake valves of cylinders No. 3 & 4. Using a 0.010 in. (0.254mm) feeler gauge, set the exhaust valves of cylinders No. 2 & 4.
   b. If working on the 2.2L engine, use a 0.016 in. (0.40mm) feeler gauge, to set the intake valve of cylinder No. 4, then the exhaust valves of cylinders No. 2, 3 & 4.

NOTE: When adjusting the valve clearance, loosen the locknut with an open-end wrench, then turn the adjuster screw with a screwdriver and retighten the locknut. The proper thickness feeler gauge should pass between the camshaft and the rocker with a slight drag when the clearance is correct.

2.0L and 2.8L

1. Remove the air cleaner and the rocker arm cover(s).
2. Rotate the crankshaft until the mark on the crankshaft pulley aligns with the **0** mark on the timing plate. Make sure that the No. 1 cylinder is positioned on the compression stroke.

NOTE: You can tell when the piston is coming up on the compression stroke by removing the spark plug and placing your thumb over the hole, you will feel the air being forced out of the spark plug hole. Stop turning the crankshaft when the TDC timing mark on the crankshaft pulley is directly aligned with the timing mark pointer.

3. With the engine in the No. 1 firing position, perform the following adjustments:
   a. If working on the 2.0L engine, adjust the intake valves of cylinders No. 1 & 2 and the exhaust valves of cylinders No. 1 & 3.
   b. If working on the 2.8L engine, adjust the intake valves of cylinders No. 1, 5 & 6 and the exhaust valves of cylinders No. 1, 2 & 3.
4. To adjust the valves, back-out the adjusting nut until lash can be felt at the push rod, then turn the nut until all of the lash is removed.

NOTE: To determine is all of the lash is removed, turn the push rod with your fingers until the movement is removed.

5. When all of the lash has been removed, turn the adjusting an additional 1½ turns; this will center the lifter plunger.
6. Rotate the crankshaft one complete revolution and realign the timing marks; the engine is now positioned on the No. 4 firing position.
7. With the engine in the No. 4 firing position, perform the following procedures:
   a. If working on the 2.0L engine, adjust the intake valves of cylinders No. 3 & 4 and the exhaust valves of cylinders No. 2 & 4.
   b. If working on the 2.8L engine, adjust the intake valves of cylinders No. 2, 3 & 4 and the exhaust valves of cylinders No. 4, 5 & 6.
8. To compete the installation, reverse the removal procedures.

2.5L Engine

Valve lash is NOT adjustable on the 2.5L engine. Check that the rocker arm bolts are tightened to 22 ft. lbs. When valve lash falls out of specification (valve tap is heard), replace the rocker arm, pushrod and hydraulic lifter on the offending cylinder.

4.3L Engine

1. To prepare the engine for valve adjustment, rotate the crankshaft until the mark on the damper pulley aligns with the 0° mark on the timing plate and the No. 1 cylinder is on the compression stroke.

NOTE: You can tell when the piston is coming up on the compression stroke by removing the spark plug and placing your thumb over the hole, you will feel the air being forced out of the spark plug hole. Stop turning the crankshaft when the TDC timing mark on the crankshaft pulley is directly aligned with the timing mark pointer.

2. With the engine on the compression stroke, adjust the exhaust valves of cylinders No. 1, 5 & 6 and the intake valves of cylinders No. 1, 2 & 3 by performing the following procedures:
   a. Back out the adjusting nut until lash can be felt at the pushrod.
   b. While rotating the pushrod, turn the adjusting nut inward until all of the lash is removed.
   c. When the play has disappeared, turn the adjusting nut inward 1 additional turn.
3. Rotate the crankshaft one complete revolution and align the mark on the damper pulley with the 0° mark on the timing plate. With the engine on the compression stroke, adjust the exhaust valves of cylinders No. 2, 3 & 4 and the intake valves of cylinders No. 4, 5 & 6, by performing the following procedures:
   a. Back out the adjusting nut until lash can be felt at the pushrod.
   b. While rotating the pushrod, turn the adjusting nut inward until all of the lash is removed.
   c. When the play has disappeared, turn the adjusting nut inward 1½ additional turns.
4. To complete the installation, reverse the removal procedures. Start the engine, the check for oil leaks and engine operation.

VALVE ARRANGEMENT

1.9L
E-I-I-E-E-I-I-E (front-to-rear)
2.0L
E-I-I-E-E-I-I-E (front-to-rear)
2.2L
E-I-I-E-E-I-I-E (front-to-rear)
2.5L
I-E-E-I-E-E-I-E-I (front-to-rear)
2.8L
E-I-I-E-I-E (right bank—front-to-rear)
E-I-E-I-I-E (left bank—front-to-rear)
4.3L
E-I-I-E-I-E (right bank—front-to-rear)
E-I-E-I-I-E (left bank—front-to-rear)

IDLE SPEED AND MIXTURE ADJUSTMENTS

CARBURETED ENGINES

1.9L Engine

In order to adjust the idle mixture you must first remove the plug that covers the mixture screw.
1. Set the parking brake, block the drive wheels and place the transmission in Neutral.
2. Refer to the Carburetor, Removal and Installation procedures in Section 4, then remove the carburetor from the engine, place it on a work bench and turn it upside down.
3. Using a screwdriver and a hammer, carefully drive the idle mixture screw metal plug from the base of the carburetor.
4. Reinstall the carburetor onto the engine. Start the engine and adjust the idle speed.
5. Allow the engine to reach normal operating temperatures, the choke must be Open and the A/C (if equipped) turned Off.

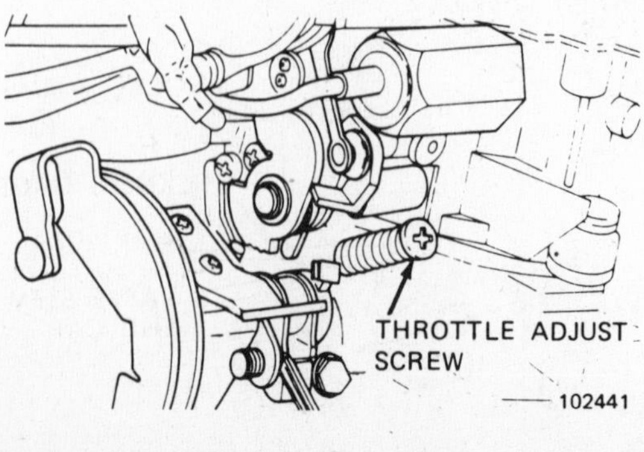
THROTTLE ADJUST
SCREW
102441
Removing the mixture screw plug — 1.9L engine

Disconnect and plug the distributor vacuum line, the EGR vacuum line and the idle compensator vacuum lines.

6. Turn the mixture screw all the way in, then back it out 1½ turns.

NOTE: After adjustment, reconnect the vacuum lines.

7. Adjust the throttle speed screw to 850 rpm (MT) or 950 rpm (AT).
8. Adjust the idle mixture screw to achieve the maximum speed.
9. Reset the throttle adjusting screw to 850 rpm (MT) or 950 rpm (AT).
10. Turn the idle mixture screw (clockwise) to until the engine speed is reduced to 800 rpm (MT) or 900 rpm (AT).
11. If equipped with A/C, perform the following procedures:
    a. Turn the A/C to Max. Cold and the blower to High.
    b. Open the throttle to ⅓ and allow it to close; this allows the speed-up solenoid to reach full travel.
    c. Adjust the speed-up controller adjusting screw to set the idle to 900 rpm.

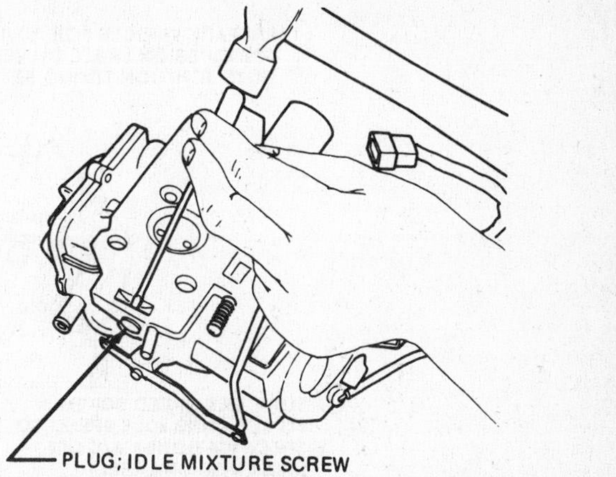
PLUG; IDLE MIXTURE SCREW
Adjusting the idle speed – 1.9L engine

2.0L and 2.8L Engines

NOTE: The idle mixture adjustments are factory set and sealed; no adjustment attempt should be made, except by an authorized GM dealer.

WITHOUT A/C

1. Refer to the emission control label on the vehicle and prepare the engine for adjustments.
2. Remove the air cleaner, set the parking brake and block the drive wheels.
3. Connect a tachometer to the distributor connector.
4. Place the transmission in Drive (AT) or Neutral (MT); make sure that the solenoid is energized.
5. Open the throttle slightly to allow the solenoid plunger to extend. Adjust the curb idle speed to the specified rpm by turning the solenoid screw.

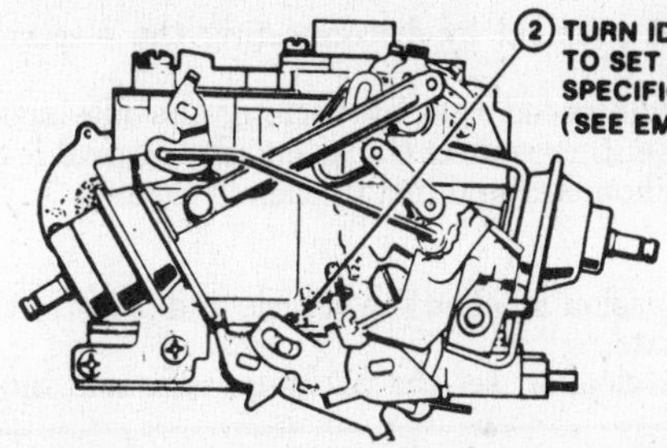
① PREPARE VEHICLE FOR ADJUSTMENTS - SEE EMISSION LABEL ON VEHICLE. NOTE: IGNITION TIMING SET PER LABEL.
② TURN IDLE SPEED SCREW TO SET CURB IDLE SPEED TO SPECIFICATIONS - (SEE EMISSION LABEL)
Adjusting the idle speed on the 2SE carburetor without air conditioning – 2.0L and 2.8L engines

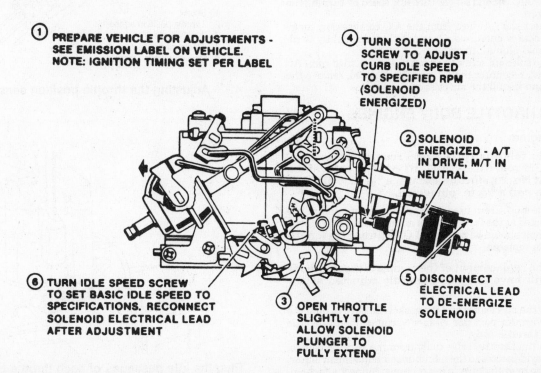

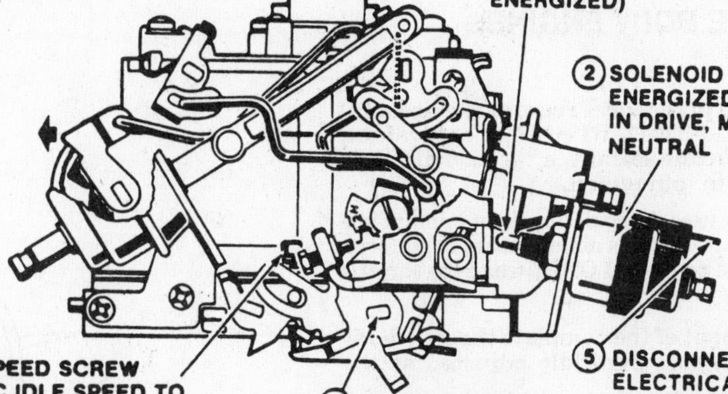
① PREPARE VEHICLE FOR ADJUSTMENTS - SEE EMISSION LABEL ON VEHICLE. NOTE: IGNITION TIMING SET PER LABEL
④ TURN SOLENOID SCREW TO ADJUST CURB IDLE SPEED TO SPECIFIED RPM (SOLENOID ENERGIZED)
② SOLENOID ENERGIZED - A/T IN DRIVE, M/T IN NEUTRAL
⑥ TURN IDLE SPEED SCREW TO SET BASIC IDLE SPEED TO SPECIFICATIONS. RECONNECT SOLENOID ELECTRICAL LEAD AFTER ADJUSTMENT
③ OPEN THROTTLE SLIGHTLY TO ALLOW SOLENOID PLUNGER TO FULLY EXTEND
⑤ DISCONNECT ELECTRICAL LEAD TO DE-ENERGIZE SOLENOID
Adjusting the idle speed on E2SE carburetors without air conditioning – 2.0L and 2.8L engines

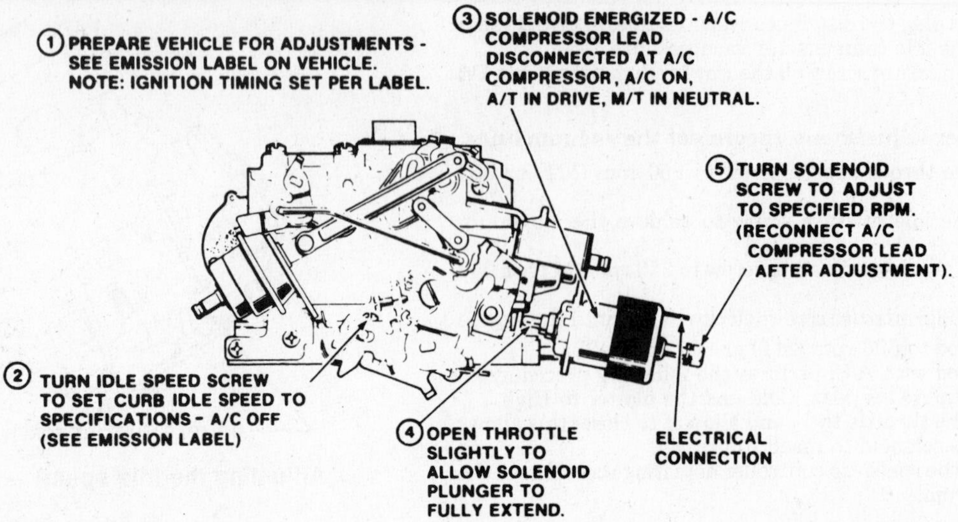

① PREPARE VEHICLE FOR ADJUSTMENTS - SEE EMISSION LABEL ON VEHICLE. NOTE: IGNITION TIMING SET PER LABEL.
③ SOLENOID ENERGIZED - A/C COMPRESSOR LEAD DISCONNECTED AT A/C COMPRESSOR, A/C ON, A/T IN DRIVE, M/T IN NEUTRAL.
⑤ TURN SOLENOID SCREW TO ADJUST TO SPECIFIED RPM. (RECONNECT A/C COMPRESSOR LEAD AFTER ADJUSTMENT).
② TURN IDLE SPEED SCREW TO SET CURB IDLE SPEED TO SPECIFICATIONS - A/C OFF (SEE EMISSION LABEL)
④ OPEN THROTTLE SLIGHTLY TO ALLOW SOLENOID PLUNGER TO FULLY EXTEND.
ELECTRICAL CONNECTION

Adjusting the idle speed on E2SE carburetors with air conditioning — 2.0L and 2.8L engines

6. De-energize the solenoid by disconnecting the electrical lead.
7. Set the basic idle speed rpm by turning the idle speed screw. After adjustment, reconnect the solenoid electrical lead.
8. Remove the tachometer and install the air cleaner.

WITH A/C

1. Refer to the emission label on the vehicle and prepare the engine for adjustments.
2. Remove the air cleaner, set the parking brake and block the drive wheels.
3. Connect a tachometer to the distributor connector.
4. Place the transmission in Drive (AT) or Neutral (MT); make sure that the solenoid is energized.
5. Turn the A/C Off and set the curb idle speed by turning the idle speed screw.
6. Disconnect the A/C lead from the A/C compressor; make sure the solenoid is energized. Open the throttle slightly to allow the solenoid plunger to extend.
7. Turn the solenoid screw to adjust to the specified rpm. After adjustment, reconnect the A/C compressor lead, remove the tachometer and install the air cleaner.

THROTTLE BODY ENGINES

2.5L EFI Engine

NOTE: The following procedures require the use a tachometer, GM tool No. J-33047, BT-8207 or equivalent, GM Torx Bit No. 20, silicone sealant, a $^5/_{32}$ in. drill bit, a prick punch and a $^1/_{16}$ in. pin punch.

The throttle stop screw, used in regulating the minimum idle speed, is adjusted at the factory and is not necessary to perform. This adjustment should be performed ONLY when the throttle body has been replaced.

NOTE: The replacement of the complete throttle body assembly will have the minimum idle adjusted at the factory.

1. Remove the air cleaner and the gasket. Be sure to plug the THERMAC vacuum port (air cleaner vacuum line-to-throttle body) on the throttle body.
2. Remove the throttle valve cable from the throttle control bracket to provide access to the minimum air adjustment screw.
3. Using the manufacturer's instructions, connect a tachometer to the engine.

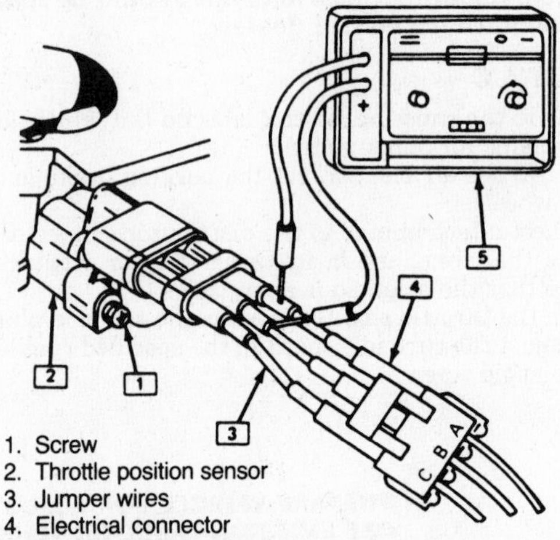

1
2
3
4
5
A
B
C

1. Screw
2. Throttle position sensor
3. Jumper wires
4. Electrical connector
5. Digital volt-ohm meter

Adjusting the throttle position sensor

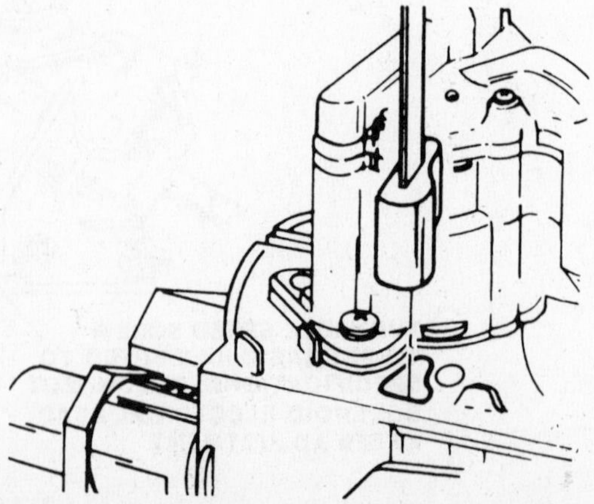

Plug the idle passages of each throttle body as shown

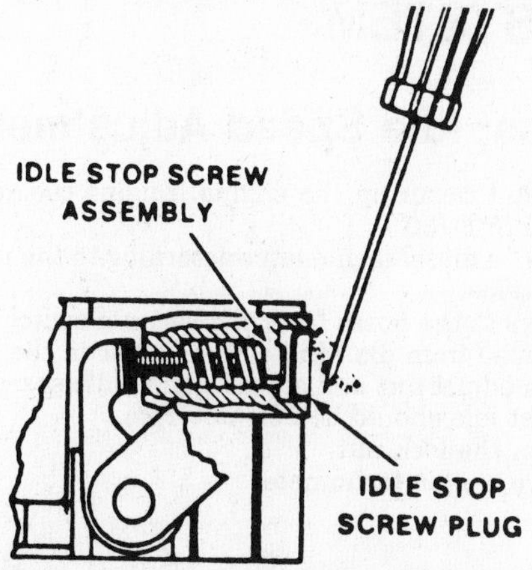
IDLE STOP SCREW ASSEMBLY
IDLE STOP SCREW PLUG

Removing the idle stop screw plug

4. Remove the electrical connector from the Idle Air Control (IAC) valve, located on the throttle body.

5. To remove the throttle stop screw cover, perform the following procedures:

a. Using a prick punch, mark the housing at the top over the center line of the throttle stop screw.

b. Using a $^5/_{32}$ in. drill bit, drill (on an angle) a hole through the casting to the hardened cover.

c. Using a $^1/_{16}$ in. pin punch, place it through the hole and drive out the cover to expose the throttle stop screw.

6. Place the transmission in Park (AT) or Neutral (MT), start the engine and allow the idle speed to stabilize.

7. Using the GM tool No. J-33047, BT-8207 or equivalent, install it into the idle air passage of the throttle body; be sure that the tool is fully seated in the opening and no air leaks exist.

8. Using the GM Torx Bit No. 20, turn the throttle stop screw until the engine speed is 475–525 rpm (AT in Park) or 750–800 rpm (MT in Neutral).

9. With the idle speed adjusted, stop the engine, remove the tool No. J-33047, BT-8207 or equivalent, from the throttle body.

10. Reconnect the Idle Air Control (IAC) electrical connector.

11. Using silicone sealant or equivalent, cover the throttle stop screw.

12. Reinstall the gasket and the air cleaner assembly.

2.8L EFI Engine

1. Remove the idle stop screw plug by piercing it with an awl.
2. With the idle air control motor connected, ground the diagnostic connector.
3. Turn the ignition On and wait 30 seconds, DO NOT start the engine.
4. Disconnect the idle air control connector with the ignition On.
5. Remove the ground from the diagnostic connector and start the engine.
6. Adjust the idle stop screw to 700 rpm with the transmission in Neutral.
7. Turn the ignition Off and reconnect the idle air control motor connector.
8. Disconnect the electrical connector from the throttle position sensor (TPS), then install jumper wires between the TPS and the electrical connector.
9. Loosen the throttle position sensor screws.
10. With the ignition switch turned On, check the voltage between terminals **B** and **C**; they should be 0.420V and 0.450V. If necessary, rotate the TPS to obtain the correct voltage.
11. With the voltage correct, tighten the mounting screws.
12. Reconnect the electrical connector and the air cleaner.

NOTE: After installing the electrical connector to the TPS, it is a good idea to recheck the TPS voltage.

Fast Idle Adjustment

CARBURETOR ENGINES

2.0L and 2.8L Engines

NOTE: Following the adjustment of the idle speed, the fast idle speed may be adjusted.

1. Place the transmission in Park (AT) or Neutral (MT) and refer to the recommendation on the emission label.
2. Place the fast idle screw on the highest step of the fast idle cam.
3. Turn the fast idle screw to obtain the specified fast idle rpm.

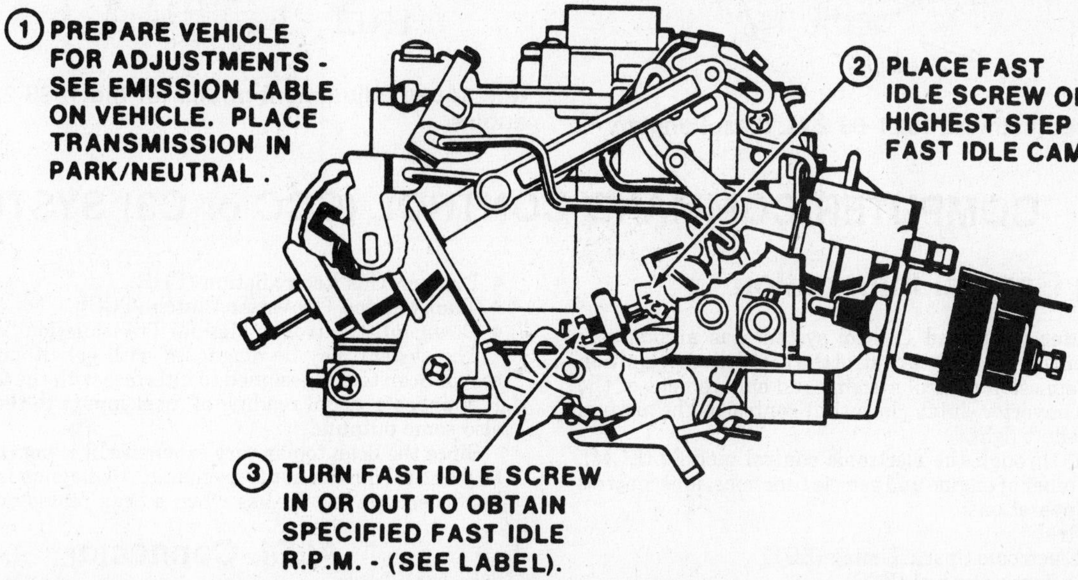
1 PREPARE VEHICLE FOR ADJUSTMENTS - SEE EMISSION LABLE ON VEHICLE. PLACE TRANSMISSION IN PARK/NEUTRAL .
2 PLACE FAST IDLE SCREW ON HIGHEST STEP OF FAST IDLE CAM.
3 TURN FAST IDLE SCREW IN OR OUT TO OBTAIN SPECIFIED FAST IDLE R.P.M. - (SEE LABEL).

Fast idle adjustment procedure

DIESEL ENGINE FUEL SYSTEM

Slow Idle Speed Adjustment

1. Set parking brake and block drive wheels.
2. Place transmission in Neutral.
3. Start and warm up the engine. Engine coolant temperature above 176°F (80°C).
4. Connect a diesel tachometer according to the manufacturer's instructions.
5. If the idle speed deviates from the specified range of 700–800 rpm, loosen the idle speed adjusting screw lock nut.
6. Turn the adjusting screw in or out until the idle speed is in the correct range. After tightening the lock nut, lock it in place.

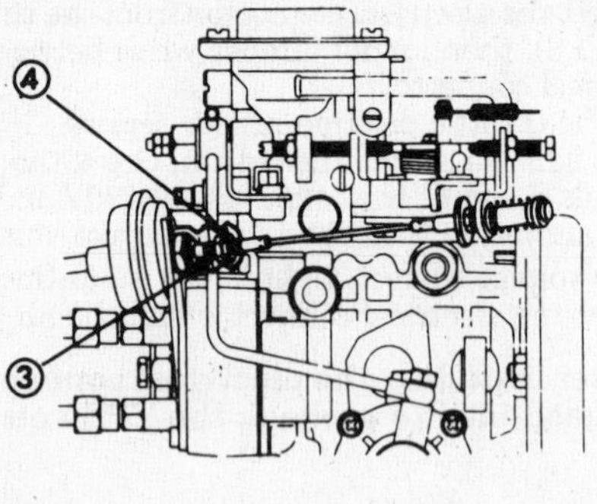
④
③

Fast idle adjustment 1983 2.2L diesel engine

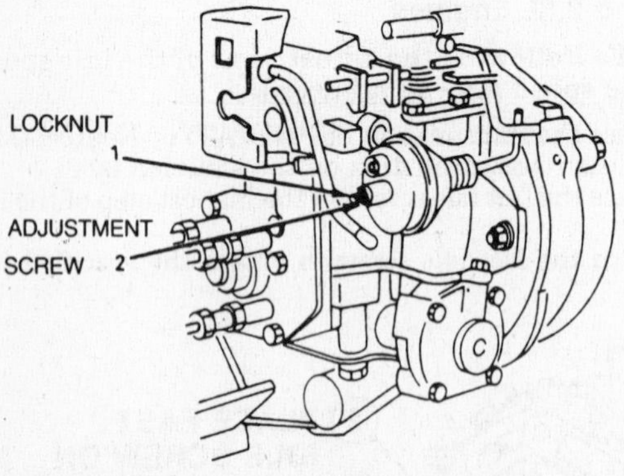
LOCKNUT
1
ADJUSTMENT
SCREW 2

Fast idle adjustment 1984–85 2.2L diesel engine

Fast Idle Speed Adjustment

1. Start and warm up the engine. Engine coolant temperature above 176°F (80°).
2. Connect a diesel tachometer according to the manufacturer's instructions.
3. Disconnect the hoses from the vacuum switch valve, then connect a pipe (4mm dia.) in position between the hoses.
4. Loosen adjust nut and adjust engine idle speed by moving the nut. Fast idle should be 900–950 rpm.
5. Tighten the lock nut.
6. Remove engine tachometer.

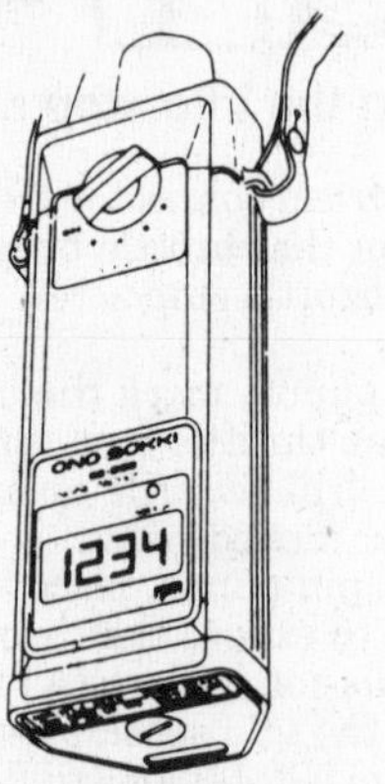
ONO SOKKI
1234

Diesel tachometer

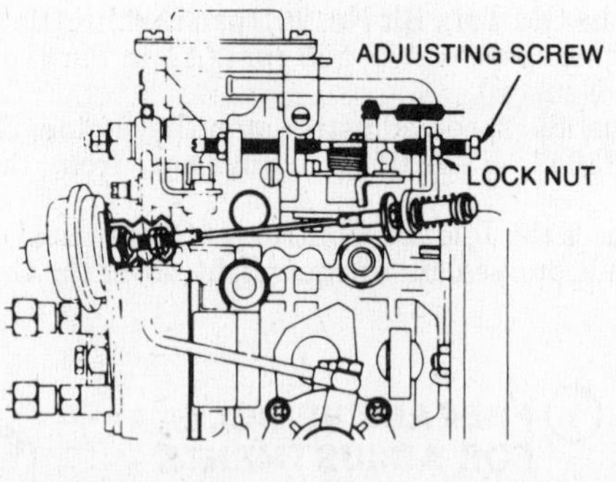
ADJUSTING SCREW
LOCK NUT

Idle speed adjustment points for the 1983 2.2L diesel engine

COMPUTER COMMAND CONTROL (CCC or C3) SYSTEM

General Information

The Computer Command Control system has a computer (Electronic Control Module) to control the fuel delivery, ignition timing, some emission control systems and engagement of the transmission converter clutch, downshift control or the manual transmission shaft light.

The system, through the electronic control module (ECM), monitors a number of engine and vehicle functions, and controls the following operations:

- Fuel Control
- Ignition/Electronic Spark Timing (EST)
- Electronic Spark Control (ESC)
- Air Management
- Exhaust Gas Recirculation (EGR)
- Transmission Converter Clutch (TCC)
- Downshift Control or Manual Transmission Shift Light

The system may be diagnosed with or without a "Scan" tool. A Scan tool is designed to interface with the CCC system. It supplies a visual reading of most inputs to the ECM, and also some outputs.

Since the Scan tool is very expensive, it is not considered to be practical for the home mechanic. All diagnostic procedures in this section are for use when a Scan tool is not available.

ALDL Connector

The Assembly Line Diagnostic Link (ALDL) is wired to the

ECM and is located under the instrument panel in the passenger compartment.

This connector has terminals that are used to diagnose the system with jumper wires. The following terminals are used:

A – This terminal provides a ground circuit to other terminals.

B – This terminal is the "diagnostic terminal" for the ECM. When grounded to terminal A with the key ON and the engine OFF, the SERVICE ENGINE SOON light will enter the Diagnostic Mode and flash codes. With the engine running, the SERVICE ENGINE SOON light will flash a Field Service Mode to determine of the system is in Closed Loop or Open Loop operation.

C – This terminal, on some air management systems is wired to the ground side of the electric air control valve. It can be used to diagnose the Air Management System.

E – This terminal is the serial data line on all engines except the 2.5L, and is used by the Scan tool to read various system data information.

F – This terminal is used to diagnose the TCC system and is wired to the ground side of the TCC solenoid.

M – This terminal is the serial data line for the 2.5L engine and is used by the Scan tool to read various system data information.

A wiring harness connects the ECM to various sensors, solenoids, relays and the ALDL connector. The ECM is located in the passenger compartment, usually behind the right side kick panel.

DIAGNOSIS

The Computer Command Control System has a diagnostic system built into the ECM to indicate a failed circuit. An amber SERVICE ENGINE SOON light on the instrument panel will illuminate if a problem has been detected when the engine and vehicle are running. This light is also used for a bulb and system check.

The system requires a tachometer, test light, ohmmeter, digital voltmeter, vacuum gage and jumper wires for diagnosis.

Bulb Check

With the ignition On and the engine OFF, the lamp should be illuminated, which indicates that the ECM has completed the circuit to turn On the light. If the SERVICE ENGINE SOON light is not illuminated, refer to Chart-A1 for diagnosis.

When the engine is started, the light will turn OFF. If the light remains ON, refer to System Check.

Code System

The ECM self-diagnosis system detects system failure and aids in finding the circuit at fault. If a sensor reading is not what the ECM thinks it should be, the ECM will illuminate the SERVICE ENGINE SOON light on the instrument panel, and will store a Fault Code in memory. The code will which circuit the trouble is in. A circuit consists of a sensor, the wiring and connectors to it, and the ECM.

An Intermittent Code is one which does not reset itself, and is not present while you are working on the vehicle. this is often caused by a loose connection.

A Hard Code is one which is present when you are working on the vehicle, and the condition still exists while working on the vehicle.

System Check

The system check provides a starting point and a method to determine if:

- The SERVICE ENGINE SOON light illuminates.
- The diagnostic system is working (Code 12).
- Any fault codes are present in memory.
- The fuel system is operating normally (Field Service Mode).

DIAGNOSTIC MODE

If the diagnostic terminal "B" is grounded with the ignition ON and the engine OFF, the system will enter the Diagnostic Mode.

With the key ON and the engine Off, jumper ALDL terminals "B" to "A" with a jumper tool or paper clip. The SERVICE ENGINE SOON light will flash Code 12 to indicate that the diagnostic system is working. Code 12 consists of one flash, followed by a pause and then two flashes. The code will repeat three times and will continue to repeat if no other codes are stored. If Code 12 does not display, refer to Chart-A2.

Any additional codes stored in memory will begin to flash after Code 12. Each code stored will flash three times. At the end of the cycle Code 12 will flash again, indicating a completed cycle. If a code is displayed, a code chart is used to diagnose the problem. The chart will determine if the problem still exists (hard failure) or if it is an intermittent problem.

FIELD SERVICE MODE

If the diagnostic terminal is grounded with the engine running, the system will enter the Field Service Mode. In this mode, the SERVICE ENGINE SOON light will show whether the system is in the Open Loop or Closed Loop and if the fuel system is operating normally.

If the engine cranks but will not start, refer to Chart-A3 for further diagnostic procedures.

With the diagnostic terminal grounded and the engine at normal operating temperature, turn the engine at 1400–1600 rpm for two minutes and note the light.

- The fuel system is operating normally and the system is in a Closed Loop operation if the light is flashing at a rate of once per second.
- The system is in Open Loop operation if the light flashes at a rate of 2.5 times per second.

Open Loop indicates that the oxygen sensor has not reached normal operating temperature and the sensor voltage signal is not usable to the ECM. Signal voltage should be at a constant between 0.35–0.55 volts.

The system will flash Open Loop from 30 seconds to 2 minutes after the engine starts or until the oxygen sensor reaches normal operating temperature. If the system fails to go Closed Loop, refer to Code 13.

- A SERVICE ENGINE SOON light that is OFF most of the time indicates that the exhaust is lean. The oxygen sensor signal voltage will be less than 0.35 volts and steady. See Code 44 for diagnosis.
- A SERVICE ENGINE SOON light that is ON most of the time indicates that the exhaust is rich. The oxygen sensor signal voltage will be above 0.55 volts and steady. See Code 45 for diagnosis.

NOTE: The ECM Closed Loop timer is bypassed and new trouble codes can not be stored while the system is in the field service mode.

Clearing Codes

When the ECM sets a code, the SERVICE ENGINE SOON light will illuminate and a code will be stored in memory. If the problem is intermittent, the light will go out after 10 seconds, when the fault goes away. However, the code will stay in the ECM memory for 50 starts or until the battery voltage to the ECM is disconnected. Removing battery voltage for 30 seconds will clear all stored codes.

Codes should be cleared after repairs have been completed. Also, some diagnostic charts will tell you to clear the codes before using the chart. This allows the ECM to set the code while going through the chart, which will help to find the cause of the problem more quickly.

CODE IDENTIFICATION

The "Service Engine Soon" light will only be "ON" if the malfunction exists under the conditions listed below. If the malfunction clears, the light will go out and the code will be stored in the ECM. Any codes stored will be erased if no problem reoccurs within 50 engine starts.

CODE AND CIRCUIT	PROBABLE CAUSE
Code 13 - O_2 Sensor Open Oxygen Sensor Circuit	Indicates that the oxygen sensor circuit or sensor was open for one minute while off idle.
Code 14 - Coolant Sensor High Temperature Indication	Sets if the sensor or signal line becomes grounded for 3 seconds.
Code 15 - Coolant Sensor Low Temperature Indication	Sets if the sensor, connections, or wires open for 3 seconds.
Code 21 - TPS Signal Voltage High	TPS voltage greater than 2.5 volts for 3 seconds with less than 1200 RPM.
Code 22 - TPS Signal Voltage Low	A shorted to ground or open signal circuit will set code in 3 seconds.
Code 23 - MAT Low Temperature Indication	Sets if the sensor, connections, or wires open for 3 seconds.
Code 24 - VSS No Vehicle Speed Indication	No vehicle speed present during a road load decel.
Code 25 - MAT High Temperature Indication	Sets if the sensor or signal line becomes grounded for 3 seconds.
Code 32 - EGR	Vacuum switch shorted to ground on start up OR Switch not closed after the ECM has commanded EGR for a specified period of time. OR EGR solenoid circuit open for a specified period of time.
Code 33 - MAP Sensor Low Vacuum	MAP sensor output to high for 5 seconds or an open signal circuit.
Code 34 - MAP Sensor High Vacuum	Low or no output from sensor with engine running.
Code 35 - IAC	IAC error
Code 42 - EST	ECM has seen an open or grounded EST or Bypass circuit.
Code 43 - ESC	Signal to the ECM has remained low for too long or the system has failed a functional check.
Code 44 Lean Exhaust Indication	Sets if oxygen sensor voltage remains below .2 volts for about 20 seconds.
Code 45 Rich Exhaust Indication	Sets if oxygen sensor voltage remains above .7 volts for about 1 minute.
Code 51	Faulty MEM-CAL, PROM, or ECM.
Code 52	Fuel CALPAK missing or faulty.
Code 53	System overvoltage. Indicates a basic generator problem.
Code 54 - Fuel Pump Low voltage	Sets when the fuel pump voltage is less than 2 volts when reference pulses are being received.
Code 55	Faulty ECM

6-25-87
7S 3337-6E

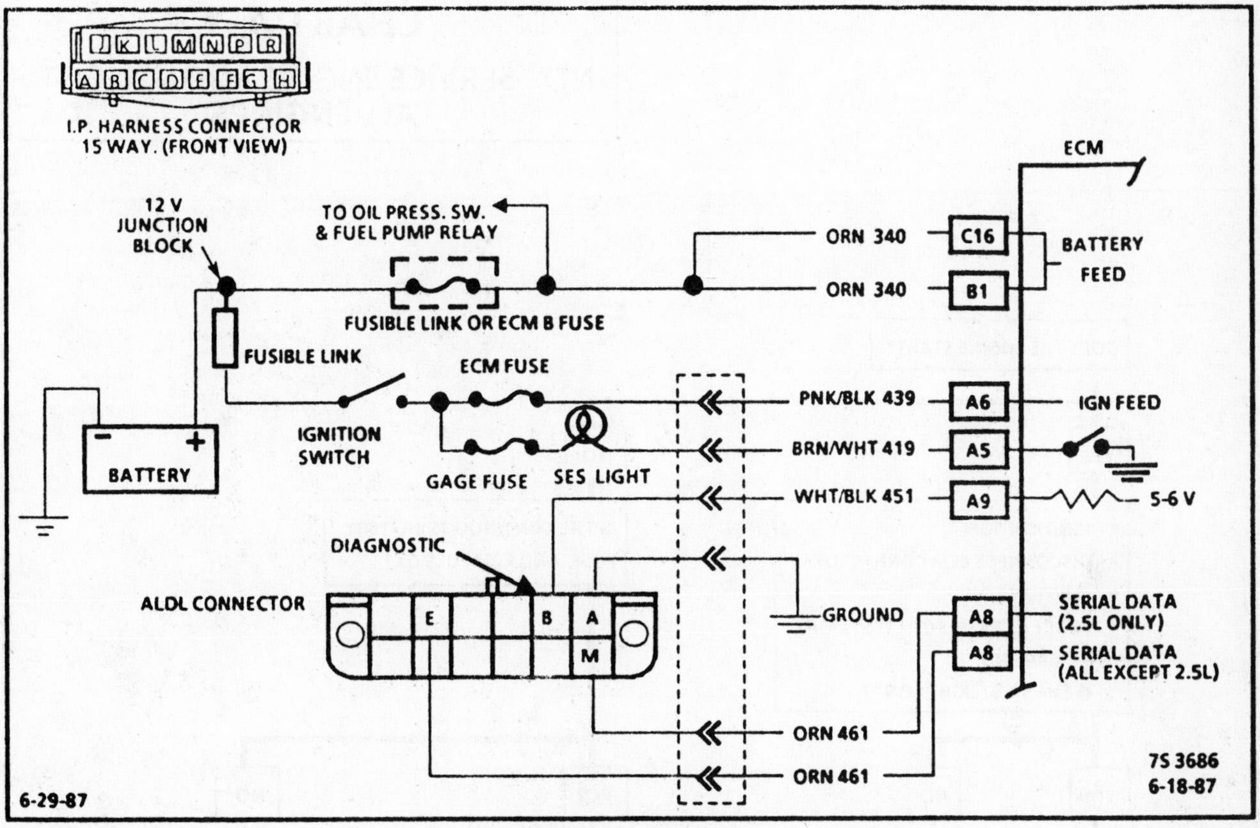
I.P. HARNESS CONNECTOR
15 WAY. (FRONT VIEW)
ECM
12 V
JUNCTION
BLOCK
TO OIL PRESS. SW.
& FUEL PUMP RELAY
ORN 340
ORN 340
C16
B1
BATTERY
FEED
FUSIBLE LINK OR ECM B FUSE
FUSIBLE LINK
ECM FUSE
PNK/BLK 439
A6
IGN FEED
BATTERY
IGNITION
SWITCH
BRN/WHT 419
A5
GAGE FUSE
SES LIGHT
WHT/BLK 451
A9
5-6 V
DIAGNOSTIC
ALDL CONNECTOR
GROUND
A8
SERIAL DATA
(2.5L ONLY)
A8
SERIAL DATA
(ALL EXCEPT 2.5L)
ORN 461
ORN 461
7S 3686
6-18-87
6-29-87

CHART A-1

NO "SERVICE ENGINE SOON" LIGHT ALL ENGINES

Circuit Description:

There should always be a steady "Service Engine Soon" light when the ignition is "ON" and engine stopped. Battery ignition voltage is supplied to the light bulb. The ECM will control the light and turn it "ON" by providing a ground path through CKT 419.

Test Description: Numbers below refer to circled numbers on the diagnostic chart.

1. If the fuse in holder is blown, refer to facing page of Code 54 for complete circuit.
2. Using a test light connected to 12 volts, probe each of the system ground circuits to be sure a good ground is present. See ECM terminal end view in front of this section for ECM pin locations of ground circuits.

Diagnostic Aids:

If the engine runs OK, check:

- Faulty light bulb.
- CKT 419 open.
- Gage fuse blown. This will result in no stop lights, oil or generator lights, seat belt reminder, etc.

If the engine cranks but will not run, check:

- Continuous battery-fuse or fusible link open.
- ECM ignition fuse open.
- Battery CKT 340 to ECM open.
- Ignition CKT 439 to ECM open.
- Poor connection to ECM.

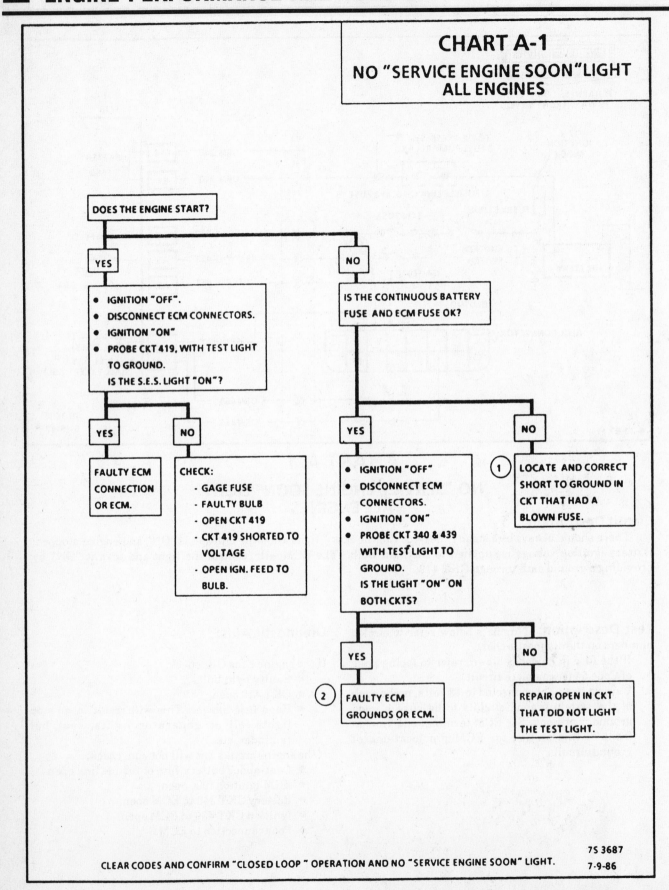

CHART A-1
NO "SERVICE ENGINE SOON" LIGHT
ALL ENGINES

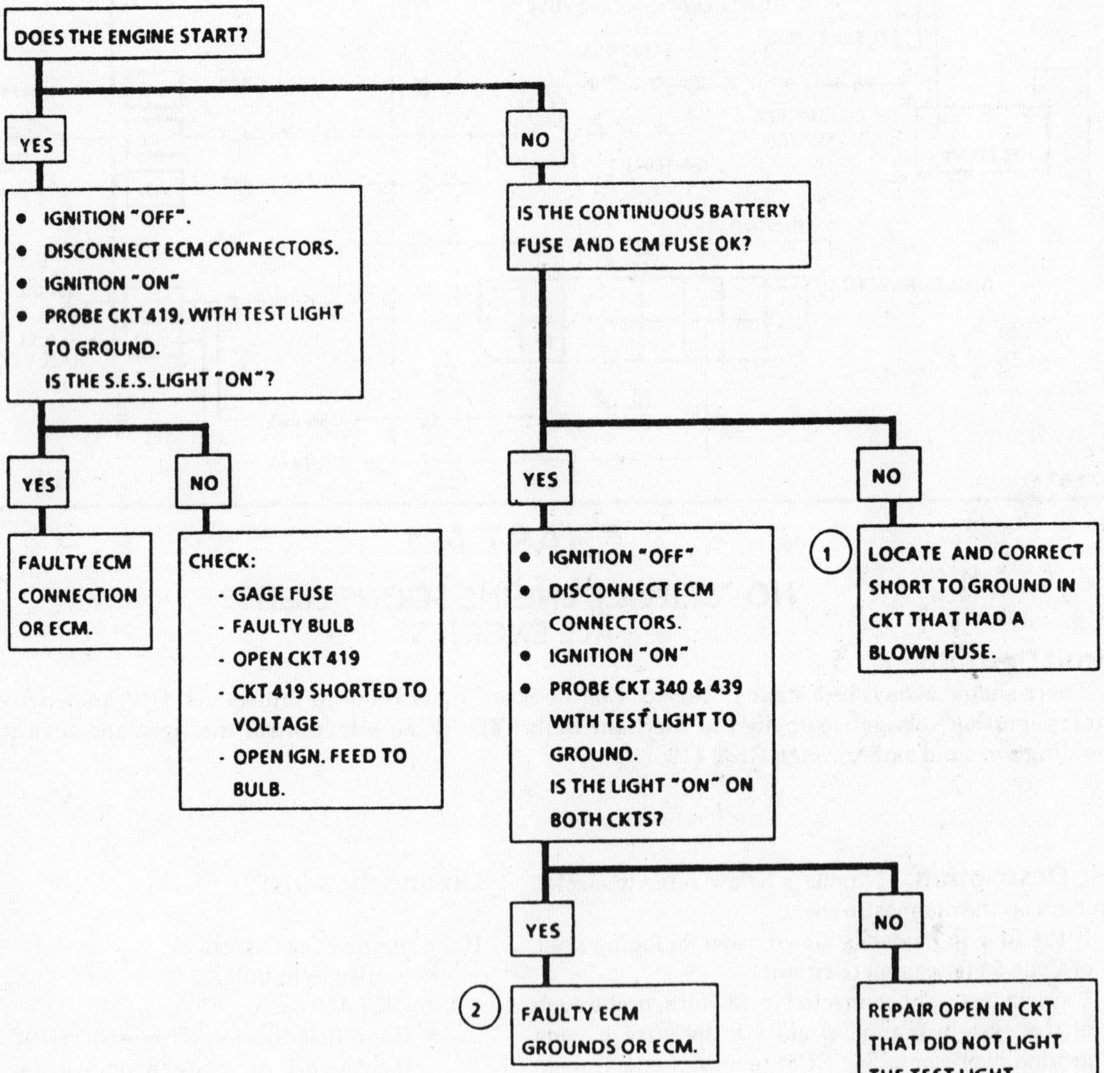
DOES THE ENGINE START?
YES
NO
• IGNITION "OFF".
• DISCONNECT ECM CONNECTORS.
• IGNITION "ON"
• PROBE CKT 419, WITH TEST LIGHT TO GROUND.
IS THE S.E.S. LIGHT "ON"?
IS THE CONTINUOUS BATTERY FUSE AND ECM FUSE OK?
YES
NO
YES
NO
FAULTY ECM CONNECTION OR ECM.
CHECK:
- GAGE FUSE
- FAULTY BULB
- OPEN CKT 419
- CKT 419 SHORTED TO VOLTAGE
- OPEN IGN. FEED TO BULB.
• IGNITION "OFF"
• DISCONNECT ECM CONNECTORS.
• IGNITION "ON"
• PROBE CKT 340 & 439 WITH TEST LIGHT TO GROUND.
IS THE LIGHT "ON" ON BOTH CKTS?
1
LOCATE AND CORRECT SHORT TO GROUND IN CKT THAT HAD A BLOWN FUSE.
YES
NO
2
FAULTY ECM GROUNDS OR ECM.
REPAIR OPEN IN CKT THAT DID NOT LIGHT THE TEST LIGHT.

7S 3687
7-9-86

CLEAR CODES AND CONFIRM "CLOSED LOOP" OPERATION AND NO "SERVICE ENGINE SOON" LIGHT.

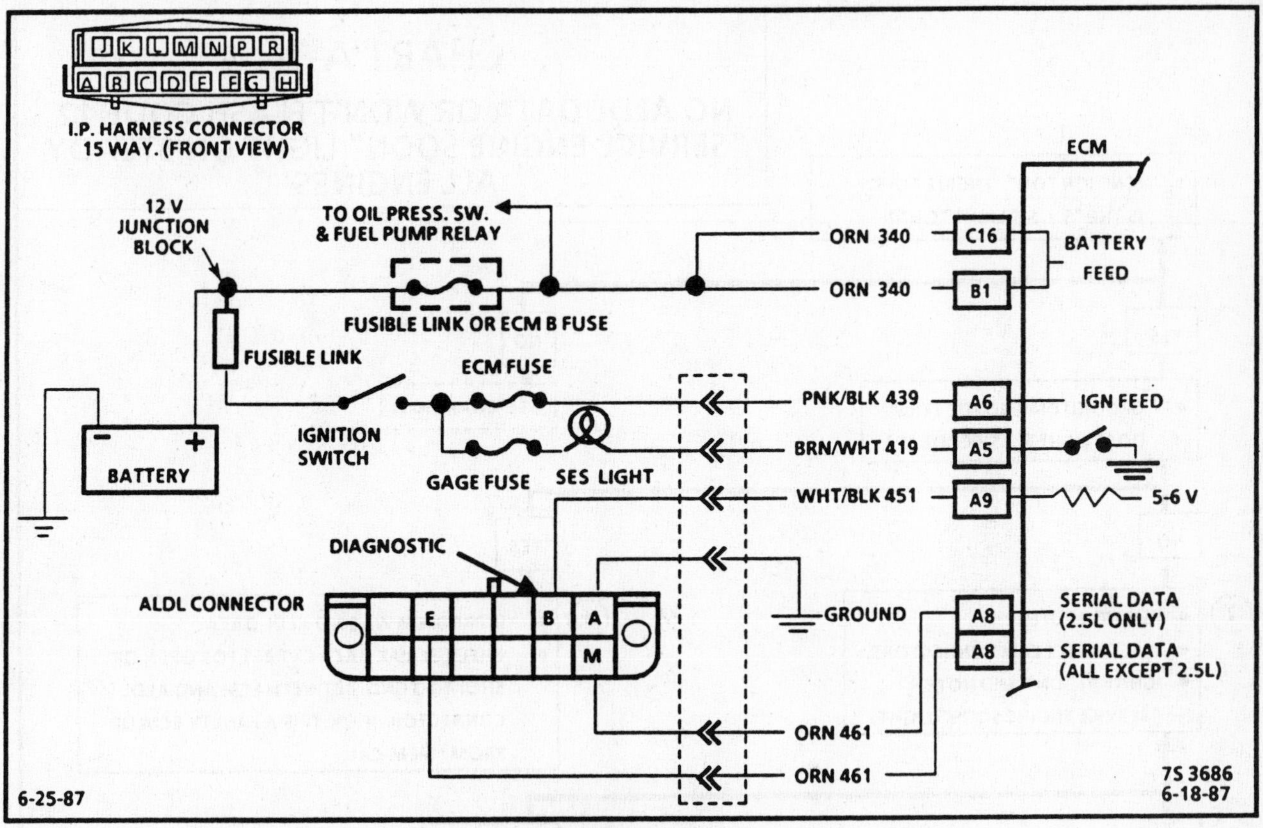

J K L M N P R
A B C D E F G H
I.P. HARNESS CONNECTOR
15 WAY. (FRONT VIEW)
ECM
12 V
JUNCTION
BLOCK
TO OIL PRESS. SW.
& FUEL PUMP RELAY
ORN 340
C16
BATTERY
FEED
ORN 340
B1
FUSIBLE LINK OR ECM B FUSE
FUSIBLE LINK
ECM FUSE
PNK/BLK 439
A6
IGN FEED
BATTERY
IGNITION
SWITCH
BRN/WHT 419
A5
GAGE FUSE
SES LIGHT
WHT/BLK 451
A9
5-6 V
DIAGNOSTIC
ALDL CONNECTOR
E
B
A
M
GROUND
A8
SERIAL DATA
(2.5L ONLY)
A8
SERIAL DATA
(ALL EXCEPT 2.5L)
ORN 461
ORN 461
6-25-87
7S 3686
6-18-87

CHART A-2

NO ALDL DATA OR WON'T FLASH CODE 12
"SERVICE ENGINE SOON" LIGHT ON STEADY
ALL ENGINES

Circuit Description:

There should always be a steady "Service Engine Soon" light when the ignition is "ON" and engine stopped. Battery ignition voltage is supplied to the light bulb. The ECM will turn the light on by grounding CKT 419.

With the diagnostic terminal grounded, the light should flash a Code 12, followed by any trouble code(s) stored in memory.

A steady light suggests a short to ground in the light control CKT 419, or an open in diagnostic CKT 451.

Test Description: Numbers below refer to circled numbers on the diagnostic chart.

1. If there is a problem with the ECM that causes a "Scan" tool to not read Serial data then the ECM should not flash a Code 12. If Code 12 does flash, be sure that the "Scan" tool is working properly on another vehicle. If the "Scan" is functioning properly and CKT 461 is OK, the PROM/Mem-Cal or ECM may be at fault for the NO ALDL symptom.
2. If the light goes "OFF" when the ECM connector is disconnected, then CKT 419 is not shorted to ground.
3. This step will check for an open diagnostic CKT 451.
4. At this point the "Service Engine Soon" light wiring is OK. The problem is a faulty ECM or PROM/Mem-Cal. If Code 12 does not flash, the ECM should be replaced using the original PROM/Mem-Cal. Replace the PROM/Mem-Cal only after trying an ECM, as a defective PROM/Mem-Cal is an unlikely cause of the problem.

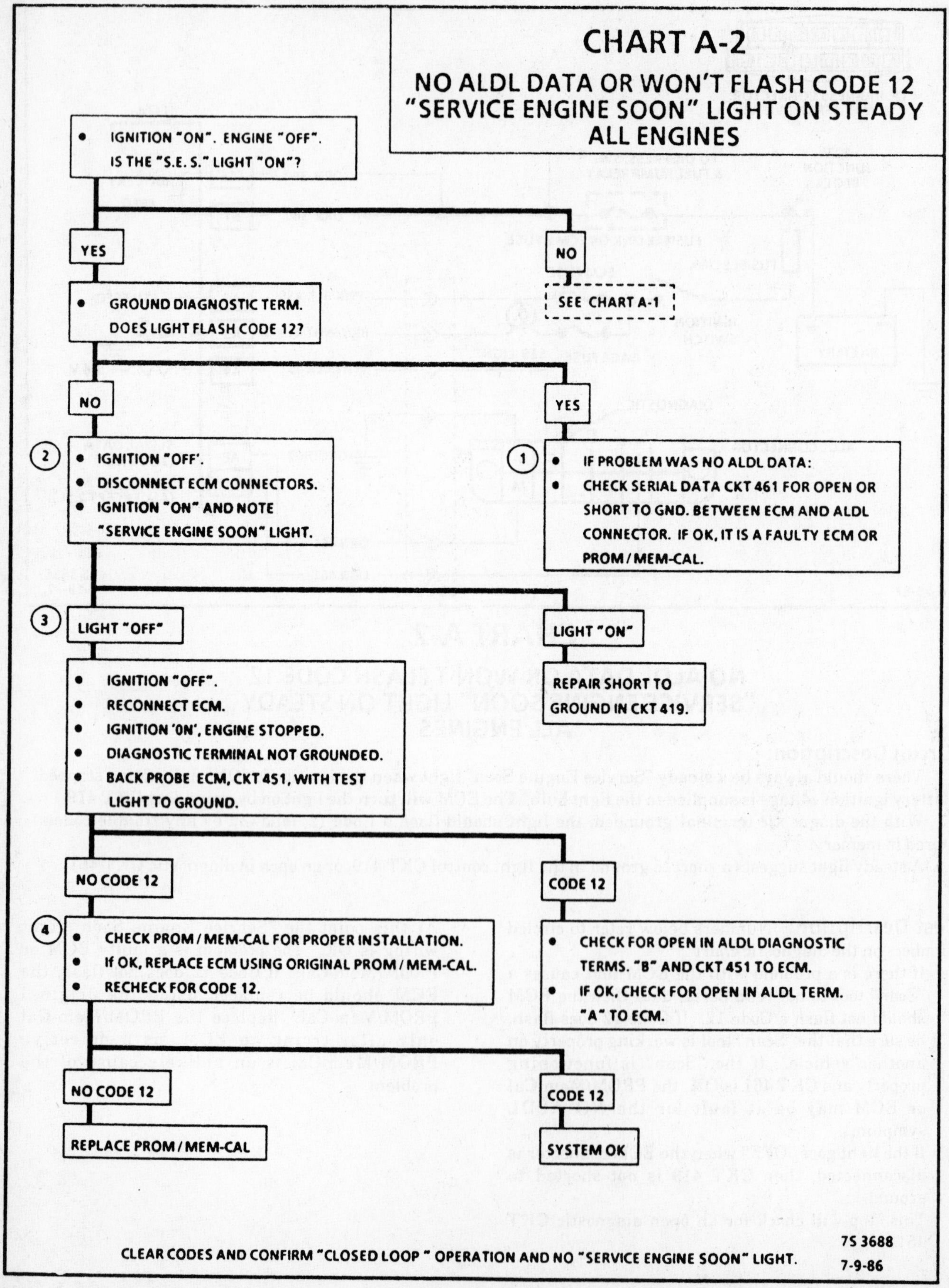
CHART A-2
NO ALDL DATA OR WON'T FLASH CODE 12
"SERVICE ENGINE SOON" LIGHT ON STEADY
ALL ENGINES
• IGNITION "ON". ENGINE "OFF". IS THE "S.E.S." LIGHT "ON"?
YES
NO
SEE CHART A-1
• GROUND DIAGNOSTIC TERM. DOES LIGHT FLASH CODE 12?
NO
YES
2
• IGNITION "OFF".
• DISCONNECT ECM CONNECTORS.
• IGNITION "ON" AND NOTE "SERVICE ENGINE SOON" LIGHT.
1
• IF PROBLEM WAS NO ALDL DATA:
• CHECK SERIAL DATA CKT 461 FOR OPEN OR SHORT TO GND. BETWEEN ECM AND ALDL CONNECTOR. IF OK, IT IS A FAULTY ECM OR PROM / MEM-CAL.
3
LIGHT "OFF"
LIGHT "ON"
REPAIR SHORT TO GROUND IN CKT 419.
• IGNITION "OFF".
• RECONNECT ECM.
• IGNITION 'ON', ENGINE STOPPED.
• DIAGNOSTIC TERMINAL NOT GROUNDED.
• BACK PROBE ECM, CKT 451, WITH TEST LIGHT TO GROUND.
NO CODE 12
CODE 12
4
• CHECK PROM / MEM-CAL FOR PROPER INSTALLATION.
• IF OK, REPLACE ECM USING ORIGINAL PROM / MEM-CAL.
• RECHECK FOR CODE 12.
• CHECK FOR OPEN IN ALDL DIAGNOSTIC TERMS. "B" AND CKT 451 TO ECM.
• IF OK, CHECK FOR OPEN IN ALDL TERM. "A" TO ECM.
NO CODE 12
CODE 12
REPLACE PROM / MEM-CAL
SYSTEM OK
CLEAR CODES AND CONFIRM "CLOSED LOOP" OPERATION AND NO "SERVICE ENGINE SOON" LIGHT.
7S 3688
7-9-86

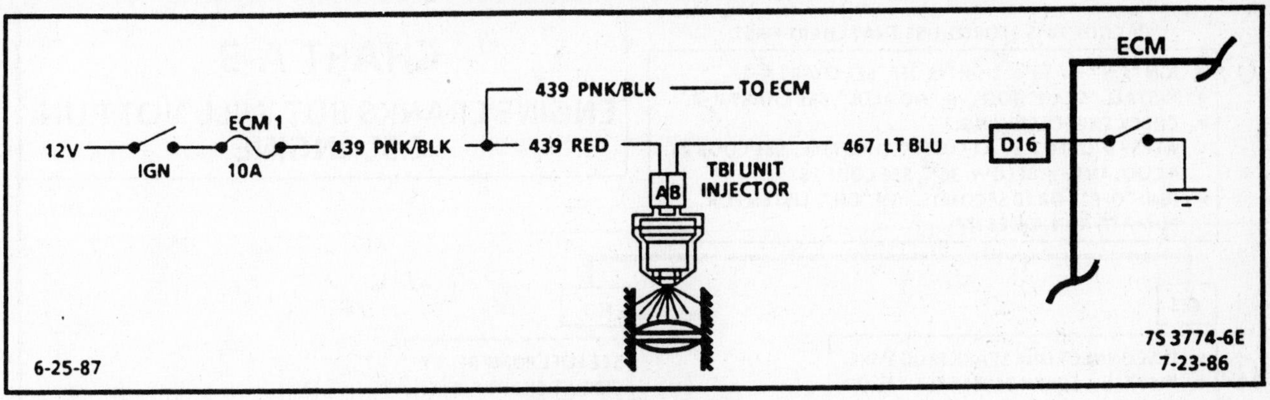
ECM
439 PNK/BLK
TO ECM
ECM 1
12V
IGN
10A
439 PNK/BLK
439 RED
467 LT BLU
D16
A B
TBI UNIT
INJECTOR
7S 3774-6E
7-23-86
6-25-87

CHART A-3

ENGINE CRANKS BUT WILL NOT RUN
2.5L ENGINE

Circuit Description:

This chart assumes that battery condition and engine cranking speed are OK, and there is adequate fuel in the tank. This chart should be used on engines using the Model 700 throttle body.

Test Description: Numbers below refer to circled numbers on the diagnostic chart.

1. A "Service Engine Soon" light "ON" is a basic test to determine if there is a 12 volt supply and ignition 12 volts to ECM. No ALDL may be due to an ECM problem and CHART A-2 will diagnose the ECM. If TPS is over 2.5 volts the engine may be in the clear flood mode which will cause starting problems. If coolant sensor is below -30°C, the ECM will provide fuel for this extremely cold temperature which will severely flood the engine.
2. Voltage at the spark plug is checked using spark tester tool ST125 (J26792) or equivalent. No spark indicates a basic ignition problem.
3. While cranking engine there should be no fuel spray with injector disconnected. Replace an injector if it sprays fuel or drips like a leaking water faucet.
4. Use an injector test light like J34730, BT8329A or equivalent, to test injector circuit. A blinking light indicates the ECM is controlling the injector.
5. This test will determine if there is fuel pressure at the injector and that the injector is operating.

Diagnostic Aids:

If no trouble is found in the fuel pump circuit or ignition system and the cause of a "Engine Cranks But Will Not Run" has not been found, check for:

- Fouled spark plugs
- EGR valve stuck open
- Low fuel pressure. See CHART A-6.
- Water or foreign material in the fuel system.
- A ground CKT 423 (EST) may cause a "No Start" or a "Start then Stall" condition.
- Basic engine problem.

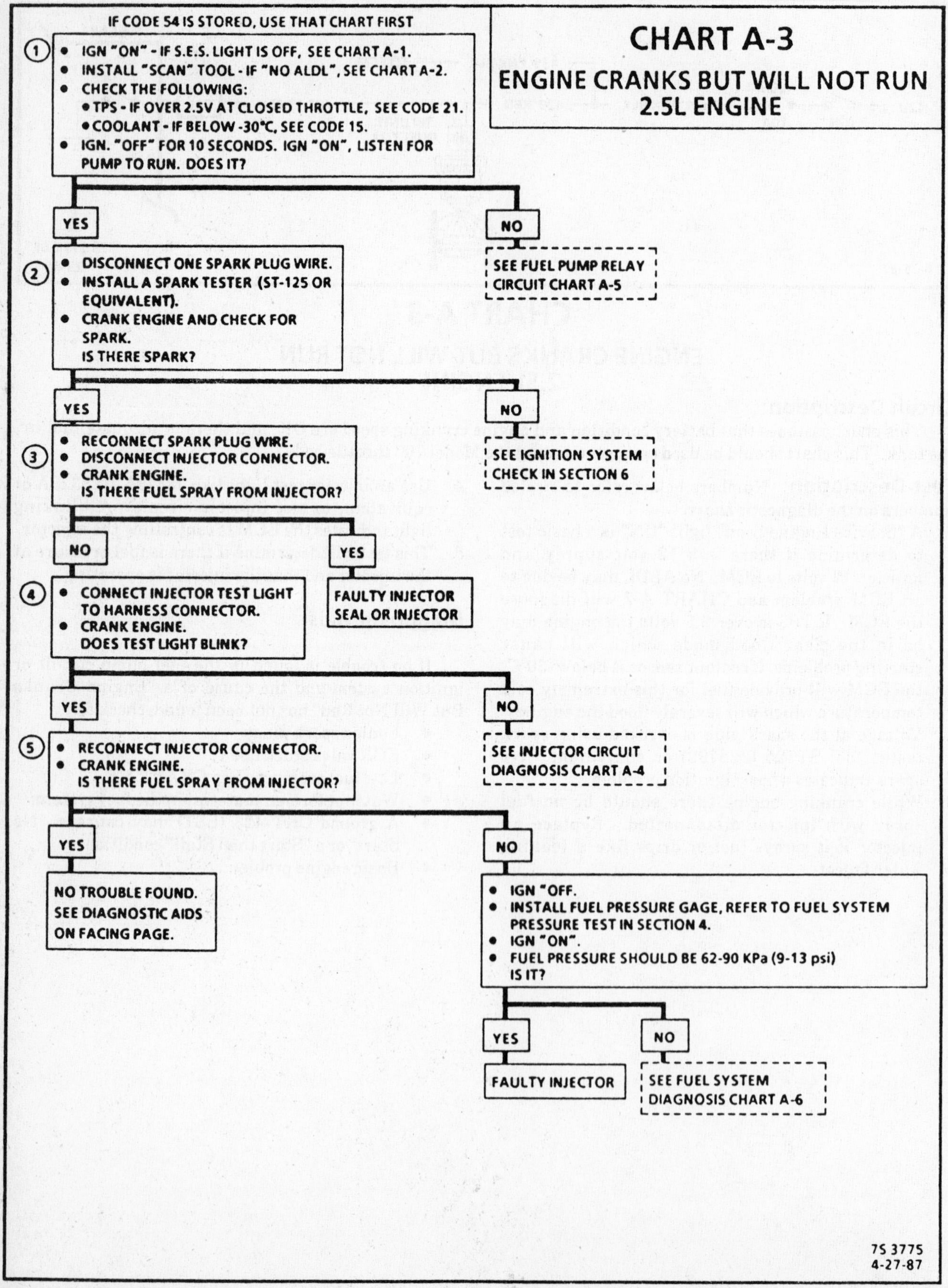
CHART A-3
ENGINE CRANKS BUT WILL NOT RUN
2.5L ENGINE
IF CODE 54 IS STORED, USE THAT CHART FIRST
1
• IGN "ON" - IF S.E.S. LIGHT IS OFF, SEE CHART A-1.
• INSTALL "SCAN" TOOL - IF "NO ALDL", SEE CHART A-2.
• CHECK THE FOLLOWING:
• TPS - IF OVER 2.5V AT CLOSED THROTTLE, SEE CODE 21.
• COOLANT - IF BELOW -30°C, SEE CODE 15.
• IGN. "OFF" FOR 10 SECONDS. IGN "ON", LISTEN FOR PUMP TO RUN. DOES IT?
YES
NO
SEE FUEL PUMP RELAY CIRCUIT CHART A-5
2
• DISCONNECT ONE SPARK PLUG WIRE.
• INSTALL A SPARK TESTER (ST-125 OR EQUIVALENT).
• CRANK ENGINE AND CHECK FOR SPARK.
IS THERE SPARK?
YES
NO
SEE IGNITION SYSTEM CHECK IN SECTION 6
3
• RECONNECT SPARK PLUG WIRE.
• DISCONNECT INJECTOR CONNECTOR.
• CRANK ENGINE.
IS THERE FUEL SPRAY FROM INJECTOR?
NO
YES
FAULTY INJECTOR SEAL OR INJECTOR
4
• CONNECT INJECTOR TEST LIGHT TO HARNESS CONNECTOR.
• CRANK ENGINE.
DOES TEST LIGHT BLINK?
YES
NO
SEE INJECTOR CIRCUIT DIAGNOSIS CHART A-4
5
• RECONNECT INJECTOR CONNECTOR.
• CRANK ENGINE.
IS THERE FUEL SPRAY FROM INJECTOR?
YES
NO
NO TROUBLE FOUND. SEE DIAGNOSTIC AIDS ON FACING PAGE.
• IGN "OFF.
• INSTALL FUEL PRESSURE GAGE, REFER TO FUEL SYSTEM PRESSURE TEST IN SECTION 4.
• IGN "ON".
• FUEL PRESSURE SHOULD BE 62-90 KPa (9-13 psi)
IS IT?
YES
NO
FAULTY INJECTOR
SEE FUEL SYSTEM DIAGNOSIS CHART A-6
7S 3775
4-27-87

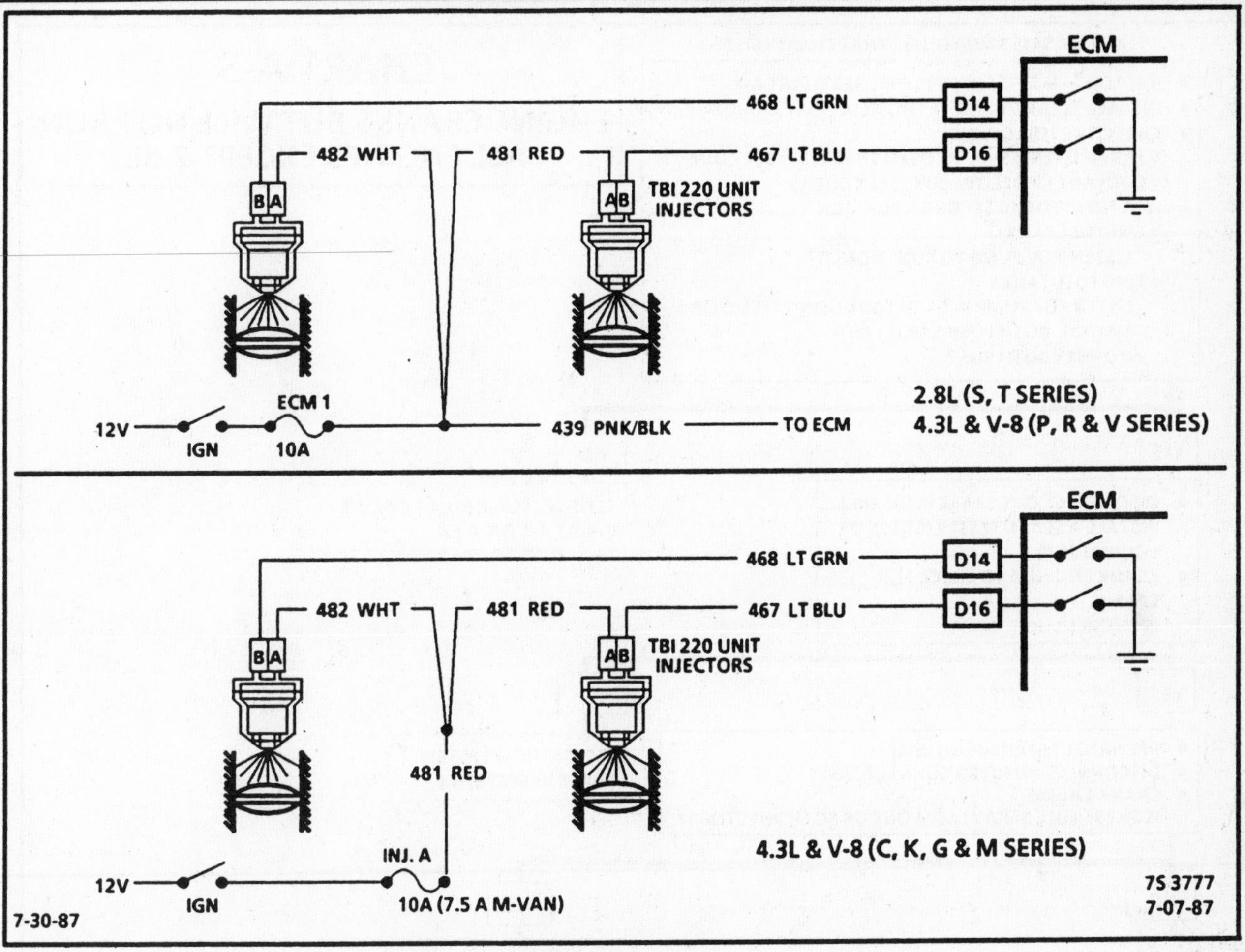
ECM
468 LT GRN
D14
482 WHT
481 RED
467 LT BLU
D16
BA
AB
TBI 220 UNIT
INJECTORS
12V
IGN
ECM 1
10A
439 PNK/BLK
TO ECM
2.8L (S, T SERIES)
4.3L & V-8 (P, R & V SERIES)
ECM
468 LT GRN
D14
482 WHT
481 RED
467 LT BLU
D16
TBI 220 UNIT
INJECTORS
481 RED
INJ. A
12V
IGN
10A (7.5 A M-VAN)
4.3L & V-8 (C, K, G & M SERIES)
7-30-87
7S 3777
7-07-87

CHART A-3

ENGINE CRANKS BUT WILL NOT RUN
ALL ENGINES EXCEPT 2.5L

Circuit Description:

This chart assumes that battery condition and engine cranking speed are OK, and there is adequate fuel in the tank. This chart should be used on engines using the Model 220 throttle body.

Test Description: Numbers below refer to circled numbers on the diagnostic chart.

1. A "Service Engine Soon" light "ON" is a basic test to determine if there is a 12 volt supply and ignition 12 volts to ECM. No ALDL may be due to an ECM problem and CHART A-2 will diagnose the ECM. If TPS is over 2.5 volts the engine may be in the clear flood mode which will cause starting problems. If coolant sensor is below -30°C, the ECM will provide fuel for this extremely cold temperature which will severely flood the engine.
2. Voltage at the spark plug is checked using Spark Tester tool ST125 (J26792) or equivalent. No spark indicates a basic ignition problem.
3. While cranking engine there should be no fuel spray with injectors disconnected. Replace an injector if it sprays fuel or drips like a leaking water faucet.
4. Use an injector test light like BT8320, or equivalent, to test each injector circuit. A blinking light indicates the ECM is controlling the injectors.
5. This test will determine if there is fuel pressure at the injectors and that the injectors are operating.

Diagnostic Aids:

If no trouble is found in the fuel pump circuit or ignition system and the cause of a "Engine Cranks But Will Not Run" has not been found, check for:

- Fouled spark plugs
- EGR valve stuck open
- Low fuel pressure. See CHART A-6.
- Water or foreign material in the fuel system.
- A grounded CKT 423 (EST) may cause a "No Start" or a "Start then Stall" condition.
- Basic engine problem.

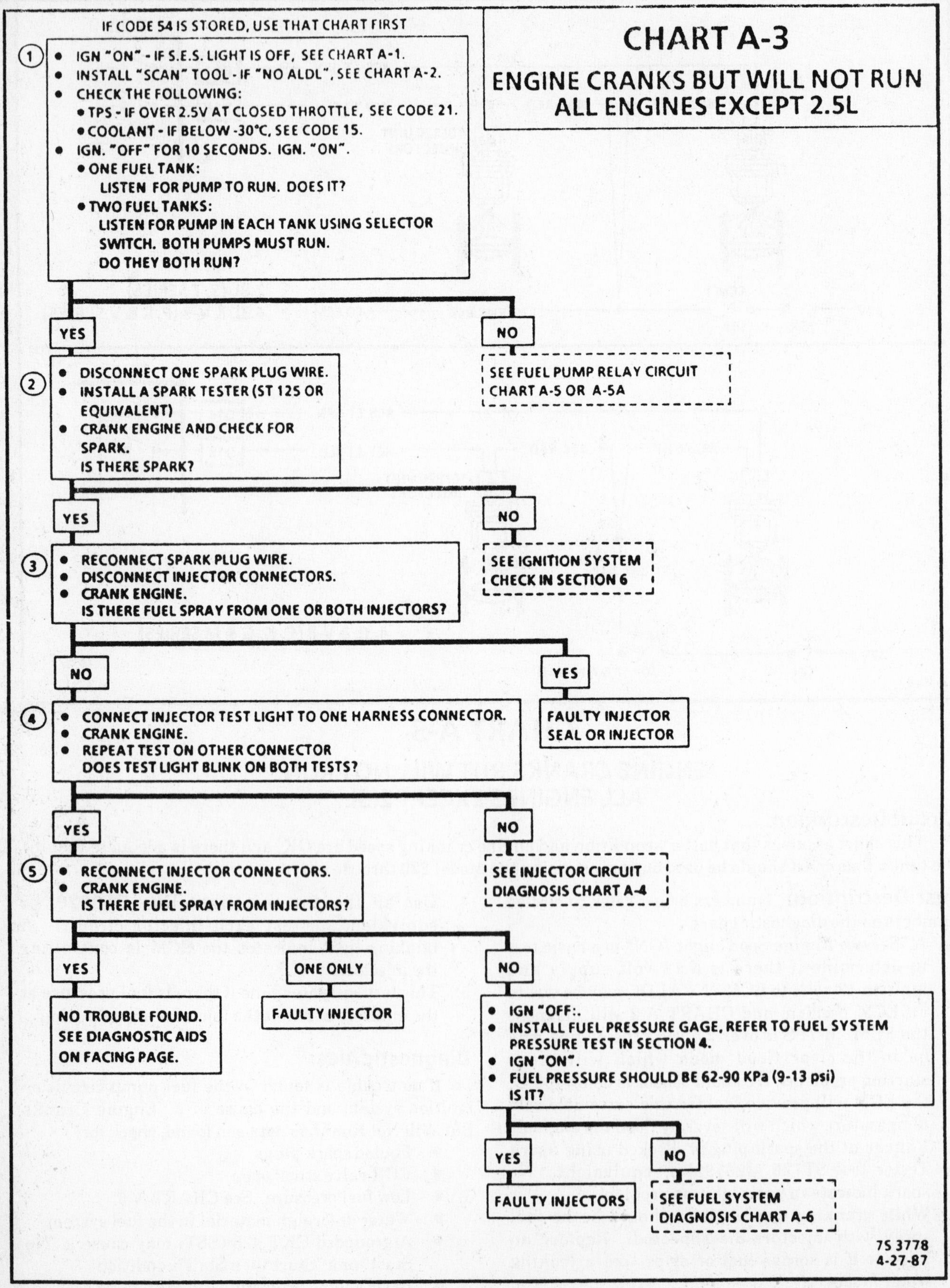
CHART A-3
ENGINE CRANKS BUT WILL NOT RUN
ALL ENGINES EXCEPT 2.5L
IF CODE 54 IS STORED, USE THAT CHART FIRST
1
• IGN "ON" - IF S.E.S. LIGHT IS OFF, SEE CHART A-1.
• INSTALL "SCAN" TOOL - IF "NO ALDL", SEE CHART A-2.
• CHECK THE FOLLOWING:
• TPS - IF OVER 2.5V AT CLOSED THROTTLE, SEE CODE 21.
• COOLANT - IF BELOW -30°C, SEE CODE 15.
• IGN. "OFF" FOR 10 SECONDS. IGN. "ON".
• ONE FUEL TANK:
LISTEN FOR PUMP TO RUN. DOES IT?
• TWO FUEL TANKS:
LISTEN FOR PUMP IN EACH TANK USING SELECTOR SWITCH. BOTH PUMPS MUST RUN.
DO THEY BOTH RUN?
YES
NO
SEE FUEL PUMP RELAY CIRCUIT CHART A-5 OR A-5A
2
• DISCONNECT ONE SPARK PLUG WIRE.
• INSTALL A SPARK TESTER (ST 125 OR EQUIVALENT)
• CRANK ENGINE AND CHECK FOR SPARK.
IS THERE SPARK?
YES
NO
SEE IGNITION SYSTEM CHECK IN SECTION 6
3
• RECONNECT SPARK PLUG WIRE.
• DISCONNECT INJECTOR CONNECTORS.
• CRANK ENGINE.
IS THERE FUEL SPRAY FROM ONE OR BOTH INJECTORS?
NO
YES
FAULTY INJECTOR SEAL OR INJECTOR
4
• CONNECT INJECTOR TEST LIGHT TO ONE HARNESS CONNECTOR.
• CRANK ENGINE.
• REPEAT TEST ON OTHER CONNECTOR
DOES TEST LIGHT BLINK ON BOTH TESTS?
YES
NO
SEE INJECTOR CIRCUIT DIAGNOSIS CHART A-4
5
• RECONNECT INJECTOR CONNECTORS.
• CRANK ENGINE.
IS THERE FUEL SPRAY FROM INJECTORS?
YES
ONE ONLY
NO
NO TROUBLE FOUND. SEE DIAGNOSTIC AIDS ON FACING PAGE.
FAULTY INJECTOR
• IGN "OFF".
• INSTALL FUEL PRESSURE GAGE, REFER TO FUEL SYSTEM PRESSURE TEST IN SECTION 4.
• IGN "ON".
• FUEL PRESSURE SHOULD BE 62-90 KPa (9-13 psi)
IS IT?
YES
NO
FAULTY INJECTORS
SEE FUEL SYSTEM DIAGNOSIS CHART A-6
7S 3778
4-27-87

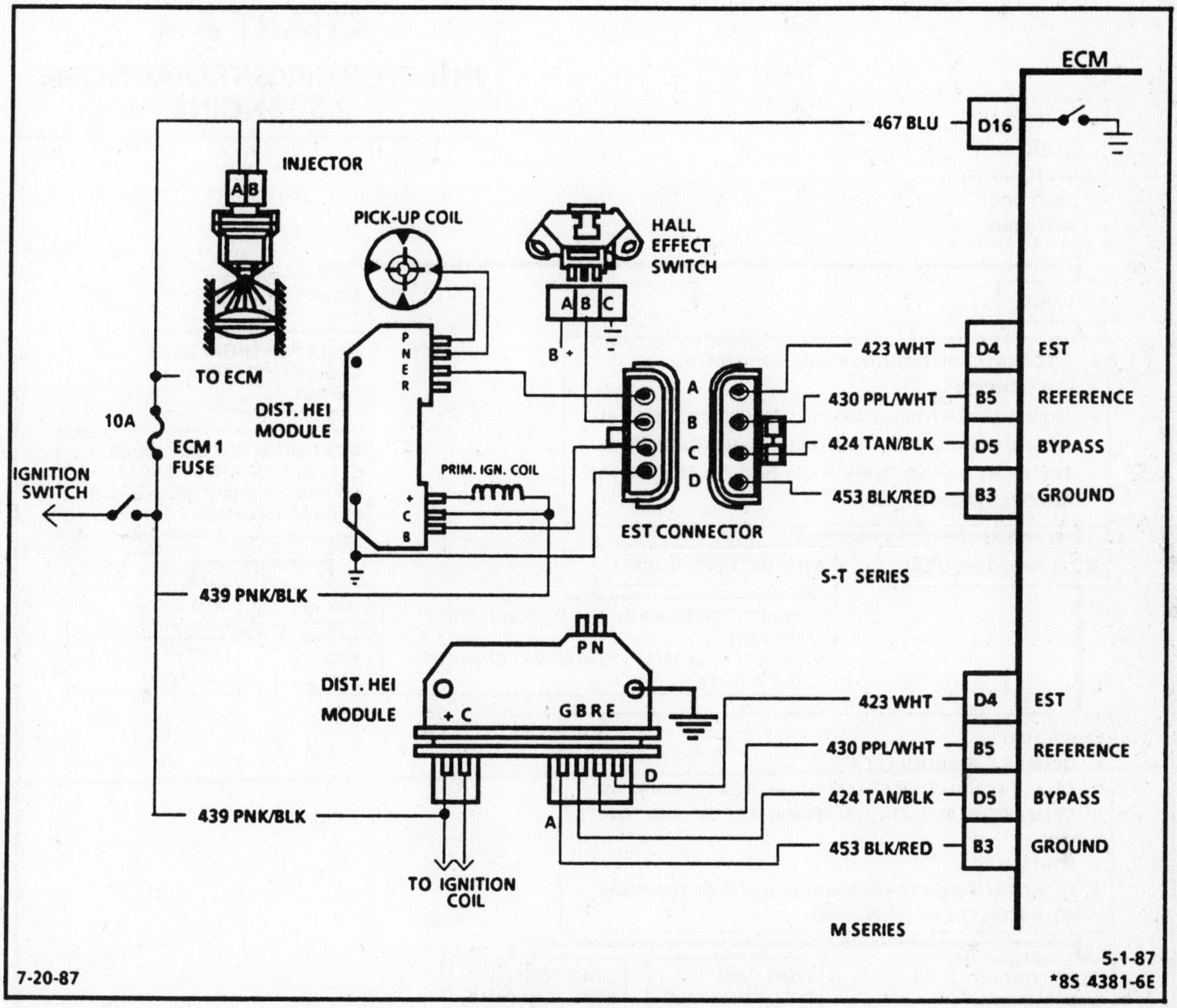
ECM
467 BLU
D16
INJECTOR
A B
PICK-UP COIL
HALL
EFFECT
SWITCH
A B C
B +
P
N
E
R
TO ECM
10A
DIST. HEI
MODULE
ECM 1
FUSE
IGNITION
SWITCH
PRIM. IGN. COIL
+
C
B
A
B
C
D
EST CONNECTOR
423 WHT
D4
EST
430 PPL/WHT
B5
REFERENCE
424 TAN/BLK
D5
BYPASS
453 BLK/RED
B3
GROUND
S-T SERIES
439 PNK/BLK
P N
DIST. HEI
MODULE
+ C
G B R E
D
A
439 PNK/BLK
TO IGNITION
COIL
423 WHT
D4
EST
430 PPL/WHT
B5
REFERENCE
424 TAN/BLK
D5
BYPASS
453 BLK/RED
B3
GROUND
M SERIES
7-20-87
5-1-87
*8S 4381-6E

CHART A-4
INJECTOR CIRCUIT DIAGNOSIS
2.5L ENGINE

Circuit Description:

This chart should only be used if diagnosis in CHART A-3 indicated an injector circuit problem.

Test Description: Numbers below refer to circled numbers on the diagnostic chart.

1. This test will determine if the ignition module is generating a reference pulse, if the wiring is at fault or if the ECM is at fault. By touching and removing a test light, connected to 12 volts, to CKT 430, a reference pulse should be generated. If injector test light blinks, the ECM and wiring are OK.
2. This step tests for 12 volts to the injector. It will also determine if there is a short to voltage on the ECM side of the circuit.
3. This test checks for continuity to the ECM.

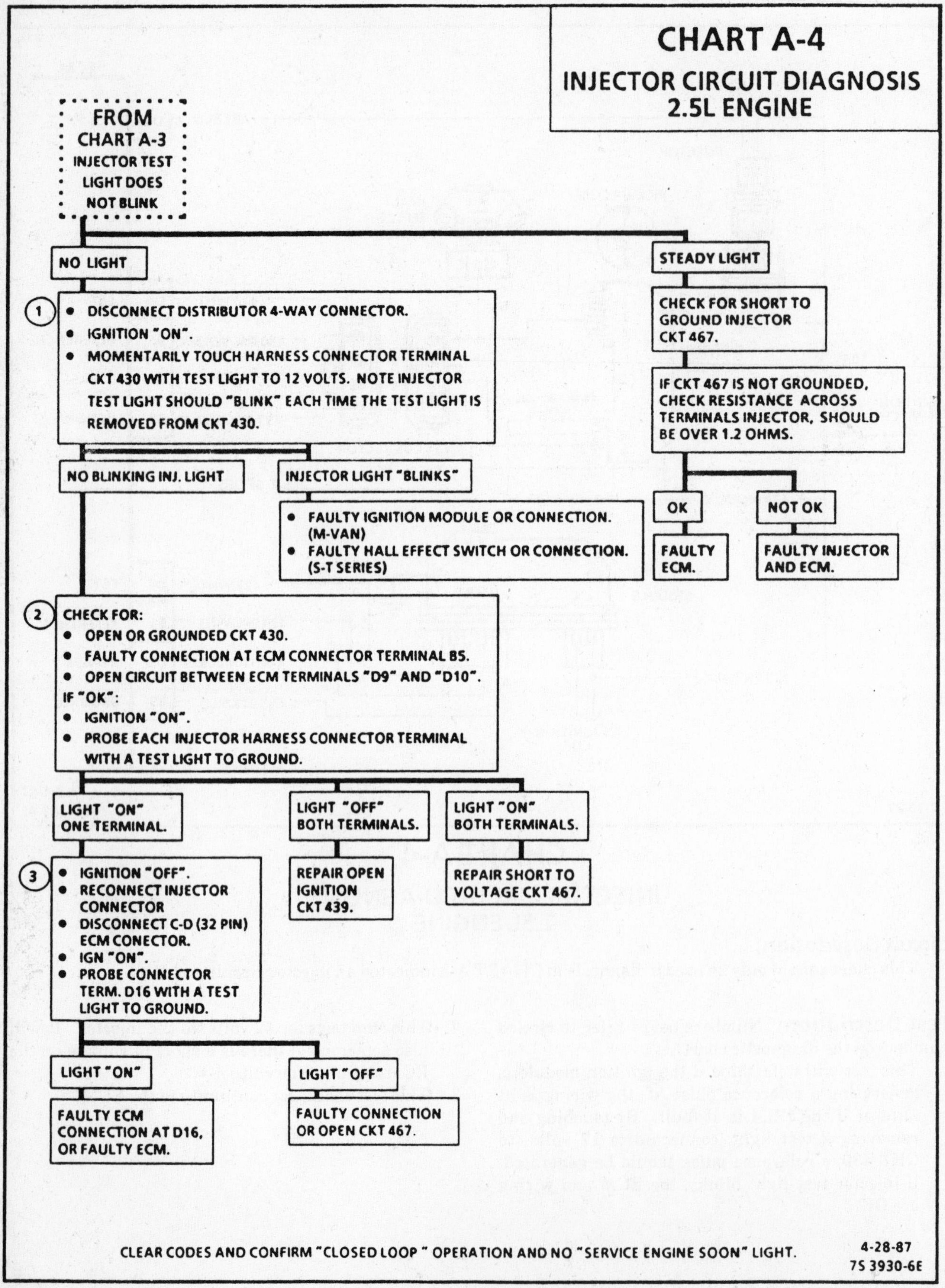
CHART A-4
INJECTOR CIRCUIT DIAGNOSIS
2.5L ENGINE
FROM CHART A-3 INJECTOR TEST LIGHT DOES NOT BLINK
NO LIGHT
STEADY LIGHT
1
• DISCONNECT DISTRIBUTOR 4-WAY CONNECTOR.
• IGNITION "ON".
• MOMENTARILY TOUCH HARNESS CONNECTOR TERMINAL CKT 430 WITH TEST LIGHT TO 12 VOLTS. NOTE INJECTOR TEST LIGHT SHOULD "BLINK" EACH TIME THE TEST LIGHT IS REMOVED FROM CKT 430.
CHECK FOR SHORT TO GROUND INJECTOR CKT 467.
IF CKT 467 IS NOT GROUNDED, CHECK RESISTANCE ACROSS TERMINALS INJECTOR, SHOULD BE OVER 1.2 OHMS.
NO BLINKING INJ. LIGHT
INJECTOR LIGHT "BLINKS"
• FAULTY IGNITION MODULE OR CONNECTION. (M-VAN)
• FAULTY HALL EFFECT SWITCH OR CONNECTION. (S-T SERIES)
OK
NOT OK
FAULTY ECM.
FAULTY INJECTOR AND ECM.
2
CHECK FOR:
• OPEN OR GROUNDED CKT 430.
• FAULTY CONNECTION AT ECM CONNECTOR TERMINAL B5.
• OPEN CIRCUIT BETWEEN ECM TERMINALS "D9" AND "D10".
IF "OK":
• IGNITION "ON".
• PROBE EACH INJECTOR HARNESS CONNECTOR TERMINAL WITH A TEST LIGHT TO GROUND.
LIGHT "ON" ONE TERMINAL.
LIGHT "OFF" BOTH TERMINALS.
LIGHT "ON" BOTH TERMINALS.
3
• IGNITION "OFF".
• RECONNECT INJECTOR CONNECTOR
• DISCONNECT C-D (32 PIN) ECM CONECTOR.
• IGN "ON".
• PROBE CONNECTOR TERM. D16 WITH A TEST LIGHT TO GROUND.
REPAIR OPEN IGNITION CKT 439.
REPAIR SHORT TO VOLTAGE CKT 467.
LIGHT "ON"
LIGHT "OFF"
FAULTY ECM CONNECTION AT D16, OR FAULTY ECM.
FAULTY CONNECTION OR OPEN CKT 467.
CLEAR CODES AND CONFIRM "CLOSED LOOP" OPERATION AND NO "SERVICE ENGINE SOON" LIGHT.
4-28-87
7S 3930-6E

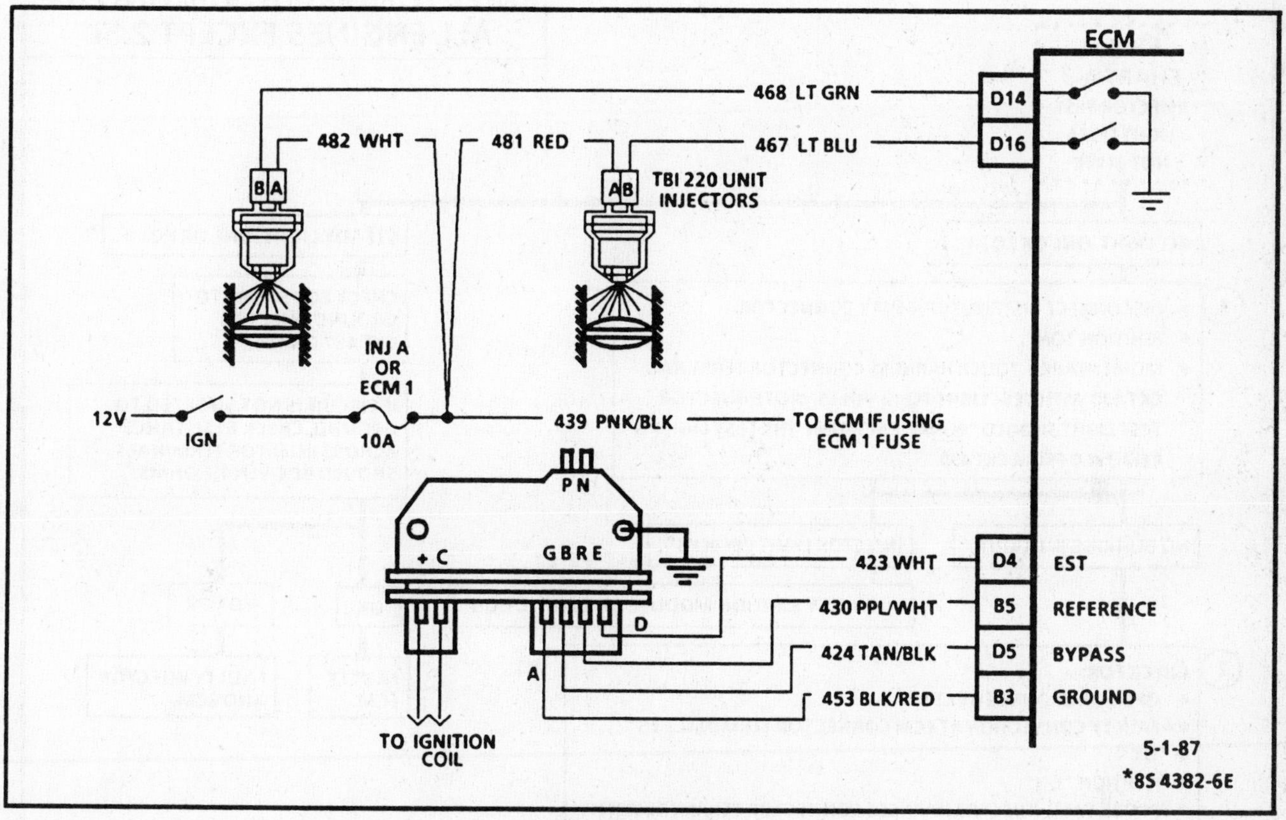
ECM
468 LT GRN
D14
482 WHT
481 RED
467 LT BLU
D16
B A
A B
TBI 220 UNIT
INJECTORS
INJ A
OR
ECM 1
12V
IGN
10A
439 PNK/BLK
TO ECM IF USING
ECM 1 FUSE
P N
+ C
G B R E
423 WHT
D4
EST
430 PPL/WHT
B5
REFERENCE
D
424 TAN/BLK
D5
BYPASS
A
453 BLK/RED
B3
GROUND
TO IGNITION
COIL
5-1-87
*8S 4382-6E

CHART A-4

INJECTOR CIRCUIT DIAGNOSIS
ALL ENGINES EXCEPT 2.5L

Circuit Description:

This chart should ony be used if diagnosis in CHART A-3 indicated an injector circuit problem. If both injector circuits fail to blink when tested, diagnose one injector circuit at a time.

Test Description: Numbers below refer to circled numbers on the diagnostic chart.

1. This test will determine if the ignition module is generting a reference pulse, if the wiring is at fault or if the ECM is at fault. By touching and removing a test light, connected to 12 volts, to CKT 430, a refernce pulse should be generated. If injector test light blinks, the ECM and wiring are OK.
2. This step tests for 12 volts to the injector. It will also determine if there is a short to voltage on the ECM side of the circuit.
3. This test checks for continuity to the ECM.

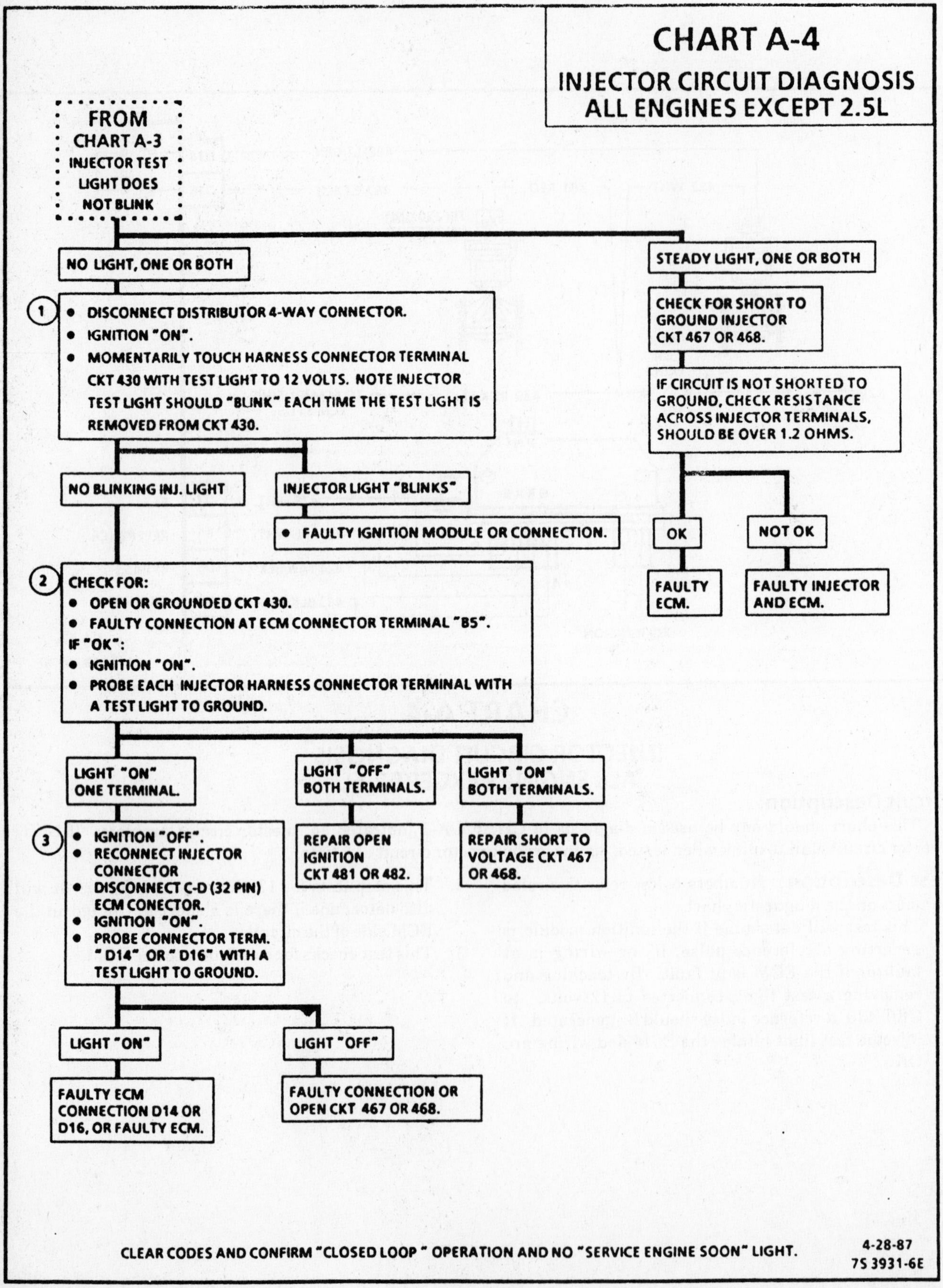
CHART A-4
INJECTOR CIRCUIT DIAGNOSIS
ALL ENGINES EXCEPT 2.5L
FROM CHART A-3 INJECTOR TEST LIGHT DOES NOT BLINK
NO LIGHT, ONE OR BOTH
1
• DISCONNECT DISTRIBUTOR 4-WAY CONNECTOR.
• IGNITION "ON".
• MOMENTARILY TOUCH HARNESS CONNECTOR TERMINAL CKT 430 WITH TEST LIGHT TO 12 VOLTS. NOTE INJECTOR TEST LIGHT SHOULD "BLINK" EACH TIME THE TEST LIGHT IS REMOVED FROM CKT 430.
NO BLINKING INJ. LIGHT
INJECTOR LIGHT "BLINKS"
• FAULTY IGNITION MODULE OR CONNECTION.
2
CHECK FOR:
• OPEN OR GROUNDED CKT 430.
• FAULTY CONNECTION AT ECM CONNECTOR TERMINAL "B5".
IF "OK":
• IGNITION "ON".
• PROBE EACH INJECTOR HARNESS CONNECTOR TERMINAL WITH A TEST LIGHT TO GROUND.
LIGHT "ON" ONE TERMINAL.
LIGHT "OFF" BOTH TERMINALS.
LIGHT "ON" BOTH TERMINALS.
3
• IGNITION "OFF".
• RECONNECT INJECTOR CONNECTOR
• DISCONNECT C-D (32 PIN) ECM CONECTOR.
• IGNITION "ON".
• PROBE CONNECTOR TERM. "D14" OR "D16" WITH A TEST LIGHT TO GROUND.
REPAIR OPEN IGNITION CKT 481 OR 482.
REPAIR SHORT TO VOLTAGE CKT 467 OR 468.
LIGHT "ON"
LIGHT "OFF"
FAULTY ECM CONNECTION D14 OR D16, OR FAULTY ECM.
FAULTY CONNECTION OR OPEN CKT 467 OR 468.
STEADY LIGHT, ONE OR BOTH
CHECK FOR SHORT TO GROUND INJECTOR CKT 467 OR 468.
IF CIRCUIT IS NOT SHORTED TO GROUND, CHECK RESISTANCE ACROSS INJECTOR TERMINALS, SHOULD BE OVER 1.2 OHMS.
OK
NOT OK
FAULTY ECM.
FAULTY INJECTOR AND ECM.
CLEAR CODES AND CONFIRM "CLOSED LOOP" OPERATION AND NO "SERVICE ENGINE SOON" LIGHT.
4-28-87
7S 3931-6E

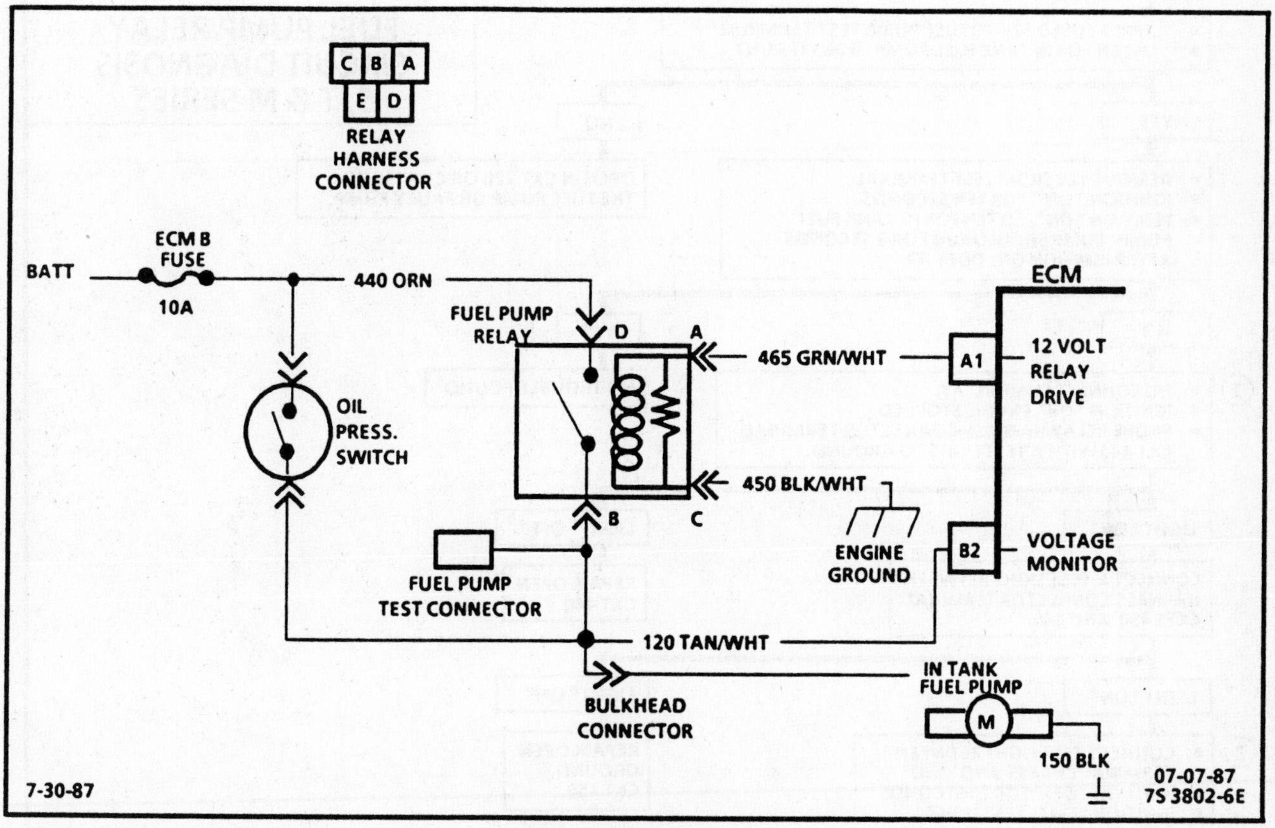
C B A
E D
RELAY HARNESS CONNECTOR
ECM B FUSE
BATT
10A
440 ORN
FUEL PUMP RELAY
D
A
465 GRN/WHT
A1
12 VOLT RELAY DRIVE
ECM
OIL PRESS. SWITCH
450 BLK/WHT
B
C
ENGINE GROUND
B2
VOLTAGE MONITOR
FUEL PUMP TEST CONNECTOR
120 TAN/WHT
IN TANK FUEL PUMP
M
BULKHEAD CONNECTOR
150 BLK
7-30-87
07-07-87
7S 3802-6E

CHART A-5

FUEL PUMP RELAY CIRCUIT DIAGNOSIS
S, T & M SERIES

Circuit Description:

When the ignition switch is turned "ON", the ECM will turn "ON" the in-tank fuel pump. It will remain "ON" as long as the engine is cranking or running, and the ECM is receiving distributor reference pulses. If there are no reference pulses, the ECM will shut "OFF" the fuel pump within 2 seconds after ignition "ON" or engine stops.

The pump will deliver fuel to the TBI unit where the system pressure is controlled to about 62 to 90 kPa (9 to 13 psi). Excess fuel is then returned to the fuel tank.

Test Description: Numbers below refer to circled numbers on the diagnostic chart.

1. Turns "ON" the fuel pump if CKT 120 wiring is OK. If the pump runs, it maybe a fuel pump relay circuit problem, which the following steps will locate.
2. The next two steps check for power and ground circuits to the relay.
3. Determines if ECM can control the relay.
4. The oil pressure switch serves as a backup for the fuel pump relay to help prevent a no start situation. If the fuel pump relay was found to be inoperative, the oil pressure switch circuit should also be tested to determine why it did not operate the fuel pump.

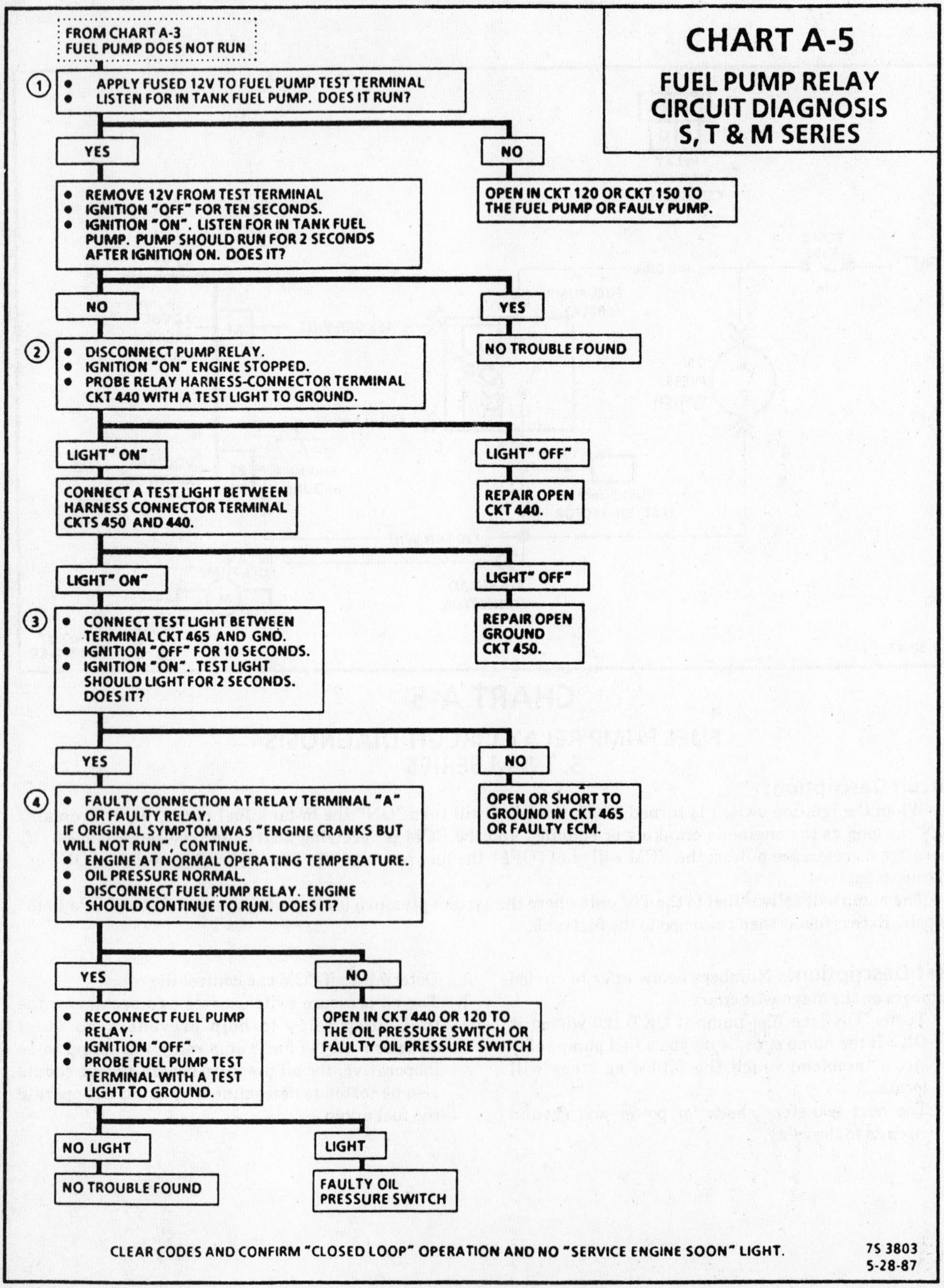
CHART A-5
FUEL PUMP RELAY
CIRCUIT DIAGNOSIS
S, T & M SERIES
FROM CHART A-3
FUEL PUMP DOES NOT RUN
1
• APPLY FUSED 12V TO FUEL PUMP TEST TERMINAL
• LISTEN FOR IN TANK FUEL PUMP. DOES IT RUN?
YES
NO
OPEN IN CKT 120 OR CKT 150 TO THE FUEL PUMP OR FAULY PUMP.
• REMOVE 12V FROM TEST TERMINAL
• IGNITION "OFF" FOR TEN SECONDS.
• IGNITION "ON". LISTEN FOR IN TANK FUEL PUMP. PUMP SHOULD RUN FOR 2 SECONDS AFTER IGNITION ON. DOES IT?
NO
YES
NO TROUBLE FOUND
2
• DISCONNECT PUMP RELAY.
• IGNITION "ON" ENGINE STOPPED.
• PROBE RELAY HARNESS-CONNECTOR TERMINAL CKT 440 WITH A TEST LIGHT TO GROUND.
LIGHT" ON"
LIGHT" OFF"
CONNECT A TEST LIGHT BETWEEN HARNESS CONNECTOR TERMINAL CKTS 450 AND 440.
REPAIR OPEN CKT 440.
LIGHT" ON"
LIGHT" OFF"
REPAIR OPEN GROUND CKT 450.
3
• CONNECT TEST LIGHT BETWEEN TERMINAL CKT 465 AND GND.
• IGNITION "OFF" FOR 10 SECONDS.
• IGNITION "ON". TEST LIGHT SHOULD LIGHT FOR 2 SECONDS. DOES IT?
YES
NO
OPEN OR SHORT TO GROUND IN CKT 465 OR FAULTY ECM.
4
• FAULTY CONNECTION AT RELAY TERMINAL "A" OR FAULTY RELAY.
IF ORIGINAL SYMPTOM WAS "ENGINE CRANKS BUT WILL NOT RUN", CONTINUE.
• ENGINE AT NORMAL OPERATING TEMPERATURE.
• OIL PRESSURE NORMAL.
• DISCONNECT FUEL PUMP RELAY. ENGINE SHOULD CONTINUE TO RUN. DOES IT?
YES
NO
OPEN IN CKT 440 OR 120 TO THE OIL PRESSURE SWITCH OR FAULTY OIL PRESSURE SWITCH
• RECONNECT FUEL PUMP RELAY.
• IGNITION "OFF".
• PROBE FUEL PUMP TEST TERMINAL WITH A TEST LIGHT TO GROUND.
NO LIGHT
LIGHT
NO TROUBLE FOUND
FAULTY OIL PRESSURE SWITCH
CLEAR CODES AND CONFIRM "CLOSED LOOP" OPERATION AND NO "SERVICE ENGINE SOON" LIGHT.
7S 3803
5-28-87

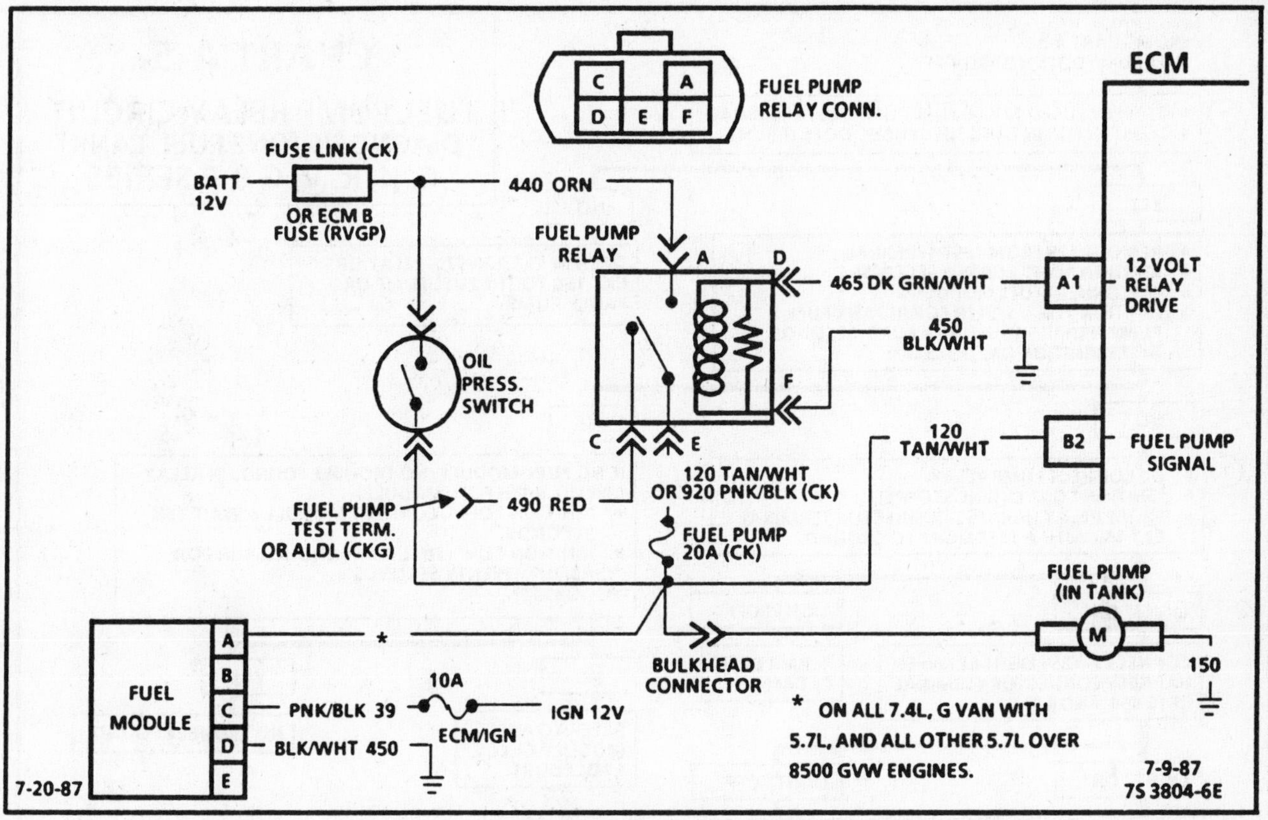
FUEL PUMP
RELAY CONN.
ECM
FUSE LINK (CK)
BATT
12V
OR ECM B
FUSE (RVGP)
440 ORN
FUEL PUMP
RELAY
465 DK GRN/WHT
A1
12 VOLT
RELAY
DRIVE
450
BLK/WHT
OIL
PRESS.
SWITCH
120
TAN/WHT
B2
FUEL PUMP
SIGNAL
120 TAN/WHT
OR 920 PNK/BLK (CK)
FUEL PUMP
TEST TERM.
OR ALDL (CKG)
490 RED
FUEL PUMP
20A (CK)
FUEL PUMP
(IN TANK)
FUEL
MODULE
BULKHEAD
CONNECTOR
150
10A
PNK/BLK 39
IGN 12V
ECM/IGN
BLK/WHT 450
* ON ALL 7.4L, G VAN WITH
5.7L, AND ALL OTHER 5.7L OVER
8500 GVW ENGINES.
7-20-87
7-9-87
7S 3804-6E

CHART A-5

FUEL PUMP RELAY CIRCUIT DIAGNOSIS (ONE FUEL TANK) C, K, R, V, G & P SERIES

Circuit Description:

When the ignition switch is turned "ON", the Electronic Control Module (ECM) will turn "ON" the in-tank fuel pump. It will remain "ON" as long as the engine is cranking or running, and the ECM is receiving distributor reference pulses. If there are no reference pulses, the ECM will shut "OFF" the fuel pump within 2 seconds after ignition "ON" or engine stops except when a fuel module is used.

The pump will deliver fuel to the TBI unit where the system pressure is controlled to about 62 to 90 kPa (9 to 13 psi). Excess fuel is then returned to the fuel tank.

A fuel module is used on all 7.4L, G van with 5.7L, and all other 5.7L over 8500 GVW engines to correct a hot restart (vapor lock) during a high ambient condition. It is designed to over-ride the ECM two second pump operation and will run the fuel pump for twenty seconds at initial ignition "ON".

Test Description: Numbers below refer to circled numbers on the diagnostic chart.

1. This procedure applies direct voltage to run the fuel pump. If the pump runs, it may be a fuel pump relay circuit problem which the following step will locate.
2. This step checks voltage from the battery and the ground circuit to the relay.
3. This test determines if there is voltage from the ECM, terminal A1, to terminal "D" on the relay connector.
4. This completes the fuel pump relay circuit but if this diagnosis was used because the engine would not run then oil pressure switch should also be diagnosed.

Diagnostic Aids:

- An inoperative fuel module may be the cause of a hot stall/no start condition. Check for power and ground circuit to the fuel module and a complete circuit to the pump from terminal "A". If OK, and the pump does not run for the specified 20 seconds at initial ignition "ON", replace the Fuel Module.

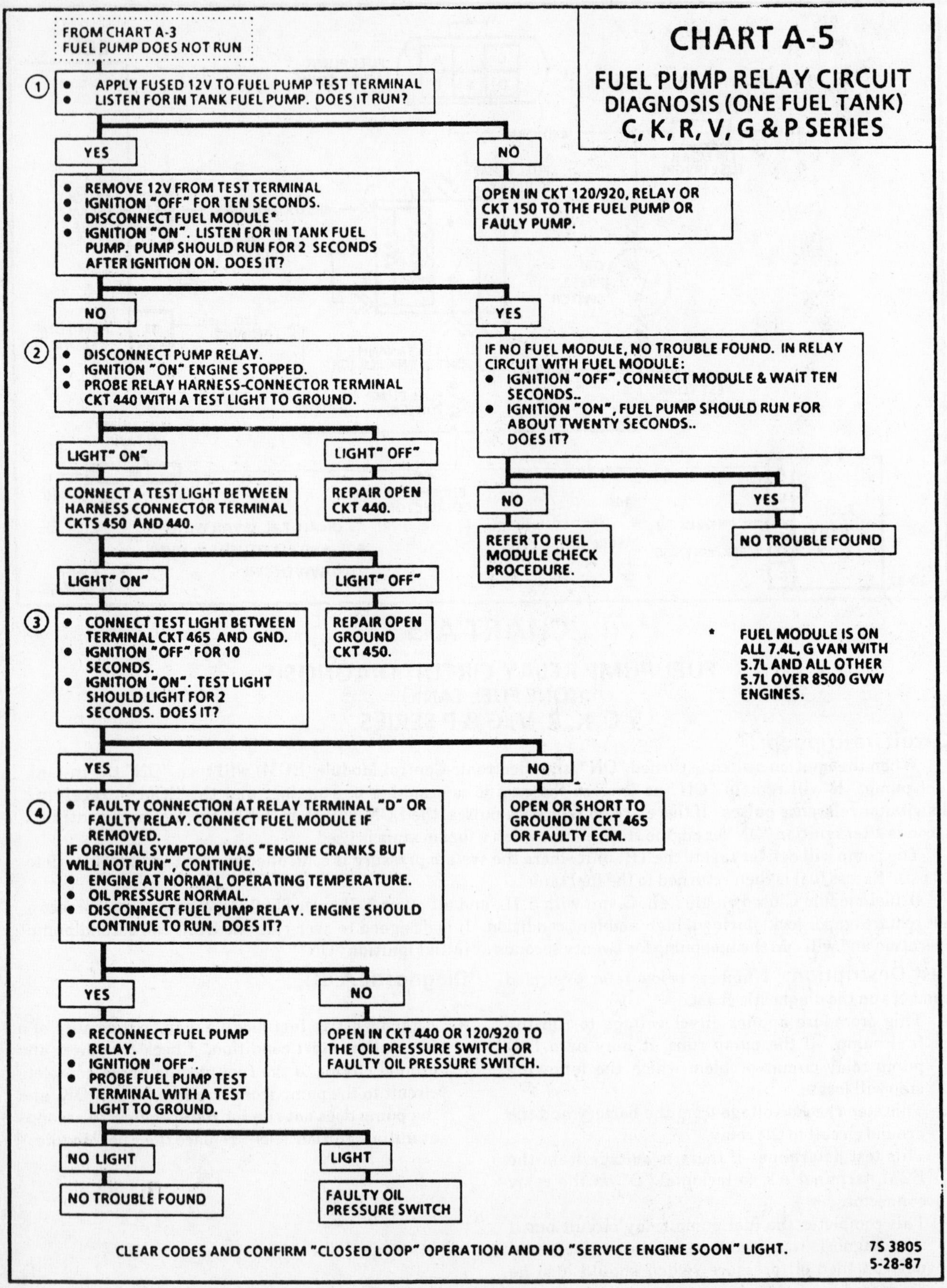
CHART A-5
FUEL PUMP RELAY CIRCUIT
DIAGNOSIS (ONE FUEL TANK)
C, K, R, V, G & P SERIES
FROM CHART A-3
FUEL PUMP DOES NOT RUN
1
• APPLY FUSED 12V TO FUEL PUMP TEST TERMINAL
• LISTEN FOR IN TANK FUEL PUMP. DOES IT RUN?
YES
NO
• REMOVE 12V FROM TEST TERMINAL
• IGNITION "OFF" FOR TEN SECONDS.
• DISCONNECT FUEL MODULE*
• IGNITION "ON". LISTEN FOR IN TANK FUEL PUMP. PUMP SHOULD RUN FOR 2 SECONDS AFTER IGNITION ON. DOES IT?
OPEN IN CKT 120/920, RELAY OR CKT 150 TO THE FUEL PUMP OR FAULY PUMP.
NO
YES
2
• DISCONNECT PUMP RELAY.
• IGNITION "ON" ENGINE STOPPED.
• PROBE RELAY HARNESS-CONNECTOR TERMINAL CKT 440 WITH A TEST LIGHT TO GROUND.
IF NO FUEL MODULE, NO TROUBLE FOUND. IN RELAY CIRCUIT WITH FUEL MODULE:
• IGNITION "OFF", CONNECT MODULE & WAIT TEN SECONDS..
• IGNITION "ON", FUEL PUMP SHOULD RUN FOR ABOUT TWENTY SECONDS.. DOES IT?
LIGHT" ON"
LIGHT" OFF"
CONNECT A TEST LIGHT BETWEEN HARNESS CONNECTOR TERMINAL CKTS 450 AND 440.
REPAIR OPEN CKT 440.
NO
YES
REFER TO FUEL MODULE CHECK PROCEDURE.
NO TROUBLE FOUND
LIGHT" ON"
LIGHT" OFF"
3
• CONNECT TEST LIGHT BETWEEN TERMINAL CKT 465 AND GND.
• IGNITION "OFF" FOR 10 SECONDS.
• IGNITION "ON". TEST LIGHT SHOULD LIGHT FOR 2 SECONDS. DOES IT?
REPAIR OPEN GROUND CKT 450.
* FUEL MODULE IS ON ALL 7.4L, G VAN WITH 5.7L AND ALL OTHER 5.7L OVER 8500 GVW ENGINES.
YES
NO
4
• FAULTY CONNECTION AT RELAY TERMINAL "D" OR FAULTY RELAY. CONNECT FUEL MODULE IF REMOVED.
IF ORIGINAL SYMPTOM WAS "ENGINE CRANKS BUT WILL NOT RUN", CONTINUE.
• ENGINE AT NORMAL OPERATING TEMPERATURE.
• OIL PRESSURE NORMAL.
• DISCONNECT FUEL PUMP RELAY. ENGINE SHOULD CONTINUE TO RUN. DOES IT?
OPEN OR SHORT TO GROUND IN CKT 465 OR FAULTY ECM.
YES
NO
• RECONNECT FUEL PUMP RELAY.
• IGNITION "OFF".
• PROBE FUEL PUMP TEST TERMINAL WITH A TEST LIGHT TO GROUND.
OPEN IN CKT 440 OR 120/920 TO THE OIL PRESSURE SWITCH OR FAULTY OIL PRESSURE SWITCH.
NO LIGHT
LIGHT
NO TROUBLE FOUND
FAULTY OIL PRESSURE SWITCH
CLEAR CODES AND CONFIRM "CLOSED LOOP" OPERATION AND NO "SERVICE ENGINE SOON" LIGHT.
7S 3805
5-28-87

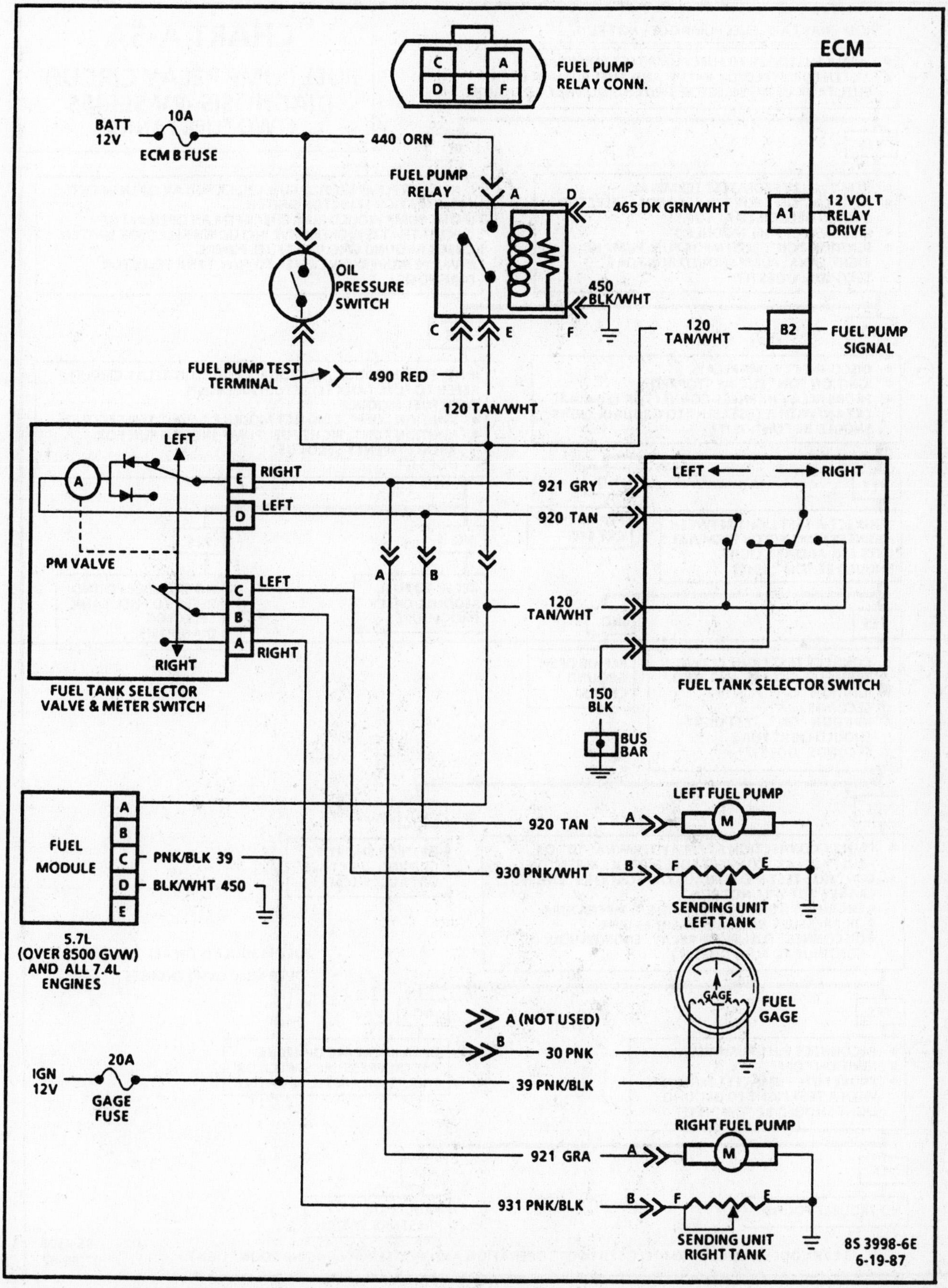
FUEL PUMP
RELAY CONN.
C
A
D
E
F
ECM
BATT
12V
10A
ECM B FUSE
440 ORN
FUEL PUMP
RELAY
A
D
465 DK GRN/WHT
A1
12 VOLT
RELAY
DRIVE
OIL
PRESSURE
SWITCH
450
BLK/WHT
C
E
F
120
TAN/WHT
B2
FUEL PUMP
SIGNAL
FUEL PUMP TEST
TERMINAL
490 RED
120 TAN/WHT
LEFT
A
E
RIGHT
D
LEFT
921 GRY
920 TAN
LEFT
RIGHT
PM VALVE
A
B
C
LEFT
B
A
RIGHT
RIGHT
120
TAN/WHT
FUEL TANK SELECTOR
VALVE & METER SWITCH
FUEL TANK SELECTOR SWITCH
150
BLK
BUS
BAR
LEFT FUEL PUMP
FUEL
MODULE
A
B
C
D
E
PNK/BLK 39
BLK/WHT 450
920 TAN
930 PNK/WHT
A
M
B
F
E
SENDING UNIT
LEFT TANK
5.7L
(OVER 8500 GVW)
AND ALL 7.4L
ENGINES
GAGE
FUEL
GAGE
A (NOT USED)
B
30 PNK
IGN
12V
20A
GAGE
FUSE
39 PNK/BLK
RIGHT FUEL PUMP
921 GRA
A
M
931 PNK/BLK
B
F
E
SENDING UNIT
RIGHT TANK
8S 3998-6E
6-19-87

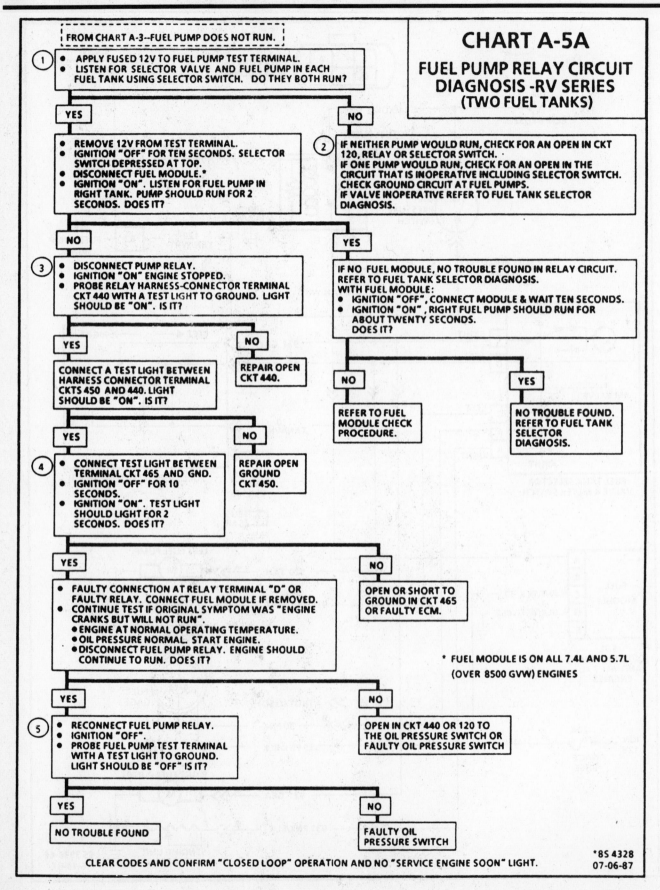

CHART A-5A

FUEL PUMP RELAY CIRCUIT DIAGNOSIS -RV SERIES (TWO FUEL TANKS)

FROM CHART A-3--FUEL PUMP DOES NOT RUN.

(1)
- APPLY FUSED 12V TO FUEL PUMP TEST TERMINAL.
- LISTEN FOR SELECTOR VALVE AND FUEL PUMP IN EACH FUEL TANK USING SELECTOR SWITCH. DO THEY BOTH RUN?

NO → (2) IF NEITHER PUMP WOULD RUN, CHECK FOR AN OPEN IN CKT 120, RELAY OR SELECTOR SWITCH. IF ONE PUMP WOULD RUN, CHECK FOR AN OPEN IN THE CIRCUIT THAT IS INOPERATIVE INCLUDING SELECTOR SWITCH. CHECK GROUND CIRCUIT AT FUEL PUMPS. IF VALVE INOPERATIVE REFER TO FUEL TANK SELECTOR DIAGNOSIS.

YES →
- REMOVE 12V FROM TEST TERMINAL.
- IGNITION "OFF" FOR TEN SECONDS. SELECTOR SWITCH DEPRESSED AT TOP.
- DISCONNECT FUEL MODULE.*
- IGNITION "ON". LISTEN FOR FUEL PUMP IN RIGHT TANK. PUMP SHOULD RUN FOR 2 SECONDS. DOES IT?

  YES → IF NO FUEL MODULE, NO TROUBLE FOUND IN RELAY CIRCUIT. REFER TO FUEL TANK SELECTOR DIAGNOSIS. WITH FUEL MODULE:
  - IGNITION "OFF", CONNECT MODULE & WAIT TEN SECONDS.
  - IGNITION "ON", RIGHT FUEL PUMP SHOULD RUN FOR ABOUT TWENTY SECONDS. DOES IT?

    NO → REFER TO FUEL MODULE CHECK PROCEDURE.

    YES → NO TROUBLE FOUND. REFER TO FUEL TANK SELECTOR DIAGNOSIS.

  NO → (3)
  - DISCONNECT PUMP RELAY.
  - IGNITION "ON" ENGINE STOPPED.
  - PROBE RELAY HARNESS-CONNECTOR TERMINAL CKT 440 WITH A TEST LIGHT TO GROUND. LIGHT SHOULD BE "ON". IS IT?

    NO → REPAIR OPEN CKT 440.

    YES → CONNECT A TEST LIGHT BETWEEN HARNESS CONNECTOR TERMINAL CKTS 450 AND 440. LIGHT SHOULD BE "ON". IS IT?

      NO → REPAIR OPEN GROUND CKT 450.

      YES → (4)
      - CONNECT TEST LIGHT BETWEEN TERMINAL CKT 465 AND GND.
      - IGNITION "OFF" FOR 10 SECONDS.
      - IGNITION "ON". TEST LIGHT SHOULD LIGHT FOR 2 SECONDS. DOES IT?

        NO → OPEN OR SHORT TO GROUND IN CKT 465 OR FAULTY ECM.

        YES →
        - FAULTY CONNECTION AT RELAY TERMINAL "D" OR FAULTY RELAY. CONNECT FUEL MODULE IF REMOVED.
        - CONTINUE TEST IF ORIGINAL SYMPTOM WAS "ENGINE CRANKS BUT WILL NOT RUN".
          - ENGINE AT NORMAL OPERATING TEMPERATURE.
          - OIL PRESSURE NORMAL. START ENGINE.
          - DISCONNECT FUEL PUMP RELAY. ENGINE SHOULD CONTINUE TO RUN. DOES IT?

          NO → OPEN IN CKT 440 OR 120 TO THE OIL PRESSURE SWITCH OR FAULTY OIL PRESSURE SWITCH

          YES → (5)
          - RECONNECT FUEL PUMP RELAY.
          - IGNITION "OFF".
          - PROBE FUEL PUMP TEST TERMINAL WITH A TEST LIGHT TO GROUND. LIGHT SHOULD BE "OFF" IS IT?

            YES → NO TROUBLE FOUND

            NO → FAULTY OIL PRESSURE SWITCH

* FUEL MODULE IS ON ALL 7.4L AND 5.7L (OVER 8500 GVW) ENGINES

CLEAR CODES AND CONFIRM "CLOSED LOOP" OPERATION AND NO "SERVICE ENGINE SOON" LIGHT.

*8S 4328
07-06-87

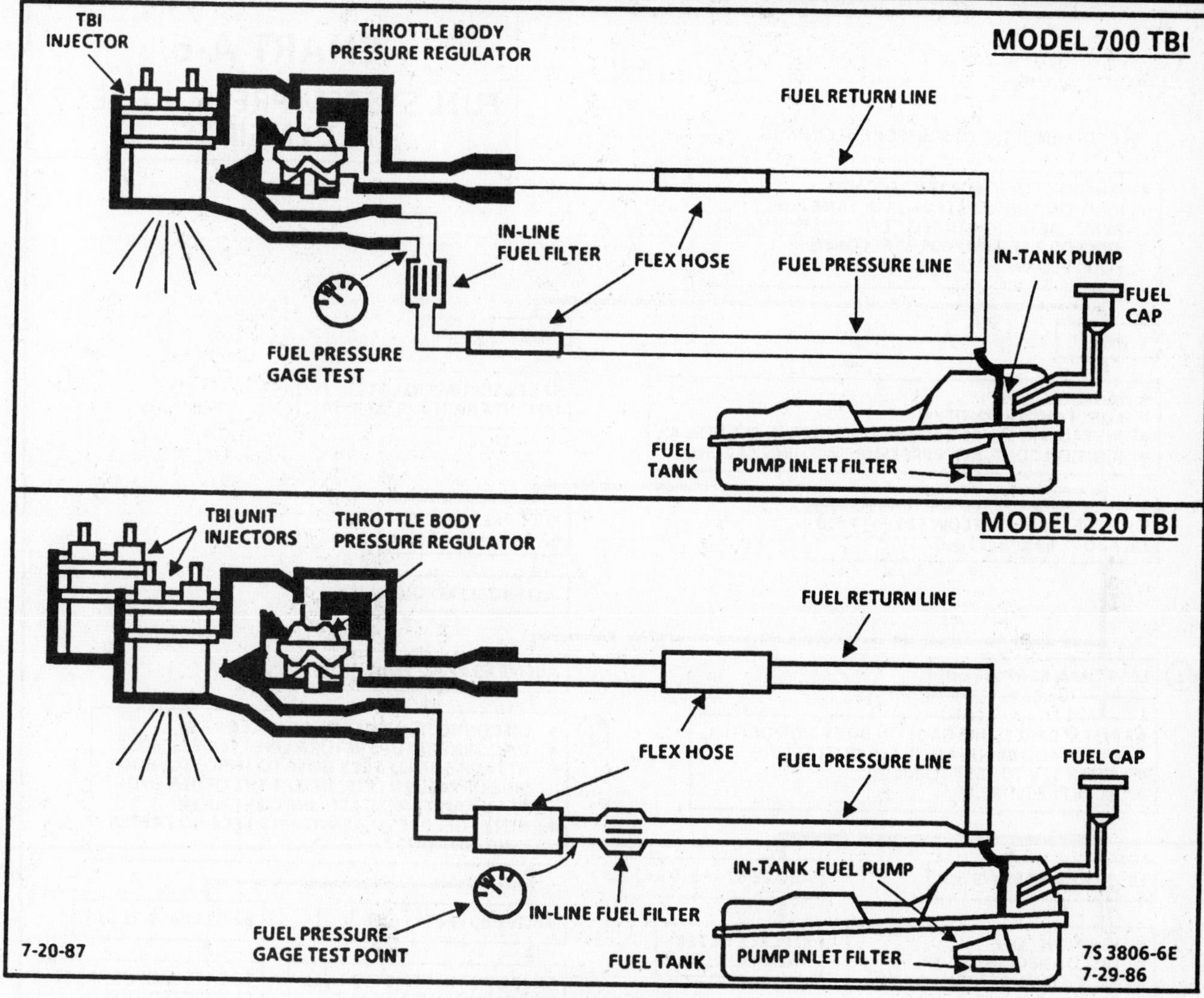
TBI INJECTOR
THROTTLE BODY PRESSURE REGULATOR
MODEL 700 TBI
FUEL RETURN LINE
IN-LINE FUEL FILTER
FLEX HOSE
FUEL PRESSURE LINE
IN-TANK PUMP
FUEL CAP
FUEL PRESSURE GAGE TEST
FUEL TANK
PUMP INLET FILTER
TBI UNIT INJECTORS
THROTTLE BODY PRESSURE REGULATOR
MODEL 220 TBI
FUEL RETURN LINE
FLEX HOSE
FUEL PRESSURE LINE
FUEL CAP
IN-TANK FUEL PUMP
IN-LINE FUEL FILTER
FUEL PRESSURE GAGE TEST POINT
7-20-87
FUEL TANK
PUMP INLET FILTER
7S 3806-6E
7-29-86

CHART A-6
FUEL SYSTEM PRESSURE TEST
ALL ENGINES

Circuit Description:

When the fuel pump is running, fuel is delivered to the injector(s) and then to the regulator where the system pressure is controlled to about 62 to 90 kPa (9 to 13 psi). Excess fuel is then returned to the fuel tank.

Test Description: Numbers below refer to circled numbers on the diagnostic chart.

1. Pressure but less than 62 kPa (9 psi) falls into two areas:
- Regulated pressure but less than 62 kPa (9 psi) - Amount of fuel to injector OK but pressure is too low. System will be lean running and may set Code 44. Also, hard starting cold and poor overall performance.
- Restricted flow causing pressure drop - Normally, a vehicle with a fuel pressure of less than 62 kPa (9 psi) at idle will not be driveable. However, if the pressure drop occurs only while driving, the engine will normally surge then stop as pressure begins to drop rapidly.

2. Restricting the fuel return line allows the fuel pump to develop its maximum pressure (dead head pressure). When battery voltage is applied to the pump test connector, pressure should be from 90 to 124 kPa (13 to 18 psi).
3. This test determines if the high fuel pressure is due to a restricted fuel return line or a throttle body pressure regulator problem.

Diagnostic Aids:

- If the vehicle is equipped with a fuel module, the module must be disconnected before performing the fuel system pressure test. Refer to Section "4".
- Fuel system is under pressure. To avoid fuel spillage, refer to procedures in Section "4" for testing or making repairs requiring disassembly of fuel lines or fittings.
- On V6 or V8 engine, the fuel pressure drops to almost zero psi after pump shuts "off".

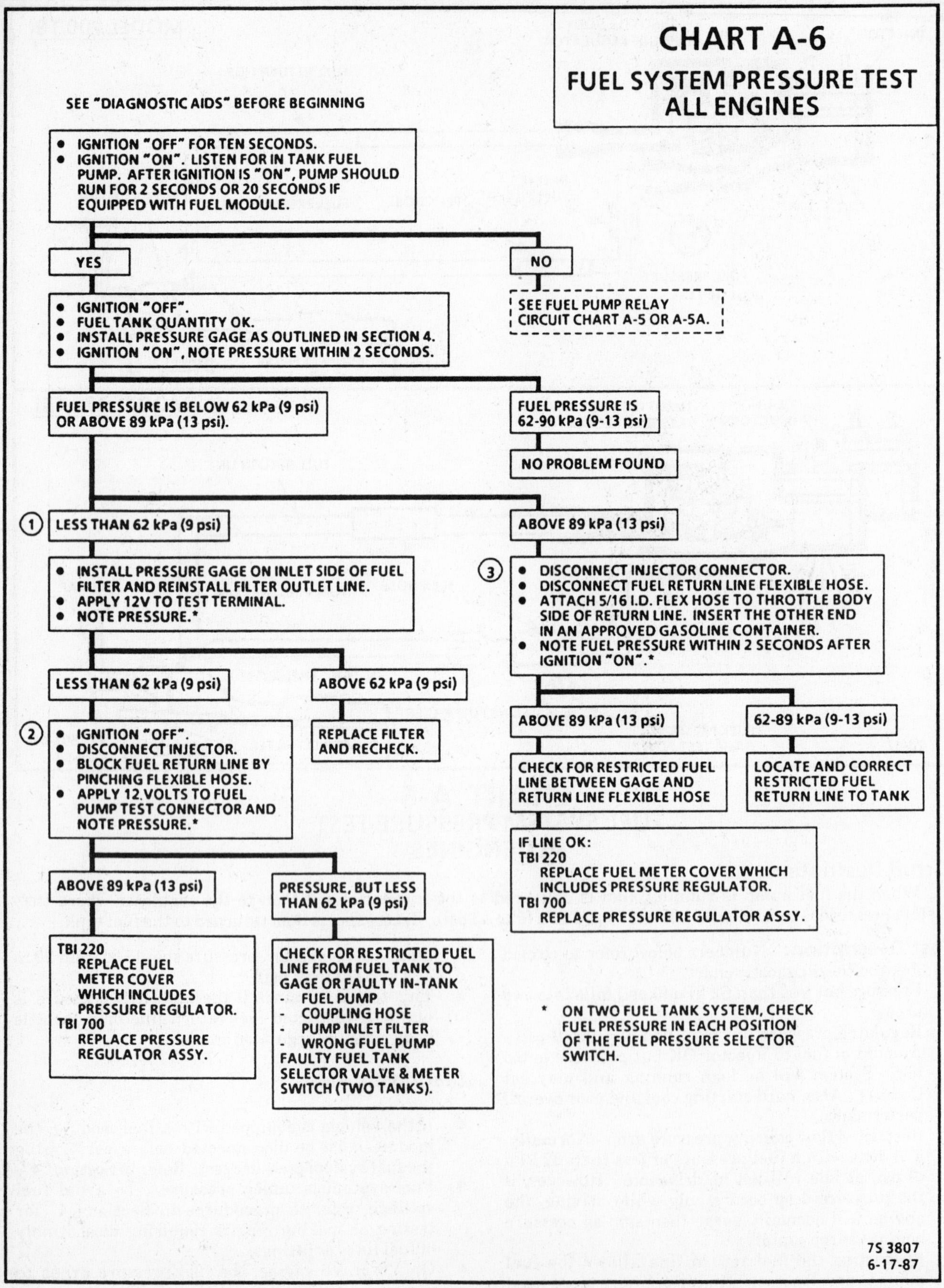
CHART A-6
FUEL SYSTEM PRESSURE TEST
ALL ENGINES
SEE "DIAGNOSTIC AIDS" BEFORE BEGINNING
• IGNITION "OFF" FOR TEN SECONDS.
• IGNITION "ON". LISTEN FOR IN TANK FUEL PUMP. AFTER IGNITION IS "ON", PUMP SHOULD RUN FOR 2 SECONDS OR 20 SECONDS IF EQUIPPED WITH FUEL MODULE.
YES
NO
SEE FUEL PUMP RELAY CIRCUIT CHART A-5 OR A-5A.
• IGNITION "OFF".
• FUEL TANK QUANTITY OK.
• INSTALL PRESSURE GAGE AS OUTLINED IN SECTION 4.
• IGNITION "ON", NOTE PRESSURE WITHIN 2 SECONDS.
FUEL PRESSURE IS BELOW 62 kPa (9 psi) OR ABOVE 89 kPa (13 psi).
FUEL PRESSURE IS 62-90 kPa (9-13 psi)
NO PROBLEM FOUND
1 LESS THAN 62 kPa (9 psi)
ABOVE 89 kPa (13 psi)
• INSTALL PRESSURE GAGE ON INLET SIDE OF FUEL FILTER AND REINSTALL FILTER OUTLET LINE.
• APPLY 12V TO TEST TERMINAL.
• NOTE PRESSURE.*
3 • DISCONNECT INJECTOR CONNECTOR.
• DISCONNECT FUEL RETURN LINE FLEXIBLE HOSE.
• ATTACH 5/16 I.D. FLEX HOSE TO THROTTLE BODY SIDE OF RETURN LINE. INSERT THE OTHER END IN AN APPROVED GASOLINE CONTAINER.
• NOTE FUEL PRESSURE WITHIN 2 SECONDS AFTER IGNITION "ON".*
LESS THAN 62 kPa (9 psi)
ABOVE 62 kPa (9 psi)
ABOVE 89 kPa (13 psi)
62-89 kPa (9-13 psi)
2 • IGNITION "OFF".
• DISCONNECT INJECTOR.
• BLOCK FUEL RETURN LINE BY PINCHING FLEXIBLE HOSE.
• APPLY 12 VOLTS TO FUEL PUMP TEST CONNECTOR AND NOTE PRESSURE.*
REPLACE FILTER AND RECHECK.
CHECK FOR RESTRICTED FUEL LINE BETWEEN GAGE AND RETURN LINE FLEXIBLE HOSE
LOCATE AND CORRECT RESTRICTED FUEL RETURN LINE TO TANK
IF LINE OK:
TBI 220
REPLACE FUEL METER COVER WHICH INCLUDES PRESSURE REGULATOR.
TBI 700
REPLACE PRESSURE REGULATOR ASSY.
ABOVE 89 kPa (13 psi)
PRESSURE, BUT LESS THAN 62 kPa (9 psi)
TBI 220
REPLACE FUEL METER COVER WHICH INCLUDES PRESSURE REGULATOR.
TBI 700
REPLACE PRESSURE REGULATOR ASSY.
CHECK FOR RESTRICTED FUEL LINE FROM FUEL TANK TO GAGE OR FAULTY IN-TANK
- FUEL PUMP
- COUPLING HOSE
- PUMP INLET FILTER
- WRONG FUEL PUMP
FAULTY FUEL TANK SELECTOR VALVE & METER SWITCH (TWO TANKS).
* ON TWO FUEL TANK SYSTEM, CHECK FUEL PRESSURE IN EACH POSITION OF THE FUEL PRESSURE SELECTOR SWITCH.
7S 3807
6-17-87

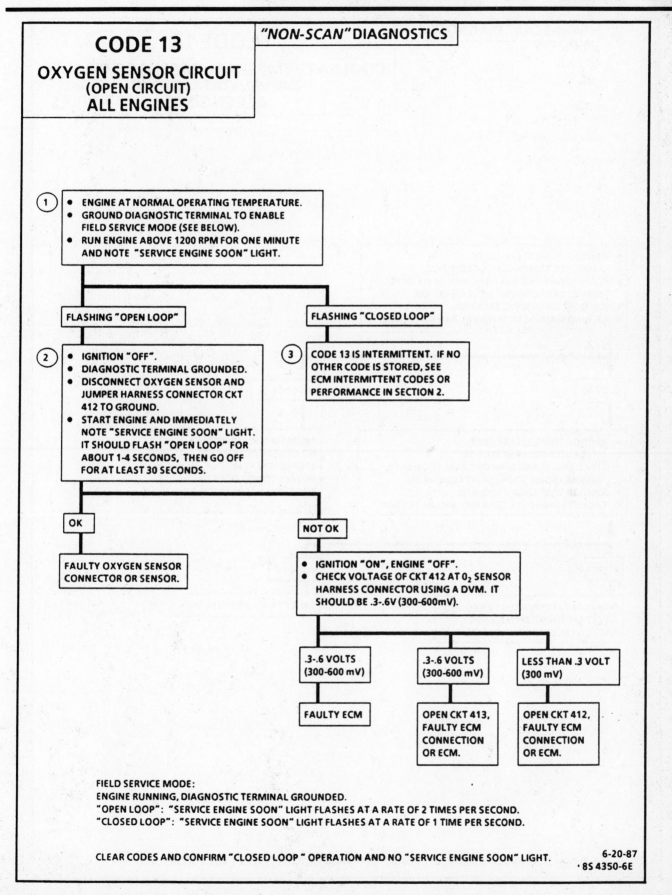

CODE 13

OXYGEN SENSOR CIRCUIT
(OPEN CIRCUIT)
ALL ENGINES

"NON-SCAN" DIAGNOSTICS

(1)
- ENGINE AT NORMAL OPERATING TEMPERATURE.
- GROUND DIAGNOSTIC TERMINAL TO ENABLE FIELD SERVICE MODE (SEE BELOW).
- RUN ENGINE ABOVE 1200 RPM FOR ONE MINUTE AND NOTE "SERVICE ENGINE SOON" LIGHT.

FLASHING "OPEN LOOP"

(2)
- IGNITION "OFF".
- DIAGNOSTIC TERMINAL GROUNDED.
- DISCONNECT OXYGEN SENSOR AND JUMPER HARNESS CONNECTOR CKT 412 TO GROUND.
- START ENGINE AND IMMEDIATELY NOTE "SERVICE ENGINE SOON" LIGHT. IT SHOULD FLASH "OPEN LOOP" FOR ABOUT 1-4 SECONDS, THEN GO OFF FOR AT LEAST 30 SECONDS.

OK

FAULTY OXYGEN SENSOR CONNECTOR OR SENSOR.

NOT OK

- IGNITION "ON", ENGINE "OFF".
- CHECK VOLTAGE OF CKT 412 AT O_2 SENSOR HARNESS CONNECTOR USING A DVM. IT SHOULD BE .3-.6V (300-600mV).

.3-.6 VOLTS (300-600 mV)

FAULTY ECM

.3-.6 VOLTS (300-600 mV)

OPEN CKT 413, FAULTY ECM CONNECTION OR ECM.

LESS THAN .3 VOLT (300 mV)

OPEN CKT 412, FAULTY ECM CONNECTION OR ECM.

FLASHING "CLOSED LOOP"

(3)
CODE 13 IS INTERMITTENT. IF NO OTHER CODE IS STORED, SEE ECM INTERMITTENT CODES OR PERFORMANCE IN SECTION 2.

FIELD SERVICE MODE:
ENGINE RUNNING, DIAGNOSTIC TERMINAL GROUNDED.
"OPEN LOOP": "SERVICE ENGINE SOON" LIGHT FLASHES AT A RATE OF 2 TIMES PER SECOND.
"CLOSED LOOP": "SERVICE ENGINE SOON" LIGHT FLASHES AT A RATE OF 1 TIME PER SECOND.

CLEAR CODES AND CONFIRM "CLOSED LOOP" OPERATION AND NO "SERVICE ENGINE SOON" LIGHT.

6-20-87
8S 4350-6E

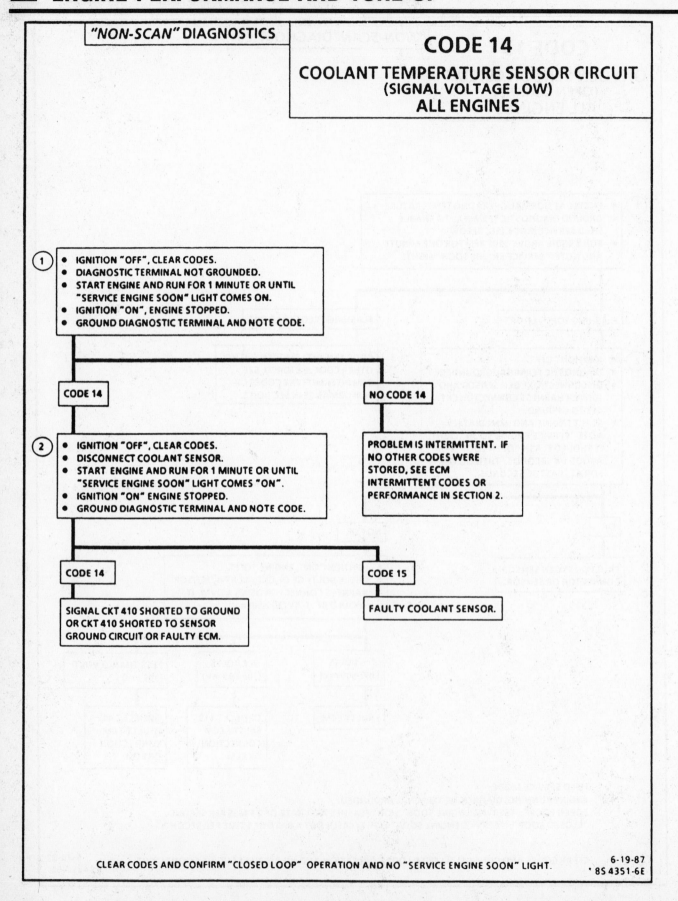

"NON-SCAN" DIAGNOSTICS

CODE 14

COOLANT TEMPERATURE SENSOR CIRCUIT
(SIGNAL VOLTAGE LOW)
ALL ENGINES

(1)
- IGNITION "OFF", CLEAR CODES.
- DIAGNOSTIC TERMINAL NOT GROUNDED.
- START ENGINE AND RUN FOR 1 MINUTE OR UNTIL "SERVICE ENGINE SOON" LIGHT COMES ON.
- IGNITION "ON", ENGINE STOPPED.
- GROUND DIAGNOSTIC TERMINAL AND NOTE CODE.

CODE 14

(2)
- IGNITION "OFF", CLEAR CODES.
- DISCONNECT COOLANT SENSOR.
- START ENGINE AND RUN FOR 1 MINUTE OR UNTIL "SERVICE ENGINE SOON" LIGHT COMES "ON".
- IGNITION "ON" ENGINE STOPPED.
- GROUND DIAGNOSTIC TERMINAL AND NOTE CODE.

CODE 14

SIGNAL CKT 410 SHORTED TO GROUND OR CKT 410 SHORTED TO SENSOR GROUND CIRCUIT OR FAULTY ECM.

CODE 15

FAULTY COOLANT SENSOR.

NO CODE 14

PROBLEM IS INTERMITTENT. IF NO OTHER CODES WERE STORED, SEE ECM INTERMITTENT CODES OR PERFORMANCE IN SECTION 2.

CLEAR CODES AND CONFIRM "CLOSED LOOP" OPERATION AND NO "SERVICE ENGINE SOON" LIGHT.

6-19-87
• 8S 4351-6E

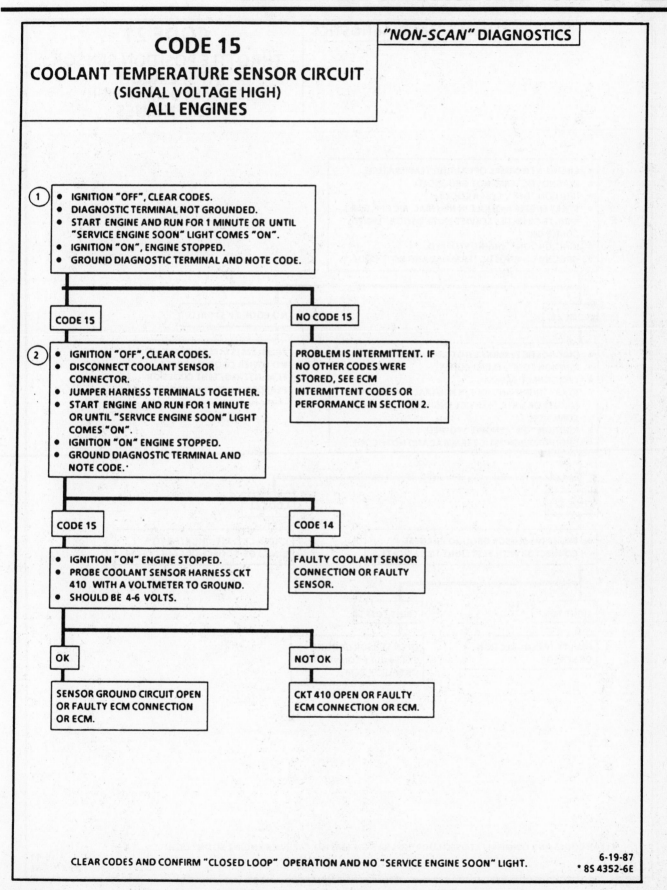

"NON-SCAN" DIAGNOSTICS

CODE 15
COOLANT TEMPERATURE SENSOR CIRCUIT
(SIGNAL VOLTAGE HIGH)
ALL ENGINES

(1)
- IGNITION "OFF", CLEAR CODES.
- DIAGNOSTIC TERMINAL NOT GROUNDED.
- START ENGINE AND RUN FOR 1 MINUTE OR UNTIL "SERVICE ENGINE SOON" LIGHT COMES "ON".
- IGNITION "ON", ENGINE STOPPED.
- GROUND DIAGNOSTIC TERMINAL AND NOTE CODE.

CODE 15

(2)
- IGNITION "OFF", CLEAR CODES.
- DISCONNECT COOLANT SENSOR CONNECTOR.
- JUMPER HARNESS TERMINALS TOGETHER.
- START ENGINE AND RUN FOR 1 MINUTE OR UNTIL "SERVICE ENGINE SOON" LIGHT COMES "ON".
- IGNITION "ON" ENGINE STOPPED.
- GROUND DIAGNOSTIC TERMINAL AND NOTE CODE.

CODE 15

- IGNITION "ON" ENGINE STOPPED.
- PROBE COOLANT SENSOR HARNESS CKT 410 WITH A VOLTMETER TO GROUND.
- SHOULD BE 4-6 VOLTS.

OK

SENSOR GROUND CIRCUIT OPEN OR FAULTY ECM CONNECTION OR ECM.

NOT OK

CKT 410 OPEN OR FAULTY ECM CONNECTION OR ECM.

CODE 14

FAULTY COOLANT SENSOR CONNECTION OR FAULTY SENSOR.

NO CODE 15

PROBLEM IS INTERMITTENT. IF NO OTHER CODES WERE STORED, SEE ECM INTERMITTENT CODES OR PERFORMANCE IN SECTION 2.

CLEAR CODES AND CONFIRM "CLOSED LOOP" OPERATION AND NO "SERVICE ENGINE SOON" LIGHT.

6-19-87
* 8S 4352-6E

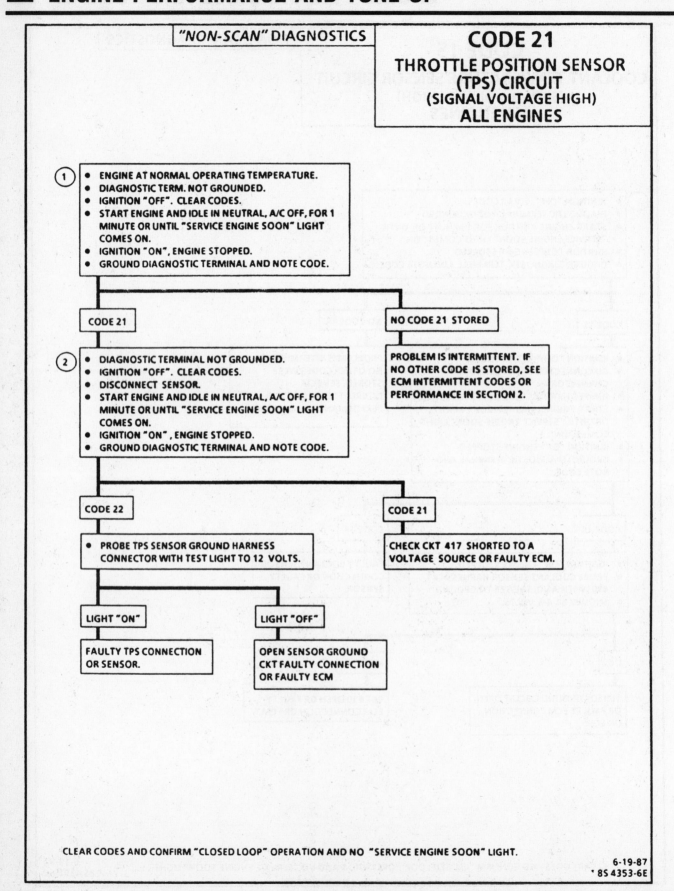

"NON-SCAN" DIAGNOSTICS

CODE 21

THROTTLE POSITION SENSOR (TPS) CIRCUIT (SIGNAL VOLTAGE HIGH) ALL ENGINES

(1)
- ENGINE AT NORMAL OPERATING TEMPERATURE.
- DIAGNOSTIC TERM. NOT GROUNDED.
- IGNITION "OFF". CLEAR CODES.
- START ENGINE AND IDLE IN NEUTRAL, A/C OFF, FOR 1 MINUTE OR UNTIL "SERVICE ENGINE SOON" LIGHT COMES ON.
- IGNITION "ON", ENGINE STOPPED.
- GROUND DIAGNOSTIC TERMINAL AND NOTE CODE.

CODE 21

NO CODE 21 STORED

PROBLEM IS INTERMITTENT. IF NO OTHER CODE IS STORED, SEE ECM INTERMITTENT CODES OR PERFORMANCE IN SECTION 2.

(2)
- DIAGNOSTIC TERMINAL NOT GROUNDED.
- IGNITION "OFF". CLEAR CODES.
- DISCONNECT SENSOR.
- START ENGINE AND IDLE IN NEUTRAL, A/C OFF, FOR 1 MINUTE OR UNTIL "SERVICE ENGINE SOON" LIGHT COMES ON.
- IGNITION "ON", ENGINE STOPPED.
- GROUND DIAGNOSTIC TERMINAL AND NOTE CODE.

CODE 22

- PROBE TPS SENSOR GROUND HARNESS CONNECTOR WITH TEST LIGHT TO 12 VOLTS.

LIGHT "ON"

FAULTY TPS CONNECTION OR SENSOR.

LIGHT "OFF"

OPEN SENSOR GROUND CKT FAULTY CONNECTION OR FAULTY ECM

CODE 21

CHECK CKT 417 SHORTED TO A VOLTAGE SOURCE OR FAULTY ECM.

CLEAR CODES AND CONFIRM "CLOSED LOOP" OPERATION AND NO "SERVICE ENGINE SOON" LIGHT.

6-19-87
* 8S 4353-6E

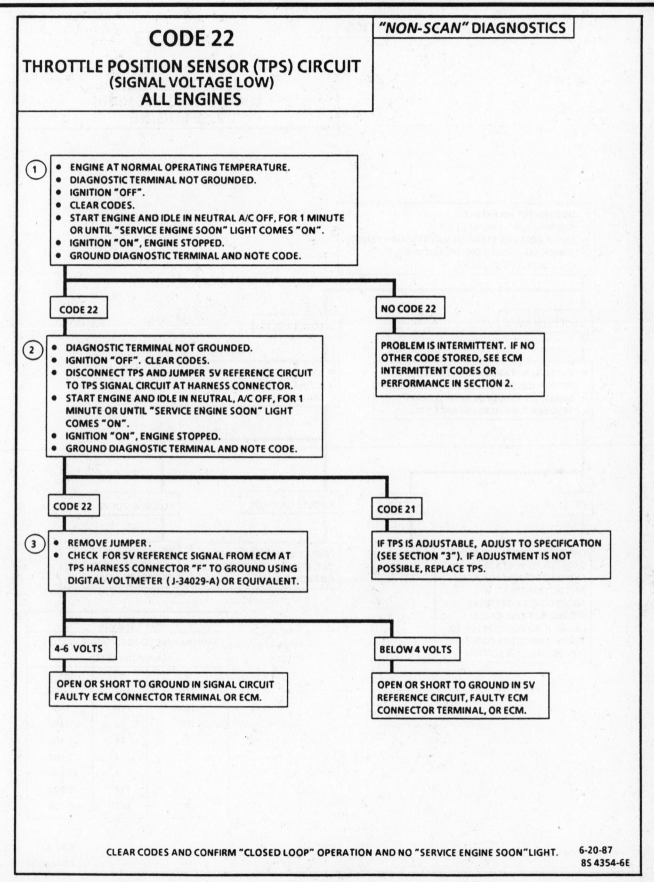

CODE 22

THROTTLE POSITION SENSOR (TPS) CIRCUIT
(SIGNAL VOLTAGE LOW)
ALL ENGINES

"NON-SCAN" DIAGNOSTICS

(1)
- ENGINE AT NORMAL OPERATING TEMPERATURE.
- DIAGNOSTIC TERMINAL NOT GROUNDED.
- IGNITION "OFF".
- CLEAR CODES.
- START ENGINE AND IDLE IN NEUTRAL A/C OFF, FOR 1 MINUTE OR UNTIL "SERVICE ENGINE SOON" LIGHT COMES "ON".
- IGNITION "ON", ENGINE STOPPED.
- GROUND DIAGNOSTIC TERMINAL AND NOTE CODE.

CODE 22

(2)
- DIAGNOSTIC TERMINAL NOT GROUNDED.
- IGNITION "OFF". CLEAR CODES.
- DISCONNECT TPS AND JUMPER 5V REFERENCE CIRCUIT TO TPS SIGNAL CIRCUIT AT HARNESS CONNECTOR.
- START ENGINE AND IDLE IN NEUTRAL, A/C OFF, FOR 1 MINUTE OR UNTIL "SERVICE ENGINE SOON" LIGHT COMES "ON".
- IGNITION "ON", ENGINE STOPPED.
- GROUND DIAGNOSTIC TERMINAL AND NOTE CODE.

CODE 22

(3)
- REMOVE JUMPER.
- CHECK FOR 5V REFERENCE SIGNAL FROM ECM AT TPS HARNESS CONNECTOR "F" TO GROUND USING DIGITAL VOLTMETER (J-34029-A) OR EQUIVALENT.

4-6 VOLTS

OPEN OR SHORT TO GROUND IN SIGNAL CIRCUIT FAULTY ECM CONNECTOR TERMINAL OR ECM.

BELOW 4 VOLTS

OPEN OR SHORT TO GROUND IN 5V REFERENCE CIRCUIT, FAULTY ECM CONNECTOR TERMINAL, OR ECM.

CODE 21

IF TPS IS ADJUSTABLE, ADJUST TO SPECIFICATION (SEE SECTION "3"). IF ADJUSTMENT IS NOT POSSIBLE, REPLACE TPS.

NO CODE 22

PROBLEM IS INTERMITTENT. IF NO OTHER CODE STORED, SEE ECM INTERMITTENT CODES OR PERFORMANCE IN SECTION 2.

CLEAR CODES AND CONFIRM "CLOSED LOOP" OPERATION AND NO "SERVICE ENGINE SOON" LIGHT.

6-20-87
8S 4354-6E

"NON-SCAN" DIAGNOSTICS

CODE 23

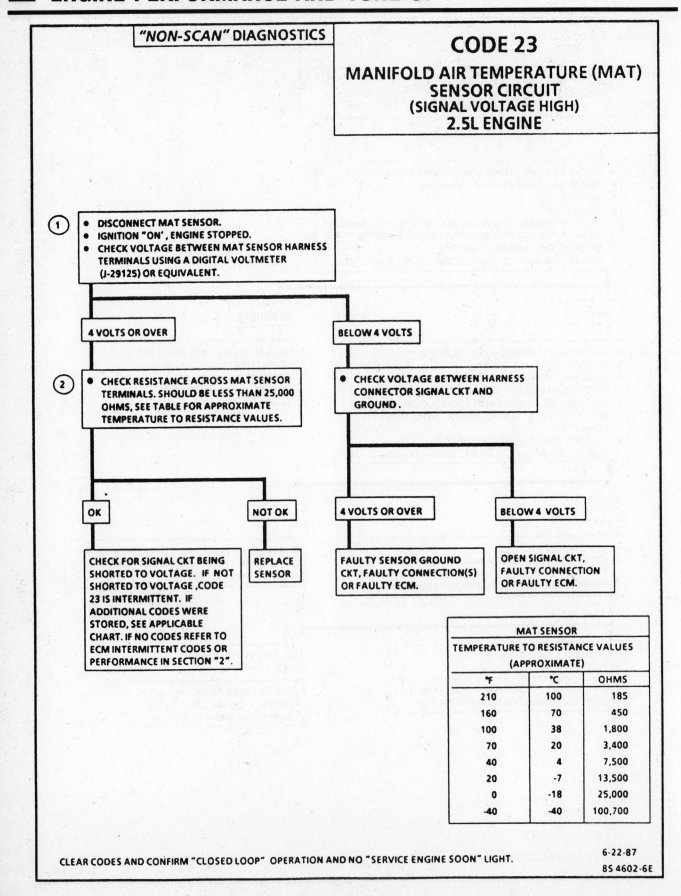

MANIFOLD AIR TEMPERATURE (MAT) SENSOR CIRCUIT
(SIGNAL VOLTAGE HIGH)
2.5L ENGINE

1
- DISCONNECT MAT SENSOR.
- IGNITION "ON", ENGINE STOPPED.
- CHECK VOLTAGE BETWEEN MAT SENSOR HARNESS TERMINALS USING A DIGITAL VOLTMETER (J-29125) OR EQUIVALENT.

4 VOLTS OR OVER

2
- CHECK RESISTANCE ACROSS MAT SENSOR TERMINALS. SHOULD BE LESS THAN 25,000 OHMS, SEE TABLE FOR APPROXIMATE TEMPERATURE TO RESISTANCE VALUES.

OK

CHECK FOR SIGNAL CKT BEING SHORTED TO VOLTAGE. IF NOT SHORTED TO VOLTAGE ,CODE 23 IS INTERMITTENT. IF ADDITIONAL CODES WERE STORED, SEE APPLICABLE CHART. IF NO CODES REFER TO ECM INTERMITTENT CODES OR PERFORMANCE IN SECTION "2".

NOT OK

REPLACE SENSOR

BELOW 4 VOLTS

- CHECK VOLTAGE BETWEEN HARNESS CONNECTOR SIGNAL CKT AND GROUND.

4 VOLTS OR OVER

FAULTY SENSOR GROUND CKT, FAULTY CONNECTION(S) OR FAULTY ECM.

BELOW 4 VOLTS

OPEN SIGNAL CKT, FAULTY CONNECTION OR FAULTY ECM.

MAT SENSOR
TEMPERATURE TO RESISTANCE VALUES
(APPROXIMATE)

°F	°C	OHMS
210	100	185
160	70	450
100	38	1,800
70	20	3,400
40	4	7,500
20	-7	13,500
0	-18	25,000
-40	-40	100,700

CLEAR CODES AND CONFIRM "CLOSED LOOP" OPERATION AND NO "SERVICE ENGINE SOON" LIGHT.

6-22-87
8S 4602-6E

"NON-SCAN" DIAGNOSTICS

CODE 24

VEHICLE SPEED SENSOR (VSS) CIRCUIT ALL ENGINES

- IDENTIFY THE TYPE OF VEHICLE SPEED SENSOR PRIOR TO USING THIS CHART TO PREVENT MISDIAGNOSIS..
- DISREGARD CODE 24 IF SET WHEN DRIVE WHEELS ARE NOT TURNING.
- SPEEDOMETER WORKING OK. IF NOT WORKING, REFER TO SECTION "8C" OF CHASSIS SERVICE MANUAL.
- LIFT DRIVE WHEELS.
- CRUISE CONTROL "OFF".
- BACK PROBE ECM CONNECTOR, VSS SIGNAL CKT 437 WITH A DIGITAL VOLTMETER TO GROUND.
- START AND IDLE ENGINE IN "DRIVE". VOLTAGE SHOULD BE VARYING FROM 1 TO 6 VOLTS.

LESS THAN 1 VOLT

CHECK:
- CKT 437 FOR SHORT TO GROUND.
- ECM FOR POOR CONNECTION.

5 TO 12 VOLTS & STEADY

CHECK:
- CKT 437 FOR OPEN

1 TO 6 VOLTS AND VARYING

CODE 24 INTERMITTENT IF NO OTHER CODES WERE STORED. CHECK PARK/NEUTRAL SWITCH DIAGNOSIS CHART IF VEHICLE EQUIPPED WITH AUTOMATIC TRANSMISSION. IF PARK/NEUTRAL SWITCH IS OK, REFER TO ECM INTERMITTENT CODES OR PERFORMANCE IN SECTION "2".

IF CKT 437 AND ECM CONNECTIONS CHECK OUT OK, CHECK FOR A FAULTY VEHICLE SPEED SENSOR OR BUFFER ASSEMBLY. SEE ELECTRICAL SECTION "8C" OF CHASSIS SERVICE MANUAL.

CLEAR CODES AND CONFIRM "CLOSED LOOP" OPERATION AND NO "SERVICE ENGINE SOON" LIGHT.

6-22-87
8S 4603-6E

"NON-SCAN" DIAGNOSTICS

CODE 25

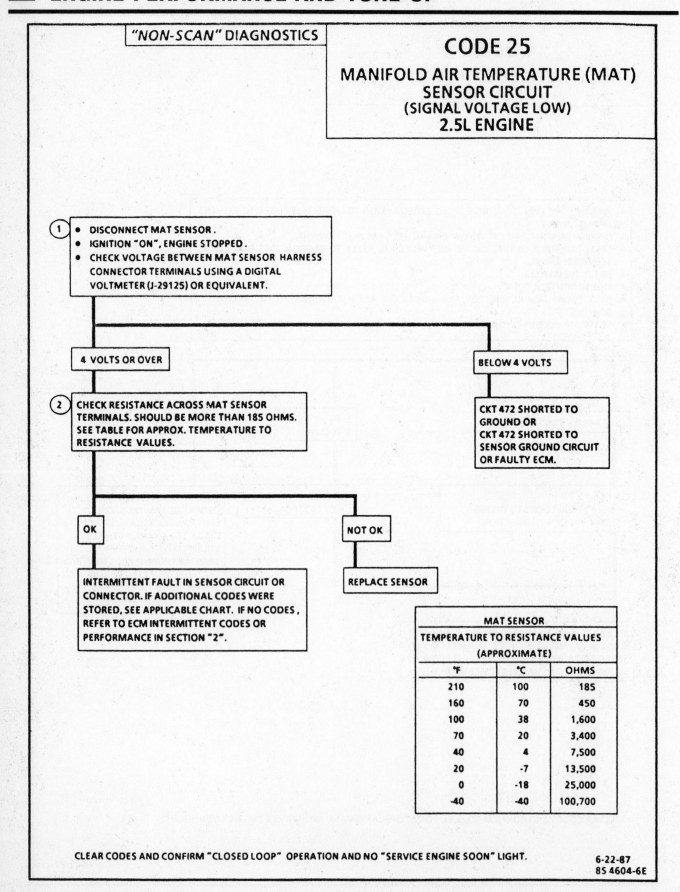

MANIFOLD AIR TEMPERATURE (MAT) SENSOR CIRCUIT
(SIGNAL VOLTAGE LOW)
2.5L ENGINE

(1)
- DISCONNECT MAT SENSOR.
- IGNITION "ON", ENGINE STOPPED.
- CHECK VOLTAGE BETWEEN MAT SENSOR HARNESS CONNECTOR TERMINALS USING A DIGITAL VOLTMETER (J-29125) OR EQUIVALENT.

4 VOLTS OR OVER

(2) CHECK RESISTANCE ACROSS MAT SENSOR TERMINALS. SHOULD BE MORE THAN 185 OHMS. SEE TABLE FOR APPROX. TEMPERATURE TO RESISTANCE VALUES.

OK

INTERMITTENT FAULT IN SENSOR CIRCUIT OR CONNECTOR. IF ADDITIONAL CODES WERE STORED, SEE APPLICABLE CHART. IF NO CODES, REFER TO ECM INTERMITTENT CODES OR PERFORMANCE IN SECTION "2".

NOT OK

REPLACE SENSOR

BELOW 4 VOLTS

CKT 472 SHORTED TO GROUND OR CKT 472 SHORTED TO SENSOR GROUND CIRCUIT OR FAULTY ECM.

MAT SENSOR
TEMPERATURE TO RESISTANCE VALUES (APPROXIMATE)

°F	°C	OHMS
210	100	185
160	70	450
100	38	1,600
70	20	3,400
40	4	7,500
20	-7	13,500
0	-18	25,000
-40	-40	100,700

CLEAR CODES AND CONFIRM "CLOSED LOOP" OPERATION AND NO "SERVICE ENGINE SOON" LIGHT.

6-22-87
8S 4604-6E

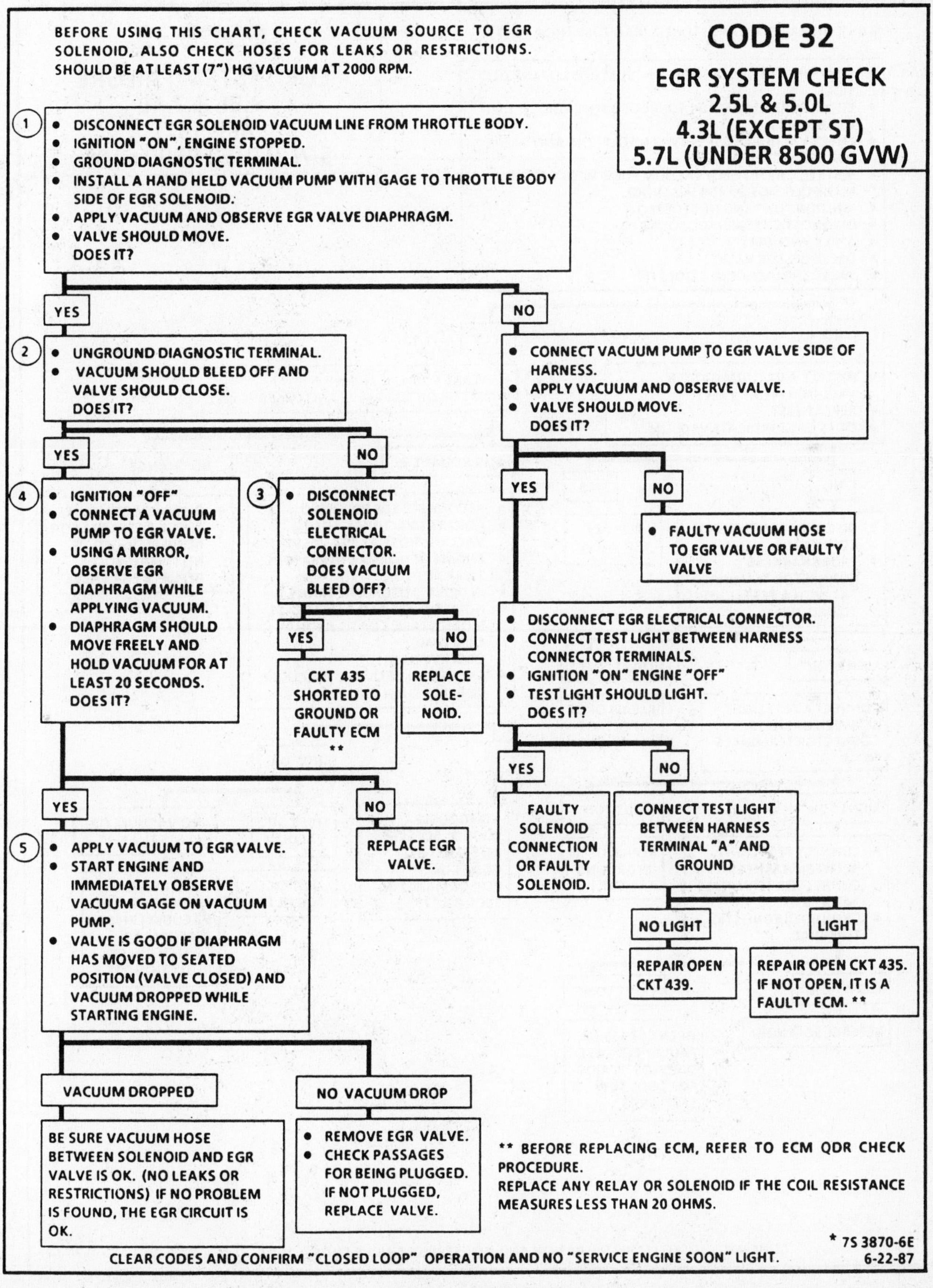
CODE 32
EGR SYSTEM CHECK
2.5L & 5.0L
4.3L (EXCEPT ST)
5.7L (UNDER 8500 GVW)
BEFORE USING THIS CHART, CHECK VACUUM SOURCE TO EGR SOLENOID, ALSO CHECK HOSES FOR LEAKS OR RESTRICTIONS. SHOULD BE AT LEAST (7") HG VACUUM AT 2000 RPM.
1
• DISCONNECT EGR SOLENOID VACUUM LINE FROM THROTTLE BODY.
• IGNITION "ON", ENGINE STOPPED.
• GROUND DIAGNOSTIC TERMINAL.
• INSTALL A HAND HELD VACUUM PUMP WITH GAGE TO THROTTLE BODY SIDE OF EGR SOLENOID.
• APPLY VACUUM AND OBSERVE EGR VALVE DIAPHRAGM.
• VALVE SHOULD MOVE. DOES IT?
YES
NO
2
• UNGROUND DIAGNOSTIC TERMINAL.
• VACUUM SHOULD BLEED OFF AND VALVE SHOULD CLOSE. DOES IT?
• CONNECT VACUUM PUMP TO EGR VALVE SIDE OF HARNESS.
• APPLY VACUUM AND OBSERVE VALVE.
• VALVE SHOULD MOVE. DOES IT?
YES
NO
YES
NO
4
• IGNITION "OFF"
• CONNECT A VACUUM PUMP TO EGR VALVE.
• USING A MIRROR, OBSERVE EGR DIAPHRAGM WHILE APPLYING VACUUM.
• DIAPHRAGM SHOULD MOVE FREELY AND HOLD VACUUM FOR AT LEAST 20 SECONDS. DOES IT?
3
• DISCONNECT SOLENOID ELECTRICAL CONNECTOR. DOES VACUUM BLEED OFF?
• FAULTY VACUUM HOSE TO EGR VALVE OR FAULTY VALVE
YES
NO
CKT 435 SHORTED TO GROUND OR FAULTY ECM **
REPLACE SOLE-NOID.
• DISCONNECT EGR ELECTRICAL CONNECTOR.
• CONNECT TEST LIGHT BETWEEN HARNESS CONNECTOR TERMINALS.
• IGNITION "ON" ENGINE "OFF"
• TEST LIGHT SHOULD LIGHT. DOES IT?
YES
NO
YES
NO
FAULTY SOLENOID CONNECTION OR FAULTY SOLENOID.
CONNECT TEST LIGHT BETWEEN HARNESS TERMINAL "A" AND GROUND
5
• APPLY VACUUM TO EGR VALVE.
• START ENGINE AND IMMEDIATELY OBSERVE VACUUM GAGE ON VACUUM PUMP.
• VALVE IS GOOD IF DIAPHRAGM HAS MOVED TO SEATED POSITION (VALVE CLOSED) AND VACUUM DROPPED WHILE STARTING ENGINE.
REPLACE EGR VALVE.
NO LIGHT
LIGHT
REPAIR OPEN CKT 439.
REPAIR OPEN CKT 435. IF NOT OPEN, IT IS A FAULTY ECM. **
VACUUM DROPPED
NO VACUUM DROP
BE SURE VACUUM HOSE BETWEEN SOLENOID AND EGR VALVE IS OK. (NO LEAKS OR RESTRICTIONS) IF NO PROBLEM IS FOUND, THE EGR CIRCUIT IS OK.
• REMOVE EGR VALVE.
• CHECK PASSAGES FOR BEING PLUGGED. IF NOT PLUGGED, REPLACE VALVE.
** BEFORE REPLACING ECM, REFER TO ECM QDR CHECK PROCEDURE.
REPLACE ANY RELAY OR SOLENOID IF THE COIL RESISTANCE MEASURES LESS THAN 20 OHMS.
* 7S 3870-6E
6-22-87
CLEAR CODES AND CONFIRM "CLOSED LOOP" OPERATION AND NO "SERVICE ENGINE SOON" LIGHT.

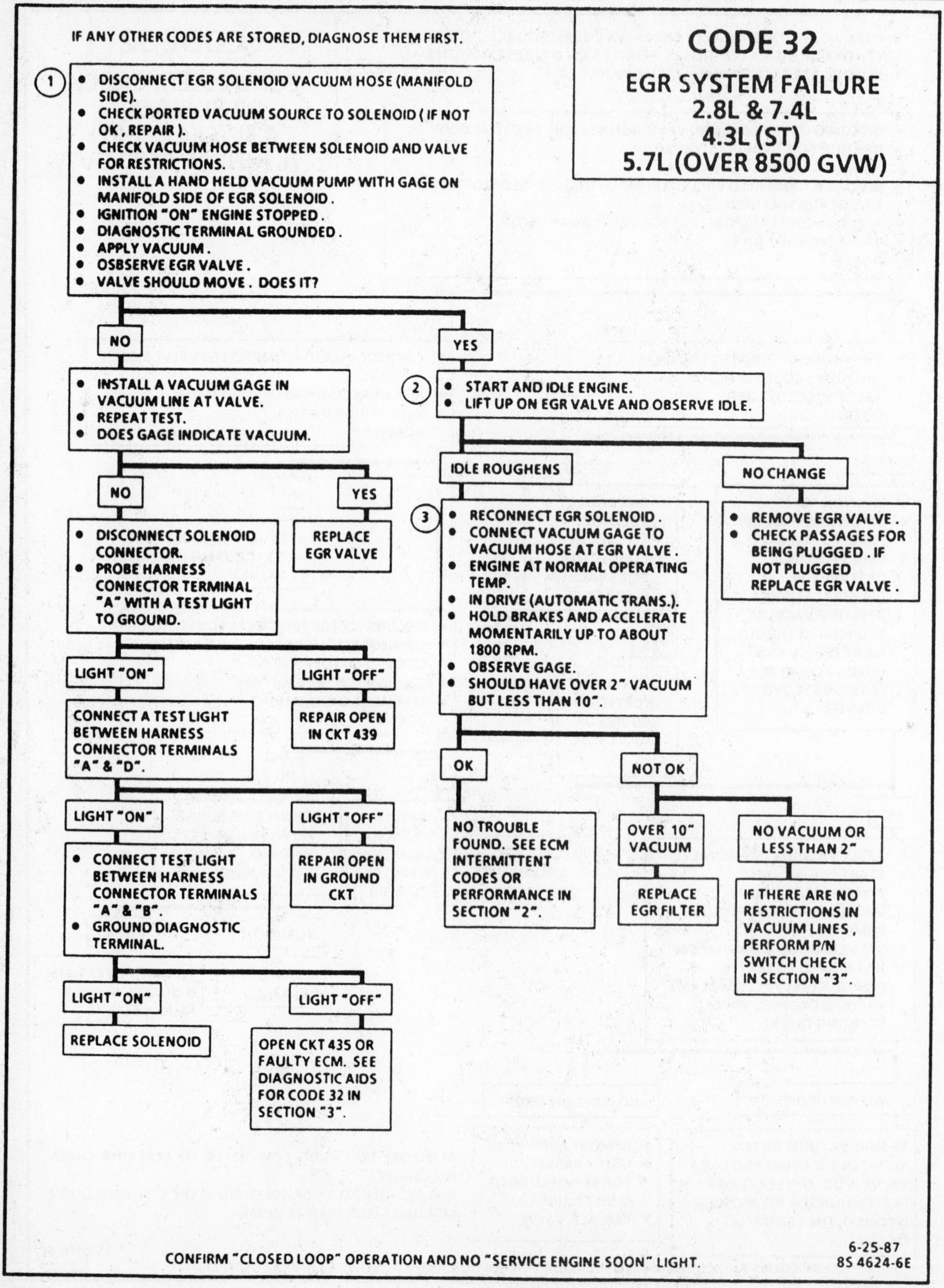
IF ANY OTHER CODES ARE STORED, DIAGNOSE THEM FIRST.
CODE 32
EGR SYSTEM FAILURE
2.8L & 7.4L
4.3L (ST)
5.7L (OVER 8500 GVW)
1
• DISCONNECT EGR SOLENOID VACUUM HOSE (MANIFOLD SIDE).
• CHECK PORTED VACUUM SOURCE TO SOLENOID (IF NOT OK, REPAIR).
• CHECK VACUUM HOSE BETWEEN SOLENOID AND VALVE FOR RESTRICTIONS.
• INSTALL A HAND HELD VACUUM PUMP WITH GAGE ON MANIFOLD SIDE OF EGR SOLENOID.
• IGNITION "ON" ENGINE STOPPED.
• DIAGNOSTIC TERMINAL GROUNDED.
• APPLY VACUUM.
• OSBSERVE EGR VALVE.
• VALVE SHOULD MOVE. DOES IT?
NO
YES
• INSTALL A VACUUM GAGE IN VACUUM LINE AT VALVE.
• REPEAT TEST.
• DOES GAGE INDICATE VACUUM.
2
• START AND IDLE ENGINE.
• LIFT UP ON EGR VALVE AND OBSERVE IDLE.
NO
YES
REPLACE EGR VALVE
IDLE ROUGHENS
NO CHANGE
• DISCONNECT SOLENOID CONNECTOR.
• PROBE HARNESS CONNECTOR TERMINAL "A" WITH A TEST LIGHT TO GROUND.
3
• RECONNECT EGR SOLENOID.
• CONNECT VACUUM GAGE TO VACUUM HOSE AT EGR VALVE.
• ENGINE AT NORMAL OPERATING TEMP.
• IN DRIVE (AUTOMATIC TRANS.).
• HOLD BRAKES AND ACCELERATE MOMENTARILY UP TO ABOUT 1800 RPM.
• OBSERVE GAGE.
• SHOULD HAVE OVER 2" VACUUM BUT LESS THAN 10".
• REMOVE EGR VALVE.
• CHECK PASSAGES FOR BEING PLUGGED. IF NOT PLUGGED REPLACE EGR VALVE.
LIGHT "ON"
LIGHT "OFF"
CONNECT A TEST LIGHT BETWEEN HARNESS CONNECTOR TERMINALS "A" & "D".
REPAIR OPEN IN CKT 439
OK
NOT OK
LIGHT "ON"
LIGHT "OFF"
• CONNECT TEST LIGHT BETWEEN HARNESS CONNECTOR TERMINALS "A" & "B".
• GROUND DIAGNOSTIC TERMINAL.
REPAIR OPEN IN GROUND CKT
NO TROUBLE FOUND. SEE ECM INTERMITTENT CODES OR PERFORMANCE IN SECTION "2".
OVER 10" VACUUM
REPLACE EGR FILTER
NO VACUUM OR LESS THAN 2"
IF THERE ARE NO RESTRICTIONS IN VACUUM LINES, PERFORM P/N SWITCH CHECK IN SECTION "3".
LIGHT "ON"
LIGHT "OFF"
REPLACE SOLENOID
OPEN CKT 435 OR FAULTY ECM. SEE DIAGNOSTIC AIDS FOR CODE 32 IN SECTION "3".
CONFIRM "CLOSED LOOP" OPERATION AND NO "SERVICE ENGINE SOON" LIGHT.
6-25-87
8S 4624-6E

CODE 33

MAP SENSOR (SIGNAL VOLTAGE HIGH) ALL ENGINES

"NON-SCAN" DIAGNOSTICS

IF ENGINE IDLE IS ROUGH, UNSTABLE, OR INCORRECT, CORRECT BEFORE USING CHART. SEE DRIVEABILITYSYMPTOMS IN SECTION "2".

(1)
- IGNITION "OFF", CLEAR CODES.
- DIAGNOSTIC TERMINAL NOT GROUNDED.
- START ENGINE AND RUN FOR 1 MINUTE OR UNTIL "SERVICE ENGINE SOON" LIGHT COMES ON.
- IGNITION "ON", ENGINE STOPPED. GROUND DIAGNOSTIC TERMINAL AND NOTE CODES.

CODE 33

(2)
- IGNITION "OFF",CLEAR CODES.
- DISCONNECT MAP SENSOR ELECTRICAL CONNECTOR.
- DIAGNOSTIC TERMINAL NOT GROUNDED.
- START ENGINE AND RUN FOR 1 MINUTE OR UNTIL "SERVICE ENGINE SOON" LIGHT COMES ON.
- IGNITION "ON" ENGINE STOPPED.
- GROUND DIAGNOSTIC TERMINAL AND NOTE CODE.

CODE 33

SIGNAL CKT SHORTED TO VOLTAGE OR FAULTY ECM.

CODE 34

CHECK FOR PLUGGED OR LEAKING SENSOR VACUUM HOSE.

IF VACUUM HOSE OK, OPEN IN SENSOR GROUND CIRCUIT OR FAULTY SENSOR.

NO CODE 33

PROBLEM IS INTERMITTENT. IF NO OTHER CODES WERE STORED, SEE ECM INTERMITTENT, CODES OR PERFORMANCE IN SECTION "2".

IGNITION "ON" ENGINE STOPPED VOLTAGES

ALTITUDE Meters	ALTITUDE Feet	VOLTAGE RANGE
Below 305	Below 1,000	3.8---5.5V
305--- 610	1,000--2,000	3.6---5.3V
610--- 914	2,000--3,000	3.5---5.1V
914--1219	3,000--4,000	3.3---5.0V
1219--1524	4,000--5,000	3.2---4.8V
1524--1829	5,000--6,000	3.0---4.6V
1829--2133	6,000--7,000	2.9---4.5V
2133--2438	7,000--8,000	2.8---4.3V
2438--2743	8,000--9,000	2.6---4.2V
2743--3048	9,000--10,000	2.5---4.0V

LOW ALTITUDE = HIGH PRESSURE = HIGH VOLTAGE

CLEAR CODES AND CONFIRM "CLOSED LOOP" OPERATION AND NO "SERVICE ENGINE SOON" LIGHT.

6-22-87
8S 4605-6E

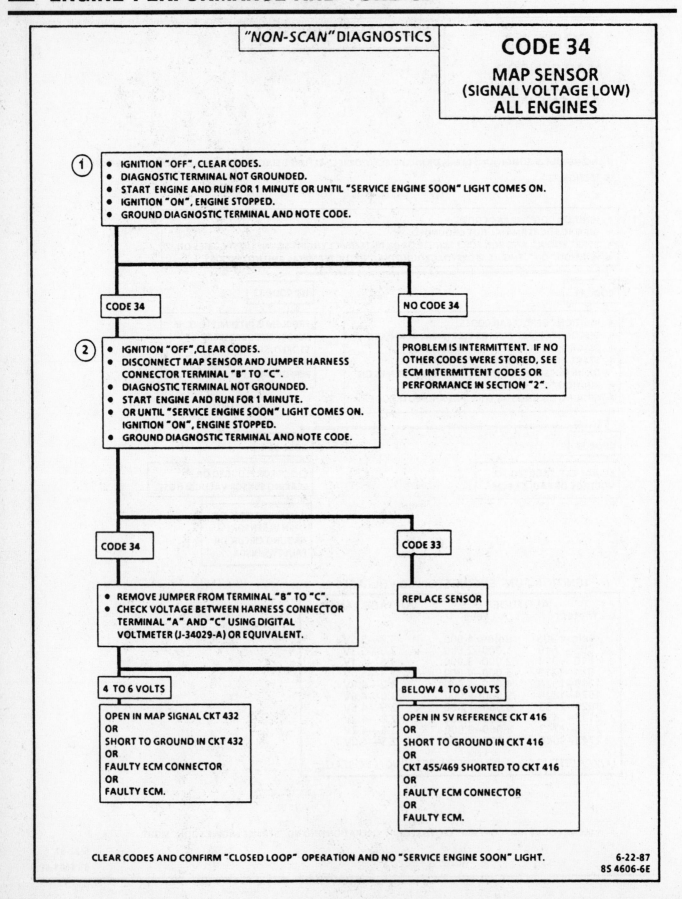

"NON-SCAN" DIAGNOSTICS

CODE 34

MAP SENSOR
(SIGNAL VOLTAGE LOW)
ALL ENGINES

(1)
- IGNITION "OFF", CLEAR CODES.
- DIAGNOSTIC TERMINAL NOT GROUNDED.
- START ENGINE AND RUN FOR 1 MINUTE OR UNTIL "SERVICE ENGINE SOON" LIGHT COMES ON.
- IGNITION "ON", ENGINE STOPPED.
- GROUND DIAGNOSTIC TERMINAL AND NOTE CODE.

CODE 34

(2)
- IGNITION "OFF", CLEAR CODES.
- DISCONNECT MAP SENSOR AND JUMPER HARNESS CONNECTOR TERMINAL "B" TO "C".
- DIAGNOSTIC TERMINAL NOT GROUNDED.
- START ENGINE AND RUN FOR 1 MINUTE.
- OR UNTIL "SERVICE ENGINE SOON" LIGHT COMES ON. IGNITION "ON", ENGINE STOPPED.
- GROUND DIAGNOSTIC TERMINAL AND NOTE CODE.

NO CODE 34

PROBLEM IS INTERMITTENT. IF NO OTHER CODES WERE STORED, SEE ECM INTERMITTENT CODES OR PERFORMANCE IN SECTION "2".

CODE 34

- REMOVE JUMPER FROM TERMINAL "B" TO "C".
- CHECK VOLTAGE BETWEEN HARNESS CONNECTOR TERMINAL "A" AND "C" USING DIGITAL VOLTMETER (J-34029-A) OR EQUIVALENT.

CODE 33

REPLACE SENSOR

4 TO 6 VOLTS

OPEN IN MAP SIGNAL CKT 432
OR
SHORT TO GROUND IN CKT 432
OR
FAULTY ECM CONNECTOR
OR
FAULTY ECM.

BELOW 4 TO 6 VOLTS

OPEN IN 5V REFERENCE CKT 416
OR
SHORT TO GROUND IN CKT 416
OR
CKT 455/469 SHORTED TO CKT 416
OR
FAULTY ECM CONNECTOR
OR
FAULTY ECM.

CLEAR CODES AND CONFIRM "CLOSED LOOP" OPERATION AND NO "SERVICE ENGINE SOON" LIGHT.

6-22-87
8S 4606-6E

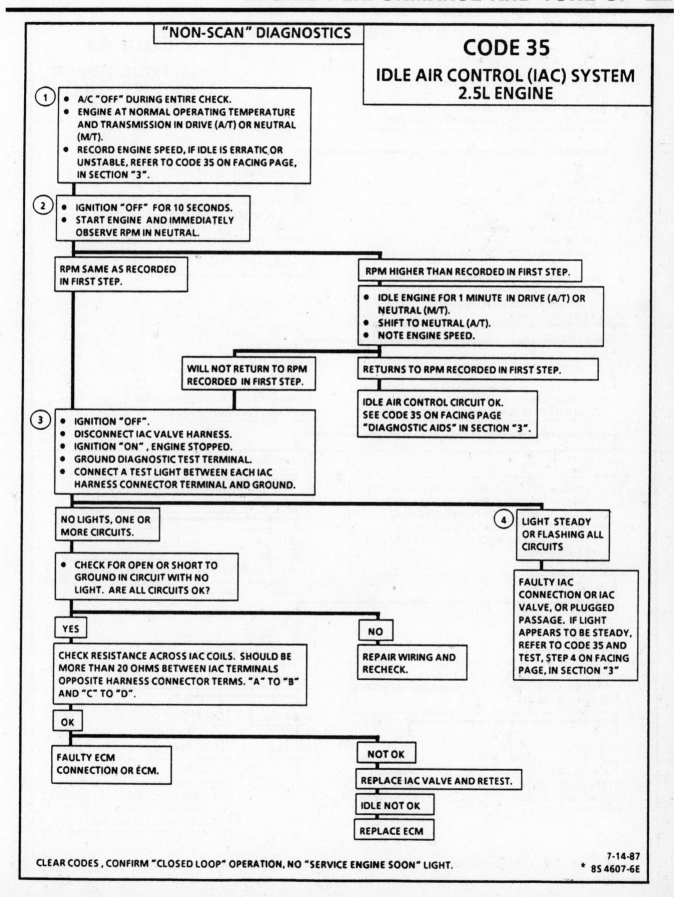

"NON-SCAN" DIAGNOSTICS

CODE 35

IDLE AIR CONTROL (IAC) SYSTEM 2.5L ENGINE

(1)
- A/C "OFF" DURING ENTIRE CHECK.
- ENGINE AT NORMAL OPERATING TEMPERATURE AND TRANSMISSION IN DRIVE (A/T) OR NEUTRAL (M/T).
- RECORD ENGINE SPEED, IF IDLE IS ERRATIC OR UNSTABLE, REFER TO CODE 35 ON FACING PAGE, IN SECTION "3".

(2)
- IGNITION "OFF" FOR 10 SECONDS.
- START ENGINE AND IMMEDIATELY OBSERVE RPM IN NEUTRAL.

RPM SAME AS RECORDED IN FIRST STEP.

RPM HIGHER THAN RECORDED IN FIRST STEP.

- IDLE ENGINE FOR 1 MINUTE IN DRIVE (A/T) OR NEUTRAL (M/T).
- SHIFT TO NEUTRAL (A/T).
- NOTE ENGINE SPEED.

WILL NOT RETURN TO RPM RECORDED IN FIRST STEP.

RETURNS TO RPM RECORDED IN FIRST STEP.

IDLE AIR CONTROL CIRCUIT OK. SEE CODE 35 ON FACING PAGE "DIAGNOSTIC AIDS" IN SECTION "3".

(3)
- IGNITION "OFF".
- DISCONNECT IAC VALVE HARNESS.
- IGNITION "ON", ENGINE STOPPED.
- GROUND DIAGNOSTIC TEST TERMINAL.
- CONNECT A TEST LIGHT BETWEEN EACH IAC HARNESS CONNECTOR TERMINAL AND GROUND.

NO LIGHTS, ONE OR MORE CIRCUITS.

- CHECK FOR OPEN OR SHORT TO GROUND IN CIRCUIT WITH NO LIGHT. ARE ALL CIRCUITS OK?

YES

CHECK RESISTANCE ACROSS IAC COILS. SHOULD BE MORE THAN 20 OHMS BETWEEN IAC TERMINALS OPPOSITE HARNESS CONNECTOR TERMS. "A" TO "B" AND "C" TO "D".

OK

FAULTY ECM CONNECTION OR ECM.

NOT OK

REPLACE IAC VALVE AND RETEST.

IDLE NOT OK

REPLACE ECM

NO

REPAIR WIRING AND RECHECK.

(4) LIGHT STEADY OR FLASHING ALL CIRCUITS

FAULTY IAC CONNECTION OR IAC VALVE, OR PLUGGED PASSAGE. IF LIGHT APPEARS TO BE STEADY, REFER TO CODE 35 AND TEST, STEP 4 ON FACING PAGE, IN SECTION "3"

CLEAR CODES, CONFIRM "CLOSED LOOP" OPERATION, NO "SERVICE ENGINE SOON" LIGHT.

7-14-87
* 8S 4607-6E

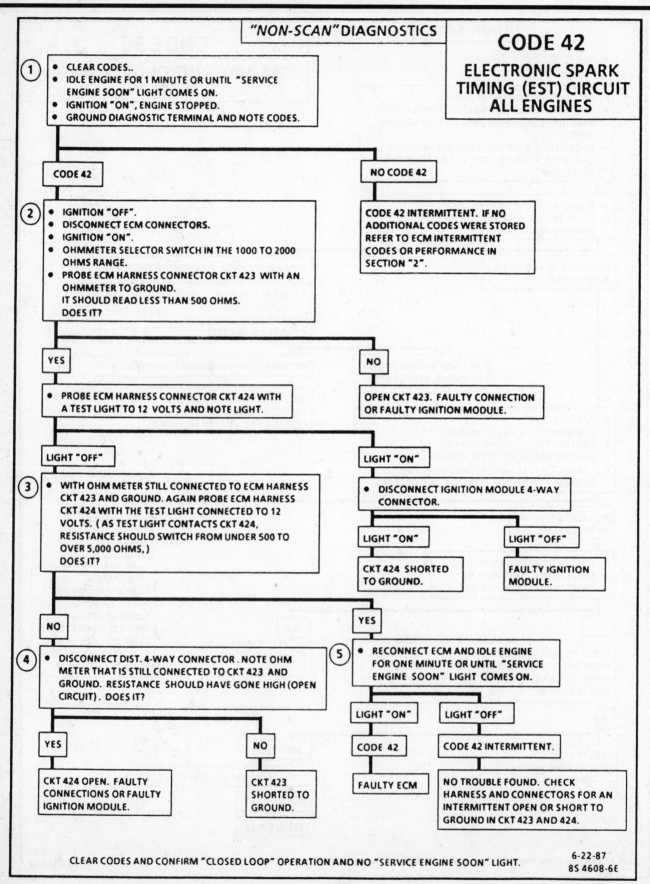

"NON-SCAN" DIAGNOSTICS

CODE 42

ELECTRONIC SPARK TIMING (EST) CIRCUIT ALL ENGINES

(1)
- CLEAR CODES..
- IDLE ENGINE FOR 1 MINUTE OR UNTIL "SERVICE ENGINE SOON" LIGHT COMES ON.
- IGNITION "ON", ENGINE STOPPED.
- GROUND DIAGNOSTIC TERMINAL AND NOTE CODES.

CODE 42

NO CODE 42

CODE 42 INTERMITTENT. IF NO ADDITIONAL CODES WERE STORED REFER TO ECM INTERMITTENT CODES OR PERFORMANCE IN SECTION "2".

(2)
- IGNITION "OFF".
- DISCONNECT ECM CONNECTORS.
- IGNITION "ON".
- OHMMETER SELECTOR SWITCH IN THE 1000 TO 2000 OHMS RANGE.
- PROBE ECM HARNESS CONNECTOR CKT 423 WITH AN OHMMETER TO GROUND.
  IT SHOULD READ LESS THAN 500 OHMS.
  DOES IT?

YES

- PROBE ECM HARNESS CONNECTOR CKT 424 WITH A TEST LIGHT TO 12 VOLTS AND NOTE LIGHT.

NO

OPEN CKT 423. FAULTY CONNECTION OR FAULTY IGNITION MODULE.

LIGHT "OFF"

(3)
- WITH OHM METER STILL CONNECTED TO ECM HARNESS CKT 423 AND GROUND. AGAIN PROBE ECM HARNESS CKT 424 WITH THE TEST LIGHT CONNECTED TO 12 VOLTS. (AS TEST LIGHT CONTACTS CKT 424, RESISTANCE SHOULD SWITCH FROM UNDER 500 TO OVER 5,000 OHMS,)
  DOES IT?

LIGHT "ON"

- DISCONNECT IGNITION MODULE 4-WAY CONNECTOR.

LIGHT "ON"

CKT 424 SHORTED TO GROUND.

LIGHT "OFF"

FAULTY IGNITION MODULE.

NO

(4)
- DISCONNECT DIST. 4-WAY CONNECTOR . NOTE OHM METER THAT IS STILL CONNECTED TO CKT 423 AND GROUND. RESISTANCE SHOULD HAVE GONE HIGH (OPEN CIRCUIT) . DOES IT?

YES

CKT 424 OPEN. FAULTY CONNECTIONS OR FAULTY IGNITION MODULE.

NO

CKT 423 SHORTED TO GROUND.

YES

(5)
- RECONNECT ECM AND IDLE ENGINE FOR ONE MINUTE OR UNTIL "SERVICE ENGINE SOON" LIGHT COMES ON.

LIGHT "ON"

CODE 42

FAULTY ECM

LIGHT "OFF"

CODE 42 INTERMITTENT.

NO TROUBLE FOUND. CHECK HARNESS AND CONNECTORS FOR AN INTERMITTENT OPEN OR SHORT TO GROUND IN CKT 423 AND 424.

CLEAR CODES AND CONFIRM "CLOSED LOOP" OPERATION AND NO "SERVICE ENGINE SOON" LIGHT.

6-22-87
8S 4608-6E

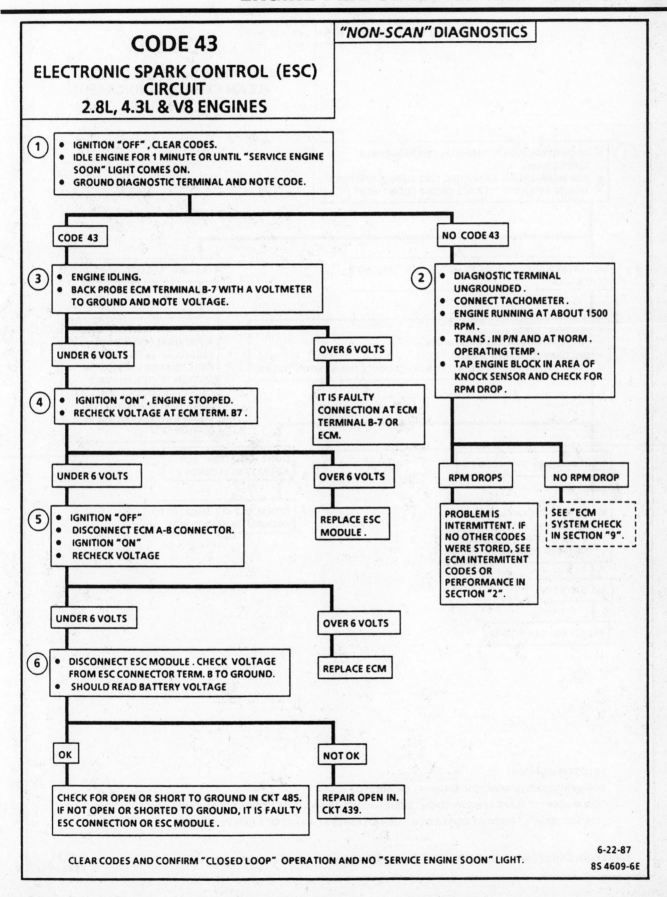

"NON-SCAN" DIAGNOSTICS

CODE 43

ELECTRONIC SPARK CONTROL (ESC) CIRCUIT 2.8L, 4.3L & V8 ENGINES

(1)
- IGNITION "OFF", CLEAR CODES.
- IDLE ENGINE FOR 1 MINUTE OR UNTIL "SERVICE ENGINE SOON" LIGHT COMES ON.
- GROUND DIAGNOSTIC TERMINAL AND NOTE CODE.

CODE 43

(3)
- ENGINE IDLING.
- BACK PROBE ECM TERMINAL B-7 WITH A VOLTMETER TO GROUND AND NOTE VOLTAGE.

UNDER 6 VOLTS

(4)
- IGNITION "ON", ENGINE STOPPED.
- RECHECK VOLTAGE AT ECM TERM. B7.

UNDER 6 VOLTS

(5)
- IGNITION "OFF"
- DISCONNECT ECM A-B CONNECTOR.
- IGNITION "ON"
- RECHECK VOLTAGE

UNDER 6 VOLTS

(6)
- DISCONNECT ESC MODULE. CHECK VOLTAGE FROM ESC CONNECTOR TERM. B TO GROUND.
- SHOULD READ BATTERY VOLTAGE

OK

CHECK FOR OPEN OR SHORT TO GROUND IN CKT 485. IF NOT OPEN OR SHORTED TO GROUND, IT IS FAULTY ESC CONNECTION OR ESC MODULE.

NOT OK

REPAIR OPEN IN. CKT 439.

OVER 6 VOLTS (step 5)

REPLACE ECM

OVER 6 VOLTS (step 4)

REPLACE ESC MODULE.

OVER 6 VOLTS (step 3)

IT IS FAULTY CONNECTION AT ECM TERMINAL B-7 OR ECM.

NO CODE 43

(2)
- DIAGNOSTIC TERMINAL UNGROUNDED.
- CONNECT TACHOMETER.
- ENGINE RUNNING AT ABOUT 1500 RPM.
- TRANS. IN P/N AND AT NORM. OPERATING TEMP.
- TAP ENGINE BLOCK IN AREA OF KNOCK SENSOR AND CHECK FOR RPM DROP.

RPM DROPS

PROBLEM IS INTERMITTENT. IF NO OTHER CODES WERE STORED, SEE ECM INTERMITENT CODES OR PERFORMANCE IN SECTION "2".

NO RPM DROP

SEE "ECM SYSTEM CHECK IN SECTION "9".

CLEAR CODES AND CONFIRM "CLOSED LOOP" OPERATION AND NO "SERVICE ENGINE SOON" LIGHT.

6-22-87
8S 4609-6E

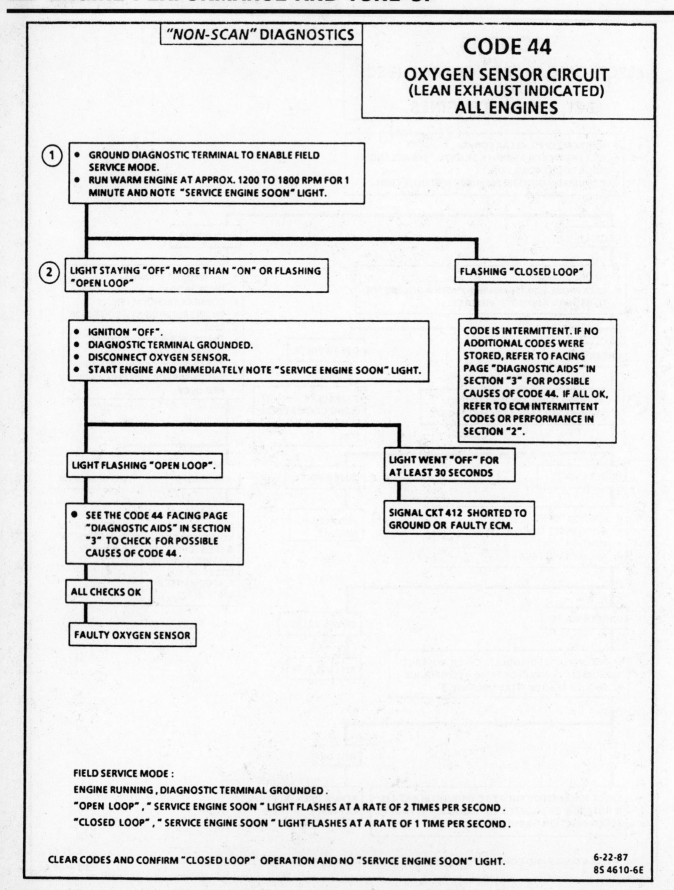

"NON-SCAN" DIAGNOSTICS

CODE 44

OXYGEN SENSOR CIRCUIT
(LEAN EXHAUST INDICATED)
ALL ENGINES

(1)
- GROUND DIAGNOSTIC TERMINAL TO ENABLE FIELD SERVICE MODE.
- RUN WARM ENGINE AT APPROX. 1200 TO 1800 RPM FOR 1 MINUTE AND NOTE "SERVICE ENGINE SOON" LIGHT.

(2) LIGHT STAYING "OFF" MORE THAN "ON" OR FLASHING "OPEN LOOP"

- IGNITION "OFF".
- DIAGNOSTIC TERMINAL GROUNDED.
- DISCONNECT OXYGEN SENSOR.
- START ENGINE AND IMMEDIATELY NOTE "SERVICE ENGINE SOON" LIGHT.

LIGHT FLASHING "OPEN LOOP".

- SEE THE CODE 44 FACING PAGE "DIAGNOSTIC AIDS" IN SECTION "3" TO CHECK FOR POSSIBLE CAUSES OF CODE 44.

ALL CHECKS OK

FAULTY OXYGEN SENSOR

LIGHT WENT "OFF" FOR AT LEAST 30 SECONDS

SIGNAL CKT 412 SHORTED TO GROUND OR FAULTY ECM.

FLASHING "CLOSED LOOP"

CODE IS INTERMITTENT. IF NO ADDITIONAL CODES WERE STORED, REFER TO FACING PAGE "DIAGNOSTIC AIDS" IN SECTION "3" FOR POSSIBLE CAUSES OF CODE 44. IF ALL OK, REFER TO ECM INTERMITTENT CODES OR PERFORMANCE IN SECTION "2".

FIELD SERVICE MODE:

ENGINE RUNNING, DIAGNOSTIC TERMINAL GROUNDED.

"OPEN LOOP", "SERVICE ENGINE SOON" LIGHT FLASHES AT A RATE OF 2 TIMES PER SECOND.

"CLOSED LOOP", "SERVICE ENGINE SOON" LIGHT FLASHES AT A RATE OF 1 TIME PER SECOND.

CLEAR CODES AND CONFIRM "CLOSED LOOP" OPERATION AND NO "SERVICE ENGINE SOON" LIGHT.

6-22-87
8S 4610-6E

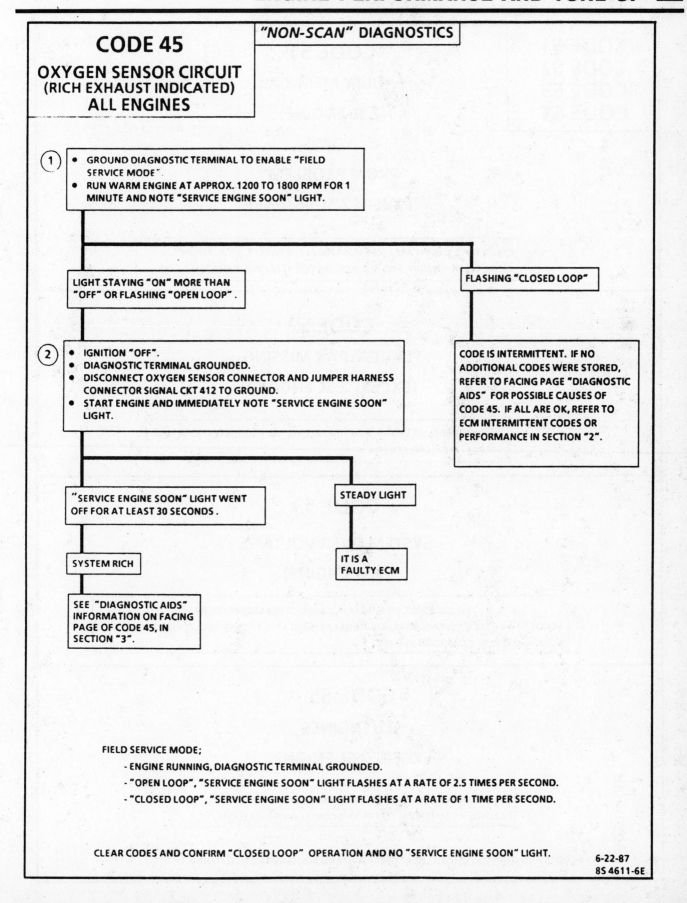

"NON-SCAN" DIAGNOSTICS

CODE 45

OXYGEN SENSOR CIRCUIT (RICH EXHAUST INDICATED) ALL ENGINES

(1)
- GROUND DIAGNOSTIC TERMINAL TO ENABLE "FIELD SERVICE MODE".
- RUN WARM ENGINE AT APPROX. 1200 TO 1800 RPM FOR 1 MINUTE AND NOTE "SERVICE ENGINE SOON" LIGHT.

LIGHT STAYING "ON" MORE THAN "OFF" OR FLASHING "OPEN LOOP".

FLASHING "CLOSED LOOP"

CODE IS INTERMITTENT. IF NO ADDITIONAL CODES WERE STORED, REFER TO FACING PAGE "DIAGNOSTIC AIDS" FOR POSSIBLE CAUSES OF CODE 45. IF ALL ARE OK, REFER TO ECM INTERMITTENT CODES OR PERFORMANCE IN SECTION "2".

(2)
- IGNITION "OFF".
- DIAGNOSTIC TERMINAL GROUNDED.
- DISCONNECT OXYGEN SENSOR CONNECTOR AND JUMPER HARNESS CONNECTOR SIGNAL CKT 412 TO GROUND.
- START ENGINE AND IMMEDIATELY NOTE "SERVICE ENGINE SOON" LIGHT.

"SERVICE ENGINE SOON" LIGHT WENT OFF FOR AT LEAST 30 SECONDS.

SYSTEM RICH

SEE "DIAGNOSTIC AIDS" INFORMATION ON FACING PAGE OF CODE 45, IN SECTION "3".

STEADY LIGHT

IT IS A FAULTY ECM

FIELD SERVICE MODE;

- ENGINE RUNNING, DIAGNOSTIC TERMINAL GROUNDED.
- "OPEN LOOP", "SERVICE ENGINE SOON" LIGHT FLASHES AT A RATE OF 2.5 TIMES PER SECOND.
- "CLOSED LOOP", "SERVICE ENGINE SOON" LIGHT FLASHES AT A RATE OF 1 TIME PER SECOND.

CLEAR CODES AND CONFIRM "CLOSED LOOP" OPERATION AND NO "SERVICE ENGINE SOON" LIGHT.

6-22-87
8S 4611-6E

CODE 51
CODE 52
CODE 53
CODE 55

CODE 51

FAULTY MEM-CAL

(2.5L ENGINE)

OR

PROM PROBLEM

(EXCEPT 2.5L ENGINE)

CHECK THAT ALL PINS ARE FULLY INSERTED IN THE SOCKET. IF OK, REPLACE PROM, CLEAR MEMORY, AND RECHECK. IF CODE 51 REAPPEARS, REPLACE ECM.

CODE 52

FUEL CALPAK MISSING

(EXCEPT 2.5L ENGINE)

CHECK FOR MISSING CALPAK AND THAT ALL PIN ARE FULLY INSERTED IN THE SOCKET - IF OK, REPLACE ECM.

CODE 53

SYSTEM OVER VOLTAGE

(2.5L ENGINE)

THIS CODE INDICATES THERE IS A BASIC GENERATOR PROBLEM.

- CODE 53 WILL SET IF VOLTAGE AT ECM TERMINAL B1 IS GREATER THAN 17.1 VOLTS FOR 2 SECONDS.
- CHECK AND REPAIR CHARGING SYSTEM.

CODE 55

ALL ENGINES

EXCEPT 2.5L ENGINE

BE SURE ECM GROUNDS ARE OK AND THAT MEM-CAL IS PROPERLY LATCHED. IF OK REPLACE ELECTRONIC CONTROL MODULE (ECM).

CLEAR CODES AND CONFIRM "CLOSED LOOP" OPERATION AND NO "SERVICE ENGINE SOON" LIGHT.

7S 3784
5-12-87

3 Engine and Engine Overhaul

QUICK REFERENCE INDEX

GENERAL INDEX

ENGINE ELECTRICAL

The engine electrical system can be broken down into three separate and distinct systems—(1) the ignition system; (2) the charging system; (3) the starting system.

Ignition System

Two different distributors are used on the S/10-S15 trucks. The first is an HEI distributor that uses mechanical and vacuum advance units to adjust the ignition spark advance curve while the engine is running. This distributor is used on the 1.9L and 2.0L engines.

The second distributor is equipped with Electronic Spark Timing. The ignition spark advance curve is controlled by the Electronic Control Unit (ECU), and no external adjustments can be made. This distributor is used on the 2.5L 4-cylinder and all 6-cylinder engines.

The Charging System

The charging system provides electrical power for operation of the vehicle's ignition, starting system and all of the electrical accessories. The battery serves as an electrical surge or storage tank, storing (in chemical form) the energy originally produced by the alternator. The system also provides a means of regulating the alternator output to protect the battery from being overcharged and the accessories from being destroyed.

The storage battery is a chemical device incorporating parallel lead plates in a tank containing a sulfuric acid-water solution. Adjacent plates are slightly dissimilar and the chemical reaction of the two dissimilar plates produces electrical energy when the battery is connected to a load such as the starter motor. The chemical reaction is reversible, so that when the alternator is producing a voltage (electrical pressure) greater than that produced by the battery, electricity is forced into the battery and it is returned to it's fully charged state.

Alternators are used on the modern vehicle for they are lighter, more efficient, rotate at higher speeds and have fewer brush problems. In an alternator, the field rotates while all of the current produced passes only through the stator windings. The brushes bear against the continuous slip rings; this causes the current produced to periodically reverse the direction of it's flow. Diodes (electrical one-way switches) block the flow of current from traveling in the wrong direction. A series of diodes are wired together to permit the alternating flow of the stator to be converted to a pulsating but unidirectional flow at the alternator output. The alternator's field is wired in series with the voltage regulator.

Battery and Starting System

The battery is the first link in the chain of mechanisms which work together to provide cranking of the engine. In most modern vehicles, the battery is a lead-acid electrochemical device consisting of six 2 volt (2V) subsections connected in series so the unit is capable of producing approximately 12V of electrical pressure. Each subsection (cell) consists of a series of positive and negative plates held a short distance apart in a solution of sulfuric acid and water. The two types of plates are of dissimilar metals. A chemical reaction takes place which produces current flow from the battery, when it's positive and negative terminals

Troubleshooting Basic Charging System Problems

Problem	Cause	Solution
Noisy alternator	• Loose mountings • Loose drive pulley • Worn bearings • Brush noise • Internal circuits shorted (High pitched whine)	• Tighten mounting bolts • Tighten pulley • Replace alternator • Replace alternator • Replace alternator
Squeal when starting engine or accelerating	• Glazed or loose belt	• Replace or adjust belt
Indicator light remains on or ammeter indicates discharge (engine running)	• Broken fan belt • Broken or disconnected wires • Internal alternator problems • Defective voltage regulator	• Install belt • Repair or connect wiring • Replace alternator • Replace voltage regulator
Car light bulbs continually burn out—battery needs water continually	• Alternator/regulator overcharging	• Replace voltage regulator/alternator
Car lights flare on acceleration	• Battery low • Internal alternator/regulator problems	• Charge or replace battery • Replace alternator/regulator
Low voltage output (alternator light flickers continually or ammeter needle wanders)	• Loose or worn belt • Dirty or corroded connections • Internal alternator/regulator problems	• Replace or adjust belt • Clean or replace connections • Replace alternator or regulator

are connected to an electrical appliance such as a lamp or motor. The continued transfer of electrons would eventually convert the sulfuric acid in the electrolyte to water and make the two plates identical in chemical composition. As electrical energy is removed from the battery, it's voltage output tends to drop. Thus, measuring battery voltage and battery electrolyte composition are two ways of checking the ability of the unit to supply power. During the starting of the engine, electrical energy is removed from the battery. However, if the charging circuit is in good condition and the operating conditions are normal, the power removed from the battery will be replaced by the alternator which will force electrons back into the battery, reversing the normal flow and restoring the battery to it's original chemical state.

The battery and starting motor are linked by very heavy electrical cables designed to minimize resistance to the flow of current. Generally, the major power supply cable that leaves the battery goes directly to the starter, while other electrical system needs are supplied by a smaller cable. During the starter operation, power flows from the battery to the starter, then is grounded through the vehicle's frame and the battery's negative ground strap.

The starting motor is a specially designed, direct current electric motor capable of producing a very great amount of power

Troubleshooting Basic Starting System Problems

Problem	Cause	Solution
Starter motor rotates engine slowly	• Battery charge low or battery defective	• Charge or replace battery
	• Defective circuit between battery and starter motor	• Clean and tighten, or replace cables
	• Low load current	• Bench-test starter motor. Inspect for worn brushes and weak brush springs.
	• High load current	• Bench-test starter motor. Check engine for friction, drag or coolant in cylinders. Check ring gear-to-pinion gear clearance.
Starter motor will not rotate engine	• Battery charge low or battery defective	• Charge or replace battery
	• Faulty solenoid	• Check solenoid ground. Repair or replace as necessary.
	• Damage drive pinion gear or ring gear	• Replace damaged gear(s)
	• Starter motor engagement weak	• Bench-test starter motor
	• Starter motor rotates slowly with high load current	• Inspect drive yoke pull-down and point gap, check for worn end bushings, check ring gear clearance
	• Engine seized	• Repair engine
Starter motor drive will not engage (solenoid known to be good)	• Defective contact point assembly	• Repair or replace contact point assembly
	• Inadequate contact point assembly ground	• Repair connection at ground screw
	• Defective hold-in coil	• Replace field winding assembly
Starter motor drive will not disengage	• Starter motor loose on flywheel housing	• Tighten mounting bolts
	• Worn drive end busing	• Replace bushing
	• Damaged ring gear teeth	• Replace ring gear or driveplate
	• Drive yoke return spring broken or missing	• Replace spring
Starter motor drive disengages prematurely	• Weak drive assembly thrust spring	• Replace drive mechanism
	• Hold-in coil defective	• Replace field winding assembly
Low load current	• Worn brushes	• Replace brushes
	• Weak brush springs	• Replace springs

for it's size. One thing that allows the motor to produce a great deal of power is it's tremendous rotating speed. It drives the engine through a tiny pinion gear (attached to the starter's armature), which drives the very large flywheel ring gear at a greatly reduced speed. Another factor allowing it to produce so much power is that only intermittent operation is required of it. Thus, little allowance for air circulation is required and the windings can be built into a very small space.

The starter solenoid is a magnetic device which employs the small current supplied by the starting switch circuit of the ignition switch. This magnetic action moves a plunger, which mechanically engages the starter and electrically closes the heavy switch which connects it to the battery. The starting switch circuit consists of the starting switch (contained within the ignition switch), a transmission neutral safety switch or clutch pedal switch and wiring necessary to connect these with the starter solenoid or relay.

The pinion (small gear) is mounted to a one-way drive clutch. This clutch is splined to the starter armature shaft. When the ignition switch is moved to the Start position, the solenoid plunger slides the pinion toward the flywheel ring rear via a collar and spring. If the teeth on the pinion and flywheel match properly, the pinion will engage the flywheel immediately. If the gear teeth butt one another, the spring will be compressed and will force the gears to mesh as soon as the starter turns far enough to allow them to do so. As the solenoid plunger reaches the end of its travel, it closes the contacts that connect the battery to the starter, then the engine is cranked.

As soon as the engine starts, the flywheel ring gear begins turning fast enough to drive the pinion at an extremely high rate of speed. At this point, the one-way clutch allows the pinion to spin faster than the starter shaft so that the starter will not operate at excessive speed(s). When the ignition switch is released from the starter position, the solenoid is de-energized, the spring (contained within the solenoid assembly) pulls the pinion out of mesh and interrupts the current flow to the starter.

Ignition Coil

The location of the ignition coil is as follows.

- 1.9L and 2.0L engines – the coil is attached to a bracket located on the inner fender at the right hand side of the engine compartment. These engines use a Non-EST distributor
- 2.5L engine – the coil is attached to the cylinder head at the right rear-side of the engine. This engine uses an EST distributor.
- 2.8L engine – the coil is attached to a valve cover bracket at the right rear-side of the engine. This engine uses an EST distributor.
- 4.3L engine – the coil is attached to a bracket attached to the intake manifold at the right rear of the engine. This engine uses an EST distributor.

TESTING

EST Distributor

NOTE: Refer to the illustration "Testing the EST Ignition Coil" for this procedure.

1. Disconnect the distributor lead and wiring from the coil.
2. Using the HIGH scale, connect an ohmmeter to the coil as shown in Step 1 of the illustration. The reading should be infinite. If not, replace the coil.
3. Using the LOW scale, connect the ohmmeter as shown in Step of the illustration.
4. The reading should be very low or zero. If not, replace the coil.
5. Using the HIGH scale, connect the ohmmeter as shown in Step 3 of the illustration.
6. The ohmmeter should **NOT** read infinite. If it does, replace the coil.
7. Reconnect the distributor lead and wiring to the coil.

Non-EST Distributor

NOTE: Refer to the illustration "Testing the Non-EST Ignition Coil" for this procedure.

1. Check the outer face of the ignition coil for cracking, rust or damage.
2. Check the resistance of the primary and secondary coils as shown in the illustration. If the resistance is not within specification, replace the coil.
   - Primary coil resistance: 0.090–1.40 ohms
   - ›Secondary coil resistance: 7.3–11.1 kilo-ohms
   - Insulation resistance: 10 megohms or more
3. When testing the insulation resistance, if the ohmmeter needle deflects even slightly, the ignition coil is poorly insulated and should be replaced.

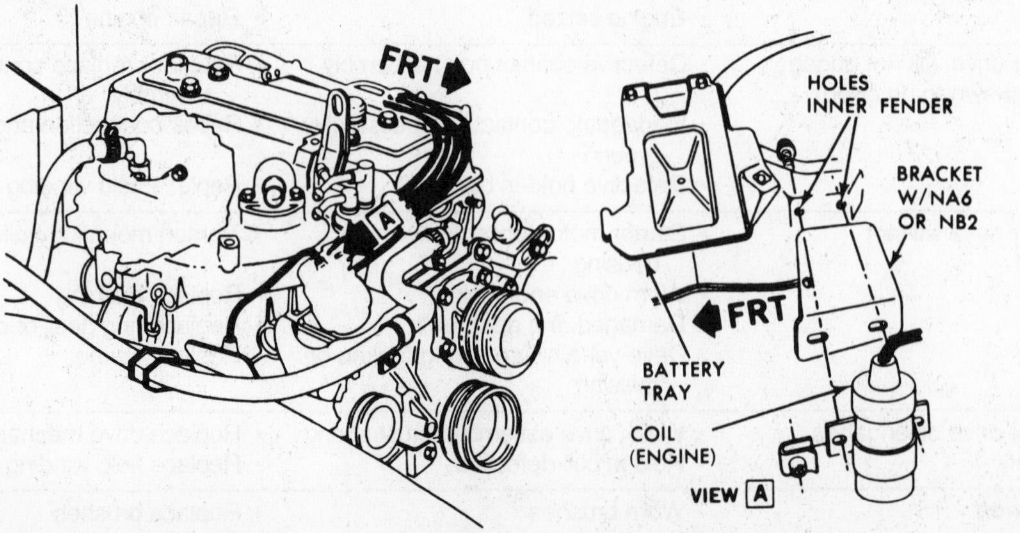
FRT
A
HOLES
INNER FENDER
BRACKET
W/NA6
OR NB2
FRT
BATTERY
TRAY
COIL
(ENGINE)
VIEW A

Ignition coil and distributor – 1.9L and 2.0L engine

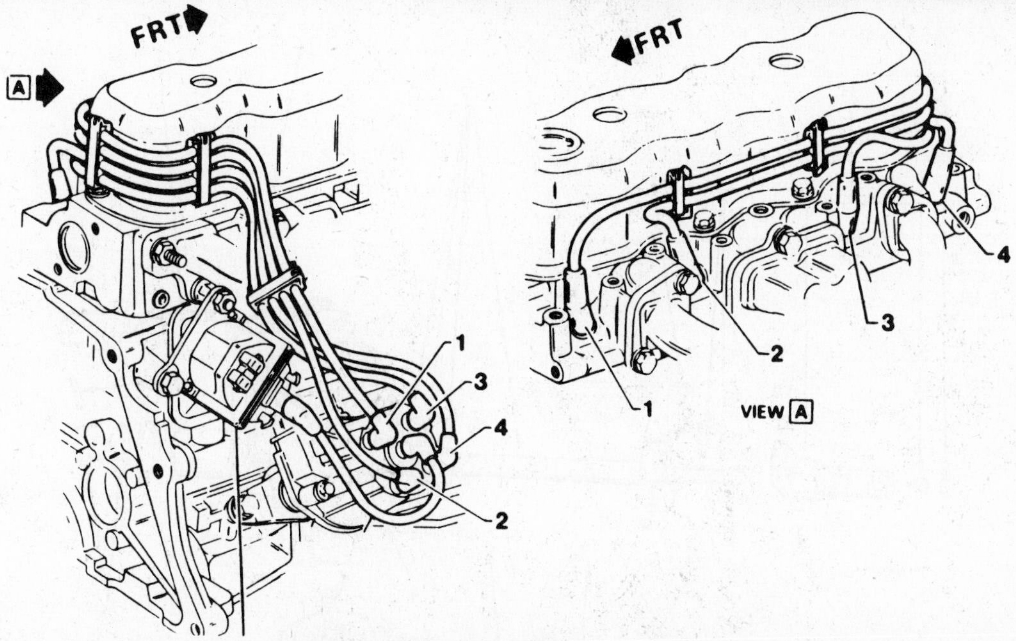
FRT
A
1
3
4
2
FRT
4
3
2
1
VIEW A

Ignition coil and distributor – 2.5L engine

REMOVAL AND INSTALLATION

1. Disconnect the negative battery terminal from the battery.
2. From the ignition coil, disconnect the primary electrical wiring connector and the coil-to-distributor high tension cable.
3. Remove the coil attaching bolts.
4. If necessary, test or replace the ignition coil.
5. Installation is the reverse of removal.

Ignition Module

REMOVAL AND INSTALLATION

Non-EST Distributor

1. Remove the distributor from the engine and place it on a work bench.
2. Remove the distributor cap, the rotor, the packing ring and the cover.
3. Remove the electrical harness-to-distributor screw, then disconnect the electrical harness connectors from the ignition module.
4. Using two medium pry bars, pry the pole piece from the distributor shaft, then remove the roll pin.

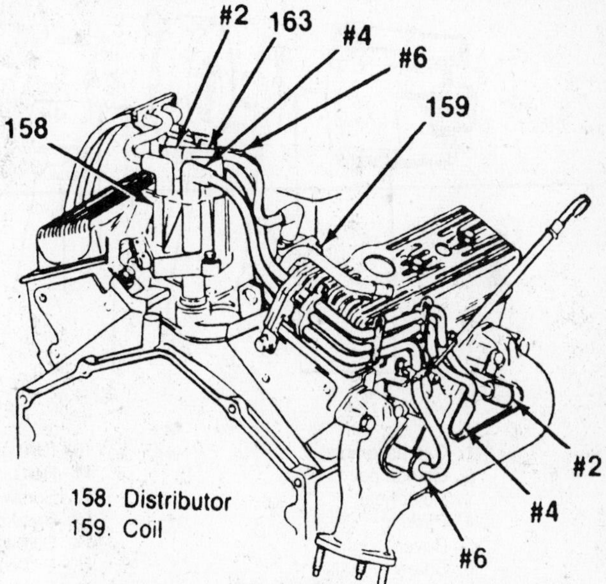
#2
163
#4
#6
159
158
#2
#4
#6
158. Distributor
159. Coil

Ignition coil and distributor – 4.3L engine

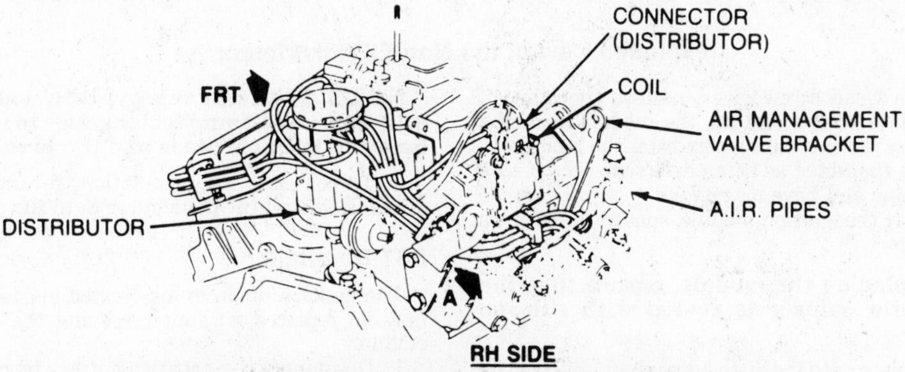
CONNECTOR
(DISTRIBUTOR)
FRT
COIL
AIR MANAGEMENT
VALVE BRACKET
A.I.R. PIPES
DISTRIBUTOR
A
RH SIDE

Ignition coil and distributor – 2.8L engine

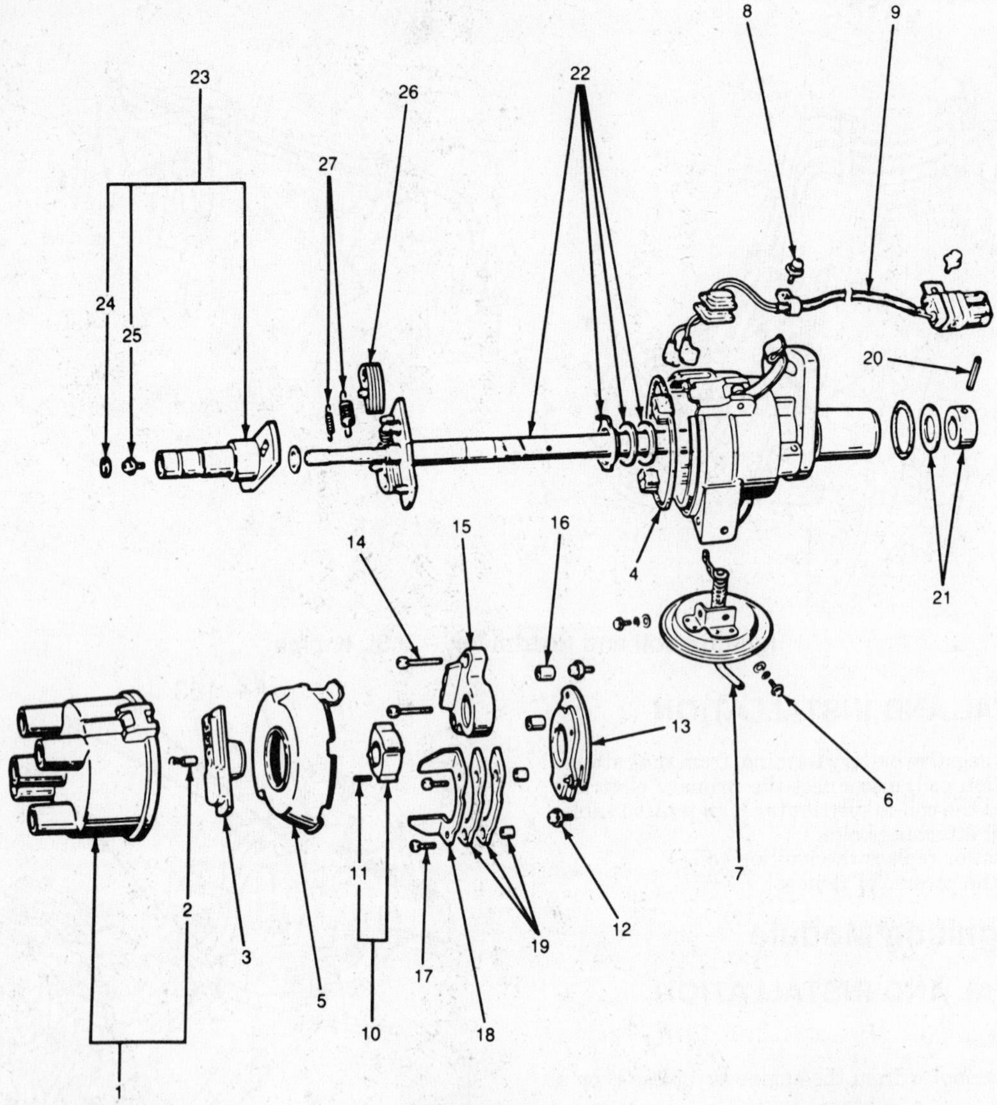
8
9
23
26
22
27
24
25
20
15
16
14
4
21
13
6
7
11
2
12
19
3
17
5
10
18
1

1. Cap assembly
2. Carbon point
3. Rotor head
4. Packing
5. Cover
6. Screw
7. Vacuum control assembly
8. Screw
9. Harness assembly
10. Pole piece
11. Roll pin
12. Screw
13. Breaker plate assembly
14. Screw
15. P/U coil module assembly
16. Spacer
17. Screw
18. Stator
19. Magnet set
20. Roll pin
21. Collar
22. Shaft assembly
23. Rotor shaft assembly
24. Packing
25. Screw
26. Governor weight
27. Governor spring

Exploded view of the Non-EST distributor

5. Using a Phillips Head screwdriver, remove the ignition module-to-breaker plate screws and lift the module from the distributor; be sure to remove the spacers from the module.
6. If the module is suspected as being defective, take it to a module testing machine and have it tested.
7. To install, replace the ignition module, spacers and screws onto the breaker plate.

NOTE: When replacing the module, ensure that the module-to-distributor surface is coated with silicone lubricant.

8. Install the pole piece onto the distributor shaft, followed by the new roll pin.

NOTE: If the breaker plate was loosened, use a 0.12–0.20 in. (3-5mm) feeler gauge to measure the air gap between the pole piece and the breaker plate stator.

9. To complete the installation, reverse the removal procedures. Reinstall the distributor onto the engine.

EST Distributor

The ignition modules are located inside the distributor; they may be replaced without removing the distributor from the engine.

1. Disconnect the negative battery terminal.
2. Remove the distributor cap and the rotor.

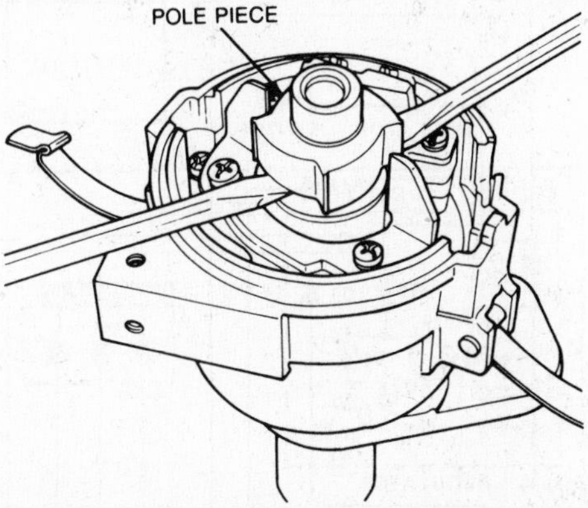
POLE PIECE

Using two pry bars to remove the pole piece from the distributor shaft on the Non-EST distributor

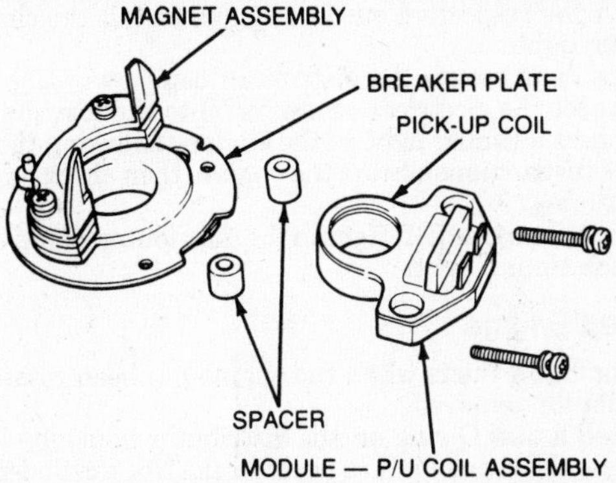
MAGNET ASSEMBLY
BREAKER PLATE
PICK-UP COIL
SPACER
MODULE — P/U COIL ASSEMBLY

Exploded view of the ignition module and the breaker plate assembly

3. If the flange, of the distributor shaft, is positioned above the module, place a socket on the crankshaft pulley bolt and rotate the crankshaft (turning the distributor shaft) to provide clearance to the ignition module.
4. Remove the ignition module-to-distributor screws, lift the module and disconnect the electrical connectors from it.
5. If the module is suspected as being defective, take it to a module testing machine and have it tested.

NOTE: When replacing the module, ensure that the module-to-distributor surface is coated with silicone lubricant.

6. To install, apply silicone lubricant to the module mounting area of the distributor and reverse the removal procedures. Install the rotor, the distributor cap and the negative battery terminal.

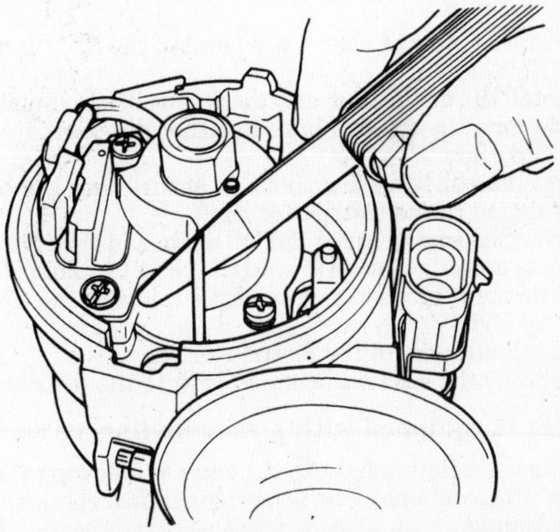

Using a non-magnetic feeler gauge, check the air gap between the pole piece and the breaker plate

Distributor

REMOVAL

1. Disconnect the negative battery terminal from the battery.
2. Tag and disconnect the electrical connector(s) from the distributor.
3. Remove the distributor cap (DO NOT remove the ignition wires) from the distributor and move it aside.
4. Using a crayon or chalk, make locating marks (for installation purposes) on the rotor, the ignition module, the distributor housing and the engine.
5. Loosen and remove the distributor clamp bolt and clamp, then lift the distributor from the engine.

NOTE: Noting the relative position of the rotor and the module alignment marks, make a second mark on the rotor to align it with the one mark on the module.

INSTALLATION

Undisturbed Engine

This condition exists if the engine has not been rotated with the distributor removed.

1. Install a new O-ring on the distributor housing.
2. Align the second mark on the rotor with the mark on the module, then install the distributor, taking care to align the mark on the housing with the one on the engine.

NOTE: It may be necessary to lift the distributor and turn the rotor slightly to align the gears and the oil pump driveshaft.

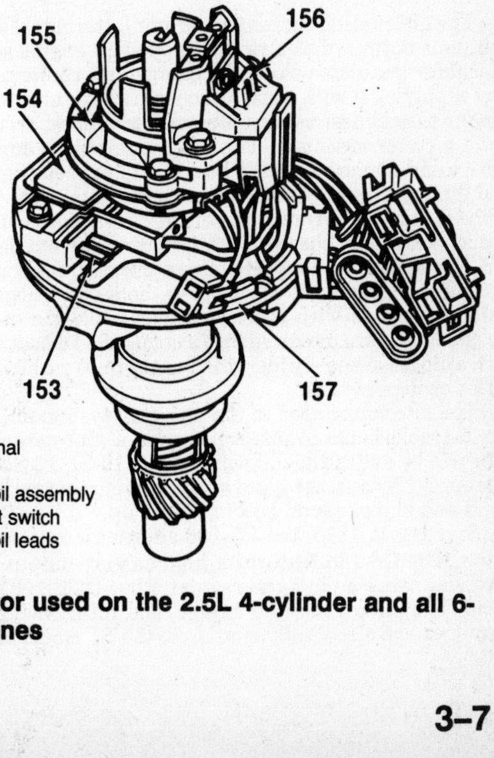
155
156
154
153
157

153. "P" terminal
154. Module
155. Pickup coil assembly
156. Hall effect switch
157. Pickup coil leads

EST distributor used on the 2.5L 4-cylinder and all 6-cylinder engines

3. With the respective marks aligned, install the clamp and bolt finger tight.
4. Install and secure the distributor cap.
5. Connect the electrical connector(s) to the distributor.
6. Connect a timing light to the engine (following the manufacturer's instructions). Start the engine, then check and/or adjust the timing.
7. Turn the engine Off, tighten the distributor clamp bolt and remove the timing light.

Disturbed Engine

This condition exists when the engine has been rotated with the distributor removed.

1. Install a new O-ring on the distributor housing.
2. Rotate the crankshaft to position the No. 1 cylinder on the TDC of it's compression stroke. This may be determined by inserting a rag into the No. 1 spark plug hole and slowly turn the engine crankshaft. When the timing mark on the crankshaft pulley aligns with the 0° mark on the timing scale and the rag is blown out by the compression, the No. 1 piston is at top-dead-center (TDC).
3. Turn the rotor so that it will point to the No. 1 terminal of the distributor cap.
4. Install the distributor into the engine block. It may be necessary to turn the rotor, a little in either direction, in order to engage the gears.
5. Tap the starter a few times to ensure that the oil pump shaft is mated to the distributor shaft.
6. Bring the engine to No. 1 TDC again and check to see that the rotor is indeed pointing toward the No. 1 terminal of the cap.
7. With the respective marks aligned, install the clamp and bolt finger tight.
8. Install and secure the distributor cap.
9. Connect the electrical connector(s) to the distributor.

NOTE: If equipped with a vacuum line, reconnect it.

10. Connect a timing light to the engine (following the manufacturer's instructions). Start the engine, then check and/or adjust the timing.
11. Turn the engine Off, tighten the distributor clamp bolt and remove the timing light.

Alternator

The alternating current generator (alternator) supplies a continuous output of electrical energy at all engine speeds. The alternator generates electrical energy and recharges the battery by supplying it with electrical current. This unit consists of four main assemblies: two end-frame assemblies, a rotor assembly and a stator assembly. The rotor assembly is supported in the drive end-frame by a roller bearing. These bearings are lubricated during assembly and require no maintenance. There are six diodes in the end-frame assembly. These diodes, used as electrical check valves, change the alternating current developed within the stator windings to direct current (DC) at the output (BAT) terminal. Three of these diodes are negative and are mounted flush with the end-frame, while the other three are positive and are mounted into a strip called a heat sink. The positive diodes are easily identified as the ones within the small cavities or depressions.

The alternator used in the charging system of 1982–86 S/10-S/15 trucks is the SI integral regulator alternator. The alternator will be one of the following types: 10-SI, 12-SI or 15-SI. Differences between the types are output current ratings, and drive end and slip ring end bearing stack up.

Starting in 1986, the CS-130 alternator was used in production. The CS-130 features a high ampere output per pound of weight. It has an integral regulator but DOES NOT use a diode trio. The stator, rectifier bridge, and rotor with slip rings and brushes are electrically similar to the SI model alternators.

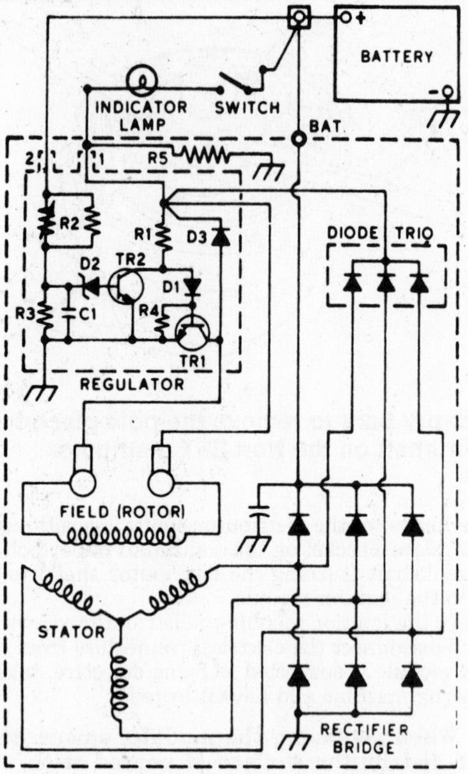
BATTERY
INDICATOR LAMP
SWITCH
BAT
R5
R2
R1
D3
D2
TR2
D1
R3
C1
R4
TR1
REGULATOR
DIODE TRIO
FIELD (ROTOR)
STATOR
RECTIFIER BRIDGE

Schematic of the SI model alternator

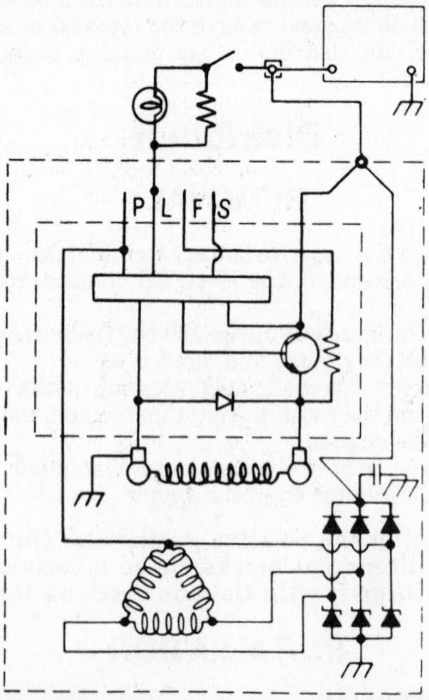
P
L
F
S

Schematic of the CS model alternator

The regulator voltage varies with temperature and limits system voltage by controlling rotor field current. It switches rotor field current on and off at a fixed frequency of about 400 cycles per second. By varying the on-off time, correct average field current for proper system voltage control is obtained. At high speeds, the on-time may be 10 percent and the off-time may be 90 percent. At low speeds, with high electrical loads, the on-off time may be 90 percent and 10 percent respectively.

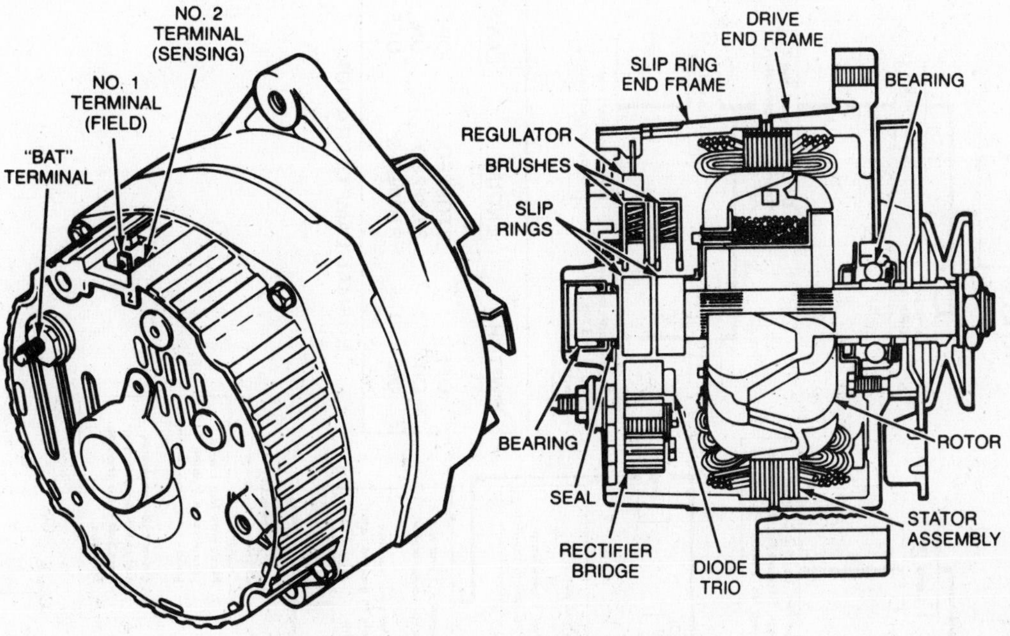
NO. 2
TERMINAL
(SENSING)
NO. 1
TERMINAL
(FIELD)
"BAT"
TERMINAL
DRIVE
END FRAME
SLIP RING
END FRAME
BEARING
REGULATOR
BRUSHES
SLIP
RINGS
BEARING
ROTOR
SEAL
STATOR
ASSEMBLY
RECTIFIER
BRIDGE
DIODE
TRIO

Sectional view of the SI model alternator

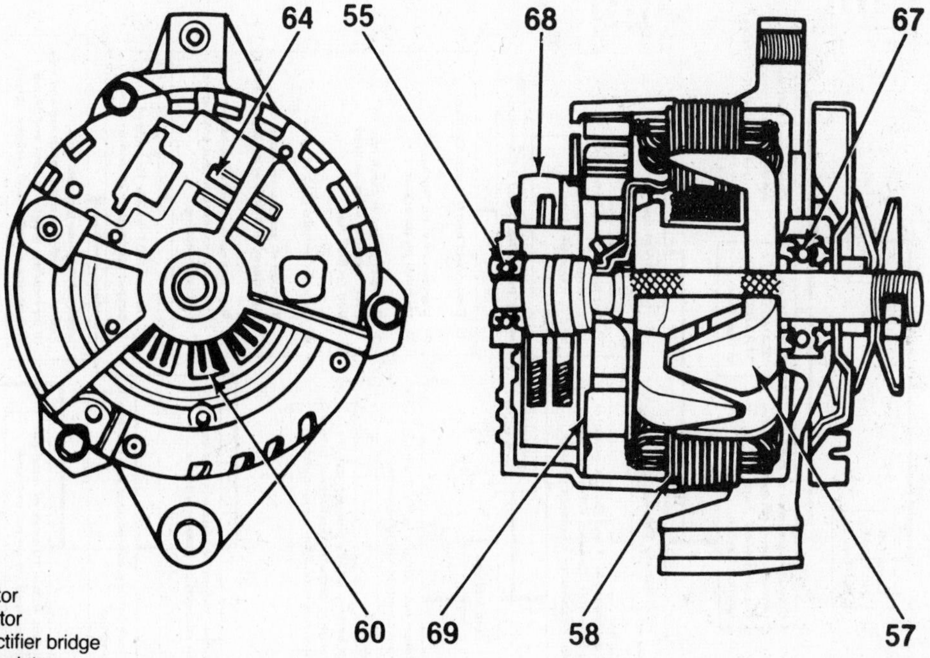
64
55
68
67
60
69
58
57

57. Rotor
58. Stator
60. Rectifier bridge
64. Regulator
67. Double sealed ball bearing
68. Terminals
69. Internal fan

Sectional view of the CS model alternator

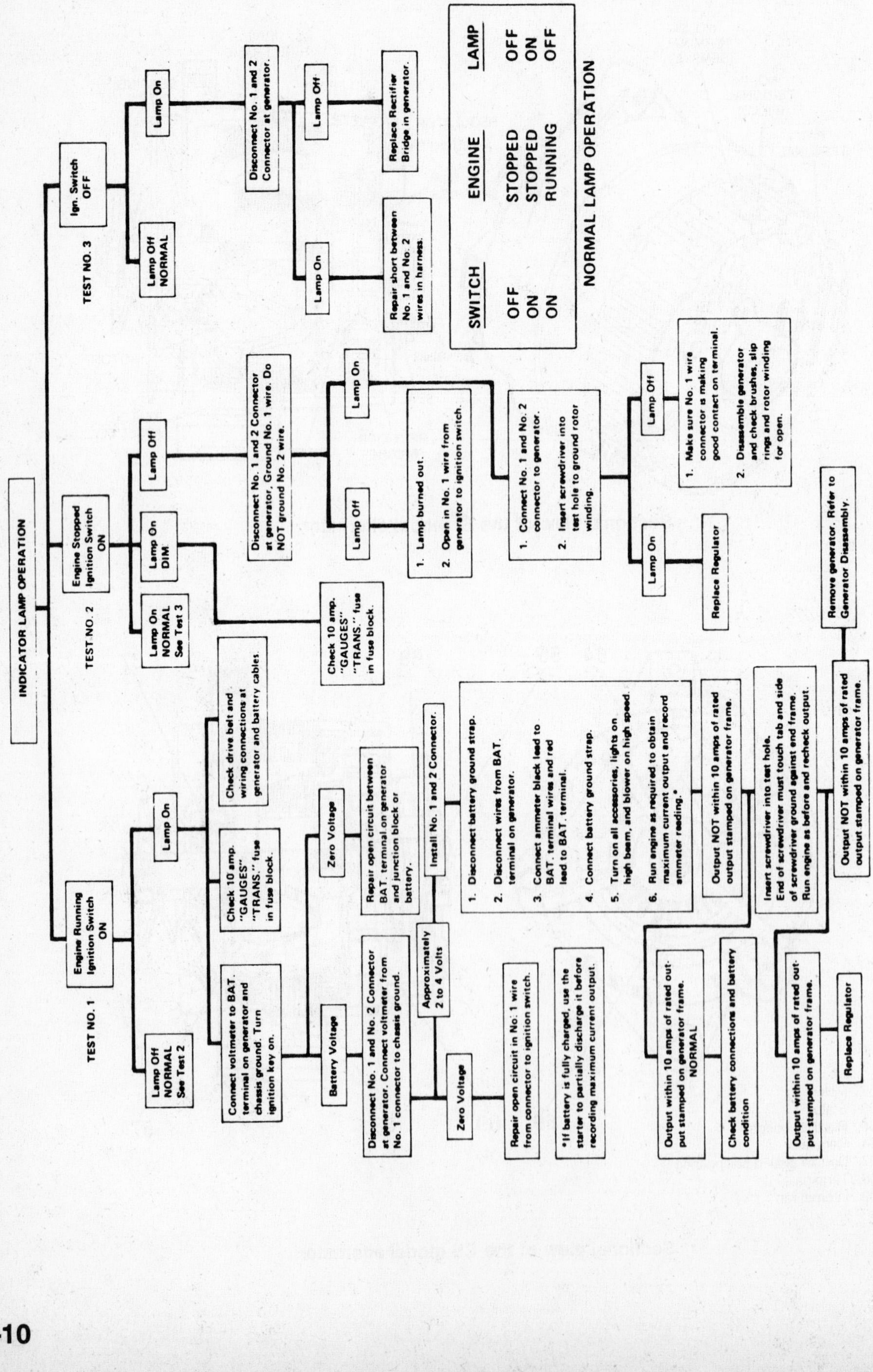
INDICATOR LAMP OPERATION
TEST NO. 1
Engine Running Ignition Switch ON
Lamp Off NORMAL See Test 2
Lamp On
Connect voltmeter to BAT. terminal on generator and chassis ground. Turn ignition key on.
Check 10 amp. "GAUGES" "TRANS." fuse in fuse block.
Check drive belt and wiring connections at generator and battery cables.
Battery Voltage
Zero Voltage
Disconnect No. 1 and No. 2 Connector at generator. Connect voltmeter from No. 1 connector to chassis ground.
Repair open circuit between BAT. terminal on generator and junction block or battery.
Zero Voltage
Approximately 2 to 4 Volts
Repair open circuit in No. 1 wire from connector to ignition switch.
Install No. 1 and 2 Connector.
1. Disconnect battery ground strap.
2. Disconnect wires from BAT. terminal on generator.
3. Connect ammeter black lead to BAT. terminal wires and red lead to BAT. terminal.
4. Connect battery ground strap.
5. Turn on all accessories, lights on high beam, and blower on high speed.
6. Run engine as required to obtain maximum current output and record ammeter reading.*
*If battery is fully charged, use the starter to partially discharge it before recording maximum current output.
Output within 10 amps of rated output stamped on generator frame. NORMAL
Output NOT within 10 amps of rated output stamped on generator frame.
Check battery connections and battery condition
Insert screwdriver into test hole. End of screwdriver must touch tab and side of screwdriver ground against end frame. Run engine as before and recheck output.
Output within 10 amps of rated output stamped on generator frame.
Output NOT within 10 amps of rated output stamped on generator frame.
Replace Regulator
Remove generator. Refer to Generator Disassembly.
TEST NO. 2
Engine Stopped Ignition Switch ON
Lamp On NORMAL See Test 3
Lamp On DIM
Lamp Off
Check 10 amp. "GAUGES" "TRANS." fuse in fuse block.
Disconnect No. 1 and 2 Connector at generator, Ground No. 1 wire. Do NOT ground No. 2 wire.
Lamp Off
Lamp On
1. Lamp burned out.
2. Open in No. 1 wire from generator to ignition switch.
1. Connect No. 1 and No. 2 connector to generator.
2. Insert screwdriver into test hole to ground rotor winding.
Lamp On
Replace Regulator
Lamp Off
1. Make sure No. 1 wire connector is making good contact on terminal.
2. Disassemble generator and check brushes, slip rings and rotor winding for open.
TEST NO. 3
Ign. Switch OFF
Lamp Off NORMAL
Lamp On
Disconnect No. 1 and 2 Connector at generator.
Lamp On
Repair short between No. 1 and No. 2 wires in harness.
Lamp Off
Replace Rectifier Bridge in generator.

SWITCH	ENGINE	LAMP
OFF	STOPPED	OFF
ON	STOPPED	ON
ON	RUNNING	OFF

NORMAL LAMP OPERATION

SI Model alternator diagnosis and testing

NOTE: The CS-130 alternator is not serviceable. If the alternator is found to be defective, replacement is the only alternative.

ALTERNATOR PRECAUTIONS

To prevent damage to the on-board computer, alternator and regulator, the following precautionary measures must be taken when working with the electrical system.

- Never reverse the battery connections. Always check the battery polarity visually. This is to be done before any connections are made to be sure that all of the connections correspond to the battery ground polarity.
- Booster batteries for starting must be connected properly. Make sure that the positive cable of the booster battery is connected to the positive terminal of the battery that is getting the boost. This applies to both negative and ground cables.
- Make sure the ignition switch is OFF when connecting or disconnecting any electrical component, especially on trucks equipped with an on-board computer control system.
- Disconnect the battery cables before using a fast charger; the charger has a tendency to force current through the diodes in the opposite direction for which they were designed. This burns out the diodes.
- Never use a fast charger as a booster for starting the vehicle.
- Never disconnect the voltage regulator while the engine is running.
- Do not ground the alternator output terminal.
- Do not attempt to polarize an alternator.

DIAGNOSIS

SI Alternator

A charge indicator lamp is used in most trucks to signal when there is a fault in the charging system. This lamp is located in the gauge package and is used in diagnosis. A voltmeter may be used instead of the charge indicator lamp in diagnosis. In this case, section "A" of the diagnosis chart should be omitted.

CS-130 Alternator

1. Check drive belt(s) for wear and tension. Check wiring for obvious damage.
2. Go to Step 5 for vehicles without a charge indicator lamp.
3. With the ignition switch ON and the engine stopped, the lamp should be ON. If not, detach the wiring harness at the generator and ground the "L" terminal lead.
4. If the lamp lights, replace the alternator. If the lamp does not light, locate the open circuit between the grounding lead and the ignition switch. Check the lamp, it may be open.
5. With the ignition switch ON, and the engine running at moderate speed, the lamp should be OFF. If not, detach the wiring harness at the alternator.
6. If the lamp goes out, replace the alternator. If the lamp stays ON, check for a grounded "L" terminal wire in the harness.
7. Determine if the battery is undercharged or overcharged.
   - An undercharged battery is evidenced by slow cranking or a dark hydrometer.
   - An overcharged battery is evidenced by excessive spewing of electrolyte from the vents.
8. Detach the wiring harness connector from the alternator.
9. With the ignition switch ON, and the engine OFF, connect a voltmeter from ground to the "L" terminal in the wiring harness, and to the "I" terminal, if used.
10. A zero reading indicates an open circuit between the terminal and the battery. Repair the circuit as necessary.
11. Connect the harness connector to the alternator and run the engine at moderate speed with accessories OFF.

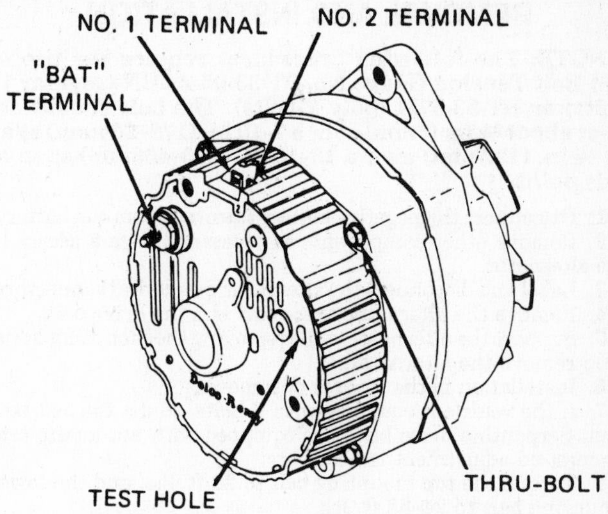
NO. 1 TERMINAL
NO. 2 TERMINAL
"BAT" TERMINAL
TEST HOLE
THRU-BOLT

Disassembling the SI Model alternator

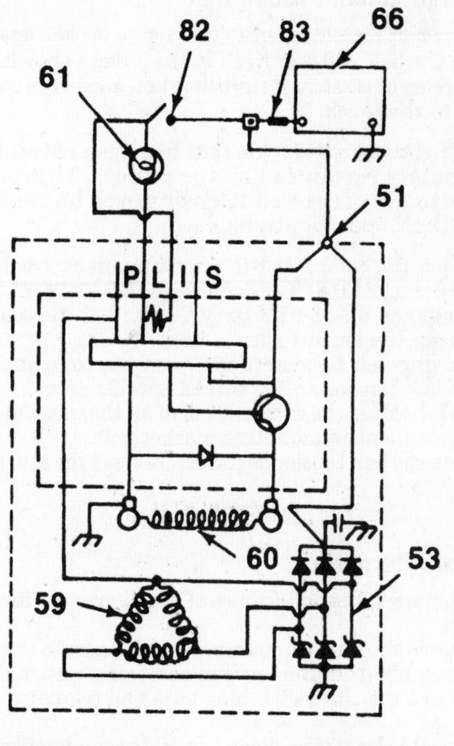
82
83
66
61
51
P L I S
60
53
59

51. BAT Terminal
53. Rectifier Bridge
59. Stator
60. Field
61. Indicator Lamp
66. Battery
82. Switch
83. Fusible Link

CS-130 diagnostic test connections

12. Measure the voltage across the battery. If above 16 volts, replace the alternator.
13. Connect an ammeter at the alternator output terminal, turn ON all the accessories and load the battery with a carbon pile to obtain maximum amperage. Maintain voltage at 13 volts or above.
14. If the output is within 15 amps of the rated output of the alternator (stamped on the alternator case), the alternator is good. If the output is not within 15 amps, replace the alternator.

REMOVAL AND INSTALLATION

NOTE: The following procedures require the use of GM Belt Tension Gauge No. BT-33-95-ACBN (regular V-belts) or BT-33-97M (poly V-belts). The belt should deflect about ¼ in. (6mm) over a 7–10 in. (178–254mm) span or ½ in. (12.7mm) over a 13–16 in. (330–406mm) span at this point.

1. Disconnect the negative battery terminal from the battery.
2. Remove other components as necessary to gain access to the alternator.
3. Label and disconnect the alternator's electrical connectors.
4. Remove the alternator brace bolt and the drive belt.
5. Support the alternator while removing the mounting bolts, then remove the alternator.
6. Installation is the reverse of removal.
7. If the vehicle is equipped with V-belts, adjust the belt tension. Serpentine drive belts are equipped with automatic tensioners; no adjustment is necessary.
8. Torque the top mounting bolt to 22 ft. lbs. and the lower mounting bolt to 24–35 ft. lbs.
9. Reconnect the negative battery terminal.

V-belt Adjustment Procedure

1. If the belt is Cold, operate the engine (at idle speed) for 15 minutes; the belt will seat itself in the pulleys allowing the belt fibers to relax or stretch. If the belt is hot, allow it to cool, until it is warm to the touch.

NOTE: A used belt is one that has been rotated at least one complete revolution on the pulleys. This begins the belt seating process and it must never be tensioned to the new belt specifications.

2. Loosen the component-to-mounting bracket bolts.
3. Place the GM Belt Tension Gauge [BT-33-95-ACBN (standard V-belts) or BT-33-97M (poly V-belts)] at the center of the belt between the longest span.
4. Applying belt tension pressure on the component, adjust the drive belt tension to the correct specifications.
5. While holding the correct tension on the component, tighten the component-to-mounting bracket bolt.
6. When the belt tension is correct, remove the tension gauge.

OVERHAUL

SI Model Alternator

1. Matchmark the end frames of the alternator for assembly reference.
2. Remove the four through-bolts and separate the drive end frame assembly from the rectifier end frame assembly.
3. Remove the three attaching nuts and regulator attaching screws.
4. Separate the stator, diode trio and regulator from the end frame.

NOTE: There are two ways of testing a regulator. The first is with an expensive regulator tester tool. This method is cost prohibitive for the average home mechanic. The second way is outlined above in diagnostic testing. It involves testing the regulator on the vehicle with the engine running.

5. Check the stator for opens with an ohmmeter as illustrated. If either reading is infinite, replace the stator.
6. Check the stator for grounds as illustrated. If the reading is close to zero, or zero, replace the stator.
7. Check the rotor for grounds with an ohmmeter. The reading should be infinite. If not, replace the rotor.
8. Check the rotor for opens. The reading should be between 2.5–3.5 ohms. If not, replace the rotor.

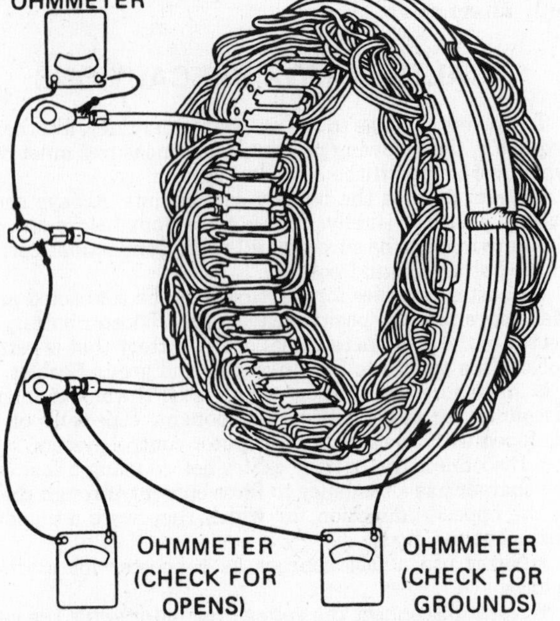
(CHECK FOR OPENS)
OHMMETER
OHMMETER
(CHECK FOR
OPENS)
OHMMETER
(CHECK FOR
GROUNDS)

Testing the stator on the SI Model alternator

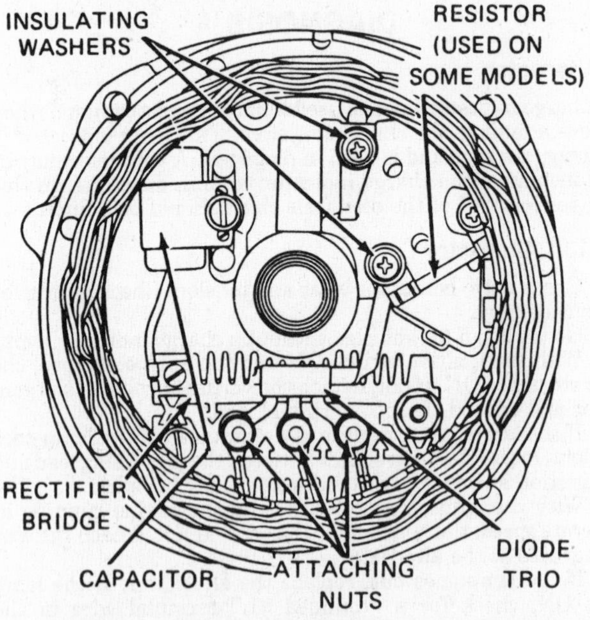
INSULATING
WASHERS
RESISTOR
(USED ON
SOME MODELS)
RECTIFIER
BRIDGE
CAPACITOR
ATTACHING
NUTS
DIODE
TRIO

SI Model alternator internal components

9. Attach an ohmmeter to the diode trio as illustrated. Then reverse the lead connections. The readings should read high one way and low the reverse way. If not, replace the diode trio.
10. Repeat the same test between the other connectors in the trio.
11. Check the rectifier bridge with an ohmmeter connected from the grounded heat sink to the flat metal on the terminal. Then, reverse the leads.
12. If both readings are the same, replace the rectifier bridge.
13. Repeat the test between the grounded heat sink and the other flat metal clips.

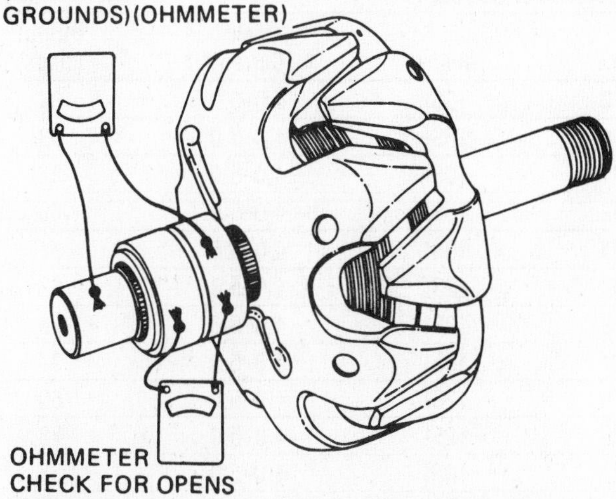
(CHECK FOR
GROUNDS)(OHMMETER)
OHMMETER
CHECK FOR OPENS

Testing the rotor on the SI Model alternator

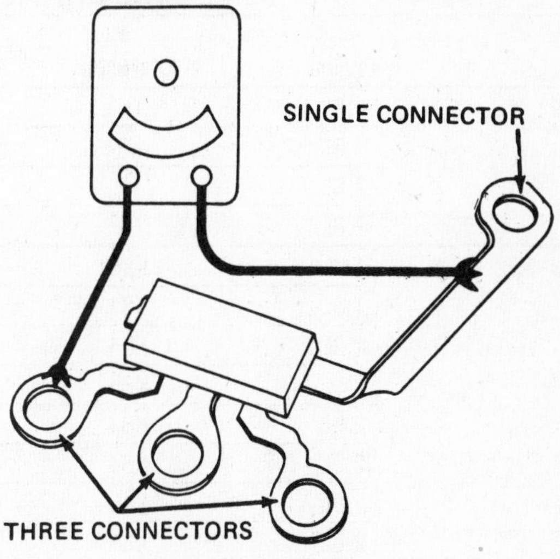
OHMMETER
SINGLE CONNECTOR
THREE CONNECTORS

Testing the diode trio on the SI Model alternator

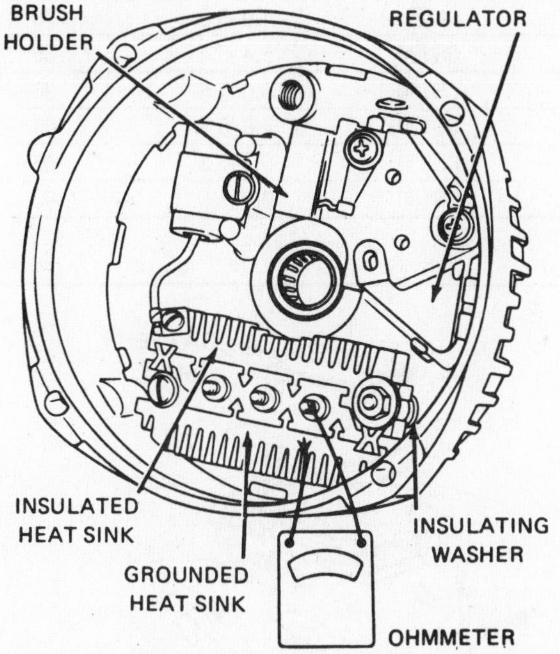
BRUSH
HOLDER
REGULATOR
INSULATED
HEAT SINK
GROUNDED
HEAT SINK
INSULATING
WASHER
OHMMETER

Testing the rectifier bridge on the SI Model alternator

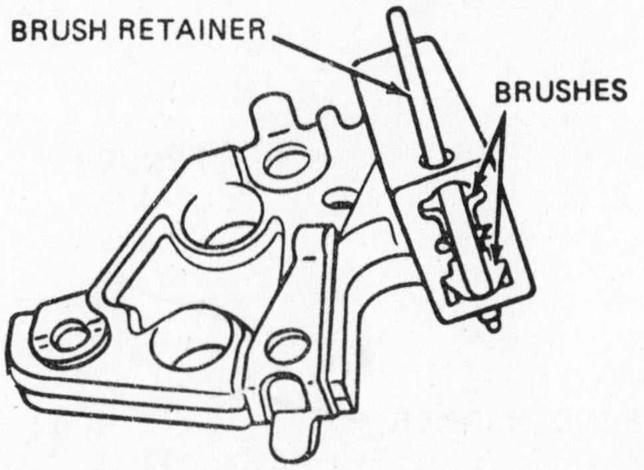
BRUSH RETAINER
BRUSHES

Installing the brushes in the holder on the SI Model alternator

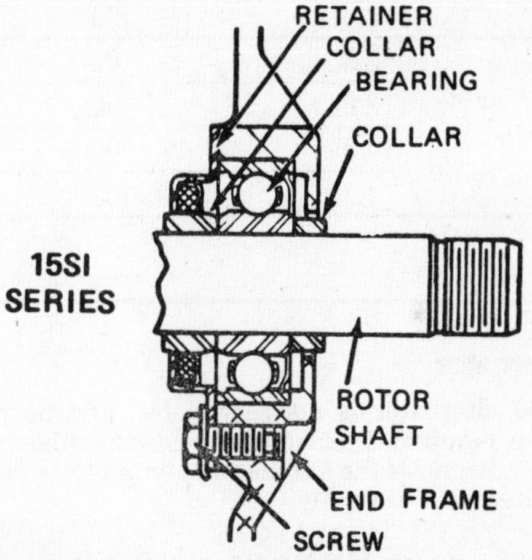
RETAINER
COLLAR
BEARING
COLLAR
15SI
SERIES
ROTOR
SHAFT
END FRAME
SCREW

Drive end bearing replacement on the SI Model alternator

14. Repeat the test between the insulated heat sink and the flat metal clips.
15. If the rectifier bridge needs replacement, remove the attaching screw and replace the assembly.
16. Install replacement brushes in the holder and retain with a tooth pick.
17. If the alternator bearings need replacement, remove the rotor and drive end bearing, remove the shaft nut, washer and pulley, fan and collar. Push the rotor from the housing.
18. Remove the retainer plate inside the drive end frame and push the bearing out. Clean all parts thoroughly.
19. Press against the outer race to push the bearing into place. Fill the cavity with lubricant.

NOTE: Late production alternators use a sealed bearing assembly that is permanently lubricated, no external lubrication is necessary.

20. Press the rotor into the end frame. Assemble the collar, fan, pulley, washer and nut. Torque the nut to 40–60 ft. lbs.
21. Assemble the remaining components in reverse order of removal.
22. Use the diagnostic tests to ensure proper operation of the overhauled alternator.

ALTERNATOR SPECIFICATIONS

Year	Engine	Alternator	Part No.	Model	Field Current	Output (amps)
1982	1.9L	—	1100140	10SI	4.0–5.0	37
	1.9L	—	1100146	15SI	4.0–5.0	63
	2.8L	—	1100201	10SI	4.0–5.0	37
	2.8L	—	1100202	15SI	4.0–5.0	66
1983–85	1.9L	K85	1105185	10SI	4.0–5.0	37
	1.9L	K81	1100207	12SI	4.0–5.0	63
	1.9L	K64	1100209	12SI	4.0–5.0	78
	2.0L	K85	1100204	10SI	4.0–5.0	37
	2.0L	K81	1100275	12SI	4.0–5.0	66
	2.0L	K64	1100276	12SI	4.0–5.0	78
	2.8L	K85	1100227	10SI	4.0–5.0	37
	2.8L	K81	1100249	12SI	4.0–5.0	66
	2.8L	K64	1100273	12SI	4.0–5.0	78
1986–87	2.5L	—	1105627	12SI	4.0–5.0	78
	2.8L	100	1105663	CS130	5.4–6.4	85
1988–91	2.5L	100	1101346	CS130	6.0–7.5	96
	2.8L	100	1101259	CS130	4.8–5.7	85
	4.3L	100	1101317	CS130	5.7–7.1	85
	4.3L	100	1101293	CS130	6.0–7.5	100

CS-130 Alternator

The CS-130 alternator is not serviceable, and no periodic maintenance is required. It should not be disassembled for any reason. If after diagnosis the alternator is found to be defective, replace the alternator assembly.

Battery

The battery is mounted in front, right-side of the engine compartment. It is a no maintenance type with side mounted terminals.

CURRENT DRAW TEST

1. Remove the negative battery cable.
2. Install a battery side terminal adapter to the negative battery terminal.
3. Connect the negative lead of a digital multimeter to the negative battery terminal.
4. Connect the positive lead of the digital multimeter to ground.
5. Set the multimeter on the DC, MA and 2000 scale. Take the reading with the engine and all accessories OFF.
6. Find the reserve capacity of the battery. This figure is usually noted on the top of the battery. If not, contact the battery manufacturer.
7. Divide the reserve capacity by 4. The current drain should not exceed this number. For example, if the battery has a reserve capacity of 100 minutes, the current draw should not exceed 25 milliamps.
8. If current draw is too high, check the system for causes such as shorted wires to a compartment lamp that does not shut off when it should.

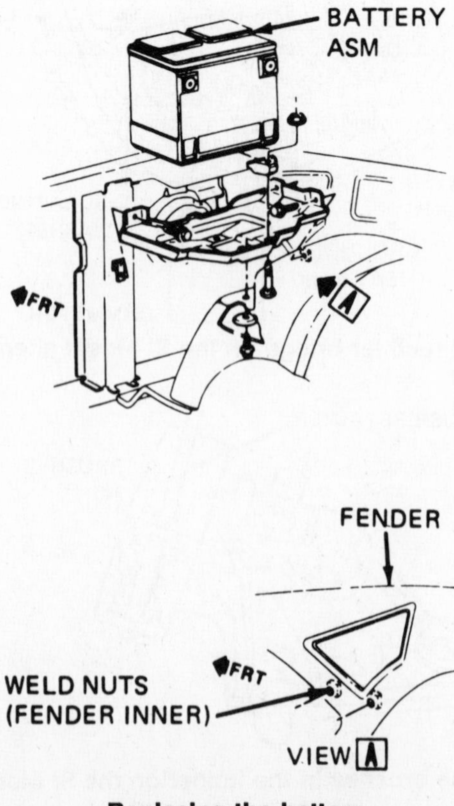
BATTERY ASM
FRT
A
FENDER
FRT
WELD NUTS (FENDER INNER)
VIEW A

Replacing the battery

REMOVAL AND INSTALLATION

1. Disconnect the negative battery terminal, then the positive battery terminal.
2. Remove the battery holddown retainer.
3. Remove the battery from the vehicle.
4. Inspect the battery, the cables and the battery carrier for damage.
5. To install, reverse the removal procedures. Torque the battery retainer to 11 ft. lbs., the top bar to 8 ft. lbs. (if equipped) and the battery cable terminals to 10 ft. lbs.

Starter

The gasoline starter is located on the lower right-side (gasoline engines) or on the lower left-side (diesel engine). The diesel engine starter is a gear reduction type.

DIAGNOSIS

Before removing the starter for repair or replacement, check the condition of all circuit wiring for damage. Inspect all connection to the starter motor, solenoid, ignition switch, and battery, including all ground connections. Clean and tighten all connections as required.

Check all switches to determine their condition. Vehicles equipped with manual transmission have a neutral start switch attached to the clutch which closes when the clutch is depressed. Vehicles equipped with automatic transmissions have a manual interlock in the steering column which does not allow the ignition switch to turn to the start position unless the transmission is in the Park or Neutral position.

Check the battery to ensure that it is fully charged. Perform battery current draw test to determine battery condition.

Check the battery cables for excessive resistance as follows:

CAUTION

To prevent possible injury from a moving vehicle or operating engine, engage the parking brakes, block the drive wheels, place the manual transmission in Neutral or the automatic transmission in Park, and disconnect the battery feed at the distributor before performing these tests.

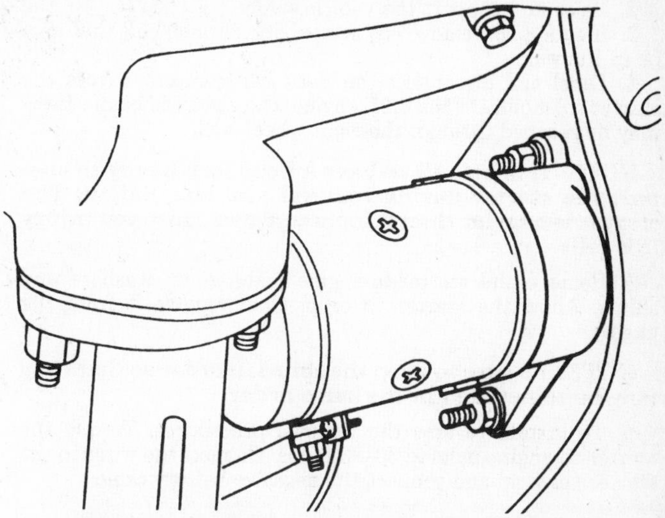

Starter mounting on the 2.2L diesel engine

- Check the voltage drop between the negative battery terminal and the vehicle frame by placing one lead of a voltmeter on the grounded battery post (not the cable clamp) and the other lead on the frame. Turn the ignition key to the START position and note the voltage drop.
- Check the voltage drop between the positive battery terminal (not the cable clamp) and the starter terminal stud. Turn the ignition key to the START position and note the voltage drop.
- Check the voltage drop between the starter housing and the frame. Turn the ignition key to the START position and note the voltage drop.
- If the voltage drop in any of the above is more than 1.0 volts, there is excessive resistance in the circuit. Clean and retest all cables not within specification. Replace as necessary.

REMOVAL AND INSTALLATION

1. Disconnect the negative battery terminal from the battery.

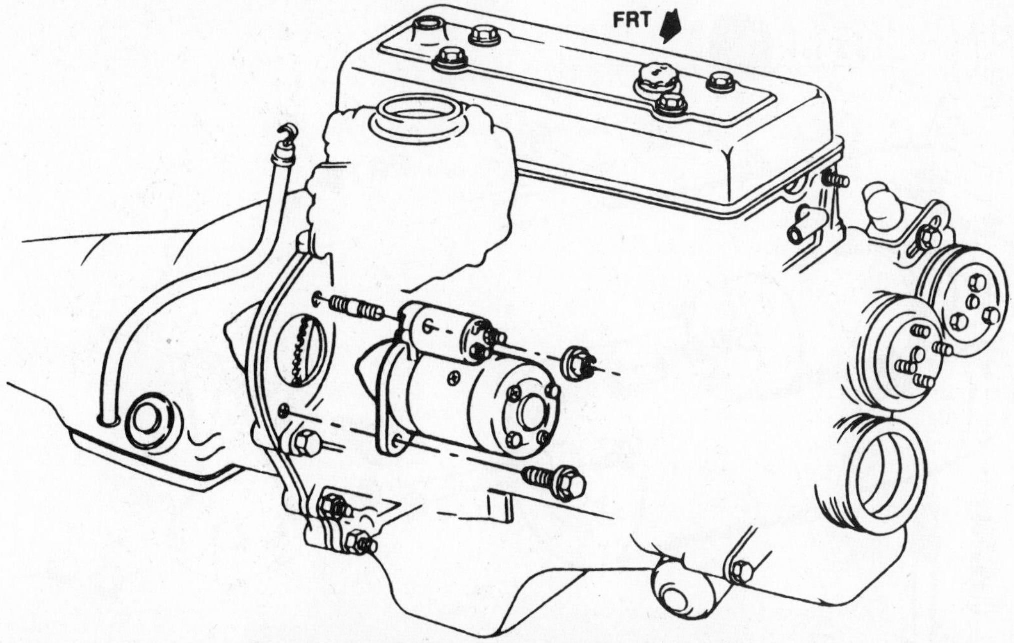
FRT

Starter mounting on the 4-cylinder engines

2. Raise and support the vehicle safely.
3. If equipped, remove any starter braces or shields that may be in the way.
4. Label and disconnect the electrical connectors from the starter solenoid. On the 4.3L engine, the electrical connections may be reached through the right wheel well.

NOTE: It is helpful to have a floor jack handy to support the starter during removal and installation. The starter is heavier than it looks and can cause you injury if it falls.

5. Remove the starter-to-engine bolts, nuts, washers and shims. Allow the starter to drop, then remove it from the engine.

NOTE: Be sure to keep the shims in order so that they may be reinstalled in the same order.

6. To install, reverse the removal procedures. Torque the starter-to-engine bolts to 30–33 ft. lbs. Connect the wires to the starter solenoid and connect the negative battery cable.

SOLENOID REPLACEMENT

Gasoline Engines

1. Remove the starter and place it on a workbench.
2. Remove the screw and the washer from the motor connector strap terminal.
3. Remove the two solenoid retaining screws.
4. Twist the solenoid housing clockwise to remove the flange key from the keyway in the housing and remove.
5. To install the solenoid, place the return spring on the plunger and place the solenoid body on the drive housing.
6. Turn solenoid counterclockwise to engage the flange key.
7. Install the two retaining screws, then install the screw and washer which secures the strap terminal.
8. Install the starter on the vehicle.

Diesel Engine

1. Remove the starter from the vehicle.
2. Remove the two screws from the drive housing and separate the drive housing from the solenoid.

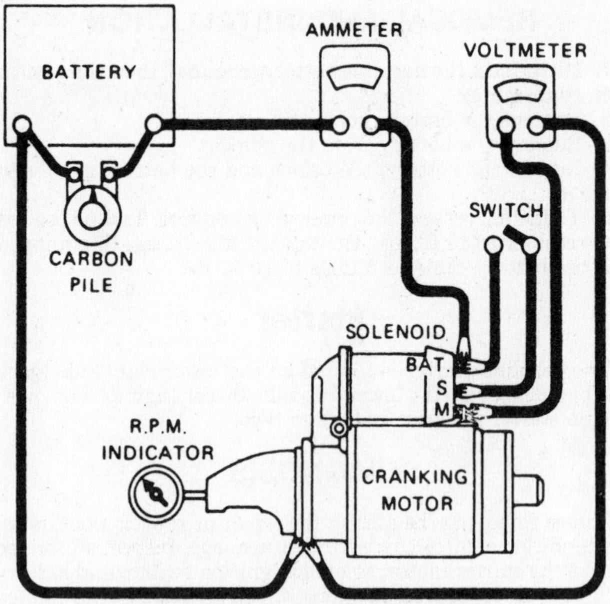
BATTERY
AMMETER
VOLTMETER
SWITCH
CARBON
PILE
SOLENOID
BAT.
S
M
R.P.M.
INDICATOR
CRANKING
MOTOR

No-Load test connections

3. Remove the two pinion gears, then remove the overrunning clutch and retainer.
4. Remove the return spring from the solenoid.
5. Remove the steel ball from the overrunning clutch.
6. Installation is the reverse of removal.

Starter Overhaul

With the starter motor removed from the engine, the pinion should be checked for freedom of operation by turning it on the screw shaft. The armature should be checked for freedom of rotation by prying the pinion with a pry bar. If the armature does not turn freely, the motor should be disassembled immediately. However, if the motor does turn freely, the motor should be given a no-load test before disassembly.

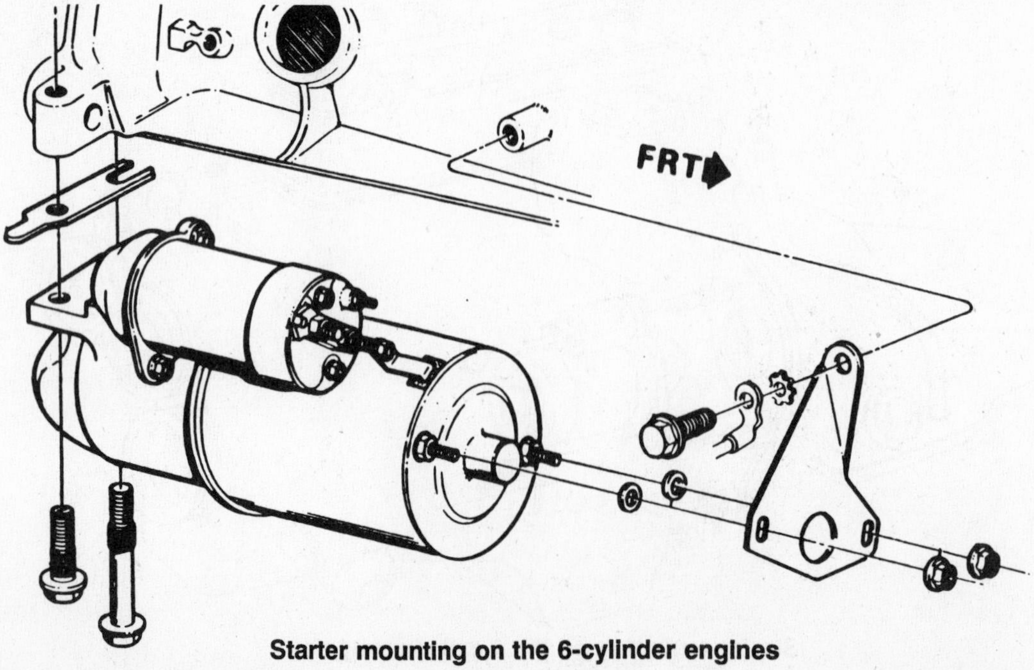
FRT

Starter mounting on the 6-cylinder engines

NO LOAD TEST

Make the connections as shown in the illustration. Close the switch and compare the rpm, current, and voltage readings with the specifications.

- Current draw and no load speed within specifications indicates normal condition of the starter motor.
- Low free speed and high current draw indicates worn bearings, a bent armature shaft, a shorted armature or grounded armature or fields.
- Failure to operate with high current draw indicates a direct ground in the terminal or fields, or frozen bearings.
- Failure to operate with no current draw indicates and open field circuit, open armature coils, broken brush springs, worn brushes or other causes which would prevent good contact between the commutator and the brushes.
- Low no load speed and low current draw indicates high internal resistance due to poor connections, defective leads, or a dirty commutator.
- High free speed and high current draw usually indicate shorted fields or a shorted armature.

DISASSEMBLY

1. Remove the screw from the field coil connector and the solenoid mounting screws. Rotate the solenoid 90° and remove along with the plunger return spring.
2. Remove the two through bolts, then remove the commutator end frame and washer.
3. Remove the field frame assembly from the drive gear housing. On the diesel starter, the armature remains in the drive end frame.
4. If it is necessary to remove the overrunning clutch from the armature shaft, remove the thrust washer or collar from the armature shaft. Slide a ⅝ deep socket over the shaft against the retainer as a driving tool. Tap the tool to move the retainer off the snapring. Remove the snapring.
5. Remove the retainer and clutch assembly (fiber washer and center bearing on diesel) from the armature shaft.
6. Disassemble the shift lever by removing the roll pin. On the diesel starter, remove the shift lever bolt.
7. On the diesel starter, remove the center bearing screws and remove the drive gear housing from the armature shaft. The shift lever and plunger as assembly will now fall away from the starter clutch.
8. If it is necessary to service the brushes, remove the brush holder from the brush support. Remove the screw to separate the brush and holder. Replace brushes as necessary.

CLEANING AND INSPECTION

9. Clean all starter motor parts.

NOTE: DO NOT use solvent for cleaning the overrunning clutch, armature or field coils.

10. Inspect the armature commutator, shaft and bushings, overrunning clutch pinion, brushes and springs for discoloration damage or wear. Replace as required.
11. Check the fit of the armature shaft in the bushings of the drive housing. The shaft should fit snugly in the bushing. If the bushing is worn, it should be replaced.
12. Inspect the armature commutator. If the commutator is rough, it should be turned down. DO NOT turn out of round commutators. Inspect the points where the armature conductors join the commutator bars to make sure they have a good connection. A burned commutator bar is usually evidence of a poor connection.
13. If a growler is available, check for a shorted armature.
14. Using a test light, place one lead on the shunt soil terminal

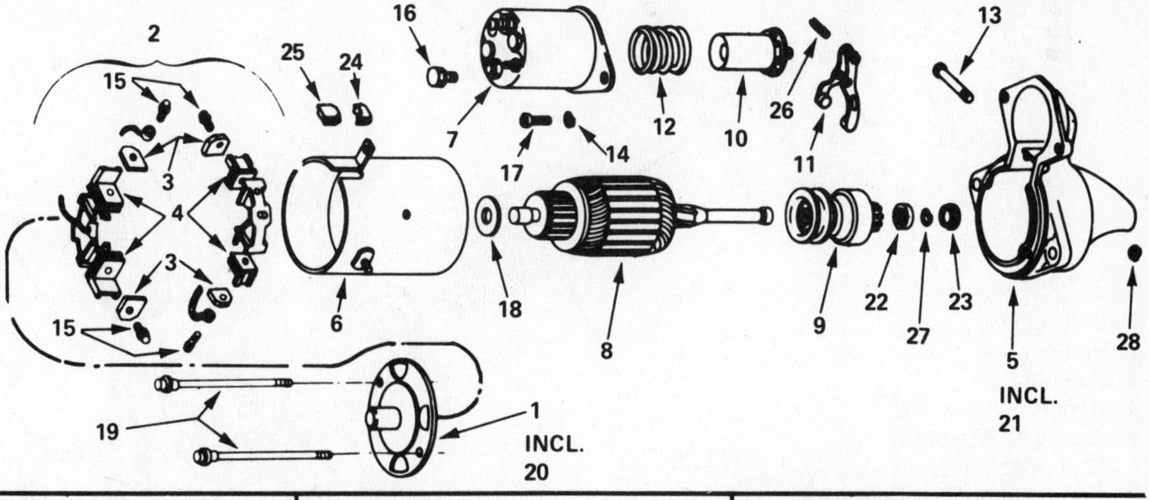
16
13
2
25
24
15
7
12
10
26
3
17
14
11
4
3
6
18
8
9
22
27
23
5
INCL.
21
28
15
19
1
INCL.
20

		19. THRU BOLT
1. FRAME–COMMUTATOR END	10. PLUNGER	20. BUSHING–COMMUTATOR END
2. BRUSH AND HOLDER PKG.	11. SHIFT LEVER	21. BUSHING–DRIVE END
3. BRUSH	12. PLUNGER RETURN SPRINGER	22. PINION STOP COLLAR
4. BRUSH HOLDER	13. SHIFT LEVER SHAFT	23. THRUST COLLAR
5. HOUSING–DRIVE END	14. LOCK WASHER	24. GROMMET
6. FRAME AND FIELD ASM.	15. SCREW–BRUSH ATTACHING	25. GROMMET
7. SOLENOID SWITCH	16. SCREW–FIELD LEAD TO SWITCH	26. PLUNGER PIN
8. ARMATURE	17. SCREW–SWITCH ATTACHING	27. PINION STOP RETAINER RING
9. DRIVE ASM.	18. LEATHER WASHER—BRAKE	28. LEVER SHAFT RETAINING RING

5MT starter — exploded view

1. Shift Lever
2. Plunger
3. Solenoid
5. Spring
9. Armature Assembly
11. Grommet
31. Housing
32. Drive
33. Brush
34. Washer
35. Bolt
36. Screw
37. Ring
38. Holder
39. Collar
40. Pin
41. Frame
42. Brushes and Holders
43. Shaft
57. Field Frame

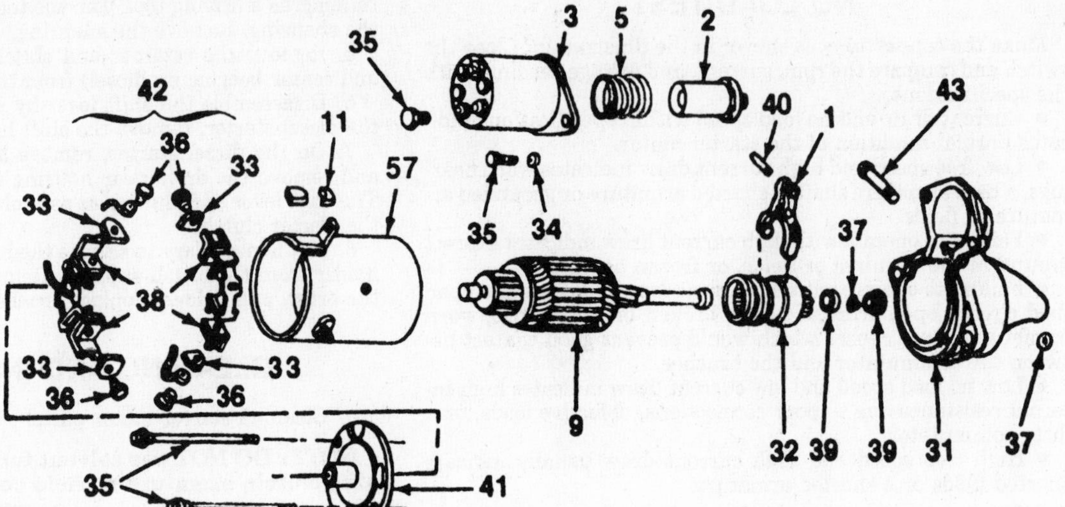

3
5
2
35
42
11
36
33
57
40
1
43
35
34
37
38
9
41
32
39
31

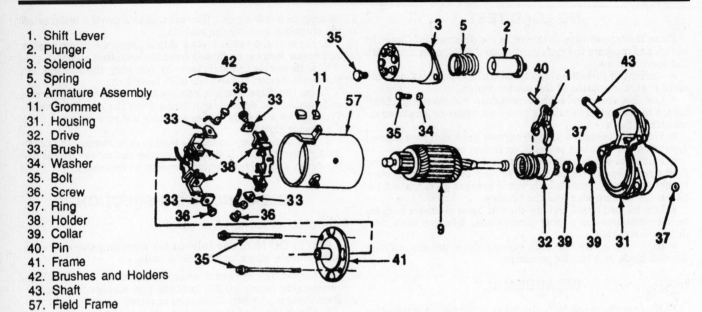

SD-200 (PGMR) starter — exploded view

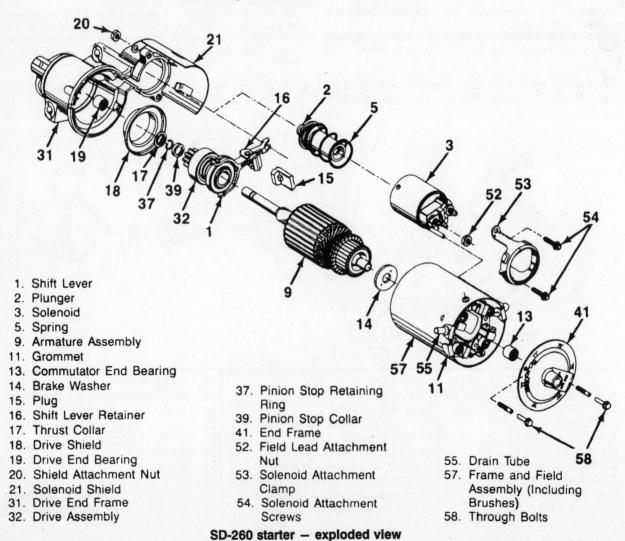

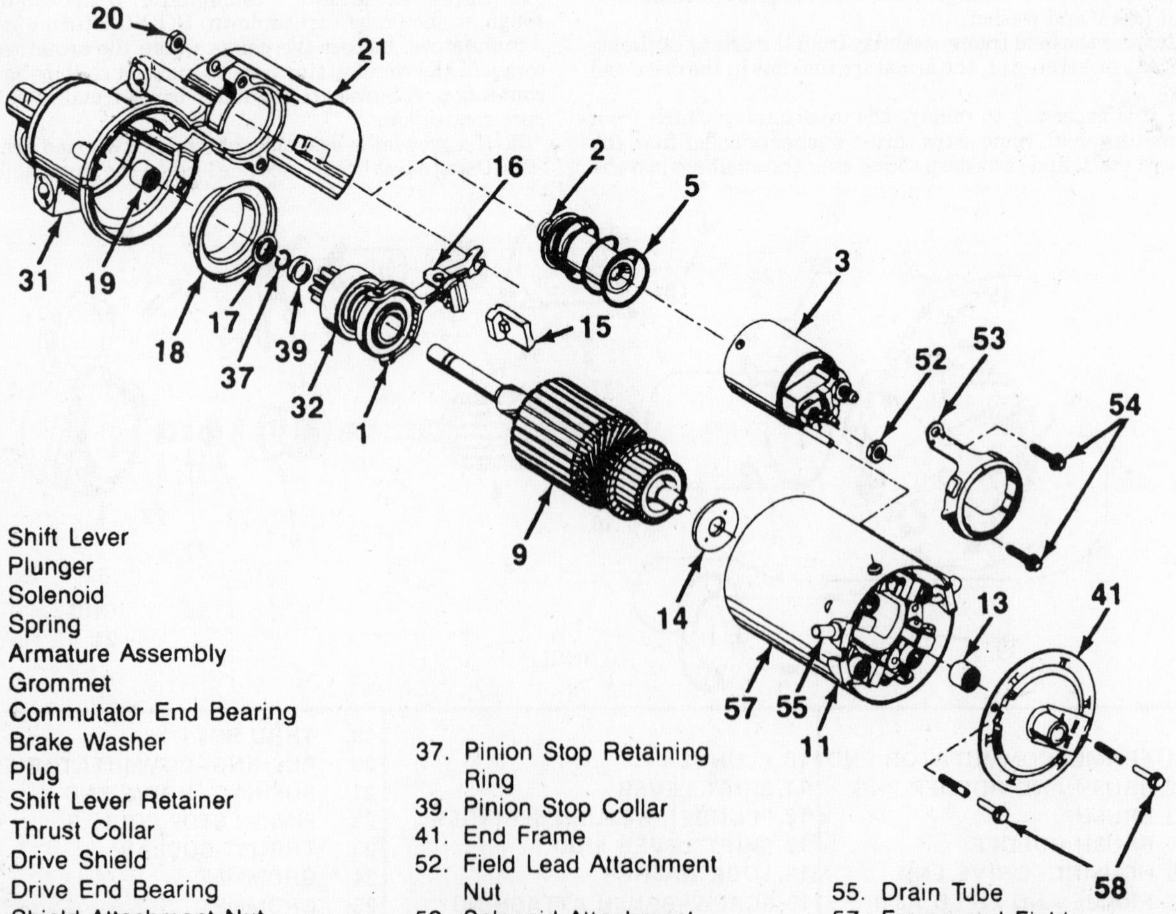

20
21
16
2
5
31
19
18
17
37
39
32
1
15
3
52
53
54
9
14
13
41
57
55
11
58

1. Shift Lever
2. Plunger
3. Solenoid
5. Spring
9. Armature Assembly
11. Grommet
13. Commutator End Bearing
14. Brake Washer
15. Plug
16. Shift Lever Retainer
17. Thrust Collar
18. Drive Shield
19. Drive End Bearing
20. Shield Attachment Nut
21. Solenoid Shield
31. Drive End Frame
32. Drive Assembly
37. Pinion Stop Retaining Ring
39. Pinion Stop Collar
41. End Frame
52. Field Lead Attachment Nut
53. Solenoid Attachment Clamp
54. Solenoid Attachment Screws
55. Drain Tube
57. Frame and Field Assembly (Including Brushes)
58. Through Bolts

SD-260 starter — exploded view

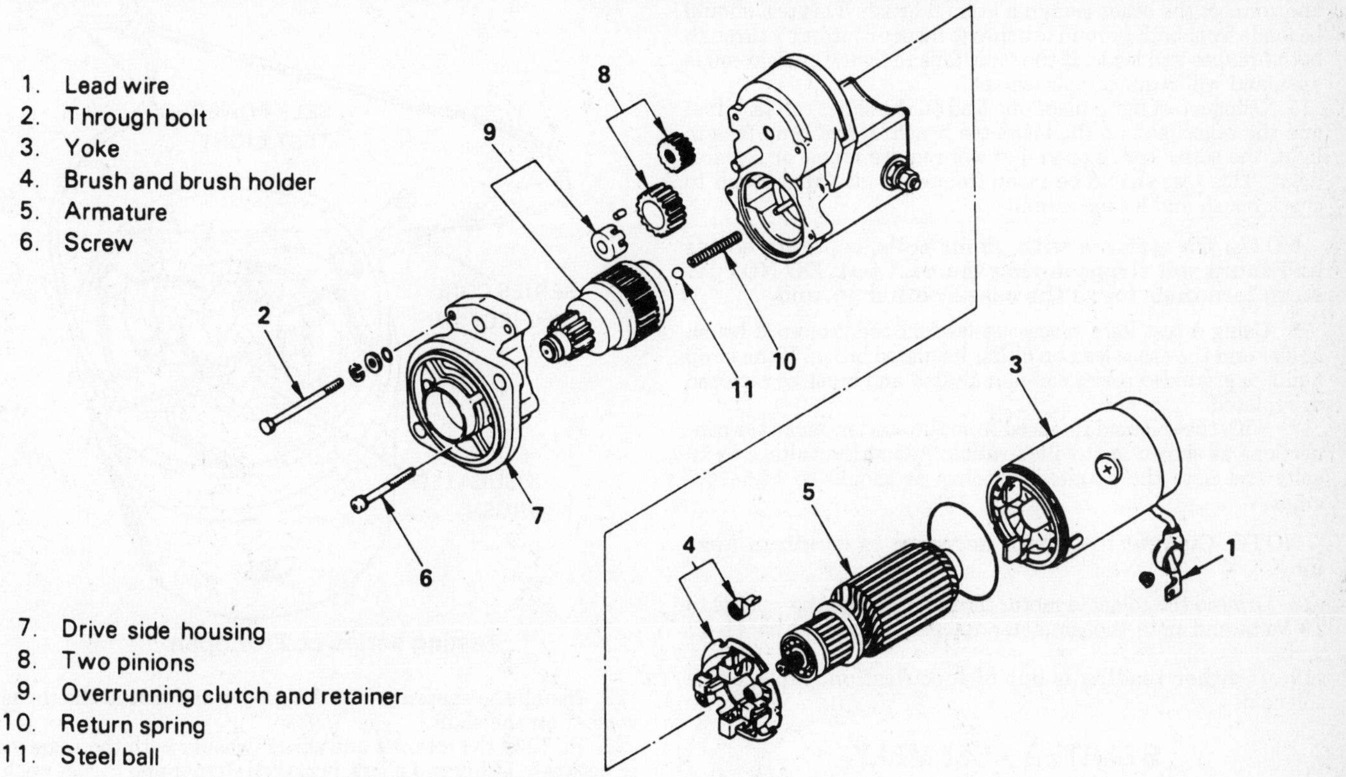
1. Lead wire
2. Through bolt
3. Yoke
4. Brush and brush holder
5. Armature
6. Screw
7. Drive side housing
8. Two pinions
9. Overrunning clutch and retainer
10. Return spring
11. Steel ball

Diesel starter – exploded view

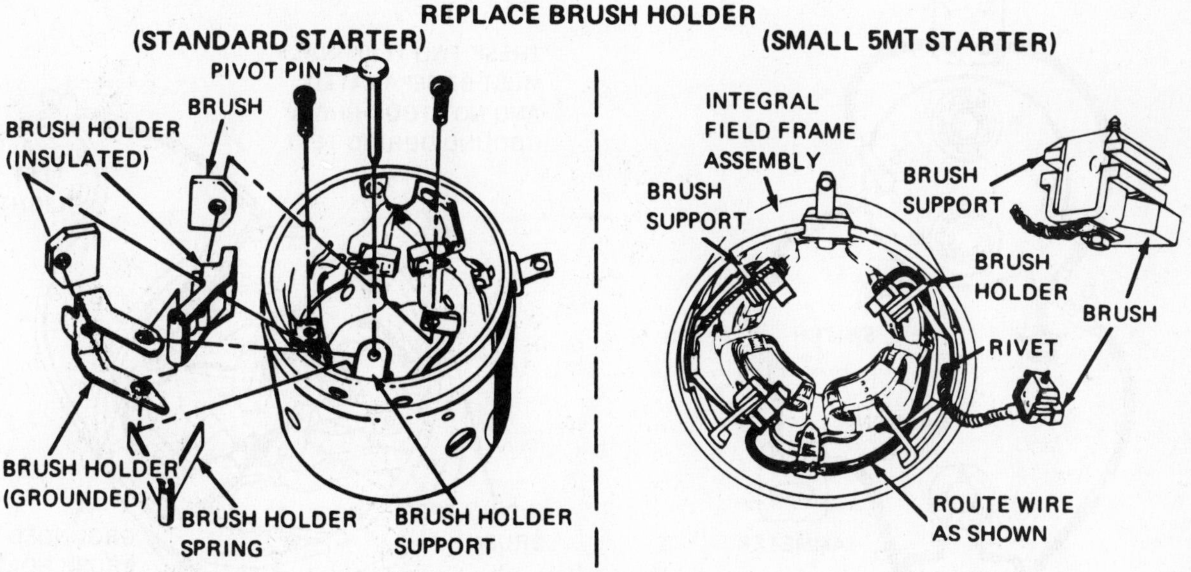
REPLACE BRUSH HOLDER
(STANDARD STARTER)
PIVOT PIN
BRUSH
BRUSH HOLDER (INSULATED)
BRUSH HOLDER (GROUNDED)
BRUSH HOLDER SPRING
BRUSH HOLDER SUPPORT
(SMALL 5MT STARTER)
INTEGRAL FIELD FRAME ASSEMBLY
BRUSH SUPPORT
BRUSH SUPPORT
BRUSH HOLDER
BRUSH
RIVET
ROUTE WIRE AS SHOWN

Replacing brush components

and connect the other lead to a ground brush. This test should be made from both ground brushes to insure continuity through both brushes and leads. If the lamp fails to light, the field coil is open and will require replacement.

15. Using a test light, place one lead on the series coil terminal and the other lead on the insulated brush. If the lamp fails to light, the series coil is open and will require repair or replacement. This test should be made from each insulated brush to check brush and lead continuity.

NOTE: On starters with shunt coils, separate series and shunt soil straps during the next test. DO NOT let strap terminals touch the case or other ground.

16. Using a test light place one lead on the grounded brush holder and the other lead on either insulated brush. If the lamp lights, a grounded series coil is indicated and must be repaired or replaced.

17. With the solenoid removed from the starter, make the connections as shown in the illustration. Adjust the voltage to 10 volts and note the ammeter reading. It should be 14.5–16.5 amps.

NOTE: Current draw will decrease as windings heat up.

18. Ground the solenoid motor terminal. Adjust the voltage to 10 volts and note the ammeter reading. It should be 41–47 amps.

19. If either reading is out of specification, replace the solenoid.

STARTER ASSEMBLY

20. Lubricate the drive end of the armature shaft and install the center bearing, washer and clutch assembly on the shaft with the pinion away from the armature.

21. Slide the retainer onto the shaft with the cupped side facing the end of the shaft.

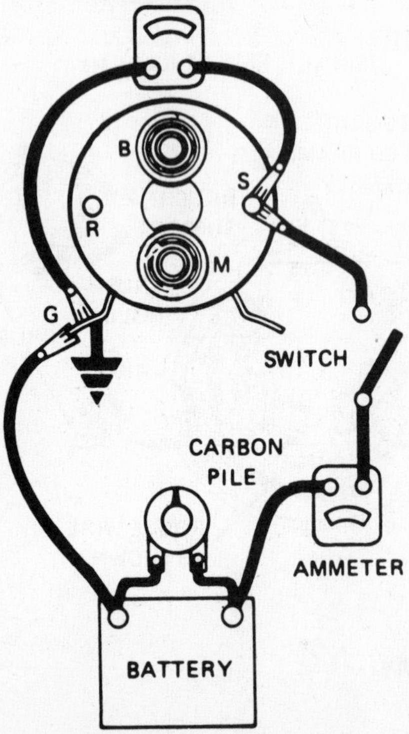
VOLTMETER
B
S
R
M
G
SWITCH
CARBON PILE
AMMETER
BATTERY
Testing solenoid windings

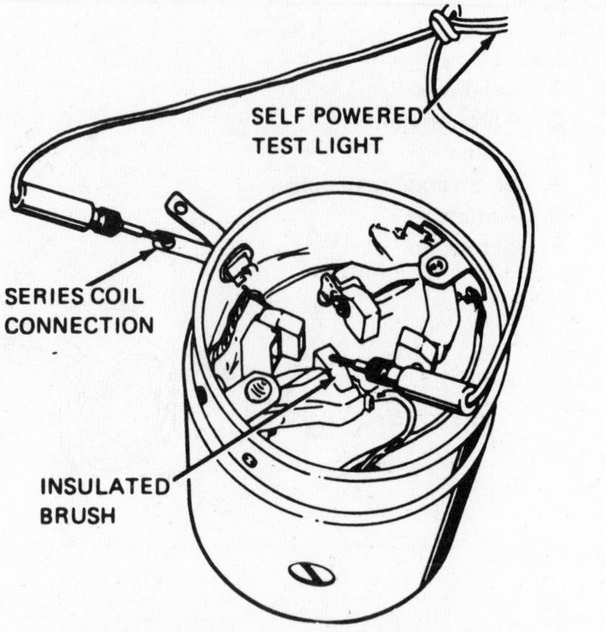
SELF POWERED TEST LIGHT
SERIES COIL CONNECTION
INSULATED BRUSH
Testing series coil for open

22. Install the snapring into the groove and install the thrust washer on the shaft.

23. Position the retainer and thrust washer with the snapring in between. Using two pliers, grip the retainer and thrust washer and squeeze until the snapring is seated.

24. Lubricate the drive gear housing bushing, engage the shift lever yoke with the clutch and slide the complete assembly into the drive gear housing.

25. Install the center bearing screws (diesel only) and shift lever pivot pin.

26. Install the solenoid assembly. Apply sealer to the solenoid flange where the field frame contacts it.

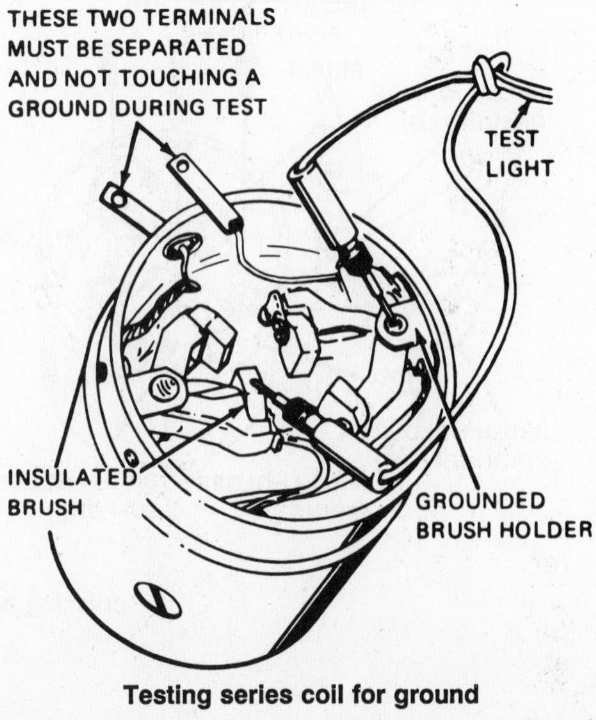
THESE TWO TERMINALS MUST BE SEPARATED AND NOT TOUCHING A GROUND DURING TEST
TEST LIGHT
INSULATED BRUSH
GROUNDED BRUSH HOLDER
Testing series coil for ground

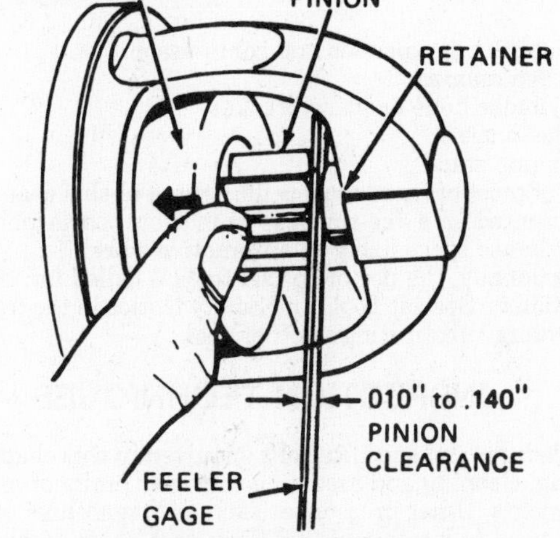
PRESS ON CLUTCH TO REMOVE SLACK
PINION
RETAINER
.010" to .140" PINION CLEARANCE
FEELER GAGE

Checking pinion clearance

27. Position the field frame against the drive gear housing on the alignment pin using care to prevent damage to the brushes.

28. Lubricate the commutator end frame bushing and install the washer on the armature shaft. Slide the end frame onto the shaft and install and tighten the through bolts. On the diesel starter, install the insulator and then the end frame onto the shaft.

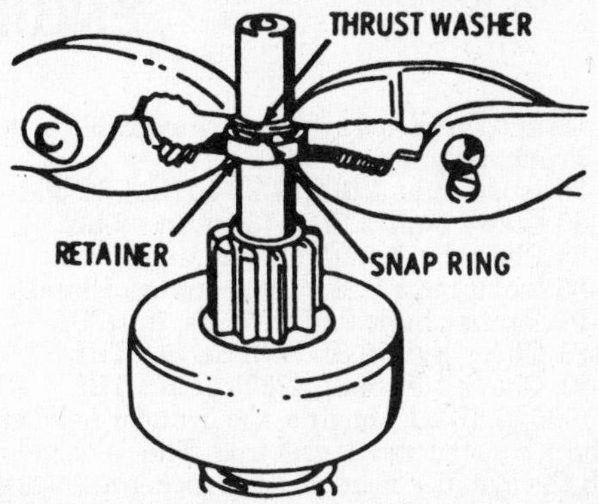
THRUST WASHER
RETAINER
SNAP RING

Installing the snapring onto the armature shaft using pliers

29. Insulate the field coil connector from the solenoid motor terminal.

30. Connect a positive battery lead (12 volt) to the solenoid switch and the ground lead to the starter frame.

31. Flash a jumper lead momentarily from the solenoid motor terminal to the starter frame. This will shift the pinion into the cranking position and it will remain there until the battery is disconnected.

32. Push the pinion back as far as possible to take up any movement, and check the clearance with a feeler gauge. The clearance should be 0.010–0.140 in.. If the clearance is not within specification, check for improper installation or worn parts.

33. Connect the field coil connector to the solenoid terminal.

34. Install the starter on the vehicle.

STARTER SPECIFICATIONS

Year	Engine	Part No.	Series	No Load Test @ 10V Amps	No Load Test @ 10V rpm
1982	2.8L	1109535	5MTPH3	45–70	7000–11900
1983	1.9L	94241705	—	—	—
	2.0L	1109561	5MTPH3	50–75	6000–11900
	2.8L	1109535	5MTPH3	45–70	7000–11900
1984–85	2.0L	1998431	5MTPH3	50–75	6000–11900
	2.8L	1998427	5MTPH3	50–75	6000–11900
1986–87	2.5L	1998532	5MT	50–75	6000–11900
	2.8L	1998524	5MT	50–75	6000–11900
1988–91	2.5L	10455018	5MT	50–70	6000–11900
	2.8L	10455016	SD200	50–75	6000–11900
	4.3L	9000735	PGMR ②	50–90	2330–2660 ①
1991	4.3L	10455013	SD260	50–62	8500–10700

① Drive speed
② SD200

3 ENGINE AND ENGINE OVERHAUL

ENGINE MECHANICAL

Six engines and three fuel systems are available to power your S-10/S-15 Truck, they are:

- 1982–85 Isuzu built 1.9L (118.9 cu. in.) 2-bbl.
- 1982–85 Chevy built 2.8L (173 cu. in.) 2-bbl.
- 1983–84 Chevy built 2.0L (121 cu. in.) 2-bbl.
- 1983–85 Isuzu built 2.2L (136.6 cu. in.) Diesel.
- 1985–91 Pontiac built 2.5L (151 cu. in.) TBI.
- 1986–91 Chevy built 2.8L (173 cu. in.) TBI.
- 1988–91 Chevy built 4.3L (262 cu. in.) TBI.

On the 1985, 2.5L EFI engine, the cylinder head and engine block are both constructed of cast iron. The valve guides are integral with the cylinder head and the rocker arms are retained by individual threaded shoulder bolts. Hydraulic roller lifters are incorporated to reduce the friction between the valve lifters and the camshaft lobes.

On the 1986–87, 2.5L TBI engine, a few changes appeared, such as: (1) the pistons were replaced with hypereutectic types (pistons embedded with silicone nodules in the walls to reduce the cylinder wall friction), (2) a reduced weight, high efficiency alternator and (3) a variable ratio A/C compressor.

The 2.8L engine, utilizes a 2-bbl (1982–85) or an TBI system (1986–87) and the use of swirl chamber heads (to increase power and fuel efficiency). The engine block and cylinder heads are constructed of cast iron. Other major features are: a wider oil pan flange, raised rails inside the cylinder heads (to improve oil return control), machined rocker cover seal surfaces, a trough along the rocker cover rails (to channel oil away from the gasket) and even distribution of the clamping loads, to make this engine one of the most leak-resistant on the road today.

In 1988, the 4.3L TBI engine was introduced. It features forged steel connecting rods and cast aluminum alloy pistons with full floating piston pins.

Engine Overhaul Tips

Most engine overhaul procedures are fairly standard. In addition to specific parts replacement procedures and complete specifications for your individual engine, this chapter also is a guide to acceptable rebuilding procedures. Examples of standard rebuilding practice are shown and should be used along with specific details concerning your particular engine.

Competent and accurate machine shop services will ensure maximum performance, reliability and engine life. Choose your machinist carefully. If the engine is not machined properly, engine failure will result within a short time period after installation.

On most instances it is more profitable for the home mechanic to remove, clean and inspect the component(s), buy the necessary parts and deliver these to a shop for actual machine work.

On the other hand, much of the rebuilding work (crankshaft, block, bearings, piston rods, and other components) is well within the scope of the home mechanic.

TOOLS

The tools required for an engine overhaul or parts replacement will depend on the depth of your involvement. With a few exceptions, they will be the tools found in a mechanic's tool kit (see Chapter 1). More in-depth work will require any or all of the following:

- A dial indicator (reading in thousandths) mounted on a universal base
- Micrometers and telescope gauges
- Jaw and screw-type pullers
- Scraper
- Valve spring compressor
- Ring groove cleaner
- Piston ring expander and compressor
- Ridge reamer
- Cylinder hone or glaze breaker
- Plastigage®
- Engine stand

Use of most of these tools is illustrated in this chapter. Many can be rented for a one-time use from a local parts jobber or tool supply house specializing in automotive work.

Occasionally, the use of special tools is called for. See the information on Special Tools and Safety Notice in the front of this book before substituting another tool.

INSPECTION TECHNIQUES

Procedures and specifications are given in this chapter for inspecting, cleaning and assessing the wear limits of most major components. Other procedures such as Magnaflux® and Zyglo® can be used to locate material flaws and stress cracks.

Magnaflux® is a magnetic process applicable only to ferrous materials. The Zyglo® process coats the material with a fluorescent dye penetrant and can be used on any material. Check for suspected surface cracks can be more readily made using spot check dye. The dye is sprayed onto the suspected area, wiped off and the area sprayed with a developer. Cracks will show up brightly.

OVERHAUL TIPS

Aluminum has become extremely popular for use in engines, due to its low weight. Observe the following precautions when handling aluminum parts:

- Never hot tank aluminum parts (the caustic hot tank solution will eat the aluminum.
- Remove all aluminum parts (identification tag, etc.) from engine parts prior to the tanking.
- Always coat threads lightly with engine oil or anti-seize compounds before installation, to prevent seizure.
- Never over-torque bolts or spark plugs especially in aluminum for you may strip the threads.

Stripped threads in any component can be repaired using any of several commercial repair kits (Heli-Coil®, Microdot®, Keenserts®, etc.).

When assembling the engine, any parts that will have frictional contact must be prelubed to provide lubrication at initial start-up. Any product specifically formulated for this purpose can be used, but engine oil is not recommended as a prelube.

When semi-permanent (locked, but removable) installation of bolts or nuts is desired, threads should be cleaned and coated with Loctite® or other similar, commercial non-hardening sealant.

REPAIRING DAMAGED THREADS

Several methods of repairing damaged threads are available. Heli-Coil® (shown here), Keenserts® and Microdot® are among the most widely used. All involve basically the same principle—drilling out stripped threads, tapping the hole and installing a prewound insert—making welding, plugging and oversize fasteners unnecessary.

Two types of thread repair inserts are usually supplied—a standard type for most Inch Coarse, Inch Fine, Metric Course and Metric Fine thread sizes and a spark lug type to fit most spark plug port sizes. Consult the individual manufacturer's catalog to determine exact applications. Typical thread repair kits will contain a selection of prewound threaded inserts, a tap (corresponding to the outside diameter threads of the insert)

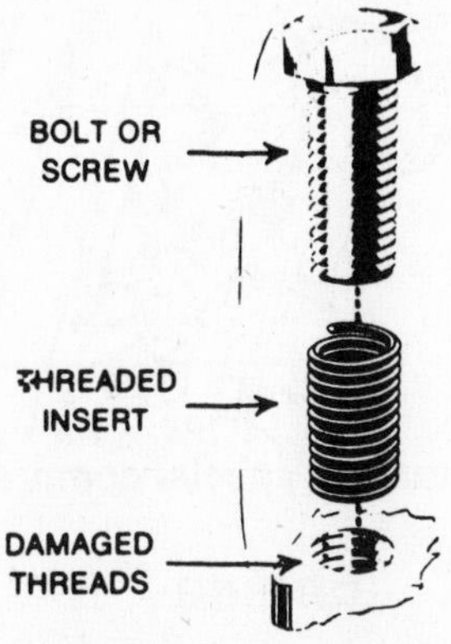
BOLT OR
SCREW
THREADED
INSERT
DAMAGED
THREADS

Using a thread insert to repair a damaged hole

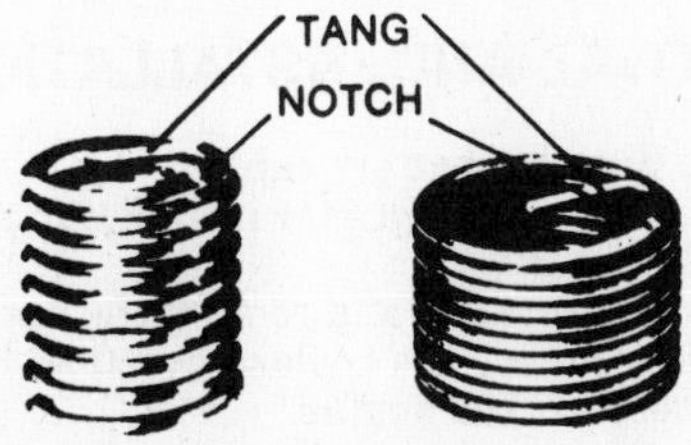
TANG
NOTCH

Standard thread repair insert (left) and the spark plug repair insert (right)

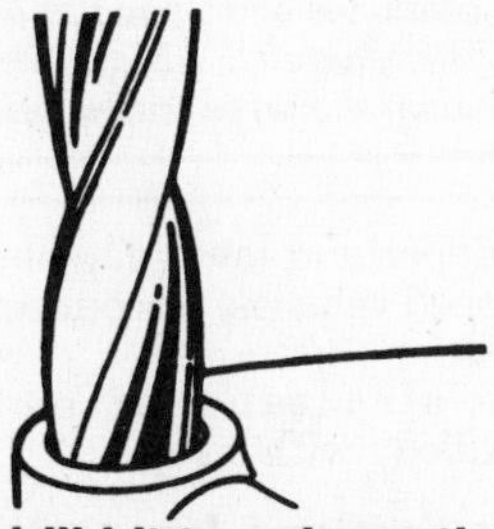

Using a specified drill bit to enlarge the damaged threads. Drill completely through the hole or to the bottom of a blind hole

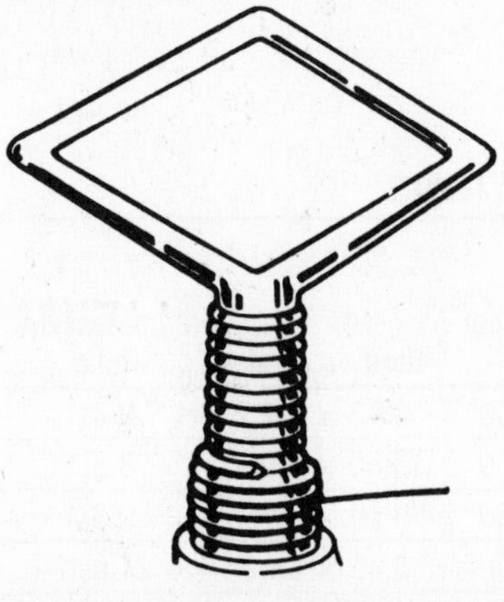

Screw the threaded insert onto the installation tool until the tang engages the slot. Screw the insert into the tapped hole until it is ¼-½ turn below the top surface. After installation, break off the tang with a hammer and punch

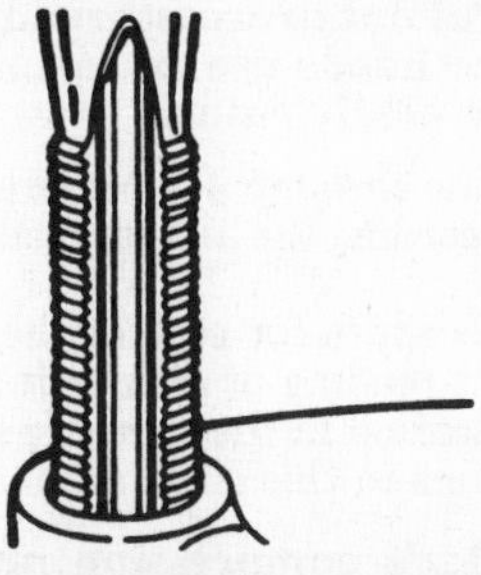

With the supplied tapping bit, tap the hole to receive the thread insert. Keep the tap well oiled and back it out frequently to avoid clogging the threads

and an installation tool. Spark plug inserts usually differ because they require a tap equipped with pilot threads and a combined reamer/tap section. Most manufacturers also supply blister-packed thread repair inserts separately in addition to a master kit containing a variety of taps and inserts plus installation tools.

Before effecting a repair to a threaded hole, remove any snapped, broken or damaged bolts or studs. Penetrating oil can be used to free frozen threads; the offending item can be removed with locking pliers or with a screw or stud extractor. After the hole is clear, the thread can be repaired, as follows:

Checking Engine Compression

A noticeable lack of engine power, excessive oil consumption and/or poor fuel mileage measured over an extended period are all indicators of internal engine wear. Worn piston rings, scored or worn cylinder bores, blown head gaskets, sticking or burnt valves and worn valve seats are all possible culprits here. A check of each cylinder's compression will help you locate the problems.

As mentioned in the "Tools and Equipment" section of Chapter 1, a screw-in type compression gauge is more accurate that the type you simply hold against the spark plug hole. Although the screw in type gauge takes slightly longer to use, it is worth the accuracy you gain.

Gasoline Engines

1. Warm up the engine to normal operating temperature.
2. Remove all spark plugs.
3. Disconnect the high tension lead from the ignition coil.
4. Fully open the throttle, either by operating the carburetor throttle linkage by hand or by having an assistant hold the accelerator pedal to the floor.
5. Screw the compression gauge into the No. 1 spark plug hole until the fitting is snug.

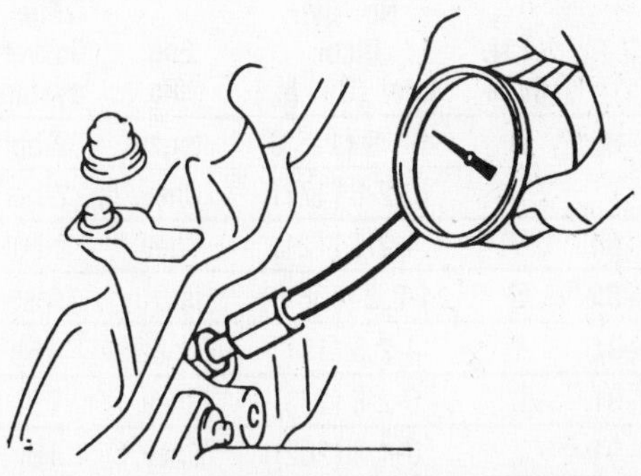

Screw-in type compression gauge

NOTE: Be careful not to crossthread the plug hole. On aluminum cylinder heads use extra care, as the threads in these heads are easily ruined.

6. Crank the engine through 4–5 compression strokes (complete revolutions) recording the highest reading on the compression gauge.
7. Repeat this procedure for each of the engine's cylinders. Compare the highest reading of each cylinder to the compression pressure specification in the Tune-Up Specifications chart in Section 2. The specs in this chart are maximum values.

NOTE: A cylinder's compression pressure is usually acceptable if it is not less than 80% of maximum. A more important measure is difference between each cylinder. The variance should be no more than 12–14 pounds.

8. If a cylinder is unusually low, pour a tablespoon of clean engine oil (30W) into the cylinder through the spark plug hole and repeat the compression test. If the compression rises after adding the oil, it appears that the cylinder's piston rings or bore are damaged or worn.
9. If the pressure remains low, the valves may not be seating properly (a valve job is needed), or the head gasket may be blown near that cylinder.
10. If compression in any two adjacent cylinders is low and if the addition of oil doesn't help the compression, there is leakage past the head gasket. Oil and coolant water in the combustion chamber can result from this problem. There may be evidence of water droplets (sometimes seen as a milky white substance) on the engine dipstick when a head gasket has blown.

Diesel Engines

Checking the cylinder compression on diesel engines is basically the same procedures as on gasoline engines, except for the following:

1. A special compression gauge adaptor suitable for diesel engines (due to greater compression pressures) must be used.
2. Remove the injector tubes and the injectors from each cylinder.

NOTE: Don't forget to remove the washer beneath each injector; otherwise, it may get lost when the engine is cranked.

3. When fitting the compression gauge adaptor to the cylinder head, make sure the bleeder of the gauge (if equipped) is closed.
4. When reinstalling the injector assemblies, install new washers beneath each injector.

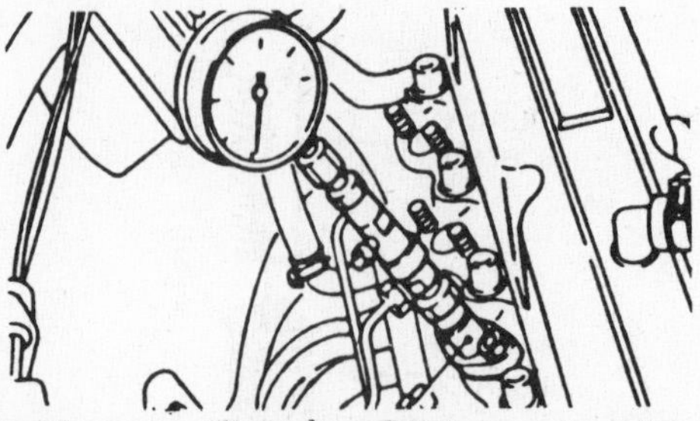

Diesel engines require a special compression gauge adaptor

Engine

NOTE: The following procedures require the use of an engine hoist with sufficient capacity to safely lift and support 500–1000 lbs.

REMOVAL AND INSTALLATION

1. Remove the negative battery cable.
2. Matchmark the hood hinges for installation reference and remove the hood.
3. Drain the cooling system and remove the upper and lower radiator hoses. Disconnect the coolant overflow hose. Disconnect the heater hoses at the engine.

CAUTION

When draining the coolant, keep in mind that cats and dogs are attracted by the ethylene glycol antifreeze, and are quite likely to drink any that is left in an uncovered container or in puddles on the ground. This will prove fatal in sufficient quantity. Always drain the coolant into a sealable container. Coolant should be reused unless it is contaminated or several years old.

4. Remove the upper and lower fan shrouds. On automatic transmission equipped vehicles, disconnect and plug the transmission cooler lines.
5. Remove the air cleaner assembly and cover the carburetor/throttle body with a rag.

NOTE: Refer to Section 5 for special procedures to release fuel system pressure.

6. Label and disconnect all necessary hoses, vacuum lines and wires from the engine, transmission and transfer case (if equipped).

GENERAL ENGINE SPECIFICATIONS

Year	V.I.N. Code	Engine No. Cyl. Displ. Liter (Cu. In.)	Eng. Mfg.	Fuel Delivery system	Horsepower @ rpm	Torque @ rpm ft. lb.	Bore × Stroke	Compression Ratio	Oil Pressure 2000 rpm
1982–85	A	4-1.9 (118.9)	Isuzu	2-bbl	84 @ 4600	101 @ 3000	3.43 × 3.23	8.4:1	57
	B	6-2.8 (173)	Chev.	2-bbl	110 @ 4800	148 @ 2000	3.50 × 2.99	8.5:1	45
1983–84	Y	4-2.0 (121)	Chev.	2-bbl	83 @ 4600	108 @ 2400	3.50 × 3.15	9.3:1	45
1983–85	S	4-2.2 (136.6)	Isuzu	Diesel	58 @ 4300	93 @ 2200	3.46 × 3.62	21.0:1	55
1985–91	E	4-2.5 (151)	Pontiac	TBI	98 @ 4400	134 @ 2800	4.00 × 3.00	9.0:1	38
1986–91	R	6-2.8 (173)	Chev.	TBI	125 @ 4800	150 @ 2200	3.50 × 2.99	8.5:1	52
1988–91	Z	6-4.3 (262)	Chev.	TBI	160 @ 4000	230 @ 2800	4.00 × 3.48	9.3:1	18

① TBI—Throttle body injection

VALVE SPECIFICATIONS

Year	V.I.N. Code	Engine No. Cyl. Displacement Liter (cu. in.)	Eng. Mfg.	Seat Angle (deg.)	Face Angle (deg.)	Spring Test Pressure (lbs. @ in.)	Spring Installed Height (in.)	Stem-to-Guide Clearance (in.) Intake	Stem-to-Guide Clearance (in.) Exhaust	Stem Diameter (in.) Intake	Stem Diameter (in.) Exhaust
1982-85	A	4-1.9 (118.9)	Isuzu	45	45	①	NA	0.0009–0.0022	0.0015–0.0031	0.3102 min.	0.3091 min.
	B	6-2.8 (173)	Chev.	46	45	195 @ 1.180	1.5748	0.0010–0.0027	0.0010–0.0027	0.3410–0.3416	0.3410–0.3416
1983-84	Y	4-2.0 (121)	Chev.	46	45	182 @ 1.330	1.5984	0.0011–0.0026	0.0014–0.0031	0.3410–0.3416	0.3410–0.3416
1983-85	S	4-2.2 (136.6)	Isuzu	45	45	②	NA	0.0015–0.0027	0.0025–0.0037	0.3150–0.3100	0.3150–0.3090
1985-91	E	4-2.5 (151)	Pontiac	46	45	82 @ 1.660	1.690	0.0010–0.0027	0.0010–0.0027	0.343–0.342	0.342–0.343
1986-91	R	6-2.8 (173)	Chev.	46	45	195 @ 1.180	1.5748	0.0010–0.0027	0.0010–0.0027	0.3410–0.2416	0.3410–0.3416
1988-91	Z	6-4.3 (262)	Chev.	46	45	195 @ 1.250	1.7187	0.0010–0.0027	0.0010–0.0027	0.3410–0.2416	0.3410–0.3416

NA—Not available
① Outer: 35 @ 1.614
Inner: 20 @ 1.516
② Outer: 145 @ 1.535
Inner: 44 @ 1.457

CRANKSHAFT AND CONNECTING ROD SPECIFICATIONS

(All measurements are given in inches)

Year	V.I.N. Code	Engine No. Cyl. Displacement Liter (cu. in.)	Eng. Mfg.	Crankshaft Main Brg. Journal Dia.	Crankshaft Main Brg. Oil Clearance	Crankshaft Shaft End-Play	Crankshaft Thrust on No.	Connecting Rod Journal Diameter	Connecting Rod Oil Clearance	Connecting Rod Side Clearance
1982-85	A	4-1.9 (118.9)	Isuzu	2.2050	0.0008–0.0025	0.0117 max.	3	1.9290	0.0007–0.0030	0.0137 max.
	B	6-2.8 (173)	Chev.	2.4940	0.0017–0.0030	0.0020–0.0067	3	1.9980	0.0014–0.0032	0.0063–0.0173
1983-84	Y	4-2.0 (121)	Chev.	①	②	0.0020–0.0071	3	1.9990	0.0010–0.0031	0.0034–0.0240
1983-85	S	4-2.2 (136.6)	Isuzu	2.3590	0.0011–0.0033	0.0018	3	2.0837	0.0016–0.0047	0.0024
1985-91	E	4-2.5 (151)	Pontiac	2.3000	0.0005–0.0022	0.0035–0.0085	5	2.000	0.0005–0.0026	0.0060–0.0220
1986-91	R	6-2.8 (173)	Chev.	③	0.0016–0.0032	0.0023–0.0082	3	1.9998–1.9983	0.0014–0.0037	0.0063–0.0173
1988-91	Z	6-4.3 (262)	Chev.	④	⑤	0.002–0.006	3	2.2487–2.2497	0.0013–0.0035	0.006–0.014

① Nos. 1, 2, 3, 4: 2.4940–2.4950
No. 5: 2.4930–2.4950
② Nos. 1, 2, 3, 4: 0.0006–0.0019
No. 5: 0.0014–0.0027
③ Nos. 1, 2, 4: 2.4937–2.4946
No. 3: 2.4934–2.4941
④ No. 1: 2.4484–2.4493
Nos. 2, 3: 2.4481–2.4490
No. 4: 2.4479–2.4488
⑤ No. 1: 0.0010–0.0015
Nos. 2, 3: 0.0010–0.0025
No. 4: 0.0025–0.0035

CAMSHAFT SPECIFICATIONS

(All measurements in inches)

Year	V.I.N. Code	Engine	Eng. Mfg.	Journal Diameter 1	2	3	4	5	Bearing Clearance	Lobe Lift Intake	Exhaust	Camshaft End Play
1982-85	A	4-1.9L (118.9)	Isuzu	1.3362–1.3370	1.3362–1.3370	1.3362–1.3370	1.3362–1.3370	1.3362–1.3370	0.0016–0.0035	NA	NA	0.0020–0.0059
	B	6-2.8L (173)	Chev.	1.8677–1.8696	1.8677–1.8696	1.8677–1.8696	1.8677–1.8696	—	0.0010–0.0039	0.231	0.262	NA
1983-84	Y	4-2.0L (121)	Chev.	1.8677–1.8696	1.8677–1.8696	1.8677–1.8696	1.8677–1.8696	1.8677–1.8696	0.0010–0.0039	0.262	0.262	NA
1983-85	S	4-2.2L (136.6)	Isuzu	1.8898–1.8741	1.8898–1.8741	1.8898–1.8741	—	—	0.0020–0.0097	NA	NA	0.0032–0.0079
1985-91	E	4-2.5L (151)	Pontiac	1.869	1.869	1.869	—	—	0.0007–0.0027	0.398	0.398	0.0015–0.0050
1986-91	R	6-2.8L (173)	Chev.	1.8677–1.8696	1.8677–1.8696	1.8677–1.8696	1.8677–1.8696	—	0.0010–0.0039	0.231	0.262	NA
1988-91	Z	6-4.3L (262)	Chev.	1.8682–1.8692	1.8682–1.8692	1.8682–1.8692	1.8682–1.8692	—	0.0010–0.0030	0.357	0.390	0.004–0.012

NA—Not available

TORQUE SPECIFICATIONS

(All readings in ft. lbs.)

Year	V.I.N. Code	Engine No. Cyl. Displacement Liter (cu. in.)	Eng. Mfg.	Cylinder Head Bolts	Rod Bearing Bolts	Main Bearing Bolts	Crankshaft Bolt	Flywheel to Crankshaft Bolts	Manifold Intake	Exhaust
1982-85	A	4-1.9 (118.9)	Isuzu	72	43	75	87	76	17	16
	B	6-2.8 (173)	Chev.	70	37	70	75	50	23	25
1983-84	Y	4-2.0 (121)	Chev.	70	37	70	75	50	23	25
1983-85	S	4-2.2 (136.6)	Isuzu	60	65	116–130	125–150	70	15	15
1985-91	E	4-2.5 (151)	Pontiac	90	32	70	160	55	①	①
1986-91	R	6-2.8 (173)	Chev.	70	39	70	70	52	23	25
1988-91	Z	6-4.3 (262)	Chev.	65	45	80	70	75	35	20②

① See text
② Except center (2) bolts 26 ft. lbs.

PISTON AND RING SPECIFICATIONS

(All measurements are given in inches. To convert inches to metric units, refer to the Metric Information section.)

Year	V.I.N. Code	Engine Type Disp. Liter (cu. in.)	Eng Mfg.	Piston-to-Bore Clearance	Ring Gap Top Compression	Ring Gap Bottom Compression	Ring Gap Oil Control	Ring Side Clearance Top Compression	Ring Side Clearance Bottom Compression	Ring Side Clearance Oil Control
1982-85	A	4-1.9 (118.9)	Isuzu	0.0018–0.0026	0.012–0.020	0.008–0.016	0.008–0.035	0.0059 max.	0.0059 max.	0.0059 max.
	B	6-2.8 (173)	Chev.	0.0017–0.0027	0.010–0.020	0.010–0.020	0.020–0.055	0.0012–0.0028	0.0016–0.0037	0.0078 max.
1983-84	Y	4-2.0 (121)	Chev.	0.0008–0.0018	0.010–0.020	0.010–0.020	0.020–0.055	0.0012–0.0027	0.0012–0.0038	0.0078 max.
1983-85	S	4-2.2 (136.6)	Isuzu	0.0062–0.0070	0.008–0.016	0.008–0.016	0.008–0.016	0.0018–0.0028	0.0012–0.0021	0.0008–0.0021
1985-91	E	4-2.5 (151)	Pontiac	0.0014–0.0022	0.010–0.020	0.010–0.020	0.020–0.060	0.002–0.003	0.001–0.003	0.0015–0.0055
1986-91	R	6-2.8 (173)	Chev.	0.0006–0.0017	0.010–0.020	0.010–0.020	0.020–0.055	0.0011–0.0027	0.0015–0.0037	0.0078 max.
1988-91	Z	6-4.3 (262)	Chev.	0.0007–0.0017	0.010–0.020	0.010–0.025	0.015–0.055	0.0012–0.0032	0.0012–0.0032	0.002–0.007

7. Disconnect the throttle cable, transmission TV cable and cruise control cable (if equipped).
8. Raise and support the vehicle safely. Disconnect the exhaust pipes at the manifold.
9. Remove the front driveshaft and skid plates on 4WD vehicles.
10. Disconnect the strut rods at the bell housing.
11. Remove the body mounting bolts. Using a floor jack, raise and support the front of the body safely. Remove the top transmission-to-engine mounting bolts. Lower the body.

NOTE: Vehicles equipped with automatic transmissions do not require transmission removal when removing the engine. Manual transmissions must be removed prior to removing the engine.

13. Remove the rear driveshaft.
14. Support the transmission with a floor jack and remove the transmission crossmember.
15. For vehicles equipped with automatic transmissions:
- Remove the torque converter cover
- Remove the torque converter to flexplate attaching bolts
- Remove the transmission shift linkage
- If equipped with 4WD, remove the transfer case shift linkage
- Remove the remaining transmission-to-engine mounting bolts, and remove the transmission and transfer case (if equipped) as an assembly

16. For vehicles equipped with manual transmissions:
- Remove the clutch slave cylinder and set aside
- Remove the transmission shift linkage and shifter
- If equipped with 4WD, remove the transfer case shift linkage and shifter
- Remove the transmission-to-bellhousing bolts and remove the transmission and transfer case (if equipped) as an assembly
- Leave the bellhousing in place to protect the clutch during engine removal

17. Remove the accessory drive belts.
18. Remove the fan.
19. If equipped, remove the power steering pump, A/C compressor and air pump with their brackets and place aside in the engine compartment.

NOTE: DO NOT disconnect the fluid or refrigerant lines.

20. Check to see that nothing else is attached to the engine.
21. Attach a suitable lifting device to the engine and remove.
22. Installation is the reverse of removal. Torque engine mounting bolts to the following:
- Engine mount-to-engine: 35 ft. lbs.
- Engine mount-to-frame mount: 52 ft. lbs.

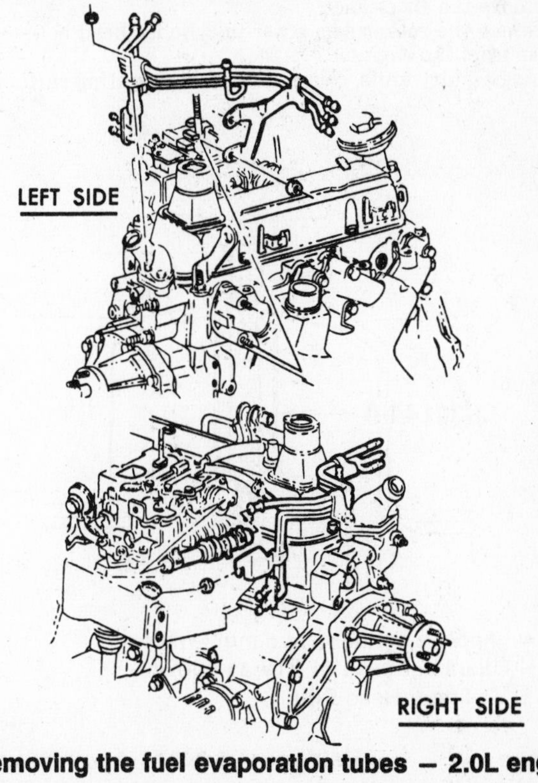
LEFT SIDE
RIGHT SIDE

Removing the fuel evaporation tubes – 2.0L engine

- Transmission mount-to-transmission: 45 ft. lbs.
- Transmission mount-to-crossmember: 24 ft. lbs.

Rocker Arm Cover

REMOVAL AND INSTALLATION

1.9L Engine

1. Remove the negative battery cable.
2. Remove the air cleaner assembly.
3. Remove the spark plug wires and the evaporator pipe.
4. Remove the rocker arm cover-to-engine nuts/washers.
5. Remove the rocker arm cover.
6. Using a putty knife, clean the gasket mounting surfaces.
7. To install, use a new gasket and reverse the removal procedures.

2.0L Engine

1. Remove the negative battery cable.
2. Remove the air cleaner assembly and the distributor cap.
3. Remove the fuel vapor canister harness tubes from the rocker arm cover.
4. Remove the accelerator cable and the PCV valve.
5. Remove the rocker arm cover-to-cylinder head bolts and the cover.

NOTE: If the cover sticks, use a rubber mallet to bump it or a prying tool to lift it from the cylinder head.

6. Using a putty knife, clean the gasket mounting surfaces.
7. To install, place an 1/8 in. bead of RTV sealant around the sealing rail of the cover and reverse the removal procedures. Torque the rocker arm cover-to-cylinder head bolts to 8 ft. lbs.

2.2L Diesel Engine

1. Remove the negative battery cable.
2. Remove the PCV valve from the rocker arm cover and the PCV valve hose.
3. Remove the air cleaner.
4. Remove the rocker arm cover-to-cylinder head bolts and the cover from the engine.
5. Using a putty knife, clean the gasket mounting surfaces.

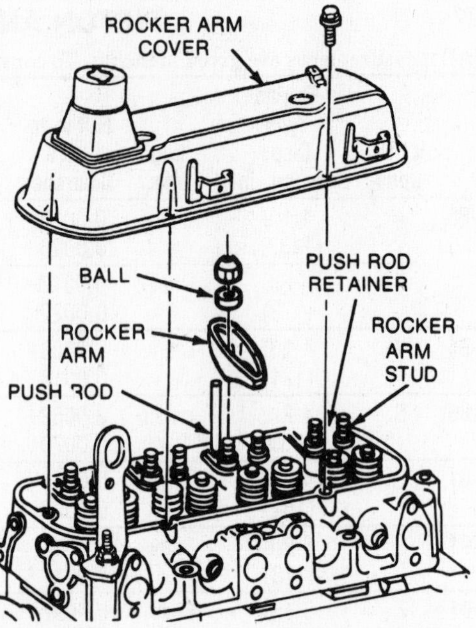
ROCKER ARM COVER
BALL
PUSH ROD RETAINER
ROCKER ARM
ROCKER ARM STUD
PUSH ROD

Exploded view of the rocker arm cover — 2.0L engine

6. To install, use a new gasket and reverse the removal procedures. Torque the rocker arm cover-to-cylinder head bolts to 9–13 ft. lbs.

2.5L Engine

NOTE: A rocker arm cover removal tool (J 34144-A) is needed to perform this procedure without damaging the sealing rail of the rocker arm cover.

1. Remove the negative battery cable.
2. Remove the air cleaner.
3. Disconnect the Positive Crankcase Ventilation (PCV) valve hose, the ignition wires from the rocker arm cover.

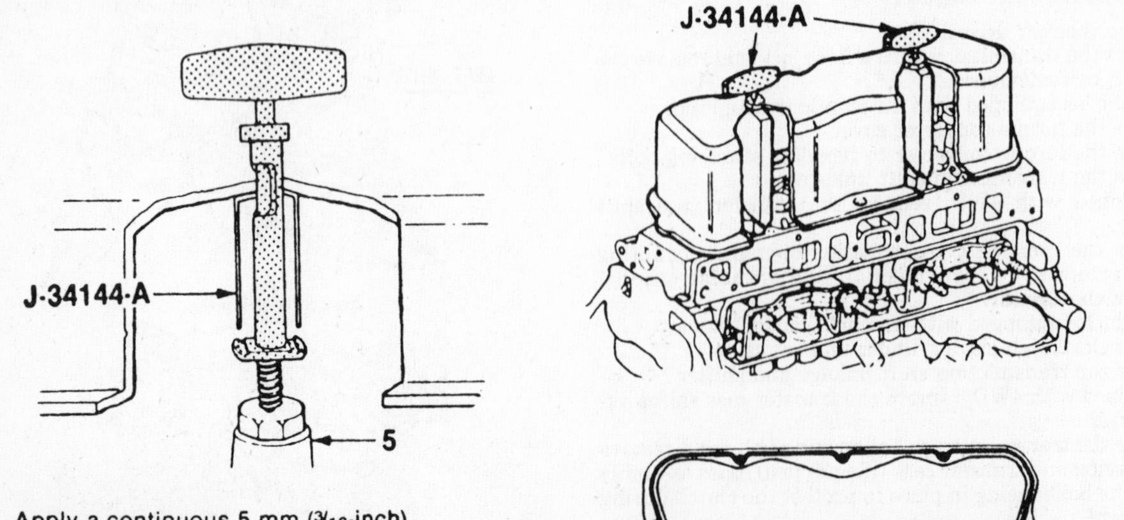
J-34144-A
5
J-34144-A
A

A. Apply a continuous 5 mm (3/16-inch) diameter bead of RTV as shown.
5. Cylinder Head Bolt

Using tool J-34144-A to remove the rocker arm cover — 2.5L engine

4. Remove the Exhaust Gas Recirculation (EGR) valve.
5. Label and disconnect the vacuum hoses.
6. Remove the rocker arm cover-to-cylinder head bolts. Remove the cover using tool J 34144-A or equivalent.
7. Using a putty knife, clean the gasket mounting surfaces.

NOTE: Be sure to use solvent to remove any oil or grease that may remain on the sealing surfaces.

8. To install, place an 1/8 in. bead of RTV sealant around the sealing rail of the cover (or use a new gasket) and reverse the removal procedures. Torque the valve cover-to-cylinder head bolts to 75 inch lbs.

2.8L Engine

LEFT-SIDE

1. Remove the negative battery cable.
2. Disconnect the air management hose, the vacuum hose(s), the electrical wires and the pipe bracket. Remove the spark plug wires and clips from the retaining stubs.
3. Disconnect the fuel line(s) from the carburetor or throttle body, if necessary.
4. Remove the rocker arm cover-to-cylinder head bolts/studs and the cover from the engine.

NOTE: If the cover will not lift, use a rubber mallet to bump it loose from the cylinder head or use a small pry bar to lift the cover.

5. Using a putty knife, clean the gasket mounting surfaces.
6. To install, place an 1/8 in. bead of RTV sealant around the sealing rail of the cover (or use a new gasket) and reverse the removal procedures. Torque the rocker arm cover-to-cylinder head bolts/studs to 72 inch lbs.

RIGHT-SIDE (1982–87)

1. Remove the negative battery cable.
2. Remove the air management and coil brackets.
3. Disconnect the air management hose, the vacuum hose(s), the electrical wires and the pipe bracket. Remove the spark plug wires and clips from the retaining stubs.
4. Disconnect the carburetor or throttle body controls and the brackets.
5. Remove the rocker arm cover-to-cylinder head bolts/studs and the cover from the engine.

NOTE: If the cover will not lift, use a rubber mallet to bump it loose from the cylinder head or use a small pry bar to lift the cover.

6. Using a putty knife, clean the gasket mounting surfaces.
7. To install, place an 1/8 in. bead of RTV sealant around the sealing rail of the cover (or use a new gasket) and reverse the removal procedures. Torque the rocker arm cover-to-cylinder head bolts/studs to 72 inch lbs.

RIGHT-SIDE (1988–91)

1. Remove the negative battery cable.
2. Remove the ignition coil and bracket.
3. Remove spark plug wires, PCV valve and vacuum pipe.
4. Remove the throttle, cruise control and TVS cables and bracket at the throttle body.
5. Remove the alternator and lay it aside.
6. Remove the rocker arm cover-to-cylinder head bolts/studs and the cover from the engine.

NOTE: If the cover will not lift, use a rubber mallet to bump it loose from the cylinder head or use a small pry bar to lift the cover.

7. Using a putty knife, clean the gasket mounting surfaces.
8. To install, place an 1/8 in. bead of RTV sealant around the sealing rail of the cover (or use a new gasket) and reverse the removal procedures. Torque the rocker arm cover-to-cylinder head bolts/studs to 72 inch lbs.

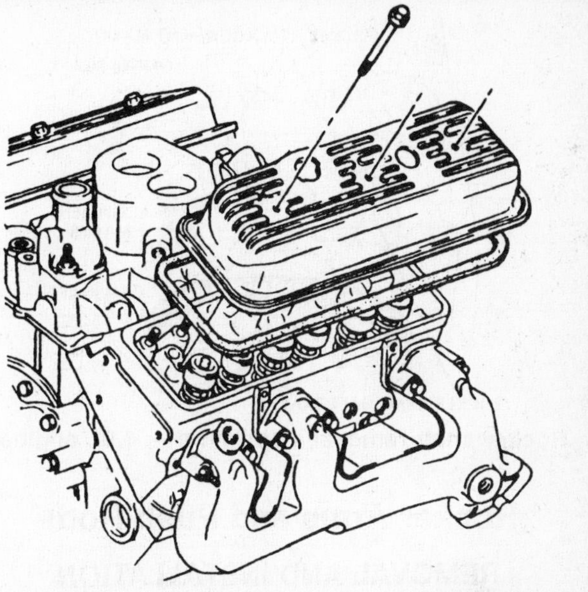

Rocker arm cover removal — 4.3L engine

4.3L Engine

RIGHT SIDE

1. Remove the negative battery cable.
2. Remove the air cleaner, PCV valve and heater pipe.
3. Remove the emissions relays with their bracket and lay them aside.
4. Remove the wiring harness and lay it aside.
5. Remove the spark plug wires and move the dipstick tube aside.
6. Remove the rocker arm cover bolts and cover.

NOTE: If the cover will not lift, use a rubber mallet to bump it loose from the cylinder head or use a small pry bar to lift the cover.

7. Using a putty knife, clean the gasket mounting surfaces.
8. To install, place an 1/8 in. bead of RTV sealant around the sealing rail of the cover (or use a new gasket) and reverse the removal procedures. Torque the rocker arm cover-to-cylinder head bolts/studs to 90 inch lbs.

LEFT SIDE

1. Remove the negative battery cable.
2. Remove the air cleaner, crankcase ventilation pipe and heater pipe.
3. Remove the fuel pipes at the throttle body and move them aside.
4. Remove the generator rear bracket.
5. Remove the spark plug wires and the power brake vacuum line.
6. Remove the rocker arm cover bolts and cover.

NOTE: If the cover will not lift, use a rubber mallet to bump it loose from the cylinder head or use a small pry bar to lift the cover.

7. Using a putty knife, clean the gasket mounting surfaces.
8. To install, place an 1/8 in. bead of RTV sealant around the sealing rail of the cover (or use a new gasket) and reverse the removal procedures. Torque the rocker arm cover-to-cylinder head bolts/studs to 90 inch lbs.

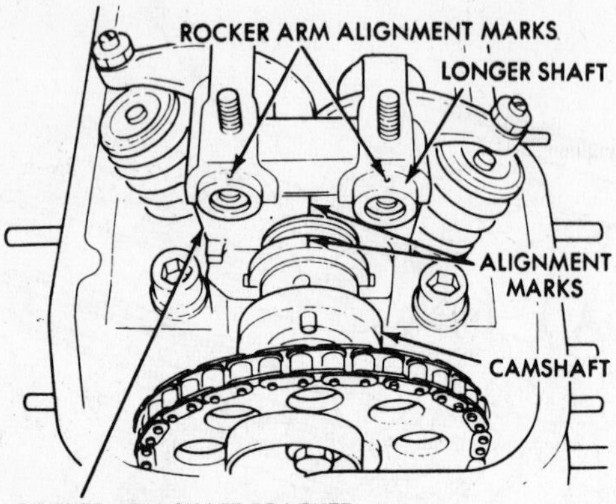
ROCKER ARM ALIGNMENT MARKS
LONGER SHAFT
ALIGNMENT MARKS
CAMSHAFT
ROCKER ARM SHAFT BRACKET

Rocker shaft removal/installation — 1.9L engine

Rocker Arms and Push Rods

REMOVAL AND INSTALLATION

1.9L Engine

1. Remove the rocker arm cover.
2. Starting with the outer rocker arm shaft bracket, loosen the bracket nuts a little at a time (in sequence), then remove the nuts.
3. To disassemble the rocker arm shaft assembly, remove the spring from the rocker arm shaft, then the rocker arm brackets and arms.
4. Inspect the rocker arm shafts for runnout. Runnout should not exceed 0.0079 in..
5. Measure the rocker arm to shaft clearance. Clearance should not exceed 0.0078 in..
6. Check the face of the rocker arms for wear and/or damage, replace the rocker arms and/or shafts if not within specification.
7. Using engine oil, lubricate all of the moving parts.
8. Assemble the rocker arm shaft brackets and rocker arms to the shaft so that the cylinder number (on the upper face of the bracket) is pointed to the front of the engine.

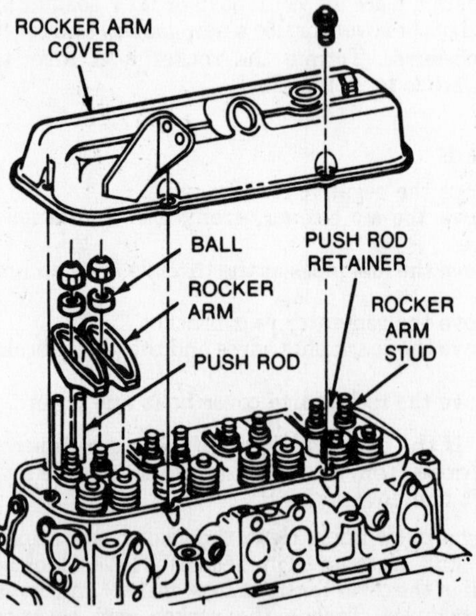
ROCKER ARM COVER
BALL
PUSH ROD RETAINER
ROCKER ARM
ROCKER ARM STUD
PUSH ROD

Rocker shaft removal/installation — 2.0L engine

9. Align the mark on the No. 1 rocker arm shaft bracket with the mark on the intake and exhaust valve side rocker arm shaft.
10. Check the amount of projection of the rocker arm shaft. The intake side should be longer when the holes in the shaft are aligned with the holes in the bracket.
11. Place the springs in position between the shaft bracket and rocker arm.
12. Check that the punch mark is turned upward, and install the shaft bracket assembly onto the head studs. Align the mark on the camshaft with the mark on the No. 1 rocker arm shaft bracket.
13. Tighten the bracket studs to 16 ft. lbs. and adjust the valves.

NOTE: The valves are adjusted with the engine Cold.

14. Using a wrench on the damper pulley bolt or a remote starter button, turn the engine's crankshaft until the No. 1 piston is at TDC of the compression stroke.

NOTE: Crank the engine until the mark on the torsional damper lines up with the 0 in. mark on the timing tab. To determine if the No. 1 cylinder is on the compression stroke, place your fingers on the number one valve as the mark on the damper comes near the 0 in. mark on the timing tab. If the rocker arms are not moving, the engine is in the number one firing position. If the rocker arms are moving, the engine is in the number four firing position. Turn the engine over one revolution. Remove the distributor cap and ensure that the rotor is pointing to the No. 1 position on the cap.

15. With the No. 1 piston at TDC of the compression stroke, use a 0.006 in. (0.152mm) feeler gauge, to set intake valves of cylinders No. 1 & 2. Using a 0.010 in. (0.254mm) feeler gauge, set the exhaust valves of cylinders No. 1 & 3.
16. Rotate the engine one complete revolution, so that cylinder No. 4 is on the TDC of its compression stroke and the timing marks are aligned.
17. With cylinder No. 4 on the TDC of the compression stroke, use a 0.006 in. (0.152mm) feeler gauge, to set intake valves of cylinders No. 3 & 18. Using a 0.010 in. (0.254mm) feeler gauge, set the exhaust valves of cylinders No. 2 & 4.

NOTE: When adjusting the valve clearance, loosen the locknut with an open-end wrench, then turn the adjuster screw with a screwdriver and retighten the locknut. The proper thickness feeler gauge should pass between the camshaft and the rocker with a slight drag when the clearance is correct.

2.0L Engine

1. Remove the rocker arm cover.
2. Remove the rocker arm nuts, the ball washers and the rocker arms off the studs, then lift out the push rods.

NOTE: Always keep the rocker arm assemblies together and install them on the same stud.

3. Coat the bearing surfaces of the rocker arms and the rocker arm ball washers with Molykote® or its equivalent.
4. Install the push rods making sure that they seat properly in the lifter.
5. Install the rocker arms, the ball washers and the nuts. Tighten the rocker arm nuts until all lash is eliminated.
6. Adjust the valves when the lifter is on the base circle of a camshaft lobe:
    a. Crank the engine until the mark on the crankshaft pulley lines up with the 0° mark on the timing tab. Make sure that the engine is in the No. 1 firing position. Place your fingers on the No. 1 rocker arms as the mark on the crank pulley comes near the 0° mark.

NOTE: If the valves are not moving, the engine is in the No. 1 firing position. If the valves move, the engine is in the No. 4 firing position; rotate the engine one complete revolution and it will be in the No. 1 position.

b. When the engine is on the No. 1 firing position, adjust the following valves:
- Exhaust—1, 3
- Intake—1, 2

c. Back the adjusting nut out until lash can be felt at the push rod, then turn the nut until all lash is removed (this can be determined by rotating the push rod while turning the adjusting nut). When all lash has been removed, turn the nut in 1½ additional turns, this will center the lifter plunger.

d. Crank the engine one complete revolution until the timing tab (0° mark) and the crankshaft pulley mark are again in alignment. Now the engine is in the No. 4 firing position. Adjust the following valves:
- Exhaust—2, 4
- Intake—3, 4

7. Install the rocker arm cover, start the engine and check the timing and the idle speed.

2.2L Diesel Engine

1. Remove the rocker cover.
2. Remove the rocker arm bracket-to-cylinder head bolts in sequence, commencing with the outer ones.
3. Remove the rocker arm, the bracket and shaft assembly.
4. Remove the snapring, the rocker arms, the springs and the brackets.

NOTE: Always keep the rocker arm assemblies together and install them on the same stud.

5. Inspect the rocker arm shafts for runnout. Runnout should not exceed 0.0079 in..
6. Measure the rocker arm to shaft clearance. Clearance should not exceed 0.0078 in..
7. Check the face of the rocker arms for wear and/or damage, replace the rocker arms and/or shafts if not within specification.
8. Using engine oil, lubricate all of the moving parts.
9. To install, position the brackets with the "F" marks facing the front of the engine. Working from the center outward, torque the bracket-to-cylinder head bolts to 9–17 ft. lbs. Adjust the valves.

NOTE: The valves are adjusted with the engine Cold.

10. Using a wrench on the damper pulley bolt or a remote starter button, turn the crankshaft until the No. 1 piston is at TDC of the compression stroke.

NOTE: Crank the engine until the mark on the torsional damper lines up with the 0 in. mark on the timing tab. To determine if the No. 1 cylinder is on the compression stroke, place your fingers on the number one valve as the mark on the damper comes near the 0 in. mark on the timing tab. If the rocker arms are not moving, the engine is in the number one firing position. If the rocker arms are moving, the engine is in the number four firing position. Turn the engine over one revolution. Remove the distributor cap and ensure that the rotor is pointing to the No. 1 position on the cap.

11. With the No. 1 piston at TDC of the compression stroke, use a 0.016 in. (0.40mm) feeler gauge, to set the intake valves of cylinders No. 1, 2 & 3, then set the exhaust valve of cylinder No. 1.
12. Rotate the engine one complete revolution, so that cylinder No. 4 is on the TDC of its compression stroke and the timing marks are aligned.
13. With cylinder No. 4 on the TDC of the compression stroke, use a 0.016 in. (0.40mm) feeler gauge, to set the intake valve of cylinder No. 4, then the exhaust valves of cylinders No. 2, 3 & 4.

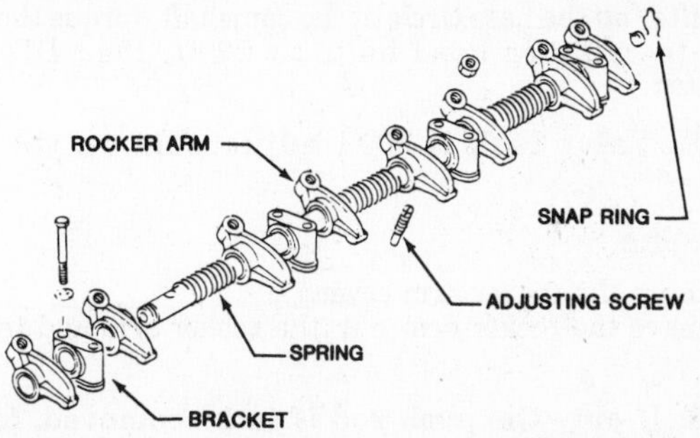
ROCKER ARM
SNAP RING
ADJUSTING SCREW
SPRING
BRACKET

Exploded view of the rocker arm assembly — 2.2L engine

NOTE: When adjusting the valve clearance, loosen the locknut with an open-end wrench, then turn the adjuster screw with a screwdriver and retighten the locknut. The proper thickness feeler gauge should pass between the camshaft and the rocker with a slight drag when the clearance is correct.

2.5L Engine

1. Remove the rocker arm cover.
2. Using a socket wrench, remove the rocker arm bolts, the ball washer and the rocker arm.

NOTE: If only the pushrod is to be removed, back off the rocker arm bolt, swing the rocker arm aside and remove the pushrod. When removing more than one assembly, at the same time, be sure to keep them in order for reassembly purposes.

3. Inspect the rocker arms and ball washers for scoring and/or other damage, replace them (if necessary).

NOTE: If replacing worn components with new ones, be sure to coat the new parts with Molykote® before installation.

4. To install, reverse the removal procedures. With the hy-

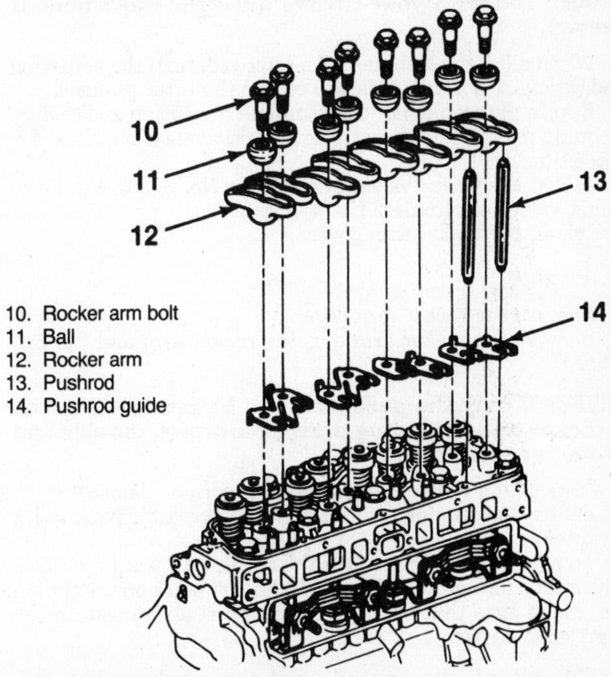
10
11
12
13
14
10. Rocker arm bolt
11. Ball
12. Rocker arm
13. Pushrod
14. Pushrod guide

Rocker shaft removal/installation — 2.5L engine

draulic lifter on the base circle of the camshaft, torque the rocker arm-to-cylinder head bolts to 22 ft. lbs.; DO NOT overtighten.

NOTE: Valve lash is NOT adjustable on the 2.5L engine.

2.8L Engine

1. Remove the rocker arm cover.
2. Remove the rocker arm nut, the rocker arm and the ball washer.

NOTE: If only the push rod is to be removed, loosen the rocker arm nut, swing the rocker arm to the side and remove the pushrod.

3. Inspect and replace components if worn or damaged.
4. Before installation, coat all of the working parts with Molykote®.
5. To adjust the valves, rotate the crankshaft until the mark on the crankshaft pulley aligns with the "0" mark on the timing plate. Make sure that the No. 1 cylinder is positioned on the compression stroke.

NOTE: Crank the engine until the mark on the torsional damper lines up with the 0 in. mark on the timing tab. To determine if the No. 1 cylinder is on the compression stroke, place your fingers on the number one valve as the mark on the damper comes near the 0 in. mark on the timing tab. If the rocker arms are not moving, the engine is in the number one firing position. If the rocker arms are moving, the engine is in the number four firing position. Turn the engine over one revolution. Remove the distributor cap and ensure that the rotor is pointing to the No. 1 position on the cap.

6. Adjust the intake valves of cylinders No. 1, 5 & 6 and the exhaust valves of cylinders No. 1, 2 & 3.
7. To adjust the valves, back-out the adjusting nut until lash can be felt at the push rod, then turn the nut until all of the lash is removed.

NOTE: To determine is all of the lash is removed, turn the push rod with your fingers until the movement is removed.

8. When all of the lash has been removed, turn the adjusting an additional 1½ turns; this will center the lifter plunger.
9. Rotate the crankshaft one complete revolution and realign the timing marks; the engine is now positioned on the No. 4 firing position.
10. Adjust the intake valves of cylinders No. 2, 3 & 4 and the exhaust valves of cylinders No. 4, 5 & 6.
11. Install the rocker arm cover.

4.3L Engine

1. Remove the rocker arm cover.
2. Remove the rocker arm nut, the rocker arm and the ball washer.

NOTE: If only the push rod is to be removed, loosen the rocker arm nut, swing the rocker arm to the side and remove the pushrod.

3. Inspect and replace components if worn or damaged.
4. Before installation, coat all of the working parts with Molykote®.
5. To adjust the valves, rotate the crankshaft until the mark on the crankshaft pulley aligns with the "0" mark on the timing plate. Make sure that the No. 1 cylinder is positioned on the compression stroke.

NOTE: Crank the engine until the mark on the torsional damper lines up with the 0 in. mark on the timing tab. To determine if the No. 1 cylinder is on the compression stroke, place your fingers on the number one valve as the mark on the damper comes near the 0 in. mark on the timing tab. If the rocker arms are not moving, the engine is in the number one firing position. If the rocker arms are moving, the engine is in the number four firing position. Turn the engine over one revolution. Remove the distributor cap and ensure that the rotor is pointing to the No. 1 position on the cap.

6. Adjust the exhaust valves of cylinders No. 1, 5 & 6 and the intake valves of cylinders No. 1, 2 & 3.
7. To adjust the valves, back-out the adjusting nut until lash can be felt at the push rod, then turn the nut until all of the lash is removed.

NOTE: To determine is all of the lash is removed, turn the push rod with your fingers until the movement is removed.

8. When all of the lash has been removed, turn the adjusting an additional 1½ turns; this will center the lifter plunger.
9. Rotate the crankshaft one complete revolution and realign the timing marks; the engine is now positioned on the No. 4 firing position.
10. Adjust the exhaust valves of cylinders No. 2, 3 & 4 and the intake valves of cylinders No. 4, 5 & 6.
11. Install the rocker arm cover.

Thermostat

DIAGNOSIS

Make an operational check of the thermostat by hanging the it on a hook in a hook in a pot of warm water. Insert a thermometer into the water and heat the water to the thermostat opening temperature (stamped on the top of the thermostat). With the temperature within 10° of the opening temperature, the thermostat should open. If not, replace the thermostat.

REMOVAL AND INSTALLATION

1.9L Engine

1. Drain the cooling system to a level below the thermostat.

CAUTION

When draining the coolant, keep in mind that cats and dogs are attracted by the ethylene glycol antifreeze, and are quite likely to drink any that is left in an uncovered container or in puddles on the ground. This will prove fatal in sufficient quantity. Always drain the coolant into a sealable container. Coolant should be reused unless it is contaminated or several years old.

2. Disconnect the PCV hose, the ECS hose, the AIR hose and the TCA hose.
3. Remove the air cleaner-to-carburetor bolts and loosen the clamp bolts, then lift the air cleaner and disconnect the TCA hose from the thermosenser (on the intake manifold). Remove the hoses from the air cleaner-to-carburetor slow actuator and the air cleaner-to-vacuum control (California), then remove the air cleaner assembly.
4. Remove the outlet pipe-to-inlet manifold bolts, the outlet pipe (with the radiator hose attached) and the thermostat from the engine.
5. Using a putty knife, clean the gasket mounting surfaces.
6. Installation is the reverse of removal. Use a new gasket and sealant. Torque the outlet pipe-to-intake manifold bolts to 21 ft. lbs.
7. Refill the cooling system with a 50% antifreeze solution. Start the engine and check for leaks.

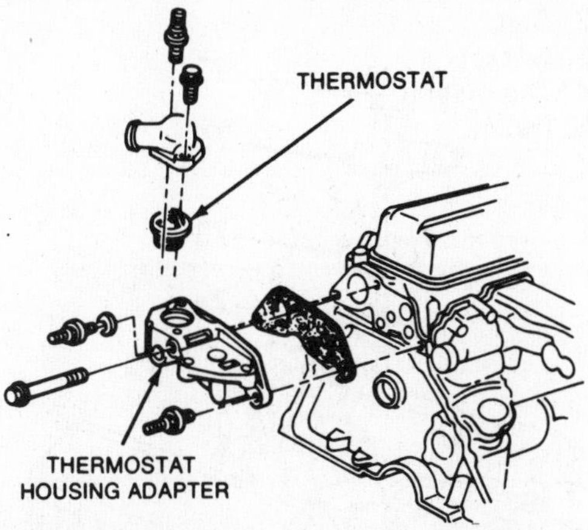
THERMOSTAT
THERMOSTAT HOUSING ADAPTER

Thermostat replacement – 2.0L engine

2.0L Engine

The thermostat is connected to the water outlet and the thermostat housing, located at the top front-side of the engine.

1. Remove the negative battery cable.
2. Drain the cooling system to a level below the thermostat.

CAUTION

When draining the coolant, keep in mind that cats and dogs are attracted by the ethylene glycol antifreeze, and are quite likely to drink any that is left in an uncovered container or in puddles on the ground. This will prove fatal in sufficient quantity. Always drain the coolant into a sealable container. Coolant should be reused unless it is contaminated or several years old.

3. Remove the steel vacuum tubes.
4. Remove the water outlet-to-thermostat housing bolts, then lift the outlet from the thermostat housing and remove the thermostat.
5. Using a putty knife, clean the gasket mounting surfaces.
6. Place an 1/8 in. bead of RTV sealant on the water outlet. Place the thermostat, with the power element down, in the housing and install water outlet while the RTV is still wet.
7. Torque the water outlet-to-thermostat housing bolts to 15–22 ft. lbs.
8. Refill the cooling system with a 50% antifreeze solution. Start the engine and check for leaks.

2.2L Diesel Engine

The thermostat is connected to the water outlet and the thermostat housing, located at the top front-side of the engine.

1. Remove the negative battery cable.
2. Drain the cooling system to a level below the thermostat.

CAUTION

When draining the coolant, keep in mind that cats and dogs are attracted by the ethylene glycol antifreeze, and are quite likely to drink any that is left in an uncovered container or in puddles on the ground. This will prove fatal in sufficient quantity. Always drain the coolant into a sealable container. Coolant should be reused unless it is contaminated or several years old.

3. Disconnect the electrical wiring.
4. Remove the water outlet-to-thermostat housing bolts, then lift the outlet from the thermostat housing and remove the thermostat.
5. Using a putty knife, clean the gasket mounting surfaces.
6. Installation is the reverse of removal. Using a new gasket and sealant, install the water outlet while the sealant is wet. Torque the water outlet-to-thermostat housing bolts to 10–17 ft. lbs.

WITH A/C

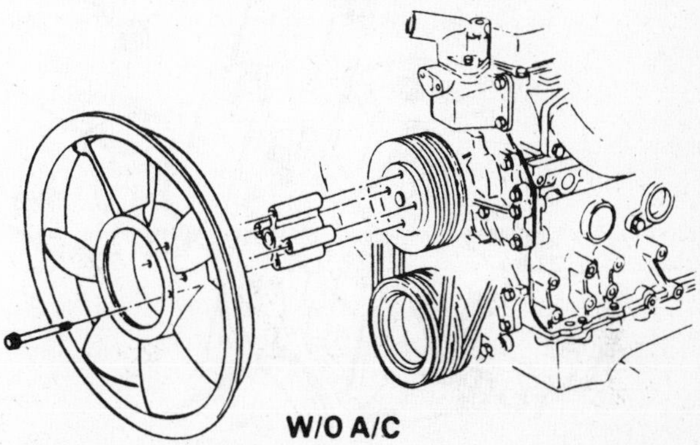

W/O A/C

Thermostat replacement – 2.2L diesel engine

7. Refill the cooling system with a 50% antifreeze solution. Start the engine and check for leaks.

2.5L Engine

The thermostat is located inside the thermostat housing, which is attached to the front of the cylinder head.

1. Remove the negative battery cable.
2. Drain the cooling system.

CAUTION

When draining the coolant, keep in mind that cats and dogs are attracted by the ethylene glycol antifreeze, and are quite likely to drink any that is left in an uncovered container or in puddles on the ground. This will prove fatal in sufficient quantity. Always drain the coolant into a sealable container. Coolant should be reused unless it is contaminated or several years old.

3. Remove the thermostat housing-to-engine bolts and the thermostat.
4. Using a putty knife, clean the gasket mounting surfaces.
5. Using RTV sealant or equivalent, place an 1/8 in. bead of sealant in the groove of the water outlet.
6. Installation is the reverse of removal. Install the housing while the sealant is still wet.
7. Torque the thermostat housing-to-engine bolts to 21 ft. lbs.
8. Refill the cooling system, start the engine and check for leaks.

2.8L and 4.3L Engine

The thermostat is located between the water outlet and the intake manifold.

1. Remove the negative battery cable.
2. Drain the cooling system.

CAUTION

When draining the coolant, keep in mind that cats and dogs are attracted by the ethylene glycol antifreeze, and are quite likely to drink any that is left in an uncovered container or in puddles on the ground. This will

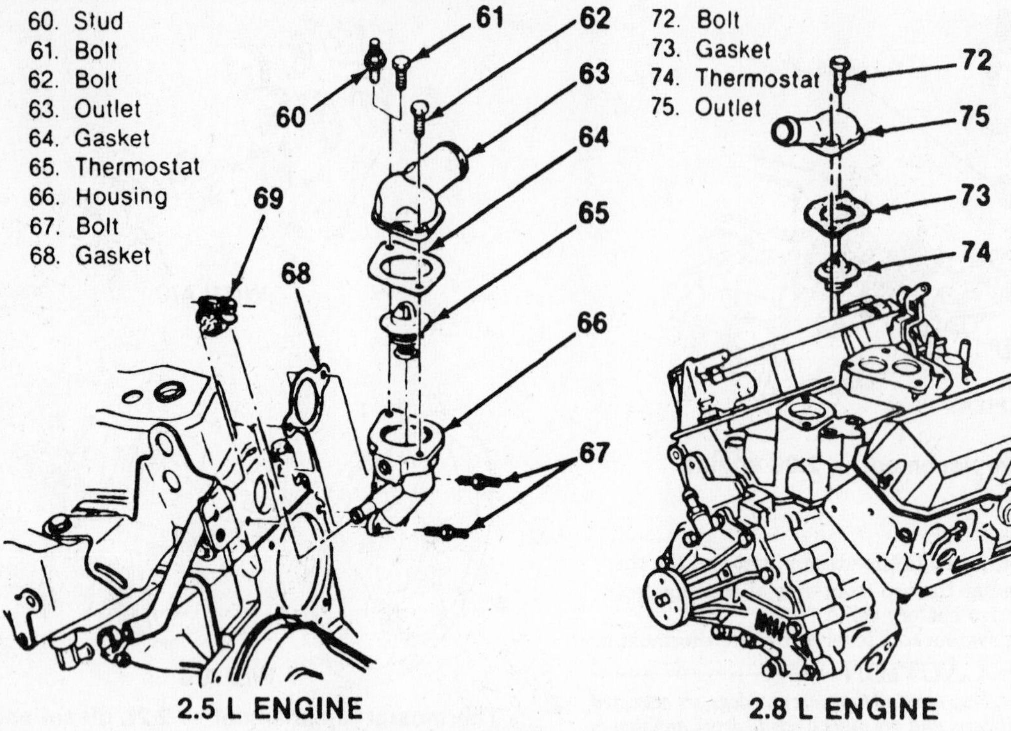
60. Stud
61. Bolt
62. Bolt
63. Outlet
64. Gasket
65. Thermostat
66. Housing
67. Bolt
68. Gasket
60
61
62
63
64
65
66
67
68
69
72. Bolt
73. Gasket
74. Thermostat
75. Outlet
72
75
73
74
2.5 L ENGINE
2.8 L ENGINE

Thermostat replacement — 2.5L and 2.8L engine

prove fatal in sufficient quantity. Always drain the coolant into a sealable container. Coolant should be reused unless it is contaminated or several years old.

---

3. Remove the thermostat housing-to-engine bolts and the thermostat.
4. Using a putty knife, clean the gasket mounting surfaces.
5. Using RTV sealant or equivalent, place an ⅛ in. bead of sealant in the groove of the water outlet.
6. Installation is the reverse of removal. Install the housing while the sealant is still wet.
7. Torque the thermostat housing-to-engine bolts to 21 ft. lbs.
8. Refill the cooling system, start the engine and check for leaks.

Intake Manifold

REMOVAL AND INSTALLATION

1.9L Engine

1. Remove the negative battery cable and the air cleaner assembly.
2. Drain the cooling system to a level below the intake manifold.

CAUTION

When draining the coolant, keep in mind that cats and dogs are attracted by the ethylene glycol antifreeze, and are quite likely to drink any that is left in an uncovered container or in puddles on the ground. This will prove fatal in sufficient quantity. Always drain the coolant into a sealable container. Coolant should be reused unless it is contaminated or several years old.

---

3. Disconnect the upper radiator hose, the vacuum hose and the heater hose (from the rear of the intake manifold).
4. Disconnect the accelerator control cable. Disconnect the automatic choke and the solenoid electrical connectors.
5. From the distributor, disconnect the vacuum advance hose and the thermo-unit wiring electrical connector.
6. Disconnect the PCV valve from the rocker arm cover, then remove the oil level gauge guide tube-to-intake manifold bolt.
7. Disconnect the EGR pipe from the EGR valve adapter, the EGR valve and the adapter. Remove the nut from under the EGR valve.

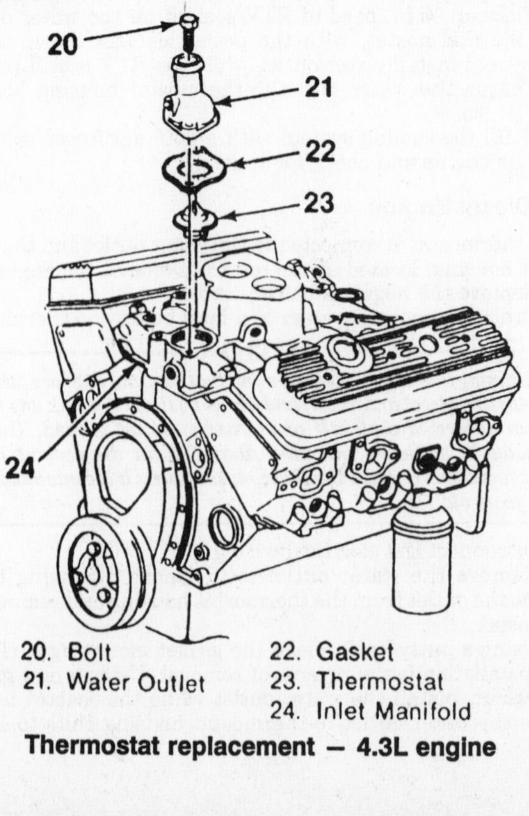
20
21
22
23
24
20. Bolt
21. Water Outlet
22. Gasket
23. Thermostat
24. Inlet Manifold

Thermostat replacement — 4.3L engine

8. Disconnect the AIR vacuum hose from the 3-way connector.
9. Remove the intake manifold-to-cylinder head nuts and the intake manifold from the engine.
10. Using a putty knife, clean the gasket mounting surfaces.
11. Inspect the manifold for cracks or damage. Using a straight edge and a feeler gauge, check manifold distortion on the sealing surfaces. Have the manifold surface ground if distortion exceeds 0.0157 in.
12. Installation is the reverse of removal. Use a new gasket and sealant. tighten intake bolts to 17 ft. lbs.

2.0L Engine

1. Remove the negative battery cable.
2. Remove the air cleaner, distributor cap, distributor holddown nut and clamp.
3. Raise and support the vehicle safely. Remove the middle right hand bellhousing to block bolt and remove the wiring harness.
4. Drain the cooling system.

CAUTION

When draining the coolant, keep in mind that cats and dogs are attracted by the ethylene glycol antifreeze, and are quite likely to drink any that is left in an uncovered container or in puddles on the ground. This will prove fatal in sufficient quantity. Always drain the coolant into a sealable container. Coolant should be reused unless it is contaminated or several years old.

5. Tag and disconnect the vacuum hose and the primary wires from the coil.
6. Remove the fuel pump-to-engine bolts and allow the pump to hang.
7. Lower the vehicle.
8. Disconnect the accelerator cable, the fuel inlet line, then the necessary vacuum hoses and wires. Remove the carburetor-to-intake manifold nuts, the carburetor and lift off the Early Fuel Evaporation (EFE) heater grid..
9. Disconnect the fuel vapor harness pipes from the cylinder head.
10. Disconnect the heater hose, bypass hose and any hoses and wires as necessary. Remove the intake manifold-to-cylinder head nuts/bolts, the intake manifold and the gasket.
11. Using a putty knife, clean the gasket mounting surfaces. Inspect the manifold for cracks, damage or distortion; if necessary, replace the intake manifold.
12. Installation is the reverse of removal. Using a new gasket and sealant, torque the intake manifold-to-cylinder head nuts/bolts to 25 ft. lbs.
13. Refill the cooling system. Adjust the drive belts. Check and/or adjust the engine timing and idle speed.

2.2L Diesel Engine

1. Remove the negative battery cable.
2. Remove the air cleaner.
3. Disconnect the heater pipe bracket, the PCV valve hose, the necessary wires and clips from the intake manifold.
4. Remove the intake manifold-to-cylinder head bolts and the intake manifold.

NOTE: In order to replace the intake manifold gasket, it is necessary to remove the exhaust manifold.

5. Using a putty knife, clean the gasket mounting surfaces.
6. Inspect the manifold for cracks, damage or distortion; if necessary, replace the intake manifold.
7. Using a new gasket, install the intake manifold onto the cylinder head. Torque the intake manifold-to-cylinder head nuts/bolts to 10–17 ft. lbs. starting from the center and working outward.

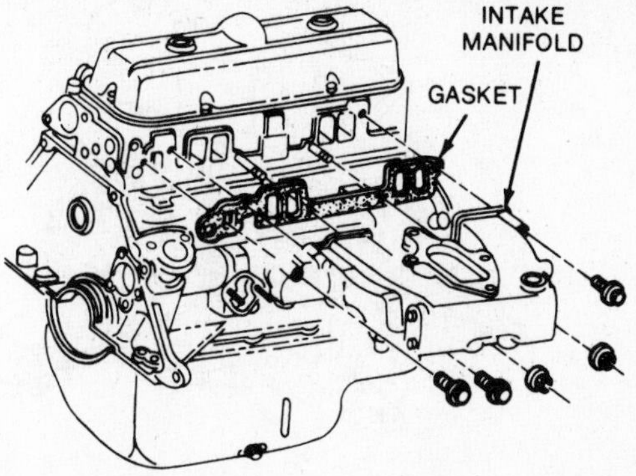
INTAKE
MANIFOLD
GASKET

Intake manifold removal/installation – 2.0L engine

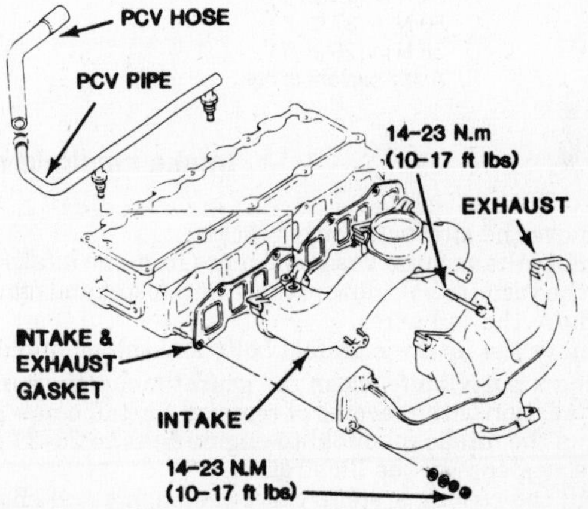
PCV HOSE
PCV PIPE
14–23 N.m
(10–17 ft lbs)
EXHAUST
INTAKE &
EXHAUST
GASKET
INTAKE
14–23 N.M
(10–17 ft lbs)

Intake manifold removal/installation – 2.2L engine

8. The remainder of the installation procedure is the reverse of removal.

2.5L Engine

The intake manifold is located on the right-side of the cylinder head.

1. Remove the negative battery cable.
2. Drain the cooling system.

CAUTION

When draining the coolant, keep in mind that cats and dogs are attracted by the ethylene glycol antifreeze, and are quite likely to drink any that is left in an uncovered container or in puddles on the ground. This will prove fatal in sufficient quantity. Always drain the coolant into a sealable container. Coolant should be reused unless it is contaminated or several years old.

3. Remove the air cleaner assembly. Label and disconnect the wiring harnesses and connectors at the intake manifold.
4. Remove the accelerator, TVS, and cruise control cables and brackets.
5. Remove the EGR vacuum line.
6. Remove the emission sensor bracket at the manifold.

CAUTION

Relieve the fuel system pressure before disconnecting any fuel line connection. Refer to Section 5 for the appropriate procedure.

7. Remove the fuel lines, vacuum lines and wiring from the TBI unit.
8. Remove the water pump bypass hose at the intake manifold.

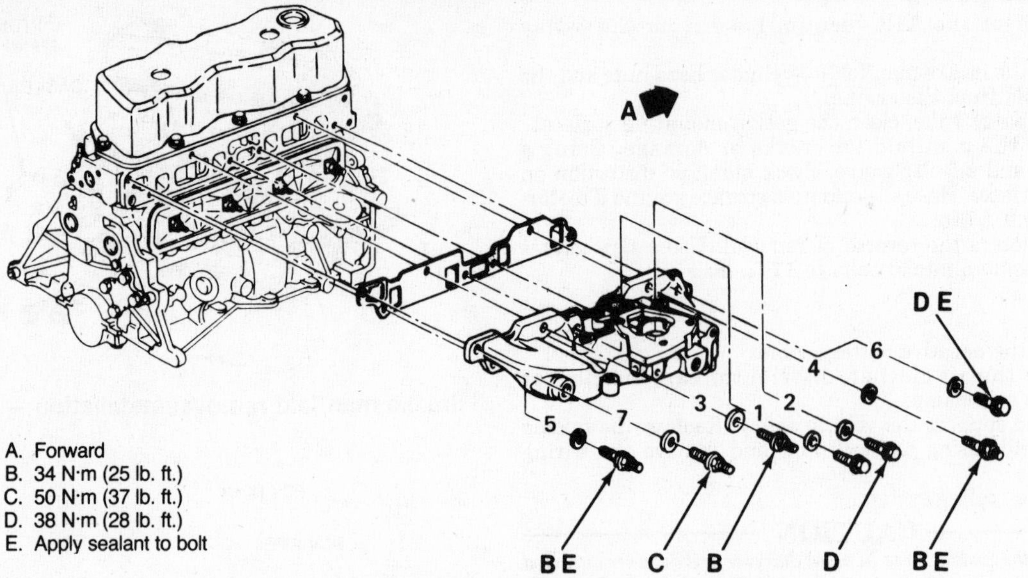
A
D E
6
4
3
1
2
5
7
A. Forward
B. 34 N·m (25 lb. ft.)
C. 50 N·m (37 lb. ft.)
D. 38 N·m (28 lb. ft.)
E. Apply sealant to bolt
B E
C
B
D
B E

Intake manifold removal/installation — 2.5L engine

9. Remove the alternator rear bracket.
10. Remove the vacuum hoses and pipes from the intake manifold and the vacuum hold down at the thermostat and manifold.
11. Remove the coil wires.
12. Remove the intake manifold bolts and the manifold.
13. Using a putty knife, clean the gasket mounting surfaces.
14. Installation is the reverse of removal. Install a new gasket and torque the intake manifold-to-engine bolts to 25–37 ft. lbs. using the sequence in the illustration.
15. Refill the cooling system. Start the engine and check for leaks.

2.8L Engine

1. Drain the cooling system.

CAUTION

When draining the coolant, keep in mind that cats and dogs are attracted by the ethylene glycol antifreeze, and are quite likely to drink any that is left in an uncovered container or in puddles on the ground. This will prove fatal in sufficient quantity. Always drain the coolant into a sealable container. Coolant should be reused unless it is contaminated or several years old.

2. Remove the negative battery cable.

CAUTION

Relieve the fuel system pressure before disconnecting any fuel line connection. Refer to Section 5 for the appropriate procedure.

3. Remove the air cleaner. Remove the electrical connectors, the vacuum hoses, the fuel lines and the accelerator cables from the carburetor or TBI unit.
4. If equipped with an AIR management system, remove the hose and the mounting bracket.
5. Label and disconnect the spark plug wires from the spark plugs and the electrical connectors from the ignition coil. Disconnect the coolant switch electrical connectors on the intake manifold.
6. Remove the distributor cap (with the wires connected). Mark the position of the rotor-to-distributor body and the distributor body-to-engine relationships, then remove the distributor from the engine.

NOTE: DO NOT crank the engine with the distributor removed.

7. Remove the EGR vacuum line and the evaporative emission hoses. Remove the pipe brackets from the rocker arm covers.
8. Remove the heater and upper radiator hoses from the intake manifold.
9. If equipped, remove the power brake vacuum hoses from the intake manifold.
10. Remove the rocker arm covers.
11. Remove the intake manifold-to-engine nuts and bolts, then the intake manifold from the engine.
11. Using a putty knife, clean the gasket mounting surfaces. Since the manifold is made from aluminum, be sure to inspect it for warpage and/or cracks; if necessary, replace it.
12. Installation is the reverse of removal. Use new intake manifold gaskets and a $^{3}/_{16}$ in. (5mm) bead of RTV sealant (applied to the front and rear of the engine block).

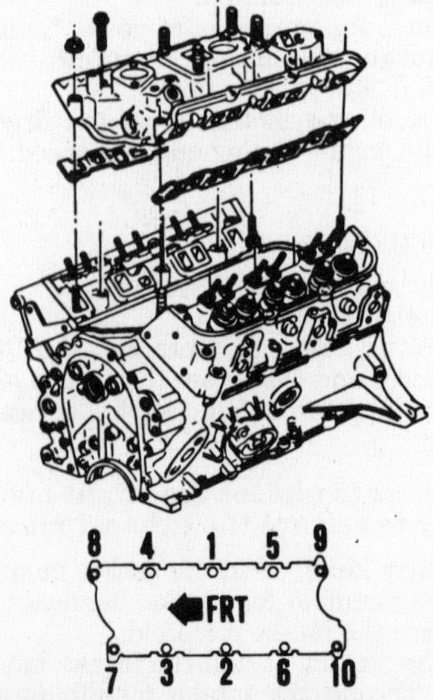
8 4 1 5 9
FRT
7 3 2 6 10

Intake manifold removal/installation with torque sequence — 2.8L engine

NOTE: The gaskets are marked "Right-Side" and "Left-Side"; DO NOT interchange them. The gaskets will have to be cut slightly to fit past the center push-rods; DO NOT cut any more material than necessary. Hold the gaskets in place by extending the ridge bead of sealer ¼ in. onto the gasket ends.

13. Torque the intake manifold-to-cylinder head nuts and bolts (in sequence) to 23 ft. lbs.
14. Refill the cooling system with a 50% solution of ethylene glycol anti-freeze.
15. Adjust the ignition timing, the idle speed (if possible) and check the coolant level after the engine has warmed up.

4.3L Engine

1. Remove the negative battery cable.
2. Drain the cooling system.

CAUTION

When draining the coolant, keep in mind that cats and dogs are attracted by the ethylene glycol antifreeze, and are quite likely to drink any that is left in an uncovered container or in puddles on the ground. This will prove fatal in sufficient quantity. Always drain the coolant into a sealable container. Coolant should be reused unless it is contaminated or several years old.

3. Remove the air cleaner and heat stove tube.
4. Remove the two braces at the rear of the fan belt tensioner.
5. Remove the upper radiator hose.
6. Remove the emissions relays, wiring harness and ground cable.

CAUTION

Relieve the fuel system pressure before disconnecting any fuel line connection. Refer to Section 5 for the appropriate procedure.

7. Remove the power brake vacuum pipe, heater hose pipe and fuel lines to the TBI unit.

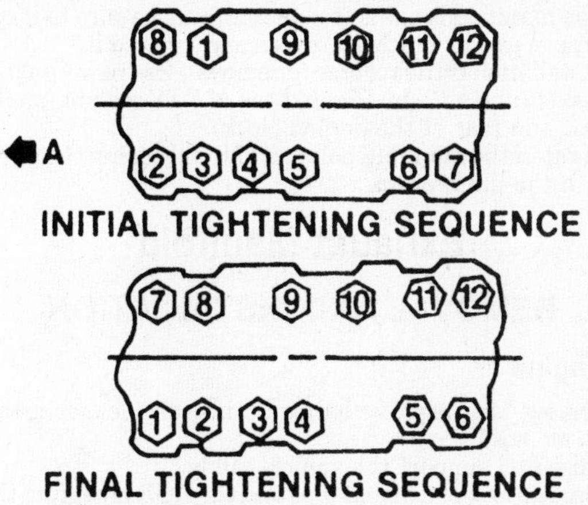
8 1 9 10 11 12
A
2 3 4 5 6 7
INITIAL TIGHTENING SEQUENCE
7 8 9 10 11 12
1 2 3 4 5 6
FINAL TIGHTENING SEQUENCE

A. Front Of Engine

Intake manifold torque sequence – 4.3L engine

8. Remove the ignition coil, and electrical connectors at the sensors on the manifold.
9. Remove the distributor cap (with the wires connected). Mark the position of the rotor-to-distributor body and the distributor body-to-engine relationships, then remove the distributor from the engine.

NOTE: DO NOT crank the engine with the distributor removed.

10. Remove the EGR hose. Remove the throttle, TVS and cruise control cables.
11. Remove the intake manifold bolts, manifold and gaskets.
12. Using a putty knife, clean the gasket mounting surfaces.

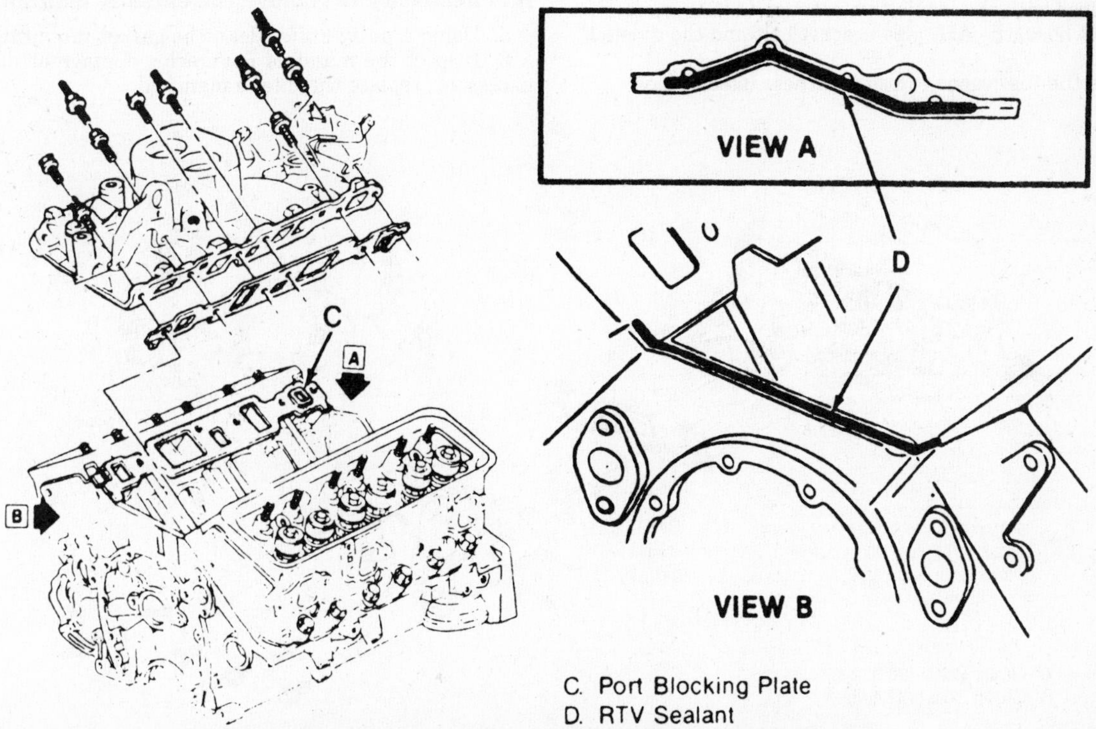
C
A
B
VIEW A
D
VIEW B

C. Port Blocking Plate
D. RTV Sealant

Intake manifold removal/installation – 4.3L engine

Since the manifold is made from aluminum, be sure to inspect it for warpage and/or cracks; if necessary, replace it.

13. Installation is the reverse of removal. Use new intake manifold gaskets and a $^3/_{16}$ in. (5mm) bead of RTV sealant (applied to the front and rear of the engine block).

14. Tighten the manifold bolts to 35 ft. lbs. using the sequence shown in the illustration.

Exhaust Manifold

REMOVAL AND INSTALLATION

1.9L Engine

1. Remove the negative battery cable, air cleaner assembly and hot air hose.
2. Raise and support the vehicle safely.
3. Disconnect the exhaust pipe and the EGR pipe from the exhaust manifold, then lower the vehicle.
4. If equipped with an A/C compressor or a P/S pump, remove the drive belt(s), the compressor/pump (move them aside) and the mounting brackets.
5. Remove the exhaust manifold shield and the heat stove (if equipped).
6. Remove the exhaust manifold-to-cylinder head nuts and the manifold from the engine.
7. Using a putty knife, clean the gasket mounting surfaces. Inspect the exhaust manifold for distortion, cracks or damage; replace it, if necessary.
8. Installation is the reverse of removal. Use a new gasket and torque the exhaust manifold-to-cylinder head nuts to 16 ft. lbs., in sequence, starting with the center and working outwards.

2.0L Engine

1. Remove the negative battery cable and air cleaner assembly.
2. Raise and support the vehicle safely.
3. Disconnect the exhaust pipe from the exhaust manifold.
4. If equipped with an air injection reaction (AIR) system, remove the AIR hose, the AIR pipe bracket bolt and the dipstick tube bracket.
5. Remove the fuel vapor canister harness (steel) pipes.

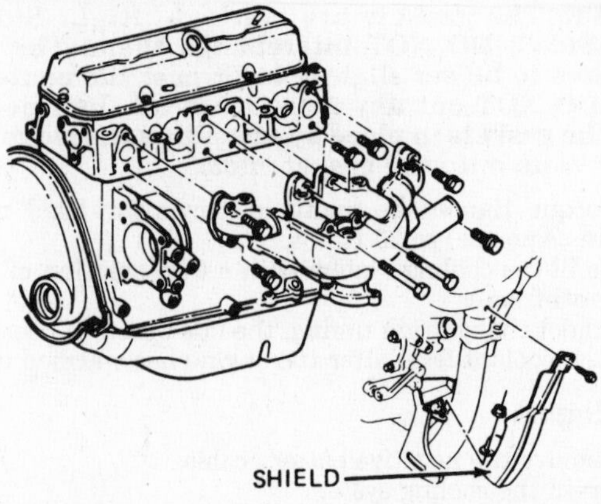
SHIELD

Exhaust manifold removal/installation – 2.0L engine

6. Remove the exhaust manifold-to-cylinder head bolts and the manifold from the engine.
7. Using a putty knife, clean the gasket mounting surfaces. Inspect the exhaust manifold for distortion, cracks or damage; replace if necessary.
8. Installation is the reverse of removal. Using a new gasket, torque the exhaust manifold-to-cylinder head bolts to 26 ft. lbs., in sequence, starting with the center and working outwards.

2.2L Diesel Engine

1. Remove the negative battery cable.
2. Remove the air cleaner and the PCV valve.
3. Disconnect the exhaust pipe from the exhaust manifold at the flange.
4. Remove the exhaust manifold-to-cylinder head nuts and the exhaust manifold from the engine.

NOTE: In order to replace the intake manifold gasket, it is necessary to remove the exhaust manifold.

5. Using a putty knife, clean the gasket mounting surfaces.
6. Inspect the manifold for cracks, damage or distortion; if necessary, replace the intake manifold.

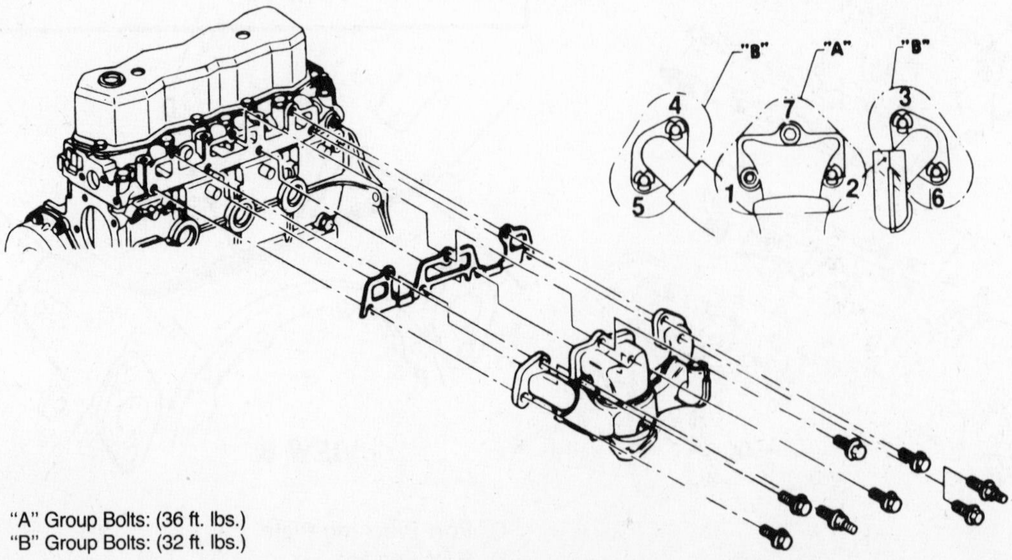
"B"
"A"
"B"
4
7
3
1
2
5
6
"A" Group Bolts: (36 ft. lbs.)
"B" Group Bolts: (32 ft. lbs.)

Exhaust manifold removal/installation – 2.5L engine

7. Using a new gasket, install the intake manifold onto the cylinder head. Torque the intake manifold-to-cylinder head nuts/bolts to 10–17 ft. lbs. starting from the center and working outward.
8. The remainder of the installation procedure is the reverse of removal.

2.5L Engine

The exhaust manifold is located on the left-side of the engine.
1. Remove the negative battery cable.
2. Remove the air cleaner and heat stove pipe.
3. Remove the A/C compressor (if equipped), drive belt, and the rear adjusting bracket (if used). Lay the compressor aside in the engine compartment.
4. Remove the dipstick tube and bracket.
5. Disconnect the exhaust pipe from the exhaust manifold.
6. Disconnect the electrical connector from the oxygen sensor.
7. Remove the exhaust manifold-to-engine bolts/washers and the manifold from the engine.
8. Using a putty knife, clean the gasket mounting surfaces.
9. Installation is the reverse of removal. Using a new gasket, torque the exhaust manifold-to-engine bolts to 36 ft. lbs. (center bolts) and 32 ft. lbs. (outer bolts).

2.8L Engine

LEFT-SIDE

1. Remove the negative battery cable.
2. Raise and support the vehicle safely.
3. Disconnect the exhaust pipe from the exhaust manifold.
4. Remove the rear exhaust manifold-to-cylinder head bolts, then lower the vehicle.
5. Disconnect the air management hoses and wiring.
6. If equipped, remove the P/S pump and bracket; DO NOT disconnect the power steering hoses.
7. Remove the front exhaust manifold-to-cylinder head bolts.
8. Using a putty knife, clean the gasket mounting surfaces. Inspect the exhaust manifold for distortion, cracks or damage; replace if necessary.
9. Installation is the reverse of removal. Using a new gasket, torque the exhaust manifold-to-cylinder head bolts to 25 ft. lbs., in a circular pattern, working from the center to the outer ends.

RIGHT-SIDE

1. Remove the negative battery cable.
2. Raise and support the vehicle safely.
3. Disconnect the exhaust pipe from the exhaust manifold.
4. Disconnect the air management hoses and wiring, then lower the vehicle.
5. Remove the exhaust manifold-to-cylinder head bolts.
6. Using a putty knife, clean the gasket mounting surfaces. Inspect the exhaust manifold for distortion, cracks or damage; replace if necessary.
7. Installation is the reverse of removal. Using a new gasket, torque the exhaust manifold-to-cylinder head bolts to 25 ft. lbs., in a circular pattern, working from the center to the outer ends.

A/C Compressor

REMOVAL AND INSTALLATION

4-Cyl Engines

NOTE: Refer to Air Conditioning in Section 1 when performing refrigerant service.

1. Discharge the A/C system.
2. Remove the negative battery cable.
3. Disconnect the electrical connectors from the compressor.
4. At the rear of the compressor, remove the bracket from the

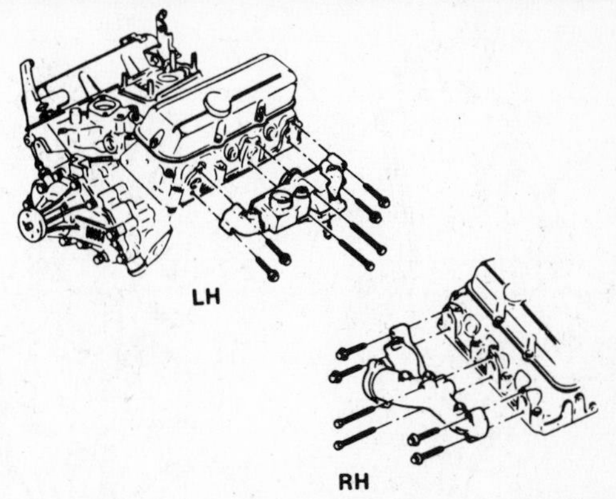
LH
RH

Exhaust manifold removal/installation — 2.8L engine

exhaust manifold. If equipped, remove the power steering pump bracket.
5. Remove the compressor-to-front bracket bolts, the drive belt and the compressor from the vehicle.
6. Installation is the reverse of removal. Torque the compressor-to-front bracket bolts to 68 ft. lbs., the manifold-to-rear compressor bolt to 47 ft. lbs. and the engine brace-to-compressor nut to 37 ft. lbs.
7. Install the accessory drive belts and adjust the tension. Refer to Section 1 for the appropriate procedure.
8. Recharge the A/C system.

V6 Engine

NOTE: Refer to Air Conditioning in Section 1 when performing refrigerant service.

1. Discharge the A/C system.
2. Remove the negative battery cable.
3. Disconnect the electrical connectors from the compressor.
4. Remove the intake manifold-to-compressor support bracket.

NOTE: If the engine is equipped with a carburetor, disconnect the vacuum brake from the carburetor for access.

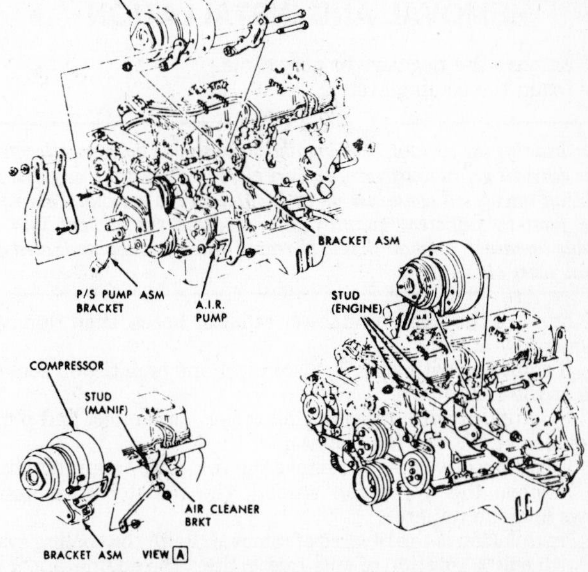
COMPRESSOR
SUPPORT
BRACKET ASM
P/S PUMP ASM
BRACKET
A.I.R.
PUMP
STUD
(ENGINE)
COMPRESSOR
STUD
(MANIF)
AIR CLEANER
BRKT
BRACKET ASM
VIEW A

Compressor replacement — 1.9L engine

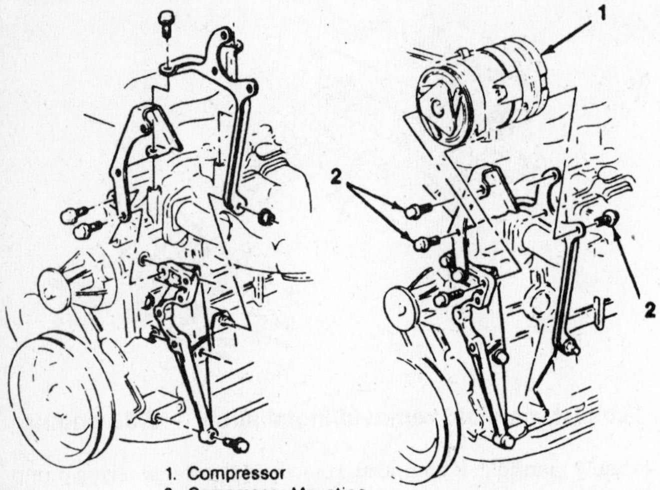
1
2
2

1. Compressor
2. Compressor Mounting Bolts

Compressor replacement – 2.5L engine

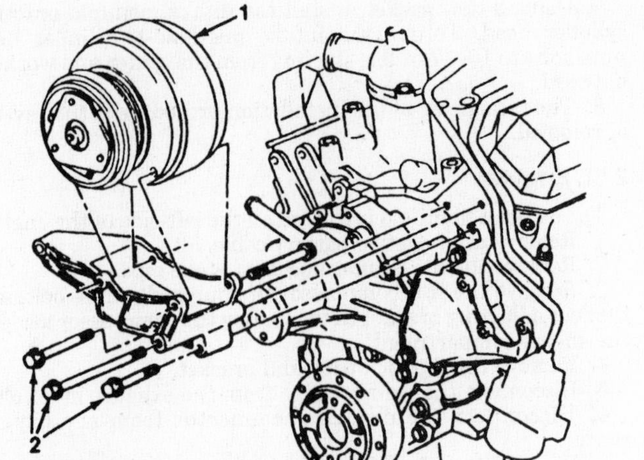
1
2

1. Compressor
2. Compressor Mounting Bolts

Compressor replacement – 2.8L engine

5. Remove the drive belt idler bracket-to-intake manifold bolts, the drive belt and the bracket from the vehicle.
6. Remove the compressor-to-mounting bracket bolts and the compressor from the vehicle.
7. Installation is the reverse of removal. Torque the compressor-to-front bracket bolts to 68 ft. lbs. and the manifold-to-compressor bolt to 47 ft. lbs.
8. Install the accessory drive belts and adjust the tension. Refer to Section 1 for the appropriate procedure.
9. Recharge the A/C system.

Radiator

DIAGNOSIS

Test for restrictions in the radiator by warming the engine to operating temperature and then turning the engine off. Feel the radiator, it should be hot along the left side and warm along the right side. The temperature should rise evenly from right to left. If cold spots are felt, have the radiator tested for clogged sections.

REMOVAL AND INSTALLATION

1. Remove the negative battery cable.
2. Drain the cooling system.

CAUTION

When draining the coolant, keep in mind that cats and dogs are attracted by the ethylene glycol antifreeze, and are quite likely to drink any that is left in an uncovered container or in puddles on the ground. This will prove fatal in sufficient quantity. Always drain the coolant into a sealable container. Coolant should be reused unless it is contaminated or several years old.

3. Remove the upper and lower radiator hoses, then remove the overflow hose.
4. If equipped with an A/T, disconnect and plug the oil cooler lines at the radiator.
5. If equipped with an engine oil cooler, disconnect and plug the oil cooler lines at the radiator.
6. If equipped with A/C, remove the A/C hose retaining clip.
7. Remove the upper fan shroud, the radiator to chassis screws and the radiator.
8. Installation is the reverse of removal. Refill the cooling system with a 50% solution of anti-freeze. Start the engine, allow it to reach normal operating temperatures and check for leaks.

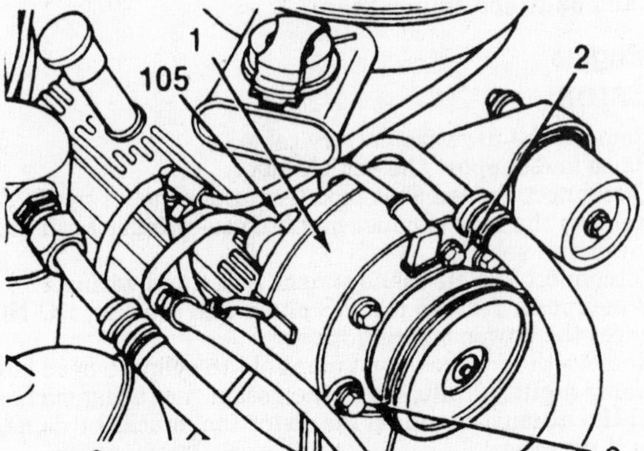
1
105
2
2

1. Compressor
2. Bolt
105. Manifold

Compressor replacement – 4.3L engine

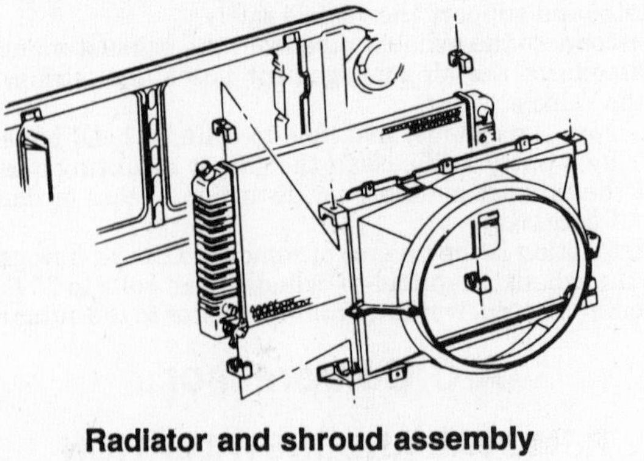

Radiator and shroud assembly

Engine Oil Cooler

REMOVAL AND INSTALLATION

1. Remove the negative battery cable.
2. Drain the cooling system.

79. Gasket
80. Bracket
81. Power Steering Pump
84. Bolt
85. Clamp
86. Bracket
87. Radiator
89. Engine
91. Oil Filter
92. Oil Cooler Lines
93. Seals
94. Adapter

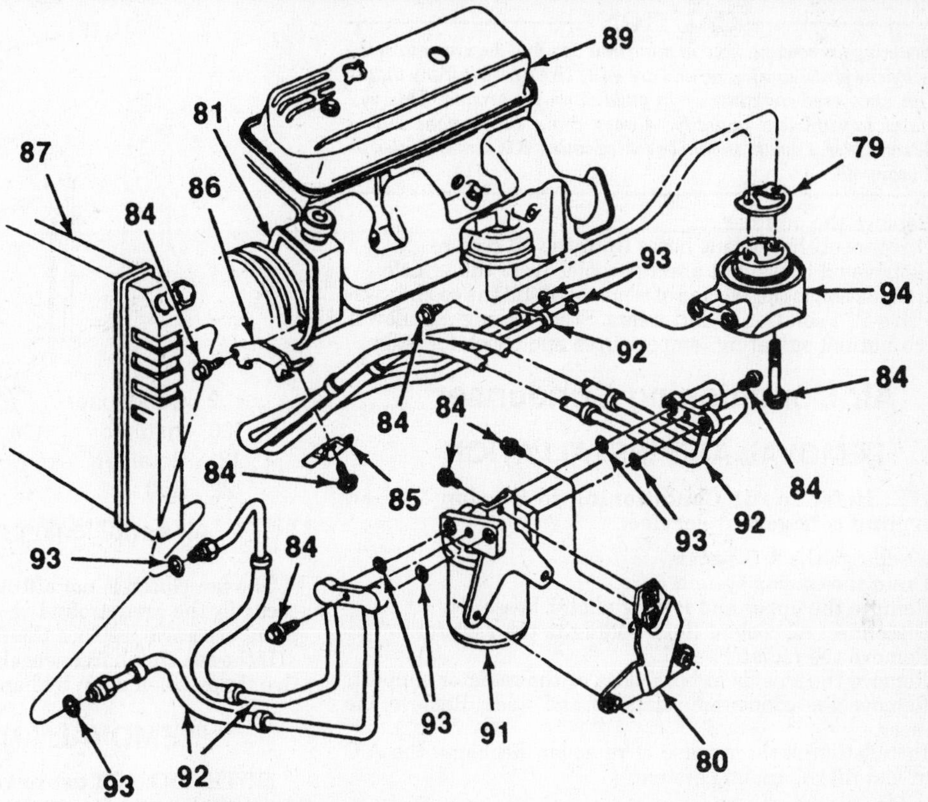
89
81
79
87
86
84
93
94
92
84
84
84
85
84
92
93
84
93
93
91
80
93
92

Engine oil cooler — 4WD

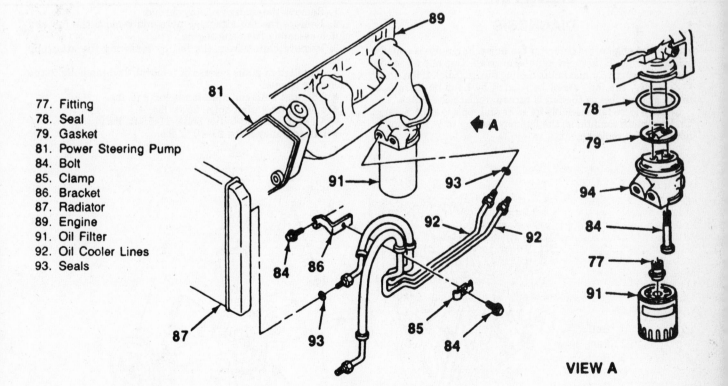

77. Fitting
78. Seal
79. Gasket
81. Power Steering Pump
84. Bolt
85. Clamp
86. Bracket
87. Radiator
89. Engine
91. Oil Filter
92. Oil Cooler Lines
93. Seals

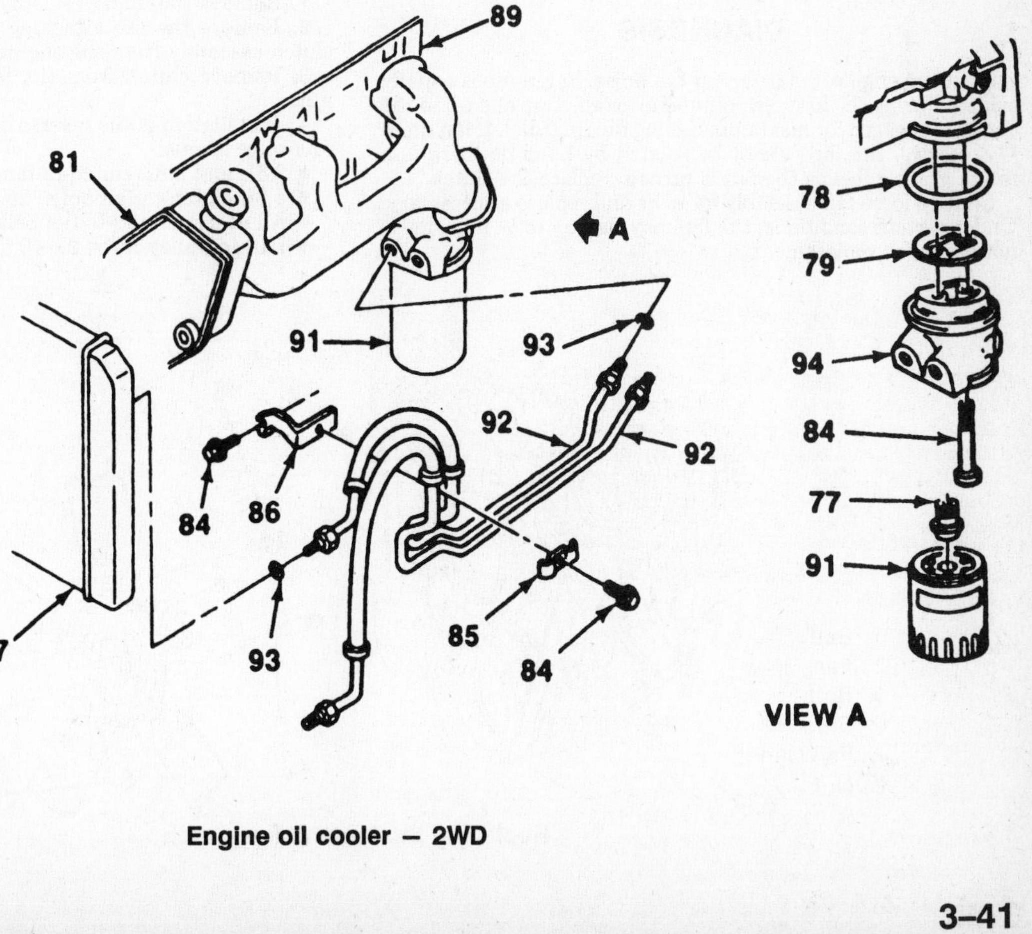
89
81
A
78
79
91
93
94
92
92
84
84
86
77
91
87
93
85
84
VIEW A

Engine oil cooler — 2WD

CAUTION

When draining the coolant, keep in mind that cats and dogs are attracted by the ethylene glycol antifreeze, and are quite likely to drink any that is left in an uncovered container or in puddles on the ground. This will prove fatal in sufficient quantity. Always drain the coolant into a sealable container. Coolant should be reused unless it is contaminated or several years old.

3. Remove the oil filter.
4. Disconnect the coolant hoses from the oil cooler.
5. Remove oil cooler nut and the cooler from the vehicle.
6. Installation is the reverse of removal. Refill the cooling system with a 50% solution of anti-freeze. Start the engine, allow it to reach normal operating temperatures and check for leaks.

Air Conditioning Condenser

REMOVAL AND INSTALLATION

NOTE: Refer to Air Conditioning in Section 1 when performing refrigerant service.

1. Discharge the A/C system.
2. Drain the cooling system.
3. Remove the upper and lower radiator hoses.
4. Disconnect all coolant lines leading to the radiator.
5. Remove the radiator.
6. Remove the shields at both sides of the radiator support.
7. Remove the condenser retainers and lines. Remove the condenser.
8. Installation is the reverse of removal. Recharge the A/C system and fill the cooling system.

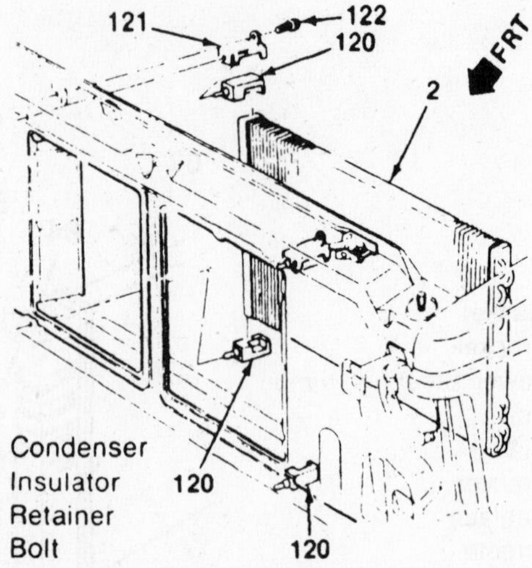

121
122
120
FRT
2
120
120
2. Condenser
120. Insulator
121. Retainer
122. Bolt

Air conditioning condenser replacement

Clutch Fan

DIAGNOSIS

Start the engine and listen for fan noise. Fan noise is usually evident during the first few minutes after start-up and when the clutch is engaged for maximum cooling (during idle). If fan noise is excessive, the fan cannot be rotated by hand or there is a rough grating feel as the fan is turned, replace the clutch.

Check a loose fan assembly for wear and replace as necessary. Under certain conditions, the fan may flex up to ¼ in.. This is not cause for replacement.

The fan clutch is not affected by small fluid leaks which may occur in the area around the bearing assembly. If leakage appears excessive, replace the fan clutch.

If the fan clutch free-wheels with no drag (revolves more than five times when spun by hand), replace the clutch.

REMOVAL AND INSTALLATION

NOTE: DO NOT use or repair a damaged fan assembly. An unbalanced fan assembly could fly apart and cause personal injury or property damage. Replace damaged assemblies with new ones.

1. Remove the upper radiator shroud.
2. Remove the fan attaching nuts and remove the fan and clutch assembly from the engine.
3. Remove clutch from the fan by removing the attaching nuts.
4. Installation is the reverse of removal. Tighten bolts to the following torque:
   - 2.5L and 2.8L clutch-to-fan bolts: 9 ft. lbs.
   - 4.3L clutch-to-fan bolts: 25 ft. lbs.
   - All others clutch-to-fan bolts: 11–16 ft. lbs.
   - Fan-to-pulley nuts: 27–40 ft. lbs.

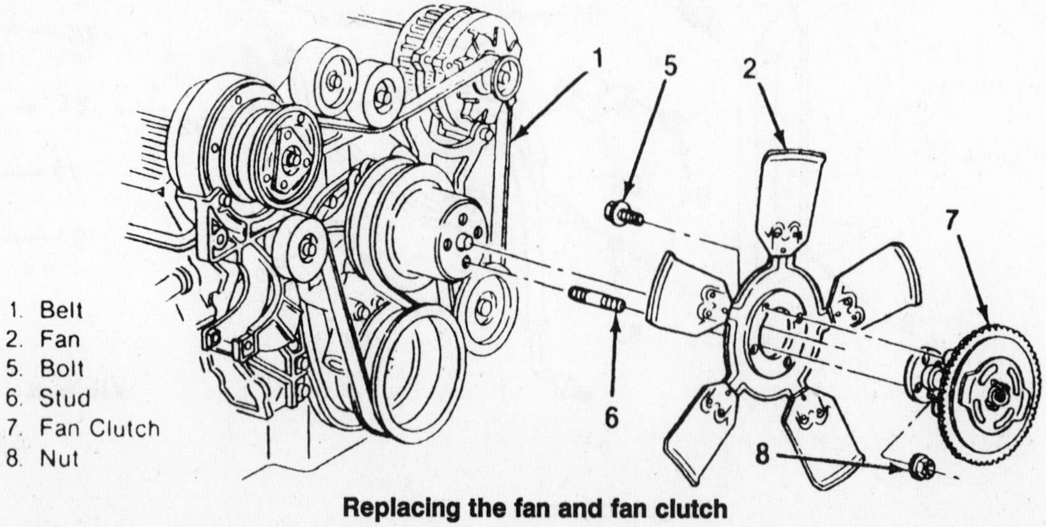

1
5
2
7
6
8
1. Belt
2. Fan
5. Bolt
6. Stud
7. Fan Clutch
8. Nut

Replacing the fan and fan clutch

Water Pump

DIAGNOSIS

Check the water pump operation by running the engine while squeezing the upper radiator hose. When the engine warms (thermostat opens) a pressure surge should be felt. Check for a plugged vent hole at the pump snout.

REMOVAL AND INSTALLATION

1.9L Engine

1. Remove the negative battery cable.
2. Raise and support the vehicle safely. Then, remove the lower fan shroud.
3. Drain the cooling system.

CAUTION

When draining the coolant, keep in mind that cats and dogs are attracted by the ethylene glycol antifreeze, and are quite likely to drink any that is left in an uncovered container or in puddles on the ground. This will prove fatal in sufficient quantity. Always drain the coolant into a sealable container. Coolant should be reused unless it is contaminated or several years old.

4. If not equipped with A/C, remove the fan-to-water pump nuts and the fan from the vehicle.
5. If equipped with A/C, perform the following procedures:
   a. Loosen the air pump and alternator adjusting bolts, pivot them toward the engine and remove the drive belt(s).
   b. Remove the fan-to-water pump nuts and the fan (with the fan and air pump drive pulley) from the vehicle.
   c. Remove the fan set plate/pulley-to-water pump bolts, then remove the set plate and the pulley.
6. Remove the coolant hoses at the water pump.
7. Remove the water pump-to-engine bolts and the water pump from the engine.
8. Using a putty knife, clean the gasket mounting surfaces.
9. Installation is the reverse of removal. Use a new gasket and sealant. tighten water pump bolts to 15–22 ft. lbs.
10. Refill the cooling system with a 50% solution of anti-freeze. Start the engine, allow it to reach normal operating temperatures and check for leaks.

2.0L Engine

1. Remove the negative battery cable.
2. Drain the cooling system.

CAUTION

When draining the coolant, keep in mind that cats and dogs are attracted by the ethylene glycol antifreeze, and are quite likely to drink any that is left in an uncovered container or in puddles on the ground. This will prove fatal in sufficient quantity. Always drain the coolant into a sealable container. Coolant should be reused unless it is contaminated or several years old.

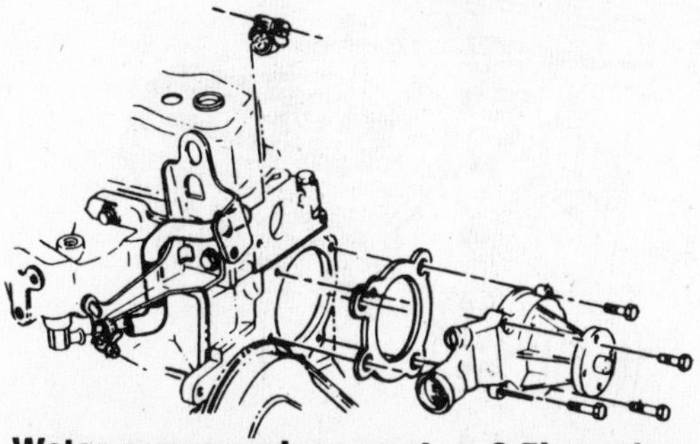

Water pump replacement – 2.5L engine

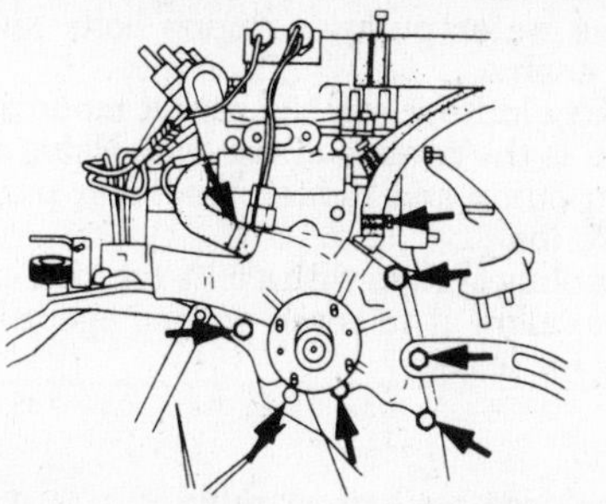

Water pump replacement – 1.9L engine. 2.2L diesel engine similar

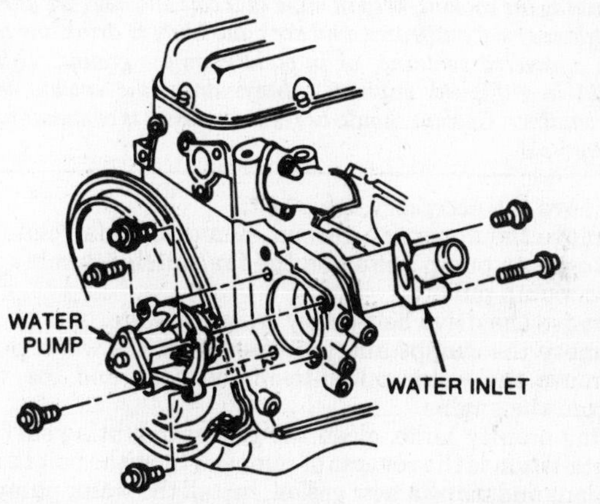
WATER PUMP
WATER INLET

Water pump replacement – 2.0L engine

3. Remove the upper fan shroud and all of the necessary drive belts.
4. Disconnect the radiator and heater hoses from the water pump.
5. Remove the water pump-to-engine bolts and the water pump from the vehicle.
6. Using a putty knife, clean the gasket mounting surfaces.
7. Installation is the reverse of removal. Use a new gasket and sealant. tighten water pump bolts to 15–22 ft. lbs.
8. Refill the cooling system with a 50% solution of anti-freeze. Start the engine, allow it to reach normal operating temperatures and check for leaks.

2.2L Diesel Engine

1. Remove the negative battery cable.
2. Disconnect the power steering reservoir. Remove the upper fan shroud.
3. Drain the cooling system.

CAUTION

When draining the coolant, keep in mind that cats and dogs are attracted by the ethylene glycol antifreeze, and are quite likely to drink any that is left in an uncovered container or in puddles on the ground. This will prove fatal in sufficient quantity. Always drain the coolant into a sealable container. Coolant should be reused unless it is contaminated or several years old.

4. Remove the drive belts, the fan and the A/C compressor (move it aside).
5. Disconnect the radiator pipe at the front cover.
6. Disconnect the radiator and heater hoses from the right-side of the water pump
7. Disconnect the PCV valve from the rocker cover. Remove the air cleaner and the heater pipe from the intake manifold.
8. Disconnect the heater hose from the left-side of the water pump, then the alternator brace.

9. Remove the water pump-to-engine bolts and the water pump from the engine.
10. Using a putty knife, clean the gasket mounting surfaces.
11. Installation is the reverse of removal. Using a new gasket install the water pump and tighten the water pump-to-engine bolts to 10–17 ft. lbs.
12. Refill the cooling system with a 50% solution of anti-freeze. Start the engine, allow it to reach normal operating temperatures and check for leaks.

2.5L Engine

1. Remove the negative battery cable.
2. Drain the cooling system.

CAUTION

When draining the coolant, keep in mind that cats and dogs are attracted by the ethylene glycol antifreeze, and are quite likely to drink any that is left in an uncovered container or in puddles on the ground. This will prove fatal in sufficient quantity. Always drain the coolant into a sealable container. Coolant should be reused unless it is contaminated or several years old.

3. Remove the accessory drive belt.
4. Remove the upper fan shroud. Remove the fan/clutch assembly-to-water pump bolts and the fan/clutch assembly from the water pump pulley.
5. Remove the drive belt pulley from the water pump.
6. Remove the clamps and the hoses from the water pump.
7. Remove the water pump-to-engine bolts and the water pump from the engine.
8. Using a putty knife, clean the gasket mounting surfaces.
9. Installation is the reverse of removal. Coat the bolt threads with sealant and using a new gasket, install the water pump and tighten the water pump-to-engine bolts to 22 ft. lbs.
10. Refill the cooling system with a 50% solution of anti-freeze. Start the engine, allow it to reach normal operating temperatures and check for leaks.

2.8L and 4.3L Engine

1. Remove the negative battery cable.
2. Drain the cooling system.

CAUTION

When draining the coolant, keep in mind that cats and dogs are attracted by the ethylene glycol antifreeze, and are quite likely to drink any that is left in an uncovered container or in puddles on the ground. This will prove fatal in sufficient quantity. Always drain the coolant into a sealable container. Coolant should be reused unless it is contaminated or several years old.

3. Remove the accessory drive belt.
4. Remove the upper fan shroud. Remove the fan/clutch assembly-to-water pump bolts and the fan/clutch assembly from the water pump pulley.
5. Remove the drive belt pulley from the water pump.

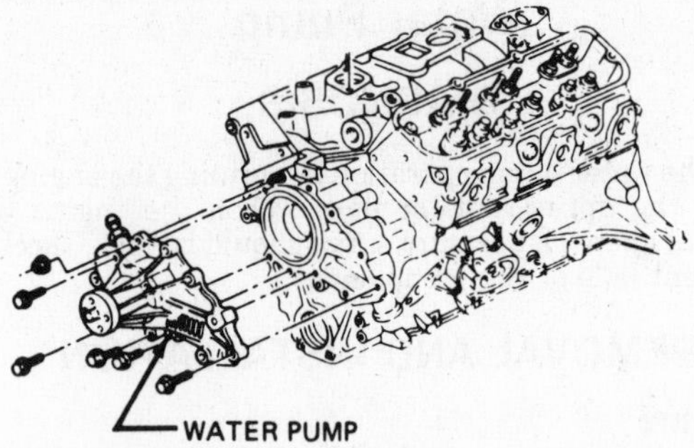
WATER PUMP

Water pump replacement – 2.8L engine

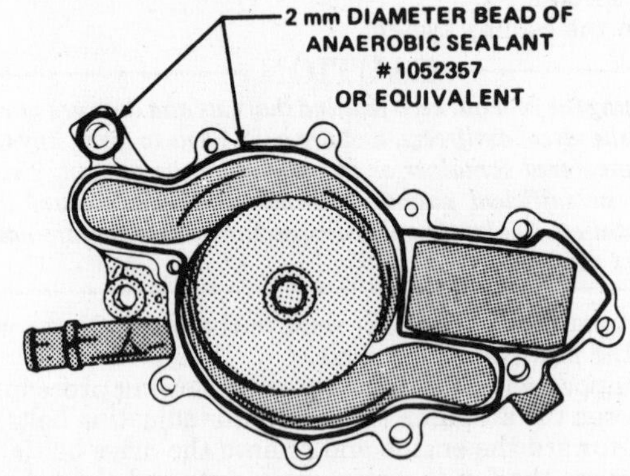
2 mm DIAMETER BEAD OF
ANAEROBIC SEALANT
1052357
OR EQUIVALENT

Applying sealer to the V6 water pump

6. Remove the clamps and the hoses from the water pump.
7. Remove the water pump-to-engine bolts and the water pump from the engine.
8. Using a putty knife, clean the gasket mounting surfaces.
9. Installation is the reverse of removal. Coat the bolt threads with sealant. Place a $^{3}/_{32}$ in. (2mm) bead of sealer on the water pump mating surface and install the water pump. Tighten the water pump-to-engine bolts to 22 ft. lbs.
10. Refill the cooling system with a 50% solution of anti-freeze. Start the engine, allow it to reach normal operating temperatures and check for leaks.

Cylinder Head

REMOVAL AND INSTALLATION

1.9L Engine

1. Remove the rocker arm cover.
2. Remove EGR pipe clamp bolt at the rear of the cylinder head.

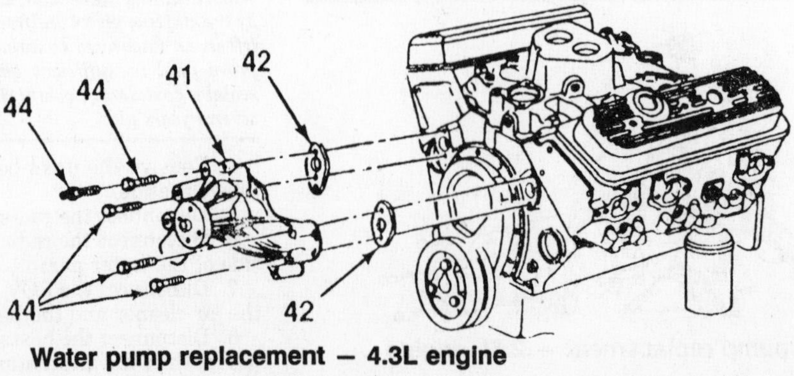
41. Water Pump
42. Gasket
44. Bolt
44
44
41
42
44
42

Water pump replacement – 4.3L engine

3. Raise and support the vehicle safely.
4. Disconnect the exhaust pipe from the exhaust manifold, then lower the vehicle.
5. Drain the cooling system.

CAUTION

When draining the coolant, keep in mind that cats and dogs are attracted by the ethylene glycol antifreeze, and are quite likely to drink any that is left in an uncovered container or in puddles on the ground. This will prove fatal in sufficient quantity. Always drain the coolant into a sealable container. Coolant should be reused unless it is contaminated or several years old.

6. Disconnect the heater hoses from the intake manifold and the front of the cylinder head.
7. If equipped with an A/C compressor and/or a P/S pump, disconnect them and lay them aside.
8. Disconnect the accelerator linkage and the fuel line from the carburetor. Disconnect all necessary electrical connections, the spark plug wires and necessary vacuum lines.
9. Rotate the camshaft until the No. 4 cylinder is in the firing position. Remove the distributor cap and mark rotor-to-housing relationship, then remove the distributor.
10. Disconnect the fuel lines from the fuel pump and remove it.
11. Using two pry bars, depress the adjuster lock lever to lock the automatic adjuster shoe in its fully retracted position.
12. Remove timing sprocket-to-camshaft bolt, the sprocket and the fuel pump drive cam from the camshaft. Keep the sprocket on the chain damper and tensioner—DO NOT remove the sprocket from the chain.
13. Disconnect the AIR hose and check valve from the air manifold.
14. Remove the cylinder head-to-timing cover bolts.
15. Using the Extension Bar Wrench tool No. J-24239-01 or equivalent, remove cylinder head-to-engine bolts; remove the bolts in a progressional sequence, beginning with the outer bolts and working inward.
16. Remove the cylinder head, intake and exhaust manifold as an assembly.
17. Using a putty knife, clean the gasket mounting surfaces.

NOTE: The gasket surfaces on both the head and block must be clean of any foreign matter and free of nicks or heavy scratches. The cylinder bolt threads in the block and thread on the bolts must be cleaned (dirt will affect the bolt torque).

18. Installation is the reverse of removal. Place the new gasket over dowel pins with "TOP" side of gasket up.

NOTE: Be sure to lubricate the cylinder head bolts with engine oil before installing them.

19. Torque the cylinder head-to-engine bolts in several steps (in the proper sequence) to 61 ft. lbs. Then retighten to 72 ft. lbs.

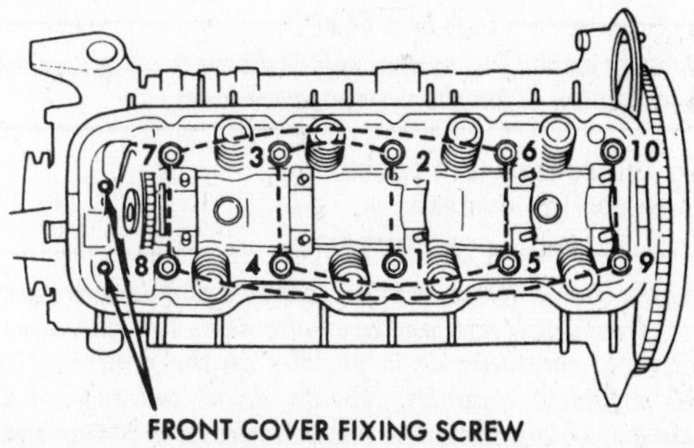
7
3
2
6
10
8
4
1
5
9
FRONT COVER FIXING SCREW

Cylinder head bolt torque sequence — 1.9L engine

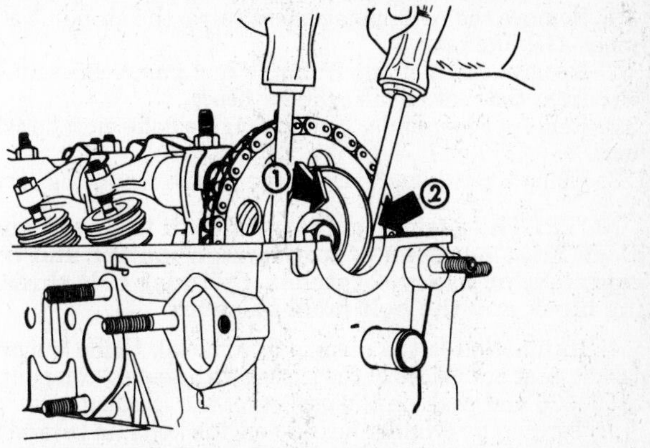
1
2

Using two pry bars to lock the automatic adjuster into position — 1.9L engine

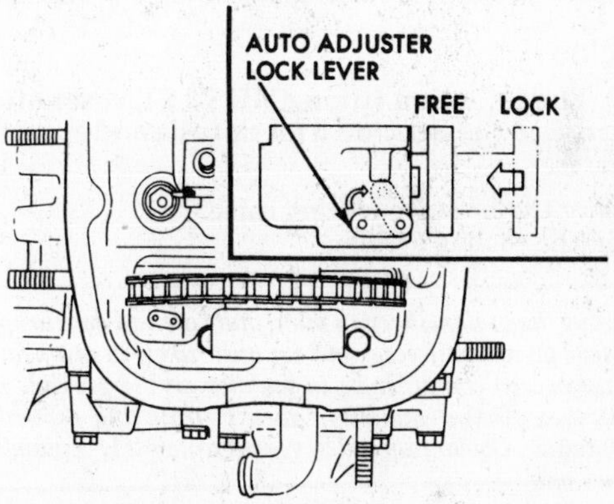
AUTO ADJUSTER
LOCK LEVER
FREE
LOCK

Locking the timing chain adjuster — 1.9L engine

20. Refill the cooling system. Start the engine, allow it to reach normal operating temperatures and check for leaks.
21. Check and/or adjust the engine timing and idle speed.

2.0L Engine

NOTE: Let the vehicle sit overnight before attempting to remove the cylinder head. The engine must be cold.

1. Remove the negative battery cable.
2. Drain the cooling system.

CAUTION

When draining the coolant, keep in mind that cats and dogs are attracted by the ethylene glycol antifreeze, and are quite likely to drink any that is left in an uncovered container or in puddles on the ground. This will prove fatal in sufficient quantity. Always drain the coolant into a sealable container. Coolant should be reused unless it is contaminated or several years old.

3. Remove the air cleaner. Raise and support the vehicle safely.
4. Remove the exhaust shield, then disconnect the exhaust pipe from the exhaust manifold. Lower the vehicle.
5. Disconnect the accelerator linkage, the necessary electrical wiring connectors and the vacuum lines.
6. Remove the fuel vapor canister harness (steel) pipes.
7. Remove the distributor cap, then mark the rotor-to-distributor housing and the distributor housing-to-engine.
8. Remove the rocker arm cover, the rocker arms and the push rods.
9. Remove the upper radiator hose, the heater hose, the upper fan shroud and the fan.

10. Remove the AIR management valve, the air pump and the upper AIR bracket.
11. Remove the fuel line from the fuel pump. Disconnect the wire from the rear of the cylinder head.
12. Remove the cylinder head-to-engine bolts and the cylinder head.
13. Using a putty knife, clean the gasket mounting surfaces.

NOTE: The gasket surfaces on both the head and the block must be clean of any foreign matter and free of any nicks or heavy scratches. Cylinder bolt threads in the block and the bolt must be clean.

14. Installation is the reverse of removal. Using a new head gasket, coat both sides of the gasket with sealing compound No. 10520026 and position the gasket on the locating pins.
15. Torque the cylinder head-to-engine bolts (in several steps) in sequence to 65–75 ft. lbs.
16. Refill the cooling system. Start the engine, allow it to reach normal operating temperatures and check for leaks.
17. Check and/or adjust the engine timing and idle speed.

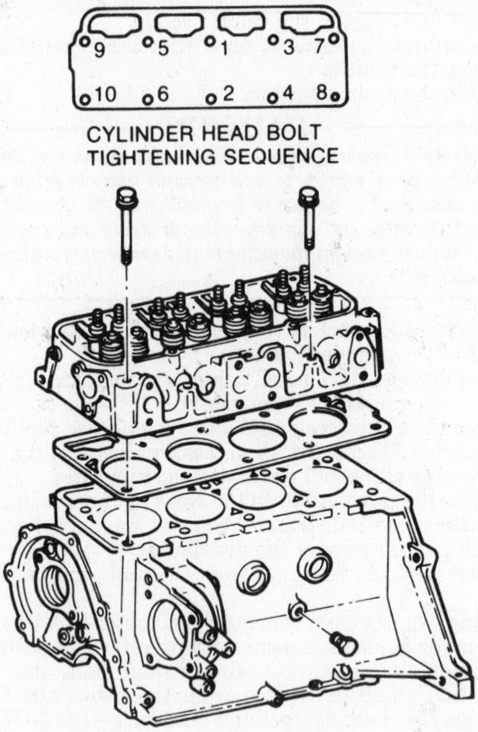
9 5 1 3 7
10 6 2 4 8
CYLINDER HEAD BOLT
TIGHTENING SEQUENCE

Cylinder head bolt torque sequence — 2.0L engine

2.2L Engine

NOTE: The injection timing MUST BE reset after this procedure. See the Section 5 for details and special tools required.

1. Remove the negative battery cable.
2. Drain the cooling system.

CAUTION

When draining the coolant, keep in mind that cats and dogs are attracted by the ethylene glycol antifreeze, and are quite likely to drink any that is left in an uncovered container or in puddles on the ground. This will prove fatal in sufficient quantity. Always drain the coolant into a sealable container. Coolant should be reused unless it is contaminated or several years old.

3. Remove the rocker arm cover, the rocker arm shaft and the pushrods.
4. Remove the upper radiator hose and the heater hose from the cylinder head.
5. Disconnect the heater tube and remove the exhaust pipe from the exhaust manifold.
6. Remove the vacuum pump and the A/C compressor (if equipped, move it aside).
7. Disconnect the heater hose/bracket, the necessary electrical wiring connectors. Disconnect the PCV valve hose from the pipe and move it aside.
8. Disconnect the dipstick tube bracket and dipstick, the breather pipe and the oil jet pipe.
9. Disconnect the fuel injection lines and cover them with protective caps.
10. Remove the air conditioning bracket and disconnect the return hose.
11. Remove the cylinder head-to-engine bolts and the cylinder head from the vehicle.

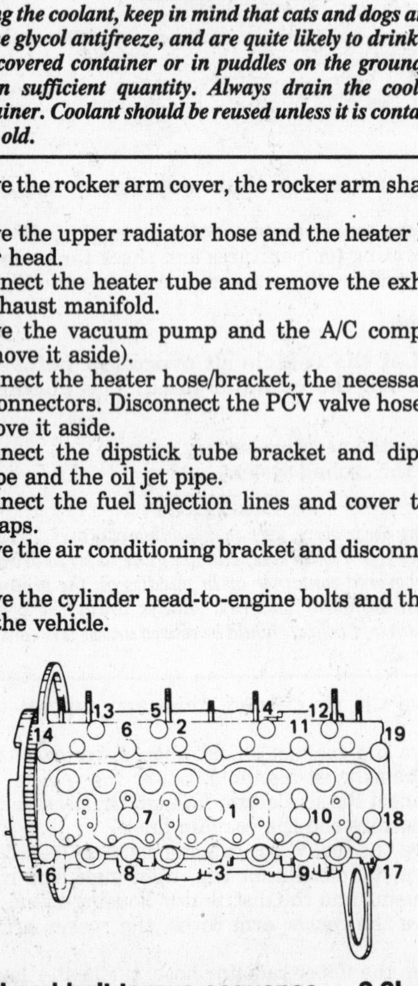
13 5 4 12
14 6 2 11 19
7 1 10 18
16 8 3 9 17

Cylinder head bolt torque sequence — 2.2L engine

12. Using a putty knife, clean the gasket mounting surfaces. Inspect the cylinder head for distortion, cracks and/or damage.

NOTE: To install, the gasket surfaces on both the head and the block must be clean of any foreign matter and free of any nicks or heavy scratches. The cylinder bolt threads in the block and the bolt must be clean.

13. Installation is the reverse of removal. Using a new head gasket with the "TOP" side facing upward, position the gasket on the locating pins, apply engine oil to the cylinder head bolt threads and torque the cylinder head-to-engine bolts (in sequence): First, to 40–47 ft. lbs. and then, to 54–61 ft. lbs. (new bolts) or 61–69 ft. lbs. (used bolts).
14. Refill the cooling system. Start the engine, allow it to reach normal operating temperatures and check for leaks.
15. Check and/or adjust the engine timing and idle speed.

2.5L Engine

NOTE: Let the vehicle sit overnight before attempting to remove the cylinder head. The engine must be cold.

CAUTION

Relieve the pressure on the fuel system before disconnecting any fuel line connection. See Section 5 for the proper procedures.

1. Remove the rocker arm cover.
2. Drain the cooling system.

CAUTION

When draining the coolant, keep in mind that cats and dogs are attracted by the ethylene glycol antifreeze, and are quite likely to drink any that is left in an uncovered container or in puddles on the ground. This will prove fatal in sufficient quantity. Always drain the coolant into a sealable container. Coolant should be reused unless it is contaminated or several years old.

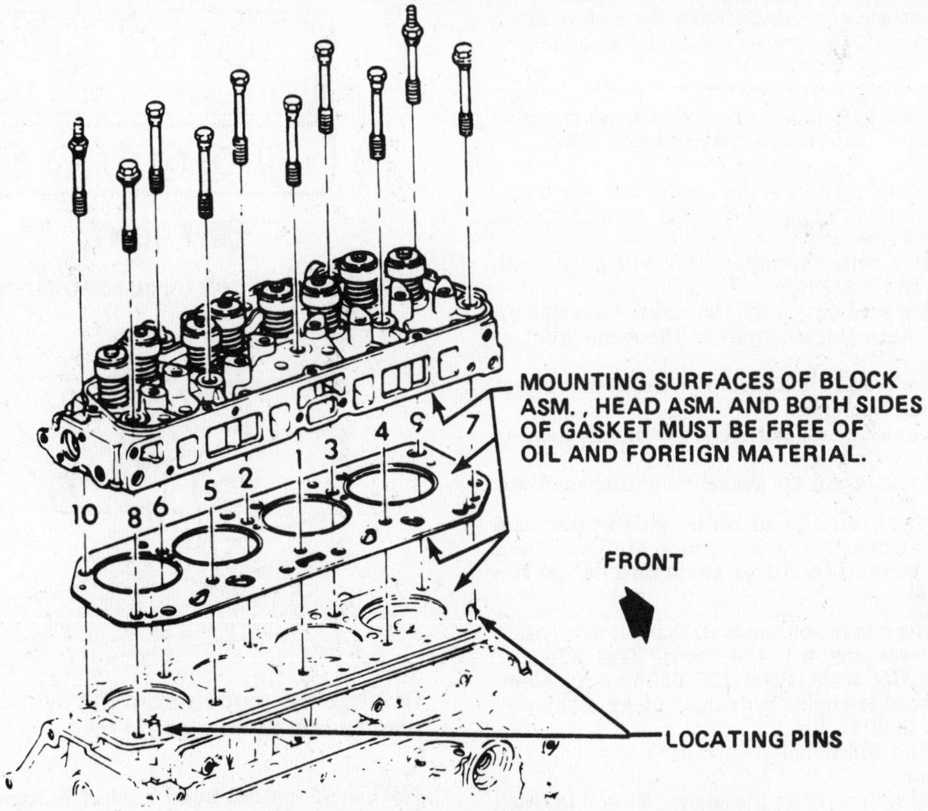
MOUNTING SURFACES OF BLOCK ASM., HEAD ASM. AND BOTH SIDES OF GASKET MUST BE FREE OF OIL AND FOREIGN MATERIAL.
FRONT
LOCATING PINS
10
8
6
5
2
1
3
4
9
7
Cylinder head bolt torque sequence – 2.5L engine

3. Disconnect the accelerator, the cruise control and the TVS cables, if equipped.
4. Remove the water pump bypass and heater hoses from the intake manifold.
5. Remove the front and rear braces from the alternator, then move it aside.
6. Disconnect the A/C compressor brackets and move the compressor aside.
7. Remove the thermostat housing-to-cylinder head bolts and the housing from the engine.
8. Remove the ground cable and any necessary electrical connectors from the cylinder head. Disconnect the wires from the spark plugs and the oxygen sensor. Disconnect and remove the ignition coil from the intake manifold and the cylinder head.
9. Remove the vacuum lines and fuel hoses from the intake manifold and the TBI unit.
10. Disconnect the exhaust pipe from the exhaust manifold.
11. Remove the rocker arm nuts, the washers, the rocker arms and the pushrods from the cylinder head.
12. Remove the cylinder head-to-engine bolts and the cylinder head from the engine (with the manifolds attached). If necessary, remove the intake and the exhaust manifolds from the cylinder head.
13. Using a putty knife, clean the gasket mounting surfaces. Using a wire brush, clean the carbon deposits from the combustion chambers.
14. Inspect the cylinder head and block for cracks, nicks, heavy scratches or other damage.
15. Installation is the reverse of removal. Using new gaskets and sealant (where necessary), torque the cylinder head bolts, in sequence, as follows:

- Torque all bolts gradually to 18 ft. lbs.
- Torque all bolts except the left front bolt (#9 in the sequence) to 26 ft. lbs. Torque number 9 to 18 ft. lbs.
- Torque all bolts an additional ¼ turn (90°).

16. Refill the cooling system, start the engine and check for leaks.

2.8L Engine

CAUTION

Relieve the pressure on the fuel system before disconnecting any fuel line connection. See Section 5 for the proper procedures.

1. Remove the intake manifold.
2. Raise and support the vehicle safely.
3. Drain the cooling system.

CAUTION

When draining the coolant, keep in mind that cats and dogs are attracted by the ethylene glycol antifreeze, and are quite likely to drink any that is left in an uncovered container or in puddles on the ground. This will

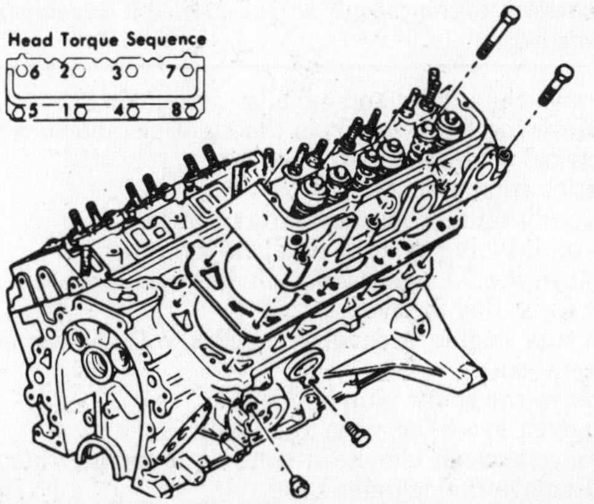
Head Torque Sequence
6 2 3 7
5 1 4 8
Cylinder head bolt torque sequence – 2.8L engine

prove fatal in sufficient quantity. Always drain the coolant into a sealable container. Coolant should be reused unless it is contaminated or several years old.

4. Disconnect the exhaust pipe from the exhaust manifold and remove the exhaust manifold-to-cylinder block bolts.
5. Lower the vehicle.
6. Remove the dipstick tube from the engine (left side only).
7. Remove the ground strap and the sensor connector from the cylinder head (left side only).
8. Remove the drive belt, alternator, and AIR pump with mounting bracket (right side only).
9. Loosen the rocker arm nuts, turn the rocker arms and remove the pushrods. Keep the pushrods in the same order as removed.
10. Remove the cylinder head bolts in stages and in the reverse order of the tightening sequence.
11. Remove the cylinder head; DO NOT pry on the head to loosen it.
12. Using a putty knife, clean the gasket mounting surfaces.

NOTE: Coat the cylinder head bolts with sealer and torque to specifications in the sequence shown. Make sure the pushrods seat in the lifter seats and adjust the valves.

13. Installation is the reverse of removal. Using a new gasket (position it on the dowel pins, with the words "This Side Up" facing upwards) and GM sealant No. 1052080 or equivalent, torque the cylinder head-to-engine bolts in sequence as follows:
- Torque all bolts to 40 ft. lbs.
- Torque all bolts an additional ¼ turn (90°).

14. Adjust the valves.
15. Refill the cooling system. Start the engine, allow it to reach normal operating temperatures and check for leaks.
16. Check and/or adjust the ignition timing and idle speed (if possible).

4.3L Engine

CAUTION

Relieve the pressure on the fuel system before disconnecting any fuel line connection. See Section 5 for the proper procedures.

1. Remove the negative battery cable.
2. Remove the rocker arm cover.
3. Drain the cooling system.

CAUTION

When draining the coolant, keep in mind that cats and dogs are attracted by the ethylene glycol antifreeze, and are quite likely to drink any that is left in an uncovered container or in puddles on the ground. This will prove fatal in sufficient quantity. Always drain the coolant into a sealable container. Coolant should be reused unless it is contaminated or several years old.

4. Remove the intake and exhaust manifolds.
5. Remove the following from the right cylinder head:
- Electrical connector at the sensor.
- Dipstick tube bracket.
- Air conditioning compressor (lay it aside).
- Air conditioning bracket and belt tensioner.

6. Remove the following from the left cylinder head:
- Alternator (lay it aside).
- Left side engine accessory bracket with power steering pump (lay it aside).

7. Remove the spark plug and wires.
8. Remove the rocker arms and pushrods.
9. Remove the cylinder head bolts by loosening them in sequence. Remove the cylinder head.
10. Using a putty knife, clean the gasket mounting surfaces.

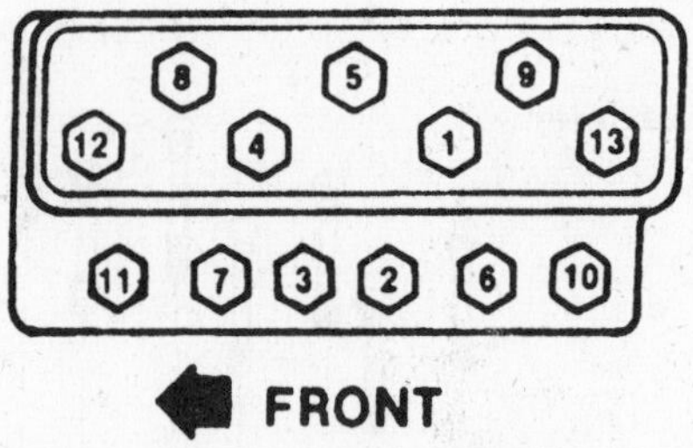
8
5
9
12
4
1
13
11
7
3
2
6
10
FRONT

Cylinder head bolt torque sequence — 4.3L engine

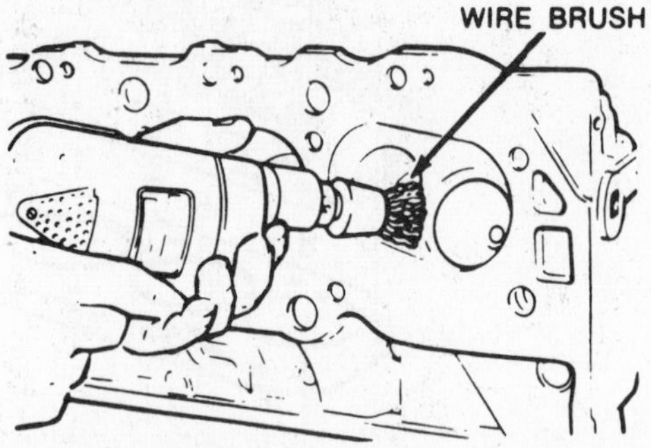
WIRE BRUSH

Remove the carbon from the cylinder head with a wire brush on an electric drill

NOTE: If a steel head gasket is used, coat both sides with sealer. If a composition head gasket is used, DO NOT use sealer.

11. Installation is the reverse of removal. Using a new gasket, position it on the dowel pins, with the words "This Side Up" facing upwards. Torque the cylinder head-to-engine bolts in sequence to 65 ft. lbs. Use three steps when torquing.

CLEANING AND INSPECTION

1. Remove the valve assemblies from the cylinder head. See the appropriate procedures in Section 3 (this section).
2. Using a small wire power brush, clean the carbon from the combustion chambers and the valve ports.
3. Inspect the cylinder head for cracks in the exhaust ports, combustion chambers or external cracks to the water chamber.
4. Thoroughly clean the valve guides using a suitable wire bore brush.

Measuring valve stem clearance with a dial indicator

NOTE: Excessive valve stem-to-bore clearance will cause excessive oil consumption and may cause valve breakage. Insufficient clearance will result in noisy and sticky functioning of the valve and disturb engine smoothness.

5. Measure the valve stem clearance as follows:
   a. Clamp a dial indicator on the cylinder head.
   b. Locate the indicator so that movement of the valve stem from side to side (horizontal to the head) will cause a direct movement of the indicator stem. The indicator stem must contact the side of the valve stem just above the valve guide.
   c. Prop the valve head about $1/16$ in. (1.6mm) off the valve seat.
   d. Move the stem of the valve from side to side using light pressure to obtain a clearance reading. If the clearance exceeds specifications, it will be necessary to ream (for oversize valves) or knurl (raise the bore for original valves) the valve guides.
6. Inspect the rocker arm studs for wear or damage.
7. Install a dial micrometer into the valve guide and check the valve seat for concentricity.

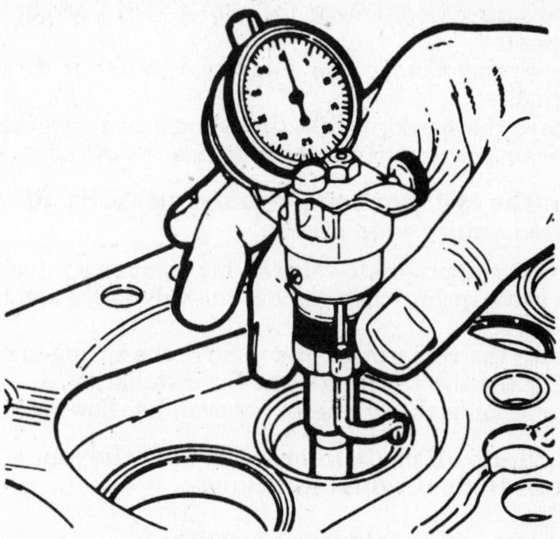

Checking valve seat concentricity with a run-out gauge

RESURFACING

1. Using a straightedge, check the cylinder head for warpage.
2. If warpage exceeds 0.003 in. in a 6 in. span, or 0.006 in. over the total length, the cylinder head must be resurfaced. Resurfacing can be performed at most machine shops.

NOTE: When resurfacing the cylinder head(s), the intake manifold mounting position is altered and must be corrected by machining a proportionate amount from the intake manifold flange.

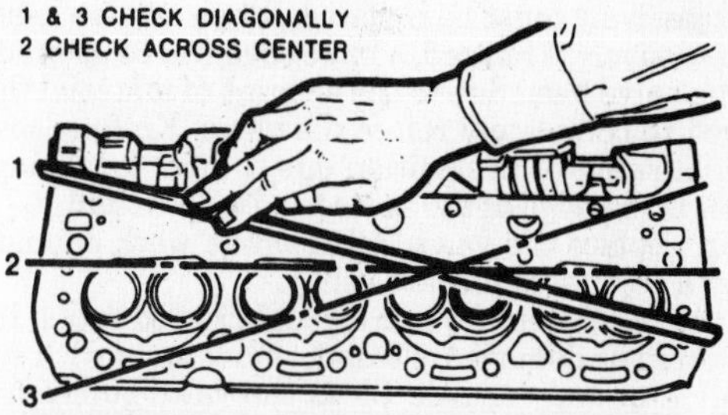
1 & 3 CHECK DIAGONALLY
2 CHECK ACROSS CENTER
1
2
3

Measuring cylinder head warpage

Valves and Valve Springs

REMOVAL AND INSTALLATION

Cylinder Head Removed

NOTE: The following procedures requires the use of a Valve Spring Compressor tool.

1. Remove the cylinder head.
2. Remove the rocker arm assemblies or rocker shaft assemblies.
3. Using a Valve Spring Compressor tool, compress the valve springs and remove the stem keys. Release the compressor tool and remove the rotators or spring caps, the oil shedders, the springs and damper assemblies, then remove the oil seals and the valve spring shims.
4. Remove the valve from the cylinder head and place them in a rack in their proper sequence so that they can be reassembled in their original positions. Discard any bent or damaged valves.
5. Installation is the reverse of removal. Always use new oil seals.
6. Adjust the valve lash (if necessary).

Removing the valve springs with the head off the engine

Cylinder Head Not Removed

This procedure requires the use of the following tools:

- GM Air Adapter tool No. J-23590 or equivalent
- Valve Spring Compressor tool No. J-5892 or equivalent (2.0L, 2.5L, 2.8L and 4.3L engines)

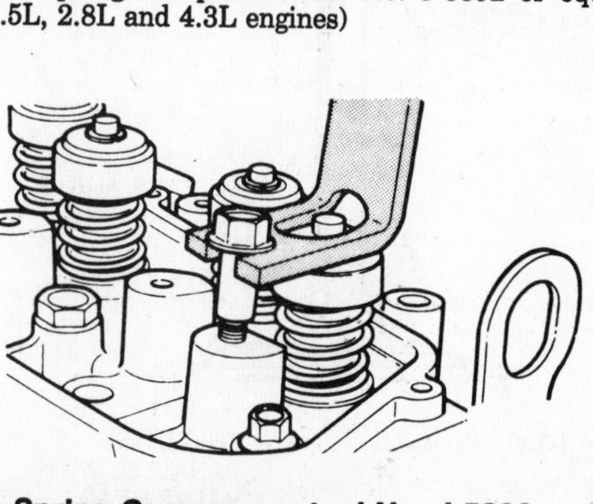

Valve Spring Compressor tool No. J-5892 — 2.0L, 2.5L, 2.8L and 4.3L engines

• Valve Spring Compressor tool No. J-26513 or equivalent (1.9L engine)
• Valve Spring Compressor tool No. J-29760 or equivalent (2.2L engine)

1. Remove the spark plug (in the cylinder being worked on). Install the air adaptor tool and pressurize the cylinder.

NOTE: The cylinder being worked on MUST BE at the TDC of its compression stroke.

2. Using the appropriate valve spring compressor tool, compress the valve spring, then remove the valve keys and the retaining ring.
3. Release the compressor and remove the spring and valve stem seal. Keep the valves in order for installation.
4. Installation is the reverse of removal. Use new valve seals.

NOTE: Keep all parts in order so that they may be assembled in their original locations.

INSPECTION

Inspect the valve faces and seats (in the head) for pits, burned spots and other evidence of poor seating. Valves that are pitted must be refaced to the proper angle (45°). Valves that are warped excessively must be replaced. When a valve head that is warped excessively is refaced, a knife edge will be ground on part or all of the valve head due to the amount of material that must be removed to completely reface the valve. Knife edges lead to breakage, burning or preignition due to heat localizing on the knife edge. If the edge of the valve head is less than $^1/_{32}$ in. after machining, replace the valve. All machine work should be performed by a reputable machine shop.

Check the valve stem for scoring and burned spots. If not noticeably scored or damaged, clean the valve stem with solvent to remove all gum and varnish. Clean the valve guides using solvent and an expanding wire-type valve guide cleaner. Use a dial indicator for measuring valve stem-to-guide clearance. Mount the dial indicator so that the stem of the indicator is at 90° to the valve stem and as close to the valve guide as possible. Move the valve off its seat, then measure the valve guide-to-stem clearance by rocking the stem back and forth to actuate the dial indicator. Measure the valve stem diameter using a micrometer and compare to specifications to determine whether the stem or guide wear is responsible for the excess clearance.

Some of the engines covered in this guide are equipped with valve rotators which double as valve spring caps. In normal operation the rotators put a certain degree of wear on the tip of the valve stem; this wear appears as concentric rings on the stem tip. However, if the rotator is not working properly, the wear

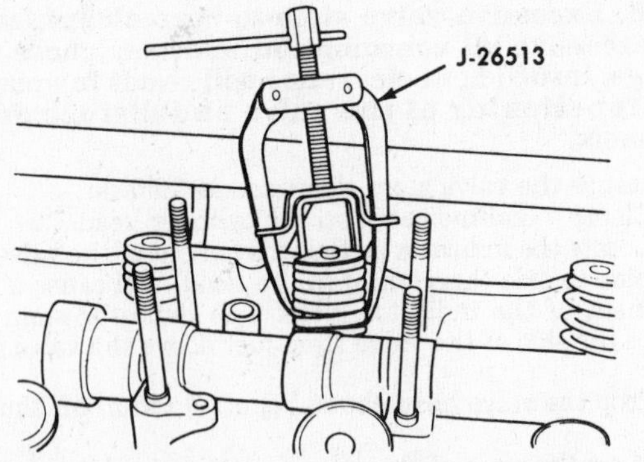
J-26513

Valve Spring Compressor tool No. J-26513 – 1.9L engine

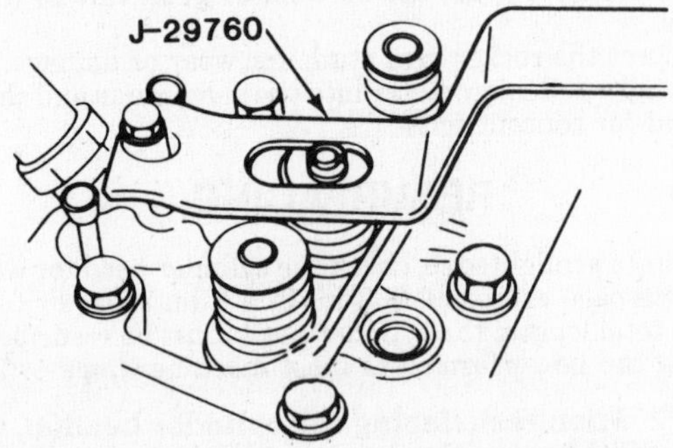
J-29760

Valve Spring Compressor tool No. J-29760 – 2.2L engine

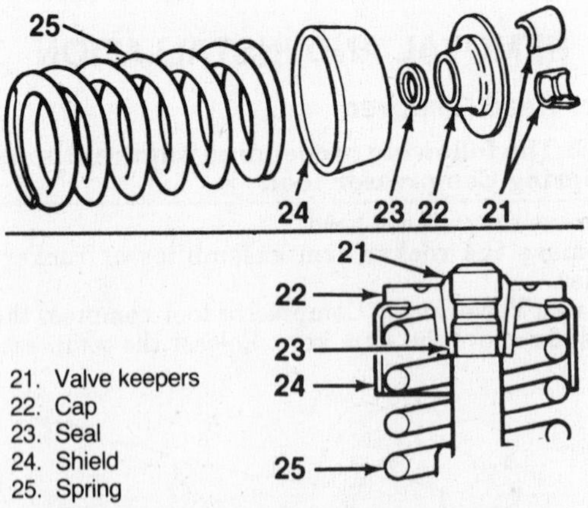
25
24
23 22
21
21
22
23
24
25
21. Valve keepers
22. Cap
23. Seal
24. Shield
25. Spring

Exploded view of the valve assembly

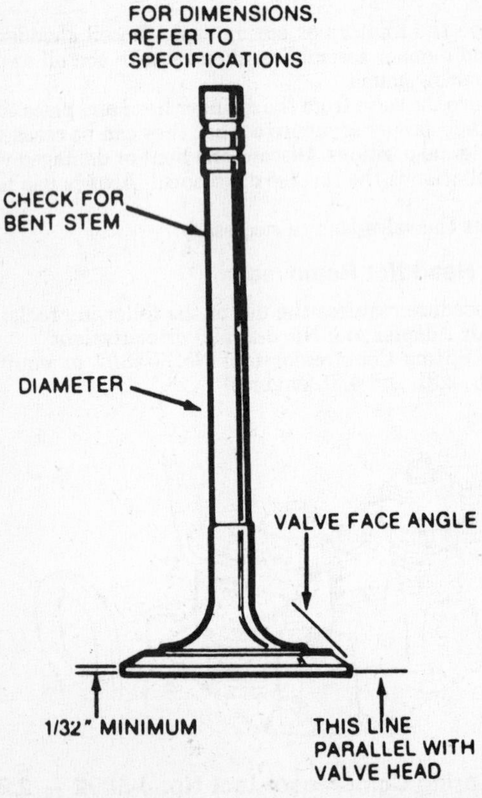
FOR DIMENSIONS, REFER TO SPECIFICATIONS
CHECK FOR BENT STEM
DIAMETER
VALVE FACE ANGLE
1/32" MINIMUM
THIS LINE PARALLEL WITH VALVE HEAD

Valve inspection and head measurement

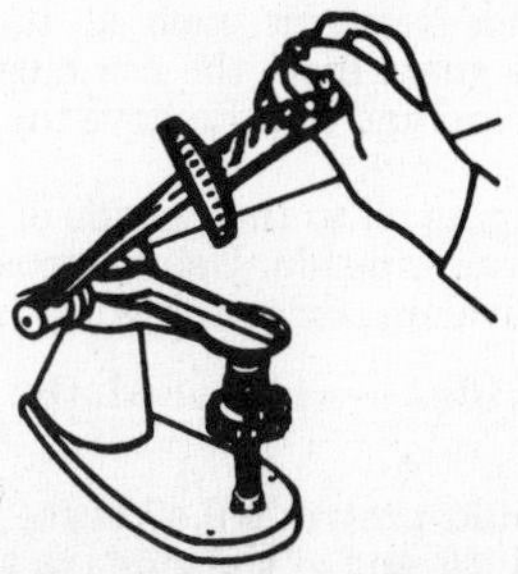

Checking the valve spring pressure

may appear as straight notches or "X" patterns across the valve stem tip. Whenever the valves are removed from the cylinder head, the tips should be inspected for improper pattern, which could indicate valve rotator problems. Valve stem tips will have to be ground flat if the rotator problems are severe.

Position the valve spring on a flat, clean surface next to a square. Measure the height of the spring and rotate it against the engine of the square to measure the distortion (out-of-roundness). If the spring height varies between the springs by more than 1/16 in. (1.6mm), replace the spring. Using a valve spring tester, check the spring pressure at the installed and compressed height.

VALVE REFACING

NOTE: All valve grinding operations should be performed by a qualified machine shop; only the valve lapping operation is recommended to be performed by the home mechanic.

Valve Lapping

When valve faces and seats have been refaced, or if they are determined to be in good condition, the valves MUST BE lapped to ensure efficient sealing when the valve closes against the seat.

1. Invert the cylinder head so that the combustion chambers are facing upward.
2. Lightly lubricate the valve stems with clean engine oil and coat the valve seats with valve lapping compound. Install the valves in the cylinder head as numbered.
3. Moisten and attach the suction cup of a valve lapping tool to a valve head.
4. Rotate the tool between your palms, changing position and lifting the tool often to prevent grooving. Lap the valve until a smooth polished seat is evident (you may have to add a bit more compound after some lapping is done).
5. Remove the valve and tool, then remove ALL traces of the grinding compound with a solvent-soaked rag or rinse the head with solvent.

Valve Seats

REMOVAL AND INSTALLATION

1.9L and 2.2L Engines

NOTE: The following procedures requires the use of an arc welder, a wire brush, a slide hammer puller, dry ice and an arbor press.

1. Weld pieces of welding rod to several points around the seat, then allow the head to cool for about 5 minutes.
2. Using a slide hammer puller, remove the valve seats attached to the welding rods.
3. Using a wire brush, clean the valve seat recess carefully.
4. Place the new valve seat in dry ice while heating the recess

Lapping the valves

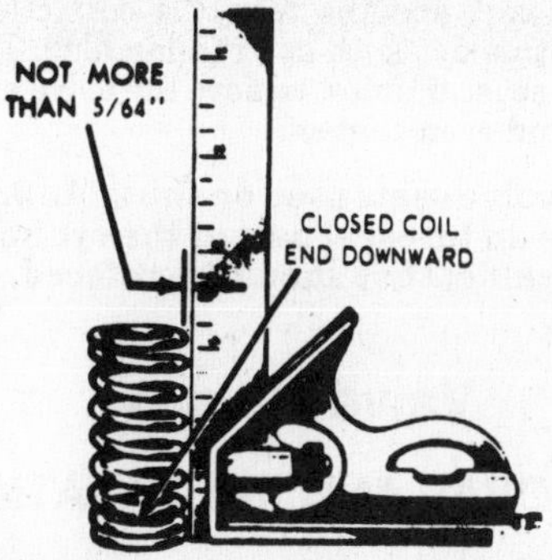
NOT MORE THAN 5/64"
CLOSED COIL END DOWNWARD

Checking the valve spring free length and squareness

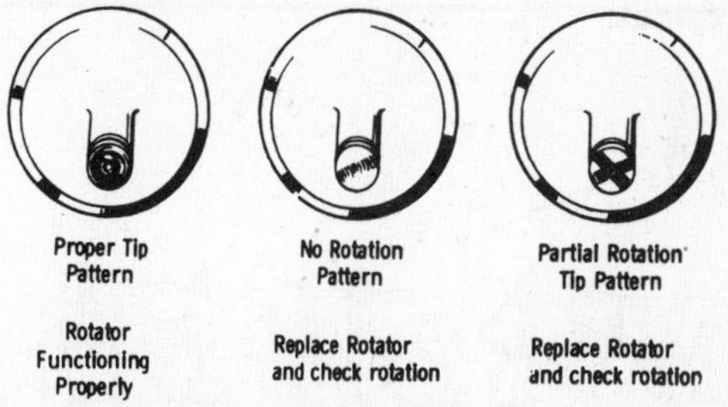
Proper Tip Pattern
Rotator Functioning Properly
No Rotation Pattern
Replace Rotator and check rotation
Partial Rotation Tip Pattern
Replace Rotator and check rotation

Valve stem wear patterns on engines using rotator cups

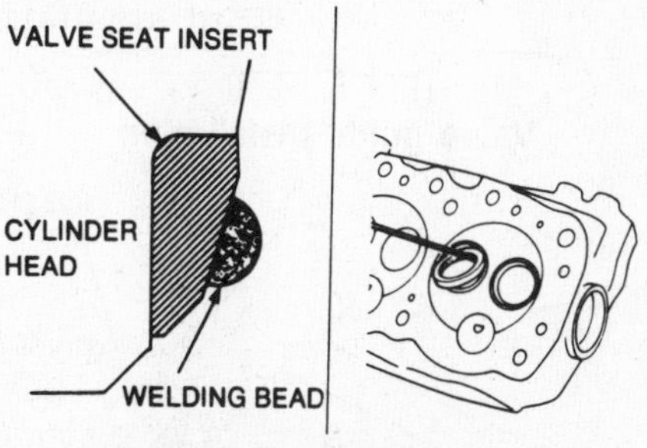
VALVE SEAT INSERT
CYLINDER HEAD
WELDING BEAD

Valve seat removal

in the head with steam. Take about 5 minutes for this procedure. Perform the heating and cooling simultaneously.

5. Using protective gloves, insert the valve seat into the cylinder head recess. The seat depth below the combustion chamber face should be 0.0031–0.0047 in. (0.08-0.12mm).
6. Cut the valve seat to the angle shown in the valve specifications chart. Valve seat contact width should be 0.0472–0.0630 in. (1.2-1.6mm).

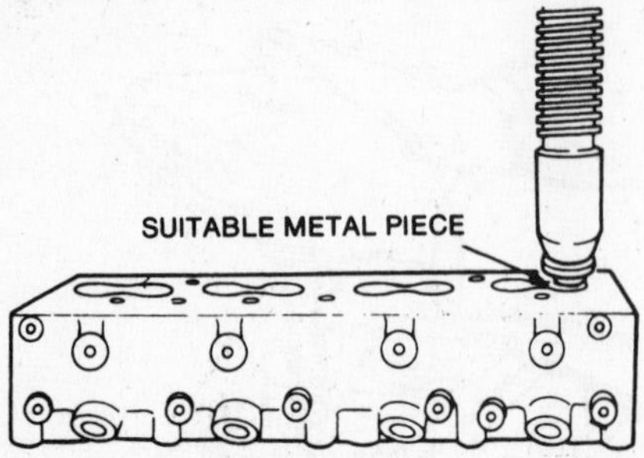
SUITABLE METAL PIECE

Valve seat installation using a bench press

7. Polish the seat using lapping compound and a suction type lapper.
8. Smear the seat and the face of a correctly ground and cleaned valve with a dye such as Prussian blue. Turn the valve against the seat several times, remove the valve and check that the dye shows and even contact.

NOTE: The valve seats used on the 2.0L, 2.5L, 2.8L and 4.3 engines are an integral part of the cylinder head and are not replaceable; they should be refaced, cleaned and lapped, ONLY.

Valve Guides

REMOVAL AND INSTALLATION

1.9L and 2.2L Engines

NOTE: The following procedures requires the use of Valve Guide Removal and Installation tool No. J-26512 or equivalent.

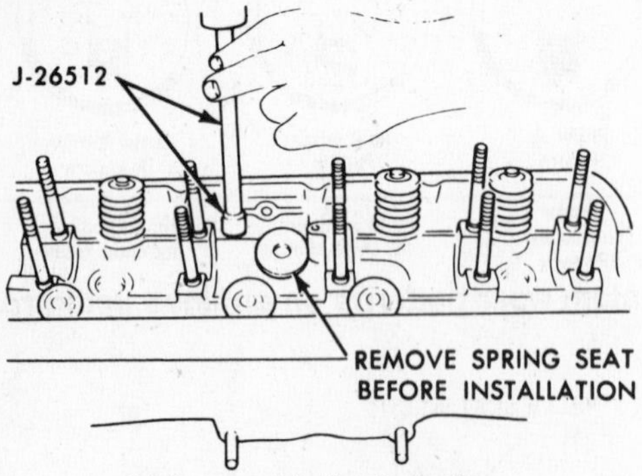
J-26512
REMOVE SPRING SEAT
BEFORE INSTALLATION

Valve guide installation

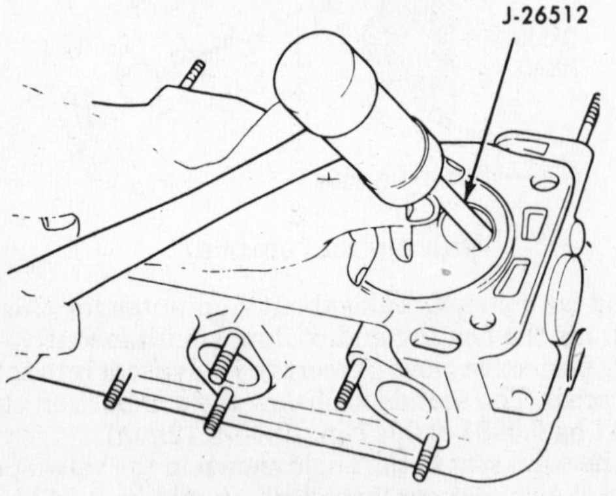
J-26512

Valve guide removal

1. Insert the guide remover such as tool No. J-26512 or equivalent, into the guide from the combustion chamber side. Drive the guide upward and out. Remove the lower valve spring seat.
2. Apply clean engine oil to the outside of the new guide and position it on the head top-side. Using opposite side of the tool No. J-26512 or equivalent, drive the guide in until it bottoms.

NOTE: If the guides are replaced, the valves should be replaced also.

3. The guide should protrude 0.4724 in. (12mm) above the head surface. Grind the end of the guide to achieve this height. Make certain that the guide has bottomed before grinding.

NOTE: Valve guides on the 2.0L, 2.5L, 2.8L and 4.3L engines are not replaceable. The guides should be reamed to accommodate valves with oversized stems. Oversized stems are available in 0.089mm, 0.394mm and 0.775mm.

KNURLING

Valve guides which are not excessively worn or distorted may, in some cases, be knurled. knurling is a process in which metal is displaced and raised, thereby reducing clearance. Knurling also provides excellent oil control.

This procedure should only be performed by a qualified machine shop.

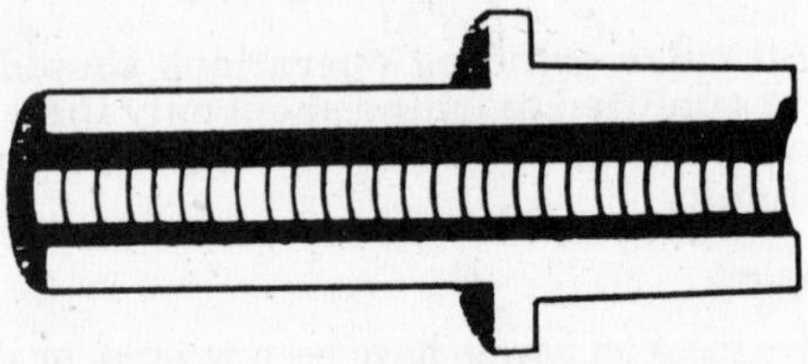

Cut-away view of a knurled valve guide

Oil Pan

In most cases it will be necessary to remove the engine in order to gain access to the oil pan. It is a difficult and tedious task to remove the oil pan with the engine in the vehicle. The chances of contaminating the bearing surfaces or damaging other internal engine components is great. Also, working under the vehicle with the engine jacked up in the frame puts you at great risk for great personal injury.

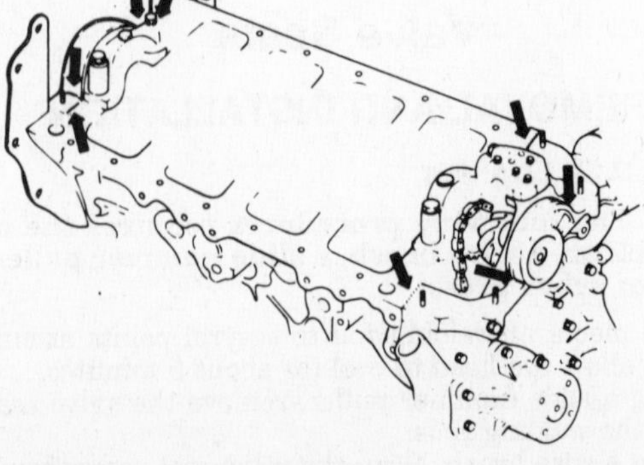

Oil pan sealer location — 1.9L engine

REMOVAL AND INSTALLATION

1.9L Engine

1. Remove the engine.
2. Remove the bolts and nuts attaching the oil pan to the cylinder block and remove the oil pan.
3. Remove the oil level gage guide tube from the intake manifold and the oil pan.
4. Using a putty knife, clean the gasket mounting surfaces. Make sure that the sealing surfaces on the pan, cylinder block and front cover are clean and free of oil.
5. Apply a thin coat of Permatex® number 2 or equivalent to the areas shown in the illustration.
6. Install the new oil pan gasket, aligning the holes, and then install the oil pan.
7. Install and tighten the bolts and nuts evenly to 4 ft. lbs.
8. Check the edge of the gasket to make certain the gasket is set in position correctly. If the projection of the gasket edge is beyond the oil pan flange is uneven, remove and reinstall.
9. Install the engine into the vehicle. Refill the crankcase with fresh oil. Start the engine, establish normal operating temperatures and check for leaks.

2.0L Engine

TWO-WHEEL DRIVE

1. Remove the negative battery cable.
2. Remove the engine from the vehicle.
3. Remove the oil pan.
4. Using a putty knife, clean the gasket mounting surfaces. Make sure that all sealing surfaces are clean and free of oil.
5. Apply a thin coat of RTV sealant to both ends of a new rear oil pan seal. Sealant must not extend beyond the tabs of the seal. Then install the seal firmly into the rear main bearing cap.
6. Apply a continuous ⅛ in. bead of RTV sealant on the oil pan side rails. This bead must be in line with the bolt holes and circled inboard at each hole location.

NOTE: DO NOT apply sealant to the rear oil pan seal mating surface.

7. Apply RTV sealant to the oil pan surface which fits to the engine front cover. Ensure the sealant meets both side rail beads.
8. Using care to avoid disturbing the RTV beads, install the oil pan onto the cylinder block. The sealant must be wet during oil pan bolt torquing. 9.Torque attaching bolts to the following:
   - Oil pan-to-cover: 6–9 ft. lbs.
   - Oil pan-to-side rail: 4–9 ft. lbs.
   - Oil pan-to-rear holes: 11–17 ft. lbs.
9. Install the engine into the vehicle. Refill the crankcase with fresh oil. Start the engine, establish normal operating temperatures and check for leaks.

FOUR-WHEEL DRIVE

1. Remove the negative battery cable.
2. Remove the starter front brace bolt.
3. Remove the motor mount through bolts.
4. Raise and support the vehicle safely.
5. Remove the front splash shield, and the brake and fuel line clip retaining bolts.
6. Remove the crossmember bolts and crossmember. Rotate the crossmember around the lines.
7. Drain the engine oil.
8. Remove the starter bolts and lay the starter aside.
9. Disconnect the steering damper at the frame.
10. Scribe the idler arm location and disconnect the idler arm and steering gear at the frame. Disconnect the front axle at the frame.

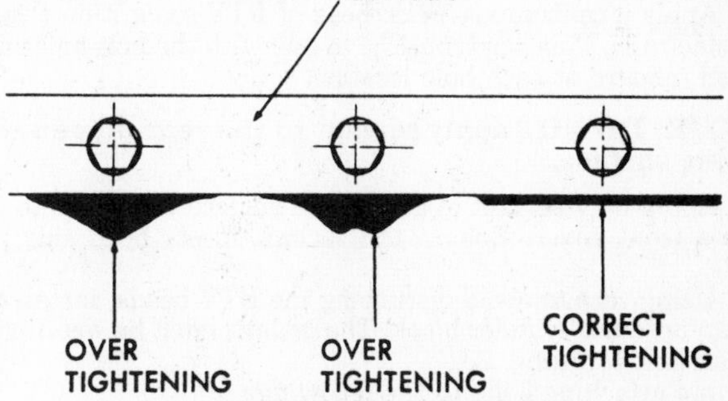
OIL PAN
OVER TIGHTENING
OVER TIGHTENING
CORRECT TIGHTENING
Oil pan gasket projection

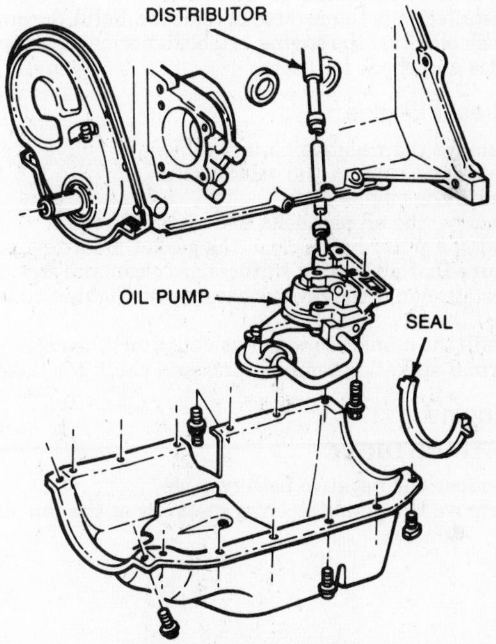
DISTRIBUTOR
OIL PUMP
SEAL
Oil pan – 2.0L engine

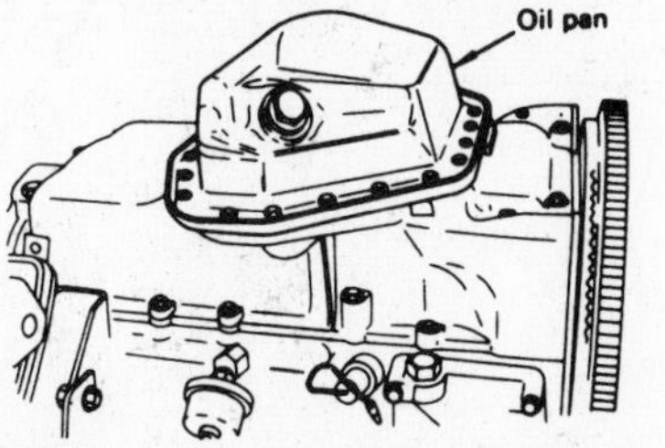
Oil pan
Oil pan – 2.2L diesel engine

11. Disconnect the front driveshaft at the front differential and slide the differential forward.
12. Remove the oil pan bolts.
13. Raise the engine slightly and remove the pan.

NOTE: Raising the engine too far could damage the EGR system.

14. Remove the oil pan.
15. Using a putty knife, clean the gasket mounting surfaces. Make sure that all sealing surfaces are clean and free of oil.
16. Apply a thin coat of RTV sealant to both ends of a new rear oil pan seal. Sealant must not extend beyond the tabs of the seal.

Then install the seal firmly into the rear main bearing cap.

17. Apply a continuous ⅛ in. bead of RTV sealant on the oil pan side rails. This bead must be in line with the bolt holes and circled inboard at each hole location.

NOTE: DO NOT apply sealant to the rear oil pan seal mating surface.

18. Apply RTV sealant to the oil pan surface which fits to the engine front cover. Ensure the sealant meets both side rail beads.

19. Using care to avoid disturbing the RTV beads, install the oil pan onto the cylinder block. The sealant must be wet during oil pan bolt torquing. 20.

Torque attaching bolts to the following:

- Oil pan-to-cover: 6–9 ft. lbs.
- Oil pan-to-side rail: 4–9 ft. lbs.
- Oil pan-to-rear holes: 11–17 ft. lbs.

21. Installation is the reverse of removal. Refill the crankcase with fresh oil. Start the engine, establish normal operating temperatures and check for leaks.

2.2L Diesel Engine

1. Remove the negative battery cable.
2. Raise and support the vehicle safely.
3. Drain the engine oil.
4. Remove the oil pan bolts and remove the pan.
5. Using a putty knife, clean the gasket mounting surfaces. Make sure that all sealing surfaces are clean and free of oil.
6. Installation is the reverse of removal. Tighten bolts to 2–4 ft. lbs.
7. Refill the crankcase with fresh oil. Start the engine, establish normal operating temperatures and check for leaks.

2.5L Engine

TWO-WHEEL DRIVE

1. Remove the negative battery cable.
2. Remove the power steering reservoir at the fan shroud.
3. Remove the radiator fan shroud.
4. Raise and support the vehicle safely.
5. Drain the engine oil.
6. Remove the strut rods.
7. Remove the exhaust pipes at the manifolds.
8. Remove the catalytic converter and exhaust pipe.
9. Remove the flywheel cover.
10. Remove the starter and brace.
11. Remove the brake line at the crossmember. Remove the engine mount through bolts.
12. Remove the oil pan bolts and pan.
13. Using a putty knife, clean the gasket mounting surfaces. Make sure that all sealing surfaces are clean and free of oil.
14. Apply RTV sealant to the oil pan flange and block as shown in the illustration.
15. Using care to avoid disturbing the RTV beads, install the oil pan onto the cylinder block. The sealant must be wet during oil pan bolt torquing.
16. Tighten oil pan bolts to 90 inch lbs.
17. The remainder of the installation procedure is the reverse of removal. Refill the crankcase with fresh oil. Start the engine, establish normal operating temperatures and check for leaks.

FOUR-WHEEL DRIVE

1. Remove the negative battery cable.
2. Remove the power steering reservoir at the fan shroud.
3. Remove the radiator fan shroud.
4. Remove the engine oil dipstick.
5. Raise and support the vehicle safely.
6. Drain the engine oil.
7. Remove the brake line at the crossmember and remove the crossmember.
9. Remove the transmission cooler lines.
10. Remove the exhaust pipes at the manifolds.
11. Remove the catalytic converter hanger.
12. Remove the flywheel cover.
13. Remove the driveshaft splash shield.
14. Remove the idler arm assembly.

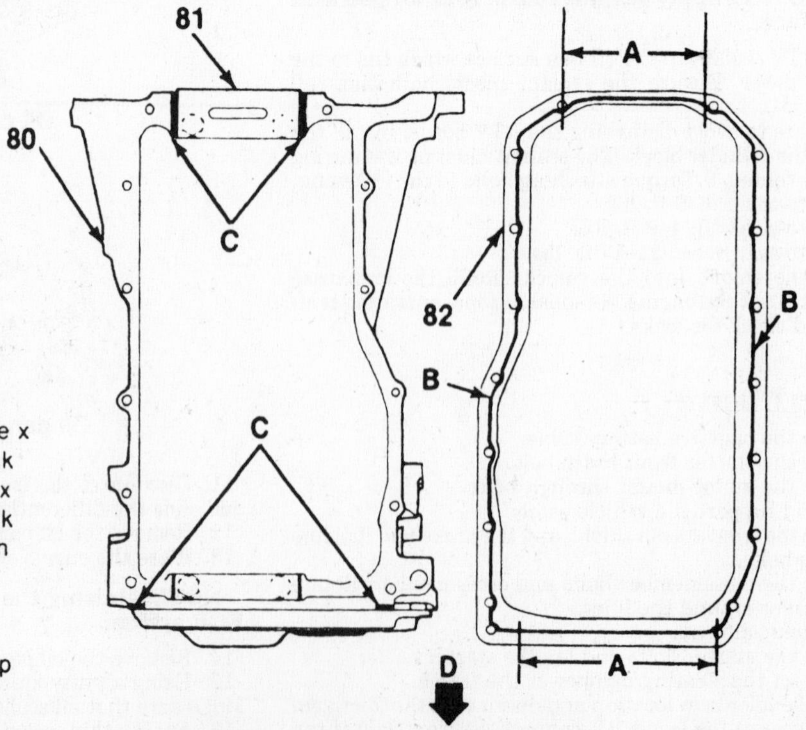
81
80
C
C
A
A
82
B
B
D

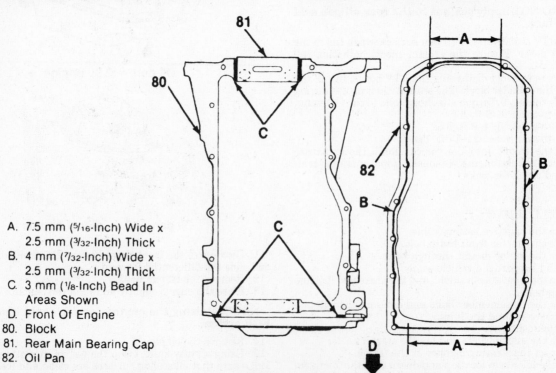

A. 7.5 mm (5/16-Inch) Wide x 2.5 mm (3/32-Inch) Thick
B. 4 mm (7/32-Inch) Wide x 2.5 mm (3/32-Inch) Thick
C. 3 mm (1/8-Inch) Bead In Areas Shown
D. Front Of Engine
80. Block
81. Rear Main Bearing Cap
82. Oil Pan

Applying RTV sealant to the oil pan and block – 2.5L engine

15. Remove the steering gear bolts. Pull the steering gear and linkage forward.
16. Remove the differential housing mounting bolts at the bracket on the right side and at the frame on the left side.
17. Remove the starter and brace.
18. Remove the engine mount through bolts.
19. Remove the oil pan bolts and pan.
21. Apply RTV sealant to the oil pan flange and block as shown in the illustration.
22. Using care to avoid disturbing the RTV beads, install the oil pan onto the cylinder block. The sealant must be wet during oil pan bolt torquing.
23. Tighten oil pan bolts to 90 inch lbs.
24. Installation is the reverse of removal. Refill the crankcase with fresh oil. Start the engine, establish normal operating temperatures and check for leaks.

2.8L and 4.3L Engine

TWO-WHEEL DRIVE

1. Remove the engine from the vehicle.
2. Remove the oil pan bolts and studs. Remove the oil pan.
3. Using a putty knife, clean the gasket mounting surfaces. Make sure that all sealing surfaces are clean and free of oil.
4. Apply RTV sealant to the rear oil pan rail where it contacts the rear bearing cap.
5. Using a new gasket, install the oil pan and tighten bolts as follows:
   - Two rear bolts: 18 ft. lbs.
   - All other bolts and nuts: 7 ft. lbs.
6. Install the engine into the vehicle. Refill the crankcase with fresh oil. Start the engine, establish normal operating temperatures and check for leaks.

FOUR-WHEEL DRIVE

1. Remove the negative battery cable.
2. Remove the dipstick.
3. Raise and support the vehicle safely.
4. Remove the drive belt splash pan, the front axle shield and the transfer case shield.
5. Remove the brake line clips from the crossmember and the 2nd crossmember from the vehicle.
6. If equipped with an A/T, remove the hanger bolt and the exhaust pipe clamp from the catalytic converter, then disconnect the exhaust pipes from the exhaust manifolds and move the exhaust pipe rearward.
7. Remove the drive shaft-to-drive pinion nuts/bolts and the drive shaft from the vehicle.
8. Remove the flywheel cover-to-engine braces and the engine-to-chassis braces.
9. Remove the flywheel cover, the starter-to-engine bolts and the starter (lay it aside).
10. Remove the steering shock absorber from the frame bracket. Using a scribing tool, mark the position of the idler arm-to-chassis, then remove the steering gear-to-chassis bolts, the steering gear, the idler arm-to-chassis bolts and the idler arm from the vehicle.
11. Remove the front differential-to-bracket bolts from the sides of the chassis, then pull the steering gear and linkage forward.
12. Remove the motor mount through bolts.
13. Drain the engine oil.
14. Raise the engine slightly, then remove the oil pan-to-engine bolts and the oil pan from the engine.
15. Apply RTV sealant to the rear oil pan rail where it contacts the rear bearing cap.
16. Using a new gasket, install the oil pan and tighten bolts as follows:
   - Two rear bolts: 18 ft. lbs.
   - All other bolts and nuts: 7 ft. lbs.

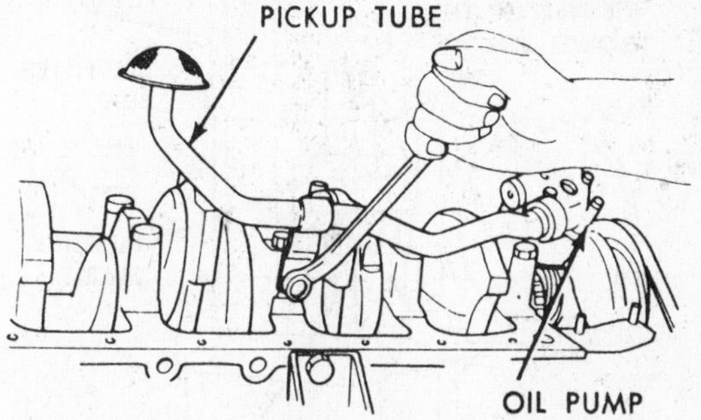
PICKUP TUBE
OIL PUMP

Oil pump and pickup tube — 1.9L engine

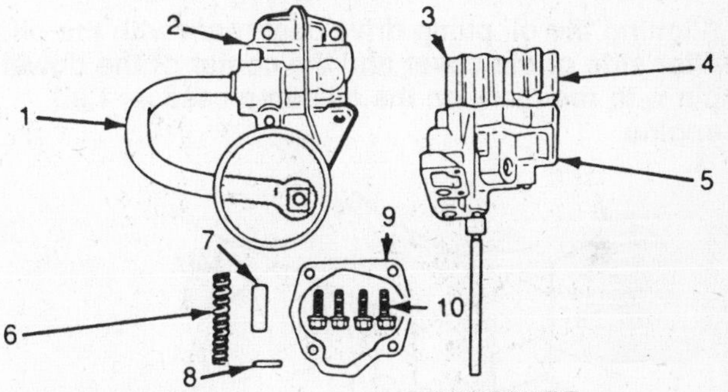
1
2
3
4
5
6
7
8
9
10
1. PICK UP TUBE AND SCREEN.
2. PUMP COVER.
3. DRIVE GEAR AND SHAFT.
4. IDLER GEAR.
5. PUMP BODY.
6. PRESSURE REGULATOR SPRING.
7. PRESSURE REGULATOR VALVE.
8. RETAINING PIN.
9. GASKET.
10. ATTACHING BOLTS.

Oil pump components — 2.0L engine shown, others similar

17. Installation is the reverse of removal. Refill the crankcase with fresh oil. Start the engine, establish normal operating temperatures and check for leaks.

Oil Pump

REMOVAL AND INSTALLATION

Except 1.9L and 2.2L Diesel

NOTE: The oil pump in the 1.9L engine is located in the front cover. See Front Cover Removal and Installation for oil pump service.

1. Remove the oil pan.
2. Remove the oil pump attaching bolt and pickup tube bolt (if necessary).
3. Ensure that the pump pickup tube is tight in the pump body. If the tube should come loose, oil pressure will be lost and oil starvation will occur.
4. Install the replacement pump aligning the pump shaft with the distributor drive gear as necessary. Tighten oil pump bolts to the following:
   - 2.0L Engine: 25–38 ft. lbs.
   - 2.5L Engine: 31 ft. lbs.
   - 2.8L Engine: 30 ft. lbs.
   - 4.3L Engine: 65 ft. lbs.

1.9L Engine

1. Remove the oil pan.

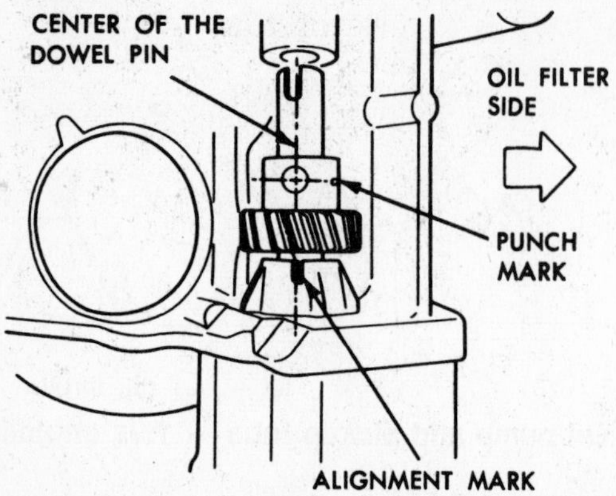
CENTER OF THE
DOWEL PIN
OIL FILTER
SIDE
PUNCH
MARK
ALIGNMENT MARK

Aligning the oil pump drive gear mark with the oil filter side of the cover and the center of the dowel pin with the mark on the oil pump case — 1.9L engine

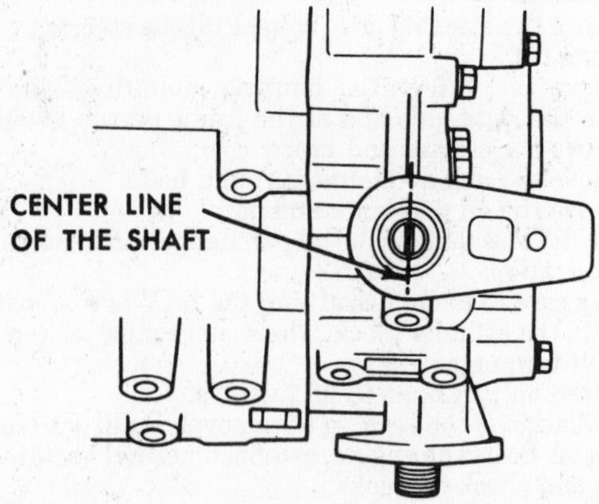
CENTER LINE
OF THE SHAFT

Checking that the slit at the end of the oil pump shaft is parallel with the front face of the block — 1.9L engine

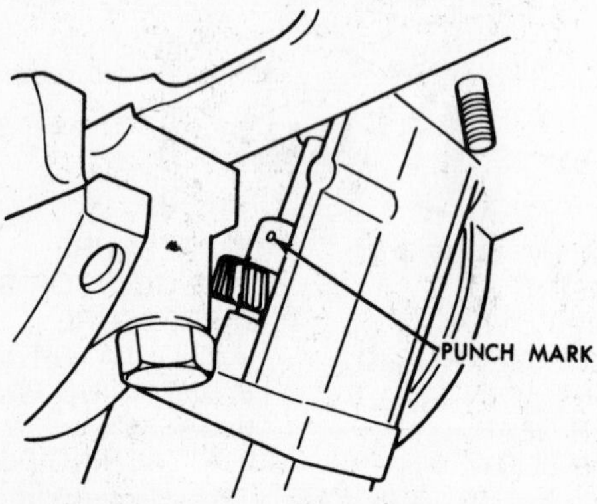
PUNCH MARK

Checking that the punch mark on the oil pump drive gear is turned to the rear side as viewed through the clearance between the front cover and the cylinder block — 1.9L engine

Oil pump — 2.2L diesel engine

2. Remove the oil pickup tube from the oil pump.
3. Remove the distributor.
4. Remove the oil pump mounting bolt and remove the pump.
5. Install the pump as follows:
   a. Align the oil pump drive gear punch mark with the oil filter side of cover; then align the center of dowel pin with alignment mark on the oil pump case.
   b. Rotate the crankshaft until the No. 1 and No. 4 cylinders are at TDC of the compression stroke.
   c. Install the pump by engaging the pinion gear with the oil pump drive gear on the crankshaft.
   d. Check that the punch mark on the oil pump drive gear is turned to the rear side as viewed through clearance between front cover and cylinder block.
   e. Check that the slit at the end of the oil pump shaft is parallel with front face of cylinder block and that it is offset forward.
6. With all parts correctly installed, the remainder of the installation procedure is the reverse the removal.
7. Check and/or adjust the engine timing. Inspect for leaks.

2.2L Diesel Engine

1. Remove the engine from the vehicle.
2. Disconnect the PCV hose at the crankcase.
3. Remove the dipstick tube.
4. Remove the oil pan.
5. Remove the crankcase bolts and using the slots provided, pry the crankcase from the engine.
6. Remove the oil pipe sleeve nut, the oil pump bolts and the oil pump.
7. Installation is the reverse of removal.

Timing (Front) Cover and Seal

On most vehicles it is possible to replace the timing cover front seal without removing the timing cover. Simply remove the torsional damper or crankshaft hub assembly and pry the seal from the cover.

REMOVAL AND INSTALLATION

1.9L Engine

1. Remove the cylinder head.
2. Remove the oil pan.
3. Remove the oil pickup tube from the oil pump.
4. Remove the crankshaft hub and pulley.
5. Remove the AIR pump drive belt.

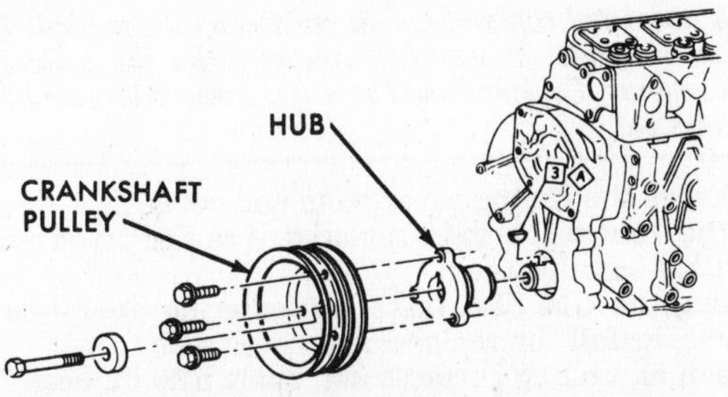
HUB
CRANKSHAFT PULLEY

Pulley and hub assembly – 2.0L engine

6. If equipped with air conditioning, remove the compressor and mounting brackets and lay aside. DO NOT remove the refrigerant lines.
7. Remove the distributor.
8. Remove the front cover attaching bolts and remove the front cover.
9. Check the front cover inner and outer faces for cracking or damage. Replace as necessary.
10. Install a new gasket onto the engine.
11. Align the oil pump drive gear punch mark with the oil filter side of cover; then align the center of dowel pin with alignment mark on the oil pump case.
12. Rotate the crankshaft until the No. 1 and No. 4 cylinders are at TDC of the compression stroke.
13. Install the front cover by engaging the pinion gear with the oil pump drive gear on the crankshaft.
14. Check that the punch mark on the oil pump drive gear is turned to the rear side as viewed through clearance between front cover and cylinder block.
15. Check that the slit at the end of the oil pump shaft is parallel with front face of cylinder block and that it is offset forward.
16. With all parts correctly installed, the remainder of the installation procedure is the reverse the removal.
17. Check and/or adjust the engine timing. Inspect for leaks.

2.0L Engine

NOTE: The following procedure requires the use of the Centering tool No. J-23042 or equivalent.

1. Remove the negative battery cable.
2. Drain the cooling system.

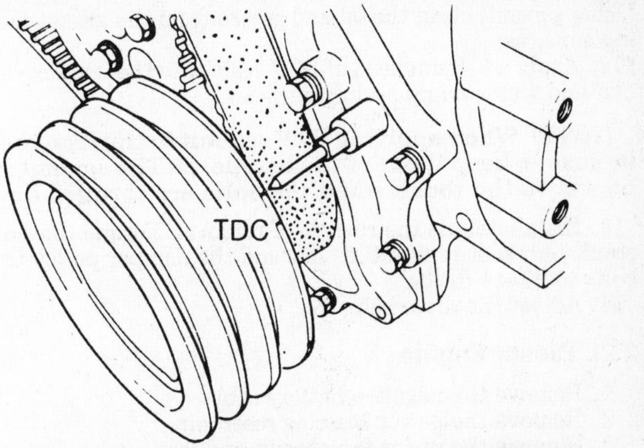
TDC

Crankshaft pulley alignment – 2.2L diesel

CAUTION

When draining the coolant, keep in mind that cats and dogs are attracted by the ethylene glycol antifreeze, and are quite likely to drink any that is left in an uncovered container or in puddles on the ground. This will prove fatal in sufficient quantity. Always drain the coolant into a sealable container. Coolant should be reused unless it is contaminated or several years old.

3. Remove the upper fan shroud.
4. Loosen the accessory drive belt adjusters and remove the drive belts from the crankshaft pulley.
5. Remove the cooling fan-to-water pump bolts and the pulley.
6. Remove the radiator hose and the heater hose from the water pump. Remove the water pump-to-engine bolts and the water pump from the engine.
7. Remove the crankshaft pulley-to-hub bolt and the pulley from the crankshaft.
8. Using the puller tool No. J-24420 or equivalent, pull the hub assembly from the crankshaft.
9. Remove the front cover-to-engine bolts and the cover from the engine.
10. Using a putty knife, clean the gasket mounting surfaces.

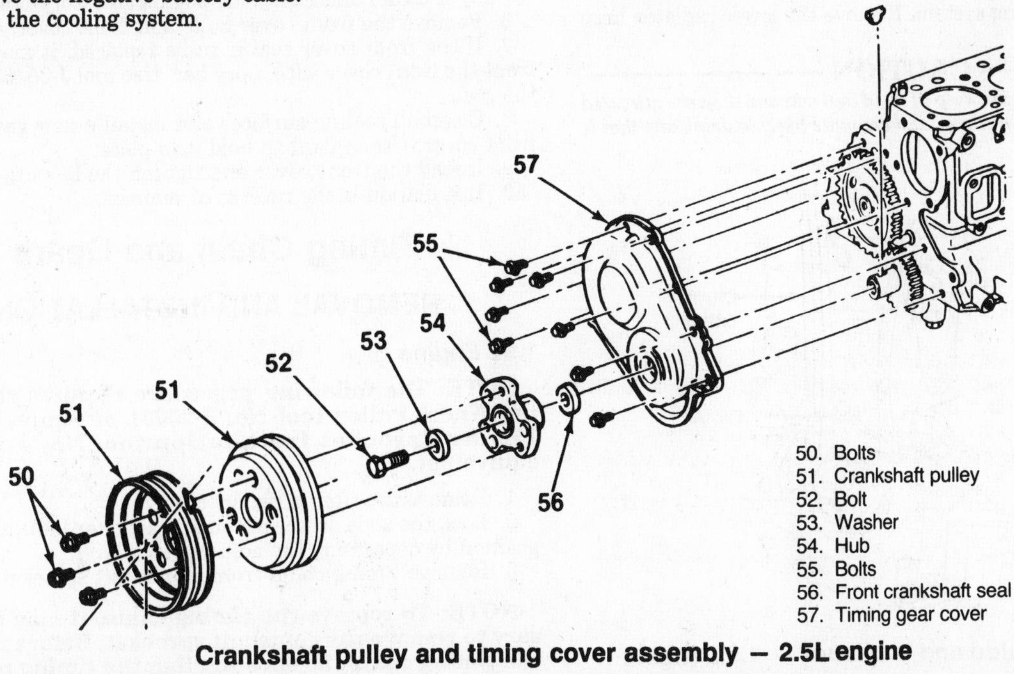
57
55
54
53
52
51
51
50
56
50. Bolts
51. Crankshaft pulley
52. Bolt
53. Washer
54. Hub
55. Bolts
56. Front crankshaft seal
57. Timing gear cover

Crankshaft pulley and timing cover assembly – 2.5L engine

Using solvent, clean the oil and grease from the gasket mounting surfaces.

12. Apply a 2–3mm bead of RTV sealant to the front cover, oil pan and water pump sealing surfaces.

NOTE: When applying RTV sealant to the front cover, be sure to keep it out of the bolt holes. The sealant must be wet to the touch when the bolts are torqued down.

13. Installation is the reverse of removal. Torque the hub-to-crankshaft bolt to 66–88 ft. lbs. and the damper pulley-to-hub bolts to 29–44 ft. lbs.
14. Adjust the drive belts.

2.2L Diesel Engine

1. Remove the negative battery cable.
2. Remove the power steering reservoir.
3. Remove the upper fan shroud and fan.
4. Loosen the drive belts and remove the fan drive pulley.
5. Remove the upper cover attaching bolts and cover.
6. Remove the alternator belt.
7. Align the crankshaft pulley and remove the attaching bolts. Remove the pulley.
8. Remove the lower cover attaching bolts and cover.
9. Installation is the reverse of removal.

2.5L and 2.8L Engine

NOTE: The following procedure requires the use of the GM Seal Installer/Centering tool No. J-34995 or equivalent.

1. Remove the negative battery cable.
2. Remove the accessory drive belts.
3. Remove the power steering reservoir from the fan shroud. Remove the fan shroud.
4. Remove the alternator and brackets (lay them aside).
5. Remove the crankshaft pulley bolt, crankshaft pulley and hub (torsional damper).

NOTE: The outer ring (weight) of the torsional damper is bonded to the hub with rubber. The damper must be removed with a puller which acts on the inner hub only. Pulling on the outer portion of the damper will break the rubber bond or destroy the tuning of the unit.

6. Drain the cooling system. Remove the lower radiator hose at the water pump.

CAUTION

When draining the coolant, keep in mind that cats and dogs are attracted by the ethylene glycol antifreeze, and are quite likely to drink any that is left in an uncovered container or in puddles on the ground. This will prove fatal in sufficient quantity. Always drain the coolant into a sealable container. Coolant should be reused unless it is contaminated or several years old.

7. Remove the timing cover bolts and cover.
8. If the front seal is to be replaced, it can be pryed out of the cover with a suitable tool.
9. Using the GM Seal Installer/Centering Tool J-34995 or equivalent, install the replacement cover seal.
10. Clean all sealing surfaces and apply a ⅜ in. bead of RTV sealant to the oil pan and timing gear cover sealing surfaces.
11. Use the GM Seal Installer/Centering Tool J-34995 or equivalent align the front cover. Install the cover while the RTV sealant is still wet.
12. Installation is the reverse of removal.
13. Tighten front cover bolts as follows:
    - 2.5L Engine: 8 ft. lbs.
    - 2.8L Engine: 18 ft. lbs.

4.3L Engine

1. Remove the torsional damper center bolts and remove the damper with suitable puller.

NOTE: The outer ring (weight) of the torsional damper is bonded to the hub with rubber. The damper must be removed with a puller which acts on the inner hub only. Pulling on the outer portion of the damper will break the rubber bond or destroy the tuning of the unit.

2. Drain the cooling system.

CAUTION

When draining the coolant, keep in mind that cats and dogs are attracted by the ethylene glycol antifreeze, and are quite likely to drink any that is left in an uncovered container or in puddles on the ground. This will prove fatal in sufficient quantity. Always drain the coolant into a sealable container. Coolant should be reused unless it is contaminated or several years old.

3. Remove the water pump.
4. Remove the oil pan.
5. Remove the upper radiator hose, air conditioner compressor (lay it aside) and right side engine accessory bracket.
6. Remove the front cover bolts and front cover.
7. If the front cover seal is to be replaced, it may be pryed front the front cover with a pry bar. Use tool J-35468 to install the seal.
8. Clean all sealing surfaces and install a new gasket to the front cover. Use sealant to hold it in place.
9. Install the front cover and tighten the bolts to 10 ft. lbs.
10. Installation is the reverse of removal.

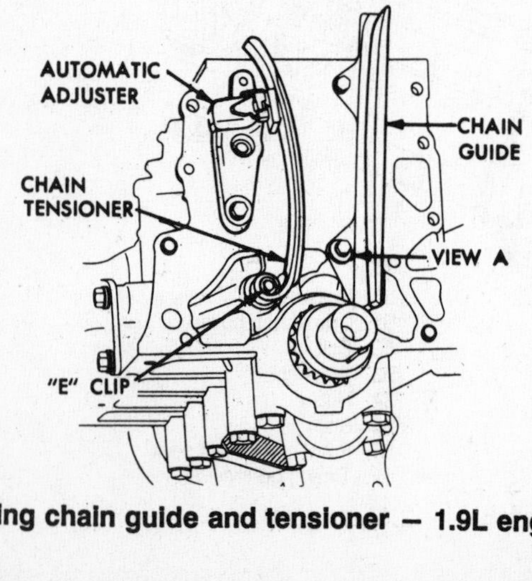
AUTOMATIC
ADJUSTER
CHAIN
GUIDE
CHAIN
TENSIONER
VIEW A
"E" CLIP

timing chain guide and tensioner – 1.9L engine

Timing Chain and Gears

REMOVAL AND INSTALLATION

1.9L Engine

NOTE: The following procedure requires the use of the Wheel Puller tool No. J-25031 or equivalent, and Timing Sprocket Installation tool No. J-26587 or equivalent.

1. Remove the timing (front) cover.
2. Lock the shoe on the automatic adjuster in fully retracted position by depressing the adjuster lock lever.
3. Remove timing chain from crankshaft sprocket.

NOTE: To remove the timing chain, it may be necessary to remove the camshaft sprocket. Before removing the timing chain, be sure to align the timing marks.

4. Check the timing sprockets for wear or damage. If crankshaft sprocket must be replaced, remove the sprocket and the pinion gear from crankshaft using the Puller tool No. J-25031 or equivalent.

5. Check timing chain for wear or damage; replace as necessary. Measure distance (L) with chain stretched with a pull of approximately 22 lbs. (98N). Standard (L) valve is 15 in. (381mm); replace chain of (L) is greater than 15.16 in. (385mm).

6. Remove the automatic chain adjuster-to-engine bolt and the adjuster.

7. To check the operation of the automatic chain adjuster, push the shoe inwards, if it becomes locked, the adjuster is working properly. The adjuster assembly must be replaced if rack teeth are found to be worn excessively.

8. To remove the chain tensioner, remove the "E" clip and the tensioner. Check the tensioner for wear or damage; if necessary, replace it.

9. Inspect the tensioner pin for wear or damage. If replacement is necessary, remove the pin from the cylinder block using a pair of locking pliers. Lubricate the NEW pin tensioner with clean engine oil. Start the pin into block, then place the tensioner over the appropriate pin. Position the E-clip onto the pin, then (using a hammer) tap it into the block until clip just clears tensioner. Check the tensioner and adjuster for freedom of rotation on the pins.

10. Inspect the guide for wear or damage and plugged lower oil jet. If replacement or cleaning is necessary, remove the guide bolts, the guide and the oil jet. Install a new guide and upper attaching bolt. Install the lower oil jet and bolt, so that the oil port is pointed toward crankshaft.

11. Install the timing sprocket and the pinion gear (groove-side toward the front cover). Align the key groove with crankshaft key, then drive it into position using Installing tool No. J-26587 or equivalent.

12. Turn the crankshaft so that key is turned toward the cylinder head-side (No. 1 and No. 4 pistons at TDC).

13. Install the timing chain, align the timing chain mark plate with the mark on the crankshaft timing sprocket. The side of the chain with the mark plate is on the front-side and the side of chain with the most links between mark plates is on the chain guide-side. Keep the timing chain engaged with the camshaft timing sprocket until the camshaft timing sprocket is installed on the camshaft.

14. Install the camshaft timing sprocket so that it's marked-side faces forward and it's triangular mark aligns with the chain mark plate.

15. Install the automatic chain adjuster.

16. Release the lock by depressing the shoe on adjuster by hand, and check to make certain the chain is properly tensioned when the lock is released.

17. Install from cover assembly as outlined previously.

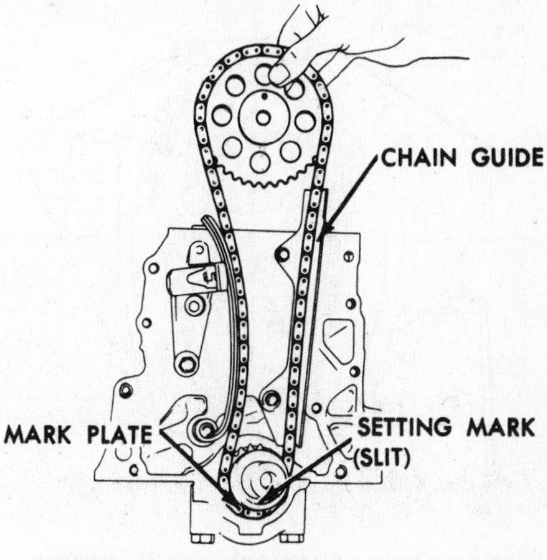
CHAIN GUIDE
MARK PLATE
SETTING MARK
(SLIT)

Timing chain alignment – 1.9L engine

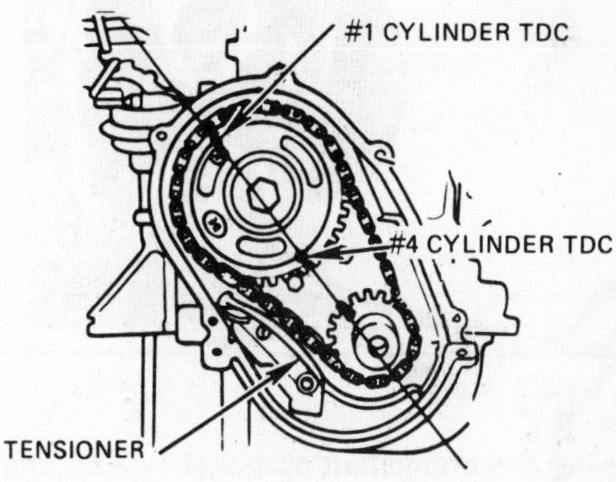
#1 CYLINDER TDC
#4 CYLINDER TDC
TENSIONER

2.0L Engine

NOTE: The following procedure requires the use of the Spring compressor tool No. J-33875 or equivalent, the Gear Puller tool No. J-22888-20 or equivalent.

1. Remove the timing cover.

2. Rotate the crankshaft to position the No. 4 piston on TDC of the compression stroke; the marks on the camshaft and crankshaft sprockets should be in alignment.

3. Loosen the timing chain tensioner nut (as far as possible) without actually removing it.

4. Remove the camshaft sprocket-to-camshaft bolts and the sprocket; remove the timing chain with the sprocket. If the sprocket does not slide from the camshaft easily, a light blow with a soft mallet at the lower edge of the sprocket will dislodge it.

5. Using the Gear Puller tool No. J-22888-20 or equivalent, remove the crankshaft sprocket.

6. Using a putty knife, clean the gasket mounting surfaces. Inspect the timing chain and the sprocket teeth for wear and/or damage; replace the parts, if necessary.

7. Install the crankshaft sprocket onto the crankshaft, position the timing chain over the camshaft sprocket and then around the crankshaft sprocket. Make sure that the marks on the two sprockets are aligned. Lubricate the thrust surface with Molykote® or equivalent.

8. Align the dowel in the camshaft with the dowel hole in the sprocket and then install the sprocket onto the camshaft. Torque the camshaft sprocket-to-camshaft bolts to 27–33 ft. lbs.

9. Lubricate the timing chain with clean engine oil. Using the Spring Compressor tool No. J-33875 or equivalent, position the tangs under the sliding block and pull the tool to compress the spring. Tighten the chain tensioner.

10. To complete the installation, reverse the removal procedures.

2.8L and 4.3L Engine

NOTE: The following procedure requires the use of the Crankshaft Sprocket Removal tool No. J-5825 or equivalent, and the Crankshaft Sprocket Installation tool No. J-5590 or equivalent.

1. Remove the timing cover.

2. Rotate the crankshaft until the No. 4 cylinder is on the TDC of it's compression stroke and the camshaft sprocket mark (No. 4 cylinder) aligns with the mark on the crankshaft sprocket (facing each other) and in line with the shaft centers.

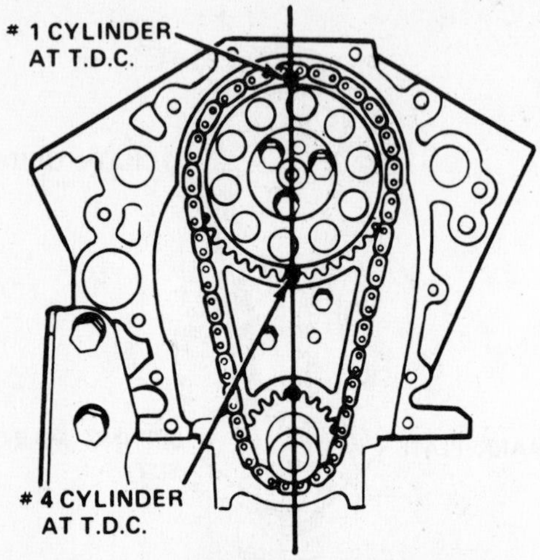

1 CYLINDER AT T.D.C.
4 CYLINDER AT T.D.C.

Timing chain alignment – 2.8L engine

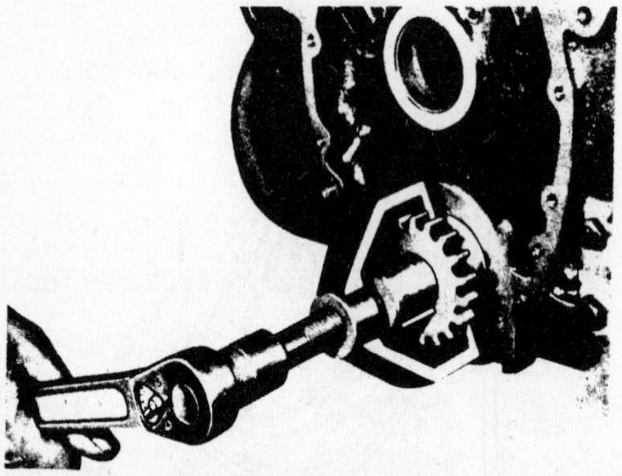

Removing the crankshaft sprocket – 2.8L engine

3. Remove the camshaft sprocket-to-camshaft bolts and the camshaft sprocket (with timing chain). If camshaft is difficult to remove, use a plastic mallet to bump the sprocket from the camshaft.

NOTE: The camshaft sprocket (located by a dowel) is lightly pressed onto the camshaft and will come off readily. The chain comes off with the camshaft sprocket.

4. Using the Crankshaft Sprocket Removal tool No. J-5825 or equivalent, remove the timing sprocket from the crankshaft.
5. Inspect the timing chain and the timing sprockets for wear or damage, replace the damaged parts (if necessary).
6. Using a putty knife, clean the gasket mounting surfaces. Using solvent, clean the oil and grease from the gasket mounting surfaces.
7. Using the Crankshaft Sprocket Installation tool No. J-5590 or equivalent, and a hammer, without disturbing the position of the engine, drive the crankshaft sprocket onto the crankshaft.
8. Position the timing chain over the camshaft sprocket. Arrange the camshaft sprocket in such a way that the timing marks will align between the shaft centers and the camshaft locating dowel will enter the dowel hole in the cam sprocket.
9. Place the cam sprocket, with its chain mounted over it, in position on the front of the camshaft and torque the camshaft sprocket-to-camshaft bolts to 17 ft. lbs.
10. With the timing chain installed, turn the crankshaft two complete revolutions, then check to make certain that the timing marks are in correct alignment between the shaft centers.
11. Install the timing cover.

Timing Belt

REMOVAL AND INSTALLATION

2.2L Diesel Engine

NOTE: The following procedure requires the use of the Belt Tension Gauge tool No. J-29771 or equivalent.

1. Remove the negative battery cable.
2. Align the mark on the crankshaft pulley with the timing pointer and remove the crankshaft pulley. Remove the front covers.

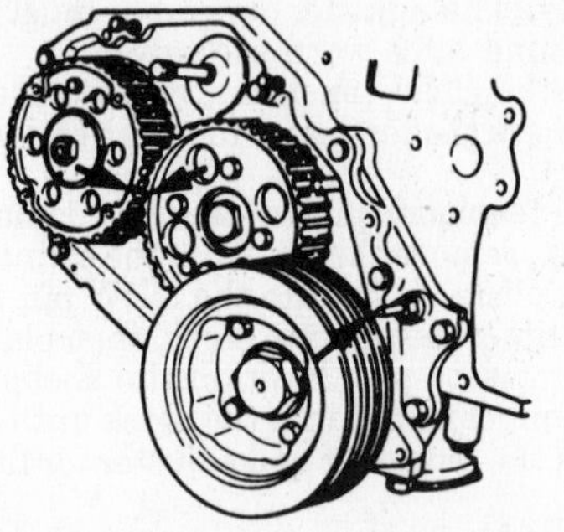

Aligning the timing marks – 2.2L diesel

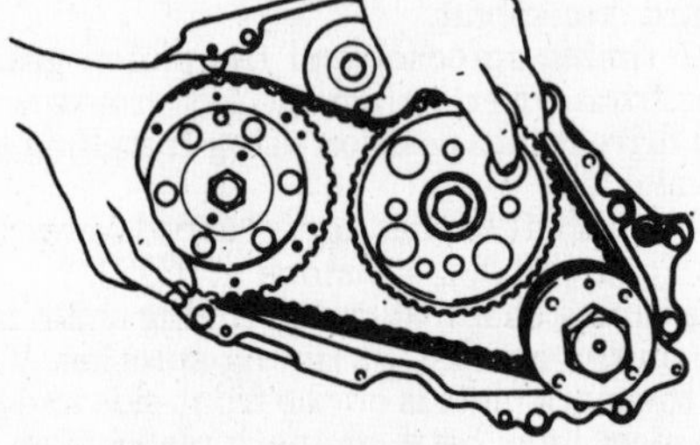

Installing the timing belt – 2.2L diesel

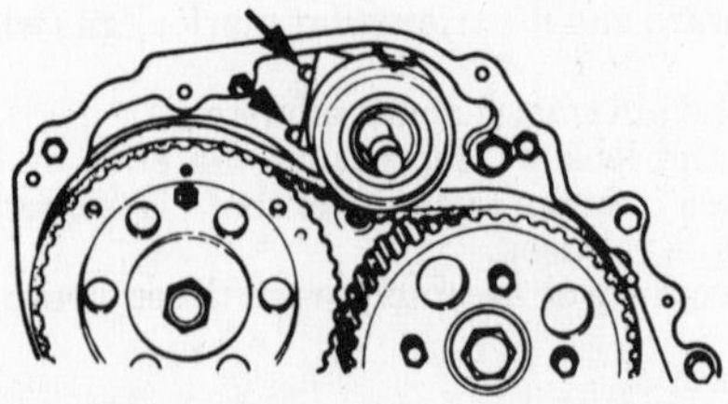

Aligning the tension pulley to make proper contact with the two housing pins – 2.2L diesel

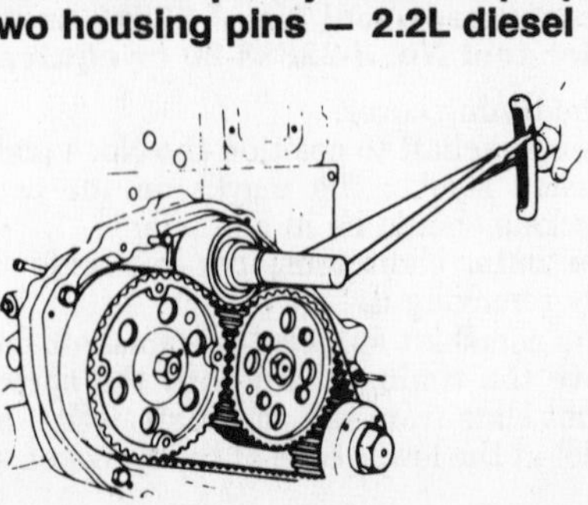

Torquing the tension pulley – 2.2L diesel

3. Remove the bolts attaching the injection pump timing pulley flange. Remove the tension spring.

NOTE: When removing tension spring, avoid using excess force, or distortion of spring will result.

4. Remove the timing belt tension pulley-to-engine fixing nut, then the tension pulley and tension center.
5. Remove the timing belt. Avoid twisting or kinking the belt and keep it free from water, oil, dust and other foreign matter.

NOTE: No attempt should be made to readjust belt tension. If the belt has been loosened through service of the timing system, it should be replaced with a new one.

6. Check that the setting marks on the crank pulley, injection pump timing pulley, and camshaft pulley are in alignment, then install the timing belt in sequence of crankshaft timing pulley, camshaft timing pulley and injection pump timing pulley.
7. Make an adjustment, so that slackness of the belt is taken up by the tension pulley. When installing the timing belt, care should be taken so as not to damage the belt.
8. Install the tension center and tension pulley, making certain the end of the tension center is in proper contact with two pins on the timing pulley housing.
9. Hand-tighten the nut, so that tension pulley can slide freely.
10. Install the tension spring correctly and semi-tighten the tension pulley fixing nut.
11. Turn the crankshaft 2 turns in normal direction of rotation to permit seating of the belt. Further rotate the crankshaft 90° beyond TDC to settle the injection pump. Never attempt to turn the crankshaft in reverse direction.

NOTE: If the engine is turned past the timing marks, keep rotating the engine in the normal direction of rotation until the marks align properly.

12. Loosen the tension pulley fixing nut completely, allowing the pulley to take up looseness of the belt. Then, tighten the nut to 78–95 ft. lbs.
13. Install the flange on the injection pump pulley. The hole in the outer circumference of the flange should be aligned with the timing mark "triangle" on the injection pump pulley.
14. Turn the crankshaft 2 (clockwise) turns to position the No. 1 cylinder on to TDC of it's compression stroke, then check that the "triangle" mark on the timing pulley is in alignment with the hole in the flange.
15. The belt tension should be checked at a point between the injection pump pulley and crankshaft pulley using tool No. J-29771 or equivalent, to 33–55 lbs. as read on the scale.
16. Adjust valve clearances and reverse the removal procedures.
17. Check the injection timing.

Timing Gear

REMOVAL AND INSTALLATION

2.5L Engine

The 2.5L engine uses a direct drive timing assembly. The sprocket on the crankshaft drives the camshaft sprocket by direct action. The timing gear (camshaft sprocket) is pressed onto the camshaft and requires the use of an arbor press to remove.

NOTE: The following procedure requires the use of an arbor press, a press plate, the GM Gear Removal tool No. J-971 or equivalent, the GM Gear Installation tool No. J-21474-13, J-21795-1 or equivalent.

1. Remove the camshaft.
2. Using an arbor press, a press plate and the GM Gear Re-

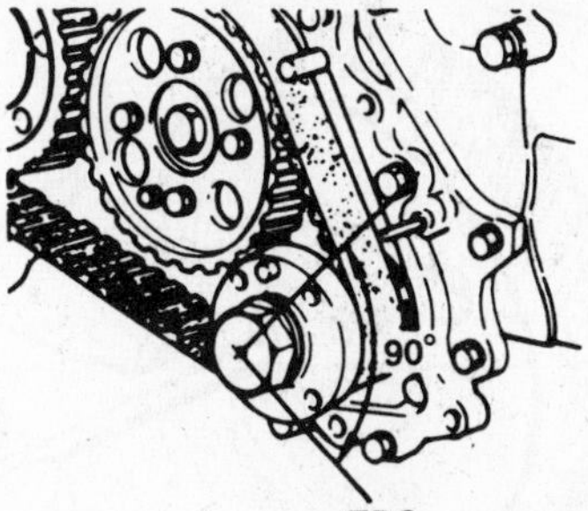
90°
TDC

Bringing the No. 1 cylinder to TDC – 2.2L diesel

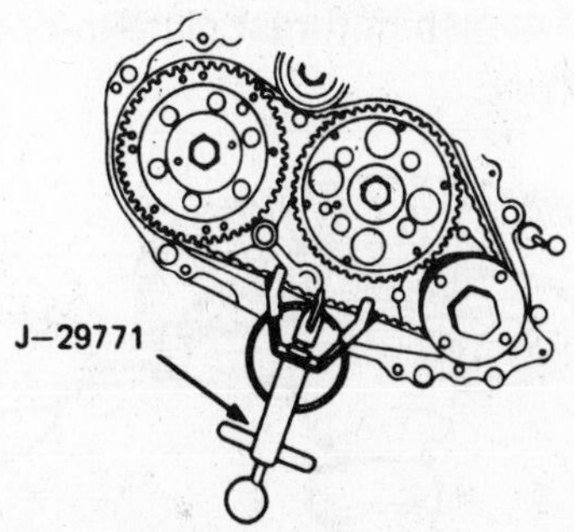
J–29771

Using tool No. J-29771 to check the belt tension – 2.2L diesel

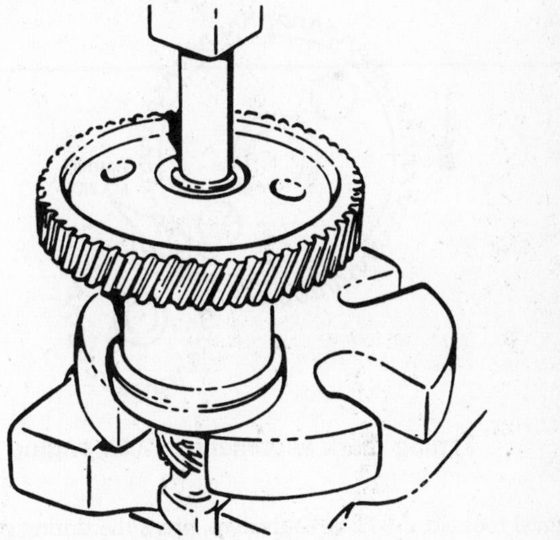

Separating the timing fear from the camshaft – 2.5L engine

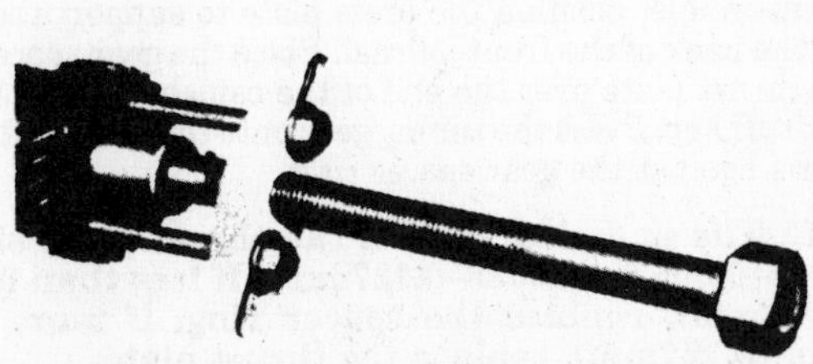

Removing the timing fear from the crankshaft – 2.5L engine

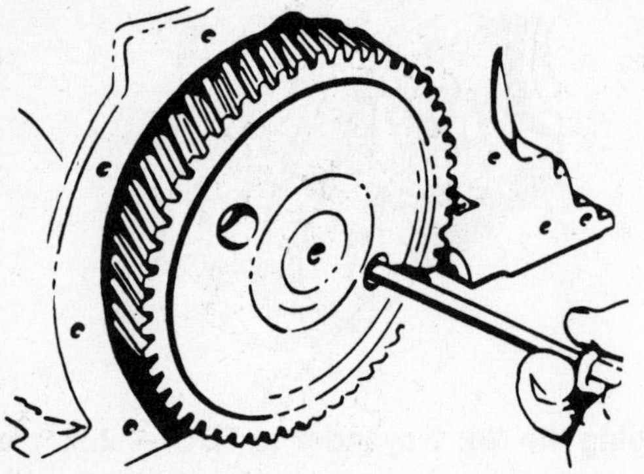

Removing the camshaft thrust plate-to-engine screws – 2.5L engine

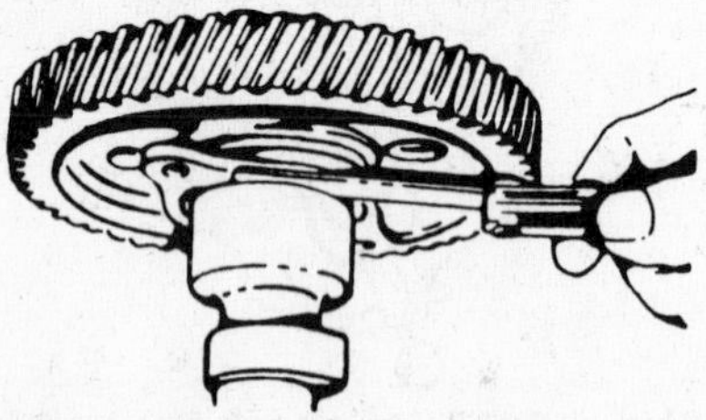

Using a feeler gauge to check thrust plate clearance – 2.5L engine

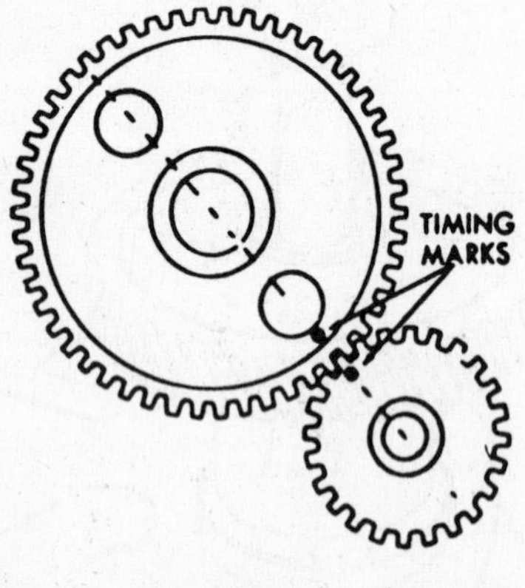
TIMING MARKS

Timing mark alignment – 2.5L engine

moval tool No. J-971 or equivalent, press the timing gear from the camshaft.

NOTE: When pressing the timing gear from the camshaft, be certain that the position of the press plate does not contact the woodruff key.

3. To assemble, position the press plate to support the camshaft at the back of the front journal. Place the gear spacer ring and the thrust plate over the end of the camshaft, then install the woodruff key. Press the timing gear onto the camshaft, until it bottoms against the gear spacer ring.

NOTE: The end clearance of the thrust plate should be 0.0015–0.005 in. (0.038–0.127mm). If less than 0.0015 in. (0.038mm), replace the spacer ring; if more than 0.005 in. (0.127mm), replace the thrust plate.

4. To complete the installation, align the marks on the timing gears and install the camshaft.

Camshaft Sprocket – OHC Engine

REMOVAL AND INSTALLATION

1.9L Engine

1. Remove timing cover.
2. Rotate camshaft until No. 4 cylinder is on the TDC of it's compression stroke.
3. Remove the distributor cap. Using a marking tool, mark the rotor-to-housing and the housing-to-engine positions, then remove the distributor from the engine.
4. Disconnect the fuel lines and remove the fuel pump from the engine.
5. Using a screwdriver or equivalent, depress the automatic shoe adjuster lock lever into the fully retracted position. After locking the automatic adjuster, check that the chain is in free state.
6. Remove the timing sprocket-to-camshaft bolt, the sprocket and the fuel pump drive cam from the camshaft. Keep the timing sprocket on the chain damper and the tensioner without removing the chain from the sprocket.
7. Check that the mark on the No. 1 rocker arm shaft bracket is in alignment with the mark on the camshaft and that the crankshaft pulley groove is aligned with the TDC mark (0°) on the front cover.
8. Assemble the timing sprocket to the camshaft by aligning it with the pin on the camshaft; use care not to remove the chain from the sprocket.
9. Install the fuel pump drive cam, the sprocket retaining bolt and washer. Remove the half-moon seal in from end of head; then install torque wrench and torque bolt to 58 ft. lbs; replace the half-moon seal in cylinder head.
10. Using the alignment marks, install the distributor.
11. Using a medium pry bar, depressing the adjuster shoe to release the lock, check the timing chain tension.
12. Check valve timing, the rotor and mark on distributor housing should be in alignment when the No. 4 cylinder on TDC. The timing mark on damper pulley should align with TDC mark (0° mark) on front cover.
13. Installation is the reverse of removal.

Valve Lifter

REMOVAL AND INSTALLATION

2.0L Engine

1. Remove the rocker arm covers.
2. Loosen the rocker arms and remove the pushrods and guide plates.
3. Using Valve Lifter Removal tool J-29834, or equivalent, remove the valve lifters.

NOTE: Keep all components in order. If reusing components, install them into their original positions.

4. For proper rotation during engine operation, the lifter bottom must be convex. Check the lifter bottom for proper shape using a straight edge. If the lifter bottom is not convex, replace the lifter. Chances are if lifters are in need of replacement, so is the camshaft.
5. Using the valve lifter tool, install the lifters into the block.
6. Installation is the reverse of removal. Adjust the valve lash.

2.2L Diesel

NOTE: The diesel engine uses solid type lifters.

1. Remove the rocker arm cover and side cover.

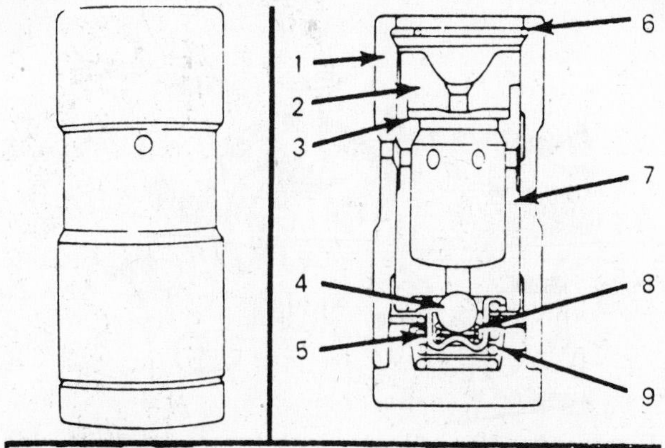
1
2
3
4
5
6
7
8
9
1. Lifter Body
2. Push Rod Seat
3. Metering Valve
4. Check Ball
5. Check Ball Retainer
6. Push Rod Seat Retainer
7. Plunger
8. Check Ball Spring
9. Plunger Spring

Valve lifter components

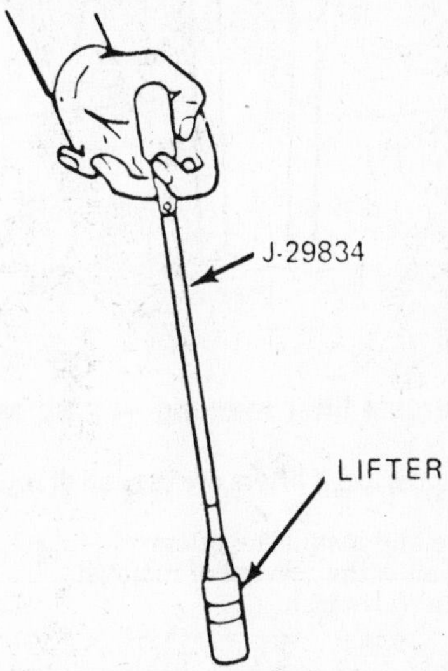
J-29834
LIFTER

Valve lifter removal/installation tool

2. Remove the rocker arm shaft assembly.
3. Remove the pushrods.
4. Remove the hydraulic lifters using an appropriate lifter removal tool.
5. Installation is the reverse of removal.
6. Adjust the valve lash.

2.5L Engine

1. Remove the rocker arm and pushrod covers.

NOTE: Keep all components in order. If reusing components, install them into their original positions. If a new hydraulic lifter is being installed, all sealer coating inside the lifter must be removed.

2. Remove the pushrods.
3. Remove the lifter studs and retainers.
4. Remove the lifter guides and lifters.
5. Inspect the lifter and lifter bore for wear and scuffing. Examine the roller for freedom of movement and/or flat spots on the roller surface.
6. Installation is the reverse of removal.

2.8L Engine

Some engines have both standard size and 0.25mm (0.010 in.) oversize valve lifters. The cylinder block will be marked with a white paint mark and 0.25mm O.S. stamp where the oversize lifters are used. If lifters replacement is necessary, use new lifters with a narrow flat along the lower ¾ of the body length. This provides additional oil to the cam lobe and lifter surfaces.

NOTE: This procedure requires the use of a Hydraulic Lifter Remover tool J-9290-1.

1. Remove the rocker arm covers.
2. Remove the intake manifold.
3. Remove the rocker arm nuts and balls.
4. Remove the rocker arms and pushrods.

NOTE: Keep all components in order. If reusing components, install them into their original positions.

5. Using the Hydraulic Lifter Remover tool, remove the lifters.
6. For proper rotation during engine operation, the lifter bottom must be convex. Check the lifter bottom for proper shape using a straight edge. If the lifter bottom is not convex, replace

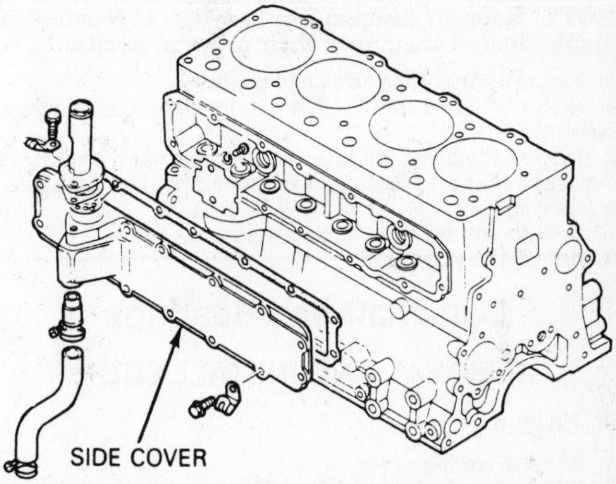
SIDE COVER

Removing the side cover – 2.2L diesel

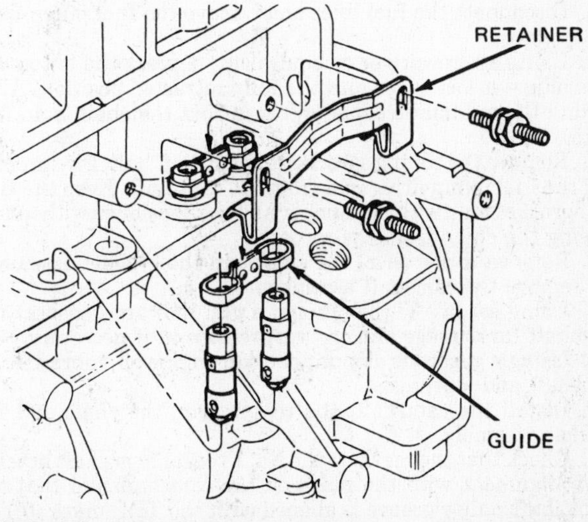
RETAINER
GUIDE

Hydraulic lifters and components – 2.5L engine

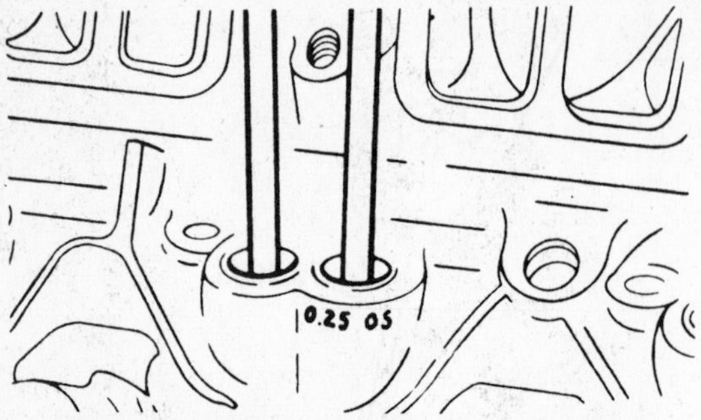
0.25 OS

Oversize lifter marking — 2.8L engine

the lifter. Chances are if lifters are in need of replacement, so is the camshaft.

7. Lubricate and install the lifters.
8. Installation is the reverse of removal.
9. Adjust the valve lash.

4.3L Engine

1. Remove the rocker arm cover.
2. Remove the intake manifold.

NOTE: Keep all components in order. If reusing components, install them into their original positions.

3. Remove the rocker arms and pushrods.
4. Remove the hydraulic lifter retainer bolts, retainers and restrictors.
5. Inspect the lifter and lifter bore for wear and scuffing. Examine the roller for freedom of movement and/or flat spots on the roller surface.
6. Installation is the reverse of removal.
7. Adjust the valve lash.

Camshaft and Bearings

REMOVAL AND INSTALLATION

1.9L Engine

1. Remove timing cover.
2. Rotate camshaft until No. 4 cylinder is on the TDC of it's compression stroke.
3. Remove the distributor cap. Using a marking tool, mark the rotor-to-housing and the housing-to-engine positions, then remove the distributor from the engine.
4. Disconnect the fuel lines and remove the fuel pump from the engine.
5. Using a screwdriver or equivalent, depress the automatic shoe adjuster lock lever into the fully retracted position. After locking the automatic adjuster, check that the chain is in free state.
6. Remove the timing sprocket-to-camshaft bolt, the sprocket and the fuel pump drive cam from the camshaft. Keep the timing sprocket on the chain damper and the tensioner without removing the chain from the sprocket.
7. Remove rocker arm, the shaft and the bracket assembly, the remove the camshaft assembly.
8. Using set of "V" blocks and a dial indicator, inspect the camshaft for damage and/or wear; replace it, if necessary.
9. Using a generous amount of clean engine oil, lubricate the camshaft and journals.
10. Install the camshaft, the rocker arm, the shaft and the bracket assembly.
11. Check that the mark on the No. 1 rocker arm shaft bracket is in alignment with the mark on the camshaft and that the crankshaft pulley groove is aligned with the TDC mark (0°) on the front cover.

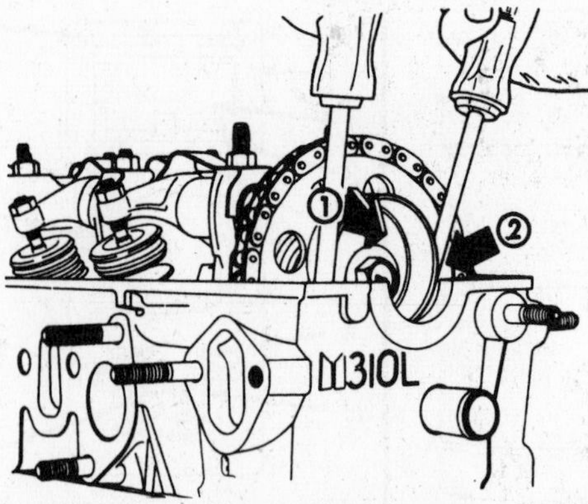
1
2

Depressing the adjuster lock lever — 1.9L engine

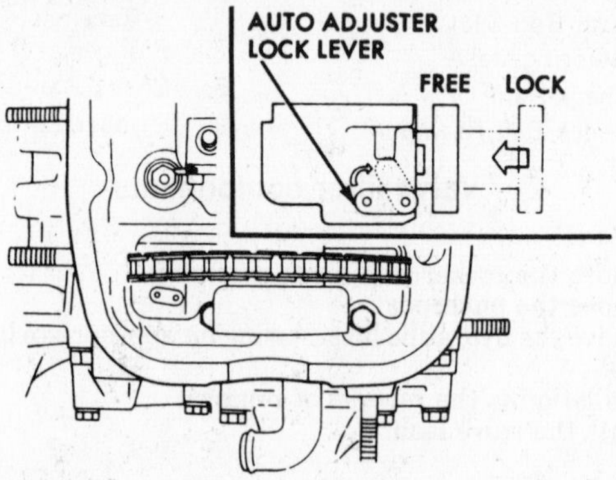
AUTO ADJUSTER
LOCK LEVER
FREE
LOCK

Locking the timing chain adapter — 1.9L engine

12. Assemble the timing sprocket to the camshaft by aligning it with the pin on the camshaft; use care not to remove the chain from the sprocket.
13. Install the fuel pump drive cam, the sprocket retaining bolt and washer. Remove the half-moon seal in from end of head; then install torque wrench and torque bolt to 58 ft. lbs; replace the half-moon seal in cylinder head.
14. Using the alignment marks, install the distributor.
15. Using a medium pry bar, depressing the adjuster shoe to release the lock, check the timing chain tension.
16. Check valve timing, the rotor and mark on distributor housing should be in alignment when the No. 4 cylinder on TDC. The timing mark on damper pulley should align with TDC mark (0° mark) on front cover.
17. To complete the installation, reverse the removal procedures. Adjust the drive belts. Refill the cooling system.

2.0L Engine

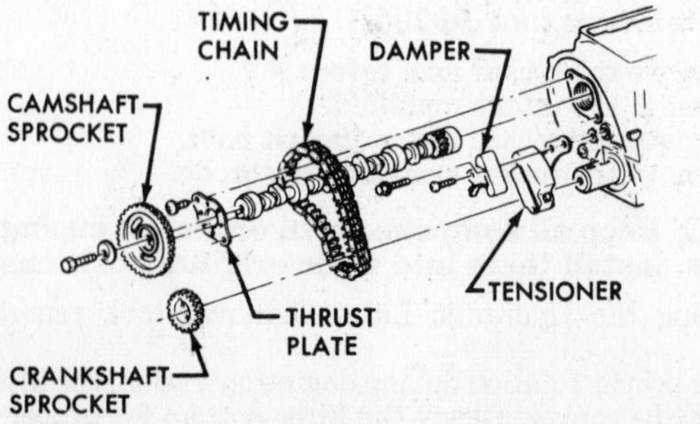
TIMING
CHAIN
DAMPER
CAMSHAFT
SPROCKET
TENSIONER
THRUST
PLATE
CRANKSHAFT
SPROCKET

Timing chain and camshaft assembly — 2.0L engine

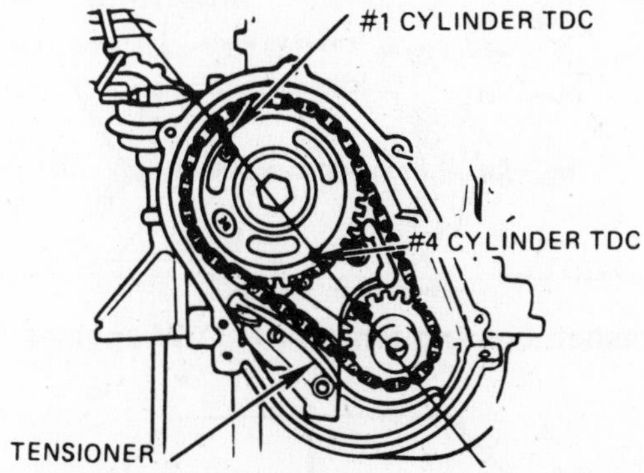
#1 CYLINDER TDC
#4 CYLINDER TDC
TENSIONER

Timing mark alignment — 2.0L engine

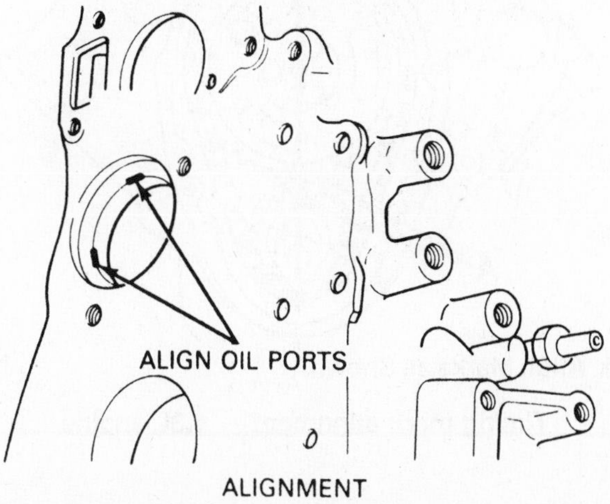
ALIGN OIL PORTS
ALIGNMENT

2.2L diesel camshaft oil hole alignment — others similar

NOTE: The following procedure requires the use of the Camshaft Bearing Removal/Installation tool No. J-6098 or equivalent.

1. Remove the timing chain and the rocker arm assemblies.
2. Drain the cooling system.

CAUTION

When draining the coolant, keep in mind that cats and dogs are attracted by the ethylene glycol antifreeze, and are quite likely to drink any that is left in an uncovered container or in puddles on the ground. This will prove fatal in sufficient quantity. Always drain the coolant into a sealable container. Coolant should be reused unless it is contaminated or several years old.

3. Remove the radiator hoses, the radiator-to-engine bolts and the radiator.
4. Remove the distributor cap, mark the rotor-to-housing and the housing-to-engine positions, then remove the distributor.
5. Raise and support the vehicle safely.
6. Disconnect the fuel lines and remove the fuel pump.
7. Lower the vehicle.
8. Remove the rocker arm studs and the push rod guides.
9. Remove the valve lifters.

NOTE: When removing the pushrods and the valve lifters, keep them in order.

10. Carefully pull the camshaft from the front of the block, being sure that the camshaft lobes do not contact the bearings.
11. If removal of camshaft bearings is necessary, use the following procedure:
    a. Using Camshaft Bearing Removal/Installation tool J-6098, install the tool with the shoulder toward the bearing. Ensure that enough threads are engaged.
    b. Using two wrenches, hold the puller screw while turning the nut. When the bearing has been released from the bore, remove the tool.
    c. Assemble the tool on the driver to remove the front and rear bearings.
    d. Install the rear and intermediate bearings with the oil hole between the 2 and 3 o'clock position. Install the front bearing with the holes at 11 o'clock and 2 o'clock.
    e. Install a fresh camshaft bearing rear cover using sealant.
12. Lubricate the camshaft journals with clean engine oil and install the camshaft into the block being extremely careful not to contact the bearings with the cam lobes.

NOTE: If installing a new camshaft, be sure to coat the lobes with GM Part No. 1051396 or equivalent.

13. Install the camshaft sprocket and timing chain. Align the timing chain and sprockets and tighten the camshaft sprocket bolt.
14. Installation is the reverse of removal.
15. Adjust the valve lash. Adjust the drive belts. Refill the cooling system.

2.2L Diesel Engine

NOTE: The following procedure requires the use of the Camshaft Bearing Removal/Installation tool No. J-29764 or equivalent.

1. Remove the engine from the vehicle and mount it on a workstand.
2. Disconnect the PCV hoses from the rocker arm cover.
3. Remove the rocker arm cover, the rocker arm shaft and the push rods.
4. Remove the upper timing housing cover. Turn the crankshaft to align the timing marks, then install a holding bolt into the injection pump gear.
5. Remove the crankshaft damper pulley and the lower timing housing cover.
6. Remove the injection pump timing gear flange, the timing belt tension spring and the pulley, then remove the timing belt.
7. Remove the camshaft sprocket, the hub and the camshaft oil seal retainer.
8. Remove the oil pump and the valve lifters.
9. Remove the camshaft from the front of the engine, using care not to damage the camshaft bearings.
10. Inspect the inner bearing faces for damage. Using an inside micrometer, measure the inside diameter of the camshaft bearings; if bearing clearance is greater than 0.0047 in. (0.12mm), replace the bearing(s).
11. Using Camshaft Bearing Removal/Installation tool No. J-29764 or equivalent, remove the camshaft bearings.
12. Using the same tool, install the replacement bearings into the engine block; be sure to align the oil ports in the bearings with those in the cylinder body.
13. Installation is the reverse of removal.

2.5L Engine

1. Remove the rocker arm cover, pushrods and valve lifters from the engine.

NOTE: When removing the pushrods and the valve lifters, be sure to keep them in order for reassembly purposes.

2. Drain the cooling system.

CAUTION

When draining the coolant, keep in mind that cats and dogs are attracted by the ethylene glycol antifreeze, and are quite likely to drink any that is left in an uncovered container or in puddles on the ground. This will prove fatal in sufficient quantity. Always drain the coolant into a sealable container. Coolant should be reused unless it is contaminated or several years old.

3. Remove the power steering reservoir from the fan shroud, then the upper fan shroud, the radiator. Remove the grille, the headlight bezel and the bumper filler panel.
4. Remove the accessory drive belts, the cooling fan and the water pump pulley.
5. If equipped with A/C, disconnect the condenser baffles and the condenser, then raise the condenser and set it aside without disconnecting the refrigerant lines.
6. Remove the crankshaft drive belt pulley and the damper hub. Remove the timing gear cover-to-engine bolts and the cover.
7. Label and disconnect the distributor electrical connectors, then the holddown bolt and the distributor from the engine. Remove the oil pump driveshaft.
8. Label and disconnect the vacuum lines from the intake manifold and the thermostat housing, then remove the Exhaust Gas Recirculation (EGR) valve from the intake manifold.
9. Remove the camshaft thrust plate-to-engine bolts. While supporting the camshaft (to prevent damaging the bearing or lobe surfaces), remove it from the front of the engine.
10. Inspect the camshaft for scratches, pitting and/or wear on the bearing and lobe surfaces. Check the timing gear teeth for damage.
11. Replace the camshaft bearings as follows:
    a. Using a Camshaft Bearing Removal/Installation tool, install the tool with the shoulder toward the bearing. Ensure that enough threads are engaged.
    b. Using two wrenches, hold the puller screw while turning the nut. When the bearing has been released from the bore, remove the tool.
    c. Assemble the tool on the driver to remove the front and rear bearings.
    d. Install the bearings at the correct clocking to ensure the oil holes in the block and bearings align.
    e. Install a fresh camshaft bearing rear cover using sealant.
12. Lubricate the camshaft with engine oil and install.
13. Torque the camshaft thrust plate-to-engine bolts to 90 inch lbs.
14. Installation is the reverse of removal. Refill the cooling system, start the engine, allow it to reach operating temperatures and check for leaks.

2.8L and 4.3L Engines

1. Remove the negative battery cable.
2. Drain the cooling system.

CAUTION

When draining the coolant, keep in mind that cats and dogs are attracted by the ethylene glycol antifreeze, and are quite likely to drink any that is left in an uncovered container or in puddles on the ground. This will prove fatal in sufficient quantity. Always drain the coolant into a sealable container. Coolant should be reused unless it is contaminated or several years old.

3. Remove the upper fan shroud and radiator.
4. Remove the intake manifold and rocker arm covers.
5. Remove the rocker arms, pushrods and lifters.
6. Remove the drive belt(s), fan and water pump.
7. Remove the torsional damper and the front (timing) cover.
8. Align the timing marks on the crankshaft and camshaft sprockets.
9. Remove the camshaft sprocket and timing chain.
10. Remove the thrust plate screws and remove the camshaft front the front of the engine. Take care not to damage the camshaft bearings when removing the camshaft.
11. If removal of camshaft bearings is necessary, use the following procedure:
    a. Using a Camshaft Bearing Removal/Installation tool, install the tool with the shoulder toward the bearing. Ensure that enough threads are engaged.
    b. Using two wrenches, hold the puller screw while turning the nut. When the bearing has been released from the bore, remove the tool.
    c. Assemble the tool on the driver to remove the front and rear bearings.
    d. Install the bearings so that the oil holes in the block and the bearing align.
    e. Install a fresh camshaft bearing rear cover using sealant.
12. Lubricate the camshaft journals with clean engine oil and install the camshaft into the block being extremely careful not to contact the bearings with the cam lobes.
13. Install the camshaft thrust plate and tighten the bolts to 105 inch lbs. Install the timing chain and camshaft sprocket. Align the timing marks an tighten the sprocket bolt to 21 ft. lbs.
14. Installation is the reverse of removal.

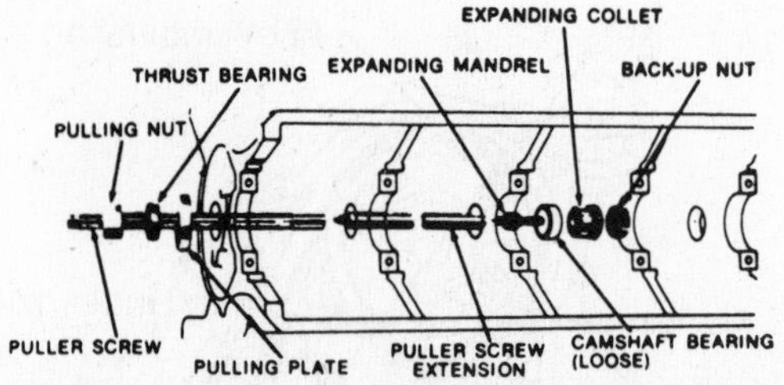
EXPANDING COLLET
THRUST BEARING
EXPANDING MANDREL
BACK-UP NUT
PULLING NUT
PULLER SCREW
PULLING PLATE
PULLER SCREW EXTENSION
CAMSHAFT BEARING (LOOSE)

Camshaft bearing removal — OHV engines only

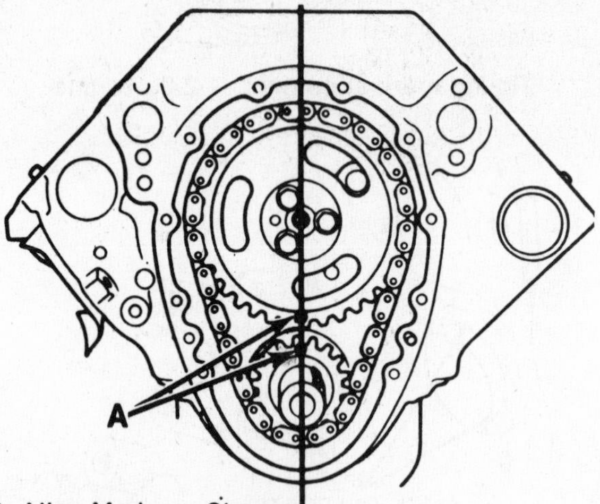
A

A. Align Marks as Shown

Timing mark alignment — 4.3L engine

INSPECTION

Using solvent, degrease the camshaft and clean out all of the oil holes. Visually inspect the cam lobes and bearing journals for excessive wear. If a lobe is questionable, check all of the lobes as indicated. If a journal or lobe is worn, the camshaft MUST BE reground or replaced.

NOTE: If a journal is worn, there is a good chance that the bearings are worn and need replacement.

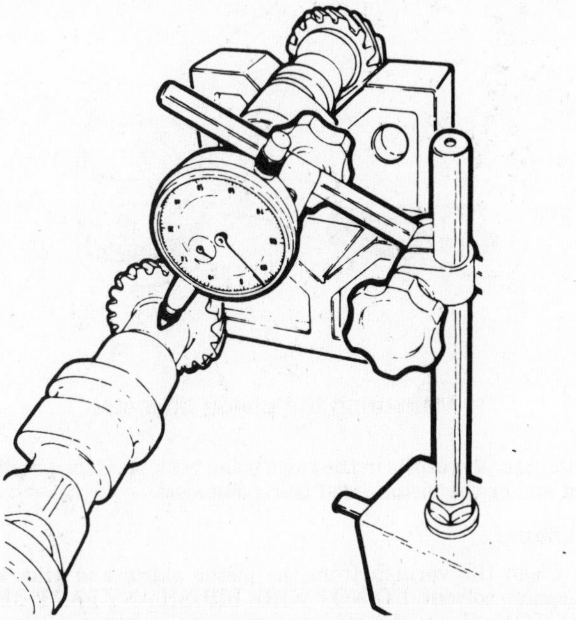

Checking the camshaft for straightness

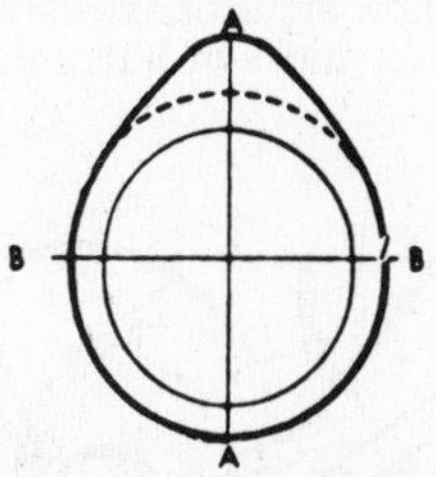
A
B
B
A

Camshaft lobe measurement

If the lobes and journals appear intact, place the front and rear journals in V-blocks and rest a dial indicator on the center journal. Rotate the camshaft to check the straightness. If deviation exceeds 0.001 in. (0.0254mm), replace the camshaft.

Check the camshaft lobes with a micrometer, by measuring the lobes from the nose to the base and again at 90° (see illustration). The lobe lift is determined by subtracting the second measurement from the first. If all of the exhaust and intake lobes are not identical, the camshaft must be reground or replace.

Pistons and Connecting Rods

REMOVAL

1. Remove the engine from the vehicle.
2. Remove the intake manifold and the cylinder head(s).
3. Remove the oil pan and the oil pump assembly.
4. Stamp the cylinder number on the machined surfaces of the bolt bosses on the connecting rod and cap for identification when reinstalling. If the pistons are to be removed from the connecting rod, mark the cylinder number on the piston with a silver pencil or quick drying paint for proper cylinder identification and cap to rod location.

NOTE: The cylinders on a 4-cylinder engine are numbered 1-2-3-4 (front-to-rear); on the V6 (2.8L and 4.3L) engine, are numbered 1-3-5 (front-to-rear) on the right-side and 2-4-6 (front-to-rear) on the left-side.

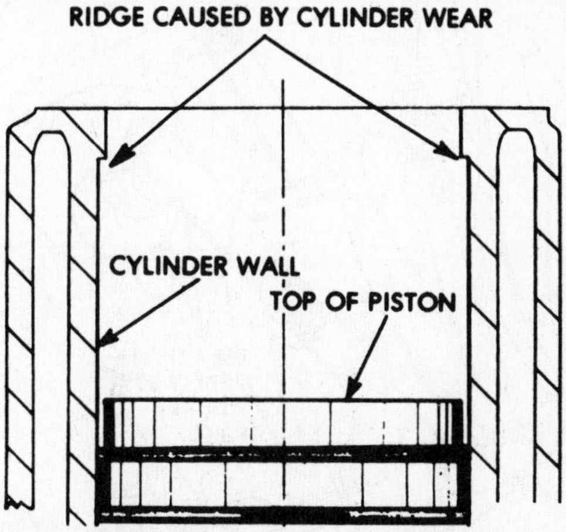
RIDGE CAUSED BY CYLINDER WEAR
CYLINDER WALL
TOP OF PISTON

The ridge at the top of the cylinder wall must be removed prior to removing the piston

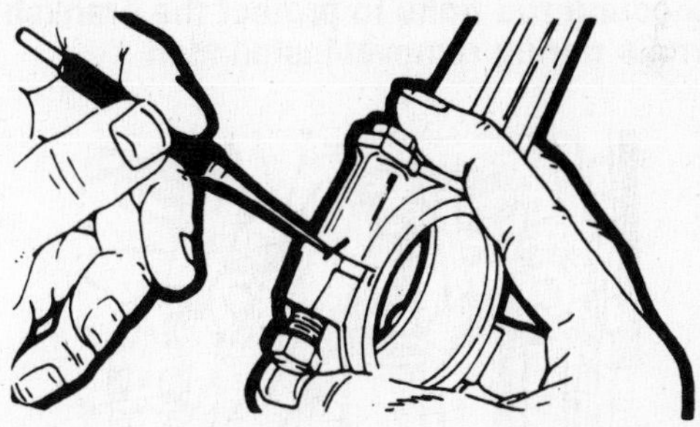

Match the connecting rods to their caps with a scribe mark

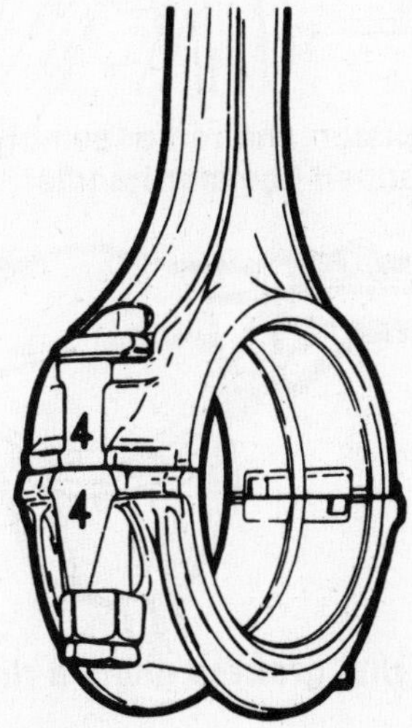
4
4

Match the connecting rods to their cylinders with a number stamp

5. Examine the cylinder bore above the ring travel. If a ridge exists, remove it with a ridge reamer before attempting to remove the piston and rod assembly.
6. Remove the connecting rod bearing cap and bearing.
7. Install a ⅜ in. rubber guide hose over the rod bolt threads; this will prevent damage to the bearing journal and rod bolt threads.

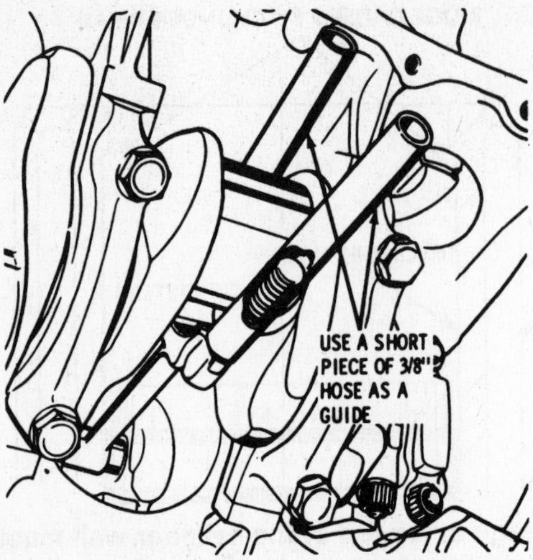
USE A SHORT
PIECE OF 3/8"
HOSE AS A
GUIDE

Install a short piece of rubber hose over the connecting rod bolts to protect the crankshaft journals during removal/installation

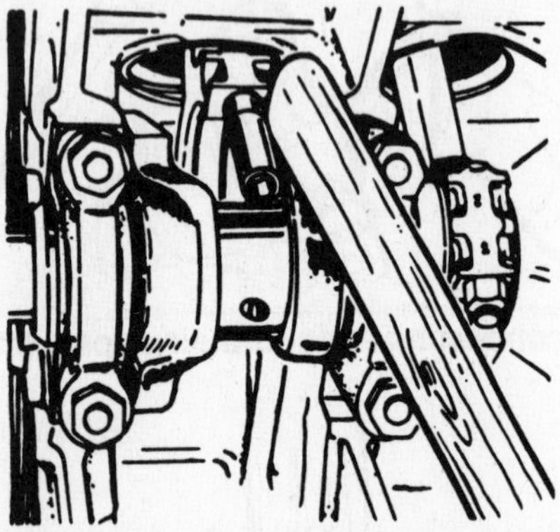

Carefully tap the piston and rod assembly out of the cylinder with a wooden hammer handle

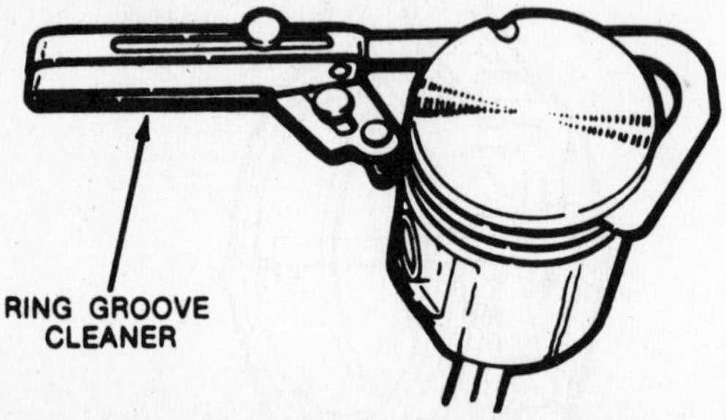
RING GROOVE
CLEANER

Clean the piston ring grooves using a ring groove cleaner

8. Remove the rod and piston assembly through the top of the cylinder bore; remove the other rod and piston assemblies in the same manner.
9. Clean and inspect the engine block, the crankshaft, the pistons and the connecting rods.

CLEANING AND INSPECTION

Using a piston ring expanding tool, remove the piston rings from the pistons; any other method (screwdriver blades, pliers, etc.) usually results in the rings being bent, scratched or distorted and/or the piston itself being damaged.

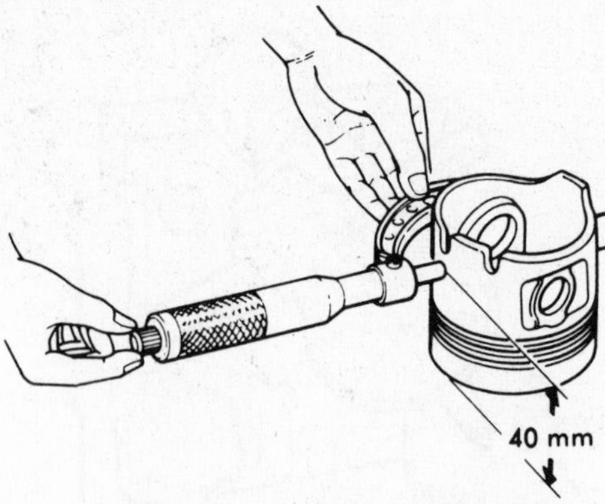
40 mm

Measuring the piston diameter

Pistons

Clean the varnish from the piston skirts and pins with a cleaning solvent. DO NOT WIRE BRUSH ANY PART OF THE PISTON. Clean the ring grooves with a groove cleaner and make sure that the oil ring holes and slots are clean.

Inspect the piston for cracked ring lands, scuffed or damaged skirts, eroded areas at the top of the piston. Replace the pistons that are damaged or show signs of excessive wear.

Inspect the grooves for nicks of burrs that might cause the rings to hang up.

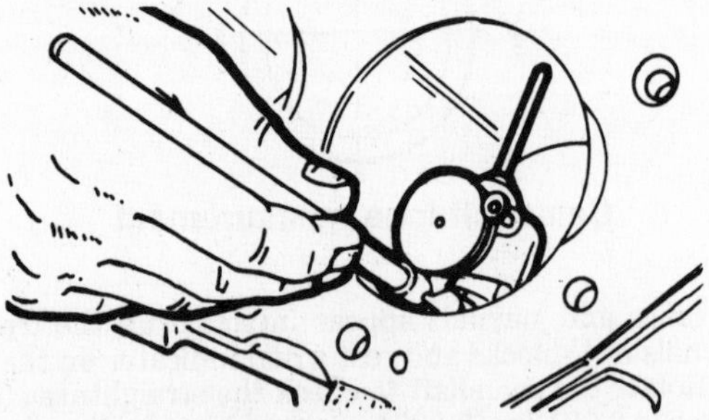

Measuring the cylinder bore with a dial gauge

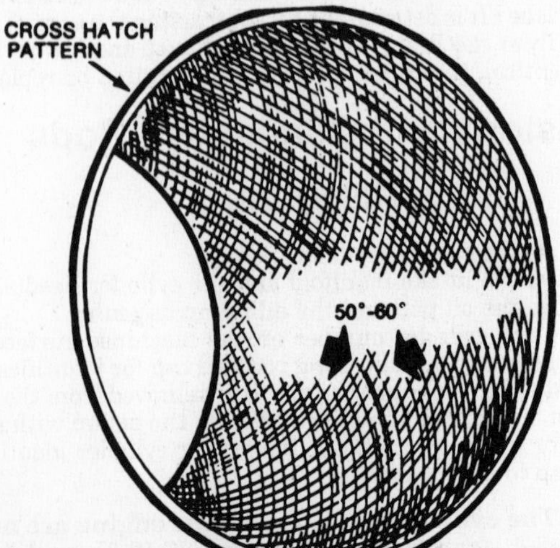
CROSS HATCH
PATTERN
50°-60°

Cylinder bore cross-hatch pattern after honing

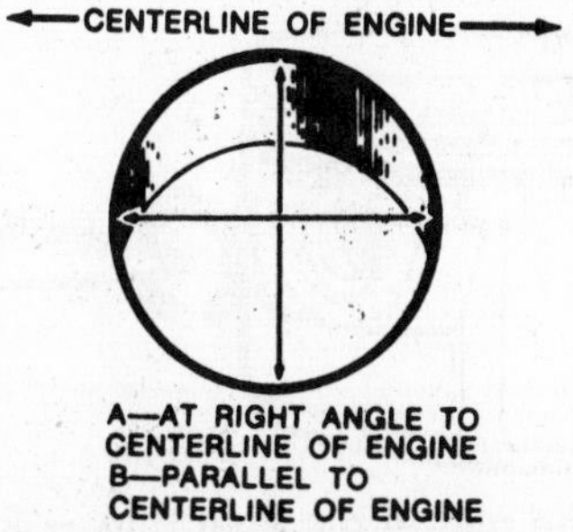
CENTERLINE OF ENGINE
A—AT RIGHT ANGLE TO CENTERLINE OF ENGINE
B—PARALLEL TO CENTERLINE OF ENGINE

Cylinder bore measuring points

Measure the piston skirt (across the center line of the piston pin) and check the piston clearance. If installing replacement pistons, follow the manufacturers recommendations on where to measure the piston.

Connecting Rods

Wash the connecting rods in cleaning solvent and dry with compressed air. Check for twisted or bent rods and inspect for nicks or cracks. Replace the connecting rods that are damaged.

Cylinder Bores

Using a telescoping gauge or an inside micrometer, measure the diameter of the cylinder bore, perpendicular (90°) to the piston pin, at 1–2½ in. below the surface of the cylinder block. The difference between the two measurements is the piston clearance.

If the clearance is within specifications or slightly below (after the cylinders have been bored or honed), finish honing is all that is necessary, If the clearance is excessive, try to obtain a slightly larger piston to bring the clearance within specifications. If this is not possible obtain the first oversize piston and hone the cylinder or (if necessary) bore the cylinder to size. Generally, if the cylinder bore is tapered more than 0.005 in. (0.127mm) or is out-of-round more than 0.003 in. (0.0762mm), it is advisable to rebore for the smallest possible oversize piston and rings. After measuring, mark the pistons with a felt-tip pen for reference and for assembly.

NOTE: Boring of the cylinder block should be performed by a reputable machine shop with the proper equipment. In some cases, clean-up honing can be done with the cylinder block in the vehicle, but most excessive honing and all cylinder boring MUST BE done with the block stripped and removed from the vehicle.

PISTON PIN REPLACEMENT

All Engines—Except 2.2L Diesel

NOTE: The following procedure requires the use of the GM Fixture/Support Assembly tool No. J-24086-20 or equivalent, the GM Piston Pin Removal tool No. J-24086-8 or equivalent, and the GM Piston Pin Installation tool No. J-24086-9 or equivalent.

Use care at all times when handling and servicing the connecting rods and pistons. To prevent possible damage to these units, DO NOT clamp the rod or piston in a vise since they may become distorted. DO NOT allow the pistons to strike one another, against hard objects or bench surfaces, since distortion of the piston contour or nicks in the soft aluminum material may result.

1. Using an arbor press, the GM Fixture/Support Assembly tool No. J-24086-20 or equivalent, and the GM Piston Pin Removal tool No. J-24086-8 or equivalent, place the piston assembly in the fixture/support tool and press the pin from the piston assembly.

NOTE: The piston and the piston pin are a matched set which are not serviced separately.

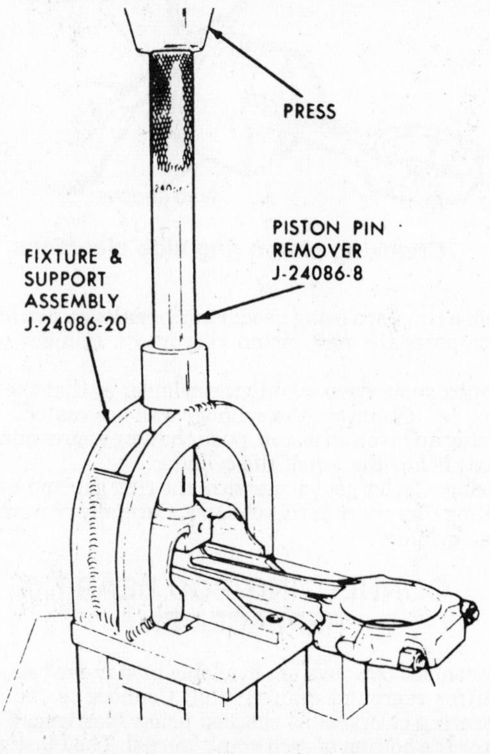
PRESS
PISTON PIN REMOVER J-24086-8
FIXTURE & SUPPORT ASSEMBLY J-24086-20

Removing the piston pin from the piston assembly

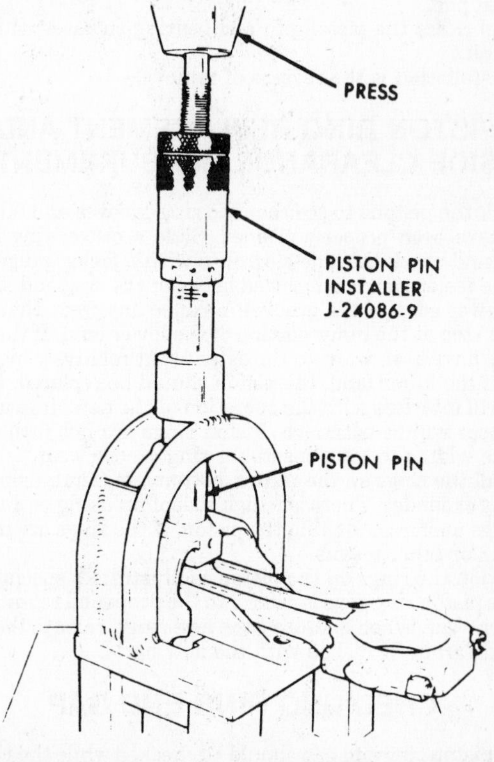
PRESS
PISTON PIN INSTALLER J-24086-9
PISTON PIN

Installing the piston pin into the piston assembly

2. Using solvent, wash the varnish and oil from the parts, then inspect the parts for scuffing or wear.
3. Using a micrometer, measure the diameter of the piston pin. Using a inside micrometer or a dial bore gauge, measure the diameter of the piston bore.

NOTE: If the piston pin-to-piston clearance is in excess of 0.001 in. (0.0254mm), replace the piston and piston pin assembly.

4. Before installation, lubricate the piston pin and the piston bore with engine oil.
5. To install the piston pin into the piston assembly, use an arbor press, the GM Fixture/Support Assembly tool No. J-24086-20 or equivalent, and the GM Piston Pin Installation tool No. J-24086-9 or equivalent, then press the piston pin into the piston/connecting rod assembly.

NOTE: When installing the piston pin into the piston/connecting rod assembly and the installation tool bottoms onto the support assembly, DO NOT exceed 5000 lbs. of pressure for structural damage may occur to the tool.

6. After installing the piston pin, make sure that the piston has freedom of movement with the piston pin. The piston/connecting rod assembly is ready for installation into the engine block.

2.2L Diesel Engine

1. Using a pair of snapring pliers, remove the piston pin snapring from the piston.
2. Slide the piston pin from the connecting rod and piston assembly.

NOTE: When separating the piston from the connecting rod, be sure to mark them for reassembly purposes.

3. Clean and inspect the piston and the connecting rod bearing surfaces for damage and/or wear; if necessary, replace the damaged part.
4. Lubricate the piston pin and bearing surfaces with clean engine oil.
5. Installation is the reverse of removal.

PISTON RING REPLACEMENT AND SIDE CLEARANCE MEASUREMENT

Check the pistons to see that the ring grooves and oil return holes have been properly cleaned. Slide a piston ring into its groove and check the side clearance with a feeler gauge. Make sure the feeler gauge is inserted between the ring and its lower land (lower edge of the groove), because any wear that occurs forms a step at the inner portion of the lower land. If the piston grooves have been worn to the extent that relatively high steps exist on the lower land, the piston should be replaced, because these will interfere with the operation of the new rings and ring clearances will be excessive. Piston rings are not furnished in oversize widths to compensate for ring groove wear.

Install the rings on the piston, bottom ring first, using a piston ring expander. There is a high risk of breaking or distorting the rings and/or scratching the piston, if the rings are installed by hand or other means.

Position the rings on the piston as illustrated; spacing of the various piston ring gaps is crucial to the proper oil retention and cylinder wear. When installing the new rings, refer to the installation diagram furnished with the new parts.

CHECKING RING END GAP

The piston ring end gap should be checked while the rings are removed from the pistons. Incorrect end gap indicates that the wrong size rings are being used; **ring breakage could result.**

1. Compress the new piston ring into a cylinder (one at a time).
2. Squirt some clean oil into the cylinder so that the ring and the top 2 in. (51mm) of the cylinder wall are coated.
3. Using an inverted piston, push the ring approximately 1 in. (25.4mm) below the top of the cylinder.
4. Using a feeler gauge, measure the ring gap and compare it to the Ring Gap chart in this chapter. Carefully remove the ring from the cylinder.

Replacing the piston pin snapring — 2.2L diesel engine

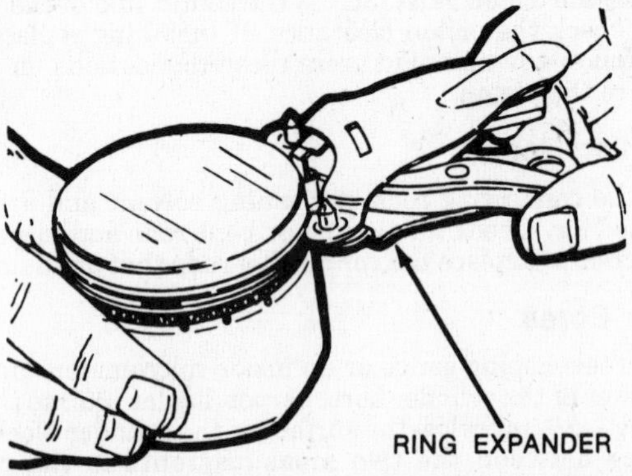
RING EXPANDER

Removing the piston rings with a piston ring expander

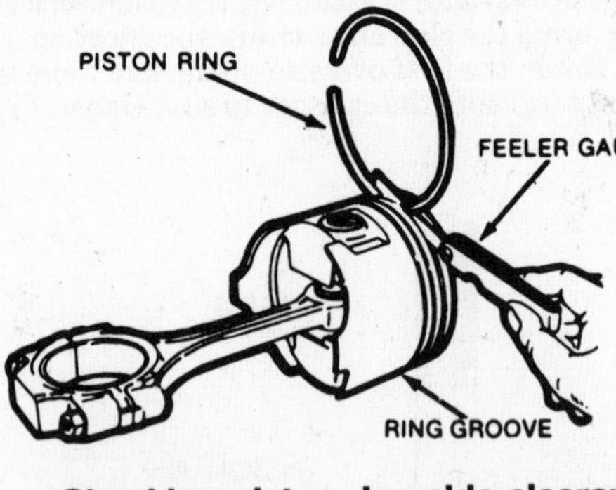
PISTON RING
FEELER GAUGE
RING GROOVE

Checking piston ring side clearance

CONNECTING ROD BEARING REPLACEMENT

Replacement bearings are available in standard size and undersize (for reground crankshafts). Connecting rod-to-crankshaft bearing clearance is checked using Plastigage® at either the top or the bottom of each crank journal. The Plastigage® has a range of 0.001–0.003 in. (0.0254–0.0762mm).

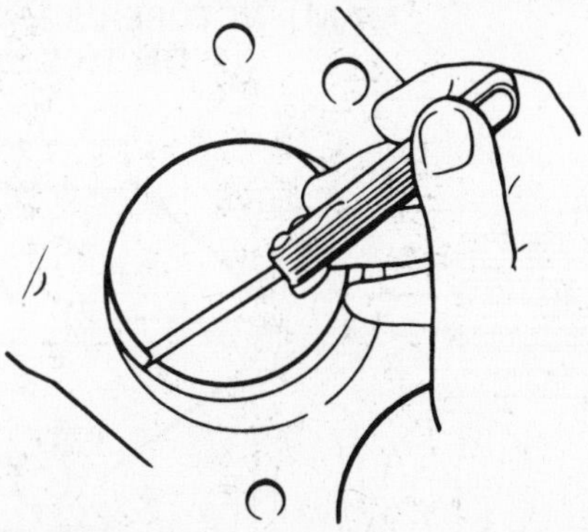

Checking piston ring end gap with a feeler gauge

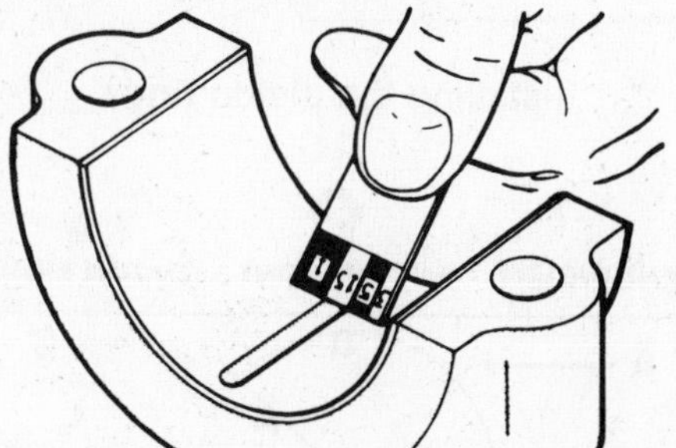

Measuring Plastigage® to determine main bearing clearance

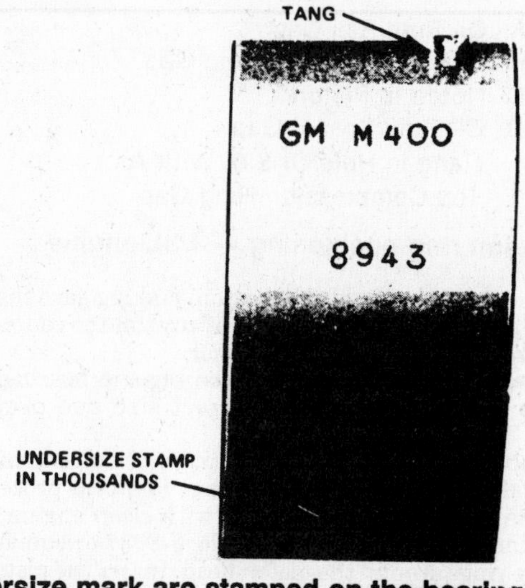
TANG
GM M400
8943
UNDERSIZE STAMP
IN THOUSANDS

Undersize mark are stamped on the bearing shells. The tang fits in the notch on the connecting rod and cap

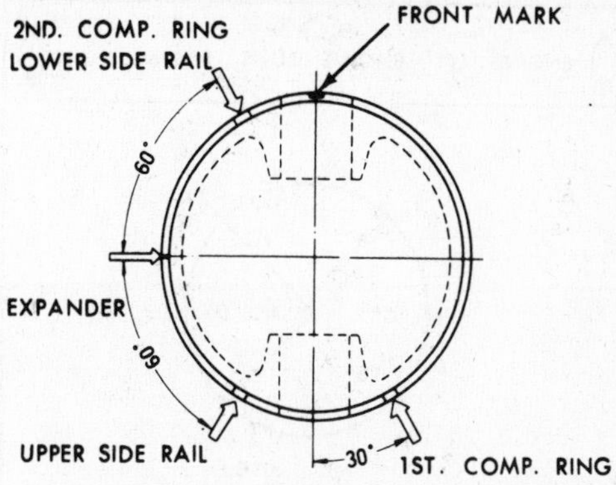
FRONT MARK
2ND. COMP. RING
LOWER SIDE RAIL
60°
EXPANDER
60°
UPPER SIDE RAIL
30°
1ST. COMP. RING

Piston ring positioning — 1.9L engine

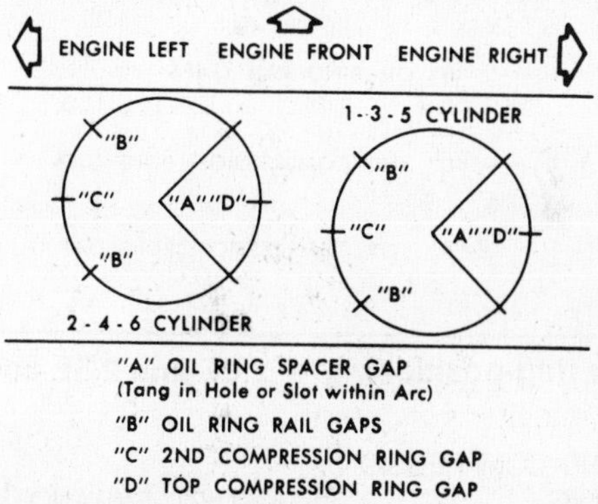
ENGINE LEFT
ENGINE FRONT
ENGINE RIGHT
1-3-5 CYLINDER
"B"
"C"
"A" "D"
"B"
2-4-6 CYLINDER
"A" OIL RING SPACER GAP
(Tang in Hole or Slot within Arc)
"B" OIL RING RAIL GAPS
"C" 2ND COMPRESSION RING GAP
"D" TOP COMPRESSION RING GAP

Piston ring positioning — 2.8L engine

1. Remove the rod cap with the bearing shell. Completely clean the bearing shell and the crank journal, blow any oil from the oil hole in the crankshaft; place the Plastigage® lengthwise along the bottom center of the lower bearing shell, then install the cap with the shell and torque the bolt or nuts to specification. DO NOT turn the crankshaft with the Plastigage® on the bearing.
2. Remove the bearing cap with the shell. The flattened Plastigage® will be found sticking to either the bearing shell or the crank journal. DO NOT remove it yet.
3. Use the scale printed on the Plastigage® envelope to measure the flattened material at its widest point. The number within the scale which most closely corresponds to the width of the Plastigage® indicates the bearing clearance in thousandths of an inch.
4. Check the specifications chart in this chapter for the desired clearance. It is advisable to install a new bearing if the clearance exceeds 0.003 in. (0.0762mm); however, if the bearing is in good condition and is not being checked because of bearing noise, bearing replacement is not necessary.
5. If you are installing new bearings, try a standard size, then each undersize in order until one is found that is within the specified limits when checked for clearance with Plastigage®; each undersize shell has its size stamped on it.
6. When the proper size shell is found, clean off the Plastigage®, oil the bearing thoroughly, reinstall the cap with its shell and torque the rod bolt nuts to specifications.

NOTE: With the proper bearing selected and the nuts torqued, it should be possible to move the connecting rod back and forth freely on the crank journal as allowed by the specified connecting rod end clearance. If the rod cannot be moved, either the rod bearing is too far undersize or the rod is misaligned.

INSTALLATION

NOTE: The following procedure requires the use of the Ring Compressor tool No. J-8037 or equivalent, and the ring installation tool.

Position the rings on the piston; **spacing of the various piston ring gaps is crucial to proper oil retention and even cylinder wear.** When installing new rings, refer to the installation diagram furnished with the new parts.

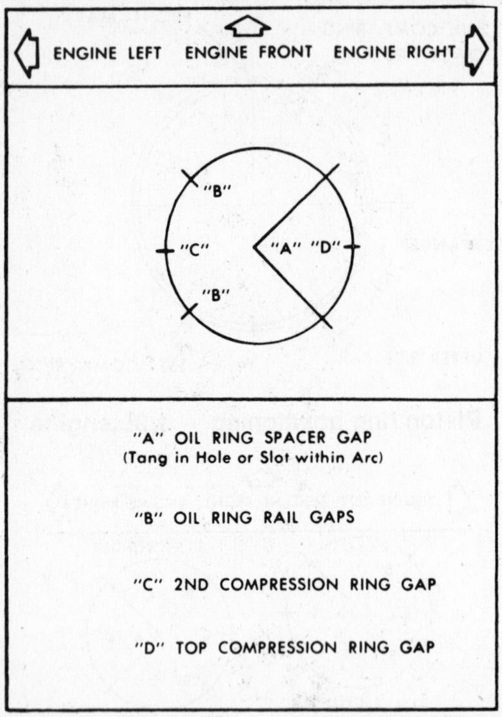
ENGINE LEFT
ENGINE FRONT
ENGINE RIGHT
"B"
"C"
"A"
"D"
"B"
"A" OIL RING SPACER GAP
(Tang in Hole or Slot within Arc)
"B" OIL RING RAIL GAPS
"C" 2ND COMPRESSION RING GAP
"D" TOP COMPRESSION RING GAP

Piston ring positioning – 2.0L and 2.5L engine

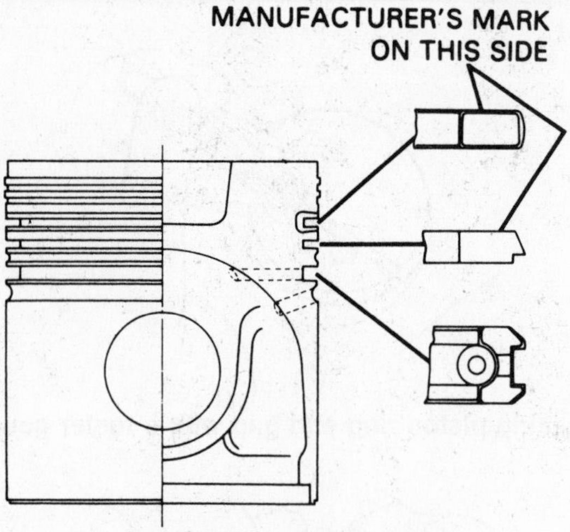
MANUFACTURER'S MARK
ON THIS SIDE

Installing the piston rings

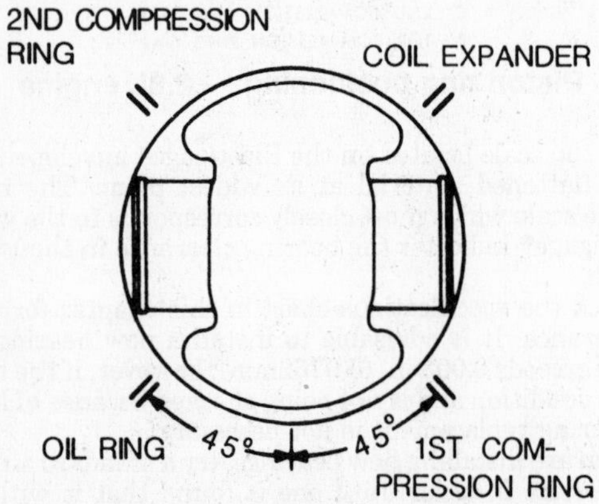
2ND COMPRESSION
RING
COIL EXPANDER
OIL RING
45°
45°
1ST COM-
PRESSION RING

Piston ring positioning – 2.2L engine

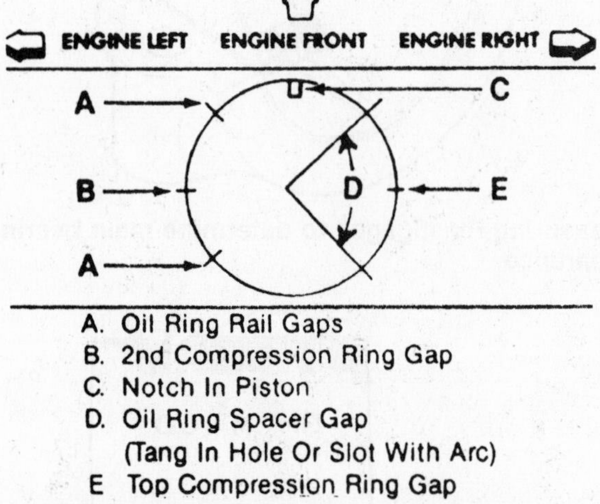
ENGINE LEFT
ENGINE FRONT
ENGINE RIGHT
A
C
B
D
E
A
A. Oil Ring Rail Gaps
B. 2nd Compression Ring Gap
C. Notch In Piston
D. Oil Ring Spacer Gap
(Tang In Hole Or Slot With Arc)
E Top Compression Ring Gap

Piston ring positioning – 4.3L engine

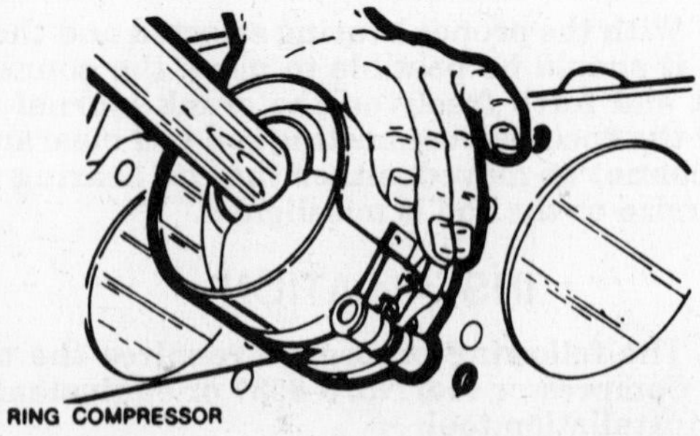
RING COMPRESSOR

Install the piston ring compressor, then tap the piston into the cylinder bore with a wooden hammer handle

Install the connecting rod to the piston, making sure that the piston installation notches and marks (if any) on the connecting rod are in proper relation to one another.

1. Make sure that the connecting rod big-end bearings (including the end cap) are of the correct size and properly installed.
2. Fit rubber hoses over the connecting rod bolts to protect the crankshaft journals, as in the Piston Removal procedure. Lubricate the connecting rod bearings with clean engine oil.
3. Using the Ring Compressor tool No. J-8037 or equivalent, compress the rings around the piston head. Insert the piston assembly into the cylinder, so that the notch (on top of the piston) faces the front of the engine.
4. From beneath the engine, coat each crank journal with clean oil. Using a hammer handle, drive the connecting rod/piston assembly into the cylinder bore. Align the connecting rod (with bearing shell) onto the crankshaft journal.
5. Remove the rubber hoses from the studs. Install the bearing cap (with bearing shell) onto the connecting rod and the cap nuts. Torque the connecting rod cap nuts to the following:

- 1.9L engine: 43 ft. lbs.
- 2.0L engine: 36 ft. lbs.
- 2.2L diesel: 62 ft. lbs.
- 2.5L engine: 32 ft. lbs.
- 2.8L engine: 39 ft. lbs.
- 4.3L engine: 45 ft. lbs.

FRONT OF ENGINE
NOTCH

Install the pistons with the notch facing the front of the engine

NOTE: When more than one connecting rod/piston assembly are being installed, the connecting rod cap nuts should only be tightened enough to keep each rod in position until the all have been installed. This will ease the installation of the remaining piston assemblies.

6. Check the clearance between the sides of the connecting rods and the crankshaft using a feeler gauge. Spread the rods slightly with a small pry bar to insert the feeler gauge. If the clearance is below the minimum tolerance, the rod may be machined to provide adequate clearance. If the clearance is excessive, substitute an unworn rod and recheck. If clearance is still outside specifications, the crankshaft must be welded and reground or replaced.
7. To complete the installation, reverse the removal procedures. Refill the cooling system. Refill the engine crankcase. Start the engine, allow it to reach normal operating temperatures and check for leaks.

Freeze Plugs

REMOVAL AND INSTALLATION

1. Remove the negative battery cable.
2. Drain the cooling system.

CAUTION

When draining the coolant, keep in mind that cats and dogs are attracted by the ethylene glycol antifreeze, and are quite likely to drink any that is left in an uncovered container or in puddles on the ground. This will prove fatal in sufficient quantity. Always drain the coolant into a sealable container. Coolant should be reused unless it is contaminated or several years old.

3. If equipped, remove the engine coolant drain plugs (located at the bottom of the block near the oil pan rail) and drain the coolant from the block. If the engine is not equipped with coolant drain plugs, drill a small hole in the leaking freeze plug and allow the coolant to drain.

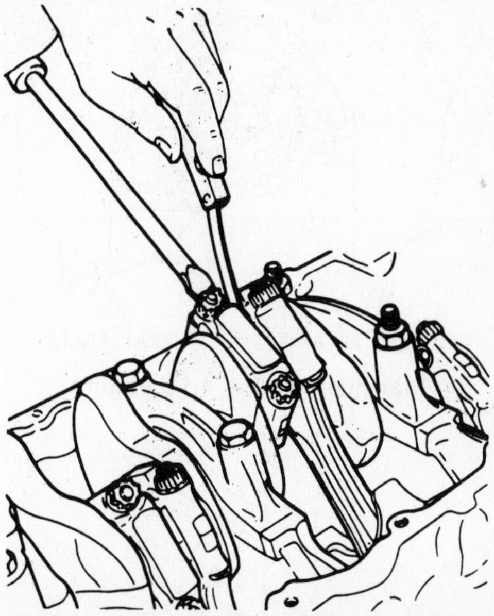

Check the connecting rod side clearance with a feeler gauge. Use a small pry bar to carefully spread the rods to specified clearance

4. Remove any components that restrict access to the freeze plug.
5. Using a chisel, tap the bottom edge of the freeze plug to cock it in the bore. Remove the plug using pliers. An alternate method is to drill an ⅛ in. hole in the plug and remove it using a dent puller.
6. Clean the freeze plug hole and using an appropriate driver tool or socket, install the freeze plug into the hole. Coat the freeze plug with sealer before installation.
7. Fill the engine with coolant, install the negative battery cable, start the engine and check for leaks.

Block Heater

REMOVAL AND INSTALLATION

1. Remove the negative battery cable.
2. Drain the cooling system.

CAUTION

When draining the coolant, keep in mind that cats and dogs are attracted by the ethylene glycol antifreeze, and are quite likely to drink any that is left in an uncovered container or in puddles on the ground. This will prove fatal in sufficient quantity. Always drain the coolant into a sealable container. Coolant should be reused unless it is contaminated or several years old.

3. If equipped, remove the engine coolant drain plugs (located at the bottom of the block near the oil pan rail) and drain the coolant from the block. If the engine is not equipped with coolant drain plugs, be ready to catch the coolant that will drain from the block when the block heater is removed.
4. Disconnect the block heater electrical connector.
5. Loosen the block heater retaining screw and remove the block heater from the engine.
6. Coat the block heater O-ring with engine oil and clean the block heater hole of rust.
7. Install the block heater and tighten the retaining screw.

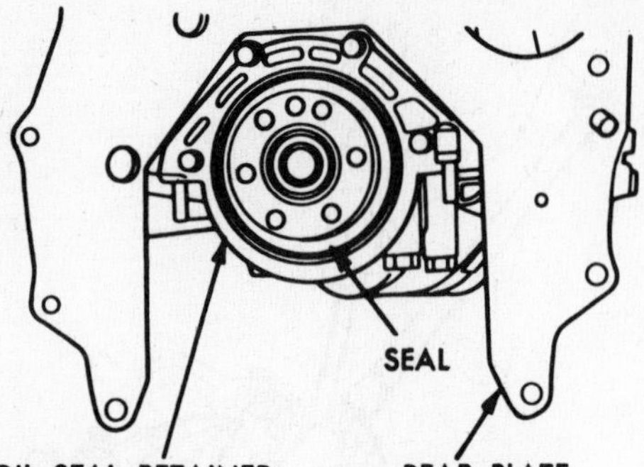
SEAL
OIL SEAL RETAINER
REAR PLATE
Rear main seal — 1.9L engine

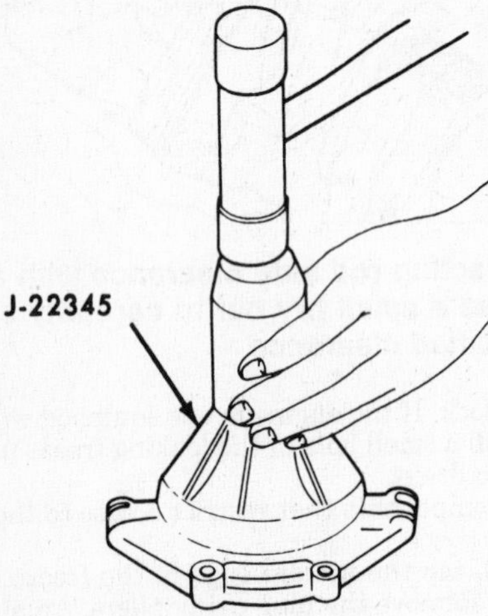
J-22345
Rear main seal installation — 1.9L engine

8. Fill the engine with coolant, install the negative battery cable, start the engine and check for leaks.

Rear Main Oil Seal

Replacing a rear main seal is a formidable task. Before replacing the seal, care should be taken in determining the exact source of the leak.

REPLACEMENT

1.9L Engine

NOTE: The following procedure requires the use of the Seal Installer tool No. J-22928-A or equivalent

1. Remove the negative battery cable.
2. Raise and support the vehicle safely.
3. Remove the starter motor and lay it aside. DO NOT allow the starter to hang by the wires.
4. Remove driveshaft.
5. Support the rear of the engine and remove the transmission.
6. If equipped with a manual transmission, remove the clutch assembly.
7. Remove the flywheel-to-crankshaft bolts and the flywheel.
8. Remove the rear main seal retainer from the engine.
9. Using a medium pry bar, remove the rear main oil seal from the retainer and discard it.
10. Lubricate the seal lips and fill the space between the seal and the crankshaft with grease.
11. Using the Seal Installer tool No. J-22928-A or equivalent, drive the new rear main oil seal into the housing.
12. Installation is the reverse of removal.

2.0L and 2.8L Engine

To determine the type of oil seal on 2.0L engines, it will be necessary to look for an identification mark (oval) stamped on the right rear side of the engine where it connects to the transmission. If the oval appears, the engine uses an 11mm second design (one-piece) seal. If the oval does not appear the engine uses a 5mm first design seal. The first design seals may come in either a one or two piece configuration.

On 2.8L engines, the year of the vehicle (engine) determines the seal used as follows:

- 1982–85 engines use a 5mm first design rear main seal.
- 1986–91 engines use an 11mm second design rear main seal.

5MM TWO PIECE

1. Remove the oil pan and pump.
2. Remove the rear main bearing cap.
3. Remove the upper and lower seal. Clean the seal channel of any oil.

NOTE: To install the replacement seal, you may need to loosen numbers 2, 3, and 4 rear main bearing caps.

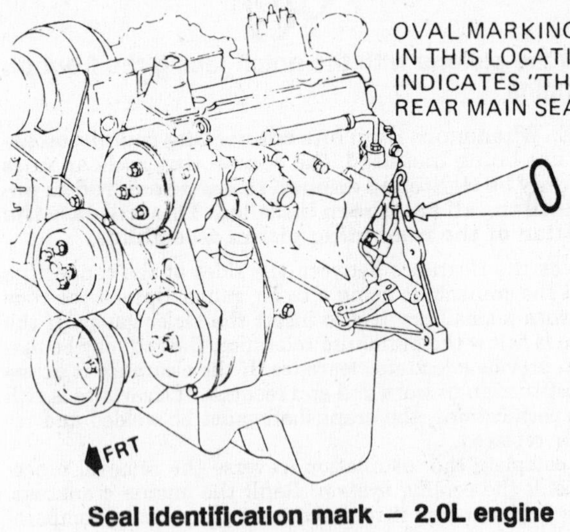
OVAL MARKING
IN THIS LOCATION
INDICATES "THICK
REAR MAIN SEAL"
FRT
Seal identification mark — 2.0L engine

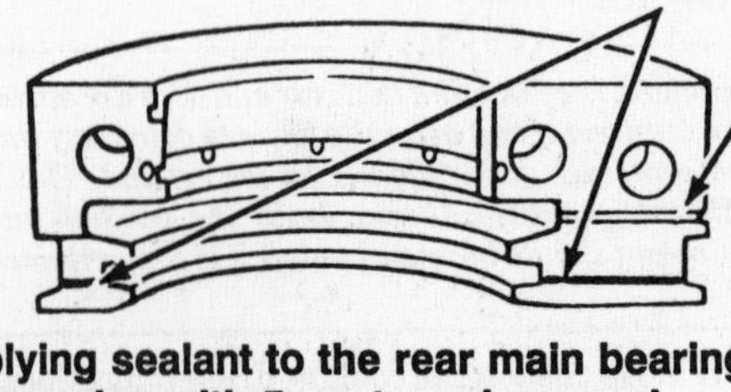
COATED AREA INDICATED
WITH #1052357 SEALER
OR EQUIVALENT.
SEALER
DRAIN
SLOT
Applying sealant to the rear main bearing — 2.0L and 2.8L engine with 5mm two-piece seal

4. Apply a very thin coat of gasket sealant to the outside diameter of the upper seal. Install the seal with the lip inward, turning the crankshaft to ease installation.
5. Install the lower seal in the rear main bearing cap after applying sealant to the outside diameter.
6. Check the bearing clearance of the rear main bearing with Plastigage®. Repair as necessary if out of specification.
7. Lightly oil the rear main bearing after removing the Plastigage®. Apply a 1mm bead of RTV to the rear main bearing cap between the rear main seal end and the oil pan rear seal groove. DO NOT allow sealant to come in contact with the rear main seal or the drain slot.
8. Lightly oil the rear main seal and install the rear main bearing cap. Torque the cap bolts to 70 ft. lbs.
9. Installation is the reverse of removal.

5MM ONE PIECE

1. Remove the engine.
2. Remove the oil pan and pump.
3. Remove the front (timing) cover and lock the chain tensioner with the pin.
4. Rotate the crankshaft until the timing marks on the cam and crank sprockets line up.
5. Remove the camshaft bolt, cam sprocket and timing chain.
6. Rotate the crankshaft to a horizontal position and remove the rod bearing nuts, caps and bearings.

NOTE: The rod bearings and caps must be replaced in order. DO NOT mix them up.

7. Remove the main bearing bolts, caps and bearings. Remove the crankshaft.
8. Remove the old rear main seal and clean the sealant from the crankshaft and block.
9. Apply a light coat of sealant to the outside diameter of the replacement seal.
10. Place a Seal Tool assembly on the rear area of the crankshaft. Position the seal tool so that the arrow points toward the engine. Place the crankshaft in the engine with the tool in this position. Remove and discard the tool.
11. Seal the rear main bearing split line (use sealant No. 1052756) and replace the rear main bearing and cap.
12. Replace the other bearings and caps. Tighten bolts to 63–75 ft. lbs.
13. Replace the rod bearings and caps. Tighten bolts to 34–50 ft. lbs.
14. Install the oil pump and tighten the bolt to 26–35 ft. lbs.
15. Align the crank sprocket timing mark and install the cam sprocket and timing chain. Tighten bolt to 66–85 ft. lbs.
16. Installation is the reverse of removal.

11MM ONE PIECE

NOTE: The following procedure requires the use of the Seal Installation tool No. J-34686 or equivalent.

1. Support the rear of the engine and remove the transmission.
2. Remove the flywheel and verify the rear main seal is leaking.
3. Remove the seal by inserting a pry bar through the dust lip and prying the seal out.
4. Check the seal bore for nicks or damage. Repair as necessary.
5. Install the new seal using a Seal Installer tool No. J-34686.
6. Install the seal over the mandrill and bottom the dust lip (back of seal) squarely against the collar of the tool.
7. Align the dowel pin of the tool with the dowel pin hole in the crankshaft and attach the tool to the crankshaft by hand.
8. Turn the handle of the tool until the collar is tight against the case. This will ensure the seal is completely seated.
9. Turn the handle of the tool out until it stops. Check the seal making sure it is seated squarely in the bore.

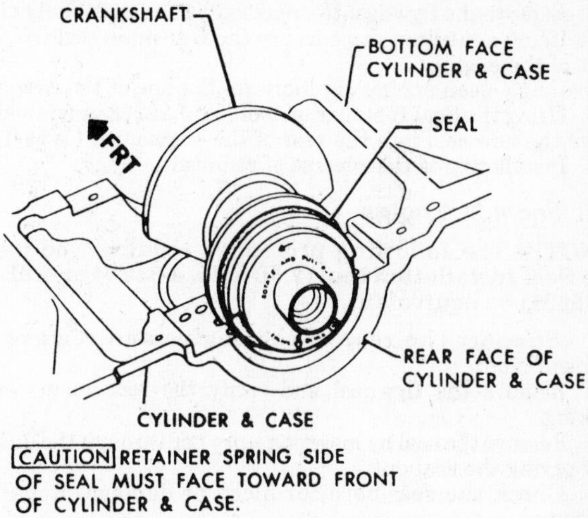
CRANKSHAFT
BOTTOM FACE CYLINDER & CASE
SEAL
FRT
REAR FACE OF CYLINDER & CASE
CYLINDER & CASE
CAUTION RETAINER SPRING SIDE OF SEAL MUST FACE TOWARD FRONT OF CYLINDER & CASE.

Installing the 5mm one-piece rear main seal – 2.0L and 2.8L engine

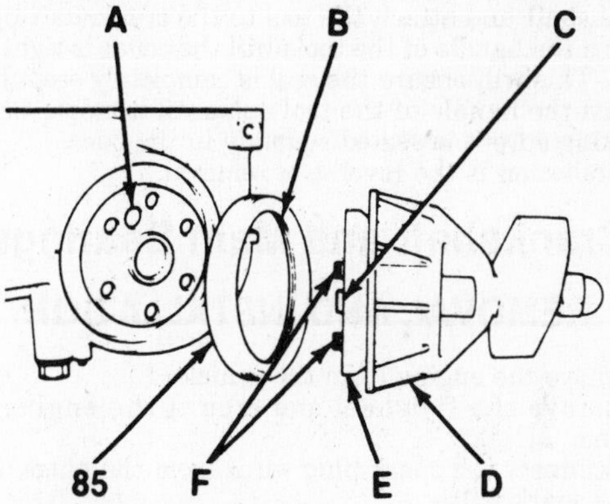
A
B
C
C
85
F
E
D

A. Alignment hole in crankshaft
B. Dust lip
C. Dowel pin
D. Collar
E. Mandrel
F. Screws
85. Crankshaft rear oil seal

Installing the 11mm one-piece rear main seal

10. Installation is the reverse of removal.

2.2L Diesel Engine

NOTE: The following procedure requires the use of the Seal Installation tool No. J-22928 or equivalent.

1. Raise and support the vehicle safely.
2. Remove the transmission. If equipped with a manual transmission, remove the clutch assembly.

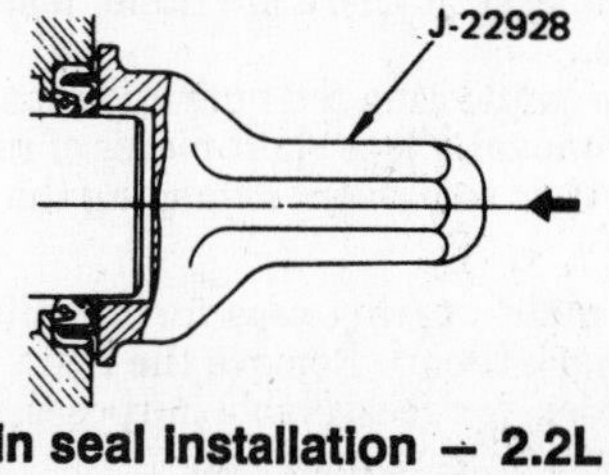
J-22928

Rear main seal installation – 2.2L diesel

3. Remove the flywheel-to-crankshaft bolts and the flywheel.
4. Using a medium pry bar, pry the rear main seal from the rear of the engine.
5. Using clean engine oil, lubricate the lips of the new seal.
6. Using the Seal Installation tool No. J-22928 or equivalent, drive the new seal into the rear of the engine until it seats.
7. Installation is the reverse of removal.

2.5L and 4.3L Engine

NOTE: The following procedure requires the use of the Seal Installation tool (2.5L–No. J-34924 or 4.3L No. J-35621) or equivalent.

1. Support the rear of the engine and remove the transmission.
2. Remove the flywheel and verify the rear main seal is leaking.
3. Remove the seal by inserting a pry bar through the dust lip and prying the seal out.
4. Check the seal bore for nicks or damage. Repair as necessary.
5. Install the new seal using a Seal Installer tool.
6. Install the seal over the mandril and bottom the dust lip (back of seal) squarely against the collar of the tool.
7. Align the dowel pin of the tool with the dowel pin hole in the crankshaft and attach the tool to the crankshaft by hand.
8. Turn the handle of the tool until the collar is tight against the case. This will ensure the seal is completely seated.
9. Turn the handle of the tool out until it stops. Check the seal making sure it is seated squarely in the bore.
10. Installation is the reverse of removal.

Crankshaft and Main Bearings

REMOVAL AND INSTALLATION

1. Remove the engine from the vehicle.
2. Remove the flywheel and mount the engine onto a workstand.
3. Disconnect the spark plug wires from the plugs, then remove the spark plugs.
4. Remove the drive belt pulley from the damper pulley/hub, the damper pulley/hub-to-crankshaft bolt, the damper pulley/hub from the crankshaft and the timing cover from the engine.

NOTE: After removing the damper pulley/hub from the crankshaft, be sure to remove the woodruff key from the crankshaft. When removing the damper pulley/hub from the crankshaft, the oil seal should be replaced.

5. Rotate the crankshaft, until the timing marks on the timing gears or sprockets align with each other, then remove the timing gear or sprocket from the crankshaft.

NOTE: After removing the timing gear or sprocket from the crankshaft, be sure to remove the woodruff key from the crankshaft.

6. Drain the engine oil.
7. Remove the oil pump as necessary.
8. Inspect the connecting rods and bearing caps for identification marks (numbers); if there are none, mark them for reassembly purposes.
9. Remove the connecting rod nuts and caps, then store them in the order of removal. Place short pieces of rubber hose on the connecting rod studs to prevent damaging the crankshaft bearing surfaces.
10. Check the main bearing caps for identification marks (if not identified, mark them). Remove the main bearing caps and store them in order, for reassembly purposes; the caps must be reinstalled in their original position.

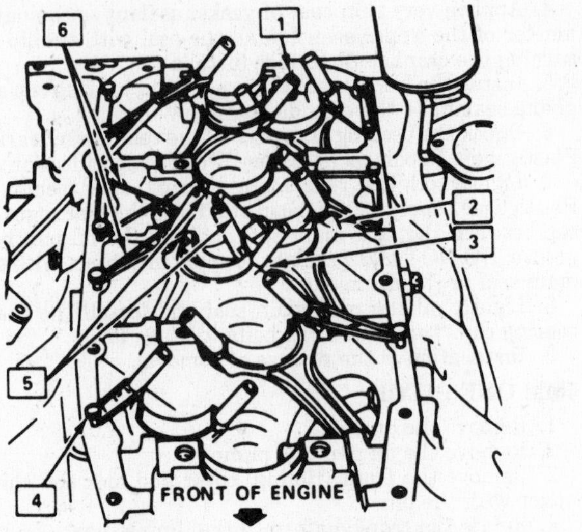
6
1
2
3
5
4
FRONT OF ENGINE

1. Rubber hose
2. #4 rod
3. #3 rod
4. Oil pan bolt
5. Note overlap of adjacent rods
6. Rubber bands

Support the connecting rods with rubber bands and install rubber rod bolt caps to protect the crankshaft during removal/installation

11. Remove the crankshaft, the main bearing inserts and the rear main oil seal.

NOTE: On engines equipped with an 11mm one-piece rear main seal, it will be necessary to remove the seal first before removing the crankshaft.

12. Using solvent, clean all of the parts and inspect for damage.
13. To install, use new bearing shell inserts and check the bearing clearances.

NOTE: If necessary, deliver the crankshaft to an automotive machine shop, have the crankshaft journals ground and new bearing shells matched.

14. Lubricate all of the parts and oil seals with clean engine oil.
15. Using a feeler gauge and a medium pry bar, move the crankshaft forward-and-rearward. Check the crankshaft endplay by inserting a feeler gauge between the crankshaft and the thrust bearing shell. An alternate method is to use a dial indicator at the crankshaft snout. Install the indicator, move the crankshaft rearward, zero the indicator and then move the crankshaft forward. the dial indicator will read the endplay. Thrust bearing location is as follows:
   - 1.9L engine: No. 3
   - 2.0L engine: No. 4
   - 2.2L engine: No. 3
   - 2.5L engine: No. 5
   - 2.8L engine: No. 3
   - 4.3L engine: No. 4
16. Tighten main bearing caps (in three steps) to the following:
   - 1.9L engine: 75 ft. lbs.
   - 2.0L engine: 70 ft. lbs.
   - 2.2L engine: 116–130 ft. lbs.
   - 2.5L engine: 70 ft. lbs.
   - 2.8L engine: 70 ft. lbs.
   - 4.3L engine: 80 ft. lbs.
17. Install connecting rod caps and torque rod bolts to the following:
   - 1.9L engine: 43 ft. lbs.
   - 2.0L engine: 37 ft. lbs.

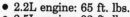

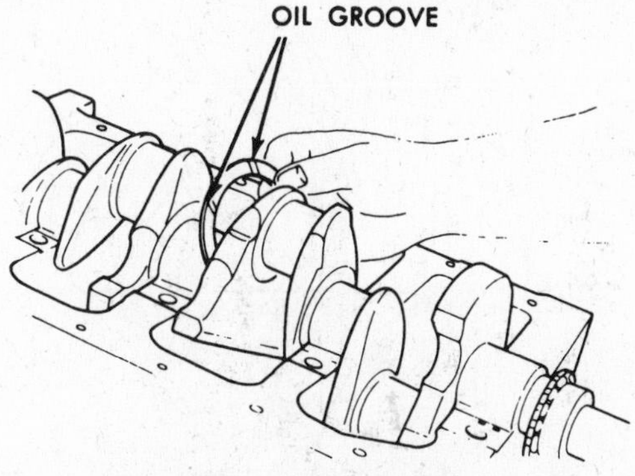
OIL GROOVE
Thrust bearing location

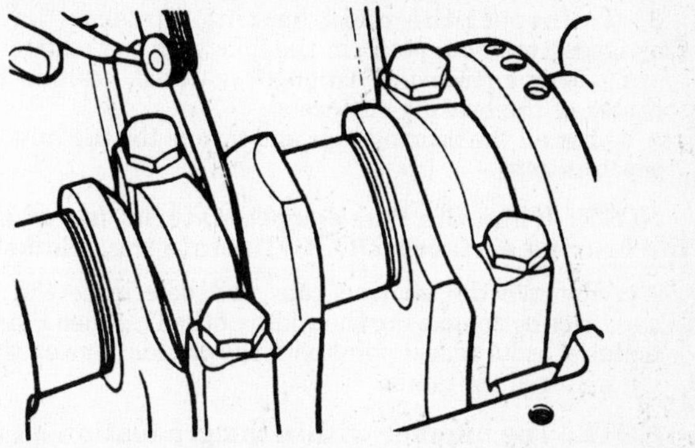
Checking crankshaft endplay with a feeler gauge

- 2.2L engine: 65 ft. lbs.
- 2.5L engine: 32 ft. lbs.
- 2.8L engine: 39 ft. lbs.
- 4.3L engine: 45 ft. lbs.

18. Check connecting rod side clearance by inserting a feeler gauge between the side of the rod and the crankshaft. If not within specification, repair as necessary.
19. The remainder of the installation procedure is the reverse of removal.
20. Fill the cooling system (with the saved coolant) and the crankcase (with new oil). Start the engine, allow it to reach normal operating temperatures and check for leaks.

CLEANING AND INSPECTION

NOTE: The following procedure requires the use of Plastigage® or a micrometer set consisting of inside and outside micrometers, and a dial indicator.

1. Remove the bearing cap and wipe the oil from the crankshaft journal and outer/inner surfaces of the bearing shell.
2. To check the crankshaft/rod bearing clearances using a micrometer, perform the following procedures:
   a. Set the crankshaft in the block with the bearings inserted. Using a dial indicator set on the center bearing journal, check the crankshaft runnout. Repair or replace the crankshaft if out of specification.
   b. Using an outside micrometer, measure the bearing journals for diameter and out-of-round conditions; if necessary, regrind the bearing journals.
   c. Install the bearings and caps and torque the nuts/bolts to specifications. Using an inside micrometer, check the bearing bores in the engine block. If out of specification, regrind the bearing bores to the next largest oversize.
   d. The difference between the two readings is the bearing clearance. If out of specification, inspect for the cause and repair as necessary.

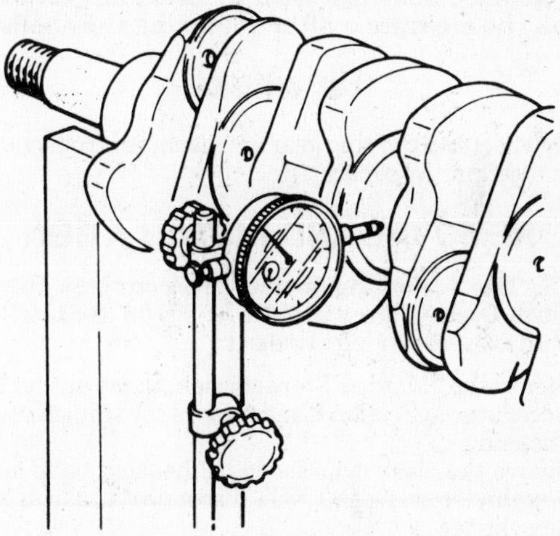
Checking crankshaft runout

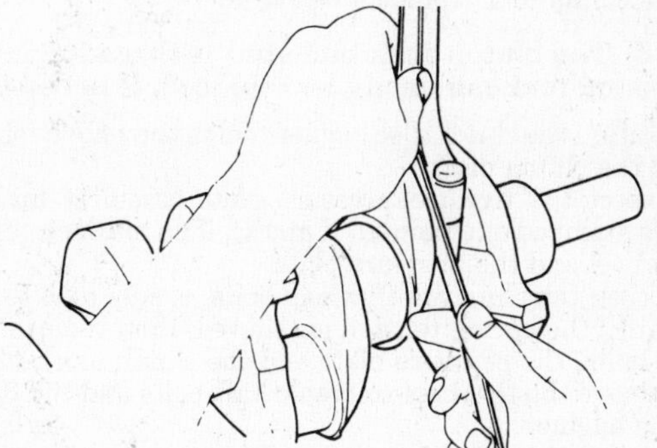
Measuring connecting rod side clearance

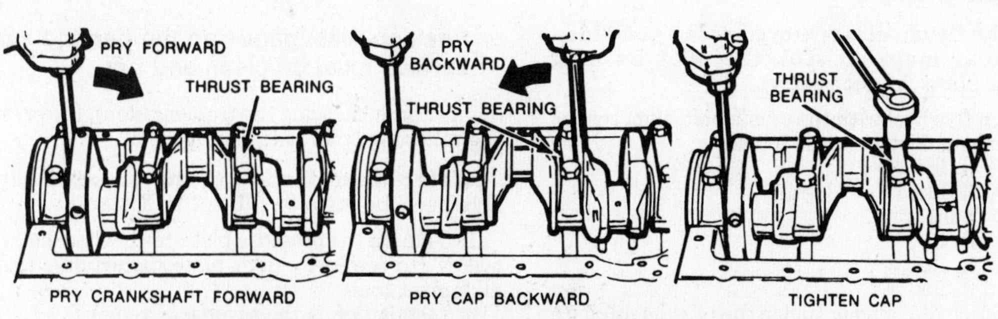
PRY FORWARD
THRUST BEARING
PRY BACKWARD
THRUST BEARING
THRUST BEARING
PRY CRANKSHAFT FORWARD
PRY CAP BACKWARD
TIGHTEN CAP
Aligning the thrust bearings and torquing the main caps

3. To inspect the main bearing surfaces, using the Plastigage® method, perform the following procedures:

a. Using a piece of Plastigage® material, position it in the center of the bearing surface(s).

b. Install the bearing caps and torque the cap nuts/bolts to specifications.

NOTE: When the Plastigage® material is installed on the bearing surfaces, DO NOT rotate the crankshaft.

c. Remove the bearing caps and determine the bearing clearance by comparing the width of the flattened Plastigage® material at its widest point with the graduations on the gauging material container.

NOTE: The number within the graduation on the envelope indicates the clearance in millimeters or thousandths of an inch. If the clearance is greater than allowed. Replace bearings with the next largest oversize. Recheck the clearance after replacing the shells.

Flywheel

The flywheel and the ring gear are machined from one piece of metal and cannot be separated.

REMOVAL AND INSTALLATION

NOTE: The following procedure requires the use of the Clutch Disc Aligner tool No. J-33169 (2.5L & 2.8L), J-33034 (all others) or equivalent.

1. Refer to the "Manual Transmission, Removal and Installation" procedures in Section 6 and remove the transmission from the bellhousing.
2. Remove the slave cylinder-to-bellhousing bolts and move the slave cylinder aside; DO NOT disconnect the hydraulic line from the cylinder.
3. Remove the bellhousing-to-engine bolts and the bellhousing from the engine. When removing the bellhousing, slide the clutch fork from the ball stud.

NOTE: The clutch fork ball stud is threaded into the bellhousing and can easily be replaced, if necessary.

4. Position the clutch disc aligner tool in the pilot bushing (to support the clutch disc).
5. Inspect the flywheel/pressure plate assembly for match marks (a stamped or a painted **X** mark); if no mark exists, mark the flywheel and the pressure plate.
6. Loosen the clutch-to-flywheel bolts, evenly (one turn at a time), until the spring tension is relieved, then remove the retaining bolts, the pressure plate and the clutch assembly.
7. Remove the flywheel-to-crankshaft bolts and the flywheel from the engine.
8. Clean the clutch disc (use a stiff brush), the pressure plate and the flywheel of all dirt, oil and grease. Inspect the flywheel, the pressure plate and the clutch disc for scoring, cracks, heat checking and/or other defects.

NOTE: When the flywheel is removed, it is a good idea to replace the rear main oil seal, the pilot bushing and/or the clutch plate (if necessary).

9. To install, align flywheel with the crankshaft, then torque the flywheel-to-crankshaft bolts to the following:
   - 1.9L engine: 76 ft. lbs.
   - 2.0L engine: 50 ft. lbs.
   - 2.2L diesel: 70 ft. lbs.
   - 2.5L engine: 55 ft. lbs.
   - 2.8L engine: 52 ft. lbs.
   - 4.3L engine: 75 ft. lbs.
10. Position the clutch disc aligner tool in the pilot bushing (to support the clutch disc), then assemble the clutch disc (the damper springs facing the transmission), the pressure plate and the retaining bolts onto the flywheel.

NOTE: When installing the pressure plate onto the flywheel, be sure to align the X marks.

11. Tighten the pressure plate-to-flywheel bolts gradually and evenly (to prevent clutch plate distortion), then remove the alignment tool.
12. Installation is the reverse of removal.
13. Lubricate the pilot bushing and the clutch release lever.

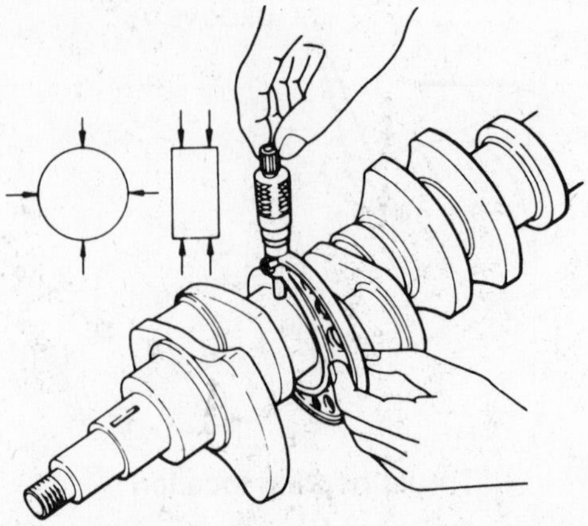

Checking main bearing journal diameter

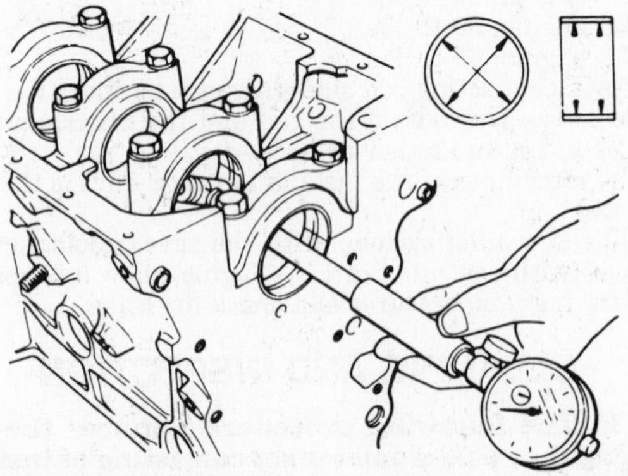

Checking main bearing bore diameter with bearings installed

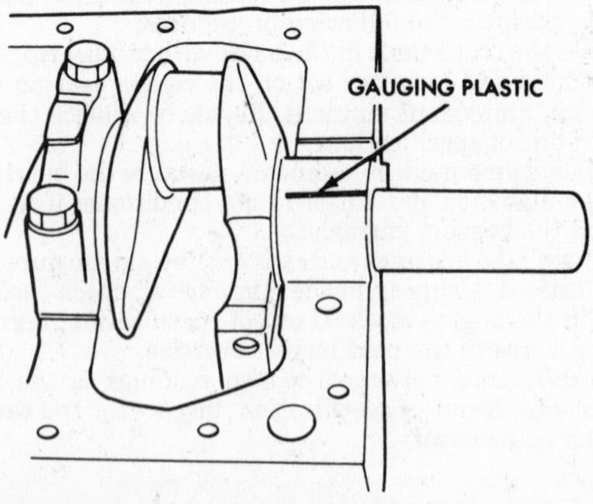
GAUGING PLASTIC

Position Plastigage® on the bearing surface. The surface must be clean and dry

Troubleshooting Engine Mechanical Problems

Problem	Cause	Solution
External oil leaks	• Fuel pump gasket broken or improperly seated	• Replace gasket
	• Cylinder head cover RTV sealant broken or improperly seated	• Replace sealant; inspect cylinder head cover sealant flange and cylinder head sealant surface for distortion and cracks
	• Oil filler cap leaking or missing	• Replace cap
External oil leaks	• Oil filter gasket broken or improperly seated	• Replace oil filter
	• Oil pan side gasket broken, improperly seated or opening in RTV sealant	• Replace gasket or repair opening in sealant; inspect oil pan gasket flange for distortion
	• Oil pan front oil seal broken or improperly seated	• Replace seal; inspect timing case cover and oil pan seal flange for distortion
	• Oil pan rear oil seal broken or improperly seated	• Replace seal; inspect oil pan rear oil seal flange; inspect rear main bearing cap for cracks, plugged oil return channels, or distortion in seal groove
	• Timing case cover oil seal broken or improperly seated	• Replace seal
	• Excess oil pressure because of restricted PCV valve	• Replace PCV valve
	• Oil pan drain plug loose or has stripped threads	• Repair as necessary and tighten
	• Rear oil gallery plug loose	• Use appropriate sealant on gallery plug and tighten
	• Rear camshaft plug loose or improperly seated	• Seat camshaft plug or replace and seal, as necessary
	• Distributor base gasket damaged	• Replace gasket
Excessive oil consumption	• Oil level too high	• Drain oil to specified level
	• Oil with wrong viscosity being used	• Replace with specified oil
	• PCV valve stuck closed	• Replace PCV valve
	• Valve stem oil deflectors (or seals) are damaged, missing, or incorrect type	• Replace valve stem oil deflectors
	• Valve stems or valve guides worn	• Measure stem-to-guide clearance and repair as necessary
	• Poorly fitted or missing valve cover baffles	• Replace valve cover
	• Piston rings broken or missing	• Replace broken or missing rings
	• Scuffed piston	• Replace piston
	• Incorrect piston ring gap	• Measure ring gap, repair as necessary
	• Piston rings sticking or excessively loose in grooves	• Measure ring side clearance, repair as necessary
	• Compression rings installed upside down	• Repair as necessary
	• Cylinder walls worn, scored, or glazed	• Repair as necessary

Troubleshooting Engine Mechanical Problems (cont.)

Problem	Cause	Solution
	• Piston ring gaps not properly staggered	• Repair as necessary
	• Excessive main or connecting rod bearing clearance	• Measure bearing clearance, repair as necessary
No oil pressure	• Low oil level	• Add oil to correct level
	• Oil pressure gauge, warning lamp or sending unit inaccurate	• Replace oil pressure gauge or warning lamp
	• Oil pump malfunction	• Replace oil pump
	• Oil pressure relief valve sticking	• Remove and inspect oil pressure relief valve assembly
	• Oil passages on pressure side of pump obstructed	• Inspect oil passages for obstruction
	• Oil pickup screen or tube obstructed	• Inspect oil pickup for obstruction
	• Loose oil inlet tube	• Tighten or seal inlet tube
Low oil pressure	• Low oil level	• Add oil to correct level
	• Inaccurate gauge, warning lamp or sending unit	• Replace oil pressure gauge or warning lamp
	• Oil excessively thin because of dilution, poor quality, or improper grade	• Drain and refill crankcase with recommended oil
	• Excessive oil temperature	• Correct cause of overheating engine
	• Oil pressure relief spring weak or sticking	• Remove and inspect oil pressure relief valve assembly
	• Oil inlet tube and screen assembly has restriction or air leak	• Remove and inspect oil inlet tube and screen assembly. (Fill inlet tube with lacquer thinner to locate leaks.)
	• Excessive oil pump clearance	• Measure clearances
	• Excessive main, rod, or camshaft bearing clearance	• Measure bearing clearances, repair as necessary
High oil pressure	• Improper oil viscosity	• Drain and refill crankcase with correct viscosity oil
	• Oil pressure gauge or sending unit inaccurate	• Replace oil pressure gauge
	• Oil pressure relief valve sticking closed	• Remove and inspect oil pressure relief valve assembly
Main bearing noise	• Insufficient oil supply	• Inspect for low oil level and low oil pressure
	• Main bearing clearance excessive	• Measure main bearing clearance, repair as necessary
	• Bearing insert missing	• Replace missing insert
	• Crankshaft end play excessive	• Measure end play, repair as necessary
	• Improperly tightened main bearing cap bolts	• Tighten bolts with specified torque
	• Loose flywheel or drive plate	• Tighten flywheel or drive plate attaching bolts
	• Loose or damaged vibration damper	• Repair as necessary

Troubleshooting Engine Mechanical Problems (cont.)

Problem	Cause	Solution
Connecting rod bearing noise	• Insufficient oil supply	• Inspect for low oil level and low oil pressure
	• Carbon build-up on piston	• Remove carbon from piston crown
	• Bearing clearance excessive or bearing missing	• Measure clearance, repair as necessary
	• Crankshaft connecting rod journal out-of-round	• Measure journal dimensions, repair or replace as necessary
	• Misaligned connecting rod or cap	• Repair as necessary
	• Connecting rod bolts tightened improperly	• Tighten bolts with specified torque
Piston noise	• Piston-to-cylinder wall clearance excessive (scuffed piston)	• Measure clearance and examine piston
	• Cylinder walls excessively tapered or out-of-round	• Measure cylinder wall dimensions, rebore cylinder
	• Piston ring broken	• Replace all rings on piston
	• Loose or seized piston pin	• Measure piston-to-pin clearance, repair as necessary
	• Connecting rods misaligned	• Measure rod alignment, straighten or replace
	• Piston ring side clearance excessively loose or tight	• Measure ring side clearance, repair as necessary
	• Carbon build-up on piston is excessive	• Remove carbon from piston
Valve actuating component noise	• Insufficient oil supply	• Check for: (a) Low oil level (b) Low oil pressure (c) Plugged push rods (d) Wrong hydraulic tappets (e) Restricted oil gallery (f) Excessive tappet to bore clearance
	• Push rods worn or bent	• Replace worn or bent push rods
	• Rocker arms or pivots worn	• Replace worn rocker arms or pivots
	• Foreign objects or chips in hydraulic tappets	• Clean tappets
	• Excessive tappet leak-down	• Replace valve tappet
	• Tappet face worn	• Replace tappet; inspect corresponding cam lobe for wear
	• Broken or cocked valve springs	• Properly seat cocked springs; replace broken springs
	• Stem-to-guide clearance excessive	• Measure stem-to-guide clearance, repair as required
	• Valve bent	• Replace valve
	• Loose rocker arms	• Tighten bolts with specified torque
	• Valve seat runout excessive	• Regrind valve seat/valves
	• Missing valve lock	• Install valve lock
	• Push rod rubbing or contacting cylinder head	• Remove cylinder head and remove obstruction in head
	• Excessive engine oil (four-cylinder engine)	• Correct oil level

Troubleshooting the Cooling System

Problem	Cause	Solution
High temperature gauge indication—overheating	• Coolant level low	• Replenish coolant
	• Fan belt loose	• Adjust fan belt tension
	• Radiator hose(s) collapsed	• Replace hose(s)
	• Radiator airflow blocked	• Remove restriction (bug screen, fog lamps, etc.)
	• Faulty radiator cap	• Replace radiator cap
	• Ignition timing incorrect	• Adjust ignition timing
	• Idle speed low	• Adjust idle speed
	• Air trapped in cooling system	• Purge air
	• Heavy traffic driving	• Operate at fast idle in neutral intermittently to cool engine
	• Incorrect cooling system component(s) installed	• Install proper component(s)
	• Faulty thermostat	• Replace thermostat
	• Water pump shaft broken or impeller loose	• Replace water pump
	• Radiator tubes clogged	• Flush radiator
	• Cooling system clogged	• Flush system
	• Casting flash in cooling passages	• Repair or replace as necessary. Flash may be visible by removing cooling system components or removing core plugs.
	• Brakes dragging	• Repair brakes
	• Excessive engine friction	• Repair engine
	• Antifreeze concentration over 68%	• Lower antifreeze concentration percentage
	• Missing air seals	• Replace air seals
	• Faulty gauge or sending unit	• Repair or replace faulty component
	• Loss of coolant flow caused by leakage or foaming	• Repair or replace leaking component, replace coolant
	• Viscous fan drive failed	• Replace unit
Low temperature indication—undercooling	• Thermostat stuck open	• Replace thermostat
	• Faulty gauge or sending unit	• Repair or replace faulty component
Coolant loss—boilover	• Overfilled cooling system	• Reduce coolant level to proper specification
	• Quick shutdown after hard (hot) run	• Allow engine to run at fast idle prior to shutdown
	• Air in system resulting in occasional "burping" of coolant	• Purge system
	• Insufficient antifreeze allowing coolant boiling point to be too low	• Add antifreeze to raise boiling point
	• Antifreeze deteriorated because of age or contamination	• Replace coolant
	• Leaks due to loose hose clamps, loose nuts, bolts, drain plugs, faulty hoses, or defective radiator	• Pressure test system to locate source of leak(s) then repair as necessary

Troubleshooting the Cooling System (cont.)

Problem	Cause	Solution
Coolant loss—boilover	• Faulty head gasket • Cracked head, manifold, or block • Faulty radiator cap	• Replace head gasket • Replace as necessary • Replace cap
Coolant entry into crankcase or cylinder(s)	• Faulty head gasket • Crack in head, manifold or block	• Replace head gasket • Replace as necessary
Coolant recovery system inoperative	• Coolant level low • Leak in system • Pressure cap not tight or seal missing, or leaking • Pressure cap defective • Overflow tube clogged or leaking • Recovery bottle vent restricted	• Replenish coolant to FULL mark • Pressure test to isolate leak and repair as necessary • Repair as necessary • Replace cap • Repair as necessary • Remove restriction
Noise	• Fan contacting shroud • Loose water pump impeller • Glazed fan belt • Loose fan belt • Rough surface on drive pulley • Water pump bearing worn • Belt alignment	• Reposition shroud and inspect engine mounts • Replace pump • Apply silicone or replace belt • Adjust fan belt tension • Replace pulley • Remove belt to isolate. Replace pump. • Check pulley alignment. Repair as necessary.
No coolant flow through heater core	• Restricted return inlet in water pump • Heater hose collapsed or restricted • Restricted heater core • Restricted outlet in thermostat housing • Intake manifold bypass hole in cylinder head restricted • Faulty heater control valve • Intake manifold coolant passage restricted	• Remove restriction • Remove restriction or replace hose • Remove restriction or replace core • Remove flash or restriction • Remove restriction • Replace valve • Remove restriction or replace intake manifold

NOTE: *Immediately after shutdown, the engine enters a condition known as heat soak. This is caused by the cooling system being inoperative while engine temperature is still high. If coolant temperature rises above boiling point, expansion and pressure may push some coolant out of the radiator overflow tube. If this does not occur frequently it is considered normal.*

Troubleshooting the Serpentine Drive Belt

Problem	Cause	Solution
Tension sheeting fabric failure (woven fabric on outside circumference of belt has cracked or separated from body of belt)	• Grooved or backside idler pulley diameters are less than minimum recommended	• Replace pulley(s) not conforming to specification
	• Tension sheeting contacting (rubbing) stationary object	• Correct rubbing condition
	• Excessive heat causing woven fabric to age	• Replace belt
	• Tension sheeting splice has fractured	• Replace belt
Noise (objectional squeal, squeak, or rumble is heard or felt while drive belt is in operation)	• Belt slippage	• Adjust belt
	• Bearing noise	• Locate and repair
	• Belt misalignment	• Align belt/pulley(s)
	• Belt-to-pulley mismatch	• Install correct belt
	• Driven component inducing vibration	• Locate defective driven component and repair
	• System resonant frequency inducing vibration	• Vary belt tension within specifications. Replace belt.
Rib chunking (one or more ribs has separated from belt body)	• Foreign objects imbedded in pulley grooves	• Remove foreign objects from pulley grooves
	• Installation damage	• Replace belt
	• Drive loads in excess of design specifications	• Adjust belt tension
	• Insufficient internal belt adhesion	• Replace belt
Rib or belt wear (belt ribs contact bottom of pulley grooves)	• Pulley(s) misaligned	• Align pulley(s)
	• Mismatch of belt and pulley groove widths	• Replace belt
	• Abrasive environment	• Replace belt
	• Rusted pulley(s)	• Clean rust from pulley(s)
	• Sharp or jagged pulley groove tips	• Replace pulley
	• Rubber deteriorated	• Replace belt
Longitudinal belt cracking (cracks between two ribs)	• Belt has mistracked from pulley groove	• Replace belt
	• Pulley groove tip has worn away rubber-to-tensile member	• Replace belt
Belt slips	• Belt slipping because of insufficient tension	• Adjust tension
	• Belt or pulley subjected to substance (belt dressing, oil, ethylene glycol) that has reduced friction	• Replace belt and clean pulleys
	• Driven component bearing failure	• Replace faulty component bearing
	• Belt glazed and hardened from heat and excessive slippage	• Replace belt
"Groove jumping" (belt does not maintain correct position on pulley, or turns over and/or runs off pulleys)	• Insufficient belt tension	• Adjust belt tension
	• Pulley(s) not within design tolerance	• Replace pulley(s)
	• Foreign object(s) in grooves	• Remove foreign objects from grooves

Troubleshooting the Serpentine Drive Belt (cont.)

Problem	Cause	Solution
"Groove jumping" (belt does not maintain correct position on pulley, or turns over and/or runs off pulleys)	• Excessive belt speed • Pulley misalignment • Belt-to-pulley profile mismatched • Belt cordline is distorted	• Avoid excessive engine acceleration • Align pulley(s) • Install correct belt • Replace belt
Belt broken (Note: identify and correct problem before replacement belt is installed)	• Excessive tension • Tensile members damaged during belt installation • Belt turnover • Severe pulley misalignment • Bracket, pulley, or bearing failure	• Replace belt and adjust tension to specification • Replace belt • Replace belt • Align pulley(s) • Replace defective component and belt
Cord edge failure (tensile member exposed at edges of belt or separated from belt body)	• Excessive tension • Drive pulley misalignment • Belt contacting stationary object • Pulley irregularities • Improper pulley construction • Insufficient adhesion between tensile member and rubber matrix	• Adjust belt tension • Align pulley • Correct as necessary • Replace pulley • Replace pulley • Replace belt and adjust tension to specifications
Sporadic rib cracking (multiple cracks in belt ribs at random intervals)	• Ribbed pulley(s) diameter less than minimum specification • Backside bend flat pulley(s) diameter less than minimum • Excessive heat condition causing rubber to harden • Excessive belt thickness • Belt overcured • Excessive tension	• Replace pulley(s) • Replace pulley(s) • Correct heat condition as necessary • Replace belt • Replace belt • Adjust belt tension

EXHAUST SYSTEM

Two types of pipe connections are used on the exhaust system, they are: the ball joint (to allow angular movement for alignment purposes) and the slip joint. Gaskets are used only with the ball joint type connections.

The system is supported by free hanging rubber mountings which permit some movement of the exhaust system but do not allow the transfer of noise and vibration into the passenger compartment. Any noise vibrations or rattles in the exhaust system are usually caused by misalignment of the parts.

CAUTION

Before performing any operation on the exhaust system, be sure to allow it to cool.

Front Pipe

REMOVAL AND INSTALLATION

NOTE: The following procedure requires the use of GM Sealing Compound No. 1051249 or equivalent, at the slip joint connection.

1. Raise and support the vehicle safely.
2. Remove the front pipe(s)-to-manifold(s) nuts and separate (pry, if necessary) the front pipe (ball joint) from the exhaust manifold(s).
3. At the catalytic converter, loosen the front pipe-to-converter clamp nuts, then slide the clamp away from the converter and separate the front pipe from the converter.

NOTE: Use a twisting motion to separate the front pipe-to-converter slip joint connection. If the front pipe cannot be removed from the catalytic converter, use a hammer (to loosen the connection) or wedge tool to separate the connection.

4. Inspect the pipe for holes, damage or deterioration; if necessary, replace the front pipe.
5. Installation is the reverse of removal.
6. Lubricate the front pipe-to-manifold(s) studs/nuts and the front pipe-to-converter clamp threads. Torque the front pipe-to-exhaust manifold bolts to 15 ft. lbs. and the front pipe-to-converter clamp nuts to 35 ft. lbs.
7. Start the engine and check for exhaust leaks.

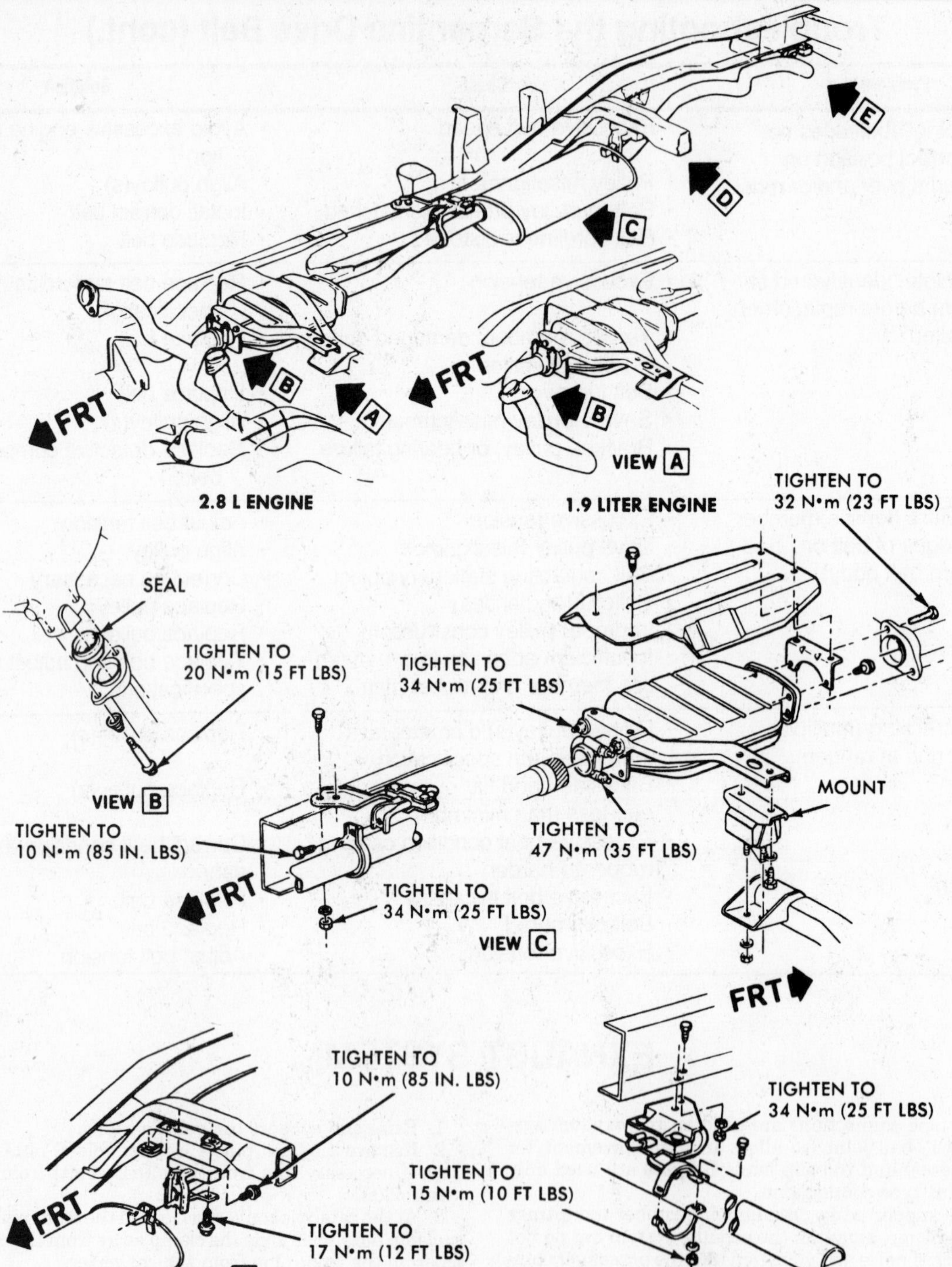
FRT
A
B
C
D
E
2.8 L ENGINE
FRT
B
VIEW A
1.9 LITER ENGINE
TIGHTEN TO
32 N•m (23 FT LBS)
SEAL
TIGHTEN TO
20 N•m (15 FT LBS)
TIGHTEN TO
34 N•m (25 FT LBS)
VIEW B
TIGHTEN TO
10 N•m (85 IN. LBS)
FRT
TIGHTEN TO
34 N•m (25 FT LBS)
VIEW C
TIGHTEN TO
47 N•m (35 FT LBS)
MOUNT
FRT
TIGHTEN TO
10 N•m (85 IN. LBS)
FRT
TIGHTEN TO
17 N•m (12 FT LBS)
VIEW D
TIGHTEN TO
34 N•m (25 FT LBS)
TIGHTEN TO
15 N•m (10 FT LBS)
VIEW E

Exhaust system components — typical

Catalytic Converter

The catalytic converter is an emission control device added to the exhaust system to reduce the emission of hydrocarbon and carbon monoxide pollutants.

NOTE: The following procedure requires the use of GM Sealing Compound No. 1051249 or equivalent, at the slip joint connection.

NOTE: When installing the catalytic converter, be sure that it is installed with adequate clearance from the floor pan, to prevent overheating of the vehicle floor.

REMOVAL AND INSTALLATION

1. Raise and support the vehicle safely.

2. Remove the catalytic converter-to-muffler bolts and separate the muffler from the converter.

NOTE: The connection between the converter and the muffler is a ball joint type, which can be easily separated.

3. Remove the catalytic converter-to-front pipe clamp nuts and move the clamp forward.
4. Remove the converter-to-mounting bracket bolts, then twist the converter to separate it from the front pipe.
5. Inspect the condition of the catalytic converter for physical damage, replace it, if necessary.
6. Align the components and reverse the removal procedures.
7. Torque the converter-to-mounting bracket bolts to 25 ft. lbs., the converter-to-front pipe clamp nuts to 35 ft. lbs. and the converter-to-muffler bolts to 23 ft. lbs. Be careful not to damage the pipe sealing surfaces when tightening the retaining clamps.
8. Start the engine and check for exhaust leaks.

Muffler

REMOVAL AND INSTALLATION

1. Remove the catalytic converter-to-muffler flange bolts and separate the items.
2. Remove the intermediate and rear tail pipe-to-bracket clamp nuts/bolts.
3. Remove the muffler bracket-to-chassis bolts and lower the muffler from the vehicle.
4. Coat the slip joints with GM Sealing Compound No. 1051249 or equivalent, and loosely install the components onto the vehicle.
5. After aligning the components, tighten the connecting bolts and clamps. Torque the muffler bracket-to-chassis bolts 12 ft. lbs., the rear tail pipe-to-bracket clamp nuts/bolts to 25 ft. lbs., the intermediate pipe-to-chassis bracket bolt to 85 inch lbs. and the muffler-to-converter bolts to 23 ft. lbs.
6. Start the engine and check for exhaust leaks.

TROUBLESHOOTING

Engine Speed Oscillates at Idle

When the engine idle speed will not remain constant, replace or repair the following items or systems, as necessary:

- A faulty fuel pump.
- A leaky Exhaust Gas Recirculation (EGR) valve.
- A blown head gasket.
- A worn camshaft.
- Worn timing gears, chain or sprockets.
- Leaking intake manifold-to-engine gasket.
- A blocked Positive Crankcase Ventilation (PCV) valve.
- Overheating of the cooling system.

Low Power Output of Engine

When the engine power output is below normal, replace or repair the following items or systems, as necessary:

- Overheating of the cooling system.
- Leaks in the vacuum system.
- Leaking of the fuel pump or hoses.
- Unadjusted valve timing.
- A blown head gasket.
- A slipping clutch disc or unadjusted pedal.
- Excessive piston-to-bore clearance.
- Worn piston rings.
- A worn camshaft.
- Sticking valve(s) or weak valve spring(s).
- A poorly operating diverter valve.
- A faulty pressure regulator valve (Auto. Trans.).
- Low fluid level (Auto. Trans.).

Poor High Speed Operation

When the engine cannot maintain high speed operations, replace or repair the following items or systems, as necessary:

- A faulty fuel pump producing low fuel volume.
- A restriction in the intake manifold.
- A worn distributor shaft.
- Unadjusted valve timing.
- Leaking valves or worn valve springs.

Poor Acceleration

When the engine experiences poor acceleration characteristics, replace or repair the following items or systems, as necessary:

- Incorrect ignition timing.
- Poorly seated valves.
- Improperly adjusted accelerator pump stroke (carburetor equipped).
- Worn accelerator pump diaphragm or piston (carburetor equipped).

Backfire – Intake Manifold

When the engine backfires through the intake manifold, replace or repair the following items or systems, as necessary:

- Incorrect ignition timing.
- Incorrect operation of the choke (carburetor equipped).
- Choke setting (initial clearance) too large (carburetor equipped).
- Defective Exhaust Gas Recirculation (EGR) valve.
- A very lean air/fuel mixture (carburetor equipped).

Backfire – Exhaust Manifold

When the engine backfires through the exhaust manifold, replace or repair the following items or systems, as necessary:

- Leaks in the vacuum hose system.
- Leaks in the exhaust system.
- Faulty choke adjustments or operation (carburetor equipped).
- Faulty vacuum diverter valve.

Engine Detonation (Dieseling)

When the engine operates beyond the controlled limits, replace or repair the following items or systems, as necessary:

- Faulty ignition electrical system components.
- The ignition timing may be too far advanced.
- Inoperative Exhaust Gas Recirculation (EGR) valve.
- Inoperative Positive Crankcase Ventilation (PCV) valve.
- Faulty or loose spark plugs.
- Clogged fuel delivery system.
- Sticking, leaking or broken valves.
- Excessive deposits in the combustion chambers.
- Leaks in the vacuum system.

Excessive Oil Leakage

When large amounts of oil are noticed under the engine after each operation, replace or repair the following items or systems, as necessary:

- Damaged or broken oil filter gasket.
- Leaking oil pressure sending switch.
- Worn rear main oil seal gasket.
- Worn front main oil seal gasket.
- Damaged or broken fuel pump gasket (mechanical pump).
- Damaged or loose valve cover gasket.
- Damaged oil pan gasket or bent oil pan.
- Improperly seated oil pan drain plug.
- Broken timing chain cover gasket.
- Blocked camshaft bearing drain hole.

Heavy Oil Consumption

When the engine is burning large amounts of oil, replace or repair the following items or systems, as necessary:

- The engine oil level may be to high.
- The engine oil may be to thin.
- Wrong size of piston rings.
- Clogged piston ring grooves or oil return slots.
- Insufficient tension of the piston rings.
- Piston rings may be sticking in the grooves.
- Excessively worn piston ring grooves.
- Reversed (up-side-down) compression rings.
- Non-staggered piston ring gaps.
- Improper Positive Crankcase Ventilation (PCV) valve operation.
- Damaged valve O-ring seals.
- Restricted oil drain back holes.
- Worn valve stem or guides.
- Damaged valve stem oil deflectors.
- Too long intake gasket dowels.
- Mismatched rail and expander of the oil ring.
- Excessive clearance of the main and connecting rods.
- Scored or worn cylinder walls.

Negative Oil Pressure

When the engine presents no oil pressure, replace or repair the following items or systems, as necessary:

- Low oil level in the crankcase.
- Broken oil pressure gauge or sender.
- Blocked oil pump passages.
- Blocked oil pickup screen or tube.
- Malfunctioning oil pump.
- Sticking oil pressure relief valve.
- Leakage of the internal oil passages.
- Worn (loose) camshaft bearings.

Low Oil Pressure

When the engine presents low oil pressure, replace or repair the following items or systems, as necessary:

- Low oil level in the crankcase.
- Blocked oil pickup screen or tube.
- Malfunctioning or excessive clearance of the oil pump.
- Sticking oil pressure relief valve.
- Very thin engine oil.
- Worn (loose) main, rod or camshaft bearings.

High Oil Pressure

When the engine presents high oil pressure, replace or repair the following items or systems, as necessary:

- Sticking (closed) oil pressure relief valve.
- Wrong grade of oil.
- Faulty oil pressure gauge or sender.

Knocking Main Bearings

When the main bearings are constantly making noise, replace or repair the following items or systems, as necessary:

- Oval shaped crankshaft journals.
- Loose torque converter or flywheel mounting bolts.
- Loose damper pulley hub.
- Excessive clearance of the main bearings.
- Excessive belt tension.
- Low oil supply to the main bearings.
- Extreme crankshaft end play.

Knocking Connecting Rods

When the connecting rod bearings are constantly making noise, replace or repair the following items or systems, as necessary:

- Misaligned connecting rod or cap.
- Missing bearing shell or excessive bearing clearance.
- Incorrectly torqued connecting rod bolts.
- Connecting rod journal of the crankshaft is out-of-round.

Knocking Pistons and Rings

When the pistons and/rings are constantly making noise, replace or repair the following items or systems, as necessary:

- Misaligned connecting rods.
- Out-of-round or tapered cylinder bore.
- Loose or tight ring side clearance.
- Build-up of carbon on the piston(s).
- Piston-to-cylinder bore clearance is excessive.
- Broken piston rings.
- Loose or seized piston pin(s).

Knocking Valve Train

When the valve train is constantly making noise, replace or repair the following items or systems, as necessary:

- Retighten any loose rocker arms.
- Remove any dirt or chips in the valve lifters.
- Excessive valve stem-to-guide clearance.
- Remove restrictions from valve lifter oil holes.
- Incorrect valve lifter may be installed in the engine.
- Valve lock(s) may be missing.
- Valve lifter check ball may be faulty.
- Valve lifter leak down may be excessive.
- Rocker arm nut may be reversed (installed up-side-down).
- Camshaft lobes may be excessively worn.
- Bent or worn pushrods.
- Excessively worn bridged pivots or rocker arms.
- Cocked or broken valve springs.
- Bent valve(s).
- Worn valve lifter face(s).
- Damaged lifter plunger or pushrod seat.

Knocking Valves

When the valves are constantly noisy, replace or repair the following items or systems, as necessary:

- Unadjusted valve lash.
- Valve springs may be broken.
- Pushrods may be bent.
- Camshaft lobes may be excessively worn.
- Dirty or worn valve lifters.
- Valve guides may be worn.
- Valve seat or face runout may be excessive.
- Loose rocker arm studs.

4 Emission Controls

QUICK REFERENCE INDEX

GENERAL INDEX

EMISSION CONTROLS

Crankcase Ventilation System

OPERATION

The Positive Crankcase Ventilation (PCV) system is used on all vehicles to evacuate the crankcase vapors. Outside vehicle air is routed through the air cleaner to the crankcase where it mixes with blow-by gases and is passed through the PCV valve. The air is then routed into the intake manifold to be burned in the combustion process. The PCV valve meters the air flow rate, which varies under engine operation, depending on manifold vacuum. In order to maintain idle quality, the PCV valve limits the air flow when intake manifold vacuum is high. If abnormal operating conditions occur, the system will allow excessive blow-by gases to back flow through the crankcase vent tube into the air cleaner. These blow-by gases will then be burned by normal combustion.

On the 1.9L engine, the blow by gases are forced back into the intake manifold through a closed loop system which consists of a baffle plate and an orifice mounted in the intake manifold.

A plugged PCV valve or hose may cause rough idle, stalling or slow idle speed, oil leaks, oil in the air cleaner or sludge in the engine. A leaking PCV valve or hose could cause rough idle, stalling or high idle speed.

Inspect the PCV system hose(s) and connections at each tune-up and replace any deteriorated hoses. Check the PCV valve at every tune-up and replace it at 30,000 mile intervals.

TESTING

1. Remove the PCV valve from the rocker arm cover.
2. Operate the engine at idle speed.
3. Place your thumb over the end of the valve to check for vacuum. If no vacuum exists, check the valve, the hoses or the manifold port for a plugged condition.
4. Remove the valve from the hose(s), then shake it and listen for a rattling of the check needle (inside the valve); the rattle means the valve is working. If no rattle is heard, replace the valve.

REMOVAL AND INSTALLATION

1. Pull the PCV valve from the rocker arm cover grommet.
2. Remove the hose(s) from the PCV valve.
3. Shake the valve to make sure that it is not plugged.
4. Installation is the reverse of removal. Always install a new PCV valve.

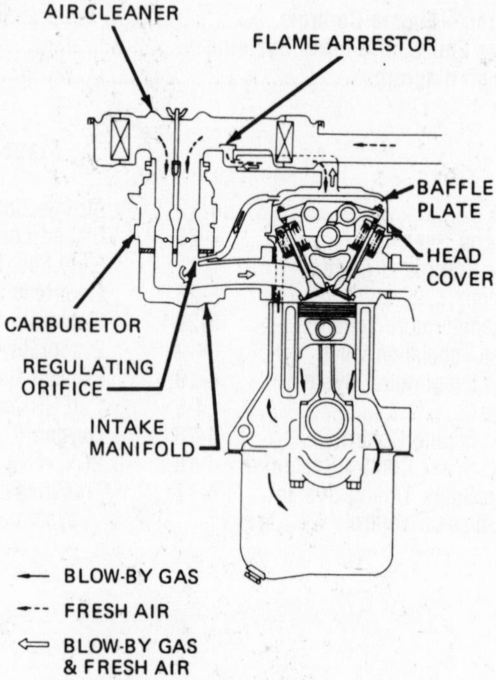
AIR CLEANER
FLAME ARRESTOR
BAFFLE PLATE
HEAD COVER
CARBURETOR
REGULATING ORIFICE
INTAKE MANIFOLD
BLOW-BY GAS
FRESH AIR
BLOW-BY GAS & FRESH AIR

PCV system — 1.9L engine

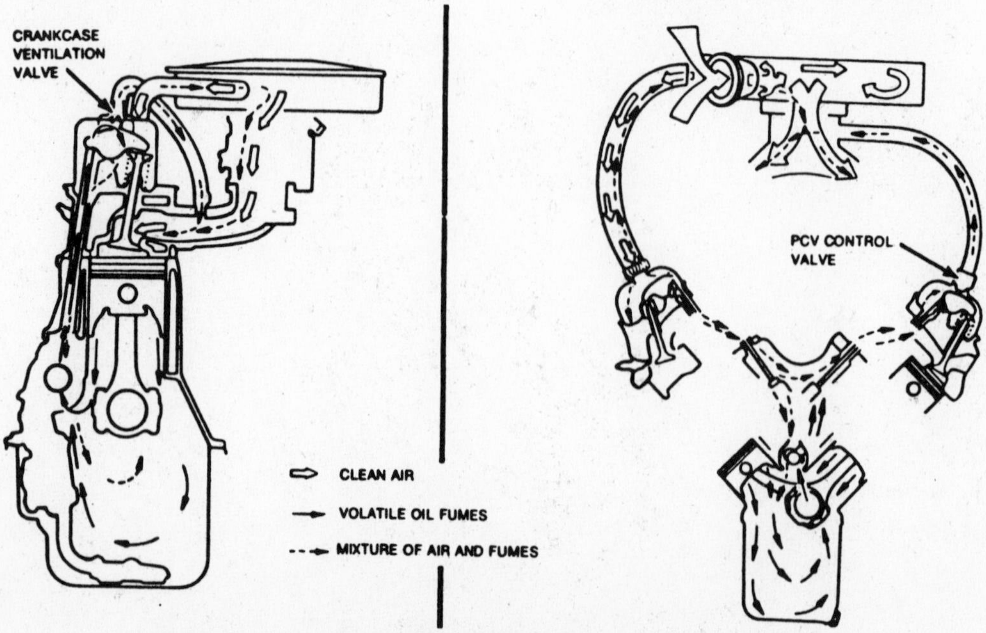
CRANKCASE VENTILATION VALVE
CLEAN AIR
VOLATILE OIL FUMES
MIXTURE OF AIR AND FUMES
PCV CONTROL VALVE

Positive crankcase ventilation (PCV) system diagram

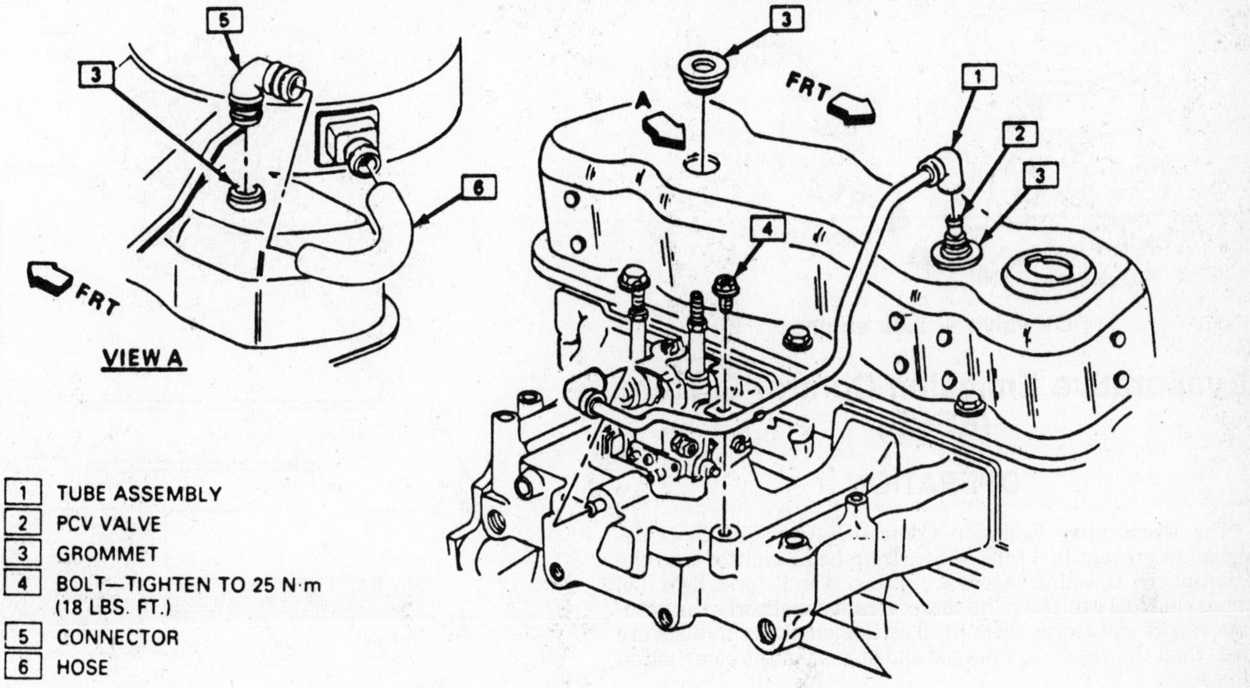
VIEW A
FRT
A
1 TUBE ASSEMBLY
2 PCV VALVE
3 GROMMET
4 BOLT—TIGHTEN TO 25 N·m (18 LBS. FT.)
5 CONNECTOR
6 HOSE

PCV system – 2.5L engine

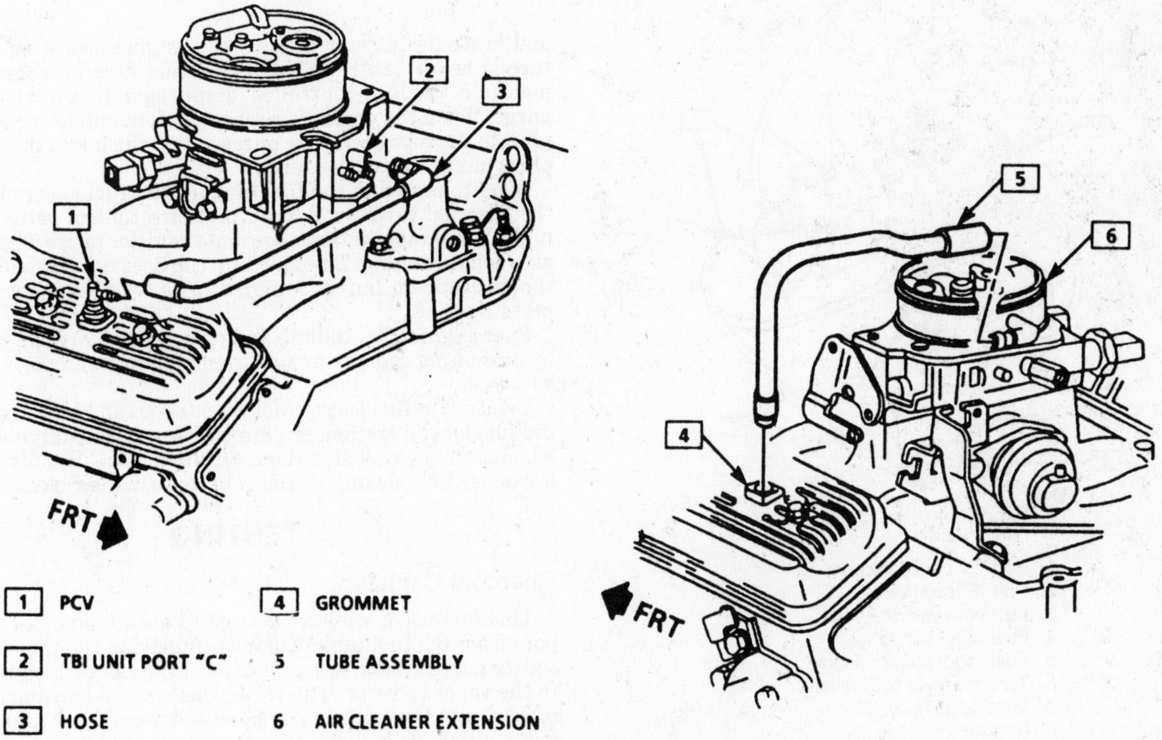
FRT
1 PCV
2 TBI UNIT PORT "C"
3 HOSE
4 GROMMET
5 TUBE ASSEMBLY
6 AIR CLEANER EXTENSION

PCV system – 4.3L engine

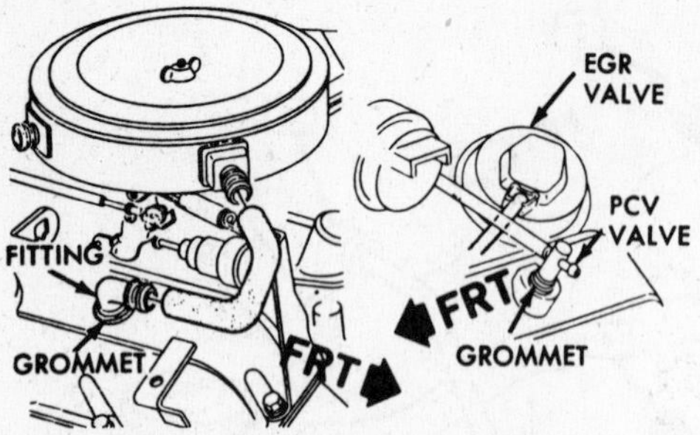
EGR
VALVE
PCV
VALVE
FITTING
GROMMET
GROMMET
FRT
FRT

PCV valve – 2.8L engine

Evaporative Emission Control System (EECS)

OPERATION

The Evaporative Emission Control System (EECS) is designed to prevent fuel tank vapors from being emitted into the atmosphere. Gasoline vapors are absorbed and stored by a fuel vapor charcoal canister. The charcoal canister absorbs the gasoline vapors and stores them until certain engine conditions are met, then the vapors are purged and burned in the combustion process.

The charcoal canister purge cycle is controlled either by a thermostatic vacuum switch or by a timed vacuum source. The thermostatic vacuum switch is installed in the coolant passage

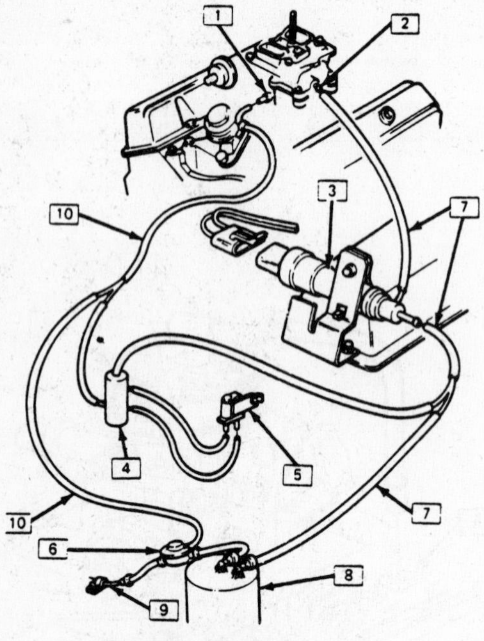

1. Port "B" ported vacuum
2. Port "F" bowl vent
3. Fuel bowl vent solenoid
4. Fuel vapor connector
5. Fuel vapor purge solenoid
6. Tank pressure control valve
7. Vent/purge hose
8. Canister
9. Tank vapor vent pipe
10. Ported vacuum line

EEC system – 2.8L engine

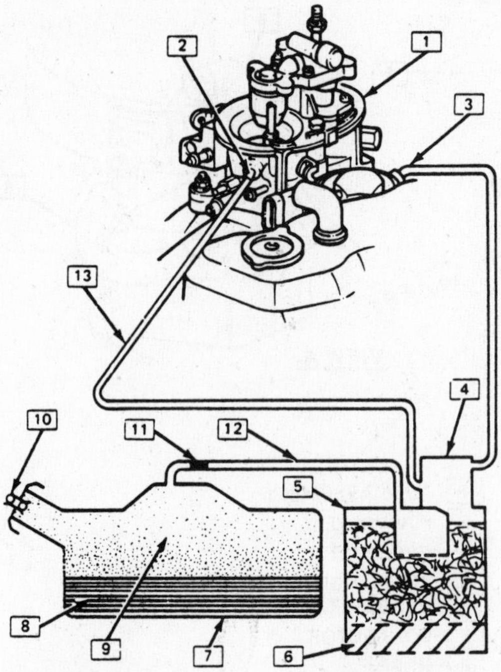

1. TBI
2. Canister purge port
3. Vacuum signal
4. Purge valve
5. Vapor storage canister
6. Purge air
7. Fuel tank
8. Fuel
9. Vapor
10. Pressure-vacuum relief gas cap
11. Vent restricter
12. Fuel tank vent
13. Purge line

EEC system – 2.5L and 4.3L engines

and prevents canister purge when engine operating temperature is below 115°F (46°C). The timed vacuum source uses a manifold vacuum-controlled diaphragm to control canister purge. When the engine is running, full manifold vacuum is applied to the top tube of the purge valve which lifts the valve diaphragm and opens the valve.

A vent, located in the fuel tank, allows fuel vapors to flow to the charcoal canister. A tank pressure control valve, used on high altitude applications, prevents canister purge when the engine is not running. The fuel tank cap does not normally vent to the atmosphere but is designed to provide both vacuum and pressure relief.

Poor engine idle, stalling and poor driveability can be caused by a damaged canister or split, damaged or improperly connected hoses.

Evidence of fuel loss or fuel vapor odor can be caused by a liquid fuel leak; a cracked or damaged vapor canister; disconnected, misrouted, kinked or damaged vapor pipe or canister hoses; a damaged air cleaner or improperly seated air cleaner gasket.

TESTING

Charcoal Canister

This fuel vapor canister is used to absorb and store fuel vapors from the fuel tank. Engines employing the timed vacuum source purge system use a canister purge valve which is integral to the vapor canister. The valve consists of a housing and tube molded into the canister cover, valve assembly, diaphragm and valve spring. The diaphragm cover has a built-in control vacuum signal tube.

NOTE: The 2.2L diesel engine is not equipped with a charcoal canister.

1. Remove the lower tube of the canister (purge valve) and install a short length of tube, then try to blow through it (little or no air should pass).
2. Using a vacuum source, apply 15 in.Hg to the upper tube of the canister (purge valve). The diaphragm should hold the vacuum for at least 20 seconds, if not replace the canister.
3. While holding the vacuum on the upper tube, blow through the lower tube (air should now pass); if not, replace the canister.

Thermostatic Vacuum Switch (TVS)

NOTE: The number stamped on the base of the switch (valve) is the calibration temperature.

1. With engine temperature below 100°F (38°C), apply vacuum to the manifold side of the switch. The switch should hold vacuum.
2. As the engine temperature increases above 122°F (50°C), vacuum should drop off.
3. Replace the switch if it fails either test.

NOTE: A leakage of up to 2 in.Hg/2 min. is allowable and does not mean that the valve is defective.

REMOVAL AND INSTALLATION

Charcoal Canister

1. Label and disconnect the hoses from the canister.
2. Loosen the retaining bolt and remove the canister from the vehicle.

NOTE: If necessary to replace the canister filter, simply pull the filter from the bottom of the charcoal filter and install a new one.

3. Installation is the reverse of removal.

Thermostatic Vacuum Switch (TVS)

The TVS is located near the engine coolant outlet housing.

1. Drain the cooling system to a level below the TVS.

CAUTION

When draining the coolant, keep in mind that cats and dogs are attracted by the ethylene glycol antifreeze, and are quite likely to drink any that is left in an uncovered container or in puddles on the ground. This will prove fatal in sufficient quantity. Always drain the coolant into a sealable container. Coolant should be reused unless it is contaminated or several years old.

2. Disconnect the vacuum hoses from the TVS.
3. Using a wrench, remove the TVS from the engine.
4. Inspect and test the TVS; if defective, replace it.
5. Apply a soft setting sealant to the TVS threads. Install the TVS and torque to 120 inch lbs.
6. Reconnect the vacuum hoses. Refill the cooling system.

NOTE: DO NOT apply sealant to the sensor end of the TVS.

Exhaust Gas Recirculation (EGR) System

OPERATION

The EGR system is used to reduce oxides of nitrogen (NOx) emission levels caused by high combustion chamber temperatures. This is accomplished by the use of an EGR valve which opens, under specific engine operating conditions, to admit a small amount of exhaust gas into the intake manifold, below the throttle plate. The exhaust gas mixes with the incoming air charge and displaces a portion of the oxygen in the air/fuel mixture entering the combustion chamber. The exhaust gas does not support combustion of the air/fuel mixture but it takes up volume, the net effect of which is to lower the temperature of the combustion process.

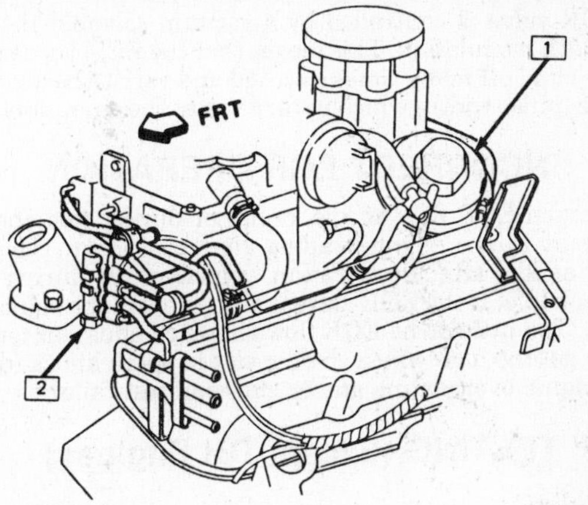
FRT
1
2

1. EGR valve
2. TVS

Location of the Thermostatic Vacuum Switch on the

The EGR valve is a mounted on the intake manifold and has an opening into the exhaust manifold. The EGR valve is opened by manifold vacuum to permit exhaust gas to flow into the intake manifold. If too much exhaust gas enters, combustion will not occur. Because of this, very little exhaust gas is allowed to pass through the valve. The EGR system will be activated once the engine reaches normal operating temperature and the EGR valve will open when engine operating conditions are above idle speed and, in some applications, below Wide Open Throttle (WOT). The EGR system is deactivated on vehicles equipped with a Transmission Converter Clutch (TCC) when the TCC is engaged. There are 2 basic types of systems as described below.

Ported EGR Valve

This valve is controlled by a flexible diaphragm. It is spring-loaded in order to hold the valve closed. When ported vacuum is applied to the top side of the diaphragm, spring pressure is overcome and the valve in the exhaust gas port is opened. This allows the exhaust gas to be pulled into the intake manifold and enter the cylinders with the air/fuel mixture. Port EGR valves have no identification stamped below the part number.

Negative Backpressure EGR Valve

The negative backpressure EGR valve is similar to the positive backpressure EGR valve, except that the bleed valve spring is moved from above the diaphragm to below and the valve is normally closed. The negative backpressure valve varies the amount of exhaust gas flow into the intake manifold depending on manifold vacuum and variations in exhaust backpressure. The diaphragm on the valve has an internal air bleed hole which is held closed by a small spring when there is no exhaust backpressure. Engine vacuum opens the EGR valve against the pressure of a spring. When manifold vacuum combines with negative exhaust backpressure, the vacuum bleed hole opens and the EGR valve closes. This valve will open if vacuum is applied with the engine not running. Negative backpressure EGR valves will have a "N" stamped on the top side of the valve below the part number and after the date built.

ELECTRONIC EGR CONTROL

On certain vehicle applications, EGR flow is regulated by an ECM-controlled Electronic Vacuum Regulator Valve (EVRV).

The EGR valve is controlled by a vacuum solenoid that uses pulse width modulation. This means that the ECM turns the solenoid on and off many times a second and varies the amount of ON time (pulse width) which in turn varies the amount of EGR.

INCORRECT EGR OPERATION

Too much EGR flow at idle, cruise or during cold operation may result in the engine stalling after cold start, the engine stalling at idle after deceleration, vehicle surge during cruise and rough idle. If the EGR valve is always open, the vehicle may not idle. Too little or no EGR flow allows combustion temperatures to get too high which could result in spark knock (detonation), engine overheating and/or emission test failure.

TESTING (Except TBI Engines)

EGR Valve

1. Check hose routing (Refer to Vehicle Emission Control Information Label).

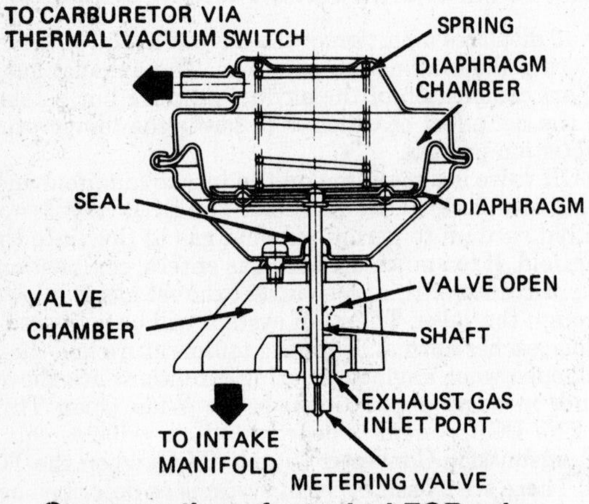
TO CARBURETOR VIA
THERMAL VACUUM SWITCH
SPRING
DIAPHRAGM
CHAMBER
SEAL
DIAPHRAGM
VALVE
CHAMBER
VALVE OPEN
SHAFT
EXHAUST GAS
INLET PORT
TO INTAKE
MANIFOLD
METERING VALVE

Cross section of a typical EGR valve

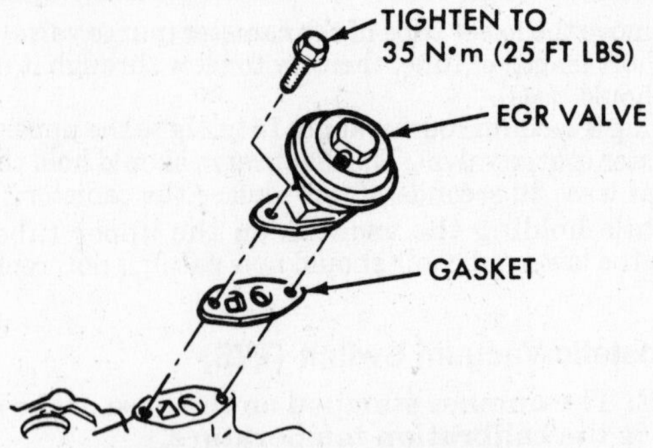
TIGHTEN TO
35 N•m (25 FT LBS)
EGR VALVE
GASKET

EGR valve — 2.8L engine

2. Check the EGR valve signal tube orifice for obstructions.
3. Connect a vacuum gauge between EGR valve and carburetor, then check the vacuum; the engine must be at operating temperature of 195°F (90°C). With the engine running at approximately 3000 rpm there should be at least 5 in.Hg.
4. Check the EGR solenoid for correct operation.
5. To check the valve, perform the following procedures:
   a. Depress the valve diaphragm.

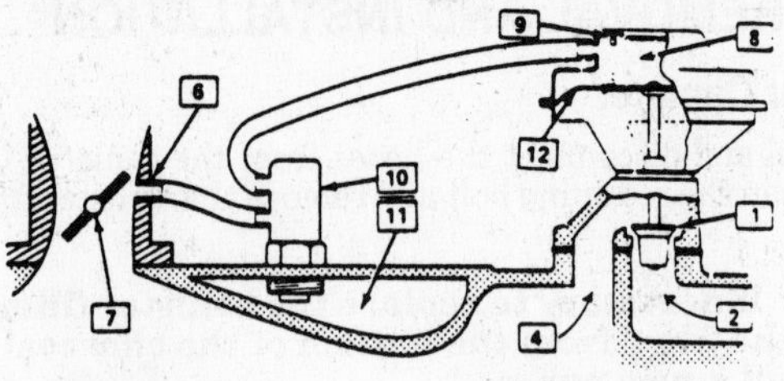
1
2
4
6
7
8
9
10
11
12

1. EGR valve
2. Exhaust gas
4. Intake flow
6. Vacuum port
7. Throttle valve
8. Vacuum chamber
9. Valve return spring
10. Thermal vacuum switch
11. Coolant
12. Diaphragm

EGR system — 2.8L carbureted engine

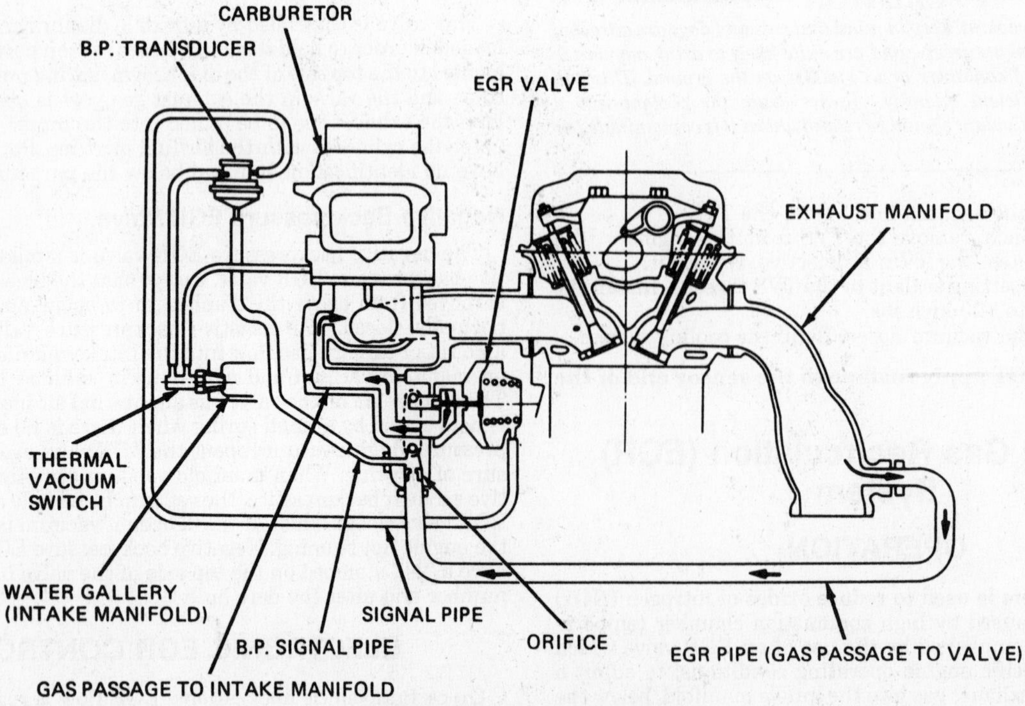
CARBURETOR
B.P. TRANSDUCER
EGR VALVE
EXHAUST MANIFOLD
THERMAL
VACUUM
SWITCH
WATER GALLERY
(INTAKE MANIFOLD)
SIGNAL PIPE
B.P. SIGNAL PIPE
ORIFICE
EGR PIPE (GAS PASSAGE TO VALVE)
GAS PASSAGE TO INTAKE MANIFOLD

EGR system — 1.9L engine

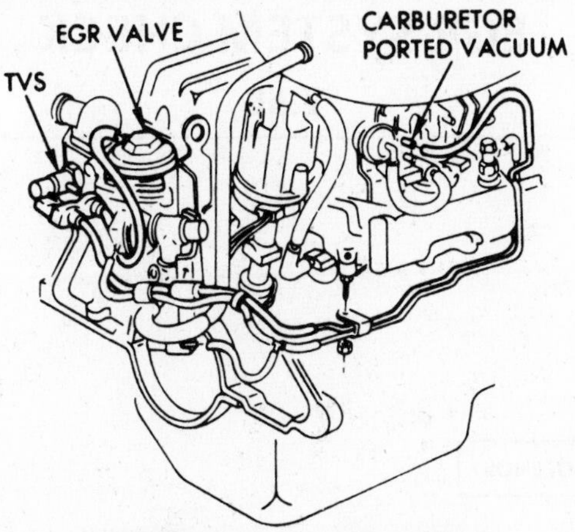
EGR VALVE
TVS
CARBURETOR
PORTED VACUUM

EGR system – 2.0L engine

b. With the diaphragm still depressed hold finger over source tube and release the diaphragm.

c. Check the diaphragm and seat for movement. The valve is good if it takes over 20 seconds for the diaphragm to move to the seated position (valve closed).

d. Replace the EGR valve if it takes less than 20 seconds to move to the seated position.

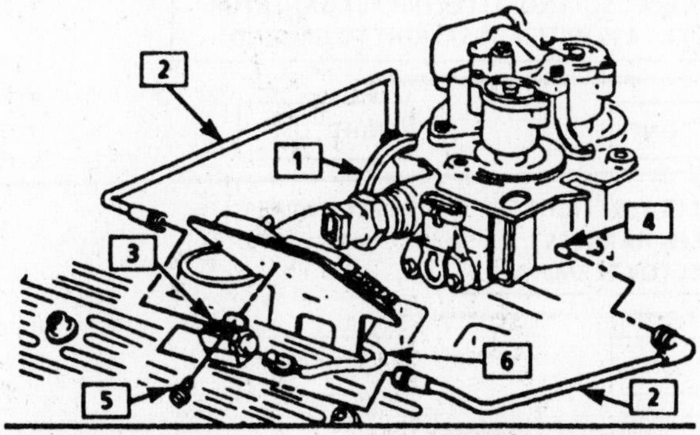
1
2
3
4
5
6

1 EGR VALVE
2 VACUUM HARNESS
3 EGR SOLENOID
4 MANIFOLD VACUUM (PORT – J)
5 BOLT – TIGHTEN TO 2 N·m (18 lb.in.)
6 HARNESS CONNECTOR

EGR system – 4.3L engine

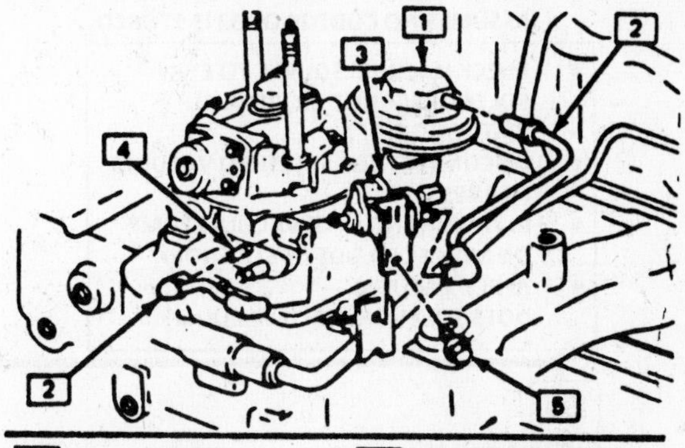
1
2
3
4
5

1 EGR VALVE
2 VACUUM HARNESS
3 EGR SOLENOID
4 PORTED MANIFOLD VACUUM (PORT F)
5 BOLT TIGHTEN TO 4 N·m (35 LBS. IN.)

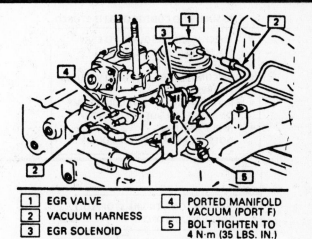

EGR system – 2.5L engine

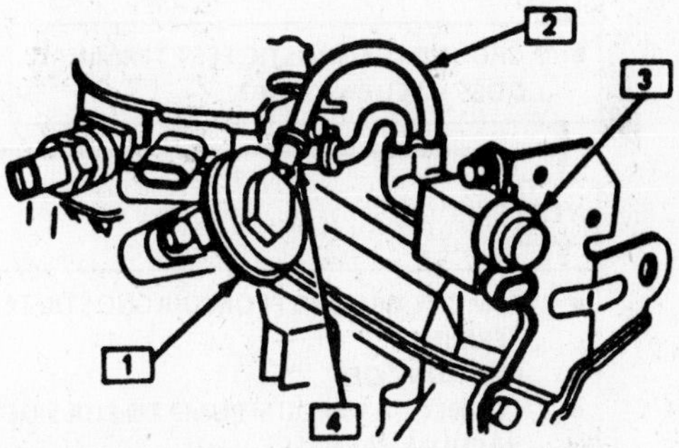
1
2
3
4

1 EGR VALVE
2 VACUUM HARNESS
3 EGR SOLENOID
4 MANIFOLD VACUUM

EGR system – 2.8L TBI engine

TESTING (TBI Engines)

EGR VALVE CLEANING

NOTE: DO NOT wash valve assembly in solvents or degreaser – permanent damage to valve diaphragm may result. Also, sand blasting of the valve is recommended since this can affect the operation of the valve.

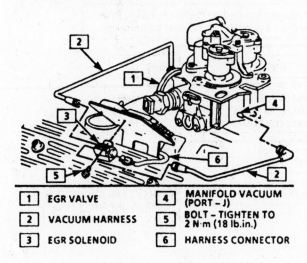

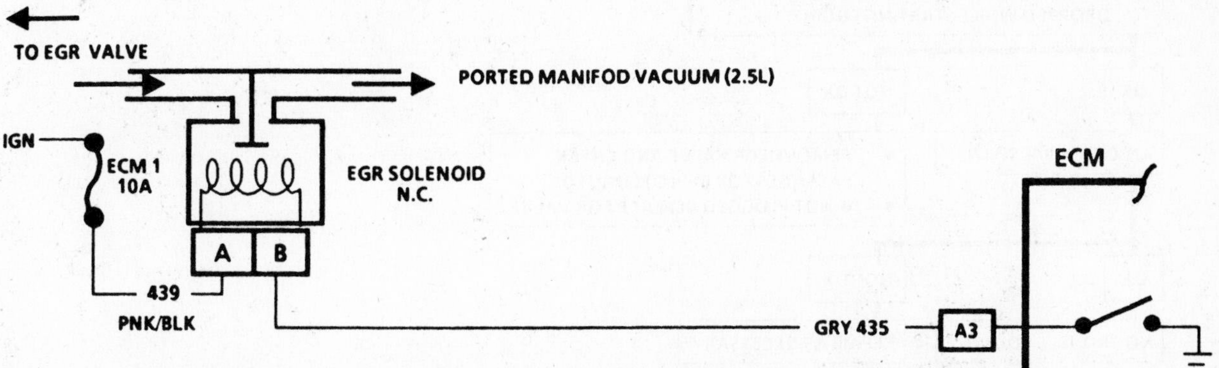
TO EGR VALVE
PORTED MANIFOD VACUUM (2.5L)
IGN
ECM 1
10A
EGR SOLENOID
N.C.
A
B
439
PNK/BLK
ECM
GRY 435
A3

EGR SYSTEM CHECK
2.5L

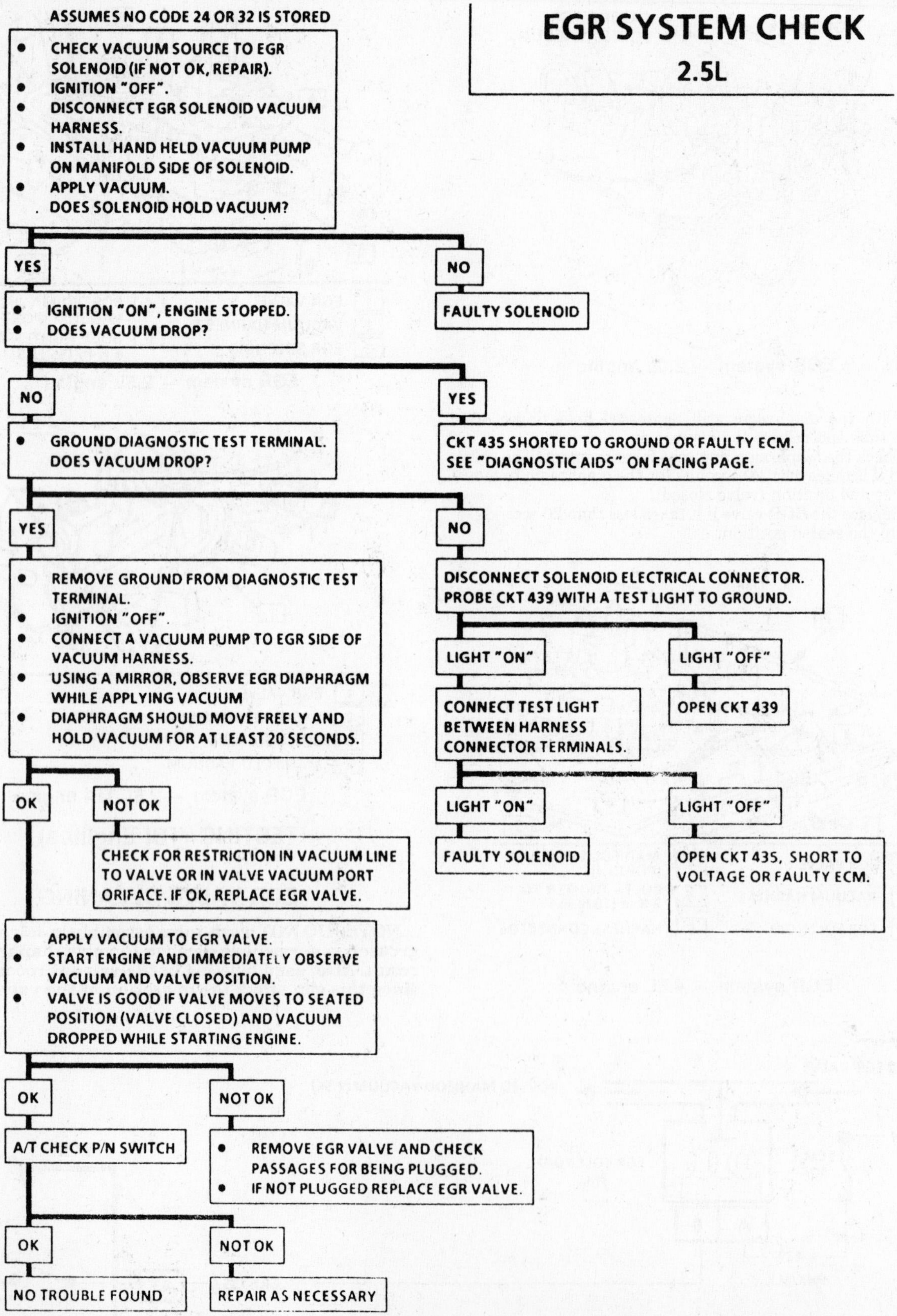
ASSUMES NO CODE 24 OR 32 IS STORED
• CHECK VACUUM SOURCE TO EGR SOLENOID (IF NOT OK, REPAIR).
• IGNITION "OFF".
• DISCONNECT EGR SOLENOID VACUUM HARNESS.
• INSTALL HAND HELD VACUUM PUMP ON MANIFOLD SIDE OF SOLENOID.
• APPLY VACUUM.
DOES SOLENOID HOLD VACUUM?
YES
NO
FAULTY SOLENOID
• IGNITION "ON", ENGINE STOPPED.
• DOES VACUUM DROP?
NO
YES
CKT 435 SHORTED TO GROUND OR FAULTY ECM. SEE "DIAGNOSTIC AIDS" ON FACING PAGE.
• GROUND DIAGNOSTIC TEST TERMINAL. DOES VACUUM DROP?
YES
NO
DISCONNECT SOLENOID ELECTRICAL CONNECTOR. PROBE CKT 439 WITH A TEST LIGHT TO GROUND.
LIGHT "ON"
LIGHT "OFF"
OPEN CKT 439
CONNECT TEST LIGHT BETWEEN HARNESS CONNECTOR TERMINALS.
LIGHT "ON"
LIGHT "OFF"
FAULTY SOLENOID
OPEN CKT 435, SHORT TO VOLTAGE OR FAULTY ECM.
• REMOVE GROUND FROM DIAGNOSTIC TEST TERMINAL.
• IGNITION "OFF".
• CONNECT A VACUUM PUMP TO EGR SIDE OF VACUUM HARNESS.
• USING A MIRROR, OBSERVE EGR DIAPHRAGM WHILE APPLYING VACUUM
• DIAPHRAGM SHOULD MOVE FREELY AND HOLD VACUUM FOR AT LEAST 20 SECONDS.
OK
NOT OK
CHECK FOR RESTRICTION IN VACUUM LINE TO VALVE OR IN VALVE VACUUM PORT ORIFACE. IF OK, REPLACE EGR VALVE.
• APPLY VACUUM TO EGR VALVE.
• START ENGINE AND IMMEDIATELY OBSERVE VACUUM AND VALVE POSITION.
• VALVE IS GOOD IF VALVE MOVES TO SEATED POSITION (VALVE CLOSED) AND VACUUM DROPPED WHILE STARTING ENGINE.
OK
NOT OK
A/T CHECK P/N SWITCH
• REMOVE EGR VALVE AND CHECK PASSAGES FOR BEING PLUGGED.
• IF NOT PLUGGED REPLACE EGR VALVE.
OK
NOT OK
NO TROUBLE FOUND
REPAIR AS NECESSARY

CONFIRM "CLOSED LOOP" OPERATION AND NO "SERVICE ENGINE SOON" LIGHT.

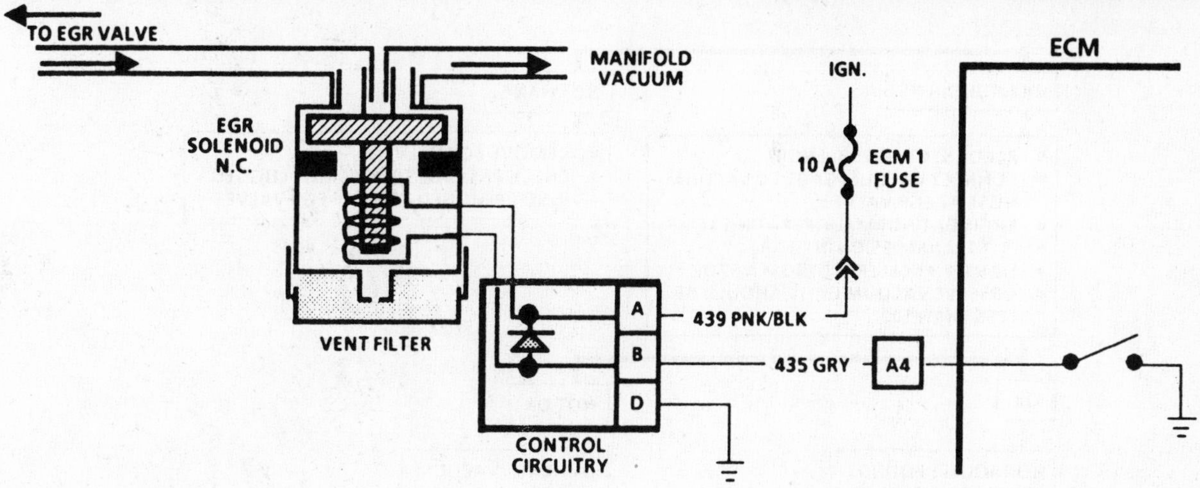
TO EGR VALVE
MANIFOLD VACUUM
EGR SOLENOID N.C.
VENT FILTER
A
B
D
CONTROL CIRCUITRY
IGN.
10 A
ECM 1 FUSE
439 PNK/BLK
435 GRY
A4
ECM

EGR SYSTEM CHECK

2.8L & 4.3L

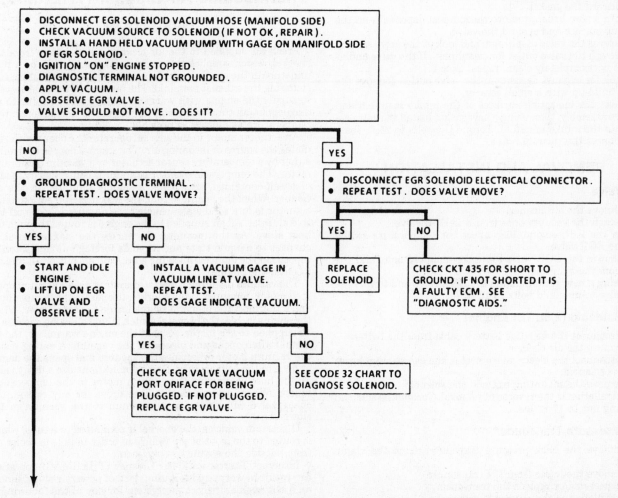

ASSUMES NO CODE 24 OR 32 IS STORED

- DISCONNECT EGR SOLENOID VACUUM HOSE (MANIFOLD SIDE)
- CHECK VACUUM SOURCE TO SOLENOID (IF NOT OK , REPAIR).
- INSTALL A HAND HELD VACUUM PUMP WITH GAGE ON MANIFOLD SIDE OF EGR SOLENOID.
- IGNITION "ON" ENGINE STOPPED.
- DIAGNOSTIC TERMINAL NOT GROUNDED.
- APPLY VACUUM.
- OSBSERVE EGR VALVE.
- VALVE SHOULD NOT MOVE. DOES IT?

NO

- GROUND DIAGNOSTIC TERMINAL.
- REPEAT TEST. DOES VALVE MOVE?

YES

- START AND IDLE ENGINE.
- LIFT UP ON EGR VALVE AND OBSERVE IDLE.

NO

- INSTALL A VACUUM GAGE IN VACUUM LINE AT VALVE.
- REPEAT TEST.
- DOES GAGE INDICATE VACUUM.

YES

CHECK EGR VALVE VACUUM PORT ORIFACE FOR BEING PLUGGED. IF NOT PLUGGED. REPLACE EGR VALVE.

NO

SEE CODE 32 CHART TO DIAGNOSE SOLENOID.

YES

- DISCONNECT EGR SOLENOID ELECTRICAL CONNECTOR.
- REPEAT TEST. DOES VALVE MOVE?

YES

REPLACE SOLENOID

NO

CHECK CKT 435 FOR SHORT TO GROUND. IF NOT SHORTED IT IS A FAULTY ECM. SEE "DIAGNOSTIC AIDS."

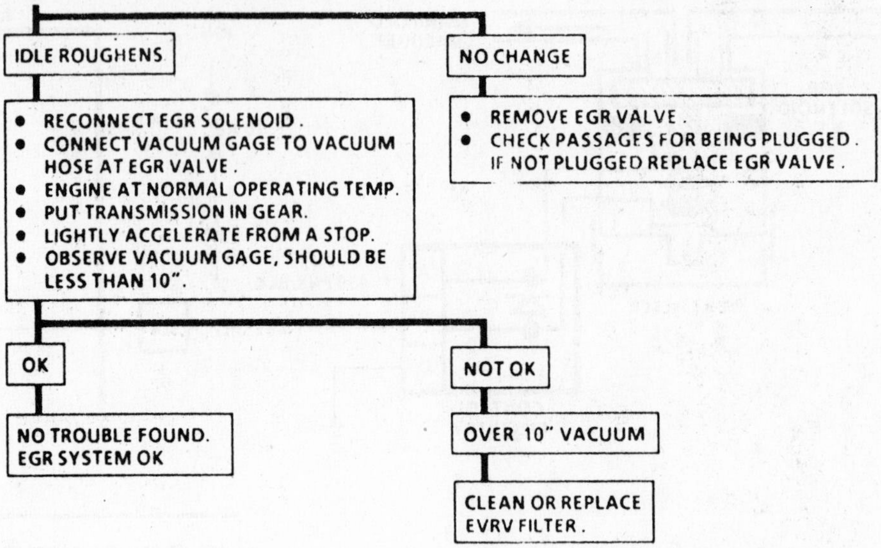
IDLE ROUGHENS
NO CHANGE
• RECONNECT EGR SOLENOID.
• CONNECT VACUUM GAGE TO VACUUM HOSE AT EGR VALVE.
• ENGINE AT NORMAL OPERATING TEMP.
• PUT TRANSMISSION IN GEAR.
• LIGHTLY ACCELERATE FROM A STOP.
• OBSERVE VACUUM GAGE, SHOULD BE LESS THAN 10".
• REMOVE EGR VALVE.
• CHECK PASSAGES FOR BEING PLUGGED. IF NOT PLUGGED REPLACE EGR VALVE.
OK
NOT OK
NO TROUBLE FOUND. EGR SYSTEM OK
OVER 10" VACUUM
CLEAN OR REPLACE EVRV FILTER.

1. Remove the EGR valve-to-intake manifold bolts and the valve, discard the gasket.
2. With a wire brush, remove the exhaust deposits from the mounting surface and around the valve.
3. Depress the valve diaphragm and look at the valve seating area through the valve outlet for cleanliness. If the valve and/or seat are not completely clean, repeat Step 2.
4. Look for exhaust deposits in the valve outlet. Remove the deposit build-up with a small scraper.
5. Clean the mounting surfaces of the intake manifold and the valve assembly, then using a new gasket install the valve assembly to the intake manifold. Torque the bolts to 25 ft. lbs.
6. Connect the vacuum hoses.

REMOVAL AND INSTALLATION

EGR Valve

1. Remove the air cleaner.
2. Detach the vacuum hose from the EGR valve.
3. On the 2.8L engine, disconnect the temperature switch from the EGR valve.
4. Remove the EGR valve-to-intake manifold bolts and the valve from the manifold.
5. Using a new gasket, install the EGR valve and torque the EGR valve-to-manifold bolts to 15 ft. lbs.

EGR Solenoid (2.8L TBI Engine)

1. Disconnect the negative battery cable from the battery.
2. Remove the air cleaner.
3. Disconnect the electrical connector and the vacuum hoses from the solenoid.
4. Remove the mounting nut and the solenoid.
5. Installation is the reverse of removal. Torque the solenoid mounting nut to 17 ft. lbs.

Back Pressure Transducer

1. Remove the back pressure transducer from the clamp bracket.
2. Remove the hoses from the transducer.
3. Inspect and/or replace the transducer.
4. Installation is the reverse of removal.

Thermostatic Air Cleaner (THERMAC)

OPERATION

Fresh air supplied to the air cleaner comes either from the snorkel, which supplies the engine with outside air, or a tube underneath the snorkel, which is connected to a heat stove surrounding the exhaust manifold. The purpose of the heat stove is to supply the engine with warm air during cold running to reduce choke-on time and bring the engine to normal operating temperature as quickly as possible.

An actuator motor in the snorkel operates the door which regulates the source of incoming air. The snorkel door is controlled either by a temperature sensor actuator or a vacuum diaphragm motor. The temperature sensor actuator is controlled by means of a self-contained, wax pellet assembly mounted in the air cleaner. When the engine is cold, the wax material sealed in the actuator is in a solid state, causing the damper to close off the cold air inlet. All air supplied to the engine is routed through the heat stove. As the incoming air warms the wax material, it changes to a liquid state and expands forcing out the piston to reposition the damper, allowing a hot/cold air mix or all cold air to enter the engine.

The vacuum diaphragm operated system uses a vacuum operated motor, mounted to the snorkel, to operate the damper door and a thermostatic bi-metal switch inside the air cleaner. When the engine is cold, the bi-metal switch is cold allowing vacuum to be supplied to the motor. As that the engine warms up, the bi-metal switch opens and bleeds off the vacuum. A spring inside the vacuum motor overcomes the vacuum and opens the damper door to the cold air inlet. Some applications use a delay valve on the hose connecting the vacuum motor to the temperature sensor. When vacuum in this hose drops for any reason, the check valve will bleed off the vacuum to the vacuum motor slowly.

On certain vehicles, the snorkel is connected to a tube, which is routed to the front of the vehicle in order to take in cooler air from outside the engine compartment.

Incorrect Thermostatic Air Cleaner (THERMAC) operation can result in warm up hesitation, lack of power or sluggishness on a hot engine. Inspect the system for any of the following:

1. Disconnected heat stove tube.

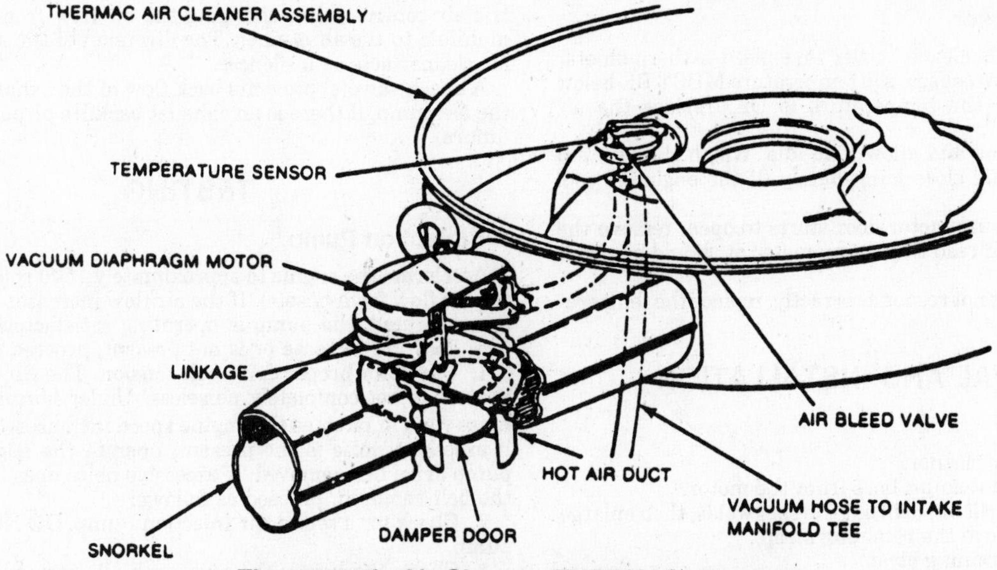
THERMAC AIR CLEANER ASSEMBLY
TEMPERATURE SENSOR
VACUUM DIAPHRAGM MOTOR
LINKAGE
AIR BLEED VALVE
HOT AIR DUCT
VACUUM HOSE TO INTAKE MANIFOLD TEE
DAMPER DOOR
SNORKEL

Thermostatic Air Cleaner (THERMAC) Assembly

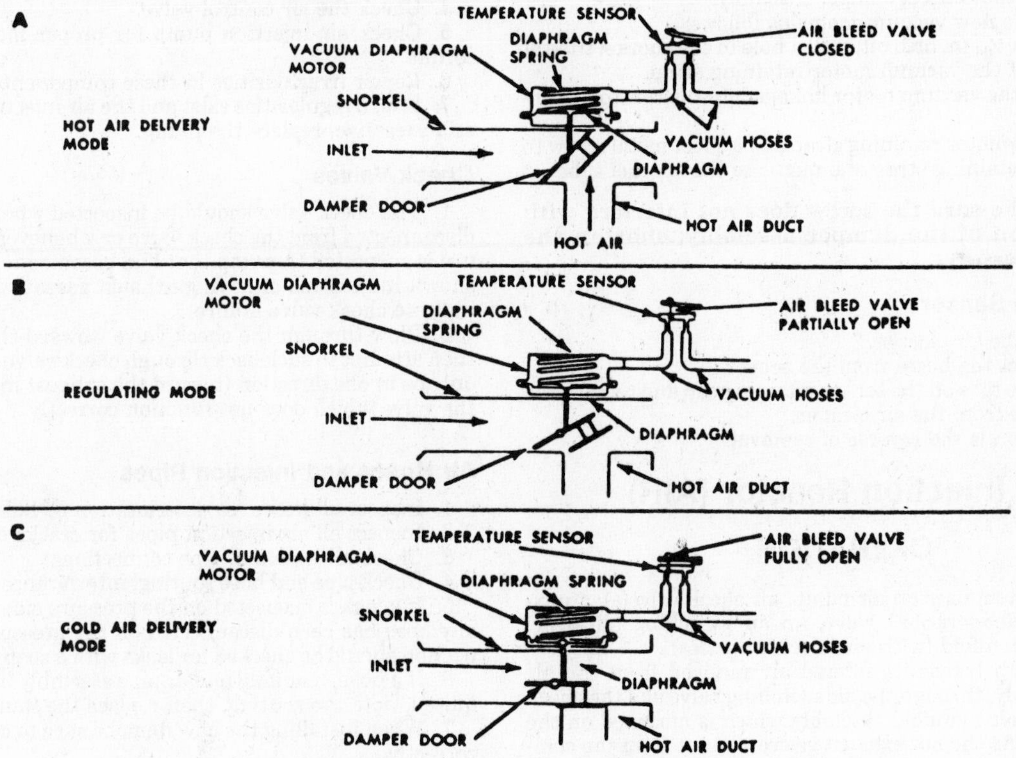
A
TEMPERATURE SENSOR
AIR BLEED VALVE CLOSED
DIAPHRAGM SPRING
VACUUM DIAPHRAGM MOTOR
SNORKEL
HOT AIR DELIVERY MODE
VACUUM HOSES
INLET
DIAPHRAGM
DAMPER DOOR
HOT AIR DUCT
HOT AIR
B
VACUUM DIAPHRAGM MOTOR
TEMPERATURE SENSOR
AIR BLEED VALVE PARTIALLY OPEN
DIAPHRAGM SPRING
SNORKEL
REGULATING MODE
VACUUM HOSES
INLET
DIAPHRAGM
DAMPER DOOR
HOT AIR DUCT
C
TEMPERATURE SENSOR
AIR BLEED VALVE FULLY OPEN
VACUUM DIAPHRAGM MOTOR
DIAPHRAGM SPRING
SNORKEL
COLD AIR DELIVERY MODE
VACUUM HOSES
INLET
DIAPHRAGM
DAMPER DOOR
HOT AIR DUCT

THERMAC vacuum door operation

2. Vacuum diaphragm motor or temperature sensor actuator inoperative.
3. No damper door operation.
4. Absence of manifold vacuum source.
5. Air cleaner not seated properly.

TESTING

Vacuum Motor

1. With the engine Off, disconnect the hose from the vacuum diaphragm motor.

2. Using a vacuum source, apply 7 in.Hg to the vacuum motor; the door should close and block off the outside air, completely.

3. Bend the vacuum hose (to trap the vacuum in the motor) and make sure that the door stays closed; if not, replace the vacuum motor.

NOTE: Before replacing the vacuum motor (if defective), be sure to check the motor linkage, for binding.

4. If the vacuum motor is OK and the problem still exists, check the temperature sensor.

Temperature Sensor

1. Remove the air cleaner cover and place a thermometer near the temperature sensor; the temperature MUST BE below 86°F (30°C). When the temperature is OK, replace the air cleaner.
2. Start the engine and allow it to idle. Watch the vacuum motor door, it should close immediately (if the engine is cool enough).
3. When the vacuum motor door starts to open, remove the air cleaner cover and read the thermometer, it should be about 131°F (55°C).
4. If the door does not respond correctly, replace the temperature sensor.

REMOVAL AND INSTALLATION

Vacuum Motor

1. Remove the air cleaner.
2. Disconnect the vacuum hose from the motor.
3. Using a ⅛ in. drill bit, drill out the spot welds, then enlarge as necessary to remove the retaining strap.
4. Remove the retaining strap.
5. Lift up the motor and cock it to one side to unhook the motor linkage at the control damper assembly.
6. Install the new vacuum motor as follows:
   a. Using a $^{7}/_{64}$ in. drill bit, drill a hole in the snorkel tube at the center of the vacuum motor retaining strap.
   b. Insert the vacuum motor linkage into the control damper assembly.
   c. Use the motor retaining strap and a sheet metal screw to secure the retaining strap and motor to the snorkel tube.

NOTE: Make sure the screw does not interfere with the operation of the damper assembly; shorten the screw, if necessary.

Temperature Sensor

1. Remove the air cleaner.
2. Disconnect the hoses from the sensor.
3. Pry up the tabs on the sensor retaining clip and remove the clip and sensor from the air cleaner.
4. Installation is the reverse of removal.

Air Injection Reactor (AIR)

OPERATION

The AIR system uses an air pump, air check valve(s), a mixture control (deceleration) valve, an air switching (diverter) valve, an air manifold (with air injector nozzles).

The air pump transmits filtered air received from the air cleaner assembly, through the air switching valve and the check valve, into an air manifold assembly which is mounted on the cylinder head. As the hot exhaust gas comes out from the combustion chamber, it meets with a blast of air from the air injection nozzle located in the exhaust port to burn some of the hydrocarbon and carbon monoxide emissions.

Upon receiving a high vacuum signal from the intake manifold, the mixture control valve introduces amnient air through the air filter into the intake manifold to dilute the momentarily rich fuel mixture that occurs on initial throttle closing. This eliminates backfire.

On California and TBI models, the Electronic Control Module (ECM) operates the electric air control valve which directs the air flow to the engine exhaust manifold ports or the the air cleaner. When the engine is cold or in wide-open throttle, the ECM energizes the solenoid to direct the air flow into the exhaust manifold check valves. When the engine warms, operating at high speeds or deceleration, the ECM de-energizes the electric air control valve, changing the air flow from the exhaust manifold to the air cleaner. The diversion of the air flow to the air cleaner acts as a silencer.

A check valve(s) prevents back flow of the exhaust gases into the air pump, if there is an exhaust backfire or pump drive belt failure.

TESTING

Air Injection Pump

Accelerate the engine to approximately 1500 rpm and observe the air flow from hose(s). If the air flow increases as the engine is accelerated, the pump is operating satisfactorily. If the air flow does not increase or is not present, proceed as follows:

1. Check for proper drive belt tension. The Air Management System is not completely noiseless. Under normal conditions, noise rises in pitch as the engine speed increases. To determine if excessive noise is the present, operate the engine with the pump drive belt removed. If excessive noise does not exist with the belt removed, proceed as follows:
2. Check for a seized Air Injection Pump. DO NOT oil the air pump.
3. Check the hoses, the pipes and all connections for leaks and proper routing.
4. Check the air control valve.
5. Check air injection pump for proper mounting and bolt torque.
6. Repair irregularities in these components, as necessary.
7. If no irregularities exist and the air injection pump noise is still excessive, replace the pump.

Check Valves

1. The check valve should be inspected whenever the hose is disconnected from the check valve or whenever check valve failure is suspected (A pump that had become inoperative and had shown indications of having exhaust gases in the pump would indicate check valve failure).
2. Blow through the check valve (toward the cylinder head) then attempt to suck back through check valve. The flow should only be in one direction (toward the exhaust manifold). Replace the valve which does not function correctly.

Air Hoses and Injection Pipes

1. Inspect all hoses for deterioration or holes.
2. Inspect all air injection pipes for cracks of holes.
3. Check all hose and pipe connections.
4. Check pipe and hose routing; interference may cause wear.
5. If a leak is suspected on the pressure side of the system or any hose has been disconnected on the pressure side, the connection should be checked for leaks with a soapy water solution.
6. If a hose, manifold and/or pipe assembly replacement is required, note the routing, then replace the item as required.
7. When installing the new item, be sure to connect the hoses correctly.

Air Switching (Diverter) Valve (ASV)

The diverter valve directs air to the exhaust ports unless there is a sudden rise in manifold vacuum due to deceleration. In such a case air is diverted to the intake manifold.

If the diverter valve is functioning properly, the secondary air will continue to blow out from the valve for a few seconds when the accelerator pedal is pressed to the floor and released quickly. If the secondary air continues to blow out for more than 5 seconds, replace the air switching valve.

Mixture Control (Deceleration) Valve

1. Install a tachometer to the engine and allow the engine to establish normal operating temperatures.

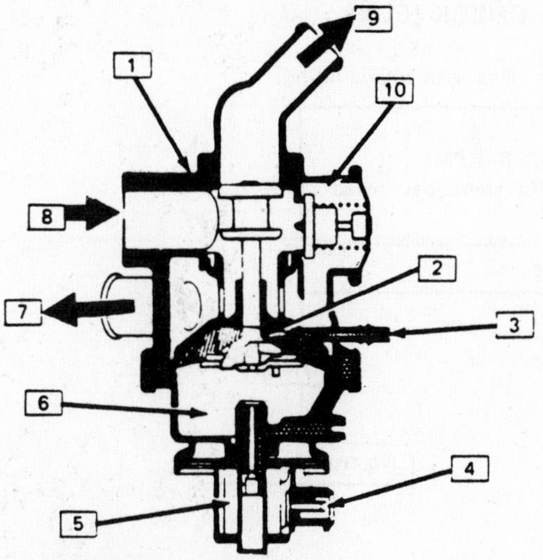
1
2
3
4
5
6
7
8
9
10

1. Electrical air control (EAC) valve
2. Decel timing assembly
3. Manifold vacuum signal tube
4. Electrical terminal
5. EAC solenoid
6. Decel Timing chamber
7. Air to air cleaner
8. Air from air pump
9. Air to exhaust ports or manifold
10. Pressure relief assembly

Electric air control valve — TBI engines

2. Remove the air cleaner and plug the air cleaner vacuum hose(s).
3. Operate the engine at idle speed, then remove the deceleration valve-to-intake manifold (diaphragm) hose.
4. Reconnect the hose and listen for a noticeable air flow (hiss) through the air cleaner-to-deceleration valve hose; there should also be a noticeable drop in idle speed.

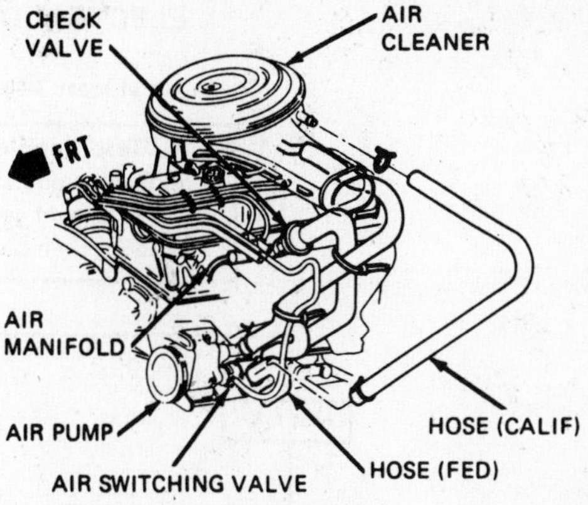
CHECK VALVE
AIR CLEANER
FRT
AIR MANIFOLD
AIR PUMP
AIR SWITCHING VALVE
HOSE (CALIF)
HOSE (FED)

Air injection reactor system — 1.9L engine

5. If the air flow does not continue for at least one second or the engine speed does not drop, check the hoses (of the deceleration valve) for restrictions or leaks.
6. If no restrictions are found, replace the deceleration valve.

REMOVAL AND INSTALLATION

Air Injection Pump

NOTE: The air pump is non-serviceable, it must be replaced as an assembly, if defective.

1. Compress the drive belt to keep the pump pulley from turning, then loosen the pump pulley bolts.
2. Loosen the pump-to-mounting brackets, release the tension on the drive belt and remove the drive belt.
3. Unscrew the mounting bolts and then remove the pump pulley.
4. If necessary, use a pair of needle nose pliers to pull the fan filter from the hub.
5. Remove the hoses, the vacuum lines, the electrical connectors (if equipped) and the air control or diverter valve.

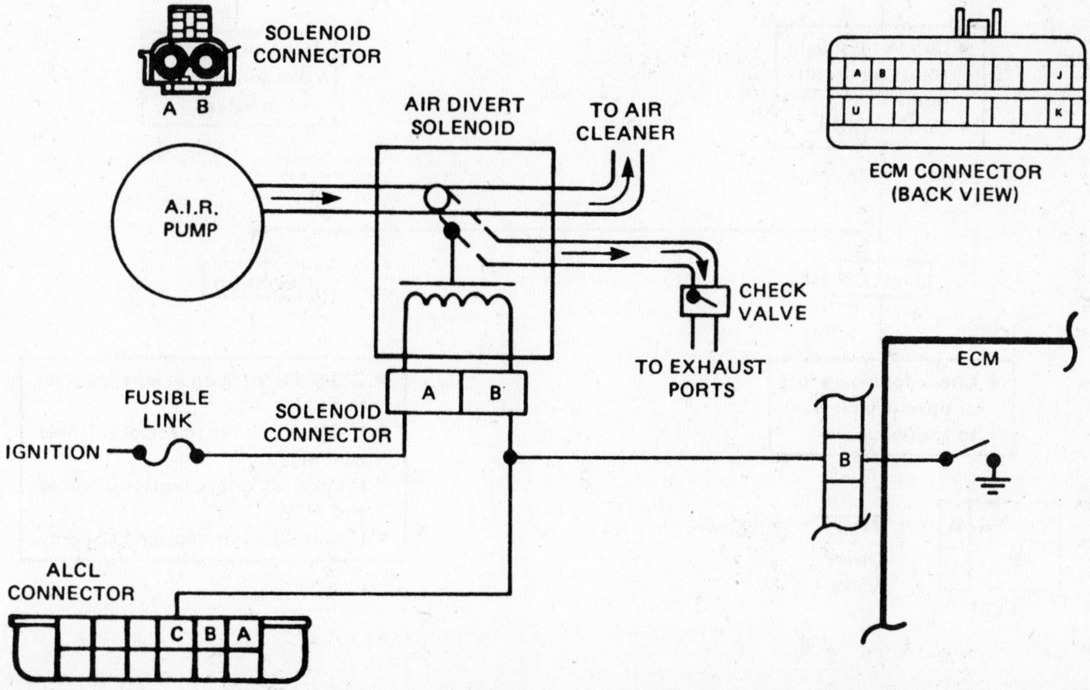
SOLENOID CONNECTOR
A B
AIR DIVERT SOLENOID
TO AIR CLEANER
A.I.R. PUMP
CHECK VALVE
TO EXHAUST PORTS
ECM CONNECTOR (BACK VIEW)
A B J
U K
ECM
FUSIBLE LINK
IGNITION
SOLENOID CONNECTOR
A B
B
ALCL CONNECTOR
C B A

ELECTRIC DIVERTER VALVE CHECK (EDV)

Check for at least 34 kPa (10") of vacuum at valve with engine idling.

(1)
- "Test" terminal ungrounded.
- Run engine at part throttle (under 2000 RPM).
- Air should go to exhaust ports until system goes closed loop, then divert to air cleaner.

OK

No trouble found

Not OK

(2)
- Test term. ungrounded.
- Ignition "ON," engine stopped.
- Remove connector from divert valve and connect a test light between connector terminals.

Light On

- Check for grounded wire from sol. to ECM.
- If not grounded, replace ECM.

Light Off

(3)
- Ground "Test" Terminal
- Note Check Engine Light.

Light On

It is faulty divert valve connections or valve.

Light Off

- Connect test light across connector terms.
- Note test light.

Light Off

- Check for blown fuse or open in pink wire to ignition.

Light On

- Check for an open in wire from sol. to ECM.
- If OK, check resistance of solenoid winding.
- If under 20 ohms, replace solenoid and ECM.
- If over 20 ohms, replace ECM only.

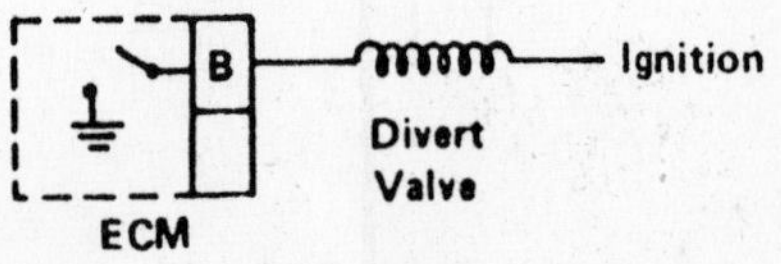
B
Ignition
Divert Valve
ECM

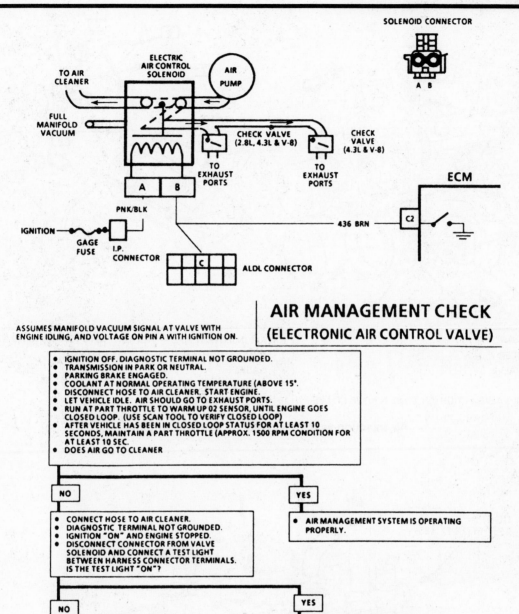

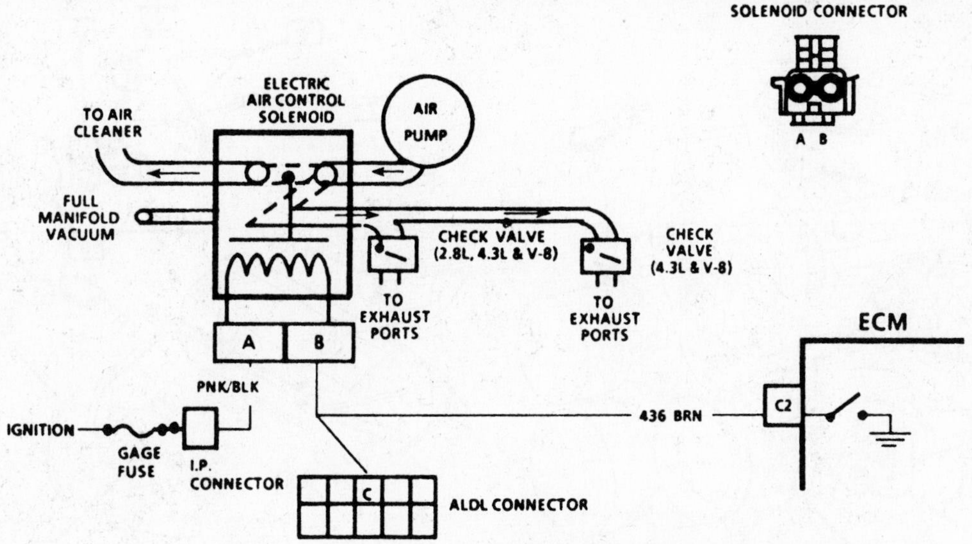
SOLENOID CONNECTOR
A B
ELECTRIC
AIR CONTROL
SOLENOID
AIR
PUMP
TO AIR
CLEANER
FULL
MANIFOLD
VACUUM
CHECK VALVE
(2.8L, 4.3L & V-8)
CHECK
VALVE
(4.3L & V-8)
TO
EXHAUST
PORTS
TO
EXHAUST
PORTS
ECM
A
B
PNK/BLK
IGNITION
GAGE
FUSE
I.P.
CONNECTOR
436 BRN
C2
C
ALDL CONNECTOR

AIR MANAGEMENT CHECK (ELECTRONIC AIR CONTROL VALVE)

ASSUMES MANIFOLD VACUUM SIGNAL AT VALVE WITH ENGINE IDLING, AND VOLTAGE ON PIN A WITH IGNITION ON.

- IGNITION OFF. DIAGNOSTIC TERMINAL NOT GROUNDED.
- TRANSMISSION IN PARK OR NEUTRAL.
- PARKING BRAKE ENGAGED.
- COOLANT AT NORMAL OPERATING TEMPERATURE (ABOVE 15°.
- DISCONNECT HOSE TO AIR CLEANER. START ENGINE.
- LET VEHICLE IDLE. AIR SHOULD GO TO EXHAUST PORTS.
- RUN AT PART THROTTLE TO WARM UP 02 SENSOR, UNTIL ENGINE GOES CLOSED LOOP. (USE SCAN TOOL TO VERIFY CLOSED LOOP)
- AFTER VEHICLE HAS BEEN IN CLOSED LOOP STATUS FOR AT LEAST 10 SECONDS, MAINTAIN A PART THROTTLE (APPROX. 1500 RPM CONDITION FOR AT LEAST 10 SEC.
- DOES AIR GO TO CLEANER

YES

- AIR MANAGEMENT SYSTEM IS OPERATING PROPERLY.

NO

- CONNECT HOSE TO AIR CLEANER.
- DIAGNOSTIC TERMINAL NOT GROUNDED.
- IGNITION "ON" AND ENGINE STOPPED.
- DISCONNECT CONNECTOR FROM VALVE SOLENOID AND CONNECT A TEST LIGHT BETWEEN HARNESS CONNECTOR TERMINALS. IS THE TEST LIGHT "ON"?

YES

- CHECK FOR GROUNDED WIRE FROM SOLENOID TO ECM.
- IF NOT GROUNDED, REPLACE ECM.

NO

- GROUND DIAGNOSTIC TERMINAL.
- IS THE TEST LIGHT "ON"?

YES

- IT IS A FAULTY VALVE SOLENOID CONNECTOR OR SOLENOID. REPLACE EAC VALVE.

NO

- CONNECT TEST LIGHT BETWEEN HARNESS TERMINAL "A" TO GROUND.
- IS THE TEST LIGHT "ON"?

NO

- CHECK FOR OPEN FUSE OR OPEN IN WIRE TO IGNITION

YES

- CHECK FOR AN OPEN IN WIRE FROM SOLENOID TO ECM.
- IF OK, CHECK RESISTANCE OF SOLENOID WINDINGS.
- IF UNDER 20 OHMS, REPLACE EAC VALVE AND PERFORM ECM QDR CHECK IN SECTION "3".
- IF OVER 20 OHMS, REPLACE ECM ONLY.

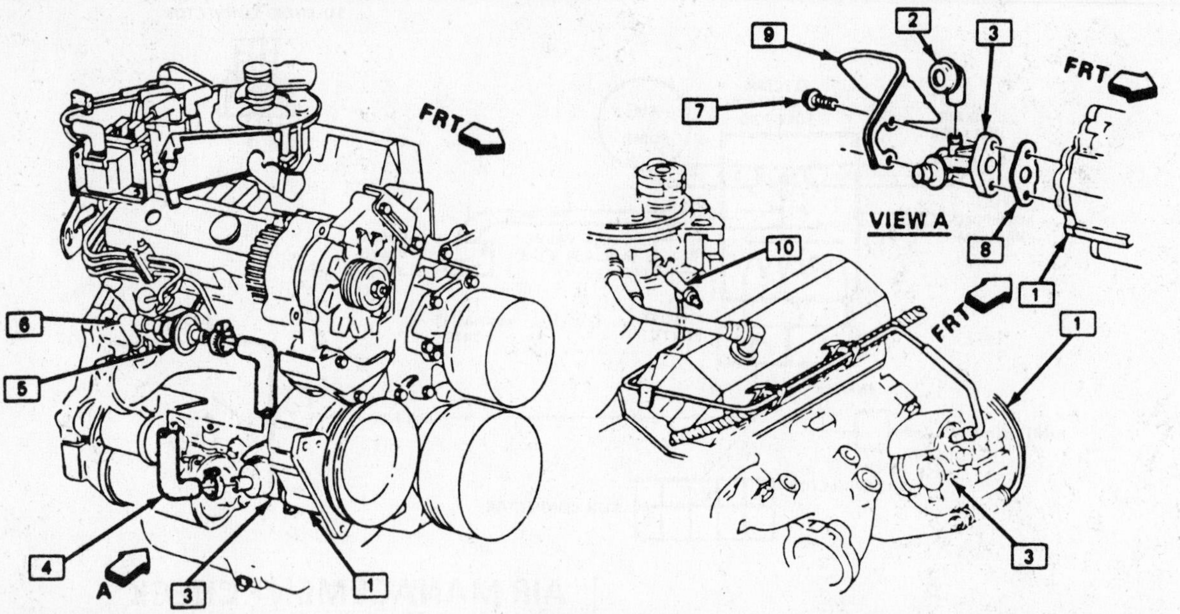
FRT
VIEW A
A
1
2
3
4
5
6
7
8
9
10

1	AIR PUMP	6	AIR INJECTION PIPE — TIGHTEN NUTS TO 28 N·m (20 FT. LBS.)
2	SILENCER	7	BOLT — TIGHTEN TO 15 N·m (11 FT. LBS.)
3	EAC VALVE	8	GASKET
4	HOSE	9	SHIELD
5	CHECK VALVE — TIGHTEN TO 85 N·m (26 FT. LBS.)	10	PORT VACUUM HARNESS

Air injection reactor system – 2.8L TBI engine

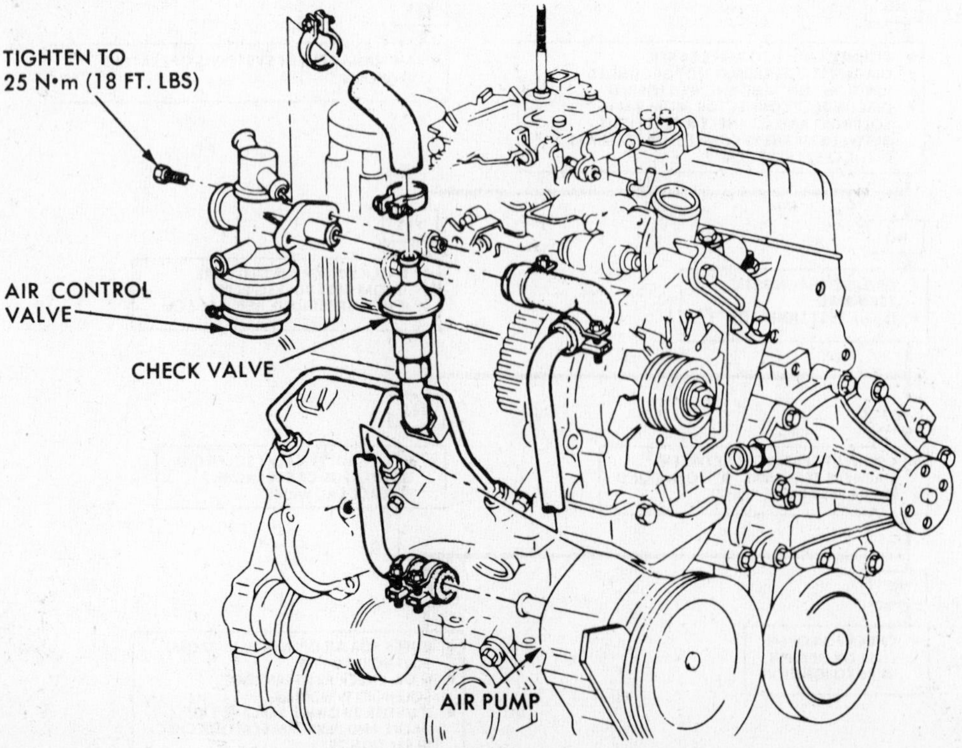
TIGHTEN TO
25 N•m (18 FT. LBS)
AIR CONTROL
VALVE
CHECK VALVE
AIR PUMP

Air injection reactor system – 2.8L engine

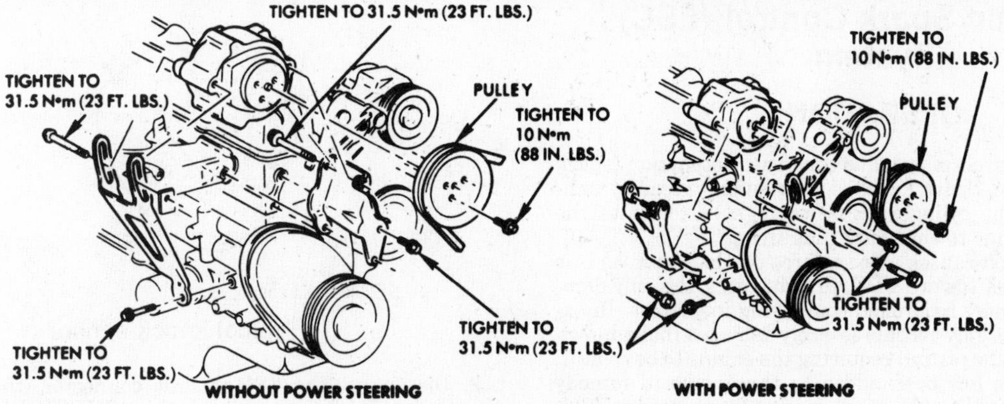
TIGHTEN TO 31.5 N•m (23 FT. LBS.)
TIGHTEN TO
31.5 N•m (23 FT. LBS.)
PULLEY
TIGHTEN TO
10 N•m
(88 IN. LBS.)
TIGHTEN TO
31.5 N•m (23 FT. LBS.)
TIGHTEN TO
31.5 N•m (23 FT. LBS.)
WITHOUT POWER STEERING
TIGHTEN TO
10 N•m (88 IN. LBS.)
PULLEY
TIGHTEN TO
31.5 N•m (23 FT. LBS.)
WITH POWER STEERING

Air injection reactor system – 2.0L engine

6. Unscrew the pump mounting bolts and then remove the pump.
7. Installation is the reverse of removal. Torque the pump pulley bolts to 90 inch lbs. and the pump-to-bracket nuts/bolts to 25 ft. lbs. Adjust the drive belt tension after installation.

Air Pump Drive Belt Adjustment and Replacement

NOTE: Vehicles using a serpentine accessory drive belt are equipped with an automatic tensioner, no adjustment is necessary.

1. Inspect the drive belt for wear, cracks or deterioration.
2. Loosen the pump adjustment and the pivot bolts.
3. Replace the drive belt, if necessary.
4. Move the air pump until the drive belt is at proper tension, then retighten bolts.
5. Check the drive belt tension using a belt tension gauge.

Air Pump Pulley Replacement

1. Hold the pump pulley from turning by compressing the drive belt, then loosen the pump pulley bolts.
2. Loosen the pump through bolt and the adjusting bolt.
3. Remove the drive belt, the pump pulley and the pulley spacer.
4. Install the pump pulley and spacer with the retaining bolts hand tight.
5. Install the drive belt and adjust to proper tension.
6. Hold the pump pulley from turning by compressing the drive belt, then torque the pump pulley bolts to 24 ft. lbs.
7. Recheck drive belt tension and adjust it, if necessary.

Air Pump Filter Fan Replacement

Before starting this operation, note the following:

- DO NOT allow any filter fragments to enter the air pump intake hole.
- DO NOT remove the filter fan by inserting a screwdriver between pump and filter fan. Air damage to the sealing lip pump will result.
- DO NOT remove the metal drive hub from the filter fan.
- It is seldom possible to remove the filter fan without destroying it.

1. Remove the drive belt, the pump pulley and spacer.
2. Insert needle nose pliers and pull the filter fan from hub.
3. Position a new filter fan onto the pump hub.
4. Position the spacer and the pump pulley against the centrifugal filter fan.
5. Install the pump pulley bolts and torque them equally to 80 inch lbs. This will compress the centrifugal filter fan into the pump hole. DO NOT drive the filter fan on with a hammer.

NOTE: A slight amount of interference with the housing bore is normal. After a new filter fan has been installed, it may squeal upon initial operation or until O.D. sealing lip has worn in. This may require a short period of pump operation at various engine speeds.

6. To complete the installation, replace the pump drive belt. Adjust the belt tension if necessary.

Check Valve(s)

1. Remove the clamp(s) and disconnect the hose from the valve(s).
2. Unscrew the valve(s) from the air injection pipe(s).
3. To test the valve(s), air should pass only in one direction only.
4. Installation is the reverse of removal.

Air Control Valve

1. Disconnect the negative battery cable.
2. Disconnect the air inlet and outlet hoses from the valve.
3. Disconnect the electrical connector (if equipped) and the vacuum hoses at the valve. Remove the electric air control or the diverter valve.
4. Installation is the reverse of removal. For California models, check the system operation.

NOTE: The air switching (diverter) valve is replaced in the same manner as the air control valve.

Mixture Control (Deceleration) Valve

1. Remove the vacuum hoses from the valve.
2. Remove the deceleration valve-to-engine bracket screws.
3. Remove the deceleration valve.
4. Installation is the reverse of removal. Torque the deceleration valve-to-engine bracket screws to 30 inch lbs.

Vacuum Switching Valve (VSV)

1. Disconnect the electrical wiring connector.
2. Remove the hoses from the valve.
3. Remove the vacuum switching valve.
4. Installation is the reverse of removal.

Electronic Spark Timing (EST) System

All HEI distributors used in S/10-S/15 vehicles are equipped to aid in spark timing changes, necessary for emissions control, economy and performance. The system used is called the Electronic Spark Timing Control (EST). For diagnostic testing and overhaul procedures, refer to Section 2 of this book.

Electronic Spark Control (ESC) System

OPERATION

Varying octane levels of gasoline can cause detonation (spark knock) in an engine. Spark knock is a condition caused by temperatures inside the cylinder rising so high as to ignite the air/fuel mixture prior to the spark plug firing.

This early ignition causes a down force on the piston as it is rising in the cylinder toward TDC. In light cases, the only damage to the engine may be broken spark plug insulators. In extreme cases, pistons may become severely damaged (holes blown through the top of the piston) requiring the engine to be rebuilt.

The ESC system has been added to the engine to remedy spark knock by retarding the spark timing by as much as 20°; this allows the engine to maximize the spark advance to improve the fuel economy and driveability.

A sensor is mounted on the left side of the block (near the cylinders) to detect the knock and send the information to the Electronic Spark Control (ESC) module. The ESC module sends a signal to the Electronic Control Module (ECM) which adjusts the Electronic Spark Timing (EST) to reduce the spark knock. If no signal is received from the ESC sensor, the ECM provides normal spark advance.

NOTE: Loss of spark knock sensor signal (through a bad ESC sensor, ESC module or a poor ground) will cause the engine to operate sluggishly and cause a Code 43 to be set.

TESTING

1. With the engine operating at 1,500 rpm, the transmission in Neutral or Park, tap on the engine block in the area of the knock sensor, the engine rpm should drop.

NOTE: If the speed does not drop, the timing is not retarding or it is retarded all of the time.

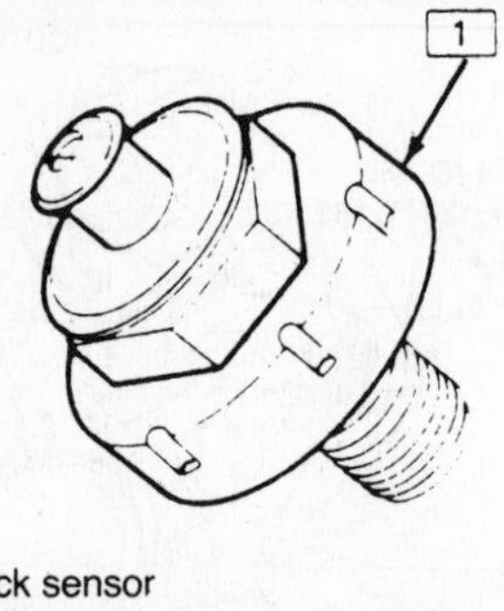
1
1. ESC knock sensor

Typical knock sensor

2. Disconnect the ESC module connector (the engine rpm should drop); after 4 seconds, the "CHECK ENGINE" light should turn ON and the Code 43 will be stored.
3. Using a digital voltmeter (set on the low AC scale), check the knock sensor voltage; low or no voltage will indicate an open circuit at terminal **E** or a bad sensor.
4. Check the CHECK ENGINE light and the Code 43 in the ESC system. If no light turns ON, the ECM is not retarding the engine spark for there may be voltage on the **C** terminal or the ECM may be faulty, replace the ECM.
5. Disconnect the electrical connector from the knock sensor; if the rpm increases with the sensor disconnected, the sensor is bad and should be replaced.

REMOVAL AND INSTALLATION

Knock Sensor

The knock sensor is mounted on the right side of the engine in front of the starter.

1. Disconnect the negative battery terminal from the battery.
2. Disconnect the electrical harness connector from the knock sensor.
3. Remove the knock sensor from the engine block.
4. Apply teflon tape to the threads. Installation is the reverse of removal.

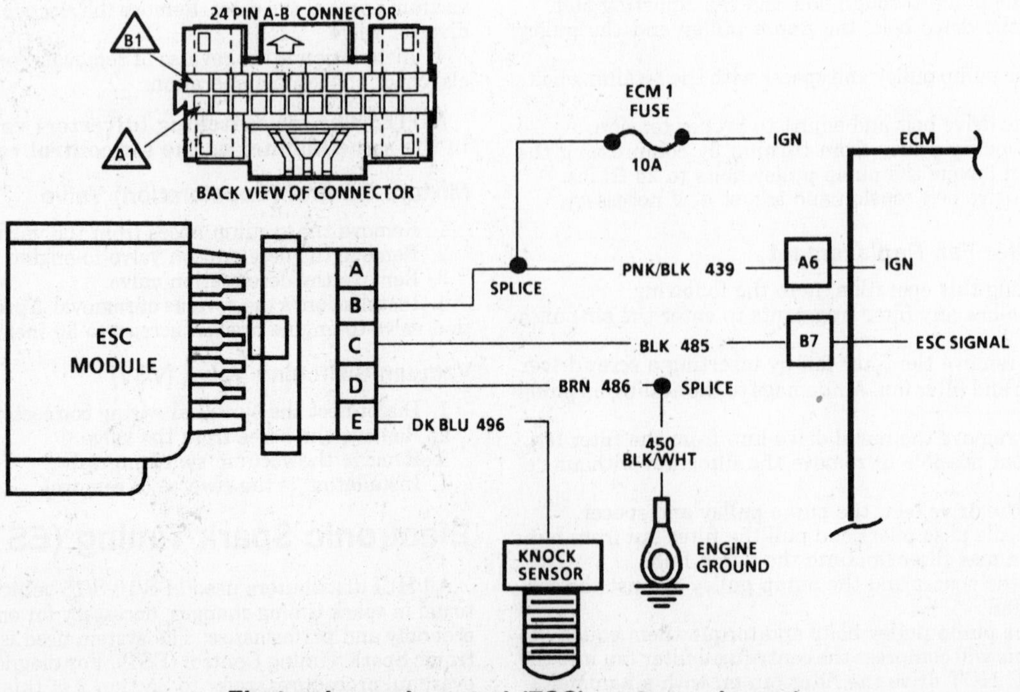
24 PIN A-B CONNECTOR
B1
A1
BACK VIEW OF CONNECTOR
ECM 1
FUSE
10A
IGN
ECM
ESC
MODULE
A
B
C
D
E
SPLICE
PNK/BLK 439
A6
IGN
BLK 485
B7
ESC SIGNAL
BRN 486
SPLICE
DK BLU 496
450
BLK/WHT
KNOCK
SENSOR
ENGINE
GROUND

Electronic spark control (ESC) system schematic

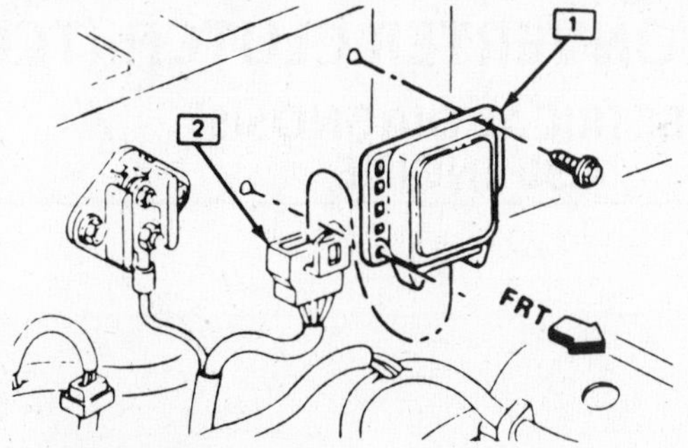
1
2
FRT

1. ESC module
2. Electrical connector

Electronic spark control (ESC) module

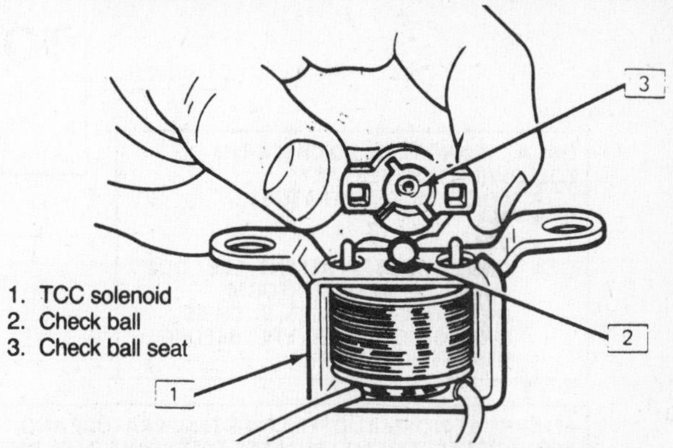
3
2
1

1. TCC solenoid
2. Check ball
3. Check ball seat

Transmission converter clutch (TCC) solenoid

ESC Module

The ESC module is located at the top-rear of the engine.

1. Disconnect the electrical harness connector from the ESC module.
2. Remove the mounting screws and the ESC module from the vehicle.
3. Installation is the reverse of removal.

Transmission Converter Clutch (TCC) System

All vehicles equipped with an automatic transmission use the TCC system. The ECM controls the converter by means of a solenoid mounted in the outdrive housing of the transmission. When the vehicle speed reaches a certain level, the ECM energizes the solenoid and allows the torque converter to mechanically couple the transmission to the engine. When the operating conditions indicate that the transmission should operate as a normal fluid coupled transmission, the ECM will de-energize the solenoid. Depressing the brake pedal will also return the transmission to normal automatic operation.

The ECM monitors the following sensors to control the transmission converter clutch operation.

- Throttle Position Sensor (TPS) – Acceleration and deceleration conditions are used to the clutch.
- Coolant Temperature Sensor – The engine MUST BE warmed before the clutch can be applied.
- Pulse Switch – During a 4-to-3 downshift condition, the clutch switch is opened momentarily.
- Brake Switch – Depressing the brake pedal will de-energize the clutch system.

Early Fuel Evaporation System Carbureted Engines

OPERATION

The early fuel evaporation system provides a rapid heat source to the engine induction system. The heat generated provides quick fuel evaporation and more uniform fuel distribution during cold starts. The system also reduces the length of carburetor choking time, thus reducing exhaust emissions.

The system consists of a ceramic heater grid (located between the carburetor and the intake manifold) and a temperature switch (non-ECM models) or a relay (ECM models) which activates the heater during cold operation. The relay, located under the right fender, is operated by the ECM.

As the coolant temperature increases, the temperature switch (non-ECM models) or the relay (ECM models) turns Off the current to the ceramic heater, allowing the engine to operate normally.

NOTE: Operational checks should be made at normal maintenance intervals.

TESTING

REMOVAL AND INSTALLATION

EFE Heater

1. Remove the air cleaner.

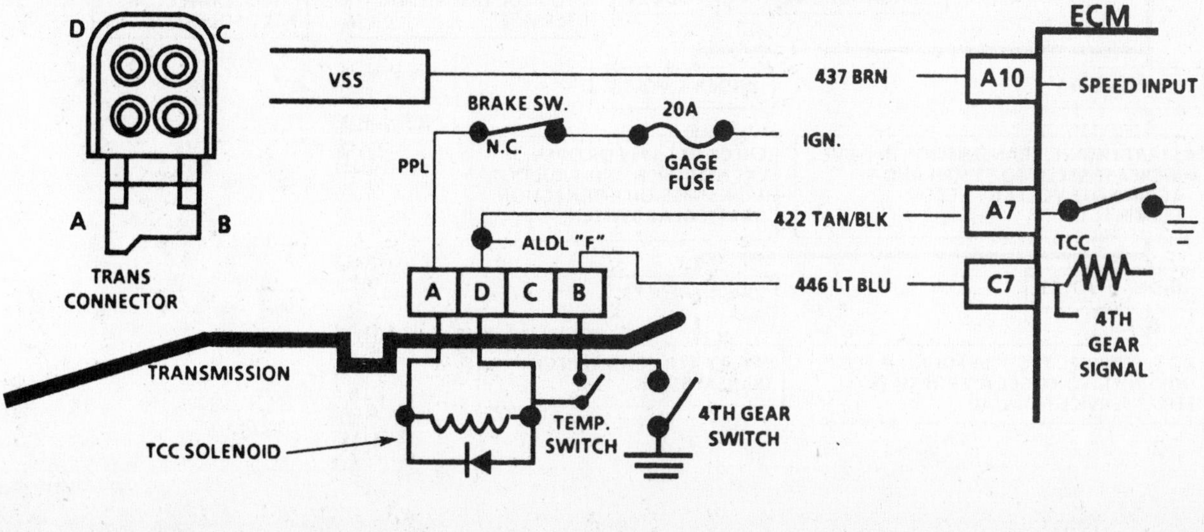
D
C
A
B
TRANS CONNECTOR
VSS
437 BRN
A10
SPEED INPUT
ECM
BRAKE SW.
N.C.
20A
GAGE FUSE
IGN.
PPL
422 TAN/BLK
A7
ALDL "F"
TCC
446 LT BLU
C7
A D C B
4TH GEAR SIGNAL
TRANSMISSION
TEMP. SWITCH
4TH GEAR SWITCH
TCC SOLENOID

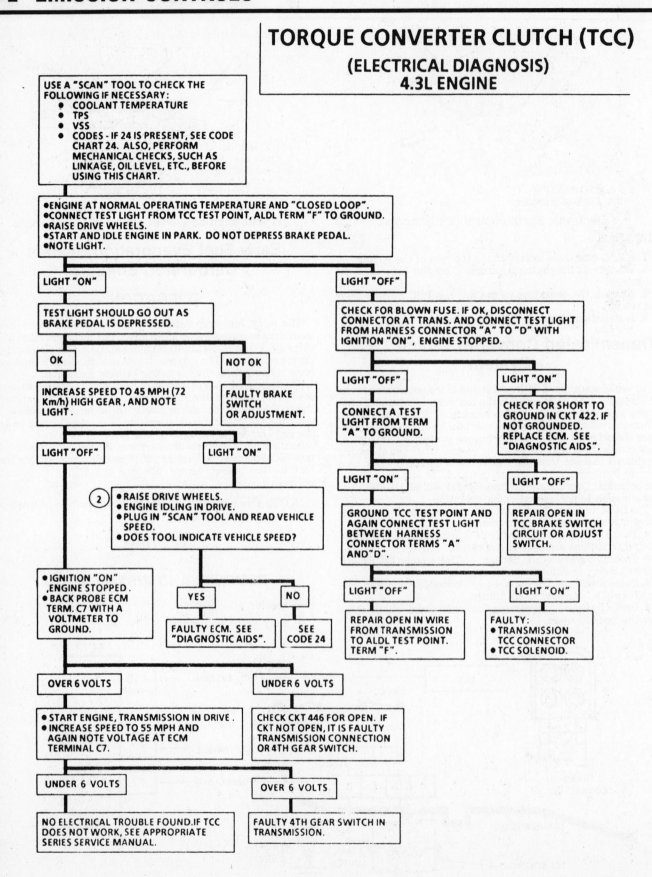

TORQUE CONVERTER CLUTCH (TCC)

(ELECTRICAL DIAGNOSIS)
4.3L ENGINE

USE A "SCAN" TOOL TO CHECK THE FOLLOWING IF NECESSARY:
- COOLANT TEMPERATURE
- TPS
- VSS
- CODES - IF 24 IS PRESENT, SEE CODE CHART 24. ALSO, PERFORM MECHANICAL CHECKS, SUCH AS LINKAGE, OIL LEVEL, ETC., BEFORE USING THIS CHART.

- ENGINE AT NORMAL OPERATING TEMPERATURE AND "CLOSED LOOP".
- CONNECT TEST LIGHT FROM TCC TEST POINT, ALDL TERM "F" TO GROUND.
- RAISE DRIVE WHEELS.
- START AND IDLE ENGINE IN PARK. DO NOT DEPRESS BRAKE PEDAL.
- NOTE LIGHT.

LIGHT "ON"

TEST LIGHT SHOULD GO OUT AS BRAKE PEDAL IS DEPRESSED.

- **OK**
  - INCREASE SPEED TO 45 MPH (72 Km/h) HIGH GEAR, AND NOTE LIGHT.
    - **LIGHT "OFF"**
      - IGNITION "ON", ENGINE STOPPED.
      - BACK PROBE ECM TERM. C7 WITH A VOLTMETER TO GROUND.
        - **OVER 6 VOLTS**
          - START ENGINE, TRANSMISSION IN DRIVE.
          - INCREASE SPEED TO 55 MPH AND AGAIN NOTE VOLTAGE AT ECM TERMINAL C7.
            - **UNDER 6 VOLTS**: NO ELECTRICAL TROUBLE FOUND. IF TCC DOES NOT WORK, SEE APPROPRIATE SERIES SERVICE MANUAL.
            - **OVER 6 VOLTS**: FAULTY 4TH GEAR SWITCH IN TRANSMISSION.
        - **UNDER 6 VOLTS**: CHECK CKT 446 FOR OPEN. IF CKT NOT OPEN, IT IS FAULTY TRANSMISSION CONNECTION OR 4TH GEAR SWITCH.
    - **LIGHT "ON"**
      - (2)
        - RAISE DRIVE WHEELS.
        - ENGINE IDLING IN DRIVE.
        - PLUG IN "SCAN" TOOL AND READ VEHICLE SPEED.
        - DOES TOOL INDICATE VEHICLE SPEED?
          - **YES**: FAULTY ECM. SEE "DIAGNOSTIC AIDS".
          - **NO**: SEE CODE 24
- **NOT OK**: FAULTY BRAKE SWITCH OR ADJUSTMENT.

LIGHT "OFF"

CHECK FOR BLOWN FUSE. IF OK, DISCONNECT CONNECTOR AT TRANS. AND CONNECT TEST LIGHT FROM HARNESS CONNECTOR "A" TO "D" WITH IGNITION "ON", ENGINE STOPPED.

- **LIGHT "OFF"**
  - CONNECT A TEST LIGHT FROM TERM "A" TO GROUND.
    - **LIGHT "ON"**
      - GROUND TCC TEST POINT AND AGAIN CONNECT TEST LIGHT BETWEEN HARNESS CONNECTOR TERMS "A" AND "D".
        - **LIGHT "OFF"**: REPAIR OPEN IN WIRE FROM TRANSMISSION TO ALDL TEST POINT. TERM "F".
        - **LIGHT "ON"**: FAULTY:
          - TRANSMISSION TCC CONNECTOR
          - TCC SOLENOID.
    - **LIGHT "OFF"**: REPAIR OPEN IN TCC BRAKE SWITCH CIRCUIT OR ADJUST SWITCH.
- **LIGHT "ON"**: CHECK FOR SHORT TO GROUND IN CKT 422. IF NOT GROUNDED. REPLACE ECM. SEE "DIAGNOSTIC AIDS".

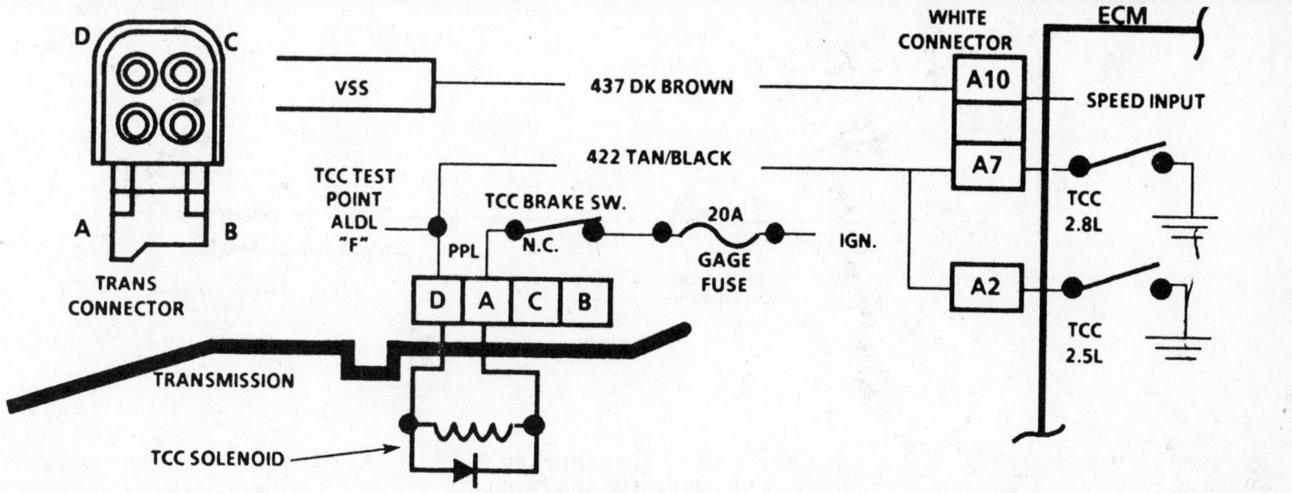
D
C
A
B
TRANS
CONNECTOR
VSS
437 DK BROWN
422 TAN/BLACK
WHITE
CONNECTOR
ECM
A10
SPEED INPUT
A7
A2
TCC
2.8L
TCC
2.5L
TCC TEST
POINT
ALDL
"F"
PPL
TCC BRAKE SW.
N.C.
20A
GAGE
FUSE
IGN.
D A C B
TRANSMISSION
TCC SOLENOID

TORQUE CONVERTER CLUTCH (TCC)

(ELECTRICAL DIAGNOSIS) 2.5L ENGINE

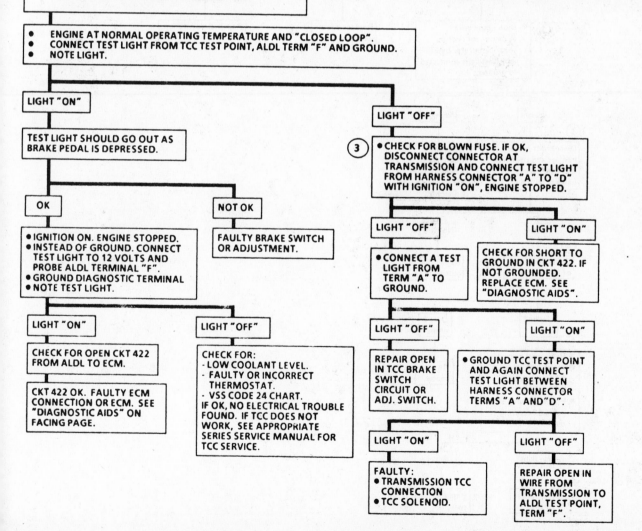

USE A "SCAN" TOOL TO CHECK THE FOLLOWING AND CORRECT IF NECESSARY:
- COOLANT TEMPERATURE
- TPS
- VSS
- CODES - IF 24 IS PRESENT, SEE CODE CHART 24. ALSO, PERFORM MECHANICAL CHECKS, SUCH AS LINKAGE, OIL LEVEL, ETC., BEFORE USING THIS CHART.

- ENGINE AT NORMAL OPERATING TEMPERATURE AND "CLOSED LOOP".
- CONNECT TEST LIGHT FROM TCC TEST POINT, ALDL TERM "F" AND GROUND.
- NOTE LIGHT.

LIGHT "ON"

TEST LIGHT SHOULD GO OUT AS BRAKE PEDAL IS DEPRESSED.

OK

- IGNITION ON. ENGINE STOPPED.
- INSTEAD OF GROUND. CONNECT TEST LIGHT TO 12 VOLTS AND PROBE ALDL TERMINAL "F".
- GROUND DIAGNOSTIC TERMINAL
- NOTE TEST LIGHT.

LIGHT "ON"

CHECK FOR OPEN CKT 422 FROM ALDL TO ECM.

CKT 422 OK. FAULTY ECM CONNECTION OR ECM. SEE "DIAGNOSTIC AIDS" ON FACING PAGE.

LIGHT "OFF"

CHECK FOR:
- LOW COOLANT LEVEL.
- FAULTY OR INCORRECT THERMOSTAT.
- VSS CODE 24 CHART.

IF OK, NO ELECTRICAL TROUBLE FOUND. IF TCC DOES NOT WORK, SEE APPROPRIATE SERIES SERVICE MANUAL FOR TCC SERVICE.

NOT OK

FAULTY BRAKE SWITCH OR ADJUSTMENT.

LIGHT "OFF"

(3)
- CHECK FOR BLOWN FUSE. IF OK, DISCONNECT CONNECTOR AT TRANSMISSION AND CONNECT TEST LIGHT FROM HARNESS CONNECTOR "A" TO "D" WITH IGNITION "ON", ENGINE STOPPED.

LIGHT "OFF"

- CONNECT A TEST LIGHT FROM TERM "A" TO GROUND.

LIGHT "OFF"

REPAIR OPEN IN TCC BRAKE SWITCH CIRCUIT OR ADJ. SWITCH.

LIGHT "ON"

- GROUND TCC TEST POINT AND AGAIN CONNECT TEST LIGHT BETWEEN HARNESS CONNECTOR TERMS "A" AND "D".

LIGHT "ON"

FAULTY:
- TRANSMISSION TCC CONNECTION
- TCC SOLENOID.

LIGHT "OFF"

REPAIR OPEN IN WIRE FROM TRANSMISSION TO ALDL TEST POINT, TERM "F".

LIGHT "ON"

CHECK FOR SHORT TO GROUND IN CKT 422. IF NOT GROUNDED. REPLACE ECM. SEE "DIAGNOSTIC AIDS".

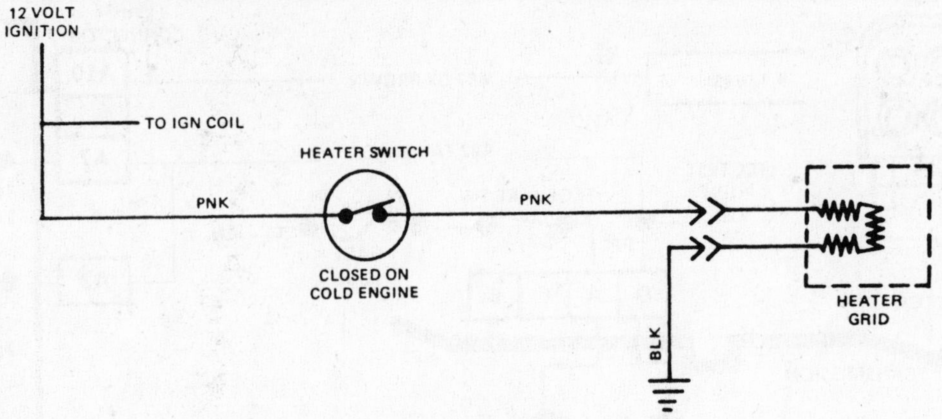
12 VOLT
IGNITION
TO IGN COIL
HEATER SWITCH
PNK
PNK
CLOSED ON
COLD ENGINE
HEATER
GRID
BLK

ELECTRIC EFE
NON-ECM CONTROLLED

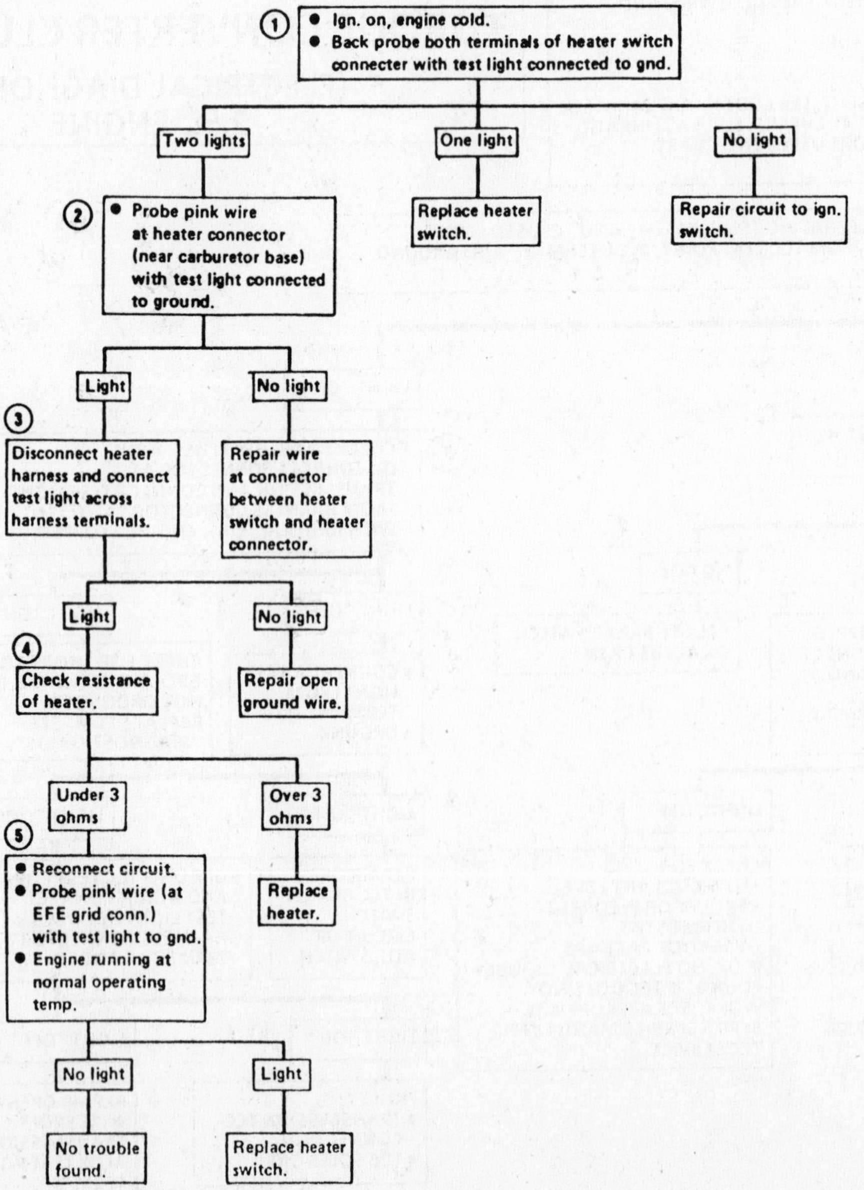
1
• Ign. on, engine cold.
• Back probe both terminals of heater switch connecter with test light connected to gnd.
Two lights
One light
No light
Replace heater switch.
Repair circuit to ign. switch.
2
• Probe pink wire at heater connector (near carburetor base) with test light connected to ground.
Light
No light
3
Disconnect heater harness and connect test light across harness terminals.
Repair wire at connector between heater switch and heater connector.
Light
No light
4
Check resistance of heater.
Repair open ground wire.
Under 3 ohms
Over 3 ohms
5
• Reconnect circuit.
• Probe pink wire (at EFE grid conn.) with test light to gnd.
• Engine running at normal operating temp.
Replace heater.
No light
Light
No trouble found.
Replace heater switch.

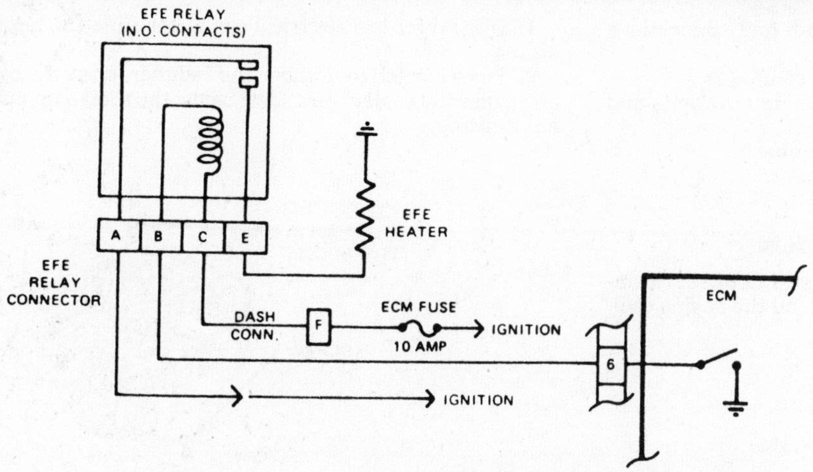
EFE RELAY
(N.O. CONTACTS)
A
B
C
E
EFE
RELAY
CONNECTOR
EFE
HEATER
DASH
CONN.
F
ECM FUSE
10 AMP
IGNITION
ECM
6
IGNITION

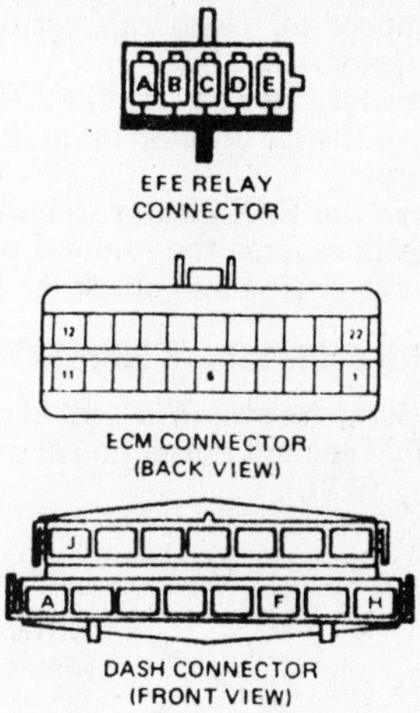
A
B
C
D
E
EFE RELAY
CONNECTOR
12
22
11
6
1
ECM CONNECTOR
(BACK VIEW)
J
A
F
H
DASH CONNECTOR
(FRONT VIEW)

EARLY FUEL EVAPORATION (EFE) CHECK (ELECTRICALLY HEATED)

An intermittent coolant sensor connection could cause the relay to click

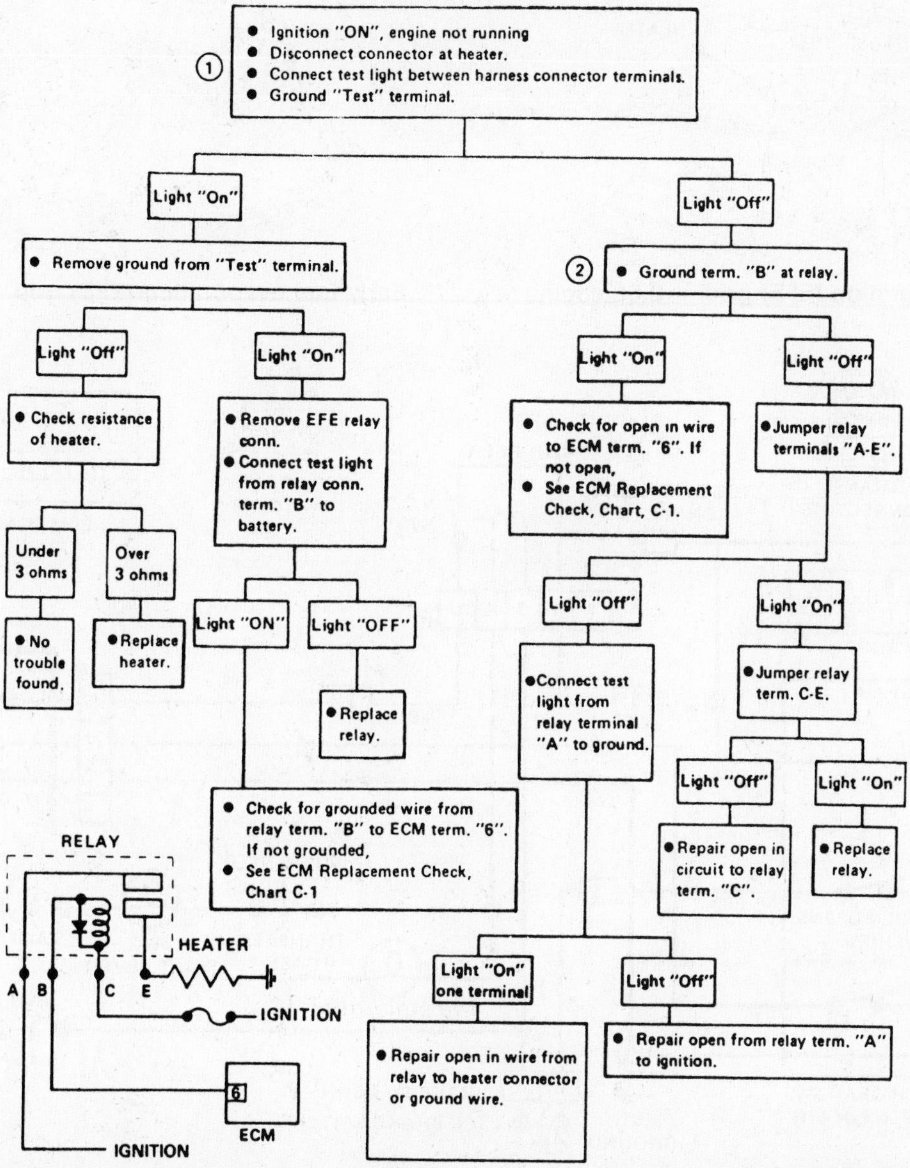
1
● Ignition "ON", engine not running
● Disconnect connector at heater.
● Connect test light between harness connector terminals.
● Ground "Test" terminal.
Light "On"
● Remove ground from "Test" terminal.
Light "Off"
● Check resistance of heater.
Under 3 ohms
● No trouble found.
Over 3 ohms
● Replace heater.
Light "On"
● Remove EFE relay conn.
● Connect test light from relay conn. term. "B" to battery.
Light "ON"
● Check for grounded wire from relay term. "B" to ECM term. "6". If not grounded,
● See ECM Replacement Check, Chart C-1
Light "OFF"
● Replace relay.
Light "Off"
2
● Ground term. "B" at relay.
Light "On"
● Check for open in wire to ECM term. "6". If not open,
● See ECM Replacement Check, Chart, C-1.
Light "Off"
● Jumper relay terminals "A-E".
Light "Off"
● Connect test light from relay terminal "A" to ground.
Light "On" one terminal
● Repair open in wire from relay to heater connector or ground wire.
Light "Off"
● Repair open from relay term. "A" to ignition.
Light "On"
● Jumper relay term. C-E.
Light "Off"
● Repair open in circuit to relay term. "C".
Light "On"
● Replace relay.
RELAY
HEATER
A
B
C
E
IGNITION
6
ECM
IGNITION

2. Disconnect all electrical, vacuum and fuel connections from carburetor.
3. Disconnect the EFE Heater electrical connector.
4. Remove the carburetor-to-intake manifold nuts/bolts and the carburetor.
5. Remove the EFE Heater isolator assembly.
6. To intall, reverse the removal procedures.
7. Start the engine and check for leaks.

Temperature Switch – Non-ECM Models

The temperature switch is located on the rear (2.0L) of the intake manifold coolant outlet housing or behind the engine coolant housing (2.8L).

1. Disconnect the electrical connector from the temperature switch.
2. Place a catch pan under the radiator, open the drain cock and drain the coolant to a level below the intake manifold coolant housing.

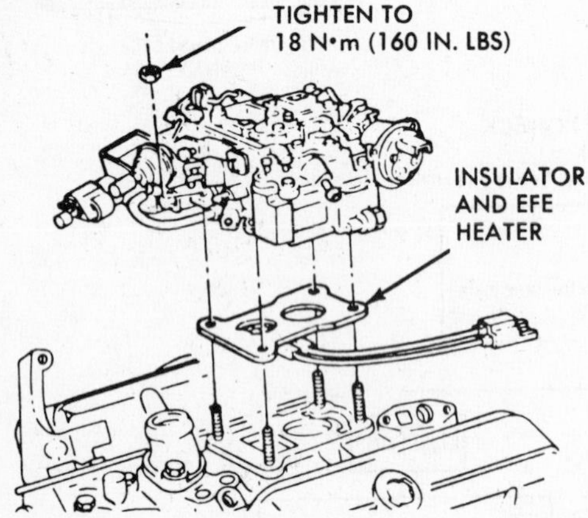
TIGHTEN TO
18 N•m (160 IN. LBS)
INSULATOR
AND EFE
HEATER

Early fuel evaporation (EFE) grid – 2.8L engine

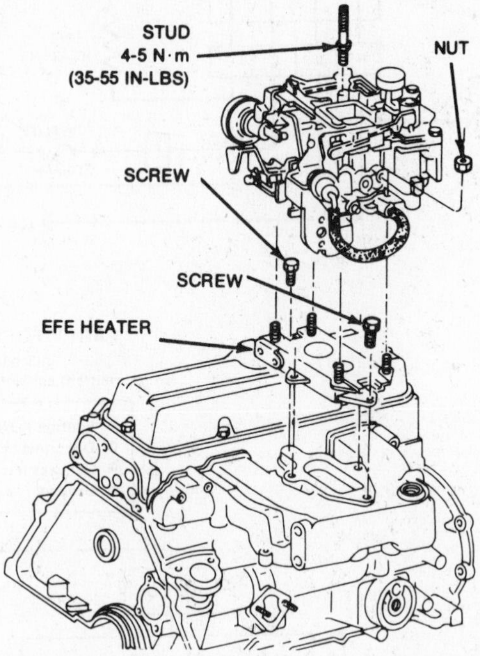
STUD
4-5 N·m
(35-55 IN-LBS)
NUT
SCREW
SCREW
EFE HEATER

Early fuel evaporation (EFE) grid – 2.0L engine

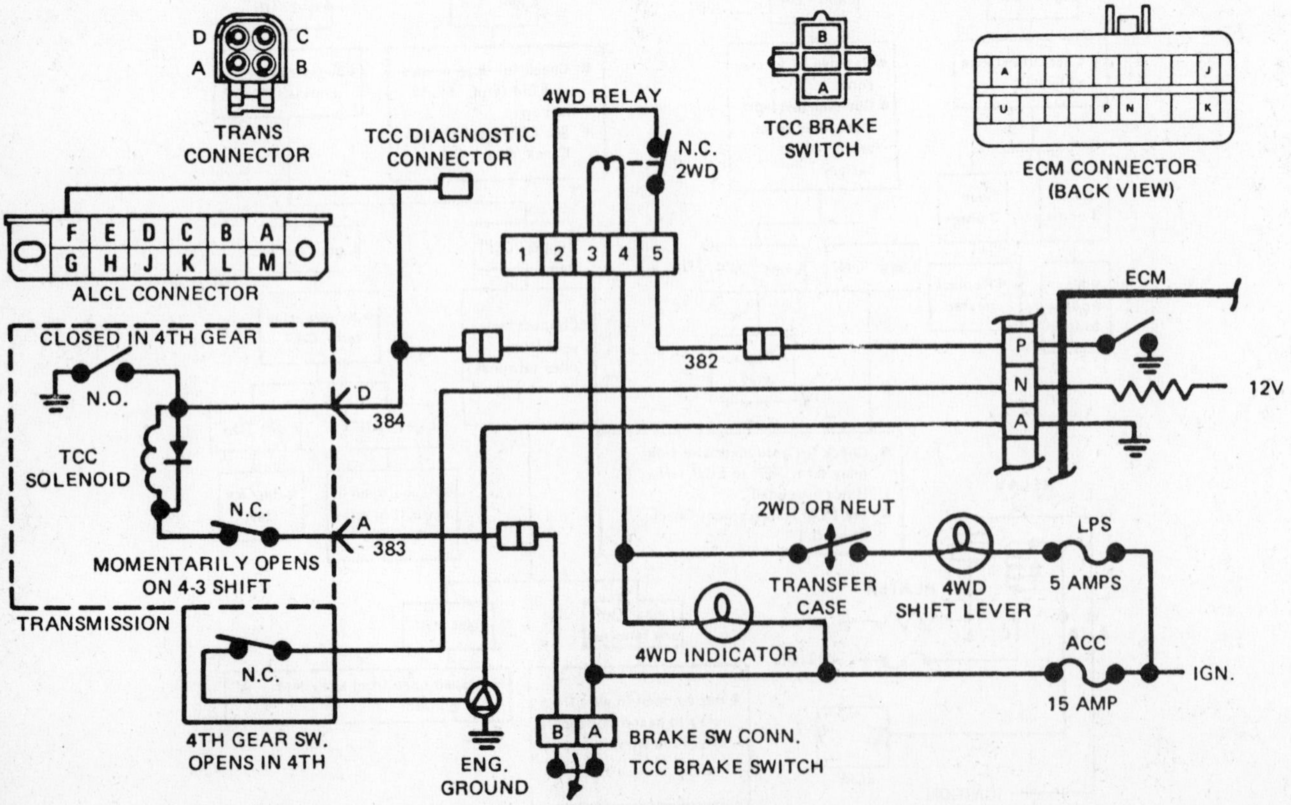
D
C
A
B
TRANS
CONNECTOR
TCC DIAGNOSTIC
CONNECTOR
4WD RELAY
N.C.
2WD
B
A
TCC BRAKE
SWITCH
A
J
U
P
N
K
ECM CONNECTOR
(BACK VIEW)
F E D C B A
G H J K L M
ALCL CONNECTOR
1 2 3 4 5
ECM
CLOSED IN 4TH GEAR
N.O.
D
384
382
P
N
A
12V
TCC
SOLENOID
N.C.
A
383
MOMENTARILY OPENS
ON 4-3 SHIFT
TRANSMISSION
2WD OR NEUT
TRANSFER
CASE
4WD
SHIFT LEVER
LPS
5 AMPS
4WD INDICATOR
ACC
IGN.
15 AMP
N.C.
4TH GEAR SW.
OPENS IN 4TH
ENG.
GROUND
B A
BRAKE SW CONN.
TCC BRAKE SWITCH

TRANSMISSION CONVERTER CLUTCH (TCC) CHECK

ELECTRICAL DIAGNOSIS

Mechanical checks, such as linkage, oil level, etc., should be performed prior to using this chart.

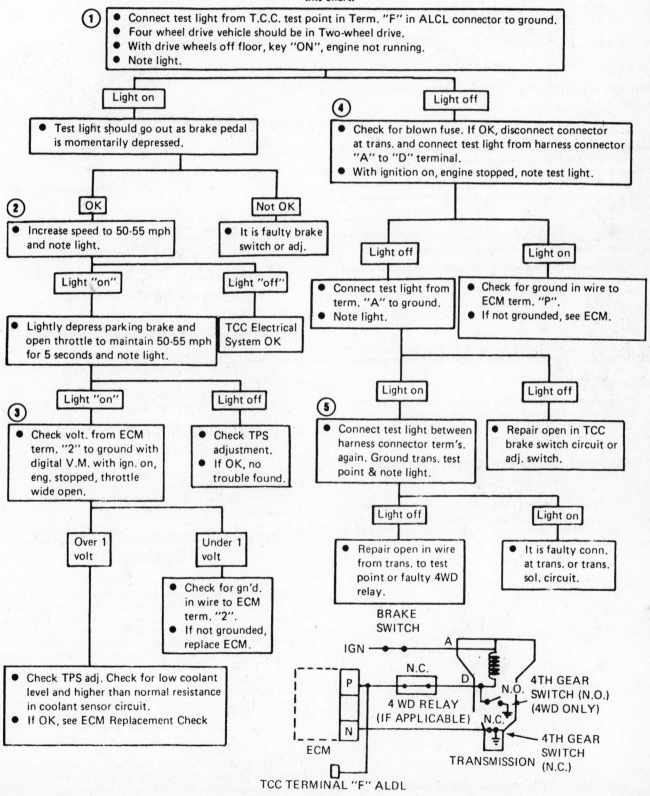

(1)
- Connect test light from T.C.C. test point in Term. "F" in ALCL connector to ground.
- Four wheel drive vehicle should be in Two-wheel drive.
- With drive wheels off floor, key "ON", engine not running.
- Note light.

Light on

- Test light should go out as brake pedal is momentarily depressed.

OK

(2)
- Increase speed to 50-55 mph and note light.

Light "on"

- Lightly depress parking brake and open throttle to maintain 50-55 mph for 5 seconds and note light.

Light "on"

(3)
- Check volt. from ECM term. "2" to ground with digital V.M. with ign. on, eng. stopped, throttle wide open.

Over 1 volt

- Check TPS adj. Check for low coolant level and higher than normal resistance in coolant sensor circuit.
- If OK, see ECM Replacement Check

Under 1 volt

- Check for gn'd. in wire to ECM term. "2".
- If not grounded, replace ECM.

Light off

- Check TPS adjustment.
- If OK, no trouble found.

Light "off"

TCC Electrical System OK

Not OK

- It is faulty brake switch or adj.

Light off

(4)
- Check for blown fuse. If OK, disconnect connector at trans. and connect test light from harness connector "A" to "D" terminal.
- With ignition on, engine stopped, note test light.

Light off

- Connect test light from term. "A" to ground.
- Note light.

Light on

(5)
- Connect test light between harness connector term's. again. Ground trans. test point & note light.

Light off

- Repair open in wire from trans. to test point or faulty 4WD relay.

Light on

- It is faulty conn. at trans. or trans. sol. circuit.

Light off

- Repair open in TCC brake switch circuit or adj. switch.

Light on

- Check for ground in wire to ECM term. "P".
- If not grounded, see ECM.

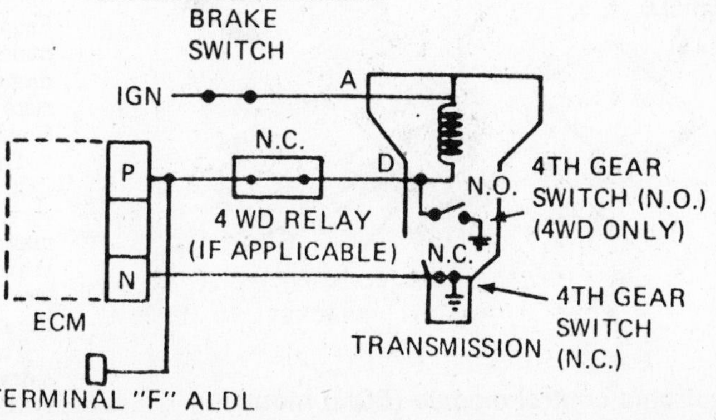

BRAKE SWITCH
IGN
A
N.C.
D
N.O.
4TH GEAR SWITCH (N.O.) (4WD ONLY)
P
N
4 WD RELAY (IF APPLICABLE)
N.C.
ECM
4TH GEAR SWITCH (N.C.)
TRANSMISSION
TCC TERMINAL "F" ALDL

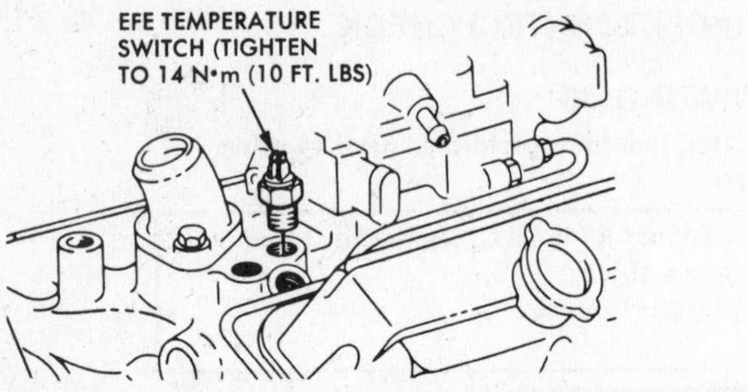
EFE TEMPERATURE
SWITCH (TIGHTEN
TO 14 N•m (10 FT. LBS)

Early fuel evaporation (EFE) temperature switch 2.8L engine

CAUTION

When draining the coolant, keep in mind that cats and dogs are attracted by the ethylene glycol antifreeze, and are quite likely to drink any that is left in an uncovered container or in puddles on the ground. This will prove fatal in sufficient quantity. Always drain the coolant into a sealable container. Coolant should be reused unless it is contaminated or several years old.

NOTE: If replacing the temperature switch, refer to the calibration number stamped on the base.

3. Apply soft setting sealant to the male threads of the temperature switch Installation is the reverse of removal.
4. Torque the temperature switch-to-intake manifold coolant housing to 10 ft. lbs. Refill the cooling system. Start the engine, run the engine to normal operating temperatures and check the operation.

NOTE: When applying sealant to the temperature switch, be sure not to coat the sensor end with sealant.

Relay – ECM Models

1. Disconnect negative battery terminal from the battery.
2. Disconnect electrical connector from the relay.
3. Remove relay-to-bracket bolts and the relay.
4. Installation is the reverse of removal.

Closed Loop Emission Control System

NOTE: When troubleshooting the system, always check the electrical and vacuum connectors which may cause the problem before testing or replacing a component.

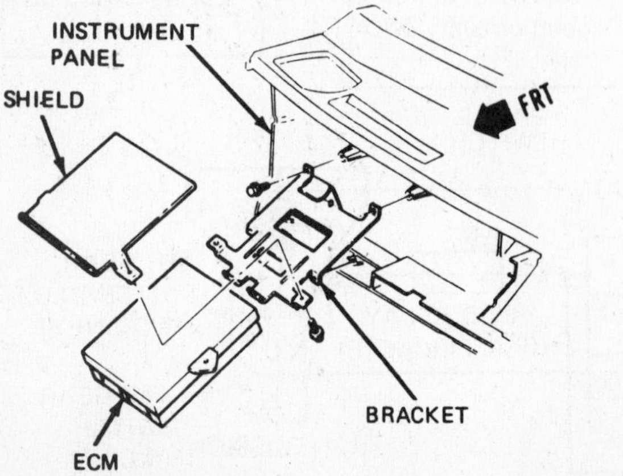
INSTRUMENT
PANEL
SHIELD
FRT
BRACKET
ECM

Electronic control module (ECM) mounting

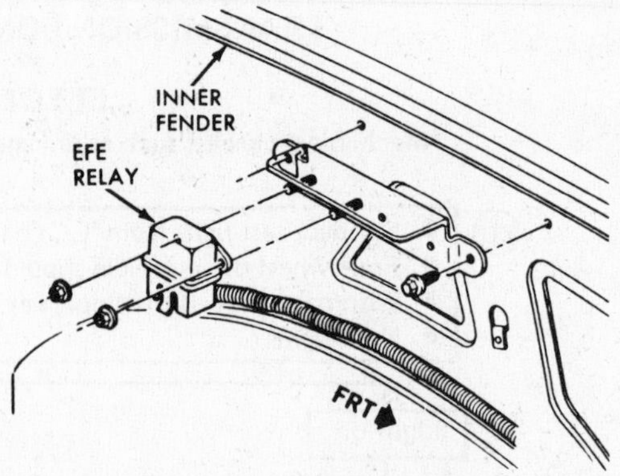
INNER
FENDER
EFE
RELAY
FRT

Early fuel evaporation (EFE) relay – 2.8L engine

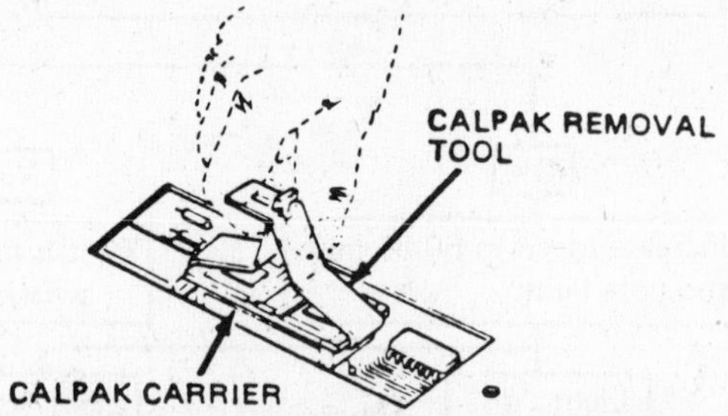
CALPAK REMOVAL
TOOL
CALPAK CARRIER

Removing the PROM from the ECM

VACUUM CONTROLLER REPLACEMENT

1. Disconnect the electrical connector.
2. Disconnect the vacuum hoses from the vacuum regulator and solenoid.
3. Remove the vacuum controller.
4. Installation is the reverse of removal.

IDLE AND WIDE OPEN THROTTLE (WOT) VACUUM SWITCH REPLACEMENT

1. Disconnect the electrical harness connector.
2. Disconnect the vacuum hoses from the sensors.
3. Remove the idle and the WOT vacuum switch.
4. Installation is the reverse of removal.

Computer Command Control (CCC) System

The Computer Command Control (CCC) System is an electronically controlled exhaust emission system that monitors many engine/vehicle operating conditions and then uses the information to control various engine related systems. The system makes constant adjustments to maintain good vehicle performance under all normal driving conditions. The system also assists the catalytic converter in effectively controlling the emissions of HC, CO and NOx.

The Electronic Control Module (ECM) is the brain of the CCC. It constantly monitors various information from the sensors and controls the systems that affect the vehicle performance. The ECM has two parts: A Controller (the ECM without the PROM) and a separate calibrator (the PROM). The ECM is located on the right side of instrument panel, accessible from the engine compartment.

To allow the Controller to be used in many different vehicles, a device called a Calibrator or Programmable Read Only Memory (PROM) is used. The PROM which is located inside the ECM, stores information such as: the vehicle's weight, engine, transmission, axle ratio and many other specifications. Since the PROM stores specific information, it is important that the correct one be used in the right vehicle.

NOTE: For diagnostic testing procedures, refer to Section 2 of this book.

REMOVAL AND INSTALLATION

Coolant Temperature Sensor (CTS)

The coolant temperature sensor is a thermistor mounted in the engine coolant stream. Low coolant temperatures produce a high resistance – 100,000Ω at 40°F (5°C) – while high temperatures cause low resistance – 70Ω at 266°F (130°C).

The ECM supplies a 5 volt signal to the CTS through a resistor in the ECM and measure the voltage. The voltage will be high when the engine is cold, and low when the engine is hot. By measuring the voltage, the ECM knows the engine coolant temperature. Engine coolant temperature affects most system controlled by the ECM

1. Remove the negative battery cable.

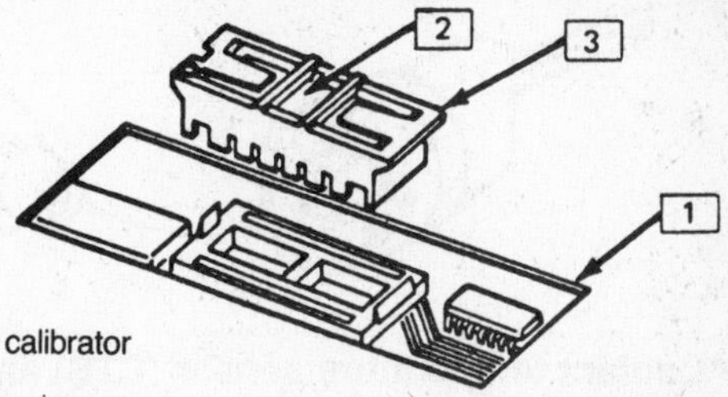
2
3
1

1. ECM
2. Prom engine calibrator
3. Prom carrier

Programmable read-only memory (PROM) chip

2. Drain the cooling system.

CAUTION

When draining the coolant, keep in mind that cats and dogs are attracted by the ethylene glycol antifreeze, and are quite likely to drink any that is left in an uncovered container or in puddles on the ground. This will prove fatal in sufficient quantity. Always drain the coolant into a sealable container. Coolant should be reused unless it is contaminated or several years old.

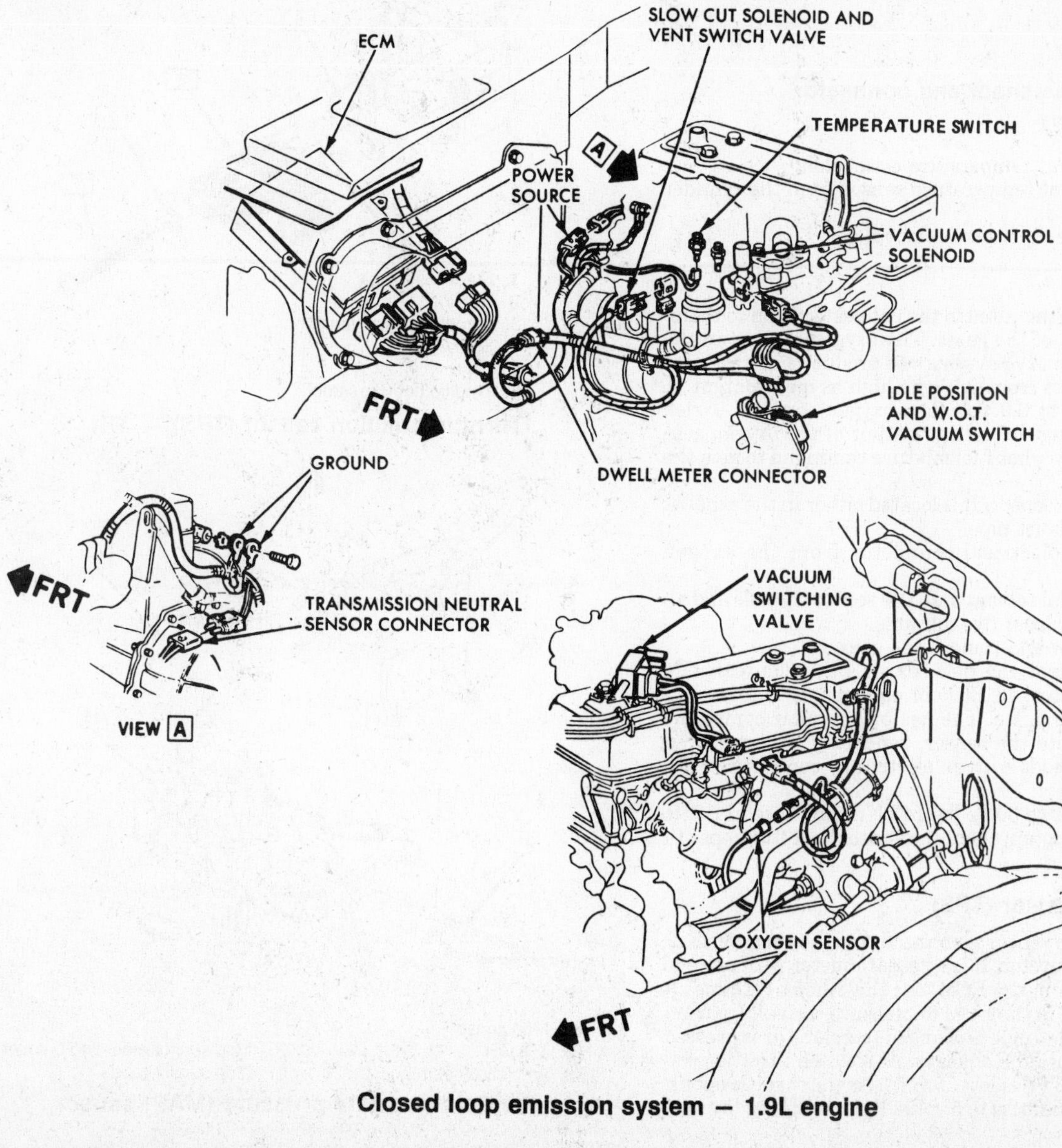
SLOW CUT SOLENOID AND VENT SWITCH VALVE
ECM
TEMPERATURE SWITCH
A
POWER SOURCE
VACUUM CONTROL SOLENOID
FRT
IDLE POSITION AND W.O.T. VACUUM SWITCH
GROUND
DWELL METER CONNECTOR
FRT
TRANSMISSION NEUTRAL SENSOR CONNECTOR
VIEW A
VACUUM SWITCHING VALVE
OXYGEN SENSOR
FRT

Closed loop emission system – 1.9L engine

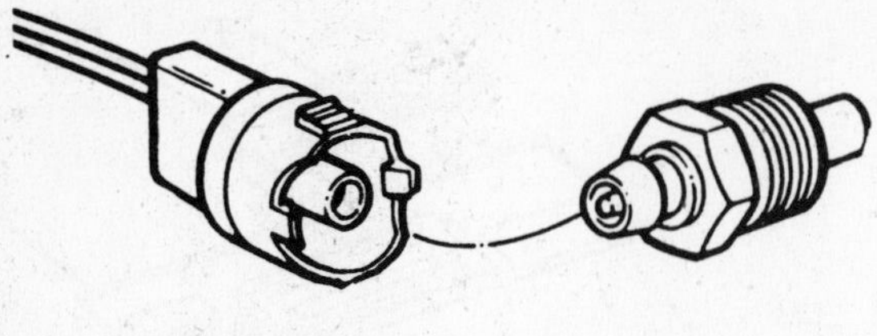

Coolant temperature sensor (CTS) and connector

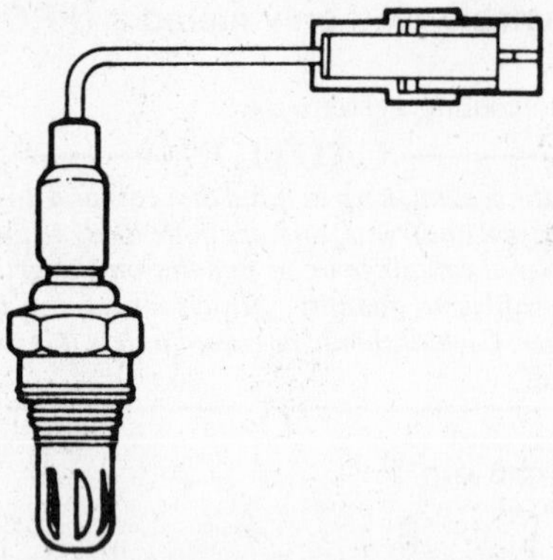

Oxygen sensor and connector

3. Remove the coolant temperature connector.
4. Remove the coolant temperature sensor from the cylinder head or intake manifold.
5. Installation is the reverse of removal.

Oxygen Sensor

The oxygen sensor is mounted in the exhaust system to monitor the oxygen content of the gases. The oxygen content in the exhaust reacts with the oxygen sensor to produce a voltage output. This voltage ranges from 0.1 volt (high oxygen content – lean air/fuel mixture) to 0.9 volt (low oxygen content – rich mixture). By monitoring the voltage output of the oxygen sensor, the ECM will know what fuel mixture command to give the injector

1. Locate the oxygen sensor. It is located either in the exhaust manifold or in the exhaust pipe.
2. Disconnect the electrical connector from the oxygen sensor.
3. Spray a commercial solvent onto the sensor threads and allow it to soak in for at least five minutes.
4. Carefully unscrew and remove the sensor.
5. To install, first coat the new sensor's threads with GM Anti-Seize Compound No. 5613695 or equivalent. This is not a conventional anti-seize paste. The use of a regular compound may electrically insulate the sensor, rendering it inoperative. You must coat the threads with an electrically conductive anti-seize compound.
6. Torque the sensor to 30 ft. lbs. (42 Nm). Be careful not to damage the electrical pigtail; check the sensor boot for proper fit and installation.

Throttle Position Sensor (TPS)

The throttle position sensor is connected to the throttle shaft of the TBI unit or carburetor. It is a potentiometer with one end connected to 5 volts from the ECM and the other to ground. A third wire is connected to the ECM to measure the voltage from the TPS. As the throttle angle is changed (accelerator is pressed down), the output of the TPS changes. At a closed throttle position, the output of the TPS is low (.5 volt). As the throttle opens, the output voltage should rise to 5 volts. By monitoring the out-

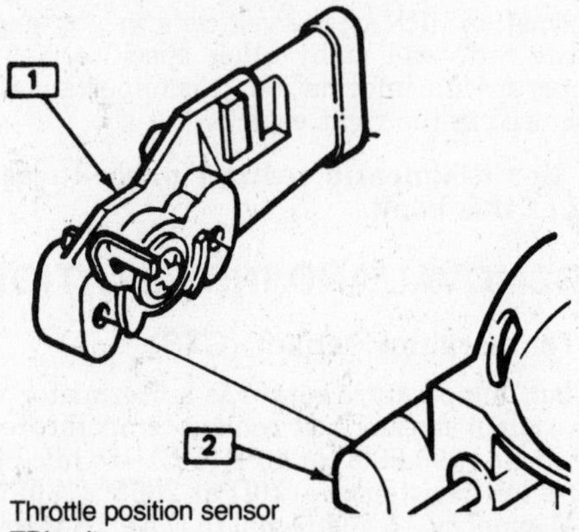
1
2

1. Throttle position sensor
2. TBI unit

Throttle position sensor (TPS) – carburetor

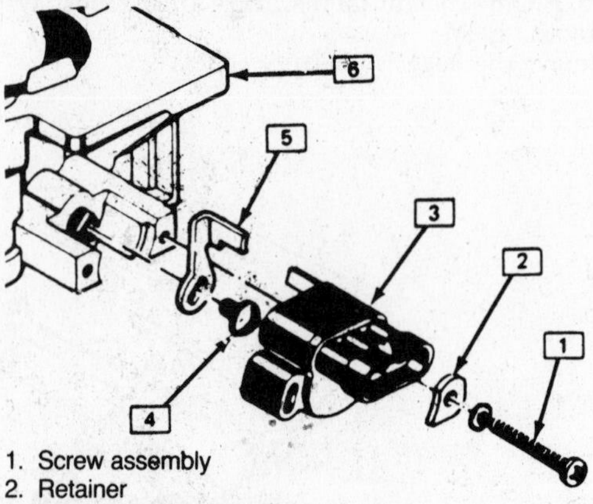
6
5
3
2
1
4

1. Screw assembly
2. Retainer
3. Throttle position sensor
4. Screw
5. Lever
6. Throttle body assembly

Throttle position sensor (TPS) – TBI

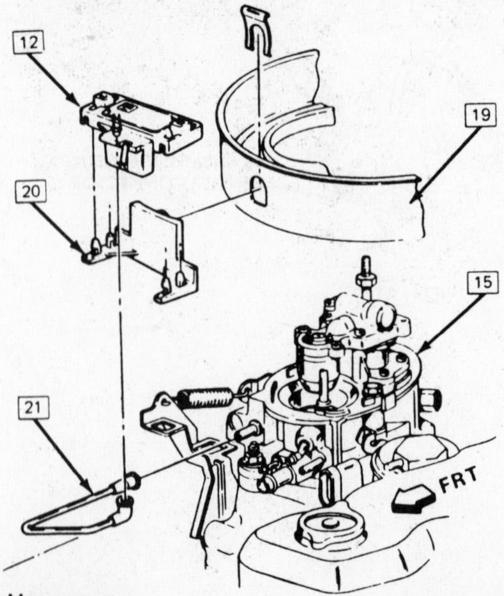
12
19
20
15
21
FRT

12. Map sensor
15. TBI unit
19. Air cleaner asm.
20. Map sensor mounting bracket
21. Map sensor tube

Manifold absolute pressure (MAP) sensor

put voltage from the TPS, the ECM can determine fuel delivery based on throttle valve angle.

1. Remove the air cleaner.
2. Disconnect the electrical connector from the Throttle Position Sensor (TPS).
3. Remove the TPS mounting screws, the lockwashers and the retainers.
4. Remove the TPS sensor.
5. To install, make sure that the throttle valve is in the closed position, then install the TPS sensor.

NOTE: Make sure that the TPS pickup lever is located ABOVE the tang on the throttle actuator lever.

6. To complete the installation, lubricate the mounting screws with Loctite® (thread locking compound) No. 262 or equivalent, then reverse the removal procedures.

Manifold Pressure Sensor (MAP)

The manifold absolute pressure sensor measures the changes in the intake manifold pressure, which result from engine load and speed changes, and converts this to a voltage output. A closed throttle on the engine coastdown will produce a relatively low MAP output, while a wide open throttle will produce a high output. This high output is produced because the pressure inside the manifold is the same as outside the manifold, so 100 percent of the outside air pressure is measured.

The MAP sensor is also used to measure barometric pressure under certain conditions, which allows the ECM to automatically adjust for different altitudes.

The ECM sends a 5 volt reference signal to the MAP sensor. As the manifold pressure changes, the electrical resistance of the sensor also changes. By monitoring the sensor output voltage, the ECM knows the manifold pressure.

By using the signal sent from the MAP sensor, the ECM can determine fuel and ignition timing requirements. A high pressure reading requires more fuel, while a low pressure reading requires less fuel.

1. Remove the sensor-to-throttle body vacuum hose.
2. Disconnect the sensor's electrical connector.
3. Remove the MAP sensor from the air cleaner mounting bracket.
4. Installation is the reverse of removal.

Manifold Air Temperature (MAT) Sensor

The manifold air temperature sensor is a thermistor which changes valve based on air cleaner temperature. Low air temperatures produce a high resistance – 100,000Ω at 40°F (5°C) – while high temperatures cause low resistance – 70Ω at 266°F (130°C).

The ECM supplies a 5 volt signal to the MAT through a resistor in the ECM and measure the voltage. The voltage will be high when the manifold air is cold, and low when the air is hot. By measuring the voltage, the ECM knows the manifold air temperature.

The MAT sensor signal is used by the ECM to delay exhaust gas recirculation (EGR valve) until the manifold air temperature reaches 40°F (5°C). The ECM also uses the signal to retard ignition timing during high air temperatures.

VACUUM DIAGRAMS

NOTE: Consult the Vehicle Emission Control Information Label in the engine compartment for vacuum hose routing specific to your vehicle.

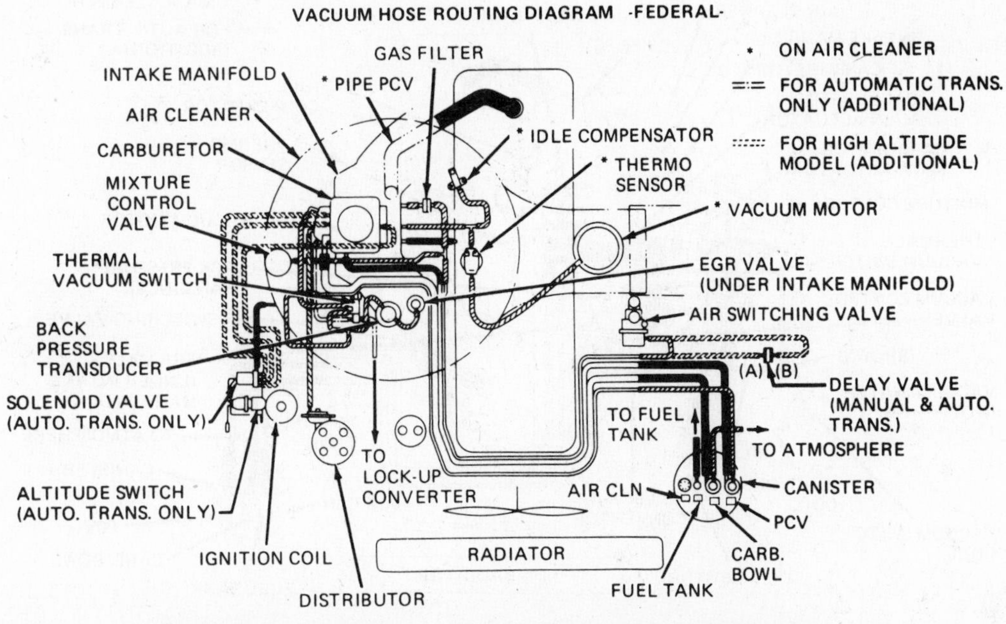
VACUUM HOSE ROUTING DIAGRAM -FEDERAL-
• ON AIR CLEANER
FOR AUTOMATIC TRANS. ONLY (ADDITIONAL)
FOR HIGH ALTITUDE MODEL (ADDITIONAL)
GAS FILTER
INTAKE MANIFOLD
* PIPE PCV
AIR CLEANER
CARBURETOR
* IDLE COMPENSATOR
* THERMO SENSOR
MIXTURE CONTROL VALVE
* VACUUM MOTOR
THERMAL VACUUM SWITCH
EGR VALVE (UNDER INTAKE MANIFOLD)
AIR SWITCHING VALVE
BACK PRESSURE TRANSDUCER
(A) (B)
DELAY VALVE (MANUAL & AUTO. TRANS.)
SOLENOID VALVE (AUTO. TRANS. ONLY)
TO FUEL TANK
TO ATMOSPHERE
TO LOCK-UP CONVERTER
AIR CLN
CANISTER
ALTITUDE SWITCH (AUTO. TRANS. ONLY)
PCV
IGNITION COIL
RADIATOR
CARB. BOWL
FUEL TANK
DISTRIBUTOR

Vacuum hose routing – 1.9L engine (except California)

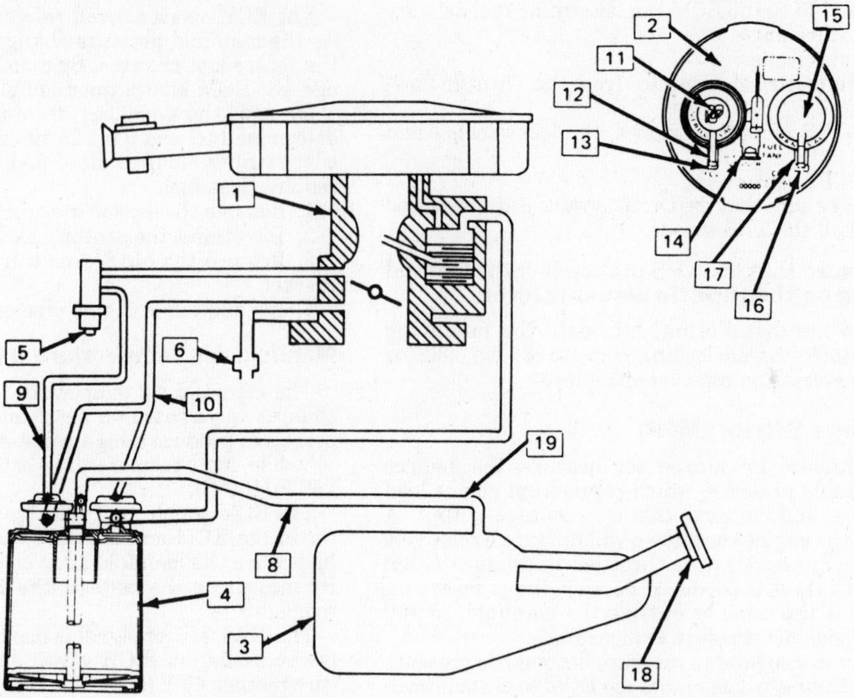

1
2
3
4
5
6
8
9
10
11
12
13
14
15
16
17
18
19

1. Carburetor
2. Top view of canister
3. Fuel tank
4. Canister
5. TVS
6. PVC
7. Carburetor bowl vent line
8. Fuel tank vapor line
9. Ported vacuum line
10. Fuel vapor purge line
11. Canister purge valve
12. Control vacuum tube (ported vac)
13. Purge tube (PCV)
14. Canister vent
15. Vapor vent valve
16. Vapor from carburetor tube
17. Control vacuum tube (manifold vac)
18. Sealed fuel tank cap
19. Fuel tank vapor line restriction

Emissions control system schematic – 2.0L and 2.8L carbureted engines

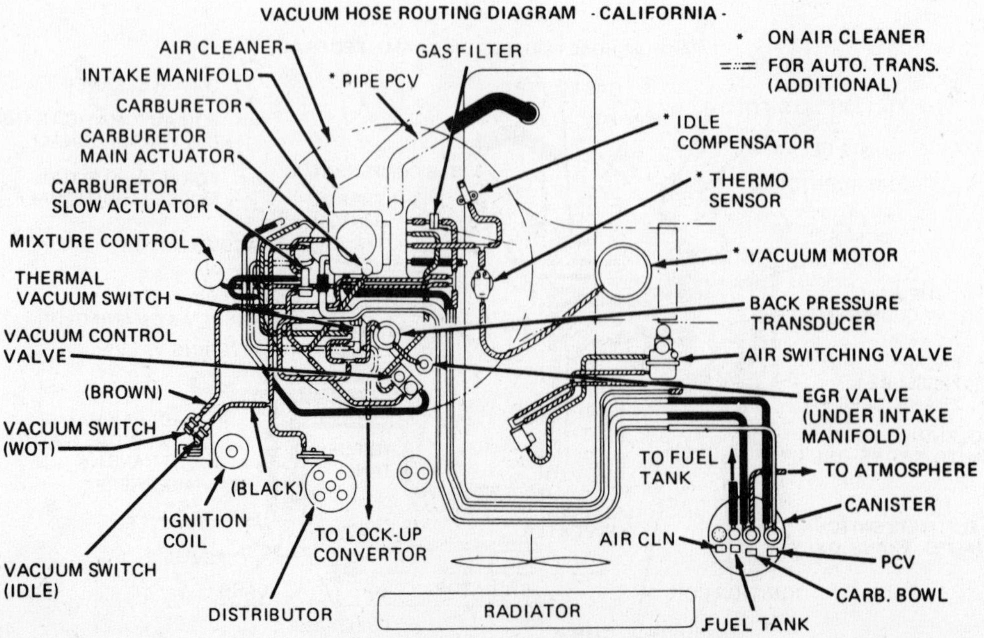

VACUUM HOSE ROUTING DIAGRAM -CALIFORNIA-
* ON AIR CLEANER
=== FOR AUTO. TRANS. (ADDITIONAL)
AIR CLEANER
GAS FILTER
INTAKE MANIFOLD
* PIPE PCV
CARBURETOR
CARBURETOR MAIN ACTUATOR
* IDLE COMPENSATOR
CARBURETOR SLOW ACTUATOR
* THERMO SENSOR
MIXTURE CONTROL
* VACUUM MOTOR
THERMAL VACUUM SWITCH
BACK PRESSURE TRANSDUCER
VACUUM CONTROL VALVE
AIR SWITCHING VALVE
(BROWN)
EGR VALVE (UNDER INTAKE MANIFOLD)
VACUUM SWITCH (WOT)
TO FUEL TANK
TO ATMOSPHERE
(BLACK)
CANISTER
IGNITION COIL
TO LOCK-UP CONVERTOR
AIR CLN
PCV
VACUUM SWITCH (IDLE)
CARB. BOWL
DISTRIBUTOR
RADIATOR
FUEL TANK

Vacuum hose routing – 1.9L engine (California)

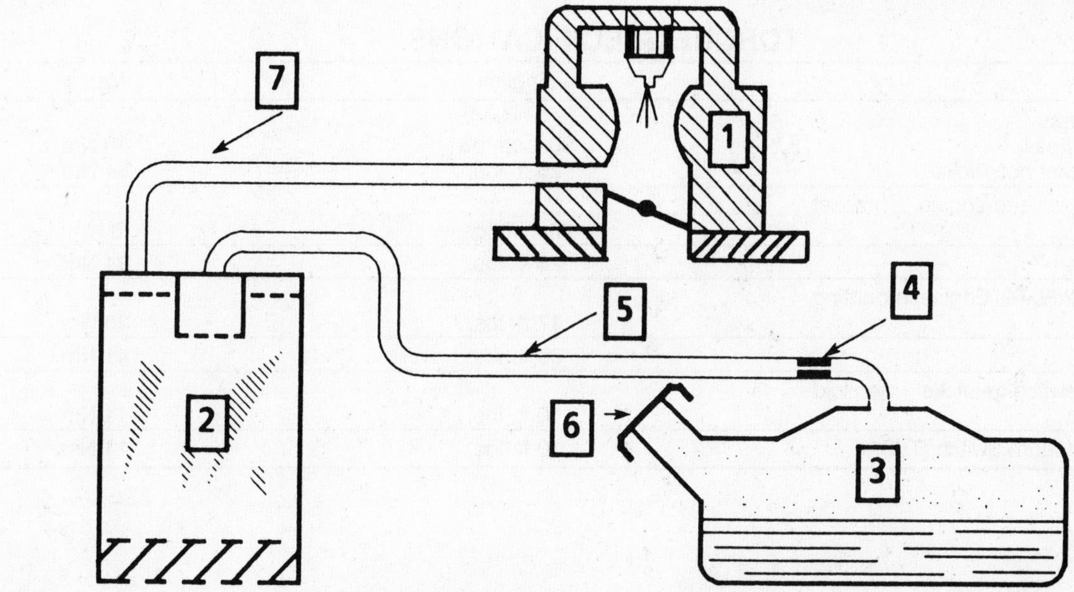
7
1
4
5
6
2
3

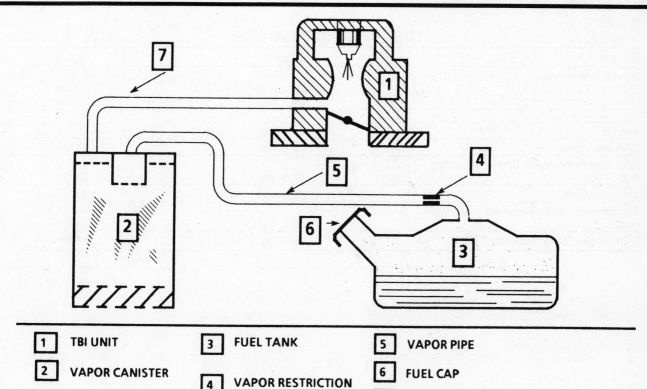

1 TBI UNIT	3 FUEL TANK	5 VAPOR PIPE
2 VAPOR CANISTER	4 VAPOR RESTRICTION	6 FUEL CAP
		7 CANISTER HOSE

Emissions control system schematic — 2.5L and 4.3L TBI engine

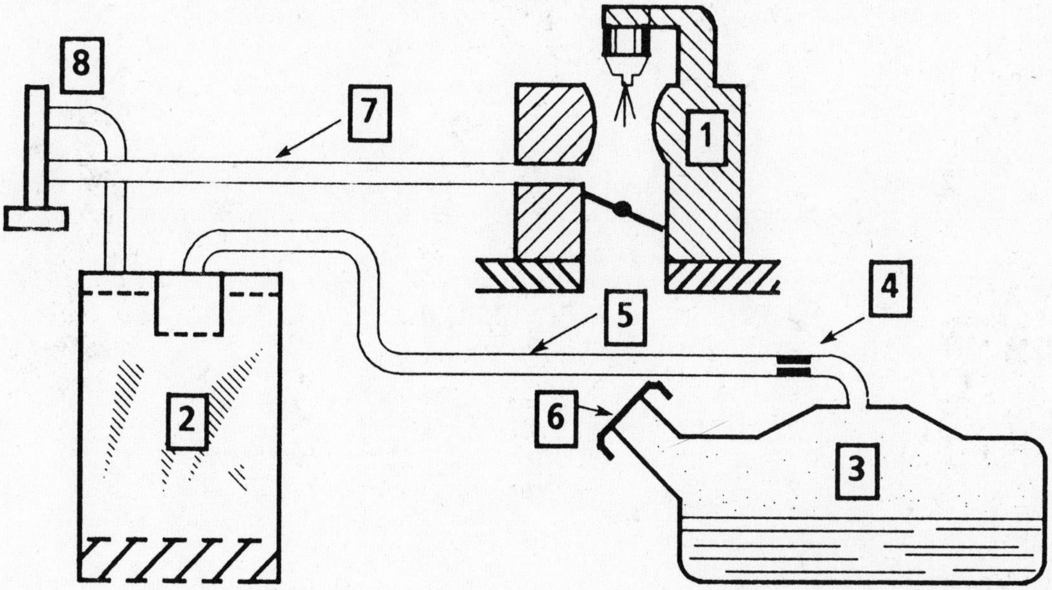
8
7
1
4
5
6
2
3

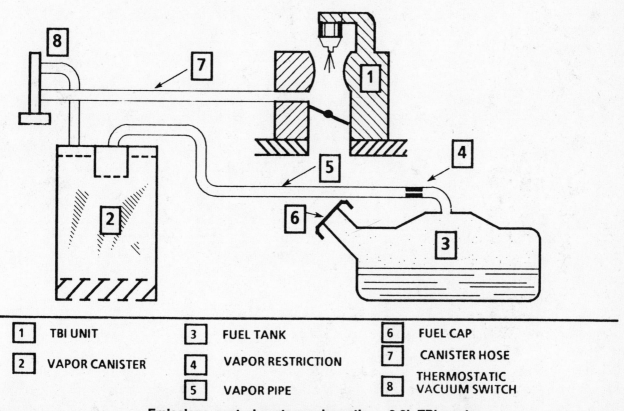

1 TBI UNIT	3 FUEL TANK	6 FUEL CAP
2 VAPOR CANISTER	4 VAPOR RESTRICTION	7 CANISTER HOSE
	5 VAPOR PIPE	8 THERMOSTATIC VACUUM SWITCH

Emissions control system schematic — 2.8L TBI engine

TORQUE SPECIFICATIONS

Component	English	Metric
Air Injection Pump		
Pump pulley bolts	90 inch lbs.	10 Nm
Pump-to-bracket nuts/bolts	25 ft. lbs.	34 Nm
Deceleration valve-to-engine bracket screws	30 inch lbs.	3 Nm
EGR Valve bolts	25 ft. lbs.	34 Nm
EGR Solenoid (2.8L TBI Engine) mounting nut	17 ft. lbs.	23 Nm
Oxygen sensor	30 ft. lbs.	41 Nm
Temperature switch-to-intake manifold coolant housing	10 ft. lbs.	14 Nm
Thermostatic Vacuum Switch (TVS)	10 ft. lbs.	14 Nm

5 Fuel System

QUICK REFERENCE INDEX

GENERAL INDEX

CARBURETED FUEL SYSTEM

Fuel Pump

All carbureted engines use a mechanical fuel pump, driven off the camshaft and located on the engine block.

REMOVAL AND INSTALLATION

1.9L and 2.0L Engines

The fuel pump is located near the front right side of the engine.

1. Disconnect the negative battery terminal from the battery.
2. Remove the distributor.
3. Disconnect the fuel hoses from the fuel pump.
4. Remove the engine lifting hook.
5. Remove the fuel pump-to-engine bolts and the fuel pump, then discard the gasket.

NOTE: Before installing the fuel pump, rotate the crankshaft so that the cam lobe is on the down stroke.

6. Use a new gasket and RTV sealant. Installation is the reverse of removal. Torque the fuel pump-to-engine bolts to 15 ft. lbs. Check and/or adjust the timing.

2.8L Engine

The fuel pump is located near the front left side of the engine.

1. Disconnect the negative battery terminal from the battery.
2. Disconnect the fuel hoses the from pump.
3. Remove the fuel pump-to-engine bolts and the fuel pump from the engine, then discard the gasket.

NOTE: Before installing the fuel pump, rotate the crankshaft so that the cam lobe is on the down stroke.

4. To install, use a new gasket, RTV sealant and reverse the removal procedures. Torque the fuel pump-to-engine bolts to 15 ft. lbs.

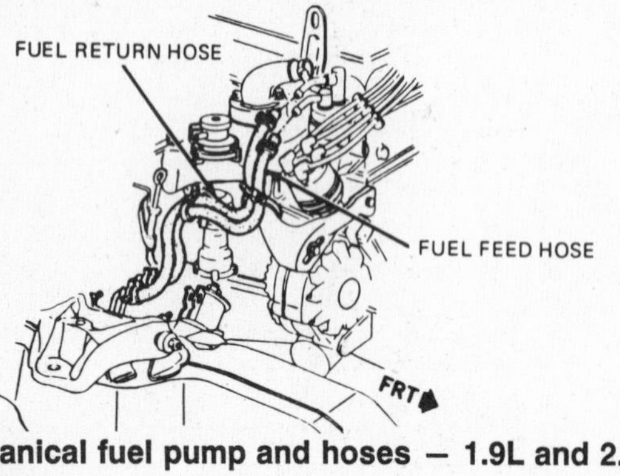
FUEL RETURN HOSE
FUEL FEED HOSE
FRT

Mechanical fuel pump and hoses — 1.9L and 2.0L engines

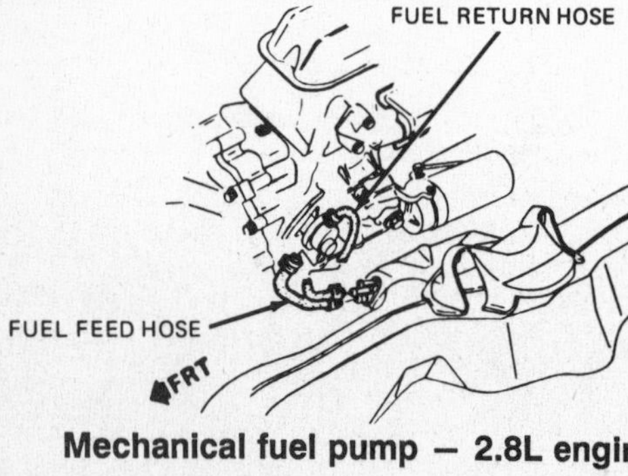
FUEL RETURN HOSE
FUEL FEED HOSE
FRT

Mechanical fuel pump — 2.8L engine

TESTING

To determine if the pump is in good condition, tests for both volume and pressure should be performed. The tests are made with the pump installed, and the engine at normal operating temperature and idle speed. Never replace a fuel pump without first performing these simple tests.

Be sure that the fuel filter has been changed at the specified interval. If in doubt, install a new filter first.

Pressure Test

1. Disconnect the fuel line from the carburetor and connect a fuel pump pressure gauge.
2. Start the engine and check the pressure with the engine at idle. If the pump has a vapor return hose, squeeze it off so that an accurate reading can be obtained. Pressure should not be below 4.5 psi.
3. If the pressure is incorrect, replace the pump. It if is OK, perform the volume test.

Volume Test

1. Disconnect the fuel line from the carburetor.
2. Place the fuel line into a graduated container.
3. Run the engine at idle until one pint of gasoline has been pumped. One pint should be delivered in 30 seconds or less. There is normally enough fuel in the carburetor float bowl to perform this test, but refill it if necessary.
4. If the delivery rate is below the minimum, check the lines for restrictions or leaks. If none are found, replace the pump.

DCH340 Carburetor

ADJUSTMENTS

NOTE: Idle Speed and Mixture Adjustment procedures are located in Section 2.

Float Level

The fuel level is normal if it is seen to be within the mark on the float bowl window. If not, Remove the top of the carburetor and bend the float seat to regulate the level.

Primary Throttle Valve

When the choke plate is completely closed, the primary throttle valve should be opened by the fast idle screw to an angle of

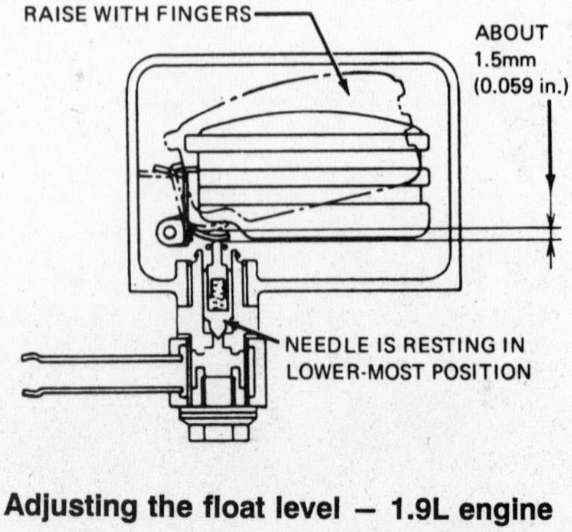
RAISE WITH FINGERS
ABOUT
1.5mm
(0.059 in.)
NEEDLE IS RESTING IN
LOWER-MOST POSITION

Adjusting the float level — 1.9L engine

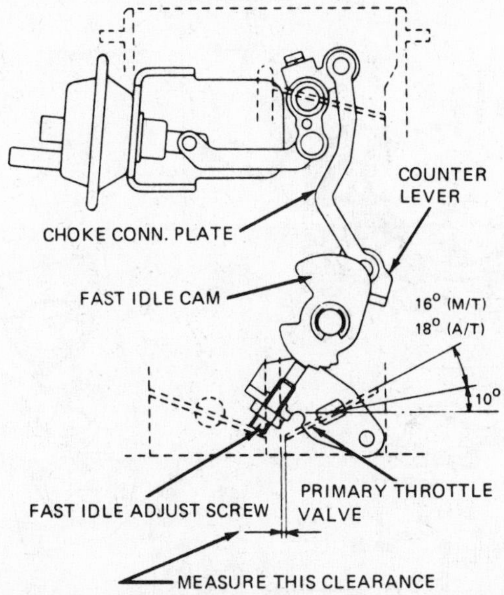
COUNTER LEVER
CHOKE CONN. PLATE
FAST IDLE CAM
16° (M/T)
18° (A/T)
10°
FAST IDLE ADJUST SCREW
PRIMARY THROTTLE VALVE
MEASURE THIS CLEARANCE

Adjusting the primary throttle valve — 1.9L engine

16° (M/T) or 18° (A/T). To check this adjustment, perform the following procedures:

1. Close the choke plate completely, then measure between the throttle plate and the air horn wall; the clearance should be 0.050–0.059 in. (1.3–1.5mm), M/T or 0.059–0.069 in. (1.50–1.75mm), A/T.

NOTE: The measurement should be made at the center point of the choke plate.

2. If necessary, adjust the opening by turning the fast idle screw.

Throttle Linkage

1. Turn the primary throttle valve plate until the adjustment plate is in contact with the kickdown lever. This is a primary throttle plate opening of about 47°.
2. Measure the clearance between the center point of the primary throttle plate and the air horn wall; the clearance should be 0.24–0.30 in. (6.0–7.6mm), if not, bend the kickdown lever tab.

Kickdown Lever

1. Turn the primary throttle lever until the plate is completely closed. Back off the throttle adjustment screw, if necessary.
2. Loosen the locknut on the kickdown lever screw and turn the screw until it just contacts the return plate, then tighten the locknut.

REMOVAL AND INSTALLATION

1.9L Engine

1. Remove the PCV valve from the rocker arm cover.
2. Disconnect the ECS hose from the air cleaner.
3. Disconnect the AIR hose from the pump.
4. On California models, disconnect the air hose from the slow carburetor.
5. Unbolt the air cleaner, lift it slightly, disconnect the hoses and remove the unit.
6. Disconnect the rubber piping from the TVS switch.
7. Disconnect the vacuum advance hose (if equipped) from the distributor.
8. If equipped with an A/T, disconnect the vacuum hose from the converter housing.

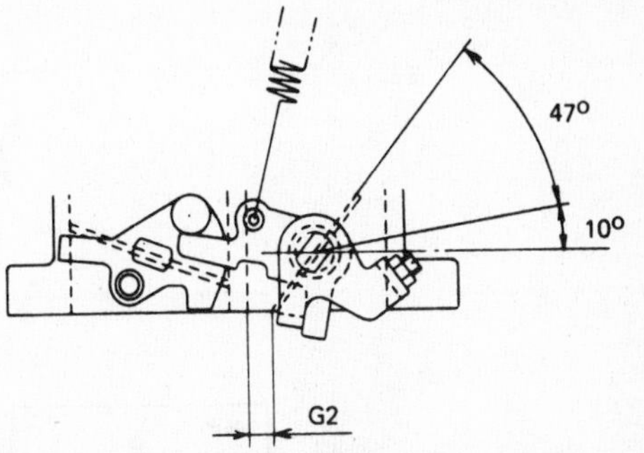
47°
10°
G2

Adjusting the throttle linkage — 1.9L engine

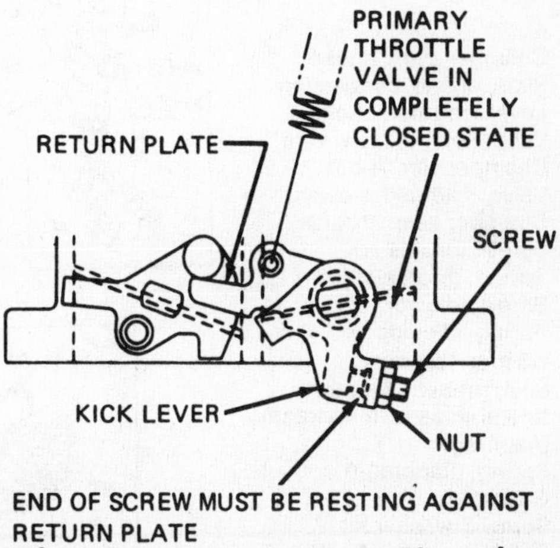
PRIMARY THROTTLE VALVE IN COMPLETELY CLOSED STATE
RETURN PLATE
SCREW
KICK LEVER
NUT
END OF SCREW MUST BE RESTING AGAINST RETURN PLATE

Adjusting the kickdown lever — 1.9L engine

9. On California models, disconnect the vacuum hoses from the slow and main actuator.
10. Disconnect the carburetor solenoid lead wire, the accelerator control cable and the cruise control cable.
11. On automatic transmission models, disconnect the control cable.
12. Disconnect the fuel line(s) from the carburetor.
13. Disconnect the ECS hose from the carburetor.
14. Remove the carburetor-to-intake manifold bolts and the carburetor; discard the mounting gasket.
15. To install, reverse the removal procedures. Make sure all of the linkage is properly adjusted and operates smoothly. Check that there are no leaks.

OVERHAUL

Disassembly

1. Remove the main and the assist return spring.
2. Disconnect the accelerator pump lever.

NOTE: On California models, disconnect the rubber pipe from the slow-actuator.

3. Remove the throttle return spring(s). Flatten the harness clips under the choke housing and at the choke chamber, then remove the lead wire from the clips.
4. Remove the connector (Federal model 3P, California model 1P) from the connector hanger and disconnect the automatic choke lead wire from the connector.

NOTE: Remove the fuel nipple and strainer carefully to avoid distortion.

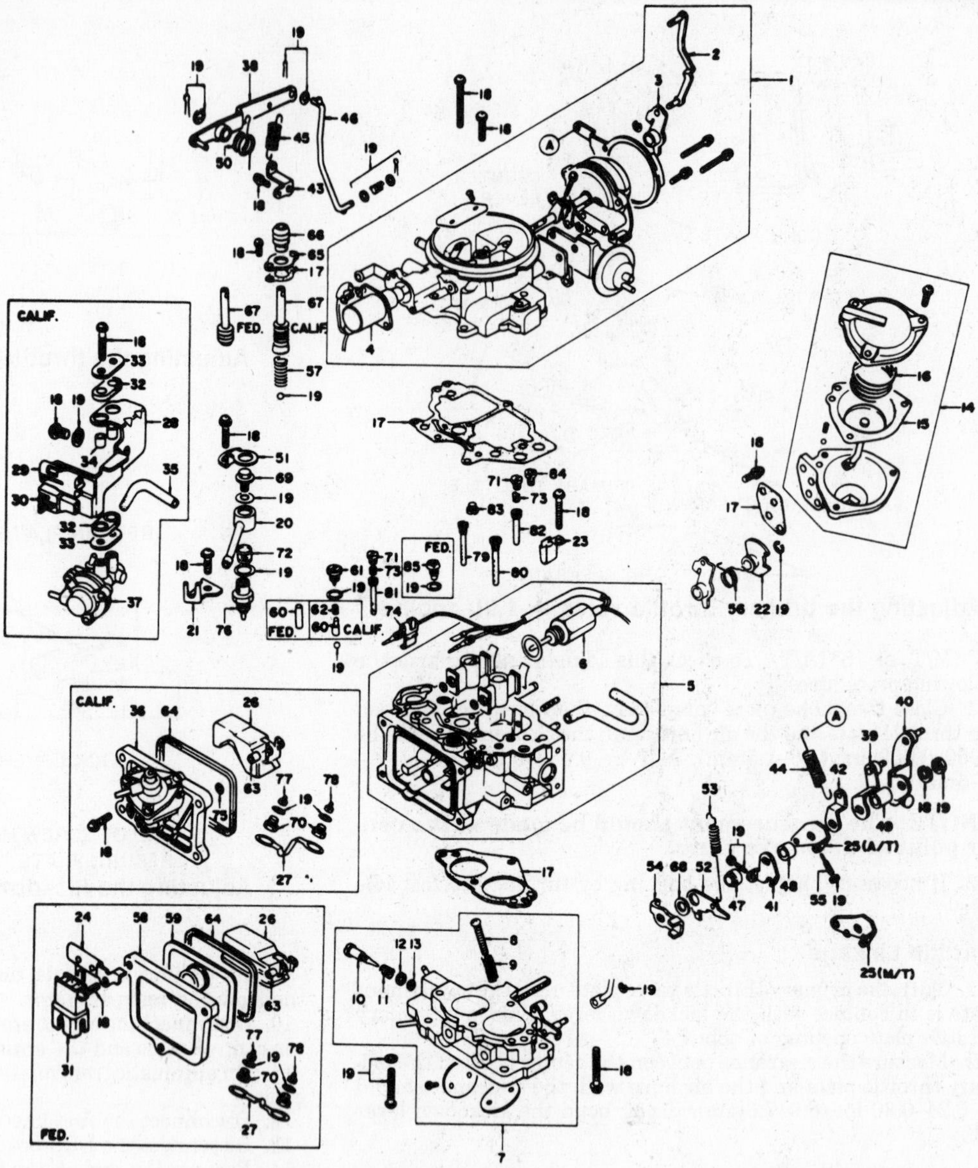

CALIF.
FED.
CALIF.
FED.
CALIF.
CALIF.
FED.
25(A/T)
25(M/T)

1. Chamber asm., choke
2. Plate, choke, connecting
3. Lever, counter, choke
4. Valve, solenoid, sw. vent.
5. Chamger asm., float
6. Valve, solenoid, slow cut
7. Chamber asm., throttle
8. Screw, throttle adj.
9. Spring, throttle adj.
10. Screw, idle adj.
11. Spring, idle adj.
12. Washer, idle adj.
13. Seal, rubber, idle adj.
14. Chamber asm., diaphragm
15. Diaphragm
16. Spring, diaphragm
17. Gasket kit
18. Screw & washer kit (A)
19. Screw & washer kit (B)
20. Nipple, fuel
21. Plate, stopping
22. Cam, fast idle
23. Holder, lead wire
24. Hanger, connector
25. Lever, fast idj.
26. Float, fuel
27. Plate, lock, drain plug
28. Hanger, connector
29. Connector
30. Connector
31. Connector
32. Rubber, mounting
33. Plate, mt. rubber
34. Collar, mt. rubber
35. Hose, rubber
36. Actuator, main
37. Actuator, slow
38. Lever, pump
39. Lever, accele
40. Lever, cruise
41. Lever, kick
42. Hanger, spring "A"
43. Hanger, spring "B"
44. Spring, main
45. Spring, assist
46. Rod, pump
47. Sleeve
48. Collar, shaft "A"
49. Collar, shaft "B"
50. Spring, pump lever
51. Lever, lock
52. Plate, return
53. Spring, throttle, "S"
54. Lever, adj.
55. Screw, fast idle
56. Spring, cam
57. Spring, piston return
58. Cover, level gauge
59. Gauge, level
60. Weight, injector
61. Screw, pump set
62. Spring, injector
63. Collar, "C"
64. Seal, rubber
65. Plate, cyl.
66. Cover, dust
67. Piston
68. Washer, throttle shaft
69. Screw, nipple set
70. Plug, drain fuel
71. Plug, taper
72. Filter
73. Spring, slow jet
74. Connector, lead wire
75. O-ring
76. Valve, needle
77. Jet, main, "P"
78. Jet, main, "S"
79. Bleed, air main. "P"
80. Bleed, air main, "S"
81. Jet, slow, "P"
82. Jet, slow, "S"
83. Bleed, air, slow, "P"
84. Bleed, air, slow, "S"
85. Valve, power

Exploded view of the DHC340 carburetor – 1.9L engine

5. Disconnect the switch vent valve lead wire from the connector.
6. Disconnect the choke connecting rod from the counter lever by removing the circuit clip.
7. Disconnect the automatic choke vacuum hose from the float chamber. Remove the choke chamber assembly-to-float chamber screws and the choke chamber assembly.
8. Remove the circuit clip between the diaphragm and the secondary throttle lever. Loosen the three diaphragm chamber attaching screws, then remove the diaphragm assembly.
9. Separate the float chamber assembly from the throttle chamber assembly.
10. Remove the slow-actuator, the accelerating pump plunger assembly and the float needle valve assembly.
11. On Federal models, remove the retaining level gauge cover screws, the level gauge and the float, be careful not to damage the rubber seal or lose the float collar.
12. On California models, remove the main actuator screws, then the main actuator and the float, be careful not to damage the rubber seal or lose the float collar.
13. Disassemble the diaphragm chamber by performing the following procedures:
   a. Remove the diaphragm cover screws.
   b. Separate the diaphragm cover, the diaphragm spring and the diaphragm; be careful not to lose the ball and spring.
14. Remove the jets from the upper part of the float chamber.
15. Remove the injector weight plug, the injector weight and the check ball.

NOTE: On California models, remove the spring.

16. Remove the power jet.

NOTE: On Federal models, be sure to place screwdriver properly in the slot to prevent damaging the valve rod.

17. Remove the two main jet plugs, the primary and the secondary main jets.
18. Remove the primary slow air bleed from choke chamber.
19. DO NOT remove the primary throttle valve screws, the secondary throttle valve or the choke valve. On California models, DO NOT remove the slow and/or the main actuators.

Inspection

CHOKE CHAMBER

1. Inspect the choke chamber for cracks and/or damage, pay particular attention to the gasket mounting surfaces of the chamber.
2. Check the shaft holes for wear.
3. Check the choke valve for smoothness of operation.
4. On Federal models, check the vacuum piston for smoothness of operation.

FLOAT CHAMBER

1. Inspect and remove the carbon deposit from inside of the body.
2. Inspect the body for cracks, the adjoining face for damage and the thread portions for damage and/or corrosion.
3. Inspect the jets mounting holes, the threaded portions and the screwdriver slots for damage.
4. Check the power valve for leaks, the power valve rod for bending and for smoothness of operation (Federal model).
5. Inspect the needle valve for sticking, dirt and/or corrosion.
6. Carefully check the float for pin hole(s) and/or wear.
7. Inspect fuel strainer in fuel inlet for dirt, corrosion and/or damage.
8. Inspect the accelerator pump plunger for damage and/or distortion. Also check for pump plunger for smooth movement within the cylinder.
9. Check the accelerating pump rubber boot for damage.

THROTTLE CHAMBER

1. Check the slow port, the idle port and others for clogging.
2. Check the primary and secondary throttle valve for the presence of carbon deposits and/or wear.
3. Check the throttle valve shaft holes for wear.
4. Check idle mixture adjusting screw seating face for step wear and the threaded portion for damage.
5. Check the diaphragm for deterioration and/or damage.

SOLENOID

Inspect for looseness of attaching parts and/or damage of wiring harness connector.

Assembly

To assemble the carburetor, reverse the disassembly procedures and perform all adjustments.

1. On Federal models, be careful not to bend valve rod when installing the power jet valve.
2. When reassembly of the accelerator pump is completed, fill the cylinder with fuel and check to be sure fuel is injected smoothly. When reassembling the accelerator pump parts be careful not to bend the piston connecting rod.
3. When reassembling the main actuator, apply grease to the O-ring, then carefully tighten the attaching screws to prevent cracking of the O-ring.

2SE and E2SE Carburetor

ADJUSTMENTS

Float Level

1. With the engine Cold, remove the top of the carburetor.
2. While holding a finger lightly but firmly, on the float retainer, press down lightly on the float tab to seat the needle valve.
3. Measure the distance between the float bowl gasket surface and the point on the float farthest from the needle valve.
4. If the measurement is not correct, remove the float and bend the tab.

Pump

1. With the throttle plate in the Closed position and the fast idle screw off the steps of the fast idle cam, measure the distance from the air horn casting to the top of the pump stem.
2. To adjust, remove the retaining screw, the washer and the pump lever. Bend the end of the lever to correct the stem height. DO NOT twist the lever or bend it sideways.
3. Install the lever, washer and screw, then check the adjustment. When correct, open and close the throttle a few times to check the linkage movement and alignment.

Fast Idle

1. Set the ignition timing and curb idle speed, then disconnect and plug the hoses as directed on the emission control decal.
2. Position the fast idle screw on the highest step of the fast idle cam.
3. Start the engine and adjust the engine speed to specification with the fast idle screw.

Choke Coil Lever

NOTE: The following procedure requires the use of the Choke Valve Angle Gauge tool No. J-26701 or BT-7704 or equivalent.

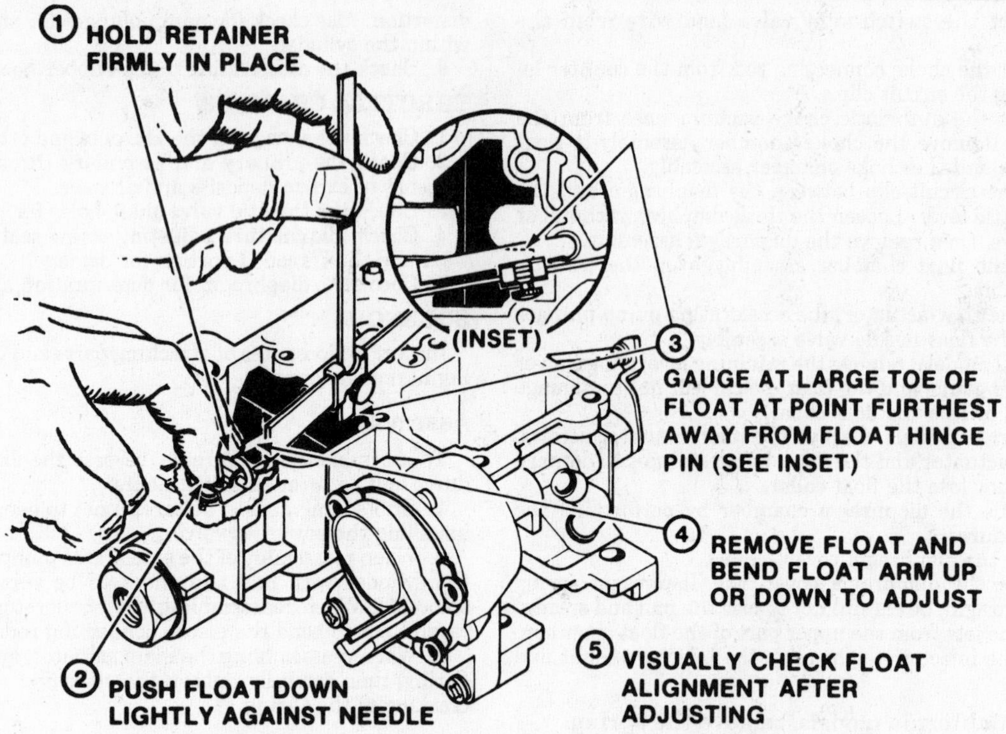

1 HOLD RETAINER FIRMLY IN PLACE
(INSET)
3 GAUGE AT LARGE TOE OF FLOAT AT POINT FURTHEST AWAY FROM FLOAT HINGE PIN (SEE INSET)
4 REMOVE FLOAT AND BEND FLOAT ARM UP OR DOWN TO ADJUST
5 VISUALLY CHECK FLOAT ALIGNMENT AFTER ADJUSTING
2 PUSH FLOAT DOWN LIGHTLY AGAINST NEEDLE

Adjusting the float level – 2.0L and 2.8L engines

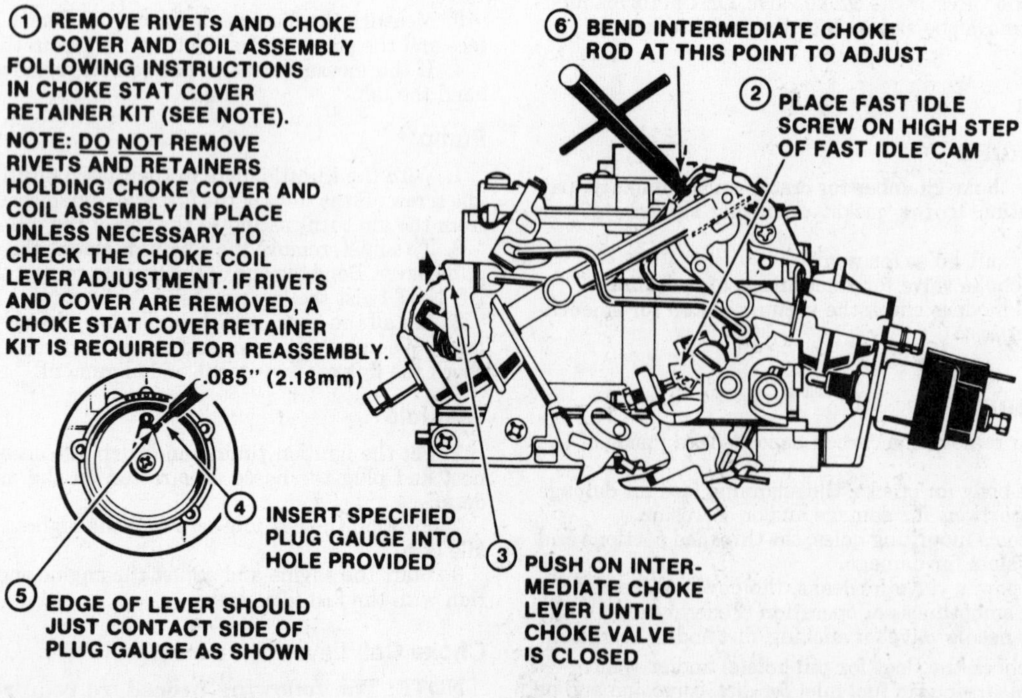

1 REMOVE RIVETS AND CHOKE COVER AND COIL ASSEMBLY FOLLOWING INSTRUCTIONS IN CHOKE STAT COVER RETAINER KIT (SEE NOTE).
NOTE: DO NOT REMOVE RIVETS AND RETAINERS HOLDING CHOKE COVER AND COIL ASSEMBLY IN PLACE UNLESS NECESSARY TO CHECK THE CHOKE COIL LEVER ADJUSTMENT. IF RIVETS AND COVER ARE REMOVED, A CHOKE STAT COVER RETAINER KIT IS REQUIRED FOR REASSEMBLY.
6 BEND INTERMEDIATE CHOKE ROD AT THIS POINT TO ADJUST
2 PLACE FAST IDLE SCREW ON HIGH STEP OF FAST IDLE CAM
.085" (2.18mm)
4 INSERT SPECIFIED PLUG GAUGE INTO HOLE PROVIDED
5 EDGE OF LEVER SHOULD JUST CONTACT SIDE OF PLUG GAUGE AS SHOWN
3 PUSH ON INTERMEDIATE CHOKE LEVER UNTIL CHOKE VALVE IS CLOSED

Adjusting the choke coil lever – 2.0L and 2.8L engines

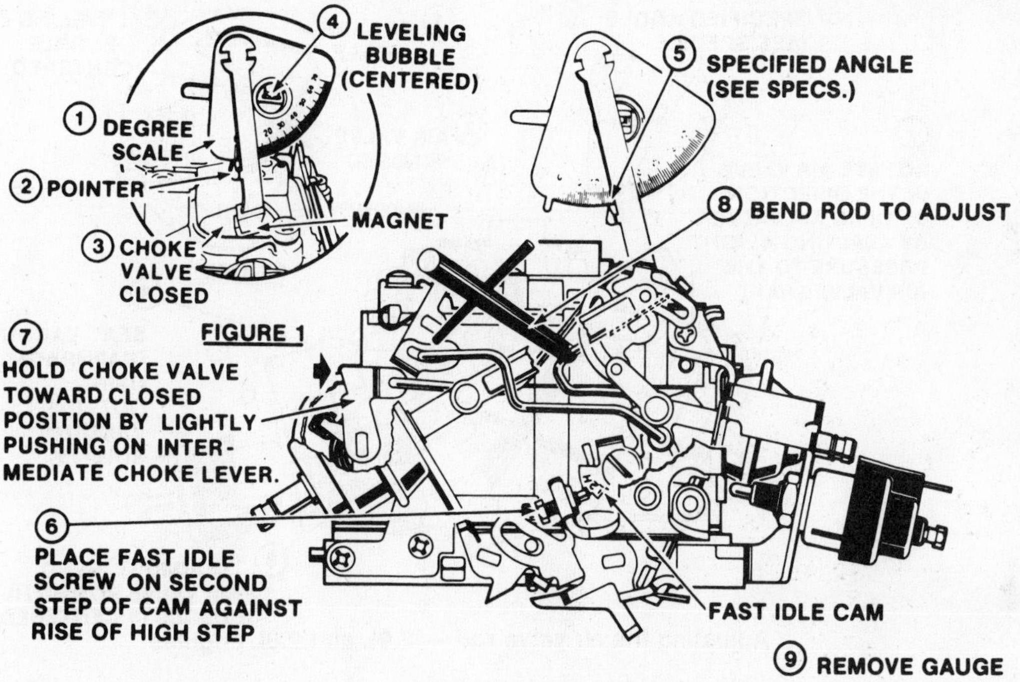

4 LEVELING BUBBLE (CENTERED)
1 DEGREE SCALE
2 POINTER
MAGNET
3 CHOKE VALVE CLOSED
FIGURE 1
7 HOLD CHOKE VALVE TOWARD CLOSED POSITION BY LIGHTLY PUSHING ON INTERMEDIATE CHOKE LEVER.
6 PLACE FAST IDLE SCREW ON SECOND STEP OF CAM AGAINST RISE OF HIGH STEP
5 SPECIFIED ANGLE (SEE SPECS.)
8 BEND ROD TO ADJUST
FAST IDLE CAM
9 REMOVE GAUGE

Adjusting the choke rod — 2.0L and 2.8L engines

1. Remove the three retaining screws, the choke cover and coil. On models with a riveted choke cover, drill out the three rivets, then remove the cover and the choke coil.

NOTE: A choke stat cover retainer kit is required for reassembly.

2. Place the fast idle screw on the high step of the fast idle cam.
3. Close the choke plate by pushing in on the intermediate choke lever.
4. Insert a drill or plug gauge, of the specified size, into the hole in the choke housing. The choke lever in the housing should be up against the side of the gauge.
5. If the lever does not just touch the gauge, bend the intermediate choke rod to adjust.

Fast Idle Cam (Choke Rod)

NOTE: The following procedure requires the use of the Choke Valve Angle Gauge tool No. J–26701 or BT–7704 or equivalent.

1. First, adjust the choke coil lever and fast idle speed.
2. Rotate the degree scale until it is zeroed.
3. Close the choke and install the degree scale onto the choke plate. Center the leveling bubble.
4. Rotate the scale so that the specified degree is opposite the scale pointer.
5. Place the fast idle screw on the second step of the cam (against the high step). Close the choke by pushing in the intermediate lever.
6. Push on the vacuum break lever, to Open the choke, until the lever is against the rear tang on the choke lever.
7. Bend the fast idle cam rod at the U to adjust the angle to specifications.

Air Valve Rod

NOTE: The following procedure requires the use of the Choke Valve Angle Gauge tool No. J–26701 or BT–7704 or equivalent.

1. Align the 0° mark with the pointer on an angle gauge.
2. Close the air valve and place a magnet on top of it.
3. Rotate the bubble until it is centered.
4. Rotate the degree scale until the specified degree mark is aligned with the pointer.
5. Seat the vacuum diaphragm using an external vacuum source.
6. On four cylinder models plug the end cover. Unplug after adjustment.
7. Apply a light pressure to the air valve shaft in the direction to open the air valve until all the slack is removed between the air link and plunger slot.
8. Bend the air valve link until the bubble is centered.

Primary Side Vacuum Break

NOTE: The following procedure requires the use of the Choke Valve Angle Gauge tool No. J–26701 or BT–7704 or equivalent.

1. Rotate the degree scale on the measuring gauge until the 0° is opposite the pointer.

NOTE: Prior to adjustment, remove the vacuum break from the carburetor. Place the bracket in a vise and using the proper safety precautions, grind off the adjustment screw cap then reinstall the vacuum break.

2. Seat the choke vacuum diaphragm by applying an external vacuum source of over 5 in.Hg to the vacuum break.

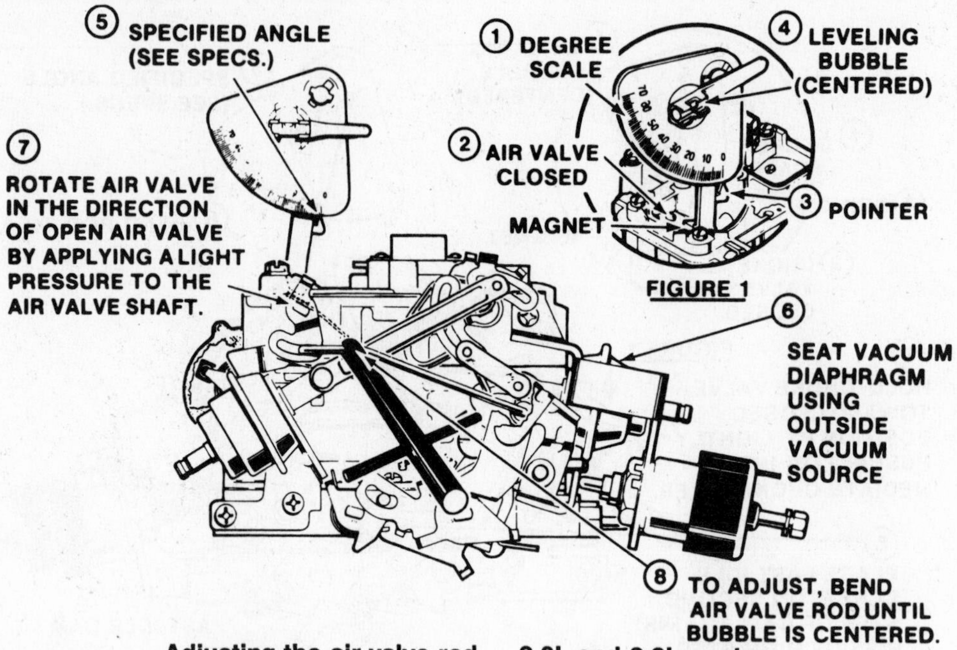

5 SPECIFIED ANGLE (SEE SPECS.)
7 ROTATE AIR VALVE IN THE DIRECTION OF OPEN AIR VALVE BY APPLYING A LIGHT PRESSURE TO THE AIR VALVE SHAFT.
1 DEGREE SCALE
2 AIR VALVE CLOSED
MAGNET
4 LEVELING BUBBLE (CENTERED)
3 POINTER
FIGURE 1
6 SEAT VACUUM DIAPHRAGM USING OUTSIDE VACUUM SOURCE
8 TO ADJUST, BEND AIR VALVE ROD UNTIL BUBBLE IS CENTERED.

Adjusting the air valve rod – 2.0L and 2.8L engines

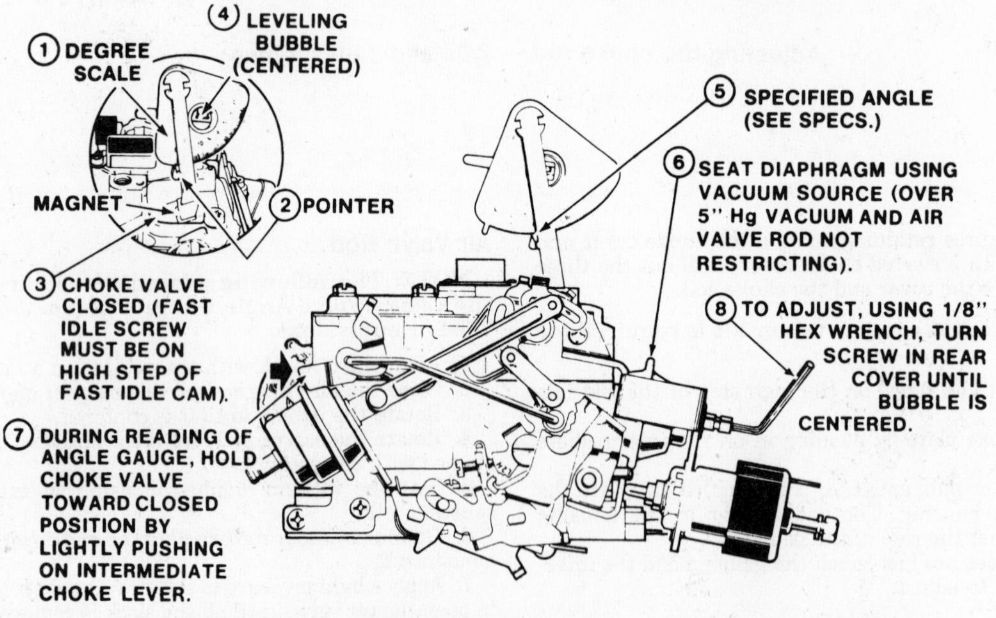

1 DEGREE SCALE
4 LEVELING BUBBLE (CENTERED)
MAGNET
2 POINTER
3 CHOKE VALVE CLOSED (FAST IDLE SCREW MUST BE ON HIGH STEP OF FAST IDLE CAM).
7 DURING READING OF ANGLE GAUGE, HOLD CHOKE VALVE TOWARD CLOSED POSITION BY LIGHTLY PUSHING ON INTERMEDIATE CHOKE LEVER.
5 SPECIFIED ANGLE (SEE SPECS.)
6 SEAT DIAPHRAGM USING VACUUM SOURCE (OVER 5" Hg VACUUM AND AIR VALVE ROD NOT RESTRICTING).
8 TO ADJUST, USING 1/8" HEX WRENCH, TURN SCREW IN REAR COVER UNTIL BUBBLE IS CENTERED.

Adjusting the primary vacuum break – 2.0L and 2.8L engines

NOTE: If the air valve rod is restricting the vacuum diaphragm from seating, it may be necessary to bend the air valve rod slightly to gain clearance. Make the air valve rod adjustment after the vacuum break adjustment.

3. Read the angle gauge while lightly pushing on the intermediate choke lever so that the choke valve is toward the Closed position.
4. Using an ⅛ in. (3mm) hex wrench, turn the screw in the rear cover until the bubble is centered. Apply a silicone sealant over the screw head to seal the setting.

Electric Choke

This procedure is only for those carburetors with choke covers retained by screws. Riveted choke covers are preset and nonadjustable.

1. Loosen the three retaining screws.
2. Place the fast idle screw on the high step of the cam.
3. Rotate the choke cover to align the cover mark with the specified housing mark.

Secondary Vacuum Break

NOTE: The following procedure requires the use of the Choke Valve Angle Gauge tool No. J-26701, BT-7704 or equivalent.

1. Rotate the degree scale on the measuring gauge until the 0° is opposite the pointer.

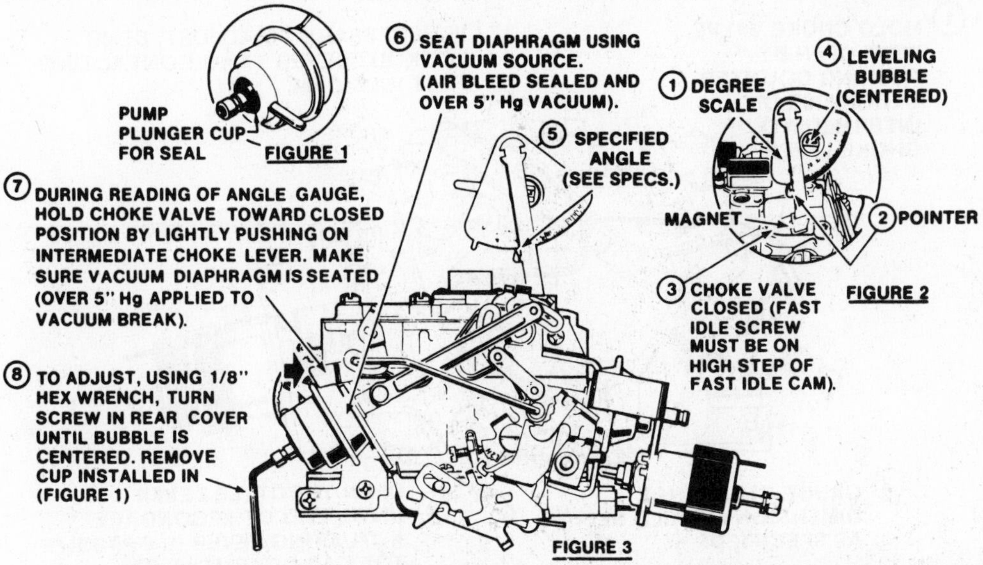
PUMP
PLUNGER CUP
FOR SEAL
FIGURE 1
6 SEAT DIAPHRAGM USING VACUUM SOURCE. (AIR BLEED SEALED AND OVER 5" Hg VACUUM).
4 LEVELING BUBBLE (CENTERED)
1 DEGREE SCALE
5 SPECIFIED ANGLE (SEE SPECS.)
7 DURING READING OF ANGLE GAUGE, HOLD CHOKE VALVE TOWARD CLOSED POSITION BY LIGHTLY PUSHING ON INTERMEDIATE CHOKE LEVER. MAKE SURE VACUUM DIAPHRAGM IS SEATED (OVER 5" Hg APPLIED TO VACUUM BREAK).
MAGNET
2 POINTER
3 CHOKE VALVE CLOSED (FAST IDLE SCREW MUST BE ON HIGH STEP OF FAST IDLE CAM).
FIGURE 2
8 TO ADJUST, USING 1/8" HEX WRENCH, TURN SCREW IN REAR COVER UNTIL BUBBLE IS CENTERED. REMOVE CUP INSTALLED IN (FIGURE 1)
FIGURE 3

Adjusting the secondary vacuum break – 2.0L and 2.8L engines

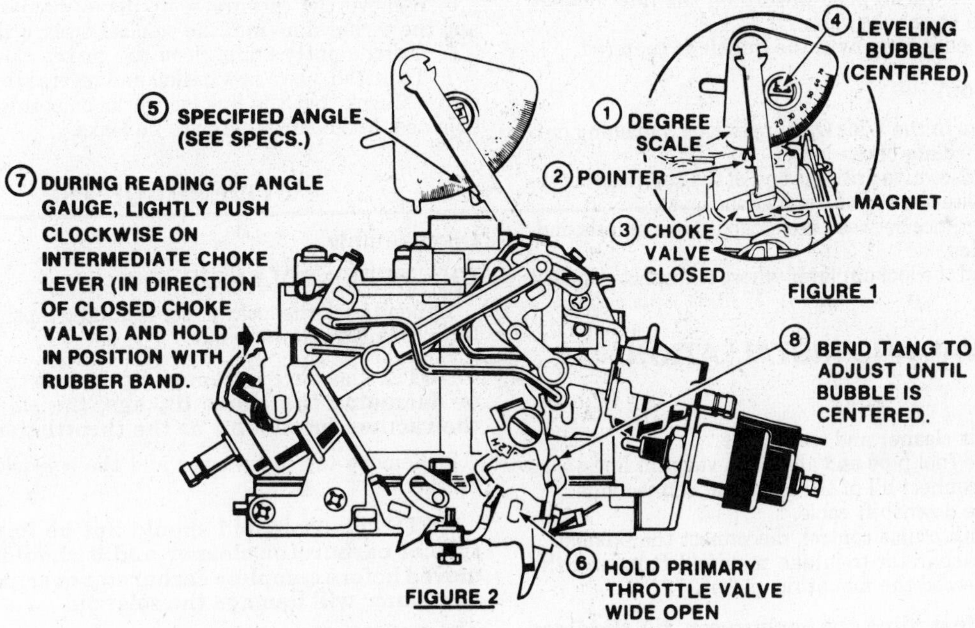
4 LEVELING BUBBLE (CENTERED)
5 SPECIFIED ANGLE (SEE SPECS.)
1 DEGREE SCALE
2 POINTER
MAGNET
7 DURING READING OF ANGLE GAUGE, LIGHTLY PUSH CLOCKWISE ON INTERMEDIATE CHOKE LEVER (IN DIRECTION OF CLOSED CHOKE VALVE) AND HOLD IN POSITION WITH RUBBER BAND.
3 CHOKE VALVE CLOSED
FIGURE 1
8 BEND TANG TO ADJUST UNTIL BUBBLE IS CENTERED.
6 HOLD PRIMARY THROTTLE VALVE WIDE OPEN
FIGURE 2

Adjusting the choke unloader – 2.0L and 2.8L engines

NOTE: Prior to adjustment, remove the vacuum break from the carburetor. Place the bracket in the vise and using the proper safety precautions, grind off the adjustment screw cap then reinstall the vacuum break. Plug the end cover using an accelerator pump plunger cup or equivalent. Remove the cup after the adjustment.

2. Seat the choke vacuum diaphragm by applying an external vacuum source of over 5 in.Hg to the vacuum break.

NOTE: If the air valve rod is restricting the vacuum diaphragm from seating it may be necessary to bend the air valve rod slightly to gain clearance. Make an air valve rod adjustment after the vacuum break adjustment.

3. Read the angle gauge while lightly pushing on the intermediate choke lever so that the choke valve is toward the Closed position.
4. Using an ⅛ in. (3mm) hex wrench, turn the screw in the rear cover until the bubble is centered. Apply silicone sealant over the screw head to seal the setting.

Choke Unloader

1. Follow Steps 1-4 of the Fast Idle Cam Adjustment.
2. If removed, install the choke cover and the coil, then align the housing marks with the cover marks, as specified.
3. Hold the primary throttle valve Wide Open.

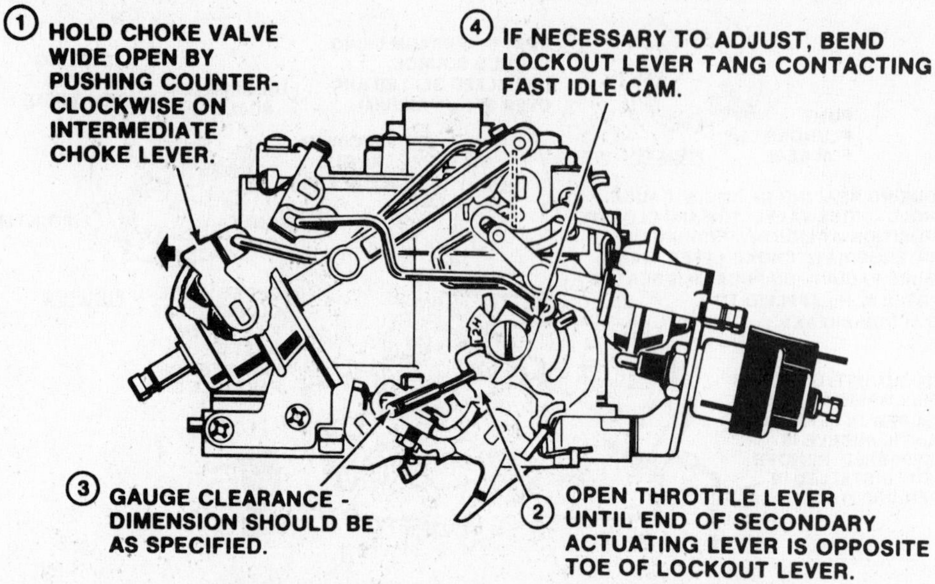
① HOLD CHOKE VALVE WIDE OPEN BY PUSHING COUNTER-CLOCKWISE ON INTERMEDIATE CHOKE LEVER.
④ IF NECESSARY TO ADJUST, BEND LOCKOUT LEVER TANG CONTACTING FAST IDLE CAM.
③ GAUGE CLEARANCE - DIMENSION SHOULD BE AS SPECIFIED.
② OPEN THROTTLE LEVER UNTIL END OF SECONDARY ACTUATING LEVER IS OPPOSITE TOE OF LOCKOUT LEVER.

Adjusting the secondary lockout — 1.9L engine

4. If the engine is Warm, push inward on the intermediate choke lever to close the choke valve.
5. Bend the unloader tang until the bubble is centered.

Secondary Lockout

1. Place the choke in the Wide Open position by pushing outward on the intermediate choke lever.
2. Open the throttle valve until the end of the secondary actuating lever is opposite the toe of the lockout lever.
3. Gauge the clearance between the lockout lever and secondary lever, as specified.
4. To adjust, bend the lockout lever where it contacts the fast idle cam.

REMOVAL AND INSTALLATION

2.0L Engine

1. Remove the air cleaner and the gasket.
2. Disconnect the fuel pipe and all of the vacuum lines.
3. Label and disconnect all of the electrical connections.
4. Disconnect the downshift cable.
5. If equipped with cruise control, disconnect the linkage.
6. Remove the carburetor-to-intake manifold bolts and the carburetor, then discard the mounting gasket.

NOTE: Before installing the carburetor, fill the float bowl with gasoline to reduce the battery strain and the possibility of backfiring when the engine is started again.

7. Inspect the EFE heater for damage. Using a putty knife, clean the gasket mounting surfaces. Be sure that the throttle body and EFE mating surfaces are clean.
8. To install, use a new gasket and the carburetor; tighten the nuts alternately.
9. To complete the installation, reverse the removal procedures.

2.8L Engine

1. Remove the air cleaner.
2. Disconnect the fuel and vacuum lines from the carburetor.
3. Disconnect all of the electrical connectors from the carburetor.
4. Disconnect all of the linkage from the carburetor.
5. Remove the carburetor-to-intake manifold nuts or bolts and the carburetor from the vehicle; discard the gasket.
6. Using a putty knife, clean the gasket mounting surfaces.
7. To install, use a new gasket and reverse the removal procedures. Check that the linkage works smoothly and is properly adjusted. Make sure there are no leaks.

OVERHAUL 2SE

Disassembly

IDLE SPEED SOLENOID

1. Bend back the lockwasher retaining taps, then remove the large solenoid retaining nut.

NOTE: Use care in removing the nut to avoid bending or damaging the choke linkage, the solenoid bracket, the vacuum break unit or the throttle lever.

2. Remove the lockwasher and the solenoid unit from the bracket.

NOTE: The solenoid should not be immersed in any type of carburetor cleaner and it should always be removed before complete carburetor overhaul. Immersion in cleaner will damage the solenoid.

AIR HORN

1. Remove the clip from the hole in the pump lever. DO NOT remove the pump lever retaining screw or the pump lever from the air horn assembly.
2. Remove the hose from the primary side vacuum break assembly.
3. Remove the primary side vacuum break bracket-to-air horn and throttle body screws, then rotate the vacuum break/bracket assembly to disengage the vacuum break link from the vacuum break slot, then disengage the choke lever and the air valve rod from air valve lever slot.

NOTE: DO NOT place the vacuum break assembly in carburetor cleaner. Immersion in cleaner will damage vacuum break diaphragm.

4. If necessary to remove the air valve rod from the vacuum break, remove and discard retaining clips from the end of the air valve rod. A new retaining clip is required for reassembly. Re-

AIR HORN PARTS
1. Screw—air horn (long) (2)
2. Screw—air horn (large)
3. Screw—air horn (short) (3)
4. Screw—air horn (medium)
5. Vent stack assembly
6. Screw—hot idle compensator (2)
7. Hot idle compensator
8. Gasket—hot idle compensator
9. Air horn assembly
10. Gasket—air horn
11. Retainer—pump link
12. Seal—pump stem
13. Retainer—stem seal

CHOKE PARTS
14. Vacuum break and bracket assembly—primary
15. Screw—vacuum break attaching
16. Bushing—air valve—link
17. Retainer—air valve link
18. Hose—vacuum break—primary
19. Link—air valve
20. Link—fast idle cam
21. Intermediate choke shaft/lever/link assembly
22. Bushing—intermediate choke shaft link
23. Retainer—intermediate choke shaft link
24. Vacuum break and bracket assembly—secondary
25. Choke cover and coil assembly
26. Screw—choke lever
27. Choke lever and contact assembly
28. Choke housing
29. Screw—choke housing (2)
30. Stat cover retainer kit
31. Screw—vacuum break attaching (2)

FLOAT BOWL PARTS
32. Float bowl assembly
33. Nut—fuel inlet
34. Gasket—fuel inlet nut
35. Filter—fuel inlet
36. Spring—fuel filter
37. Float assembly
38. Hinge pin—float
39. Insert—float bowl
40. Needle and seat assembly
41. Spring—pump return
42. Pump—assembly
43. Jet—main metering
44. Rod—main metering assembly
45. Ball—pump discharge
46. Spring—pump discharge
47. Retainer—pump discharge spring
48. Power piston assembly
49. Spring—power piston

THROTTLE BODY PARTS
50. Gasket—throttle body
51. Throttle body assembly
52. Pump rod
53. Clip—cam screw
54. Screw—cam
55. Spring—throttle stop screw
56. Screw—throttle stop
57. Idle needle and spring
58. Screw—throttle body attaching (4)
59. Nut—idle solenoid
60. Retainer—idle solenoid
61. Idle solenoid

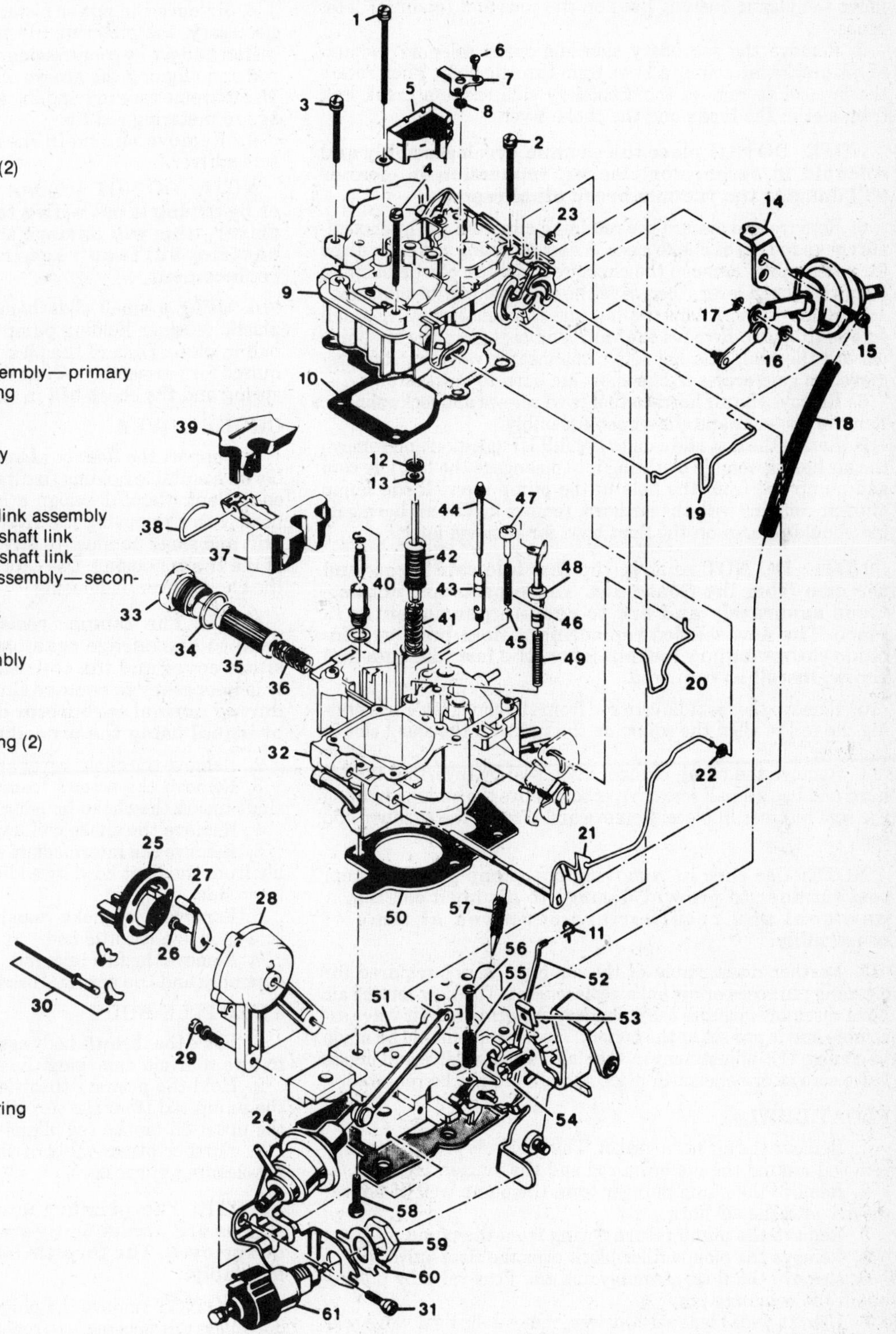
1
6
7
5
8
3
2
4
14
23
9
17
16
15
10
18
39
12
13
19
44
47
38
42
37
40
43
48
33
41
46
45
34
35
49
20
36
32
22
21
25
27
28
50
57
11
56
55
52
26
51
53
30
29
54
24
58
59
60
61
31

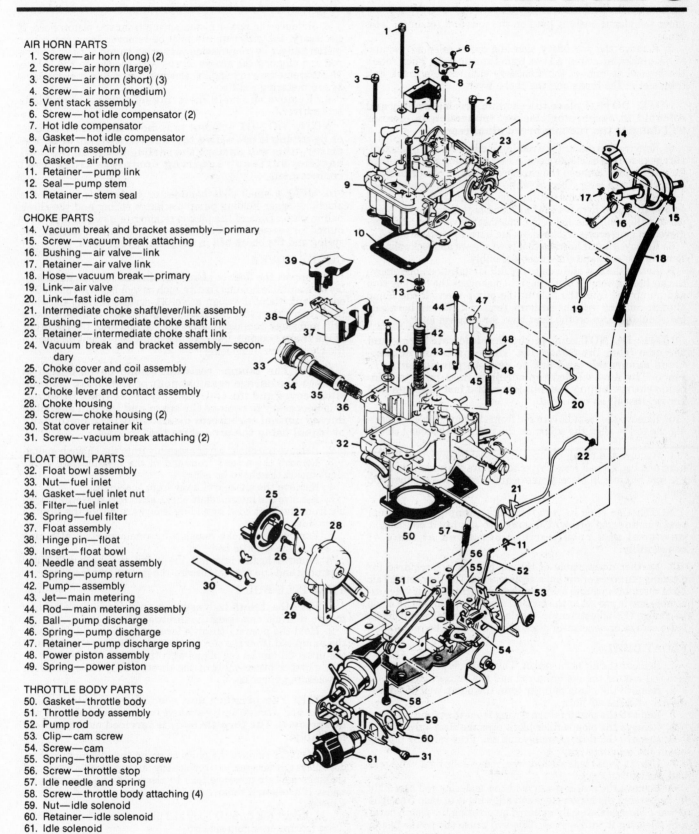

Exploded view of the 2SE carburetor – 2.0L and 2.8L engines

move the plastic bushing used on the rods and retain for later reuse.

5. Remove the secondary side idle speed solenoid vacuum break bracket attaching screws from throttle body. Then rotate the bracket to remove the secondary side vacuum break link from slot in the break and the choke lever.

NOTE: DO NOT place the vacuum break assembly and solenoid in carburetor cleaner. Immersion in cleaner will damage the vacuum break diaphragm.

6. Remove and discard the retaining clip from the intermediate choke rod at the choke lever. A new retaining clip is required for reassembly. Remove the choke rod and the plastic bushing from the choke lever, then save the the bushing for later use.

7. Remove and retain the hot idle compensator valve small screws (if used). Remove the valve and seal from the air horn; discard the seal. The hot idle compensator valve must be removed to gain access to the short air horn-to-bowl screw.

8. Remove the air horn-to-fuel bowl screws and lockwashers. Remove the vent and the screen assembly.

9. Rotate the fast idle cam to the full UP position and remove the air horn assembly by tilting it to disengage the fast idle cam and pump rod from the hole in the pump lever. If the pump plunger remains with the air horn, remove it. The air horn gasket should remain on the float bowl for removal later.

NOTE: DO NOT remove the fast idle cam screw and the cam from the float bowl. These parts are not serviced separately and are to remain permanently in place. The new service replacement float bowl will include the secondary lockout lever, the fast idle cam and screw, install as required.

10. Remove the fast idle cam rod from the choke lever by rotating the rod to align the squirt on the rod with the small slot in the lever.

11. Remove the pump plunger stem seal by inverting the air horn and use a small screwdriver to remove the staking holding the seal retainer in place. Remove and discard the retainer and seal.

NOTE: Use care in removing the pump plunger stem seal retainer to prevent damage to air horn casting. A new seal and retainer are required at time of reassembly.

12. Further disassembly of the air horn is not required for cleaning purposes or air horn replacement. The new service air horn assembly includes the secondary metering rod-air valve assembly and is pre-set at the factory. No attempt should be made to change this adjustment in the field. The air valve and choke valve screws are staked in place and should not be removed.

FLOAT BOWL

1. Remove the air horn gasket. The gasket is pre-cut for easy removal around the metering rod and the hanger assembly.

2. Remove the pump plunger from the pump well (if not removed with the air horn).

3. Remove the pump return spring from the pump well.

4. Remove the plastic filler block over the float valve.

5. Remove the float assembly and the float valve by pulling up on the retaining pin.

6. Using a wide blade screwdriver, remove the float valve seat and gasket.

7. Remove the power piston and the metering rod assembly by depressing the piston stem and allowing it to snap free. The power piston can be easily removed by pressing the piston down and releasing it with a snap. This will cause the power piston spring to snap the piston up against the plastic retainer. This procedure may have to be repeated several times. DO NOT remove the power piston by using pliers on the metering rod holder.

8. Remove the power piston spring from the piston bore. If necessary, the metering rod may be removed from the power piston hanger by compressing the spring on top of the metering rod and aligning the groove on rod with the slot in the holder. Use extreme care in handling the metering rod to prevent damage to metering rod tip.

9. Remove the main metering jet using a wide blade screwdriver.

NOTE: DO NOT attempt to remove the plastic retainer by prying it out with a tool such as a punch or screwdriver–this will damage the sealing beads on the bowl casting surface requiring complete float bowl replacement.

10. Using a small slide hammer or equivalent, remove the plastic retainer holding pump discharge spring and the check ball in place. Discard the plastic retainer (a new retainer is required for reassembly). Turn the bowl upside down catching the spring and the check ball in the palm of your hand.

CHOKE COVER

1. Support the float bowl and the throttle body as an assembly on a suitable holding fixture such as tool No. J09789–118 or equivalent. Carefully align a No. 21 drill to remove the rivet head. After removing the rivet heads and the retainers, use a drift and small hammer to drive the remainder of the rivets out of the choke housing. Use care in drilling to prevent damage to the choke cover or housing.

NOTE: The tamper resistant choke cover design is used to discourage readjustment of the choke thermostatic cover and the coil assembly in the field. However, it is necessary to remove the cover and the coil assembly during normal carburetor disassembly for cleaning and overhaul using the procedure that follows.

2. Remove the choke cover assembly from the choke housing.

3. Remove the screws from end of the intermediate choke shaft inside the choke housing.

4. Remove the choke coil lever from the shaft.

5. Remove the intermediate choke shaft and the lever assembly from the float bowl by sliding it forward out of the throttle lever side.

6. Remove the choke housing by removing two attaching screws in the throttle body.

7. Remove the fuel inlet nut, the gasket, the check valve/filter assembly and the spring. Discard the gasket and the filter.

THROTTLE BODY

1. Place the throttle body assembly onto a carburetor holding fixture to avoid damaging the throttle valves.

2. Hold the primary throttle lever wide-open and disengage the pump rod from the throttle lever by rotating the rod until the upset on on the rod aligns with the slot in the lever.

3. Further disassembly of the throttle body is not required for cleaning purposes.

NOTE: The primary and secondary throttle valve screws are permanently staked in place and should not be removed. The throttle body is serviced as a complete assembly.

4. DO NOT remove the plugs covering the idle mixture needle unless it is necessary to replace the mixture needle or normal soakings and air pressure fails to clean the idle mixture passages. If necessary, remove the idle mixture plug and needle as follows:

a. Invert the throttle body and place it on carburetor holding fixture, manifold-side up.

b. Make two parallel cuts into the throttle body on the side of the locator points, beneath the idle mixture needle plug (manifold-side), with a hack saw. The cut should reach down to the steel plug but should not extend more than ⅛ in.

(3mm) beyond the locator points. The distance between the saw marks depends on the size of the punch to be used.

c. Place a flat punch at a point near the ends of the saw marks in the throttle body. Holding the punch at a 45° angle, drive it into the throttle body until the casting breaks way, exposing the steel plug.

d. Holding a center punch vertical, drive it into the steel plug. Then, holding the punch at a 45° angle, drive the plug out of the casting.

NOTE: Hardened plug will shatter rather than remaining intact. It is not necessary to remove the plug completely; remove loose pieces.

5. Using tool No. J–29030, BT–7610B or equivalent, remove idle mixture needle and spring from throttle body.

Cleaning

The carburetor parts should be cleaned in a cold immersion-type cleaner such as Carbon X (X–55) or equivalent.

NOTE: The idle speed solenoid, mixture control solenoid, throttle position sensor, electric choke, rubber parts, plastic parts, diaphragms, pump plunger, plastic filler, should NOT be immersed in carburetor cleaner as they will swell, harden or distort. The plastic bushing in the throttle lever will withstand normal cleaning in carburetor cleaner.

1. Thoroughly clean all metal parts and blow dry with compressed air. Make sure all fuel passages and metering parts are free of burrs and dirt. Do not pass drills or wires through jets and passages.
2. Inspect upper and lower surface of carburetor casting for damage.
3. Inspect holes in levers for excessive wear or out of round conditions. If worn, levers should be replaced. Inspect plastic bushings for damage and excessive wear. Replace as required.

Inspection

Check, repair or replace parts if the following problems are encountered:

FLOODING

1. Inspect float valve and seat for dirt, deep wear grooves, scores and proper seating.
2. Inspect float valve pull clip for proper installation. Be careful not to bend pull clip.
3. Inspect float, float arms and hinge pin for distortion, binds, and burrs. Check density of material in the float; if heavier than normal, replace float.
4. Clean or replace fuel inlet filter and check valve assembly.

HESITATION

1. Inspect pump plunger and cup for cracks, scores or cup excessive wear. A used pump cup will shrink when dry. If dried out, soak in fuel for 8 hours before testing.
2. Inspect pump duration and return springs for being weak or distorted.
3. Check all pump passages and jet for dirt, improper seating of discharge check ball and scores in pump well. Check condition of pump discharge check ball spring, then replace as necessary.
4. Check pump linkage for excessive wear; repair or replace as necessary.

HARD STARTING – POOR COLD OPERATION

1. Check choke valve and linkage for excessive wear, binds or distortion.
2. Inspect choke vacuum diaphragms for leaks.
3. Replace carburetor fuel filter.
4. Inspect float valve for sticking, dirt, etc.
5. Also check items under "Flooding".

POOR PERFORMANCE – POOR GAS MILEAGE

1. Clean all fuel and vacuum passages in the castings.
2. Check the choke valve for freedom of movement.
3. Check the Mixture Control Solenoid for sticking, binding or leaking as follows:

a. Connect one end of a jumper wire to either terminal of the solenoid connector and the other end to the positive (+) terminal of a 12V battery source.

b. Connect a jumper wire to the other terminal of the solenoid connector and the other end to a known good ground.

c. With the rubber seal, retainer and the spacer removed from the end of the solenoid stem, attach a hose from a hand vacuum pump.

d. With the solenoid fully energized (lean position), apply 25 in.Hg and time the leak-down rate should not exceed 5 in.Hg in 5 seconds. If leakage exceeds that amount, replace the solenoid.

e. To check the solenoid for sticking in the down position, remove the jumper lead from the 12V source and observe hand vacuum pump reading. The reading should go to 0 in less than one second.

4. Inspect the metering jet for dirt, loose parts or damage.

NOTE: DO NOT attempt to readjust the mixture screw located inside the metering jet. The screw is factory adjusted and a change can upset the fuel system calibration. NO ATTEMPT should be made to change this adjustment in the field except as the result of a Computer Command Control system performance check.

5. Check the air valve and the secondary metering rod for binding conditions. If the air valve or metering rod is damaged or the metering rod adjustment is changed from the factory setting, the air horn assembly must be replaced. Also check the air valve spring for proper installation (tension against the air valve shaft pin).

ROUGH IDLE

1. Inspect gasket and gasket mating surfaces on castings for nicks, burrs or damage to the sealing beads.
2. Check operation and sealing of mixture control solenoid.
3. Clean all idle fuel passages.
4. If removed, inspect idle mixture needle for ridges, burrs or being bent.
5. Check the throttle lever and valves for bind, nicks and other damage.
6. Check all diaphragms for possible ruptures or leaks.

NOTE: When cleaning plastic parts, only use low volatile cleaning solvent – never in gasoline.

Assembly

THROTTLE BODY

1. Holding the primary throttle lever wide open, install lower end of pump rod in throttle lever by aligning the squirt on rod with the slot in the lever. The end of the rod should point outward toward the throttle lever.
2. If removed, install idle mixture needle and spring using the tool No. J–29030–B or equivalent. Lightly seat needle and then back out 3 turns as a preliminary idle mixture adjustment. Final idle mixture adjustment must be made on the vehicle. Refer to the "On-Vehicle Service" section for idle mixture adjustment procedures.

FLOAT BOWL

1. Install new throttle body to bowl insulator gasket over two locating dowels on the bowl.

NOTE: If a new float bowl assembly is used, stamp or engrave the model number on the new float bowl.

2. Rotate the fast idle cam so that the steps face fast idle

screw on throttle lever when properly installed, install the throttle body making certain the throttle body is properly located over dowels on float bowl; then install the throttle body-to-bowl screws and lockwashers, then tighten evenly and securely.

NOTE: Inspect the linkage to insure lockout tang is located properly to engage slot in the secondary lockout lever and that linkage moves freely and does not bind.

3. Place the carburetor on a proper fixture tool No. J-9789-118 or equivalent.
4. Install fuel inlet filter spring, new filter assembly, new gasket and inlet nut, then torque the nut to 18 ft. lbs.

NOTE: When properly installed, the hole in filter faces the inlet nut. Ribs on closed end of filter element prevent filter from being installed incorrectly unless forced. Tightening beyond specified torque can damage the nylon gasket and cause fuel leakage. When installing a service replacement filter, make sure the filter is the type that includes a check valve to meet U.S. Motor Vehicle Safety Standards (MVSS).

5. Install the choke housing onto the throttle body, making sure raised boss and locating lug on rear of housing fit into recesses in float bowl casting. Install the choke housing attaching screws and lockwashers onto the throttle body, then tighten the screws evenly and securely.
6. Install the intermediate choke shaft assembly into the float bowl by pushing the shaft through from throttle lever side.
7. With the intermediate choke lever in the UP (12 o'clock) position, install the choke coil lever inside the choke housing onto the flats on the intermediate choke shaft. The choke coil lever is properly aligned when the coil pick-up tang is in the UP position. Install the choke coil lever retaining screw into the end of intermediate choke shaft and tighten securely.
8. Install the pump discharge steel check ball, spring and plastic retainer into the float bowl. Tap lightly into place until the top of the retainer is flush with bowl casting surface.
9. Using a wide-blade screwdriver, install the main metering jet and the float valve seat (with gasket) into the bottom of the float bowl. Tighten and seat securely.
10. To make the adjustment easier, carefully bend float arm upward at the notch in arm before assembly.
11. Install the float valve onto the float arm by sliding the float lever under the pull clip. Correct installation of the pull clip is to hook the clip over the edge of the float on the float arm facing the float pontoon.
12. Install the float hinge pin into float arm with the end of the loop of the pin facing the pump well. Then, install the float assembly by aligning the valve in the seat and the float hinge pin into the locating channels in float bowl.
13. To adjust the float level, perform the following procedures:
    a. Hold the float hinge pin firmly in place and push down lightly on the float arm at outer end against the top of the float valve.
    b. Using an adjustable "T" scale, measure from top of float bowl casting surface (air horn gasket removed) to top of float at the toe.
    c. Bend the float arm (as necessary, for proper adjustment) by pushing on pontoon (see adjustment chart for specifications).
    d. Visually check the float alignment after adjustment.
14. Install the plastic filler block over the float valve pressing downward until properly seated (flush with the bowl casting surface).
15. Install the Throttle Position Sensor return spring into the bottom of the float bowl well.
16. Install the Throttle Position Sensor (TPS) and connector assembly in the float bowl by aligning the groove in the electrical connector with the "V" in the float bowl casting, push down on the connector and sensor assembly so that the connector wires and sensor are located below the bowl casting surface.

NOTE: Care must be taken when installing the throttle position sensor to assure that the electrical integrity is maintained. Make sure that the wires between the connector and the sensor assembly are not pinched or insulation broken upon final assembly. Accidental electrical grounding of the TPS must be avoided.

17. Install the air horn gasket onto the float bowl by locating the gasket over the two dowel locating pins on the bowl.
18. Install the pump return spring into the pump well.
19. Install the pump plunger assembly into the pump well.

AIR HORN

1. Install the new pump plunger stem seal and retainer into the air horn casting. Lightly stake the seal retainer in three places, choosing locations different from the original stakings.
2. Install the new Throttle Position Sensor (TPS) actuator plunger seal and retainer into the air horn casting. Lightly stake the seal retainer in three places, choosing location different from the original stakings.
3. Install the vent/screen assembly by installing the two small attaching screws; tighten securely.
4. Inspect the air valve shaft pin for lubrication, apply a liberal quantity of lithium base grease to the air valve shaft pin. Make sure to lubricate the pin surface contact by windup spring.
5. Install the fast idle cam rod into the lower hole of the choke lever, aligning the squirt on the rod with small slot in lever.
6. Install the TPS plunger through seal in the air horn until about ½ of the plunger extends above the surface of the air horn casing. The seal pressure should hold the plunger in place during the air horn installation on the float bowl.

FINAL ASSEMBLY

1. Rotate the fast idle cam to the the full UP position and tilt the air horn assembly to engage the lower end of the fast idle cam rod in the slot of the fast idle cam and install the pump rod end into hole of the pump lever. Then, holding down on the pump plunger assembly, carefully lower the air horn assembly onto the float bowl, guiding the pump plunger stem through the hole in the air horn casting. DO NOT force the air horn assembly onto the bowl but rather lightly lower it into place.
2. Install the vent and screen assembly over the vent stack in the air horn. Then, install the air horn-to-bowl screws and the lockwashers – tighten evenly and securely.
3. Install new the retainer clip through the hole in end of the pump rod.
4. Install the new seal in the recess of the air horn, then install the hot idle compensator valve and retain it with the small screws; tighten the screws securely.
5. Install the plastic bushing in the upper hole in the vacuum break and choke lever, making sure the small end of the bushing faces the retaining clip when installed. With the inner coil lever and the intermediate choke lever at the 12 o'clock position, install the intermediate choke rod into the bushing; retain it with needle-nose pliers. Make sure the clip has full contact on the rod but is not seated tightly against the bushing. The rod-to-bushing clearance should be 0.030 in. (0.8mm).
6. Install the idle speed solenoid, the lockwasher and the retaining nut on the secondary side vacuum break; tighten the nut securely. Then, bend back two (2) retaining tabs on the lockwasher to fit slots in the bracket.
7. Rotate the secondary side vacuum break and the bracket assembly, then insert the end ("T" pin) of the vacuum break link into the upper slot of the vacuum break and the choke lever. Install the bracket onto the throttle body and the countersunk screws; tighten the screws securely.
8. If the air valve rod has been removed from primary side vacuum break plunger, install the plastic bushings in the hole in the primary side vacuum break plunger, making sure the small end of the bushing faces the retaining clip when installed. Then, insert the end of the air valve rod through the bushing. Retain

with the new clip, by it pressing the clip in place using needle-nose pliers. Make sure the clip has full contact on the rod but is not sealed tightly against the bushing. The rod-to-bushing clearance should be 0.030 in. (0.8mm).

9. Rotate the primary side vacuum break assembly and the bracket, then insert the end of the air valve rod into the slot of the air valve lever and the end of the "T" pin of the vacuum break link into the lower slot of the vacuum break and choke lever. Position the bracket over the locating lug on the air horn and install the (2) countersunk screws and tighten securely.

10. Reinstall the hose onto the primary-side vacuum break assembly and the throttle body tube.

11. Perform the choke coil lever adjustment procedure as specified in the carburetor adjustment section.

12. Install the choke cover and the coil assembly in the choke housing, aligning the notch in cover with raised casting projection on the housing cover flange. Make sure the choke coil lever is located inside the "trapped stat" coil tang when installing the choke cover and the coil assembly.

13. The ground contact for the electric choke is provided by a metal plate located at the rear of the choke cover assembly. DO NOT install a choke cover gasket between the electric choke assembly and the choke housing.

14. A choke cover retainer kit is required to attach choke cover to choke housing. Install the proper retainers and rivets contained in the kit, using a suitable blind rivet installation tool.

OVERHAUL E2SE

Disassembly

SECONDARY VACUUM BREAK

Remove the secondary vacuum break/bracket assembly-to-throttle body screws. Then, rotate the assembly to disengage the vacuum break link ("T" Pin) from the choke lever slot.

DO NOT immerse the idle speed solenoid or the vacuum break units in any type of carburetor cleaner. These items must always be removed before complete cleaning or damage to the components will result.

AIR HORN

1. Remove the clip from the hole in the pump rod.

NOTE: DO NOT remove the pump lever retaining screw or the pump lever from the air horn assembly.

2. Remove and discard the retaining clip from the intermediate choke link at the choke lever. A new retaining clip is required for reassembly. Remove the choke link and the plastic bushing from the choke lever, then save the bushing for later reuse.

3. Remove the mixture control solenoid-to-air horn screws; then, using a slight twisting motion, carefully lift the solenoid out of the air horn. Remove and discard the solenoid gasket.

4. Remove the seal retainer and the rubber seal from the end of the solenoid stem, being careful not to damage or nick end of the solenoid stem. Discard the seal and retainer. Retain the spacer for use at time of reassembly.

5. Remove the air horn-to-fuel bowl screws and lockwashers.

6. Rotate the fast idle cam to the full UP position and remove the air horn assembly by tilting to disengage the fast idle cam rod from the slot in the fast idle cam and the pump rod from the pump lever hole. If the pump plunger comes out of the float bowl with the air horn removal, remove the pump plunger from the air horn. The air horn gasket should remain on the float bowl for removal later. DO NOT remove the fast idle cam screw and the cam from the float bowl. These parts are not serviced separately and are to remain permanently in place as installed by the factory. The new service replacement float bowl will include the secondary lockout lever, the fast idle cam and screw installed as required.

7. Remove the fast idle cam link from the choke lever by rotating the rod to align the upset on the link with the small slot in the lever.

8. Remove the Throttle Position Sensor (TPS) plunger by pushing it downward through the air horn seal.

NOTE: Use your fingers ONLY to remove the plunger to prevent damage to the sealing surface of the plunger.

9. Remove the TPS seal by inverting the air horn and use a small screwdriver to remove the staking, holding the seal retainer in place. Remove and discard the retainer and seal.

10. Remove the pump plunger stem seal by inverting the air horn and using a small screwdriver to remove the staking, holding the seal retainer in place. Remove and discard the retainer and seal.

NOTE: Use care in removing the TPS plunger seal retainer and the pump plunger stem seal retainer to prevent damage to the air horn casting. New seals and retainers are required for reassembly.

11. Remove the vent/screen assembly by removing the two small attaching screws.

12. Further disassembly of the air horn is not required for cleaning purposes or air horn replacement. A new service air horn assembly includes the secondary metering rod-air valve assembly with adjustments pre-set to factory specifications. No attempt should be made to change the air valve settings. The air valve and the choke valve attaching screws are staked in place and are not removable. A new service air horn assembly will also include a TPS adjustment screw (refer to "on Vehicle Service," section or proper adjustment procedure for the TPS). The new service air horn assembly will also have the thermostatic pump bypass assembly installed, this temperature sensitive device is pressed permanently into place and is not serviceable, separately.

FLOAT BOWL

1. Remove the air horn gasket.

2. Remove the pump plunger from the pump well (if not removed with the air horn).

3. Remove the pump return spring from the pump well.

4. Push up from the bottom on the electrical connector and remove the Throttle Position Sensor (TPS) and the connector assembly from the float bowl. Remove the spring from the bottom of TPS well in the bowl.

NOTE: Use care in removing the sensor and connector assembly to prevent damage to this critical electrical part.

5. Remove the plastic filler block over the float valve.

6. Remove the float assembly and the float valve by pulling up the hinge pin (hold the float valve clip in place with your finger while tilting the float to clear the bowl vapor purge tube).

7. Using a removal tool or a wide-blade screwdriver, remove the float valve seat (with gasket) and the extended metering jet from the float bowl.

NOTE: DO NOT remove or change the adjustment of the small calibration screw located deep inside the metering jet during routine servicing. The adjustment screw is pre-set at the factory and no attempt should be made to change this adjustment in the field except as the result of a Computer Command Control system performance check.

8. Using a small slidehammer or equivalent, remove the plastic retainer holding the pump discharge spring and check ball in place. Discard the plastic retainer (a new retainer is required for reassembly).

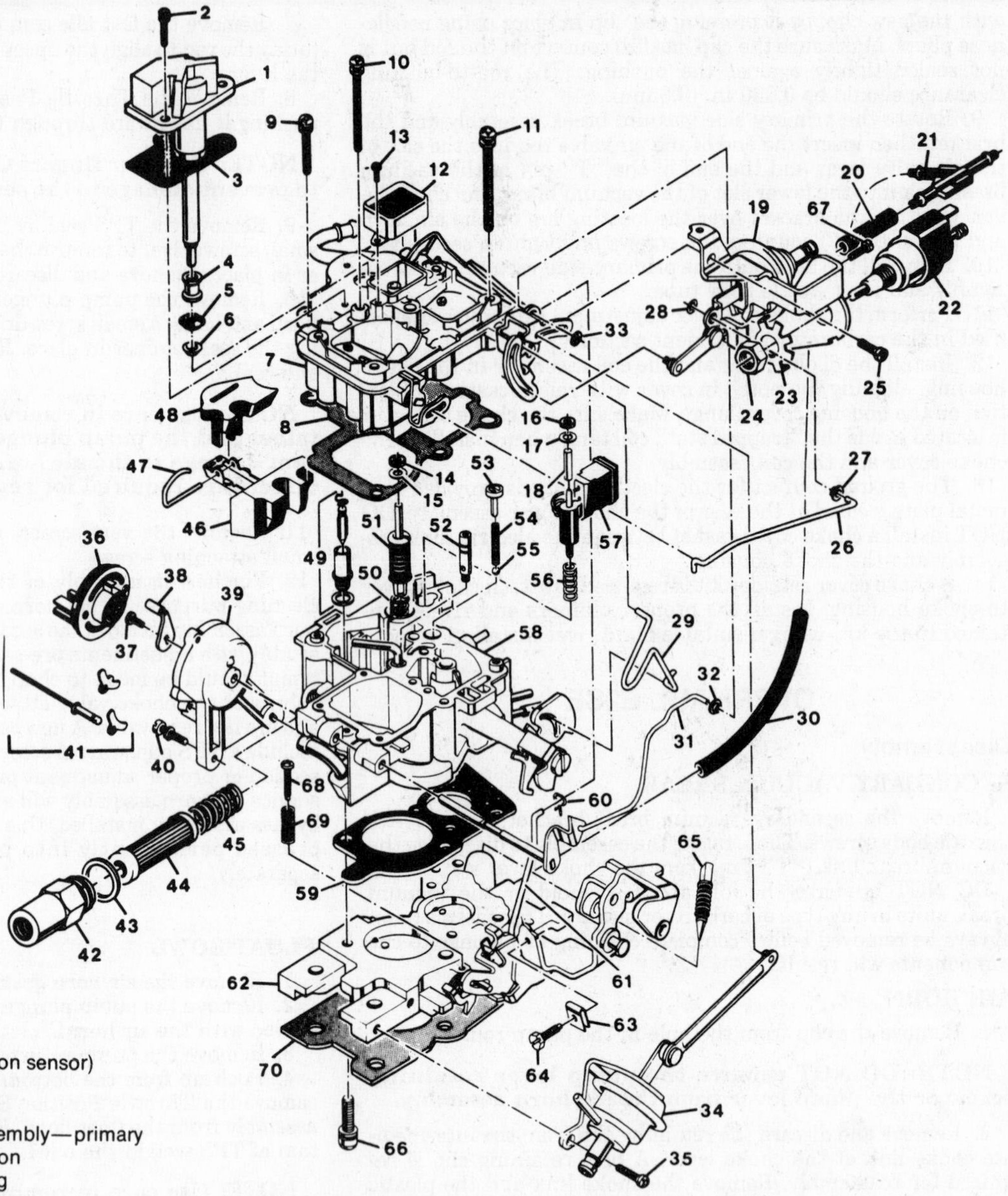

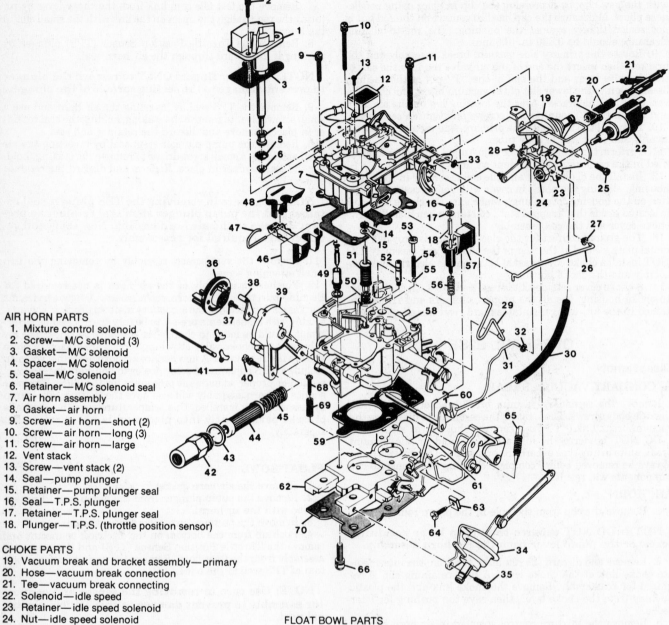

AIR HORN PARTS
1. Mixture control solenoid
2. Screw—M/C solenoid (3)
3. Gasket—M/C solenoid
4. Spacer—M/C solenoid
5. Seal—M/C solenoid
6. Retainer—M/C solenoid seal
7. Air horn assembly
8. Gasket—air horn
9. Screw—air horn—short (2)
10. Screw—air horn—long (3)
11. Screw—air horn—large
12. Vent stack
13. Screw—vent stack (2)
14. Seal—pump plunger
15. Retainer—pump plunger seal
16. Seal—T.P.S. plunger
17. Retainer—T.P.S. plunger seal
18. Plunger—T.P.S. (throttle position sensor)

CHOKE PARTS
19. Vacuum break and bracket assembly—primary
20. Hose—vacuum break connection
21. Tee—vacuum break connecting
22. Solenoid—idle speed
23. Retainer—idle speed solenoid
24. Nut—idle speed solenoid
25. Screw—vacuum break bracket attaching
26. Link—air valve
27. Bushing—air valve link
28. Retainer—air valve link
29. Link—fast idle cam
30. Hose—vacuum break
31. Intermediate choke shaft/lever/link assembly
32. Bushing—intermediate choke link
33. Retainer—intermediate choke link
34. Vacuum break and bracket assembly—secondary
35. Screw—vacuum break attaching (2)
36. Choke—cover and coil assembly
37. Screw—choke lever attaching
38. Choke lever and contract assembly
39. Choke housing
40. Screw—choke housing attaching (2)
41. Stat cover retainer kit

FLOAT BOWL PARTS
42. Nut—fuel inlet
43. Gasket—fuel inlet nut
44. Filter—fule inlet
45. Spring—fuel filter
46. Float assembly
47. Hinge pin—float
48. Insert—float bowl
49. Needle and seat assembly
50. Spring—pump return
51. Pump—assembly
52. Metering jet
53. Retainer—pump spring and check ball
54. Spring—pump check ball
55. Ball—pump check
56. Spring—T.P.S.
57. T.P.S.—(throttle position sensor)
58. Float bowl assembly
59. Gasket—float bowl

THROTTLE BODY PARTS
60. Clip—pump rod
61. Pump rod
62. Throttle body assembly
63. Clip—cam screw
64. Screw—fast idle cam
65. Idle needle and spring
66. Screw—throttle body attaching
67. Screw—vacuum break bracket attaching (new)
68. Screw—idle stop
69. Spring—idle stop screw
70. Gasket—intake manifold

Exploded view of the E2SE carburetor – 2.0L and 2.8L engines

NOTE: DO NOT attempt to remove the plastic retainer by prying it out with a tool such as a punch or screwdriver as this will damage the sealing beads on the bowl casting surface and require complete float bowl replacement.

9. Turn the fuel bowl upside down catching the pump discharge spring and the check ball in palm of your hand. Return the bowl to the upright position.
10. Remove the fuel inlet nut, the gasket, the check valve filter assembly and the spring.

CHOKE ASSEMBLY

A tamper resistant choke cover design is used to discourage readjustment of the choke thermostatic coil assembly in the field. However, it is necessary to remove the cover and coil assembly during normal carburetor disassembly for cleaning and overhaul using the following procedures:

1. Support the float bowl and the throttle body as an assembly on a suitable holding fixture.
2. Carefully align a No. 21 drill (0.159 in.) on the rivet head and drill only enough to remove the rivet head. After removing the rivet heads and retainers, use a drift and a small hammer to drive the remainder of the rivets out of the choke housing.

NOTE: Use care in drilling to prevent damage to the choke cover or housing.

3. Remove the screw from the end of the intermediate choke shaft inside the choke housing.
4. Remove the choke coil lever from the end of the shaft.
5. Remove the intermediate choke shaft assembly from the float bowl by sliding the shaft rearward and out of the throttle lever side.
6. Remove the choke housing by removing the two attaching screws.

THROTTLE BODY

1. Remove the throttle body-to-bowl screws and the throttle body assembly from the float bowl.
2. Remove the throttle body gasket.
3. Place the throttle body assembly on the carburetor holding fixture to avoid damaging the throttle valves.
4. Hold the primary throttle lever wide-open and disengage the pump rod from the throttle lever by rotating the rod until the upset on the rod aligns with slot in the lever.
5. Further disassembly of the throttle body is not required for cleaning purposes.

NOTE: The primary and secondary throttle valve screws are permanently staked in place and should not be removed. The throttle body is serviced as a complete assembly.

6. DO NOT remove the plugs covering the idle mixture needle unless it is necessary to replace the mixture needle or normal soakings and air pressure fails to clean the idle mixture passages. If necessary, remove the idle mixture plug and needle as follows:
   a. Invert the throttle body and place it on a suitable holding fixture — manifold side up.
   b. Make two parallel cuts into the throttle body on either side of the locator point beneath the idle mixture needle plug (manifold side) with a hacksaw. The cuts should reach down to the steel plug but should not extend more than ⅛ in. (3mm) beyond the locator point. The distance between the saw marks depends on the size of the punch to be used.
   c. Place a flat punch at a point near the ends of the saw marks in the throttle body. Holding the punch at a 45° angle, drive it into the throttle body until the casting breaks away, exposing the steel plug.
   d. Holding a center punch vertical, drive it into the steel plug. Then holding the punch at a 45° angle, drive the plug out of the casting.

NOTE: The hardened plug will break rather than remaining intact. It is not necessary to remove the plug whole; instead, remove loose pieces to allow use of Idle Mixture Adjusting tool No. J-29030, BT-7610B or equivalent.

7. Using the tool No. J-29030, BT-7610B or equivalent, remove the idle mixture needle and spring from the throttle body.

Cleaning

The carburetor parts should be cleaned in a cold immersion-type cleaner such as Carbon X (X-55) or its equivalent.

NOTE: The idle speed solenoid, the mixture control solenoid, the throttle position sensor, the electric choke, the rubber parts, the plastic parts, the diaphragms, the pump plunger, the plastic filler block, should NOT be immersed in carburetor cleaner as they will harden, swell or distort.

The plastic bushing in the throttle lever will withstand normal cleaning in the carburetor cleaner.

1. Thoroughly clean all of the metal parts and blow dry with shop air. Make sure all the fuel passages and metering parts are free of burrs and dirt. DO NOT pass the drills or wires through the jets and passages.
2. Inspect the upper and lower surface of the carburetor castings for damage.
3. Inspect the holes in the levers for excessive wear or out of round conditions. If worn, the levers should be replaced. Inspect the plastic bushings in the levers for damage and excessive wear, replace as required.

Inspection

Check, repair or replace parts if the following problems are encountered:

FLOODING

1. Inspect float valve and seat for dirt, deep wear grooves, scores and proper seating.
2. Inspect float valve pull clip for proper installation. Be careful not to bend pull clip.
3. Inspect float, float arms and hinge pin for distortion, binds, and burrs. Check density of material in the float; if heavier than normal, replace float.
4. Clean or replace fuel inlet filter and check valve assembly.

HESITATION

1. Inspect pump plunger and cup for cracks, scores or cup excessive wear. A used pump cup will shrink when dry. If dried out, soak in fuel for 8 hours before testing.
2. Inspect pump duration and return springs for being weak or distorted.
3. Check all pump passages and jet for dirt, improper seating of discharge check ball and scores in pump well. Check condition of pump discharge check ball spring, then replace as necessary.
4. Check pump linkage for excessive wear; repair or replace as necessary.

HARD STARTING – POOR COLD OPERATION

1. Check choke valve and linkage for excessive wear, binds or distortion.
2. Inspect choke vacuum diaphragms for leaks.
3. Replace carburetor fuel filter.
4. Inspect float valve for sticking, dirt, etc.
5. Also check items under "Flooding".

POOR PERFORMANCE – POOR GAS MILEAGE

1. Clean all fuel and vacuum passages in the castings.
2. Check the choke valve for freedom of movement.

3. Check the Mixture Control Solenoid for sticking, binding or leaking as follows:

a. Connect one end of a jumper wire to either terminal of the solenoid connector and the other end to the positive (+) terminal of a 12V battery source.

b. Connect a jumper wire to the other terminal of the solenoid connector and the other end to a known good ground.

c. With the rubber seal, retainer and the spacer removed from the end of the solenoid stem, attach a hose from a hand vacuum pump.

d. With the solenoid fully energized (lean position), apply 25 in.Hg and time the leak-down rate should not exceed 5 in.Hg in 5 seconds. If leakage exceeds that amount, replace the solenoid.

e. To check the solenoid for sticking in the down position, remove the jumper lead from the 12V source and observe hand vacuum pump reading. The reading should go to 0 in less than one second.

4. Inspect the metering jet for dirt, loose parts or damage.

NOTE: DO NOT attempt to readjust the mixture screw located inside the metering jet. The screw is factory adjusted and a change can upset the fuel system calibration. NO ATTEMPT should be made to change this adjustment in the field except as the result of a Computer Command Control system performance check.

5. Check the air valve and the secondary metering rod for binding conditions. If the air valve or metering rod is damaged or the metering rod adjustment is changed from the factory setting, the air horn assembly must be replaced. Also check the air valve spring for proper installation (tension against the air valve shaft pin).

ROUGH IDLE

1. Inspect gasket and gasket mating surfaces on castings for nicks, burrs or damage to the sealing beads.
2. Check operation and sealing of mixture control solenoid.
3. Clean all idle fuel passages.
4. If removed, inspect idle mixture needle for ridges, burrs or being bent.
5. Check the throttle lever and valves for bind, nicks and other damage.
6. Check all diaphragms for possible ruptures or leaks.

NOTE: When cleaning plastic parts, only use low volatile cleaning solvent – never in gasoline.

Assembly

THROTTLE BODY

1. Holding the primary throttle lever wide-open, install the lower end of the pump rod in the throttle lever by aligning the squirt on the rod with the slot in the lever. End of the rod should point outward toward the throttle lever.

2. If removed, install the idle mixture needle and spring using tool No. J029030 or equivalent. Lightly seat the needle and then back out three turns as a preliminary idle mixture adjustment. Final idle mixture adjustment must be made on-vehicle. Refer to the "On-Vehicle Service" section for the idle mixture adjustment procedures.

FLOAT BOWL

1. Install a new throttle-to-bowl gasket over the two locating dowels on the bowl.

NOTE: If a new float bowl assembly is used, stamp or engrave the model number on the new float bowl.

2. Rotate the fast idle cam so that the steps face fast the idle screw on the throttle lever when properly installed, install the throttle body making certain the throttle body is properly located over the dowels on the float bowl; then install the throttle body-to-bowl screws and lockwashers, then tighten evenly and securely.

NOTE: Inspect the linkage to insure the lockout tang is located properly to engage the slot in the secondary lockout lever and that the linkage moves freely and does not bind.

3. Place the carburetor on suitable holding fixture.

4. Install the fuel inlet filter spring, the filter assembly, a new gasket and inlet nut, then tighten the nut to 18 ft. lbs.

5. When installing a service replacement filter, make sure the filter is the type that includes the check valve to need U.S. Motor Vehicle Safety Standards (MVSS).

6. When properly installed, the hole (check valve end) in the filter faces toward the inlet nut.

NOTE: Tightening beyond the specified torque can damage the nylon gasket to cause a fuel leak.

7. Install the choke housing on the throttle body, making sure the raised boss and locating lug on the rear of the housing fit into the recesses in the float bowl casting. Install the choke housing attaching screws and lockwashers, then tighten the screws evenly and securely.

8. Install the immediate choke shaft assembly in the float bowl by pushing the shaft through from the throttle lever side.

9. With the intermediate choke lever in the UP (12 o'clock) position, install the choke coil lever inside the choke housing onto flats on the intermediate choke shaft. The choke coil lever is properly aligned when the coil pick-up tang is in the UP position. Install the choke coil lever retaining screws into the end of the intermediate choke shaft and tighten securely.

10. Install the pump discharge check ball, the spring and a new plastic retainer in the float bowl. Tap lightly into place until the top of retainer is flush with the bowl casting surface.

11. Using a wide-blade screwdriver, install the float valve seat (with gasket) and the metering jet; tighten securely.

12. To make the adjustment easier, carefully bend the float arm upward at the notch in the arm before assembly.

13. Install the float valve onto the float arm by sliding the float lever under the pull clip. The correct installation of the pull clip is to hook the clip over the edge of the float on the float arm facing the float pontoon.

14. Install the float hinge pin into the float arm with the end of loop of pin facing the pump well. Then, install the float assembly by aligning the valve in the seat and the float hinge pin into locating channels in the float bowl.

15. To adjust the float level, perform the following procedures:

a. Hold the float hinge pin firmly in place and push down lightly on the arm at the outer end against the top of the float valve.

b. Using adjustment "T" scale, measure from the top of the float bowl casting surface (air horn gasket removed) to the top of the float at the toe.

c. Bend the float arm as necessary for proper adjustment by pushing on the pontoon (see Adjustment Chart for specifications).

d. Visually check the float alignment after adjustment.

16. Install the plastic filler block over the float valve by pressing downward until properly seated (flush with the bowl casting surface).

17. Install the Throttle Position Sensor (TPS) return spring in the bottom of the well in the float bowl.

18. Install the Throttle Position Sensor (TPS) and the connector assembly in the float bowl by aligning the groove in the electrical connector with the "V" in the float bowl casting, push down on the connector and sensor assembly so that the connector wires and sensor are located below the bowl casting surface.

NOTE: Care must be taken when installing the throttle position sensor to assure that the electrical integrity is maintained. Make sure that the wires between the connector and sensor assembly are not pinched or the insulation broken upon final assembly. Accidental electrical grounding of the TPS must be avoided.

19. Install the air horn gasket on the float bowl, locating the gasket over the two dowel locating pins on the bowl.
20. Install the pump return spring and plunger in the pump well.

AIR HORN

1. Install the new pump plunger stem seal and retainer in the air horn casting. Lightly stake the seal retainer in three places, choosing locations different from the original stakings.
2. Install new Throttle Position Sensor (TPS) actuator plunger seal and retainer in the air horn casting. Lightly stake the seal retainer in three places, choosing locations different from the original stakings.
3. Install the vent/screen assembly by installing the two small attaching screws; tighten securely.
4. Inspect the air valve shaft pin for lubrication, apply a liberal quantity of lithium base grease to the air valve shaft pin. Make sure to lubricate the pin surface contacted by the windup spring.
5. Install the fast idle cam rod in lower hole of the choke lever, aligning the squirt on the rod with small slot in the lever.
6. Install the TPS plunger through seal in the air horn until about ½ of the plunger extends above the surface of the air horn casting. Seal pressure should hold the plunger in place during the air horn installation on the float bowl.

FINAL ASSEMBLY

1. Rotate the fast idle cam to the full UP position and tilt the air horn assembly to engage the lower end of the fast idle cam rod in the slot in the fast idle cam and install the pump rod end into hole in the pump lever; check the intermediate choke rod for position, then, holding down on the the pump plunger assembly, carefully lower the air horn assembly onto the float bowl, guiding the pump plunger stem through the seal in the air horn casting.

NOTE: DO NOT force the air horn assembly onto the bowl but rather lightly lower it into place. Make sure the TPS actuator plunger engages the sensor plunger in the bowl by checking the plunger movement.

2. Install the air horn-to-bowl screws and lockwashers, tighten evenly and securely.
3. Install a new retainer clip through the hole in the end of the pump rod extending through the pump lever, making sure the clip is securely locked in place.

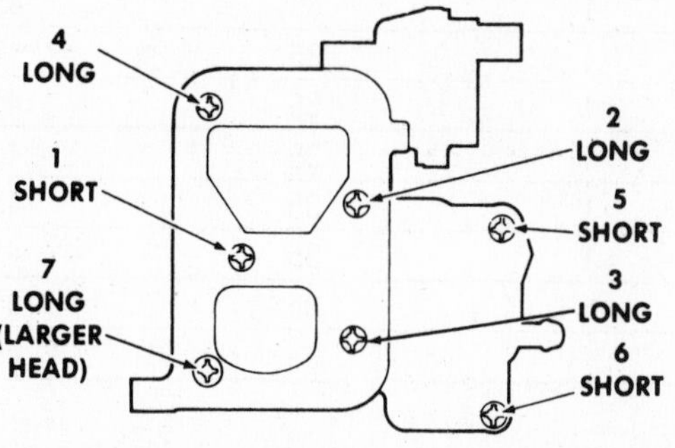
4
LONG
1
SHORT
7
LONG
(LARGER
HEAD)
2
LONG
5
SHORT
3
LONG
6
SHORT

Air horn tightening sequence — 2SE and E2SE carburetors

4. If not tested previously, test the mixture control solenoid for sticking, binding or leaking, following the steps noted in the cleaning and inspection procedure. Then, install the spacer and new rubber seal on the mixture control solenoid stem making sure the seal is up against the spacer. Then, using a $^{3}/_{16}$ in. socket and light hammer, carefully drive a new retainer on the stem. Drive the retainer onto the stem only far enough to retain the rubber seal on the stem leaving a slight clearance between the retainer and seal to allow for seal expansion.
5. Prior to installing the mixture control solenoid, lightly coat the rubber seal on the end of the solenoid stem with a silicone grease or light engine oil. Using a new mounting gasket, install the mixture control solenoid on the air horn, carefully aligning the solenoid stem with recess in bottom of the bowl. Use a slight twisting motion of the solenoid during installation to ensure the rubber seal on stem is guided into the recess in the bottom of the bowl, to prevent distortion or damage to the rubber seal. Install the solenoid attaching screws and tighten securely.
6. Install the plastic bushing in the hole in the choke lever, making sure the small end of bushing faces the retaining clip, when installed. With the inner coil lever and intermediate choke lever at the 12 o'clock position, install the intermediate choke rod in the bushing. Retain the rod with new clip, pressing the clip securely in place with needle nose pliers. Make sure the clip has full contact on the rod but is not seated tightly against the bushing. The rod-to-bushing clearance should be 0.030 in. (0.8mm).
7. Install the secondary vacuum break assembly. Rotate the assembly and insert the end ("T" Pin) of the vacuum break link into the upper slot of the choke lever. Attach the bracket-to-throttle body with countersunk screws and tighten the screws securely.
8. If the air valve rod has been removed from the primary-side vacuum break plunger, install a plastic bushing in the hole in the primary-side vacuum break plunger, making sure the small end of the bushing faces the retaining clip when installed. Then insert the end of the air valve rod through the bushing. Retain with a new clip, pressing the clip into place using needle-nose pliers. Make sure the clip has full contact on the rod but is not seated tightly against the bushing. The rod-to-bushing clearance should be 0.030 in. (0.8mm).
9. Rotate the primary-side vacuum break assembly (with the idle speed solenoid and bracket), then insert the end of the air valve rod into the slot of the air valve lever and end ("T" Pin) of the vacuum break link into the lower slot of the choke lever. Connect the primary vacuum break hose-to-tube on the throttle body and tube on the vacuum break unit. Position the bracket over the locating lug on the air horn and install the two countersunk screws on the air horn and screw with lockwasher in the throttle body; tighten the screws securely.
10. Perform the choke coil lever adjustment procedure as specified in carburetor adjustment section.
11. Install the choke cover and coil assembly in the choke housing, aligning the notch in the cover with the raised casting projection on the housing cover flange. Make sure the coil pick-up tang engages the inside choke coil lever.
12. The tang on the thermostatic coil is the "trapped stat" design. This means that the coil tang is formed so that it will completely encircle the coil pick-up lever. Make sure the coil pick-up lever is located inside the coil tang when installing the choke cover and coil assembly.

NOTE: The ground contact for the electric choke is provided by a metal plate located at the rear of the choke cover assembly. DO NOT install a choke cover gasket between the electric choke assembly and the choke housing. A choke cover retainer kit is required to attach the choke cover-to-choke housing. Install the proper retainers and rivets contained in kit, using a blind rivet installation tool.

5 FUEL SYSTEM

CARBURETOR SPECIFICATIONS

Type DCH340 4-1.9L Engine

Primary Throttle Plate Gap (in.)	Primary Main Jet Number	Secondary Main Jet Number	Primary Slow Jet Number	Secondary Slow Jet Number	Power Jet Number	Primary Main Air Bleed Number	Secondary Main Air Bleed Number	Slow Air Bleed Number
.050–.059 (MT) .059–.069 (AT)	114 Fed. 85 Cal.	170	50 Fed. 54 Cal.	100	50	120 Fed. 110 Cal.	70 Fed. 90 Cal.	150 Fed. 130 Cal.

Type E2SE 6-2.8L (Code B) (California)

Carb. Number	Float Level (in.)	Fast Idle Cam. (deg.)	Primary Vacuum Break (deg.)	Air Valve Rod (deg.)	Secondary Vacuum Break (deg.)	Choke Unloader (deg.)
17082356	13/32	22	25	1	30	30
17082357	13/32	22	25	1	32	30
17082358	13/32	22	25	1	30	30
17082359	13/32	22	25	1	32	30
17072683	9/32	28	25	1	35	45
17074812	9/32	28	25	1	35	45
17084356	9/32	22	25	1	30	30
17084357	9/32	22	25	1	30	30
17084358	9/32	22	25	1	30	30
17084359	9/32	22	25	1	30	30
17084368	1/8	22	25	1	30	30
17084370	1/8	22	25	1	30	30
17084430	11/32	15	26	1	38	42
17084431	11/32	15	26	1	38	42
17084434	11/32	15	26	1	38	42
17084435	11/32	15	26	1	38	42
17084452	5/32	28	25	1	35	45
17084453	5/32	28	25	1	35	45
17084455	5/32	28	25	1	35	45
17084456	5/32	28	25	1	35	45
17084458	5/32	28	25	1	35	45
17084532	5/32	28	25	1	35	45
17084534	5/32	28	25	1	35	45
17084535	5/32	28	25	1	35	45
17084537	5/32	28	25	1	35	45
17084538	5/32	28	25	1	35	45
17084540	5/32	28	25	1	35	45
17084542	1/8	28	25	1	35	45
17084632	9/32	28	25	1	35	45
17084633	9/32	28	25	1	35	45
17084635	9/32	28	25	1	35	45
17084636	9/32	28	25	1	35	45

Type 2SE 6-2.8L (Code B) (excluding California)

Carb. Number	Float Level (in.)	Fast Idle Cam. (deg.)	Primary Vacuum Break (deg.)	Air Valve Rod (deg.)	Secondary Vacuum Break (deg.)	Choke Unloader (deg.)
17082348	7/16	22	26	1	32	40
17082349	7/16	22	28	1	32	40
17082350	7/16	22	26	1	32	40
17082351	7/16	22	28	1	32	40
17082353	7/16	22	28	1	35	30
17082355	7/16	22	28	1	35	30
17083348	7/16	22	30	1	32	40
17083349	7/16	22	30	1	32	40
17083350	7/16	22	30	1	32	40
17083351	7/16	22	30	1	32	40
17083352	7/16	22	30	1	35	40
17083353	7/16	22	30	1	35	40
17083354	7/16	22	30	1	35	40
17083355	7/16	22	30	1	35	40
17083360	7/16	22	30	1	32	40
17083361	7/16	22	28	1	32	40
17083362	7/16	22	30	1	32	40
17083363	7/16	22	28	1	32	40
17083364	7/16	22	30	1	35	40
17083365	7/16	22	30	1	35	40
17083366	7/16	22	30	1	35	40
17083367	7/16	22	30	1	35	40
17083390	13/32	28	30	1	35	38
17083391	13/32	28	30	1	35	38
17083392	13/32	28	30	1	35	38
17083393	13/32	28	30	1	35	38
17083394	13/32	28	30	1	35	38
17083395	13/32	28	30	1	35	38
17083396	13/32	28	30	1	35	38
17083397	13/32	28	30	1	35	38
17084410	11/32	15	23	1	38	42
17084412	11/32	15	23	1	38	42
17084425	11/32	15	26	1	36	40
17084427	11/32	15	26	1	36	40
17084560	11/32	15	24	1	34	38
17084562	11/32	15	24	1	34	38
17084569	11/32	15	24	1	34	38

GASOLINE FUEL INJECTION SYSTEM

Operation

The Throttle Body Injection (TBI) system provides a means of fuel distribution for controlling exhaust emissions within legislated limits by precisely controlling the air/fuel mixture and under all operating conditions for, as near as possible, complete combustion.

This is accomplished by using an Electronic Control Module (ECM) (a small on-board microcomputer) that receives electrical inputs from various sensors about engine operating conditions. An oxygen sensor in the main exhaust stream functions to provide feedback information to the ECM as to the oxygen content (lean or rich) in the exhaust. The ECM uses this information from the oxygen sensor, and other sensors, to modify fuel delivery to achieve, as near as possible, an ideal air/fuel ratio of 14.7:1. This air/fuel ratio allows the 3-way catalytic converter to be more efficient in the conversion process of reducing exhaust emissions while at the same time providing acceptable levels of driveability and fuel economy.

The ECM program electronically signals the fuel injector in the TBI assembly to provide the correct quantity of fuel for a wide range of operating conditions. Several sensors are used to determine existing operating conditions and the ECM then signals the injector to provide the precise amount of fuel required.

The TBI assembly is centrally located on the intake manifold where air and fuel are distributed through a single bore in the throttle body, similar to a carbureted engine. Air for combustion is controlled by a single throttle valve which is connected to the accelerator pedal linkage by a throttle shaft and lever assembly. A special plate is located directly beneath the throttle valve to aid in mixture distribution.

Fuel for combustion is supplied by 1 or 2 fuel injector(s), mounted on the TBI assembly, whose metering tip is located directly above the throttle valve. The injector is pulsed or timed open or closed by an electronic output signal received from the ECM. The ECM receives inputs concerning engine operating conditions from the various sensors (coolant temperature sensor, oxygen sensor, etc.). The ECM, using this information, performs high speed calculations of engine fuel requirements and pulses or times the injector, open or closed, thereby controlling fuel and air mixtures to achieve, as near as possible, ideal air/fuel mixture ratios.

When the ignition key is turned ON, the ECM will initialize (start program running) and energize the fuel pump relay. The fuel pump pressurizes the system to approximately 10 psi. If the ECM does not receive a distributor reference pulse (telling the ECM the engine is turning) within 2 seconds, the ECM will then de-energize the fuel pump relay, turning off the fuel pump. If a distributor reference pulse is later received, the ECM will turn the fuel pump back on.

CRANKING MODE

During engine crank, for each distributor reference pulse the ECM will deliver an injector pulse. The crank air/fuel ratio will be used if the throttle position is less than 80% open. Crank air fuel is determined by the ECM and ranges from 1.5:1 at −33°F (−36°C) to 14.7:1 at 201°F (94°C).

The lower the coolant temperature, the longer the pulse width (injector on-time) or richer the air/fuel ratio. The higher the coolant temperature, the less pulse width (injector on-time) or the leaner the air/fuel ratio.

CLEAR FLOOD MODE

If for some reason the engine should become flooded, provisions have been made to clear this condition. To clear the flood, the driver must depress the accelerator pedal enough to open to wide-open throttle position. The ECM then issues injector pulses at a rate that would be equal to an air/fuel ratio of 20:1. The ECM maintains this injector rate as long as the throttle remains wide open and the engine rpm is below 600. If the throttle position becomes less than 80%, the ECM then would immediately start issuing crank pulses to the injector calculated by the ECM based on the coolant temperature.

RUN MODE

There are 2 different run modes. When the engine rpm is above 400, the system goes into open loop operation. In open loop operation, the ECM will ignore the signal from the oxygen sensor and calculate the injector on-time based upon inputs from the coolant and manifold absolute pressure sensors.

During open loop operation, the ECM analyzes the following items to determine when the system is ready to go to the closed loop mode:

1. The oxygen sensor varying voltage output. (This is dependent on temperature).
2. The coolant sensor must be above specified temperature.
3. A specific amount of time must elapse after starting the engine. These values are stored in the PROM.

When these conditions have been met, the system goes into closed loop operation In closed loop operation, the ECM will modify the pulse width (injector on-time) based upon the signal from the oxygen sensor. The ECM will decrease the on-time if the air/fuel ratio is too rich, and will increase the on-time if the air/fuel ratio is too lean.

The pulse width, thus the amount of enrichment, is determined by manifold pressure change, throttle angle change, and coolant temperature. The higher the manifold pressure and the wider the throttle opening, the wider the pulse width. The acceleration enrichment pulses are delivered non-synchronized. Any reduction in throttle angle will cancel the enrichment pulses. This way, quick movements of the accelerator will not over-enrich the mixture.

ACCELERATION ENRICHMENT MODE

When the engine is required to accelerate, the opening of the throttle valve(s) causes a rapid increase in Manifold Absolute Pressure (MAP). This rapid increase in the manifold pressure causes fuel to condense on the manifold walls. The ECM senses this increase in throttle angle and MAP, and supplies additional fuel for a short period of time. This prevents the engine from stumbling due to too lean a mixture.

DECELERATION MODE

Upon deceleration, a leaner fuel mixture is required to reduce emission of hydrocarbons (HC) and carbon monoxide (CO). To adjust the injection on-time, the ECM uses the decrease in manifold pressure and the decrease in throttle position to calculate a decrease in pulse width. To maintain an idle fuel ratio of 14.7:1, fuel output is momentarily reduced. This is done because of the fuel remaining in the intake manifold during deceleration.

BATTERY VOLTAGE CORRECTION MODE

The purpose of battery voltage correction is to compensate for variations in battery voltage to fuel pump and injector response. The ECM modifies the pulse width by a correction factor in the PROM. When battery voltage decreases, pulse width increases.

Battery voltage correction takes place in all operating modes. When battery voltage is low, the spark delivered by the distributor may be low. To correct this low battery voltage problem, the ECM can do any or all of the following:

1. Increase injector pulse width (increase fuel)
2. Increase idle rpm
3. Increase ignition dwell time

FUEL CUT-OFF MODE

When the ignition is OFF, the ECM will not energize the injector. Fuel will also be cut off if the ECM does not receive a reference pulse from the distributor. To prevent dieseling, fuel delivery is completely stopped as soon as the engine is stopped. The ECM will not allow any fuel supply until it receives distributor reference pulses which prevents flooding.

Basic Troubleshooting

NOTE: The following explains how to activate the trouble code signal light in the instrument cluster and gives an explanation of what each code means. This is not a full system troubleshooting and isolation procedure. See Electronic Engine Controls in Section 2 for further troubleshooting procedures.

Before suspecting the system or any of its components as faulty, check the ignition system including distributor, timing, spark plugs and wires. Check the engine compression, air cleaner, and emission control components not controlled by the ECM. Also check the intake manifold, vacuum hoses and hose connectors for leaks.

The following symptoms could indicate a possible problem with the system:

1. Detonation
2. Stalls or rough idle-cold
3. Stalls or rough idle-hot
4. Missing
5. Hesitation
6. Surges
7. Poor gasoline mileage
8. Sluggish or spongy performance
9. Hard starting-cold
10. Objectionable exhaust odors (rotten egg smell)
11. Cuts out
12. Improper idle speed

As a bulb and system check, the CHECK ENGINE light will come on when the ignition switch is turned to the ON position but the engine is not started. The CHECK ENGINE light will also produce the trouble code or codes by a series of flashes which translate as follows. When the diagnostic test terminal under the dash is grounded, with the ignition in the ON position and the engine not running, the CHECK ENGINE light will flash once, pause, then flash twice in rapid succession. This is a Code 12, which indicates that the diagnostic system is working. After a long pause, the Code 12 will repeat itself 2 more times. The cycle will then repeat itself until the engine is started or the ignition is turned off.

When the engine is started, the CHECK ENGINE light will remain on for a few seconds, then turn off. If the CHECK ENGINE light remains on, the self-diagnostic system has detected a problem. If the test terminal is then grounded, the trouble code will flash 3 times. If more than 1 problem is found, each trouble code will flash 3 times. Trouble codes will flash in numerical order (lowest code number to highest). The trouble codes series will repeat as long as the test terminal is grounded.

A trouble code indicates a problem with a given circuit. For example, trouble Code 14 indicates a problem in the cooling sensor circuit. This includes the coolant sensor, its electrical harness, and the ECM. Since the self-diagnostic system cannot diagnose every possible fault in the system, the absence of a trouble code does not mean the system is trouble-free. To determine problems within the system which do not activate a trouble code, a system performance check must be made.

In the case of an intermittent fault in the system, the CHECK ENGINE light will go out when the fault goes away, but the trouble code will remain in the memory of the ECM. Therefore, it a trouble code can be obtained even though the CHECK ENGINE light is not on, the trouble code must be evaluated. It must be determined if the fault is intermittent or if the engine must be at certain operating conditions (under load, etc.) before the CHECK ENGINE light will come on. Some trouble codes will not be recorded in the ECM until the engine has been operated at part throttle for about 5–18 minutes. On the CCC System, a trouble code will be stored until terminal R of the ECM has been disconnected from the battery for 10 seconds.

An easy way to erase the computer memory on the CCC System is to disconnect the battery terminals from the battery. If this method is used, don't forget to reset clocks and electronic pre-programmable radios. Another method is to remove the fuse marked ECM in the fuse panel. Not all models have such a fuse.

Fuel Pressure Relief

Prior to servicing any component of the fuel injection system, the fuel pressure must relieved. If fuel pressure is not relieved, serious injury could result.

2.5L TBI ENGINE

1. From the fuse block, located in the passenger compartment, remove the fuse labeled, Fuel Pump.
2. Start the engine.

NOTE: The engine will start and run, for a short period of time, until the remaining fuel is used up.

3. Engage the starter, a few more times, to relieve any remaining pressure.
4. Turn the ignition switch Off and install the Fuel Pump fuse into the fuse block.

2.8L and 4.3L TBI ENGINE

Allow the engine to set for 5–10 minutes; this will allow the orifice (in the fuel system) to bleed off the pressure.

Electric Fuel Pump

The electric fuel pump is attached to the fuel sending unit, located in the fuel tank.

REMOVAL AND INSTALLATION

NOTE: The following procedure requires the use of the GM Fuel Gauge Sending Unit Retaining Cam tool No. J-24187 or equivalent, a brass drift and a hammer.

1. Relieve the system fuel pressure.
2. Disconnect the negative battery terminal from the battery.

NOTE: Be sure to keep a Class B (dry chemical) fire extinguisher nearby.

CAUTION

Due to the possibility of fire or explosion, never drain or store gasoline in an open container.

3. Using a hand pump or a siphon hose, drain the gasoline into an approved container.
4. Raise and support the vehicle on jackstands.
5. Support the fuel tank and remove the fuel tank-to-vehicle straps.

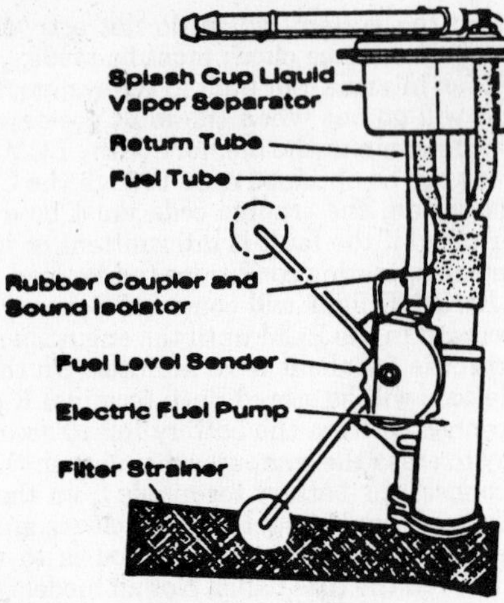

Splash Cup Liquid Vapor Separator
Return Tube
Fuel Tube
Rubber Coupler and Sound Isolator
Fuel Level Sender
Electric Fuel Pump
Filter Strainer

TBI fuel pump and fuel gauge sender assembly

6. Lower the tank slightly, then remove the sender unit wires, the hoses and the ground strap.
7. Remove the fuel tank from the vehicle.
8. Using the GM Fuel Gauge Sending Unit Retaining Cam tool No. J-24187 (or equivalent) or a brass drift and a hammer, remove the cam locking ring (fuel sending unit) counterclockwise, then lift the sending unit from the fuel tank.
9. Remove the fuel pump from the fuel sending unit, by performing the following procedures:

a. Pull the fuel pump up into the mounting tube, while pulling outward (away) from the bottom support.

NOTE: When removing the fuel pump from the sending unit, be careful not to damage the rubber insulator and the strainer.

b. When the pump assembly is clear of the bottom support, pull it out of the rubber connector.

10. Inspect the fuel pump hose and bottom sound insulator for signs of deterioration, then replace it, if necessary.
11. Push the fuel pump onto the sending tube.
12. Using a new sending unit-to-fuel tank O-ring, install the sending unit into the fuel tank.

NOTE: When installing the sending unit, be careful not to fold or twist the fuel strainer, for it will restrict the fuel flow.

13. Using the GM Fuel Gauge Sending Unit Retaining Cam tool No. J-24187 (or equivalent) or a brass drift and a hammer, turn the sending unit-to-fuel tank locking ring clockwise.
14. To install the fuel tank, align the insulator strips and reverse the removal procedures. Torque the inner fuel tank strap-to-vehicle bolts to 26 ft. lbs. and the outer fuel tank strap-to-vehicle nuts/bolts to 26 ft. lbs.

TESTING AND ADJUSTMENTS

Flow Test

1. Remove the fuel pump-to-throttle body line from the throttle body.
2. Place the fuel line in a clean container.
3. Turn the ignition switch On; approximately ½ pint of the fuel should be delivered in 15 seconds.
4. If the fuel flow is below minimum, inspect the fuel system for restrictions; if no restrictions are found, replace the fuel pump.

Pressure Test

NOTE: The following procedure requires the use of a GM Fuel Pressure Gauge tool No. J-29658-A or equivalent.

1. If equipped with an EFI equipped engine, refer to the Fuel Pressure Relief procedures in this section and relieve the fuel pressure.
2. Remove the air cleaner, then disconnect and plug the THERMAC vacuum port on the throttle body unit.
3. Place a rag (to catch excess fuel) under the fuel line-to-throttle body connection. Disconnect the fuel line from the throttle body.

NOTE: When disconnecting the fuel line, use a back-up wrench to hold the fuel nut on the throttle body.

4. Using a GM Fuel Pressure Gauge tool No. J-29658-A or equivalent, install it into the fuel line.
5. Start the engine and observe the fuel pressure, it should be 9–13 psi.

NOTE: If the fuel pressure does not meet specifications, inspect the fuel system for restrictions or replace the fuel pump.

6. Turn the engine Off, relieve the fuel pressure and remove the GM Fuel Pressure Gauge tool No. J-29658-A or equivalent.
7. Install a new fuel line-to-throttle body O-ring and reverse the removal procedures. Unplug from the THERMAC vacuum port. Start the engine and check for fuel leaks.

Fuel Pump Relay

The fuel pump relay is mounted on the left front fender in the engine compartment. Check for loose electrical connections; no other service is possible, except replacement.

REMOVAL AND INSTALLATION

1. Disconnect the negative battery terminal from the battery.
2. Disconnect the relay/electrical connector assembly from the bracket.
3. Pull the fuel pump relay from the electrical connector.
4. If necessary, use a new fuel pump and reverse the removal procedures.

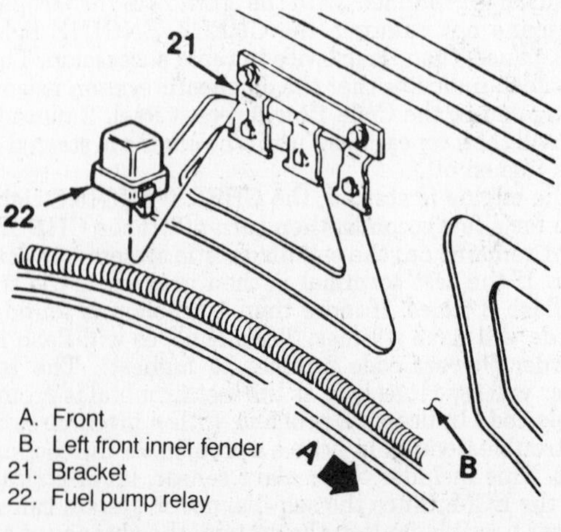

21
22
A
B
A. Front
B. Left front inner fender
21. Bracket
22. Fuel pump relay

Fuel pump relay location

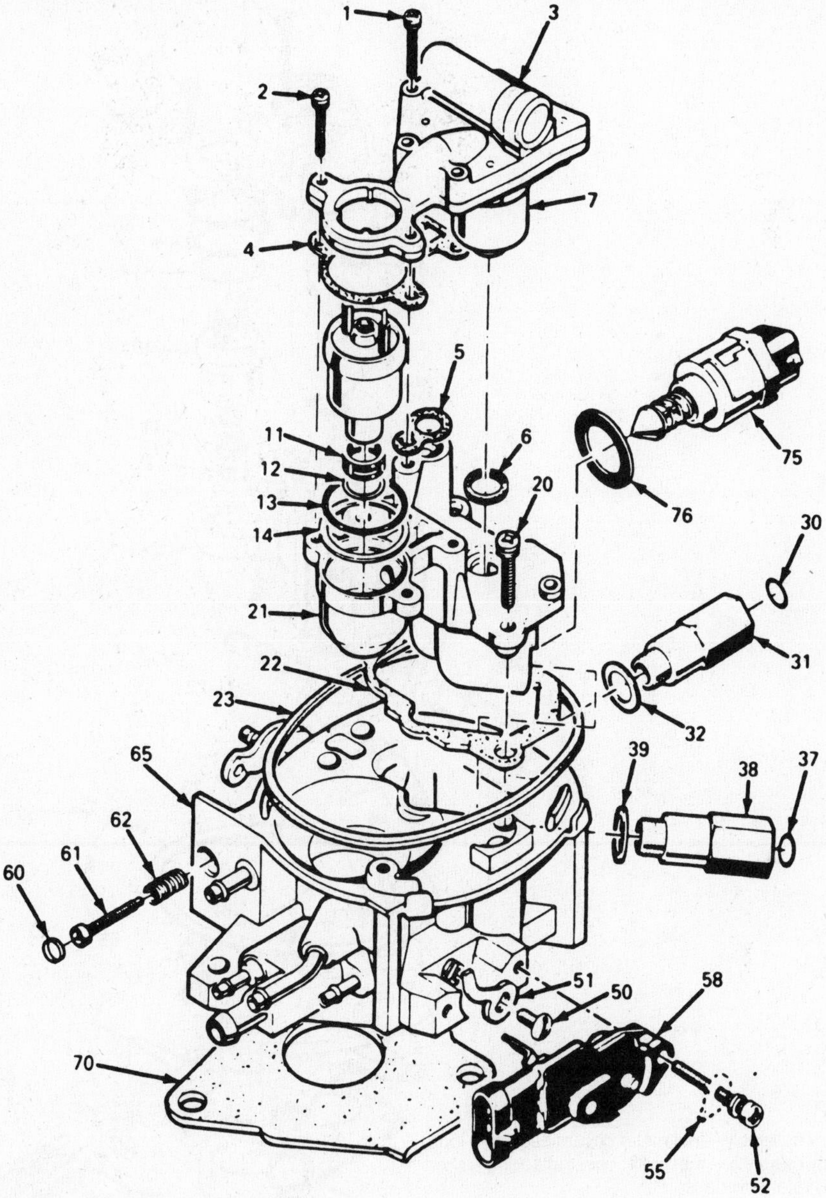
1
2
3
4
5
6
7
11
12
13
14
20
21
22
23
30
31
32
37
38
39
50
51
52
55
58
60
61
62
65
70
75
76

1. Screw & washer assembly
2. Screw & washer assembly
3. Fuel meter cover assembly
4. Gasket—fuel meter cover
5. Gasket—fuel meter outlet
6. Dust seal—pressure regulator
7. Pressure regulator
11. Filter—fuel injector nozzle
12. Lower "O" ring
13. Upper "O" ring
14. Back-up washer—fuel injector
20. Screw & washer assembly
21. Fuel meter body assembly
22. Gasket—fuel meter body
23. Gasket—air filter
30. Fuel return line "O" ring
31. Nut—fuel return
32. Gasket—fuel return nut
37. Fuel inlet line "O" ring
38. Nut—fuel inlet
39. Gasket—fuel inlet nut
50. Screw—TPS lever attaching
51. Lever—TPS
52. Screw & washer assembly
55. Retainer—TPS attaching screw
58. Sensor—throttle position
60. Plug—idle stop screw
61. Screw—throttle stop
62. Spring—throttle stop screw
65. Throttle body assembly
70. Gasket—flange mounting
75. Idle air control assembly
76. Gasket—IAC to throttle body

Exploded view of the model 300 TBI unit – early 2.5L engines

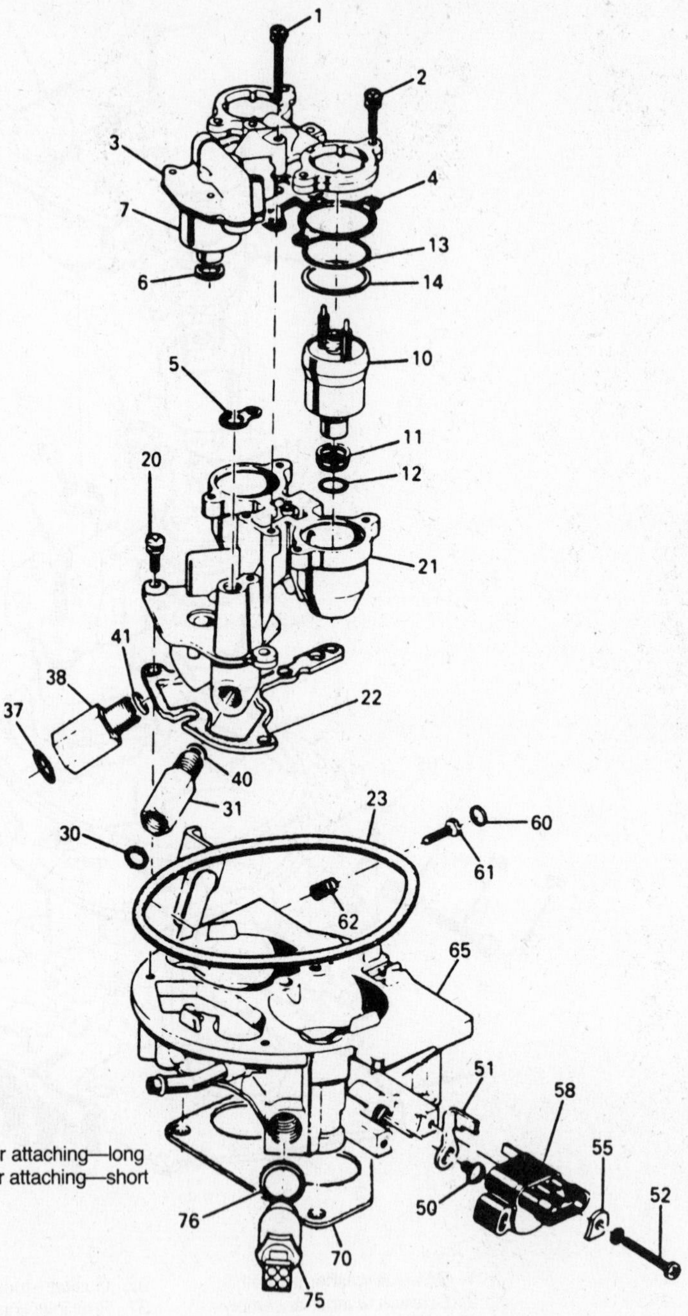
1
2
3
4
7
13
6
14
10
5
11
20
12
21
41
38
22
37
40
31
23
30
60
61
62
65
51
58
55
52
50
76
70
75

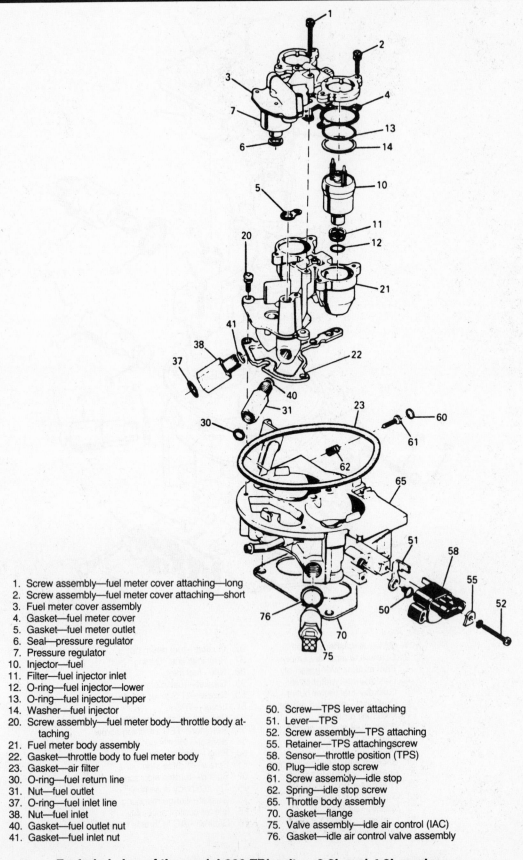

1. Screw assembly—fuel meter cover attaching—long
2. Screw assembly—fuel meter cover attaching—short
3. Fuel meter cover assembly
4. Gasket—fuel meter cover
5. Gasket—fuel meter outlet
6. Seal—pressure regulator
7. Pressure regulator
10. Injector—fuel
11. Filter—fuel injector inlet
12. O-ring—fuel injector—lower
13. O-ring—fuel injector—upper
14. Washer—fuel injector
20. Screw assembly—fuel meter body—throttle body attaching
21. Fuel meter body assembly
22. Gasket—throttle body to fuel meter body
23. Gasket—air filter
30. O-ring—fuel return line
31. Nut—fuel outlet
37. O-ring—fuel inlet line
38. Nut—fuel inlet
40. Gasket—fuel outlet nut
41. Gasket—fuel inlet nut
50. Screw—TPS lever attaching
51. Lever—TPS
52. Screw assembly—TPS attaching
55. Retainer—TPS attachingscrew
58. Sensor—throttle position (TPS)
60. Plug—idle stop screw
61. Screw assembly—idle stop
62. Spring—idle stop screw
65. Throttle body assembly
70. Gasket—flange
75. Valve assembly—idle air control (IAC)
76. Gasket—idle air control valve assembly

Exploded view of the model 220 TBI unit – 2.8L and 4.3L engines

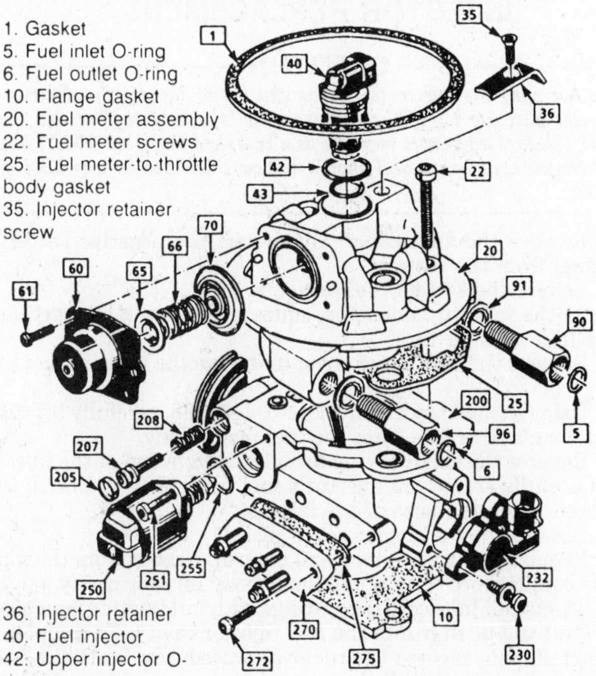

1
35
40
36
42
22
43
70
66
20
60
65
61
91
90
200
25
208
96
5
207
6
205
255
251
232
250
10
270
272
275
230

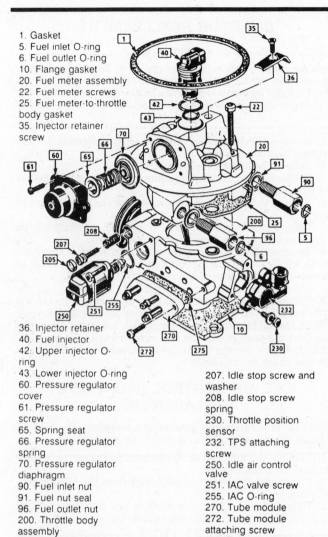

1. Gasket
5. Fuel inlet O-ring
6. Fuel outlet O-ring
10. Flange gasket
20. Fuel meter assembly
22. Fuel meter screws
25. Fuel meter-to-throttle body gasket
35. Injector retainer screw
36. Injector retainer
40. Fuel injector
42. Upper injector O-ring
43. Lower injector O-ring
60. Pressure regulator cover
61. Pressure regulator screw
65. Spring seat
66. Pressure regulator spring
70. Pressure regulator diaphragm
90. Fuel inlet nut
91. Fuel nut seal
96. Fuel outlet nut
200. Throttle body assembly
205. Idle stop screw plug
207. Idle stop screw and washer
208. Idle stop screw spring
230. Throttle position sensor
232. TPS attaching screw
250. Idle air control valve
251. IAC valve screw
255. IAC O-ring
270. Tube module
272. Tube module attaching screw
275. Tube module gasket

Exploded view of the model 700 TBI unit – late 2.5L engines

Throttle Body

The Model 220 throttle body assembly is used on the 2.8L and 4.3L engines. It consists of three major casting assemblies:

- Fuel pressure cover with pressure regulator.
- Fuel metering body with fuel injectors.
- Throttle body with an Idle Speed Control (IAC) Valve and a Throttle Position Sensor (TPS).

The Model 300 throttle body assembly is used on early 2.5L engines. It consists of three major casting assemblies:

- Fuel pressure cover with pressure regulator.
- Fuel metering body with fuel injectors.
- Throttle body with an Idle Speed Control (IAC) Valve and a Throttle Position Sensor (TPS).

The Model 700 throttle body assembly is used on later 2.5L engines. It consists of two major casting assemblies:

- Fuel metering assembly with pressure regulator and fuel injector.
- Throttle body with an Idle Speed Control (IAC) Valve and a Throttle Position Sensor (TPS).

The Throttle Position Sensor (TPS) is a variable resistor used to convert the degree of throttle plate opening to an electrical signal to the ECM. The ECM uses this signal as a reference point of throttle valve position. In addition, an Idle Air Control (IAC) assembly, mounted in the throttle body is used to control idle speeds. A cone-shaped valve in the IAC assembly is located in an air passage in the throttle body that leads from the point beneath the air cleaner to below the throttle valve. The ECM monitors idle speeds and, depending on engine load, moves the IAC cone in the air passage to increase or decrease air bypassing the throttle valve to the intake manifold for control of idle speeds.

The operation of all throttle bodies is basically the same. Each is constantly monitored by the ECM to produce a 14.7:1 air/fuel ratio, which is vital to the catalytic converter operation.

REMOVAL AND INSTALLATION

1. Relieve the system fuel pressure.
2. Remove the air cleaner. Disconnect the negative battery cable from the battery.
3. Disconnect the electrical connectors from the idle air control valve, the throttle position sensor and the fuel injector(s).
4. Remove the throttle return spring(s), the cruise control (if equipped) and the throttle linkage.
5. Label and disconnect the vacuum hoses from the throttle body.
6. Place a rag (to catch the excess fuel) under the fuel line-to-throttle body connection, then disconnect the fuel line from the throttle body.
7. Remove the attaching hardware, the throttle body-to-intake manifold bolts, the throttle body and the gasket.

NOTE: Be sure to place a cloth in the intake manifold to prevent dirt from entering the engine.

8. Using a putty knife (if necessary), clean the gasket mounting surfaces.

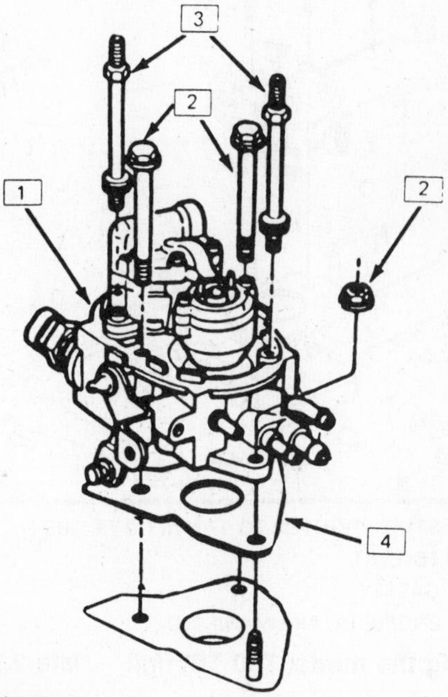

3
2
1
2
4

1. TBI unit
2. Bolts and nut—tighten to 18 N·m (13 ft. lbs.)
3. Stud—tighten to 5 N·m (45 in. lbs.)
4. Gasket

Removing the model 300 TBI unit – early 2.5L engine

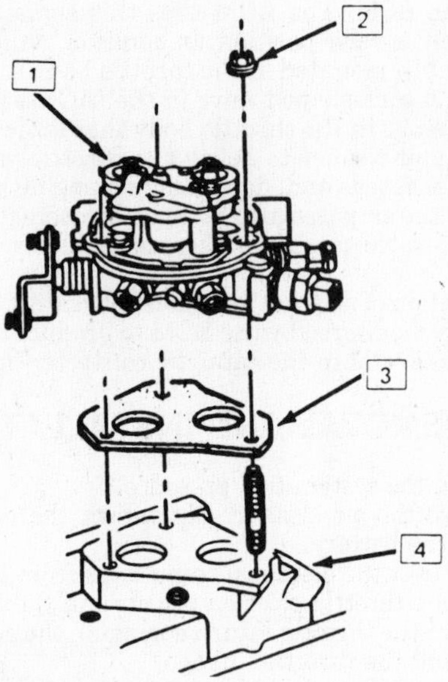
1
2
3
4

1. TBI unit
2. Nut-tighten to 25 N·m (18 ft. lbs.)
3. Gasket
4. Engine inlet manifold

Removing the model 220 TBI unit – 2.8L and 4.3L engine

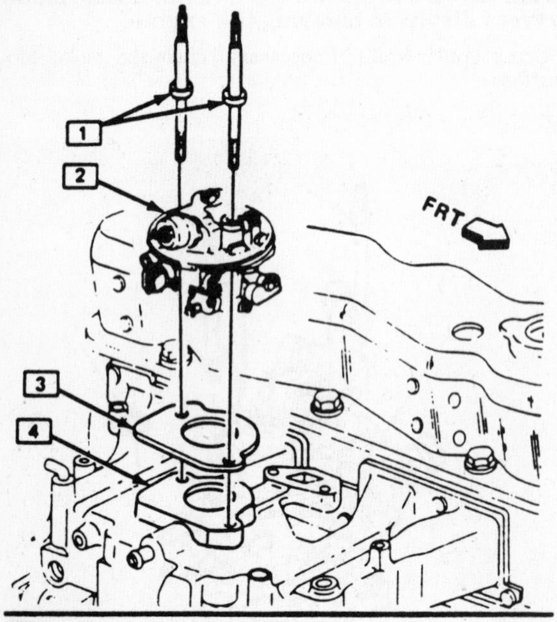
1
2
3
4
FRT

1 STUD - TIGHTEN TO 17 N·m (12 FT. LBS.)
2 TBI UNIT
3 GASKET
4 ENGINE INTAKE MANIFOLD

Removing the model 700 TBI unit – late 2.5L engine

9. To install, use a new gasket and reverse the removal procedures. Torque the throttle body-to-intake manifold nuts/bolts to 13 ft. lbs. Depress the accelerator pedal to the floor and release it, to see if the pedal returns freely. Turn the ignition switch On and check for fuel leaks.

INJECTOR REPLACEMENT

CAUTION

When removing the injector(s), be careful not to damage the electrical connector pins (on top of the injector), the injector fuel filter and the nozzle. The fuel injector is serviced as a complete assembly ONLY, it is an electrical component and should not be immersed in any kind of cleaner.

1. Remove the air cleaner. Disconnect the negative battery terminal from the battery.
2. Relieve the system fuel pressure.
3. At the injector connector, squeeze the two tabs together and pull it straight up.
4. Remove the fuel meter cover and leave the cover gasket in place.
5. Using a small pry bar or tool No. J–26868, carefully lift the injector until it is free from the fuel meter body.
6. Remove the small O-ring form the nozzle end of the injector. Carefully rotate the injector's fuel filter back-and-forth to remove it from the base of the injector.
7. Discard the fuel meter cover gasket.
8. Remove the large O-ring and back-up washer from the top of the counterbore of the fuel meter body injector cavity.
9. To install, lubricate the O-rings with automatic transmission fluid and push it into the fuel injector cavity. To complete the installation, reverse the removal procedures. Start the engine and check for fuel leaks.

IDLE AIR CONTROL (IAC) VALVE REPLACEMENT

NOTE: The following procedure requires the use of the GM Removal tool No. J–33031 or equivalent.

1. Remove the air cleaner. Disconnect the negative battery terminal from the battery.
2. Disconnect the electrical connector from the idle air control valve.
3. Using a 1¼ in. (32mm) wrench or the GM Removal tool No. J–33031, remove the idle air control valve.

CAUTION

Before installing a new idle air control valve, measure the distance that the valve extends (from the motor housing to the end of the cone); the distance should be no greater than 1⅛ in. (28mm). If it extends to far, damage will occur to the valve when it is installed.

4. To install, use a new gasket and reverse the removal procedures. Start the engine and allow it to reach normal operating temperatures.

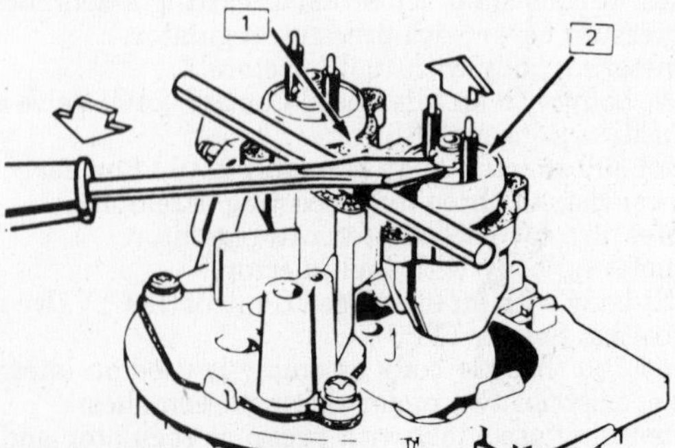
1
2

1. Fuel meter cover gasket
2. Removing fuel injector

Fuel injector removal – model 220

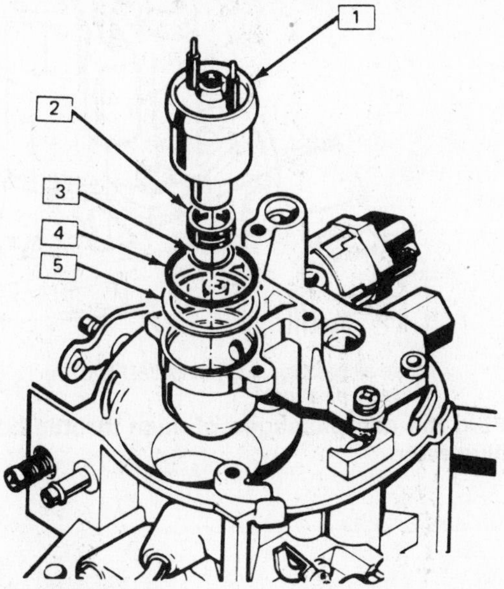
1
2
3
4
5

1. Fuel injector
2. Filter
3. Small "O" ring
4. Large "O" ring
5. Steel back-up washer

Fuel injector removal – model 300

1. Fuel meter body
2. Fuel injector
A. Suitable prybar
B. Fulcrum

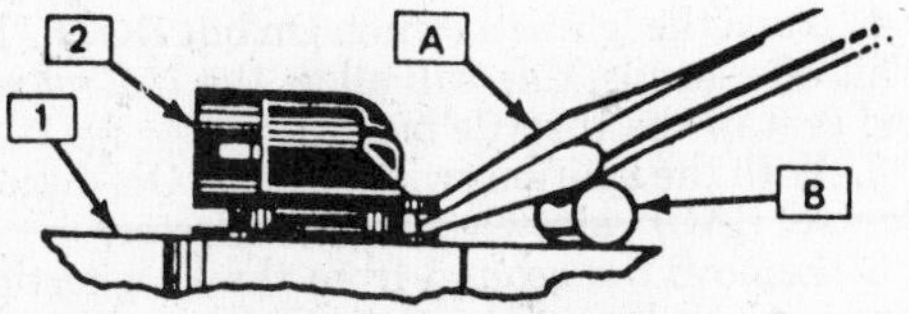
2
A
1
B

Fuel injector removal – model 700

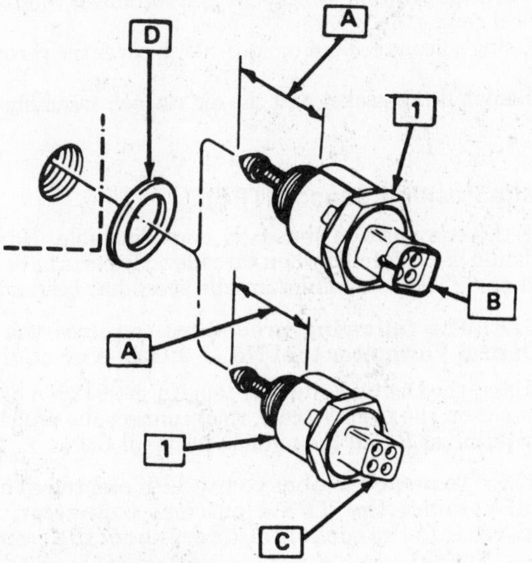
D
A
1
B
A
1
C

1. Idle air control valve
A. Less than 28mm (1⅛ in.)
B. Type I (with collar)
C. Type II (without collar)
D. Gasket (part of IAC valve service kit)

Idle air control valve

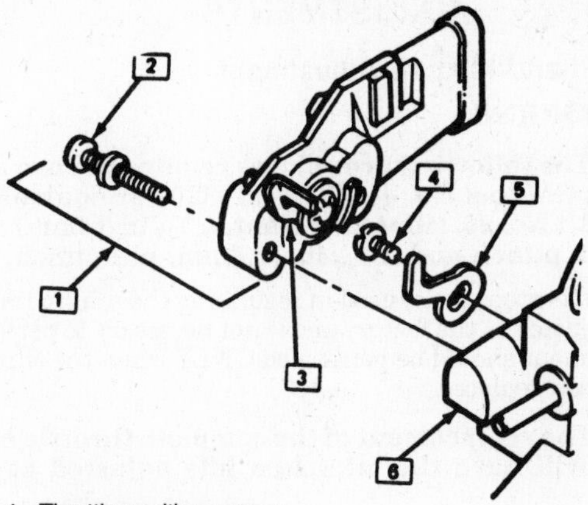
2
4
5
1
3
6

1. Throttle position sensor
2. Screw & washer
3. TPS pick up lever
4. Screw
5. Lever
6. Throttle body assembly

Throttle position sensor – 2.5L engine

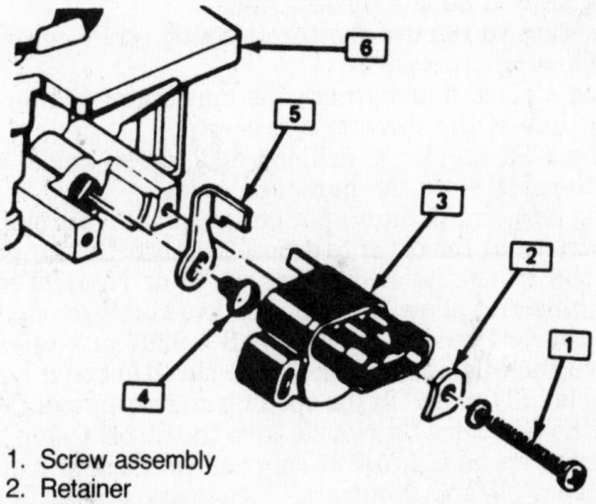
6
5
3
2
1
4

1. Screw assembly
2. Retainer
3. Throttle position sensor
4. Screw
5. Lever
6. Throttle body assembly

Throttle position sensor – 2.8L and 4.3L engines

NOTE: The ECM will reset the idle speed when the vehicle is driven at 30 mph.

THROTTLE POSITION SENSOR (TPS)

1. Remove the air cleaner.
2. Disconnect the electrical connector from the throttle position sensor (TPS).
3. Remove the TPS mounting screws, the lockwashers and the retainers.
4. Remove the TPS sensor.
5. To install, make sure that the throttle valve is in the closed position, then install the TPS sensor.

NOTE: Make sure the the TPS pickup lever is located ABOVE the tang on the throttle actuator lever.

6. To complete the installation, lubricate the mounting screws with Loctite® (thread locking compound) No. 262 or equivalent, then reverse the removal procedures.

ADJUSTMENTS

Idle Speed and Mixture Adjustment

2.5L TBI ENGINE

NOTE: The following procedures require the use a tachometer, GM tool No. J–33047, BT–8207 or equivalent, GM Torx Bit No. 20, silicone sealant, a $^{5}/_{32}$ in. (4mm) drill bit, a prick punch and a $^{1}/_{16}$ in. (1.5mm) pin punch.

The throttle stop screw, used in regulating the minimum idle speed, is adjusted at the factory and is not necessary to perform. This adjustment should be performed ONLY when the throttle body has been replaced.

NOTE: The replacement of the complete throttle body assembly will have the minimum idle adjusted at the factory.

1. Remove the air cleaner and the gasket. Be sure to plug the THERMAC vacuum port (air cleaner vacuum line-to-throttle body) on the throttle body.
2. Remove the throttle valve cable from the throttle control bracket to provide access to the minimum air adjustment screw.
3. Using the manufacturer's instructions, connect a tachometer to the engine.
4. Remove the electrical connector from the Idle Air Control (IAC) valve, located on the throttle body.
5. If necessary to remove the throttle stop screw cover, perform the following procedures:
   a. Using a prick punch, mark the housing at the top over the center line of the throttle stop screw.
   b. Using a $^{5}/_{32}$ in. (4mm) drill bit, drill (on an angle) a hole through the casting to the hardened cover.
   c. Using a $^{1}/_{16}$ in. (1.5mm) pin punch, place it through the hole and drive out the cover to expose the throttle stop screw.
6. Place the transmission in Park (A/T) or Neutral (M/T), start the engine and allow the idle speed to stabilize.
7. Using the GM tool No. J–33047, BT–8207 or equivalent, install it into the idle air passage of the throttle body; be sure that the tool is fully seated in the opening and no air leaks exist.
8. Using the GM Torx Bit No. 20, turn the throttle stop screw until the engine speed is 475–525 rpm (A/T in Park or Neutral) or 750–800 rpm (M/T in Neutral).
9. With the idle speed adjusted, stop the engine, remove the tool No. J–33047, BT–8207 or equivalent, from the throttle body.
10. Reconnect the Idle Air Control (IAC) electrical connector.
11. Using silicone sealant or equivalent, cover the throttle stop screw.
12. Reinstall the gasket and the air cleaner assembly.

2.8L TBI ENGINE

NOTE: The following procedure requires the use of a tachometer, a prick punch, a $^{5}/_{32}$ in. (4mm) drill bit, a $^{1}/_{16}$ in. (1.5mm) pin punch, a grounding wire and silicone sealant.

1. Remove the air cleaner and the gasket.
2. If necessary to remove the throttle stop screw cover, perform the following procedures:
   a. Using a prick punch, mark the housing at the top over the center line of the throttle stop screw.
   b. Using a $^{5}/_{32}$ in. (4mm) drill bit, drill (on an angle) a hole through the casting to the hardened cover.
   c. Using a $^{1}/_{16}$ in. (1.5mm) pin punch, place it through the hole and drive out the cover to expose the throttle stop screw.

NOTE: The following adjustment should be performed ONLY when the throttle body assembly has been replaced; the engine should be at normal operating temperatures before making this adjustment.

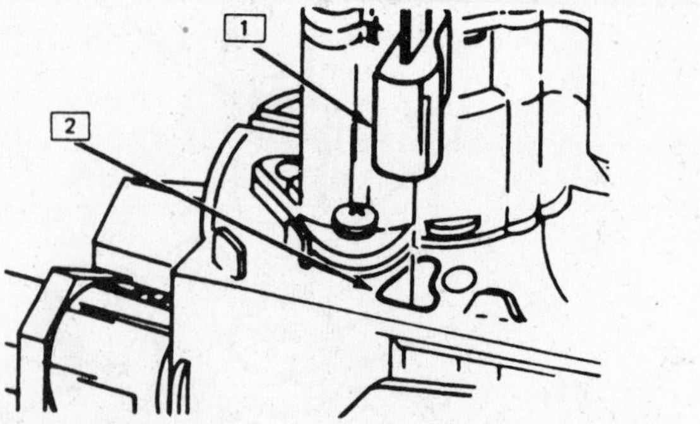
1
2

1. Idle air passage plug (J33047/BT 8207-A)
2. Idle air passage

Plug the idle passages of each throttle body as illustrated

3. With the Idle Air Control (IAC) connected, ground the diagnostic terminal of the Assembly Line Communications Link (ALCL) connector.

NOTE: The Assembly Line Communications Link (ALCL) connector is located in the engine compartment on the left side firewall.

4. Turn the ignition switch On but DO NOT start the engine. Wait 30 seconds, this will allow the IAC valve pintle to extend and seat in the throttle body.
5. With the ignition switch turned On, disconnect the Idle Air Control (IAC) valve electrical connector.
6. Remove the ground from the Diagnostic Terminal ALCL connector and start the engine.
7. Adjust the idle stop screw to obtain 700 rpm (M/T) or 400–450 rpm (A/T in Drive).
8. Turn the ignition switch Off and reconnect the IAC valve electrical connector.
9. Using silicone sealant or equivalent, cover the throttle stop screw.
10. Reinstall the gasket and the air cleaner assembly.

Throttle Position Sensor (TPS)

The throttle position sensor is non-adjustable. However, a test should be performed when throttle body parts have been replaced or AFTER the minimum idle speed has been adjusted.

NOTE: The following procedure requires the use of the Digital Voltmeter tool No. J–29125–A or equivalent.

1. Using the Digital Voltmeter tool No. J–29125–A or equivalent, set it on the 0–5.0V scale, then connect the probes to the center terminal **B** and the outside terminal **C**.

NOTE: To attach probes to the TPS electrical connector, disconnect the TPS electrical connector, install thin wires into the sockets and reconnect the connector.

2. Turn the ignition On (engine stopped).
3. On the Model 220 and 700 throttle body units, the output voltage should be 1.25V. If the voltage is more that 1.25V, replace the TPS.
4. On the Model 300 throttle body unit, the output voltage should be 0.420–0.450V; if not, rotate the TPS to obtain the correct voltage.
5. Remove the voltmeter and the jumper wires.

DIESEL ENGINE FUEL SYSTEM – 2.2L ENGINE

CAUTION

The following procedures should not be attempted unless all tools necessary to adjust the injection pump timing are available.

Fuel Injectors

The primary function of the nozzles is to distribute the fuel in the combustion chamber, which effects the combustion efficiency and engine performance.

REMOVAL AND INSTALLATION

1. Disconnect the negative battery terminal from the battery.
2. From the fuel injector nozzle(s), disconnect the fuel return line(s).
3. From the fuel injector nozzle(s), disconnect the fuel injection line(s).
4. Remove the fuel injector nozzle(s) from the engine.
5. Inspect and test the fuel injector nozzle(s).
6. To install, reverse the removal procedures.

TESTING

NOTE: The following procedure requires the use of a reliable pressure tester and Calibrating Oil No. SAE J9670 or equivalent (70°F).

CAUTION

DO NOT use diesel fuel; it is unstable with the respect to corrosion inhibition and may cause skin problems.

Opening Pressure

1. Using a reliable pressure tester, connect the test line to a fuel nozzle and tighten the fittings.

CAUTION

Exercise extreme care, when using the pressure tester, not to damage the gauge with excessive pressure during the test procedure. When testing the nozzle(s), be sure not to position your hands or arms near the nozzle tip. The atomized high pressure fuel spray has enough penetrating power to puncture the flesh and destroy tissue and may also cause blood poisoning. The nozzle tip should always be enclosed in a transparent receptacle, to contain the spray.

2. Close the gauge valve and operate the handle several times, then check for proper nozzle spray pattern.
3. Open the gauge valve and operate the handle slowly to determine the injector opening pressure. Observe the gauge reading just before the oil is sprayed from the tip; a buzzing noise will occur when the spray is injected. The minimum opening pressure is 1493 psi.

Spray Pattern

1. Close the pressure gauge.
2. Operate the handle slowly, one stroke every 2 seconds, and observe the spray pattern.
3. The spray should be uniform and injected at the correct angle of the nozzle being tested.

Leakage

1. Operate the handle to increase the fuel pressure to 284 psi.
2. Observe the nozzle tip, it should remain dry without an accumulation of fuel at the spray holes; a slight wetting is permitted after 10 seconds, if no droplets are formed.

Injection Pump

REMOVAL

1. Raise the hood.
2. Disconnect the negative battery terminal from the battery. Remove the battery.
3. Remove the undercover.
4. Place a drain pan under the radiator, open the drain cock and on the cylinder block, then drain the cooling system.

CAUTION

When draining the coolant, keep in mind that cats and dogs are attracted by the ethylene glycol antifreeze, and are quite likely to drink any that is left in an uncovered container or in puddles on the ground. This will prove fatal in sufficient quantity. Always drain the coolant into a sealable container. Coolant should be reused unless it is contaminated or several years old.

5. Disconnect the upper water hose from the engine side.
6. Loosen the compressor drive belt by moving the power steering oil pump or idler, if equipped.
7. Remove the cooling fan and the fan shroud.

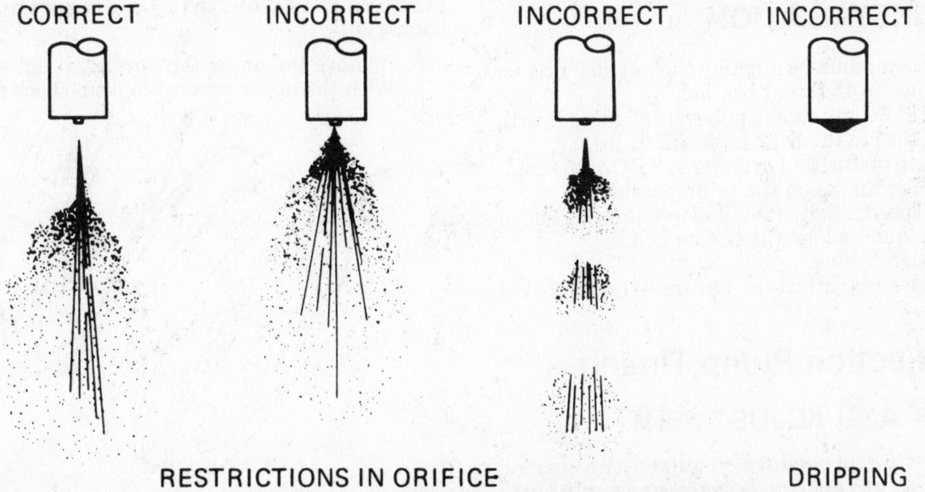
CORRECT
INCORRECT
INCORRECT
INCORRECT
RESTRICTIONS IN ORIFICE
DRIPPING

Description of the fuel nozzle spray pattern – 2.2L diesel engine

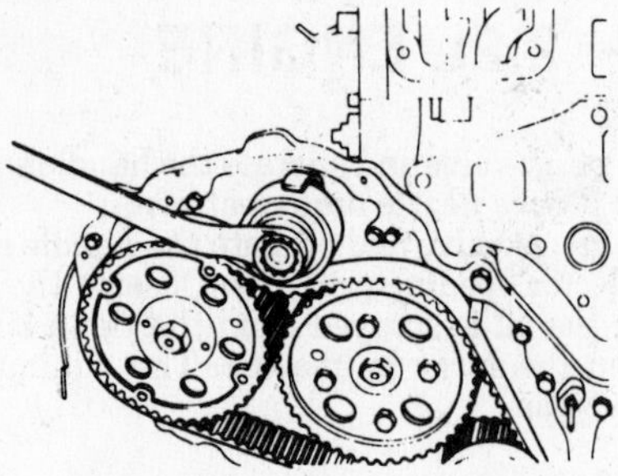

Loosen the tension pulley

J-29801

Removing the tension pulley

8. Disconnect the lower water hose from the engine side.
9. Remove the air conditioner compressor, if equipped.
10. Remove the fan belt, the crankshaft pulley and the timing pulley housing covers.
11. Remove the tension spring and the fixing bolt, then remove the tension center and pulley.
12. Remove the timing belt, the engine control cable and the wiring harness of the fuel cut solenoid.
13. Remove the fuel hoses and the injection pipes. Using a wrench to hold the delivery holder, loosen the sleeve nuts on the injection pump side.
14. Install a 6mm bolt (with pitch of 1.25) into threaded hole in the timing pulley housing through the hole in pulley to prevent turning of the pulley.
15. Remove the bolt fixing the injection pump timing pulley, then remove the pulley using pulley puller.
16. Remove injection pump flange fixing nuts and rear bracket bolts, then remove the injection pump.

INSTALLATION

1. Install the injection pump by aligning the notched line on the flange with the line on the front bracket.
2. Install the injection pump timing pulley by aligning it with the key groove, then torque the bolts to 42–52 ft. lbs.
3. Position the piston of the No. 1 cylinder to TDC of the compression stoke and align marks on the timing pulleys.
4. Refer to the "Timing Belt, Installation" procedures in Chapter 3, then install and adjust the timing belt.
5. Check the injection timing.
6. To complete the installation, reverse the removal procedures.

Diesel Injection Pump Timing

CHECK AND ADJUSTMENT

NOTE: The following procedure requires the use of the Static Timing Gauge tool No. J-29763 or equivalent.

1. Check that notched line on the injection pump flange is in alignment with notched line on the injection pump front bracket.
2. Position the No. 1 piston on TDC of the compression stroke by turning crankshaft as necessary.

NOTE: Make sure No. 1 cylinder is on the compression stroke; it is possible to align the timing marks incorrectly.

3. Remove the upper fan shroud, if not already done.
4. With the upper cover removed, check that the timing belt

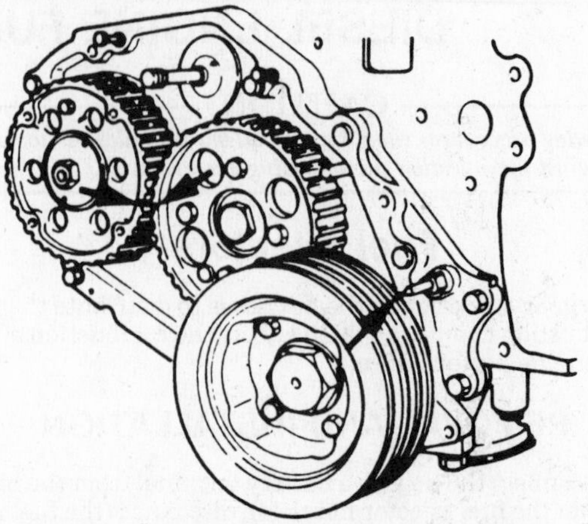

Correct timing mark alignment at TDC

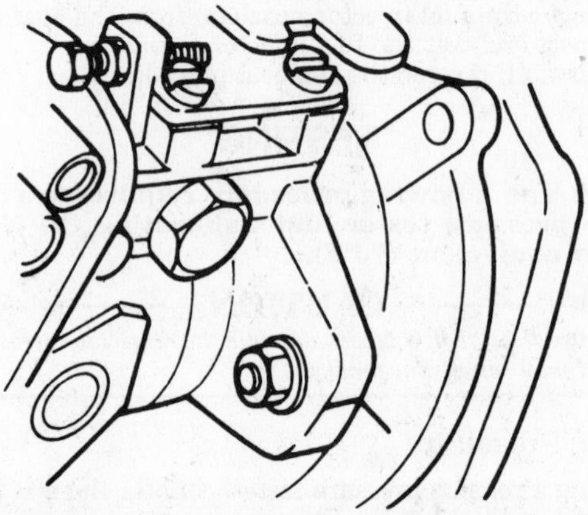

Injection pump and flange alignment

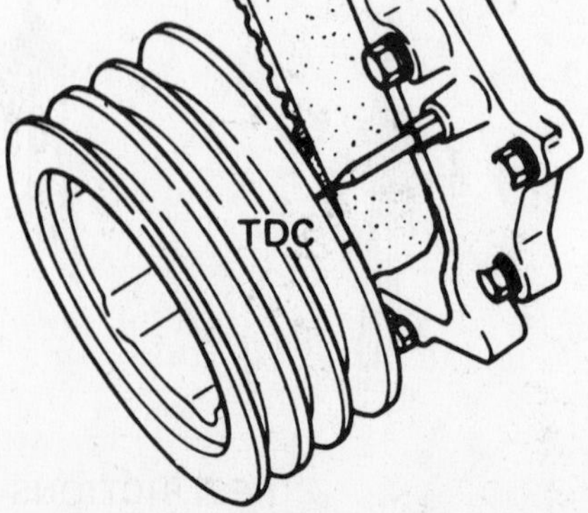
TDC

No. 1 piston at TDC

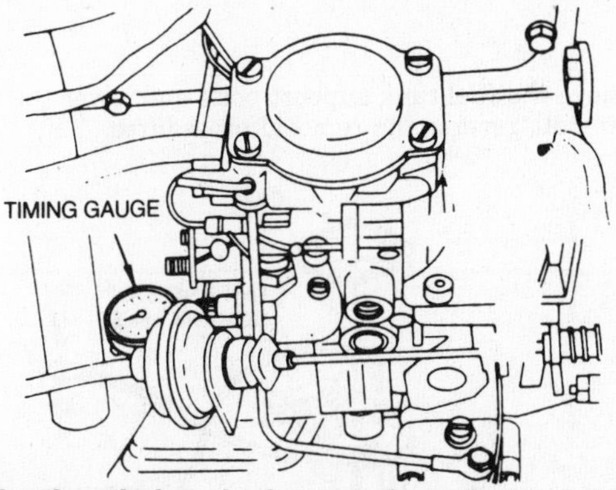
TIMING GAUGE
Injection timing dual gauge installed in injection pump

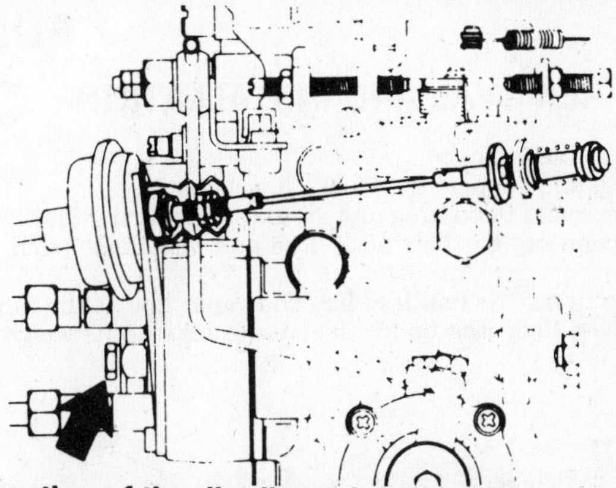
Location of the distributor head screw (arrow) that must be removed to install the dial gauge

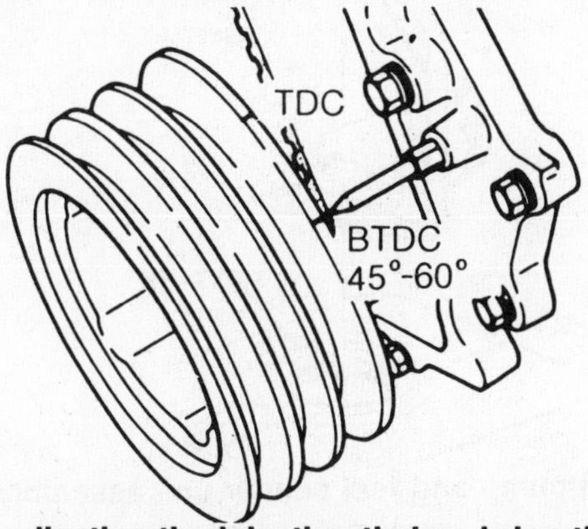
TDC
BTDC
45°-60°
Before adjusting the injection timing, bring the No. 1 piston to 45-60° BTDC and then zero the dial gauge

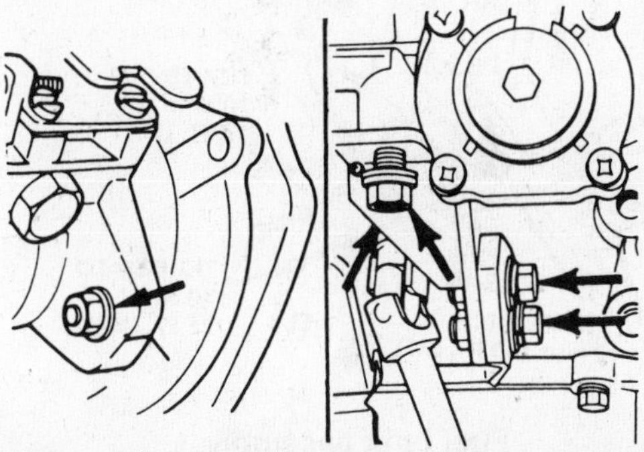
Location of the injection pump flange and bracket bolts

is properly tensioned and that the timing marks are properly aligned. If the marks are not aligned properly, the timing belt will have to be removed and readjusted.

5. With the injection lines removed, remove the distributor head screws and washer from the injection pump.

6. Install the Static Timing Gauge tool No. J–29763 or equivalent, and set the lift to approximately 0.04 in. (1mm) from the plunger.

7. Position the piston, of the No. 1 cylinder, to a point 45–60° BTDC by turning the crankshaft, then calibrate the dial indicator to 0°. Turn the crankshaft pulley slightly in both directions and check that the gauge indication is stable.

8. Turn the crankshaft in the normal direction of rotation and record the reading of the dial indicator when the timing mark (15°) on the crankshaft pulley is in alignment with the TDC pointer. The dial indicator should read 0.020 in. (0.5mm).

9. If the reading of the dial indicator is not as described, hold the crankshaft in position (15°) before TDC and loosen two nuts on the injection pump flange. Move the injection pump to a point where the dial indicator gives reading of 0.020 in. (0.5mm), then tighten pump flange nuts.

10. Recheck the dial indicator reading and readjust the injection pump as necessary. Remove the dial indicator from the pump.

11. Install the distributor screw and washer into injection pump, then tighten.

12. Install the injection lines; DO NOT overtighten the connections.

13. To complete the installation, reverse the removal procedures. Adjust the idle speed and the fast idle speed as described in Chapter 2. Check for leaks in the fuel system and correct, if necessary.

FUEL TANK

REMOVAL AND INSTALLATION

1. Drain the tank.
2. Raise and support the truck on jackstands.
3. Disconnect the wiring and ground strap at the tank.
4. Disconnect the filler neck hose and vent hose from the tank.
5. Disconnect the fuel feed line and vapor line at the tank.
6. Place a floor jack under the tank to take up its weight.
7. Remove the fuel tank support bolts and lower the tank.
8. To install, reverse the removal procedures.

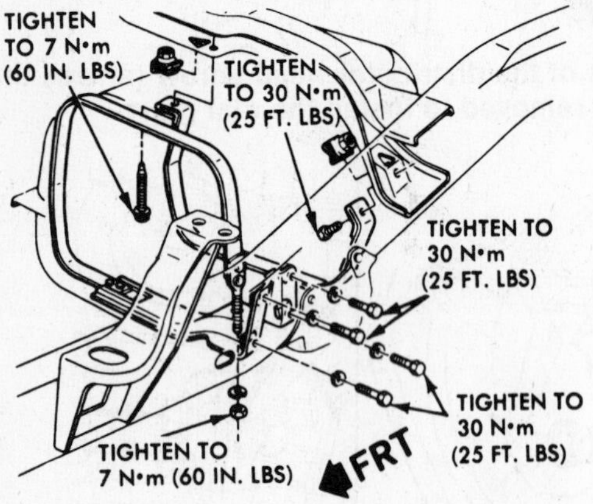
TIGHTEN TO 7 N•m (60 IN. LBS)
TIGHTEN TO 30 N•m (25 FT. LBS)
TIGHTEN TO 30 N•m (25 FT. LBS)
TIGHTEN TO 30 N•m (25 FT. LBS)
TIGHTEN TO 7 N•m (60 IN. LBS)
FRT

Fuel tank assembly

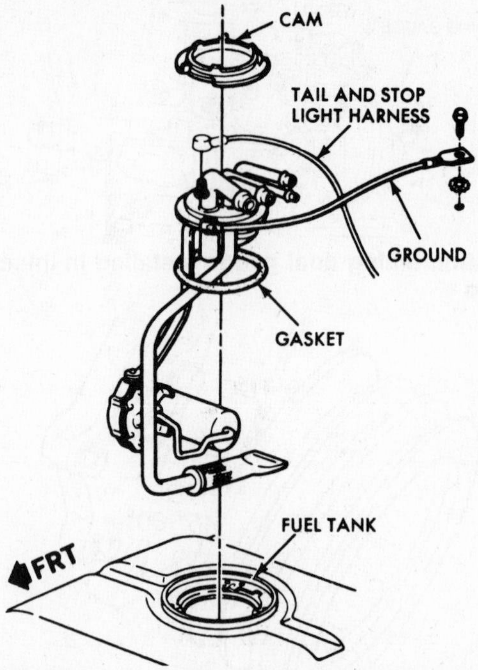
CAM
TAIL AND STOP LIGHT HARNESS
GROUND
GASKET
FUEL TANK
FRT

Fuel pump and fuel sender unit assembly

6 Chassis Electrical

QUICK REFERENCE INDEX

GENERAL INDEX

6 CHASSIS ELECTRICAL

UNDERSTANDING AND TROUBLESHOOTING ELECTRICAL SYSTEMS

At the rate which both import and domestic manufacturers are incorporating electronic control systems into their production lines, it won't be long before every new vehicle is equipped with one or more on-board computer, like the unit installed on your truck. These electronic components (with no moving parts) should theoretically last the life of the vehicle, provided nothing external happens to damage the circuits or memory chips.

While it is true that electronic components should never wear out, in the real world malfunctions do occur. It is also true that any computer-based system is extremely sensitive to electrical voltages and cannot tolerate careless or haphazard testing or service procedures. An inexperienced individual can literally do major damage looking for a minor problem by using the wrong kind of test equipment or connecting test leads or connectors with the ignition switch ON. When selecting test equipment, make sure the manufacturers instructions state that the tester is compatible with whatever type of electronic control system is being serviced. Read all instructions carefully and double check all test points before installing probes or making any test connections.

The following section outlines basic diagnosis techniques for dealing with computerized automotive control systems. Along with a general explanation of the various types of test equipment available to aid in servicing modern electronic automotive systems, basic repair techniques for wiring harnesses and connectors is given. Read the basic information before attempting any repairs or testing on any computerized system, to provide the background of information necessary to avoid the most common and obvious mistakes that can cost both time and money. Although the replacement and testing procedures are simple in themselves, the systems are not, and unless one has a thorough understanding of all components and their function within a particular computerized control system, the logical test sequence these systems demand cannot be followed. Minor malfunctions can make a big difference, so it is important to know how each component affects the operation of the overall electronic system to find the ultimate cause of a problem without replacing good components unnecessarily. It is not enough to use the correct test equipment; the test equipment must be used correctly.

Safety Precautions

CAUTION

Whenever working on or around any computer based microprocessor control system, always observe these general precautions to prevent the possibility of personal injury or damage to electronic components.

- Never install or remove battery cables with the key ON or the engine running. Jumper cables should be connected with the key OFF to avoid power surges that can damage electronic control units. Engines equipped with computer controlled systems should avoid both giving and getting jump starts due to the possibility of serious damage to components from arcing in the engine compartment when connections are made with the ignition ON.
- Always remove the battery cables before charging the battery. Never use a high output charger on an installed battery or attempt to use any type of "hot shot" (24 volt) starting aid.
- Exercise care when inserting test probes into connectors to insure good connections without damaging the connector or spreading the pins. Always probe connectors from the rear (wire) side, NOT the pin side, to avoid accidental shorting of terminals during test procedures.
- Never remove or attach wiring harness connectors with the ignition switch ON, especially to an electronic control unit.
- Do not drop any components during service procedures and never apply 12 volts directly to any component (like a solenoid or relay) unless instructed specifically to do so. Some component electrical windings are designed to safely handle only 4 or 5 volts and can be destroyed in seconds if 12 volts are applied directly to the connector.
- Remove the electronic control unit if the vehicle is to be placed in an environment where temperatures exceed approximately 176°F (80°C), such as a paint spray booth or when arc or gas welding near the control unit location in the car.

ORGANIZED TROUBLESHOOTING

When diagnosing a specific problem, organized troubleshooting is a must. The complexity of a modern automobile demands that you approach any problem in a logical, organized manner. There are certain troubleshooting techniques that are standard:

1. Establish when the problem occurs. Does the problem appear only under certain conditions? Were there any noises, odors, or other unusual symptoms?
2. Isolate the problem area. To do this, make some simple tests and observations; then eliminate the systems that are working properly. Check for obvious problems such as broken wires, dirty connections or split or disconnected vacuum hoses. Always check the obvious before assuming something complicated is the cause.
3. Test for problems systematically to determine the cause once the problem area is isolated. Are all the components functioning properly? Is there power going to electrical switches and motors? Is there vacuum at vacuum switches and/or actuators? Is there a mechanical problem such as bent linkage or loose mounting screws? Doing careful, systematic checks will often turn up most causes on the first inspection without wasting time checking components that have little or no relationship to the problem.
4. Test all repairs after the work is done to make sure that the problem is fixed. Some causes can be traced to more than one component, so a careful verification of repair work is important to pick up additional malfunctions that may cause a problem to reappear or a different problem to arise. A blown fuse, for example, is a simple problem that may require more than another fuse to repair. If you don't look for a problem that caused a fuse to blow, for example, a shorted wire may go undetected.

Experience has shown that most problems tend to be the result of a fairly simple and obvious cause, such as loose or corroded connectors or air leaks in the intake system; making careful inspection of components during testing essential to quick and accurate troubleshooting. Special, hand held computerized testers designed specifically for diagnosing the system are available from a variety of after market sources, as well as from the vehicle manufacturer, but care should be taken that any test equipment being used is designed to diagnose that particular computer controlled system accurately without damaging the control unit (ECU) or components being tested.

NOTE: Pinpointing the exact cause of trouble in an electrical system can sometimes only be accomplished by the use of special test equipment. The following describes commonly used test equipment and explains how to put it to best use in diagnosis. In addition to the information covered below, the manufacturer's instructions booklet provided with the tester should be read and clearly understood before attempting any test procedures.

TEST EQUIPMENT

Jumper Wires

Jumper wires are simple, yet extremely valuable, pieces of test equipment. Jumper wires are merely wires that are used to bypass sections of a circuit. The simplest type of jumper wire is merely a length of multistrand wire with an alligator clip at each end. Jumper wires are usually fabricated from lengths of standard automotive wire and whatever type of connector (alligator clip, spade connector or pin connector) that is required for the particular vehicle being tested. The well equipped tool box will have several different styles of jumper wires in several different lengths. Some jumper wires are made with three or more terminals coming from a common splice for special purpose testing. In cramped, hard-to-reach areas it is advisable to have insulated boots over the jumper wire terminals in order to prevent accidental grounding, sparks, and possible fire, especially when testing fuel system components.

Jumper wires are used primarily to locate open electrical circuits, on either the ground (−) side of the circuit or on the hot (+) side. If an electrical component fails to operate, connect the jumper wire between the component and a good ground. If the component operates only with the jumper installed, the ground circuit is open. If the ground circuit is good, but the component does not operate, the circuit between the power feed and component is open. You can sometimes connect the jumper wire directly from the battery to the hot terminal of the component, but first make sure the component uses 12 volts in operation. Some electrical components, such as fuel injectors, are designed to operate on about 4 volts and running 12 volts directly to the injector terminals can burn out the wiring. By inserting an inline fuse holder between a set of test leads, a fused jumper wire can be used for bypassing open circuits. Use a 5 amp fuse to provide protection against voltage spikes. When in doubt, use a voltmeter to check the voltage input to the component and measure how much voltage is being applied normally. By moving the jumper wire successively back from the lamp toward the power source, you can isolate the area of the circuit where the open is located. When the component stops functioning, or the power is cut off, the open is in the segment of wire between the jumper and the point previously tested.

CAUTION

Never use jumpers made from wire that is of lighter gauge than used in the circuit under test. If the jumper wire is of too small gauge, it may overheat and possibly melt. Never use jumpers to bypass high resistance loads (such as motors) in a circuit. Bypassing resistances, in effect, creates a short circuit which may, in turn, cause damage and fire. Never use a jumper for anything other than temporary bypassing of components in a circuit.

12 Volt Test Light

The 12 volt test light is used to check circuits and components while electrical current is flowing through them. It is used for voltage and ground tests. Twelve volt test lights come in different styles but all have three main parts; a ground clip, a probe, and a light. The most commonly used 12 volt test lights have pick-type probes. To use a 12 volt test light, connect the ground clip to a good ground and probe wherever necessary with the pick. The pick should be sharp so that it can penetrate wire insulation to make contact with the wire, without making a large hole in the insulation. The wrap-around light is handy in hard to reach areas or where it is difficult to support a wire to push a probe pick into it. To use the wrap around light, hook the wire to probed with the hook and pull the trigger. A small pick will be forced through the wire insulation into the wire core.

CAUTION

Do not use a test light to probe electronic ignition spark plug or coil wires. Never use a pick-type test light to probe wiring on computer controlled systems unless specifically instructed to do so. Any wire insulation that is pierced by the test light probe should be taped and sealed with silicone after testing.

Like the jumper wire, the 12 volt test light is used to isolate opens in circuits. But, whereas the jumper wire is used to bypass the open to operate the load, the 12 volt test light is used to locate the presence of voltage in a circuit. If the test light glows, you know that there is power up to that point; if the 12 volt test light does not glow when its probe is inserted into the wire or connector, you know that there is an open circuit (no power). Move the test light in successive steps back toward the power source until the light in the handle does glow. When it does glow, the open is between the probe and point previously probed.

NOTE: The test light does not detect that 12 volts (or any particular amount of voltage) is present; it only detects that some voltage is present. It is advisable before using the test light to touch its terminals across the battery posts to make sure the light is operating properly.

Self-Powered Test Light

The self-powered test light usually contains a 1.5 volt penlight battery. One type of self-powered test light is similar in design to the 12 volt test light. This type has both the battery and the light in the handle and pick-type probe tip. The second type has the light toward the open tip, so that the light illuminates the contact point. The self-powered test light is dual purpose piece of test equipment. It can be used to test for either open or short circuits when power is isolated from the circuit (continuity test). A powered test light should not be used on any computer controlled system or component unless specifically instructed to do so. Many engine sensors can be destroyed by even this small amount of voltage applied directly to the terminals.

Open Circuit Testing

To use the self-powered test light to check for open circuits, first isolate the circuit from the vehicle's 12 volt power source by disconnecting the battery or wiring harness connector. Connect the test light ground clip to a good ground and probe sections of the circuit sequentially with the test light. (start from either end of the circuit). If the light is out, the open is between the probe and the circuit ground. If the light is on, the open is between the probe and end of the circuit toward the power source.

Short Circuit Testing

By isolating the circuit both from power and from ground, and using a self-powered test light, you can check for shorts to ground in the circuit. Isolate the circuit from power and ground. Connect the test light ground clip to a good ground and probe any easy-to-reach test point in the circuit. If the light comes on, there is a short somewhere in the circuit. To isolate the short, probe a test point at either end of the isolated circuit (the light should be on). Leave the test light probe connected and open connectors, switches, remove parts, etc., sequentially, until the light goes out. When the light goes out, the short is between the last circuit component opened and the previous circuit opened.

NOTE: The 1.5 volt battery in the test light does not provide much current. A weak battery may not provide enough power to illuminate the test light even when a complete circuit is made (especially if there are high re-

sistances in the circuit). Always make sure that the test battery is strong. To check the battery, briefly touch the ground clip to the probe; if the light glows brightly the battery is strong enough for testing. Never use a self-powered test light to perform checks for opens or shorts when power is applied to the electrical system under test. The 12 volt vehicle power will quickly burn out the 1.5 volt light bulb in the test light.

Voltmeter

A voltmeter is used to measure voltage at any point in a circuit, or to measure the voltage drop across any part of a circuit. It can also be used to check continuity in a wire or circuit by indicating current flow from one end to the other. Voltmeters usually have various scales on the meter dial and a selector switch to allow the selection of different voltages. The voltmeter has a positive and a negative lead. To avoid damage to the meter, always connect the negative lead to the negative (–) side of circuit (to ground or nearest the ground side of the circuit) and connect the positive lead to the positive (+) side of the circuit (to the power source or the nearest power source). Note that the negative voltmeter lead will always be black and that the positive voltmeter will always be some color other than black (usually red). Depending on how the voltmeter is connected into the circuit, it has several uses.

A voltmeter can be connected either in parallel or in series with a circuit and it has a very high resistance to current flow. When connected in parallel, only a small amount of current will flow through the voltmeter current path; the rest will flow through the normal circuit current path and the circuit will work normally. When the voltmeter is connected in series with a circuit, only a small amount of current can flow through the circuit. The circuit will not work properly, but the voltmeter reading will show if the circuit is complete or not.

Available Voltage Measurement

Set the voltmeter selector switch to the 20V position and connect the meter negative lead to the negative post of the battery. Connect the positive meter lead to the positive post of the battery and turn the ignition switch ON to provide a load. Read the voltage on the meter or digital display. A well charged battery should register over 12 volts. If the meter reads below 11.5 volts, the battery power may be insufficient to operate the electrical system properly. This test determines voltage available from the battery and should be the first step in any electrical trouble diagnosis procedure. Many electrical problems, especially on computer controlled systems, can be caused by a low state of charge in the battery. Excessive corrosion at the battery cable terminals can cause a poor contact that will prevent proper charging and full battery current flow.

Normal battery voltage is 12 volts when fully charged. When the battery is supplying current to one or more circuits it is said to be "under load". When everything is off the electrical system is under a "no-load" condition. A fully charged battery may show about 12.5 volts at no load; will drop to 12 volts under medium load; and will drop even lower under heavy load. If the battery is partially discharged the voltage decrease under heavy load may be excessive, even though the battery shows 12 volts or more at no load. When allowed to discharge further, the battery's available voltage under load will decrease more severely. For this reason, it is important that the battery be fully charged during all testing procedures to avoid errors in diagnosis and incorrect test results.

Voltage Drop

When current flows through a resistance, the voltage beyond the resistance is reduced (the larger the current, the greater the reduction in voltage). When no current is flowing, there is no voltage drop because there is no current flow. All points in the circuit which are connected to the power source are at the same voltage as the power source. The total voltage drop always equals the total source voltage. In a long circuit with many connectors, a series of small, unwanted voltage drops due to corrosion at the connectors can add up to a total loss of voltage which impairs the operation of the normal loads in the circuit.

INDIRECT COMPUTATION OF VOLTAGE DROPS

1. Set the voltmeter selector switch to the 20 volt position.
2. Connect the meter negative lead to a good ground.
3. Probe all resistances in the circuit with the positive meter lead.
4. Operate the circuit in all modes and observe the voltage readings.

DIRECT MEASUREMENT OF VOLTAGE DROPS

1. Set the voltmeter switch to the 20 volt position.
2. Connect the voltmeter negative lead to the ground side of the resistance load to be measured.
3. Connect the positive lead to the positive side of the resistance or load to be measured.
4. Read the voltage drop directly on the 20 volt scale.

Too high a voltage indicates too high a resistance. If, for example, a blower motor runs too slowly, you can determine if there is too high a resistance in the resistor pack. By taking voltage drop readings in all parts of the circuit, you can isolate the problem. Too low a voltage drop indicates too low a resistance. If, for example, a blower motor runs too fast in the MED and/or LOW position, the problem can be isolated in the resistor pack by taking voltage drop readings in all parts of the circuit to locate a possibly shorted resistor. The maximum allowable voltage drop under load is critical, especially if there is more than one high resistance problem in a circuit because all voltage drops are cumulative. A small drop is normal due to the resistance of the conductors.

HIGH RESISTANCE TESTING

1. Set the voltmeter selector switch to the 4 volt position.
2. Connect the voltmeter positive lead to the positive post of the battery.
3. Turn on the headlights and heater blower to provide a load.
4. Probe various points in the circuit with the negative voltmeter lead.
5. Read the voltage drop on the 4 volt scale. Some average maximum allowable voltage drops are:

FUSE PANEL–7 volts
IGNITION SWITCH–5 volts
HEADLIGHT SWITCH–7 volts
IGNITION COIL (+)–5 volts
ANY OTHER LOAD–1.3 volts

NOTE: Voltage drops are all measured while a load is operating; without current flow, there will be no voltage drop.

Ohmmeter

The ohmmeter is designed to read resistance (ohms) in a circuit or component. Although there are several different styles of ohmmeters, all will usually have a selector switch which permits the measurement of different ranges of resistance (usually the selector switch allows the multiplication of the meter reading by 10, 100, 1000, and 10,000). A calibration knob allows the meter to be set at zero for accurate measurement. Since all ohmmeters are powered by an internal battery (usually 9 volts), the ohmmeter can be used as a self-powered test light. When the ohmmeter is connected, current from the ohmmeter flows through the circuit or component being tested. Since the ohmmeter's internal resistance and voltage are known values, the amount of current flow through the meter depends on the resistance of the circuit or component being tested.

The ohmmeter can be used to perform continuity test for opens or shorts (either by observation of the meter needle or as a self-powered test light), and to read actual resistance in a circuit. It should be noted that the ohmmeter is used to check the resistance of a component or wire while there is no voltage applied to the circuit. Current flow from an outside voltage source (such as the vehicle battery) can damage the ohmmeter, so the circuit or component should be isolated from the vehicle electrical system before any testing is done. Since the ohmmeter uses its own voltage source, either lead can be connected to any test point.

NOTE: When checking diodes or other solid state components, the ohmmeter leads can only be connected one way in order to measure current flow in a single direction. Make sure the positive (+) and negative (–) terminal connections are as described in the test procedures to verify the one-way diode operation.

In using the meter for making continuity checks, do not be concerned with the actual resistance readings. Zero resistance, or any resistance readings, indicate continuity in the circuit. Infinite resistance indicates an open in the circuit. A high resistance reading where there should be none indicates a problem in the circuit. Checks for short circuits are made in the same manner as checks for open circuits except that the circuit must be isolated from both power and normal ground. Infinite resistance indicates no continuity to ground, while zero resistance indicates a dead short to ground.

RESISTANCE MEASUREMENT

The batteries in an ohmmeter will weaken with age and temperature, so the ohmmeter must be calibrated or "zeroed" before taking measurements. To zero the meter, place the selector switch in its lowest range and touch the two ohmmeter leads together. Turn the calibration knob until the meter needle is exactly on zero.

NOTE: All analog (needle) type ohmmeters must be zeroed before use, but some digital ohmmeter models are automatically calibrated when the switch is turned on. Self-calibrating digital ohmmeters do not have an adjusting knob, but its a good idea to check for a zero readout before use by touching the leads together. All computer controlled systems require the use of a digital ohmmeter with at least 10 megohms impedance for testing. Before any test procedures are attempted, make sure the ohmmeter used is compatible with the electrical system or damage to the on-board computer could result.

To measure resistance, first isolate the circuit from the vehicle power source by disconnecting the battery cables or the harness connector. Make sure the key is OFF when disconnecting any components or the battery. Where necessary, also isolate at least one side of the circuit to be checked to avoid reading parallel resistances. Parallel circuit resistances will always give a lower reading than the actual resistance of either of the branches. When measuring the resistance of parallel circuits, the total resistance will always be lower than the smallest resistance in the circuit. Connect the meter leads to both sides of the circuit (wire or component) and read the actual measured ohms on the meter scale. Make sure the selector switch is set to the proper ohm scale for the circuit being tested to avoid misreading the ohmmeter test value.

CAUTION

Never use an ohmmeter with power applied to the circuit. Like the self-powered test light, the ohmmeter is designed to operate on its own power supply. The normal 12 volt automotive electrical system current could damage the meter.

Ammeters

An ammeter measures the amount of current flowing through a circuit in units called amperes or amps. Amperes are units of electron flow which indicate how fast the electrons are flowing through the circuit. Since Ohms Law dictates that current flow in a circuit is equal to the circuit voltage divided by the total circuit resistance, increasing voltage also increases the current level (amps). Likewise, any decrease in resistance will increase the amount of amps in a circuit. At normal operating voltage, most circuits have a characteristic amount of amperes, called "current draw" which can be measured using an ammeter. By referring to a specified current draw rating, measuring the amperes, and comparing the two values, one can determine what is happening within the circuit to aid in diagnosis. An open circuit, for example, will not allow any current to flow so the ammeter reading will be zero. More current flows through a heavily loaded circuit or when the charging system is operating.

An ammeter is always connected in series with the circuit being tested. All of the current that normally flows through the circuit must also flow through the ammeter; if there is any other path for the current to follow, the ammeter reading will not be accurate. The ammeter itself has very little resistance to current flow and therefore will not affect the circuit, but it will measure current draw only when the circuit is closed and electricity is flowing. Excessive current draw can blow fuses and drain the battery, while a reduced current draw can cause motors to run slowly, lights to dim and other components to not operate properly. The ammeter can help diagnose these conditions by locating the cause of the high or low reading.

Multimeters

Different combinations of test meters can be built into a single unit designed for specific tests. Some of the more common combination test devices are known as Volt/Amp testers, Tach/Dwell meters, or Digital Multimeters. The Volt/Amp tester is used for charging system, starting system or battery tests and consists of a voltmeter, an ammeter and a variable resistance carbon pile. The voltmeter will usually have at least two ranges for use with 6, 12 and 24 volt systems. The ammeter also has more than one range for testing various levels of battery loads and starter current draw and the carbon pile can be adjusted to offer different amounts of resistance. The Volt/Amp tester has heavy leads to carry large amounts of current and many later models have an inductive ammeter pickup that clamps around the wire to simplify test connections. On some models, the ammeter also has a zero-center scale to allow testing of charging and starting systems without switching leads or polarity. A digital multimeter is a voltmeter, ammeter and ohmmeter combined in an instrument which gives a digital readout. These are often used when testing solid state circuits because of their high input impedance (usually 10 megohms or more).

The tach/dwell meter combines a tachometer and a dwell (cam angle) meter and is a specialized kind of voltmeter. The tachometer scale is marked to show engine speed in rpm and the dwell scale is marked to show degrees of distributor shaft rotation. In most electronic ignition systems, dwell is determined by the control unit, but the dwell meter can also be used to check the duty cycle (operation) of some electronic engine control systems. Some tach/dwell meters are powered by an internal battery, while others take their power from the car battery in use. The battery powered testers usually require calibration much like an ohmmeter before testing.

Special Test Equipment

A variety of diagnostic tools are available to help troubleshoot and repair computerized engine control systems. The most sophisticated of these devices are the console type engine analyzers that usually occupy a garage service bay, but there are several types of aftermarket electronic testers available that will allow quick circuit tests of the engine control system by plugging directly into a special connector located in the engine compartment or under the dashboard. Several tool and equipment manufacturers offer simple, hand held testers that measure various circuit voltage levels on command to check all system components for proper operation. Although these testers usually cost about $300–500, consider that the average computer control unit (or ECM) can cost just as much and the money saved by not replacing perfectly good sensors or components in an attempt to correct a problem could justify the purchase price of a special diagnostic tester the first time it's used.

These computerized testers can allow quick and easy test measurements while the engine is operating or while the car is being driven. In addition, the on-board computer memory can be read to access any stored trouble codes; in effect allowing the computer to tell you where it hurts and aid trouble diagnosis by pinpointing exactly which circuit or component is malfunctioning. In the same manner, repairs can be tested to make sure the problem has been corrected. The biggest advantage these special testers have is their relatively easy hookups that minimize or eliminate the chances of making the wrong connections and getting false voltage readings or damaging the computer accidentally.

NOTE: It should be remembered that these testers check voltage levels in circuits; they don't detect mechanical problems or failed components if the circuit voltage falls within the preprogrammed limits stored in the tester PROM unit. Also, most of the hand held testers are designed to work only on one or two systems made by a specific manufacturer.

A variety of after market testers are available to help diagnose different computerized control systems. Owatonna Tool Company (OTC), for example, markets a device called the OTC Monitor which plugs directly into the assembly line diagnostic link (ALDL). The OTC tester makes diagnosis a simple matter of pressing the correct buttons and, by changing the internal PROM or inserting a different diagnosis cartridge, it will work on any model from full size to subcompact, over a wide range of years. An adapter is supplied with the tester to allow connection to all types of ALDL links, regardless of the number of pin terminals used. By inserting an updated PROM into the OTC tester, it can be easily updated to diagnose any new modifications of computerized control systems.

Wiring Harnesses

The average automobile contains about ½ mile of wiring, with hundreds of individual connections. To protect the many wires from damage and to keep them from becoming a confusing tangle, they are organized into bundles, enclosed in plastic or taped together and called wire harnesses. Different wiring harnesses serve different parts of the vehicle. Individual wires are color coded to help trace them through a harness where sections are hidden from view.

A loose or corroded connection or a replacement wire that is too small for the circuit will add extra resistance and an additional voltage drop to the circuit. A ten percent voltage drop can result in slow or erratic motor operation, for example, even though the circuit is complete. Automotive wiring or circuit conductors can be in any one of three forms:

1. Single strand wire
2. Multistrand wire
3. Printed circuitry

Single strand wire has a solid metal core and is usually used inside such components as alternators, motors, relays and other devices. Multistrand wire has a core made of many small strands of wire twisted together into a single conductor. Most of the wiring in an automotive electrical system is made up of multistrand wire, either as a single conductor or grouped together in a harness. All wiring is color coded on the insulator, either as a solid color or as a colored wire with an identification stripe. A printed circuit is a thin film of copper or other conductor that is printed on an insulator backing. Occasionally, a printed circuit is sandwiched between two sheets of plastic for more protection and flexibility. A complete printed circuit, consisting of conductors, insulating material and connectors for lamps or other components is called a printed circuit board. Printed circuitry is used in place of individual wires or harnesses in places where space is limited, such as behind instrument panels.

Wire Gauge

Since computer controlled automotive electrical systems are very sensitive to changes in resistance, the selection of properly sized wires is critical when systems are repaired. The wire gauge number is an expression of the cross section area of the conductor. The most common system for expressing wire size is the American Wire Gauge (AWG) system.

Wire cross section area is measured in circular mils. A mil is 1/000″ (0.001″); a circular mil is the area of a circle one mil in diameter. For example, a conductor ¼″ in diameter is 0.250 in. or 250 mils. The circular mil cross section area of the wire is 250 squared (250″) or 62,500 circular mils. Imported car models usually use metric wire gauge designations, which is simply the cross section area of the conductor in square millimeters (mm).

Gauge numbers are assigned to conductors of various cross section areas. As gauge number increases, area decreases and the conductor becomes smaller. A 5 gauge conductor is smaller than a 1 gauge conductor and a 10 gauge is smaller than a 5 gauge. As the cross section area of a conductor decreases, resistance increases and so does the gauge number. A conductor with a higher gauge number will carry less current than a conductor with a lower gauge number.

NOTE: Gauge wire size refers to the size of the conductor, not the size of the complete wire. It is possible to have two wires of the same gauge with different diameters because one may have thicker insulation than the other.

12 volt automotive electrical systems generally use 10, 12, 14, 16 and 18 gauge wire. Main power distribution circuits and larger accessories usually use 10 and 12 gauge wire. Battery cables are usually 4 or 6 gauge, although 1 and 2 gauge wires are occasionally used. Wire length must also be considered when making repairs to a circuit. As conductor length increases, so does resistance. An 18 gauge wire, for example, can carry a 10 amp load for 10 feet without excessive voltage drop; however if a 15 foot wire is required for the same 10 amp load, it must be a 16 gauge wire.

An electrical schematic shows the electrical current paths when a circuit is operating properly. It is essential to understand how a circuit works before trying to figure out why it doesn't. Schematics break the entire electrical system down into individual circuits and show only one particular circuit. In a schematic, no attempt is made to represent wiring and components as they physically appear on the vehicle; switches and other components are shown as simply as possible. Face views of harness connectors show the cavity or terminal locations in all multi-pin connectors to help locate test points.

If you need to backprobe a connector while it is on the component, the order of the terminals must be mentally reversed. The wire color code can help in this situation, as well as a keyway, lock tab or other reference mark.

NOTE: Wiring diagrams are not included in this book. As trucks have become more complex and available with longer option lists, wiring diagrams have grown in size and complexity. It has become almost impossible to provide a readable reproduction of a wiring diagram in a

book this size. Information on ordering wiring diagrams from the vehicle manufacturer can be found in the owner's manual.

WIRING REPAIR

Soldering is a quick, efficient method of joining metals permanently. Everyone who has the occasion to make wiring repairs should know how to solder. Electrical connections that are soldered are far less likely to come apart and will conduct electricity much better than connections that are only "pig-tailed" together. The most popular (and preferred) method of soldering is with an electrical soldering gun. Soldering irons are available in many sizes and wattage ratings. Irons with higher wattage ratings deliver higher temperatures and recover lost heat faster. A small soldering iron rated for no more than 50 watts is recommended, especially on electrical systems where excess heat can damage the components being soldered.

There are three ingredients necessary for successful soldering; proper flux, good solder and sufficient heat. A soldering flux is necessary to clean the metal of tarnish, prepare it for soldering and to enable the solder to spread into tiny crevices. When soldering, always use a resin flux or resin core solder which is non-corrosive and will not attract moisture once the job is finished. Other types of flux (acid core) will leave a residue that will attract moisture and cause the wires to corrode. Tin is a unique metal with a low melting point. In a molten state, it dissolves and alloys easily with many metals. Solder is made by mixing tin with lead. The most common proportions are 40/60, 50/50 and 60/40, with the percentage of tin listed first. Low priced solders usually contain less tin, making them very difficult for a beginner to use because more heat is required to melt the solder. A common solder is 40/60 which is well suited for all-around general use, but 60/40 melts easier, has more tin for a better joint and is preferred for electrical work.

Soldering Techniques

Successful soldering requires that the metals to be joined be heated to a temperature that will melt the solder—usually 360–460°F (182–238°C). Contrary to popular belief, the purpose of the soldering iron is not to melt the solder itself, but to heat the parts being soldered to a temperature high enough to melt the solder when it is touched to the work. Melting flux-cored solder on the soldering iron will usually destroy the effectiveness of the flux.

NOTE: Soldering tips are made of copper for good heat conductivity, but must be "tinned" regularly for quick transference of heat to the project and to prevent the solder from sticking to the iron. To "tin" the iron, simply heat it and touch the flux-cored solder to the tip; the solder will flow over the hot tip. Wipe the excess off with a clean rag, but be careful as the iron will be hot.

After some use, the tip may become pitted. If so, simply dress the tip smooth with a smooth file and "tin" the tip again. An old saying holds that "metals well cleaned are half soldered." Flux-cored solder will remove oxides but rust, bits of insulation and oil or grease must be removed with a wire brush or emery cloth. For maximum strength in soldered parts, the joint must start off clean and tight. Weak joints will result in gaps too wide for the solder to bridge.

If a separate soldering flux is used, it should be brushed or swabbed on only those areas that are to be soldered. Most solders contain a core of flux and separate fluxing is unnecessary. Hold the work to be soldered firmly. It is best to solder on a wooden board, because a metal vise will only rob the piece to be soldered of heat and make it difficult to melt the solder. Hold the soldering tip with the broadest face against the work to be soldered. Apply solder under the tip close to the work, using enough solder to give a heavy film between the iron and the piece being soldered, while moving slowly and making sure the solder melts properly. Keep the work level or the solder will run to the lowest part and favor the thicker parts, because these require more heat to melt the solder. If the soldering tip overheats (the solder coating on the face of the tip burns up), it should be retinned. Once the soldering is completed, let the soldered joint stand until cool. Tape and seal all soldered wire splices after the repair has cooled.

Wire Harness and Connectors

The on-board computer (ECM) wire harness electrically connects the control unit to the various solenoids, switches and sensors used by the control system. Most connectors in the engine compartment or otherwise exposed to the elements are protected against moisture and dirt which could create oxidation and deposits on the terminals. This protection is important because of the very low voltage and current levels used by the computer and sensors. All connectors have a lock which secures the male and female terminals together, with a secondary lock holding the seal and terminal into the connector. Both terminal locks must be released when disconnecting ECM connectors.

These special connectors are weather-proof and all repairs require the use of a special terminal and the tool required to service it. This tool is used to remove the pin and sleeve terminals. If removal is attempted with an ordinary pick, there is a good chance that the terminal will be bent or deformed. Unlike standard blade type terminals, these terminals cannot be straightened once they are bent. Make certain that the connectors are properly seated and all of the sealing rings in place when connecting leads. On some models, a hinge-type flap provides a backup or secondary locking feature for the terminals. Most secondary locks are used to improve the connector reliability by retaining the terminals if the small terminal lock tangs are not positioned properly.

Molded-on connectors require complete replacement of the connection. This means splicing a new connector assembly into the harness. All splices in on-board computer systems should be soldered to insure proper contact. Use care when probing the connections or replacing terminals in them as it is possible to short between opposite terminals. If this happens to the wrong terminal pair, it is possible to damage certain components. Always use jumper wires between connectors for circuit checking and never probe through weatherproof seals.

Open circuits are often difficult to locate by sight because corrosion or terminal misalignment are hidden by the connectors. Merely wiggling a connector on a sensor or in the wiring harness may correct the open circuit condition. This should always be considered when an open circuit or a failed sensor is indicated. Intermittent problems may also be caused by oxidized or loose connections. When using a circuit tester for diagnosis, always probe connections from the wire side. Be careful not to damage sealed connectors with test probes.

All wiring harnesses should be replaced with identical parts, using the same gauge wire and connectors. When signal wires are spliced into a harness, use wire with high temperature insulation only. With the low voltage and current levels found in the system, it is important that the best possible connection at all wire splices be made by soldering the splices together. It is seldom necessary to replace a complete harness. If replacement is necessary, pay close attention to insure proper harness routing. Secure the harness with suitable plastic wire clamps to prevent vibrations from causing the harness to wear in spots or contact any hot components.

NOTE: Weatherproof connectors cannot be replaced with standard connectors. Instructions are provided with replacement connector and terminal packages. Some wire harnesses have mounting indicators (usually pieces of colored tape) to mark where the harness is to be secured.

In making wiring repairs, it's important that you always replace damaged wires with wires that are the same gauge as the wire being replaced. The heavier the wire, the smaller the gauge number. Wires are color-coded to aid in identification and whenever possible the same color coded wire should be used for replacement. A wire stripping and crimping tool is necessary to install solderless terminal connectors. Test all crimps by pulling on the wires; it should not be possible to pull the wires out of a good crimp.

Wires which are open, exposed or otherwise damaged are repaired by simple splicing. Where possible, if the wiring harness is accessible and the damaged place in the wire can be located, it is best to open the harness and check for all possible damage. In an inaccessible harness, the wire must be bypassed with a new insert, usually taped to the outside of the old harness.

When replacing fusible links, be sure to use fusible link wire, NOT ordinary automotive wire. Make sure the fusible segment is of the same gauge and construction as the one being replaced and double the stripped end when crimping the terminal connector for a good contact. The melted (open) fusible link segment of the wiring harness should be cut off as close to the harness as possible, then a new segment spliced in as described. In the case of a damaged fusible link that feeds two harness wires, the harness connections should be replaced with two fusible link wires so that each circuit will have its own separate protection.

NOTE: Most of the problems caused in the wiring harness are due to bad ground connections. Always check all vehicle ground connections for corrosion or looseness before performing any power feed checks to eliminate the chance of a bad ground affecting the circuit.

Repairing Hard Shell Connectors

Unlike molded connectors, the terminal contacts in hard shell connectors can be replaced. Weatherproof hard-shell connectors with the leads molded into the shell have non-replaceable terminal ends. Replacement usually involves the use of a special terminal removal tool that depress the locking tangs (barbs) on the connector terminal and allow the connector to be removed from the rear of the shell. The connector shell should be replaced if it shows any evidence of burning, melting, cracks, or breaks. Replace individual terminals that are burnt, corroded, distorted or loose.

NOTE: The insulation crimp must be tight to prevent the insulation from sliding back on the wire when the wire is pulled. The insulation must be visibly compressed under the crimp tabs, and the ends of the crimp should be turned in for a firm grip on the insulation.

The wire crimp must be made with all wire strands inside the crimp. The terminal must be fully compressed on the wire strands with the ends of the crimp tabs turned in to make a firm grip on the wire. Check all connections with an ohmmeter to insure a good contact. There should be no measurable resistance between the wire and the terminal when connected.

Mechanical Test Equipment

Vacuum Gauge

Most gauges are graduated in inches of mercury (in.Hg), although a device called a manometer reads vacuum in inches of water (in. H_2O). The normal vacuum reading usually varies between 18 and 22 in.Hg at sea level. To test engine vacuum, the vacuum gauge must be connected to a source of manifold vacuum. Many engines have a plug in the intake manifold which can be removed and replaced with an adapter fitting. Connect the vacuum gauge to the fitting with a suitable rubber hose or, if no manifold plug is available, connect the vacuum gauge to any device using manifold vacuum, such as EGR valves, etc. The vacuum gauge can be used to determine if enough vacuum is reaching a component to allow its actuation.

Hand Vacuum Pump

Small, hand-held vacuum pumps come in a variety of designs. Most have a built-in vacuum gauge and allow the component to be tested without removing it from the vehicle. Operate the pump lever or plunger to apply the correct amount of vacuum required for the test specified in the diagnosis routines. The level of vacuum in inches of Mercury (in.Hg) is indicated on the pump gauge. For some testing, an additional vacuum gauge may be necessary.

Intake manifold vacuum is used to operate various systems and devices on late model vehicles. To correctly diagnose and solve problems in vacuum control systems, a vacuum source is necessary for testing. In some cases, vacuum can be taken from the intake manifold when the engine is running, but vacuum is normally provided by a hand vacuum pump. These hand vacuum pumps have a built-in vacuum gauge that allow testing while the device is still attached to the component. For some tests, an additional vacuum gauge may be necessary.

HEATING AND AIR CONDITIONING

Blower Motor

REMOVAL AND INSTALLATION

1. Disconnect the negative battery terminal from the battery.
2. Disconnect the electrical connectors from the blower motor.

NOTE: On some earlier models equipped with A/C, it may be necessary to remove the A/C vacuum tank and move it aside.

3. Remove the blower motor-to-case screws, then lift the blower motor from the case.
4. To install, reverse the removal procedures. Torque the blower motor-to-case screws to 18 ft. lbs.

Heater Core

The heater core is removable from under the right side of the instrument panel.

REMOVAL AND INSTALLATION

1. Disconnect the negative battery terminal from the battery.
2. Position a drain pan under the radiator, open the drain cock and drain the cooling system to a level below the heater core.

CAUTION

When draining the coolant, keep in mind that cats and dogs are attracted by the ethylene glycol antifreeze, and are quite likely to drink any that is left in an uncovered container or in puddles on the ground. This will

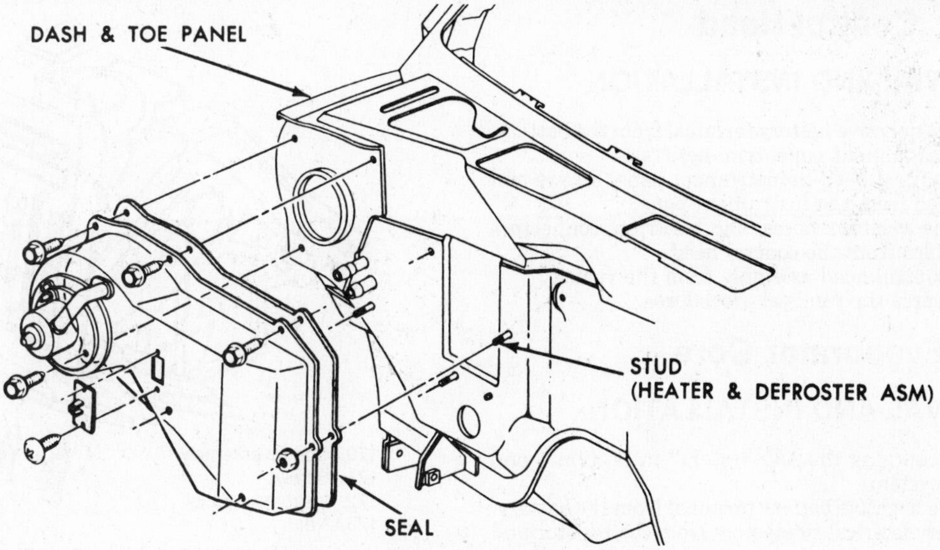
DASH & TOE PANEL
STUD
(HEATER & DEFROSTER ASM)
SEAL

Heater case and blower motor

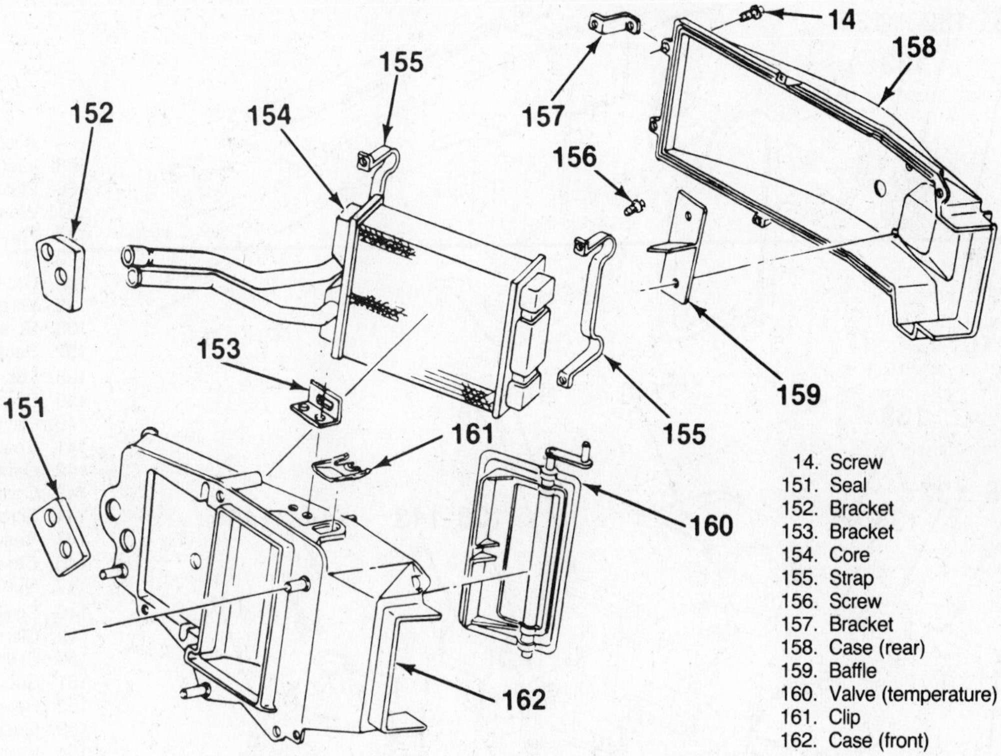
14
158
155
152
154
157
156
153
151
161
155
159
160
162
14. Screw
151. Seal
152. Bracket
153. Bracket
154. Core
155. Strap
156. Screw
157. Bracket
158. Case (rear)
159. Baffle
160. Valve (temperature)
161. Clip
162. Case (front)

Exploded view of the heater core assembly

prove fatal in sufficient quantity. Always drain the coolant into a sealable container. Coolant should be reused unless it is contaminated or several years old.

3. Disconnect the heater-to-engine coolant hoses from the core tubes on the fire wall, in the engine compartment.

NOTE: Plug the heater core tubes to avoid spilling coolant in the passenger compartment during removal.

4. Remove the heater core cover-to-cowl screws and the cover from the vehicle.
5. Remove the brackets from each end of the heater core.
6. Lift out the heater core.
7. To install, reverse the removal procedures. Torque the rear cover-to-case screws to 27 inch lbs. Refill the cooling system, the start the engine, allow the engine to reach normal operating temperatures, then check for leaks.

Control Head

REMOVAL AND INSTALLATION

1. Disconnect the negative battery terminal from the battery.
2. Remove the instrument panel trim bezel(s).
3. Remove the control head-to-instrument panel screws and pull the control head from the instrument panel.
4. Disconnect the vacuum hoses, the electrical connectors and the control cables from the control head.
5. Remove the control head assembly from the vehicle.
6. To install, reverse the removal procedures.

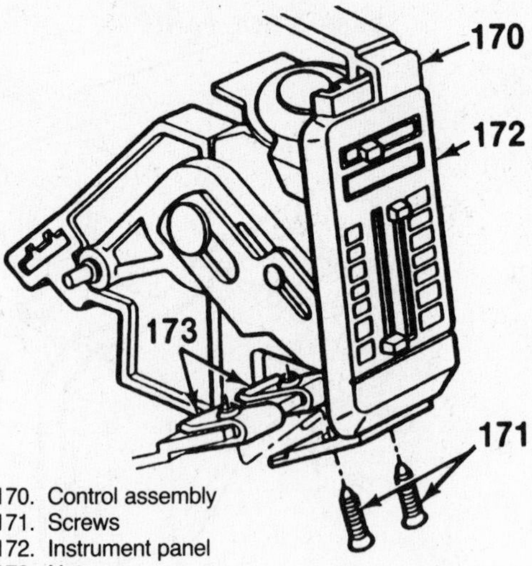
170
172
173
171

170. Control assembly
171. Screws
172. Instrument panel
173. Nuts

Heater and A/C control head

Evaporator Core

REMOVAL AND INSTALLATION

1. Refer to "Discharging the A/C System" in Section 1 and discharge the A/C system.
2. Disconnect the negative battery terminal from the battery.
3. Disconnect the electrical connectors from the resistor and the blower motor.

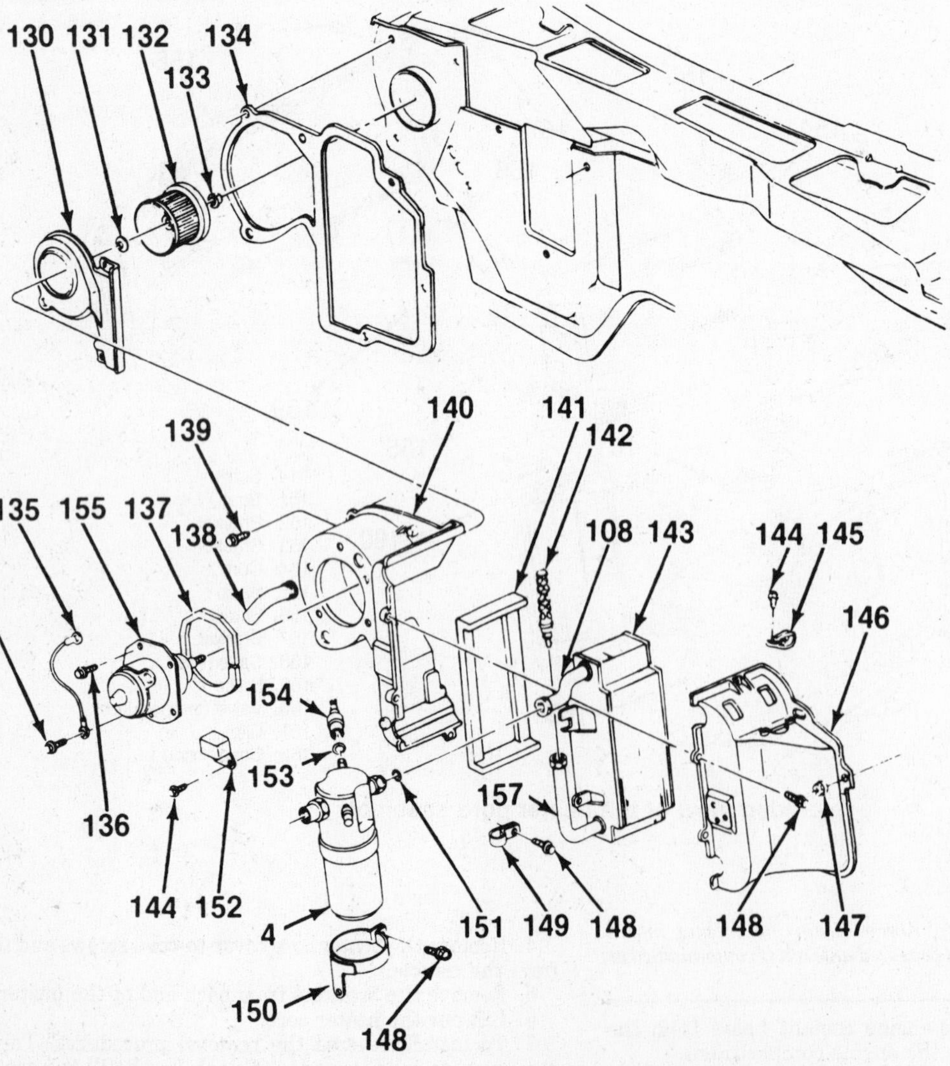
130 131 132 134
133
139
140
141
142
135 155 137
156
138
108 143
144 145
146
154
153
157
136
144 152
4
151 149 148
148 147
150
148

4. Accumulator
108. Inlet line (accumulator)
130. Plate
131. Washer
132. Fan
133. Nut
134. Gasket
135. Wire
136. Screw
137. Seal
138. Tube
139. Screw
140. Case
141. Seal
142. Orifice
143. Core
144. Screw
145. Resistor
146. Case
147. Nut
148. Screw
149. Clamp
150. Clamp
151. Seal
152. Relay
153. Gasket
154. Switch
155. Motor
156. Screw
157. Inlet (evaporator)

Exploded view of the A/C evaporator

4. Remove the inlet line from the A/C evaporator.
5. Remove the blower motor-to-case nuts/screws and the blower motor assembly from the vehicle.
6. Remove the accumulator inlet line from the evaporator and the accumulator.
7. Remove the blower motor case-to-evaporator case screws and separate the cases, then remove the evaporator core.
8. To install, reverse the removal procedures. Recharge the A/C system.

Expansion Tube

REMOVAL AND INSTALLATION

NOTE: An orifice tube removal and installation tool (J–26549–D) is required to perform this procedure.

1. Refer to Section 1 and evacuate the refrigerant from the A/C system.
2. Disconnect the refrigerant inlet line at the accumulator.
3. Remove the orifice from the refrigerant line using tool J–26549–D.
4. Install the new orifice into the inlet line with the shorter screen end toward the expansion tube.
5. Install the refrigerant line onto the accumulator and tighten to 18 ft. lbs.
6. Recharge the A/C system and check for leaks.

Accumulator

The accumulator assembly has a service replacement kit which includes two seals for the inlet and outlet connections. The desiccant is not serviced separately, it is part of the sealed accumulator assembly. Replace the accumulator only when:

- A physical perforation produces a leak.
- The orifice screen experiences continued or repeated plugging.
- An evaporator fail because of internal and external corrosion.

REMOVAL AND INSTALLATION

1. Remove the negative battery cable.
2. Refer to Section 1 and evacuate the refrigerant from the A/C system.
3. Disconnect the electrical connector from the dual pressure switch.
4. Remove the inlet line at the accumulator. Remove the evaporator outlet line at the accumulator and cap or plug both lines.
5. Remove the accumulator attaching screw and clamp. Remove the accumulator.
6. Drain excess refrigerant into a clean container. Measure to determine how much oil needs to be added to the system.
7. Install the accumulator attaching clamp and screw.
8. Add 2 oz. of clean refrigerant oil plus an amount equal to the oil drained from the system. Use clean 525 viscosity refrigerant oil on the seals.
9. Install the inlet and outlet lines and tighten to 18 ft. lbs.
10. Install the electrical connector. Install the negative battery cable.
11. Evacuate, charge and leak test the system.

RADIO

Receiver

REMOVAL AND INSTALLATION

1. Disconnect the negative battery terminal from the battery.
2. Remove the ash tray and any necessary wires.
3. Remove the instrument panel center bezel and the support clip nuts.
4. Remove the radio bracket-to-instrument panel bracket screws and pull the radio forward.
5. Disconnect the antenna, the clock connector, the speaker connectors and any electrical wires, then remove the radio.

WARNING: DO NOT let the antenna cable touch the clock connector. It is very important when changing speakers or performing any radio work to avoid pinching the wires. A short circuit-to-ground from any wire will cause damage to the output circuit in the radio.

6. Installation is the reverse of removal.

NOTE: In order to prevent damage to the receiver, always connect the speaker wire to the receiver before applying power to it.

WINDSHIELD WIPERS

The windshield wiper units are of the 2-speed, non-depressed park type, a washer pump mounted under the washer bottle and turn signal type wiper/washer switch. A single wiper motor operates both wiper blades. Rotating the switch to either **LO** or **HI** speed position completes the circuit and the wiper motor runs at that speed.

The pulse/demand wash functions are controlled by a plug-in printed circuit board enclosed in the wiper housing cover.

Blade and Arm

REMOVAL AND INSTALLATION

NOTE: The following procedure requires the use of GM Windshield Wiper Blade/Arm Removal tool No. J–8966 or equivalent.

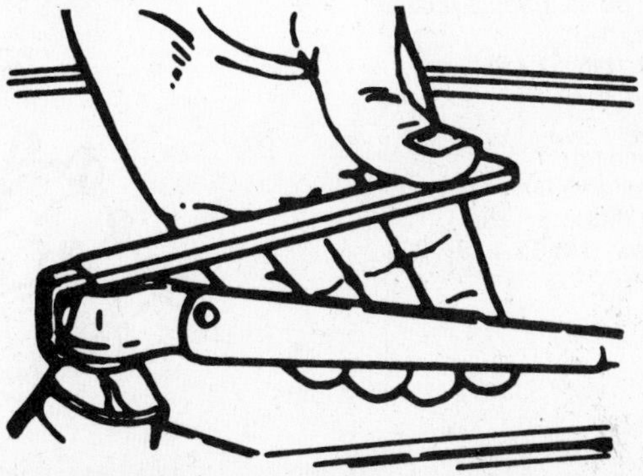

Using the GM Windsheild Wiper Blade/Arm Removal tool No. J-8966 to remove the wiper arms

If the wiper assembly has a press type release tab at the center, simply depress the tab and remove the blade. If the blade has no release tab, use a screwdriver to depress the spring at the center; this will release the assembly. To install the assembly, position the blade over the pin (at the tip of the arm) and press until the spring retainer engages the groove in the pin.

To remove the element, either depress the release button or squeeze the spring type retainer clip (at the outer end) together and slide the blade element out. To install, slide the new element in until it latches.

1. Insert the tool under the wiper arm and lever the arm off the shaft.
2. Disconnect the washer hose from the arm (if equipped), then remove the arm.
3. To install, operate the wiper motor (momentarily) to position the pivot shafts into the Park position and reverse the removal procedures. The proper Park position for the arms is with the blades approximately 2 in. (51mm) on the driver's side, or 2¾ in. (70mm) on the passenger's side, above the lower windshield molding.

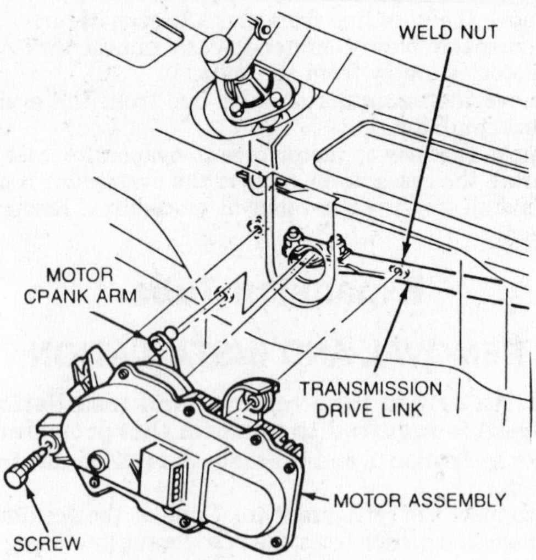
WELD NUT
MOTOR
CPANK ARM
TRANSMISSION
DRIVE LINK
MOTOR ASSEMBLY
SCREW

Windshield wiper motor

Wiper Motor

REMOVAL AND INSTALLATION

1. Disconnect the negative battery terminal from the battery.
2. Using the GM Windshield Wiper Blade/Arm Removal tool No. J-8966 or equivalent, remove the wiper arms.
3. Remove the cowl, vent and grille.
4. Loosen but DO NOT remove the nuts which hold the drive link to the motor crank arm.
5. Detach the drive link from the crank arm.
6. Disconnect the wiring from the wiper motor.
7. Remove the wiper motor-to-cowl screws. Turn the motor upward, then move it outward and remove it from the vehicle.
8. To install, reverse the removal procedures. Torque the wiper motor-to-cowl screws to 50–75 inch lbs.

1. Arm, windshield wiper
2. Blade
   insert
3. Nozzle
4. Spacer, nozzle
5. Nut, type R stamped (M16)
6. Transmission, left hand
   transmission, right hand
7. Lever
8. Module
9. Lens, pulse switch
10. Knob, pulse switch
11. Nut, pulse module retaining
12. Reserovir
13. Bolt, (M6 × 1 × 25)
14. Hose, (5/32" ID)
15. Strap
16. Connector
17. Motor assembly
18. Bolt (M5 × .8 × 28)
19. Screw, (M6.3 × 1.69 × 20)
20. Pump

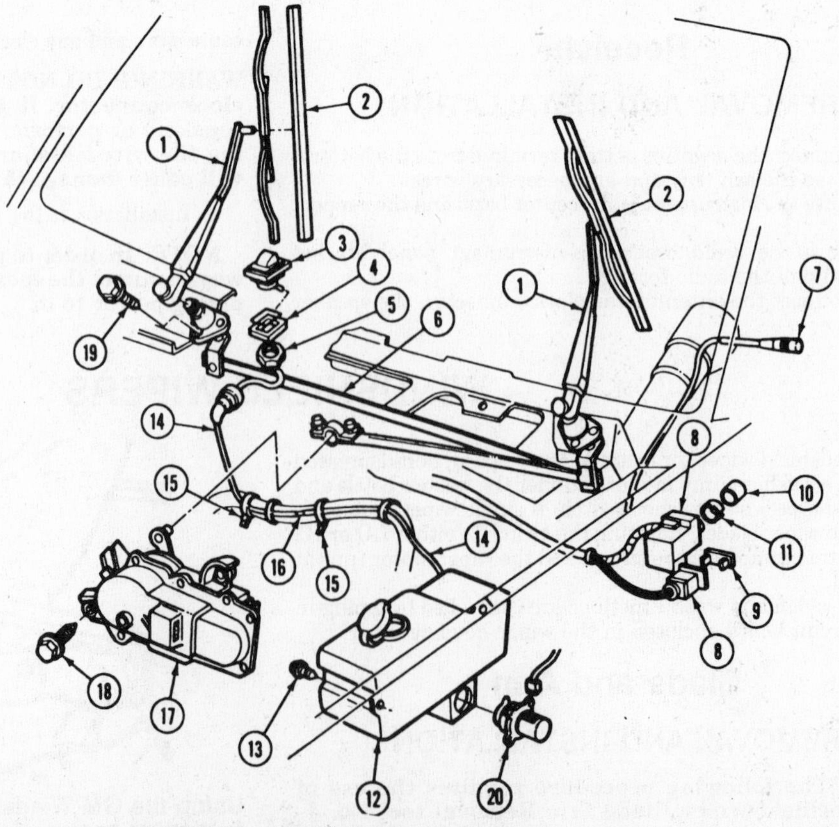
1
2
3
4
5
6
7
8
9
10
11
12
13
14
15
16
17
18
19
20

Exploded view of the windshield wiper assembly

Wiper Linkage

REMOVAL AND INSTALLATION

1. Disconnect the negative battery terminal from the battery.
2. Using the GM Windshield Wiper Blade/Arm Removal tool No. J-8966 or equivalent, remove the wiper arms.
3. Remove the cowl vent and the grille.
4. Remove the wiper linkage-to-motor clamp.
5. Remove the wiper linkage-to-cowl panel screws.
6. To install, reverse the removal procedures. Torque the wiper linkage-to-panel screws to 50–80 inch lbs.

INSTRUMENTS AND SWITCHES

Instrument Cluster

REMOVAL AND INSTALLATION

1. Disconnect the negative battery terminal from the battery.
2. Remove the lamp switch trim plate-to-instrument panel screws and the trim plate, then disconnect the electrical connector from the lamp switch.
3. Remove the air conditioning/heater control assembly-to-instrument panel screws and the assembly, the disconnect the electrical connector from the lamp switch.
4. Remove the filler panel (under the steering column) to instrument panel screws and the filler panel.
5. Remove the instrument cluster-to-instrument panel nuts, the instrument cluster, the nuts and the instrument cluster.
6. Disconnect the speedometer drive cable from the instrument cluster.
7. Disconnect the cluster electrical connectors and remove the instrument cluster.
8. To install, reverse the removal procedures.

Oil Pressure Gage

The oil pressure gauge is an electrical gage which measures current flow from a variable resistance sender. The sender is located on the right side of the 4-cylinder engines, below the intake manifold. On the 2.8L engine, the sender is located above or on the oil filter adapter. On the 4.3L engine, the sender is located on the top of the engine block near the distributor.

Fuel Gage

The fuel gage is an electrical instrument that measures an electrical current from a variable resistance in the fuel tank. The variable resistance is controlled by a float. When the fuel tank is full, the resistance is high, the fuel gage pointer is moved to its maximum position which is FULL on the gage face.

The fuel gage sender is attached to the top of the fuel tank. The sender is retained with a cam lock ring. A seal is used between the tank and the sender.

The sender will have two or three places to attach hoses. One line is for the fuel feed line. The second line is connected to the

1. Instrument panel
10. Nut
11. Instrument cluster
12. Instrument cluster housing
13. Screw
14. Filler panel

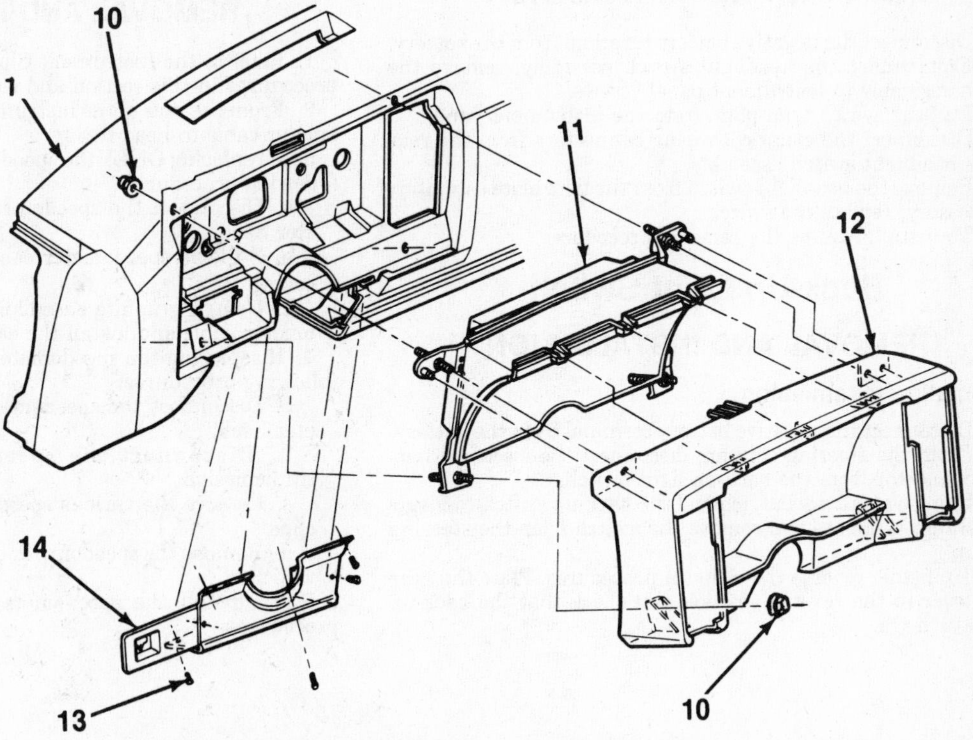
10
1
11
12
14
13
10

Exploded view of the instrument panel

vapor canister. The third line is used as a fuel return line to the fuel tank. On some senders a short connector lead is used, while on other senders the connector attaches directly to the sender.

Coolant Temperature Warning System

The coolant temperature warning system consists of a temperature switch and a warning lamp in the instrument panel. When the coolant becomes too hot, the switch closes and the lamp comes ON. The switch closes when the coolant temperature reaches 257°F (125°C).

Voltmeter

The voltmeter measures the voltage levgel of the electrical system. The voltmeter uses an internal shunt.

Windshield Wiper Switch

The windshield wiper switch is located on the end of the combination switch, attached to the steering column. Refer to the Combination Switch Removal and Installation procedures in Section 8 for servicing procedures.

Headlight Switch

The headlight switch, a push button switch to turn the lights On and Off, is located on the left side of the instrument panel. A rheostat dial, located just above the headlight/parking light switch, is used to control the illumination of the instrument panel.

A dimmer switch (part of the combination switch), to control the HI and LO beam operation, is located on the steering column; the lights are changed by pulling the combination switch lever toward the driver.

REMOVAL AND INSTALLATION

1. Disconnect the negative battery terminal from the battery.
2. From under the headlight switch assembly, remove the switch assembly-to-instrument panel screws.
3. Pull the switch trim plate from the instrument panel.
4. Disconnect the electrical wiring connectors from the rear of the headlight switch assembly.
5. Remove the headlight switch from the trim plate assembly; if necessary, replace the switch.
6. To install, reverse the removal procedures.

Back-Up Light Switch

REMOVAL AND INSTALLATION

Automatic Transmission

1. Disconnect the negative battery terminal from the battery.
2. From the steering column, disconnect the electrical harness connector from the back-up light switch.
3. Using a small pry bar, expand the back-up switch-to-steering column retainers and remove the switch from the steering column.
4. To install, reverse the removal procedures. Place the gear shift lever in the reverse position and check that the back-up lights turn On.

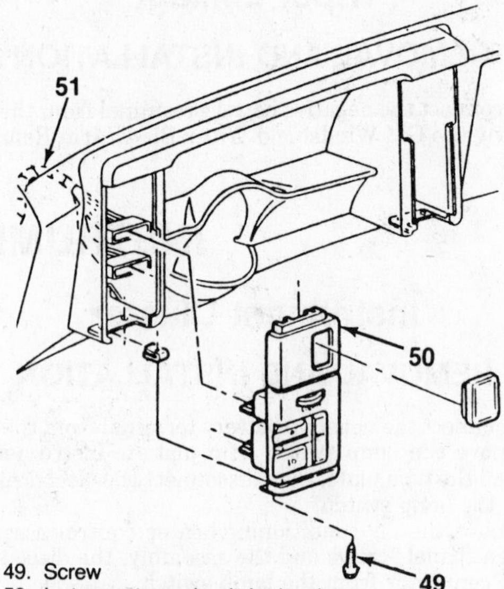
51
50
49

49. Screw
50. Instrument panel switch trim plate
51. Instrument panel harness

Headlight switch assembly

Manual Transmission

To replace the back-up light switch, refer to the Back-Up Light Switch, Removal and Installation procedures in Section 7.

Speedometer Cable

REMOVAL AND INSTALLATION

1. Refer to the Instrument Cluster Removal and Installation procedures in this section and remove the instrument cluster.
2. From the rear of the instrument cluster, remove the speedometer cable-to-head fitting.
3. If replacing ONLY the speedometer cable core, perform the following procedures:
   a. Disconnect the speedometer casing from the speedometer head.
   b. Pull the speedometer cable core from the speedometer casing.
   c. Using a graphite-based lubricant, lubricate a new speedometer cable and install the cable into the casing.
4. If replacing the speedometer cable assembly, perform the following procedures:
   a. Disconnect the speedometer casing from the speedometer head.
   b. Disconnect the speedometer casing from the transmission.
   c. Remove the various speedometer cable/casing retaining clips.
   d. Remove the speedometer cable/casing assembly from the vehicle.
5. To install the speedometer cable, reverse the removal procedures.

DIAGNOSIS OF THE ELECTRONIC DIGITAL INSTRUMENT CLUSTER

PROBLEM	POSSIBLE CAUSE	CORRECTION
Cluster Display Does Not Light	1. No ignition feed to the cluster. 2. Inoperative cluster.	1. Remove the large 34 pin connector from the cluster. Using a digital volt-OHM meter, measure the voltage from pin A15 to B-7 with the ignition in run. The meter should read battery voltage. If the meter reads less than battery voltage, or zero, repair the pink/white wire from the ignition switch. 2. Replace the cluster.
Cluster Display Does Not Dim With Lights On	1. Park lamp feed open or shorted. 2. Park lamp switch feed open or shorted. 3. Cluster inoperative.	1. Measure between pin A6 of the large 34 pin connector, and ground using a digital volt-OHM meter. Ignition in run, parking lamps on. If the reading is less than battery voltage, repair the open or short at the brown wire. 2. Measure between pin A6 of the large 34 pin connector, and ground using a digital volt-OHM meter. Ignition in run, parking lamps on. Adjust the panel lamp switch from high intensity to low intensity. The voltmeter should read between 0 to battery voltage. If this reading is not obtained, repair the brown wire and/or the park lamp switch. 3. If the previous 2 steps are OK, replace the instrument cluster.
Cluster Display Always Dim	1. Inoperative cluster.	1. Replace the cluster.
Speedometer Inoperative or Inaccurate, Odometer Operates Correctly	1. Inoperative instrument cluster.	1. Replace the cluster.
One or Both Odometers Do Not Operate Properly but the Speedometer Operates Properly	1. Inoperative instrument cluster.	1. Replace the cluster.
Speedometer and Odometers Do Not Operate	1. No vehicle speed sensor signal.	1. Disconnect the large 34 pin connector from the cluster, and the connector from the digital ratio adapter. Measure the resistance between the wire at pin A-11 of the harness and the wire at pin B of the digital ratio adapter harness. If the resistance is above zero OHMs, and the vehicle speed sensor circuit is working properly, replace the instrument cluster.

DIAGNOSIS OF THE ELECTRONIC DIGITAL INSTRUMENT CLUSTER (CONT.)

PROBLEM	POSSIBLE CAUSE	CORRECTION
Fuel Gage Is Inaccurate	1. Shorts or opens in the wiring from the fuel tank sender, or an inoperative fuel sender unit.	1. Disconnect the fuel gage sender at the tank and connect one lead of J 33431 to the pink wire and the other to ground. Turn the ignition to the run position, and set the resistance dials of J 33431 to zero OHMs. The fuel gage should read empty. Set the resistance dials to 35 OHMs. The fuel gage should read half full (7 to 8 segments lit). Set the resistance dials to 90 OHMs. The fuel gage should read full. If the gage responds correctly, check the black wire to ground at the fuel sender unit. If the black wire is OK replace the fuel tank sender. If the gage does not respond correctly to the test, check the pink wire from the fuel sender to A-12 of the cluster. If this wire is OK replace the cluster.
Low Fuel Indicator Does Not Light With Low Fuel Level	1. Inoperative cluster.	1. Replace the cluster.
Temperature Gage Is Inaccurate	1. Shorts or opens in the wiring from the temperature sender, or an inoperative temperature sending unit.	1. Disconnect the temperature sender and connect one lead of J 33431 to the dark green wire and the other to ground. Turn the ignition to the run position, and set the resistance dials of J 33431 to 1400 OHMs. The temperature gage should read cold. Set the resistance dials to 400 OHMs. The fuel gage should read half (7 to 8 segments lit). Set the resistance dials to 55 OHMs. The fuel gage should read hot. If the gage responds correctly, replace the temperature gage sender. If the gage does not respond correctly to the test, check the dark green wire from the temperature sender to the cluster A-1. If this wire is OK, replace the cluster.
Temperature Indicator Does Not Light With the Engine Coolant Overheated	1. Inoperative cluster.	1. Replace the instrument cluster.

DIAGNOSIS OF THE ELECTRONIC DIGITAL INSTRUMENT CLUSTER (CONT.)

PROBLEM	POSSIBLE CAUSE	CORRECTION
Oil Pressure Gage Is Inaccurate	1. Shorts or opens in the wire from the oil pressure sender, or an inoperative oil pressure sending unit.	1. Disconnect the oil pressure sender and connect one lead of J 33431 to the tan wire and the other to ground. Turn the ignition to the run position, and set the resistance dials of J 33431 to zero OHMs. The oil gage should read low. Set the resistance dials to 35 OHMs. The oil gage should read half (7 to 8 segments lit). Set the resistance dials to 90 OHMs. The oil gage should read high. If the gage responds correctly, replace the oil gage sender. If the gage does not respond correctly to the test, check the tan wire from the oil sender to the cluster A-2. If this wire is OK replace the cluster.
Oil Pressure Indicator Does Not Light	1. Inoperative cluster.	1. Replace the instrument cluster.
Voltmeter Is Inaccurate	1. Short, open or high resistance in the brown wire from the generator.	1. Measure the voltage between the battery terminals. Then measure the voltage between the PNK/BLK (A-15) wire, and a good chassis ground. If the readings are different, repair the PNK/BLK wire. If the readings are the same, check the black wire A-9 and B-7 for high resistance to ground. If the black wires at the cluster are OK replace the instrument cluster.

DIAGNOSIS OF THE VOLTMETER

PROBLEM	POSSIBLE CAUSE	CORRECTION
Voltmeter Reads At 9 Or Below	1. Discharged battery. 2. High resistance in the voltmeter connections. 3. Faulty voltmeter.	1. Measure the voltage across the battery. Recharge the battery. Read the dash voltmeter with the charger working. The voltage should come up to at least 12 volts. Find and correct the cause of the battery discharging. 2. Clean and tighten the connections. 3. Apply 12 volts directly to the voltmeter. If the voltmeter doesn't respond accurately, replace the voltmeter.

DIAGNOSIS OF THE VEHICLE SPEED SENSOR AND DIGITAL RATIO ADAPTER CONTROLLER

PROBLEM	POSSIBLE CAUSE	CORRECTION
Speedometer and Odometer Are Inaccurate	1. Incorrect digital ratio adapter.	1. Check for the correct digital ratio adapter.
Speedometer and Odometer Do Not Operate Properly	1. Inoperative digital ratio adapter.	1. Disconnect the digital ratio adapter, and place the ignition in run. Check for voltage between the pink/black wire in the harness and a good chassis ground. If the voltage is less than the battery voltage, check 15 amp brake fuse or for an open or short in the pink/black wire.
	2. Poor ground path from the digital ratio adapter.	2. Check for voltage between the LT BLU/BLK wire #15 in the DRAC harness and the black wire #8. If the voltage is less than battery voltage, check for an open or short in the black wire.
	3. No signal from the vehicle speed sensor.	3. Raise and support the vehicle, start the engine, and place the transmission in drive. Check for AC voltage that changes with the engine rpm between the purple/white wire #12, and the light green/black wire #7 at the digital ratio adapter controller. If there is not AC voltage at these wires, check for opens in the purple/white wire and the light green wire. If there are not shorts or opens, replace the vehicle speed sensor.
	4. Inoperative digital ratio adapter (speedometer output).	4. Raise and support the vehicle, start the engine, and place the transmission in drive. Check for AC voltage that changes with the engine rpm between the light blue/black #15 and the black wires #8 at the digital ratio adapter connector (connector attached) if AC voltage varies with rpm, replace the digital ratio adapter.
	5. Inoperative digital ratio adapter (cruise output).	5. Raise and support the vehicle, start the engine, and place the transmission in drive. Check for AC voltage that changes with the engine rpm between the yellow and the black wires at the digital ratio adapter connector (connector attached) if AC voltage varies with rpm, replace the digital ratio adapter.
	6. Inoperative instrument cluster.	6. Refer to DIAGNOSIS OF THE ELECTRONIC INSTRUMENT CLUSTER in this section.

DIAGNOSIS OF THE FUEL GAGE

PROBLEM	POSSIBLE CAUSE	CORRECTION
Gage Stays At "E"	1. No fuel. 2. Circuit is grounded.	1. Fill the fuel tank. 2. Disconnect the lead at the fuel tank. The gage should read past the "F". If the gage does not read past the "F", replace the fuel tank sender. If the gage stays at "E", find the ground in the circuit between the gage and the fuel tank.
Gage Stays At "F" Or Beyond	Open circuit between the gage and the sender.	Disconnect the sender lead at the fuel tank. Ground the lead. The fuel gage should read at "E". If the gage reads at "E", replace the sender. If the gage still reads at "F" or beyond, find the open between the gage and the fuel tank.
Gage Reads Wrong	1. Corrosion or a loose connection. 2. Faulty sender. 3. Faulty gage.	1. Clean the terminals. Tighten the terminals. 2. Remove the sender. Test the sender with an ohmmeter. The empty position should read 1 ohm. The full position should read 88 ohms. 3. Disconnect the front body connector. Connect J 33431 tester to the lead that goes to the gage. Turn the engine control switch ON. If the gage responds accurately, check the wiring between the rear compartment and the front body connector. If the gage reads between one fourth and one half with the J 33431 set at 90 ohms, remove the gage and check for loose nuts at the gage terminals. Tighten the nuts and replace the gage. If the gage doesn't read according to the J 33431 settings, replace the gage.

DIAGNOSIS OF THE OIL PRESSURE WARNING SYSTEM

PROBLEM	POSSIBLE CAUSE	CORRECTION
Lamp Won't Light With The Engine Not Running And The Engine Control Switch Turned To On	1. Lamp bulb is burned out. 2. Open in the oil pressure switch lead circuit.	1. Check the bulb. Replace the bulb if necessary. 2. Remove the oil pressure switch lead from the switch. Ground the switch lead. If the lamp does not light, find and correct the open in the circuit. If the lamp does light, replace the switch.

DIAGNOSIS OF THE COOLANT TEMPERATURE GAGE

PROBLEM	POSSIBLE CAUSE	CORRECTION
Gage Does Not Move From "Cold" When The Engine Is "Hot"	1. Blown fuse. 2. Open circuit. 3. Bad sender.	1. Check fuse and replace if blown. Turn engine control switch key "on." Do not start engine. 2&3. Remove the lead at the sender unit. Short the sender lead to ground. Gage should indicate "260." Connect the sender lead. If the gage indicates "100," check the connector on the sender. If OK, replace the sender. If the gage indicates "100," the gage is stuck. Replace the gage. If the lamp does not glow, check for continuity between the sender unit terminal at the gage and ground, and between the ignition terminal and ground. Also check the case ground. If all checks "OK," replace the gage.
Gage Indicates "Hot" With Cold Engine	Shorted or grounded circuit.	Remove the sender lead at the sender unit. The gage should swing to "100." If the gage does not swing to "100," check the sender unit for an external short. If there is no external short, replace the sender. If the gage stays "260," check for a short circuit in the gage to sender wiring. If there is no short, replace the gage.
Gage Reads Low	1. Resistance in the circuit due to corrosion or a loose connection. 2. Bad sender.	1. Clean and tighten the terminals and connections in the circuit. Check for resistance in the ground path of the sender. 2. Remove the lead at the sender. Measure the resistance with an ohmmeter. At 40°C (104°F) the resistance is 1365 ohms. At 125°C (257°F) the resistance is 55.1 ohms. If the sender does not have approximately these values, replace the sender.
Gage Reads High	1. Faulty sender. 2. Circuit has a high resistance ground.	1. Measure the sender's resistance as described in the previous step. 2. Disconnect the sender lead at the gage and sender. Check for a high resistance ground with an ohmmeter. Repair the circuit.

DIAGNOSIS OF THE OIL PRESSURE GAGE

PROBLEM	POSSIBLE CAUSE	CORRECTION
Gage Reads At "0"	1. Low oil level.	1. Check oil level. Add oil if necessary.
	2. The circuit is grounded between the gage and the sender.	2. Remove the sender lead at the sender. The gage should read "80." If the gage stays at "0", remove the sender lead at the gage. The gage should read "80." If the gage reads "80", find the ground in the circuit between the gage and the sender. If the gage reads "0", replace the gage.
Gage Reads At "0" (Continued)	3. Faulty sender.	3. Remove the sender lead at the sender. Connect an ohmmeter to the sender. With the engine stopped, the resistance should be one ohm. With the engine running, the resistance should be about 44 ohms at 40 psi (275 kPa). If the sender reads one ohm with the engine running, replace the sender.
Gage Reads "80" PSI Or Above	The sender circuit has an open.	Disconnect the sender lead from the sender. Ground the sender lead. The gage should read "0" psi. If the gage reads "0" psi, replace the sender. If the gage stays at "80" psi, find the open in the circuit between the gage and the sender.
Gage Readings Are In Error	Gage is faulty.	Remove the sender lead from the sender. Connect the J 33431 Tester to the sender lead and ground. If the gage responds accurately to the tester, replace the sender. If the gage does not respond accurately to the tester, replace the gage.

DIAGNOSIS OF THE COOLANT TEMPERATURE WARNING SYSTEM

PROBLEM	POSSIBLE CAUSE	CORRECTION
Lamp Won't Light During Bulb Check	1. Lamp bulb is burned out. 2. Open in the temperature switch lead circuit.	1. Check the bulb. Replace the bulb if necessary. 2. Remove the temperature switch lead from the switch. Ground the switch lead. If the lamp does not light, find and correct the open in the circuit. If the lamp does light, replace the switch.

DIAGNOSIS OF THE BRAKE WARNING SYSTEM

PROBLEM	POSSIBLE CAUSE	CORRECTION
Warning Lamp Won't Light During Bulb Check	1. Lamp bulb is burned out. 2. Open in the brake warning circuit.	1. Replace the bulb. 2. Remove the switch lead at the switch. Refer to BRAKES Ground the switch lead with a jumper. If the lamp comes on, replace the switch.

DIAGNOSIS OF THE "CHECK GAGES" LAMP (Gages Cluster Only)

PROBLEM	POSSIBLE CAUSE	CORRECTION
	TEMPERATURE GAGE	
"Check Gages" Telltale Lamp Does Not Light With High Temperature	1. Burned out bulb. 2. Inoperative check gages circuit.	1. Replace "Check Gages" telltale bulb. 2. Replace temperature gage. 3. Exchange instrument cluster.
	OIL GAGE	
"Check Gages" Telltale Lamp Does Not Light With Low Oil Pressure	1. Burned out bulb. 2. Inoperative check gages circuit.	1. Replace "Check Gages" telltale bulb. 2. Replace temperature gage. 3. Exchange instrument cluster.
	CHECK GAGES TELLTALE	
Check Gages Telltale Lights at All Times	1. Verify temperature gage circuit works correctly. 2. Verify oil pressure gage circuit works correctly.	1. Replace faulty temperature gage. 2. Replace faulty temperature gage. 3. Exchange instrument cluster.

LIGHTING

Headlights

REMOVAL AND INSTALLATION

1. Disconnect the negative battery terminal from the battery.
2. Remove the headlight-to-fender bezel and the retaining spring.
3. Rotate the headlight to the right and remove it from the adjusters.
4. Disconnect the electrical harness connector from the rear of the headlight and remove the headlight from the vehicle.
5. To install, reverse the removal procedures.

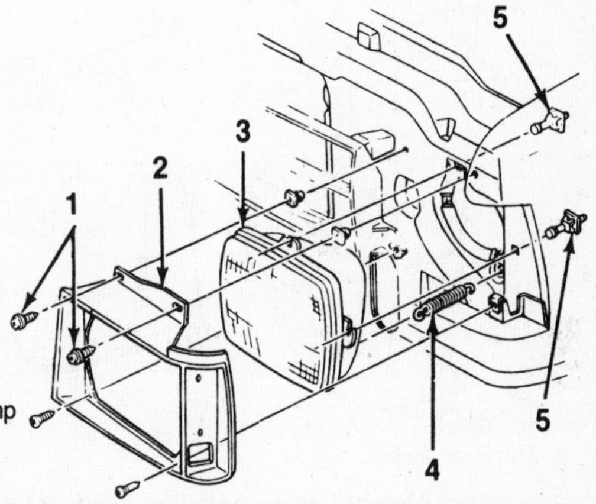
5
3
2
1
5
4

1. Screws
2. Bezel
3. Headlamp
4. Spring
5. Adjuster

Exploded view of the headlight assembly

Signal and Marker Lights

REMOVAL AND INSTALLATION

Front Turn Signal/Marker Lights

1. Disconnect the negative battery terminals from the battery.
2. Remove the headlight bezel-to-fender screws and the bezel; allow the bezel to hang by the turn signal/marker light wires.
3. At the rear of the headlight bezel, turn the turn signal/marker bulb socket ¼ turn and remove it from the headlight bezel.
4. Remove the bulb from the turn signal/marker bulb socket; if necessary, replace the bulb.
5. To install, use a new bulb (if necessary) and reverse the removal procedures. Check the turn signal/marker light operations.

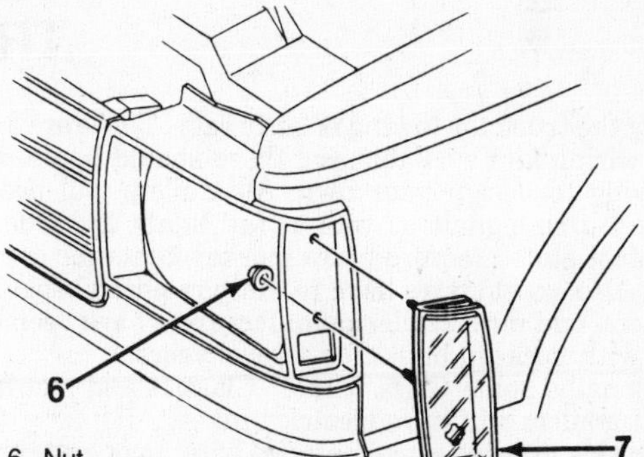
6
7

6. Nut
7. Front marker lamp

Turn signal/marker light assembly

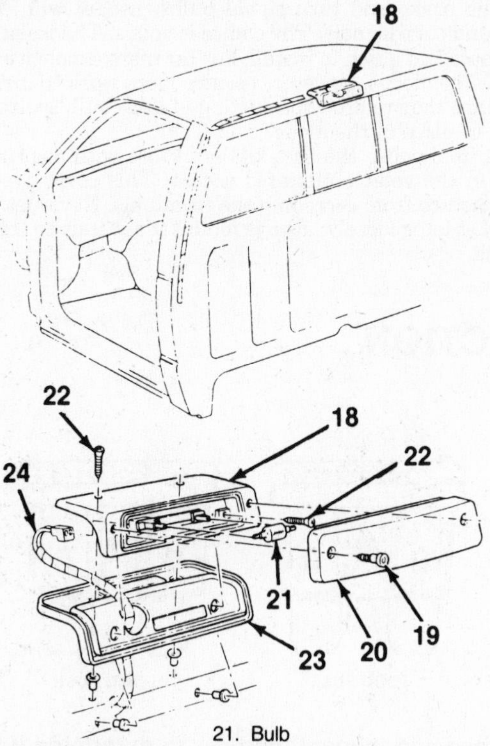
18
22
18
22
24
21
19
23
20

18. Lamp assembly
19. Screw
20. Lens
21. Bulb
22. Screw
23. Insulator
24. Wire assembly

Exploded view of the cargo light assembly

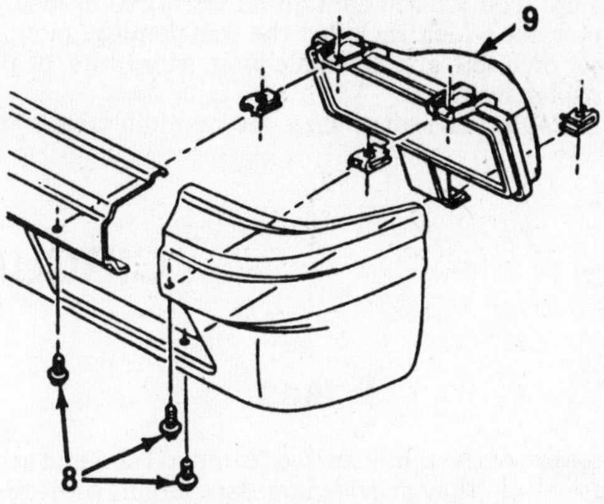
9
8

Parking light assembly

Parking Lights

1. Disconnect the negative battery terminal from the battery.
2. At the rear of the front bumper, turn the bulb socket ¼ turn and remove the socket from the parking brake housing.
3. Remove the bulb from the socket; if necessary, replace the bulb.
4. To install, reverse the removal procedures. Check the parking light operations.

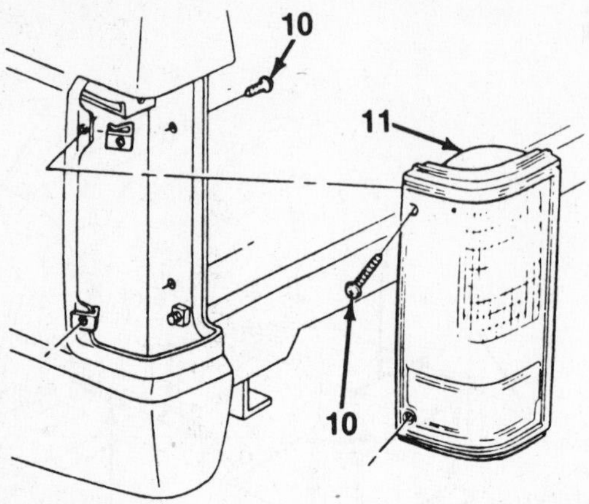

10
11
10

10. Screw
11. Rear lamp

Rear turn signal/brake/parking light assembly

Rear Turn Signal, Brake and Parking Lights

1. Disconnect the negative battery terminal from the battery.
2. Remove the rear turn signal/brake/parking lamp-to-vehicle screws and the lamp housing from the vehicle.
3. Turn the bulb socket ¼ turn and remove the socket from the lamp housing.
4. Remove the bulb from the bulb socket; if necessary, replace the bulb.
5. To install, reverse the removal procedures. Check the turn signal/brake/parking light operations.

Cargo Light

REMOVAL AND INSTALLATION

1. Disconnect the negative battery terminal from the battery.
2. Remove the lens-to-housing screws and the lens.
3. Remove the bulb from the cargo light housing; if necessary, replace the bulb.
4. To install, reverse the removal procedures.

TRAILER WIRING

Wiring the truck for towing is fairly easy. There are a number of good wiring kits available and these should be used, rather than trying to design your own. All trailers will need brake lights and turn signals as well as tail lights and side marker lights. Most states require extra marker lights for overly wide trailers. Also, most states have recently required back-up lights for trailers, and most trailer manufacturers have been building trailers with back-up lights for several years.

Additionally, some Class I, most Class II and just about all Class III trailers will have electric brakes.

Add to this number an accessories wire, to operate trailer internal equipment or to charge the trailer's battery, and you can have as many as seven wires in the harness.

Determine the equipment on your trailer and buy the wiring kit necessary. The kit will contain all the wires needed, plus a plug adapter set which included the female plug, mounted on the bumper or hitch, and the male plug, wired into, or plugged into the trailer harness.

When installing the kit, follow the manufacturer's instructions. The color coding of the wires is standard throughout the industry.

One point to note: some domestic vehicles, and most imported vehicles, have separate turn signals. On most domestic vehicles, the brake lights and rear turn signals operate with the same bulb. For those vehicles with separate turn signals, you can purchase an isolation unit so that the brake lights won't blink whenever the turn signals are operated, or you can go to your local electronics supply house and buy four diodes to wire in series with the brake and turn signal bulbs. Diodes will isolate the brake and turn signals. The choice is yours. The isolation units are simple and quick to install, but far more expensive than the diodes. The diodes, however, require more work to install properly, since they require the cutting of each bulb's wire and soldering in place of the diode.

One, final point, the best kits are those with a spring loaded cover on the vehicle mounted socket. This cover prevent dirt and moisture from corroding the terminals. Never let the vehicle socket hang loosely; always mount it securely to the bumper or hitch.

CIRCUIT PROTECTION

Fuses

The fuses are of the miniaturized (compact) size and are located on a fuse block, they provide increased circuit protection and reliability. Access to the fuse block is gained through a swing-down unit at the far left side of the dash panel. Each fuse receptacle is marked as to the circuit it protects and the correct amperage of the fuse.

REPLACEMENT

1. Pull the fuse from the fuse block.
2. Inspect the fuse element (through the clear plastic body) to the blade terminal for defects.

NOTE: When replacing the fuse, DO NOT use one of a higher amperage.

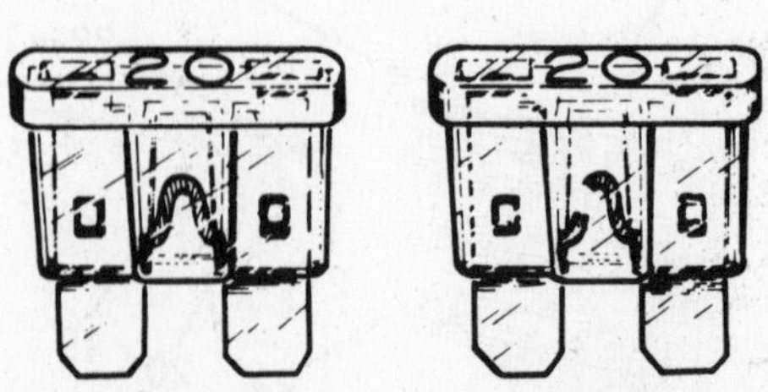

20
20
GOOD FUSE
BLOWN FUSE

Remove and inspect the fuse to determine if the element is broken or burned. If so, determine the reason why the fuse blew and replace the fuse with one of the same rating.

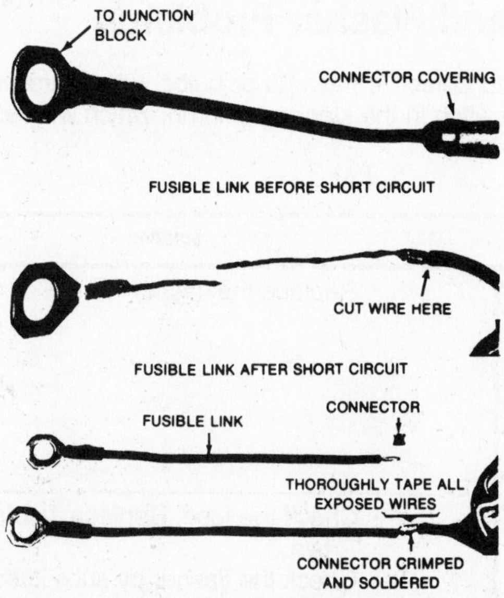
TO JUNCTION BLOCK
CONNECTOR COVERING
FUSIBLE LINK BEFORE SHORT CIRCUIT
CUT WIRE HERE
FUSIBLE LINK AFTER SHORT CIRCUIT
FUSIBLE LINK
CONNECTOR
THOROUGHLY TAPE ALL EXPOSED WIRES
CONNECTOR CRIMPED AND SOLDERED

New fusible links are spliced into the wire

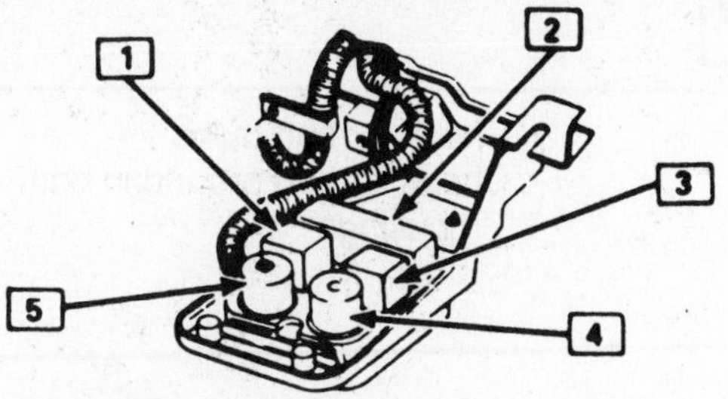
1
2
3
4
5

1. Horn relay
2. Seat belt–ignition key–headlight buzzer
3. Choke relay (vacant w/EFI)
4. Hazard flasher
5. Signal flasher

Convenience center and components

3. To install, reverse the removal procedures.

Convenience Center

The Convenience Center is a swing-down unit located on the underside of the instrument panel, near the steering column. The swing-down feature provides central location and easy access to buzzers, relays and flasher units. All units are serviced by plug-in replacement.

Fusible Links

In addition to fuses, the wiring harness incorporates fusible links (in the battery feed circuits) to protect the wiring. Fusible links are 4 in. (102mm) sections of copper wire, 4 gauges smaller than the circuit(s) they are protecting, designed to melt under electrical overload. There are four different gauge sizes used. The fusible links are color coded so that they may be installed in their original positions.

REPLACEMENT

1. Disconnect the negative battery terminal from the battery.
2. Locate the burned out link.
3. Strip away the melted insulation and cut the burned link ends from the wire.

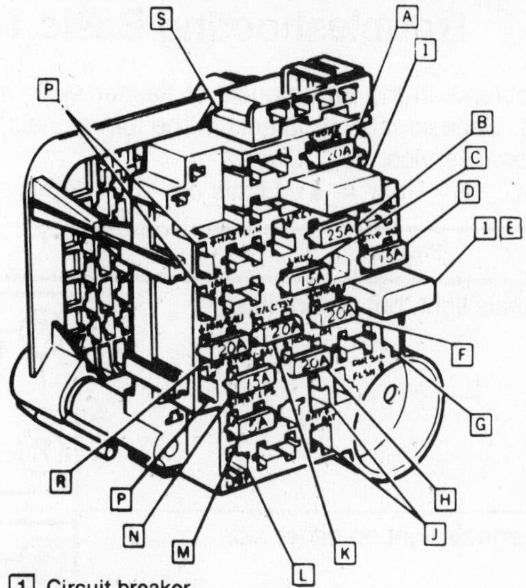
S
A
I
P
B
C
D
I E
F
G
R
P
H
N
M
J
K
L

- 1 Circuit breaker
- A Fuse—choke
- B Fuse—heater or air condition
- C Fuse—radio
- D Fuse—stop, hazard lamps
- E Power accessory
- F Fuse—windshield wiper
- G Receptacle—power door locks
- H Fuse—horn
- J Receptacle—clock, courtesy lamp, dome lamp, I/P compt lamp & hdlp wrng buzzer
- K Fuse—tail & ctsy lamps
- L Receptacle—headlamp on warning
- M Fuse—instrument panel lamps
- N Fuse—turn & back up lamps
- P Receptacle—cruise control & auto trans
- R Fuse—ignition & gauges
- S Connector—seat belt warning buzzer & timer

Fuse box

4. Strip the wire back ½ in. (13mm) to allow soldering of the new link.
5. Using a new fusible link 4 gauges smaller than the protected circuit – approx. 10 in. (254mm) long – solder it into the circuit.

NOTE: Whenever splicing a new wire, always bond the splice with rosin core solder, then cover with electrical tape. Using acid core solder may cause corrosion.

6. Tape and seal all splices with silicone to weatherproof repairs.
7. After taping the wire, tape the electrical harness leaving an exposed 5 in. (127mm) loop of wire.
8. Reconnect the battery.

Circuit Breakers

A circuit breaker is an electrical switch which breaks the circuit in case of an overload. The circuit breaker is located on the lower center of the fuse block. The circuit breaker will remain open until the short or overload condition in the circuit is corrected.

RESETTING

Locate the circuit breaker on the fuse block, then push the circuit breaker in until it locks. If the circuit breaker kicks itself Off again, locate and correct the problem in the electrical circuit.

Troubleshooting Basic Turn Signal and Flasher Problems

Most problems in the turn signals or flasher system can be reduced to defective flashers or bulbs, which are easily replaced. Occasionally, problems in the turn signals are traced to the switch in the steering column, which will require professional service.

F = Front R = Rear ● = Lights off o = Lights on

Problem		Solution
Turn signals light, but do not flash	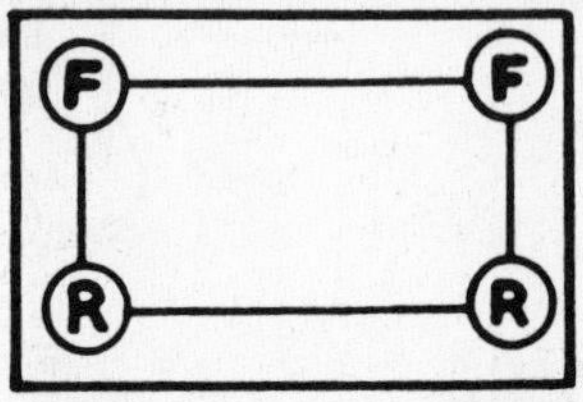F F R R	• Replace the flasher
No turn signals light on either side	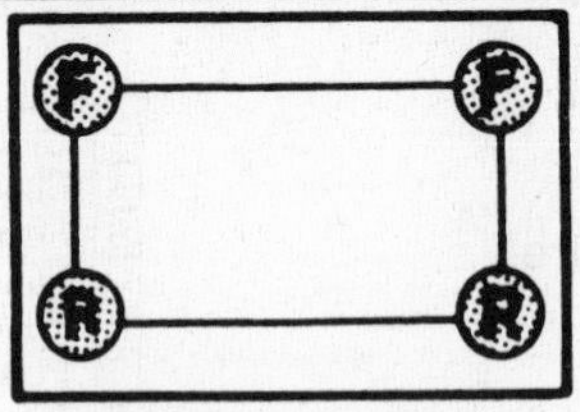F F R R	• Check the fuse. Replace if defective. • Check the flasher by substitution • Check for open circuit, short circuit or poor ground
Both turn signals on one side don't work	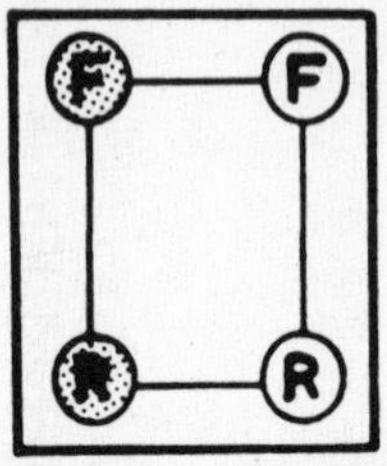F F R R	• Check for bad bulbs • Check for bad ground in both housings
One turn signal light on one side doesn't work	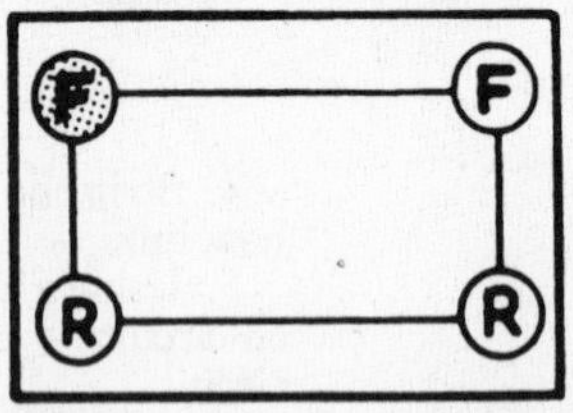F F R R	• Check and/or replace bulb • Check for corrosion in socket. Clean contacts. • Check for poor ground at socket
Turn signal flashes too fast or too slow	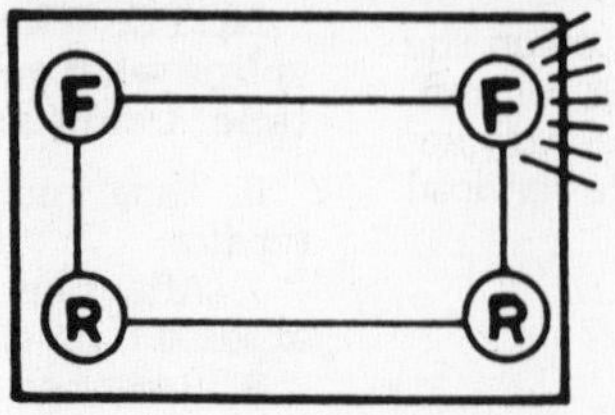F F R R	• Check any bulb on the side flashing too fast. A heavy-duty bulb is probably installed in place of a regular bulb. • Check the bulb flashing too slow. A standard bulb was probably installed in place of a heavy-duty bulb. • Check for loose connections or corrosion at the bulb socket
Indicator lights don't work in either direction		• Check if the turn signals are working • Check the dash indicator lights • Check the flasher by substitution

Troubleshooting Basic Turn Signal and Flasher Problems

Most problems in the turn signals or flasher system can be reduced to defective flashers or bulbs, which are easily replaced. Occasionally, problems in the turn signals are traced to the switch in the steering column, which will require professional service.

F = Front R = Rear ● = Lights off o = Lights on

Problem		Solution
One indicator light doesn't light		• On systems with 1 dash indicator: See if the lights work on the same side. Often the filaments have been reversed in systems combining stoplights with taillights and turn signals. Check the flasher by substitution • On systems with 2 indicators: Check the bulbs on the same side Check the indicator light bulb Check the flasher by substitution

Troubleshooting the Heater

Problem	Cause	Solution
Blower motor will not turn at any speed	• Blown fuse • Loose connection • Defective ground • Faulty switch • Faulty motor • Faulty resistor	• Replace fuse • Inspect and tighten • Clean and tighten • Replace switch • Replace motor • Replace resistor
Blower motor turns at one speed only	• Faulty switch • Faulty resistor	• Replace switch • Replace resistor
Blower motor turns but does not circulate air	• Intake blocked • Fan not secured to the motor shaft	• Clean intake • Tighten security
Heater will not heat	• Coolant does not reach proper temperature • Heater core blocked internally • Heater core air-bound • Blend-air door not in proper position	• Check and replace thermostat if necessary • Flush or replace core if necessary • Purge air from core • Adjust cable
Heater will not defrost	• Control cable adjustment incorrect • Defroster hose damaged	• Adjust control cable • Replace defroster hose

Troubleshooting Basic Lighting Problems

Problem	Cause	Solution
Lights		
One or more lights don't work, but others do	• Defective bulb(s) • Blown fuse(s) • Dirty fuse clips or light sockets • Poor ground circuit	• Replace bulb(s) • Replace fuse(s) • Clean connections • Run ground wire from light socket housing to car frame
Lights burn out quickly	• Incorrect voltage regulator setting or defective regulator • Poor battery/alternator connections	• Replace voltage regulator • Check battery/alternator connections
Lights go dim	• Low/discharged battery • Alternator not charging • Corroded sockets or connections • Low voltage output	• Check battery • Check drive belt tension; repair or replace alternator • Clean bulb and socket contacts and connections • Replace voltage regulator
Lights flicker	• Loose connection • Poor ground • Circuit breaker operating (short circuit)	• Tighten all connections • Run ground wire from light housing to car frame • Check connections and look for bare wires
Lights "flare"—Some flare is normal on acceleration—if excessive, see "Lights Burn Out Quickly"	• High voltage setting	• Replace voltage regulator
Lights glare—approaching drivers are blinded	• Lights adjusted too high • Rear springs or shocks sagging • Rear tires soft	• Have headlights aimed • Check rear springs/shocks • Check/correct rear tire pressure
Turn Signals		
Turn signals don't work in either direction	• Blown fuse • Defective flasher • Loose connection	• Replace fuse • Replace flasher • Check/tighten all connections
Right (or left) turn signal only won't work	• Bulb burned out • Right (or left) indicator bulb burned out • Short circuit	• Replace bulb • Check/replace indicator bulb • Check/repair wiring
Flasher rate too slow or too fast	• Incorrect wattage bulb • Incorrect flasher	• Flasher bulb • Replace flasher (use a variable load flasher if you pull a trailer)
Indicator lights do not flash (burn steadily)	• Burned out bulb • Defective flasher	• Replace bulb • Replace flasher
Indicator lights do not light at all	• Burned out indicator bulb • Defective flasher	• Replace indicator bulb • Replace flasher

Troubleshooting Basic Dash Gauge Problems

Problem	Cause	Solution
Coolant Temperature Gauge		
Gauge reads erratically or not at all	• Loose or dirty connections • Defective sending unit	• Clean/tighten connections • Bi-metal gauge: remove the wire from the sending unit. Ground the wire for an instant. If the gauge registers, replace the sending unit.
	• Defective gauge	• Magnetic gauge: disconnect the wire at the sending unit. With ignition ON gauge should register COLD. Ground the wire; gauge should register HOT.
Ammeter Gauge—Turn Headlights ON (do not start engine). Note reaction		
Ammeter shows charge	• Connections reversed on gauge	• Reinstall connections
Ammeter shows discharge	• Ammeter is OK	• Nothing
Ammeter does not move	• Loose connections or faulty wiring • Defective gauge	• Check/correct wiring • Replace gauge
Oil Pressure Gauge		
Gauge does not register or is inaccurate	• On mechanical gauge, Bourdon tube may be bent or kinked	• Check tube for kinks or bends preventing oil from reaching the gauge
	• Low oil pressure	• Remove sending unit. Idle the engine briefly. If no oil flows from sending unit hole, problem is in engine.
	• Defective gauge	• Remove the wire from the sending unit and ground it for an instant with the ignition ON. A good gauge will go to the top of the scale.
	• Defective wiring	• Check the wiring to the gauge. If it's OK and the gauge doesn't register when grounded, replace the gauge.
	• Defective sending unit	• If the wiring is OK and the gauge functions when grounded, replace the sending unit
All Gauges		
All gauges do not operate	• Blown fuse • Defective instrument regulator	• Replace fuse • Replace instrument voltage regulator
All gauges read low or erratically	• Defective or dirty instrument voltage regulator	• Clean contacts or replace
All gauges pegged	• Loss of ground between instrument voltage regulator and car • Defective instrument regulator	• Check ground • Replace regulator

Troubleshooting Basic Dash Gauge Problems

Problem	Cause	Solution
Warning Lights		
Light(s) do not come on when ignition is ON, but engine is not started	• Defective bulb • Defective wire • Defective sending unit	• Replace bulb • Check wire from light to sending unit • Disconnect the wire from the sending unit and ground it. Replace the sending unit if the light comes on with the ignition ON.
Light comes on with engine running	• Problem in individual system • Defective sending unit	• Check system • Check sending unit (see above)

Troubleshooting Basic Windshield Wiper Problems

Problem	Cause	Solution
Electric Wipers		
Wipers do not operate— Wiper motor heats up or hums	• Internal motor defect • Bent or damaged linkage • Arms improperly installed on linking pivots	• Replace motor • Repair or replace linkage • Position linkage in park and reinstall wiper arms
Electric Wipers		
Wipers do not operate— No current to motor	• Fuse or circuit breaker blown • Loose, open or broken wiring • Defective switch • Defective or corroded terminals • No ground circuit for motor or switch	• Replace fuse or circuit breaker • Repair wiring and connections • Replace switch • Replace or clean terminals • Repair ground circuits
Wipers do not operate— Motor runs	• Linkage disconnected or broken	• Connect wiper linkage or replace broken linkage
Vacuum Wipers		
Wipers do not operate	• Control switch or cable inoperative • Loss of engine vacuum to wiper motor (broken hoses, low engine vacuum, defective vacuum/fuel pump) • Linkage broken or disconnected • Defective wiper motor	• Repair or replace switch or cable • Check vacuum lines, engine vacuum and fuel pump • Repair linkage • Replace wiper motor
Wipers stop on engine acceleration	• Leaking vacuum hoses • Dry windshield • Oversize wiper blades • Defective vacuum/fuel pump	• Repair or replace hoses • Wet windshield with washers • Replace with proper size wiper blades • Replace pump

1982–85 WIRING DIAGRAMS

Circuit Number	Circuit Color	Circuit Name
2	Red	Feed, Battery - Unfused
3	Pink	Feed, Ign. Sw. "On & Crank" Controlled, Unfused
4	Brown	Feed, Ign. Sw. "Accsy & On" Controlled, Unfused
5	Yellow	Neutral Safety Start Sw. or Start Relay Feed
6	Purple	Starter Solenoid Feed
7	Yellow	Primary Ignition Resistance By-Pass
8	Gray	Instrument and Panel Lights (Fused No. 44 Cir.)
9	Brown	Tail, License, Park and Side Marker Lamp Feed
10	Yellow	Dimmer Sw. Feed
11	Light Green	Headlamp Feed, Hi-Beam
12	Tan	Headlamp Feed, Lo-Beam
13	Purple	Front Parking Lamps
14	Light Blue	L.H. Indicator and Front Directional Lamps
15	Dark Blue	R.H. Indicator and Front Directional Lamps
16	Purple	Directional Signal Sw., Feed From Flasher
17	White	Directional Signal Sw., Feed From Stop Sw.
18	Yellow	Stop and Directional Lamp or Directional Lamp Only - Rear L.H.
19	Dark Green	Stop and Directional Lamp or Directional Lamp Only - Rear R.H.
20	Light Blue	Stop Lamp (Only)
21	Pink	Spot Light
22	White	Direct Ground - Trailer
24	Light Green	Back Up Lamp Feed
25	Brown	Feed, Voltage Regulator Controlled
26	Dark Blue	Field Circuit (F) (Gen/Reg.)
27	Brown	Traffic Hazard Sw., Feed From Hazard Flasher
28	Black	Ground, Horn Sw. Controlled
29	Dark Green	Horn Feed
30	Pink	Fuel Gauge to Tank Unit
31	Tan	Oil Pressure, Engine
32	Yellow	Map Light Feed
33	Tan-White	Warning Light - Brake
34	Purple	Fog or Drive Lamp
35	Dark Green	Ground, Eng. Coolant Temp. Sw. or ECM Controlled (Hot)
36	Light Green	Ground, Eng. Temp. Sw. Controlled (Cold)
37	Light Green	Ground, Eng. Metal Temp. Sw. Controlled (Hot)
38	Dark Blue	Flasher Fused Feed
39	Pink-Black	Feed, Ign. Sw. "On and Crank" Controlled - Fused
40	Orange	Feed, Battery - Fused
41	Brown-White	Feed, Ign. Sw. "Accsy and On" Controlled - Fused
42	Yellow	Feed, A/C Auto Relay Controlled
43	Yellow	Radio Feed
44	Dark Green	I.P. and Lights Feed (Usually Light Sw. to Fuse)
45	Black	Marker and Clearance Lamps (Trailers)
46	Dark Blue	Rear Seat Speaker Feed From Single Radio or Right Stereo
47	Dark Blue	Auxiliary Circuit (Trailer)
48	Gray	Tail Lp. - Headlamp Sw. "On" - or Dir. Signal and Stop - Headlamp Sw. "Off" Rear L.H.
49	Dark Blue	Tail Lp. - Headlamp Sw. "On" - or Dir. Signal and Stop - Headlamp Sw. "Off" Rear R.H.
50	Brown	Feed, Ign. Sw. "On" Controlled - Fused
51	Yellow	Blower Resistor Feed - Low
52	Orange	Feed, Blow Sw. "Hi" or Selector Sw. "Max Cold" Controlled
53	Light Green	Valve Release Solenoid to Control Box
54	Dark Green	Control to Shield
55	Orange	Kick Down Solenoid Feed
56	Tan	Amplifier to Transducer
57	Orange	L.H. Cornering Lamp Feed
58	Black	R.H. Cornering Lamp Feed
59	Dark Green	Compressor Feed
60	Orange-Black	Feed, Battery, Circuit Breaker Protected
61	Yellow	Ground, Resistive, Auto A/C Amb. Sensor Controlled
62	Light Green	Ground, Resistive, Auto A/C Feed Back Pot Conrolled
63	Tan	Feed, Blower Sw. "Medium 1" Controlled
64	Brown	Blower Sw. Feed From A/C Selector Sw.
65	Purple	Blower Motor Feed
66	Light Green	Feed, A/C Selector Sw. Controlled (Comp. Ct.)
67	Light Blue	Feed, A/C Freon Press, Cut-Out Sw. Controlled

1982–85 WIRING DIAGRAMS (CONT.)

ELECTRICAL CIRCUIT IDENTIFICATION FOR WIRING DIAGRAMS (Cont'd)

Circuit Number	Circuit Color	Circuit Name
68	Yellow-Black	Ground, Resistive, Low Coolant Probe Controlled
69	Gray	Ground Low Coolant Module Controlled
70	Pink	Feed, Relay Controlled, Ign. Sw. Controlled
71	Black	Ground, A/C Selector Sw. "Def" Controlled
72	Light Blue	Feed, Blower Sw. "Medium 2" Controlled
73	Purple-White	Feed, Blower Sw. "Medium 3" Controlled
74	Light Green	Feed to Throttle Switch
75	Dark Blue	Feed, Ign. Sw. "On and Crank" Controlled - Fused
76	Pink	Feed, Ign. Sw. Controlled
78	Light Blue	Electric Choke Feed
80	Light Green	Ground Key Warning Buzzer
81	Nat. White	Electric Remote Mirror, Right
82	Light Blue	Electric Remote Mirror, Left
83	Dark Green	Feed, Cruise Engage Sw. "Retard" Controlled
84	Dark Blue	Feed, Cruise Engage Sw. "Engage" Controlled
85	White	Ground, Cruise Indicator Regulator Controlled
86	Brown	Feed, Cruise Brake Release Sw. Controlled
87	Gray-Black	Feed, Resume Solenoid, Brake Switch Controlled
88	Yellow	Electric Remote Mirror, Up
89	Light Green	Electric Remote Mirror, Down
90	Pink	Feed, Cutout Sw. Controlled, Cir. Brkr. Protected
91	Gray	Windshield Wiper - Low
92	Purple	Windshield Wiper - Hi
93	White	Windshield Wiper Motor Feed
94	Pink	Windshield Washer Sw. to Washer
95	Dark Green	Ground, Pulse Wiper Sw. Controlled
96	Brown	Feed, Pulse Wiper Rheostat Sw. Controlled
97	Light Blue	Windshield Wiper, Pulse Low
98	Orange	Feed, Dynamic Break, "B-Plus" Switch Wiper Motor
99	Black-White	Windshield Washer Low Fluid
101	Dark Blue	Resistor Output to Blower Relay
102	White	SL Alternator - Regulator Sensing Circuit
105	Black	Ammeter - Generator
106	Gray	Ammeter - Battery

Circuit Number	Circuit Color	Circuit Name
107	Dark Blue	Over Speed Warning Light
111	Black	Ground, Anti-Ski Low Air Sw. Controlled
112	Dark Green	Telltale Temperature Gauge (Hot)
115	Light Blue	Speaker Return, RT rr Stereo
116	Yellow	Speaker Return, LF rr Stereo
117	Dark Green	Speaker Return, RT Frt. Stereo
118	Gray	Speaker Return, LF Frt. Stereo
119	White	Generator (Alternator) to Regulator
120	Purple	Electric Fuel Pump Feed
121	White	Tachometer to Coil
125	Yellow	Door Jamb Switch
126	Black	Seat Back Lock Feed
130	Brown-White	Generator (Alternator) Ext. Resist. 2 Ohms/Foot
131	Black-Pink	Generator (Alternator) Ext. Resist. 1 Ohm/Foot
132	White	Ground, Fuel Economy Sw. Controlled, Amber Telltale
133	Yellow	Ground, Fuel Economy Sw. Controlled, Grn. Telltale
135	Dark Green White	Ground, Resistive, Temp. Gauge Sensor Controlled
136	Dark Blue	Ground, Vacuum Switch Controlled, Turbo Boost Telltale
137	Natural-White	Ground, Vacuum Switch Controlled, Turbo Boost Economy Telltale
139	Pink-Black	Feed, Ign. Sw. "On and Crank" Controlled - Fused
140	Orange	Feed, Battery - Fused
141	Brown-White	Feed, Ign. Sw., "Accsy and On" Controlled
142	Black	Rr Compartment Lid Lock Release
143	Pink	Feed Radio Sw. "On" Controlled
144	Yellow	Feed to Pwr Ant Sw.
145	Dark Green	Feed, Pwr Ant Up, Relay Controlled
146	Dark Green	Ground, Trunk Release Tell-Tale
150	Black	Ground Circuit - Direct
151	Black	Ground Circuit - Direct
152	Black	Ground Circuit - Direct
153	Black	Ground Circuit - Direct
154	Black	Ground Circuit - Direct
155	Black	Ground Circuit - Direct

1982–85 WIRING DIAGRAMS (CONT.)

ELECTRICAL CIRCUIT IDENTIFICATION FOR WIRING DIAGRAMS (Cont'd)

Circuit Number	Circuit Color	Circuit Name
156	White	Ground Circuit - Sw. Controlled Body Interior Lamps - Such as Dome, Courtesy, Map, Warning, etc.
157	Gray	Ground Circuit - Sw. Controlled - Body Interior Lamps - Such as Dome, Courtesy, Map, Warning etc.
158	Black-Orange	Ground Circuit - Sw. Controlled - Body Interior Lamps - Such as Dome, Courtesy, Map, Warning etc.
159	Tan	Ground, Key Warning Buzzer
160	White	Power Antenna Down
161	Black	Power Antenna Up
162	Gray	Power Top - Up
163	Purple	Power Top - Down
164	Dark Blue	Window Control LF Up
165	Brown	Window Control LF Down
166	Dark Blue-White	Window Control RF Up
167	Tan	Window Control RF Down
168	Dark Green	Window Control LR Up
169	Purple	Window Control LR Down
170	Light Green	Window Control RR Up
171	Purple-White	Window Control RR Down
172	Light Green	Vent Control LF Close
173	Yellow	Vent Control LF Open
174	Dark Green	Vent Control RF Close
175	Purple	Vent Control RF Open
176	Dark Green	Power Seat Fore
177	Yellow	Power Seat Aft or Recline
178	Dark Green	Power Seat - 6-Way Fore and Aft
179	Tan	Power Seat - 6-Way Solenoid - Rear - Up and Down
180	Light Green	Power Seat - 6-Way Solenoid - Front - Up and Down
181	Light Blue	Power - Solenoid - Fore and Aft
182	Yellow	Power Seat - 6-Way - Aft and Down
183	Light Blue	Tailgate or Center Partition Window Up
184	Tan-White	Tailgate or Center Partition Window Down
185	Tan	Vent Control LR Open
186	Gray	Vent Control LR Close
187	Dark Blue	Vent Control RR Open
188	Light Blue	Vent Control RR Close
189	Dark Green	Power Seat - 4-Way - Fore and Down

Circuit Number	Circuit Color	Circuit Name
190	Yellow	Power Seat - 4-Way - Aft and Up
191	Light Green	Power Seat - 4-Way Solenoid - Up and Down
192	Purple	Defogger - Hi or Single Speed
193	Purple-White	Defogger - Low Speed - 0.38 Ohms per foot
194	Black	Electric Door Lock - Unlock
195	Light Blue	Electric Door Lock - Lock
198	Light Green Black	Ground, Resistive, A/C In-Car Sensor Controlled
199	Brown	Rear Seat Speaker - Feed from Radio Left Stereo
200	Light Green	Front Speaker - Feed from Radio Single or Right Stereo
201	Tan	Front Speaker - Feed from Radio Left Stereo
202	Black	Ground, Compressor over Heat Sw. Controlled
203	Light Blue	Rear A/C Potentiometer Feed
204	Dark Blue	Thermal Limiter Feed
205	White-Black	Seat Belt Seat Sensor to Belt Retractor (Grd)
206	Dark Blue	Neutral Start Sw. to Buzzer and Lamp
207	Yellow	Seat Sensor to Neutral Start Sw. (Lamp and Buzzer Grd)
208	Gray	Sw. Controlled Ground (TCS)
209	Purple	Park Brake Warning Lamp
210	White	Power Seat - 6-Way - Fore and Down - "A" Body
211	Dark Blue	Power Seat - 6-Way - Aft and Up - "A" Body
212	Yellow-Black Stripe	LH Seat Sensor
213	Dark Blue	Center Seat Sensor
214	Gray	RH Seat Sensor
215	Tan-Black	LH Sw.
216	Dark Blue-White	Center Buckle Sw. (Feed)
217	Gray-White	RH Sw.
218	Dark Green	Interlock Relay - Ground (Provided by Electronics)
219	Light Green-Black	Starter Interlock Controlled Starter Feed
220	Yellow	Starter Interlock Buz and Lp Feed
221	Brown	Passenger Initiator Feed, Low Level, IR
222	Dark Blue	Passenger Initiator Return, Low Level, IR

1982–85 WIRING DIAGRAMS (CONT.)

ELECTRICAL CIRCUIT IDENTIFICATION FOR WIRING DIAGRAMS (Cont'd)

Circuit Number	Circuit Color	Circuit Name
223	Light Blue	Sensor Detector Hi Return, Low Level, IR
224	Light Green	Sensor Detector Lo Feed, Lo Feed, Low Level, IR
225	Dark Green	Warning Lamp Ground IR
226	Orange	Warning Lamp Sensor
227	Tan	Recorder to Sensor Power Feed
228	Yellow	Warning Lamp Feed
229	Pink	Sensor Detector Hi Feed, Lo Level IR
230	Pink	Recorder Power Feed
231	Orange	Driver Initiator Feed, IR
232	White	Driver Initiator Return, IR
233	Dark Green	Hi Level Actuation Passenger (Inactive)
234	Yellow	IR Feed, Ign. Sw. Controlled, Unfused
235	Yellow	Sensor Detector Hi Feed - Hi Level IR
236	Gray	Sensor Detector Hi Return - Hi Level IR
237	Yellow	Feed, Belt Warn Timer Controlled (Timed 39 Ct.)
238	Black	Seat Belt Warn System - Buzzer Ground to Belt Assy Sw.
239	Pink-Black	Feed, Ign. Sw. "On & Crank" Controlled - Fused
240	Orange	Feed, Battery - Fused
241	Purple	Sensor Detector Lo Feed, Hi Level, IR
242	Tan	Feed, Throttle Control Spark Valve Controlled
243	Black-White	Feed, Drive Selector Sw. Controlled
244	Purple	Feed, LT F/D Solenoid Relay Controlled
245	Dark Blue	Feed, RT F/D Solenoid Relay Controlled
246	Dark Green	Feed, ADL Lock Relay Coil
247	Brown	Feed, to A/C Shut-Off Relay
248	Dark Blue	Feed, to A/C Compressor Harn Relay Controlled
249	Dark Green	Feed, From A/C Harn
250	Brown	Feed, Ign. Sw. on Controlled, Fused
251	Orange	Passenger Initiator Feed
252	Yellow	Ground, ADL Module Unlock Output Controlled
253	Dark Brown	Ground, ADL Module Lock Output Controlled
254	Light Green	Ground, ADL LT Unlock Relay Coil

Circuit Number	Circuit Color	Circuit Name
255	Yellow	Ground, ADL RT Unlock Relay Coil
256	Dark Blue	Ground, Module Controlled, Lamp Out Indicator
257	Brown	Ground, A/C Press, Sw. Controlled
258	White	Passenger Initiator Return Hi Level, IR
259	Purple	IR Crank Start Signal - Fused 6 Cir.
260	Black	Theft Deterrent - Hood Sw.
261	Yellow	Theft Deterrent - Alarm Arm
262	Light Green	Theft Deterrent - Key - Door Unlock and Alarm Disarm
263	Light Blue	Theft Deterrent - Alarm
264	Dark Green	Theft Deterrent - Arm Indication
265	Black-White	Theft Deterrent - Alarm Output
266	Pink	Theft Deterrent - Alarm Arm Abort
267	Dark Green	Pwr Seat - Fore and Up Recliner
268	Yellow	Pwr Seat - Aft and Down Recliner
269	Light Green	Pwr Seat - Sol Up and Down Recliner
270	Black-Yellow	Feed, Amplifier to Potentiometer
271	Purple	Ground, Potentiometer Controlled
272	Light Green	Feed, Potentiometer Rheostat Controlled
273	Orange	Feed, Hdlp Sw. to Amplifier, Hdlp Sw. Controlled
274	Dark Green-White	Feed, Hdlp Sw. to Amplifier
275	Light Green	Feed, Neut. Saf. Start Sw. "Park" Controlled
276	Light Green	Recl. Mtr. Feed, Power St. Fwd.
277	Light Blue	Recl. Mtr. Feed, Power St. Recliner
278	White	Amplifier to Photocell
279	Black	Headlamp Sw. to Photocell
280	Pink	Feed, P.M. Motor Up Cycle (Deck Lid Pull Down)
281	White	Ground, Relay Coil Down Cycle (Deck Lid Pull Down)
282	Yellow	Power Seat, Rear Vert Up - Motor
283	Light Blue	Power Seat, Rear Vert Down - Motor
284	Light Green	Power Seat, Aft Motor
285	Tan	Power Seat, Fore Motor
286	Dark Green	Power Seat, Front Vert Up - Motor
287	Dark Blue	Power Seat, Front Vert Down - Motor

1982–85 WIRING DIAGRAMS (CONT.)

ELECTRICAL CIRCUIT IDENTIFICATION FOR WIRING DIAGRAMS (Cont'd)

Circuit Number	Circuit Color	Circuit Name
288	Yellow-Black	Power Seat, Rear Vert Up Relay
289	Light Blue-Black	Power Seat, Rear Vert Down Relay
290	Light Green-Black	Power Seat, Aft Relay
291	Dark Blue	Ground, Heated Glass Timer, On-Off Sw. Controlled
292	Light Blue	Feed, Heated Glass Timer, On-Off Sw. Controlled
293	Purple-White	Feed, Heated Glass Timer Controlled
294	Tan	Door Lock Motor - Unlock
295	Gray	Door Lock Motor - Lock
296	Brown	Power Seat, Fore Relay
297	Gray	Power Seat, Front Vert Up Relay
298	Purple	Power Seat, Front Vert Down Relay
300	Orange	Feed, Ign. Sw., "On" Controlled - Unfused
318	Yellow-Black Stripe	Relay Activated Left Directional Lamp
319	Dark Green-White	Relay Activated Right Directional Lamp
339	Pink-Black	Feed, Ign. Sw. On and Crank Controlled Fused
340	Orange	Feed, Battery - Fused
350	Pink-White	Feed, Ign. Sw. "On" Controlled - Fused
351	Dark Blue	Feed, Inverter to Opera Lamp
352	White	Opera Lamp to Inverter Return
370	Pink	Feed, Avl
382	Light Blue-Black	Low Vacuum Switch to Four Wheel Drive Relay
383	Light Blue	Convert Clutch Release Sw. to Vac. Sw.
384	Light Green	Vac. Sw. to Transmission Sw. Sol
385	Purple	Hi Vac Sw. to Transmission Sw. Sol
386	Yellow	Exhaust Gas Recirculation Bleed Solenoid to Torque Converter Clutch Pressure Switch
387	Orange	Torque Converter Clutch Pressure Switch to Transmission Solenoid
390	Tan	Feed to Side Marker and License Lamp - Export Only
391	Gray	Rear Window Wiper Low
392	Dark Green	Feed, Rear Window Wiper Switch to Washer
393	White	Feed, Rear Window Wiper
394	Light Green Black	Ground, LT F/D Remote Handle Sw. Controlled

Circuit Number	Circuit Color	Circuit Name
395	Light Blue	Ground, RT F/D Remote Handle Sw. Controlled
402	Light Green	Feed, Electronic Cruise Control Valve
403	Dark Blue	Feed, Electronic Cruise Shut-Off Valve
404	Light Green	EST Pickup Coil to HEI Module, High
405	White	EST Pickup Coil to HEI Module, Low
406	White-Green	ESC Module to HEI Module, Signal Lead
407	Black	Emergency Signal Lead, ECM to HEI Module
408	Tan-White	ECM to ESC Bypass
410	Yellow	ECM to Coolant Temp Sensor
411	Light Blue	ECM to Fuel Metering Sol
412	Purple	O_2 Sensor Sig
413	Tan	O_2 Sensor Low
414	Pink	O_2 Sensor Heater High
415	Light Green	ECM to Enrichment Sw.
416	Gray	ECM 5V Reference Voltage
417	Dark Blue	ECM to Throttle Position Sensor Signal
418	Brown	ECM to Adaptive Sw.
419	Brown-White	ECM to Check Eng Lp
420	Purple	ECM to Break Sw.
421	Dark Blue-White	ECM to Cold Start Program Modifier
422	Tan-Black	ECM to TCC Solenoid
423	White	EST Signal
424	Tan-Black	EST Bypass
425	Light Blue	ECM to ISC-Motor Extend
426	Dark Blue	ECM to ESC-Motor Retract
427	Pink	ECM to ISC-Sw.
428	Dark Green-Yellow	ECM to Canister Purge
429	Black-Pink	ECM to Air Control Solenoid
430	Purple-White	ECM Ref Pulse High
431	Light Green-Black	8V Ref Voltage
432	Light Green	ECM to Map Sig
433	Gray-Black	ECM to Baro Sig
434	Orange-Black	ECM to Neutral Park Sw
435	Gray	Electronic Control Module to Exhaust Gas Recirculation Solenoid
436	Brown	ECM to Air Switch Solenoid
437	Brown	ECM to Vehicle Speed Sensor
438	Dark Green-White	ECM to High Gear Switch

1982–85 WIRING DIAGRAMS (CONT.)

ELECTRICAL CIRCUIT IDENTIFICATION FOR WIRING DIAGRAMS (Cont'd)

Circuit Number	Circuit Color	Circuit Name
439	Pink-Black	Feed Ign. Sw. "On & Crank" Controlled - Fused
440	Orange	Feed, Battery - Fused
441	Light Blue-Red	Electronic Control Module to Idle Air Control Coil A, High
442	Light Blue-Black	Electronic Control Module to Idle Air Control, Coil A, Low
443	Light Green-Red	Electronic Control Module to Idle Air Control, Coil B, High
444	Light Green-Black	Electronic Control Module to Idle Air Control, Coil B, Low
450	Black-White	CLCC ECM Power Grd
451	White-Black	Diagnostic Enable
452	Black	Low Level Ground
453	Black-Red	EST Ref Pulse Low
454	Black-White	Critical Ground Circuit
460	Black-Orange	Feed, Battery Circuit Breaker Protected
461	Orange	IMC to ECC, Serial Data for MPG or Diagnostics
462	Pink-Black	Ground, IMC, Set Timing
463	Black-Orange	IMC to Trip Computer Signal, Fuel Flow Data (Injector on Time)
464	Tan-Black	MPG Reset Signal
465	Dark Green-White	Feed, Electric Fuel
466	Gray	IMC to Trip Computer, RPM Data
467	Light Blue	Low Side of Injector "A" IMC Controlled
468	Light Green	Low Side of Injector "B" IMC Controlled
469	Black-Orange	Map Return, Low Level Ground
470	Black	Coolant Temp and Manifold Temp Return, Low Level Grd
471	Pink-Black	Baro Reference Voltage, 5V
472	Tan	Manifold Air Temp Sig
473	Black-Light Blue	Baro Return, Low Level Ground
474	Gray	Throttle Position Sensor Excitation, 5V
475	Pink-White	Map Reference Voltage, 5V
476	Black-Pink	Throttle Position Sensor Return, Low Level Grd
477	Brown	MPG Request Signal
478	Purple	Fuel Economy Indicator (Grn), IMC Controlled
479	Light Green-Black	Fuel Economy Indicator (Amber), IMC Controlled
480	Orange	Feed, IMC Battery Controlled, Fused
481	Red	Feed, for Injector "A" Fused
482	White	Feed, for Injector "B" Fused
483	Green	ESC Reference Pulse High
484	White	ESC Reference Pulse Low
485	Black	ESC Signal
486	Brown	ESC Distributor Grd
496	Dark Blue	ESC Denotation Sensor Input
500	Black-White	Module - PTC, Ground Plane
501	Purple	Sensor, Secondary PTC
502	Gray	Sensor, Primary PTC
503	Orange	Glow Plug, Feed or Sensor
504	Brown-White	Feed, Voltage Regulator Control (Diode Isolated)
505	Yellow	Feed, Glow Plug Relay
506	Light Blue	Return, Glow Plug Relay
507	Dark Blue	Wait Lamp
508	Yellow-Black	Switched Grd for "Water-in-Tank" Indicator
509	Orange-Black	Glow Plug, Feed or Sense, Passenger Side
610	Tan	Power Seat - 6-Way - Fore and Down Relay to Motor
611	Light Blue	Power Seat - 6-Way - Aft and Up, Relay to Motor
618	Yellow-Black	Feed, Lt Side Trailer and Direction
619	Green-White	Feed, Rt Side Trailer and Direction
666	Dark Blue	Wdo Control Rf Up - Passenger Sw.
667	Brown	Wdo Control Rf Down - Passenger Sw.
668	Dark Blue	Wdo Control Lr Up - Lr Sw.
669	Brown	Wdo Control Lr Down - Lr Sw.
670	Dark Blue	Wdo Control RR Up - RR Sw.
671	Brown	Wdo Control RR Down - RR Sw.
756	Dark Green-White	Feed, Vac Sol Controlled (For Electronic Distributor)
801	Brown	Feed, EFI Battery Controlled, Fusible Link Protected
804	Purple	Feed, EFI, Ign. Sw. "Crank" Controlled, Fusible Link Protected
807	Purple	Feed, EFI Battery Controlled, Fused
808	Dark Blue	Feed, EFI Module Fast Idle Valve Output and 3 Circuit Controlled - Fused
810	Tan	Feed, Distributor Electronics Controlled
811	White	Feed, EFI Module Group Two Injector Output Controlled Fusible Link Protected
812	Pink	Feed, EFI Module Group One Injector Output Controlled Fusible Link Protected

1982–85 WIRING DIAGRAMS (CONT.)

ELECTRICAL CIRCUIT IDENTIFICATION FOR WIRING DIAGRAMS (Cont'd)

Circuit Number	Circuit Color	Circuit Name
813	White	Feed, EFI Distributor Trigger and 815 Circuit Controlled, Fused
814	Yellow	Feed, EFI Distributor Trigger and 815 Circuit Controlled, Fused
815	Black	Feed, EFI Module Distributor Trigger Output Controlled, Fused
816	Pink	Accelerator Enrichment Input #2
817	Tan	Accelerator Enrichment Input #1
818	Light Green	Accelerator Enrichment Sw. Supply Voltage
819	Black-White	Clossed Throttle Sw.
820	Orange	Wide Open Throttle Switch

Circuit Number	Circuit Color	Circuit Name
821	Dark Green	Ground, EFI Module Coolant Temp. Sensor Output Controlled
822	Dark Blue	Ground Resistive, Coolant Temp. Sensor Controlled
823	Gray	Ground, EFI Module Air Temp. Sensor Output Controlled
824	Orange	Ground, Resistive Air Temp. Sensor Controlled
827	Dark Green	Feed, EFI Module Elec Fuel Pump Output Controlled - Fused
828	Gray	Feed, EFI, Ign. Sw. "On & Crank" Controlled Fused
831	Brown	Feed, EFI Module EGR Solenoid Output Controlled, Fused

1987 S/T TRUCK

SECTION	DESCRIPTION
	FUSE BLOCK DETAILS
1	FORWARD LAMP
2	ENGINE LN8 L4 W/TBI
3	ENGINE C60&MB2&NA5/NA6
4	I/P ALL EXCEPT BLAZER W/GAGES
5	I/P ALL EXCEPT BLAZER
6	I/P BLAZER ONLY
7	I/P BLAZER W/GAGES
8	INSTRUMENT CLUSTER W/O GAGES INSTRUMENT CLUSTER W/GAGES TACHOMETER U16
9	CRUISE CONTROL AUTOMATIC K34
10	CRUISE CONTROL MANUAL K34
11	AIR CONDITIONING C60&LL2
12	AIR CONDITIONING C60&LN8
13	RADIO EQUIPMENT STEREO UM2/UM3/U58 HEATER HARNESS

SECTION	DESCRIPTION
14	ASH TRAY LAMP I/P COMPT BOX LAMP 4 WHEEL DRIVE INDICATOR
15	POWER WINDOWS & POWER LOCKS A31-AU3
16	POWER WINDOWS A31
17	POWER LOCKS AU3
18	DOME LAMP C91 ST000(03)
19	CARGO LAMP UF2
20	LIFT GATE RELEASE AUTO TRANS CONV CLUTCH FEED MD8
21	HEATED LIFTGATE C49
22	REAR LAMP & BODY ALL BODIES EXCEPT BLAZER
23	REAR LAMP & BODY W/BLAZER
24	TRAILER WIRING W/BLAZER U89
25	TRAILER WIRING U89 03-53
26	HEAVY DUTY TRAILERING UY7

1986–87 WIRING DIAGRAMS (CONT.)

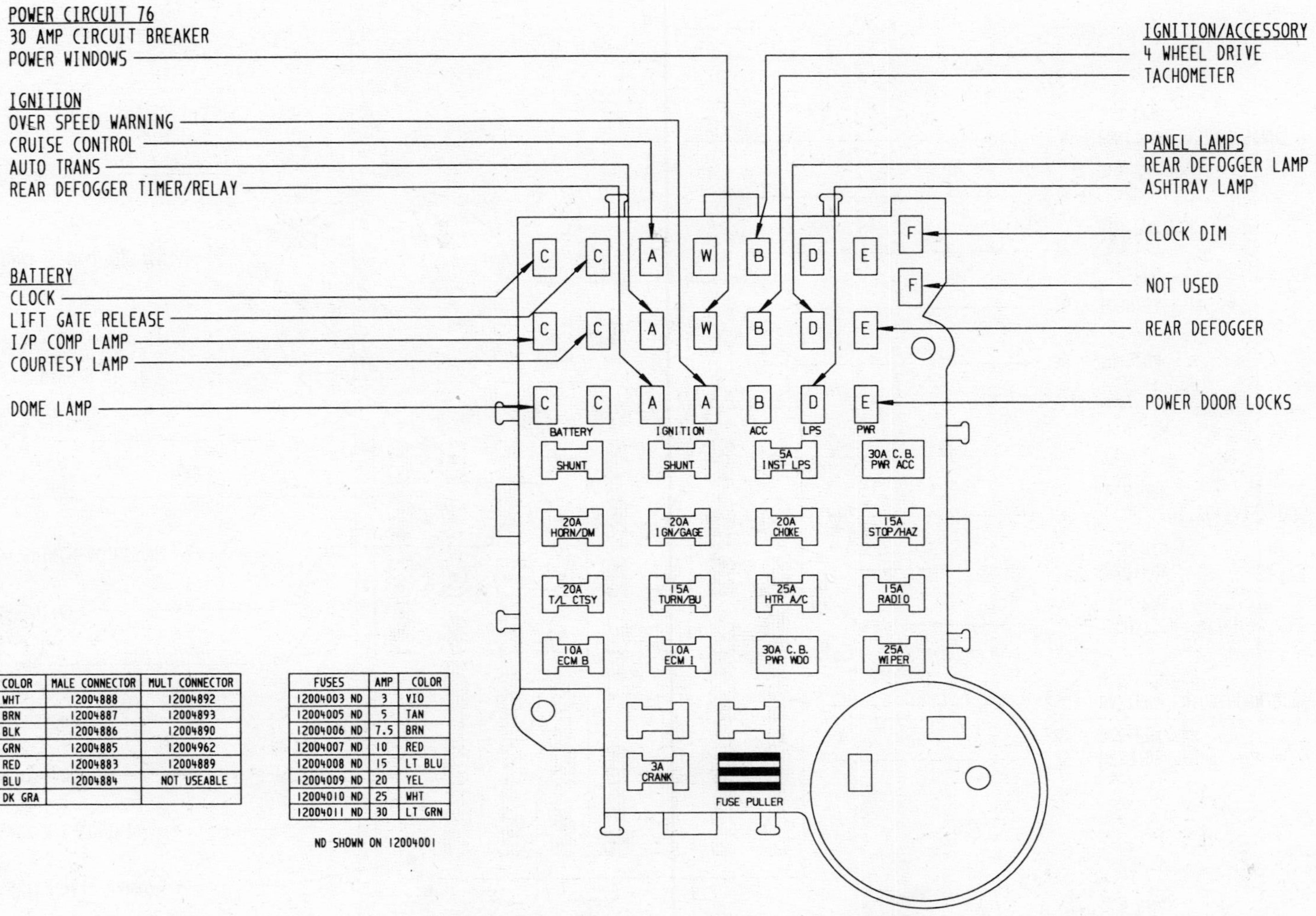
POWER CIRCUIT 76
30 AMP CIRCUIT BREAKER
POWER WINDOWS
IGNITION
OVER SPEED WARNING
CRUISE CONTROL
AUTO TRANS
REAR DEFOGGER TIMER/RELAY
BATTERY
CLOCK
LIFT GATE RELEASE
I/P COMP LAMP
COURTESY LAMP
DOME LAMP
IGNITION/ACCESSORY
4 WHEEL DRIVE
TACHOMETER
PANEL LAMPS
REAR DEFOGGER LAMP
ASHTRAY LAMP
CLOCK DIM
NOT USED
REAR DEFOGGER
POWER DOOR LOCKS
BATTERY
IGNITION
ACC
LPS
PWR
SHUNT
SHUNT
5A INST LPS
30A C.B. PWR ACC
20A HORN/DM
20A IGN/GAGE
20A CHOKE
15A STOP/HAZ
20A T/L CTSY
15A TURN/BU
25A HTR A/C
15A RADIO
10A ECM B
10A ECM I
30A C.B. PWR WDO
25A WIPER
3A CRANK
FUSE PULLER

	COLOR	MALE CONNECTOR	MULT CONNECTOR
A	WHT	12004888	12004892
B	BRN	12004887	12004893
C	BLK	12004886	12004890
D	GRN	12004885	12004962
E	RED	12004883	12004889
W	BLU	12004884	NOT USEABLE
F	DK GRA		

FUSES	AMP	COLOR
12004003 ND	3	VIO
12004005 ND	5	TAN
12004006 ND	7.5	BRN
12004007 ND	10	RED
12004008 ND	15	LT BLU
12004009 ND	20	YEL
12004010 ND	25	WHT
12004011 ND	30	LT GRN

ND SHOWN ON 12004001

12052632 FUSE BLOCK

1986–87 WIRING DIAGRAMS (CONT.)

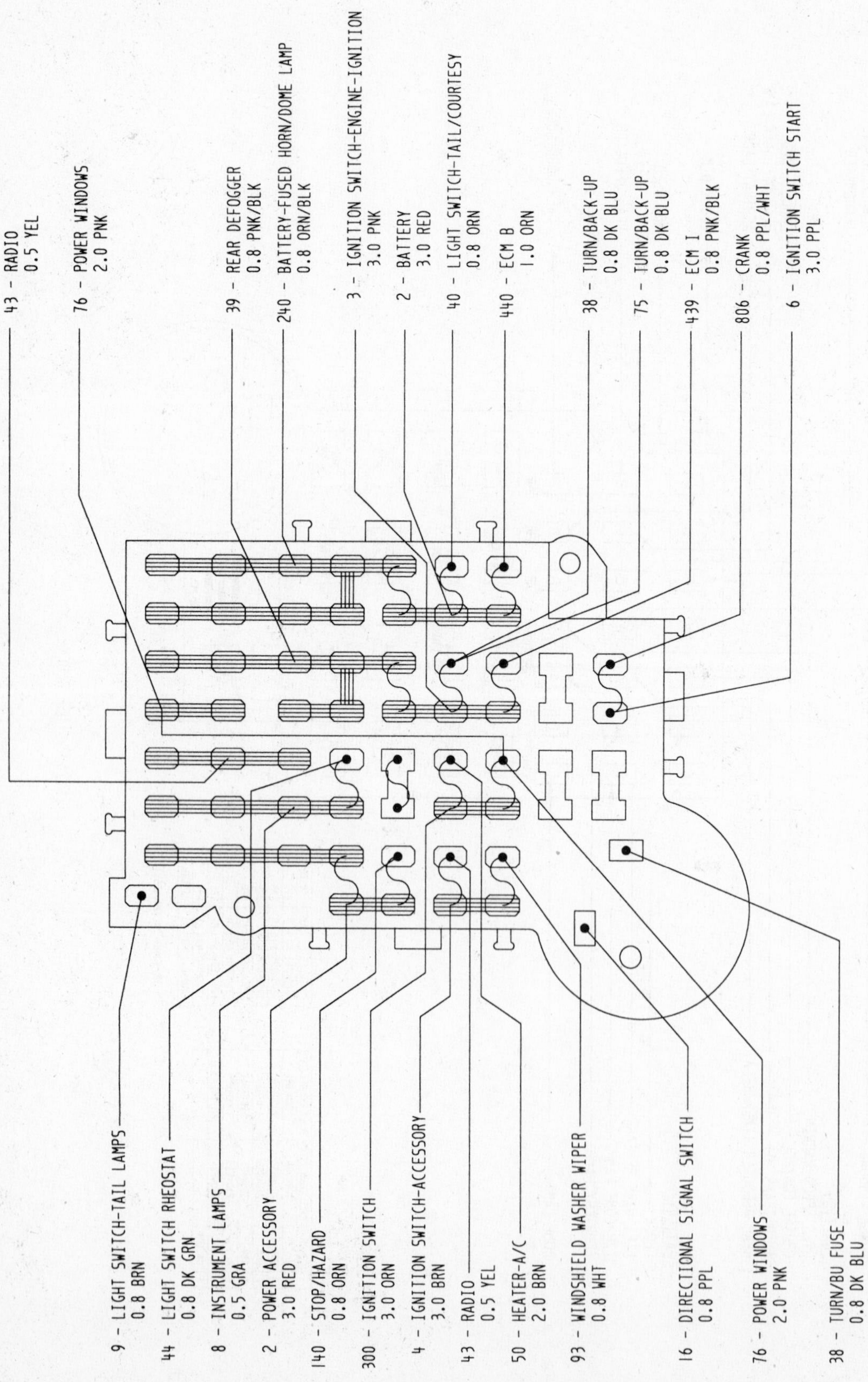
43 - RADIO 0.5 YEL
76 - POWER WINDOWS 2.0 PNK
39 - REAR DEFOGGER 0.8 PNK/BLK
240 - BATTERY-FUSED HORN/DOME LAMP 0.8 ORN/BLK
3 - IGNITION SWITCH-ENGINE-IGNITION 3.0 PNK
2 - BATTERY 3.0 RED
40 - LIGHT SWITCH-TAIL/COURTESY 0.8 ORN
440 - ECM B 1.0 ORN
38 - TURN/BACK-UP 0.8 DK BLU
75 - TURN/BACK-UP 0.8 DK BLU
439 - ECM I 0.8 PNK/BLK
806 - CRANK 0.8 PPL/WHT
6 - IGNITION SWITCH START 3.0 PPL
9 - LIGHT SWITCH-TAIL LAMPS 0.8 BRN
44 - LIGHT SWITCH RHEOSTAT 0.8 DK GRN
8 - INSTRUMENT LAMPS 0.5 GRA
2 - POWER ACCESSORY 3.0 RED
140 - STOP/HAZARD 0.8 ORN
300 - IGNITION SWITCH 3.0 ORN
4 - IGNITION SWITCH-ACCESSORY 3.0 BRN
43 - RADIO 0.5 YEL
50 - HEATER-A/C 2.0 BRN
93 - WINDSHIELD WASHER WIPER 0.8 WHT
16 - DIRECTIONAL SIGNAL SWITCH 0.8 PPL
76 - POWER WINDOWS 2.0 PNK
38 - TURN/BU FUSE 0.8 DK BLU

S/T TRUCK FUSE BLOCK

1986–87 WIRING DIAGRAMS

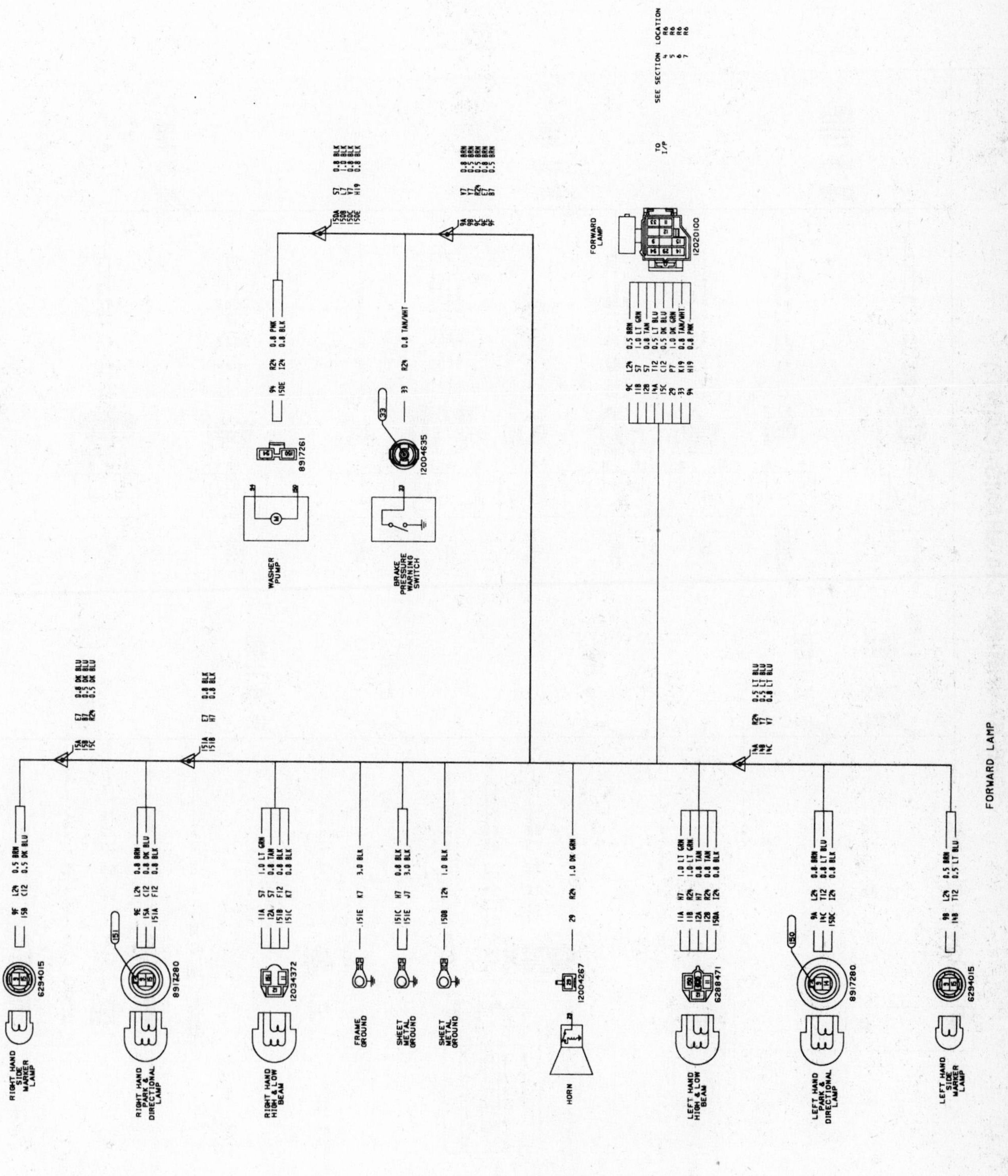
RIGHT HAND SIDE MARKER LAMP
RIGHT HAND PARK & DIRECTIONAL LAMP
RIGHT HAND HIGH & LOW BEAM
FRAME GROUND
SHEET METAL GROUND
SHEET METAL GROUND
HORN
LEFT HAND HIGH & LOW BEAM
LEFT HAND PARK & DIRECTIONAL LAMP
LEFT HAND SIDE MARKER LAMP
WASHER PUMP
BRAKE PRESSURE WARNING SWITCH
FORWARD LAMP
TO I/P
SEE SECTION LOCATION
FORWARD LAMP

1986–87 WIRING DIAGRAMS (CONT.)

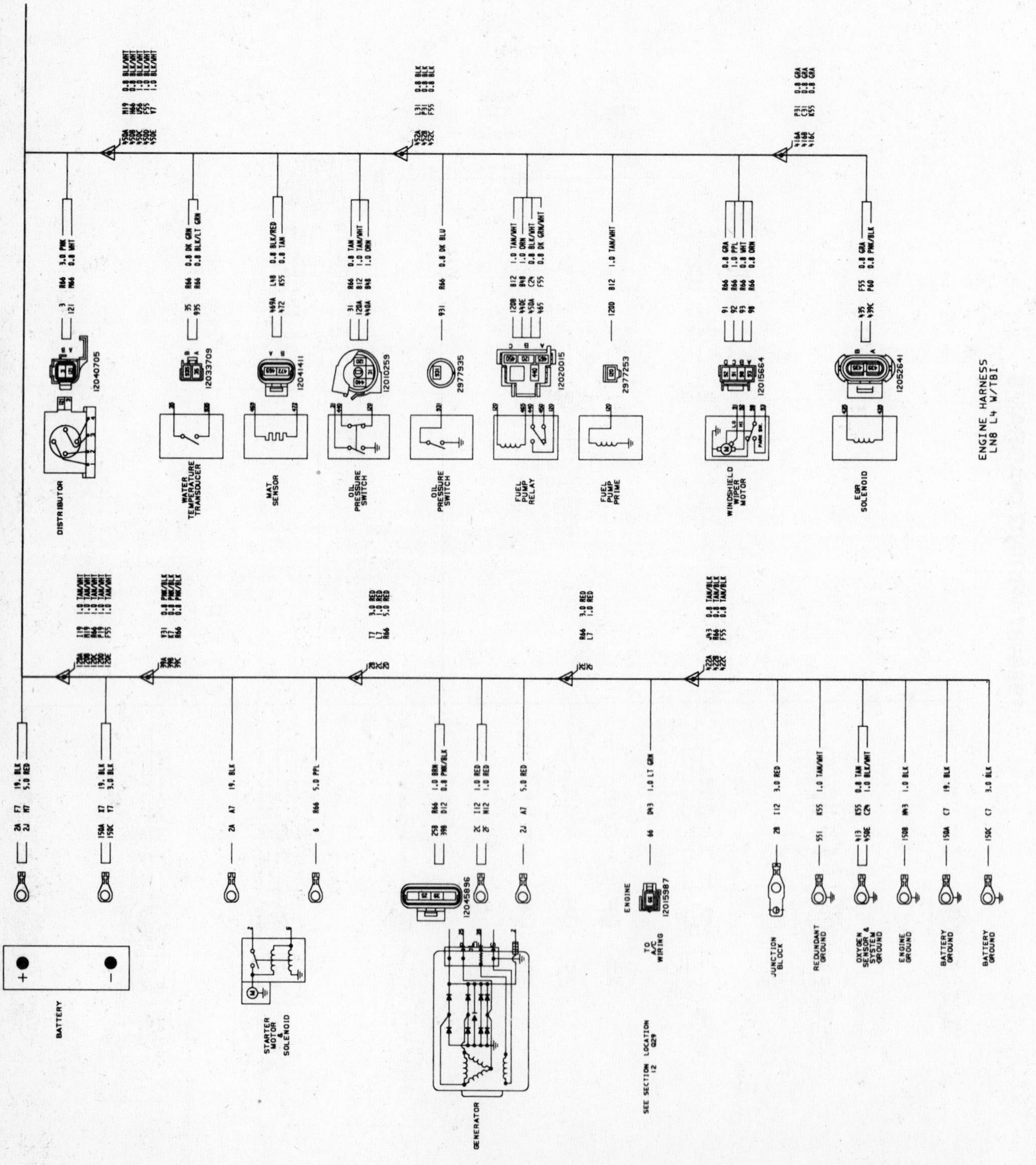

BATTERY
STARTER MOTOR & SOLENOID
12045896
GENERATOR
ENGINE
12015987
TO A/C WIRING
SEE SECTION 12 LOCATION G29
JUNCTION BLOCK
REDUNDANT GROUND
OXYGEN SENSOR & SYSTEM GROUND
ENGINE GROUND
BATTERY GROUND
BATTERY GROUND
12040705
DISTRIBUTOR
12033709
WATER TEMPERATURE TRANSDUCER
12041411
MAT SENSOR
12010259
OIL PRESSURE SWITCH
2977935
OIL PRESSURE SWITCH
12020015
FUEL PUMP RELAY
2977253
FUEL PUMP PRIME
12015664
WINDSHIELD WIPER MOTOR
12052641
EGR SOLENOID
ENGINE HARNESS
LN8 L4 W/TBI

1986–87 WIRING DIAGRAMS (CONT.)

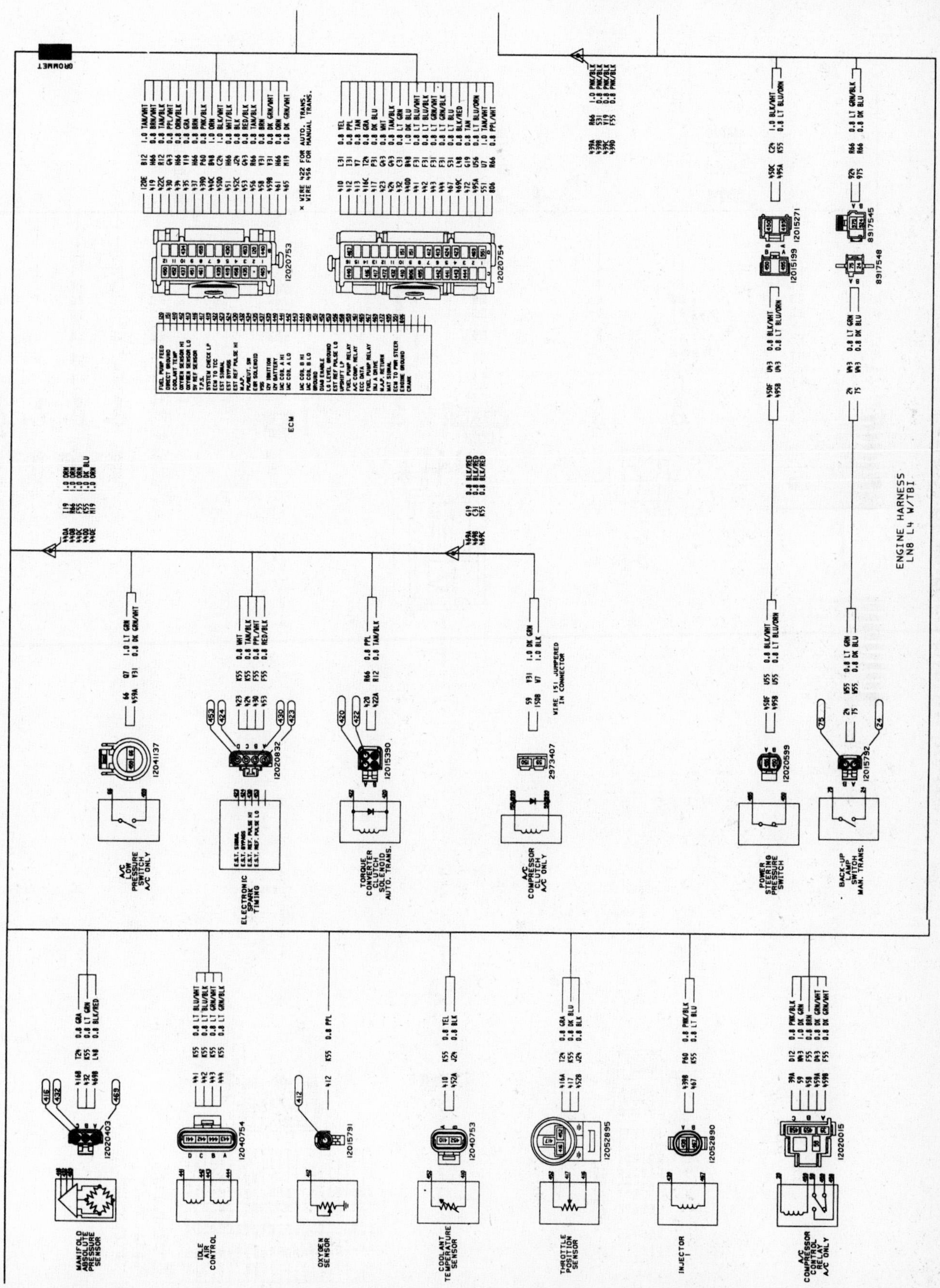

GROMMET
ECM
ENGINE HARNESS LN8 L4 W/TBI
A/C LOW PRESSURE SWITCH A/C ONLY
ELECTRONIC SPARK TIMING
TORQUE CONVERTER CLUTCH SOLENOID AUTO. TRANS.
A/C COMPRESSOR CLUTCH A/C ONLY
POWER STEERING PRESSURE SWITCH
BACK-UP LAMP SWITCH MAN. TRANS.
MANIFOLD ABSOLUTE PRESSURE SENSOR
IDLE AIR CONTROL
OXYGEN SENSOR
COOLANT TEMPERATURE SENSOR
THROTTLE POSITION SENSOR
INJECTOR
A/C COMPRESSOR CONTROL RELAY A/C ONLY
WIRE 151 JUMPERED IN CONNECTOR

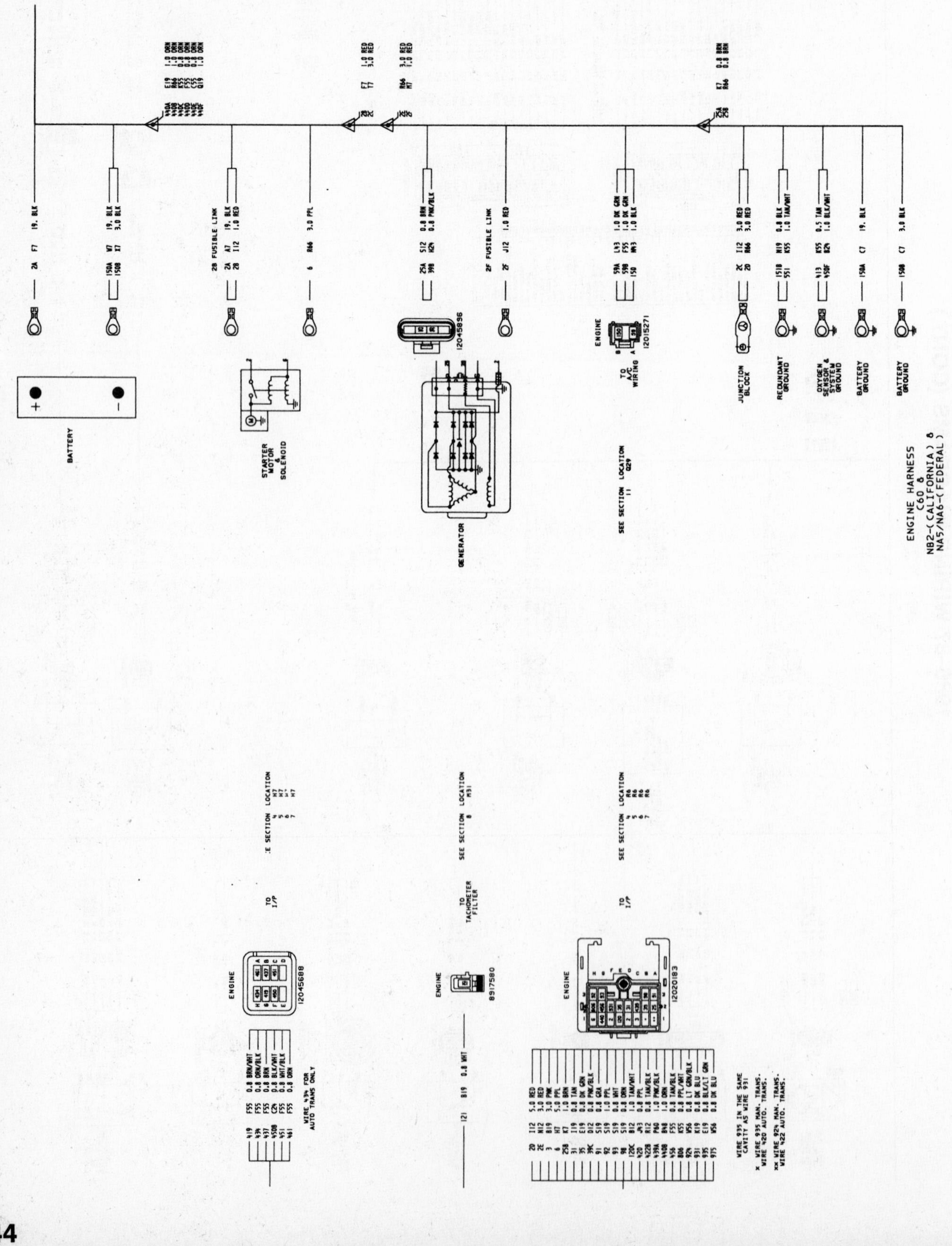
BATTERY
STARTER MOTOR & SOLENOID
GENERATOR
12045896
2B FUSIBLE LINK
2F FUSIBLE LINK
ENGINE
TO A/C WIRING
12015271
JUNCTION BLOCK
REDUNDANT GROUND
OXYGEN SENSOR & SYSTEM GROUND
BATTERY GROUND
BATTERY GROUND
ENGINE HARNESS
C60 &
NB2-(CALIFORNIA) &
NA5/NA6-(FEDERAL)
TO I/P
12045688
WIRE 434 FOR AUTO TRANS ONLY
TO TACHOMETER FILTER
8917580
TO I/P
12020183

1986–87 WIRING DIAGRAMS (CONT.)

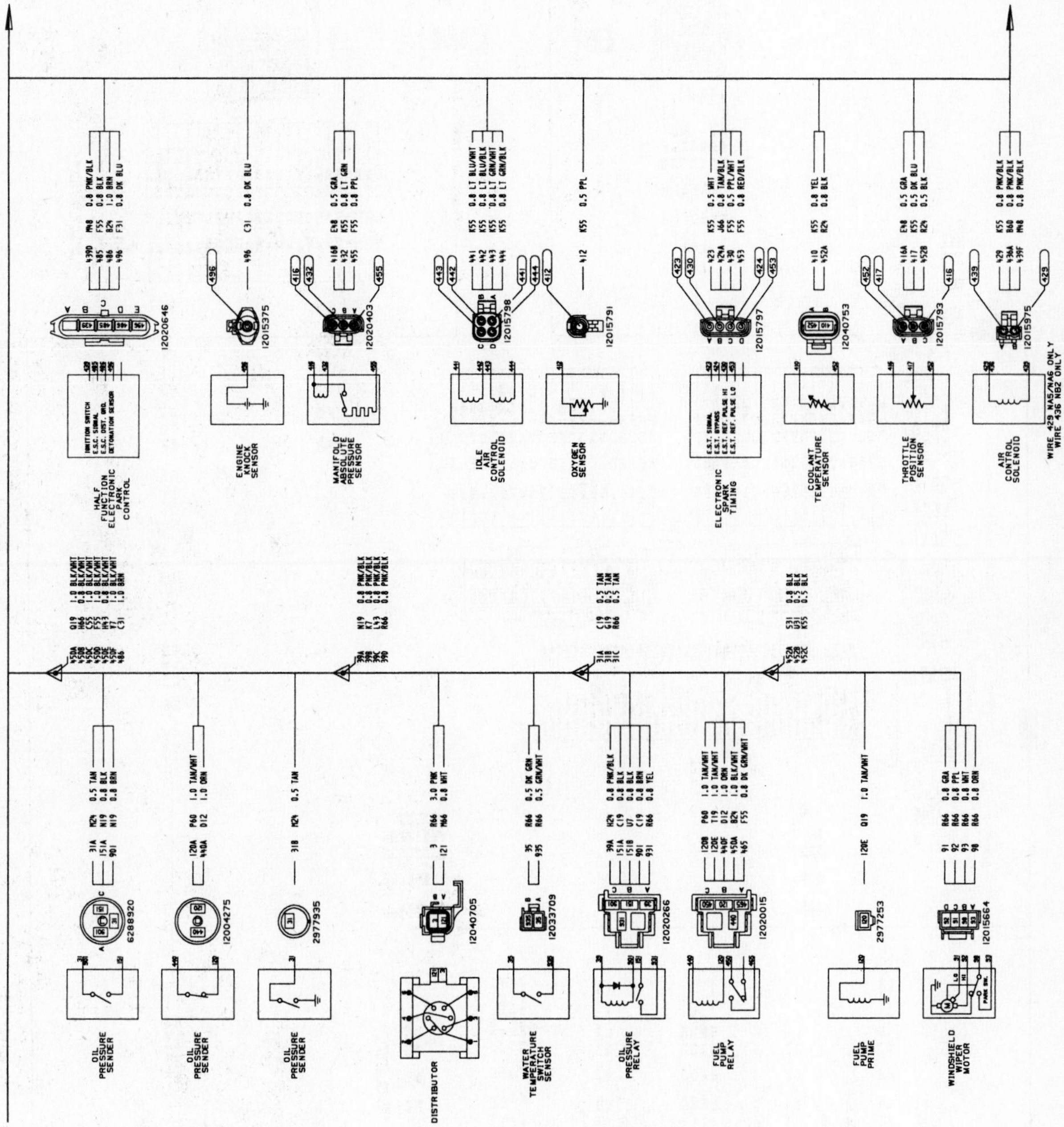
OIL PRESSURE SENDER
OIL PRESSURE SENDER
OIL PRESSURE SENDER
DISTRIBUTOR
WATER TEMPERATURE SWITCH SENSOR
OIL PRESSURE RELAY
FUEL PUMP RELAY
FUEL PUMP PRIME
WINDSHIELD WIPER MOTOR
HALF FUNCTION ELECTRONIC PARK CONTROL
ENGINE KNOCK SENSOR
MANIFOLD ABSOLUTE PRESSURE SENSOR
IDLE AIR CONTROL SOLENOID
OXYGEN SENSOR
ELECTRONIC SPARK TIMING
COOLANT TEMPERATURE SENSOR
THROTTLE POSITION SENSOR
AIR CONTROL SOLENOID
WIRE 429 NA5/NA6 ONLY
WIRE 436 NB2 ONLY

1986–87 WIRING DIAGRAMS (CONT.)

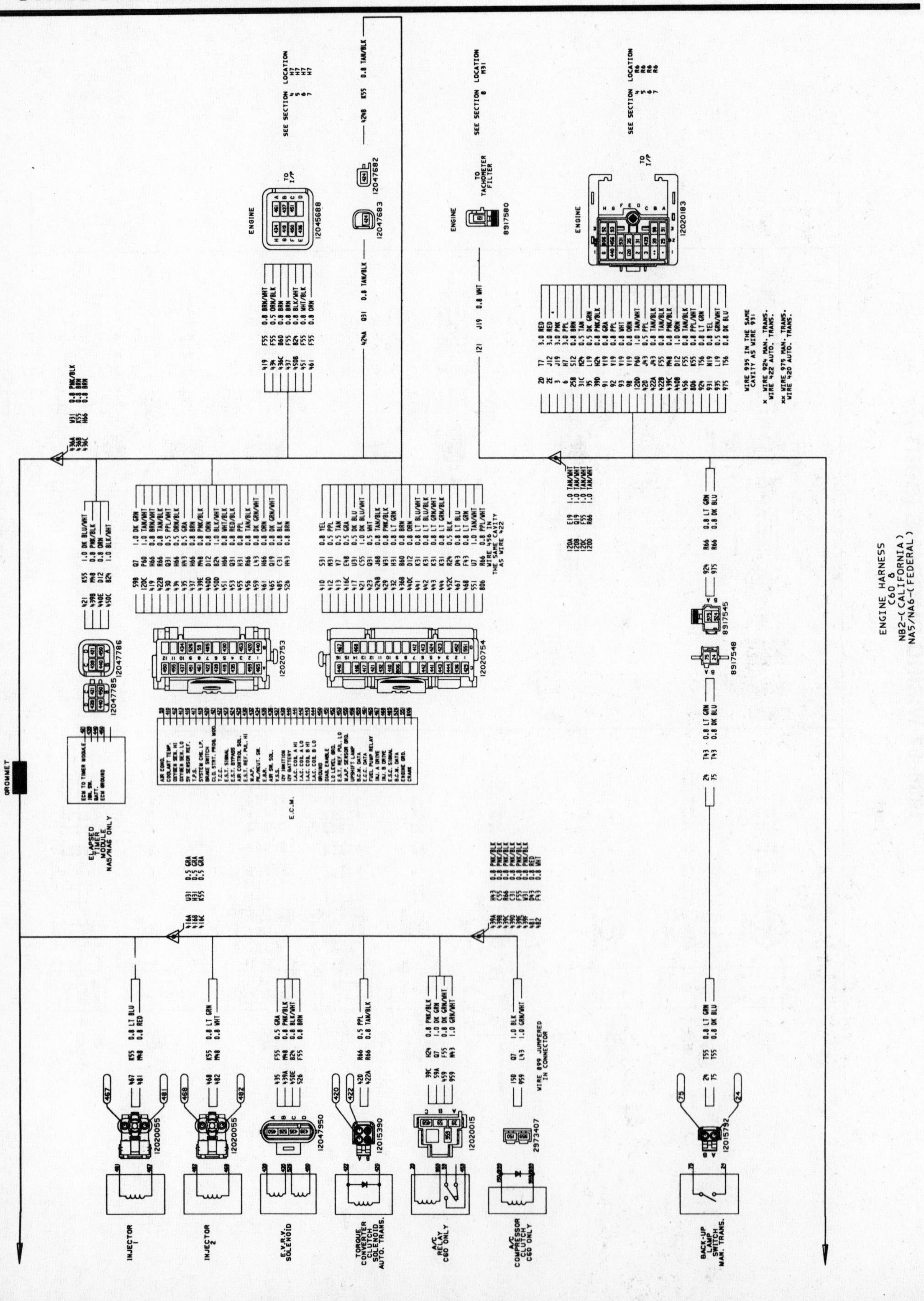
GROMMET
ELAPSED TIMER MODULE NA5/NA6 ONLY
E.C.M.
INJECTOR 1
INJECTOR 2
E.V.R.V. SOLENOID
TORQUE CONVERTER CLUTCH SOLENOID AUTO. TRANS.
A/C RELAY C60 ONLY
A/C COMPRESSOR CLUTCH C60 ONLY
BACK-UP LAMP SWITCH MAN. TRANS.
ENGINE
TO I/P
TO TACHOMETER FILTER
ENGINE HARNESS
C60 &
NB2-(CALIFORNIA)
NA5/NA6-(FEDERAL)

1986–87 WIRING DIAGRAMS (CONT.)

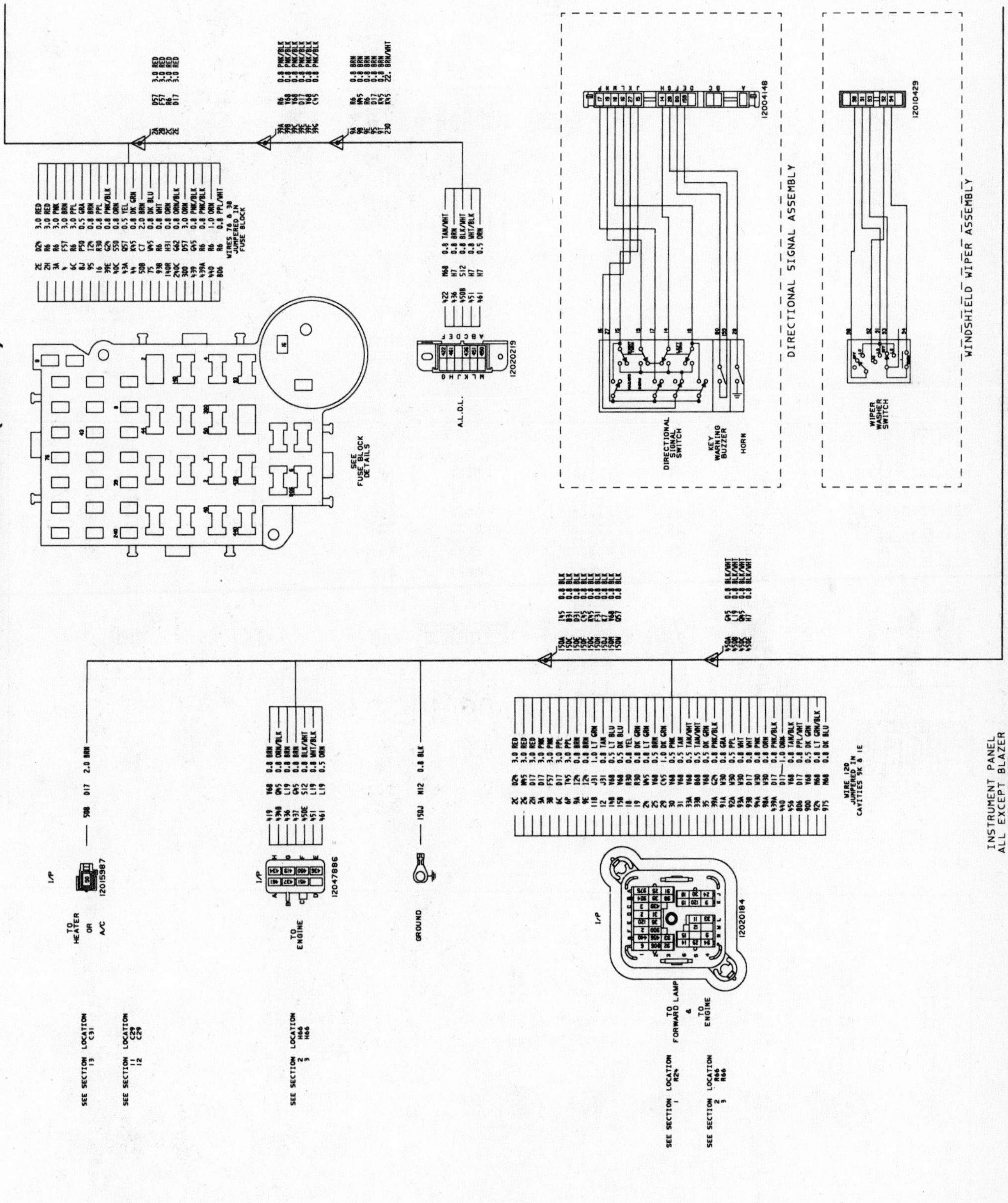
DIRECTIONAL SIGNAL ASSEMBLY
WINDSHIELD WIPER ASSEMBLY
DIRECTIONAL SIGNAL SWITCH
KEY WARNING BUZZER
HORN
WIPER WASHER SWITCH
SEE FUSE BLOCK DETAILS
A.L.D.L.
12020219
12004148
12010429
12015987
12047886
12020184
TO HEATER OR A/C
TO ENGINE
GROUND
TO FORWARD LAMP & TO ENGINE
SEE SECTION 13 LOCATION C31
SEE SECTION 11 12 LOCATION C29 C29
SEE SECTION 2 3 LOCATION H66 H66
SEE SECTION 1 LOCATION R24
SEE SECTION 2 3 LOCATION R66 R66
WIRES 76 & 78 JUMPERED IN FUSE BLOCK
WIRE 120 JUMPERED IN CAVITIES 5K & 1E
INSTRUMENT PANEL ALL EXCEPT BLAZER WITH GAGES

1986–87 WIRING DIAGRAMS (CONT.)

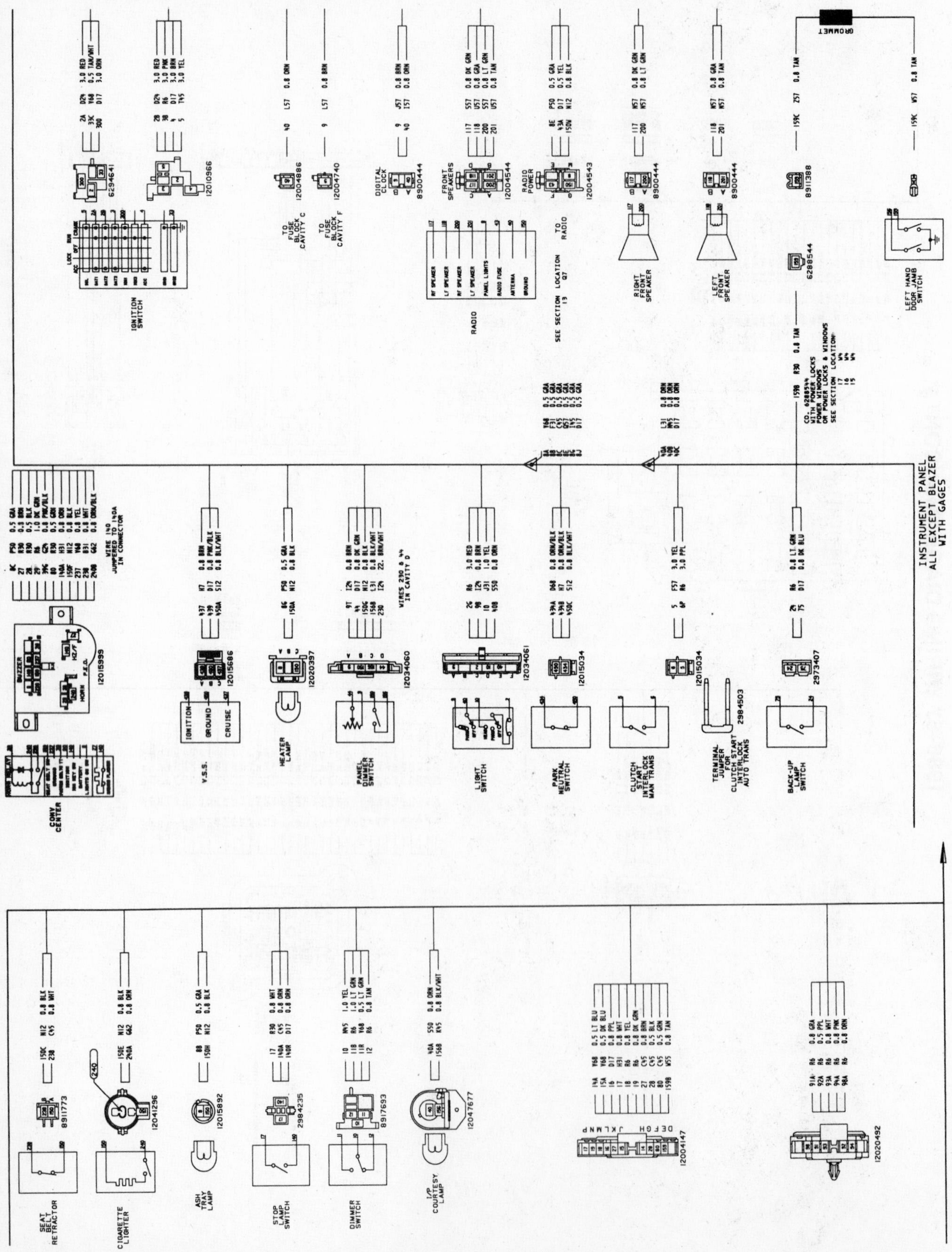

1986–87 WIRING DIAGRAMS (CONT.)

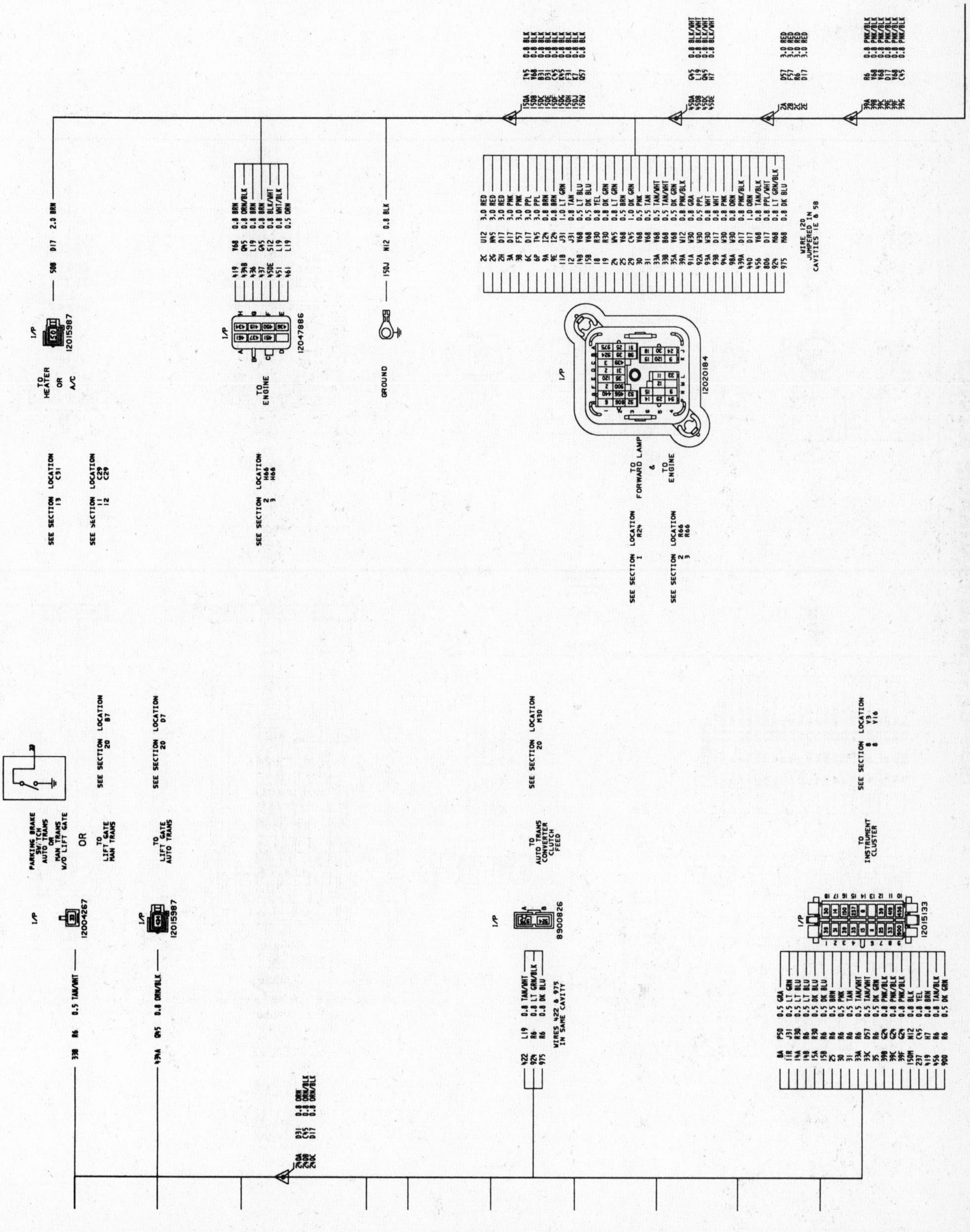

1986–87 WIRING DIAGRAMS (CONT.)

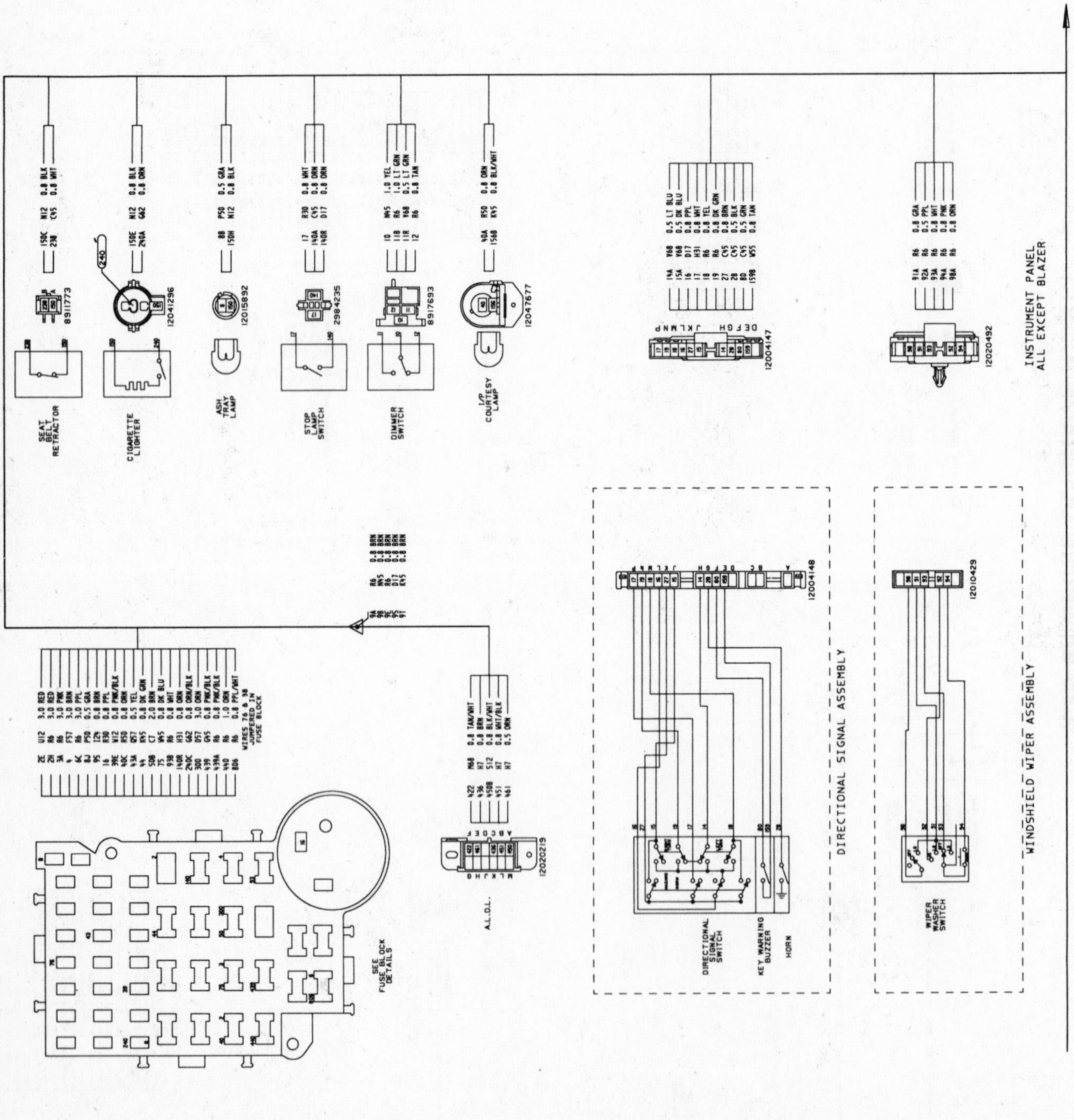
SEAT BELT RETRACTOR
8911773
CIGARETTE LIGHTER
12041296
ASH TRAY LAMP
12015892
STOP LAMP SWITCH
2984235
DIMMER SWITCH
8917693
I/P COURTESY LAMP
12047677
12004147
12020492
INSTRUMENT PANEL ALL EXCEPT BLAZER
SEE FUSE BLOCK DETAILS
A.L.D.L.
12020219
WIRES 7A & 9B JUMPERED IN FUSE BLOCK
DIRECTIONAL SIGNAL SWITCH
KEY WARNING BUZZER
HORN
12004148
DIRECTIONAL SIGNAL ASSEMBLY
WIPER WASHER SWITCH
12010429
WINDSHIELD WIPER ASSEMBLY

1986–87 WIRING DIAGRAMS (CONT.)

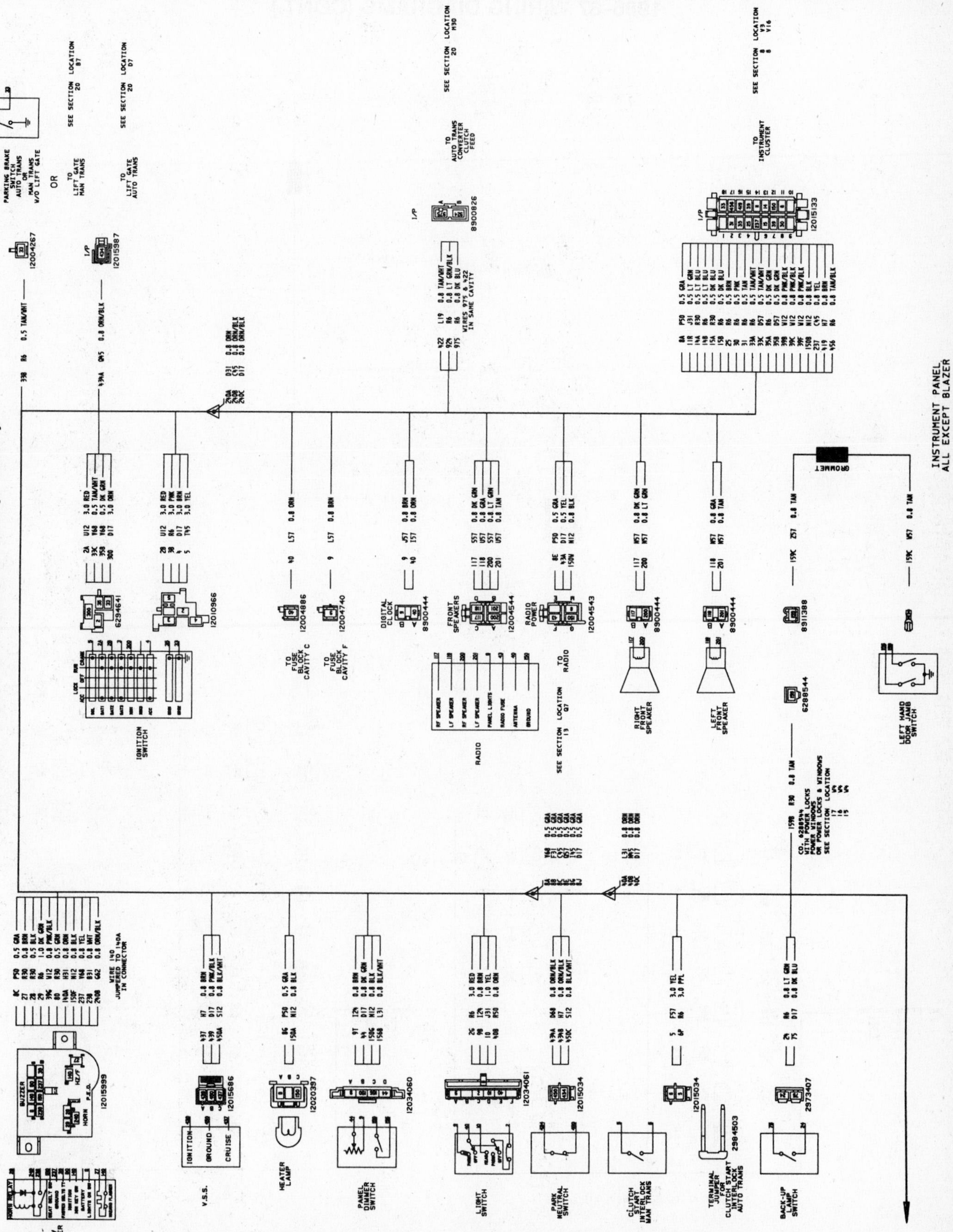
INSTRUMENT PANEL
ALL EXCEPT BLAZER
IGNITION SWITCH
RADIO
RIGHT FRONT SPEAKER
LEFT FRONT SPEAKER
LEFT HAND DOOR JAMB SWITCH
CONV CENTER
V.S.S.
HEATER LAMP
PANEL DIMMER SWITCH
LIGHT SWITCH
PARK NEUTRAL SWITCH
CLUTCH START INTERLOCK MAN TRANS
TERMINAL JUMPER FOR CLUTCH START INTERLOCK AUTO TRANS
BACK-UP LAMP SWITCH
GROMMET
TO INSTRUMENT CLUSTER

1986–87 WIRING DIAGRAMS (CONT.)

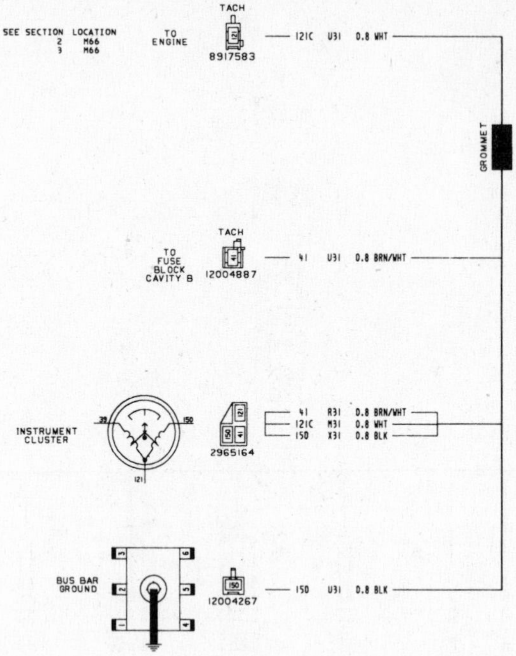
SEE SECTION LOCATION
2 M66
3 M66
TACH
TO ENGINE
8917583
121C U31 0.8 WHT
GROMMET
TACH
TO FUSE BLOCK CAVITY B
12004887
41 U31 0.8 BRN/WHT
INSTRUMENT CLUSTER
2965164
41 R31 0.8 BRN/WHT
121C M31 0.8 WHT
150 X31 0.8 BLK
BUS BAR GROUND
12004267
150 U31 0.8 BLK

TACHOMETER
U16

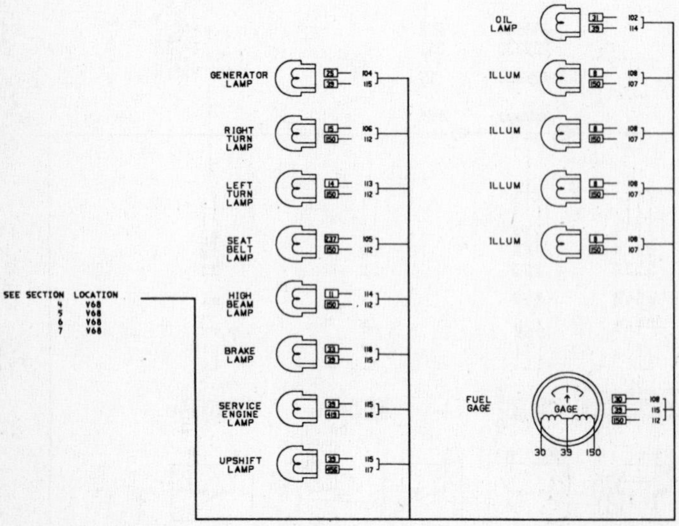
SEE SECTION LOCATION
4 V68
5 V68
6 V68
7 V68
GENERATOR LAMP
RIGHT TURN LAMP
LEFT TURN LAMP
SEAT BELT LAMP
HIGH BEAM LAMP
BRAKE LAMP
SERVICE ENGINE LAMP
UPSHIFT LAMP
OIL LAMP
ILLUM
FUEL GAGE
GAGE

INSTRUMENT CLUSTER WITHOUT GAGES

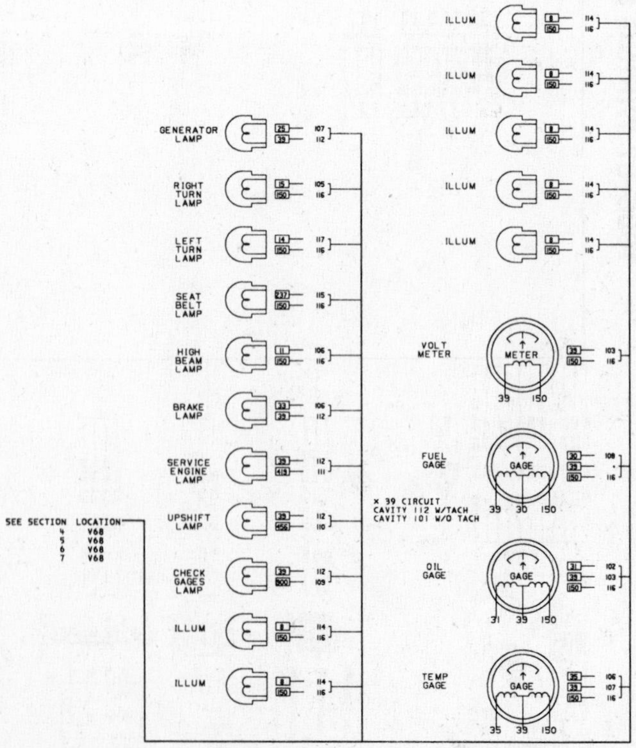
SEE SECTION LOCATION
4 V68
5 V68
6 V68
7 V68
GENERATOR LAMP
RIGHT TURN LAMP
LEFT TURN LAMP
SEAT BELT LAMP
HIGH BEAM LAMP
BRAKE LAMP
SERVICE ENGINE LAMP
UPSHIFT LAMP
CHECK GAGES LAMP
ILLUM
VOLT METER
FUEL GAGE
× 39 CIRCUIT CAVITY 112 W/TACH CAVITY 101 W/O TACH
OIL GAGE
TEMP GAGE

INSTRIMENT CLUSTER WITH GAGES

1986–87 WIRING DIAGRAMS (CONT.)

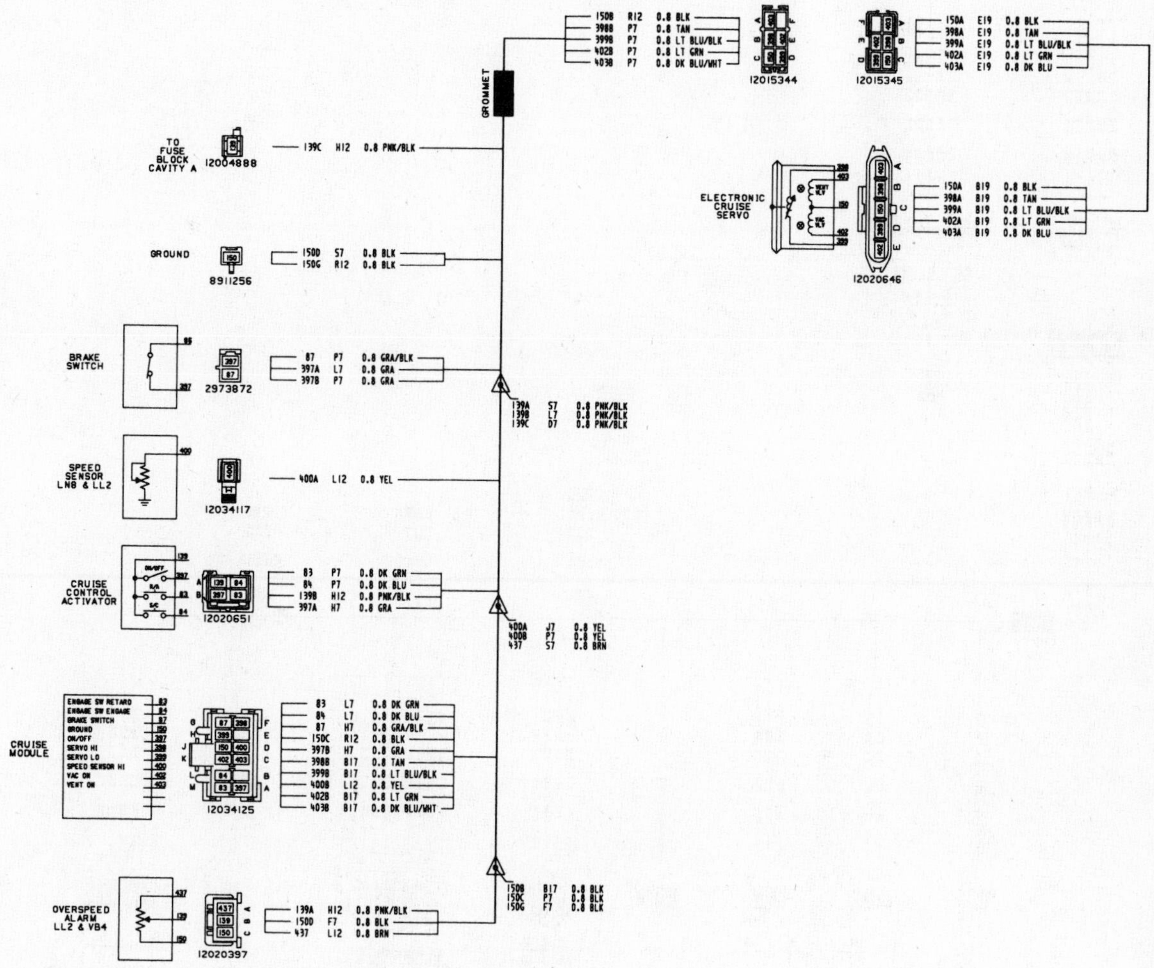
150B R12 0.8 BLK
398B P7 0.8 TAN
399B P7 0.8 LT BLU/BLK
402B P7 0.8 LT GRN
403B P7 0.8 DK BLU/WHT
12015344
12015345
150A E19 0.8 BLK
398A E19 0.8 TAN
399A E19 0.8 LT BLU/BLK
402A E19 0.8 LT GRN
403A E19 0.8 DK BLU
GROMMET
TO FUSE BLOCK CAVITY A
12004888
139C H12 0.8 PNK/BLK
ELECTRONIC CRUISE SERVO
VENT VLV
VAC VLV
12020646
150A B19 0.8 BLK
398A B19 0.8 TAN
399A B19 0.8 LT BLU/BLK
402A B19 0.8 LT GRN
403A B19 0.8 DK BLU
GROUND
8911256
150D S7 0.8 BLK
150G R12 0.8 BLK
BRAKE SWITCH
2973872
87 P7 0.8 GRA/BLK
397A L7 0.8 GRA
397B P7 0.8 GRA
139A S7 0.8 PNK/BLK
139B L7 0.8 PNK/BLK
139C D7 0.8 PNK/BLK
SPEED SENSOR LN8 & LL2
12034117
400A L12 0.8 YEL
CRUISE CONTROL ACTIVATOR
ON/OFF
R/A
S/C
12020651
83 P7 0.8 DK GRN
84 P7 0.8 DK BLU
139B H12 0.8 PNK/BLK
397A H7 0.8 GRA
400A J7 0.8 YEL
400B P7 0.8 YEL
437 S7 0.8 BRN
CRUISE MODULE
ENGAGE SW RETARD
ENGAGE SW ENGAGE
BRAKE SWITCH
GROUND
ON/OFF
SERVO HI
SERVO LO
SPEED SENSOR HI
VAC ON
VENT ON
12034125
83 L7 0.8 DK GRN
84 L7 0.8 DK BLU
87 H7 0.8 GRA/BLK
150C R12 0.8 BLK
397B H7 0.8 GRA
398B B17 0.8 TAN
399B B17 0.8 LT BLU/BLK
400B L12 0.8 YEL
402B B17 0.8 LT GRN
403B B17 0.8 DK BLU/WHT
150B B17 0.8 BLK
150C P7 0.8 BLK
150G F7 0.8 BLK
OVERSPEED ALARM LL2 & VB4
12020397
139A H12 0.8 PNK/BLK
150D F7 0.8 BLK
437 L12 0.8 BRN

CRUISE CONTROL
AUTOMATIC TRANSMISSION
K34

1986–87 WIRING DIAGRAMS (CONT.)

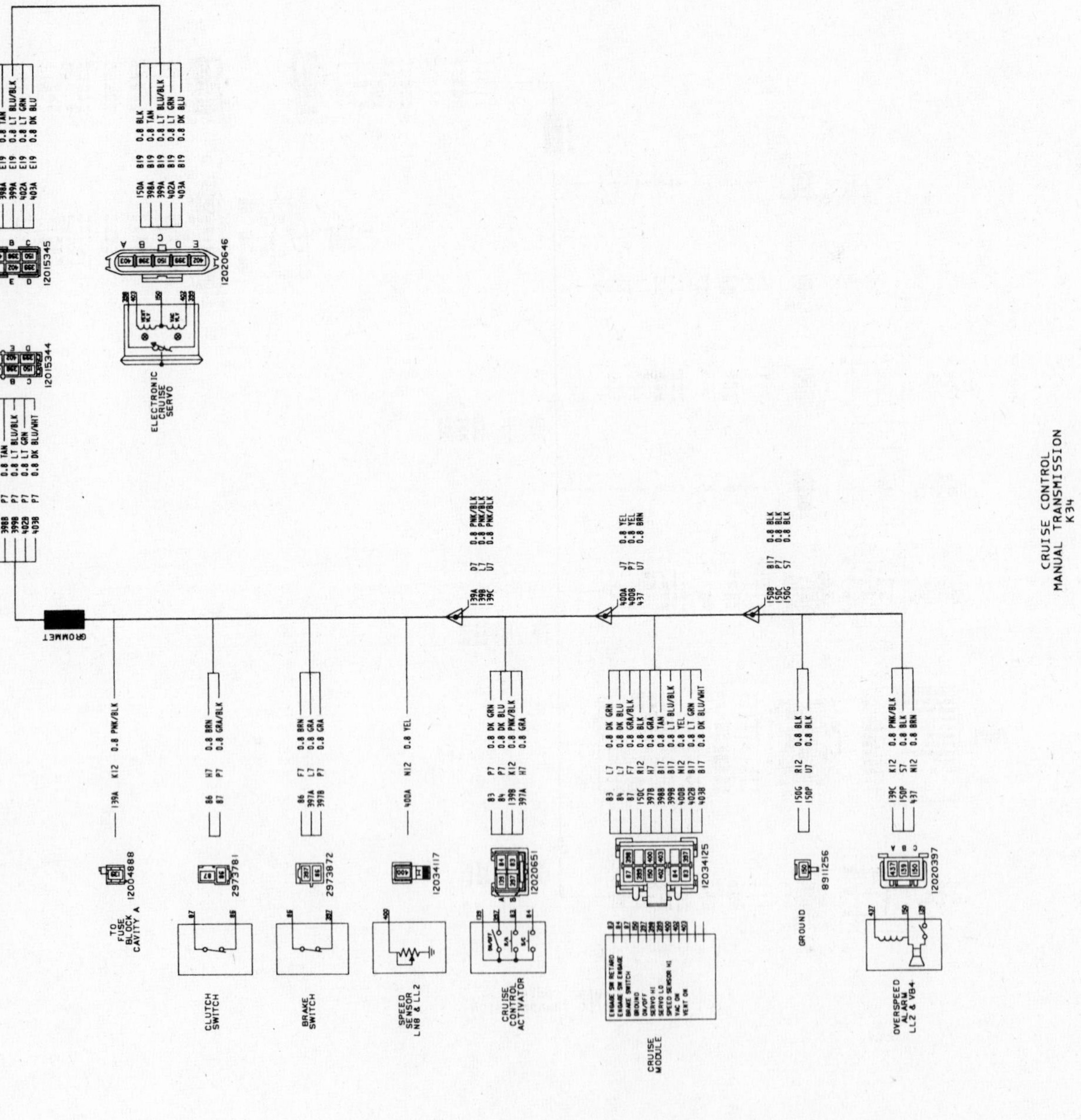
GROMMET
TO FUSE BLOCK CAVITY A
CLUTCH SWITCH
BRAKE SWITCH
SPEED SENSOR LNB & LL2
CRUISE CONTROL ACTIVATOR
CRUISE MODULE
GROUND
OVERSPEED ALARM LL2 & VB4
ELECTRONIC CRUISE SERVO
12004888
2973781
2973872
12034117
12020651
12034125
8911256
12020397
12015344
12015345
12020646

CRUISE CONTROL
MANUAL TRANSMISSION
K34

1986–87 WIRING DIAGRAMS (CONT.)

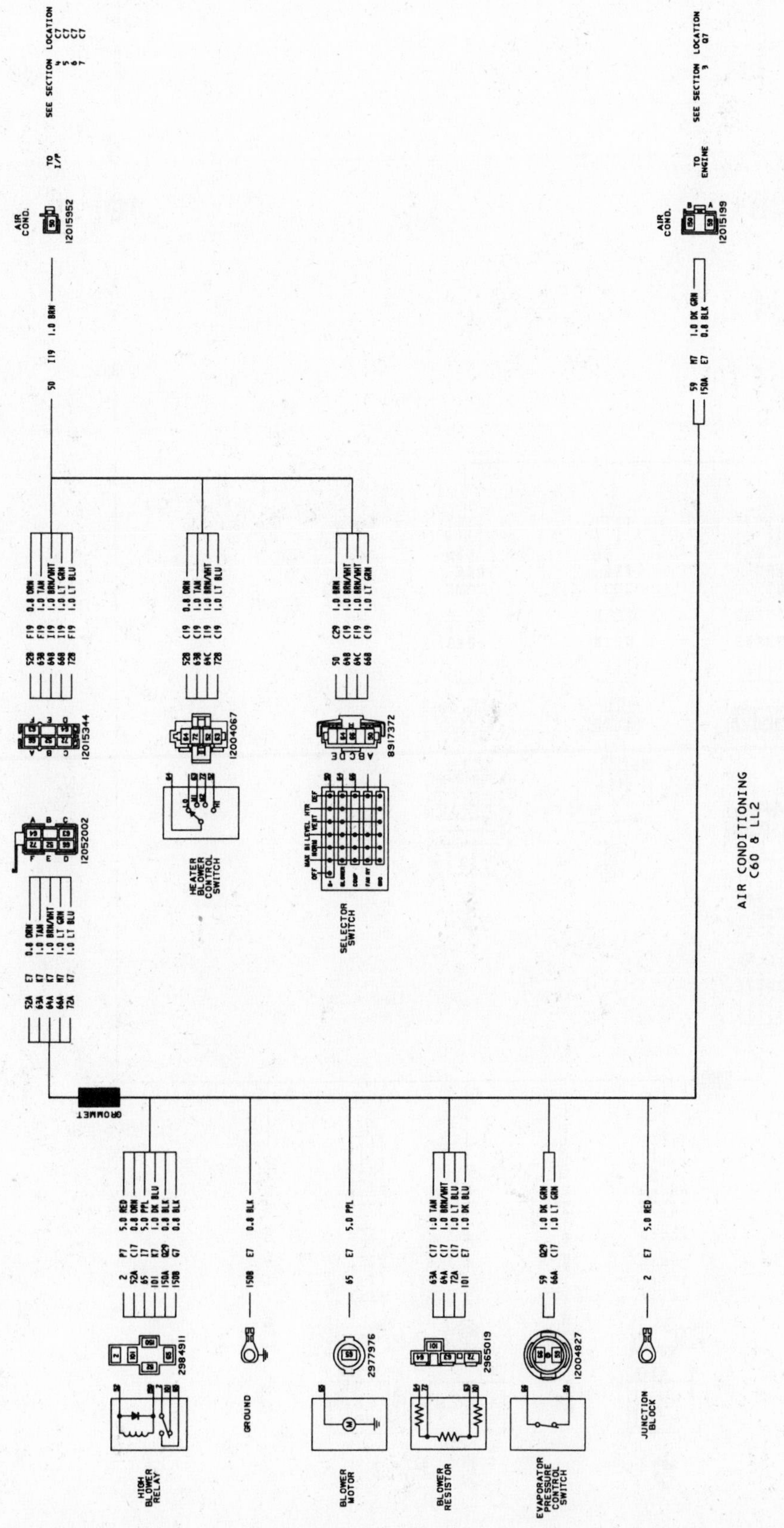
AIR CONDITIONING
C60 & LL2
HIGH BLOWER RELAY
GROUND
BLOWER MOTOR
BLOWER RESISTOR
EVAPORATOR PRESSURE CONTROL SWITCH
JUNCTION BLOCK
GROMMET
HEATER BLOWER CONTROL SWITCH
SELECTOR SWITCH
AIR COND.
TO I/P
TO ENGINE
SEE SECTION LOCATION

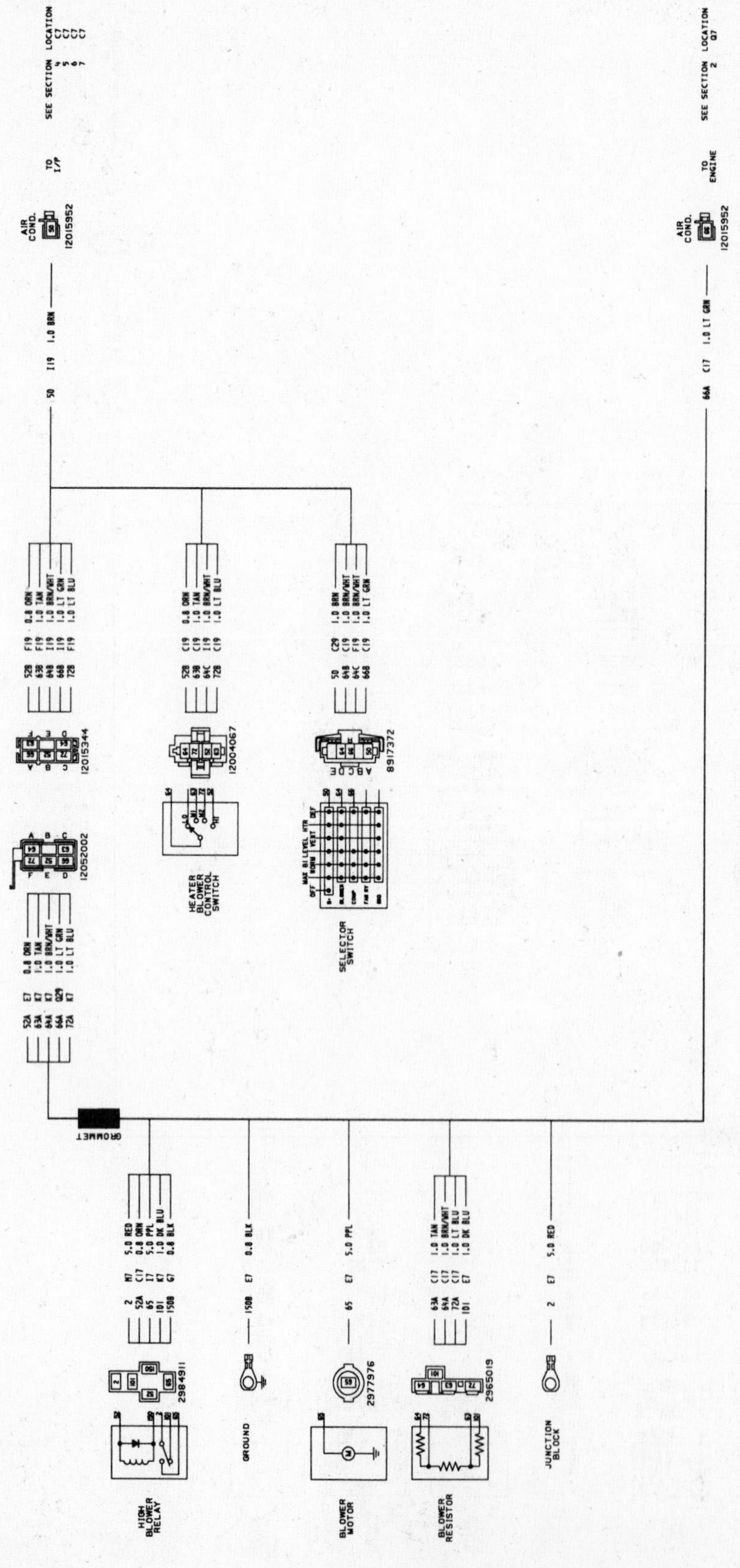

AIR CONDITIONING
C60 & LN8

1986–87 WIRING DIAGRAMS (CONT.)

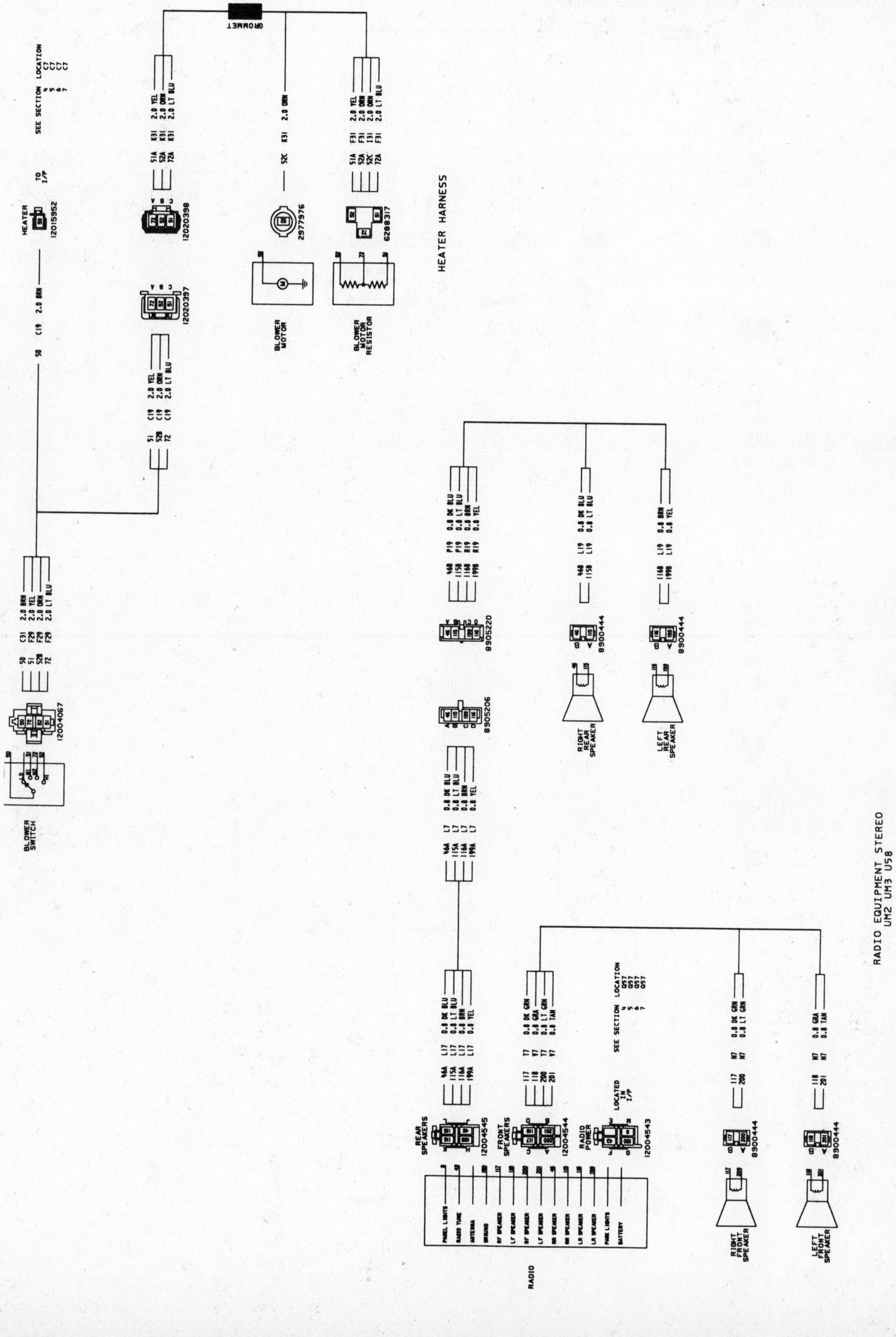
HEATER HARNESS
BLOWER SWITCH
BLOWER MOTOR
BLOWER MOTOR RESISTOR
GROMMET
HEATER
RADIO EQUIPMENT STEREO
UM2 UM3 U58
RADIO
RIGHT REAR SPEAKER
LEFT REAR SPEAKER
RIGHT FRONT SPEAKER
LEFT FRONT SPEAKER
REAR SPEAKERS
FRONT SPEAKERS
RADIO POWER

1986–87 WIRING DIAGRAMS (CONT.)

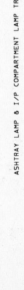

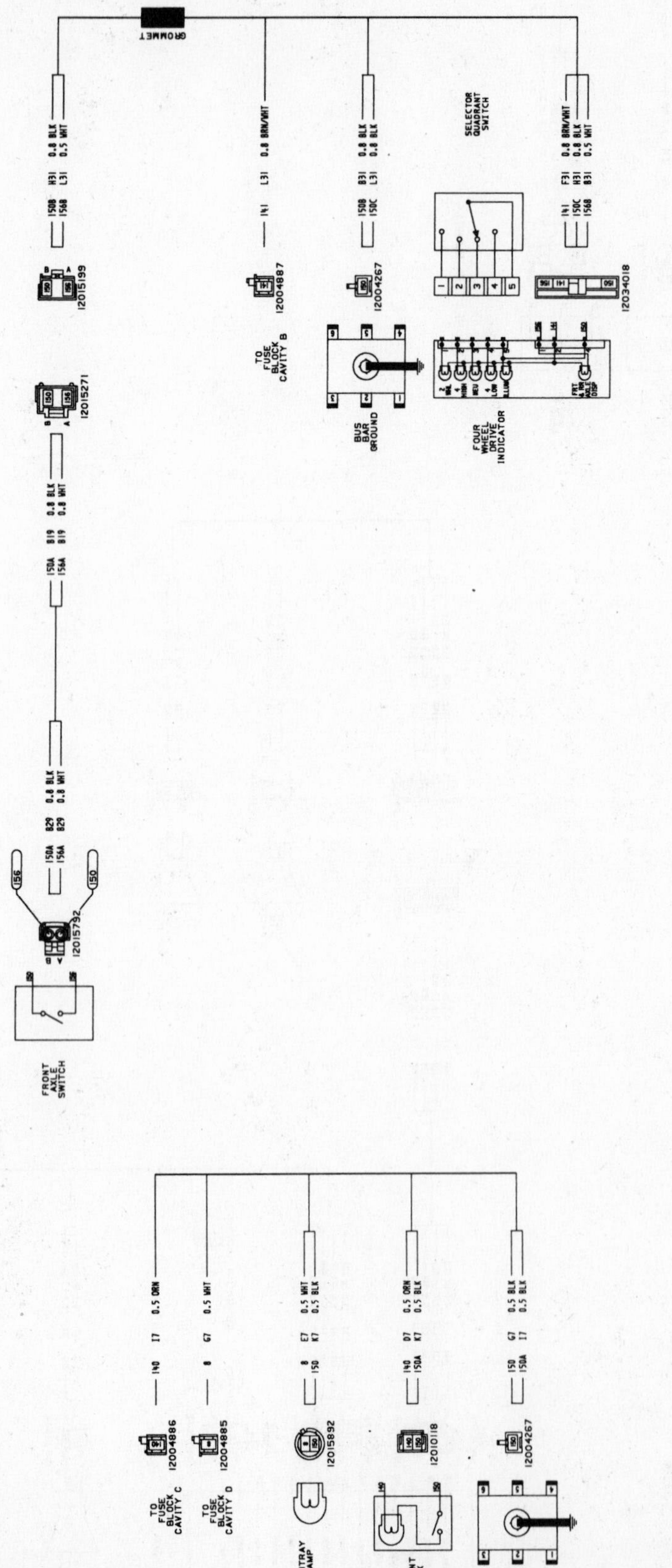
GROMMET
FRONT AXLE SWITCH
12015792
12015271
12015199
TO FUSE BLOCK CAVITY B
12004887
BUS BAR GROUND
12004267
FOUR WHEEL DRIVE INDICATOR
SELECTOR QUADRANT SWITCH
12034018
TO FUSE BLOCK CAVITY C
12004886
TO FUSE BLOCK CAVITY D
12004885
ASHTRAY LAMP
12015892
I/P COMPARTMENT GLOVE BOX LAMP
12010118
BUS BAR GROUND
12004267

FOUR WHEEL DRIVE INDICATOR

ASHTRAY LAMP & I/P COMPARTMENT LAMP TR9

1986–87 WIRING DIAGRAMS (CONT.)

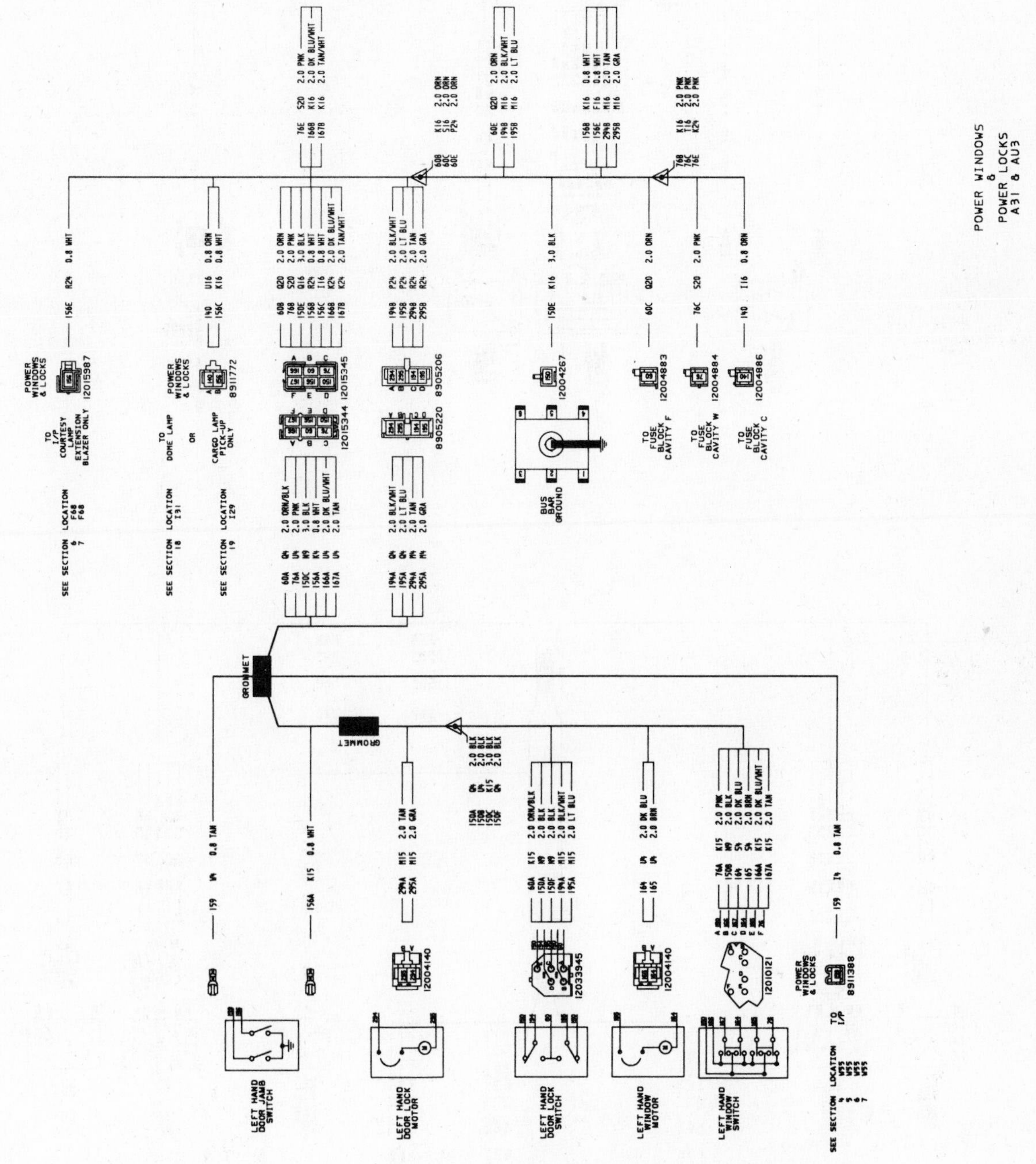
POWER WINDOWS & POWER LOCKS A31 & AU3
GROMMET
LEFT HAND DOOR JAMB SWITCH
LEFT HAND DOOR LOCK MOTOR
LEFT HAND DOOR LOCK SWITCH
LEFT HAND WINDOW MOTOR
LEFT HAND WINDOW SWITCH
BUS BAR GROUND

1986–87 WIRING DIAGRAMS (CONT.)

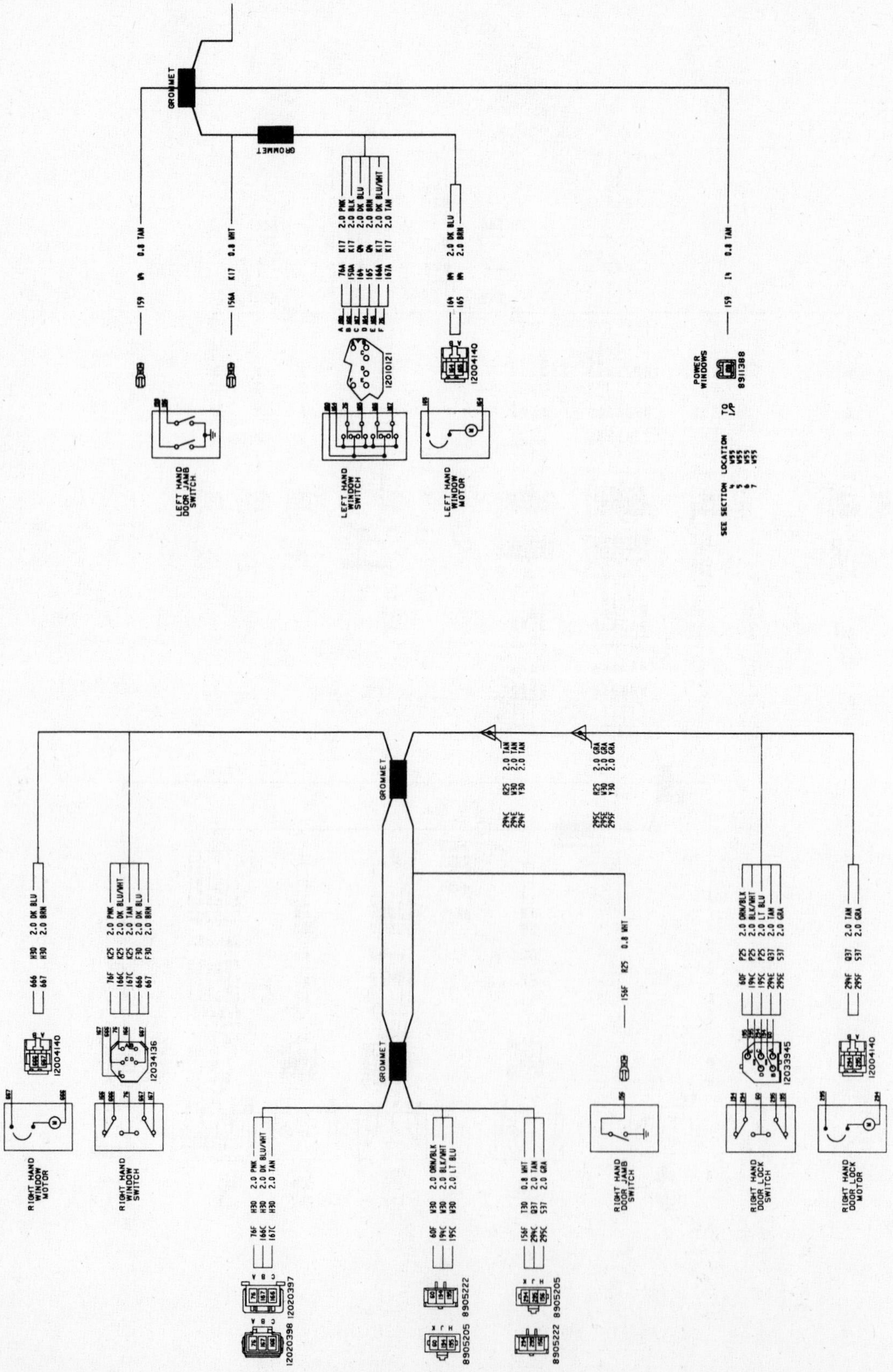
GROMMET
LEFT HAND DOOR JAMB SWITCH
LEFT HAND WINDOW SWITCH
LEFT HAND WINDOW MOTOR
POWER WINDOWS
8911388
12010121
12004140
SEE SECTION LOCATION TO I/P
RIGHT HAND WINDOW MOTOR
RIGHT HAND WINDOW SWITCH
12034136
RIGHT HAND DOOR JAMB SWITCH
RIGHT HAND DOOR LOCK SWITCH
12033945
RIGHT HAND DOOR LOCK MOTOR
12020398 12020397
8905205 8905222
8905222 8905205

1986–87 WIRING DIAGRAMS (CONT.)

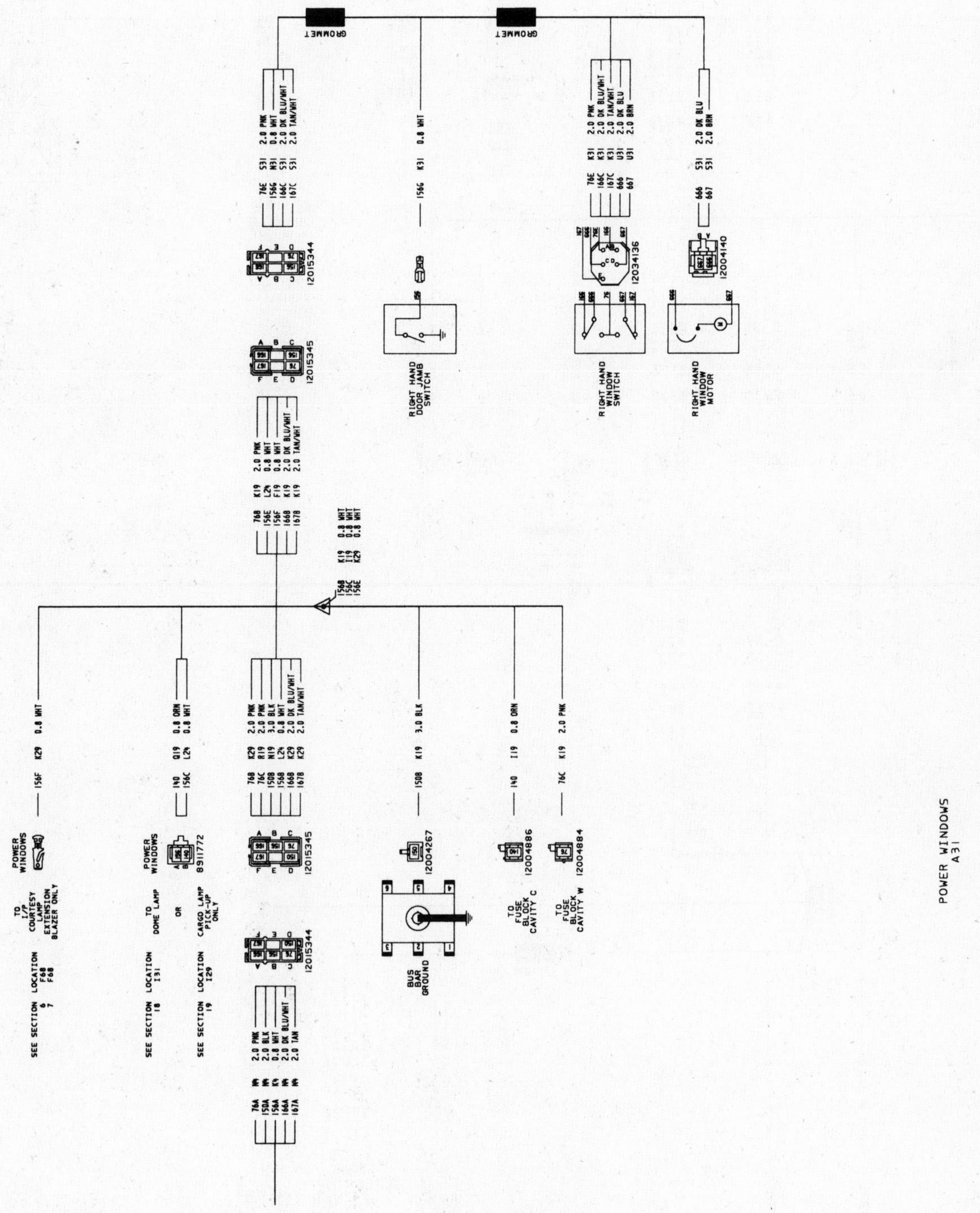
GROMMET
GROMMET
RIGHT HAND DOOR JAMB SWITCH
RIGHT HAND WINDOW SWITCH
RIGHT HAND WINDOW MOTOR
BUS BAR GROUND
POWER WINDOWS A31

1986–87 WIRING DIAGRAMS (CONT.)

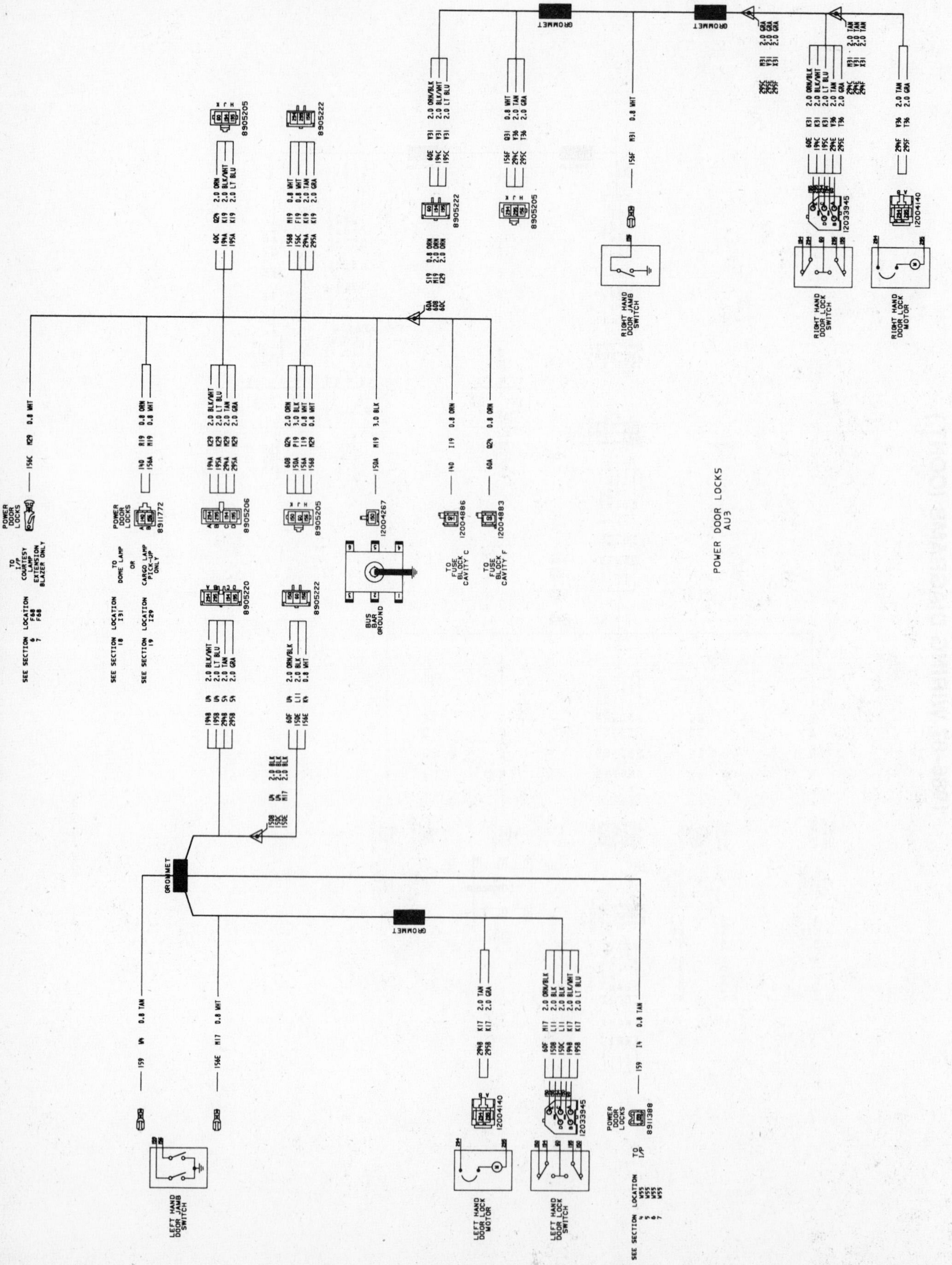
POWER DOOR LOCKS
AU3
GROMMET
BUS BAR GROUND
LEFT HAND DOOR JAMB SWITCH
LEFT HAND DOOR LOCK MOTOR
LEFT HAND DOOR LOCK SWITCH
RIGHT HAND DOOR JAMB SWITCH
RIGHT HAND DOOR LOCK SWITCH
RIGHT HAND DOOR LOCK MOTOR

1986–87 WIRING DIAGRAMS (CONT.)

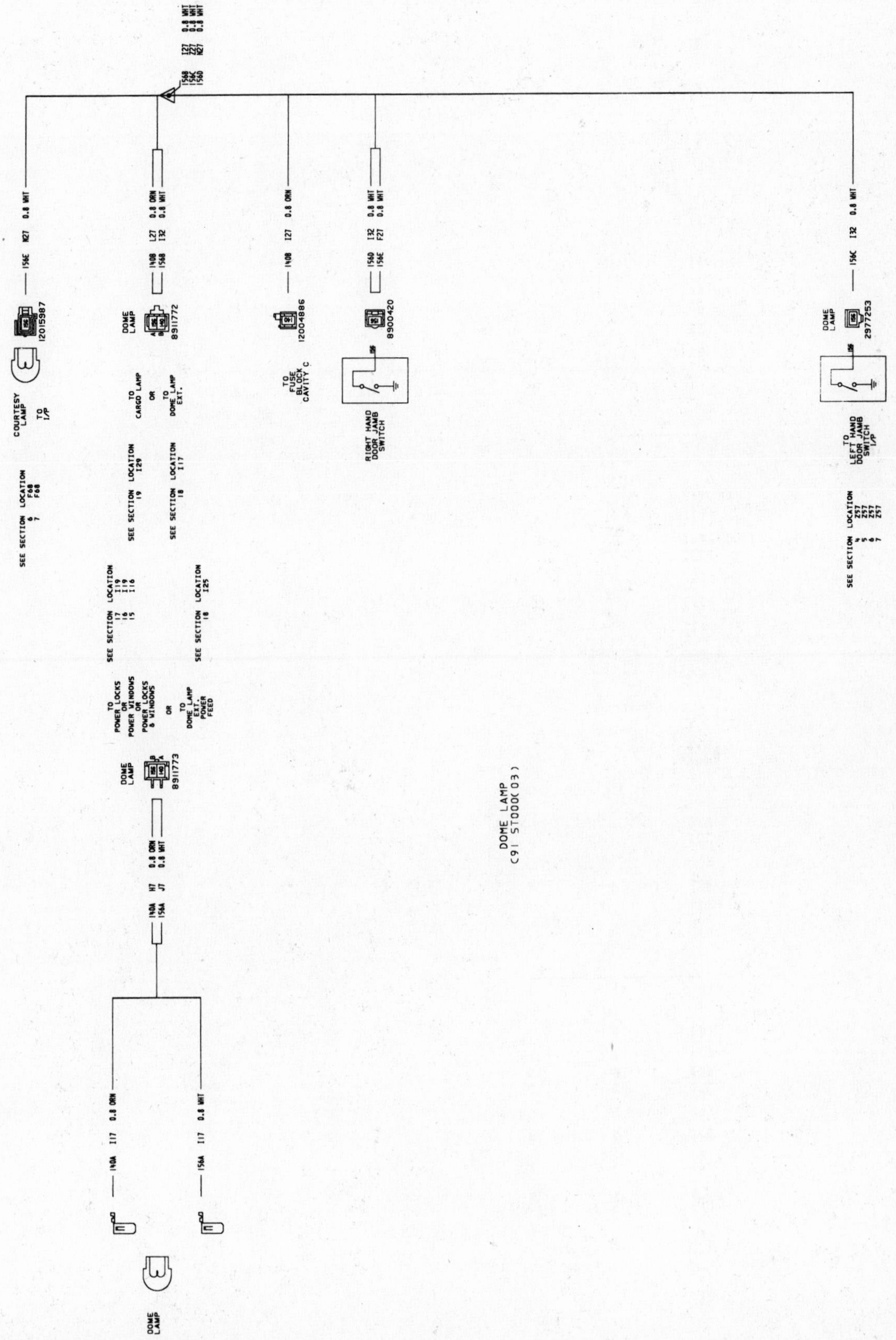
COURTESY LAMP
TO I/P
12015987
DOME LAMP
8911772
TO CARGO LAMP OR TO DOME LAMP EXT.
12004886
TO FUSE BLOCK CAVITY C
8900420
RIGHT HAND DOOR JAMB SWITCH
DOME LAMP
2977253
TO LEFT HAND DOOR JAMB SWITCH I/P
DOME LAMP
8911773
TO POWER LOCKS OR POWER WINDOWS OR POWER LOCKS & WINDOWS
OR
TO DOME LAMP EXT. POWER FEED
DOME LAMP

1986–87 WIRING DIAGRAMS (CONT.)

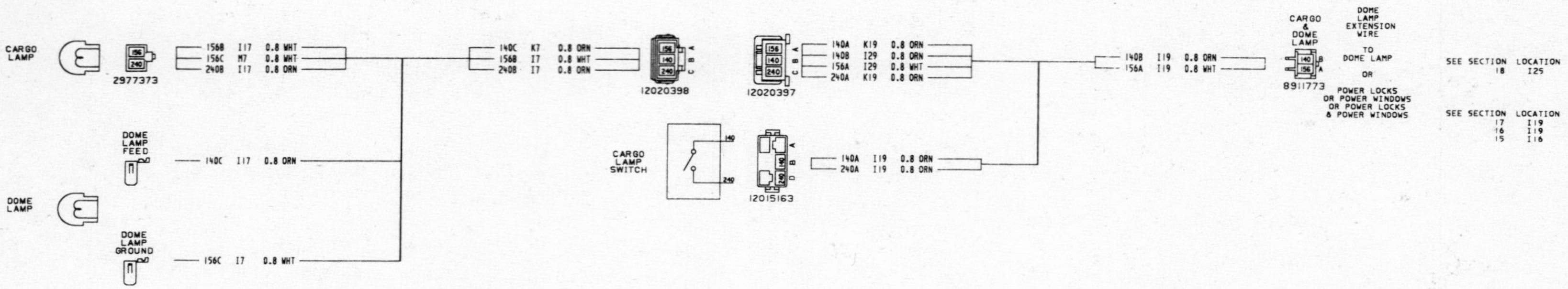
CARGO LAMP
2977373
156B I17 0.8 WHT
156C M7 0.8 WHT
240B I17 0.8 ORN
DOME LAMP FEED
140C I17 0.8 ORN
DOME LAMP
DOME LAMP GROUND
156C I7 0.8 WHT
140C K7 0.8 ORN
156B I7 0.8 WHT
240B I7 0.8 ORN
12020398
12020397
140A K19 0.8 ORN
140B I29 0.8 ORN
156A I29 0.8 WHT
240A K19 0.8 ORN
CARGO LAMP SWITCH
12015163
140A I19 0.8 ORN
240A I19 0.8 ORN
140B I19 0.8 ORN
156A I19 0.8 WHT
CARGO & DOME LAMP
8911773
DOME LAMP EXTENSION WIRE
TO
DOME LAMP
OR
POWER LOCKS
OR POWER WINDOWS
OR POWER LOCKS
& POWER WINDOWS
SEE SECTION LOCATION
18 I25
SEE SECTION LOCATION
17 I19
16 I19
15 I16

CARGO LAMP
UF2

1986–87 WIRING DIAGRAMS (CONT.)

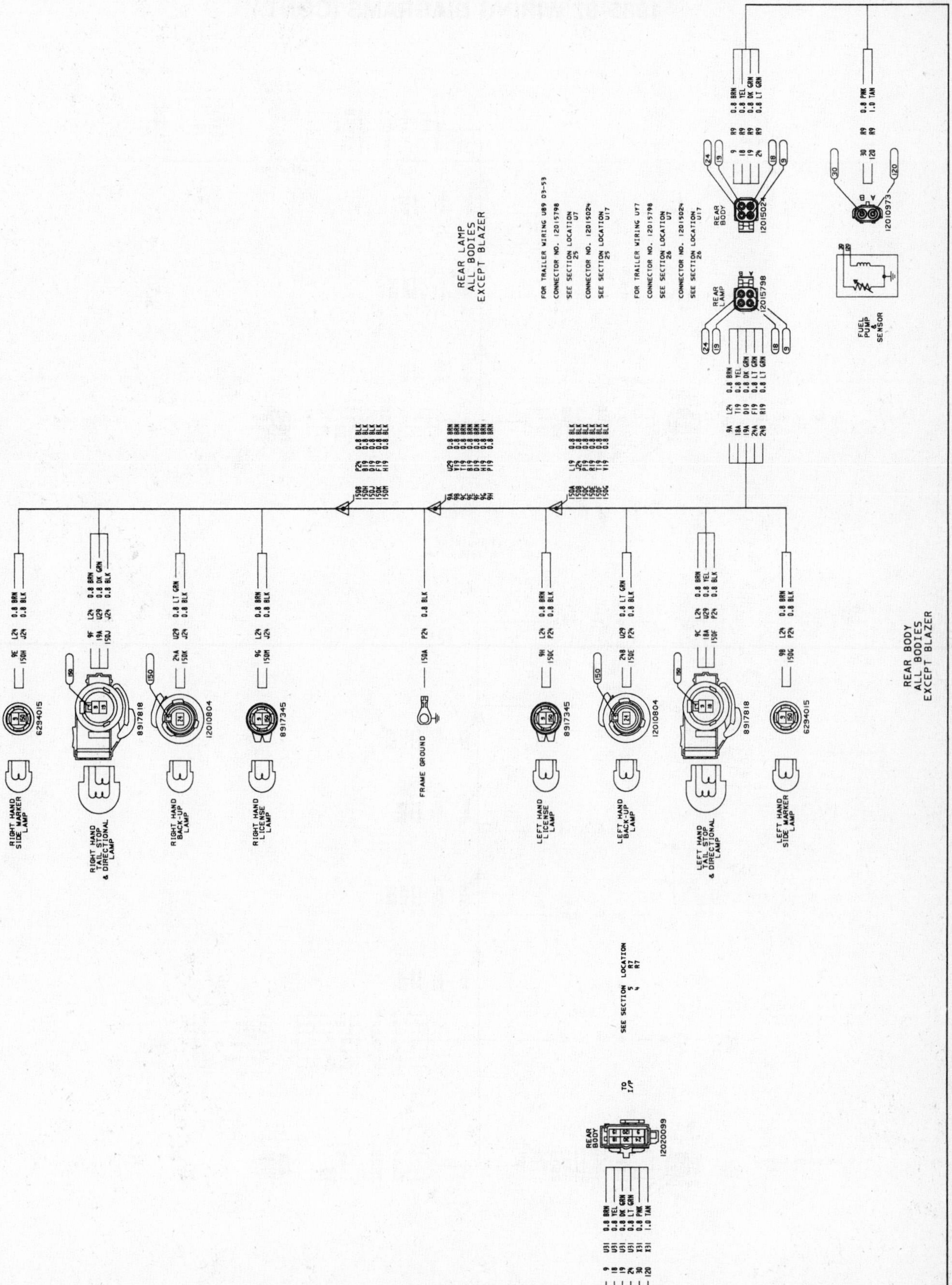
RIGHT HAND SIDE MARKER LAMP
6294015
RIGHT HAND TAIL STOP & DIRECTIONAL LAMP
8917818
RIGHT HAND BACK-UP LAMP
12010804
RIGHT HAND LICENSE LAMP
8917345
FRAME GROUND
LEFT HAND LICENSE LAMP
8917345
LEFT HAND BACK-UP LAMP
12010804
LEFT HAND TAIL STOP & DIRECTIONAL LAMP
8917818
LEFT HAND SIDE MARKER LAMP
6294015
REAR BODY ALL BODIES EXCEPT BLAZER
REAR LAMP ALL BODIES EXCEPT BLAZER
FOR TRAILER WIRING U89 D3-53
CONNECTOR NO. 12015798
SEE SECTION LOCATION 25 U7
CONNECTOR NO. 12015024
SEE SECTION LOCATION 25 U17
FOR TRAILER WIRING UY7
CONNECTOR NO. 12015798
SEE SECTION LOCATION 26 U7
CONNECTOR NO. 12015024
SEE SECTION LOCATION 26 U17
REAR LAMP
12015798
REAR BODY
12015024
FUEL PUMP & SENSOR
12010973
SEE SECTION LOCATION 5 R7 4 R7
TO I/P
REAR BODY
12020099

1986–87 WIRING DIAGRAMS (CONT.)

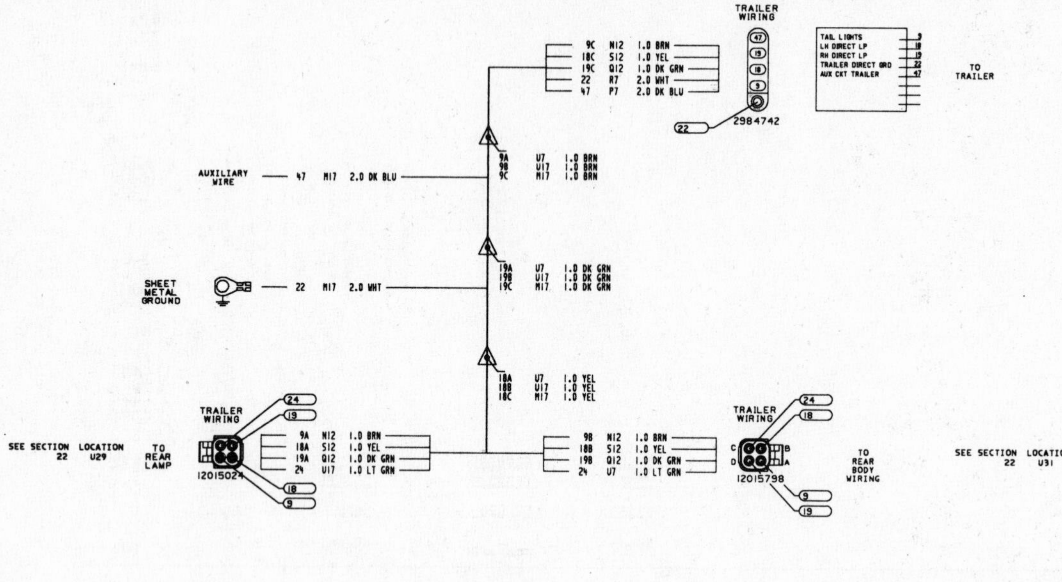
TRAILER WIRING
TAIL LIGHTS
LH DIRECT LP
RH DIRECT LP
TRAILER DIRECT GRD
AUX CKT TRAILER
TO TRAILER
2984742
AUXILIARY WIRE
47 M17 2.0 DK BLU
SHEET METAL GROUND
22 M17 2.0 WHT
SEE SECTION 22 LOCATION U29
TO REAR LAMP
12015024
SEE SECTION 22 LOCATION U31
TO REAR BODY WIRING
12015798

TRAILER WIRING
U89 03-53

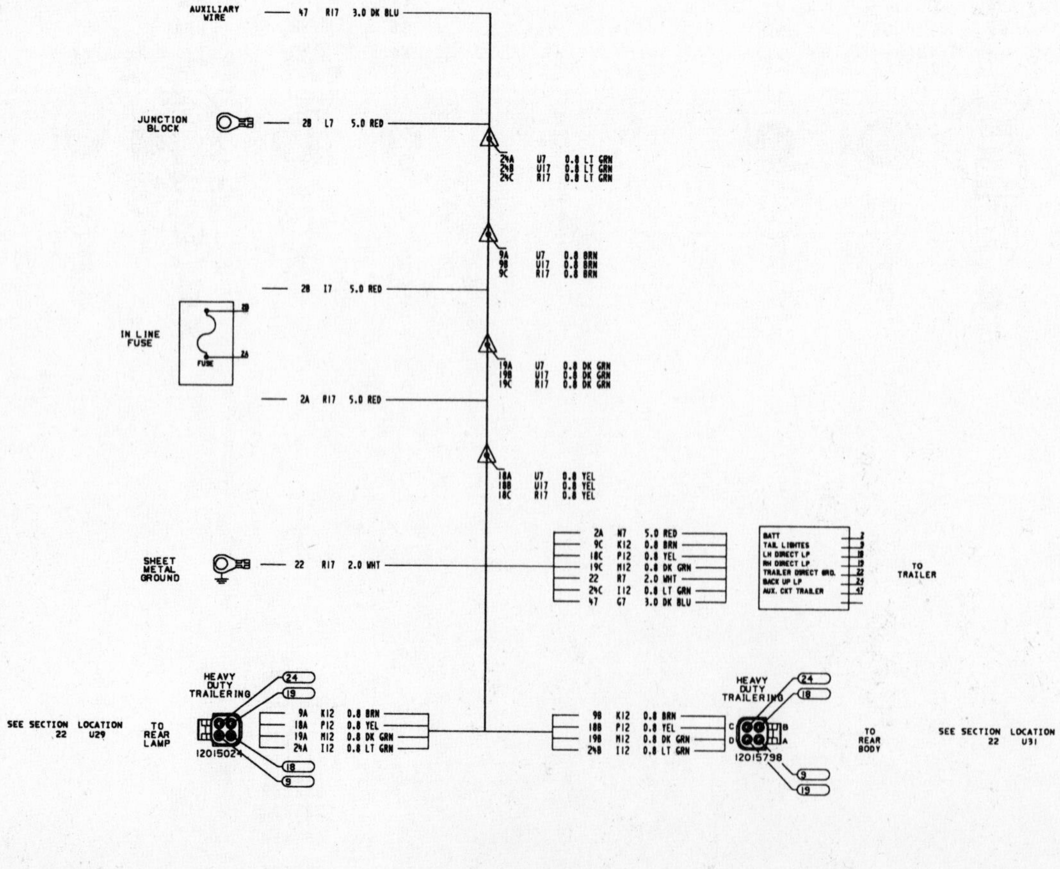
AUXILIARY WIRE
47 R17 3.0 DK BLU
JUNCTION BLOCK
2B L7 5.0 RED
IN LINE FUSE
FUSE
2A R17 5.0 RED
SHEET METAL GROUND
22 R17 2.0 WHT
BATT
TAIL LIGHTS
LH DIRECT LP
RH DIRECT LP
TRAILER DIRECT GRD.
BACK UP LP
AUX. CKT TRAILER
TO TRAILER
HEAVY DUTY TRAILERING
SEE SECTION 22 LOCATION U29
TO REAR LAMP
12015024
TO REAR BODY
12015798
SEE SECTION 22 LOCATION U31

HEAVY DUTY TRAILERING
UY7

1988–91 WIRING DIAGRAMS

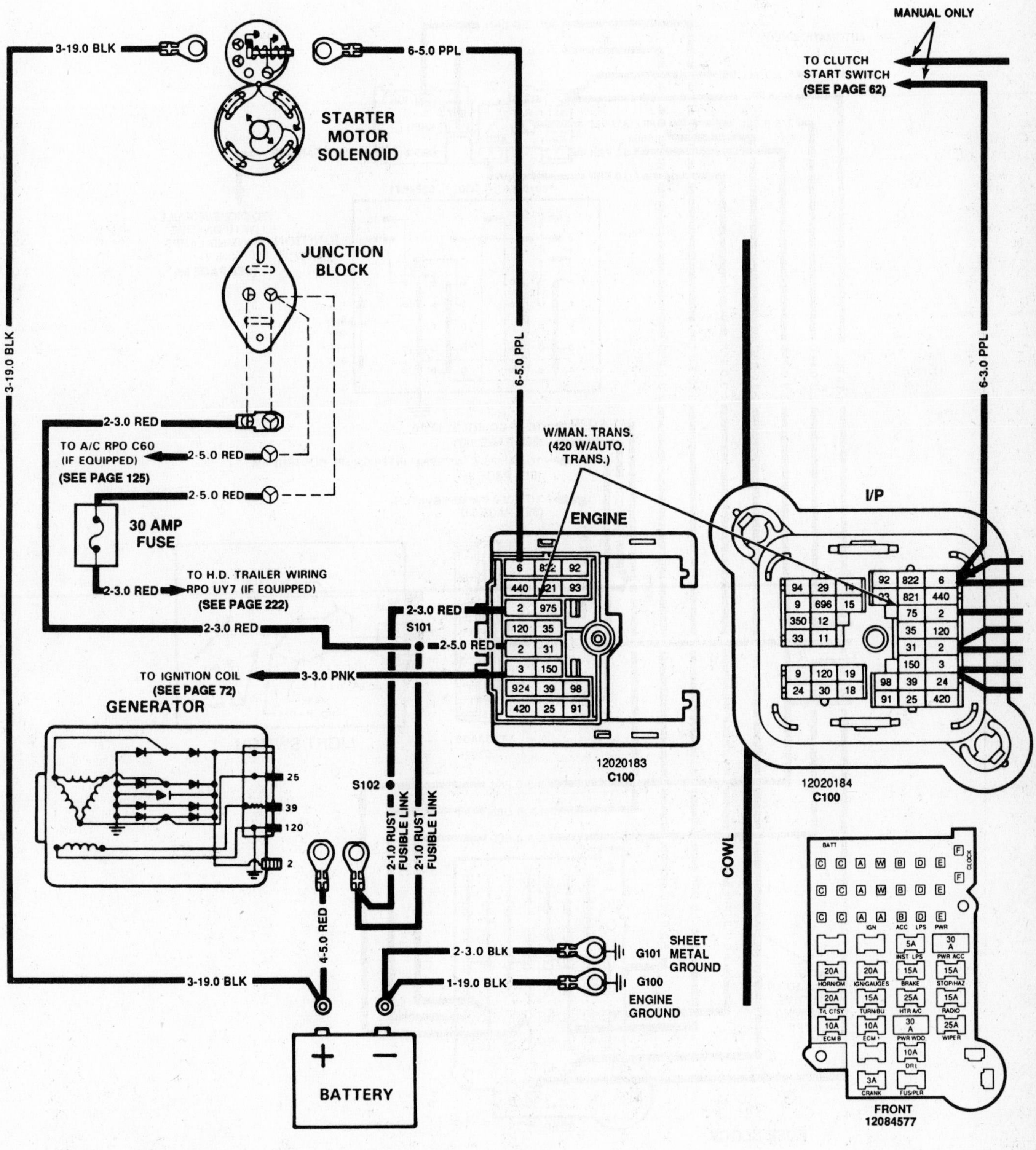

3-19.0 BLK
6-5.0 PPL
STARTER MOTOR SOLENOID
MANUAL ONLY
TO CLUTCH START SWITCH (SEE PAGE 62)
JUNCTION BLOCK
6-3.0 PPL
2-3.0 RED
TO A/C RPO C60 (IF EQUIPPED) (SEE PAGE 125)
2-5.0 RED
W/MAN. TRANS. (420 W/AUTO. TRANS.)
30 AMP FUSE
ENGINE
I/P
TO H.D. TRAILER WIRING RPO UY7 (IF EQUIPPED) (SEE PAGE 222)
S101
TO IGNITION COIL (SEE PAGE 72)
3-3.0 PNK
GENERATOR
12020183 C100
12020184 C100
S102
2-1.0 RUST FUSIBLE LINK
COWL
4-5.0 RED
2-3.0 BLK
G101 SHEET METAL GROUND
1-19.0 BLK
G100 ENGINE GROUND
BATTERY
FRONT 12084577

POWER DISTRIBUTION - 2.5L (151 CID) ENGINE

1988–91 WIRING DIAGRAMS (CONT.)

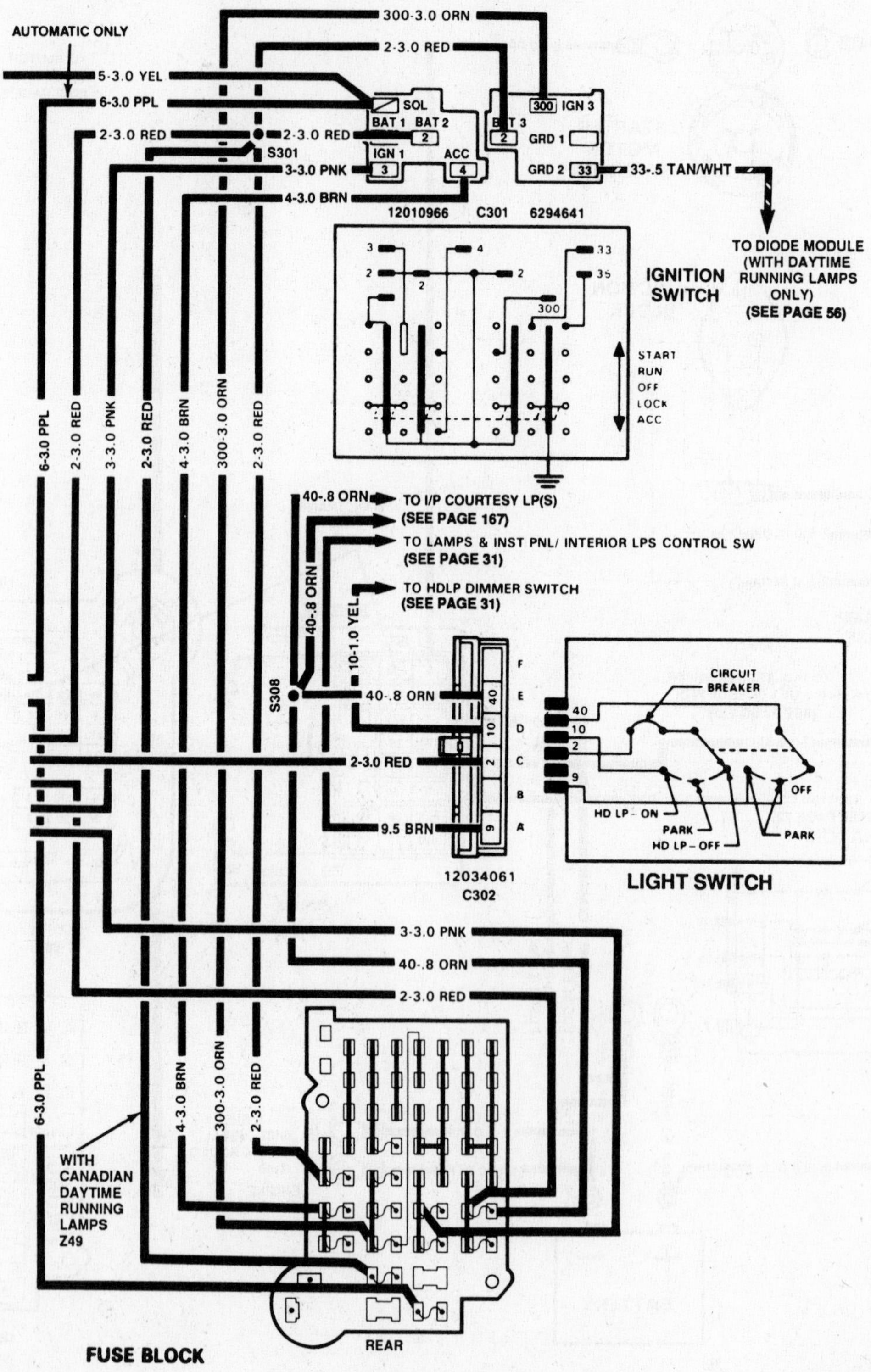
AUTOMATIC ONLY
300-3.0 ORN
2-3.0 RED
5-3.0 YEL
6-3.0 PPL
2-3.0 RED
S301
3-3.0 PNK
4-3.0 BRN
SOL
BAT 1
BAT 2
IGN 1
ACC
BAT 3
IGN 3
GRD 1
GRD 2
33-.5 TAN/WHT
12010966
C301
6294641
TO DIODE MODULE (WITH DAYTIME RUNNING LAMPS ONLY) (SEE PAGE 56)
IGNITION SWITCH
START
RUN
OFF
LOCK
ACC
40-.8 ORN
TO I/P COURTESY LP(S) (SEE PAGE 167)
TO LAMPS & INST PNL/ INTERIOR LPS CONTROL SW (SEE PAGE 31)
TO HDLP DIMMER SWITCH (SEE PAGE 31)
10-1.0 YEL
S308
9.5 BRN
12034061
C302
CIRCUIT BREAKER
HD LP - ON
PARK
HD LP - OFF
OFF
LIGHT SWITCH
WITH CANADIAN DAYTIME RUNNING LAMPS Z49
REAR
FUSE BLOCK

1988–91 WIRING DIAGRAMS (CONT.)

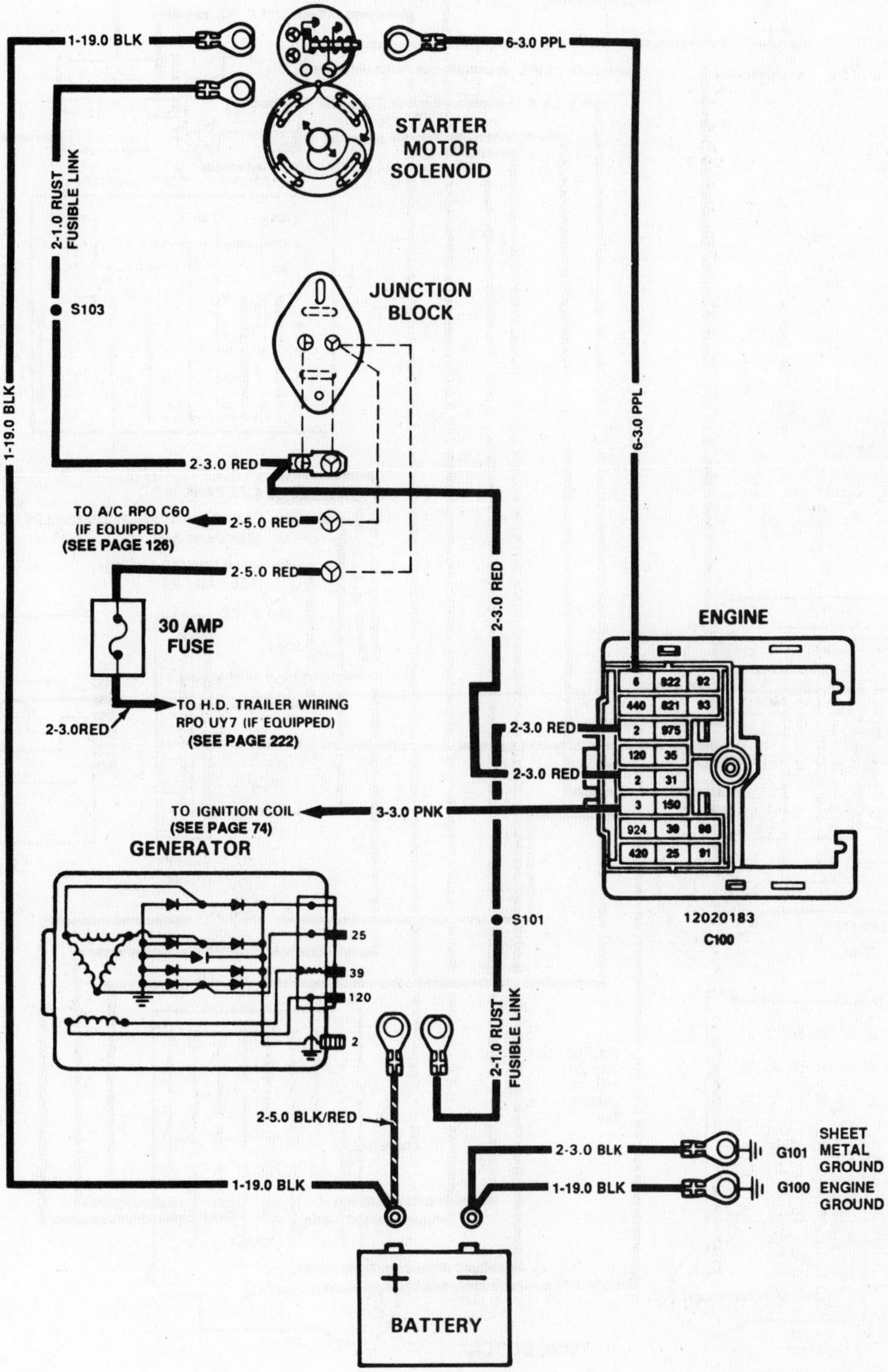
1-19.0 BLK
6-3.0 PPL
STARTER MOTOR SOLENOID
2-1.0 RUST FUSIBLE LINK
S103
JUNCTION BLOCK
1-19.0 BLK
6-3.0 PPL
2-3.0 RED
TO A/C RPO C60 (IF EQUIPPED) (SEE PAGE 126)
2-5.0 RED
2-5.0 RED
2-3.0 RED
30 AMP FUSE
ENGINE
TO H.D. TRAILER WIRING RPO UY7 (IF EQUIPPED) (SEE PAGE 222)
2-3.0RED
2-3.0 RED
2-3.0 RED
TO IGNITION COIL (SEE PAGE 74)
3-3.0 PNK
GENERATOR
S101
12020183
C100
25
39
120
2
2-1.0 RUST FUSIBLE LINK
2-5.0 BLK/RED
2-3.0 BLK
G101 SHEET METAL GROUND
1-19.0 BLK
1-19.0 BLK
G100 ENGINE GROUND
BATTERY

1988–91 WIRING DIAGRAMS (CONT.)

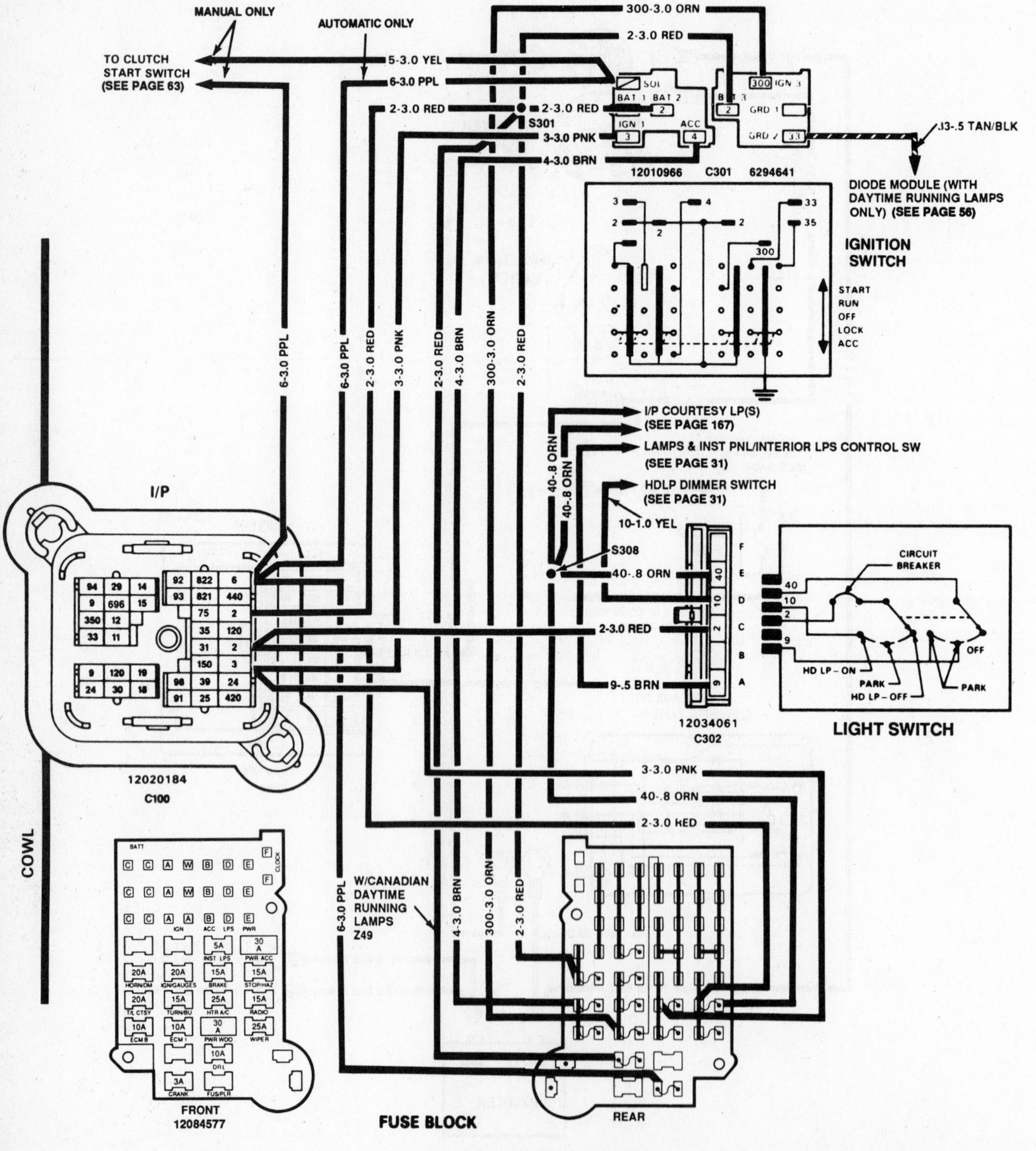
MANUAL ONLY
AUTOMATIC ONLY
TO CLUTCH START SWITCH (SEE PAGE 63)
300-3.0 ORN
2-3.0 RED
5-3.0 YEL
6-3.0 PPL
2-3.0 RED
2-3.0 RED
S301
3-3.0 PNK
4-3.0 BRN
12010966
C301
6294641
33-.5 TAN/BLK
DIODE MODULE (WITH DAYTIME RUNNING LAMPS ONLY) (SEE PAGE 56)
IGNITION SWITCH
START
RUN
OFF
LOCK
ACC
6-3.0 PPL
6-3.0 PPL
2-3.0 RED
3-3.0 PNK
2-3.0 RED
4-3.0 BRN
300-3.0 ORN
2-3.0 RED
I/P COURTESY LP(S) (SEE PAGE 167)
LAMPS & INST PNL/INTERIOR LPS CONTROL SW (SEE PAGE 31)
HDLP DIMMER SWITCH (SEE PAGE 31)
40-.8 ORN
40-.8 ORN
10-1.0 YEL
S308
40-.8 ORN
2-3.0 RED
9-.5 BRN
12034061
C302
CIRCUIT BREAKER
HD LP – ON
PARK
HD LP – OFF
PARK
OFF
LIGHT SWITCH
I/P
12020184
C100
COWL
3-3.0 PNK
40-.8 ORN
2-3.0 RED
W/CANADIAN DAYTIME RUNNING LAMPS Z49
6-3.0 PPL
4-3.0 BRN
300-3.0 ORN
2-3.0 RED
FRONT
12084577
FUSE BLOCK
REAR

POWER DISTRIBUTION - 2.8L (173 CID) ENGINE

1988–91 WIRING DIAGRAMS (CONT.)

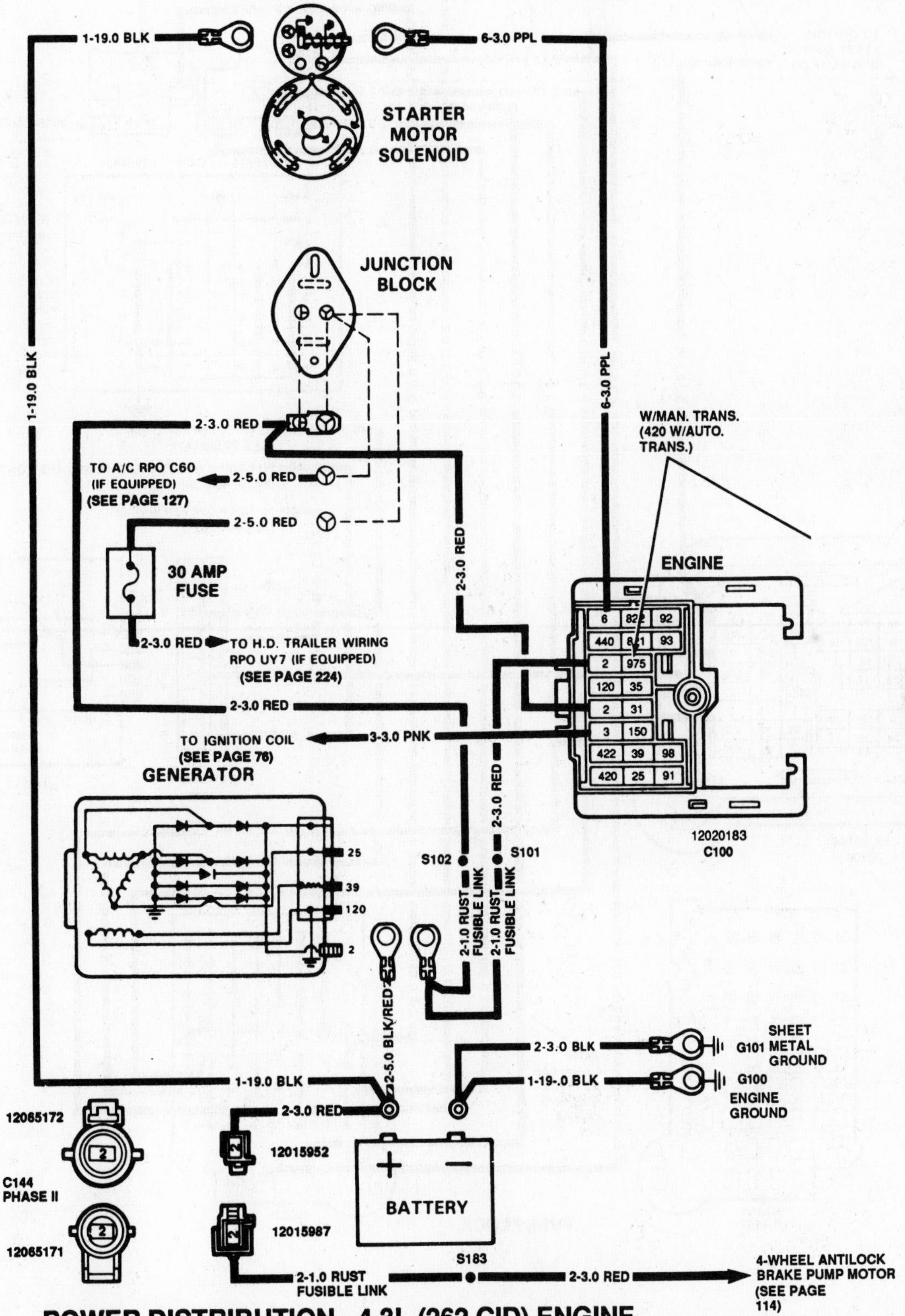
1-19.0 BLK
6-3.0 PPL
STARTER MOTOR SOLENOID
JUNCTION BLOCK
1-19.0 BLK
6-3.0 PPL
2-3.0 RED
TO A/C RPO C60 (IF EQUIPPED) (SEE PAGE 127)
2-5.0 RED
2-5.0 RED
30 AMP FUSE
2-3.0 RED
W/MAN. TRANS. (420 W/AUTO. TRANS.)
ENGINE
2-3.0 RED
TO H.D. TRAILER WIRING RPO UY7 (IF EQUIPPED) (SEE PAGE 224)
2-3.0 RED
TO IGNITION COIL (SEE PAGE 76)
3-3.0 PNK
GENERATOR
2-3.0 RED
6
822
92
440
821
93
2
975
120
35
2
31
3
150
422
39
98
420
25
91
12020183 C100
25
39
120
2
S102
S101
2-1.0 RUST FUSIBLE LINK
2-1.0 RUST FUSIBLE LINK
2-5.0 BLK/RED
2-3.0 BLK
G101 SHEET METAL GROUND
1-19.0 BLK
1-19.0 BLK
G100 ENGINE GROUND
2-3.0 RED
12065172
12015952
C144 PHASE II
BATTERY
12065171
12015987
S183
2-1.0 RUST FUSIBLE LINK
2-3.0 RED
4-WHEEL ANTILOCK BRAKE PUMP MOTOR (SEE PAGE 114)

POWER DISTRIBUTION - 4.3L (262 CID) ENGINE

1988–91 WIRING DIAGRAMS (CONT.)

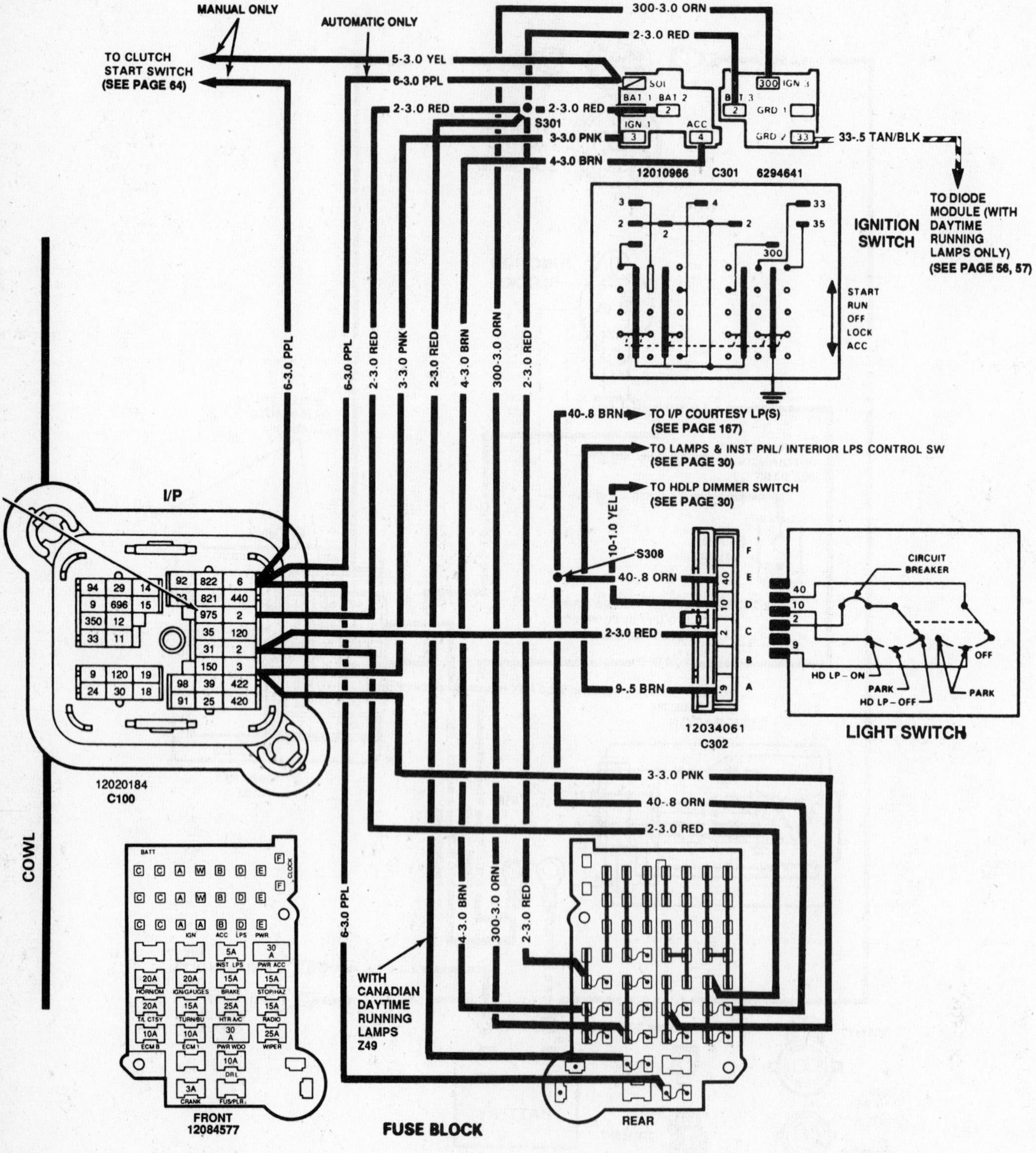
MANUAL ONLY
AUTOMATIC ONLY
TO CLUTCH
START SWITCH
(SEE PAGE 64)
300-3.0 ORN
2-3.0 RED
5-3.0 YEL
6-3.0 PPL
2-3.0 RED
2-3.0 RED
S301
3-3.0 PNK
4-3.0 BRN
SOI
BAT 1
BAT 2
IGN 1
ACC
BAT 3
IGN 3
GRD 1
GRD 2
33-.5 TAN/BLK
12010966
C301
6294641
TO DIODE
MODULE (WITH
DAYTIME
RUNNING
LAMPS ONLY)
(SEE PAGE 56, 57)
IGNITION
SWITCH
START
RUN
OFF
LOCK
ACC
6-3.0 PPL
6-3.0 PPL
2-3.0 RED
3-3.0 PNK
2-3.0 RED
4-3.0 BRN
300-3.0 ORN
2-3.0 RED
40-.8 BRN
TO I/P COURTESY LP(S)
(SEE PAGE 167)
TO LAMPS & INST PNL/ INTERIOR LPS CONTROL SW
(SEE PAGE 30)
TO HDLP DIMMER SWITCH
(SEE PAGE 30)
10-1.0 YEL
S308
40-.8 ORN
2-3.0 RED
9-.5 BRN
12034061
C302
CIRCUIT
BREAKER
HD LP – ON
PARK
HD LP – OFF
PARK
OFF
LIGHT SWITCH
I/P
12020184
C100
COWL
3-3.0 PNK
40-.8 ORN
2-3.0 RED
6-3.0 PPL
4-3.0 BRN
300-3.0 ORN
2-3.0 RED
WITH
CANADIAN
DAYTIME
RUNNING
LAMPS
Z49
BATT
CLOCK
IGN
ACC
LPS
PWR
5A
INST LPS
30 A
PWR ACC
20A
HORN/DM
20A
IGN/GAUGES
15A
BRAKE
15A
STOP/HAZ
20A
T/L CTSY
15A
TURN/BU
25A
HTR A/C
15A
RADIO
10A
ECM B
10A
ECM I
30 A
PWR WDO
25A
WIPER
10A
DRL
3A
CRANK
FUS/PLR
FRONT
12084577
FUSE BLOCK
REAR

1988–91 WIRING DIAGRAMS (CONT.)

CAUTION: Determine if non-cycling circuit breakers are hot before removing them. Hot non-cycling circuit breakers can cause personal injury.

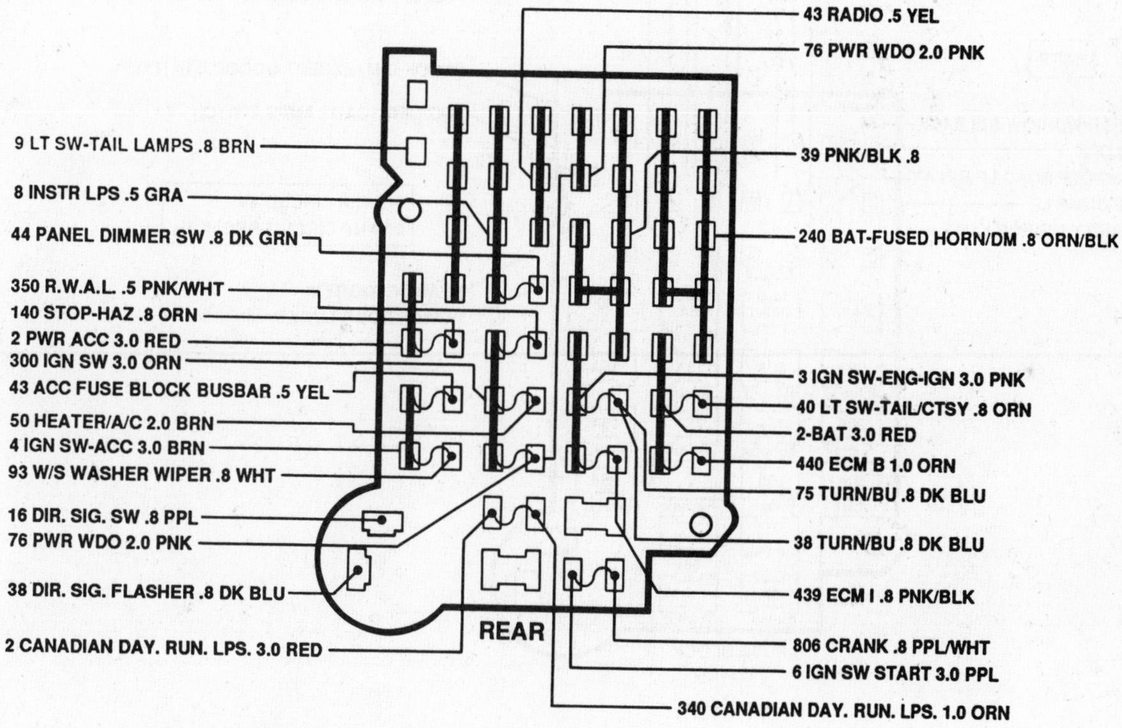

43 RADIO .5 YEL
76 PWR WDO 2.0 PNK
9 LT SW-TAIL LAMPS .8 BRN
39 PNK/BLK .8
8 INSTR LPS .5 GRA
44 PANEL DIMMER SW .8 DK GRN
240 BAT-FUSED HORN/DM .8 ORN/BLK
350 R.W.A.L. .5 PNK/WHT
140 STOP-HAZ .8 ORN
2 PWR ACC 3.0 RED
300 IGN SW 3.0 ORN
43 ACC FUSE BLOCK BUSBAR .5 YEL
3 IGN SW-ENG-IGN 3.0 PNK
40 LT SW-TAIL/CTSY .8 ORN
50 HEATER/A/C 2.0 BRN
2-BAT 3.0 RED
4 IGN SW-ACC 3.0 BRN
440 ECM B 1.0 ORN
93 W/S WASHER WIPER .8 WHT
75 TURN/BU .8 DK BLU
16 DIR. SIG. SW .8 PPL
76 PWR WDO 2.0 PNK
38 TURN/BU .8 DK BLU
38 DIR. SIG. FLASHER .8 DK BLU
439 ECM I .8 PNK/BLK
REAR
2 CANADIAN DAY. RUN. LPS. 3.0 RED
806 CRANK .8 PPL/WHT
6 IGN SW START 3.0 PPL
340 CANADIAN DAY. RUN. LPS. 1.0 ORN

FUSE INFORMATION

FUSES	AMP	COLOR
12004005	5	TAN
12004007	10	RED
12004008	15	LT BLU
12004009	20	YEL
12004010	25	WHT
12004003	3	VIOLET
12004006	7.5	BROWN
12004011	30	LT GRN

POWER DISTRIBUTION - FUSE BLOCK W/GAGES I/P

1988–91 WIRING DIAGRAMS (CONT.)

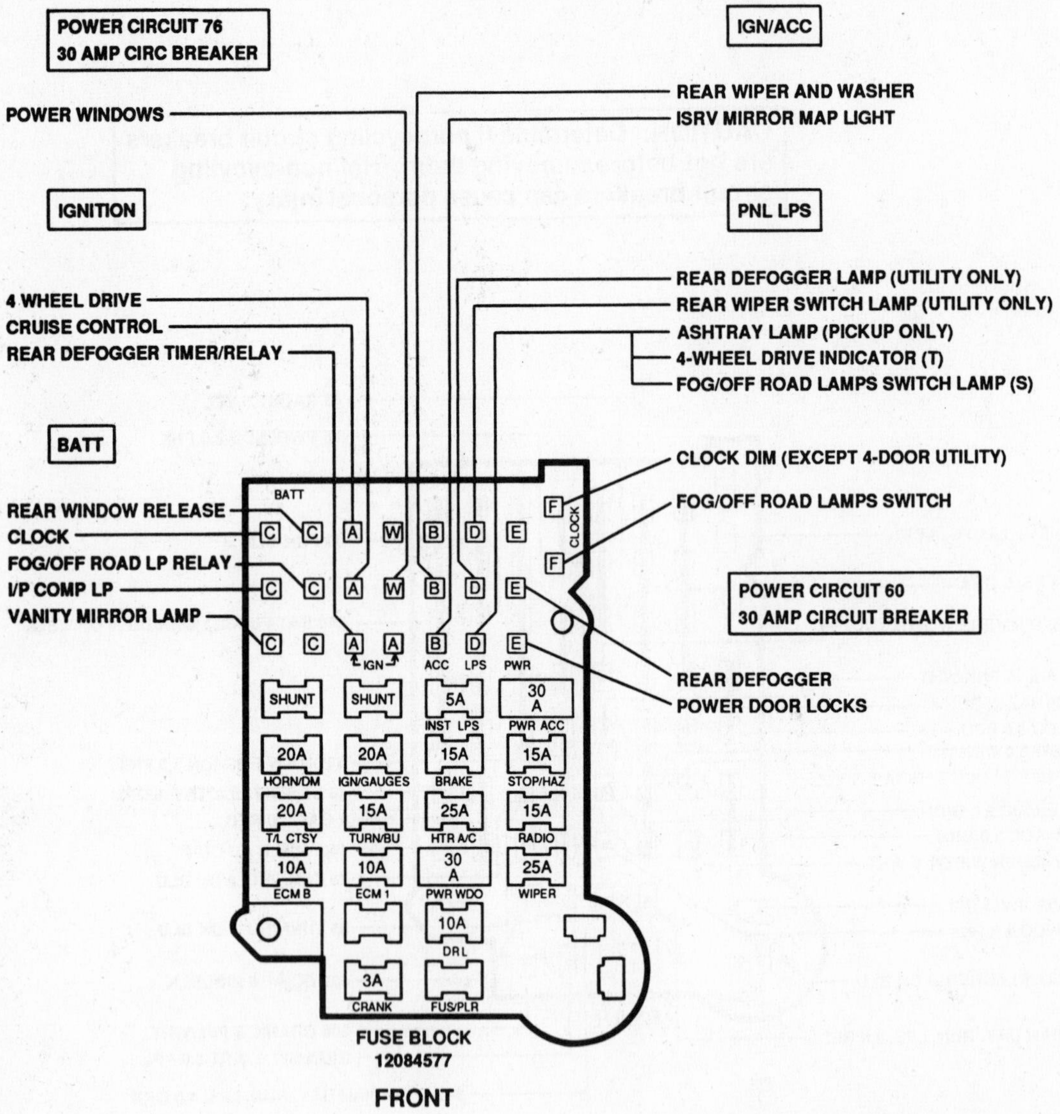
POWER CIRCUIT 76
30 AMP CIRC BREAKER
IGN/ACC
REAR WIPER AND WASHER
POWER WINDOWS
ISRV MIRROR MAP LIGHT
IGNITION
PNL LPS
REAR DEFOGGER LAMP (UTILITY ONLY)
4 WHEEL DRIVE
REAR WIPER SWITCH LAMP (UTILITY ONLY)
CRUISE CONTROL
ASHTRAY LAMP (PICKUP ONLY)
REAR DEFOGGER TIMER/RELAY
4-WHEEL DRIVE INDICATOR (T)
FOG/OFF ROAD LAMPS SWITCH LAMP (S)
BATT
CLOCK DIM (EXCEPT 4-DOOR UTILITY)
FOG/OFF ROAD LAMPS SWITCH
REAR WINDOW RELEASE
CLOCK
FOG/OFF ROAD LP RELAY
I/P COMP LP
VANITY MIRROR LAMP
POWER CIRCUIT 60
30 AMP CIRCUIT BREAKER
REAR DEFOGGER
POWER DOOR LOCKS
BATT
CLOCK
IGN
ACC
LPS
PWR
SHUNT
SHUNT
5A
INST LPS
30 A
PWR ACC
20A
HORN/DM
20A
IGN/GAUGES
15A
BRAKE
15A
STOP/HAZ
20A
T/L CTSY
15A
TURN/BU
25A
HTR A/C
15A
RADIO
10A
ECM B
10A
ECM 1
30 A
PWR WDO
25A
WIPER
10A
DRL
3A
CRANK
FUS/PLR

FUSE BLOCK
12084577

FRONT

FUSE BLOCK ACCESSORY CONNECTORS

	COLOR	MALE CONN	MULT CONN
A	NAT	12004888	12004892
B	BRN	12004887	12004893
C	BLK	12004886	12004890
D	GRN	12004885	12004962
E	RED	12004883	12004889
W	BLU	12004884	NOT USABLE
F	DK GRA	12004740	

1988–91 WIRING DIAGRAMS (CONT.)

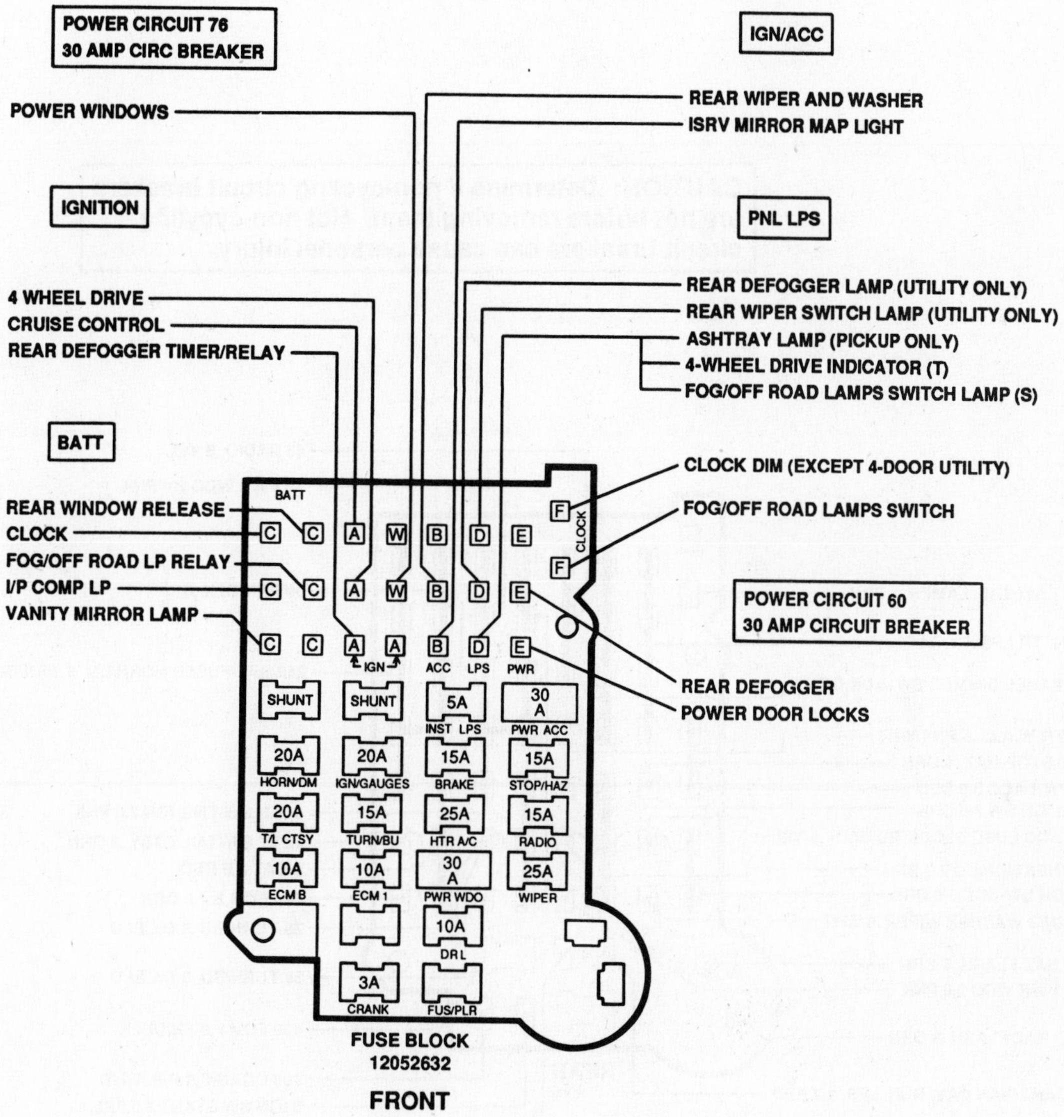
POWER CIRCUIT 76
30 AMP CIRC BREAKER
IGN/ACC
POWER WINDOWS
REAR WIPER AND WASHER
ISRV MIRROR MAP LIGHT
IGNITION
PNL LPS
4 WHEEL DRIVE
CRUISE CONTROL
REAR DEFOGGER TIMER/RELAY
REAR DEFOGGER LAMP (UTILITY ONLY)
REAR WIPER SWITCH LAMP (UTILITY ONLY)
ASHTRAY LAMP (PICKUP ONLY)
4-WHEEL DRIVE INDICATOR (T)
FOG/OFF ROAD LAMPS SWITCH LAMP (S)
BATT
CLOCK DIM (EXCEPT 4-DOOR UTILITY)
FOG/OFF ROAD LAMPS SWITCH
REAR WINDOW RELEASE
CLOCK
FOG/OFF ROAD LP RELAY
I/P COMP LP
VANITY MIRROR LAMP
POWER CIRCUIT 60
30 AMP CIRCUIT BREAKER
IGN ACC LPS PWR
REAR DEFOGGER
POWER DOOR LOCKS
SHUNT
SHUNT
5A INST LPS
30 A PWR ACC
20A HORN/DM
20A IGN/GAUGES
15A BRAKE
15A STOP/HAZ
20A T/L CTSY
15A TURN/BU
25A HTR A/C
15A RADIO
10A ECM B
10A ECM 1
30 A PWR WDO
25A WIPER
10A DRL
3A CRANK
FUS/PLR
FUSE BLOCK
12052632
FRONT

FUSE BLOCK ACCESSORY CONNECTORS

	COLOR	MALE CONN	MULT CONN
A	NAT	12004888	12004892
B	BRN	12004887	12004893
C	BLK	12004886	12004890
D	GRN	12004885	12004962
E	RED	12004883	12004889
W	BLU	12004884	NOT USABLE
F	DK GRA	12004740	

POWER DISTRIBUTION - FUSE BLOCK W/DIGITAL I/P

1988–91 WIRING DIAGRAMS (CONT.)

CAUTION: Determine if non-cycling circuit breakers are hot before removing them. Hot non-cycling circuit breakers can cause personal injury.

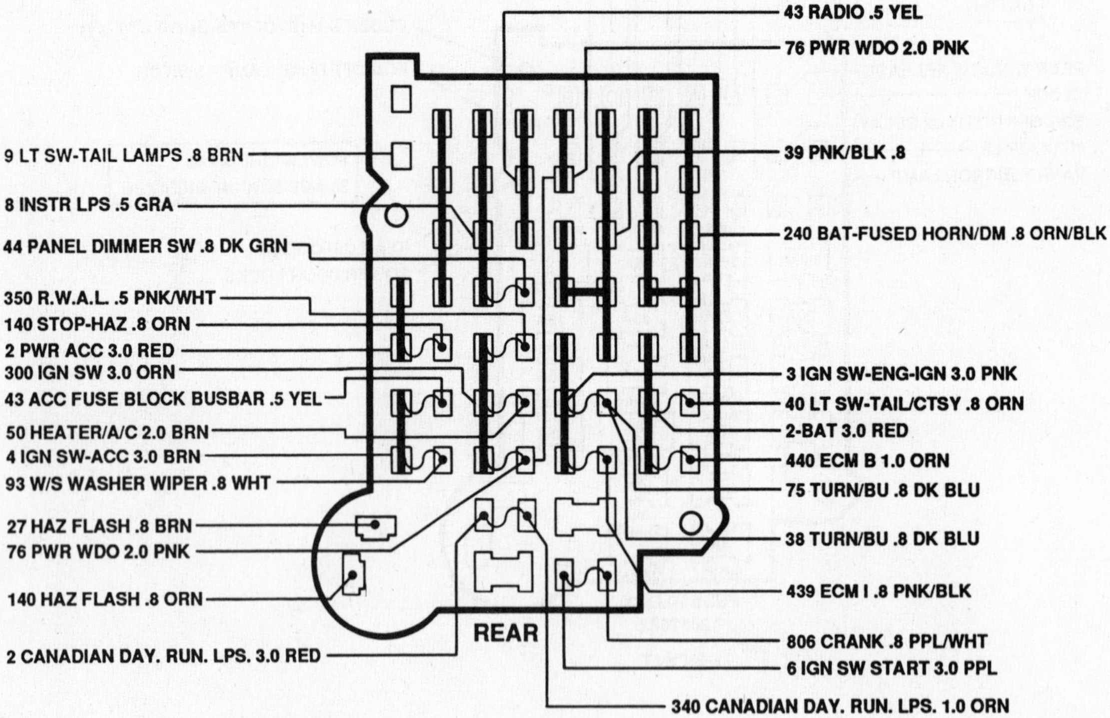

43 RADIO .5 YEL
76 PWR WDO 2.0 PNK
9 LT SW-TAIL LAMPS .8 BRN
39 PNK/BLK .8
8 INSTR LPS .5 GRA
240 BAT-FUSED HORN/DM .8 ORN/BLK
44 PANEL DIMMER SW .8 DK GRN
350 R.W.A.L. .5 PNK/WHT
140 STOP-HAZ .8 ORN
2 PWR ACC 3.0 RED
300 IGN SW 3.0 ORN
3 IGN SW-ENG-IGN 3.0 PNK
43 ACC FUSE BLOCK BUSBAR .5 YEL
40 LT SW-TAIL/CTSY .8 ORN
50 HEATER/A/C 2.0 BRN
2-BAT 3.0 RED
4 IGN SW-ACC 3.0 BRN
440 ECM B 1.0 ORN
93 W/S WASHER WIPER .8 WHT
75 TURN/BU .8 DK BLU
27 HAZ FLASH .8 BRN
38 TURN/BU .8 DK BLU
76 PWR WDO 2.0 PNK
140 HAZ FLASH .8 ORN
439 ECM I .8 PNK/BLK
REAR
806 CRANK .8 PPL/WHT
2 CANADIAN DAY. RUN. LPS. 3.0 RED
6 IGN SW START 3.0 PPL
340 CANADIAN DAY. RUN. LPS. 1.0 ORN

FUSE INFORMATION

FUSES	AMP	COLOR
12004005	5	TAN
12004007	10	RED
12004008	15	LT BLU
12004009	20	YEL
12004010	25	WHT
12004003	3	VIOLET
12004006	7.5	BROWN
12004011	30	LT GRN

1988–91 WIRING DIAGRAMS (CONT.)

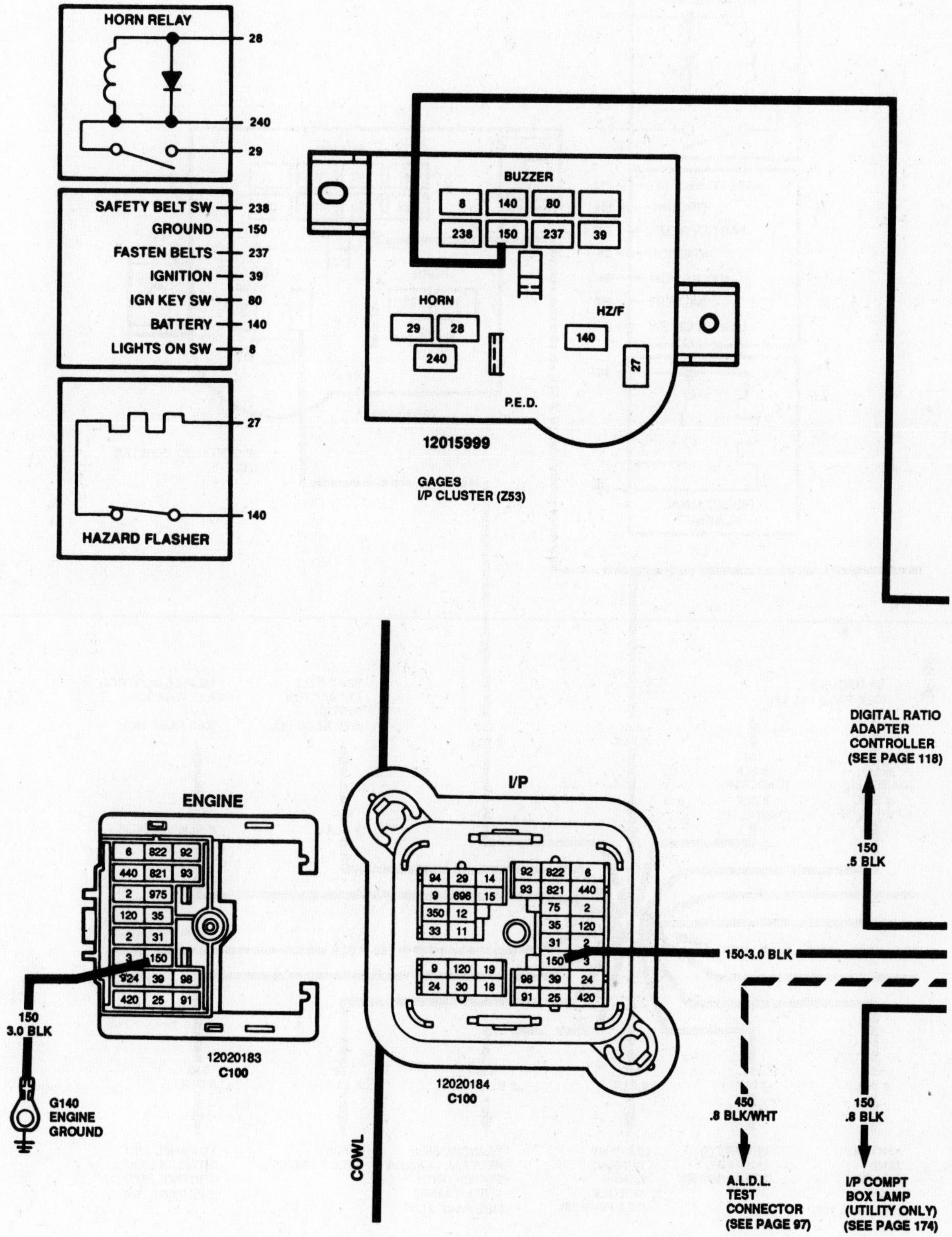
HORN RELAY
28
240
29
SAFETY BELT SW 238
GROUND 150
FASTEN BELTS 237
IGNITION 39
IGN KEY SW 80
BATTERY 140
LIGHTS ON SW 8
27
140
HAZARD FLASHER
BUZZER
8
140
80
238
150
237
39
HORN
29
28
240
HZ/F
140
27
P.E.D.
12015999
GAGES
I/P CLUSTER (Z53)
ENGINE
12020183
C100
150
3.0 BLK
G140
ENGINE
GROUND
I/P
12020184
C100
COWL
150-3.0 BLK
DIGITAL RATIO
ADAPTER
CONTROLLER
(SEE PAGE 118)
150
.5 BLK
450
.8 BLK/WHT
A.L.D.L.
TEST
CONNECTOR
(SEE PAGE 97)
150
.8 BLK
I/P COMPT
BOX LAMP
(UTILITY ONLY)
(SEE PAGE 174)

1988–91 WIRING DIAGRAMS (CONT.)

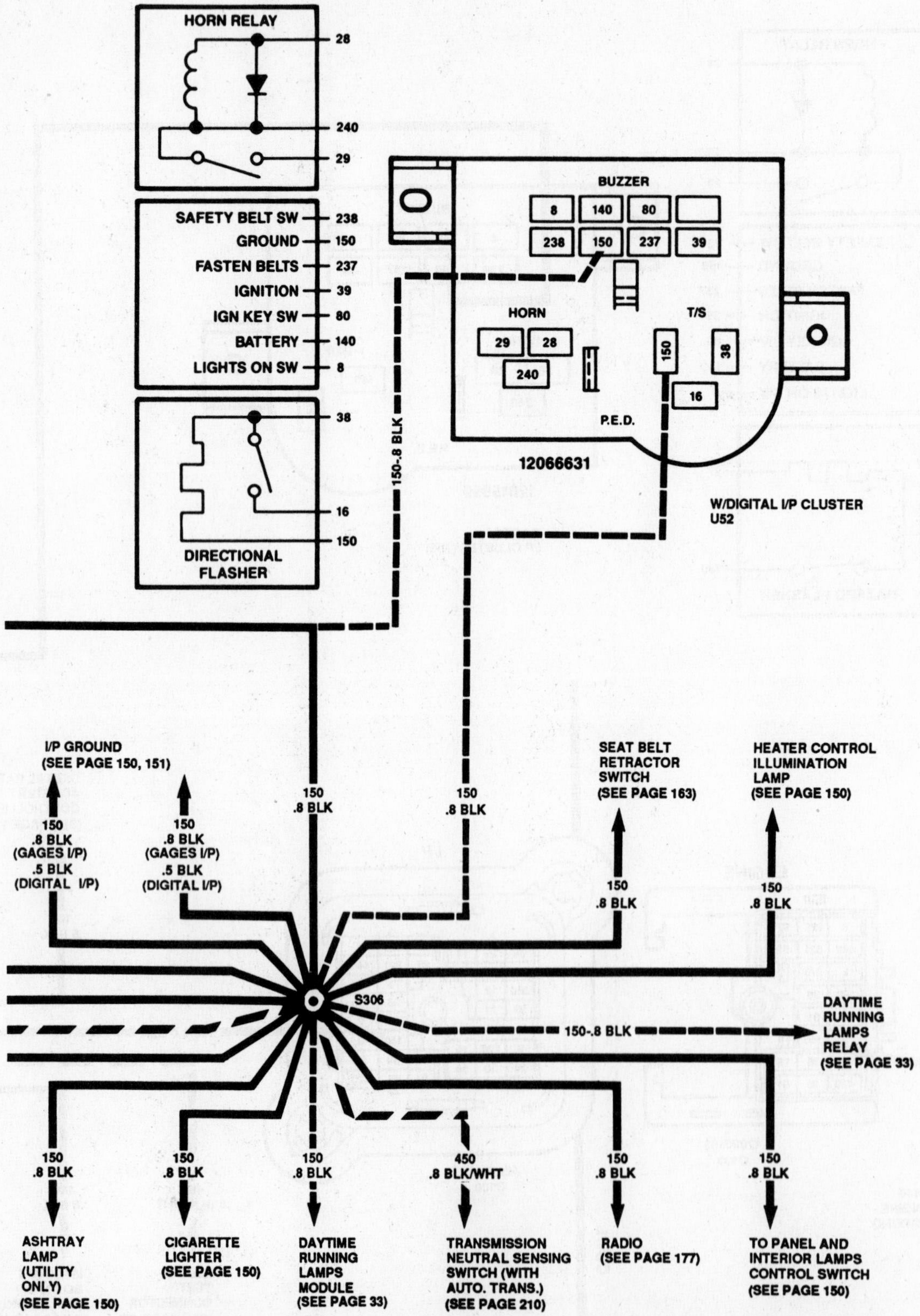
HORN RELAY
28
240
29
SAFETY BELT SW 238
GROUND 150
FASTEN BELTS 237
IGNITION 39
IGN KEY SW 80
BATTERY 140
LIGHTS ON SW 8
38
16
150
DIRECTIONAL FLASHER
BUZZER
8 140 80
238 150 237 39
HORN
29 28
240
T/S
150
38
16
P.E.D.
12066631
150-.8 BLK
W/DIGITAL I/P CLUSTER U52
I/P GROUND (SEE PAGE 150, 151)
150 .8 BLK (GAGES I/P) .5 BLK (DIGITAL I/P)
150 .8 BLK (GAGES I/P) .5 BLK (DIGITAL I/P)
150 .8 BLK
150 .8 BLK
SEAT BELT RETRACTOR SWITCH (SEE PAGE 163)
150 .8 BLK
HEATER CONTROL ILLUMINATION LAMP (SEE PAGE 150)
150 .8 BLK
S306
150-.8 BLK
DAYTIME RUNNING LAMPS RELAY (SEE PAGE 33)
150 .8 BLK
150 .8 BLK
150 .8 BLK
450 .8 BLK/WHT
150 .8 BLK
150 .8 BLK
ASHTRAY LAMP (UTILITY ONLY) (SEE PAGE 150)
CIGARETTE LIGHTER (SEE PAGE 150)
DAYTIME RUNNING LAMPS MODULE (SEE PAGE 33)
TRANSMISSION NEUTRAL SENSING SWITCH (WITH AUTO. TRANS.) (SEE PAGE 210)
RADIO (SEE PAGE 177)
TO PANEL AND INTERIOR LAMPS CONTROL SWITCH (SEE PAGE 150)

POWER DISTRIBUTION - CONVENIENCE CENTER

1988–91 WIRING DIAGRAMS (CONT.)

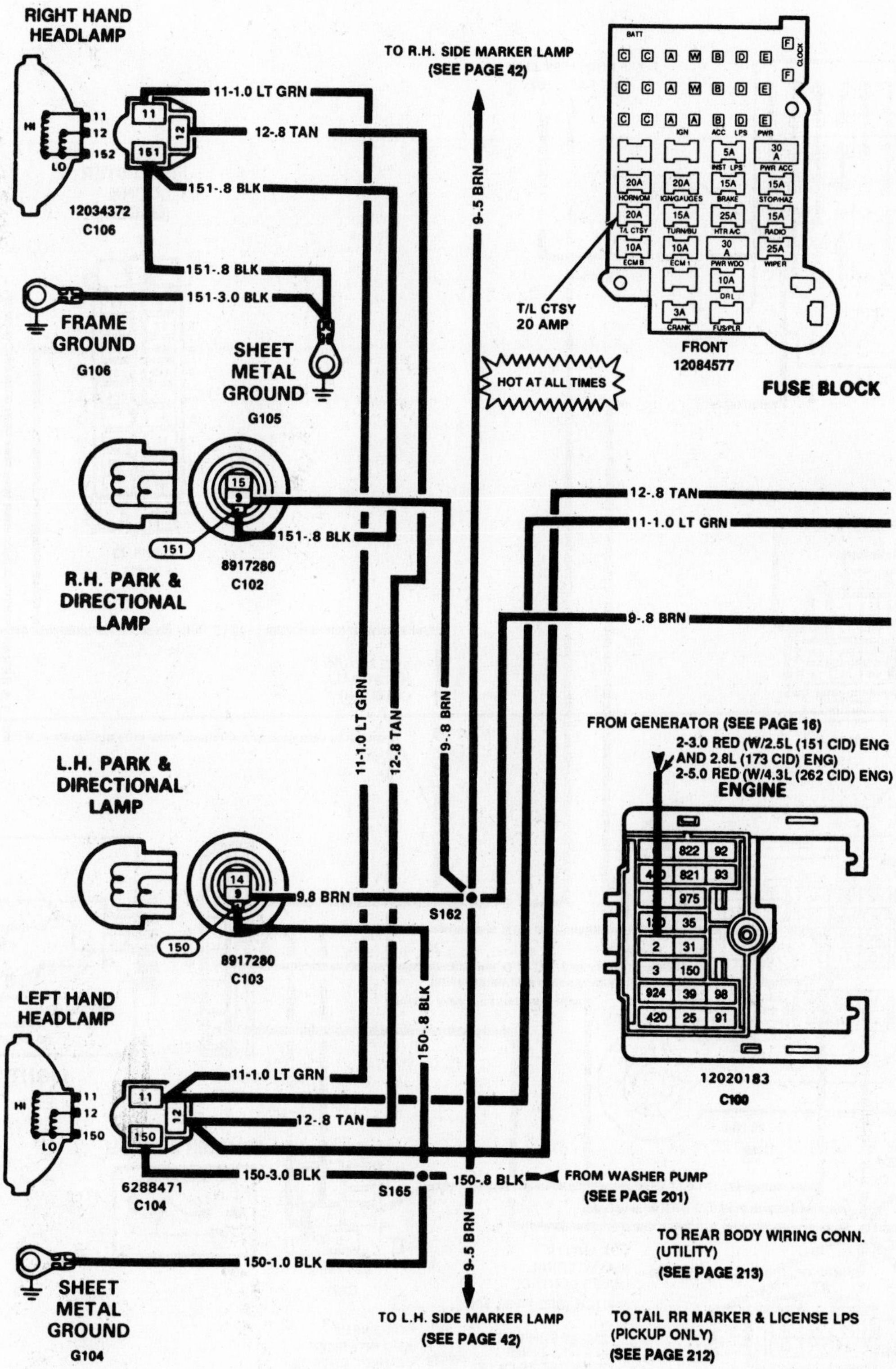

RIGHT HAND HEADLAMP
12034372
C106
11-1.0 LT GRN
12-.8 TAN
151-.8 BLK
151-.8 BLK
151-3.0 BLK
FRAME GROUND
G106
SHEET METAL GROUND
G105
TO R.H. SIDE MARKER LAMP (SEE PAGE 42)
9-.5 BRN
HOT AT ALL TIMES
T/L CTSY 20 AMP
FRONT
12084577
FUSE BLOCK
R.H. PARK & DIRECTIONAL LAMP
8917280
C102
151-.8 BLK
12-.8 TAN
11-1.0 LT GRN
9-.8 BRN
11-1.0 LT GRN
12-.8 TAN
9-.8 BRN
FROM GENERATOR (SEE PAGE 16)
2-3.0 RED (W/2.5L (151 CID) ENG AND 2.8L (173 CID) ENG)
2-5.0 RED (W/4.3L (262 CID) ENG)
ENGINE
L.H. PARK & DIRECTIONAL LAMP
9.8 BRN
S162
8917280
C103
150-.8 BLK
12020183
C100
LEFT HAND HEADLAMP
11-1.0 LT GRN
12-.8 TAN
6288471
C104
150-3.0 BLK
S165
150-.8 BLK
FROM WASHER PUMP (SEE PAGE 201)
TO REAR BODY WIRING CONN. (UTILITY) (SEE PAGE 213)
150-1.0 BLK
9-.5 BRN
SHEET METAL GROUND
G104
TO L.H. SIDE MARKER LAMP (SEE PAGE 42)
TO TAIL RR MARKER & LICENSE LPS (PICKUP ONLY) (SEE PAGE 212)

HEADLAMPS AND PARKING LAMPS - W/O CANADIAN DAYTIME RUNNING LAMPS Z49 - PICKUP AND 2-DOOR UTILITY

1988–91 WIRING DIAGRAMS (CONT.)

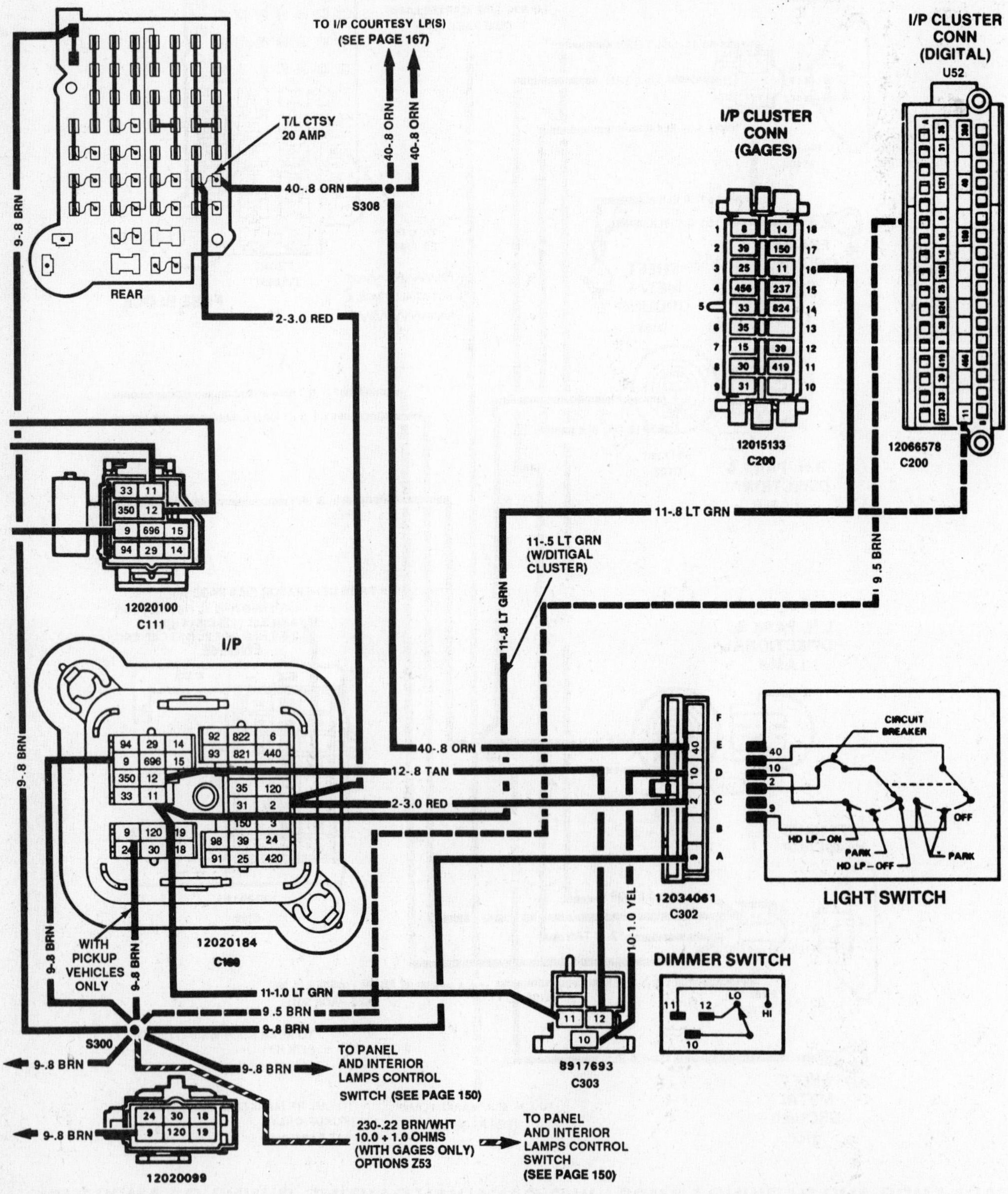
TO I/P COURTESY LP(S) (SEE PAGE 167)
I/P CLUSTER CONN (DIGITAL)
U52
I/P CLUSTER CONN (GAGES)
T/L CTSY 20 AMP
40-.8 ORN
S308
9-.8 BRN
REAR
2-3.0 RED
12015133
C200
12066578
C200
11-.8 LT GRN
11-.5 LT GRN (W/DITIGAL CLUSTER)
9.5 BRN
11-.8 LT GRN
12020100
C111
I/P
12-.8 TAN
CIRCUIT BREAKER
HD LP-ON
PARK
HD LP-OFF
OFF
LIGHT SWITCH
12034061
C302
10-1.0 YEL
DIMMER SWITCH
LO
HI
WITH PICKUP VEHICLES ONLY
12020184
C100
11-1.0 LT GRN
9.5 BRN
9-.8 BRN
S300
8917693
C303
TO PANEL AND INTERIOR LAMPS CONTROL SWITCH (SEE PAGE 150)
230-.22 BRN/WHT 10.0 + 1.0 OHMS (WITH GAGES ONLY) OPTIONS Z53
TO PANEL AND INTERIOR LAMPS CONTROL SWITCH (SEE PAGE 150)
12020099

1988–91 WIRING DIAGRAMS (CONT.)

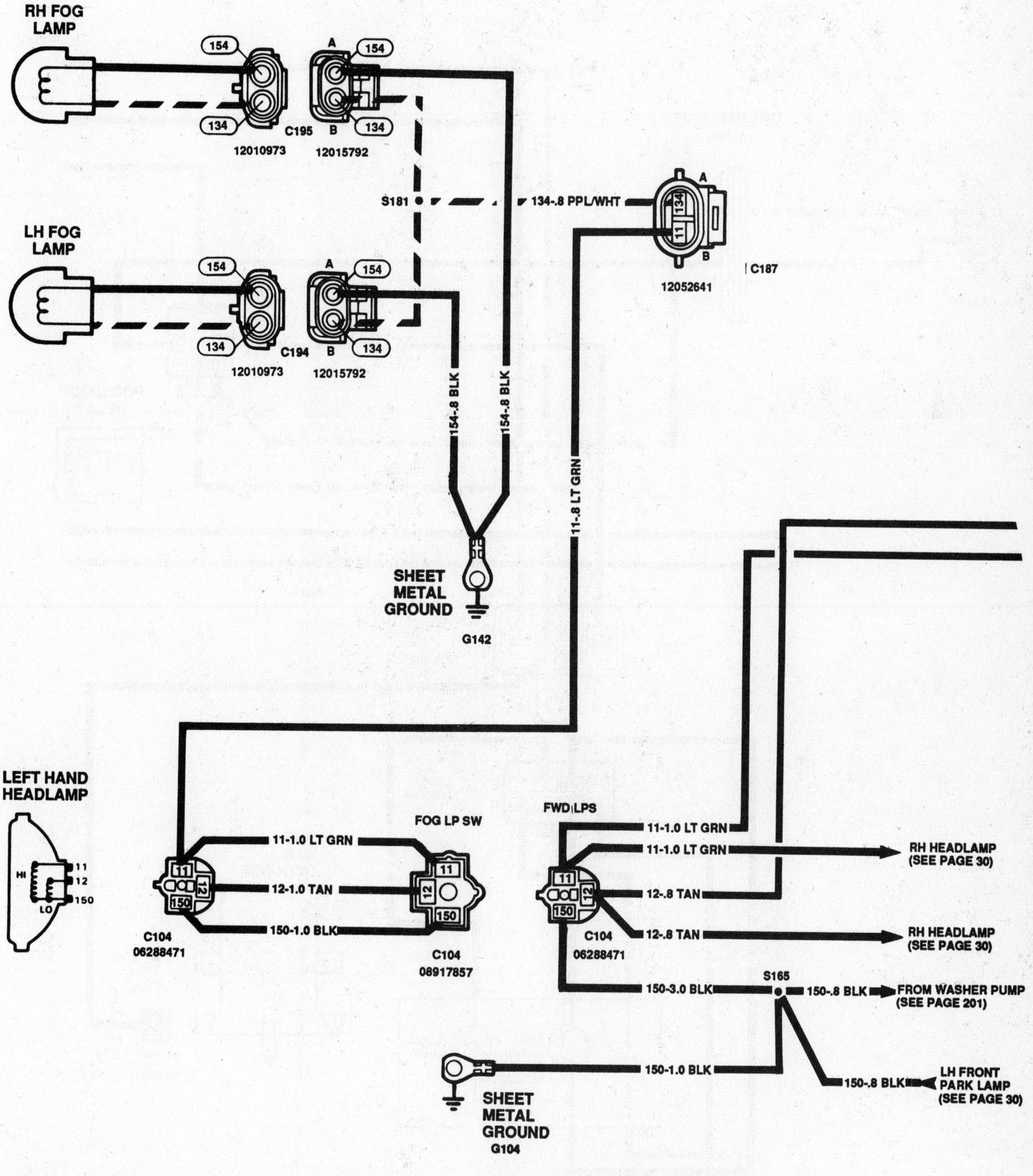
RH FOG LAMP
154
134
C195
12010973
A
154
B
134
12015792
S181
134-.8 PPL/WHT
A
134
11
B
C187
12052641
LH FOG LAMP
154
134
C194
12010973
A
154
B
134
12015792
154-.8 BLK
154-.8 BLK
11-.8 LT GRN
SHEET METAL GROUND
G142
LEFT HAND HEADLAMP
HI
LO
11
12
150
11-1.0 LT GRN
12-1.0 TAN
150-1.0 BLK
C104
06288471
FOG LP SW
C104
08917857
FWD LPS
11-1.0 LT GRN
11-1.0 LT GRN
12-.8 TAN
12-.8 TAN
C104
06288471
RH HEADLAMP (SEE PAGE 30)
RH HEADLAMP (SEE PAGE 30)
150-3.0 BLK
S165
150-.8 BLK
FROM WASHER PUMP (SEE PAGE 201)
150-1.0 BLK
150-.8 BLK
LH FRONT PARK LAMP (SEE PAGE 30)
SHEET METAL GROUND
G104

FOG LAMPS (ANL) - W/O CANADIAN DAYTIME RUNNING LAMPS Z49

1988–91 WIRING DIAGRAMS (CONT.)

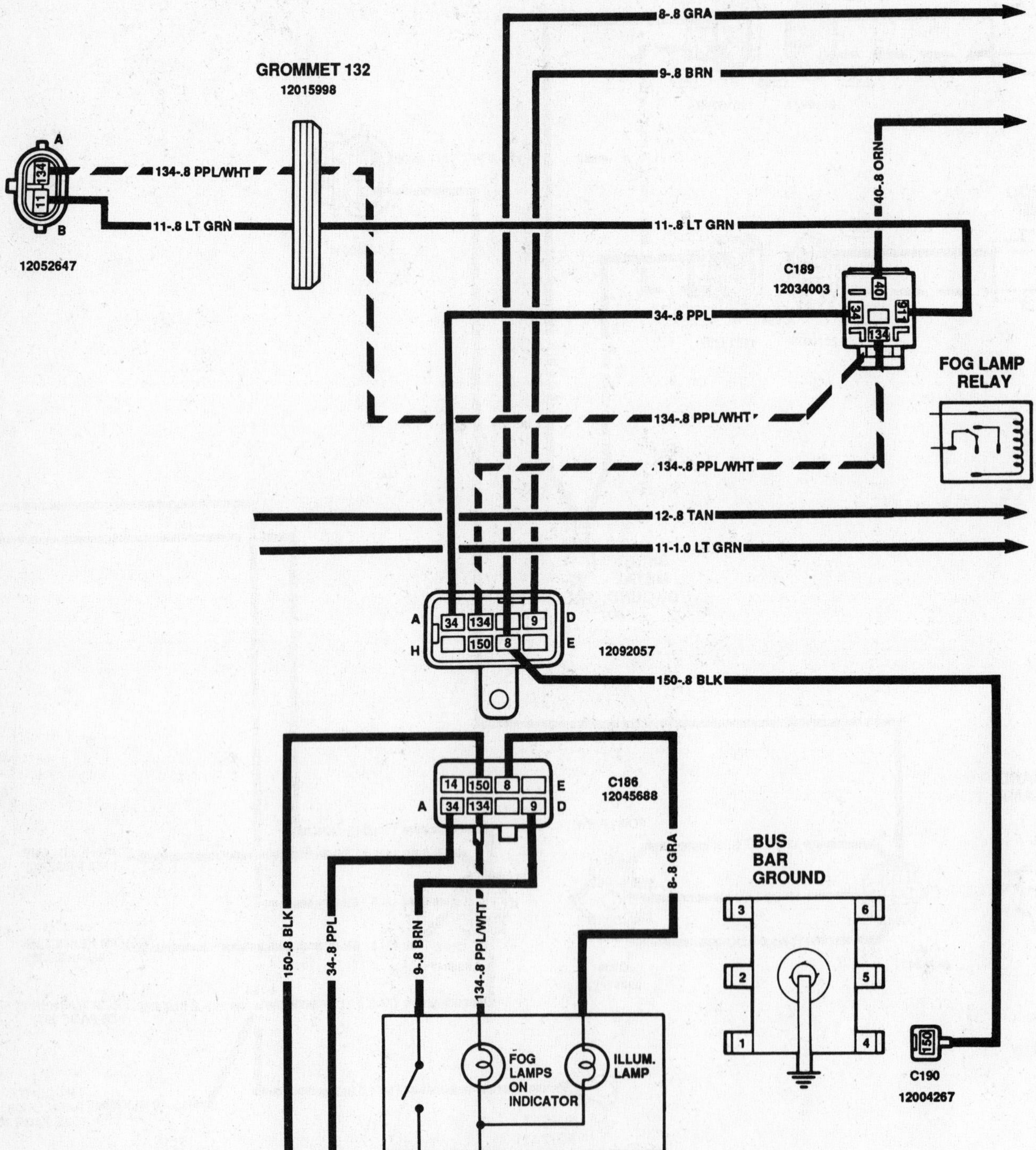

8-.8 GRA
9-.8 BRN
GROMMET 132
12015998
A
134
11
B
134-.8 PPL/WHT
11-.8 LT GRN
12052647
40-.8 ORN
11-.8 LT GRN
C189
12034003
40
34
11
134
34-.8 PPL
FOG LAMP
RELAY
134-.8 PPL/WHT
134-.8 PPL/WHT
12-.8 TAN
11-1.0 LT GRN
A
34
134
9
D
H
150
8
E
12092057
150-.8 BLK
14
150
8
E
A
34
134
9
D
C186
12045688
8-.8 GRA
150-.8 BLK
34-.8 PPL
9-.8 BRN
134-.8 PPL/WHT
BUS
BAR
GROUND
3
6
2
5
1
4
FOG
LAMPS
ON
INDICATOR
ILLUM.
LAMP
150
C190
12004267

1988–91 WIRING DIAGRAMS (CONT.)

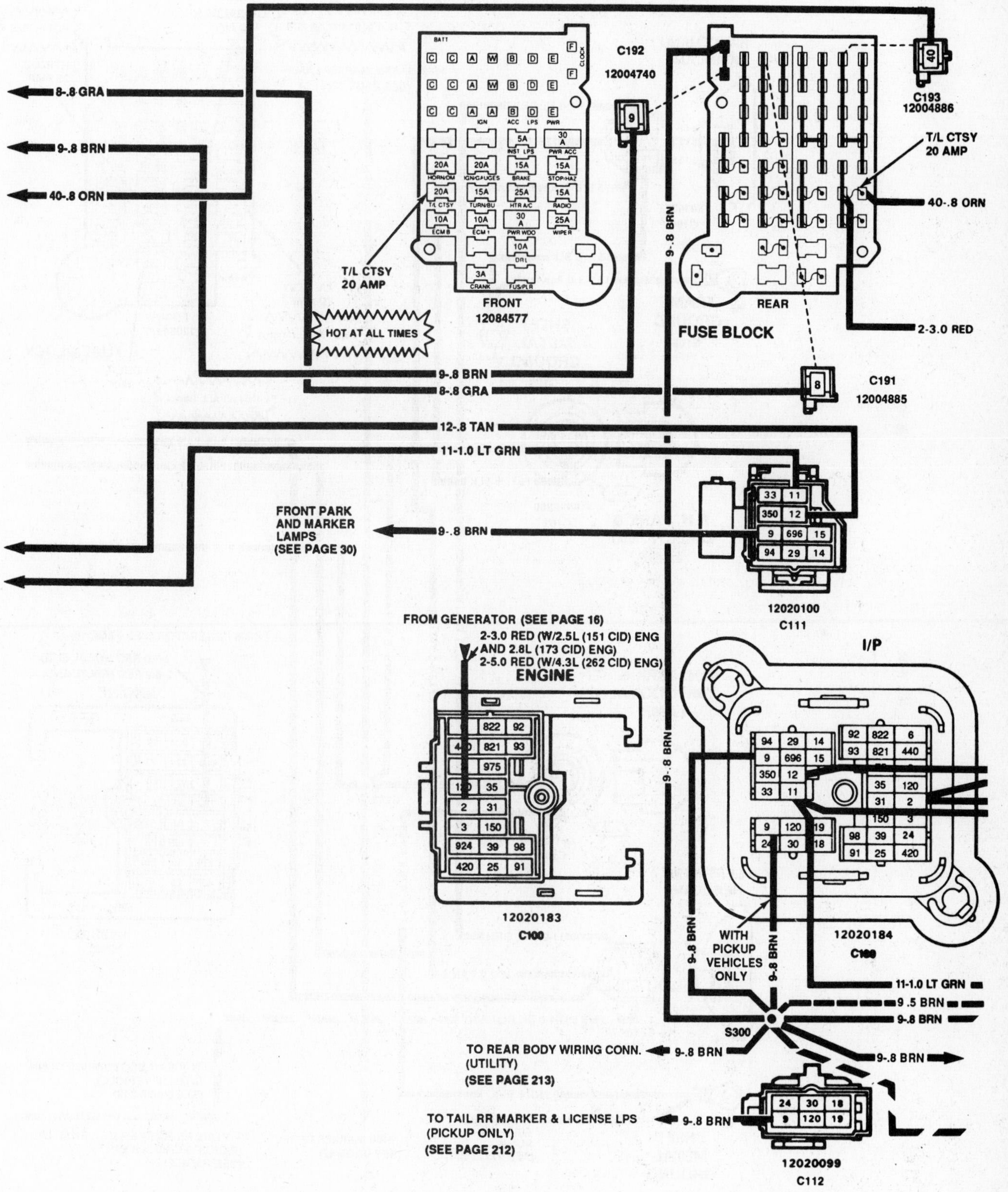

8-.8 GRA
9-.8 BRN
40-.8 ORN
T/L CTSY
20 AMP
HOT AT ALL TIMES
FRONT
12084577
C192
12004740
C193
12004886
T/L CTSY
20 AMP
40-.8 ORN
REAR
FUSE BLOCK
2-3.0 RED
9-.8 BRN
8-.8 GRA
C191
12004885
12-.8 TAN
11-1.0 LT GRN
FRONT PARK
AND MARKER
LAMPS
(SEE PAGE 30)
12020100
C111
FROM GENERATOR (SEE PAGE 16)
2-3.0 RED (W/2.5L (151 CID) ENG
AND 2.8L (173 CID) ENG)
2-5.0 RED (W/4.3L (262 CID) ENG)
ENGINE
I/P
12020183
C100
12020184
C100
WITH
PICKUP
VEHICLES
ONLY
11-1.0 LT GRN
9.5 BRN
9-.8 BRN
S300
TO REAR BODY WIRING CONN.
(UTILITY)
(SEE PAGE 213)
9-.8 BRN
TO TAIL RR MARKER & LICENSE LPS
(PICKUP ONLY)
(SEE PAGE 212)
12020099
C112

1988–91 WIRING DIAGRAMS (CONT.)

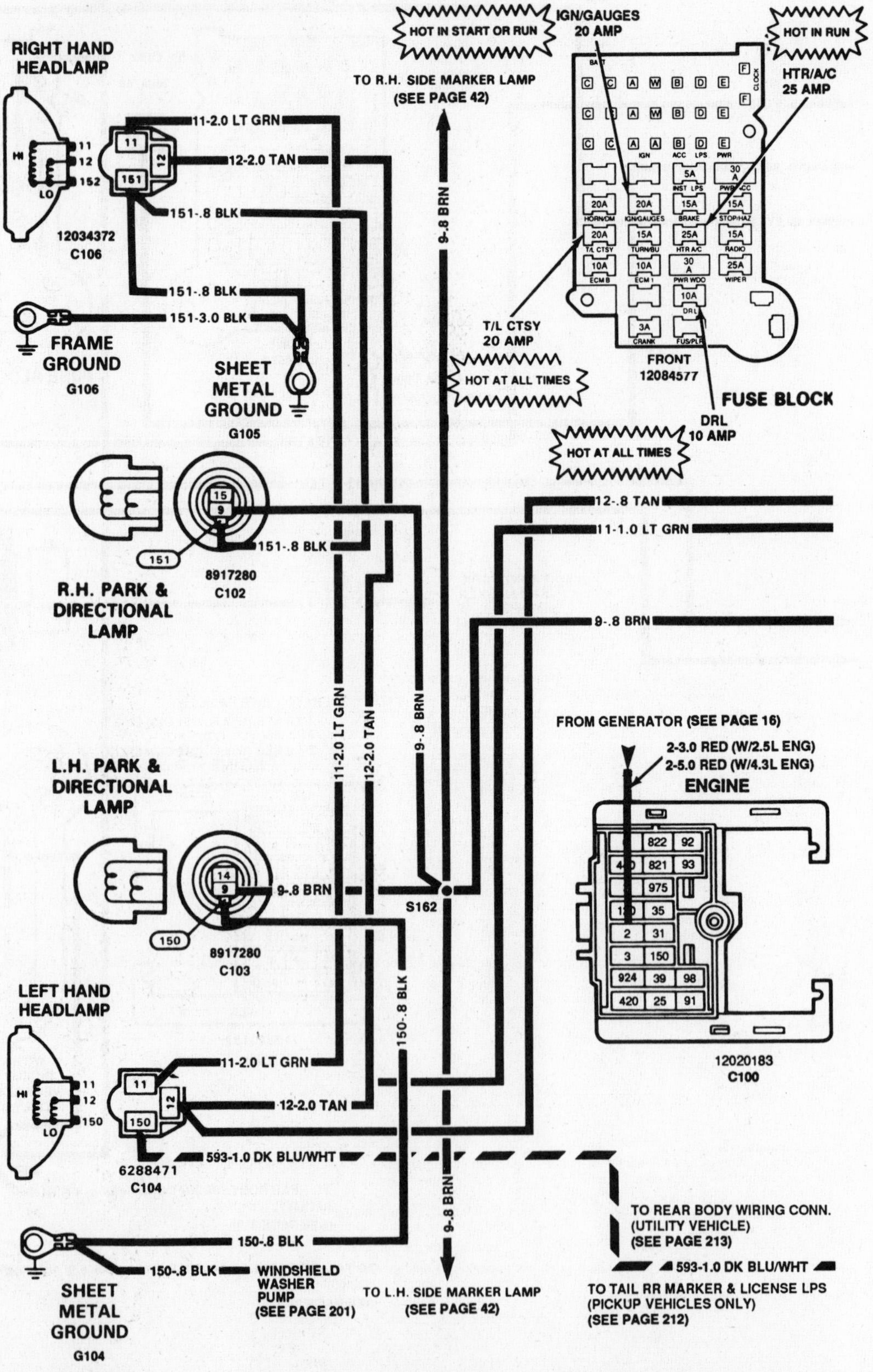

HOT IN START OR RUN
IGN/GAUGES 20 AMP
HOT IN RUN
HTR/A/C 25 AMP
RIGHT HAND HEADLAMP
TO R.H. SIDE MARKER LAMP (SEE PAGE 42)
11-2.0 LT GRN
12-2.0 TAN
151-.8 BLK
12034372 C106
151-.8 BLK
151-3.0 BLK
FRAME GROUND G106
SHEET METAL GROUND G105
9-.8 BRN
T/L CTSY 20 AMP
HOT AT ALL TIMES
FRONT 12084577
FUSE BLOCK
DRL 10 AMP
HOT AT ALL TIMES
12-.8 TAN
11-1.0 LT GRN
151-.8 BLK
8917280 C102
R.H. PARK & DIRECTIONAL LAMP
9-.8 BRN
11-2.0 LT GRN
12-2.0 TAN
9-.8 BRN
FROM GENERATOR (SEE PAGE 16)
2-3.0 RED (W/2.5L ENG)
2-5.0 RED (W/4.3L ENG)
ENGINE
L.H. PARK & DIRECTIONAL LAMP
9-.8 BRN
S162
8917280 C103
150-.8 BLK
12020183 C100
LEFT HAND HEADLAMP
11-2.0 LT GRN
12-2.0 TAN
593-1.0 DK BLU/WHT
6288471 C104
9-.8 BRN
TO REAR BODY WIRING CONN. (UTILITY VEHICLE) (SEE PAGE 213)
150-.8 BLK
593-1.0 DK BLU/WHT
150-.8 BLK
WINDSHIELD WASHER PUMP (SEE PAGE 201)
TO L.H. SIDE MARKER LAMP (SEE PAGE 42)
TO TAIL RR MARKER & LICENSE LPS (PICKUP VEHICLES ONLY) (SEE PAGE 212)
SHEET METAL GROUND G104

32 HEADLAMPS AND PARKING LAMPS - W/CANADIAN DAYTIME

1988–91 WIRING DIAGRAMS (CONT.)

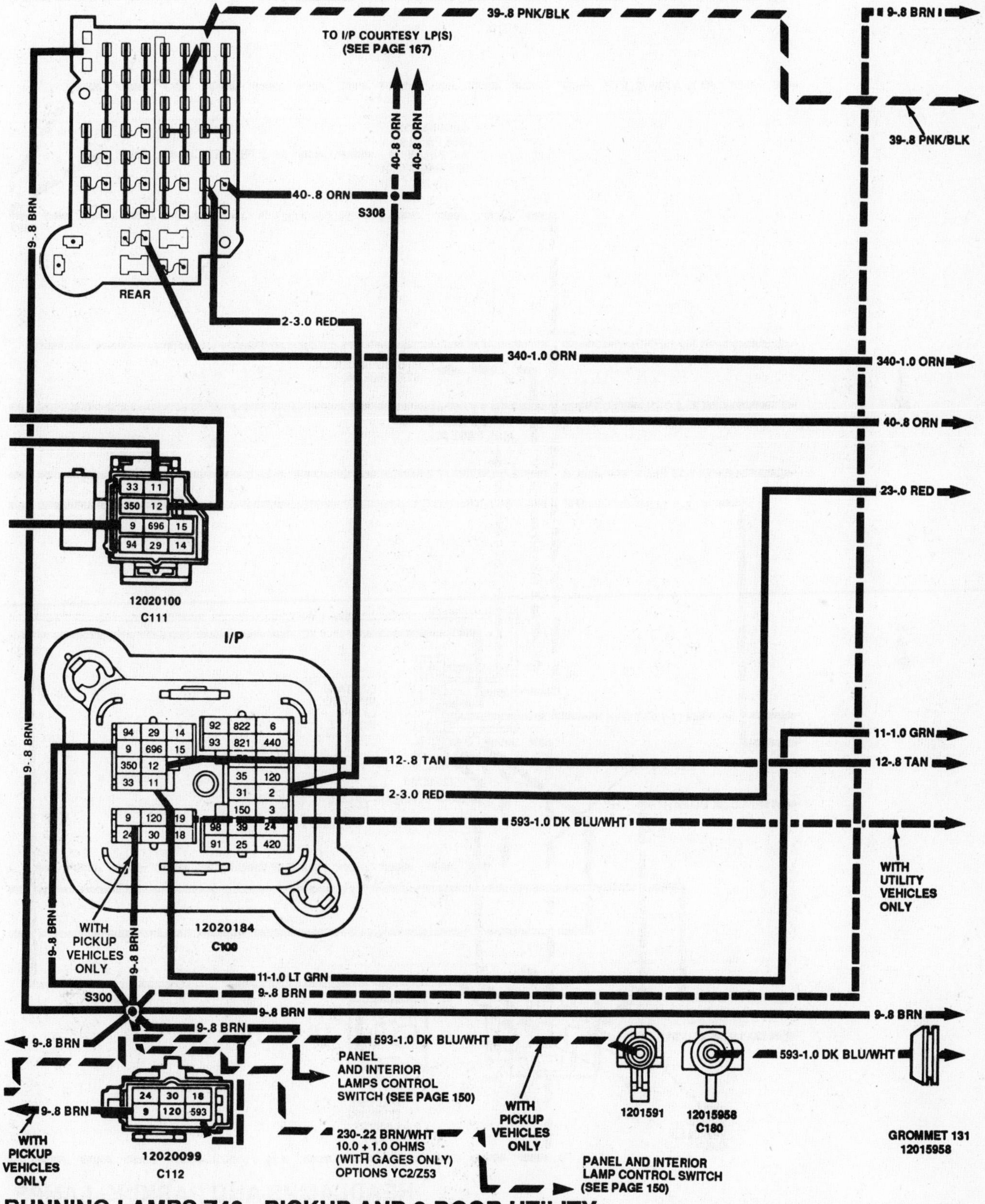
39-.8 PNK/BLK
TO I/P COURTESY LP(S) (SEE PAGE 167)
9-.8 BRN
39-.8 PNK/BLK
40-.8 ORN
40-.8 ORN
40-.8 ORN
S308
9-.8 BRN
REAR
2-3.0 RED
340-1.0 ORN
340-1.0 ORN
40-.8 ORN
23-.0 RED
12020100
C111
I/P
11-1.0 GRN
12-.8 TAN
12-.8 TAN
2-3.0 RED
593-1.0 DK BLU/WHT
WITH UTILITY VEHICLES ONLY
WITH PICKUP VEHICLES ONLY
12020184
C109
11-1.0 LT GRN
S300
9-.8 BRN
9-.8 BRN
9-.8 BRN
9-.8 BRN
9-.8 BRN
593-1.0 DK BLU/WHT
PANEL AND INTERIOR LAMPS CONTROL SWITCH (SEE PAGE 150)
593-1.0 DK BLU/WHT
9-.8 BRN
WITH PICKUP VEHICLES ONLY
12020099
C112
230-.22 BRN/WHT
10.0 + 1.0 OHMS
(WITH GAGES ONLY)
OPTIONS YC2/Z53
WITH PICKUP VEHICLES ONLY
1201591
12015958
C180
PANEL AND INTERIOR LAMP CONTROL SWITCH (SEE PAGE 150)
GROMMET 131
12015958

RUNNING LAMPS Z49 - PICKUP AND 2-DOOR UTILITY

1988–91 WIRING DIAGRAMS (CONT.)

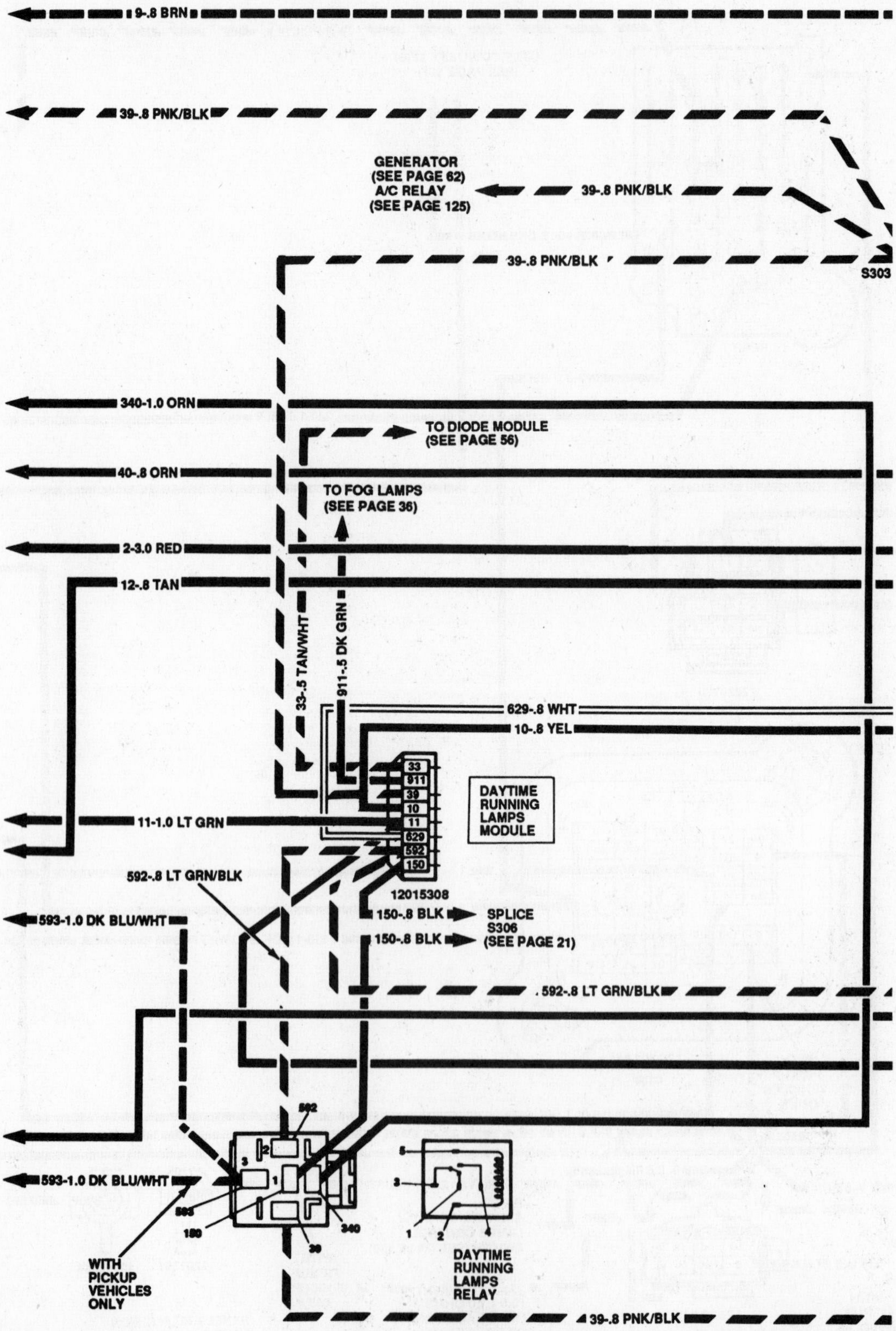
9-.8 BRN
39-.8 PNK/BLK
GENERATOR
(SEE PAGE 62)
A/C RELAY
(SEE PAGE 125)
39-.8 PNK/BLK
39-.8 PNK/BLK
S303
340-1.0 ORN
TO DIODE MODULE
(SEE PAGE 56)
40-.8 ORN
TO FOG LAMPS
(SEE PAGE 36)
2-3.0 RED
12-.8 TAN
33-.5 TAN/WHT
911-.5 DK GRN
629-.8 WHT
10-.8 YEL
33
911
39
10
11
629
592
150
DAYTIME
RUNNING
LAMPS
MODULE
11-1.0 LT GRN
12015308
592-.8 LT GRN/BLK
593-1.0 DK BLU/WHT
150-.8 BLK
150-.8 BLK
SPLICE
S306
(SEE PAGE 21)
592-.8 LT GRN/BLK
592
593-1.0 DK BLU/WHT
593
150
39
340
WITH
PICKUP
VEHICLES
ONLY
DAYTIME
RUNNING
LAMPS
RELAY
39-.8 PNK/BLK

HEADLAMPS AND PARKING LAMPS

1988–91 WIRING DIAGRAMS (CONT.)

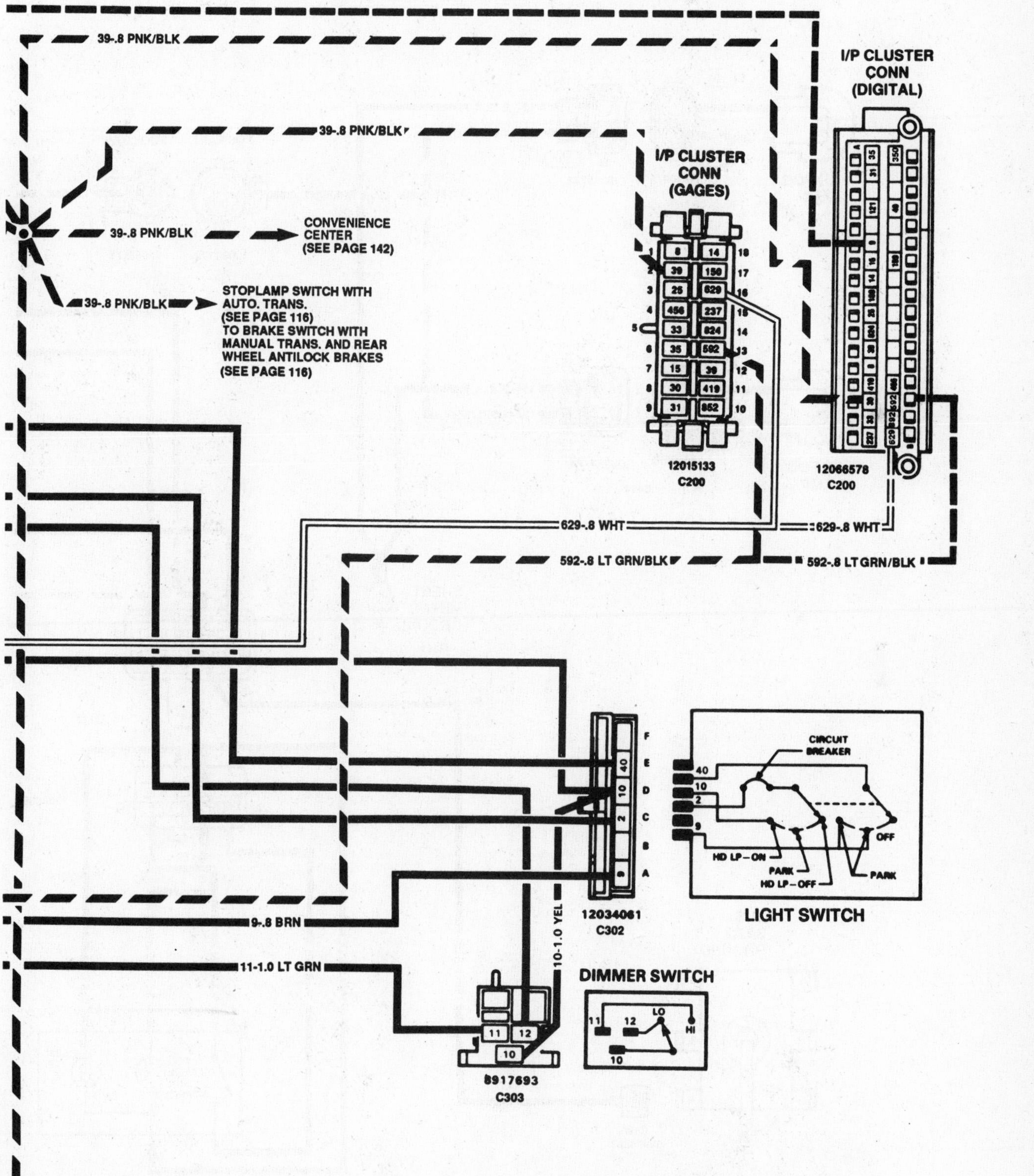
39-.8 PNK/BLK
39-.8 PNK/BLK
I/P CLUSTER CONN (DIGITAL)
I/P CLUSTER CONN (GAGES)
39-.8 PNK/BLK
CONVENIENCE CENTER (SEE PAGE 142)
39-.8 PNK/BLK
STOPLAMP SWITCH WITH AUTO. TRANS. (SEE PAGE 116) TO BRAKE SWITCH WITH MANUAL TRANS. AND REAR WHEEL ANTILOCK BRAKES (SEE PAGE 116)
12015133
C200
12066578
C200
629-.8 WHT
629-.8 WHT
592-.8 LT GRN/BLK
592-.8 LT GRN/BLK
CIRCUIT BREAKER
HD LP-ON
PARK
HD LP-OFF
PARK
OFF
LIGHT SWITCH
12034061
C302
9-.8 BRN
10-1.0 YEL
11-1.0 LT GRN
DIMMER SWITCH
LO
HI
8917693
C303

- W/CANADIAN DAYTIME RUNNING LAMPS Z49 - PICKUP AND 2-DOOR UTILITY 33

1988–91 WIRING DIAGRAMS (CONT.)

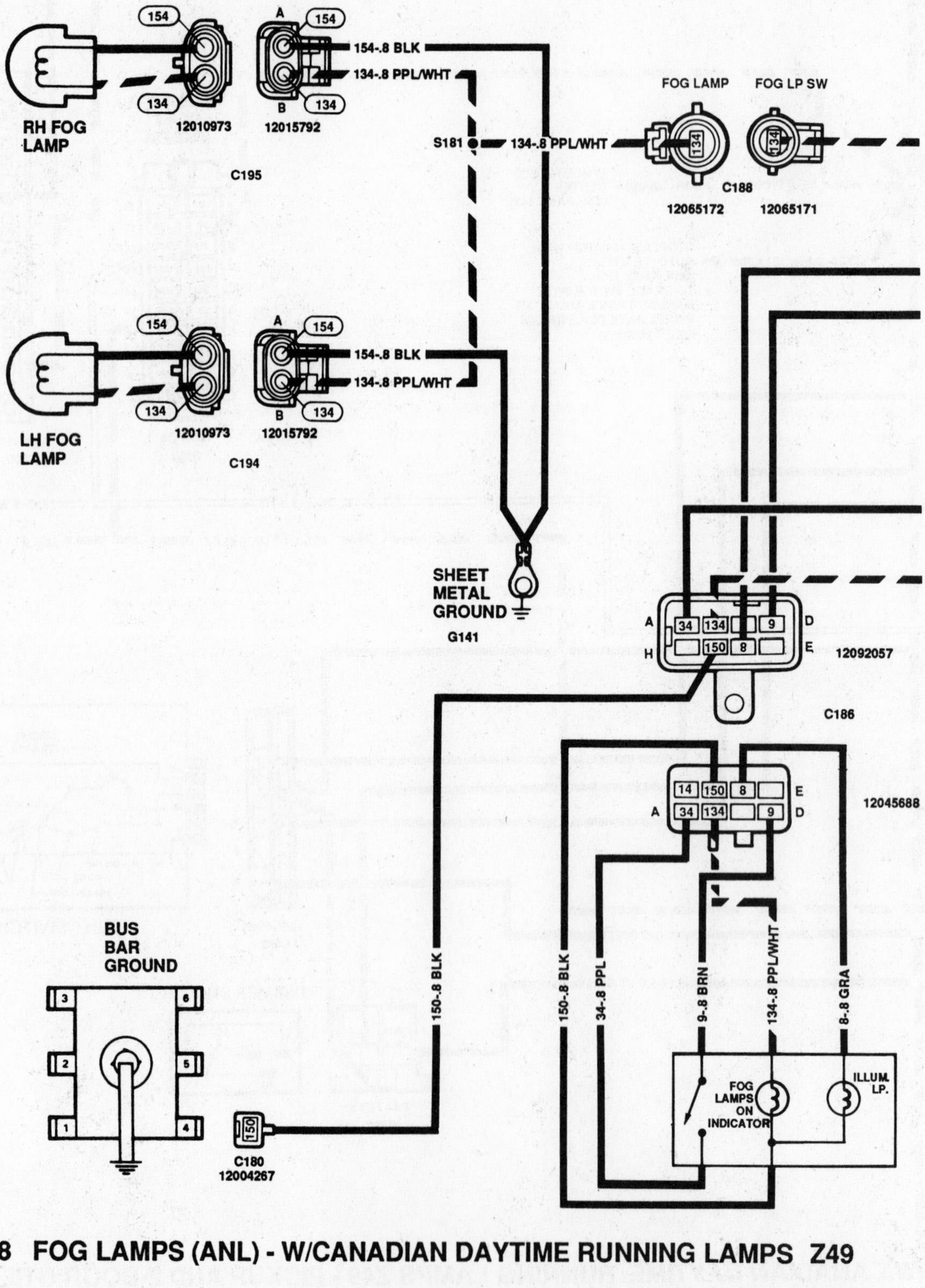
154
134
RH FOG LAMP
12010973
A
154
B
134
12015792
154-.8 BLK
134-.8 PPL/WHT
C195
S181
134-.8 PPL/WHT
FOG LAMP
FOG LP SW
134
134
C188
12065172
12065171
154
134
LH FOG LAMP
12010973
A
154
B
134
12015792
154-.8 BLK
134-.8 PPL/WHT
C194
SHEET METAL GROUND
G141
A
34
134
9
D
H
150
8
E
12092057
C186
14
150
8
E
A
34
134
9
D
12045688
BUS BAR GROUND
3
6
2
5
1
4
150
C180
12004267
150-.8 BLK
150-.8 BLK
34-.8 PPL
9-.8 BRN
134-.8 PPL/WHT
8-.8 GRA
FOG LAMPS ON INDICATOR
ILLUM. LP.

38 FOG LAMPS (ANL) - W/CANADIAN DAYTIME RUNNING LAMPS Z49

1988–91 WIRING DIAGRAMS (CONT.)

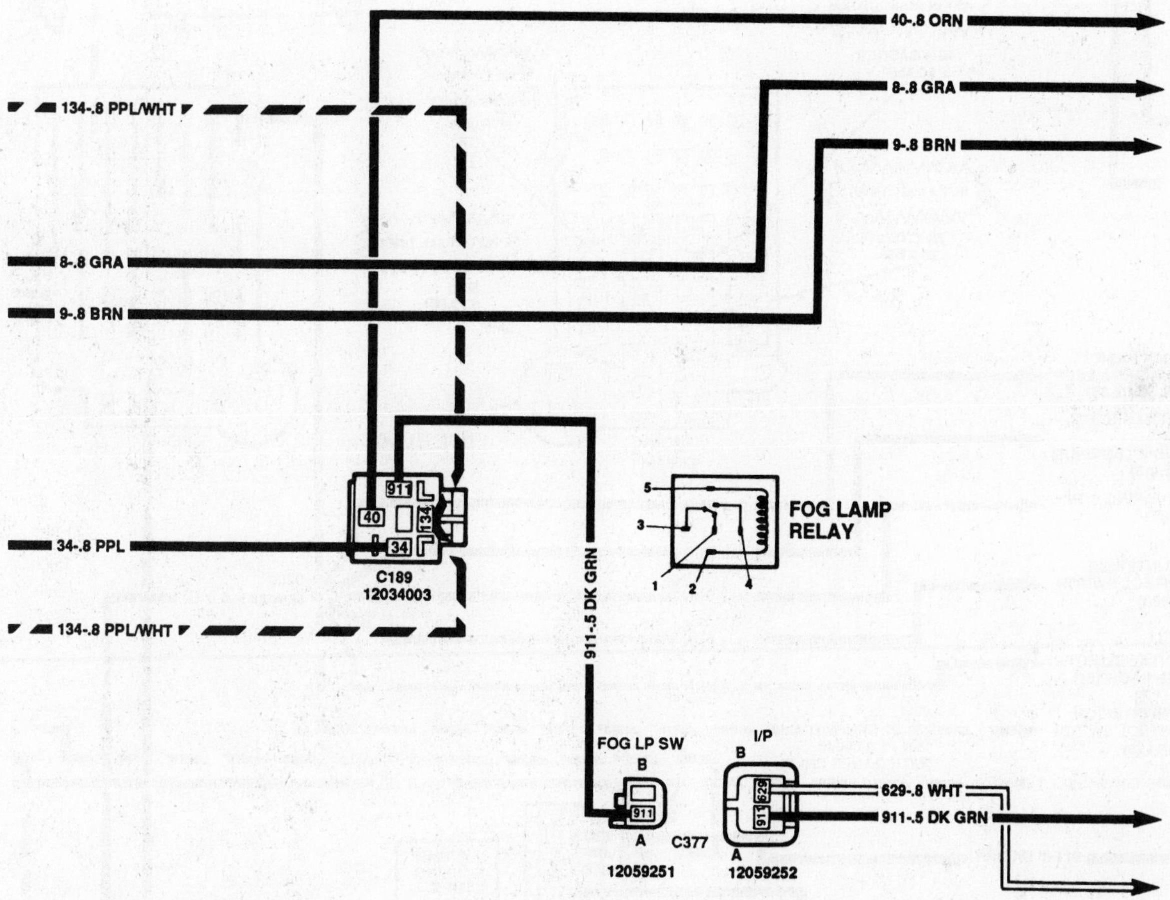
40-.8 ORN
8-.8 GRA
9-.8 BRN
134-.8 PPL/WHT
8-.8 GRA
9-.8 BRN
911
40
134
34
34-.8 PPL
C189
12034003
134-.8 PPL/WHT
911-.5 DK GRN
5
3
1
2
4
FOG LAMP
RELAY
FOG LP SW
B
911
A
C377
12059251
I/P
B
629
911
A
12059252
629-.8 WHT
911-.5 DK GRN

1988–91 WIRING DIAGRAMS (CONT.)

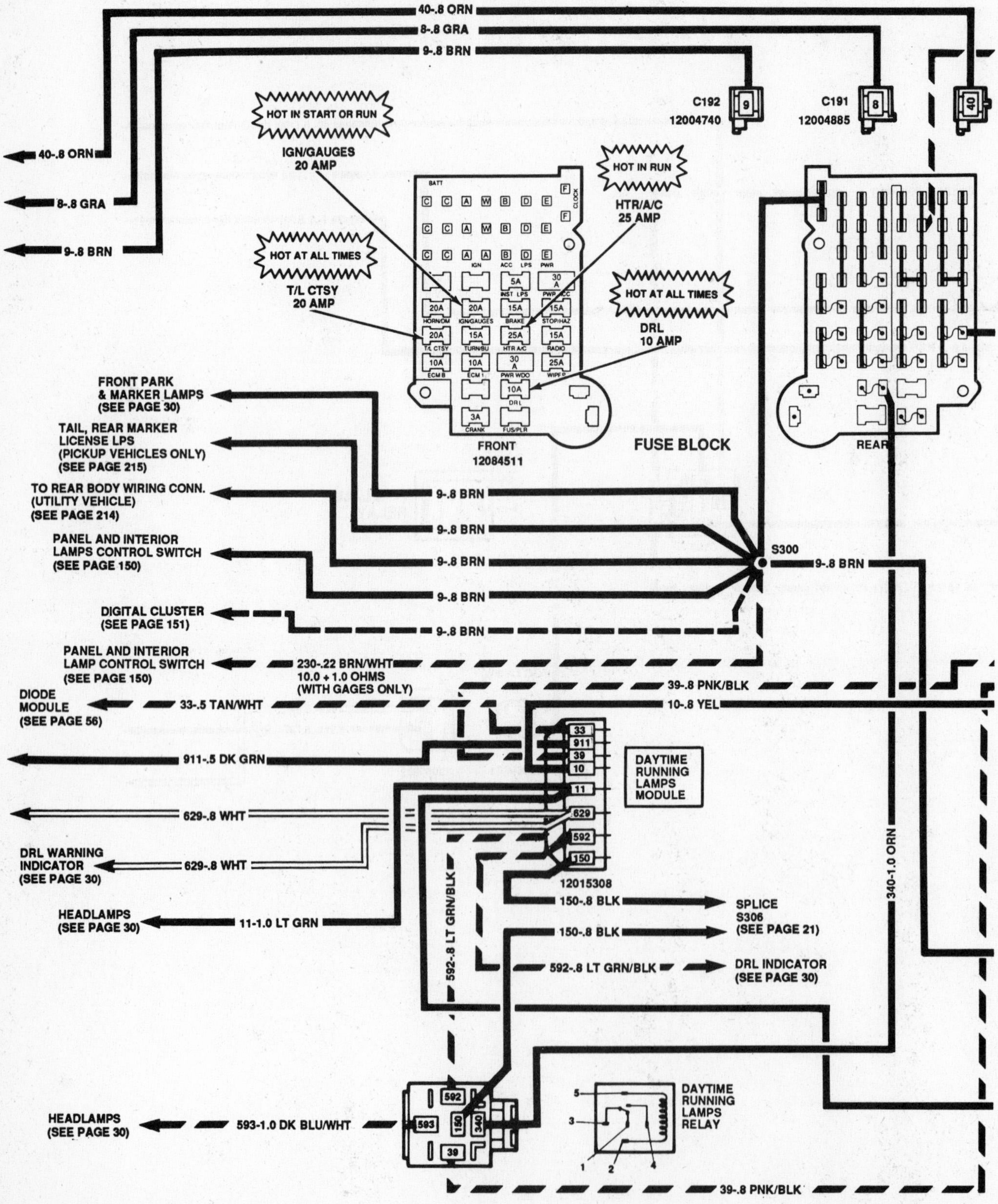
40-.8 ORN
8-.8 GRA
9-.8 BRN
C192
12004740
C191
12004885
HOT IN START OR RUN
IGN/GAUGES
20 AMP
HOT IN RUN
HTR/A/C
25 AMP
HOT AT ALL TIMES
T/L CTSY
20 AMP
HOT AT ALL TIMES
DRL
10 AMP
FRONT
12084511
FUSE BLOCK
REAR
FRONT PARK & MARKER LAMPS (SEE PAGE 30)
TAIL, REAR MARKER LICENSE LPS (PICKUP VEHICLES ONLY) (SEE PAGE 215)
TO REAR BODY WIRING CONN. (UTILITY VEHICLE) (SEE PAGE 214)
PANEL AND INTERIOR LAMPS CONTROL SWITCH (SEE PAGE 150)
DIGITAL CLUSTER (SEE PAGE 151)
S300
PANEL AND INTERIOR LAMP CONTROL SWITCH (SEE PAGE 150)
230-.22 BRN/WHT
10.0 + 1.0 OHMS
(WITH GAGES ONLY)
39-.8 PNK/BLK
DIODE MODULE (SEE PAGE 56)
33-.5 TAN/WHT
10-.8 YEL
911-.5 DK GRN
DAYTIME RUNNING LAMPS MODULE
629-.8 WHT
DRL WARNING INDICATOR (SEE PAGE 30)
12015308
150-.8 BLK
SPLICE S306 (SEE PAGE 21)
HEADLAMPS (SEE PAGE 30)
11-1.0 LT GRN
592-.8 LT GRN/BLK
DRL INDICATOR (SEE PAGE 30)
340-1.0 ORN
HEADLAMPS (SEE PAGE 30)
593-1.0 DK BLU/WHT
DAYTIME RUNNING LAMPS RELAY
39-.8 PNK/BLK

1988–91 WIRING DIAGRAMS (CONT.)

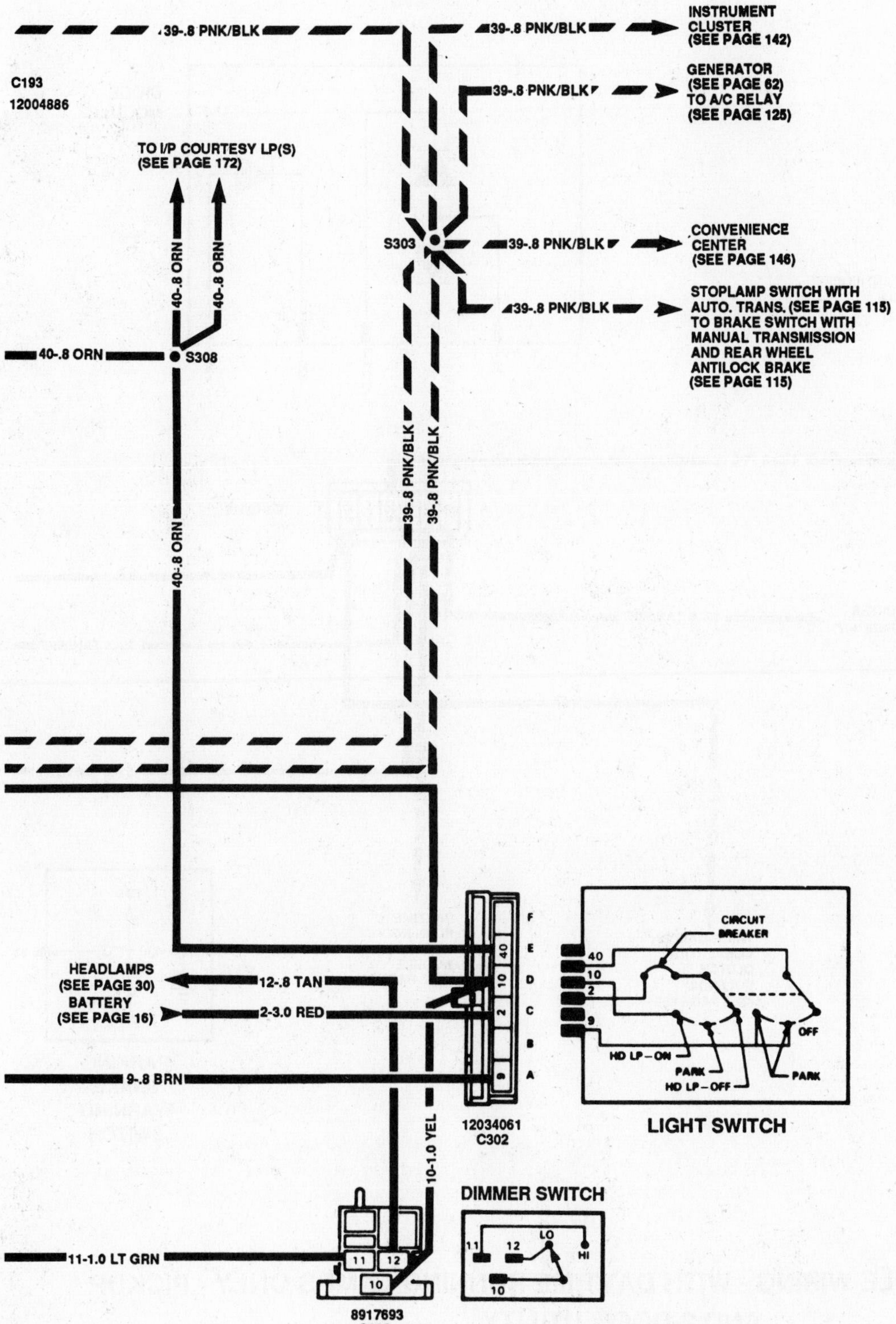
39-.8 PNK/BLK
39-.8 PNK/BLK
INSTRUMENT CLUSTER (SEE PAGE 142)
C193
12004886
39-.8 PNK/BLK
GENERATOR (SEE PAGE 62) TO A/C RELAY (SEE PAGE 125)
TO I/P COURTESY LP(S) (SEE PAGE 172)
S303
39-.8 PNK/BLK
CONVENIENCE CENTER (SEE PAGE 146)
40-.8 ORN
40-.8 ORN
39-.8 PNK/BLK
STOPLAMP SWITCH WITH AUTO. TRANS. (SEE PAGE 115) TO BRAKE SWITCH WITH MANUAL TRANSMISSION AND REAR WHEEL ANTILOCK BRAKE (SEE PAGE 115)
40-.8 ORN
S308
39-.8 PNK/BLK
39-.8 PNK/BLK
40-.8 ORN
HEADLAMPS (SEE PAGE 30)
12-.8 TAN
BATTERY (SEE PAGE 16)
2-3.0 RED
9-.8 BRN
CIRCUIT BREAKER
HD LP – ON
PARK
HD LP – OFF
OFF
PARK
12034061
C302
LIGHT SWITCH
10-1.0 YEL
DIMMER SWITCH
LO
HI
11-1.0 LT GRN
8917693
C303

FOG LAMPS (ANL) - W/CANADIAN DAYTIME RUNNING LAMPS Z49 39

1988–91 WIRING DIAGRAMS (CONT.)

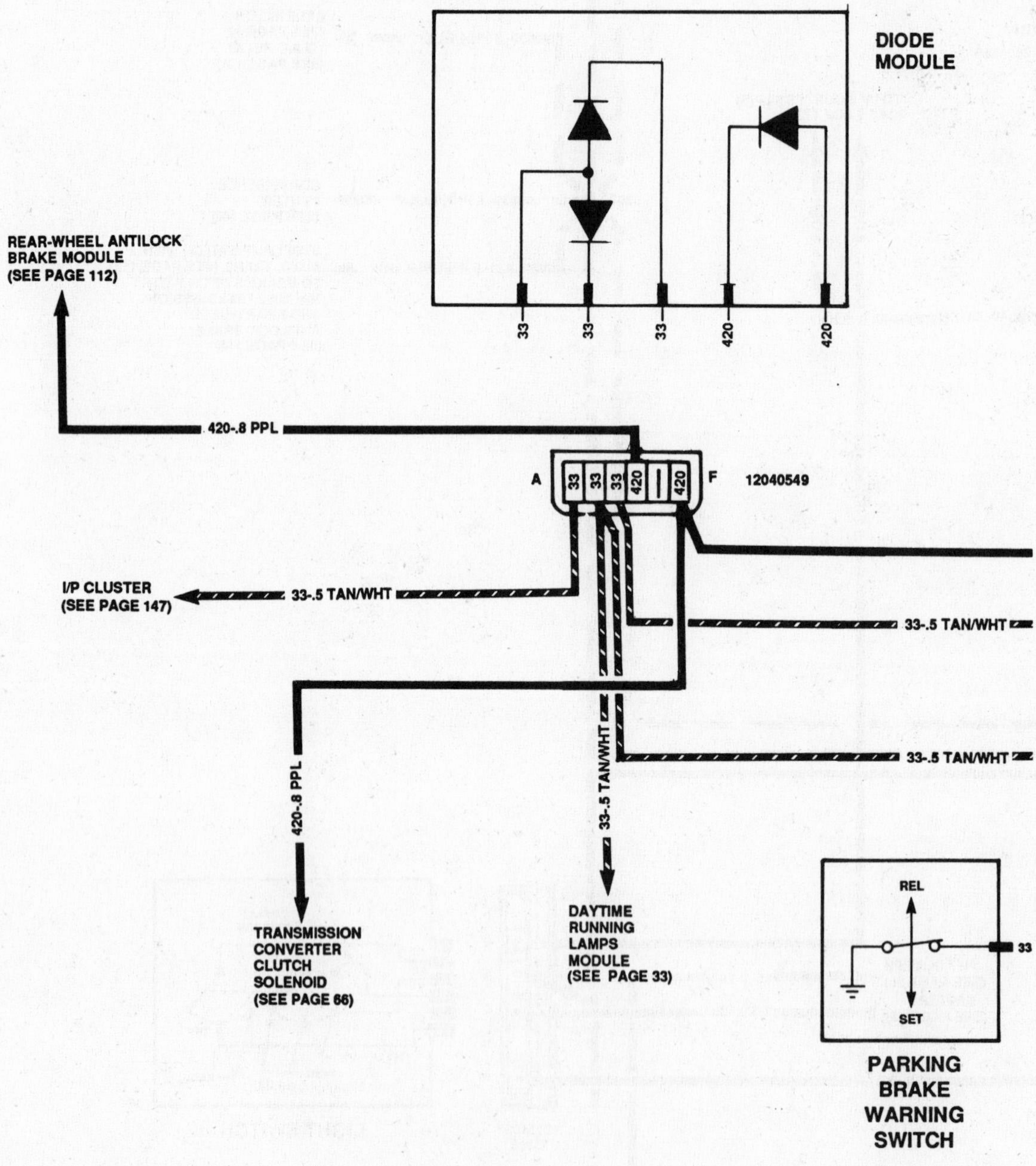

DIODE MODULE
33
33
33
420
420
REAR-WHEEL ANTILOCK BRAKE MODULE (SEE PAGE 112)
420-.8 PPL
A
33
33
33
420
420
F
12040549
I/P CLUSTER (SEE PAGE 147)
33-.5 TAN/WHT
33-.5 TAN/WHT
420-.8 PPL
33-.5 TAN/WHT
33-.5 TAN/WHT
TRANSMISSION CONVERTER CLUTCH SOLENOID (SEE PAGE 66)
DAYTIME RUNNING LAMPS MODULE (SEE PAGE 33)
REL
SET
33
PARKING BRAKE WARNING SWITCH

56 DIODE MODULE WIRING - WITH DAYTIME RUNNING LAMPS ONLY - PICKUP AND 2-DOOR UTILITY

1988–91 WIRING DIAGRAMS (CONT.)

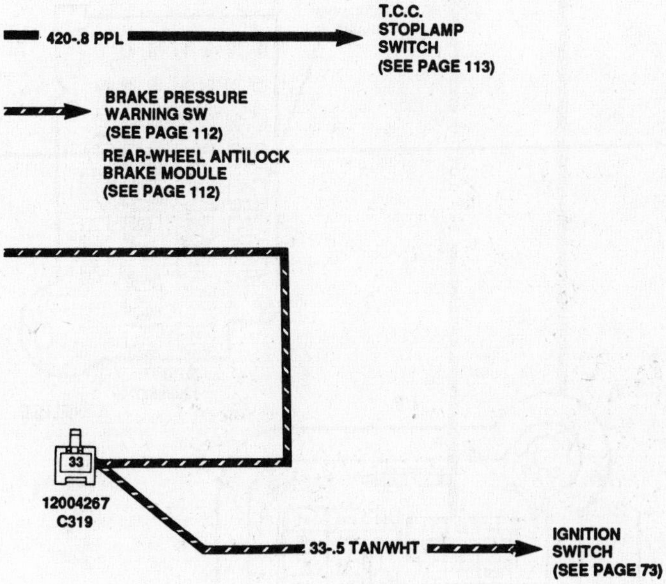
420-.8 PPL
T.C.C.
STOPLAMP
SWITCH
(SEE PAGE 113)
BRAKE PRESSURE
WARNING SW
(SEE PAGE 112)
REAR-WHEEL ANTILOCK
BRAKE MODULE
(SEE PAGE 112)
33
12004267
C319
33-.5 TAN/WHT
IGNITION
SWITCH
(SEE PAGE 73)

1988–91 WIRING DIAGRAMS (CONT.)

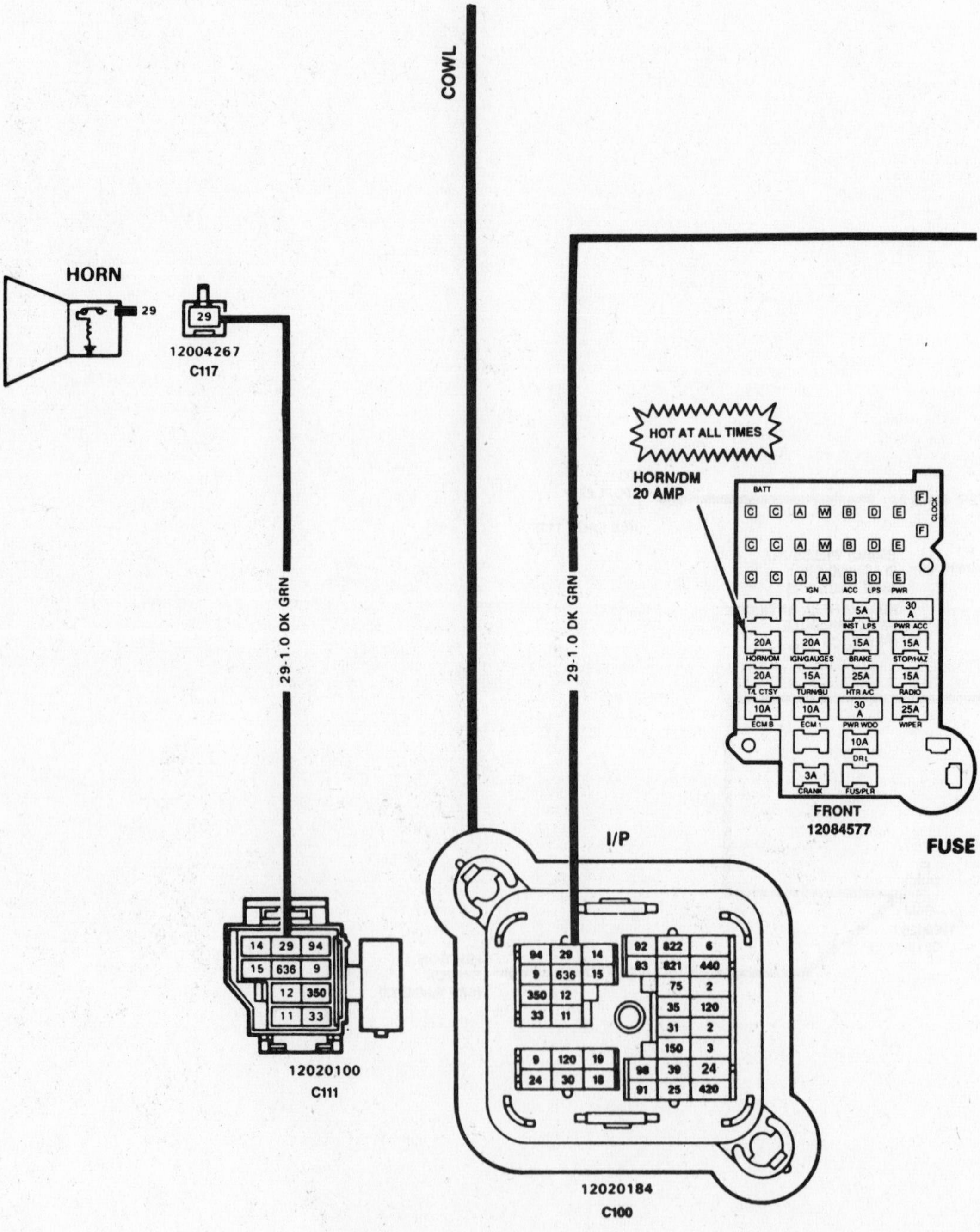
COWL
HORN
29
12004267
C117
29-1.0 DK GRN
29-1.0 DK GRN
HOT AT ALL TIMES
HORN/DM
20 AMP
FRONT
12084577
FUSE
I/P
12020100
C111
12020184
C100

1988–91 WIRING DIAGRAMS (CONT.)

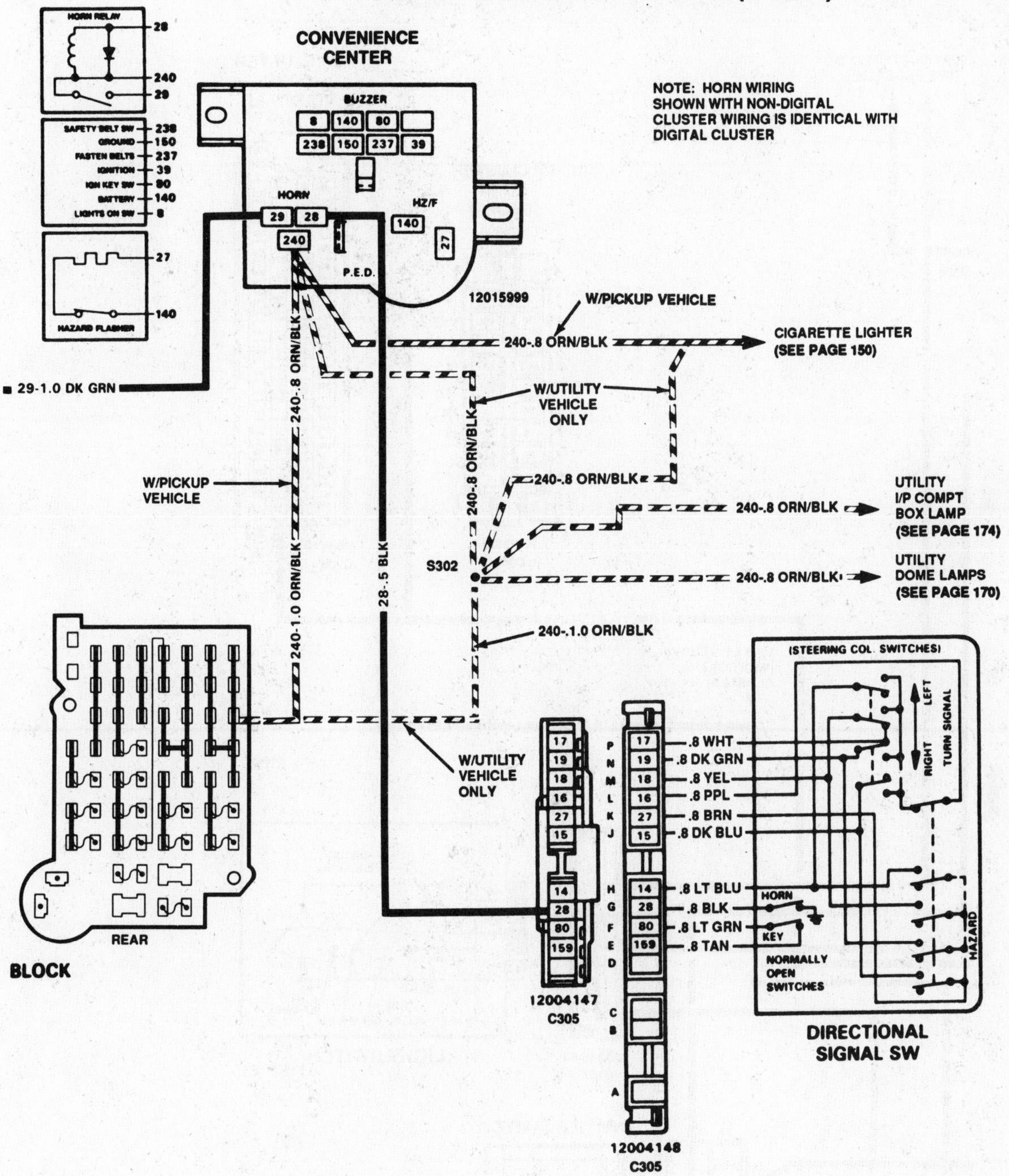
HORN RELAY
28
240
29
SAFETY BELT SW 238
GROUND 150
FASTEN BELTS 237
IGNITION 39
IGN KEY SW 80
BATTERY 140
LIGHTS ON SW 8
27
140
HAZARD FLASHER
CONVENIENCE CENTER
BUZZER
8 140 80
238 150 237 39
HORN
29 28
240
HZ/F
140
27
P.E.D.
12015999
NOTE: HORN WIRING SHOWN WITH NON-DIGITAL CLUSTER WIRING IS IDENTICAL WITH DIGITAL CLUSTER
W/PICKUP VEHICLE
240-.8 ORN/BLK
CIGARETTE LIGHTER (SEE PAGE 150)
29-1.0 DK GRN
W/UTILITY VEHICLE ONLY
240-.8 ORN/BLK
W/PICKUP VEHICLE
240-.8 ORN/BLK
240-.8 ORN/BLK
UTILITY I/P COMPT BOX LAMP (SEE PAGE 174)
S302
240-1.0 ORN/BLK
28-.5 BLK
240-.8 ORN/BLK
UTILITY DOME LAMPS (SEE PAGE 170)
240-.1.0 ORN/BLK
W/UTILITY VEHICLE ONLY
REAR
BLOCK
17 19 18 16 27 15 14 28 80 159
P N M L K J H G F E D C B A
.8 WHT
.8 DK GRN
.8 YEL
.8 PPL
.8 BRN
.8 DK BLU
.8 LT BLU
.8 BLK
.8 LT GRN
.8 TAN
12004147 C305
12004148 C305
(STEERING COL. SWITCHES)
LEFT
RIGHT
TURN SIGNAL
HORN
KEY
NORMALLY OPEN SWITCHES
HAZARD
DIRECTIONAL SIGNAL SW

HORN 59

1988–91 WIRING DIAGRAMS (CONT.)

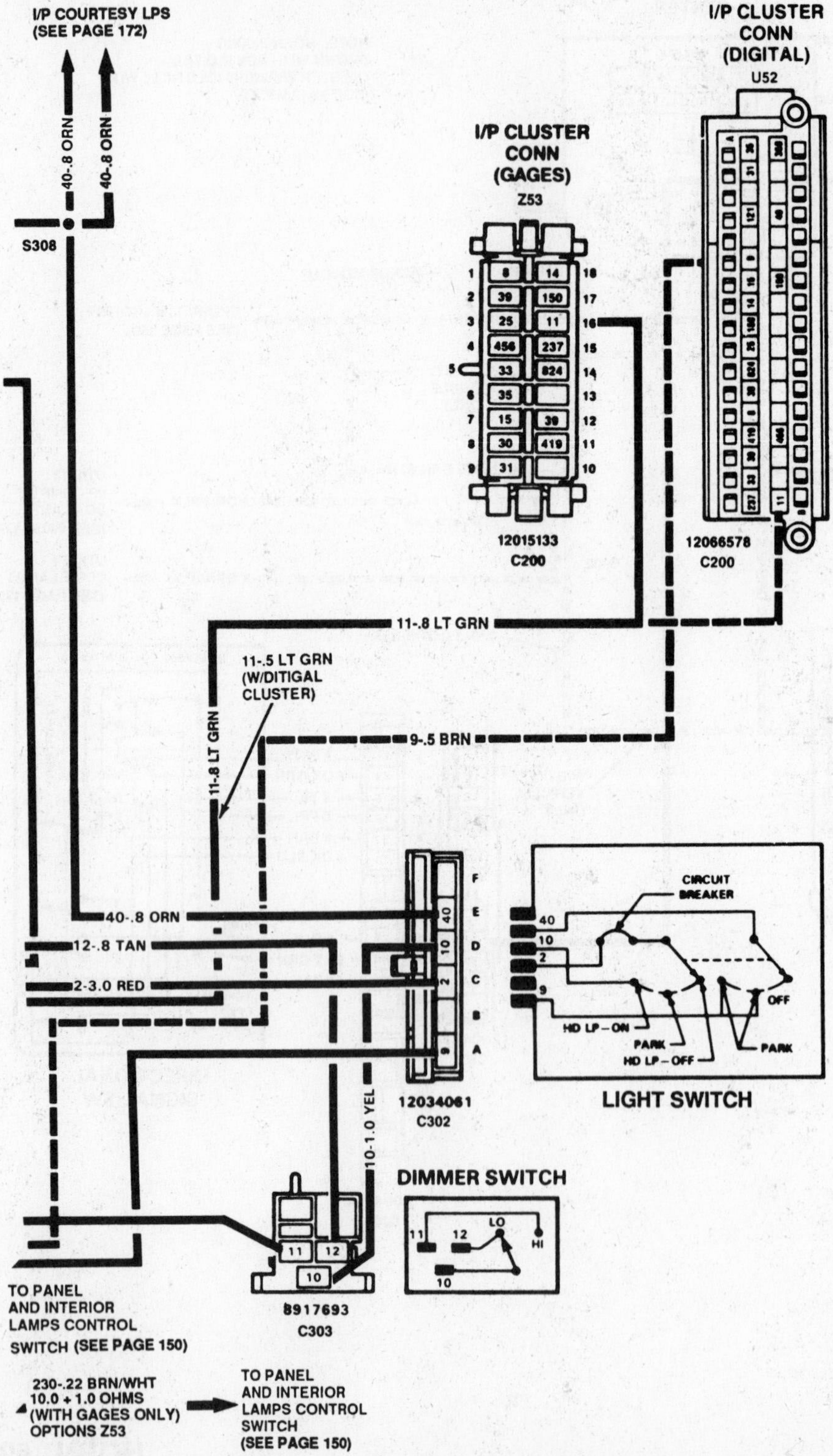

I/P COURTESY LPS (SEE PAGE 172)
40-.8 ORN
40-.8 ORN
S308
I/P CLUSTER CONN (GAGES)
Z53
12015133
C200
I/P CLUSTER CONN (DIGITAL)
U52
12066578
C200
11-.8 LT GRN
11-.5 LT GRN (W/DITIGAL CLUSTER)
11-.8 LT GRN
9-.5 BRN
40-.8 ORN
12-.8 TAN
2-3.0 RED
12034061
C302
CIRCUIT BREAKER
HD LP – ON
PARK
HD LP – OFF
OFF
PARK
LIGHT SWITCH
10-1.0 YEL
DIMMER SWITCH
LO
HI
8917693
C303
TO PANEL AND INTERIOR LAMPS CONTROL SWITCH (SEE PAGE 150)
230-.22 BRN/WHT 10.0 + 1.0 OHMS (WITH GAGES ONLY) OPTIONS Z53
TO PANEL AND INTERIOR LAMPS CONTROL SWITCH (SEE PAGE 150)

FOG LAMPS (ANL) - W/O CANADIAN DAYTIME RUNNING LAMPS Z49

1988–91 WIRING DIAGRAMS (CONT.)

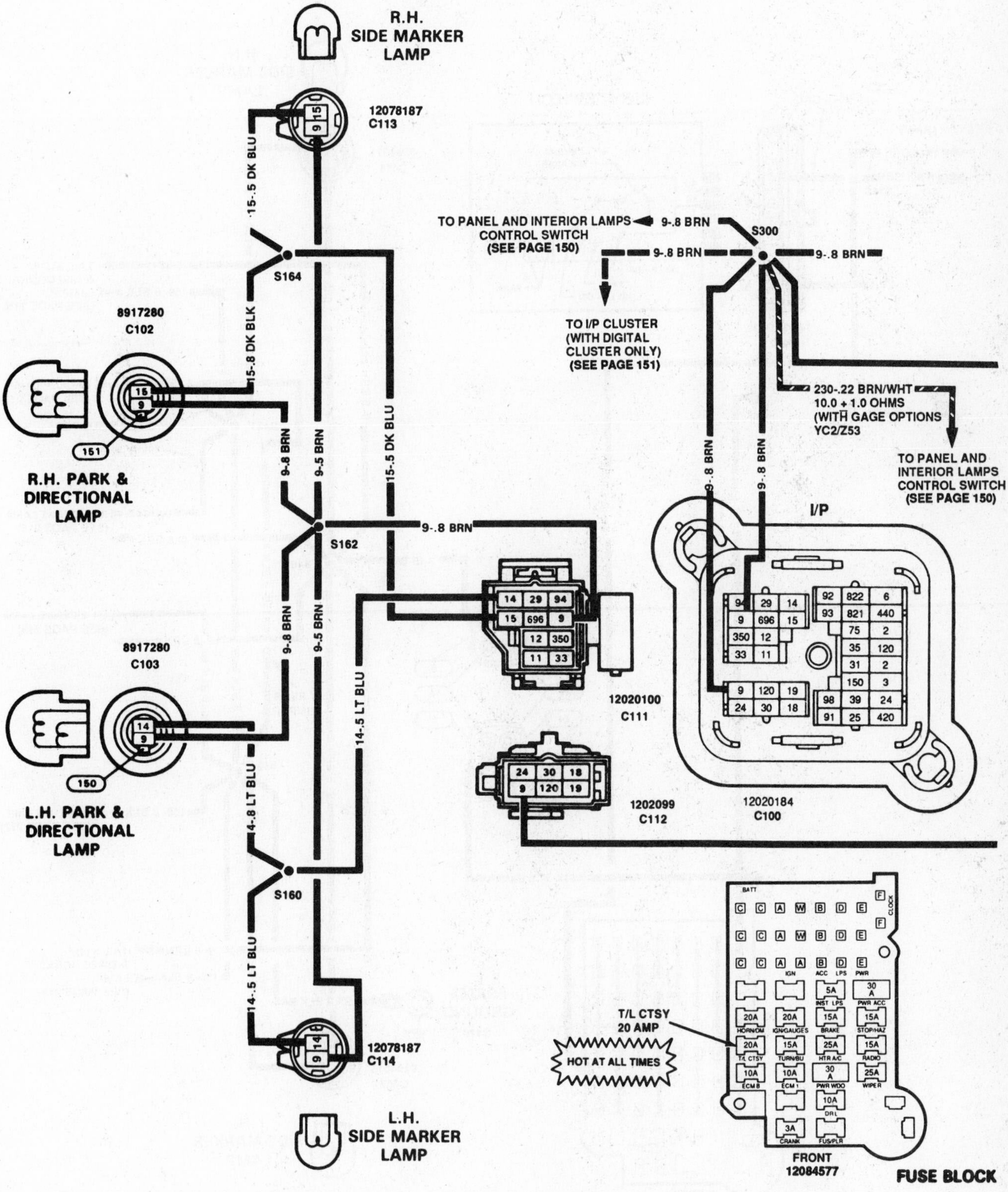
R.H. SIDE MARKER LAMP
12078187 C113
15-.5 DK BLU
TO PANEL AND INTERIOR LAMPS CONTROL SWITCH (SEE PAGE 150)
9-.8 BRN
S300
TO I/P CLUSTER (WITH DIGITAL CLUSTER ONLY) (SEE PAGE 151)
S164
8917280 C102
15-.8 DK BLK
R.H. PARK & DIRECTIONAL LAMP
9-.8 BRN
9-.5 BRN
15-.5 DK BLU
230-.22 BRN/WHT 10.0 + 1.0 OHMS (WITH GAGE OPTIONS YC2/Z53
TO PANEL AND INTERIOR LAMPS CONTROL SWITCH (SEE PAGE 150)
I/P
S162
12020100 C111
8917280 C103
14-.5 LT BLU
L.H. PARK & DIRECTIONAL LAMP
14-.8 LT BLU
1202099 C112
12020184 C100
S160
T/L CTSY 20 AMP
HOT AT ALL TIMES
12078187 C114
L.H. SIDE MARKER LAMP
FRONT 12084577
FUSE BLOCK

1988–91 WIRING DIAGRAMS (CONT.)

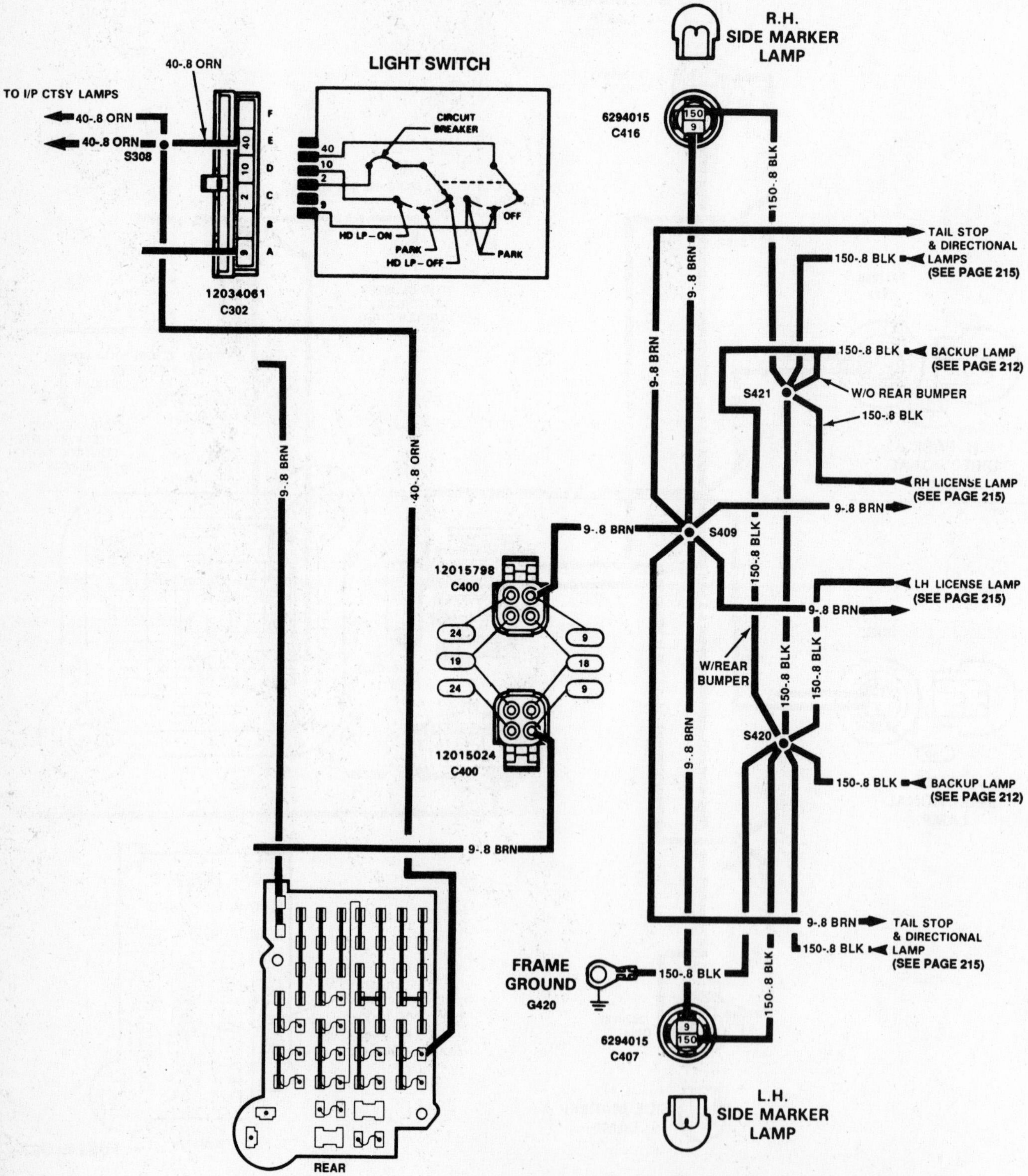
R.H.
SIDE MARKER
LAMP
40-.8 ORN
LIGHT SWITCH
TO I/P CTSY LAMPS
40-.8 ORN
40-.8 ORN
S308
CIRCUIT BREAKER
40
10
2
9
F
E
D
C
B
A
HD LP – ON
PARK
HD LP – OFF
OFF
PARK
12034061
C302
6294015
C416
150
150-.8 BLK
TAIL STOP
& DIRECTIONAL
LAMPS
(SEE PAGE 215)
150-.8 BLK
9-.8 BRN
150-.8 BLK
BACKUP LAMP
(SEE PAGE 212)
S421
W/O REAR BUMPER
150-.8 BLK
RH LICENSE LAMP
(SEE PAGE 215)
9-.8 BRN
9-.8 BRN
9-.8 BRN
S409
40-.8 ORN
12015798
C400
LH LICENSE LAMP
(SEE PAGE 215)
9-.8 BRN
24
19
24
9
18
9
W/REAR
BUMPER
S420
12015024
C400
150-.8 BLK
BACKUP LAMP
(SEE PAGE 212)
9-.8 BRN
9-.8 BRN
TAIL STOP
& DIRECTIONAL
LAMP
(SEE PAGE 215)
150-.8 BLK
FRAME
GROUND
G420
150-.8 BLK
6294015
C407
L.H.
SIDE MARKER
LAMP
REAR

MARKER LAMPS - PICKUP

1988–91 WIRING DIAGRAMS (CONT.)

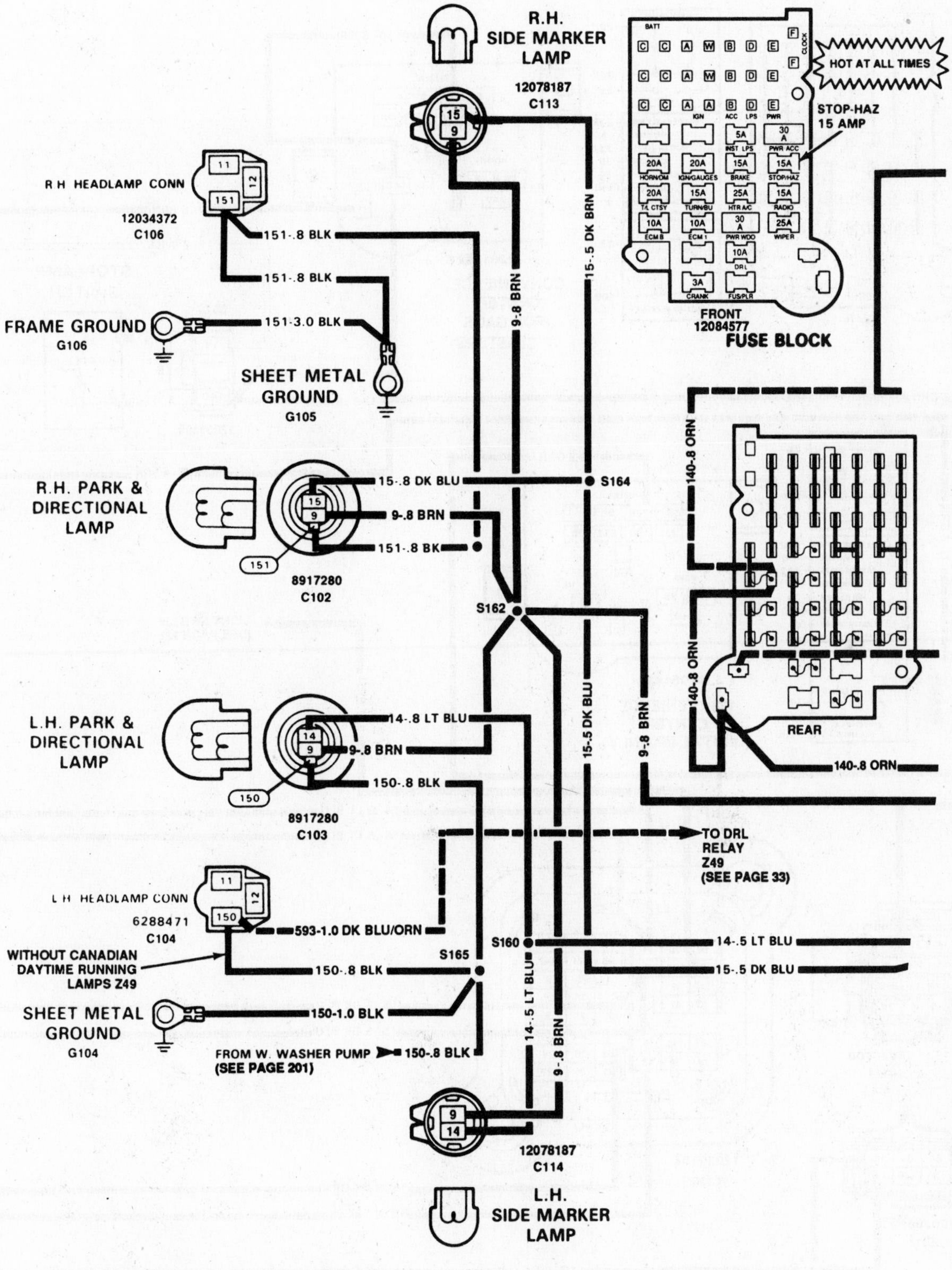
R.H. SIDE MARKER LAMP
12078187
C113
HOT AT ALL TIMES
STOP-HAZ 15 AMP
FRONT
12084577
FUSE BLOCK
REAR
R H HEADLAMP CONN
12034372
C106
151-.8 BLK
151-.8 BLK
FRAME GROUND
G106
151-3.0 BLK
SHEET METAL GROUND
G105
9-.8 BRN
15-.5 DK BRN
R.H. PARK & DIRECTIONAL LAMP
15-.8 DK BLU
S164
9-.8 BRN
151-.8 BK
8917280
C102
S162
140-.8 ORN
140-.8 ORN
140-.8 ORN
L.H. PARK & DIRECTIONAL LAMP
14-.8 LT BLU
9-.8 BRN
150-.8 BLK
8917280
C103
15-.5 DK BLU
9-.8 BRN
TO DRL RELAY Z49 (SEE PAGE 33)
L H HEADLAMP CONN
6288471
C104
593-1.0 DK BLU/ORN
WITHOUT CANADIAN DAYTIME RUNNING LAMPS Z49
S165
150-.8 BLK
S160
14-.5 LT BLU
15-.5 DK BLU
SHEET METAL GROUND
G104
150-1.0 BLK
FROM W. WASHER PUMP
(SEE PAGE 201)
150-.8 BLK
14-.5 LT BLU
9-.8 BRN
12078187
C114
L.H. SIDE MARKER LAMP

HAZARD LAMPS - PICKUP

1988–91 WIRING DIAGRAMS (CONT.)

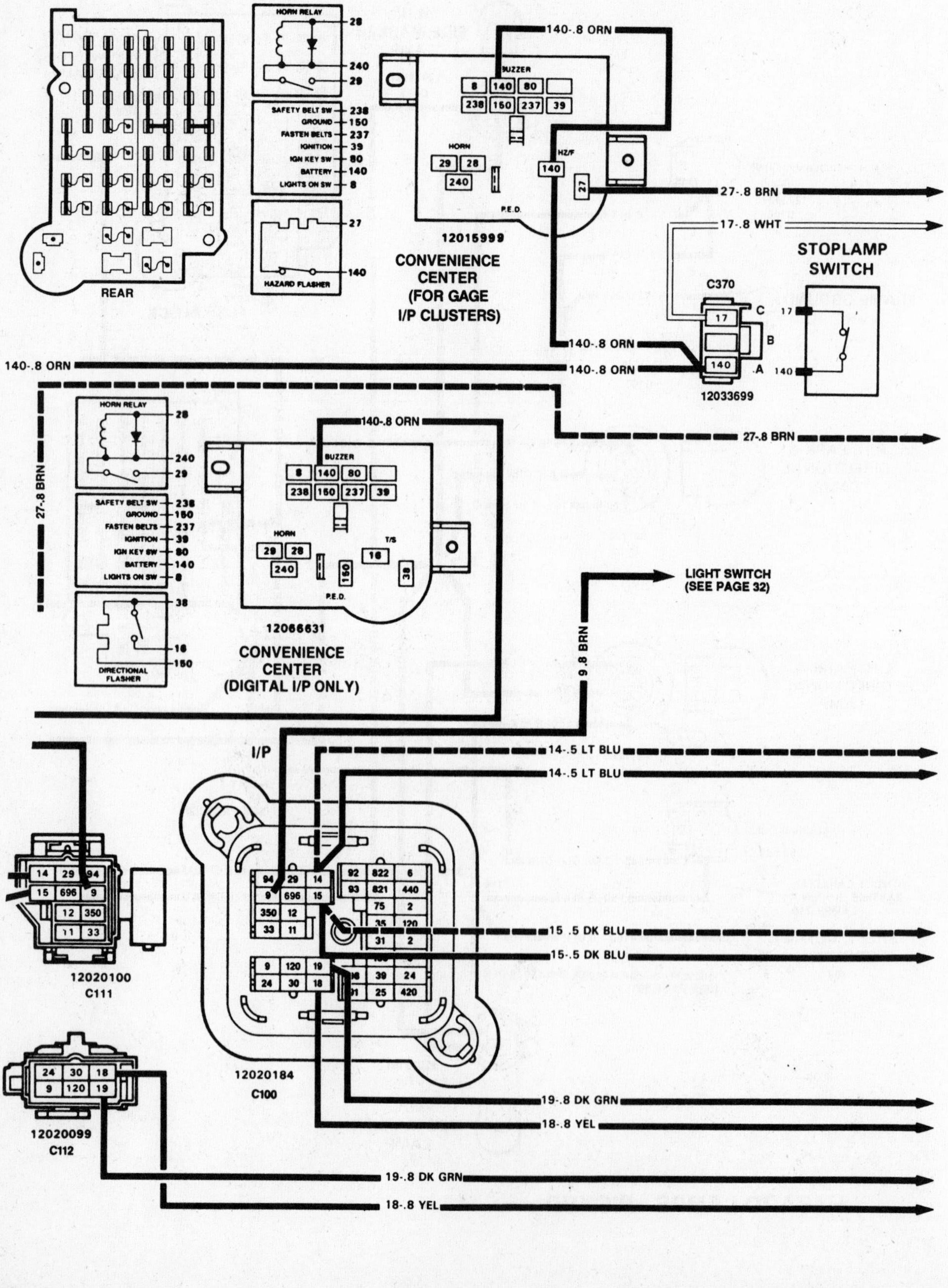

HORN RELAY
28
240
29
SAFETY BELT SW
GROUND
FASTEN BELTS
IGNITION
IGN KEY SW
BATTERY
LIGHTS ON SW
238
150
237
39
80
140
8
27
140
HAZARD FLASHER
REAR
140-.8 ORN
BUZZER
HORN
HZ/F
P.E.D.
12015999
CONVENIENCE CENTER (FOR GAGE I/P CLUSTERS)
27-.8 BRN
17-.8 WHT
STOPLAMP SWITCH
C370
C
B
A
12033699
140-.8 ORN
140-.8 ORN
140-.8 ORN
27-.8 BRN
27-.8 BRN
38
18
150
DIRECTIONAL FLASHER
T/S
12066631
CONVENIENCE CENTER (DIGITAL I/P ONLY)
LIGHT SWITCH (SEE PAGE 32)
9-.8 BRN
I/P
14-.5 LT BLU
14-.5 LT BLU
15 .5 DK BLU
15-.5 DK BLU
12020100
C111
12020184
C100
19-.8 DK GRN
18-.8 YEL
12020099
C112
19-.8 DK GRN
18-.8 YEL

1988–91 WIRING DIAGRAMS (CONT.)

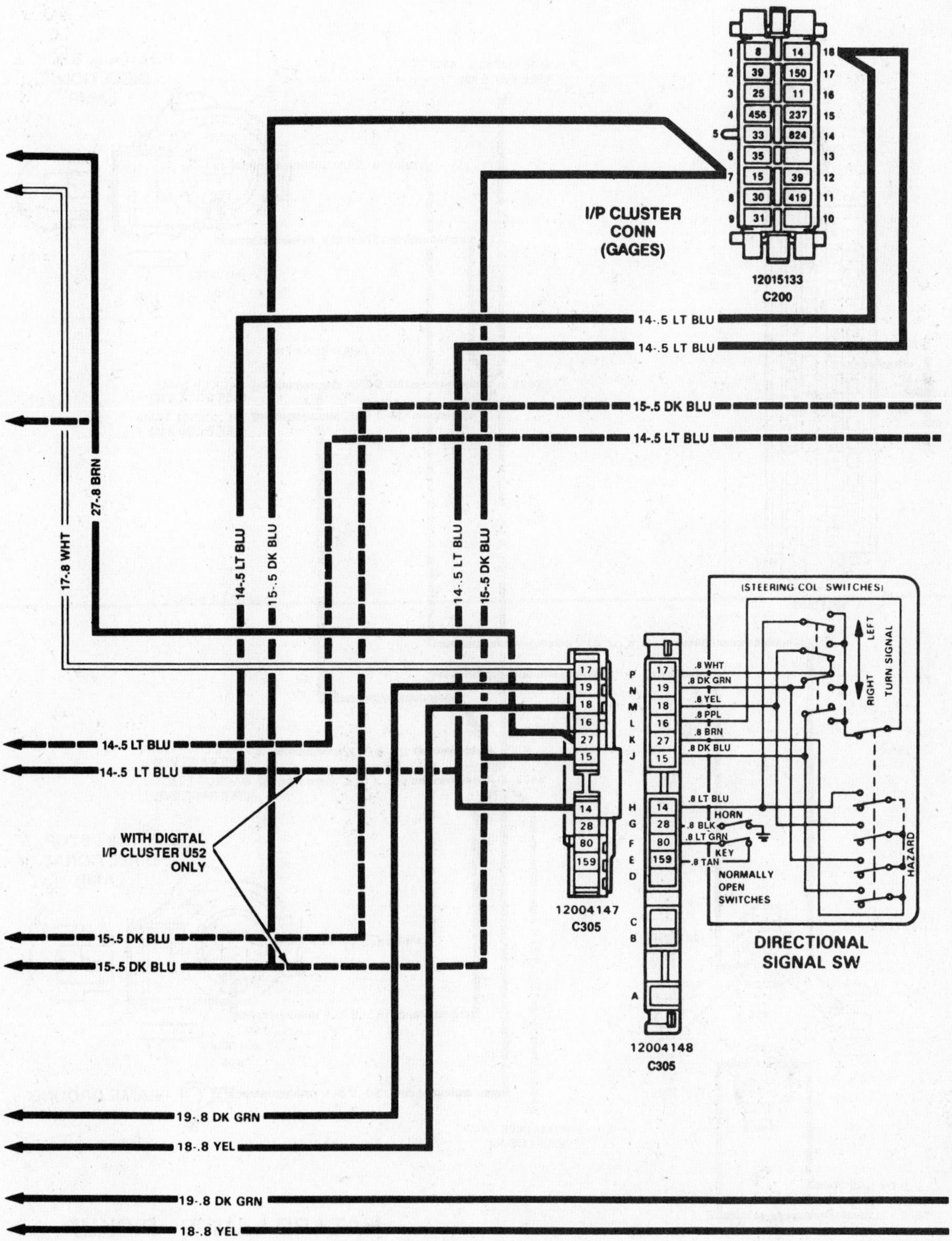
I/P CLUSTER
CONN
(GAGES)
12015133
C200
14-.5 LT BLU
14-.5 LT BLU
15-.5 DK BLU
14-.5 LT BLU
17-.8 WHT
27-.8 BRN
14-.5 LT BLU
15-.5 DK BLU
14-.5 LT BLU
15-.5 DK BLU
14-.5 LT BLU
14-.5 LT BLU
WITH DIGITAL
I/P CLUSTER U52
ONLY
15-.5 DK BLU
15-.5 DK BLU
12004147
C305
12004148
C305
.8 WHT
.8 DK GRN
.8 YEL
.8 PPL
.8 BRN
.8 DK BLU
.8 LT BLU
HORN
.8 BLK
.8 LT GRN
KEY
.8 TAN
NORMALLY
OPEN
SWITCHES
(STEERING COL SWITCHES)
LEFT
RIGHT
TURN SIGNAL
HAZARD
DIRECTIONAL
SIGNAL SW
19-.8 DK GRN
18-.8 YEL
19-.8 DK GRN
18-.8 YEL

1988–91 WIRING DIAGRAMS (CONT.)

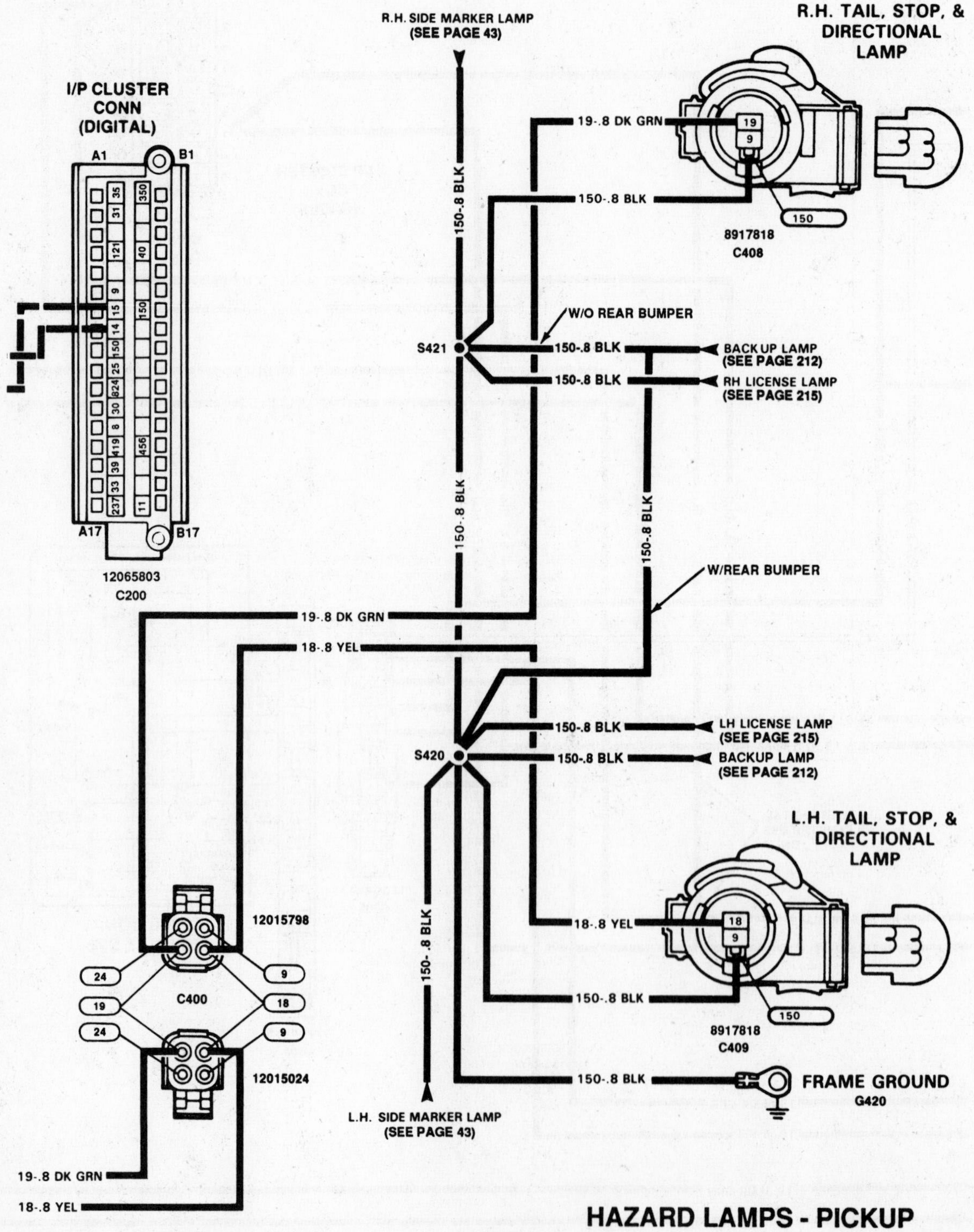
R.H. SIDE MARKER LAMP
(SEE PAGE 43)
R.H. TAIL, STOP, &
DIRECTIONAL
LAMP
I/P CLUSTER
CONN
(DIGITAL)
A1
B1
A17
B17
12065803
C200
19-.8 DK GRN
150-.8 BLK
8917818
C408
W/O REAR BUMPER
S421
BACK UP LAMP
(SEE PAGE 212)
RH LICENSE LAMP
(SEE PAGE 215)
W/REAR BUMPER
18-.8 YEL
S420
LH LICENSE LAMP
(SEE PAGE 215)
BACKUP LAMP
(SEE PAGE 212)
L.H. TAIL, STOP, &
DIRECTIONAL
LAMP
12015798
C400
12015024
8917818
C409
FRAME GROUND
G420
L.H. SIDE MARKER LAMP
(SEE PAGE 43)

HAZARD LAMPS - PICKUP

1988–91 WIRING DIAGRAMS (CONT.)

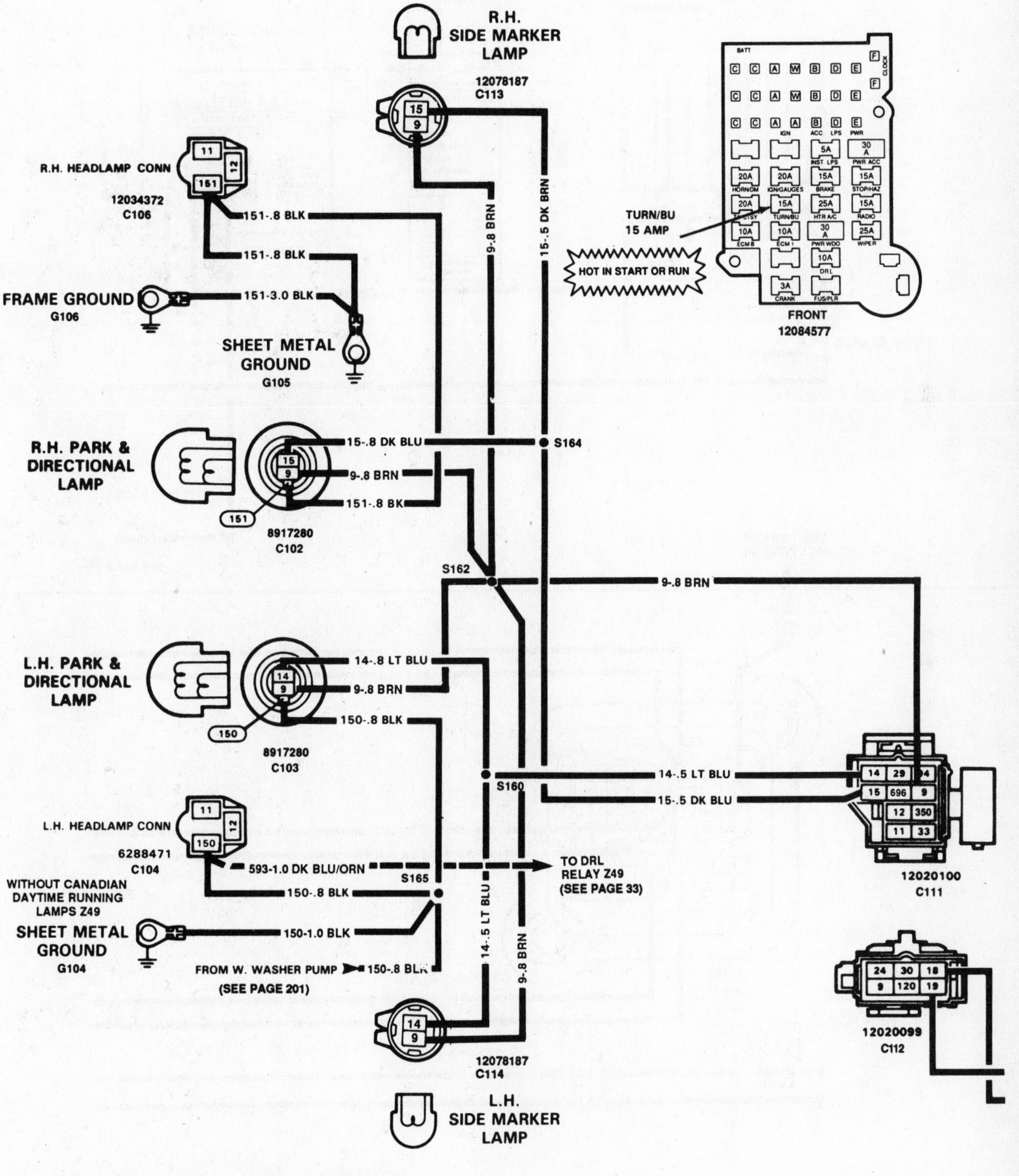

R.H. SIDE MARKER LAMP
12078187
C113
15
9
R.H. HEADLAMP CONN
11
12
151
12034372
C106
151-.8 BLK
151-.8 BLK
FRAME GROUND
G106
151-3.0 BLK
SHEET METAL GROUND
G105
9-.8 BRN
15-.5 DK BRN
TURN/BU
15 AMP
HOT IN START OR RUN
FRONT
12084577
R.H. PARK & DIRECTIONAL LAMP
15-.8 DK BLU
S164
9-.8 BRN
151-.8 BK
151
8917280
C102
S162
9-.8 BRN
L.H. PARK & DIRECTIONAL LAMP
14-.8 LT BLU
9-.8 BRN
150-.8 BLK
150
8917280
C103
S160
14-.5 LT BLU
15-.5 DK BLU
12020100
C111
L.H. HEADLAMP CONN
6288471
C104
593-1.0 DK BLU/ORN
S165
TO DRL RELAY Z49 (SEE PAGE 33)
WITHOUT CANADIAN DAYTIME RUNNING LAMPS Z49
150-.8 BLK
SHEET METAL GROUND
G104
150-1.0 BLK
FROM W. WASHER PUMP
150-.8 BLK
(SEE PAGE 201)
14-.5 LT BLU
9-.8 BRN
12020099
C112
14
9
12078187
C114
L.H. SIDE MARKER LAMP

DIRECTIONAL LAMPS - PICKUP

1988–91 WIRING DIAGRAMS (CONT.)

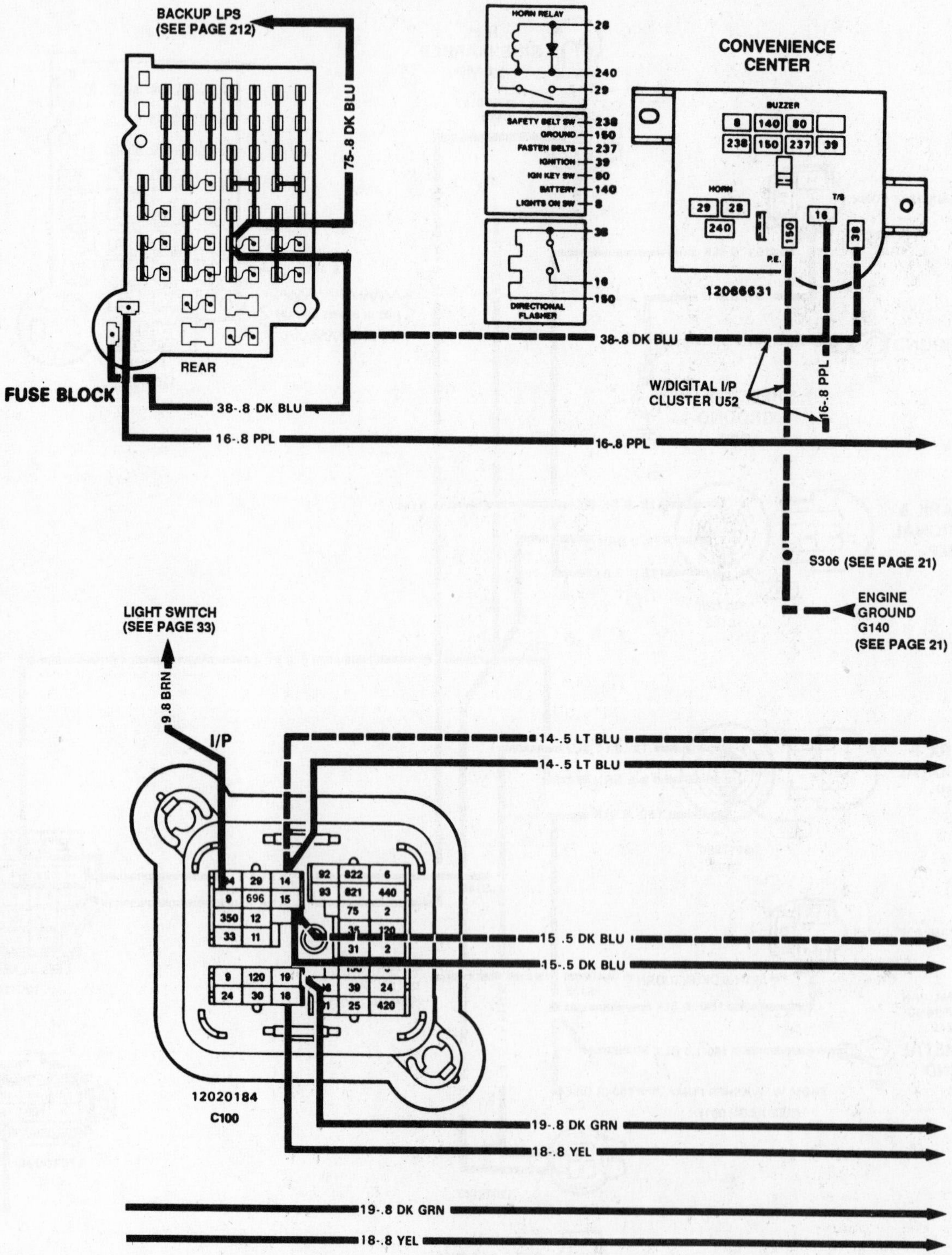
BACKUP LPS
(SEE PAGE 212)
75-.8 DK BLU
HORN RELAY
28
240
29
SAFETY BELT SW 238
GROUND 150
FASTEN BELTS 237
IGNITION 39
IGN KEY SW 90
BATTERY 140
LIGHTS ON SW 8
38
16
150
DIRECTIONAL FLASHER
CONVENIENCE CENTER
BUZZER
8 140 90
238 150 237 39
HORN
29 28
240
150
T/S
16
38
P.E.
12066631
REAR
FUSE BLOCK
38-.8 DK BLU
38-.8 DK BLU
W/DIGITAL I/P CLUSTER U52
16-.8 PPL
16-.8 PPL
16-.8 PPL
S306 (SEE PAGE 21)
ENGINE GROUND G140 (SEE PAGE 21)
LIGHT SWITCH
(SEE PAGE 33)
9-.8 BRN
I/P
14-.5 LT BLU
14-.5 LT BLU
15 .5 DK BLU
15-.5 DK BLU
12020184
C100
19-.8 DK GRN
18-.8 YEL
19-.8 DK GRN
18-.8 YEL

1988–91 WIRING DIAGRAMS (CONT.)

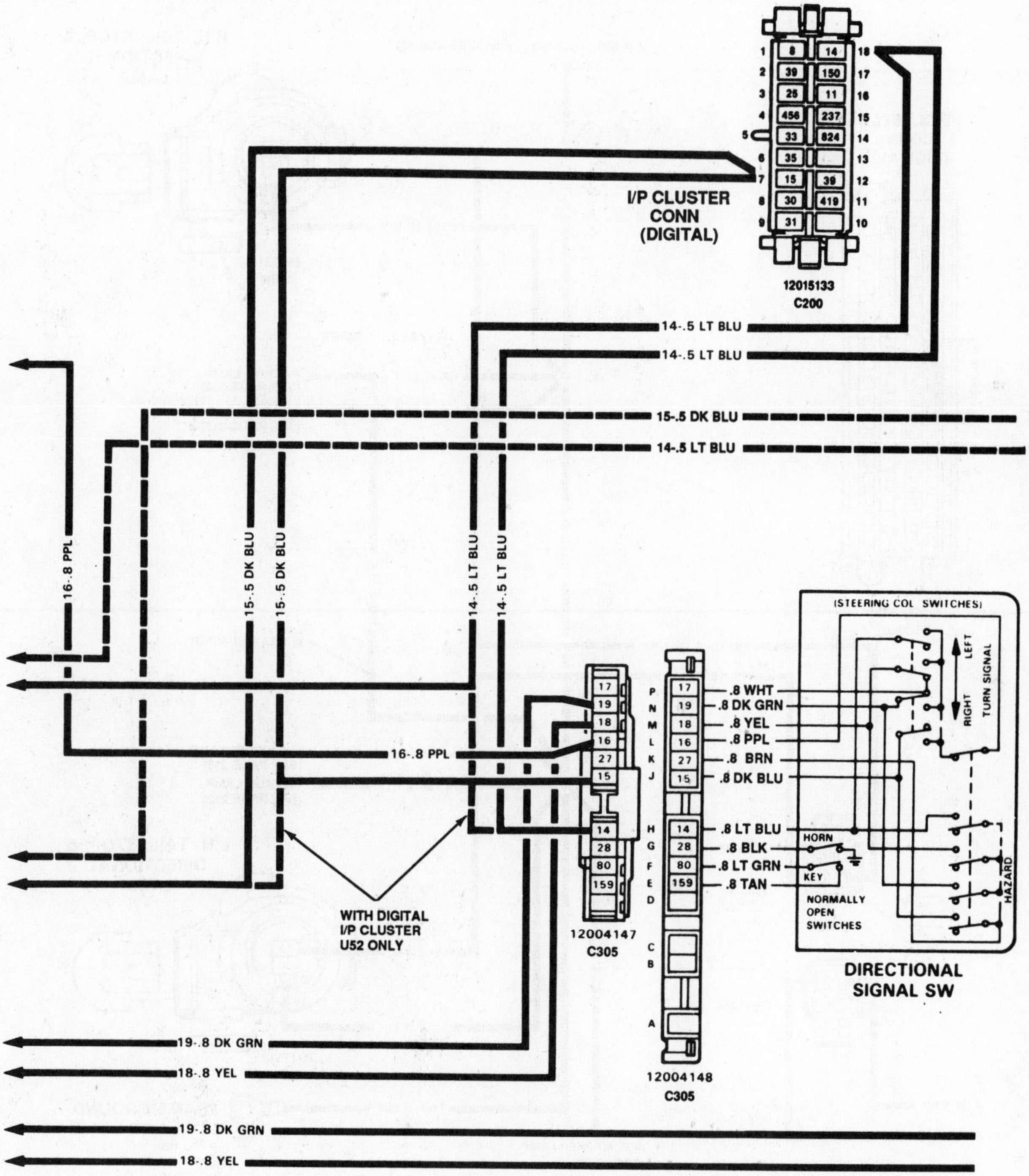
I/P CLUSTER
CONN
(DIGITAL)
12015133
C200
14-.5 LT BLU
14-.5 LT BLU
15-.5 DK BLU
14-.5 LT BLU
16-.8 PPL
15-.5 DK BLU
15-.5 DK BLU
14-.5 LT BLU
14-.5 LT BLU
16-.8 PPL
WITH DIGITAL
I/P CLUSTER
U52 ONLY
12004147
C305
.8 WHT
.8 DK GRN
.8 YEL
.8 PPL
.8 BRN
.8 DK BLU
.8 LT BLU
.8 BLK
.8 LT GRN
.8 TAN
12004148
C305
(STEERING COL SWITCHES)
LEFT
RIGHT
TURN SIGNAL
HORN
KEY
NORMALLY
OPEN
SWITCHES
HAZARD
DIRECTIONAL
SIGNAL SW
19-.8 DK GRN
18-.8 YEL
19-.8 DK GRN
18-.8 YEL

1988–91 WIRING DIAGRAMS (CONT.)

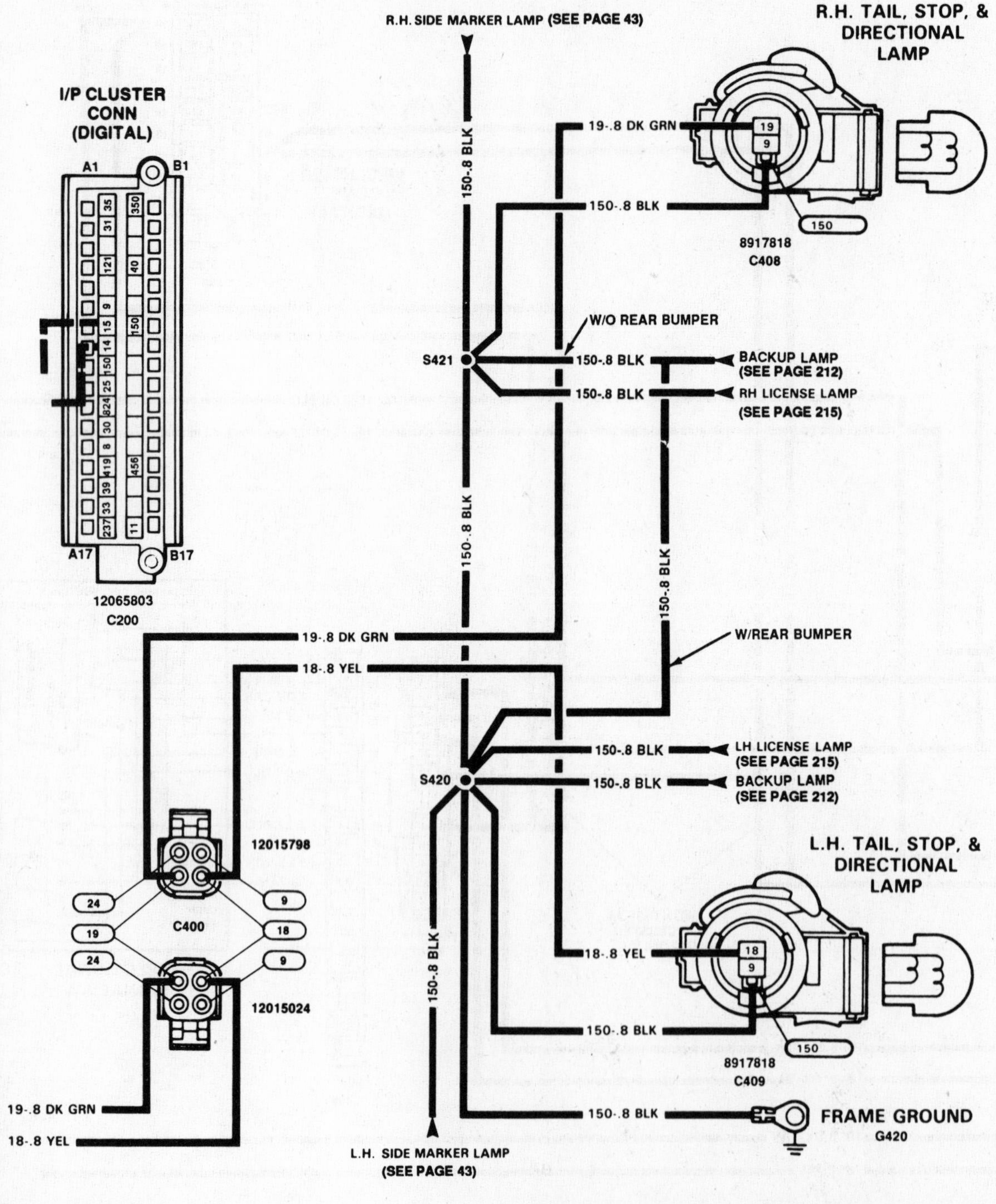
R.H. SIDE MARKER LAMP (SEE PAGE 43)
R.H. TAIL, STOP, & DIRECTIONAL LAMP
I/P CLUSTER CONN (DIGITAL)
A1
B1
A17
B17
12065803
C200
19-.8 DK GRN
150-.8 BLK
150
8917818
C408
W/O REAR BUMPER
S421
BACKUP LAMP (SEE PAGE 212)
RH LICENSE LAMP (SEE PAGE 215)
W/REAR BUMPER
18-.8 YEL
LH LICENSE LAMP (SEE PAGE 215)
S420
BACKUP LAMP (SEE PAGE 212)
L.H. TAIL, STOP, & DIRECTIONAL LAMP
12015798
C400
12015024
8917818
C409
FRAME GROUND
G420
L.H. SIDE MARKER LAMP (SEE PAGE 43)

DIRECTIONAL LAMPS - PICKUP

1988–91 WIRING DIAGRAMS (CONT.)

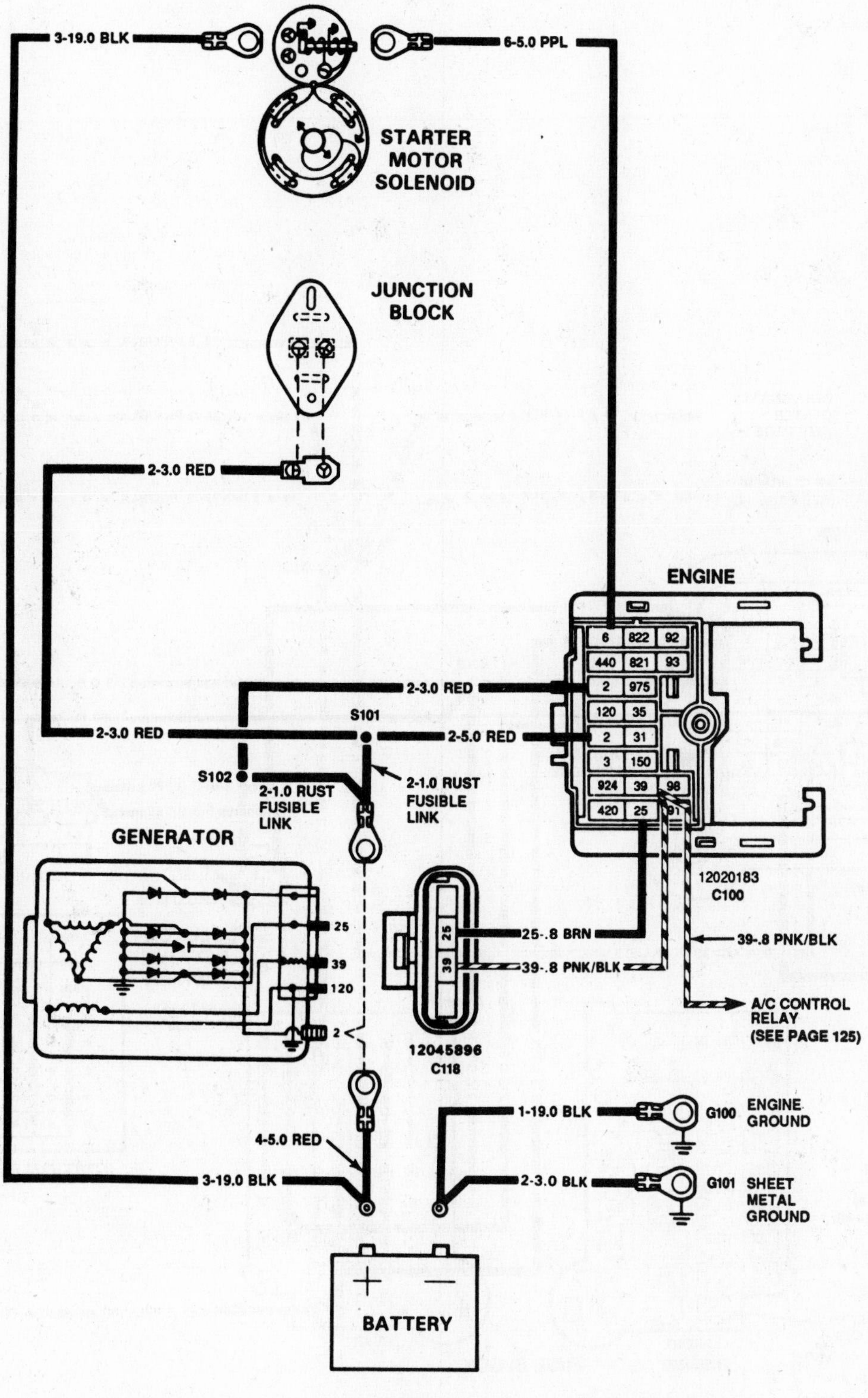
3-19.0 BLK
6-5.0 PPL
STARTER MOTOR SOLENOID
JUNCTION BLOCK
2-3.0 RED
ENGINE
6
822
92
440
821
93
2
975
120
35
2
31
3
150
924
39
98
420
25
91
2-3.0 RED
S101
2-3.0 RED
2-5.0 RED
S102
2-1.0 RUST FUSIBLE LINK
2-1.0 RUST FUSIBLE LINK
GENERATOR
25
39
120
2
12020183
C100
25-.8 BRN
39-.8 PNK/BLK
39-.8 PNK/BLK
A/C CONTROL RELAY (SEE PAGE 125)
12045896
C118
1-19.0 BLK
G100
ENGINE GROUND
4-5.0 RED
3-19.0 BLK
2-3.0 BLK
G101
SHEET METAL GROUND
BATTERY

STARTING AND CHARGING - 2.5L (151 CID) ENGINE

1988–91 WIRING DIAGRAMS (CONT.)

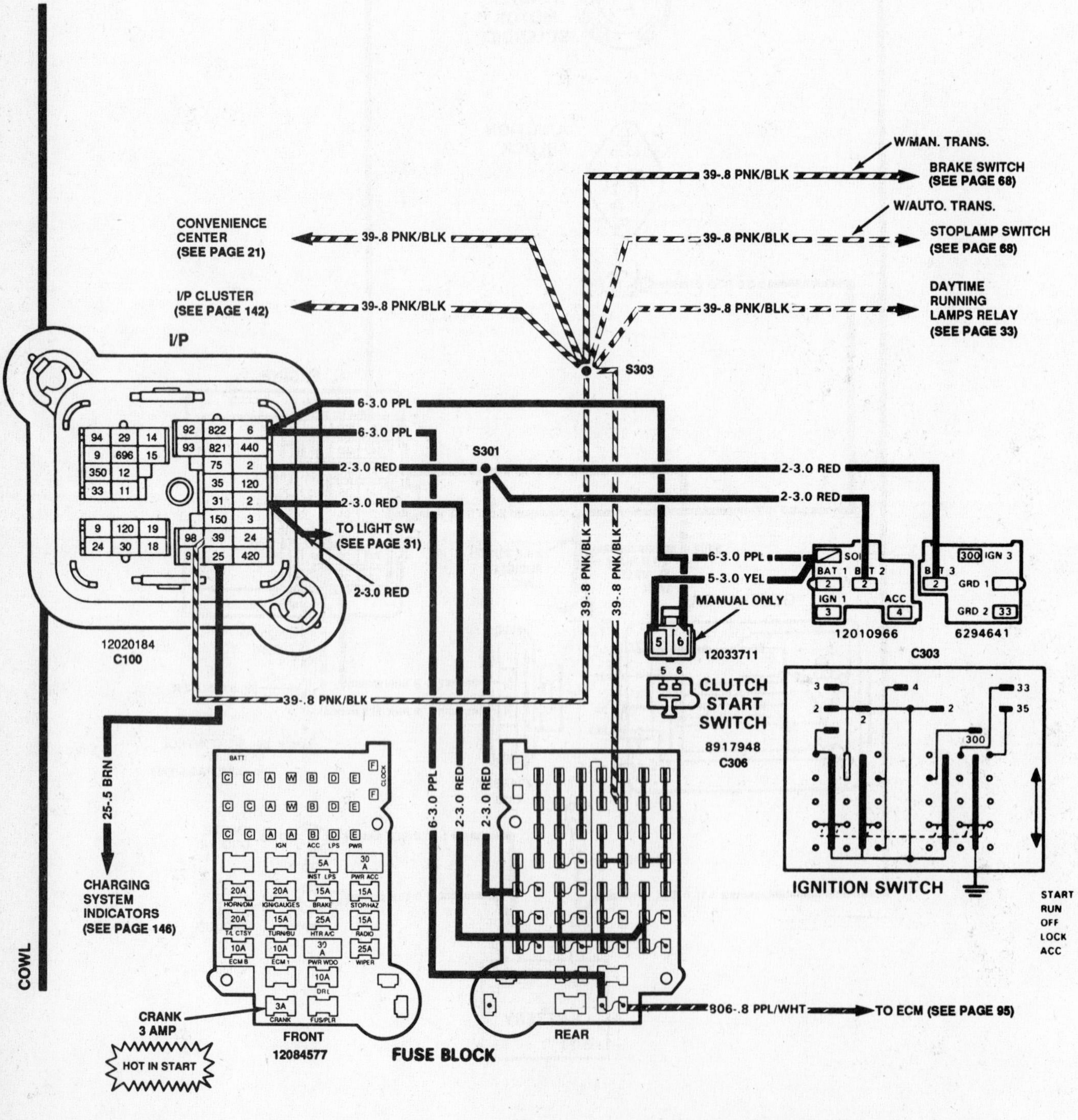
W/MAN. TRANS.
39-.8 PNK/BLK
BRAKE SWITCH (SEE PAGE 68)
W/AUTO. TRANS.
CONVENIENCE CENTER (SEE PAGE 21)
STOPLAMP SWITCH (SEE PAGE 68)
I/P CLUSTER (SEE PAGE 142)
DAYTIME RUNNING LAMPS RELAY (SEE PAGE 33)
I/P
S303
6-3.0 PPL
S301
2-3.0 RED
TO LIGHT SW (SEE PAGE 31)
12020184
C100
39-.8 PNK/BLK
5-3.0 YEL
MANUAL ONLY
12033711
CLUTCH START SWITCH
8917948
C306
SOL
BAT 1
BAT 2
IGN 1
ACC
12010966
C303
BAT 3
IGN 3
GRD 1
GRD 2
6294641
IGNITION SWITCH
START
RUN
OFF
LOCK
ACC
25-.5 BRN
CHARGING SYSTEM INDICATORS (SEE PAGE 146)
COWL
CRANK 3 AMP
HOT IN START
FRONT
12084577
FUSE BLOCK
REAR
806-.8 PPL/WHT
TO ECM (SEE PAGE 95)

1988–91 WIRING DIAGRAMS (CONT.)

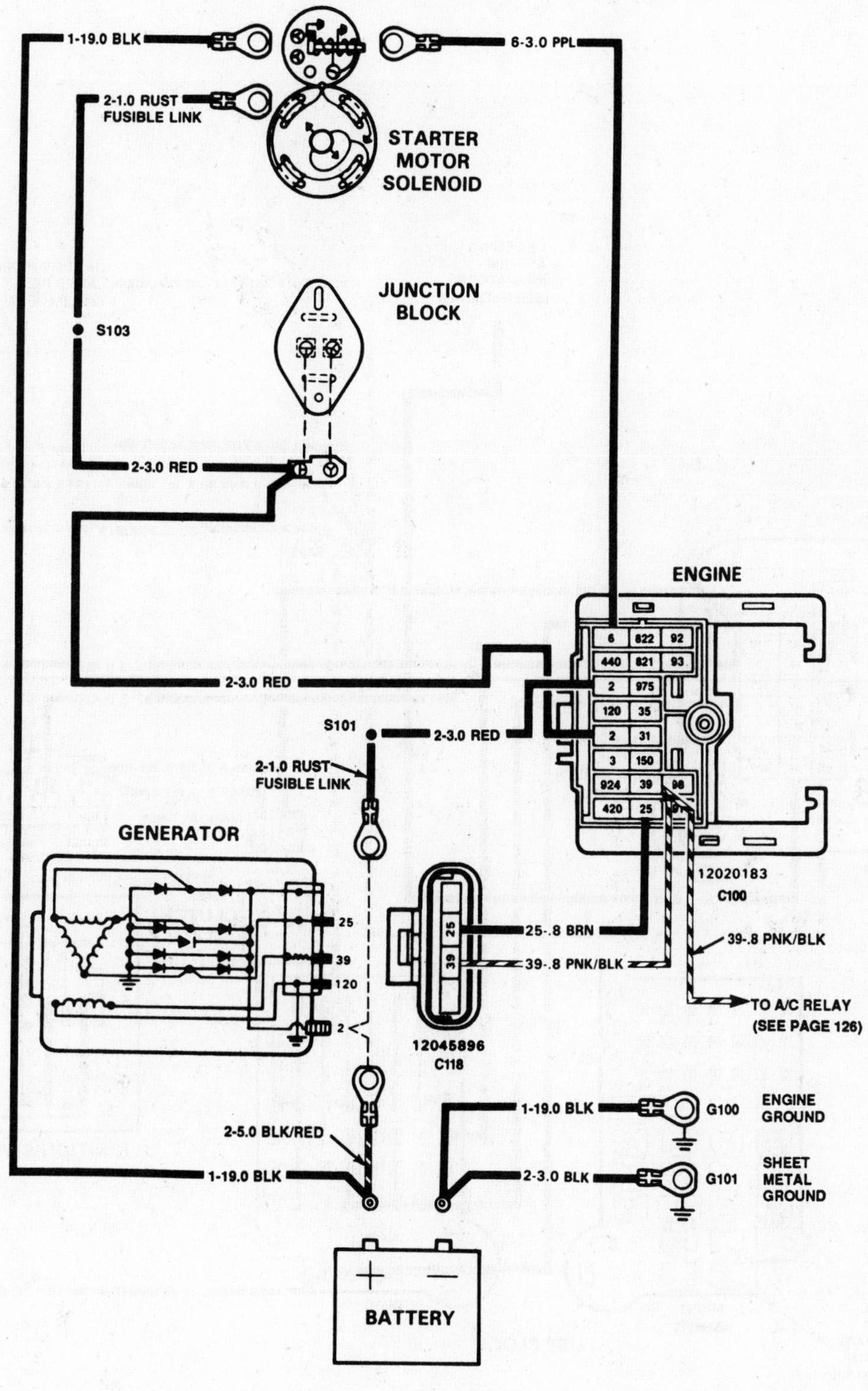
1-19.0 BLK
6-3.0 PPL
2-1.0 RUST
FUSIBLE LINK
STARTER
MOTOR
SOLENOID
JUNCTION
BLOCK
S103
2-3.0 RED
ENGINE
6
822
92
440
821
93
2
975
120
35
2
31
3
150
924
39
98
420
25
2-3.0 RED
S101
2-3.0 RED
2-1.0 RUST
FUSIBLE LINK
GENERATOR
25
39
120
2
12020183
C100
25-.8 BRN
39-.8 PNK/BLK
39-.8 PNK/BLK
TO A/C RELAY
(SEE PAGE 126)
12045896
C118
1-19.0 BLK
G100
ENGINE
GROUND
2-5.0 BLK/RED
1-19.0 BLK
2-3.0 BLK
G101
SHEET
METAL
GROUND
BATTERY

1988–91 WIRING DIAGRAMS (CONT.)

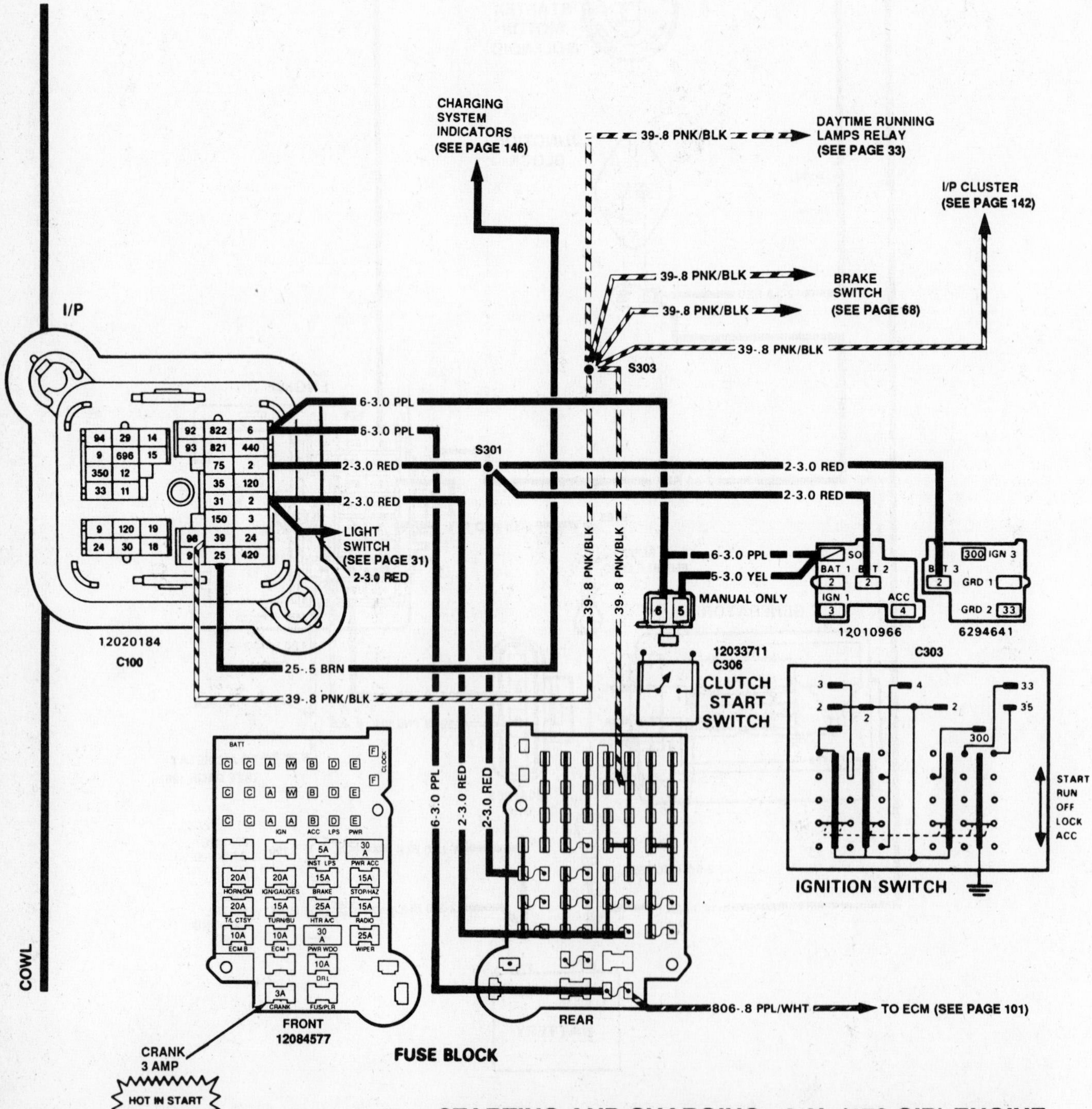

CHARGING SYSTEM INDICATORS (SEE PAGE 146)
39-.8 PNK/BLK
DAYTIME RUNNING LAMPS RELAY (SEE PAGE 33)
I/P CLUSTER (SEE PAGE 142)
BRAKE SWITCH (SEE PAGE 68)
S303
I/P
6-3.0 PPL
S301
2-3.0 RED
LIGHT SWITCH (SEE PAGE 31)
12020184
C100
25-.5 BRN
6-5.0 YEL
MANUAL ONLY
BAT 1
BAT 2
IGN 1
ACC
BAT 3
IGN 3
GRD 1
GRD 2
12010966
6294641
C303
12033711
C306
CLUTCH START SWITCH
START
RUN
OFF
LOCK
ACC
IGNITION SWITCH
COWL
FRONT
12084577
REAR
FUSE BLOCK
806-.8 PPL/WHT
TO ECM (SEE PAGE 101)
CRANK 3 AMP
HOT IN START

STARTING AND CHARGING - 2.8L (173 CID) ENGINE

1988–91 WIRING DIAGRAMS (CONT.)

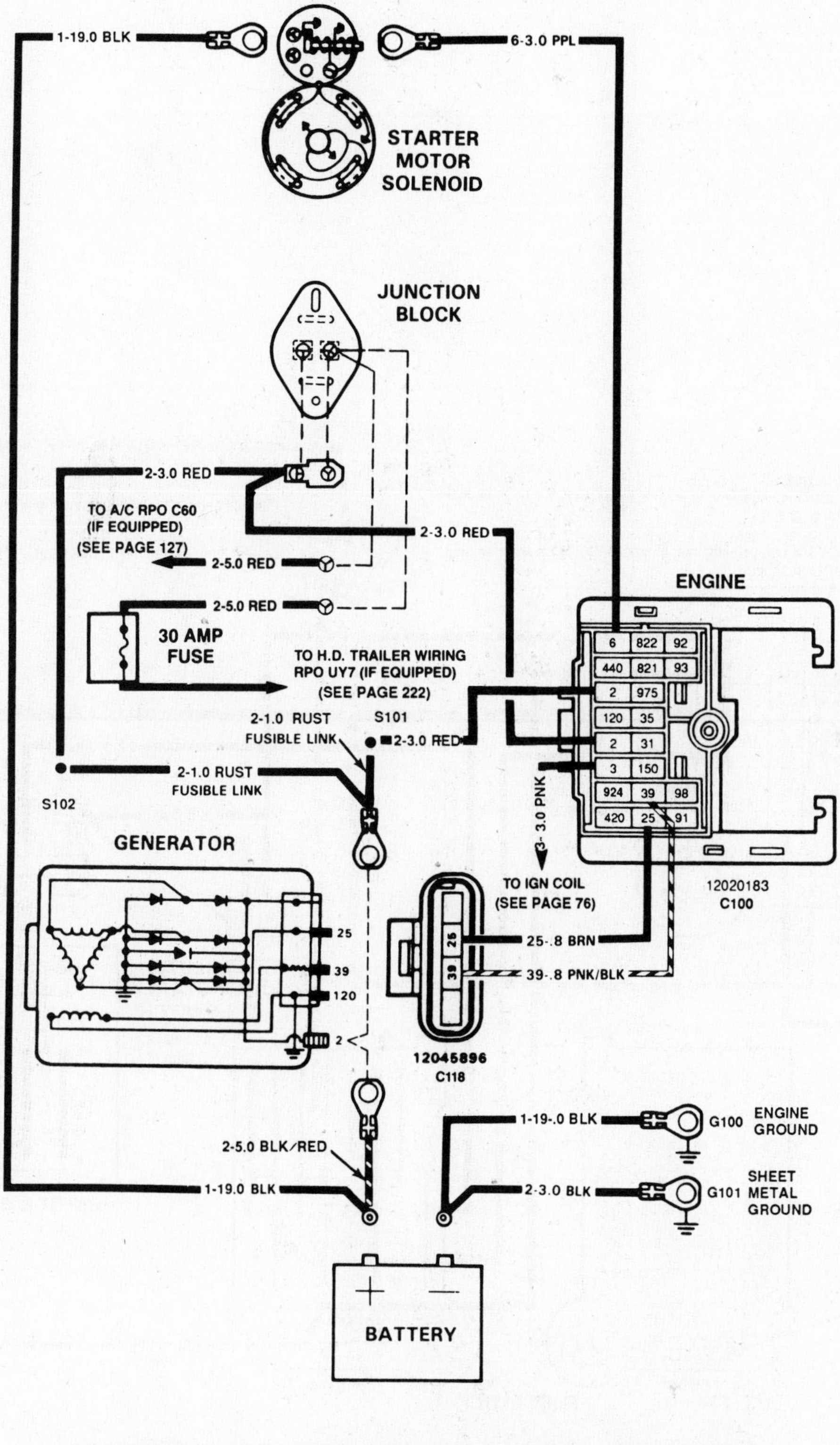
1-19.0 BLK
6-3.0 PPL
STARTER MOTOR SOLENOID
JUNCTION BLOCK
2-3.0 RED
TO A/C RPO C60 (IF EQUIPPED) (SEE PAGE 127)
2-3.0 RED
2-5.0 RED
ENGINE
2-5.0 RED
30 AMP FUSE
TO H.D. TRAILER WIRING RPO UY7 (IF EQUIPPED) (SEE PAGE 222)
2-1.0 RUST FUSIBLE LINK
S101
2-3.0 RED
2-1.0 RUST FUSIBLE LINK
S102
3-3.0 PNK
GENERATOR
TO IGN COIL (SEE PAGE 76)
12020183 C100
25-.8 BRN
39-.8 PNK/BLK
25
39
120
2
12045896 C118
1-19-.0 BLK
G100 ENGINE GROUND
2-5.0 BLK/RED
SHEET METAL GROUND
1-19.0 BLK
2-3.0 BLK
G101
BATTERY

STARTING AND CHARGING - 4.3L (262 CID) ENGINE

1988–91 WIRING DIAGRAMS (CONT.)

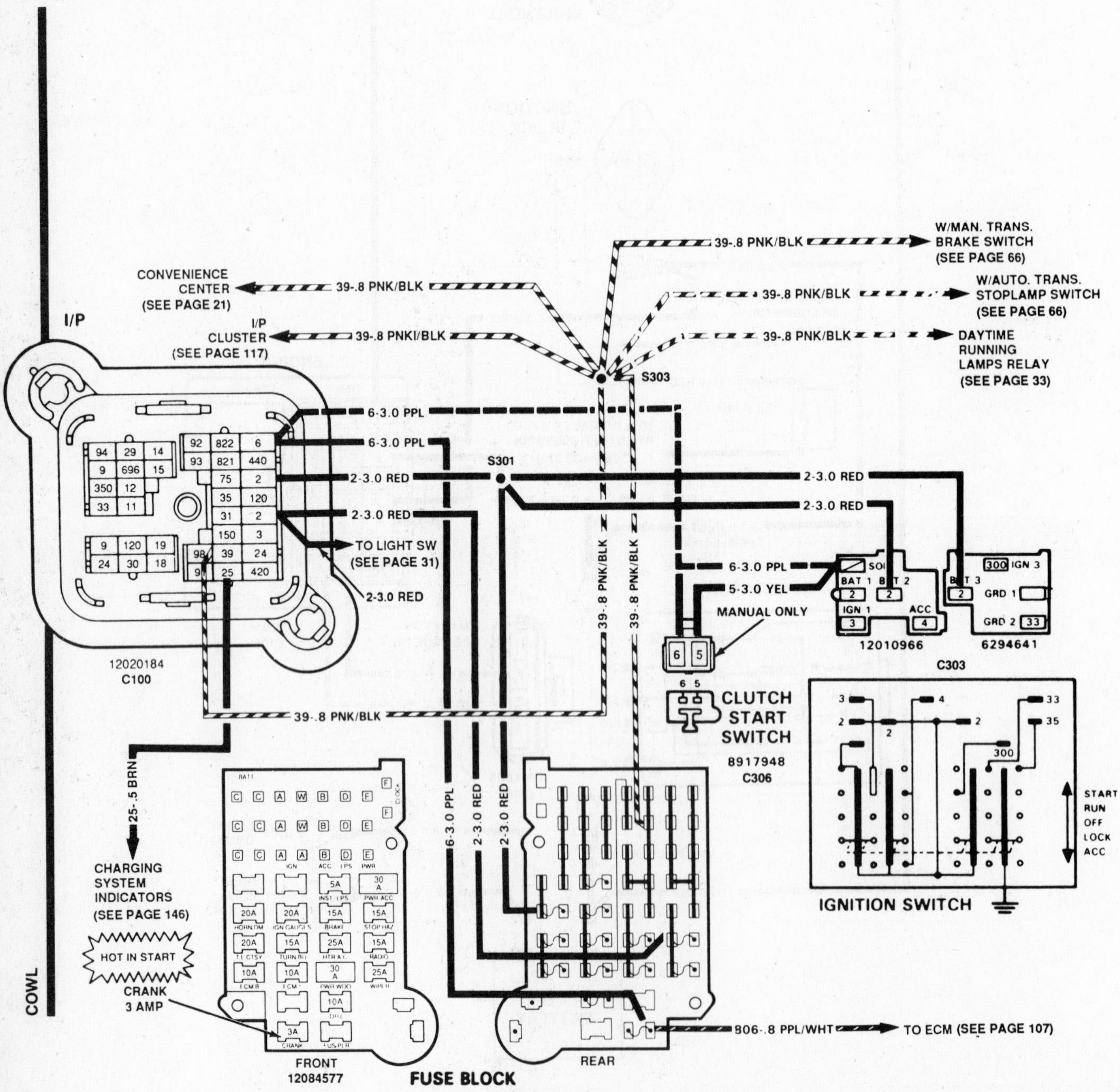

CONVENIENCE CENTER (SEE PAGE 21)
39-.8 PNK/BLK
I/P CLUSTER (SEE PAGE 117)
39-.8 PNKI/BLK
W/MAN. TRANS. BRAKE SWITCH (SEE PAGE 66)
W/AUTO. TRANS. STOPLAMP SWITCH (SEE PAGE 66)
DAYTIME RUNNING LAMPS RELAY (SEE PAGE 33)
S303
I/P
6-3.0 PPL
2-3.0 RED
S301
TO LIGHT SW (SEE PAGE 31)
5-3.0 YEL
MANUAL ONLY
12010966
6294641
C303
12020184
C100
CLUTCH START SWITCH
8917948
C306
IGNITION SWITCH
START
RUN
OFF
LOCK
ACC
25-.5 BRN
CHARGING SYSTEM INDICATORS (SEE PAGE 146)
HOT IN START
CRANK 3 AMP
806-.8 PPL/WHT
TO ECM (SEE PAGE 107)
FRONT
12084577
FUSE BLOCK
REAR
COWL

1988–91 WIRING DIAGRAMS (CONT.)

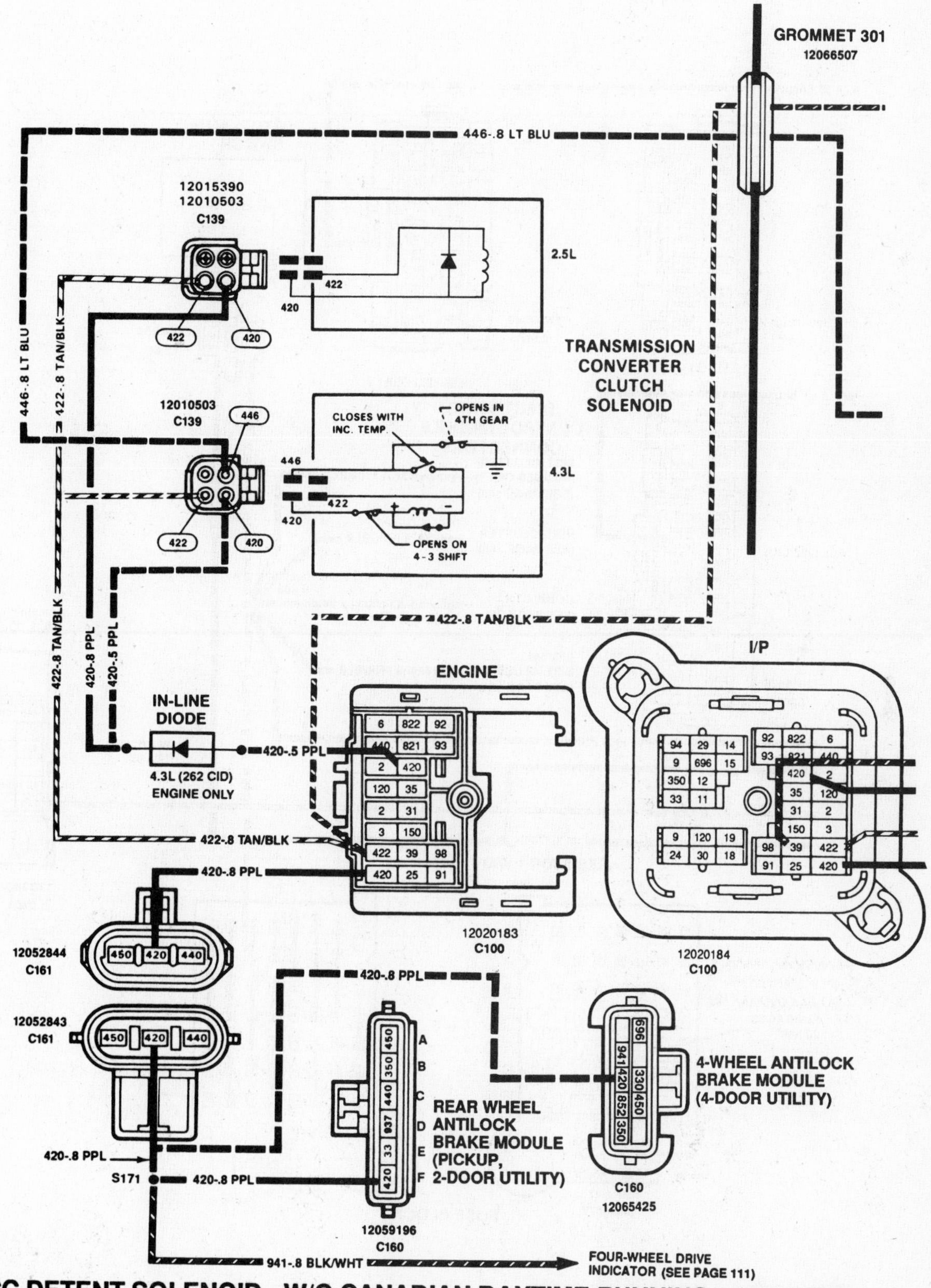
GROMMET 301
12066507
446-.8 LT BLU
12015390
12010503
C139
422
420
2.5L
TRANSMISSION
CONVERTER
CLUTCH
SOLENOID
446-.8 LT BLU
422-.8 TAN/BLK
12010503
C139
446
CLOSES WITH
INC. TEMP.
OPENS IN
4TH GEAR
4.3L
OPENS ON
4-3 SHIFT
422-.8 TAN/BLK
I/P
ENGINE
420-.8 PPL
420-.5 PPL
IN-LINE
DIODE
4.3L (262 CID)
ENGINE ONLY
420-.5 PPL
422-.8 TAN/BLK
420-.8 PPL
12020183
C100
12020184
C100
12052844
C161
12052843
C161
420-.8 PPL
REAR WHEEL
ANTILOCK
BRAKE MODULE
(PICKUP,
2-DOOR UTILITY)
4-WHEEL ANTILOCK
BRAKE MODULE
(4-DOOR UTILITY)
S171
12059196
C160
C160
12065425
941-.8 BLK/WHT
FOUR-WHEEL DRIVE
INDICATOR (SEE PAGE 111)

TCC DETENT SOLENOID - W/O CANADIAN DAYTIME RUNNING LAMPS Z49

1988–91 WIRING DIAGRAMS (CONT.)

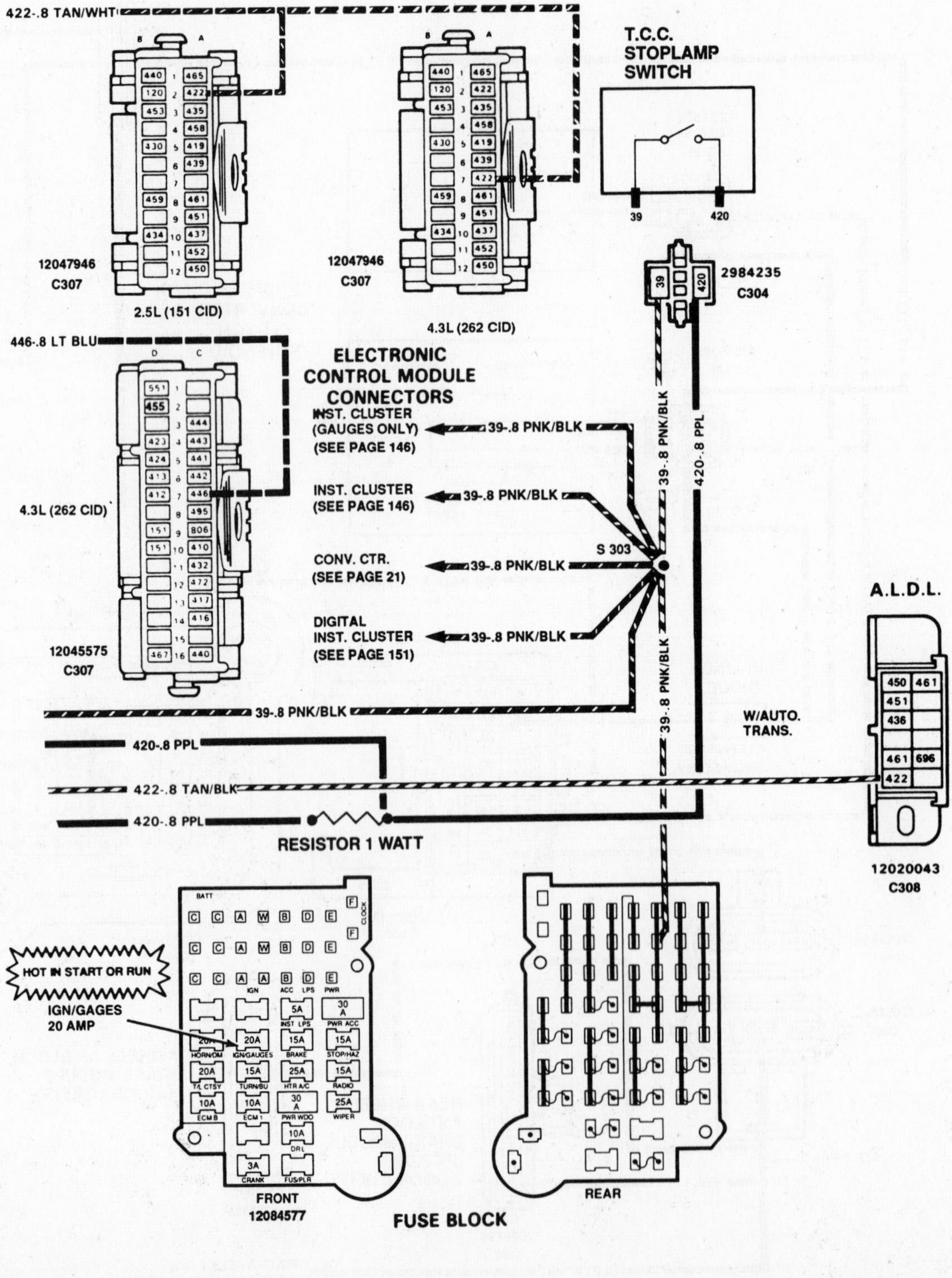
422-.8 TAN/WHT
12047946
C307
2.5L (151 CID)
12047946
C307
4.3L (262 CID)
T.C.C.
STOPLAMP
SWITCH
39
420
2984235
C304
446-.8 LT BLU
4.3L (262 CID)
12045575
C307
ELECTRONIC
CONTROL MODULE
CONNECTORS
INST. CLUSTER
(GAUGES ONLY)
(SEE PAGE 146)
39-.8 PNK/BLK
INST. CLUSTER
(SEE PAGE 146)
39-.8 PNK/BLK
CONV. CTR.
(SEE PAGE 21)
39-.8 PNK/BLK
S 303
DIGITAL
INST. CLUSTER
(SEE PAGE 151)
39-.8 PNK/BLK
39-.8 PNK/BLK
420-.8 PPL
A.L.D.L.
W/AUTO.
TRANS.
39-.8 PNK/BLK
420-.8 PPL
422-.8 TAN/BLK
420-.8 PPL
RESISTOR 1 WATT
12020043
C308
HOT IN START OR RUN
IGN/GAGES
20 AMP
FRONT
12084577
REAR
FUSE BLOCK

1988–91 WIRING DIAGRAMS (CONT.)

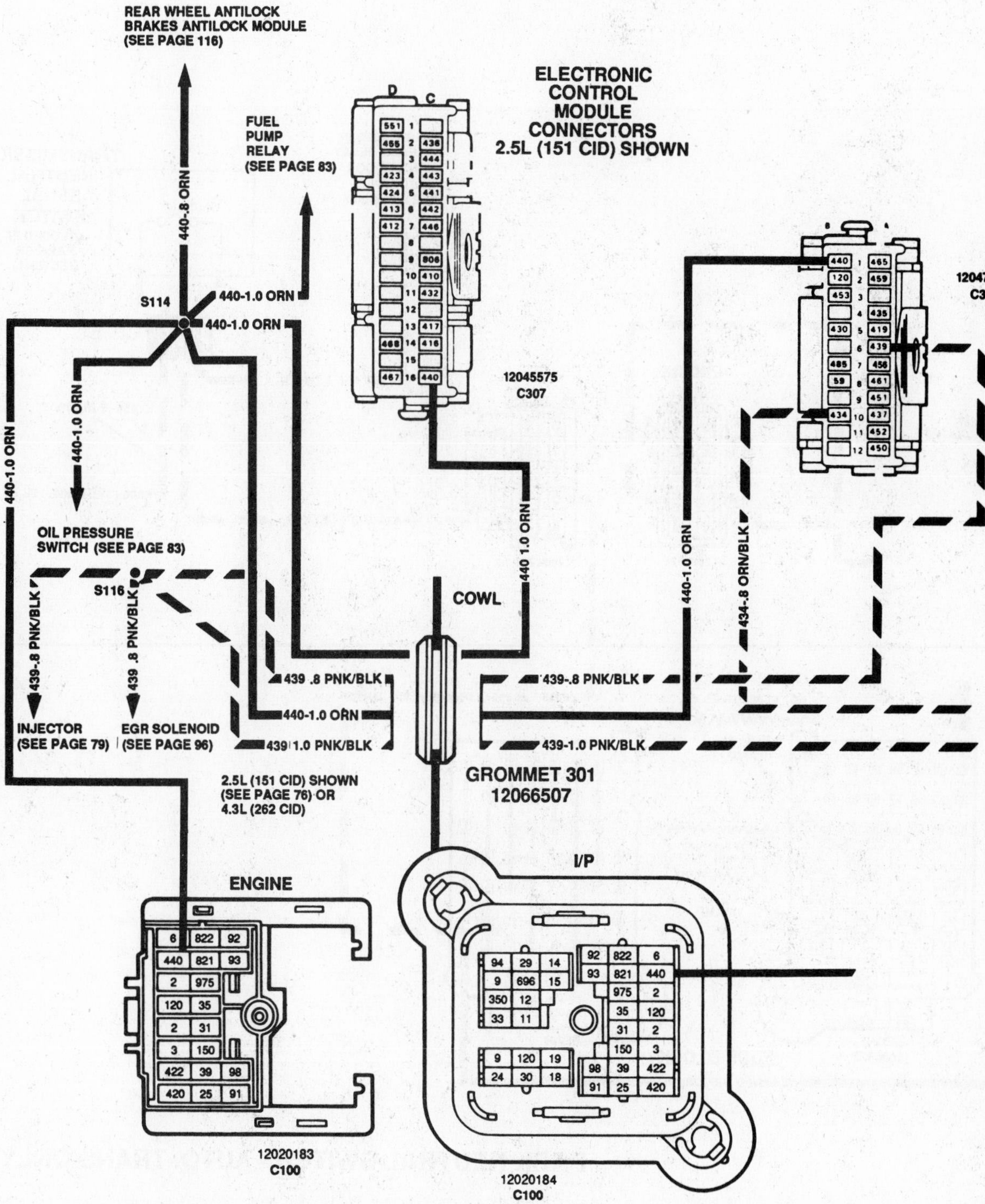
REAR WHEEL ANTILOCK BRAKES ANTILOCK MODULE (SEE PAGE 116)
FUEL PUMP RELAY (SEE PAGE 83)
ELECTRONIC CONTROL MODULE CONNECTORS 2.5L (151 CID) SHOWN
440-.8 ORN
S114
440-1.0 ORN
12045575 C307
12047946 C307
OIL PRESSURE SWITCH (SEE PAGE 83)
S116
439-.8 PNK/BLK
439 .8 PNK/BLK
INJECTOR (SEE PAGE 79)
EGR SOLENOID (SEE PAGE 96)
440 1.0 ORN
COWL
434-.8 ORN/BLK
439-1.0 PNK/BLK
GROMMET 301 12066507
2.5L (151 CID) SHOWN (SEE PAGE 76) OR 4.3L (262 CID)
ENGINE
I/P
12020183 C100
12020184 C100

1988–91 WIRING DIAGRAMS (CONT.)

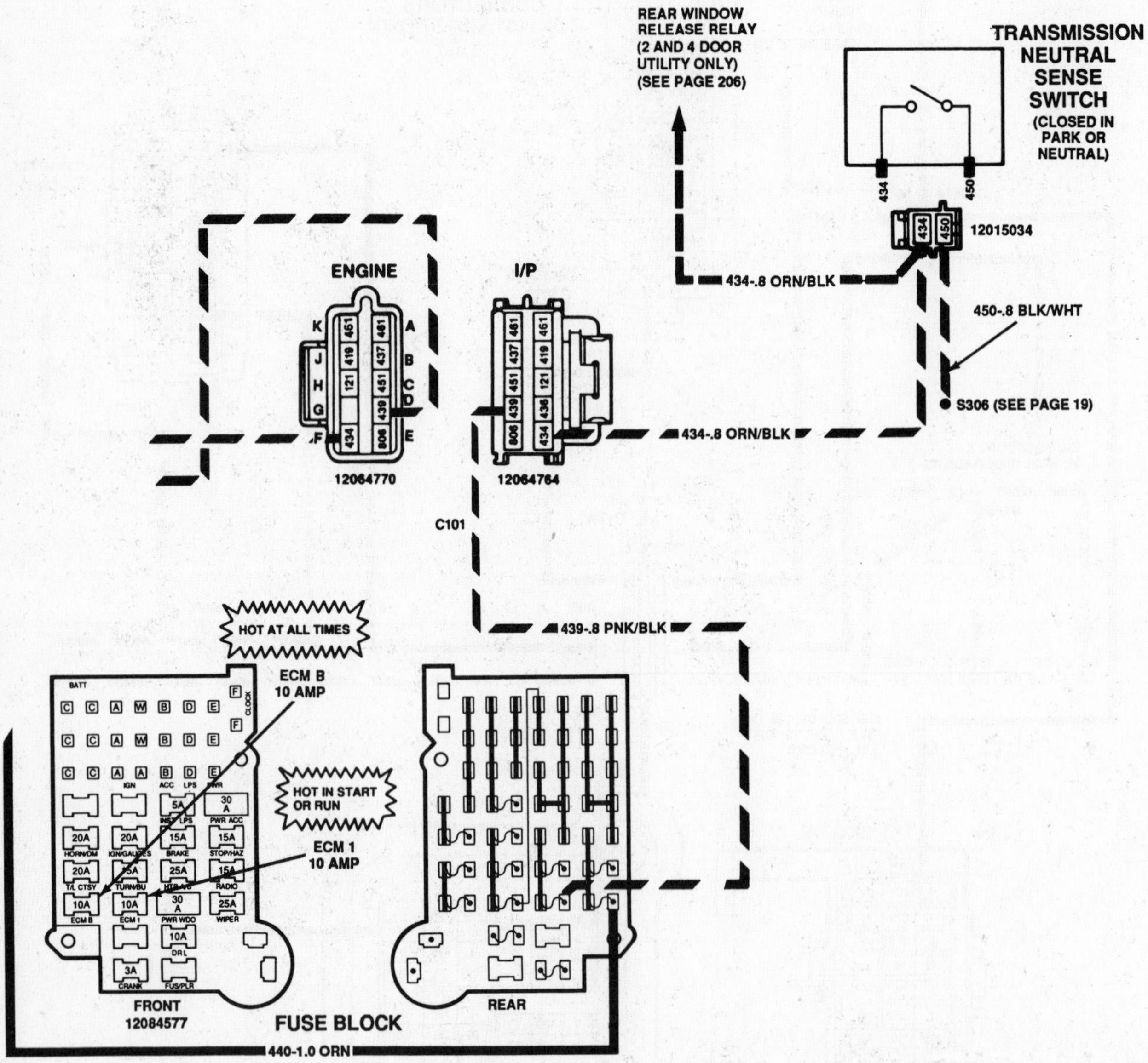
REAR WINDOW RELEASE RELAY (2 AND 4 DOOR UTILITY ONLY) (SEE PAGE 206)
TRANSMISSION NEUTRAL SENSE SWITCH
(CLOSED IN PARK OR NEUTRAL)
434
450
12015034
434-.8 ORN/BLK
450-.8 BLK/WHT
S306 (SEE PAGE 19)
ENGINE
I/P
12064770
12064764
C101
439-.8 PNK/BLK
HOT AT ALL TIMES
ECM B 10 AMP
HOT IN START OR RUN
ECM 1 10 AMP
FRONT 12084577
FUSE BLOCK
REAR
440-1.0 ORN

PARK NEUTRAL SWITCH - AUTO. TRANS ONLY

1988–91 WIRING DIAGRAMS (CONT.)

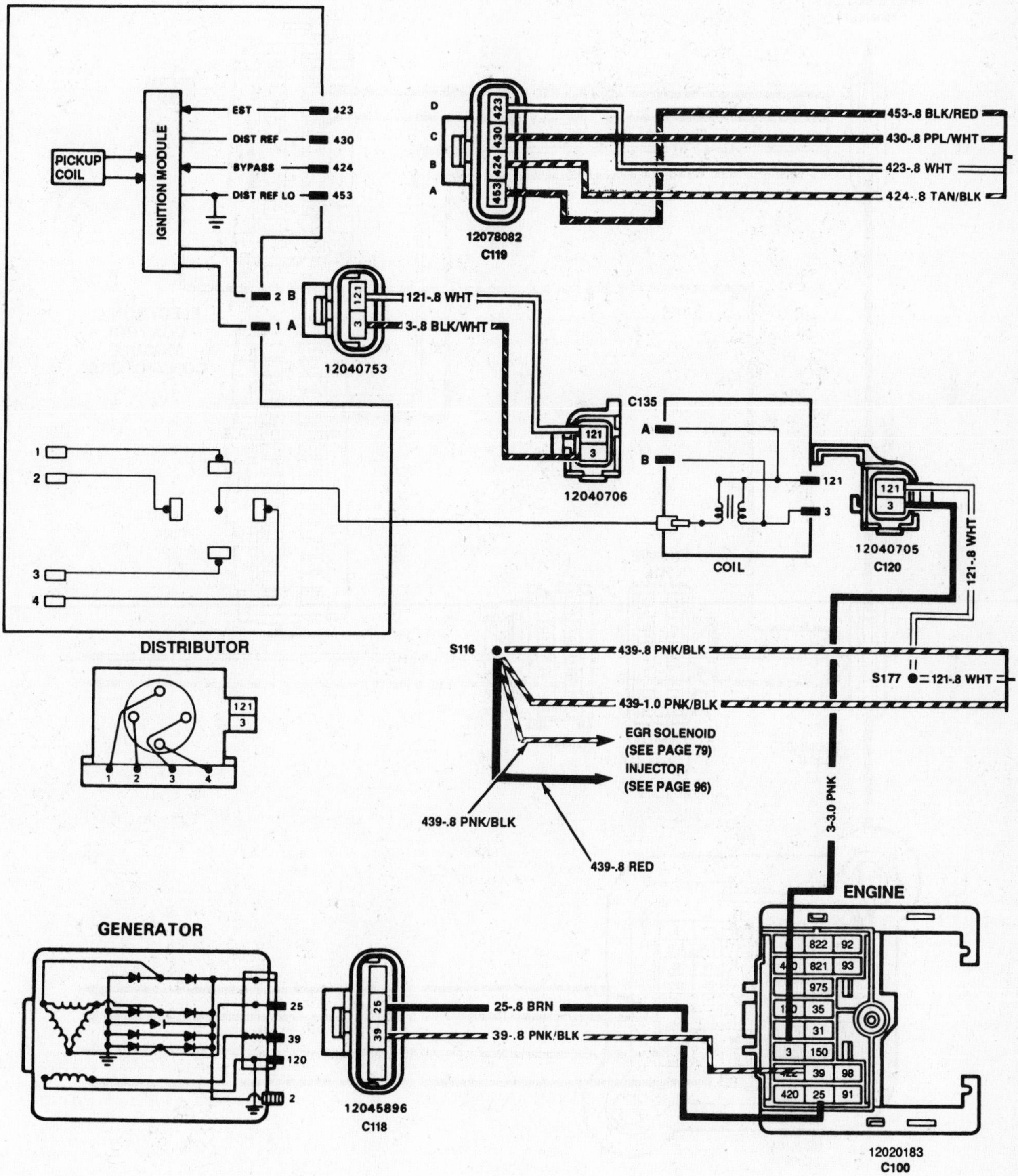
IGNITION MODULE
PICKUP COIL
EST
DIST REF
BYPASS
DIST REF LO
423
430
424
453
12078082
C119
453-.8 BLK/RED
430-.8 PPL/WHT
423-.8 WHT
424-.8 TAN/BLK
121-.8 WHT
3-.8 BLK/WHT
12040753
C135
12040706
COIL
12040705
C120
DISTRIBUTOR
S116
439-.8 PNK/BLK
439-1.0 PNK/BLK
S177
121-.8 WHT
EGR SOLENOID
(SEE PAGE 79)
INJECTOR
(SEE PAGE 96)
439-.8 RED
3-3.0 PNK
ENGINE
GENERATOR
25-.8 BRN
39-.8 PNK/BLK
12045896
C118
12020183
C100

IGNITION - 2.5L (151 CID) ENGINE

1988–91 WIRING DIAGRAMS (CONT.)

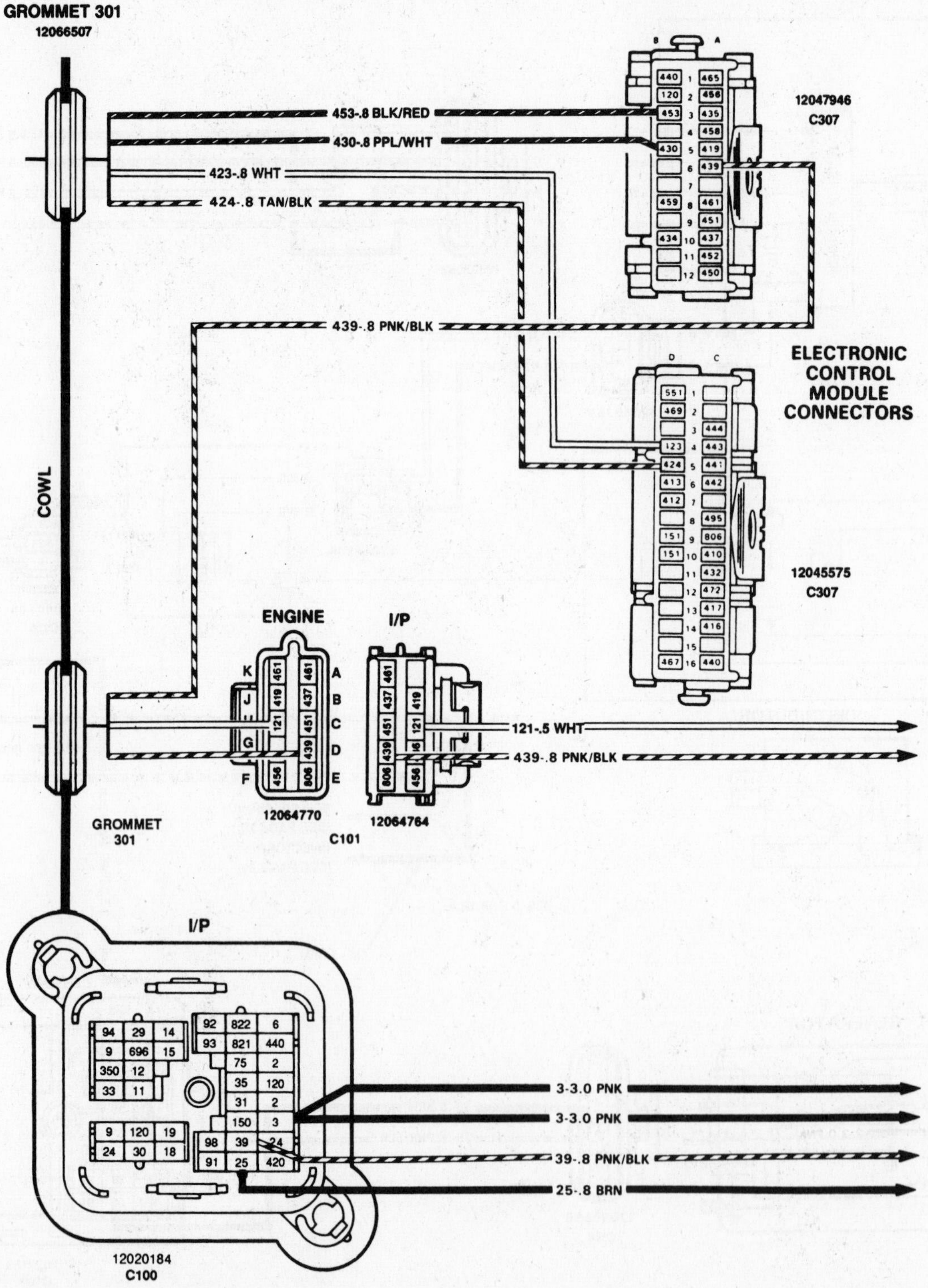
GROMMET 301
12066507
453-.8 BLK/RED
430-.8 PPL/WHT
423-.8 WHT
424-.8 TAN/BLK
12047946
C307
439-.8 PNK/BLK
ELECTRONIC CONTROL MODULE CONNECTORS
12045575
C307
COWL
ENGINE
I/P
121-.5 WHT
439-.8 PNK/BLK
GROMMET 301
12064770
C101
12064764
I/P
3-3.0 PNK
3-3.0 PNK
39-.8 PNK/BLK
25-.8 BRN
12020184
C100

1988–91 WIRING DIAGRAMS (CONT.)

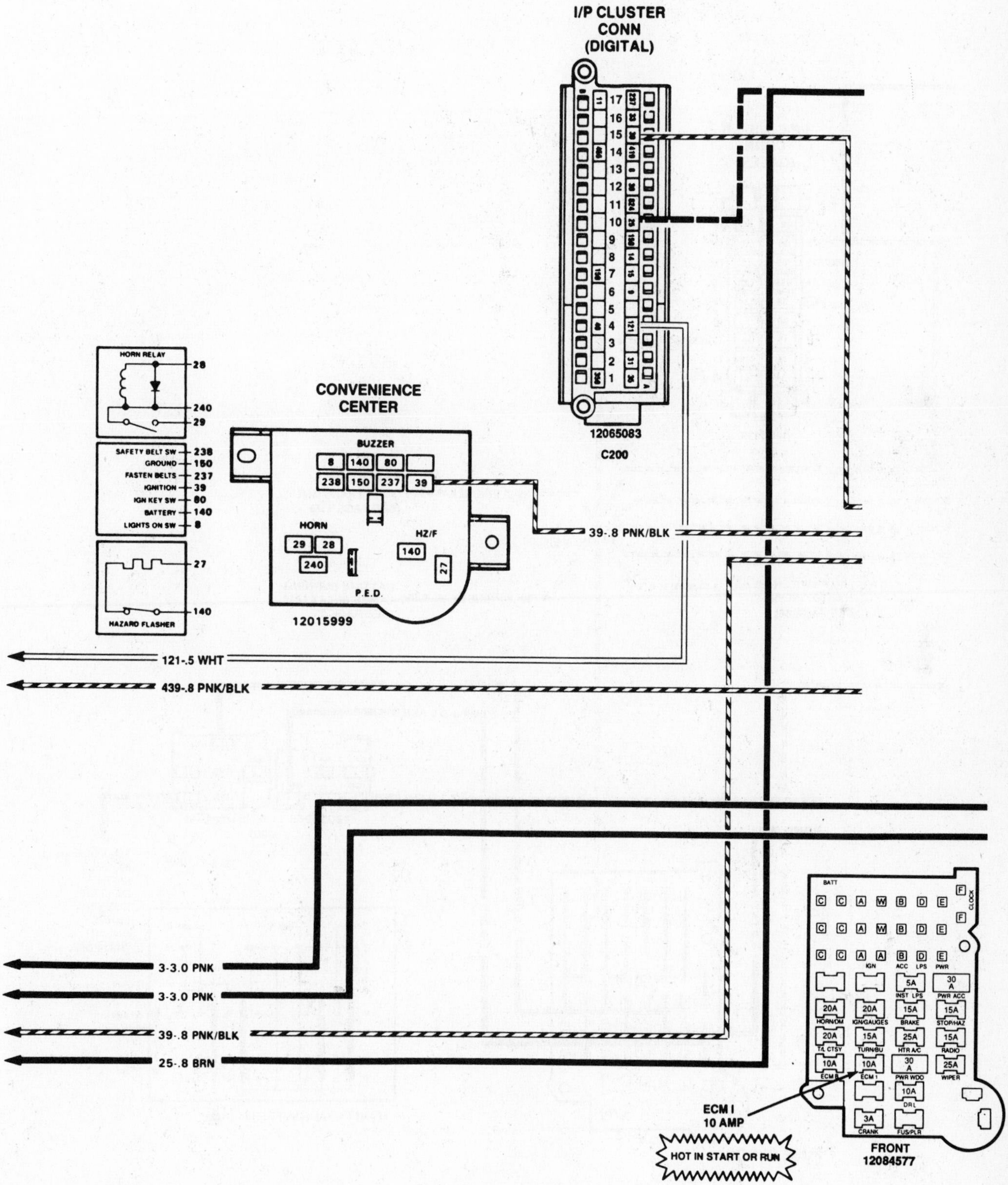
I/P CLUSTER
CONN
(DIGITAL)
12065083
C200
HORN RELAY
28
240
29
SAFETY BELT SW
GROUND
FASTEN BELTS
IGNITION
IGN KEY SW
BATTERY
LIGHTS ON SW
238
150
237
39
80
140
8
27
140
HAZARD FLASHER
CONVENIENCE
CENTER
BUZZER
HORN
HZ/F
P.E.D.
12015999
39-.8 PNK/BLK
121-.5 WHT
439-.8 PNK/BLK
3-3.0 PNK
3-3.0 PNK
39-.8 PNK/BLK
25-.8 BRN
ECM I
10 AMP
HOT IN START OR RUN
FRONT
12084577

1988–91 WIRING DIAGRAMS (CONT.)

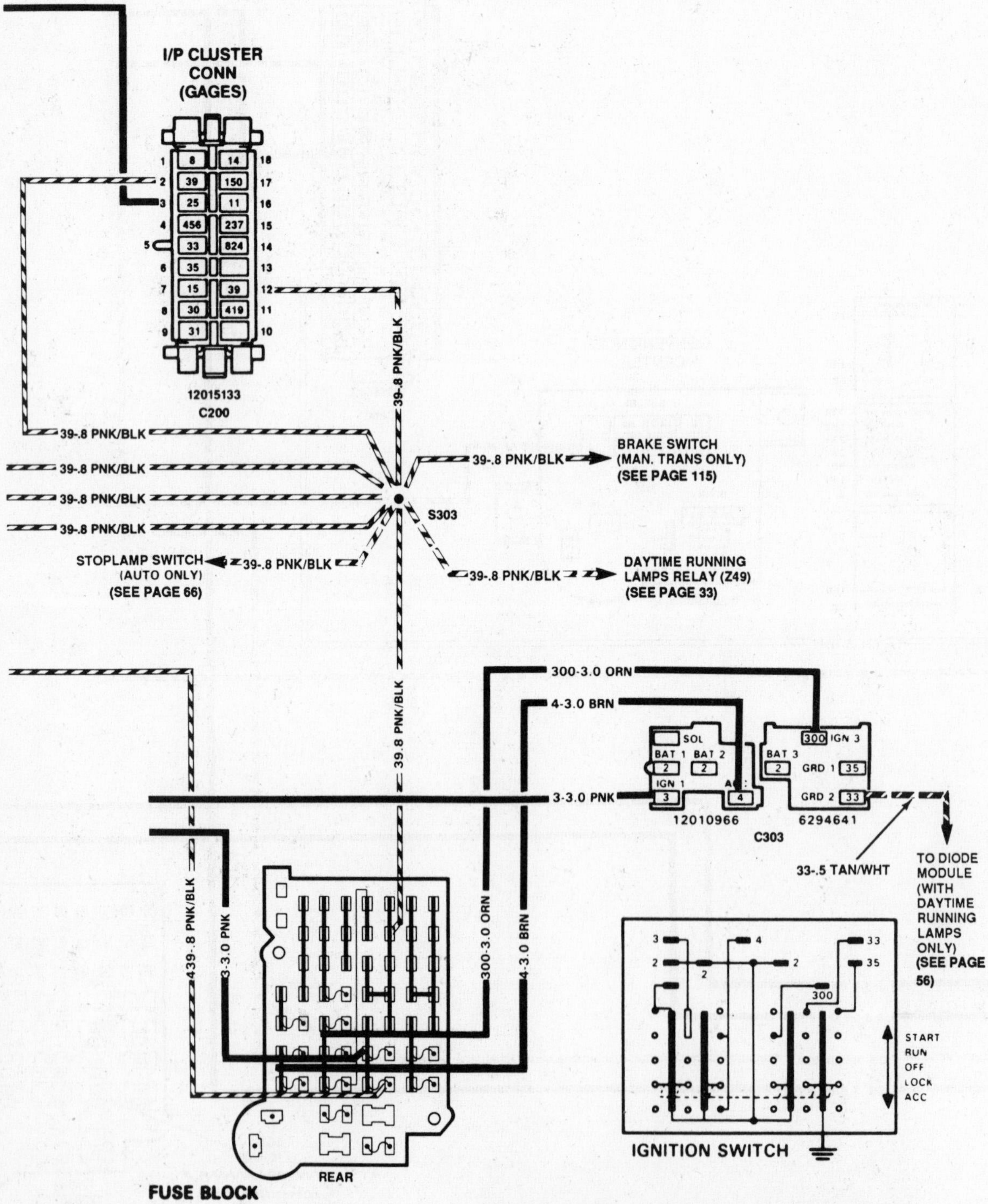

I/P CLUSTER
CONN
(GAGES)
12015133
C200
39-.8 PNK/BLK
S303
BRAKE SWITCH
(MAN. TRANS ONLY)
(SEE PAGE 115)
STOPLAMP SWITCH
(AUTO ONLY)
(SEE PAGE 66)
DAYTIME RUNNING
LAMPS RELAY (Z49)
(SEE PAGE 33)
39.8 PNK/BLK
300-3.0 ORN
4-3.0 BRN
3-3.0 PNK
SOL
BAT 1
BAT 2
IGN 1
BAT 3
IGN 3
GRD 1
GRD 2
12010966
6294641
C303
33-.5 TAN/WHT
TO DIODE
MODULE
(WITH
DAYTIME
RUNNING
LAMPS
ONLY)
(SEE PAGE
56)
439-.8 PNK/BLK
3-3.0 PNK
START
RUN
OFF
LOCK
ACC
IGNITION SWITCH
REAR
FUSE BLOCK

IGNITION - 2.5L (151 CID) ENGINE

1988–91 WIRING DIAGRAMS (CONT.)

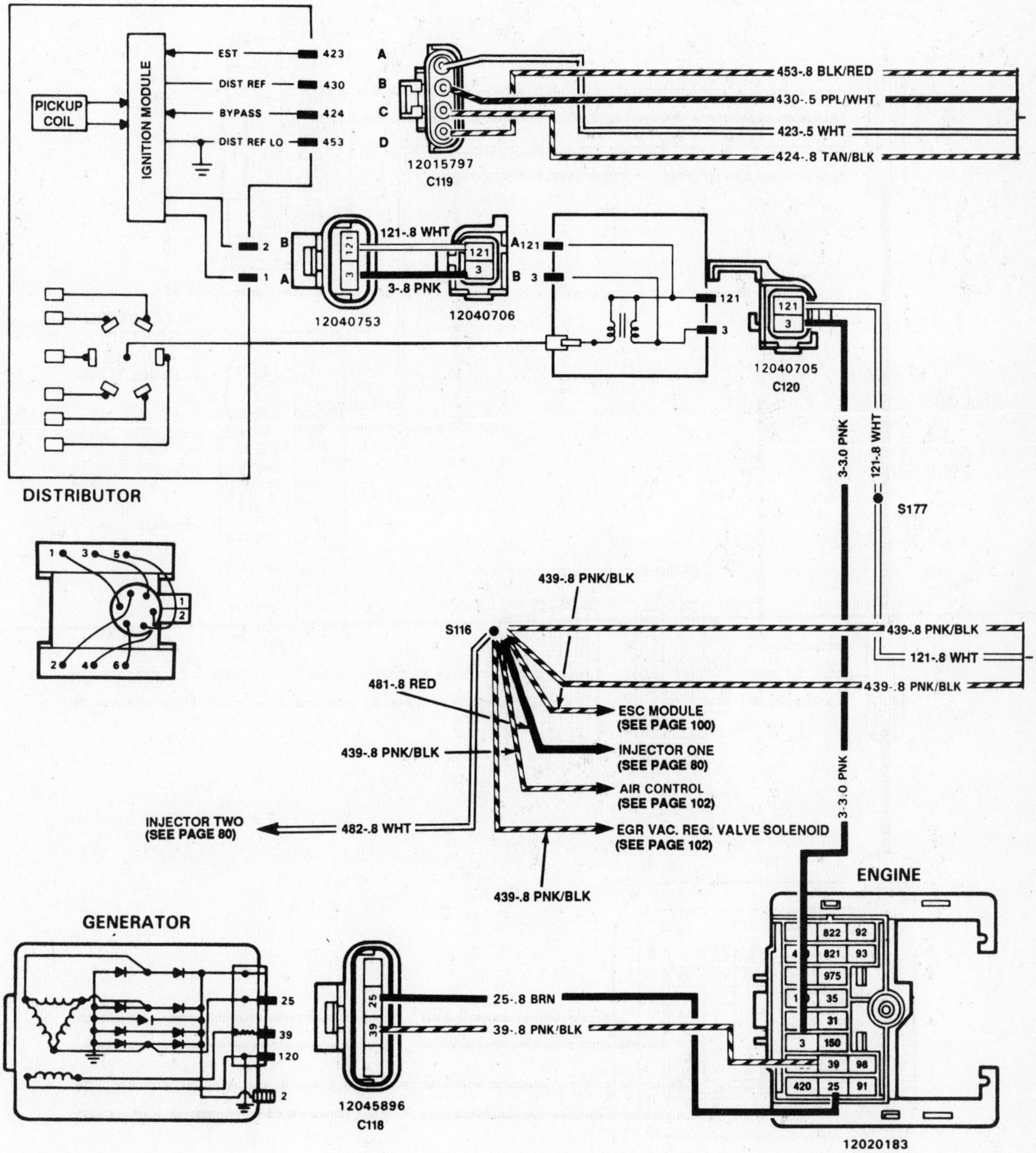

PICKUP COIL
IGNITION MODULE
EST
DIST REF
BYPASS
DIST REF LO
423
430
424
453
A
B
C
D
12015797
C119
453-.8 BLK/RED
430-.5 PPL/WHT
423-.5 WHT
424-.8 TAN/BLK
121-.8 WHT
3-.8 PNK
12040753
12040706
12040705
C120
DISTRIBUTOR
3-3.0 PNK
121-.8 WHT
S177
439-.8 PNK/BLK
S116
121-.8 WHT
481-.8 RED
ESC MODULE (SEE PAGE 100)
INJECTOR ONE (SEE PAGE 80)
AIR CONTROL (SEE PAGE 102)
EGR VAC. REG. VALVE SOLENOID (SEE PAGE 102)
INJECTOR TWO (SEE PAGE 80)
482-.8 WHT
ENGINE
GENERATOR
25-.8 BRN
39-.8 PNK/BLK
12045896
C118
12020183
C100

IGNITION - 2.8L (173 CID) ENGINE

1988–91 WIRING DIAGRAMS (CONT.)

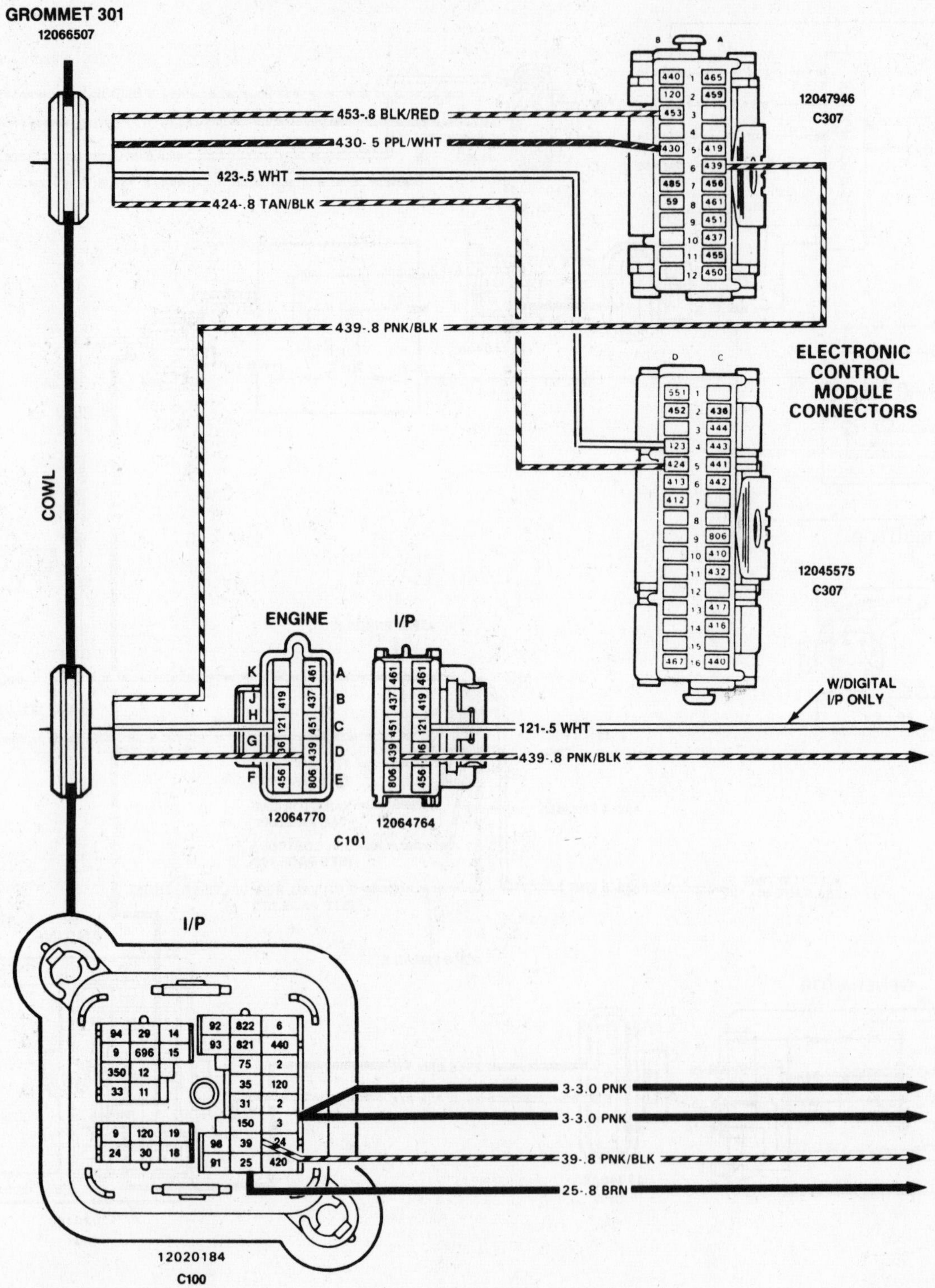
GROMMET 301
12066507
453-.8 BLK/RED
430-.5 PPL/WHT
423-.5 WHT
424-.8 TAN/BLK
12047946
C307
439-.8 PNK/BLK
ELECTRONIC CONTROL MODULE CONNECTORS
12045575
C307
COWL
ENGINE
I/P
12064770
12064764
C101
W/DIGITAL I/P ONLY
121-.5 WHT
439-.8 PNK/BLK
I/P
3-3.0 PNK
3-3.0 PNK
39-.8 PNK/BLK
25-.8 BRN
12020184
C100

1988–91 WIRING DIAGRAMS (CONT.)

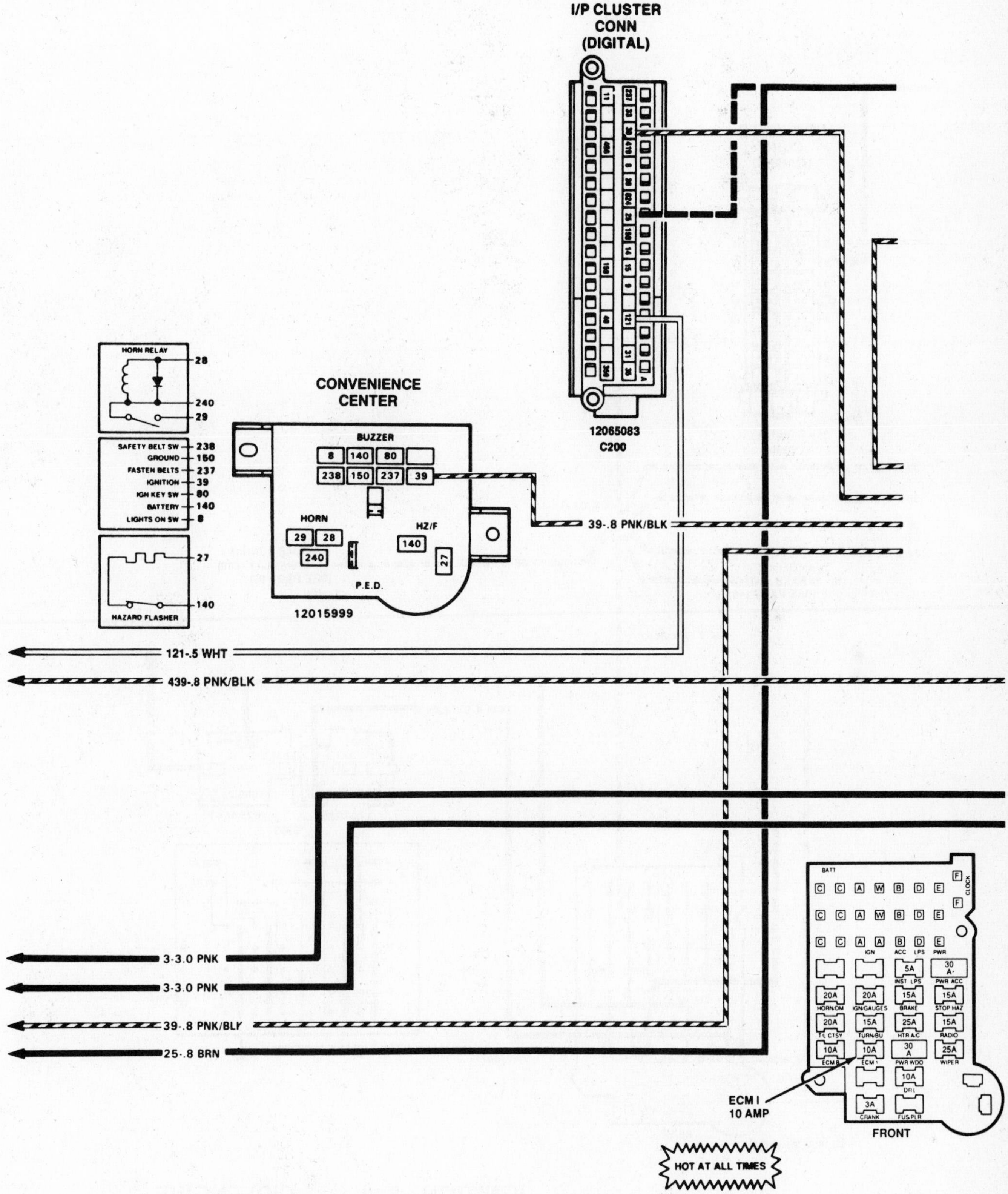
I/P CLUSTER CONN (DIGITAL)
12065083
C200
HORN RELAY
28
240
29
SAFETY BELT SW 238
GROUND 150
FASTEN BELTS 237
IGNITION 39
IGN KEY SW 80
BATTERY 140
LIGHTS ON SW 8
27
140
HAZARD FLASHER
CONVENIENCE CENTER
BUZZER
8 140 80
238 150 237 39
HORN
29 28
240
HZ/F
140
27
P.E.D.
12015999
39-.8 PNK/BLK
121-.5 WHT
439-.8 PNK/BLK
3-3.0 PNK
3-3.0 PNK
39-.8 PNK/BLK
25-.8 BRN
ECM I
10 AMP
FRONT
HOT AT ALL TIMES

1988–91 WIRING DIAGRAMS (CONT.)

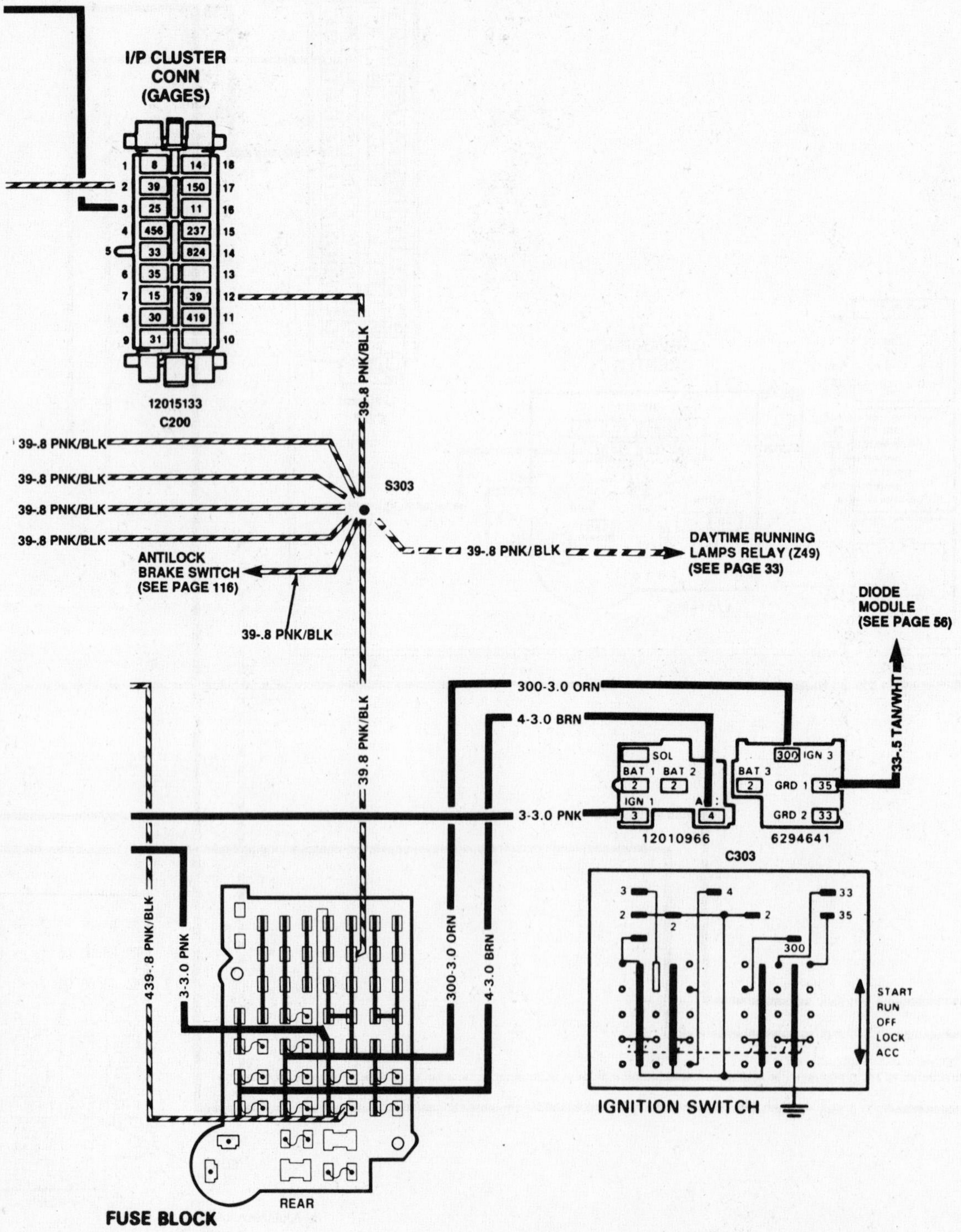
I/P CLUSTER CONN (GAGES)
12015133
C200
39-.8 PNK/BLK
S303
ANTILOCK BRAKE SWITCH (SEE PAGE 116)
DAYTIME RUNNING LAMPS RELAY (Z49) (SEE PAGE 33)
DIODE MODULE (SEE PAGE 56)
33-.5 TAN/WHT
39.8 PNK/BLK
300-3.0 ORN
4-3.0 BRN
3-3.0 PNK
439-.8 PNK/BLK
SOL
BAT 1
BAT 2
IGN 1
IGN 3
BAT 3
GRD 1
GRD 2
12010966
6294641
C303
START
RUN
OFF
LOCK
ACC
IGNITION SWITCH
REAR
FUSE BLOCK

IGNITION - 2.8L (173 CID) ENGINE

1988–91 WIRING DIAGRAMS (CONT.)

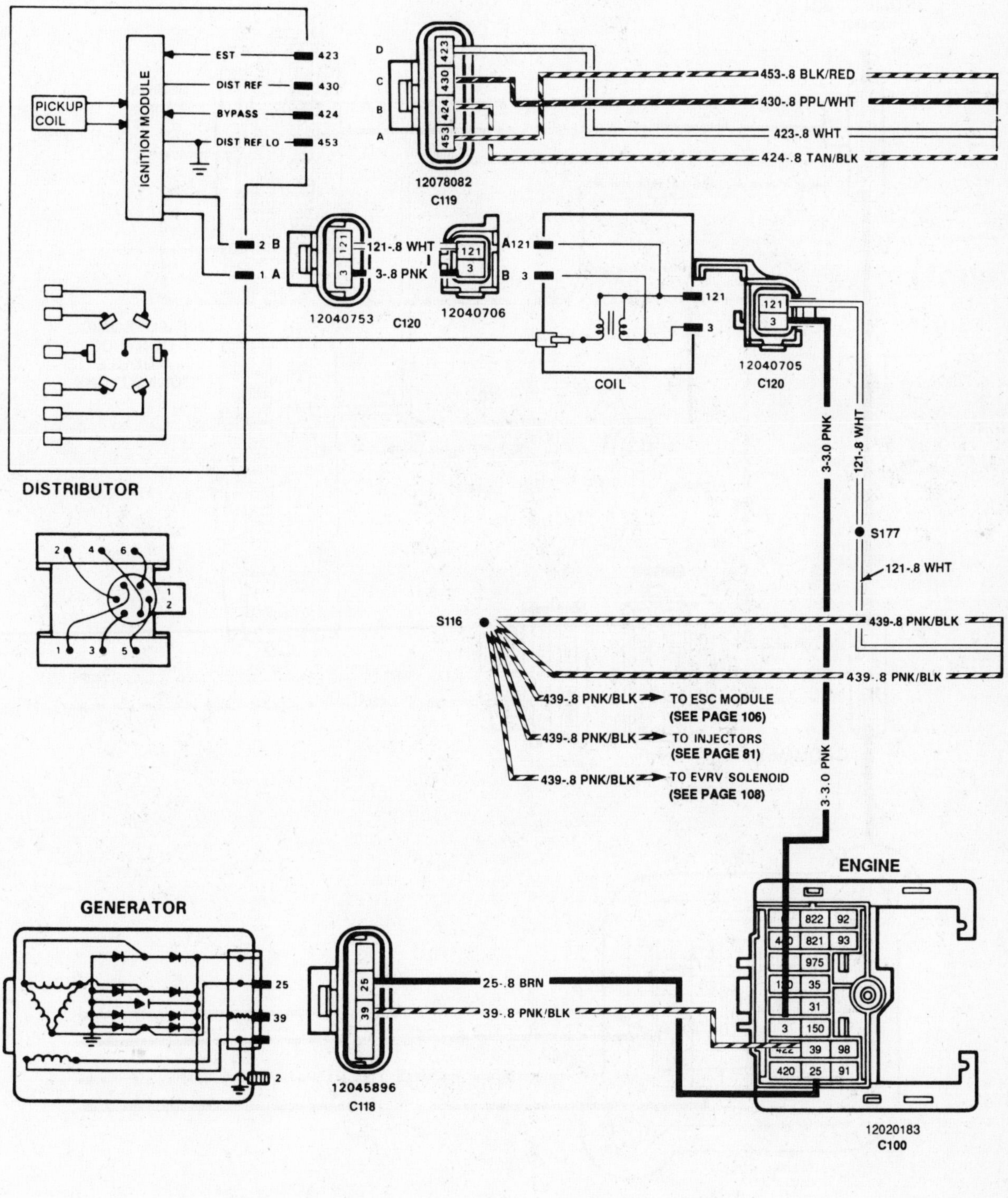

PICKUP COIL
IGNITION MODULE
EST
DIST REF
BYPASS
DIST REF LO
423
430
424
453
D
C
B
A
12078082
C119
453-.8 BLK/RED
430-.8 PPL/WHT
423-.8 WHT
424-.8 TAN/BLK
2 B
1 A
121-.8 WHT
3-.8 PNK
12040753
C120
12040706
A 121
B 3
121
3
COIL
12040705
C120
DISTRIBUTOR
3-3.0 PNK
121-.8 WHT
S177
121-.8 WHT
S116
439-.8 PNK/BLK
439-.8 PNK/BLK
439-.8 PNK/BLK TO ESC MODULE (SEE PAGE 106)
439-.8 PNK/BLK TO INJECTORS (SEE PAGE 81)
439-.8 PNK/BLK TO EVRV SOLENOID (SEE PAGE 108)
3-3.0 PNK
ENGINE
GENERATOR
25
39
2
25-.8 BRN
39-.8 PNK/BLK
12045896
C118
822 92
821 93
975
35
31
150
39 98
420 25 91
12020183
C100

IGNITION - 4.3L (262 CID) ENGINE

1988–91 WIRING DIAGRAMS (CONT.)

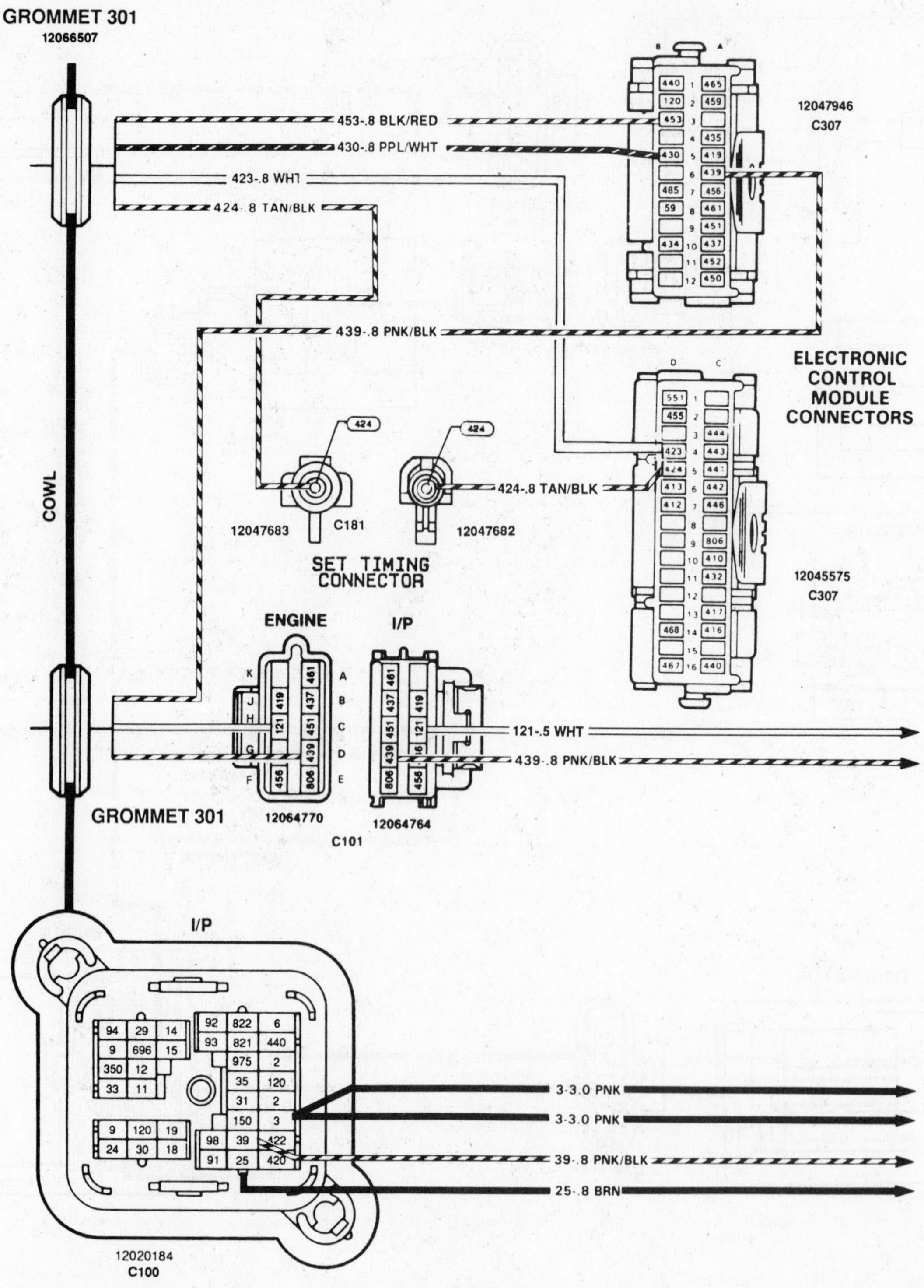

GROMMET 301
12066507
453-.8 BLK/RED
430-.8 PPL/WHT
423-.8 WHT
424-.8 TAN/BLK
12047946
C307
439-.8 PNK/BLK
ELECTRONIC CONTROL MODULE CONNECTORS
COWL
424
12047683
C181
12047682
424-.8 TAN/BLK
SET TIMING CONNECTOR
12045575
C307
ENGINE
I/P
GROMMET 301
12064770
C101
12064764
121-.5 WHT
439-.8 PNK/BLK
I/P
3-3.0 PNK
3-3.0 PNK
39-.8 PNK/BLK
25-.8 BRN
12020184
C100

1988–91 WIRING DIAGRAMS (CONT.)

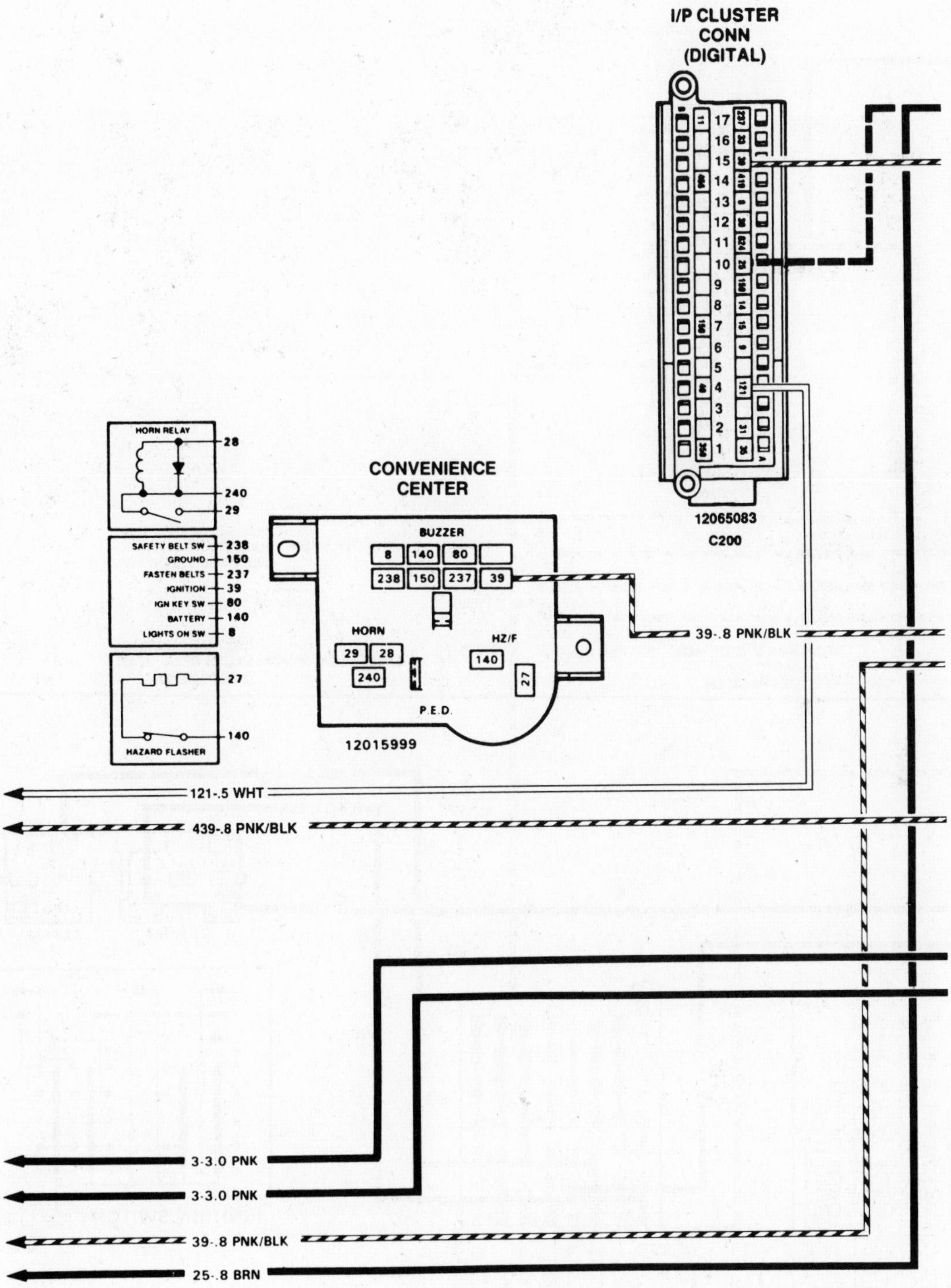

I/P CLUSTER CONN (DIGITAL)
17
16
15
14
13
12
11
10
9
8
7
6
5
4
3
2
1
12065083
C200
HORN RELAY
28
240
29
SAFETY BELT SW 238
GROUND 150
FASTEN BELTS 237
IGNITION 39
IGN KEY SW 80
BATTERY 140
LIGHTS ON SW 8
27
140
HAZARD FLASHER
CONVENIENCE CENTER
BUZZER
8
140
80
238
150
237
39
HORN
29
28
240
HZ/F
140
27
P.E.D.
12015999
39-.8 PNK/BLK
121-.5 WHT
439-.8 PNK/BLK
3-3.0 PNK
3-3.0 PNK
39-.8 PNK/BLK
25-.8 BRN

1988–91 WIRING DIAGRAMS (CONT.)

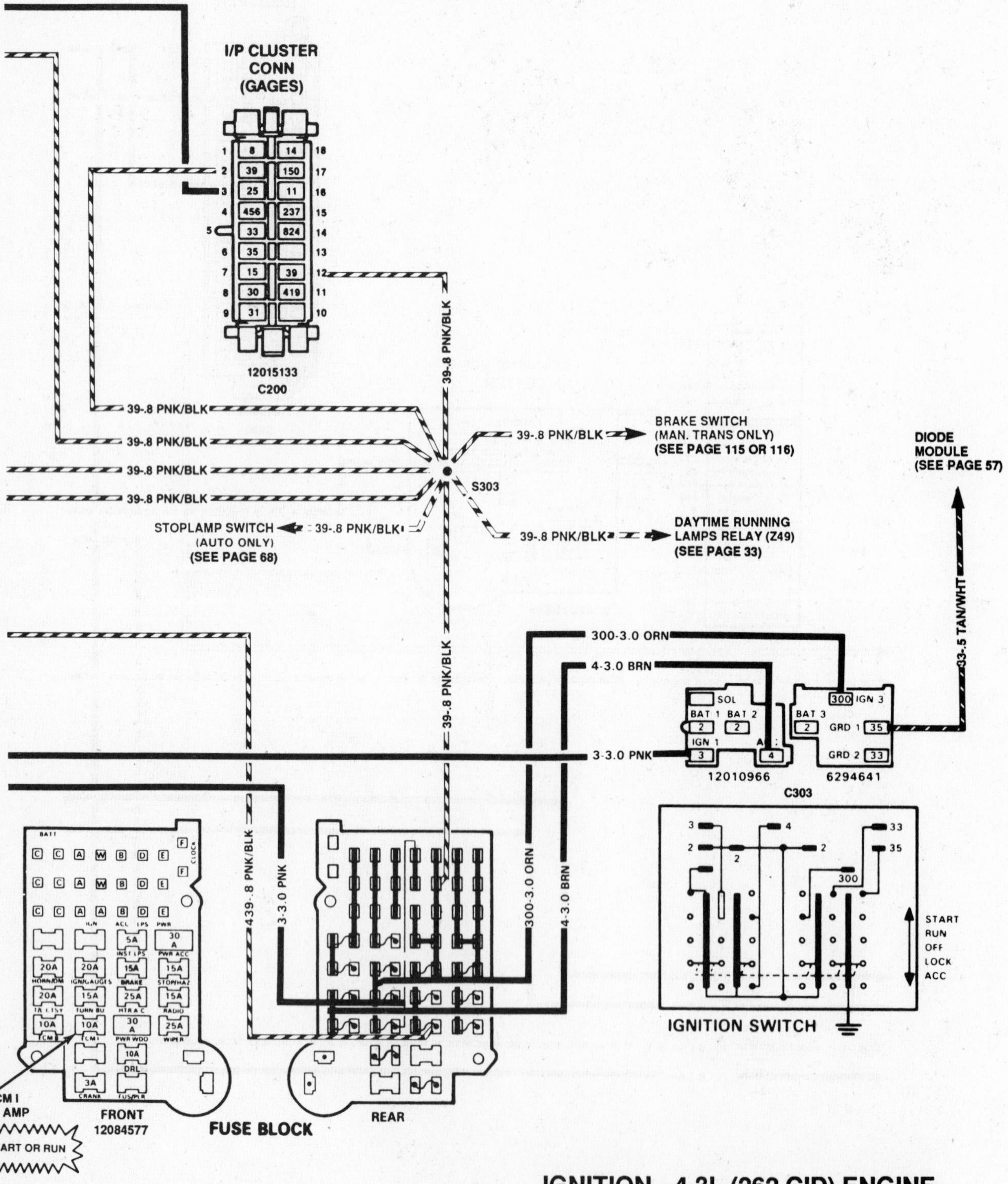
I/P CLUSTER
CONN
(GAGES)
12015133
C200
39-.8 PNK/BLK
S303
BRAKE SWITCH
(MAN. TRANS ONLY)
(SEE PAGE 115 OR 116)
STOPLAMP SWITCH
(AUTO ONLY)
(SEE PAGE 68)
DAYTIME RUNNING
LAMPS RELAY (Z49)
(SEE PAGE 33)
DIODE
MODULE
(SEE PAGE 57)
33-.5 TAN/WHT
300-3.0 ORN
4-3.0 BRN
3-3.0 PNK
439-.8 PNK/BLK
SOL
BAT 1
BAT 2
IGN 1
IGN 3
BAT 3
GRD 1
GRD 2
12010966
6294641
C303
START
RUN
OFF
LOCK
ACC
IGNITION SWITCH
ECM I
10 AMP
HOT IN START OR RUN
FRONT
12084577
FUSE BLOCK
REAR

IGNITION - 4.3L (262 CID) ENGINE

1988–91 WIRING DIAGRAMS (CONT.)

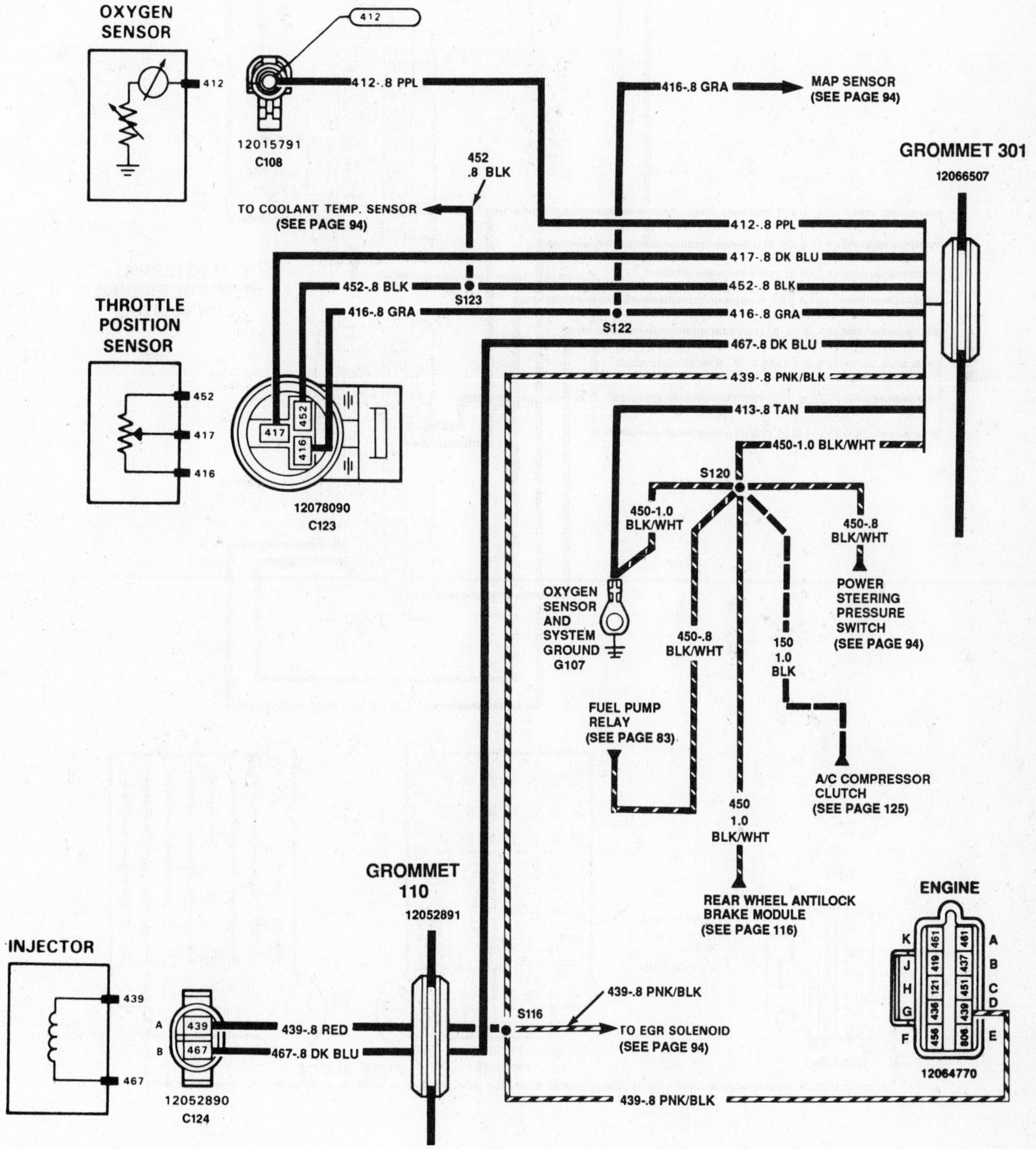
OXYGEN
SENSOR
412
412
12015791
C108
412-.8 PPL
416-.8 GRA
MAP SENSOR
(SEE PAGE 94)
GROMMET 301
12066507
452
.8 BLK
TO COOLANT TEMP. SENSOR
(SEE PAGE 94)
412-.8 PPL
417-.8 DK BLU
452-.8 BLK
452-.8 BLK
S123
416-.8 GRA
416-.8 GRA
S122
467-.8 DK BLU
439-.8 PNK/BLK
413-.8 TAN
450-1.0 BLK/WHT
THROTTLE
POSITION
SENSOR
452
417
416
417
452
416
12078090
C123
S120
450-1.0
BLK/WHT
450-.8
BLK/WHT
POWER
STEERING
PRESSURE
SWITCH
(SEE PAGE 94)
OXYGEN
SENSOR
AND
SYSTEM
GROUND
G107
450-.8
BLK/WHT
150
1.0
BLK
FUEL PUMP
RELAY
(SEE PAGE 83)
A/C COMPRESSOR
CLUTCH
(SEE PAGE 125)
450
1.0
BLK/WHT
REAR WHEEL ANTILOCK
BRAKE MODULE
(SEE PAGE 116)
GROMMET
110
12052891
ENGINE
INJECTOR
439
467
A
B
439
467
439-.8 RED
467-.8 DK BLU
12052890
C124
439-.8 PNK/BLK
S116
TO EGR SOLENOID
(SEE PAGE 94)
439-.8 PNK/BLK
K
J
H
G
F
A
B
C
D
E
461
419
121
436
456
461
437
451
439
806
12064770

1988–91 WIRING DIAGRAMS (CONT.)

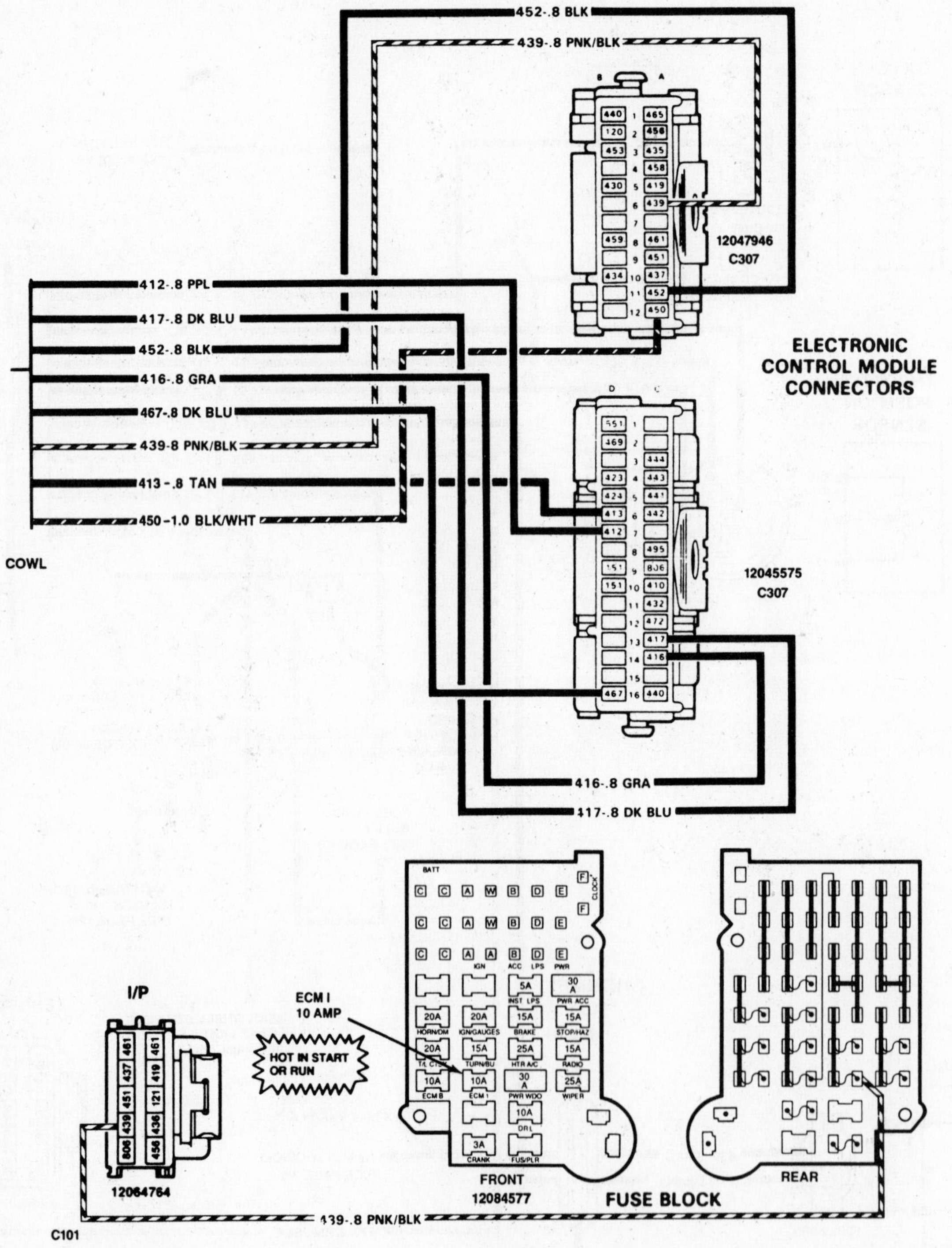
452-.8 BLK
439-.8 PNK/BLK
12047946
C307
412-.8 PPL
417-.8 DK BLU
452-.8 BLK
416-.8 GRA
467-.8 DK BLU
439-8 PNK/BLK
413-.8 TAN
450-1.0 BLK/WHT
COWL
ELECTRONIC CONTROL MODULE CONNECTORS
12045575
C307
416-.8 GRA
417-.8 DK BLU
I/P
ECM I 10 AMP
HOT IN START OR RUN
12064764
C101
FRONT
12084577
FUSE BLOCK
REAR
439-.8 PNK/BLK

THROTTLE BODY INJECTION - 2.5L (151 CID) ENGINE

1988–91 WIRING DIAGRAMS (CONT.)

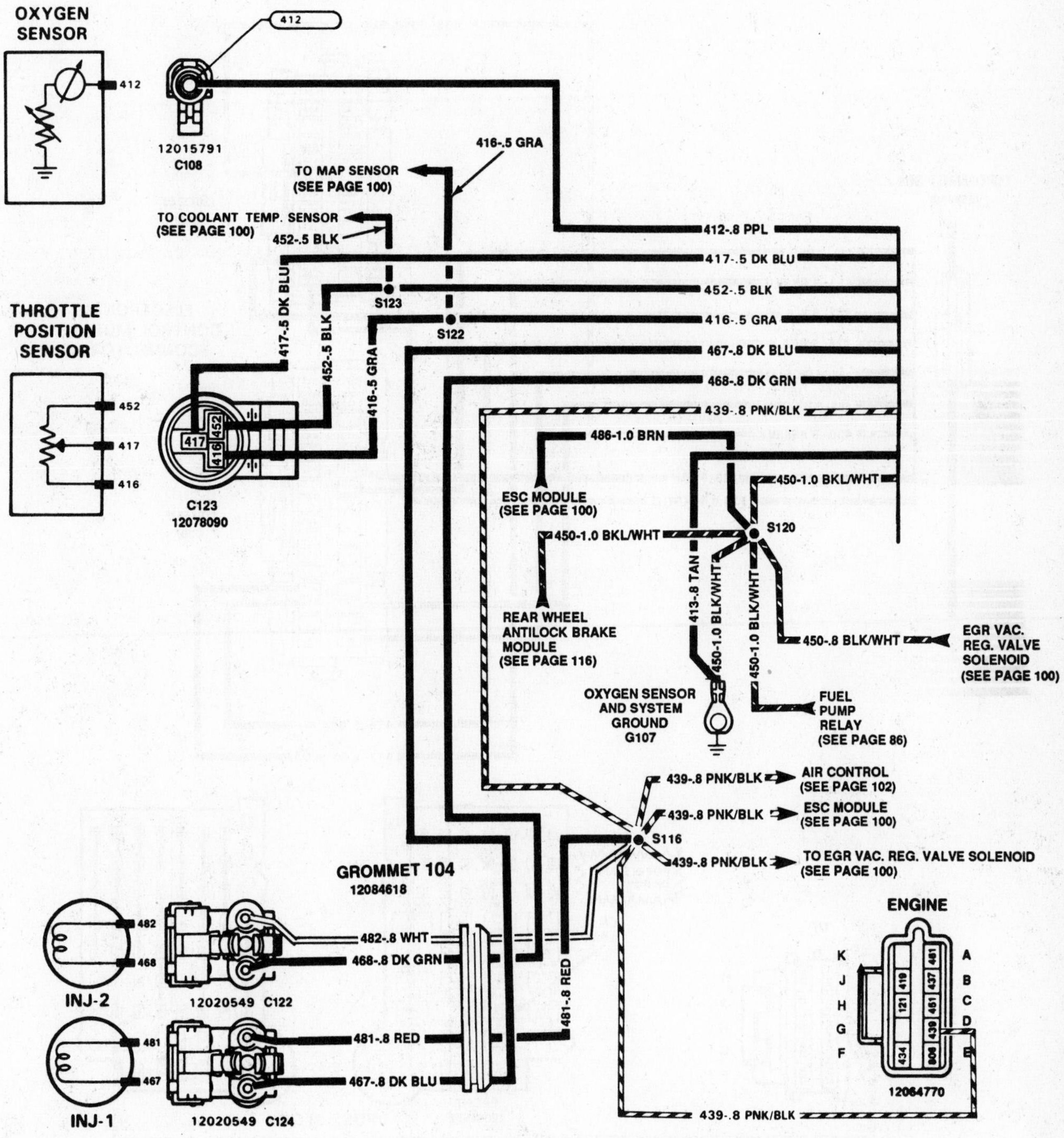
OXYGEN SENSOR
412
12015791
C108
TO MAP SENSOR (SEE PAGE 100)
416-.5 GRA
TO COOLANT TEMP. SENSOR (SEE PAGE 100)
452-.5 BLK
412-.8 PPL
417-.5 DK BLU
452-.5 BLK
S123
416-.5 GRA
S122
467-.8 DK BLU
468-.8 DK GRN
439-.8 PNK/BLK
THROTTLE POSITION SENSOR
452
417
416
C123
12078090
486-1.0 BRN
450-1.0 BKL/WHT
ESC MODULE (SEE PAGE 100)
450-1.0 BKL/WHT
S120
413-.8 TAN
450-1.0 BLK/WHT
450-.8 BLK/WHT
EGR VAC. REG. VALVE SOLENOID (SEE PAGE 100)
REAR WHEEL ANTILOCK BRAKE MODULE (SEE PAGE 116)
OXYGEN SENSOR AND SYSTEM GROUND G107
FUEL PUMP RELAY (SEE PAGE 86)
439-.8 PNK/BLK
AIR CONTROL (SEE PAGE 102)
ESC MODULE (SEE PAGE 100)
S116
TO EGR VAC. REG. VALVE SOLENOID (SEE PAGE 100)
GROMMET 104
12084618
ENGINE
482
468
INJ-2
482-.8 WHT
468-.8 DK GRN
12020549 C122
481-.8 RED
481
467
INJ-1
467-.8 DK BLU
12020549 C124
K J H G F
A B C D E
12064770

THROTTLE BODY INJECTION - 2.8L (173 CID) ENGINE

1988–91 WIRING DIAGRAMS (CONT.)

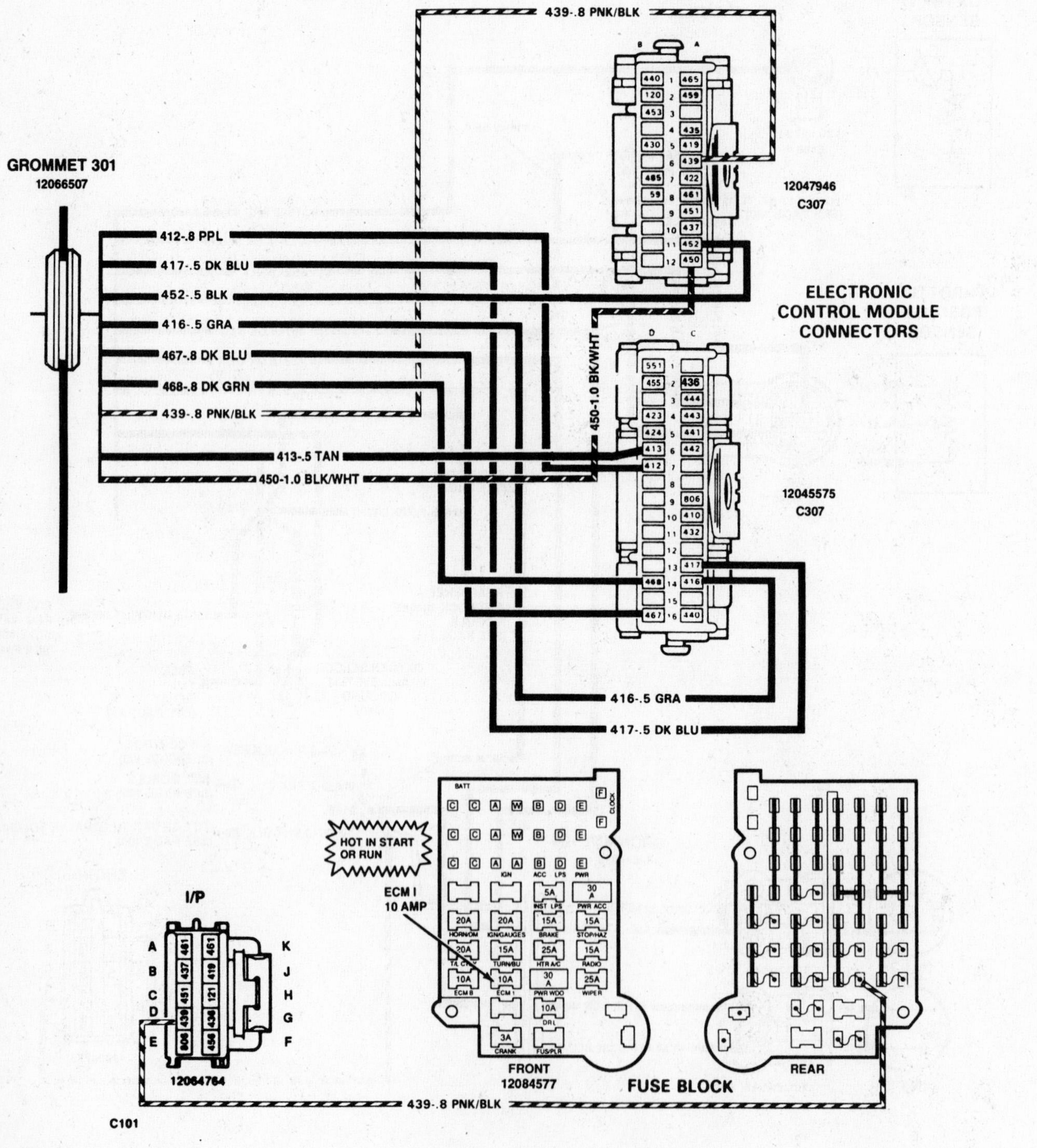
439-.8 PNK/BLK
GROMMET 301
12066507
412-.8 PPL
417-.5 DK BLU
452-.5 BLK
416-.5 GRA
467-.8 DK BLU
468-.8 DK GRN
439-.8 PNK/BLK
413-.5 TAN
450-1.0 BLK/WHT
450-1.0 BK/WHT
12047946
C307
ELECTRONIC
CONTROL MODULE
CONNECTORS
12045575
C307
416-.5 GRA
417-.5 DK BLU
HOT IN START
OR RUN
ECM I
10 AMP
I/P
12064764
C101
FRONT
12084577
FUSE BLOCK
REAR
439-.8 PNK/BLK

1988–91 WIRING DIAGRAMS (CONT.)

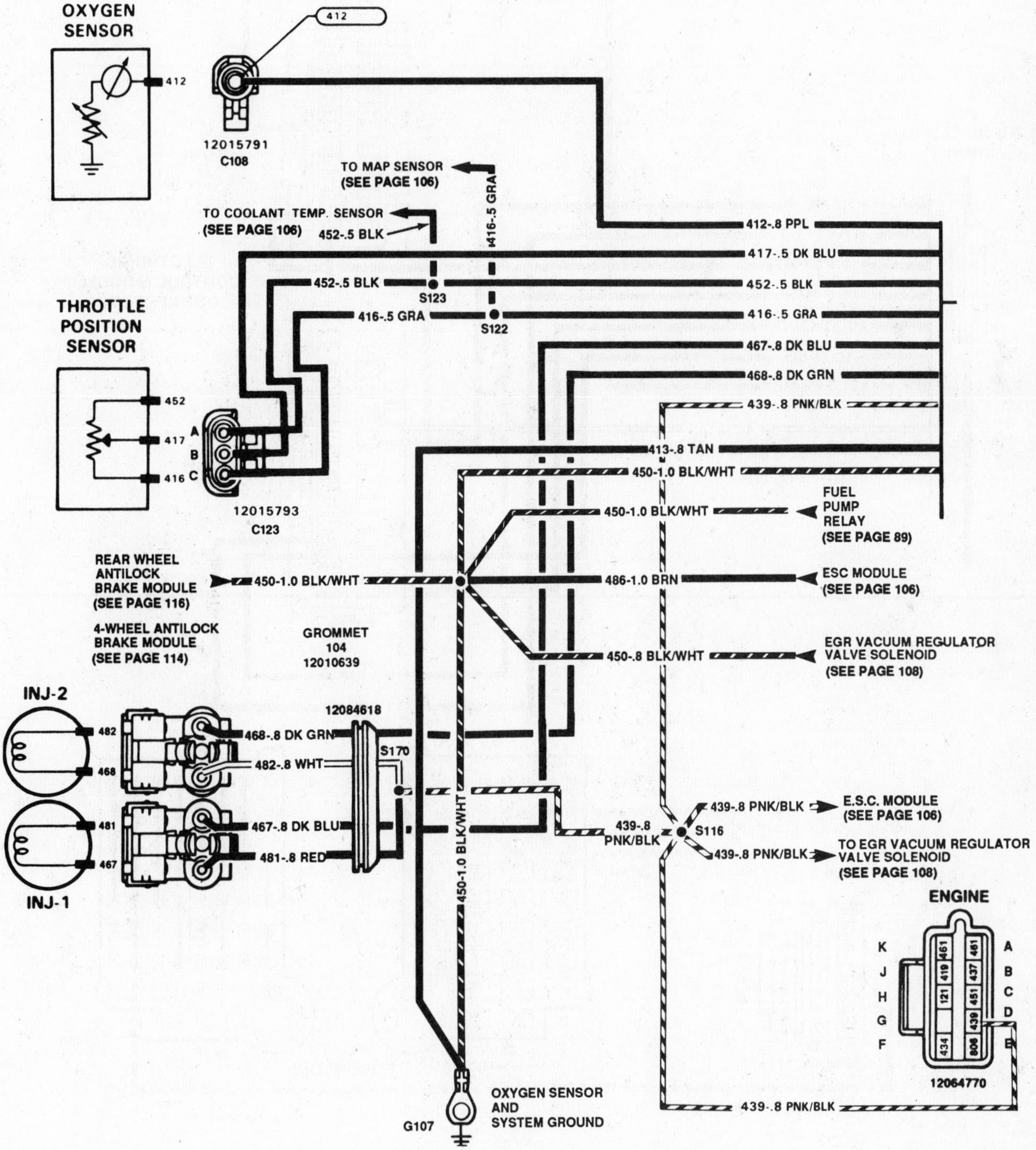

OXYGEN SENSOR
412
12015791
C108
TO MAP SENSOR (SEE PAGE 106)
TO COOLANT TEMP. SENSOR (SEE PAGE 106)
452-.5 BLK
416-.5 GRA
412-.8 PPL
417-.5 DK BLU
452-.5 BLK
S123
416-.5 GRA
S122
THROTTLE POSITION SENSOR
452
417
416
A
B
C
12015793
C123
467-.8 DK BLU
468-.8 DK GRN
439-.8 PNK/BLK
413-.8 TAN
450-1.0 BLK/WHT
FUEL PUMP RELAY (SEE PAGE 89)
REAR WHEEL ANTILOCK BRAKE MODULE (SEE PAGE 116)
4-WHEEL ANTILOCK BRAKE MODULE (SEE PAGE 114)
486-1.0 BRN
ESC MODULE (SEE PAGE 106)
GROMMET 104 12010639
450-.8 BLK/WHT
EGR VACUUM REGULATOR VALVE SOLENOID (SEE PAGE 108)
INJ-2
482
468
12084618
468-.8 DK GRN
S170
482-.8 WHT
INJ-1
481
467
467-.8 DK BLU
481-.8 RED
450-1.0 BLK/WHT
439-.8 PNK/BLK
S116
439-.8 PNK/BLK
E.S.C. MODULE (SEE PAGE 106)
TO EGR VACUUM REGULATOR VALVE SOLENOID (SEE PAGE 108)
ENGINE
K
J
H
G
F
A
B
C
D
E
461
419
121
434
461
437
451
439
806
12064770
OXYGEN SENSOR AND SYSTEM GROUND
G107
439-.8 PNK/BLK

1988–91 WIRING DIAGRAMS (CONT.)

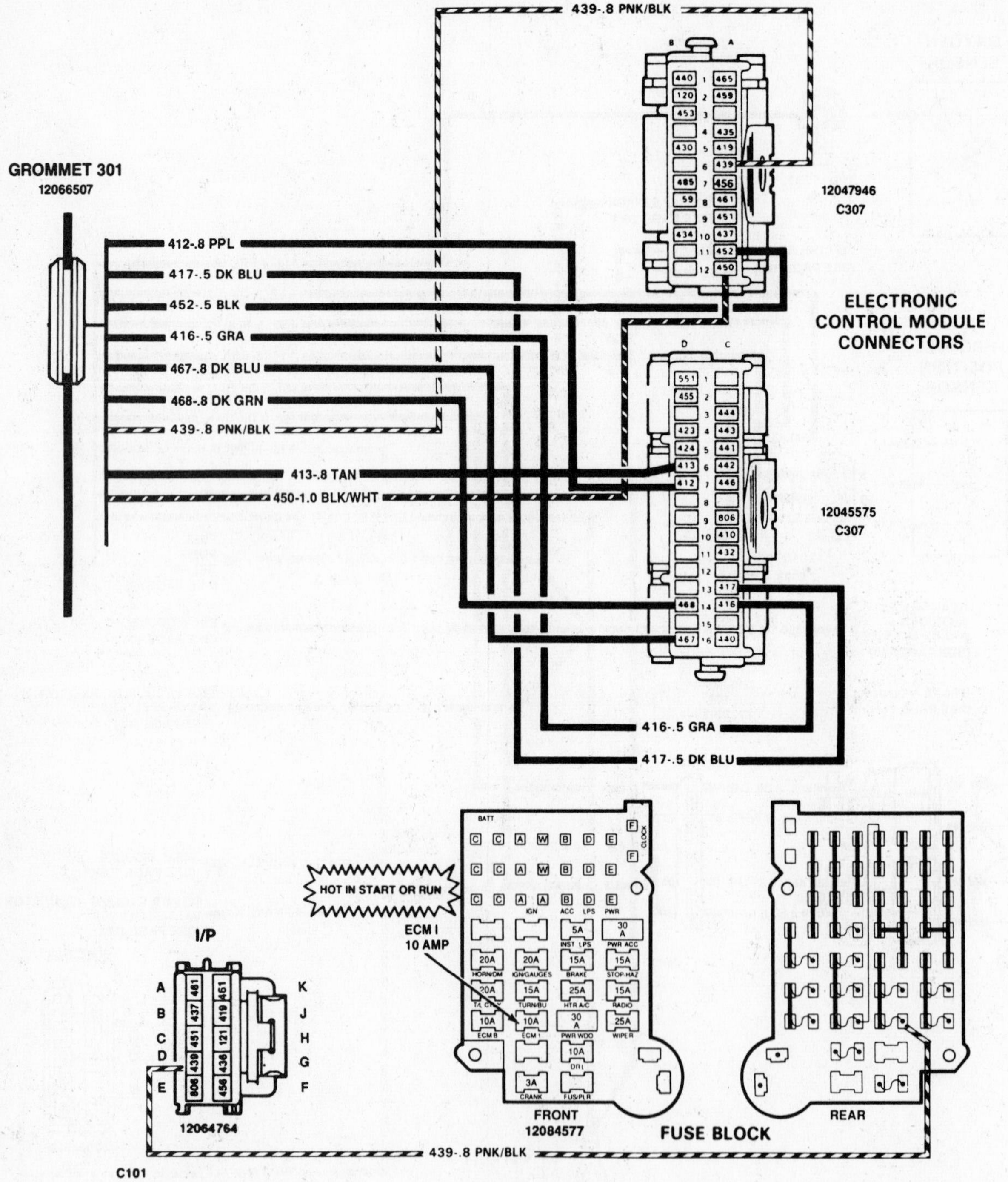
439-.8 PNK/BLK
GROMMET 301
12066507
412-.8 PPL
417-.5 DK BLU
452-.5 BLK
416-.5 GRA
467-.8 DK BLU
468-.8 DK GRN
439-.8 PNK/BLK
413-.8 TAN
450-1.0 BLK/WHT
12047946
C307
ELECTRONIC
CONTROL MODULE
CONNECTORS
12045575
C307
416-.5 GRA
417-.5 DK BLU
HOT IN START OR RUN
ECM I
10 AMP
I/P
12064764
FRONT
12084577
FUSE BLOCK
REAR
439-.8 PNK/BLK
C101

THROTTLE BODY INJECTION - 4.3L (262 CID) ENGINE

1988–91 WIRING DIAGRAMS (CONT.)

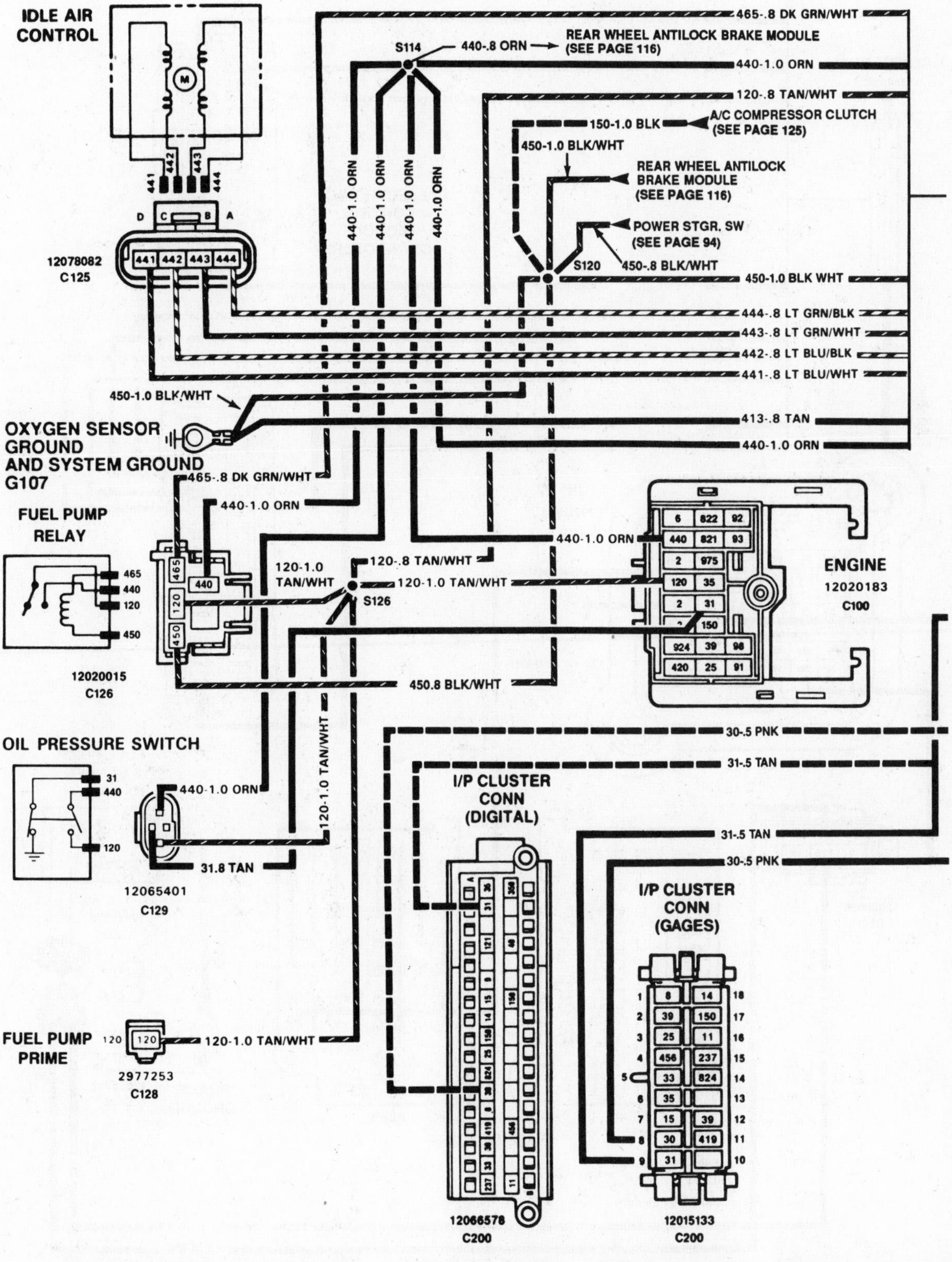
IDLE AIR CONTROL
441
442
443
444
D C B A
12078082
C125
465-.8 DK GRN/WHT
S114
440-.8 ORN
REAR WHEEL ANTILOCK BRAKE MODULE (SEE PAGE 116)
440-1.0 ORN
120-.8 TAN/WHT
150-1.0 BLK
A/C COMPRESSOR CLUTCH (SEE PAGE 125)
450-1.0 BLK/WHT
REAR WHEEL ANTILOCK BRAKE MODULE (SEE PAGE 116)
POWER STGR. SW (SEE PAGE 94)
S120
450-.8 BLK/WHT
450-1.0 BLK WHT
444-.8 LT GRN/BLK
443-.8 LT GRN/WHT
442-.8 LT BLU/BLK
441-.8 LT BLU/WHT
450-1.0 BLK/WHT
OXYGEN SENSOR GROUND AND SYSTEM GROUND G107
413-.8 TAN
440-1.0 ORN
465-.8 DK GRN/WHT
440-1.0 ORN
FUEL PUMP RELAY
465
440
120
450
12020015
C126
120-1.0 TAN/WHT
120-.8 TAN/WHT
120-1.0 TAN/WHT
S126
440-1.0 ORN
450.8 BLK/WHT
ENGINE
12020183
C100
OIL PRESSURE SWITCH
31
440
120
440-1.0 ORN
31.8 TAN
120-1.0 TAN/WHT
12065401
C129
30-.5 PNK
31-.5 TAN
I/P CLUSTER CONN (DIGITAL)
31-.5 TAN
30-.5 PNK
I/P CLUSTER CONN (GAGES)
FUEL PUMP PRIME
120
120-1.0 TAN/WHT
2977253
C128
12066578
C200
12015133
C200

FUEL CONTROL AND IDLE AIR CONTROL - 2.5L (151 CID) ENGINE - PICKUP

1988–91 WIRING DIAGRAMS (CONT.)

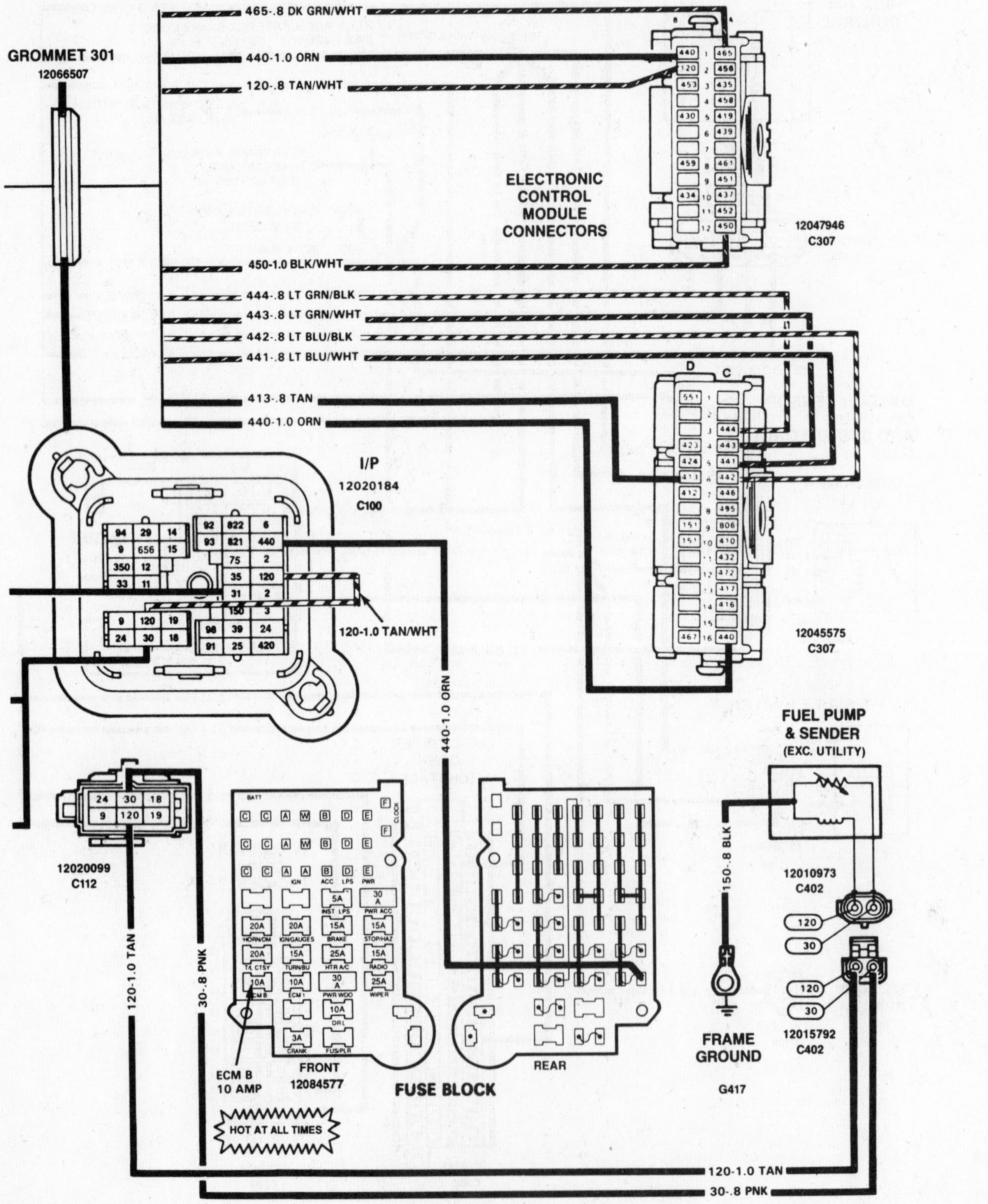
465-.8 DK GRN/WHT
440-1.0 ORN
120-.8 TAN/WHT
GROMMET 301
12066507
ELECTRONIC CONTROL MODULE CONNECTORS
12047946
C307
450-1.0 BLK/WHT
444-.8 LT GRN/BLK
443-.8 LT GRN/WHT
442-.8 LT BLU/BLK
441-.8 LT BLU/WHT
413-.8 TAN
440-1.0 ORN
I/P
12020184
C100
120-1.0 TAN/WHT
12045575
C307
440-1.0 ORN
FUEL PUMP & SENDER
(EXC. UTILITY)
12020099
C112
150-.8 BLK
12010973
C402
120-1.0 TAN
30-.8 PNK
FRONT
12084577
FUSE BLOCK
REAR
ECM B
10 AMP
HOT AT ALL TIMES
FRAME GROUND
G417
12015792
C402
120-1.0 TAN
30-.8 PNK

1988–91 WIRING DIAGRAMS (CONT.)

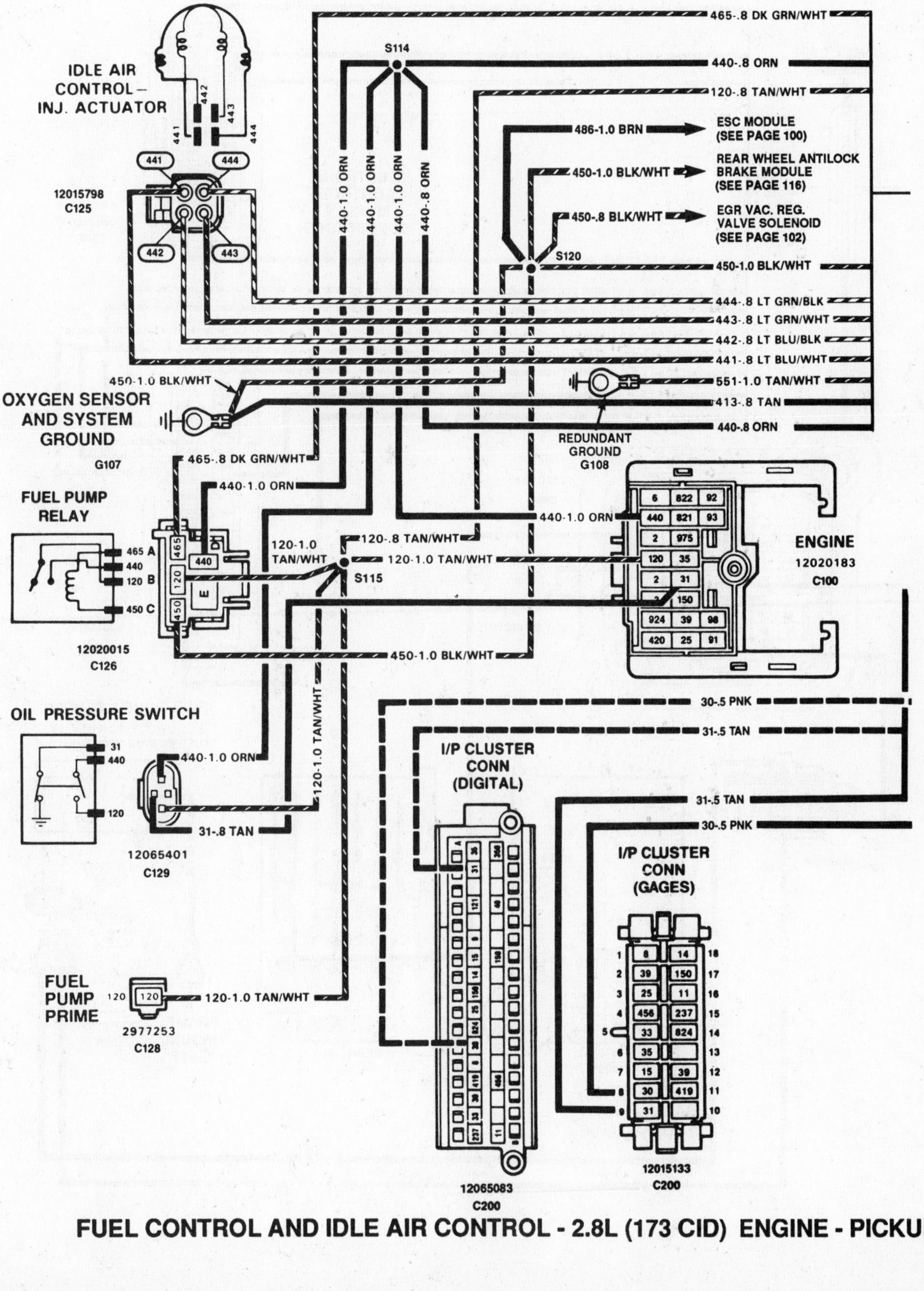

IDLE AIR CONTROL – INJ. ACTUATOR
12015798
C125
465-.8 DK GRN/WHT
S114
440-.8 ORN
120-.8 TAN/WHT
486-1.0 BRN
ESC MODULE (SEE PAGE 100)
450-1.0 BLK/WHT
REAR WHEEL ANTILOCK BRAKE MODULE (SEE PAGE 116)
450-.8 BLK/WHT
EGR VAC. REG. VALVE SOLENOID (SEE PAGE 102)
S120
440-1.0 ORN
440-.8 ORN
444-.8 LT GRN/BLK
443-.8 LT GRN/WHT
442-.8 LT BLU/BLK
441-.8 LT BLU/WHT
551-1.0 TAN/WHT
413-.8 TAN
OXYGEN SENSOR AND SYSTEM GROUND
G107
REDUNDANT GROUND
G108
FUEL PUMP RELAY
12020015
C126
120-1.0 TAN/WHT
120-.8 TAN/WHT
S115
ENGINE
12020183
C100
450-1.0 BLK/WHT
OIL PRESSURE SWITCH
12065401
C129
31-.8 TAN
30-.5 PNK
31-.5 TAN
I/P CLUSTER CONN (DIGITAL)
I/P CLUSTER CONN (GAGES)
FUEL PUMP PRIME
2977253
C128
12065083
C200
12015133
C200

FUEL CONTROL AND IDLE AIR CONTROL - 2.8L (173 CID) ENGINE - PICKUP

1988–91 WIRING DIAGRAMS (CONT.)

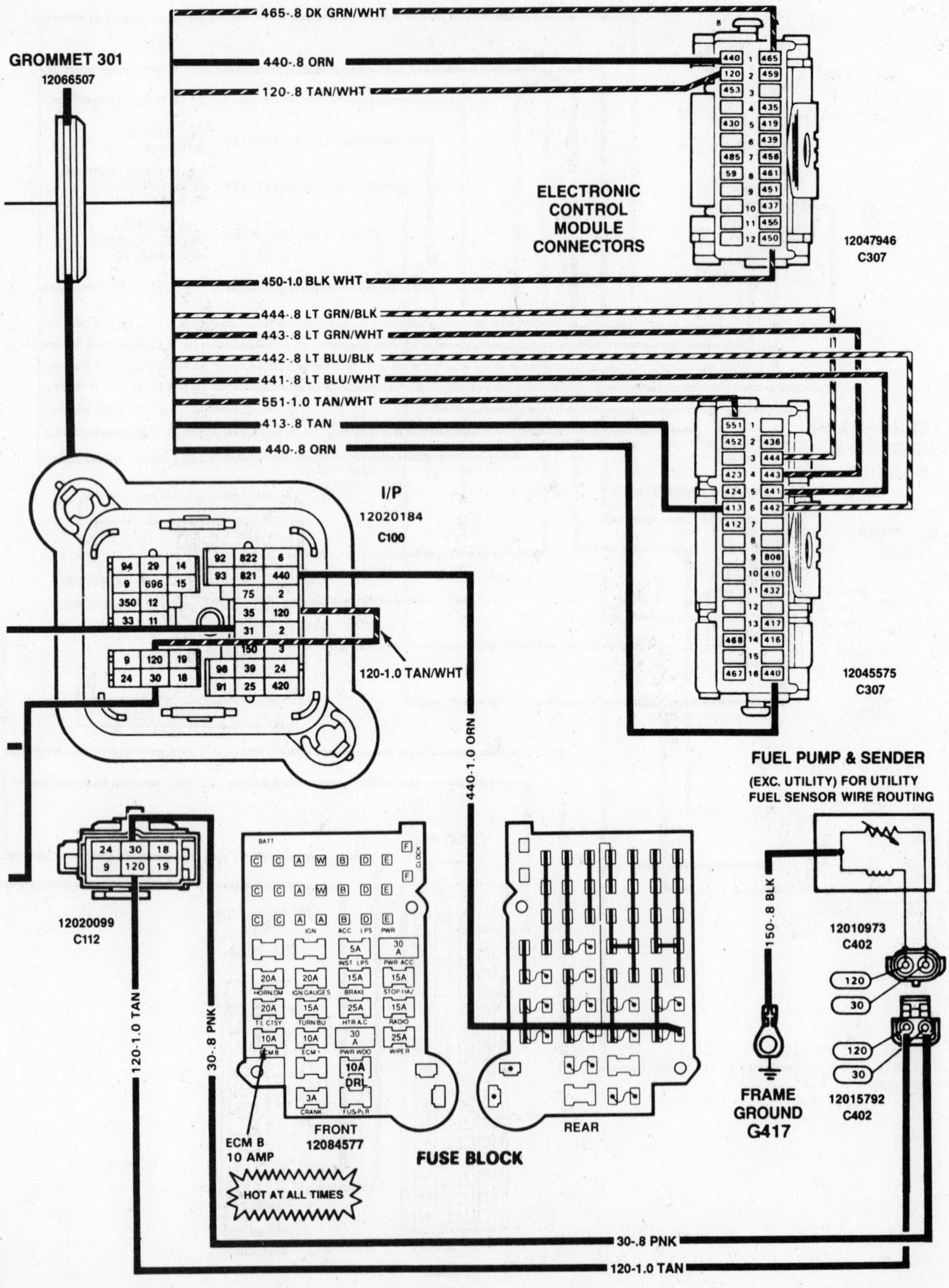
465-.8 DK GRN/WHT
440-.8 ORN
120-.8 TAN/WHT
GROMMET 301
12066507
ELECTRONIC CONTROL MODULE CONNECTORS
12047946
C307
450-1.0 BLK WHT
444-.8 LT GRN/BLK
443-.8 LT GRN/WHT
442-.8 LT BLU/BLK
441-.8 LT BLU/WHT
551-1.0 TAN/WHT
413-.8 TAN
440-.8 ORN
I/P
12020184
C100
120-1.0 TAN/WHT
12045575
C307
440-1.0 ORN
FUEL PUMP & SENDER
(EXC. UTILITY) FOR UTILITY FUEL SENSOR WIRE ROUTING
12020099
C112
150-.8 BLK
12010973
C402
120
30
12015792
C402
FRAME GROUND G417
120-1.0 TAN
30-.8 PNK
FRONT
12084577
REAR
ECM B
10 AMP
HOT AT ALL TIMES
FUSE BLOCK
30-.8 PNK
120-1.0 TAN

1988–91 WIRING DIAGRAMS (CONT.)

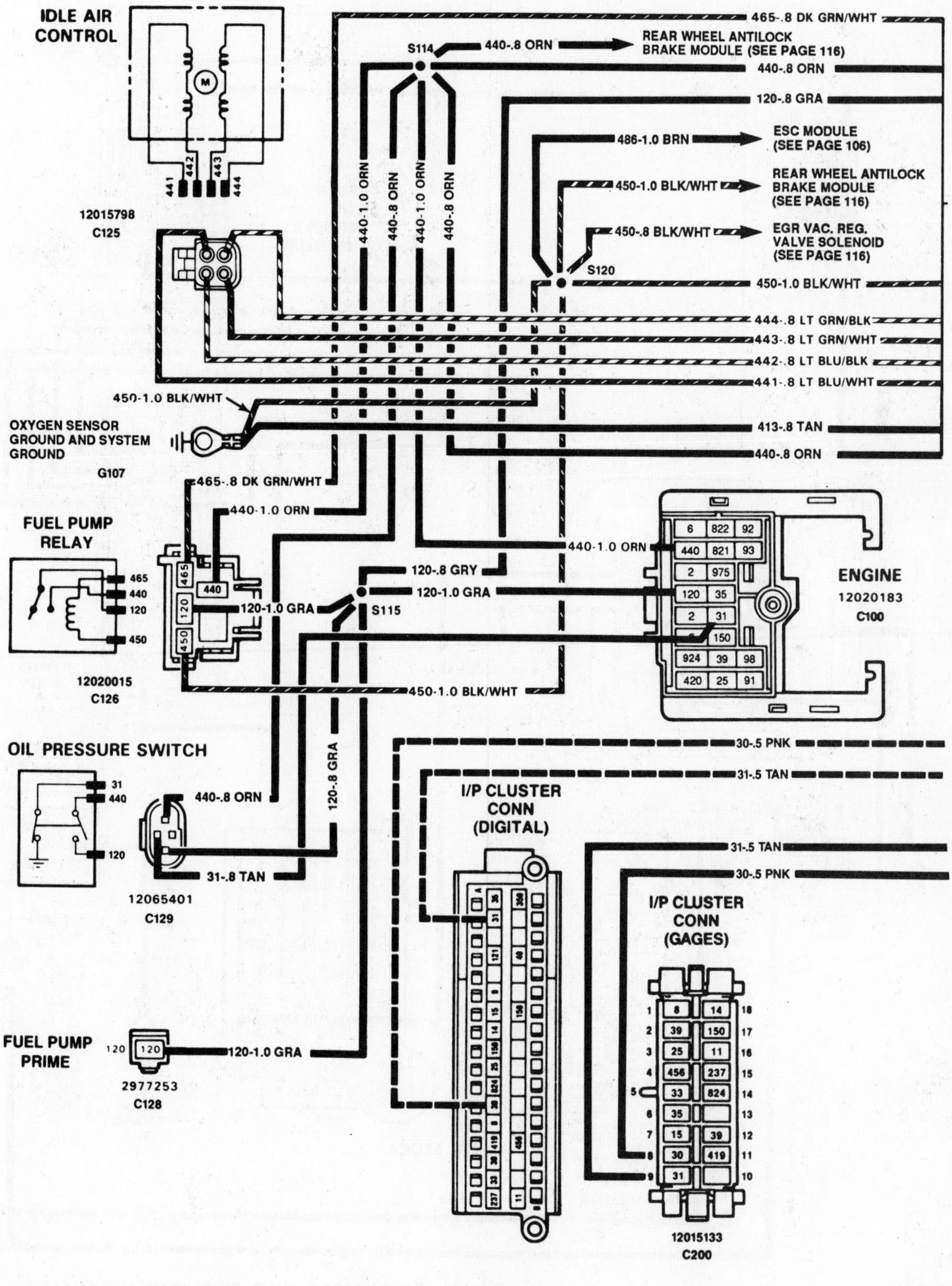
IDLE AIR CONTROL
M
441
442
443
444
12015798
C125
465-.8 DK GRN/WHT
S114
440-.8 ORN
REAR WHEEL ANTILOCK BRAKE MODULE (SEE PAGE 116)
440-.8 ORN
120-.8 GRA
486-1.0 BRN
ESC MODULE (SEE PAGE 106)
450-1.0 BLK/WHT
REAR WHEEL ANTILOCK BRAKE MODULE (SEE PAGE 116)
450-.8 BLK/WHT
EGR VAC. REG. VALVE SOLENOID (SEE PAGE 116)
S120
450-1.0 BLK/WHT
440-1.0 ORN
440-.8 ORN
440-1.0 ORN
440-.8 ORN
444-.8 LT GRN/BLK
443-.8 LT GRN/WHT
442-.8 LT BLU/BLK
441-.8 LT BLU/WHT
450-1.0 BLK/WHT
OXYGEN SENSOR GROUND AND SYSTEM GROUND
G107
413-.8 TAN
440-.8 ORN
465-.8 DK GRN/WHT
440-1.0 ORN
FUEL PUMP RELAY
465
440
120
450
12020015
C126
440-1.0 ORN
120-.8 GRY
120-1.0 GRA
120-1.0 GRA
S115
450-1.0 BLK/WHT
ENGINE
12020183
C100
6
822
92
440
821
93
2
975
120
35
2
31
150
924
39
98
420
25
91
OIL PRESSURE SWITCH
31
440
120
440-.8 ORN
31-.8 TAN
120-.8 GRA
12065401
C129
30-.5 PNK
31-.5 TAN
I/P CLUSTER CONN (DIGITAL)
31-.5 TAN
30-.5 PNK
I/P CLUSTER CONN (GAGES)
FUEL PUMP PRIME
120
120-1.0 GRA
2977253
C128
12015133
C200

1988–91 WIRING DIAGRAMS (CONT.)

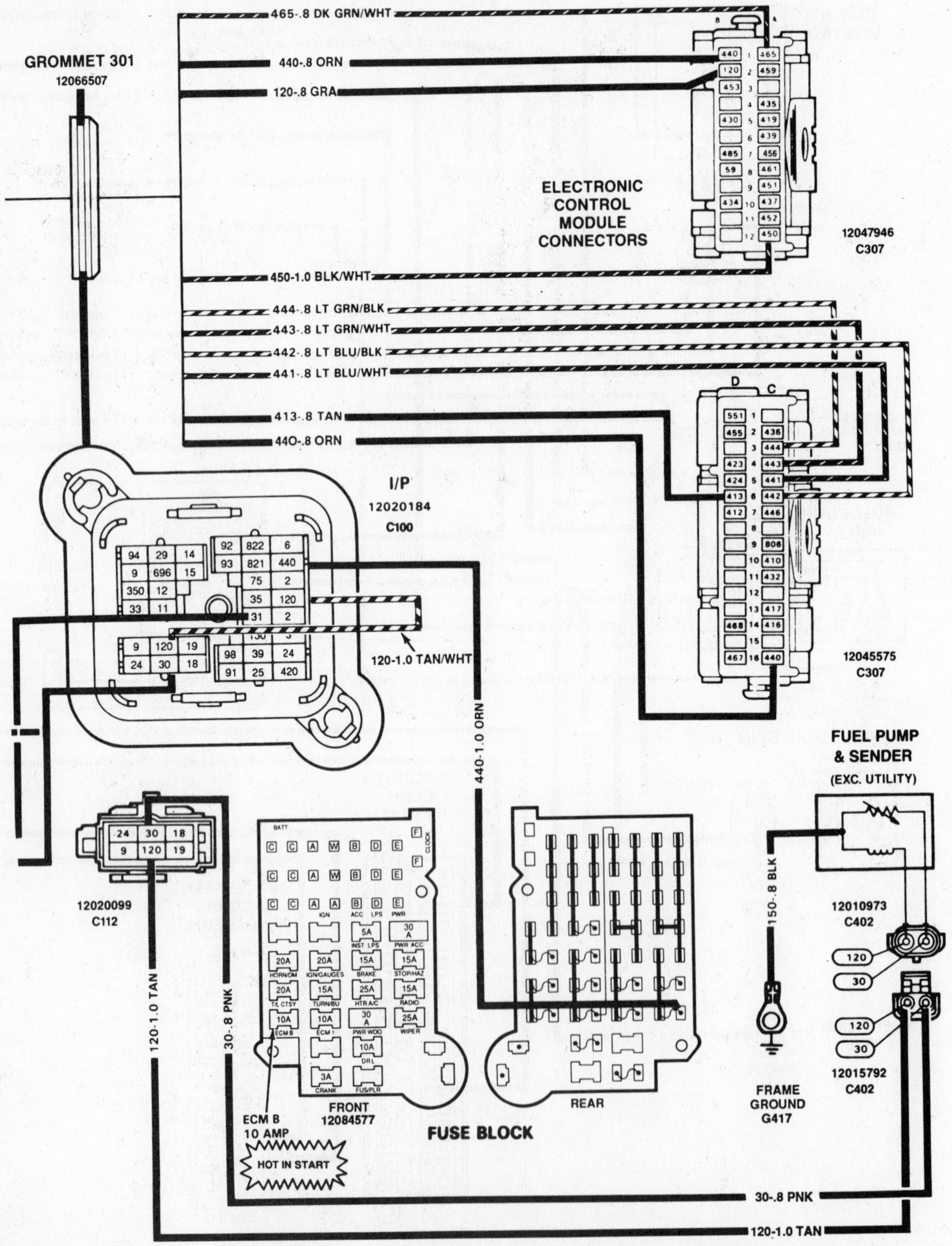
465-.8 DK GRN/WHT
440-.8 ORN
120-.8 GRA
GROMMET 301
12066507
ELECTRONIC CONTROL MODULE CONNECTORS
12047946
C307
450-1.0 BLK/WHT
444-.8 LT GRN/BLK
443-.8 LT GRN/WHT
442-.8 LT BLU/BLK
441-.8 LT BLU/WHT
413-.8 TAN
440-.8 ORN
I/P
12020184
C100
120-1.0 TAN/WHT
12045575
C307
440-1.0 ORN
FUEL PUMP & SENDER
(EXC. UTILITY)
12020099
C112
150-.8 BLK
12010973
C402
12015792
C402
120-1.0 TAN
30-.8 PNK
ECM B
10 AMP
HOT IN START
FRONT
12084577
FUSE BLOCK
REAR
FRAME GROUND
G417
30-.8 PNK
120-1.0 TAN

FUEL CONTROL AND IDLE AIR CONTROL - 4.3L (262 CID) ENGINE - PICKUP

1988–91 WIRING DIAGRAMS (CONT.)

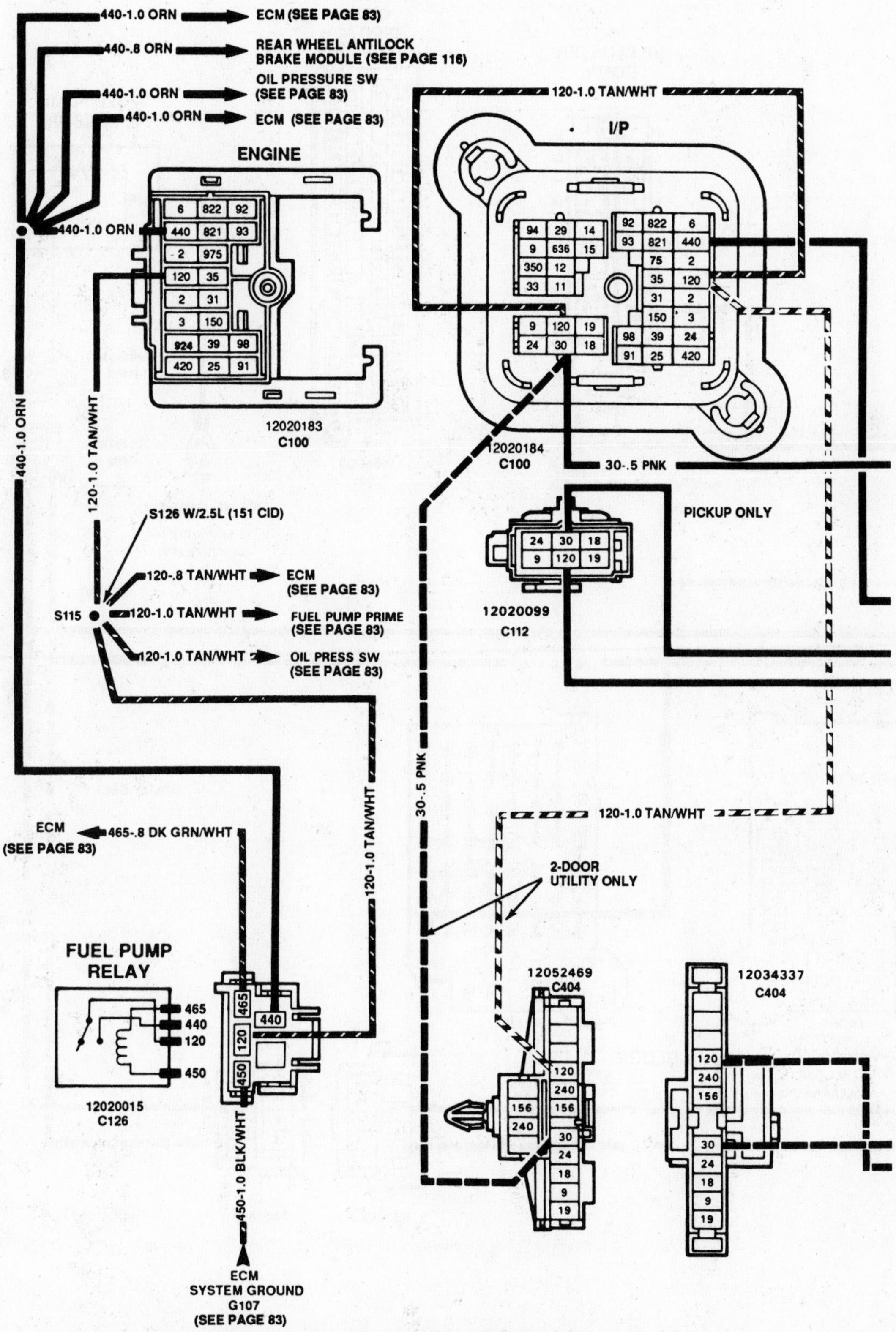

440-1.0 ORN
ECM (SEE PAGE 83)
440-.8 ORN
REAR WHEEL ANTILOCK BRAKE MODULE (SEE PAGE 116)
440-1.0 ORN
OIL PRESSURE SW (SEE PAGE 83)
440-1.0 ORN
ECM (SEE PAGE 83)
ENGINE
440-1.0 ORN
12020183
C100
120-1.0 TAN/WHT
I/P
12020184
C100
30-.5 PNK
PICKUP ONLY
12020099
C112
440-1.0 ORN
120-1.0 TAN/WHT
S126 W/2.5L (151 CID)
120-.8 TAN/WHT
ECM (SEE PAGE 83)
S115
120-1.0 TAN/WHT
FUEL PUMP PRIME (SEE PAGE 83)
120-1.0 TAN/WHT
OIL PRESS SW (SEE PAGE 83)
120-1.0 TAN/WHT
30-.5 PNK
120-1.0 TAN/WHT
ECM (SEE PAGE 83)
465-.8 DK GRN/WHT
2-DOOR UTILITY ONLY
FUEL PUMP RELAY
465
440
120
450
12020015
C126
450-1.0 BLK/WHT
12052469
C404
12034337
C404
ECM SYSTEM GROUND G107 (SEE PAGE 83)

FUEL SENSOR - PICKUP AND 2-DOOR UTILITY

1988–91 WIRING DIAGRAMS (CONT.)

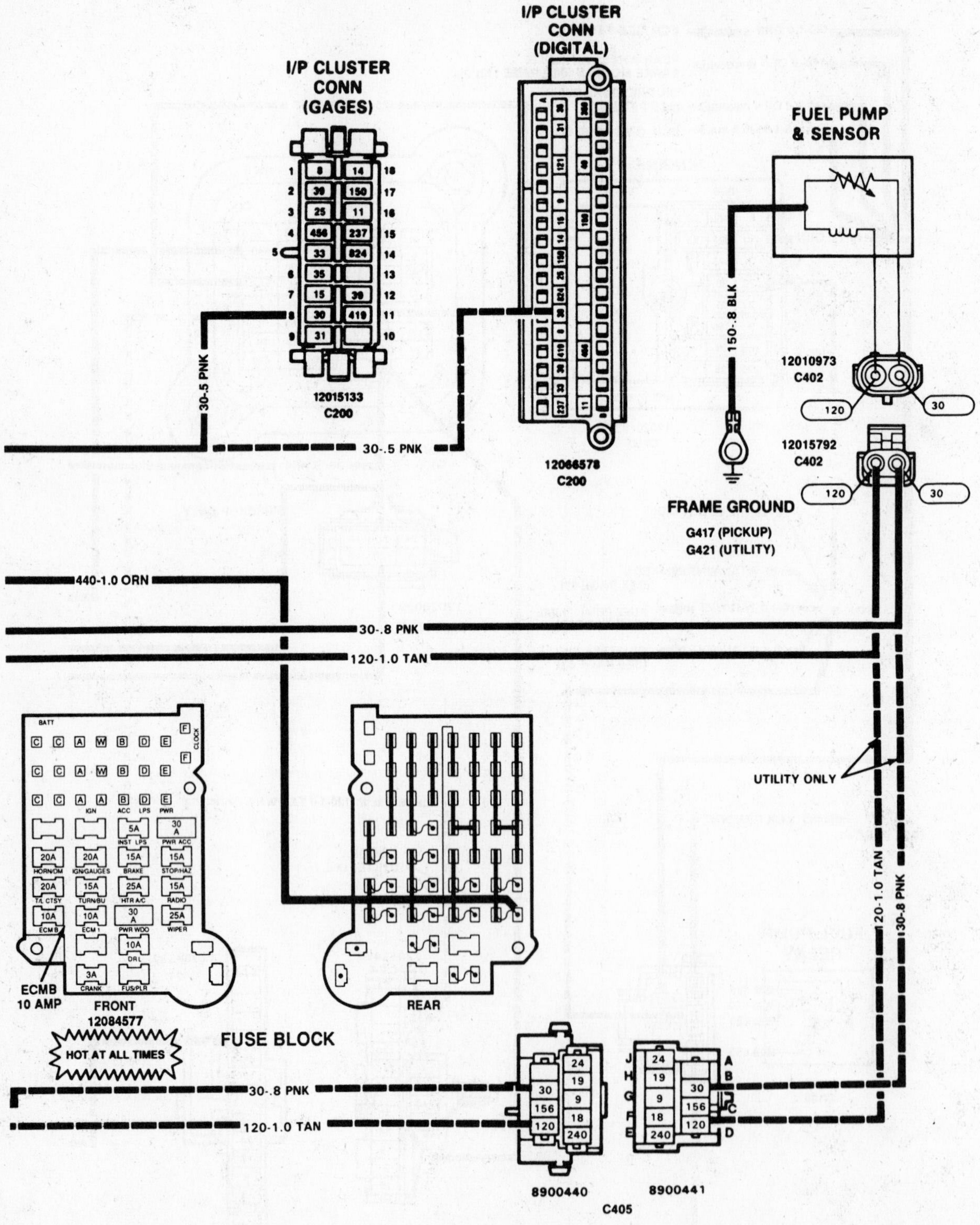
I/P CLUSTER CONN (GAGES)
12015133
C200
I/P CLUSTER CONN (DIGITAL)
12066578
C200
FUEL PUMP & SENSOR
150-.8 BLK
12010973
C402
120
30
12015792
C402
FRAME GROUND
G417 (PICKUP)
G421 (UTILITY)
30-.5 PNK
440-1.0 ORN
30-.8 PNK
120-1.0 TAN
UTILITY ONLY
ECMB 10 AMP
FRONT
12084577
REAR
HOT AT ALL TIMES
FUSE BLOCK
8900440
8900441
C405

1988–91 WIRING DIAGRAMS (CONT.)

CIRCUIT NO.	WIRE SIZE	COLOR	CAVITY	DESCRIPTION
465	.8	DK GRN/WHT	A1	FUEL PUMP RELAY DRIVE
✱ 422	.8	TAN/BLK	A2	TORQUE CONVERTER CLUTCH CONTROL
□ 456	.8	TAN/BLK	A2	UPSHIFT LAMP CONTROL
435	.8	GRA	A3	EGR SOLENOID CONTROL
458	.8	DK BLU	A4	A/C RELAY CONTROL
419	.8	BRN/WHT	A5	SERVICE ENGINE SOON LAMP
439	.8	PNK/BLK	A6	12V IGNITION (FUSED)
			A7	NOT USED
461	.8	ORN	A8	ALDL SERIAL DATA
451	.8	WHT/BLK	A9	ALDL DIAGNOSTIC TEST
437	.8	BRN	A10	DIGITAL RATIO ADAPTER SIGNAL
452	.8	BLK	A11	COOLANT TEMP SENSOR AND TPS GROUND
450	1.0	BLK/WHT	A12	SYSTEM GROUND
440	1.0	ORN	B1	12V BATTERY (FUSED)
120	.8	TAN/WHT	B2	FUEL PUMP SIGNAL
453	.8	BLK/RED	B3	DISTRIBUTOR REF LOW
			B4	NOT USED
430	.8	PPL/WHT	B5	DISTRIBUTOR REF HIGH
			B6	NOT USED
			B7	NOT USED
459	.8	DK GRN/WHT	B8	A/C SIGNAL
			B9	NOT USED
△ 434	.8	ORN/BLK	B10	PARK/NEUTRAL SWITCH SIGNAL
			B11	NOT USED
			B12	NOT USED

✱ 422—AUTO TRANS ONLY
□ 456—MAN TRANS ONLY
△ AUTO TRANS ONLY

ELECTRONIC CONTROL MODULE - 2.5L (151 CID) ENGINE

1988–91 WIRING DIAGRAMS (CONT.)

CIRCUIT NO.	WIRE SIZE	COLOR	CAVITY	DESCRIPTION
			C1	NOT USED
			C2	NOT USED
444	.8	LT GRN/BLK	C3	IAC COIL B LOW
443	.8	LT GRN/WHT	C4	IAC COIL B HIGH
441	.8	LT BLU/WHT	C5	IAC COIL A HIGH
442	.8	LT BLU/BLK	C6	IAC COIL A LOW
			C7	NOT USED
495	.8	LT BLU	C8	PWR STRG PRESSURE SW SIGNAL
806	.8	PPL	C9	CRANK SIGNAL (FUSED)
410	.8	YEL	C10	COOLANT TEMPERATURE SIGNAL
432	.8	LT GRN	C11	MAP SIGNAL
472	.8	TAN	C12	MANIFOLD AIR TEMP SIGNAL
417	.8	DK BLU	C13	TPS SIGNAL
416	.8	GRA	C14	5V SENSOR REFERENCE
			C15	NOT USED
440	1.0	ORN	C16	12V BATTERY (FUSED)
551	1.0	TAN/WHT	D1	SYSTEM GROUND
469	.8	BLK/RED	D2	5V RETURN
			D3	NOT USED
423	.8	NAT/WHT	D4	EST SPARK TIMING SIGNAL
424	.8	TAN/BLK	D5	EST BYPASS
413	.8	TAN	D6	OXYGEN SENSOR GROUND
412	.8	PPL	D7	OXYGEN SENSOR SIGNAL
			D8	NOT USED
151	.8	BLK	D9	GROUND
151	.8	BLK	D10	GROUND
			D11	NOT USED
			D12	NOT USED
			D13	NOT USED
			D14	NOT USED
			D15	NOT USED
467	.8	DK BLU	D16	INJECTOR DRIVER

1988–91 WIRING DIAGRAMS (CONT.)

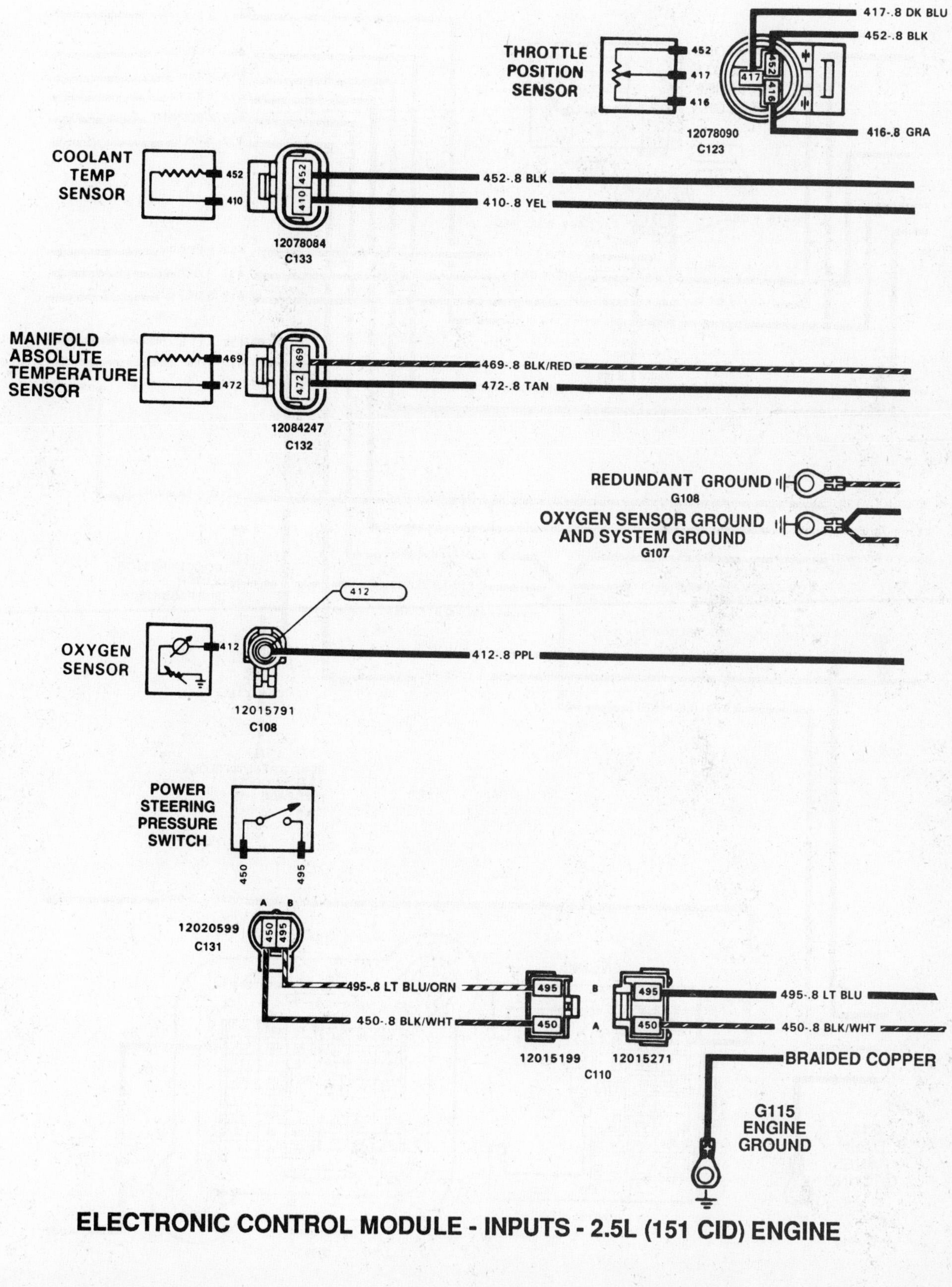

THROTTLE POSITION SENSOR
452
417
416
12078090
C123
417-.8 DK BLU
452-.8 BLK
416-.8 GRA
COOLANT TEMP SENSOR
452
410
12078084
C133
452-.8 BLK
410-.8 YEL
MANIFOLD ABSOLUTE TEMPERATURE SENSOR
469
472
12084247
C132
469-.8 BLK/RED
472-.8 TAN
REDUNDANT GROUND
G108
OXYGEN SENSOR GROUND AND SYSTEM GROUND
G107
OXYGEN SENSOR
412
12015791
C108
412-.8 PPL
POWER STEERING PRESSURE SWITCH
450
495
A B
12020599
C131
495-.8 LT BLU/ORN
450-.8 BLK/WHT
12015199
C110
12015271
495-.8 LT BLU
450-.8 BLK/WHT
BRAIDED COPPER
G115 ENGINE GROUND

ELECTRONIC CONTROL MODULE - INPUTS - 2.5L (151 CID) ENGINE

1988–91 WIRING DIAGRAMS (CONT.)

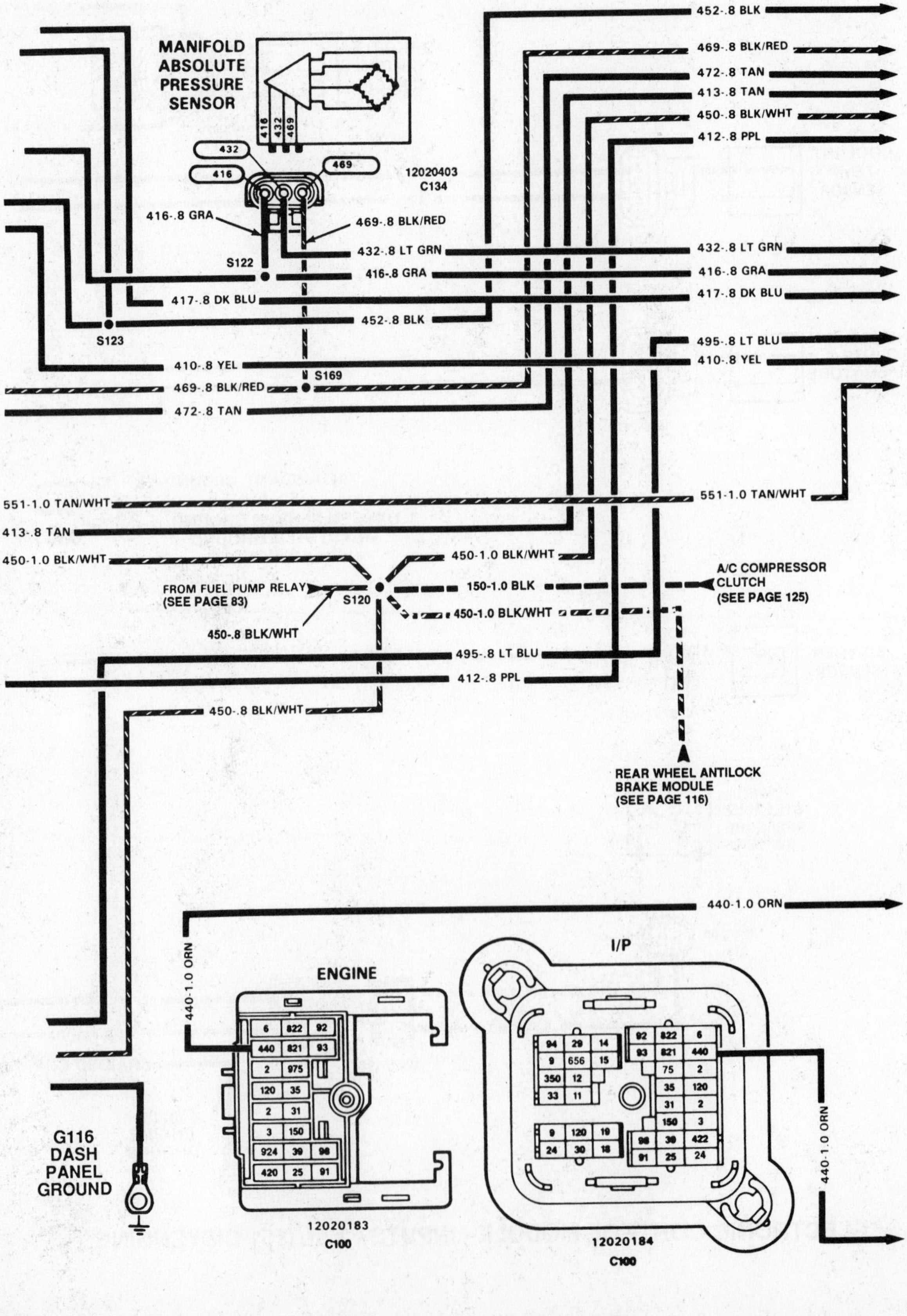
MANIFOLD ABSOLUTE PRESSURE SENSOR
416
432
469
12020403
C134
416-.8 GRA
469-.8 BLK/RED
432-.8 LT GRN
S122
416-.8 GRA
417-.8 DK BLU
452-.8 BLK
S123
410-.8 YEL
469-.8 BLK/RED
S169
472-.8 TAN
452-.8 BLK
469-.8 BLK/RED
472-.8 TAN
413-.8 TAN
450-.8 BLK/WHT
412-.8 PPL
432-.8 LT GRN
416-.8 GRA
417-.8 DK BLU
495-.8 LT BLU
410-.8 YEL
551-1.0 TAN/WHT
413-.8 TAN
450-1.0 BLK/WHT
551-1.0 TAN/WHT
450-1.0 BLK/WHT
FROM FUEL PUMP RELAY (SEE PAGE 83)
S120
150-1.0 BLK
A/C COMPRESSOR CLUTCH (SEE PAGE 125)
450-1.0 BLK/WHT
450-.8 BLK/WHT
495-.8 LT BLU
412-.8 PPL
450-.8 BLK/WHT
REAR WHEEL ANTILOCK BRAKE MODULE (SEE PAGE 116)
440-1.0 ORN
440-1.0 ORN
ENGINE
I/P
G116 DASH PANEL GROUND
12020183
C100
12020184
C100
440-1.0 ORN

1988–91 WIRING DIAGRAMS (CONT.)

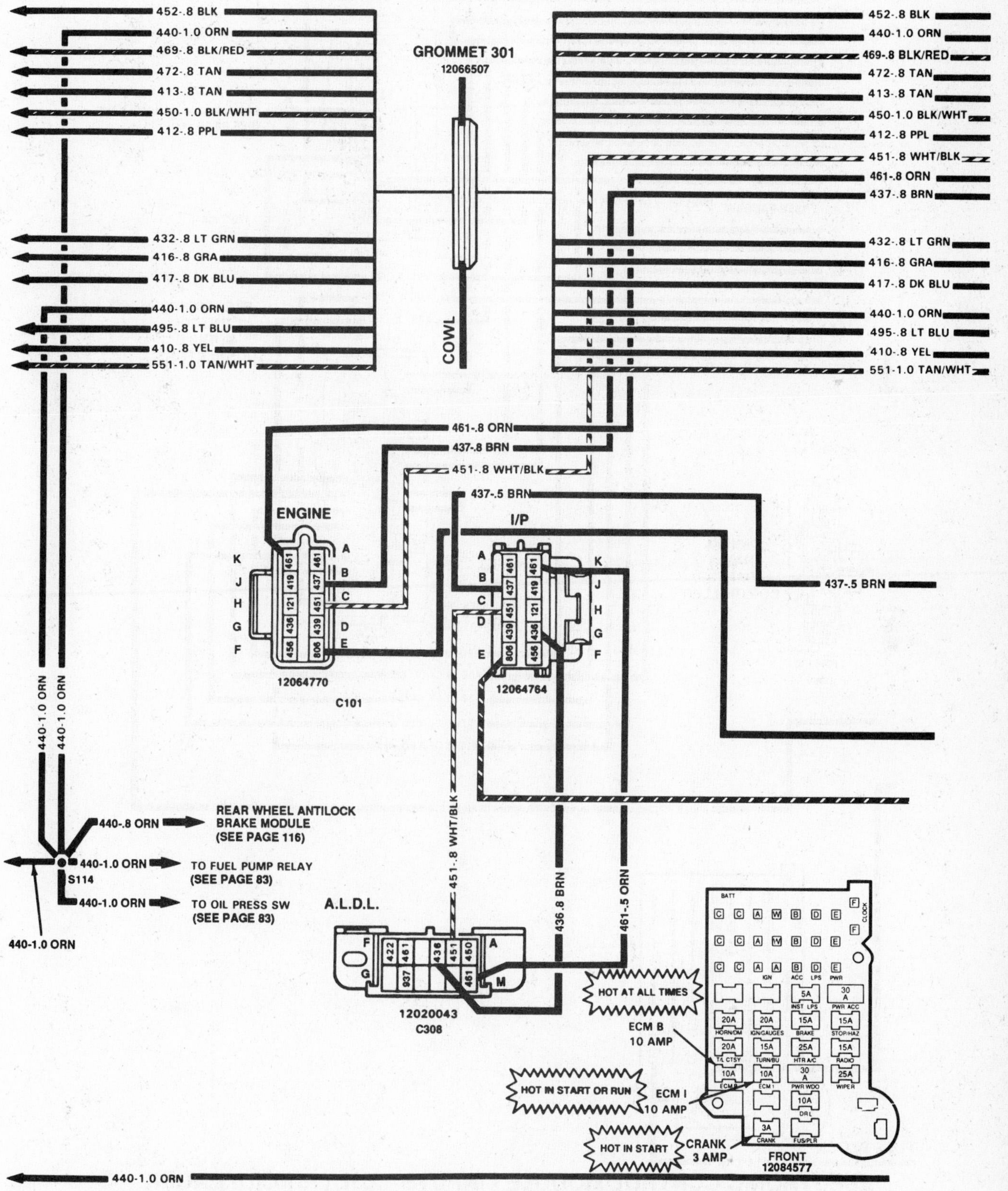

452-.8 BLK
440-1.0 ORN
469-.8 BLK/RED
472-.8 TAN
413-.8 TAN
450-1.0 BLK/WHT
412-.8 PPL
451-.8 WHT/BLK
461-.8 ORN
437-.8 BRN
432-.8 LT GRN
416-.8 GRA
417-.8 DK BLU
440-1.0 ORN
495-.8 LT BLU
410-.8 YEL
551-1.0 TAN/WHT
GROMMET 301
12066507
COWL
461-.8 ORN
437-.8 BRN
451-.8 WHT/BLK
437-.5 BRN
ENGINE
I/P
12064770
C101
12064764
437-.5 BRN
440-1.0 ORN
440-.8 ORN
REAR WHEEL ANTILOCK BRAKE MODULE (SEE PAGE 116)
440-1.0 ORN
TO FUEL PUMP RELAY (SEE PAGE 83)
S114
440-1.0 ORN
TO OIL PRESS SW (SEE PAGE 83)
440-1.0 ORN
451-.8 WHT/BLK
436-.8 BRN
461-.5 ORN
A.L.D.L.
12020043
C308
HOT AT ALL TIMES
ECM B 10 AMP
HOT IN START OR RUN
ECM I 10 AMP
HOT IN START
CRANK 3 AMP
FRONT
12084577
440-1.0 ORN

1988–91 WIRING DIAGRAMS (CONT.)

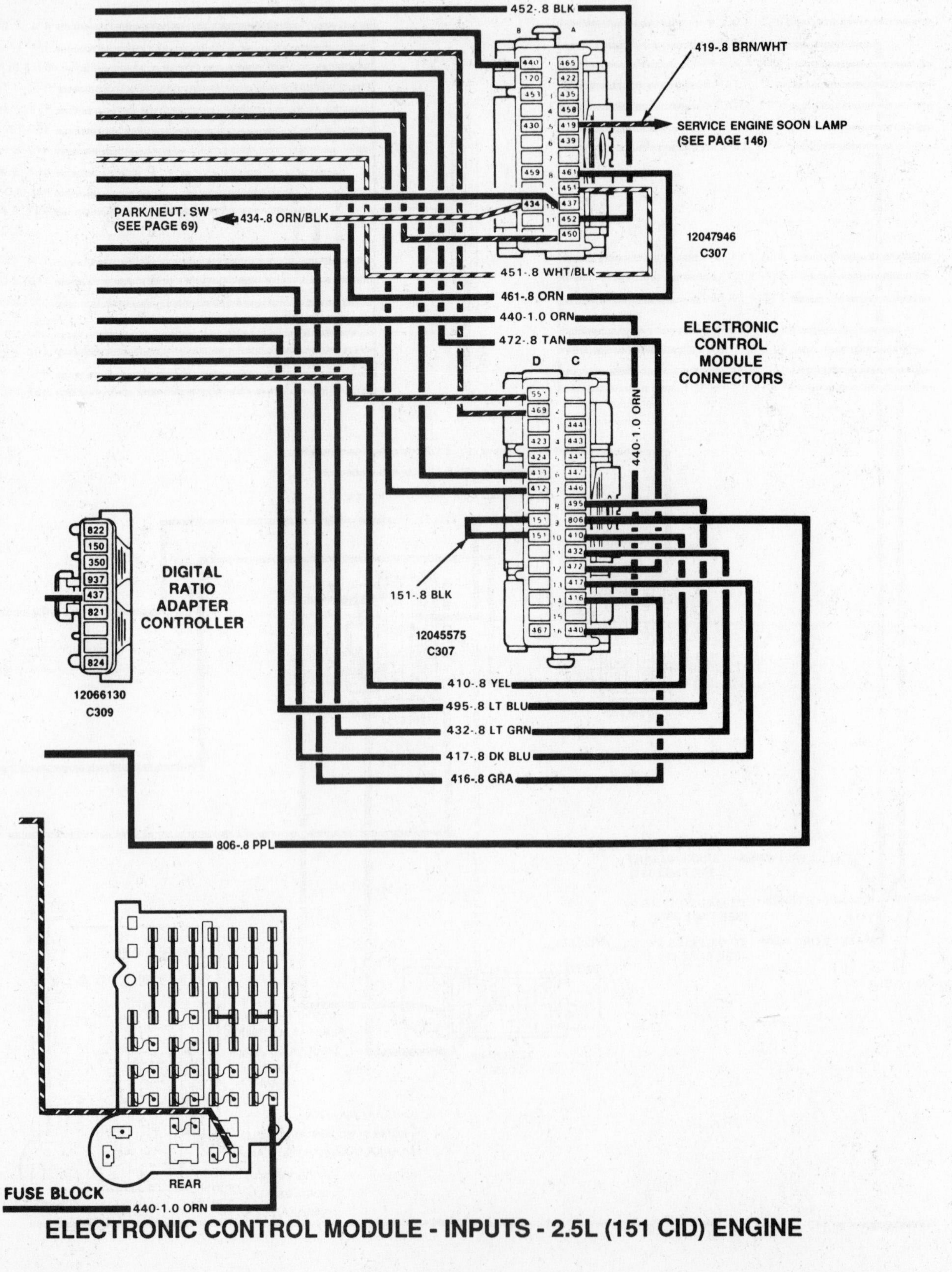
452-.8 BLK
419-.8 BRN/WHT
SERVICE ENGINE SOON LAMP
(SEE PAGE 146)
PARK/NEUT. SW
(SEE PAGE 69)
434-.8 ORN/BLK
12047946
C307
451-.8 WHT/BLK
461-.8 ORN
440-1.0 ORN
472-.8 TAN
ELECTRONIC
CONTROL
MODULE
CONNECTORS
D C
151-.8 BLK
12045575
C307
DIGITAL
RATIO
ADAPTER
CONTROLLER
12066130
C309
410-.8 YEL
495-.8 LT BLU
432-.8 LT GRN
417-.8 DK BLU
416-.8 GRA
806-.8 PPL
REAR
FUSE BLOCK

ELECTRONIC CONTROL MODULE - INPUTS - 2.5L (151 CID) ENGINE

1988–91 WIRING DIAGRAMS (CONT.)

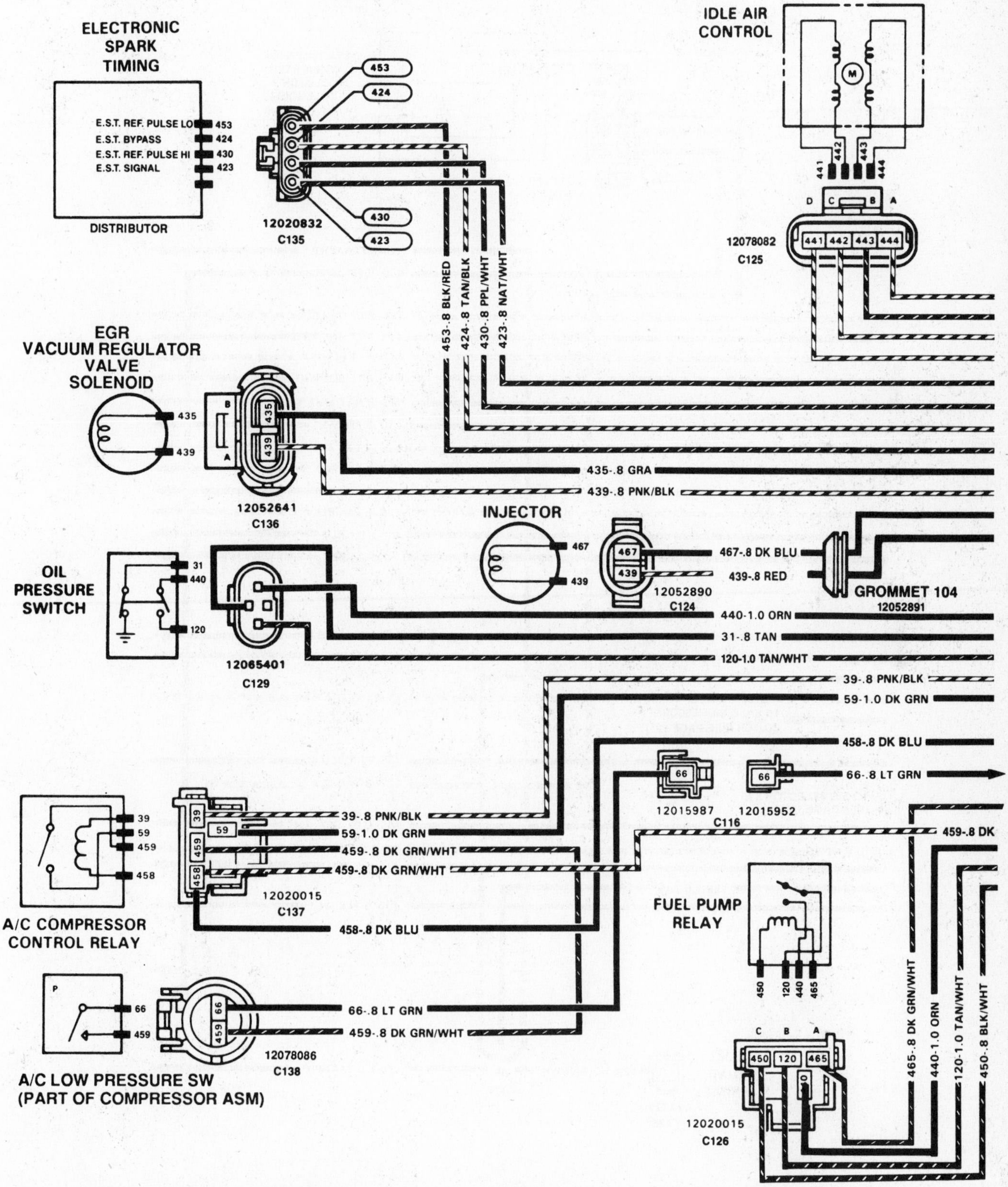
ELECTRONIC SPARK TIMING
E.S.T. REF. PULSE LO 453
E.S.T. BYPASS 424
E.S.T. REF. PULSE HI 430
E.S.T. SIGNAL 423
DISTRIBUTOR
12020832
C135
453-.8 BLK/RED
424-.8 TAN/BLK
430-.8 PPL/WHT
423-.8 NAT/WHT
IDLE AIR CONTROL
M
441 442 443 444
D C B A
12078082
C125
EGR VACUUM REGULATOR VALVE SOLENOID
435
439
B
A
12052641
C136
435-.8 GRA
439-.8 PNK/BLK
INJECTOR
467
439
12052890
C124
467-.8 DK BLU
439-.8 RED
GROMMET 104
12052891
OIL PRESSURE SWITCH
31
440
120
12065401
C129
440-1.0 ORN
31-.8 TAN
120-1.0 TAN/WHT
39-.8 PNK/BLK
59-1.0 DK GRN
458-.8 DK BLU
66
12015987
12015952
C116
66-.8 LT GRN
459-.8 DK
A/C COMPRESSOR CONTROL RELAY
39
59
459
458
39-.8 PNK/BLK
59-1.0 DK GRN
459-.8 DK GRN/WHT
459-.8 DK GRN/WHT
12020015
C137
458-.8 DK BLU
FUEL PUMP RELAY
450
120
440
465
A/C LOW PRESSURE SW (PART OF COMPRESSOR ASM)
P
66
459
66-.8 LT GRN
459-.8 DK GRN/WHT
12078086
C138
C B A
450 120 465
12020015
C126
465-.8 DK GRN/WHT
440-1.0 ORN
120-1.0 TAN/WHT
450-.8 BLK/WHT

ELECTRONIC CONTROL MODULE - OUTPUTS - 2.5L (151 CID) ENGINE

1988–91 WIRING DIAGRAMS (CONT.)

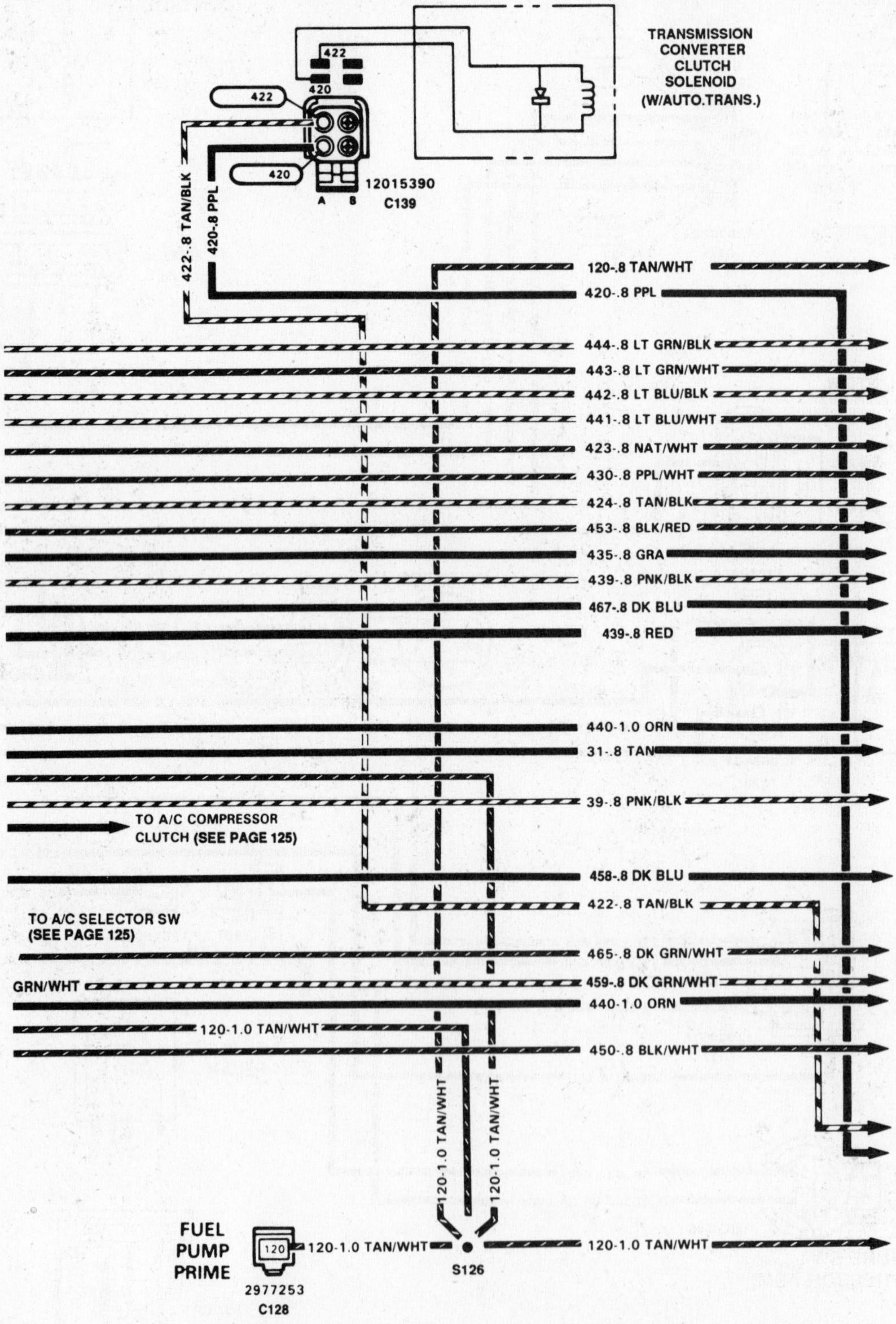
TRANSMISSION
CONVERTER
CLUTCH
SOLENOID
(W/AUTO.TRANS.)
422
420
422
420
12015390
C139
A B
422-.8 TAN/BLK
420-.8 PPL
120-.8 TAN/WHT
420-.8 PPL
444-.8 LT GRN/BLK
443-.8 LT GRN/WHT
442-.8 LT BLU/BLK
441-.8 LT BLU/WHT
423-.8 NAT/WHT
430-.8 PPL/WHT
424-.8 TAN/BLK
453-.8 BLK/RED
435-.8 GRA
439-.8 PNK/BLK
467-.8 DK BLU
439-.8 RED
440-1.0 ORN
31-.8 TAN
39-.8 PNK/BLK
TO A/C COMPRESSOR
CLUTCH (SEE PAGE 125)
458-.8 DK BLU
422-.8 TAN/BLK
TO A/C SELECTOR SW
(SEE PAGE 125)
465-.8 DK GRN/WHT
GRN/WHT
459-.8 DK GRN/WHT
440-1.0 ORN
120-1.0 TAN/WHT
450-.8 BLK/WHT
120-1.0 TAN/WHT
120-1.0 TAN/WHT
FUEL
PUMP
PRIME
120
120-1.0 TAN/WHT
S126
120-1.0 TAN/WHT
2977253
C128

1988–91 WIRING DIAGRAMS (CONT.)

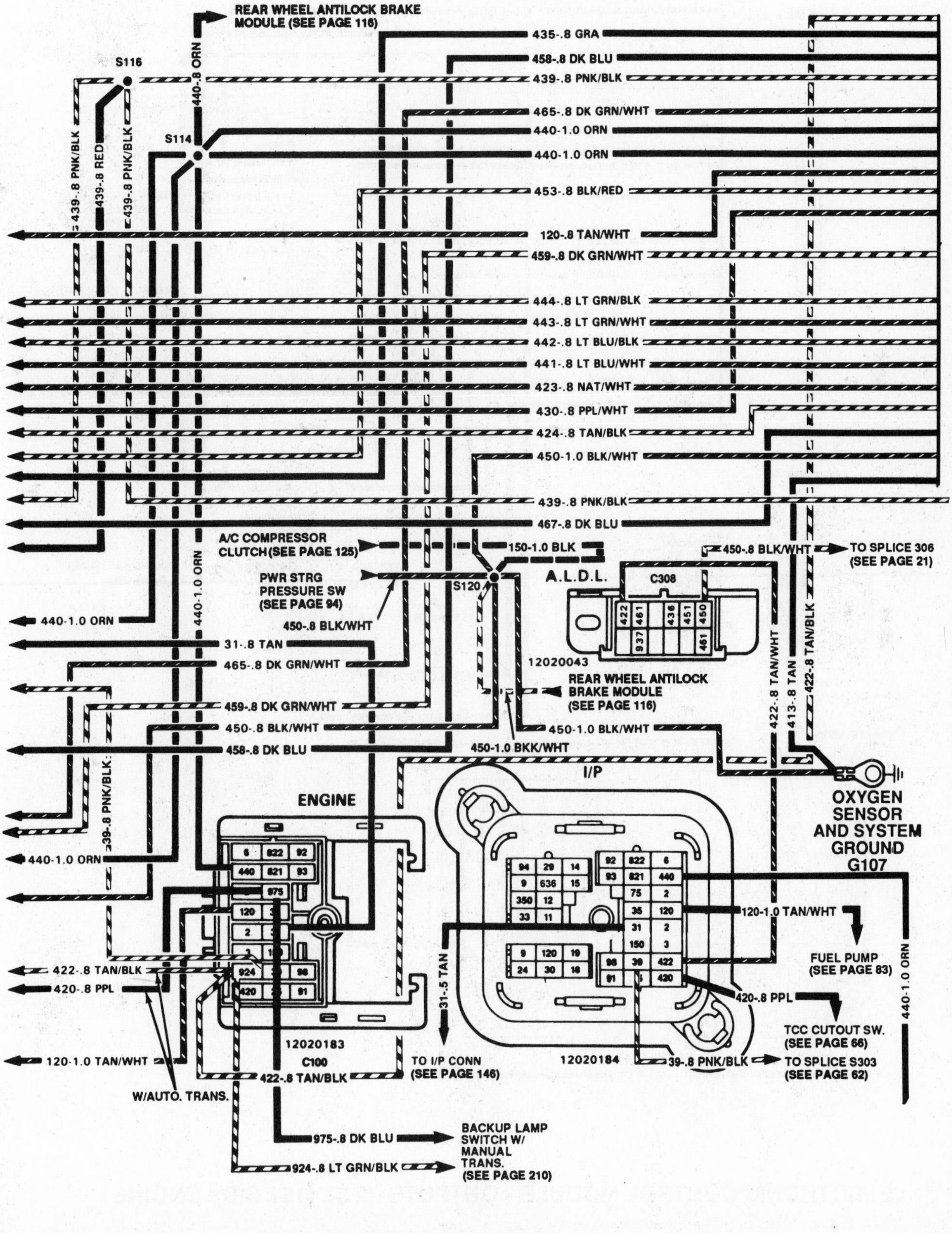
REAR WHEEL ANTILOCK BRAKE MODULE (SEE PAGE 116)
S116
S114
435-.8 GRA
458-.8 DK BLU
439-.8 PNK/BLK
465-.8 DK GRN/WHT
440-1.0 ORN
440-1.0 ORN
453-.8 BLK/RED
120-.8 TAN/WHT
459-.8 DK GRN/WHT
444-.8 LT GRN/BLK
443-.8 LT GRN/WHT
442-.8 LT BLU/BLK
441-.8 LT BLU/WHT
423-.8 NAT/WHT
430-.8 PPL/WHT
424-.8 TAN/BLK
450-1.0 BLK/WHT
439-.8 PNK/BLK
467-.8 DK BLU
A/C COMPRESSOR CLUTCH (SEE PAGE 125)
150-1.0 BLK
450-.8 BLK/WHT
TO SPLICE 306 (SEE PAGE 21)
PWR STRG PRESSURE SW (SEE PAGE 94)
S120
A.L.D.L.
C308
450-.8 BLK/WHT
440-1.0 ORN
31-.8 TAN
465-.8 DK GRN/WHT
12020043
REAR WHEEL ANTILOCK BRAKE MODULE (SEE PAGE 116)
459-.8 DK GRN/WHT
450-.8 BLK/WHT
450-1.0 BLK/WHT
458-.8 DK BLU
450-1.0 BKK/WHT
I/P
ENGINE
OXYGEN SENSOR AND SYSTEM GROUND G107
440-1.0 ORN
120-1.0 TAN/WHT
FUEL PUMP (SEE PAGE 83)
422-.8 TAN/BLK
420-.8 PPL
420-.8 PPL
TCC CUTOUT SW. (SEE PAGE 66)
12020183
C100
120-1.0 TAN/WHT
TO I/P CONN (SEE PAGE 146)
12020184
39-.8 PNK/BLK
TO SPLICE S303 (SEE PAGE 62)
422-.8 TAN/BLK
W/AUTO. TRANS.
975-.8 DK BLU
BACKUP LAMP SWITCH W/ MANUAL TRANS. (SEE PAGE 210)
924-.8 LT GRN/BLK
31-.5 TAN
440-1.0 ORN
422-.8 TAN/WHT
413-.8 TAN
422-.8 TAN/BLK
439-.8 PNK/BLK
439-.8 RED

1988–91 WIRING DIAGRAMS (CONT.)

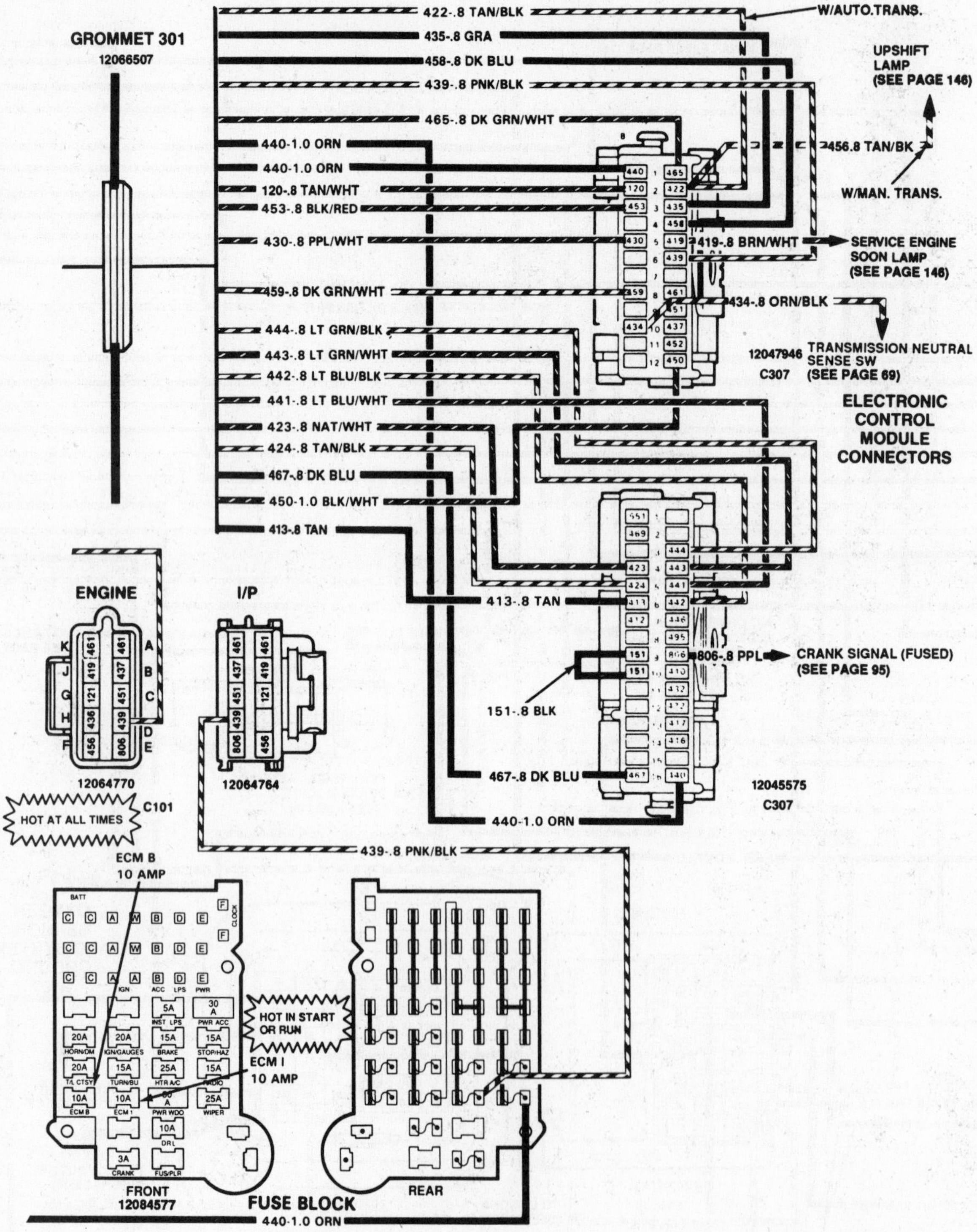

GROMMET 301
12066507
422-.8 TAN/BLK
W/AUTO.TRANS.
435-.8 GRA
458-.8 DK BLU
439-.8 PNK/BLK
UPSHIFT LAMP (SEE PAGE 146)
465-.8 DK GRN/WHT
440-1.0 ORN
440-1.0 ORN
456.8 TAN/BK
120-.8 TAN/WHT
453-.8 BLK/RED
W/MAN. TRANS.
430-.8 PPL/WHT
419-.8 BRN/WHT
SERVICE ENGINE SOON LAMP (SEE PAGE 146)
459-.8 DK GRN/WHT
434-.8 ORN/BLK
444-.8 LT GRN/BLK
443-.8 LT GRN/WHT
12047946
C307
TRANSMISSION NEUTRAL SENSE SW (SEE PAGE 69)
442-.8 LT BLU/BLK
441-.8 LT BLU/WHT
ELECTRONIC CONTROL MODULE CONNECTORS
423-.8 NAT/WHT
424-.8 TAN/BLK
467-.8 DK BLU
450-1.0 BLK/WHT
413-.8 TAN
ENGINE
I/P
413-.8 TAN
806-.8 PPL
CRANK SIGNAL (FUSED) (SEE PAGE 95)
151-.8 BLK
12064770
12064764
467-.8 DK BLU
12045575
C307
HOT AT ALL TIMES
C101
440-1.0 ORN
ECM B 10 AMP
439-.8 PNK/BLK
HOT IN START OR RUN
ECM I 10 AMP
FRONT
12084577
FUSE BLOCK
REAR
440-1.0 ORN

ELECTRONIC CONTROL MODULE - OUTPUTS - 2.5L (151 CID) ENGINE

1988–91 WIRING DIAGRAMS (CONT.)

CIRCUIT NO.	WIRE SIZE	COLOR	CAVITY	DESCRIPTION
			C1	NOT USED
436	.8	BRN	C2	AIR CONTROL SOLENOID CONTROL
444	.8	LT GRN/BLK	C3	IAC COIL B LOW
443	.8	LT GRN/WHT	C4	IAC COIL B HIGH
441	.8	LT BLU/WHT	C5	IAC COIL A HIGH
442	.8	LT BLU/BLK	C6	IAC COIL A LOW
			C7	NOT USED
			C8	NOT USED
806	.8	PPL/WHT	C9	CRANK SIGNAL
410	.8	YEL	C10	COOLANT TEMP SIGNAL
432	.8	LT GRN	C11	MAP SENSOR SIGNAL
			C12	NOT USED
417	.5	DK BLU	C13	TPS SIGNAL
416	.5	GRA	C14	5V SENSOR REFERENCE
			C15	NOT USED
440	.8	ORN	C16	12V BATTERY (FUSED)
551	1.0	TAN/WHT	D1	SYSTEM GROUND
452	.8	BLK	D2	COOLANT TEMP SENSOR AND TPS GROUND
			D3	NOT USED
423	.5	WHT	D4	EST SPARK TIMING CONTROL
424	.8	TAN/BLK	D5	EST BYPASS
413	.8	TAN	D6	OXYGEN SENSOR GROUND
412	.5	PPL	D7	OXYGEN SENSOR SIGNAL
			D8	NOT USED
			D9	NOT USED
			D10	NOT USED
			D11	NOT USED
			D12	NOT USED
			D13	NOT USED
468	.8	DK GRN	D14	INJECTOR 2 DRIVE
			D15	NOT USED
467	.8	DK BLU	D16	INJECTOR 1 DRIVE

ELECTRONIC CONTROL MODULE - 2.8L (173 CID) ENGINE

1988–91 WIRING DIAGRAMS (CONT.)

CIRCUIT NO.	WIRE SIZE	COLOR	CAVITY	DESCRIPTION
465	.8	DK GRN/WHT	A1	FUEL PUMP RELAY DRIVE
459	.8	BRN	A2	A/C RELAY CONTROL
			A3	NOT USED
435	.5	GRA	A4	EVRV SOLENOID CONTROL
419	.8	BRN/WHT	A5	SERVICE ENGINE SOON LAMP CONTROL
439	.8	PNK/BLK	A6	12V IGNITION (FUSED)
456	.8	TAN/BLK	A7	UPSHIFT LAMP CONTROL
461	.8	ORN	A8	ALDL SERIAL DATA
451	.8	WHT/BLK	A9	ALDL DIAGNOSTIC TEST
437	.8	BRN	A10	DIGITAL RATIO ADAPTER SIGNAL
455	.8	PPL	A11	MAP SENSOR GROUND
450	1.0	BLK/WHT	A12	SYSTEM GROUND
440	.8	ORN	B1	12V BATTERY (FUSED)
120	.8	TAN/WHT	B2	FUEL PUMP SIGNAL
453	.8	RED/BLK	B3	DISTRIBUTOR REF LOW
			B4	NOT USED
430	.5	PPL/WHT	B5	DISTRIBUTOR REF HIGH
			B6	NOT USED
485	.8	BLK	B7	SPARK RETARD SIGNAL
59	.8	DK BRN	B8	A/C SIGNAL
			B9	NOT USED
			B10	NOT USED
			B11	NOT USED
			B12	NOT USED

1988–91 WIRING DIAGRAMS (CONT.)

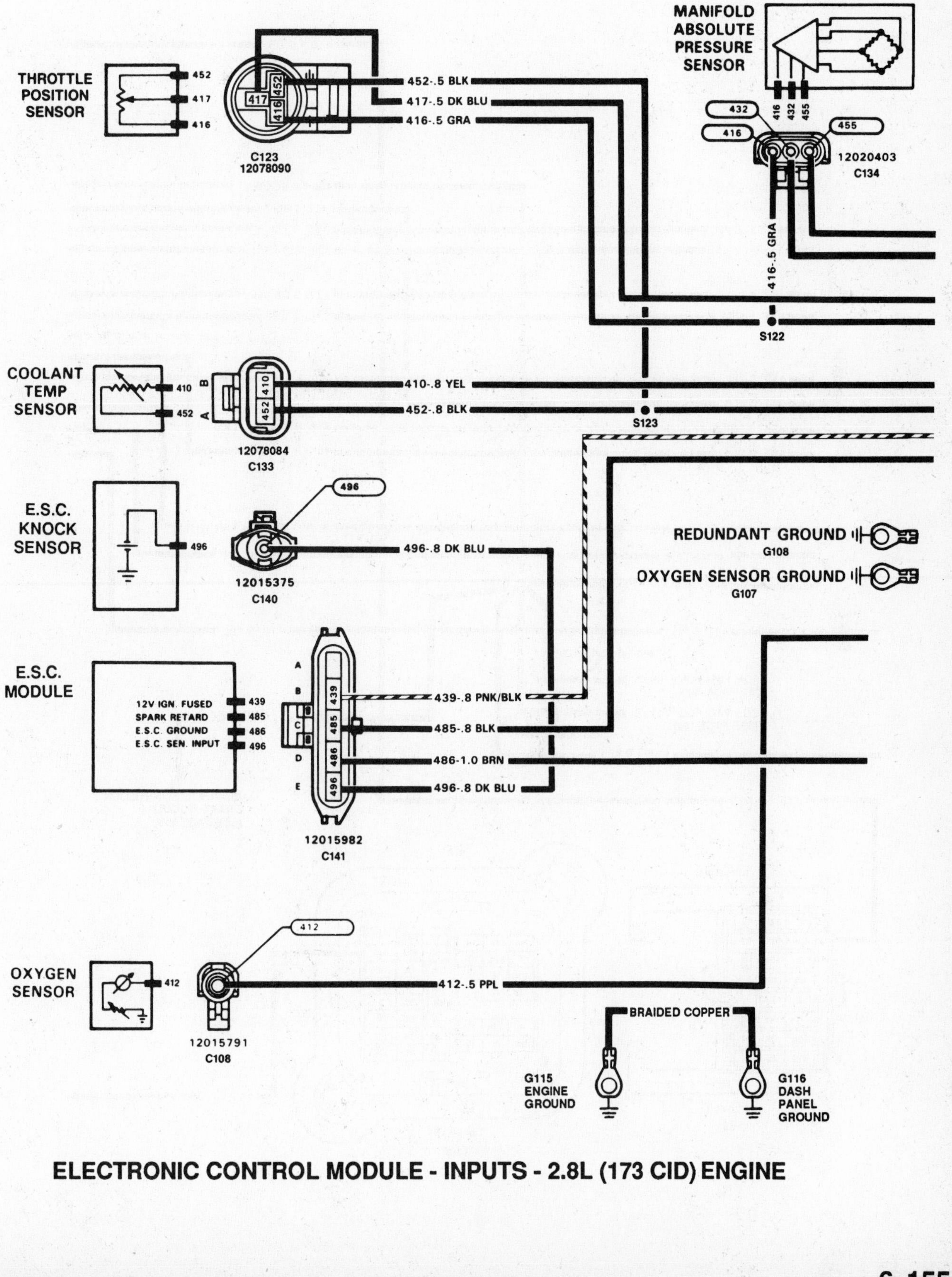

MANIFOLD ABSOLUTE PRESSURE SENSOR
THROTTLE POSITION SENSOR
452
417
416
C123
12078090
452-.5 BLK
417-.5 DK BLU
416-.5 GRA
432
416
455
12020403
C134
416-.5 GRA
S122
COOLANT TEMP SENSOR
410
452
12078084
C133
410-.8 YEL
452-.8 BLK
S123
E.S.C. KNOCK SENSOR
496
12015375
C140
496-.8 DK BLU
REDUNDANT GROUND
G108
OXYGEN SENSOR GROUND
G107
E.S.C. MODULE
12V IGN. FUSED
SPARK RETARD
E.S.C. GROUND
E.S.C. SEN. INPUT
439
485
486
439-.8 PNK/BLK
485-.8 BLK
486-1.0 BRN
496-.8 DK BLU
12015982
C141
OXYGEN SENSOR
412
412-.5 PPL
12015791
C108
BRAIDED COPPER
G115 ENGINE GROUND
G116 DASH PANEL GROUND

ELECTRONIC CONTROL MODULE - INPUTS - 2.8L (173 CID) ENGINE

1988–91 WIRING DIAGRAMS (CONT.)

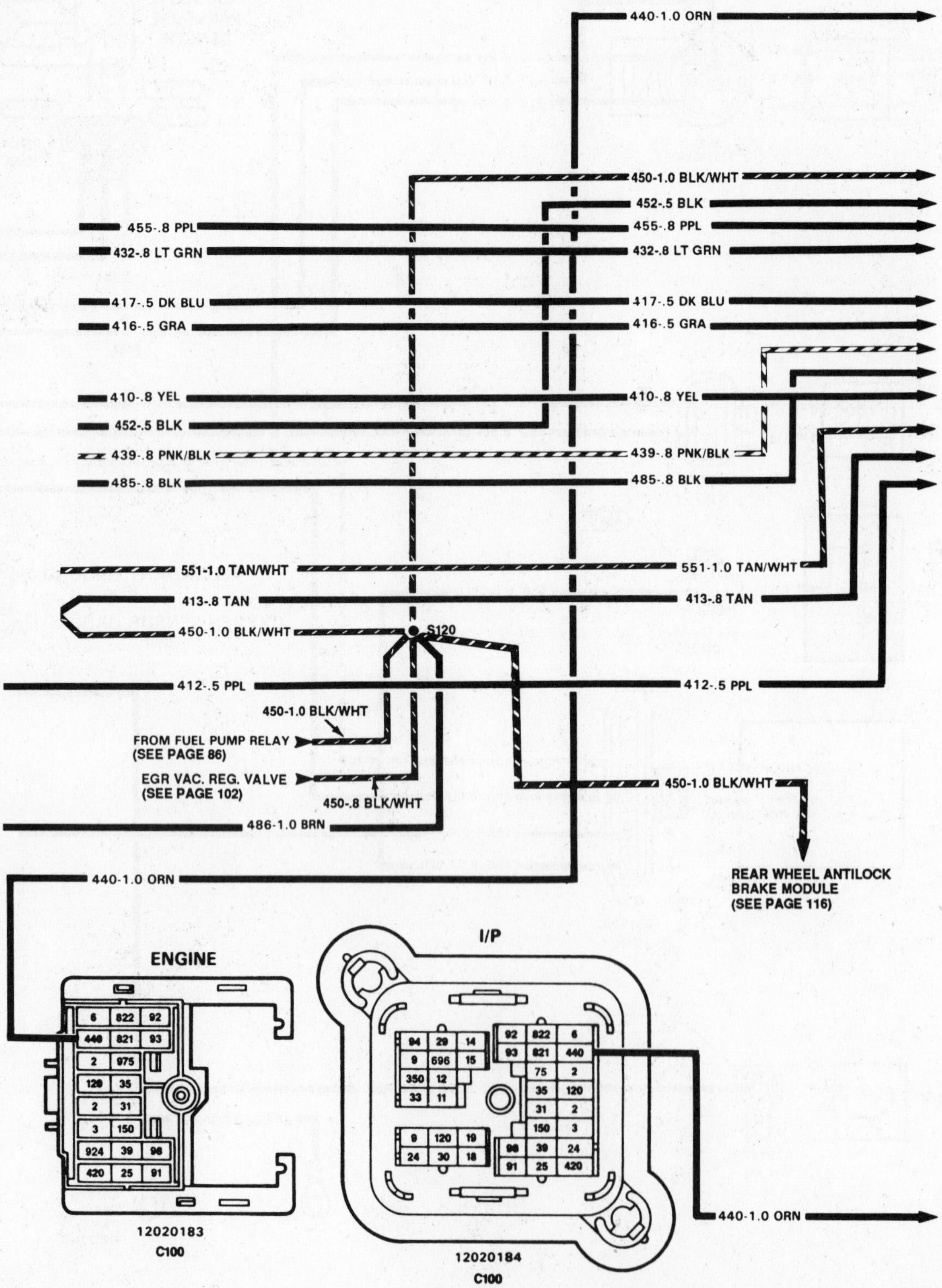
440-1.0 ORN
450-1.0 BLK/WHT
452-.5 BLK
455-.8 PPL
455-.8 PPL
432-.8 LT GRN
432-.8 LT GRN
417-.5 DK BLU
417-.5 DK BLU
416-.5 GRA
416-.5 GRA
410-.8 YEL
410-.8 YEL
452-.5 BLK
439-.8 PNK/BLK
439-.8 PNK/BLK
485-.8 BLK
485-.8 BLK
551-1.0 TAN/WHT
551-1.0 TAN/WHT
413-.8 TAN
413-.8 TAN
450-1.0 BLK/WHT
S120
412-.5 PPL
412-.5 PPL
450-1.0 BLK/WHT
FROM FUEL PUMP RELAY
(SEE PAGE 86)
EGR VAC. REG. VALVE
(SEE PAGE 102)
450-.8 BLK/WHT
450-1.0 BLK/WHT
486-1.0 BRN
440-1.0 ORN
REAR WHEEL ANTILOCK
BRAKE MODULE
(SEE PAGE 116)
ENGINE
I/P
12020183
C100
12020184
C100
440-1.0 ORN

1988–91 WIRING DIAGRAMS (CONT.)

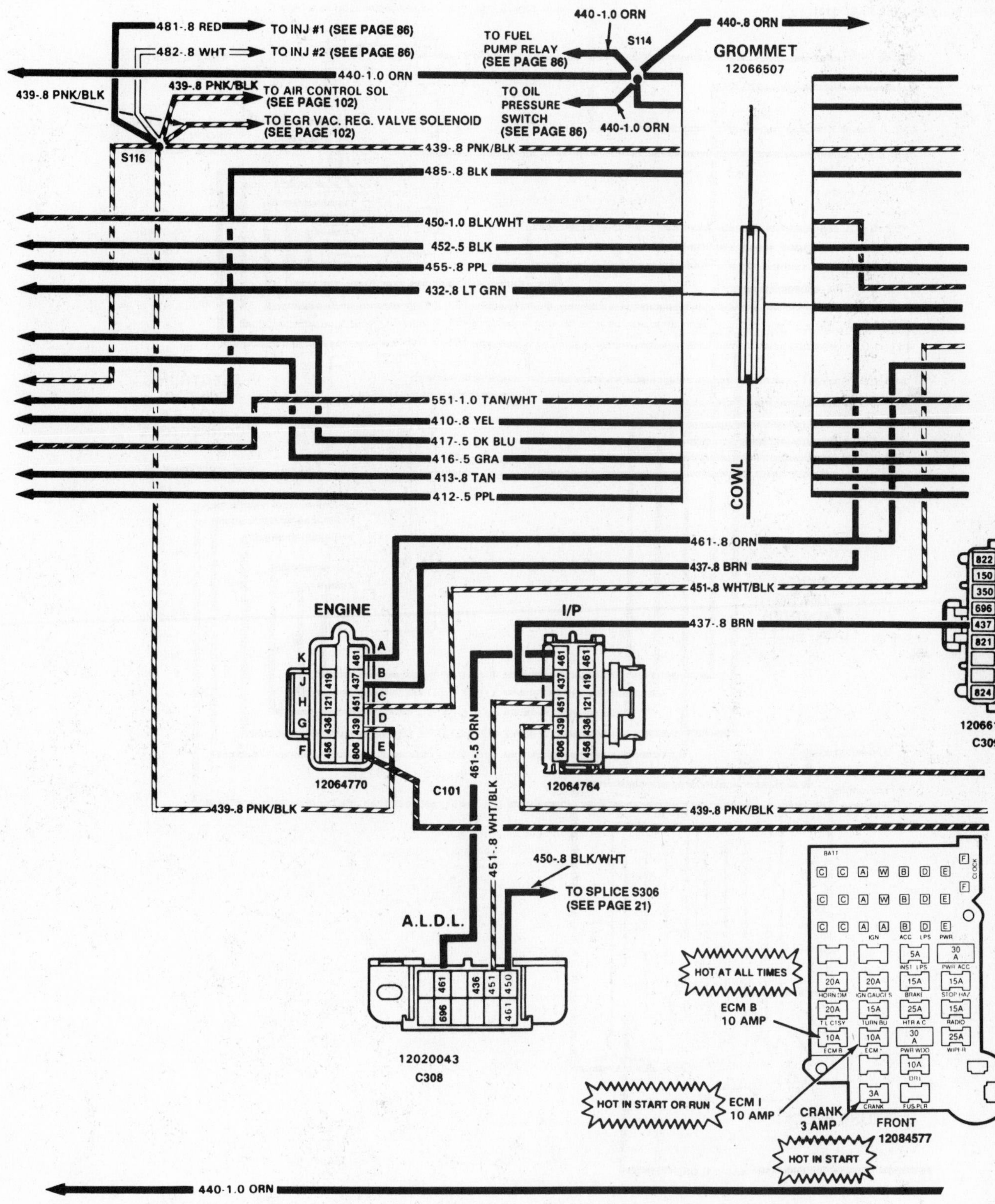
481-.8 RED
TO INJ #1 (SEE PAGE 86)
482-.8 WHT
TO INJ #2 (SEE PAGE 86)
440-1.0 ORN
TO FUEL PUMP RELAY (SEE PAGE 86)
S114
440-.8 ORN
GROMMET 12066507
439-.8 PNK/BLK
TO AIR CONTROL SOL (SEE PAGE 102)
TO EGR VAC. REG. VALVE SOLENOID (SEE PAGE 102)
TO OIL PRESSURE SWITCH (SEE PAGE 86)
S116
485-.8 BLK
450-1.0 BLK/WHT
452-.5 BLK
455-.8 PPL
432-.8 LT GRN
551-1.0 TAN/WHT
410-.8 YEL
417-.5 DK BLU
416-.5 GRA
413-.8 TAN
412-.5 PPL
COWL
461-.8 ORN
437-.8 BRN
451-.8 WHT/BLK
ENGINE
I/P
12066130
C309
12064770
C101
12064764
461-.5 ORN
451-.8 WHT/BLK
450-.8 BLK/WHT
TO SPLICE S306 (SEE PAGE 21)
A.L.D.L.
12020043
C308
HOT AT ALL TIMES
ECM B 10 AMP
HOT IN START OR RUN
ECM I 10 AMP
CRANK 3 AMP
FRONT 12084577
HOT IN START
440-1.0 ORN

1988–91 WIRING DIAGRAMS (CONT.)

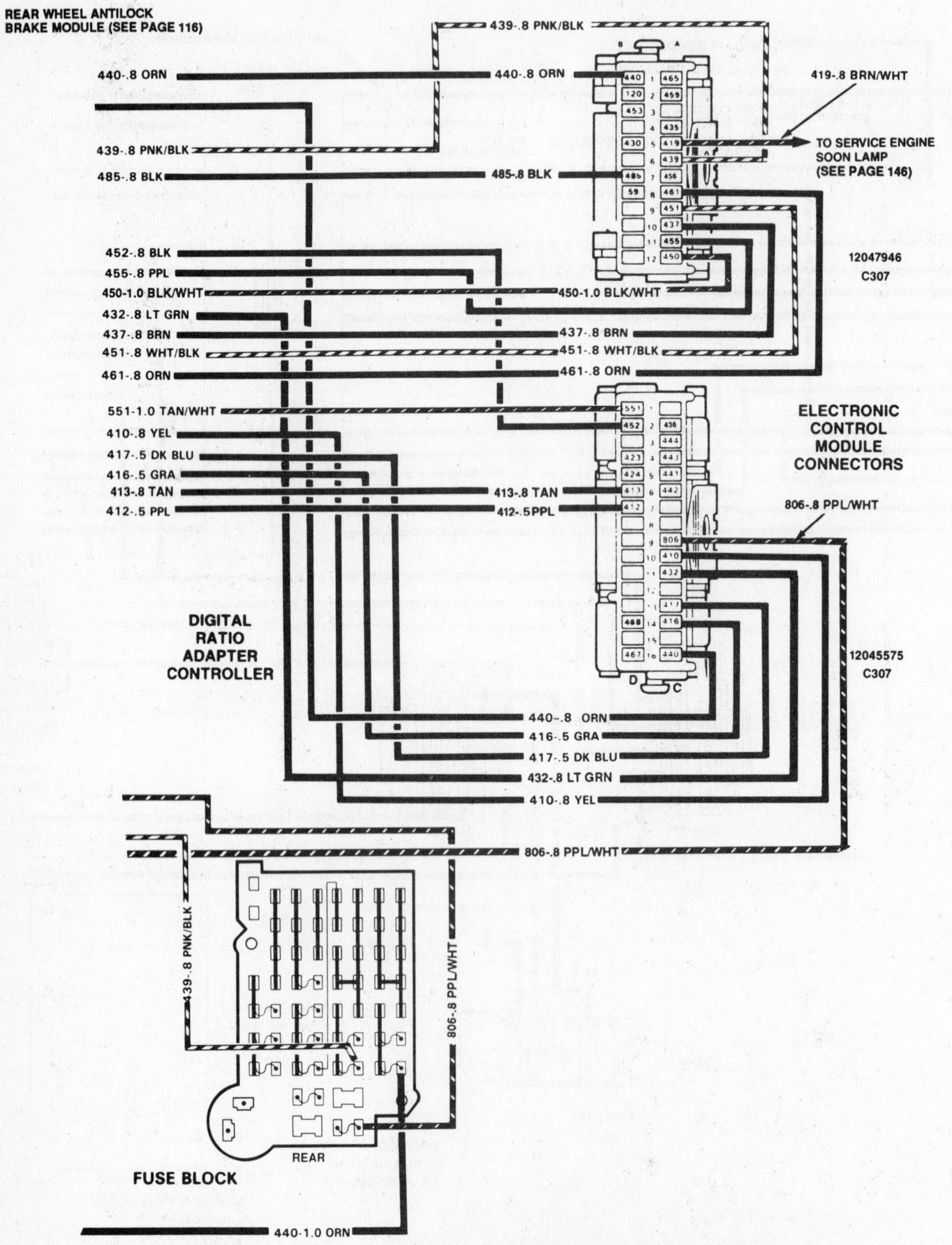
REAR WHEEL ANTILOCK BRAKE MODULE (SEE PAGE 116)
440-.8 ORN
439-.8 PNK/BLK
485-.8 BLK
452-.8 BLK
455-.8 PPL
450-1.0 BLK/WHT
432-.8 LT GRN
437-.8 BRN
451-.8 WHT/BLK
461-.8 ORN
551-1.0 TAN/WHT
410-.8 YEL
417-.5 DK BLU
416-.5 GRA
413-.8 TAN
412-.5 PPL
419-.8 BRN/WHT
TO SERVICE ENGINE SOON LAMP (SEE PAGE 146)
12047946
C307
ELECTRONIC CONTROL MODULE CONNECTORS
806-.8 PPL/WHT
12045575
C307
DIGITAL RATIO ADAPTER CONTROLLER
440-.8 ORN
416-.5 GRA
417-.5 DK BLU
432-.8 LT GRN
410-.8 YEL
FUSE BLOCK
REAR
440-1.0 ORN

ELECTRONIC CONTROL MODULE - INPUTS - 2.8L (173 CID) ENGINE

1988–91 WIRING DIAGRAMS (CONT.)

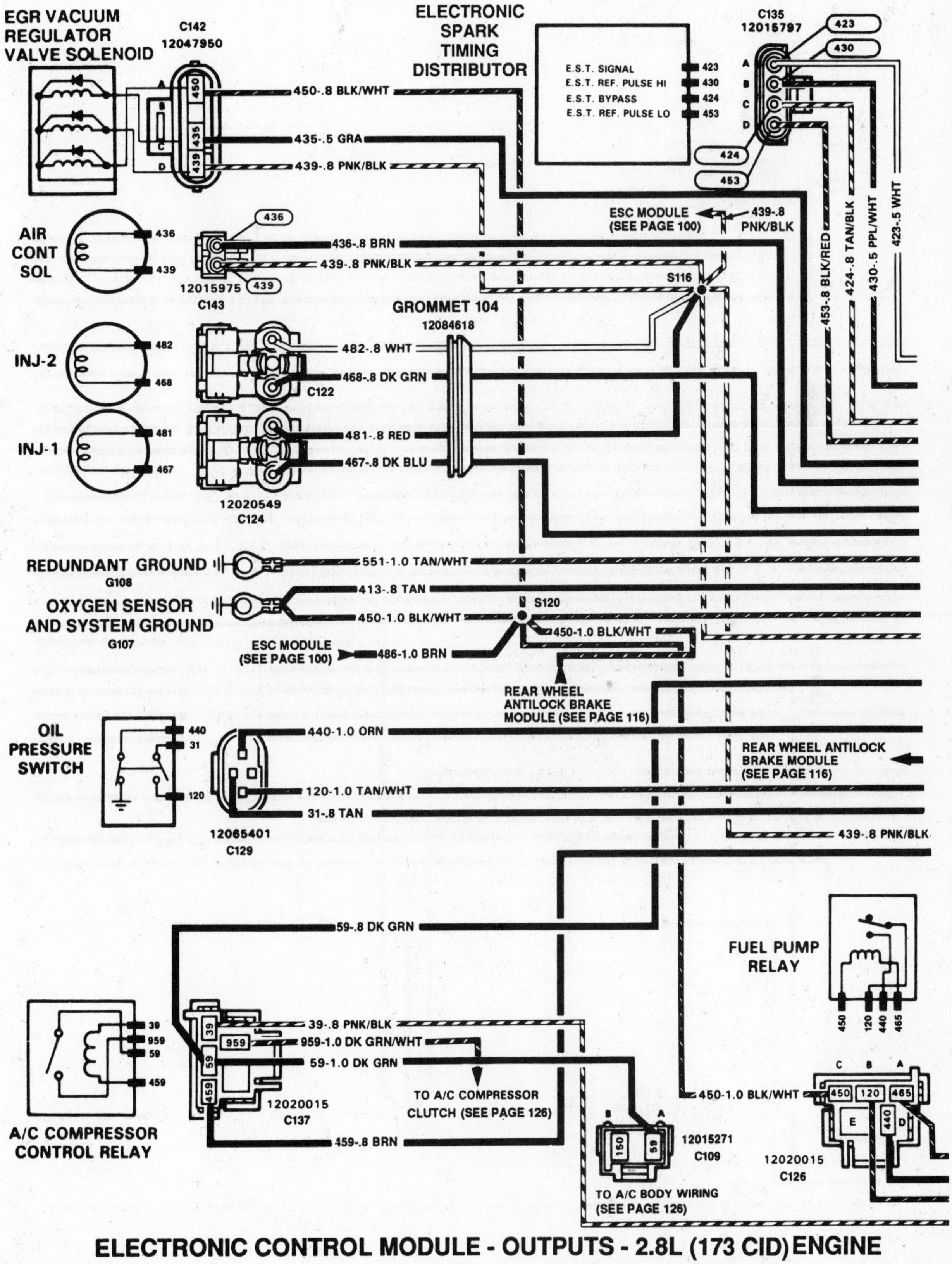
EGR VACUUM REGULATOR VALVE SOLENOID
C142
12047950
450-.8 BLK/WHT
435-.5 GRA
439-.8 PNK/BLK
ELECTRONIC SPARK TIMING DISTRIBUTOR
E.S.T. SIGNAL
E.S.T. REF. PULSE HI
E.S.T. BYPASS
E.S.T. REF. PULSE LO
C135
12015797
423
430
424
453
ESC MODULE (SEE PAGE 100)
439-.8 PNK/BLK
453-.8 BLK/RED
424-.8 TAN/BLK
430-.5 PPL/WHT
423-.5 WHT
AIR CONT SOL
436
439
436-.8 BRN
439-.8 PNK/BLK
12015975
C143
S116
GROMMET 104
12084618
INJ-2
482
468
482-.8 WHT
468-.8 DK GRN
C122
INJ-1
481
467
481-.8 RED
467-.8 DK BLU
12020549
C124
REDUNDANT GROUND
G108
551-1.0 TAN/WHT
OXYGEN SENSOR AND SYSTEM GROUND
G107
413-.8 TAN
450-1.0 BLK/WHT
S120
450-1.0 BLK/WHT
ESC MODULE (SEE PAGE 100)
486-1.0 BRN
REAR WHEEL ANTILOCK BRAKE MODULE (SEE PAGE 116)
OIL PRESSURE SWITCH
440
31
120
440-1.0 ORN
120-1.0 TAN/WHT
31-.8 TAN
12065401
C129
REAR WHEEL ANTILOCK BRAKE MODULE (SEE PAGE 116)
439-.8 PNK/BLK
59-.8 DK GRN
FUEL PUMP RELAY
450
120
440
465
A/C COMPRESSOR CONTROL RELAY
39
959
59
459
39-.8 PNK/BLK
959-1.0 DK GRN/WHT
59-1.0 DK GRN
459-.8 BRN
12020015
C137
TO A/C COMPRESSOR CLUTCH (SEE PAGE 126)
150
12015271
C109
TO A/C BODY WIRING (SEE PAGE 126)
450-1.0 BLK/WHT
12020015
C126

ELECTRONIC CONTROL MODULE - OUTPUTS - 2.8L (173 CID) ENGINE

1988–91 WIRING DIAGRAMS (CONT.)

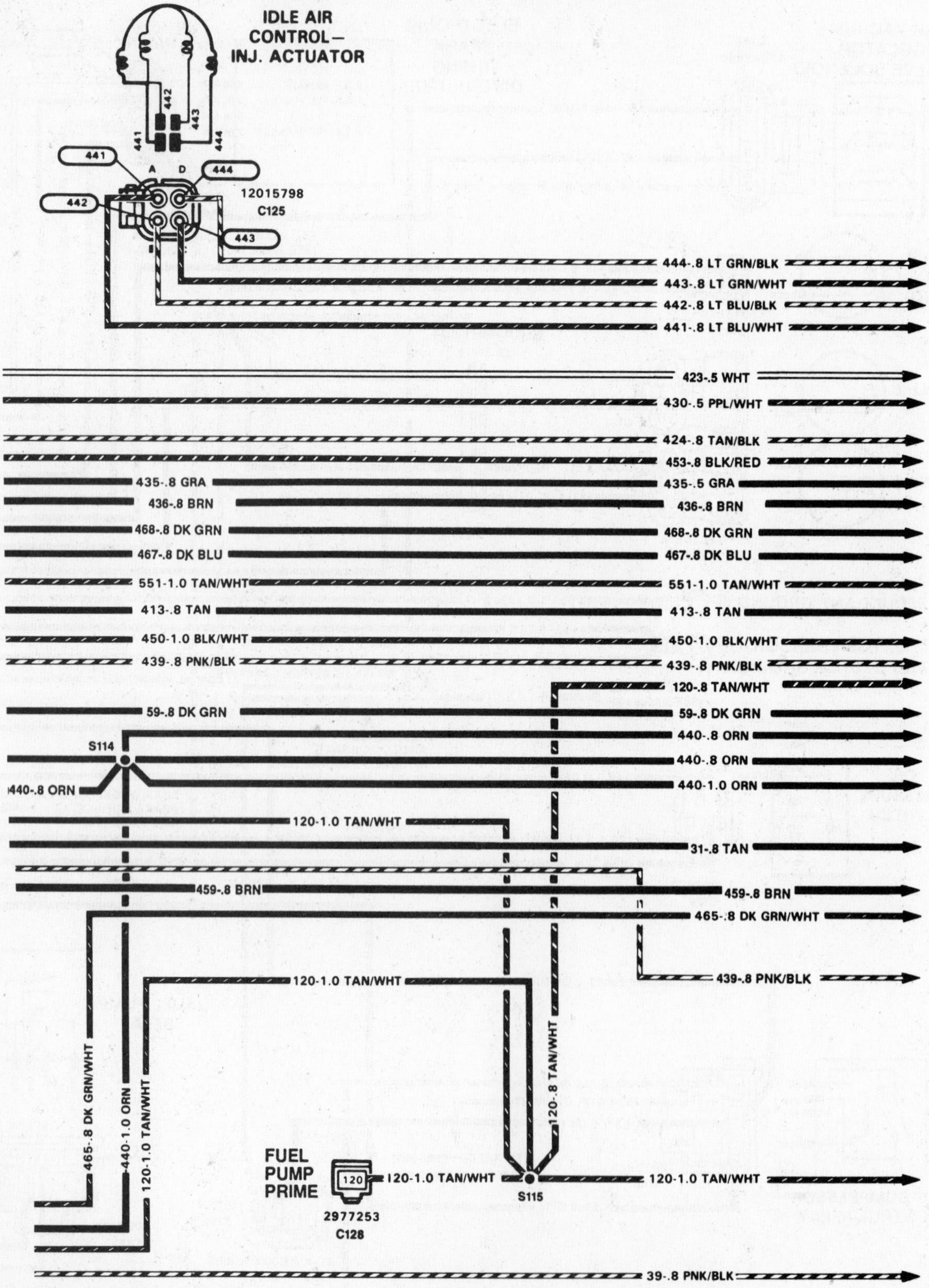
IDLE AIR
CONTROL—
INJ. ACTUATOR
441
442
443
444
A
D
12015798
C125
444-.8 LT GRN/BLK
443-.8 LT GRN/WHT
442-.8 LT BLU/BLK
441-.8 LT BLU/WHT
423-.5 WHT
430-.5 PPL/WHT
424-.8 TAN/BLK
453-.8 BLK/RED
435-.8 GRA
435-.5 GRA
436-.8 BRN
468-.8 DK GRN
467-.8 DK BLU
551-1.0 TAN/WHT
413-.8 TAN
450-1.0 BLK/WHT
439-.8 PNK/BLK
120-.8 TAN/WHT
59-.8 DK GRN
440-.8 ORN
S114
440-1.0 ORN
120-1.0 TAN/WHT
31-.8 TAN
459-.8 BRN
465-.8 DK GRN/WHT
440-1.0 ORN
120-1.0 TAN/WHT
FUEL
PUMP
PRIME
120
2977253
C128
S115
39-.8 PNK/BLK

1988–91 WIRING DIAGRAMS (CONT.)

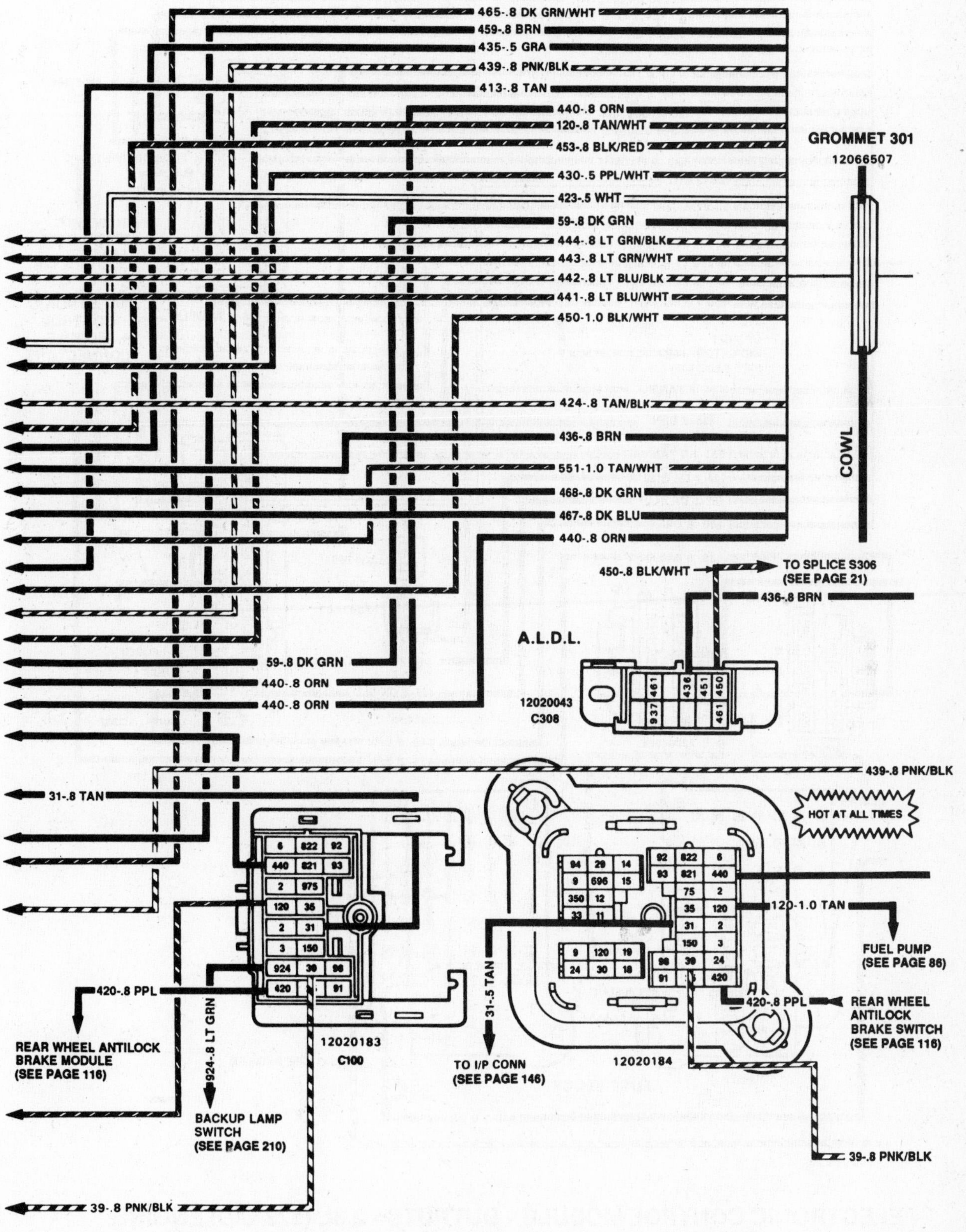
465-.8 DK GRN/WHT
459-.8 BRN
435-.5 GRA
439-.8 PNK/BLK
413-.8 TAN
440-.8 ORN
120-.8 TAN/WHT
453-.8 BLK/RED
430-.5 PPL/WHT
423-.5 WHT
59-.8 DK GRN
444-.8 LT GRN/BLK
443-.8 LT GRN/WHT
442-.8 LT BLU/BLK
441-.8 LT BLU/WHT
450-1.0 BLK/WHT
GROMMET 301
12066507
424-.8 TAN/BLK
436-.8 BRN
551-1.0 TAN/WHT
468-.8 DK GRN
467-.8 DK BLU
440-.8 ORN
COWL
450-.8 BLK/WHT
TO SPLICE S306
(SEE PAGE 21)
436-.8 BRN
A.L.D.L.
12020043
C308
59-.8 DK GRN
440-.8 ORN
440-.8 ORN
439-.8 PNK/BLK
HOT AT ALL TIMES
31-.8 TAN
120-1.0 TAN
FUEL PUMP
(SEE PAGE 86)
420-.8 PPL
REAR WHEEL ANTILOCK BRAKE MODULE (SEE PAGE 116)
924-.8 LT GRN
31-.5 TAN
420-.8 PPL
REAR WHEEL ANTILOCK BRAKE SWITCH (SEE PAGE 116)
12020183
C100
TO I/P CONN
(SEE PAGE 146)
12020184
BACKUP LAMP SWITCH
(SEE PAGE 210)
39-.8 PNK/BLK
39-.8 PNK/BLK

1988–91 WIRING DIAGRAMS (CONT.)

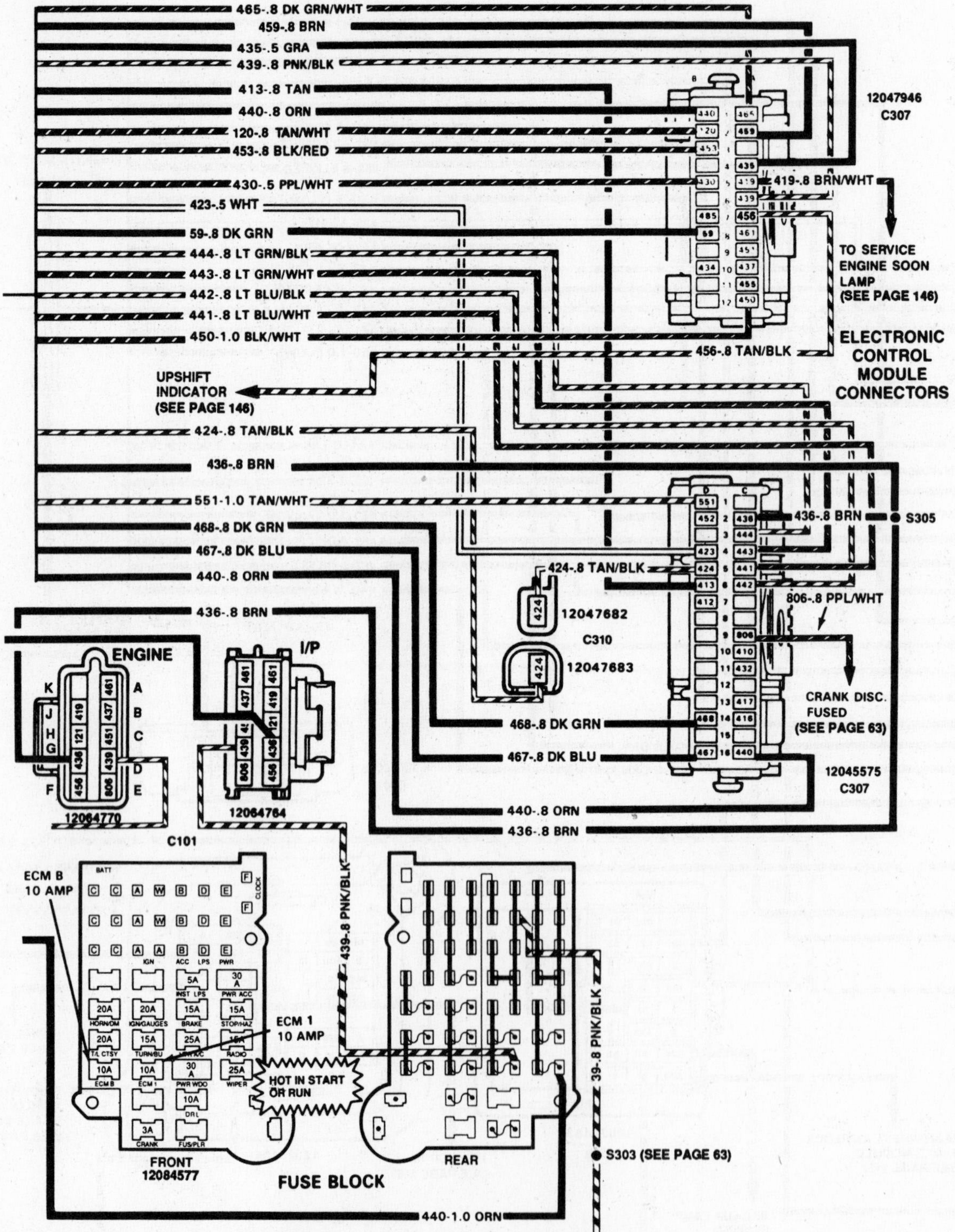
465-.8 DK GRN/WHT
459-.8 BRN
435-.5 GRA
439-.8 PNK/BLK
413-.8 TAN
440-.8 ORN
120-.8 TAN/WHT
453-.8 BLK/RED
430-.5 PPL/WHT
423-.5 WHT
59-.8 DK GRN
444-.8 LT GRN/BLK
443-.8 LT GRN/WHT
442-.8 LT BLU/BLK
441-.8 LT BLU/WHT
450-1.0 BLK/WHT
UPSHIFT INDICATOR (SEE PAGE 146)
424-.8 TAN/BLK
436-.8 BRN
551-1.0 TAN/WHT
468-.8 DK GRN
467-.8 DK BLU
440-.8 ORN
436-.8 BRN
12047946
C307
419-.8 BRN/WHT
TO SERVICE ENGINE SOON LAMP (SEE PAGE 146)
456-.8 TAN/BLK
ELECTRONIC CONTROL MODULE CONNECTORS
436-.8 BRN
S305
424-.8 TAN/BLK
12047682
C310
12047683
806-.8 PPL/WHT
CRANK DISC. FUSED (SEE PAGE 63)
468-.8 DK GRN
467-.8 DK BLU
12045575
C307
440-.8 ORN
436-.8 BRN
ENGINE
12064770
I/P
12064764
C101
ECM B 10 AMP
ECM 1 10 AMP
HOT IN START OR RUN
439-.8 PNK/BLK
39-.8 PNK/BLK
S303 (SEE PAGE 63)
FRONT
12084577
REAR
FUSE BLOCK
440-1.0 ORN

ELECTRONIC CONTROL MODULE - OUTPUTS - 2.8L (173 CID) ENGINE

1988–91 WIRING DIAGRAMS (CONT.)

CIRCUIT NO.	WIRE SIZE	COLOR	CAVITY	DESCRIPTION
465	.8	DK GRN/WHT	A1	FUEL PUMP RELAY DRIVE
459	.8	DK GRN/BLK	A2	A/C RELAY CONTROL
			A3	NOT USED
435	.5	GRA	A4	EVRV SOLENOID CONTROL
419	.8	BRN/WHT	A5	SERVICE ENGINE SOON LAMP CONTROL
439	.8	PNK/BLK	A6	12V IGNITION (FUSED)
✱422	.8	TAN/BLK	A7	TCC SOLENOID CONTROL
□456	.8	TAN/BLK	A7	UPSHIFT LAMP CONTROL
461	.8	ORN	A8	ALDL SERIAL DATA
451	.8	WHT/BLK	A9	ALDL DIAGNOSTIC TEST
437	.8	BRN	A10	DIGITAL RATIO ADAPTER SIGNAL
452	.8	BLK	A11	COOLANT TEMP SENSOR AND TPS GROUND
450	1.0	BLK/WHT	A12	SYSTEM GROUND
440	.8	ORN	B1	12V BATTERY (FUSED)
120	.8	GRA	B2	FUEL PUMP SIGNAL
453	.8	BLK/RED	B3	DISTRIBUTOR REF LOW
			B4	NOT USED
430	.5	PPL/WHT	B5	DISTRIBUTOR REF HIGH
			B6	NOT USED
485	.8	BLK	B7	SPARK RETARD SIGNAL
59	.8	DK GRN	B8	A/C SIGNAL
			B9	NOT USED
△ 434	.5	ORN/BLK	B10	PARK/NEUTRAL SWITCH SIGNAL
			B11	NOT USED
			B12	NOT USED

✱ 422—AUTO TRANS ONLY

□ 456—MAN TRANS ONLY

△ AUTO TRANS ONLY

ELECTRONIC CONTROL MODULE - 4.3L (262 CID) ENGINE

1988–91 WIRING DIAGRAMS (CONT.)

CIRCUIT NO.	WIRE SIZE	COLOR	CAVITY	DESCRIPTION
			C1	NOT USED
			C2	NOT USED
444	.8	LT GRN/BLK	C3	IAC COIL B LOW
443	.8	LT GRN/WHT	C4	IAC COIL B HIGH
441	.8	LT BLU/WHT	C5	IAC COIL A HIGH
442	.8	LT BLU/BLK	C6	IAC COIL A LOW
△ 446	.8	LT BLU	C7	TCC SOLENOID SIGNAL
			C8	NOT USED
806	.8	PPL/WHT	C9	CRANK SIGNAL
410	.8	YEL	C10	COOLANT TEMP SENSOR SIGNAL
432	.8	LT GRN	C11	MAP SENSOR SIGNAL
			C12	NOT USED
417	.5	DK BLU	C13	TPS SIGNAL
416	.5	GRA	C14	5V SENSOR REFERENCE
			C15	NOT USED
440	.8	ORN	C16	12V BATTERY (FUSED)
551	1.0	TAN/WHT	D1	SYSTEM GROUND
455	.8	PPL	D2	MAP SENSOR GROUND
			D3	NOT USED
423	.5	NAT/WHT	D4	EST SPARK TIMING CONTROL
424	.8	TAN/BLK	D5	EST BYPASS
413	.5	TAN	D6	OXYGEN SENSOR GROUND
412	.5	PPL	D7	OXYGEN SENSOR SIGNAL
			D8	NOT USED
			D9	NOT USED
			D10	NOT USED
			D11	NOT USED
			D12	NOT USED
			D13	NOT USED
468	.8	DK GRN	D14	INJECTOR 2 DRIVE
			D15	NOT USED
467	.8	DK BLU	D16	INJECTOR 1 DRIVE

1988–91 WIRING DIAGRAMS (CONT.)

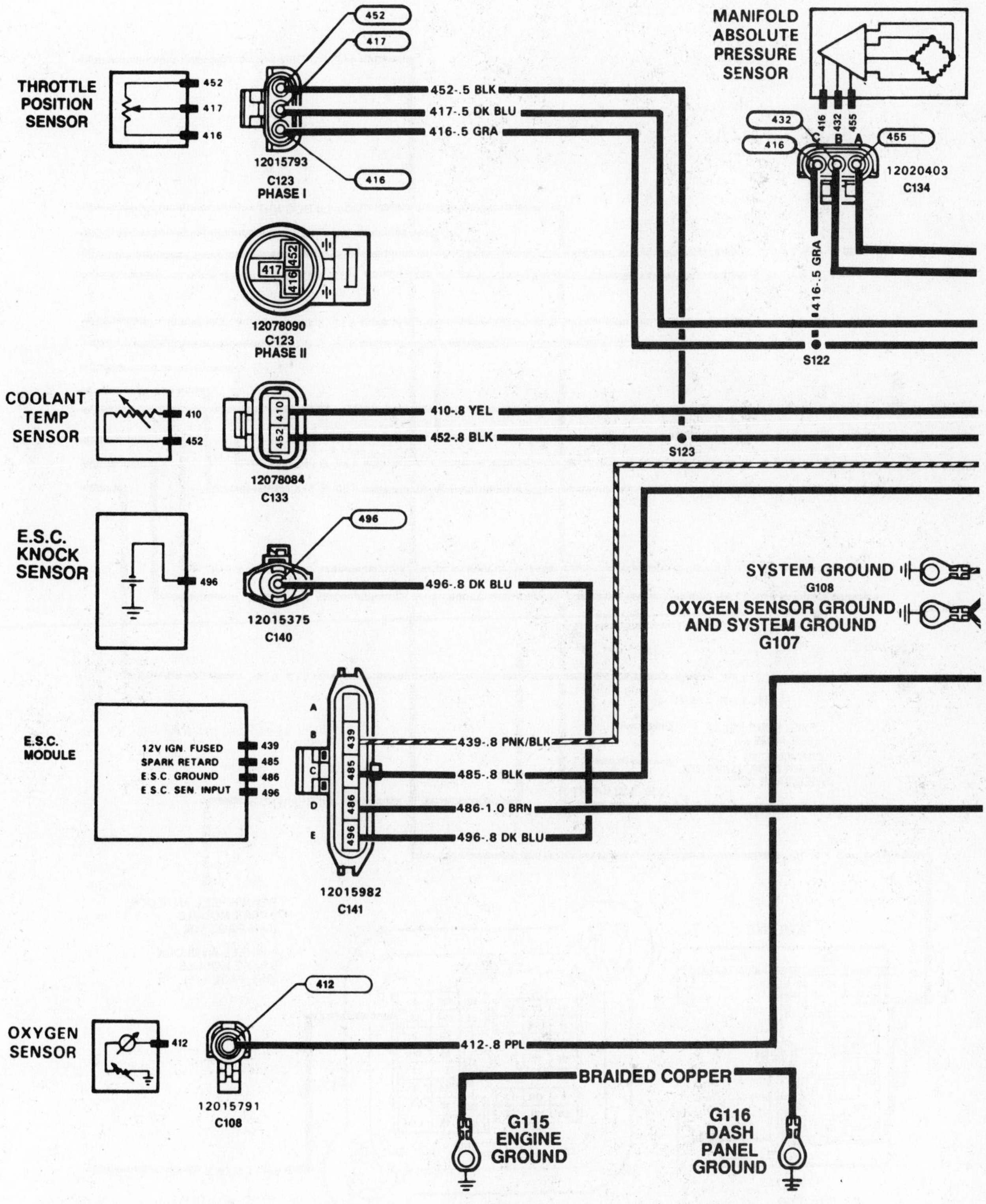
THROTTLE POSITION SENSOR
452
417
416
12015793
C123
PHASE I
452-.5 BLK
417-.5 DK BLU
416-.5 GRA
12078090
C123
PHASE II
MANIFOLD ABSOLUTE PRESSURE SENSOR
432
416
455
12020403
C134
416-.5 GRA
S122
COOLANT TEMP SENSOR
410
452
12078084
C133
410-.8 YEL
452-.8 BLK
S123
E.S.C. KNOCK SENSOR
496
12015375
C140
496-.8 DK BLU
SYSTEM GROUND
G108
OXYGEN SENSOR GROUND AND SYSTEM GROUND
G107
E.S.C. MODULE
12V IGN. FUSED
SPARK RETARD
E.S.C. GROUND
E.S.C. SEN. INPUT
439
485
486
496
439-.8 PNK/BLK
485-.8 BLK
486-1.0 BRN
496-.8 DK BLU
12015982
C141
OXYGEN SENSOR
412
12015791
C108
412-.8 PPL
BRAIDED COPPER
G115 ENGINE GROUND
G116 DASH PANEL GROUND

ELECTRONIC CONTROL MODULE - INPUTS - 4.3L (262 CID) ENGINE

1988–91 WIRING DIAGRAMS (CONT.)

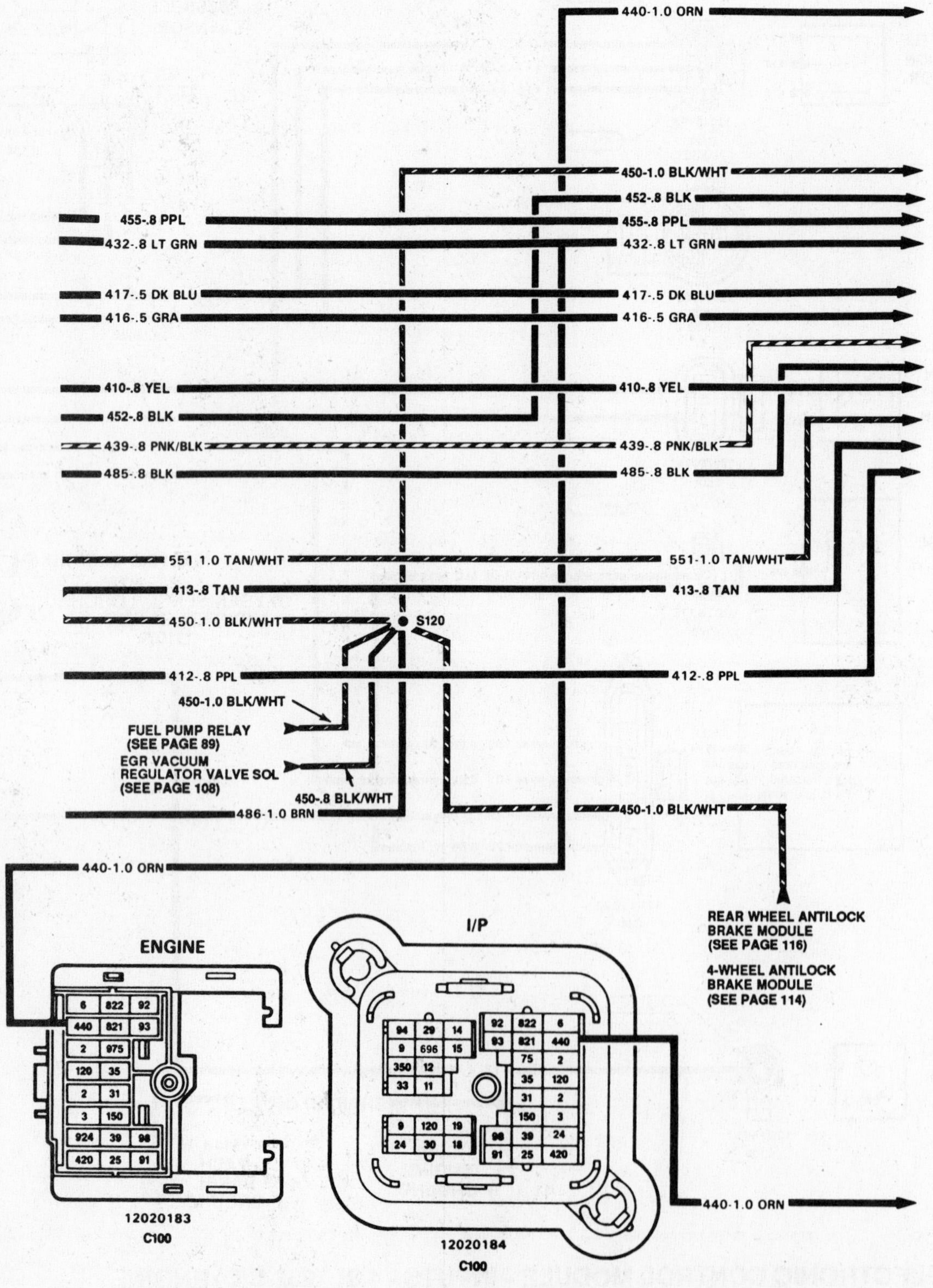
440-1.0 ORN
450-1.0 BLK/WHT
452-.8 BLK
455-.8 PPL
455-.8 PPL
432-.8 LT GRN
432-.8 LT GRN
417-.5 DK BLU
417-.5 DK BLU
416-.5 GRA
416-.5 GRA
410-.8 YEL
410-.8 YEL
452-.8 BLK
439-.8 PNK/BLK
439-.8 PNK/BLK
485-.8 BLK
485-.8 BLK
551 1.0 TAN/WHT
551-1.0 TAN/WHT
413-.8 TAN
413-.8 TAN
450-1.0 BLK/WHT
S120
412-.8 PPL
412-.8 PPL
450-1.0 BLK/WHT
FUEL PUMP RELAY (SEE PAGE 89)
EGR VACUUM REGULATOR VALVE SOL (SEE PAGE 108)
450-.8 BLK/WHT
486-1.0 BRN
450-1.0 BLK/WHT
440-1.0 ORN
REAR WHEEL ANTILOCK BRAKE MODULE (SEE PAGE 116)
4-WHEEL ANTILOCK BRAKE MODULE (SEE PAGE 114)
ENGINE
I/P
440-1.0 ORN
12020183
C100
12020184
C100

1988–91 WIRING DIAGRAMS (CONT.)

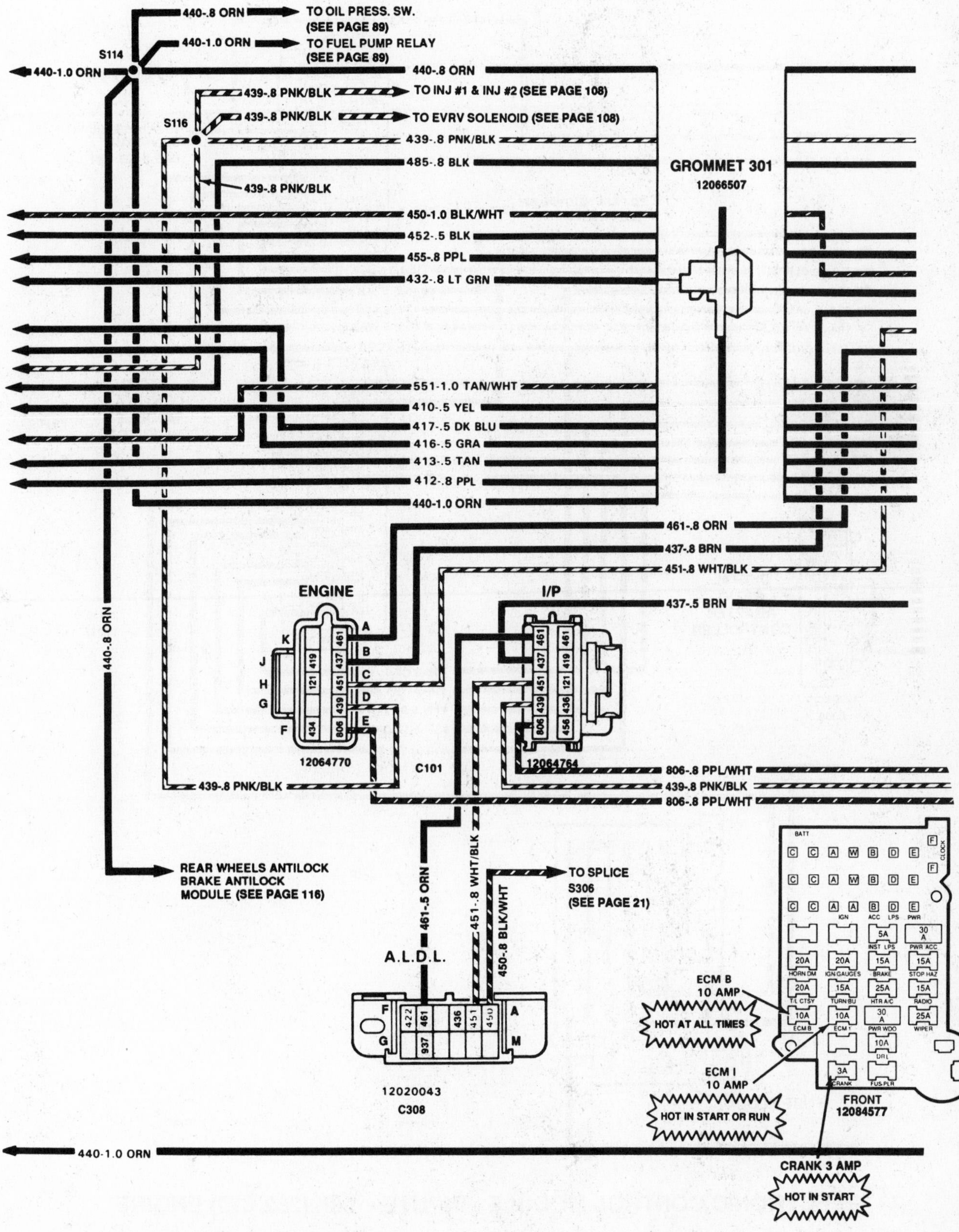
440-.8 ORN
TO OIL PRESS. SW. (SEE PAGE 89)
440-1.0 ORN
TO FUEL PUMP RELAY (SEE PAGE 89)
S114
440-1.0 ORN
440-.8 ORN
439-.8 PNK/BLK
TO INJ #1 & INJ #2 (SEE PAGE 108)
S116
439-.8 PNK/BLK
TO EVRV SOLENOID (SEE PAGE 108)
439-.8 PNK/BLK
485-.8 BLK
GROMMET 301
12066507
439-.8 PNK/BLK
450-1.0 BLK/WHT
452-.5 BLK
455-.8 PPL
432-.8 LT GRN
551-1.0 TAN/WHT
410-.5 YEL
417-.5 DK BLU
416-.5 GRA
413-.5 TAN
412-.8 PPL
440-1.0 ORN
461-.8 ORN
437-.8 BRN
451-.8 WHT/BLK
ENGINE
I/P
437-.5 BRN
440-.8 ORN
12064770
C101
12064764
806-.8 PPL/WHT
439-.8 PNK/BLK
439-.8 PNK/BLK
806-.8 PPL/WHT
REAR WHEELS ANTILOCK BRAKE ANTILOCK MODULE (SEE PAGE 116)
461-.5 ORN
451-.8 WHT/BLK
450-.8 BLK/WHT
TO SPLICE S306 (SEE PAGE 21)
A.L.D.L.
12020043
C308
ECM B 10 AMP
HOT AT ALL TIMES
ECM I 10 AMP
HOT IN START OR RUN
FRONT
12084577
CRANK 3 AMP
HOT IN START
440-1.0 ORN

1988–91 WIRING DIAGRAMS (CONT.)

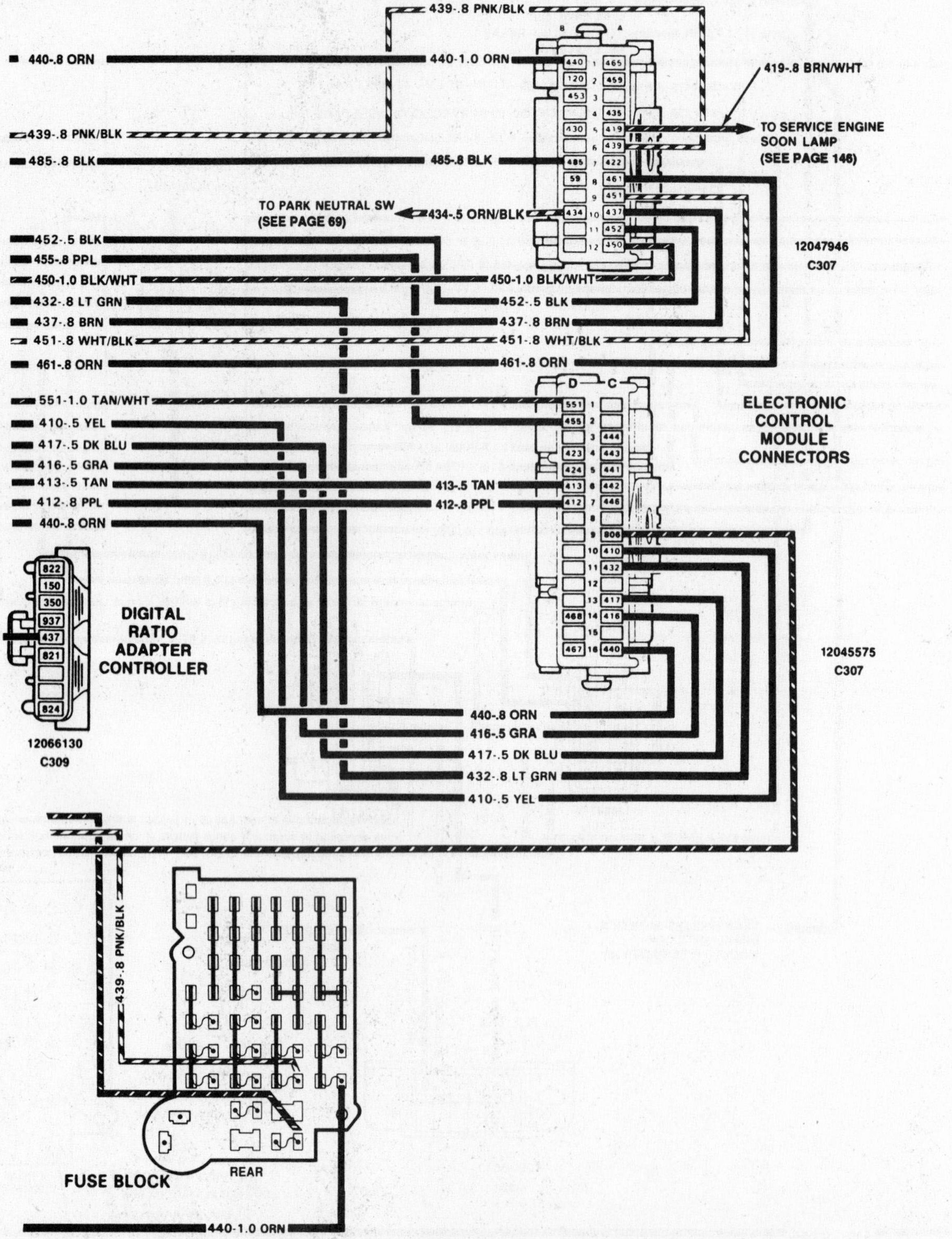
439-.8 PNK/BLK
440-.8 ORN
440-1.0 ORN
419-.8 BRN/WHT
TO SERVICE ENGINE SOON LAMP (SEE PAGE 146)
439-.8 PNK/BLK
485-.8 BLK
485-.8 BLK
TO PARK NEUTRAL SW (SEE PAGE 69)
434-.5 ORN/BLK
452-.5 BLK
455-.8 PPL
450-1.0 BLK/WHT
450-1.0 BLK/WHT
432-.8 LT GRN
452-.5 BLK
437-.8 BRN
437-.8 BRN
451-.8 WHT/BLK
451-.8 WHT/BLK
461-.8 ORN
461-.8 ORN
12047946
C307
551-1.0 TAN/WHT
410-.5 YEL
417-.5 DK BLU
416-.5 GRA
413-.5 TAN
413-.5 TAN
412-.8 PPL
412-.8 PPL
440-.8 ORN
ELECTRONIC CONTROL MODULE CONNECTORS
DIGITAL RATIO ADAPTER CONTROLLER
12066130
C309
12045575
C307
440-.8 ORN
416-.5 GRA
417-.5 DK BLU
432-.8 LT GRN
410-.5 YEL
439-.8 PNK/BLK
FUSE BLOCK
REAR
440-1.0 ORN

ELECTRONIC CONTROL MODULE - INPUTS - 4.3L (262 CID) ENGINE

1988–91 WIRING DIAGRAMS (CONT.)

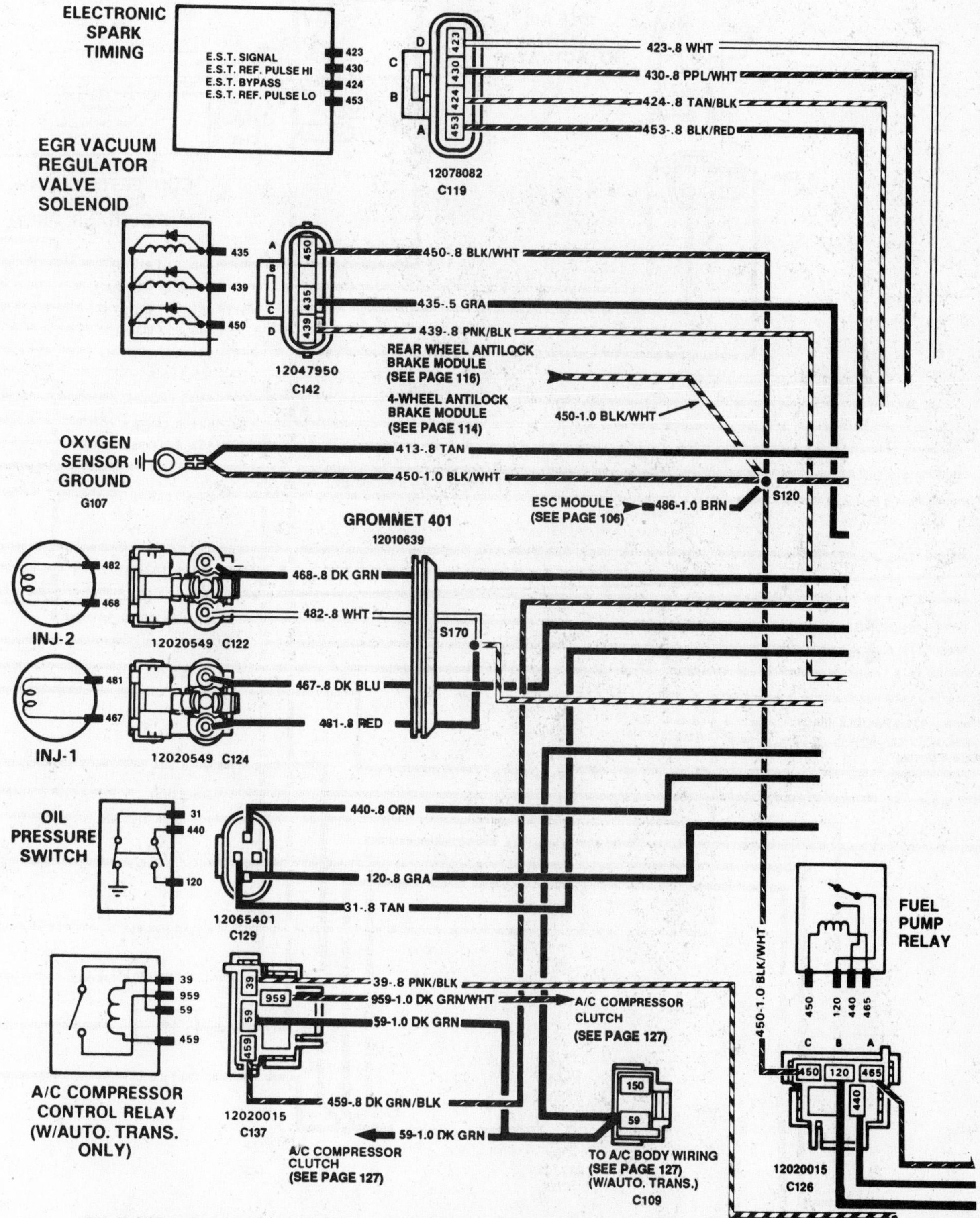
ELECTRONIC SPARK TIMING
E.S.T. SIGNAL
E.S.T. REF. PULSE HI
E.S.T. BYPASS
E.S.T. REF. PULSE LO
423
430
424
453
12078082
C119
423-.8 WHT
430-.8 PPL/WHT
424-.8 TAN/BLK
453-.8 BLK/RED
EGR VACUUM REGULATOR VALVE SOLENOID
435
439
450
12047950
C142
450-.8 BLK/WHT
435-.5 GRA
439-.8 PNK/BLK
REAR WHEEL ANTILOCK BRAKE MODULE (SEE PAGE 116)
4-WHEEL ANTILOCK BRAKE MODULE (SEE PAGE 114)
450-1.0 BLK/WHT
OXYGEN SENSOR GROUND
G107
413-.8 TAN
450-1.0 BLK/WHT
ESC MODULE (SEE PAGE 106)
486-1.0 BRN
S120
GROMMET 401
12010639
482
468
INJ-2
12020549 C122
468-.8 DK GRN
482-.8 WHT
S170
481
467
INJ-1
12020549 C124
467-.8 DK BLU
481-.8 RED
OIL PRESSURE SWITCH
31
440
120
12065401
C129
440-.8 ORN
120-.8 GRA
31-.8 TAN
FUEL PUMP RELAY
450
120
440
465
450-1.0 BLK/WHT
39
959
59
459
A/C COMPRESSOR CONTROL RELAY (W/AUTO. TRANS. ONLY)
12020015
C137
39-.8 PNK/BLK
959-1.0 DK GRN/WHT
59-1.0 DK GRN
A/C COMPRESSOR CLUTCH (SEE PAGE 127)
459-.8 DK GRN/BLK
59-1.0 DK GRN
A/C COMPRESSOR CLUTCH (SEE PAGE 127)
150
59
TO A/C BODY WIRING (SEE PAGE 127) (W/AUTO. TRANS.)
C109
C B A
12020015
C126

ELECTRONIC CONTROL MODULE - OUTPUTS - 4.3L (262 CID) ENGINE

1988–91 WIRING DIAGRAMS (CONT.)

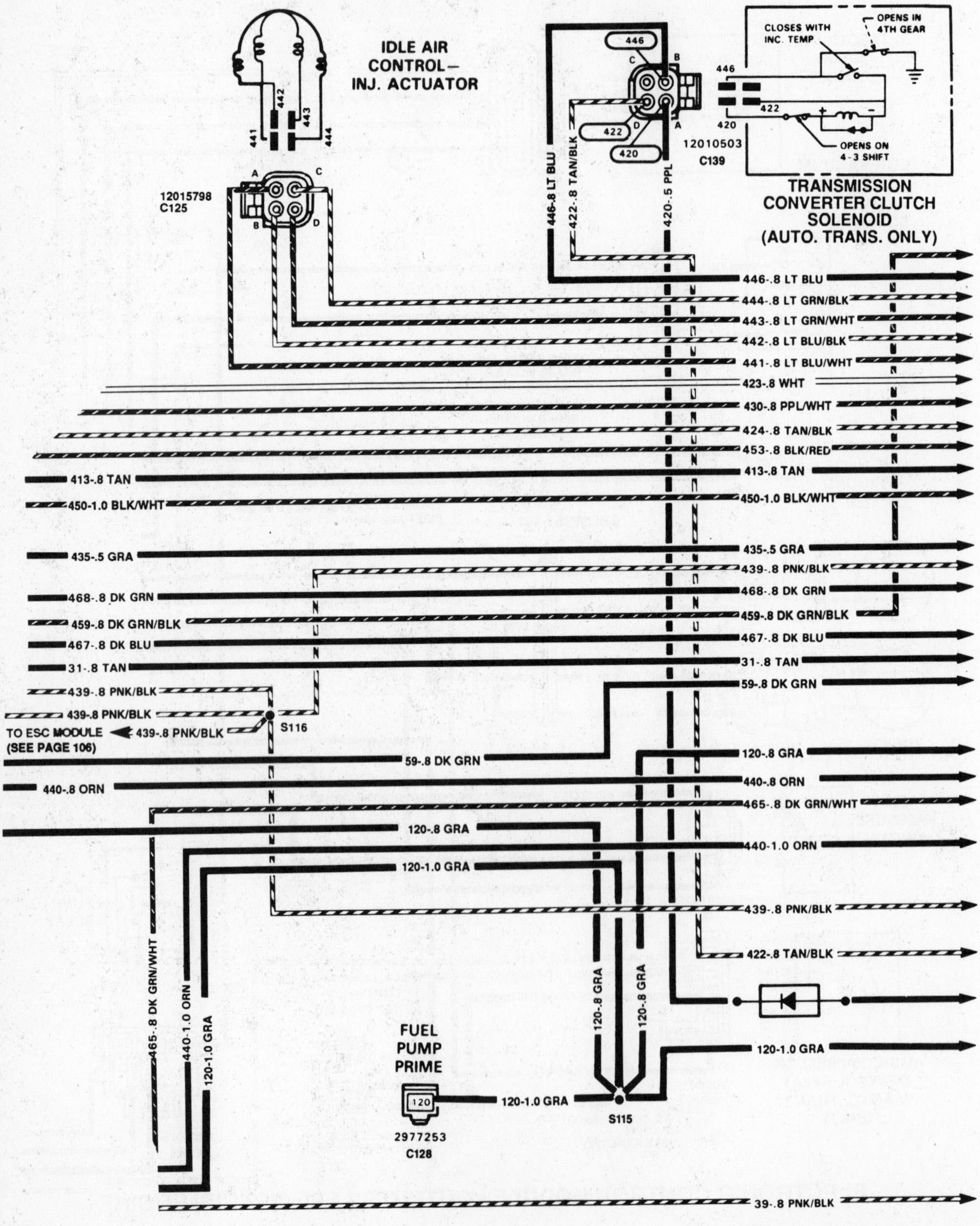
IDLE AIR
CONTROL–
INJ. ACTUATOR
12015798
C125
12010503
C139
CLOSES WITH INC. TEMP
OPENS IN 4TH GEAR
OPENS ON 4-3 SHIFT
TRANSMISSION
CONVERTER CLUTCH
SOLENOID
(AUTO. TRANS. ONLY)
446-.8 LT BLU
422-.8 TAN/BLK
420-.5 PPL
444-.8 LT GRN/BLK
443-.8 LT GRN/WHT
442-.8 LT BLU/BLK
441-.8 LT BLU/WHT
423-.8 WHT
430-.8 PPL/WHT
424-.8 TAN/BLK
453-.8 BLK/RED
413-.8 TAN
450-1.0 BLK/WHT
435-.5 GRA
439-.8 PNK/BLK
468-.8 DK GRN
459-.8 DK GRN/BLK
467-.8 DK BLU
31-.8 TAN
59-.8 DK GRN
TO ESC MODULE
(SEE PAGE 106)
S116
120-.8 GRA
440-.8 ORN
465-.8 DK GRN/WHT
440-1.0 ORN
120-1.0 GRA
FUEL
PUMP
PRIME
2977253
C128
S115
39-.8 PNK/BLK

1988–91 WIRING DIAGRAMS (CONT.)

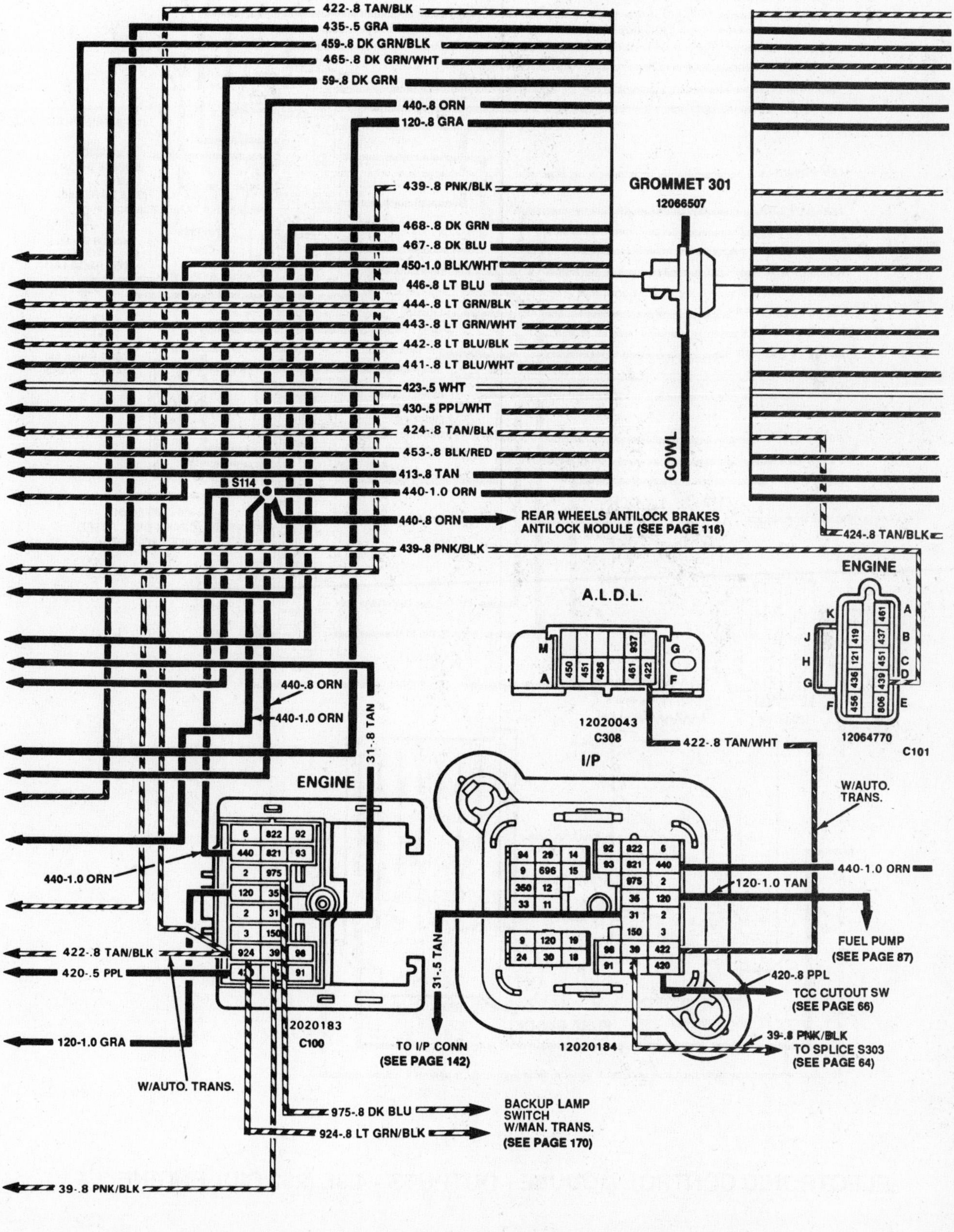
422-.8 TAN/BLK
435-.5 GRA
459-.8 DK GRN/BLK
465-.8 DK GRN/WHT
59-.8 DK GRN
440-.8 ORN
120-.8 GRA
439-.8 PNK/BLK
GROMMET 301
12066507
468-.8 DK GRN
467-.8 DK BLU
450-1.0 BLK/WHT
446-.8 LT BLU
444-.8 LT GRN/BLK
443-.8 LT GRN/WHT
442-.8 LT BLU/BLK
441-.8 LT BLU/WHT
423-.5 WHT
430-.5 PPL/WHT
424-.8 TAN/BLK
453-.8 BLK/RED
413-.8 TAN
S114
440-1.0 ORN
COWL
440-.8 ORN
REAR WHEELS ANTILOCK BRAKES
ANTILOCK MODULE (SEE PAGE 116)
424-.8 TAN/BLK
439-.8 PNK/BLK
ENGINE
A.L.D.L.
12020043
C308
422-.8 TAN/WHT
12064770
C101
I/P
W/AUTO. TRANS.
440-.8 ORN
440-1.0 ORN
31-.8 TAN
ENGINE
440-1.0 ORN
120-1.0 TAN
FUEL PUMP
(SEE PAGE 87)
422-.8 TAN/BLK
420-.5 PPL
31-.5 TAN
420-.8 PPL
TCC CUTOUT SW
(SEE PAGE 66)
120-1.0 GRA
12020183
C100
TO I/P CONN
(SEE PAGE 142)
12020184
39-.8 PNK/BLK
TO SPLICE S303
(SEE PAGE 64)
W/AUTO. TRANS.
975-.8 DK BLU
924-.8 LT GRN/BLK
BACKUP LAMP
SWITCH
W/MAN. TRANS.
(SEE PAGE 170)
39-.8 PNK/BLK

1988–91 WIRING DIAGRAMS (CONT.)

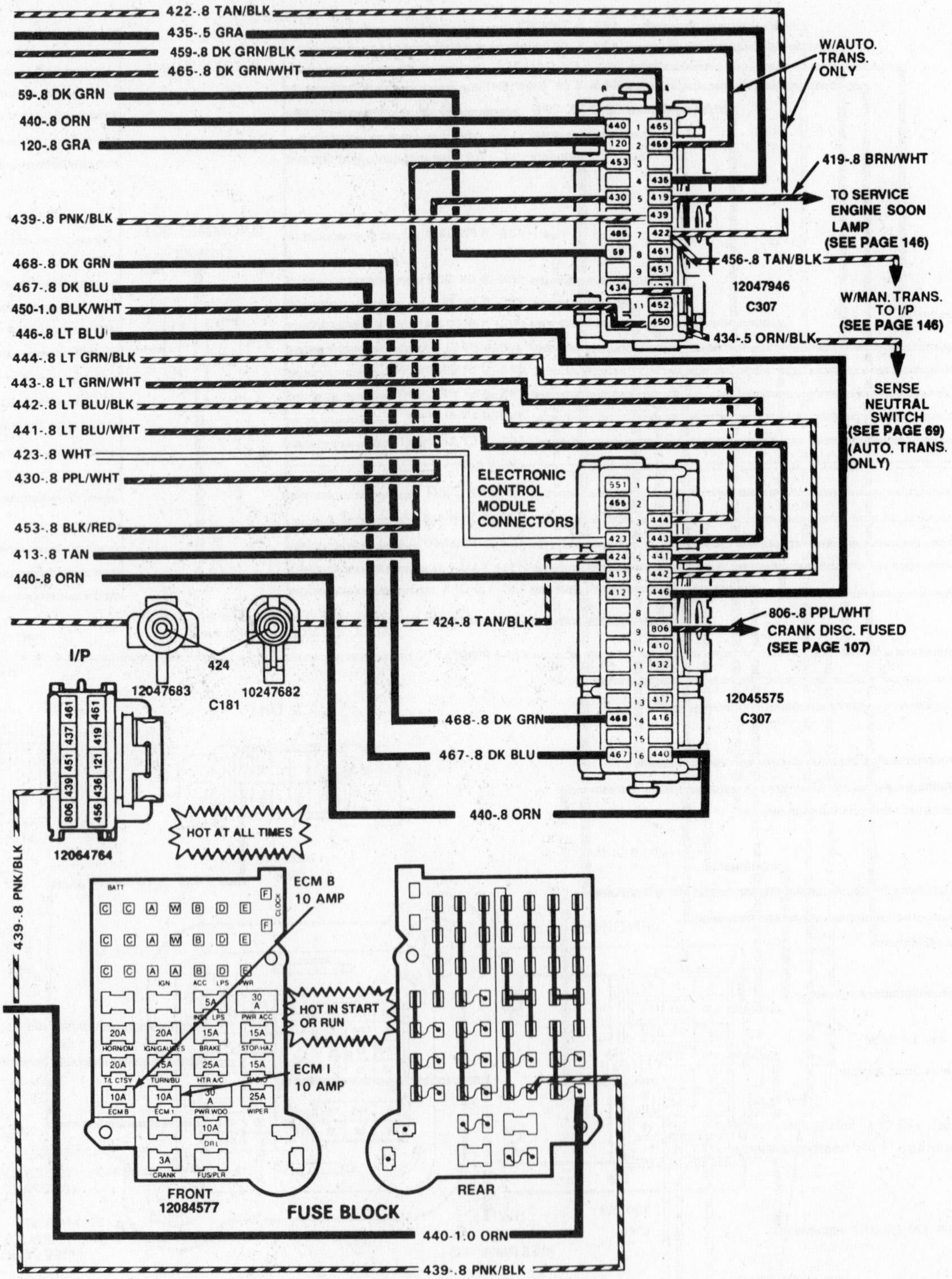
422-.8 TAN/BLK
435-.5 GRA
459-.8 DK GRN/BLK
465-.8 DK GRN/WHT
59-.8 DK GRN
440-.8 ORN
120-.8 GRA
W/AUTO. TRANS. ONLY
419-.8 BRN/WHT
TO SERVICE ENGINE SOON LAMP (SEE PAGE 146)
439-.8 PNK/BLK
456-.8 TAN/BLK
12047946
C307
W/MAN. TRANS. TO I/P (SEE PAGE 146)
434-.5 ORN/BLK
468-.8 DK GRN
467-.8 DK BLU
450-1.0 BLK/WHT
446-.8 LT BLU
444-.8 LT GRN/BLK
443-.8 LT GRN/WHT
442-.8 LT BLU/BLK
441-.8 LT BLU/WHT
423-.8 WHT
430-.8 PPL/WHT
SENSE NEUTRAL SWITCH (SEE PAGE 69) (AUTO. TRANS. ONLY)
ELECTRONIC CONTROL MODULE CONNECTORS
453-.8 BLK/RED
413-.8 TAN
440-.8 ORN
424-.8 TAN/BLK
806-.8 PPL/WHT CRANK DISC. FUSED (SEE PAGE 107)
I/P
424
12047683
C181
10247682
12045575
C307
468-.8 DK GRN
467-.8 DK BLU
440-.8 ORN
12064764
HOT AT ALL TIMES
ECM B 10 AMP
HOT IN START OR RUN
ECM I 10 AMP
439-.8 PNK/BLK
FRONT
12084577
FUSE BLOCK
REAR
440-1.0 ORN
439-.8 PNK/BLK

ELECTRONIC CONTROL MODULE - OUTPUTS - 4.3L (262 CID) ENGINE

1988–91 WIRING DIAGRAMS (CONT.)

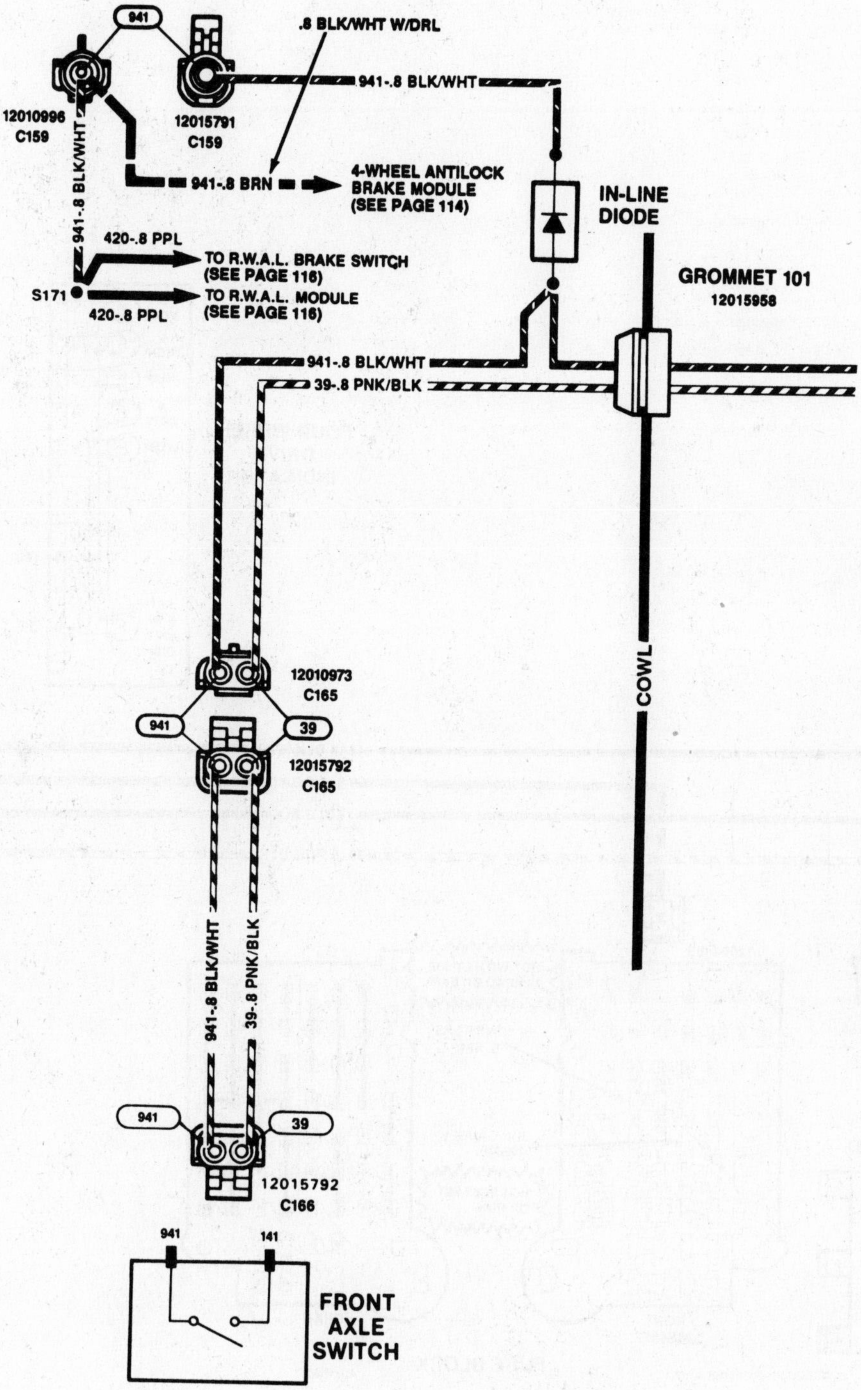
941
.8 BLK/WHT W/DRL
941-.8 BLK/WHT
12010996
C159
12015791
C159
941-.8 BLK/WHT
941-.8 BRN
4-WHEEL ANTILOCK
BRAKE MODULE
(SEE PAGE 114)
IN-LINE
DIODE
420-.8 PPL
TO R.W.A.L. BRAKE SWITCH
(SEE PAGE 116)
S171
TO R.W.A.L. MODULE
(SEE PAGE 116)
420-.8 PPL
GROMMET 101
12015958
941-.8 BLK/WHT
39-.8 PNK/BLK
12010973
C165
941
39
12015792
C165
COWL
941-.8 BLK/WHT
39-.8 PNK/BLK
941
39
12015792
C166
941
141
FRONT
AXLE
SWITCH

1988–91 WIRING DIAGRAMS (CONT.)

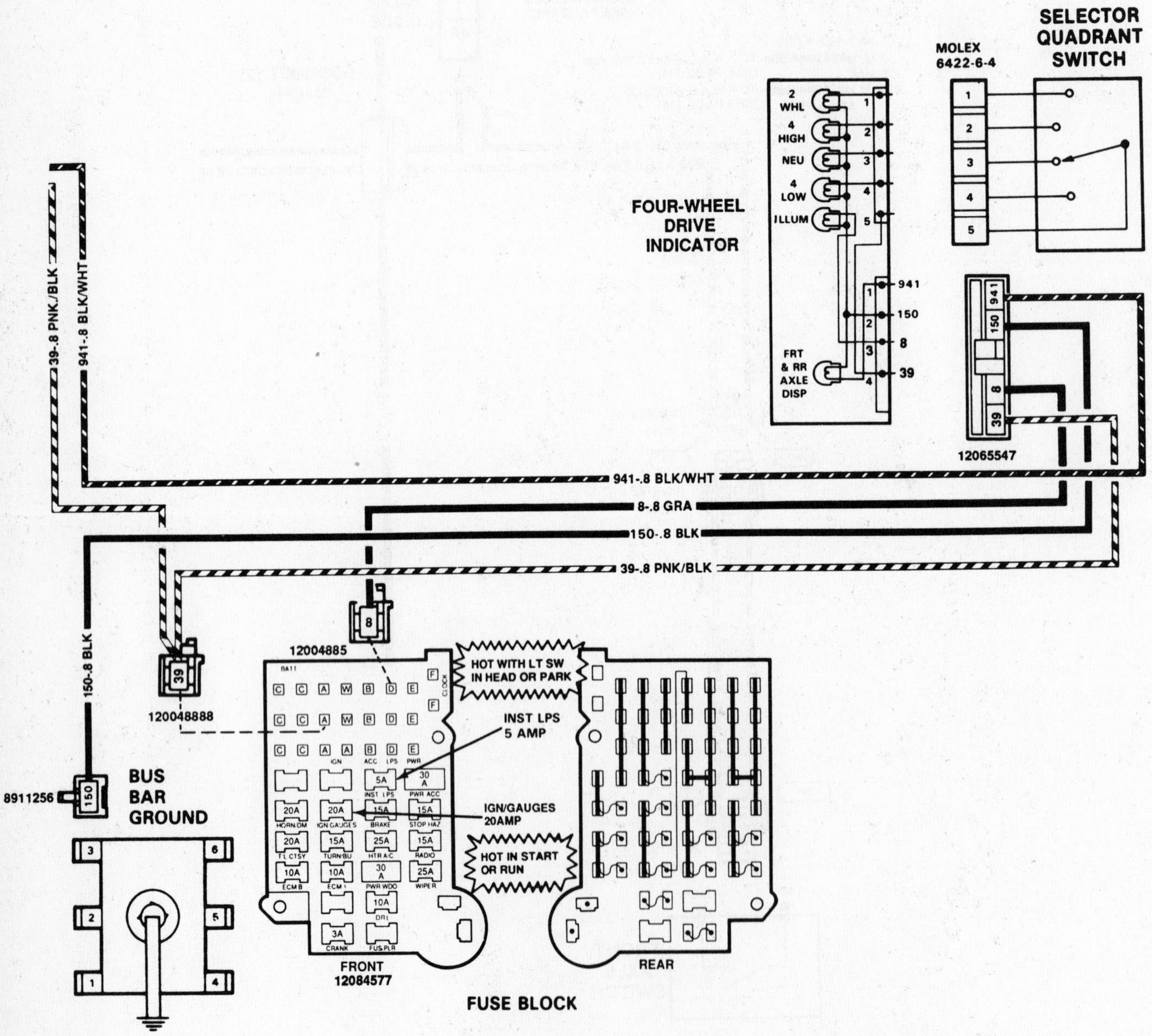
SELECTOR QUADRANT SWITCH
MOLEX 6422-6-4
FOUR-WHEEL DRIVE INDICATOR
2 WHL
4 HIGH
NEU
4 LOW
ILLUM
FRT & RR AXLE DISP
941
150
8
39
12065547
941-.8 BLK/WHT
8-.8 GRA
150-.8 BLK
39-.8 PNK/BLK
39-.8 PNK./BLK
941-.8 BLK/WHT
150-.8 BLK
12004885
120048888
8911256
BUS BAR GROUND
HOT WITH LT SW IN HEAD OR PARK
INST LPS 5 AMP
IGN/GAUGES 20AMP
HOT IN START OR RUN
FRONT 12084577
REAR
FUSE BLOCK

FOUR-WHEEL DRIVE INDICATOR

1988–91 WIRING DIAGRAMS (CONT.)

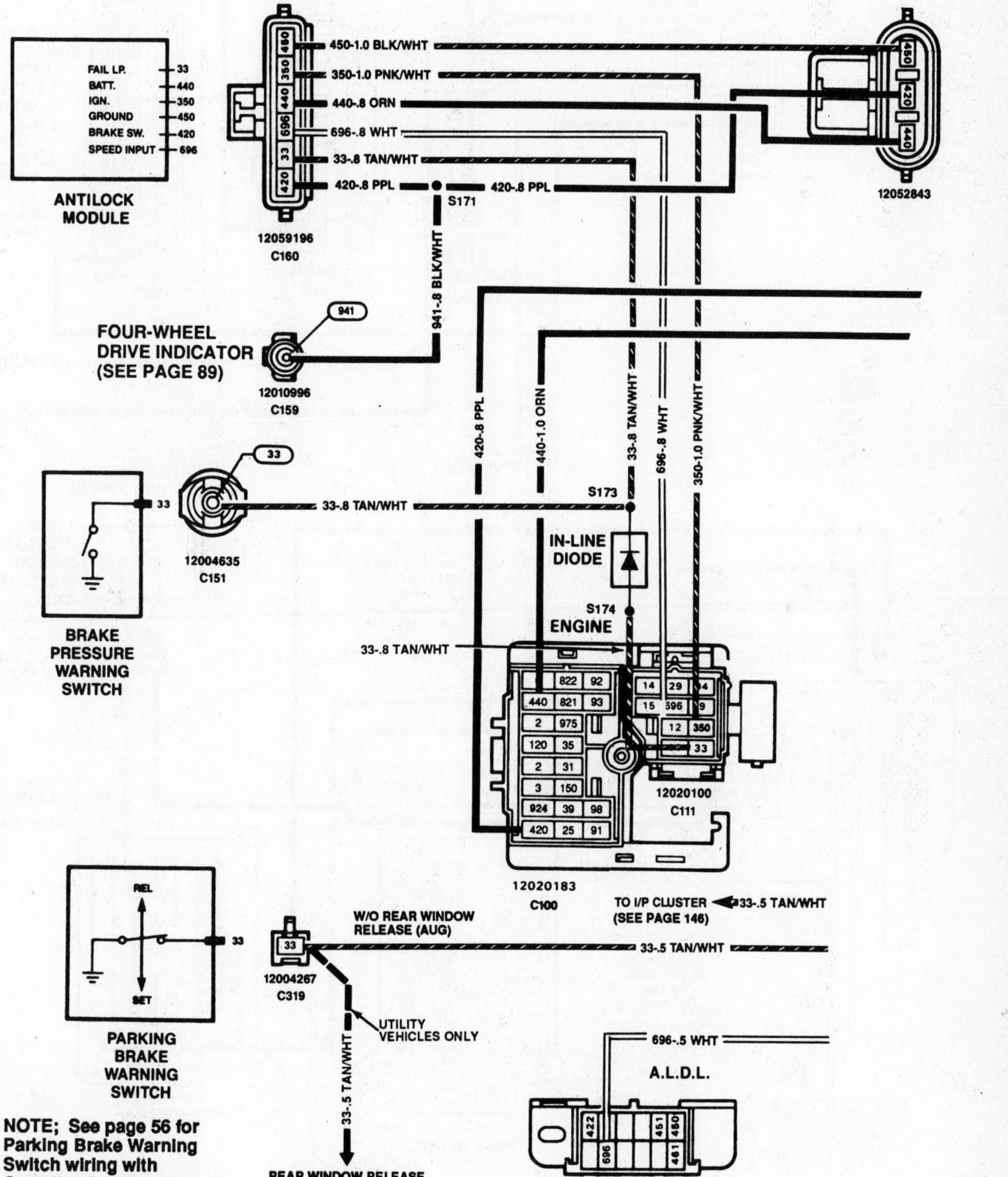

FAIL LP. 33
BATT. 440
IGN. 350
GROUND 450
BRAKE SW. 420
SPEED INPUT 696
ANTILOCK MODULE
12059196
C160
450-1.0 BLK/WHT
350-1.0 PNK/WHT
440-.8 ORN
696-.8 WHT
33-.8 TAN/WHT
420-.8 PPL
S171
420-.8 PPL
12052843
941-.8 BLK/WHT
941
FOUR-WHEEL DRIVE INDICATOR (SEE PAGE 89)
12010996
C159
420-.8 PPL
440-1.0 ORN
33-.8 TAN/WHT
696-.8 WHT
350-1.0 PNK/WHT
33
33
33-.8 TAN/WHT
S173
12004635
C151
IN-LINE DIODE
S174
ENGINE
BRAKE PRESSURE WARNING SWITCH
33-.8 TAN/WHT
12020100
C111
12020183
C100
REL
SET
33
33
PARKING BRAKE WARNING SWITCH
12004267
C319
W/O REAR WINDOW RELEASE (AUG)
33-.5 TAN/WHT
TO I/P CLUSTER
(SEE PAGE 146)
33-.5 TAN/WHT
UTILITY VEHICLES ONLY
33-.5 TAN/WHT
REAR WINDOW RELEASE RELAY (SEE PAGE 206)
696-.5 WHT
A.L.D.L.
12020043
C308

NOTE; See page 56 for Parking Brake Warning Switch wiring with Canadian Daytime Running Lamps.

REAR WHEEL ANTILOCK BRAKE WARNING SYSTEM

1988–91 WIRING DIAGRAMS (CONT.)

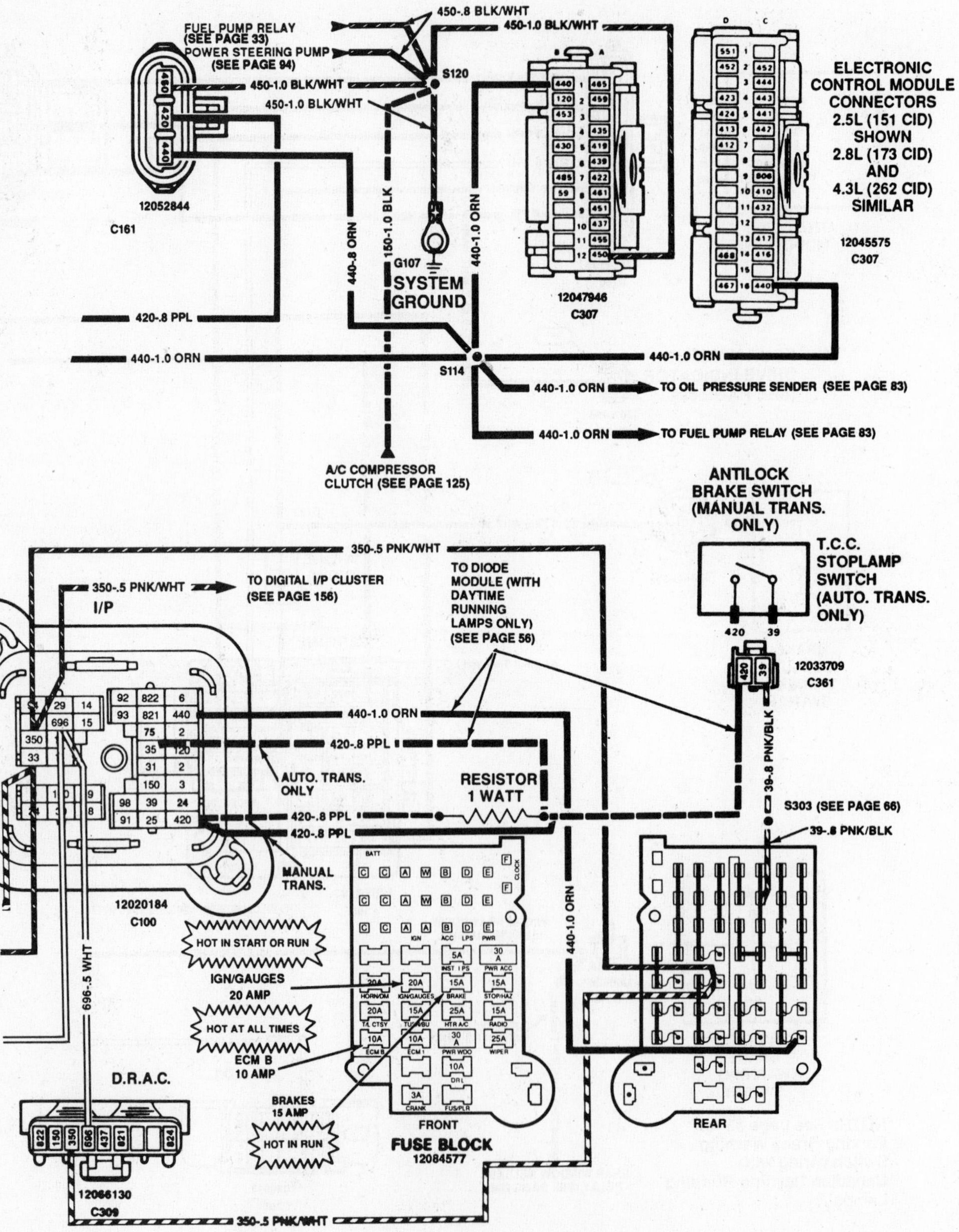

FUEL PUMP RELAY
(SEE PAGE 33)
POWER STEERING PUMP
(SEE PAGE 94)
450-.8 BLK/WHT
450-1.0 BLK/WHT
450-1.0 BLK/WHT
450-1.0 BLK/WHT
S120
12052844
C161
440-.8 ORN
150-1.0 BLK
G107
SYSTEM GROUND
440-1.0 ORN
12047946
C307
ELECTRONIC CONTROL MODULE CONNECTORS
2.5L (151 CID) SHOWN
2.8L (173 CID) AND 4.3L (262 CID) SIMILAR
12045575
C307
420-.8 PPL
440-1.0 ORN
S114
440-1.0 ORN
440-1.0 ORN
TO OIL PRESSURE SENDER (SEE PAGE 83)
440-1.0 ORN
TO FUEL PUMP RELAY (SEE PAGE 83)
A/C COMPRESSOR CLUTCH (SEE PAGE 125)
ANTILOCK BRAKE SWITCH (MANUAL TRANS. ONLY)
T.C.C. STOPLAMP SWITCH (AUTO. TRANS. ONLY)
350-.5 PNK/WHT
350-.5 PNK/WHT
TO DIGITAL I/P CLUSTER (SEE PAGE 156)
I/P
TO DIODE MODULE (WITH DAYTIME RUNNING LAMPS ONLY) (SEE PAGE 56)
12033709
C361
440-1.0 ORN
420-.8 PPL
AUTO. TRANS. ONLY
RESISTOR 1 WATT
420-.8 PPL
420-.8 PPL
39-.8 PNK/BLK
S303 (SEE PAGE 66)
39-.8 PNK/BLK
MANUAL TRANS.
12020184
C100
HOT IN START OR RUN
IGN/GAUGES 20 AMP
HOT AT ALL TIMES
ECM B 10 AMP
BRAKES 15 AMP
HOT IN RUN
696-.5 WHT
440-1.0 ORN
D.R.A.C.
12066130
C309
350-.5 PNK/WHT
FRONT
FUSE BLOCK
12084577
REAR

1988–91 WIRING DIAGRAMS (CONT.)

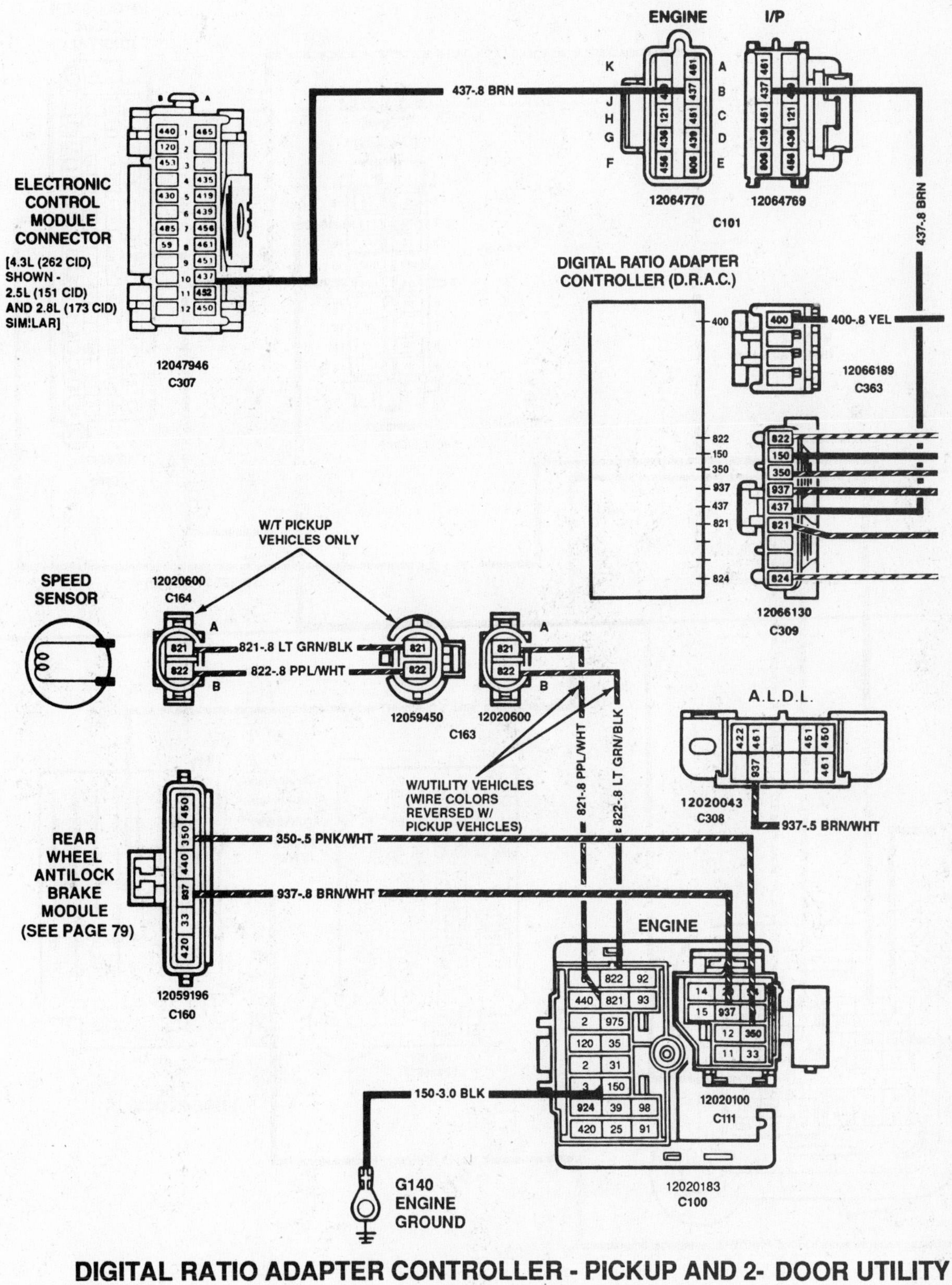

ENGINE
I/P
K
J
H
G
F
A
B
C
D
E
12064770
12064769
C101
437-.8 BRN
ELECTRONIC CONTROL MODULE CONNECTOR
[4.3L (262 CID) SHOWN - 2.5L (151 CID) AND 2.8L (173 CID) SIMILAR]
12047946
C307
DIGITAL RATIO ADAPTER CONTROLLER (D.R.A.C.)
400-.8 YEL
12066189
C363
12066130
C309
W/T PICKUP VEHICLES ONLY
SPEED SENSOR
12020600
C164
821-.8 LT GRN/BLK
822-.8 PPL/WHT
12059450
12020600
C163
W/UTILITY VEHICLES (WIRE COLORS REVERSED W/ PICKUP VEHICLES)
821-.8 PPL/WHT
822-.8 LT GRN/BLK
A.L.D.L.
12020043
C308
937-.5 BRN/WHT
REAR WHEEL ANTILOCK BRAKE MODULE (SEE PAGE 79)
350-.5 PNK/WHT
937-.8 BRN/WHT
12059196
C160
ENGINE
12020100
C111
150-3.0 BLK
G140 ENGINE GROUND
12020183
C100

DIGITAL RATIO ADAPTER CONTROLLER - PICKUP AND 2- DOOR UTILITY

1988–91 WIRING DIAGRAMS (CONT.)

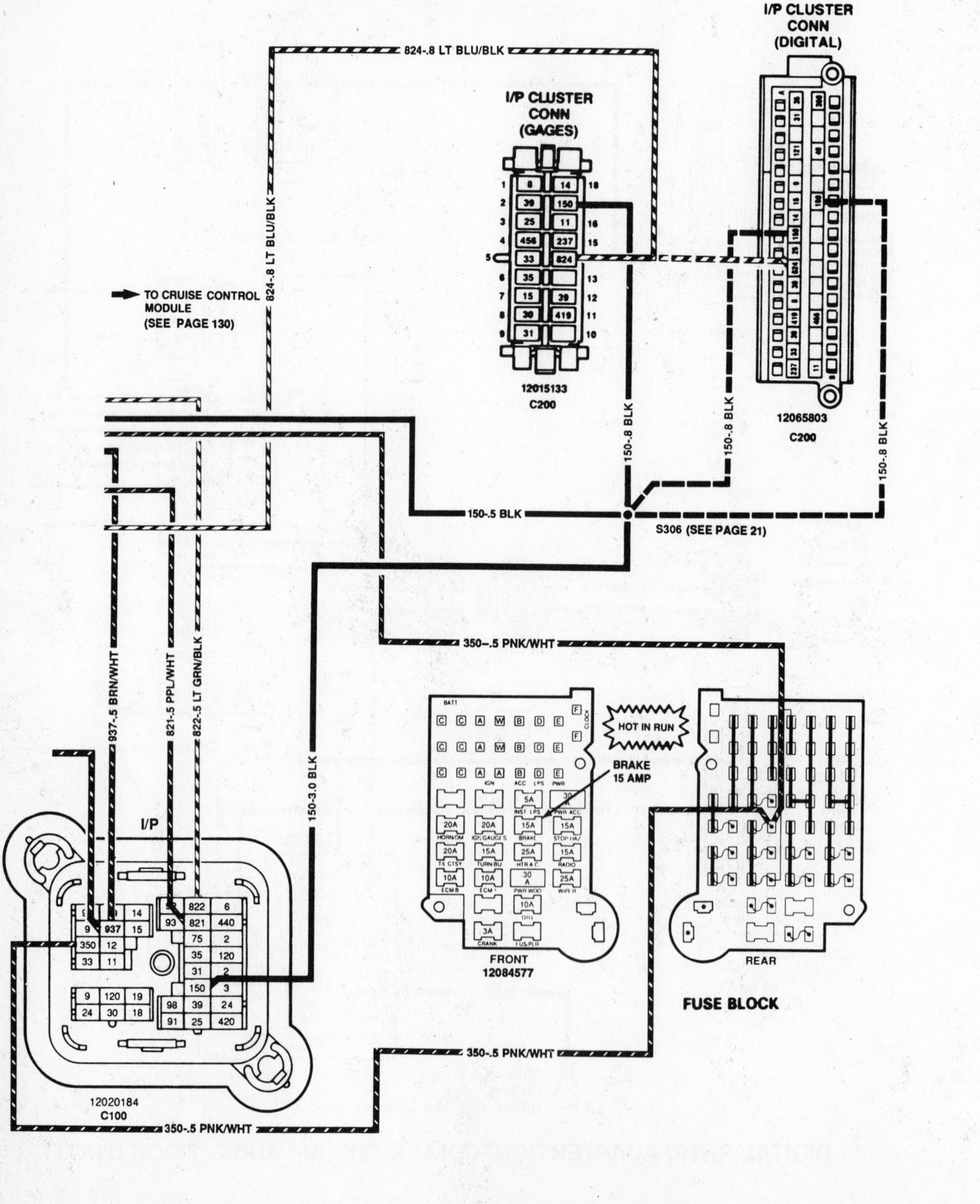
I/P CLUSTER CONN (DIGITAL)
824-.8 LT BLU/BLK
I/P CLUSTER CONN (GAGES)
TO CRUISE CONTROL MODULE (SEE PAGE 130)
824-.8 LT BLU/BLK
12015133
C200
12065803
C200
150-.8 BLK
150-.8 BLK
150-.8 BLK
150-.5 BLK
S306 (SEE PAGE 21)
350-.5 PNK/WHT
937-.5 BRN/WHT
821-.5 PPL/WHT
822-.5 LT GRN/BLK
150-3.0 BLK
I/P
HOT IN RUN
BRAKE 15 AMP
FRONT
12084577
REAR
FUSE BLOCK
350-.5 PNK/WHT
12020184
C100
350-.5 PNK/WHT

1988–91 WIRING DIAGRAMS (CONT.)

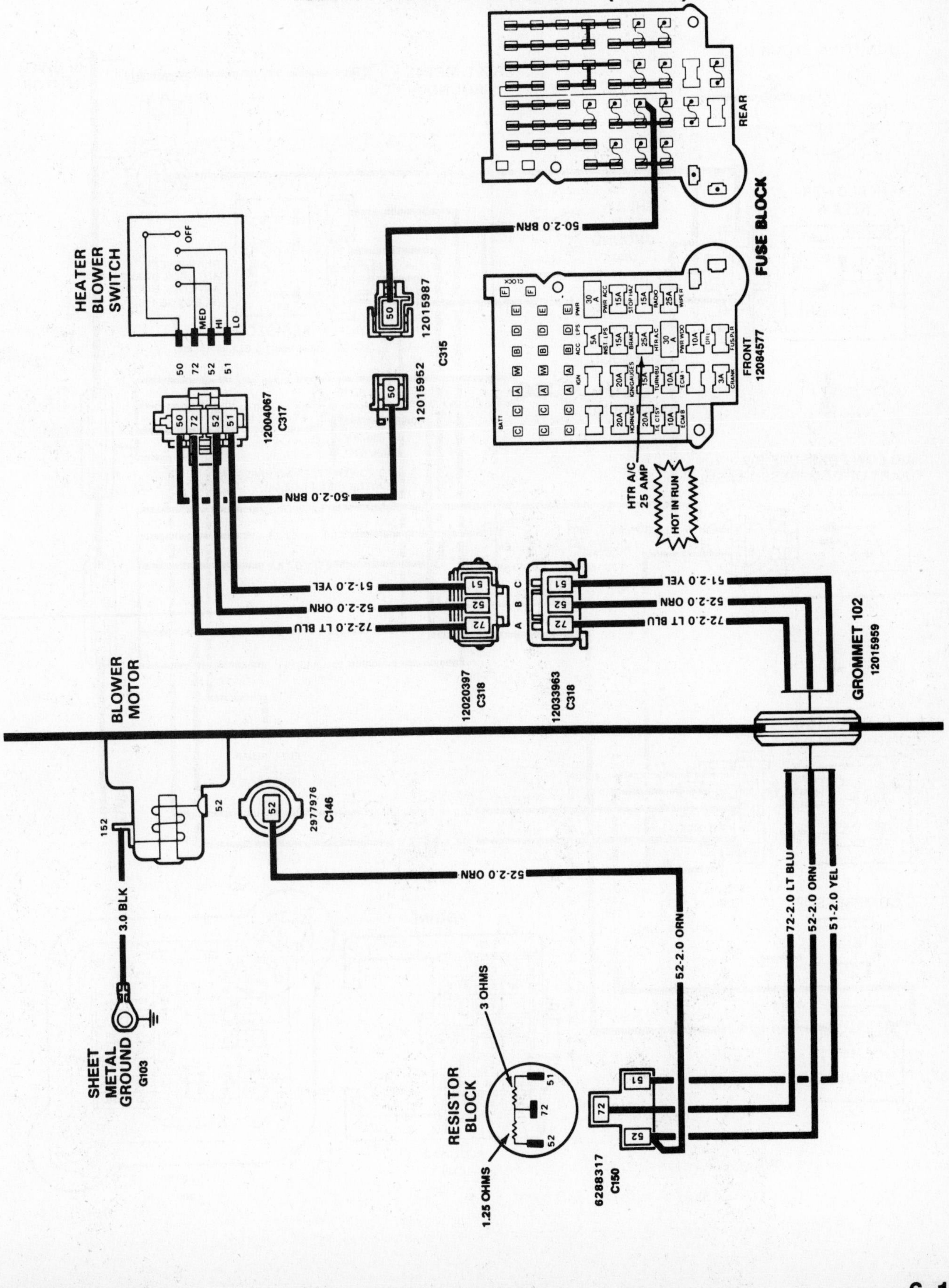
HEATER BLOWER SWITCH
OFF
MED
HI
LO
50
72
52
51
12004067
C317
12015952
12015987
C315
50-2.0 BRN
REAR
FUSE BLOCK
FRONT
12084577
HTR A/C
25 AMP
HOT IN RUN
51-2.0 YEL
52-2.0 ORN
72-2.0 LT BLU
12020397
C318
12033963
C318
GROMMET 102
12015959
BLOWER MOTOR
152
2977976
C146
3.0 BLK
SHEET METAL GROUND
G103
52-2.0 ORN
RESISTOR BLOCK
3 OHMS
1.25 OHMS
6288317
C150

1988–91 WIRING DIAGRAMS (CONT.)

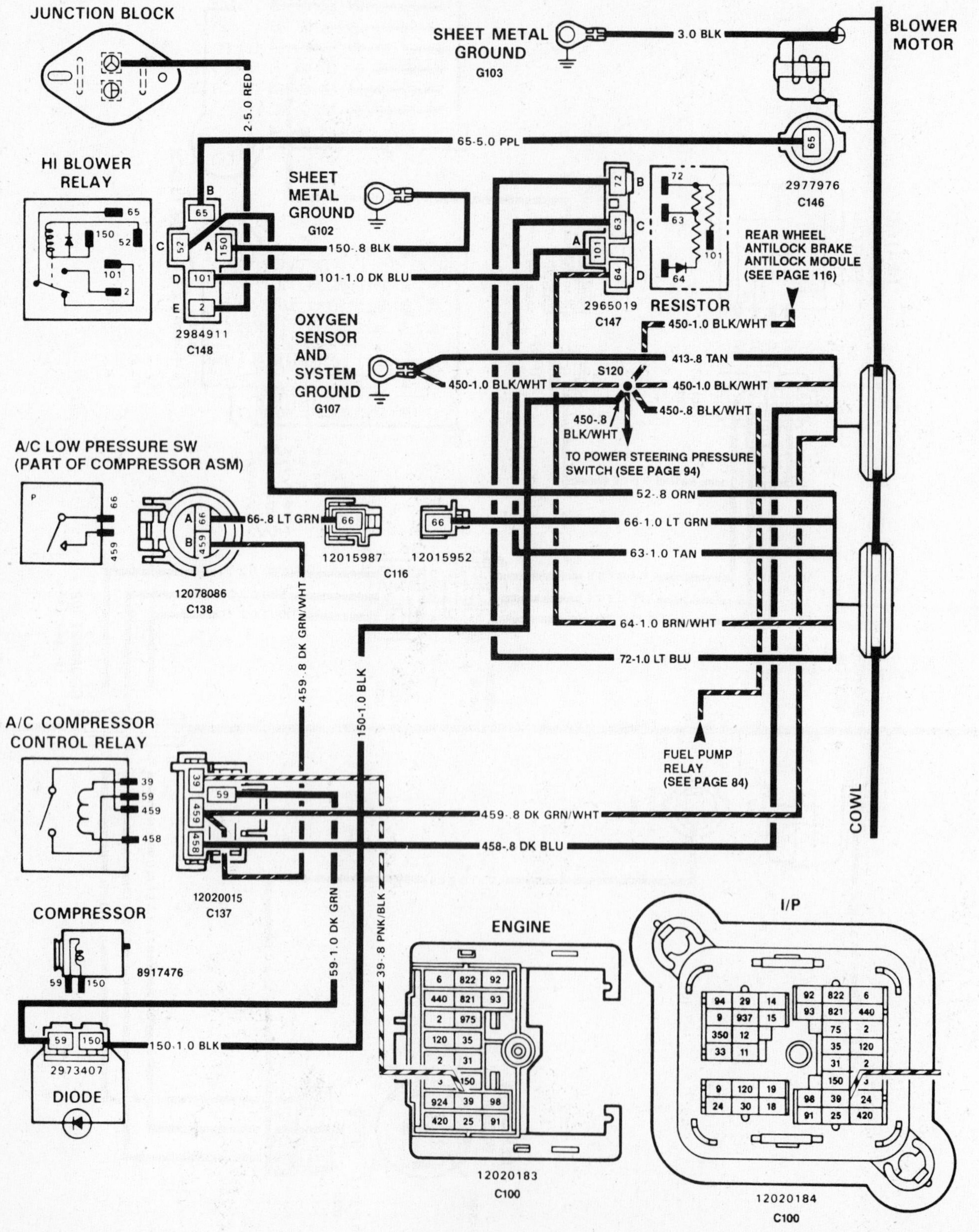
JUNCTION BLOCK
2-5.0 RED
SHEET METAL GROUND
G103
3.0 BLK
BLOWER MOTOR
HI BLOWER RELAY
65-5.0 PPL
2977976
C146
SHEET METAL GROUND
G102
150-.8 BLK
101-1.0 DK BLU
2984911
C148
2965019
C147
RESISTOR
REAR WHEEL ANTILOCK BRAKE ANTILOCK MODULE (SEE PAGE 116)
450-1.0 BLK/WHT
OXYGEN SENSOR AND SYSTEM GROUND
G107
413-.8 TAN
S120
450-1.0 BLK/WHT
450-.8 BLK/WHT
450-.8 BLK/WHT
TO POWER STEERING PRESSURE SWITCH (SEE PAGE 94)
A/C LOW PRESSURE SW (PART OF COMPRESSOR ASM)
52-.8 ORN
66-.8 LT GRN
66-1.0 LT GRN
63-1.0 TAN
12078086
C138
12015987
12015952
C116
64-1.0 BRN/WHT
72-1.0 LT BLU
459-.8 DK GRN/WHT
150-1.0 BLK
FUEL PUMP RELAY (SEE PAGE 84)
A/C COMPRESSOR CONTROL RELAY
459-.8 DK GRN/WHT
458-.8 DK BLU
COWL
12020015
C137
COMPRESSOR
8917476
59-1.0 DK GRN
39-.8 PNK/BLK
150-1.0 BLK
2973407
DIODE
ENGINE
12020183
C100
I/P
12020184
C100

1988–91 WIRING DIAGRAMS (CONT.)

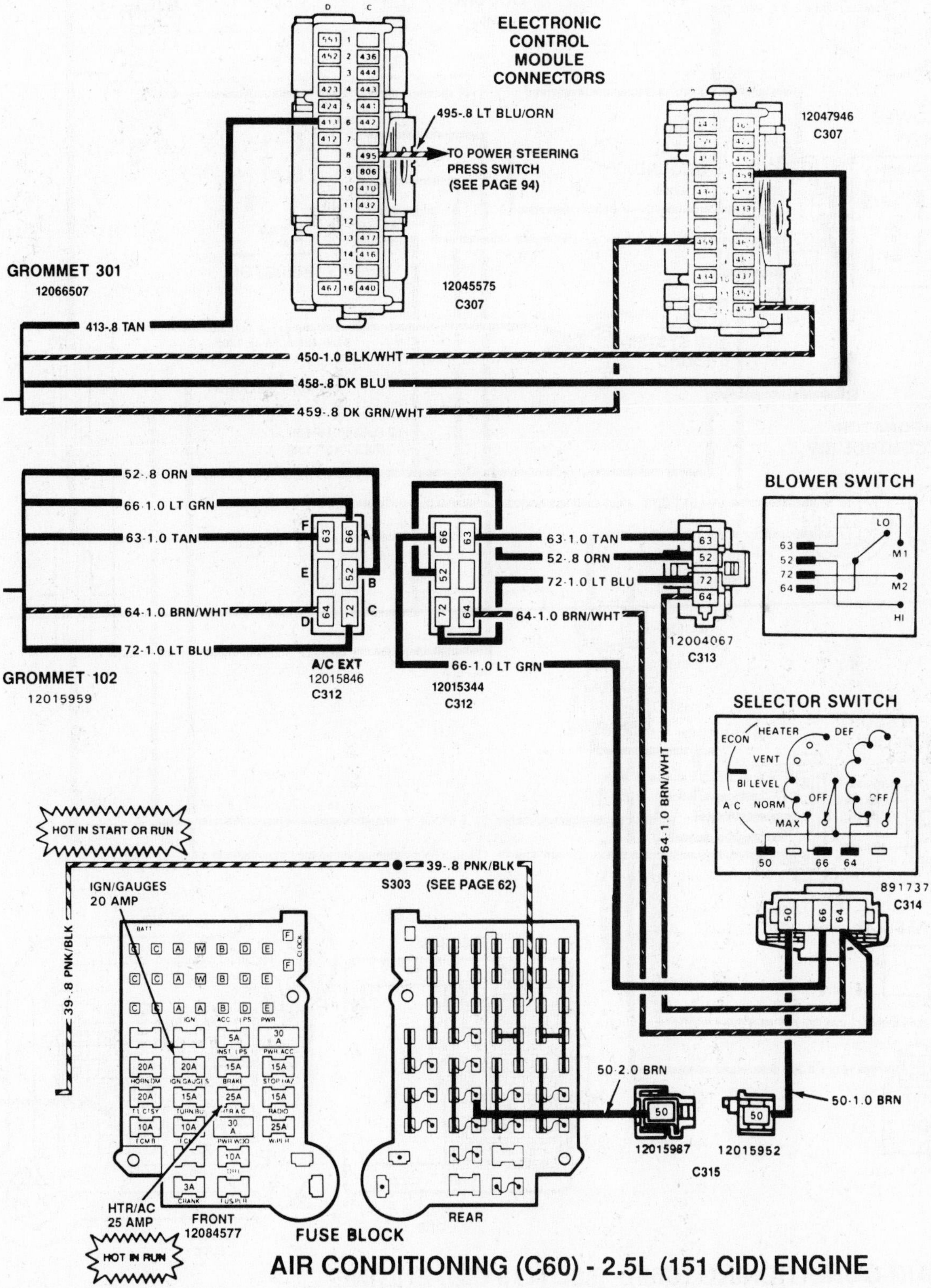
ELECTRONIC CONTROL MODULE CONNECTORS
495-.8 LT BLU/ORN
TO POWER STEERING PRESS SWITCH (SEE PAGE 94)
12047946 C307
12045575 C307
GROMMET 301
12066507
413-.8 TAN
450-1.0 BLK/WHT
458-.8 DK BLU
459-.8 DK GRN/WHT
52-.8 ORN
66-1.0 LT GRN
63-1.0 TAN
64-1.0 BRN/WHT
72-1.0 LT BLU
GROMMET 102
12015959
A/C EXT
12015846
C312
12015344
C312
BLOWER SWITCH
LO
M1
M2
HI
12004067
C313
SELECTOR SWITCH
ECON
HEATER
DEF
VENT
BI LEVEL
A C
NORM
MAX
OFF
89 17372
C314
64-1.0 BRN/WHT
HOT IN START OR RUN
39-.8 PNK/BLK
S303
(SEE PAGE 62)
IGN/GAUGES 20 AMP
50-2.0 BRN
50-1.0 BRN
12015987
12015952
C315
HTR/AC 25 AMP
HOT IN RUN
FRONT
12084577
REAR
FUSE BLOCK

AIR CONDITIONING (C60) - 2.5L (151 CID) ENGINE

1988–91 WIRING DIAGRAMS (CONT.)

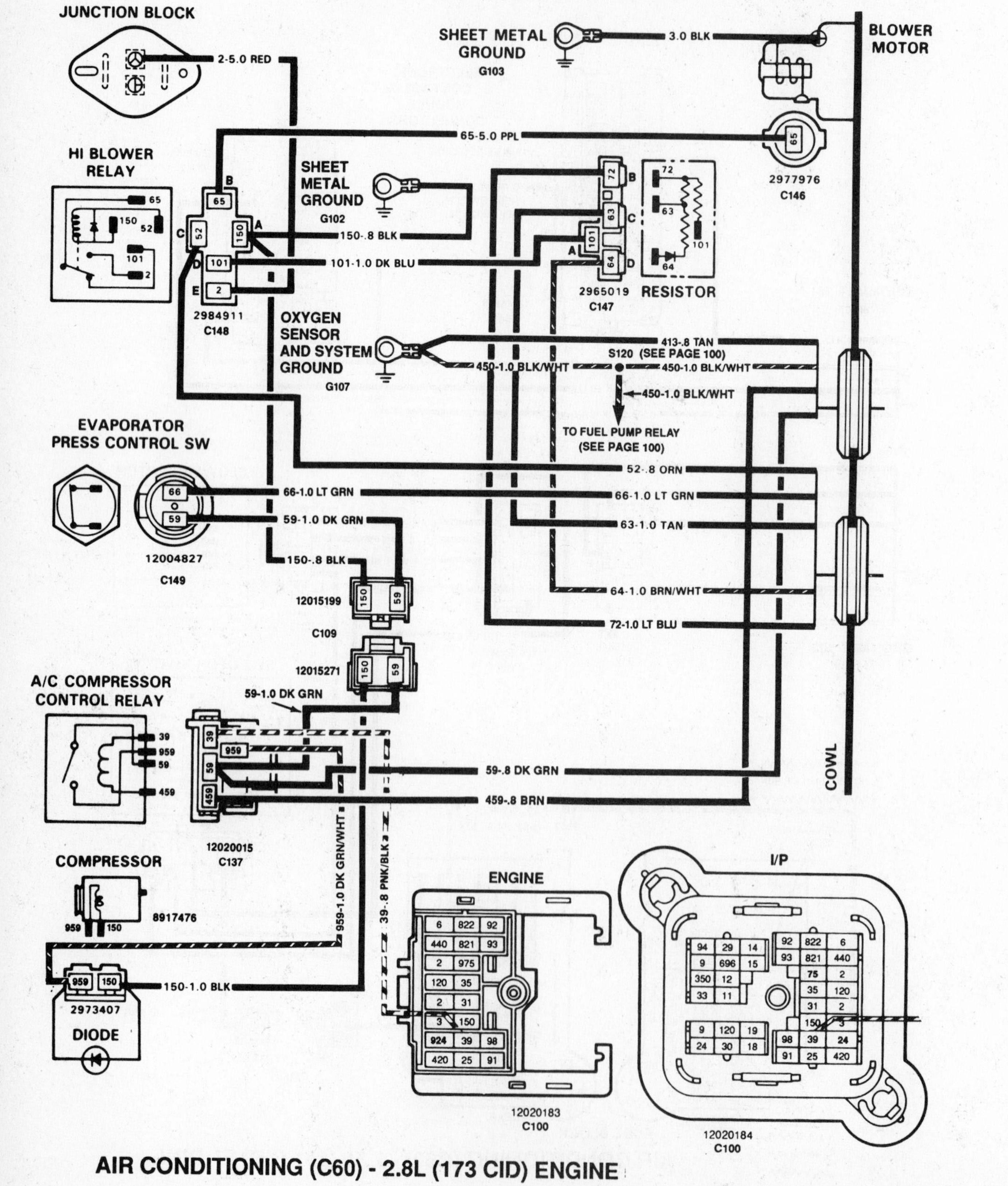
JUNCTION BLOCK
2-5.0 RED
SHEET METAL GROUND
G103
3.0 BLK
BLOWER MOTOR
HI BLOWER RELAY
65-5.0 PPL
2977976
C146
SHEET METAL GROUND
G102
150-.8 BLK
101-1.0 DK BLU
2984911
C148
2965019
C147
RESISTOR
OXYGEN SENSOR AND SYSTEM GROUND
G107
413-.8 TAN
S120 (SEE PAGE 100)
450-1.0 BLK/WHT
TO FUEL PUMP RELAY (SEE PAGE 100)
EVAPORATOR PRESS CONTROL SW
52-.8 ORN
66-1.0 LT GRN
59-1.0 DK GRN
63-1.0 TAN
12004827
C149
150-.8 BLK
12015199
C109
64-1.0 BRN/WHT
72-1.0 LT BLU
12015271
A/C COMPRESSOR CONTROL RELAY
59-1.0 DK GRN
59-.8 DK GRN
459-.8 BRN
COWL
12020015
C137
COMPRESSOR
8917476
959-1.0 DK GRN/WHT
39-.8 PNK/BLK
150-1.0 BLK
2973407
DIODE
ENGINE
I/P
12020183
C100
12020184
C100

AIR CONDITIONING (C60) - 2.8L (173 CID) ENGINE

1988–91 WIRING DIAGRAMS (CONT.)

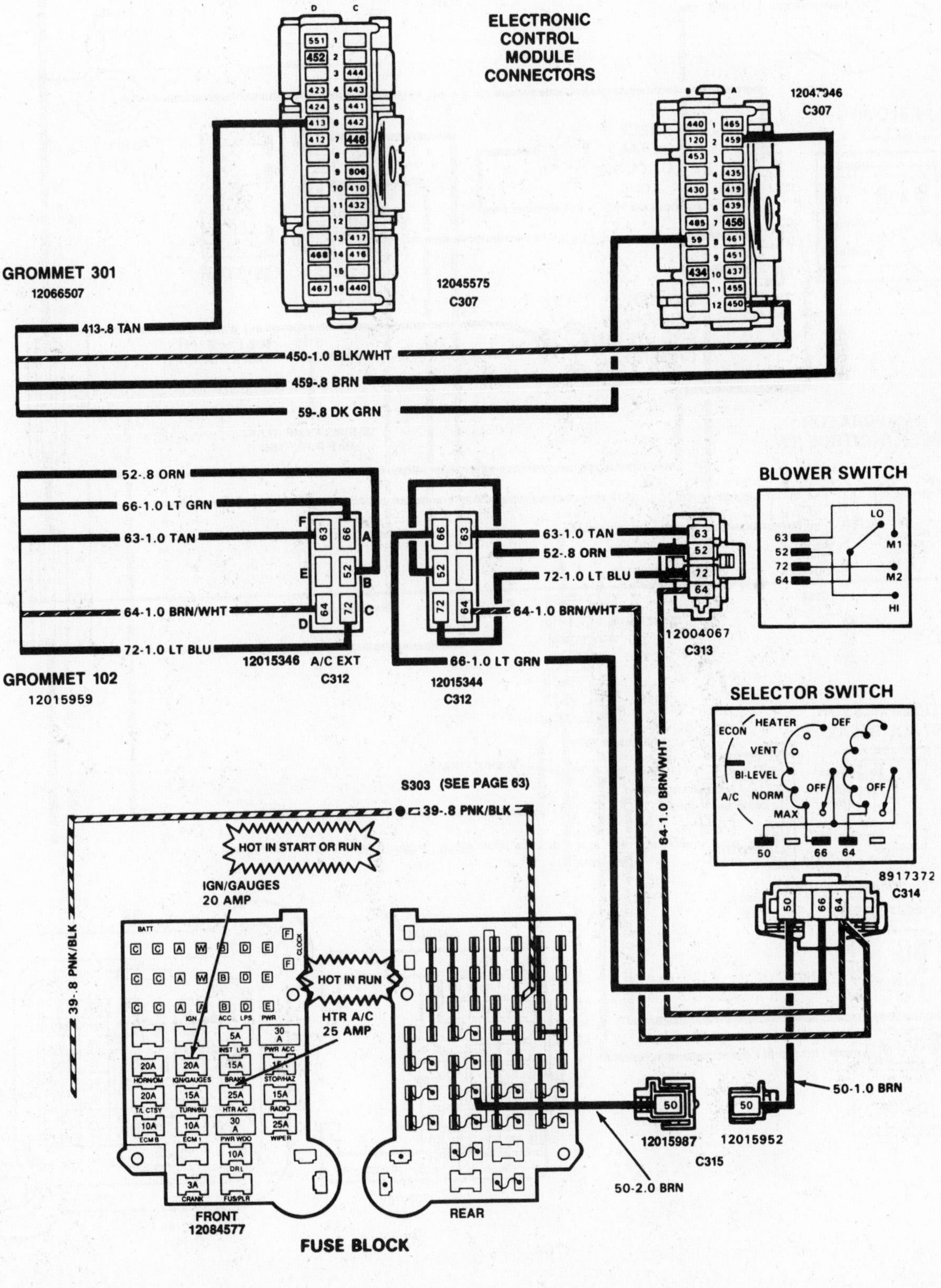
ELECTRONIC CONTROL MODULE CONNECTORS
12045575
C307
12047946
C307
GROMMET 301
12066507
413-.8 TAN
450-1.0 BLK/WHT
459-.8 BRN
59-.8 DK GRN
52-.8 ORN
66-1.0 LT GRN
63-1.0 TAN
64-1.0 BRN/WHT
72-1.0 LT BLU
GROMMET 102
12015959
12015346 A/C EXT
C312
12015344
C312
BLOWER SWITCH
LO
M1
M2
HI
12004067
C313
SELECTOR SWITCH
ECON
HEATER
DEF
VENT
BI-LEVEL
A/C
NORM
MAX
OFF
8917372
C314
S303 (SEE PAGE 63)
39-.8 PNK/BLK
HOT IN START OR RUN
IGN/GAUGES
20 AMP
HOT IN RUN
HTR A/C
25 AMP
64-1.0 BRN/WHT
50-1.0 BRN
12015987
12015952
C315
50-2.0 BRN
FRONT
12084577
REAR
FUSE BLOCK

1988–91 WIRING DIAGRAMS (CONT.)

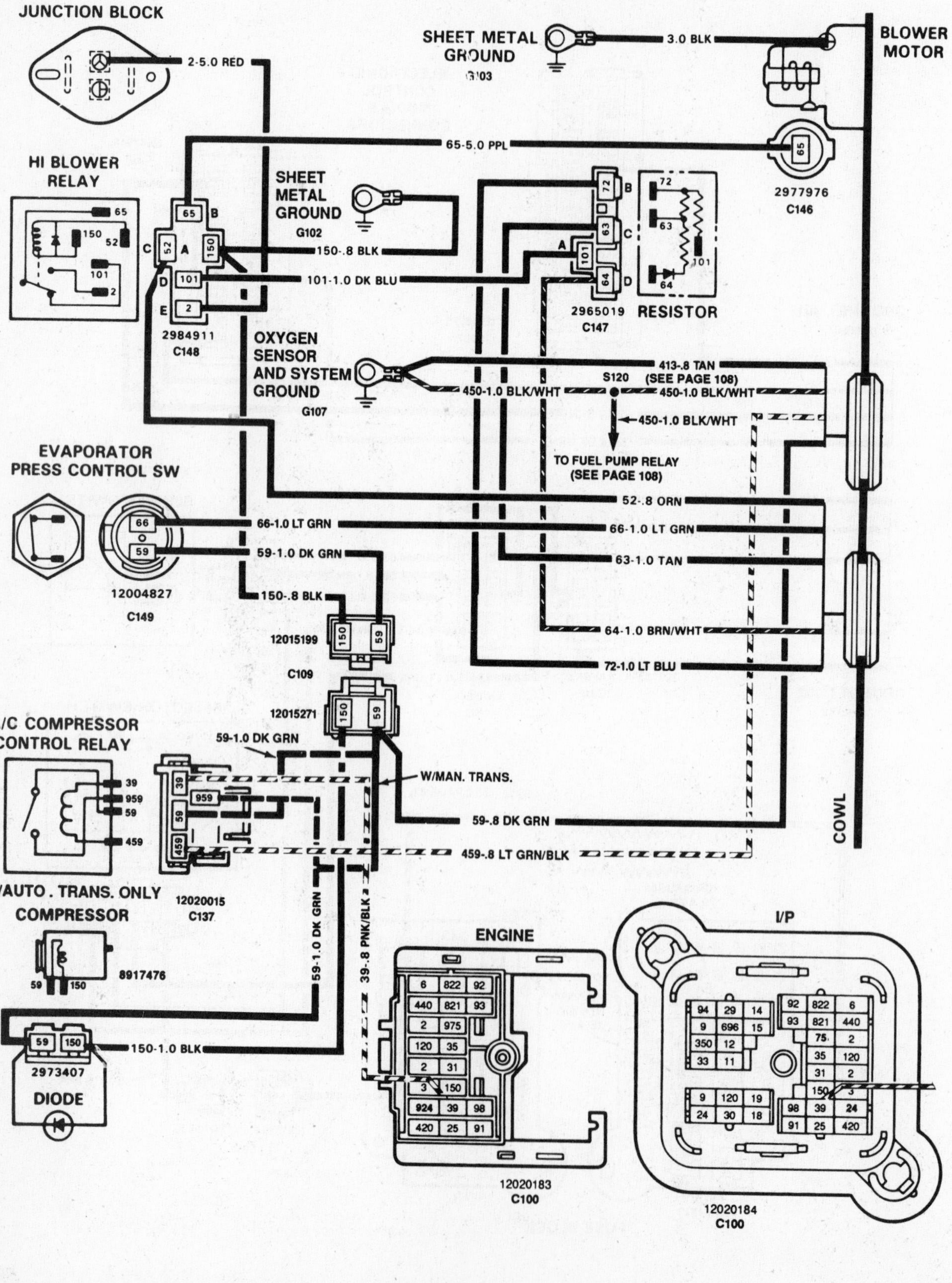
JUNCTION BLOCK
2-5.0 RED
SHEET METAL GROUND
G103
3.0 BLK
BLOWER MOTOR
HI BLOWER RELAY
65-5.0 PPL
2977976
C146
SHEET METAL GROUND
G102
150-.8 BLK
101-1.0 DK BLU
2984911
C148
2965019
C147
RESISTOR
OXYGEN SENSOR AND SYSTEM GROUND
G107
413-.8 TAN
(SEE PAGE 108)
S120
450-1.0 BLK/WHT
450-1.0 BLK/WHT
450-1.0 BLK/WHT
TO FUEL PUMP RELAY
(SEE PAGE 108)
EVAPORATOR PRESS CONTROL SW
52-.8 ORN
66-1.0 LT GRN
66-1.0 LT GRN
59-1.0 DK GRN
63-1.0 TAN
12004827
C149
150-.8 BLK
12015199
64-1.0 BRN/WHT
72-1.0 LT BLU
C109
12015271
A/C COMPRESSOR CONTROL RELAY
59-1.0 DK GRN
W/MAN. TRANS.
59-.8 DK GRN
COWL
459-.8 LT GRN/BLK
W/AUTO. TRANS. ONLY
12020015
C137
COMPRESSOR
8917476
59-1.0 DK GRN
39-.8 PNK/BLK
ENGINE
I/P
150-1.0 BLK
2973407
DIODE
12020183
C100
12020184
C100

1988–91 WIRING DIAGRAMS (CONT.)

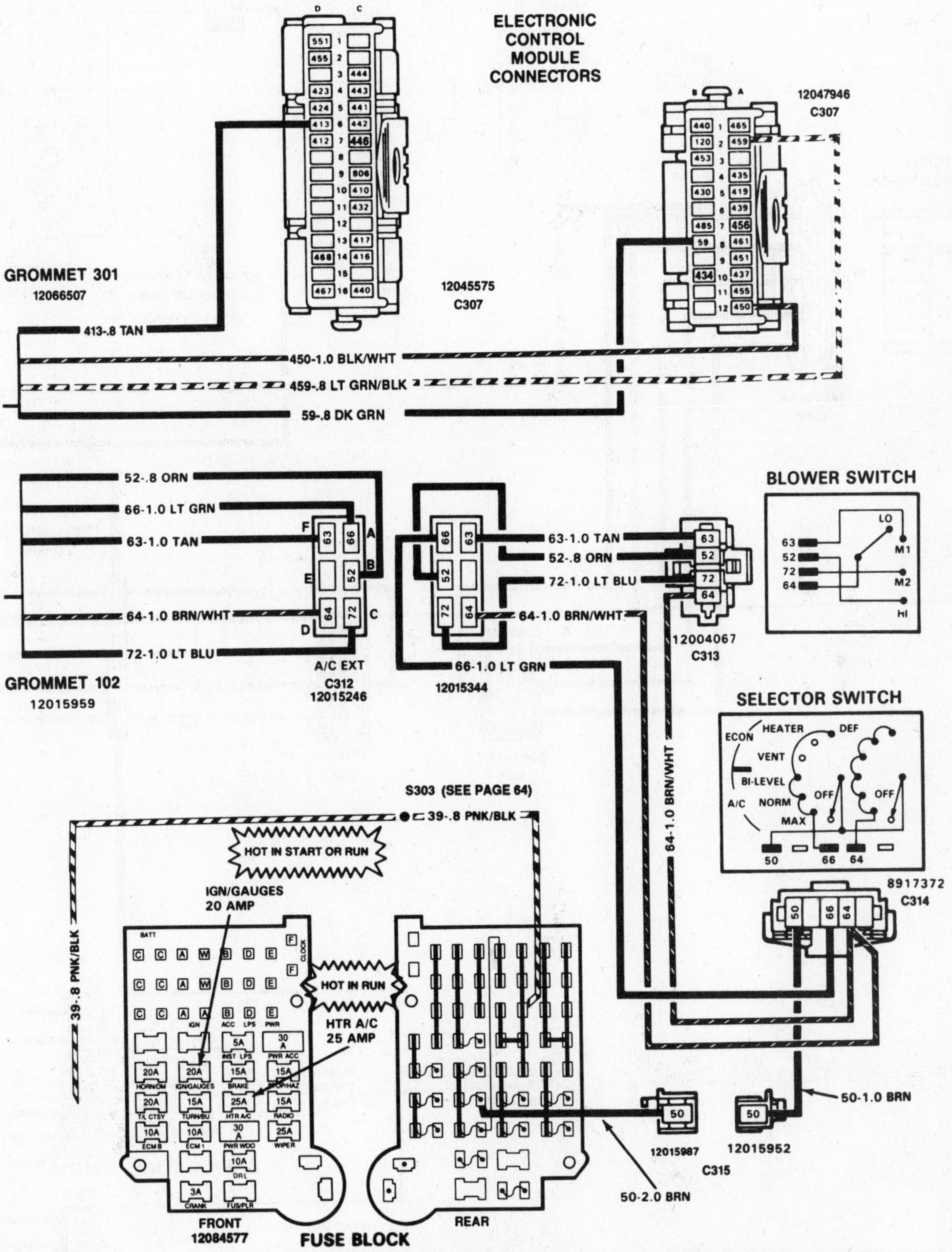
ELECTRONIC CONTROL MODULE CONNECTORS
12045575
C307
12047946
C307
GROMMET 301
12066507
413-.8 TAN
450-1.0 BLK/WHT
459-.8 LT GRN/BLK
59-.8 DK GRN
52-.8 ORN
66-1.0 LT GRN
63-1.0 TAN
64-1.0 BRN/WHT
72-1.0 LT BLU
GROMMET 102
12015959
A/C EXT
C312
12015246
12015344
BLOWER SWITCH
LO
M1
M2
HI
12004067
C313
SELECTOR SWITCH
ECON
HEATER
DEF
VENT
BI-LEVEL
A/C
NORM
MAX
OFF
8917372
C314
S303 (SEE PAGE 64)
39-.8 PNK/BLK
HOT IN START OR RUN
IGN/GAUGES 20 AMP
HOT IN RUN
HTR A/C 25 AMP
50-1.0 BRN
12015987
12015952
C315
50-2.0 BRN
FRONT
12084577
REAR
FUSE BLOCK

AIR CONDITIONING (C60) - 4.3L (262 CID) ENGINE

1988–91 WIRING DIAGRAMS (CONT.)

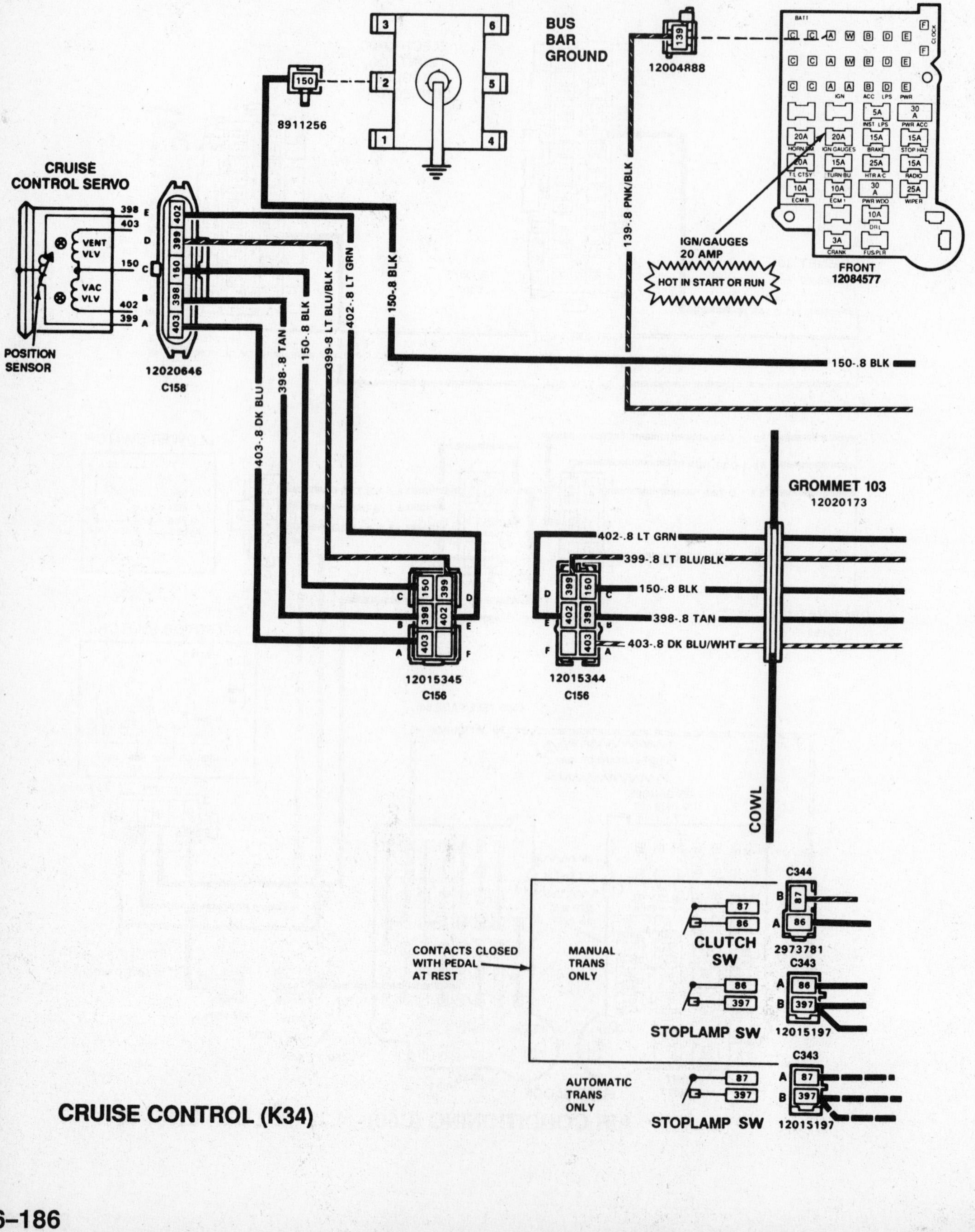
BUS
BAR
GROUND
12004888
8911256
CRUISE
CONTROL SERVO
VENT
VLV
VAC
VLV
POSITION
SENSOR
12020646
C158
139-.8 PNK/BLK
150-.8 BLK
402-.8 LT GRN
399-.8 LT BLU/BLK
150-.8 BLK
398-.8 TAN
403-.8 DK BLU
IGN/GAUGES
20 AMP
HOT IN START OR RUN
FRONT
12084577
GROMMET 103
12020173
402-.8 LT GRN
399-.8 LT BLU/BLK
150-.8 BLK
398-.8 TAN
403-.8 DK BLU/WHT
12015345
C156
12015344
C156
COWL
C344
CLUTCH
SW
2973781
C343
CONTACTS CLOSED
WITH PEDAL
AT REST
MANUAL
TRANS
ONLY
STOPLAMP SW
12015197
C343
AUTOMATIC
TRANS
ONLY
STOPLAMP SW
12015197

CRUISE CONTROL (K34)

1988–91 WIRING DIAGRAMS (CONT.)

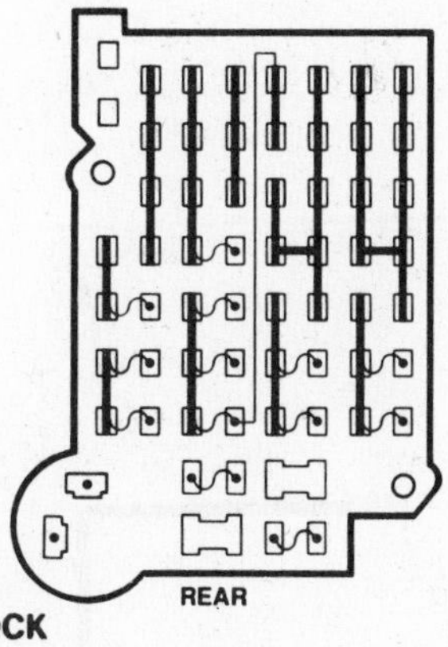
REAR

FUSE BLOCK

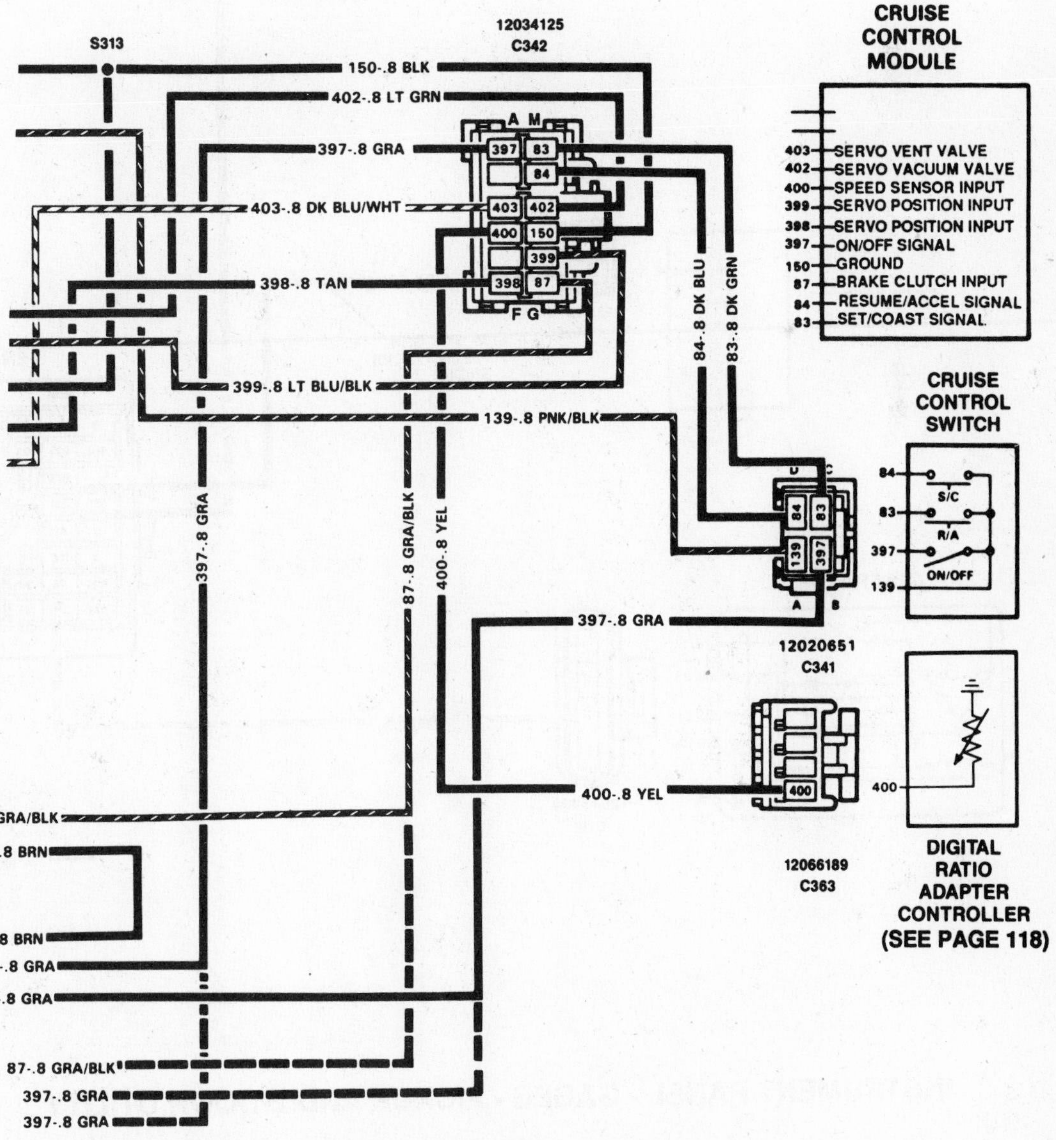
S313
12034125
C342
150-.8 BLK
402-.8 LT GRN
397-.8 GRA
403-.8 DK BLU/WHT
398-.8 TAN
399-.8 LT BLU/BLK
139-.8 PNK/BLK
84-.8 DK BLU
83-.8 DK GRN
397-.8 GRA
87-.8 GRA/BLK
400-.8 YEL
CRUISE CONTROL MODULE
403 SERVO VENT VALVE
402 SERVO VACUUM VALVE
400 SPEED SENSOR INPUT
399 SERVO POSITION INPUT
398 SERVO POSITION INPUT
397 ON/OFF SIGNAL
150 GROUND
87 BRAKE CLUTCH INPUT
84 RESUME/ACCEL SIGNAL
83 SET/COAST SIGNAL
CRUISE CONTROL SWITCH
S/C
R/A
ON/OFF
12020651
C341
12066189
C363
DIGITAL RATIO ADAPTER CONTROLLER (SEE PAGE 118)
87-.8 GRA/BLK
86-.8 BRN
86-.8 BRN
397-.8 GRA
397-.8 GRA
87-.8 GRA/BLK
397-.8 GRA
397-.8 GRA

1988–91 WIRING DIAGRAMS (CONT.)

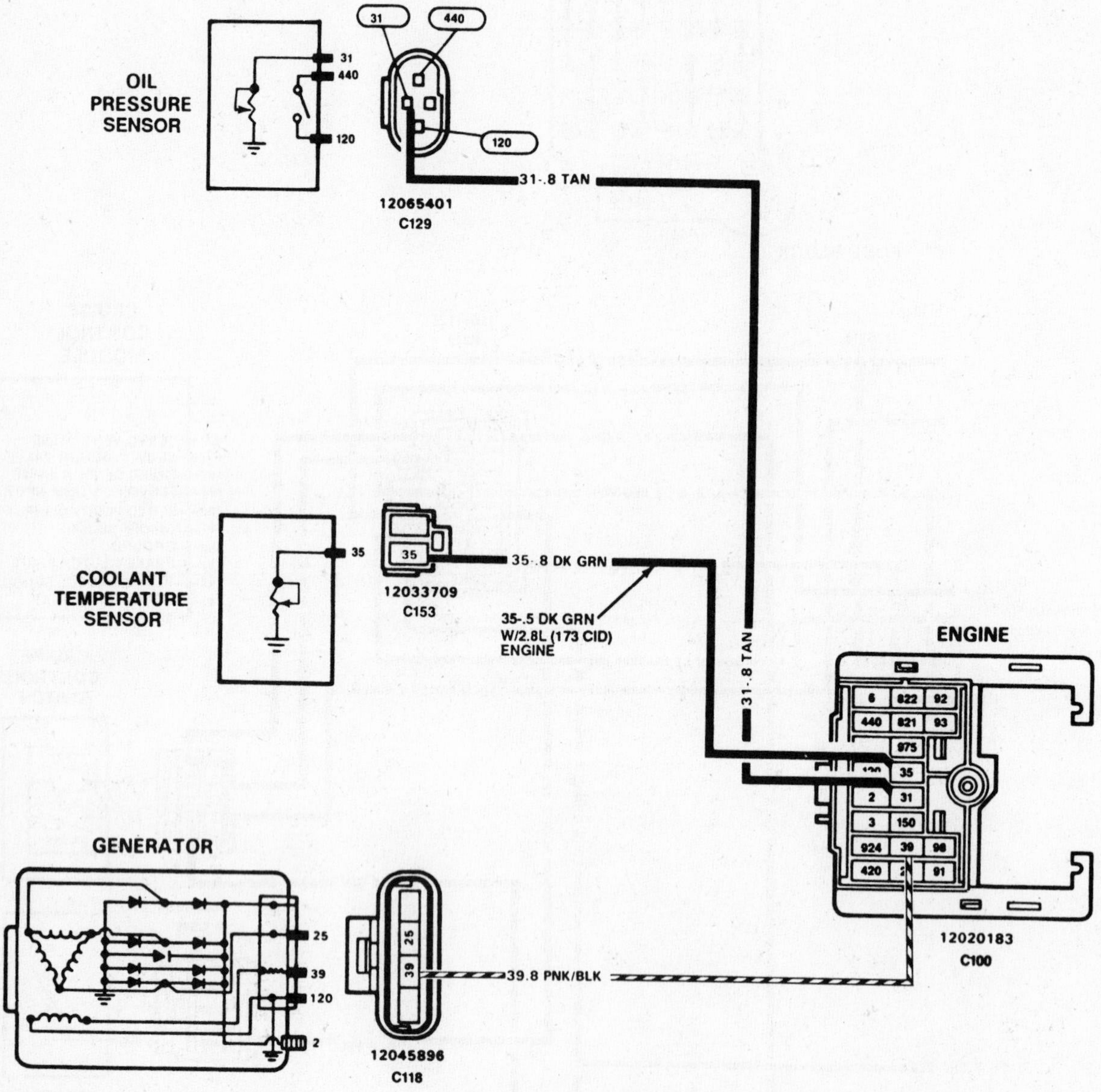

OIL PRESSURE SENSOR
31
440
120
12065401
C129
31-.8 TAN
COOLANT TEMPERATURE SENSOR
35
12033709
C153
35-.8 DK GRN
35-.5 DK GRN W/2.8L (173 CID) ENGINE
31-.8 TAN
ENGINE
6
822
92
440
821
93
975
35
2
31
3
150
924
39
96
420
91
12020183
C100
GENERATOR
25
39
120
2
12045896
C118
39.8 PNK/BLK

INSTRUMENT PANEL - GAGES - PICKUP AND 2-DOOR UTILITY

1988–91 WIRING DIAGRAMS (CONT.)

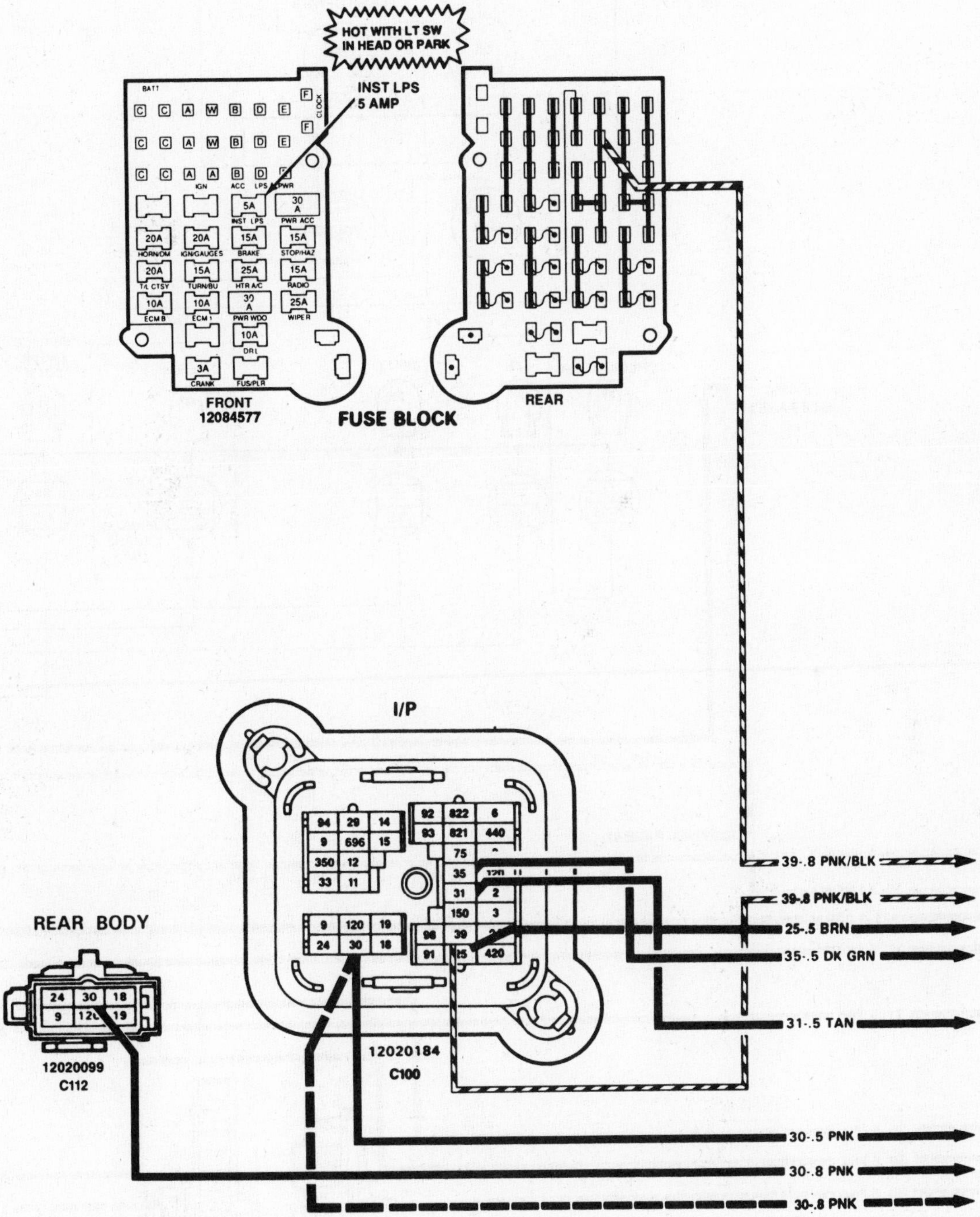
HOT WITH LT SW IN HEAD OR PARK
INST LPS 5 AMP
FRONT
12084577
FUSE BLOCK
REAR
I/P
REAR BODY
12020099
C112
12020184
C100
39-.8 PNK/BLK
39-.8 PNK/BLK
25-.5 BRN
35-.5 DK GRN
31-.5 TAN
30-.5 PNK
30-.8 PNK
30-.8 PNK

1988–91 WIRING DIAGRAMS (CONT.)

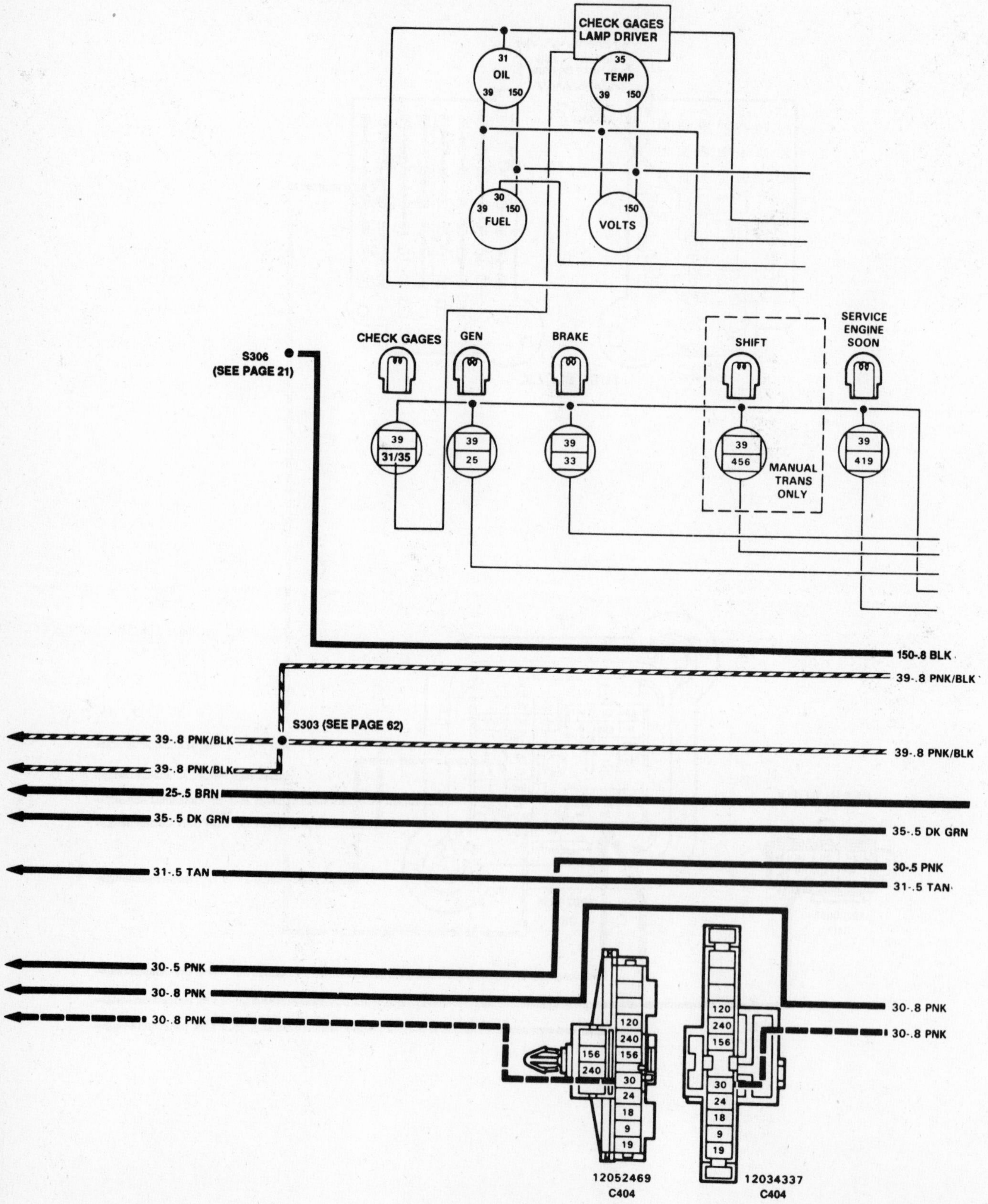
CHECK GAGES LAMP DRIVER
31 OIL 39 150
35 TEMP 39 150
30 39 150 FUEL
150 VOLTS
CHECK GAGES
GEN
BRAKE
SHIFT
SERVICE ENGINE SOON
S306 (SEE PAGE 21)
39 31/35
39 25
39 33
39 456
MANUAL TRANS ONLY
39 419
150-.8 BLK
39-.8 PNK/BLK
S303 (SEE PAGE 62)
39-.8 PNK/BLK
39-.8 PNK/BLK
39-.8 PNK/BLK
25-.5 BRN
35-.5 DK GRN
35-.5 DK GRN
30-.5 PNK
31-.5 TAN
31-.5 TAN
30-.5 PNK
30-.8 PNK
30-.8 PNK
30-.8 PNK
30-.8 PNK
120 240 156 156 240 30 24 18 9 19
120 240 156 30 24 18 9 19
12052469 C404
12034337 C404

1988–91 WIRING DIAGRAMS (CONT.)

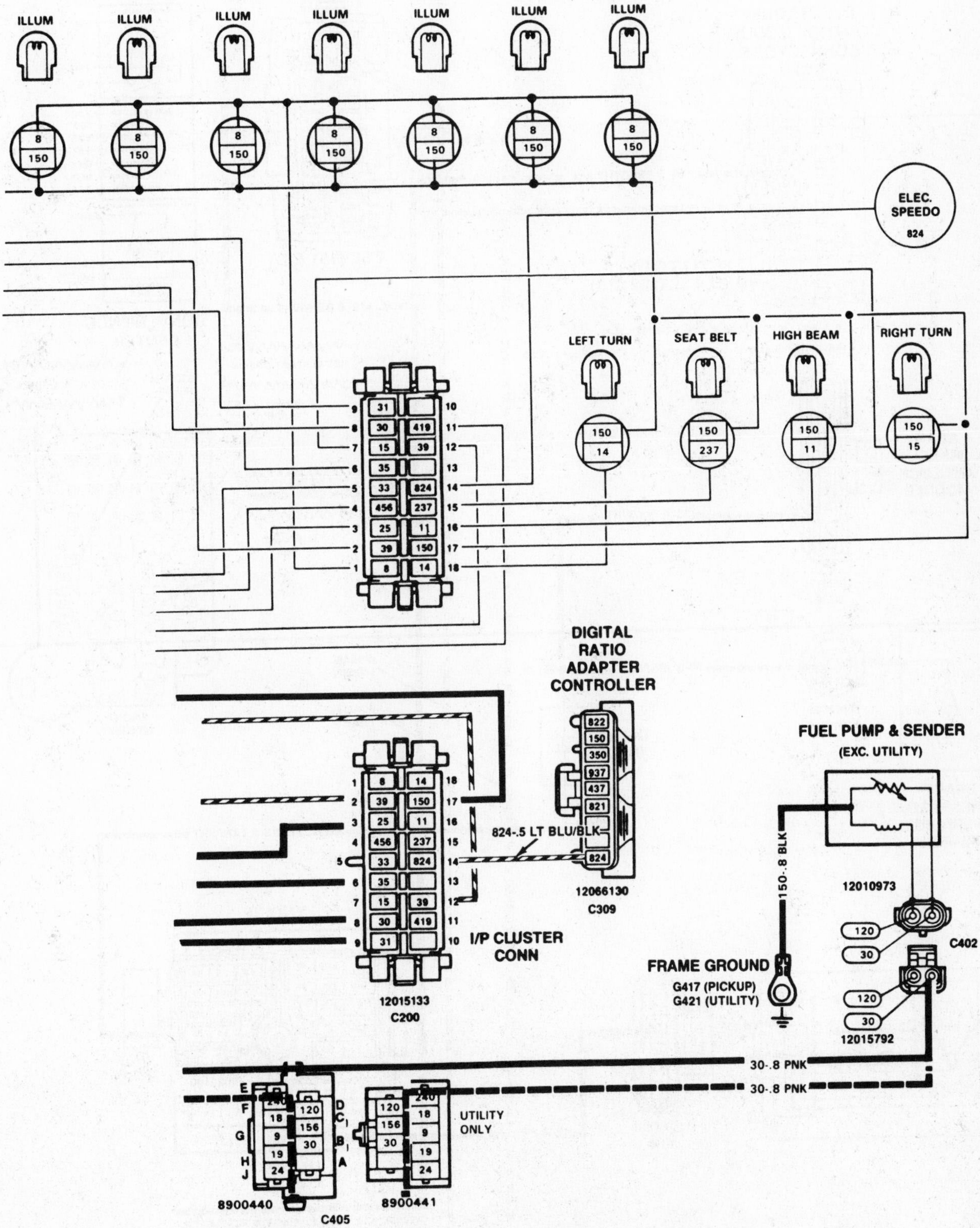

ILLUM
ILLUM
ILLUM
ILLUM
ILLUM
ILLUM
ILLUM
ELEC. SPEEDO
824
LEFT TURN
SEAT BELT
HIGH BEAM
RIGHT TURN
DIGITAL RATIO ADAPTER CONTROLLER
FUEL PUMP & SENDER
(EXC. UTILITY)
824-.5 LT BLU/BLK
150-.8 BLK
12066130
C309
12010973
C402
I/P CLUSTER CONN
FRAME GROUND
G417 (PICKUP)
G421 (UTILITY)
12015792
12015133
C200
30-.8 PNK
30-.8 PNK
UTILITY ONLY
8900440
8900441
C405

INSTRUMENT PANEL - GAGES - PICKUP AND 2-DOOR UTILITY

1988–91 WIRING DIAGRAMS (CONT.)

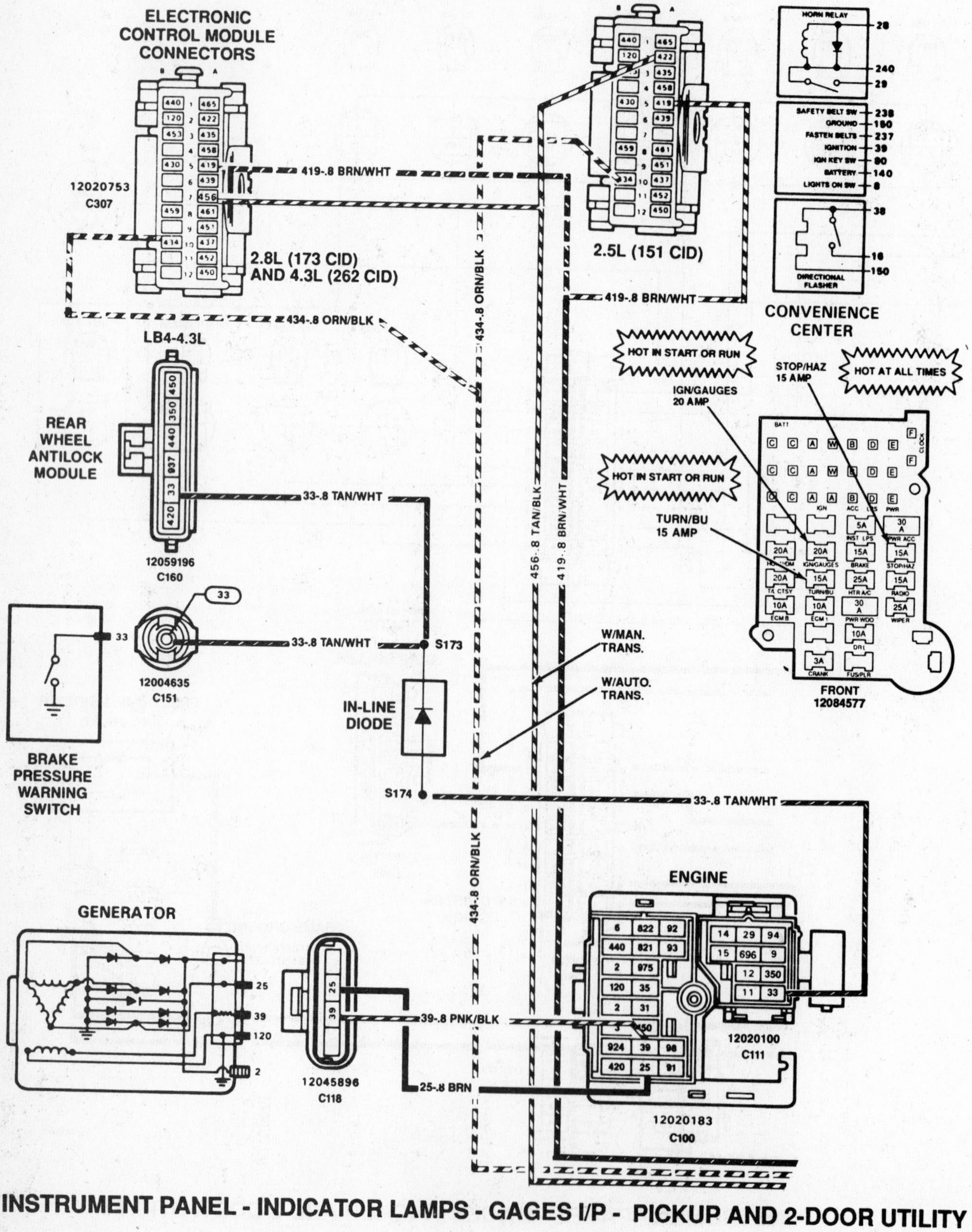
ELECTRONIC
CONTROL MODULE
CONNECTORS
12020753
C307
2.8L (173 CID)
AND 4.3L (262 CID)
2.5L (151 CID)
419-.8 BRN/WHT
434-.8 ORN/BLK
456-.8 TAN/BLK
419-.8 BRN/WHT
LB4-4.3L
REAR
WHEEL
ANTILOCK
MODULE
12059196
C160
33-.8 TAN/WHT
12004635
C151
S173
S174
IN-LINE
DIODE
BRAKE
PRESSURE
WARNING
SWITCH
W/MAN.
TRANS.
W/AUTO.
TRANS.
HORN RELAY
SAFETY BELT SW
GROUND
FASTEN BELTS
IGNITION
IGN KEY SW
BATTERY
LIGHTS ON SW
DIRECTIONAL
FLASHER
CONVENIENCE
CENTER
HOT IN START OR RUN
HOT AT ALL TIMES
STOP/HAZ
15 AMP
IGN/GAUGES
20 AMP
TURN/BU
15 AMP
FRONT
12084577
ENGINE
12020100
C111
12020183
C100
GENERATOR
12045896
C118
39-.8 PNK/BLK
25-.8 BRN

INSTRUMENT PANEL - INDICATOR LAMPS - GAGES I/P - PICKUP AND 2-DOOR UTILITY

1988–91 WIRING DIAGRAMS (CONT.)

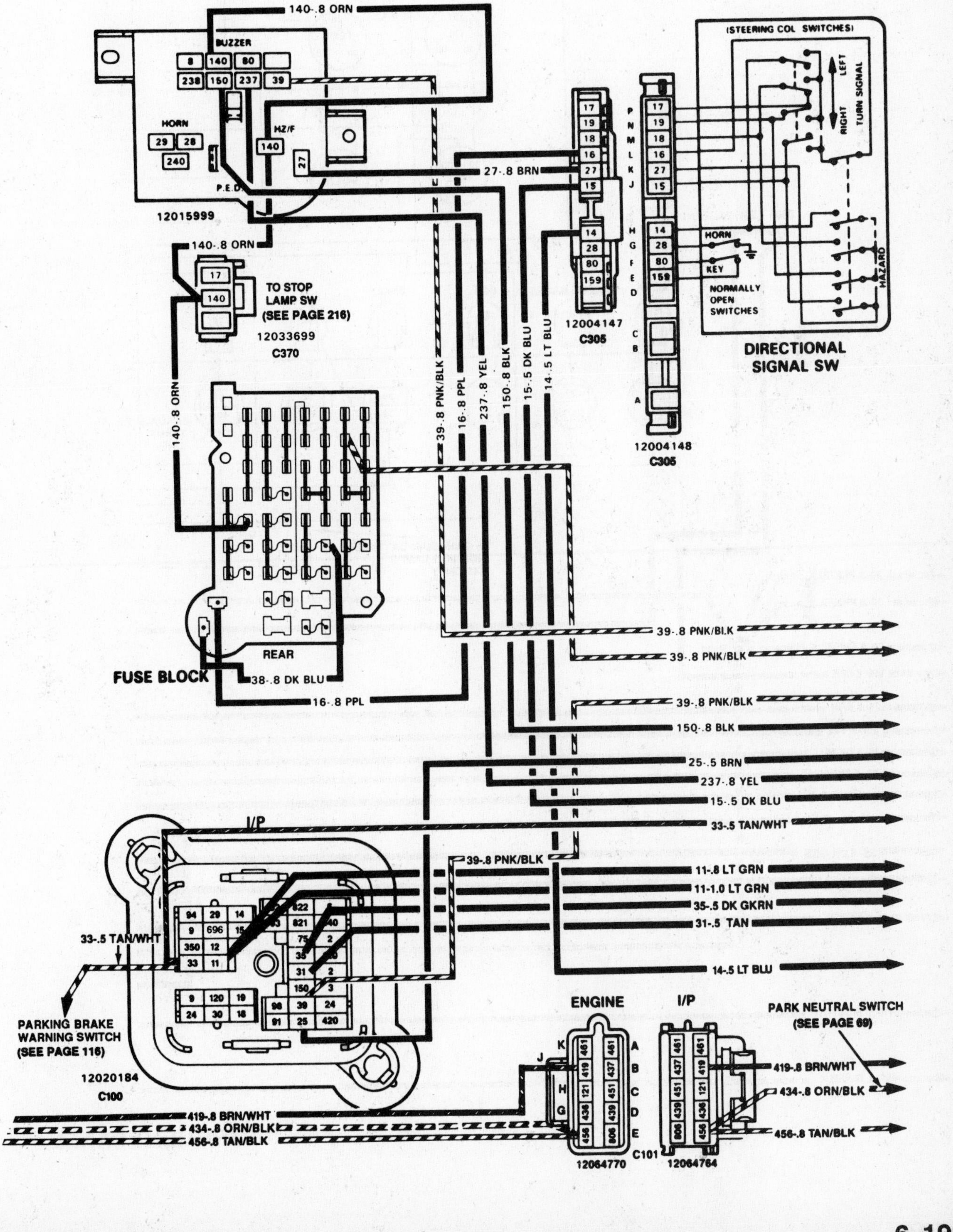

140-.8 ORN
BUZZER
HORN
HZ/F
P.E.D.
12015999
140-.8 ORN
TO STOP LAMP SW (SEE PAGE 216)
12033699
C370
140-.8 ORN
27-.8 BRN
12004147
C305
12004148
C305
(STEERING COL SWITCHES)
LEFT
RIGHT
TURN SIGNAL
HORN
KEY
NORMALLY OPEN SWITCHES
HAZARD
DIRECTIONAL SIGNAL SW
39-.8 PNK/BLK
16-.8 PPL
237-.8 YEL
150-.8 BLK
15-.5 DK BLU
14-.5 LT BLU
REAR
FUSE BLOCK
38-.8 DK BLU
16-.8 PPL
39-.8 PNK/BLK
39-.8 PNK/BLK
39-.8 PNK/BLK
150-.8 BLK
25-.5 BRN
237-.8 YEL
15-.5 DK BLU
I/P
33-.5 TAN/WHT
39-.8 PNK/BLK
11-.8 LT GRN
11-1.0 LT GRN
35-.5 DK GKRN
31-.5 TAN
14-.5 LT BLU
33-.5 TAN/WHT
PARKING BRAKE WARNING SWITCH (SEE PAGE 116)
12020184
C100
ENGINE
I/P
PARK NEUTRAL SWITCH (SEE PAGE 69)
419-.8 BRN/WHT
434-.8 ORN/BLK
456-.8 TAN/BLK
419-.8 BRN/WHT
434-.8 ORN/BLK
456-.8 TAN/BLK
C101
12064770
12064764

1988–91 WIRING DIAGRAMS (CONT.)

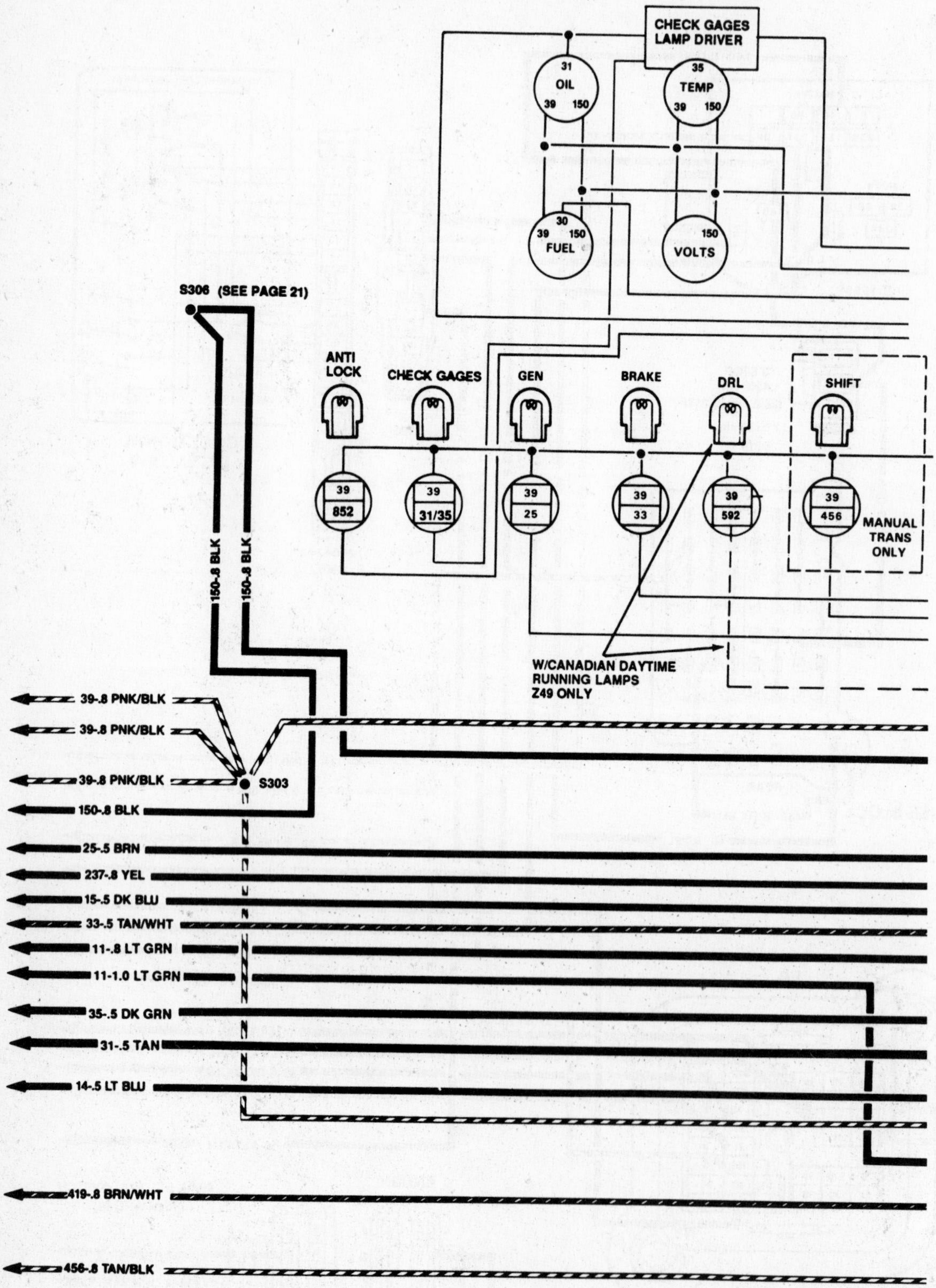
CHECK GAGES
LAMP DRIVER
31
OIL
39 150
35
TEMP
39 150
30
39 150
FUEL
150
VOLTS
S306 (SEE PAGE 21)
ANTI
LOCK
CHECK GAGES
GEN
BRAKE
DRL
SHIFT
39
852
39
31/35
39
25
39
33
39
592
39
456
MANUAL
TRANS
ONLY
150-.8 BLK
150-.8 BLK
W/CANADIAN DAYTIME
RUNNING LAMPS
Z49 ONLY
39-.8 PNK/BLK
39-.8 PNK/BLK
39-.8 PNK/BLK
S303
150-.8 BLK
25-.5 BRN
237-.8 YEL
15-.5 DK BLU
33-.5 TAN/WHT
11-.8 LT GRN
11-1.0 LT GRN
35-.5 DK GRN
31-.5 TAN
14-.5 LT BLU
419-.8 BRN/WHT
456-.8 TAN/BLK

INSTRUMENT PANEL -

1988–91 WIRING DIAGRAMS (CONT.)

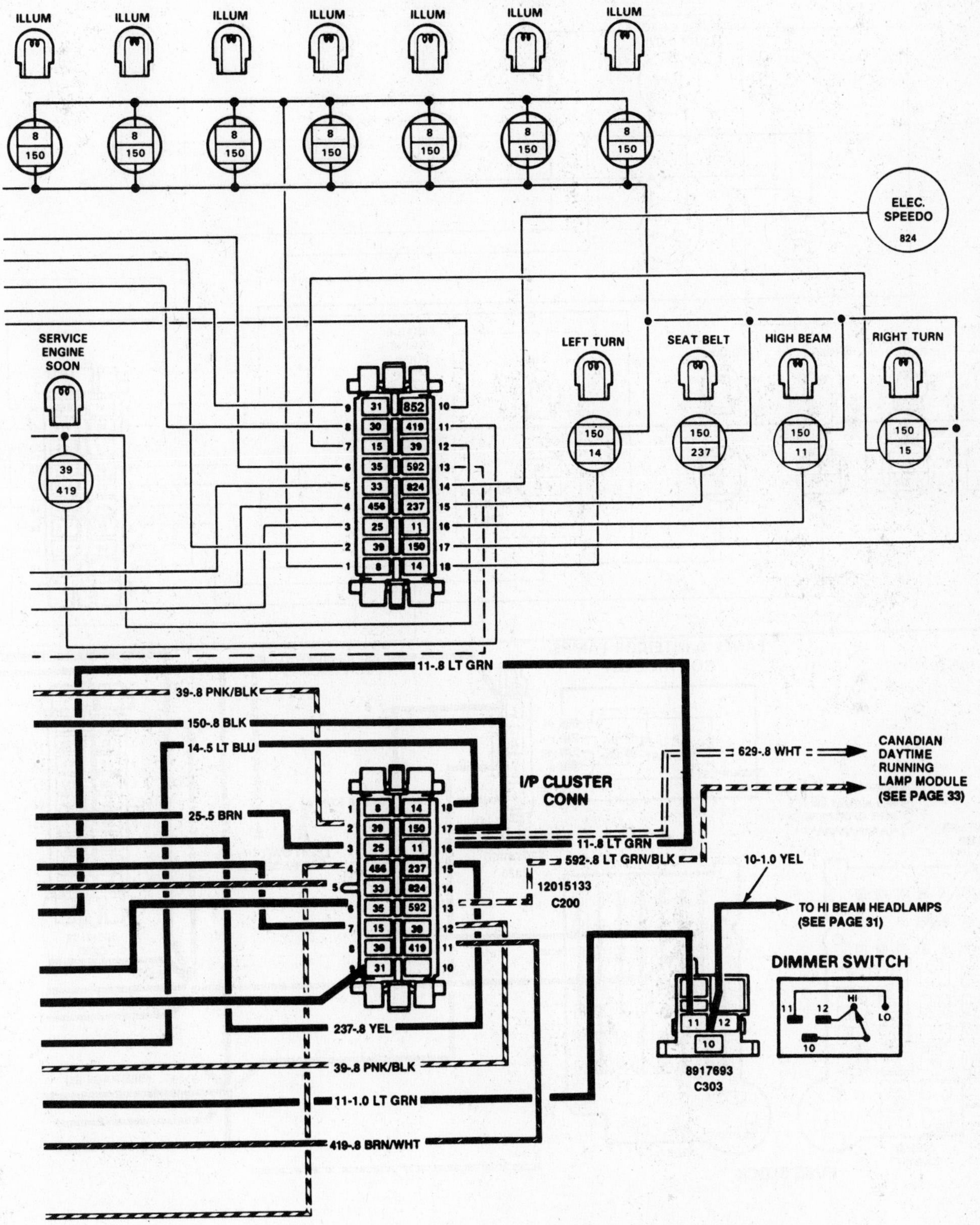
ILLUM
8
150
ELEC. SPEEDO
824
SERVICE ENGINE SOON
39
419
LEFT TURN
150
14
SEAT BELT
237
HIGH BEAM
11
RIGHT TURN
15
31
852
30
419
15
39
35
592
33
824
456
237
25
11
39
150
8
14
11-.8 LT GRN
39-.8 PNK/BLK
150-.8 BLK
14-.5 LT BLU
25-.5 BRN
I/P CLUSTER CONN
629-.8 WHT
CANADIAN DAYTIME RUNNING LAMP MODULE (SEE PAGE 33)
11-.8 LT GRN
592-.8 LT GRN/BLK
12015133
C200
10-1.0 YEL
TO HI BEAM HEADLAMPS (SEE PAGE 31)
DIMMER SWITCH
HI
LO
8917693
C303
237-.8 YEL
39-.8 PNK/BLK
11-1.0 LT GRN
419-.8 BRN/WHT

INDICATOR LAMPS - GAGES I/P - PICKUP AND 2-DOOR UTILITY

1988–91 WIRING DIAGRAMS (CONT.)

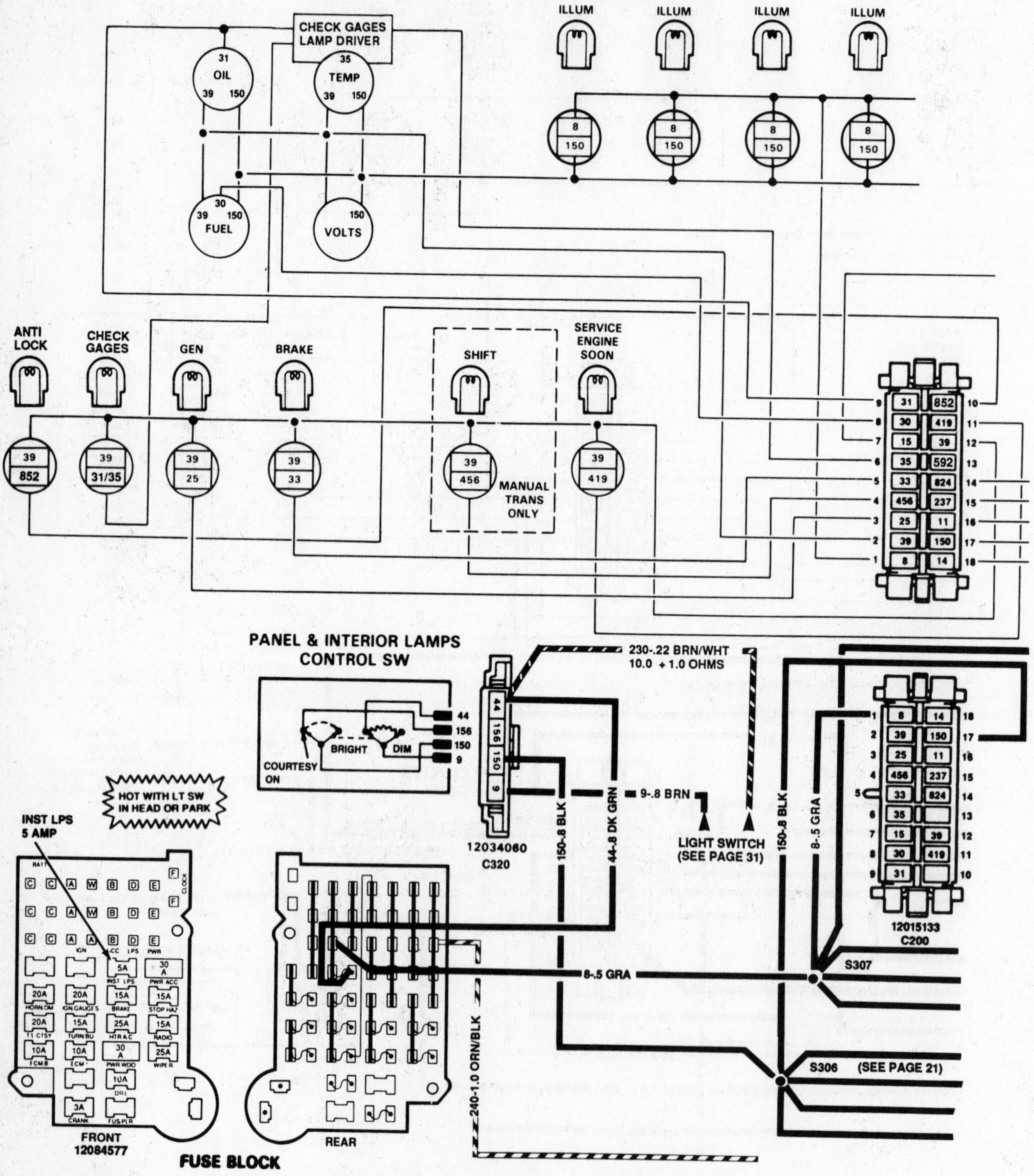
CHECK GAGES
LAMP DRIVER
OIL
TEMP
FUEL
VOLTS
ILLUM
ILLUM
ILLUM
ILLUM
ANTI LOCK
CHECK GAGES
GEN
BRAKE
SHIFT
SERVICE ENGINE SOON
MANUAL TRANS ONLY
PANEL & INTERIOR LAMPS CONTROL SW
COURTESY ON
BRIGHT
DIM
230-.22 BRN/WHT
10.0 + 1.0 OHMS
HOT WITH LT SW IN HEAD OR PARK
INST LPS 5 AMP
12034060
C320
150-.8 BLK
44-.8 DK GRN
9-.8 BRN
LIGHT SWITCH (SEE PAGE 31)
150-.8 BLK
8-.5 GRA
12015133
C200
8-.5 GRA
S307
S306 (SEE PAGE 21)
240-1.0 ORN/BLK
FRONT
12084577
FUSE BLOCK
REAR

INSTRUMENT PANEL - ILLUMINATION LAMPS - GAGES I/P

1988–91 WIRING DIAGRAMS (CONT.)

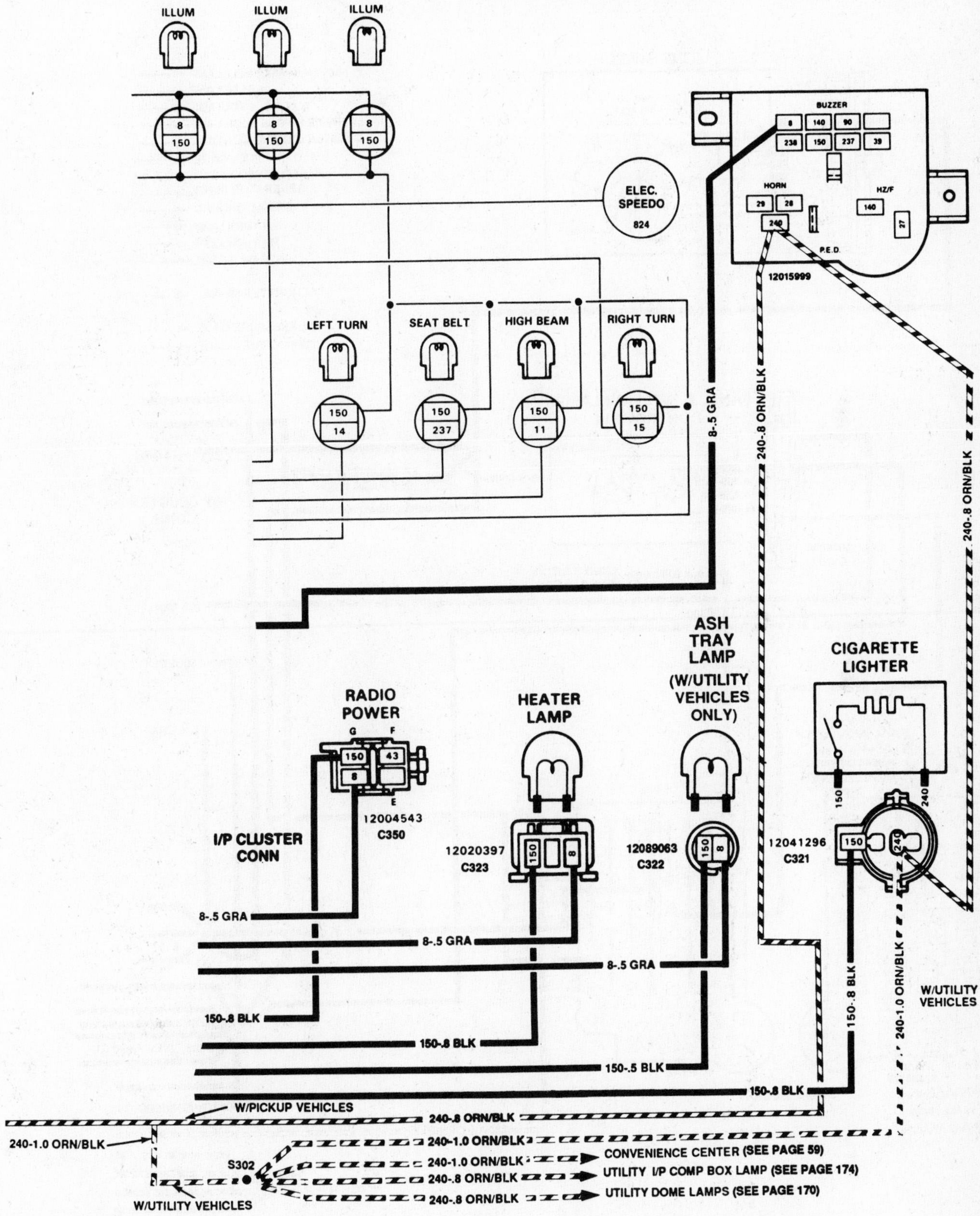
ILLUM
ILLUM
ILLUM
8
150
ELEC. SPEEDO
824
BUZZER
HORN
HZ/F
P.E.D.
12015999
LEFT TURN
SEAT BELT
HIGH BEAM
RIGHT TURN
150 14
150 237
150 11
150 15
8-.5 GRA
240-.8 ORN/BLK
ASH TRAY LAMP (W/UTILITY VEHICLES ONLY)
CIGARETTE LIGHTER
RADIO POWER
HEATER LAMP
12004543
C350
I/P CLUSTER CONN
12020397
C323
12089063
C322
12041296
C321
150-.8 BLK
150-.5 BLK
240-1.0 ORN/BLK
W/UTILITY VEHICLES
W/PICKUP VEHICLES
S302
CONVENIENCE CENTER (SEE PAGE 59)
UTILITY I/P COMP BOX LAMP (SEE PAGE 174)
UTILITY DOME LAMPS (SEE PAGE 170)

1988–91 WIRING DIAGRAMS (CONT.)

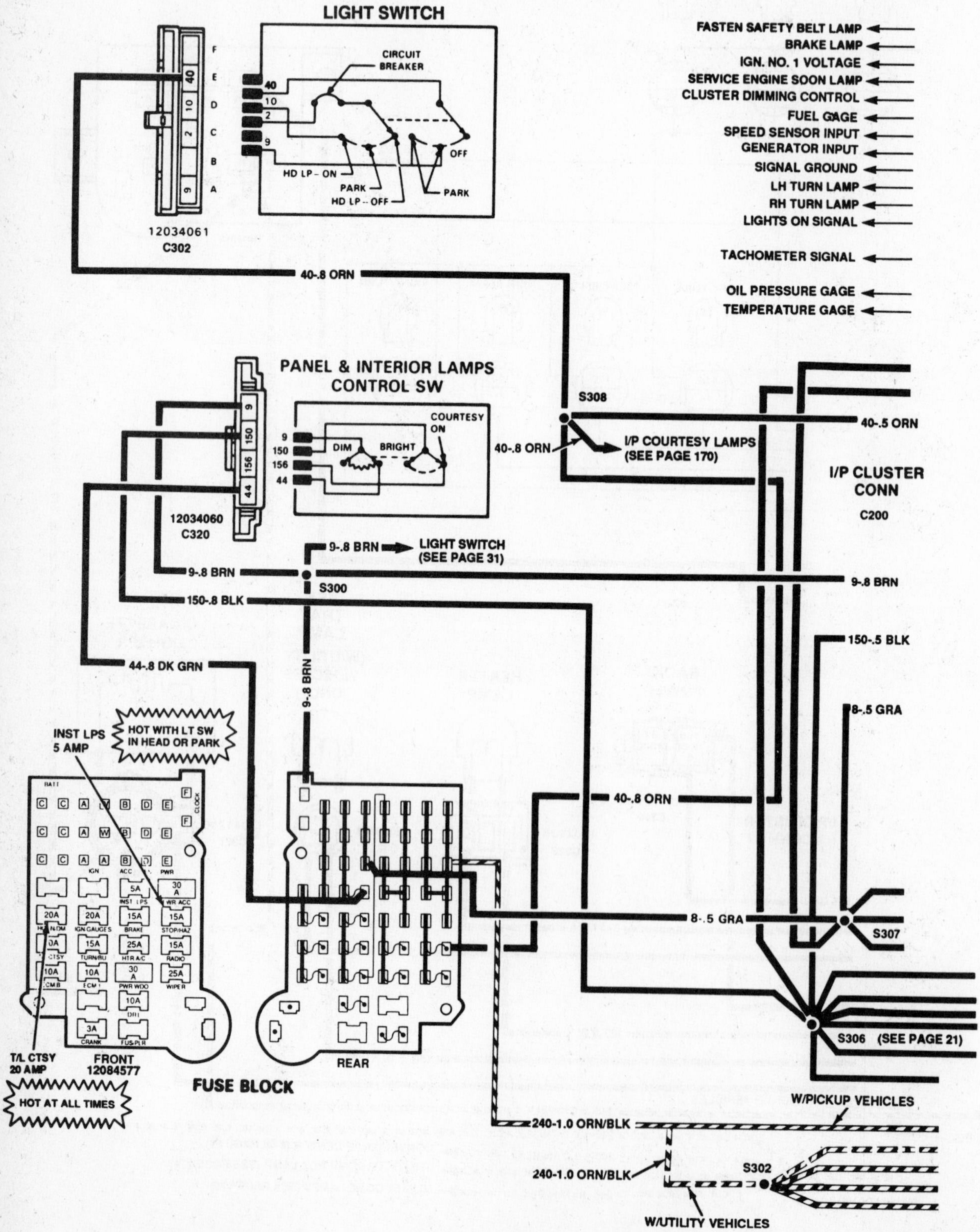
LIGHT SWITCH
CIRCUIT BREAKER
HD LP - ON
PARK
HD LP - OFF
OFF
PARK
12034061
C302
FASTEN SAFETY BELT LAMP
BRAKE LAMP
IGN. NO. 1 VOLTAGE
SERVICE ENGINE SOON LAMP
CLUSTER DIMMING CONTROL
FUEL GAGE
SPEED SENSOR INPUT
GENERATOR INPUT
SIGNAL GROUND
LH TURN LAMP
RH TURN LAMP
LIGHTS ON SIGNAL
TACHOMETER SIGNAL
OIL PRESSURE GAGE
TEMPERATURE GAGE
40-.8 ORN
PANEL & INTERIOR LAMPS CONTROL SW
COURTESY ON
DIM
BRIGHT
12034060
C320
S308
40-.8 ORN
I/P COURTESY LAMPS (SEE PAGE 170)
40-.5 ORN
I/P CLUSTER CONN
C200
9-.8 BRN
LIGHT SWITCH (SEE PAGE 31)
9-.8 BRN
S300
9-.8 BRN
150-.8 BLK
150-.5 BLK
44-.8 DK GRN
9-.8 BRN
8-.5 GRA
INST LPS 5 AMP
HOT WITH LT SW IN HEAD OR PARK
40-.8 ORN
8-.5 GRA
S307
S306 (SEE PAGE 21)
T/L CTSY 20 AMP
FRONT 12084577
REAR
FUSE BLOCK
HOT AT ALL TIMES
W/PICKUP VEHICLES
240-1.0 ORN/BLK
240-1.0 ORN/BLK
S302
W/UTILITY VEHICLES

1988–91 WIRING DIAGRAMS (CONT.)

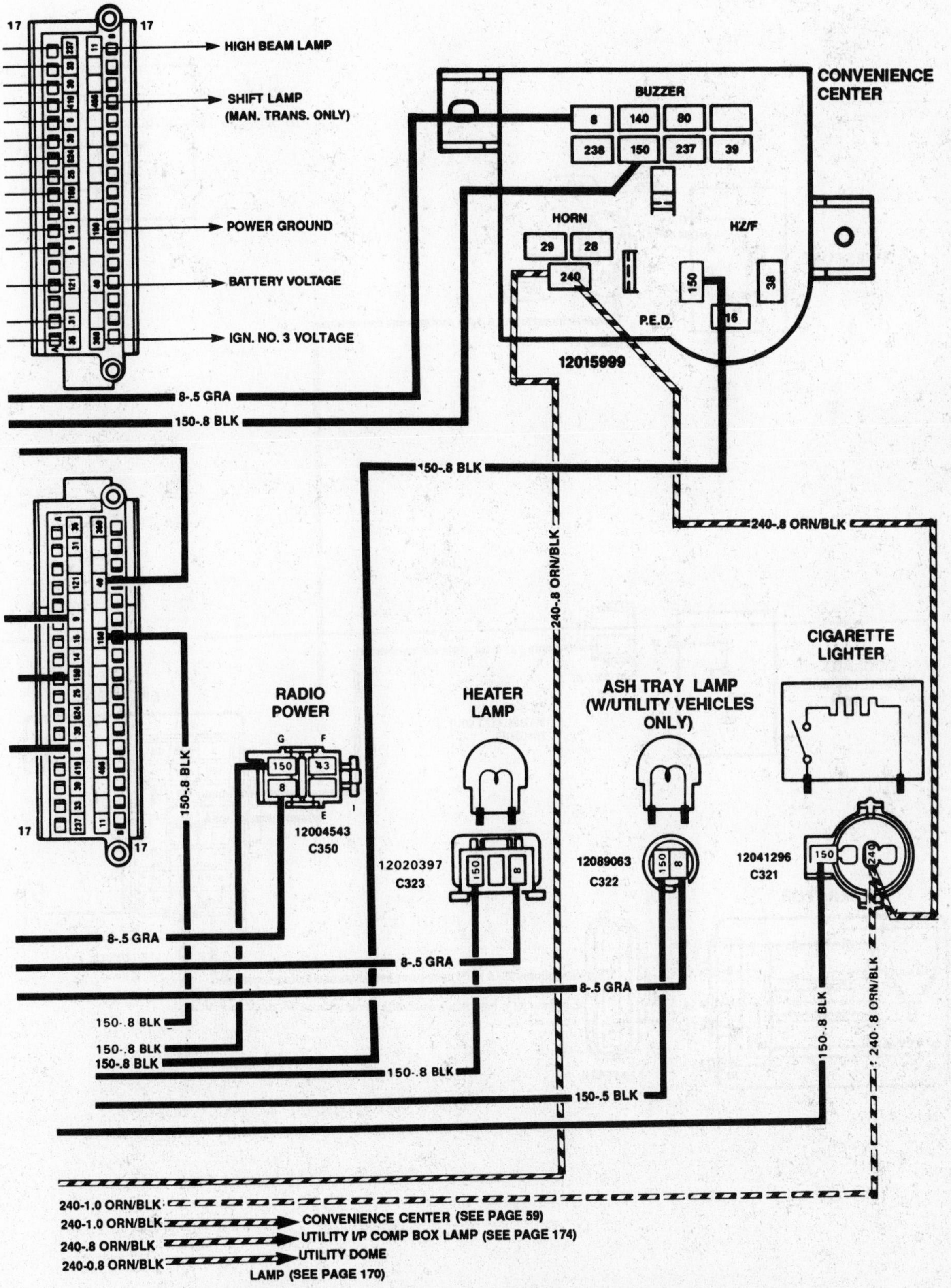

HIGH BEAM LAMP
SHIFT LAMP (MAN. TRANS. ONLY)
POWER GROUND
BATTERY VOLTAGE
IGN. NO. 3 VOLTAGE
CONVENIENCE CENTER
BUZZER
HORN
HZ/F
P.E.D.
12015999
8-.5 GRA
150-.8 BLK
240-.8 ORN/BLK
CIGARETTE LIGHTER
RADIO POWER
HEATER LAMP
ASH TRAY LAMP (W/UTILITY VEHICLES ONLY)
12004543
C350
12020397
C323
12089063
C322
12041296
C321
150-.5 BLK
240-1.0 ORN/BLK
240-0.8 ORN/BLK
CONVENIENCE CENTER (SEE PAGE 59)
UTILITY I/P COMP BOX LAMP (SEE PAGE 174)
UTILITY DOME LAMP (SEE PAGE 170)

INSTRUMENT PANEL - ILLUMINATION LAMPS - DIGITAL I/P

1988–91 WIRING DIAGRAMS (CONT.)

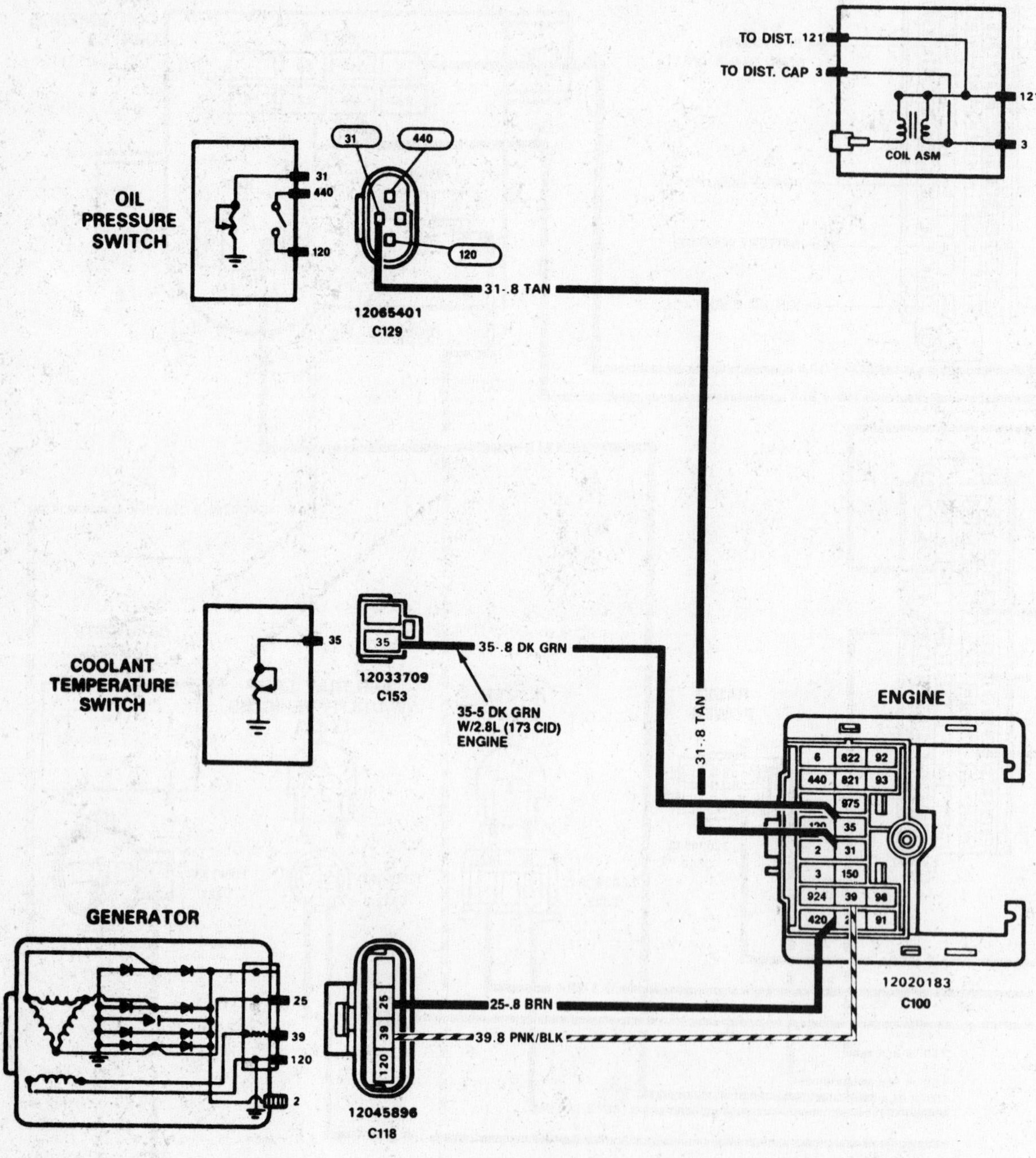

TO DIST. 121
TO DIST. CAP 3
121
3
COIL ASM
OIL PRESSURE SWITCH
31
440
120
12065401
C129
31-.8 TAN
COOLANT TEMPERATURE SWITCH
35
12033709
C153
35-.8 DK GRN
35-5 DK GRN W/2.8L (173 CID) ENGINE
31-.8 TAN
ENGINE
6
822
92
440
821
93
975
35
2
31
3
150
924
39
96
420
91
12020183
C100
GENERATOR
25
39
120
2
25-.8 BRN
39.8 PNK/BLK
12045896
C118

1988–91 WIRING DIAGRAMS (CONT.)

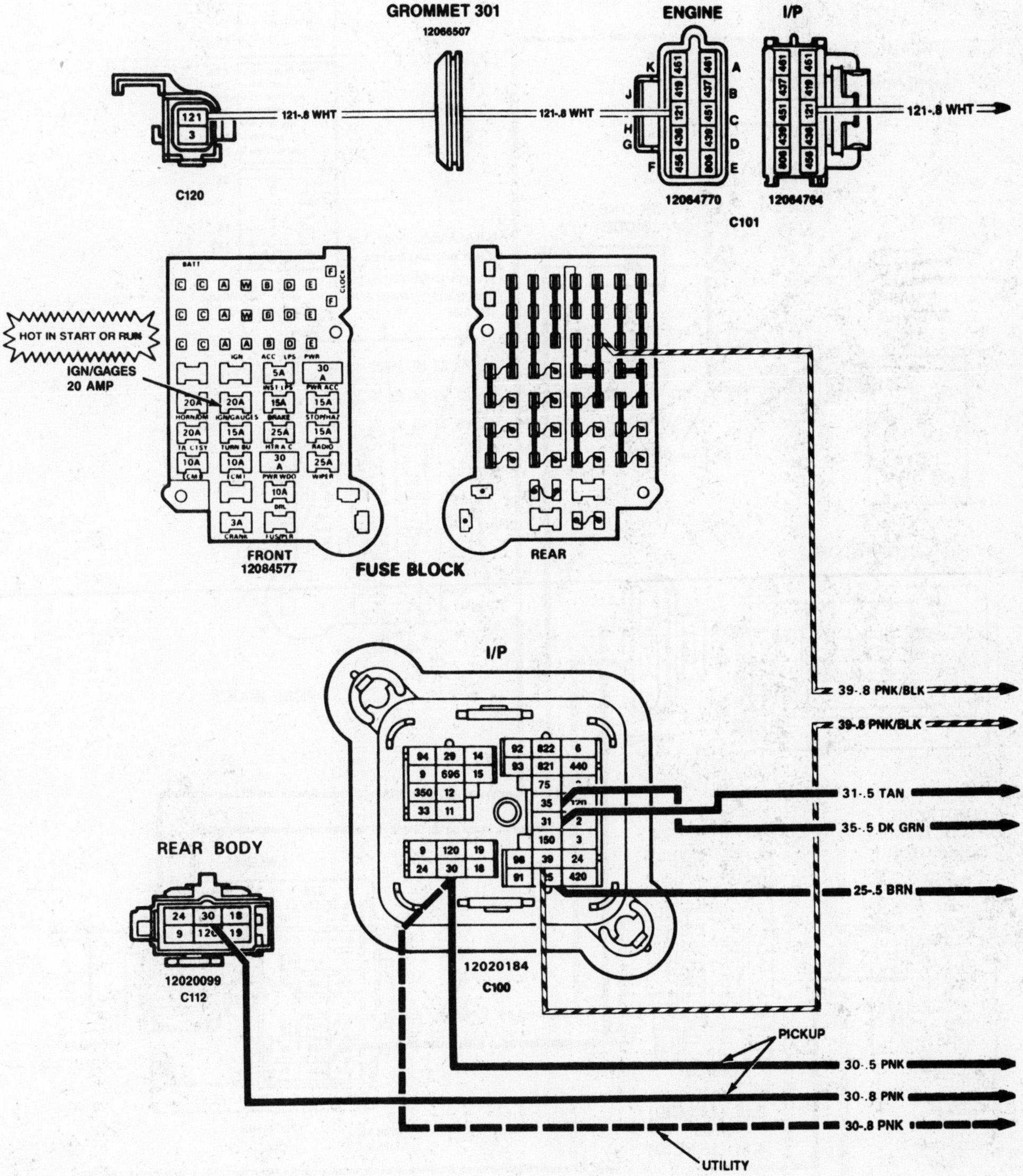
GROMMET 301
12066507
ENGINE
I/P
121-.8 WHT
121-.8 WHT
121-.8 WHT
C120
12064770
12064764
C101
HOT IN START OR RUN
IGN/GAGES
20 AMP
FRONT
12084577
FUSE BLOCK
REAR
I/P
39-.8 PNK/BLK
39-.8 PNK/BLK
31-.5 TAN
35-.5 DK GRN
25-.5 BRN
REAR BODY
12020099
C112
12020184
C100
PICKUP
30-.5 PNK
30-.8 PNK
30-.8 PNK
UTILITY

1988–91 WIRING DIAGRAMS (CONT.)

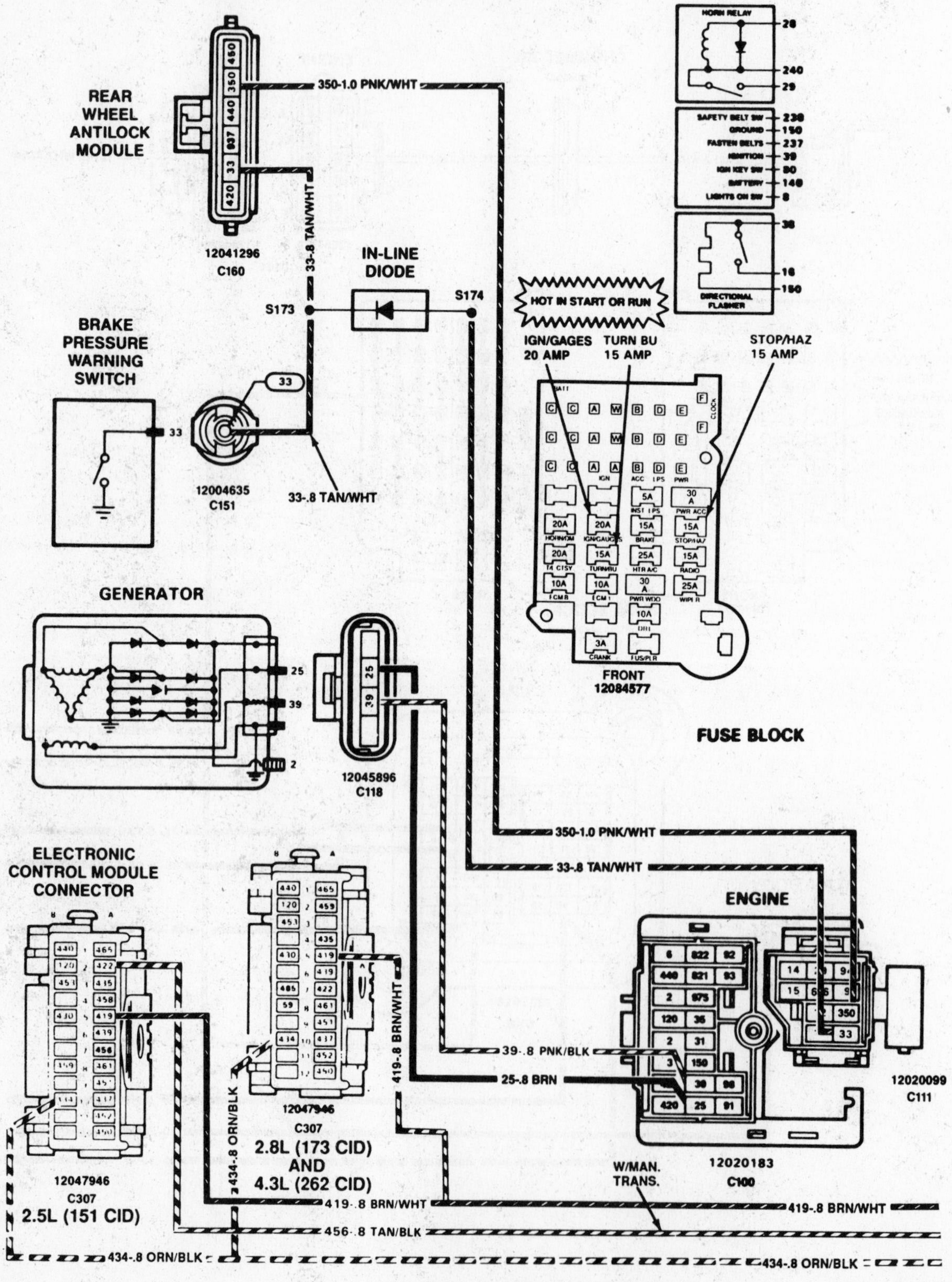

REAR WHEEL ANTILOCK MODULE
12041296
C160
350-1.0 PNK/WHT
33-.8 TAN/WHT
IN-LINE DIODE
S173
S174
HOT IN START OR RUN
IGN/GAGES 20 AMP
TURN BU 15 AMP
STOP/HAZ 15 AMP
BRAKE PRESSURE WARNING SWITCH
12004635
C151
33-.8 TAN/WHT
HORN RELAY
DIRECTIONAL FLASHER
FRONT
12084577
FUSE BLOCK
GENERATOR
12045896
C118
350-1.0 PNK/WHT
33-.8 TAN/WHT
ELECTRONIC CONTROL MODULE CONNECTOR
ENGINE
12047946
C307
2.5L (151 CID)
12047946
C307
2.8L (173 CID) AND 4.3L (262 CID)
39-.8 PNK/BLK
25-.8 BRN
419-.8 BRN/WHT
434-.8 ORN/BLK
12020099
C111
12020183
C100
W/MAN. TRANS.
419-.8 BRN/WHT
456-.8 TAN/BLK
434-.8 ORN/BLK

1988–91 WIRING DIAGRAMS (CONT.)

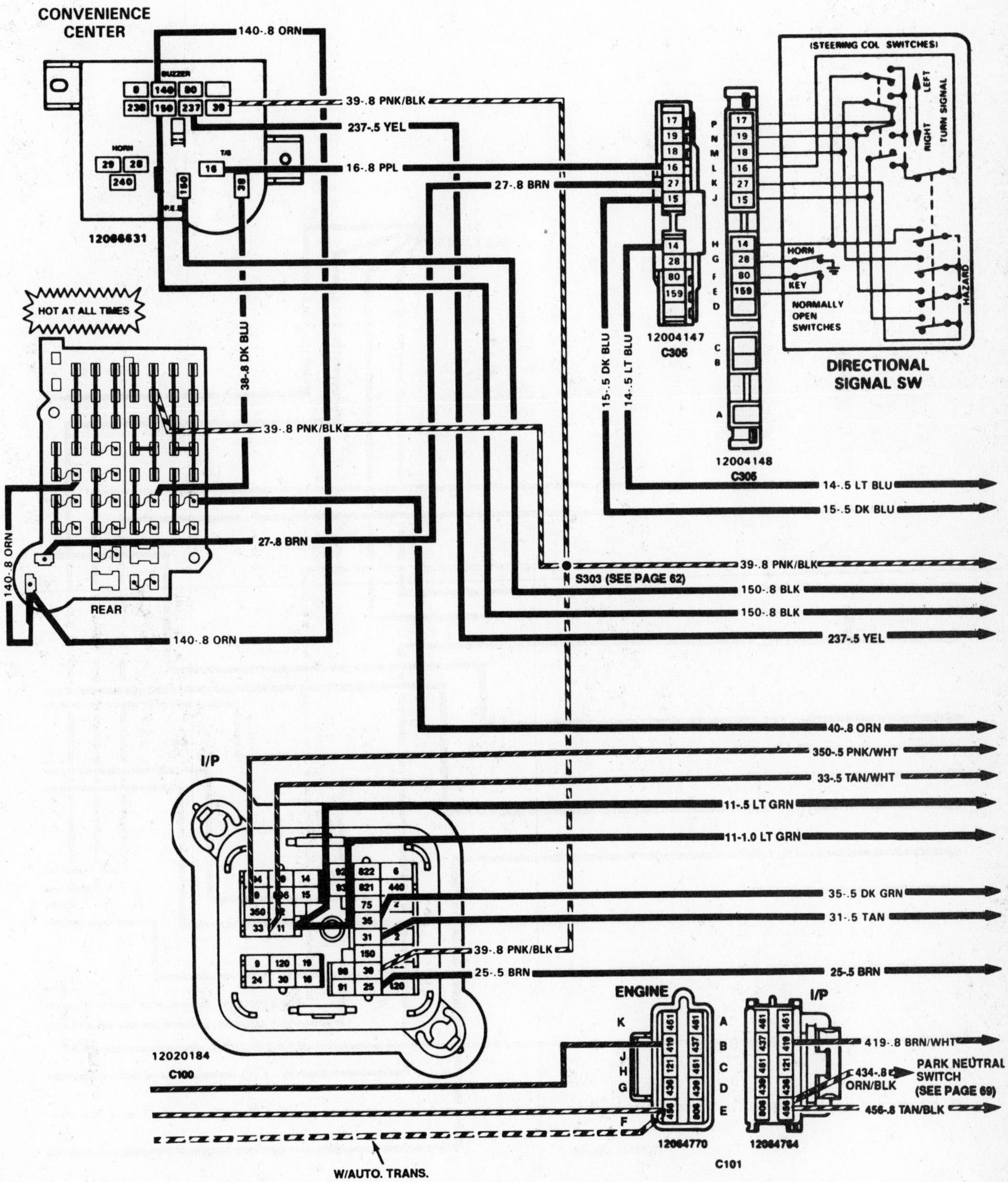

CONVENIENCE CENTER
140-.8 ORN
BUZZER
HORN
T/S
P.E.B.
12066631
39-.8 PNK/BLK
237-.5 YEL
16-.8 PPL
27-.8 BRN
38-.8 DK BLU
HOT AT ALL TIMES
REAR
140-.8 ORN
27-.8 BRN
(STEERING COL SWITCHES)
LEFT
TURN SIGNAL
RIGHT
HORN
KEY
NORMALLY OPEN SWITCHES
HAZARD
DIRECTIONAL SIGNAL SW
15-.5 DK BLU
14-.5 LT BLU
12004147
C305
12004148
C305
14-.5 LT BLU
15-.5 DK BLU
39-.8 PNK/BLK
S303 (SEE PAGE 62)
150-.8 BLK
150-.8 BLK
237-.5 YEL
40-.8 ORN
I/P
350-.5 PNK/WHT
33-.5 TAN/WHT
11-.5 LT GRN
11-1.0 LT GRN
35-.5 DK GRN
31-.5 TAN
39-.8 PNK/BLK
25-.5 BRN
25-.5 BRN
12020184
C100
ENGINE
I/P
419-.8 BRN/WHT
434-.8 ORN/BLK
PARK NEUTRAL SWITCH (SEE PAGE 69)
456-.8 TAN/BLK
12064770
12064764
C101
W/AUTO. TRANS.

1988–91 WIRING DIAGRAMS (CONT.)

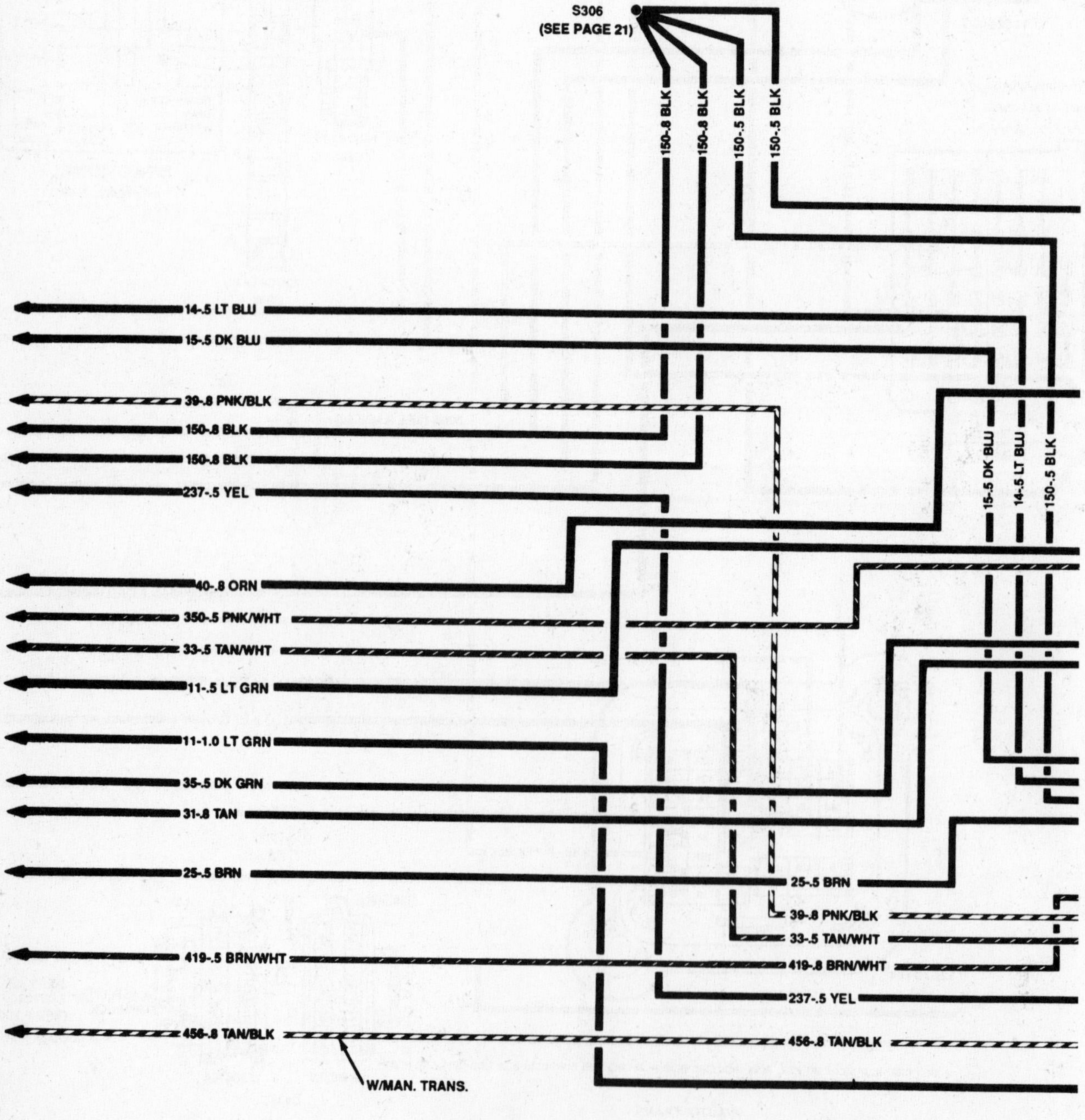
S306
(SEE PAGE 21)
150-.8 BLK
150-.8 BLK
150-.5 BLK
150-.5 BLK
14-.5 LT BLU
15-.5 DK BLU
39-.8 PNK/BLK
150-.8 BLK
150-.8 BLK
237-.5 YEL
15-.5 DK BLU
14-.5 LT BLU
150-.5 BLK
40-.8 ORN
350-.5 PNK/WHT
33-.5 TAN/WHT
11-.5 LT GRN
11-1.0 LT GRN
35-.5 DK GRN
31-.8 TAN
25-.5 BRN
25-.5 BRN
39-.8 PNK/BLK
33-.5 TAN/WHT
419-.5 BRN/WHT
419-.8 BRN/WHT
237-.5 YEL
456-.8 TAN/BLK
456-.8 TAN/BLK
W/MAN. TRANS.

1988–91 WIRING DIAGRAMS (CONT.)

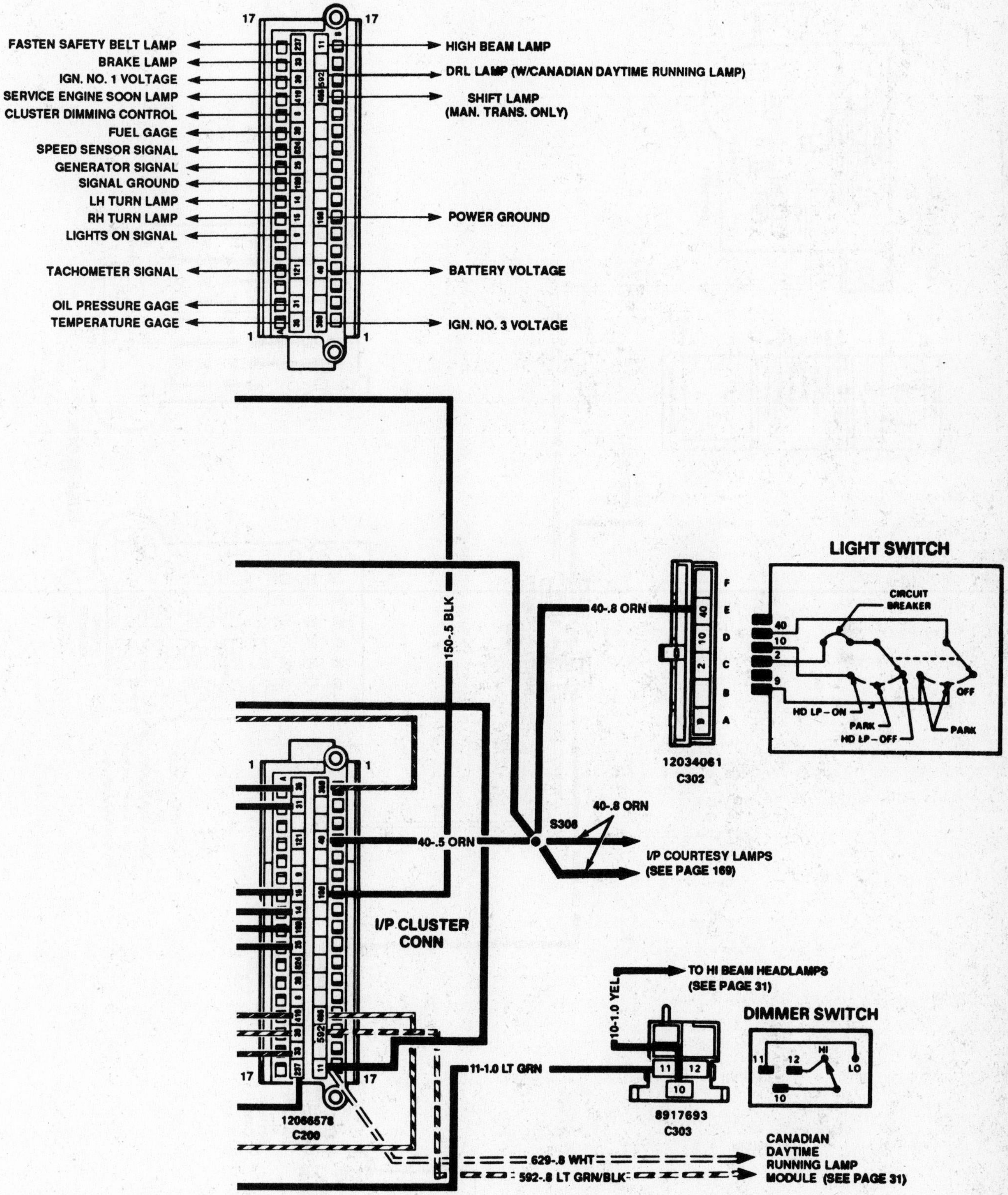
FASTEN SAFETY BELT LAMP
BRAKE LAMP
IGN. NO. 1 VOLTAGE
SERVICE ENGINE SOON LAMP
CLUSTER DIMMING CONTROL
FUEL GAGE
SPEED SENSOR SIGNAL
GENERATOR SIGNAL
SIGNAL GROUND
LH TURN LAMP
RH TURN LAMP
LIGHTS ON SIGNAL
TACHOMETER SIGNAL
OIL PRESSURE GAGE
TEMPERATURE GAGE
HIGH BEAM LAMP
DRL LAMP (W/CANADIAN DAYTIME RUNNING LAMP)
SHIFT LAMP
(MAN. TRANS. ONLY)
POWER GROUND
BATTERY VOLTAGE
IGN. NO. 3 VOLTAGE
150-.5 BLK
40-.8 ORN
LIGHT SWITCH
CIRCUIT BREAKER
HD LP – ON
PARK
HD LP – OFF
OFF
PARK
12034061
C302
40-.8 ORN
S308
40-.5 ORN
I/P COURTESY LAMPS
(SEE PAGE 169)
I/P CLUSTER
CONN
TO HI BEAM HEADLAMPS
(SEE PAGE 31)
10-1.0 YEL
DIMMER SWITCH
HI
LO
11-1.0 LT GRN
8917693
C303
12066578
C200
629-.8 WHT
592-.8 LT GRN/BLK
CANADIAN
DAYTIME
RUNNING LAMP
MODULE (SEE PAGE 31)

1988–91 WIRING DIAGRAMS (CONT.)

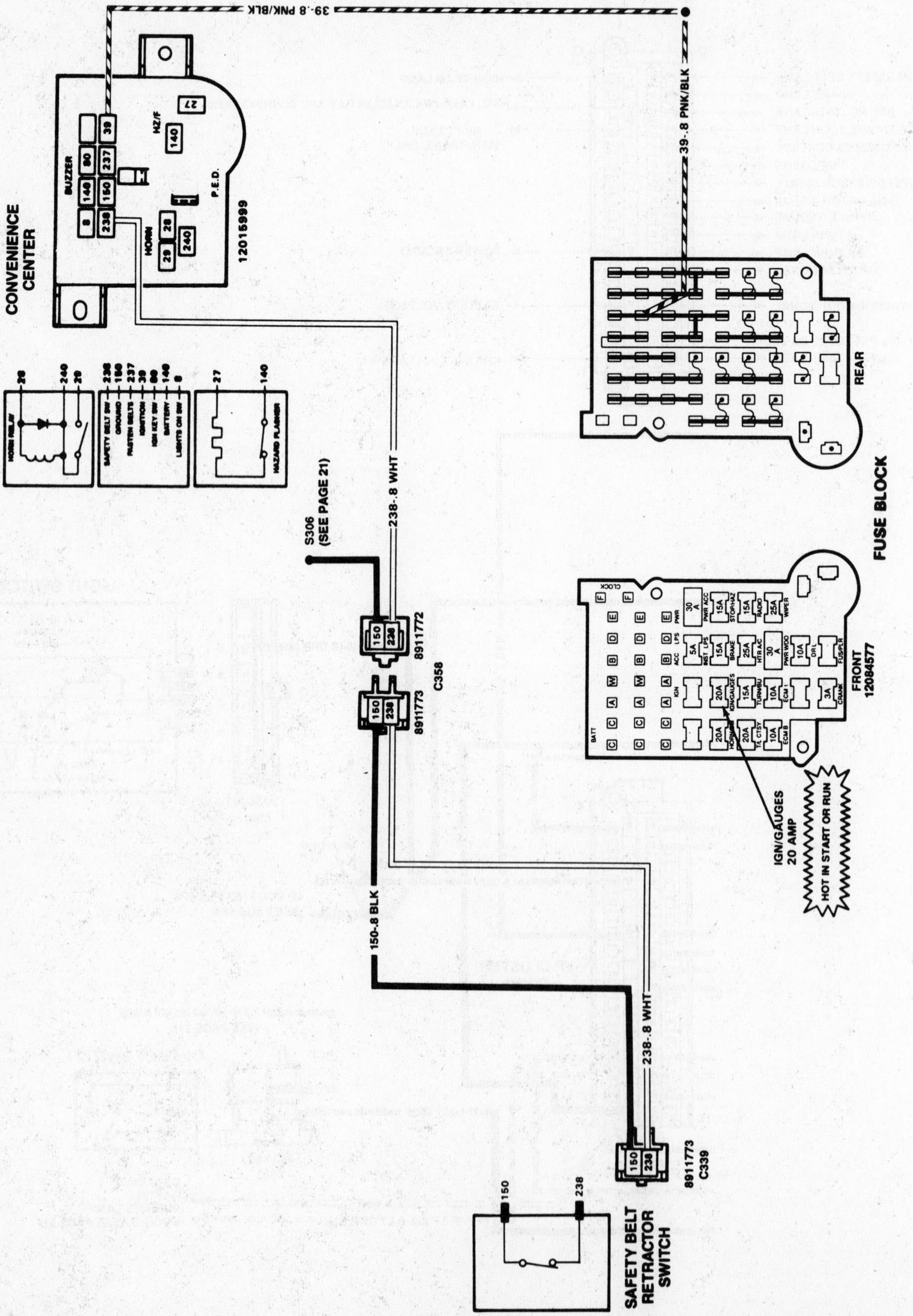

S303
39-.8 PNK/BLK
39-.8 PNK/BLK
CONVENIENCE CENTER
12015999
BUZZER
HORN
HZ/F
P.E.D.
HORN RELAY
SAFETY BELT SW
GROUND
FASTEN BELTS
IGNITION
IGN KEY SW
BATTERY
LIGHTS ON SW
HAZARD FLASHER
S306 (SEE PAGE 21)
238-.8 WHT
8911772
C358
8911773
150-.8 BLK
238-.8 WHT
FUSE BLOCK
REAR
FRONT 12084577
IGN/GAUGES 20 AMP
HOT IN START OR RUN
8911773
C339
SAFETY BELT RETRACTOR SWITCH

1988–91 WIRING DIAGRAMS (CONT.)

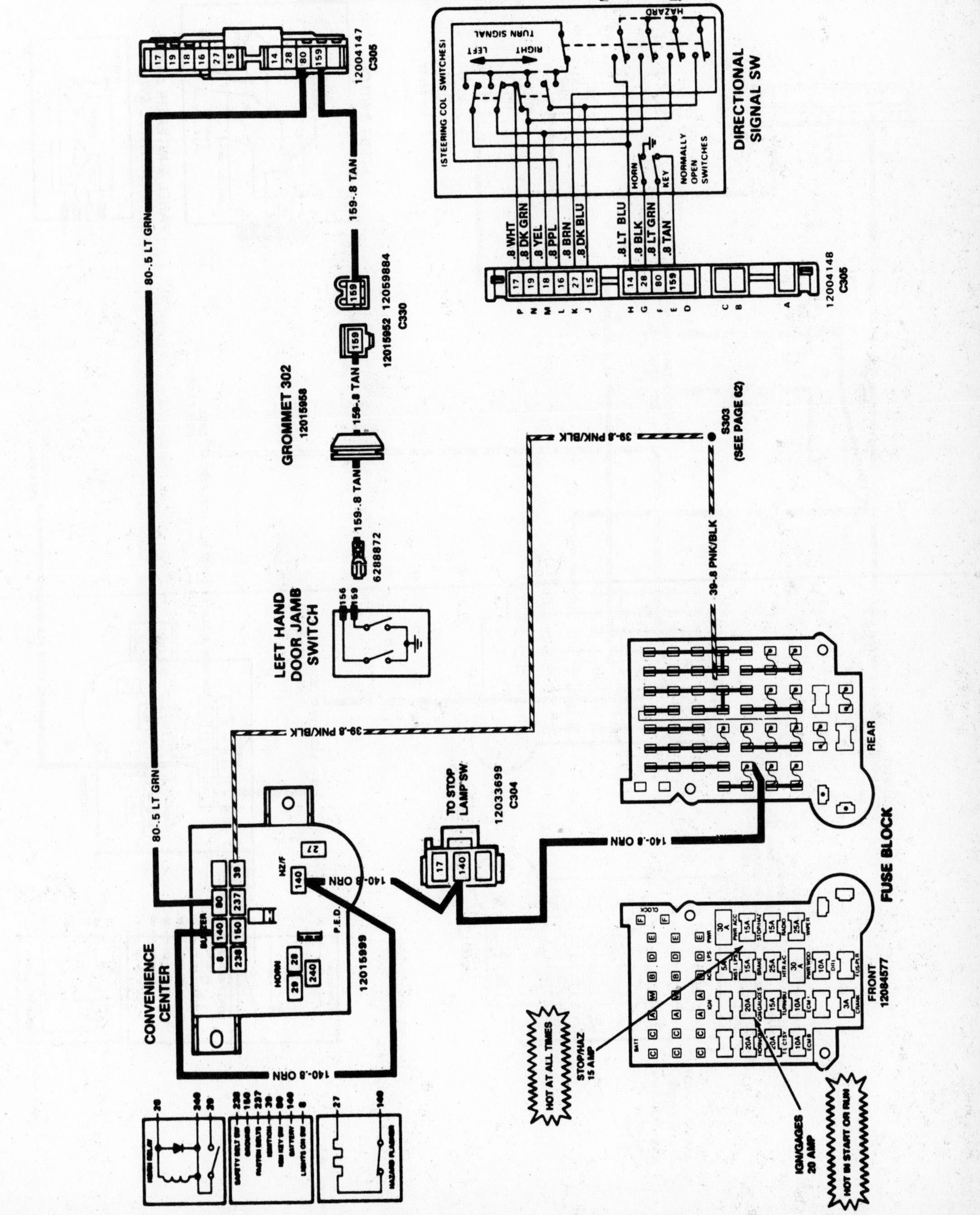
CONVENIENCE CENTER
12015999
HORN
P.E.D.
HZ/F
BUZZER
140-.8 ORN
80-.5 LT GRN
39-.8 PNK/BLK
LEFT HAND DOOR JAMB SWITCH
6288872
159-.8 TAN
GROMMET 302
12015958
12015952
12059884
C330
12004147
C305
DIRECTIONAL SIGNAL SW
(STEERING COL SWITCHES)
TURN SIGNAL
RIGHT
LEFT
HAZARD
HORN
KEY
NORMALLY OPEN SWITCHES
.8 WHT
.8 DK GRN
.8 YEL
.8 PPL
.8 BRN
.8 DK BLU
.8 LT BLU
.8 BLK
.8 LT GRN
.8 TAN
12004148
C305
S303
(SEE PAGE 62)
TO STOP LAMP SW
12033699
C304
FUSE BLOCK
REAR
FRONT
12084577
HOT AT ALL TIMES
STOP/HAZ
15 AMP
IGN/GAGES
20 AMP
HOT IN START OR RUN

1988–91 WIRING DIAGRAMS (CONT.)

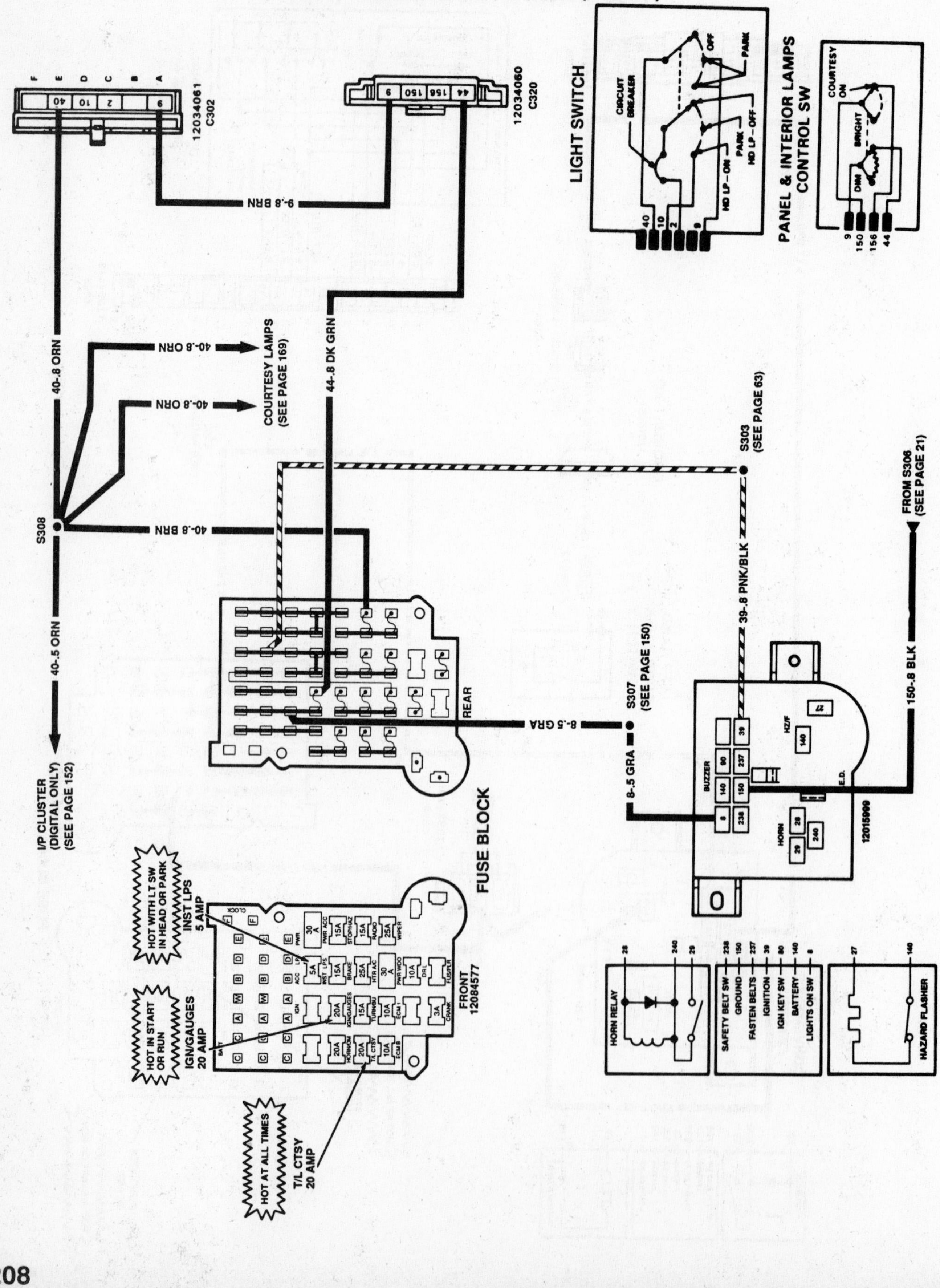

LIGHT SWITCH
CIRCUIT BREAKER
OFF
PARK
HD LP – ON
HD LP – OFF
PANEL & INTERIOR LAMPS CONTROL SW
COURTESY ON
BRIGHT
DIM
12034061
C302
12034060
C320
9-.8 BRN
40-.8 ORN
COURTESY LAMPS (SEE PAGE 169)
44-.8 DK GRN
S303 (SEE PAGE 63)
S308
40-.8 BRN
40-.5 ORN
I/P CLUSTER (DIGITAL ONLY) (SEE PAGE 152)
39-.8 PNK/BLK
FROM S306 (SEE PAGE 21)
150-.8 BLK
S307 (SEE PAGE 150)
8-.5 GRA
REAR
FUSE BLOCK
BUZZER
HZ/F
HORN
12015999
FRONT
12084577
HOT WITH LT SW IN HEAD OR PARK
INST LPS 5 AMP
HOT IN START OR RUN
IGN/GAUGES 20 AMP
HOT AT ALL TIMES
T/L CTSY 20 AMP
HORN RELAY
SAFETY BELT SW
GROUND
FASTEN BELTS
IGNITION
IGN KEY SW
BATTERY
LIGHTS ON SW
HAZARD FLASHER

1988–91 WIRING DIAGRAMS (CONT.)

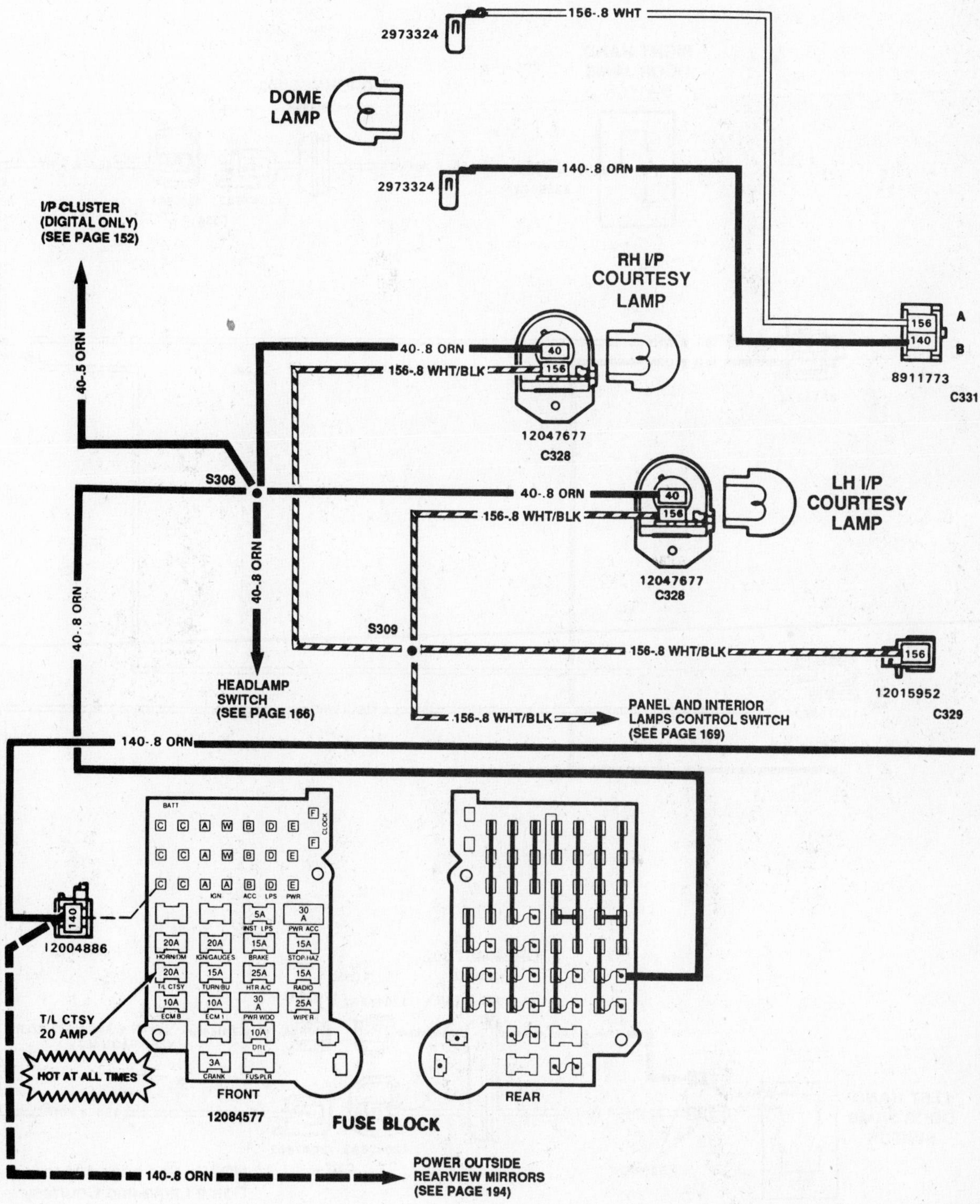
156-.8 WHT
2973324
DOME LAMP
140-.8 ORN
2973324
I/P CLUSTER (DIGITAL ONLY) (SEE PAGE 152)
RH I/P COURTESY LAMP
40-.5 ORN
40-.8 ORN
156-.8 WHT/BLK
40
156
12047677
C328
156
140
A
B
8911773
C331
S308
40-.8 ORN
LH I/P COURTESY LAMP
156-.8 WHT/BLK
40
156
12047677
C328
40-.8 ORN
40-.8 ORN
S309
156-.8 WHT/BLK
156
12015952
C329
HEADLAMP SWITCH (SEE PAGE 166)
156-.8 WHT/BLK
PANEL AND INTERIOR LAMPS CONTROL SWITCH (SEE PAGE 169)
140-.8 ORN
140
12004886
T/L CTSY 20 AMP
HOT AT ALL TIMES
FRONT
12084577
FUSE BLOCK
REAR
140-.8 ORN
POWER OUTSIDE REARVIEW MIRRORS (SEE PAGE 194)

1988–91 WIRING DIAGRAMS (CONT.)

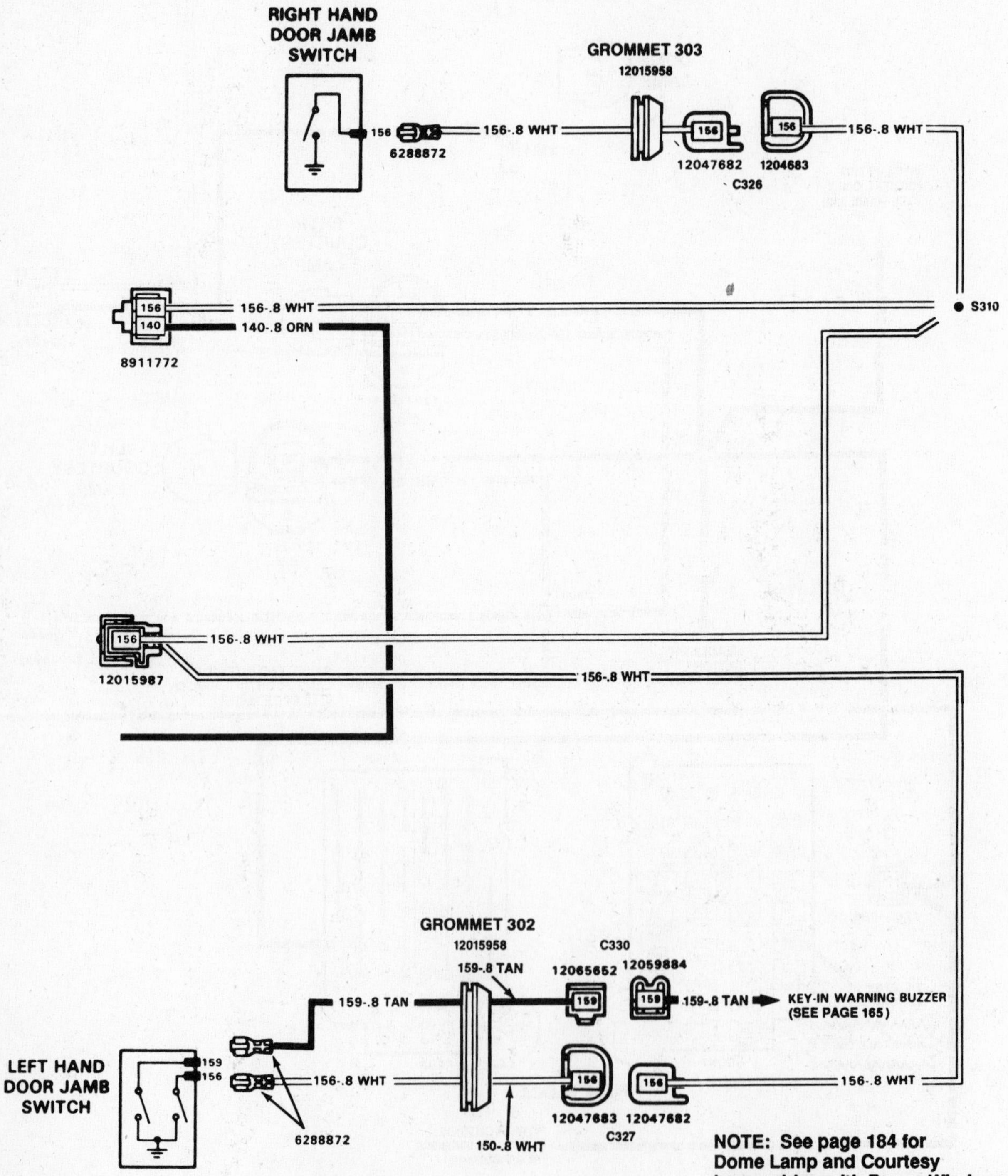

RIGHT HAND
DOOR JAMB
SWITCH
156
6288872
156-.8 WHT
GROMMET 303
12015958
156
12047682
156
1204683
C326
156-.8 WHT
156
140
156-.8 WHT
140-.8 ORN
8911772
S310
156
156-.8 WHT
12015987
156-.8 WHT
GROMMET 302
12015958
159-.8 TAN
C330
12065652
12059884
159-.8 TAN
159
159
159-.8 TAN
KEY-IN WARNING BUZZER
(SEE PAGE 165)
LEFT HAND
DOOR JAMB
SWITCH
159
156
156-.8 WHT
156
156
156-.8 WHT
6288872
150-.8 WHT
12047683
12047682
C327

NOTE: See page 184 for Dome Lamp and Courtesy Lamp wiring with Power Windows and Door Locks.

1988–91 WIRING DIAGRAMS (CONT.)

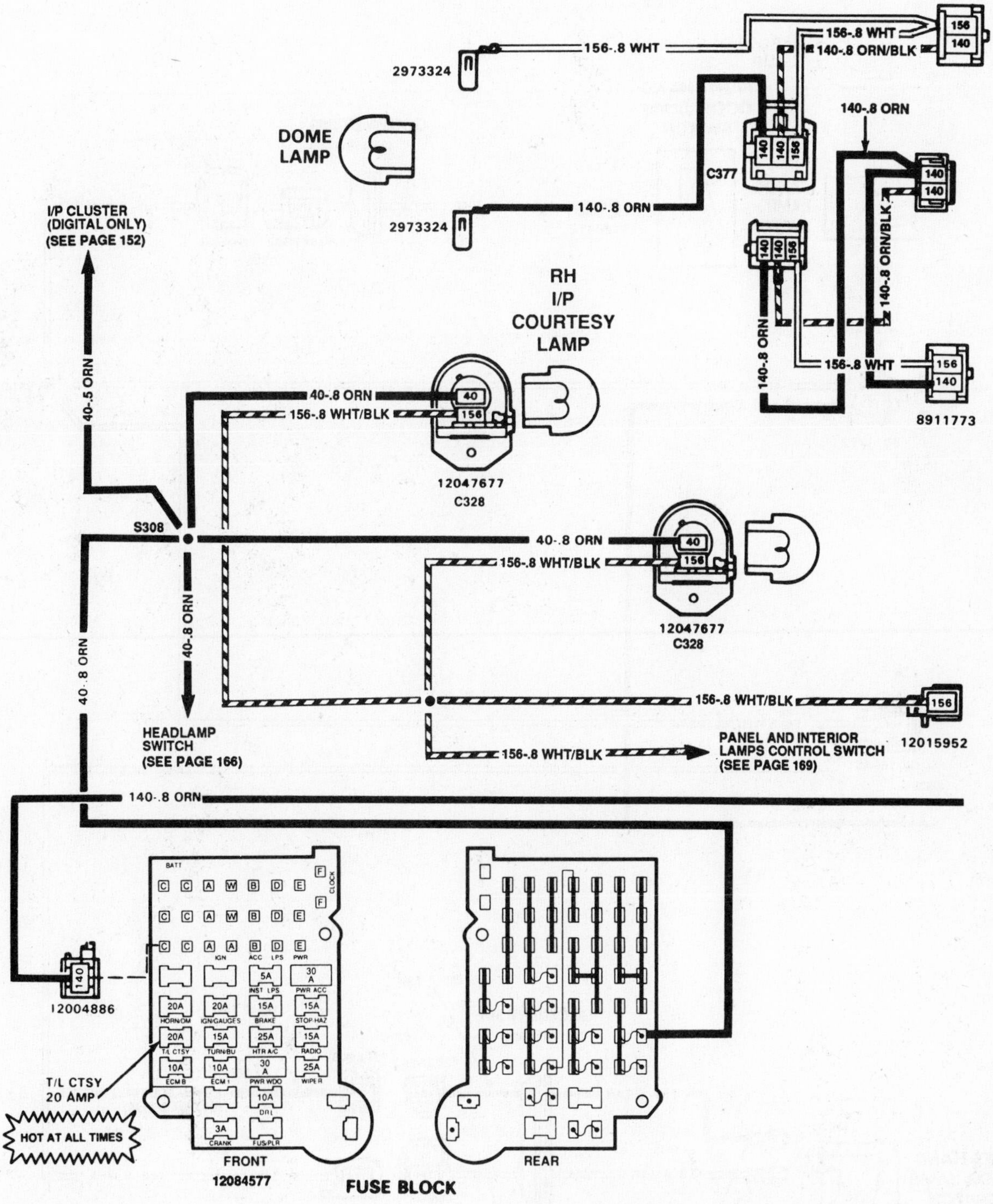
156-.8 WHT
140-.8 ORN/BLK
2973324
DOME LAMP
C377
140-.8 ORN
2973324
I/P CLUSTER (DIGITAL ONLY) (SEE PAGE 152)
RH I/P COURTESY LAMP
140-.8 ORN/BLK
140-.8 ORN
156-.8 WHT
8911773
40-.5 ORN
40-.8 ORN
156-.8 WHT/BLK
12047677
C328
S308
40-.8 ORN
156-.8 WHT/BLK
12047677
C328
40-.8 ORN
40-.8 ORN
156-.8 WHT/BLK
12015952
HEADLAMP SWITCH (SEE PAGE 166)
156-.8 WHT/BLK
PANEL AND INTERIOR LAMPS CONTROL SWITCH (SEE PAGE 169)
140-.8 ORN
12004886
T/L CTSY 20 AMP
HOT AT ALL TIMES
FRONT
12084577
FUSE BLOCK
REAR

1988–91 WIRING DIAGRAMS (CONT.)

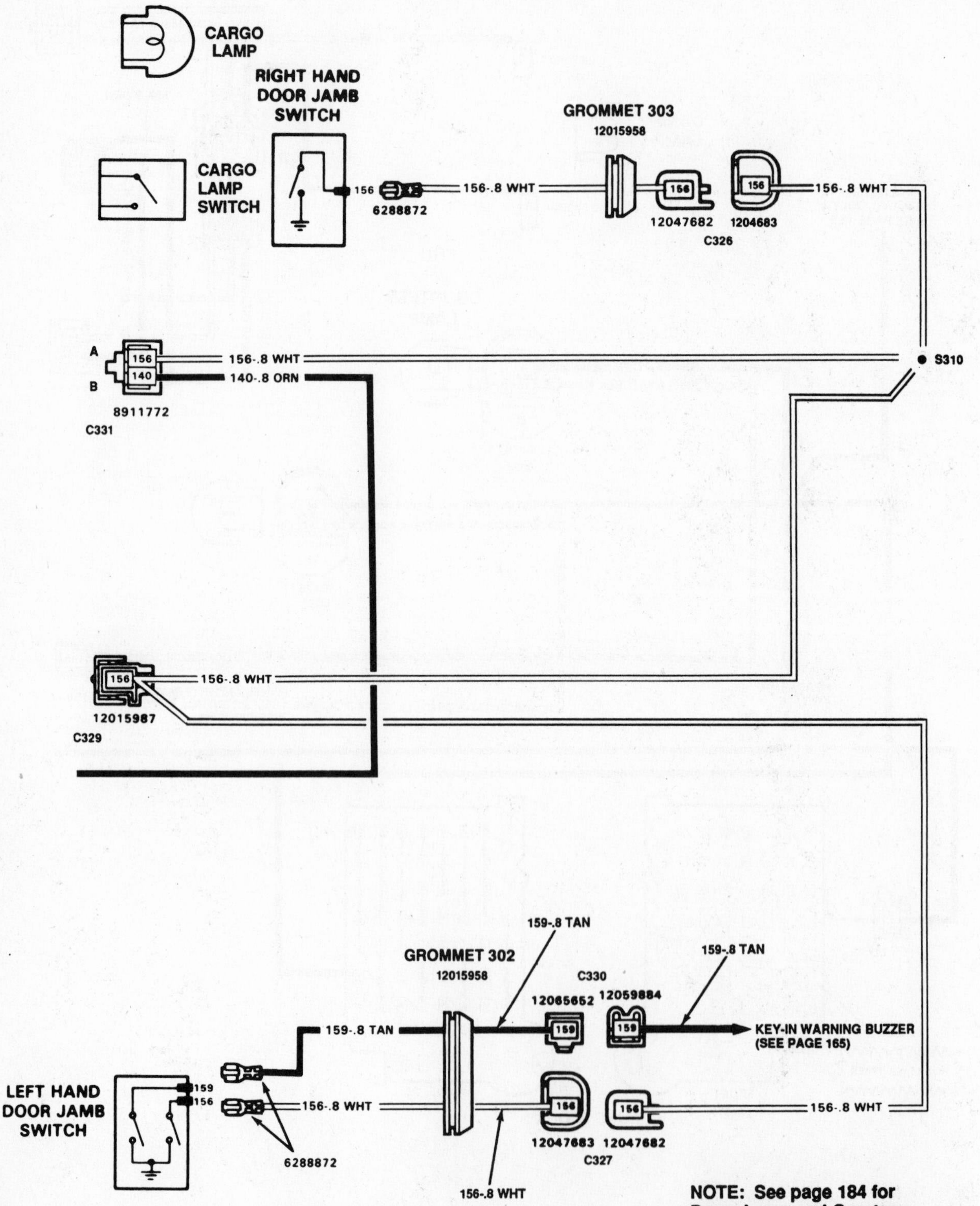
CARGO LAMP
RIGHT HAND DOOR JAMB SWITCH
CARGO LAMP SWITCH
156
6288872
156-.8 WHT
GROMMET 303
12015958
156
12047682
156
1204683
C326
156-.8 WHT
A
B
156
140
156-.8 WHT
140-.8 ORN
8911772
C331
S310
156
156-.8 WHT
12015987
C329
159-.8 TAN
GROMMET 302
12015958
159-.8 TAN
C330
12065652
12059884
159-.8 TAN
159
159
KEY-IN WARNING BUZZER (SEE PAGE 165)
LEFT HAND DOOR JAMB SWITCH
159
156
156-.8 WHT
156
156
12047683
12047682
C327
156-.8 WHT
6288872
156-.8 WHT

NOTE: See page 184 for Dome Lamp and Courtesy Lamp wiring with Power Windows and Door Locks.

1988–91 WIRING DIAGRAMS (CONT.)

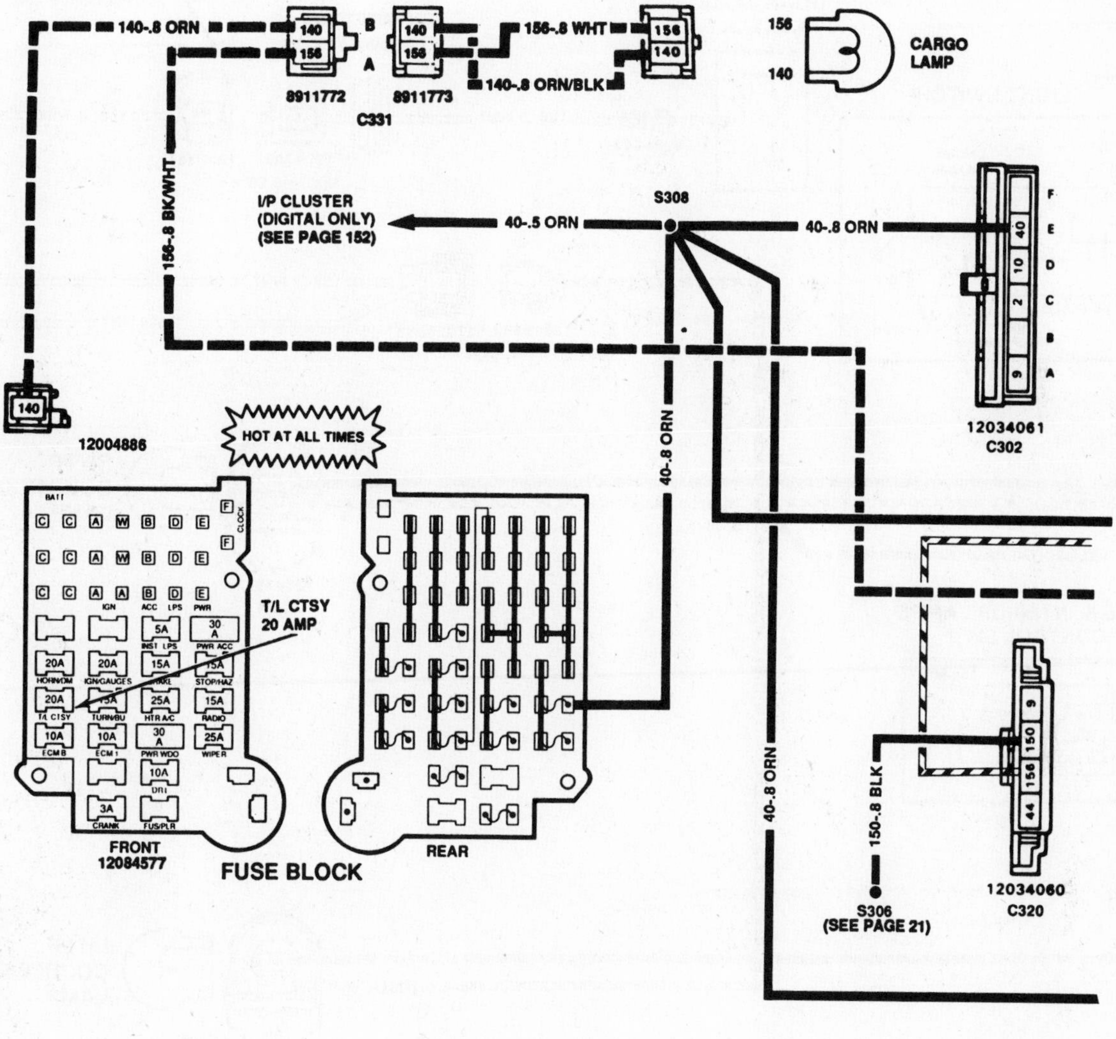
140-.8 ORN
140
156
B
A
8911772
8911773
C331
156-.8 WHT
140-.8 ORN/BLK
156
140
CARGO LAMP
156-.8 BK/WHT
I/P CLUSTER (DIGITAL ONLY) (SEE PAGE 152)
40-.5 ORN
S308
40-.8 ORN
F
E
D
C
B
A
40
10
2
9
12034061
C302
140
12004886
HOT AT ALL TIMES
40-.8 ORN
T/L CTSY 20 AMP
BATT
CLOCK
IGN
ACC
LPS
PWR
5A
30 A
INST LPS
PWR ACC
20A
15A
HORN/DM
IGN/GAUGES
STOP/HAZ
25A
T/L CTSY
TURN/BU
HTR A/C
RADIO
10A
ECM B
ECM 1
PWR WDO
WIPER
DRL
3A
CRANK
FUS/PLR
FRONT 12084577
FUSE BLOCK
REAR
40-.8 ORN
150-.8 BLK
150
156
44
S306 (SEE PAGE 21)
12034060
C320

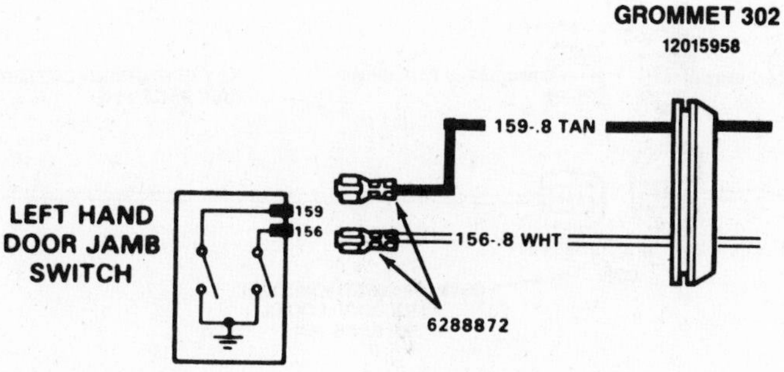
GROMMET 302
12015958
159-.8 TAN
LEFT HAND DOOR JAMB SWITCH
159
156
156-.8 WHT
6288872

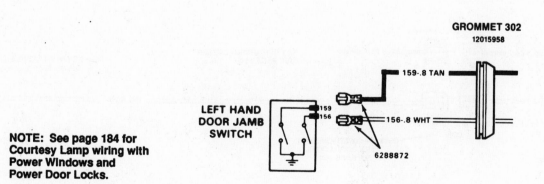

NOTE: See page 184 for Courtesy Lamp wiring with Power Windows and Power Door Locks.

1988–91 WIRING DIAGRAMS (CONT.)

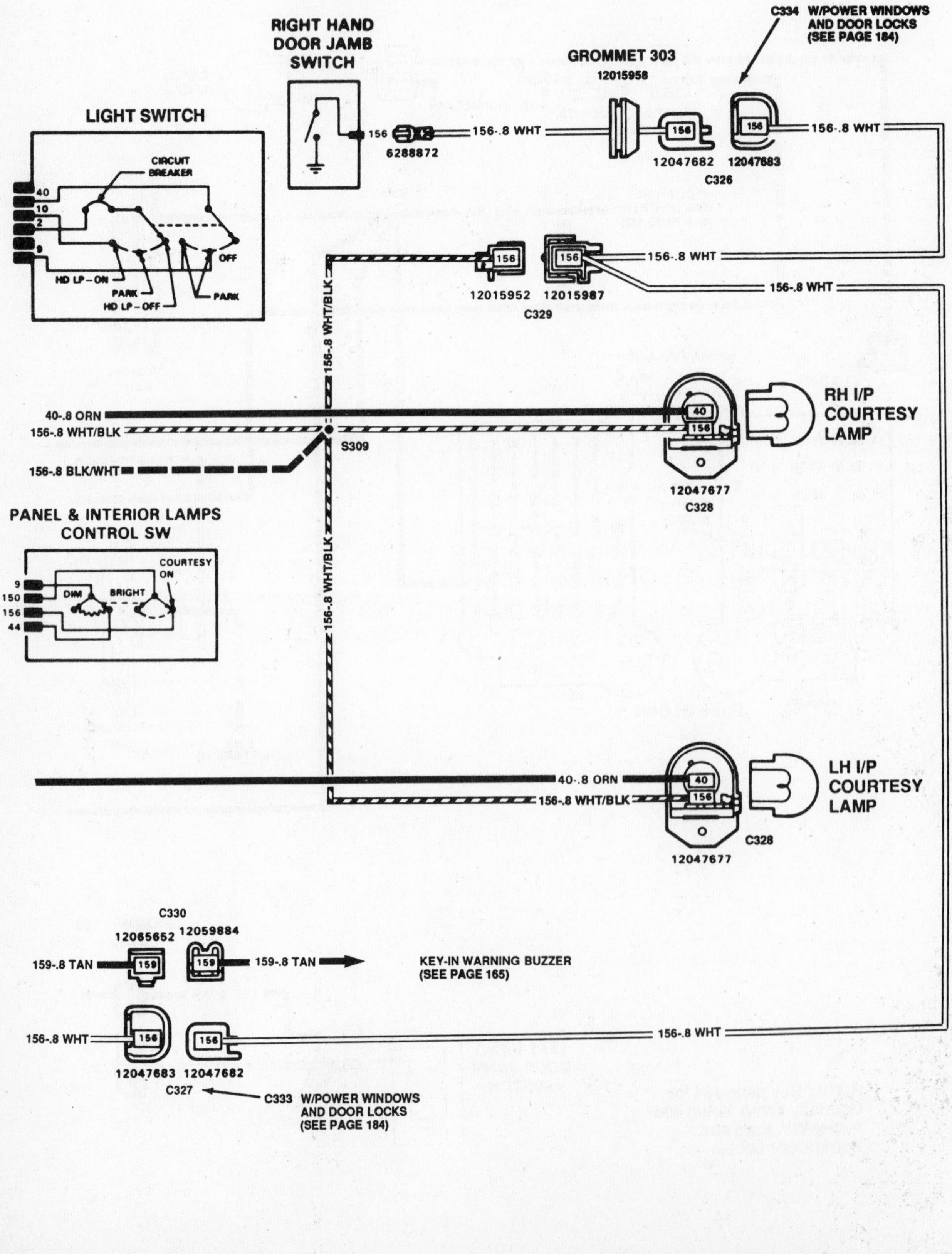
RIGHT HAND DOOR JAMB SWITCH
C334 W/POWER WINDOWS AND DOOR LOCKS (SEE PAGE 184)
GROMMET 303
12015958
LIGHT SWITCH
CIRCUIT BREAKER
40
10
2
9
OFF
HD LP – ON
PARK
HD LP – OFF
PARK
156
6288872
156-.8 WHT
156
12047682
156
12047683
C326
156-.8 WHT
156
12015952
156
12015987
C329
156-.8 WHT
156-.8 WHT
156-.8 WHT/BLK
40-.8 ORN
156-.8 WHT/BLK
S309
156-.8 BLK/WHT
40
156
12047677
C328
RH I/P COURTESY LAMP
PANEL & INTERIOR LAMPS CONTROL SW
COURTESY ON
DIM
BRIGHT
9
150
156
44
156-.8 WHT/BLK
40-.8 ORN
156-.8 WHT/BLK
40
156
C328
12047677
LH I/P COURTESY LAMP
C330
12065652
12059884
159-.8 TAN
159
159
159-.8 TAN
KEY-IN WARNING BUZZER (SEE PAGE 165)
156-.8 WHT
156
156
156-.8 WHT
12047683
12047682
C327
C333 W/POWER WINDOWS AND DOOR LOCKS (SEE PAGE 184)

1988–91 WIRING DIAGRAMS (CONT.)

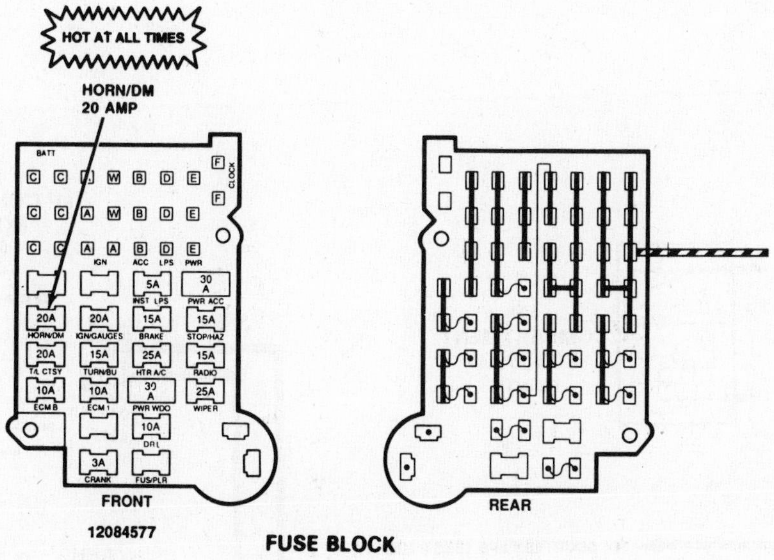
HOT AT ALL TIMES
HORN/DM
20 AMP
FRONT
12084577
REAR
FUSE BLOCK

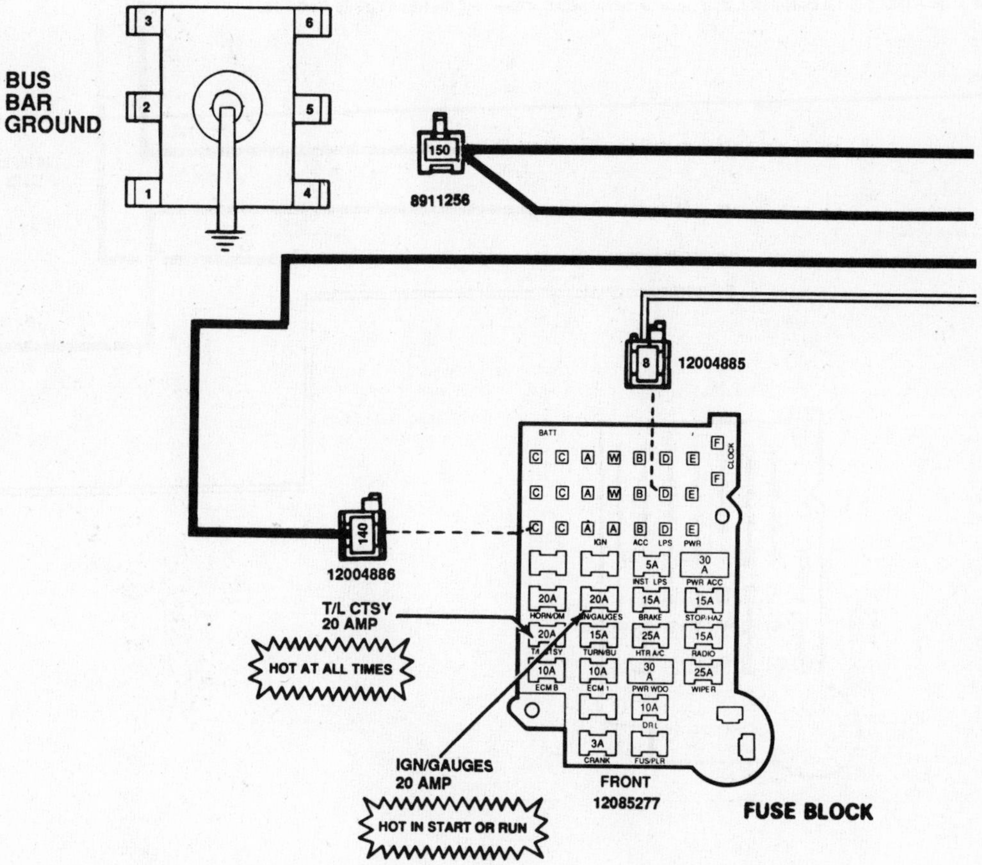
BUS BAR GROUND
150
8911256
8
12004885
140
12004886
T/L CTSY
20 AMP
HOT AT ALL TIMES
IGN/GAUGES
20 AMP
HOT IN START OR RUN
FRONT
12085277
FUSE BLOCK

1988–91 WIRING DIAGRAMS (CONT.)

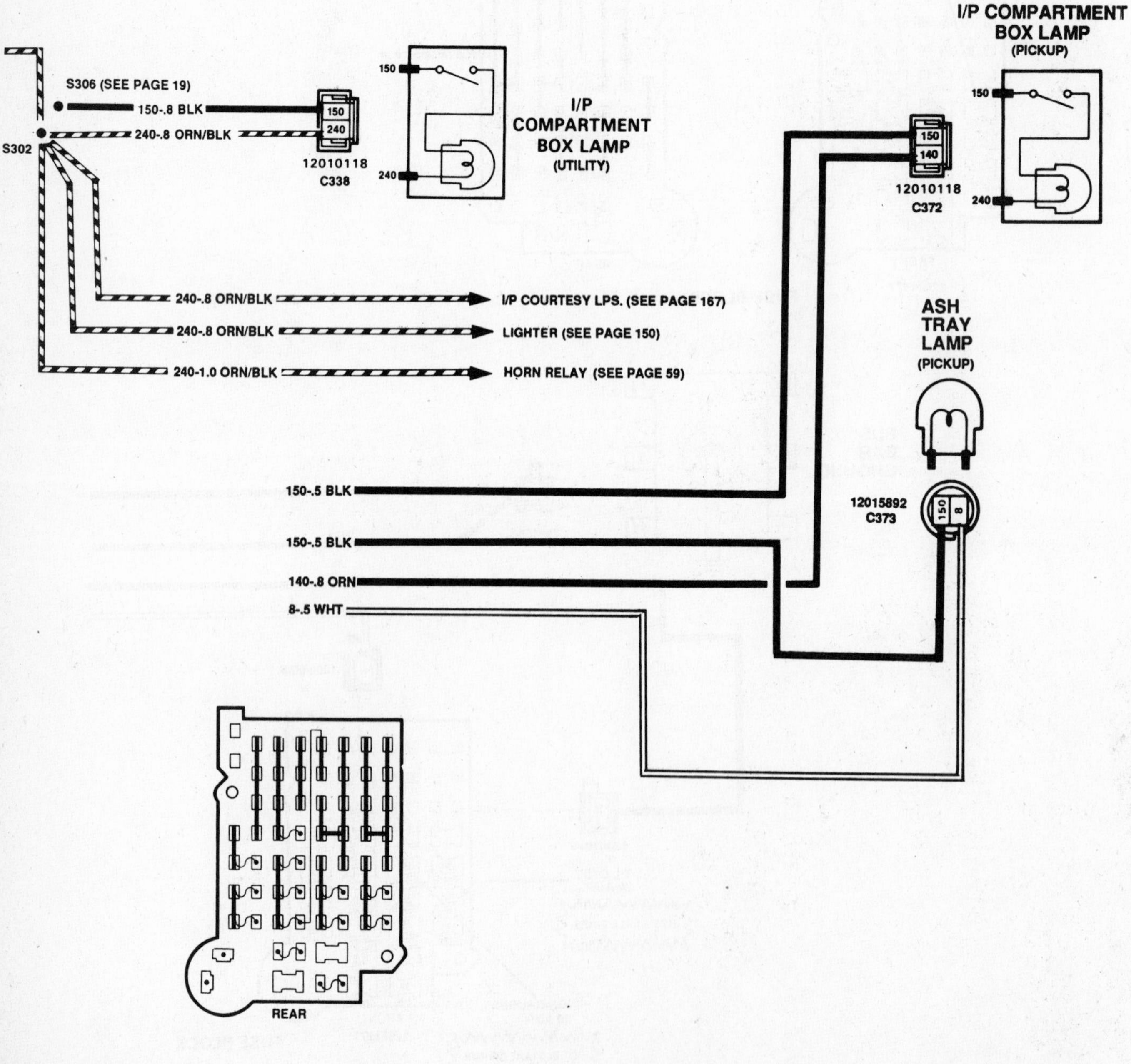
S306 (SEE PAGE 19)
150-.8 BLK
240-.8 ORN/BLK
S302
150
240
12010118
C338
I/P COMPARTMENT BOX LAMP
(UTILITY)
240-.8 ORN/BLK
I/P COURTESY LPS. (SEE PAGE 167)
240-.8 ORN/BLK
LIGHTER (SEE PAGE 150)
240-1.0 ORN/BLK
HORN RELAY (SEE PAGE 59)
I/P COMPARTMENT BOX LAMP
(PICKUP)
150
140
12010118
C372
240
ASH TRAY LAMP
(PICKUP)
12015892
C373
150
8
150-.5 BLK
150-.5 BLK
140-.8 ORN
8-.5 WHT
REAR

1988–91 WIRING DIAGRAMS (CONT.)

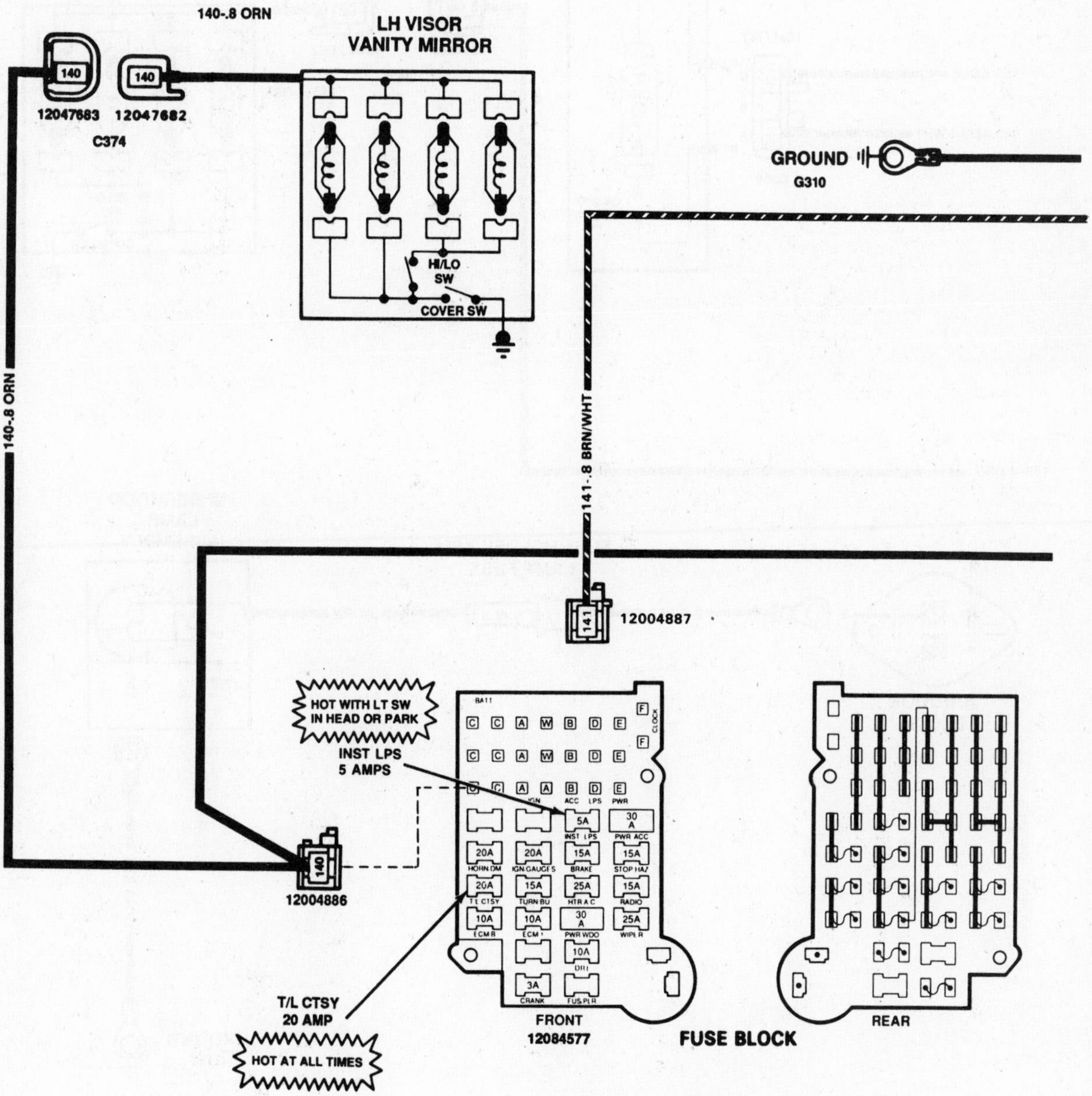
140-.8 ORN
LH VISOR
VANITY MIRROR
140
12047683
12047682
C374
HI/LO
SW
COVER SW
GROUND
G310
140-.8 ORN
141-.8 BRN/WHT
141
12004887
HOT WITH LT SW
IN HEAD OR PARK
INST LPS
5 AMPS
140
12004886
T/L CTSY
20 AMP
HOT AT ALL TIMES
FRONT
12084577
FUSE BLOCK
REAR

1988–91 WIRING DIAGRAMS (CONT.)

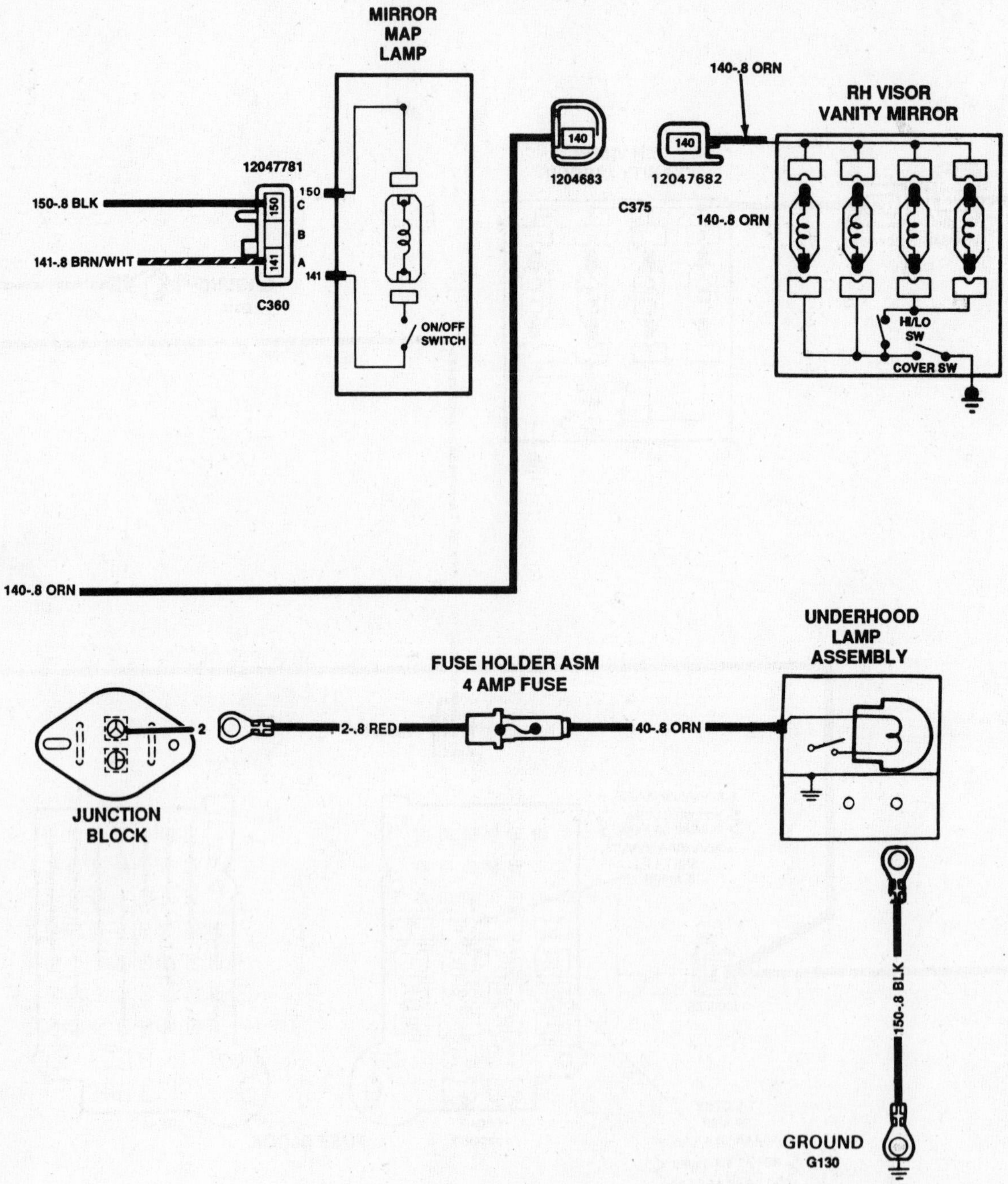
MIRROR
MAP
LAMP
12047781
150-.8 BLK
141-.8 BRN/WHT
150
C
B
A
141
C360
ON/OFF
SWITCH
140
1204683
140
12047682
C375
140-.8 ORN
140-.8 ORN
RH VISOR
VANITY MIRROR
HI/LO
SW
COVER SW
140-.8 ORN
UNDERHOOD
LAMP
ASSEMBLY
FUSE HOLDER ASM
4 AMP FUSE
2
2-.8 RED
40-.8 ORN
JUNCTION
BLOCK
150-.8 BLK
GROUND
G130

1988–91 WIRING DIAGRAMS (CONT.)

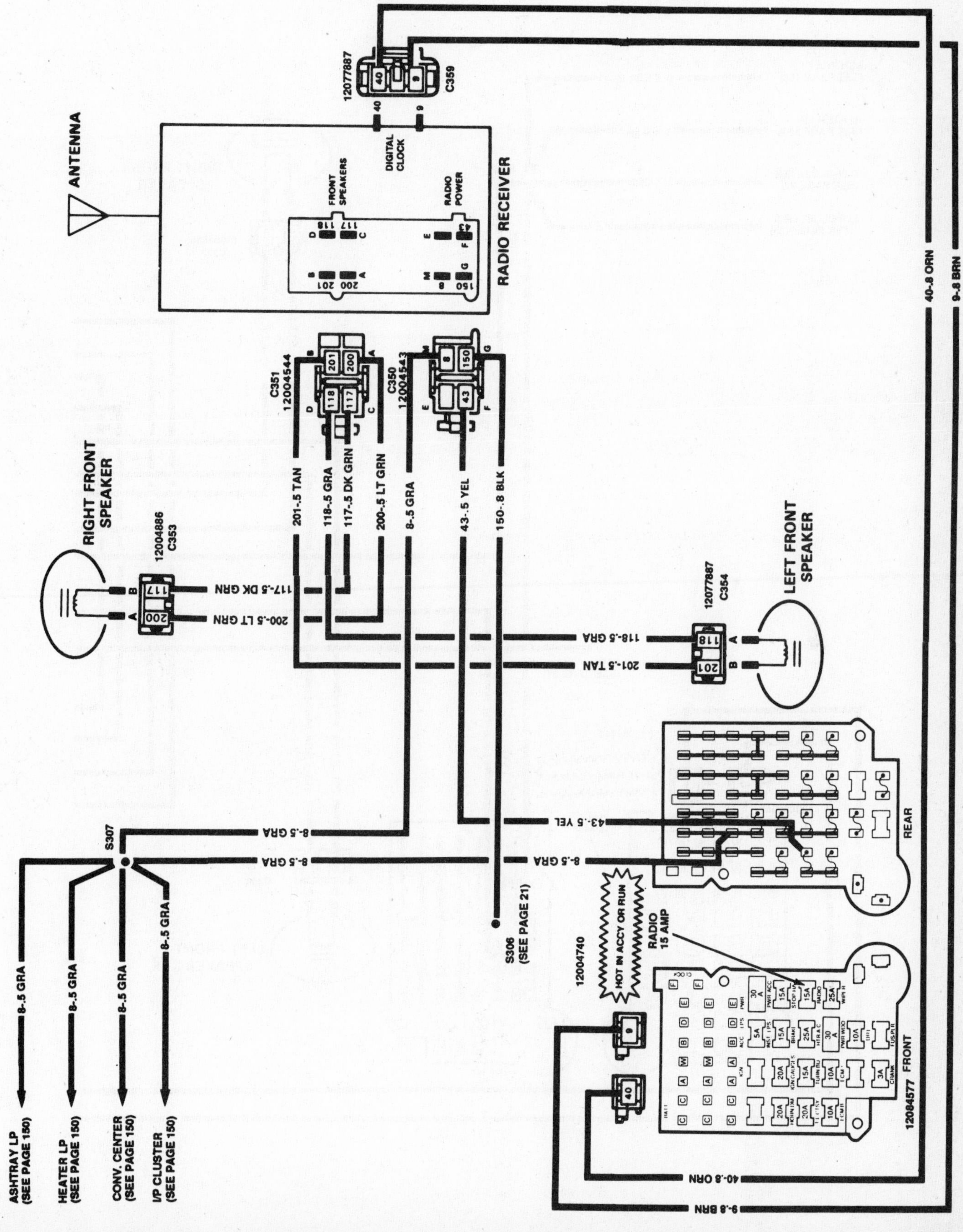
ANTENNA
RADIO RECEIVER
FRONT SPEAKERS
DIGITAL CLOCK
RADIO POWER
12077887
C359
C351
12004544
C350
12004543
RIGHT FRONT SPEAKER
12004886
C353
LEFT FRONT SPEAKER
12077887
C354
201-.5 TAN
118-.5 GRA
117-.5 DK GRN
200-.5 LT GRN
8-.5 GRA
43-.5 YEL
150-.8 BLK
40-.8 ORN
9-.8 BRN
S307
S306 (SEE PAGE 21)
HOT IN ACCY OR RUN
RADIO 15 AMP
12004740
REAR
FRONT
12084577
ASHTRAY LP (SEE PAGE 150)
HEATER LP (SEE PAGE 150)
CONV. CENTER (SEE PAGE 150)
I/P CLUSTER (SEE PAGE 150)

1988–91 WIRING DIAGRAMS (CONT.)

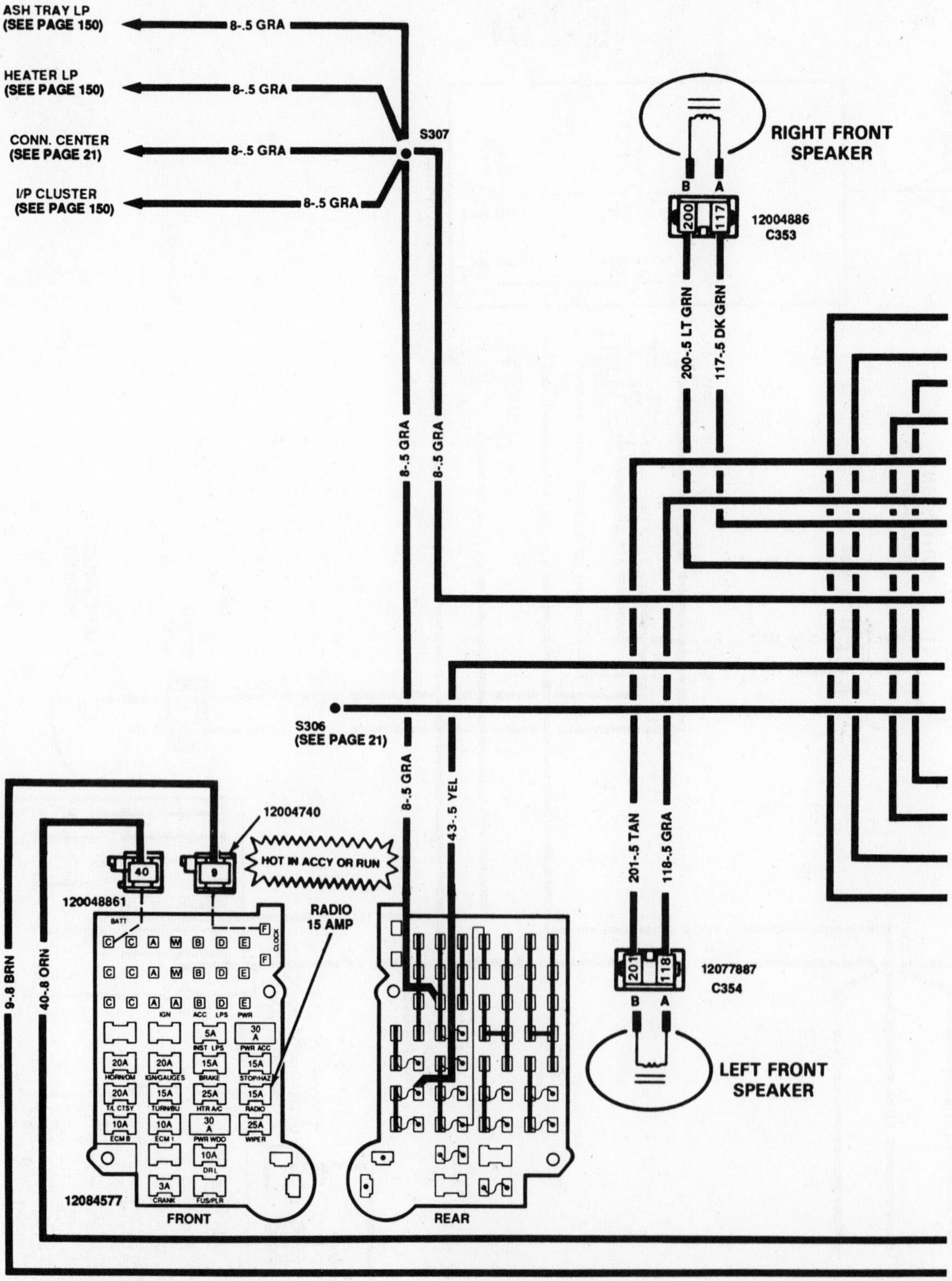

ASH TRAY LP (SEE PAGE 150)
8-.5 GRA
HEATER LP (SEE PAGE 150)
8-.5 GRA
CONN. CENTER (SEE PAGE 21)
8-.5 GRA
I/P CLUSTER (SEE PAGE 150)
8-.5 GRA
S307
8-.5 GRA
8-.5 GRA
RIGHT FRONT SPEAKER
B A
200 117
12004886
C353
200-.5 LT GRN
117-.5 DK GRN
S306 (SEE PAGE 21)
8-.5 GRA
43-.5 YEL
201-.5 TAN
118-.5 GRA
12004740
HOT IN ACCY OR RUN
40
9
120048861
RADIO 15 AMP
9-.8 BRN
40-.8 ORN
BATT
CLOCK
IGN ACC LPS PWR
5A
30 A
INST LPS
PWR ACC
20A 20A 15A 15A
HORN/DM IGN/GAUGES BRAKE STOP/HAZ
20A 15A 25A 15A
T/L CTSY TURN/BU HTR A/C RADIO
10A 10A 30 A 25A
ECM B ECM 1 PWR WDO WIPER
10A
DRL
3A
CRANK FUS/PLR
12084577
FRONT
REAR
201 118
12077887
C354
B A
LEFT FRONT SPEAKER

1988–91 WIRING DIAGRAMS (CONT.)

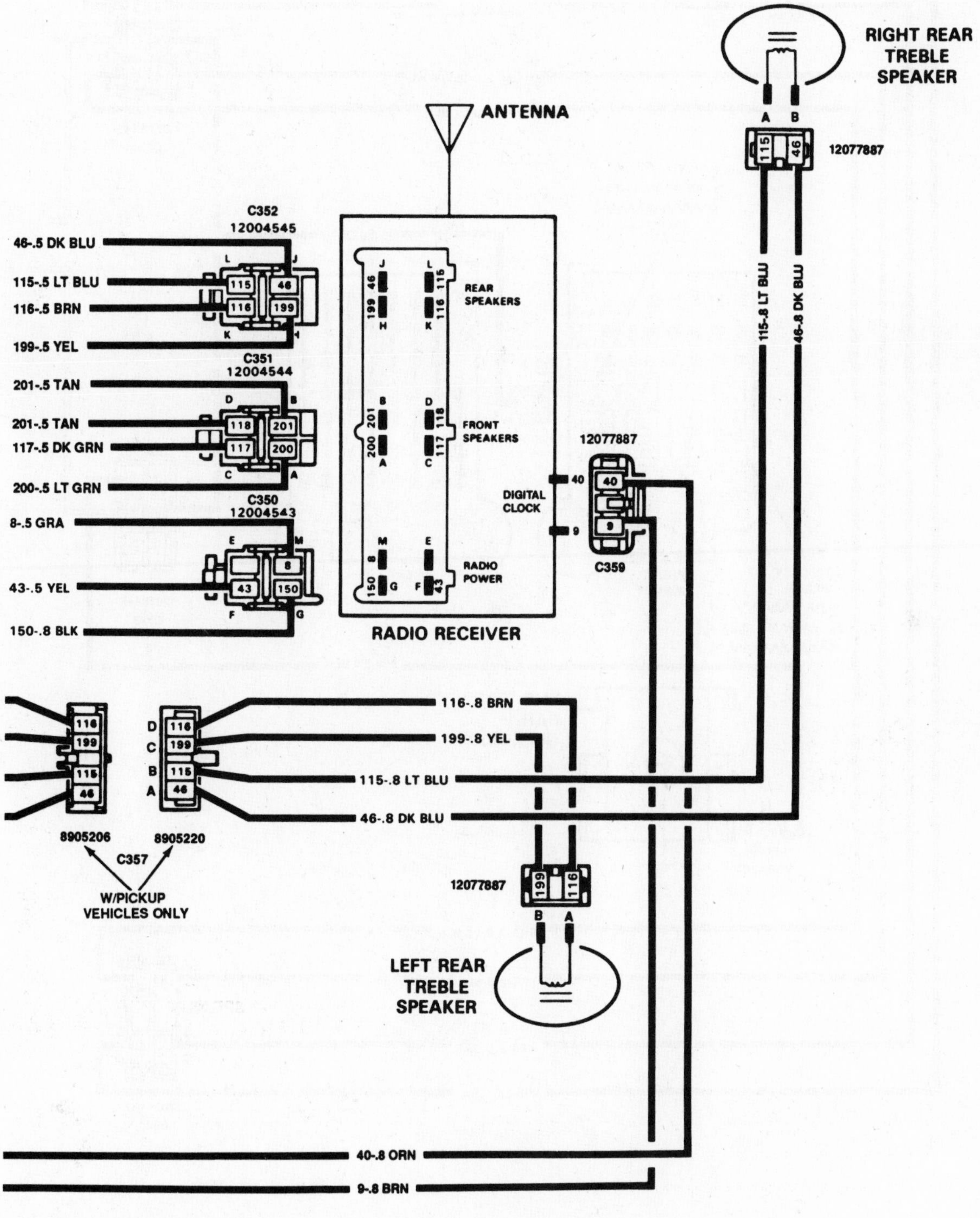
RIGHT REAR TREBLE SPEAKER
ANTENNA
12077887
C352
12004545
46-.5 DK BLU
115-.5 LT BLU
116-.5 BRN
199-.5 YEL
C351
12004544
201-.5 TAN
201-.5 TAN
117-.5 DK GRN
200-.5 LT GRN
C350
12004543
8-.5 GRA
43-.5 YEL
150-.8 BLK
REAR SPEAKERS
FRONT SPEAKERS
DIGITAL CLOCK
RADIO POWER
RADIO RECEIVER
C359
115-.8 LT BLU
46-.8 DK BLU
116-.8 BRN
199-.8 YEL
115-.8 LT BLU
46-.8 DK BLU
8905206
8905220
C357
W/PICKUP VEHICLES ONLY
LEFT REAR TREBLE SPEAKER
40-.8 ORN
9-.8 BRN

1988–91 WIRING DIAGRAMS (CONT.)

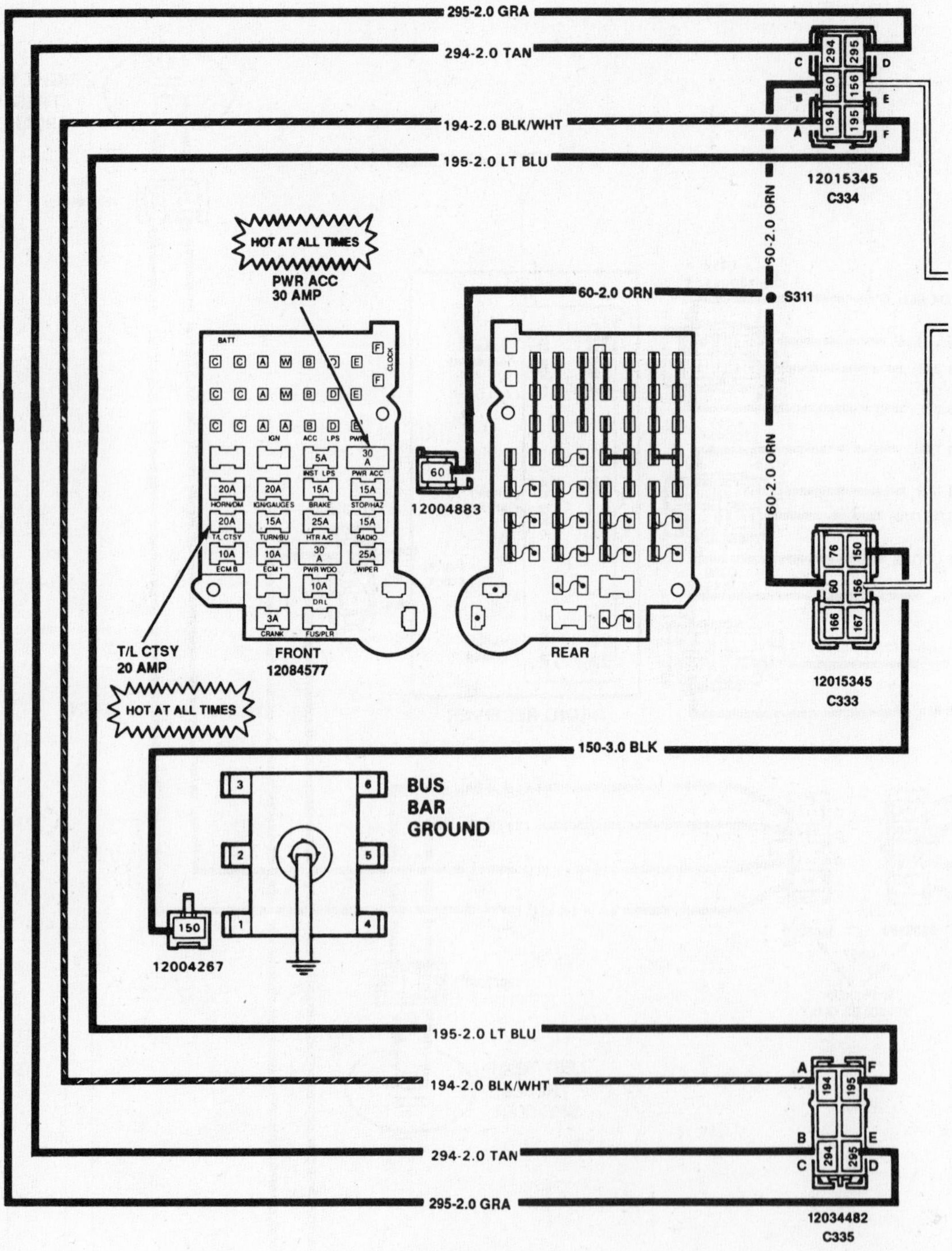

295-2.0 GRA
294-2.0 TAN
194-2.0 BLK/WHT
195-2.0 LT BLU
12015345
C334
HOT AT ALL TIMES
PWR ACC
30 AMP
60-2.0 ORN
S311
12004883
T/L CTSY
20 AMP
HOT AT ALL TIMES
FRONT
12084577
REAR
12015345
C333
150-3.0 BLK
BUS
BAR
GROUND
12004267
195-2.0 LT BLU
194-2.0 BLK/WHT
294-2.0 TAN
295-2.0 GRA
12034482
C335

1988–91 WIRING DIAGRAMS (CONT.)

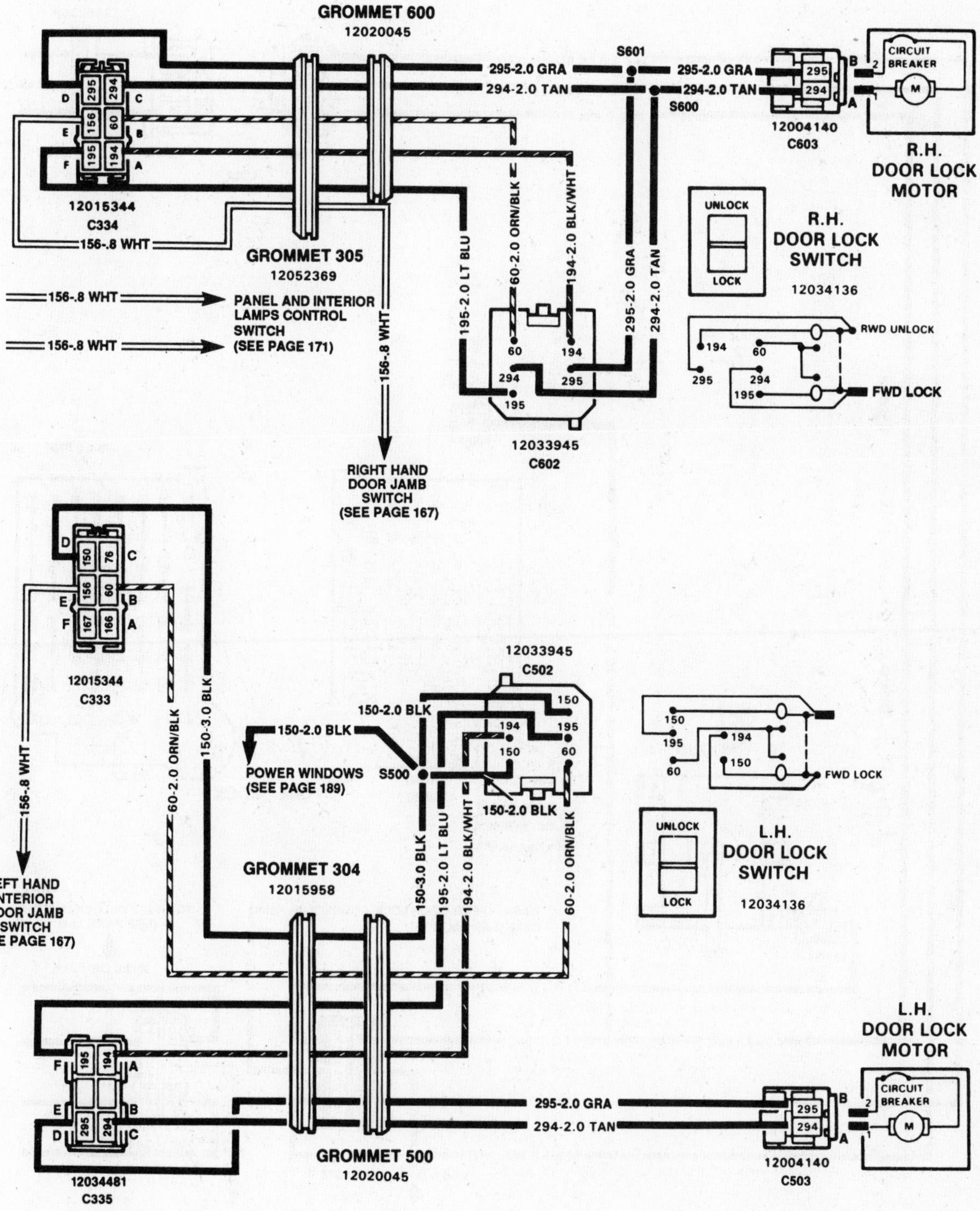
GROMMET 600
12020045
S601
295-2.0 GRA
294-2.0 TAN
S600
12004140
C603
CIRCUIT BREAKER
R.H. DOOR LOCK MOTOR
12015344
C334
156-.8 WHT
GROMMET 305
12052369
PANEL AND INTERIOR LAMPS CONTROL SWITCH (SEE PAGE 171)
195-2.0 LT BLU
60-2.0 ORN/BLK
194-2.0 BLK/WHT
295-2.0 GRA
294-2.0 TAN
156-.8 WHT
12033945
C602
RIGHT HAND DOOR JAMB SWITCH (SEE PAGE 167)
UNLOCK
LOCK
R.H. DOOR LOCK SWITCH
12034136
RWD UNLOCK
FWD LOCK
12015344
C333
156-.8 WHT
60-2.0 ORN/BLK
150-3.0 BLK
LEFT HAND INTERIOR DOOR JAMB SWITCH (SEE PAGE 167)
12033945
C502
150-2.0 BLK
POWER WINDOWS (SEE PAGE 189)
S500
GROMMET 304
12015958
150-3.0 BLK
195-2.0 LT BLU
194-2.0 BLK/WHT
60-2.0 ORN/BLK
FWD LOCK
L.H. DOOR LOCK SWITCH
12034136
L.H. DOOR LOCK MOTOR
12034481
C335
GROMMET 500
12020045
295-2.0 GRA
294-2.0 TAN
12004140
C503

1988–91 WIRING DIAGRAMS (CONT.)

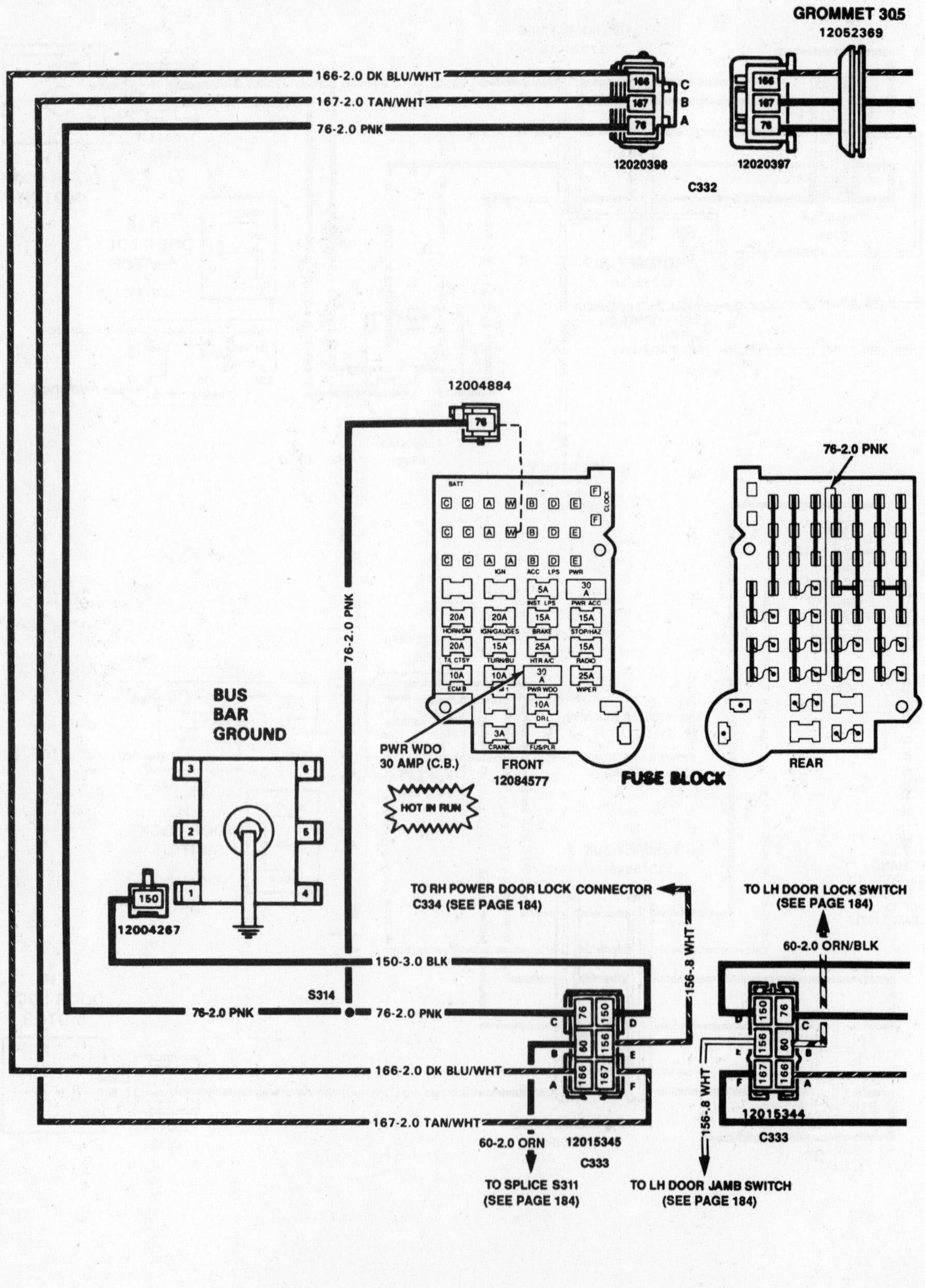
GROMMET 305
12052369
166-2.0 DK BLU/WHT
167-2.0 TAN/WHT
76-2.0 PNK
166
167
76
C
B
A
12020398
12020397
C332
12004884
76-2.0 PNK
BATT
CLOCK
IGN
ACC
LPS
PWR
5A
INST LPS
30 A
PWR ACC
20A
HORN/DM
20A
IGN/GAUGES
15A
BRAKE
15A
STOP/HAZ
20A
T/L CTSY
15A
TURN/BU
25A
HTR A/C
15A
RADIO
10A
ECM B
10A
30 A
PWR WDO
25A
WIPER
10A
DRL
3A
CRANK
FUS/PLR
PWR WDO
30 AMP (C.B.)
HOT IN RUN
FRONT
12084577
FUSE BLOCK
REAR
BUS
BAR
GROUND
150
12004267
TO RH POWER DOOR LOCK CONNECTOR
C334 (SEE PAGE 184)
TO LH DOOR LOCK SWITCH
(SEE PAGE 184)
60-2.0 ORN/BLK
150-3.0 BLK
156-.8 WHT
S314
76-2.0 PNK
76-2.0 PNK
166-2.0 DK BLU/WHT
167-2.0 TAN/WHT
60-2.0 ORN
12015345
C333
12015344
C333
TO SPLICE S311
(SEE PAGE 184)
TO LH DOOR JAMB SWITCH
(SEE PAGE 184)

1988–91 WIRING DIAGRAMS (CONT.)

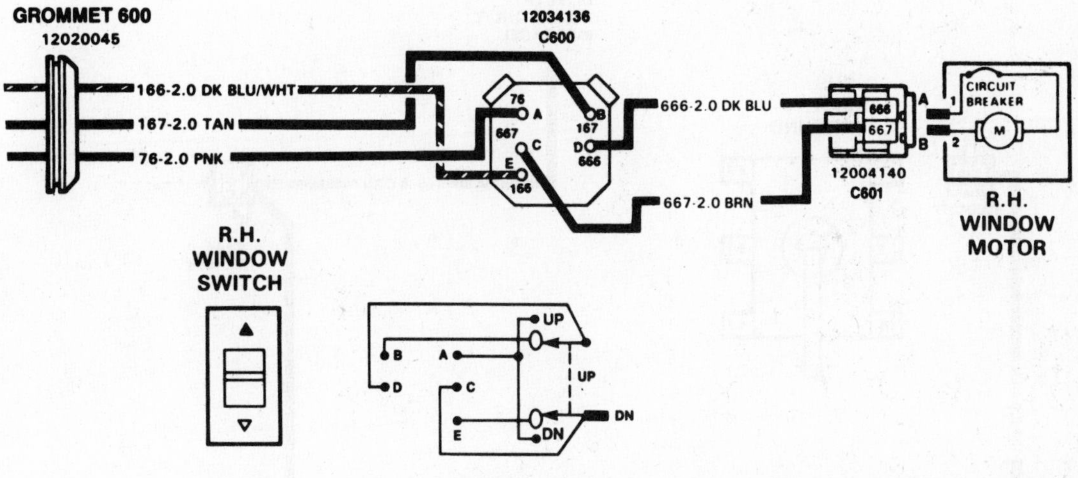
GROMMET 600
12020045
12034136
C600
166-2.0 DK BLU/WHT
167-2.0 TAN
76-2.0 PNK
666-2.0 DK BLU
667-2.0 BRN
12004140
C601
CIRCUIT BREAKER
M
R.H. WINDOW MOTOR
R.H. WINDOW SWITCH
UP
DN

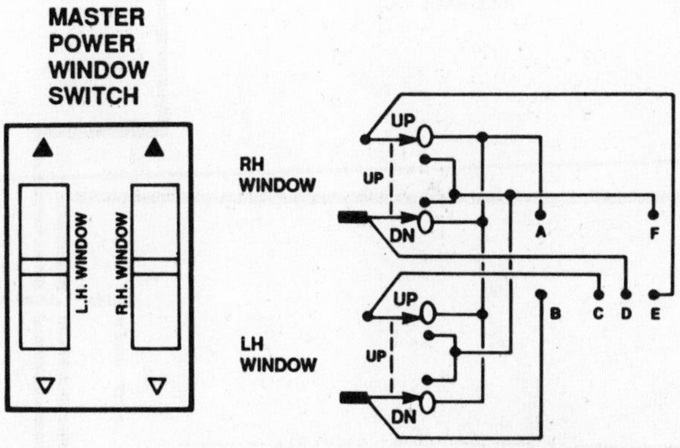
MASTER POWER WINDOW SWITCH
L.H. WINDOW
R.H. WINDOW
RH WINDOW
LH WINDOW
UP
DN

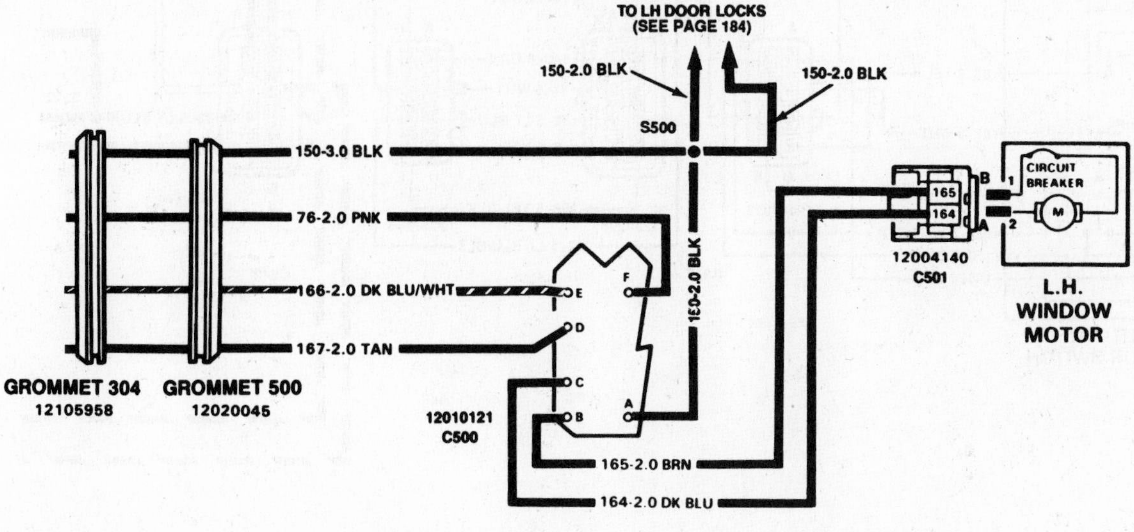
TO LH DOOR LOCKS (SEE PAGE 184)
150-2.0 BLK
150-2.0 BLK
S500
150-3.0 BLK
76-2.0 PNK
166-2.0 DK BLU/WHT
167-2.0 TAN
150-2.0 BLK
GROMMET 304
12105958
GROMMET 500
12020045
12010121
C500
165-2.0 BRN
164-2.0 DK BLU
12004140
C501
CIRCUIT BREAKER
M
L.H. WINDOW MOTOR

1988–91 WIRING DIAGRAMS (CONT.)

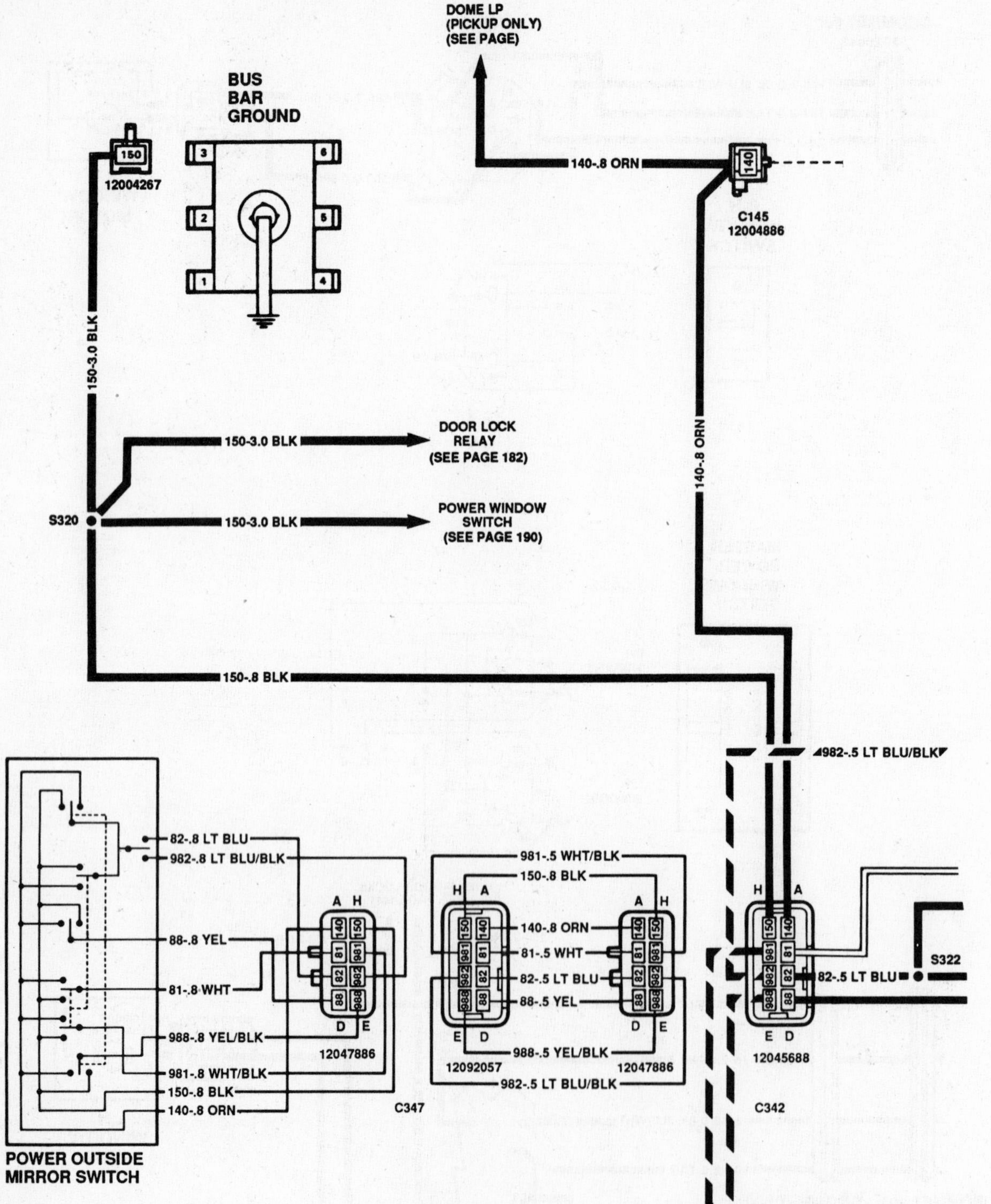
DOME LP
(PICKUP ONLY)
(SEE PAGE)
BUS
BAR
GROUND
150
12004267
140-.8 ORN
140
C145
12004886
150-3.0 BLK
150-3.0 BLK
DOOR LOCK
RELAY
(SEE PAGE 182)
S320
150-3.0 BLK
POWER WINDOW
SWITCH
(SEE PAGE 190)
140-.8 ORN
150-.8 BLK
982-.5 LT BLU/BLK
82-.8 LT BLU
982-.8 LT BLU/BLK
88-.8 YEL
81-.8 WHT
988-.8 YEL/BLK
981-.8 WHT/BLK
150-.8 BLK
140-.8 ORN
12047886
C347
981-.5 WHT/BLK
150-.8 BLK
140-.8 ORN
81-.5 WHT
82-.5 LT BLU
88-.5 YEL
988-.5 YEL/BLK
982-.5 LT BLU/BLK
12092057
12047886
12045688
82-.5 LT BLU
S322
C342
POWER OUTSIDE
MIRROR SWITCH

1988–91 WIRING DIAGRAMS (CONT.)

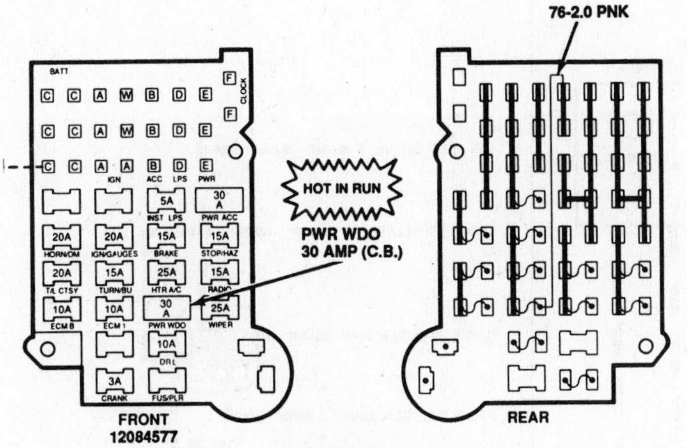
76-2.0 PNK
BATT
CLOCK
IGN
ACC LPS
PWR
5A
30 A
INST LPS
PWR ACC
HOT IN RUN
PWR WDO
30 AMP (C.B.)
20A
20A
15A
15A
HORN/DM
IGN/GAUGES
BRAKE
STOP/HAZ
20A
15A
25A
15A
T/L CTSY
TURN/BU
HTR A/C
RADIO
10A
10A
30 A
25A
ECM B
ECM 1
PWR WDO
WIPER
10A
DRL
3A
CRANK
FUS/PLR
FRONT
12084577
REAR

FUSE BLOCK
12084577

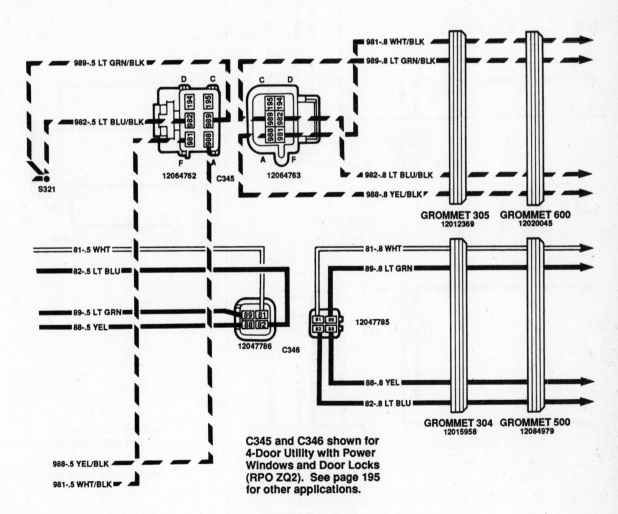

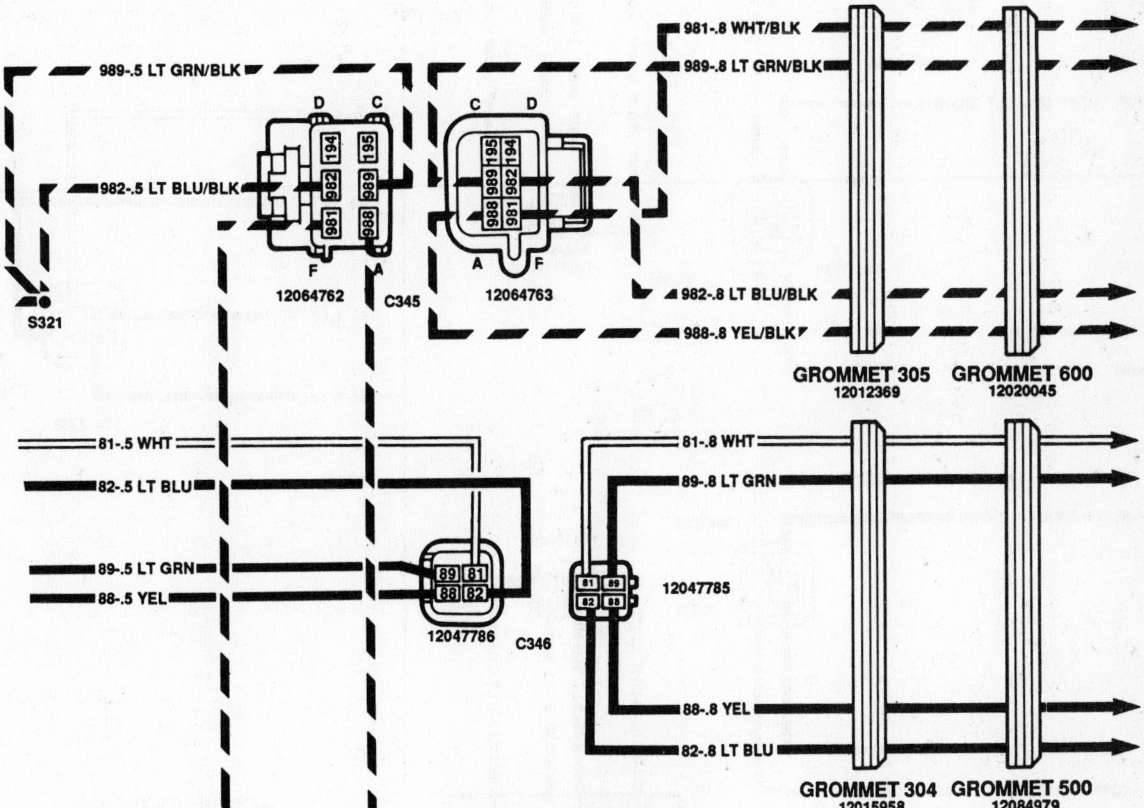
981-.8 WHT/BLK
989-.5 LT GRN/BLK
989-.8 LT GRN/BLK
D C
C D
194
195
982
989
981
988
982-.5 LT BLU/BLK
F A
A F
S321
12064762
C345
12064763
982-.8 LT BLU/BLK
988-.8 YEL/BLK
GROMMET 305
12012369
GROMMET 600
12020045
81-.5 WHT
82-.5 LT BLU
89-.5 LT GRN
88-.5 YEL
81-.8 WHT
89-.8 LT GRN
89 81
88 82
12047786
C346
12047785
88-.8 YEL
82-.8 LT BLU
GROMMET 304
12015958
GROMMET 500
12084979
988-.5 YEL/BLK
981-.5 WHT/BLK

C345 and C346 shown for 4-Door Utility with Power Windows and Door Locks (RPO ZQ2). See page 195 for other applications.

1988–91 WIRING DIAGRAMS (CONT.)

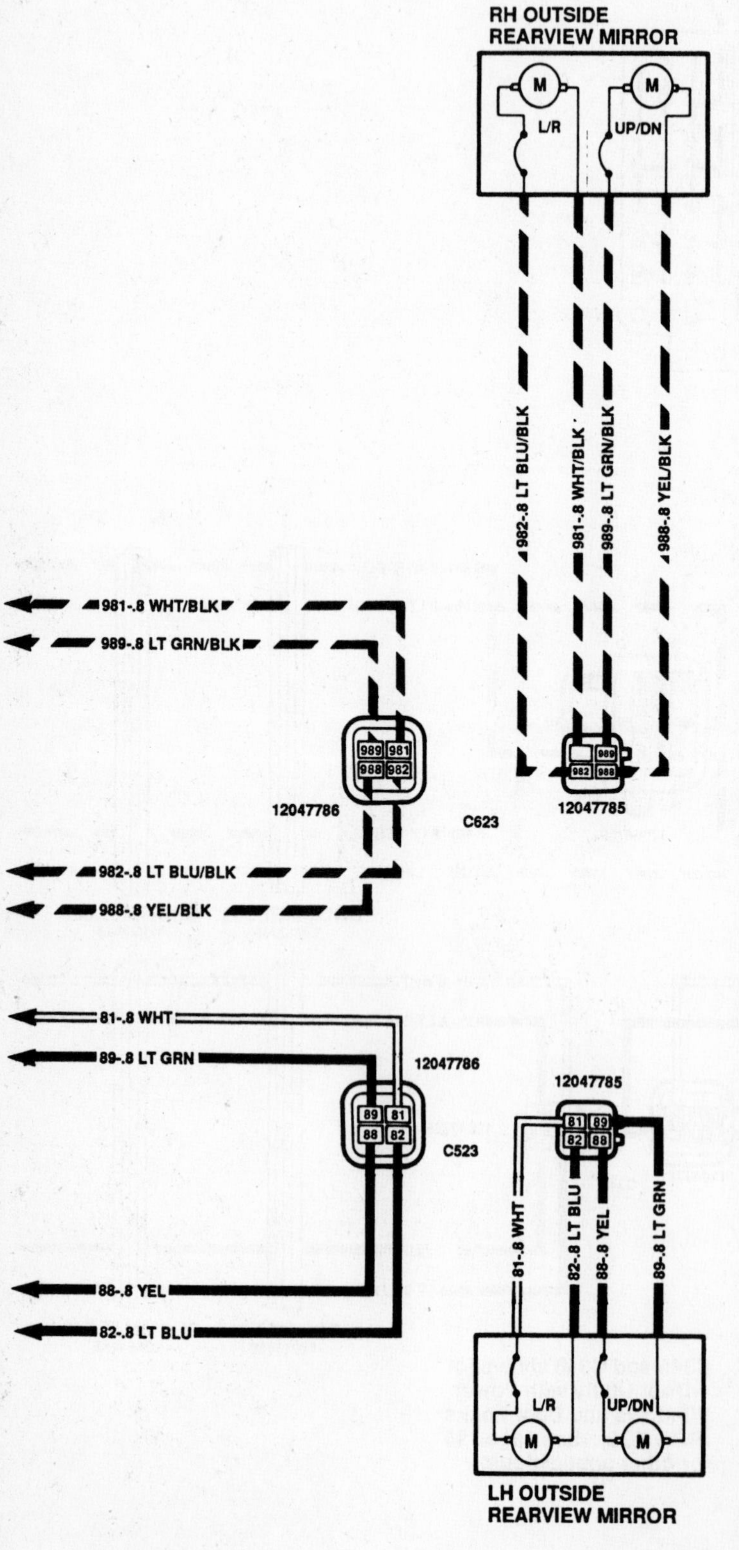
RH OUTSIDE
REARVIEW MIRROR
M
M
L/R
UP/DN
982-.8 LT BLU/BLK
981-.8 WHT/BLK
989-.8 LT GRN/BLK
988-.8 YEL/BLK
981-.8 WHT/BLK
989-.8 LT GRN/BLK
989
981
988
982
12047786
C623
982
988
989
12047785
982-.8 LT BLU/BLK
988-.8 YEL/BLK
81-.8 WHT
89-.8 LT GRN
12047786
89
81
88
82
C523
12047785
81
89
82
88
81-.8 WHT
82-.8 LT BLU
88-.8 YEL
89-.8 LT GRN
88-.8 YEL
82-.8 LT BLU
L/R
UP/DN
M
M
LH OUTSIDE
REARVIEW MIRROR

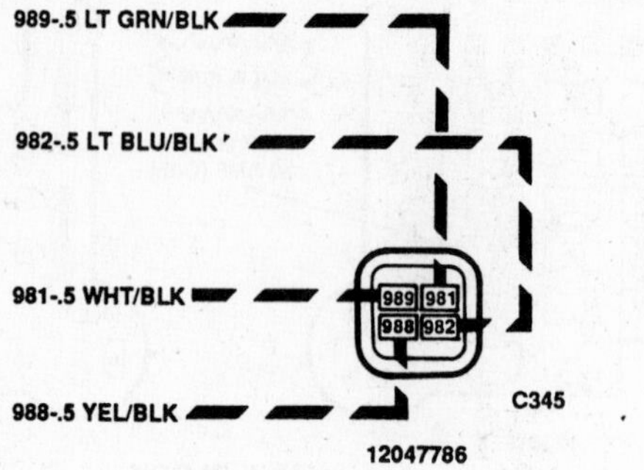
989-.5 LT GRN/BLK
982-.5 LT BLU/BLK
981-.5 WHT/BLK
988-.5 YEL/BLK
989
981
988
982
C345
12047786

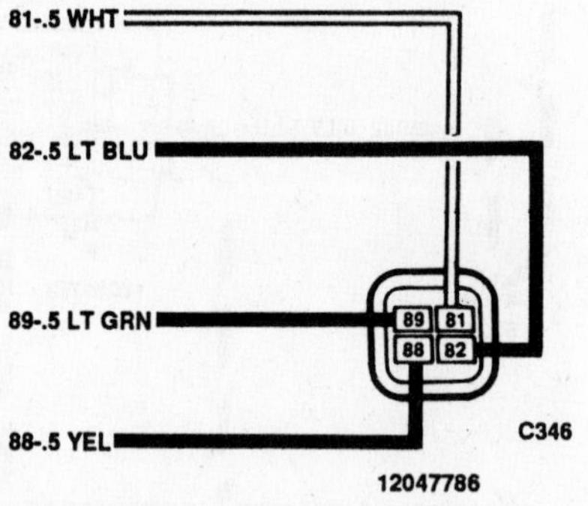
81-.5 WHT
82-.5 LT BLU
89-.5 LT GRN
88-.5 YEL
89
81
88
82
C346
12047786

4-DOOR UTILITY W/O POWER WINDOWS AND DOOR LOCKS

2-DOOR UTILITY AND PICKUP WITH POWER WINDOWS AND DOOR LOCKS

1988–91 WIRING DIAGRAMS (CONT.)

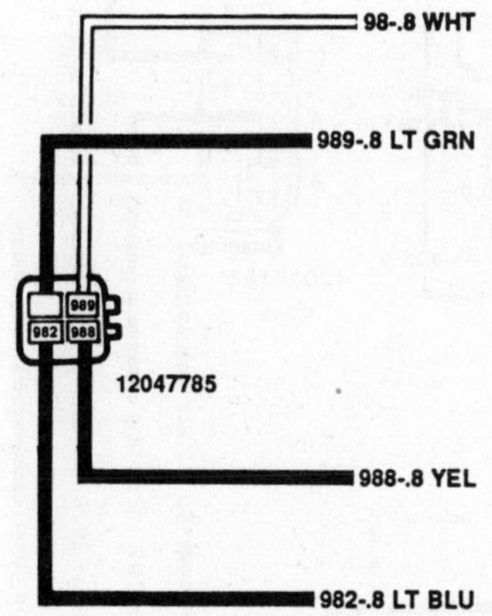
98-.8 WHT
989-.8 LT GRN
989
982 988
12047785
988-.8 YEL
982-.8 LT BLU

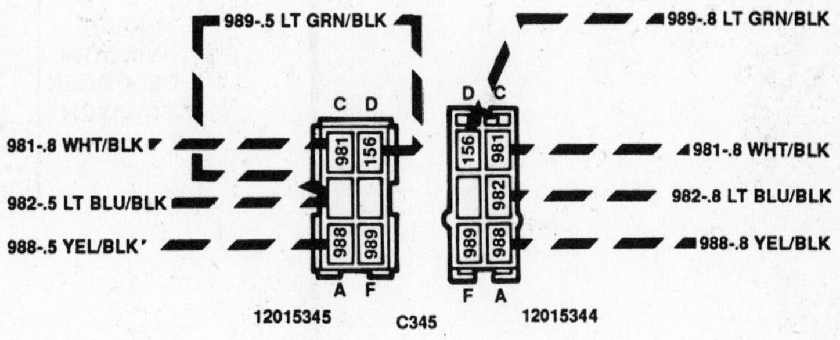
989-.5 LT GRN/BLK
989-.8 LT GRN/BLK
C D
D C
981-.8 WHT/BLK
982-.5 LT BLU/BLK
988-.5 YEL/BLK
981-.8 WHT/BLK
982-.8 LT BLU/BLK
988-.8 YEL/BLK
981 156
988 989
156 981
982
989 988
A F
F A
12015345
C345
12015344

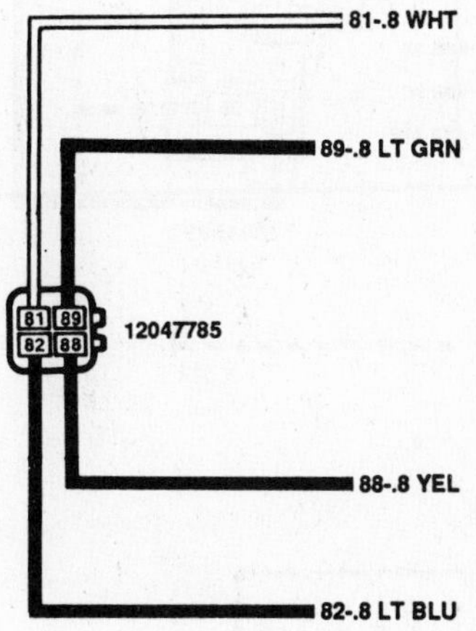
81-.8 WHT
89-.8 LT GRN
81 89
82 88
12047785
88-.8 YEL
82-.8 LT BLU

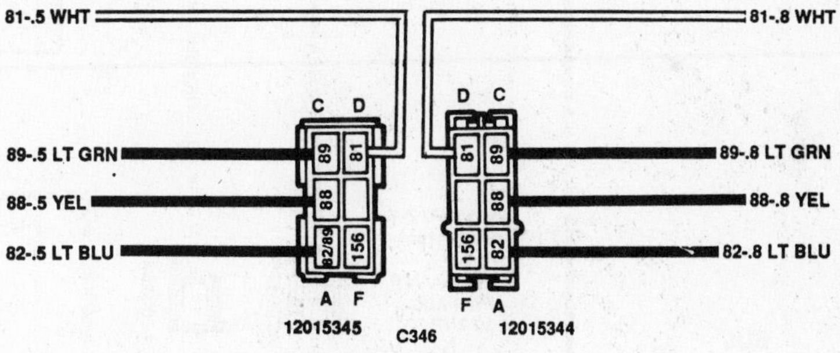
81-.5 WHT
81-.8 WHT
C D
D C
89-.5 LT GRN
88-.5 YEL
82-.5 LT BLU
89-.8 LT GRN
88-.8 YEL
82-.8 LT BLU
89 81
88
82/89 156
81 89
88
156 82
A F
F A
12015345
C346
12015344

2-DOOR UTILITY AND PICKUP
W/O POWER WINDOWS AND DOOR LOCKS

1988–91 WIRING DIAGRAMS (CONT.)

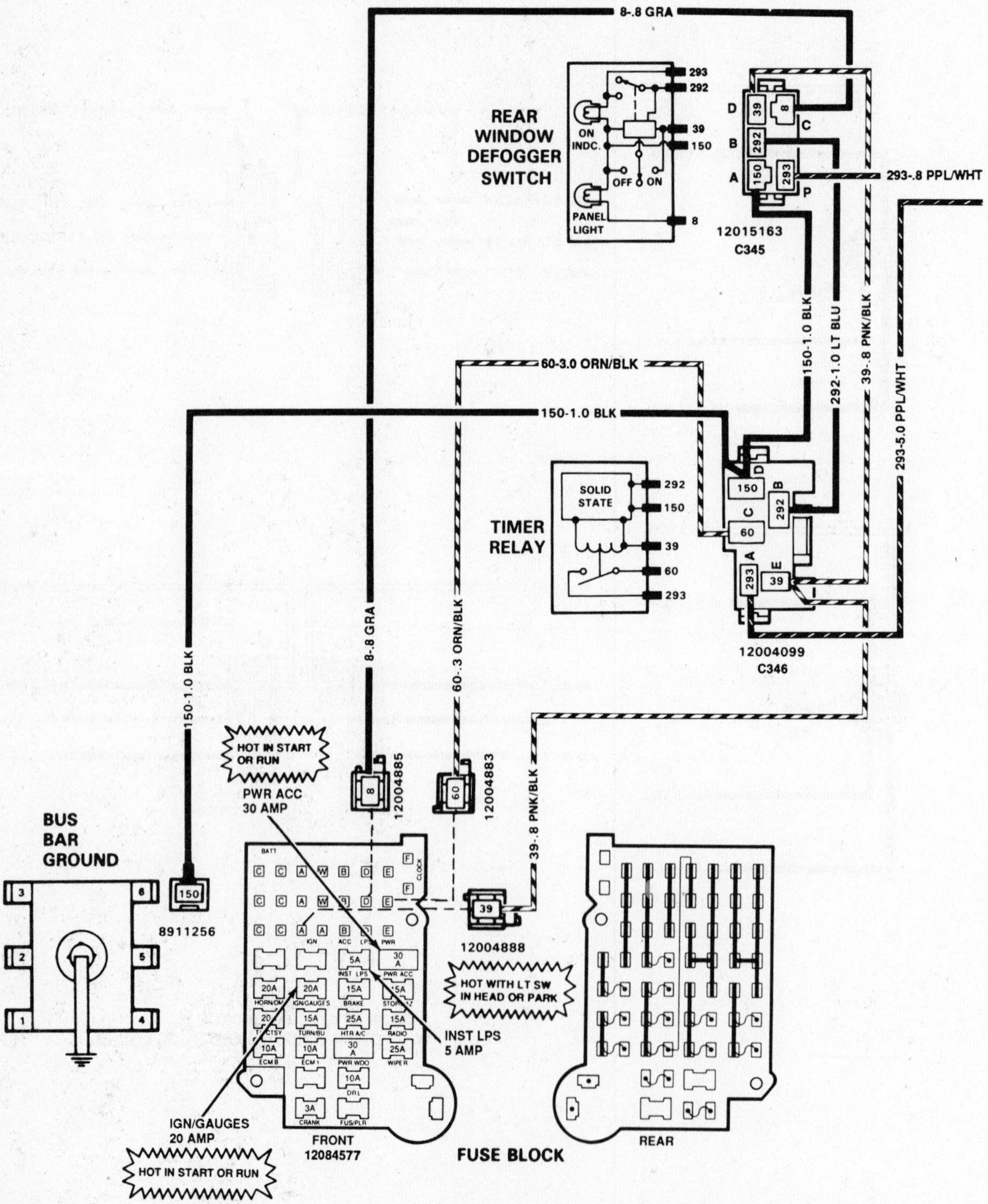
8-.8 GRA
REAR WINDOW DEFOGGER SWITCH
ON INDC.
OFF ON
PANEL LIGHT
293
292
39
150
8
D
B
A
C
P
12015163
C345
293-.8 PPL/WHT
150-1.0 BLK
292-1.0 LT BLU
39-.8 PNK/BLK
293-5.0 PPL/WHT
60-3.0 ORN/BLK
150-1.0 BLK
SOLID STATE
TIMER RELAY
60
12004099
C346
8-.8 GRA
60-.3 ORN/BLK
39-.8 PNK/BLK
HOT IN START OR RUN
PWR ACC 30 AMP
12004885
12004883
BUS BAR GROUND
8911256
12004888
HOT WITH LT SW IN HEAD OR PARK
INST LPS 5 AMP
IGN/GAUGES 20 AMP
HOT IN START OR RUN
FRONT
12084577
FUSE BLOCK
REAR

1988–91 WIRING DIAGRAMS (CONT.)

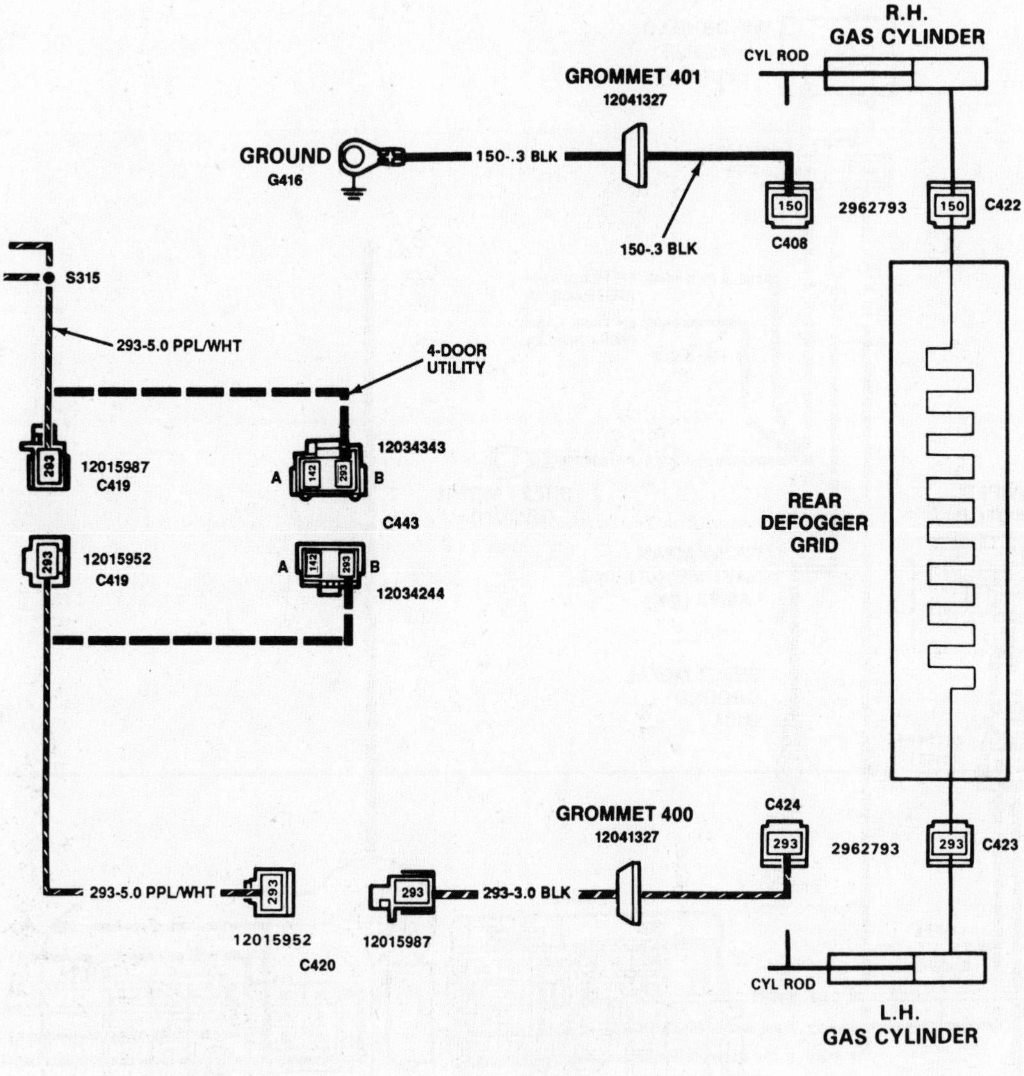
R.H.
GAS CYLINDER
CYL ROD
GROMMET 401
12041327
GROUND
G416
150-.3 BLK
150
C408
150-.3 BLK
2962793
150
C422
S315
293-5.0 PPL/WHT
4-DOOR
UTILITY
293
12015987
C419
A
142
293
B
12034343
C443
293
12015952
C419
A
142
293
B
12034244
REAR
DEFOGGER
GRID
GROMMET 400
12041327
C424
293
2962793
293
C423
293-5.0 PPL/WHT
293
12015952
C420
293
12015987
293-3.0 BLK
CYL ROD
L.H.
GAS CYLINDER

1988–91 WIRING DIAGRAMS (CONT.)

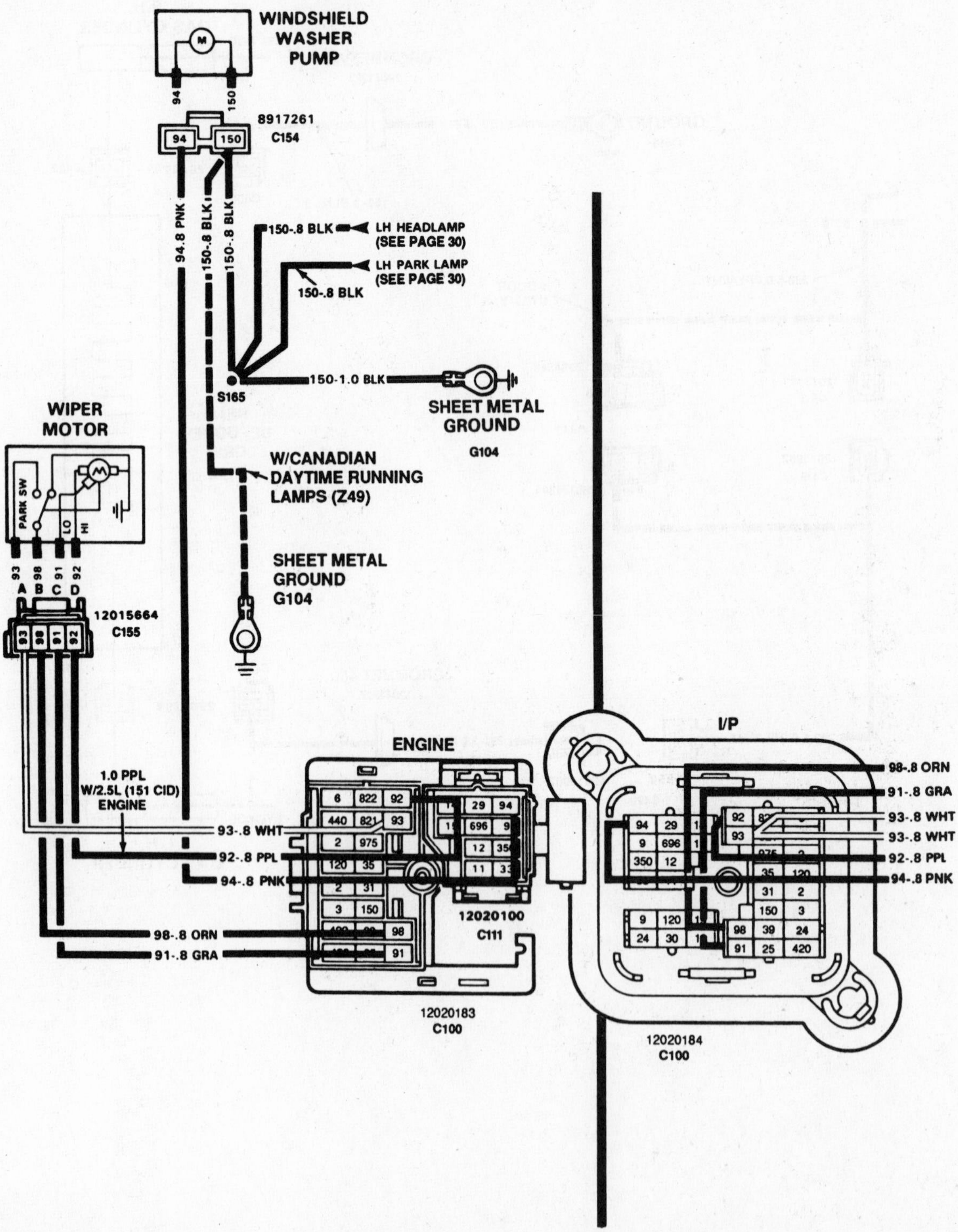

WINDSHIELD WASHER PUMP
M
94
150
8917261
C154
94.8 PNK
150-.8 BLK
150-.8 BLK
150-.8 BLK
LH HEADLAMP (SEE PAGE 30)
LH PARK LAMP (SEE PAGE 30)
150-.8 BLK
S165
150-1.0 BLK
SHEET METAL GROUND
G104
WIPER MOTOR
PARK SW
LO
HI
93 98 91 92
A B C D
12015664
C155
W/CANADIAN DAYTIME RUNNING LAMPS (Z49)
SHEET METAL GROUND
G104
1.0 PPL
W/2.5L (151 CID) ENGINE
93-.8 WHT
92-.8 PPL
94-.8 PNK
98-.8 ORN
91-.8 GRA
ENGINE
12020100
C111
12020183
C100
I/P
98-.8 ORN
91-.8 GRA
93-.8 WHT
93-.8 WHT
92-.8 PPL
94-.8 PNK
12020184
C100

1988–91 WIRING DIAGRAMS (CONT.)

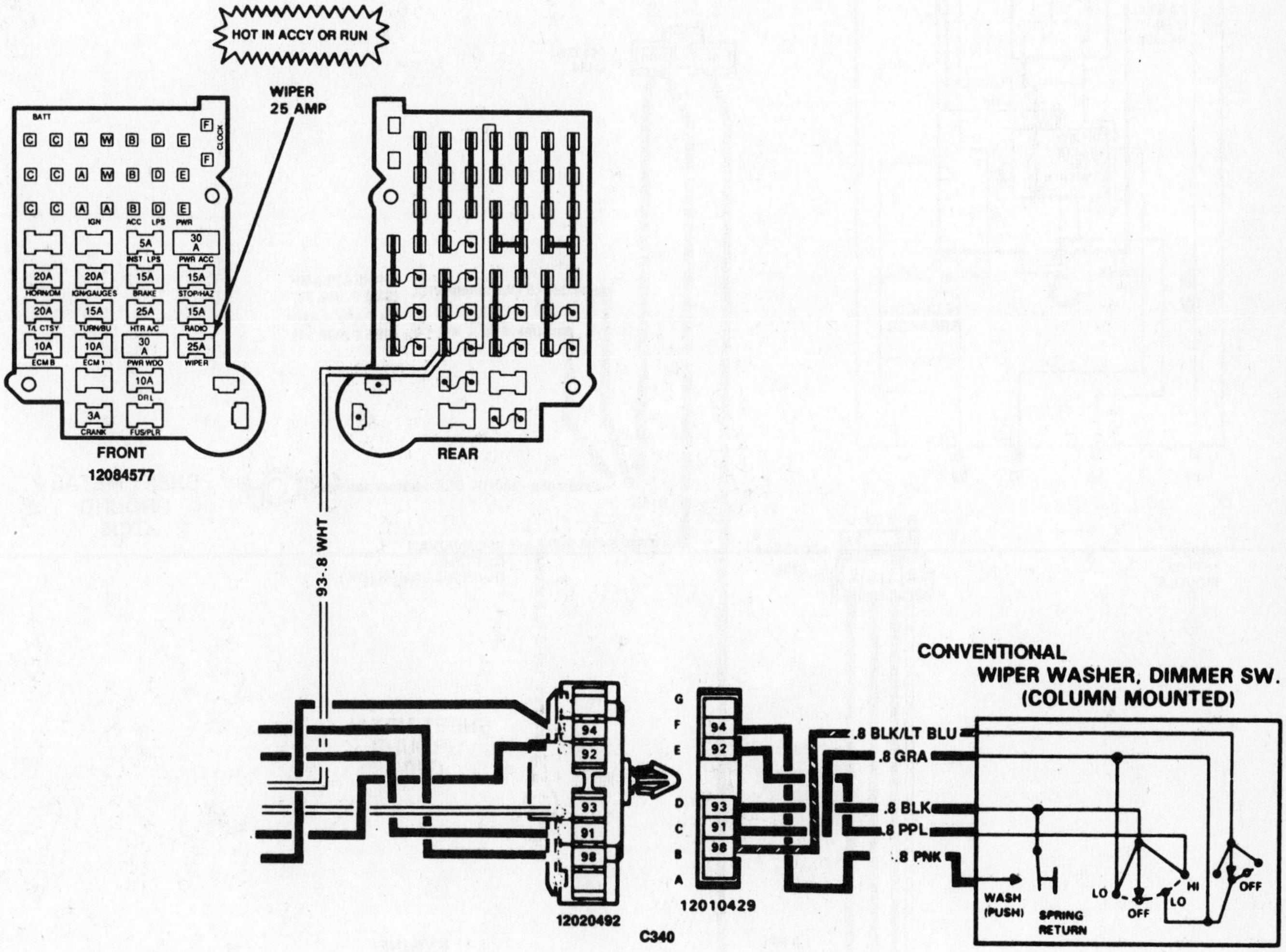
HOT IN ACCY OR RUN
WIPER
25 AMP
BATT
CLOCK
IGN
ACC
LPS
PWR
5A
INST LPS
30 A
PWR ACC
20A
HORN/DM
20A
IGN/GAUGES
15A
BRAKE
15A
STOP/HAZ
20A
T/L CTSY
15A
TURN/BU
25A
HTR A/C
15A
RADIO
10A
ECM B
10A
ECM 1
30 A
PWR WDO
25A
WIPER
10A
DRL
3A
CRANK
FUS/PLR
FRONT
12084577
REAR
93 .8 WHT
94
92
93
91
98
12020492
C340
G
F
E
D
C
B
A
12010429
.8 BLK/LT BLU
.8 GRA
.8 BLK
.8 PPL
.8 PNK
CONVENTIONAL
WIPER WASHER, DIMMER SW.
(COLUMN MOUNTED)
WASH
(PUSH)
SPRING
RETURN
LO
OFF
HI
LO
OFF

1988–91 WIRING DIAGRAMS (CONT.)

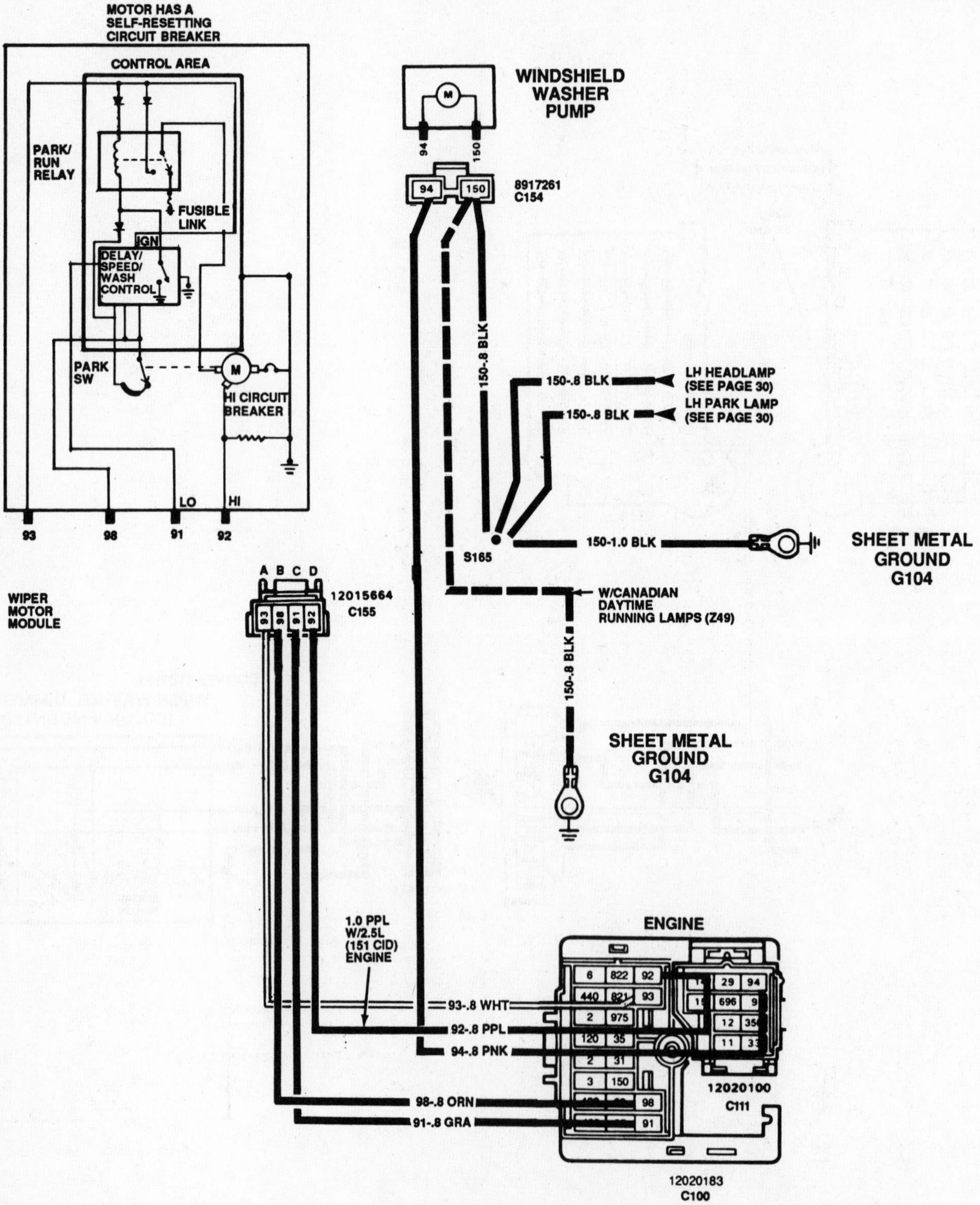
MOTOR HAS A SELF-RESETTING CIRCUIT BREAKER
CONTROL AREA
PARK/ RUN RELAY
FUSIBLE LINK
IGN
DELAY/ SPEED/ WASH CONTROL
PARK SW
M
HI CIRCUIT BREAKER
LO
HI
93
98
91
92
WIPER MOTOR MODULE
A B C D
12015664 C155
WINDSHIELD WASHER PUMP
94
150
8917261 C154
150-.8 BLK
150-.8 BLK
LH HEADLAMP (SEE PAGE 30)
150-.8 BLK
LH PARK LAMP (SEE PAGE 30)
S165
150-1.0 BLK
SHEET METAL GROUND G104
W/CANADIAN DAYTIME RUNNING LAMPS (Z49)
150-.8 BLK
SHEET METAL GROUND G104
1.0 PPL W/2.5L (151 CID) ENGINE
93-.8 WHT
92-.8 PPL
94-.8 PNK
98-.8 ORN
91-.8 GRA
ENGINE
12020100 C111
12020183 C100

1988–91 WIRING DIAGRAMS (CONT.)

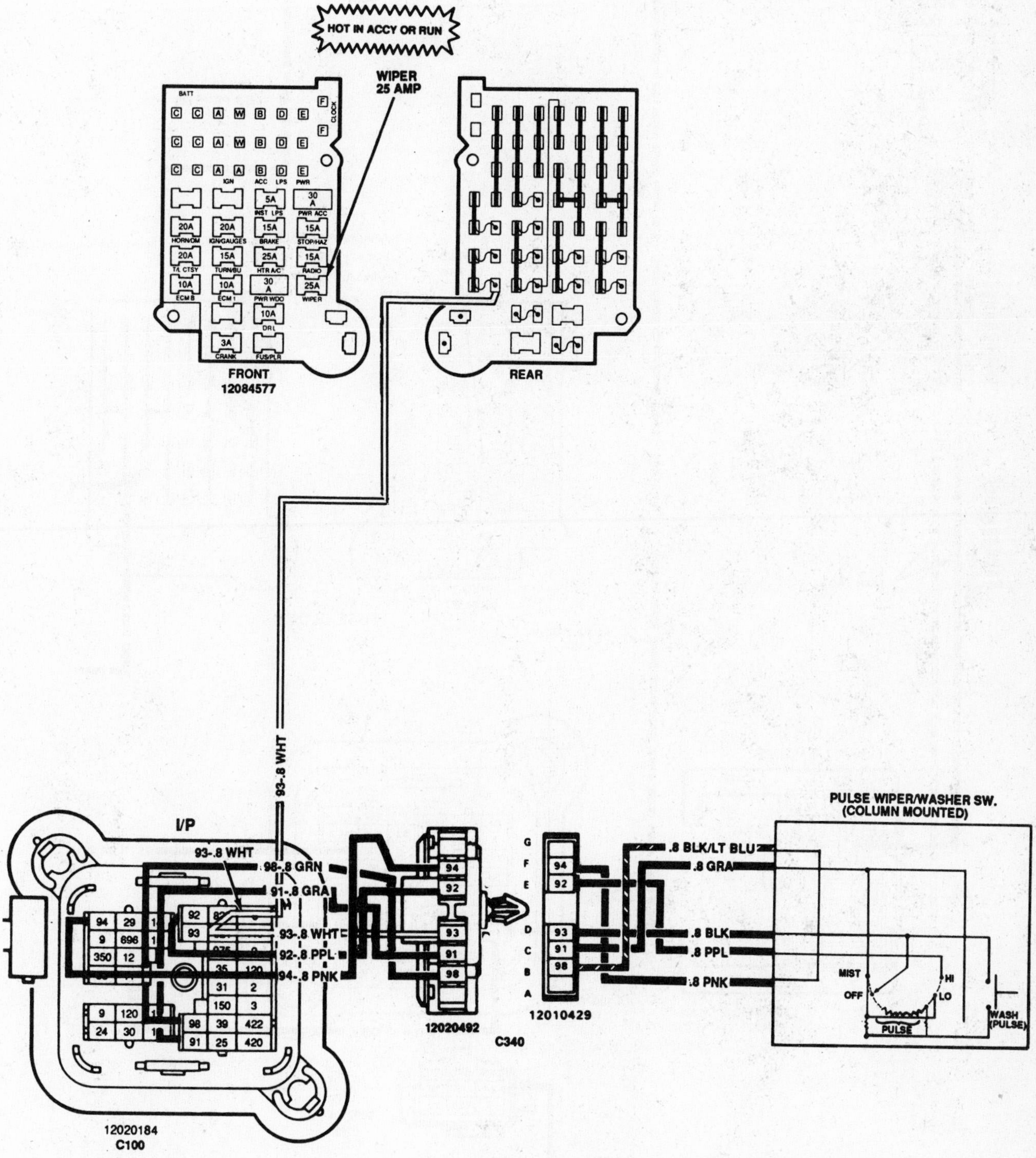
HOT IN ACCY OR RUN
WIPER
25 AMP
BATT
CLOCK
IGN
ACC
LPS
PWR
5A
INST LPS
30 A
PWR ACC
20A
HORN/DM
20A
IGN/GAUGES
15A
BRAKE
15A
STOP/HAZ
20A
T/L CTSY
15A
TURN/BU
25A
HTR A/C
15A
RADIO
10A
ECM B
10A
ECM I
30 A
PWR WDO
25A
WIPER
10A
DRL
3A
CRANK
FUS/PLR
FRONT
12084577
REAR
93-.8 WHT
I/P
93-.8 WHT
98-.8 GRN
91-.8 GRA
93-.8 WHT
92-.8 PPL
94-.8 PNK
12020184
C100
12020492
C340
12010429
.8 BLK/LT BLU
.8 GRA
.8 BLK
.8 PPL
.8 PNK
PULSE WIPER/WASHER SW.
(COLUMN MOUNTED)
MIST
OFF
HI
LO
PULSE
WASH
(PULSE)

1988–91 WIRING DIAGRAMS (CONT.)

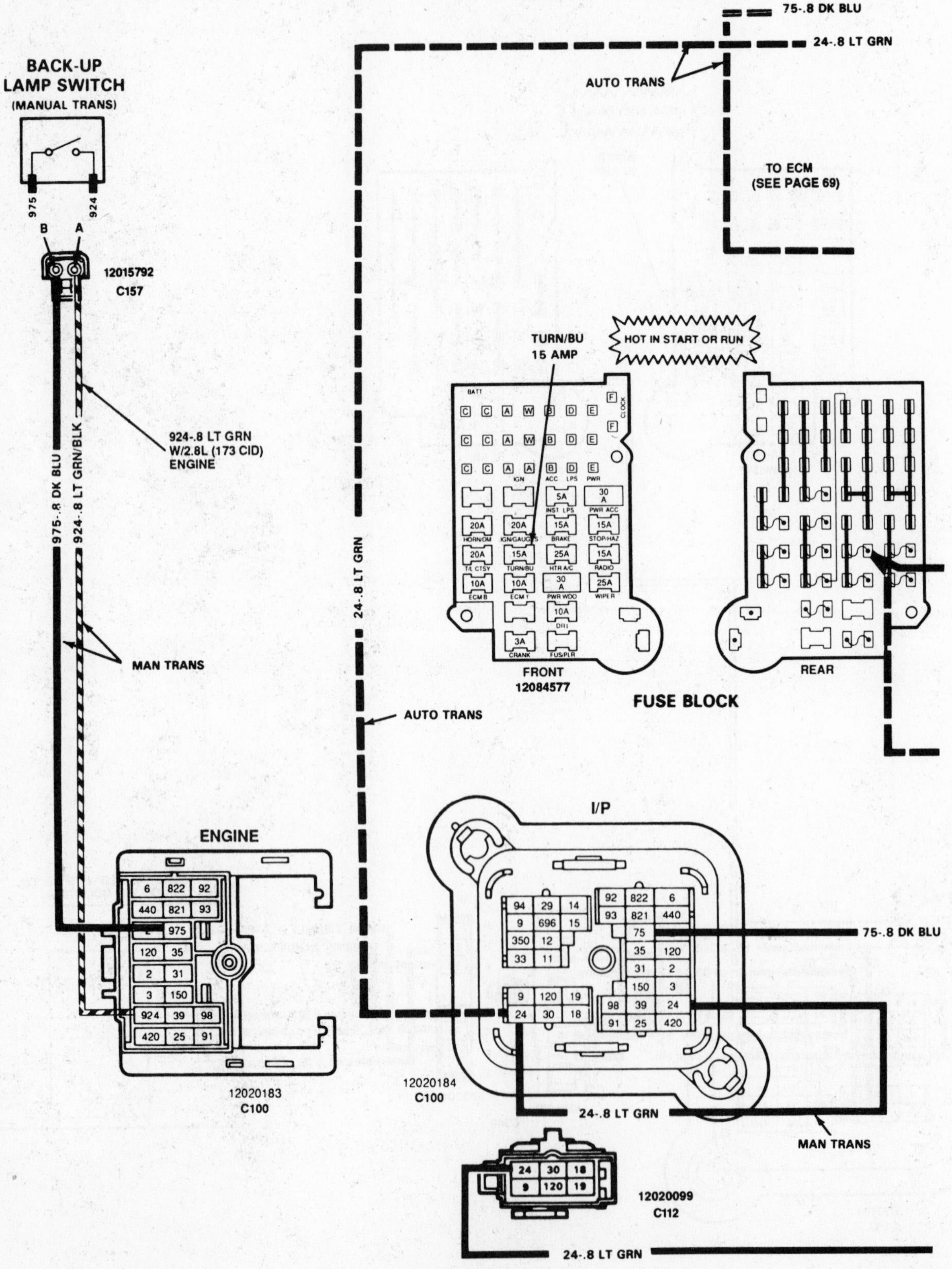

75-.8 DK BLU
24-.8 LT GRN
AUTO TRANS
TO ECM
(SEE PAGE 69)
BACK-UP
LAMP SWITCH
(MANUAL TRANS)
975
924
B
A
12015792
C157
924-.8 LT GRN
W/2.8L (173 CID)
ENGINE
975-.8 DK BLU
924-.8 LT GRN/BLK
MAN TRANS
TURN/BU
15 AMP
HOT IN START OR RUN
24-.8 LT GRN
AUTO TRANS
FRONT
12084577
REAR
FUSE BLOCK
ENGINE
12020183
C100
I/P
12020184
C100
75-.8 DK BLU
24-.8 LT GRN
MAN TRANS
12020099
C112
24-.8 LT GRN

1988–91 WIRING DIAGRAMS (CONT.)

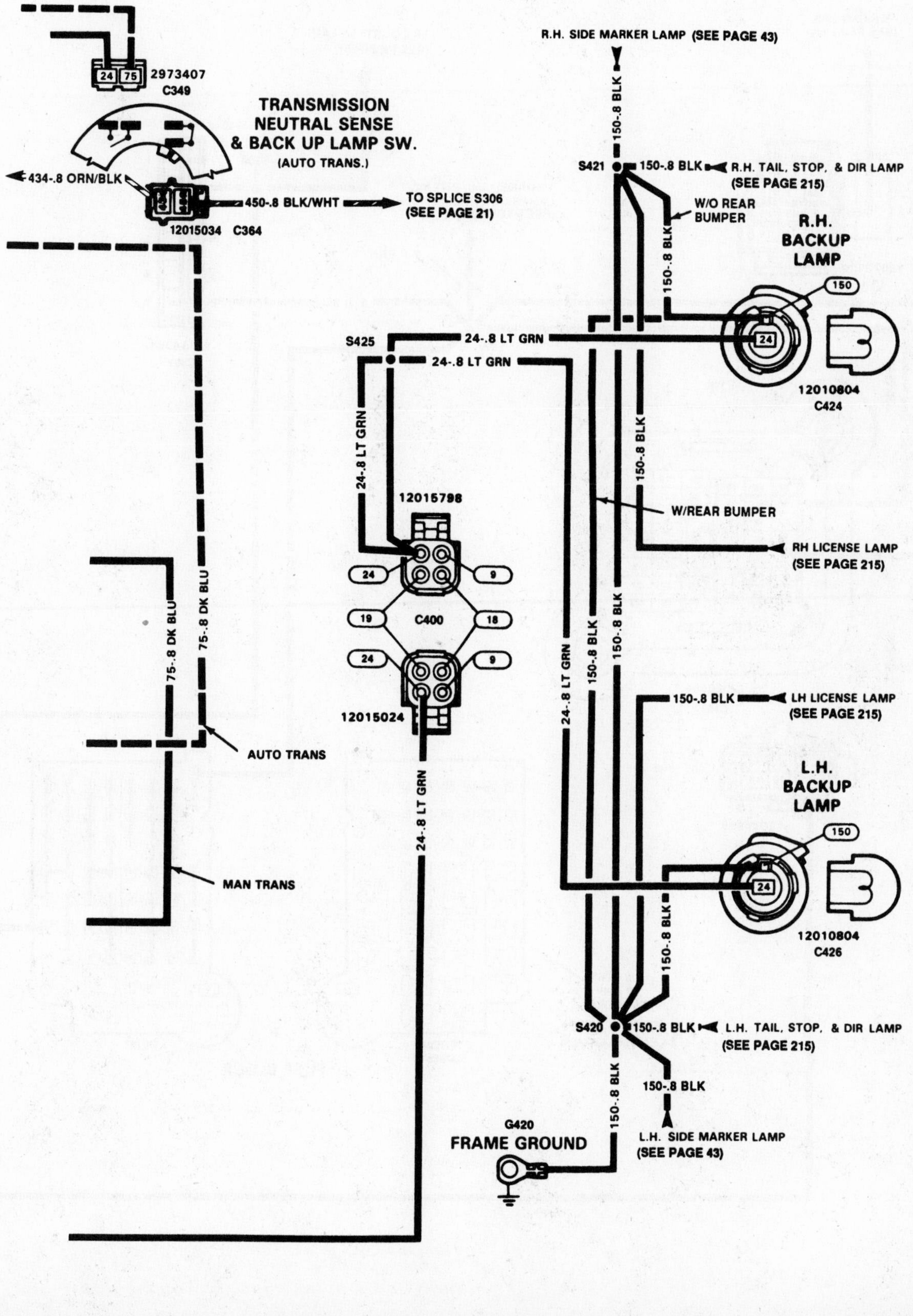

24
75
2973407
C349
TRANSMISSION NEUTRAL SENSE & BACK UP LAMP SW.
(AUTO TRANS.)
434-.8 ORN/BLK
450-.8 BLK/WHT
TO SPLICE S306 (SEE PAGE 21)
12015034 C364
75-.8 DK BLU
75-.8 DK BLU
AUTO TRANS
MAN TRANS
S425
24-.8 LT GRN
24-.8 LT GRN
24-.8 LT GRN
12015798
24
9
19
C400
18
24
9
12015024
24-.8 LT GRN
R.H. SIDE MARKER LAMP (SEE PAGE 43)
150-.8 BLK
S421
150-.8 BLK
R.H. TAIL, STOP, & DIR LAMP (SEE PAGE 215)
W/O REAR BUMPER
150-.8 BLK
R.H. BACKUP LAMP
150
24
12010804
C424
150-.8 BLK
W/REAR BUMPER
RH LICENSE LAMP (SEE PAGE 215)
24-.8 LT GRN
150-.8 BLK
150-.8 BLK
150-.8 BLK
LH LICENSE LAMP (SEE PAGE 215)
L.H. BACKUP LAMP
150
24
12010804
C426
150-.8 BLK
S420
150-.8 BLK
L.H. TAIL, STOP, & DIR LAMP (SEE PAGE 215)
150-.8 BLK
150-.8 BLK
L.H. SIDE MARKER LAMP (SEE PAGE 43)
G420
FRAME GROUND

1988–91 WIRING DIAGRAMS (CONT.)

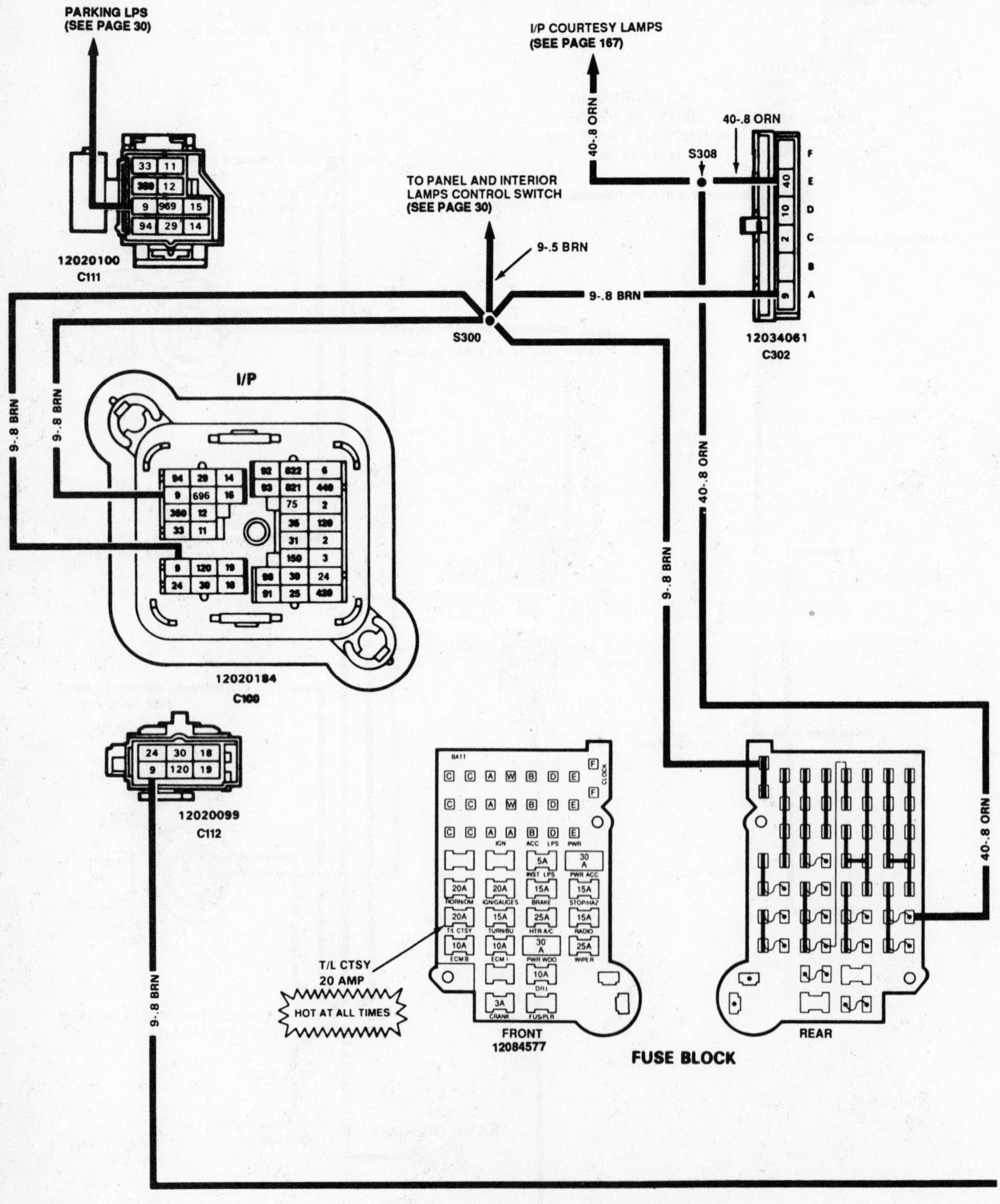
PARKING LPS
(SEE PAGE 30)
I/P COURTESY LAMPS
(SEE PAGE 167)
40-.8 ORN
40-.8 ORN
S308
TO PANEL AND INTERIOR
LAMPS CONTROL SWITCH
(SEE PAGE 30)
9-.5 BRN
9-.8 BRN
12020100
C111
S300
12034061
C302
I/P
9-.8 BRN
9-.8 BRN
40-.8 ORN
9-.8 BRN
12020184
C100
12020099
C112
T/L CTSY
20 AMP
HOT AT ALL TIMES
9-.8 BRN
FRONT
12084577
REAR
FUSE BLOCK
40-.8 ORN

1988–91 WIRING DIAGRAMS (CONT.)

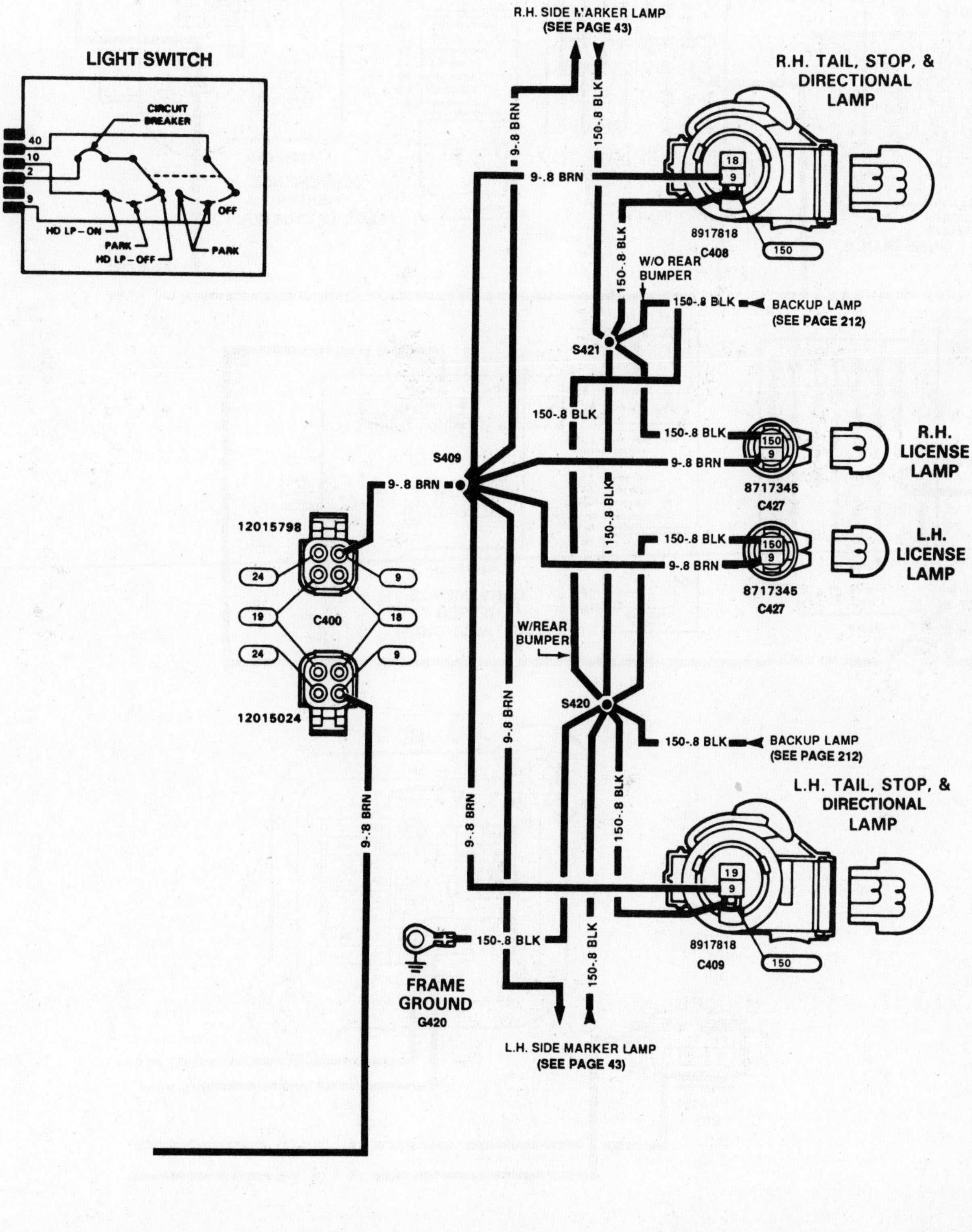
LIGHT SWITCH
CIRCUIT BREAKER
40
10
2
9
OFF
HD LP–ON
PARK
HD LP–OFF
PARK
R.H. SIDE MARKER LAMP (SEE PAGE 43)
9-.8 BRN
150-.8 BLK
R.H. TAIL, STOP, & DIRECTIONAL LAMP
18
9
8917818
C408
150
W/O REAR BUMPER
BACKUP LAMP (SEE PAGE 212)
S421
R.H. LICENSE LAMP
8717345
C427
S409
L.H. LICENSE LAMP
12015798
24
19
C400
18
12015024
W/REAR BUMPER
S420
L.H. TAIL, STOP, & DIRECTIONAL LAMP
19
C409
FRAME GROUND
G420
L.H. SIDE MARKER LAMP (SEE PAGE 43)

1988–91 WIRING DIAGRAMS (CONT.)

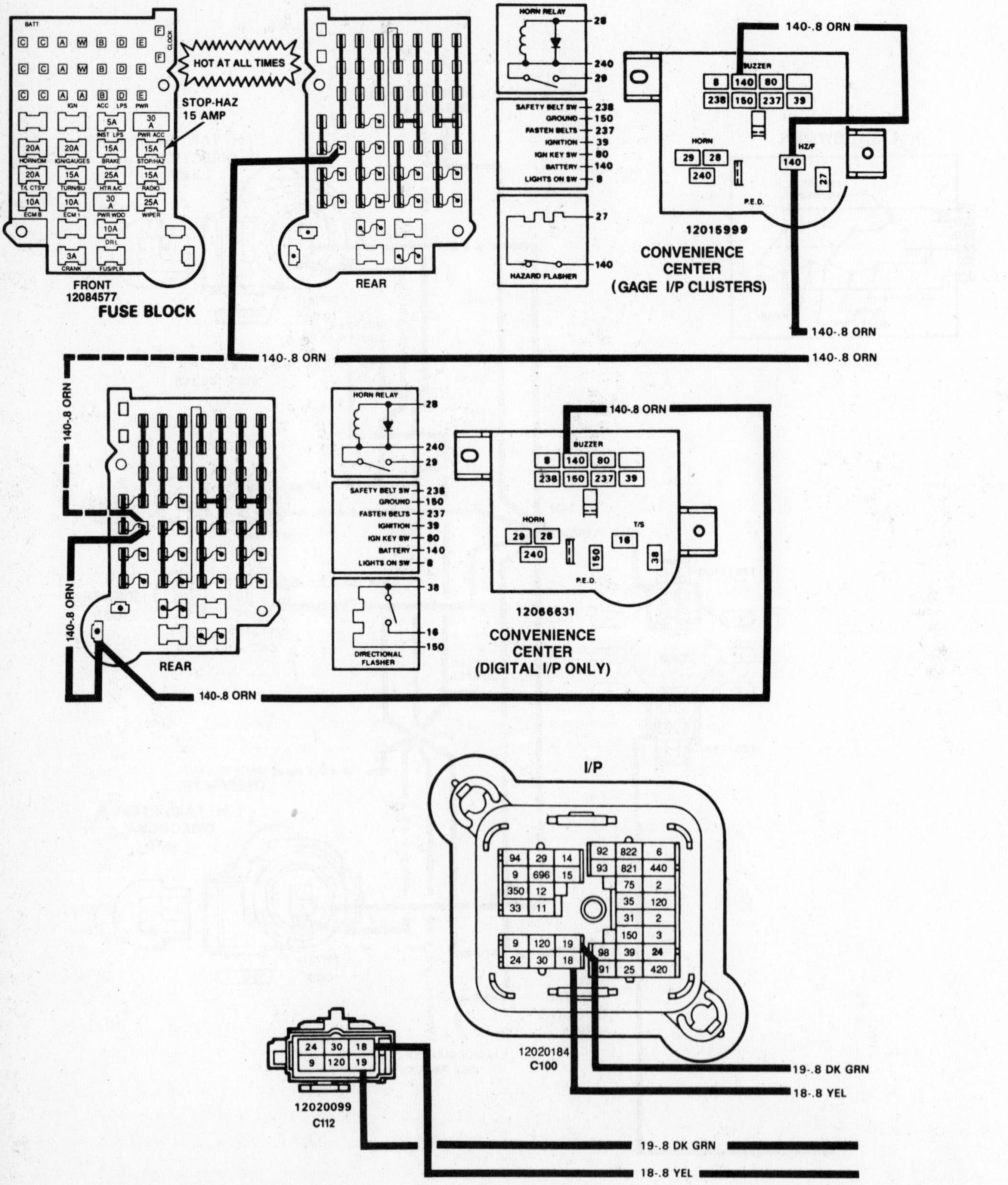

HOT AT ALL TIMES
STOP-HAZ 15 AMP
FRONT
12084577
FUSE BLOCK
REAR
HORN RELAY
28
240
29
SAFETY BELT SW 238
GROUND 150
FASTEN BELTS 237
IGNITION 39
IGN KEY SW 80
BATTERY 140
LIGHTS ON SW 8
27
HAZARD FLASHER
140
140-.8 ORN
BUZZER
HORN
HZ/F
P.E.D.
12015999
CONVENIENCE CENTER
(GAGE I/P CLUSTERS)
140-.8 ORN
REAR
38
16
150
DIRECTIONAL FLASHER
T/S
12066631
CONVENIENCE CENTER
(DIGITAL I/P ONLY)
I/P
12020184
C100
19-.8 DK GRN
18-.8 YEL
12020099
C112

1988–91 WIRING DIAGRAMS (CONT.)

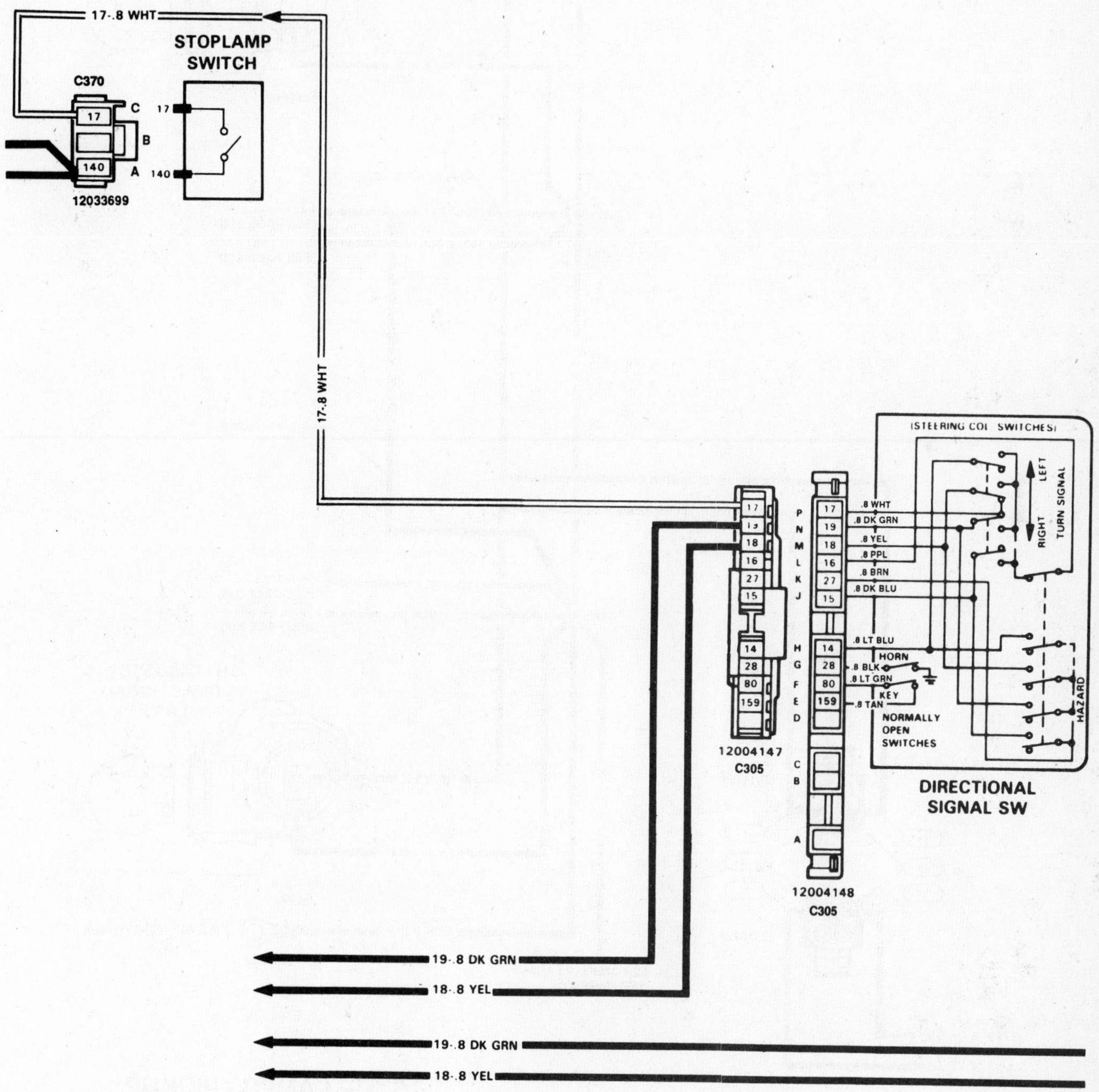

17-.8 WHT
STOPLAMP SWITCH
C370
17
C
B
140
A
12033699
17
140
17-.8 WHT
(STEERING COL SWITCHES)
LEFT
RIGHT
TURN SIGNAL
HAZARD
.8 WHT
.8 DK GRN
.8 YEL
.8 PPL
.8 BRN
.8 DK BLU
.8 LT BLU
HORN
.8 BLK
.8 LT GRN
KEY
.8 TAN
NORMALLY OPEN SWITCHES
P N M L K J H G F E D C B A
12004147
C305
12004148
C305
DIRECTIONAL SIGNAL SW
19-.8 DK GRN
18-.8 YEL
19-.8 DK GRN
18-.8 YEL

1988–91 WIRING DIAGRAMS (CONT.)

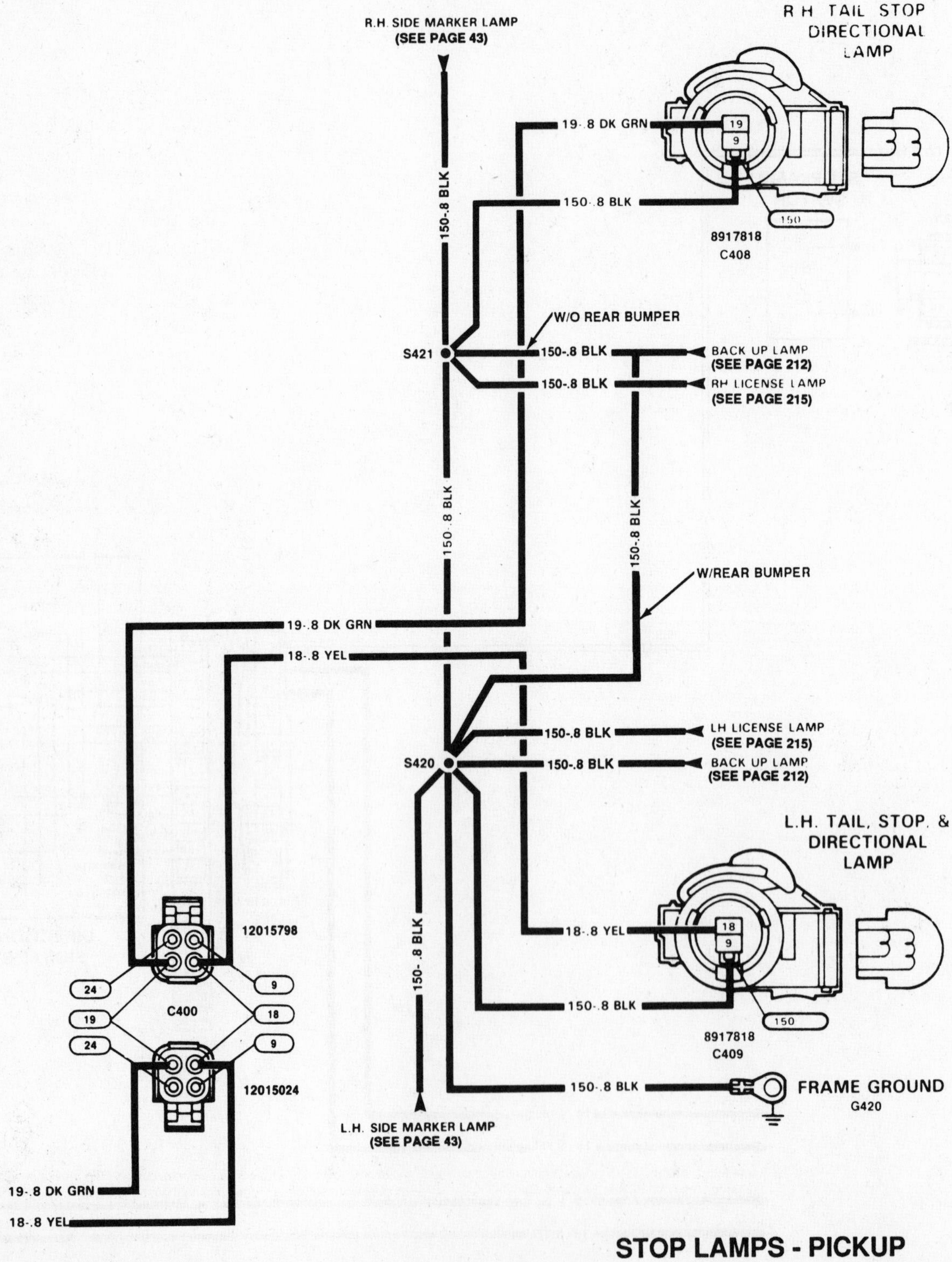
R.H. SIDE MARKER LAMP
(SEE PAGE 43)
R.H. TAIL STOP DIRECTIONAL LAMP
19-.8 DK GRN
19
9
150-.8 BLK
150
8917818
C408
150-.8 BLK
W/O REAR BUMPER
S421
150-.8 BLK
BACK UP LAMP
(SEE PAGE 212)
150-.8 BLK
RH LICENSE LAMP
(SEE PAGE 215)
150-.8 BLK
150-.8 BLK
W/REAR BUMPER
19-.8 DK GRN
18-.8 YEL
150-.8 BLK
LH LICENSE LAMP
(SEE PAGE 215)
S420
150-.8 BLK
BACK UP LAMP
(SEE PAGE 212)
L.H. TAIL, STOP, & DIRECTIONAL LAMP
12015798
18-.8 YEL
18
9
24
9
C400
19
18
24
9
150-.8 BLK
150-.8 BLK
150
8917818
C409
12015024
150-.8 BLK
FRAME GROUND
G420
L.H. SIDE MARKER LAMP
(SEE PAGE 43)
19-.8 DK GRN
18-.8 YEL

STOP LAMPS - PICKUP

1988–91 WIRING DIAGRAMS (CONT.)

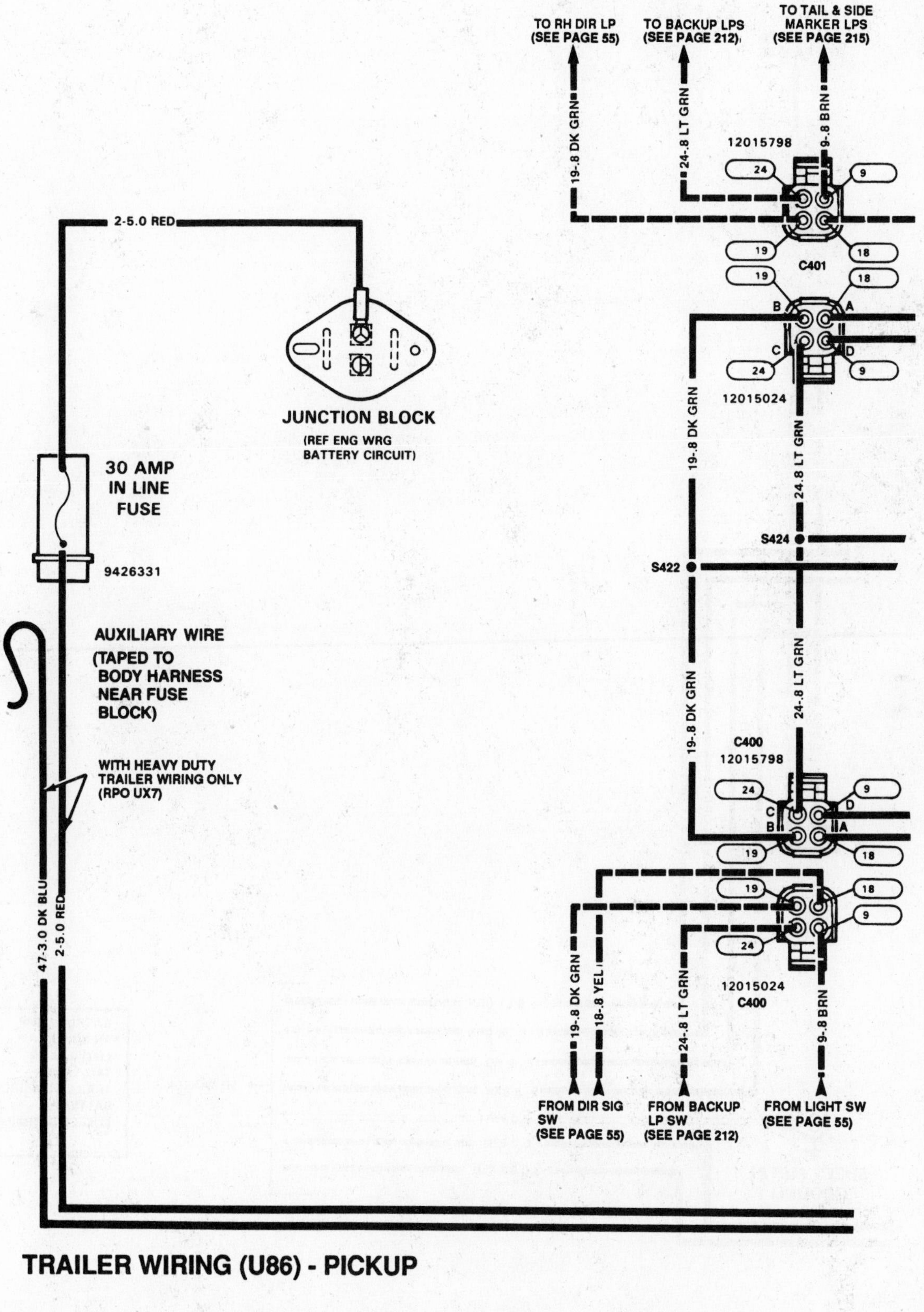
TO RH DIR LP
(SEE PAGE 55)
TO BACKUP LPS
(SEE PAGE 212)
TO TAIL & SIDE
MARKER LPS
(SEE PAGE 215)
19-.8 DK GRN
24-.8 LT GRN
9-.8 BRN
12015798
24
9
19
18
C401
B
A
C
D
12015024
2-5.0 RED
JUNCTION BLOCK
(REF ENG WRG
BATTERY CIRCUIT)
30 AMP
IN LINE
FUSE
9426331
S424
S422
AUXILIARY WIRE
(TAPED TO
BODY HARNESS
NEAR FUSE
BLOCK)
WITH HEAVY DUTY
TRAILER WIRING ONLY
(RPO UX7)
C400
12015798
47-3.0 DK BLU
2-5.0 RED
18-.8 YEL
12015024
C400
FROM DIR SIG
SW
(SEE PAGE 55)
FROM BACKUP
LP SW
(SEE PAGE 212)
FROM LIGHT SW
(SEE PAGE 55)

TRAILER WIRING (U86) - PICKUP

1988–91 WIRING DIAGRAMS (CONT.)

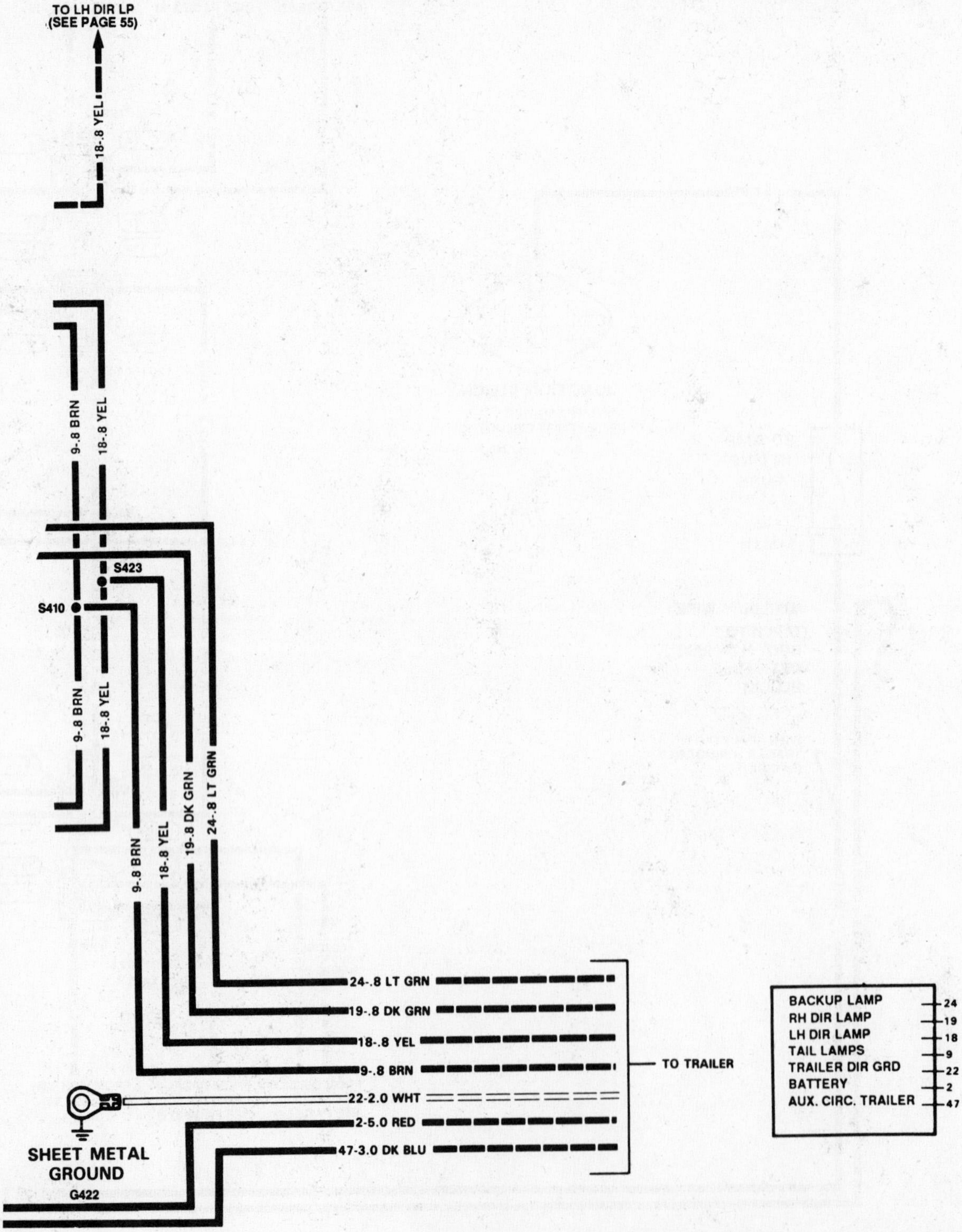
TO LH DIR LP (SEE PAGE 55)
18-.8 YEL
9-.8 BRN
18-.8 YEL
S423
S410
9-.8 BRN
18-.8 YEL
9-.8 BRN
18-.8 YEL
19-.8 DK GRN
24-.8 LT GRN
24-.8 LT GRN
19-.8 DK GRN
18-.8 YEL
9-.8 BRN
22-2.0 WHT
2-5.0 RED
47-3.0 DK BLU
TO TRAILER
SHEET METAL GROUND
G422
BACKUP LAMP 24
RH DIR LAMP 19
LH DIR LAMP 18
TAIL LAMPS 9
TRAILER DIR GRD 22
BATTERY 2
AUX. CIRC. TRAILER 47

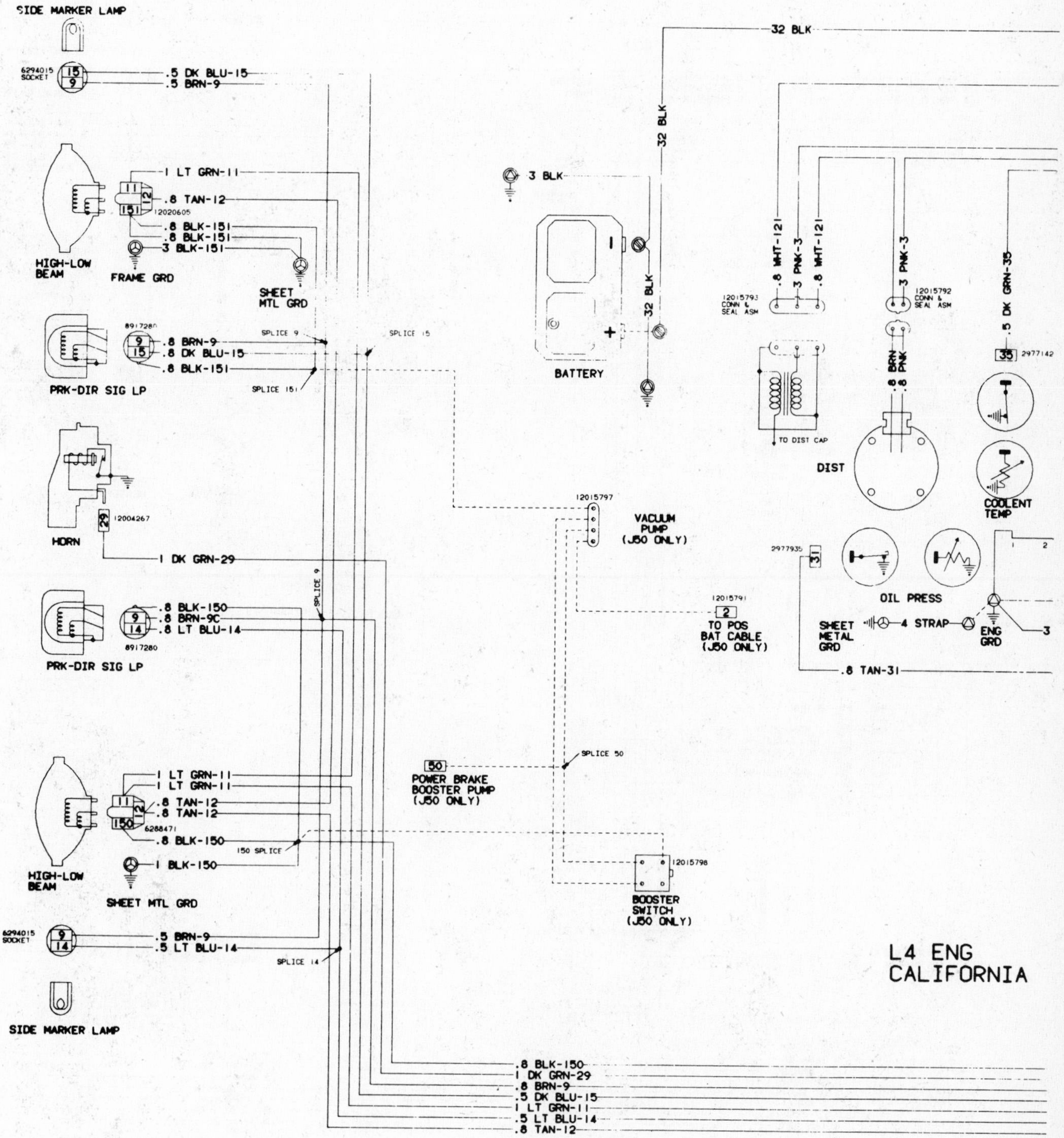
SIDE MARKER LAMP
6294015 SOCKET
.5 DK BLU-15
.5 BRN-9
1 LT GRN-11
.8 TAN-12
12020605
.8 BLK-151
.8 BLK-151
3 BLK-151
HIGH-LOW BEAM
FRAME GRD
SHEET MTL GRD
8917280
.8 BRN-9
.8 DK BLU-15
.8 BLK-151
SPLICE 9
SPLICE 15
SPLICE 151
PRK-DIR SIG LP
12004267
HORN
1 DK GRN-29
.8 BLK-150
.8 BRN-9C
.8 LT BLU-14
8917280
PRK-DIR SIG LP
1 LT GRN-11
1 LT GRN-11
.8 TAN-12
.8 TAN-12
6288471
.8 BLK-150
150 SPLICE
1 BLK-150
HIGH-LOW BEAM
SHEET MTL GRD
6294015 SOCKET
.5 BRN-9
.5 LT BLU-14
SPLICE 14
SIDE MARKER LAMP
32 BLK
3 BLK
32 BLK
32 BLK
BATTERY
.8 WHT-121
.3 PNK-3
.8 WHT-121
12015793 CONN & SEAL ASM
.3 PNK-3
12015792 CONN & SEAL ASM
.5 DK GRN-35
2977142
.8 BRN
.8 PNK
TO DIST CAP
DIST
COOLENT TEMP
12015797
VACUUM PUMP (J50 ONLY)
2977935
OIL PRESS
12015791
TO POS BAT CABLE (J50 ONLY)
SHEET METAL GRD
4 STRAP
ENG GRD
.8 TAN-31
SPLICE 50
POWER BRAKE BOOSTER PUMP (J50 ONLY)
12015798
BOOSTER SWITCH (J50 ONLY)
.8 BLK-150
1 DK GRN-29
.8 BRN-9
.5 DK BLU-15
1 LT GRN-11
.5 LT BLU-14
.8 TAN-12

L4 ENG
CALIFORNIA

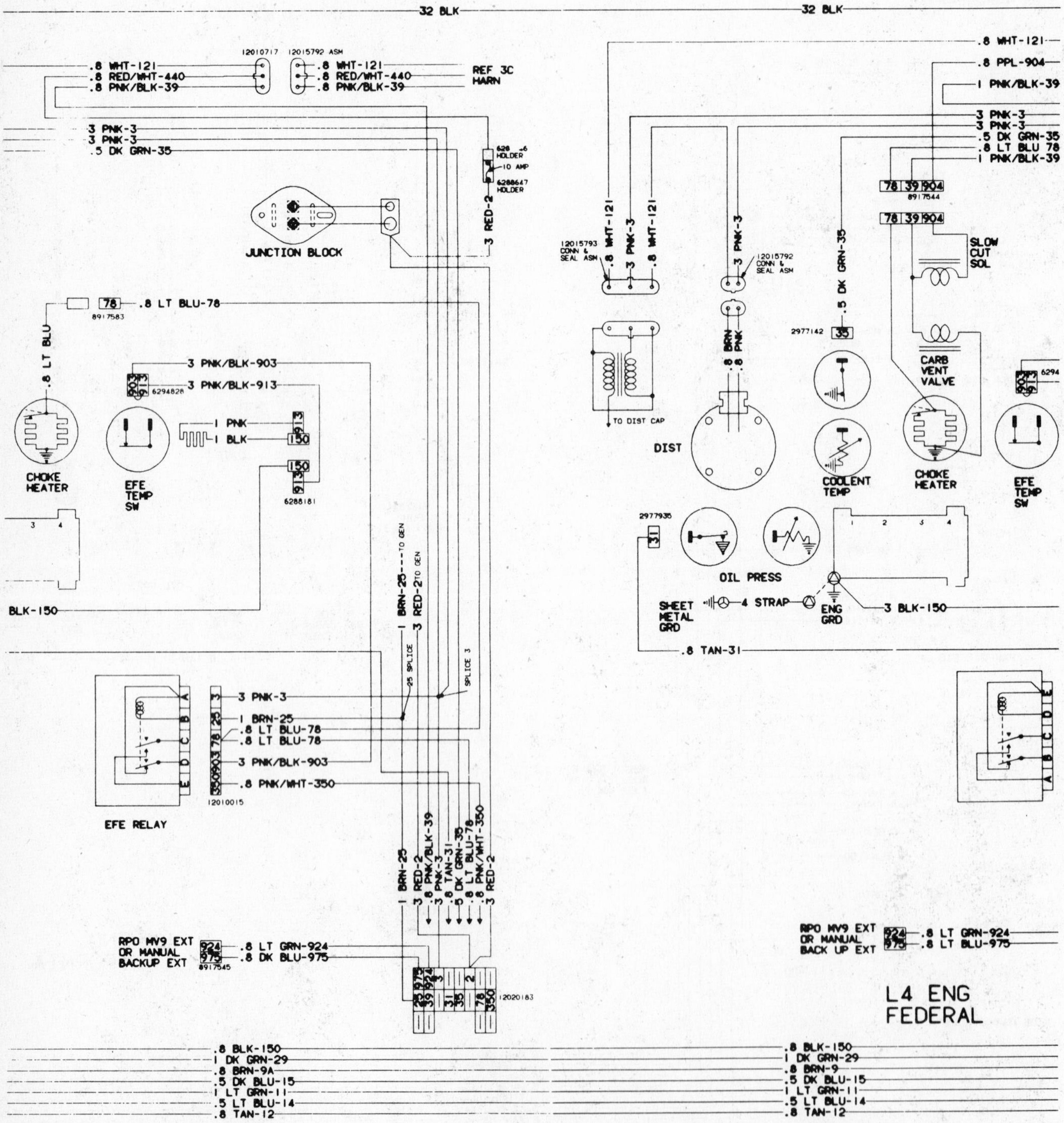
32 BLK
.8 WHT-121
.8 RED/WHT-440
.8 PNK/BLK-39
12010717
12015792 ASM
REF 3C HARN
3 PNK-3
.5 DK GRN-35
10 AMP
3 RED-2
JUNCTION BLOCK
.8 LT BLU-78
8917583
.8 LT BLU
3 PNK/BLK-903
3 PNK/BLK-913
6294828
1 PNK
1 BLK
6288181
CHOKE HEATER
EFE TEMP SW
BLK-150
1 BRN-25
3 RED-2
25 SPLICE
SPLICE 3
3 PNK-3
1 BRN-25
.8 LT BLU-78
3 PNK/BLK-903
.8 PNK/WHT-350
12010015
EFE RELAY
.8 PNK/BLK-39
.8 TAN-31
.5 DK GRN-35
.8 LT BLU-78
RPO MV9 EXT OR MANUAL BACKUP EXT
.8 LT GRN-924
.8 DK BLU-975
8917545
12020183
.8 BLK-150
1 DK GRN-29
.8 BRN-9A
.5 DK BLU-15
1 LT GRN-11
.5 LT BLU-14
.8 TAN-12
.8 PPL-904
1 PNK/BLK-39
.8 LT BLU 78
8917544
SLOW CUT SOL
12015793 CONN & SEAL ASM
12015792 CONN & SEAL ASM
.8 BRN
.8 PNK
TO DIST CAP
DIST
2977142
COOLENT TEMP
CARB VENT VALVE
CHOKE HEATER
EFE TEMP SW
2977935
OIL PRESS
SHEET METAL GRD
4 STRAP
ENG GRD
3 BLK-150
.8 TAN-31
RPO MV9 EXT OR MANUAL BACK UP EXT
.8 LT GRN-924
.8 LT BLU-975
.8 BRN-9
L4 ENG FEDERAL

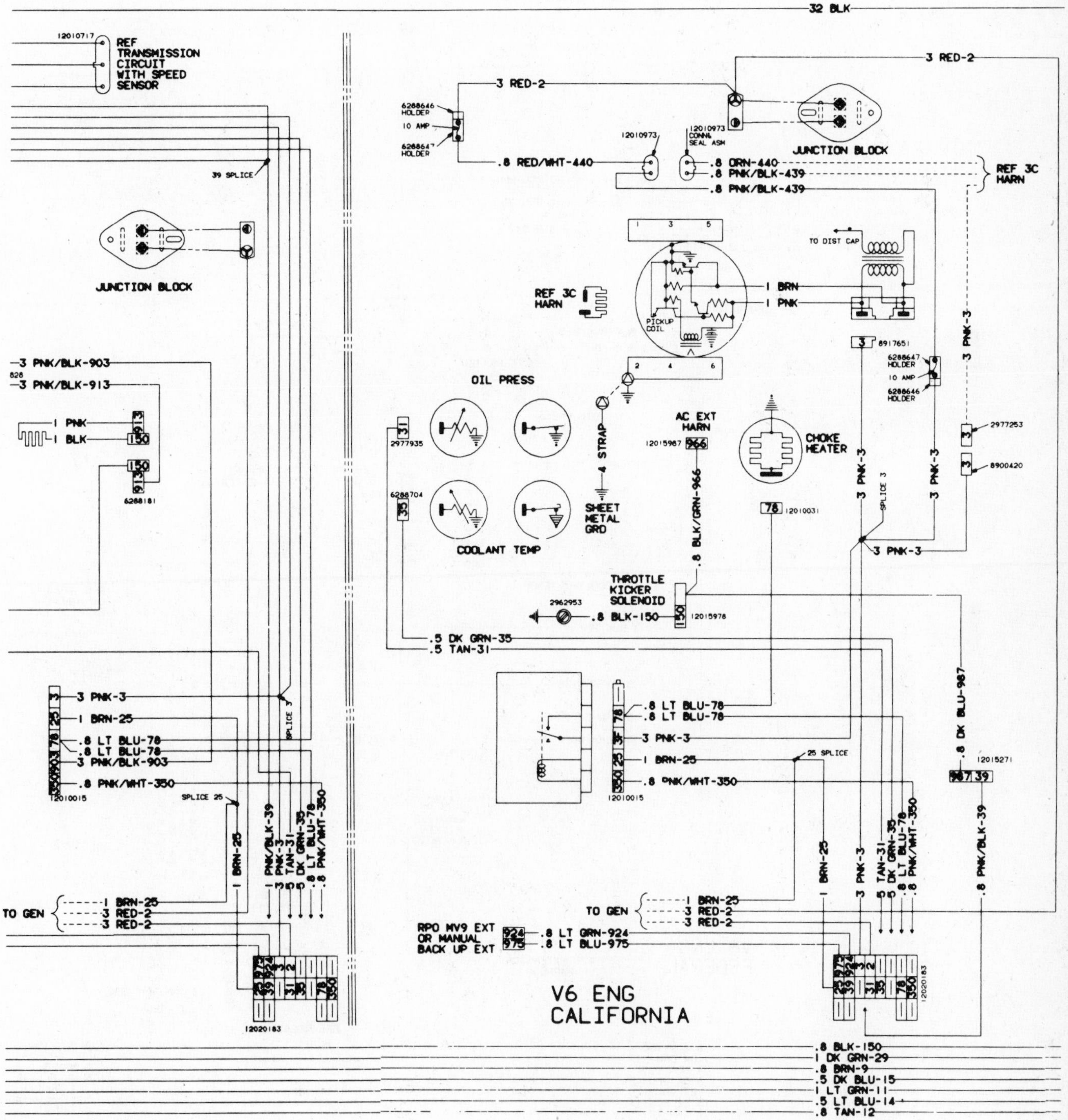

32 BLK
REF TRANSMISSION CIRCUIT WITH SPEED SENSOR
12010717
3 RED-2
6288646 HOLDER
10 AMP
6288647 HOLDER
.8 RED/WHT-440
12010973
12010973 CONN& SEAL ASM
.8 ORN-440
.8 PNK/BLK-439
REF 3C HARN
JUNCTION BLOCK
39 SPLICE
TO DIST CAP
1 BRN
1 PNK
REF 3C HARN
PICKUP COIL
8917651
3 PNK-3
2977253
8900420
OIL PRESS
COOLANT TEMP
2977935
6288704
4 STRAP
SHEET METAL GRD
AC EXT HARN
12015987
.8 BLK/GRN-966
CHOKE HEATER
12010031
SPLICE 3
3 PNK-3
THROTTLE KICKER SOLENOID
2962953
.8 BLK-150
12015978
.5 DK GRN-35
.5 TAN-31
-3 PNK/BLK-903
828
-3 PNK/BLK-913
1 PNK
1 BLK
6288181
1 BRN-25
.8 LT BLU-78
3 PNK/BLK-903
.8 PNK/WHT-350
12010015
SPLICE 25
.8 DK BLU-987
12015271
25 SPLICE
1 BRN-25
.8 PNK/BLK-39
TO GEN
1 BRN-25
3 RED-2
RPO MV9 EXT OR MANUAL BACK UP EXT
.8 LT GRN-924
.8 LT BLU-975
12020183
V6 ENG CALIFORNIA
.8 BLK-150
1 DK GRN-29
.8 BRN-9
.5 DK BLU-15
1 LT GRN-11
.5 LT BLU-14
.8 TAN-12

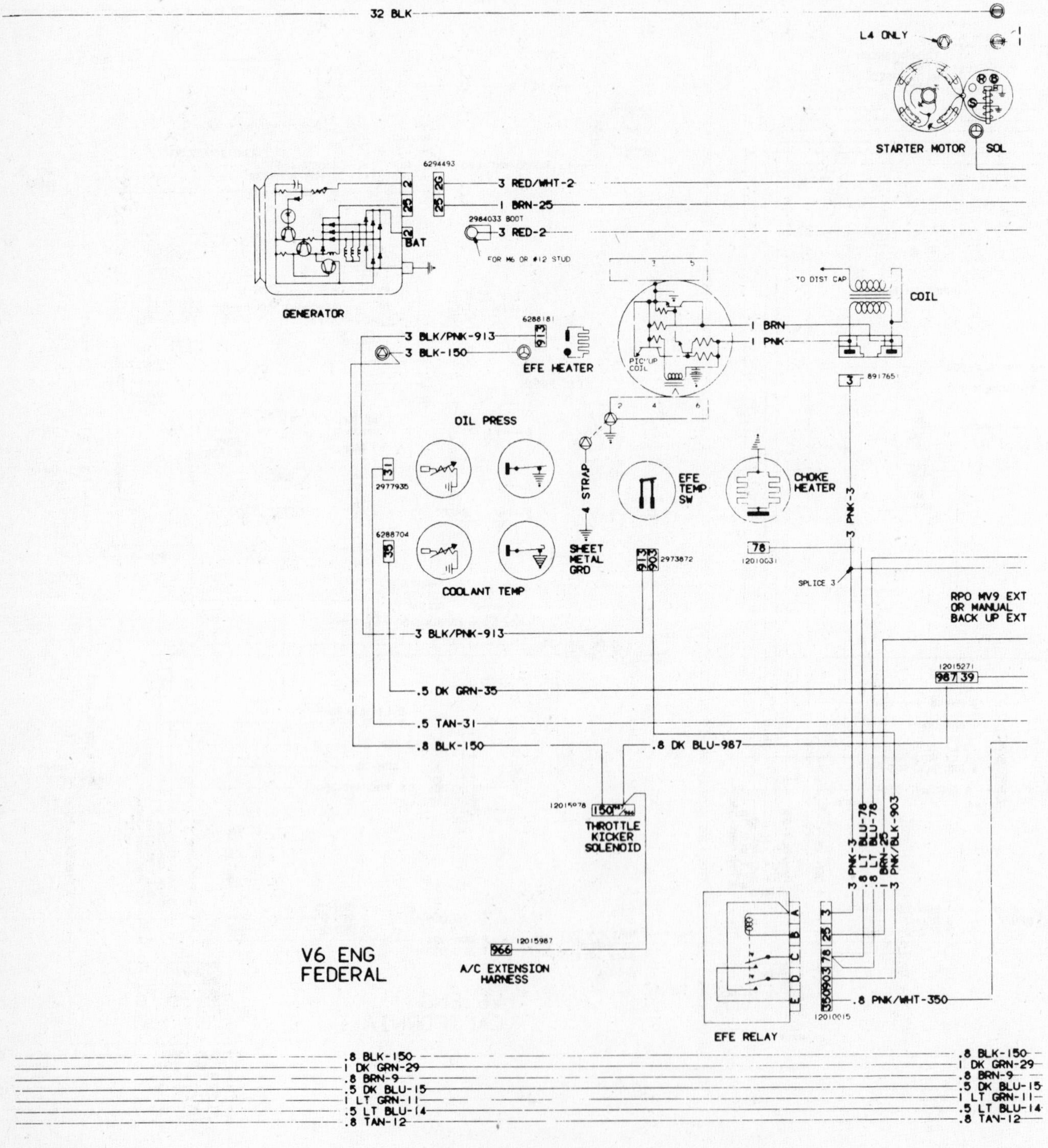

32 BLK
L4 ONLY
STARTER MOTOR
SOL
6294493
3 RED/WHT-2
1 BRN-25
2984033 BOOT
3 RED-2
FOR M6 OR #12 STUD
BAT
GENERATOR
TO DIST CAP
COIL
1 BRN
1 PNK
PIC'UP COIL
6288181
3 BLK/PNK-913
3 BLK-150
EFE HEATER
8917651
OIL PRESS
2977935
4 STRAP
EFE TEMP SW
CHOKE HEATER
3 PNK-3
6288704
SHEET METAL GRD
2973872
12010031
SPLICE 3
COOLANT TEMP
RPO MV9 EXT OR MANUAL BACK UP EXT
3 BLK/PNK-913
12015271
.5 DK GRN-35
.5 TAN-31
.8 BLK-150
.8 DK BLU-987
12015978
THROTTLE KICKER SOLENOID
3 PNK-3
.8 LT BLU-78
.8 LT BLU-78
1 BRN-25
3 PNK/BLK-903
12015987
V6 ENG FEDERAL
A/C EXTENSION HARNESS
.8 PNK/WHT-350
12010015
EFE RELAY
.8 BLK-150
1 DK GRN-29
.8 BRN-9
.5 DK BLU-15
1 LT GRN-11
.5 LT BLU-14
.8 TAN-12

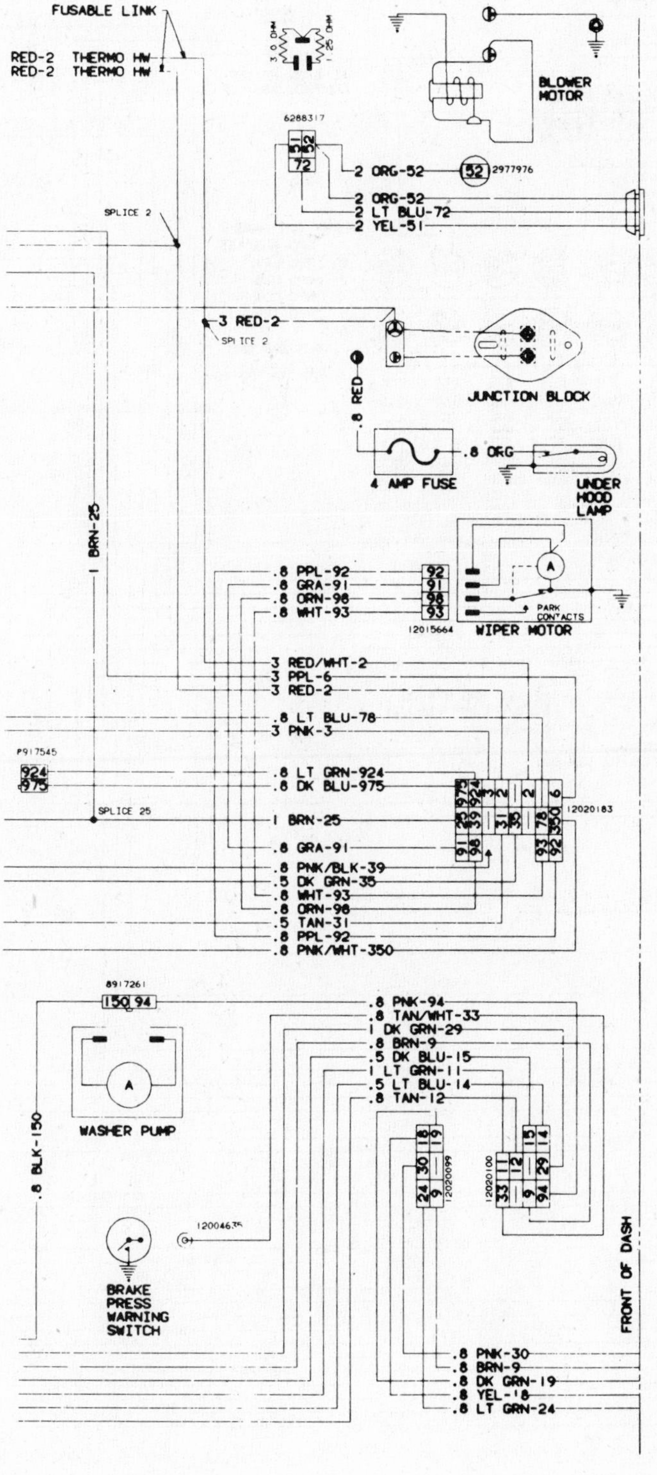
FUSABLE LINK
RED-2 THERMO HW
RED-2 THERMO HW
BLOWER MOTOR
6288317
2 ORG-52
2977976
2 ORG-52
2 LT BLU-72
2 YEL-51
SPLICE 2
3 RED-2
SPLICE 2
.8 RED
JUNCTION BLOCK
4 AMP FUSE
.8 ORG
UNDER HOOD LAMP
1 BRN-25
.8 PPL-92
.8 GRA-91
.8 ORN-98
.8 WHT-93
12015664
WIPER MOTOR
PARK CONTACTS
3 RED/WHT-2
3 PPL-6
3 RED-2
.8 LT BLU-78
3 PNK-3
P917545
.8 LT GRN-924
.8 DK BLU-975
SPLICE 25
1 BRN-25
12020183
.8 GRA-91
.8 PNK/BLK-39
.5 DK GRN-35
.8 WHT-93
.8 ORN-98
.5 TAN-31
.8 PPL-92
.8 PNK/WHT-350
8917261
.8 PNK-94
.8 TAN/WHT-33
1 DK GRN-29
.8 BRN-9
.5 DK BLU-15
1 LT GRN-11
.5 LT BLU-14
.8 TAN-12
WASHER PUMP
.8 BLK-150
12020099
12020100
12004635
BRAKE PRESS WARNING SWITCH
FRONT OF DASH
.8 PNK-30
.8 BRN-9
.8 DK GRN-19
.8 YEL-18
.8 LT GRN-24

CS-TS 100	TS-TT 100
BODY STYLE-ALL	

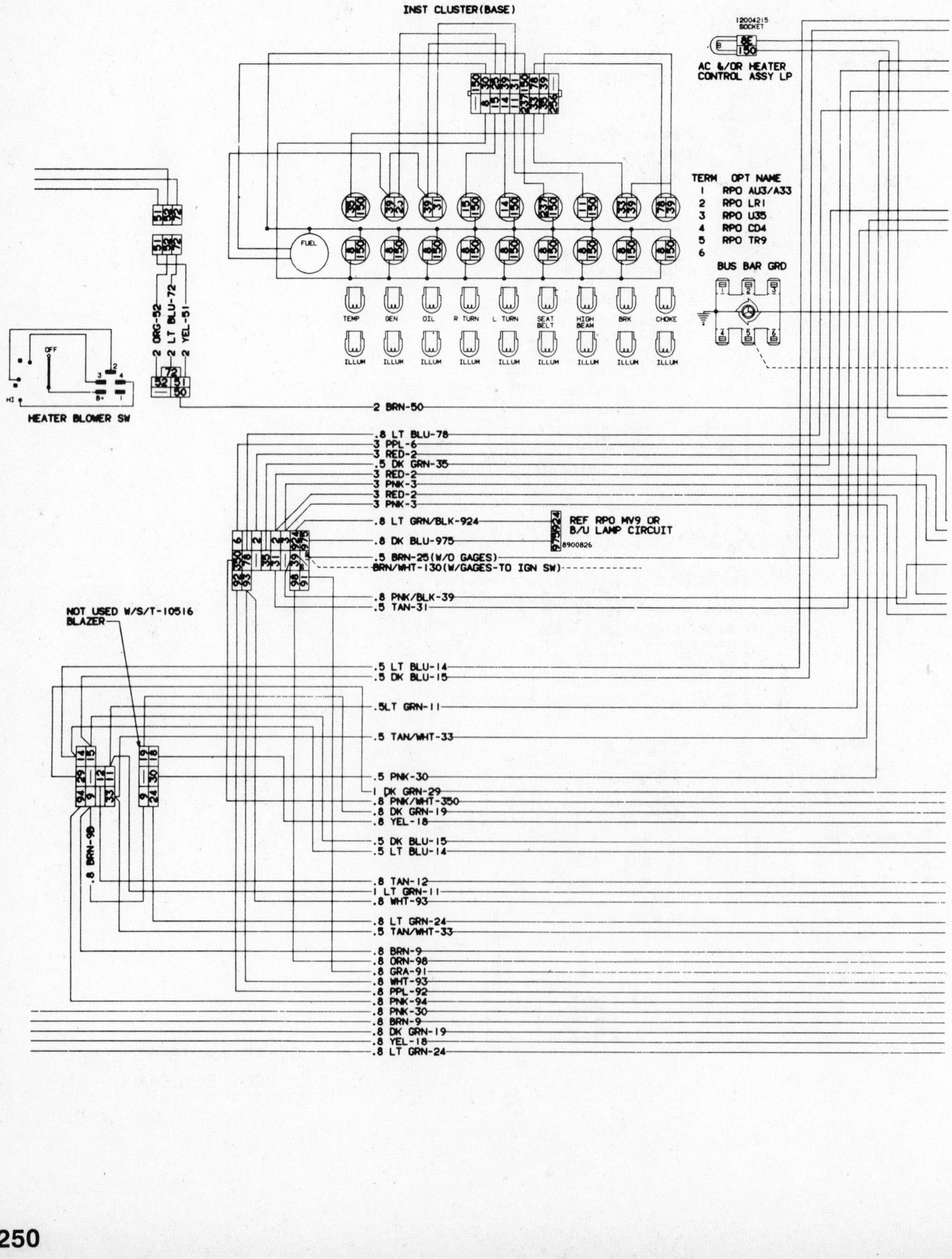
INST CLUSTER(BASE)
12004215 SOCKET
AC &/OR HEATER CONTROL ASSY LP
FUEL
TEMP
GEN
OIL
R TURN
L TURN
SEAT BELT
HIGH BEAM
BRK
CHOKE
ILLUM
TERM OPT NAME
1 RPO AU3/A33
2 RPO LR1
3 RPO U35
4 RPO CD4
5 RPO TR9
6
BUS BAR GRD
2 ORG-52
2 LT BLU-72
2 YEL-51
OFF
HI
B+
HEATER BLOWER SW
2 BRN-50
.8 LT BLU-78
3 PPL-6
3 RED-2
.5 DK GRN-35
3 RED-2
3 PNK-3
3 RED-2
3 PNK-3
.8 LT GRN/BLK-924
.8 DK BLU-975
REF RPO MV9 OR B/U LAMP CIRCUIT
8900826
.5 BRN-25(W/O GAGES)
BRN/WHT-130(W/GAGES-TO IGN SW)
.8 PNK/BLK-39
.5 TAN-31
NOT USED W/S/T-10516 BLAZER
.5 LT BLU-14
.5 DK BLU-15
.5LT GRN-11
.5 TAN/WHT-33
.5 PNK-30
1 DK GRN-29
.8 PNK/WHT-350
.8 DK GRN-19
.8 YEL-18
.5 DK BLU-15
.5 LT BLU-14
.8 BRN-98
.8 TAN-12
1 LT GRN-11
.8 WHT-93
.8 LT GRN-24
.5 TAN/WHT-33
.8 BRN-9
.8 ORN-98
.8 GRA-91
.8 WHT-93
.8 PPL-92
.8 PNK-94
.8 PNK-30
.8 BRN-9
.8 DK GRN-19
.8 YEL-18
.8 LT GRN-24

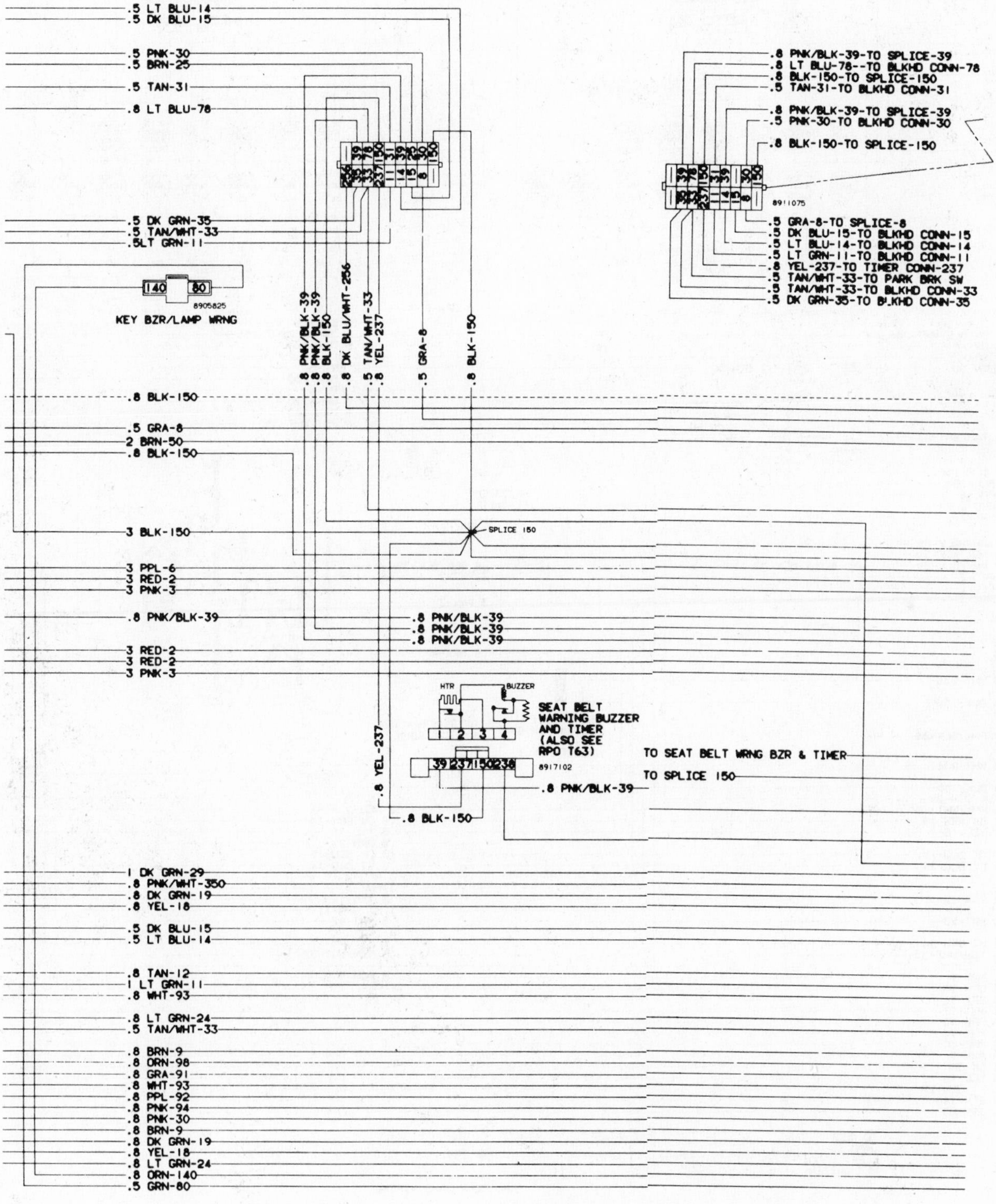
.5 LT BLU-14
.5 DK BLU-15
.5 PNK-30
.5 BRN-25
.5 TAN-31
.8 LT BLU-78
.5 DK GRN-35
.5 TAN/WHT-33
.5LT GRN-11
140
80
8905825
KEY BZR/LAMP WRNG
.8 PNK/BLK-39
.8 PNK/BLK-39
.8 BLK-150
.8 DK BLU/WHT-256
.5 TAN/WHT-33
.8 YEL-237
.5 GRA-8
.8 BLK-150
.8 PNK/BLK-39-TO SPLICE-39
.8 LT BLU-78--TO BLKHD CONN-78
.8 BLK-150-TO SPLICE-150
.5 TAN-31-TO BLKHD CONN-31
.8 PNK/BLK-39-TO SPLICE-39
.5 PNK-30-TO BLKHD CONN-30
.8 BLK-150-TO SPLICE-150
8911075
.5 GRA-8-TO SPLICE-8
.5 DK BLU-15-TO BLKHD CONN-15
.5 LT BLU-14-TO BLKHD CONN-14
.5 LT GRN-11-TO BLKHD CONN-11
.8 YEL-237-TO TIMER CONN-237
.5 TAN/WHT-33-TO PARK BRK SW
.5 TAN/WHT-33-TO BLKHD CONN-33
.5 DK GRN-35-TO BLKHD CONN-35
.8 BLK-150
.5 GRA-8
2 BRN-50
.8 BLK-150
3 BLK-150
SPLICE 150
3 PPL-6
3 RED-2
3 PNK-3
.8 PNK/BLK-39
.8 PNK/BLK-39
.8 PNK/BLK-39
.8 PNK/BLK-39
3 RED-2
3 RED-2
3 PNK-3
HTR
BUZZER
SEAT BELT WARNING BUZZER AND TIMER (ALSO SEE RPO T63)
1 2 3 4
39 237 150 238
8917102
.8 YEL-237
TO SEAT BELT WRNG BZR & TIMER
TO SPLICE 150
.8 PNK/BLK-39
.8 BLK-150
1 DK GRN-29
.8 PNK/WHT-350
.8 DK GRN-19
.8 YEL-18
.5 DK BLU-15
.5 LT BLU-14
.8 TAN-12
1 LT GRN-11
.8 WHT-93
.8 LT GRN-24
.5 TAN/WHT-33
.8 BRN-9
.8 ORN-98
.8 GRA-91
.8 WHT-93
.8 PPL-92
.8 PNK-94
.8 PNK-30
.8 BRN-9
.8 DK GRN-19
.8 YEL-18
.8 LT GRN-24
.8 ORN-140
.5 GRN-80

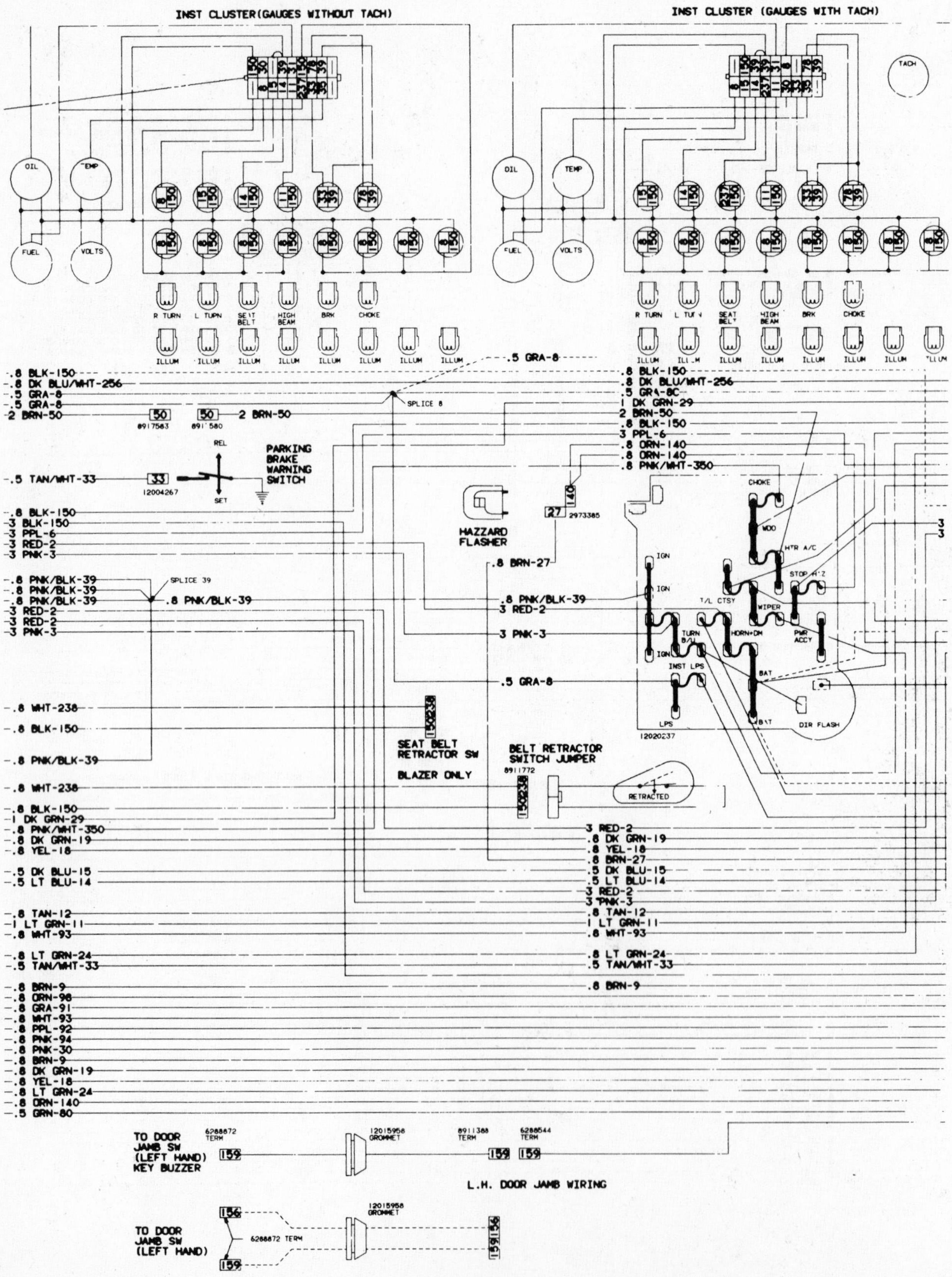
INST CLUSTER(GAUGES WITHOUT TACH)
INST CLUSTER (GAUGES WITH TACH)
TACH
OIL
TEMP
FUEL
VOLTS
R TURN
L TURN
SEAT BELT
HIGH BEAM
BRK
CHOKE
ILLUM
.5 GRA-8
.8 BLK-150
.8 DK BLU/WHT-256
.5 GRA-8
.5 GRA-8
2 BRN-50
8917583
8911580
SPLICE 8
1 DK GRN-29
3 PPL-6
.8 ORN-140
.8 PNK/WHT-350
PARKING BRAKE WARNING SWITCH
REL
SET
.5 TAN/WHT-33
12004267
HAZZARD FLASHER
2973385
.8 BRN-27
3 BLK-150
3 RED-2
3 PNK-3
.8 PNK/BLK-39
SPLICE 39
CHOKE
WDO
HTR A/C
IGN
STOP H'Z
T/L CTSY
WIPER
TURN B/U
HORN+DM
PWR ACCY
INST LPS
BAT
DIR FLASH
LPS
12020237
.8 WHT-238
SEAT BELT RETRACTOR SW
BLAZER ONLY
BELT RETRACTOR SWITCH JUMPER
8911772
RETRACTED
.8 DK GRN-19
.8 YEL-18
.5 DK BLU-15
.5 LT BLU-14
.8 TAN-12
1 LT GRN-11
.8 WHT-93
.8 LT GRN-24
.8 BRN-9
.8 ORN-98
.8 GRA-91
.8 PPL-92
.8 PNK-94
.8 PNK-30
.8 ORN-140
.5 GRN-80
TO DOOR JAMB SW (LEFT HAND) KEY BUZZER
6288872 TERM
12015958 GROMMET
8911388 TERM
6288544 TERM
L.H. DOOR JAMB WIRING
TO DOOR JAMB SW (LEFT HAND)
6288872 TERM
12015958 GROMMET

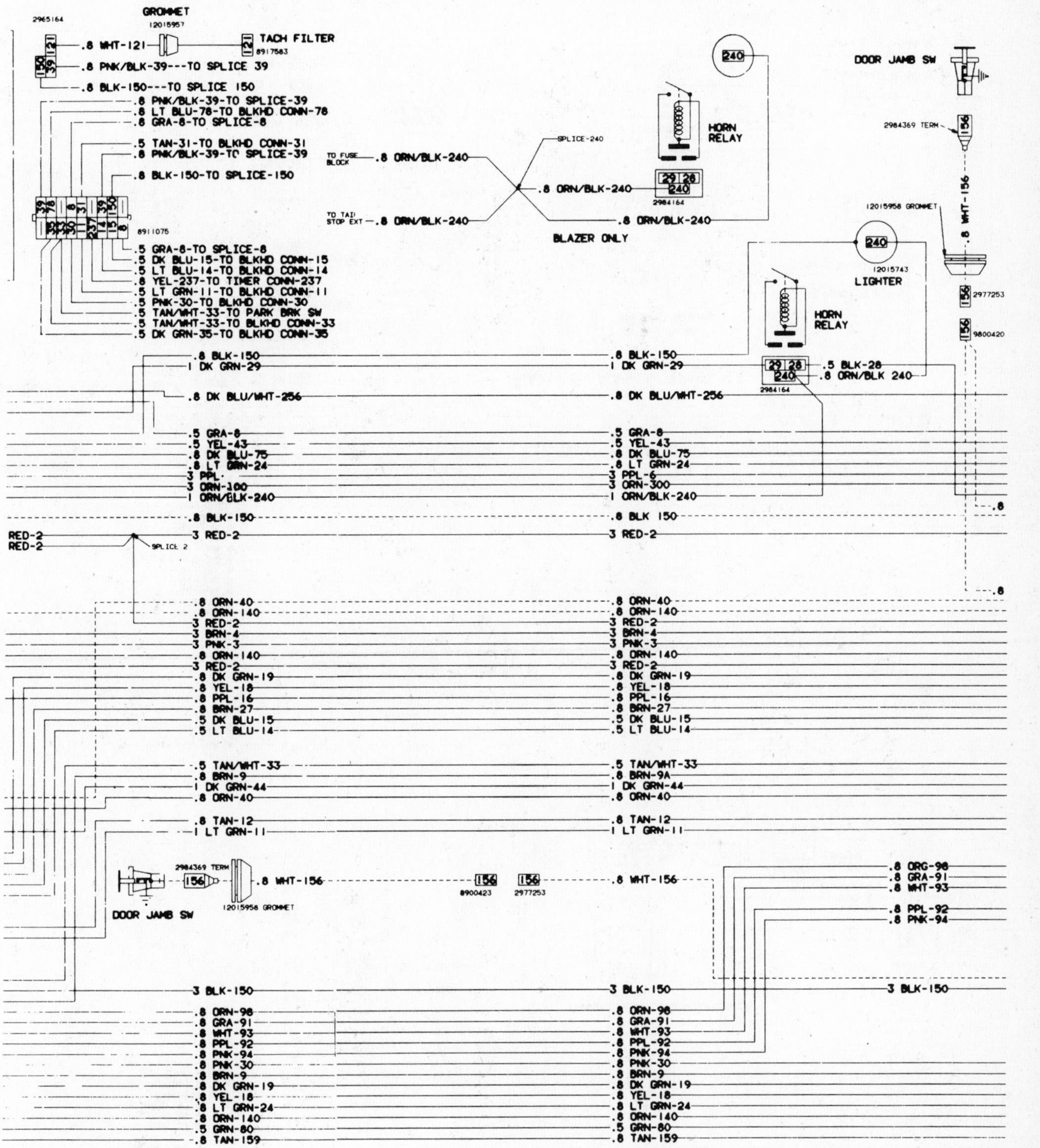
GROMMET
TACH FILTER
TO SPLICE 39
TO SPLICE 150
HORN RELAY
DOOR JAMB SW
SPLICE-240
TO FUSE BLOCK
TO TAIL STOP EXT
BLAZER ONLY
LIGHTER
SPLICE 2
DOOR JAMB SW
.8 WHT-156
3 BLK-150

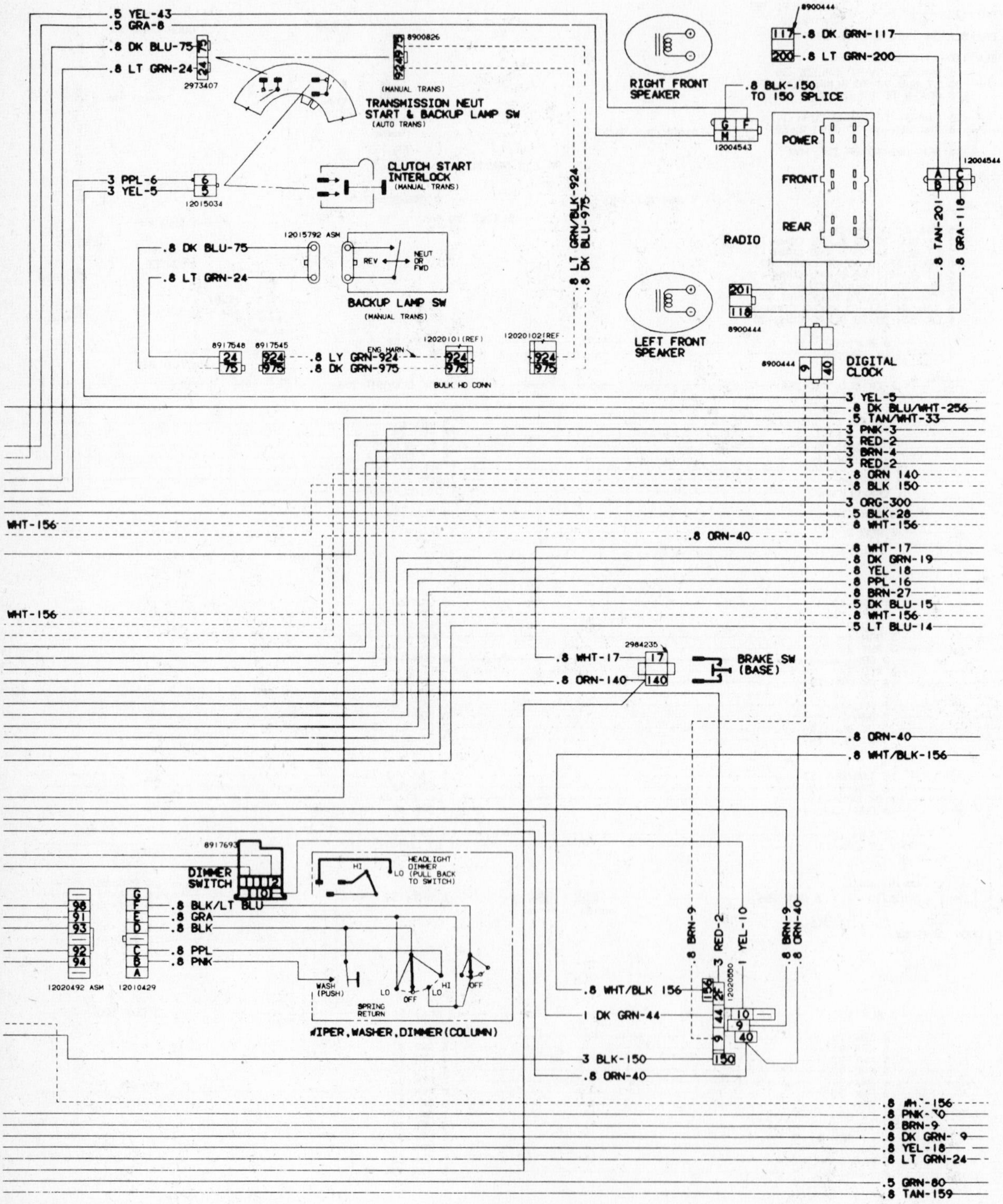
.5 YEL-43
.5 GRA-8
.8 DK BLU-75
.8 LT GRN-24
2973407
8900826
(MANUAL TRANS)
TRANSMISSION NEUT START & BACKUP LAMP SW
(AUTO TRANS)
CLUTCH START INTERLOCK
(MANUAL TRANS)
3 PPL-6
3 YEL-5
12015034
12015792 ASM
NEUT OR FWD
REV
BACKUP LAMP SW
(MANUAL TRANS)
8917548
8917545
.8 LY GRN-924
.8 DK GRN-975
ENG HARN
12020101 (REF)
12020102 (REF)
BULK HD CONN
.8 LT GRN/BLK-924
.8 DK BLU-975
RIGHT FRONT SPEAKER
.8 BLK-150 TO 150 SPLICE
12004543
8900444
.8 DK GRN-117
.8 LT GRN-200
POWER
FRONT
REAR
RADIO
12004544
.8 TAN-201
.8 GRA-118
LEFT FRONT SPEAKER
DIGITAL CLOCK
3 YEL-5
.8 DK BLU/WHT-256
.5 TAN/WHT-33
3 PNK-3
3 RED-2
3 BRN-4
3 RED-2
.8 ORN 140
.8 BLK 150
3 ORG-300
.5 BLK-28
.8 WHT-156
WHT-156
.8 ORN-40
.8 WHT-17
.8 DK GRN-19
.8 YEL-18
.8 PPL-16
.8 BRN-27
.5 DK BLU-15
.8 WHT-156
.5 LT BLU-14
2984235
.8 WHT-17
.8 ORN-140
BRAKE SW (BASE)
.8 ORN-40
.8 WHT/BLK-156
8917693
DIMMER SWITCH
HEADLIGHT DIMMER
HI
LO (PULL BACK TO SWITCH)
.8 BLK/LT BLU
.8 GRA
.8 BLK
.8 PPL
.8 PNK
12020492 ASM
12010429
WASH (PUSH)
SPRING RETURN
LO
OFF
HI
WIPER, WASHER, DIMMER (COLUMN)
.8 BRN-9
3 RED-2
1 YEL-10
.8 BRN-9
.8 ORN-40
12020550
.8 WHT/BLK 156
1 DK GRN-44
3 BLK-150
.8 ORN-40
.8 BRN-9
.8 YEL-18
.8 LT GRN-24
.5 GRN-80
.8 TAN-159

CS-TS 100	TS-TT 100
BODY STYLE-ALL	

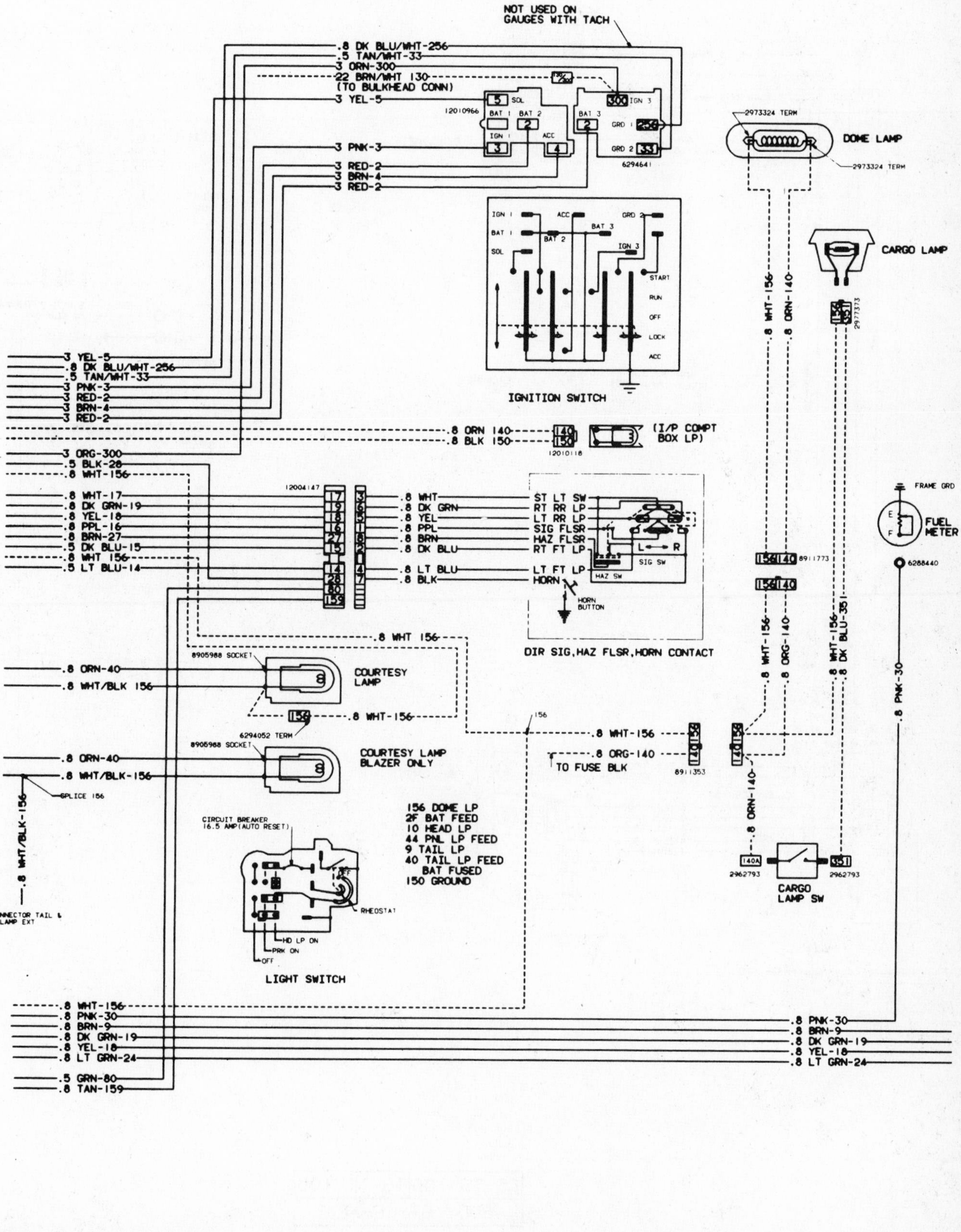
NOT USED ON GAUGES WITH TACH
IGNITION SWITCH
DOME LAMP
CARGO LAMP
(I/P COMPT BOX LP)
DIR SIG, HAZ FLSR, HORN CONTACT
FUEL METER
FRAME GRD
COURTESY LAMP
COURTESY LAMP BLAZER ONLY
TO FUSE BLK
CARGO LAMP SW
LIGHT SWITCH
CIRCUIT BREAKER 16.5 AMP (AUTO RESET)
RHEOSTAT
SPLICE 156
TO CONNECTOR TAIL & STOP LAMP EXT
156 DOME LP
2F BAT FEED
10 HEAD LP
44 PNL LP FEED
9 TAIL LP
40 TAIL LP FEED BAT FUSED
150 GROUND

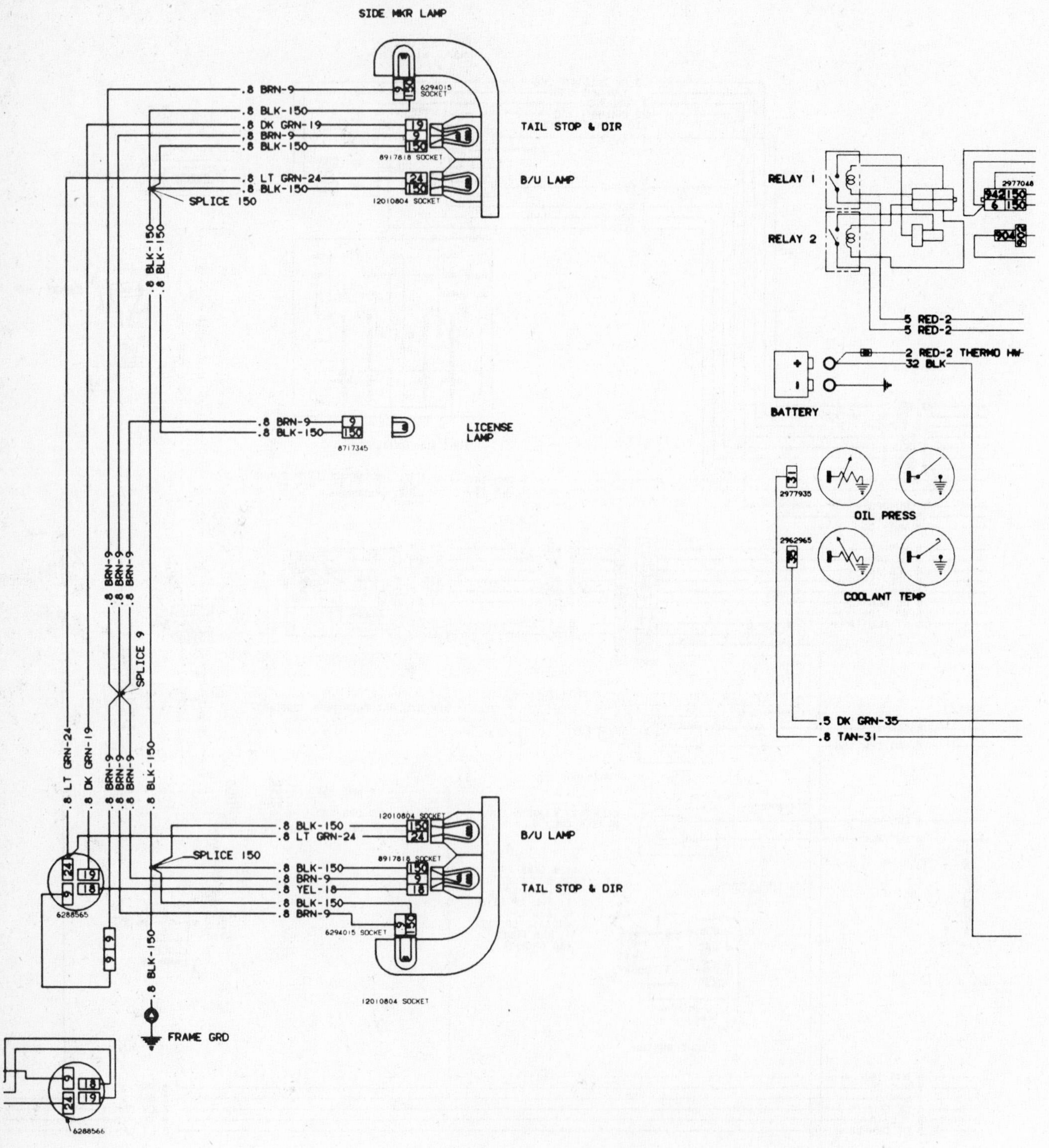
SIDE MKR LAMP
.8 BRN-9
6294015 SOCKET
.8 BLK-150
.8 DK GRN-19
.8 BRN-9
.8 BLK-150
TAIL STOP & DIR
8917818 SOCKET
.8 LT GRN-24
.8 BLK-150
B/U LAMP
SPLICE 150
12010804 SOCKET
.8 BLK-150
.8 BLK-150
.8 BRN-9
.8 BLK-150
LICENSE LAMP
8717345
.8 BRN-9
.8 BRN-9
.8 BRN-9
SPLICE 9
.8 LT GRN-24
.8 DK GRN-19
.8 BRN-9
.8 BRN-9
.8 BRN-9
.8 BLK-150
12010804 SOCKET
.8 BLK-150
.8 LT GRN-24
B/U LAMP
SPLICE 150
8917818 SOCKET
.8 BLK-150
.8 BRN-9
.8 YEL-18
TAIL STOP & DIR
.8 BLK-150
.8 BRN-9
6294015 SOCKET
6288565
12010804 SOCKET
.8 BLK-150
FRAME GRD
6288566
RELAY 1
RELAY 2
2977048
5 RED-2
5 RED-2
2 RED-2 THERMO HW
32 BLK
BATTERY
2977935
OIL PRESS
2962965
COOLANT TEMP
.5 DK GRN-35
.8 TAN-31

CS-TS 100	TS-TT 100
BODY STYLE-ALL	

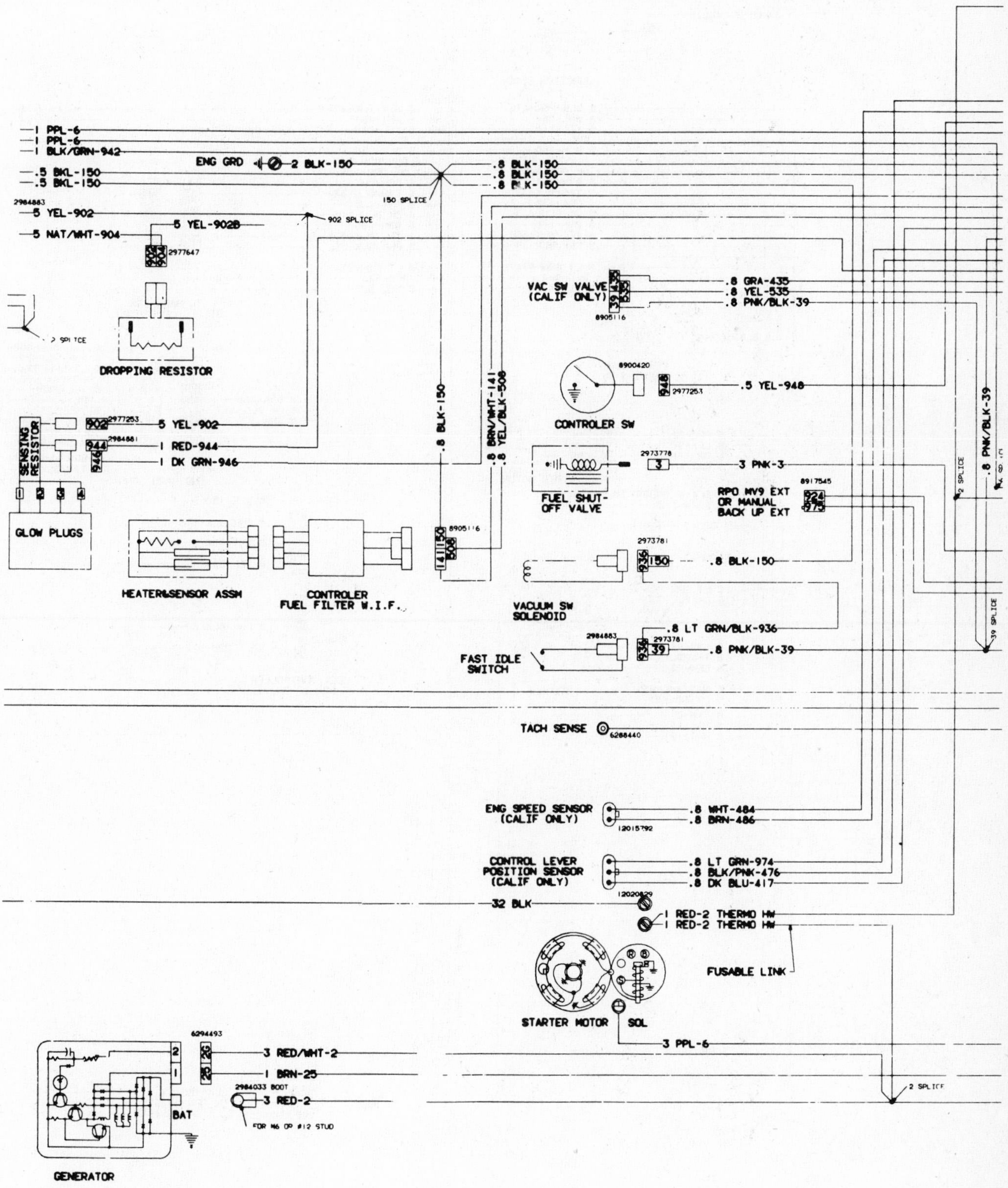
1 PPL-6
1 PPL-6
1 BLK/GRN-942
ENG GRD
2 BLK-150
.5 BKL-150
.5 BKL-150
.8 BLK-150
.8 BLK-150
150 SPLICE
2984883
5 YEL-902
902 SPLICE
5 YEL-902B
5 NAT/WHT-904
2977647
DROPPING RESISTOR
VAC SW VALVE
(CALIF ONLY)
8905116
.8 GRA-435
.8 YEL-535
.8 PNK/BLK-39
8900420
2977253
.5 YEL-948
CONTROLER SW
.8 BLK-150
.8 BRN/WHT-141
.8 YEL/BLK-508
SENSING RESISTOR
2977253
5 YEL-902
2984881
1 RED-944
1 DK GRN-946
2973778
3 PNK-3
FUEL SHUT-OFF VALVE
RPO MV9 EXT
OR MANUAL
BACK UP EXT
8917545
GLOW PLUGS
8905116
HEATER&SENSOR ASSM
CONTROLER
FUEL FILTER W.I.F.
2973781
.8 BLK-150
VACUUM SW
SOLENOID
.8 LT GRN/BLK-936
2984883
2973781
.8 PNK/BLK-39
FAST IDLE
SWITCH
.8 PNK/BLK-39
2 SPLICE
39 SPLICE
TACH SENSE
6288440
ENG SPEED SENSOR
(CALIF ONLY)
12015792
.8 WHT-484
.8 BRN-486
CONTROL LEVER
POSITION SENSOR
(CALIF ONLY)
.8 LT GRN-974
.8 BLK/PNK-476
.8 DK BLU-417
32 BLK
1 RED-2 THERMO HW
1 RED-2 THERMO HW
FUSABLE LINK
STARTER MOTOR
SOL
3 PPL-6
6294493
3 RED/WHT-2
1 BRN-25
2984033 BOOT
3 RED-2
FOR M6 OR #12 STUD
BAT
2 SPLICE
GENERATOR

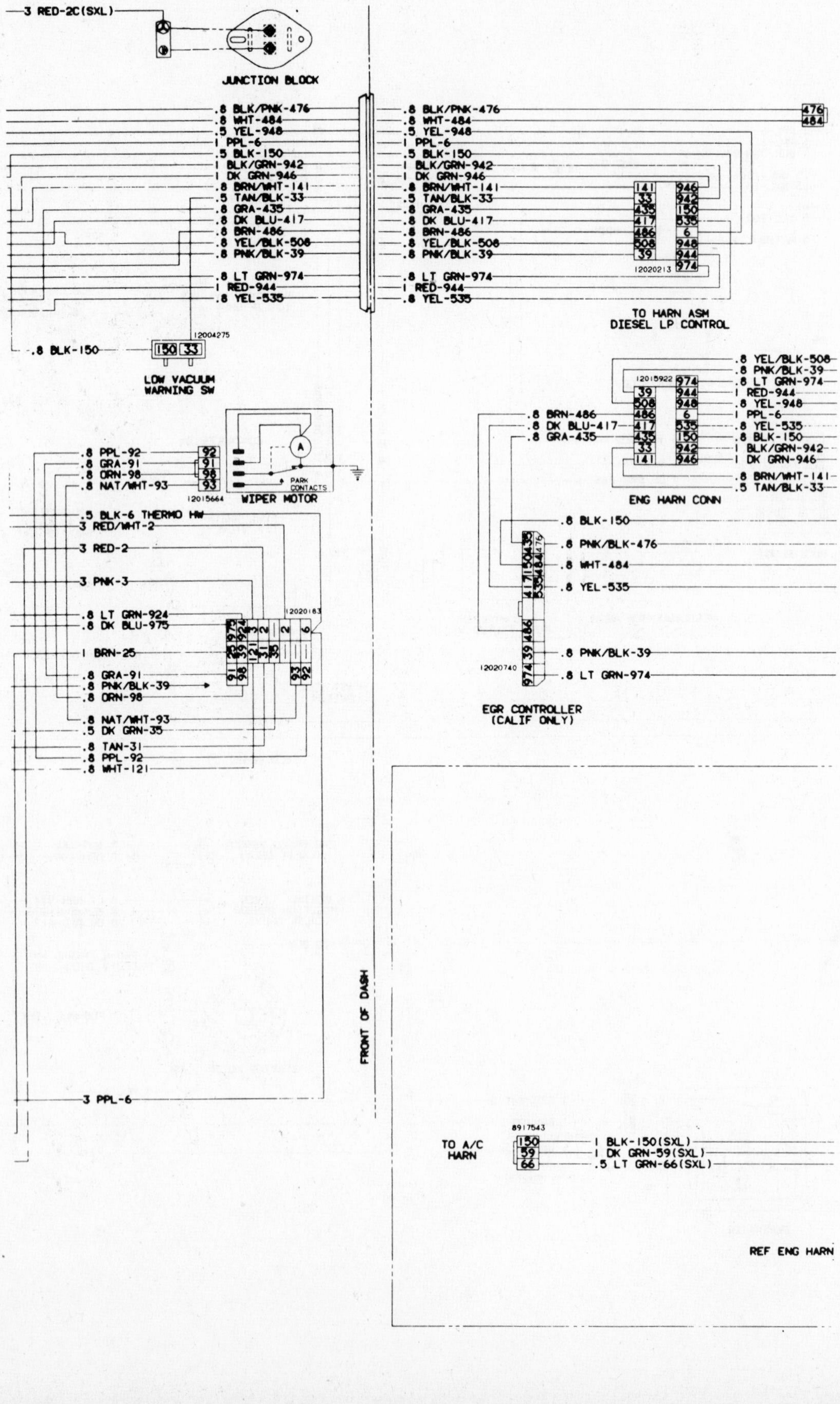
3 RED-2C(SXL)
JUNCTION BLOCK
.8 BLK/PNK-476
.8 WHT-484
.5 YEL-948
1 PPL-6
.5 BLK-150
1 BLK/GRN-942
1 DK GRN-946
.8 BRN/WHT-141
.5 TAN/BLK-33
.8 GRA-435
.8 DK BLU-417
.8 BRN-486
.8 YEL/BLK-508
.8 PNK/BLK-39
.8 LT GRN-974
1 RED-944
.8 YEL-535
12020213
TO HARN ASM DIESEL LP CONTROL
12004275
.8 BLK-150
LOW VACUUM WARNING SW
12015922
ENG HARN CONN
.8 PPL-92
.8 GRA-91
.8 ORN-98
.8 NAT/WHT-93
12015664
WIPER MOTOR
PARK CONTACTS
.5 BLK-6 THERMO HW
3 RED/WHT-2
3 RED-2
3 PNK-3
.8 LT GRN-924
.8 DK BLU-975
1 BRN-25
.8 PNK/BLK-39
.8 ORN-98
.5 DK GRN-35
.8 TAN-31
.8 WHT-121
12020183
.8 PNK/BLK-476
12020740
EGR CONTROLLER (CALIF ONLY)
3 PPL-6
FRONT OF DASH
8917543
TO A/C HARN
1 BLK-150(SXL)
1 DK GRN-59(SXL)
.5 LT GRN-66(SXL)
REF ENG HARN

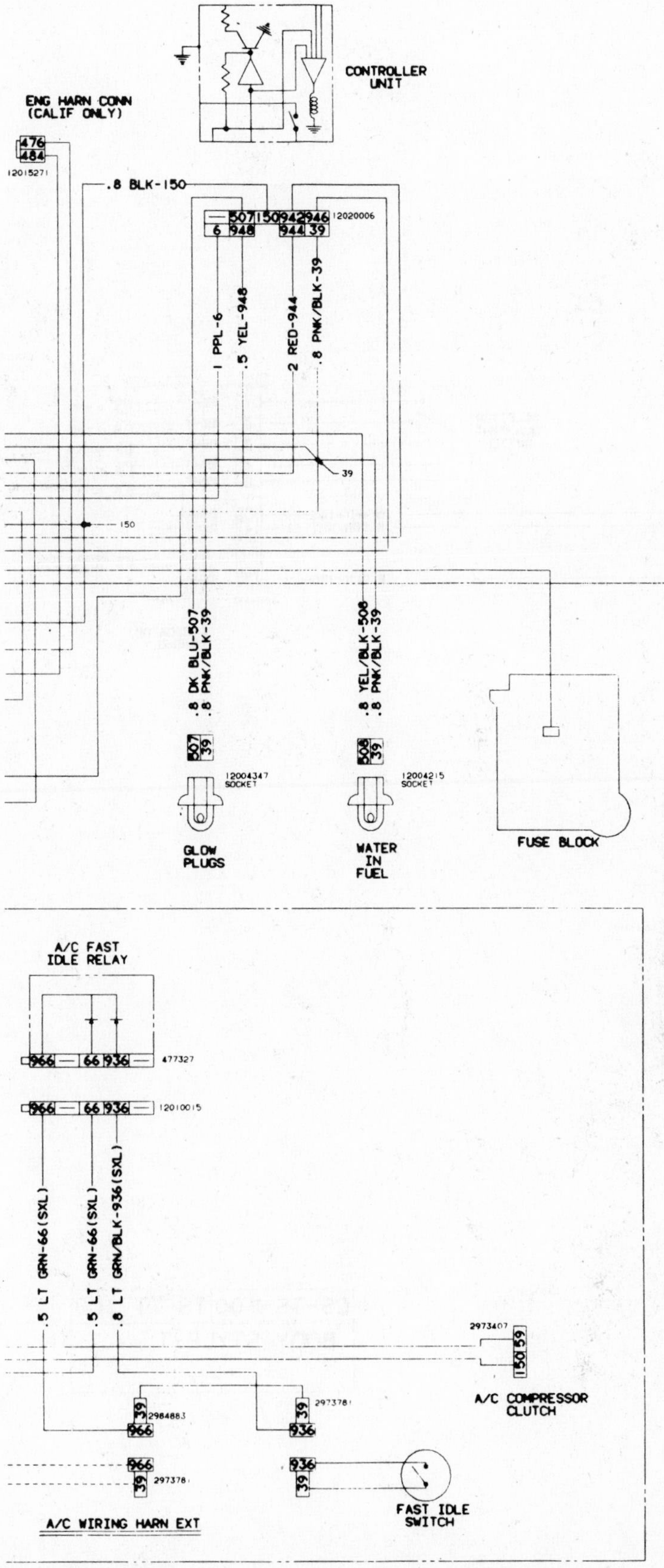
CONTROLLER UNIT
ENG HARN CONN (CALIF ONLY)
476
484
12015271
.8 BLK-150
507
150
942
946
6
948
944
39
12020006
1 PPL-6
.5 YEL-948
2 RED-944
.8 PNK/BLK-39
39
150
33
PARK BRK SWITCH
.8 DK BLU-507
.8 PNK/BLK-39
.8 YEL/BLK-508
.8 PNK/BLK-39
33
507
39
508
39
12004347 SOCKET
12004215 SOCKET
GLOW PLUGS
WATER IN FUEL
FUSE BLOCK
A/C FAST IDLE RELAY
966
66
936
477327
12010015
.5 LT GRN-66(SXL)
.5 LT GRN-66(SXL)
.8 LT GRN/BLK-936(SXL)
2973407
150
59
A/C COMPRESSOR CLUTCH
2984883
2973781
297378
FAST IDLE SWITCH
A/C WIRING HARN EXT

CS 100	TS 100
BODY STYLE-ALL	

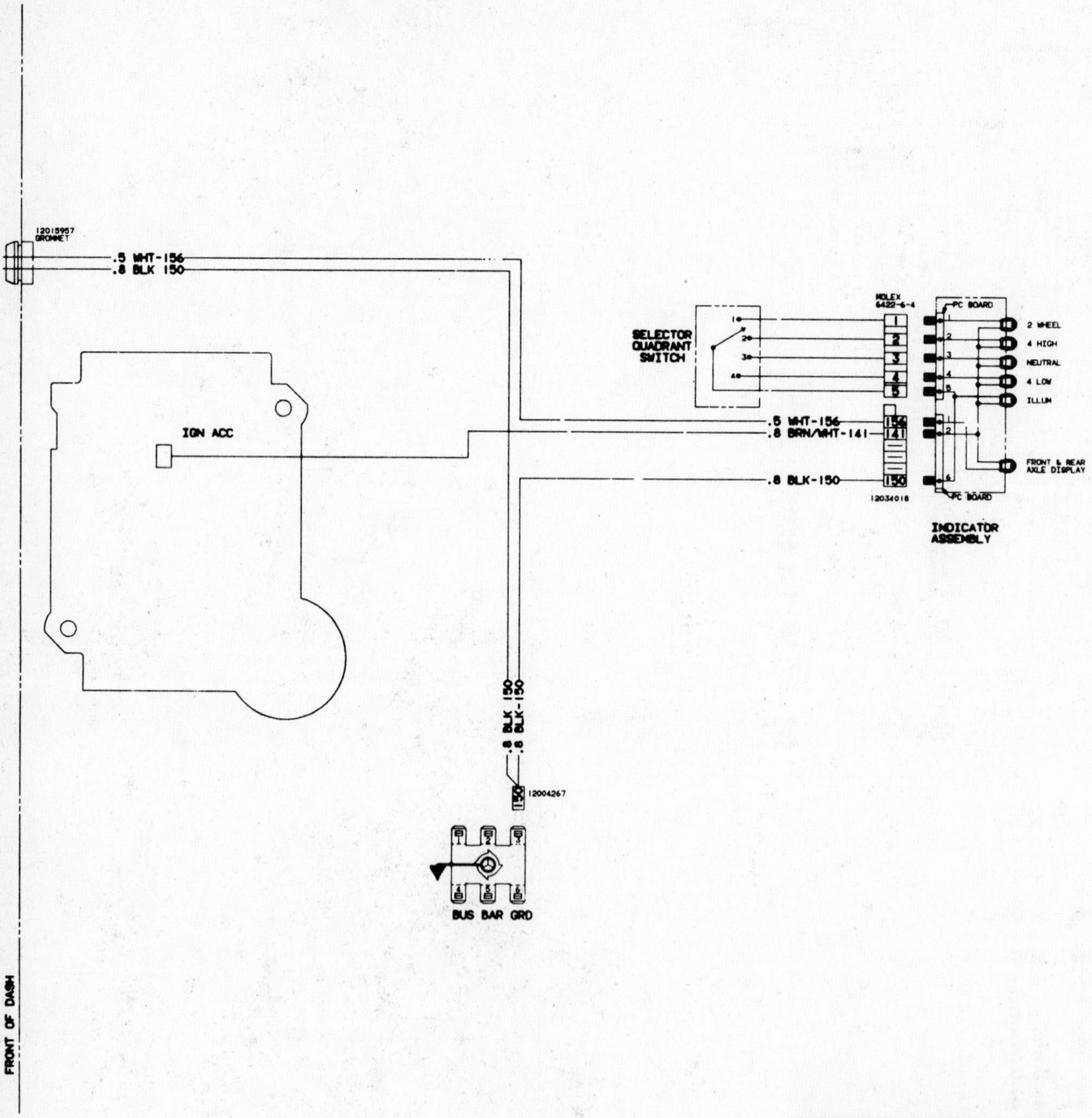
12015957
GROMMET
.5 WHT-156
.8 BLK 150
SELECTOR
QUADRANT
SWITCH
MOLEX
6422-6-4
PC BOARD
2 WHEEL
4 HIGH
NEUTRAL
4 LOW
ILLUM
IGN ACC
.5 WHT-156
.8 BRN/WHT-141
.8 BLK-150
12034018
FRONT & REAR
AXLE DISPLAY
PC BOARD
INDICATOR
ASSEMBLY
.8 BLK 150
.8 BLK-150
12004267
BUS BAR GRD
FRONT OF DASH

CS-TS 100	TS-TT 100
BODY STYLE-T	

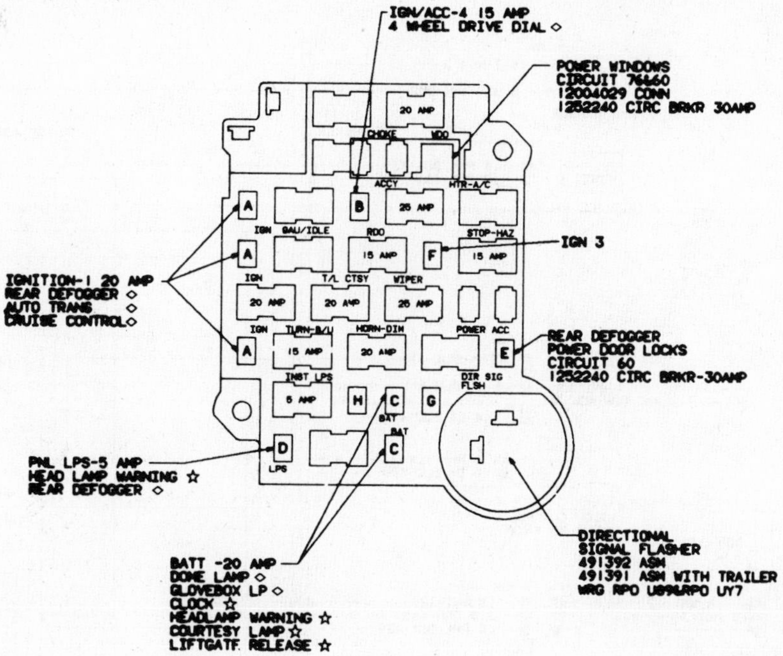
IGN/ACC-4 15 AMP
4 WHEEL DRIVE DIAL ◇
POWER WINDOWS
CIRCUIT 76&60
12004029 CONN
1252240 CIRC BRKR 30AMP
20 AMP
CHOKE
WDO
ACCY
HTR-A/C
A
B
25 AMP
IGN
GAU/IDLE
RDO
STOP-HAZ
15 AMP
F
15 AMP
IGN 3
IGNITION-1 20 AMP
REAR DEFOGGER ◇
AUTO TRANS ◇
CRUISE CONTROL◇
IGN
T/L CTSY
WIPER
20 AMP
20 AMP
25 AMP
IGN
TURN-B/U
HORN-DIM
POWER ACC
15 AMP
20 AMP
E
REAR DEFOGGER
POWER DOOR LOCKS
CIRCUIT 60
1252240 CIRC BRKR-30AMP
INST LPS
DIR SIG FLSH
5 AMP
H
C
G
BAT
BAT
D
LPS
PNL LPS-5 AMP
HEAD LAMP WARNING ☆
REAR DEFOGGER ◇
DIRECTIONAL
SIGNAL FLASHER
491392 ASM
491391 ASM WITH TRAILER
WRG RPO U89&RPO UY7
BATT -20 AMP
DOME LAMP ◇
GLOVEBOX LP ◇
CLOCK ☆
HEADLAMP WARNING ☆
COURTESY LAMP ☆
LIFTGATE RELEASE ☆

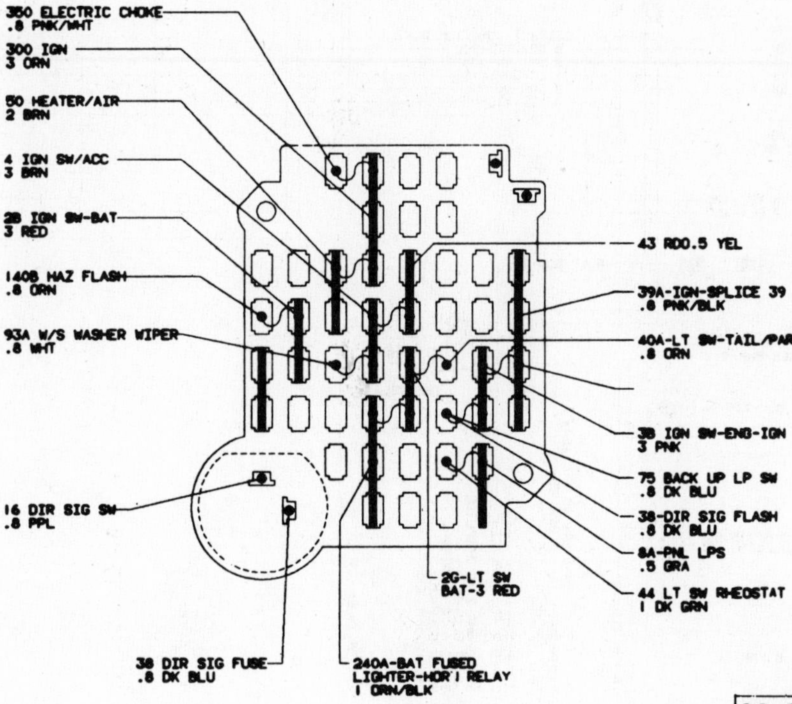
350 ELECTRIC CHOKE
.8 PNK/WHT
300 IGN
3 ORN
50 HEATER/AIR
2 BRN
4 IGN SW/ACC
3 BRN
2B IGN SW-BAT
3 RED
140B HAZ FLASH
.8 ORN
93A W/S WASHER WIPER
.8 WHT
16 DIR SIG SW
.8 PPL
38 DIR SIG FUSE
.8 DK BLU
240A-BAT FUSED
LIGHTER-HOR'I RELAY
1 ORN/BLK
2G-LT SW
BAT-3 RED
43 RDO.5 YEL
39A-IGN-SPLICE 39
.8 PNK/BLK
40A-LT SW-TAIL/PARK LPS
.8 ORN
3B IGN SW-ENG-IGN 1
3 PNK
75 BACK UP LP SW
.8 DK BLU
38-DIR SIG FLASH
.8 DK BLU
8A-PNL LPS
.5 GRA
44 LT SW RHEOSTAT
1 DK GRN

CS-CT 100	TS-TT 100
BODY STYLE-ALL	

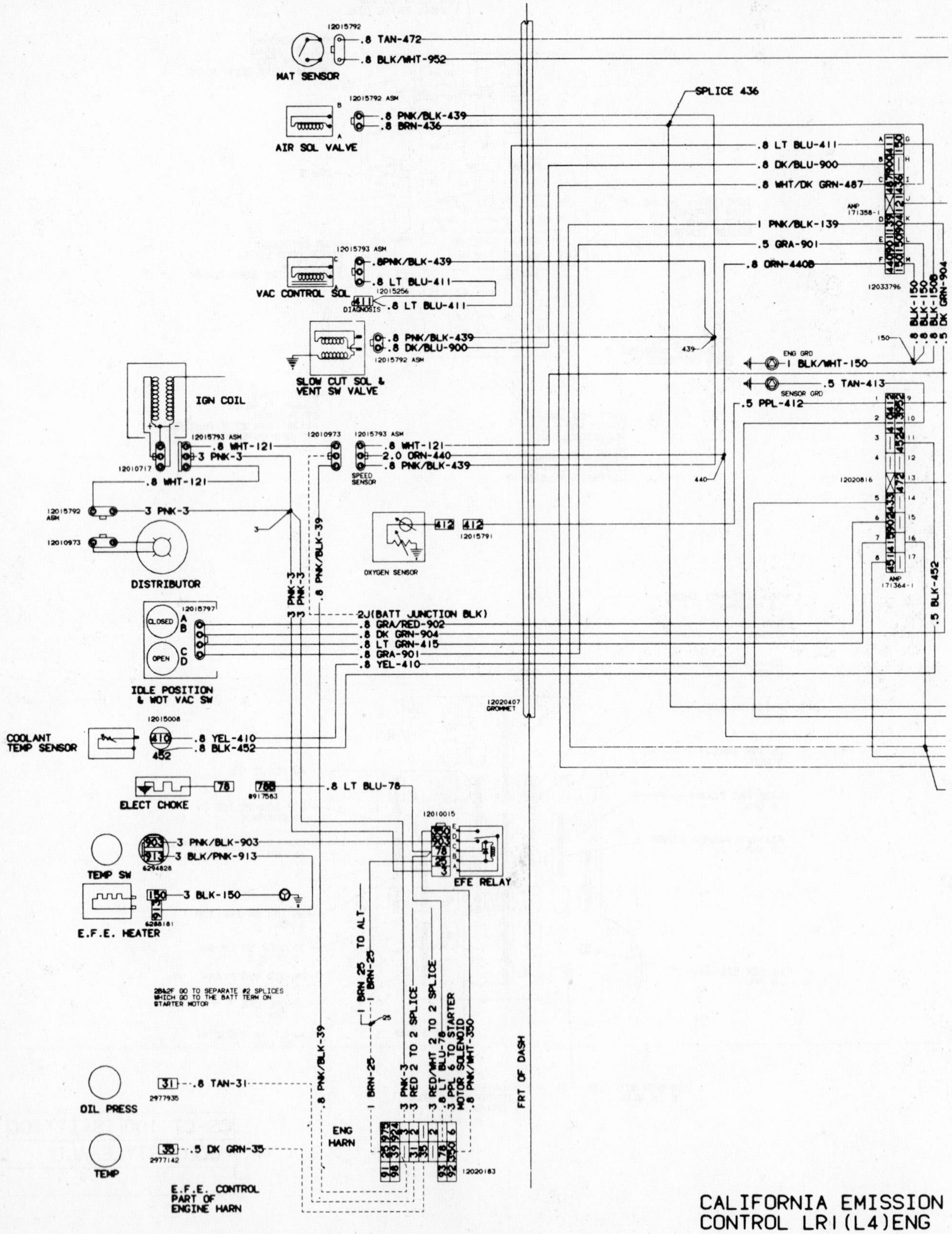
MAT SENSOR
.8 TAN-472
.8 BLK/WHT-952
SPLICE 436
AIR SOL VALVE
.8 PNK/BLK-439
.8 BRN-436
.8 LT BLU-411
.8 DK/BLU-900
.8 WHT/DK GRN-487
1 PNK/BLK-139
.5 GRA-901
.8 ORN-440B
VAC CONTROL SOL
DIAGNOSIS
SLOW CUT SOL & VENT SW VALVE
.8 DK/BLU-900
ENG GRD
1 BLK/WHT-150
.5 TAN-413
SENSOR GRD
.5 PPL-412
IGN COIL
.8 WHT-121
3 PNK-3
2.0 ORN-440
SPEED SENSOR
DISTRIBUTOR
OXYGEN SENSOR
2J(BATT JUNCTION BLK)
.8 GRA/RED-902
.8 DK GRN-904
.8 LT GRN-415
.8 GRA-901
.8 YEL-410
IDLE POSITION & WOT VAC SW
CLOSED
OPEN
GROMMET
COOLANT TEMP SENSOR
.8 YEL-410
.8 BLK-452
.5 BLK-452
ELECT CHOKE
.8 LT BLU-78
EFE RELAY
TEMP SW
3 PNK/BLK-903
3 BLK/PNK-913
E.F.E. HEATER
3 BLK-150
TO ALT
1 BRN-25
2&2F GO TO SEPARATE #2 SPLICES WHICH GO TO THE BATT TERM ON STARTER MOTOR
.8 PNK/BLK-39
1 BRN-25
3 PNK-3 TO 2 SPLICE
3 RED 2 TO 2 SPLICE
3 RED/WHT 2 TO 2 SPLICE
.8 LT BLU-78
3 PPL 6 TO STARTER MOTOR SOLENOID
.8 PNK/WHT-350
FRT OF DASH
OIL PRESS
.8 TAN-31
ENG HARN
TEMP
.5 DK GRN-35
E.F.E. CONTROL PART OF ENGINE HARN

CALIFORNIA EMISSION CONTROL LR1(L4)ENG

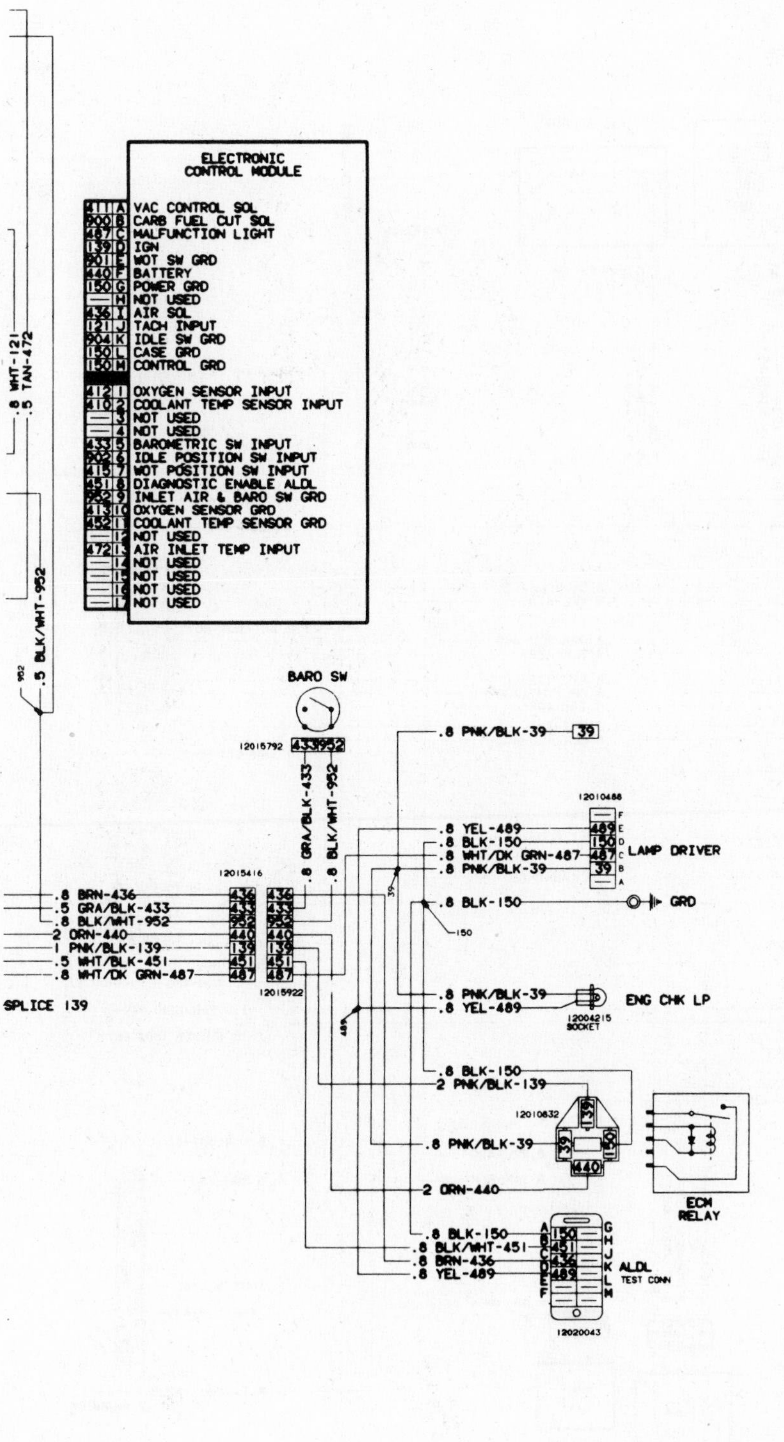
ELECTRONIC CONTROL MODULE
411 A VAC CONTROL SOL
900 B CARB FUEL CUT SOL
487 C MALFUNCTION LIGHT
139 D IGN
901 E WOT SW GRD
440 F BATTERY
150 G POWER GRD
H NOT USED
436 I AIR SOL
121 J TACH INPUT
904 K IDLE SW GRD
150 L CASE GRD
150 M CONTROL GRD
412 1 OXYGEN SENSOR INPUT
410 2 COOLANT TEMP SENSOR INPUT
3 NOT USED
4 NOT USED
433 5 BAROMETRIC SW INPUT
902 6 IDLE POSITION SW INPUT
415 7 WOT POSITION SW INPUT
451 8 DIAGNOSTIC ENABLE ALDL
952 9 INLET AIR & BARO SW GRD
413 10 OXYGEN SENSOR GRD
452 11 COOLANT TEMP SENSOR GRD
12 NOT USED
472 13 AIR INLET TEMP INPUT
14 NOT USED
15 NOT USED
16 NOT USED
17 NOT USED
.8 WHT-121
.5 TAN-472
.5 BLK/WHT-952
BARO SW
12015792
.8 GRA/BLK-433
.8 BLK/WHT-952
.8 PNK/BLK-39
12010488
.8 YEL-489
.8 BLK-150
.8 WHT/DK GRN-487
.8 PNK/BLK-39
LAMP DRIVER
12015416
.8 BRN-436
.5 GRA/BLK-433
.8 BLK/WHT-952
2 ORN-440
1 PNK/BLK-139
.5 WHT/BLK-451
.8 WHT/DK GRN-487
12015922
SPLICE 139
.8 BLK-150
GRD
.8 PNK/BLK-39
.8 YEL-489
ENG CHK LP
12004215 SOCKET
.8 BLK-150
2 PNK/BLK-139
12010832
.8 PNK/BLK-39
2 ORN-440
ECM RELAY
.8 BLK-150
.8 BLK/WHT-451
.8 BRN-436
.8 YEL-489
ALDL TEST CONN
12020043

CS-TS 100	TS-TT 100
BODY STYLE-ALL	

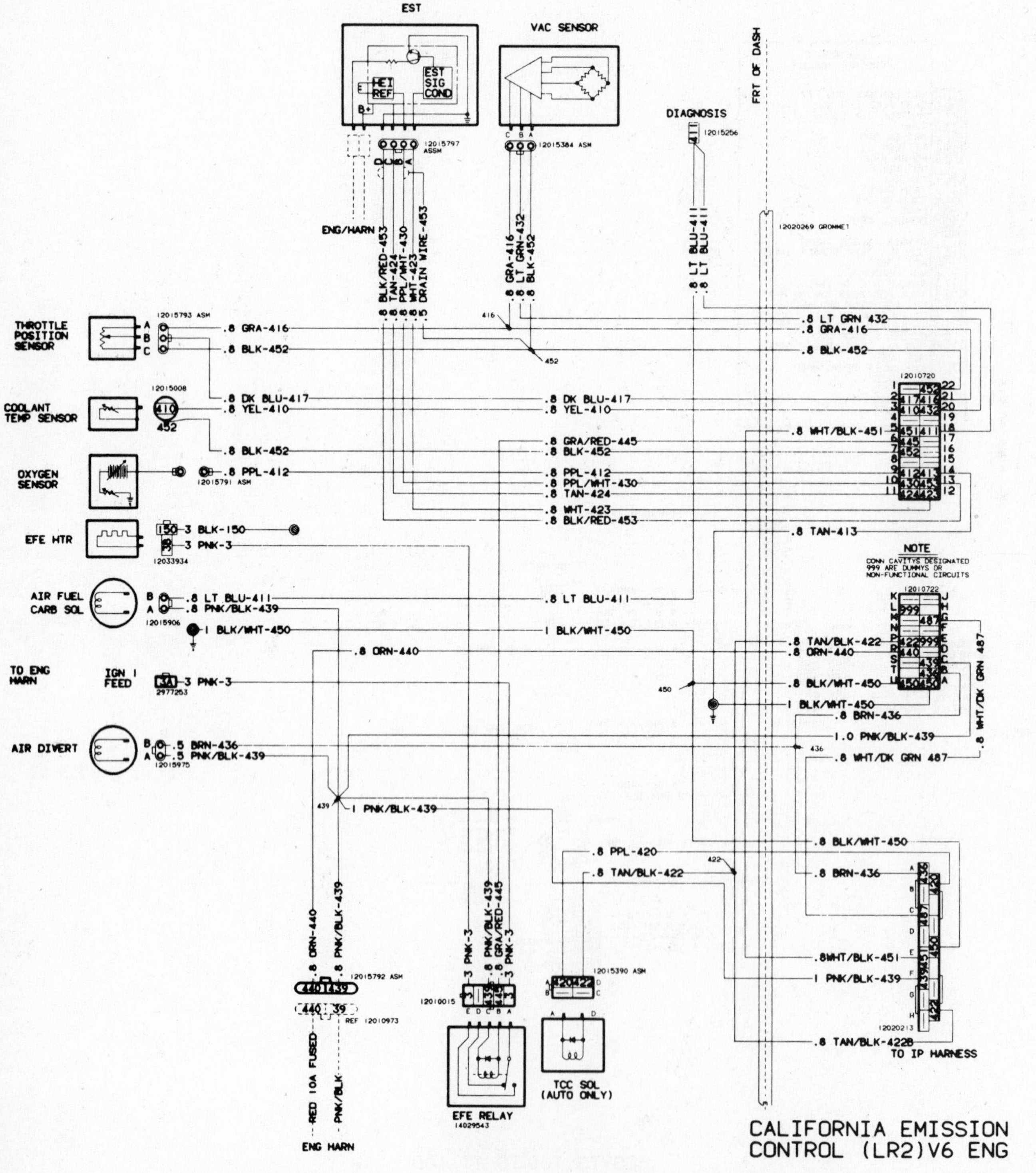
EST
VAC SENSOR
DIAGNOSIS
FRT OF DASH
HEI REF
EST SIG COND
ENG/HARN
THROTTLE POSITION SENSOR
COOLANT TEMP SENSOR
OXYGEN SENSOR
EFE HTR
AIR FUEL CARB SOL
TO ENG HARN
IGN I FEED
AIR DIVERT
.8 GRA-416
.8 BLK-452
.8 DK BLU-417
.8 YEL-410
.8 PPL-412
3 BLK-150
3 PNK-3
.8 LT BLU-411
.8 PNK/BLK-439
I BLK/WHT-450
.8 ORN-440
.5 BRN-436
.5 PNK/BLK-439
I PNK/BLK-439
.8 LT GRN 432
.8 GRA/RED-445
.8 PPL/WHT-430
.8 TAN-424
.8 WHT-423
.8 BLK/RED-453
.5 DRAIN WIRE-453
.8 WHT/BLK-451
.8 TAN-413
.8 TAN/BLK-422
.8 BRN-436
1.0 PNK/BLK-439
.8 WHT/DK GRN 487
.8 PPL-420
.8WHT/BLK-451
.8 TAN/BLK-422B
TO IP HARNESS
NOTE
CONN CAVITYS DESIGNATED 999 ARE DUMMYS OR NON-FUNCTIONAL CIRCUITS
RED 10A FUSED
PNK/BLK
ENG HARN
EFE RELAY
TCC SOL (AUTO ONLY)
12020269 GROMMET

CALIFORNIA EMISSION CONTROL (LR2) V6 ENG

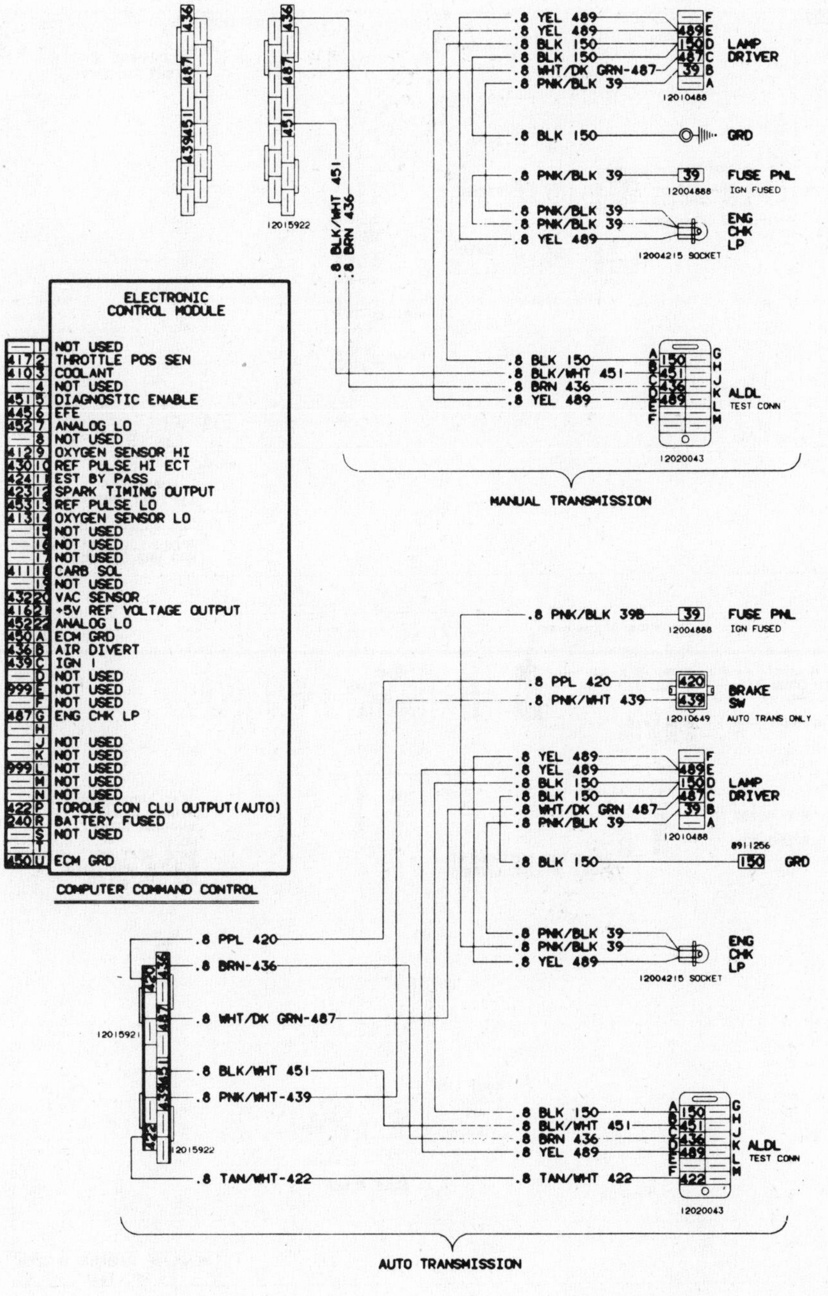
ELECTRONIC CONTROL MODULE
1 NOT USED
417 2 THROTTLE POS SEN
410 3 COOLANT
4 NOT USED
451 5 DIAGNOSTIC ENABLE
445 6 EFE
452 7 ANALOG LO
8 NOT USED
412 9 OXYGEN SENSOR HI
430 10 REF PULSE HI ECT
424 11 EST BY PASS
423 12 SPARK TIMING OUTPUT
453 13 REF PULSE LO
413 14 OXYGEN SENSOR LO
15 NOT USED
16 NOT USED
17 NOT USED
411 18 CARB SOL
19 NOT USED
432 20 VAC SENSOR
416 21 +5V REF VOLTAGE OUTPUT
452 22 ANALOG LO
450 A ECM GRD
436 B AIR DIVERT
439 C IGN 1
D NOT USED
999 E NOT USED
F NOT USED
487 G ENG CHK LP
H
J NOT USED
K NOT USED
999 L NOT USED
M NOT USED
N NOT USED
422 P TORQUE CON CLU OUTPUT(AUTO)
240 R BATTERY FUSED
S NOT USED
T
450 U ECM GRD
COMPUTER COMMAND CONTROL
12015922
.8 BLK/WHT 451
.8 BRN 436
.8 YEL 489
.8 BLK 150
.8 WHT/DK GRN-487
.8 PNK/BLK 39
LAMP DRIVER
12010488
GRD
FUSE PNL
IGN FUSED
12004888
ENG CHK LP
12004215 SOCKET
ALDL
TEST CONN
12020043
MANUAL TRANSMISSION
.8 PNK/BLK 39B
.8 PPL 420
.8 PNK/WHT 439
BRAKE SW
12010649
AUTO TRANS ONLY
8911256
.8 TAN/WHT 422
12015921
AUTO TRANSMISSION

CS-TS 100	TS-TT 100
BODY STYLE-ALL	

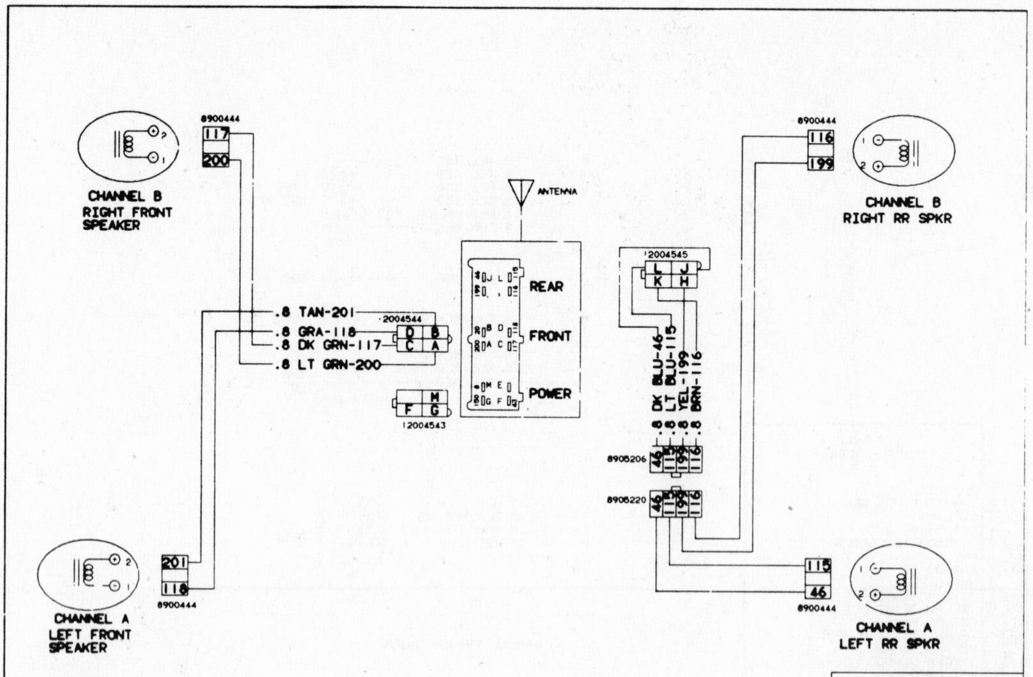
8900444
117
200
CHANNEL B
RIGHT FRONT
SPEAKER
ANTENNA
REAR
FRONT
POWER
.8 TAN-201
.8 GRA-118
.8 DK GRN-117
.8 LT GRN-200
2004544
12004543
12004545
.8 DK BLU-46
.8 LT BLU-115
.8 YEL-199
.8 BRN-116
8905206
8905220
116
199
CHANNEL B
RIGHT RR SPKR
201
118
CHANNEL A
LEFT FRONT
SPEAKER
115
46
CHANNEL A
LEFT RR SPKR

RADIO EQUIPMENT STEREO
RPO UM2,UN3,U58

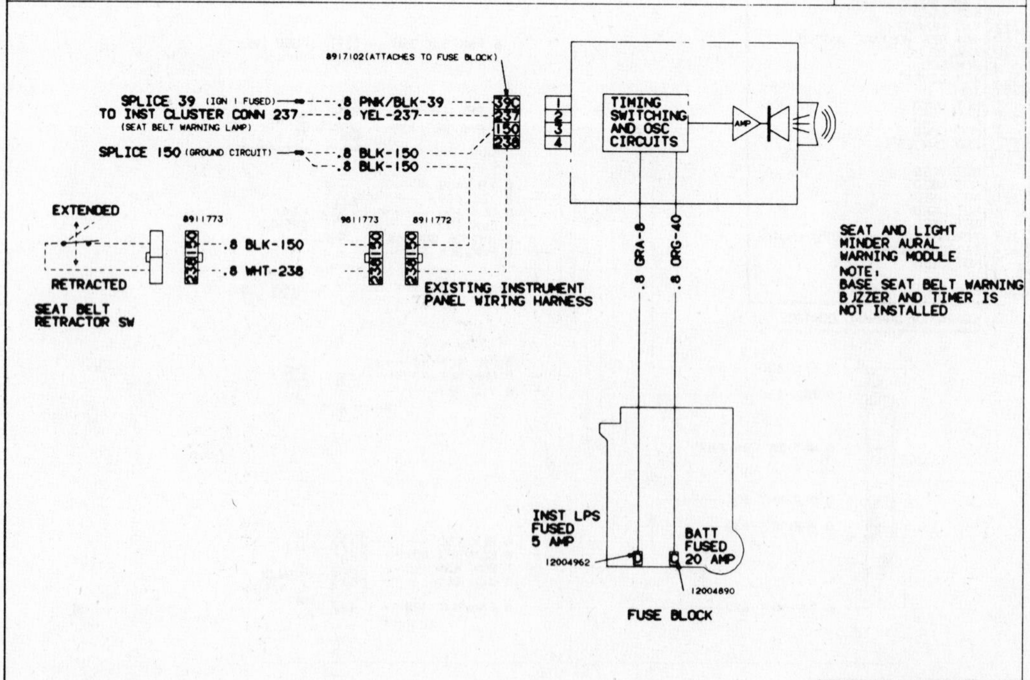
8917102(ATTACHES TO FUSE BLOCK)
SPLICE 39 (IGN 1 FUSED)
TO INST CLUSTER CONN 237
(SEAT BELT WARNING LAMP)
SPLICE 150 (GROUND CIRCUIT)
.8 PNK/BLK-39
.8 YEL-237
.8 BLK-150
.8 BLK-150
TIMING
SWITCHING
AND OSC
CIRCUITS
AMP
EXTENDED
RETRACTED
SEAT BELT
RETRACTOR SW
8911773
9811773
8911772
.8 BLK-150
.8 WHT-238
EXISTING INSTRUMENT
PANEL WIRING HARNESS
.8 GRA-8
.8 ORG-40
SEAT AND LIGHT
MINDER AURAL
WARNING MODULE
NOTE:
BASE SEAT BELT WARNING
BUZZER AND TIMER IS
NOT INSTALLED
INST LPS
FUSED
5 AMP
12004962
BATT
FUSED
20 AMP
12004890
FUSE BLOCK

HEADLAMP WARNING BUZZER
RPO T63

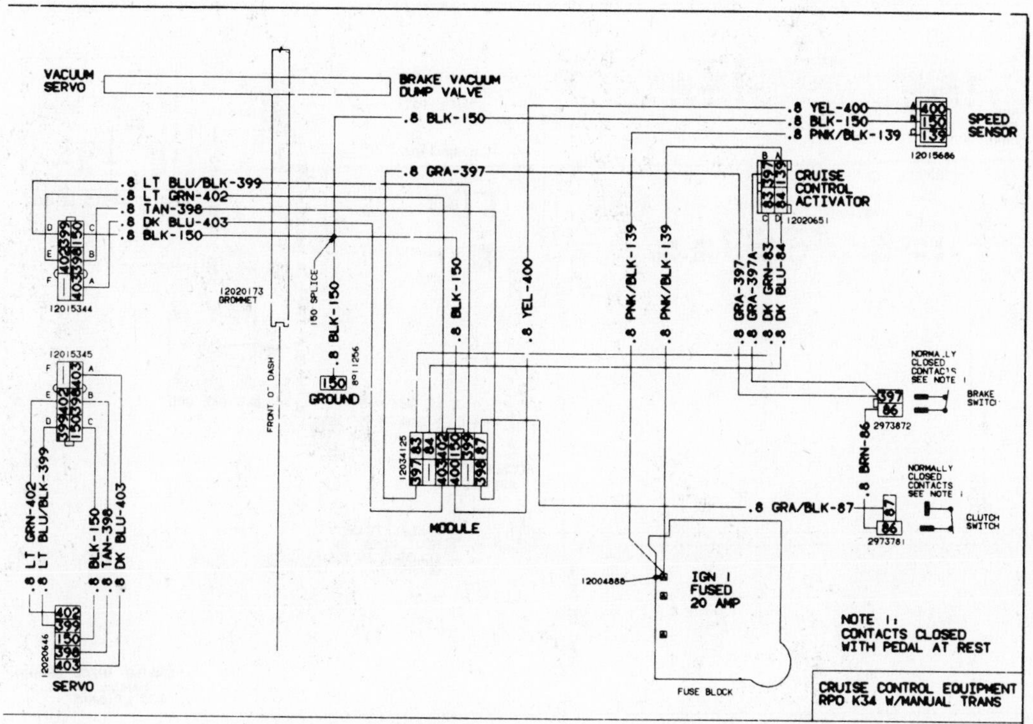
VACUUM SERVO
BRAKE VACUUM DUMP VALVE
.8 BLK-150
.8 YEL-400
.8 BLK-150
.8 PNK/BLK-139
SPEED SENSOR
12015686
.8 GRA-397
CRUISE CONTROL ACTIVATOR
12020651
.8 LT BLU/BLK-399
.8 LT GRN-402
.8 TAN-398
.8 DK BLU-403
.8 BLK-150
12015344
12020173 GROMMET
150 SPLICE
.8 BLK-150
8911256
150 GROUND
FRONT OF DASH
12015345
MODULE
12034125
.8 PNK/BLK-139
.8 GRA-397
.8 GRA-397A
.8 DK GRN-83
.8 DK BLU-84
NORMALLY CLOSED CONTACTS SEE NOTE 1
BRAKE SWITCH
2973872
.8 BRN-86
.8 GRA/BLK-87
CLUTCH SWITCH
2973781
12004888
IGN 1 FUSED 20 AMP
FUSE BLOCK
NOTE 1: CONTACTS CLOSED WITH PEDAL AT REST
SERVO
12020646

CRUISE CONTROL EQUIPMENT RPO K34 W/MANUAL TRANS

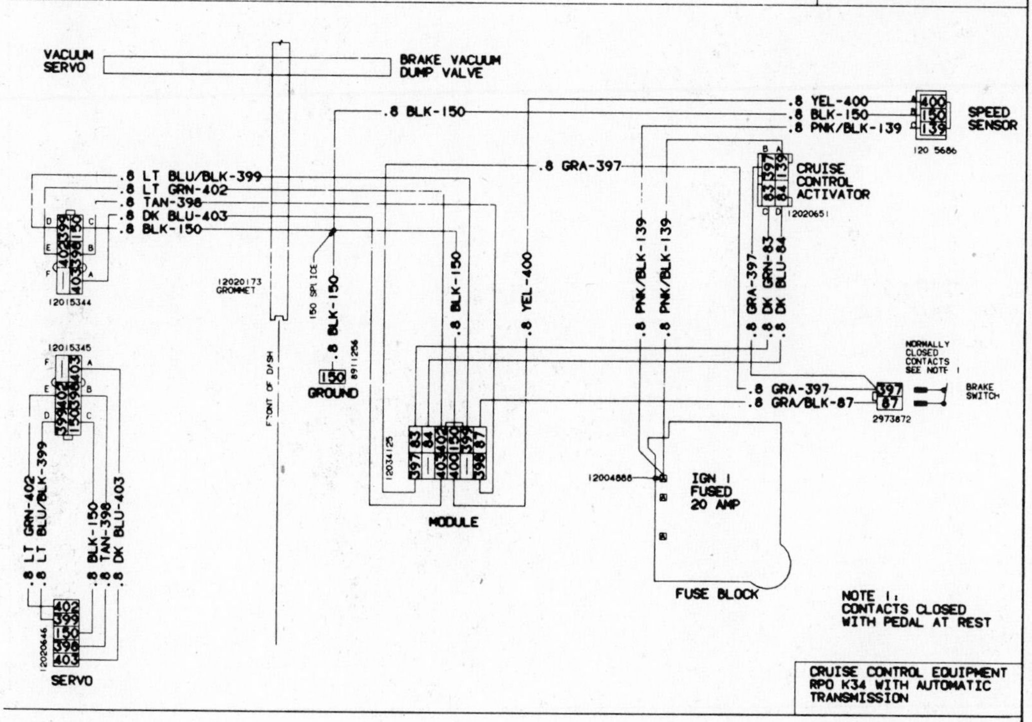
VACUUM SERVO
BRAKE VACUUM DUMP VALVE
.8 BLK-150
.8 YEL-400
.8 BLK-150
.8 PNK/BLK-139
SPEED SENSOR
.8 GRA-397
CRUISE CONTROL ACTIVATOR
12020651
.8 LT BLU/BLK-399
.8 LT GRN-402
.8 TAN-398
.8 DK BLU-403
.8 BLK-150
12015344
12020173 GROMMET
150 SPLICE
8911256
150 GROUND
FRONT OF DASH
12015345
MODULE
12034125
.8 PNK/BLK-139
.8 DK GRN-83
.8 DK BLU-84
NORMALLY CLOSED CONTACTS SEE NOTE 1
.8 GRA-397
.8 GRA/BLK-87
BRAKE SWITCH
2973872
12004888
IGN 1 FUSED 20 AMP
FUSE BLOCK
NOTE 1: CONTACTS CLOSED WITH PEDAL AT REST
SERVO
12020646

CRUISE CONTROL EQUIPMENT RPO K34 WITH AUTOMATIC TRANSMISSION

CS-TS 100	TS-TT 100
BODY STYLE-ALL	

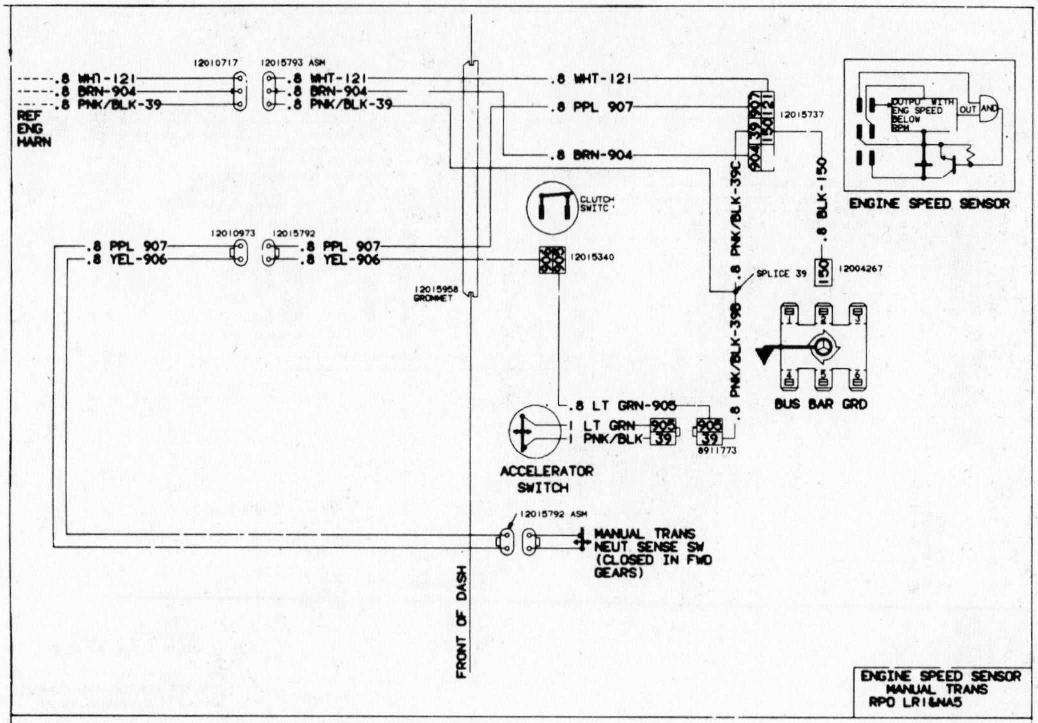
REF ENG HARN
.8 WHT-121
.8 BRN-904
.8 PNK/BLK-39
.8 PPL 907
.8 YEL-906
.8 BRN-904
CLUTCH SWITCH
ENGINE SPEED SENSOR
.8 PNK/BLK-39C
.8 BLK-150
SPLICE 39
.8 PNK/BLK-39B
BUS BAR GRD
.8 LT GRN-905
1 LT GRN
1 PNK/BLK
ACCELERATOR SWITCH
MANUAL TRANS NEUT SENSE SW (CLOSED IN FWD GEARS)
12015958 GROMMET
FRONT OF DASH
ENGINE SPEED SENSOR MANUAL TRANS RPO LR1&NA5

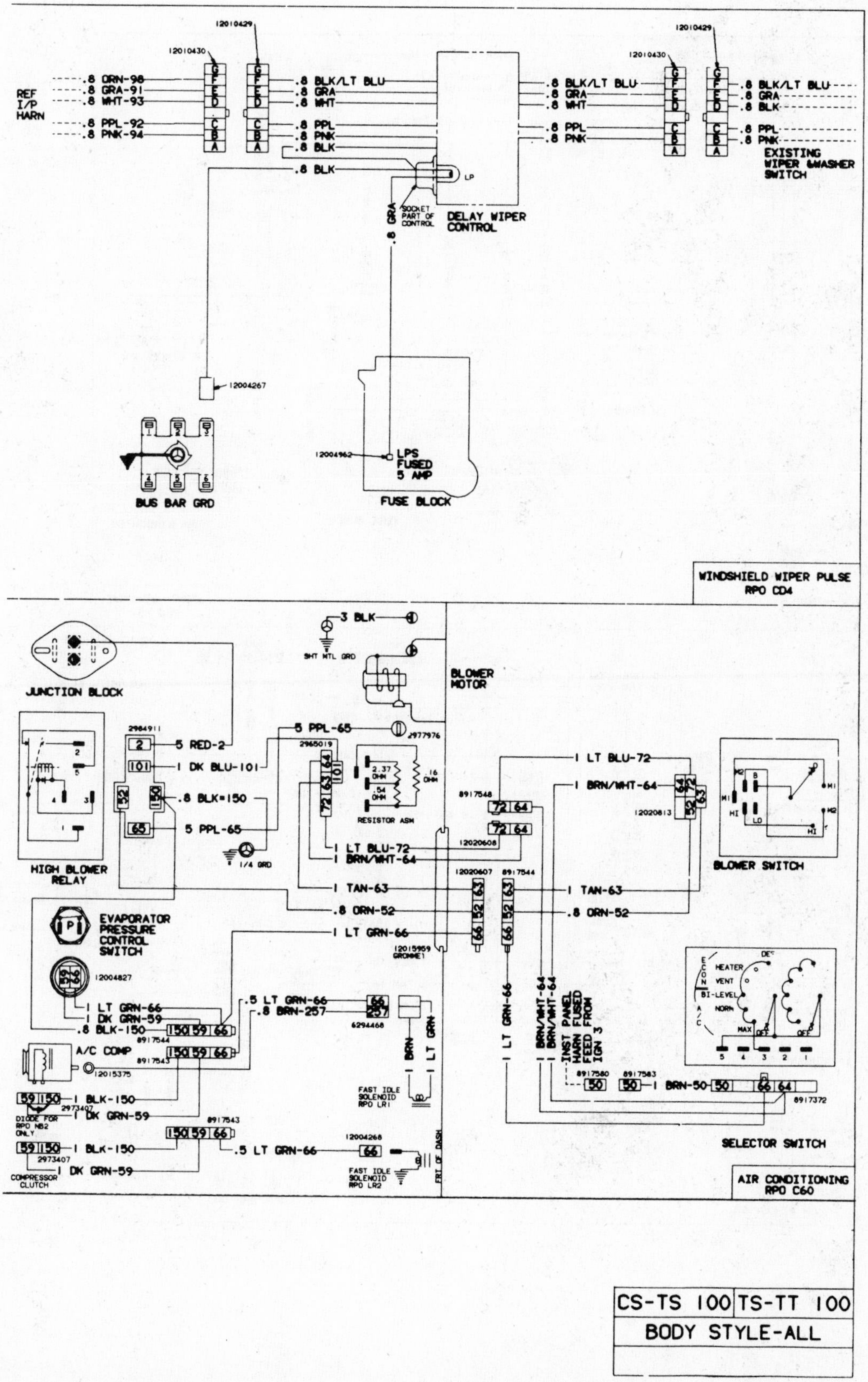
REF I/P HARN
.8 ORN-98
.8 GRA-91
.8 WHT-93
.8 PPL-92
.8 PNK-94
12010430
12010429
.8 BLK/LT BLU
.8 GRA
.8 WHT
.8 PPL
.8 PNK
.8 BLK
.8 BLK
.8 GRA
SOCKET PART OF CONTROL
LP
DELAY WIPER CONTROL
EXISTING WIPER &WASHER SWITCH
12004267
BUS BAR GRD
12004962
LPS FUSED 5 AMP
FUSE BLOCK
WINDSHIELD WIPER PULSE RPO CD4
3 BLK
SHT MTL GRD
BLOWER MOTOR
JUNCTION BLOCK
2984911
5 RED-2
1 DK BLU-101
.8 BLK=150
5 PPL-65
5 PPL-65
1/4 GRD
2977976
2965019
RESISTOR ASM
HIGH BLOWER RELAY
1 LT BLU-72
1 BRN/WHT-64
8917548
12020608
12020813
BLOWER SWITCH
1 TAN-63
.8 ORN-52
1 LT GRN-66
12020607
8917544
12015959 GROMMET
EVAPORATOR PRESSURE CONTROL SWITCH
12004827
1 LT GRN-66
1 DK GRN-59
.8 BLK-150
.5 LT GRN-66
.8 BRN-257
6294468
A/C COMP
12015375
1 BLK-150
1 DK GRN-59
2973407
DIODE FOR RPO NB2 ONLY
FAST IDLE SOLENOID RPO LR1
BRN
LT GRN
LT GRN-66
BRN/WHT-64
BRN/WHT-64
INST PANEL HARN FUSED FEED FROM IGN 3
HEATER
VENT
BI-LEVEL
NORM
MAX
OFF
DEF
8917580
8917583
1 BRN-50
8917372
SELECTOR SWITCH
8917543
12004268
.5 LT GRN-66
FAST IDLE SOLENOID RPO LR2
FRT OF DASH
COMPRESSOR CLUTCH
AIR CONDITIONING RPO C60
CS-TS 100
TS-TT 100
BODY STYLE-ALL

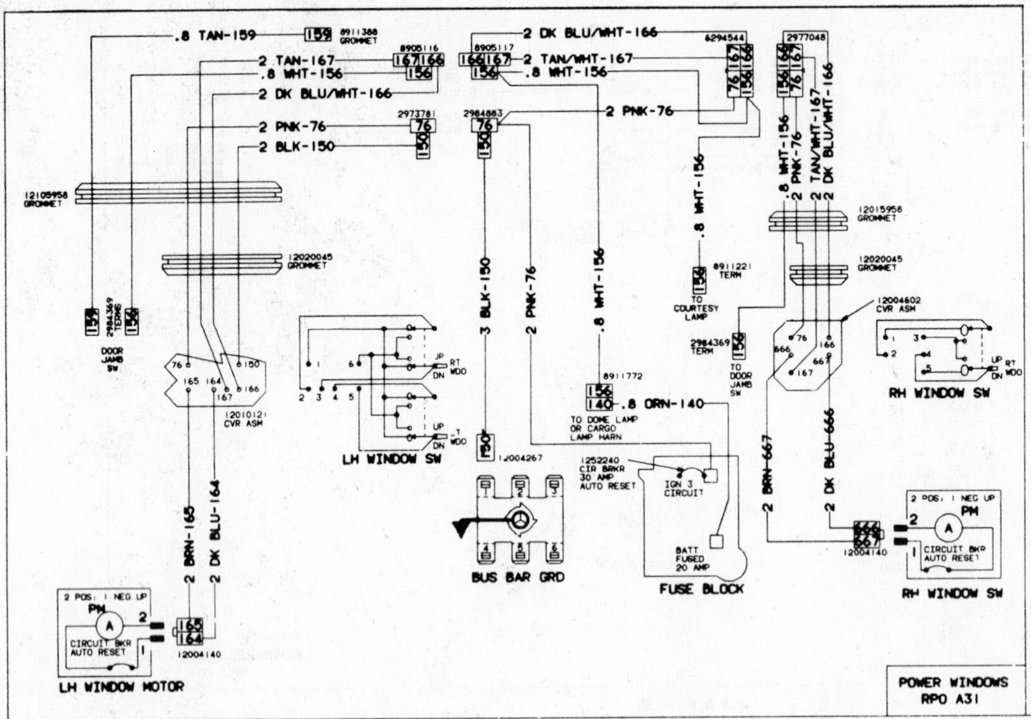

.8 TAN-159
2 TAN-167
.8 WHT-156
2 DK BLU/WHT-166
2 PNK-76
2 BLK-150
2 TAN/WHT-167
.8 WHT-156
12105958 GROMMET
12020045 GROMMET
12015958 GROMMET
DOOR JAMB SW
12010121 CVR ASM
LH WINDOW SW
3 BLK-150
2 PNK-76
.8 WHT-156
.8 ORN-140
TO DOME LAMP OR CARGO LAMP HARN
TO COURTESY LAMP
TO DOOR JAMB SW
12004602 CVR ASM
RH WINDOW SW
1252240 CIR BRKR 30 AMP AUTO RESET
IGN 3 CIRCUIT
BATT FUSED 20 AMP
FUSE BLOCK
BUS BAR GRD
2 BRN-165
2 DK BLU-164
2 BRN-667
2 DK BLU-666
2 POS; 1 NEG UP
CIRCUIT BKR AUTO RESET
LH WINDOW MOTOR
RH WINDOW SW
POWER WINDOWS RPO A31

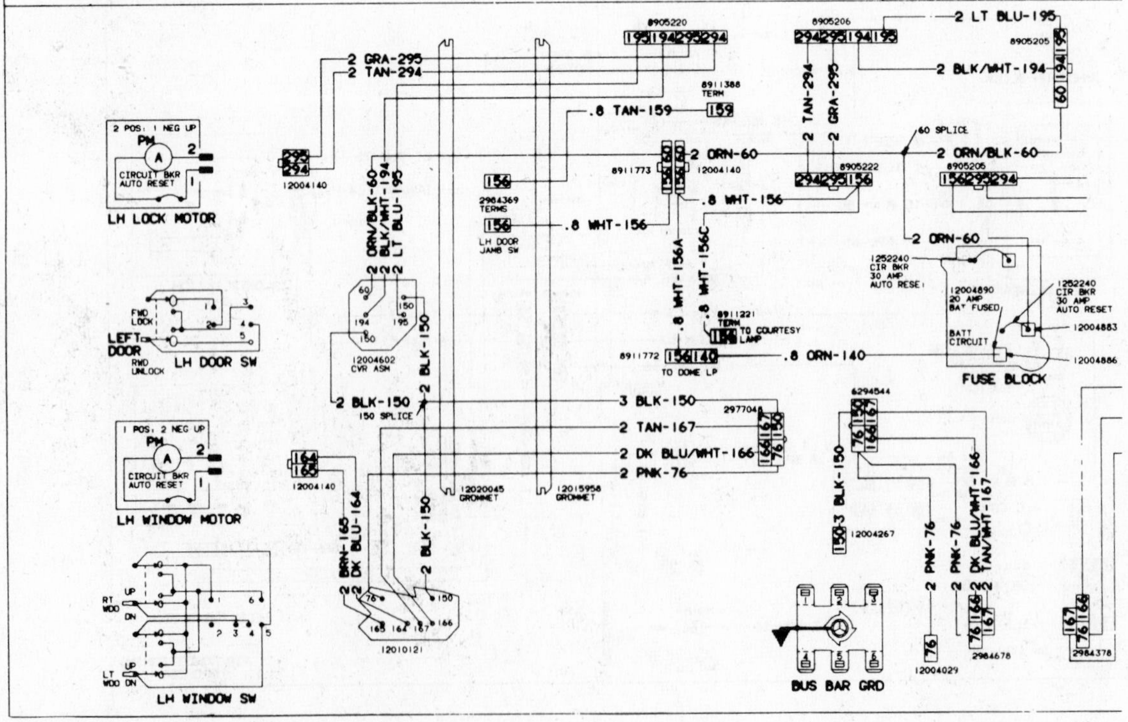

2 GRA-295
2 TAN-294
2 LT BLU-195
2 BLK/WHT-194
.8 TAN-159
2 ORN-60
60 SPLICE
2 ORN/BLK-60
.8 WHT-156
LH DOOR JAMB SW
LH LOCK MOTOR
FWD LOCK
LEFT DOOR
RWD UNLOCK
LH DOOR SW
12004602 CVR ASM
2 BLK-150
150 SPLICE
3 BLK-150
2 TAN-167
2 DK BLU/WHT-166
2 PNK-76
TO COURTESY LAMP
TO DOME LP
.8 ORN-140
1252240 CIR BKR 30 AMP AUTO RESET
12004890 20 AMP BAT FUSED
BATT CIRCUIT
FUSE BLOCK
1 POS; 2 NEG UP
CIRCUIT BKR AUTO RESET
LH WINDOW MOTOR
12020045 GROMMET
12015958 GROMMET
LH WINDOW SW
BUS BAR GRD

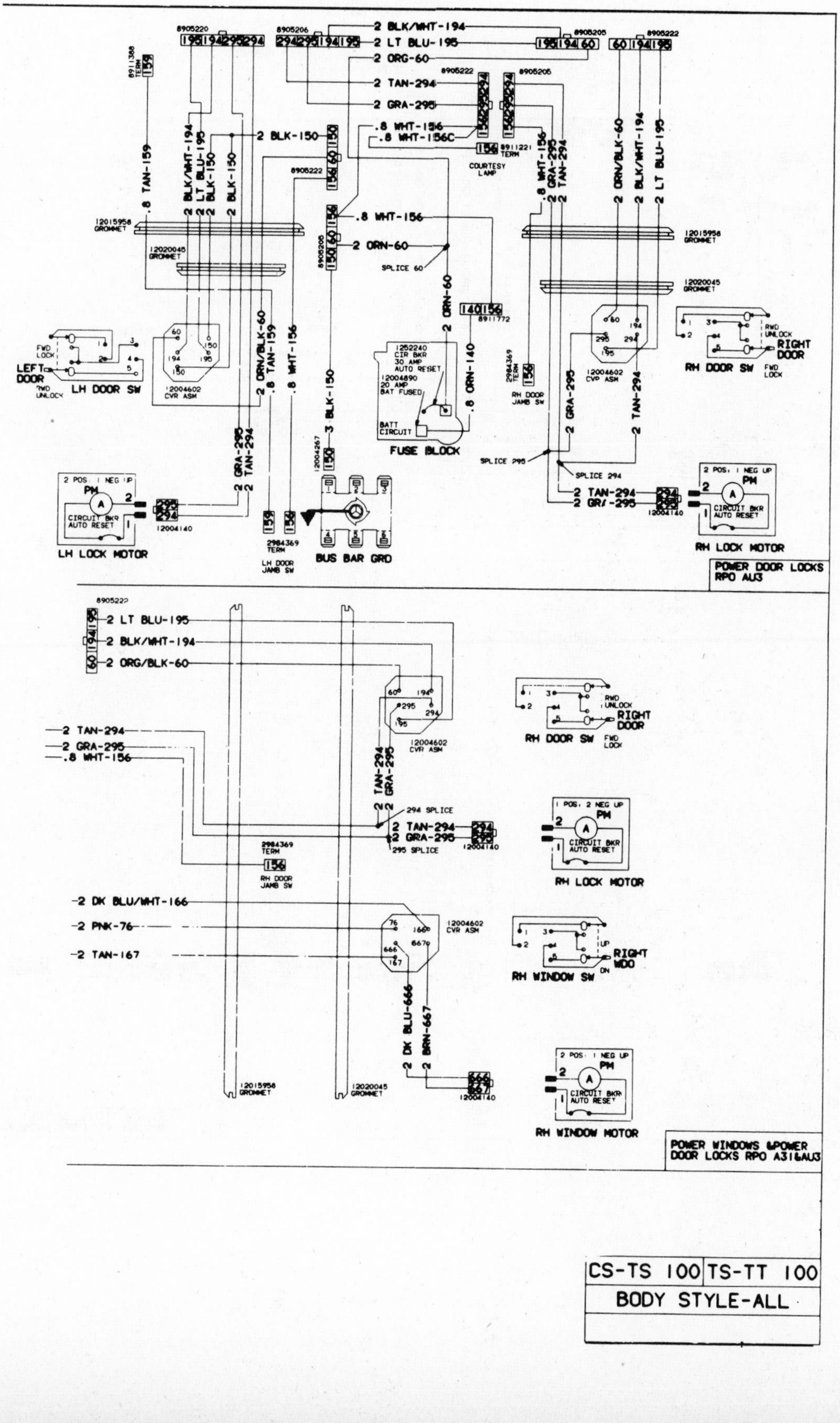

LH DOOR SW
LEFT DOOR
LH LOCK MOTOR
BUS BAR GRD
FUSE BLOCK
COURTESY LAMP
RH DOOR SW
RIGHT DOOR
RH LOCK MOTOR
POWER DOOR LOCKS RPO AU3
RH WINDOW SW
RIGHT WDO
RH WINDOW MOTOR
POWER WINDOWS &POWER DOOR LOCKS RPO A31&AU3
CS-TS 100
TS-TT 100
BODY STYLE-ALL

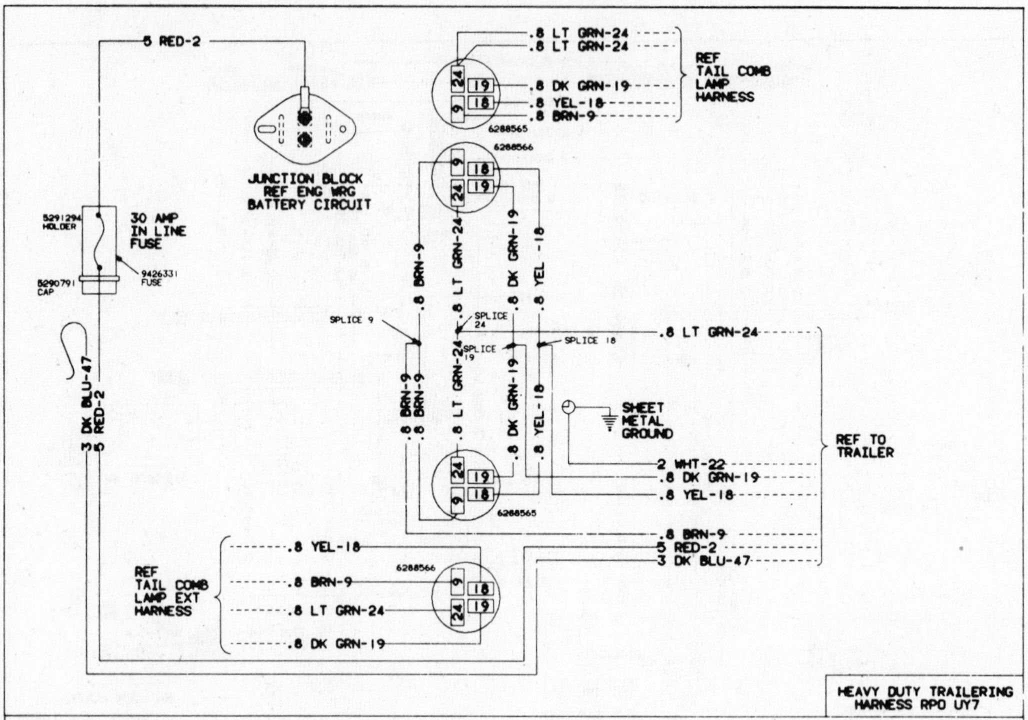
5 RED-2
JUNCTION BLOCK REF ENG WRG BATTERY CIRCUIT
5291294 HOLDER
30 AMP IN LINE FUSE
9426331 FUSE
5290791 CAP
3 DK BLU-47
5 RED-2
.8 LT GRN-24
.8 DK GRN-19
.8 YEL-18
.8 BRN-9
REF TAIL COMB LAMP HARNESS
6288565
6288566
SPLICE 9
SPLICE 24
SPLICE 19
SPLICE 18
SHEET METAL GROUND
2 WHT-22
REF TO TRAILER
REF TAIL COMB LAMP EXT HARNESS
HEAVY DUTY TRAILERING HARNESS RPO UY7

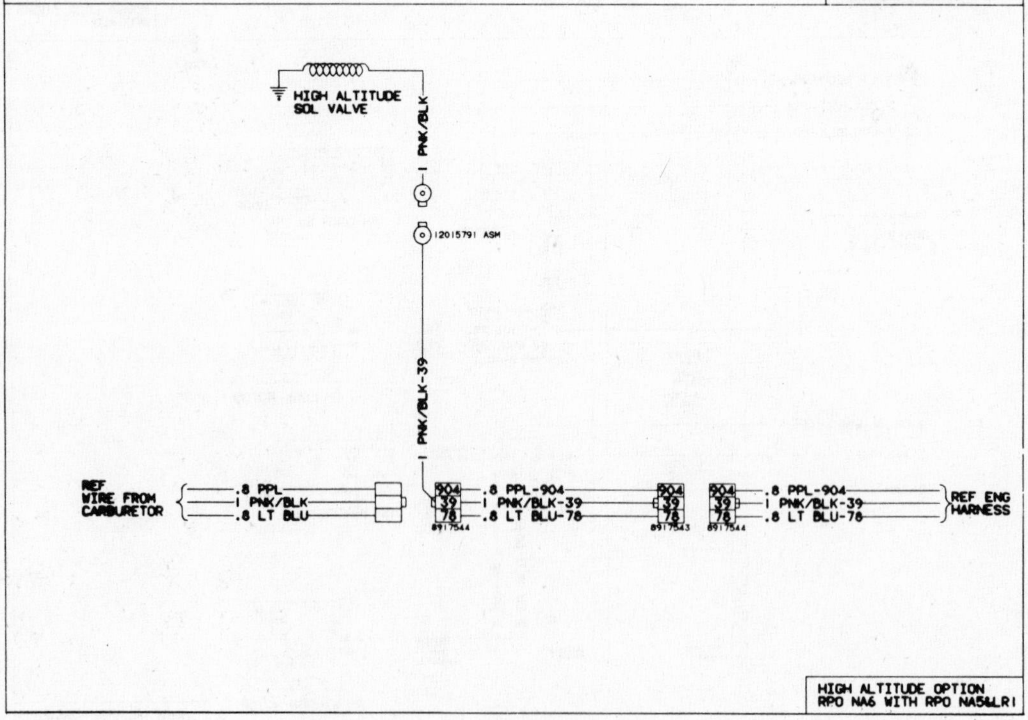
HIGH ALTITUDE SOL VALVE
1 PNK/BLK
12015791 ASM
1 PNK/BLK-39
REF WIRE FROM CARBURETOR
.8 PPL
1 PNK/BLK
.8 LT BLU
.8 PPL-904
1 PNK/BLK-39
.8 LT BLU-78
8917544
8917543
REF ENG HARNESS
HIGH ALTITUDE OPTION RPO NA6 WITH RPO NA5&LR1

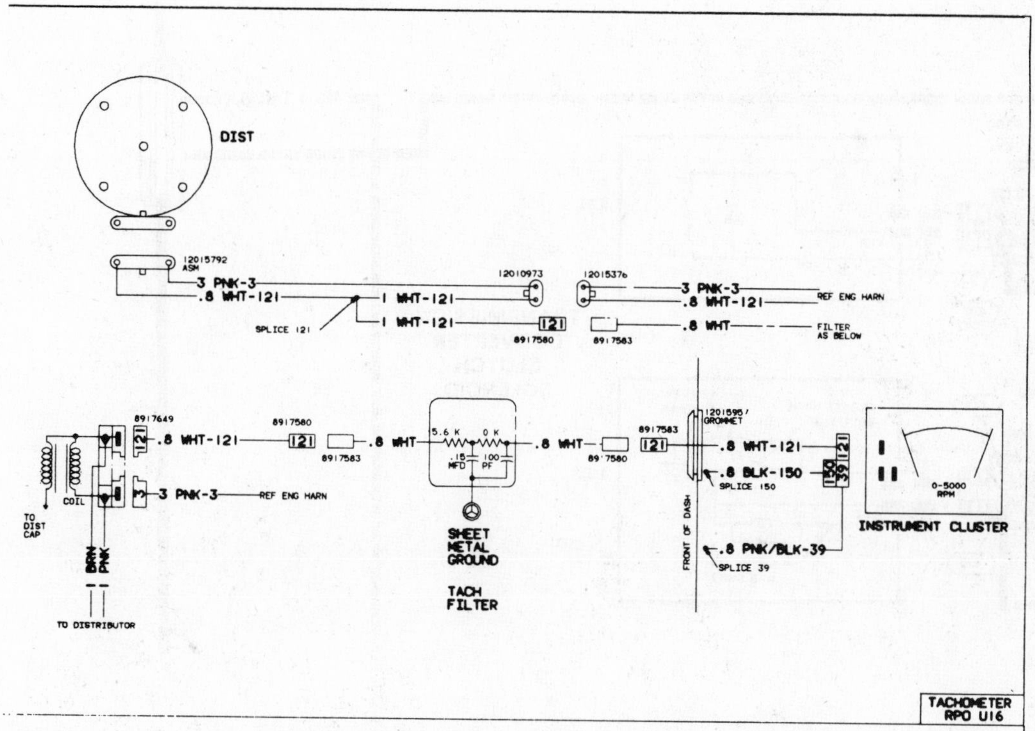
DIST
12015792 ASM
3 PNK-3
.8 WHT-121
SPLICE 121
1 WHT-121
1 WHT-121
12010973
12015376
121
8917580
8917583
3 PNK-3
.8 WHT-121
REF ENG HARN
.8 WHT
FILTER AS BELOW
8917649
121
.8 WHT-121
8917580
121
8917583
.8 WHT
5.6 K
0 K
.15 MFD
100 PF
.8 WHT
8917580
8917583
121
3 PNK-3
REF ENG HARN
COIL
TO DIST CAP
BRN
PNK
TO DISTRIBUTOR
SHEET METAL GROUND
TACH FILTER
12015957/ GROMMET
.8 WHT-121
.8 BLK-150
SPLICE 150
FRONT OF DASH
.8 PNK/BLK-39
SPLICE 39
121
150
39
0-5000 RPM
INSTRUMENT CLUSTER
TACHOMETER RPO U16

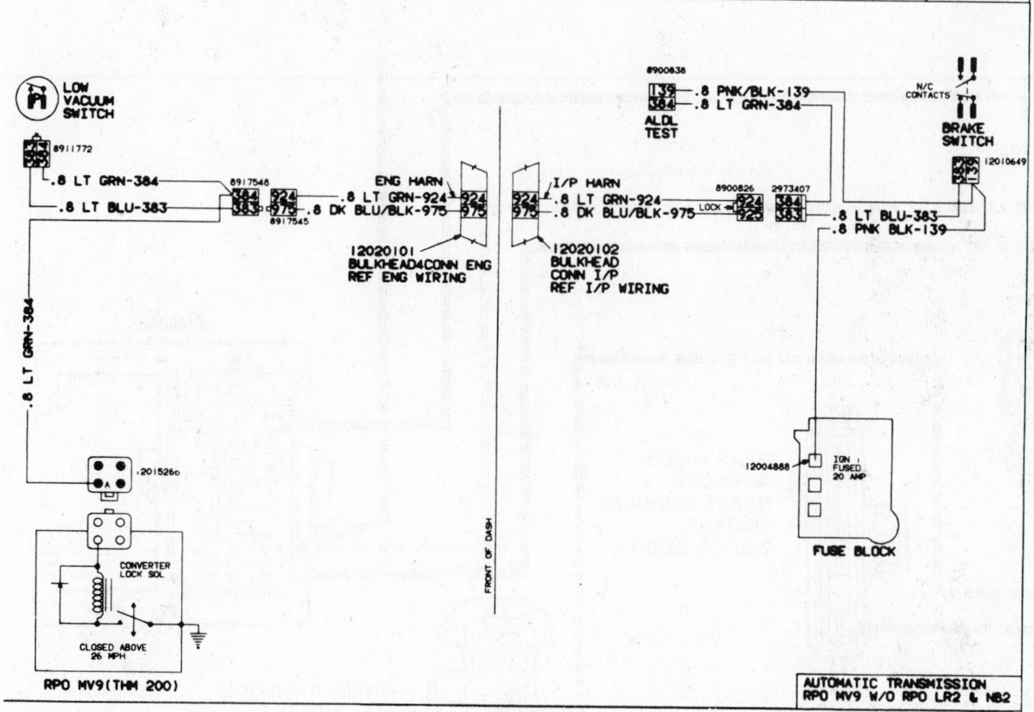
LOW VACUUM SWITCH
8911772
.8 LT GRN-384
.8 LT BLU-383
8917546
384
383
924
975
8917545
ENG HARN
.8 LT GRN-924
.8 DK BLU/BLK-975
924
975
12020101
BULKHEAD4CONN ENG
REF ENG WIRING
FRONT OF DASH
I/P HARN
.8 LT GRN-924
.8 DK BLU/BLK-975
12020102
BULKHEAD
CONN I/P
REF I/P WIRING
8900838
139
384
.8 PNK/BLK-139
.8 LT GRN-384
ALDL TEST
8900826
2973407
LOCK
924
925
384
383
.8 LT BLU-383
.8 PNK BLK-139
N/C CONTACTS
BRAKE SWITCH
12010649
.8 LT GRN-384
.1201526
CONVERTER LOCK SOL
CLOSED ABOVE 26 MPH
RPO MV9(THM 200)
12004888
IGN FUSED 20 AMP
FUSE BLOCK
AUTOMATIC TRANSMISSION
RPO MV9 W/O RPO LR2 & NB2

CS-TS 100	TS-TT 100
BODY STYLE-ALL	

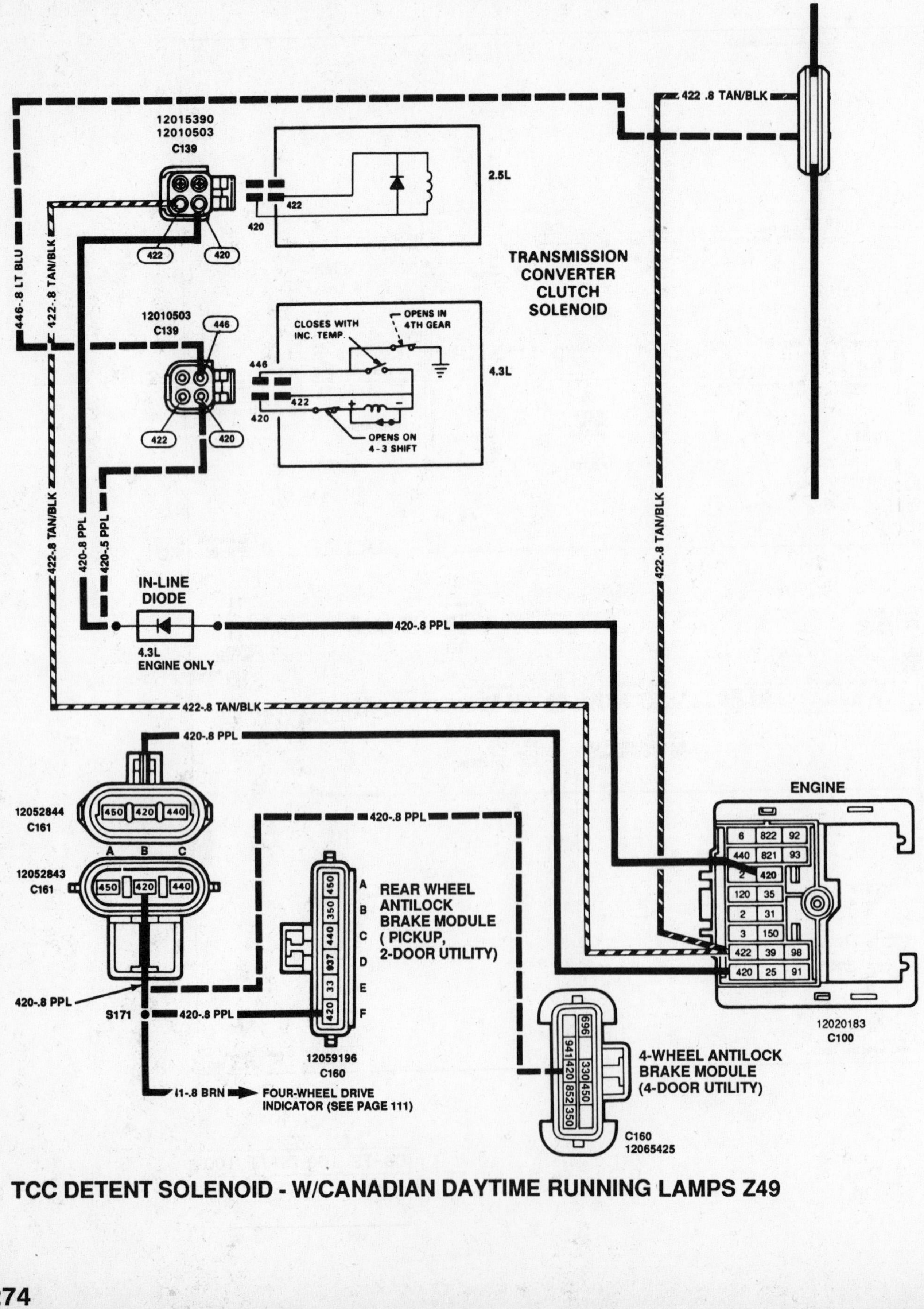
422 .8 TAN/BLK
12015390
12010503
C139
422
420
422
420
2.5L
TRANSMISSION
CONVERTER
CLUTCH
SOLENOID
446-.8 LT BLU
422-.8 TAN/BLK
12010503
C139
446
CLOSES WITH
INC. TEMP.
OPENS IN
4TH GEAR
446
422
420
OPENS ON
4-3 SHIFT
422
420
4.3L
422-.8 TAN/BLK
420-.8 PPL
420-.5 PPL
422-.8 TAN/BLK
IN-LINE
DIODE
4.3L
ENGINE ONLY
420-.8 PPL
422-.8 TAN/BLK
420-.8 PPL
12052844
C161
450
420
440
420-.8 PPL
A
B
C
12052843
C161
450
420
440
REAR WHEEL
ANTILOCK
BRAKE MODULE
(PICKUP,
2-DOOR UTILITY)
450
350
440
937
33
420
D
E
F
420-.8 PPL
S171
420-.8 PPL
12059196
C160
11-.8 BRN
FOUR-WHEEL DRIVE
INDICATOR (SEE PAGE 111)
ENGINE
6
822
92
440
821
93
2
420
120
35
2
31
3
150
422
39
98
420
25
91
12020183
C100
696
941
420
852
350
330
450
4-WHEEL ANTILOCK
BRAKE MODULE
(4-DOOR UTILITY)
C160
12065425

TCC DETENT SOLENOID - W/CANADIAN DAYTIME RUNNING LAMPS Z49

7 Drive Train

QUICK REFERENCE INDEX

GENERAL INDEX

Troubleshooting the Manual Transmission and Transfer Case

Problem	Cause	Solution
Transmission shifts hard	• Clutch adjustment incorrect • Clutch linkage or cable binding • Shift rail binding • Internal bind in transmission caused by shift forks, selector plates, or synchronizer assemblies • Clutch housing misalignment • Incorrect lubricant • Block rings and/or cone seats worn	• Adjust clutch • Lubricate or repair as necessary • Check for mispositioned selector arm roll pin, loose cover bolts, worn shift rail bores, worn shift rail, distorted oil seal, or extension housing not aligned with case. Repair as necessary. • Remove, dissemble and inspect transmission. Replace worn or damaged components as necessary. • Check runout at rear face of clutch housing • Drain and refill transmission • Blocking ring to gear clutch tooth face clearance must be 0.030 inch or greater. If clearance is correct it may still be necessary to inspect blocking rings and cone seats for excessive wear. Repair as necessary.
Gear clash when shifting from one gear to another	• Clutch adjustment incorrect • Clutch linkage or cable binding • Clutch housing misalignment • Lubricant level low or incorrect lubricant • Gearshift components, or synchronizer assemblies worn or damaged	• Adjust clutch • Lubricate or repair as necessary • Check runout at rear of clutch housing • Drain and refill transmission and check for lubricant leaks if level was low. Repair as necessary. • Remove, disassemble and inspect transmission. Replace worn or damaged components as necessary.
Transmission noisy	• Lubricant level low or incorrect lubricant • Clutch housing-to-engine, or transmission-to-clutch housing bolts loose • Dirt, chips, foreign material in transmission • Gearshift mechanism, transmission gears, or bearing components worn or damaged • Clutch housing misalignment	• Drain and refill transmission. If lubricant level was low, check for leaks and repair as necessary. • Check and correct bolt torque as necessary • Drain, flush, and refill transmission • Remove, disassemble and inspect transmission. Replace worn or damaged components as necessary. • Check runout at rear face of clutch housing

Troubleshooting the Manual Transmission and Transfer Case (cont.)

Problem	Cause	Solution
Jumps out of gear	• Clutch housing misalignment	• Check runout at rear face of clutch housing
	• Gearshift lever loose	• Check lever for worn fork. Tighten loose attaching bolts.
	• Offset lever nylon insert worn or lever attaching nut loose	• Remove gearshift lever and check for loose offset lever nut or worn insert. Repair or replace as necessary.
	• Gearshift mechanism, shift forks, selector plates, interlock plate, selector arm, shift rail, detent plugs, springs or shift cover worn or damaged	• Remove, disassemble and inspect transmission cover assembly. Replace worn or damaged components as necessary.
	• Clutch shaft or roller bearings worn or damaged	• Replace clutch shaft or roller bearings as necessary
Jumps out of gear (cont.)	• Gear teeth worn or tapered, synchronizer assemblies worn or damaged, excessive end play caused by worn thrust washers or output shaft gears	• Remove, disassemble, and inspect transmission. Replace worn or damaged components as necessary.
	• Pilot bushing worn	• Replace pilot bushing
Will not shift into one gear	• Gearshift selector plates, interlock plate, or selector arm, worn, damaged, or incorrectly assembled	• Remove, disassemble, and inspect transmission cover assembly. Repair or replace components as necessary.
	• Shift rail detent plunger worn, spring broken, or plug loose	• Tighten plug or replace worn or damaged components as necessary
	• Gearshift lever worn or damaged	• Replace gearshift lever
	• Synchronizer sleeves or hubs, damaged or worn	• Remove, disassemble and inspect transmission. Replace worn or damaged components.
Locked in one gear—cannot be shifted out	• Shift rail(s) worn or broken, shifter fork bent, setscrew loose, center detent plug missing or worn	• Inspect and replace worn or damaged parts
	• Broken gear teeth on countershaft gear, clutch shaft, or reverse idler gear	• Inspect and replace damaged part
	Gearshift lever broken or worn, shift mechanism in cover incorrectly assembled or broken, worn damaged gear train components	• Disassemble transmission. Replace damaged parts or assemble correctly.

Troubleshooting the Manual Transmission and Transfer Case (cont.)

Problem	Cause	Solution
Transfer case difficult to shift or will not shift into desired range	• Vehicle speed too great to permit shifting	• Stop vehicle and shift into desired range. Or reduce speed to 3–4 km/h (2–3 mph) before attempting to shift.
	• If vehicle was operated for extended period in 4H mode on dry paved surface, driveline torque load may cause difficult shifting	• Stop vehicle, shift transmission to neutral, shift transfer case to 2H mode and operate vehicle in 2H on dry paved surfaces
	• Transfer case external shift linkage binding	• Lubricate or repair or replace linkage, or tighten loose components as necessary
	• Insufficient or incorrect lubricant	• Drain and refill to edge of fill hole
	• Internal components binding, worn, or damaged	• Disassemble unit and replace worn or damaged components as necessary
Transfer case noisy in all drive modes	• Insufficient or incorrect lubricant	• Drain and refill to edge of fill hole Check for leaks and repair if necessary. Note: If unit is still noisy after drain and refill, disassembly and inspection may be required to locate source of noise.
Noisy in—or jumps out of four wheel drive low range	• Transfer case not completely engaged in 4L position	• Stop vehicle, shift transfer case in Neutral, then shift back into 4L position
	• Shift linkage loose or binding	• Tighten, lubricate, or repair linkage as necessary
	• Shift fork cracked, inserts worn, or fork is binding on shift rail	• Disassemble unit and repair as necessary
Lubricant leaking from output shaft seals or from vent	• Transfer case overfilled	• Drain to correct level
	• Vent closed or restricted	• Clear or replace vent if necessary
Lubricant leaking from output shaft seals or from vent (cont.)	• Output shaft seals damaged or installed incorrectly	• Replace seals. Be sure seal lip faces interior of case when installed. Also be sure yoke seal surfaces are not scored or nicked. Remove scores, nicks with fine sandpaper or replace yoke(s) if necessary.
Abnormal tire wear	• Extended operation on dry hard surface (paved) roads in 4H range	• Operate in 2H on hard surface (paved) roads

MANUAL TRANSMISSION

Identification

Manual transmissions are officially identified by using the following descriptions:

a. The number of forward gears.

b. The measured distance between the center lines of the mainshaft and the countergear.

The 4-speed (77.5mm) transmission is a fully synchronized unit with blocker ring synchronizers and a sliding mesh reverse gear. It is contained in an aluminum alloy case with an integral clutch housing, a center support and an extension housing, which houses some of the gears, bearings and shafts. The shift lever is mounted on top of the extension housing. Tis transmission is used with the 2.8L 6 cylinder and the 1.9L 4 cylinder engines. The easiest way to identify the 77.5mm transmission is that the gear box and bell housing are one casting.

The 4-speed (77mm) and 5-speed (77mm) model transmissions are fully synchronized units with blocker ring synchronizers and a sliding mesh reverse gear. They have the more familiar aluminum gear box type of transmission case that houses the various gears, bearings and shafts. The floor-mounted gearshift lever assembly is located on top of the extension housing. The ML2 model is used with the 2.5L 4 cylinder engine; the ML3 model is used with the V6 engine. The easiest way to identify 77mm transmissions is that the gear box can be removed from the bell housing.

Adjustments

CLUTCH SWITCH

A clutch switch is located under the instrument panel and attached to the top of the clutch pedal. Its function is to prevent starter operation unless the clutch pedal is depressed. On some vehicles, the switch must be adjusted for reliable starter operation.

1. Remove the lower steering column-to-instrument panel cover.
2. Disconnect the electrical connector from the clutch switch.
3. Be sure to leave any carpets and floor mats in place when making the adjustment.

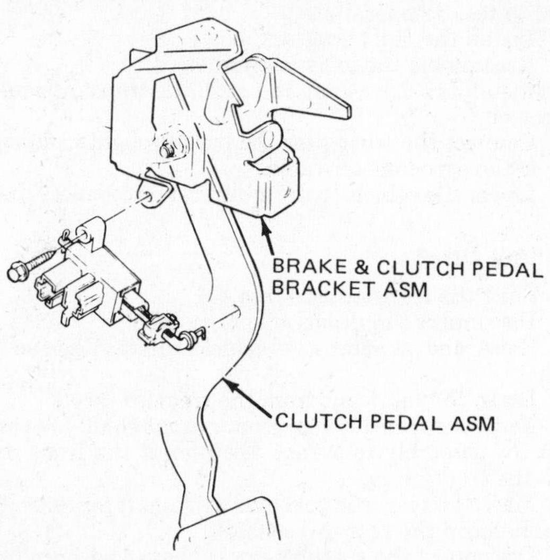
BRAKE & CLUTCH PEDAL
BRACKET ASM
CLUTCH PEDAL ASM

On some models the clutch safety start switch is adjustable

4. At the clutch switch, move the slider (A) rearward (towards the clutch switch) on the clutch switch shaft (B).
5. Push the clutch pedal to the floor. A clicking noise will be heard as the switch adjusts itself.
6. Release the clutch pedal; the adjustment is complete.
7. Reconnect the switch and test it.

Shift Lever

REMOVAL AND INSTALLATION

1. With the transmission in Neutral, loosen the lock nut under the shift knob and unscrew the knob from the lever.
2. Unscrew and remove the shifter boot.
3, On 1984–91 models, there is another lock nut which can be loosened to remove upper portion of the lever.
4. Remove the bolts to remove the shift lever from the housing assembly.
5. When reassembling, lightly lubricate the shifter with moly grease and use a new gasket or silicone sealer. Torque the bolts to 10 ft. lbs. (13 Nm).

Back-Up Light Switch

REMOVAL AND INSTALLATION

1. Disconnect the negative battery terminal from the battery.
2. At the left-rear of the transmission, the back-up light switch is threaded into the transmission case. The speed sensor is held in with a separate bracket. Disconnect the electrical connector from the back-up light switch.
3. Remove the back-up light switch from the transmission.
4. To install, reverse the removal procedures. Place the gear shift lever in the reverse position and check the back-up lights work.

Extension Housing Seal

REMOVAL AND INSTALLATION

2-Wheel Drive

This seal controls transmission oil leakage around the driveshaft. Continued failure of this seal usually indicates a worn output shaft bushing. If so, there will be signs of the same wear on the driveshaft where it contacts the seal and bushing. The seal is available and is fairly simple to install, with the proper tool.

1. Raise and safely support rear of the vehicle to minimumize transmission oil loss when the driveshaft is removed.
2. Unbolt the driveshaft from the differential and center support bearing, if equipped. Wrap tape around the bearing cups to keep them in place on the universal joint and slide the shaft out of the transmission.
3. Use a small pry tool to carefully pry out the old seal. Be carefull not to insert the tool too far into the housing or the bushing will be damaged.
4. Use an oil seal installation tool to evenly drive the new seal into the housing. Make sure the tool only contacts the outer metal portion of the seal.
5. Install the driveshaft. Torque the universal bearing cup retainer bolts to 15 ft. lbs. Torque the center bearing bolts to 25 ft. lbs.

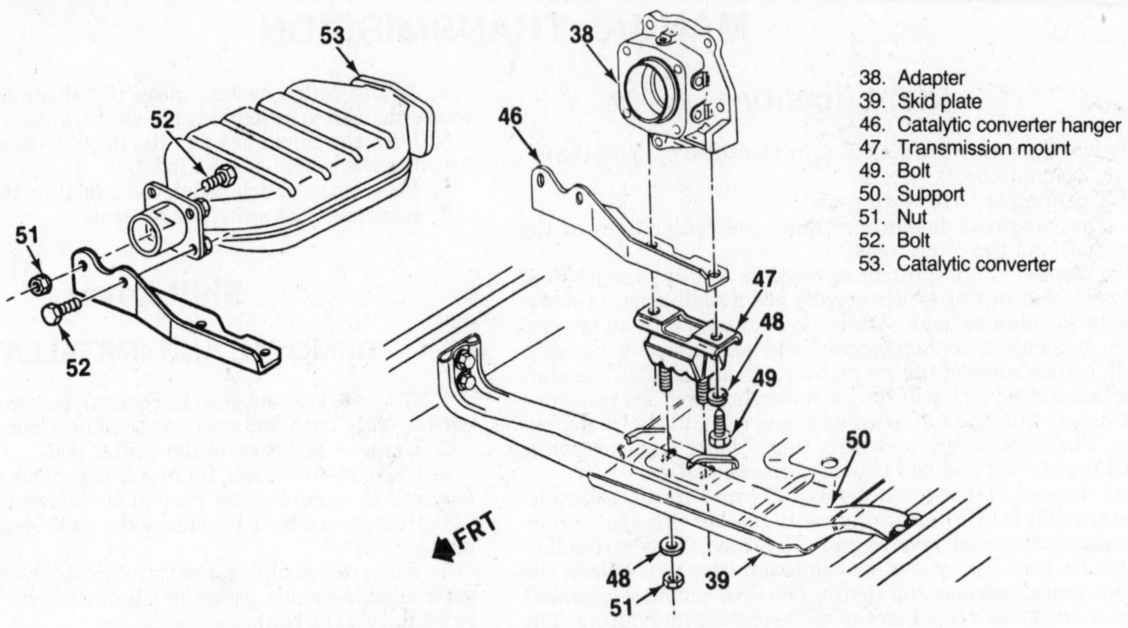
53
38
52
46
51
52
47
48
49
50
FRT
48
39
51
38. Adapter
39. Skid plate
46. Catalytic converter hanger
47. Transmission mount
49. Bolt
50. Support
51. Nut
52. Bolt
53. Catalytic converter

Catalytic converter hanger assembly under transmission

Transmission

REMOVAL AND INSTALLATION

2-Wheel Drive

1. Disconnect the negative battery terminal from the battery.
2. If the bell housing is being removed with the transmission (77.5mm 4-speed) remove the starter. The 77mm 4- and 5-speed can be removed without removing the bellhousing.
3. Shift the transmission into Neutral. Remove the shift lever boot-to-console screws and slide the boot up the shift lever.
4. Remove the shift lever.
5. Raise and safely support the truck on jackstands. Remove the drain plug and drain the oil. Dispose of old oil properly at a reclaimation center, such as a gas station or parts retailer.
6. Disconnect the speedometer cable and/or the electrical wiring connectors from the transmission.
7. Remove the driveshaft(s). Refer to the Driveline section if necessary.
8. Disconnect the exhaust pipe-to-exhaust manifold nuts and separate the exhaust pipe from the manifold.
9. On the 1982–83 models, disconnect the clutch cable from the clutch lever. On the 1984–91 models, remove the clutch slave cylinder from the clutch release lever. It can be secured out of the way without disconnecting the hydraulic line.
10. Position a floor jack under the transmission and support the transmission. Secure the jack to the transmission so it won't slip
11. Remove the transmission-to-crossmember mount bolts.
12. Remove the catalytic converter-to-chassis hanger bolts.
13. Remove the crossmember-to-chassis bolts and the crossmember from the vehicle.
14. If the bellhousing is being removed, remove the clutch cover from the front of the housing.
15. Unbolt the bellhousing from the engine, or the transmission from the bellhousing and carefully roll the floor jack straight back away from the engine. Carefully lower it from the vehicle.

To install

16. Lightly coat the input shaft spline with high temperature or molyebdenum grease. Don't use too much or the clutch disc will be ruined.
17. If the clutch was removed, make sure it is properly aligned or it will be impossible to install the transmission.
18. Put the transmission into high gear.
19. With the transmission properly placed behind the engine, turn the output shaft slowly to engage the splines of the input shaft into the clutch while pushing the transmission forward into place. Don't force it, the transmission will easily fall into place when everything is properly aligned.
20. On 4 cylinder engines with the 77.5mm transmission, torque the bellhousing-to-engine bolts to 25 ft. lbs. On all others, torque all the bolts to 55 ft. lbs.
21. Install the cross member and torque the bolts to 25 ft. lbs.
22. Install the support braces and catalyst hanger and torque the nuts and bolts to 35 ft. lbs.
23. Install the clutch inspection cover and starter.
24. On 1984–91 models, install the slave cylinder and if necessary, attach the hydraulic line and bleed the system.
25. On earlier models, attach the clutch cable and push the pedal to test its operation.
26. Install the shift lever and boot.
27. Reassemble the exhaust system.
28. Install the driveshaft and refill the transmission with the proper oil.
20. Connect the wiring for the back-up lights and speed sensor, or the speedometer cable.
30. Lower the vehicle to the ground and reconnect the battery.

4-Wheel Drive

1. Shift the transfer case into **4H**.
2. Disconnect the negative battery cable.
3. Raise and support the vehicle safely. Remove the skid plate.
4. Drain the lubricant from the transfer case.
5. Mark the transfer case front output shaft yoke and driveshaft for assembly reference. Disconnect the front driveshaft from the transfer case.
6. Mark the rear axle yoke and driveshaft for assembly reference. Remove the rear driveshaft.
7. Disconnect the speedometer cable and vacuum harness at the transfer case. Remove the shift lever from the transfer case.
8. Remove the catalytic converter hanger bolts at the converter.

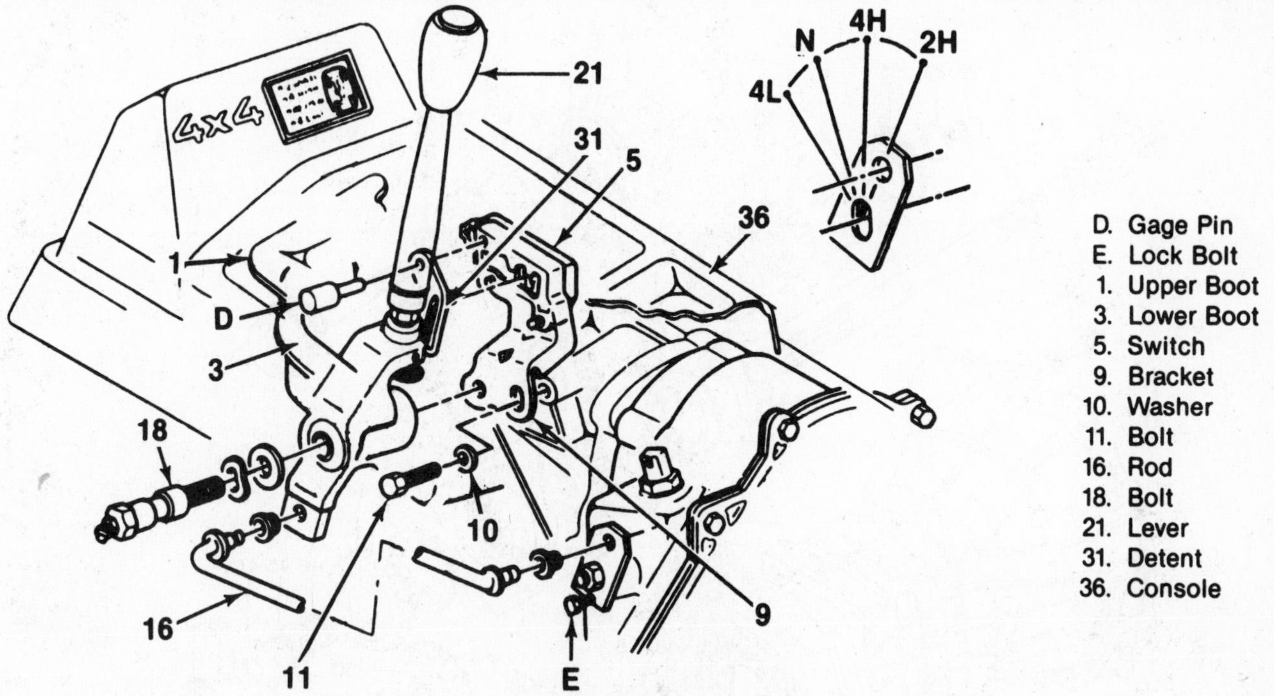
4H
N
2H
4L
21
31
5
36
1
D
3
18
10
16
11
E
9
4x4
D. Gage Pin
E. Lock Bolt
1. Upper Boot
3. Lower Boot
5. Switch
9. Bracket
10. Washer
11. Bolt
16. Rod
18. Bolt
21. Lever
31. Detent
36. Console

Transfer case shift linkage

9. Raise the transmission and transfer case and remove the transmission mount attaching bolts. Remove the mount and catalytic converter hanger and lower the transmission and transfer case.

10. If the bellhousing is being removed, remove the clutch cover from the front of the housing.

11. Unbolt the bellhousing from the engine, or the transmission from the bellhousing and carefully roll the floor jack straight back away from the engine. Carefully lower it from the vehicle.

To install

12. Lightly coat the input shaft spline with high temperature or molyebdenum grease. Don't use too much or the clutch disc will be ruined.

13. If the clutch was removed, make sure it is properly aligned or it will be impossible to install the transmission.

14. Put the transmission into high gear.

15. With the transmission properly placed behind the engine, turn the output shaft slowly to engage the splines of the input shaft into the clutch while pushing the transmission forward into place. Don't force it, the transmission will easily fall into place when everything is properly aligned.

16. On 4 cylinder engines with the 77.5mm transmission, torque the bellhousing-to-engine bolts to 25 ft. lbs. On all others, torque all the bolts to 55 ft. lbs.

17. Install the cross member and torque the bolts to 25 ft. lbs.

18. Install the support braces and catalyst hanger and torque the nuts and bolts to 35 ft. lbs.

19. Install the clutch inspection cover and starter.

20. On 1984–91 models, install the slave cylinder and if necessary, attach the hydraulic line and bleed the system.

21. On earlier models, attach the clutch cable and push the pedal to test its operation.

22. Install the transmission shift lever and transfer case shift linkage.

23. Reassemble the exhaust system.

24. Install the driveshafts. Note the alignment marks and make sure the shafts are installed the same way.

25. Refill the transmission and transfer case with the proper fluids.

26. Connect the wiring for the back-up lights and speed sensor, or the speedometer cable. Connect the transfer case vacuum lines.

27. Lower the vehicle to the ground and reconnect the battery.

77.5mm 4-Speed Overhaul

Cleanliness is an important factor in the overhaul of the transmission. Before attempting any disassembly operation, the exterior of the transmission should be thoroughly cleaned. During inspection and reassembly, all parts should be thoroughly cleaned and then air dried. Wiping cloths or rags should not be used to dry parts. All oil passages should be blown out and checked to make sure that they are not obstructed. All parts should be inspected to determine which parts are to be replaced.

DISASSEMBLY

1. Throughly clean the exterior of the transmission.
2. In the bell housing, disconnect the retaining clips and remove the clutch release bearing, fork and boot.
3. If not already done, drain the oil. Remove the bolts to remove the front bearing retainer. Remove the ball stud, if equipped.
4. Remove the speedometer drive and back-up light switch.
5. Remove the shift cover and gasket.
6. Remove the rear extension housing and gasket.
7. Remove the speedometer drive gear from the mainshaft.
8. Support the shift rods with a block of wood. Using a punch, carefully drive the pin from the reverse shift block.
9. Remove the reverse block retaining bolts. Remove the reverse shifter shaft, shift block, shift fork and reverse gear as an assembly.
10. Remove the retaining rings from the counter shaft and drive gear shaft bearings.

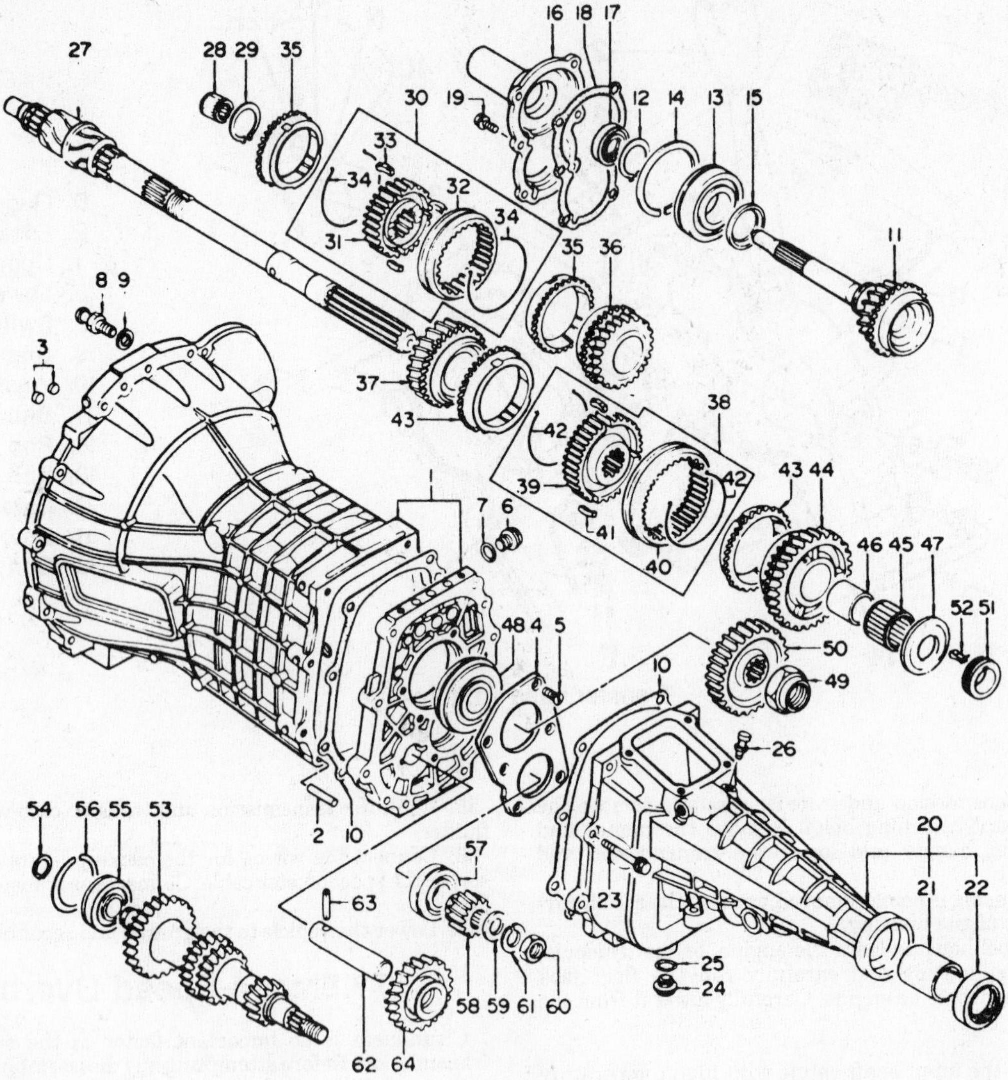

1. Transmission case and center support
2. Dowel
3. Plug
4. Rear bearing retainer
5. Screw
6. Oil filler plug
7. Gasket
8. Ball stud
9. Washer
10. Gasket
11. Drive gear shaft
12. Retaining ring
13. Bearing
14. Retaining ring
15. Spacer
16. Front bearing retainer
17. Oil seal
18. Gasket
19. Bolt and spring washer
20. Extension housing
21. Bushing
22. Rear oil seal
23. Bolt, plain washer and spring washer
24. Oil drain plug
25. Gasket
26. Ventilator
27. Mainshaft
28. Needle roller bearing
29. Retaining ring
30. 3rd/4th sychronizer
31. Clutch hub
32. Sleeve
33. Insert
34. Spring
35. Blocker ring
36. 3rd gear
37. 2nd gear
38. 1st/2nd synchronizer
39. Clutch hub
40. Sleeve
41. Insert
42. Spring
43. Blocker ring
44. 1st gear
45. Needle roller bearing
46. Bearing collar
47. Thrust washer
48. Bearing
49. Nut
50. Reverse gear
51. Speedometer drive gear
52. Clip
53. Counter shaft
54. Retaining ring
55. Bearing
56. Retaining ring
57. Bearing
58. Reverse gear
59. Plain washer
60. Nut
61. Spring washer
62. Reverse idler shaft
63. Spring pin
64. Reverse idler gear

Exploded view of the 77.5mm four speed transmission

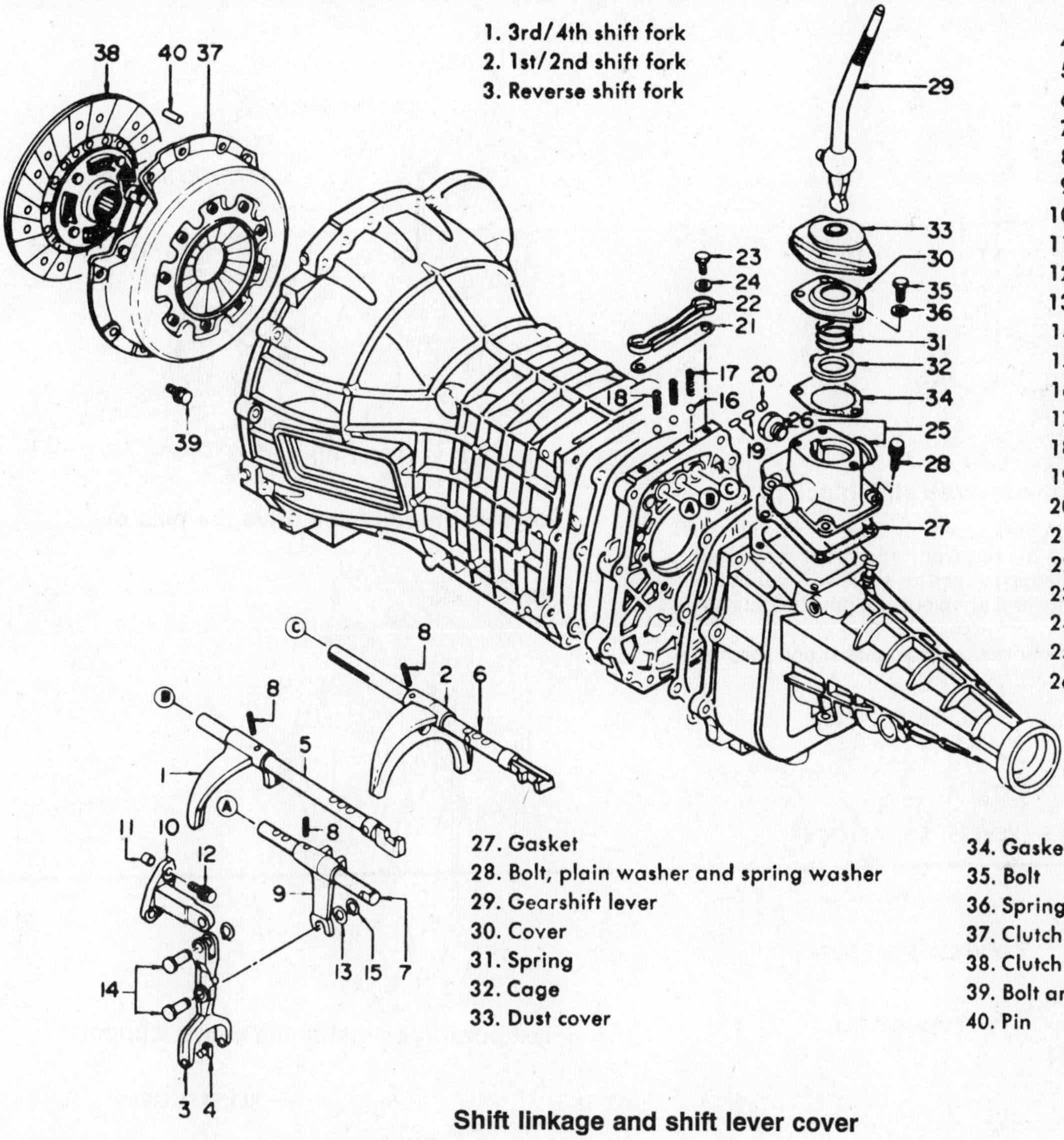

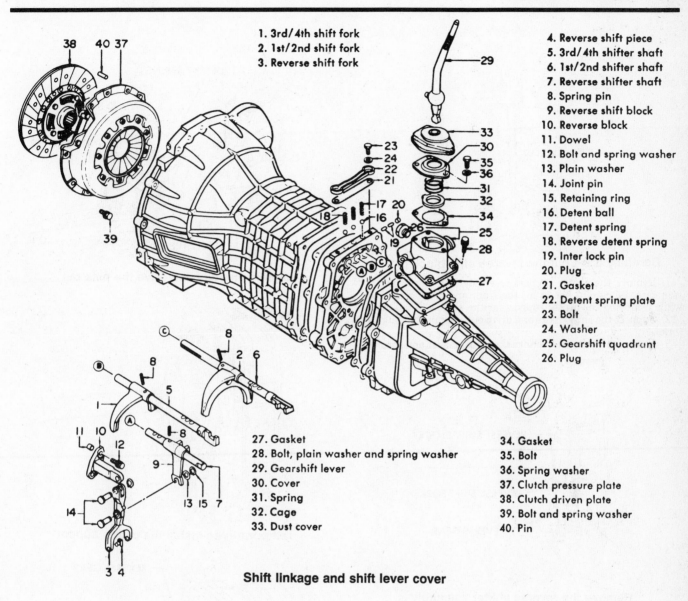

1. 3rd/4th shift fork
2. 1st/2nd shift fork
3. Reverse shift fork
4. Reverse shift piece
5. 3rd/4th shifter shaft
6. 1st/2nd shifter shaft
7. Reverse shifter shaft
8. Spring pin
9. Reverse shift block
10. Reverse block
11. Dowel
12. Bolt and spring washer
13. Plain washer
14. Joint pin
15. Retaining ring
16. Detent ball
17. Detent spring
18. Reverse detent spring
19. Inter lock pin
20. Plug
21. Gasket
22. Detent spring plate
23. Bolt
24. Washer
25. Gearshift quadrant
26. Plug
27. Gasket
28. Bolt, plain washer and spring washer
29. Gearshift lever
30. Cover
31. Spring
32. Cage
33. Dust cover
34. Gasket
35. Bolt
36. Spring washer
37. Clutch pressure plate
38. Clutch driven plate
39. Bolt and spring washer
40. Pin

Shift linkage and shift lever cover

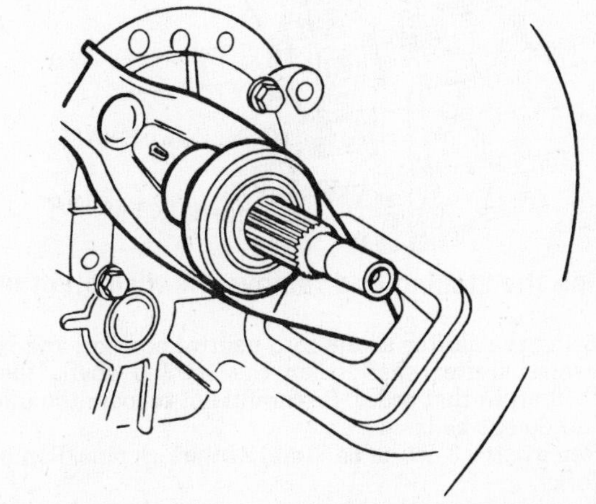

Remove the clutch release bearing and fork

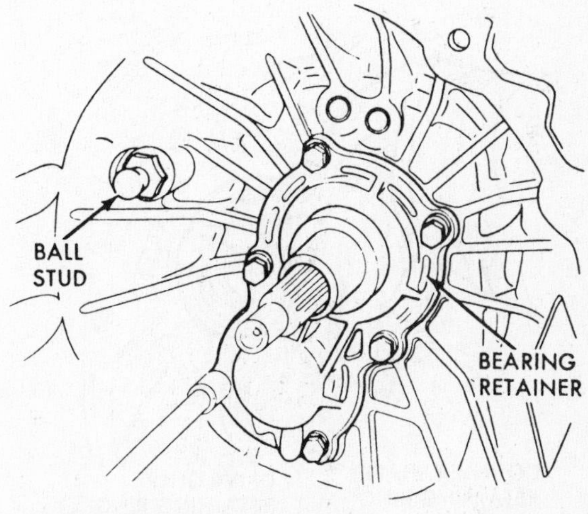
BALL
STUD
BEARING
RETAINER

Remove the ball stud and bearing retainer

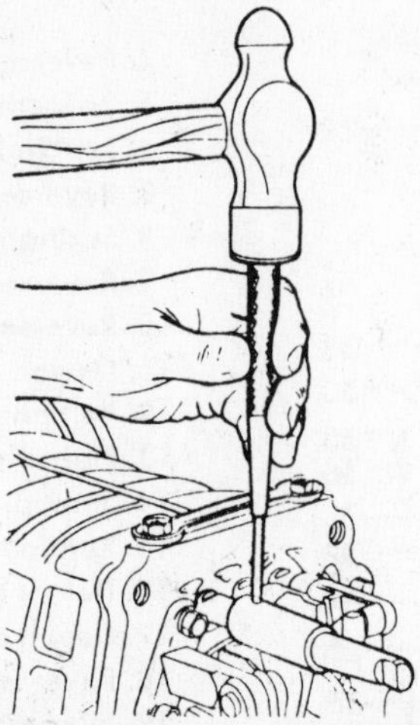

Carefully drive out the reverse shift block pin

11. Remove the center support assembly fron the transmission case. Be careful not to hit the front end drive gear shaft while removing the center support, or the shaft will fall out.
12. Support the shift shafts and drive out the pins holding the forks.
13. Loosen the bolts and remove the plate, gasket and springs.

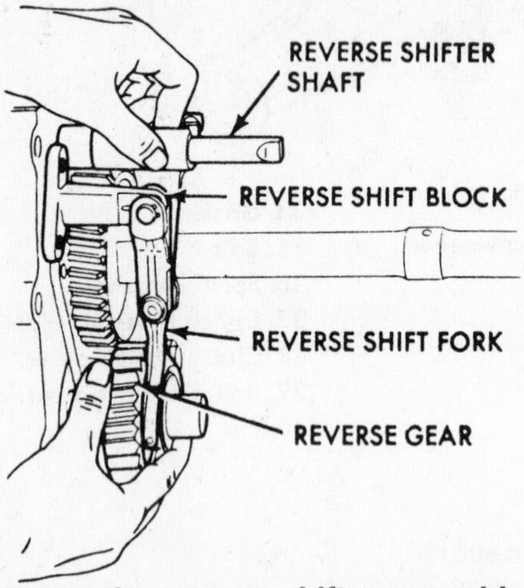
REVERSE SHIFTER SHAFT
REVERSE SHIFT BLOCK
REVERSE SHIFT FORK
REVERSE GEAR

Remove the reverse shifter assembly

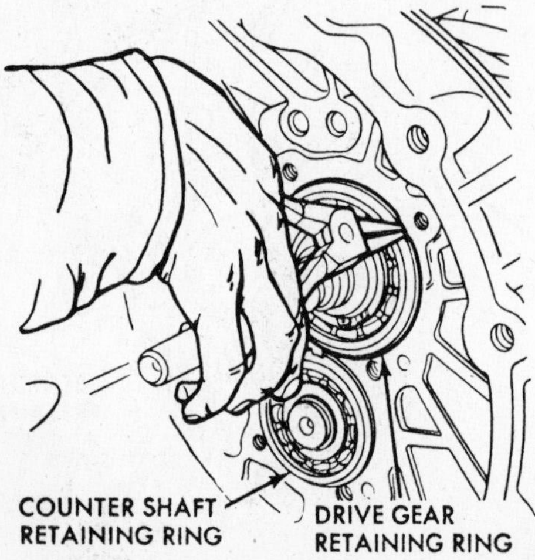
COUNTER SHAFT RETAINING RING
DRIVE GEAR RETAINING RING

Remove the bearing race retaining rings

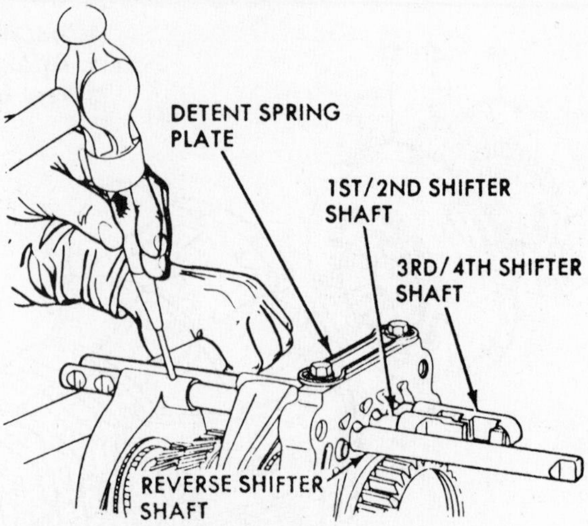
DETENT SPRING PLATE
1ST/2ND SHIFTER SHAFT
3RD/4TH SHIFTER SHAFT
REVERSE SHIFTER SHAFT

Support the rails and drive the pins out

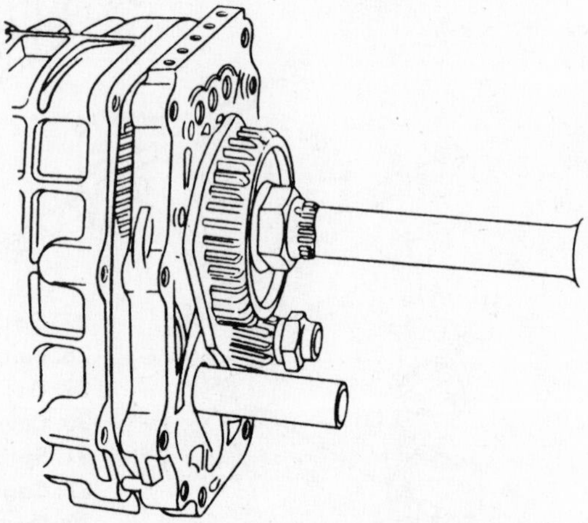

Temporarily re-install the center support

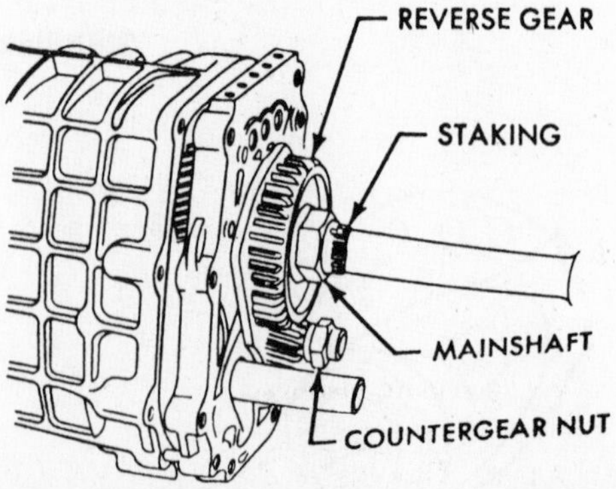
REVERSE GEAR
STAKING
MAINSHAFT
COUNTERGEAR NUT

Raise the staking and remove the mainshaft nut

14. Bring the shifter shafts into neutral position and remove the reverse shifter shaft, then the 1st/2nd shaft, then the 3rd/4th shaft in that order. Be careful not to loose the interlock pins and detent balls.
15. Remove the 3 detent balls and 2 interlock pins. Remove the shift forks.
16. Engage the synchronizers to prevent the mainshaft from turning. Temporarily install the center support section onto the transmission case.

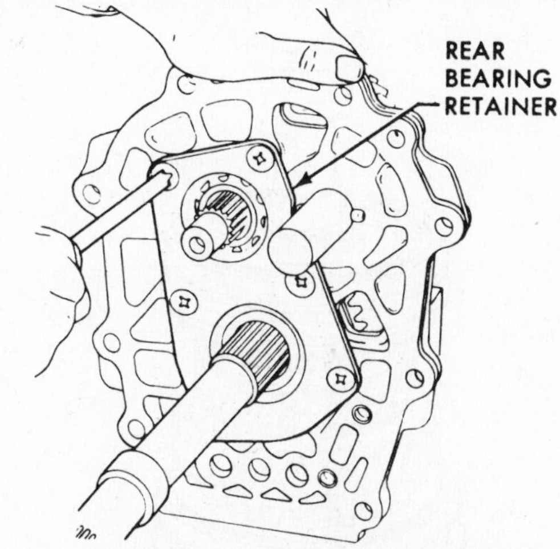
REAR
BEARING
RETAINER

Remove the rear bearing retainer

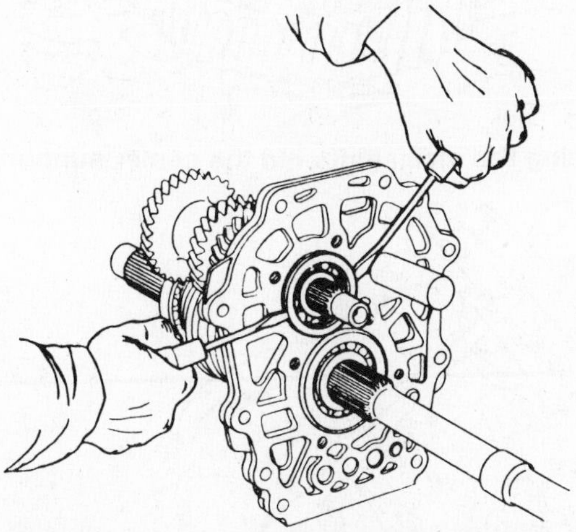

Carefully pry the bearing race out of the center support

17. Use a punch to raise the staking on the mainshaft rear nut, then remove the nut. The reverse gear can now be removed fron the mainshaft.
18. Remove the nut and reverse counter gear from the counter shaft.
19. Remove the center support section from the transmission.
20. Set the synchronizers in neutral and remove the rear bearing retainer.
21. Carefully move the counter shaft back and forth to push the outer bearing race out far enough to be able to pry it out.
22. Remove the race, then remove the countershaft.
23. To remove the mainshaft, install special tool J-22912-01 or an equivilant gear puller on the rear face of 2nd gear. Press the mainshaft out of the center support, being careful not to loose the sychronizers and bearings as the shaft is slid out.
24. Remove the snapring from the other end of the mainshaft. Install the gear puller onto 3rd gear and press the shaft out of the case.

INSPECTION

Clean all parts and the case. Carefully inspect the case for signs of cracking or burrs, especially near the bearing areas. If the front bearing oil seal has been leaking, check the shaft for rust or wear in the seal area. While the transmission is apart, it is usually advisable to change the shaft seals at both ends. Clean

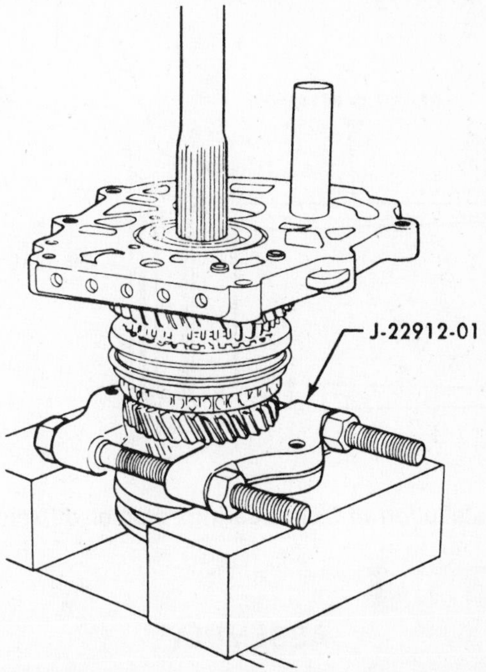
J-22912-01

The mainshaft must be pressed out of the center support

and blow dry the bearings. Do not spin the bearings with air, this will cause damage to the bearing or to your hands. Inspect the bearings for signs of wear, then lightly oil them and slowly rotate, feeling for any roughness that may not be visible. Closely inspect the gears for uneven or heavy wear patterns, chips or cracks. If a gear shows enough wear or damage to warrent replacement, make sure the countershaft is still usable. Synchronizer hubs and sleeves must be replaced as an assembly, but the springs and keys may be replaced separately.

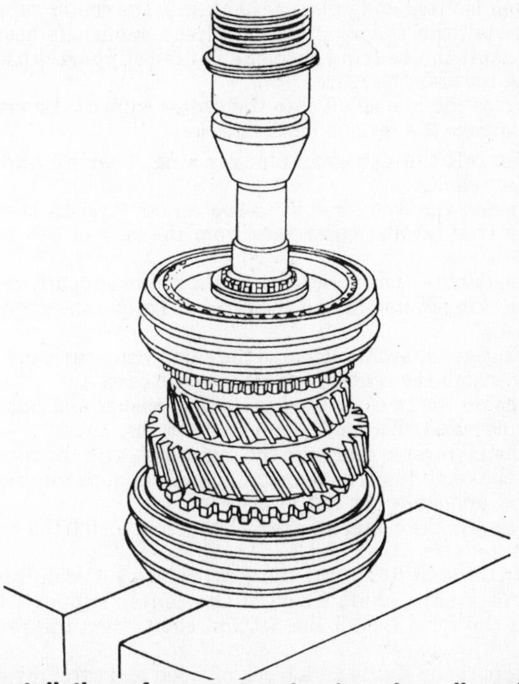

Installation of rear extension housing oil seal

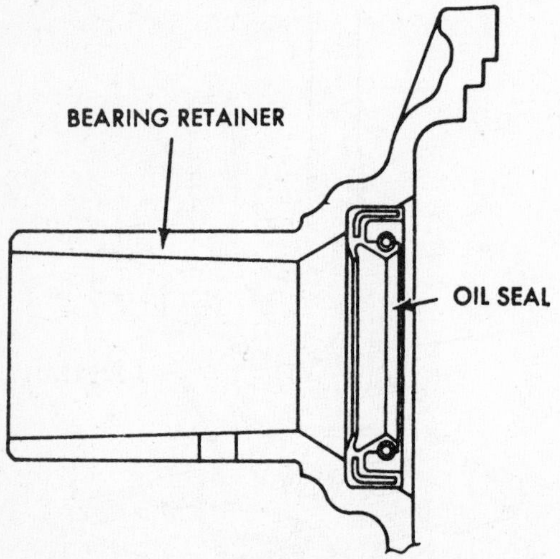
BEARING RETAINER
OIL SEAL

Installation of front bearing retainer oil seal

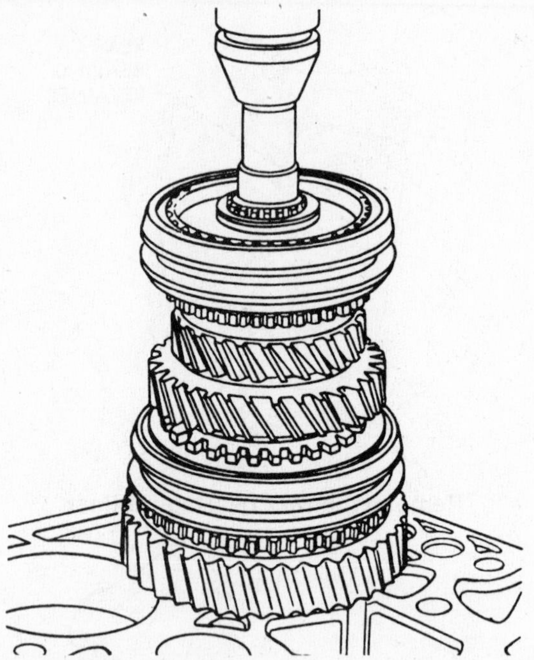

Pressing the mainshaft onto the center support

ASSEMBLY

25. To assemble the mainshaft, install 3rd gear and the 3rd gear blocker ring onto the shaft.
26. When installing the 3rd/4th synchronizer onto the shaft, make sure the hub is supported on the press blocks while pressing the shaft.
27. Install the retaining ring to the front of the mainshaft.
28. Install the 2nd gear and blocker ring to the mainshaft.
29. Press the 1st/2nd sychronizer assembly onto the shaft, making sure to press against the sychronizer hub.
30. Press the 1st gear bearing collar to the mainshaft using a suitable spacer.
31. Install the blocker ring, gear, bearing and thrust washer, with the grooves in the washer towards the gear.
32. If the reverse idler shaft was removed, make sure the spring pin is fitted and press the shaft into the center support.
33. Install the snapring onto the rear mainshaft bearing, then install the bearing into the center support with the snapring towards the rear.
34. Press the mainshaft into the center support. Be careful not to damage the reverse block dowels.
35. Install the 4th gear blocker ring, bearing and 4th gear/input shaft.
36. Install the countershaft to the center support, then install the rear bearing outer race from the rear of the center support.
37. Install the bearing retainer on the center support, using a thread locking compound on the screws. Torque the screws to 15 ft. lbs.
38. Engage the sychronizers so the shafts can't turn and temporarily install the center support into the case.
39. Install the reverse, washer, spring washer and nut onto the countershaft. Torque the nut to 80 ft. lbs.
40. Install reverse gear onto the mainshaft with the rounded edge of the teeth towards the rear. Install the nut, torque it to 95 ft. lbs. and stake the nut in place.
41. Remove the center support. Grease and install the 2 inter lock pins.
42. Lay the shift forks onto the synchronizers. Carefully slide the 3dr/4th shift shaft through the center support, then through the fork. Install the 1st/2nd shaft, then the reverse shaft.
43. Support the shafts on a block of wood and carefully drive the spring pins into the forks.

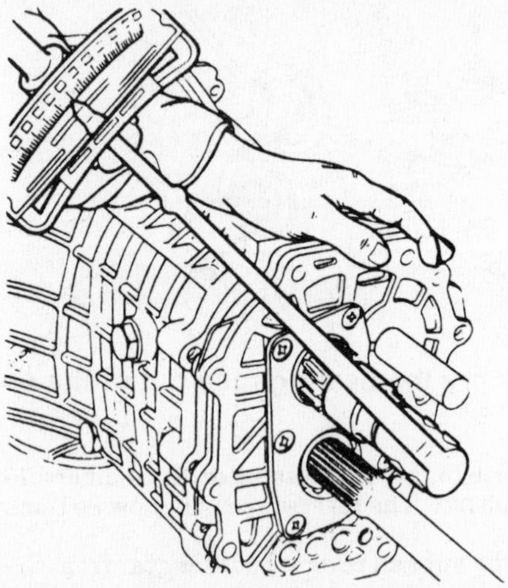

Use a torque wrench when installing the shaft nuts

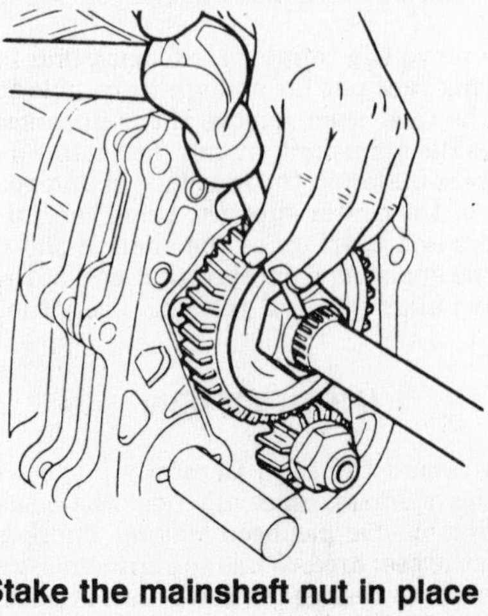

Stake the mainshaft nut in place

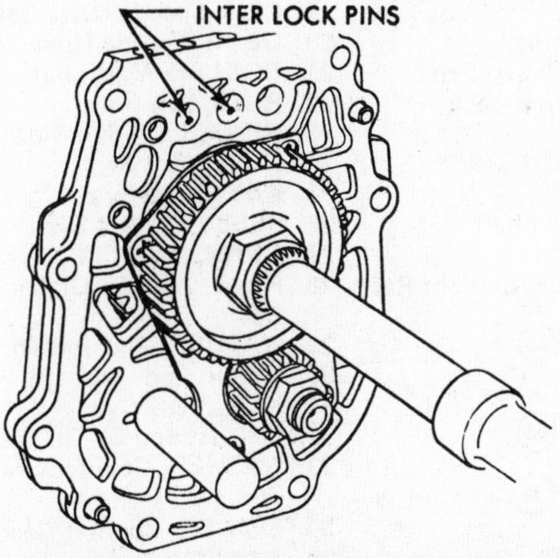
INTER LOCK PINS

Grease the inter lock pins before installing them

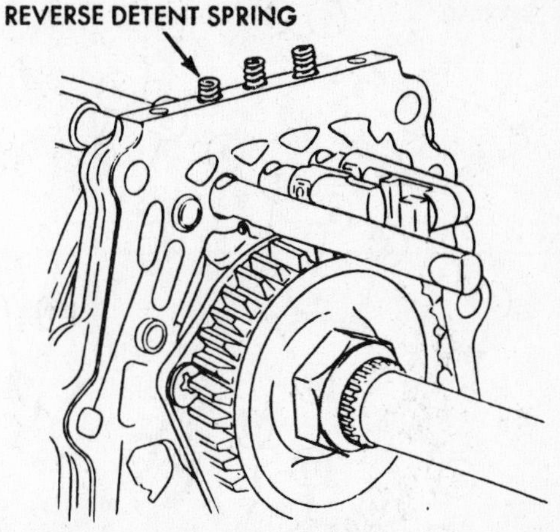
REVERSE DETENT SPRING

The reverse detent spring is the short one

44. Drop the detent balls into their holes, put in a few drops of oil and install the springs. The reverse spring is the shorter one.
45. Install the gasket and detent spring retainer plate and torque the bolts to 15 ft. lbs.
46. Install the gasket and carefully install the center support onto the case. Install the retaining rings on the bearing races in the bell housing.
47. Assemble the reverse shift block, reverse block and reverse shift fork using the pins and snaprings.
48. Install the shift block assembly to the reverse shift fork,

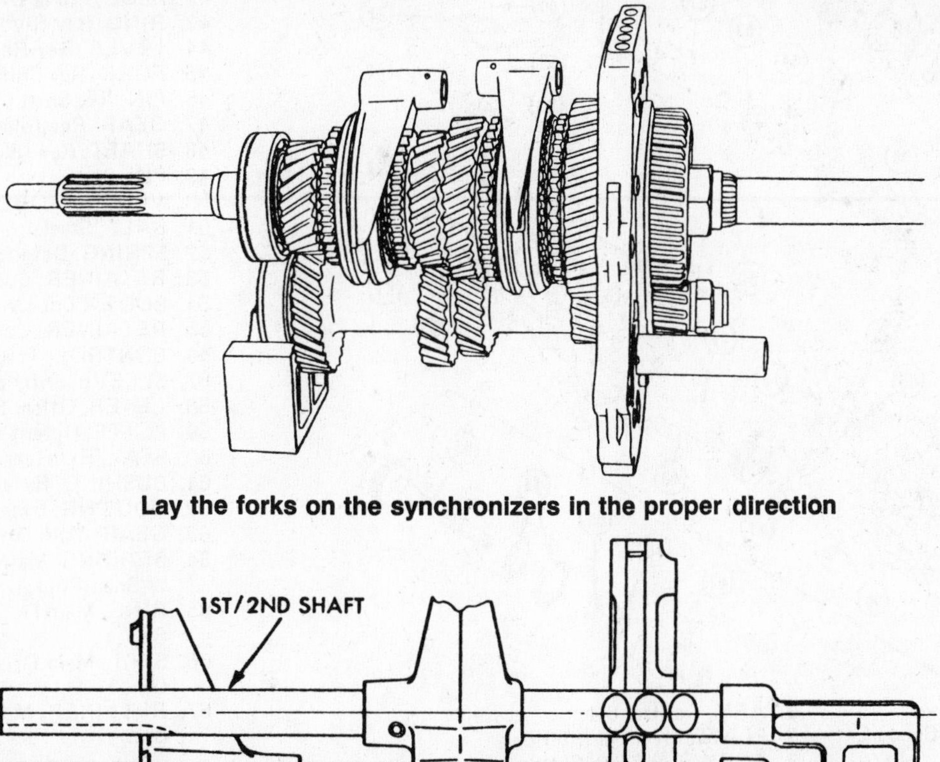

Lay the forks on the synchronizers in the proper direction

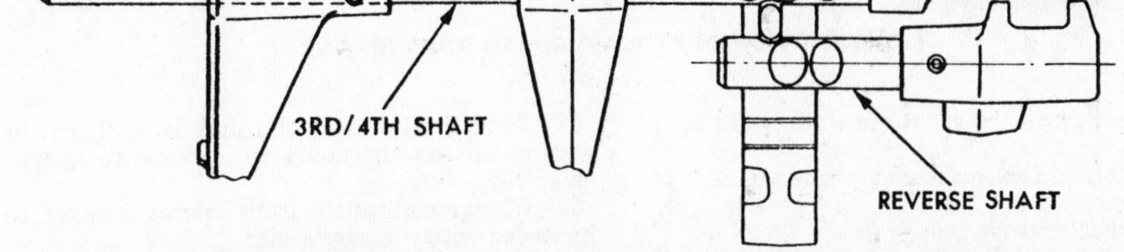
1ST/2ND SHAFT
3RD/4TH SHAFT
REVERSE SHAFT

Make sure the shafts are in neutral when installing the pins

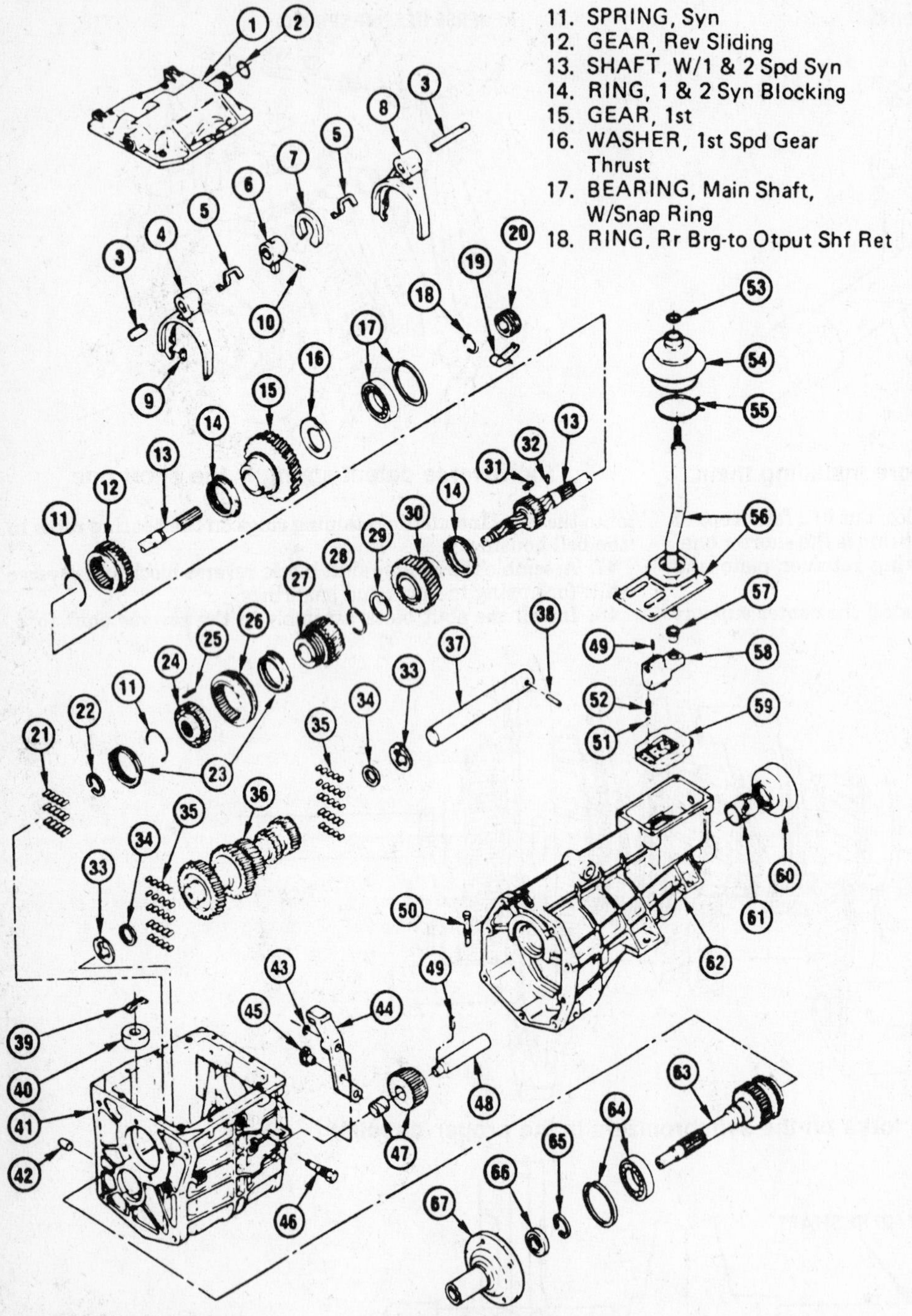

1. COVER, Trans Case
2. SEAL, "O" Ring, Cvr to Ext
3. SHAFT, Shift
4. FORK, 3 & 4 Spd Shift
5. PLATE, Shift Fork
6. ARM, Control Sel
7. PLATE, Gear Sel Interlock
8. FORK, 1 & 2 Spd Shift
9. INSERT, Shift Fork
10. PIN, Roll
11. SPRING, Syn
12. GEAR, Rev Sliding
13. SHAFT, W/1 & 2 Spd Syn
14. RING, 1 & 2 Syn Blocking
15. GEAR, 1st
16. WASHER, 1st Spd Gear Thrust
17. BEARING, Main Shaft, W/Snap Ring
18. RING, Rr Brg-to Otput Shf Ret
19. CLIP, Speedo Drive Gear
20. GEAR, Speedo Drive
21. ROLLER, Main Shaft
22. RING, Syn Ret
23. RING, 3 & 4 Syn Blocking
24. HUB, 3 & 4 Syn
25. KEY, 3 & 4 Syn
26. SLEEVE, 3 & 4 Syn
27. GEAR, 3rd
28. RING, 2nd Spd Gr Thr Wa Ret
29. WASHER, 2nd Spd Thrust
30. GEAR, 2nd
31. KEY, 1 & 2 Syn
32. PIN, 1st Spd Gr Thr Wa Ret
33. WASHER, Counter Gear Thrust
34. SPACER, Counter Gear Rlr
35. ROLLER, Counter Gear
36. GEAR, Counter
37. SHAFT, Counter Gear
38. PIN, Spring
39. NUT, Spring
40. MAGNET
41. CASE
42. PLUG, Fill & Drain
43. RING, Rev Rly Lvr Ret
44. LEVER, Rev Relay
45. FORK, Rev Shift Lvr
46. PIN, Rev Shift Lvr Pivot
47. GEAR, Rev Idler, W/Bushing
48. SHAFT, Rev Idler Gear
49. PIN, Spr
50. VENTILATOR, Ext
51. BALL, Steel
52. SPRING, Detent
53. RETAINER, Cont Lvr Boot
54. BOOT, Cont Lvr
55. RETAINER, Cont Lvr Boot
56. CONTROL, Trans Lvr & Hsg
57. SLEEVE, Shift Lvr Damper
58. LEVER, Offset Shift
59. PLATE, Detent & Guide
60. SEAL, Ext Rear Oil
61. BUSHING, Extension Housing
62. HOUSING, Extension
63. GEAR, Main Drive
64. BEARING, Main Drive Gear, W/Snap Ring
65. RING, Main Dr Gr Brg to Shf Ret
66. SEAL, Main Drive Gear Brg Oil
67. RETAINER, Main Drive Gear Brg

Exploded view of 77mm 4 speed transmission

then insert the shift fork into the groove in the reverse idler gear.

49. Install the assembly to the shafts and torque the reverse block bolts to 15 ft. lbs.

50. Install the speedometer drive gear.

51. Using a new gasket, install the extension housing and torque the bolts to 30 ft. lbs.

52. Temporarily install the shift lever. Turn the input shaft while shifting the gears to make sure everything works smoothly.

53. When installing the front bearing retainer, the bolts must be sealed with a gasket sealer.

54. Install the clutch release parts. Torque the ball stud to 30 ft. lbs. (40 Nm).

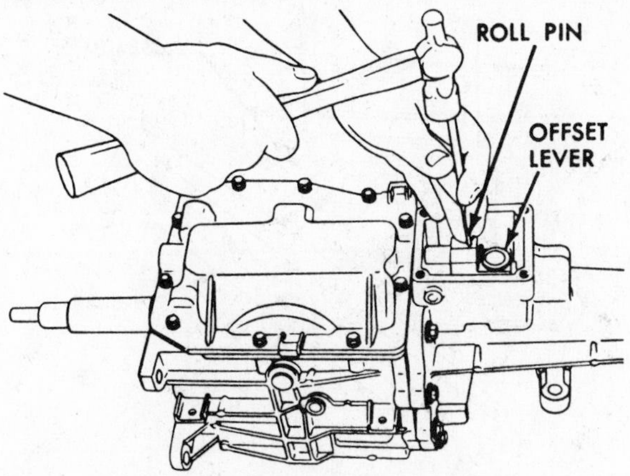
ROLL PIN
OFFSET LEVER
Removing offset lever roll pin

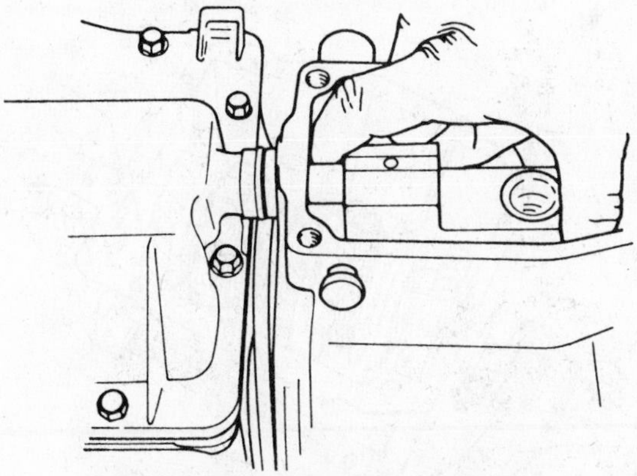
Remove the extension housing

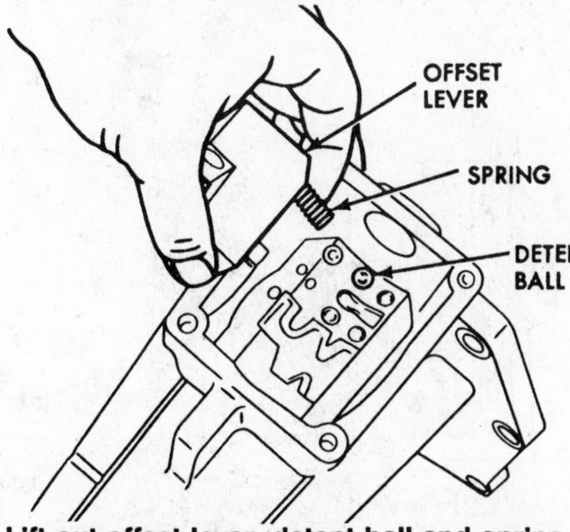
OFFSET LEVER
SPRING
DETENT BALL
Lift out offset lever, detent ball and spring

55. The gear shift lever must be removed to install the transmission. When installing it in the vehicle, use a new gasket and torque the bolts to 15 ft. lbs. (20Nm).

77mm 4-Speed Overhaul

Cleanliness is an important factor in the overhaul of the transmission. Before attempting any disassembly operation, the exterior of the transmission should be thoroughly cleaned. During inspection and reassembly, all parts should be thoroughly

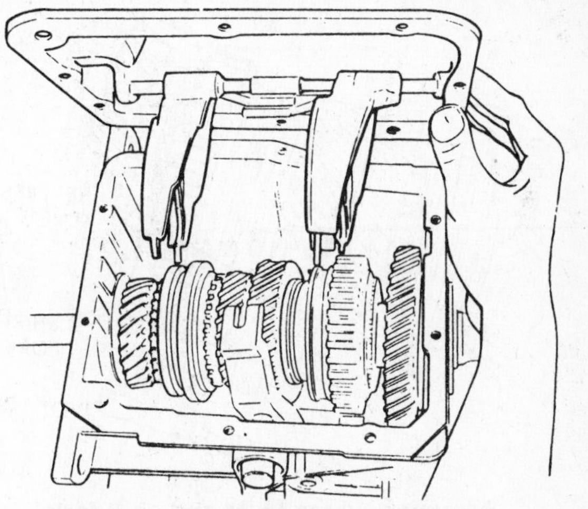
Remove top cover and shift forks

cleaned and then air dried. Wiping cloths or rags should not be used to dry parts. All oil passages should be blown out and checked to make sure that they are not obstructed. All parts should be inspected to determine which parts are to be replaced.

DISASSEMBLY

1. Remove drain plug and drain lubricant from transmission.
2. Thoroughly clean the exterior of the transmission assembly.
3. Using a hammer and punch, remove the roll pin that retains the offset lever to shift rail.
4. Remove extension housing attaching bolts. Separate the extension housing from the transmission case and remove housing and offset lever as an assembly.
5. Remove detent ball and spring from offset lever and remove roll pin from extension housing or offset lever.
6. Remove transmission shift cover attaching bolts. Pry the shift cover loose and remove cover from transmission case.
7. Remove clip that retains reverse lever to reverse lever pivot bolt.
8. Remove reverse lever pivot bolt and remove reverse lever and fork as an assembly.
9. Using a hammer and punch, mark position of front bearing cap to transmission case. Remove front bearing cap bolts and remove bearing cap.
10. Remove small retaining and large locating snaprings from front drive gear bearing.
11. Install bearing puller J-22912-01 or equivalent, on front bearing and puller J-8433-1 or equivalent, with 2 bolts on end

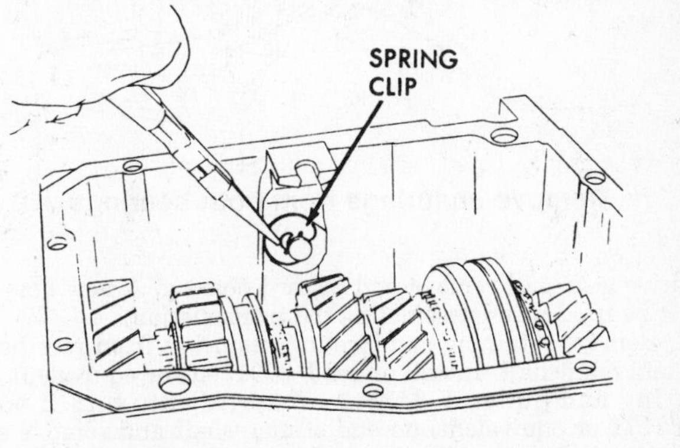
SPRING CLIP
Remove reverse lever retainer clip

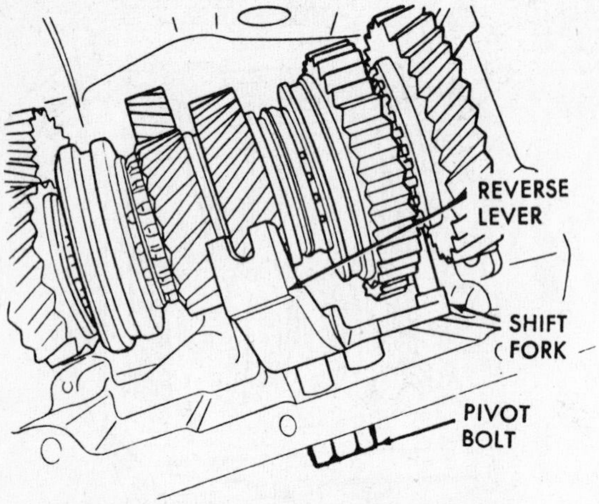
REVERSE
LEVER
SHIFT
FORK
PIVOT
BOLT

Remove reverse lever and shift fork

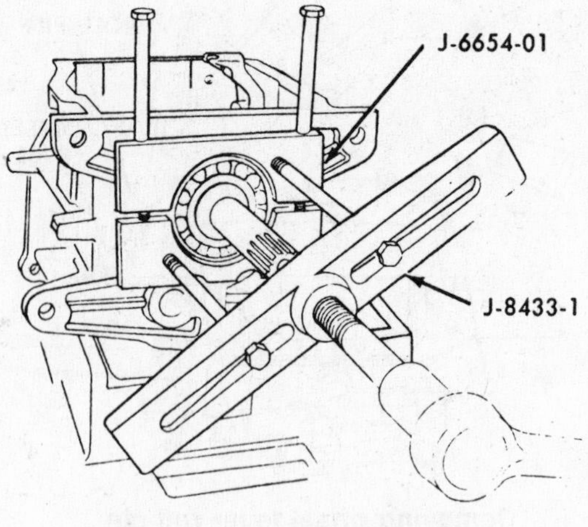
J-6654-01
J-8433-1

Bearings must be replaced

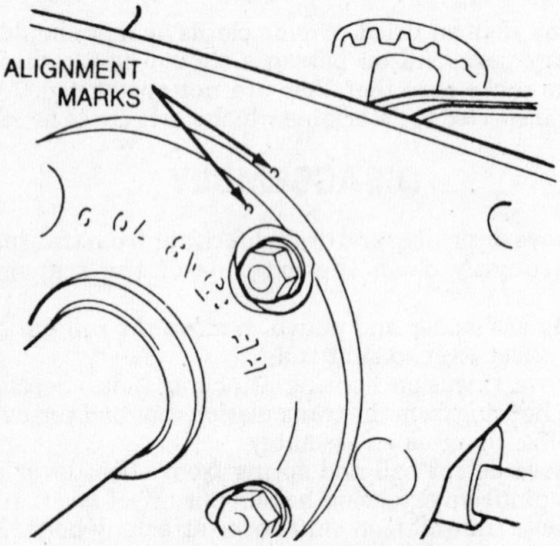
ALIGNMENT
MARKS

Mark the front bearing retainer

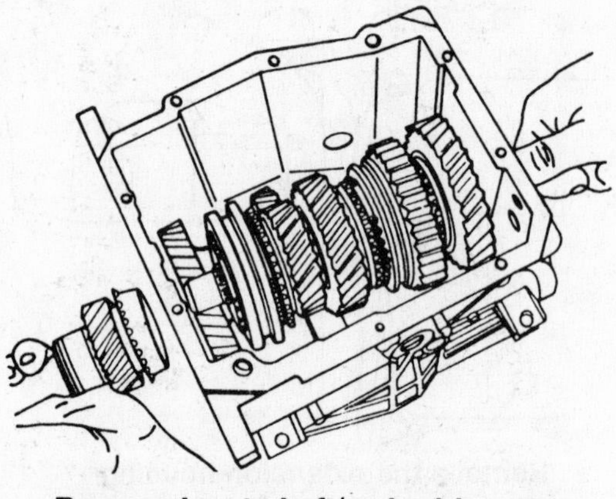

Remove input shaft/main drive gear

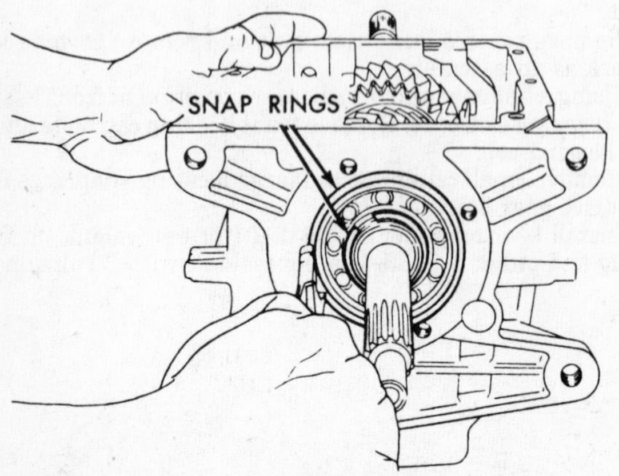
SNAP RINGS

Remove snaprings from both bearings

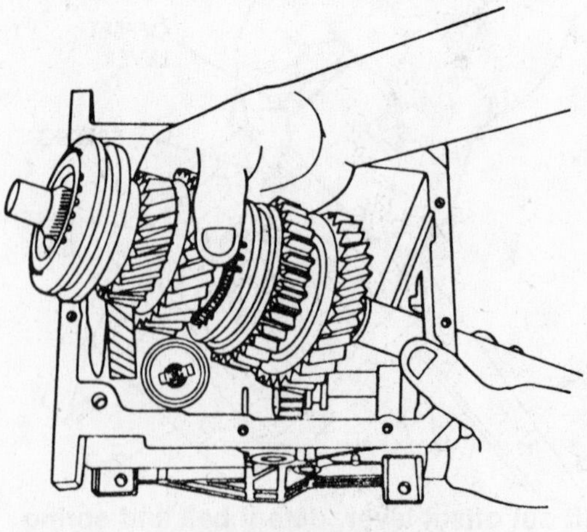

Lift the mainshaft out

of drive gear and remove and discard bearing. A new bearing must be used when assembling the transmission.

12. Remove retaining and locating snaprings from rear bearing and mainshaft. Install puller J–22912–01 or equivalent, on bearing and puller J–8433–1 or equivalent, with 2 bolts (J–33171 or equivalent) on end of mainshaft and remove and discard used bearing. A new bearing must be used when assembling transmission.

13. Remove drive gear from mainshaft and transmission case.

14. Remove mainshaft from transmission case by tipping mainshaft down at the rear and lifting shaft out through shift cover opening.

15. Using a hammer and punch, remove roll pin retaining reverse idler gear shaft in transmission case. Remove idler gear and shaft from case.

16. Remove countershaft from rear of case using loading tool

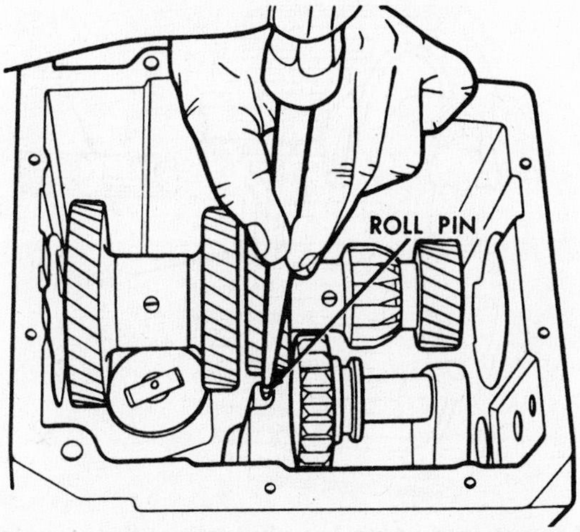
ROLL PIN
Remove roll pin from reverse idler shaft

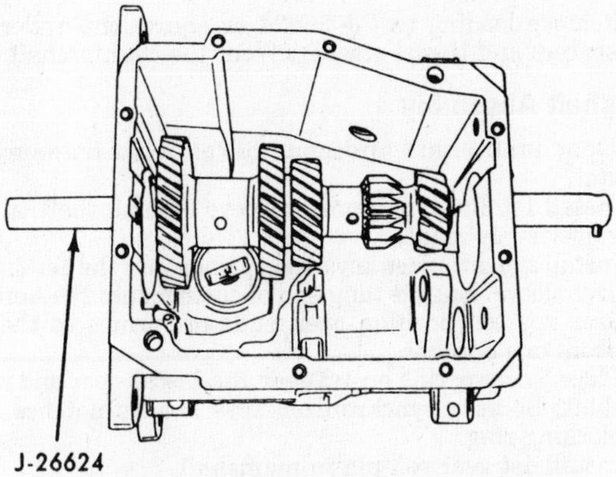
J-26624
Use alignment tool to remove countershaft

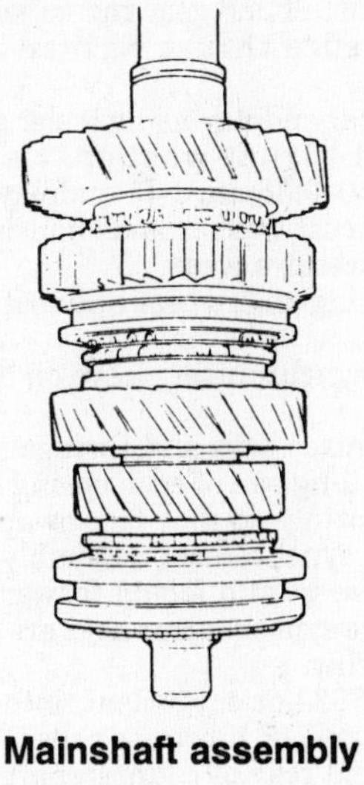
Mainshaft assembly

J–26624. Remove countershaft gear and loading tool as an assembly from case along with thrust washers.

Mainshaft Disassembly

1. Scribe an alignment mark on 3rd/4th synchronizer hub

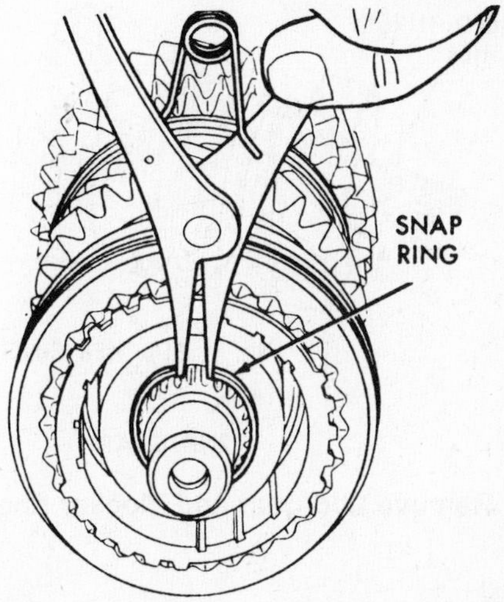
SNAP
RING
Remove 3dr/4th synchronizer snapring

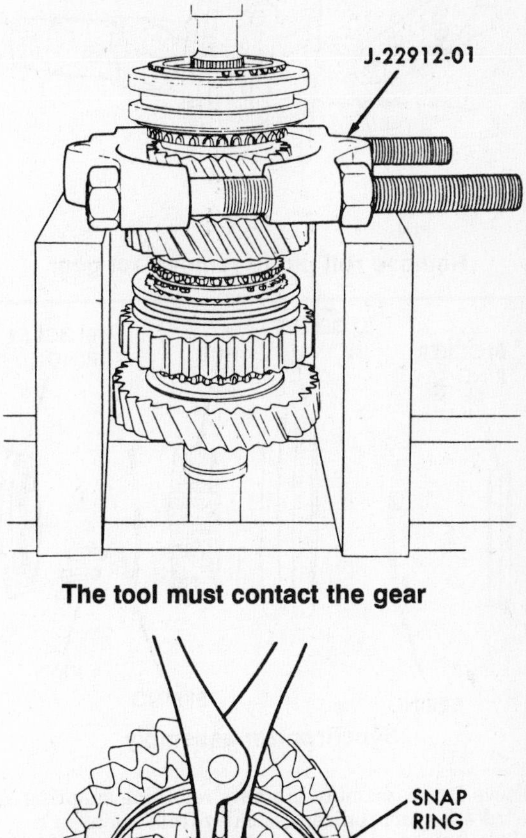
J-22912-01
The tool must contact the gear

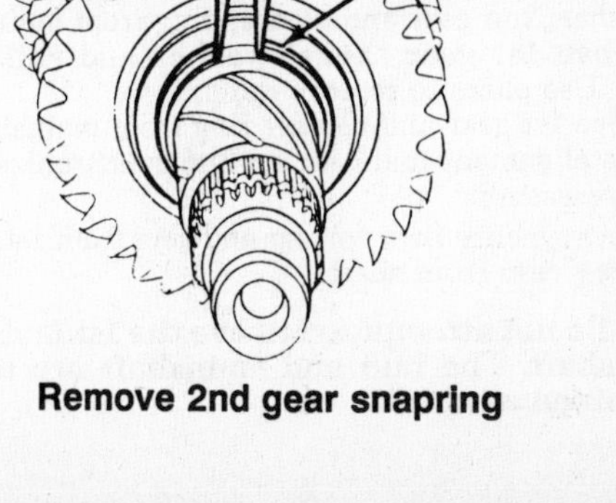
SNAP
RING
Remove 2nd gear snapring

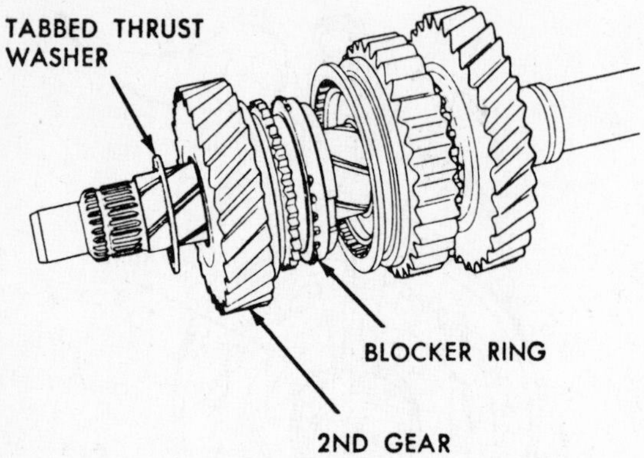
TABBED THRUST WASHER
BLOCKER RING
2ND GEAR

Remove 2nd gear and blocker ring

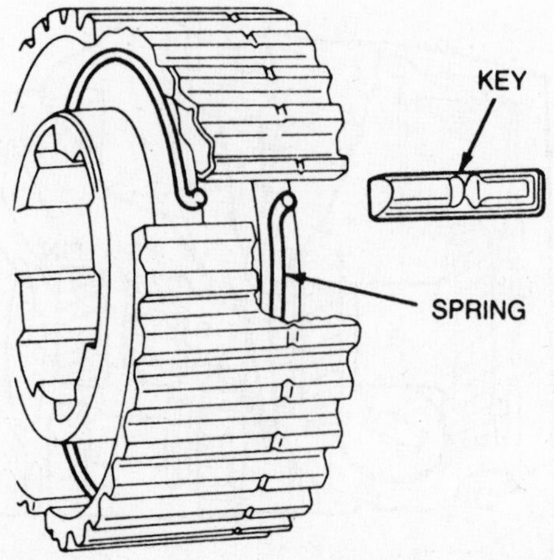
KEY
SPRING

Put tangs into same key, but offset the openings

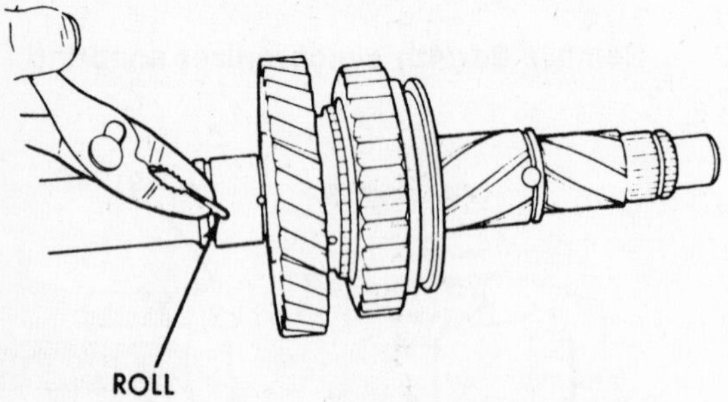
ROLL PIN

Remove roll pin to remove 1st gear

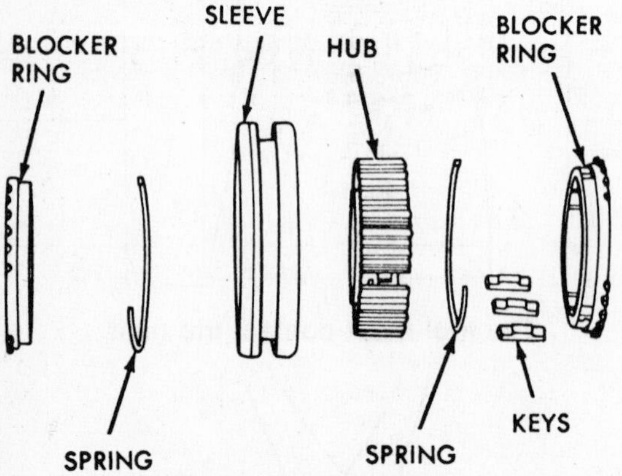
BLOCKER RING
SLEEVE
HUB
BLOCKER RING
KEYS
SPRING
SPRING

Synchronizer assembly

and sleeve for reassembly. Remove retaining snapring and remove 3rd/4th synchronizer assembly from mainshaft.

2. Slide 3rd gear off mainshaft.

3. Remove 2nd gear retaining snapring. Remove tabbed thrust washer, 2nd gear and blocker ring from mainshaft.

4. Remove 1st gear thrust washer and roll pin from mainshaft. Use pliers to remove roll pin.

5. Remove 1st gear and blocker ring from mainshaft.

6. Scribe alignment mark on 1st/2nd synchronizer hub and sleeve for reassembly.

7. Remove synchronizer springs and keys from 1st/2nd sleeve and remove sleeve from shaft.

NOTE: Do not attempt to remove the 1st/2nd hub from the mainshaft. The hub and mainshaft are assembled and machined as a unit.

8. Remove loading tool J–26624 or equivalent, roller bearings, spacers and thrust washers from the countershaft gear.

Mainshaft Assembly

1. Coat mainshaft and gear bores with transmission lubricant.

2. Install 1st/2nd synchronizer sleeve on mainshaft, aligning marks previously made.

3. Install synchronizer keys and springs into the 1st/2nd synchronizer sleeve. Engage tang end of springs into the same synchronizer key but position open ends of springs so they face away from one another.

4. Place blocking ring on 1st gear and install gear and ring on mainshaft. Be sure synchronizer keys engage notches in 1st gear blocking ring.

5. Install 1st gear roll pin in mainshaft.

6. Place blocking ring on 2nd gear and install gear and ring on mainshaft. Be sure synchronizer keys engage notches in 2nd gear blocking ring. Install 2nd gear thrust washer and snapring on mainshaft. Be sure thrust washer tab is engaged in mainshaft notch.

7. Measure 2nd gear endplay using feeler gauge. Insert gauge between gear and thrust washer. Endplay should be 0.004–0.014 in. (0.10–0.36mm). If endplay is over 0.014 in. (0.36mm), replace thrust washer and snapring and inspect synchronizer hub for excessive wear.

8. Place blocking ring on 3rd gear and install gear and ring on mainshft.

9. Install 3rd/4th synchronizer sleeve on hub, aligning marks previously made.

10. Install synchronizer keys and springs in 3rd/4th synchronizer sleeve. Engage tang end of each spring in same key but position open ends of springs so they face away from one another.

11. Install 3rd/4th synchronizer assembly on the mainshaft with machined groove in hub facing forward. Install snapring on mainshaft. Be sure synchronizer keys are engaged in notches in 3rd gear blocker ring.

12. Install tool J–26624 or equivalent, into countershaft gear. Using a light weight grease, lubricate roller bearings and install into bores at front and rear of countershaft gear. Install roller bearing retainers on tool J–26624 or equivalent.

Transmission Cover Disassembly

1. Place selector arm plates and shift rail in neutral position (centered).

2. Rotate shift rail until selector arm disengages from selector arm plates and roll pin is accessible.

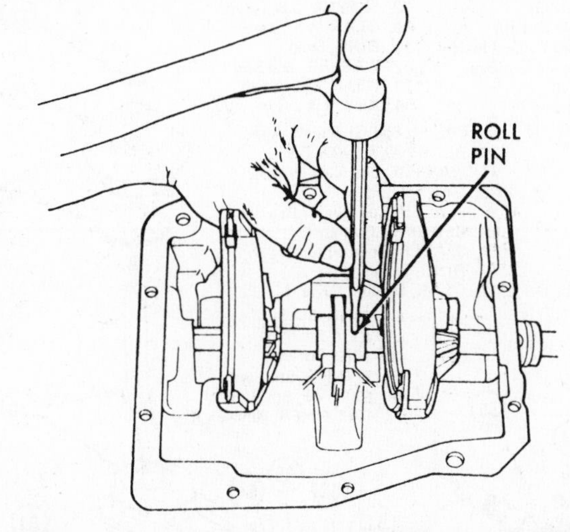
ROLL
PIN

Remove roll pin to disassemble the shift forks

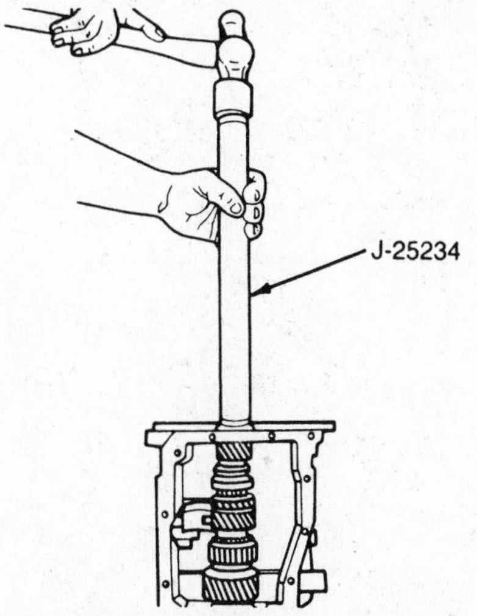
J-25234

The bearing is driven onto the shaft

3. Remove selector arm roll pin using a pin punch and hammer.
4. Remove shift rail, shift forks, selector arm plates, selector arm, interlock plate and roll pin.
5. Remove shift cover to extension housing O-ring seal using a suitable tool.
6. Remove nylon inserts and selector arm plates from shift forks. Note position of inserts and plates for assembly reference.

Inspection

1. Inspect the shift rail for wear.
2. Inspect the shift forks and selector arm for wear.
3. Inspect the selector arm plates and interlock plate for wear.

Cover Assembly

1. Install nylon inserts and selector arm plates in shift forks.
2. If removed, install shift rail plug. Coat edges of plug with sealer before installing.
3. Coat shift rail and rail bores with light weight grease and insert shift rail in cover. Install rail until flush with inside edge of cover.
4. Place 1st/2nd shift fork in cover with fork offset facing rear of cover and push shift rail through fork. The 1st/2nd shift fork is the larger of the 2 forks.
5. Position selector arm and C-shaped interlock plate in cover and insert shift rail through arm. Widest part of interlock plate must face away from cover and selector arm roll pin hole must face downward and toward rear of cover.
6. Position 3rd/4th shift fork in cover with fork offset facing rear of cover. The 3rd/4th shift fork selector arm plate must be under 1st/2nd shift for selector arm plate.
7. Push shift rail through 3rd/4th shift fork and into front bore in cover.
8. Rotate shift rail until selector arm plate at forward end of rail faces away from, but is parallel to cover.
9. Align roll pin holes in selector arm and shift rail and install roll pin. Roll pin must be flush with surface of selector arm to prevent pin from contacting selector arm plates during shifts.
10. Install a new shift cover to extension housing O-ring seal. Coat O-ring seal with transmission lubricant.

TRANSMISSION ASSEMBLY

1. Coat countershaft gear thrust washers with petroleum jelly and position washer in case.
2. Position countershaft gear in case and install countershaft from rear of case. Be sure that thrust washers stay in place during installation of countershaft and gear.
3. Position reverse idler gear in case with shift lever groove facing rear of case and install reverse idler shaft from rear of case. Install roll pin in shaft and center pin in shaft.
4. Install mainshaft assembly into the case. Do not disturb position of synchronizer assemblies during installation.
5. Install 4th gear blocking ring in 3rd/4th synchronizer sleeve. Be sure synchronizer keys engaged in notches in blocker ring.
6. Install input shaft/drive gear into case and engage with mainshaft.
7. Position mainshaft 1st gear against the rear of the case. Using a new bearing, start front bearing onto input shaft/drive gear. Align bearing with bearing bore in case and drive bearing onto drive gear and into case using tool J-25234 or equivalent.
8. Install front bearing retaining and locating snaprings.
9. Apply a ⅛ in. (3mm) diameter bead of RTV sealant, No. 732 or equivalent, on case mating surface of front bearing cap. Install bearing cap aligning marks previously made. Apply non-hardening sealer on attaching bolts and install bolts. Torque bolts to 15 ft. lbs. (20 Nm).
10. Install 1st gear thrust washer with oil grove facing 1st gear on mainshaft, aligning slot in washer with 1st gear roll pin.
11. Using a new bearing, position rear bearing on mainshaft. Align bearing with bearing bore in case and drive bearing into case using tool J-25234 or equivalent.
12. Install locating and retaining snaprings on rear bearing.
13. Install speedometer gear and retaining clip on mainshaft.
14. Apply non-hardening sealer to threads of reverse lever pivot bolt and start bolt into case. Engage reverse lever fork in the reverse idler gear and reverse lever on pivot bolt. Torque bolt to 20 ft. lbs. (27 Nm) and install retaining clip.
15. Rotate drive gear and mainshaft gear. If blocker rings tend to stick on gears, release the rings by gently prying them off the cones.
16. Apply a ⅛ in. (3mm) diameter bead or RTV sealant, No. 732 or equivalent, on the cover mating surface of transmission. Place reverse lever in neutral and position cover on case.
17. Install 2 dowel type bolts first to align cover on case. Install remaining cover bolts and torque to 10 ft. lbs. (13 Nm). The offset lever to shift rail roll pin hole must be in the vertical position after cover installation.
18. Apply a ⅛ in. (3mm) diameter bead of RTV sealant, No. 732 or equivalent, on the extension housing to transmission case mating surface.

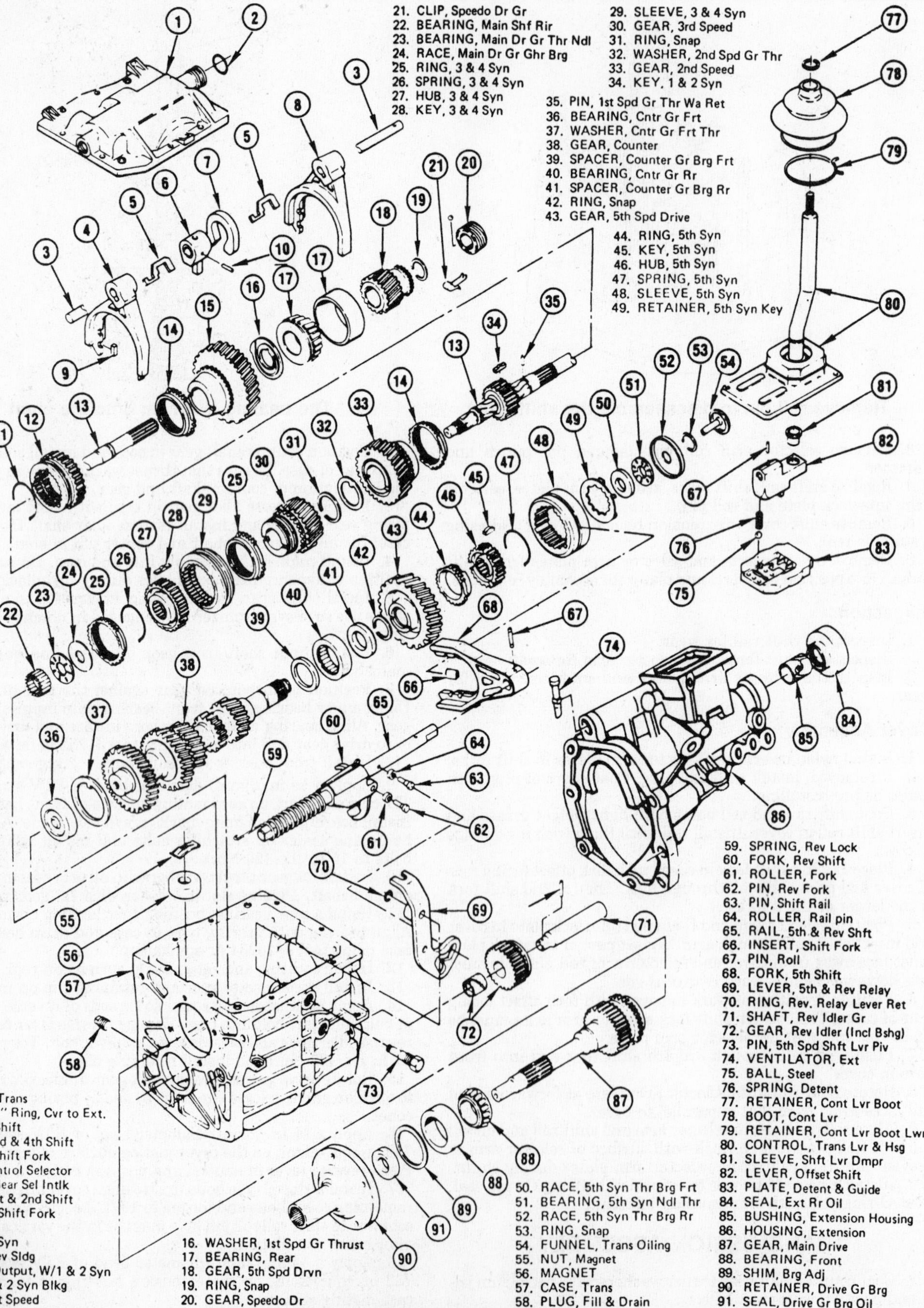

1. COVER, Trans
2. SEAL, "O" Ring, Cvr to Ext.
3. SHAFT, Shift
4. FORK, 3rd & 4th Shift
5. PLATE, Shift Fork
6. ARM, Control Selector
7. PLATE, Gear Sel Intlk
8. FORK, 1st & 2nd Shift
9. INSERT, Shift Fork
10. PIN, Roll
11. SPRING, Syn
12. GEAR, Rev Sldg
13. SHAFT, Output, W/1 & 2 Syn
14. RING, 1 & 2 Syn Blkg
15. GEAR, 1st Speed
16. WASHER, 1st Spd Gr Thrust
17. BEARING, Rear
18. GEAR, 5th Spd Drvn
19. RING, Snap
20. GEAR, Speedo Dr
21. CLIP, Speedo Dr Gr
22. BEARING, Main Shf Rlr
23. BEARING, Main Dr Gr Thr Ndl
24. RACE, Main Dr Gr Ghr Brg
25. RING, 3 & 4 Syn
26. SPRING, 3 & 4 Syn
27. HUB, 3 & 4 Syn
28. KEY, 3 & 4 Syn
29. SLEEVE, 3 & 4 Syn
30. GEAR, 3rd Speed
31. RING, Snap
32. WASHER, 2nd Spd Gr Thr
33. GEAR, 2nd Speed
34. KEY, 1 & 2 Syn
35. PIN, 1st Spd Gr Thr Wa Ret
36. BEARING, Cntr Gr Frt
37. WASHER, Cntr Gr Frt Thr
38. GEAR, Counter
39. SPACER, Counter Gr Brg Frt
40. BEARING, Cntr Gr Rr
41. SPACER, Counter Gr Brg Rr
42. RING, Snap
43. GEAR, 5th Spd Drive
44. RING, 5th Syn
45. KEY, 5th Syn
46. HUB, 5th Syn
47. SPRING, 5th Syn
48. SLEEVE, 5th Syn
49. RETAINER, 5th Syn Key
50. RACE, 5th Syn Thr Brg Frt
51. BEARING, 5th Syn Ndl Thr
52. RACE, 5th Syn Thr Brg Rr
53. RING, Snap
54. FUNNEL, Trans Oiling
55. NUT, Magnet
56. MAGNET
57. CASE, Trans
58. PLUG, Fill & Drain
59. SPRING, Rev Lock
60. FORK, Rev Shift
61. ROLLER, Fork
62. PIN, Rev Fork
63. PIN, Shift Rail
64. ROLLER, Rail pin
65. RAIL, 5th & Rev Shft
66. INSERT, Shift Fork
67. PIN, Roll
68. FORK, 5th Shift
69. LEVER, 5th & Rev Relay
70. RING, Rev. Relay Lever Ret
71. SHAFT, Rev Idler Gr
72. GEAR, Rev Idler (Incl Bshg)
73. PIN, 5th Spd Shft Lvr Piv
74. VENTILATOR, Ext
75. BALL, Steel
76. SPRING, Detent
77. RETAINER, Cont Lvr Boot
78. BOOT, Cont Lvr
79. RETAINER, Cont Lvr Boot Lwr
80. CONTROL, Trans Lvr & Hsg
81. SLEEVE, Shft Lvr Dmpr
82. LEVER, Offset Shift
83. PLATE, Detent & Guide
84. SEAL, Ext Rr Oil
85. BUSHING, Extension Housing
86. HOUSING, Extension
87. GEAR, Main Drive
88. BEARING, Front
89. SHIM, Brg Adj
90. RETAINER, Drive Gr Brg
91. SEAL, Drive Gr Brg Oil

Exploded view of 77mm 5 speed transmission

19. Place extension housing over mainshaft to a position where shift rail is in shift cover opening.
20. Install detent spring in offset lever. Place ball in neutral guide plate detent position. Apply pressure on the offset lever, slide offset lever onto shift rail and seat extension housing to transmission case.
21. Install extension housing retaining bolts. Torque bolts to 25 ft. lbs. (30 Nm).
22. Align hole in offset lever and shift rail and install roll pin.
23. Temporarily install the shift lever. Rotate the input shaft while shifting gears to make sure the unit works.

77mm 5-Speed Overhaul

Cleanliness is an important factor in the overhaul of the transmission. Before attempting any disassembly operation, the exterior of the transmission should be thoroughly cleaned to prevent the possibility of dirt entering the transmission internal mechanism. During inspection and reassembly, all parts should be thoroughly cleaned with cleaning fluid and then air dried. Wiping cloths or rags should not be used to dry parts. All oil passages should be blown out and checked to make sure that they are not obstructed. Small passages should be checked with tag wire. All parts should be inspected to determine which parts are to be replaced.

DISASSEMBLY

1. Remove drain plug on transmission case and drain lubricant.

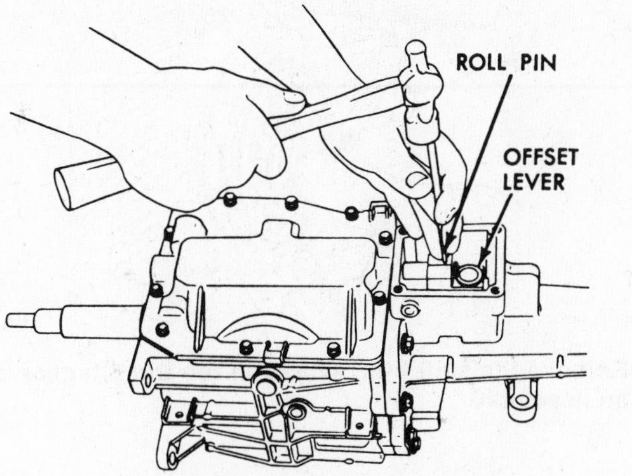
ROLL PIN
OFFSET
LEVER
Remove offset lever roll pin only

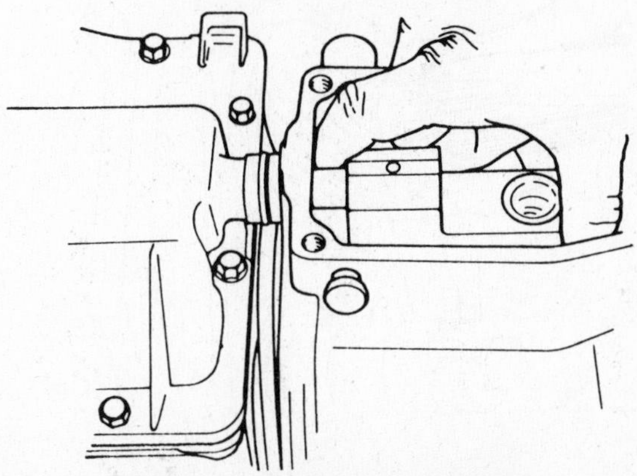
Remove extension housing

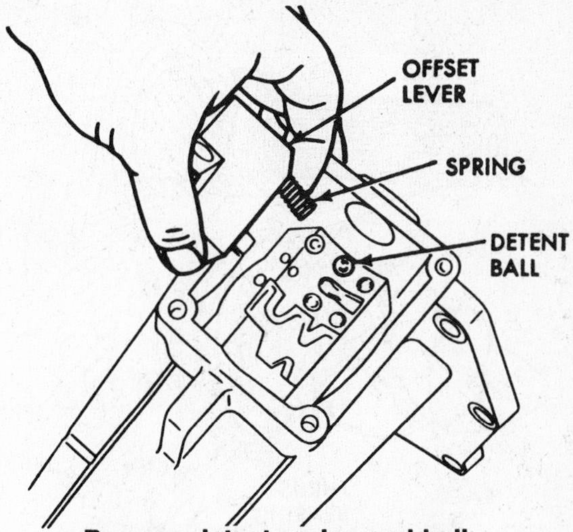
OFFSET
LEVER
SPRING
DETENT
BALL
Remove detent spring and ball

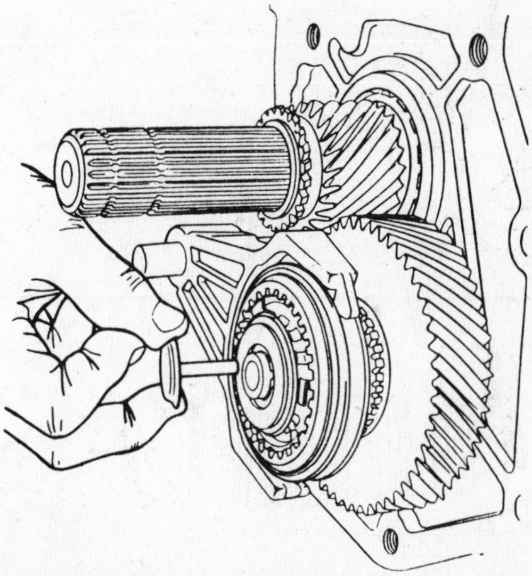
Plastic funnel on rear of the countershaft

2. Thoroughly clean the exterior of the transmission assembly.
3. Using pin punch and hammer, remove roll pin attaching offset lever to shift rail.
4. Remove extension housing to transmission case bolts and remove housing and offset lever as an assembly. Do not attempt to remove the offset lever while the extension housing is still bolted in place. The lever has a positioning lug engaged in the housing detent plate which prevents moving the lever far enough for removal.
5. Remove detent ball and spring from offset lever and remove roll pin from extension housing or offset lever.
6. Remove plastic funnel, thrust bearing race and thrust bearing from rear of countershaft. The countershaft rear thrust bearing, bearing washer and plastic funnel may be found inside the extension housing.
7. Remove bolts attaching transmission cover and shift fork assembly and remove cover. Two of the transmission cover attaching bolts are alignment-type dowel bolts. Note the location of these bolts for assembly reference.
8. Using a punch and hammer, drive the roll pin from the 5th gearshift fork while supporting the end of the shaft with a block of wood.

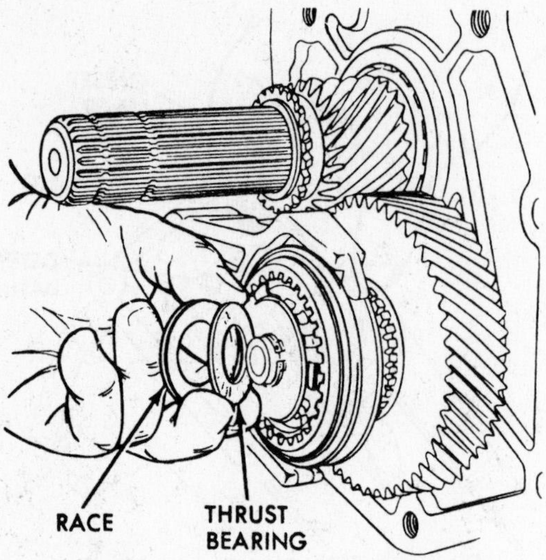
RACE
THRUST BEARING

Remove the thrust bearing and race

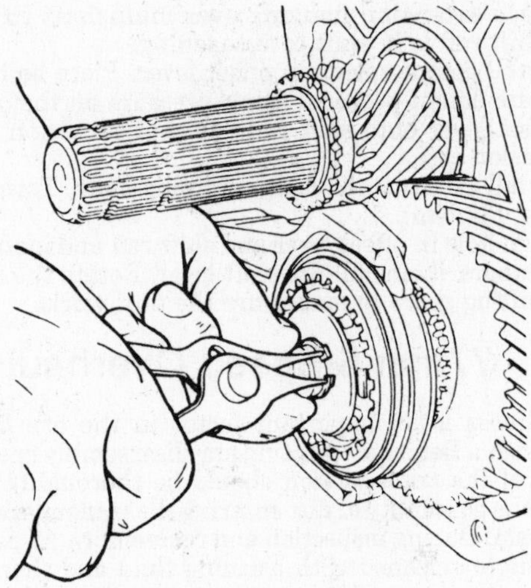

Remove the snapring

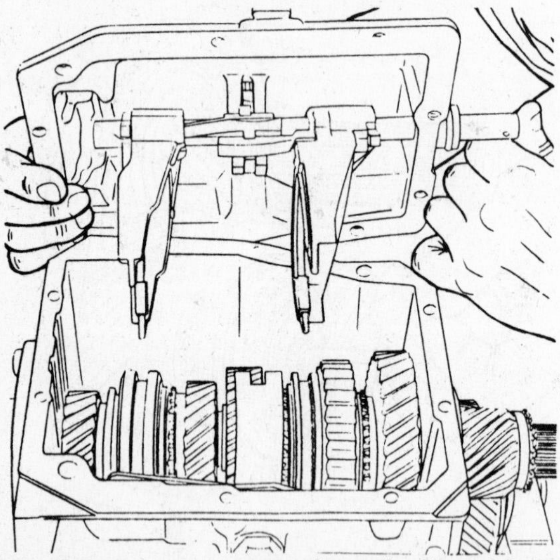

Remove the top cover, note where the dowel bolts go

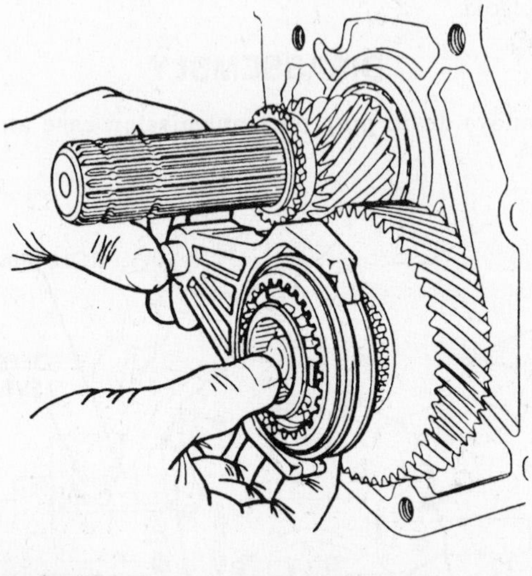

Remove the shift fork, synchronizer and 5th gear as an assembly

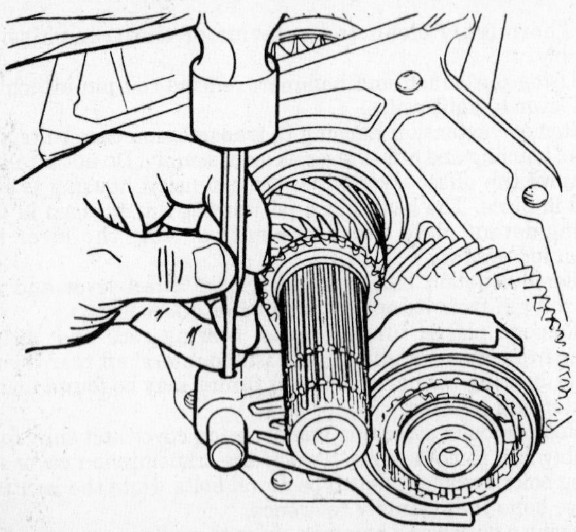

Support the shaft and drive out the 5th gear shift fork roll pin

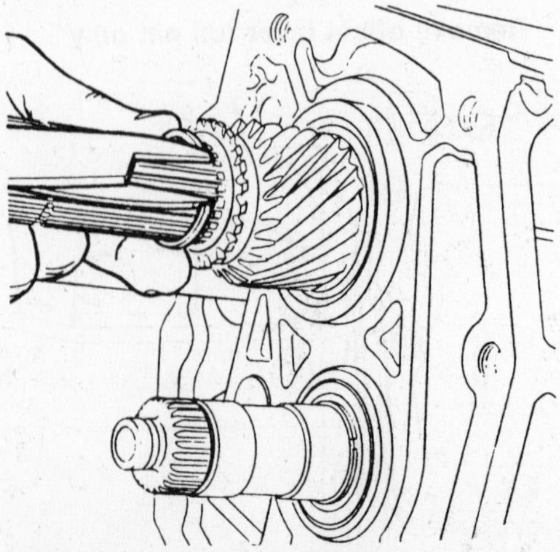

Snapring for 5th gear driven gear

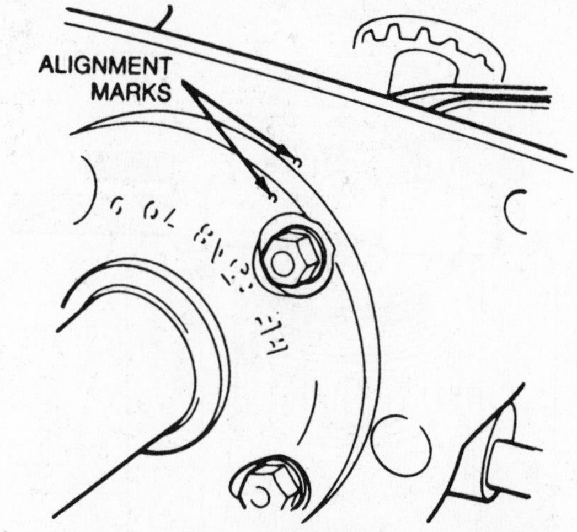
ALIGNMENT
MARKS
Mark front bearing cap for installation

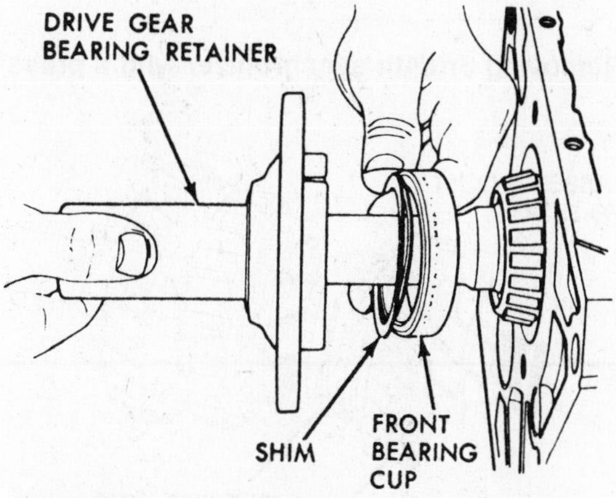
DRIVE GEAR
BEARING RETAINER
SHIM
FRONT
BEARING
CUP
Keep the cap, shims and race together

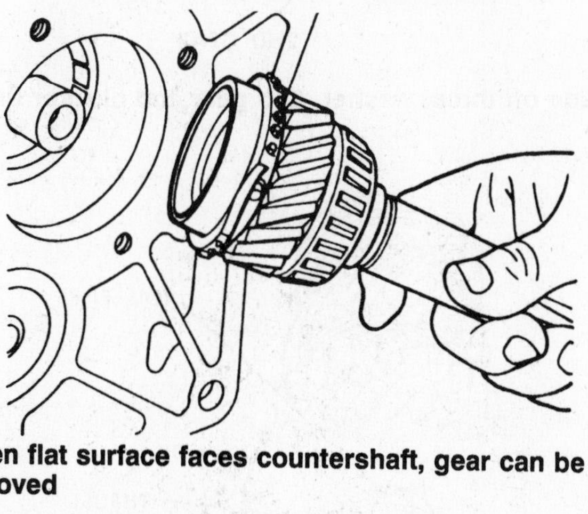
When flat surface faces countershaft, gear can be removed

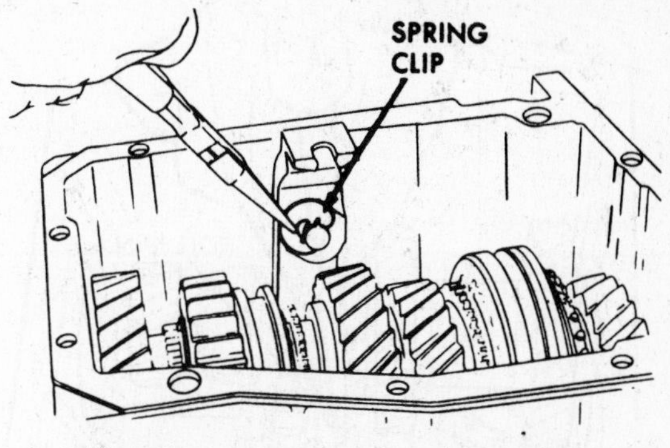
SPRING
CLIP
Remove reverse lever spring clip

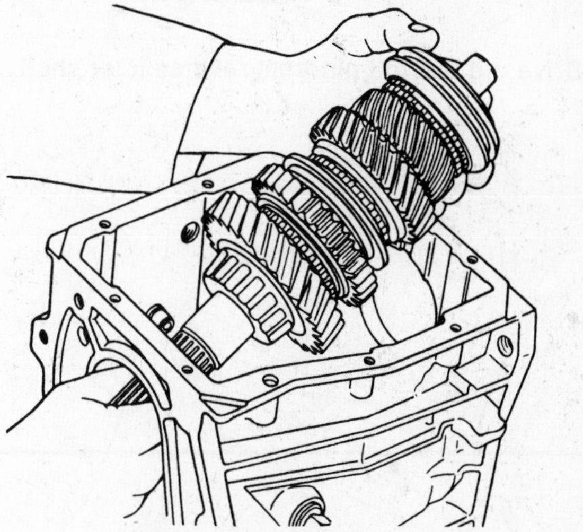
Lift out the main shaft

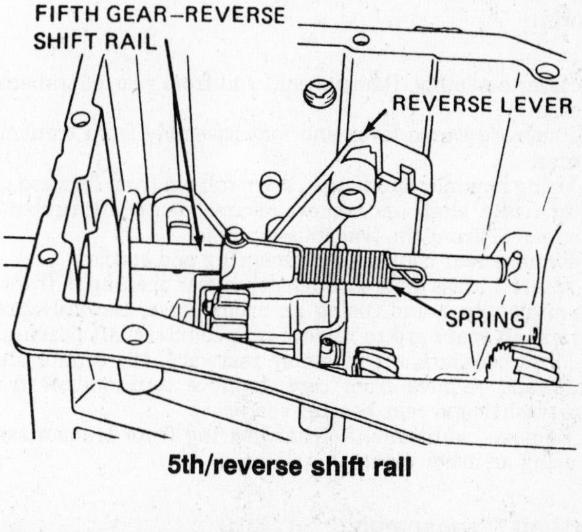
FIFTH GEAR–REVERSE
SHIFT RAIL
REVERSE LEVER
SPRING
5th/reverse shift rail

9. Remove 5th synchronizer gear snapring, shift fork, 5th gear synchronizer sleeve, blocking ring and 5th speed drive gear from rear of countershaft.
10. Remove snapring from 5th speed driven gear.
11. Using a hammer and punch, mark both bearing cap and case for assembly reference.
12. Remove front bearing cap bolts and remove front bearing cap. Remove front bearing race and endplay shims from front bearing cap.
13. Rotate drive gear until flat surface faces counter shaft and remove drive gear from transmission case.
14. Remove reverse lever C-clip and pivot bolt.
15. Remove mainshaft rear bearing race and then tilt mainshaft assembly upward and remove assembly from transmission case.
16. Unhook overcenter link spring from front of transmission case.
17. Rotate 5th gear/reverse shift rail to disengage rail from re-

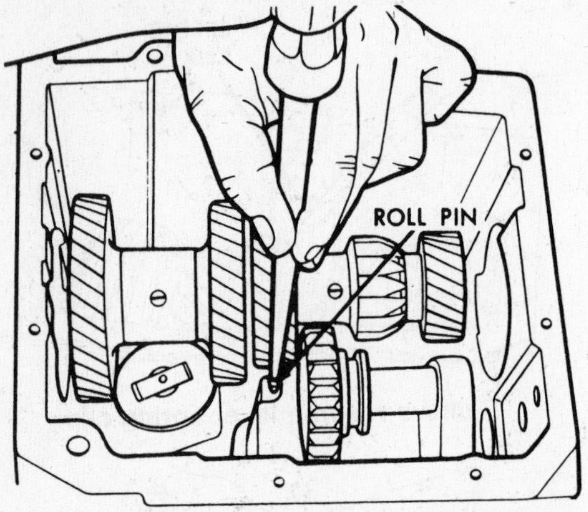
ROLL PIN

Drive out the roll pin from reverse idler shaft

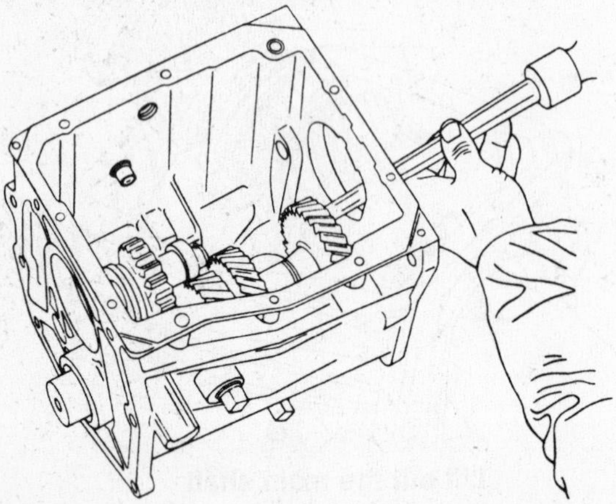

The countershaft is pressed out to remove the rear bearing

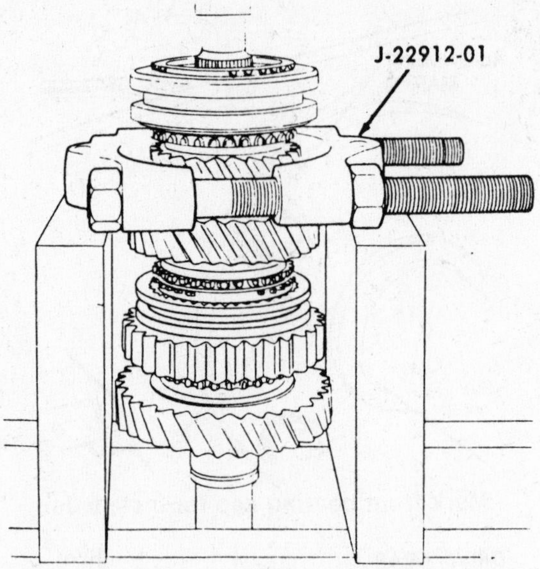
J-22912-01

Removing 3rd/4th synchronizer with a press

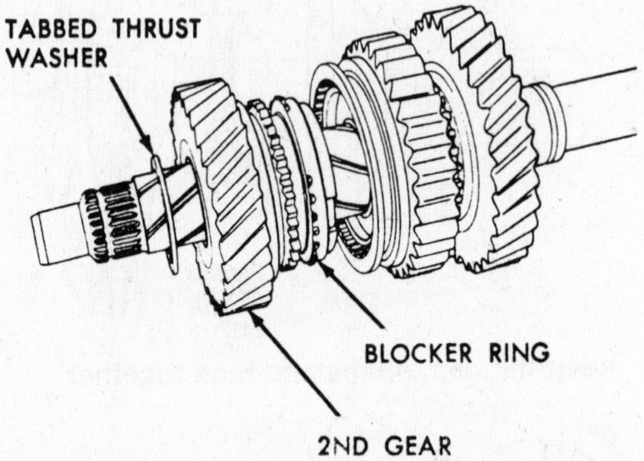
TABBED THRUST
WASHER
BLOCKER RING
2ND GEAR

Slide off thrust washer, 2nd gear and blocker ring

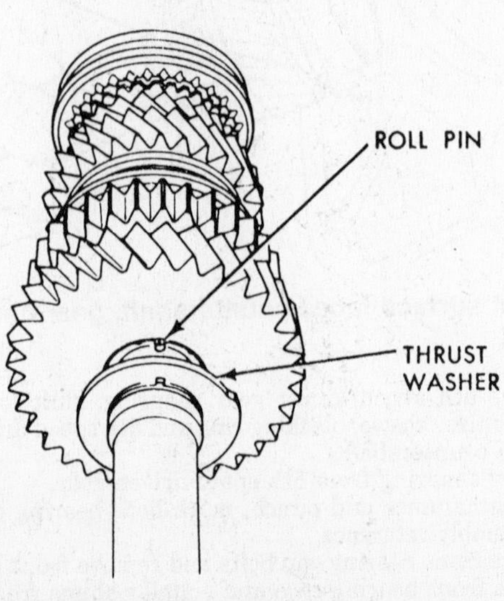
ROLL PIN
THRUST
WASHER

First gear thrust washer and roll pin

verse lever assembly. Remove shift rail from rear of transmission case.

18. Remove reverse lever and fork assembly from transmission case.

19. Using hammer and punch, drive roll pin from forward end of reverse idler shaft and remove reverse idler shaft, rubber O-ring and gear from the transmission case.

20. Remove rear countershaft snapring and spacer.

21. Insert a brass drift through drive gear opening in front of transmission case and, using an arbor press, carefully press countershaft rearward to remove rear countershaft bearing.

22. Move countershaft assembly rearward, tilt countershaft upward and remove from case. Remove countershaft front thrust washer and rear bearing spacer.

23. Remove countershaft front bearing from transmission case using an arbor press.

Mainshaft Disassembly

1. Remove thrust bearing washer from front end of mainshaft.
2. Scribe a reference mark on 3rd/4th synchronizer hub and sleeve for reassembly.
3. Remove 3rd/4th synchronizer blocking ring, sleeve, hub and 3rd gear as an assembly from mainshaft.
4. Remove snapring, tabbed thrust washer and 2nd gear from mainshaft.

5. Remove 5th gear with tool J-22912-01 or equivalent and arbor press. Slide rear bearing off mainshaft.
6. Remove 1st gear thrust washer, roll pin, 1st gear and synchronizer ring from mainshaft.
7. Scribe a reference mark on 1st/2nd synchronizer hub and sleeve for reassembly.
8. Remove synchronizer spring and keys from 1st/reverse sliding gear and remove gear from mainshaft hub. Do not attempt to remove the 1st/2nd reverse hub from mainshaft. The hub and shaft are assembled and machined as a matched set.

Mainshaft Assembly

1. Coat mainshaft and gear bores with transmission lubricant.
2. Install 1st/2nd synchronizer sleeve on mainshaft hub aligning marks made at disassembly.
3. Install 1st/2nd synchronizer keys and springs. Engage tang end of each spring in same synchronizer key but position open end of springs opposite of each other.
4. Install blocker ring and 2nd gear on mainshaft. Install tabbed thrust washer and 2nd gear retaining snapring on mainshaft. Be sure washer tab is properly seated in mainshaft notch.

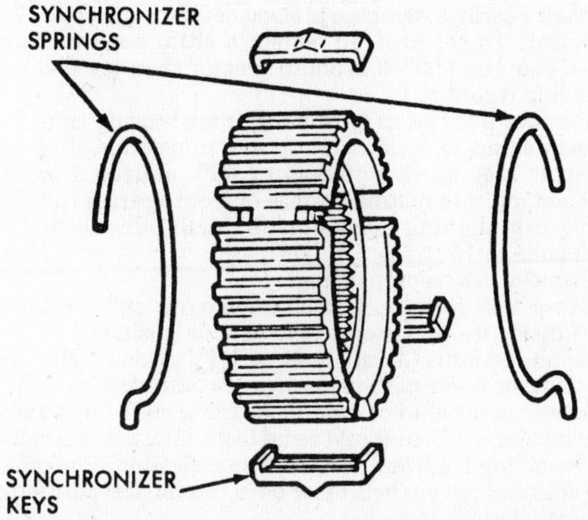
SYNCHRONIZER SPRINGS
SYNCHRONIZER KEYS

Install synchronizer spring tangs into the same key with the springs facing opposite directions

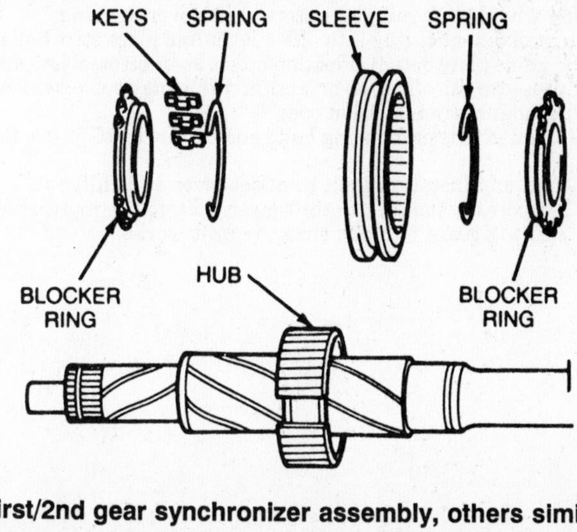
KEYS
SPRING
SLEEVE
SPRING
BLOCKER RING
HUB
BLOCKER RING

First/2nd gear synchronizer assembly, others similar

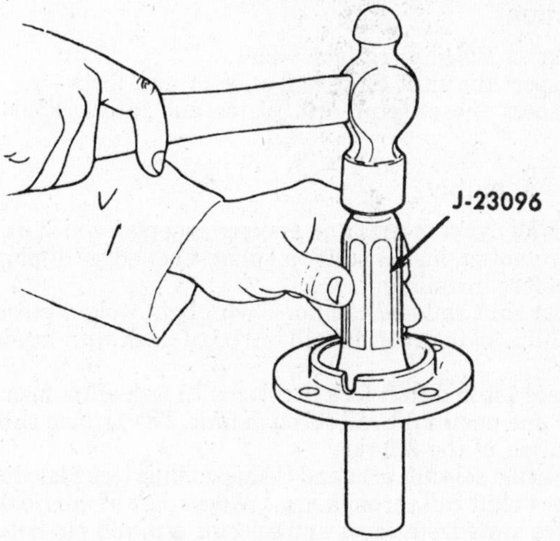
J-23096

Exploded view of transmission cover

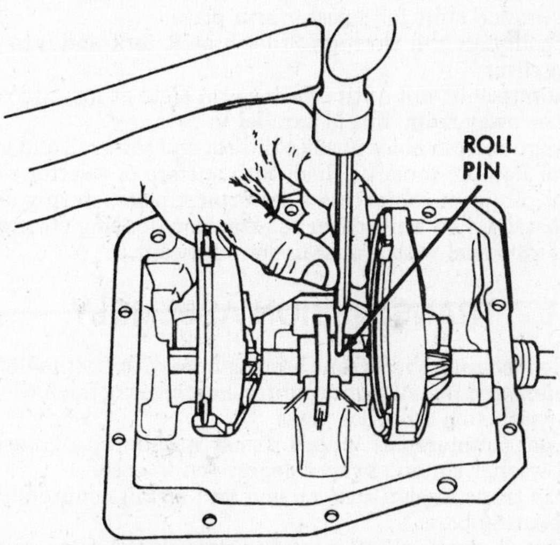
ROLL PIN

Remove selector arm roll pin

5. Install blocker ring and 1st gear on mainshaft. Install 1st gear roll pin and then 1st gear thrust washer.
6. Slide rear bearing on mainshaft.
7. Install 5th speed gear on mainshaft using tool J-22912-01 or equivalent and arbor press. Install snapring on mainshaft.
8. Install 3rd gear, 3rd/4th synchronizer assembly and thrust bearing on mainshaft. Synchronizer hub offset must face forward.

Transmission Cover Disassembly

1. Place selector arm plates and shift rail in neutral position (centered).
2. Rotate shift rail until selector arm disengages from selector arm plates and roll pin is accessible.
3. Remove selector arm roll pin using a pin punch and hammer.
4. Remove shift rail, shift forks, selector arm plates, selector arm, interlock plate and roll pin.
5. Remove shift cover to extension housing O-ring seal using a suitable tool.
6. Remove nylon inserts and selector arm plates from shift forks. Note position of inserts and plates for assembly reference.

Inspection

1. Inspect the shift rail for wear.
2. Inspect the shift forks and selector arm for wear.
3. Inspect the selector arm plates and interlock plate for wear.

Cover Assembly

1. Install nylon inserts and selector arm plates in shift forks.
2. If removed, install shift rail plug. Coat edges of plug with sealer before installing.
3. Coat shift rail and rail bores with light weight grease and insert shift rail in cover. Install rail until flush with inside edge of cover.
4. Place 1st/2nd shift fork in cover with fork offset facing rear of cover and push shift rail through fork. The 1st/2nd shift fork is the larger of the 2 forks.
5. Position selector arm and C-shaped interlock plate in cover and insert shift rail through arm. Widest part of interlock plate must face away from cover and selector arm roll pin hole must face downward and toward rear of cover.
6. Position 3rd/4th shift fork in cover with fork offset facing rear of cover. The 3rd/4th shift fork selector arm plate must be under 1st/2nd shift for selector arm plate.
7. Push shift rail through 3rd/4th shift fork and into front bore in cover.
8. Rotate shift rail until selector arm plate at forward end of rail faces away from, but is parallel to cover.
9. Align roll pin holes in selector arm and shift rail and install roll pin. Roll pin must be flush with surface of selector arm to prevent pin from contacting selector arm plates during shifts.
10. Install a new shift cover to extension housing O-ring seal. Coat O-ring seal with transmission lubricant.

TRANSMISSION ASSEMBLY

1. Coat countershaft front bearing bore with Loctite® 601, or equivalent and install front countershaft bearing flush with facing of case using an arbor press.
2. Coat countershaft tabbed thrust washer with grease and install washer so tab engages depression in case.
3. Tip transmission case on end and install countershaft in front bearing bore.
4. Install countershaft rear bearing spacer. Coat countershaft rear bearing with grease and install bearing using tool J-29895 or equivalent and sleeve J-33032, or its equivalent. The bearing when correctly installed will extend beyond the case surface 0.125 in. (3mm).
5. Position reverse idler gear in case with shift lever groove facing rear of case and install reverse idler shaft from rear of case. Install roll pin in idler shaft.
6. Install assembled mainshaft in transmission case. Install rear mainshaft bearing race in case.
7. Install drive gear in case and engage in 3rd/4th synchronizer sleeve and blocker ring.
8. Install front bearing race in front bearing cap. Do not install shims in front bearing cap at this time.
9. Temporarily install front bearing cap.
10. Install 5th speed/reverse lever, pivot bolt and retaining clip. Coat pivot bolt threads with non-hardening sealer and torque to 20 ft. lbs. (27 Nm). Be sure to engage reverse lever fork in reverse idler gear.
11. Install countershaft rear bearing spacer and retaining snapring.
12. Install 5th speed gear on countershaft.
13. Insert 5th speed/reverse rail in rear of case and install into reverse 5th speed lever. Rotate rail during installation to simplify engagement with lever. Connect spring to front of case.
14. Position 5th gear shift fork on 5th gear synchronizer assembly and install synchronizer on countershaft and shift fork on shift rail. Make sure roll pin hole in shift fork and shift rail are aligned.
15. Support 5th gear shift rail and fork on a block of wood and install roll pin.
16. Install thrust race against 5th speed synchronizer hub and install snapring. Install thrust bearing against race on countershaft. Coat both bearing and race with petroleum jelly.
17. Install lipped thrust race over needle-type thrust bearing and install plastic funnel into hole in end of countershaft gear.
18. Temporarily install extension housing and attaching bolts. Turn transmission case on end and mount a dial indicator on extension housing with indicator on the end of mainshaft.
19. Rotate mainshaft and zero the dial indicator. Pull upward on mainshaft until endplay is removed and record reading. Mainshaft bearings require a preload of 0.001–0.005 in. (0.025–0.125mm). To set preload, select a shim pack measuring 0.001–0.005 in. (0.025–0.125mm) greater than the dial indicator reading recorded.
20. Remove front bearing cap and front bearing race. Install necessary shims to obtain preload and reinstall bearing race.
21. Apply a ⅛ in. (3mm) bead of RTV sealant, No. 732 or equivalent, on case mating surface of front bearing cap. Install bearing cap aligning marks made during disassembly and torque bolts to 15 ft. lbs. (20 Nm).
22. Remove extension housing.
23. Move shift forks on transmission cover and synchronizer sleeves inside transmission to the neutral position.
24. Apply a ⅛ in. (3mm) bead of RTV sealant, No. 732 or equivalent, or cover mating surface of transmission.
25. Lower cover onto case while aligning shift forks and synchronizer sleeves. Center cover and install the 2 dowel bolts. Install remaining bolts and torque to specification. The offset lever to shift rail roll pin hole must be in the vertical position after cover installation.
26. Apply a ⅛ in. (3mm) bead of RTV sealant, No. 732 or equivalent, on extension housing to transmission case mating surface.
27. Install extension housing over mainshaft and shift rail to a position where shift rail just enters shift cover opening.
28. Install detent spring into offset lever and place steel ball in neutral guide plate detent. Position offset lever on steel ball and apply pressure on offset lever and at the time seat extension housing against transmission case.
29. Install extension housing bolts and torque to 25 ft. lbs. (30 Nm).
30. Align and install roll pin in offset lever and shift rail.
31. Temporarily install the shift lever. Rotate the input shaft while shifting gears to make sure the unit works.

Troubleshooting Basic Clutch Problems

Problem	Cause
Excessive clutch noise	Throwout bearing noises are more audible at the lower end of pedal travel. The usual causes are: • Riding the clutch • Too little pedal free-play • Lack of bearing lubrication A bad clutch shaft pilot bearing will make a high pitched squeal, when the clutch is disengaged and the transmission is in gear or within the first 2" of pedal travel. The bearing must be replaced. Noise from the clutch linkage is a clicking or snapping that can be heard or felt as the pedal is moved completely up or down. This usually requires lubrication. Transmitted engine noises are amplified by the clutch housing and heard in the passenger compartment. They are usually the result of insufficient pedal free-play and can be changed by manipulating the clutch pedal.
Clutch slips (the car does not move as it should when the clutch is engaged)	This is usually most noticeable when pulling away from a standing start. A severe test is to start the engine, apply the brakes, shift into high gear and SLOWLY release the clutch pedal. A healthy clutch will stall the engine. If it slips it may be due to: • A worn pressure plate or clutch plate • Oil soaked clutch plate • Insufficient pedal free-play
Clutch drags or fails to release	The clutch disc and some transmission gears spin briefly after clutch disengagement. Under normal conditions in average temperatures, 3 seconds is maximum spin-time. Failure to release properly can be caused by: • Too light transmission lubricant or low lubricant level • Improperly adjusted clutch linkage
Low clutch life	Low clutch life is usually a result of poor driving habits or heavy duty use. Riding the clutch, pulling heavy loads, holding the car on a grade with the clutch instead of the brakes and rapid clutch engagement all contribute to low clutch life.

CLUTCH

The 1984–91 trucks use a hydraulic clutch system which consists of a master and a slave cylinder. When pressure is applied to the clutch pedal (pedal depressed), the push rod contacts the plunger and pushes it up the bore of the master cylinder. In the first $\frac{1}{32}$ in. (0.8mm) of movement, the center valve seal closes the port to the fluid reservoir tank and as the plunger continues to move up the bore of the cylinder, the fluid is forced through the outlet line to the slave cylinder mounted on the clutch housing. As fluid is pushed down the pipe from the master cylinder, this in turn forces the piston in the slave cylinder outward. A push rod is connected to the slave cylinder and rides in the pocket of the clutch fork. As the slave cylinder piston moves rearward the push rod forces the clutch fork and the release bearing to disengage the pressure plate from the clutch disc. On the return stroke (pedal released), the plunger moves back as a result of the return pressure of the clutch. Fluid returns to the master cylinder and the final movement of the plunger lifts the valve seal off the seat, allowing an unrestricted flow of fluid between the system and the reservoir.

A piston return spring in the slave cylinder preloads the clutch linkage and assures contact of the release bearing with the clutch release fingers at all times. As the driven disc wears, the diaphragm spring fingers move rearward forcing the release bearing, fork and push rod to move. This movement forces the slave cylinder piston forward in its bore, displacing hydraulic fluid up into the master cylinder reservoir, thereby providing the self-adjusting feature of the hydraulic clutch linkage system.

Before attempting to repair the clutch, transmission, hydraulic system or related linkages for any reason other than an obvious failure, the problem and probable cause should be identified. A large percentage of clutch and manual transmission problems are manifested by shifting difficulties such as high shift effort, gear clash and grinding or transmission blockout. When any of these problems occur, a careful analysis of these difficulties should be made, then the basic checks and adjustments performed before removing the clutch or transmission for repairs. Run the engine at a normal idle with the transmis-

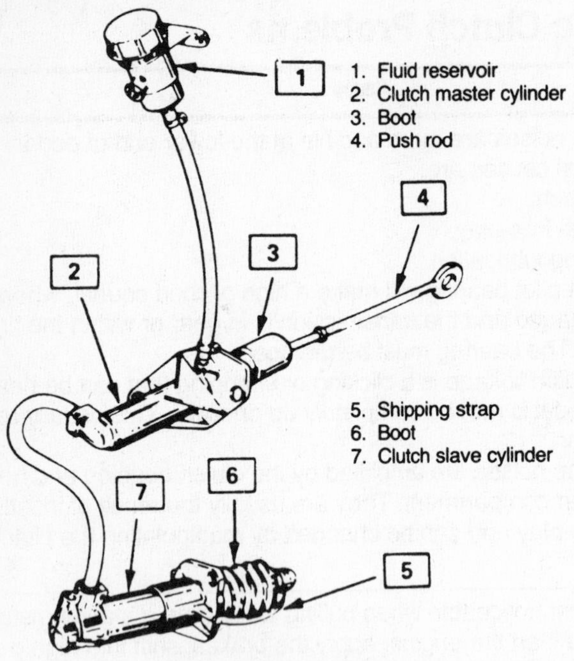
1
2
3
4
5
6
7
1. Fluid reservoir
2. Clutch master cylinder
3. Boot
4. Push rod
5. Shipping strap
6. Boot
7. Clutch slave cylinder

Hydraulic clutch system

sion in Neutral (clutch engaged). Disengage the clutch, wait about 10 seconds and shift the transmission into Reverse (no grinding noise should be heard). A grinding noise indicates incorrect clutch travel, lost motion, clutch misalignment or internal problems such as failed dampers, facings, cushion springs, diaphragm spring fingers, pressure plate drive straps, pivot rings or etc.

Adjustment

Since the hydraulic system provides automatic clutch adjustment, no adjustment of the clutch linkage or pedal height is required.

CLUTCH CABLE – 1982–83

1. Lift up on the pedal to allow the self adjuster to adjust the cable length.
2. Depress the pedal several times to set the pawl into mesh with the detent teeth.
3. Check the linkage for lost motion caused by loose or worn swivels, mounting brackets or a damaged cable.

Clutch Disc and Pressure Plate

REMOVAL AND INSTALLATION

CAUTION

The clutch plate contains asbestos, which has been determined to be a cancer causing agent. Never clean the clutch surfaces with compressed air! Avoid inhaling any dust from any clutch surface! When cleaning clutch surfaces, use a commercially available brake cleaning fluid.

1. Refer to the "Transmission, Removal and Installation" procedures in this section and remove the transmission.

NOTE: If equipped with a clutch cable (1982–83), disconnect the cable from the clutch lever and move it aside. If equipped with a hydraulic clutch system (1984–87), disconnect the slave cylinder from the clutch release fork and move it aside.

2. If the bellhousing was not removed with the transmission, remove it.

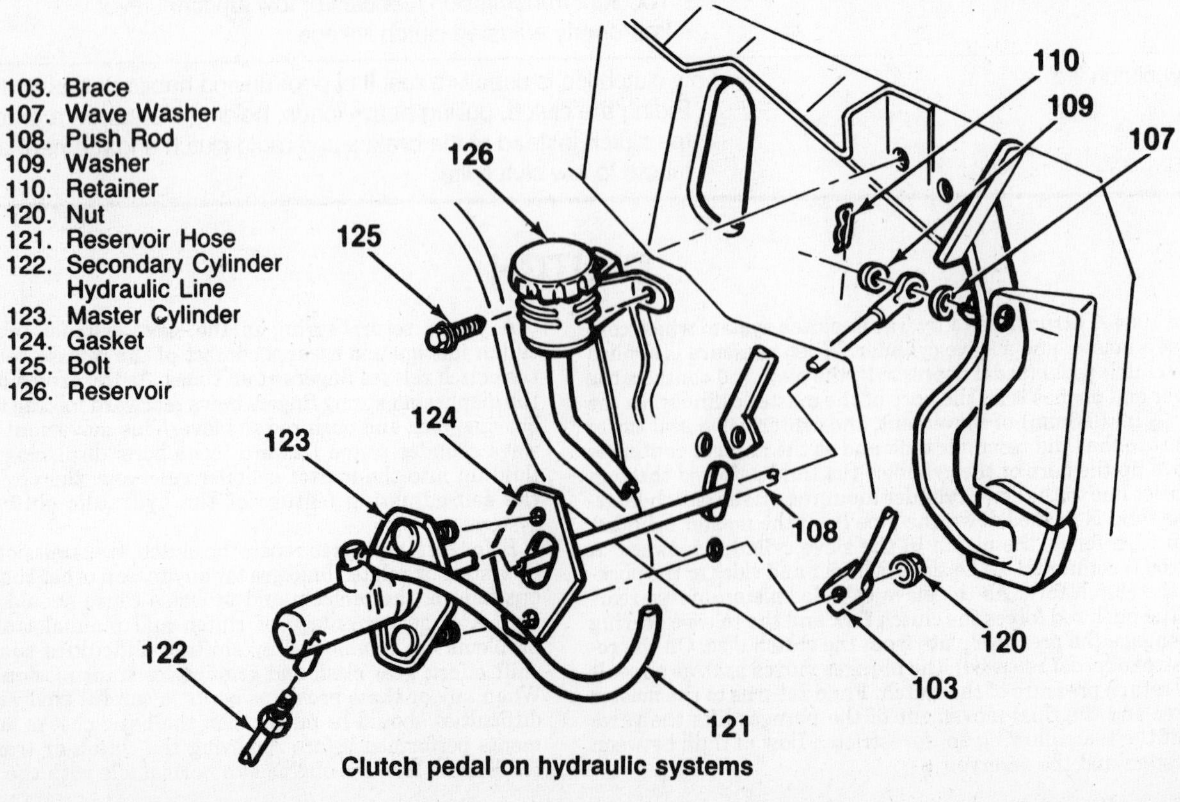
103. Brace
107. Wave Washer
108. Push Rod
109. Washer
110. Retainer
120. Nut
121. Reservoir Hose
122. Secondary Cylinder Hydraulic Line
123. Master Cylinder
124. Gasket
125. Bolt
126. Reservoir
110
109
107
126
125
124
123
108
120
122
103
121

Clutch pedal on hydraulic systems

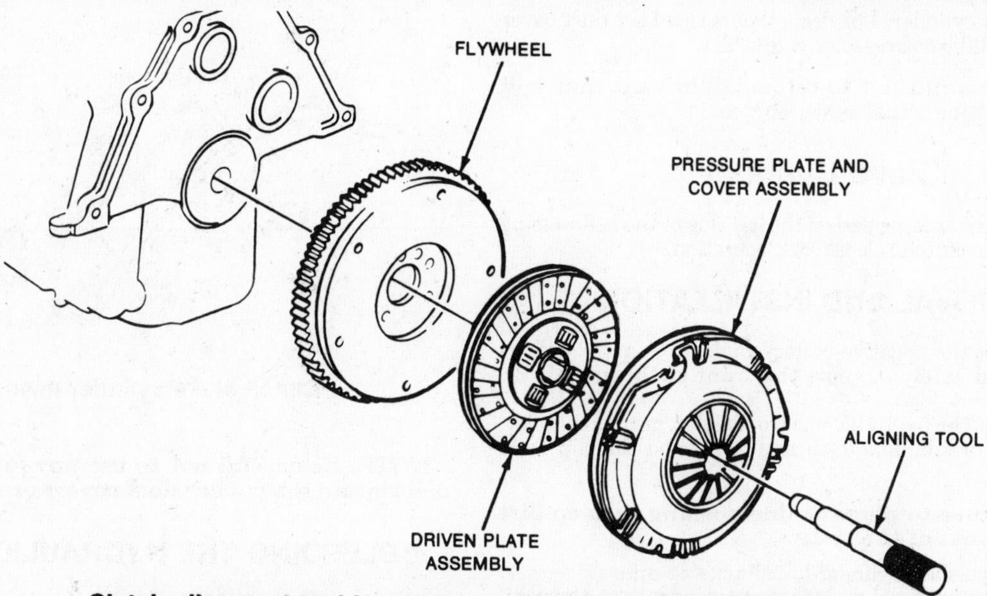
FLYWHEEL
PRESSURE PLATE AND COVER ASSEMBLY
ALIGNING TOOL
DRIVEN PLATE ASSEMBLY

Clutch alignment tool is required to install the clutch assembly

3. Remove the clutch fork from the ball stud and the dust boot.
4. Using the Clutch Alignment tool No. J-33169 (V6) or J-33034 (4-cyl), insert it into the crankshaft pilot bearing to support the clutch assembly.
5. Check for an "X" or other painted mark on the pressure plate and flywheel. If there isn't a mark, mark the assembly for installation purposes.
6. Loosen the pressure plate-to-flywheel bolts, evenly and alternately, a little at a time, until the spring tension is released. Remove the pressure plate and the driven clutch plate.
7. Check the flywheel for cracks, wear, scoring or other damage. Check the pilot bearing for wear. Replace it by removing it with a slide-type bearing puller and driving in a new one with a wood or plastic hammer.
8. To install, use the clutch assembly alignment tool and reverse the removal procedures. The raised hub of the driven plate faces the transmission. Align the mating marks and torque the pressure plate-to-flywheel bolts (evenly and alternately) to 20 ft. lbs.

NOTE: If equipped with a clutch cable (1982–83), install and/or adjust the clutch cable.

Master Cylinder

The clutch master cylinder is located in the engine compartment, on the left-side of the firewall, above the steering column.

REMOVAL AND INSTALLATION

1. Disconnect negative battery terminal from the battery.
2. Remove hush panel from under the dash.
3. Disconnect push rod from clutch pedal.
4. Disconnect hydraulic line from the clutch master cylinder.
5. Remove the master cylinder-to-cowl brace nuts. Remove master cylinder and overhaul (if necessary).
6. Using a putty knife, clean the master cylinder and cowl mounting surfaces.
7. To install, reverse the removal procedures. Torque the master cylinder-to-cowl brace nuts to 10–15 ft. lbs. (14–20 Nm). Fill master cylinder with new hydraulic fluid conforming to DOT 3 specifications. Bleed and check the hydraulic clutch system for leaks.

OVERHAUL

1. Remove the filler cap and drain fluid from the master cylinder.
2. Remove the reservoir and seal from the master cylinder. Pull back the dust cover and remove the snapring.
3. Remove the push rod assembly. Using a block of wood, tap the master cylinder on it to eject the plunger assembly from the cylinder bore.
4. Remove the seal (carefully) from the front of the plunger assembly, ensuring no damage occurs to the plunger surfaces.
5. From the rear of the plunger assembly, remove the spring, the support, the seal and the shim.
6. Using clean brake fluid, clean all of the parts.
7. Inspect the cylinder bore and the plunger for ridges, pitting and/or scratches, the dust cover for wear and cracking; replace the parts if any of the conditions exist.
8. To install, use new seals, lubricate all of the parts in clean brake fluid, fit the plunger seal to the plunger and reverse the removal procedures.
9. Insert the plunger assembly, valve end leading into the cylinder bore (easing the entrance of the plunger seal).
10. Position the push rod assembly into the cylinder bore, then install a new snapring to retain the push rod. Install dust cover

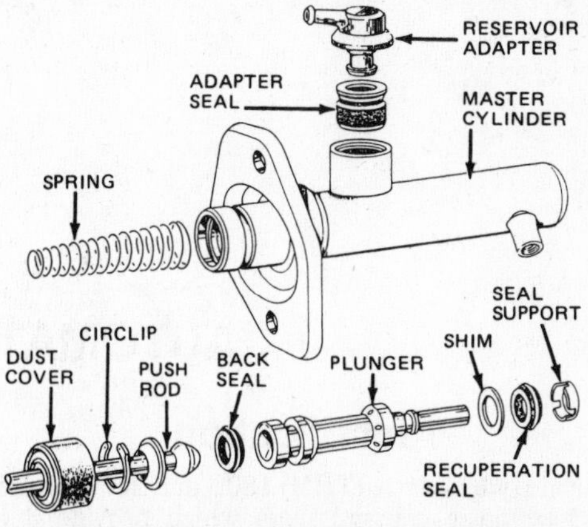
RESERVOIR ADAPTER
ADAPTER SEAL
MASTER CYLINDER
SPRING
SEAL SUPPORT
SHIM
CIRCLIP
DUST COVER
PUSH ROD
BACK SEAL
PLUNGER
RECUPERATION SEAL

Clutch master cylinder assembly

onto the master cylinder. Lubricate the inside of the dust cover with Girling® Rubber Grease or equivalent.

NOTE: Be careful not to use any lubricant that will deteriorate rubber dust covers or seals.

Slave Cylinder

The slave cylinder is located on the left side of the bellhousing and controls the clutch release fork operation.

REMOVAL AND INSTALLATION

1. Disconnect the negative battery cable.
2. Raise and safely support the front of the vehicle on jackstands.
3. Disconnect the hydraulic line from clutch master cylinder. Remove the hydraulic line-to-chassis screw and the clip from the chassis.

NOTE: Be sure to plug the line opening to keep dirt and moisture out of the system.

4. Remove the slave cylinder-to-bellhousing nuts.
5. Remove the push rod and the slave cylinder from the vehicle, then overhaul it (if necessary).
6. To install, reverse the removal procedures. Lubricate leading end of the slave cylinder with Girling® Rubber Lube or equivalent. Torque the slave cylinder-to-bellhousing nuts to 10–15 ft. lbs. (14–20 Nm). Fill the master cylinder with new brake fluid conforming to DOT 3 specifications. Bleed the hydraulic system.

OVERHAUL

1. Remove the shield, the pushrod and dust cover from the slave cylinder, then inspect the cover for damage or deterioration.
2. Remove the snapring from the end of the cylinder bore.
3. Using a block of wood, tap the slave cylinder on it to eject the plunger, then remove the seal and the spring.
4. Using clean brake fluid, clean all of the parts.
5. Inspect the cylinder bore and the plunger for ridges, pitting and/or scratches, the dust cover for wear and cracking; replace the parts if any of the conditions exist.
6. To install, use new seals and lubricate all of the parts in clean brake fluid. Install the spring, the plunger seal and the plunger into the cylinder bore, then install a new snapring.
7. Lubricate the inside of the dust cover with Girling® Rubber Grease or equivalent, then install it into the slave cylinder.

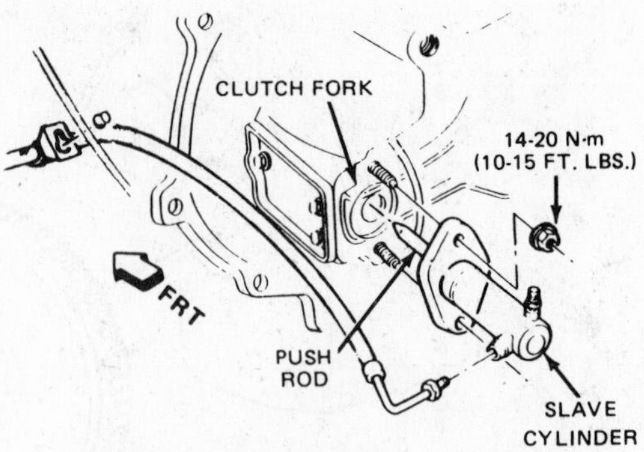
CLUTCH FORK
14-20 N·m
(10-15 FT. LBS.)
FRT
PUSH
ROD
SLAVE
CYLINDER

Clutch slave cylinder assembly

NOTE: Be careful not to use any lubricant that will deteriorate the rubber dust covers or seals.

BLEEDING THE HYDRAULIC CLUTCH

Bleeding air from the hydraulic clutch system is necessary whenever any part of the system has been disconnected or the fluid level (in the reservoir) has been allowed to fall so low, that air has been drawn into the master cylinder.

1. Fill master cylinder reservoir with new brake fluid conforming to Dot 3 specifications.

CAUTION

Never, under any circumstances, use fluid which has been bled from a system to fill the reservoir as it may be aerated, have too much moisture content and possibly be contaminated.

2. Raise and safely support the front of the vehicle on jackstands.
3. Remove the slave cylinder attaching bolts.
4. Hold slave cylinder at approximately 45° with the bleeder at highest point. Fully depress clutch pedal and open the bleeder screw.
5. Close the bleeder screw and release clutch pedal.
6. Repeat the procedure until all of the air is evacuated from the system. Check and refill master cylinder reservoir as required to prevent air from being drawn through the master cylinder.

NOTE: Never release a depressed clutch pedal with the bleeder screw open or air will be drawn into the system.

AUTOMATIC TRANSMISSION

Identification

The Turbo Hydra-Matic (THM) 180C and 200C transmission are fully automatic transmissions which provide 3 forward gears and a reverse gear.

The Turbo Hydra-Matic (THM) 700-R4 and 4L60 transmission is a fully automatic transmission which provides 4 forward gears and a reverse gear. The oil pressure and shifting points are controlled by the throttle opening, via a Throttle Valve (TV) cable.

Troubleshooting Basic Automatic Transmission Problems

Problem	Cause	Solution
Fluid leakage	• Defective pan gasket • Loose filler tube • Loose extension housing to transmission case • Converter housing area leakage	• Replace gasket or tighten pan bolts • Tighten tube nut • Tighten bolts • Have transmission checked professionally
Fluid flows out the oil filler tube	• High fluid level • Breather vent clogged • Clogged oil filter or screen • Internal fluid leakage	• Check and correct fluid level • Open breather vent • Replace filter or clean screen (change fluid also) • Have transmission checked professionally
Transmission overheats (this is usually accompanied by a strong burned odor to the fluid)	• Low fluid level • Fluid cooler lines clogged • Heavy pulling or hauling with insufficient cooling • Faulty oil pump, internal slippage	• Check and correct fluid level • Drain and refill transmission. If this doesn't cure the problem, have cooler lines cleared or replaced. • Install a transmission oil cooler • Have transmission checked professionally
Buzzing or whining noise	• Low fluid level • Defective torque converter, scored gears	• Check and correct fluid level • Have transmission checked professionally
No forward or reverse gears or slippage in one or more gears	• Low fluid level • Defective vacuum or linkage controls, internal clutch or band failure	• Check and correct fluid level • Have unit checked professionally
Delayed or erratic shift	• Low fluid level • Broken vacuum lines • Internal malfunction	• Check and correct fluid level • Repair or replace lines • Have transmission checked professionally

Lockup Torque Converter Service Diagnosis

Problem	Cause	Solution
No lockup	• Faulty oil pump • Sticking governor valve • Valve body malfunction (a) Stuck switch valve (b) Stuck lockup valve (c) Stuck fail-safe valve • Failed locking clutch • Leaking turbine hub seal • Faulty input shaft or seal ring	• Replace oil pump • Repair or replace as necessary • Repair or replace valve body or its internal components as necessary • Replace torque converter • Replace torque converter • Repair or replace as necessary

Lockup Torque Converter Service Diagnosis

Problem	Cause	Solution
Will not unlock	· Sticking governor valve · Valve body malfunction (a) Stuck switch valve (b) Stuck lockup valve (c) Stuck fail-safe valve	· Repair or replace as necessary · Repair or replace valve body or its internal components as necessary
Stays locked up at too low a speed in direct	· Sticking governor valve · Valve body malfunction (a) Stuck switch valve (b) Stuck lockup valve (c) Stuck fail-safe valve	· Repair or replace as necessary · Repair or replace valve body or its internal components as necessary
Locks up or drags in low or second	· Faulty oil pump · Valve body malfunction (a) Stuck switch valve (b) Stuck fail-safe valve	· Replace oil pump · Repair or replace valve body or its internal components as necessary
Sluggish or stalls in reverse	· Faulty oil pump · Plugged cooler, cooler lines or fittings · Valve body malfunction (a) Stuck switch valve (b) Faulty input shaft or seal ring	· Replace oil pump as necessary · Flush or replace cooler and flush lines and fittings · Repair or replace valve body or its internal components as necessary
Loud chatter during lockup engagement (cold)	· Faulty torque converter · Failed locking clutch · Leaking turbine hub seal	· Replace torque converter · Replace torque converter · Replace torque converter
Vibration or shudder during lockup engagement	· Faulty oil pump · Valve body malfunction · Faulty torque converter · Engine needs tune-up	· Repair or replace oil pump as necessary · Repair or replace valve body or its internal components as necessary · Replace torque converter · Tune engine
Vibration after lockup engagement	· Faulty torque converter · Exhaust system strikes underbody · Engine needs tune-up · Throttle linkage misadjusted	· Replace torque converter · Align exhaust system · Tune engine · Adjust throttle linkage
Vibration when revved in neutral	· Torque converter out of balance	· Replace torque converter
Overheating: oil blows out of dip stick tube or pump seal	· Plugged cooler, cooler lines or fittings · Stuck switch valve	· Flush or replace cooler and flush lines and fittings · Repair switch valve in valve body or replace valve body

Lockup Torque Converter Service Diagnosis

Problem	Cause	Solution
Shudder after lockup engagement	• Faulty oil pump	• Replace oil pump
	• Plugged cooler, cooler lines or fittings	• Flush or replace cooler and flush lines and fittings
	• Valve body malfunction	• Repair or replace valve body or its internal components as necessary
	• Faulty torque converter	• Replace torque converter
	• Fail locking clutch	• Replace torque converter
	• Exhaust system strikes underbody	• Align exhaust system
	• Engine needs tune-up	• Tune engine
	• Throttle linkage misadjusted	• Adjust throttle linkage

Transmission Fluid Indications

The appearance and odor of the transmission fluid can give valuable clues to the overall condition of the transmission. Always note the appearance of the fluid when you check the fluid level or change the fluid. Rub a small amount of fluid between your fingers to feel for grit and smell the fluid on the dipstick.

If the fluid appears:	It indicates:
Clear and red colored	• Normal operation
Discolored (extremely dark red or brownish) or smells burned	• Band or clutch pack failure, usually caused by an overheated transmission. Hauling very heavy loads with insufficient power or failure to change the fluid, often result in overheating. Do not confuse this appearance with newer fluids that have a darker red color and a strong odor (though not a burned odor).
Foamy or aerated (light in color and full of bubbles)	• The level is too high (gear train is churning oil) • An internal air leak (air is mixing with the fluid). Have the transmission checked professionally.
Solid residue in the fluid	• Defective bands, clutch pack or bearings. Bits of band material or metal abrasives are clinging to the dipstick. Have the transmission checked professionally.
Varnish coating on the dipstick	• The transmission fluid is overheating

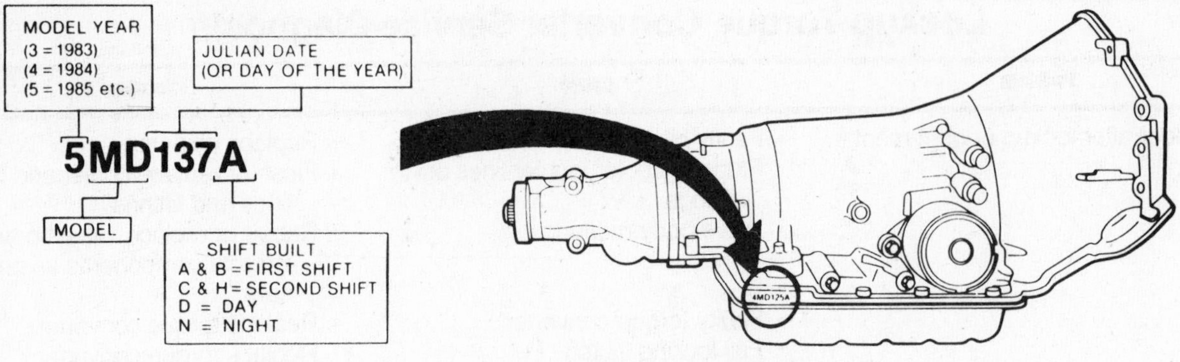
MODEL YEAR
(3 = 1983)
(4 = 1984)
(5 = 1985 etc.)
JULIAN DATE
(OR DAY OF THE YEAR)
5MD137A
MODEL
SHIFT BUILT
A & B = FIRST SHIFT
C & H = SECOND SHIFT
D = DAY
N = NIGHT

Four speed automatic transmission

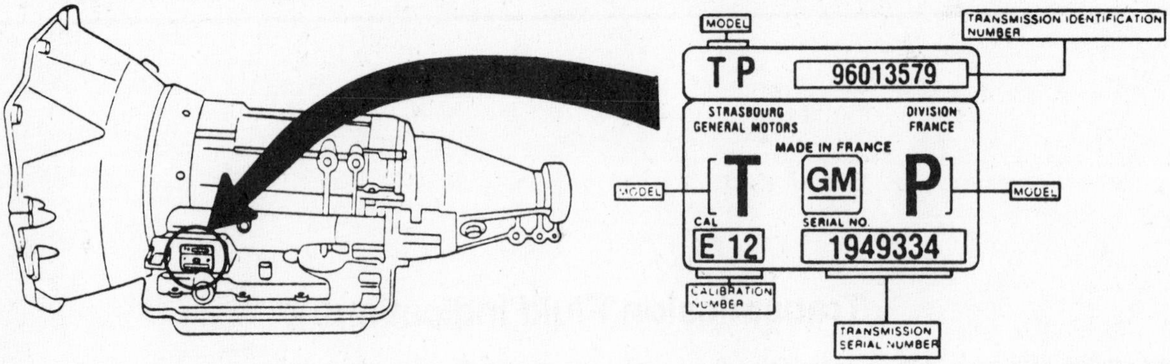
MODEL
TRANSMISSION IDENTIFICATION NUMBER
T P
96013579
STRASBOURG
GENERAL MOTORS
DIVISION
FRANCE
MADE IN FRANCE
MODEL
T
GM
P
MODEL
CAL
SERIAL NO.
E 12
1949334
CALIBRATION NUMBER
TRANSMISSION SERIAL NUMBER

Three speed automatic transmission

Fluid Pan

REMOVAL AND INSTALLATION

NOTE: The fluid should be drained when the transmission is warm.

1. Raise and safely support the front of the vehicle with jackstands.
2. Place a drain catch pan under the transmission oil pan.
3. Remove the pan bolts from the front and sides of the pan, then loosen the rear bolts 4 turns.
4. Using a small pry bar, pry the oil pan loose and allow the pan to partially drain. Remove the remaining pan bolts and carefully lower the pan away from the transmission.

NOTE: If the transmission fluid is dark or has a burnt smell, transmission damage is indicated. Have the transmission checked professionally.

CAUTION

If the pan sticks, carefully tap sideways on the pan with a rubber or plastic mallet to break it loose; DO NOT dent the pan.

5. Empty and wash the pan in solvent, then blow dry with compressed air.
6. Using a putty knife, clean the gasket mounting surfaces.
7. To install, use a new filter, a new gasket and reverse the removal procedures. Torque the pan-to-transmission bolts to 12–14 ft. lbs. (in a criss-cross pattern). Recheck the bolt torque after all of the bolts have been tightened once. Add Dexron®II automatic transmission fluid through the filler tube.

CAUTION

***DO NOT OVERFILL** the transmission; foaming of the fluid and subsequent transmission damage due to slippage will result.*

8. With the gear selector lever in the Park position, start the engine and let it idle; DO NOT race the engine.
9. Move the gear selector lever through each position, holding the brakes. Return the lever to Park and check the fluid level with the engine idling. The level should be between the two dimples on the dipstick, about ¼ in. (6mm) below the ADD mark. Add fluid, if necessary.
10. Check the fluid level after the vehicle has been driven enough to thoroughly warm the transmission. Details are given

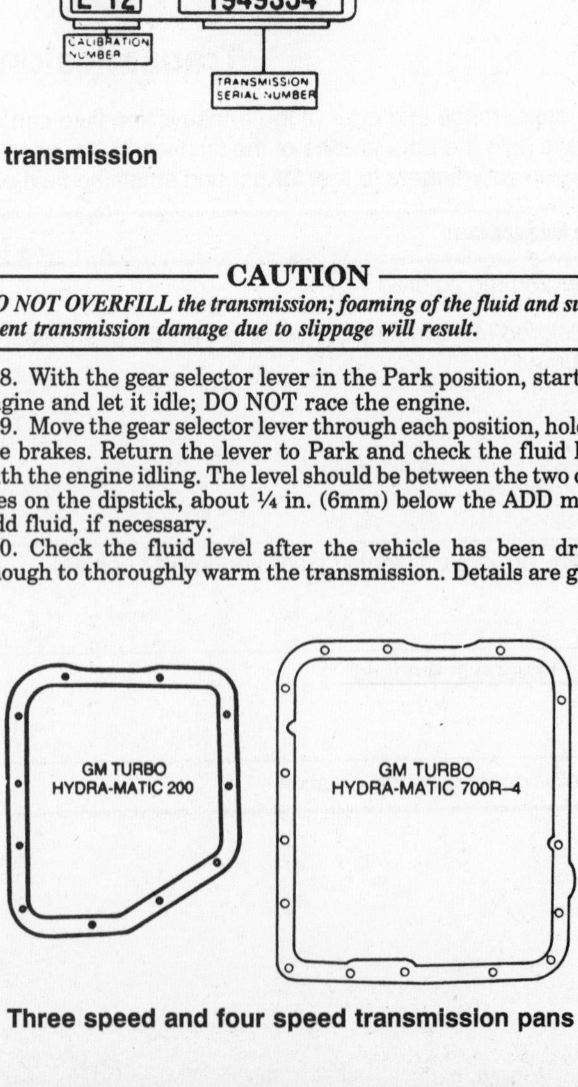
GM TURBO
HYDRA-MATIC 200
GM TURBO
HYDRA-MATIC 700R–4

Three speed and four speed transmission pans

under "Fluid Level Checks" earlier in Chapter 1. If the transmission is overfilled, the excess must be drained off. Use a suction pump, if necessary.

FILTER SERVICE

1. Refer to the "Fluid Pan, Removal and Installation" procedures in this section and remove the fluid pan.
2. Remove the transmission filter screws or clips and the filter from the valve body. The filter may have either a fibrous or screen filtering element and is retained by one or two fasteners.

NOTE: If the transmission uses a filter having a fully exposed screen, it may be cleaned and reused.

3. To install, use a new filter, a new gasket and reverse the removal procedures. Torque the pan-to-transmission bolts to 12–14 ft. lbs. (in a criss-cross pattern). Recheck the bolt torque after all of the bolts have been tightened once. Add Dexron®II automatic transmission fluid through the filler tube.

Adjustments

SHIFT LINKAGE

The shift linkage should be adjusted so that the engine will start when the transmission is in the Park and Neutral positions only.

1. Firmly apply the parking brake and chock the rear wheels.
2. Raise and safely support the front of the vehicle on jackstands.
3. At the left-side of the transmission, loosen the shift rod swivel-to-equalizer lever nut.
4. Rotate the transmission shift lever clockwise (forward) to the last detent (Park) position, then turn it counterclockwise (rearward) to the rear of the 2nd detent (Neutral) position.
5. At the steering column, place the gear selector lever into the Neutral position.

NOTE: When positioning the gear selector lever, DO NOT use the steering column indicator to find the Neutral position.

6. Tightly, hold the shifting rod (swivel) against the equalizer lever, then torque the adjusting nut to 11 ft. lbs.
7. Using the gear selector lever (on the steering column), place it in the Park position and check the adjustment. Move the gear selector lever into the various positions; the engine must start in the Park and the Neutral positions.

NOTE: If the engine will not start in the Neutral and/or Park positions, refer to Back-Up Light Switch adjustment procedures in Chapter 5 and adjust the switch.

CAUTION

With the gear selector lever in the Park position, the parking pawl should engage the rear internal gear lugs or output ring gear lugs to prevent the vehicle from rolling and causing personal injury.

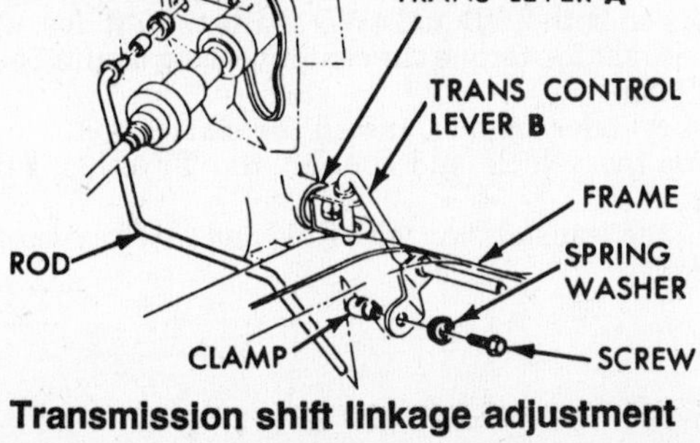
TRANS LEVER A
TRANS CONTROL LEVER B
FRAME
ROD
SPRING WASHER
CLAMP
SCREW

Transmission shift linkage adjustment

8. Align the gear selector lever indicator, if necessary. Lower the vehicle and release the parking brake.

THROTTLE VALVE (TV) CABLE

If the TV cable is broken, sticking, misadjusted or using an incorrect part for the model, the vehicle may exhibit various malfunctions, such as: delayed or full throttle shifts.

Preliminary Checks

1. Inspect and/or correct the transmission fluid level.
2. Make sure that the brakes are not dragging and that the engine is operating correctly.
3. Make sure that the cable is connected at both ends.
4. Make sure that the correct cable is installed.

Adjustment

1. If necessary, remove the air cleaner.
2. If the cable has been removed and installed, check to see that the cable slider is in the zero or the fully adjusted position; if not, perform the following procedures:
   a. Depress and hold the readjust tab.
   b. Move the slider back through the fitting (away from the throttle lever) until it stops against the fitting.
   c. Release the readjust tab.
3. Rotate the throttle lever to the Full Throttle Stop position to obtain a minimum of 1 click.
4. Release the throttle lever.

Neutral Safety Switch

The Neutral Safety Switch is a part of the Back-Up Light Switch. For the replacement or adjustment procedures, refer to the "Back-Up Light Switch, Removal and Installation" procedures in Section 6, Chassis Electrical.

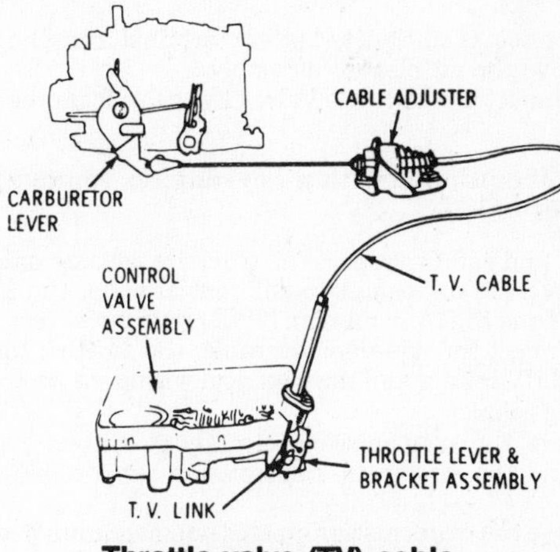
CABLE ADJUSTER
CARBURETOR LEVER
CONTROL VALVE ASSEMBLY
T. V. CABLE
THROTTLE LEVER & BRACKET ASSEMBLY
T. V. LINK

Throttle valve (TV) cable

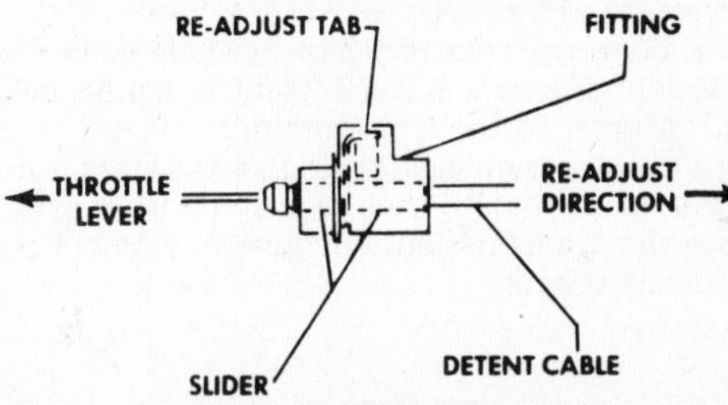
RE-ADJUST TAB
FITTING
THROTTLE LEVER
RE-ADJUST DIRECTION
DETENT CABLE
SLIDER

TV cable adjustment

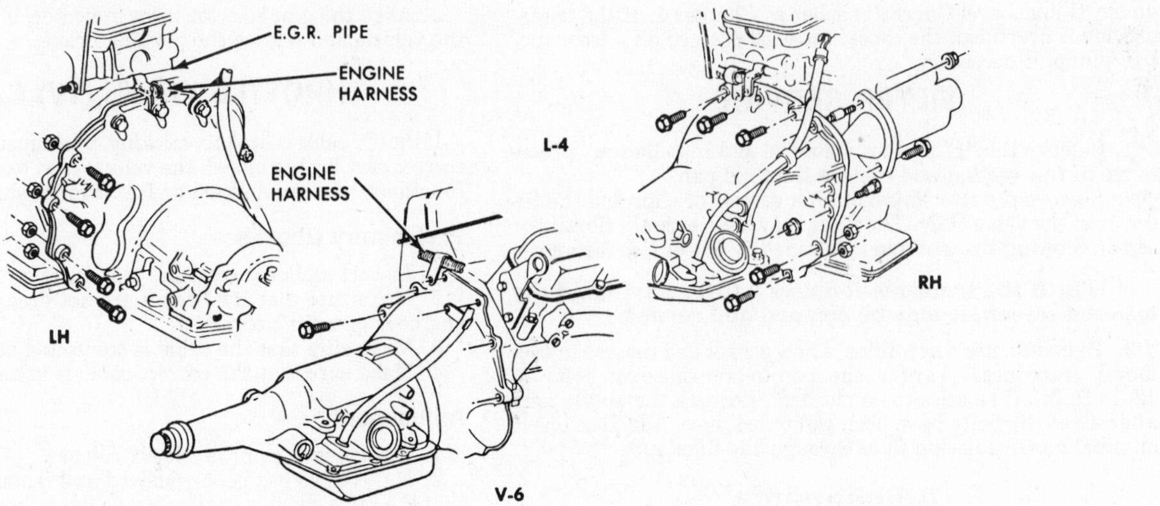
E.G.R. PIPE
ENGINE HARNESS
ENGINE HARNESS
L-4
LH
RH
V-6
Removal of automatic transmission

Back-Up Light Switch

NOTE: The back-up light switch is located on the steering column. To replace the back-up light switch, refer to the "Back-Up Light Switch, Removal and Installation" procedures in Section 6, Chassis Electrical.

Transmission

REMOVAL AND INSTALLATION

NOTE: The following procedure requires the use of the Torque Converter Holding Strap tool No. J-21366 or equivalent.

1. Disconnect the negative battery terminal from the battery.
2. Remove the air cleaner assembly.
3. Disconnect the Throttle Valve (TV) cable from the throttle linkage.

NOTE: If equipped with a 4-cyl engine, remove the upper starter bolt.

4. Raise and safely support the truck on jackstands.
5. Remove the driveshaft-to-differential bolts, the slide the driveshaft from the transmission (2WD) or transfer case (4WD).
6. Disconnect the speedometer cable, the dipstick tube (and seal), the shift linkage and the electrical wiring connectors from the transmission.
7. Remove the transmission-to-catalytic converter support brackets and the engine–to–transmission support brackets, if equipped.
8. Remove the transmission-to-crossmember nuts/bolts, slide the crossmember rearward and remove it from the vehicle.
9. Remove the torque converter cover, then match-mark the torque converter-to-flywheel.
10. Remove the torque converter-to-flywheel bolts. Using the Converter Holding Strap tool No. J-21366 or equivalent, secure the torque converter to the transmission.
11. Using a transmission jack, position and secure it to the underside of the transmission, then to take up its weight.
12. Remove the transmission-to-engine mount bolts and the mounts from the vehicle.
13. Lower the transmission slightly to gain access to the fluid cooler lines, then disconnect and cap the fluid lines.
14. Disconnect the Throttle Valve (TV) cable from the transmission.
15. Position a floor jack or jackstand under the engine and support it.
16. Remove the transmission-to-engine bolts and then the transmission from the engine; pull the transmission rearward to disengage it and lower it from the truck.

NOTE: When removing the transmission, be careful not to allow the transmission to hang from the pilot shaft, for it could become bent.

To install:

17. Carefully position the transmission behind the engine and push it foreward to engage the pilot shaft.
18. Install the transmission–to–engine bolts. On 4–cylinder engines, torque the bolts to 25 ft. lbs. (30 Nm). On V6 engines, torque the bolts to 55 ft. lbs. (75 Nm).
19. Connect the fluid coolant lines and the TV cable.
20. Install the transmission mount bolts and torque to 25 ft. lbs. Make sure the torque converter turns freely by hand.
21. Install the crossmember bolts and torque to 25 ft. lbs. (35 Nm).
23. Install all the converter–to–flywheel bolts finger tight, then torque to 35 ft. lbs. (50 Nm). Install the converter cover.
24. Install the transmission–to–engine bracket bolts, if equipped and torque to 41 ft. lbs. (55 Nm) at the transmission end and 52 ft. lbs. (70 Nm) at the engine end.
25. Install the catalyst support bracket and torque to 50 Ft. lbs. (68 Nm).
26. Install the dipstick tube, speedometer cable and wiring.
27. Attach and adjust the shift linkage as required.
28. Install the driveshaft(s). Torque the shaft bearing cap retainer bolts on both 2WD and 4WD shafts to 17 ft. lbs. (23 Nm). On two piece shafts, torque the center bearing mount bolts to 25 ft. lbs. (39 Nm).
29. On 4 cylinder engines, install the starter bolt.
30. Lower the vehicle and connect the TV cable. Adjust as necessary.
31. Refill the transmission with fluid and check as described in Filter Service.

TRANSFER CASE

Identification

An identification tag, which is attached to the rear half of the case, gives the model number, low range reduction ratio and assembly number. The vehicles use two units: the New Process 207 and the New Process 231.

The Model 207 transfer case is an aluminum case, chain drive, 4 position unit providing 4WD High and Low ranges, a 2WD High range and a Neutral position. The 207 is a part-time 4WD unit. Range positions are selected by a floor mounted shift lever. Dexron® II automatic transmission fluid, or equivalent, is the recommended lubricant.

The Model 231 is a part-time transfer case with a bulit in low range gear reduction system. A front axle disconnect mechanism is used for 2-wheel drive operation. The 231 has three operating ranges – 2-wheel drive High and 4-wheel drive High and Low, plus Neutral. The 4-wheel drive operating ranges are undifferentiated. Dexron® II automatic transmission fluid, or equivalent, is used as a lubricant.

Adjustment

SHIFT LEVER

Model 207 and 231

1. Loosen the switch-to-transfer case bolt and the shift lever-to-transfer case pivot bolt.
2. Using the shift lever, shift the transfer case to the 4WD High position.
3. Remove the console and slide the upper boot Up the shift lever.
4. Loosen the lower transfer case shift lever-to-transfer case lock bolt.
5. Using a $^5/_{16}$ in. (8mm) drill bit, insert it through the shift lever and into the switch bracket.
6. Install the lower transfer case shift lever-to-transfer case lock bolt to lock the lever into position; this will lock the transfer case into 4WD High position.
7. Torque the switch bracket bolt to 30 ft. lbs. and the shifter pivot bolt to 96 ft. lbs.
8. Remove the lower transfer case shift lever-to-transfer case lock bolt, which was installed to lock the lever.
9. Remove the drill bit and check the shifting action.

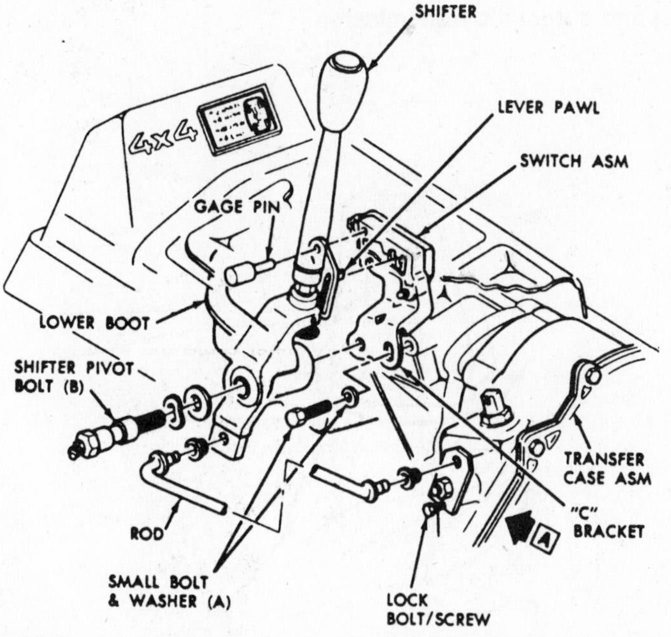
SHIFTER
LEVER PAWL
SWITCH ASM
GAGE PIN
LOWER BOOT
SHIFTER PIVOT BOLT (B)
TRANSFER CASE ASM
"C" BRACKET
A
ROD
SMALL BOLT & WASHER (A)
LOCK BOLT/SCREW

Shift lever adjustment on Model 207 and 231 transfer case

Transfer Case

REMOVAL AND INSTALLATION

1. Disconnect the negative battery cable from the battery.
2. Shift the transfer case into the 4WD High range.
3. Raise and safely support the vehicle on jackstands.
4. From under the transmission/transfer case assembly, remove the skid plate bolts and the skid plate.
5. Remove the front/rear driveshaft-to-transfer case nuts/bolts and lower the driveshafts from the transfer case.
6. Remove the speedometer cable, the vacuum harness and/or the electrical connectors from the transmission.
7. Remove console cover from the console; slide the upper boot up the shift lever and remove the shift boot.
8. Remove the shift lever-to-transfer case bolt and shift lever from the case.
9. Remove the catalytic converter hanger-to-catalytic converter bolts.
10. Remove the transmission/transfer case assembly mount-to-crossmember bolts.
11. Using a transmission jack, secure it to the transmission/transfer case assembly, then raise the assembly.
12. Remove the crossmember-to-chassis bolts and the crossmember from the vehicle.
13. Lower the transmission/transfer case assembly, then remove transfer case-to-transmission bolts, the transfer case from the adapter (A/T) or extension housing (M/T).

To install:

14. Use a new transfer case-to-transmission gasket and mount the unit to the transmission. Torque the bolts to 23 ft. lbs. (31 Nm).
15. Lower the transmission enough to install the shift lever bracket bolts, if removed.
16. Raise the transmission to install the catalytic converter hanger and crossmember. Torque the crossmember and the converter hanger–to–transmission bolts to 22 ft. lbs. (30 Nm). Torque the converter bolts to 40 ft. lbs. (53 Nm).
17. Install the driveshafts and torque the bearing cap retainer bolts to 15 ft. lbs. (20 Nm).
18. Connect the speedometer cable and shift linkage. Adjust as required.
19. Install the skid plate if equipped, fill the transfer case with Dexron®II transmission fluid and road test the vehicle.

New Process 207 Overhaul

CASE DISASSEMBLY

1. Remove fill and drain plugs.
2. Remove front yoke. Discard yoke seal washer and yoke nut.
3. Turn transfer case on end and position front case on wood blocks.
4. Shift transfer case to 4-Low.
5. Remove extension housing attaching bolts. Using a hammer, tap the shoulder on the extension housing to break sealer loose.

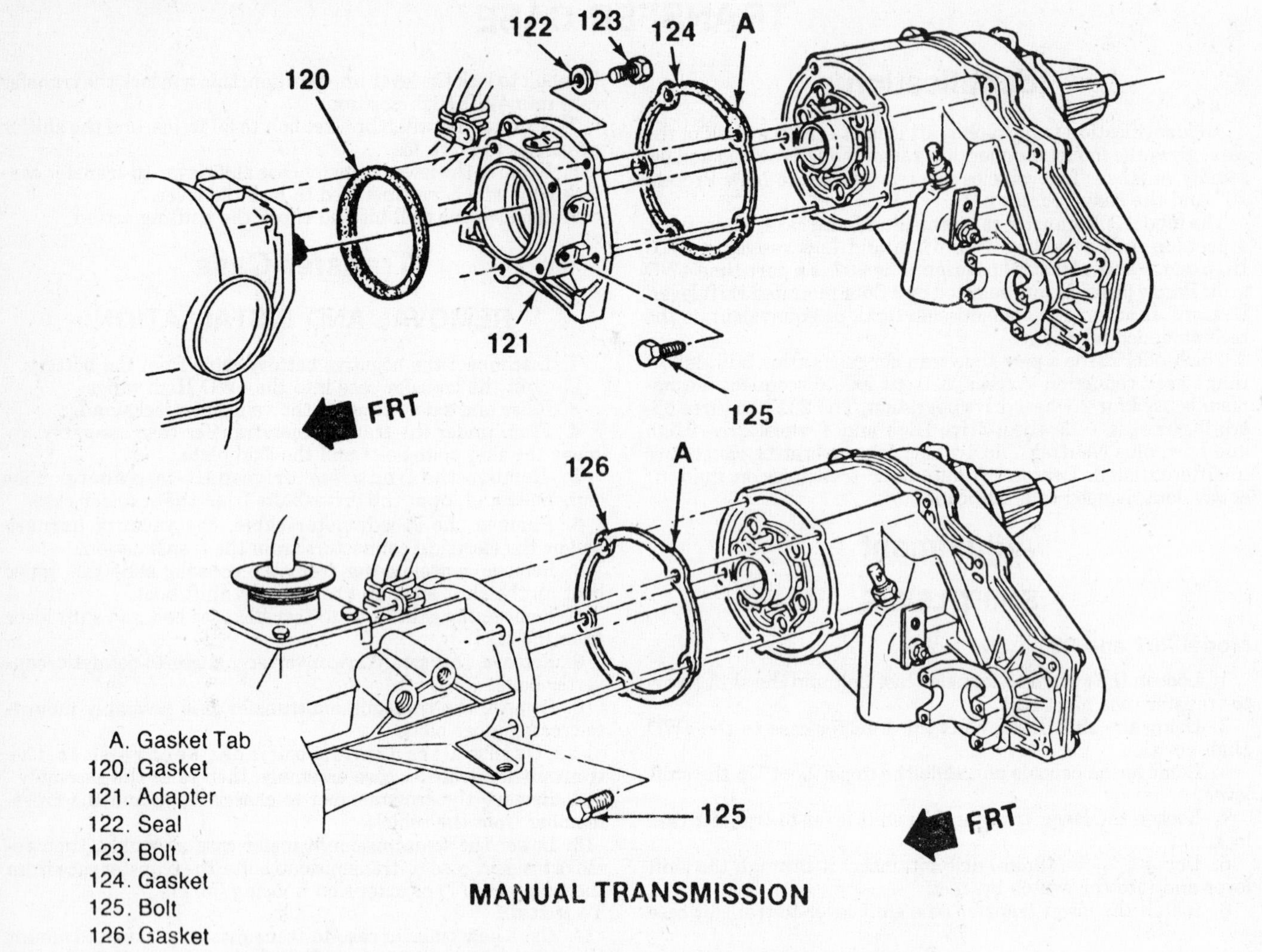
120
121
122
123
124
A
125
FRT
126
A
125
FRT
A. Gasket Tab
120. Gasket
121. Adapter
122. Seal
123. Bolt
124. Gasket
125. Bolt
126. Gasket
MANUAL TRANSMISSION

Removing transfer case from manual and automatic transmission

6. Remove the snapring for the rear bearing from the main shaft and discard.
7. Remove the rear retainer attaching bolts. Using a hammer, tap the shoulder on the retainer to break sealer loose.
8. Remove the rear retainer and pump housing from the transfer case.
9. Remove the pump seal from the pump housing and discard.
10. Remove the speedometer drive gear from the main shaft.
11. Remove the pump gear from the main shaft.
12. Remove the bolts attaching the rear case to the front case and remove rear case. To separate the case, insert a pry bar into the slots cast into the case ends and pry upward. DO NOT attempt to wedge the case halves apart at any point on the mating surfaces.
13. Remove the front output shaft and drive chain as an assembly. It may be necessary to raise the main shaft slightly for the output shaft to clear the case.
14. Pull up on the mode fork rail until rail clears range fork and rotate mode fork and rail and remove from transfer case.
15. Pull up on the main shaft until it separates from the planetary assembly. Remove the main shaft from the transfer case.

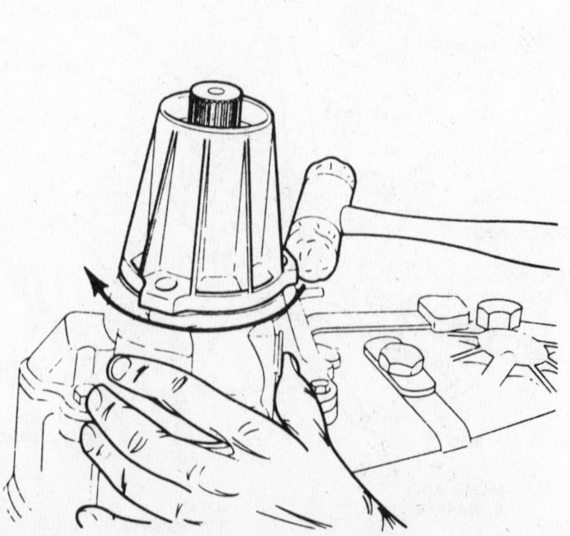

Tap the extension housing sideways to break the seal

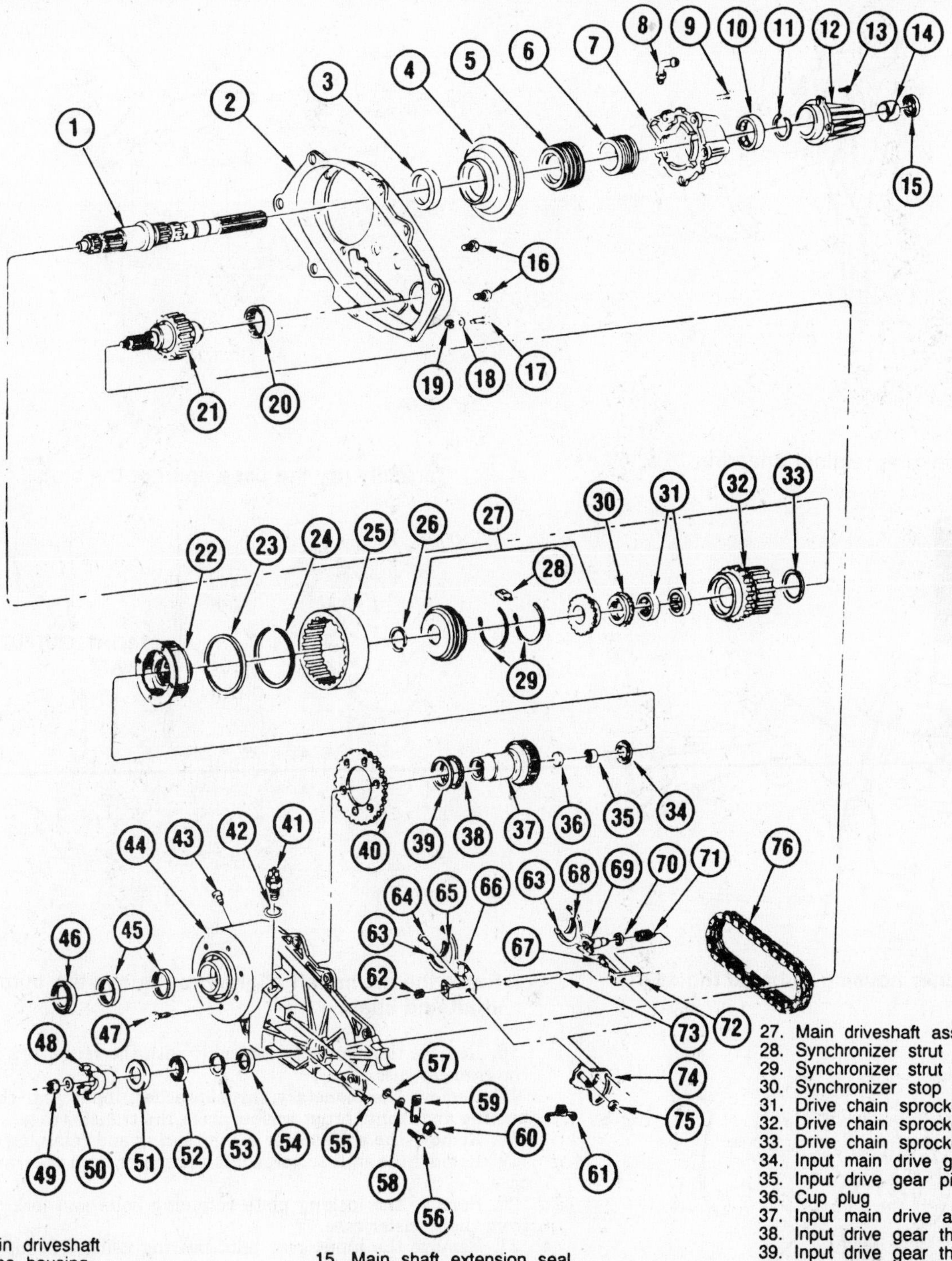
1
2
3
4
5
6
7
8
9
10
11
12
13
14
15
16
17
18
19
20
21
22
23
24
25
26
27
28
29
30
31
32
33
34
35
36
37
38
39
40
41
42
43
44
45
46
47
48
49
50
51
52
53
54
55
56
57
58
59
60
61
62
63
64
65
66
67
68
69
70
71
72
73
74
75
76

1. Main driveshaft
2. Case housing
3. Oil pump housing seal
4. Oil pump housing
5. Oil pump
6. Speed drive gear
7. Mainshaft rear bearing retaining ring
8. Case vent connector
9. Bolt
10. Mainshaft rear bearing
11. Mainshaft rear bearing retaining ring
12. Mainshaft extension
13. Hex bolt
14. Case mainshaft extension bushing
15. Main shaft extension seal
16. Case oil plug
17. Hex (m10' x 1.5mm x 35mm) (2 req'd) bolt
18. Alignment dowel washer housing; alignment
19. Housing alignment dowel
20. Front output shaft pilot bearing
21. Front output shaft
22. Planet gear assembly carrier
23. Planet gear carrier retaining ring thrust washer
24. Planet gear carrier retaining ring
25. Planet gear carrier annulus gear
26. Main driveshaft synchronizer retaining ring
27. Main driveshaft assembly synchronizer
28. Synchronizer strut
29. Synchronizer strut spring
30. Synchronizer stop ring
31. Drive chain sprocket bearing
32. Drive chain sprocket
33. Drive chain sprocket thrust washer
34. Input main drive gear thrust washer
35. Input drive gear pilot bearing
36. Cup plug
37. Input main drive assembly gear
38. Input drive gear thrust bearing
39. Input drive gear thrust bearing washer
40. Low range lockplate
41. Vacuum four wheel switch
42. Four wheel drive indicator light switch
43. Oil access hole plug
44. Case (front half) housing
45. Input drive bearing

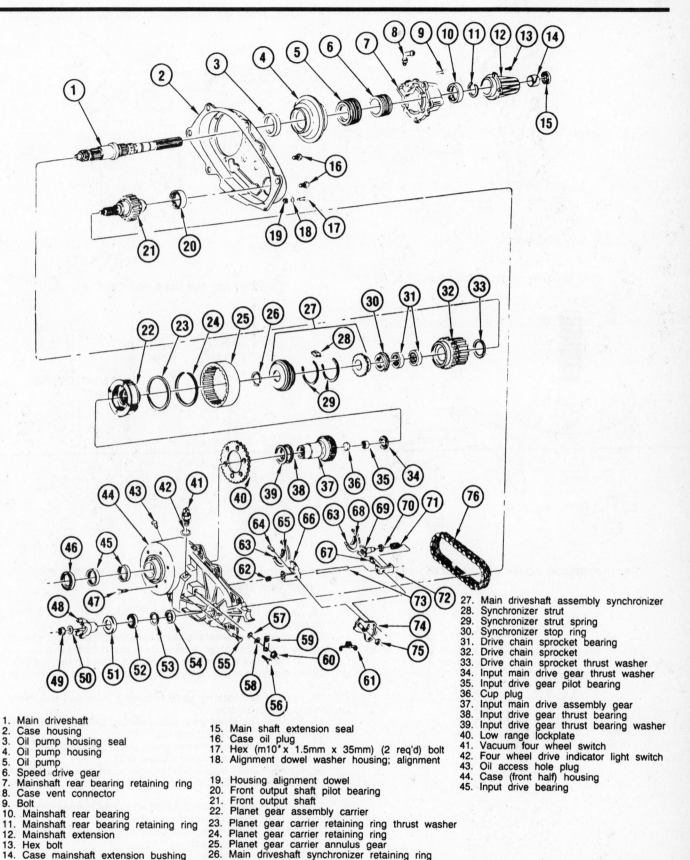

Exploded view of New Process transfer case

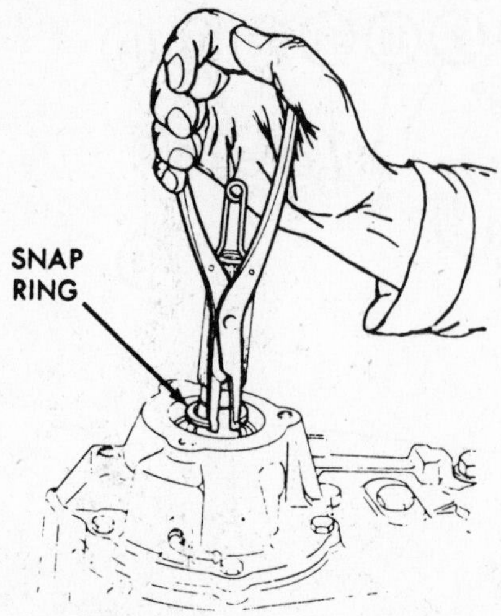
SNAP
RING

Rear bearing retainer snapring

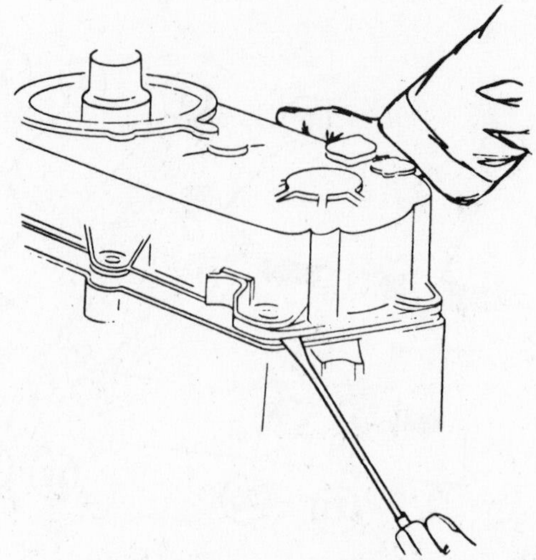

Carefully pry the case apart at the slots

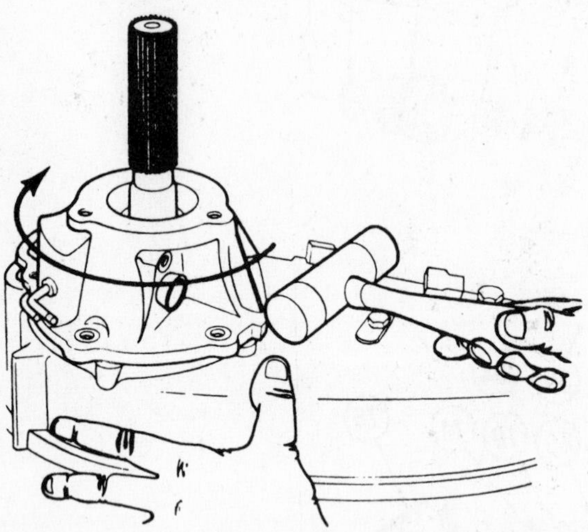

Tap the retainer housing to break the seal

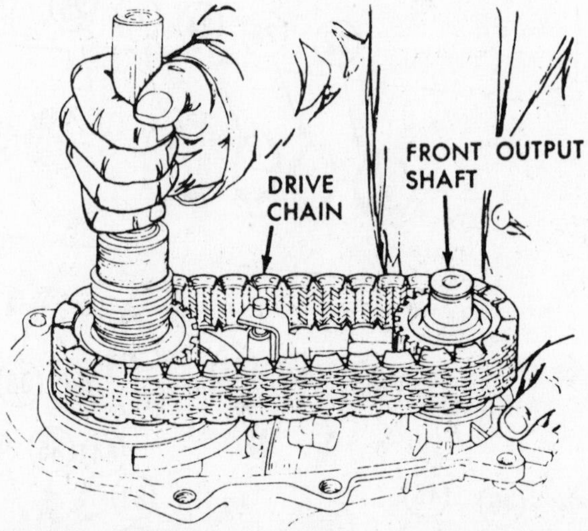
FRONT OUTPUT
SHAFT
DRIVE
CHAIN

Raise the mainshaft slightly to remove the output shaft and chain

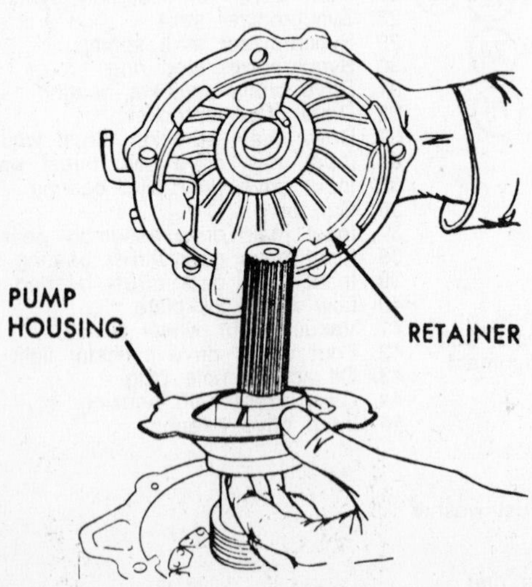
PUMP
HOUSING
RETAINER

Remove the pump housing and retainer

16. Remove the planetary assembly with the range fork from the transfer case.
17. Remove the planetary thrust washer, input gear thrust bearing and front thrust washer from the transfer case.
18. Remove the shift sector detent spring and retaining bolt.
19. Remove the shift sector, shaft and spacer from the transfer case.
20. Remove the locking plate retaining bolts and lock plate from the transfer case.
21. Remove the input gear pilot bearing using J-29369-1 or equivalent with a slide hammer.
22. Remove the front output shaft seal, input shaft seal and the rear extension seal using a brass drift.
23. Using J-33841 with J-8092 or equivalent, press the 2 caged roller bearings for the front input shaft gear from the transfer case.
24. Using J-29369-2 with J-33367 or a slide hammer, remove the rear bearing for the front output shaft.
25. Using a hammer and drift, remove the rear main shaft bearing from the rear retainer.
26. Using an awl, remove the snapring retaining the front output shaft bearing. Using a hammer and drift, remove the bearing from the case.

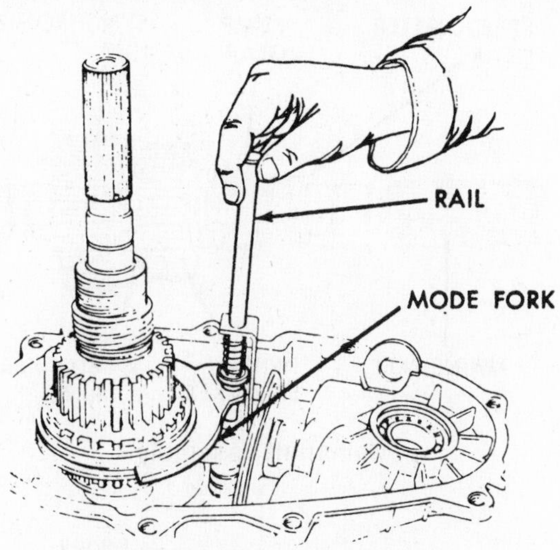
RAIL
MODE FORK

Remove the rail and mode fork

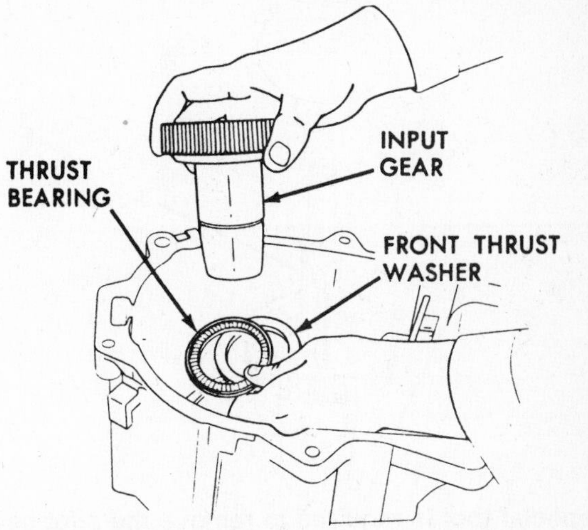
THRUST
BEARING
INPUT
GEAR
FRONT THRUST
WASHER

Lift out the input gear and thrust bearing

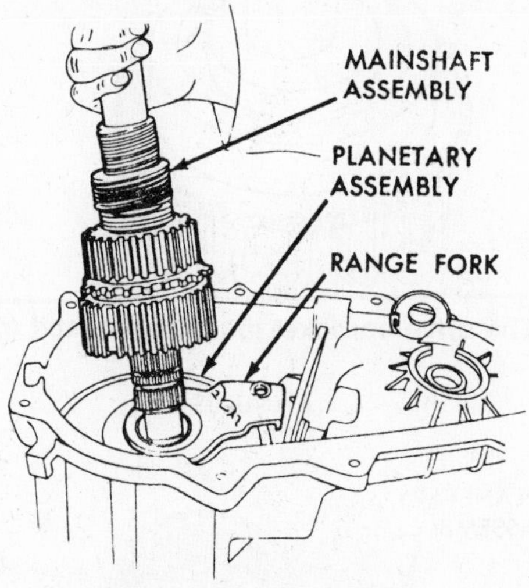
MAINSHAFT
ASSEMBLY
PLANETARY
ASSEMBLY
RANGE FORK

Remove the mainshaft

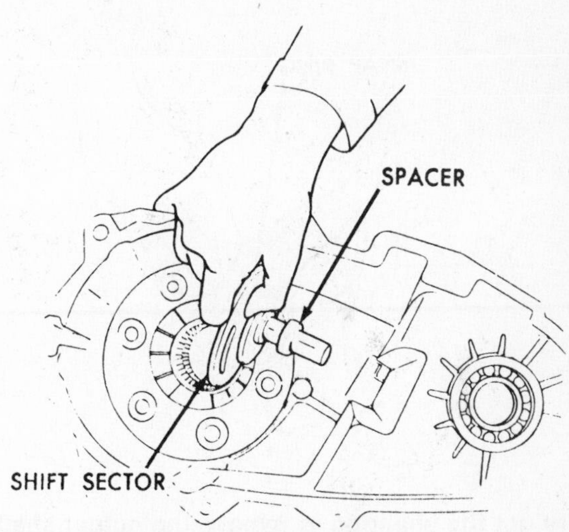
SPACER
SHIFT SECTOR

Remove the shift selector

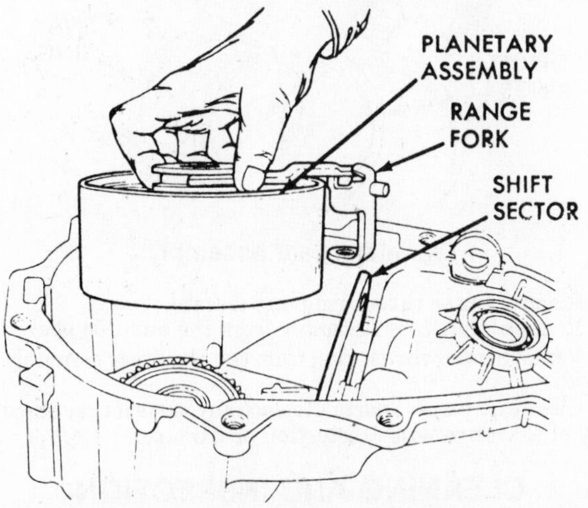
PLANETARY
ASSEMBLY
RANGE
FORK
SHIFT
SECTOR

Lift out the planetary assembly

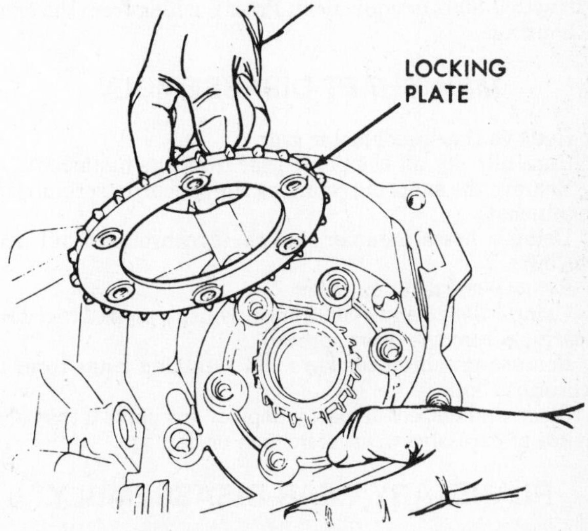
LOCKING
PLATE

Remove the locking plate

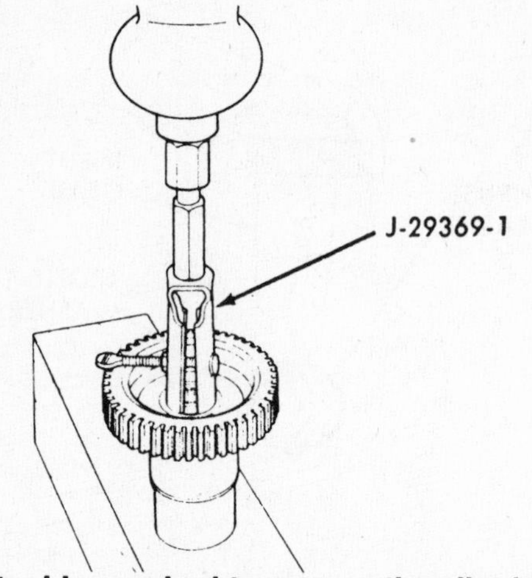
J-29369-1

A special tool is required to remove the pilot bearing

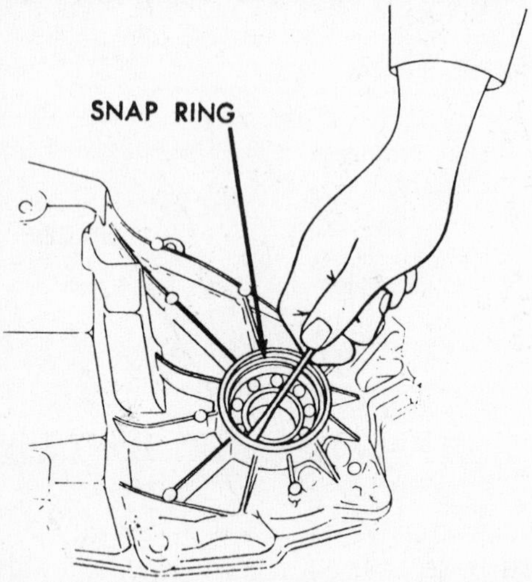
SNAP RING

Pry out the snapring to remove the output shaft bearing

27. Remove the bushing from the extension housing using J-33839 with J-8092 or equivalent. Press bushing from the extension housing.

MAINSHAFT DISASSEMBLY

1. Remove the speedometer gear.
2. Carefully pry off the pump gear from the mainshaft.
3. Remove the snapring retaining the synchronizer hub from the mainshaft.
4. Using a brass hammer, tap the synchronizer hub from mainshaft.
5. Remove the drive sprocket.
6. Using J-33826 and J-8092 or equivalent, press 2 caged roller bearings from the drive sprocket.
7. Remove synchronizer keys and retaining rings from the synchronizer hub.
8. Clean and inspect all parts. Replace any parts if they show evidence of excessive wear, distortion or damage.

PLANETARY GEAR DISASSEMBLY

1. Remove the snapring retaining the planetary gear in the annulus gear.

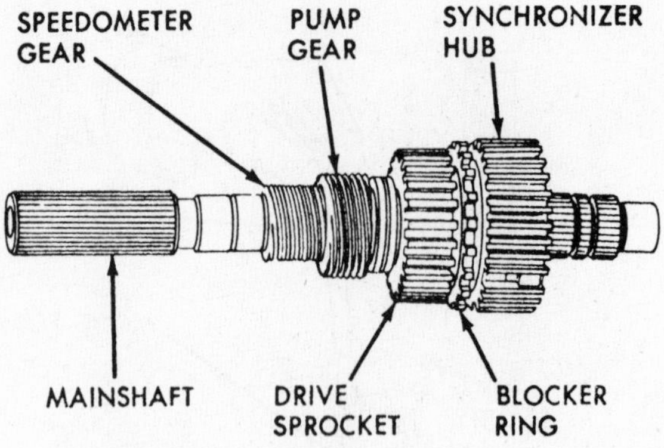
SPEEDOMETER GEAR
PUMP GEAR
SYNCHRONIZER HUB
MAINSHAFT
DRIVE SPROCKET
BLOCKER RING

Mainshaft assembly

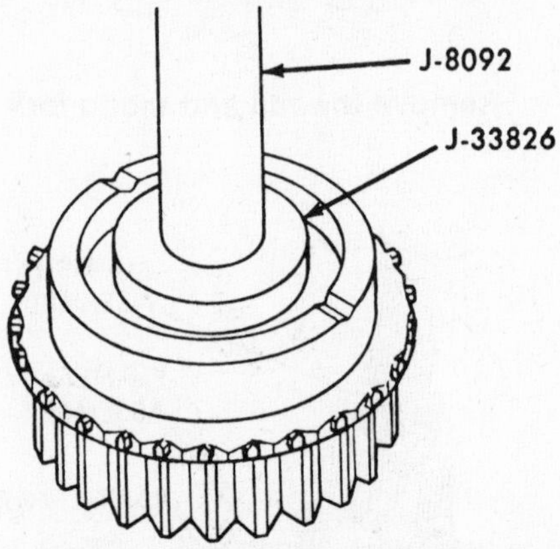
J-8092
J-33826

The drive sprocket must be pressed off

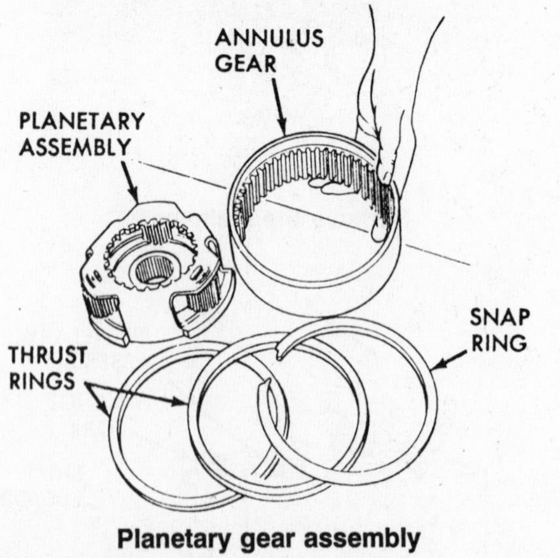
ANNULUS GEAR
PLANETARY ASSEMBLY
THRUST RINGS
SNAP RING

Planetary gear assembly

2. Remove outer thrust ring and discard.
3. Remove planetary assembly from the annulus gear.
4. Remove inner thrust ring from the planetary assembly and discard.
5. Clean and inspect parts. Replace any parts if they show evidence of excessive wear, distortion or damage.

CLEANING AND INSPECTION

Wash all parts thoroughly in clean solvent. Be sure all old lubricant, metallic particles, dirt, or foreign material are removed from the surfaces of every part. Apply compressed air to each oil feed port and channel in each case half to remove any obstructions or cleaning solvent residue.

Inspect all gear teeth for signs of excessive wear or damage and check all gear splines for burrs, nicks, wear or damage. Remove minor nicks or scratches with an oil stone. Replace any part exhibiting excessive wear or damage.

Inspect all snaprings and thrust washers for evidence of excessive wear, distortion or damage. Replace any of these parts if they exhibit these conditions.

Inspect the two case halves for cracks, porosity, damaged mating surfaces, stripped bolt threads, or distortion. Replace any part that exhibits these conditions. Inspect the low range lock plate in the front case. If the lock plate teeth or the plate hub is cracked, broken, chipped, or excessively worn, replace the lock plate and the lock plate attaching bolts.

Inspect the condition of all needle, roller and thrust bearings in the front and rear case halves and the input gear. Also, check the condition of the bearing bores in both cases and in the input gear, rear output shaft and rear retainer. Replace any part that exhibits signs of excessive wear or damage.

PLANETARY GEAR ASSEMBLY

1. Install the inner thrust ring on planetary assembly.
2. Install the planetary assembly into the annulus gear.
3. Install the outer thrust ring and then the snapring.

MAINSHAFT ASSEMBLY

1. Using J-33828 and J-8092 or equivalent, install the front drive sprocket bearing. Press bearing until tool bottoms out. Bearing should be flush with front surface. Reverse tool on J-8092 or equivalent and press rear bearing into sprocket until tool bottoms out. The rear bearing should be recessed after installation.
2. Install thrust washer on the mainshaft.
3. Install drive sprocket on the mainshaft.
4. Install blocker ring and synchronizer hub on the mainshaft. Seat hub on main shaft and install a new snapring to retain.
5. Install pump gear on the mainshaft. Tap the gear with a hammer to seat on mainshaft.
6. Install speedometer gear on the mainshaft.

CASE ASSEMBLY

All of the bearings used in the transfer case must be correctly positioned to avoid covering the bearing oil feed holes. After installation of bearings, check the bearing position to be sure the feed hole is not obstructed or blocked by a bearing.

1. Install the lock plate in the transfer case. Coat case and lock plate surfaces around bolt holes with Loctite®515 or equivalent.
2. Position the lock plate to the case and align bolt holes in lock plate with case. Install attaching bolts and torque to 25 ft. lbs. (34 Nm).
3. Install the roller bearings for the input shaft into the transfer case using J-33830 and J-8092 or equivalent. Press bearings until tool bottoms in bore.
4. Install the front output shaft rear bearing, using J-33832 and J-8092 or equivalent. Press bearing until tool bottoms in case.
5. Install the front output shaft front bearing using J-33833 and J-8092 or equivalent. Press bearing until tool bottoms in bore.
6. Install the snapring that retains the front output shaft bearing in case.
7. Install the front output shaft seal using J-33834 or equivalent.
8. Install the input shaft seal using J-33831 or equivalent.
9. Install spacer on shift sector shaft and install sector in transfer case. Install shift lever and retaining nut. Torque to 20 ft. lbs. (27 Nm).
10. Install shift sector detent spring and retaining bolt.
11. Install the pilot bearing into the input gear using J-33829 and J-8092 or equivalent. Press bearing until tool bottoms out.
12. Install the input gear front thrust bearing and input gear in transfer case.
13. Install the planetary gear thrust washer on the input gear. Position range fork on planetary assembly and install planetary assembly into the transfer case.
14. Install the mainshaft into the transfer case. Make sure the thrust washer is aligned with the input gear and planetary assembly before installing mainshaft.
15. Install mode fork on synchronizer sleeve and rotate until mode fork is aligned with range fork. Slide mode fork rail down through range fork until rail is seated in bore of transfer case.
16. Position drive chain on front output shaft and install chain on drive sprocket. Install front output shaft in the transfer case. It may be necessary to slightly raise the main shaft to seat the output shaft in the case.
17. Install the magnet into pocket of transfer case.
18. Apply ⅛ in. (3mm) bead of Loctite®515 or equivalent to the mating surface of the front case. Install rear case on the front case aligning dowel pins. Install bolts and torque to 20–25 ft. lbs.(27–34Nm). Install the two bolts with washers into the dowel pin holes.
19. Install the output bearing into the rear retainer using J-33833 and J-8092 or equivalent. Press bearing until seated in bore.
20. Install pump seal in pump housing using J-33835 or equivalent. Apply petroleum jelly to pump housing tabs and install housing in rear retainer.
21. Apply ⅛ in. (3mm) bead of Loctite®515 or equivalent to mating surface of rear retainer. Align retainer to case and install retaining bolts. Torque bolts to 20 ft. lbs.(27 Nm).
22. Using a new snapring, install snapring on mainshaft. Pull up on mainshaft and seat snapring in its groove.
23. Install bushing in extension housing using J-33826 and J-8092 or equivalent. Press bushing until tool bottoms in bore.
24. Install a new seal in the extension housing using J-33843 or equivalent.
25. Apply ⅛ in. (3mm) bead of Loctite®515 or equivalent to mating surface of extension housing. Align extension housing to the rear retainer and install attaching bolts. Torque bolts to specification 25 ft. lbs. (34 Nm).
26. Install front yoke on output shaft. Install a new yoke seal washer with a new nut and torque to 90–130 ft. lbs. (122–176 Nm).
27. Install drain and fill plugs.

New Process 231 Overhaul

DISASSEMBLY

1. Remove the transfer case from the vehicle and clean it before disassembly.
2. Remove the attaching nuts from the front and rear output yokes. Remove the yokes and sealing washers.
3. Move the range lever to 4-LOW. Remove the bolts and tap the extension housing off of the rear retainer.

NOTE: To avoid damaging the sealing surfaces of the extension housing, DO NOT attempt to pry or wedge the housing off the retainer.

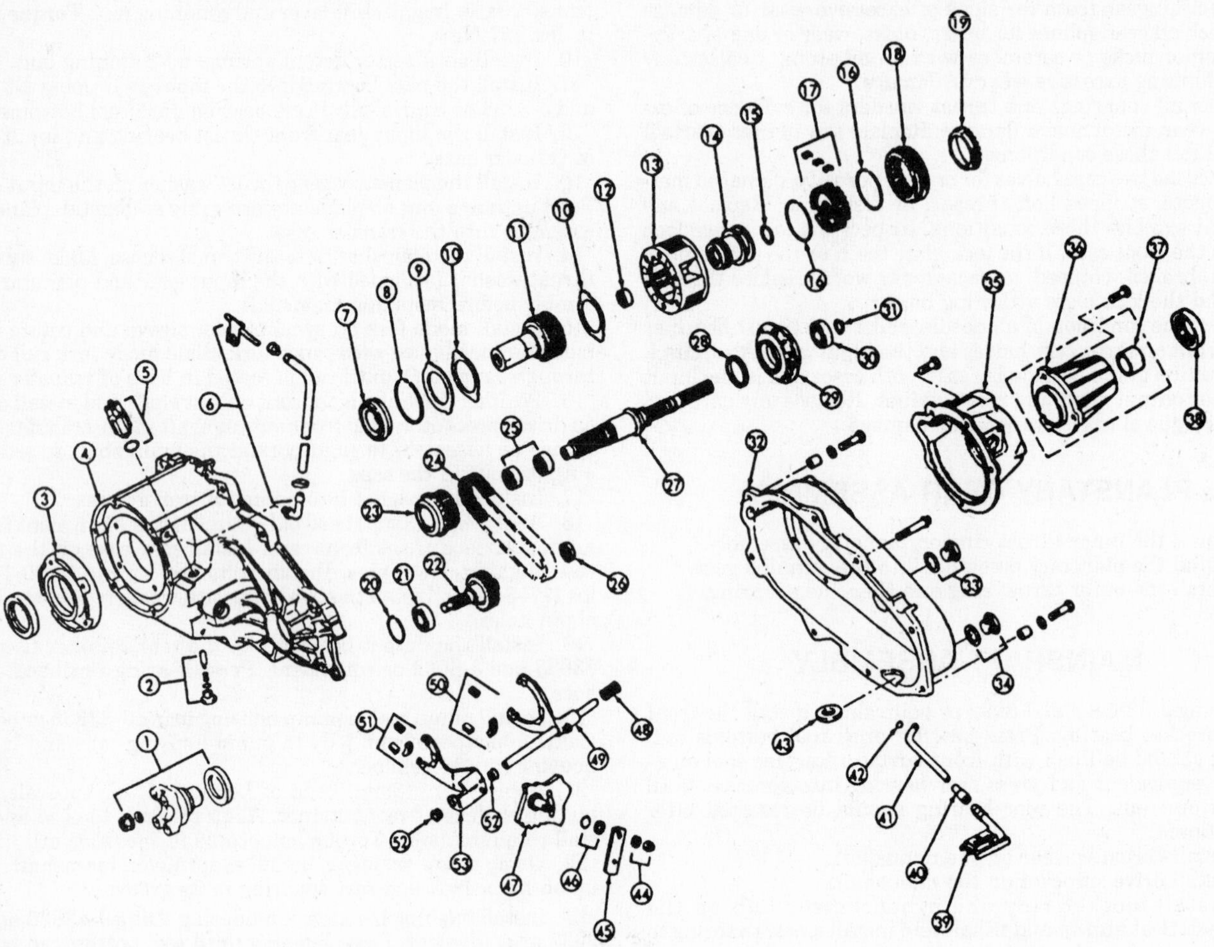

1. Front yoke, nut, seal washer, and oil seal
2. Shift detent plug, spring and pin
3. Front retainer and seal
4. Front case
5. Vacuum switch and seal
6. Vent assembly
7. Input gear bearing and snap ring
8. Low range gear snap ring
9. Input gear retainer
10. Low range gear thrust washers
11. Input gear
12. Input gear pilot bearing
13. Low range gear
14. Range fork shift hub
15. Synchro hub snap ring
16. Synchro hub springs
17. Synchro hub and inserts
18. Synchro sleeve
19. Stop ring
20. Snap ring
21. Output shaft front bearing
22. Output shaft (front)
23. Drive sprocket
24. Drive chain
25. Drive sprocket bearings
26. Output shaft rear bearing
27. Mainshaft
28. Oil seal
29. Oil pump assembly
30. Rear bearing
31. Snap ring
32. Rear case
33. Fill plug and gasket
34. Drain plug and gasket
35. Rear retainer
36. Extension housing
37. Bushing
38. Oil seal
39. Oil pickup screen
40. Tube connector
41. Oil pickup tube
42. Pickup tube O–ring
43. Magnet
44. Range lever nut and washer
45. Range lever
46. O–ring and seal
47. Sector
48. Mode spring
49. Mode fork
50. Mode fork inserts
51. Range fork inserts
52. Range fork bushings
53. Range fork

Exploded view of New Process 231 transfer case

4. Remove the snapring from the rear bearing, then, remove the four bolts and separate the rear bearing retainer from the rear case half.
5. Remove the case attaching bolts, and separate the case halves by inserting a small pry bar in the pry slots on the case.
6. Remove the oil pump and rear case as an assembly. Remove the oil screen and pick-up tube. Remove the oil pump from the rear case. Remove the pickup tube O-ring.
7. Mark the position of the oil pump housings for referance. Separate the two halves of the pump. Remove the feed housing from the gear housing. Note the position of the pump gears and remove.

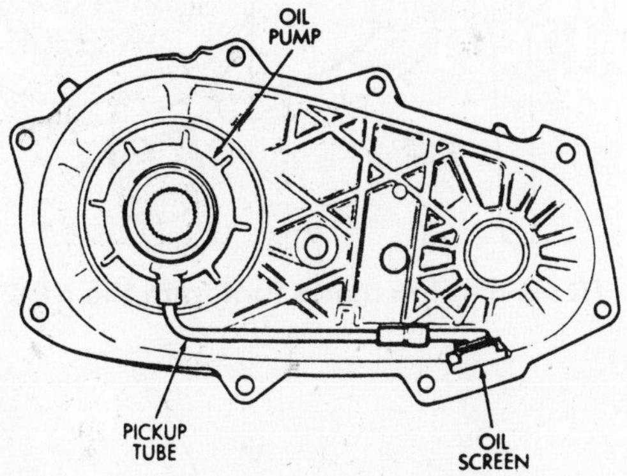
OIL
PUMP
PICKUP
TUBE
OIL
SCREEN
Removing the oil screen and pickup tube from the NP-231

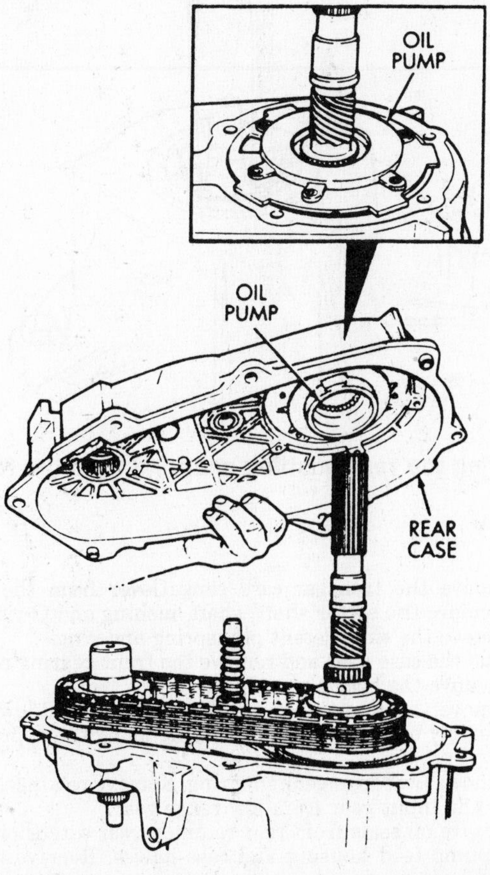
OIL
PUMP
OIL
PUMP
REAR
CASE
Removing the rear case and oil pump from the NP-231

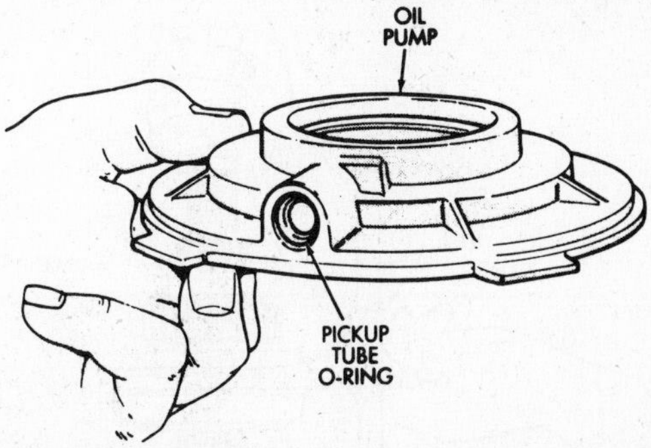
OIL
PUMP
PICKUP
TUBE
O-RING
Removing the pick-up tube oil ring from the NP-231

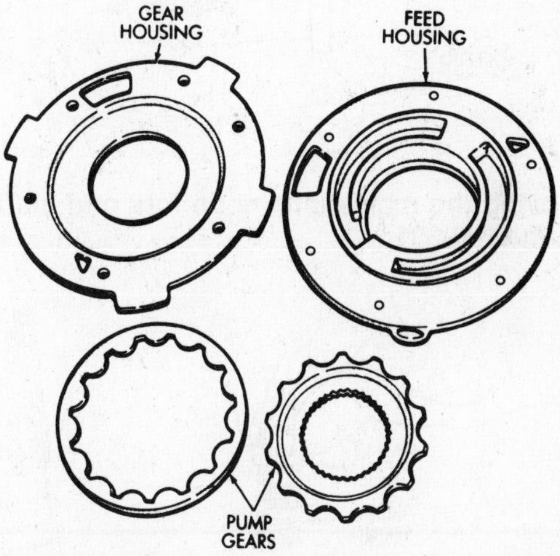
GEAR
HOUSING
FEED
HOUSING
PUMP
GEARS
Disassembling the oil pump from the NP-231

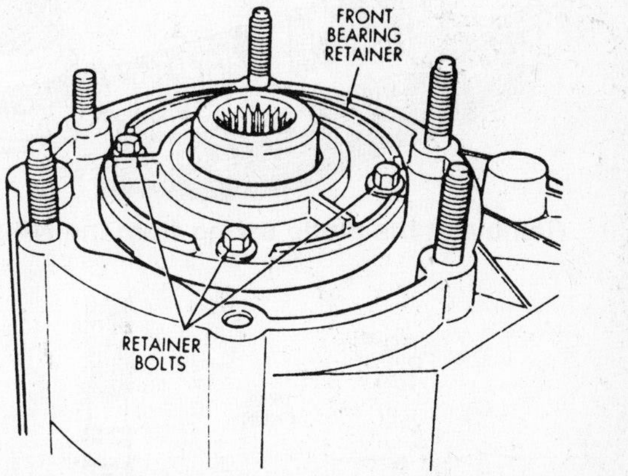
FRONT
BEARING
RETAINER
RETAINER
BOLTS
Removing the bearing retainer bolts from the NP-231

8. Remove the mode spring from the shift rail.
9. Remove the output shaft and drive chain by pushing the front input shaft inward and by angling the gear slightly to obtain adequate clearance to remove the chain.
10. Remove the mainshaft assembly, mode fork and shift rail from the front case half. Remove the mode fork and shift rail from the synchro sleeve.
11. Remove the synchro sleeve from the mainshaft. Remove the synchro hub snapring and stop ring.
12. Remove the drive sprocket. Slide the range fork pin out of the shift sector and remove the range fork and shift hub.

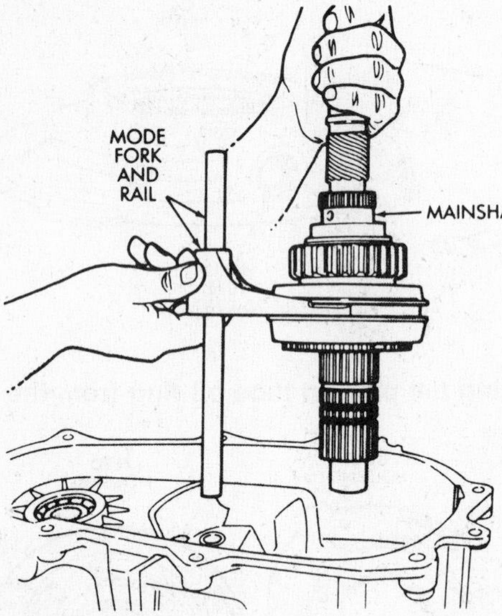
MODE
FORK
AND
RAIL
MAINSHAFT
Removing the mainshaft, mode fork and shift rail from the NP-231

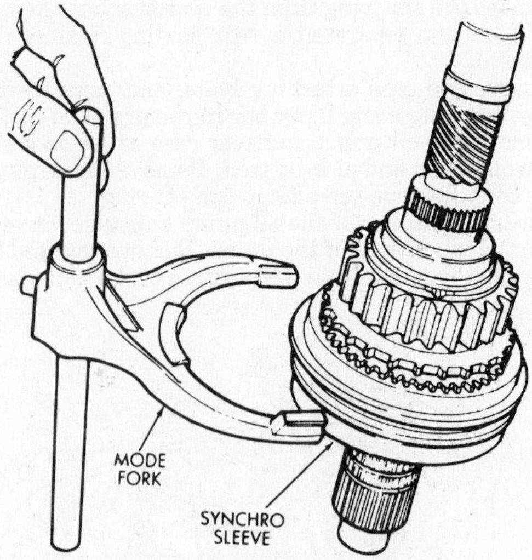
MODE
FORK
SYNCHRO
SLEEVE
Removing the mode fork from the NP-231

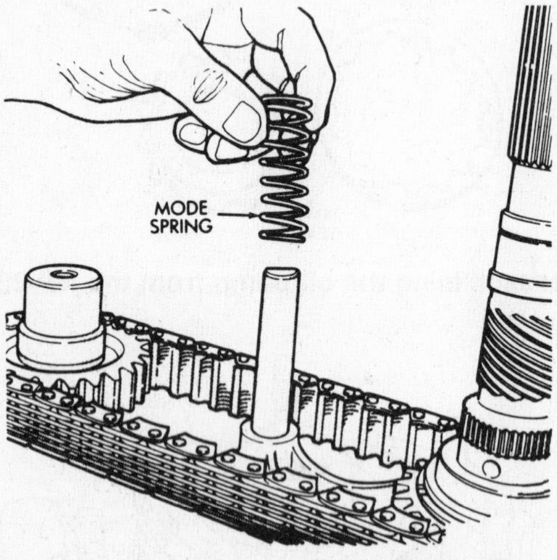
MODE
SPRING
Removing the mode spring from the NP-231

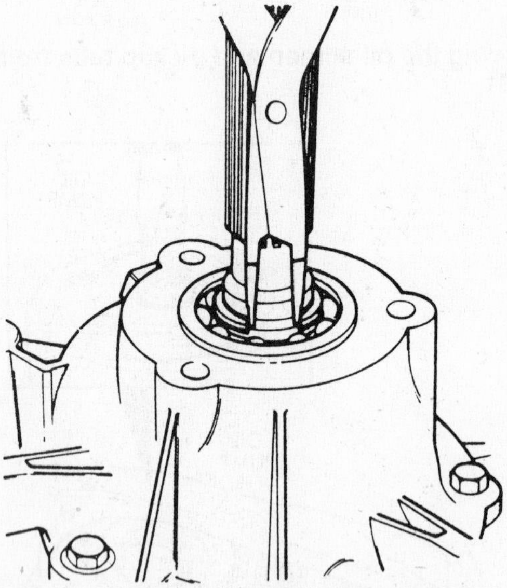
Removing the rear bushing snapring from the NP-231

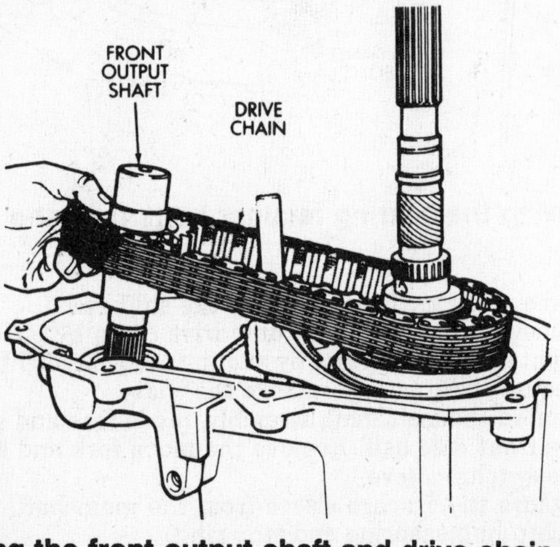
FRONT
OUTPUT
SHAFT
DRIVE
CHAIN
Removing the front output shaft and drive chain from the NP-231

13. Remove the transger case range lever from the sector shaft. Remove the sector shaft, shaft bushing and O-ring.
14. Remove the shift detent pin, spring and plug.
15. Turn the case over and remove the front bearing retainer bolts. Remove the bearing retainer.
16. Remove the input gear snapring. Press inlut/low range gear assembly out of input gear bearing using the appropriate tools.
17. Remove low range gear snapring. Remove retainer, thrust washers and input gear from low range gear.
18. Remove oil seals from rear retainer, rear extension housing, oil pump feed housing and case halves. Remove magnet from front case.
19. Remove speedometer gear, seals and adaptor.
20. Remove output shaft snapring, oil seal and bearing.

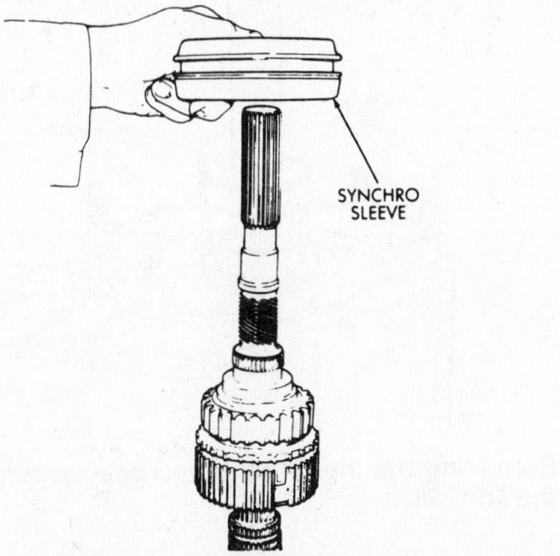
SYNCHRO
SLEEVE

Removing the synchronizer sleeve from the NP-231

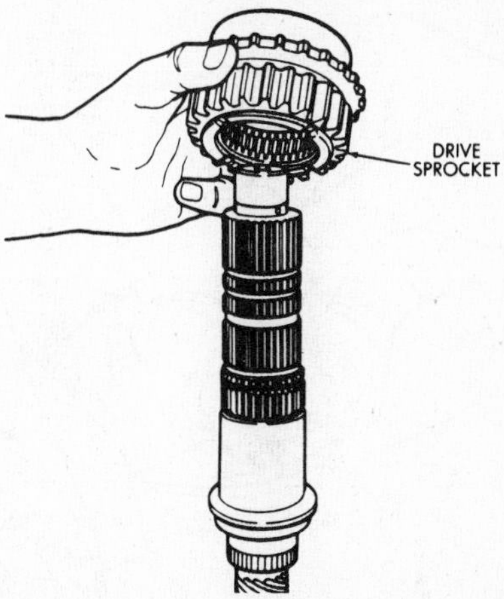
DRIVE
SPROCKET

Removing the drive sprocket from the NP-231

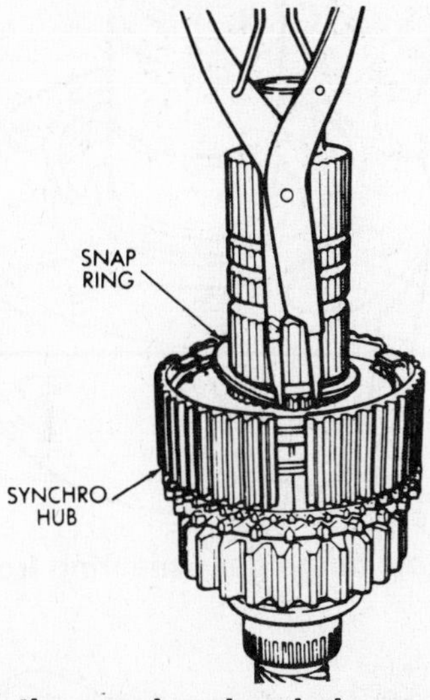
SNAP
RING
SYNCHRO
HUB

Removing the synchronizer hub snapring from the NP-231

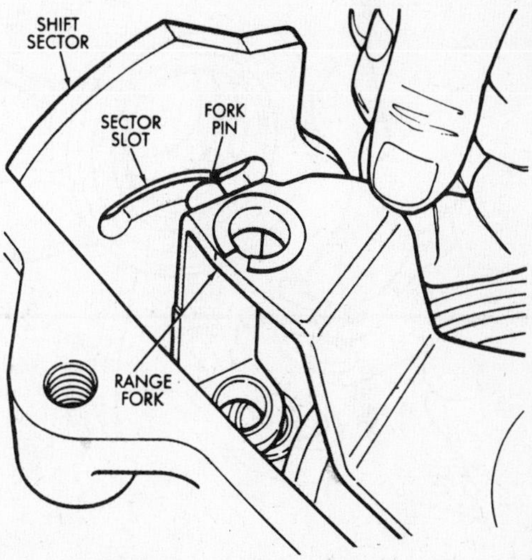
SHIFT
SECTOR
SECTOR
SLOT
FORK
PIN
RANGE
FORK

Disengaging the range fork on the NP-231

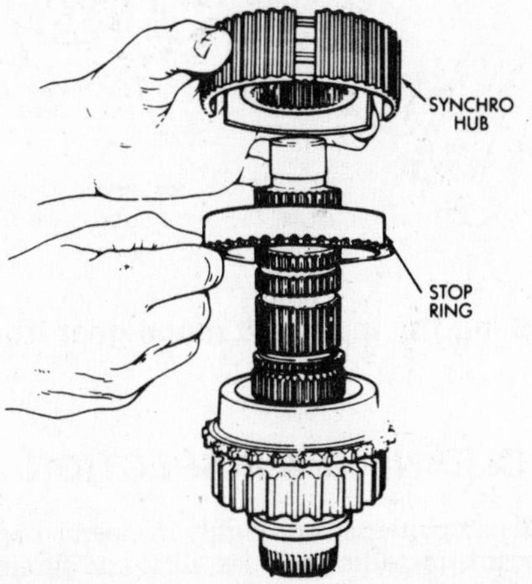
SYNCHRO
HUB
STOP
RING

Removing the hub and stop ring from the NP-231

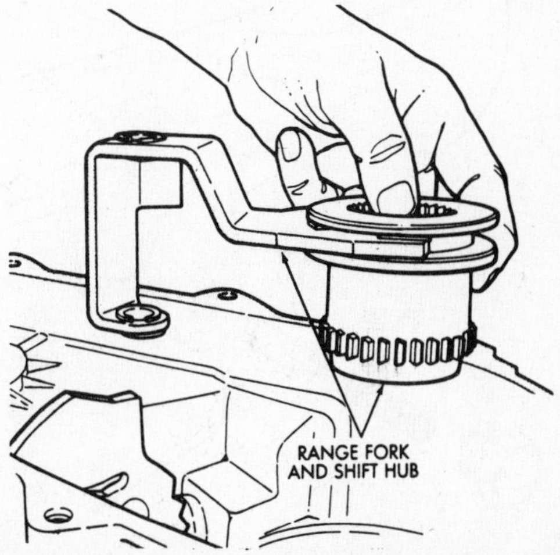
RANGE FORK
AND SHIFT HUB

Removing the range fork and hub from the NP-231

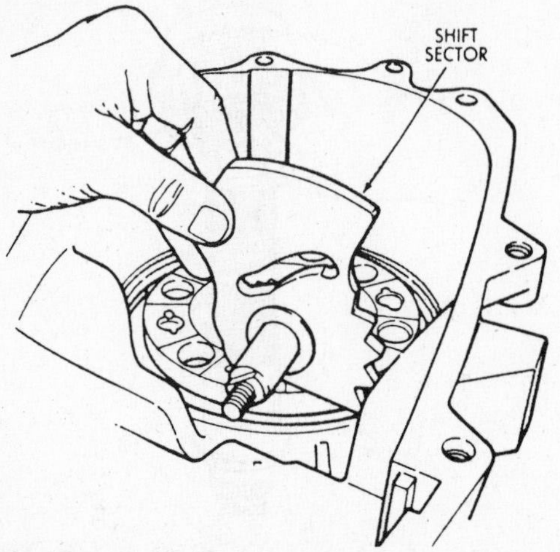
SHIFT
SECTOR

Removing the shift selector from the NP-231

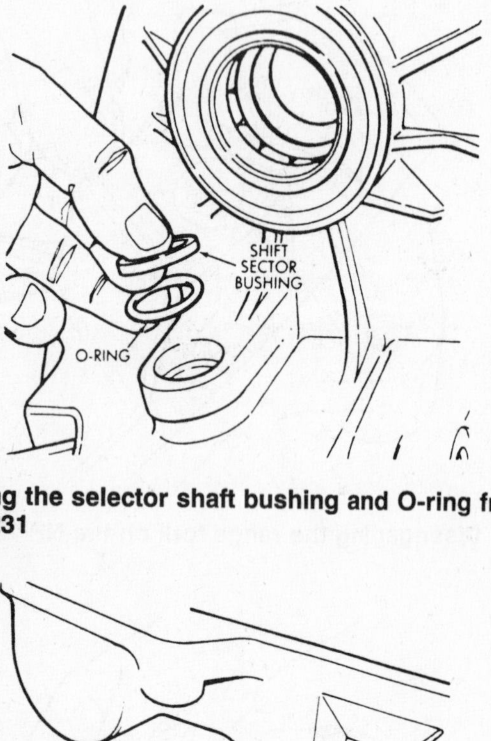
SHIFT
SECTOR
BUSHING
O-RING

Removing the selector shaft bushing and O-ring from the NP-231

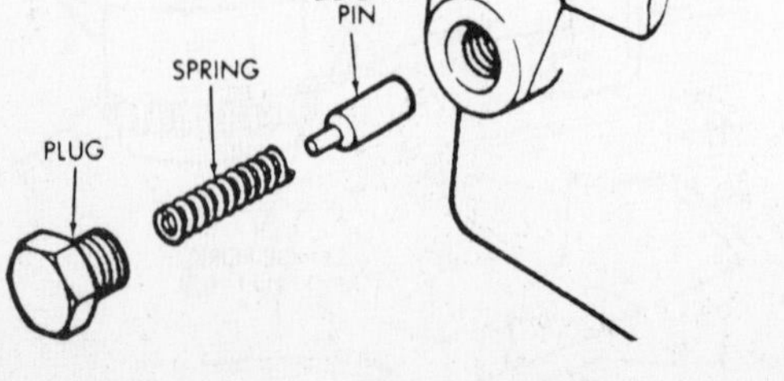
DETENT
PIN
SPRING
PLUG

Removing the detent pin, spring and plug from the NP-231

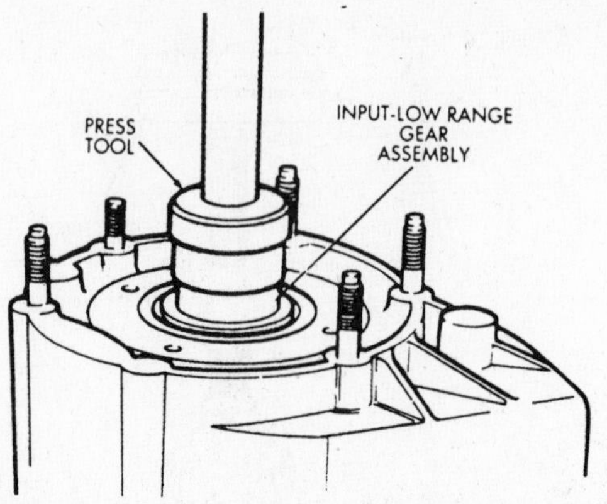
PRESS
TOOL
INPUT-LOW RANGE
GEAR
ASSEMBLY

Removing the input/low range gear assembly from the NP-231

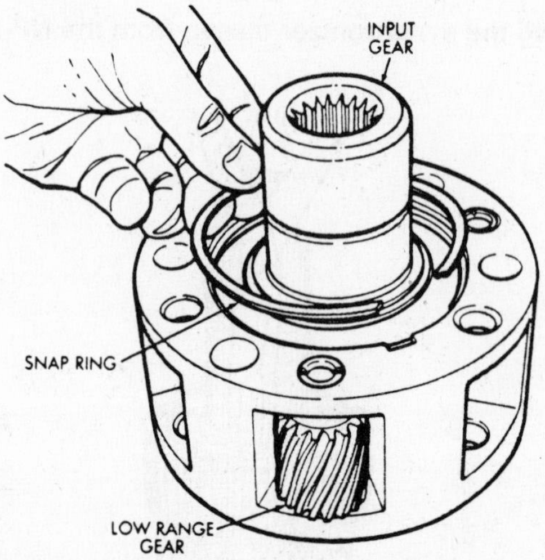
INPUT
GEAR
SNAP RING
LOW RANGE
GEAR

Removing the low range gear snapring from the NP-231

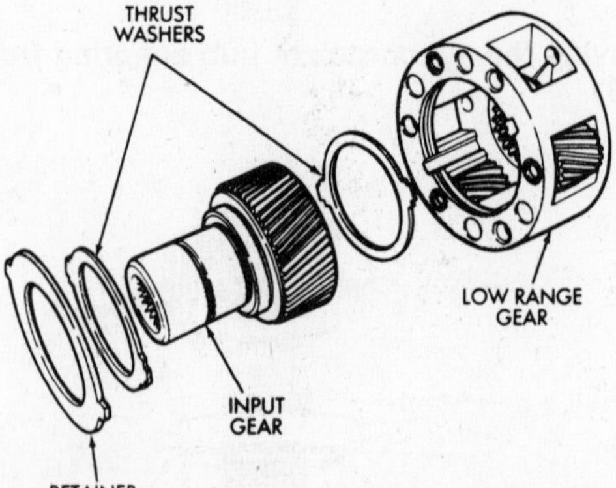
THRUST
WASHERS
LOW RANGE
GEAR
INPUT
GEAR
RETAINER

Disassembling the input/low range gear from the NP-231

CLEANING & INSPECTION

1. Wash all components thoroughly in clean solvent. Ensure that all lubricant, metallic particles, dirt, and foreign material are removed from the surfaces of every component.

2. Apply compressed air to each oil supply port and channel in

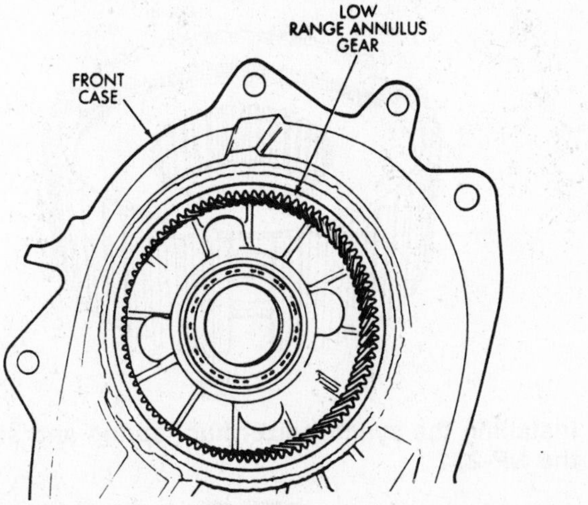
LOW
RANGE ANNULUS
GEAR
FRONT
CASE

Inspecting the low range annulus gear on the NP-231

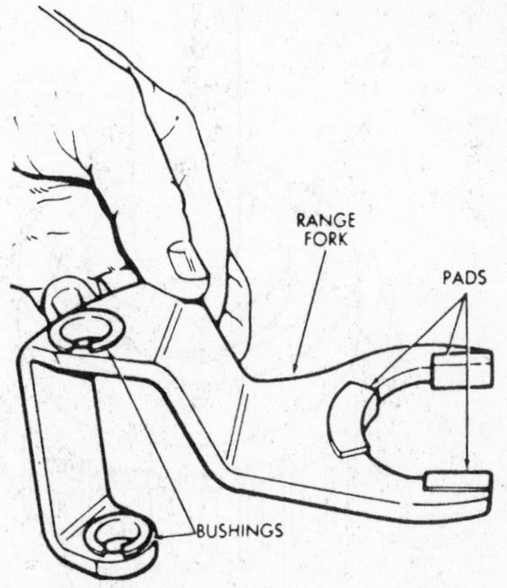
RANGE
FORK
PADS
BUSHINGS

Installing new pads and bushings in the range fork on the NP-231

each transfer case half to remove any obstructions or cleaning solvent residue.

3. Inspect all gear teeth for excessive wear or damage. Inspect all gear splines for burrs, nicks, wear or damage.

4. Inspect the low range annulus gear. If the gear is damaged, replace the gear and front case as an assembly. Do not attempt to remove the gear.

5. Remove minor nicks or scratches using an oilstone. Replace any component exhibiting excessive wear or damage.

6. Inspect all snaprings and thrust washers for excessive wear, distortion and damage. Replace any component exhibiting these conditions.

7. Inspect the transfer case halves and rear retainer for cracks, porosity, damaged mating surfaces, stripped bolt threads and distortion. Replace any component exhibiting these conditions.

8. Inspect the condition of all needle, roller, ball and thrust bearings in the front and rear transfer case halves. Also inspect to determine the condition of the bearing bores in both transfer case halves and in the input gear, rear output shaft, side gear, and rear retainer.

9. Replace any component that is excessively worn or damaged.

ASSEMBLY

NOTE: The bearing bores in various transfer case components contain oil feed holes. Ensure replacement bearings do not block these feed holes.

1. Install new output shaft bearing, snapring and oil seal.

2. Press the input gear bearing from the front case with a remover tool. Install a snapring on the new bearing and install the bearing into the case so the snapring seats against the case.

3. Install a new input gear pilot bearing.

4. Assemble the low range gear, input gear thrust washers, input gear and input gear retainer. Install the low range gear snapring.

5. Press the input gear into the front bearing and install a new snapring.

NOTE: Use a proper sized tool to press the input gear into the front bearing. DO NOT press against the end surfaces of the low range gear. The gear case and thrust washers could be damaged.

6. Install a new oil seal in the front bearing retainer. Apply an ⅛ in. (3mm) bead of RTV sealer to the front bearing retainter sealing surfaces.

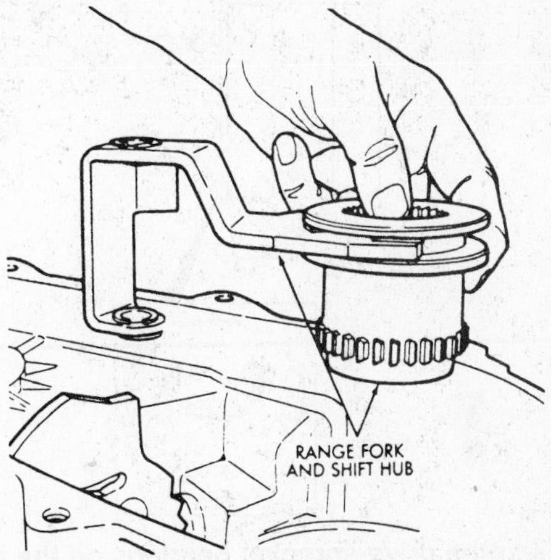
RANGE FORK
AND SHIFT HUB

Assembling the range fork and shift hub on the NP-231

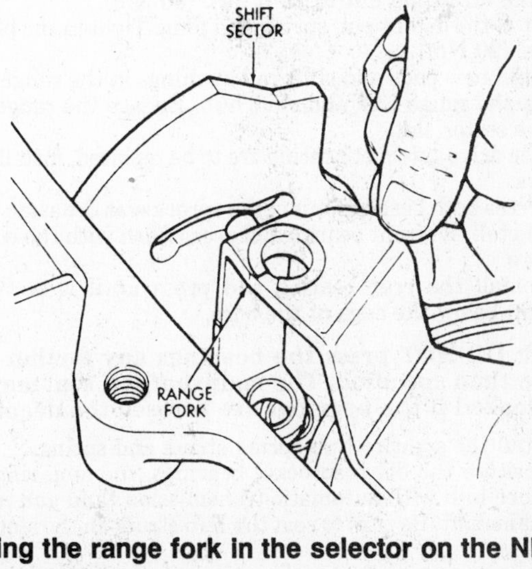
SHIFT
SECTOR
RANGE
FORK

Seating the range fork in the selector on the NP-231

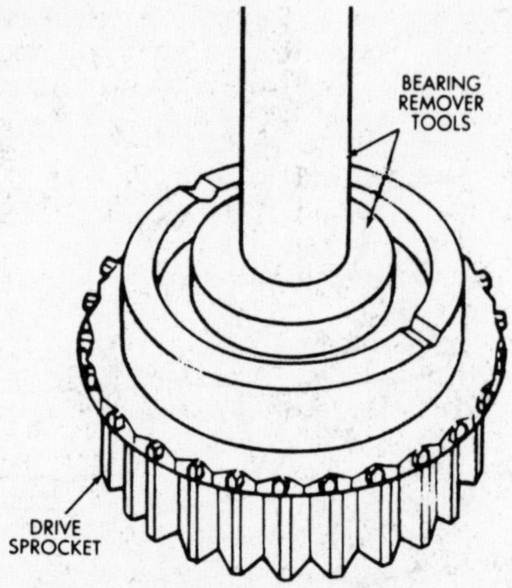
BEARING
REMOVER
TOOLS
DRIVE
SPROCKET
Removing the drive sprocket bearings on the NP-231

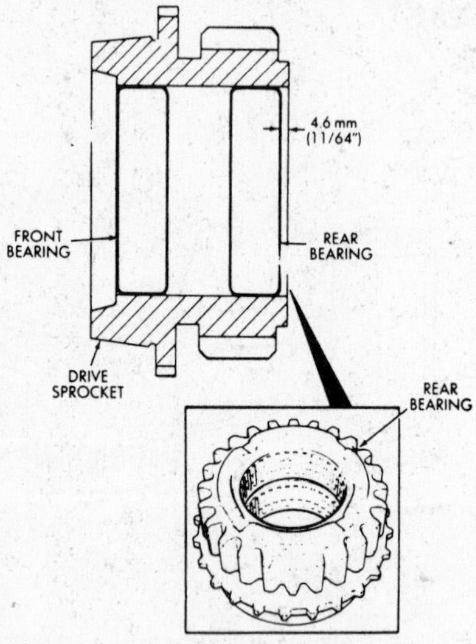
4.6 mm
(11/64")
FRONT
BEARING
REAR
BEARING
DRIVE
SPROCKET
REAR
BEARING
Installing the drive sprocket bearings on the NP-231

7. Install the front bearing retainer on the front case and tighten the bolts to 16 ft. lbs.(23 Nm).
8. Install a new sector shaft O-ring and bushing. Install the shift sector. Then install the range lever on the shift sector and tighten the attaching nut to 22 ft. lbs. (30 Nm).
9. Install the detent pin, spring and plug. Tighten the plug to 15 ft. lbs. (20 Nm).
10. Install new pads and shift rail bushings in the range fork. Assemble the range fork and shift hub. Engage the range fork pin in the sector slot.
11. If the drive sprocket bearing are to be replaced, install then as follows:
   a. Press both bearings out of the sprocket at the same time.
   b. Install the front bearingand press flush with the edge of the bore.
   c. Install the rear bearing and press until it is 1/16 in. (1.6mm) below the edge of the bore.

NOTE: DO NOT press the bearings any farther into the bore than specified. The mainshaft oil seal may become blocked if the bearings are pressed too deeply.

12. Install the synchro hub spring struts and spring.
13. Lubricate the drive sprocket bearings, the stop ring and the synchro hub with automatic transmission fluid and install on the mainshaft. Be sure to seat the hub struts on the stop ting lugs.

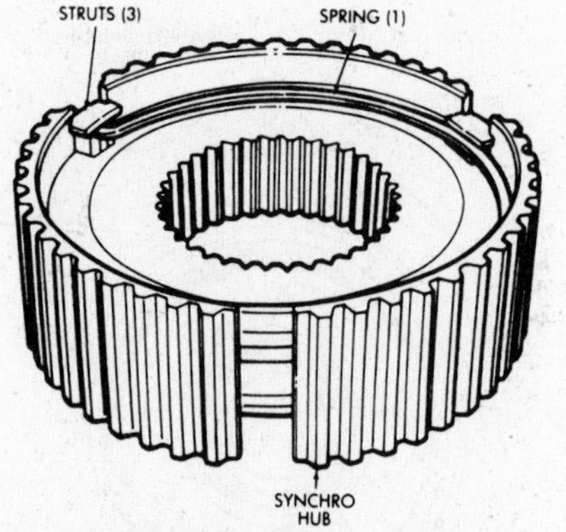
STRUTS (3)
SPRING (1)
SYNCHRO
HUB
Installing the synchronizer hub, spring and struts on the NP-231

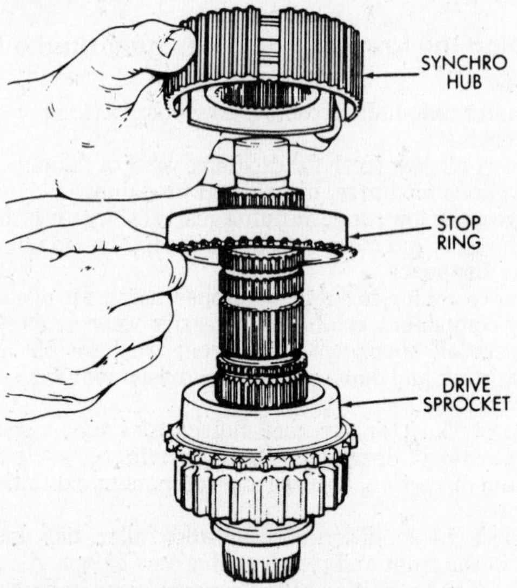
SYNCHRO
HUB
STOP
RING
DRIVE
SPROCKET
Installing the drive sprocket, stop ring and synchronizer hub on the NP-231

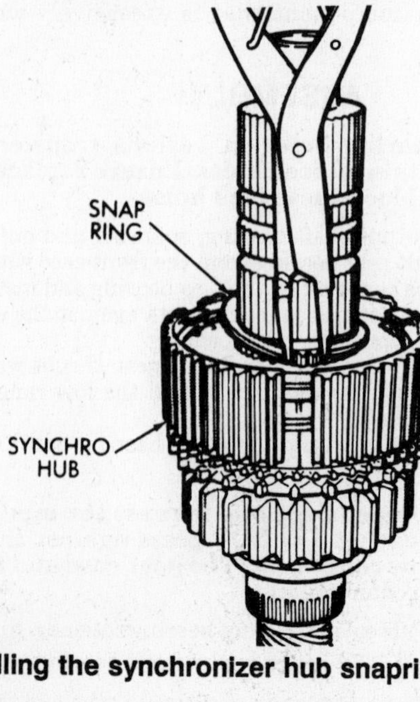
SNAP
RING
SYNCHRO
HUB
Installing the synchronizer hub snapring on the NP-231

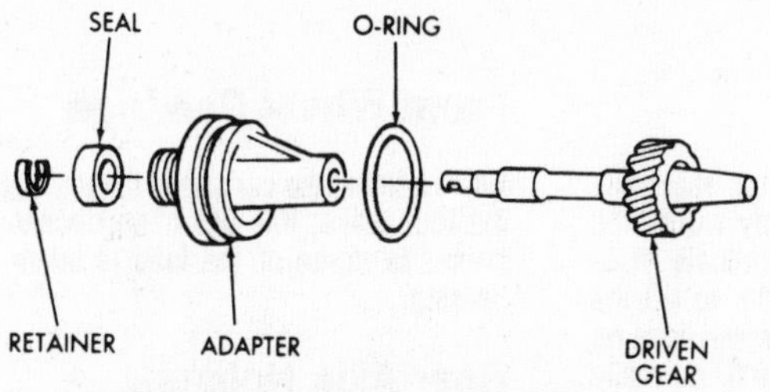
SEAL
O-RING
RETAINER
ADAPTER
DRIVEN GEAR

NP-231 speedometer gears

14. Install new synchro hub snapring. Install the sleeve on the synchro hub with the beveled spline ends facing the stop ring.
15. Install new pads on the mode fork and install the shift rail in the fork.
16. Engage the mode fork in the synchro sleeve. Install the mode fork mainshaft assembly in the case. Be sure the mode fork rail is seated in both of the range fork bushings.
17. Assemble and install the output shaft and drive chain. Lift the mainshaft slightle to ease chain and shaft installation.
18. Install the mode spring on the shift rail.
19. Install new output shaft rear bearing.
20. Install new seal in oil pump feed housing. Assemble the oil pump and install. Tighten screws to 14 inch lbs. Install new pick-up tube O-ring and install the pick-up tube. Attach the oil screen and connecting hose to the pick-up tube.
21. Install the assembled oil pump in the rear case.
22. Install the magnet in the from case.
23. Apply an ⅛ in. (3mm) bead of RTV sealer to the sealing surface of the front case. Align the case halves and join. Ensure locating dowels are inplace and that mainshaft splines are engaged in the oil pump inner gear.
24. Install and tighten attaching bolts/washers to 30 ft. lbs. (41 Nm).
25. Install new rear retainer bearing.
26. Apply an ⅛ in. (3mm) bead of RTV sealer to the flange of the rear retainer. Install the locating dowels and install retainer on case. Tighten bolts to 18 ft. lbs. (25 Nm).
27. Install a new rear bearing snapring. Lift the mainshaft to seat the snapring in the shaft groove.
28. Install new extension housing bushing and seal.
29. Apply an ⅛ in. (3mm) bead of RTV sealer to the flange of the extension housing. Mate the extension housing to the case and tighten bolts to 30 ft. lbs. (41 Nm).
30. Install front yoke and seal washer. Tighten nut to 110 ft. lbs. 150 Nm).
31. Install a replacement gasket on the vacuum switch and install switch.
32. Install drain plug and tighten to 35 ft. lbs. (47 Nm). Install speedometer gear, seals and adaptor.
33. Fill the case with lubricant and install fill plug. Tighten fill plug to 35 ft. lbs. (47 Nm).

DRIVELINE

Troubleshooting Basic Driveshaft and Rear Axle Problems

When abnormal vibrations or noises are detected in the driveshaft area, this chart can be used to help diagnose possible causes. Remember that other components such as wheels, tires, rear axle and suspension can also produce similar conditions.

BASIC DRIVESHAFT PROBLEMS

Problem	Cause	Solution
Shudder as car accelerates from stop or low speed	• Loose U-joint • Defective center bearing	• Replace U-joint • Replace center bearing
Loud clunk in driveshaft when shifting gears	• Worn U-joints	• Replace U-joints
Roughness or vibration at any speed	• Out-of-balance, bent or dented driveshaft • Worn U-joints • U-joint clamp bolts loose	• Balance or replace driveshaft • Replace U-joints • Tighten U-joint clamp bolts
Squeaking noise at low speeds	• Lack of U-joint lubrication	• Lubricate U-joint; if problem persists, replace U-joint
Knock or clicking noise	• U-joint or driveshaft hitting frame tunnel • Worn CV joint	• Correct overloaded condition • Replace CV joint

BASIC REAR AXLE PROBLEMS

First, determine when the noise is most noticeable.

Drive Noise – Produced under vehicle acceleration.

Coast Noise – Produced while the car coast with a closed throttle.

Float Noise – Occurs while maintaining constant car speed (just enough to keep speed constant) on a level road.

Road Noise

Brick or rough surfaced concrete roads produce noises that seem to come from the rear axle. Road noise is usually identical in Drive or Coast and driving on a different type of road will tell whether the road is the problem.

Tire Noise

Tire noises are often mistaken for rear axle problems. Snow treads or unevenly worn tires produce vibrations seeming to originate elsewhere. Temporarily inflating the tire to 40 lbs will significantly alter tire noise, but will have no effect on rear axle noises (which normally cease below about 30 mph).

Engine/Transmission Noise

Determine at what speed the noise is more pronounced, then stop the car in a quiet place. With the transmission in Neutral, run the engine through speeds corresponding to road speeds where the noise was noticed. Noises produced with the car standing still are coming from the engine or transmission.

Front Wheel Bearings

While holding the car speed steady, lightly apply the foot brake; this will often decease bearing noise, as some of the load is taken from the bearing.

Rear Axle Noises

Eliminating other possible sources can narrow the cause to the rear axle, which normally produces noise from worn gears or bearings. Gear noises tend to peak in a narrow speed range, while bearing noises will usually vary in pitch with engine speeds.

NOISE DIAGNOSIS

The Noise Is	Most Probably Produced By
• Identical under Drive or Coast	• Road surface, tires or front wheel bearings
• Different depending on road surface	• Road surface or tires
• Lower as the car speed is lowered	• Tires
• Similar with car standing or moving	• Engine or transmission
• A vibration	• Unbalanced tires, rear wheel bearing, unbalanced driveshaft or worn U-joint
• A knock or click about every 2 tire revolutions	• Rear wheel bearing
• Most pronounced on turns	• Damaged differential gears
• A steady low-pitched whirring or scraping, starting at low speeds	• Damaged or worn pinion bearing
• A chattering vibration on turns	• Wrong differential lubricant or worn clutch plates (limited slip rear axle)
• Noticed only in Drive, Coast or Float conditions	• Worn ring gear and/or pinion gear

DRIVELINE

On all models, conventional, open type driveshafts are used. Located at either end of the driveshaft is a universal joint (U-joint), which allows the driveshaft to move up and down to match the motion of the rear axle.

Since the truck can be obtained in 2WD and 4WD, three types of driveshafts may be employed. On the 2WD model, a one-piece driveshaft is used. On some 4WD models is a two-piece rear driveshaft with a center bearing, and the front shaft is a two piece telescope type with internal splines.

On the front of the one-piece driveshaft (2WD) or the two-piece driveshaft (4WD), the U-joints connect the driveshaft to a slip-jointed yoke. This yoke is internally splined and allows the driveshaft to move in and out on the transmission splines.

On the rear of the one-piece driveshaft (2WD) or the two-piece driveshaft (4WD), the U-joint is clamped to the rear axle pinion. It is attached to the rear axle pinion by use of bolted straps.

On the front driveshaft (4WD), the U-joints are secured to the transfer case and the front differential by the use of bolted straps. Located in the center of the driveshaft is a slip-joint, which allows the driveshaft to move in and out on its own splines.

On production U-joints, nylon is injected through a small hole in the yoke during manufacture and flows along a circular groove between the U-joint and the yoke, creating a non-metallic snapring.

Bad U-joints, requiring replacement, will produce a clunking sound when the vehicle is put into gear and when the transmission shifts from gear-to-gear. This is due to worn needle bearings or scored trunnion ends. U-joints require no periodic maintenance and therefore have no lubrication fittings.

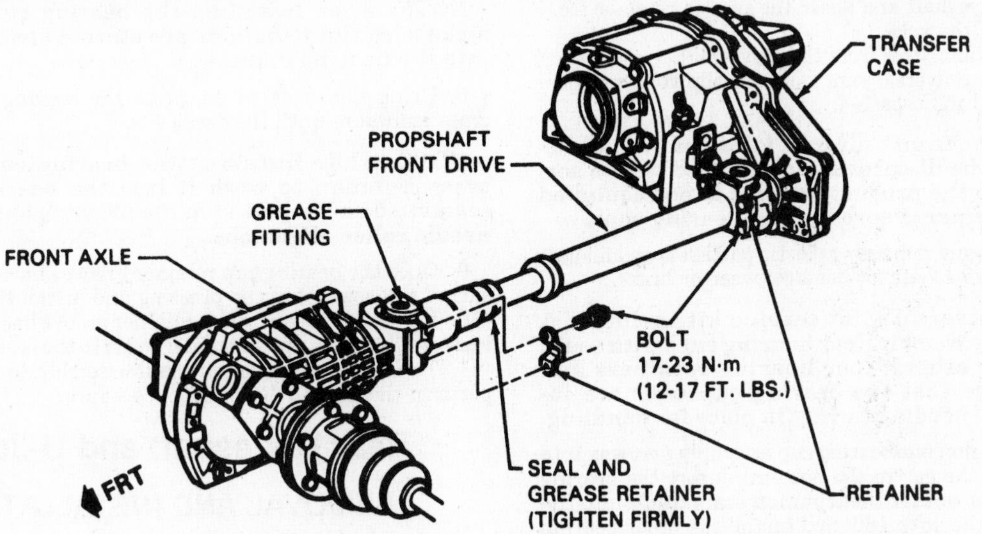
TRANSFER
CASE
PROPSHAFT
FRONT DRIVE
GREASE
FITTING
FRONT AXLE
BOLT
17-23 N·m
(12-17 FT. LBS.)
FRT
SEAL AND
GREASE RETAINER
(TIGHTEN FIRMLY)
RETAINER

Front drive shaft assembly on Blazer and Jimmy; Bravada similar

Front driveshaft and U-Joints

REMOVAL AND INSTALLATION

NOTE: DO NOT pound on the original driveshaft ears or the injected nylon U-joints may fracture.

1. Raise and safely support the front of the truck on jackstands.
2. Mark the relationship of the driveshaft to the front axle and the transfer case flanges.
3. Remove the driveshaft-to-retainer bolts and the retainers.
4. Collapse the driveshaft so it may be disengaged from the transfer case flange.
5. Move the driveshaft rearward (between the transfer case and the chassis) to disengage it from the front axle.

NOTE: Use care when handling the driveshaft to avoid dropping the U-joint cap assemblies.

6. Using tape, wrap it around the loose caps (if necessary) to hold them in place.
7. To install, use the alignment marks and reverse the removal procedures. Torque the retainer-to-transfer case/front axle bolts to 12–17 ft. lbs.

U-JOINT OVERHAUL

A universal type U-joint is used: it uses an internal snapring (production is plastic injected).

NOTE: The following procedure requires the use of an Arbor Press, the GM Cross Press tool No. J-9522-3 or equivalent, the GM Spacer tool No. J-9522-5 or equivalent, and a 1⅛ in. (29mm) socket.

1. While supporting the driveshaft, in the horizontal position, position it so that the lower ear of the front universal joint's shaft yoke is supported on a 1⅛ in. (29mm) socket.

NOTE: DO NOT clamp the driveshaft tube in a vise, for the tube may become damaged.

2. Using the GM Cross Press tool No. J-9522-3 or equivalent, place it on the horizontal bearing cups and press the lower bearing cup out of the yoke ear; the pressing action will shear the plastic retaining ring from the lower bearing cup. If the bearing cup was not completely removed, insert the GM Spacer tool No. J-9522-5 or equivalent, onto the universal joint, then complete the pressing procedure to remove the joint.

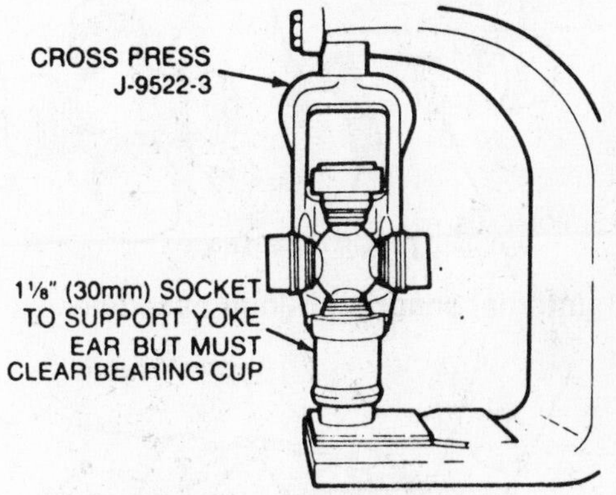
CROSS PRESS
J-9522-3
1⅛" (30mm) SOCKET
TO SUPPORT YOKE
EAR BUT MUST
CLEAR BEARING CUP

Pressing out the old U-joint

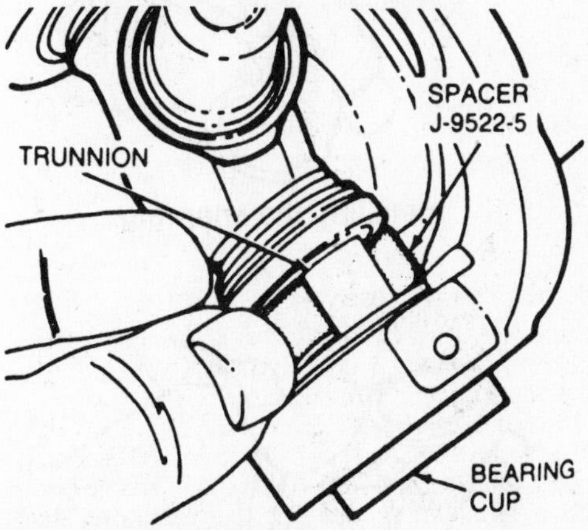
SPACER
J-9522-5
TRUNNION
BEARING
CUP

Spacer tool used to push the cup out all the way

3. Rotate the driveshaft and shear the plastic retainer from the opposite side of the yoke.
4. Disengage the slip yoke from the driveshaft.
5. To remove the universal joint from the slip yoke, perform the procedures used in Steps 1–4.

NOTE: When the front universal joint has been disassembled, it must be discarded and replaced with a service kit joint, for the production joint is not equipped with bearing retainer grooves on the bearing cups.

6. Clean (remove any remaining plastic particles) and inspect the slip yoke and driveshaft for damage, wear or burrs.

NOTE: The universal joint service kit includes: A pregreased cross assembly, four bearing cups with seals, needle rollers, washers, four bearing retainers and grease. Make sure that the bearing cup seals are installed to hold the needle bearings in place for handling.

7. To install, position one bearing cup assembly part way into the yoke ear (turn the ear to the bottom), insert the bearing cross (into the yoke) so that the trunnion seats freely into the bearing cup. Turn the yoke 180° and install the other bearing cup assembly.

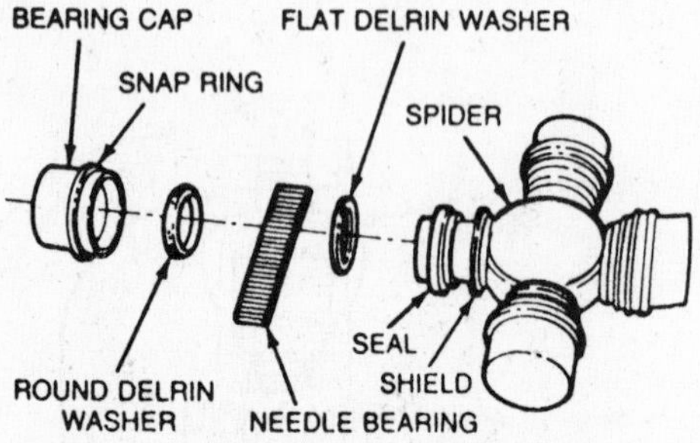
BEARING CAP
FLAT DELRIN WASHER
SNAP RING
SPIDER
SEAL
SHIELD
ROUND DELRIN WASHER
NEEDLE BEARING

Internal snapring U-joint assembly

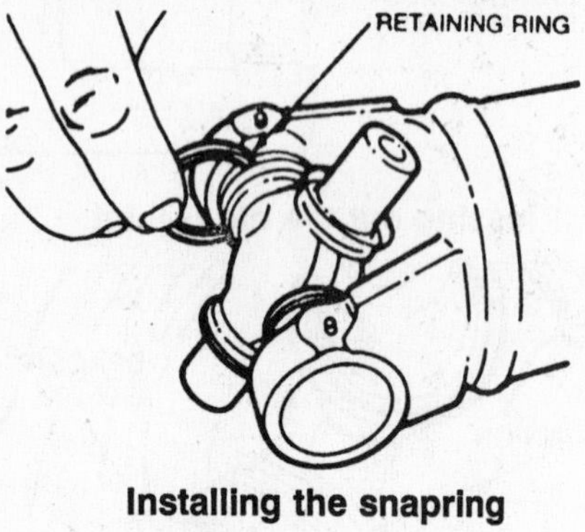
RETAINING RING

Installing the snapring

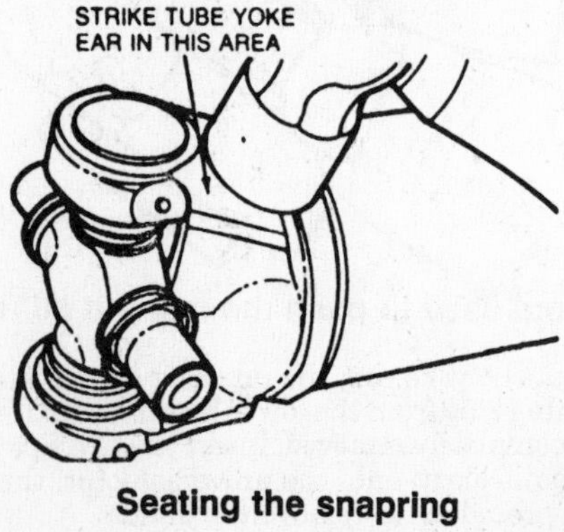
STRIKE TUBE YOKE EAR IN THIS AREA

Seating the snapring

NOTE: When installing the bearing cup assemblies, make sure the trunnions are started straight and true into the bearing cups.

8. Using the arbor press, press the bearing cups onto the cross trunnion, until they seat.

NOTE: While installing the bearing cups, twist the cross trunnion to work it into the bearings. If there seems to be a hangup, stop the pressing and recheck the needle roller alignment.

9. Once the bearing cup retainer grooves have cleared the inside of the yoke, stop the pressing and install the snaprings.
10. If the other bearing cup retainer groove has not cleared the inside of the yoke, use a hammer to aid in the seating procedure.
11. To install the yoke/universal assembly to the driveshaft, perform the Steps 7–10 of this procedure.

Rear Driveshaft and U-Joints

REMOVAL AND INSTALLATION

NOTE: DO NOT pound on the original propeller shaft yoke ears for the injected nylon joints may fracture.

1. Raise and safely support the rear of the vehicle on jackstands.
2. Mark relationship of the driveshaft-to-pinion flange and disconnect the rear universal joint by removing retainers. If the bearing cups are loose, tape them together to prevent dropping and loss of bearing rollers.
3. If equipped with a one-piece driveshaft, perform the following procedures:
   a. Slide the driveshaft forward to disengage it from the rear axle flange.
   b. Move the driveshaft rearward to disengage it from the transmission slip-joint, passing it under the axle housing.
4. If equipped with a two-piece driveshaft, perform the following procedures:
   a. Slide the driveshaft forward to disengage it from the rear axle flange.
   b. Slide the driveshaft rearward to disengage it from slip-joint of the front half-shaft, passing it under the axle housing.
   c. Remove the center bearing-to-support nuts and bolts.
   d. Slide the front half-shaft rearward to disengage it from the transfer case slip-joint.

NOTE: DO NOT allow the driveshaft to drop or allow the universal joints to bend to extreme angles, as this might fracture injected joint internally. Support propeller shaft during removal.

5. Inspect the slip-joint splines for damage, burrs or wear, for this will damage the transmission seal. Apply engine oil to all splined propeller shaft yokes.
6. DO NOT use a hammer to force the driveshaft into place. Check for burrs on transmission output shaft spline, twisted slip yoke splines or possibly the wrong U-joint. Make sure the splines agree in number and fit. To prevent trunnion seal damage, DO NOT place any tool between yoke and splines.
7. If installing a one-piece driveshaft, perform the following procedures:
   a. Slide driveshaft into the transmission.
   b. Align the rear universal joint-to-rear axle pinion flange, make sure the bearings are properly seated in the pinion flange yoke.
   c. Install the rear driveshaft-to-pinion fasteners. Torque the fasteners to 15 ft. lbs. (20 Nm).
8. If installing a two-piece drivehaft, perform the following procedures:
   a. Install the front half-shaft into the transmission and

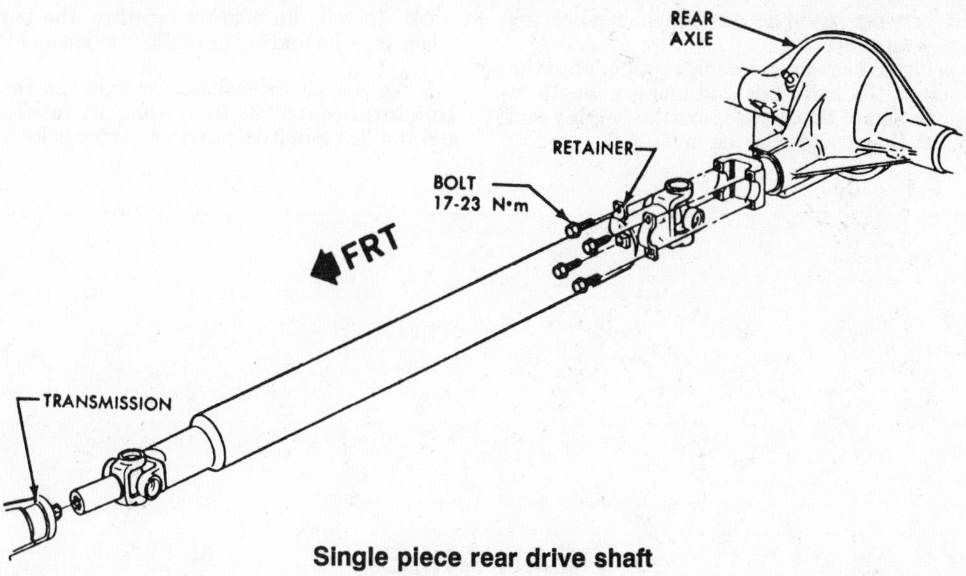
REAR AXLE
RETAINER
BOLT 17-23 N•m
FRT
TRANSMISSION

Single piece rear drive shaft

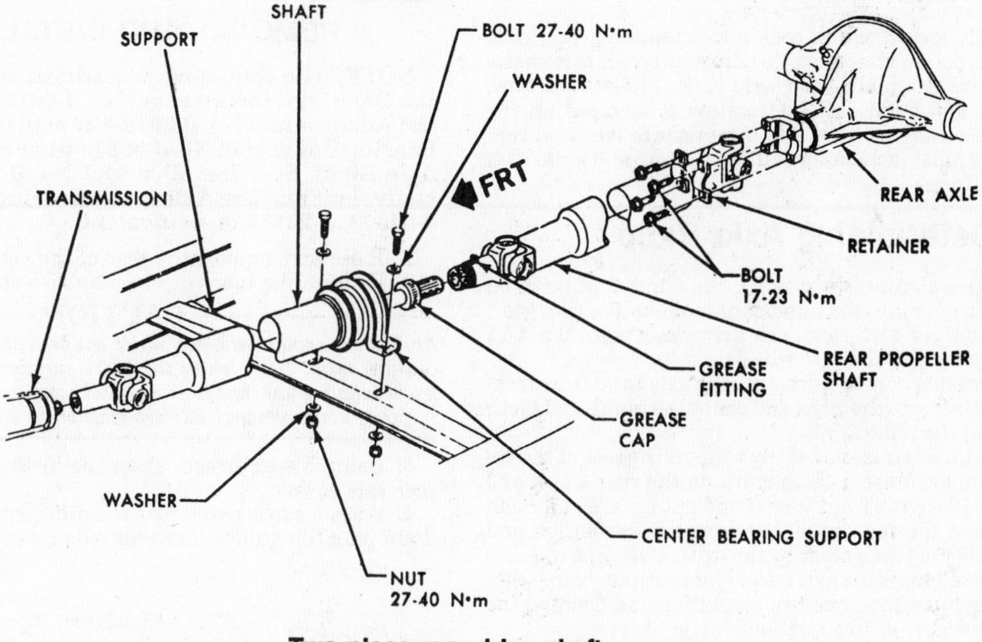
FRONT PROPELLER SHAFT
SUPPORT
BOLT 27-40 N•m
WASHER
FRT
TRANSMISSION
REAR AXLE
RETAINER
BOLT 17-23 N•m
REAR PROPELLER SHAFT
GREASE FITTING
GREASE CAP
WASHER
CENTER BEARING SUPPORT
NUT 27-40 N•m

Two-piece rear drive shaft

bolt the center bearing-to-support. Torque the center bearing to support nuts and bolts to 25 ft. lbs. (34 Nm).

NOTE: The front half-shaft yoke must be bottomed out in the transmission (fully forward) before installation to the support.

b. Rotate the shaft so that the front U-joint trunnion is in the correct position.

NOTE: Before installing the rear driveshaft, align the U-joint trunnions (a "key" in the output spline of the front half-shaft will align with a missing spline in the rear yoke).

c. Attach the rear U-joint to axle. Torque the retainers to 15 ft. lbs. (20 Nm).

9. Road test the vehicle.

Center Support Bearing

REMOVAL AND INSTALLATION

1. Refer to the "Rear Driveshaft, Removal and Installation" procedures in this section and remove the driveshaft.
2. Remove the strap retaining the rubber cushion from the bearing support.
3. Pull the support bracket from the rubber cushion and the cushion from the bearing.
4. Press the bearing assembly from half-shaft.
5. To assemble the bearing support, perform the following procedures:

a. If removed, install the inner deflector onto the half-shaft and prick punch the deflector at 2 opposite points to make sure it is tight on the shaft.

b. Fill the space between the inner dust shield and bearing with lithium soap grease.

c. Start the bearing and slinger assembly straight onto the shaft journal. Support the half-shaft and using a length of pipe over the splined end of the shaft, press the bearing and inner slinger against the shoulder of the half-shaft.

d. Install the bearing retainer, the rubber cushion onto bearing, the bracket onto the cushion and the retaining strap.

6. To install driveshaft, reverse the removal procedures. Torque the center bearing-to-support nuts/bolts to 20–30 ft. lbs. and the driveshaft-to-pinion retainer bolts to 12–17 ft. lbs.

REAR AXLE

Identification

The rear axle identification code and manufacturer's code must be known before attempting to adjust or repair axle shafts or rear axle case assembly. Rear axle ratio, differential type, manufacturer, and build date information is stamped on the right axle tube on the forward side. Any reports made on rear axle assemblies must include the full code letters and build date numbers.

Determining Axle Ratio

An axle ratio is obtained by dividing the number of teeth on the drive pinion gear into the number of teeth on the ring gear. For instance, on a 4.11:1 ratio, the driveshaft will turn 4.11 times for every turn of the rear wheels.

The most accurate way to determine the axle ratio is to drain the differential, remove the cover and count the number of teeth on the ring and the pinion.

An easier method is raise and safely support the rear of the vehicle on jackstands. Make a chalk mark on the rear wheel and the driveshaft. Block the front wheels and put the transmission in Neutral. Turn the rear wheel one complete revolution and count the number of turns made by the driveshaft. The number of driveshaft rotations is the axle ratio. More accuracy can be obtained by going more than one tire revolution and dividing the result by the number of tire rotations.

The axle ratio is also identified by the axle serial number prefix on the axle; the axle ratios are listed in the dealer's parts books according to the prefix number.

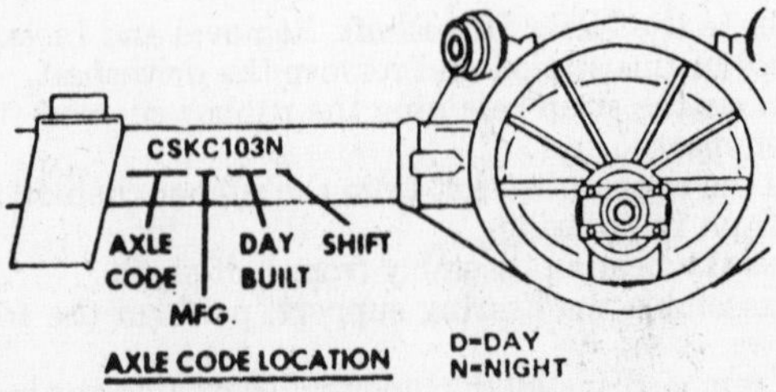
CSKC103N
AXLE CODE
DAY BUILT
SHIFT
MFG.
AXLE CODE LOCATION
D-DAY
N-NIGHT

Axle data on the rear axle housing

Axle Shaft, Bearing and Seal

REMOVAL AND INSTALLATION

NOTE: The following procedures requires the use of the GM Slide Hammer tool No. J-2619 or equivalent, the GM Adapter tool No. J-2619-4 or equivalent, the GM Axle Bearing Puller tool No. J-22813-01 or equivalent, the GM Axle Shaft Seal Installer tool No. J-33782, J-23771 or equivalent and the Axle Shaft Bearing Installer tool No. J-34974, J-23765 or equivalent.

1. Raise and support the rear of the vehicle on jackstands.
2. Remove the rear wheel assemblies and the brake drums.

CAUTION

Brake shoes contain asbestos, which has been determined to be a cancer causing agent. Never clean the brake surfaces with compressed air! Avoid inhaling any dust from any brake surface! When cleaning brake surfaces, use a commercially available brake cleaning fluid.

3. Using a wire brush, clean the dirt/rust from around the rear axle cover.
4. Place a catch pan under the differential, then remove the drain plug (if equipped) or rear axle cover and drain the oil.

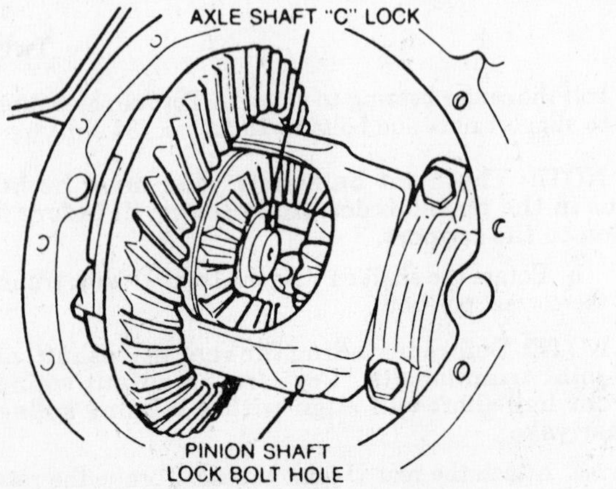
AXLE SHAFT "C" LOCK
PINION SHAFT
LOCK BOLT HOLE

Removing the axle shaft C-lock

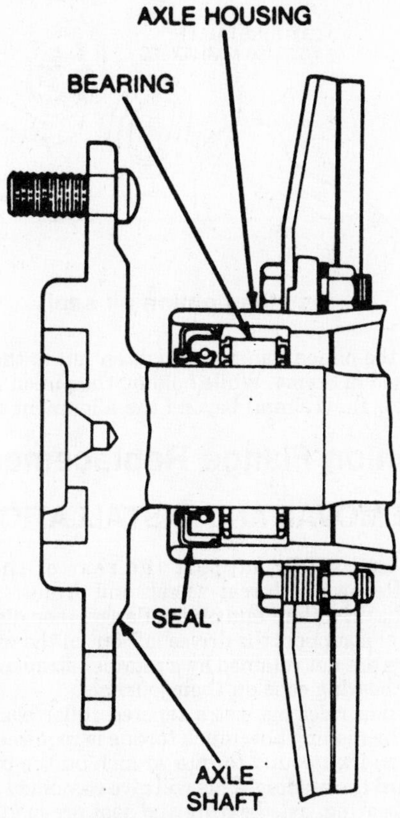
AXLE HOUSING
BEARING
SEAL
AXLE
SHAFT
Axle bearing and seal

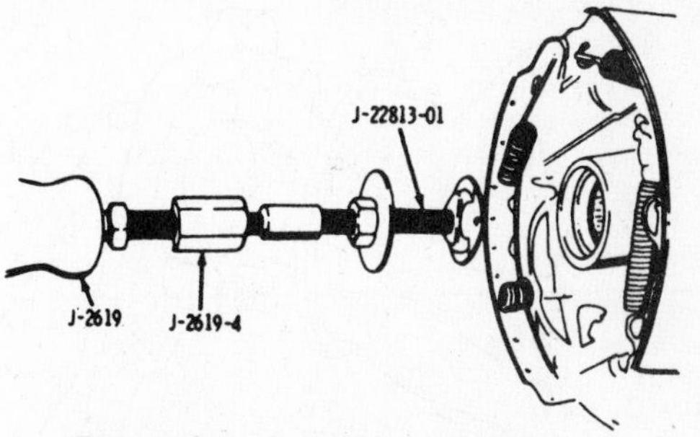
J-22813-01
J-2619
J-2619-4
Removing the axle bearing

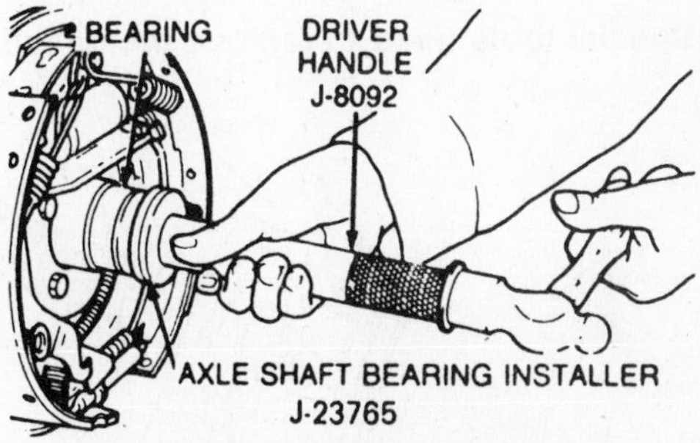
BEARING
DRIVER
HANDLE
J-8092
AXLE SHAFT BEARING INSTALLER
J-23765
Installing the axle bearing

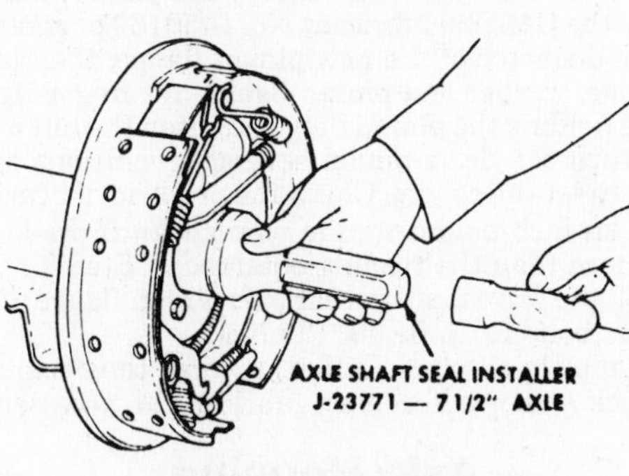
AXLE SHAFT SEAL INSTALLER
J-23771 — 7 1/2" AXLE
Installing the axle seal

5. At the differential, remove the rear pinion shaft lock bolt and the pinion shaft.
6. Push the axle shaft inward and remove the C-lock from the button end of the axle shaft.
7. Remove the axle shaft from the axle housing, be careful not to damage the oil seal.
8. Using a putty knife, clean the gasket mounting surfaces.

NOTE: It is recommended, when the axle shaft is removed, to replace the oil seal.

9. To replace the oil seal, perform the following procedures:
   a. Using a medium pry bar, pry the oil seal from the end of the rear axle housing; DO NOT damage the housing oil seal surface.
   b. Clean and inspect the axle tube housing.
   c. Using the GM Axle Shaft Seal Installer tool No. J-33782, J-23771 or equivalent, drive the new seal into the housing until it is flush with the axle tube.
   d. Using gear oil, lubricate the new seal lips.
10. If replacing the wheel bearing, perform the following procedures:
   a. Using the GM Slide Hammer tool No. J-2619 or equivalent, the GM Adapter tool No. J-2619-4 or equivalent and the GM Axle Bearing Puller tool No. J-22813-01 or equivalent, install the tool assembly so that the tangs engage the outer race of the bearing.
   b. Using the action of the slide hammer, pull the wheel bearing from the axle housing.
   c. Using solvent, throughly clean the wheel bearing, then blow dry with compressed air. Inspect the wheel bearing for excessive wear or damage. If it feels rough, replace it.
   d. With a new or the reused bearing, place a blob of heavy grease in the palm of your hand, then work the bearing into the grease until it is thoroughly lubricated.
   e. Using the Axle Shaft Bearing Installer tool No. J-34974, J-23765 or equivalent, drive the bearing into the axle housing until it bottoms against the seat. Install a new seal.
11. To install, slide the axle shaft into the rear axle housing and engage the splines of the axle shaft with the splines of the rear axle side gear, then install the C-lock retainer on the axle shaft button end. After the C-lock is installed, pull the axle shaft outward to seat the C-lock retainer in the counterbore of the side gears.

NOTE: When installing the axle shaft(s), be careful not to cut the oil seal lips.

12. Install the pinion shaft through the case and the pinions, then install a new pinion shaft lock bolt. Torque the new lock bolt to 25 ft. lbs. (34 Nm).
13. To complete the installation, use a new rear axle cover gasket and reverse the removal procedures. Torque the carrier cover-to-rear axle housing bolts to 20 ft. lbs. (27 Nm). Refill the housing with SAE-80W or SAE-80W-90 GL-5 oil to a level ⅜ in. (10mm) below the filler plug hole.

NOTE: When adding oil to the rear axle, be aware that some locking differentials require the use of a special gear lubricant additive GM No. Seal Replacement

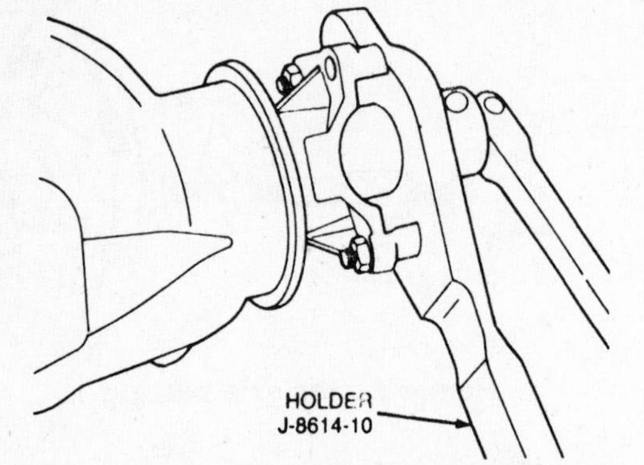
HOLDER
J-8614-10

Special tools used to remove the pinion nut

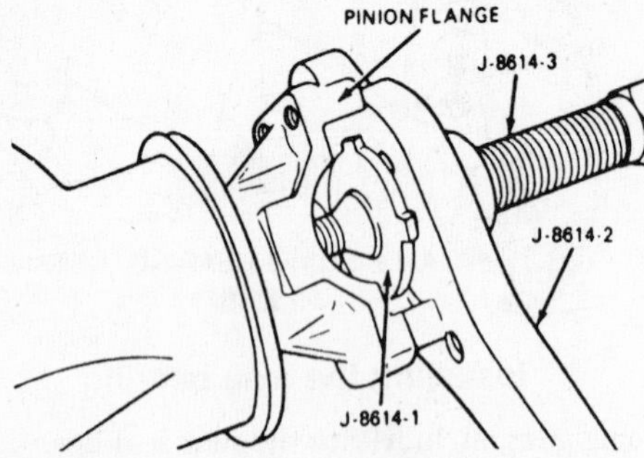
PINION FLANGE
J-8614-3
J-8614-2
J-8614-1

Puller used to remove pinion flange

Pinion Oil Seal Replacement

REMOVAL AND INSTALLATION

NOTE: The following procedure requires the use of the Pinion Holding tool No. J-8614-10 or equivalent, the Pinion Flange Removal tool No. J-8614-1, J-8614-2, J-8614-3 or equivalent, and the Pinion Oil Seal Installation tool No. J-23911 or equivalent.

1. Mark the driveshaft and pinion flange so they can be reassembled in the same position.
2. Disconnect the driveshaft from rear axle pinion flange and support the shaft up in body tunnel by wiring the driveshaft to the exhaust pipe. If the U-joint bearings are not retained by a retainer strap, use a piece of tape to hold bearings on their journals.
3. Mark the position of the pinion flange, the pinion shaft and nut so the proper pinion bearing pre-load can be maintained.
4. Using the Pinion Holding tool No. J-8614-10 or equivalent, the Pinion Flange Removal tool No. J-8614-1, J-8614-2, J-8614-3 or equivalent, remove the pinion flange nut and washer.
5. With suitable container in place to hold any fluid that may drain from rear axle, remove the pinion flange.
6. Remove the oil seal by driving it out of the differential with a blunt chisel; DO NOT damage the carrier.
7. Examine the seal surface of pinion flange for tool marks, nicks or damage, such as a groove worn by the seal. If damaged, replace flange as outlined under PINION FLANGE REPLACEMENT.
8. Examine the carrier bore and remove any burrs that might cause leaks around the O.D. of the seal.
9. To install a new seal, apply GM Seal Lubricant No. 1050169 or equivalent, to the outside diameter of the pinion flange and sealing lip of new seal. Drive the new seal into place with the correct size tool.

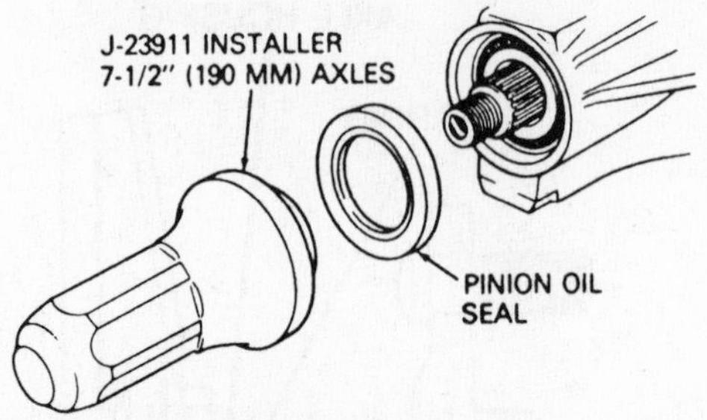
J-23911 INSTALLER
7-1/2" (190 MM) AXLES
PINION OIL
SEAL

Installing pinion oil seal

10. Install the pinion flange and tighten nut to the same position as marked in Step 4. While holding the pinion flange tighten the nut $^{1}/_{16}$ in. (1.6mm) beyond the alignment marks.

Pinion Flange Replacement

REMOVAL AND INSTALLATION

1. Raise and safely support the rear of the truck on jackstands. Remove both rear wheels and drums.
2. Mark the driveshaft and pinion flange, then disconnect the rear U-joint and support the driveshaft out of the way. If the U-joint bearings are not retained by a retainer strap, use a piece of tape to hold bearing caps on their journals.
3. The pinion rides against a tapered roller bearing. Check the pre-load by reading how much torque is required to turn the pinion. Use an inch pound torque wrench on the pinion flange nut and record the reading. This will give combined pinion bearing, carrier bearing, axle bearing and seal pre-load.
4. Remove pinion flange nut and washer.
5. With a suitable container in place to hold any fluid that may drain from the rear axle, remove the pinion flange.
6. Apply the GM Seal lubricant No. 1050169 or equivalent, to the outside diameter of the new pinion flange, then install the pinion flange, washer and pinion flange nut finger tight.
7. While holding the pinion flange, tighten the nut a little at a time and turn the drive pinion several revolutions after each tightening to set the rollers. Check the pre-load of bearings each time with an inch pound torque wrench until pre-load is 3–5 inch lbs. more than the reading obtained in Step 3.
8. Install the driveshaft-to-rear axle pinion flange and torque the retainer bolts to 15 ft. lbs. (20 Nm).
9. To complete the installation, reverse the removal procedures. Check and/or add correct lubricant as necessary.

Axle Housing

REMOVAL AND INSTALLATION

1. Refer to the "Driveshaft, Removal and Installation" procedures in this section and disconnect the driveshaft from the rear axle housing; the driveshaft may either be removed or supported on a wire. Using a floor jack, position it under and support the rear axle housing.

NOTE: When supporting the rear of the vehicle, be sure to place the jackstands under the frame.

2. Remove the rear wheel assemblies.
3. Remove the shock absorber-to-axle housing nuts/bolts, then swing the shock absorbers away from the axle housing.
4. Disconnect the brake lines from the axle housing clips and the backing plates (wheel cylinders).

NOTE: When disconnecting the brake lines from the wheel cylinders, be sure to plug the lines to keep dirt from entering the lines.

1. Nut
2. Shock absorber
3. Bolt
4. Retainer
5. Pinion flange
6. U-bolts
7. Vent hose
8. Nut
10. Axle housing

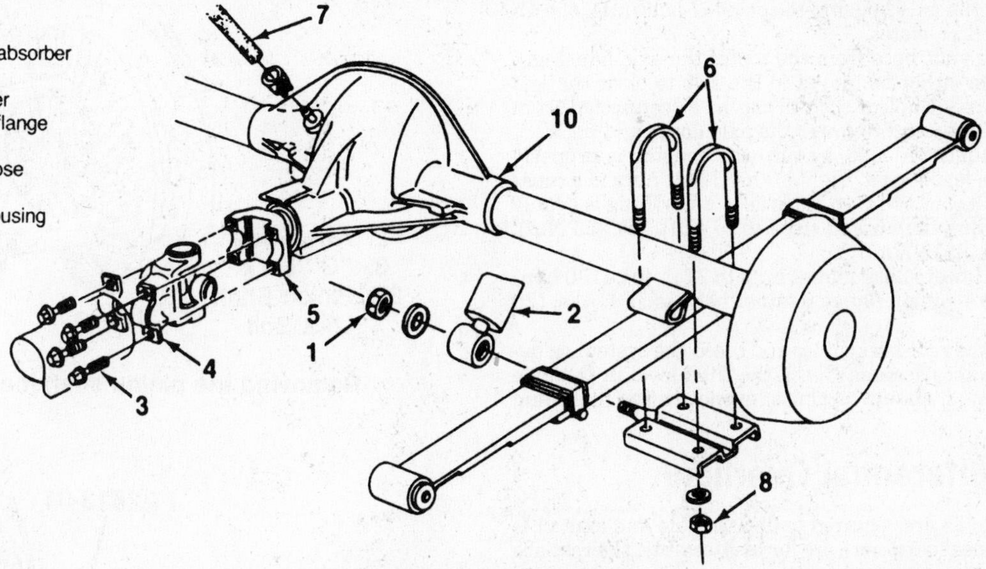

7
6
10
5
2
1
4
3
8

Removing the rear axle

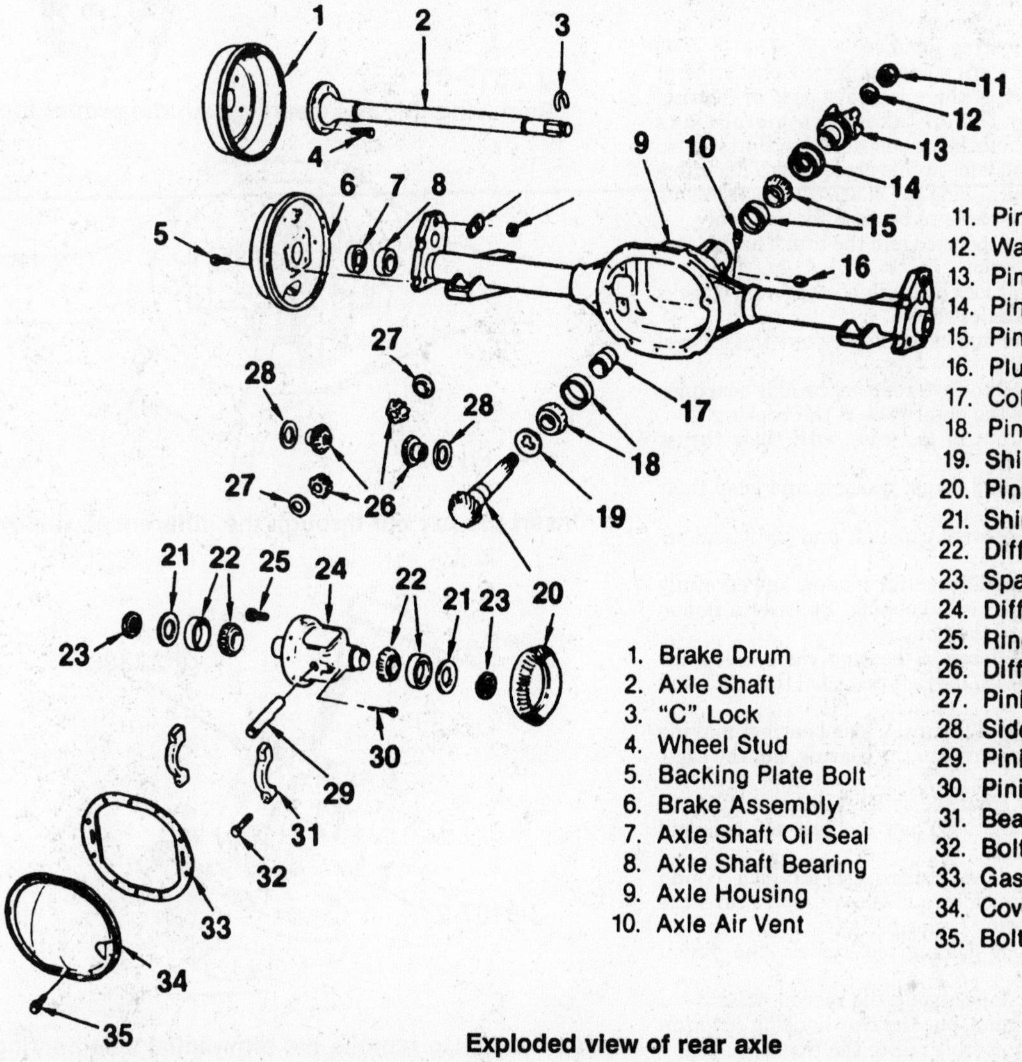

1
2
3
4
5
6
7
8
9
10
11
12
13
14
15
16
17
18
19
20
21
22
23
24
25
26
27
28
29
30
31
32
33
34
35

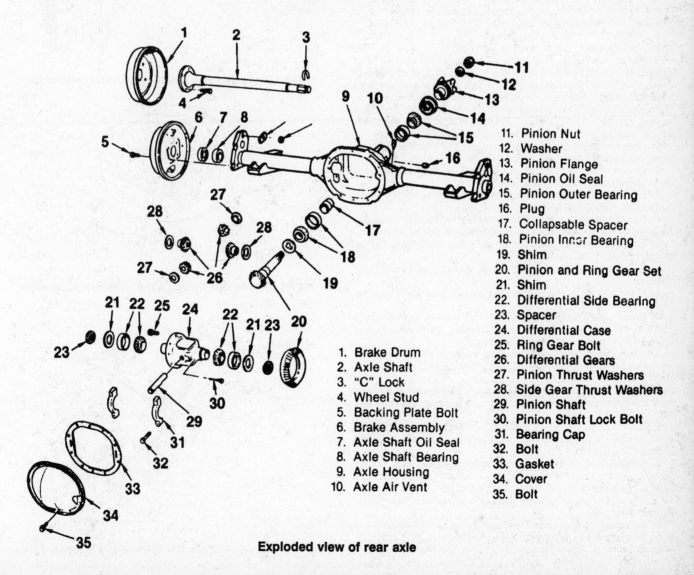

1. Brake Drum
2. Axle Shaft
3. "C" Lock
4. Wheel Stud
5. Backing Plate Bolt
6. Brake Assembly
7. Axle Shaft Oil Seal
8. Axle Shaft Bearing
9. Axle Housing
10. Axle Air Vent
11. Pinion Nut
12. Washer
13. Pinion Flange
14. Pinion Oil Seal
15. Pinion Outer Bearing
16. Plug
17. Collapsable Spacer
18. Pinion Inner Bearing
19. Shim
20. Pinion and Ring Gear Set
21. Shim
22. Differential Side Bearing
23. Spacer
24. Differential Case
25. Ring Gear Bolt
26. Differential Gears
27. Pinion Thrust Washers
28. Side Gear Thrust Washers
29. Pinion Shaft
30. Pinion Shaft Lock Bolt
31. Bearing Cap
32. Bolt
33. Gasket
34. Cover
35. Bolt

Exploded view of rear axle

5. Disconnect the axle housing-to-spring U-bolt nuts, the U-bolts and the anchor plates.

6. Remove the vent hose from the top of the axle housing.

7. The axle can either be moved to the side to clear the leaf spring or, if desired, the leaf springs can be disconnected from the frame at the rear end to lower the axle down and back.

8. When installing the axle, be sure the housing is properly positioned on the leaf spring. Tighten the U-bolt nuts in a cross pattern to 18 ft. lbs. (25 Nm) to made sure everything is evenly seated. Then torque the nuts in stepa to to 41 ft. lbs. (55 Nm), then to 85 ft. lbs. (115 Nm).

9. Torque the lower shock mount nuts to 74 ft. lbs. (100 Nm) and the U-joint–to–pinion flange retainer bolts to 15 ft. lbs. (20 Nm).

10. Reconnect the rear brake lines and bleed the system as described in the Brakes section. Check the fluid level in the axle before test driving: it should be almost even with the filler plug hole.

Differential Overhaul

Some special tools are required to disassemble and assemble the rear axle. Those listed here are for disassembly, the rest are listed with the assembly procedure.

- J-2619-01 Slide Hammer
- J-22813-01 Axle Bearing Puller
- J-8107-2 Differential Side Bearing Remover Plug
- J-22888 Side Bearing Remover
- J-8614-01 Pinion Flange Remover
- J-25320 Rear Pinion Bearing Remover

Before disassembly, there are some things to check. First drain the oil and examine it. If there is heavy gear or bearing wear in the axle, usually the oil takes on a metal-flake appearence from the worn metal being suspended in the oil. Also check the backlash, described later in this procedure. This information can be useful in determining the cause of axle problems and in deciding on the shim packs to be used for assembly.

1. With the axle properly supported and the brake backplates removed, remove the rear cover.

2. Remove the pinion shaft lock bolt, pinion shaft and C locks from the button end of the axles shafts.

3. Remove the axle shafts and carefully pry out the oil seal from each end of the housing.

4. Use the bearing removal tools to remove the axle bearings. Make sure the tool engages the outer race of the bearing.

5. Roll the pinion gears out of the case with their thrust washers. Label their position.

6. Remove the side gears and thrust washers and label their position.

7. Mark the differential bearing caps left and right and remove them.

8. Insert a pry bar into the differential window and carefully pry the differential out of the axle housing. Be careful not to damage the gasket surface of the housing.

9. When removing the differential bearing races, keep the shims and spacers together with the race and label them left and right.

10. Install the puller on the differential side bearing, making sure the jaws contact the inner race of the bearing, not the cage. Remove the bearings.

11. Remove the ring gear from the differential case. The 10 bolts are left hand thread. DO NOT pry the gear off, this will damage the gear and the case.

12. Before removing the drive pinion, use an inch pound torque wrench to see how much torque is required to turn the pinion. This checks the bearing preload.

13. Install the pinion flange holding tool removė the pinion flange nut.

14. To remove the pinion flange using the special puller.

15. To remove the drive pinion, put the rear housing cover on with 2 screws so the pinion doesn't fall to the floor.

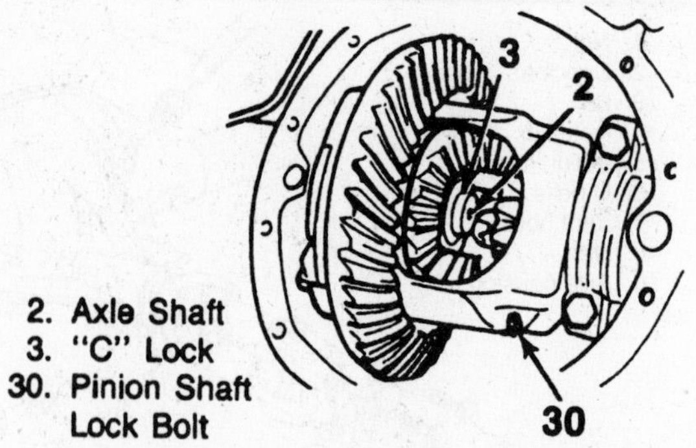
3
2
2. Axle Shaft
3. "C" Lock
30. Pinion Shaft
Lock Bolt
30

Removing the pinion shaft lock bolt

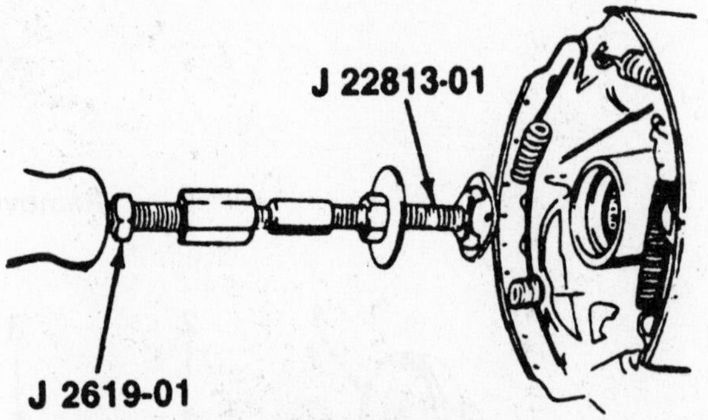
J 22813-01
J 2619-01

Removing the axle bearing with the proper tool

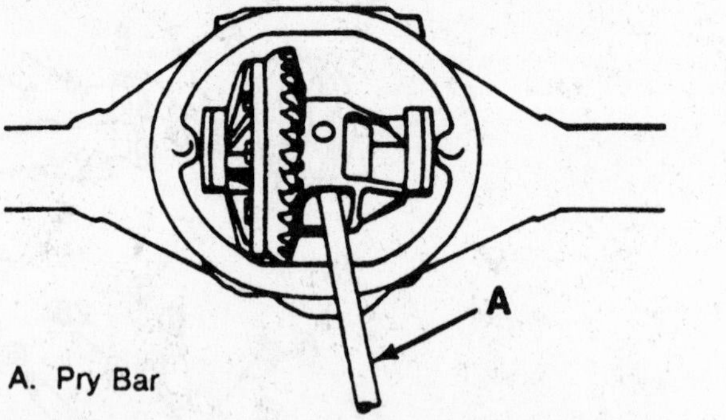
A
A. Pry Bar

Insert the pry bar through the differential window

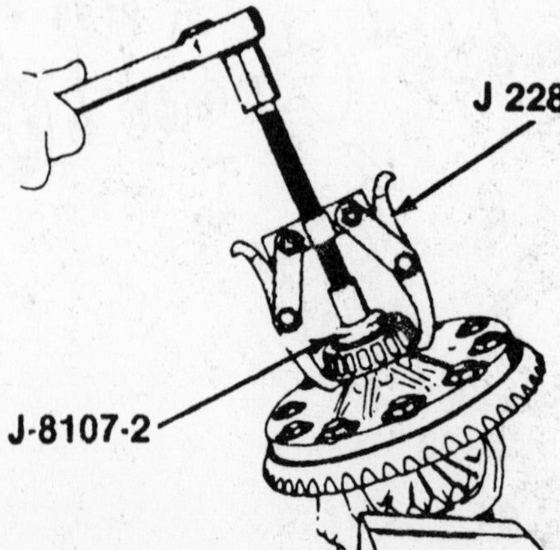
J 22888
J-8107-2

Use a puller to remove the differential side bearings

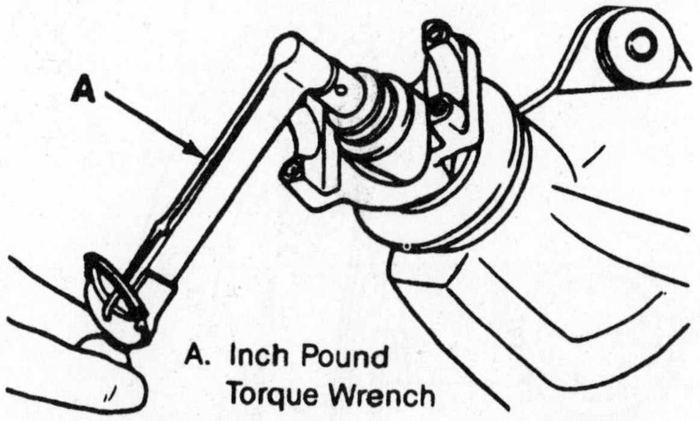
A
A. Inch Pound
Torque Wrench

Check the bearing preload before removing the pinion

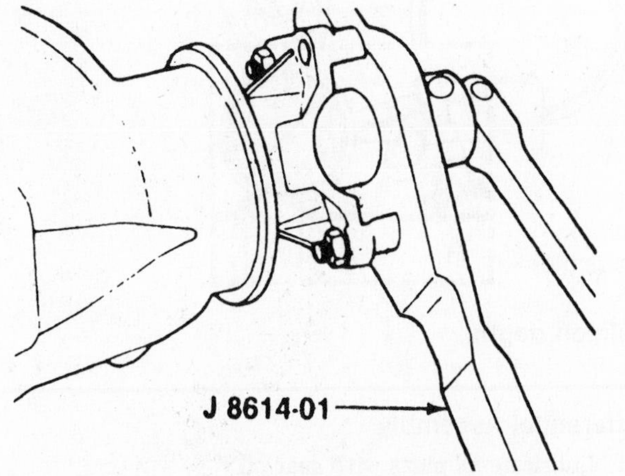
J 8614-01

Removing the pinion nut with the holding tool

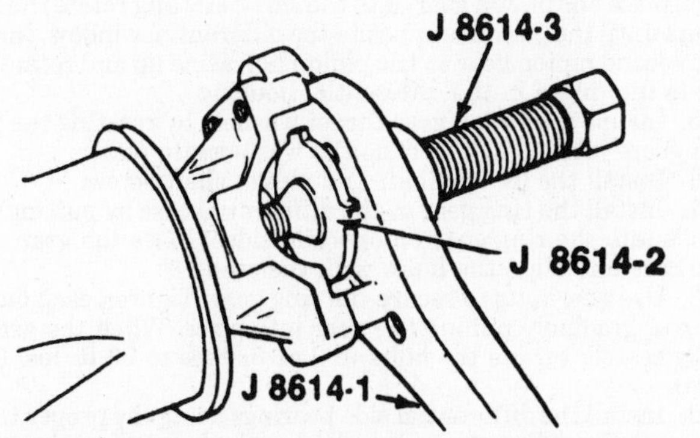
J 8614-3
J 8614-2
J 8614-1

Removing the pinion with the special puller

16. Put the flange nut onto the pinion a few threads and use a hammer and soft drift pin to drive the pinion out of the housing.
17. With the pinion out, remove the collapsible spacer.
18. Remove the oil seal and outer pinion bearing.
19. To remove the inner pinion bearing, use the bearing pulling tool J25320 and a press. Keep track of the shims under the bearing.
20. Remove the pinion drive bearing races from the case with a hammer and drift pin.

INSPECTION

Clean all parts in a clean solvent and dry with air. Carefully inspect the housing for damage to the sealing areas and the bearing areas for burrs or nicks that may interfere with assembly. Remove any imperfections that are found. Throughly clean the housing using solvent, not steam or water. Any metal chips or rust left in the housing will damage the gears and bearings. Check the housing for cracks.

Check the differential gears, shafts and thrust washers for uneven or heavy wear patterns. Check the differential case for cracks and signs of heat damage or scoring. Check the fit of the gears on the axle shafts and in the differential case. If in doubt, replace the parts.

Inspect the pinion shaft splines for wear and check the fit with the pinion flange. If the sealing surface on the flange is nicked or worn, replace the flange. Compare the wear patterns on the ring and pinion gears for excessive wear or signs of heat damage. A ring and pinion gear are a matched set and must be replaced together.

Inspect the bearings for signs of heat damage or contamination. The big end of tapered rollers is where signs of wear or damage will appear first. Low milage units will show some scratches on the bearings from initial preload. If the (oiled) bearing still feels smooth, it need not be replaced. If the axle was used for an extended period with very loose bearings, the ring and pinion should be replaced. When replacing bearings, also replace the outer race.

ASSEMBLY

Note: Several special assembly tools are required for correct measurement and positioning of the ring and pinion.

- J-21777-40 Rear pilot washer
- J-21777-42 Front pilot washer
- J-21777-43 Stud
- J-21777-45 Side bearing discs
- J-23597-1 Arbor
- J-23597-11 Gage plate
- J-8001 Dial indicator

Pinion Depth Adjustment

1. Clean all gage parts.
2. Lubricate the front and rear pinion bearings with gear oil.

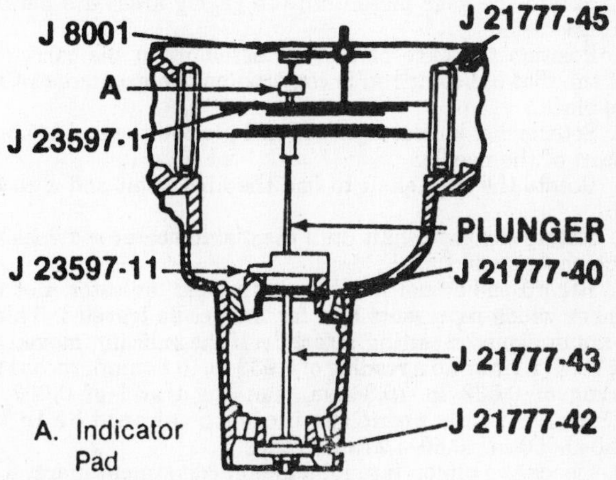
J 8001
J 21777-45
A
J 23597-1
PLUNGER
J 23597-11
J 21777-40
J 21777-43
A. Indicator
Pad
J 21777-42

Secure the bearings in place with the adjustment tools

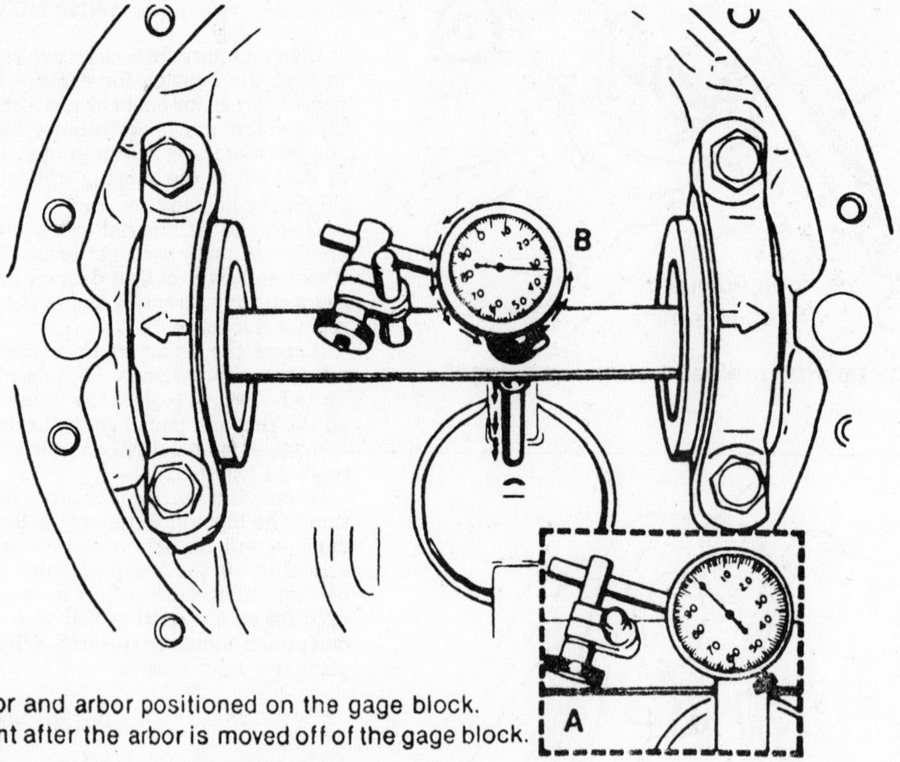
B
A

A. Dial indicator and arbor positioned on the gage block.
B. Measurement after the arbor is moved off of the gage block.

Checking nominal pinion depth

3. With the outer races installed into the axle housing, place the bearings into the outer races and secure them in place with the pilot washers and stud assembly tool and gage plate as shown.
4. Torque the J 21777-43 stud assembly to 20 inch lbs. (2.2 Nm).
5. Rotate the gage plate and bearings several revolutions to seat the bearings.
6. Retorque the stud assembly.
7. Install the arbor, side bearing disks and dial indicator as shown.
8. Install the side bearing caps and finger tighten the bolts.
9. Rotate the gage plate until the gaging areas are parallel with the disks.
10. Position the gage plate shaft assembly in the carrier so that the dial indicator rod is centered on the gage area of the gage block.
11. Set the dial indicator at zero and preload the dial to about ¾ turn of the needle.
12. Rotate the gage shaft to find the high point and zero the dial.
13. Rotate the gage shaft until the dial indicator rod does not touch the gage block.
14. Record the actual number on the dial indicator, not the number which represents how far the needle traveled. This is the nominal pinion setting. Example: If the indicator moved left 0.067 in. (1.7mm) to a reading of 0.033 in. (0.84mm), record the reading of 0.033 in. (0.84mm), not the travel of 0.067 in. (1.7mm). At this point the indicator should be in the 0.020–0.050 in. (0.50–1.27mm) range.
15. Check the pinion face for a pinion adjustment mark. This mark is the best running position for the pinion from the nominal setting.
16. Remove the measuring tools and install the pinion shim according to the measurements taken.

Differential Assembly

1. Lubricate all parts with gear oil.
2. Install the side gear thrust washers to the side gears.
3. Install the side gears into the same side that they were removed from.
4. Install the pinion gears without the thrust washers. To do this, place one pinion gear onto the side gears ang rotate the side gears until the pinion is opposite the differential window. Install the second pinion gear so the pinion holes line up and rotate the gears into place in the differential housing.
5. Install the pinion gear thrust washers by rotating the pinion gears just enough to slide the washer into place.
6. Install the pinion shaft and pinion shaft screw.
7. Install the ring gear to the differential case by putting two studs into the ring gear on opposite sides. Place the gear onto the case and align the holes with the studs.
8. Use new bolts to secure the ring gear. Tighten each one in stages, gradually pulling the gear into place. When the gear is fully seated, torque the bolts in 2 or 3 steps to 90 ft. lbs. (120 Nm).
9. Install the differential side bearings using the proper tools. Support the differential when driving the bearing on the opposite side so the bearing does not take the load.

Setting Side Bearing Pre-load Adjustment

Note: This procedure requires a special gaging tool, J 22779.

The adjustment is to position the differential properly side-to-side in the axle housing so the bearings are properly loaded. This is done by changing the shim thickness on both sides equally so the original backlash is maintained. Production shims are made of cast iron and must not be reused. Measure the shims and spacers one at a time and add the numbers to

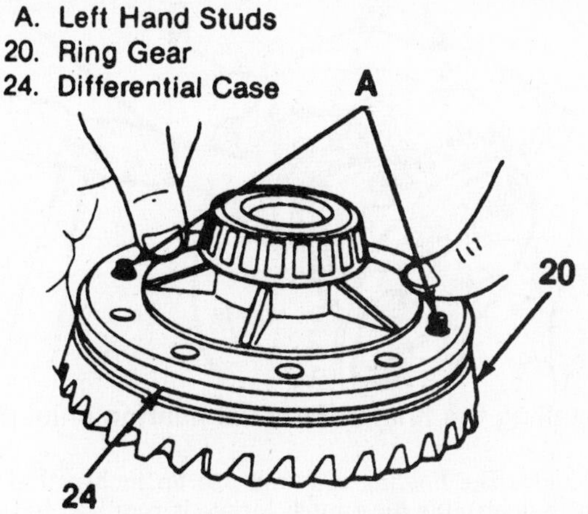
A. Left Hand Studs
20. Ring Gear
24. Differential Case
A
20
24
Align the ring gear studs

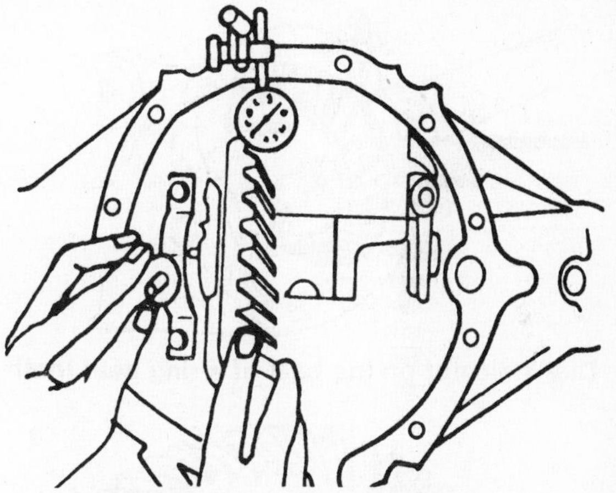
Install the side bearing gaging tool

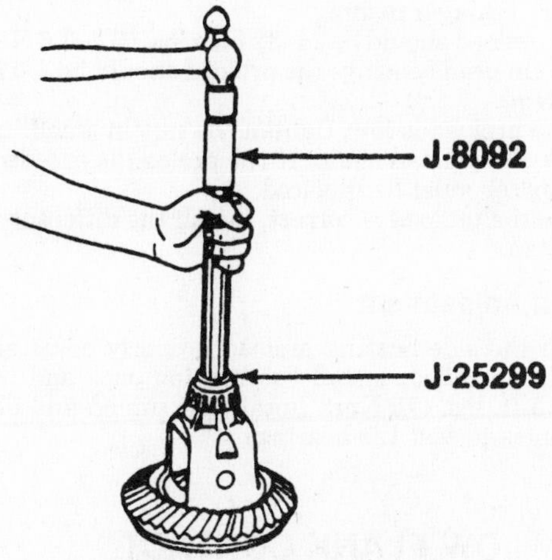
J-8092
J-25299
Installing the side bearings

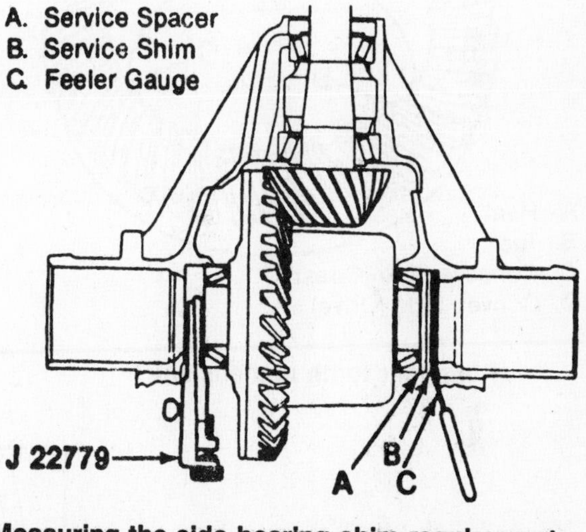
A. Service Spacer
B. Service Shim
C. Feeler Gauge
J 22779
A
B
C
Measuring the side bearing shim requirements

optain the original shim pack thickness. The new service spacer thickness is 0.170 in. (4.32mm). The shims are available in increments of 0.004 in. (0.101mm) in sizes from 0.040–0.100 in. (1.02–2.54mm).

1. With the bearing races installed and lubricated, set the differential case into the axle housing to set the side bearing preload adjustment.
2. Insert the gaging tool between the axle housing and the left bearing cup.
3. Move the tool back and forth in the bore while turning the adjusting nut to the right until a noticeable drag is produced. Tighten the lock bolt on the side of the tool and leave the tool in place.
4. Install a new spacer and a shim between the right bearing race and the axle housing.
5. Determine the bearing preload by inserting progressively larger feeler gages between the carrier and the shim. Push the gage down so it contacts the shim at the top and bottom, then contacts the axle housing. The point just before additional drag begins is the correct feeler gage thickness. This is the zero setting without preload.
6. Remove the gaging tool, spacer, shim, feeler gage and differential from the axle housing.
7. Measure the gaging tool in 3 places using a micrometer and average the readings.
8. Add the dimensions of the right side spacer, shim and feeler gage.
9. For an initial backlash setting, move the ring gear away from the pinion by subtracting 0.010 in. (0.04mm) from the ring gear side of the shim pack and adding the same to the opposite side.
10. To obtain the proper preload on the side bearings, add 0.010 in. (0.04mm) to the measurement of each shim pack.
11. The differential is ready for installation.

Pinion Installation

1. The bearing races should already be installed from the pinion depth adjustment done earlier. Install the pinion inner bearing onto the pinion; drive the inner race until it is seated on the shims.
2. Install a new collapsible spacer.
3. Install the pinion into the axle housing.
4. While holding the pinion in place, carefully drive the outer bearing onto the pinion shaft.
5. Install a new pinion oil seal.
6. Install the pinion flange by tapping it with a soft mallet until enough threads show to start the nut.
7. Install the flange holding tool and install the washer and a new nut. DO NOT tighten the nut. The bearing preload must be adjusted.

Pinion Bearing Preload Adjustment

1. Tighten the pinion nut just until the end play is taken out.

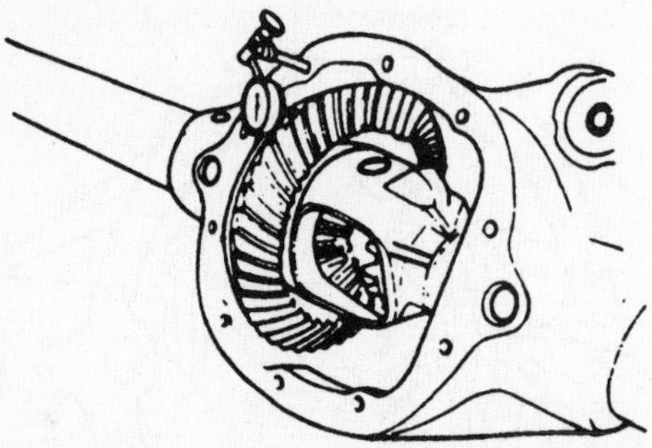

Dial indicator on the heel of a ring gear tooth

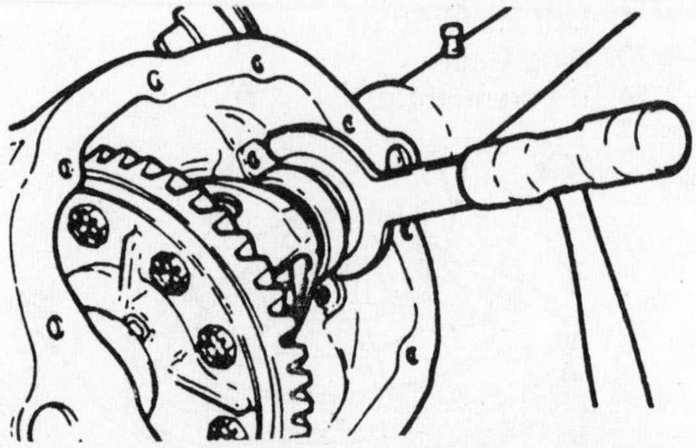

Installing the final differential bearing shim pack

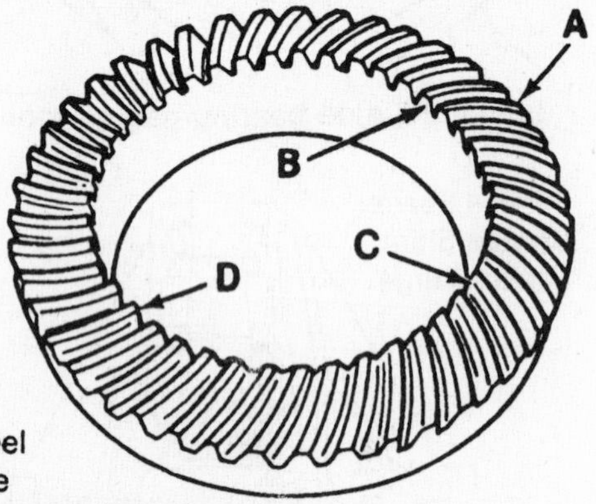
A
B
C
D

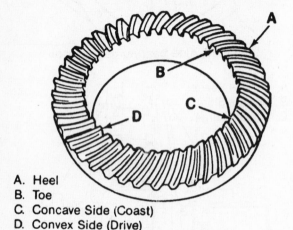

A. Heel
B. Toe
C. Concave Side (Coast)
D. Convex Side (Drive)

Ring gear tooth nomenclature

2. Remove the holding tool and use an inch pound torque wrench to determine how much torque is required to turn the pinion. This is bearing preload. Some of the resistance to turning the pinion shaft comes from the seal, so make sure it is properly lubricated. Turn the pinion several times to seat the bearings before taking a reading.

3. The preload should be 24–32 inch lbs. (2.7–3.6 Nm) on new bearings. On used bearings the preload should be 8–12 inch lbs. (1.0–1.4 Nm).

4. If the preload is low, tighten the nut in small increments and check the preload again. If the preload is exceded, the collapsible spacer must be replaced.

5. Once the proload is correct, install the differential and set the backlash.

Backlash Adjustment

1. With the side bearing preload properly adjusted and the differential installed, install the bearing caps and torque the bolts to 55 ft. lbs. (75 Nm). Rotate the pinion and differential several times to seat the bearings.

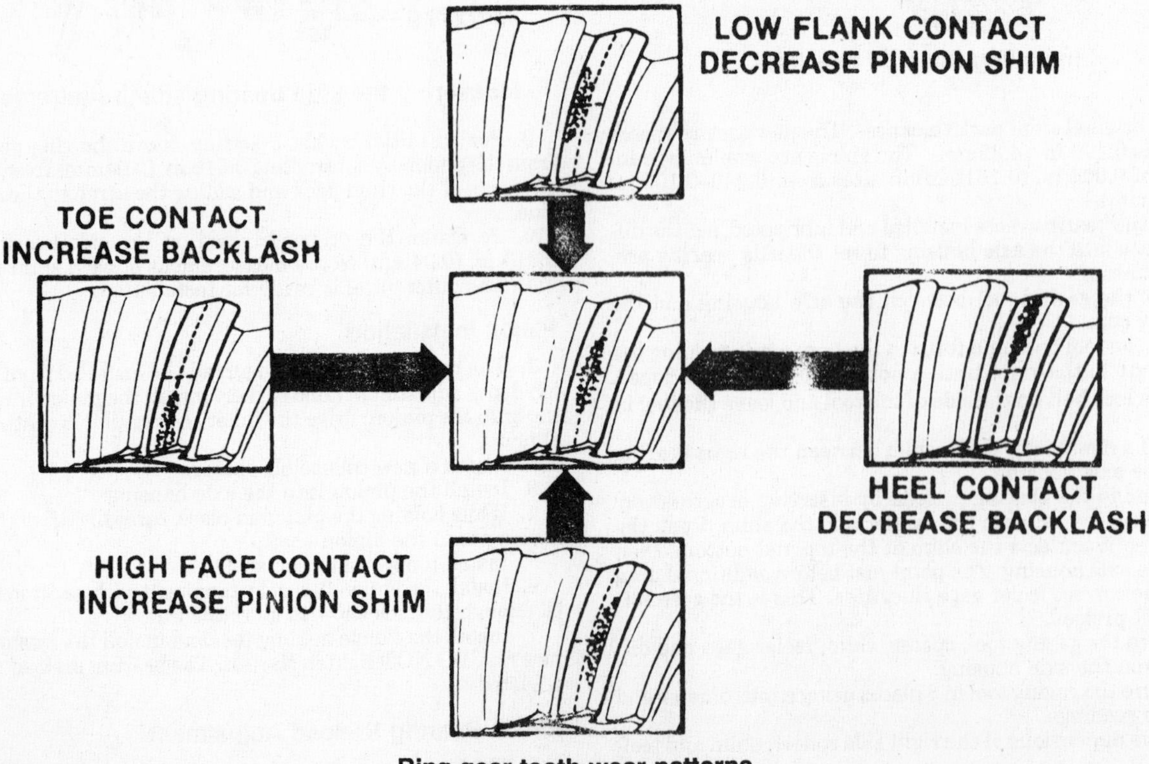
LOW FLANK CONTACT
DECREASE PINION SHIM
TOE CONTACT
INCREASE BACKLASH
HEEL CONTACT
DECREASE BACKLASH
HIGH FACE CONTACT
INCREASE PINION SHIM

Ring gear tooth wear patterns

2. Install a dial indicator to the axle housing. A unit with a magnetic base is acceptable.
3. Touch the stem to the heel of a tooth on the ring gear. That's the outer edge of the convex or drive side.
4. Hold the pinion fast and rock the ring gear to see how much play there is between the gear teeth; backlash. Record the reading and check 3 or 4 more places around the ring gear.
5. The readings should all be within 0.002 in. (0.05mm). If the readings vary more than this, check for burrs, a distorted case flange or uneven torque of the ring gear bolts.
6. The correct backlash is 0.005–0.009 in. (0.13–0.23mm) for new gear sets.
7. To adjust backlash, remove shim thickness from one side of the differential and add the same amount to the other side. This moves the ring gear to one side while maintaining the side bearing preload. Moving 0.002 in. (0.05mm) of shim changes the backlash by 0.001 in. (0.03mm).
8. When the backlash is correctly adjusted, remove the side bearing caps and shim packs.
9. Add 0.004 in. (0.10mm) of shim to the left side shim pack and install it. Install the left bearing cap but do not tighten the bolts yet.
10. Add 0.004 in. (0.10mm) of shim to the right side shim pack and drive the shim pack into place. Install the bearing cap and torque the bolts to 55 ft. lbs. (75 Nm).
11. Recheck the backlash and adjust as needed.

Final Assembly

1. Install new axle bearings and oil them with gear oil.
2. Install new axle seals and oil the lips with gear oil.
3. Install the axle shafts and edgage the splines with the side gears in the differential.
4. Install the C locks on the end of the shafts. Pull out on the shafts to seat the C locks in the side gears.
5. Install the pinion shaft into the differential gears and install the lock bolt. DO NOT over tighten the lock bolt. Torque it to 25 ft. lbs. (34 Nm).
6. Install the rear cover with a new gasket and torque the bolts to 20 ft. lbs. (27 Nm). Refill with lubricant.

FRONT DRIVE AXLE

Identification

The front axle assembly, used on the 4WD models, utilizes a central disconnect type front axle/transfer case system which allows shifting in and out of 4WD when the vehicle is moving under most driving conditions. The axle has an aluminum carrier which includes a vacuum activated center lock feature.

The drive axles employ completely flexible assemblies which consist of inner and outer constant velocity (CV) joints connect-

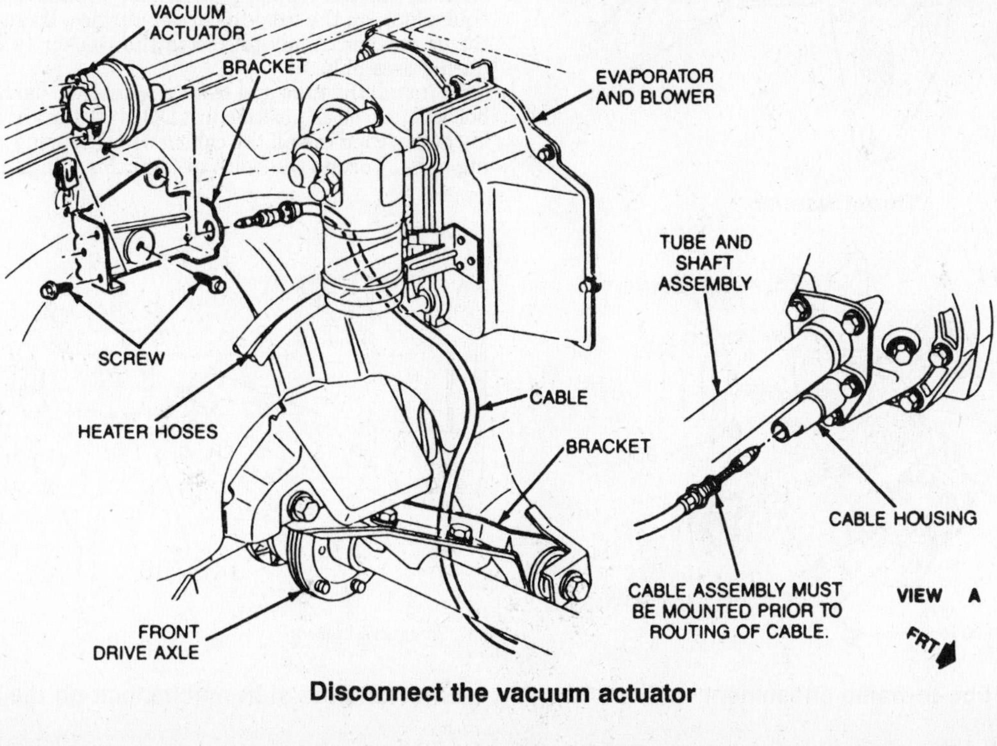
VACUUM ACTUATOR
BRACKET
EVAPORATOR AND BLOWER
TUBE AND SHAFT ASSEMBLY
SCREW
HEATER HOSES
CABLE
BRACKET
CABLE HOUSING
CABLE ASSEMBLY MUST BE MOUNTED PRIOR TO ROUTING OF CABLE.
VIEW A
FRT
FRONT DRIVE AXLE

Disconnect the vacuum actuator

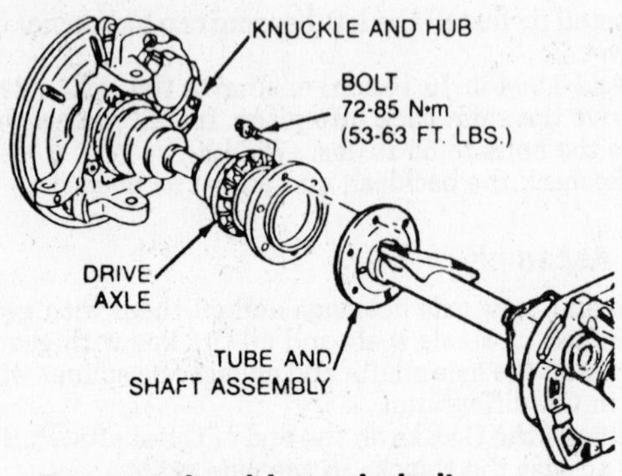

KNUCKLE AND HUB
BOLT
72-85 N·m
(53-63 FT. LBS.)
DRIVE
AXLE
TUBE AND
SHAFT ASSEMBLY

Remove the drive axle bolts

ed by an axle shaft. The inner CV joint is a "tri-pot" design, which is completely flexible and can move in and out. The outer CV joint is a "Rzeppa" design which is also flexible but cannot move in or out.

Axle Tube and Shaft Assembly

REMOVAL AND INSTALLATION

NOTE: The following procedure requires the use of the Shift Cable Housing Seal Installer tool No. J-33799 or equivalent.

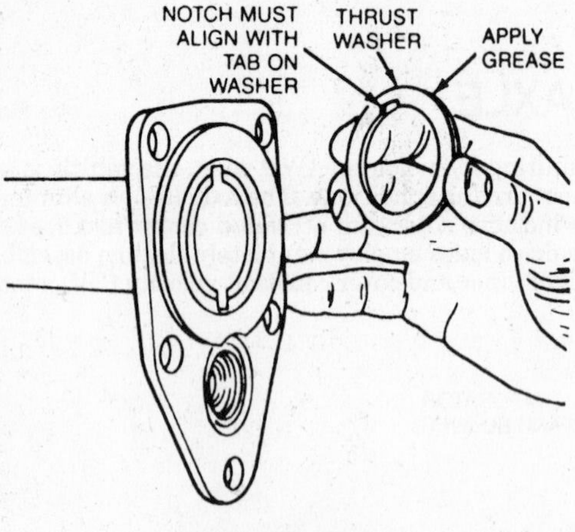

NOTCH MUST
ALIGN WITH
TAB ON
WASHER
THRUST
WASHER
APPLY
GREASE

Thrust washer

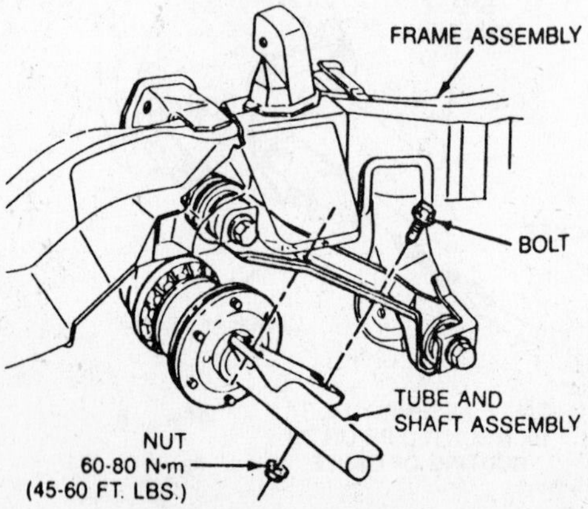

FRAME ASSEMBLY
BOLT
TUBE AND
SHAFT ASSEMBLY
NUT
60-80 N·m
(45-60 FT. LBS.)

Tube-to-frame attachment

1. Disconnect the negative battery terminal from the battery.
2. Disconnect the shift cable from the vacuum actuator by disengaging the locking spring. Then push the actuator diaphragm in to release the cable.
3. Unlock the steering wheel at steering column so the linkage is free to move.
4. Raise and safely support the front of the truck on jackstands.

NOTE: If a twin post hoist is used, place the jackstands under frame and lower front post hoist.

5. Remove the front wheel assemblies, the engine drive belt shield and the front axle skid plate (if equipped).
6. Place a support under right-side lower control arm and disconnect right-side upper ball joint, then remove the support so the control arm will hang free.

NOTE: To keep the axle from turning, insert a drift through the opening in the top of the brake caliper, into the corresponding vane of the brake rotor.

7. Remove the right-side drive axle shaft-to-tube assembly bolts and separate the drive axle from the tube assembly, then remove the drift from the brake caliper and rotor.
8. Disconnect the four wheel drive indicator lamp electrical connector from the switch.
9. Remove the three bolts securing the cable and switch housing-to-carrier and pull the housing away to gain access to the cable locking spring. DO NOT unscrew the cable coupling nut unless the cable is being replaced.
10. Disconnect the cable from the shift fork shaft by lifting spring over slot in shift fork.
11. Remove the two bolts securing the tube bracket to the frame.
12. Remove the remaining upper bolts securing the tube assembly to the carrier.
13. Remove the tube assembly by working around the drive axle. Be careful not to allow the sleeve, thrust washers, connector and output shaft to fall out of carrier or be damaged when removing the tube.

To install:

14. Install the sleeve, thrust washers, connector and output shaft in carrier. Apply Sealant No. 1052357, Loctite® 514 or equivalent, on the tube-to-carrier surface. Be sure to install the thrust washer. Apply grease to the washer to hold it in place during assembly.
15. Install the tube and shaft assembly-to-carrier and install a bolt at one o'clock position but DO NOT torque. Pull the assembly down, then install the cable/switch housing and the remaining bolts. Torque the bolts to 55 ft. lbs. (75 Nm).

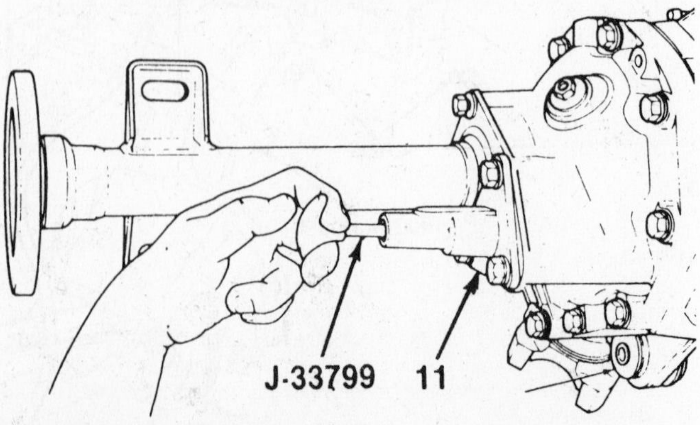

J-33799
11

11. Shift cable housing

Checking the shift mechanism on the front axle

16. Install the tube-to-frame nuts/bolts and torque to the bolts to 36 ft. lbs. (48 Nm) and the nuts to 55 ft. lbs. (75 Nm).
17. Using the Shift Cable Housing Seal Installer tool No. J-33799 or equivalent, check the operation of the 4WD mechanism. Insert tool into the shift fork and check for the rotation of the axle shaft.
18. Remove the Shift Cable Housing Seal Installer tool No. J-33799 or equivalent, and install the shift cable switch housing by pushing the cable through into fork shaft hole. The cable will automatically snap into place (Refer to Shift Cable Replacement).
19. Connect 4WD indicator light electrical connector to the switch.
20. Install the support under the right-side lower control arm to raise arm and connect upper ball joint.
21. Install right-side drive axle-to-axle tube by installing one bolt first, then, rotate the axle to install remaining bolts. Torque the bolts to 60 ft. lbs. (80 Nm).

NOTE: To hold the axle from turning, insert a drift through the opening in the top of the brake caliper into the corresponding vane of the brake rotor.

22. To complete the installation, reverse the removal procedures. Connect the shift cable-to-vacuum actuator by pushing the cable end into the vacuum actuator shaft hole. The cable will snap into place, automatically; Refer to the Shift Cable Replacement.

Differential Output Shaft Pilot Bearing

REMOVAL AND INSTALLATION

NOTE: The following procedures requires the use of the Pilot Bearing Remover tool No. J-34011 or equivalent, and the Pilot Bearing Installer tool No. J-33842 or equivalent.

1. Refer to the "Tube and Shaft Assembly, Removal and Installation" procedures in this section and remove the tube and shaft.
2. Using the Pilot Bearing Remover tool No. J-34011 or equivalent, remove the pilot bearing.
3. Using axle fluid, lubricate the new bearing.
4. Using the Pilot Bearing Installer tool No. J-33842 or equivalent, install the new pilot bearing.

Differential Carrier

REMOVAL AND INSTALLATION

1. Raise and safely support the front of the truck on jackstands.

NOTE: If a twin post hoist is used, place jackstands under the frame and lower front post.

2. Refer to the "Tube and Shaft Assembly, Removal and Installation" procedures in this section and remove the tube and shaft assembly.
3. Remove the stabilizer-to-frame bolts.
4. Using a scribing tool, mark the location of the steering idler arm-to-frame, then remove the steering arm-to-frame bolts.
5. Push the steering linkage towards the front of the truck.
6. Remove the axle vent hose from the carrier fitting.
7. Remove the left-side drive axle shaft-to-carrier bolts and the drive axle shaft.

NOTE: To keep the axle from turning, insert a drift through top opening of the brake caliper, then through the corresponding vane of the brake rotor.

8. Disconnect the front driveshaft.
9. Remove the differential carrier-to-frame bolts; use an 18mm combination wrench to hold the upper nut from turning, by holding it through the frame.
10. To remove the differential carrier, tip it counterclockwise while lifting it up to gain clearance from the mounting ears.
11. To install, reverse the removal procedures. Torque the left-side drive axle shaft-to-differential carrier bolts to 60 ft. lbs. (80 Nm). Check and/or add axle lubricant, fill to level of fill plug hole. Lower vehicle, test drive and recheck the lubricant.

Shift Cable

REMOVAL AND INSTALLATION

1. Disengage the shift cable from the vacuum actuator by disengaging the locking spring, then, push the actuator diaphragm in to release the cable. Using a pair of pliers, squeeze the two cable locking fingers, then pull the cable out of the bracket hole.
2. Raise and safely support the front of the truck on jackstands, then remove cable/switch housing-to-carrier bolts and pull housing away to gain access to the cable locking spring. Disconnect the cable from the shift fork shaft by lifting the spring over shift fork slot.
3. Unscrew the cable from the housing.
4. Remove the cable from the truck.
5. To install the cable, observe the proper routing.
6. Install the cable/switch housing-to-carrier bolts. Torque the bolts to 36 ft. lbs. (48 Nm).
7. Guide the cable through the switch housing into the fork shaft hole and push the cable inward; the cable will automatically snap into place. Start turning the coupling nut by hand, to avoid cross threading, then torque the nut to 71–106 inch lbs. DO NOT overtorque the nut as this will cause thread damage to the plastic housing.
8. Lower the vehicle.
9. Connect the shift cable-to-vacuum actuator by pressing the cable into the bracket hole. The cable and housing will snap into place, automatically.
10. Check the cable operation.

Differential Carrier Overhaul

Note: Several special tools are required for dissassembly of the carrier case.

- J-8614-01 Pinion flange remover.
- J-21551 Bearing remover.
- J-22912-01 Pinion bearing cone remover.
- J-29307 Slide hammer.
- J-33791 Bushing remover.
- J-33792 Side bearing adjuster wrench.
- J-33837 Pinion cup remover kit.
- J-29369-2 Countershaft roller bearing remover.
- J-33970 Bearing installation tool.

DISASSEMBLY

1. Remove the right axle shaft, deflector and retaining ring by striking the inside of the shaft flange to pop the retaining ring out of its groove.
2. Unbolt the axle tube and remove it.
3. If the seal and bearing are to be replaced, use the special tools to remove them.
4. Remove the shaft and deflector from the left side.
5. Remove the bolts and the bearing cover from the left side.
6. Remove the bolts to separate the carrier case. Pry the case halves apart only at the tabs provided.
7. Lift out the differential case.

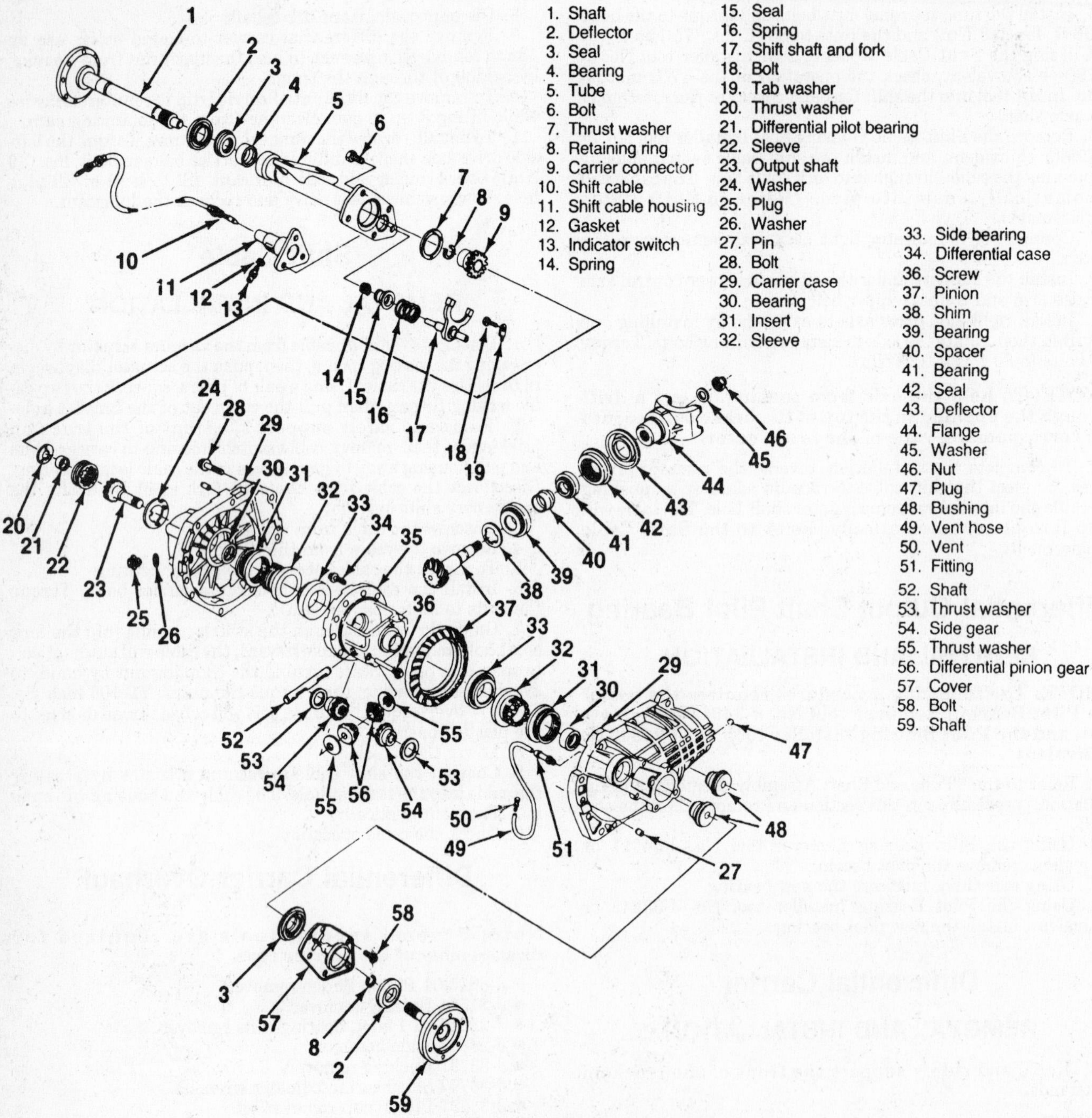
1. Shaft
2. Deflector
3. Seal
4. Bearing
5. Tube
6. Bolt
7. Thrust washer
8. Retaining ring
9. Carrier connector
10. Shift cable
11. Shift cable housing
12. Gasket
13. Indicator switch
14. Spring
15. Seal
16. Spring
17. Shift shaft and fork
18. Bolt
19. Tab washer
20. Thrust washer
21. Differential pilot bearing
22. Sleeve
23. Output shaft
24. Washer
25. Plug
26. Washer
27. Pin
28. Bolt
29. Carrier case
30. Bearing
31. Insert
32. Sleeve
33. Side bearing
34. Differential case
36. Screw
37. Pinion
38. Shim
39. Bearing
40. Spacer
41. Bearing
42. Seal
43. Deflector
44. Flange
45. Washer
46. Nut
47. Plug
48. Bushing
49. Vent hose
50. Vent
51. Fitting
52. Shaft
53. Thrust washer
54. Side gear
55. Thrust washer
56. Differential pinion gear
57. Cover
58. Bolt
59. Shaft

Exploded view of front drive axle

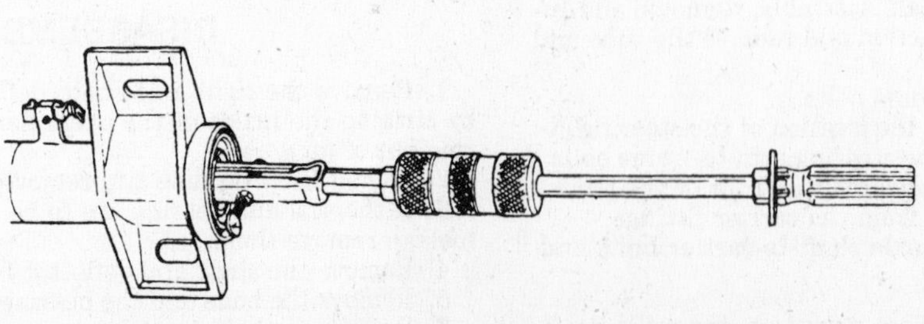

Removing the right side axle tube seal and bearing

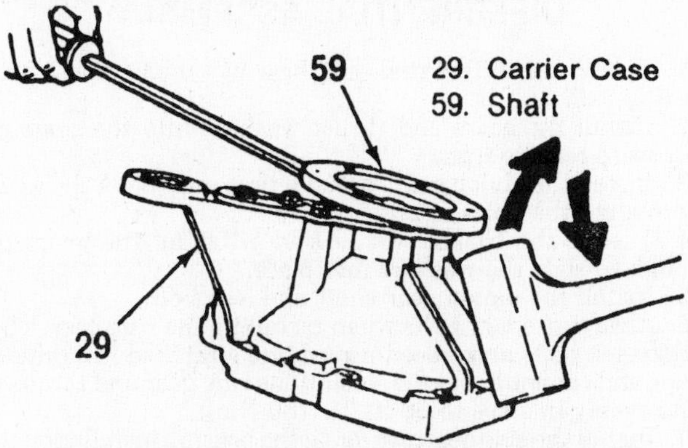
59
29. Carrier Case
59. Shaft
29
Removing the output shaft from the left side

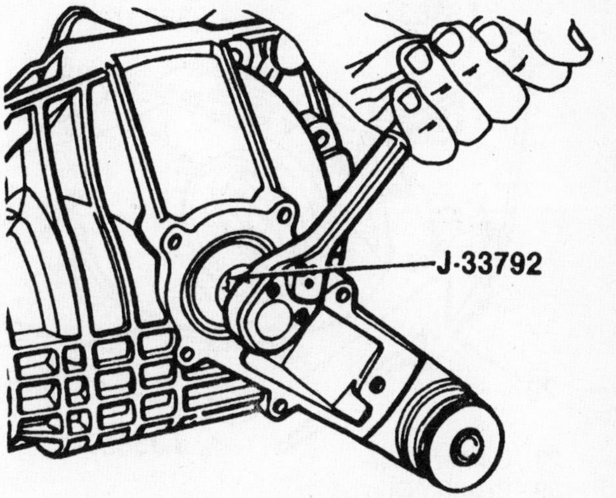
J-33792
Removing the side bearing cup

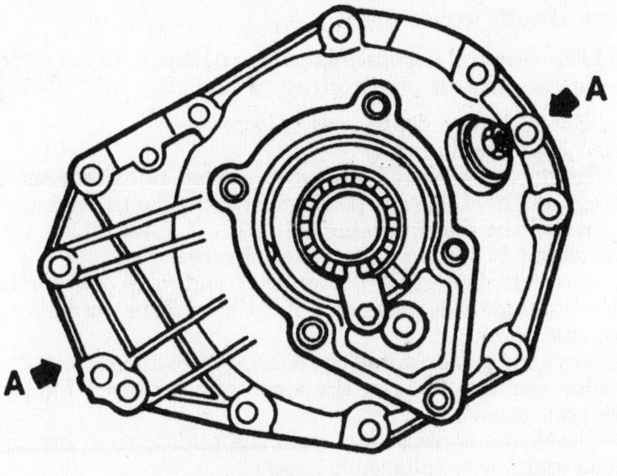
A
A
A. Carrier Pry Points
Pry the carrier case apart at the indicated points

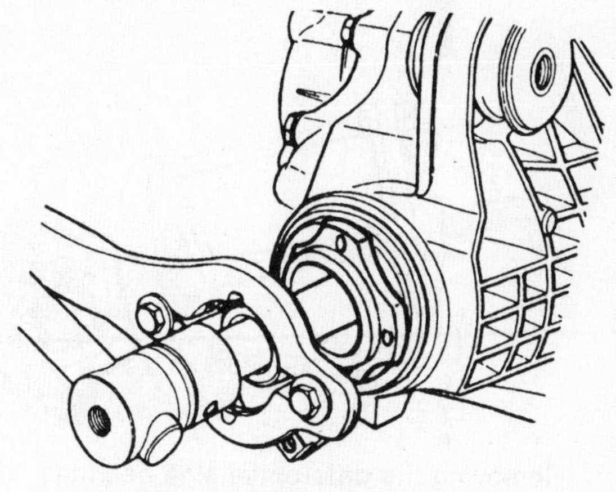
Removing the pinion nut

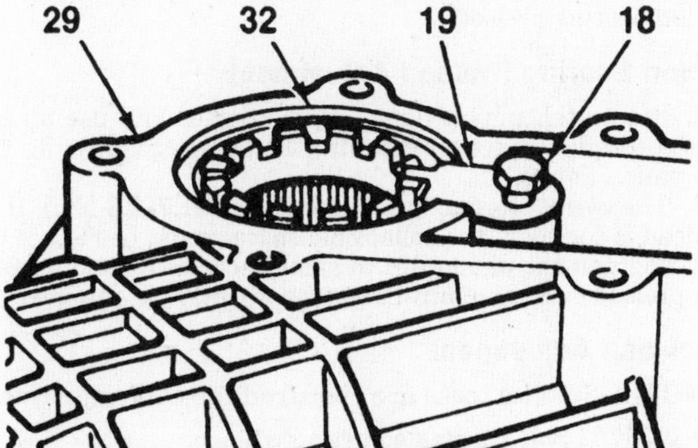
29
32
19
18
18. Bolt
19. Lock Tab
29. Carrier Case
32. Sleeve
Remove the lock tabs

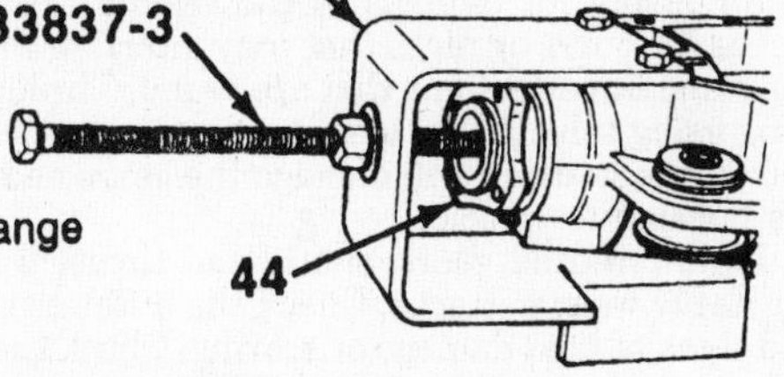
J 33837-1
J 33837-3
44. Flange
44
Removing the pinion flange

8. Remove the bolts and lock tabs from the side bearing adjuster sleeves.
9. Remove the bearing cups and sleeves from the case using the special tool.
10. Remove the input flange nut and washer and use the special puller to remove the flange.
11. Remove the pinion and use a press to remove the pinion bearing.
12. To remove the bearing race from the case, attach the special tools as shown. Thread the J 33837-3 screw into the puller and turn the screw to draw the parts out of the case.
13. Remove the bolt and shaft from the differential case to remove the pinion gears and thrust washers. Label the gears and washers for installation.
14. Remove the differential side gears and thrust washers. Label the gears and washers for installation.
15. Unbolt the ring gear and carefully drive it off with a brass drift pin.
16. Using the special puller, remove the side bearings from the differential.

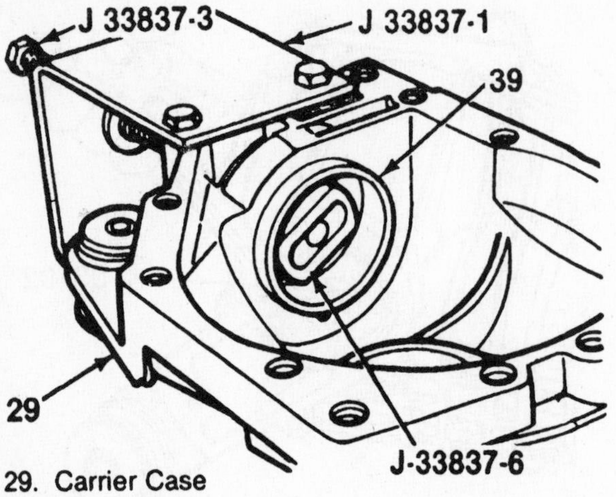
J 33837-3
J 33837-1
39
29
J-33837-6

29. Carrier Case
39. Bearing Cup

Removing the pinion bearing race from the case

Removing the differential side bearings

INSPECTION

Clean all parts in a clean solvent and dry with air. Carefully inspect the housing for damage to the sealing areas and the bearing areas for burrs or nicks that may interfere with assembly. Remove any imperfections that are found. Throughly clean the housing using solvent, not steam or water. Any metal chips or rust left in the housing will damage the gears and bearings. Check the housing for cracks.

Check the differential gears, shafts and thrust washers for uneven or heavy wear patterns. Check the differential case for cracks and signs of heat damage or scoring. Check the fit of the gears on the axle shafts and in the differential case. If in doubt, replace the parts.

Inspect the pinion shaft splines for wear and check the fit with the pinion flange. If the sealing surface on the flange is nicked or worn, replace the flange. Compare the wear patterns on the ring and pinion gears for excessive wear or signs of heat damage. A ring and pinion gear are a matched set and must be replaced together.

Inspect the bearings for signs of heat damage or contamination. The big end of tapered rollers is where signs of wear or damage will appear first. Low milage units will show some scratches on the bearings from initial preload. If the (oiled) bearing still feels smooth, it need not be replaced. If the axle was used for an extended period with very loose bearings, the ring and pinion should be replaced. When replacing bearings, also replace the outer race.

DIFFERENTIAL ASSEMBLY

1. Install the differential side bearings using the J 33970 bearing tool.
2. Install the gears and thrust washers into the same side they were remove from.
3. Install the pinion gears one at a time and rotate the assembly to align the holes.
4. Install the thrust washers by rotating the gears just enough to slide the washers into place.
5. Install the pinion gear shaft and lock bolt.
6. Always use new bolts when installing the ring gear. These are stretch bolts and, once torqued, are stretched to a different shape and cannot be reused. Install the ring gear and torque the bolts evenly in steps to 60 ft. lbs. (80 Nm).
7. Install the side bearings using the bearing installation tool.
8. Using the pinion bearing tools, install the pinion bearing race into the housing.

Pinion Depth Adjustment

NOTE: Special assembly tools are required for correct measurement and positioning of the ring and pinion.

- J-33838 Pinion depth setting gage.
- J-29763 Dial indicator.

1. Pinion depth is adjusted with shims. Lubricate the axle bearings and hold them in position with the depth setting gage.
2. Install the dial indicator and push it down til the needle moves about ¾ turn. Tighten the set screw.
3. Move the depth gage button back and forth over the bearing bore to find the lowest point of the bore. Zero the dial indicator at this point.
4. Move the button out of the bearing bore and record the dial indicator reading. This is the size shim required for pinion depth adjustment.
5. Install the correct shim onto the pinion, then install the bearing and a new collapsible spacer.
6. Install the bearing and seal into the case.
7. Lubricate the seal and install the pinion into the case.
8. Apply a sealing compound to the threads and both sides of the washer, then install the deflector, flange, washer and nut. Tighten the nut only enough to remove end play, then set the pinion bearing preload.

Pinion Bearing Preload Adjustment

1. Rotate teh pinion flange seversl times and use an inch pound torque wrench to measure the torque required to turn the pinion flange.
2. The correct torque is 15–25 inch lbs. (1.7–2.8 Nm). If the preload is too high, the collapsible spacer must be replaced.
3. Tighten the pinion nut in small increments and measure the preload each time until the proper torque is obtained.

Backlash Adjustment

NOTE: Special tools are required for this adjustment:

- J-33792 Side bearing adjusting wrench.
- J-34047 Dial indicator adapter.
- J-25025-1 Dial indicator stand.
- J-8001-1 Dial indicator clamp

1. With the bearings and adjusting sleeves installed into the case, install the differential into the case with the pinion.
2. Temporarily assemble the case halves. If they don't make full contact, back out the right hand adjusting sleeve.
3. Torque the case bolts to 37 ft. lbs. (50 Nm).
4. Torque the right, then the left bearing sleeve to 100 ft. lbs. (140 Nm) using the side bearing adjusting wrench.
5. Mark the position of the sleeves to the case so the notches can be counted during adjustment.
6. Turn the right sleeve OUT 2 notches, and the left sleeve IN 1 notch.

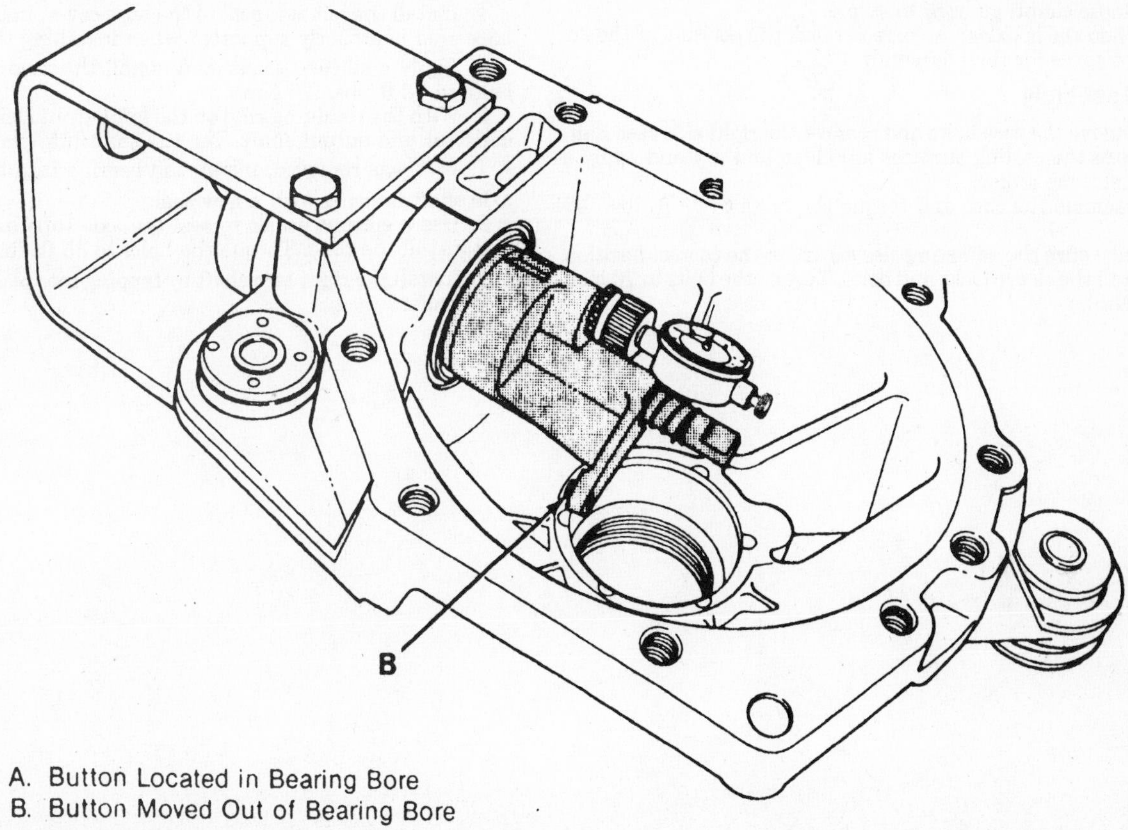
B
A. Button Located in Bearing Bore
B. Button Moved Out of Bearing Bore

Install the pinion depth setting gage and dial indicator with the button A in the bore

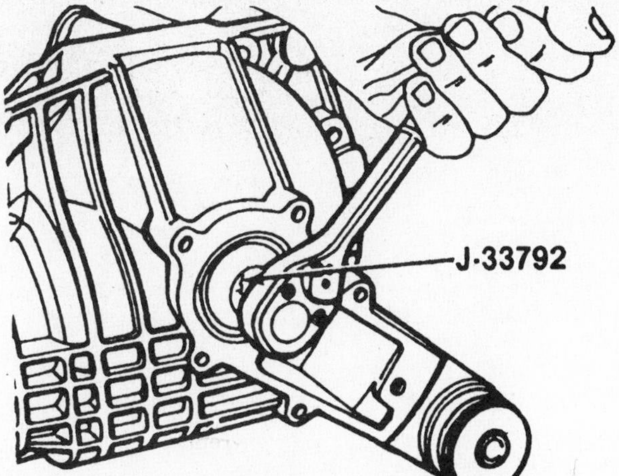
J-33792

Installing the adjusting sleeve

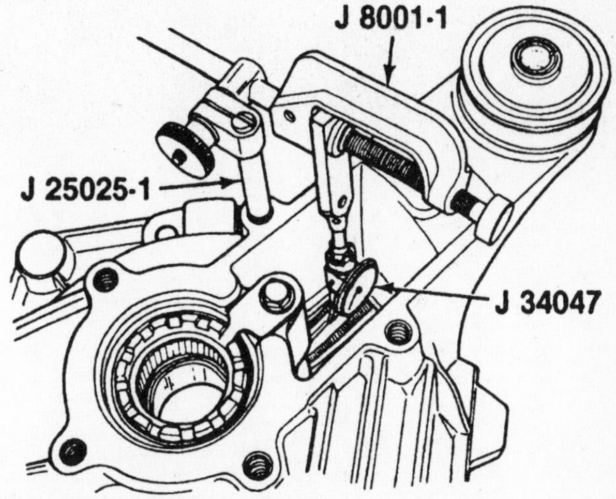
J 8001-1
J 25025-1
J 34047

Touch the stem to the heel of a ring gear tooth

7. Rotate the pinion several times to seat the bearings.
8. Install the dial indicator tools and place the stem of the indicator at the heel end of a tooth on the ring gear.
9. Hold the pinion steady and measure the gear backlash. Take measurements at 3 or 4 places on the ring gear.
10. The backlash should be within 0.002 in. (0.05mm) at all points. If the readings vary more than this, check for a distorted case flange, uneven bolting of the case or ring gear or improper seating of the ring gear on the differential.
11. Backlash should be 0.006 ± 0.003 in. (0.16 ± 0.08mm).
12. To adjust backlash, turn both sleeves the same number of notches: one side IN, the other side OUT. To increase backlash, move the left sleeve IN, to decrease, move the left side OUT. Always be sure to move both sleeves the same number of notches.

If you loose count, go back to step 4.

13. When the backlash is correct, mark the position of the adjusting sleeves for final assembly.

Final Assembly

1. Remove the case bolts and remove the right side case half. Make sure the sealing surfaces are clean and dry and apply a bead of silicone sealer.
2. Assemble the case and torque the bolts to 35 ft. lbs. (47 Nm).
3. Make sure the adjusting sleeves are in the correct position and install the sleeve locks and bolts. Torque the bolts to 70 inch lbs. (8 Nm).
4. Install the left side seal to the bore cover, making sure the bore area is properly supported when installing the seal.
5. Apply a silicone sealer and install the cover. Torque the bolts to 18 ft. lbs. (25 Nm).
6. With the retaining ring on the left output shaft, install the deflector and output shaft. Tap the shaft into place.
7. If it was removed, install the bearing into the right side axle shaft housing with a new seal.
8. Use a silicone sealer to seal the axle tube to the housing and install the tube. Torque the bolts to 35 ft. lbs. (48 Nm).
9. Install the right axle shaft by tapping into place with a soft face mallet.

8 Suspension and Steering

QUICK REFERENCE INDEX

GENERAL INDEX

WHEELS

2- and 4-Wheel Drive

REMOVAL AND INSTALLATION

These vehicles use a variety of wheel styles, but from the factory they are all one piece rims with 5 bolt holes in a 4.75 in. (120.6mm) bolt circle. Standard sizes are 14 × 6 in. (355.6mm × 152.4mm) and 15 × 7 in. (381mm × 177.8mm). A space saver spare for emergency use only comes in a 16 × 4 in. (406.4mm × 101.6mm) size.

1. When removing a wheel, loosen all the lug nuts with the wheel on the ground, then raise and safely support the vehicle.
2. If the wheel is stuck or rusted on the hub, make all the lug nuts finger tight, then back each one off 2 turns. Put the truck back on the ground and rock it side to side. Get another person to help if necessary. This is far safer than hitting a stuck wheel with the vehicle on a jack or lift.
3. When installing a wheel, tighten the lug nuts in a rotation, skipping every other one. If the nuts are numbered 1 through 5 in a circle, the tigntening sequence will be 1-3-5-2-4.
4. Always use a torque wrench to avoid uneven tightening, which will distort the brake drum or disc. On steel wheels, torque the nuts to 73 ft. lbs. (100Nm). On aluminum alloy wheels, torque the nuts to 90 ft. lbs. (120Nm).

INSPECTION

Wheels can be distorted or bent and not effect dry road handling to a noticable degree. Out of round wheels will show up as uneven tire wear, or will make it difficult to balance the tire. Runout can be checked with the wheel on or off the truck, with the tire on or off the rim, but off is better.

1. If the tire is on the wheel, set a dial indicator to touch the wheel in position "A" in the illustration to measure lateral runout.
2. To measure radial runout, set the dial indicator to position "B".
3. If the tire is not on the wheel, use the same positions on the inside of the rim. This is usually more accurate and easier to get a clean surface for the indicator stem.

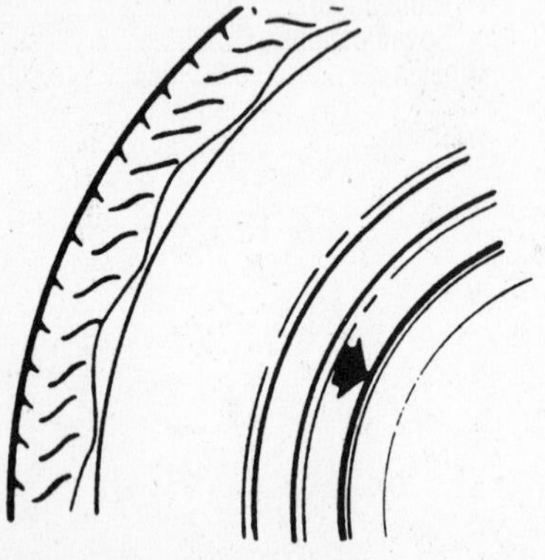

Use a dial indicator to measure radial and lateral runout with or without the tire on the rim

4. For steel wheels, the radial runout limit is 0.040 in. (1mm), the lateral runout limit is 0.045 in. (1.1mm).
5. For aluminum alloy wheels, the limit for both runout directions is 0.030 in. (0.8mm).

Wheel Lug Studs

REMOVAL AND INSTALLATION

2-Wheel Drive Front Wheels

1. Raise and safely support the vehicle and remove the wheel.
2. Remove the brake pads and caliper. Refer to the section on brakes if necessary.
3. Remove the outer wheel bearing and lift the rotor off the axle. Refer to **Front Wheel Bearings** later in this section, if necessary.
4. Properly support the rotor and press the stud out.
5. Clean the stud hole with a wire brush and start the new stud with a hammer and drift pin. Do not use any lubricant or thread sealer.
6. Finish installing the stud with the press.
7. Install the rotor, adjust the wheel bearing and install the brake caliper and pads.

4-Wheel Drive Front and 2- and 4-Wheel Drive Rear

1. Raise and safely support the vehicle and remove the wheel.
2. On front wheels, remove the brake, caliper and rotor. On rear wheels, remove the brake drum. Refer to the section on brakes if necessary.
3. Do not hammer the wheel stud to remove it. This will ruin the wheel bearing. Use the stud press tool J6627A or equivalvent to press the stud out of the hub.
4. Clean the hole with a wire brush and start the new stud into the hole. Do not use any lubricant or thread sealer.
5. Stack 4 or 5 washers onto the stud and then put the nut on. Tighten the nut to draw the stud into place.It should be easy to feel when the stud is seated.
6. Reinstall the rotor and caliper or drum and use a torque wrench when installing the wheel.

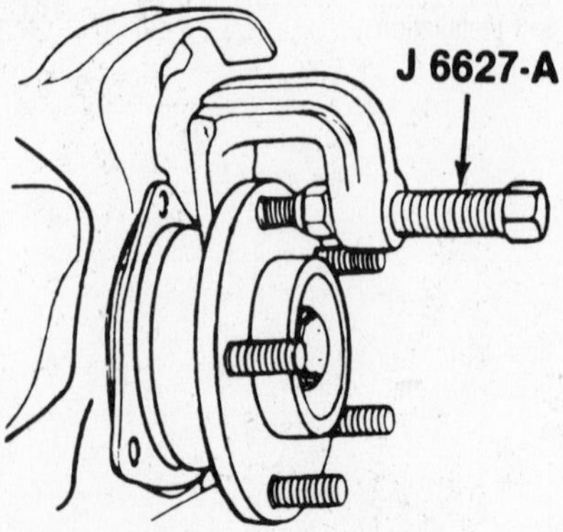
J 6627-A

Pressing the old stud off

FRONT SUSPENSION

Coil Spring – 2WD

REMOVAL

NOTE: The following procedure requires the use of the Coil Spring Removal and Installation tool No. J-23028 or equivalent.

1. Raise and safely support the front of the vehicle so that the front wheels hang free.
2. Remove the shock absorber-to-lower control arm bolts, then push the shock up through the control arm and into the spring.
3. Using the Coil Spring Removal and Installation tool No. J-23028 or equivalent, secured to the end of a jack, cradle the inner control arm bushings.
4. Remove the stabilizer bar link from the lower control arm.
5. To remove the lower control arm pivot bolts, perform the following procedures:
   a. Raise the jack to remove the tension from the lower control arm pivot bolts.
   b. Install a chain around the spring and through the control arm as a safety measure.

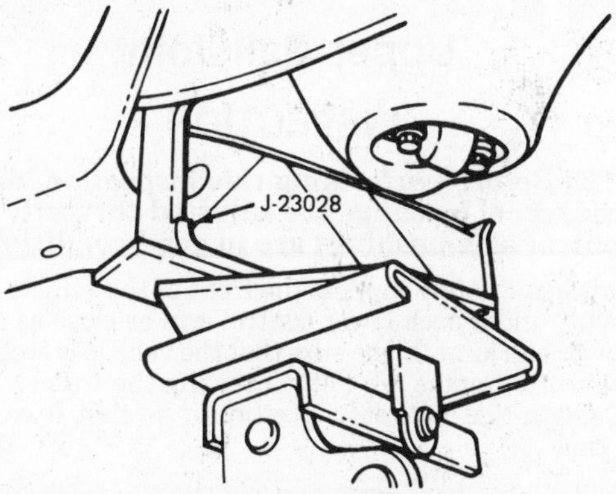
J-23028

With the spring compressor secured to the jack, lift the control arm to take the tension off the spring

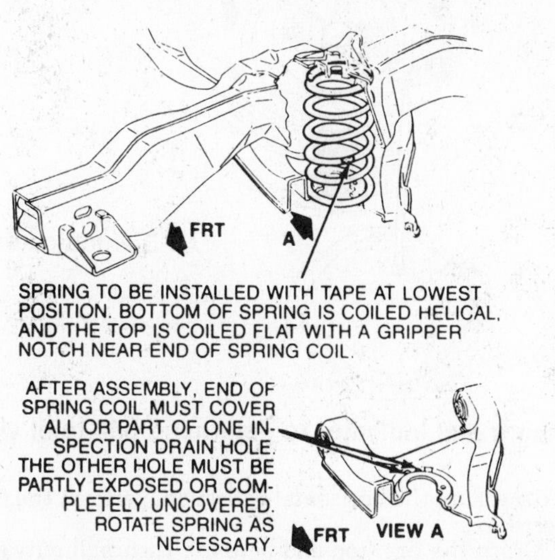
FRT
A
SPRING TO BE INSTALLED WITH TAPE AT LOWEST POSITION. BOTTOM OF SPRING IS COILED HELICAL, AND THE TOP IS COILED FLAT WITH A GRIPPER NOTCH NEAR END OF SPRING COIL.
AFTER ASSEMBLY, END OF SPRING COIL MUST COVER ALL OR PART OF ONE INSPECTION DRAIN HOLE. THE OTHER HOLE MUST BE PARTLY EXPOSED OR COMPLETELY UNCOVERED. ROTATE SPRING AS NECESSARY.
FRT
VIEW A

Front control arms and components on 2WD

   c. Remove the lower control arm-to-frame pivot nuts and bolts – remove the rear pivot bolt first.
   d. Lower the control arm by slowly lowering the jack.
6. When all of the compression is removed from the spring, remove the safety chain and the spring.

NOTE: DO NOT apply force to the lower control arm and/or ball joint to remove the spring. Proper maneuvering of the spring will allow for easy removal.

7. To install, properly position the spring on the control arm, make sure the spring insulator is in place.
8. Using the Coil Spring Removal and Installation tool No. J-23028 or equivalent, raise the control arm and spring assembly into position.
9. To complete the installation, align the control arm with the frame and install the pivot bolts (front bolt first) and nuts, then reverse the removal procedures. Torque the lower control arm-to-frame pivot nuts/bolts to 45 ft. lbs., the stabilizer bar-to-lower control arm link to 13 ft. lbs. and the shock absorber-to-lower control arm bolts to 20 ft. lbs. Road test the vehicle.

Torsion Bar – 4WD

REMOVAL AND INSTALLATION

NOTE: The following procedure requires the use of the Torsion Bar Unloader tool No. J-22517-C or equivalent.

1. Raise and safely support the front of the vehicle on jackstands.
2. Using the Torsion Bar Unloader tool No. J-22517-C or equivalent, attach it and apply pressure (to relax the tension) to the torsion bar adjusting arm screw; remove the adjusting screw by counting the number of turns necessary to remove the screw.
3. Remove the torsion support-to-insulator nut/bolt, the support insulator-to-frame nuts/bolts, the insulator retainer and the insulator from the support.
4. Slide the torsion bar(s) forward into the control arm(s) to clear the support.

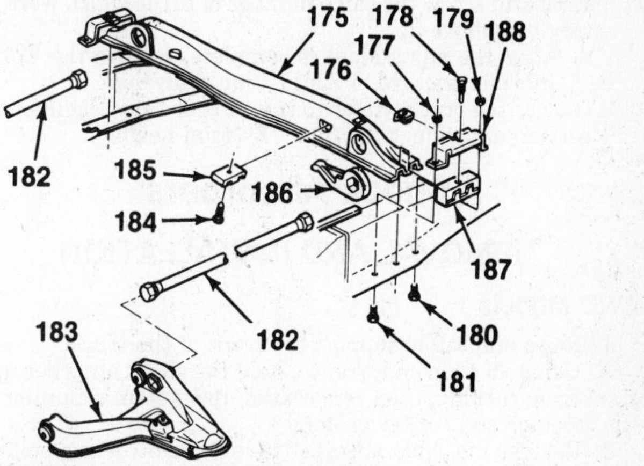
175
178
179
188
177
176
182
185
186
184
187
183
182
180
181

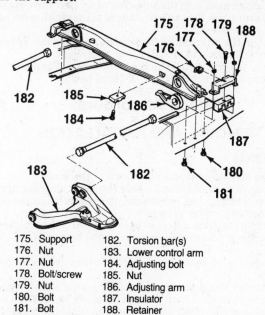

175. Support
176. Nut
177. Nut
178. Bolt/screw
179. Nut
180. Bolt
181. Bolt
182. Torsion bar(s)
183. Lower control arm
184. Adjusting bolt
185. Nut
186. Adjusting arm
187. Insulator
188. Retainer

Torsion bar front suspension on 4WD

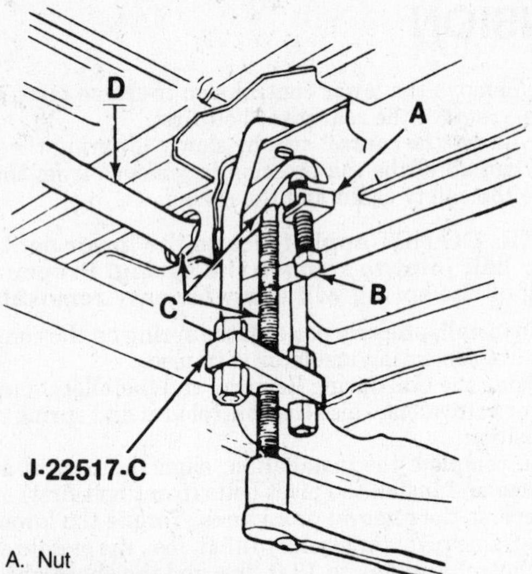
D
A
B
C
J-22517-C

A. Nut
B. Torsion bar adjusting bolt
C. Apply lubricant at points to ease installation
D. Torsion bar

Using the torsion bar unloader tool

5. Remove the adjusting arm, the adjusting arm screw and the nut from the support.
6. Remove the torsion bar from the control arm and the support.
7. To install the support insulator, reverse the removal procedures. Torque the insulator-to-frame nuts/bolts to 26 ft. lbs. and the torsion support-to-insulator nut/bolt to 25 ft. lbs.
8. To install the torsion bar, perform the following procedures:
   a. Slide the torsion bar into the lower control arm.
   b. Raise and slide the torsion bar into the adjusting arm.

NOTE: Be sure the torsion bar clearance at the support is 0.236 in. (6mm).

   c. Using the Torsion Bar Unloader tool No. J-22517-C or equivalent, install it to the adjusting arm, then turn the adjusting arm screw the same number of turns which were necessary to remove it.
   d. After the adjustment is complete, remove the Torsion Bar Unloader tool No. J-22517-C or equivalent.
9. Lower the truck. Refer to the "Front End Alignment" in this section and adjust the final "Z" trim height.

Shock Absorbers

REMOVAL AND INSTALLATION

2WD Models

1. Raise and safely support the front of the truck.
2. Using an open end wrench, hold the shock absorber upper stem from turning, then remove the upper stem retaining nut, the retainer and rubber grommet.
3. Remove the shock absorber-to-lower control arm bolts and lower the shock absorber assembly from the bottom of the control arm.
4. Inspect and test the shock absorber; replace it, if necessary.
5. To install the shock absorber, fully extend the shock absorber stem, then push it up through the lower control arm and spring, so that the upper stem passes through the mounting hole in the upper control arm frame bracket.
6. Torque the upper shock absorber nut to 8 ft. lbs. If desired, use the old nut as a jam nut. Be careful not to crush the rubber bushing.
7. Torque the shock absorber-to-lower control arm bolts to 20 ft. lbs.

4WD Models

1. Raise and safely support the front of the truck.
2. Remove the shock absorber-to-lower control arm nut and bolt, then collapse the shock absorber.
3. Remove the upper shock absorber-to-frame nut and bolt.
4. Inspect and test the shock absorber; replace it, if necessary.
5. To install, reverse the removal procedures. Torque the upper and lower mounting bolts to 54 ft. lbs.

TESTING

Visually inspect the shock absorber. If there is evidence of leakage and the shock absorber is covered with oil, the shock is defective and should be replaced.

If there is no sign of excessive leakage (a small amount of weeping is normal) bounce the truck at one corner by pressing down on the bumper and releasing it. When you have the truck bouncing as much as you can, release the bumper. The truck should stop bouncing after the first rebound. If the bouncing continues past the center point of the bounce more than once, the shock absorbers are worn and should be replaced.

Upper Ball Joint

INSPECTION

NOTE: Before performing this inspection, make sure that the wheel bearings are adjusted correctly and that the control arm bushings are in good condition.

1. Raise and safely support the front of the vehicle by placing jackstands under each lower control arm as close as possible to each lower ball joint. Make sure that the vehicle is stable and the control arm bumpers are not contacting the frame.
2. Using a dial indicator, position it so that it contacts the wheel rim.

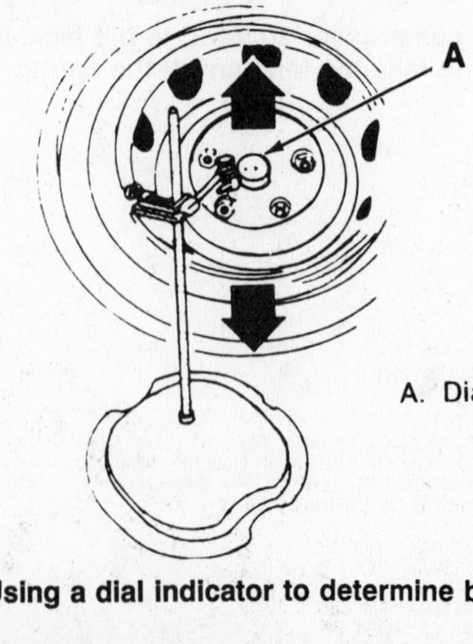
A

A. Dial Indicator

Using a dial indicator to determine ball joint ware

3. To measure the horizontal deflection, perform the following procedures:
   a. Grasp the tire (top and bottom), then pull outward on the top and push inward on the bottom; record the reading on the dial indicator.

b. Grasp the tire (top and bottom), then pull outward on the bottom and push inward on the top; record the reading on the dial indicator.

c. If the difference in the dial indicator reading is more than 0.125 in. (3mm), or if the rubber seal is cut or appears damaged, the ball joint must be replaced.

REMOVAL AND INSTALLATION

NOTE: The following procedure requires the use of the GM Ball Joint Remover tool No. J-23742 or equivalent.

1. Raise and safely support the front of the vehicle by placing jackstands under the frame, not the lower control arms.
2. Place the floor jack under the lower control arm spring seat and raise it slightly to retain the spring and the lower control arm in position.

CAUTION

With the ball joint nut removed, the floor jack is holding the lower control arm in place against the coil spring. Make sure the jack is firmly engaged with the spring seat and cannot move, or personal injury could result.

3. Remove the wheel and brake caliper. Without disconnecting the hydraulic line, hang the caliper from the body with wire so it does not hang on the line.
5. From the upper ball joint, remove the cotter pin, the nut and the grease fitting.
6. Using the GM Ball Joint Remover tool No. J-23742 or equivalent, separate the upper ball joint from the steering knuckle. Pull the steering knuckle free of the ball joint after removal.

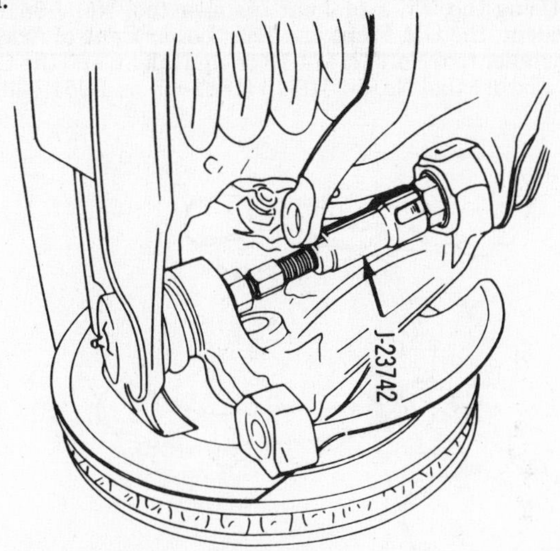
J-23742

Use a ball joint removal tool to press the ball joint out of the steering knuckle

NOTE: After separating the steering knuckle from the upper ball joint, be sure to support the steering knuckle/hub assembly to prevent damaging the brake hose.

7. To remove the upper ball joint from the upper control arm, perform the following procedures:

a. Using a ⅛ in. (3mm) drill bit, drill a ¼ in. (6mm) deep hole into each rivet.

b. Using a ½ in. (13mm) drill bit, drill off the rivet heads.

c. Using a pin punch and the hammer, drive the rivets from the upper ball joint-to-upper control arm assembly and remove the upper ball joint.

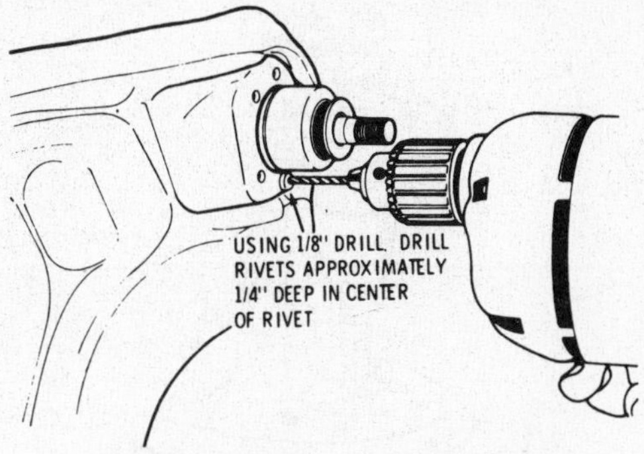
USING 1/8" DRILL, DRILL RIVETS APPROXIMATELY 1/4" DEEP IN CENTER OF RIVET

Drill the upper ball joint rivets

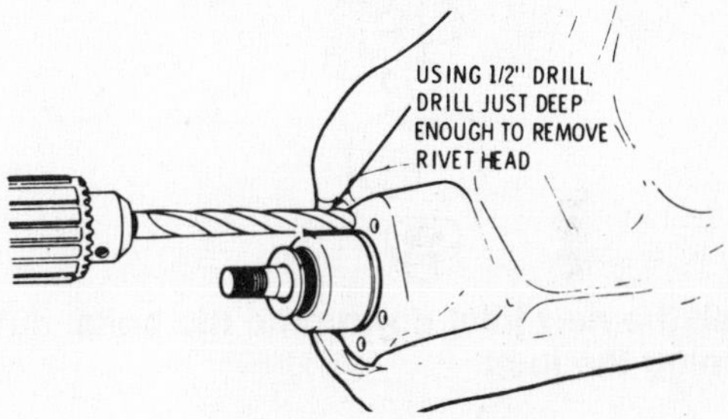
USING 1/2" DRILL, DRILL JUST DEEP ENOUGH TO REMOVE RIVET HEAD

Drill the rivet heads

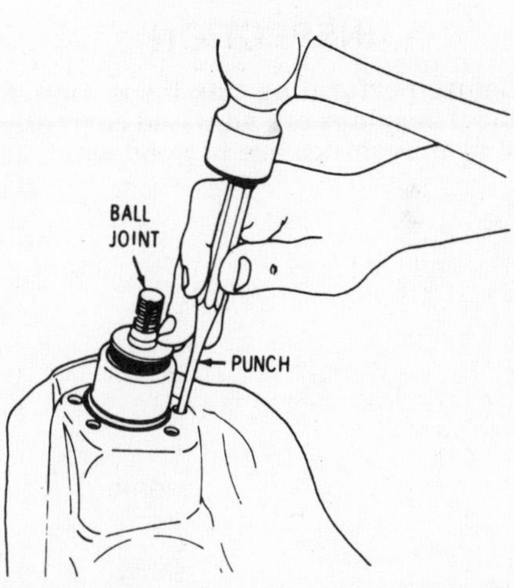
BALL JOINT
PUNCH

Punch the rivets out to remove the ball joint

8. Clean and inspect the steering knuckle hole. Replace the steering knuckle if the hole is out of round.

To install:

9. When installing the new joint, put the bolts up through the control arm and install the joint down onto the bolts. Torque the nuts to 17 ft. lbs.
10. To complete the installation, seat the upper ball joint into the steering knuckle and install the nut. Torque the upper ball joint-to-steering knuckle nut to 65 ft. lbs. and install a new cotter pin.

NOTE: When installing the cotter pin, never loosen the castle nut to expose the cotter pin hole.

11. Use a grease gun to lubricate the upper ball joint.
12. Install the brake caliper and pads and the wheel. When a ball joint is replaced, a front end alignment is strongly recommended.

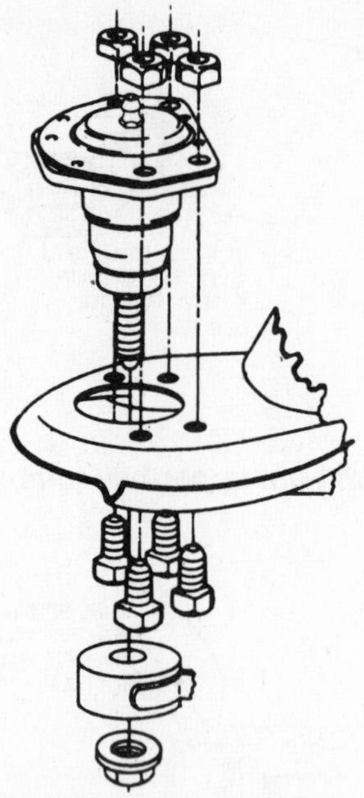

Install the new joint down onto the bolts, nuts touching the joint

Lower Ball Joint

INSPECTION

NOTE: Before performing this inspection, make sure that the wheel bearings are adjusted correctly and that the control arm bushings are in good condition.

Visually check the wear indicator, the small nub that the grease fitting screws into. If it is flush or inside the ball joint cover surface, replace the ball joint. If the rubber grease seal is broken, the ball joint must be replaced.

REMOVAL AND INSTALLATION

NOTE: The following procedure requires the use of the GM Ball Joint Separator tool No. J-23742 or equivalent, the GM Front and Rear Lower Control Arm Bushing Installer tool No. J-21474-13 or equivalent, the GM Ball Joint Installer tool No. J-9519-9 or equivalent, the GM Ball Joint Installer tool No. J-9519-16 or equivalent, and the GM Ball Joint Fixture tool No. J-9519-10 (1982-85) or J-9519-30 (1986-91) or equivalent.

1. Raise and safely support the front of the vehicle on jackstands. Remove the wheel and brake caliper.
2. Using a floor jack, place it under the spring seat of the lower control arm, then raise the jack to support the arm.

NOTE: The floor jack MUST remain under the lower control arm, during the removal and installation procedures, to retain the arm and spring positions.

3. Remove the cotter pin (discard it) and the ball joint nut.
4. Using the GM Ball Joint Separator tool No. J-23742 or equivalent, disconnect the lower ball joint from the steering knuckle. Pull the steering knuckle away from the lower control arm, place a block of wood between the frame and the upper control arm; make sure that the brake hose is free of tension.
5. From the lower ball joint, remove the rubber grease seal and the grease fitting.
6. Using the GM Ball Joint Installer tool No. J-9519-16 or equivalent, the GM Front and Rear Lower Control Arm Bushing Installer tool No. J-21474-13 or equivalent, and the GM Ball Joint Fixture tool No. J-9519-10 (1982-85) or J-9519-30 (1986-

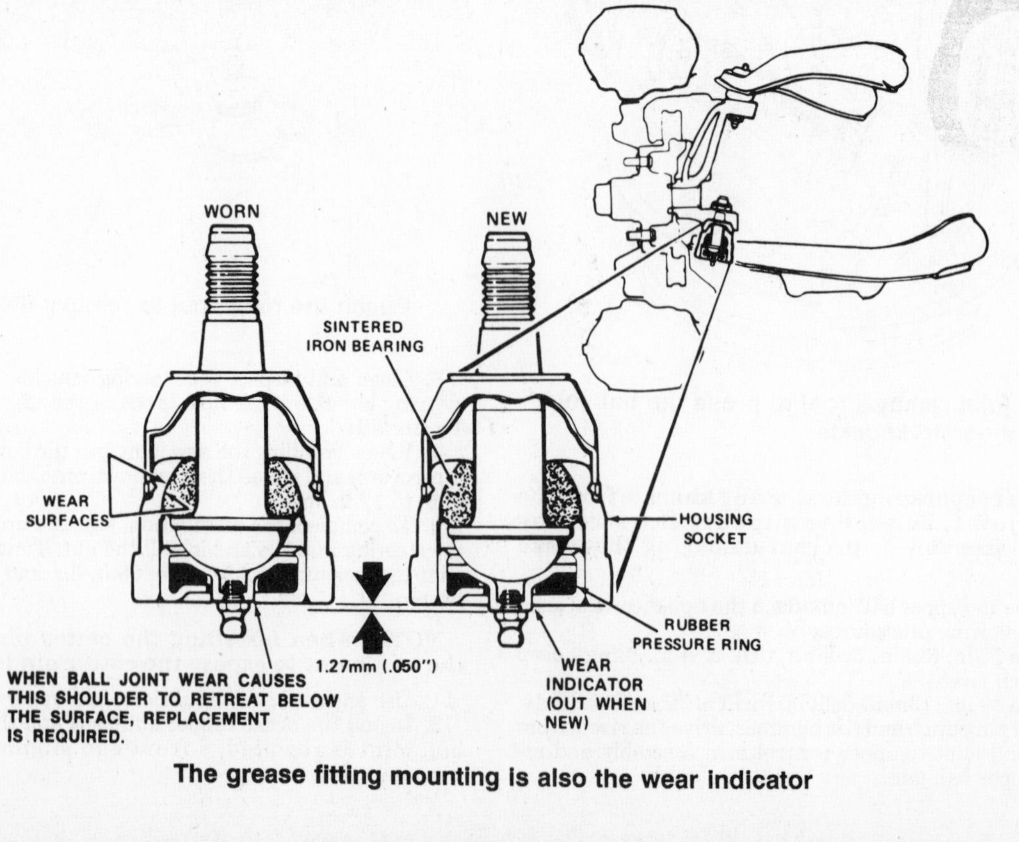
WORN
NEW
SINTERED IRON BEARING
WEAR SURFACES
HOUSING SOCKET
RUBBER PRESSURE RING
1.27mm (.050")
WHEN BALL JOINT WEAR CAUSES THIS SHOULDER TO RETREAT BELOW THE SURFACE, REPLACEMENT IS REQUIRED.
WEAR INDICATOR (OUT WHEN NEW)

The grease fitting mounting is also the wear indicator

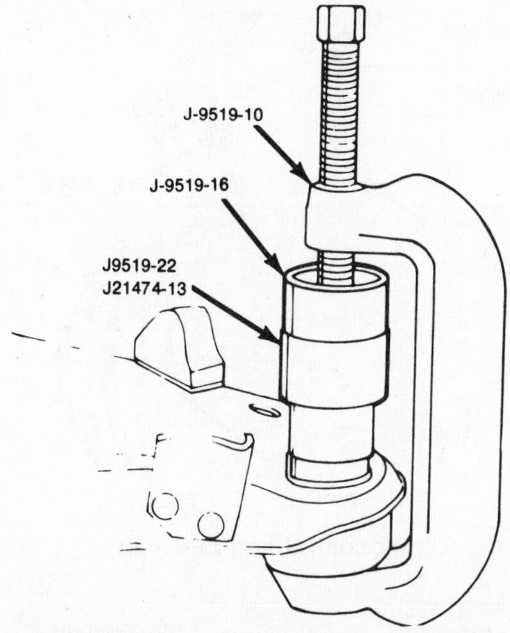
J-9519-10
J-9519-16
J9519-22
J21474-13
Pressing the lower ball joint out of the control arm

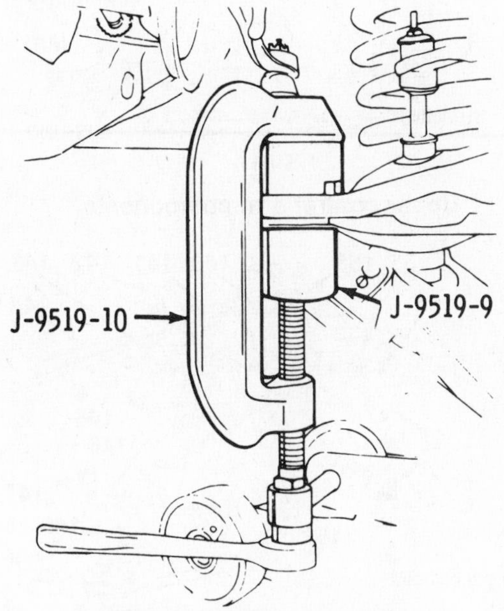
J-9519-10
J-9519-9
Installing the new ball joint

91) or equivalent, remove the lower ball joint from the lower control arm.

7. To install, position the new lower ball joint into the lower control arm. Using the GM Ball Joint Installer tool No. J-9519-9 or equivalent, and the GM Ball Joint Fixture tool No. J-9519-10 (1982-85) or J-9519-30 (1986-91) or equivalent, press the new lower ball joint into the lower control arm.
8. Install the grease fitting and the grease seal onto the lower ball joint; the grease seal MUST BE fully seated on the ball joint and the grease purge hole MUST face inboard.
9. To complete the installation, reverse the removal procedures. Torque the ball joint-to-steering knuckle nut to 90 ft. lbs.
10. Install a new cotter pin to the lower ball joint stud.

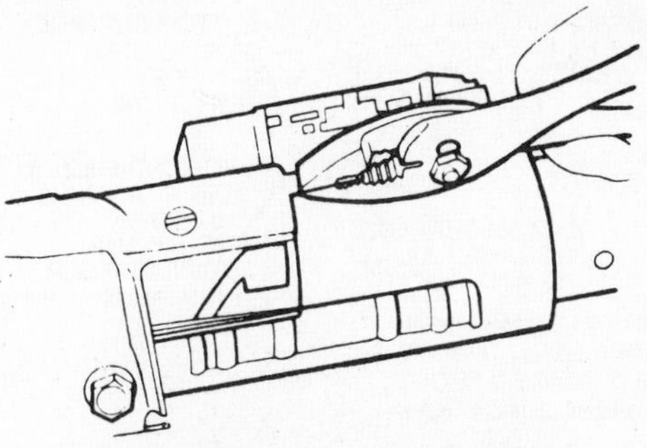
Removing the wire protector

NOTE: When installing the cotter pin, never loosen the castle nut to expose the cotter pin hole.

11. Use a grease gun to lubricate the ball joint.
12. Install the brake caliper and pads and the wheel. When a ball joint is replaced, a front end alignment is strongly recommended.

Stabilizer Bar

REMOVAL AND INSTALLATION

1. Raise and safely support the front of the vehicle on jackstands. Remove the wheels.
2. Disconnect the stabilizer bar link nuts from the lower control arms.
3. Remove the stabilizer bar-to-frame clamps.
4. Remove the stabilizer bar from the vehicle.
5. To install, reverse the removal procedures. Torque the stabilizer bar link-to-lower control arm nuts/bolts to 13 ft. lbs. (2WD) or 24 ft. lbs. (4WD) and the stabilizer retainer-to-frame nuts/bolts to 24 ft. lbs. (2WD) or 35 ft. lbs. (4WD).

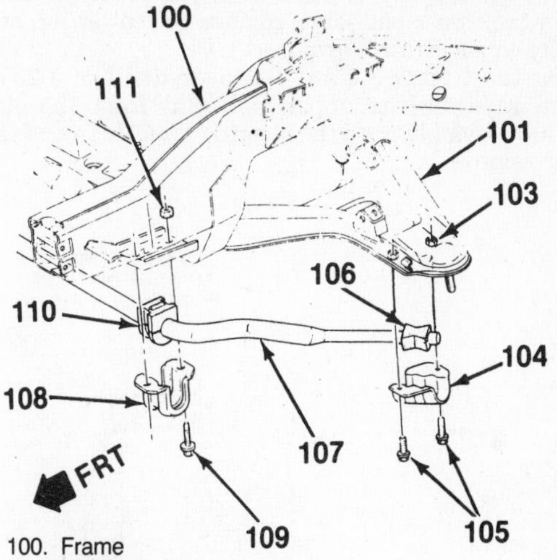
100
111
101
103
106
110
104
108
107
FRT
109
105

100. Frame
101. Lower control arm
103. Weld nut
104. Clamp
105. Bolts
106. Insulator
107. Stabilizer shaft
108. Clamp
109. Bolt
110. Insulator
111. Nut

Front stabilizer bar mounting on 4WD

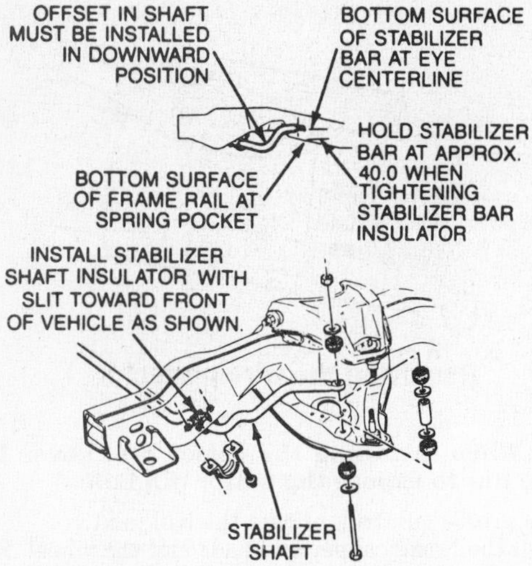
OFFSET IN SHAFT MUST BE INSTALLED IN DOWNWARD POSITION
BOTTOM SURFACE OF STABILIZER BAR AT EYE CENTERLINE
HOLD STABILIZER BAR AT APPROX. 40.0 WHEN TIGHTENING STABILIZER BAR INSULATOR
BOTTOM SURFACE OF FRAME RAIL AT SPRING POCKET
INSTALL STABILIZER SHAFT INSULATOR WITH SLIT TOWARD FRONT OF VEHICLE AS SHOWN.
STABILIZER SHAFT

Front stabilizer bar mounting on 2WD

Upper Control Arm

REMOVAL AND INSTALLATION

NOTE: The following procedure requires the use of the GM Ball Joint Remover tool No. J-23742 or equivalent.

1. Raise and safely support the front of the vehicle by placing jackstands under the frame.

NOTE: Allow the floor jack to remain under the lower control arm seat, to retain the spring and the lower control arm position.

2. Remove the wheels and brake caliper. Hang the caliper from the body with wire to avoid straining the hydraulic line.
3. From the upper ball joint, remove the cotter pin and the ball joint-to-upper control arm nut.
4. Using the GM Ball Joint Remover tool No. J-23742 or equivalent, separate the upper ball joint from the steering knuckle/hub assembly. Pull the steering knuckle free of the ball joint after removal.

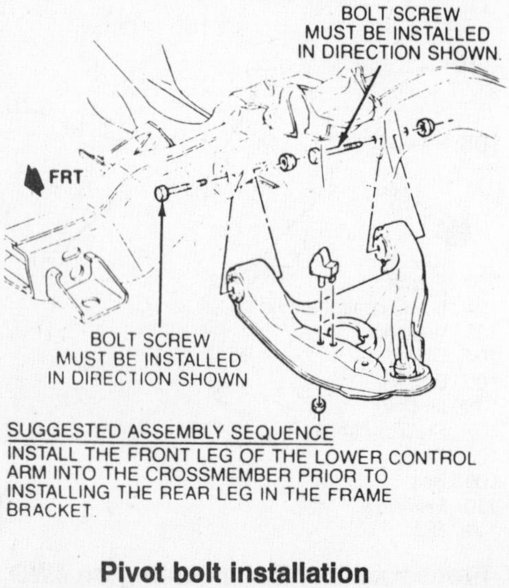
BOLT SCREW MUST BE INSTALLED IN DIRECTION SHOWN.
FRT
BOLT SCREW MUST BE INSTALLED IN DIRECTION SHOWN
SUGGESTED ASSEMBLY SEQUENCE
INSTALL THE FRONT LEG OF THE LOWER CONTROL ARM INTO THE CROSSMEMBER PRIOR TO INSTALLING THE REAR LEG IN THE FRAME BRACKET.

Pivot bolt installation

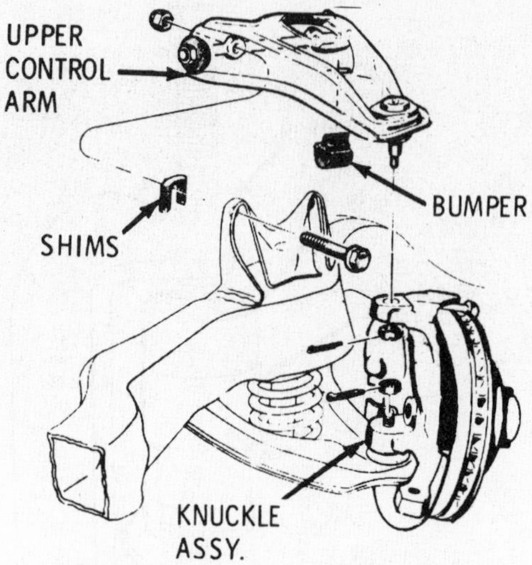
UPPER CONTROL ARM
BUMPER
SHIMS
KNUCKLE ASSY.

Upper control arm removal

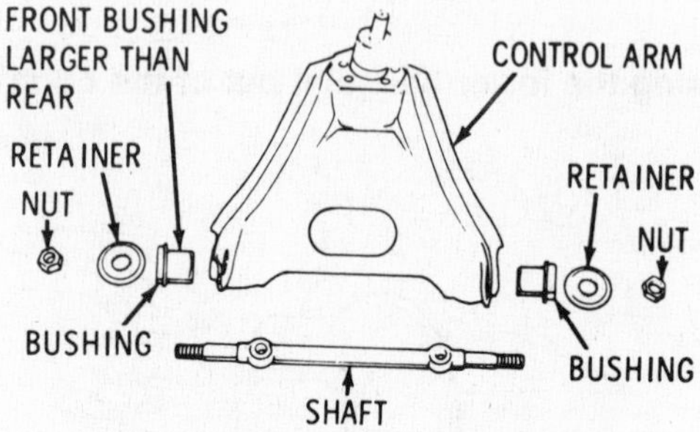
FRONT BUSHING LARGER THAN REAR
CONTROL ARM
RETAINER
NUT
RETAINER
NUT
BUSHING
BUSHING
SHAFT

Upper control arm components

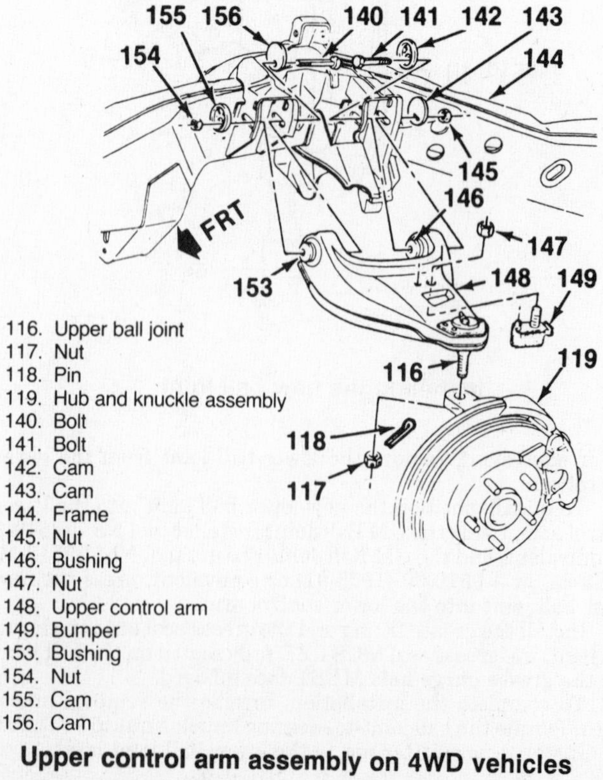
155 156
140 141 142 143
154
144
145
146
FRT
147
153
148 149
116
119
118
117
116. Upper ball joint
117. Nut
118. Pin
119. Hub and knuckle assembly
140. Bolt
141. Bolt
142. Cam
143. Cam
144. Frame
145. Nut
146. Bushing
147. Nut
148. Upper control arm
149. Bumper
153. Bushing
154. Nut
155. Cam
156. Cam

Upper control arm assembly on 4WD vehicles

NOTE: After separating the steering knuckle from the upper ball joint, be sure to support steering knuckle/hub assembly to prevent damaging the brake hose.

5. Remove the upper control arm-to-frame nuts and bolts, then lift and remove the upper control arm from the vehicle.

NOTE: On 2WD, tape the shims together and identify them so that they can be re-installed in the same place

6. Clean and inspect the steering knuckle hole. Replace the steering knuckle, if any out of roundness is noted.

To install

7. Attach the upper control arm to the frame, insert the shims in their proper positions, and torque the upper control arm bolts to 45 ft. lbs. (2WD) or 70 ft. lbs. (4WD).
8. Seat the upper ball joint into the steering knuckle, install the nut and torque it to 61 ft. lbs.
9. Install a new cotter pin to the upper ball joint stud.

NOTE: When installing the cotter pin, never loosen the castle nut to expose the cotter pin hole.

10. Use a grease gun to lubricate the upper ball joint.
11. Install the brake caliper and pads and the wheel. On 4WD, when a control arm is removed, a front end alignment is escential.

Lower Control Arm

REMOVAL AND INSTALLATION

2WD Models

NOTE: The following procedure requires the use of the GM Ball Joint Remover tool No. J-23742 or equivalent.

1. Refer to the "Coil Spring, Removal and Installation" procedures in this section and remove the coil spring.
2. Remove the cotter pin (discard it) and the ball joint nut.
3. Using the GM Ball Joint Remover tool No. J-23742 or equivalent, disconnect the lower ball joint from the steering knuckle and the lower control arm from the vehicle.

NOTE: Place a block of wood between the frame and the upper control arm; make sure that the brake hose is free of tension.

4. To install, position the lower ball joint stud into the steering knuckle and finger tignten it for now.
5. Install the control arm bolts, making sure the bolt goes in from the front of the vehicle. Torque the front nut and bolt to 94 ft. lbs., and the rear nut and bolt to 66 ft. lbs. Torque the ball joint-to-steering knuckle nut to 81 ft. lbs.
6. Install a new cotter pin to the lower ball joint stud.

NOTE: When installing the cotter pin, never loosen the castle nut to expose the cotter pin hole.

7. Pull the shock absorber down, then install the shock absorber-to-lower control arm nuts/bolts. Torque the nuts and bolts to 20 ft. lbs.
8. Remove the lower control arm support and lower the vehicle.

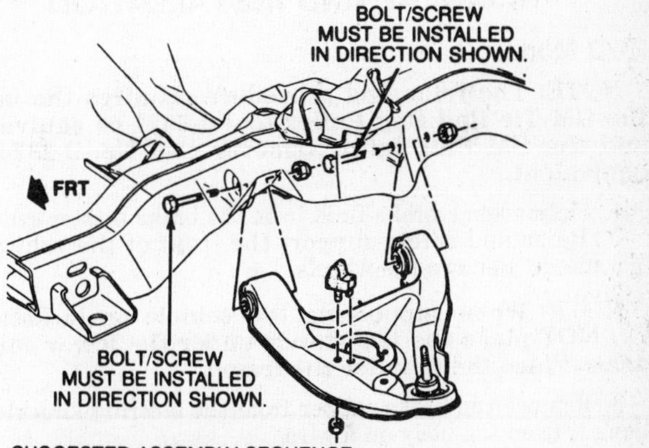
BOLT/SCREW
MUST BE INSTALLED
IN DIRECTION SHOWN.
FRT
BOLT/SCREW
MUST BE INSTALLED
IN DIRECTION SHOWN.
SUGGESTED ASSEMBLY SEQUENCE
INSTALL THE FRONT LEG OF THE LOWER CONTROL ARM INTO THE CROSSMEMBER PRIOR TO INSTALLING THE REAR LEG IN THE FRAME BRACKET.

Lower control arm installation on 2WD

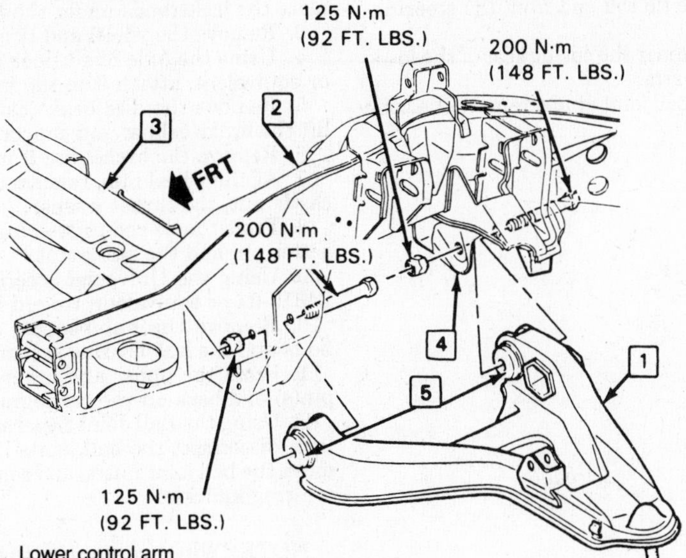
125 N·m
(92 FT. LBS.)
200 N·m
(148 FT. LBS.)
3
2
FRT
200 N·m
(148 FT. LBS.)
4
5
1
125 N·m
(92 FT. LBS.)

1. Lower control arm
2. Frame
3. Crossmember
4. Frame bracket
5. Bushing

Lower control arm on 4WD

4WD Models

1. Refer to the "Torsion Bar, Removal and Installation" procedures in this section, then remove the torsion bar and support assembly.
2. Remove the stabilizer bar-to-lower control arm nuts/bolts.
3. Remove the shock absorber-to-lower control arm nuts/bolts and push the shock absorber upward.
4. Remove the lower control arm-to-frame nuts/bolts and the lower control arm from the truck.
5. To install, reverse the removal procedures. Torque the lower control arm-to-frame bolts to 148 ft. lbs., the lower control arm-to-frame nuts to 92 ft. lbs., the shock absorber-to-lower control arm nut/bolt to 54 ft. lbs., the stabilizer bar-to-lower control arm nuts/bolts to 24 ft. lbs. and the lower control arm ball joint-to-steering knuckle nut to 83 ft. lbs.

Steering Knuckle and Spindle

REMOVAL AND INSTALLATION

2WD Model

NOTE: The following procedure requires the use of the GM Tie Rod End Puller tool J-6627 or equivalent, and the GM Ball Joint Remover tool No. J-23742 or equivalent.

1. Siphon some brake fluid from the brake master cylinder.
2. Raise and safely support the front of the vehicle on jackstands. Remove the wheels.

NOTE: When supporting the vehicle on jackstands, DO NOT place the jackstands under the lower control arms. Place them under the frame.

3. Remove the brake caliper from the steering knuckle and hang it from the body on a wire.
4. Remove the grease cup, the cotter pin, the castle nut and the hub-and-rotor assembly.
5. Remove the splash shield-to-steering knuckle bolts and the shield.
6. At the tie rod end-to-steering knuckle stud, remove the cotter pin and the nut. Using the GM Tie Rod End Puller tool J-6627 or equivalent, separate the tie rod end from the steering knuckle.
7. Using a floor jack, place it under the spring seat of the lower control arm and support the arm.
8. From the upper and lower ball joint studs, remove the cotter pins and the nuts.

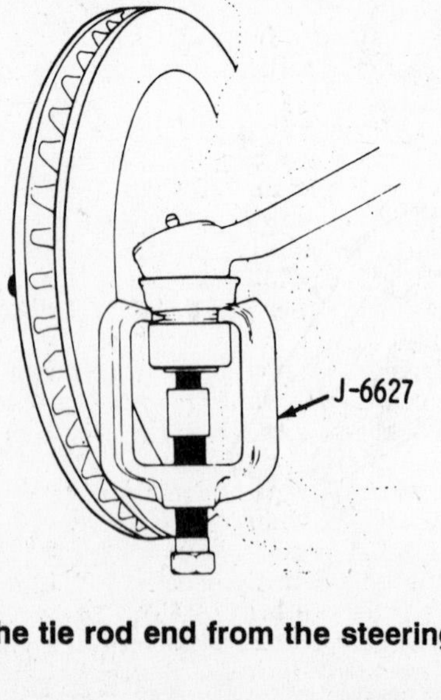
J-6627

Removing the tie rod end from the steering knuckle

9. Using the GM Ball Joint Remover tool No. J-23742 or equivalent, separate the upper ball joint from the steering knuckle.
10. Raise the upper control arm to separate it from the steering knuckle.
11. Using the GM Ball Joint Remover tool No. J-23742 or equivalent, separate the lower ball joint from the steering knuckle, then lift the steering knuckle from the lower control arm.
12. Clean and inspect the steering knuckle and spindle for signs of wear or damage; if necessary, replace the steering knuckle.
13. To install the steering knuckle, position it onto the lower ball joint stud, then lift the upper control arm to insert the upper ball joint stud into the steering knuckle. Torque the upper ball joint-to-steering knuckle nut to 65 ft. lbs. and the lower ball joint-to-steering knuckle nut to 90 ft. lbs. Remove the floor jack from under the lower control arm.
14. Install a new cotter pin into the upper and lower ball joint studs.

NOTE: When installing the cotter pin, never loosen the castle nut to expose the cotter pin hole.

15. To complete the installation, reverse the removal procedures. Torque the tie rod end-to-steering knuckle nut to 40 ft. lbs., the splash shield-to-steering knuckle bolts to 10 ft. lbs. Check and/or adjust the wheel bearing and the front end alignment.
16. Remove the jackstands and lower the vehicle. Refill the brake master cylinder.

4WD Model

NOTE: The following procedure requires the use of the Universal Steering Linkage Puller tool No. J-24319-01 or equivalent, the Axle Shaft Boot Seal Protector tool No. J-28712 or equivalent, the Ball Joint Separator tool No. J-34026 or equivalent, and the Steering Knuckle Seal Installation tool No. J-28574 or equivalent.

1. Refer to the "Torsion Bar, Removal and Installation" procedures in this section and relieve the torsion bar pressure.
2. Raise and support the front of the truck on jackstands; place the jackstands under the frame.
3. Remove the wheel and tire.
4. Using the Axle Shaft Boot Seal Protector tool No. J-28712 or equivalent, attach it to the tripot axle joint.
5. Remove the disc brake caliper-to-steering knuckle bolts, lift the brake caliper and support it (out of the way) on a wire.
6. Remove the brake disc from the wheel hub.
7. At the wheel hub, remove the cotter pin, the retainer, the castle nut, the thrust washer.
8. From the tie-rod-to-steering knuckle assembly, remove the cotter pin and the castle nut.
9. Using the Universal Steering Linkage Puller tool No. J-24319-01 or equivalent, tie-rod from the steering knuckle.
10. Remove the hub/bearing assembly-to-steering knuckle bolts and the hub/bearing assembly from the steering knuckle.
11. From the upper and lower ball joints, remove the cotter pin(s) and back off the castle nut(s).
12. Using the Ball Joint Separator tool No. J-34026 or equivalent, disconnect the ball joints from the steering knuckle. Remove the ball joint nut(s) and separate the ball joint(s) from the steering knuckle.

NOTE: When removing the steering knuckle from the wheel hub, be careful not to damage the splined surface of the half shaft.

13. Remove the spacer and the seal from the steering knuckle.
14. Clean and inspect the parts for nicks, scores and/or damage, then replace them as necessary.

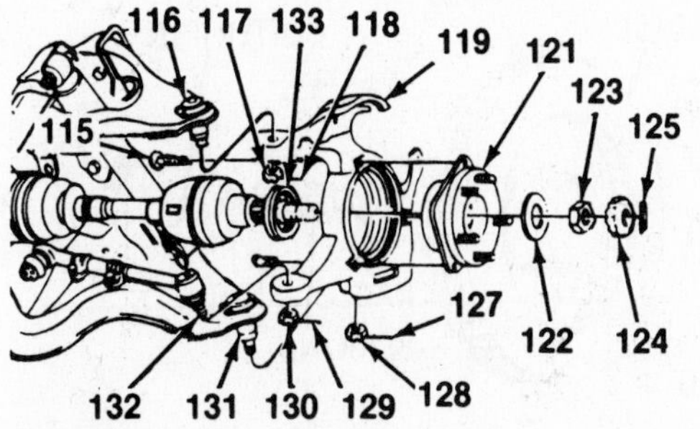
116 117 133 118
119
121
123
125
115
127
122 124
132 131 130 129 128

115. Bolt
116. Upper control arm ball joint
117. Nut
118. Pin
119. Knuckle
121. Hub and bearing assembly
122. Washer
123. Nut
124. Retainer
125. Pin
127. Pin
128. Nut
129. Pin
130. Nut
131. Lower control arm ball joint
132. Tie rod end
133. Seal

Steering knuckle and hub assembly on 4WD

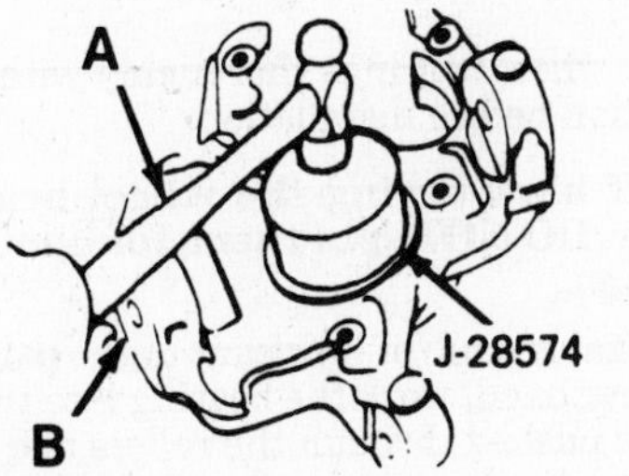
A
J-28574
B

A. Hammer
B. Knuckle

Installing the new steering knuckle seal on 4WD

15. Using the Steering Knuckle Seal Installation tool No. J-28574 or equivalent, install a new seal into the steering knuckle.
16. Install the spacer, then the upper and lower ball joints to the steering knuckle. Torque the upper ball joint-to-steering knuckle nut to 61 ft. lbs. and the lower ball joint-to-steering knuckle nut to 83 ft. lbs. DO NOT loosen the nut for the cotter pin installation, simply turn the nut a 1/6 turn further; bend the pin ends against the nut flats.
17. Install the wheel hub/bearing assembly-to-steering knuckle, be careful to align the threads and splines carefully. Torque the hub/bearing assembly-to-steering knuckle bolts to 86 ft. lbs.
18. Install the tie-rod end-to-steering knuckle, then torque the tie-rod end nut to 35 ft. lbs. Install the cotter pin and bend the ends against the nut flats.
19. To complete the installation, reverse the removal procedures. Before torquing the wheel hub/bearing, put the vehicle on the ground. The torque is high enough to cause the truck to fall off the jack stands. Torque the wheel hub/bearing assembly-to-half shaft nut to 181 ft. lbs. Check and/or adjust the front end alignment.

Front Wheel Bearings

The proper functioning of the front suspension cannot be maintained unless the front wheel taper roller bearings are correctly adjusted. The cones must be a slip fit on the spindle and the inside diameter should be lubricated to insure that the cones will creep. The spindle nut must be a free-running fit on threads.

2-WHEEL DRIVE ADJUSTMENT

1. Raise and support the front of the vehicle on jackstands, then remove the grease cap from the hub.
2. Remove the cotter pin from axle spindle and spindle nut.
3. Tighten the spindle nut to 12 ft. lbs. while turning the wheel assembly forward by hand to fully seat the bearings. This will remove any grease or burrs which could cause excessive wheel bearing play later.
4. Back off the nut to the "just loose" position.
5. Hand tighten the spindle nut. Loosen the spindle nut until either hole in the spindle aligns with a slot in the nut; not more than ½ flat.
6. Install a new cotter pin; bend the ends against nut flat, cut off extra length to ensure ends will not interfere with the grease cap.
7. Measure the looseness in the wheel hub assembly. There will be from 0.001-0.005 in. (0.03-0.13mm) end play when properly adjusted.
8. Install the grease cap onto the wheel hub.

REMOVAL AND INSTALLATION

2WD Models

NOTE: The following procedure requires the use of the Wheel Bearing Removal tool No. J-29117 or equivalent, the Wheel Bearing Installation tools No. J-8092 and J-8850 or equivalent.

1. Remove to the "Disc Brake Caliper, Removal and Installation" procedures in the brake section and remove the disc brake caliper.

CAUTION

Brake shoes and pads contain asbestos, which has been determined to be a cancer causing agent. Never clean the brake surfaces with compressed air! Avoid inhaling any dust from any brake surface! When cleaning brake surfaces, use a commercially available brake cleaning fluid.

2. Remove the grease cup from wheel hub.
3. Remove the cotter pin, the castle nut and the thrust washer from the spindle.
4. Carefully pull wheel hub assembly from the spindle.
5. Remove the outer wheel bearing from the wheel hub. The inner wheel bearing will remain in the hub and may be removed after prying out the inner wheel bearing grease seal; discard the seal.
6. Using the Wheel Bearing Removal tool No. J-29117 or equivalent, remove the inner and outer wheel bearing races from the wheel hub.
7. Clean all of the parts in clean solvent and air dry.
8. Inspect the bearings for cracks, worn or pitted rollers.
9. Inspect the bearing races for cracks, scores or a brinelled condition.
10. If the the outer races were removed, use the Wheel Bearing Installation tools No. J-8092 and J-8850 or equivalent, drive or press the races into the hub.
11. Clean off any grease in the hub/spindle and thoroughly clean out any grease in the bearings. Use clean solvent and a small brush, with no loose bristles, to clean out all old grease.

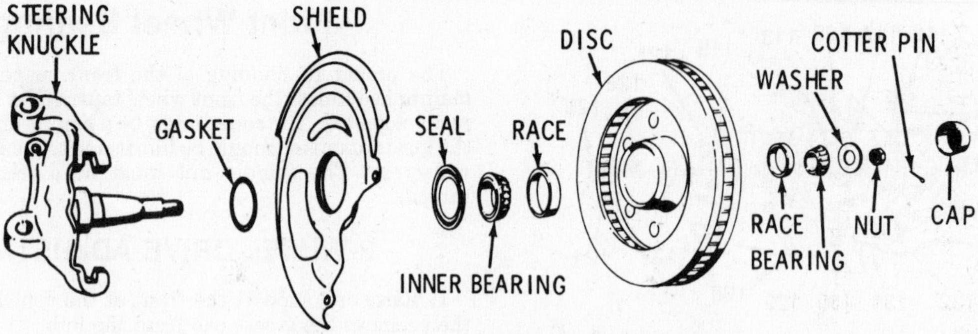
STEERING KNUCKLE
SHIELD
GASKET
SEAL
RACE
DISC
COTTER PIN
WASHER
RACE
NUT
CAP
BEARING
INNER BEARING

Front rotor and wheel bearings, 2WD

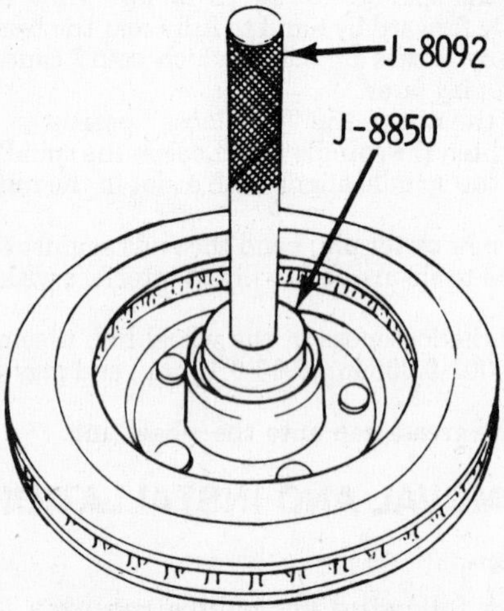
J-8092
J-8850

Installing inner bearing race

DO NOT spin the bearing with compressed air while drying it or the bearing may be damaged.

12. Use an approved high temperature front wheel bearing grease.

NOTE: DO NOT mix greases as mixing may change the grease properties and result in poor performance.

13. Apply a thin film of grease to the spindle at the outer bearing seat and at the inner bearing seat, the shoulder and the seal seat.

14. Put a small quantity of grease inboard of each bearing cup in the hub. This can be applied with your finger, forming a dam to provide extra grease availability to the bearing and to keep thinned grease from flowing out of the bearing.

15. Fill the bearing cone and roller assemblies full of grease.

NOTE: A preferred method for doing this is with a cone type grease machine that forces grease into the bearing. If a cone greaser is not available, the bearings can be packed by hand. If hand packing is used, it is extremely important to work the grease thoroughly into the bearings between the rollers, cone and the cage. Failure to do this could result in premature bearing failure.

16. Place the inner bearing cone and roller assembly in the hub. Then using your finger, put an additional quantity of grease outboard of the bearing.

17. Install a new grease seal using a flat plate until the seal is flush with the hub. Lubricate the seal lip with a thin layer of grease.

18. Carefully install the hub and rotor assembly. Place the outer bearing cone and roller assembly in the outer bearing cup. Install the washer and nut and initially tighten the nut to 12 ft. lbs. while turning the wheel assembly forward by hand. Put an additional quantity of grease outboard the bearing. This provides extra grease availability to the bearing.

19. Check and/or adjust the wheel bearing.

4WD Models

NOTE: The wheel bearing is installed in the wheel hub assembly and is serviced by replacement only.

CAUTION

Brake shoes and pads contain asbestos, which has been determined to be a cancer causing agent. Never clean the brake surfaces with compressed air! Avoid inhaling any dust from any brake surface! When cleaning brake surfaces, use a commercially available brake cleaning fluid.

Refer to the "Steering Knuckle, Removal and Installation" procedures in this section and replace the wheel hub assembly.

PACKING

Clean the wheel bearings thoroughly with solvent and check their condition before installation.

NOTE: If blow drying the wheel bearings with compressed air, DO NOT spin them, for damage may occur to the bearings.

Apply a sizable daub of lubricant to the palm of one hand. Using your other hand, work the bearing into the lubricant so that the grease is pushed through the rollers and out the other side. Keep rotating the bearing while continuing to push the lubricant through it.

Front End Alignment

CASTER

Caster is the tilting of the front steering axis either forward or backward from the vertical. A backward tilt is said to be positive (+) and a forward tilt is said to be negative (−).

CAMBER

Camber is the inward or outward tilting of the front wheels from the vertical. When the wheels tilt outward at the top, the camber is said to be positive (+). When the wheels tilt inward at the top, the camber is said to be negative (−). The amount of tilt is measured in degrees from the vertical and this measurement is called the camber angle.

TOE-IN

Toe-in is the turning in of the front wheels. The actual amount of toe-in is normally only a fraction of a degree. The purpose of toe-in is to ensure parallel rolling of the front wheels. Excessive toe-in or toe-out will cause tire wear.

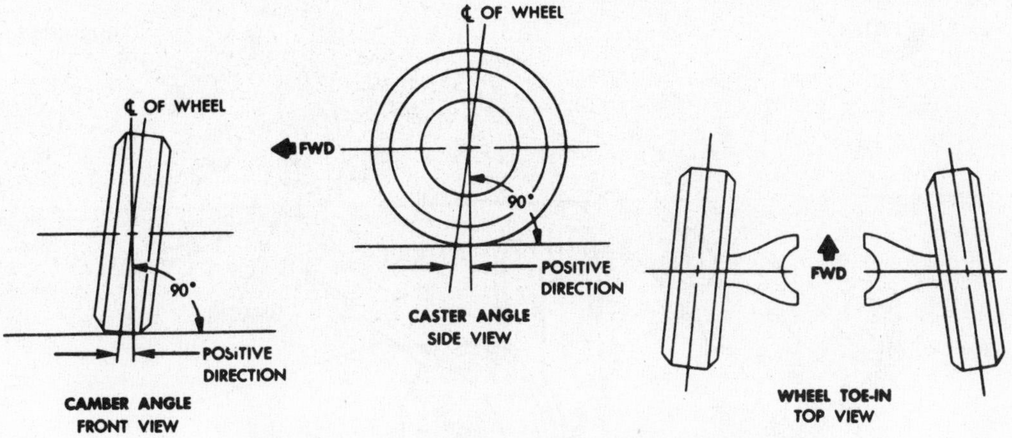
℄ OF WHEEL
90°
POSITIVE DIRECTION
CAMBER ANGLE FRONT VIEW
FWD
℄ OF WHEEL
90°
POSITIVE DIRECTION
CASTER ANGLE SIDE VIEW
FWD
WHEEL TOE-IN TOP VIEW

Camber, caster and toe are adjusted in degrees

WHEEL ALIGNMENT SPECIFICATIONS

Toe-in		Camber		Caster	
Range (in.)	Preferred (in.)	Range (deg.)	Preferred (deg.)	Range (deg.)	Preferred (deg.)
$^{1}/_{16}$P–$^{1}/_{4}$P	$^{1}/_{8}$P	0–1$^{5}/_{8}$P	$^{13}/_{16}$P	1P–3P	2P

REAR SUSPENSION

The rear suspension system consists of several major components: The double acting shock absorbers, variable rate multi-leaf springs and various attachment parts. The multi-leaf springs are connected to the frame by a hanger assembly with integral bushings in the front and a shackle assembly with integral bushings in the rear. The shackle assembly, in response to different road and payload conditions, allows the leaf spring to "change its length". The rear axle is connected to both the leaf springs and the shock absorbers by various attaching parts.

Leaf Springs

REMOVAL AND INSTALLATION

NOTE: The following procedure requires the use of two sets of jackstands.

1. Raise and safely support the rear frame of the vehicle on jackstands. support the rear axle with the second set of jackstands.

NOTE: When supporting the rear of the vehicle, support the axle and the body separately to relieve the load on the rear spring.

2. Remove the wheel and tire assembly.
3. At the rear of the spring, loosen (DO NOT remove) the shackle-to-frame bolt and the shackle-to-spring bolt.
4. Remove the shock absorber.
5. Remove the axle U-bolt-to-anchor plate nuts, the lower plate-to-anchor plate nuts, the U-bolts and the lower plate, then jack up the axle on that side only just enough to lift off of the spring.
6. At the front of the spring, remove the retainer-to-hanger assembly nuts, the washers and the retainer(s).
7. At the rear of the spring, remove the spring-to-shackle nut, washer and bolt. Remove the spring from the vehicle.

To install:

8. When installing a new spring, it is usually easier to put the rear end up first. Put the bolts through one of the shackle plates, hang the shackle on the frame, hang the spring on the shackle and put on the other shackle plate. Install the nuts finger tight.
9. It should be possible to move the spring enough on the shackle to line up the holes for the front mounting bolt. Install the washers and nut finger tight.
10. Lower the axle to rest on the spring and install the U-bolts

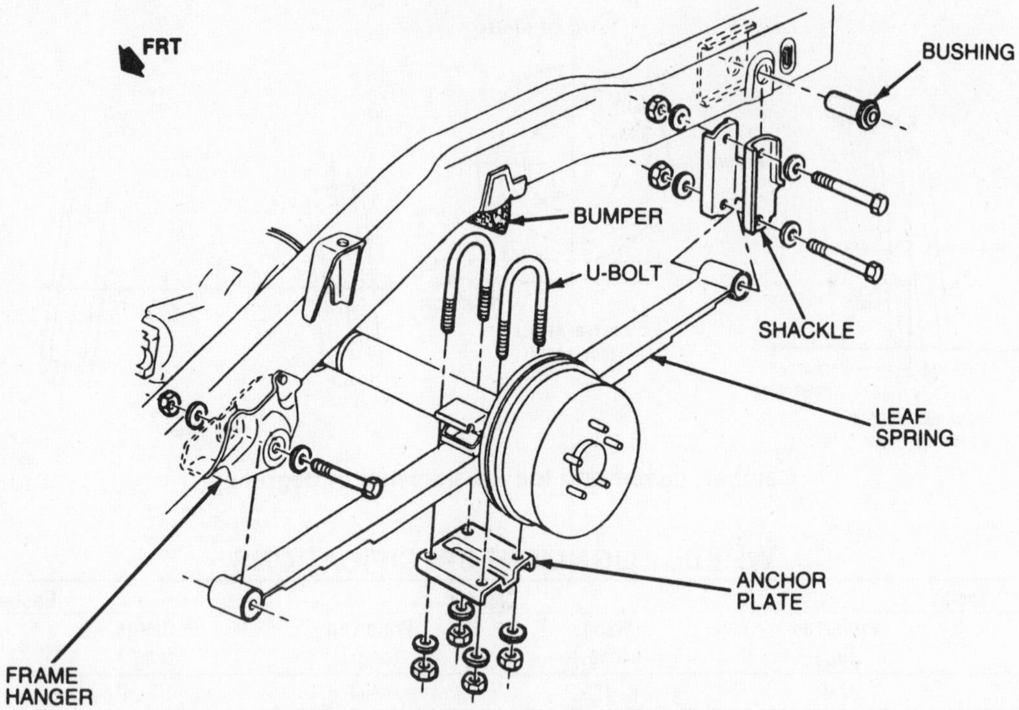
FRT
BUSHING
BUMPER
U-BOLT
SHACKLE
LEAF SPRING
ANCHOR PLATE
FRAME HANGER

Rear leaf spring and axle attachment

and anchor plates. Torque the nuts in a cross pattern first to 18 ft. lbs., then to 85 ft. lbs. It is important that the U-bolts are tigntened evenly.

11. Raise the axle so there is about 6.75 in. (170mm) between the axle housing and the frame of the truck. Measure from the housing between the U-bolts to the metal part of the rubber bump stop on the frame.

12. Torque the front spring mounting bolt and the rear shackle bolts to 92 ft. lbs. Install the shock absorber and wheel.

Shock Absorbers

REMOVAL AND INSTALLATION

1. Raise and support the rear of the truck on jackstands; support the rear axle.
2. At the upper mounting location, disconnect shock absorber bolts.
3. At the lower mounting location, remove the nut and washer.
4. Remove the shock absorber(s) from the vehicle.
5. To install the shock absorber, place it into position and reattach at upper mounting location.
6. Align the lower-end of the shock absorber with the anchor plate stud and install the washer and nut.
7. Torque the shock absorber-to-body bolts to 15 ft. lbs. and the shock absorber-to-axle nut to 50 ft. lbs.
8. Lower vehicle and remove from hoist.

TESTING

Visually inspect the shock absorber. If there is evidence of leakage and the shock absorber is covered with oil, the shock is defective and should be replaced.

If there is no sign of excessive leakage (a small amount of weeping is normal) bounce the truck at one corner by pressing down on the bumper and releasing it. When you have the truck bouncing as much as you can, release the bumper. The truck should stop bouncing after the first rebound. If the bouncing continues past the center point of the bounce more than once, the shock absorbers are worn and should be replaced.

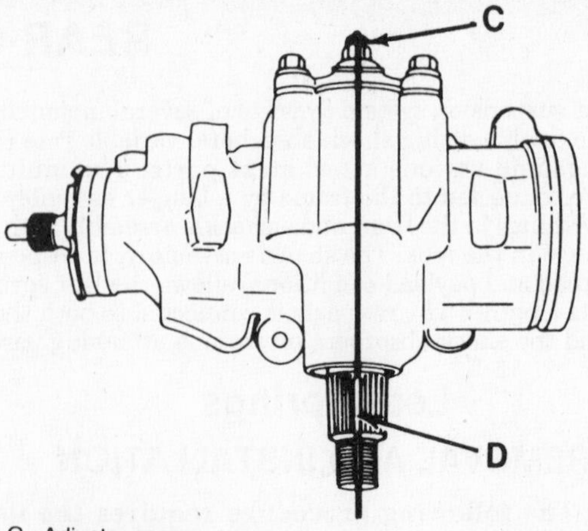
C
D

C. Adjuster screw
D. Master spline on the Pitman shaft

Align the pitman arm shaft master spline

STEERING

The steering box (manual or power) consists of a recirculating balls, which transmits force from the worm gear to the sector gear. A relay type steering linkage is used with a pitman arm connected to one end of the relay rod. The relay rod is supported by two idler arms; the idler arms pivot on a support which is attached to the frame. The relay rod is connected to the steering arms by two adjustable tie rods. The trucks are equipped with a collapsible steering column designed to collapse on impact, thereby reducing possible chest injuries during accidents. When making any repairs to the steering column or steering wheel, excessive pressure or force capable of collapsing the column must be avoided. The ignition lock, ignition switch and an antitheft system are built into each column.

On the automatic transmission, the ignition key cannot be removed unless the shift lever is in the Park position and the ignition switch in the Lock position. Placing the key in the Lock position activates a rod within the column which locks the steering wheel and shift lever.

Steering Wheel

REMOVAL AND INSTALLATION

NOTE: The following procedure requires the use of the GM Steering Wheel Puller tool No. J-1859-03 or equivalent.

1. Disconnect the negative battery cable from the battery.
2. Position the steering wheel so that it is in the horizontal position and the front wheel are straight.
3. If equipped with a horn cap, pry the cap from the center of the steering wheel. If equipped with a steering wheel shroud, remove the screw from the rear of the steering wheel and remove the shroud.

NOTE: If the horn cap or shroud is equipped with an electrical connector, disconnect it.

4. Remove the steering wheel-to-steering shaft retainer (snapring) and nut.

NOTE: Since the steering column is designed to collapse upon impact, it is recommended NEVER to hammer on it!

5. Matchmark the relationship of the steering wheel to the steering shaft.

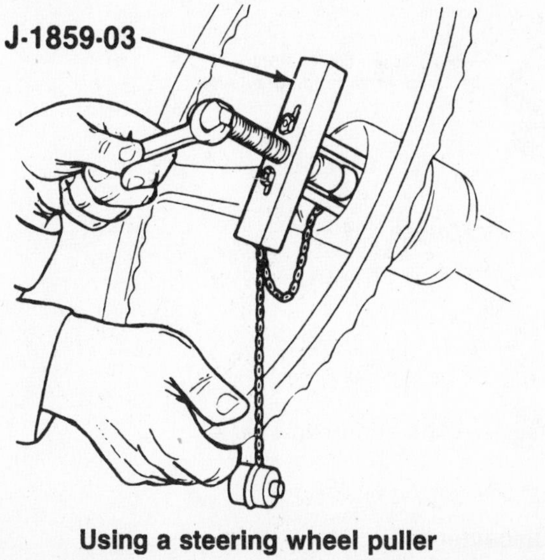
J-1859-03

Using a steering wheel puller

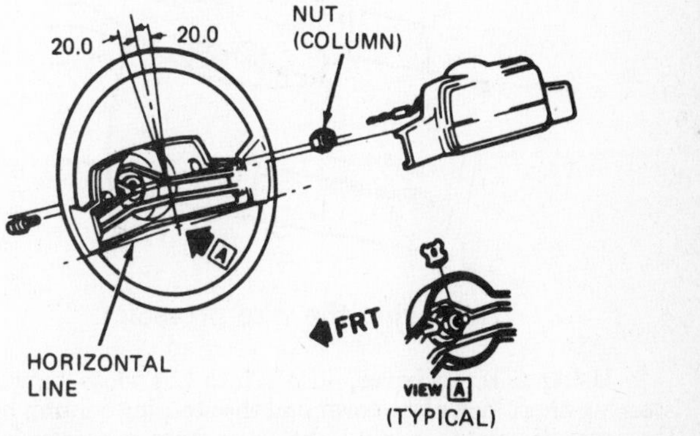
20.0
20.0
NUT
(COLUMN)
HORIZONTAL
LINE
FRT
VIEW A
(TYPICAL)

Make sure the wheel is properly aligned when installing it

6. Using the GM Steering Wheel Puller tool No. J-1859-03 or equivalent, press the steering wheel from the steering column.

NOTE: Before installing the steering wheel, be sure that the turn signal switch is in the Neutral position. DO NOT misalign the steering wheel more than 1 in. (25mm) from the horizontal centerline.

7. To install the steering wheel, align the matchmarks and push it onto the steering shaft splines, torque the steering wheel-to-steering shaft nut to 30 ft. lbs. Install the horn cap or pad.

Combination Switch

The combination switch is a combination of the turn signal, the windshield wiper/washer, the dimmer and the cruise control switches.

REMOVAL AND INSTALLATION

NOTE: The following procedure requires the use of the GM Lock Plate Compressor tool No. J-23653 or equivalent.

1. Disconnect the negative battery cable. Refer to the "Steering Wheel, Removal and Installation" procedures in this section and remove the steering wheel.
2. If necessary, remove the steering column-to-lower instrument panel cover. Disconnect the electrical harness connector from the steering column jacket (under the dash).

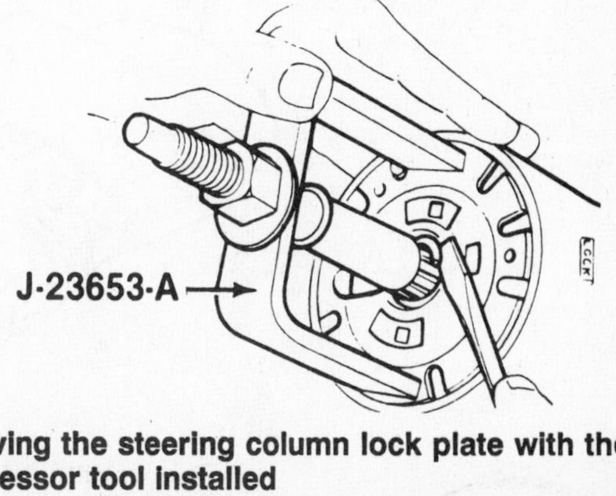
J-23653-A

Removing the steering column lock plate with the compressor tool installed

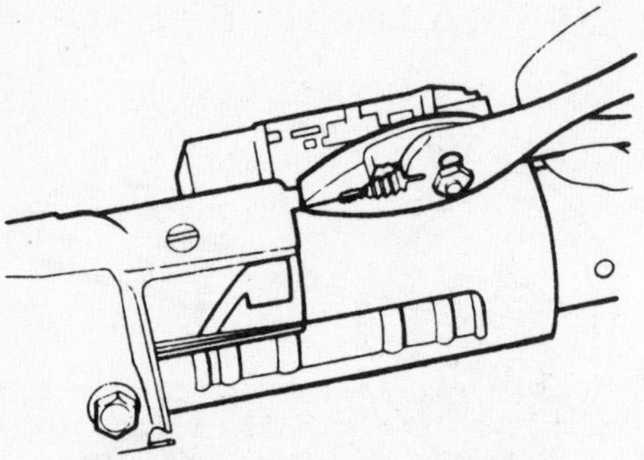

Removing the wire protector

3. Using a screwdriver, insert into the slots between the steering shaft lock plate cover and the steering column housing, then pry upward to remove the cover from the lock plate.
4. Using the GM Lock Plate Compressor tool No. J-23653-A or equivalent, screw the center shaft onto the steering shaft (as far as it will go), then screw the center post nut clockwise until the lock plate is compressed.
5. Pry the snapring from the steering shaft slot.

NOTE: If the steering column is being disassembled on a bench, the steering shaft will slide out of the mast jacket when the snapring is removed.

6. Remove the GM Lock Plate Compressor tool No. J-23653 or equivalent, and the lock plate.
7. Remove the multi-function lever-to-switch screw and the lever.
8. To remove the hazard warning switch, press the knob inward and unscrew it.
9. Remove the combination switch assembly-to-steering column screws.
10. Lift the combination switch assembly from the steering column, then slide the electrical connector through the column housing and the protector.

NOTE: If the steering column is the tilting type, position the steering housing into the Low position.

11. To remove the harness cover, pull it toward the lower end of the column; be careful not to damage the wires.
12. To remove the wire protector, grab the protector's tab with a pair of pliers, then pull the protector downward, out of the steering column.

NOTE: When assembling the steering column, use only fasteners of the correct length; overlength fasteners could prevent a portion of the assembly from compressing under impact.

To install:

13. To install the combination switch electrical connector, perform the following procedures:
   a. On the non-tilt columns, be sure that the electrical connector is on the protector, then feed it and the cover down through the housing and under the mounting bracket.
   b. On the tilt columns, feed the electrical connector down through the housing and under the mounting bracket, then install the cover onto the housing.
14. Install the clip on the electrical connector to the clip on the jacket, the combination switch-to-steering column mounting screws, the lower instrument trim panel, the turn signal lever/screws and the hazard warning knob.

NOTE: With the multi-function lever installed, place it into the Neutral position. With the hazard warning knob installed, pull it Outward.

15. Onto the upper end of the steering shaft, install the washer, the upper bearing preload spring, the canceling cam, the lock plate and a new retaining ring (snapring). Using the GM Lock Plate Compressor tool No. J-23653 or equivalent, compress the lock plate and slide the new retaining ring into the steering shaft groove.
16. To complete the installation, reverse the removal procedures. Torque the multi-function switch-to-steering column screws to 35 inch lbs. and the steering wheel nut to 30 ft. lbs.

Ignition Switch

The ignition switch, for anti-theft reasons, is located inside the channel section of the brake pedal support and is completely inaccessible without first lowering the steering column. The switch is actuated by a rod and rack assembly. A gear on the end of the lock cylinder engages the toothed upper end of the actuator rod.

REMOVAL AND INSTALLATION

1. Remove the lower instrument panel-to-steering column cover. Remove the steering column-to-dash bolts and lower the steering column; be sure to properly support it.
2. Place the ignition switch in the Locked position.

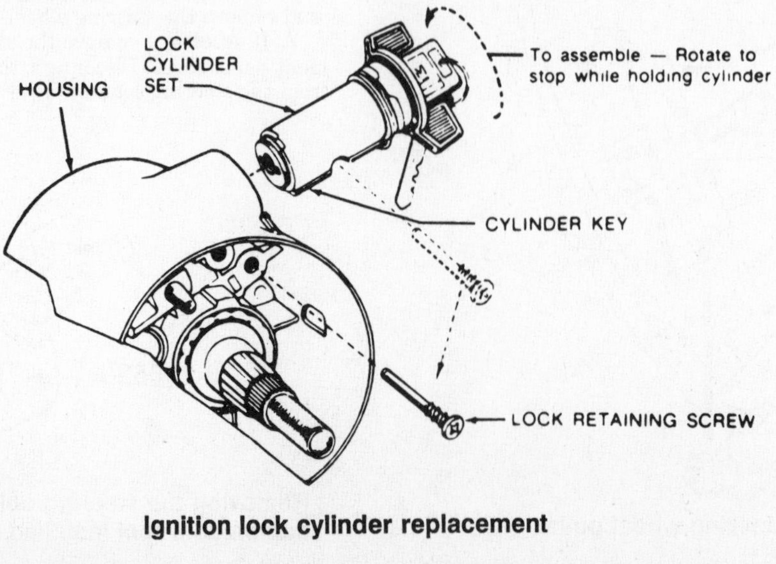
LOCK CYLINDER SET
HOUSING
To assemble — Rotate to stop while holding cylinder
CYLINDER KEY
LOCK RETAINING SCREW

Ignition lock cylinder replacement

NOTE: If the lock cylinder was removed, the actuating rod should be pulled up until it stops, then moved down one detent; the switch is now in the Lock position.

3. Remove the two ignition switch-to-steering column screws and the switch assembly.
4. Before installing the ignition switch, place it in the Locked position, then make sure that the lock cylinder and actuating rod are in the Locked position (1st detent from the top).
5. Install the activating rod into the ignition switch and assemble the switch onto the steering column. Torque the ignition switch-to-steering column screws to 35 inch lbs.

NOTE: When installing the ignition switch, use only the specified screws since overlength screws could impair the collapsibility of the column.

6. To complete the installation, install the steering column and the lower instrument panel cover. Torque the steering column-to-instrument bolts to 22 ft. lbs.

Ignition Lock Cylinder

REMOVAL AND INSTALLATION

1. Disconnect the negative battery cable. Refer to the "Combination Switch, Removal and Installation" procedures in this section and remove the combination switch.
2. Place the lock cylinder in the **Run** position.
3. Remove the buzzer switch, the lock cylinder screw and the lock cylinder.

CAUTION

If the screw is dropped upon removal, it could fall into the steering column, requiring complete disassembly to retrieve the screw.

4. To install, rotate the lock cylinder clockwise to align the cylinder key with the keyway in the housing.
5. Push the lock cylinder all the way in.
6. Install the cylinder lock-to-housing screw. Tighten the screw to 14 inch lbs.

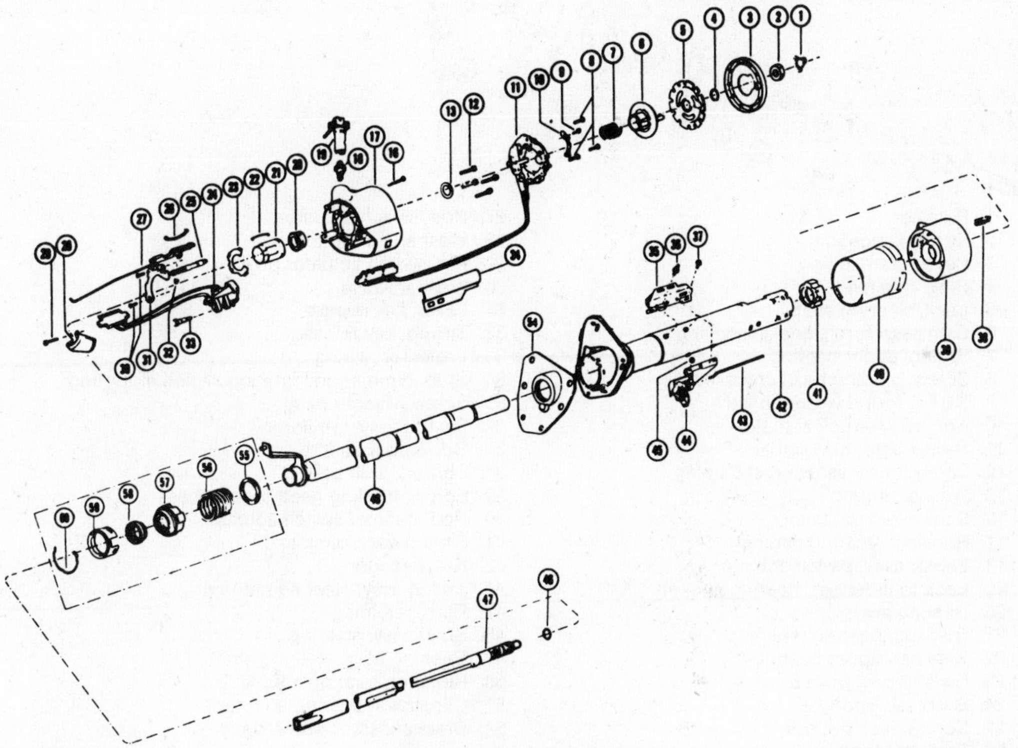

1. Retainer
2. Nut, hexagon
3. Cover, shaft lock
4. Ring, retaining
5. Lock, steering shaft
6. Cam assy, turn signal cancelling
7. Spring, upper bearing
8. Screw, binding head cross recess
9. Screw, round washer head
10. Arm assy, switch actuator
11. Switch assy, turn signal
12. Screw, hex washer head tapping
13. Washer, thrust
16. Screw, lock retaining
17. Housing, steering column
18. Sector assy, switch actuator
19. Lock cylinder set, steering column
20. Bearing assy
21. Bushing, bearing retaining
22. Contact, horn circuit
23. Retainer, upper bearing
24. Switch assy, pivot &
25. Bolt assy, spring &
26. Spring, rack preload
27. Rack assy, switch actuator rod &
28. Cover, housing
29. Screw, binding head cross recess
30. Screw, flat head cross recess
31. Gate, shift lever
32. Washer, spring thrust
33. Pin, switch actuator pivot
34. Protector, wiring
35. Switch assy, ignition
36. Stud, dimmer & ignition switch mounting
37. Screw, washer head
38. Spring, upper shift lever
39. Bowl, gearshift lever
40. Shroud, gearshift bowl
41. Bearing, bowl lower
42. Jacket assy, steering column
43. Rod, dimmer switch actuator
44. Switch assy, dimmer
45. Nut, hexagon
46. Ring, retaining
47. Shaft assy, steering
48. Tube assy, shift
54. Seal, dash
55. Washer spring thrust
56. Spring shift tube return
57. Adapter, lower bearing
58. Bearing assembly
59. Retainer bearing adapter
60. Clip, lower bearing adapter

Standard steering column components

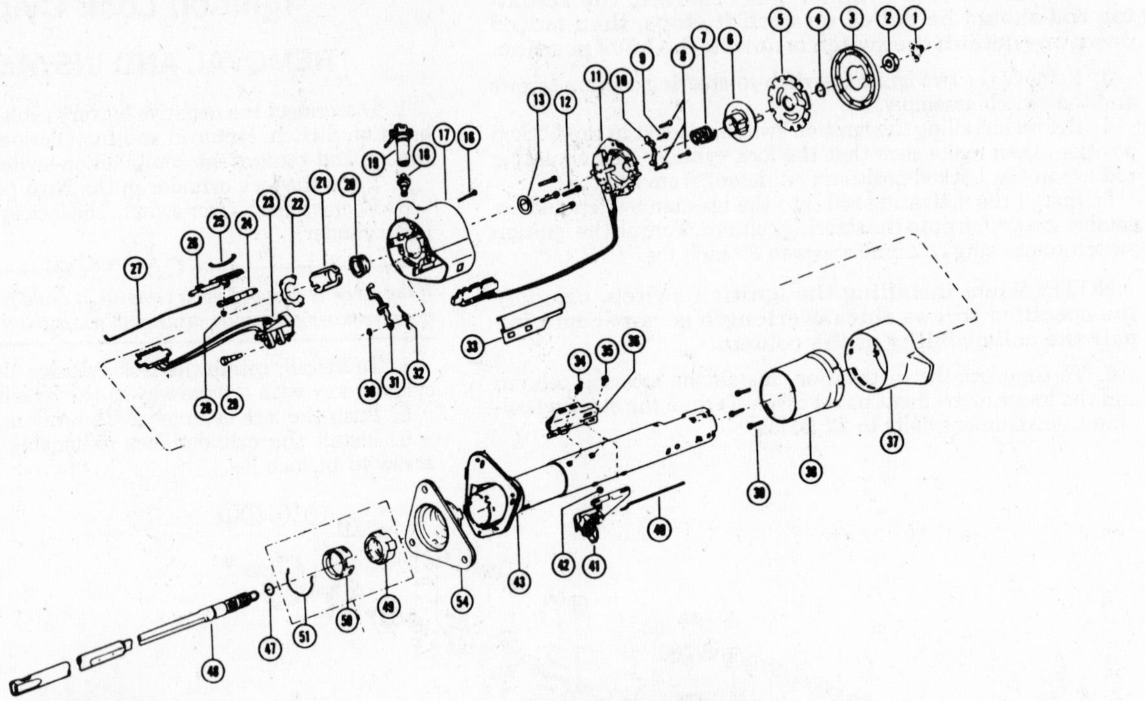

1. Retainer
2. Nut, hexagon jam
3. Cover, shaft lock
4. Ring, retaining
5. Lock, steering shaft
6. Cam assy, turn signal cancelling
7. Spring, upper bearing
8. Screw, binding head cross recess
9. Screw, round washer head
10. Arm assy, switch actuator
11. Switch assy, turn signal
12. Screw, hex washer head tapping
13. Washer, thrust
16. Screw, lock retaining
17. Housing, steering column
18. Sector assy, switch actuator
19. Lock cylinder set, steering column
20. Bearing assy
21. Bushing, bearing retaining
22. Retainer, upper bearing
23. Switch assy, pivot &
24. Bolt assy, spring &
25. Spring, rack preload
26. Rack, switch actuator
27. Rod, switch actuator
28. Washer, spring thrust
29. Pin, switch actuator pivot
30. Washer, wave
31. Lever, key release
32. Spring, key release
33. Protector, wiring
34. Stud, dimmer and ignition switch mounting
35. Screw, washer head
36. Switch assy, ignition
37. Bowl, floor shift
38. Shroud, shift bowl
39. Screw, binding head cross recess
40. Rod, dimmer switch actuator
41. Switch assy, dimmer
42. Nut, hexagon
43. Jacket assy, steering column
47. Ring, retaining
48. Shaft assy, steering
49. Bushing assy. steering shaft
50. Retainer, bearing adapter
51. Clip, lower bearing adapter
54. Bracket assy, column dash

Key release standard steering column components

Steering Column

REMOVAL AND INSTALLATION

NOTE: The following procedure requires the use of the Steering Column Holding Fixture tool No. J-23074 or equivalent.

1. Disconnect the negative battery cable. Refer to the "Steering Wheel, Removal and Installation" procedures in this section and remove the steering wheel.
2. Disconnect the negative battery terminal from the battery.
3. If equipped with a column shift, disconnect the transmission control linkage from the column shift tube levers.
4. From inside the engine compartment, remove the intermediate shaft-to-steering column shaft (pot-joint) bolt.

NOTE: Before separating the intermediate shaft from the steering column shaft, mark the relationship of the two shafts.

5. Remove the lower instrument panel-to-steering column cover, the steering column bracket-to-dash nuts/bolts (support the steering column) and the steering column-to-firewall cover (if necessary).
6. From under the dash, disconnect the electrical harness connectors from the steering column.

NOTE: Some models are equipped with a back-up light switch and a neutral/start switch, be sure to disconnect the electrical connectors from them.

7. Remove the steering column from the vehicle.

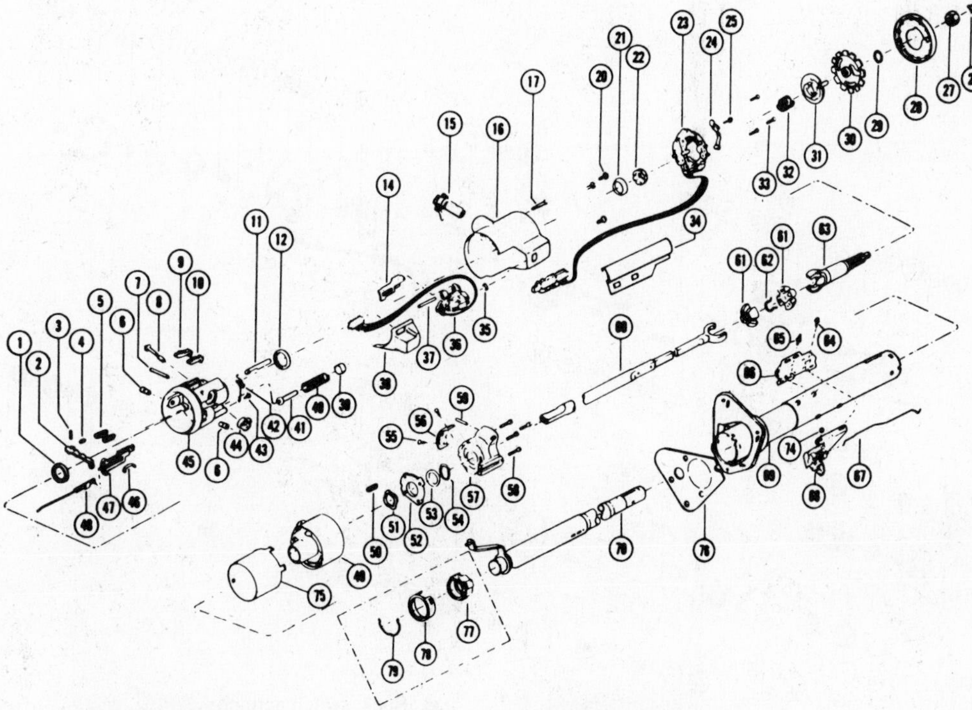

1. Bearing assy
2. Lever, shoe release
3. Pin, release lever
4. Spring, release lever
5. Spring, shoe
6. Pin, pivot
7. Pin, dowel
8. Shaft, drive
9. Shoe, steering wheel lock
10. Shoe, steering wheel lock
11. Bolt, lock
12. Bearing assy
14. Actuator, dimmer switch rod
15. Lock cylinder set, strg column
16. Cover, lock housing
17. Screw, lock retaining
20. Screw, pan head cross recess
21. Race, inner
22. Seat, upper bearing inner race
23. Switch assy, turn signal
24. Arm assy, signal switch
25. Screw, round washer head
26. Retainer
27. Nut, hex jam
28. Cover, shaft lock
29. Ring, retaining
30. Lock, shaft
31. Cam assy, turn signal cancelling
32. Spring, upper bearing
33. Screw, binding head cross recess
34. Protector, wiring
35. Spring, pin preload
36. Switch assy, pivot &
37. Pin, switch actuator pivot
38. Cap, column housing cover end
39. Retainer, spring
40. Spring, wheel tilt
41. Guide, spring
42. Spring, lock bolt
43. Screw, hex washer head
44. Sector, switch actuator
45. Housing, steering column
46. Spring, rack preload
47. Rack, switch actuator
48. Actuator assy, ignition switch
49. Bowl, gearshift lever
50. Spring, shift lever
51. Washer, wave
52. Plate, lock
53. Washer, thrust
54. Ring, shift tube retaining
55. Screw, oval head cross recess
56. Gate, shift lever
57. Support, strg column housing
58. Screw, support
59. Pin, dowel
60. Shaft assy, lower steering
61. Sphere, centering
62. Spring, joint preload
63. Shaft assy, race & upper
64. Screw, washer head
65. Stud, dimmer & ignition switch mounting
66. Switch assy, ignition
67. Rod, dimmer switch
68. Switch assy, dimmer
69. Jacket assy, steering column
70. Tube assy, shift
74. Nut, hexagon
75. Shroud, gearshift bowl
76. Seal, dash
77. Bushing assy, steering shaft
78. Retainer, bearing adapter
79. Clip, lower bearing adapter

Tilt steering column components

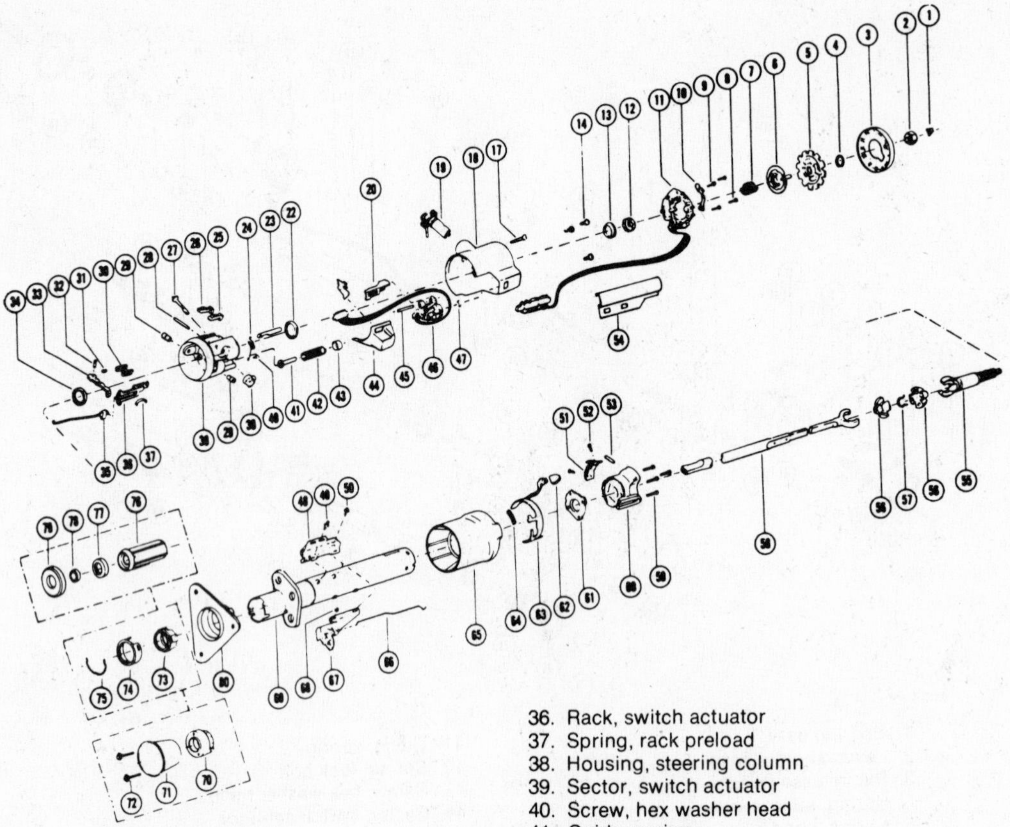

1. Retainer
2. Nut, hexagon jam
3. Cover, shaft lock
4. Ring, retaining
5. Lock, shaft
6. Cam assy, turn signal cancelling
7. Spring, upper bearing
8. Screw, binding head cross recess
9. Screw, round washer head
10. Arm assy, signal switch
11. Switch assy, turn signal
12. Seat, upper bearing inner race
13. Race, inner
14. Screw, pan head cross recess
17. Screw, lock retaining
18. Cover, lock housing
19. Lock cylinder set, steering column
20. Actuator, dimmer switch rod
22. Bearing assy
23. Bolt, lock
24. Spring, lock bolt
25. Shoe, steering wheel lock
26. Shoe, steering wheel lock
27. Shaft, drive
28. Pin, dowel
29. Pin, pivot
30. Spring, shoe
31. Spring, release lever
32. Pin, release lever
33. Lever, shoe release
34. Bearing assy
35. Actuator assy, ignition switch
36. Rack, switch actuator
37. Spring, rack preload
38. Housing, steering column
39. Sector, switch actuator
40. Screw, hex washer head
41. Guide, spring
42. Spring, wheel tilt
43. Retainer, spring
44. Cap, column housing cover end
45. Pin, switch actuator pivot
46. Switch assy, pivot &
47. Spring, pin preload
48. Switch assy, ignition
49. Stud, dimmer & ignition switch mounting
50. Screw, washer head
51. Plate, shroud retaining
52. Screw, oval head cross recess
53. Pin, dowel
54. Protector, wiring
55. Shaft assy,race & upper
56. Sphere, centering
57. Spring, joint preload
58. Shaft assy, lower steering
59. Screw, support
60. Support, steering column housing
61. Plate, lock
62. Finger pad, release lever
63. Lever, key release
64. Spring, key release
65. Shroud, steering column housing
66. Rod, dimmer switch
67. Switch assy, dimmer
68. Nut, hexagon
69. Jacket assy, steering column
73. Bushing assy, steering shaft
74. Retainer, bearing adapter
75. Clip, lower bearing adapter
80. Bracket assy, column dash

Tilt steering column with key release components

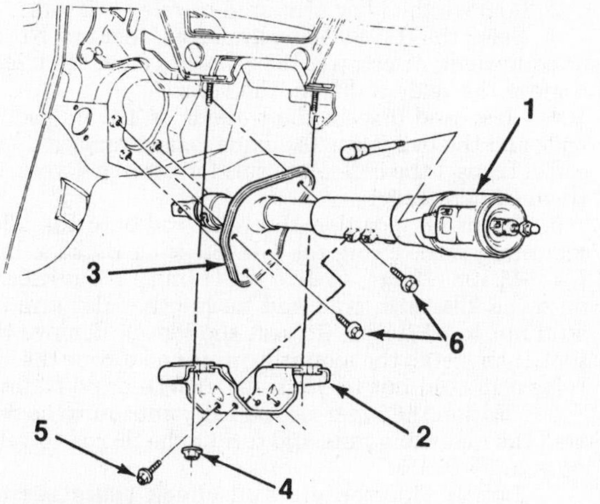
1
3
6
5
2
4

1. Steering column
2. Support bracket
3. Seal
4. Nut
5. Bolt
6. Screws

Steering column removal

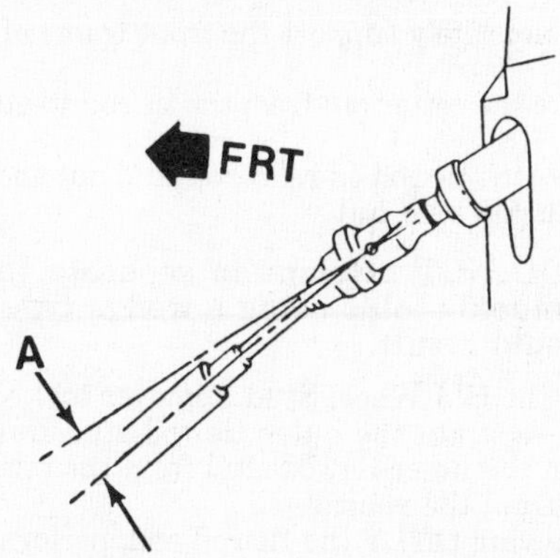
FRT
A

Pot joint angle not to exceed 12.5 degrees

NOTE: If equipped with a column shifter, rotate the steering column so that the shift lever clears the dash opening.

8. To install, align the matchmarks of the steering column shaft and the intermediate shaft, tighten the fasteners finger tight and reverse the removal procedures.
9. Torque the intermediate shaft-to-steering column shaft (pot-joint) pinch bolt to 30 ft. lbs., the steering column bracket-to-dash nuts to 25 ft. lbs. and the steering column-to-firewall screws to 7 ft. lbs.
10. Reconnect the electrical harness-to-steering column connectors. Reinstall the steering wheel and the negative battery terminal.

NOTE: If equipped with steering column shifter, reconnect the transmission-to-steering column linkage.

Steering Linkage

The steering linkage consists of: a forward mounted linkage, crimp nuts at the inner pivots, castellated nuts at the steering knuckle arm, an idler arm, a steering gear pitman arm, a relay rod and a steering damper (manual steering). Grease fittings are equipped with each joint, for durability.

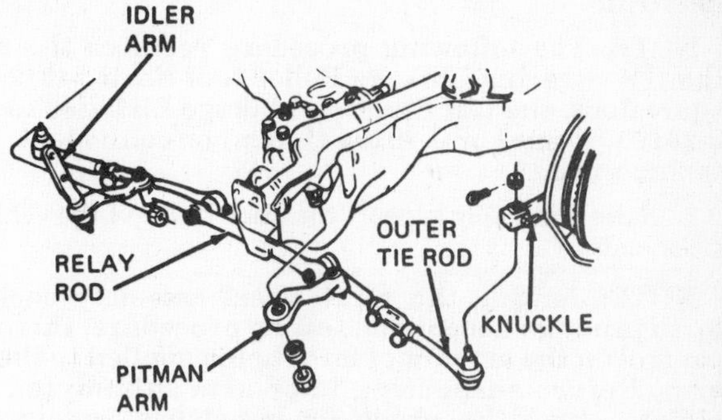
IDLER
ARM
RELAY
ROD
OUTER
TIE ROD
KNUCKLE
PITMAN
ARM

Steering linkage

REMOVAL AND INSTALLATION

Pitman Arm

NOTE: The following procedure requires the use of the GM Steering Linkage Puller tool No. J-24319-01 or equivalent, the GM Pitman Arm Remover tool No. J-6632 or equivalent, and the GM Steering Linkage Installer tool No. J-29193 (12mm) or J-29194 (14mm) or equivalent.

1. Raise and safely support the front frame of the vehicle on jackstands.
2. Disconnect the nut from the pitman arm ball joint stud.
3. Using the GM Steering Linkage Puller tool No. J-24319-01 or equivalent, separate the relay rod from the pitman arm. Pull down on the relay rod and separate it from the stud.
4. Remove the pitman arm-to-pitman shaft nut, mark the relationship the arm to the shaft. Using the GM Pitman Arm Remover tool No. J-6632 or equivalent, separate the pitman arm from the pitman shaft.

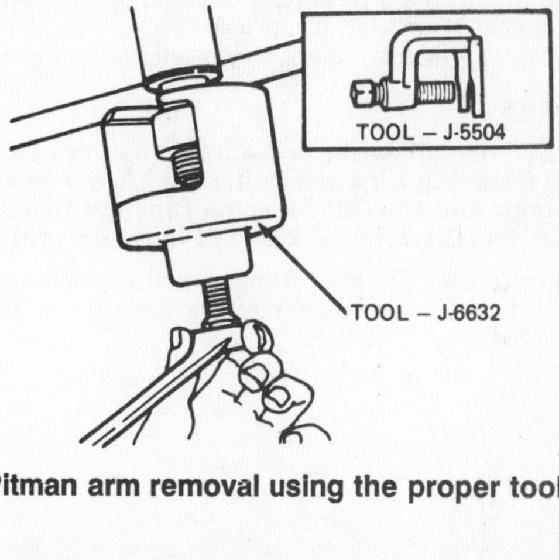
TOOL – J-5504
TOOL – J-6632

Pitman arm removal using the proper tool

NOTE: When separating the pitman arm from the shaft, DO NOT use a hammer or apply heat to the arm.

5. To install, align the pitman arm-to-pitman shaft matchmark and the pitman shaft nut; torque the pitman arm-to-pitman shaft nut to 185 ft. lbs.
6. Connect the pitman arm to the relay rod ball stud (make sure that the seal is on the stud). Using the GM Steering Linkage Installer tool No. J-29193 (12mm) or J-29194 (14mm) or equivalent, install the correct one onto the ball stud and torque it to 40 ft. lbs. to seat the taper.
7. After seating, remove the tool, install the lock washer and nut and torque to 60 ft. lbs.

Idler Arm

NOTE: The following procedure requires the use of the GM Steering Linkage Puller tool No. J-24319-01 or equivalent, the GM Steering Linkage Installer tool No. J-29193 (12mm) or J-29194 (14mm) or equivalent, and a spring scale.

1. Raise and safely support the front frame of the vehicle on jackstands.

NOTE: Jerking the right wheel assembly back and forth is not an acceptable testing procedure; there is no control on the amount of force being applied to the idler arm. Before suspecting idler arm shimmying complaints, check the wheels for imbalance, runout, force variation and/or road surface irregularities.

2. To inspect for a defective idler arm, perform the following procedures:
   a. Position the wheels in the straight ahead position.
   b. Using a spring scale, position it near the relay rod end of the idler arm, then exert 25 lbs. of force upward and then downward.
   c. Measure the distance between the upward and downward directions that the idler arm moves. The allowable deflection is 1/8 in. (3mm) for each direction; a total difference of 1/4 in. (6mm); if the idler arm deflection is beyond the allowable limits, replace it.
3. Remove the idler arm-to-frame bolts and the idler arm-to-relay rod ball joint nut.
4. Using the GM Steering Linkage Puller tool No. J-24319-01 or equivalent, separate the relay rod from the ball joint stud.
5. Inspect and/or replace (if necessary) the idler arm.
6. Install the idler arm-to-frame bolts and torque them to 60 ft. lbs.
7. Connect the relay rod to the idler arm ball joint stud. Using the GM Steering Linkage Installer tool No. J-29193 (12mm) or J-29194 (14mm) or equivalent, seat (torque) the relay rod-to-idler arm ball joint stud to 40 ft. lbs., then remove the tool.
8. Install the idler arm-to-relay rod stud nut and torque it to 35 ft. lbs. (2WD) or 60 ft. lbs. (4WD).
9. Lower the vehicle. Check and/or adjust the toe-in.

Relay Rod

NOTE: The following procedure requires the use of the GM Steering Linkage Puller tool No. J-24319-01 or equivalent, and the GM Steering Linkage Installer tool No. J-29193 (12mm) or J-29194 (14mm) or equivalent.

1. Refer to the "Tie Rod, Removal and Installation" procedures in this section and disconnect the inner tie rod ends from the relay rod.

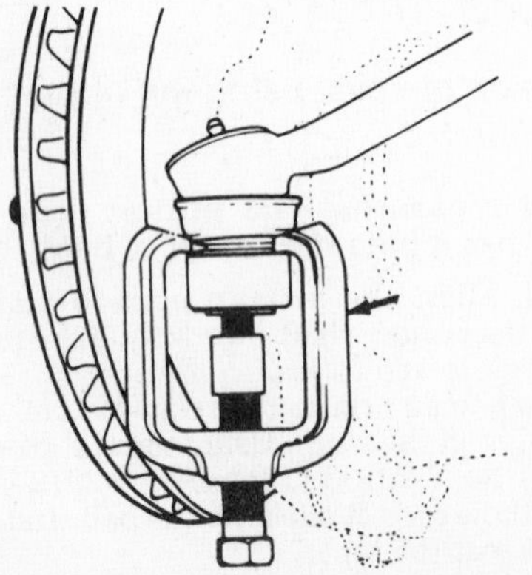

Disconnecting the tie rod end with the proper tool

2. Remove the idler arm stud-to-relay rod nut.
3. Using the GM Steering Linkage Puller tool No. J-24319-01 or equivalent, disconnect the relay rod from the idler arm, then remove the relay rod from the vehicle.
4. Clean and inspect the threads on the tie rod, the tie rod ends and the ball joints for damage, and replace them (if necessary). Inspect the ball joint seals for excessive wear, and replace them (if necessary).
5. To install, position the relay rod onto the idler arm (no mounting nut). Using the GM Steering Linkage Installer tool No. J-29193 (12mm) or J-29194 (14mm) or equivalent, install it onto the idler arm stud and torque the idler arm-to-relay rod stud nut to 35 ft. lbs. (to seat the taper). Remove the installer tool, then install the mounting nuts and torque the idler arm-to-relay arm stud nut to 35 ft. lbs. (2WD) or 60 ft. lbs. (4WD).
6. Position the inner tie rod ball joints onto the relay rod. Install the mounting nuts and torque the tie rod-to-relay rod stud nuts to 35 ft. lbs.
7. Lower the vehicle and check the steering linkage performance.

Tie Rod

NOTE: The following procedure requires the use of the Steering Linkage Installer tool No. J-29193 (12mm) or J-29194 (14mm) or equivalent, and the GM Wheel Stud and Tie Rod Remover tool No. J-6627-A or equivalent.

1. Raise and safely support the front frame of the vehicle on jackstands.
2. Remove the cotter pin from the tie rod-to-steering knuckle stud.
3. Remove the tie rod-to-relay rod stud nut and the tie rod-to-steering knuckle stud nut.

NOTE: DO NOT attempt to separate the tie rod-to-steering knuckle joint using a wedge type tool for seal damage could result.

4. Using the GM Wheel Stud Remover tool No. J-6627-A or equivalent, separate the outer tie rod stud from the steering knuckle and the inner tie rod stud from the relay rod. Remove the tie rod from the vehicle.
5. If removing ONLY the tie rod end, perform the following procedures:
   a. Disconnect the defective ball joint end of the tie rod.
   b. Loosen the adjuster tube clamp bolt.
   c. Unscrew the tie rod end from the adjuster tube; count the number of turns necessary to remove the tie rod end.
   d. Clean, inspect and lubricate the adjuster tube threads.
   e. To install a new tie rod end, screw it into the adjuster tube using the same number of turns necessary to remove it.
   f. Position the clamp bolts between the adjuster tube dimples (located at each end) and in the proper location (see illustration). Torque the adjuster tube clamp bolt 13 ft. lbs.
6. To install, position the tie rod onto the steering knuckle and the relay rod. Using the Steering Linkage Installer tool No. J-29193 (12mm) or J-29194 (14mm) or equivalent, install them onto the studs and torque them to 35 ft. lbs. (to seat the tapers). After seating the tapers, remove the tool.
7. At the tie rod-to-steering knuckle stud, tighten the nut until the castle nut slot aligns with the hole in the stud, then install a new cotter pin.
8. Lower the vehicle and check the steering linkage performance.

Damper Assembly

The damper assembly is used to the remove steering wheel vibration and vehicle wonder; not all vehicles are equipped with it.

NOTE: The following procedure requires the use of the Steering Linkage Puller tool No. J-24319-01 or equivalent.

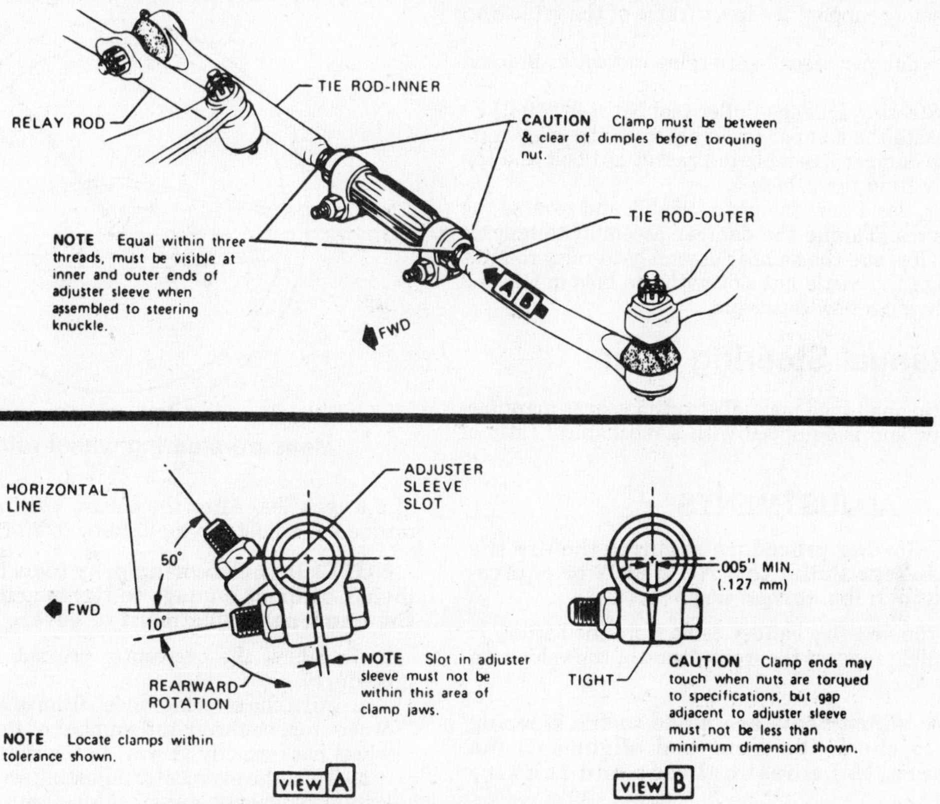
TIE ROD-INNER
RELAY ROD
CAUTION Clamp must be between & clear of dimples before torquing nut.
TIE ROD-OUTER
NOTE Equal within three threads, must be visible at inner and outer ends of adjuster sleeve when assembled to steering knuckle.
FWD
HORIZONTAL LINE
ADJUSTER SLEEVE SLOT
50°
FWD
10°
REARWARD ROTATION
NOTE Slot in adjuster sleeve must not be within this area of clamp jaws.
NOTE Locate clamps within tolerance shown.
VIEW A
.005" MIN. (.127 mm)
TIGHT
CAUTION Clamp ends may touch when nuts are torqued to specifications, but gap adjacent to adjuster sleeve must not be less than minimum dimension shown.
VIEW B

Tie rod clamp and sleeve positioning

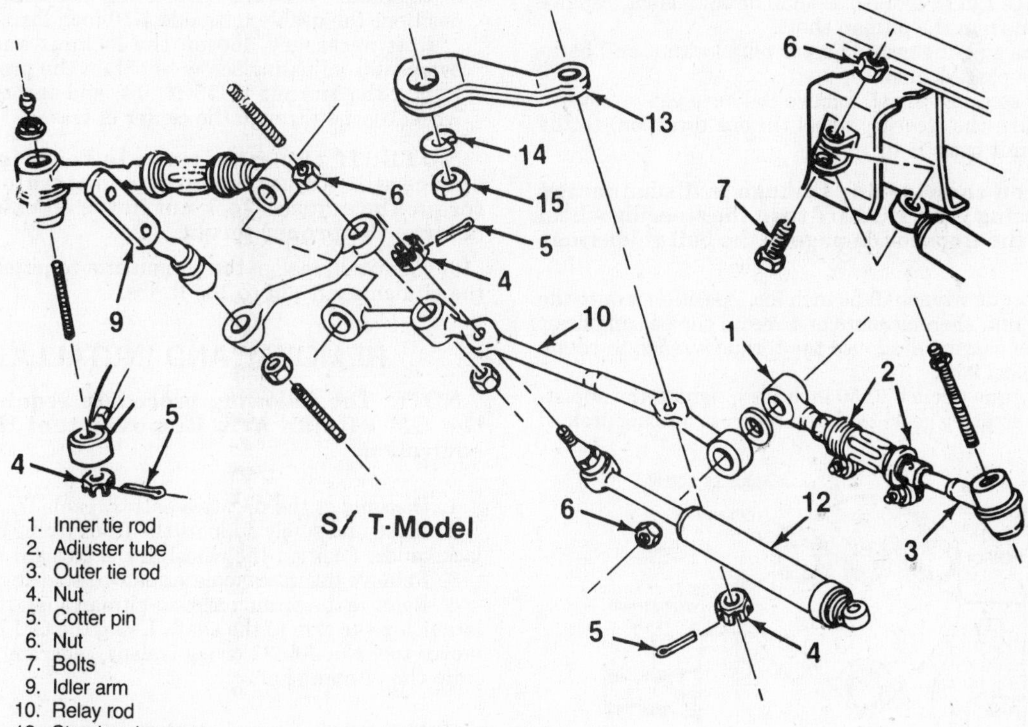
S/ T-Model

1. Inner tie rod
2. Adjuster tube
3. Outer tie rod
4. Nut
5. Cotter pin
6. Nut
7. Bolts
9. Idler arm
10. Relay rod
12. Steering dampner
13. Pitman arm
14. Washer
15. Nut

Steering linkage with damper

1. Raise and safely support the front frame of the vehicle on jackstands.
2. Remove the damper assembly-to-relay rod cotter pin and nut.
3. Using the Steering Linkage Puller tool No. J-24319-01 or equivalent, separate the damper assembly from the relay rod.
4. Remove the damper assembly-to-bracket nut/bolt and the damper assembly from the vehicle.
5. If necessary, use a new damper assembly and reverse the removal procedures. Torque the damper assembly-to-bracket nut/bolt to 26 ft. lbs. and the damper assembly-to-relay rod nut to 45 ft. lbs. Align the castle nut slot with the hole in the ball joint stud and install a new cotter pin.

Manual Steering Gear

The recirculating ball type manual steering gear is manufactured by Saginaw and is equipped with a mechanical ratio of 24:1.

ADJUSTMENTS

NOTE: The following procedure requires the use the GM Steering Linkage Puller tool No. J-6632 or equivalent, and a 0-50 inch lbs. torque wrench.

1. Disconnect the negative battery cable from the battery.
2. Raise and safely support the front frame of the vehicle on jackstands.

NOTE: Before adjustments are made to the steering gear, be sure to check the front end alignment, the shock absorbers, the wheel balance and the tire pressure.

3. Remove the pitman arm-to-pitman shaft nut and matchmark the pitman arm to the pitman shaft. Using the GM Steering Linkage Puller tool No. J-6632 or equivalent, remove the pitman arm from the pitman shaft.
4. Loosen the steering gear adjuster plug locknut and back-off the adjuster plug ¼ turn.
5. From the steering wheel, remove the horn cap or cover.
6. Gently, turn the steering wheel (in one direction) to the stop; then, turn it back ½ turn.

NOTE: When the steering linkage is disconnected from the steering gear, DO NOT turn the steering wheel hard against the stops for damage to the ball guides may result.

7. Using a torque wrench (0-50 inch lbs.), position it onto the steering wheel nut, then measure and record the bearing drag. To measure the bearing drag, use the torque wrench to rotate the steering wheel 90°.
8. Using a torque wrench (0-50 inch lbs.), tighten the adjuster plug (on the steering gear) to obtain a thrust bearing preload of 5-8 inch lbs. After the thrust bearing preload is obtained, torque the adjuster plug locknut to 25 ft. lbs.

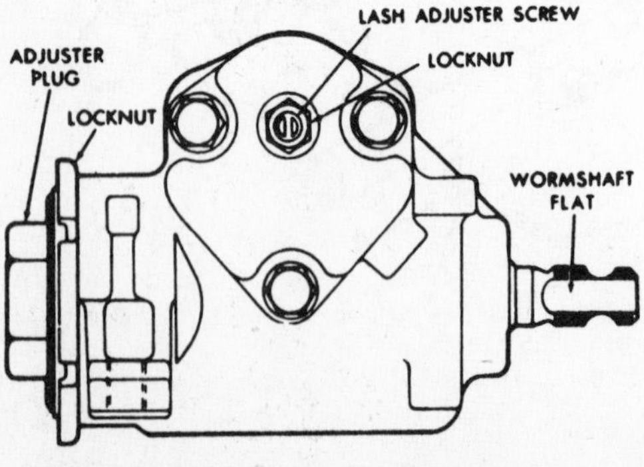
LASH ADJUSTER SCREW
ADJUSTER PLUG
LOCKNUT
LOCKNUT
WORMSHAFT FLAT
Manual steering gear adjustment

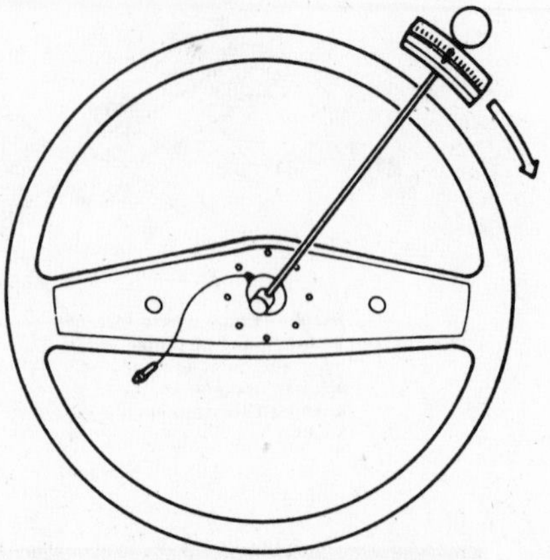
Measure steering wheel rotation effort

NOTE: If the steering gear feels lumpy (after adjustment), suspect damage to the bearings, probably due to the improper adjustment or severe impact.

9. To adjust the overcenter preload, perform the following procedures:
   a. Turn the steering wheel, from one stop all the way to the other stop, counting the number of turns. Turn the steering wheel back exactly ½ way, to the center position.
   b. Turn the overcenter adjusting screw clockwise, until the lash is removed between the ball nut and the pitman shaft sector teeth, then tighten the locknut.
   c. Using a torque wrench (0-50 inch lbs.), check the highest force necessary to turn the steering wheel through the center position; the usable torque is 4-10 inch lbs.
   d. If necessary, loosen the locknut and readjust the overcenter adjusting screw to obtain the proper torque. Retorque the locknut to 25 ft. lbs. and recheck the steering wheel torque through the center of travel.

NOTE: If the maximum is too high, turn the overcenter adjuster screw counterclockwise, then torque the adjuster lock nut in the clockwise motion to achieve the proper torque.

10. To install, realign the pitman arm-to-pitman shaft, torque the pitman shaft nut to 185 ft. lbs.

REMOVAL AND INSTALLATION

NOTE: The following procedure requires the use of the GM Pitman Arm Remover tool No. J-6632 or equivalent.

1. Disconnect the negative battery cable from the battery.
2. Raise and safely support the front frame of the vehicle on jackstands. Position the wheel in the straight ahead direction.
3. Remove the intermediate shaft-to-steering gear pinch bolt.
4. Remove the pitman arm-to-pitman shaft nut, mark the relationship the arm to the shaft. Using the GM Pitman Arm Remover tool No. J-6632 or equivalent, separate the pitman arm from the pitman shaft.

NOTE: When separating the pitman arm from the shaft, DO NOT use a hammer or apply heat to the arm.

5. Remove the steering gear-to-frame bolts and the gear from the vehicle.

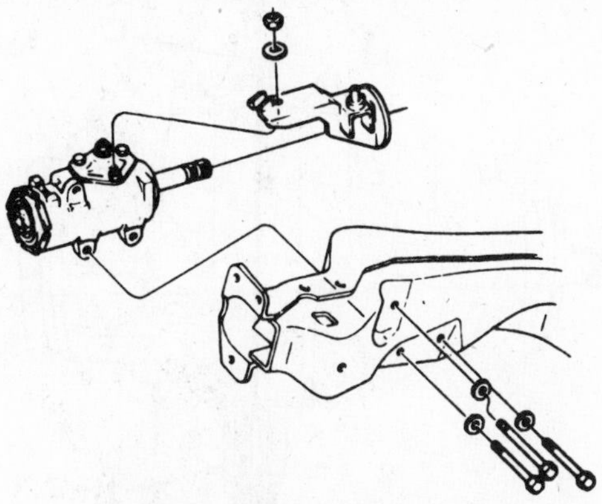

Steering gear mounting

NOTE: When installing the steering gear, be sure that the intermediate shaft bottoms on the worm shaft, so that the pinch bolt passes through the undercut on the worm shaft. Check and/or adjust the alignment of the pitman arm-to-pitman shaft.

6. To install, align the matchmarks and reverse the removal procedures. Torque the steering gear-to-frame bolts to 60 ft. lbs., the pitman arm-to-pitman shaft nut to 185 ft. lbs. and the intermediate steering shaft-to-steering gear bolt to 30 ft. lbs.

Power Steering Gear

The recirculating ball type power steering gear is basically the same as the manual steering gear, except that it uses a hydraulic assist on the rack piston.

The power steering gear control valve directs the power steering fluid to either side of the rack piston, which rides up and down the worm shaft. The steering rack converts the hydraulic pressure into mechanical force. Should the vehicle loose the hydraulic pressure, it can still be controlled mechanically.

ADJUSTMENTS

NOTE: To perform adjustments to the power steering gear, it is recommended to remove the power steering gear from the vehicle and place it in a vise. Before adjustments are performed to the system, be sure to check problems relating to hydraulic pressures and performance.

Worm Bearing Preload

NOTE: The following procedure requires the use of the GM Adjustable Spanner Wrench tool No. J-7624 or equivalent.

1. Refer to the "Power Steering Gear, Removal and Installation" procedures in this section, remove the steering gear from the vehicle and position it in a vise.
2. Using a hammer and a brass punch, drive the adjuster plug lock nut counterclockwise and remove it from the end of the steering gear.
3. Using the GM Adjustable Spanner Wrench tool No. J-7624 or equivalent, turn the adjuster plug inward, until it firmly bottoms in the housing with a torque of 20 ft. lbs.
4. Using a scribing tool, place a matchmark (on the housing) next to the one of the spanner wrench holes in the adjuster plug.
5. Using a ruler, measure ½ in. (12.7mm) counterclockwise from the scribed mark (on the housing) and place another mark.
6. Using the GM Adjustable Spanner Wrench tool No. J-7624 or equivalent, turn the adjuster plug (counterclockwise) until the hole in the adjuster plug aligns with the 2nd scribed mark.

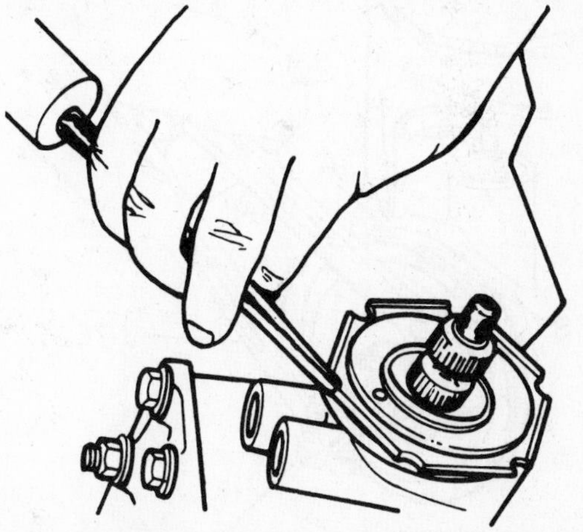

Removing the adjuster plug lock nut from the power steering gear

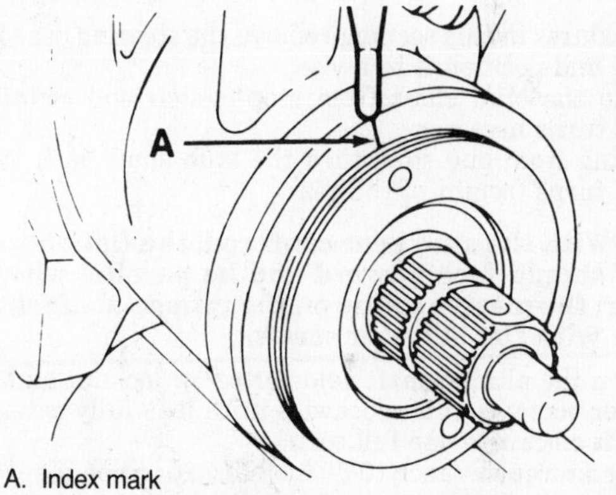
A

A. Index mark

Marking the housing with the adjuster plug hole

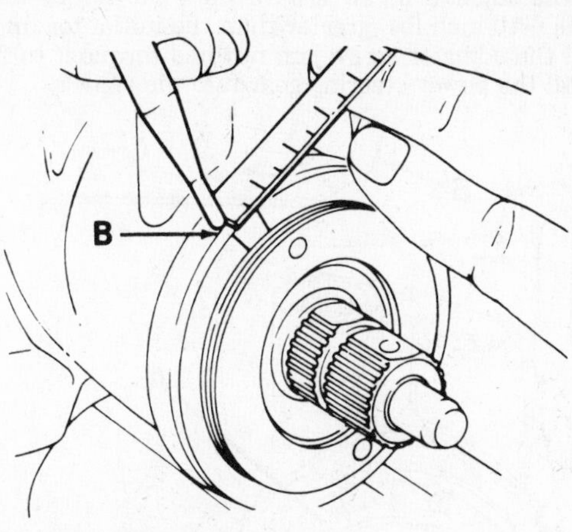
B

B. Second index mark

Make the second index mark

7. While holding the adjuster plug in alignment, install and tighten the adjuster plug lock nut.
8. Perform the overcenter preload adjustment.

Overcenter Preload

1. Refer to the "Power Steering Gear, Removal and Installa-

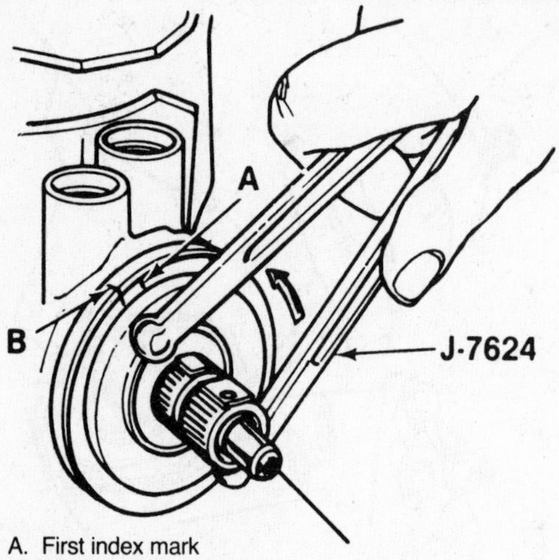
A
B
J-7624

A. First index mark
B. Second index mark

Using the spanner to align the adjuster plug with the second mark

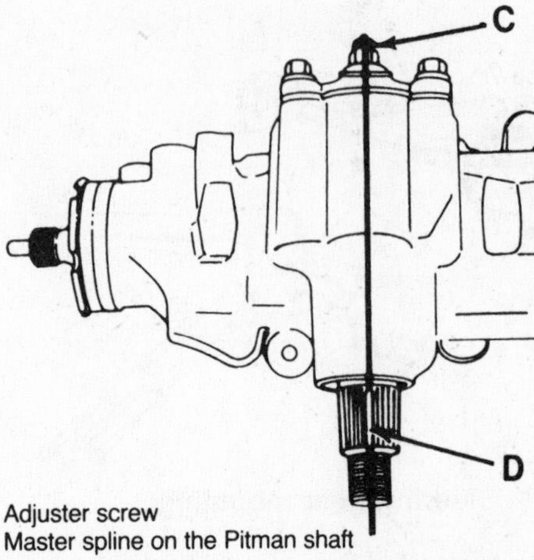
C
D

C. Adjuster screw
D. Master spline on the Pitman shaft

Align the pitman arm shaft master spline

tion" procedures in this section, remove the steering gear from the vehicle and position it in a vise.

2. Rotate the stud shaft from stop-to-stop and count the number of turns necessary.

3. Starting from one stop, turn the stub shaft back ½ the number of turns (center of the gear).

NOTE: With the stub gear centered, the flat on top of the shaft should face upward and be parallel with the side cover; the master spline on the pitman shaft should be in line with the adjuster screw.

4. Loosen the pitman shaft adjuster screw locknut and turn the adjuster screw counterclockwise until it is fully extended, then turn it clockwise one full turn.

5. Using a torque wrench (0-50 inch lbs.), position it onto the stub shaft, rotate it 45° (to each side) and record the highest drag measured near or on the center.

6. Turn the adjuster screw inward until the torque on the stub shaft is 6-10 inch lbs. greater than the initial reading.

7. Install the adjuster screw jam nut and torque it to 20 ft. lbs. Reinstall the power steering gear into the vehicle.

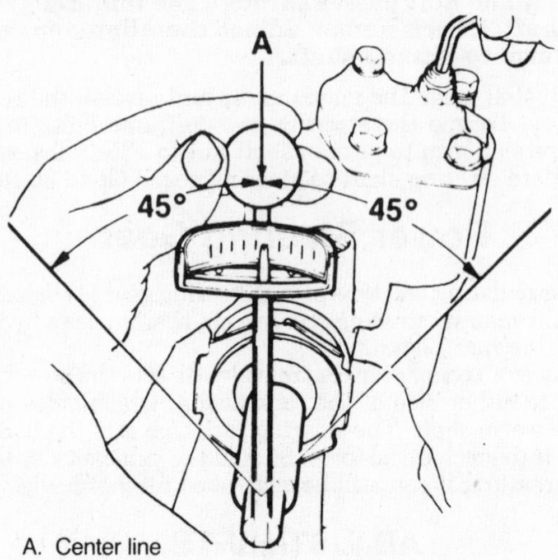
A
45°
45°

A. Center line

Reading over center rotation torque

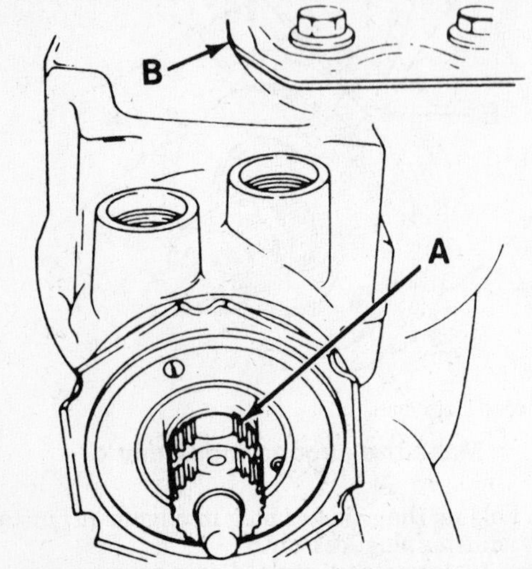
B
A

A. Stub shaft flat
B. Side cover

Alining the stub shaft with the side cover

REMOVAL AND INSTALLATION

1. Refer to the "Pitman Arm, Removal and Installation" procedures in this section and disconnect the pitman arm from the power steering gear.

2. Position a fluid catch pan under the power steering gear.

3. At the power steering gear, disconnect and plug the pressure hoses; any excess fluid will be caught by the catch pan.

NOTE: Be sure to plug the pressure hoses and the openings of the power steering pump to keep dirt out of the system.

4. Remove the intermediate shaft-to-steering gear bolt. Matchmark the intermediate shaft-to-power steering gear and separate the shaft from the gear.

5. Remove the power steering gear-to-frame bolts, washers and the steering gear from the vehicle.

6. To install, reverse the removal procedures. Torque the power steering gear-to-frame bolts to 55 ft. lbs., the intermediate shaft-to-power steering gear bolt to 30 ft. lbs. and the pitman arm-to-pitman shaft nut to 185 ft. lbs.

7. Connect the pressure hoses to the power steering gear, refill the power steering reservoir and bleed the power steering system.

8. Road test the vehicle.

Power Steering Pump

Two types of power steering pumps are offered, they are: The submerged and the non-submerged. The submerged pump has a housing and internal parts which are inside the reservoir and operate submerged in oil. The non-submerged pump functions the same as the submerged pump except the reservoir is separate from the housing and internal parts.

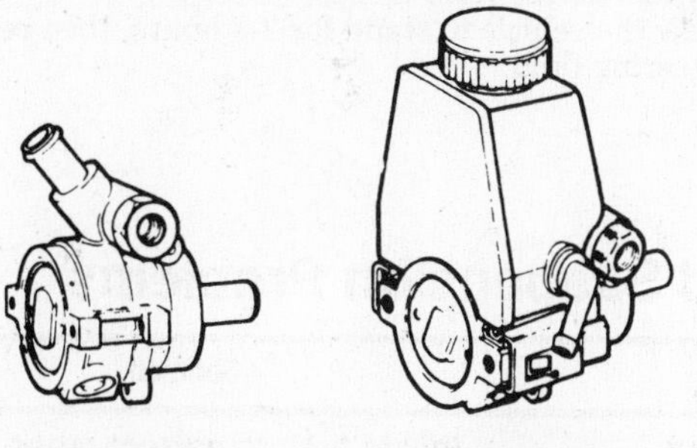
NONSUBMERGED
SUBMERGED

Two pumps are in production

REMOVAL AND INSTALLATION

NOTE: The following procedure requires the use of the GM Puller tool No. J-29785-A or equivalent, and the GM Pulley Installer tool No. J-25033-B or equivalent.

1. Position a fluid catch pan under the power steering pump.
2. Remove the pressure hoses from the power steering pump and drain the excess fluid into the catch pan.

NOTE: On models equipped with a remote fluid reservoir, disconnect and plug the hose(s).

3. Loosen the power steering pump adjusting bolt, the washer and the pivot bolt, then remove the drive belt.
4. Using the GM Puller tool No. J-29785-A or equivalent, install it onto the power steering pump pulley. While holding the tool body, turn the pilot bolt counterclockwise to press the drive pulley from the pump.

NOTE: When installing the puller tool onto the power steering pump pulley, be sure that the pilot bolt bottoms in the pump shaft by turning the head of the pilot bolt.

5. Remove the power steering pump-to-bracket bolts and the pump from the vehicle.
6. To install, reverse the removal procedures. Torque the power steering pump-to-bracket bolts to 18 ft. lbs.
7. Using the GM Pulley Installer tool No. J-25033-B or equivalent, press the drive pulley onto the power steering pump. While holding the tool body, turn the pilot bolt clockwise to press the drive pulley onto the pump.

NOTE: When installing the installer tool onto the power steering pump pulley, be sure that the pilot bolt bottoms in the pump shaft by turning the head of the pilot bolt.

8. Hand tighten the pivot bolt, the adjusting bolt and the washer.
9. Install the drive belt and adjust the drive belt tension. Torque the mounting bolts and nut to 36 ft. lbs. (submerged type) or 20 ft. lbs. (nonsubmerged type). Install the pressure hoses (to the pump), refill the power steering reservoir and bleed the system.

NOTE: Be sure to secure any hoses which may get in the way or rub other components.

10. Test drive the vehicle.

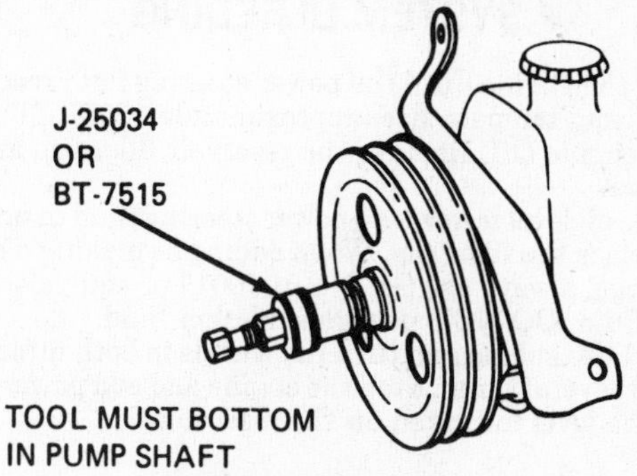
J-25034
OR
BT-7515
TOOL MUST BOTTOM
IN PUMP SHAFT

Installing pilot bolt

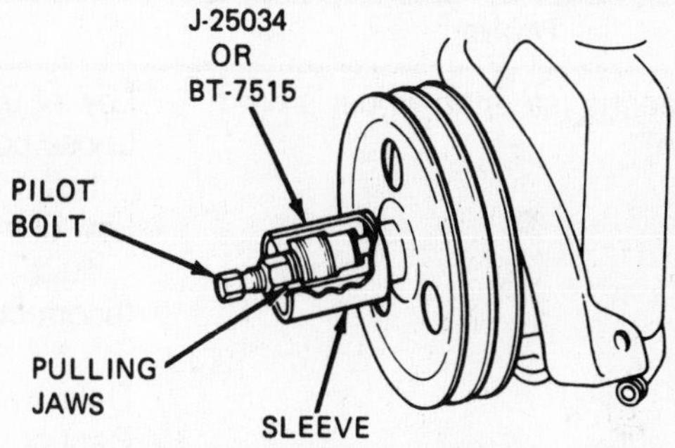
J-25034
OR
BT-7515
PILOT
BOLT
PULLING
JAWS
SLEEVE

Installing the puller

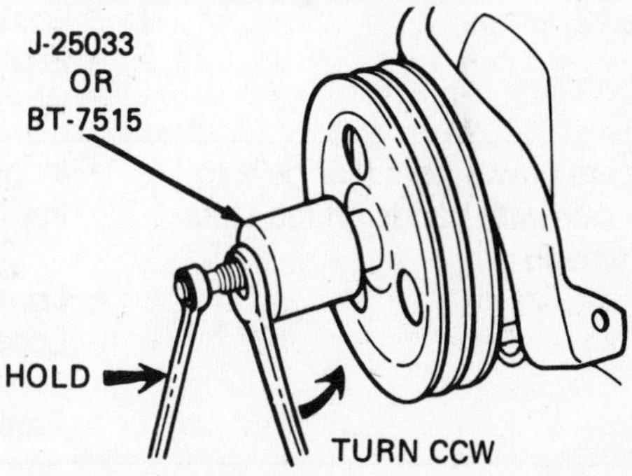
J-25033
OR
BT-7515
HOLD
TURN CCW

Removing the power steering pump pulley

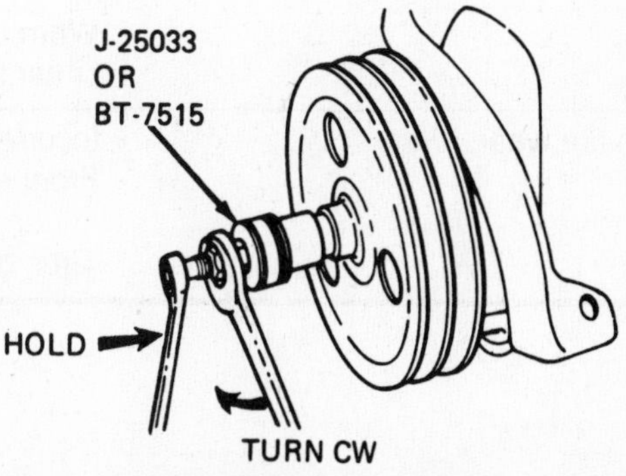
J-25033
OR
BT-7515
HOLD
TURN CW

Installing the pulley

SYSTEM BLEEDING

1. Run the engine until the power steering fluid reaches normal operating temperature, approximately 170°F (76°C), then shut the engine Off. Remove the reservoir filler cap and check the oil level.

2. If the oil level is low, add power steering fluid to proper level and replace the filler cap. When adding or making a complete fluid change, always use GM No. 1050017 or equivalent, power steering fluid. DO NOT use transmission fluid.

3. Start the engine and turn the wheels in both directions (to the stops) several times. Stop the engine and add power steering fluid to the level indicated on the reservoir.

NOTE: Maintain the fluid level just above the internal pump casting. Fluid with air in it will have a light tan or milky appearance. This air must be eliminated from the fluid before normal steering action can be obtained.

4. Return the wheels to the center position and continue to run it for 2-3 minutes, then shut the engine Off.

5. Road test the vehicle to make sure the steering functions normally and is free from noise.

6. Allow the vehicle to stand for 2-3 hours, then recheck the power steering fluid.

Troubleshooting Basic Steering and Suspension Problems

Problem	Cause	Solution
Hard steering (steering wheel is hard to turn)	• Low or uneven tire pressure	• Inflate tires to correct pressure
	• Loose power steering pump drive belt	• Adjust belt
	• Low or incorrect power steering fluid	• Add fluid as necessary
	• Incorrect front end alignment	• Have front end alignment checked/adjusted
	• Defective power steering pump	• Check pump
	• Bent or poorly lubricated front end parts	• Lubricate and/or replace defective parts
Loose steering (too much play in the steering wheel)	• Loose wheel bearings	• Adjust wheel bearings
	• Loose or worn steering linkage	• Replace worn parts
	• Faulty shocks	• Replace shocks
	• Worn ball joints	• Replace ball joints
Car veers or wanders (car pulls to one side with hands off the steering wheel)	• Incorrect tire pressure	• Inflate tires to correct pressure
	• Improper front end alignment	• Have front end alignment checked/adjusted
	• Loose wheel bearings	• Adjust wheel bearings
	• Loose or bent front end components	• Replace worn components
	• Faulty shocks	• Replace shocks
Wheel oscillation or vibration transmitted through steering wheel	• Improper tire pressures	• Inflate tires to correct pressure
	• Tires out of balance	• Have tires balanced
	• Loose wheel bearings	• Adjust wheel bearings
	• Improper front end alignment	• Have front end alignment checked/adjusted
	• Worn or bent front end components	• Replace worn parts
Uneven tire wear	• Incorrect tire pressure	• Inflate tires to correct pressure
	• Front end out of alignment	• Have front end alignment checked/adjusted
	• Tires out of balance	• Have tires balanced

Troubleshooting the Steering Column

Problem	Cause	Solution
Will not lock	• Lockbolt spring broken or defective	• Replace lock bolt spring
High effort (required to turn ignition key and lock cylinder)	• Lock cylinder defective • Ignition switch defective • Rack preload spring broken or deformed • Burr on lock sector, lock rack, housing, support or remote rod coupling • Bent sector shaft • Defective lock rack • Remote rod bent, deformed • Ignition switch mounting bracket bent • Distorted coupling slot in lock rack (tilt column)	• Replace lock cylinder • Replace ignition switch • Replace preload spring • Remove burr • Replace shaft • Replace lock rack • Replace rod • Straighten or replace • Replace lock rack
Will stick in "start"	• Remote rod deformed • Ignition switch mounting bracket bent	• Straighten or replace • Straighten or replace
Key cannot be removed in "off-lock"	• Ignition switch is not adjusted correctly • Defective lock cylinder	• Adjust switch • Replace lock cylinder
Lock cylinder can be removed without depressing retainer	• Lock cylinder with defective retainer • Burr over retainer slot in housing cover or on cylinder retainer	• Replace lock cylinder • Remove burr
High effort on lock cylinder between "off" and "off-lock"	• Distorted lock rack • Burr on tang of shift gate (automatic column) • Gearshift linkage not adjusted	• Replace lock rack • Remove burr • Adjust linkage
Noise in column	• One click when in "off-lock" position and the steering wheel is moved (all except automatic column) • Coupling bolts not tightened • Lack of grease on bearings or bearing surfaces • Upper shaft bearing worn or broken • Lower shaft bearing worn or broken • Column not correctly aligned • Coupling pulled apart • Broken coupling lower joint • Steering shaft snap ring not seated	• Normal—lock bolt is seating • Tighten pinch bolts • Lubricate with chassis grease • Replace bearing assembly • Replace bearing. Check shaft and replace if scored. • Align column • Replace coupling • Repair or replace joint and align column • Replace ring. Check for proper seating in groove.

Troubleshooting the Steering Column (cont.)

Problem	Cause	Solution
Noise in column	• Shroud loose on shift bowl. Housing loose on jacket—will be noticed with ignition in "off-lock" and when torque is applied to steering wheel.	• Position shroud over lugs on shift bowl. Tighten mounting screws.
High steering shaft effort	• Column misaligned • Defective upper or lower bearing • Tight steering shaft universal joint • Flash on I.D. of shift tube at plastic joint (tilt column only) • Upper or lower bearing seized	• Align column • Replace as required • Repair or replace • Replace shift tube • Replace bearings
Lash in mounted column assembly	• Column mounting bracket bolts loose • Broken weld nuts on column jacket • Column capsule bracket sheared	• Tighten bolts • Replace column jacket • Replace bracket assembly
Lash in mounted column assembly (cont.)	• Column bracket to column jacket mounting bolts loose • Loose lock shoes in housing (tilt column only) • Loose pivot pins (tilt column only) • Loose lock shoe pin (tilt column only) • Loose support screws (tilt column only)	• Tighten to specified torque • Replace shoes • Replace pivot pins and support • Replace pin and housing • Tighten screws
Housing loose (tilt column only)	• Excessive clearance between holes in support or housing and pivot pin diameters • Housing support-screws loose	• Replace pivot pins and support • Tighten screws
Steering wheel loose—every other tilt position (tilt column only)	• Loose fit between lock shoe and lock shoe pivot pin	• Replace lock shoes and pivot pin
Steering column not locking in any tilt position (tilt column only)	• Lock shoe seized on pivot pin • Lock shoe grooves have burrs or are filled with foreign material • Lock shoe springs weak or broken	• Replace lock shoes and pin • Clean or replace lock shoes • Replace springs
Noise when tilting column (tilt column only)	• Upper tilt bumpers worn • Tilt spring rubbing in housing	• Replace tilt bumper • Lubricate with chassis grease
One click when in "off-lock" position and the steering wheel is moved	• Seating of lock bolt	• None. Click is normal characteristic sound produced by lock bolt as it seats.
High shift effort (automatic and tilt column only)	• Column not correctly aligned • Lower bearing not aligned correctly • Lack of grease on seal or lower bearing areas	• Align column • Assemble correctly • Lubricate with chassis grease

Troubleshooting the Steering Column (cont.)

Problem	Cause	Solution
Improper transmission shifting—automatic and tilt column only	• Sheared shift tube joint • Improper transmission gearshift linkage adjustment • Loose lower shift lever	• Replace shift tube • Adjust linkage • Replace shift tube

Troubleshooting the Ignition Switch

Problem	Cause	Solution
Ignition switch electrically inoperative	• Loose or defective switch connector • Feed wire open (fusible link) • Defective ignition switch	• Tighten or replace connector • Repair or replace • Replace ignition switch
Engine will not crank	• Ignition switch not adjusted properly	• Adjust switch
Ignition switch wil not actuate mechanically	• Defective ignition switch • Defective lock sector • Defective remote rod	• Replace switch • Replace lock sector • Replace remote rod
Ignition switch cannot be adjusted correctly	• Remote rod deformed	• Repair, straighten or replace

Troubleshooting the Turn Signal Switch

Problem	Cause	Solution
Turn signal will not cancel	• Loose switch mounting screws • Switch or anchor bosses broken • Broken, missing or out of position detent, or cancelling spring	• Tighten screws • Replace switch • Reposition springs or replace switch as required
Turn signal difficult to operate	• Turn signal lever loose • Switch yoke broken or distorted • Loose or misplaced springs • Foreign parts and/or materials in switch • Switch mounted loosely	• Tighten mounting screws • Replace switch • Reposition springs or replace switch • Remove foreign parts and/or material • Tighten mounting screws
Turn signal will not indicate lane change	• Broken lane change pressure pad or spring hanger • Broken, missing or misplaced lane change spring • Jammed wires	• Replace switch • Replace or reposition as required • Loosen mounting screws, reposition wires and retighten screws
Turn signal will not stay in turn position	• Foreign material or loose parts impeding movement of switch yoke • Defective switch	• Remove material and/or parts • Replace switch

Troubleshooting the Turn Signal Switch (cont.)

Problem	Cause	Solution
Hazard switch cannot be pulled out	• Foreign material between hazard support cancelling leg and yoke	• Remove foreign material. No foreign material impeding function of hazard switch—replace turn signal switch.
No turn signal lights	• Inoperative turn signal flasher	• Replace turn signal flasher
	• Defective or blown fuse	• Replace fuse
	• Loose chassis to column harness connector	• Connect securely
	• Disconnect column to chassis connector. Connect new switch to chassis and operate switch by hand. If vehicle lights now operate normally, signal switch is inoperative	• Replace signal switch
	• If vehicle lights do not operate, check chassis wiring for opens, grounds, etc.	• Repair chassis wiring as required
Instrument panel turn indicator lights on but not flashing	• Burned out or damaged front or rear turn signal bulb	• Replace bulb
	• If vehicle lights do not operate, check light sockets for high resistance connections, the chassis wiring for opens, grounds, etc.	• Repair chassis wiring as required
	• Inoperative flasher	• Replace flasher
	• Loose chassis to column harness connection	• Connect securely
	• Inoperative turn signal switch	• Replace turn signal switch
	• To determine if turn signal switch is defective, substitute new switch into circuit and operate switch by hand. If the vehicle's lights operate normally, signal switch is inoperative.	• Replace turn signal switch
Stop light not on when turn indicated	• Loose column to chassis connection	• Connect securely
	• Disconnect column to chassis connector. Connect new switch into system without removing old.	• Replace signal switch
Stop light not on when turn indicated (cont.)	Operate switch by hand. If brake lights work with switch in the turn position, signal switch is defective.	
	• If brake lights do not work, check connector to stop light sockets for grounds, opens, etc.	• Repair connector to stop light circuits using service manual as guide

Troubleshooting the Turn Signal Switch (cont.)

Problem	Cause	Solution
Turn indicator panel lights not flashing	• Burned out bulbs • High resistance to ground at bulb socket • Opens, ground in wiring harness from front turn signal bulb socket to indicator lights	• Replace bulbs • Replace socket • Locate and repair as required
Turn signal lights flash very slowly	• High resistance ground at light sockets • Incorrect capacity turn signal flasher or bulb • If flashing rate is still extremely slow, check chassis wiring harness from the connector to light sockets for high resistance • Loose chassis to column harness connection • Disconnect column to chassis connector. Connect new switch into system without removing old. Operate switch by hand. If flashing occurs at normal rate, the signal switch is defective.	• Repair high resistance grounds at light sockets • Replace turn signal flasher or bulb • Locate and repair as required • Connect securely • Replace turn signal switch
Hazard signal lights will not flash—turn signal functions normally	• Blow fuse • Inoperative hazard warning flasher • Loose chassis-to-column harness connection • Disconnect column to chassis connector. Connect new switch into system without removing old. Depress the hazard warning lights. If they now work normally, turn signal switch is defective. • If lights do not flash, check wiring harness "K" lead for open between hazard flasher and connector. If open, fuse block is defective	• Replace fuse • Replace hazard warning flasher in fuse panel • Conect securely • Replace turn signal switch • Repair or replace brown wire or connector as required

Troubleshooting the Manual Steering Gear

Problem	Cause	Solution
Hard or erratic steering	• Incorrect tire pressure	• Inflate tires to recommended pressures
	• Insufficient or incorrect lubrication	• Lubricate as required (refer to Maintenance Section)
	• Suspension, or steering linkage parts damaged or misaligned	• Repair or replace parts as necessary
	• Improper front wheel alignment	• Adjust incorrect wheel alignment angles
	• Incorrect steering gear adjustment	• Adjust steering gear
	• Sagging springs	• Replace springs
Play or looseness in steering	• Steering wheel loose	• Inspect shaft spines and repair as necessary. Tighten attaching nut and stake in place.
	• Steering linkage or attaching parts loose or worn	• Tighten, adjust, or replace faulty components
	• Pitman arm loose	• Inspect shaft splines and repair as necessary. Tighten attaching nut and stake in place
	• Steering gear attaching bolts loose	• Tighten bolts
	• Loose or worn wheel bearings	• Adjust or replace bearings
	• Steering gear adjustment incorrect or parts badly worn	• Adjust gear or replace defective parts
Wheel shimmy or tramp	• Improper tire pressure	• Inflate tires to recommended pressures
	• Wheels, tires, or brake rotors out-of-balance or out-of-round	• Inspect and replace or balance parts
	• Inoperative, worn, or loose shock absorbers or mounting parts	• Repair or replace shocks or mountings
	• Loose or worn steering or suspension parts	• Tighten or replace as necessary
	• Loose or worn wheel bearings	• Adjust or replace bearings
	• Incorrect steering gear adjustments	• Adjust steering gear
	• Incorrect front wheel alignment	• Correct front wheel alignment
Tire wear	• Improper tire pressure	• Inflate tires to recommended pressures
	• Failure to rotate tires	• Rotate tires
	• Brakes grabbing	• Adjust or repair brakes
	• Incorrect front wheel alignment	• Align incorrect angles
	• Broken or damaged steering and suspension parts	• Repair or replace defective parts
	• Wheel runout	• Replace faulty wheel
	• Excessive speed on turns	• Make driver aware of conditions

Troubleshooting the Manual Steering Gear

Problem	Cause	Solution
Vehicle leads to one side	• Improper tire pressures	• Inflate tires to recommended pressures
	• Front tires with uneven tread depth, wear pattern, or different cord design (i.e., one bias ply and one belted or radial tire on front wheels)	• Install tires of same cord construction and reasonably even tread depth, design, and wear pattern
	• Incorrect front wheel alignment	• Align incorrect angles
	• Brakes dragging	• Adjust or repair brakes
	• Pulling due to uneven tire construction	• Replace faulty tire

Troubleshooting the Power Steering Gear

Problem	Cause	Solution
Hissing noise in steering gear	• There is some noise in all power steering systems. One of the most common is a hissing sound most evident at standstill parking. There is no relationship between this noise and performance of the steering. Hiss may be expected when steering wheel is at end of travel or when slowly turning at standstill.	• Slight hiss is normal and in no way affects steering. Do not replace valve unless hiss is extremely objectionable. A replacement valve will also exhibit slight noise and is not always a cure. Investigate clearance around flexible coupling rivets. Be sure steering shaft and gear are aligned so flexible coupling rotates in a flat plane and is not distorted as shaft rotates. Any metal-to-metal contacts through flexible coupling will transmit valve hiss into passenger compartment through the steering column.
Rattle or chuckle noise in steering gear	• Gear loose on frame	• Check gear-to-frame mounting screws.
	• Steering linkage looseness	• Check linkage pivot points for wear. Replace if necessary.
	• Pressure hose touching other parts of car	• Adjust hose position. Do not bend tubing by hand.
	• Loose pitman shaft over center adjustment **NOTE:** A slight rattle may occur on turns because of increased clearance off the "high point." This is normal and clearance must not be reduced below specified limits to eliminate this slight rattle.	• Adjust to specifications
	• Loose pitman arm	• Tighten pitman arm nut to specifications

Troubleshooting the Power Steering Gear (cont.)

Problem	Cause	Solution
Squawk noise in steering gear when turning or recovering from a turn	• Damper O-ring on valve spool cut	• Replace damper O-ring
Poor return of steering wheel to center	• Tires not properly inflated • Lack of lubrication in linkage and ball joints • Lower coupling flange rubbing against steering gear adjuster plug • Steering gear to column misalignment • Improper front wheel alignment • Steering linkage binding • Ball joints binding • Steering wheel rubbing against housing • Tight or frozen steering shaft bearings • Sticking or plugged valve spool • Steering gear adjustments over specifications • Kink in return hose	• Inflate to specified pressure • Lube linkage and ball joints • Loosen pinch bolt and assemble properly • Align steering column • Check and adjust as necessary • Replace pivots • Replace ball joints • Align housing • Replace bearings • Remove and clean or replace valve • Check adjustment with gear out of car. Adjust as required. • Replace hose
Car leads to one side or the other (keep in mind road condition and wind. Test car in both directions on flat road)	• Front end misaligned • Unbalanced steering gear valve **NOTE:** If this is cause, steering effort will be very light in direction of lead and normal or heavier in opposite direction	• Adjust to specifications • Replace valve
Momentary increase in effort when turning wheel fast to right or left	• Low oil level • Pump belt slipping • High internal leakage	• Add power steering fluid as required • Tighten or replace belt • Check pump pressure. (See pressure test)
Steering wheel surges or jerks when turning with engine running especially during parking	• Low oil level • Loose pump belt • Steering linkage hitting engine oil pan at full turn • Insufficient pump pressure • Pump flow control valve sticking	• Fill as required • Adjust tension to specification • Correct clearance • Check pump pressure. (See pressure test). Replace relief valve if defective. • Inspect for varnish or damage, replace if necessary

Troubleshooting the Power Steering Gear (cont.)

Problem	Cause	Solution
Excessive wheel kickback or loose steering	• Air in system	• Add oil to pump reservoir and bleed by operating steering. Check hose connectors for proper torque and adjust as required.
	• Steering gear loose on frame	• Tighten attaching screws to specified torque
	• Steering linkage joints worn enough to be loose	• Replace loose pivots
	• Worn poppet valve	• Replace poppet valve
	• Loose thrust bearing preload adjustment	• Adjust to specification with gear out of vehicle
	• Excessive overcenter lash	• Adjust to specification with gear out of car
Hard steering or lack of assist	• Loose pump belt	• Adjust belt tension to specification
	• Low oil level **NOTE:** Low oil level will also result in excessive pump noise	• Fill to proper level. If excessively low, check all lines and joints for evidence of external leakage. Tighten loose connectors.
	• Steering gear to column misalignment	• Align steering column
	• Lower coupling flange rubbing against steering gear adjuster plug	• Loosen pinch bolt and assemble properly
	• Tires not properly inflated	• Inflate to recommended pressure
Foamy milky power steering fluid, low fluid level and possible low pressure	• Air in the fluid, and loss of fluid due to internal pump leakage causing overflow	• Check for leak and correct. Bleed system. Extremely cold temperatures will cause system aeriation should the oil level be low. If oil level is correct and pump still foams, remove pump from vehicle and separate reservoir from housing. Check welsh plug and housing for cracks. If plug is loose or housing is cracked, replace housing.
Low pressure due to steering pump	• Flow control valve stuck or inoperative	• Remove burrs or dirt or replace. Flush system.
	• Pressure plate not flat against cam ring	• Correct
Low pressure due to steering gear	• Pressure loss in cylinder due to worn piston ring or badly worn housing bore	• Remove gear from car for disassembly and inspection of ring and housing bore
	• Leakage at valve rings, valve body-to-worm seal	• Remove gear from car for disassembly and replace seals

Troubleshooting the Power Steering Pump

Problem	Cause	Solution
Chirp noise in steering pump	• Loose belt	• Adjust belt tension to specification
Belt squeal (particularly noticeable at full wheel travel and stand still parking)	• Loose belt	• Adjust belt tension to specification
Growl noise in steering pump	• Excessive back pressure in hoses or steering gear caused by restriction	• Locate restriction and correct. Replace part if necessary.
Growl noise in steering pump (particularly noticeable at stand still parking)	• Scored pressure plates, thrust plate or rotor • Extreme wear of cam ring	• Replace parts and flush system • Replace parts
Groan noise in steering pump	• Low oil level • Air in the oil. Poor pressure hose connection.	• Fill reservoir to proper level • Tighten connector to specified torque. Bleed system by operating steering from right to left—full turn.
Rattle noise in steering pump	• Vanes not installed properly • Vanes sticking in rotor slots	• Install properly • Free up by removing burrs, varnish, or dirt
Swish noise in steering pump	• Defective flow control valve	• Replace part
Whine noise in steering pump	• Pump shaft bearing scored	• Replace housing and shaft. Flush system.
Hard steering or lack of assist	• Loose pump belt • Low oil level in reservoir **NOTE:** Low oil level will also result in excessive pump noise • Steering gear to column misalignment • Lower coupling flange rubbing against steering gear adjuster plug • Tires not properly inflated	• Adjust belt tension to specification • Fill to proper level. If excessively low, check all lines and joints for evidence of external leakage. Tighten loose connectors. • Align steering column • Loosen pinch bolt and assemble properly • Inflate to recommended pressure
Foaming milky power steering fluid, low fluid level and possible low pressure	• Air in the fluid, and loss of fluid due to internal pump leakage causing overflow	• Check for leaks and correct. Bleed system. Extremely cold temperatures will cause system aeriation should the oil level be low. If oil level is correct and pump still foams, remove pump from vehicle and separate reservoir from body. Check welsh plug and body for cracks. If plug is loose or body is cracked, replace body.

Troubleshooting the Power Steering Pump (cont.)

Problem	Cause	Solution
Low pump pressure	• Flow control valve stuck or inoperative • Pressure plate not flat against cam ring	• Remove burrs or dirt or replace. Flush system. • Correct
Momentary increase in effort when turning wheel fast to right or left	• Low oil level in pump • Pump belt slipping • High internal leakage	• Add power steering fluid as required • Tighten or replace belt • Check pump pressure. (See pressure test)
Steering wheel surges or jerks when turning with engine running especially during parking	• Low oil level • Loose pump belt • Steering linkage hitting engine oil pan at full turn • Insufficient pump pressure	• Fill as required • Adjust tension to specification • Correct clearance • Check pump pressure. (See pressure test). Replace flow control valve if defective.
Steering wheel surges or jerks when turning with engine running especially during parking (cont.)	• Sticking flow control valve	• Inspect for varnish or damage, replace if necessary
Excessive wheel kickback or loose steering	• Air in system	• Add oil to pump reservoir and bleed by operating steering. Check hose connectors for proper torque and adjust as required.

TORQUE SPECIFICATIONS

Component	English	Metric
	WHEELS	
Aluminum alloy wheels	90 ft. lbs.	120Nm
Steel wheels	73 ft. lbs.	100Nm
	FRONT SUSPENSION	
Lower ball joint-to-steering knuckle nut	90 ft. lbs.	122 Nm
Lower Control Arm-to-frame		
2WD Models		
Front nut and bolt	94 ft. lbs.	128 Nm
Rear nut and bolt	66 ft. lbs.	90 Nm
4WD Models		
Control arm-to-frame bolts	148 ft. lbs.	201 Nm
Control arm-to-frame nuts	92 ft. lbs.	125 Nm
Shock Absorbers		
2WD Models		
Upper shock absorber nut	8 ft. lbs.	11 Nm
Shock absorber-to-lower control arm bolts	20 ft. lbs.	27 Nm
4WD Models		
Upper and lower mounting bolts	54 ft. lbs.	73 Nm

TORQUE SPECIFICATIONS

Component	English	Metric
Stabilzer Bar		
Stabilizer bar link-to-lower control arm nuts/bolts		
2WD	13 ft. lbs.	18 Nm
4WD	24 ft. lbs.	33 Nm
Stabilizer retainer-to-frame nuts/bolts		
2WD	24 ft. lbs.	33 Nm
4WD	35 ft. lbs.	48 Nm
Torsion bar insulator-to-frame nuts/bolts	26 ft. lbs.	35 Nm
Torsion bar support-to-insulator nut/bolt	25 ft. lbs.	34 Nm
Upper Ball Joint		
Ball joint-to-control arm nuts	17 ft. lbs.	23 Nm
Ball joint-to-steering knuckle nut	65 ft. lbs.	88 Nm
4WD hub/bearing assembly-to-steering knuckle bolts	86 ft. lbs.	117 Nm
4WD hub/bearing assembly-to-half shaft nut	181 ft. lbs.	246 Nm
REAR SUSPENSION		
Shock absorber-to-axle nut	50 ft. lbs.	68 Nm
Shock absorber-to-body bolts	15 ft. lbs.	20 Nm
Spring front bolt	92 ft. lbs.	125 Nm
Spring rear shackle bolts	92 ft. lbs.	125 Nm
Spring U-bolt nuts		
Step 1:	18 ft. lbs.	24 Nm
Step 2:	85 ft. lbs.	116 Nm
STEERING		
Cylinder lock-to-housing screw	14 inch lbs.	1.6 Nm
Damper assembly-to-bracket nut/bolt	26 ft. lbs.	35 Nm
Damper assembly-to-relay rod nut	45 ft. lbs.	61 Nm
Idler arm-to-frame bolts	60 ft. lbs.	82 Nm
Idler arm-to-relay rod stud nut		
2WD	35 ft. lbs.	48 Nm
4WD	60 ft. lbs.	82 Nm
Ignition switch-to-steering column screws	35 inch lbs.	4 Nm
Intermediate shaft-to-steering column shaft pinch bolt	30 ft. lbs.	41 Nm
Manual steering gear-to-frame bolts	60 ft. lbs.	82 Nm
Multi-function switch-to-steering column screws	35 inch lbs.	4 Nm
Pitman arm-to-pitman shaft nut	185 ft. lbs.	252 Nm
Pitman arm-to-relay rod ball stud nut	60 ft. lbs.	82 Nm
Power steering gear-to-frame bolts	55 ft. lbs.	75 Nm
Power steering pump-to-bracket bolts	18 ft. lbs.	25 Nm
Power steering pump mounting bolts		
Submerged type	36 ft. lbs.	49 Nm
Nonsubmerged type	20 ft. lbs.	27 Nm
Steering wheel-to-steering shaft nut	30 ft. lbs.	41 Nm
Steering column-to-instrument panel bolts	22 ft. lbs.	30 Nm
Steering column-to-firewall screws	7 ft. lbs.	0.8 Nm
Tie rod adjuster tube clamp bolt	13 ft. lbs.	18 Nm
Tie rod-to-steering knuckle and the relay rod	35 ft. lbs.	48 Nm

9 Brakes

QUICK REFERENCE INDEX

GENERAL INDEX

Troubleshooting the Brake System

Problem	Cause	Solution
Low brake pedal (excessive pedal travel required for braking action.)	• Excessive clearance between rear linings and drums caused by inoperative automatic adjusters	• Make 10 to 15 alternate forward and reverse brake stops to adjust brakes. If brake pedal does not come up, repair or replace adjuster parts as necessary.
	• Worn rear brakelining	• Inspect and replace lining if worn beyond minimum thickness specification
	• Bent, distorted brakeshoes, front or rear	• Replace brakeshoes in axle sets
	• Air in hydraulic system	• Remove air from system. Refer to Brake Bleeding.
Low brake pedal (pedal may go to floor with steady pressure applied.)	• Fluid leak in hydraulic system	• Fill master cylinder to fill line; have helper apply brakes and check calipers, wheel cylinders, differential valve tubes, hoses and fittings for leaks. Repair or replace as necessary.
	• Air in hydraulic system	• Remove air from system. Refer to Brake Bleeding.
	• Incorrect or non-recommended brake fluid (fluid evaporates at below normal temp).	• Flush hydraulic system with clean brake fluid. Refill with correct-type fluid.
	• Master cylinder piston seals worn, or master cylinder bore is scored, worn or corroded	• Repair or replace master cylinder
Low brake pedal (pedal goes to floor on first application—o.k. on subsequent applications.)	• Disc brake pads sticking on abutment surfaces of anchor plate. Caused by a build-up of dirt, rust, or corrosion on abutment surfaces	• Clean abutment surfaces
Fading brake pedal (pedal height decreases with steady pressure applied.)	• Fluid leak in hydraulic system	• Fill master cylinder reservoirs to fill mark, have helper apply brakes, check calipers, wheel cylinders, differential valve, tubes, hoses, and fittings for fluid leaks. Repair or replace parts as necessary.
	• Master cylinder piston seals worn, or master cylinder bore is scored, worn or corroded	• Repair or replace master cylinder

Troubleshooting the Brake System (cont.)

Problem	Cause	Solution
Decreasing brake pedal travel (pedal travel required for braking action decreases and may be accompanied by a hard pedal.)	• Caliper or wheel cylinder pistons sticking or seized	• Repair or replace the calipers, or wheel cylinders
	• Master cylinder compensator ports blocked (preventing fluid return to reservoirs) or pistons sticking or seized in master cylinder bore	• Repair or replace the master cylinder
	• Power brake unit binding internally	• Test unit according to the following procedure: (a) Shift transmission into neutral and start engine (b) Increase engine speed to 1500 rpm, close throttle and fully depress brake pedal (c) Slow release brake pedal and stop engine (d) Have helper remove vacuum check valve and hose from power unit. Observe for backward movement of brake pedal. (e) If the pedal moves backward, the power unit has an internal bind—replace power unit
Grabbing brakes (severe reaction to brake pedal pressure.)	• Brakelining(s) contaminated by grease or brake fluid	• Determine and correct cause of contamination and replace brakeshoes in axle sets
	• Parking brake cables incorrectly adjusted or seized	• Adjust cables. Replace seized cables.
	• Incorrect brakelining or lining loose on brakeshoes	• Replace brakeshoes in axle sets
	• Caliper anchor plate bolts loose	• Tighten bolts
	• Rear brakeshoes binding on support plate ledges	• Clean and lubricate ledges. Replace support plate(s) if ledges are deeply grooved. Do not attempt to smooth ledges by grinding.
	• Incorrect or missing power brake reaction disc	• Install correct disc
	• Rear brake support plates loose	• Tighten mounting bolts
Spongy brake pedal (pedal has abnormally soft, springy, spongy feel when depressed.)	• Air in hydraulic system	• Remove air from system. Refer to Brake Bleeding.
	• Brakeshoes bent or distorted	• Replace brakeshoes
	• Brakelining not yet seated with drums and rotors	• Burnish brakes
	• Rear drum brakes not properly adjusted	• Adjust brakes

Troubleshooting the Brake System (cont.)

Problem	Cause	Solution
Hard brake pedal (excessive pedal pressure required to stop vehicle. May be accompanied by brake fade.)	• Loose or leaking power brake unit vacuum hose	• Tighten connections or replace leaking hose
	• Incorrect or poor quality brake-lining	• Replace with lining in axle sets
	• Bent, broken, distorted brakeshoes	• Replace brakeshoes
	• Calipers binding or dragging on mounting pins. Rear brakeshoes dragging on support plate.	• Replace mounting pins and bushings. Clean rust or burrs from rear brake support plate ledges and lubricate ledges with molydisulfide grease. **NOTE:** If ledges are deeply grooved or scored, do not attempt to sand or grind them smooth—replace support plate.
	• Caliper, wheel cylinder, or master cylinder pistons sticking or seized	• Repair or replace parts as necessary
	• Power brake unit vacuum check valve malfunction	• Test valve according to the following procedure: (a) Start engine, increase engine speed to 1500 rpm, close throttle and immediately stop engine (b) Wait at least 90 seconds then depress brake pedal (c) If brakes are not vacuum assisted for 2 or more applications, check valve is faulty
	• Power brake unit has internal bind	• Test unit according to the following procedure: (a) With engine stopped, apply brakes several times to exhaust all vacuum in system (b) Shift transmission into neutral, depress brake pedal and start engine (c) If pedal height decreases with foot pressure and less pressure is required to hold pedal in applied position, power unit vacuum system is operating normally. Test power unit. If power unit exhibits a bind condition, replace the power unit.

Troubleshooting the Brake System (cont.)

Problem	Cause	Solution
Hard brake pedal (excessive pedal pressure required to stop vehicle. May be accompanied by brake fade.)	• Master cylinder compensator ports (at bottom of reservoirs) blocked by dirt, scale, rust, or have small burrs (blocked ports prevent fluid return to reservoirs).	• Repair or replace master cylinder **CAUTION:** Do not attempt to clean blocked ports with wire, pencils, or similar implements. Use compressed air only.
	• Brake hoses, tubes, fittings clogged or restricted	• Use compressed air to check or unclog parts. Replace any damaged parts.
	• Brake fluid contaminated with improper fluids (motor oil, transmission fluid, causing rubber components to swell and stick in bores	• Replace all rubber components, combination valve and hoses. Flush entire brake system with DOT 3 brake fluid or equivalent.
	• Low engine vacuum	• Adjust or repair engine
Dragging brakes (slow or incomplete release of brakes)	• Brake pedal binding at pivot	• Loosen and lubricate
	• Power brake unit has internal bind	• Inspect for internal bind. Replace unit if internal bind exists.
	• Parking brake cables incorrrectly adjusted or seized	• Adjust cables. Replace seized cables.
	• Rear brakeshoe return springs weak or broken	• Replace return springs. Replace brakeshoe if necessary in axle sets.
	• Automatic adjusters malfunctioning	• Repair or replace adjuster parts as required
	• Caliper, wheel cylinder or master cylinder pistons sticking or seized	• Repair or replace parts as necessary
	• Master cylinder compensating ports blocked (fluid does not return to reservoirs).	• Use compressed air to clear ports. Do not use wire, pencils, or similar objects to open blocked ports.
Vehicle moves to one side when brakes are applied	• Incorrect front tire pressure	• Inflate to recommended cold (reduced load) inflation pressure
	• Worn or damaged wheel bearings	• Replace worn or damaged bearings
	• Brakelining on one side contaminated	• Determine and correct cause of contamination and replace brakelining in axle sets
	• Brakeshoes on one side bent, distorted, or lining loose on shoe	• Replace brakeshoes in axle sets
	• Support plate bent or loose on one side	• Tighten or replace support plate
	• Brakelining not yet seated with drums or rotors	• Burnish brakelining
	• Caliper anchor plate loose on one side	• Tighten anchor plate bolts
	• Caliper piston sticking or seized	• Repair or replace caliper
	• Brakelinings water soaked	• Drive vehicle with brakes lightly applied to dry linings
	• Loose suspension component attaching or mounting bolts	• Tighten suspension bolts. Replace worn suspension components.
	• Brake combination valve failure	• Replace combination valve

Troubleshooting the Brake System (cont.)

Problem	Cause	Solution
Chatter or shudder when brakes are applied (pedal pulsation and roughness may also occur.)	• Brakeshoes distorted, bent, contaminated, or worn	• Replace brakeshoes in axle sets
	• Caliper anchor plate or support plate loose	• Tighten mounting bolts
	• Excessive thickness variation of rotor(s)	• Refinish or replace rotors in axle sets
Noisy brakes (squealing, clicking, scraping sound when brakes are applied.)	• Bent, broken, distorted brakeshoes	• Replace brakeshoes in axle sets
	• Excessive rust on outer edge of rotor braking surface	• Remove rust
Noisy brakes (squealing, clicking, scraping sound when brakes are applied.) (cont.)	• Brakelining worn out—shoes contacting drum of rotor	• Replace brakeshoes and lining in axle sets. Refinish or replace drums or rotors.
	• Broken or loose holdown or return springs	• Replace parts as necessary
	• Rough or dry drum brake support plate ledges	• Lubricate support plate ledges
	• Cracked, grooved, or scored rotor(s) or drum(s)	• Replace rotor(s) or drum(s). Replace brakeshoes and lining in axle sets if necessary.
	• Incorrect brakelining and/or shoes (front or rear).	• Install specified shoe and lining assemblies
Pulsating brake pedal	• Out of round drums or excessive lateral runout in disc brake rotor(s)	• Refinish or replace drums, re-index rotors or replace

BRAKE SYSTEM

These trucks are equipped with independent front and rear brake systems. The systems consist of a power booster, a master cylinder, a combination valve, front disc and rear drum assemblies.

The master cylinder, mounted on the left-firewall or power booster, consists of two fluid reservoirs, a primary (rear) cylinder, a secondary (front) cylinder and springs. The reservoirs, being independent of one another, are contained within the same housing; fluid cannot pass from one to the other. The rear reservoir supplies fluid to the front brakes while the front reservoir supplies fluid to the rear brakes.

During operation, fluid drains from the reservoirs to the master cylinder. When the brake pedal is applied, fluid from the master cylinder is sent to the combination valve (mounted on a bracket, directly under the master cylinder), here it is monitored and proportionally distributed to the front or rear brake systems. Should a loss of pressure occur in one system, the other system will provide enough braking pressure to stop the vehicle. Also, should a loss of pressure in one system occur, the differential warning switch (located on the combination valve) will turn ON the brake warning light (located on the dash board).

As the fluid enters each brake caliper or wheel cylinder, the pistons are forced outward. The outward movement of the pistons force the brake pads against a round flat disc or the brake shoes against a round metal drum. The brake lining attached to the pads or shoes comes in contact with the revolving disc or drum, causing friction, which brings the wheel to a stop.

In time, the brake linings wear down. If not replaced, their metal support plates (bonded type) or rivet heads (riveted type) will come in contact with the disc or drum; damage to the disc or drum will occur. Never use brake pads or shoes with a lining thickness less than $\frac{1}{32}$ in. (0.8mm).

Most manufacturers provide a wear sensor, a piece of spring steel, attached to the rear edge of the inner brake pad. When the pad wears to the replacement thickness, the sensor will contact the disc and produce a high pitched squeal.

Adjustments

FRONT DISC BRAKES

Disc brakes are not adjustable. They are, in effect, self adjusting.

ADJUSTMENT OF REAR BRAKES

Normal adjustments of the rear drum brakes are automatic and are made during the reverse applications of the brakes. ONLY, if the lining has been renewed, should the following procedure be performed.

NOTE: The following procedure requires the use of the GM Brake Adjustment tool No. J-4735 or equivalent.

1. Raise and support the vehicle safely.
2. Using a punch and a hammer, at the rear of the backing plate, knock out the lanced metal area near the starwheel assembly.

NOTE: When knocking out the lanced metal area from the backing plate, the wheels must be removed and all of the metal pieces discarded.

3. Using the GM Brake Adjustment tool No. J-4735 or equivalent, insert it into the slot and engage the lowest possible tooth on the starwheel. Move the end of the brake tool downward to move the starwheel upward and expand the adjusting screw. Repeat this operation until the brakes just lock the wheel.
4. Insert a small screwdriver or piece of firm wire (coathanger wire) into the adjusting slot and push the automatic adjuster lever out and free of the starwheel on the adjusting screw.
5. While holding the adjusting lever out of the way, engage the top-most tooth possible on the starwheel (with the brake tool). Move the end of the adjusting tool upward to move the adjusting screw starwheel downward and contact the adjusting screw. Back off the adjusting screw starwheel until the wheel spins freely with a minimum of drag. Keep track of the number of turns the starwheel is backed off.
6. Repeat this operation for the other side. When backing off the brakes on the other side, the adjusting lever must be backed off the same number of turns to prevent side-to-side brake pull.

NOTE: Backing off the starwheel 12 notches (clicks) is usually enough to eliminate brake drag.

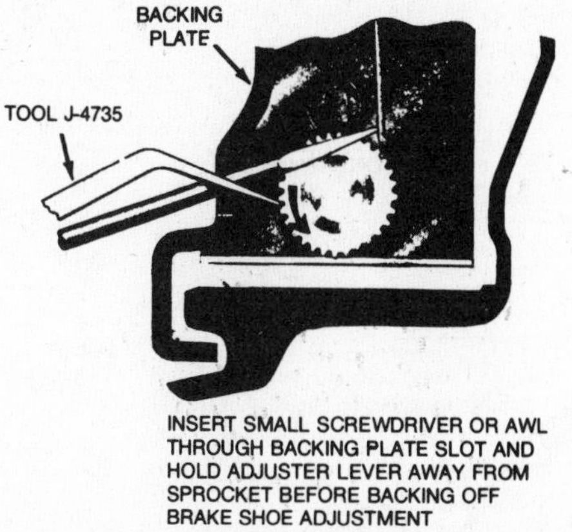
BACKING PLATE
TOOL J-4735
INSERT SMALL SCREWDRIVER OR AWL THROUGH BACKING PLATE SLOT AND HOLD ADJUSTER LEVER AWAY FROM SPROCKET BEFORE BACKING OFF BRAKE SHOE ADJUSTMENT

Adjusting the rear brake star wheel

7. Repeat this operation on the other side of the rear brake system.
8. After the brakes are adjusted, install a rubber hole cover into the backing plate slot. To complete the brake adjustment operation, make several stops while backing the truck to equalize the adjustment.
9. Road test the vehicle.

BRAKE PEDAL TRAVEL

The brake pedal travel is the distance the pedal moves toward the floor from the fully released position. Inspection should be made with 100 lbs. pressure on the brake pedal, when the brake system is Cold. The brake pedal travel should be 4¾ in. (120mm) for manual, or 2½ in. (61mm) for power.

NOTE: If equipped with power brakes, be sure to pump the brake pedal at least 3 times with the engine Off, before making the brake pedal check.

1. From under the dash, remove the pushrod-to-pedal clevis pin and separate the pushrod from the brake pedal.
2. Loosen the pushrod adjuster lock nut, then adjust the pushrod.
3. After the correct travel is established, reverse the removal procedure.

Brake Light Switch

REMOVAL AND INSTALLATION

1. Remove the negative battery cable.
2. Disconnect the electrical connector from the brake light switch.
3. Turn the brake light switch retainer (to align the key with the bracket slot), then remove the switch with the retainer.
4. Installation is the reverse of removal. Adjust the brake light switch.

ADJUSTMENT

1. Depress the brake pedal and press the brake light switch inward until it seats firmly against the clip.

NOTE: As the switch is being pushed into the clip, audible clicks can be heard.

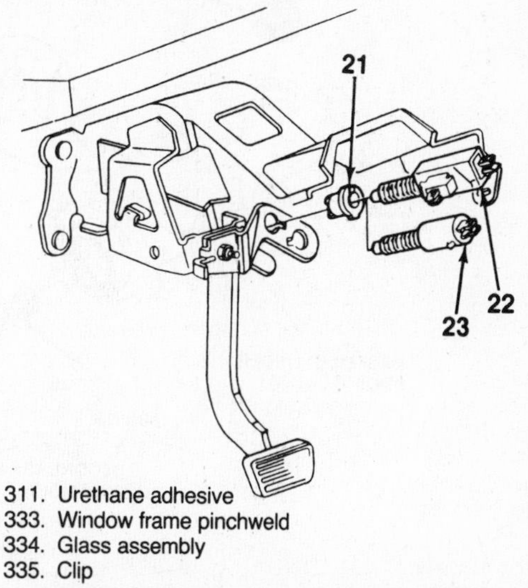
21
22
23
311. Urethane adhesive
333. Window frame pinchweld
334. Glass assembly
335. Clip

Adjusting the brake light switch

2. Release the brake pedal, then pull it back against the pedal stop until the audible click can no longer be heard.
3. The brake light switch will operate when the pedal is depressed 0.53 in. (13mm) from the fully released position.

Master Cylinder

REMOVAL AND INSTALLATION

1. Apply the parking brakes and block the wheels.
2. Use a line wrench to disconnect the hydraulic lines from the master cylinder. Plug the lines to prevent contamination.
3. If equipped with non-power brakes, disconnect the pushrod from the brake pedal.
4. Remove the master cylinder attachment nuts, then separate the combination valve/bracket from the master cylinder.
5. Remove the master cylinder, the gasket and the rubber boot from the vehicle.

To install:

6. Fill the master cylinder with new brake fluid and operate the pushrod to bench bleed the master cylinder.
7. Install the master cylinder and torque the mounting nuts to 20 ft. lbs.
8. Install the combination valve and connect the brake lines. Torque the line nuts to 120 in. lbs. (13.5 Nm).
9. Refill the master cylinder with clean brake fluid, bleed the brake system and check the brake pedal travel.

NOTE: If equipped with manual brakes, be sure to reconnect the pushrod to the brake pedal.

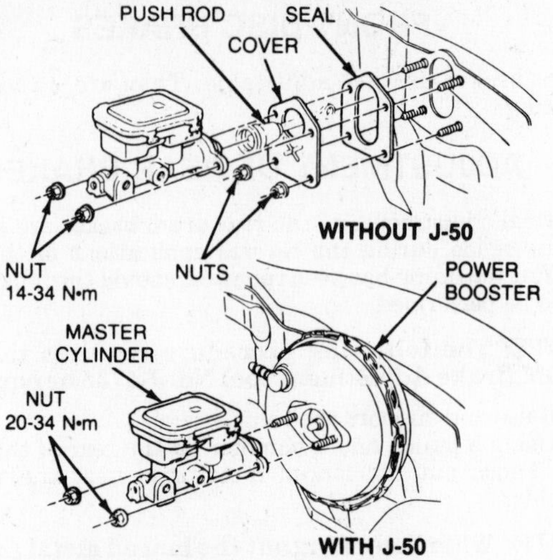
PUSH ROD
SEAL
COVER
WITHOUT J-50
NUT
14-34 N·m
NUTS
POWER
BOOSTER
MASTER
CYLINDER
NUT
20-34 N·m
WITH J-50

Master cylinder attachment

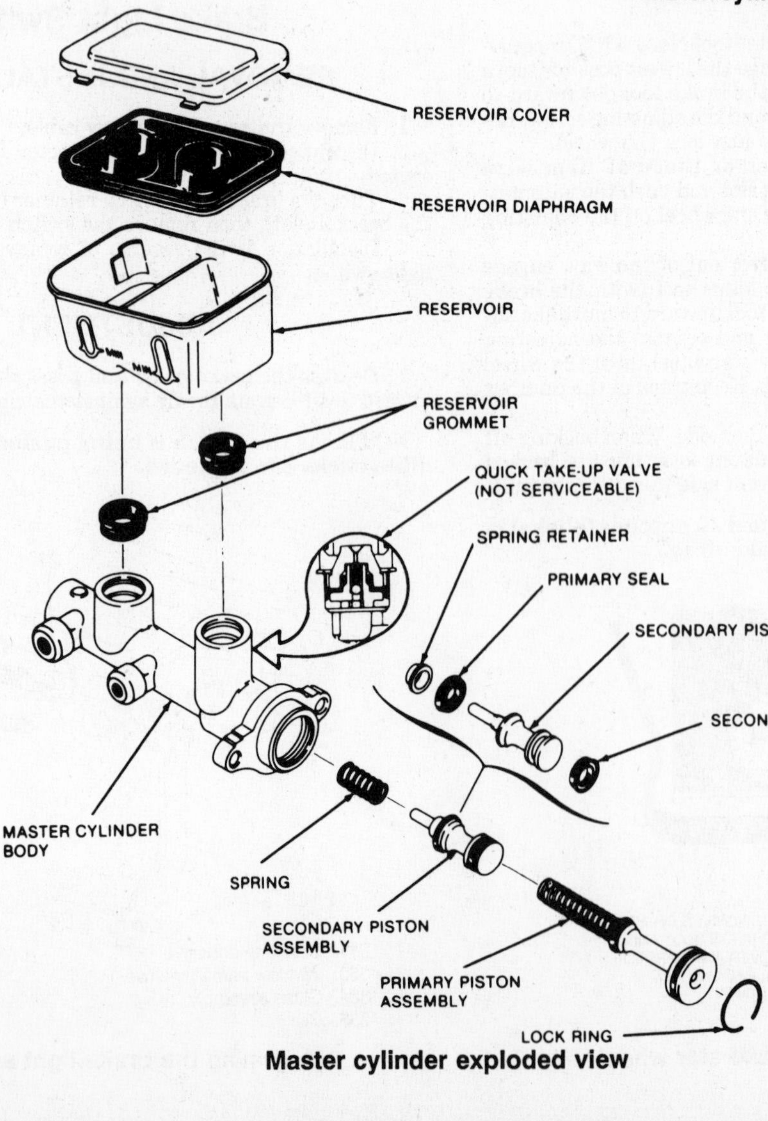
RESERVOIR COVER
RESERVOIR DIAPHRAGM
RESERVOIR
RESERVOIR
GROMMET
QUICK TAKE-UP VALVE
(NOT SERVICEABLE)
SPRING RETAINER
PRIMARY SEAL
SECONDARY PISTON
SECONDARY SEAL
MASTER CYLINDER
BODY
SPRING
SECONDARY PISTON
ASSEMBLY
PRIMARY PISTON
ASSEMBLY
LOCK RING

Master cylinder exploded view

OVERHAUL

1. Remove the master cylinder from the vehicle.
2. At the rear of the master cylinder, depress the primary piston and remove the lock ring.
3. Block the rear outlet hole on the master cylinder. Using compressed air, gently direct it into the front outlet hole to remove the primary and secondary pistons from the master cylinder. If compressed air is not available, use a hooked wire to pull out the secondary piston.

CAUTION

If using compressed air to remove the pistons from the master cylinder, DO NOT stand in front of the pistons, for too much air will cause the pistons to be fired from the master cylinder, causing bodily harm.

4. From the secondary piston, remove the spring retainer and the seals.
5. Using the mounting flange (ear) on the master cylinder, clamp it into a vise.
6. Using a medium pry bar, pry the reservoirs from the master cylinder. Remove the reservoir grommets.

NOTE: DO NOT attempt to remove the quick take-up valve from the master cylinder body; the valve is not serviceable separately.

7. Using denatured alcohol, clean and blow dry all of the master cylinder parts.
8. Inspect the master cylinder bore for corrosion or scratches; if damaged, replace the master cylinder with a new one.

To install:

9. Use new reservoir grommets (lubricated with brake fluid) and press them into the master cylinder body. Install new seals onto the primary and secondary pistons.
10. Position the reservoirs on flat, hard surfaces (block of wood), then press the master cylinder onto the reservoirs, using a rocking motion.
11. Using heavy duty brake fluid, meeting Dot 3 specifications, lubricate the primary and secondary pistons, then install them into the master cylinder. While depressing the primary piston, install the lock ring.
12. Install new diaphragms onto the reservoir covers.
13. Install the master cylinder on the vehicle, fill with new brake fluid and bleed the brakes.

Power Brake Booster

The power brake booster is a tandem vacuum suspended unit, equipped with a single or dual function vacuum switch that activates a brake warning light should low booster vacuum be present. Under normal operation, vacuum is present on both sides of the diaphragms. When the brakes are applied, atmospheric air is admitted to one side of the diaphragms to provide power assistance.

REMOVAL AND INSTALLATION

1. Apply the parking brake and block the wheels.
2. Remove the master cylinder-to-power brake booster nuts and move the master cylinder out of the way; if necessary, support the master cylinder on a wire.

NOTE: When removing the master cylinder from the

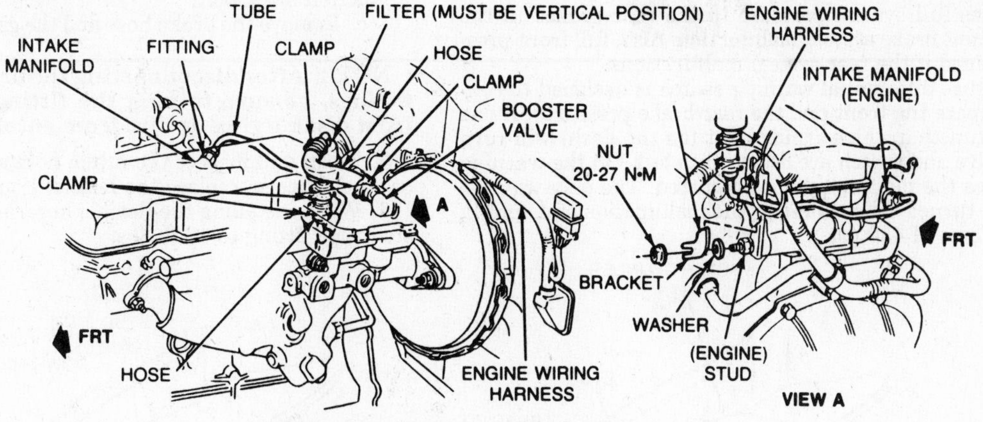
TUBE
FILTER (MUST BE VERTICAL POSITION)
ENGINE WIRING HARNESS
INTAKE MANIFOLD
FITTING
CLAMP
HOSE
CLAMP
INTAKE MANIFOLD (ENGINE)
BOOSTER VALVE
NUT 20-27 N•M
CLAMP
A
FRT
BRACKET
WASHER
FRT
HOSE
ENGINE WIRING HARNESS
(ENGINE) STUD
VIEW A

4-cylinder engine vacuum lines

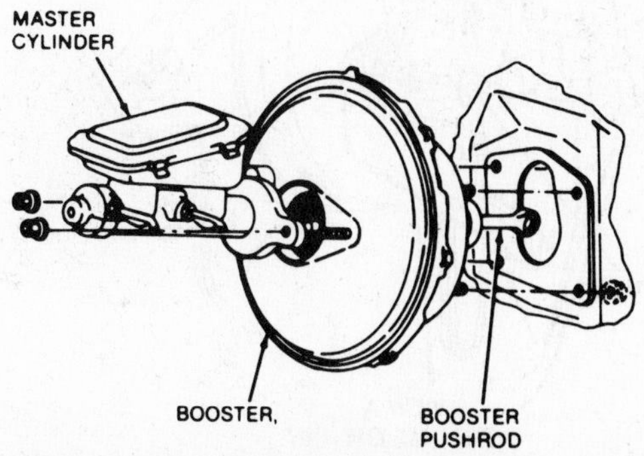
MASTER CYLINDER
BOOSTER,
BOOSTER PUSHROD

Power brake booster attachment

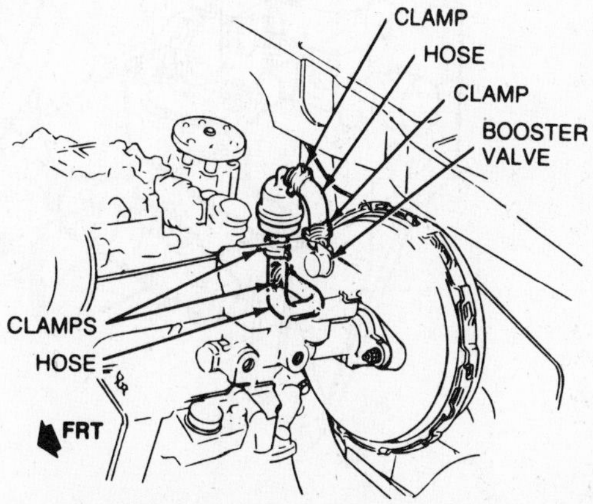
CLAMP
HOSE
CLAMP
BOOSTER VALVE
CLAMPS
HOSE
FRT

6-cylinder engine vacuum lines

power brake booster, it is not necessary to disconnect the hydraulic lines.

3. Disconnect the vacuum hose from the power brake booster.
4. From under the dash, disconnect the pushrod from the brake pedal.
5. From under the dash, remove the power brake booster-to-cowl nuts.
6. From the engine compartment, remove the power brake booster and the gasket from the vehicle.

To install:

7. Install the booster to the firewall with a new gasket and torque the nuts to 15 ft. lbs. (20 Nm).
8. Connect the pedal pushrod.
9. Install the master cylinder, connect the vacuum hose and run the engine to test the system.

Combination Valve

The combination valve is located in the engine compartment, directly under the master cylinder. It consists of three sections: the metering valve, the warning switch and the proportioning valve.

The metering section limits the pressure to the front disc brakes until a predetermined front input pressure is reached, enough to overcome the rear shoe retractor springs. Under 3 psi, there is no restriction of the inlet pressures; the pressures are allowed to equalize during the no brake period.

The proportioning section controls the outlet pressure to the rear brakes after a predetermined rear input pressure has been reached; this feature is provided for vehicles with light loads, to help prevent rear wheel lock-up. The by-pass feature of this valve assures full system pressure to the rear brakes in the event of a front brake system malfunction. Also, full front pressure is retained if the rear system malfunctions.

The pressure differential warning switch is designed to constantly compare the front and the rear brake pressures; if one should malfunction, the warning light (on the dash) will turn On. The valve and switch are designed to lock On the warning position once the malfunction has occurred. The only way the light can be turned Off is to repair the malfunction and apply a brake line force of 450 psi.

REMOVAL AND INSTALLATION

1. Disconnect and plug the hydraulic lines from the combination valve to prevent the loss of brake fluid or dirt from entering the system.
2. Disconnect the electrical connector from the combination valve.
3. Remove the combination valve-to-bracket nuts and the combination valve from the vehicle.

NOTE: The combination valve is not repairable and must be replaced as a complete assembly.

4. Using a new combination valve (if defective), torque the combination valve-to-bracket nuts to 12 ft. lbs. Reconnect the electrical connector to the combination valve.
5. Bleed the brake system.

Brake Pipes and Hoses

REMOVAL AND INSTALLATION

Flexible Hoses

Flexible hoses are installed between the frame-to-front calipers and the frame-to-rear differential.

1. Using a wire brush, clean the dirt and/or grease from both ends of the hose fittings.
2. Disconnect the steel pipes from the flexible hose.
3. To remove the brake hose from the front brake caliper or the rear differential, perform the following procedures:
   a. Remove the brake hose-to-frame bracket retaining clip.
   b. Remove the brake hose-to-brake caliper or differential junction block bolt.
   c. Remove the brake hose and the gaskets from the vehicle.

NOTE: After disconnecting the brake hose(s) from the fittings, be sure to plug the fittings to keep the fluid from discharging or dirt from entering the system.

5. Clean and inspect the brake hose(s) for cracking, chafing or road damage; replace the hose(s) if any signs are observed.
6. When installing the flexible hose, and torque the hose–to–steel pipe fitting to 13 ft. lbs.

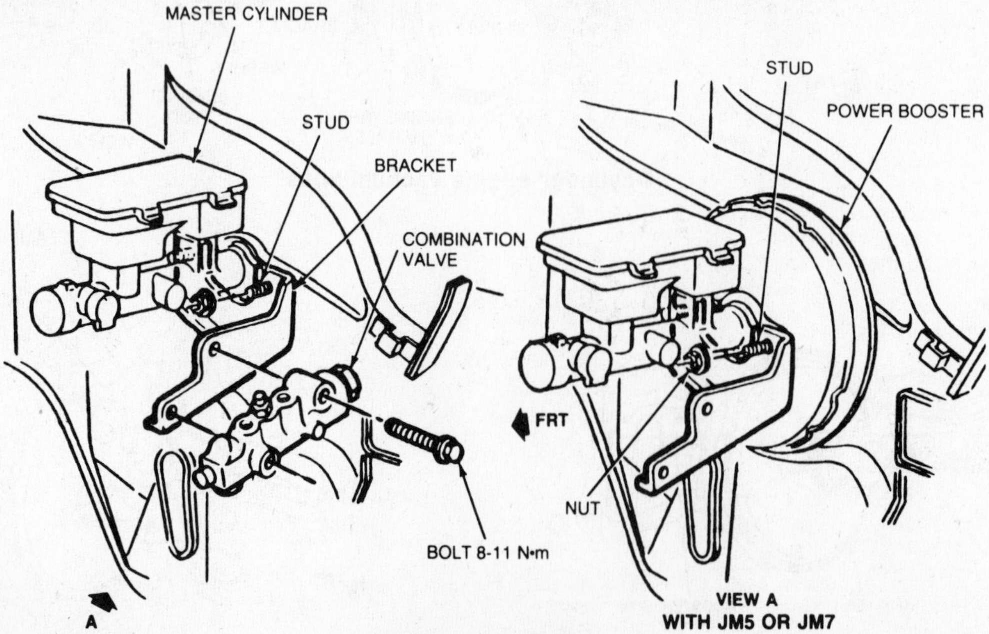
MASTER CYLINDER
STUD
BRACKET
COMBINATION VALVE
BOLT 8-11 N•m
A
STUD
POWER BOOSTER
FRT
NUT
VIEW A
WITH JM5 OR JM7

Combination valve

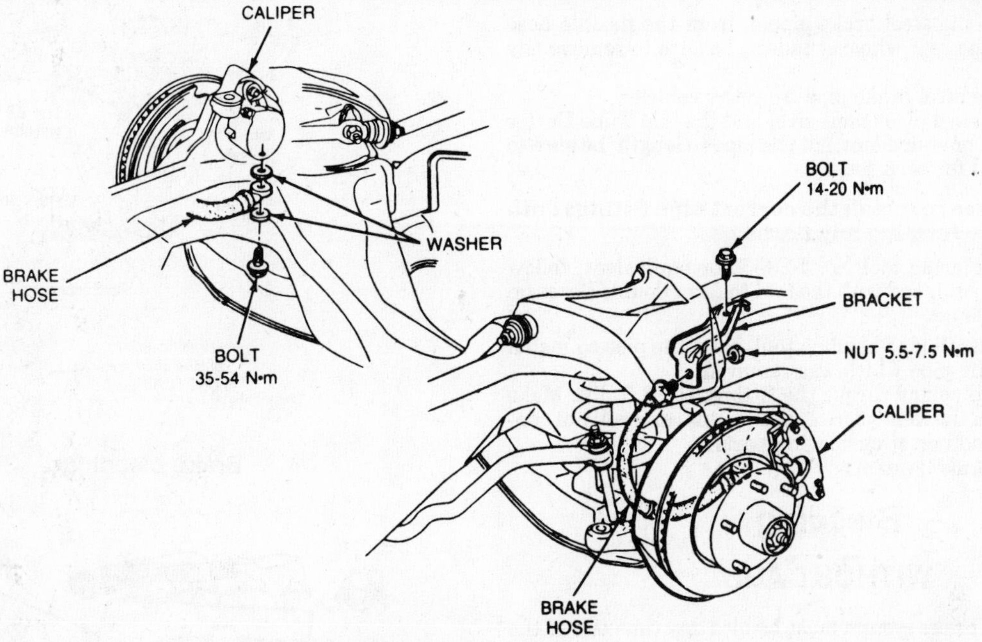
CALIPER
WASHER
BRAKE HOSE
BOLT 35-54 N•m
BOLT 14-20 N•m
BRACKET
NUT 5.5-7.5 N•m
CALIPER
BRAKE HOSE

Front brake hoses

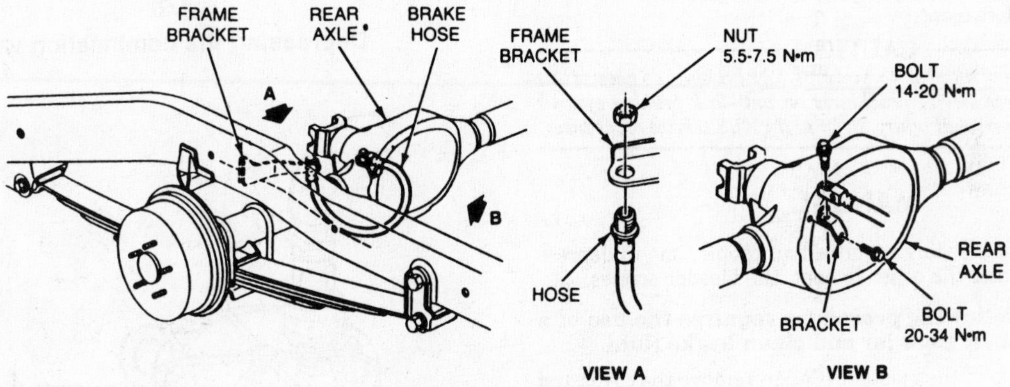
FRAME BRACKET
REAR AXLE
BRAKE HOSE
A
B
FRAME BRACKET
NUT 5.5-7.5 N•m
BOLT 14-20 N•m
HOSE
REAR AXLE
BRACKET
BOLT 20-34 N•m
VIEW A
VIEW B

Rear brake hoses

7. Use new copper gaskets to install the hose to the front caliper and torque the fitting to 32 ft. lbs.
8. Install the line retaining clips and bleed the brake system.

NOTE: Be sure that the hoses do not make contact with any of the suspension components.

Steel Pipes

When replacing the steel brake pipes, always use steel piping which is designed to withstand high pressure, resist corrosion and is of the same size.

CAUTION

Never use copper tubing. It is subject to fatigue, cracking, and/or corrosion, which will result in brake line failure.

NOTE: The following procedure requires the use of the GM Tube Cutter tool No. J-23533 or equivalent, and the GM Flaring tool No. J-23530 or equivalent.

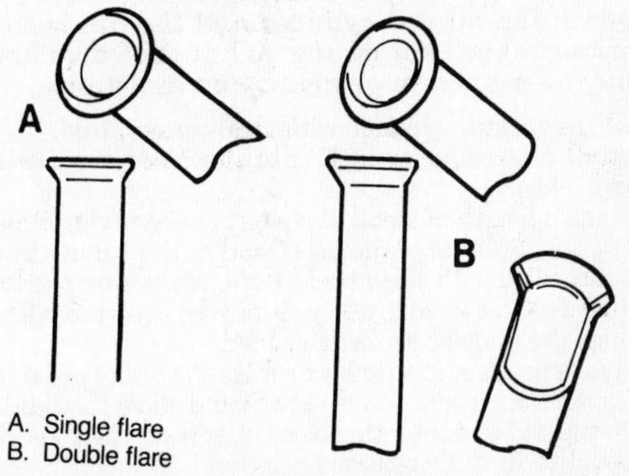
A
B
A. Single flare
B. Double flare

Single and double flare tube ends

1. Disconnect the steel brake pipe(s) from the flexible hose connections or the rear wheel cylinders; be sure to remove any retaining clips.
2. Remove the steel brake pipe from the vehicle.
3. Using new steel pipe (same size) and the GM Tube Cutter tool No. J-23533 or equivalent, cut the pipe to length; be sure to add ⅛ in. (3mm) for each flare.

NOTE: Be sure to install the correct pipe fittings onto the tube before forming any flares.

4. Using the Flaring tool No. J-23530 or equivalent, follow the instructions equipped with the tool to form double flares on the ends of the pipes.
5. Using the small pipe bending tool, bend the pipe to match the contour of the pipe which was removed.
6. Install the pipe and torque the fittings to 13 ft. lbs. Make sure the pipe is in the same place as the original and will not contact any syspension or other moving parts.
7. Bleed the brake system.

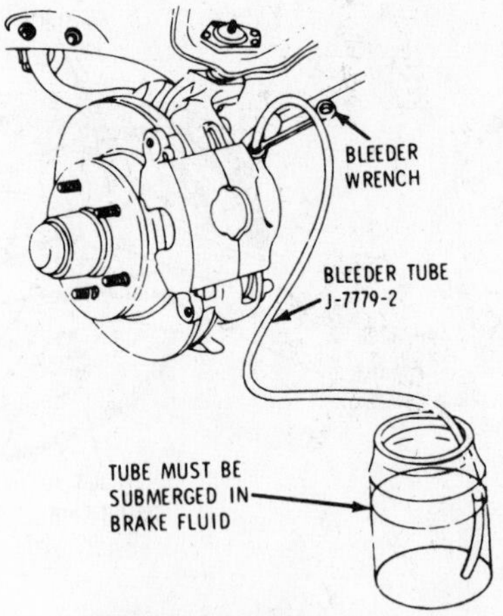
BLEEDER
WRENCH
BLEEDER TUBE
J-7779-2
TUBE MUST BE
SUBMERGED IN
BRAKE FLUID
Brake bleeding

Bleeding

WITHOUT ABS

The hydraulic brake system must be bled any time one of the lines is disconnected or any time air enters the system. If the brake pedal feels spongy upon application, and goes almost to the floor but regains height when pumped, air has entered the system. It must be bled out. Check for leaks that would have allowed the entry of air and repair them before bleeding the system. The correct bleeding sequence is; right-rear, left-rear, right-front and left-front.

CAUTION

If the vehicle has rear wheel or 4 wheel anti-lock braking, do not use this procedure. Improper service procedures on anti-lock braking systems can cause serious personal injury. Refer to the ABS service procedures.

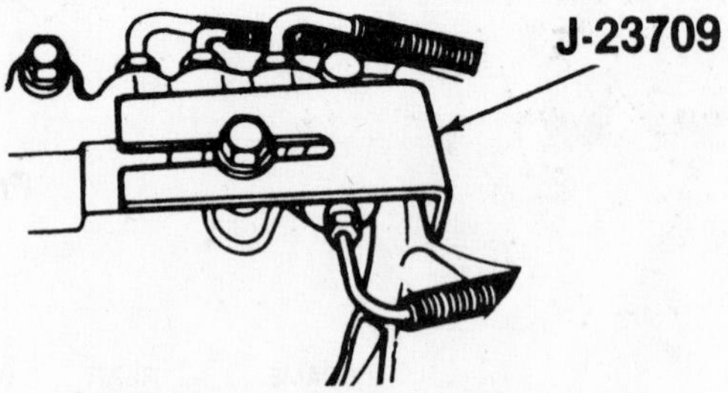
J-23709
Depressing the combination valve

MANUAL

This method of bleeding requires two people, one to depress the brake pedal and the other to open the bleeder screws.

NOTE: The following procedure requires the use of a clear vinyl hose, a glass jar and clean brake fluid.

1. Clean the top of the master cylinder, remove the cover and fill the reservoirs with clean fluid. To prevent squirting fluid, replace the cover.

NOTE: On vehicles equipped with front disc brakes, it will be necessary to hold in the metering valve pin during the bleeding procedure. The metering valve is located beneath the master cylinder and the pin is situated under the rubber boot on the end of the valve housing. This may be tapped in or held by an assistant.

2. Fill the master cylinder with clean brake fluid.
3. Install a box end wrench onto the bleeder screw on the right rear wheel.
4. Attach a length of small diameter, clear vinyl tubing to the bleeder screw. Submerge the other end of the tubing in a glass jar partially filled with clean brake fluid. Make sure the tube fits on the bleeder screw snugly or you may be squirted with brake fluid when the bleeder screw is opened.
5. Have your assistant slowly depress the brake pedal. As this is done, open the bleeder screw ½ turn and allow the fluid to run through the tube. Close the bleeder screw, then return the brake pedal to its fully released position.
6. Repeat this procedure until no bubbles appear in the jar. Refill the master cylinder.

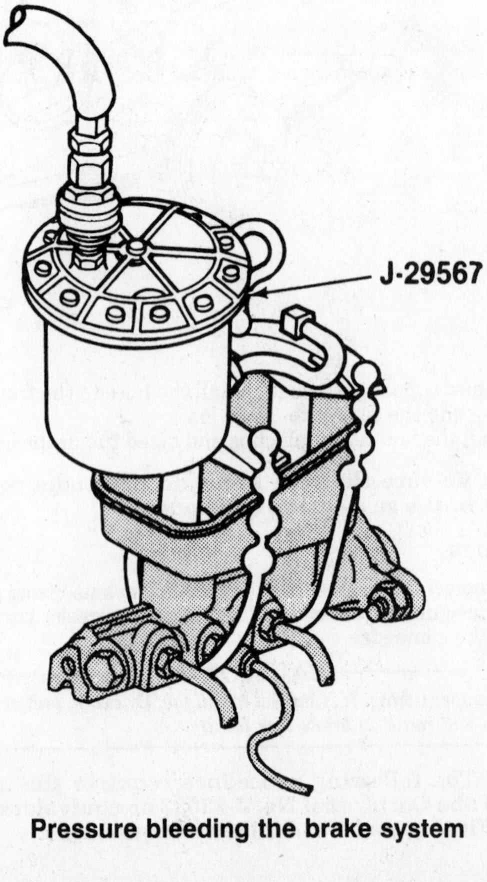
J-29567
Pressure bleeding the brake system

7. Repeat this procedure on the left-rear, right-front and the left-front wheels, in that order. Periodically, refill the master cylinder so that it does not run dry.

8. If the brake warning light is On, depress the brake pedal firmly. If there is no air in the system, the dash light will turn Off.

PRESSURE

NOTE: The following procedure requires the use of the GM Brake Bleeder Adapter tool No. J-29567 or equivalent, and the GM Combination Valve Depressor tool No. J-23709 or equivalent.

1. Using the GM Brake Bleeder Adapter tool No. J-29567 or equivalent, fill the pressure tank to at least ⅓ full of brake fluid. Using compressed air, charge the pressure tank to 20–25 psi., then install it onto the master cylinder.

2. Using the GM Combination Valve Depressor tool No. J-35856 or equivalent, install it onto the combination valve to hold the valve open during the bleeding operation.

3. Bleed each wheel cylinder or caliper in the following sequence: right-rear, left-rear, right-front and left-front.

4. Connect a hose from the bleeder tank to the adapter at the master cylinder, then open the tank valve.

5. Attach a clear vinyl hose to the brake bleeder screw, then immerse the opposite end into a container partially filled with clean brake fluid.

6. Open the bleeder screw ¾ turn and allow the fluid to flow until no air bubbles are seen in the fluid, then close the bleeder screw.

7. Repeat the bleeding process to each wheel.

8. Inspect the brake pedal for sponginess and if necessary, repeat the entire bleeding procedure.

9. Remove the depressor tool from the combination valve and the bleeder adapter from the master cylinder.

10. Refill the master cylinder to the proper level with brake fluid.

FRONT DISC BRAKES

CAUTION

Brake shoes contain asbestos, which has been determined to be a cancer causing agent. Never clean the brake surfaces with compressed air! Avoid inhaling any dust from any brake surface! When cleaning brake surfaces, use a commercially available brake cleaning fluid.

CAUTION

The insertion of thicker replacement pads will push the piston back into its bore and will cause a full master cylinder reservoir to overflow, possibly causing paint damage. In addition to siphoning off fluid, it would be wise to keep the reservoir cover on during pad replacement.

Brake Pads

INSPECTION

Brake pads should be inspected once a year or at 7,500 miles, which ever occurs first. Check both ends of the outboard shoe, looking in at each end of the caliper; then check the lining thickness on the inboard shoe, looking down through the inspection hole. The lining should be more than 0.032 in. (0.8mm) thick above the rivet (so that the lining is thicker than the metal backing). Keep in mind that any applicable state inspection standards that are more stringent, take precedence. All four pads must be replaced if one shows excessive wear.

NOTE: All models have a wear indicator that makes a noise when the linings wear to a degree where replacement is necessary. The spring clip is an integral part of the inboard shoe and lining. When the brake pad reaches a certain degree of wear, the clip will contact the rotor and produce a warning noise.

REMOVAL AND INSTALLATION

NOTE The following procedure requires the use of a C-clamp and channel lock pliers.

1. If the fluid reservoir is full, siphon off about ⅔ of the brake fluid from the master cylinder reservoirs.

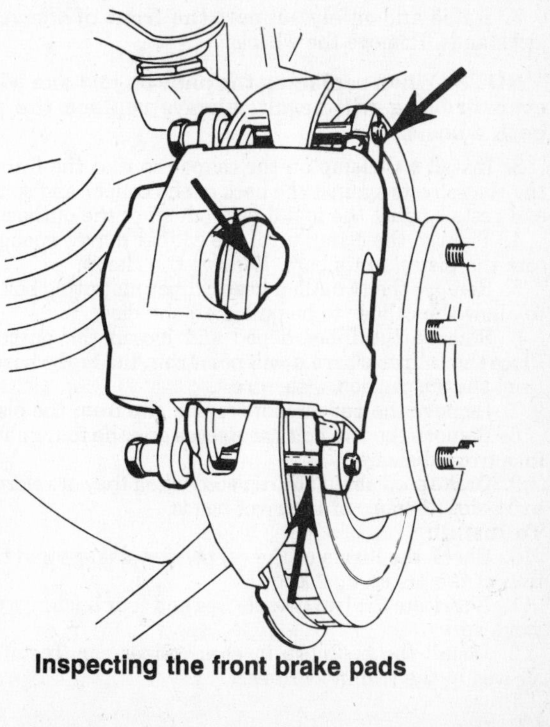

Inspecting the front brake pads

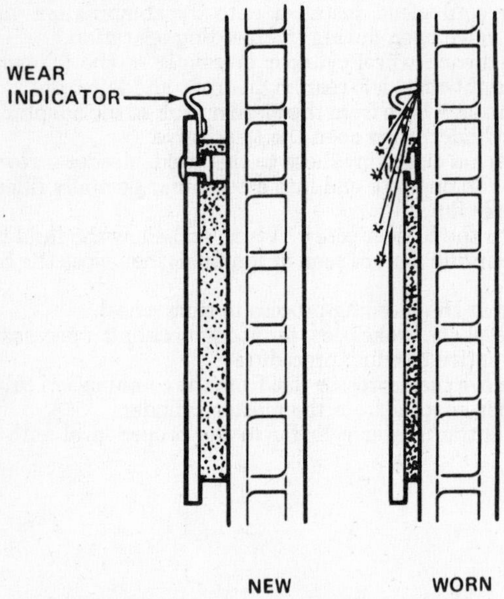
WEAR
INDICATOR
NEW
WORN
Disk brake pad wear indicator operation

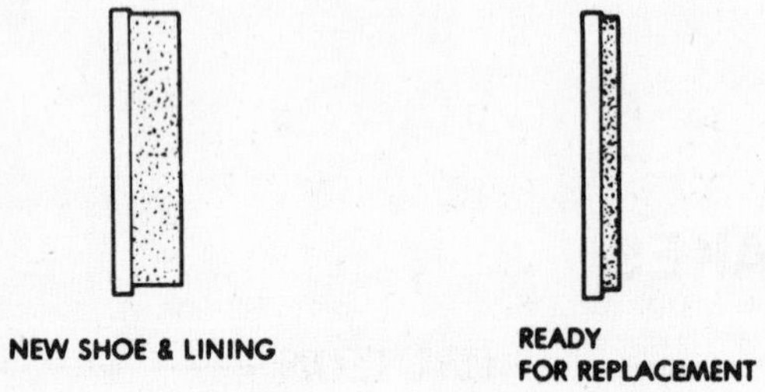
NEW SHOE & LINING
READY
FOR REPLACEMENT
New and worn brake pads

2. Raise and safely support the front of the vehicle on jackstands. Remove the wheels.

NOTE: When replacing the pads on just one wheel, uneven braking will result; always replace the pads on both wheels.

3. Install a C-clamp on the caliper so that the frame side of the clamp rests against the back of the caliper and so the screw end rests against the metal part (shoe) of the outboard pad.
4. Tighten the clamp until the caliper moves enough to bottom the piston in its bore. Remove the clamp.
5. Remove the two Allen head caliper mounting bolts enough to allow the caliper to be pulled off the disc.
6. Remove the inboard pad and loosen the outboard pad. Place the caliper where it will not strain the brake hose; hang it from the suspension with wire.
7. Remove the pad support spring clip from the piston.
8. Remove the two bolt ear sleeves and the four rubber bushings from the ears.
9. Brake pads should be replaced when they are worn to within $^{1}/_{32}$ in. (0.8mm) of the rivet heads.

To install:

10. Check the inside of the caliper for leakage and the condition of the piston dust boot.
11. Lubricate the two new sleeves and four bushings with a silicone spray.
12. Install the bushings in each caliper ear. Install the two sleeves in the two inboard ears.

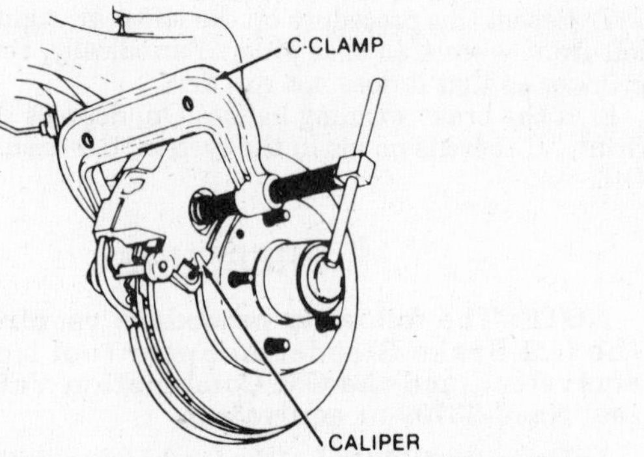
C-CLAMP
CALIPER
Using a C-clamp to bottom the brake caliper piston

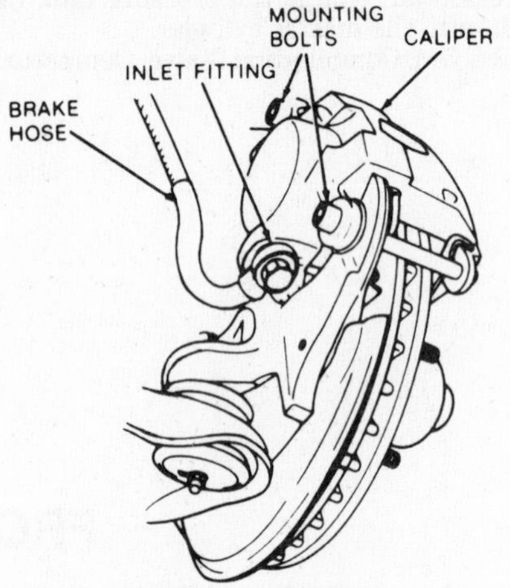
MOUNTING
BOLTS
CALIPER
INLET FITTING
BRAKE
HOSE
Caliper mounting

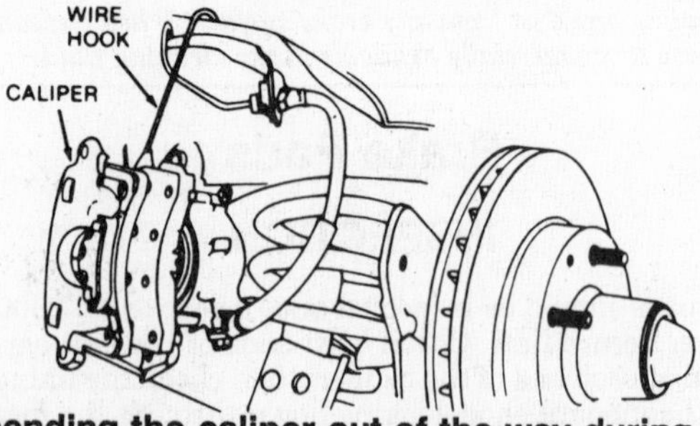
WIRE
HOOK
CALIPER
Suspending the caliper out of the way during brake servicing

13. Install the pad support spring clip and the old pad into the center of the piston. You will then push this pad down to get the piston flat against the caliper. This part of the job is a hassle and requires an assistant. While the assistant holds the caliper and loosens the bleeder valve to relieve the pressure, obtain a medium pry bar and try to force the old pad inward, making the piston flush with the caliper surface. When it is flush, close the bleeder valve so that no air gets into the system.

NOTE: Make sure that the wear sensor is facing toward the rear of the caliper.

14. Place the outboard pad in the caliper with its top ears over the caliper ears and the bottom tab engaged in the caliper cutout.
15. After both pads are installed, lift the caliper and place the bottom edge of the outboard pad on the outer edge of the disc to

make sure that there is no clearance between the tab on the bottom of the shoes and the caliper abutment.

16. Place the caliper over the disc, lining up the hole in the caliper ears with the hole in the mounting bracket. Make sure that the brake hose is not kinked.

17. Start the caliper-to-mounting bracket bolts through the sleeves in the inboard caliper ears and through the mounting bracket, making sure that the ends of the bolts pass under the retaining ears of the inboard shoe.

18. Push the mounting bolts through to engage the holes in the outboard shoes and the outboard caliper ears and then thread them into the mounting bracket.

19. Torque the mounting bolts to 37 ft. lbs. Pump the brake pedal to seat the linings against the rotors.

20. Using a pair of channel lock pliers, place them on the notch on the caliper housing, bend the caliper upper ears until no clearance exists between the shoe and the caliper housing.

21. Install the wheels, lower the vehicle and refill the master cylinder reservoirs with brake fluid. Pump the brake pedal to make sure that it is firm. If it is not, bleed the brakes.

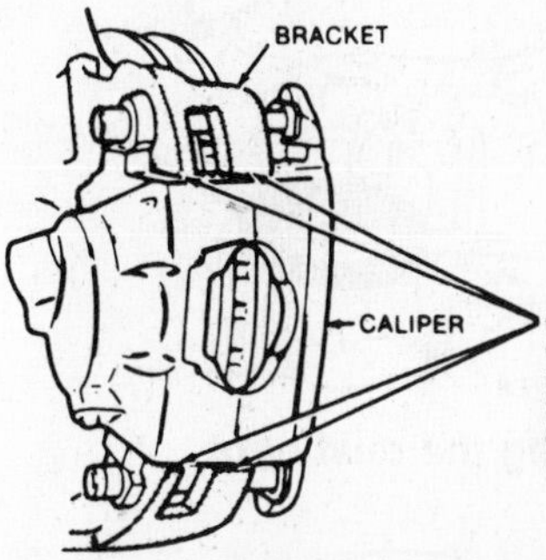
BRACKET
CALIPER
CLEARANCE BETWEEN
CALIPER AND
BRACKET STOPS
SHALL BE 0.13-0.30 MM
(0.005-0.012 IN.)
FOUR PLACES

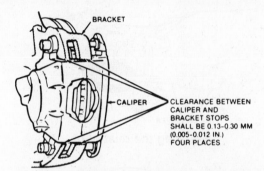

Checking caliper-to-bracket stop clearance

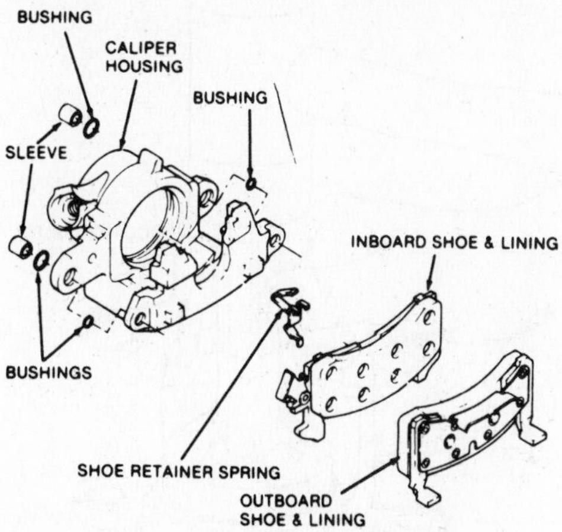
BUSHING
CALIPER
HOUSING
BUSHING
SLEEVE
INBOARD SHOE & LINING
BUSHINGS
SHOE RETAINER SPRING
OUTBOARD
SHOE & LINING

Removing the pads from the caliper

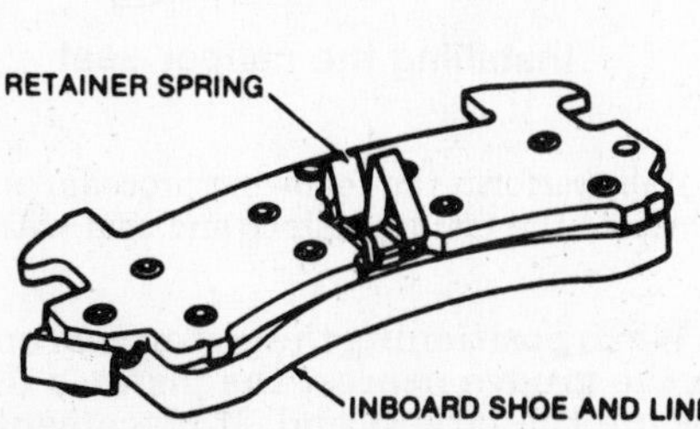
SHOE RETAINER SPRING
INBOARD SHOE AND LINING

Installing the shoe retainer spring

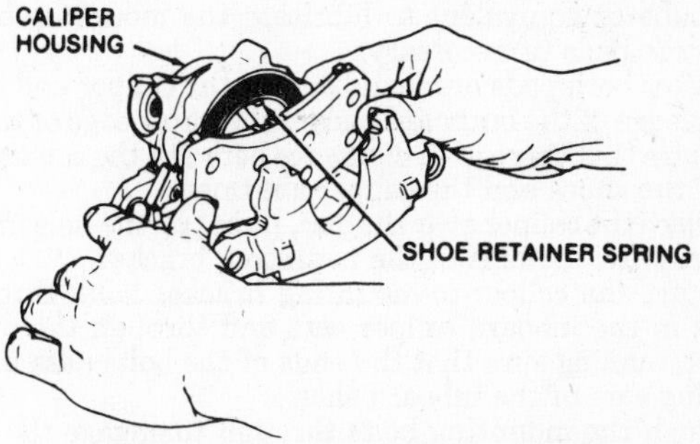
CALIPER
HOUSING
SHOE RETAINER SPRING

Installing the pads in the caliper

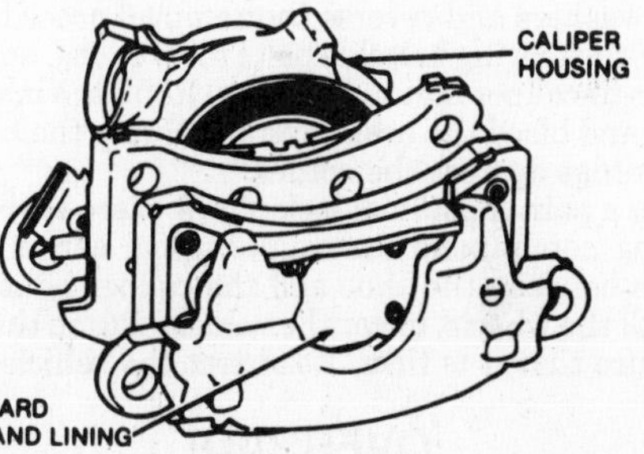
CALIPER
HOUSING
OUTBOARD
SHOE AND LINING

Positioning the shoe in the caliper

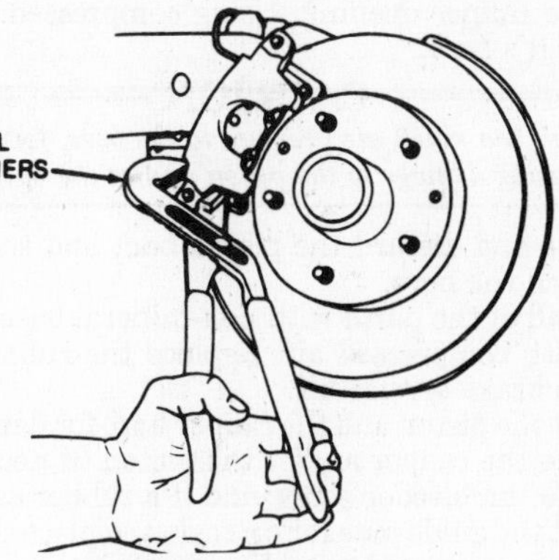
CHANNEL
LOCK PLIERS

Seating the caliper

Brake Caliper

REMOVAL AND INSTALLATION

1. Remove the brake caliper from the steering knuckle.
2. Disconnect the flexible brake hose-to-caliper bolt, discard the pressure fitting washers, then remove the brake caliper from the vehicle and place it on a work bench.
3. To inspect the caliper assembly, perform the following procedures:
   a. Check the inside of the caliper assembly for signs of leakage; if necessary, replace or rebuild the caliper.
   b. Check the mounting bolts and sleeves for signs of corrosion; if necessary, replace the bolts.

NOTE: If the mounting bolts have signs of corrosion, DO NOT attempt to polish away the corrosion.

4. Using new caliper bushings and sleeves, apply Delco® Sili-

cone Lube or equivalent to lubricate the mounting bolts and new brake pads (if necessary).

5. After both pads are installed, lift the caliper and place the bottom edge of the outboard pad on the outer edge of the disc to make sure that there is no clearance between the tab on the bottom of the shoes and the caliper abutment.

6. Place the caliper over the disc, lining up the hole in the caliper ears with the hole in the mounting bracket.

7. Start the caliper-to-mounting bracket bolts through the sleeves in the inboard caliper ears and through the mounting bracket, making sure that the ends of the bolts pass under the retaining ears of the inboard shoe.

8. Push the mounting bolts through to engage the holes in the outboard shoes and the outboard caliper ears, then thread them into the mounting bracket.

9. To complete the installation, use new flexible brake hose-to-caliper washers and reverse the removal procedures. Torque the caliper-to-steering knuckle bolts to 37 ft. lbs. and the flexible brake hose-to-caliper bolt to 32 ft. lbs. Refill the master cylinder reservoirs and bleed the brake system. Pump the brake pedal to seat the linings against the rotors.

10. Using a pair of channel lock pliers, place them on the caliper housing notch, bend the caliper upper ears until no clearance exists between the shoe and the caliper housing.

11. Install the wheels, lower the vehicle. Pump the brake pedal to make sure that it is firm. Road test the vehicle.

OVERHAUL

1. Remove the brake caliper from the vehicle.
2. Remove the inlet fitting from the brake caliper.
3. Position the caliper on a work bench and place clean shop cloths in the caliper opening. Using compressed air, force the piston from it's bore.

CAUTION

DO NOT apply too much air pressure to the bore, for the piston may jump out, causing damage to the piston and/or the operator.

4. Remove and discard the piston boot and seal. Be careful not to scratch the bore.
5. Clean all of the parts with non-mineral based solvent and blow dry with compressed air. Replace the rubber parts with those in the brake service kit.
6. Inspect the piston and the caliper bore for damage or corrosion. Replace the caliper and/or the piston (if necessary).
7. Remove the bleeder screw and it's rubber cap.
8. Inspect the guide pins for corrosion, replace them (if necessary). When installing the guide pins, coat them with silicone grease.

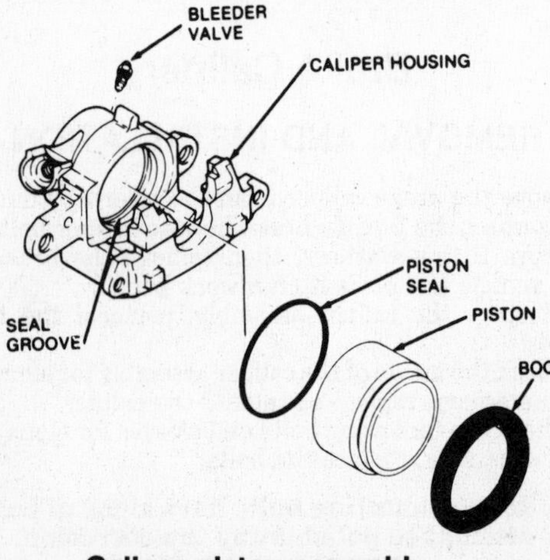
BLEEDER VALVE
CALIPER HOUSING
PISTON SEAL
PISTON
BOOT
SEAL GROOVE

Caliper piston assembly

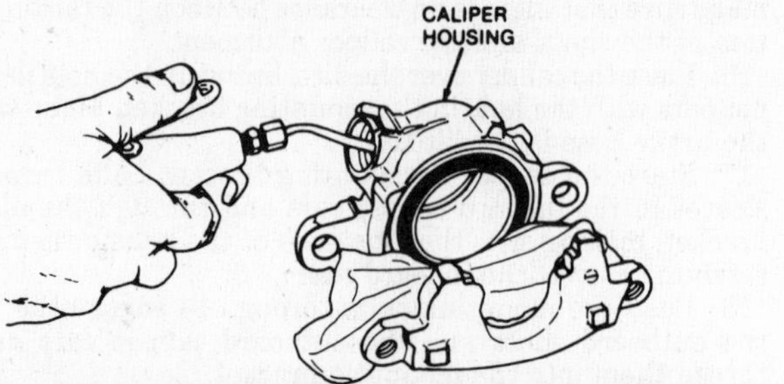
CALIPER HOUSING

Place a clean rag as shown to catch the caliper piston when using compressed air to remove the piston from the bore

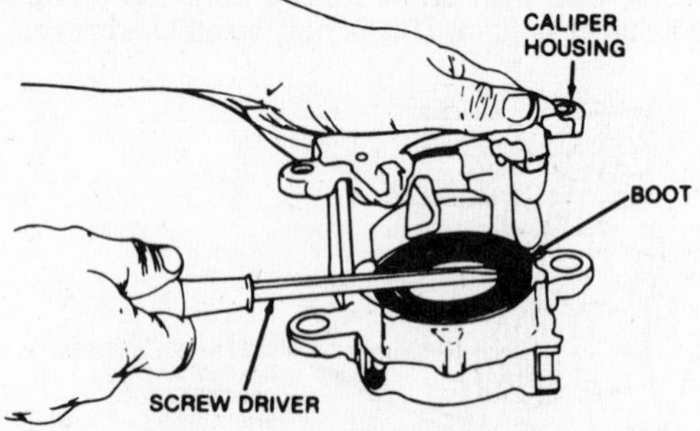
CALIPER HOUSING
BOOT
SCREW DRIVER

Removing the dust boot

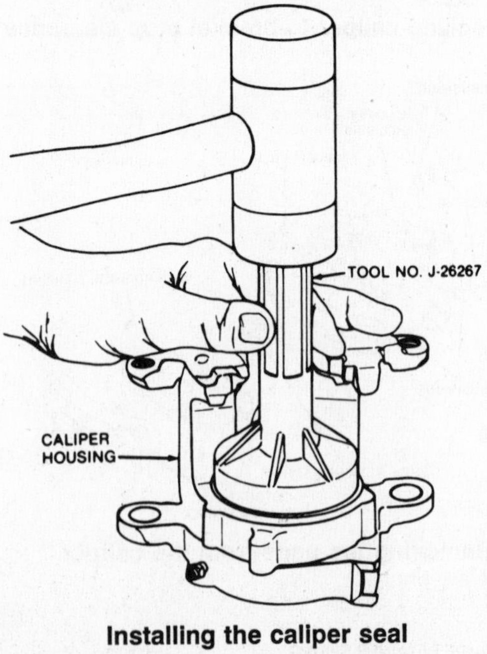
TOOL NO. J-26267
CALIPER HOUSING

Installing the caliper seal

9. To install, perform the following procedures:

a. Lubricate the piston, caliper and seal with clean brake fluid.

NOTE: When positioning the piston seal on the piston, it goes in the groove nearest the piston's flat end with the lap facing the largest end. If placement is correct, the seal lips will be in the groove and not extend over the groove's step.

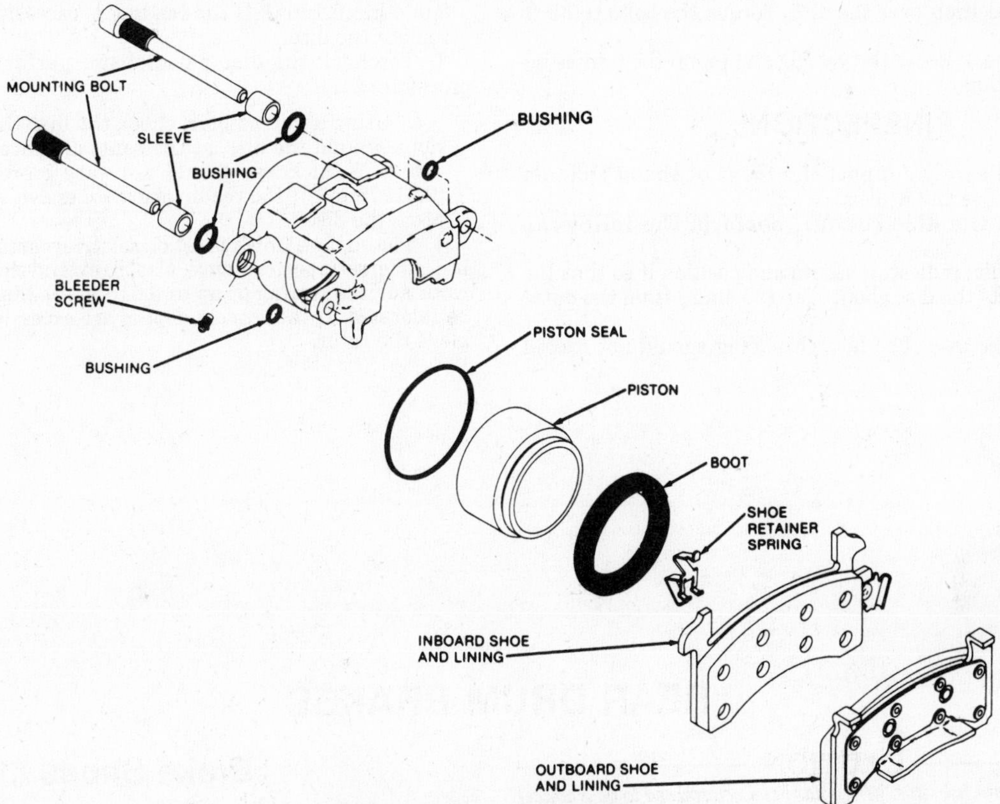
MOUNTING BOLT
SLEEVE
BUSHING
BUSHING
BLEEDER SCREW
BUSHING
PISTON SEAL
PISTON
BOOT
SHOE RETAINER SPRING
INBOARD SHOE AND LINING
OUTBOARD SHOE AND LINING

Caliper and pad assembly

b. Replace the caliper-to-steering knuckle bolts and torque the bolts to 37 ft. lbs.

10. To complete the installation, reverse the removal procedures. Bleed the brake system after installation.

Brake Disc (Rotor)

REMOVAL AND INSTALLATION

2WD Model

1. Siphon some brake fluid from the brake master cylinder.
2. Raise and safely support the front of the vehicle on jackstands. Remove the wheels.
3. Remove the brake caliper from the steering knuckle and hang it on a wire.
4. Remove the grease cup, the cotter pin, the castle nut and the hub assembly.
5. Inspect the brake discs for signs of wear or damage; if necessary, replace the brake disc.
6. If installing a new disc, drive the outer bearing race out of the disc hub and carefully install it into the new disc using a suitable installation tool. Refer to the section on Front Suspension.
7. Grease the inner and outer bearings, install the inner bearing and seal and place the disc onto the axle.
8. Install the outer bearing, thrust washer and nut. Torque the nut to 12 ft. lbs. while turning the wheel. Loosen the nut again, then make it as tight as possible using just fingers, no other tools. Loosen the nut as required to install the cotter pin, no more than ½ turn.
7. Install the wheel, refil the brake fluid and road test the vehicle.

4WD Model

1. Raise and safely support the front of the truck on jackstands; place the jackstands under the frame.
2. Remove the wheel and tire assembly.
3. Remove the disc brake caliper and hang it out of the way on a wire.4. Remove the brake disc from the wheel hub.
5.Inspect the disc for nicks, scores and/or damage, then replace it if necessary.
6.When installing the caliper, spread the brake pads to slide the

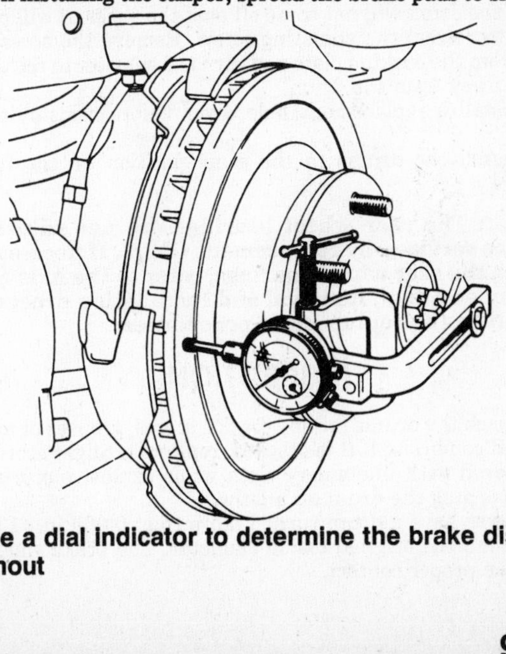

Use a dial indicator to determine the brake disc runout

caliper into position over the disc. Torque the bolts to 35 ft. lbs.

7. Install the wheel, lower the vehicle and pump the brakes before road testing.

INSPECTION

1. Raise and safely support the front of the vehicle on jackstands. Remove the wheels.
2. To check the disc runout, perform the following procedures:
   a. Using a dial indicator, secure and position it so that the button contacts the disc about 1 in. (25.4mm) from the outer edge.
   b. Rotate the disc. The lateral reading should not exceed 0.004 in. (0.1mm). If the reading is excessive, recondition or replace the disc.
3. To check the disc parallelism, perform the following procedures:
   a. Using a micrometer, check the disc thickness at 4 locations around the disc, at the same distance from the edge.
   b. The thickness should not vary more than 0.0005 in. (0.0127mm). If the readings are excessive, recondition or replace the disc.
4. The surface finish must be relatively smooth to avoid pulling and erratic performance, also, to extend the lining life. Light rotor surface scoring of up to 0.015 in. (0.38mm) in depth, can be tolerated. If the scoring depths are excessive, refinish or replace the rotor.

REAR DRUM BRAKES

CAUTION

Brake shoes contain asbestos, which has been determined to be a cancer causing agent. Never clean the brake surfaces with compressed air! Avoid inhaling any dust from any brake surface! When cleaning brake surfaces, use a commercially available brake cleaning fluid.

Brake Drums

REMOVAL AND INSTALLATION

1. Raise and safely support the rear of the vehicle on jackstands.
2. Remove the wheel and tire assemblies.
3. Pull the brake drum off. It may by necessary to gently tap the rear edges of the drum to start it off the studs.
4. If the drum will not come off past the shoes, it will be necessary to retract the adjusting screw. Remove the access hole cover from the backing plate and turn the adjuster to retract the linings away from the drum.
5. Install a replacement hole cover before reinstalling the drum.
6. Install the drums in the same position on the hub as removed.

NOTE: The rear wheel bearings are not adjustable, they are serviced by replacement ONLY. If necessary to replace the rear wheel bearings, refer to the Axle Shaft, Bearing and Seal, Removal and Installation procedures and follow the replacement procedures.

INSPECTION

1. Check the drums for any cracks, scores, grooves or an out-of-round condition; if it is cracked, replace it. Slight scores can be removed with fine emery cloth while extensive scoring requires turning the drum on a lathe.
2. Never have a drum turned more than 0.060 in. (1.5mm) larger than the original inside diameter. The brake shoes will not make proper contact.

Brake Shoes

INSPECTION

Remove the drum and inspect the lining thickness of both brake shoes. The rear brake shoes should be replaced if the lining is less than $^1/_{16}$ in. (1.5mm) at the lowest point (bonded linings) or above the rivet heads (riveted linings) on the brake shoe. However, these lining thickness measurements may disagree with your state inspections laws.

NOTE: Brake shoes should always be replaced in sets.

REMOVAL AND INSTALLATION

NOTE: The following procedure requires the use of the GM Brake Spring Pliers tool No. J-8057 or equivalent.

1. Raise and safely support the rear of the vehicle on jackstands.
2. Slacken the parking brake cable.
3. Remove the rear wheels and the brake drum.
4. Using the GM Brake Spring Pliers tool No. J-8057 or equivalent, disconnect the brake shoe return springs, the actuator pullback spring, the holddown pins/springs and the actuator assembly.

NOTE: Special brake spring tools are available from the auto supply stores, which will ease the replacement of the spring and anchor pin, but the job may still be performed with common hand tools.

5. Disconnect the adjusting mechanism and spring, then remove the primary shoe. The primary shoe has a shorter lining than the secondary and is mounted at the front of the wheel.
6. Disconnect the parking brake lever from the secondary shoe and remove the shoe.
7. Clean and inspect all of the brake parts.
8. Check the wheel cylinders for seal condition and leaking.
9. Inspect the axle seal for leakage and replace, if necessary.

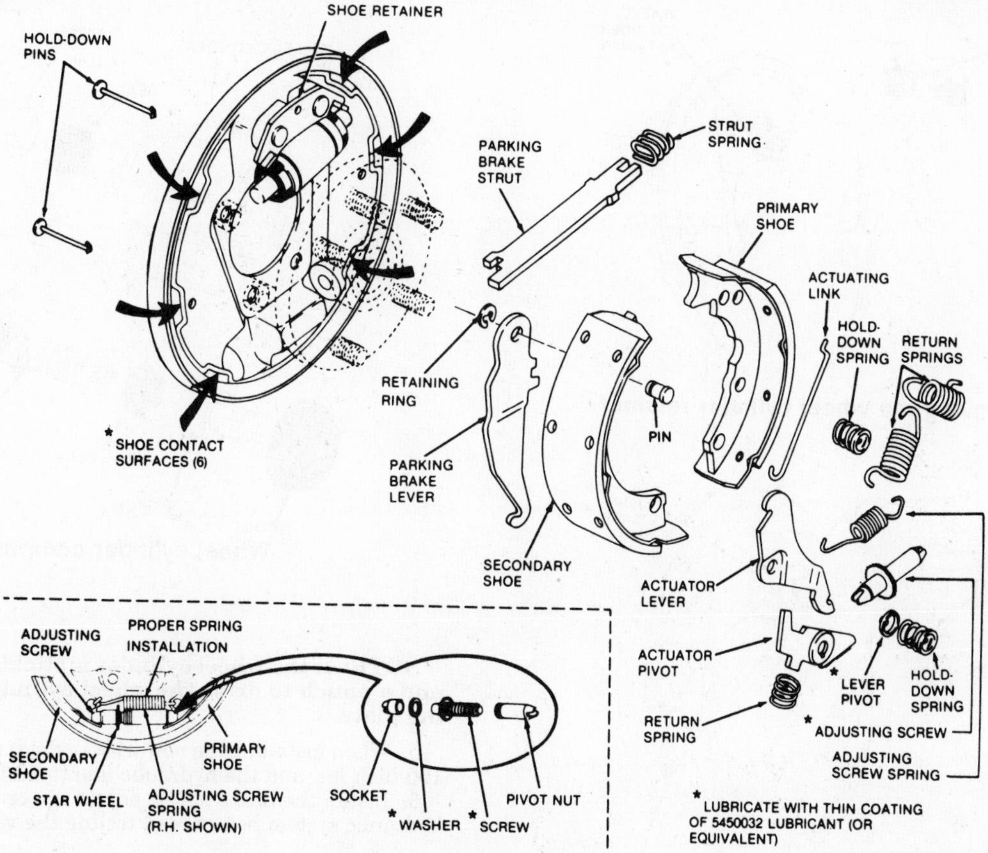
SHOE RETAINER
HOLD-DOWN PINS
STRUT SPRING
PARKING BRAKE STRUT
PRIMARY SHOE
ACTUATING LINK
HOLD-DOWN SPRING
RETURN SPRINGS
RETAINING RING
PIN
* SHOE CONTACT SURFACES (6)
PARKING BRAKE LEVER
SECONDARY SHOE
ACTUATOR LEVER
ACTUATOR PIVOT
LEVER PIVOT
HOLD-DOWN SPRING
RETURN SPRING
* ADJUSTING SCREW
ADJUSTING SCREW SPRING
ADJUSTING SCREW
PROPER SPRING INSTALLATION
SECONDARY SHOE
PRIMARY SHOE
STAR WHEEL
ADJUSTING SCREW SPRING (R.H. SHOWN)
SOCKET
* WASHER
* SCREW
PIVOT NUT
* LUBRICATE WITH THIN COATING OF 5450032 LUBRICANT (OR EQUIVALENT)

Rear brake assembly

10. Inspect the replacement shoes for nicks or burrs, lightly lubricate the backing plate contact points, the brake cable, the levers and adjusting screws with brake grease, then reassemble them.
11. Make sure that the right and left hand adjusting screws are not mixed. You can prevent this by working on one side at a time. This will also provide you with a reference for reassembly. The star wheel should be nearest to the secondary shoe when correctly installed.
12. Install the parking brake lever to the secondary shoe.
13. Connect the parking brake cable to the lever and lightly lubricate the shoe contact areas of the back plate with brake grease.
14. Install the shoes to the backplate with the hold down springs.
15. Install the parking brake strut and spring, making sure the strut properly engages the parking brake lever.
16. Install the self adjusting screw, spring, actuating lever and spring.
17. Install the actuating link, lift up on the actuating lever and hook it to the link.
18. Install the return springs. Lightly sandpaper the shoes to make sure they are clean before installing the drum.
19. Adjust the brakes as previously described and road test the vehicle.

Wheel Cylinders

REMOVAL AND INSTALLATION

1. Remove the brake shoe assembly from the backing plate.
2. Clean away all of the dirt, crud and foreign material from around the wheel cylinder. It is important that dirt be kept away from the brake line when the cylinder is disconnected.
3. Disconnect and plug the hydraulic line at the wheel cylinder.

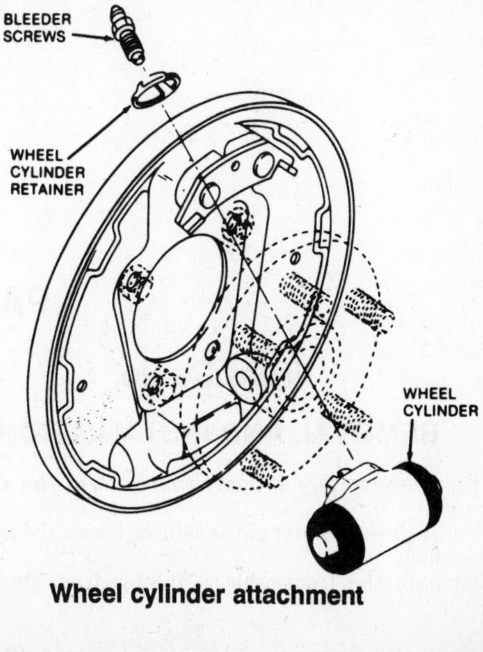
BLEEDER SCREWS
WHEEL CYLINDER RETAINER
WHEEL CYLINDER

Wheel cylinder attachment

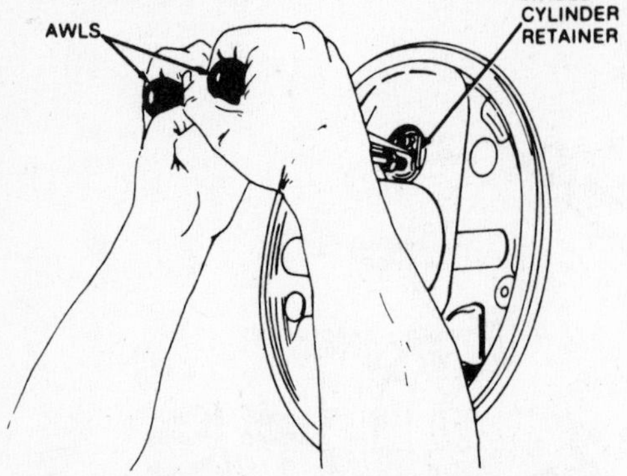
AWLS
WHEEL
CYLINDER
RETAINER
Removing the wheel cylinder retainer

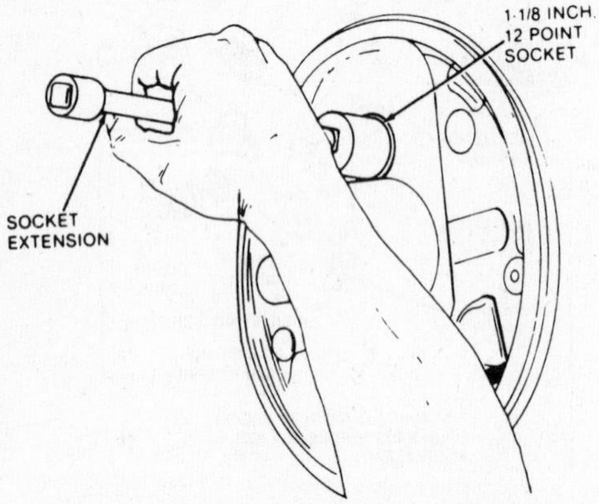
1-1/8 INCH.
12 POINT
SOCKET
SOCKET
EXTENSION
Installing the wheel cylinder retainer

4. Remove the wheel cylinder-to-backing plate bolts and the wheel cylinder from the backing plate.

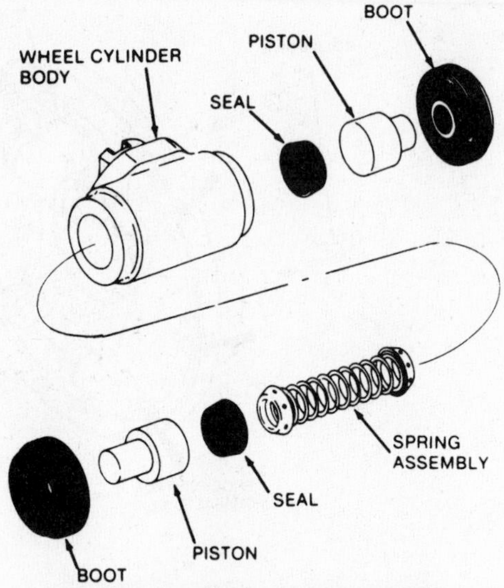
BOOT
PISTON
WHEEL CYLINDER
BODY
SEAL
SPRING
ASSEMBLY
SEAL
PISTON
BOOT
Wheel cylinder components

NOTE: If the wheel cylinder is sticking, use a hammer and a punch to drive the wheel cylinder from the backing plate.

5. When installing the new wheel cylinder, torque the bolts to 160 inch lbs. and the hydraulic line to 13 ft. lbs.
6. Install the brake shoes, adjust the brakes, then bleed the hydraulic system before road testing the vehicle.

OVERHAUL

1. Remove the boots, pistons, seals and spring.
2. Dry the bore and pistons, then check for wear, scoring, pitting or corrosion. GM does not recommend honing of the bore. If light corrosion exists it may be removed with crocus cloth. If crocus cloth does not do the job, replace the cylinder.
3. To assemble, use new seals/boots, coat all of the parts with clean silicone brake fluid and reverse the removal procedures.

PARKING BRAKE

Front Cable

REMOVAL AND INSTALLATION

1. Raise and safely support the front of the vehicle on jackstands.
2. Under the left-center of the vehicle, loosen the cable equalizer assembly.
3. Separate the front-cable connector from the equalizer cable.
4. Remove the front-cable retaining bolts and clips, then bend the retaining fingers.
5. Disconnect the front cable from the parking pedal assembly and the cable from the vehicle.

NOTE: On some models, it may be necessary to remove the dash trim panels to gain access to the brake pedal.

6. To install the front-cable, attach a piece of wire to the ca-

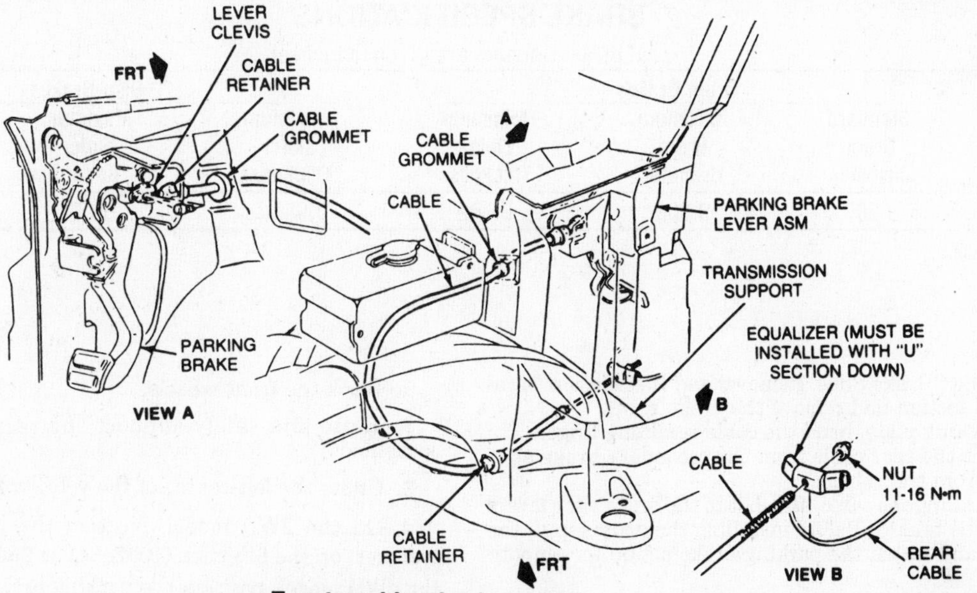
LEVER
CLEVIS
FRT
CABLE
RETAINER
CABLE
GROMMET
CABLE
GROMMET
A
CABLE
PARKING BRAKE
LEVER ASM
TRANSMISSION
SUPPORT
EQUALIZER (MUST BE
INSTALLED WITH "U"
SECTION DOWN)
PARKING
BRAKE
VIEW A
B
CABLE
NUT
11-16 N•m
CABLE
RETAINER
FRT
VIEW B
REAR
CABLE

Front parking brake cable

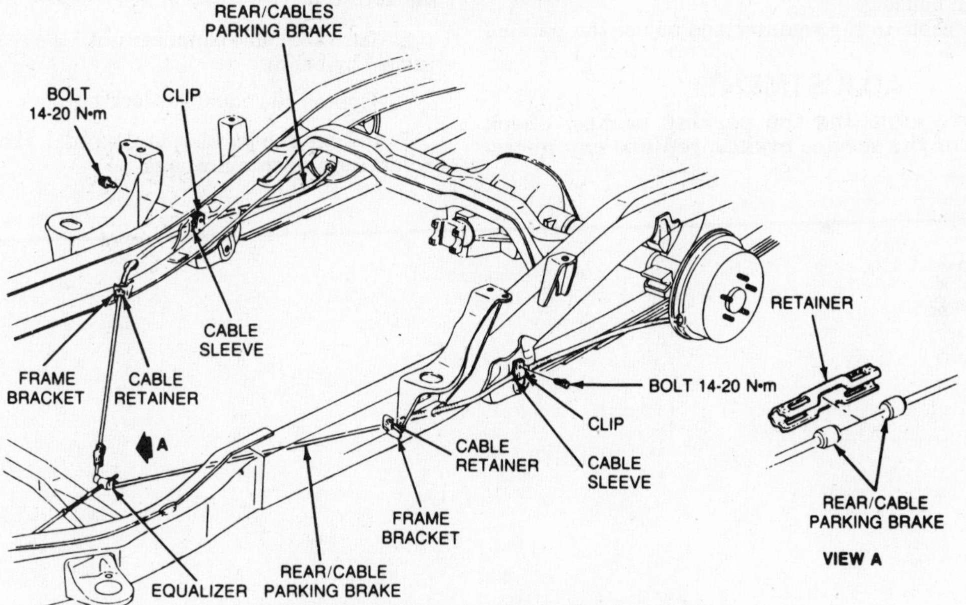
REAR/CABLES
PARKING BRAKE
BOLT
14-20 N•m
CLIP
CABLE
SLEEVE
FRAME
BRACKET
CABLE
RETAINER
A
RETAINER
BOLT 14-20 N•m
CLIP
CABLE
RETAINER
CABLE
SLEEVE
FRAME
BRACKET
REAR/CABLE
PARKING BRAKE
VIEW A
EQUALIZER
REAR/CABLE
PARKING BRAKE

Intermediate rear parking brake cable

ble, fish it through the cowl and connect it to the pedal assembly.

7. Attach the cable to the equalizer and secure it to the frame before adjusting the parking brake.

Rear Cable

REMOVAL AND INSTALLATION

Left and Right Rear Cables

1. Raise and safely support the rear of the vehicle on jackstands.
2. Under the left-center of the vehicle, loosen the cable equalizer assembly.
3. Separate the front-cable connector from the equalizer cable.

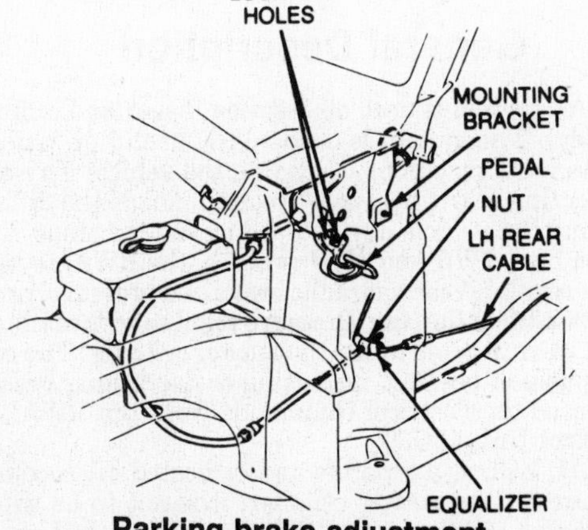
LOCATOR
HOLES
MOUNTING
BRACKET
PEDAL
NUT
LH REAR
CABLE
EQUALIZER

Parking brake adjustment

BRAKE SPECIFICATIONS

(All measurements are given in inches)

Master Cylinder Bore	Drum Brakes: Standard Drum Diameter	Drum Brakes: Maximum Drum Diameter	Drum Brakes: Minimum Lining Thickness	Disc Brakes: Minimum Rotor Thickness	Disc Brakes: Maximum Rotor Runout	Disc Brakes: Minimum Lining Thickness
0.945	9.500	9.560	0.062	0.980 ①	0.004	0.030

① Discard at 0.965

4. Refer to the "Brake Shoe, Removal and Installation" procedures in this section and remove the brake shoes.
5. At the backing plate, bend the cable retaining fingers.
6. Disconnect the rear cable from the secondary brake shoe and the cable from the vehicle.
7. When installing the cable, attach it to the brake shoe levers and assemble the brakes. Before installing the drums, pull the cable by hand and watch the parking brake action for smooth operation.
8. Secure the cable retainers at the frame brackets and the clips to the cable housing.
9. Attach the cable to the equilizer and adjust the parking brake.

ADJUSTMENT

NOTE: Before adjusting the parking brakes, check the condition of the service brakes; replace any necessary parts.

1. Block the front wheels.
2. Raise and safely support the rear of the vehicle on jackstands.
3. Under the left-center of the vehicle, loosen the equalizer.
4. On the 2WD model, position the parking brake pedal (ratchet) on the 8th click (1982–84) or 2nd click (1985–91); on the 4WD model, position the parking brake pedal (ratchet) on the 10th click (1983–84) or the 3rd click (1985–91).
5. Turn the cable equalizer until the rear wheel drags (when turned by hand).
6. Tighten the equalizer lock nut.
7. Release the parking brake pedal, then test it; the correct adjustment to specifications.

REAR WHEEL ANTILOCK (RWAL) SYSTEM

General Description

The RWAL system is used on S-series Blazer and Jimmy (S-10/S-15 body). The system is particularly useful on trucks because of the wide variations of loading the vehicle may experience. Preventing rear wheel lock-up often makes the difference in controlling the vehicle during hard or sudden stops.

Found on both 2WD and 4WD vehicles, the RWAL system is designed to regulate rear hydraulic brake line pressure, preventing wheel lock-up at the rear. Pressure regulation is managed by the control valve, located under the master cylinder. The control valve is capable of holding, increasing or decreasing brake line pressure based on electrical commands from the RWAL Electronic Control Unit (ECU).

The RWAL ECU is a separate and dedicated microcomputer mounted next to the master cylinder; it is not to be confused with the engine management ECU. The RWAL ECU receives signals from the speed sensor. The speed sensor sends its signals to the Digital Ratio Adapter Controller (DRAC) within the instrument cluster. The RWAL ECU reads this signal and commands the control valve to function. If commanded to release pressure, the dump valve within the control valve releases pressurized fluid into the accumulator where it is held under pressure. If a pressure increase is called for, the isolator valve within the control valve pulses, releasing pressurized fluid into the system.

The RWAL system is connected to the BRAKE warning lamp on the instrument cluster. A RWAL self-check and a bulb test are performed every time the ignition switch is turned to **ON**. The BRAKE warning lamp should illuminate for about 2 seconds and then go off. Problems within the RWAL system will be indicated by the BRAKE warning lamp staying illuminated.

If a fault is detected within the system, the RWAL ECU will

assign a fault code and store the code in memory. The code may be read to aid in diagnosis.

SYSTEM COMPONENTS

No component of the RWAL system can be disassembled or repaired. Should the RWAL ECU, the control valve containing the isolation/dump valve or the speed sensor fail, it must be replaced as an assembly. If the axle ratio or tire size is changed on the vehicle, the speedometer must be recalibrated.

Circuit Maintenance

All electrical connections must be kept clean and tight. Make certain that all connectors are properly seated and all of the sealing rings on weather-proof connectors are in place. The low current and/or voltage found in some circuits require that every connection be the best possible. Special tools are required for servicing the GM Weather–Pack and Metri–Pack connectors. Use terminal remover tool J–28742 or equivalent for Weather–Pack and J–35689-A or equivalent for Metri–Pack connectors.

If removal of a terminal is attempted with a regular pick, there is a good chance that the terminal will be bent or deformed. Once damaged, these connectors cannot be straightened.

Use care when probing the connections or replacing terminals; it is possible to short between adjacent terminals, causing component damage. Always use jumper wires between circuit connectors for testing circuits; never probe through weatherproof seals on connectors.

Oxidation or terminal misalignment may be hidden by the connector shell. When diagnosing open or intermittent circuits, wiggling the wire harness at the connector or component may reveal or correct the condition. When the location of the fault is identified, the connector should be separated and the problem corrected. Never disconnect a harness connector with the ignition **ON**.

NOTE: When working with the RWAL ECU connectors, do not touch the connections or pins with the fingers. Do not allow the connectors or pins to contact brake fluid; internal damage to the RWAL ECU will occur.

Diagnosis and Testing

SYSTEM PRECAUTIONS

- If the vehicle is equipped with airbag (SIR) system, always properly disable the system before commencing work on the ABS system.
- Certain components within the RWAL system are not intended to be serviced or repaired. Only those components with removal and installation procedures should be serviced.
- Do not use rubber hoses or other parts not specifically specified for the RWAL system. When using repair kits, replace all parts included in the kit. Partial or incorrect repair may lead to functional problems.
- Lubricate rubber parts with clean, fresh brake fluid to ease assembly. Do not use lubricated shop air to clean parts; damage to rubber components may result.
- Use only brake fluid from an unopened container. Use of suspect or contaminated brake fluid can reduce system performance and/or durability.
- A clean repair area is essential. Perform repairs after components have been thoroughly cleaned; use only denatured alcohol to clean components. Do not allow components to come into contact with any substance containing mineral oil; this includes used shop rags.
- The RWAL ECU is a microprocessor similar to other computer units in the vehicle. Insure that the ignition switch is **OFF** before removing or installing controller harnesses. Avoid static electricity discharge at or near the controller.
- Never disconnect any electrical connection with the ignition switch **ON** unless instructed to do so in a test.
- Always wear a grounded wrist strap when servicing any control module or component labeled with a Electrostatic Discharge (ESD) symbol.
- Avoid touching module connector pins.
- Leave new components and modules in the shipping package until ready to install them.
- To avoid static discharge, always touch a vehicle ground after sliding across a vehicle seat or walking across carpeted or vinyl floors.
- Never allow welding cables to lie on, near or across any vehicle electrical wiring. When doing any electric welding on the

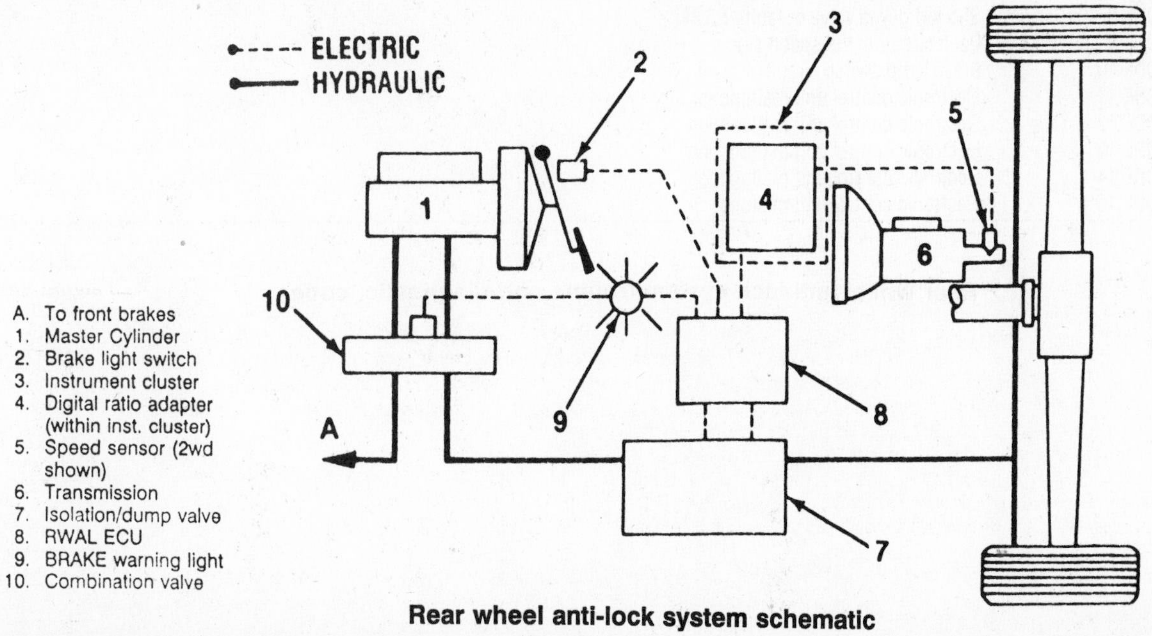
ELECTRIC
HYDRAULIC
1
2
3
4
5
6
7
8
9
10
A
A. To front brakes
1. Master Cylinder
2. Brake light switch
3. Instrument cluster
4. Digital ratio adapter (within inst. cluster)
5. Speed sensor (2wd shown)
6. Transmission
7. Isolation/dump valve
8. RWAL ECU
9. BRAKE warning light
10. Combination valve

Rear wheel anti-lock system schematic

vehicle, disconnect the negative battery cable and all ECUs connectors.

- Do not allow extension cords for power tools or droplights to lie on, near or across any vehicle electrical wiring.

PRELIMINARY DIAGNOSIS

Before reading trouble codes, perform the Diagnostic Circuit Check according to the chart. This test will aid in separating RWAL system problems from common problems in the hydraulic brake system. The diagnostic circuit check will direct the reading of trouble codes as necessary.

READING TROUBLE CODES

The RWAL ECU will assign a code to the first fault found in the system. If there is more than 1 fault, only the first recognized code will the stored and transmitted.

Trouble codes are read by connecting a jumper wire from pin H on ALDL to pin A; the fault code will be displayed through the flashing of the BRAKE warning lamp on the dash. The terminals must be connected for about 20 seconds before the display begins. The display will begin with 1 long flash followed by shorter ones—count the long flash as part of the display.

NOTE: Sometimes the first display sequence will be inaccurate or short; subsequent displays will be accurate.

SYSTEM FILLING

The master cylinder is filled in the usual manner with no special procedures being necessary. Only DOT 3 brake fluid must be used; silicone or DOT 5 fluid is specifically prohibited. Do not use any fluid which contains a petroleum base; these fluids will cause swelling and distortion of the rubber parts within the system. Do not use old or contaminated brake fluid.

SYSTEM BLEEDING

The brake system is bled in the usual manner with no special procedures required because of the RWAL system. The use of a power bleeder is recommended but the system may also be bled manually. If a power bleeder is used, it must be of the diaphragm type and provide isolation of the fluid from air and moisture.

Do not pump the pedal rapidly when bleeding; this can make the circuits very difficult to bleed. Instead, press the brake pedal slowly 1 time and hold it down while bleeding takes place. Tighten the bleeder screw, release the pedal and wait 15 seconds before repeating the sequence. Because of the length of the brake lines and other factors, it may take 10 or more repetitions of the sequence to bleed each line properly. When necessary to bleed all 4 wheels, the correct order is right rear, left rear, right front and left front.

CAUTION

Do not move the vehicle until a firm brake pedal is achieved. Failure to properly bleed the system may cause impaired braking and the possibility of injury and/or property damage

CODE	SYSTEM PROBLEM
CODE 1	Electronic control unit malfunction
CODE 2	Open isolation valve or faulty ECU
CODE 3	Open dump valve or faulty ECU
CODE 4	Grounded antilock valve switch
CODE 5	Excessive actuations of dump valve during an antilock stop
CODE 6	Erratic speed signal
CODE 7	Shorted isolation valve or faulty ECU
CODE 8	Shorted dump valve or faulty ECU
CODE 9	Open circuit to the speed signal
CODE 10	Brake lamp switch circuit
CODE 11	Electronic control unit malfunction
CODE 12	Electronic control unit malfunction
CODE 13	Electronic control unit malfunction
CODE 14	Electronic control unit malfunction
CODE 15	Electronic control unit malfunction

Rear wheel anti-lock system trouble and diagnostic codes

DIAGNOSTIC CIRCUIT CHECK

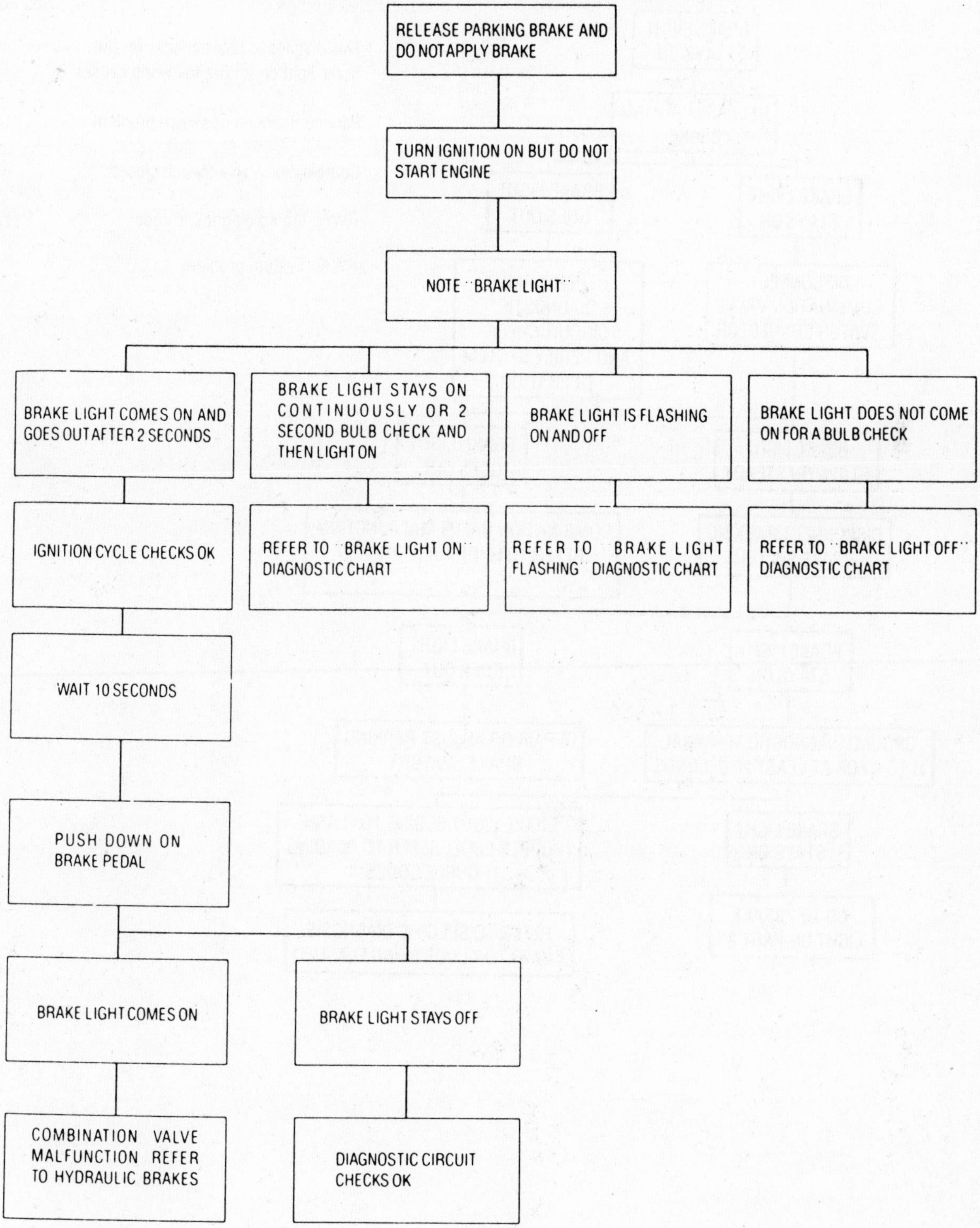
RELEASE PARKING BRAKE AND DO NOT APPLY BRAKE
TURN IGNITION ON BUT DO NOT START ENGINE
NOTE "BRAKE LIGHT"
BRAKE LIGHT COMES ON AND GOES OUT AFTER 2 SECONDS
BRAKE LIGHT STAYS ON CONTINUOUSLY OR 2 SECOND BULB CHECK AND THEN LIGHT ON
BRAKE LIGHT IS FLASHING ON AND OFF
BRAKE LIGHT DOES NOT COME ON FOR A BULB CHECK
IGNITION CYCLE CHECKS OK
REFER TO "BRAKE LIGHT ON" DIAGNOSTIC CHART
REFER TO "BRAKE LIGHT FLASHING" DIAGNOSTIC CHART
REFER TO "BRAKE LIGHT OFF" DIAGNOSTIC CHART
WAIT 10 SECONDS
PUSH DOWN ON BRAKE PEDAL
BRAKE LIGHT COMES ON
BRAKE LIGHT STAYS OFF
COMBINATION VALVE MALFUNCTION REFER TO HYDRAULIC BRAKES
DIAGNOSTIC CIRCUIT CHECKS OK

BRAKE LIGHT ON — PART 1

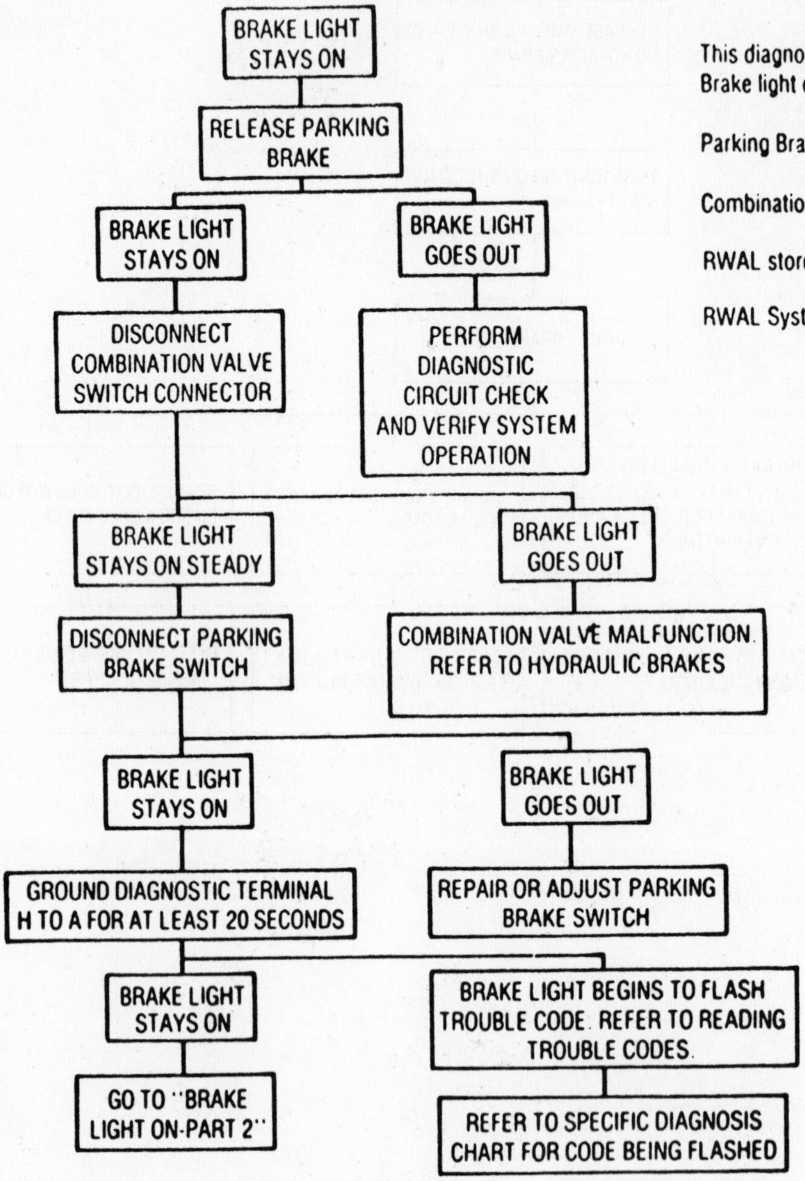
BRAKE LIGHT STAYS ON
RELEASE PARKING BRAKE
BRAKE LIGHT STAYS ON
BRAKE LIGHT GOES OUT
DISCONNECT COMBINATION VALVE SWITCH CONNECTOR
PERFORM DIAGNOSTIC CIRCUIT CHECK AND VERIFY SYSTEM OPERATION
BRAKE LIGHT STAYS ON STEADY
BRAKE LIGHT GOES OUT
DISCONNECT PARKING BRAKE SWITCH
COMBINATION VALVE MALFUNCTION. REFER TO HYDRAULIC BRAKES
BRAKE LIGHT STAYS ON
BRAKE LIGHT GOES OUT
GROUND DIAGNOSTIC TERMINAL H TO A FOR AT LEAST 20 SECONDS
REPAIR OR ADJUST PARKING BRAKE SWITCH
BRAKE LIGHT STAYS ON
BRAKE LIGHT BEGINS TO FLASH TROUBLE CODE. REFER TO READING TROUBLE CODES.
GO TO "BRAKE LIGHT ON-PART 2"
REFER TO SPECIFIC DIAGNOSIS CHART FOR CODE BEING FLASHED

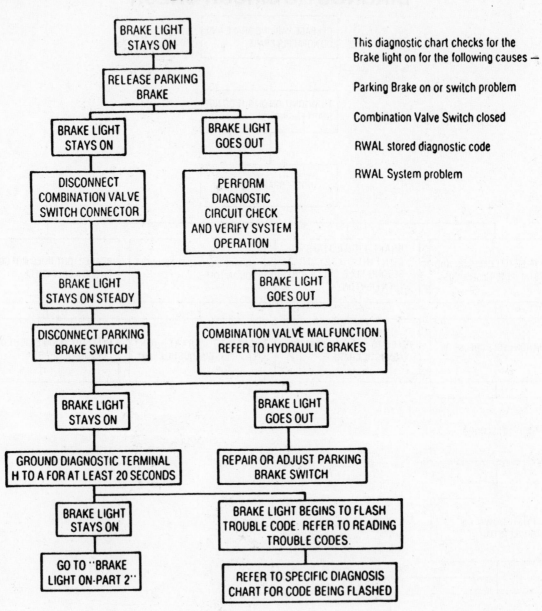

This diagnostic chart checks for the Brake light on for the following causes —

Parking Brake on or switch problem

Combination Valve Switch closed

RWAL stored diagnostic code

RWAL System problem

BRAKE LIGHT ON — PART 2

This diagnostic chart checks for the Brake light on for the following causes —

No Speed Signal voltage to ECU

RWAL system or wiring problem

Faulty ECU

NOTE: If voltage readings are low or varying, check battery and charging system or check for intermittent connections

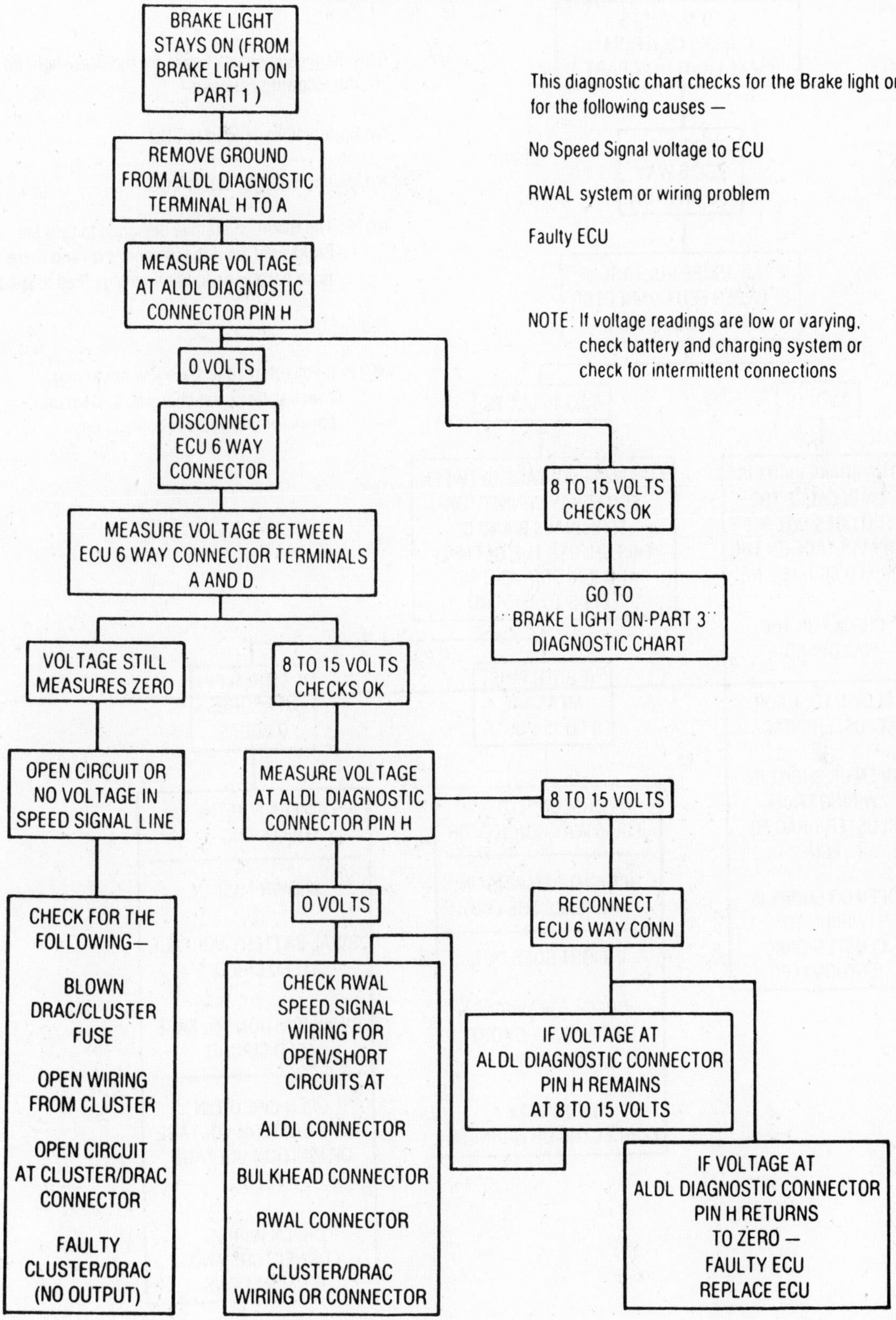
BRAKE LIGHT STAYS ON (FROM BRAKE LIGHT ON PART 1)
REMOVE GROUND FROM ALDL DIAGNOSTIC TERMINAL H TO A
MEASURE VOLTAGE AT ALDL DIAGNOSTIC CONNECTOR PIN H
0 VOLTS
8 TO 15 VOLTS CHECKS OK
GO TO "BRAKE LIGHT ON-PART 3" DIAGNOSTIC CHART
DISCONNECT ECU 6 WAY CONNECTOR
MEASURE VOLTAGE BETWEEN ECU 6 WAY CONNECTOR TERMINALS A AND D
VOLTAGE STILL MEASURES ZERO
8 TO 15 VOLTS CHECKS OK
OPEN CIRCUIT OR NO VOLTAGE IN SPEED SIGNAL LINE
MEASURE VOLTAGE AT ALDL DIAGNOSTIC CONNECTOR PIN H
8 TO 15 VOLTS
0 VOLTS
RECONNECT ECU 6 WAY CONN
CHECK FOR THE FOLLOWING—
BLOWN DRAC/CLUSTER FUSE
OPEN WIRING FROM CLUSTER
OPEN CIRCUIT AT CLUSTER/DRAC CONNECTOR
FAULTY CLUSTER/DRAC (NO OUTPUT)
CHECK RWAL SPEED SIGNAL WIRING FOR OPEN/SHORT CIRCUITS AT
ALDL CONNECTOR
BULKHEAD CONNECTOR
RWAL CONNECTOR
CLUSTER/DRAC WIRING OR CONNECTOR
IF VOLTAGE AT ALDL DIAGNOSTIC CONNECTOR PIN H REMAINS AT 8 TO 15 VOLTS
IF VOLTAGE AT ALDL DIAGNOSTIC CONNECTOR PIN H RETURNS TO ZERO — FAULTY ECU REPLACE ECU

BRAKE LIGHT ON — PART 3

This diagnostic chart checks for the Brake light on for the following causes –

No Battery voltage feed to ECU

No Ignition voltage feed to ECU

NOTE: The RWAL system is designed to turn the Brake light on if the ignition is on and there is no battery or ignition voltage feed to the ECU.

Faulty ECU

NOTE: If voltage readings are low or varying, check battery and charging system or check for intermittent connections

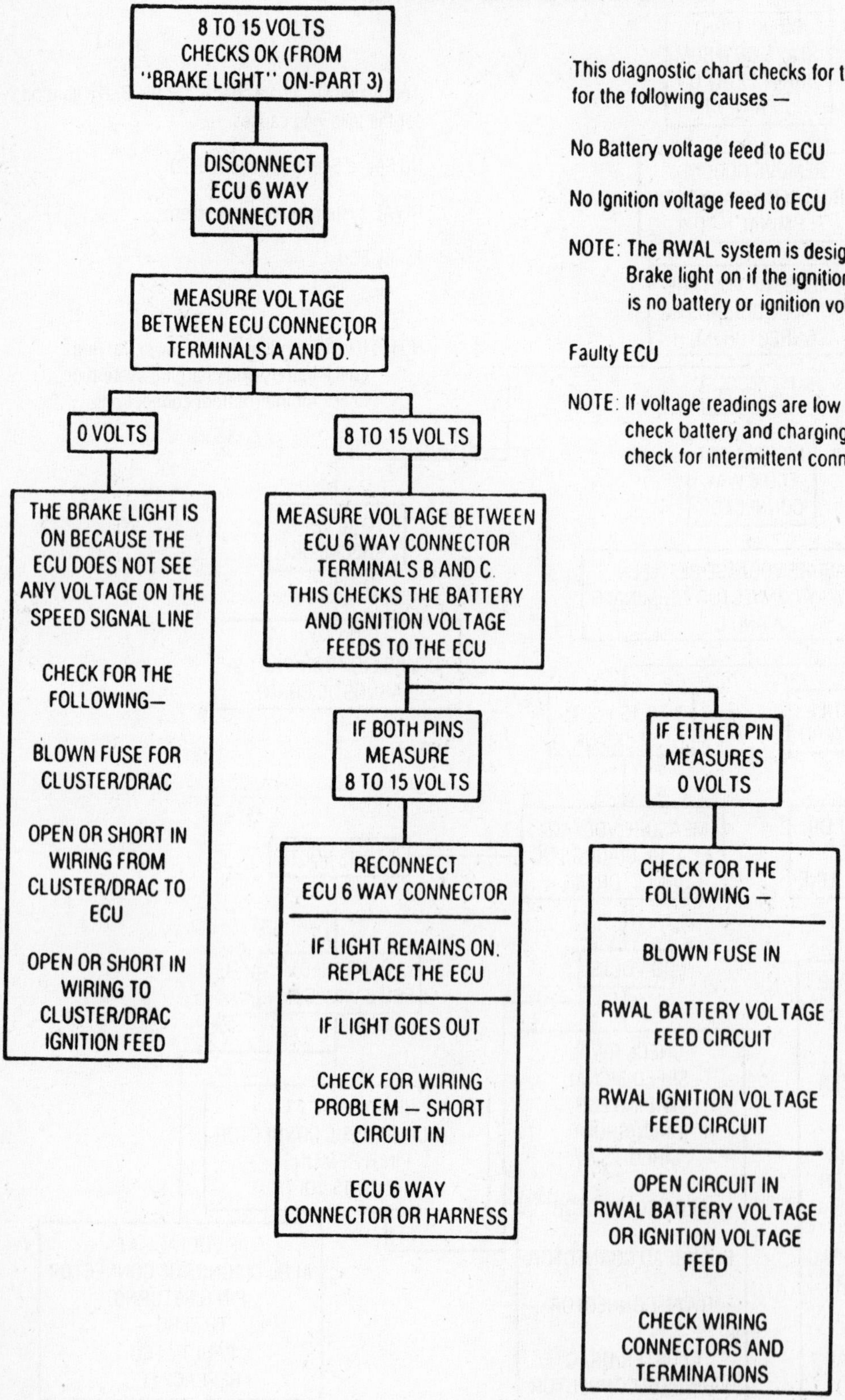
8 TO 15 VOLTS CHECKS OK (FROM "BRAKE LIGHT" ON-PART 3)
DISCONNECT ECU 6 WAY CONNECTOR
MEASURE VOLTAGE BETWEEN ECU CONNECTOR TERMINALS A AND D.
0 VOLTS
8 TO 15 VOLTS
THE BRAKE LIGHT IS ON BECAUSE THE ECU DOES NOT SEE ANY VOLTAGE ON THE SPEED SIGNAL LINE
CHECK FOR THE FOLLOWING–
BLOWN FUSE FOR CLUSTER/DRAC
OPEN OR SHORT IN WIRING FROM CLUSTER/DRAC TO ECU
OPEN OR SHORT IN WIRING TO CLUSTER/DRAC IGNITION FEED
MEASURE VOLTAGE BETWEEN ECU 6 WAY CONNECTOR TERMINALS B AND C. THIS CHECKS THE BATTERY AND IGNITION VOLTAGE FEEDS TO THE ECU
IF BOTH PINS MEASURE 8 TO 15 VOLTS
IF EITHER PIN MEASURES 0 VOLTS
RECONNECT ECU 6 WAY CONNECTOR
IF LIGHT REMAINS ON, REPLACE THE ECU
IF LIGHT GOES OUT
CHECK FOR WIRING PROBLEM – SHORT CIRCUIT IN
ECU 6 WAY CONNECTOR OR HARNESS
CHECK FOR THE FOLLOWING –
BLOWN FUSE IN
RWAL BATTERY VOLTAGE FEED CIRCUIT
RWAL IGNITION VOLTAGE FEED CIRCUIT
OPEN CIRCUIT IN RWAL BATTERY VOLTAGE OR IGNITION VOLTAGE FEED
CHECK WIRING CONNECTORS AND TERMINATIONS

BRAKE LIGHT FLASHING

This diagnostic chart checks for the Brake light flashing for the following causes -

Intermittent Speed Signal voltage tothe ECU

RWAL system problem (stored code)

NOTE: If voltage readings are low or varying, check battery and charging system or check for intermittent connections

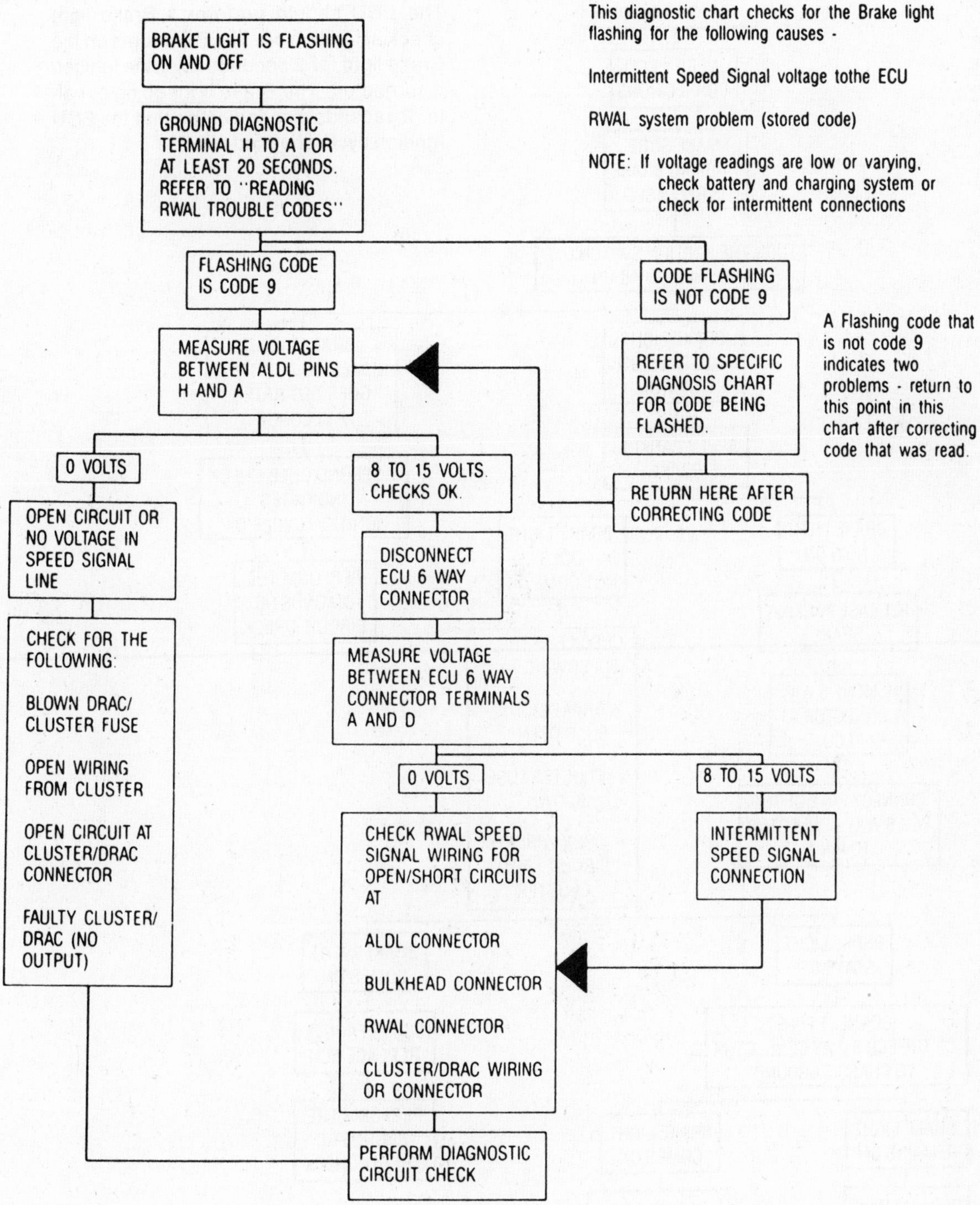
BRAKE LIGHT IS FLASHING ON AND OFF
GROUND DIAGNOSTIC TERMINAL H TO A FOR AT LEAST 20 SECONDS. REFER TO "READING RWAL TROUBLE CODES"
FLASHING CODE IS CODE 9
CODE FLASHING IS NOT CODE 9
REFER TO SPECIFIC DIAGNOSIS CHART FOR CODE BEING FLASHED.
A Flashing code that is not code 9 indicates two problems - return to this point in this chart after correcting code that was read.
RETURN HERE AFTER CORRECTING CODE
MEASURE VOLTAGE BETWEEN ALDL PINS H AND A
0 VOLTS
8 TO 15 VOLTS. CHECKS OK.
OPEN CIRCUIT OR NO VOLTAGE IN SPEED SIGNAL LINE
CHECK FOR THE FOLLOWING:
BLOWN DRAC/ CLUSTER FUSE
OPEN WIRING FROM CLUSTER
OPEN CIRCUIT AT CLUSTER/DRAC CONNECTOR
FAULTY CLUSTER/ DRAC (NO OUTPUT)
DISCONNECT ECU 6 WAY CONNECTOR
MEASURE VOLTAGE BETWEEN ECU 6 WAY CONNECTOR TERMINALS A AND D
0 VOLTS
8 TO 15 VOLTS
CHECK RWAL SPEED SIGNAL WIRING FOR OPEN/SHORT CIRCUITS AT
ALDL CONNECTOR
BULKHEAD CONNECTOR
RWAL CONNECTOR
CLUSTER/DRAC WIRING OR CONNECTOR
INTERMITTENT SPEED SIGNAL CONNECTION
PERFORM DIAGNOSTIC CIRCUIT CHECK

BRAKE LIGHT OFF

The ECU should perform a Brake light check at Ignition on. The ECU turns on the Brake light for 2 seconds after the ignition is turned on. The Brake light going out after 2 seconds also indicates that the ECU Ignition cycle checked ok.

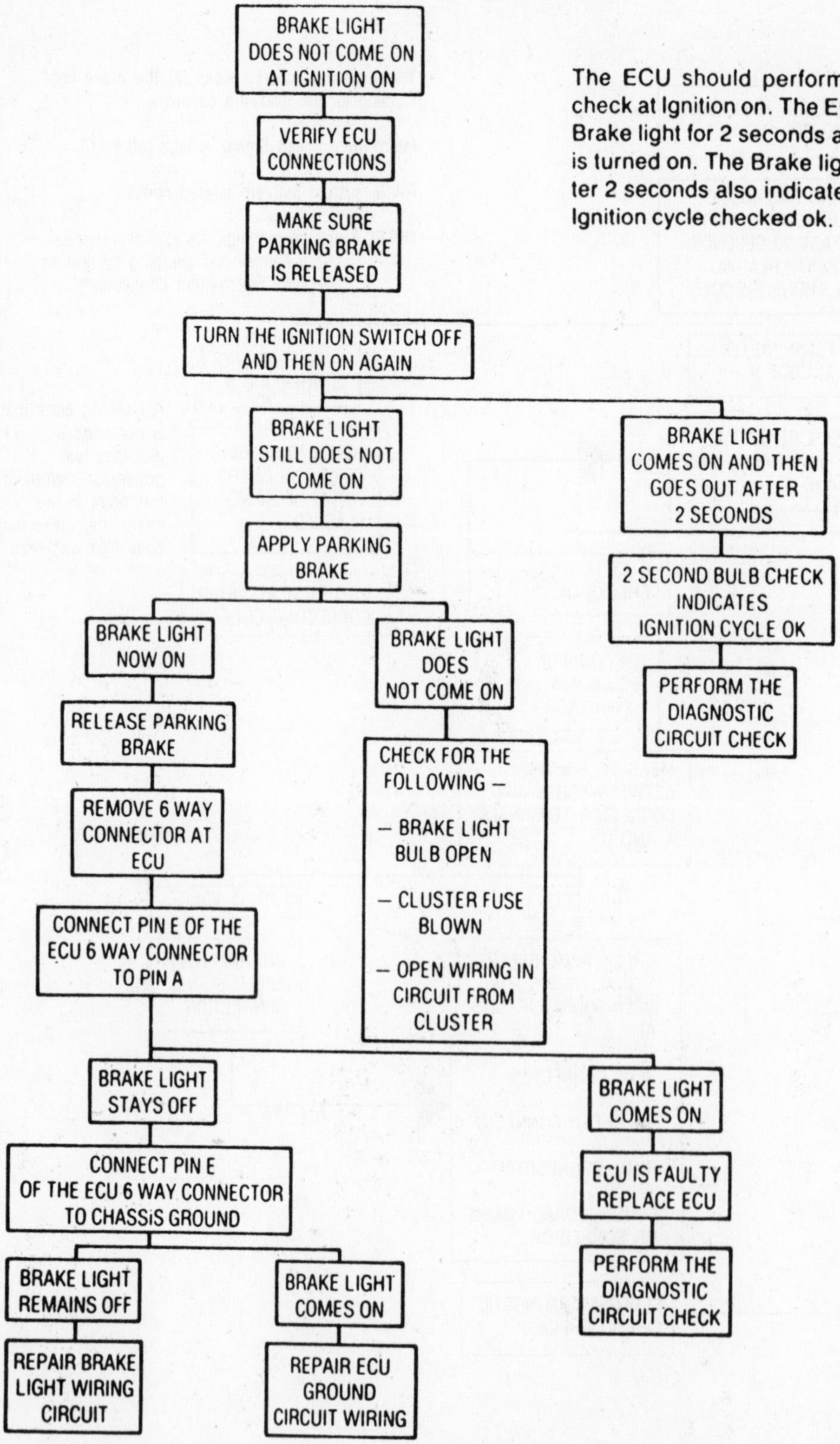
BRAKE LIGHT DOES NOT COME ON AT IGNITION ON
VERIFY ECU CONNECTIONS
MAKE SURE PARKING BRAKE IS RELEASED
TURN THE IGNITION SWITCH OFF AND THEN ON AGAIN
BRAKE LIGHT STILL DOES NOT COME ON
BRAKE LIGHT COMES ON AND THEN GOES OUT AFTER 2 SECONDS
2 SECOND BULB CHECK INDICATES IGNITION CYCLE OK
PERFORM THE DIAGNOSTIC CIRCUIT CHECK
APPLY PARKING BRAKE
BRAKE LIGHT NOW ON
BRAKE LIGHT DOES NOT COME ON
RELEASE PARKING BRAKE
REMOVE 6 WAY CONNECTOR AT ECU
CONNECT PIN E OF THE ECU 6 WAY CONNECTOR TO PIN A
CHECK FOR THE FOLLOWING –
– BRAKE LIGHT BULB OPEN
– CLUSTER FUSE BLOWN
– OPEN WIRING IN CIRCUIT FROM CLUSTER
BRAKE LIGHT STAYS OFF
BRAKE LIGHT COMES ON
CONNECT PIN E OF THE ECU 6 WAY CONNECTOR TO CHASSIS GROUND
ECU IS FAULTY REPLACE ECU
PERFORM THE DIAGNOSTIC CIRCUIT CHECK
BRAKE LIGHT REMAINS OFF
BRAKE LIGHT COMES ON
REPAIR BRAKE LIGHT WIRING CIRCUIT
REPAIR ECU GROUND CIRCUIT WIRING

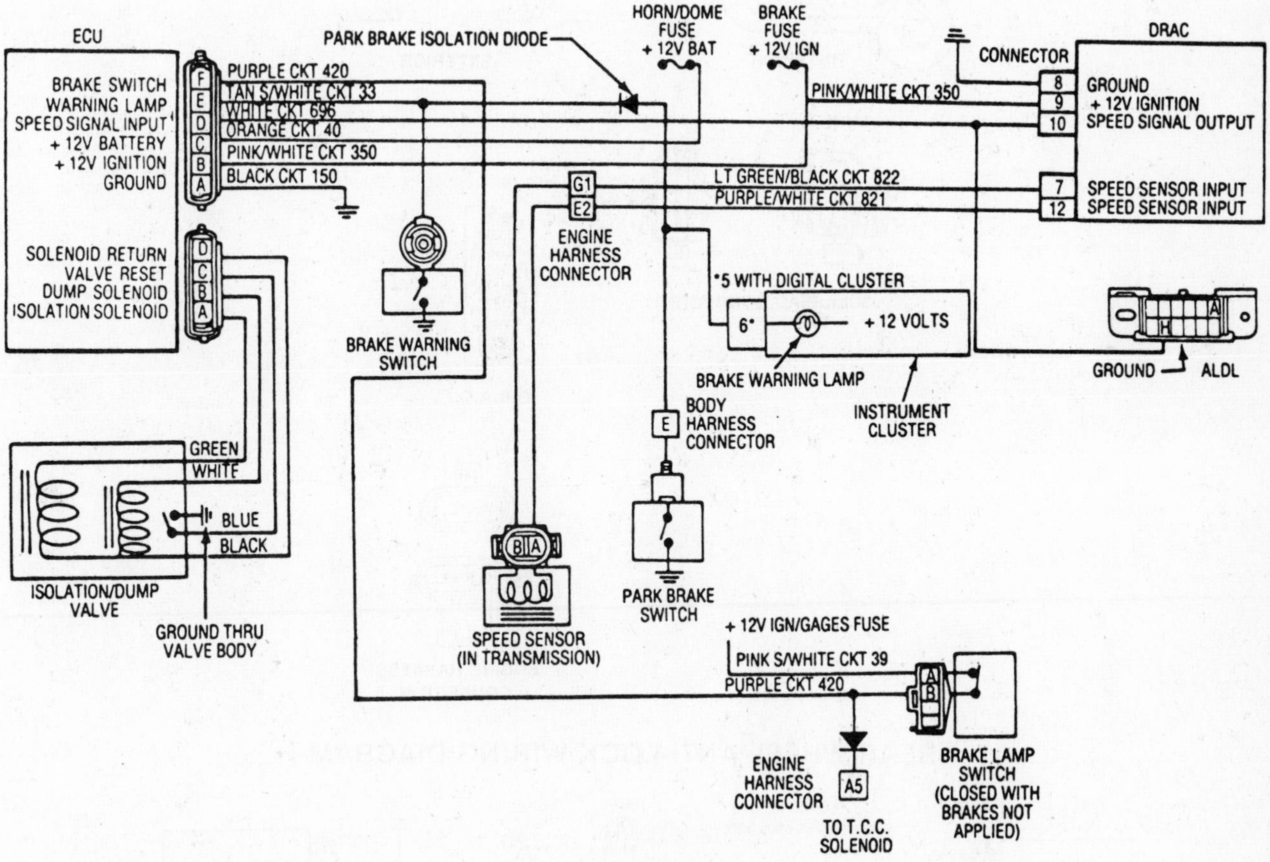
ECU
BRAKE SWITCH
WARNING LAMP
SPEED SIGNAL INPUT
+ 12V BATTERY
+ 12V IGNITION
GROUND
F
E
D
C
B
A
PURPLE CKT 420
TAN S/WHITE CKT 33
WHITE CKT 696
ORANGE CKT 40
PINK/WHITE CKT 350
BLACK CKT 150
PARK BRAKE ISOLATION DIODE
HORN/DOME FUSE + 12V BAT
BRAKE FUSE + 12V IGN
CONNECTOR
DRAC
PINK/WHITE CKT 350
8
9
10
GROUND
+ 12V IGNITION
SPEED SIGNAL OUTPUT
G1
E2
LT GREEN/BLACK CKT 822
PURPLE/WHITE CKT 821
7
12
SPEED SENSOR INPUT
SPEED SENSOR INPUT
SOLENOID RETURN
VALVE RESET
DUMP SOLENOID
ISOLATION SOLENOID
ENGINE HARNESS CONNECTOR
*5 WITH DIGITAL CLUSTER
6*
+ 12 VOLTS
BRAKE WARNING SWITCH
BRAKE WARNING LAMP
INSTRUMENT CLUSTER
GROUND
ALDL
BODY HARNESS CONNECTOR
E
GREEN
WHITE
BLUE
BLACK
ISOLATION/DUMP VALVE
GROUND THRU VALVE BODY
PARK BRAKE SWITCH
SPEED SENSOR (IN TRANSMISSION)
+ 12V IGN/GAGES FUSE
PINK S/WHITE CKT 39
PURPLE CKT 420
ENGINE HARNESS CONNECTOR
A5
TO T.C.C. SOLENOID
BRAKE LAMP SWITCH (CLOSED WITH BRAKES NOT APPLIED)

Rear wheel anti-lock wiring diagram

REAR WHEEL ANTI-LOCK CONNECTORS

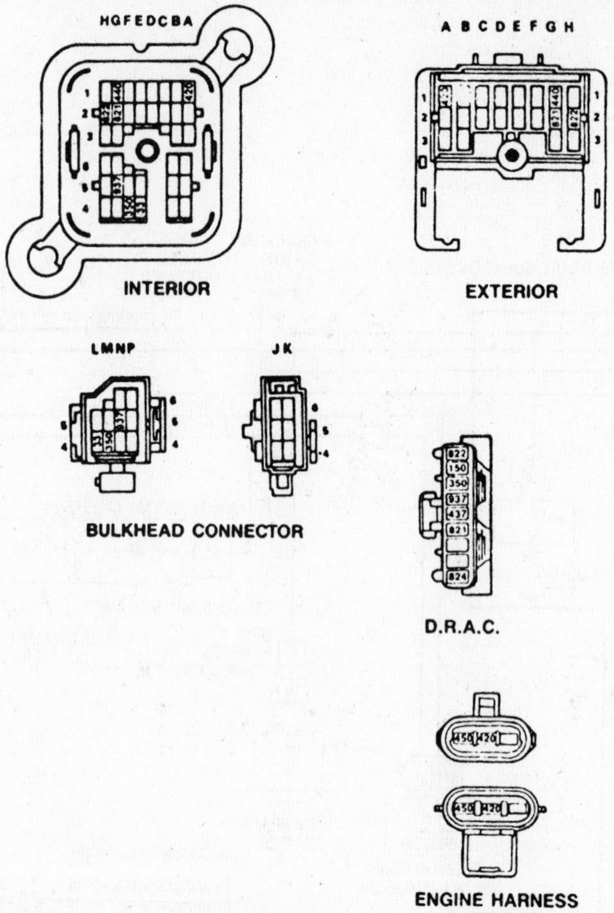
HGFEDCBA
ABCDEFGH
INTERIOR
EXTERIOR
LMNP
JK
BULKHEAD CONNECTOR
D.R.A.C.
ENGINE HARNESS CONNECTOR

REAR WHEEL ANTI-LOCK WIRING DIAGRAM

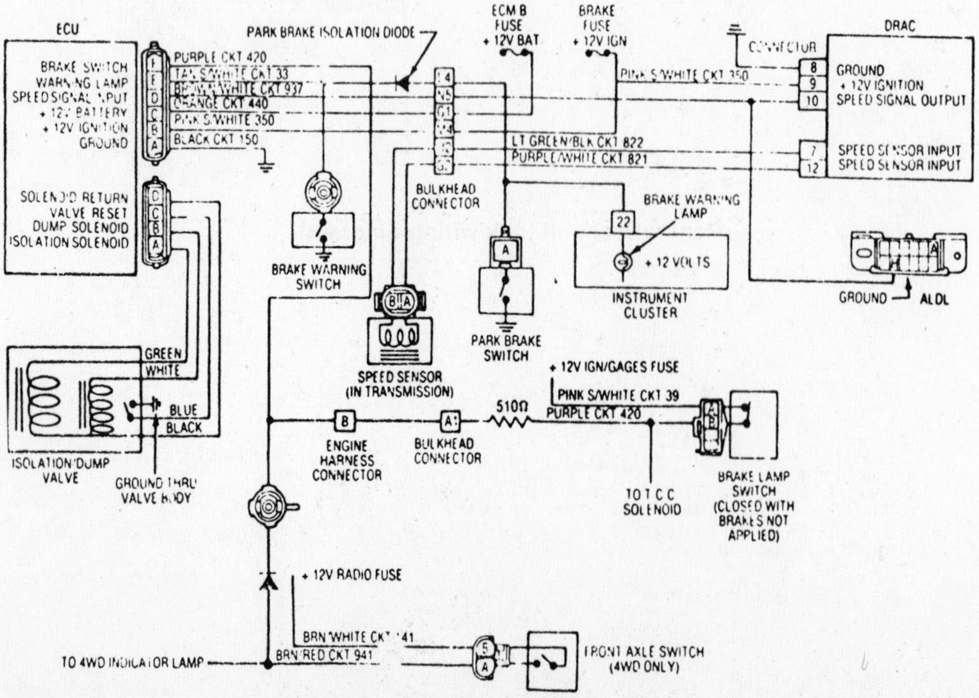
ECU
PARK BRAKE ISOLATION DIODE
ECM B FUSE + 12V BAT
BRAKE FUSE + 12V IGN
DRAC
BRAKE SWITCH
SPEED SIGNAL INPUT
+ 12V IGNITION
GROUND
PURPLE CKT 420
ORANGE CKT 440
PINK S/WHITE 350
BLACK CKT 150
GROUND
+ 12V IGNITION
SPEED SIGNAL OUTPUT
LT GREEN/BLK CKT 822
PURPLE/WHITE CKT 821
SPEED SENSOR INPUT
SPEED SENSOR INPUT
VALVE RESET
DUMP SOLENOID
ISOLATION SOLENOID
BULKHEAD CONNECTOR
BRAKE WARNING LAMP
+ 12 VOLTS
INSTRUMENT CLUSTER
BRAKE WARNING SWITCH
SPEED SENSOR (IN TRANSMISSION)
PARK BRAKE SWITCH
GROUND
ALDL
GREEN
WHITE
BLUE
BLACK
+ 12V IGN/GAGES FUSE
PINK S/WHITE CKT 39
PURPLE CKT 420
510Ω
ISOLATION/DUMP VALVE
ENGINE HARNESS CONNECTOR
BULKHEAD CONNECTOR
TO T C C SOLENOID
BRAKE LAMP SWITCH (CLOSED WITH BRAKES NOT APPLIED)
+ 12V RADIO FUSE
BRN/RED CKT 941
TO 4WD INDICATOR LAMP
FRONT AXLE SWITCH (4WD ONLY)

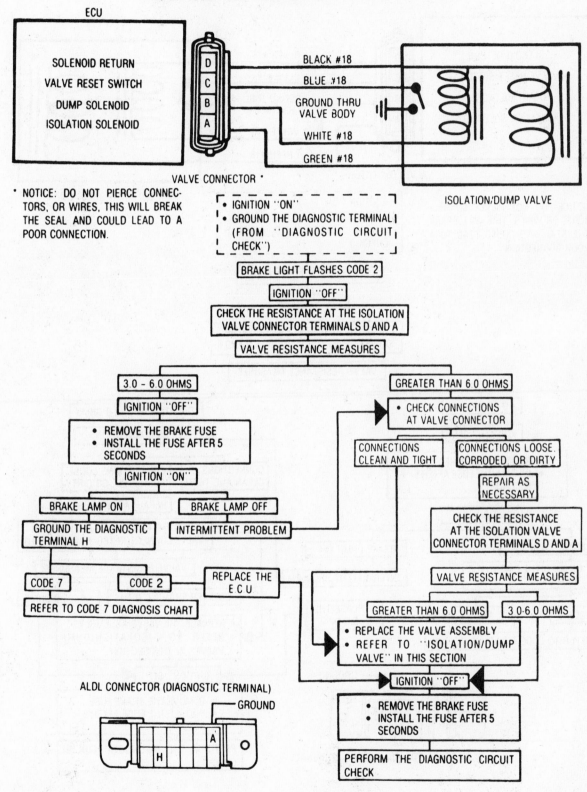

CODE 2
OPEN ISOLATION VALVE OR MALFUNCTIONING ECU

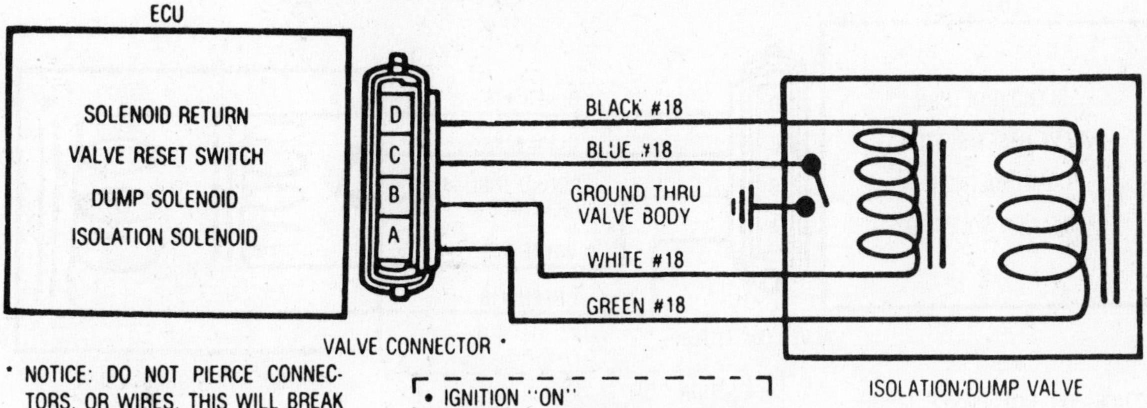
ECU
SOLENOID RETURN
VALVE RESET SWITCH
DUMP SOLENOID
ISOLATION SOLENOID
D
C
B
A
BLACK #18
BLUE #18
GROUND THRU VALVE BODY
WHITE #18
GREEN #18
VALVE CONNECTOR *
ISOLATION/DUMP VALVE

* NOTICE: DO NOT PIERCE CONNECTORS, OR WIRES, THIS WILL BREAK THE SEAL AND COULD LEAD TO A POOR CONNECTION.

- IGNITION "ON"
- GROUND THE DIAGNOSTIC TERMINAL (FROM "DIAGNOSTIC CIRCUIT CHECK")

BRAKE LIGHT FLASHES CODE 2

IGNITION "OFF"

CHECK THE RESISTANCE AT THE ISOLATION VALVE CONNECTOR TERMINALS D AND A

VALVE RESISTANCE MEASURES

3.0 - 6.0 OHMS

IGNITION "OFF"

- REMOVE THE BRAKE FUSE
- INSTALL THE FUSE AFTER 5 SECONDS

IGNITION "ON"

BRAKE LAMP ON → GROUND THE DIAGNOSTIC TERMINAL H
- CODE 7 → REFER TO CODE 7 DIAGNOSIS CHART
- CODE 2 → REPLACE THE E C U → IGNITION "OFF"

BRAKE LAMP OFF → INTERMITTENT PROBLEM → CHECK CONNECTIONS AT VALVE CONNECTOR

GREATER THAN 6.0 OHMS

- CHECK CONNECTIONS AT VALVE CONNECTOR

CONNECTIONS CLEAN AND TIGHT → REPLACE THE VALVE ASSEMBLY

CONNECTIONS LOOSE, CORRODED, OR DIRTY → REPAIR AS NECESSARY

CHECK THE RESISTANCE AT THE ISOLATION VALVE CONNECTOR TERMINALS D AND A

VALVE RESISTANCE MEASURES

GREATER THAN 6.0 OHMS:
- REPLACE THE VALVE ASSEMBLY
- REFER TO "ISOLATION/DUMP VALVE" IN THIS SECTION

3.0-6.0 OHMS → IGNITION "OFF"

IGNITION "OFF"

- REMOVE THE BRAKE FUSE
- INSTALL THE FUSE AFTER 5 SECONDS

PERFORM THE DIAGNOSTIC CIRCUIT CHECK

ALDL CONNECTOR (DIAGNOSTIC TERMINAL)

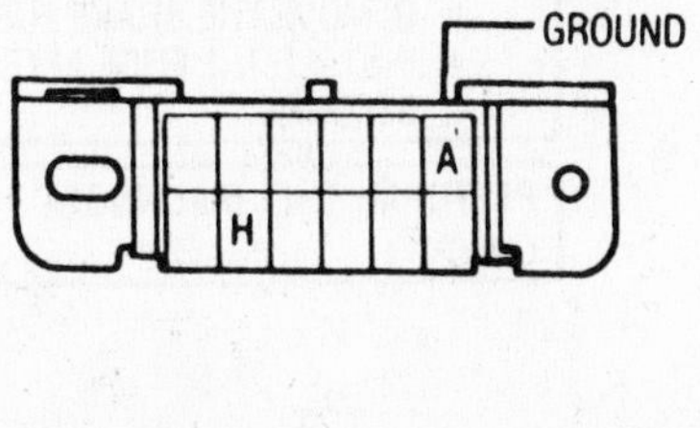
GROUND
A
H

CODE 3
OPEN DUMP VALVE OR MALFUNCTIONING ECU

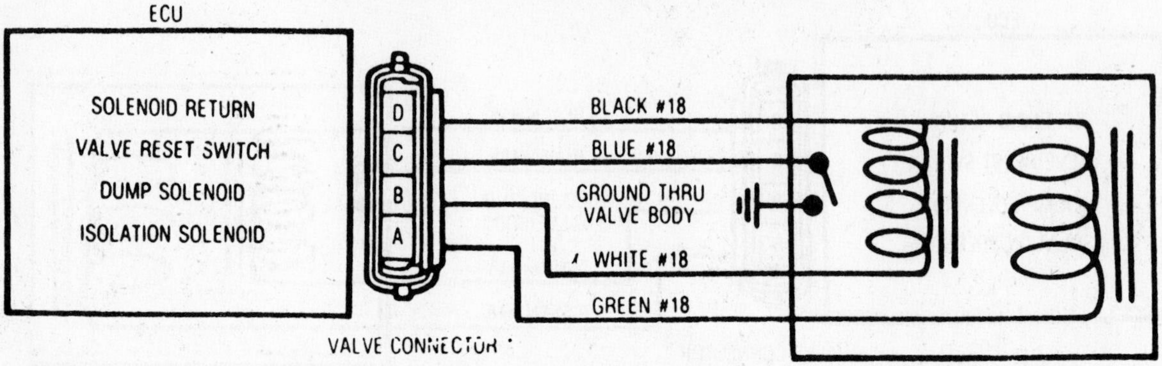
ECU
SOLENOID RETURN
VALVE RESET SWITCH
DUMP SOLENOID
ISOLATION SOLENOID
D
C
B
A
BLACK #18
BLUE #18
GROUND THRU VALVE BODY
WHITE #18
GREEN #18
VALVE CONNECTOR
ISOLATION/DUMP VALVE

NOTICE: DO NOT PIERCE CONNECTORS, OR WIRES, THIS WILL BREAK THE SEAL AND COULD LEAD TO A POOR CONNECTION.

- IGNITION "ON"
- GROUND THE DIAGNOSTIC TERMINAL (FROM "DIAGNOSTIC CIRCUIT CHECK")

BRAKE LIGHT FLASHES CODE 3

IGNITION "OFF"

CHECK THE RESISTANCE AT THE DUMP VALVE CONNECTOR TERMINALS D AND B

VALVE RESISTANCE MEASURES

1.0 - 3.0 OHMS

IGNITION "OFF"

- REMOVE THE BRAKE FUSE
- INSTALL THE FUSE AFTER 5 SECONDS

IGNITION "ON"

- BRAKE LAMP ON
  - GROUND THE DIAGNOSTIC TERMINAL
    - CODE 7: REFER TO CODE 7 DIAGNOSIS CHART
    - CODE 3: REPLACE THE E.C.U. → IGNITION "OFF"
- BRAKE LAMP OFF
  - INTERMITTENT PROBLEM → CHECK CONNECTIONS

GREATER THAN 3.0 OHMS

- CHECK CONNECTIONS

- CONNECTIONS CLEAN AND TIGHT → REPLACE THE VALVE ASSEMBLY
- CONNECTIONS LOOSE, CORRODED, OR DIRTY
  - REPAIR AS NECESSARY
  - CHECK THE RESISTANCE AT THE DUMP VALVE CONNECTOR TERMINALS D AND B
  - VALVE RESISTANCE MEASURES
    - GREATER THAN 3.0 OHMS:
      - REPLACE THE VALVE ASSEMBLY
      - REFER TO "ISOLATION/DUMP VALVE" IN THIS SECTION
    - 1.0 - 3.0 OHMS → IGNITION "OFF"

IGNITION "OFF"

- REMOVE THE BRAKE FUSE
- INSTALL THE FUSE AFTER 5 SECONDS

PERFORM THE DIAGNOSTIC CIRCUIT CHECK

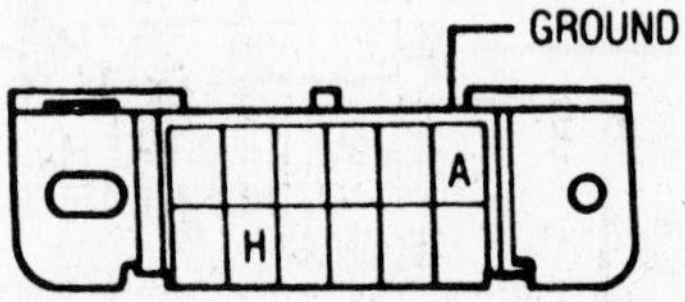
GROUND
A
H

ALDL CONNECTOR (DIAGNOSTIC TERMINAL)

CODE 4
GROUNDED ANTI-LOCK VALVE SWITCH

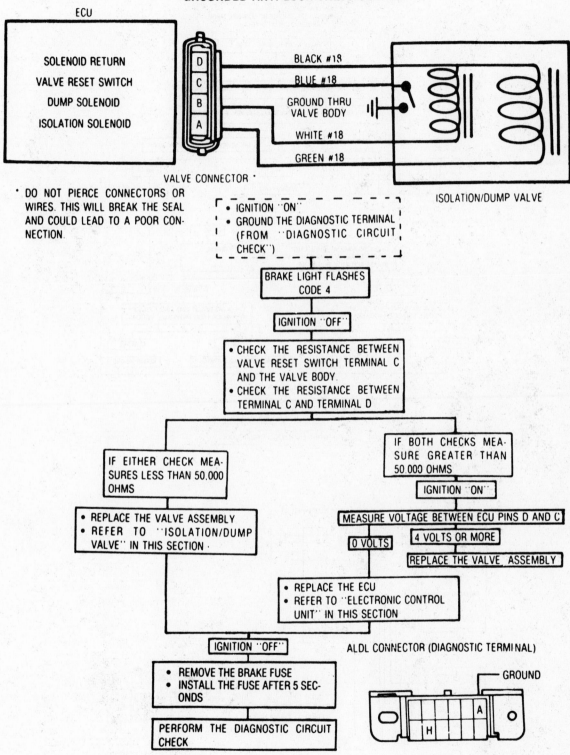

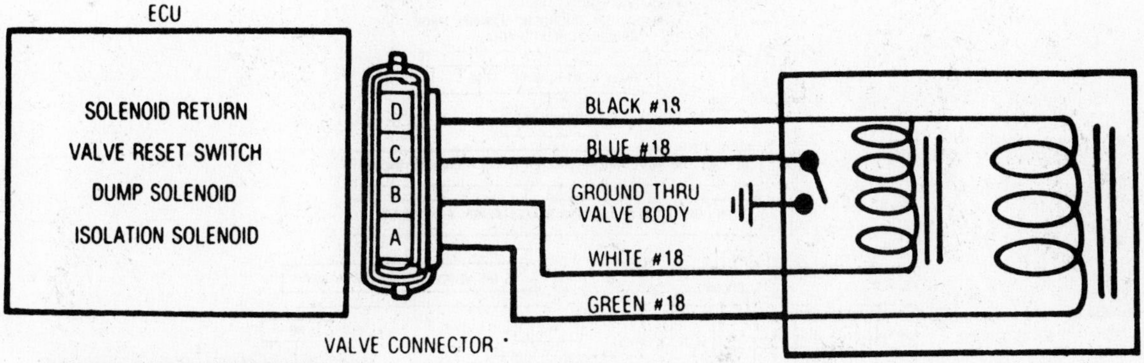
ECU
SOLENOID RETURN
VALVE RESET SWITCH
DUMP SOLENOID
ISOLATION SOLENOID
D
C
B
A
BLACK #18
BLUE #18
GROUND THRU VALVE BODY
WHITE #18
GREEN #18
VALVE CONNECTOR *
ISOLATION/DUMP VALVE

* DO NOT PIERCE CONNECTORS OR WIRES. THIS WILL BREAK THE SEAL AND COULD LEAD TO A POOR CONNECTION.

- IGNITION "ON"
- GROUND THE DIAGNOSTIC TERMINAL (FROM "DIAGNOSTIC CIRCUIT CHECK")

BRAKE LIGHT FLASHES CODE 4

IGNITION "OFF"

- CHECK THE RESISTANCE BETWEEN VALVE RESET SWITCH TERMINAL C AND THE VALVE BODY.
- CHECK THE RESISTANCE BETWEEN TERMINAL C AND TERMINAL D

IF EITHER CHECK MEASURES LESS THAN 50,000 OHMS

- REPLACE THE VALVE ASSEMBLY
- REFER TO "ISOLATION/DUMP VALVE" IN THIS SECTION

IF BOTH CHECKS MEASURE GREATER THAN 50,000 OHMS

IGNITION "ON"

MEASURE VOLTAGE BETWEEN ECU PINS D AND C

4 VOLTS OR MORE

REPLACE THE VALVE ASSEMBLY

0 VOLTS

- REPLACE THE ECU
- REFER TO "ELECTRONIC CONTROL UNIT" IN THIS SECTION

IGNITION "OFF"

- REMOVE THE BRAKE FUSE
- INSTALL THE FUSE AFTER 5 SECONDS

PERFORM THE DIAGNOSTIC CIRCUIT CHECK

ALDL CONNECTOR (DIAGNOSTIC TERMINAL)

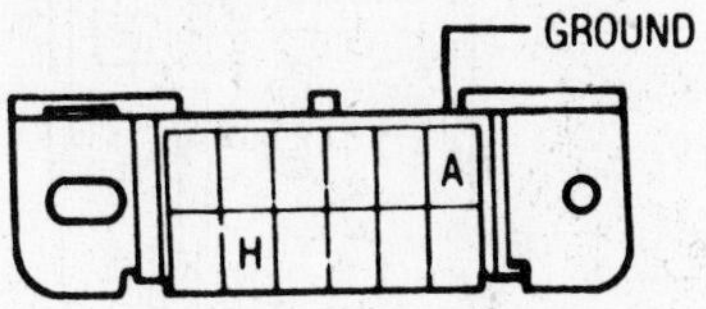
GROUND
A
H

CODE 5—EXCESSIVE ACTUATION OF DUMP VALVE DURING ANTI-LOCK STOP

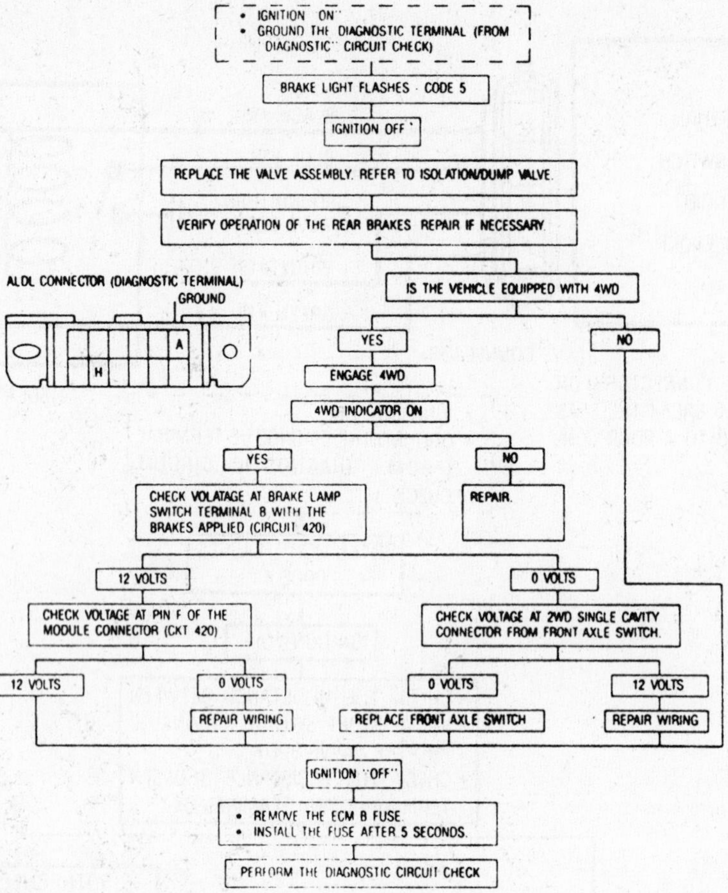
• IGNITION "ON"
• GROUND THE DIAGNOSTIC TERMINAL (FROM "DIAGNOSTIC" CIRCUIT CHECK)
BRAKE LIGHT FLASHES - CODE 5
IGNITION "OFF"
REPLACE THE VALVE ASSEMBLY. REFER TO ISOLATION/DUMP VALVE.
VERIFY OPERATION OF THE REAR BRAKES. REPAIR IF NECESSARY.
ALDL CONNECTOR (DIAGNOSTIC TERMINAL)
GROUND
A
H
IS THE VEHICLE EQUIPPED WITH 4WD
YES
NO
ENGAGE 4WD
4WD INDICATOR ON
YES
NO
CHECK VOLATAGE AT BRAKE LAMP SWITCH TERMINAL B WITH THE BRAKES APPLIED (CIRCUIT 420)
REPAIR.
12 VOLTS
0 VOLTS
CHECK VOLTAGE AT PIN F OF THE MODULE CONNECTOR (CKT 420)
CHECK VOLTAGE AT 2WD SINGLE CAVITY CONNECTOR FROM FRONT AXLE SWITCH.
12 VOLTS
0 VOLTS
REPAIR WIRING
0 VOLTS
REPLACE FRONT AXLE SWITCH
12 VOLTS
REPAIR WIRING
IGNITION "OFF"
• REMOVE THE ECM B FUSE.
• INSTALL THE FUSE AFTER 5 SECONDS.
PERFORM THE DIAGNOSTIC CIRCUIT CHECK

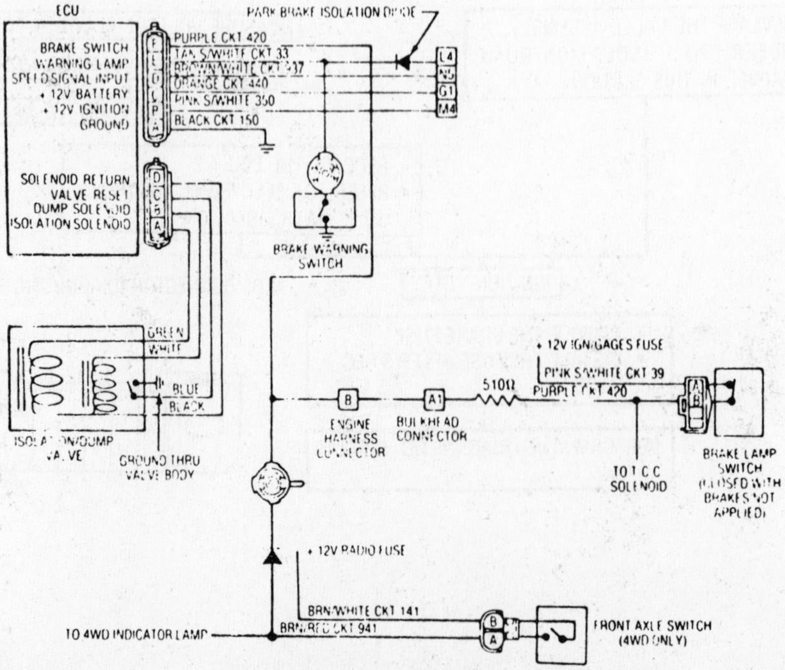
ECU
BRAKE SWITCH
WARNING LAMP
SPEED SIGNAL INPUT
+ 12V BATTERY
+ 12V IGNITION
GROUND
PARK BRAKE ISOLATION DIODE
PURPLE CKT 420
TAN S/WHITE CKT 33
ORANGE CKT 440
PINK S/WHITE 350
BLACK CKT 150
L4
G1
M4
SOLENOID RETURN
VALVE RESET
DUMP SOLENOID
ISOLATION SOLENOID
BRAKE WARNING SWITCH
GREEN
WHITE
BLUE
BLACK
ISOLATION/DUMP VALVE
GROUND THRU VALVE BODY
+ 12V IGN/GAGES FUSE
PINK S/WHITE CKT 39
510Ω
PURPLE CKT 420
B
A1
ENGINE HARNESS CONNECTOR
BULKHEAD CONNECTOR
TO T.C.C SOLENOID
BRAKE LAMP SWITCH (CLOSED WITH BRAKES NOT APPLIED)
+ 12V RADIO FUSE
BRN/WHITE CKT 141
TO 4WD INDICATOR LAMP
FRONT AXLE SWITCH (4WD ONLY)

CODE 5
EXCESSIVE ACTUATIONS OF THE DUMP VALVE DURING AN ANTI-LOCK STOP

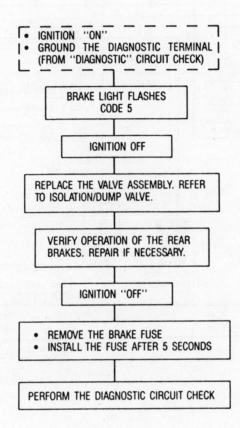

- IGNITION "ON"
- GROUND THE DIAGNOSTIC TERMINAL (FROM "DIAGNOSTIC" CIRCUIT CHECK)

BRAKE LIGHT FLASHES CODE 5

IGNITION OFF

REPLACE THE VALVE ASSEMBLY. REFER TO ISOLATION/DUMP VALVE.

VERIFY OPERATION OF THE REAR BRAKES. REPAIR IF NECESSARY.

IGNITION "OFF"

- REMOVE THE BRAKE FUSE
- INSTALL THE FUSE AFTER 5 SECONDS

PERFORM THE DIAGNOSTIC CIRCUIT CHECK

ALDL CONNECTOR (DIAGNOSTIC TERMINAL)

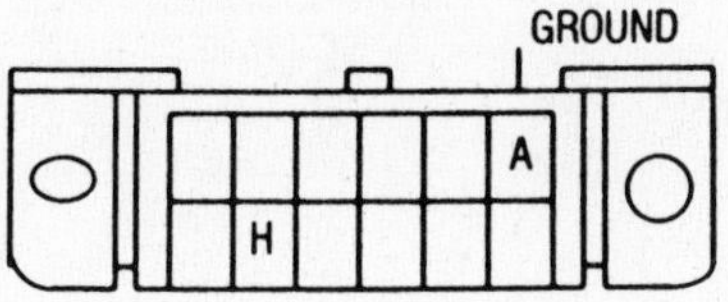
GROUND
A
H

CODE 6
ERRATIC SPEED SIGNAL

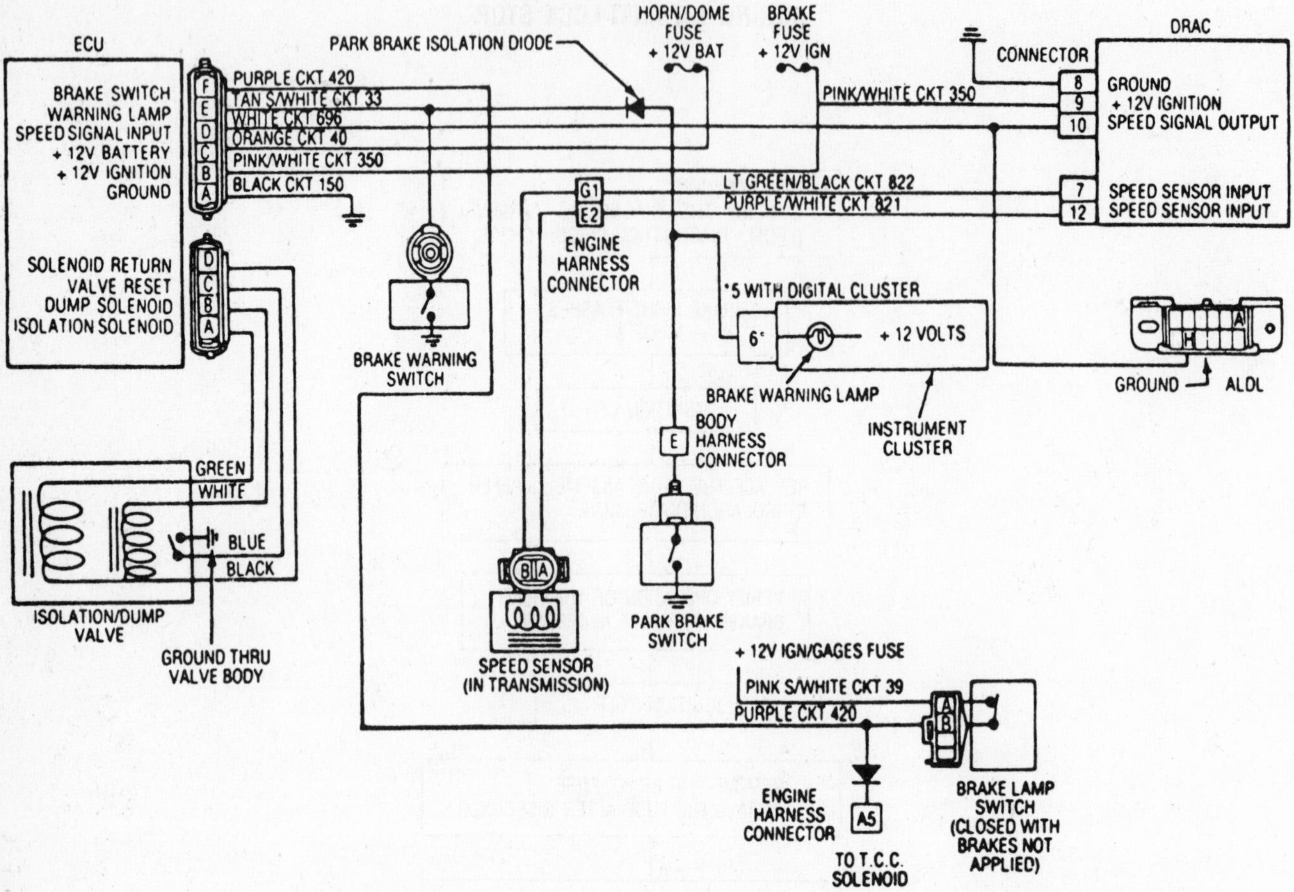

ECU
BRAKE SWITCH
WARNING LAMP
SPEED SIGNAL INPUT
+ 12V BATTERY
+ 12V IGNITION
GROUND
PURPLE CKT 420
TAN S/WHITE CKT 33
WHITE CKT 696
ORANGE CKT 40
PINK/WHITE CKT 350
BLACK CKT 150
SOLENOID RETURN
VALVE RESET
DUMP SOLENOID
ISOLATION SOLENOID
PARK BRAKE ISOLATION DIODE
HORN/DOME FUSE + 12V BAT
BRAKE FUSE + 12V IGN
PINK/WHITE CKT 350
DRAC
CONNECTOR
GROUND
+ 12V IGNITION
SPEED SIGNAL OUTPUT
LT GREEN/BLACK CKT 822
PURPLE/WHITE CKT 821
SPEED SENSOR INPUT
SPEED SENSOR INPUT
ENGINE HARNESS CONNECTOR
BRAKE WARNING SWITCH
*5 WITH DIGITAL CLUSTER
+ 12 VOLTS
BRAKE WARNING LAMP
INSTRUMENT CLUSTER
GROUND
ALDL
BODY HARNESS CONNECTOR
GREEN
WHITE
BLUE
BLACK
ISOLATION/DUMP VALVE
GROUND THRU VALVE BODY
SPEED SENSOR (IN TRANSMISSION)
PARK BRAKE SWITCH
+ 12V IGN/GAGES FUSE
PINK S/WHITE CKT 39
PURPLE CKT 420
ENGINE HARNESS CONNECTOR
TO T.C.C. SOLENOID
BRAKE LAMP SWITCH (CLOSED WITH BRAKES NOT APPLIED)

CODE 6
ERRATIC SPEED SIGNAL

This diagnostic chart checks for the Brake light flashing a code 6 for the following causes:

Erratic Speed Signal to the ECU

Intermittent/erratic Speed signal connection

Faulty ECU

NOTE: If voltage readings are low or varying, check battery and charging system or check for intermittent connections.

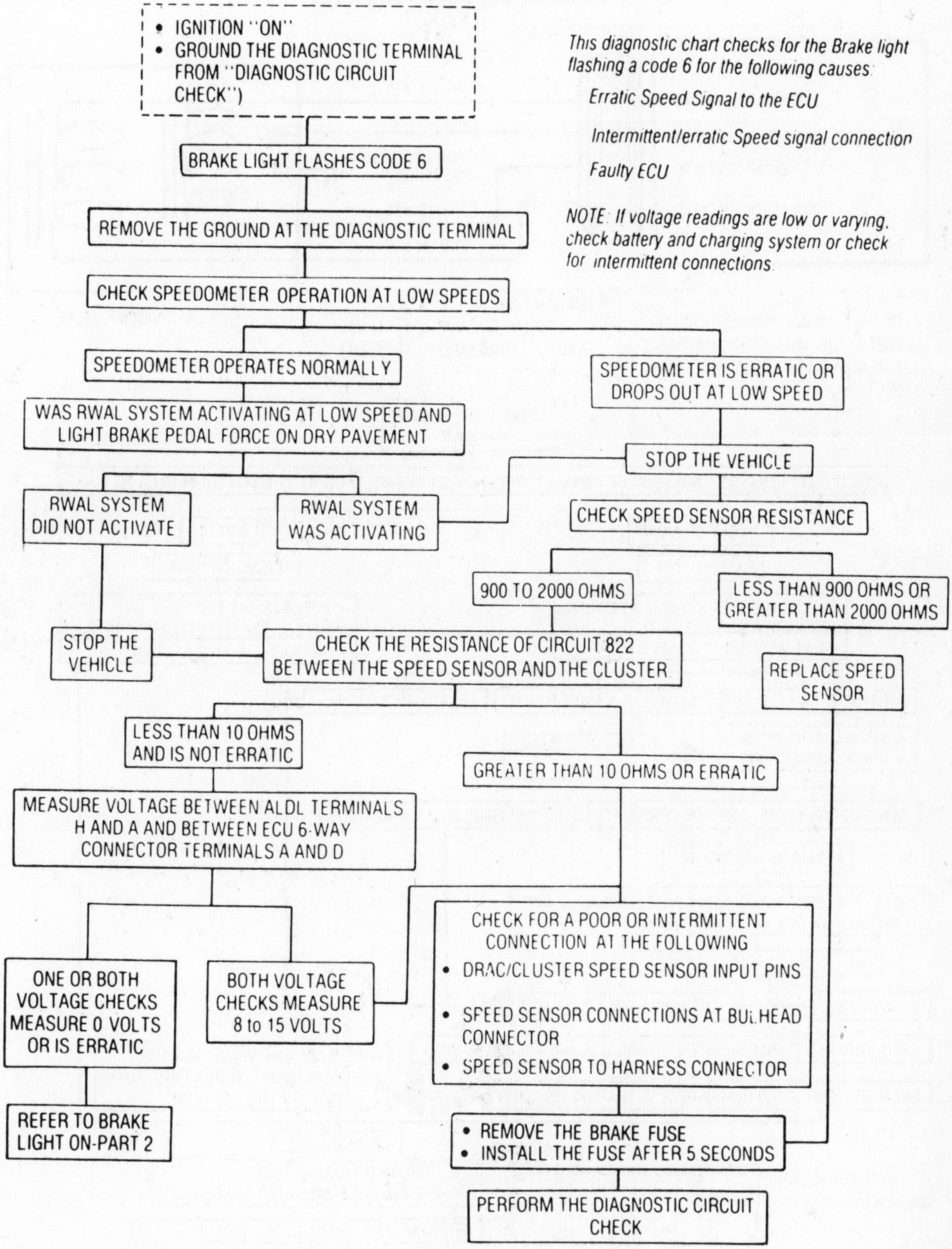
• IGNITION "ON"
• GROUND THE DIAGNOSTIC TERMINAL FROM "DIAGNOSTIC CIRCUIT CHECK")
BRAKE LIGHT FLASHES CODE 6
REMOVE THE GROUND AT THE DIAGNOSTIC TERMINAL
CHECK SPEEDOMETER OPERATION AT LOW SPEEDS
SPEEDOMETER OPERATES NORMALLY
SPEEDOMETER IS ERRATIC OR DROPS OUT AT LOW SPEED
WAS RWAL SYSTEM ACTIVATING AT LOW SPEED AND LIGHT BRAKE PEDAL FORCE ON DRY PAVEMENT
STOP THE VEHICLE
RWAL SYSTEM DID NOT ACTIVATE
RWAL SYSTEM WAS ACTIVATING
CHECK SPEED SENSOR RESISTANCE
900 TO 2000 OHMS
LESS THAN 900 OHMS OR GREATER THAN 2000 OHMS
STOP THE VEHICLE
CHECK THE RESISTANCE OF CIRCUIT 822 BETWEEN THE SPEED SENSOR AND THE CLUSTER
REPLACE SPEED SENSOR
LESS THAN 10 OHMS AND IS NOT ERRATIC
GREATER THAN 10 OHMS OR ERRATIC
MEASURE VOLTAGE BETWEEN ALDL TERMINALS H AND A AND BETWEEN ECU 6-WAY CONNECTOR TERMINALS A AND D
CHECK FOR A POOR OR INTERMITTENT CONNECTION AT THE FOLLOWING
• DRAC/CLUSTER SPEED SENSOR INPUT PINS
• SPEED SENSOR CONNECTIONS AT BULHEAD CONNECTOR
• SPEED SENSOR TO HARNESS CONNECTOR
ONE OR BOTH VOLTAGE CHECKS MEASURE 0 VOLTS OR IS ERRATIC
BOTH VOLTAGE CHECKS MEASURE 8 to 15 VOLTS
REFER TO BRAKE LIGHT ON-PART 2
• REMOVE THE BRAKE FUSE
• INSTALL THE FUSE AFTER 5 SECONDS
PERFORM THE DIAGNOSTIC CIRCUIT CHECK

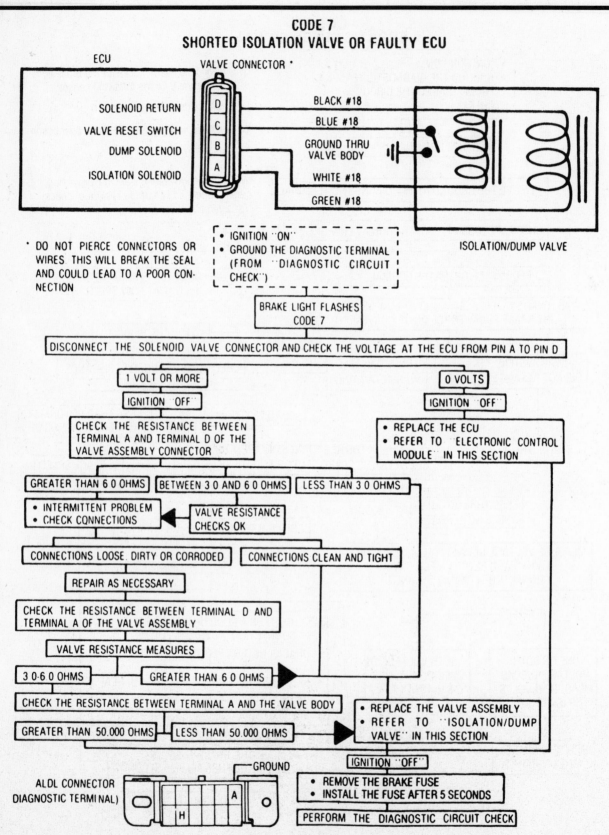

CODE 7
SHORTED ISOLATION VALVE OR FAULTY ECU

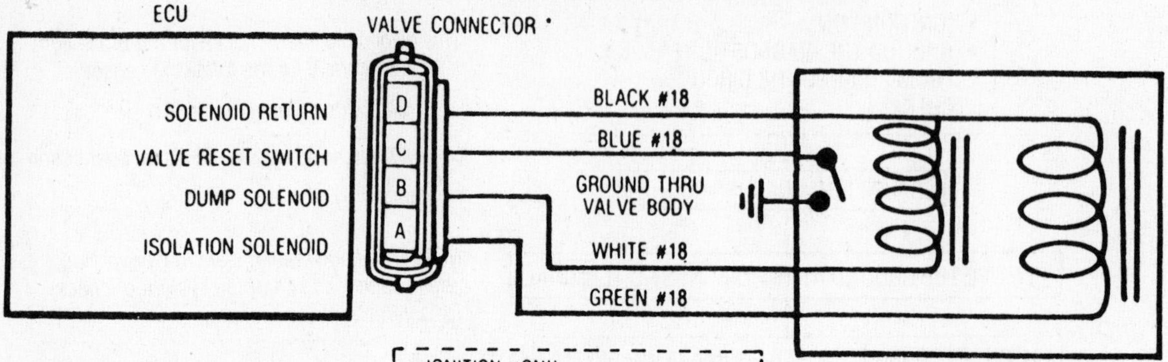
ECU
VALVE CONNECTOR *
SOLENOID RETURN
VALVE RESET SWITCH
DUMP SOLENOID
ISOLATION SOLENOID
D
C
B
A
BLACK #18
BLUE #18
GROUND THRU VALVE BODY
WHITE #18
GREEN #18
ISOLATION/DUMP VALVE

* DO NOT PIERCE CONNECTORS OR WIRES. THIS WILL BREAK THE SEAL AND COULD LEAD TO A POOR CONNECTION

- IGNITION "ON"
- GROUND THE DIAGNOSTIC TERMINAL (FROM "DIAGNOSTIC CIRCUIT CHECK")

BRAKE LIGHT FLASHES CODE 7

DISCONNECT THE SOLENOID VALVE CONNECTOR AND CHECK THE VOLTAGE AT THE ECU FROM PIN A TO PIN D

- 1 VOLT OR MORE
  - IGNITION "OFF"
  - CHECK THE RESISTANCE BETWEEN TERMINAL A AND TERMINAL D OF THE VALVE ASSEMBLY CONNECTOR
    - GREATER THAN 6.0 OHMS
    - BETWEEN 3.0 AND 6.0 OHMS → VALVE RESISTANCE CHECKS OK
      - INTERMITTENT PROBLEM
      - CHECK CONNECTIONS
        - CONNECTIONS LOOSE, DIRTY OR CORRODED
          - REPAIR AS NECESSARY
          - CHECK THE RESISTANCE BETWEEN TERMINAL D AND TERMINAL A OF THE VALVE ASSEMBLY
          - VALVE RESISTANCE MEASURES
            - 3.0-6.0 OHMS
              - CHECK THE RESISTANCE BETWEEN TERMINAL A AND THE VALVE BODY
                - GREATER THAN 50,000 OHMS
                - LESS THAN 50,000 OHMS
            - GREATER THAN 6.0 OHMS
        - CONNECTIONS CLEAN AND TIGHT
    - LESS THAN 3.0 OHMS
  - (GREATER THAN 6.0 OHMS / CONNECTIONS CLEAN AND TIGHT / LESS THAN 3.0 OHMS / LESS THAN 50,000 OHMS):
    - REPLACE THE VALVE ASSEMBLY
    - REFER TO "ISOLATION/DUMP VALVE" IN THIS SECTION
- 0 VOLTS
  - IGNITION "OFF"
  - REPLACE THE ECU
  - REFER TO "ELECTRONIC CONTROL MODULE" IN THIS SECTION

IGNITION "OFF"

- REMOVE THE BRAKE FUSE
- INSTALL THE FUSE AFTER 5 SECONDS

PERFORM THE DIAGNOSTIC CIRCUIT CHECK

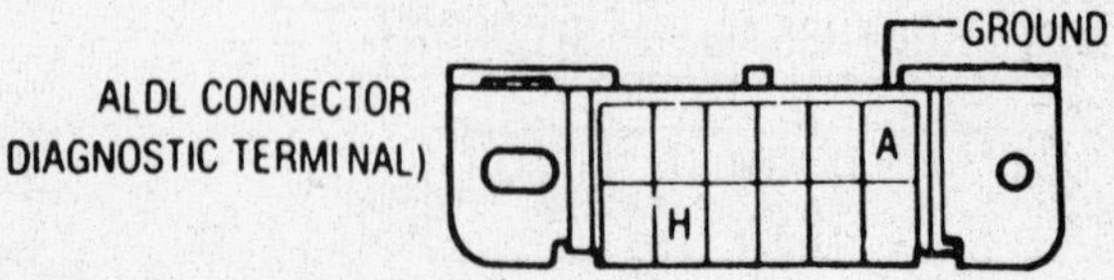
GROUND
ALDL CONNECTOR
DIAGNOSTIC TERMINAL)
A
H

CODE 8
SHORTED DUMP VALVE OR FAULTY ECU

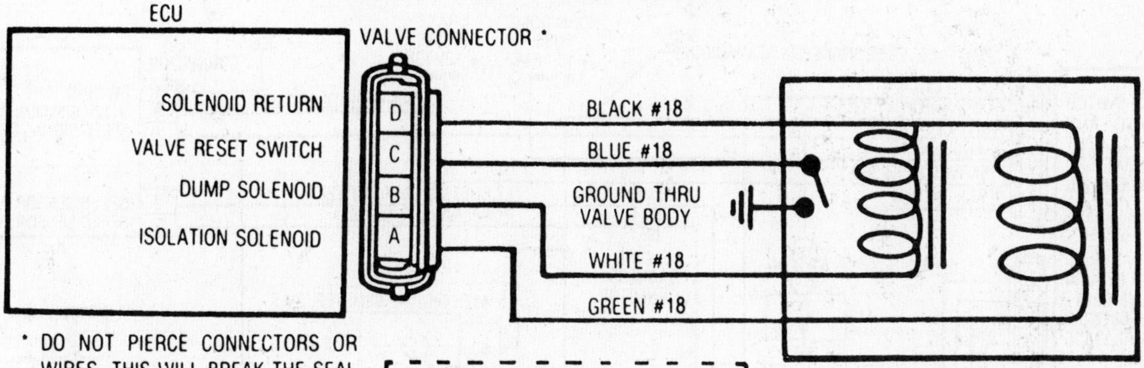
ECU
SOLENOID RETURN
VALVE RESET SWITCH
DUMP SOLENOID
ISOLATION SOLENOID
VALVE CONNECTOR *
D
C
B
A
BLACK #18
BLUE #18
GROUND THRU VALVE BODY
WHITE #18
GREEN #18
ISOLATION/DUMP VALVE

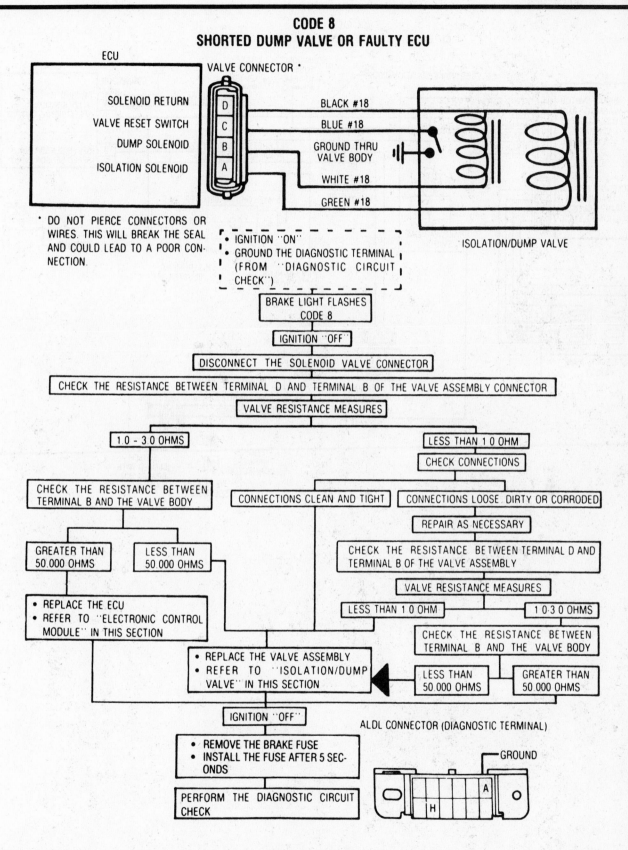

* DO NOT PIERCE CONNECTORS OR WIRES. THIS WILL BREAK THE SEAL AND COULD LEAD TO A POOR CONNECTION.

- IGNITION "ON"
- GROUND THE DIAGNOSTIC TERMINAL (FROM "DIAGNOSTIC CIRCUIT CHECK")

BRAKE LIGHT FLASHES CODE 8

IGNITION "OFF"

DISCONNECT THE SOLENOID VALVE CONNECTOR

CHECK THE RESISTANCE BETWEEN TERMINAL D AND TERMINAL B OF THE VALVE ASSEMBLY CONNECTOR

VALVE RESISTANCE MEASURES

1.0 - 3.0 OHMS → CHECK THE RESISTANCE BETWEEN TERMINAL B AND THE VALVE BODY

- GREATER THAN 50.000 OHMS →
  - REPLACE THE ECU
  - REFER TO "ELECTRONIC CONTROL MODULE" IN THIS SECTION
- LESS THAN 50.000 OHMS → REPLACE THE VALVE ASSEMBLY

LESS THAN 1.0 OHM → CHECK CONNECTIONS

- CONNECTIONS CLEAN AND TIGHT → REPLACE THE VALVE ASSEMBLY
- CONNECTIONS LOOSE, DIRTY OR CORRODED → REPAIR AS NECESSARY → CHECK THE RESISTANCE BETWEEN TERMINAL D AND TERMINAL B OF THE VALVE ASSEMBLY → VALVE RESISTANCE MEASURES
  - LESS THAN 1.0 OHM → REPLACE THE VALVE ASSEMBLY
  - 1.0-3.0 OHMS → CHECK THE RESISTANCE BETWEEN TERMINAL B AND THE VALVE BODY
    - LESS THAN 50.000 OHMS → REPLACE THE VALVE ASSEMBLY
    - GREATER THAN 50.000 OHMS → IGNITION "OFF"

- REPLACE THE VALVE ASSEMBLY
- REFER TO "ISOLATION/DUMP VALVE" IN THIS SECTION

IGNITION "OFF"

- REMOVE THE BRAKE FUSE
- INSTALL THE FUSE AFTER 5 SECONDS

PERFORM THE DIAGNOSTIC CIRCUIT CHECK

ALDL CONNECTOR (DIAGNOSTIC TERMINAL)

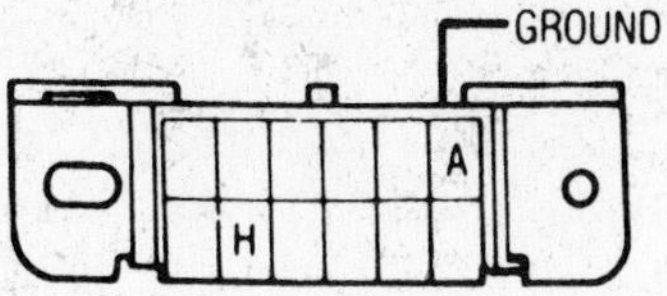
GROUND
A
H

CODE 9
OPEN CIRCUIT TO THE SPEED SIGNAL

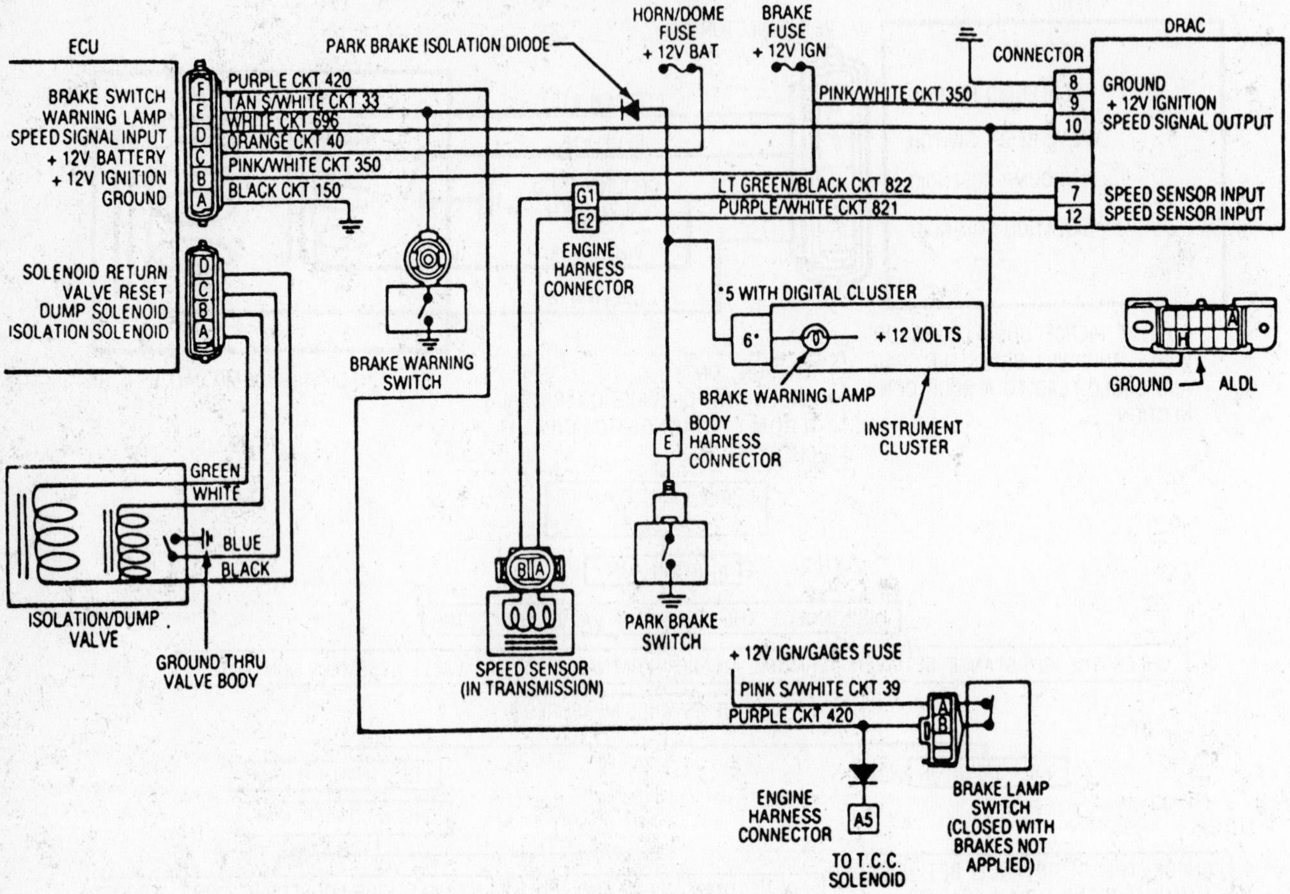
ECU
BRAKE SWITCH
WARNING LAMP
SPEED SIGNAL INPUT
+ 12V BATTERY
+ 12V IGNITION
GROUND
F
E
D
C
B
A
PURPLE CKT 420
TAN S/WHITE CKT 33
WHITE CKT 696
ORANGE CKT 40
PINK/WHITE CKT 350
BLACK CKT 150
PARK BRAKE ISOLATION DIODE
HORN/DOME FUSE + 12V BAT
BRAKE FUSE + 12V IGN
PINK/WHITE CKT 350
CONNECTOR
DRAC
8
9
10
GROUND
+ 12V IGNITION
SPEED SIGNAL OUTPUT
LT GREEN/BLACK CKT 822
PURPLE/WHITE CKT 821
7
12
SPEED SENSOR INPUT
SPEED SENSOR INPUT
G1
E2
ENGINE HARNESS CONNECTOR
SOLENOID RETURN
VALVE RESET
DUMP SOLENOID
ISOLATION SOLENOID
BRAKE WARNING SWITCH
*5 WITH DIGITAL CLUSTER
6*
+ 12 VOLTS
BRAKE WARNING LAMP
INSTRUMENT CLUSTER
GROUND
ALDL
BODY HARNESS CONNECTOR
E
GREEN
WHITE
BLUE
BLACK
ISOLATION/DUMP VALVE
GROUND THRU VALVE BODY
SPEED SENSOR (IN TRANSMISSION)
PARK BRAKE SWITCH
+ 12V IGN/GAGES FUSE
PINK S/WHITE CKT 39
PURPLE CKT 420
ENGINE HARNESS CONNECTOR
A5
TO T.C.C. SOLENOID
BRAKE LAMP SWITCH (CLOSED WITH BRAKES NOT APPLIED)

CODE 9
OPEN CIRCUIT TO THE SPEED SIGNAL

THIS DIAGNOSTIC CHART CHECKS FOR THE BRAKE LIGHT FLASHING FOR THE FOLLOWING CAUSES -

- OPEN/SHORT CONDITION IN SPEED SIGNAL CIRCUIT TO ECU
- INTERMITTENT SPEED SIGNAL VOLTAGE TO ECU
- FAULTY INSTRUMENT CLUSTER

NOTE: IF VOLTAGE READINGS ARE LOW OR VARYING, CHECK BATTERY AND CHARGING SYSTEM OR CHECK FOR INTERMITTENT/POOR CONNECTIONS.

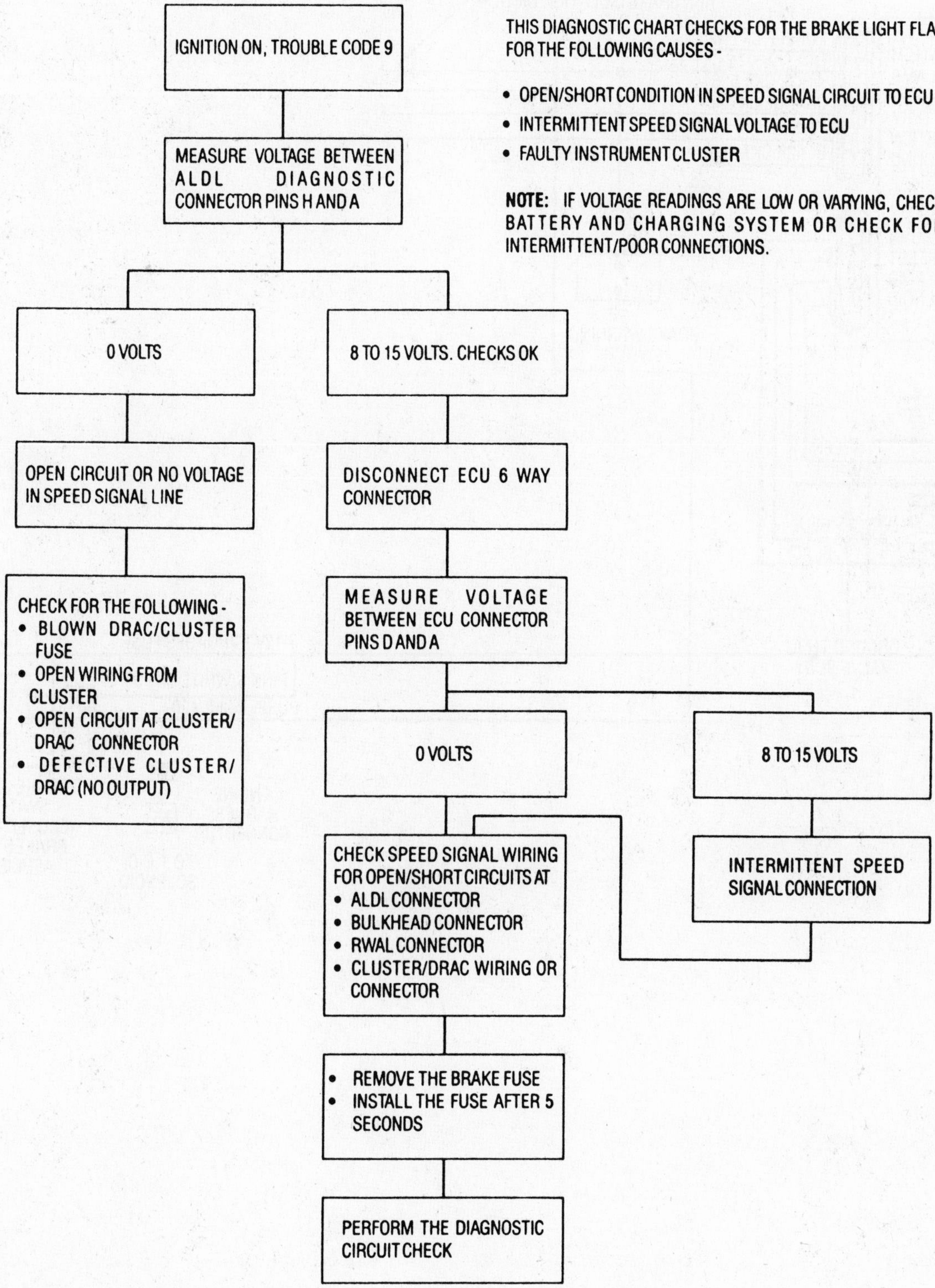
IGNITION ON, TROUBLE CODE 9
MEASURE VOLTAGE BETWEEN ALDL DIAGNOSTIC CONNECTOR PINS H AND A
0 VOLTS
8 TO 15 VOLTS. CHECKS OK
OPEN CIRCUIT OR NO VOLTAGE IN SPEED SIGNAL LINE
DISCONNECT ECU 6 WAY CONNECTOR
CHECK FOR THE FOLLOWING - • BLOWN DRAC/CLUSTER FUSE • OPEN WIRING FROM CLUSTER • OPEN CIRCUIT AT CLUSTER/DRAC CONNECTOR • DEFECTIVE CLUSTER/DRAC (NO OUTPUT)
MEASURE VOLTAGE BETWEEN ECU CONNECTOR PINS D AND A
0 VOLTS
8 TO 15 VOLTS
CHECK SPEED SIGNAL WIRING FOR OPEN/SHORT CIRCUITS AT • ALDL CONNECTOR • BULKHEAD CONNECTOR • RWAL CONNECTOR • CLUSTER/DRAC WIRING OR CONNECTOR
INTERMITTENT SPEED SIGNAL CONNECTION
• REMOVE THE BRAKE FUSE • INSTALL THE FUSE AFTER 5 SECONDS
PERFORM THE DIAGNOSTIC CIRCUIT CHECK

CODE 10
BRAKE LAMP SWITCH CIRCUIT

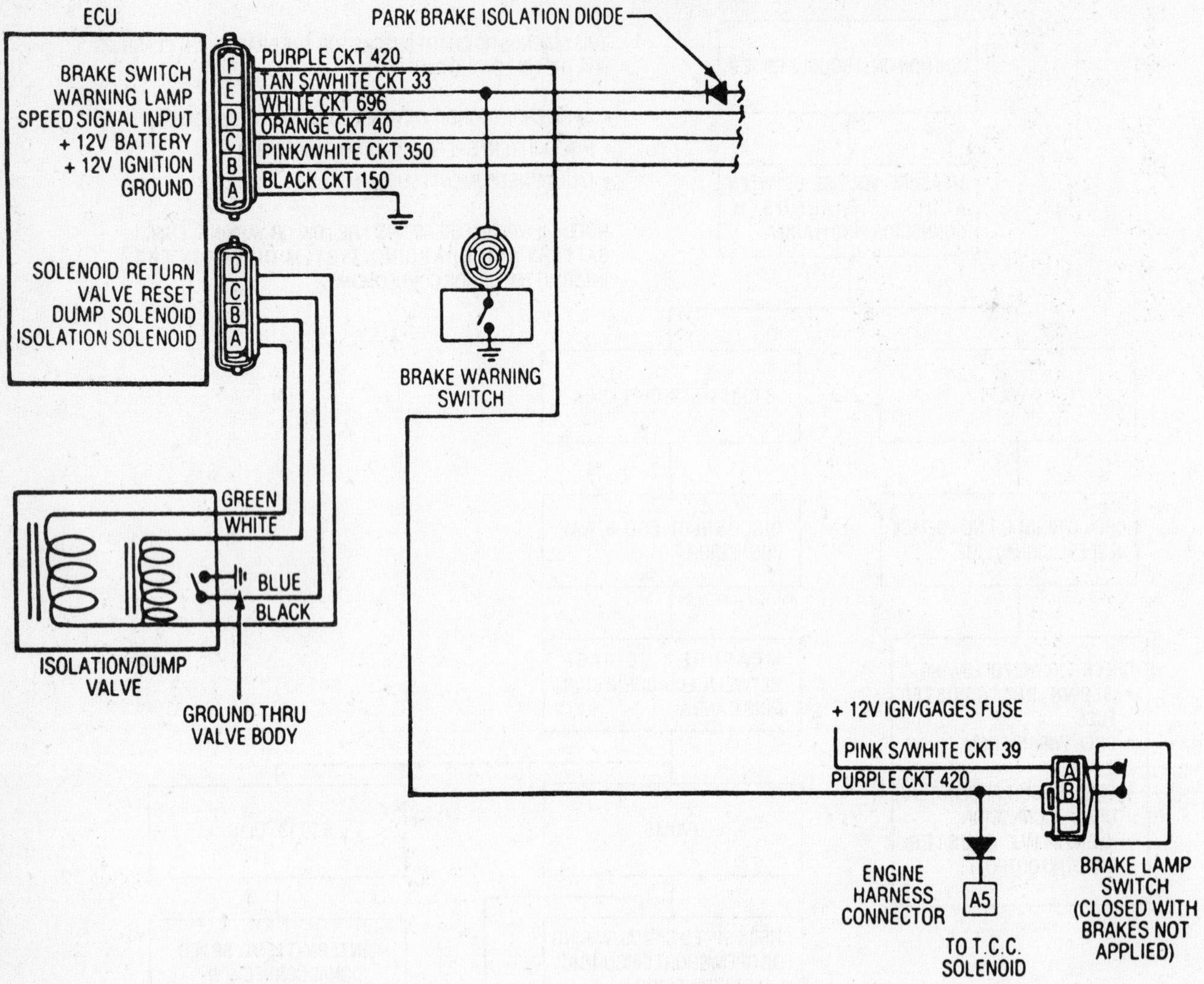
ECU
PARK BRAKE ISOLATION DIODE
BRAKE SWITCH
WARNING LAMP
SPEED SIGNAL INPUT
+ 12V BATTERY
+ 12V IGNITION
GROUND
F
E
D
C
B
A
PURPLE CKT 420
TAN S/WHITE CKT 33
WHITE CKT 696
ORANGE CKT 40
PINK/WHITE CKT 350
BLACK CKT 150
SOLENOID RETURN
VALVE RESET
DUMP SOLENOID
ISOLATION SOLENOID
BRAKE WARNING SWITCH
GREEN
WHITE
BLUE
BLACK
ISOLATION/DUMP VALVE
GROUND THRU VALVE BODY
+ 12V IGN/GAGES FUSE
PINK S/WHITE CKT 39
PURPLE CKT 420
ENGINE HARNESS CONNECTOR
A5
TO T.C.C. SOLENOID
BRAKE LAMP SWITCH (CLOSED WITH BRAKES NOT APPLIED)

CODES 10-BRAKE LAMP SWITCH CIRCUIT*

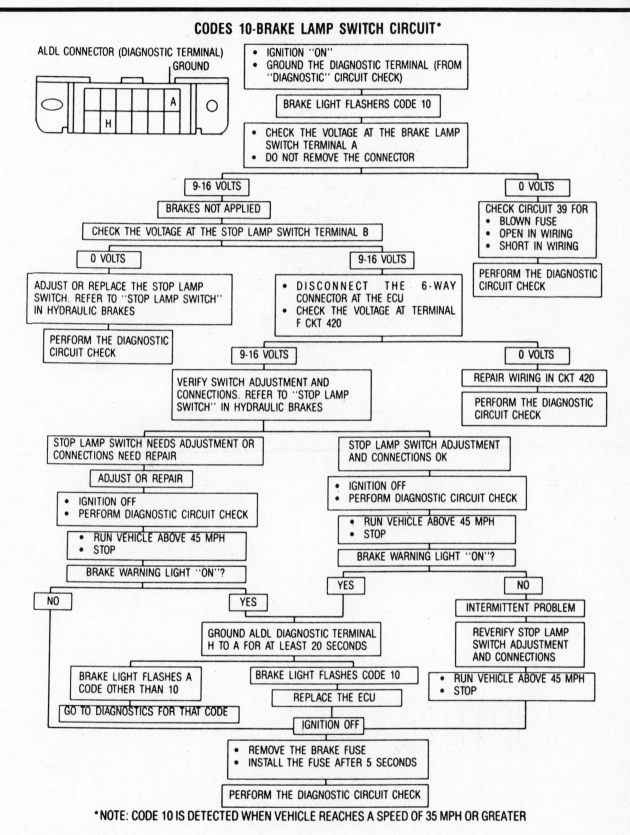

ALDL CONNECTOR (DIAGNOSTIC TERMINAL)

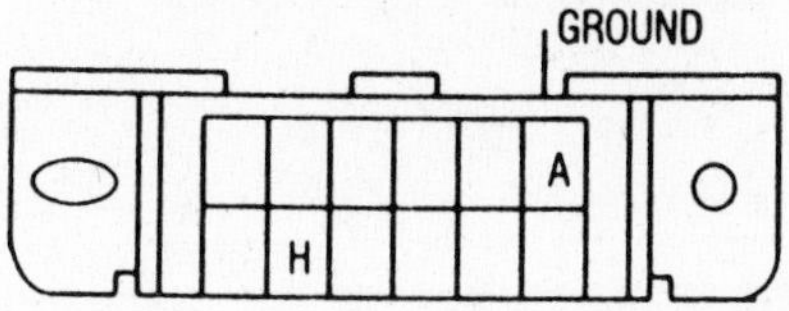
GROUND
A
H

- IGNITION "ON"
- GROUND THE DIAGNOSTIC TERMINAL (FROM "DIAGNOSTIC" CIRCUIT CHECK)

BRAKE LIGHT FLASHERS CODE 10

- CHECK THE VOLTAGE AT THE BRAKE LAMP SWITCH TERMINAL A
- DO NOT REMOVE THE CONNECTOR

9-16 VOLTS

BRAKES NOT APPLIED

CHECK THE VOLTAGE AT THE STOP LAMP SWITCH TERMINAL B

0 VOLTS

ADJUST OR REPLACE THE STOP LAMP SWITCH. REFER TO "STOP LAMP SWITCH" IN HYDRAULIC BRAKES

PERFORM THE DIAGNOSTIC CIRCUIT CHECK

9-16 VOLTS

- DISCONNECT THE 6-WAY CONNECTOR AT THE ECU
- CHECK THE VOLTAGE AT TERMINAL F CKT 420

9-16 VOLTS

VERIFY SWITCH ADJUSTMENT AND CONNECTIONS. REFER TO "STOP LAMP SWITCH" IN HYDRAULIC BRAKES

STOP LAMP SWITCH NEEDS ADJUSTMENT OR CONNECTIONS NEED REPAIR

ADJUST OR REPAIR

- IGNITION OFF
- PERFORM DIAGNOSTIC CIRCUIT CHECK

- RUN VEHICLE ABOVE 45 MPH
- STOP

BRAKE WARNING LIGHT "ON"?

NO

YES

STOP LAMP SWITCH ADJUSTMENT AND CONNECTIONS OK

- IGNITION OFF
- PERFORM DIAGNOSTIC CIRCUIT CHECK

- RUN VEHICLE ABOVE 45 MPH
- STOP

BRAKE WARNING LIGHT "ON"?

YES

GROUND ALDL DIAGNOSTIC TERMINAL H TO A FOR AT LEAST 20 SECONDS

BRAKE LIGHT FLASHES A CODE OTHER THAN 10

GO TO DIAGNOSTICS FOR THAT CODE

BRAKE LIGHT FLASHES CODE 10

REPLACE THE ECU

NO

INTERMITTENT PROBLEM

REVERIFY STOP LAMP SWITCH ADJUSTMENT AND CONNECTIONS

- RUN VEHICLE ABOVE 45 MPH
- STOP

0 VOLTS

REPAIR WIRING IN CKT 420

PERFORM THE DIAGNOSTIC CIRCUIT CHECK

0 VOLTS

CHECK CIRCUIT 39 FOR
- BLOWN FUSE
- OPEN IN WIRING
- SHORT IN WIRING

PERFORM THE DIAGNOSTIC CIRCUIT CHECK

IGNITION OFF

- REMOVE THE BRAKE FUSE
- INSTALL THE FUSE AFTER 5 SECONDS

PERFORM THE DIAGNOSTIC CIRCUIT CHECK

*NOTE: CODE 10 IS DETECTED WHEN VEHICLE REACHES A SPEED OF 35 MPH OR GREATER

CODE 13, 14, AND 15
ELECTRONIC CONTROL UNIT MALFUNCTION

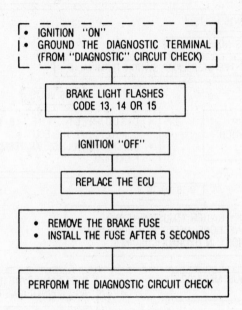

- IGNITION "ON"
- GROUND THE DIAGNOSTIC TERMINAL (FROM "DIAGNOSTIC" CIRCUIT CHECK)

↓

BRAKE LIGHT FLASHES CODE 13, 14 OR 15

↓

IGNITION "OFF"

↓

REPLACE THE ECU

↓

- REMOVE THE BRAKE FUSE
- INSTALL THE FUSE AFTER 5 SECONDS

↓

PERFORM THE DIAGNOSTIC CIRCUIT CHECK

ALDL CONNECTOR (DIAGNOSTIC TERMINAL)

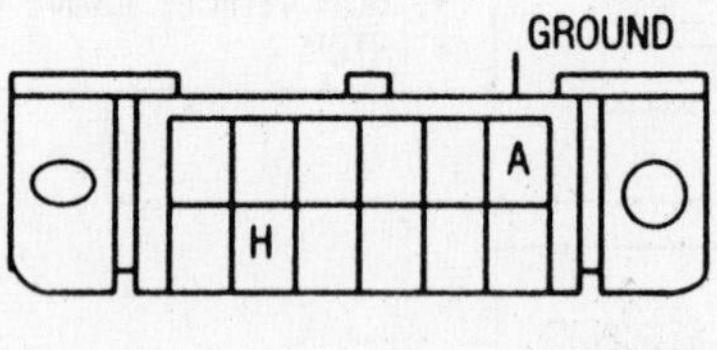
GROUND
A
H

REAR WHEEL ANTI-LOCK WIRING DIAGRAM AND CONNECTORS

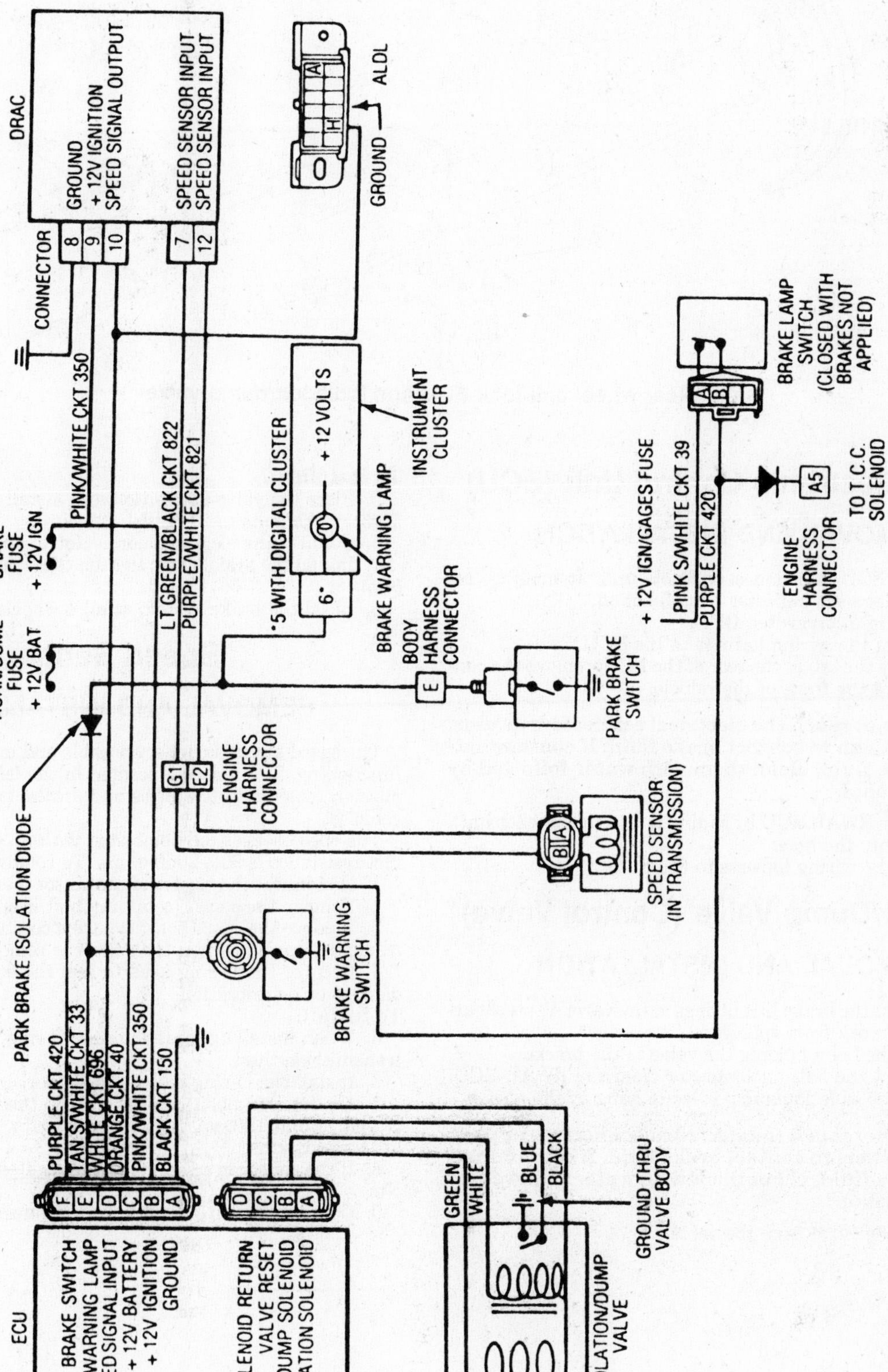
DRAC
GROUND
+12V IGNITION
SPEED SIGNAL OUTPUT
SPEED SENSOR INPUT
SPEED SENSOR INPUT
CONNECTOR
8
9
10
7
12
ALDL
GROUND
PINK/WHITE CKT 350
LT GREEN/BLACK CKT 822
PURPLE/WHITE CKT 821
+12 VOLTS
INSTRUMENT CLUSTER
*5 WITH DIGITAL CLUSTER
6*
BRAKE WARNING LAMP
BRAKE FUSE +12V IGN
HORN/DOME FUSE +12V BAT
BODY HARNESS CONNECTOR
E
PARK BRAKE SWITCH
PARK BRAKE ISOLATION DIODE
G1
E2
ENGINE HARNESS CONNECTOR
SPEED SENSOR (IN TRANSMISSION)
BRAKE WARNING SWITCH
+12V IGN/GAGES FUSE
PINK S/WHITE CKT 39
PURPLE CKT 420
ENGINE HARNESS CONNECTOR
A5
TO T.C.C. SOLENOID
BRAKE LAMP SWITCH (CLOSED WITH BRAKES NOT APPLIED)
PURPLE CKT 420
TAN S/WHITE CKT 33
WHITE CKT 696
ORANGE CKT 40
PINK/WHITE CKT 350
BLACK CKT 150
ECU
BRAKE SWITCH
WARNING LAMP
SPEED SIGNAL INPUT
+12V BATTERY
+12V IGNITION
GROUND
SOLENOID RETURN
VALVE RESET
DUMP SOLENOID
ISOLATION SOLENOID
GREEN
WHITE
BLUE
BLACK
GROUND THRU VALVE BODY
ISOLATION/DUMP VALVE

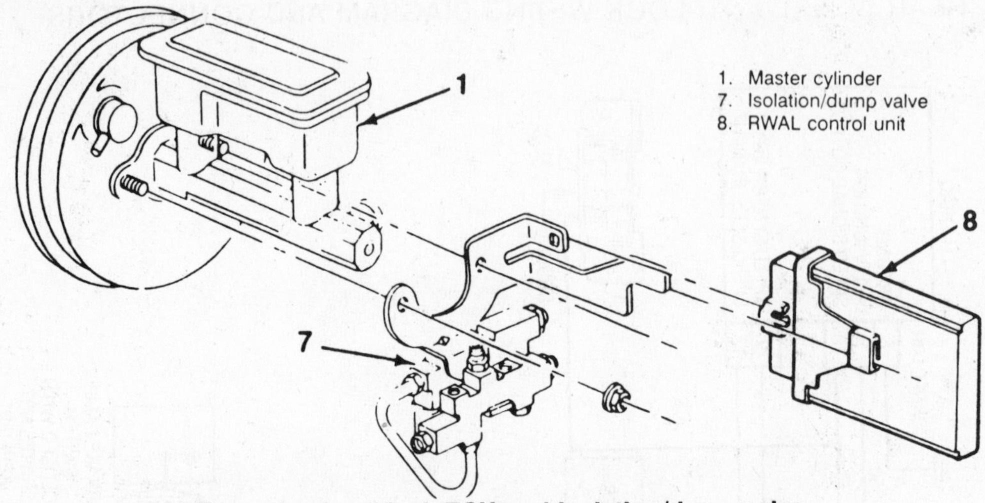
1
8
7
1. Master cylinder
7. Isolation/dump valve
8. RWAL control unit

Rear wheel anti-lock ECU and isolation/dump valve

RWAL Electronic Control Unit (ECU)

REMOVAL AND INSTALLATION

The RWAL ECU is a non-serviceable unit. It must be replaced when diagnosis indicates a malfunction.

1. Turn the ignition switch **OFF**.
2. Disconnect the wiring harness to the ECU.
3. Gently pry the tab at the rear of the ECU; remove the control unit toward the front of the vehicle.

NOTE: Do not touch the electrical connectors or pins; do not allow them to contact brake fluid. If contaminated with brake fluid, clean them with water followed by isopropyl alcohol.

4. Install the RWAL ECU by sliding it into the bracket until the tab locks into the hole.
5. Connect the wiring harness to the ECU.

Isolation/Dump Valve (Control Valve)

REMOVAL AND INSTALLATION

1. Disconnect the brake line fittings at the valve. Protect surrounding paintwork from spillage.
2. Remove the bolts holding the valve to the bracket.
3. Disconnect the bottom connector from the RWAL ECU. Do not allow the isolation/dump valve to hang by the wiring.

NOTE: Do not touch the electrical connectors or pins; do not allow them to contact brake fluid. If contaminated with brake fluid, clean them with water followed by isopropyl alcohol.

4. Remove the valve from the vehicle.

To install:

5. Place the valve in position and install the retaining bolts. Tighten the bolts to 21 ft. lbs. (29 Nm).
6. Connect the electrical connector to the RWAL ECU.
7. Install the brake lines; tighten the fittings to 18 ft. lbs. (24 Nm)
8. Bleed the brake system at all 4 wheels.

Speed Sensor

REMOVAL AND INSTALLATION

The speed sensor is not serviceable and must replaced if malfunctioning. The sensor is located in the left rear of the transmission case on 2wd vehicles and on the transfer case of 4wd vehicles.

The speed sensor may be tested with an ohmmeter; the correct resistance is 900–2000 ohms. To remove the speed sensor:

1. Disconnect the electrical connector from the speed sensor.
2. Remove the sensor retaining bolt if one is used.
3. Remove the speed sensor; have a container handy to catch transmission fluid when the sensor is removed.
4. Recover the O-ring used to seal the sensor; inspect it for damage or deterioration.

To install:

5. When installing, coat the new O-ring with a thin film of transmission fluid.
6. Install the O-ring and speed sensor.
7. If a retaining bolt is used, tighten the bolt to 8 ft. lbs. (11 Nm) in automatic transmissions or 9 ft. lbs. (12 Nm) for all other transmissions.
8. If the sensor is a screw-in unit, tighten it to 32 ft. lbs. (43 Nm).
9. Connect the wire harness to the sensor.

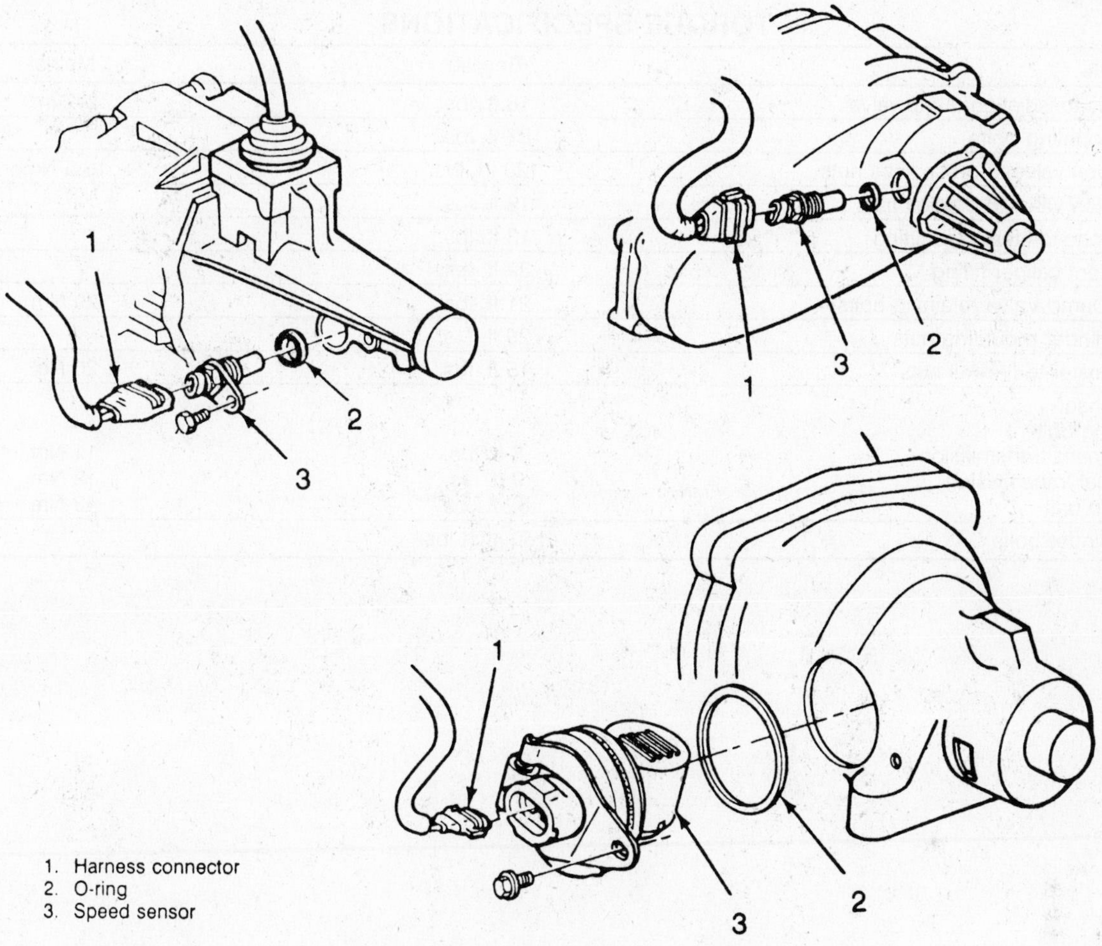
1
2
3
1
3
2
1
2
3
1. Harness connector
2. O-ring
3. Speed sensor

Speed sensor locations and installation

TORQUE SPECIFICATIONS

Component	English	Metric
Brake lines-to-isolation/dump valve	18 ft. lbs.	24 Nm
Caliper mounting bolts	37 ft. lbs.	
Combination valve-to-brake lines nuts	120 in. lbs.	13.5 Nm
Combination valve-to-bracket nuts	12 ft. lbs.	
Flexible hose-to-steel pipe fitting	13 ft. lbs.	
Hose-to-front caliper fitting	32 ft. lbs.	
Isolation/Dump Valve retaining bolts	21 ft. lbs.	29 Nm
Master cylinder mounting nuts	20 ft. lbs.	
Power booster-to-firewall nuts	15 ft. lbs.	20 Nm
Speed sensor		
Retaining bolt		
Automatic transmission	8 ft. lbs.	11 Nm
Manual transmission	9 ft. lbs.	12 Nm
Screw-in unit	32 ft. lbs.	43 Nm
Wheel cylinder bolts	160 inch lbs.	

10 Body

QUICK REFERENCE INDEX

GENERAL INDEX

EXTERIOR

Doors

REMOVAL AND INSTALLATION

NOTE: The following procedure requires the use of the GM Door Hinge Spring Compressor tool No. J-28625-A or equivalent.

1. If equipped with power door components, perform the following procedures:
   a. Disconnect the negative battery cable from the battery.
   b. Remove the door trim panel.
   c. Disconnect the electrical harness connector from the power door lock motor and/or the power window regulator.
   d. Remove the electrical harness from the door.

CAUTION

Before removing the hinge spring from the door, cover the spring with a towel to prevent the spring from flying and possibly causing personal injury.

2. Using the GM Door Hinge Spring Compressor tool No. J-28625-A or equivalent, compress the door hinge spring and remove it.
3. To remove the door hinge pin clips, spread the clips and move them above the recess on the pin; when the pin is removed, the clip will ride on the pin and fall free of it.
4. Using a soft-head hammer and a pair of locking pliers, remove the lower pin from the door hinge; then, install a bolt (in the lower pin hole) to hold the door in place until the upper hinge pin is removed.
5. Remove the upper door hinge pin and support the door, then remove the bolt from the lower hinge pin hole and the door from the truck.
6. To install the door, position it on the hinges and insert a bolt through the lower hinge pin hole.
7. Using a new hinge pin clip, install the upper hinge pin.

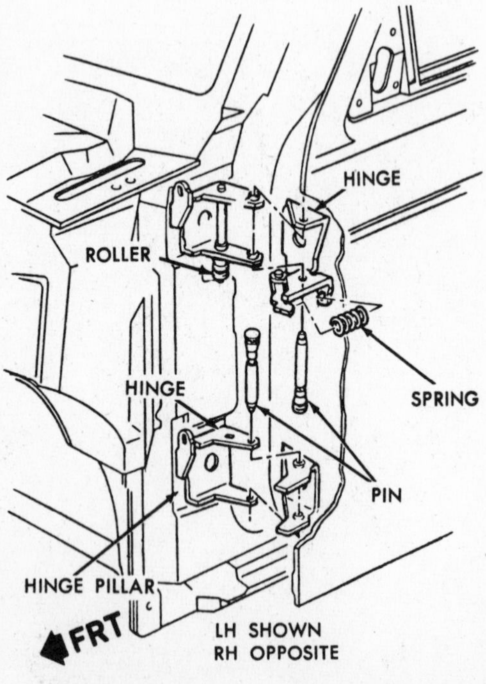
HINGE
ROLLER
HINGE
SPRING
PIN
HINGE PILLAR
FRT
LH SHOWN
RH OPPOSITE

Door hinge pins — exploded view

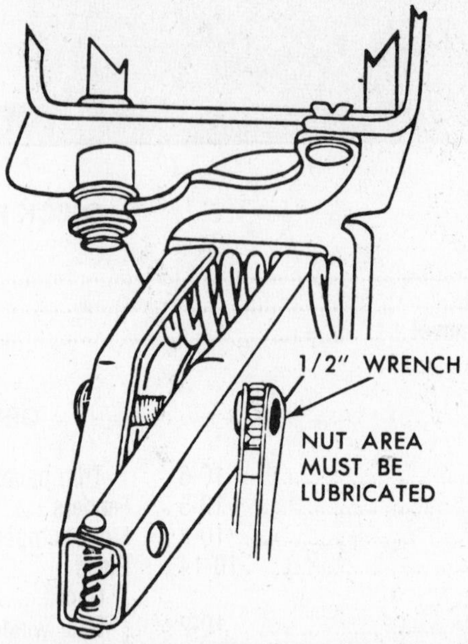
1/2" WRENCH
NUT AREA
MUST BE
LUBRICATED

Using a spring compressor to replace the door hinge pins

8. Remove the bolt from the lower hinge pin hole. Using a new hinge pin, install it into the lower hinge pin holes.
9. Using the GM Door Hinge Spring Compressor tool No. J-28625-A or equivalent, compress the door hinge spring and install it into the door hinge.
10. If equipped with power door components, reconnect the electrical harness connector(s), install the door panel and the reconnect the negative battery terminal.

ADJUSTMENTS

Factory installed hinges are welded in place, so no adjustment of the system is necessary or recommended.

Door Hinges

NOTE: The following procedure requires the use of an ⅛ in. (3mm) drill bit, ½ in. (13mm) drill bit, a center punch, a cold chisel, a portable body grinder, a putty knife and a scribing tool.

REMOVAL AND INSTALLATION

1. Remove the door(s), then place the door on a padded workbench.
2. Using a putty knife, remove the sealant from the around the edge of the hinge.
3. Using a scribing tool, outline the position of the hinge(s) on the door and the body pillar.
4. Using a center punch, mark the center position of the hinge-to-door and the hinge-to-body pillar welds.
5. Using a ⅛ in. (3mm) drill bit, drill a pilot hole completely through each weld.

NOTE: When drilling the holes through the hinge welds, DO NOT drill through the door or the body pillar.

6. Using a ½ in. (13mm) drill bit, drill a hole through the hinge base, following the ⅛ in. (3mm) pilot hole.

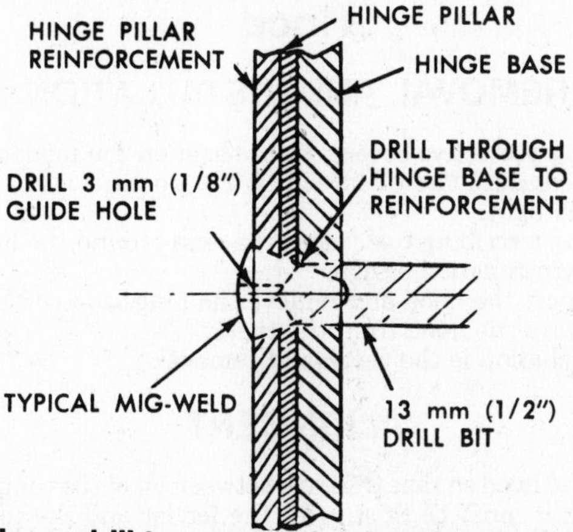
HINGE PILLAR REINFORCEMENT
HINGE PILLAR
HINGE BASE
DRILL THROUGH HINGE BASE TO REINFORCEMENT
DRILL 3 mm (1/8") GUIDE HOLE
TYPICAL MIG-WELD
13 mm (1/2") DRILL BIT

Using a drill to remove the door hinge welds

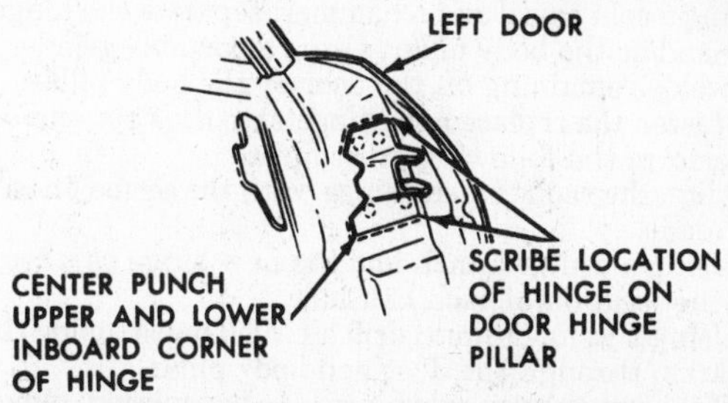
LEFT DOOR
SCRIBE LOCATION OF HINGE ON DOOR HINGE PILLAR
CENTER PUNCH UPPER AND LOWER INBOARD CORNER OF HINGE

Marking the door hinges for replacement

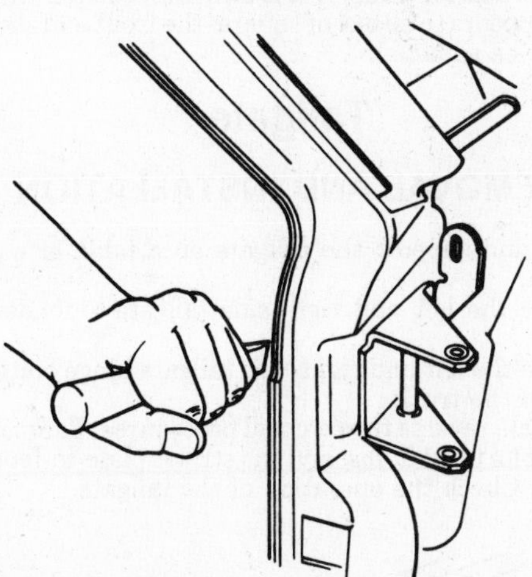

Using a cold chisel to open the door pillar pinch weld

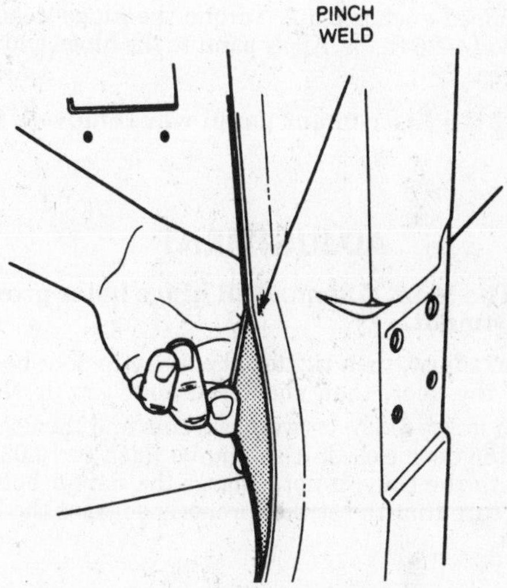
PINCH WELD

Opening the door pillar to insert the tapped anchor plate

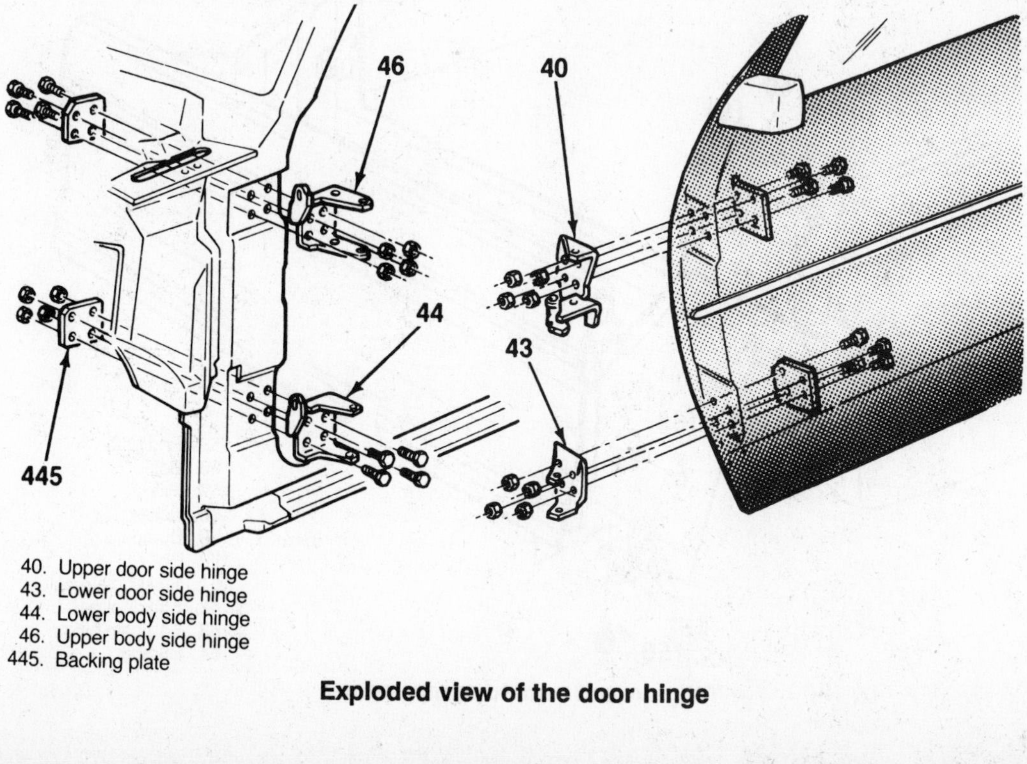
46
40
44
43
445

40. Upper door side hinge
43. Lower door side hinge
44. Lower body side hinge
46. Upper body side hinge
445. Backing plate

Exploded view of the door hinge

7. Using a cold chisel and a hammer, separate the hinge from the door and/or the body pillar. Using a portable grinder, clean off any welds remaining on the door or the body pillar.
8. To fasten the replacement hinge(s) to the door and/or body pillar, perform the following procedures:
   a. Align the replacement hinge, with the scribe lines, previously made.
   b. Using a center punch and the new hinge as a template, mark the location of each bolt hole.
   c. Using a ½ in. (13mm) drill bit, drill holes (using the center marks) through the door and body pillar.
   d. If the upper body-side hinge is to be replaced, remove the instrument panel fasteners, pull the panel outwards and support it. Using a cold chisel, open the door pillar pinch weld to install the tapped anchor plate.
9. To install, use medium body sealant (apply it to the hinge-to-door or body pillar surface), the hinge-to-door/body pillar bolts and tapped anchor plate. Torque the hinge-to-door/body pillar bolts to 14–26 ft. lbs. Apply paint to the hinge and the surrounding area.

NOTE: If the instrument panel was removed, replace it.

ADJUSTMENT

NOTE: The ½ in. (13mm) drill hinge holes provide for some adjustment.

1. Loosen, adjust, then tighten the hinge-to-door/body pillar bolts; close the door, then check the door gap, it should be 0.157–0.235 in. (4–6mm) between the door and the door frame.
2. With the door closed, it should be flush (± 0.039 in. [± 1.0mm]) with the body; if not, enlarge the striker hole.
3. Make sure that the striker properly engages the lock fork bolt.

Hood

REMOVAL AND INSTALLATION

1. Using protective covers, place them on the fenders.
2. Disconnect the electrical wiring connector from the underhood light.
3. Using a scribing tool, mark the area around the hinges to make the installation easier.
4. Support the hood and remove the hinge-to-hood bolts.
5. Remove the hood from the truck.
6. Installation is the reverse of removal.

ALIGNMENT

Align the hood so that the gaps between all of the components are equal; it must be flush with the fender and the cowl vent grille. Center the hood in the opening between the fenders, the cowl and the radiator grille. If it is difficult to center the hood or if the hood appears to be out of square, the front end sheet metal may need to be adjusted.

Tailgate

REMOVAL AND INSTALLATION

1. Lower and support the tailgate on a table or equivalent support.
2. Remove the left and right-side tailgate-to-fender striker bolts.
3. Remove the left and right-side tailgate hinge bolts and the tailgate from the truck.
4. To install, reverse the removal procedures. Torque the tailgate hinge bolts to 20 ft. lbs. and the striker plate-to-fender bolts to 20 ft. lbs. Check the operation of the tailgate.

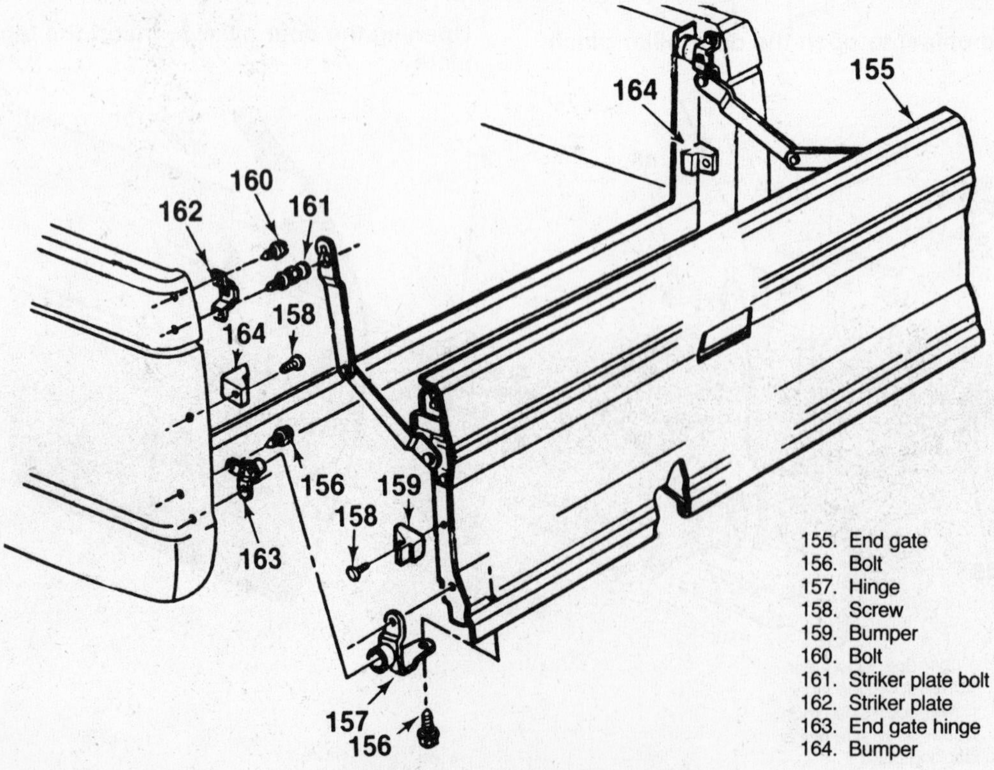

155
164
160
162
161
158
164
156
159
158
163
157
156
155. End gate
156. Bolt
157. Hinge
158. Screw
159. Bumper
160. Bolt
161. Striker plate bolt
162. Striker plate
163. End gate hinge
164. Bumper

Tailgate and related components

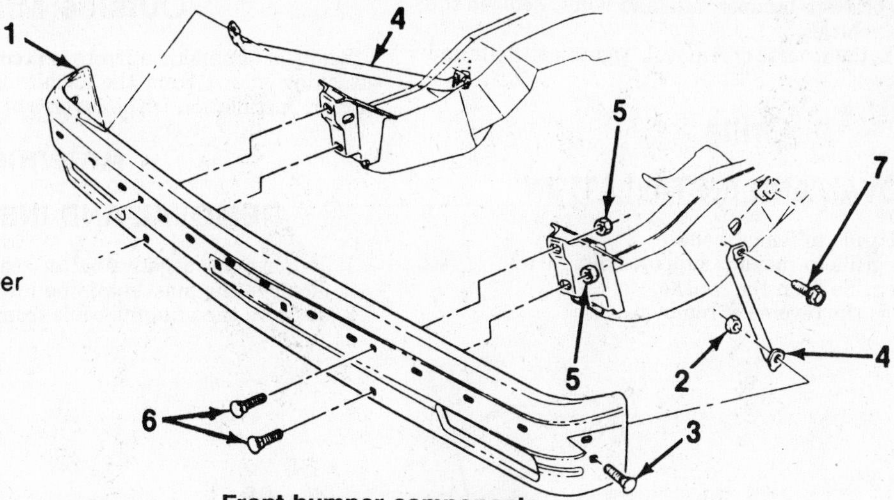
1
4
5
7
5
2
4
6
3

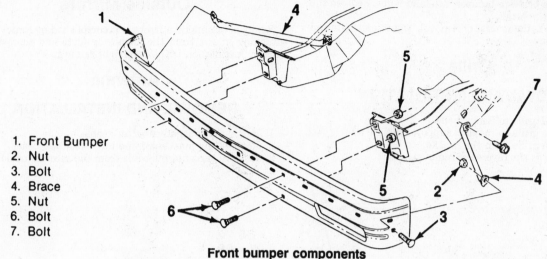

1. Front Bumper
2. Nut
3. Bolt
4. Brace
5. Nut
6. Bolt
7. Bolt

Front bumper components

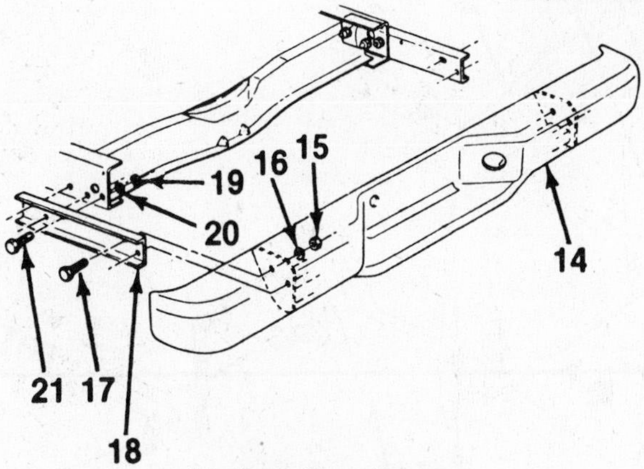
19
16
15
20
14
21
17
18

14. Rear Step Bumper
15. Nut
16. Washer
17. Bolt
18. Brace
19. Nut
20. Washer
21. Bolt

Rear step bumper components

ALIGNMENT

Align the tailgate so the gaps between all of the components are equal; it must be flush with the fenders. Center the tailgate in the opening between the fenders by adjusting the hinges and/or the striker bolts.

Bumper

REMOVAL AND INSTALLATION

Front

1. Remove the bumper to air dam bolts and support the air dam in the center.
2. Remove the brace to bumper nut and bolt.
3. Disconnect the parking lamp connectors.
4. Remove the bumper to frame nuts and bolts. Remove the bumper from the vehicle.
5. Installation is the reverse of removal. Tighten all nuts to 20 ft. lbs. and all bolts to 37ft. lbs.

Rear

1. On vehicles equipped with standard rear bumpers, remove the bracket to bumper nuts and bolts.

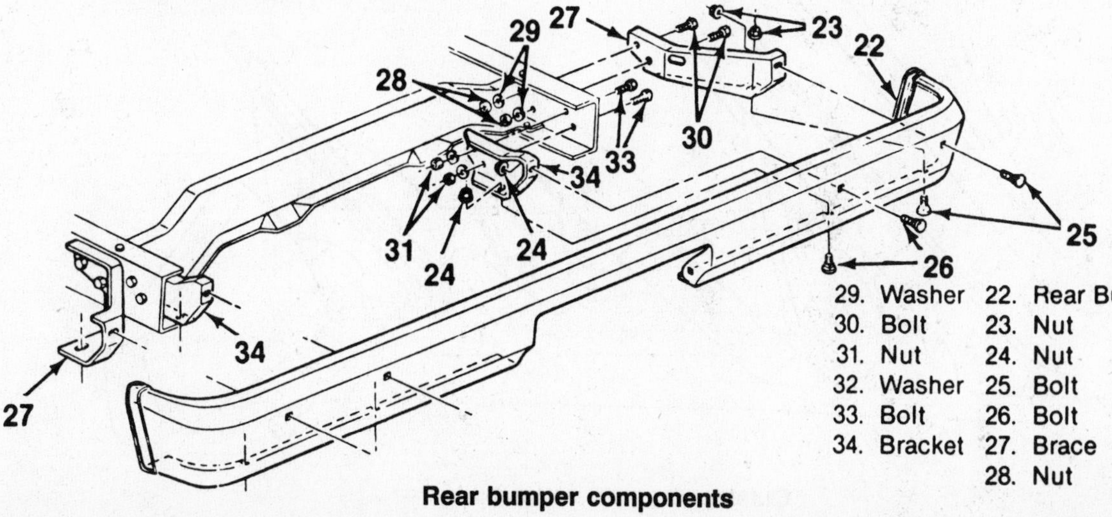
29
27
23
22
28
30
33
34
31
24
24
25
26
34
27

29. Washer
30. Bolt
31. Nut
32. Washer
33. Bolt
34. Bracket

22. Rear Bumper
23. Nut
24. Nut
25. Bolt
26. Bolt
27. Brace
28. Nut

Rear bumper components

2. Remove the brace to bumper nuts and bolts. Remove the bumper from the vehicle.
3. Installation is the reverse of removal. Tighten all bolts and nuts to 70 ft. lbs.

Grille

REMOVAL AND INSTALLATION

1. Remove the grille to fender bolts.
2. Remove the grille to radiator support bolts.
3. Remove the grille from the vehicle.
4. Installation is the reverse of removal.

Outside Mirrors

Removal of outside mirrors is accomplished by removing the attaching screws from the anchoring plate and removing the mirror. Installation is the reverse of removal.

Antenna

REMOVAL AND INSTALLATION

1. Remove the negative battery cable.
2. Remove the mast retaining nut, mast and bezel.
3. Remove the antenna cable from the receiver cable.

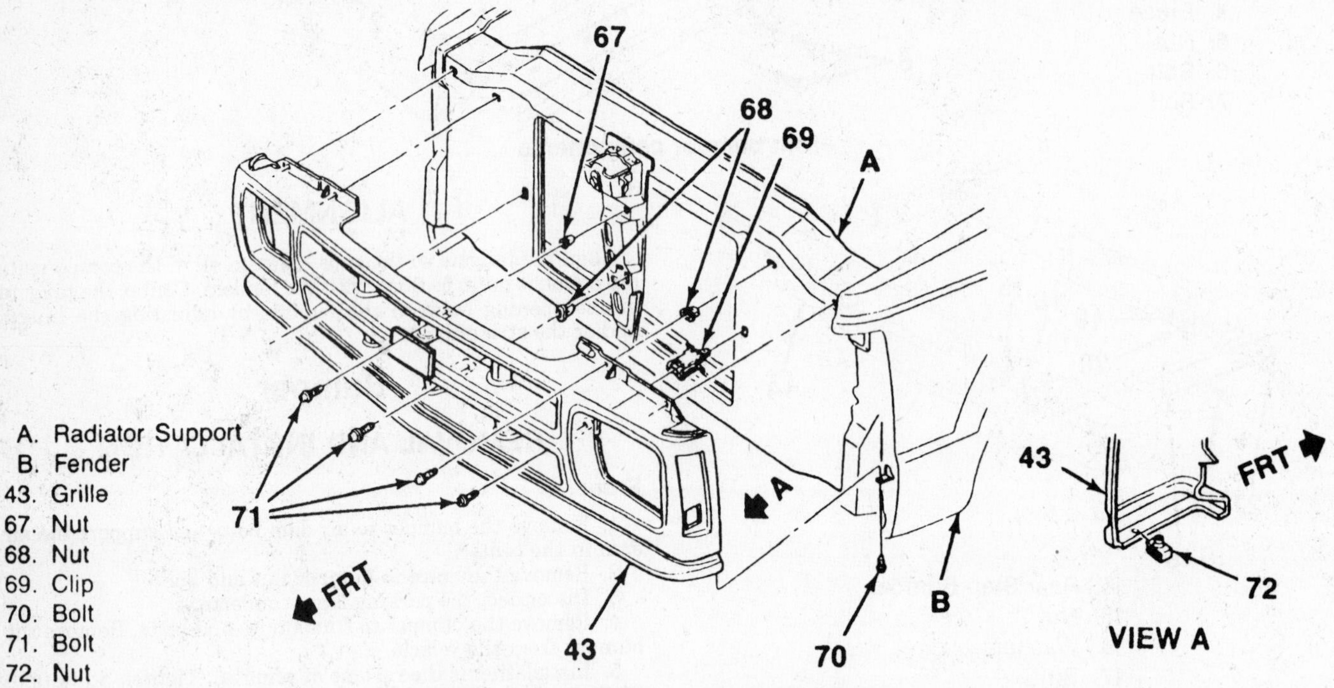

A. Radiator Support
B. Fender
43. Grille
67. Nut
68. Nut
69. Clip
70. Bolt
71. Bolt
72. Nut
67
68
69
A
71
FRT
A
43
70
B
43
FRT
72
VIEW A

1991 radiator grille — others similar

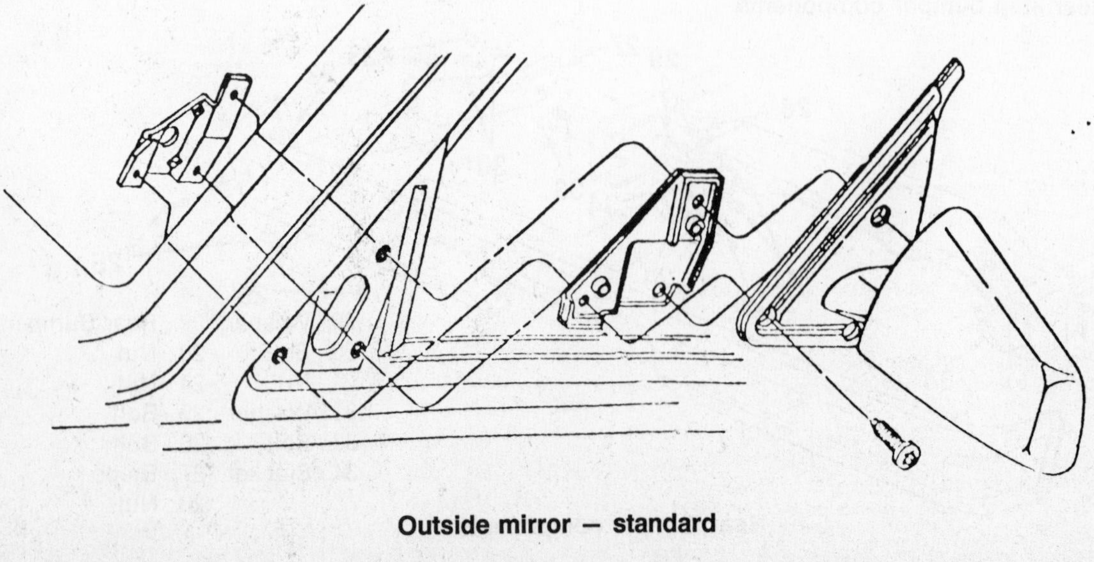

Outside mirror — standard

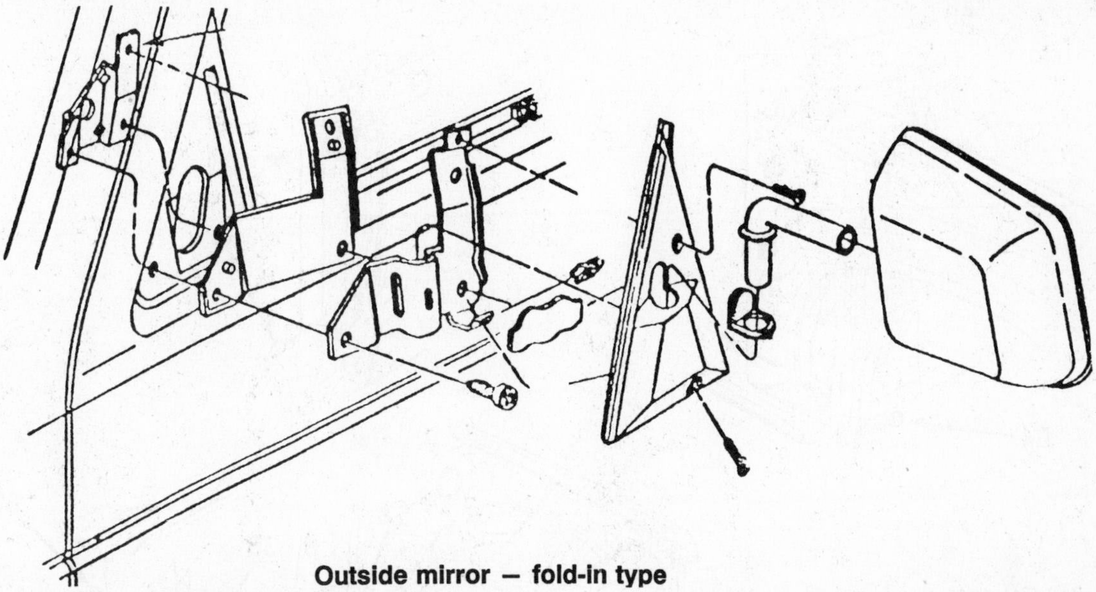

Outside mirror — fold-in type

4. Remove the screw and star washer attaching the antenna to the fender.
5. Remove the antenna.
6. Installation is the reverse of removal.

Fenders

REMOVAL AND INSTALLATION

Right

1. Remove the headlight bezels and radiator grille.
2. Remove the front bumper and filler panel.
3. Remove the battery, battery tray and radiator coolant bottle.
4. Remove the antenna mast and base.
5. Remove the windshield wiper arms and cowl vent grille.
6. Remove the hood hinge to fender nut and support the hood at the rear corner.
7. Remove the fender to radiator bolts, fender to reinforcement bolts, fender to door frame bolts and fender to door hinge bolts.
8. Remove the fender from the vehicle.
9. Installation is the reverse of removal. DO NOT tighten the bolts until the fender is aligned.
10. Align the fender so that all clearances are even. Tighten bolts securely.

Left

1. Remove the headlight bezels and radiator grille.
2. Remove the front bumper and filler panel.
3. Remove the radiator coolant bottle (if present) and the windshield wiper bottle.
4. Remove the hood latch cable.
5. Remove the windshield wiper arms and cowl vent grille.
6. Remove the hood hinge to fender nut and support the hood at the rear corner.
7. Remove the fender to radiator bolts, fender to reinforcement bolts, fender to door frame bolts and fender to door hinge bolts.
8. Remove the fender from the vehicle.
9. Installation is the reverse of removal. DO NOT tighten the bolts until the fender is aligned.
10. Align the fender so that all clearances are even. Tighten bolts securely.

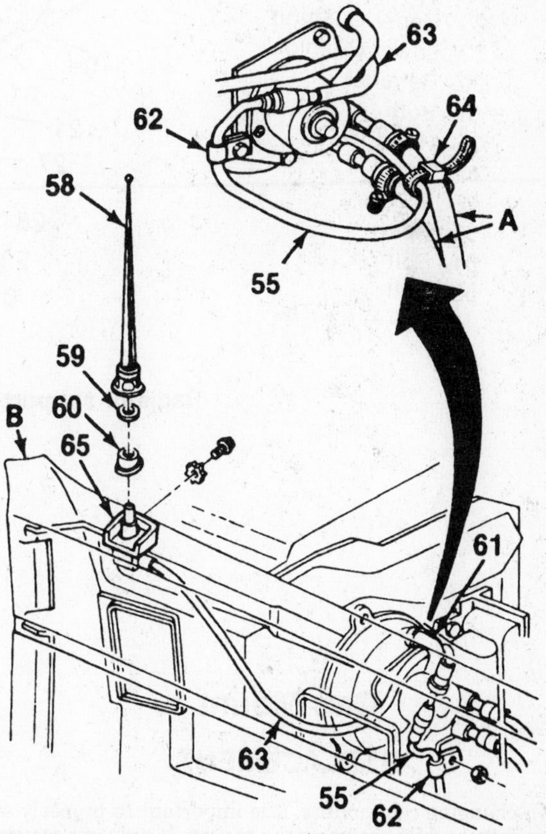
63
62
64
58
A
55
59
B
60
65
61
63
55
62

55. Antenna Cable, Receiver
58. Antenna
59. Nut
60. Bezel
61. Heater Vent Pipe
62. Clamp
63. Antenna Cable
64. Strap
65. Antenna Cable
A. Heater Hoses
B. Right Fender

Radio antenna components

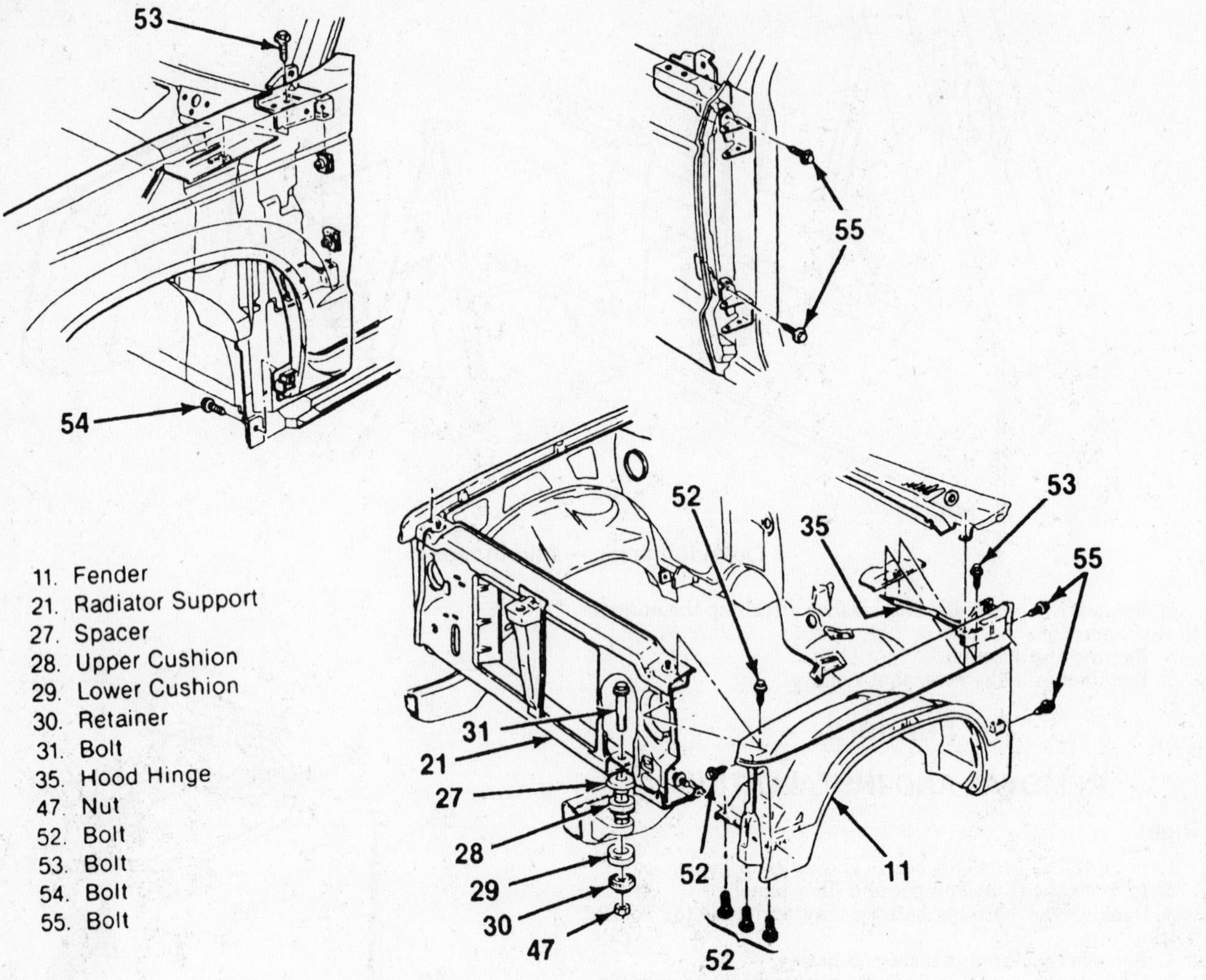
53
55
54
52
35
53
55
11. Fender
21. Radiator Support
27. Spacer
28. Upper Cushion
29. Lower Cushion
30. Retainer
31. Bolt
35. Hood Hinge
47. Nut
52. Bolt
53. Bolt
54. Bolt
55. Bolt
31
21
27
28
29
30
47
52
11
52

Radiator support and fender — exploded view

Cab Mount

REPLACEMENT

When changing cab mounts, it is important to properly support the frame while changing the mount. If only one mount is to be changed, the entire side on which the mount is placed must be lowered enough to provide clearance for the mount. Shims are available in various sizes to level the cab. The shim stack should not exceed ¼ in. (6mm).

1. Raise and support the vehicle safely. Place jackstands under the side of the body where the mounts will be replaced.
2. Remove the mount bolt, retainer and lower cushion.
3. Lower the vehicle enough to leave the body supported by the jackstands.
4. Remove the upper cushion, spacer and shims.
5. Installation is the reverse of removal. Tighten the bolts to 52 ft. lbs.

Spare Tire Carrier

REPLACEMENT

1. Lower the spare tire and remove it.
2. Remove the cotter pin and bolts attaching the spare tire hoist to the frame.
3. Remove the spare tire hoist.
4. Installation is the reverse of removal. Tighten bolts to 11 ft. lbs.

A. Shim Stack (Not to Exceed 6 mm [0.24 inch])
46. Spacer
47. Upper Cushion
48. Lower Cushion
49. Retainer
50. Bolt
51. Nut

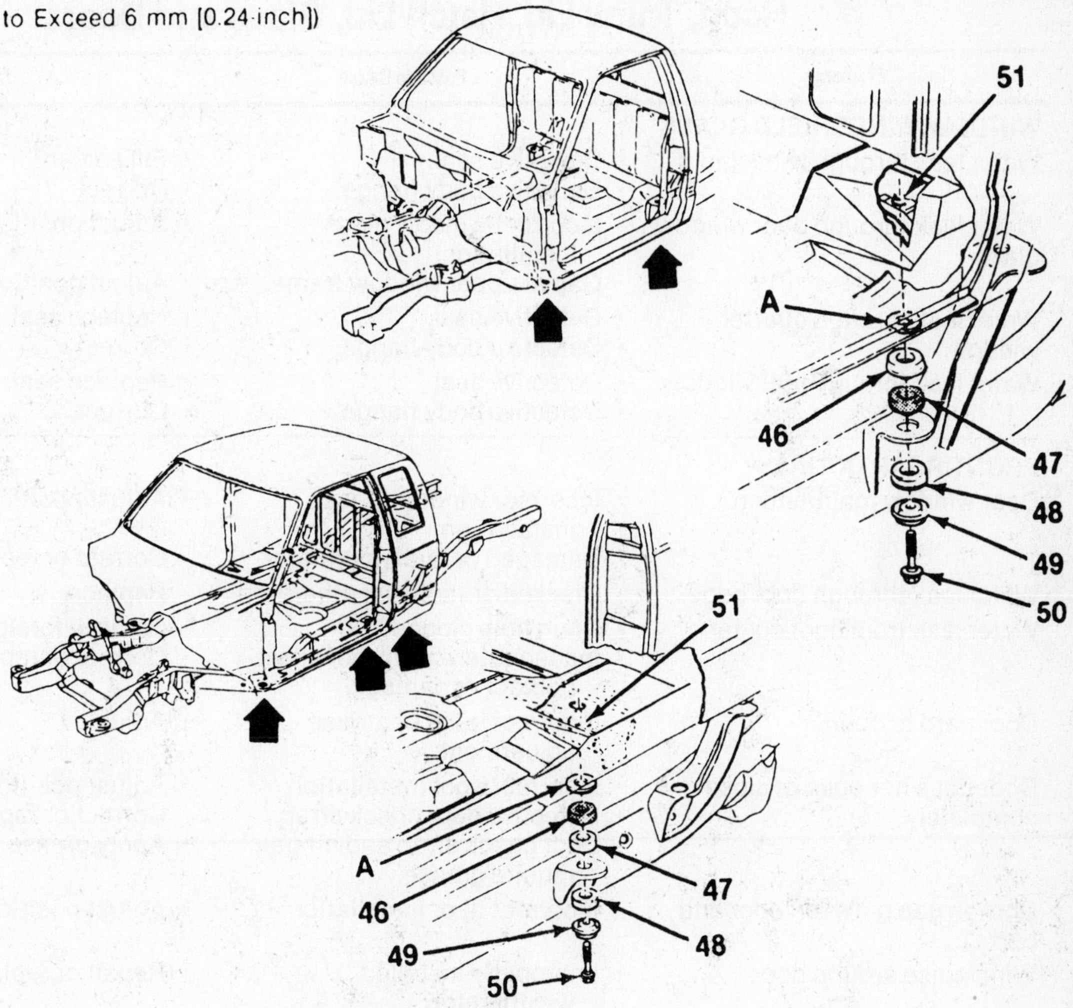

51
A
46
47
48
49
50
51
A
46
47
49
48
50

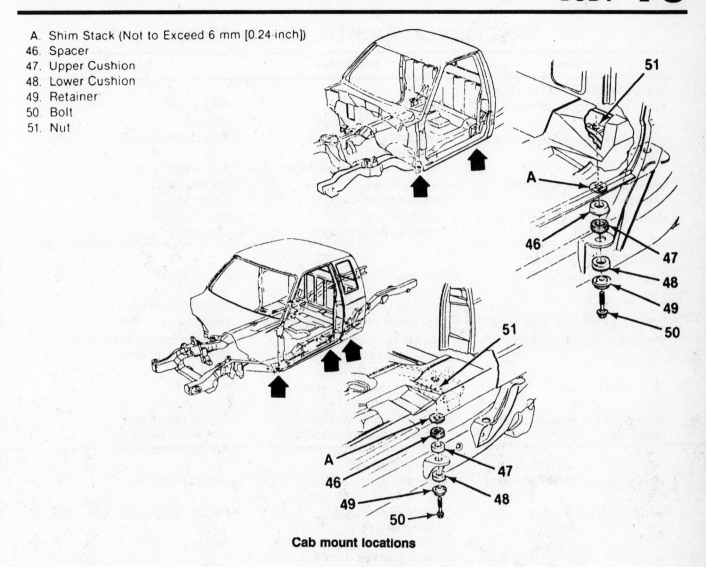

Cab mount locations

Hood, Trunk Lid, Hatch Lid, Glass and Doors

Problem	Possible Cause	Correction
HOOD/TRUNK/HATCH LID		
Improper closure.	• Striker and latch not properly aligned.	• Adjust the alignment.
Difficulty locking and unlocking.	• Striker and latch not properly aligned.	• Adjust the alignment.
Uneven clearance with body panels.	• Incorrectly installed hood or trunk lid.	• Adjust the alignment.

Hood, Trunk Lid, Hatch Lid, Glass and Doors

Problem	Possible Cause	Correction
WINDOW/WINDSHIELD GLASS		
Water leak through windshield	• Defective seal. • Defective body flange.	• Fill sealant • Correct.
Water leak through door window glass.	• Incorrect window glass installation. • Gap at upper window frame.	• Adjust position. • Adjust position.
Water leak through quarter window.	• Defective seal. • Defective body flange.	• Replace seal. • Correct.
Water leak through rear window.	• Defective seal. • Defective body flange.	• Replace seal. • Correct.
FRONT/REAR DOORS		
Door window malfunction.	• Incorrect window glass installation. • Damaged or faulty regulator.	• Adjust position. • Correct or replace.
Water leak through door edge.	• Cracked or faulty weatherstrip.	• Replace.
Water leak from door center.	• Drain hole clogged. • Inadequate waterproof skeet contact or damage.	• Remove foreign objects. • Correct or replace.
Door hard to open.	• Incorrect latch or striker adjustment.	• Adjust.
Door does not open or close completely.	• Incorrect door installation. • Defective door check strap. • Door check strap and hinge require grease.	• Adjust position. • Correct or replace. • Apply grease.
Uneven gap between door and body.	• Incorrect door installation.	• Adjust position.
Wind noise around door.	• Improperly installed weatherstrip. • Improper clearance between door glass and door weatherstrip. • Deformed door.	• Repair or replace. • Adjust. • Repair or replace.

INTERIOR

Door Handles

REMOVAL AND INSTALLATION

NOTE: The following procedure requires the use of the Window Handle Spring Removal tool No. J-9886 or equivalent.

Outside Handle

NOTE: Be sure the window is in the Full Up position.

1. Remove the door panel.
2. Remove the water deflector.
3. Remove the outside handle-to-lock rod from the door handle.

4. Remove the outside handle-to-door nuts and the door handle from the door.
5. Installation is the reverse of removal. Roll window down and check for proper operation of door handle.

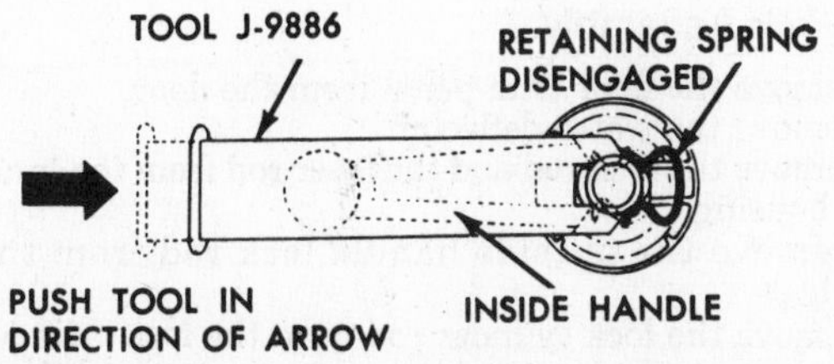
TOOL J-9886
RETAINING SPRING
DISENGAGED
PUSH TOOL IN
DIRECTION OF ARROW
INSIDE HANDLE

Removing the window regulator handle retaining spring

Inside Handle

1. Remove the door handle bezel-to-door screws and the bezel from the door.
2. Using the Window Handle Spring Removal tool No. J-9886 or equivalent, remove the window handle spring clip and the door handle.
3. Remove the armrest-to-door screws and the armrest.
4. Remove the door trim panel-to-door screws and the door trim panel from the door.
5. Remove the inner door handle housing-to-door screws, then slide the housing forward and pull it from the door.
6. Remove the control rods from the handle and the door lock.
7. Installation is the reverse of removal. Check the door handle operation.

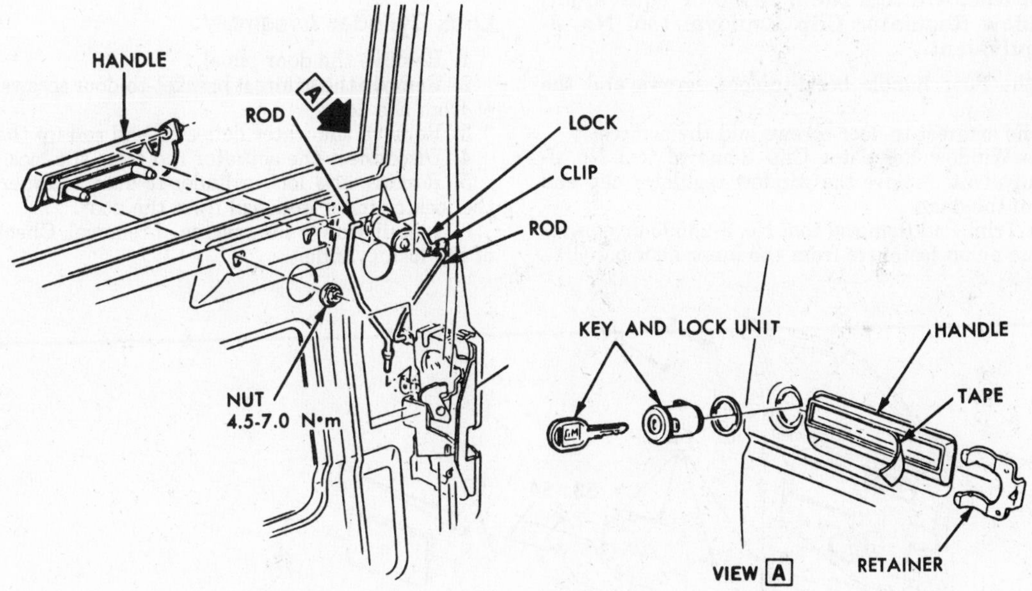
HANDLE
ROD
A
LOCK
CLIP
ROD
NUT
4.5-7.0 N•m
KEY AND LOCK UNIT
HANDLE
TAPE
VIEW A
RETAINER

Outside door handle and cylinder lock assembly – exploded view

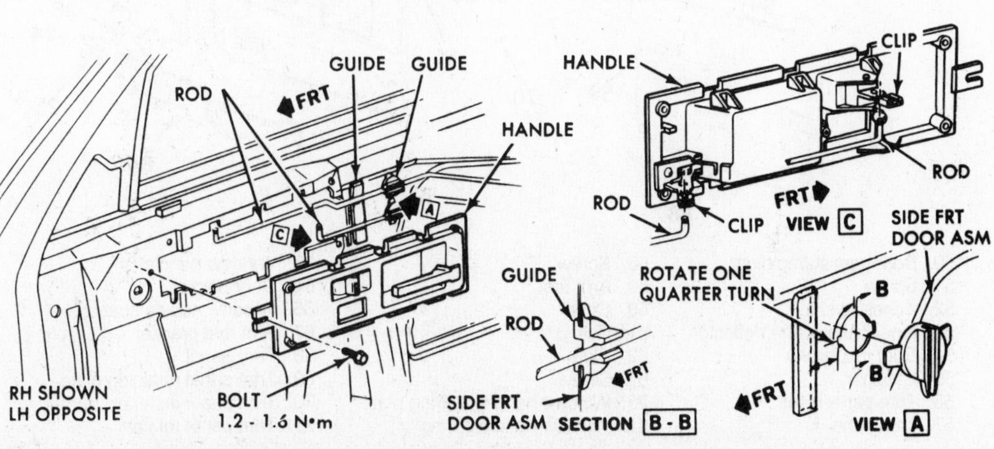
ROD
GUIDE
GUIDE
FRT
HANDLE
A
C
RH SHOWN
LH OPPOSITE
BOLT
1.2 - 1.6 N•m
HANDLE
CLIP
ROD
ROD
CLIP
FRT
VIEW C
SIDE FRT
DOOR ASM
GUIDE
ROD
ROTATE ONE
QUARTER TURN
B
B
FRT
SIDE FRT
DOOR ASM
SECTION B - B
FRT
VIEW A

Inner door handle and lock assembly – exploded view

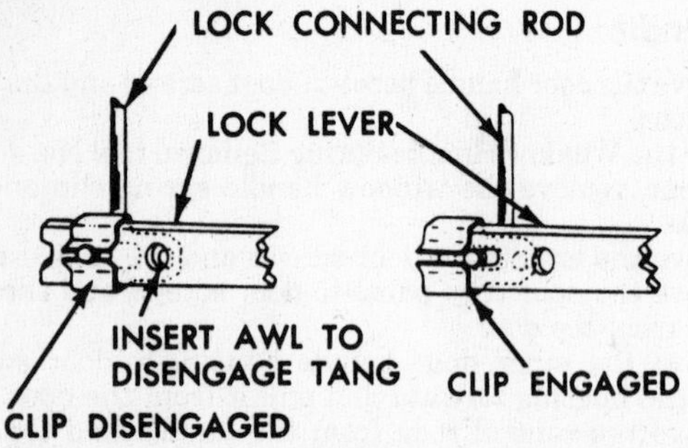
LOCK CONNECTING ROD
LOCK LEVER
INSERT AWL TO DISENGAGE TANG
CLIP ENGAGED
CLIP DISENGAGED

Disengaging and engaging the connecting rod retaining clip

Door Trim Panel

REMOVAL AND INSTALLATION

NOTE: The following procedure requires the use of the Trim Pad Removal tool No. J-24595 or equivalent, and the Window Regulator Clip Removal tool No. J-9886-01 or equivalent.

1. Remove the door handle bezel-to-door screws and the bezel.
2. Remove the armrest-to-door screws and the armrest.
3. Using the Window Regulator Clip Removal tool No. J-9886-01 or equivalent, remove the window regulator clip and the handle from the door.
4. Using the Trim Pad Removal tool No. J-24595 or equivalent, remove the nylon fasteners from the inner door panel.
5. If equipped with power windows, disconnect the electrical connector.
6. Installation is the reverse of removal.

Door Locks

REMOVAL AND INSTALLATION

Door Lock Assembly

1. Remove the door trim panel from the door.
2. Remove the water deflector.
3. Remove the lock rod and the lever rod from the inner door handle housing.
4. Remove the outside handle lock rod from the lock assembly.
5. Remove the lock cylinder rod from the lock cylinder.
6. Remove the lock assembly-to-door screws and the assembly from the door.
7. Installation is the reverse of removal. Check the operation of the lock assembly.

Lock Cylinder Assembly

1. Remove the door panel.
2. Remove the armrest bracket-to-door screws and the bracket from the door.
3. Remove the water deflector and roll up the window.
4. Disconnect the actuator rod from the lock cylinder.
5. Remove the lock cylinder-to-door retainer, then remove the lock cylinder and seal from the door.
6. Installation is the reverse of removal. Check the operation of the lock cylinder.

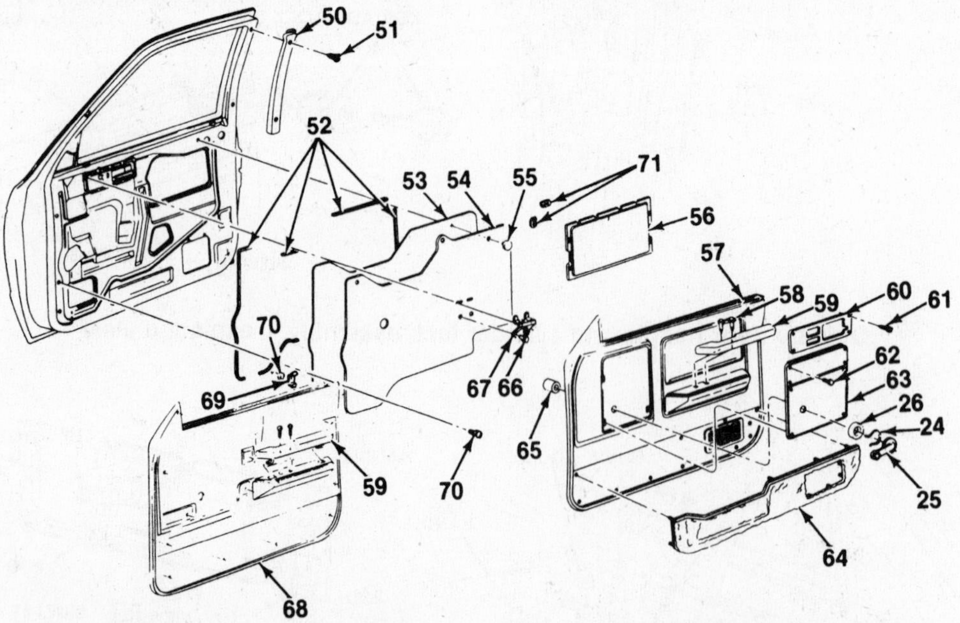
50
51
52
53
54
55
71
56
57
58
59
60
61
62
63
26
24
25
64
65
67
66
70
69
59
70
68

50. Door garnish molding
51. Screw
52. Adhesive strip
53. Inner panel water deflector
54. Door insulator
55. Retainer
56. Trim panel insert
57. Trim panel
58. Screw
59. Arm rest
60. Cover
61. Bolt
62. Plate
63. Screw
26. Window handle bearing plate
24. Window handle spring
25. Window handle
64. Door pocket
65. Window handle spacer
67. Arm rest bracket
68. Trim panel
69. Trim panel retaining plate
70. Trim panel fastener
71. Trim panel retainer

Door trim panel and related components

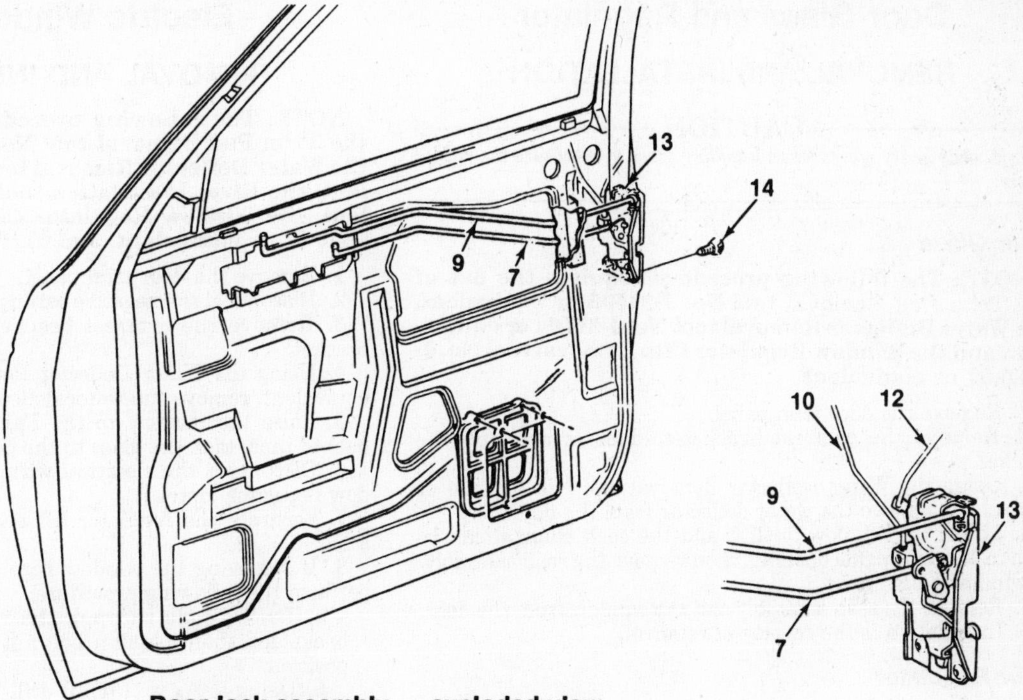
13
14
9
7
10
12
9
13
7

7. Door handle rod
9. Lock handle rod
10. Outside handle rod
12. Lock cylinder rod
13. Lock mechanism
14. Screw

Door lock assembly – exploded view

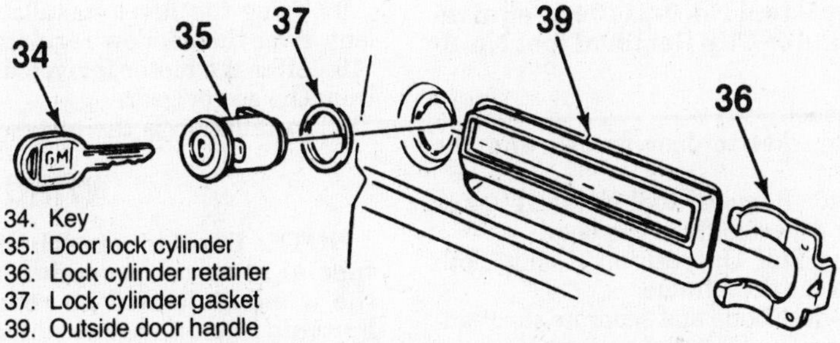
34
35
37
39
36
GM

34. Key
35. Door lock cylinder
36. Lock cylinder retainer
37. Lock cylinder gasket
39. Outside door handle

Lock Cylinder assembly – exploded view

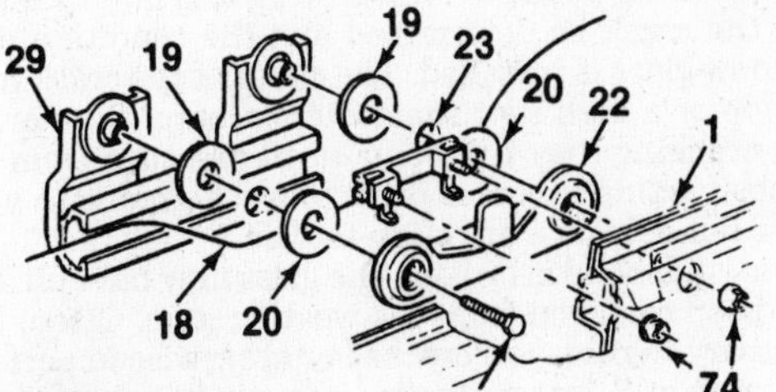
29
19
19
23
20
22
1
18
20
21
74

1. Door
18. Glass
19. Window glass mount washer
20. Window mount bushing
21. Bolt
22. Window mount sash
23. Side window retainer
29. Window mount sash
74. Nut

Window sash components

18. Glass
27. Bolt
28. Window Regulator
29. Window Mount Sash

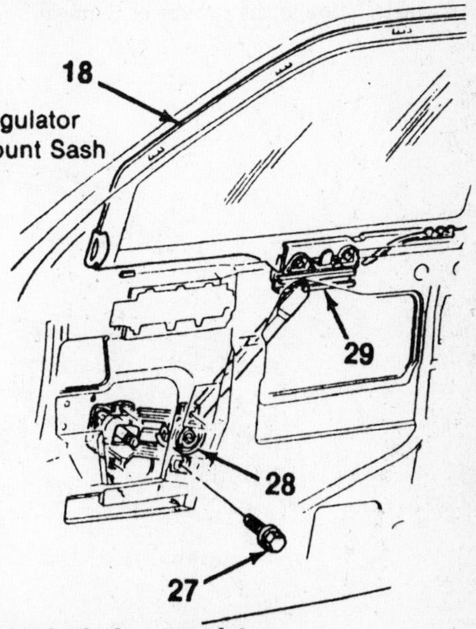
18
29
28
27

Standard window regulator

Door Glass and Regulator

REMOVAL AND INSTALLATION

CAUTION

Always wear heavy gloves when handling glass to minimize the risk of injury.

Door Glass

NOTE: The following procedure requires the use of the Trim Pad Removal tool No. J-24595 or equivalent, the Water Deflector Removal tool No. J-21104 or equivalent, and the Window Regulator Clip Removal tool No. J-9886-01 or equivalent.

1. Remove the door trim panel.
2. Remove the armrest bracket-to-door screws and the bracket.
3. Using the Water Deflector Removal tool No. J-21104 or equivalent, remove the water deflector from the door.
4. Lower the window until it and the sash channel can be seen in the door panel opening, then remove the sash assembly-to-window bolts.
5. Remove the sash assembly and the window from the door.
6. Installation is the reverse of removal.

Door Regulator

NOTE: The following procedure requires the use of the Trim Pad Removal tool No. J-24595 or equivalent, the Water Deflector Removal tool No. J-21104 or equivalent, and the Window Regulator Clip Removal tool No. J-9886-01 or equivalent.

1. Remove the door trim panel.
2. Remove the armrest bracket-to-door screws and the bracket.
3. Using the Water Deflector Removal tool No. J-21104 or equivalent, remove the water deflector from the door.
4. Raise the window to the Full Up position. Using cloth backed tape, tape the glass to the door frame.
5. Remove the regulator-to-door bolts and separate the regulator lift arm roller from the window sash, then remove the regulator from the door.
6. Installation is the reverse of removal.

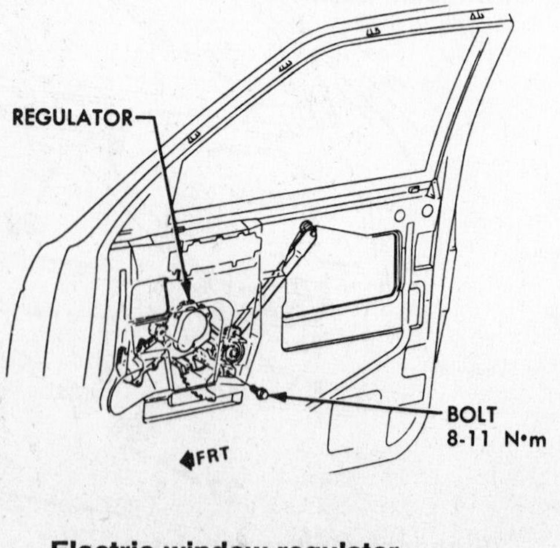
REGULATOR
BOLT
8-11 N•m
FRT

Electric window regulator

Electric Window Motor

REMOVAL AND INSTALLATION

NOTE: The following procedure requires the use of the Trim Pad Removal tool No. J-24595 or equivalent, the Water Deflector Removal tool No. J-21104 or equivalent, the Rivet Installation tool No. J-29022 or equivalent, the Window Regulator Clip Removal tool No. J-9886-01 or equivalent, and $^{3}/_{16}$ in. (5mm) rivets.

1. Remove the door trim panel.
2. Disconnect the negative battery terminal from the battery.
3. Remove the armrest bracket-to-door screws and the bracket.
4. Using the Water Deflector Removal tool No. J-21104 or equivalent, remove the water deflector from the door.
5. Raise the window to the Full Up position. Using cloth backed tape, tape the glass to the door frame.
6. Disconnect the electrical wiring connector from the window regulator motor.
7. Separate the regulator lift arm roller from the window sash.
8. If removing the window regulator motor from the door, perform the following procedure:
   a. Drill a hole through the regulator sector gear and backplate, then install a bolt/nut to lock the sector gear in position.
   b. Using a $^{3}/_{16}$ in. (5mm) drill bit, drill out the motor-to-door rivets.
   c. Remove the motor from the door.
9. Using the Rivet Installation tool No. J-29022 or equivalent, rivet the window regulator motor to the door.
10. After the motor is riveted to the door, remove the nut/bolt from the sector gear.
11. Installation is the reverse of removal.

Windshield

NOTE: Bonded windshields require special tools and special removal procedures to be performed to ensure the windshield will be removed without being broken. For this reason we recommend that you refer all removal and installation to a qualified technician.

CAUTION

Always wear heavy gloves when handling glass to reduce the risk of injury.

When replacing a cracked windshield, it is important that the cause of the crack be determined and the condition corrected, before a new glass is installed. The cause of the crack may be an obstruction or a high spot somewhere around the flange of the opening; cracking may not occur until pressure from the high spot or obstruction becomes particularly high due to winds, extremes of temperature or rough terrain.

When a windshield is broken, the glass may have already have fallen or been removed from the weatherstrip. Often, however, it is necessary to remove a cracked or otherwise imperfect windshield that is still intact. In this case, it is a good practice to crisscross the glass with strips of masking tape before removing the it; this will help hold the glass together and minimize the risk of injury.

If a crack extends to the edge of the glass, mark the point where the crack meets the weather strip. (Use a piece of chalk to mark the point on the cab, next to the weatherstrip.) Later, examining the window flange for a cause of the crack which started at the point marked.

The higher the temperature of the work area, the more pliable the weather strip will be. The more pliable the weather strip, the more easily the windshield can be removed.

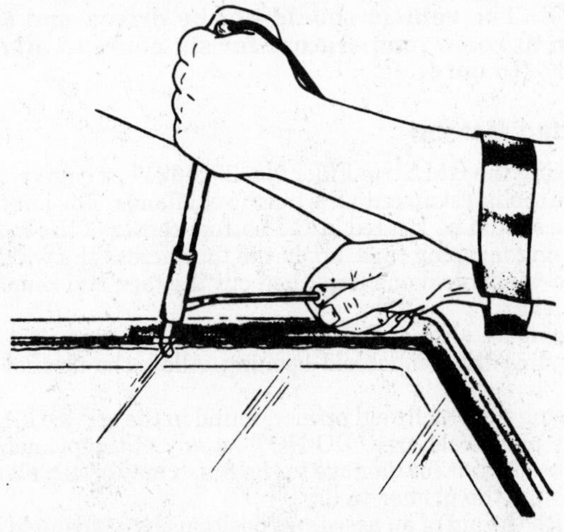

Using an electric knife to cut the window seal

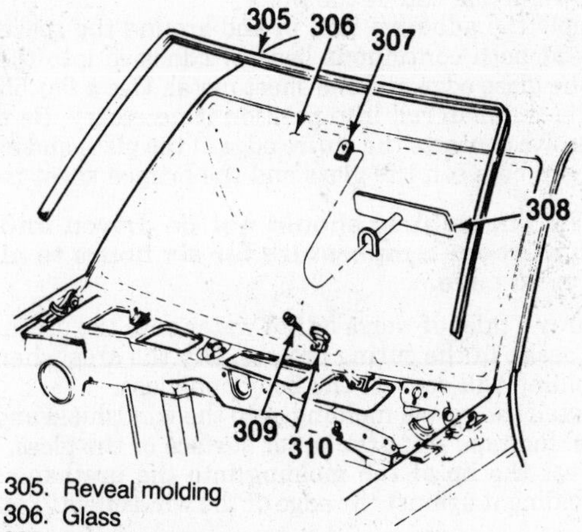
305
306
307
308
309
310

305. Reveal molding
306. Glass
307. Rear view mirror support
308. Rear view mirror
309. Screw
310. Support

Windshield components

There are two methods of windshield removal, depending on the method of windshield replacement chosen. When using the short method of installation, it is important to cut the glass from the urethane adhesive as close to the glass as possible. This is due to the fact that the urethane adhesive will be used to provide a base for the replacement windshield.

When using the extended method of windshield replacement, all the urethane adhesive must be removed from the pinchweld flange so, the process of cutting the window from the adhesive is less critical.

REMOVAL AND INSTALLATION

NOTE: The following procedure requires the use of the Urethane Glass Sealant Remover (hot knife) tool No. J-24709-1 or equivalent, the Glass Sealant Remover Knife tool No. J-24402-A or equivalent.

1. Place the protective covering around the area where the glass will be removed.
2. Remove the windshield wiper arms, the cowl vent grille, the windshield supports, the rear view mirror and the interior garnish moldings.

NOTE: If equipped with a radio antenna, embedded in the windshield, disconnect the electrical connector from the windshield.

3. Remove the exterior reveal molding from the urethane adhesive by prying one end of the molding from the adhesive. Pull the free end of the molding away from the windshield or the pinchweld flange until the molding is completely free of the windshield.
4. Using the Urethane Glass Sealant Remover (hot knife) tool No. J-24709-1 or equivalent, and the Glass Sealant Remover Knife tool No. J-24402-A or equivalent, cut the windshield from the urethane adhesive. If the short method of glass replacement is to be used, keep the knife as close to the glass as possible in order to leave a base for the replacement glass.
5. With the help of an assistant, remove the glass.
6. If the original glass is to be reinstalled, place it on a protected bench or a holding or holding fixture. Remove any remaining adhesive with a razor blade or a sharp scraper. Any remaining traces of adhesive material can be removed with denatured alcohol or lacquer thinner.

NOTE: When cleaning the windshield glass, avoid contacting the edge of the plastic laminate material (on the edge of the glass) with a volatile cleaner. Contact may cause discoloration and deterioration of the plastic laminate. DO NOT use a petroleum based solvent such as gasoline or kerosene; the presence of oil will prevent the adhesion of new material.

INSPECTION

Inspection of the windshield opening, the weather strip and the glass may reveal the cause of a broken windshield; this can help prevent future breakage. If there is no apparent cause of breakage, the weatherstrip should be removed from the flange and the flange inspected. Look for high weld or solder spots, hardened spot welds sealer, or any other obstruction or irregularity in the flange. Check the weatherstrip for irregularities or obstructions in it.

Check the windshield to be installed to make sure that it does not have chipped edges. Chipped edges can be ground off, restoring a smooth edge to the glass and minimizing concentrations of pressure that cause breakage. Remove no more than necessary, in an effort to maintain the original shape of the glass and the proper clearance between it and the flange of the opening.

INSTALLATION

To replace a urethane adhered windshield, the GM Adhesive Service Kit No. 9636067 contains some of the materials needed and must be used to insure the original integrity of the windshield design. Materials in this kit include:

1. One tube of adhesive material.
2. One dispensing nozzle.
3. Steel music wire.
4. Rubber cleaner.
5. Rubber Primer.
6. Pinchweld primer.
7. Blackout primer.
8. Filler strip (for use on windshield installations of vehicles equipped with an embedded windshield antenna).
9. Primer applicators.

Other materials required for windshield installation which are not included in the service kit, are:

1. GM rubber lubricant No. 1051717.
2. Alcohol for cleaning the edge of the glass.
3. Adhesive dispensing gun No. J-24811 or equivalent.
4. A commercial type razor knife.
5. Two rubber support spacers.

Short Method

1. Using masking tape, apply the tape across the windshield pillar-to-windshield opening, then cut the tape and remove the windshield.
2. Using an alcohol dampened cloth, clean the metal flange surrounding the windshield opening. Allow the alcohol to air dry.
3. Using the pinchweld primer, found in the service kit, apply it to the pinchweld area. DO NOT let any of the primer touch the exposed paint for damage to the finish may occur; allow five minutes for the primer to dry.
4. Cut the tip of the adhesive cartridge approximately $^3/_{16}$ in. (5mm) from the end of the tip.
5. Apply the adhesive first in and around the spacer blocks. Apply a smooth continuous bead of adhesive into the gap between the glass edge and the sheet metal. Use a flat bladed tool to paddle the material into position if necessary. Be sure that the adhesive contacts the entire edge of the glass and extends to fill the gap between the glass and the solidified urethane base.
6. With the aid of a helper, position the windshield on the filler strips against the two support spacers.

NOTE: The vehicle should not be driven and should remain at room temperature for six hours to allow the adhesive to cure.

7. Spray a mist of water onto the urethane. Water will assist in the curing process. Dry the area where the reveal molding will contact the body and glass.
8. Install new reveal moldings. Remove the protective tape covering the butyl adhesive on the underside of the molding. Push the molding caps onto each end of one of the reveal moldings. Press the lip of the molding into the urethane adhesive while holding it against the edge of the windshield. Take care to seat the molding in the corners. The lip must fully contact the adhesive and the gap must be entirely covered by the crown of the molding. Slide the molding caps onto the adjacent moldings. Use tape to hold the molding in position until the adhesive cures.
9. Install the wiper arms and the interior garnish moldings.

NOTE: The vehicle should not be driven and should remain at room temperature for six hours to allow the adhesive to cure.

Extended Method

1. Using the GM Strip Filler No. 20146247 or equivalent, install the sealing strip onto the pinchweld flange. The joint of the molding should be located at the bottom center of the molding.
2. Using masking tape, apply the tape across the windshield pillar-to-windshield opening, then cut the tape and remove the windshield.
3. Using an alcohol dampened cloth, clean the metal flange surrounding the windshield opening. Allow the alcohol to air dry.
4. Using the pinchweld primer, found in the service kit, apply it to the pinchweld area. DO NOT let any of the primer touch the exposed paint for damage to the finish may occur; allow five minutes for the primer to dry.
5. With the aid of an assistant, position the windshield on the filler strips against the two support spacers.
6. Cut the tip of the adhesive cartridge approximately $^3/_8$ in. (10mm) from the end of the tip.
7. Apply the adhesive first in and around the spacer blocks. Apply a smooth continuous bead of adhesive into the gap between the glass edge and the sheet metal. Use a flat bladed tool to paddle the material into position if necessary. Be sure that the adhesive contacts the entire edge of the glass and extends to fill the gap between the glass and the primed sheet metal.

NOTE: The vehicle should not be driven and should remain at room temperature for six hours to allow the adhesive to cure.

8. Spray a mist of warm or hot water onto the urethane. Water will assist in the curing process. Dry the area where the reveal molding will contact the body and glass.
9. Install the reveal molding onto the windshield and remove the masking tape from the inner surface of the glass.
10. Press the lip of the molding into the urethane adhesive while holding it against the edge of the windshield. Take care to

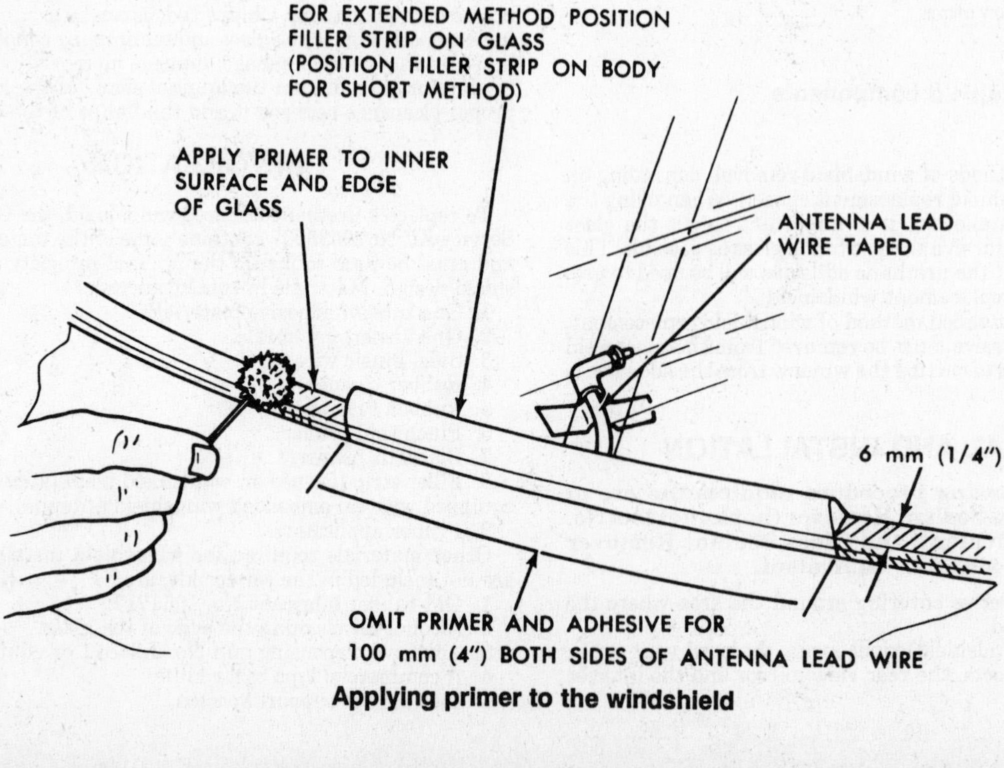
FOR EXTENDED METHOD POSITION FILLER STRIP ON GLASS (POSITION FILLER STRIP ON BODY FOR SHORT METHOD)
APPLY PRIMER TO INNER SURFACE AND EDGE OF GLASS
ANTENNA LEAD WIRE TAPED
6 mm (1/4")
OMIT PRIMER AND ADHESIVE FOR 100 mm (4") BOTH SIDES OF ANTENNA LEAD WIRE

Applying primer to the windshield

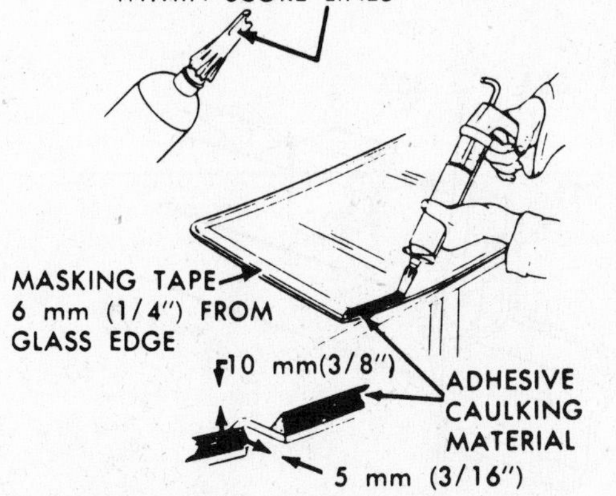
FOR EXTENDED METHOD ENLARGE NOZZLE BY CUTTING OUT MATERIAL WITHIN SCORE LINES
MASKING TAPE 6 mm (1/4") FROM GLASS EDGE
10 mm(3/8")
ADHESIVE CAULKING MATERIAL
5 mm (3/16")

Applying sealant to the windshield

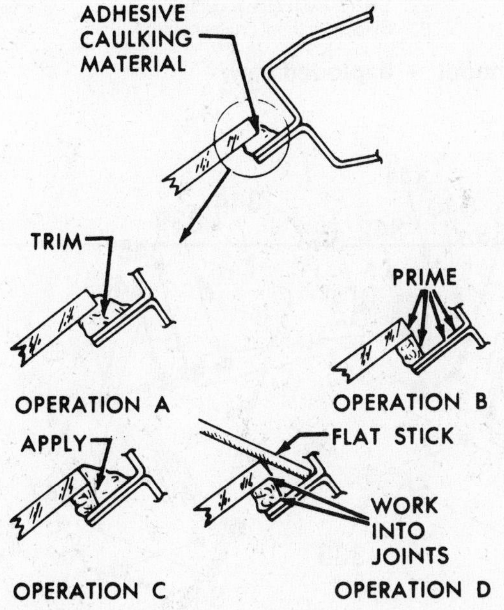
ADHESIVE CAULKING MATERIAL
TRIM
PRIME
OPERATION A
OPERATION B
APPLY
FLAT STICK
WORK INTO JOINTS
OPERATION C
OPERATION D

Trimming the sealant to accept the reveal trim molding

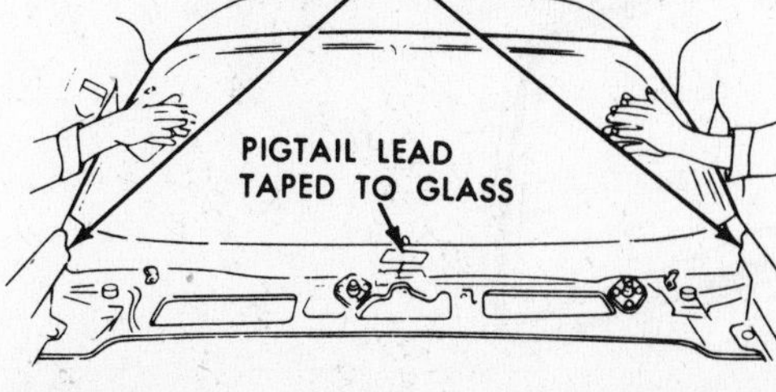
GUIDE GLASS ALONG REAR EDGE OF FRONT FENDER
PIGTAIL LEAD TAPED TO GLASS

Installing the glass onto the window frame

seat the molding in the corners. The lip must fully contact the adhesive and the gap must be entirely covered by the crown of the molding. Use tape to hold the molding in position until the adhesive cures.

11. Install the wiper arms and the interior garnish moldings.

Side Window – Extended Cab

REMOVAL AND INSTALLATION

Stationary

NOTE: The following procedure requires the use of the Urethane Glass Sealant Remover (hot knife) tool No. J-24709-1 or equivalent, and the Glass Sealant Remover Knife tool No. J-24402-A or equivalent.

1. Remove the upper quarter trim molding.
2. Remove the retaining clips.

NOTE: If the glass is cracked, it should be crisscrossed with masking tape to reduce the risk of damage to the vehicle. If a crack extends to the edge of the glass, mark the cab with a piece of chalk at the point where the crack meets the cab; this will aid the inspection later.

3. Working from inside the vehicle, use the Urethane Glass Sealant Remover (hot knife) tool No. J-24709-1 or equivalent, or the Glass Sealant Remover Knife tool No. J-24402-A or equivalent, separate the window glass and molding.
4. Remove the molding and the glass from the window frame.
5. Using a scraper or a chisel, remove the adhesive from the pinchweld flange; be sure to remove all of the mounds or loose adhesive.
6. Using alcohol and a clean cloth, clean the pinchweld flange. Allow the alcohol to air dry.
7. Using the pinchweld primer, found in the service kit, apply it to the pinchweld area. DO NOT let any of the primer touch the exposed paint for damage to the finish may occur; allow five minutes for the primer to dry.
8. Apply a smooth continuous bead of adhesive around the molding edge. Be sure that the adhesive contacts the entire edge of the molding and extends to fill the gap between the glass and the primed sheet metal.
9. Using hand pressure, press the glass/molding assembly onto the pinchweld flange. Using retaining clips, secure the glass/molding assembly to the pinchweld.
10. Spray a mist of warm or hot water onto the urethane. Water will assist in the curing process. Dry the area where the reveal molding will contact the body and glass.

Latched

NOTE: The following procedure requires the use of a pin punch and a mallet.

1. Using a pin punch and a mallet, drive the pin from the latch assembly.
2. Remove the glass-to-hinge retaining screws and the glass from the vehicle.
3. Installation is the reverse of removal.

Rear Window Glass

REMOVAL AND INSTALLATION

NOTE: The following procedure requires the use of a ¼ in. (6mm) cord, a putty knife and an assistant.

1. Using a putty knife, run it between the weatherstrip and the flange on both sides.
2. Position an assistant on the outside of the cab by the window, to catch the window.

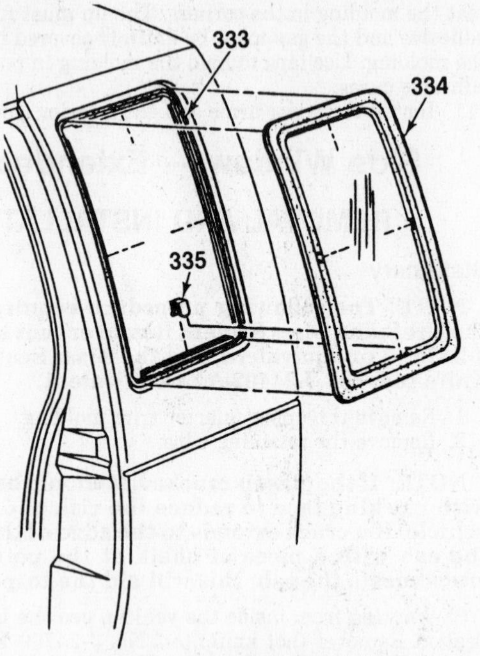
333
334
335

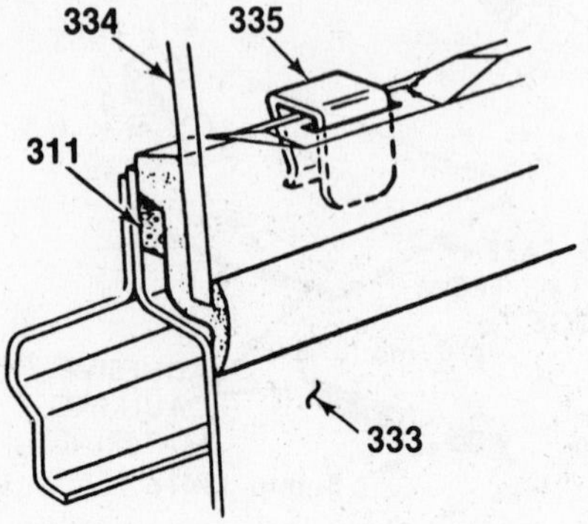
334
335
311
333

21. Clip
22. Switch (with cruise control)
23. Switch (without cruise control)

Stationary side window on the extended cab model – exploded view

336. Hinge
337. Rivet
338. Seal
339. Bolt
340. Screw
341. Pin
342. Latch
343. Retainer
344. Glass
345. Bearing
346. Bushing
347. Nut
348. Shim

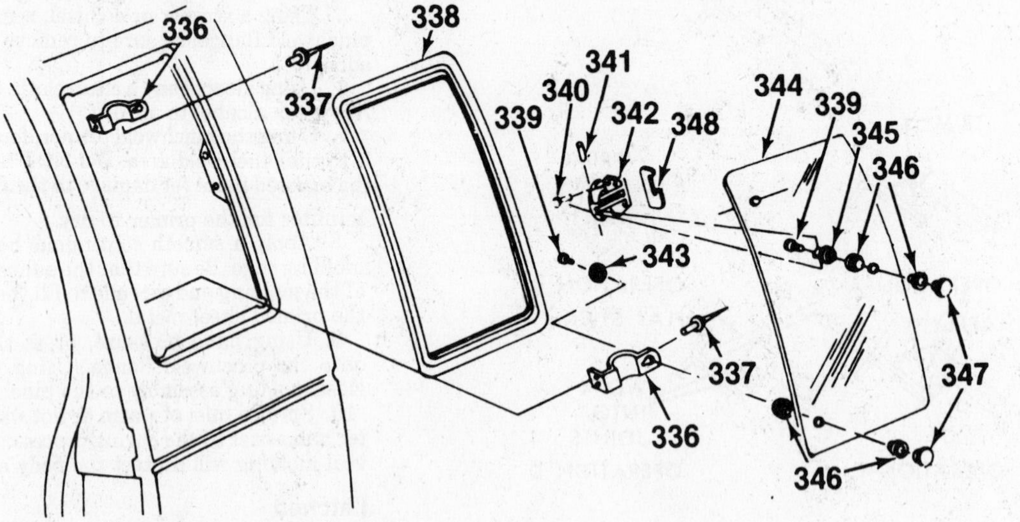
336
338
337
341
340
339
342
348
344
339
345
346
343
337
347
336
346

Latched side window on the extended cab model – exploded view

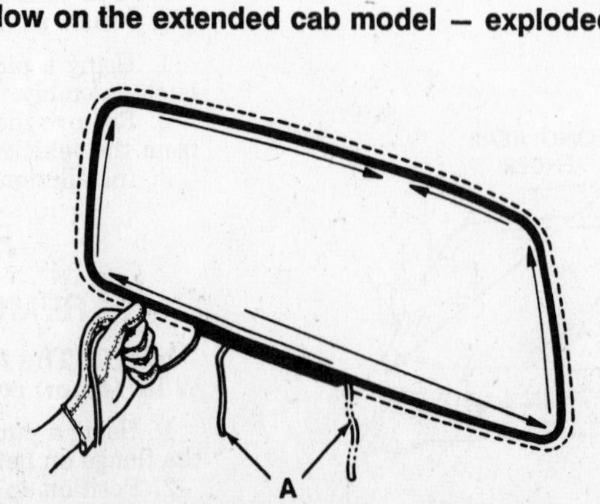
A

A. Overlap

Using a cord to install the rear window

3. Using a putty knife, on the inside of the rear window, force the weatherstrip/glass assembly, from the flange.
4. Separate the glass from the weatherstrip.

NOTE: To ease the weatherstrip installation, heat it with a non-flame source heater; at higher temperatures the weatherstrip is more pliable. DO NOT heat it above 125°F (52°C) or for more than 1½ hours.

5. To install, position the rear window glass in the weatherstrip.
6. Using a ¼ in. (6mm) cord, place it in the weatherstrip groove; the ends should overlap 6 in. (152mm) at the bottom of the window.
7. Using soapy water, lubricate the flange and the weatherstrip.
8. Position an assistant inside the cab, install the weatherstrip/glass assembly and have the assistant pull the cord to seat the weatherstrip on the window flange.
9. Apply a light mist of water to the window to check for leaks. If leak(s) are present, use urethane sealant to remedy the problem(s).

Inside Rear View Mirror

REPLACEMENT

1. Determine the location of the rear view mirror and using a wax pencil, draw a centerline on the outside of the glass from the roof panel to the windshield base.
2. Draw a line intersecting the centerline 23 in. (584mm) from the base of the glass. THe base of the support will be located at the intersection of these lines.
3. Clean the inside glass within 3 in. (76mm) of the intersecting lines. Using a glass cleaning solution rub the area until completely dry. Reclean with a towel saturated with alcohol.
4. Sand the bonding surface of the rear view mirror support with 320 grit sandpaper. Remove all traces of the factory adhesive if reusing the old support. Wipe the mirror support with alcohol and allow to dry.
5. Apply Loctite® Minuit Bond Adhesive 312, or equivalent to the mirror support bonding surfaces.
6. Place the bottom of the support at the premarked line. The rounded edge of the support should face upward.
7. Press the support against the glass for 30–60 seconds with a steady pressure. Allow the adhesive to dry 5 minutes to dry before cleaning.
8. Clean all traces of adhesive and wax from the windshield with alcohol.

Seats

REMOVAL AND INSTALLATION

To remove the front bench seat, simply remove the seat retaining nuts and lift the seat assembly from the body. Installation is the reverse of removal. Tighten the seat retaining nuts to 24 ft. lbs.

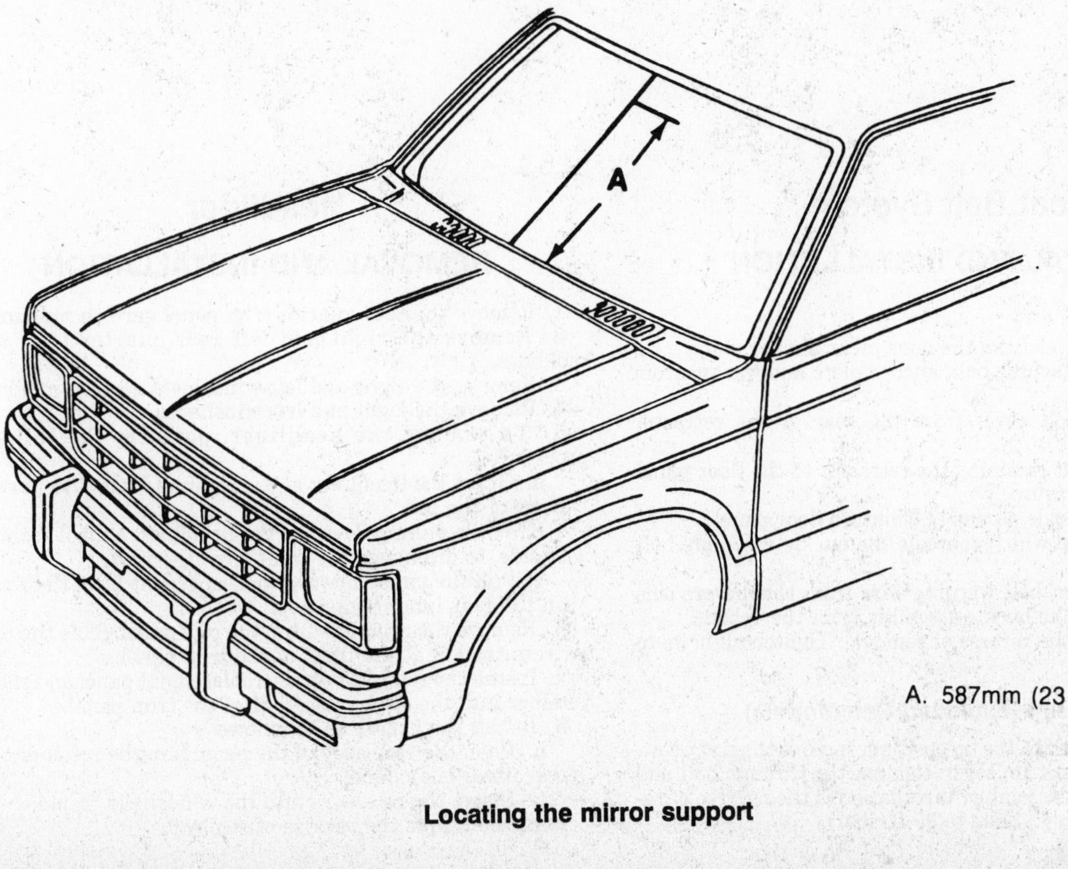
A

A. 587mm (23 1/8")

Locating the mirror support

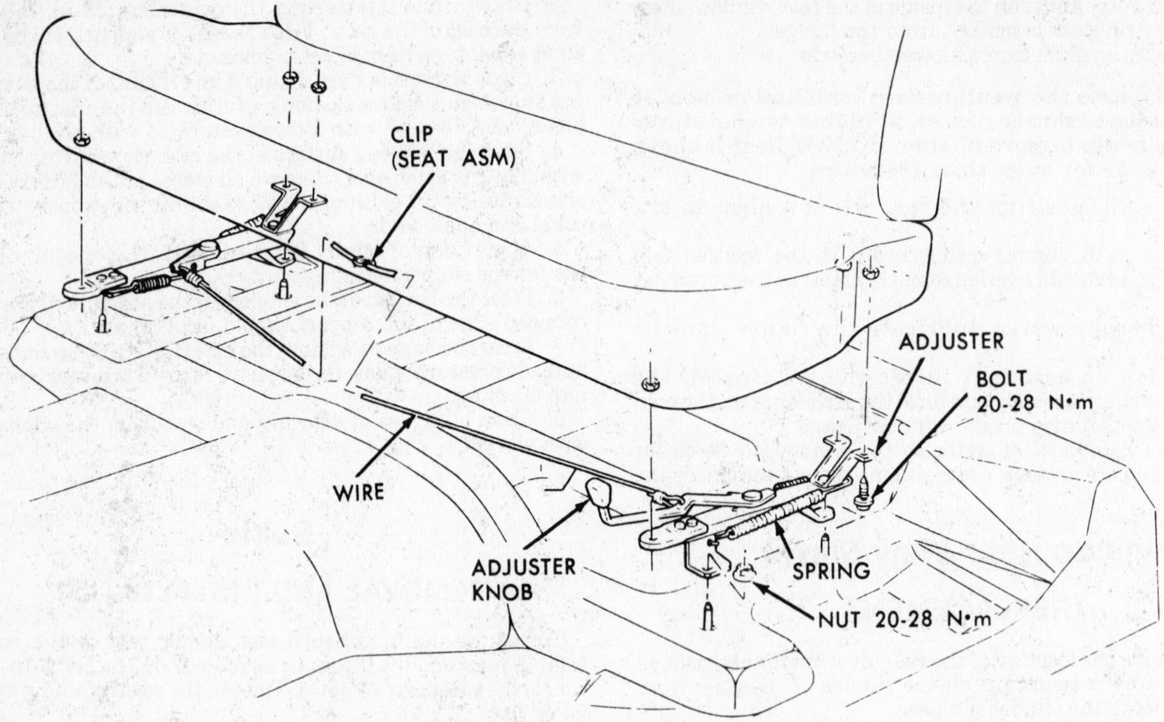
CLIP
(SEAT ASM)
ADJUSTER
BOLT
20-28 N•m
WIRE
ADJUSTER
KNOB
SPRING
NUT 20-28 N•m

Front bench seat and adjuster assembly

Seat Belt System

REMOVAL AND INSTALLATION

Front Seat Belt

1. Remove the cover from the door pillar anchor plate.
2. Remove the attaching bolt, anchor plate and washer from the door pillar.
3. Remove the bolt cover from the rear of the retractor assembly.
4. Remove the bolt retaining the retractor to the floor panel and remove the retractor.
5. Remove the buckle assembly from the floor panel.
6. Remove the cap which conceals the buckle assembly bolt and remove the bolt.
7. Remove the seat belt warning wire from the drivers side buckle and remove the buckle assembly from the vehicle.
8. Installation is the reverse of removal. Tighten all bolts to 39 ft. lbs.

Rear Jump Seat Belt (Extended Cab Models)

With the seat folded to the up position, remove the screws attaching the jump seat trim cover. Remove the through bolt and remove the seat belt assembly. Installation is the reverse of removal. Tighten through bolts to 35 ft. lbs.

Headliner

REMOVAL AND INSTALLATION

1. Remove the rear-quarter trim panel garnish molding.
2. Remove the right and left rear-quarter trim upper moldings.
3. Remove the right and left windshield garnish molding.
4. Remove the right and left sunshades.
5. To remove the headliner, perform the following procedures:
   a. Grasp the headliner at the right and left-sides, near the front of the cab.
   b. While pulling down on the headliner, shift it from side-to-side, to disengage the front from the roof.
   c. Pull the panel forward to disengage it from the retainer on the rear inner body panel.
6. Remove the retainers from the roof panel. Slide the retainer from the slit at the front of the trim panel.
7. Install the retainers on the replacement panel and slide the retainer into the slit at the front of the trim panel.
8. Install the headliner as follows:
   a. Push the rear edge of the panel into the retainer on the rear inner body panel.
   b. Insert the retainers into the windsheild frame.

9.Installation is the reverse of removal.

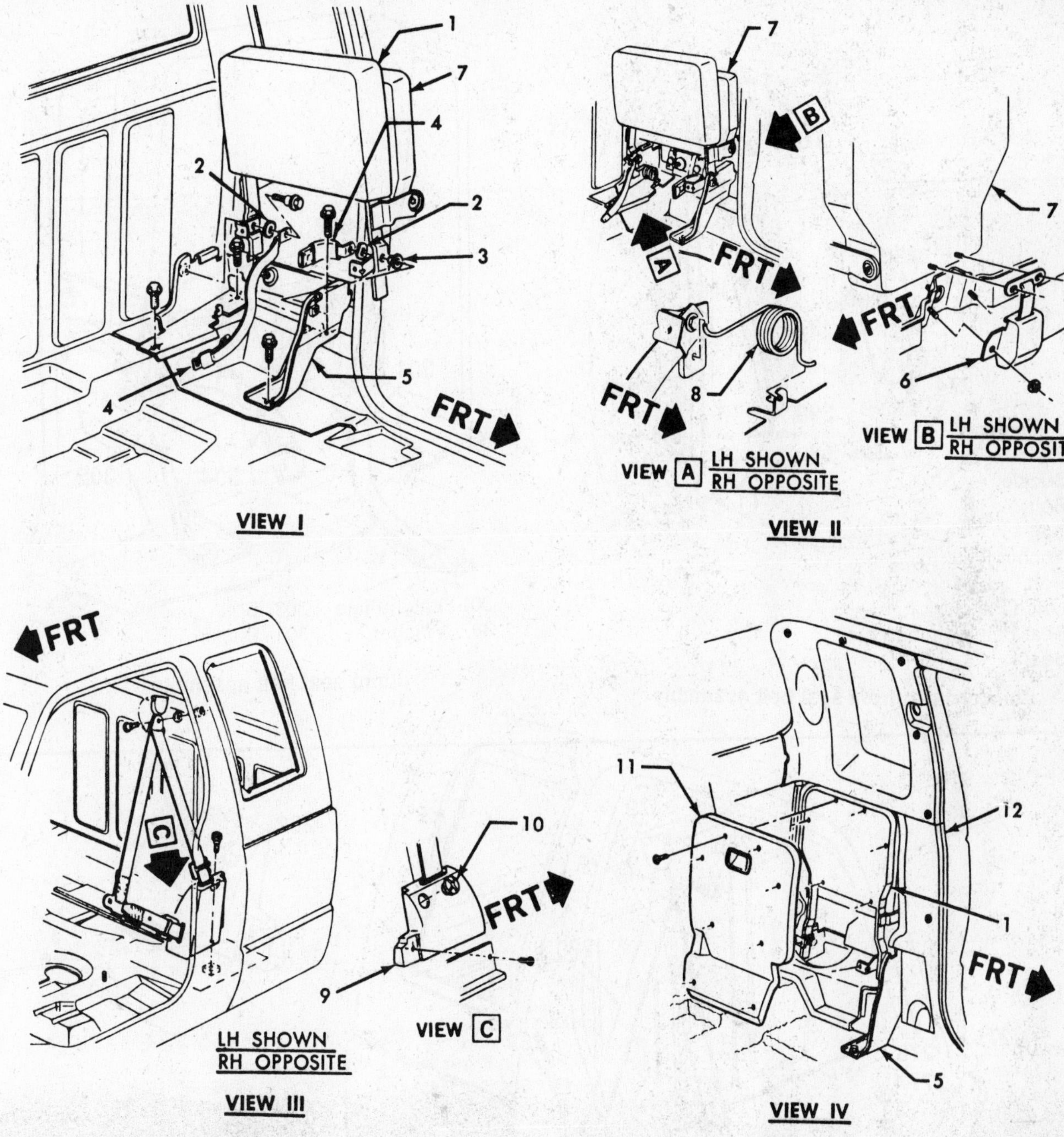

VIEW I
VIEW A LH SHOWN RH OPPOSITE
VIEW B LH SHOWN RH OPPOSITE
VIEW II
LH SHOWN RH OPPOSITE
VIEW C
VIEW III
VIEW IV
FRT

1. SEAT CUSHION ASSEMBLY
2. SPRING WASHER
3. PIVOT BUSHING
4. SEAT LAP BELT
5. SEAT MOUNTING SUPPORT BRACKET
6. SEAT BACK LOCK-ASSEMBLY
7. SEAT BACK ASSEMBLY
8. TENSIONER SPRING
9. FRONT SEAT BELT ASSEMBLY
10. PLUG
11. SEAT CUSHION BOTTOM TRIM PANEL
12. BODY SIDE LOWER TRIM PANEL

Folding jump seat components

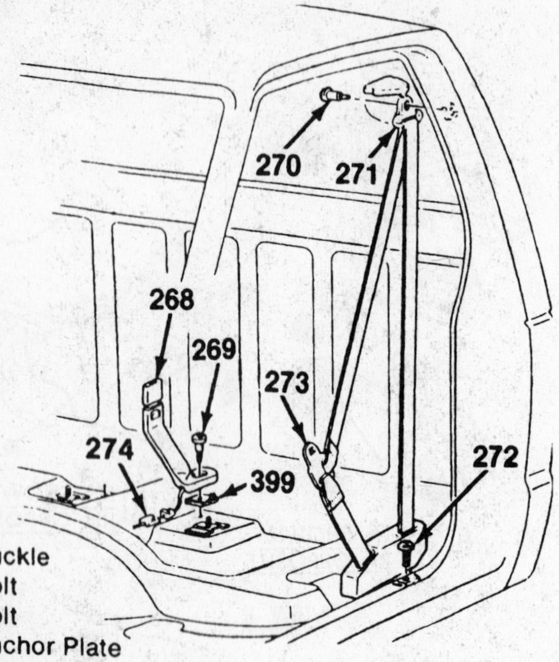
270
271
268
269
273
274
399
272

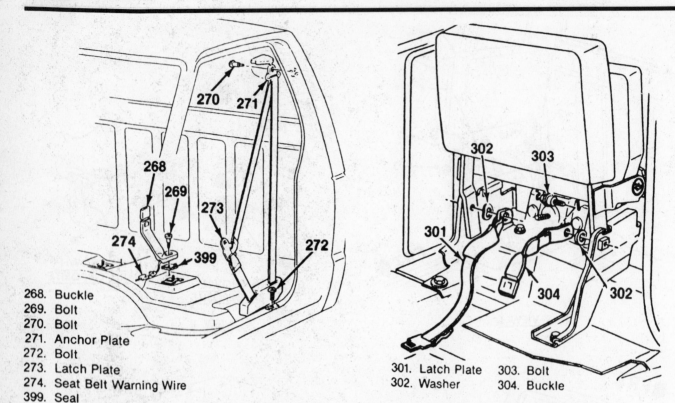

268. Buckle
269. Bolt
270. Bolt
271. Anchor Plate
272. Bolt
273. Latch Plate
274. Seat Belt Warning Wire
399. Seal

Standard cab front seat belt assembly

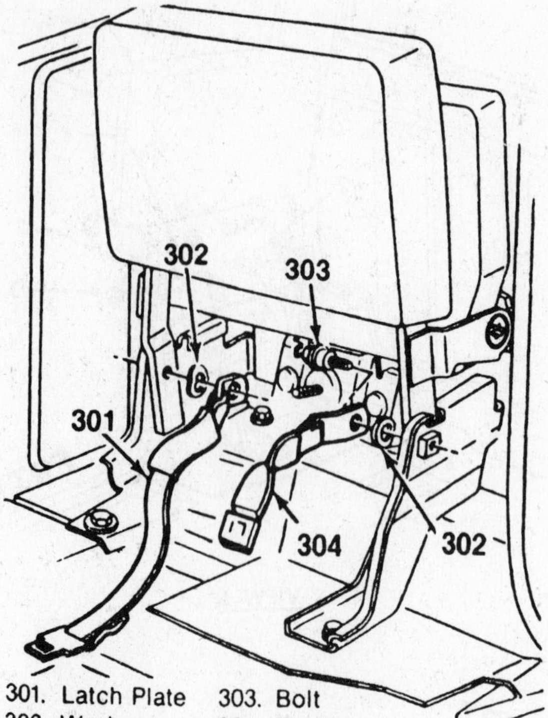
302
303
301
304
302

301. Latch Plate
302. Washer
303. Bolt
304. Buckle

Jump seat belt assembly

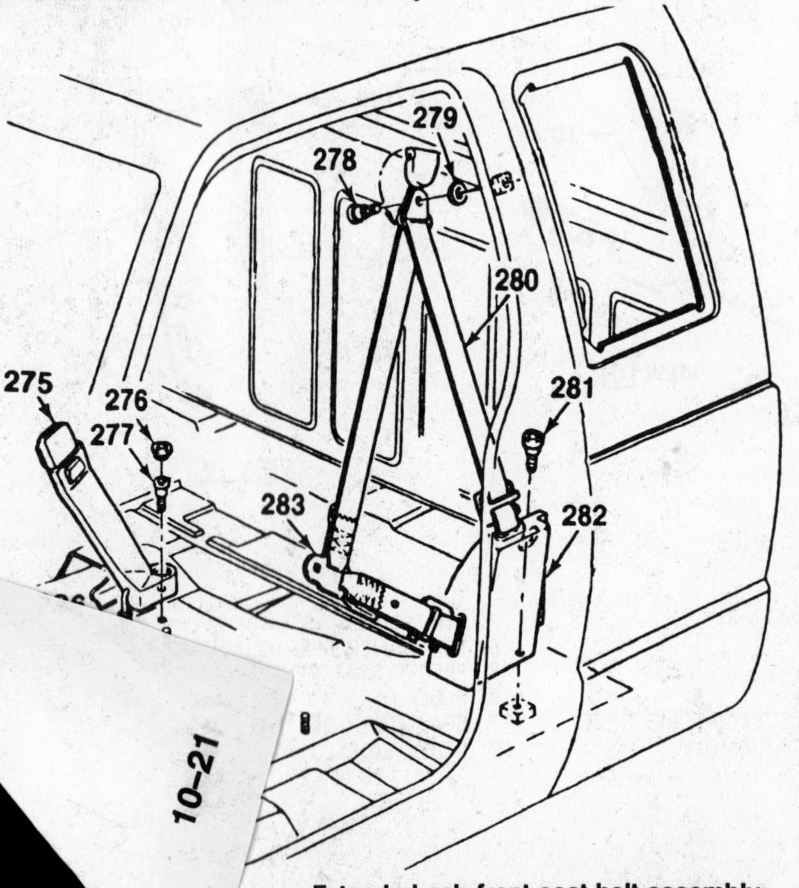
279
278
280
275
276
277
281
283
282

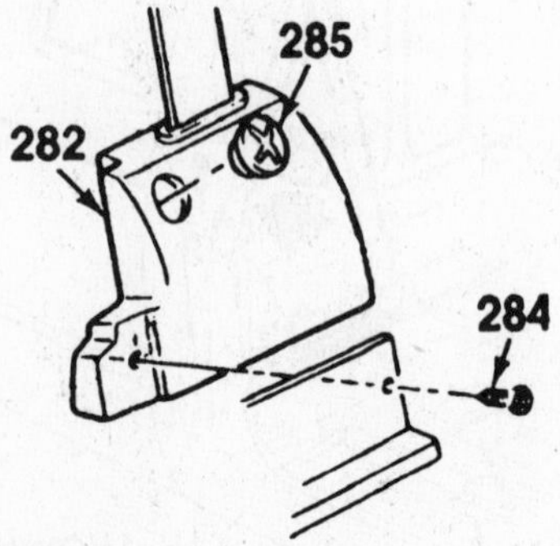
285
282
284

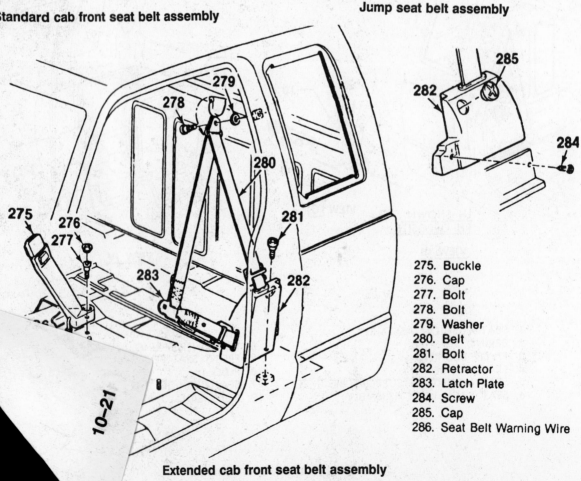

275. Buckle
276. Cap
277. Bolt
278. Bolt
279. Washer
280. Belt
281. Bolt
282. Retractor
283. Latch Plate
284. Screw
285. Cap
286. Seat Belt Warning Wire

Extended cab front seat belt assembly

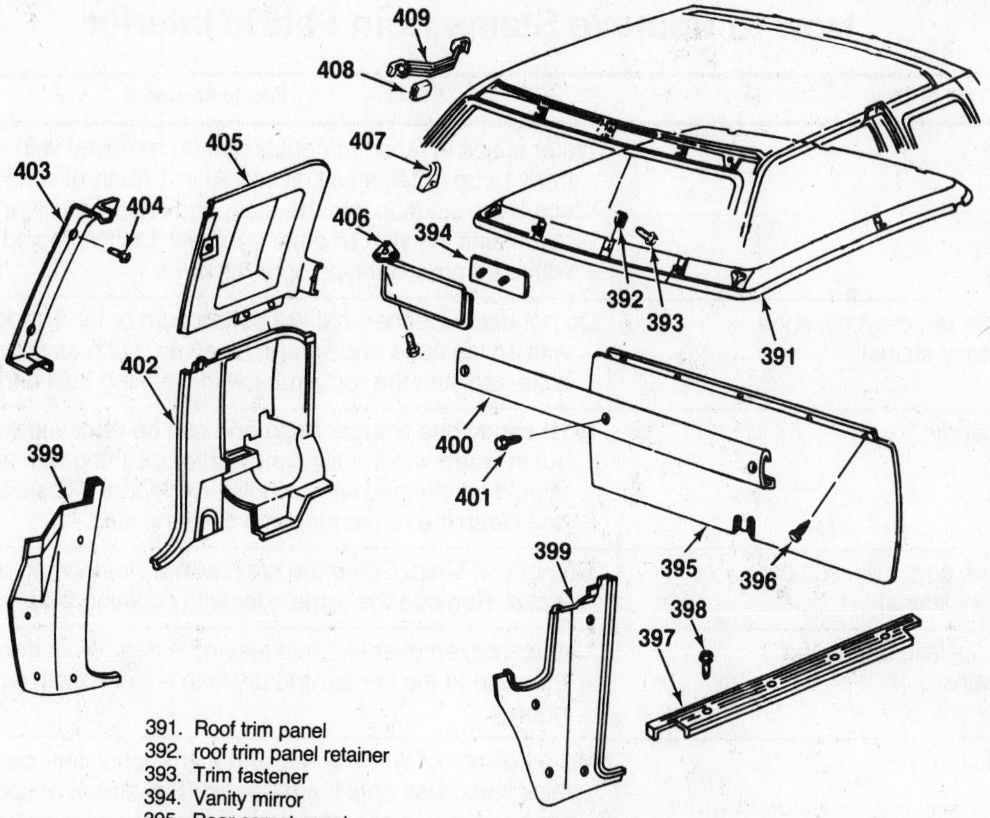
409
408
405
407
403
404
406
394
392
393
391
402
400
401
399
399
395
396
398
397

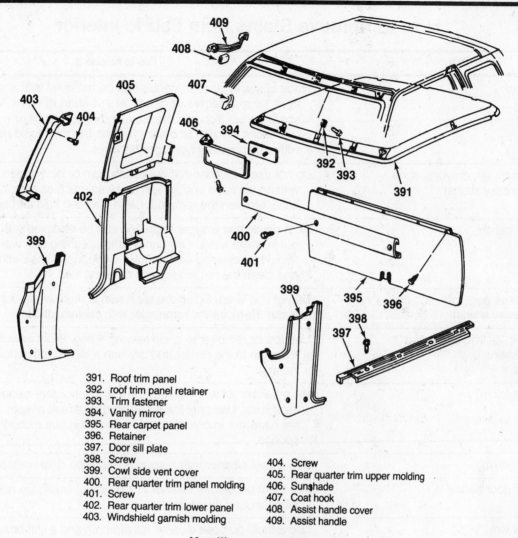

391. Roof trim panel
392. roof trim panel retainer
393. Trim fastener
394. Vanity mirror
395. Rear carpet panel
396. Retainer
397. Door sill plate
398. Screw
399. Cowl side vent cover
400. Rear quarter trim panel molding
401. Screw
402. Rear quarter trim lower panel
403. Windshield garnish molding
404. Screw
405. Rear quarter trim upper molding
406. Sunshade
407. Coat hook
408. Assist handle cover
409. Assist handle

Headliner assembly

How to Remove Stains from Fabric Interior

For best results, spots and stains should be removed as soon as possible. Never use gasoline, lacquer thinner, acetone, nail polish remover or bleach. Use a 3′ x 3″ piece of cheesecloth. Squeeze most of the liquid from the fabric and wipe the stained fabric from the outside of the stain toward the center with a lifting motion. Turn the cheesecloth as soon as one side becomes soiled. When using water to remove a stain, be sure to wash the entire section after the spot has been removed to avoid water stains. Encrusted spots can be broken up with a dull knife and vacuumed before removing the stain.

Type of Stain	How to Remove It
Surface spots	Brush the spots out with a small hand brush or use a commercia preparation such as K2R to lift the stain.
Mildew	Clean around the mildew with warm suds. Rinse in cold wa soak the mildew area in a solution of 1 part table salt a water. Wash with upholstery cleaner.

How to Remove Stains from Fabric Interior

Type of Stain	How to Remove It
Water stains	Water stains in fabric materials can be removed with a solution made from 1 cup of table salt dissolved in 1 quart of water. Vigorously scrub the solution into the stain and rinse with clear water. Water stains in nylon or other synthetic fabrics should be removed with a commercial type spot remover.
Chewing gum, tar, crayons, shoe polish (greasy stains)	Do not use a cleaner that will soften gum or tar. Harden the deposit with an ice cube and scrape away as much as possible with a dull knife. Moisten the remainder with cleaning fluid and scrub clean.
Ice cream, candy	Most candy has a sugar base and can be removed with a cloth wrung out in warm water. Oily candy, after cleaning with warm water, should be cleaned with upholstery cleaner. Rinse with warm water and clean the remainder with cleaning fluid.
Wine, alcohol, egg, milk, soft drink (non-greasy stains)	Do not use soap. Scrub the stain with a cloth wrung out in warm water. Remove the remainder with cleaning fluid.
Grease, oil, lipstick, butter and related stains	Use a spot remover to avoid leaving a ring. Work from the outisde of the stain to the center and dry with a clean cloth when the spot is gone.
Headliners (cloth)	Mix a solution of warm water and foam upholstery cleaner to give thick suds. Use only foam—liquid may streak or spot. Clean the entire headliner in one operation using a circular motion with a natural sponge.
Headliner (vinyl)	Use a vinyl cleaner with a sponge and wipe clean with a dry cloth.
Seats and door panels	Mix 1 pint upholstery cleaner in 1 gallon of water. Do not soak the fabric around the buttons.
Leather or vinyl fabric	Use a multi-purpose cleaner full strength and a stiff brush. Let stand 2 minutes and scrub thoroughly. Wipe with a clean, soft rag.
Nylon or synthetic fabrics	For normal stains, use the same procedures you would for washing cloth upholstery. If the fabric is extremely dirty, use a multi-purpose cleaner full strength with a stiff scrub brush. Scrub thoroughly in all directions and wipe with a cotton towel or soft rag.

Glossary

AIR/FUEL RATIO: The ratio of air to gasoline by weight in the fuel mixture drawn into the engine.

AIR INJECTION: One method of reducing harmful exhaust emissions by injecting air into each of the exhaust ports of an engine. The fresh air entering the hot exhaust manifold causes any remaining fuel to be burned before it can exit the tailpipe.

ALTERNATOR: A device used for converting mechanical energy into electrical energy.

AMMETER: An instrument, calibrated in amperes, used to measure the flow of an electrical current in a circuit. Ammeters are always connected in series with the circuit being tested.

AMPERE: The rate of flow of electrical current present when one volt of electrical pressure is applied against one ohm of electrical resistance.

ANALOG COMPUTER: Any microprocessor that uses similar (analogous) electrical signals to make its calculations.

ARMATURE: A laminated, soft iron core wrapped by a wire that converts electrical energy to mechanical energy as in a motor or relay. When rotated in a magnetic field, it changes mechanical energy into electrical energy as in a generator.

ATMOSPHERIC PRESSURE: The pressure on the Earth's surface caused by the weight of the air in the atmosphere. At sea level, this pressure is 14.7 psi at 32°F (101 kPa at 0°C).

ATOMIZATION: The breaking down of a liquid into a fine mist that can be suspended in air.

AXIAL PLAY: Movement parallel to a shaft or bearing bore.

BACKFIRE: The sudden combustion of gases in the intake or exhaust system that results in a loud explosion.

BACKLASH: The clearance or play between two parts, such as meshed gears.

BACKPRESSURE: Restrictions in the exhaust system that slow the exit of exhaust gases from the combustion chamber.

BAKELITE: A heat resistant, plastic insulator material commonly used in printed circuit boards and transistorized components.

BALL BEARING: A bearing made up of hardened inner and outer races between which hardened steel balls roll.

BALLAST RESISTOR: A resistor in the primary ignition circuit that lowers voltage after the engine is started to reduce wear on ignition components.

BEARING: A friction reducing, supportive device usually located between a stationary part and a moving part.

BIMETAL TEMPERATURE SENSOR: Any sensor or switch made of two dissimilar types of metal that bend when heated or cooled due to the different expansion rates of the alloys. These types of sensors usually function as an on/off switch.

BLOWBY: Combustion gases, composed of water vapor and unburned fuel, that leak past the piston rings into the crankcase during normal engine operation. These gases are removed by the PCV system to prevent the buildup of harmful acids in the crankcase.

BRAKE PAD: A brake shoe and lining assembly used with disc brakes.

BRAKE SHOE: The backing for the brake lining. The term is, however, usually applied to the assembly of the brake backing and lining.

BUSHING: A liner, usually removable, for a bearing; an anti-friction liner used in place of a bearing.

BYPASS: System used to bypass ballast resistor during engine cranking to increase voltage supplied to the coil.

CALIPER: A hydraulically activated device in a disc brake system, which is mounted straddling the brake rotor (disc). The caliper contains at least one piston and two brake pads. Hydraulic pressure on the piston(s) forces the pads against the rotor.

CAMSHAFT: A shaft in the engine on which are the lobes (cams) which operate the valves. The camshaft is driven by the crankshaft, via a belt, chain or gears, at one half the crankshaft speed.

CAPACITOR: A device which stores an electrical charge.

CARBON MONOXIDE (CO): A colorless, odorless gas given off as a normal byproduct of combustion. It is poisonous and extremely dangerous in confined areas, building up slowly to toxic levels without warning if adequate ventilation is not available.

CARBURETOR: A device, usually mounted on the intake manifold of an engine, which mixes the air and fuel in the proper proportion to allow even combustion.

CATALYTIC CONVERTER: A device installed in the exhaust system, like a muffler, that converts harmful byproducts o combustion into carbon dioxide and water vapor by means o heat-producing chemical reaction.

CENTRIFUGAL ADVANCE: A mechanical method vancing the spark timing by using flyweights in the di that react to centrifugal force generated by the distri rotation.

CHECK VALVE: Any one-way valve installe flow of air, fuel or vacuum in one direction o

GLOSSARY

CHOKE: A device, usually a moveable valve, placed in the intake path of a carburetor to restrict the flow of air.

CIRCUIT: Any unbroken path through which an electrical current can flow. Also used to describe fuel flow in some instances.

CIRCUIT BREAKER: A switch which protects an electrical circuit from overload by opening the circuit when the current flow exceeds a predetermined level. Some circuit breakers must be reset manually, while most reset automatically

COIL (IGNITION): A transformer in the ignition circuit which steps up the voltage provided to the spark plugs.

COMBINATION MANIFOLD: An assembly which includes both the intake and exhaust manifolds in one casting.

COMBINATION VALVE: A device used in some fuel systems that routes fuel vapors to a charcoal storage canister instead of venting them into the atmosphere. The valve relieves fuel tank pressure and allows fresh air into the tank as the fuel level drops to prevent a vapor lock situation.

COMPRESSION RATIO: The comparison of the total volume of the cylinder and combustion chamber with the piston at BDC and the piston at TDC.

CONDENSER: 1. An electrical device which acts to store an electrical charge, preventing voltage surges.
2. A radiator-like device in the air conditioning system in which refrigerant gas condenses into a liquid, giving off heat.

CONDUCTOR: Any material through which an electrical current can be transmitted easily.

CONTINUITY: Continuous or complete circuit. Can be checked with an ohmmeter.

COUNTERSHAFT: An intermediate shaft which is rotated by a mainshaft and transmits, in turn, that rotation to a working part.

CRANKCASE: The lower part of an engine in which the crankshaft and related parts operate.

CRANKSHAFT: The main driving shaft of an engine which receives reciprocating motion from the pistons and converts it to rotary motion.

CYLINDER: In an engine, the round hole in the engine block in which the piston(s) ride.

CYLINDER BLOCK: The main structural member of an engine in which is found the cylinders, crankshaft and other principal parts.

...EAD: The detachable portion of the engine, fas- ...on of the cylinder block, containing all or ...ers. On overhead valve engines, it ... parts. On overhead cam

... bottom of the piston

...ion of the air/fuel mixture ... excess heat and compres- ...ean mixture. Also referred

DIAPHRAGM: A thin, flexible wall separating two cavities, such as in a vacuum advance unit.

DIESELING: A condition in which hot spots in the combustion chamber cause the engine to run on after the key is turned off.

DIFFERENTIAL: A geared assembly which allows the transmission of motion between drive axles, giving one axle the ability to turn faster than the other.

DIODE: An electrical device that will allow current to flow in one direction only.

DISC BRAKE: A hydraulic braking assembly consisting of a brake disc, or rotor, mounted on an axle, and a caliper assembly containing, usually two brake pads which are activated by hydraulic pressure. The pads are forced against the sides of the disc, creating friction which slows the vehicle.

DISTRIBUTOR: A mechanically driven device on an engine which is responsible for electrically firing the spark plug at a predetermined point of the piston stroke.

DOWEL PIN: A pin, inserted in mating holes in two different parts allowing those parts to maintain a fixed relationship.

DRUM BRAKE: A braking system which consists of two brake shoes and one or two wheel cylinders, mounted on a fixed backing plate, and a brake drum, mounted on an axle, which revolves around the assembly. Hydraulic action applied to the wheel cylinders forces the shoes outward against the drum, creating friction, slowing the vehicle.

DWELL: The rate, measured in degrees of shaft rotation, at which an electrical circuit cycles on and off.

ELECTRONIC CONTROL UNIT (ECU): Ignition module, module, amplifier or igniter. See Module for definition.

ELECTRONIC IGNITION: A system in which the timing and firing of the spark plugs is controlled by an electronic control unit, usually called a module. These systems have no points or condenser.

ENDPLAY: The measured amount of axial movement in a shaft.

ENGINE: A device that converts heat into mechanical energy.

EXHAUST MANIFOLD: A set of cast passages or pipes which conduct exhaust gases from the engine.

FEELER GAUGE: A blade, usually metal, of precisely predetermined thickness, used to measure the clearance between two parts. These blades usually are available in sets of assorted thicknesses.

F-Head: An engine configuration in which the intake valves are in the cylinder head, while the camshaft and exhaust valves are located in the cylinder block. The camshaft operates the intake valves via lifters and pushrods, while it operates the exhaust valves directly.

FIRING ORDER: The order in which combustion occurs in the cylinders of an engine. Also the order in which spark is distributed to the plugs by the distributor.

FLATHEAD: An engine configuration in which the camshaft and all the valves are located in the cylinder block.

FLOODING: The presence of too much fuel in the intake manifold and combustion chamber which prevents the air/fuel mixture from firing, thereby causing a no-start situation.

FLYWHEEL: A disc shaped part bolted to the rear end of the crankshaft. Around the outer perimeter is affixed the ring gear. The starter drive engages the ring gear, turning the flywheel, which rotates the crankshaft, imparting the initial starting motion to the engine.

FOOT POUND (ft.lb. or sometimes, ft. lbs.): The amount of energy or work needed to raise an item weighing one pound, a distance of one foot.

FUSE: A protective device in a circuit which prevents circuit overload by breaking the circuit when a specific amperage is present. The device is constructed around a strip or wire of a lower amperage rating than the circuit it is designed to protect. When an amperage higher than that stamped on the fuse is present in the circuit, the strip or wire melts, opening the circuit.

GEAR RATIO: The ratio between the number of teeth on meshing gears.

GENERATOR: A device which converts mechanical energy into electrical energy.

HEAT RANGE: The measure of a spark plug's ability to dissipate heat from its firing end. The higher the heat range, the hotter the plug fires.

HUB: The center part of a wheel or gear.

HYDROCARBON (HC): Any chemical compound made up of hydrogen and carbon. A major pollutant formed by the engine as a byproduct of combustion.

HYDROMETER: An instrument used to measure the specific gravity of a solution.

INCH POUND (in.lb. or sometimes, in. lbs.): One twelfth of a foot pound.

INDUCTION: A means of transferring electrical energy in the form of a magnetic field. Principle used in the ignition coil to increase voltage.

INJECTION PUMP: A device, usually mechanically operated, which meters and delivers fuel under pressure to the fuel injector.

INJECTOR: A device which receives metered fuel under relatively low pressure and is activated to inject the fuel into the engine under relatively high pressure at a predetermined time.

INPUT SHAFT: The shaft to which torque is applied, usually carrying the driving gear or gears.

INTAKE MANIFOLD: A casting of passages or pipes used to conduct air or a fuel/air mixture to the cylinders.

JOURNAL: The bearing surface within which a shaft operates.

KEY: A small block usually fitted in a notch between a shaft and a hub to prevent slippage of the two parts.

MANIFOLD: A casting of passages or set of pipes which connect the cylinders to an inlet or outlet source.

MANIFOLD VACUUM: Low pressure in an engine intake manifold formed just below the throttle plates. Manifold vacuum is highest at idle and drops under acceleration.

MASTER CYLINDER: The primary fluid pressurizing device in a hydraulic system. In automotive use, it is found in brake and hydraulic clutch systems and is pedal activated, either directly or, in a power brake system, through the power booster.

MODULE: Electronic control unit, amplifier or igniter of solid state or integrated design which controls the current flow in the ignition primary circuit based on input from the pick-up coil. When the module opens the primary circuit, the high secondary voltage is induced in the coil.

NEEDLE BEARING: A bearing which consists of a number (usually a large number) of long, thin rollers.

OHM: (Ω) The unit used to measure the resistance of conductor to electrical flow. One ohm is the amount of resistance that limits current flow to one ampere in a circuit with one volt of pressure.

OHMMETER: An instrument used for measuring the resistance, in ohms, in an electrical circuit.

OUTPUT SHAFT: The shaft which transmits torque from a device, such as a transmission.

OVERDRIVE: A gear assembly which produces more shaft revolutions than that transmitted to it.

OVERHEAD CAMSHAFT (OHC): An engine configuration in which the camshaft is mounted on top of the cylinder head and operates the valve either directly or by means of rocker arms.

OVERHEAD VALVE (OHV): An engine configuration in which all of the valves are located in the cylinder head and the camshaft is located in the cylinder block. The camshaft operates the valves via lifters and pushrods.

OXIDES OF NITROGEN (NOx): Chemical compounds of nitrogen produced as a byproduct of combustion. They combine with hydrocarbons to produce smog.

OXYGEN SENSOR: Used with the feedback system to sense the presence of oxygen in the exhaust gas and signal the computer which can reference the voltage signal to an air/fuel ratio.

PINION: The smaller of two meshing gears.

PISTON RING: An open ended ring which fits into a groove on the outer diameter of the piston. Its chief function is to form a seal between the piston and cylinder wall. Most automotive pistons have three rings: two for compression sealing; one for oil sealing.

PRELOAD: A predetermined load placed on a bearing during assembly or by adjustment.

PRIMARY CIRCUIT: Is the low voltage side of the ig system which consists of the ignition switch, ballast re resistance wire, bypass, coil, electronic control unit a coil as well as the connecting wires and harnesses.

PRESS FIT: The mating of two parts under p the inner diameter of one being smaller than th of the other, or vice versa; an interference f

GLOSSARY

RACE: The surface on the inner or outer ring of a bearing on which the balls, needles or rollers move.

REGULATOR: A device which maintains the amperage and/or voltage levels of a circuit at predetermined values.

RELAY: A switch which automatically opens and/or closes a circuit.

RESISTANCE: The opposition to the flow of current through a circuit or electrical device, and is measured in ohms. Resistance is equal to the voltage divided by the amperage.

RESISTOR: A device, usually made of wire, which offers a preset amount of resistance in an electrical circuit.

RING GEAR: The name given to a ring-shaped gear attached to a differential case, or affixed to a flywheel or as part a planetary gear set.

ROLLER BEARING: A bearing made up of hardened inner and outer races between which hardened steel rollers move.

ROTOR: 1. The disc-shaped part of a disc brake assembly, upon which the brake pads bear; also called, brake disc.
2. The device mounted atop the distributor shaft, which passes current to the distributor cap tower contacts.

SECONDARY CIRCUIT: The high voltage side of the ignition system, usually above 20,000 volts. The secondary includes the ignition coil, coil wire, distributor cap and rotor, spark plug wires and spark plugs.

SENDING UNIT: A mechanical, electrical, hydraulic or electromagnetic device which transmits information to a gauge.

SENSOR: Any device designed to measure engine operating conditions or ambient pressures and temperatures. Usually electronic in nature and designed to send a voltage signal to an on-board computer, some sensors may operate as a simple on/off switch or they may provide a variable voltage signal (like a potentiometer) as conditions or measured parameters change.

SHIM: Spacers of precise, predetermined thickness used between parts to establish a proper working relationship.

SLAVE CYLINDER: In automotive use, a device in the hydraulic clutch system which is activated by hydraulic force, disengaging the clutch.

SOLENOID: A coil used to produce a magnetic field, the effect of which is produce work.

SPARK PLUG: A device screwed into the combustion chamber of a spark ignition engine. The basic construction is a conduc- [illegible] core inside of a ceramic insulator, mounted in an outer con- [illegible] An electrical charge from the spark plug wire trav- [illegible] ductive core and jumps a preset air gap to a [illegible] the end of the conductive base. The [illegible] mixture in the combustion [illegible]

[illegible] to the outer diameter of a shaft or inner diameter of a bore to enable parts to mate without rotation.

TACHOMETER: A device used to measure the rotary speed of an engine, shaft, gear, etc., usually in rotations per minute.

THERMOSTAT: A valve, located in the cooling system of an engine, which is closed when cold and opens gradually in response to engine heating, controlling the temperature of the coolant and rate of coolant flow.

TOP DEAD CENTER (TDC): The point at which the piston reaches the top of its travel on the compression stroke.

TORQUE: The twisting force applied to an object.

TORQUE CONVERTER: A turbine used to transmit power from a driving member to a driven member via hydraulic action, providing changes in drive ratio and torque. In automotive use, it links the driveplate at the rear of the engine to the automatic transmission.

TRANSDUCER: A device used to change a force into an electrical signal.

TRANSISTOR: A semi-conductor component which can be actuated by a small voltage to perform an electrical switching function.

TUNE-UP: A regular maintenance function, usually associated with the replacement and adjustment of parts and components in the electrical and fuel systems of a vehicle for the purpose of attaining optimum performance.

TURBOCHARGER: An exhaust driven pump which compresses intake air and forces it into the combustion chambers at higher than atmospheric pressures. The increased air pressure allows more fuel to be burned and results in increased horsepower being produced.

VACUUM ADVANCE: A device which advances the ignition timing in response to increased engine vacuum.

VACUUM GAUGE: An instrument used to measure the presence of vacuum in a chamber.

VALVE: A device which control the pressure, direction of flow or rate of flow of a liquid or gas.

VALVE CLEARANCE: The measured gap between the end of the valve stem and the rocker arm, cam lobe or follower that activates the valve.

VISCOSITY: The rating of a liquid's internal resistance to flow.

VOLTMETER: An instrument used for measuring electrical force in units called volts. Voltmeters are always connected parallel with the circuit being tested.

WHEEL CYLINDER: Found in the automotive drum brake assembly, it is a device, actuated by hydraulic pressure, which, through internal pistons, pushes the brake shoes outward against the drums.